The Pocket Oxford-Duden
German Dictionary

D0594931

STEELE

The Pocket
Oxford-Duden
German
Dictionary

English—German
German—English

Edited by the Dudenredaktion
and the German Section of the
Oxford University Press
Dictionary Department

Chief Editors

M. CLARK

O. THYEN

CLARENDON PRESS · OXFORD

1992

Oxford University Press, Walton Street, Oxford OX2 6DP

Oxford New York Toronto
Delhi Bombay Calcutta Madras Karachi
Kuala Lumpur Singapore Hong Kong Tokyo
Nairobi Dar es Salaam Cape Town
Melbourne Auckland Madrid
and associated companies in
Berlin Ibadan

Oxford is a trade mark of Oxford University Press

Published in the United States by
Oxford University Press, New York

The word 'DUDEN' is a registered trade mark of the
Bibliographisches Institut for books of any kind

British Library Cataloguing in Publication Data
Data available

ISBN 0-19-864194 X
ISBN 0-19-864200-8 (pb: u.s.)

Library of Congress Cataloging in Publication Data
Data available

Printed in Great Britain by
Richard Clay Ltd, Bungay, Suffolk

Foreword

The *Pocket Oxford–Duden German Dictionary* has been designed to meet the needs of students, tourists, and all those who require quick and reliable answers to their translation questions. It provides clear guidance on selecting the most appropriate translation, numerous illustrative examples to help with problems of construction and usage, and precise information on grammar, style, and pronunciation.

Based on the much acclaimed *Oxford–Duden German Dictionary*, this easy-to-use pocket dictionary carries the authority of two of the world's foremost dictionary publishers, Oxford University Press and the Dudenverlag, making use of the unparalleled databases maintained and continually expanded by the two publishers for their celebrated native-speaker dictionaries. Its reliability and clarity make it an invaluable aid to understanding, speaking, and writing everyday idiomatic German in the nineteen nineties.

MICHAEL CLARK
Oxford University Press

Editors and Contributors

in Oxford	in Mannheim
Michael Clark	Olaf Thyen
Bernadette Mohan	Werner Scholze-Stubenrecht
Maurice Waite	Brigitte Alsleben
Ursula Lang	Ulrike Röhrenbeck
Trish Stableford	Magdalena Seubel
Tim Connell	Eva Vennebusch

Contents

Phonetic symbols used in transcriptions /
Die bei den Ausspracheangaben verwendeten
Zeichen der Lautschrift   7

English abbreviations used in the Dictionary /
Im Wörterverzeichnis verwendete englische
Abkürzungen   9

German abbreviations used in the Dictionary /
Im Wörterverzeichnis verwendete deutsche
Abkürzungen   10

English–German Dictionary /
Englisch–deutsches Wörterverzeichnis   13

German–English Dictionary /
Deutsch–englisches Wörterverzeichnis   403

Englische unregelmäßige Verben   793

German irregular verbs   795

Weights and Measures /
Maße und Gewichte   799

Inside front cover / Innendeckel vorn:
Key to English–German entries /
Erläuterungen zum englisch-deutschen Text

Inside back cover / Innendeckel hinten:
Key to German–English entries /
Erläuterungen zum deutsch–englischen Text

Proprietary Names

Die für das Englische verwendeten Zeichen der Lautschrift

ɑ:	barb	bɑ:b		m	mat	mæt
ã	séance	'seiãs		n	not	nɒt
æ	fat	fæt		ŋ	sing	sıŋ
æ̃	lingerie	'læ̃ʒərı		ɒ	got	gɒt
aı	fine	faın		ɔ:	paw	pɔ:
aʊ	now	naʊ		ɔı	boil	bɔıl
b	bat	bæt		p	pet	pet
d	dog	dɒg		r	rat	ræt
dʒ	jam	dʒæm		s	sip	sıp
e	met	met		ʃ	ship	ʃıp
eı	fate	feıt		t	tip	tıp
eə	fairy	'feərı		tʃ	chin	tʃın
əʊ	goat	gəʊt		θ	thin	θın
ə	ago	ə'gəʊ		ð	the	ðə
ɜ:	fur	fɜ:(r)		u:	boot	bu:t
f	fat	fæt		ʊ	book	bʊk
g	good	gʊd		ʊə	tourist	'tʊərıst
h	hat	hæt		ʌ	dug	dʌg
ı	bit, lately	bıt, 'leıtlı		v	van	væn
ıə	nearly	'nıəlı		w	win	wın
i:	meet	mi:t		x	loch	lɒx
j	yet	jet		z	zip	zıp
k	kit	kıt		ʒ	vision	'vıʒn
l	lot	lɒt				

:   Längezeichen, bezeichnet Länge des unmittelbar davor stehenden Vokals, z. B. boot [bu:t].

'   Betonung, steht unmittelbar vor einer betonten Silbe, z. B. ago [ə'gəʊ].

(r)   Ein „r" in runden Klammern wird nur gesprochen, wenn im Textzusammenhang ein Vokal unmittelbar folgt, z. B. pare [peə(r)]; pare away [peər ə'weı].

Phonetic information given in the German-English section

The pronunciation of German is largely regular, and phonetic transcriptions have only been given where additional help is needed. In all other cases only the position of the stressed syllable and the length of the vowel in that syllable are shown: a long vowel is indicated by an underline, e.g. Maß, a short vowel by a dot placed underneath, e.g. Masse.

Phonetic symbols used in transcriptions of German words

a	hat	hat	ŋ	lang	laŋ
a:	Bahn	ba:n	o	Moral	mo'ra:l
ɐ	Ober	'o:bɐ	o:	Boot	bo:t
ɐ̯	Uhr	u:ɐ̯	ɔ	loyal	lɔa'ja:l
ã	Ensemble	ã'sã:bl̩	õ	Fondue	fõ'dy:
ã:	Abonnement	abɔnə'mã:	õ:	Fond	fõ:
ai	weit	vait	ɔ	Post	pɔst
au	Haut	haut	ø	Ökonom	øko'no:m
b	Ball	bal	ø:	Öl	ø:l
ç	ich	ɪç	œ	göttlich	'gœtlɪç
d	dann	dan	œ̃:	Parfum	par'fœ̃:
dʒ	Gin	dʒɪn	ɔy	Heu	hɔy
e	egal	e'ga:l	p	Pakt	pakt
e:	Beet	be:t	pf	Pfahl	pfa:l
ɛ	mästen	'mɛstn̩	r	Rast	rast
ɛ:	wählen	'vɛ:lən	s	Hast	hast
ɛ̃	Mannequin	'manəkɛ̃	ʃ	schal	ʃa:l
ɛ̃:	Cousin	ku'zɛ̃:	t	Tal	ta:l
ə	Nase	'na:zə	ts	Zahl	tsa:l
f	Faß	fas	tʃ	Matsch	matʃ
g	Gast	gast	u	kulant	ku'lant
h	hat	hat	u:	Hut	hu:t
i	vital	vi'ta:l	u̯	aktuell	ak'tu̯ɛl
i:	viel	fi:l	ʊ	Pult	pʊlt
i̯	Studie	'ʃtu:di̯ə	v	was	vas
ɪ	Birke	'bɪrkə	x	Bach	bax
j	ja	ja:	y	Physik	fy'zi:k
k	kalt	kalt	y:	Rübe	'ry:bə
l	Last	last	y̆	Nuance	'nỹã:sə
l̩	Nabel	'na:bl̩	ʏ	Fülle	'fʏlə
m	Mast	mast	z	Hase	'ha:zə
n	Naht	na:t	ʒ	Genie	ʒe'ni:
n̩	baden	'ba:dn̩			

'   Glottal stop, e. g. beachten [bə'|axtn̩].

:   Length sign, indicating that the preceding vowel is long, e. g. Chrom [kro:m].

~   Indicates a nasal vowel, e. g. Fond [fõ:].

'   Stress mark, immediately preceding a stressed syllable, e. g. Ballon [ba'lɔn].

English abbreviations used in the Dictionary/ Im Wörterverzeichnis verwendete englische Abkürzungen

abbr(s).	abbreviation(s)	Footb.	Football
abs.	absolute	Gastr.	Gastronomy
adj(s).	adjective(s)	Geog.	Geography
Admin.	Administration, Administrative	Geol.	Geology
adv.	adverb	Geom.	Geometry
Aeronaut.	Aeronautics	Her.	Heraldry
Agric.	Agriculture	Hist.	History, Historical
Amer.	American, America	Hort.	Horticulture
Anat.	Anatomy	imper.	imperative
arch.	archaic	impers.	impersonal
Archaeol.	Archaeology	incl.	including
Archit.	Architecture	indef.	indefinite
art.	article	Information Sci.	Information Science
Astrol.	Astrology	int.	interjection
Astron.	Astronomy	interrog.	interrogative
Astronaut.	Astronautics	Ir.	Irish, Ireland
attrib.	attributive	iron.	ironical
Austral.	Australian, Australia	joc.	jocular
Biol.	Biology	Journ.	Journalism
Bookk.	Bookkeeping	lang.	language
Bot.	Botany	Ling.	Linguistics
Brit.	British, Britain	Lit.	Literature
Chem.	Chemistry	lit.	literal
Cinemat.	Cinematography	masc.	masculine
coll.	colloquial	Math.	Mathematics
collect.	collective	Mech.	Mechanics
comb.	combination	Mech. Engin.	Mechanical Engineering
Commerc.	Commerce, Commercial	Med.	Medicine
compar.	comparative	Metalw.	Metalwork
condit.	conditional	Meteorol.	Meteorology
conj.	conjunction	Mil.	Military
def.	definite	Min.	Mineralogy
Dent.	Dentistry	Motor Veh.	Motor Vehicles
derog.	derogatory	Mus.	Music
dial.	dialect	Mythol.	Mythology
Diplom.	Diplomacy	n.	noun
Dressm.	Dressmaking	Naut.	Nautical
Eccl.	Ecclesiastical	neg.	negative
Ecol.	Ecology	N. Engl.	Northern English
Econ.	Economics	ns.	nouns
Educ.	Education	Nucl. Phys.	Nuclear Physics
Electr.	Electricity	obj.	object
ellipt.	elliptical	Ornith.	Ornithology
emphat.	emphatic	P	Proprietary name
esp.	especially	Parl.	Parliament
euphem.	euphemistic	pass.	passive
excl.	exclamation, exclamatory	Pharm.	Pharmacy
		Philos.	Philosophy
expr.	expressing	Photog.	Photography
fem.	feminine	phr(s).	phrase(s)
fig.	figurative	Phys.	Physics

Physiol.	Physiology	Scot.	Scottish, Scotland
pl.	plural	sing.	singular
poet.	poetical	sl.	slang
Polit.	Politics	Sociol.	Sociology
poss.	possessive	St. Exch.	Stock Exchange
postpos.	postpositive	sth.	something
p.p.	past participle	subord.	subordinate
pred.	predicative	suf.	suffix
pref.	prefix	superl.	superlative
prep.	preposition	Surv.	Surveying
pres.	present	symb.	symbol
pres. p.	present participle	tech.	technical
pr. n.	proper noun	Teleph.	Telephony
pron.	pronoun	Telev.	Television
prov.	proverbial	Theol.	Theology
Psych.	Psychology	Univ.	University
p.t.	past tense	usu.	usually
Railw.	Railways	v. aux.	auxiliary verb
RC Ch.	Roman Catholic	Vet. Med.	Veterinary Medicine
	Church	v.i.	intransitive verb
refl.	reflexive	v. refl.	reflexive verb
rel.	relative	v.t.	transitive verb
Relig.	Religion	v.t. & i.	transitive and
rhet.	rhetorical		intransitive verb
sb.	somebody	Woodw.	Woodwork
Sch.	School	Zool.	Zoology
Sci.	Science		

German abbreviations used in the Dictionary/ Im Wörterverzeichnis verwendete deutsche Abkürzungen

a.	anderes; andere	berlin.	berlinisch
ä.	ähnliches; ähnliche	bes.	besonders
Abk.	Abkürzung	Bez.	Bezeichnung
adj.	adjektivisch	bibl.	biblisch
Adj.	Adjektiv	bild. Kunst	bildende Kunst
adv.	adverbial	Biol.	Biologie
Adv.	Adverb	Börsenw.	Börsenwesen
Akk.	Akkusativ	Bot.	Botanik
amerik.	amerikanisch	BRD	Bundesrepublik
Amtsspr.	Amtssprache		Deutschland
Anat.	Anatomie	brit.	britisch
Anthrop.	Anthropologie	Bruchz.	Bruchzahl
Archäol.	Archäologie	Buchf.	Buchführung
Archit.	Architektur	Buchw.	Buchwesen
Art.	Artikel	Bürow.	Bürowesen
Astrol.	Astrologie	chem.	chemisch
Astron.	Astronomie	christl.	christlich
A.T.	Altes Testament	Dat.	Dativ
attr.	attributiv	DDR	Deutsche
Bauw.	Bauwesen		Demokratische
Bergmannsspr.	Bergmannssprache		Republik

Dekl.	Deklination	jur.	juristisch
Demonstrativ-	Demonstrativ-	Kardinalz.	Kardinalzahl
pron.	pronomen	kath.	katholisch
d.h.	das heißt	Kaufmannsspr.	Kaufmannssprache
dichter.	dichterisch	Kfz-W.	Kraftfahrzeugwesen
Druckerspr.	Druckersprache	Kinderspr.	Kindersprache
Druckw.	Druckwesen	Kochk.	Kochkunst
dt.	deutsch	Konj.	Konjunktion
DV	Datenverarbeitung	Kunstwiss.	Kunstwissenschaft
ehem.	ehemals, ehemalig	landsch.	landschaftlich
Eisenb.	Eisenbahn	Landw.	Landwirtschaft
elektr.	elektrisch	Literaturw.	Literaturwissenschaft
Elektrot.	Elektrotechnik	Luftf.	Luftfahrt
engl.	englisch	ma.	mittelalterlich
etw.	etwas	MA.	Mittelalter
ev.	evangelisch	marx.	marxistisch
fachspr.	fachsprachlich	Math.	Mathematik
fam.	familiär	Med.	Medizin
Ferns.	Fernsehen	Meeresk.	Meereskunde
Fernspr.	Fernsprechwesen	Met.	Meteorologie
fig.	figurativ	Metall.	Metallurgie
Finanzw.	Finanzwesen	Metallbearb.	Metallbearbeitung
Flugw.	Flugwesen	Milit.	Militär
Forstw.	Forstwesen	Mineral.	Mineralogie
Fot.	Fotografie	mod.	modifizierend
Frachtw.	Frachtwesen	Modalv.	Modalverb
Funkw.	Funkwesen	Münzk.	Münzkunde
Gastr.	Gastronomie	Mus.	Musik
Gattungsz.	Gattungszahl	Mythol.	Mythologie
Gaunerspr.	Gaunersprache	Naturw.	Naturwissenschaft
geh.	gehoben	Neutr.	Neutrum
Gen.	Genitiv	niederdt.	niederdeutsch
Geneal.	Genealogie	Nom.	Nominativ
Geogr.	Geographie	nordamerik.	nordamerikanisch
Geol.	Geologie	nordd.	norddeutsch
Geom.	Geometrie	nordostd.	nordostdeutsch
Handarb.	Handarbeit	nordwestd.	nordwestdeutsch
Handw.	Handwerk	ns.	nationalsozialistisch
Her.	Heraldik	N.T.	Neues Testament
hess.	hessisch	o.	ohne; oben
Hilfsv.	Hilfsverb	o.ä.	oder ähnliches;
hist.	historisch		oder ähnliche
Hochschulw.	Hochschulwesen	od.	oder
Holzverarb.	Holzverarbeitung	Ordinalz.	Ordinalzahl
Indefinitpron.	Indefinitpronomen	ostd.	ostdeutsch
indekl.	indeklinabel	österr.	österreichisch
Indik.	Indikativ	Päd.	Pädagogik
Inf.	Infinitiv	Papierdt.	Papierdeutsch
Informationst.	Informationstechnik	Parapsych.	Parapsychologie
Interj.	Interjektion	Parl.	Parlament
iron.	ironisch	Part.	Partizip
intr.	intransitiv	Perf.	Perfekt
Jagdw.	Jagdwesen	Pers.	Person
Jägerspr.	Jägersprache	pfälz.	pfälzisch
jmd.	jemand	Pharm.	Pharmazie
jmdm.	jemandem	Philos.	Philosophie
jmdn.	jemanden	Physiol.	Physiologie
jmds.	jemandes	Pl.	Plural
Jugendspr.	Jugendsprache	Plusq.	Plusquamperfekt

Postw.	Postwesen	Sup.	Superlativ
präd.	prädikativ	Textilw.	Textilwesen
Präp.	Präposition	Theol.	Theologie
Präs.	Präsens	thüring.	thüringisch
Prät.	Präteritum	Tiermed.	Tiermedizin
Pron.	Pronomen	tr.	transitiv
Psych.	Psychologie	Trenn.	Trennung
Raumf.	Raumfahrt	u.	und
Rechtsspr.	Rechtssprache	u. a.	und andere[s]
Rechtsw.	Rechtswesen	u. ä.	und ähnliches
refl.	reflexiv	ugs.	umgangssprachlich
regelm.	regelmäßig	unbest.	unbestimmt
Rel.	Religion	unpers.	unpersönlich
Relativpron.	Relativpronomen	unr.	unregelmäßig
rhein.	rheinisch	usw.	und so weiter
Rhet.	Rhetorik	v.	von
röm.	römisch	V.	Verb
röm.-kath.	römisch-katholisch	verächtl.	verächtlich
Rundf.	Rundfunk	veralt.	veraltet; veraltend
s.	siehe	Verhaltensf.	Verhaltensforschung
S.	Seite	verhüll.	verhüllend
scherzh.	scherzhaft	Verkehrsw.	Verkehrswesen
schles.	schlesisch	Versiche-	Versicherungswesen
schott.	schottisch	rungsw.	
Schülerspr.	Schülersprache	vgl.	vergleiche
Schulw.	Schulwesen	Vkl.	Verkleinerungsform
schwäb.	schwäbisch	Völkerk.	Völkerkunde
schweiz.	schweizerisch	Völkerr.	Völkerrecht
Seemannsspr.	Seemannssprache	Volksk.	Volkskunde
Seew.	Seewesen	volkst.	volkstümlich
Sexualk.	Sexualkunde	vulg.	vulgär
Sg.	Singular	Werbespr.	Werbesprache
s. o.	siehe oben	westd.	westdeutsch
Soldatenspr.	Soldatensprache	westfäl.	westfälisch
Sozialvers.	Sozialversicherung	Wieder-	Wiederholungs-
Soziol.	Soziologie	holungsz.	zahlwort
spött.	spöttisch	wiener.	wienerisch
Spr.	Sprichwort	Winzerspr.	Winzersprache
Sprachw.	Sprachwissenschaft	Wirtsch.	Wirtschaft
Steuerw.	Steuerwesen	Wissensch.	Wissenschaft
Stilk.	Stilkunde	Wz.	Warenzeichen
Studentenspr.	Studentensprache	Zahnmed.	Zahnmedizin
s. u.	siehe unten	z. B.	zum Beispiel
Subj.	Subjekt	Zeitungsw.	Zeitungswesen
subst.	substantivisch;	Zollw.	Zollwesen
	substantiviert	Zool.	Zoologie
Subst.	Substantiv	Zus.	Zusammensetzung
südd.	süddeutsch	Zusschr.	Zusammenschreibung
südwestd.	südwestdeutsch		

A

A, ¹a [eɪ] n. A, a, das

²a [ə, stressed eɪ] indef. art. ein/eine/ ein; **he is a gardener/a Frenchman** er ist Gärtner/Franzose; **she did not say a word** sie sagte kein Wort

AA abbr. (Brit.) Automobile Association britischer Automobilklub

aback [ə'bæk] adv. **be taken ~:** erstaunt sein

abandon [ə'bændən] v.t. verlassen ⟨Ort, Person⟩; aufgeben ⟨Prinzip⟩

abase [ə'beɪs] v.t. erniedrigen

abashed [ə'bæʃt] adj. beschämt

abate [ə'beɪt] v.i. nachlassen

abattoir ['æbətwɑː(r)] n. Schlachthof, der

abbey ['æbɪ] n. Abtei, die

abbot ['æbət] n. Abt, der

abbreviate [ə'briːvɪeɪt] v.t. abkürzen.
abbreviation [əbriːvɪ'eɪʃn] n. Abkürzung, die

abdicate ['æbdɪkeɪt] v.t. abdanken.
abdication [æbdɪ'keɪʃn] n. Abdankung, die

abdomen ['æbdəmɪn] n. Bauch, der.
abdominal [æb'dɒmɪnl] adj. Bauch-

abduct [əb'dʌkt] v.t. entführen. **abduction** [əb'dʌkʃn] n. Entführung, die

aberration [æbə'reɪʃn] n. Abweichung, die

abet [ə'bet] v.t., **-tt-** helfen (+ Dat.);
aid and ~: Beihilfe leisten (+ Dat.)

abhor [əb'hɔː(r)] v.t., **-rr-** verabscheuen. **abhorrent** [əb'hɒrənt] adj. abscheulich

abide [ə'baɪd] **1.** v.i. **~ by** befolgen ⟨Gesetz, Vorschrift⟩; [ein]halten ⟨Versprechen⟩. **2.** v.t. ertragen; **I can't ~ dogs** ich kann Hunde nicht ausstehen

ability [ə'bɪlɪtɪ] n. **a)** (capacity) Fähigkeit, die; **have the ~ to do sth.** etw. können; **b)** (cleverness) Intelligenz, die; **c)** (talent) Begabung, die

abject ['æbdʒekt] adj. elend; bitter ⟨Armut⟩; demütig ⟨Entschuldigung⟩

ablaze [ə'bleɪz] adj. **be ~:** in Flammen stehen

able ['eɪbl] adj. **a) be ~ to do sth.** etw. können; **b)** (competent) fähig. **ablebodied** ['eɪblbɒdɪd] adj. kräftig; tauglich ⟨Soldat, Matrose⟩. **ably** ['eɪblɪ] adv. geschickt; gekonnt

abnormal [æb'nɔːml] adj. abnorm; a[b]normal ⟨Interesse, Verhalten⟩. **abnormality** [æbnɔː'mælɪtɪ] n. Abnormität, die

aboard [ə'bɔːd] **1.** adv. an Bord. **2.** prep. an Bord (+ Gen.); **~ the bus** im Bus; **~ ship** an Bord

abode [ə'bəʊd] n. **of no fixed ~:** ohne festen Wohnsitz

abolish [ə'bɒlɪʃ] v.t. abschaffen.
abolition [æbə'lɪʃn] n. Abschaffung, die

abominable [ə'bɒmɪnəbl] adj. abscheulich; scheußlich

aborigine [æbə'rɪdʒɪnɪ] n. Ureinwohner, der

abort [ə'bɔːt] v.t. abtreiben ⟨Baby⟩.
abortion [ə'bɔːʃn] n. Abtreibung, die. **abortive** [ə'bɔːtɪv] adj. mißlungen ⟨Plan⟩; fehlgeschlagen ⟨Versuch⟩

abound [ə'baʊnd] v.i. **~ in sth.** an etw. (Dat.) reich sein

about [ə'baʊt] **1.** adv. **a)** (all around) rings[her]um; (here and there) überall; **all ~:** ringsumher; **b)** (near) **be ~:** dasein; hiersein; **c) be ~ to do sth.** gerade etw. tun wollen; **d) be out and ~:** aktiv sein; **e)** (approximately) ungefähr. **2.** prep. **a)** (all round) um [... herum]; **b)** (concerning) über (+ Akk.); **know ~ sth.** von etw. wissen; **a question ~ sth.** eine Frage zu etw.; **what was it ~?** worum ging es?

above [ə'bʌv] **1.** adv. **a)** (position) oben; (higher up) darüber; **b)** (direction) nach oben. **2.** prep. (position) über (+ Dat.); (direction, more than) über (+ Akk.); **~ all** vor allem. **a'bovementioned** adj. oben genannt

abrasion [ə'breɪʒn] n. *(graze)* Hautab-
schürfung, *die*

abrasive [ə'breɪsɪv] **1.** *adj.* **a)** scheu-
ernd; Scheuer-; **b)** *(fig.: harsh)* aggressiv. **2.** *n.* Scheuermittel, *das*

abreast [ə'brest] *adv.* **a)** nebeneinander; **b)** *(fig.)* keep ~ of sth. sich über
etw. *(Akk.)* auf dem laufenden halten

abroad [ə'brɔːd] *adv.* **a)** im Ausland;
(direction) ins Ausland

abrupt [ə'brʌpt] *adj.,* **a'bruptly** *adv.*
a) *(sudden[ly])* abrupt; plötzlich; **b)**
(brusque[ly]) schroff

abscess ['æbsɪs] n. Abszeß, *der*

abscond [əb'skɒnd] v. t. sich entfernen

absence ['æbsəns] n. Abwesenheit,
die; the ~ of sth. der Mangel an etw.
(Dat.)

absent ['æbsənt] *adj.* abwesend; be ~
from school/work in der Schule/am
Arbeitsplatz fehlen. **absentee** [æb-
sən'tiː] n. Fehlende, *der/die;* Abwe-
sende, *der/die.* **absent-minded** [æb-
sənt'maɪndɪd] *adj.* geistesabwesend;
(habitually) zerstreut

absolute ['æbsəluːt] *adj.* absolut; ausgemacht *(Lüge, Skandal).* **abso-
'lutely** *adv.* absolut; völlig *(verrückt);* **you're ~ right!** du hast völlig
recht; ~ **not!** auf keinen Fall!

absolve [əb'zɒlv] v. t. ~ from entbinden von *(Pflichten);* lossprechen von
(Schuld)

absorb [əb'sɔːb] v. t. **a)** aufsaugen
(Flüssigkeit); **b)** abfangen *(Schlag,
Stoß);* **c)** *(fig.: engross)* ausfüllen. **ab-
sorbent** [əb'sɔːbənt] *adj.* saugfähig.
ab'sorbing *adj.* faszinierend

abstain [əb'steɪn] v. i. ~ from sth. sich
einer Sache *(Gen.)* enthalten; ~ [from
voting] sich der Stimme enthalten

abstemious [əb'stiːmɪəs] *adj.* enthaltsam

abstention [əb'stenʃn] n. *(from voting)* Stimmenthaltung, *die*

abstinence ['æbstɪnəns] n. Abstinenz,
die

abstract ['æbstrækt] **1.** *adj.* abstrakt.
2. *n.* Zusammenfassung, *die*

absurd [əb'sɜːd] *adj.* absurd; *(ridiculous)* lächerlich. **absurdity** [əb'sɜːdɪ-
tɪ] n. Absurdität, *die.* **ab'surdly** *adv.*
lächerlich

abundance [ə'bʌndəns] n. [an] ~ of
sth. eine Fülle von etw.

abundant [ə'bʌndənt] *adj.* reich (in an
+ *Dat.*)

abuse 1. [ə'bjuːz] v. t. beschimpfen. **2.**
[ə'bjuːs] n. Beschimpfungen Pl. **ab-
usive** [ə'bjuːsɪv] *adj.* beleidigend;
become ~: ausfallend werden

abysmal [ə'bɪzml] *adj.* *(coll.: bad)* katastrophal *(ugs.)*

abyss [ə'bɪs] n. Abgrund, *der*

AC *abbr.* **alternating current** Ws

academic [ækə'demɪk] *adj.* akademisch

academy [ə'kædəmɪ] n. Akademie,
die

accede [æk'siːd] v. i. **a)** zustimmen (to
Dat.); **b)** ~ [to the throne] den Thron
besteigen

accelerate [ək'seləreɪt] **1.** v. t. beschleunigen. **2.** v. i. sich beschleunigen; *(Auto, Fahrer:)* beschleunigen.
acceleration [əkselə'reɪʃn] n. Beschleunigung, *die.* **accelerator** [ək-
'seləreɪtə(r)] n. ~ [pedal] Gas[pedal],
das

accent ['æksənt] n. Akzent, *der.* **ac-
centuate** [ək'sentjʊeɪt] v. t. betonen

accept [ək'sept] v. t. **a)** annehmen;
entgegennehmen *(Dank, Spende);*
übernehmen *(Verantwortung);* **b)** *(acknowledge)* akzeptieren. **acceptable**
[ək'septəbl] *adj.* akzeptabel; annehmbar *(Preis, Gehalt).* **acceptance** [ək-
'septəns] n. **a)** Annahme, *die;* **b)** *(acknowledgement)* Anerkennung, *die*

access ['ækses] n. **a)** *(admission)* gain
~: Einlaß finden; **b)** *(opportunity to
use or approach)* Zugang, *der* (to zu).
accessible [ək'sesɪbl] *adj.* **a)** *(reach-
able)* erreichbar; **b)** *(available, understandable)* zugänglich (to für)

accession [ək'seʃn] n. Amtsantritt,
der; ~ [to the throne] Thronbestei-
gung, *die*

accessory [ək'sesərɪ] n. **a)** accessories
pl. Zubehör, *das;* **b)** *(dress article)* Ac-
cessoire, *das*

accident ['æksɪdənt] n. **a)** Unfall, *der;*
b) *(chance)* Zufall, *der;* by ~: zufällig;
c) *(mistake)* Versehen, *das;* by ~: versehentlich. **accidental** [æksɪ'dentl]
adj. *(chance)* zufällig; *(unintended)*
unbeabsichtigt. **acci'dentally** *adv.*
(by chance) zufällig; *(by mistake)* versehentlich

acclaim [ə'kleɪm] v. t. feiern

acclimatize [ə'klaɪmətaɪz] v. t. get or
become ~d sich akklimatisieren

accolade ['ækəleɪd] n. *(praise)* ~[s]
Lob, *das*

accommodate [ə'kɒmədeɪt] v. t. **a)**
unterbringen; *(hold)* Platz bieten
(+ *Dat.*); **b)** *(oblige)* gefällig sein

(+ *Dat.*). **accommodating** [ə'kɒmədeɪtɪŋ] *adj.* zuvorkommend. **accommodation** [əkɒmə'deɪʃn] *n.* Unterkunft, *die*

accompaniment [ə'kʌmpənɪmənt] *n.* Begleitung, *die*

accompanist [ə'kʌmpənɪst] *n.* Begleiter, *der*/Begleiterin, *die*

accompany [ə'kʌmpənɪ] *v.t.* begleiten

accomplice [ə'kʌmplɪs] *n.* Komplize, *der*/Komplizin, *die*

accomplish [ə'kʌmplɪʃ] *v.t.* vollbringen ⟨*Tat*⟩; erfüllen ⟨*Aufgabe*⟩. **accomplished** [ə'kʌmplɪʃt] *adj.* fähig; **he is an ~ speaker/dancer** er ist ein erfahrener Redner/vollendeter Tänzer. **ac'complishment** *n.* a) *(completion)* Vollendung, *die;* b) *(achievement)* Leistung, *die; (skill)* Fähigkeit, *die*

accord [ə'kɔ:d] **1.** *n.* Übereinstimmung, *die; of one's own* ~: aus eigenem Antrieb; **with one** ~: geschlossen. **2.** *v.t.* ~ **sb. sth.** jmdm. etw. gewähren. **accordance** [ə'kɔ:dəns] *n.* **in** ~ **with** in Übereinstimmung mit. **ac'cording** *adv.* ~ **to** nach; ~ **to him** nach seiner Aussage. **ac'cordingly** *adv. (as appropriate)* entsprechend; *(therefore)* folglich

accordion [ə'kɔ:dɪən] *n.* Akkordeon, *das*

accost [ə'kɒst] *v.t.* ansprechen

account [ə'kaʊnt] *n.* a) *(Finance)* Rechnung, *die; (at bank, shop)* Konto, *das;* b) *(consideration)* **take ~ of sth.**, **take sth. into** ~: etw. berücksichtigen; **take no ~ of sth./sb.** etw./jmdn. unberücksichtigt lassen; **don't change your plans on my** ~: ändert nicht meinetwegen eure Pläne; **on** ~ **of** wegen; **on no** ~: auf [gar] keinen Fall; c) *(report)* Bericht, *der;* d) **call sb. to** ~: jmdn. zur Rechenschaft ziehen. **ac'count for** *v.t.* Rechenschaft ablegen über; *(explain)* erklären

accountable [ə'kaʊntəbl] *adj.* verantwortlich

accountancy [ə'kaʊntənsɪ] *n.* Buchhaltung, *die*

accountant [ə'kaʊntənt] *n.* [Bilanz]buchhalter, *der*/-halterin, *die*

ac'count number *n.* Kontonummer, *die*

accrue [ə'kru:] *v.i.* ⟨*Zinsen:*⟩ auflaufen; ~ **to sb.** ⟨*Reichtümer, Einnahmen:*⟩ jmdm. zufließen

accumulate [ə'kju:mjʊleɪt] **1.** *v.t.*

sammeln. **2.** *v.i.* ⟨*Menge, Staub:*⟩ sich ansammeln; ⟨*Geld:*⟩ sich anhäufen. **accumulation** [əkju:mjʊ'leɪʃn] *n.* [An]sammeln, *das; (being accumulated)* Anhäufung, *die*

accuracy ['ækjʊrəsɪ] *n.* Genauigkeit, *die*

accurate ['ækjʊrət] *adj.,* '**accurately** *adv.* genau; *(correct[ly])* richtig

accusation [ækju:'zeɪʃn] *n.* Anschuldigung, *die; (Law)* Anklage, *die*

accusative [ə'kju:zətɪv] *adj. & n.* ~ |*case*| Akkusativ, *der*

accuse [ə'kju:z] *v.t.* beschuldigen; *(Law)* anklagen (of wegen + *Gen.*)

accustom [ə'kʌstəm] *v.t.* gewöhnen (to an + *Akk.*); **grow/be ~ed to sth.** sich an etw. *(Akk.)* gewöhnen/an etw. *(Akk.)* gewöhnt sein. **accustomed** [ə'kʌstəmd] *attrib. adj.* gewohnt; üblich

ace [eɪs] *n.* As, *das*

ache [eɪk] **1.** *v.i.* schmerzen; weh tun. **2.** *n.* Schmerz, *der*

achieve [ə'tʃi:v] *v.t.* zustande bringen; erreichen ⟨*Ziel, Standard*⟩. **a'chievement** *n.* a) *see* achieve: Zustandebringen, *das;* Erreichen, *das;* b) *(thing accomplished)* Leistung, *die*

acid ['æsɪd] **1.** *adj.* sauer. **2.** *n.* Säure, *die.* **acidic** [ə'sɪdɪk] *adj.* säuerlich. **acidity** [ə'sɪdɪtɪ] *n.* Säuregehalt, *der*

acid: ~ **'rain** *n.* saurer Regen; ~ **test** *n. (fig.)* Feuerprobe, *die*

acknowledge [ək'nɒlɪdʒ] *v.t.* a) zugeben ⟨*Tatsache, Fehler, Schuld*⟩; b) sich erkenntlich zeigen für ⟨*Dienste, Bemühungen*⟩; erwidern ⟨*Gruß*⟩; c) bestätigen ⟨*Empfang, Bewerbung*⟩; ~ **a letter** den Empfang eines Briefes bestätigen. **acknowledg[e]ment** [ək'nɒlɪdʒmənt] *n.* a) *(admission)* Eingeständnis, *das;* b) *(thanks)* Dank, *der* (of für); c) *(of letter)* Bestätigung [des Empfangs]

acne ['æknɪ] *n.* Akne, *die*

acorn ['eɪkɔ:n] *n.* Eichel, *die*

acoustic [ə'ku:stɪk] *adj.* akustisch. **a'coustics** *n. pl.* Akustik, *die*

acquaint [ə'kweɪnt] *v.t.* **be ~ed with sb.** mit jmdm. bekannt sein. **acquaintance** [ə'kweɪntəns] *n.* a) ~ **with sb.** Bekanntschaft mit jmdm.; **make sb.'s** ~: jmds. Bekanntschaft machen; b) *(person)* Bekannte, *der/die*

acquiesce [ækwɪ'es] *v.i.* einwilligen (in in + *Akk.*)

acquire [ə'kwaɪə(r)] *v.t.* sich *(Dat.)* anschaffen ⟨*Gegenstände*⟩; erwerben

⟨*Besitz, Kenntnisse*⟩. **acquisition** [ækwɪ'zɪʃn] *n.* Erwerb, *der;* ⟨*thing*⟩ Anschaffung, *die.* **acquisitive** [ə'kwɪzɪtɪv] *adj.* raffsüchtig

acquit [ə'kwɪt] *v. t.,* -tt- freisprechen. **acquittal** [ə'kwɪtl] *n.* Freispruch, *der*

acre ['eɪkə(r)] *n.* Acre, *der*

acrid ['ækrɪd] *adj.* beißend ⟨*Geruch, Rauch*⟩; bitter ⟨*Geschmack*⟩

acrimonious [ækrɪ'məʊnɪəs] *adj.* bitter; erbittert ⟨*Streit*⟩

acrobat ['ækrəbæt] *n.* Akrobat, *der/*Akrobatin, *die.* **acrobatic** [ækrə'bætɪk] *adj.* akrobatisch. **acrobatics** [ækrə'bætɪks] *n.* Akrobatik, *die*

acronym ['ækrənɪm] *n.* Akronym, *das*

across [ə'krɒs] 1. *adv. (from one side to the other)* darüber; *(from here to there)* hinüber; be 9 miles ~: 9 Meilen breit sein. 2. *prep.* über (+ *Akk.*); *(on the other side of)* auf der anderen Seite (+ *Gen.*)

act [ækt] 1. *n.* a) *(deed)* Tat, *die;* b) *(Theatre)* Akt, *der;* c) *(pretence)* Theater, *das;* put on an ~ : Theater spielen; d) *(Law)* Gesetz, *das.* 2. *v. t.* spielen ⟨*Stück*⟩. 3. *v. i.* a) *(perform actions)* handeln; b) *(behave)* sich verhalten; ~ as fungieren als; c) *(perform play)* spielen; d) *(have effect)* ~ on sth. auf etw. *(Akk.)* wirken. '**acting** 1. *n.* *(Theatre etc.)* die Schauspielerei. 2. *adj. (temporary)* stellvertretend

action ['ækʃn] *n.* a) *(doing sth.)* Handeln, *das;* take ~ : Schritte od. etwas unternehmen; put a plan into ~ : einen Plan in die Tat umsetzen; put sth. out of ~ : etw. außer Betrieb setzen; b) *(act)* Tat, *die;* c) *(legal process)* [Gerichts]verfahren, *das;* d) die in ~ : im Kampf fallen. **action** '**replay** *n.* Wiederholung [in Zeitlupe]

activate ['æktɪveɪt] *v. t.* a) in Gang setzen; b) *(Chem., Phys.)* aktivieren

active ['æktɪv] *adj.,* '**actively** *adv.* aktiv

activist ['æktɪvɪst] *n.* Aktivist, *der/*Aktivistin, *die*

activity [æk'tɪvɪtɪ] *n.* Aktivität, *die*

actor ['æktə(r)] *n.* Schauspieler, *der*

actress ['æktrɪs] *n.* Schauspielerin, *die*

actual ['æktʃʊəl] *adj.* eigentlich; wirklich ⟨*Name*⟩. '**actually** *adv. (in fact)* eigentlich; *(by the way)* übrigens; *(believe it or not)* sogar

acumen ['ækjʊmen] *n.* Scharfsinn, *der;* business ~: Geschäftssinn, *der*

acupuncture ['ækjʊpʌnktʃə(r)] *n.* Akupunktur, *die*

acute [ə'kjuːt] *adj.* a) spitz ⟨*Winkel*⟩; b) *(critical; Med.)* akut

AD *abbr.* **Anno Domini** n. Chr.

ad [æd] *n. (coll.)* Annonce, *die*

adamant ['ædəmənt] *adj.* unnachgiebig; be ~ that ...: darauf bestehen, daß ...

adapt [ə'dæpt] *v. t.* a) anpassen (to *Dat.*); ~ oneself to sth. sich an etw. *(Akk.)* gewöhnen; b) bearbeiten ⟨*Text, Theaterstück*⟩. **adaptable** [ə'dæptəbl] *adj.* anpassungsfähig. **adaptation** [ædəp'teɪʃn] *n.* a) Anpassung, *die;* b) *(version)* Adap[ta]tion, *die;* ⟨*of story, text*⟩ Bearbeitung, *die.* **adapter, adaptor** [ə'dæptə(r)] *n.* Adapter, *der*

add [æd] 1. *v. t.* hinzufügen (to *Dat.*); ~ two and two zwei und zwei zusammenzählen. 2. *v. i.* ~ to vergrößern ⟨*Schwierigkeiten, Einkommen*⟩. **add** '**up** 1. *v. i.* ~ up to sth. *(fig.)* auf etw. *(Akk.)* hinauslaufen. 2. *v. t.* zusammenzählen

adder ['ædə(r)] *n.* Viper, *die*

addict 1. ['ædɪkt] *v. t.* be ~ed süchtig sein (to nach). 2. ['ædɪkt] *n.* Süchtige, *der/die.* **addiction** [ə'dɪkʃn] *n.* Sucht, *die* (to nach). **addictive** [ə'dɪktɪv] *adj.* be ~ : süchtig machen

addition [ə'dɪʃn] *n.* a) Hinzufügen, *das;* *(adding up)* Addieren, *das;* *(process)* Addition, *die;* in ~ : außerdem; in ~ to zusätzlich zu; b) *(thing added)* Ergänzung, *die* (to zu). **additional** [ə'dɪʃənl] *adj.* zusätzlich

additive ['ædɪtɪv] *n.* Zusatz, *der*

address [ə'dres] 1. *v. t.* a) *(mark with ~)* adressieren (to an + *Akk.*); *(speak to)* anreden; sprechen zu ⟨*Zuhörern*⟩. 2. *n.* a) *(on letter)* Adresse, *die;* b) *(speech)* Ansprache, *die.* **addressee** [ædre'siː] *n.* Adressat, *der/*Adressatin, *die*

adept ['ædept] *adj.* geschickt (in, at in + *Dat.*)

adequate ['ædɪkwət] *adj.* a) angemessen (to *Dat.*); *(suitable)* passend; b) *(sufficient)* ausreichend. '**adequately** *adv.* a) *(sufficiently)* ausreichend; b) *(suitably)* angemessen ⟨*gekleidet, qualifiziert usw.*⟩

adhere [əd'hɪə(r)] *v. i.* haften, *(by glue)* kleben (to an + *Dat.*). **adhesion** [əd'hiːʒn] *n.* Haften, *das.* **adhesive** [əd'hiːsɪv] 1. *adj.* gummiert ⟨*Briefmarke*⟩; Klebe⟨*band*⟩. 2. *n.* Klebstoff, *der*

adjacent [ə'dʒeɪsənt] *adj.* angrenzend; ~ to neben *(position:* + *Dat.; direction:* + *Akk.)*

adjective ['ædʒɪktɪv] *n.* Adjektiv, *das*
adjoin [ə'dʒɔɪn] *v.t.* grenzen an (+ *Akk.*)
adjourn [ə'dʒɜːn] **1.** *v.t.* (*break off*) unterbrechen; (*put off*) aufschieben. **2.** *v.i.* sich vertagen; ~ **for lunch/half an hour** eine Mittagspause/halbstündige Pause einlegen. **a'djournment** *n.* (*of court*) Vertagung, *die;* (*of meeting*) Unterbrechung, *die*
adjudicate [ə'dʒuːdɪkeɪt] *v.i.* (*in court, tribunal*) das Urteil fällen; (*in contest*) entscheiden
adjust [ə'dʒʌst] **1.** *v.t.* einstellen; ~ **sth. |to sth.|** etw. [an etw. (*Akk.*)] anpassen. **2.** *v.i.* ⟨*Person:*⟩ sich anpassen (**to** an + *Akk.*). **adjustable** [ə'dʒʌstəbl] *adj.* einstellbar; verstellbar ⟨*Gerät*⟩. **a'djustment** *n.* Einstellung, *die;* (*to situation etc.*) Anpassung, *die*
ad-lib [æd'lɪb] **1.** *adj.* improvisiert. **2.** *v.i., -bb-* improvisieren
administer [æd'mɪnɪstə(r)] **a)** (*manage*) verwalten; **b)** leisten ⟨*Hilfe*⟩; verabreichen ⟨*Medikamente*⟩. **administration** [ədmɪnɪ'streɪʃn] *n.* Verwaltung, *die.* **administrative** [əd'mɪnɪstrətɪv] *adj.* Verwaltungs-. **administrator** [əd'mɪnɪstreɪtə(r)] *n.* Administrator, *der;* Verwalter, *der*
admirable ['ædmərəbl] *adj.* bewundernswert
admiral ['ædmərəl] *n.* Admiral, *der*
admiration [ædmə'reɪʃn] *n.* Bewunderung, *die* (**of, for** für)
admire [əd'maɪə(r)] *v.t.* bewundern. **admirer** [əd'maɪərə(r)] *n.* Bewunderer, *der*/Bewunderin, *die*
admission [əd'mɪʃn] *n.* **a)** (*entry*) Zutritt, *der;* **b)** (*charge*) Eintritt, *der;* **c)** (*confession*) Eingeständnis, *das*
admit [əd'mɪt] *v.t., -tt-:* **a)** (*let in*) hinein-/hereinlassen; **b)** (*acknowledge*) zugeben. **admittance** [əd'mɪtəns] *n.* Zutritt, *der.* **admittedly** [əd'mɪtɪdlɪ] *adv.* zugegeben[ermaßen]
admonish [əd'mɒnɪʃ] *v.t.* ermahnen
ado [ə'duː] *n.* **without more ~:** ohne weiteres Aufheben
adolescence [ædə'lesns] *n.* die Zeit des Erwachsenwerdens. **adolescent** [ædə'lesnt] **1.** *n.* Heranwachsende, *der/die.* **2.** *adj.* heranwachsend
adopt [ə'dɒpt] *v.t.* **a)** adoptieren; **b)** (*take over*) annehmen ⟨*Glaube, Kultur*⟩; **c)** (*take up*) übernehmen ⟨*Methode*⟩; ⟨*Standpunkt, Haltung*⟩. **adoption** [ə'dɒpʃn] *n.* **a)** Adoption, *die;* **b)** (*taking over*) Annahme,

die; **c)** (*taking up*) Übernahme, *die;* (*of point of view*) Einnahme, *die*
adorable [ə'dɔːrəbl] *adj.* bezaubernd
adoration [ædə'reɪʃn] *n.* Verehrung, *die*
adore [ə'dɔː(r)] *v.t.* verehren
adorn [ə'dɔːn] *v.t.* schmücken. **a'dornment** *n.* Verzierung, *die;* ~**s** Schmuck, *der*
adrenalin [ə'drenəlɪn] *n.* Adrenalin, *das*
Adriatic [eɪdrɪ'ætɪk] *pr. n.* ~ **[Sea]** Adriatisches Meer
adrift [ə'drɪft] *adj.* **be ~:** treiben
adroit [ə'drɔɪt] *adj.* geschickt
adulation [ædjʊ'leɪʃn] *n.* Vergötterung, *die*
adult ['ædʌlt, ə'dʌlt] **1.** *adj.* erwachsen. **2.** *n.* Erwachsene, *der/die*
adulterate [ə'dʌltəreɪt] *v.t.* verunreinigen
adultery [ə'dʌltərɪ] *n.* Ehebruch, *der*
advance [əd'vɑːns] **1.** *v.t.* **a)** (*also Mil.*) vorrücken lassen; **b)** (*put forward*) vorbringen ⟨*Plan, Meinung*⟩; **c)** (*further*) fördern; **d)** (*pay before due date*) vorschießen; ⟨*Bank:*⟩ leihen. **2.** *v.i.* **a)** (*also Mil.*) vorrücken; ⟨*Prozession:*⟩ sich vorwärts bewegen; **b)** (*fig.: make progress*) vorankommen. **3.** *n.* **a)** Vorrücken, *das;* (*fig.: progress*) Fortschritt, *der;* **b)** *usu. in pl.* (*personal approach*) Annäherungsversuch, *der;* **c)** (*on salary*) Vorschuß, *der;* **d) in ~:** im voraus. **advanced** [əd'vɑːnst] *adj.* fortgeschritten
advantage [əd'vɑːntɪdʒ] *n.* Vorteil, *der;* **take ~ of sb.** jmdn. ausnutzen; **be to one's ~:** für jmdn. von Vorteil sein; **turn sth. to [one's] ~:** etw. ausnutzen. **advantageous** [ædvən'teɪdʒəs] *adj.* vorteilhaft
advent ['ædvent] *n.* Beginn, *der;* **A~:** Advent, *der*
adventure [əd'ventʃə(r)] *n.* Abenteuer, *das.* **adventurous** [əd'ventʃərəs] *adj.* abenteuerlustig
adverb ['ædvɜːb] *n.* Adverb, *das*
adversary ['ædvəsərɪ] *n.* (*enemy*) Widersacher, *der*/Widersacherin, *die;* (*opponent*) Kontrahent, *der*/Kontrahentin, *die*
adverse ['ædvɜːs] *adj.* **a)** (*unfavourable*) ungünstig; **b)** (*contrary*) widrig ⟨*Wind, Umstände*⟩. **adversity** [əd'vɜːsɪtɪ] *n.* **a)** *no pl.* Not, *die;* **b)** *usu. in pl.* Widrigkeit, *die*
advert ['ædvɜːt] *n.* (*Brit. coll.*) *see* **advertisement**

advertise ['ædvətaɪz] **1.** *v.t.* werben für; *(by small ad)* inserieren; ausschreiben ⟨*Stelle*⟩. **2.** *v.i.* werben; *(in newspaper)* inserieren; annoncieren. **advertisement** [əd'vɜːtɪsmənt] *n.* Anzeige, *die;* TV ~: Fernsehspot, *der.* **advertiser** ['ædvətaɪzə(r)] *n. (in newspaper)* Inserent, *der/*Inserentin, *die.* **advertising** ['ædvətaɪzɪŋ] *n.* Werbung, *die; attrib.* Werbe-

advice [əd'vaɪs] *n.* Rat, *der;* **take sb.'s** ~: jmds. Rat *(Dat.)* folgen

advisable [əd'vaɪzəbl] *adj.* ratsam

advise [əd'vaɪz] *v.t.* beraten; ~ **sth.** zu etw. raten; *(inform)* unterrichten (of über + *Akk.*). **adviser, advisor** [əd'vaɪzə(r)] *n.* Berater, *der/*Beraterin, *die.* **advisory** [əd'vaɪzərɪ] *adj.* beratend

advocate 1. ['ædvəkət] *n. (of a cause)* Befürworter, *der/*Befürworterin, *die; (Law)* [Rechts]anwalt, *der/-*anwältin, *die.* **2.** ['ædvəkeɪt] *v.t.* befürworten

aerial ['eərɪəl] **1.** *adj.* Luft-. **2.** *n.* Antenne, *die*

aero- [eərəʊ] *in comb.* Aero-

aerody'namic *adj.* aerodynamisch

aeronautics [eərə'nɔːtɪks] *n.* Aeronautik, *die*

aeroplane ['eərəpleɪn] *n. (Brit.)* Flugzeug, *das*

aerosol ['eərəsɒl] *n. (spray)* Spray, *der od. das; (container)* ~ [spray] Spraydose, *die*

aesthetic [iːs'θetɪk] *adj.* ästhetisch

afar [ə'fɑː] *adv.* from ~: aus der Ferne

affable ['æfəbl] *adj.* freundlich

affair [ə'feə(r)] *n.* **a)** *(concern)* Angelegenheit, *die;* **b)** *in pl. (business)* Geschäfte *Pl.;* **c)** *(love* ~*)* Affäre, *die*

affect [ə'fekt] *v.t.* **a)** sich auswirken auf (+ *Akk.*); **b)** *(emotionally)* betroffen machen

affectation [æfek'teɪʃn] *n. (studied display)* Verstellung, *die; (artificiality)* Affektiertheit, *die*

affected [ə'fektɪd] *adj.* affektiert; gekünstelt ⟨*Sprache, Stil*⟩

affection [ə'fekʃn] *n.* Zuneigung, *die.* **affectionate** [ə'fekʃənət] *adj.* anhänglich; liebevoll ⟨*Umarmung*⟩. **af'fectionately** *adv.* liebevoll

affiliate [ə'fɪlɪeɪt] *v.t.* be ~d to sth. an etw. *(Akk.)* angegliedert sein

affinity [ə'fɪnɪtɪ] *n.* **a)** *(relationship)* Verwandtschaft, *die* (to mit); **b)** *(liking)* Neigung, *die* (for zu); feel an ~ to or for sb./sth. sich zu jmdm./etw. hingezogen fühlen

affirm [ə'fɜːm] *v.t. (assert)* bekräftigen ⟨*Absicht*⟩; beteuern ⟨*Unschuld*⟩; *(state as a fact)* bestätigen. **affirmation** [æfə'meɪʃn] *n. (of intention)* Bekräftigung, *die; (of fact)* Bestätigung, *die.* **affirmative** [ə'fɜːmətɪv] **1.** *adj.* affirmativ; bejahend ⟨*Antwort*⟩. **2.** *n.* answer in the ~: bejahend antworten

afflict [ə'flɪkt] *v.t. (physically)* plagen; *(mentally)* quälen; peinigen; be ~ed with sth. von etw. befallen sein. **affliction** [ə'flɪkʃn] *n.* Leiden, *das*

affluence ['æflʊəns] *n.* Reichtum, *der.* **affluent** ['æflʊənt] *adj.* reich

afford [ə'fɔːd] *v.t.* **a)** sich *(Dat.)* leisten; **b)** *(provide)* bieten; gewähren ⟨*Schutz*⟩

affray [ə'freɪ] *n.* Schlägerei, *die*

affront [ə'frʌnt] **1.** *v.t.* beleidigen. **2.** *n.* Beleidigung, *die*

afield [ə'fiːld] *adv.* far ~ *(direction)* weit hinaus; *(place)* weit draußen

afloat [ə'fləʊt] *pred. adj.* **a)** *(floating)* über Wasser; flott ⟨*Schiff*⟩; **b)** *(at sea)* auf See; be ~: auf dem Meer treiben

afoot [ə'fʊt] *pred. adj.* im Gange

aforementioned [ə'fɔːmenʃnd], **aforesaid** [ə'fɔːsed] *adjs.* obenerwähnt *od. -*genannt

afraid [ə'freɪd] *adj.* be ~ [of sb./sth.] [vor jmdm./etw.] Angst haben; be ~ to do sth. Angst davor haben, etw. zu tun; I'm ~ so/not ich fürchte ja/nein

afresh [ə'freʃ] *adv.* von neuem

Africa ['æfrɪkə] *pr. n.* Afrika *(das).* **African** ['æfrɪkən] **1.** *adj.* afrikanisch. **2.** *n.* Afrikaner, *der/*Afrikanerin, *die*

after ['ɑːftə(r)] **1.** *adv.* **a)** *(later)* danach; **b)** *(behind)* hinterher. **2.** *prep.* **a)** *(in time)* nach; two days ~ zwei Tage danach; **b)** *(behind)* hinter (+ *Dat.*); **c)** ask ~ sb./sth. nach jmdm./etw. fragen; **d)** ~ all schließlich. **3.** *conj.* nachdem. '**after-care** *n. (Med.)* Nachbehandlung, *die.* '**after-effect** *n.* Nachwirkung, *die*

aftermath ['ɑːftəmæθ, 'ɑːftəmɑːθ] *n.* Nachwirkungen *Pl.*

after: ~'noon *n.* Nachmittag, *der;* this/tomorrow ~: heute/morgen nachmittag; in the ~: am Nachmittag; *(regularly)* nachmittags; ~shave *n.* After-shave, *das;* ~'thought *n.* nachträglicher Einfall

afterwards ['ɑːftəwədz] *adv.* danach

again [ə'gen, ə'geɪn] *adv.* wieder; *(one more time)* noch einmal; ~ and ~, time and [time] ~: immer wieder; back ~: wieder zurück

against [ə'genst, ə'geɪnst] *prep.* gegen
age [eɪdʒ] 1. *n.* a) Alter, *das; what ~ are you?* wie alt bist du?; *at the ~ of* im Alter von; *come of ~:* volljährig werden; *be under ~:* zu jung sein; b) *(great period)* Zeitalter, *das; ~s (coll.: a long time)* eine Ewigkeit. 2. *v.t.* altern lassen. 3. *v.i.* altern. **aged** *adj.* a) [eɪdʒd] *be ~ five* fünf Jahre alt sein; *a boy ~ five* ein fünfjähriger Junge; b) ['eɪdʒɪd] *(elderly)* bejahrt
age: ~**-group** *n.* Altersgruppe, *die;* ~ **limit** *n.* Altersgrenze, *die*
agency ['eɪdʒənsɪ] *n.* a) *(business establishment)* Geschäftsstelle, *die; (news/ advertising ~)* Agentur, *die*
agenda [ə'dʒendə] *n.* Tagesordnung, *die*
agent ['eɪdʒənt] *n.* Vertreter, *der/*Vertreterin, *die; (spy)* Agent, *der/*Agentin, *die*
aggravate ['ægrəveɪt] *v.t.* a) *(make worse)* verschlimmern; b) *(annoy)* aufregen; ärgern. **aggravating** ['ægrə-veɪtɪŋ] *adj.* ärgerlich. **aggravation** [ægrə'veɪʃn] *n.* a) Verschlimmerung, *die;* b) *(annoyance)* Ärger, *der*
aggregate ['ægrɪgət] 1. *n.* Gesamtmenge, *die.* 2. *adj.* gesamt
aggression [ə'greʃn] *n.* Aggression, *die*
aggressive [ə'gresɪv] *adj.,* ag'**gressively** *adv.* aggressiv. ag'**gressiveness** *n.* Aggressivität, *die*
aggressor [ə'gresə(r)] *n.* Aggressor, *der*
aggrieved [ə'griːvd] *v.t.* a) *(resentful)* verärgert; *(offended)* gekränkt
aghast [ə'gɑːst] *pred. adj.* bestürzt
agile ['ædʒaɪl] *adj.* beweglich; flink *⟨Bewegung⟩.* **agility** [ə'dʒɪlɪtɪ] *n.* Beweglichkeit, *die; (of movement)* Flinkheit, *die*
agitate ['ædʒɪteɪt] 1. *v.t.* a) *(shake)* schütteln; b) *(disturb)* erregen. 2. *v.i.* agitieren. **agitation** [ædʒɪ'teɪʃn] *n.* a) *(shaking)* Schütteln, *das;* b) *(emotional)* Erregung, *die.* **agitator** ['ædʒɪteɪtə(r)] *n.* Agitator, *der*
agnostic [æg'nɒstɪk] *n.* Agnostiker, *der/*Agnostikerin, *die*
ago [ə'gəʊ] *adv.* *ten years ~:* vor zehn Jahren; *[not] long ~:* vor [nicht] langer Zeit
agog [ə'gɒg] *pred. adj.* gespannt
agonize ['ægənaɪz] *v.i.* ~ *over sth.* sich *(Dat.)* den Kopf über etw. *(Akk.)* zermartern
agony ['ægənɪ] *n.* Todesqualen *Pl.*

agree [ə'griː] 1. *v.i.* a) *(consent)* einverstanden sein **(to, with** mit); b) *(hold similar opinion)* einer Meinung sein; **they ~d [with me]** sie waren derselben Meinung [wie ich]; c) *(reach similar opinion)* ~ **on** sth. sich über etw. *(Akk.)* einigen; d) *(harmonize)* übereinstimmen; e) ~ **with** sb. *(suit)* jmdm. bekommen. 2. *v.t.* vereinbaren. **agreeable** [ə'griːəbl] *adj.* a) *(pleasing)* angenehm; b) **be ~ [to** sth.] [mit etw.] einverstanden sein. **agreeably** [ə'griːəblɪ] *adv.* angenehm. **agreed** [ə'griːd] *adj.* einig; vereinbart *⟨Summe, Zeit⟩.* a'**greement** *n.* Übereinstimmung, *die; be in ~* **[about** sth.] sich *(Dat.)* [über etw. *(Akk.)*] einig sein
agricultural [ægrɪ'kʌltʃərl] *adj.* landwirtschaftlich
agriculture ['ægrɪkʌltʃə(r)] *n.* Landwirtschaft, *die*
aground [ə'graʊnd] *adj.* **go** *or* **run ~:** auf Grund laufen
ahead [ə'hed] *adv.* voraus; ~ **of** vor *(+ Dat.);* **be ~ of the others** *(fig.)* den anderen voraus sein
aid [eɪd] 1. *v.t.* a) ~ sb. **[to do** sth.] jmdm. helfen[, etw. zu tun]; ~**ed by** unterstützt von; b) *(promote)* fördern. 2. *n.* a) *(help)* Hilfe, *die; with the ~ of* sth./sb. mit Hilfe einer Sache *(Gen.)/*mit jmds. Hilfe; *in ~ of* sb./sth. zugunsten von jmdm./etw.; b) *(source of help)* Hilfsmittel, *das* (zu für)
aide [eɪd] *n.* Berater, *der/*Beraterin, *die*
Aids [eɪdz] *n.* Aids *(das)*
ailment ['eɪlmənt] *n.* Gebrechen, *das*
aim [eɪm] 1. *v.t.* ausrichten *⟨Schußwaffe, Rakete⟩;* ~ **at** sb./sth. etw. auf jmdn./etw. richten. 2. *v.i.* a) zielen **(at** auf *+ Akk.);* b) ~ **to do** sth. beabsichtigen, etw. zu tun; ~ **at** *or* **for** sth. *(fig.)* etwas anstreben. 3. *n.* Ziel, *das;* **take ~ [at** sth./sb.] [auf etw./jmdn.] zielen. '**aimless** *adj.,* '**aimlessly** *adv.* ziellos
air [eə(r)] 1. *n.* a) Luft, *die; be/go on the ~:* senden; *(Programm:)* gesendet werden; **by ~:** mit dem Flugzeug; *(by ~ mail)* mit Luftpost; b) *(facial expression)* Miene, *die;* c) **put on ~s** sich aufspielen. 2. *v.t.* *(ventilate)* lüften; *(make public)* [öffentlich] darlegen
air: ~**-bed** *n.* Luftmatratze, *die;* ~**borne** *adj.* **be ~borne** sich in der Luft befinden; ~**-conditioned** *adj.* klimatisiert; ~**-conditioning** *n.* Klimaanlage, *die;* ~**craft** *n., pl.* same

Flugzeug, *das*; ~**craft-carrier** *n.* Flugzeugträger, *der*; ~ **fare** *n.* Flugpreis, *der*; ~**field** *n.* Flugplatz, *der*; ~ **force** *n.* Luftwaffe, *die*; ~**gun** *n.* Luftgewehr, *das*; ~ **hostess** *n.* Stewardeß, *die*; ~ **letter** *n.* Aerogramm, *das*; ~**line** *n.* Fluggesellschaft, *die*; ~ **mail** *n.* Luftpost, *die*; **by** ~ **mail** mit Luftpost; ~**man** ['eəmən] *n., pl.* ~**men** [~mən] Flieger, *der*; ~**plane** *n.* (*Amer.*) Flugzeug, *das*; ~**port** *n.* Flughafen, *der*; ~ **raid** *n.* Luftangriff, *der*; ~-**raid shelter** *n.* Luftschutzraum, *der*; ~**ship** *n.* Luftschiff, *das*; ~**sick** *adj.* luftkrank; ~**tight** *adj.* luftdicht; ~-**traffic controller** *n.* Fluglotse, *der*

airy *adj.* luftig ⟨*Büro, Zimmer*⟩

aisle [aɪl] *n.* Gang, *der*; (*of church*) Seitenschiff, *das*

ajar [ə'dʒɑː(r)] *adj.* **be** ~: einen Spaltbreit offenstehen

akin [ə'kɪn] *adj.* **be** ~ **to sth.** einer Sache (*Dat.*) ähnlich sein

alarm [ə'lɑːm] **1.** *n.* **a)** Alarm, *der*; **give or raise the** ~: Alarm schlagen; **b)** (*fear*) Angst, *die.* **2.** *v. t.* aufschrecken. **a'larm clock** *n.* Wecker, *der*

alas [ə'læs] *int.* ach

albatross ['ælbətrɒs] *n.* Albatros, *der*

album ['ælbəm] *n.* Album, *das*

alcohol ['ælkəhɒl] *n.* Alkohol, *der.* **al'coholic** [ælkə'hɒlɪk] **1.** *adj.* alkoholisch. **2.** *n.* Alkoholiker, *der*/Alkoholikerin, *die.* **alcoholism** ['ælkəhɒlɪzm] *n.* Alkoholismus, *der*

alcove ['ælkəʊv] *n.* Alkoven, *der*

ale [eɪl] *n.* Ale, *das*

alert [ə'lɜːt] **1.** *adj.* wachsam. **2.** *n.* Alarmbereitschaft, *die*; **on the** ~: auf der Hut. **3.** *v. t.* alarmieren; ~ **sb.** [**to sth.**] jmdn. [vor etw. (*Dat.*)] warnen

'A level *n.* (*Brit. Sch.*) ≈ Abitur, *das*

algebra ['ældʒɪbrə] *n.* Algebra, *die*

Algeria [æl'dʒɪərɪə] *pr. n.* Algerien (*das*)

alias ['eɪlɪəs] **1.** *adv.* alias. **2.** *n.* angenommener Name

alibi ['ælɪbaɪ] *n.* Alibi, *das*

alien ['eɪlɪən] **1.** *adj.* **a)** (*strange*) fremd; **b)** (*foreign*) ausländisch. **2.** *n.* **a)** (*from another world*) Außerirdische, *der*/*die*; **b)** (*Admin.: foreigner*) Ausländer, *der*/Ausländerin, *die.* **alienate** ['eɪlɪəneɪt] *v. t.* befremden. **alienation** [eɪlɪə'neɪʃn] *n.* Entfremdung, *die*

¹alight [ə'laɪt] *v. i.* **a)** aussteigen (*from* aus); **b)** ⟨*Vogel:*⟩ sich niedersetzen

²alight *adj.* **be/catch** ~: brennen; **set sth.** ~: etw. in Brand setzen

align [ə'laɪn] *v. t.* **a)** (*place in a line*) ausrichten; **b)** (*bring into line*) in eine Linie bringen. **a'lignment** *n.* Ausrichtung, *die*; **out of** ~: nicht richtig ausgerichtet

alike [ə'laɪk] *pred. adj.* ähnlich; (*indistinguishable*) gleich

alimony ['ælɪmənɪ] *n.* Unterhaltszahlung, *die*

alive [ə'laɪv] *pred. adj.* **a)** lebendig; **b)** (*aware*) **be** ~ **to sth.** sich (*Dat.*) einer Sache (*Gen.*) bewußt sein; **c)** (*swarming*) **be** ~ **with** wimmeln von

alkali ['ælkəlaɪ] *n., pl.* ~**s** *or* ~**es** Alkali, *das*

all [ɔːl] **1.** *attrib. adj.* **a)** (*entire extent or quantity of*) ganz; ~ **day** den ganzen Tag; ~ **my money** all mein Geld; **mein ganzes Geld; b)** (*entire number of*) alle; ~ **the books** alle Bücher; ~ **my books** all[e] meine Bücher; ~ **the others** alle anderen; **c)** (*any whatever*) jeglicher/jegliche/jegliches; **d)** (*greatest possible*) **in** ~ **innocence** in aller Unschuld. **2.** *n.* **a)** (~ *persons*) alle; ~ **of us** wir alle; **the happiest of** ~: der/die Glücklichste unter *od.* von allen; **b)** (*every bit*) ~ **of it** alles; ~ **of the money** das ganze Geld; **c)** ~ **of** (*coll.: as much as*) **be** ~ **of seven feet tall** gut sieben Fuß groß sein; **d)** (~ *things*) alles; ~ **I need is the money** ich brauche nur das Geld; **that is** ~: das ist alles; **the most beautiful of** ~: der/die/das Schönste von allen; **most of** ~: am meisten; **it was** ~ **but impossible** es war fast unmöglich; **it's** ~ **the same to me** es ist mir ganz egal; **can I help you at** ~? kann ich Ihnen irgendwie behilflich sein?; **she has no talent at** ~: sie hat überhaupt kein Talent; **nothing at** ~: gar nichts; **not at** ~ **happy/well** überhaupt nicht glücklich/gesund; **not at** ~! überhaupt nicht!; (*acknowledging thanks*) gern geschehen!; **if at** ~: wenn überhaupt; **in** ~: insgesamt; **e)** (*Sport*) **two** [**goals**] ~: zwei zu zwei; (*Tennis*) **thirty** ~: dreißig beide. **3.** *adv.* ganz; ~ **but** fast; ~ **the better/worse** [**for that**] um so besser/schlimmer; ~ **at once** (*suddenly*) plötzlich; **be** ~ **'in** (*exhausted*) total erledigt sein (*ugs.*); **sth. is** ~ **right** etw. ist in Ordnung; (*tolerable*) etw. ist ganz gut; **I'm** ~ **right** mir geht es ganz gut; **yes,** ~ **right** ja, gut; **it's** ~ **right by me** das ist mir recht

allay [əˈleɪ] *v. t.* zerstreuen ⟨*Besorgnis, Befürchtungen*⟩
all-'clear *n.* Entwarnung, *die*
allegation [ælɪˈgeɪʃn] *n.* Behauptung, *die*
allege [əˈledʒ] *v. t.* behaupten. **alleged** [əˈledʒd] *adj.,* **allegedly** [əˈledʒɪdlɪ] *adv.* angeblich
allegiance [əˈliːdʒəns] *n.* Loyalität, *die* (to gegenüber)
allegory [ˈælɪgərɪ] *n.* Allegorie, *die*
allergic [əˈlɜːdʒɪk] *adj.* allergisch (to gegen)
allergy [ˈælədʒɪ] *n.* Allergie, *die*
alleviate [əˈliːvɪeɪt] *v. t.* abschwächen
alley [ˈælɪ] *n.* [schmale] Gasse
alliance [əˈlaɪəns] *n.* Bündnis, *das; (league)* Allianz, *die*
allied [ˈælaɪd] *adj.* be ~ to or with sb./ sth. mit jmdm./etw. verbündet sein
alligator [ˈælɪgeɪtə(r)] *n.* Alligator, *der*
'all-in *adj.* Pauschal-
allocate [ˈæləkeɪt] *v. t.* zuweisen, zuteilen (to *Dat.*). **allocation** [ælə-ˈkeɪʃn] *n.* Zuweisung, *die; (ration)* Zuteilung, *die*
allot [əˈlɒt] *v. t.,* -tt-: ~ sth. to sb. jmdm. etw. zuteilen. **al'lotment** *n. (Brit.: plot of land)* ≈ Schrebergarten, *der*
allow [əˈlaʊ] 1. *v. t.* erlauben; zulassen; ~ sb. to do sth. jmdm. erlauben, etw. zu tun; be ~ed to do sth. etw. tun dürfen. 2. *v. i.* ~ for sth. etw. berücksichtigen. **allowance** [əˈlaʊəns] *n.* a) Zuteilung, *die; (for special expenses)* Zuschuß, *der;* b) make ~s for sth./sb. etw./jmdn. berücksichtigen
alloy [ˈælɔɪ] *n.* Legierung, *die*
all: **~-round** *adj.* Allround-; **~-'rounder** *n.* Allroundtalent, *das;* **~-time** *adj.* **~-time record** absoluter Rekord
allude [əˈluːd] *v. i.* ~ to sich beziehen auf (+ *Akk.*); *(indirectly)* anspielen auf (+ *Akk.*). **allusion** [əˈluːʒn] *n.* Hinweis, *der; (indirect)* Anspielung, *die*
ally [ˈælaɪ] *n.* Verbündete, *der/die;* the Allies die Alliierten
almighty [ɔːlˈmaɪtɪ] *adj.* allmächtig; the A~: der Allmächtige
almond [ˈɑːmənd] *n.* Mandel, *die*
almost [ˈɔːlməʊst] *adv.* fast; beinahe
alms [ɑːmz] *n.* Almosen, *das*
alone [əˈləʊn] 1. *pred. adj.* allein; alleine *(ugs.).* 2. *adv.* allein
along [əˈlɒŋ] 1. *prep.* entlang *(position:* + *Dat.; direction:* + *Akk.).* 2. *adv.*

weiter; **I'll be ~ shortly** ich komme gleich; **all ~:** die ganze Zeit [über].
along'side 1. *adv.* daneben. 2. *prep.* neben *(position:* + *Dat.; direction:* + *Akk.)*
aloof [əˈluːf] 1. *adv.* abseits; **hold ~ from sb.** sich von jmdm. fernhalten. 2. *adj.* distanziert
aloud [əˈlaʊd] *adv.* laut; **read [sth.] ~:** [etw.] vorlesen
alphabet [ˈælfəbet] *n.* Alphabet, *das.* **alphabetical** [ælfəˈbetɪkl] *adj.,* **alpha'betically** *adv.* alphabetisch
alpine [ˈælpaɪn] *adj.* alpin
Alps [ælps] *pr. n. pl.* the ~: die Alpen
already [ɔːlˈredɪ] *adv.* schon
Alsation [ælˈseɪʃn] *n.* [deutscher] Schäferhund
also [ˈɔːlsəʊ] *adv.* auch; *(moreover)* außerdem
altar [ˈɔːltə(r), ˈɒltə(r)] *n.* Altar, *der*
alter [ˈɔːltə(r), ˈɒltə(r)] 1. *v. t.* ändern. 2. *v. i.* sich verändern. **alteration** [ɔːltə-ˈreɪʃn, ɒltəˈreɪʃn] *n.* Änderung, *die*
alternate 1. [ɔːlˈtɜːnət] *adj.* sich abwechselnd. 2. [ˈɔːltəneɪt] *v. t.* abwechseln lassen. 3. [ˈɔːltəneɪt] *v. i.* sich abwechseln. **al'ternately** *adv.* abwechselnd
alternative [ɔːlˈtɜːnətɪv] 1. *adj.* alternativ; Alternativ-. 2. *n.* a) *(choice)* Alternative, *die;* b) *(possibility)* Möglichkeit, *die.* **al'ternatively** *adv.* oder aber; or ~: oder aber auch
although [ɔːlˈðəʊ] *conj.* obwohl
altitude [ˈæltɪtjuːd] *n.* Höhe, *die*
altogether [ɔːltəˈgeðə(r)] *adv.* völlig; *(on the whole)* im großen und ganzen; *(in total)* insgesamt; **not ~** [true/convincing] nicht ganz [wahr/überzeugend]
altruistic [æltrʊˈɪstɪk] *adj.* altruistisch
aluminium [æljʊˈmɪnɪəm] *(Brit.),* **aluminum** [əˈluːmɪnəm] *(Amer.)* ns. Aluminium, *das*
always [ˈɔːlweɪz] *adv.* immer; *(repeatedly)* ständig
AM *abbr.* **amplitude modulation** AM
am *see* be
a.m. [eɪˈem] *adv.* vormittags; [at] one/ four ~: [um] ein/vier Uhr früh
amalgamate [əˈmælgəmeɪt] 1. *v. t.* vereinigen. 2. *v. i.* sich vereinigen; ⟨*Firmen:*⟩ fusionieren. **amalgamation** [əmælgəˈmeɪʃn] *n.* Vereinigung, *die; (of firms)* Fusion, *die*
amass [əˈmæs] *v. t.* anhäufen
amateur [ˈæmətə(r)] *n.* Amateur, *der; attrib.* Amateur-; Laien-. **amateur-**

ish ['æmətərɪʃ] *adj.* laienhaft; amateurhaft

amaze [ə'meɪz] *v. t.* verblüffen; verwundern. **a'mazement** *n.* Verblüffung, *die*; Verwunderung, *die.* **amazing** [ə'meɪzɪŋ] *adj. (remarkable)* erstaunlich; *(astonishing)* verblüffend

Amazon ['æməzən] *pr. n.* the ~: der Amazonas

ambassador [æm'bæsədə(r)] *n.* Botschafter, *der*/Botschafterin, *die*

amber ['æmbə(r)] **1.** *n.* a) Bernstein, *der*; b) *(traffic light)* Gelb, *das.* **2.** *adj.* Bernstein-; *(colour)* bernsteinfarben; gelb ⟨*Verkehrslicht*⟩

ambiguity [æmbɪ'gjuːɪtɪ] *n.* Zweideutigkeit, *die*

ambiguous [æm'bɪgjʊəs] *adj.* zweideutig

ambition [æm'bɪʃn] *n.* Ehrgeiz, *der*; *(aspiration)* Ambition, *die.* **ambitious** [æm'bɪʃəs] *adj.* ehrgeizig

ambivalent [æm'bɪvələnt] *adj.* ambivalent

amble ['æmbl] *v. i.* schlendern

ambulance ['æmbjʊləns] *n.* Krankenwagen, *der*; Ambulanz, *die*

ambush ['æmbʊʃ] **1.** *n.* Hinterhalt, *der*; lie in ~: im Hinterhalt liegen. **2.** *v. t.* [aus dem Hinterhalt] überfallen

amen [ɑː'men, eɪ'men] **1.** *int.* amen. **2.** *n.* Amen, *das*

amenable [ə'miːnəbl] *adj.* zugänglich, aufgeschlossen (**to** *Dat.*)

amend [ə'mend] *v. t.* berichtigen; abändern ⟨*Gesetzentwurf, Antrag*⟩. **a'mendment** *n.* *(to motion)* Abänderungsantrag, *der*; *(to bill)* Änderungsantrag, *der*

amends [ə'mendz] *n. pl.* make ~ [to sb.] es [bei jmdm.] wiedergutmachen; make ~ for sth. etw. wiedergutmachen

amenity [ə'miːnɪtɪ] *n., usu. in pl.* amenities *(of town)* kulturelle und Freizeiteinrichtungen

America [ə'merɪkə] *pr. n.* Amerika *(das).* **American** [ə'merɪkən] **1.** *adj.* amerikanisch; **sb. is** ~: jmd. ist Amerikaner/Amerikanerin. **2.** *n. (person)* Amerikaner, *der*/Amerikanerin, *die*. **Americanize** [ə'merɪkənaɪz] *v. t.* amerikanisieren

amiable ['eɪmɪəbl] *adj.* umgänglich

amicable ['æmɪkəbl] *adj.* freundschaftlich; gütlich ⟨*Einigung*⟩. **amicably** ['æmɪkəblɪ] *adv.* in [aller] Freundschaft

amid[st] [ə'mɪd(st)] *prep.* inmitten; *(fig.: during)* bei

amiss [ə'mɪs] **1.** *pred. adj.* verkehrt; **is anything** ~? stimmt irgend etwas nicht? **2.** *adv.* **take sth.** ~: etw. übelnehmen

ammonia [ə'məʊnɪə] *n.* Ammoniak, *das*

ammunition [æmjʊ'nɪʃn] *n.* Munition, *die*

amnesia [æm'niːzɪə] *n.* Amnesie, *die*

amnesty ['æmnɪstɪ] *n.* Amnestie, *die*

amok [ə'mɒk] *adv.* **run** ~: Amok laufen

among[st] [ə'mʌŋ(st)] *prep.* unter (+ *Dat.*); ~ **other things** unter anderem; **they often quarrel** ~ **themselves** sie streiten oft miteinander

amoral [eɪ'mɒrl] *adj.* amoralisch

amorphous [ə'mɔːfəs] *adj.* formlos; amorph ⟨*Masse*⟩

amount [ə'maʊnt] **1.** *v. i.* ~ **to sth.** sich auf etw. *(Akk.)* belaufen; *(fig.)* etw. bedeuten. **2.** *n.* a) *(total)* Betrag, *der*; Summe, *die*; b) *(quantity)* Menge, *die*

amp [æmp] *n.* Ampere, *das*

amphibian [æm'fɪbɪən] **1.** *adj.* amphibisch. **2.** *n.* Amphibie, *die.* **amphibious** [æm'fɪbɪəs] *adj.* amphibisch

amphitheatre ['æmfɪθɪətə(r)] *n.* Amphitheater, *das*

ample ['æmpl] *adj.* a) *(spacious)* weitläufig ⟨*Garten, Räume*⟩; reichhaltig ⟨*Mahl*⟩; b) *(enough)* ~ **room/food** reichlich Platz/zu essen

amplifier ['æmplɪfaɪə(r)] *n.* Verstärker, *der*

amplify ['æmplɪfaɪ] *v. t.* verstärken; *(enlarge on)* weiter ausführen

amputate ['æmpjʊteɪt] *v. t.* amputieren. **amputation** [æmpjʊ'teɪʃn] *n.* Amputation, *die*

amuse [ə'mjuːz] *v. t.* a) *(interest)* unterhalten; ~ **oneself by doing sth.** sich *(Dat.)* die Zeit damit vertreiben, etw. zu tun; b) *(make laugh or smile)* amüsieren. **a'musement** *n.* Belustigung, *die*; ~ **arcade** Spielhalle, *die.* **amusing** [ə'mjuːzɪŋ] *adj.* amüsant

an [ən, *stressed* æn] *indef. art. see also* ²**a**: ein/eine/ein

anaemia [ə'niːmɪə] *n.* Blutarmut, *die*; Anämie, *die.* **anaemic** [ə'niːmɪk] *adj.* blutarm; anämisch

anaesthetic [ænɪs'θetɪk] *n.* Anästhetikum, *das*; general ~: Narkosemittel, *das*; local ~: Lokalanästhetikum, *das*

anagram ['ænəgræm] *n.* Anagramm, *das*

analogy [ə'nælədʒɪ] *n.* Analogie, *die*

analyse ['ænəlaɪz] *v. t.* analysieren.

analysis [ə'nælɪsɪs] *n., pl.* **analyses** [ə'nælɪsi:z] Analyse, *die.* **analyst** ['ænəlɪst] *n.* **a)** (*Psych.*) Analytiker, *der*/Analytikerin, *die;* **b)** (*Econ., Polit., etc.*) Experte, *der.* **analytic** [ænə'lɪtɪk], **analytical** [ænə'lɪtɪkl] *adj.* analytisch. **analyze** (*Amer.*) *see* **analyse**

anarchist ['ænəkɪst] *n.* Anarchist, *der*/Anarchistin, *die*

anarchy ['ænəkɪ] *n.* Anarchie, *die*

anatomical [ænə'tɒmɪkl] *adj.* anatomisch

anatomy [ə'nætəmɪ] *n.* Anatomie, *die*

ancestor ['ænsestə(r)] *n.* Vorfahr, *der.*

ancestry ['ænsestrɪ] *n.* Abstammung, *die*

anchor ['æŋkə(r)] **1.** *n.* Anker, *der.* **2.** *v. t.* verankern. **3.** *v. i.* ankern. **anchorage** ['æŋkərɪdʒ] *n.* Ankerplatz, *der*

anchovy ['æntʃəvɪ] *n.* Sardelle, *die*

ancient ['eɪnʃənt] *adj.* alt; historisch ⟨*Gebäude usw.*⟩; (*of antiquity*) antik

and [ənd, *stressed* ænd] *conj.* und; **for weeks ~ weeks** wochenlang; **better ~ better** immer besser

anecdote ['ænɪkdəʊt] *n.* Anekdote, *die*

anemia, anemic (*Amer.*) *see* **anaemia**

angel ['eɪndʒl] *n.* Engel, *der.* **angelic** [æn'dʒelɪk] *adj.* engelhaft

anger ['æŋgə(r)] **1.** *n.* Zorn, *der* (**at** über + *Akk.*); (*fury*) Wut, *die* (**at** über + *Akk.*). **2.** *v. t.* verärgern; (*infuriate*) wütend machen

¹angle ['æŋgl] *n.* **a)** (*Geom.*) Winkel, *der;* **at an ~ of 60°** im Winkel von 60°; **at an ~:** schief; **b)** (*fig.*) Gesichtspunkt, *der*

²angle *v. i.* angeln; (*fig.*) **~ for sth.** sich um etw. bemühen. **angler** ['æŋglə(r)] *n.* Angler, *der*/Anglerin, *die*

Anglican ['æŋglɪkən] **1.** *adj.* anglikanisch. **2.** *n.* Anglikaner, *der*/Anglikanerin, *die*

Anglo- ['æŋgləʊ] *in comb.* anglo-/Anglo-. **Anglo-Saxon** [~'sæksn] **1.** *n.* Angelsachse, *der*/Angelsächsin, *die;* (*language*) Angelsächsisch, *das.* **2.** *adj.* angelsächsisch

angrily ['æŋgrɪlɪ] *adv.* verärgert; (*stronger*) zornig

angry ['æŋgrɪ] *adj.* böse; verärgert ⟨*Person, Stimme, Geste*⟩; (*stronger*) zornig; wütend; **be ~ at** *or* **about sth.** wegen etw. böse sein; **be ~ with** *or* **at sb.** mit jmdm. *od.* auf jmdn. böse sein; **get ~:** böse werden

anguish ['æŋgwɪʃ] *n.* Qualen *Pl.*

angular ['æŋgjʊlə(r)] *adj.* eckig ⟨*Gebäude, Struktur*⟩; kantig ⟨*Gesicht*⟩

animal ['ænɪml] **1.** *n.* Tier, *das.* **2.** *adj.* tierisch

animate 1. ['ænɪmeɪt] *v. t.* beleben. **2.** ['ænɪmət] *adj.* beseelt ⟨*Leben, Körper*⟩; belebt ⟨*Objekt, Welt*⟩. **animated** ['ænɪmeɪtɪd] *adj.* lebhaft ⟨*Diskussion, Gebärde*⟩; **~ cartoon** Zeichentrickfilm, *der.* **animation** [ænɪ'meɪʃn] *n.* **a)** Lebhaftigkeit, *die;* **b)** (*Cinemat.*) Animation, *die*

animosity [ænɪ'mɒsɪtɪ] *n.* Feindseligkeit, *die*

aniseed ['ænɪsi:d] *n.* Anis(samen), *der*

ankle ['æŋkl] *n.* Fußgelenk, *das*

annex 1. [ə'neks] *v. t.* annektieren ⟨*Land, Territorium*⟩. **2.** ['æneks] *n.* Anbau, *der.* **annexe** *see* **annex 2**

annihilate [ə'naɪɪleɪt] *v. t.* vernichten. **annihilation** [ənaɪ'leɪʃn] *n.* Vernichtung, *die*

anniversary [ænɪ'vɜ:sərɪ] *n.* Jahrestag, *der;* **wedding ~:** Hochzeitstag, *der*

annotate ['ænəteɪt] *v. t.* kommentieren

announce [ə'naʊns] *v. t.* bekanntgeben; ansagen ⟨*Programm*⟩; (*over Tannoy etc.*) durchsagen; (*in newspaper*) anzeigen ⟨*Heirat usw.*⟩. **announcement** *n.* Bekanntgabe, *die;* (*over Tannoy etc.*) Durchsage, *die;* (*in newspaper*) Anzeige, *die.* **announcer** *n.* Ansager, *der*/Ansagerin, *die*

annoy [ə'nɔɪ] *v. t.* **a)** ärgern; **b)** (*harass*) schikanieren. **annoyance** [ə'nɔɪəns] *n.* Verärgerung, *die;* (*nuisance*) Plage, *die.* **annoyed** [ə'nɔɪd] *adj.* **be ~** |**at** *or* **with sb./sth.**| ärgerlich [auf *od.* über jmdn./über etw.] sein; **he got very ~:** er hat sich darüber sehr geärgert. **annoying** *adj.* ärgerlich; lästig ⟨*Gewohnheit, Person*⟩

annual [ænjʊəl] **1.** *adj.* **a)** (*reckoned by the year*) Jahres-; **~ rainfall** jährliche Regenmenge; **b)** (*recurring yearly*) [all]jährlich ⟨*Ereignis, Feier*⟩; Jahres- ⟨*bericht, -hauptversammlung*⟩. **2.** *n.* **a)** Jahrbuch, *das;* (*of comic etc.*) Jahresalbum, *das;* **b)** (*plant*) einjährige Pflanze. **annually** *adv.* jährlich

annul [ə'nʌl] *v. t.,* -ll- annullieren; auflösen ⟨*Vertrag*⟩

anonymous [ə'nɒnɪməs] *adj.* anonym

anorak ['ænəræk] *n.* Anorak, *der*

anorexia [ænə'reksɪə] *n.* Anorexie, *die* (*Med.*); Magersucht, *die* (*volkst.*)

another [ə'nʌðə(r)] **1.** *pron.* **a)** (*an*

additional one) noch einer/eine/eins;
ein weiterer/eine weitere/ein weiteres; **b)** *(counterpart)* wieder einer/ei-
ne/eins; **c)** *(a different one)* ein ande-
rer/eine andere/ein anderes. **2.** *adj.* **a)**
(additional) noch ein/eine; ein weite-
rer/eine weitere/ein weiteres; **after ~
six weeks** nach weiteren sechs Wochen; **b)** *(different)* ein anderer/eine
andere/ein anderes
answer ['ɑːnsə(r)] **1.** *n.* **a)** *(reply)* Antwort, *die* (**to** auf + *Akk.*); **b)** *(to problem)* Lösung, *die* (**to** Gen.); **c)** *(to calculation)* Ergebnis, *das.* **2.** *v. t.* **a)** beantworten ⟨*Brief, Frage*⟩; antworten auf
(+ *Akk.*) ⟨*Frage, Hilferuf, Einladung,
Inserat*⟩; eingehen auf (+ *Akk.*)
⟨*Angebot, Vorschlag*⟩; sich stellen zu
⟨*Beschuldigung*⟩; erhören ⟨*Gebet*⟩; erfüllen ⟨*Bitte, Wunsch*⟩; **~ sb.** jmdm.
antworten; **b)** **~ the door/bell** an die
Tür gehen. **3.** *v. i.* **a)** *(reply)* antworten;
~ to sth. sich zu etw. äußern; **b)** *(be responsible)* **~ for sth.** für etw. die Verantwortung übernehmen; **c)** **~ to a description** einer Beschreibung *(Dat.)*
entsprechen. **answerable** ['ɑːnsə-
rəbl] *adj.* verantwortlich (**for** für; **to**
Dat.). **'answering machine** *n.* An-
rufbeantworter, *der*
ant [ænt] *n.* Ameise, *die*
antagonism [æn'tægənɪzm] *n.* Feindseligkeit, *die* (**towards, against** gegenüber). **antagonist** [æn'tægənɪst] *n.*
Gegner, *der*/Gegnerin, *die.* **anta-
gonistic** [æntægə'nɪstɪk] *adj.* feindlich. **antagonize** [æn'tægənaɪz] *v. t.*
~ sb. sich *(Dat.)* jmdn. zum Feind machen
antarctic [ænt'ɑːktɪk] **1.** *adj.* antarktisch. **2.** *n.* **the A~:** die Antarktis
antelope ['æntɪləʊp] *n.* Antilope, *die*
antenna [æn'tenə] *n.* **a)** *pl.* **~e** [æn-
'teniː] *(Zool.)* Fühler, *der*; **b)** *pl.* **~s**
(Amer.: aerial) Antenne, *die*
anthem ['ænθəm] *n.* Chorgesang, *der*
anthology [æn'θɒlədʒɪ] *n.* Antholo-
gie, *die*
anthropology [ænθrə'pɒlədʒɪ] *n.* An-
thropologie, *die*
anti- [æntɪ] *pref.* anti-/Anti-
anti·aircraft *adj.* *(Mil.)* Flugab-
wehr-; **~ gun** Flak, *die*
antibiotic [æntɪbaɪ'ɒtɪk] *n.* Antibiotikum, *das*
antic ['æntɪk] *n.* *(trick)* Mätzchen, *das*
(ugs.); *(of clown)* Possen, *der*
anticipate [æn'tɪsɪpeɪt] *v. t.* **a)** *(expect)*
erwarten; *(foresee)* voraussehen; **~**

trouble mit Ärger rechnen; **b)** *(consider before due time)* vorwegnehmen.
anticipation [æntɪsɪ'peɪʃn] *n.* Erwartung, *die*
anti·climax *n.* Abstieg, *der*
anti·clockwise *adv., adj.* gegen den
Uhrzeigersinn
anti·cyclone *n.* Hochdruckgebiet,
das
antidote ['æntɪdəʊt] *n.* Gegenmittel,
das (**for, against, to** gegen)
'antifreeze *n.* Frostschutzmittel, *das*
antiquated ['æntɪkweɪtɪd] *adj.* antiquiert; veraltet
antique [æn'tiːk] **1.** *adj.* antik ⟨*Möbel,
Schmuck usw.*⟩. **2.** *n.* Antiquität, *die*;
~ shop Antiquitätenladen, *der*
antiquity [æn'tɪkwɪtɪ] *n.* Altertum,
das; Antike, *die*
anti·septic 1. *adj.* antiseptisch. **2.** *n.*
Antiseptikum, *das*
anti·social *adj.* asozial
antithesis [æn'tɪθəsɪs] *n., pl.* **anti-
theses** [æn'tɪθəsiːz] Gegenstück, *das*
(**of, to** zu)
antler ['æntlə(r)] *n.* Geweihsprosse,
die; **|pair of|~s** Geweih, *das*
anvil ['ænvɪl] *n.* Amboß, *der*
anxiety [æŋ'zaɪətɪ] *n.* Angst, *die*; *(concern about future)* Sorge, *die* (**about**
wegen)
anxious ['æŋkʃəs] *adj.* **a)** *(troubled)*
besorgt (**about** um); **b)** *(eager)* sehn-
lich; **be ~ for sth.** sich nach etw. sehnen. **'anxiously** *adv.* **a)** besorgt; **b)**
(eagerly) sehnsüchtig
any ['enɪ] **1.** *adj.* **a)** *(some)* |irgend|ein/
eine; **not ~:** kein/keine; **have you ~
wool/wine?** haben Sie Wolle/Wein?; **b)**
(one) ein/eine; **c)** *(all, every)* jeder/
jede/jedes; **|at| ~ time** jederzeit; **d)**
(whichever) jeder/jede/jedes |beliebi-
ge|; **choose ~ |one| book/~ books** you
like suchen Sie sich *(Dat.)* irgendein
Buch/irgendwelche Bücher aus. **2.**
pron. **a)** *(some)* in condit., interrog., or
neg. sentence *(replacing sing. n.)* einer/
eine/ein|e|s; *(replacing collect. n.)* wel-
cher/welche/welches; *(replacing pl.
n.)* welche; **not ~:** keiner/keine/
kein|e|s/*Pl.* keine; **without ~:** ohne; **b)**
(no matter which) irgendeiner/irgend-
eine/irgend|ein|es; irgendwelche *Pl.* **3.**
adv. **do you feel ~ better today?** fühlen
Sie sich heute |etwas| besser?; **if it gets
~ colder** wenn es noch kälter wird; **I
can't wait ~ longer** ich kann nicht
|mehr| länger warten
'anybody *n. & pron.* **a)** *(whoever)* je-

der; b) *(somebody)* [irgend]jemand; *after neg.* niemand

'**anyhow** *adv.* a) *see* **anyway;** b) *(haphazardly)* irgendwie

'**anyone** *see* **anybody**

'**anything** 1. *n. & pron.* a) *(whatever thing)* was [immer]; alles, was; b) *(something)* irgend etwas; *after neg.* nichts; c) *(a thing of any kind)* alles. 2. *adv.* not ~ like as ... as keineswegs so ... wie

'**anyway** *adv.* a) *(in any case, besides)* sowieso; b) *(at any rate)* jedenfalls

'**anywhere** *adv.* a) *(in any place)* *(wherever)* überall, wo; wo [immer]; *(somewhere)* irgendwo; not ~ near as ... as *(coll.)* nicht annähernd so ... wie; b) *(to any place)(wherever)* wohin [auch immer]; *(somewhere)* irgendwohin

apart [ə'pɑːt] *adv.* a) *(separately)* getrennt; ~ **from** ...: außer ...; b) *(into pieces)* auseinander

apartheid [ə'pɑːteɪt] *n.* Apartheid, *die*

apartment [ə'pɑːtmənt] *n.* a) *(room)* Apartment, *das;* b) *(Amer.: flat)* Wohnung, *die*

apathetic [æpə'θetɪk] *adj.* apathisch *(about* gegenüber*)*

apathy ['æpəθɪ] *n.* Apathie, *die (about* gegenüber*)*

ape [eɪp] 1. *n.* [Menschen]affe, *der.* 2. *v.t.* nachahmen

aperitif [əperɪ'tiːf] *n.* Aperitif, *der*

aperture ['æpətʃə(r)] *n.* Öffnung, *die*

apex ['eɪpeks] *n.* Spitze, *die*

aphrodisiac [æfrə'dɪzɪæk] *n.* Aphrodisiakum, *das*

apiece [ə'piːs] *adv.* je; **they cost a penny ~:** sie kosten einen Penny das Stück

apologetic [əpɒlə'dʒetɪk] *adj.* entschuldigend; **be ~:** sich entschuldigen

apologize [ə'pɒlədʒaɪz] *v.i.* sich entschuldigen (to bei)

apology [ə'pɒlədʒɪ] *n.* Entschuldigung, *die;* **make an ~:** sich entschuldigen (to bei)

apoplectic [æpə'plektɪk] *adj.* apoplektisch; ~ **fit** Schlaganfall, *der*

apostle [ə'pɒsl] *n.* Apostel, *der*

apostrophe [ə'pɒstrəfɪ] *n.* Apostroph, *der;* Auslassungszeichen, *das*

appal *(Amer.:* **appall)** [ə'pɔːl] *v.t.,* **-ll-** entsetzen. **ap'palling** *adj.* entsetzlich

apparatus [æpə'reɪtəs] *n.* *(equipment)* Gerät, *das; (gymnastic* ~*)* Geräte *Pl.; (machinery, lit. or fig.)* Apparat, *der;* **a piece of ~:** ein Gerät

apparent [ə'pærənt] *adj.* a) *(clear)* offensichtlich; offenbar ⟨*Bedeutung, Wahrheit*⟩; b) *(seeing)* scheinbar.

ap'parently *adv.* a) *(clearly)* offensichtlich; b) *(seemingly)* scheinbar

apparition [æpə'rɪʃn] *n.* [Geister]erscheinung, *die*

appeal [ə'piːl] 1. *v.i.* a) *(Law etc.)* Einspruch einlegen; *(make earnest request)* ~ **to sb. for sth./to do sth.** jmdn. um etw. ersuchen/jmdn. ersuchen, etw. zu tun; c) *(address oneself)* ~ **to sb./sth.** an jmdn./etw. appellieren; d) *(be attractive)* ~ **to sb.** jmdm. zusagen. 2. *n.* a) *(Law etc.)* Einspruch, *der* (to bei); *(to higher court)* Berufung, *die* (to bei); b) *(request)* Appell, *der;* **an ~ to sb. for sth.** eine Bitte an jmdn. um etw.; c) *(attraction)* Reiz, *der.* **ap'pealing** *adj.* a) *(imploring)* flehend; b) *(attractive)* ansprechend; verlockend ⟨*Idee*⟩

appear [ə'pɪə(r)] *v.i.* a) *(become visible, arrive)* erscheinen; ⟨*Licht, Mond:*⟩ auftauchen; *(present oneself)* auftreten; b) *(occur)* vorkommen; c) *(seem)* ~ [to be] ...: scheinen ... [zu sein]. **appearance** [ə'pɪərəns] *n.* a) *(becoming visible)* Auftauchen, *das; (arrival)* Erscheinen, *das; (of performer etc.)* Auftritt, *der;* b) *(look)* Äußere, *das;* **to all ~s** allem Anschein nach; c) *(semblance)* Anschein, *der;* d) *(occurrence)* Vorkommen, *das*

appease [ə'piːz] *v.t.* besänftigen; *(Polit.)* beschwichtigen

append [ə'pend] *v.t.* anhängen (to an + Akk.); *(add)* anfügen (+ Dat.). **ap'pendage** [ə'pendɪdʒ] *n.* Anhängsel, *das; (addition)* Anhang, *der*

appendicitis [əpendɪ'saɪtɪs] *n.* Blinddarmentzündung, *die*

appendix [ə'pendɪks] *n., pl.* **appendices** [ə'pendɪsiːz] *or* **-es** a) Anhang, *der* (to zu); b) *(Anat.)* Blinddarm, *der*

appetite ['æpɪtaɪt] *n.* a) Appetit, *der* (for auf + Akk.); b) *(fig.)* Verlangen, *das* (for nach). **appetizer** ['æpɪtaɪzə(r)] *n.* Appetitanreger, *der.* **appetizing** ['æpɪtaɪzɪŋ] *adj.* appetitlich

applaud [ə'plɔːd] 1. *v.i.* applaudieren; [Beifall] klatschen. 2. *v.t.* applaudieren (+ Dat.). **applause** [ə'plɔːz] *n.* Beifall, *der;* Applaus, *die*

apple ['æpl] *n.* Apfel, *der*

appliance [ə'plaɪəns] *n.* Gerät, *das*

applicable [ə'plɪkəbl] *adj.* a) anwendbar (to auf + Akk.); b) *(appropriate)* geeignet; zutreffend ⟨*Fragebogenteil*⟩

applicant ['æplɪkənt] *n.* Bewerber, *der*/Bewerberin, *die* (for um); *(claimant)* Antragsteller, *der*/-stellerin, *die*

application [æplɪ'keɪʃn] *n.* **a)** *(request)* Bewerbung, *die* (for um); **b)** *(for passport, licence, etc.)* Antrag, *der* (for auf + *Akk.*); ~ **form** Antragsformular, *das*; **b)** *(putting)* Auftragen, *das* (to auf + *Akk.*); **c)** *(use)* Anwendung, *die*

apply [ə'plaɪ] **1.** *v.t.* **a)** auftragen ⟨*Creme, Farbe*⟩ (to auf + *Akk.*); **b)** *(make use of)* anwenden. **2.** *v.i.* **a)** *(have relevance)* zutreffen (to auf + *Akk.*); **b)** ~ [to sb.] for sth. [jmdn.] um etw. bitten; *(for passport etc.)* [bei jmdn.] etw. beantragen; *(for job)* sich [bei jmdm.] um etw. bewerben

appoint [ə'pɔɪnt] *v.t.* **a)** *(fix)* bestimmen; festlegen ⟨*Zeitpunkt, Ort*⟩; **b)** *(to job)* einstellen; *(to office)* ernennen. **ap'pointment** *n.* **a)** *(to job)* Einstellung, *die*; *(to office)* Ernennung, *die* (as zum/zur); **b)** *(job)* Stelle, *die*; **c)** *(arrangement)* Termin, *der*; **make an** ~ **with sb.** sich *(Dat.)* von jmdm. einen Termin geben lassen; **by** ~: nach Anmeldung

appreciable [ə'priːʃəbl] *adj.* **a)** *(perceptible)* nennenswert ⟨*Unterschied, Einfluß*⟩; spürbar ⟨*Veränderung, Wirkung*⟩; merklich ⟨*Verringerung, Anstieg*⟩; **b)** *(considerable)* beträchtlich. **appreciably** [ə'priːʃəblɪ] *adv.* **a)** *(perceptibly)* spürbar ⟨*verändern*⟩; merklich ⟨*sich unterscheiden*⟩; **b)** *(considerably)* beträchtlich

appreciate [ə'priːʃɪeɪt] **1.** *v.t.* **a)** *([correctly] estimate)* [richtig] einschätzen; *(understand)* verstehen; *(be aware of)* sich *(Dat.)* bewußt sein (+ *Gen.*); **b)** *(be grateful for)* schätzen; *(enjoy)* genießen. **2.** *v.i.* im Wert steigen. **appreciation** [əpriːʃɪ'eɪʃn] *n.* **a)** *([correct] estimation)* [richtige] Einschätzung; *(understanding)* Verständnis, *das* (of für); *(awareness)* Bewußtsein, *das*; **b)** *(gratefulness)* Dankbarkeit, *die*; *(enjoyment)* Gefallen, *das* (of an + *Dat.*). **appreciative** [ə'priːʃətɪv] *adj.* *(grateful)* dankbar (of für); *(approving)* anerkennend

apprehend [æprɪ'hend] *v.t.* **a)** *(arrest)* festnehmen; **b)** *(understand)* erfassen. **apprehension** [æprɪ'henʃn] *n.* Besorgnis, *die*. **apprehensive** [æprɪ'hensɪv] *adj.* besorgt

apprentice [ə'prentɪs] *n.* Lehrling, *der* (to bei). **ap'prenticeship** *n.*

(training) Lehre, *die; (learning period)* Lehrzeit, *die*

approach [ə'prəʊtʃ] **1.** *v.i.* sich nähern; *(in time)* nahen. **2.** *v.t.* **a)** *(come near to)* sich nähern (+ *Dat.*); **b)** *(approximate to)* nahekommen (+ *Dat.*); **c)** *(appeal to)* sich wenden an (+ *Akk.*). **3.** *n.* **a)** [Heran]nahen, *das;* **b)** *(approximation)* Annäherung, *die* (to an + *Akk.*); **c)** *(appeal)* Herantreten, *das* (to an + *Akk.*); **d)** *(access)* Zugang, *der; (road)* Zufahrtsstraße, *die*. **approachable** [ə'prəʊtʃəbl] *adj.* **a)** *(friendly)* umgänglich; **b)** *(accessible)* zugänglich

appropriate **1.** [ə'prəʊprɪət] *adj.* geeignet (to, for für). **2.** [ə'prəʊprɪeɪt] *v.t.* sich *(Dat.)* aneignen. **appropriately** [ə'prəʊprɪətlɪ] *adv.* gebührend; passend ⟨*gekleidet, genannt*⟩

approval [ə'pruːvl] *n.* **a)** *(sanctioning)* Genehmigung, *die; (of proposal)* Billigung, *die; (agreement)* Zustimmung, *die*; **b)** **on** ~ *(Commerc.)* zur Probe

approve [ə'pruːv] **1.** *v.t.* **a)** *(sanction)* genehmigen ⟨*Plan, Projekt*⟩; billigen ⟨*Vorschlag*⟩; **b)** *(find good)* gutheißen. **2.** *v.i.* ~ **of** billigen; zustimmen (+ *Dat.*) ⟨*Plan*⟩. **approving** [ə'pruːvɪŋ] *adj.* zustimmend ⟨*Worte*⟩; anerkennend ⟨*Blicke*⟩

approximate [ə'prɒksɪmət] *adj.* ungefähr *attr.* **ap'proximately** *adv.* ungefähr. **approximation** [əprɒksɪ'meɪʃn] *n.* **a)** Annäherung, *die* (to an + *Dat.*); **b)** *(estimate)* Annäherungswert, *der*

Apr. *abbr.* April Apr.

apricot ['eɪprɪkɒt] *n.* Aprikose, *die*

April ['eɪprəl] *n.* April, *der;* ~ **fool** April[s]narr, *der; see also* **August**

apron ['eɪprən] *n.* Schürze, *die*

apt [æpt] *adj.* **a)** *(suitable)* passend; treffend ⟨*Bemerkung*⟩; **b)** **be** ~ **to do sth.** dazu neigen, etw. zu tun

aptitude ['æptɪtjuːd] *n.* Begabung, *die*. **'aptly** *adv.* passend

aqualung ['ækwəlʌŋ] *n.* Tauchgerät, *das*

aquarium [ə'kweərɪəm] *n., pl.* ~s **or** **aquaria** [ə'kweərɪə] Aquarium, *das*

Aquarius [ə'kweərɪəs] *n.* der Wassermann

aquatic [ə'kwætɪk] *adj.* aquatisch; Wasser-; ~ **plant** Wasserpflanze, *die*. **aqueduct** ['ækwɪdʌkt] *n.* Aquädukt, *der od. das*

Arab ['ærəb] **1.** *adj.* arabisch. **2.** *n.* Araber, *der*/Araberin, *die*

Arabian [ə'reɪbɪən] 1. *adj.* arabisch. 2. *n.* Araber, *der*/Araberin, *die*

Arabic ['ærəbɪk] 1. *adj.* arabisch. 2. *n.* Arabisch, *das; see also* **English 2 a**

arbitrary ['ɑ:bɪtrərɪ] *adj.* willkürlich

arbitrate ['ɑ:bɪtreɪt] 1. *v. t.* schlichten ⟨Streit⟩. 2. *v. i.* ~ [upon sth.] [in einer Sache] vermitteln. **arbitration** [ɑ:bɪ-'treɪʃn] *n.* Vermittlung, *die; (in industry)* Schlichtung, *die;* **arbitrator** ['ɑ:bɪtreɪtə(r)] *n.* Vermittler, *der; (in industry)* Schlichter, *der*

arc [ɑ:k] *n.* [Kreis]bogen, *der*

arcade [ɑ:'keɪd] *n.* Arkade, *die*

arch [ɑ:tʃ] 1. *n.* Bogen, *der; (of foot)* Wölbung, *die.* 2. *v. t.* beugen ⟨Rücken⟩; ~ **its back** ⟨Katze:⟩ einen Buckel machen

arch- *pref.* Erz-

archaeological [ɑ:kɪə'lɒdʒɪkl] *adj.* archäologisch

archaeologist [ɑ:kɪ'ɒlədʒɪst] *n.* Archäologe, *der*/Archäologin, *die*

archaeology [ɑ:kɪ'ɒlədʒɪ] *n.* Archäologie, *die*

archaic [ɑ:'keɪɪk] *adj.* veraltet

archbishop *n.* Erzbischof, *der*

archeology *etc. (Amer.) see* **archaeology** *etc.*

archery ['ɑ:tʃərɪ] *n.* Bogenschießen, *das*

archetype ['ɑ:kɪtaɪp] *n. (original)* Urfassung, *die; (typical specimen)* Prototyp, *der*

architect ['ɑ:kɪtekt] *n.* Architekt, *der*/Architektin, *die*

architectural [ɑ:kɪ'tektʃərl] *adj.* architektonisch

architecture ['ɑ:kɪtektʃə(r)] *n.* Architektur, *die*

archive ['ɑ:kaɪv] 1. *n., usu. in pl.* Archiv, *das.* 2. *v. t.* archivieren

arctic ['ɑ:ktɪk] 1. *adj.* arktisch; A~ **Circle** nördlicher Polarkreis; A~ **Ocean** Nordpolarmeer, *das.* 2. *n.* the A~: die Arktis

ardent ['ɑ:dənt] *adj.* leidenschaftlich; brennend ⟨Wunsch⟩; *(eager)* begeistert

ardor *(Amer.),* **ardour** *(Brit.)* ['ɑ:də(r)] *n.* Leidenschaft, *die*

arduous ['ɑ:djʊəs] *adj.* anstrengend

are *see* **be**

area ['eərɪə] *n.* a) *(surface measure)* Fläche, *die;* Flächeninhalt, *der;* b) *(region)* Gelände, *das; (of wood, marsh, desert)* Gebiet, *das; (of city, country)* Gegend, *die;* **parking/picnic ~:** Park-/Picknickplatz, *der;* c) *(subject field)* Gebiet, *das*

arena [ə'ri:nə] *n.* Arena, *die*

aren't [ɑ:nt] *(coll.)* = **are not;** *see* **be**

Argentina [ɑ:dʒən'ti:nə] *pr. n.* Argentinien *(das).* **Argentinian** [ɑ:dʒən-'tɪnɪən] 1. *adj.* argentinisch. 2. *n.* Argentinier, *der*/Argentinierin, *die*

arguable ['ɑ:gjʊəbl] *adj. (questionable)* fragwürdig. **arguably** ['ɑ:gjʊəblɪ] *adv.* möglicherweise

argue ['ɑ:gju:] 1. *v. t.* a) *(maintain)* ~ **that ...:** die Ansicht vertreten, daß ...; b) *(with reasoning)* darlegen ⟨Grund, Standpunkt⟩. 2. *v. i.* ~ **with sb.** sich mit jmdm. streiten; ~ **for/against sth.** für/gegen etw. eintreten; ~ **about sth.** sich über/um etw. *(Akk.)* streiten. **argument** ['ɑ:gjʊmənt] *n.* a) *(reason)* Begründung, *die;* ~**s for/against sth.** Argumente für/gegen etw.; b) *(reasoning process)* Argumentieren, *das;* c) *(disagreement, quarrel)* Auseinandersetzung, *die.* **argumentative** [ɑ:gjʊ-'mentətɪv] *adj.* widerspruchsfreudig

arid ['ærɪd] *adj.* trocken

Aries ['eəri:z] *n.* der Widder

arise [ə'raɪz] *v. i.,* **arose** [ə'rəʊz], **arisen** [ə'rɪzn] a) *(originate)* entstehen; b) *(present itself)* auftreten; ⟨Gelegenheit:⟩ sich bieten; c) *(result)* ~ **from** *or* **out of sth.** von etw. herrühren

aristocracy [ærɪ'stɒkrəsɪ] *n.* Aristokratie, *die*

aristocrat ['ærɪstəkræt] *n.* Aristokrat, *der*/Aristokratin, *die.* **aristocratic** [ærɪstə'krætɪk] *adj.* aristokratisch

arithmetic [ə'rɪθmətɪk] *n.* Arithmetik, *die*

¹**arm** [ɑ:m] *n.* Arm, *der*

²**arm** 1. *n.* a) *usu. in pl. (weapon)* Waffe, *die;* **up in ~s** *(fig.)* in Harnisch **(about** wegen); b) *in pl. (heraldic device)* Wappen, *das.* 2. *v. t.* bewaffnen

armada [ɑ:'mɑ:də] *n.* Armada, *die*

arm: ~band *n.* Armbinde, *die;* **~chair** *n.* Sessel, *der*

armed [ɑ:md] *adj.* bewaffnet; ~ **forces** Streitkräfte *Pl.*

armistice ['ɑ:mɪstɪs] *n.* Waffenstillstand, *der*

armor *(Amer.),* **armour** *(Brit.)* ['ɑ:mə(r)] *n.* a) *(Hist.)* Rüstung, *die;* b) *(steel plates)* Panzerung, *die*

¹**armpit** *n.* Achselhöhle, *die*

army ['ɑ:mɪ] *n.* Heer, *das;* **join the ~:** zum Militär gehen

aroma [ə'rəʊmə] *n.* Duft, *der.* **aromatic** [ærə'mætɪk] *adj.* aromatisch

arose *see* **arise**

around [ə'raʊnd] 1. *adv.* a) *(on every*

side) |all| ~: überall; b) *(round)* herum; c) *(in various places)* **ask/look** ~: herumfragen/sich umsehen. 2. *prep.* a) um [... herum]; b) *(approximately)* ~ 3 o'clock gegen 3 Uhr; **sth.** [costing] ~ £2 etw. für ungefähr 2 Pfund

arouse [ə'raʊz] *v.t.* a) *(awake)* [auf]wecken; b) *(excite)* erregen; erwecken ⟨Interesse, Begeisterung⟩; ~ **suspicion** Verdacht erregen

arrange [ə'reɪndʒ] **1.** *v.t.* a) *(order)* anordnen; b) *(settle, agree)* ausmachen, vereinbaren ⟨Termin⟩; planen ⟨Urlaub⟩; **they** ~**d to meet the following day** sie verabredeten sich für den nächsten Tag. **2.** *v.i.* *(plan)* sorgen (**for** für). **ar'rangement** *n.* a) *(ordering, order)* Anordnung, *die*; b) *(settling, agreement)* Vereinbarung, *die*; c) *in pl.* *(plans)* Vorkehrungen; **make** ~**s** Vorkehrungen treffen

arrears [ə'rɪəz] *n. pl.* Schulden *Pl.*; **be in** ~ **with sth.** mit etw. im Rückstand sein

arrest [ə'rest] **1.** *v.t.* a) verhaften, *(temporarily)* festnehmen ⟨Person⟩; b) *(stop)* aufhalten. **2.** *n.* Verhaftung, *die*; **under** ~: festgenommen

arrival [ə'raɪvl] *n.* Ankunft, *die*; **new** ~**s** Neuankömmlinge

arrive [ə'raɪv] *v.i.* a) ankommen; ~ **at a conclusion/an agreement** zu einem Schluß/einer Einigung kommen; b) ⟨Stunde, Tag, Augenblick:⟩ kommen

arrogance [ˈærəgəns] *n.* Arroganz, *die*

arrogant [ˈærəgənt] *adj.* arrogant

arrow [ˈærəʊ] *n.* Pfeil, *der*

arse [ɑːs] *n.* *(coarse)* Arsch, *der (derb)*

arsenal [ˈɑːsənl] *n.* Waffenlager, *das*

arsenic [ˈɑːsənɪk] *n.* a) Arsenik, *das*; b) *(element)* Arsen, *das*

arson [ˈɑːsn] *n.* Brandstiftung, *die.* **arsonist** [ˈɑːsənɪst] *n.* Brandstifter, *der/* Brandstifterin, *die*

art [ɑːt] *n.* a) Kunst, *die;* **works of** ~: Kunstwerke *Pl.;* ~ **college** *or* **school** Kunsthochschule, *die;* ~**s and crafts** Kunsthandwerk, *das;* b) *in pl.* *(branch of study)* Geisteswissenschaften

artery [ˈɑːtərɪ] *n.* *(Anat.)* Schlagader, *die;* Arterie, *die (bes. fachspr.)*

artful [ˈɑːtfl] *adj.* schlau

'art gallery *n.* Kunstgalerie, *die*

arthritic [ɑːˈθrɪtɪk] *adj.* arthritisch.

arthritis [ɑːˈθraɪtɪs] *n.* Arthritis, *die (fachspr.);* Gelenkentzündung, *die*

artichoke [ˈɑːtɪtʃəʊk] *n.* [globe] ~: Artischocke, *die*

article [ˈɑːtɪkl] *n.* a) *(in magazine,*

newspaper; Ling.) Artikel, *der;* b) **an** ~ **of furniture/clothing** ein Möbel-/Kleidungsstück; **an** ~ **of value** ein Wertgegenstand

articulate [ɑːˈtɪkjʊlət] *adj.* redegewandt; **be** ~**/not very** ~: sich gut/nicht sehr gut ausdrücken [können]

articulated [ɑːˈtɪkjʊleɪtɪd] *adj.* ~ **'lorry** Sattelzug, *der*

artificial [ɑːtɪˈfɪʃl] *adj.* a) künstlich; Kunst-; *(not real)* unecht; ~ **limb** Prothese, *die;* b) *(affected)* gekünstelt

artificial: ~ **insemi'nation** *n.* künstliche Besamung; ~ **in'telligence** *n.* künstliche Intelligenz; ~ **respira'tion** *n.* künstliche Beatmung

artillery [ɑːˈtɪlərɪ] *n.* Artillerie, *die*

artisan [ˈɑːtɪzn, ɑːtɪˈzæn] *n.* [Kunst]handwerker, *der*

artist [ˈɑːtɪst] *n.* Künstler, *der/* Künstlerin, *die*

artiste [ɑːˈtiːst] *n.* Artist, *der/*Artistin, *die*

artistic [ɑːˈtɪstɪk] *adj.* a) *(of art)* Kunst-; künstlerisch; b) *(naturally skilled in person)* künstlerisch veranlagt

'artless *adj.* arglos

as [əz, *stressed* æz] **1.** *adv., conj.* a) **he is as tall as I am** er ist so groß wie ich; **as quickly as you can/as possible** so schnell du kannst/wie möglich; b) *(though)* **small as he was** obwohl er klein war; c) *(however much)* **try as he might/would, he could not concentrate** sosehr er sich auch bemühte, er konnte sich nicht konzentrieren; d) *expr. manner* wie; **as you may already have heard, ...:** wie Sie vielleicht schon gehört haben, ...; **as it were** sozusagen; e) *expr. time* als; während; **as we climbed the stairs** als wir die Treppe hinaufgingen; **as we were talking** während wir uns unterhielten; f) *expr. reason* da. **2.** *prep.* a) *(in the function of)* als; **as an artist** als Künstler; **speaking as a mother ...:** als Mutter ...; b) *(like)* wie; c) **the same as ...:** der-/die-/dasselbe wie ...; **such as** wie zum Beispiel. **3. as for ...:** was ... angeht *od.* betrifft; **as** [it] **is** wie die Dinge liegen; **the place is untidy enough as it is** es ist hier [so] schon unordentlich genug; **as of ...** *(Amer.)* von ... an; **as to** hinsichtlich (+ *Gen.*); **as yet** bis jetzt; noch

asbestos [æzˈbestɒs] *n.* Asbest, *der*

ascend [əˈsend] **1.** *v.i.* a) *(go up)* hinaufsteigen; *(climb up)* hinaufklettern; *(by vehicle)* hinauffahren; *(rise)* aufsteigen; ⟨Hubschrauber:⟩ höhersteigen; c) *(slope upwards)* ⟨*Hügel, Straße:*⟩ ansteigen. **2.** *v. t.* **a)** *(go up)* hinaufsteigen ⟨*Treppe, Leiter, Berg:*⟩ **b)** ~ **the throne** den Thron besteigen

A'scension Day n. Himmelfahrtstag, *der*

ascent [ə'sent] *n.* Aufstieg, *der*

ascertain [æsə'teɪn] *v. t.* feststellen; ermitteln ⟨*Fakten, Daten*⟩

ascribe [ə'skraɪb] *v. t.* zuschreiben (to *Dat.*)

¹**ash** [æʃ] *n. (tree)* Esche, *die*

²**ash** *n. (from fire etc.)* Asche, *die*

ashamed [ə'ʃeɪmd] *adj.* beschämt; **be** ~: sich schämen (of wegen)

ashen ['æʃn] *adj.* aschfahl ⟨*Gesicht*⟩

ashore [ə'ʃɔ:(r)] *adv.* an Land

'ash-tray *n.* Aschenbecher, *der*

Ash 'Wednesday *n.* Aschermittwoch, *der*

Asia ['eɪʃə] *pr. n.* Asien *(das)*. **Asian** ['eɪʃən] **1.** *adj.* asiatisch. **2.** *n.* Asiat, *der*/Asiatin, *die*

aside [ə'saɪd] *adv.* beiseite; zur Seite

ask [ɑ:sk] **1.** *v. t.* **a)** fragen; ~ **sb. |sth.|** jmdn. [nach etw.] fragen; **b)** *(seek to obtain)* ~ sth. um etw. bitten; **how much are you ~ing for that car?** wieviel verlangen Sie für das Auto?; ~ **sb. to do sth.** jmdn. [darum] bitten, etw. zu tun; **c)** *(invite)* einladen. **2.** *v. i.* ~ **after sb./sth.** nach jmdm./etw. fragen; ~ **for sth./sb.** etw./jmdn. verlangen

askance [ə'skæns, ə'skɑ:ns] *adv.* **look** ~ **at sb.** jmdn. befremdet ansehen

askew [ə'skju:] *adv., pred. adj.* schief

asleep [ə'sli:p] *pred. adj.* schlafend; **be/lie** ~: schlafen; **fall** ~: einschlafen

asparagus [ə'spærəgəs] *n.* Spargel, *der*

aspect ['æspekt] *n.* Aspekt, *der*

aspersion [ə'spɜ:ʃn] *n.* **cast** ~**s on sb.**/ sth. jmdn./etw. in den Schmutz ziehen

asphalt ['æsfælt] *n.* Asphalt, *der*

asphyxiate [æs'fɪksɪeɪt] *v. t. & i.* ersticken

aspiration [æspə'reɪʃn] *n.* Streben, *das*

aspire [ə'spaɪə(r)] *v. i.* ~ **to** *or* **after sth.** nach etw. streben

aspirin ['æspərɪn] *n.* Aspirin Ⓦ, *das;* Kopfschmerztablette, *die*

ass [æs] *n.* Esel, *der*

assailant [ə'seɪlənt] *n.* Angreifer, *der*/ Angreiferin, *die*

assassin [ə'sæsɪn] *n.* Mörder, *der*/ Mörderin, *die*. **assassinate** [ə'sæsɪneɪt] *v. t.* ermorden; **be** ~**d** einem Attentat zum Opfer fallen. **assassina-**

tion [əsæsɪ'neɪʃn] *n.* Mord, *der* (of an + *Dat.*); ~ **attempt** Attentat, *das* (on auf + *Akk.*)

assault [ə'sɔ:lt] **1.** *n.* Angriff, *der; (fig.)* Anschlag, *der.* **2.** *v. t.* angreifen

assemble [ə'sembl] **1.** *v. t.* **a)** zusammentragen; zusammenrufen ⟨*Menschen*⟩; **b)** *(fit together)* zusammenbauen. **2.** *v. i.* sich versammeln. **assembly** [ə'semblɪ] *n.* **a)** *(meeting)* Versammlung, *die; (in school)* Morgenandacht, *die;* **b)** *(fitting together)* Zusammenbau, *der.* **as'sembly line** *n.* Fließband, *das*

assent [ə'sent] **1.** *v. i.* zustimmen (to *Dat.*). **2.** *n.* Zustimmung, *die*

assert [ə'sɜ:t] *v. t.* **a)** geltend machen; ~ **oneself** sich durchsetzen; **b)** *(declare)* behaupten; beteuern ⟨*Unschuld*⟩. **assertion** [ə'sɜ:ʃn] *n.* **a)** Geltendmachen, *das; b) (declaration)* Behauptung, *die.* **assertive** [ə'sɜ:tɪv] *adj.* energisch ⟨*Person*⟩; bestimmt ⟨*Ton, Verhalten*⟩

assess [ə'ses] *v. t.* einschätzen; festsetzen ⟨*Steuer*⟩ (at auf + *Akk.*). **as'sessment** *n.* **a)** Einschätzung, *die; b) (tax to be paid)* Steuerbescheid, *der*

asset ['æset] *n.* **a)** Vermögenswert, *der; b) (useful quality)* Vorzug, *der* (to für); *(person)* Stütze, *die; (thing)* Hilfe, *die*

assiduous [ə'sɪdjʊəs] *adj.* **a)** *(diligent)* eifrig; **b)** *(conscientious)* gewissenhaft

assign [ə'saɪn] *v. t.* **a)** *(allot)* zuweisen (to *Dat.*); **b)** *(appoint)* zuteilen; ~ **sb. to do sth.** jmdn. damit betrauen, etw. zu tun. **as'signment** *n.* **a)** *(allotment)* Zuweisung, *die; (appointment)* Zuteilung, *die; b) (task)* Aufgabe, *die*

assimilate [ə'sɪmɪleɪt] *v. t.* angleichen (to, with an + *Akk.*). **assimilation** [əsɪmɪ'leɪʃn] *n.* Angleichung, *die* (to, with an + *Akk.*)

assist [ə'sɪst] **1.** *v. t.* helfen (+ *Dat.*). **2.** *v. i.* helfen; ~ **with sth./in doing sth.** bei etw. helfen/helfen, etw. zu tun. **assistance** [ə'sɪstəns] *n.* Hilfe, *die.* **assistant** [ə'sɪstənt] *n. (helper)* Helfer, *der*/Helferin, *die; (subordinate)* Mitarbeiter, *der*/Mitarbeiterin, *die; (of professor, artist)* Assistent, *der*/Assistentin, *die; (in shop)* Verkäufer, *der*/Verkäuferin, *die*

associate 1. [ə'səʊʃɪət, ə'səʊsɪət] *n. (partner)* Partner, *der*/Partnerin, *die; (colleague)* Kollege, *der*/Kollegin, *die.* **2.** [ə'səʊʃɪeɪt, ə'səʊsɪeɪt] *v. t.* in Verbindung bringen; **be** ~**d** in Verbindung stehen. **3.** [əˈsəʊʃɪeɪt, əˈsəʊsɪeɪt] *v. i.* ~ **with sb.** mit jmdm. Umgang haben. **association** [əsəʊsɪˈeɪʃn] *n.* **a)** *(organization)* Vereinigung, *die;* **b)** *(mental connection)* Assoziation, *die;* **c)** *(connection)* Verbindung, *die*

assorted [əˈsɔːtɪd] *adj.* gemischt

assortment [əˈsɔːtmənt] *n.* Sortiment, *das;* **a good ~ of hats |to choose from|** eine gute Auswahl an Hüten

assume [əˈsjuːm] *v. t.* **a)** voraussetzen; **assuming that ...:** vorausgesetzt, daß ...; **b)** *(undertake)* übernehmen ⟨*Amt, Pflichten*⟩; **c)** *(take on)* annehmen ⟨*Namen, Rolle*⟩. **assumption** [əˈsʌmpʃn] *n.* Annahme, *die;* **going on the ~ that ...:** vorausgesetzt, daß ...

assurance [əˈʃʊərəns] *n.* **a)** Zusicherung, *die;* **b)** *(self-confidence)* Selbstsicherheit, *die*

assure [əˈʃʊə(r)] *v. t.* **a)** versichern (+ *Dat.*); **b)** *(convince)* ~ **sb./oneself** jmdn./sich überzeugen; **c)** *(make certain or safe)* gewährleisten. **assured** [əˈʃʊəd] *adj.* gewährleistet ⟨*Erfolg*⟩; **be ~ of sth.** sich *(Dat.)* einer Sache *(Gen.)* sicher sein

asterisk [ˈæstərɪsk] *n.* Sternchen, *das*

astern [əˈstɜːn] *adv.* *(Naut., Aeronaut.)* achtern; *(towards the rear)* achterwärts

asteroid [ˈæstərɔɪd] *n.* Asteroid, *der*

asthma [ˈæsmə] *n.* Asthma, *das.* **asthmatic** [æsˈmætɪk] **1.** *adj.* asthmatisch. **2.** *n.* Asthmatiker, *der*/Asthmatikerin, *die*

astonish [əˈstɒnɪʃ] *v. t.* erstaunen. **a'stonishing** *adj.* erstaunlich. **a'stonishment** *n.* Erstaunen, *das*

astound [əˈstaʊnd] *v. t.* verblüffen. **a'stounding** *adj.* erstaunlich

astray [əˈstreɪ] *adv.* **sth. goes ~** *(is mislaid)* etw. wird verlegt; *(is lost)* etw. geht verloren; **go/lead ~** *(fig.)* in die Irre geraten/führen

astride [əˈstraɪd] **1.** *adv.* rittlings ⟨*sitzen*⟩. **2.** *prep.* rittlings auf (+ *Dat.*)

astringent [əˈstrɪndʒənt] *adj.* scharf

astrologer [əˈstrɒlədʒə(r)] *n.* Astrologe, *der*/Astrologin, *die*

astrological [æstrəˈlɒdʒɪkl] *adj.* astrologisch

astrology [əˈstrɒlədʒɪ] *n.* Astrologie, *die*

astronaut [ˈæstrənɔːt] *n.* Astronaut, *der*/Astronautin, *die*

astronomer [əˈstrɒnəmə(r)] *n.* Astronom, *der*/Astronomin, *die*

astronomical [æstrəˈnɒmɪkl] *adj.* astronomisch

astronomy [əˈstrɒnəmɪ] *n.* Astronomie, *die*

astute [əˈstjuːt] *adj.* scharfsinnig

asylum [əˈsaɪləm] *n.* Asyl, *das*

at [ət, *stressed* æt] *prep.* **a)** *expr. place* **an** (+ *Dat.*); **at the station** an Bahnhof; **at the baker's/butcher's/grocer's** beim Bäcker/Fleischer/Kaufmann; **at the chemist's** in der Apotheke/Drogerie; **at the supermarket** im Supermarkt; **at the party** auf der Party; **at the office/hotel** im Büro/Hotel; **at Dover** in Dover; **b)** *expr. time* **at Christmas** [zu *od.* an] Weihnachten; **at six o'clock** um sechs Uhr; **at midnight** um Mitternacht; **at midday** am Mittag; **at |the age of|** 40 mit 40; im Alter von 40; **at this/the moment** in diesem/im Augenblick *od.* Moment; **c)** *expr. price* **at £2.50 |each|** zu *od.* für |je| 2,50 Pfund; **d)** *expr. speed* **at 30 m. p. h.** *etc.* mit dreißig Meilen pro Stunde *usw.;* **e)** **at that** *(at that point)* dabei; *(at that provocation)* daraufhin; *(moreover)* noch dazu.

ate *see* **eat**

atheism [ˈeɪθɪɪzm] *n.* Atheismus, *der.* **atheist** [ˈeɪθɪɪst] *n.* Atheist, *der*/Atheistin, *die*

Athens [ˈæθɪnz] *pr. n.* Athen *(das)*

athlete [ˈæθliːt] *n.* Athlet, *der*/Athletin, *die;* *(runner, jumper)* Leichtathlet, *der*/Leichtathletin, *die.* **athletic** [æθˈletɪk] *adj.* sportlich. **ath'letics** *n.* Leichtathletik, *die*

Atlantic [ətˈlæntɪk] **1.** *adj.* atlantisch; **~ Ocean** Atlantischer Ozean. **2.** *pr. n.* Atlantik, *der*

atlas [ˈætləs] *n.* Atlas, *der*

atmosphere [ˈætməsfɪə(r)] *n.* Atmosphäre, *die.* **atmospheric** [ætməsˈferɪk] *adj.* atmosphärisch

atom [ˈætəm] *n.* Atom, *das.* **'atom bomb** *n.* Atombombe, *die*

atomic [əˈtɒmɪk] *adj.* Atom-

atomizer [ˈætəmaɪzə(r)] *n.* Zerstäuber, *der*

atone [əˈtəʊn] *v. i.* ~ es wiedergutmachen; **~ for sth.** etw. wiedergutmachen. **a'tonement** *n.* Buße, *die*

atrocious [əˈtrəʊʃəs] *adj.* grauenhaft; scheußlich ⟨*Wetter, Benehmen*⟩. **a'trociously** *adv.* grauenhaft; scheußlich *(sich benehmen)*. **atrocity** [əˈtrɒsɪtɪ] *n.* **a)** *(wickedness)* Grauenhaftigkeit, *die;* **b)** *(deed)* Greueltat, *die*

attach [əˈtætʃ] *v. t.* **a)** *(fasten)* befestigen (**to** an + *Dat.*); **please find ~ed** a copy of the letter beigeheftet ist eine

Kopie des Briefes; **b)** *(fig.)* ~ **importance to sth.** einer Sache *(Dat.)* Gewicht beimessen

attaché [ə'tæʃeɪ] *n.* Attaché, *der.* at'**taché case** *n.* Diplomatenkoffer, *der*

attached [ə'tætʃt] *adj. (emotionally)* be ~ **to sb./sth.** an jmdm./etw. hängen

at'tachment *n.* **a)** *(act or means of fastening)* Befestigung, *die;* **b)** *(affection)* Anhänglichkeit, *die* **(to an +** *Akk.)*; **c)** *(accessory)* Zusatzgerät, *das*

attack [ə'tæk] **1.** *v.t.* **a)** angreifen; *(ambush, raid)* überfallen; *(fig.: criticize)* attackieren; **b)** *(affect)* ⟨*Krankheit:*⟩ befallen. **2.** *v.i.* angreifen. **3.** *n.* Angriff, *der; (ambush)* Überfall, *der; (fig.: criticism)* Attacke, *die; (of illness)* Anfall, *der.* at'**tacker** *n.* Angreifer, *der/*Angreiferin, *die*

attain [ə'teɪn] *v.t.* erreichen. at'**tainment** *n.* Verwirklichung, *die*

attempt [ə'tempt] **1.** *v.t.* versuchen. **2.** *n.* Versuch, *der*

attend [ə'tend] **1.** *v.i.* **a)** *(give care and thought)* aufpassen; *(apply oneself)* ~ **to sth.** *(deal with sth.)* sich um etw. kümmern; **b)** *(be present)* anwesend sein (**at** bei). **2.** *v.t.* **a)** *(be present at)* teilnehmen an (+ *Dat.*); *(go regularly to)* besuchen; **b)** *(wait on)* bedienen (+ *Dat.*); **c)** ⟨*Arzt:*⟩ behandeln. at'**tendance** [ə'tendəns] *n.* Anwesenheit, *die; (number of people)* Teilnehmerzahl, *die.* **attendant** [ə'tendənt] *n.* **a)** |**lavatory**| ~: Toilettenmann, *der/*-frau, *die;* |**cloakroom**| ~: Garderobenmann, *der/*-frau, *die;* **museum** ~: Museumswärter, *der/*-wärterin, *die;* **b)** *(member of entourage)* Begleiter, *der/*Begleiterin, *die*

attention [ə'tenʃn] **1.** *n.* **a)** Aufmerksamkeit, *die;* **attract** |**sb.'s**| ~: [jmdn.] auf sich *(Akk.)* aufmerksam machen; **pay** ~ **to sb./sth.** jmdn./etw. beachten; **pay** ~ **I** gib acht!; paß auf!; **hold sb.'s** ~: jmds. Interesse wachhalten; ~ **Miss Jones** *(on letter)* zu Händen [von] Miss Jones; **b)** *(Mil.)* **stand to** ~: stillstehen. **2.** *int.* **a)** Achtung; **b)** *(Mil.)* stillgestanden

attentive [ə'tentɪv] *adj.* aufmerksam

attic ['ætɪk] *n. (room)* Dachboden, *der; (habitable)* Dachkammer, *die*

attire [ə'taɪə(r)] *n.* Kleidung, *die*

attitude ['ætɪtjuːd] *n.* **a)** Haltung, *die;* **b)** *(mental* ~*)* Einstellung, *die*

attorney [ə'tɜːnɪ] *n.* **a)** Bevollmächtigte, *der/die;* **power of** ~: Vollmacht,

die; **b)** *(Amer.: lawyer)* [Rechts]anwalt, *der/*-anwältin, *die*

attract [ə'trækt] *v.t.* **a)** *(draw)* anziehen; auf sich *(Akk.)* ziehen ⟨*Interesse, Blick, Kritik*⟩; **b)** *(arouse pleasure in)* anziehend wirken auf + *Akk.*); **c)** *(arouse interest in)* reizen (**about** an + *Dat.*). **attraction** [ə'trækʃn] *n.* **a)** Anziehung, *die; (force, lit. or fig.)* Anziehung[skraft], *die;* **b)** *(fig.: thing that attracts)* Attraktion, *die; (charm)* Verlockung, *die;* Reiz, *der.* **attractive** [ə'træktɪv] *adj.* **a)** anziehend; **b)** *(fig.)* attraktiv; reizvoll ⟨*Vorschlag, Möglichkeit, Idee*⟩

attribute **1.** ['ætrɪbjuːt] *n.* Eigenschaft, *die.* **2.** [ə'trɪbjuːt] *v.t.* zuschreiben (**to** *Dat.*). **attributive** [ə'trɪbjʊtɪv] *adj. (Ling.)* attributiv

aubergine ['əʊbəʒiːn] *n.* Aubergine, *die*

auburn ['ɔːbən] *adj.* rötlichbraun

auction ['ɔːkʃn] **1.** *n.* Versteigerung, *die.* **2.** *v.t.* versteigern. **auctioneer** [ɔːkʃə'nɪə(r)] *n.* Auktionator, *der/*Auktionatorin, *die*

audacious [ɔː'deɪʃəs] *adj.* **a)** *(daring)* kühn; verwegen; **b)** *(impudent)* dreist. **audacity** [ɔː'dæsɪtɪ] *n.* **a)** *(daringness)* Kühnheit, *die;* Verwegenheit, *die;* **b)** *(impudence)* Dreistigkeit, *die*

audible ['ɔːdɪbl] *adj.* hörbar

audience ['ɔːdɪəns] *n.* **a)** Publikum, *das;* **b)** *(formal interview)* Audienz, *die* (**with** bei)

audio ['ɔːdɪəʊ] *adj.* Ton-. '**audio typist** *n.* Phonotypist, *der/*-typistin, *die.* **audio'visual** *adj.* audiovisuell

audit ['ɔːdɪt] **1.** *n.* ~ |**of the accounts**| Rechnungsprüfung, *die.* **2.** *v.t.* prüfen

audition [ɔː'dɪʃn] **1.** *n. (singing)* Vorsingen, *das; (dancing)* Vortanzen, *das; (acting)* Vorsprechen, *das.* **2.** *v.i. (sing)* vorsingen; *(dance)* vortanzen; *(act)* vorsprechen. **3.** *v.t.* vorsingen/vortanzen/vorsprechen lassen

auditor ['ɔːdɪtə(r)] *n.* Buchprüfer, *der/*-prüferin, *die*

auditorium [ɔːdɪ'tɔːrɪəm] *n.* Zuschauerraum, *der*

Aug. *abbr.* **August** Aug.

augment [ɔːg'ment] *v.t.* verbessern ⟨*Einkommen*⟩; aufstocken ⟨*Fonds*⟩

augur ['ɔːgə(r)] **1.** *v.t.* bedeuten; versprechen ⟨*Erfolg*⟩. **2.** *v.i.* ~ **well/ill for sth./sb.** ein gutes/schlechtes Zeichen für etw./jmdn. sein

August ['ɔːgəst] *n.* August, *der;* **in** ~: im August; **last/next** ~: letzten/näch-

sten August; **the first of/on the first of**
~: der erste/am ersten August
aunt [ɑːnt] *n.* Tante, *die*
auntie, aunty ['ɑːntɪ] *n. (coll.)* Tänt-
chen, *das; (with name)* Tante, *die*
au pair [əʊ 'peə(r)] *n.* Au-pair-Mäd-
chen, *das*
aura ['ɔːrə] *n.* Aura, *die*
auspices ['ɔːspɪsɪz] *n. pl.* **under the ~**
of sb./sth. unter jmds./einer Sache
Schirmherrschaft
auspicious [ɔː'spɪʃəs] *adj.* günstig;
vielversprechend (*Anfang*)
austere [ɒ'stɪə(r)] *adj.* **a)** *(strict, stern)*
streng; **b)** *(severely simple)* karg. **aus-
terity** [ɒ'sterɪtɪ] *n.* **a)** *(strictness)*
Strenge, *die;* **b)** *(severe simplicity)*
Kargheit, *die;* **c)** *(lack of luxuries)*
wirtschaftliche Einschränkung
Australia [ɒ'streɪlɪə] *pr. n.* Australien
(das). **Australian** [ɒ'streɪlɪən] **1.** *adj.*
australisch. **2.** *n.* Australier, *der/*Au-
stralierin, *die*
Austria ['ɒstrɪə] *pr. n.* Österreich
(das). **Austrian** ['ɒstrɪən] **1.** *adj.*
österreichisch. **2.** *n.* Österreicher,
*der/*Österreicherin, *die*
authentic [ɔː'θentɪk] *adj.* authentisch.
authenticity [ɔːθen'tɪsɪtɪ] *n.* Authen-
tizität, *die*
author ['ɔːθə(r)] *n.* Autor, *der/*Autorin, *die; (profession)* Schriftsteller,
*der/*Schriftstellerin, *die*
authoritarian [ɔːθɒrɪ'teərɪən] **1.** *adj.*
autoritär. **2.** *n.* autoritäre Person
authoritative [ɔː'θɒrɪtətɪv] *adj.* maß-
gebend; zuverlässig (*Bericht, Information*)
authority [ɔː'θɒrɪtɪ] *n.* **a)** Autorität,
die; **in ~:** verantwortlich; **b) the authorities** die Behörde[n]
authorization [ɔːθəraɪ'zeɪʃn] *n.* Genehmigung, *die*
authorize ['ɔːθəraɪz] *v. t.* **a)** ermächtigen; bevollmächtigen; **b)** *(sanction)*
genehmigen
auto ['ɔːtəʊ] *n., pl.* ~s *(Amer. coll.)* Auto, *das*
auto- [ɔːtəʊ] *in comb.* auto-/Auto-
autobio'graphical *adj.* autobiogra-
phisch
autobi'ography *n.* Autobiographie,
die
autocratic [ɔːtə'krætɪk] *adj.* autokra-
tisch
autograph ['ɔːtəɡrɑːf] **1.** *n.* Auto-
gramm, *das.* **2.** *v. t.* signieren
automate ['ɔːtəmeɪt] *v. t.* automatisieren

automatic [ɔːtə'mætɪk] **1.** *adj.* automatisch. **2.** *n. (weapon)* automatische
Waffe; *(vehicle)* Fahrzeug mit Auto-
matikgetriebe. **automatically** [ɔːtə-
'mætɪkəlɪ] *adv.* automatisch
automation [ɔːtə'meɪʃn] *n.* Automation, *die*
automobile ['ɔːtəməbiːl] *n. (Amer.)*
Auto, *das*
autonomous [ɔː'tɒnəməs] *adj.* auto-
nom. **autonomy** [ɔː'tɒnəmɪ] *n.* Auto-
nomie, *die*
autopsy ['ɔːtɒpsɪ] *n.* Autopsie, *die*
autumn ['ɔːtəm] *n.* Herbst, *der;* **in [the]**
~: im Herbst. **autumnal** [ɔː'tʌmnl]
adj. herbstlich
auxiliary [ɔːɡ'zɪljərɪ] **1.** *adj.* Hilfs-. **2.**
n. **a)** Hilfskraft, *die;* **b)** *(Ling.)* Hilfsverb, *das*
avail [ə'veɪl] **1.** *n.* **be of no** ~: nichts
nützen; **to no** ~: vergebens. **2.** *v. refl.*
~ **oneself of sth.** von etw. Gebrauch
machen
available [ə'veɪləbl] *adj.* **a)** *(at one's
disposal)* verfügbar; **b)** *(obtainable)*
erhältlich; lieferbar (*Waren*)
avalanche ['ævəlɑːnʃ] *n.* Lawine, *die*
avarice ['ævərɪs] *n.* Geldgier, *die;*
Habsucht, *die.* **avaricious** [ævə'rɪ-
ʃəs] *adj.* geldgierig; habsüchtig
avenge [ə'vendʒ] *v. t.* rächen
avenue ['ævənjuː] *n.* Allee, *die; (fig.)*
Weg, *der* (to zu)
average ['ævərɪdʒ] **1.** *n.* Durchschnitt,
der; **on** ~: im Durchschnitt; durchschnittlich. **2.** *adj.* durchschnittlich. **3.**
v. t. **a)** *(find the* ~ *of)* den Durchschnitt ermitteln von; **b)** *(amount on* ~
to) durchschnittlich betragen. **4.** *v. i.*
~ **out at** im Durchschnitt betragen
averse [ə'vɜːs] *adj.* **be** ~ **to sth.** einer
Sache *(Dat.)* abgeneigt sein. **aver-
sion** [ə'vɜːʃn] *n.* Abneigung, *die* (to
gegen)
avert [ə'vɜːt] *v. t.* abwenden; verhüten
(*Unfall*)
aviary ['eɪvɪərɪ] *n.* Vogelhaus, *das*
aviation [eɪvɪ'eɪʃn] *n.* Luftfahrt, *die*
avid ['ævɪd] *adj. (enthusiastic)* begeistert; **be** ~ **for sth.** *(eager, greedy)* begierig auf etw. *(Akk.)* sein
avocado [ævə'kɑːdəʊ] *n., pl.* ~s: ~
[pear] Avocado[birne], *die*
avoid [ə'vɔɪd] *v. t.* **a)** meiden (*Ort*); ~ **a**
cyclist einem Radfahrer ausweichen;
~ **the boss when he's in a temper** geh
dem Chef aus dem Weg, wenn er
schlechte Laune hat; **b)** *(refrain from,
escape)* vermeiden. **avoidable** [ə'vɔɪ-

dəbl] *adj.* vermeidbar. **avoidance** [ə'vɔɪdəns] *n.* Vermeidung, *die*

await [ə'weɪt] *v.t.* erwarten

awake [ə'weɪk] **1.** *v.i.*, awoke [ə'wəʊk], awoken [ə'wəʊkn] erwachen. **2.** *v.t.*, awoke, awoken wecken. **3.** *pred. adj.* wach; **wide ~:** hellwach

awaken [ə'weɪkn] *v.t. & i. (esp. fig.)* *see* **awake 1, 2**

award [ə'wɔːd] **1.** *v.t.* verleihen 〈*Preis, Auszeichnung*〉; zusprechen 〈*Sorgerecht, Entschädigung*〉; gewähren 〈*Zahlung, Gehaltserhöhung*〉. **2.** *n. (prize)* Auszeichnung, *die*

aware [ə'weə(r)] *adj.* **be ~ of sth.** sich (*Dat.*) einer Sache (*Gen.*) bewußt sein; **be ~ that …:** sich (*Dat.*) [dessen] bewußt sein, daß … **a'wareness** *n.* Bewußtsein, *das*

awash [ə'wɒʃ] *adj.* **be ~ (flooded)** unter Wasser stehen

away [ə'weɪ] **1.** *adv.* **a)** *(at a distance)* entfernt; **play ~** *(Sport)* auswärts spielen; **b)** *(to a distance)* weg; fort; **c)** *(absent)* nicht da. **2.** *adj. (Sport)* auswärts präd.; Auswärts-

awe [ɔː] *n.* Ehrfurcht, *die* (**of** vor + *Dat.*)

awful ['ɔːfl] *adj.*, **'awfully** *adv.* furchtbar

awkward ['ɔːkwəd] *adj.* **a)** *(difficult to use)* ungünstig; **be ~ to use** unhandlich sein; **b)** *(clumsy)* unbeholfen; **c)** *(embarrassing)* peinlich; **d)** *(difficult)* schwierig; ungünstig 〈*Zeitpunkt*〉

awning ['ɔːnɪŋ] *n. (on house)* Markise, *die;* (*of tent*) Vordach, *das*

awoke, awoken *see* **awake**

awry [ə'raɪ] *adv.* schief; **go ~** *(fig.)* schiefgehen *(ugs.);* 〈*Plan:*〉 fehlschlagen

axe [æks] *n.* Axt, *die;* Beil, *das*

axis ['æksɪs] *n., pl.* **axes** ['æksiːz] Achse, *die*

axle ['æksl] *n.* Achse, *die*

B

B, b [biː] *n.* B, b, *das*

BA *abbr.* Bachelor of Arts

babble ['bæbl] *v.i.* **a)** *(talk incoherently)* stammeln; **b)** *(talk foolishly)*

[dumm] schwatzen; **c)** 〈*Bach:*〉 plätschern

baboon [bə'buːn] *n.* Pavian, *der*

baby ['beɪbɪ] *n.* **a)** Baby, *das;* **have a ~/be going to have a ~:** ein Kind bekommen; **b)** *(childish person)* **be a ~:** sich wie ein kleines Kind benehmen. **'baby-carriage** *n. (Amer.)* Kinderwagen, *der*

'babyish *adj.* kindlich 〈*Aussehen*〉; kindisch 〈*Benehmen, Person*〉

baby: ~-minder *n.* Tagesmutter, *die;* **~-sit** *v.i.*, forms as **sit 1** babysitten *(ugs.);* auf das Kind/die Kinder aufpassen; **~-sitter** *n.* Babysitter, *der*

bachelor ['bætʃələ(r)] *n.* **a)** Junggeselle, *der;* **b)** *(Univ.)* **B~** of Arts/Science Bakkalaureus der philosophischen Fakultät/der Naturwissenschaften

back [bæk] **1.** *n.* **a)** *(of person, animal)* Rücken, *der;* (*of house, cheque*) Rückseite, *die;* (*of vehicle*) Heck, *das;* (*inside car*) Rücksitz, *der;* **stand ~ to ~:** Rücken an Rücken stehen; **~ to front** verkehrt rum; **turn one's ~ on sb.** jmdm. den Rücken zuwenden; *(fig.)* jmdn. im Stich lassen; **turn one's ~ on sth.** *(fig.)* sich um etw. nicht kümmern; **get or put sb.'s ~ up** *(fig.)* jmdn. wütend machen; **be glad to see the ~ of sb./sth.** *(fig.)* froh sein, jmdn./etw. nicht mehr sehen zu müssen; **have one's ~ to the wall** *(fig.)* mit dem Rücken vor Wand stehen; **put one's ~ into sth.** *(fig.)* sich für etw. mit allen Kräften einsetzen; **with the ~ of one's hand** mit dem Handrücken; **at the ~ [of the book]** hinten [im Buch]; **b)** *(Sport: player)* Verteidiger, *der.* **2.** *adj.* hinter-. **3.** *adv.* zurück; **two miles ~:** vor zwei Meilen; **~ and forth** hin und her; **there and ~:** hin und zurück; **a week/month ~:** vor einer Woche/vor einem Monat. **4.** *v.t.* **a)** *(assist)* unterstützen; **b)** *(bet on)* wetten *od.* setzen auf (+ *Akk.*); **c)** zurücksetzen [mit] 〈*Fahrzeug*〉. **5.** *v.i.* zurücksetzen; **~ into/out of sth.** rückwärts in etw. (*Akk.*)/aus etw. fahren; **~ on to sth.** hinten an etw. (*Akk.*) grenzen. **back 'down** *v.i.* nachgeben. **back 'out** *v.i.* rückwärts herausfahren; **~ out of sth.** *(fig.)* von etw. zurücktreten. **back 'up** *v.t.* unterstützen; untermauern 〈*Anspruch, These*〉

back: ~ache *n.* Rückenschmerzen *Pl.;* **~-bencher** [bæk'bentʃə(r)] *n. (Brit. Parl.)* [einfacher] Abgeordneter/ [einfache] Abgeordnete; **~bone** *n.*

Rückgrat, *das;* ~**chat** *n. (coll.)* [freche] Widerrede; ~**date** *v. t.* zurückdatieren (**to auf** + *Akk.*); ~ '**door** *n.* Hintertür, *die*

'**backer** *n.* Geldgeber, *der*

back: ~·'**fire** *v. i.* knallen; *(fig.)* fehlschlagen; **it** ~**fired on me/him** *etc.* der Schuß ging nach hinten los *(ugs.);* ~**ground** *n.* Hintergrund, *der; (social status)* Herkunft, *die;* ~**hand** *(Tennis etc.)* **1.** *adj.* Rückhand-; **2.** *n.* Rückhand, *die;* ~·'**handed** *adj.* **a)** *(Tennis etc.)* Rückhand-; **b)** *(fig.)* indirekt; zweifelhaft ⟨*Kompliment*⟩; ~'**hander** *n. (sl.: bribe)* Schmiergeld, *das*

'**backing** *n. (support)* Unterstützung, *die*

back: ~**lash** *n. (fig.)* Gegenreaktion, *die;* ~**log** *n.* Rückstand, *der;* ~**number** *n.* alte Nummer; ~**pedal** *v. i.* die Pedale rückwärts treten; ~ '**seat** *n.* Rücksitz, *der;* ~**side** *n.* Hintern, *das (ugs.);* ~'**stage** *adv.* **go** ~**stage** hinter die Bühne gehen; ~ **street** *n.* kleine Seitenstraße; ~**stroke** *n.* Rückenschwimmen, *das*

backward ['bækwəd] **1.** *adj.* **a)** rückwärts gerichtet; Rückwärts-; **b)** *(reluctant, shy)* zurückhaltend; **c)** *(underdeveloped)* rückständig ⟨*Land, Region*⟩. **2.** *adv.* **see backwards**

backwards ['bækwədz] *adv.* **a)** nach hinten; **the child fell** [**over**] ~ **into the water** das Kind fiel rückwärts ins Wasser; **bend** *or* **lean over** ~ **to do sth.** *(fig. coll.)* sich zerreißen, um etw. zu tun *(ugs.);* **b)** *(oppositely to normal direction)* rückwärts; ~ **and forwards** hin und her

back: ~**water** *n. (fig.)* Kaff, *das (ugs.);* ~ '**yard** *n.* Hinterhof, *der*

bacon ['beɪkn] *n.* [Frühstücks]speck, *der*

bacterium [bæk'tɪərɪəm] *n., pl.* **bacteria** [bæk'tɪərɪə] Bakterie, *die*

bad [bæd] *adj., worse* [wɜːs], *worst* [wɜːst] **a)** schlecht; *(rotten)* schlecht, verdorben ⟨*Fleisch, Fisch, Essen*⟩; **not** ~ *(coll.)* nicht schlecht; nicht übel; **b)** *(naughty)* ungezogen, böse ⟨*Kind, Hund*⟩; **c)** *(offensive)* [**use**] ~ **language** Kraftausdrücke [benutzen]; **d)** *(regretful)* **feel** ~ **about sth.** etw. bedauern; **I feel** ~ **about him** ich habe seinetwegen ein schlechtes Gewissen; **e)** *(serious)* schlimm ⟨*Sturz, Krise*⟩; schwer ⟨*Fehler, Krankheit, Unfall;* **f)** *(Commerc.)* **a** ~ **debt** eine uneinbringliche Schuld

bade *see* **bid 1 b**

badge [bædʒ] *n.* Abzeichen, *das*

badger ['bædʒə(r)] *n.* Dachs, *der*

'**badly** *adv.,* **worse** [wɜːs], **worst** [wɜːst] **a)** schlecht; **b)** schwer ⟨*verletzt, beschädigt*⟩; **c)** *(urgently)* dringend

bad-mannered [bæd'mænəd] *adj.* **be** ~: schlechte Manieren haben

badminton ['bædmɪntn] *n.* Federball, *der; (als Sport)* Badminton, *das*

bad-tempered [bæd'tempəd] *adj.* griesgrämig

baffle ['bæfl] *v. t.* ~ **sb.** jmdm. unverständlich sein. **baffling** ['bæflɪŋ] *adj.* rätselhaft

bag [bæg] **1.** *n.* Tasche, *die; (sack)* Sack, *der; (hand~)* Handtasche, *die; (plastic ~)* Beutel, *der; (small paper ~)* Tüte, *die;* ~**s of** *(sl.: large amount)* jede Menge. **2.** *v. t.,* **-gg-: a)** in Säcke/Beutel/Tüten füllen; **b)** *(claim possession of)* sich *(Dat.)* schnappen *(ugs.)*

baggage ['bægɪdʒ] *n.* Gepäck, *das.* '**baggage reclaim** *n.* Gepäckausgabe, *die*

baggy ['bægɪ] *adj.* weit [geschnitten] ⟨*Kleid, Hose*⟩; *(through long use)* ausgebeult ⟨*Hose*⟩

'**bagpipe[s]** *n.* Dudelsack, *der*

Bahamas [bə'hɑːməz] *pr. n. pl.* **the** ~: die Bahamas

¹**bail** [beɪl] **1.** *n.* Kaution, *die;* **be** [**out**] **on** ~: gegen Kaution auf freiem Fuß sein. **2.** *v. t.* ~ **sb. out** jmdn. gegen Kaution freibekommen; *(fig.)* jmdm. aus der Klemme helfen *(ugs.)*

²**bail** *v. t. (scoop)* ~ **out** ausschöpfen. '**bail out** *v. i.* ⟨*Pilot:*⟩ abspringen

bailiff ['beɪlɪf] *n.* ≈ Gerichtsvollzieher, *der*

bait [beɪt] **1.** *v. t.* mit einem Köder versehen. **2.** *n.* Köder, *der*

bake [beɪk] *v. t. & i.* backen. '**baker** *n.* Bäcker, *der.* **bakery** ['beɪkərɪ] *n.* Bäckerei, *die*

baking: ~**powder** *n.* Backpulver, *das;* ~**tin** *n.* Backform, *die;* ~**tray** *n.* Kuchenblech, *das*

balance ['bæləns] **1.** *n.* **a)** *(instrument)* Waage, *die;* **b)** *(fig.)* **be** *or* **hang in the** ~: in der Schwebe sein; **c)** *(steady position)* Gleichgewicht, *das;* **keep/lose one's** ~: das Gleichgewicht halten/verlieren; *(fig.)* sein Gleichgewicht bewahren/verlieren; **strike a** ~ **between** *(fig.)* den Mittelweg finden zwischen *(+ Dat.);* **d)** *(difference)* Bilanz, *die; (state of bank account)* Kontostand, *der;* **on** ~ *(fig.)* al-

les in allem; ~ **sheet** Bilanz, *die;* **e)**
(Econ.) ~ **of payments** Zahlungsbi-
lanz, *die;* **f)** *(remainder)* Rest, *der* **2.**
v. t. **a)** *(weigh up)* abwägen; **b)** *(bring
into or keep in* ~) balancieren; aus-
wuchten *⟨Rad⟩;* **c)** *(equal, neutralize)*
ausgleichen; ~ **each other, be** ~**d** sich
(Dat.) die Waage halten. '**balanced**
adj. ausgewogen; ausgeglichen *⟨Per-
son, Team, Gemüt⟩*

balcony ['bælkənɪ] *n.* Balkon, *der*

bald [bɔːld] *adj.* kahl *⟨Kopf⟩;* kahlköp-
fig, glatzköpfig *(Person)*

bale [beɪl] *n.* Ballen, *der*

balk [bɔːlk] **1.** *v. i.* **they were ~ed in
their plan** ihr Plan wurde blockiert. **2.**
v. i. sich sträuben (**at** gegen)

Balkan [bɔːlkn] **1.** *adj.* Balkan-. **2.**
pl. **the** ~**s** der Balkan

¹**ball** [bɔːl] *n.* **a)** Ball, *der;* (*Billiards etc.,
Croquet*) Kugel, *die;* **be on the** ~ *(coll.:
be alert)* auf Zack sein *(ugs.);* **b)** *(of
wool, string, fluff, etc.)* Knäuel, *das*

²**ball** *n. (dance)* Ball, *der*

ballad ['bæləd] *n.* Ballade, *die*

ballast ['bæləst] *n.* Ballast, *der*

ball-'bearing *n.* Kugellager, *das*

ballerina [bælə'riːnə] *n.* Ballerina, *die*

ballet ['bæleɪ] *n.* Ballett, *das;* ~ **dancer**
Ballettänzer, *der/*Ballettänzerin, *die*

balloon [bə'luːn] *n.* **a)** Ballon, *der;*
hot-air ~: Heißluftballon, *der;* **b)**
(toy) Luftballon, *der*

ballot ['bælət] *n.* Abstimmung, *die;*
[**secret**] ~: geheime Wahl

ball: ~**-pen, ~-point 'pen** *ns.* Kugelschreiber, *der;* ~**room** *n.* Tanzsaal,
der

balm [bɑːm] *n.* Balsam, *der*

balmy ['bɑːmɪ] *adj. (mild)* mild

Baltic ['bɔːltɪk] **1.** *pr. n.* Ostsee, *die.* **2.**
adj. ~ **Sea** Ostsee, *die*

balustrade [bælə'streɪd] *n.* Balustrade, *die*

bamboo [bæm'buː] *n.* Bambus, *der*

ban [bæn] **1.** *v. t.,* -nn- verbieten; ~ **sb.
from doing sth.** jmdm. verbieten, etw.
zu tun. **2.** *n.* Verbot, *das*

banal [bə'nɑːl] *adj.* banal

banana [bə'nɑːnə] *n.* Banane, *die*

band [bænd] **1.** *n.* **a)** Band, *das;* **a** ~ **of
light/colour** ein Streifen Licht/Farbe;
b) *(range of values)* Bandbreite, *die;* **c)**
(organized group) Gruppe, *die;* (*of rob-
bers, outlaws, etc.*) Bande, *die;* **d)**
(Mus.) [Musik]kapelle, *die;* (*pop
group, jazz* ~) Band, *die.* **2.** *v. i.* ~
together [**with sb.**] sich [mit jmdm.] zusammenschließen

bandage ['bændɪdʒ] **1.** *n.* Verband,
der; (*as support*) Bandage, *die.* **2.** *v. t.*
verbinden; bandagieren *⟨verstauch-
tes⟩ Gelenk usw.⟩*

bandit ['bændɪt] *n.* Bandit, *der*

band: ~**stand** *n.* Musiktribüne, *die;*
~**wagon** *n.* **climb** or **jump on** [**to**] **the**
~**wagon** *(fig.)* auf den fahrenden Zug
aufspringen *(fig.)*

¹**bandy** ['bændɪ] *v. t.* **they were ~ing
words/insults** sie stritten sich/be-
schimpften sich gegenseitig

²**bandy** *adj.* krumm; **he is ~-legged** er
hat O-Beine *(ugs.)*

bang [bæŋ] **1.** *v. t.* knallen *(ugs.);*
schlagen; zuknallen *(ugs.) ⟨Tür, Fenster, Deckel⟩;* ~ **one's head on sth.** mit
dem Kopf an etw. *(Akk.)* knallen
(ugs.). **2.** *v. i. (strike)* ~ [**against sth.**]
[gegen etw.] knallen *(ugs.);* ~ **shut**
⟨Tür:⟩ zuknallen *(ugs.).* **3.** *n.* **a)** *(blow)*
Schlag, *der;* **b)** *(noise)* Knall, *der.* **4.**
adv. **go** ~ *⟨Gewehr, Feuerwerkskörper:⟩* krachen

'**banger** *n. (sl.)* **a)** *(sausage)* Würstchen, *das;* **b)** *(firework)* Kracher, *der
(ugs.);* **c)** *(car)* Klapperkiste, *die (ugs.)*

bangle ['bæŋgl] *n.* Armreif, *der*

banish ['bænɪʃ] *v. t.* verbannen (**from**
aus)

banister ['bænɪstə(r)] *n.* [Treppen]ge-
länder, *das*

banjo ['bændʒəʊ] *n., pl.* ~**s** or ~**es**
Banjo, *das*

¹**bank** [bæŋk] *n.* **a)** *(slope)* Böschung,
die; **b)** *(of river)* Ufer, *das*

²**bank** **1.** *n. (Finance)* Bank, *die.* **2.** *v. i.*
~ **at/with ...:** ein Konto haben bei ...;
~ **on sth.** *(fig.)* auf etw. *(Akk.)* zählen.
3. *v. t.* zur Bank bringen

bank: ~ **account** *n.* Bankkonto, *das;*
~ **card** *n.* Scheckkarte, *die;* ~ **clerk**
n. Bankangestellte, *der/die*

'**banker** *n.* Bankier, *der*

bank 'holiday *n. (Brit.)* Feiertag, *der*

'**banking** *n.* Bankwesen, *das*

bank: ~ **manager** *n.* Zweigstellenlei-
ter/-leiterin [einer/der Bank]; ~**note**
n. Banknote, *die*

bankrupt ['bæŋkrʌpt] **1.** *n.* Bankrot-
teur, *der.* **2.** *adj.* **go** ~: Bankrott machen. **3.** *v. t.* bankrott machen. **bankruptcy** ['bæŋkrʌptsɪ] *n.* Konkurs,
der; Bankrott, *der*

banner ['bænə(r)] *n.* Banner, *das;* (*on
two poles*) Spruchband, *das*

banns [bænz] *n. pl.* Aufgebot, *das*

banquet ['bæŋkwɪt] *n.* Bankett, *das*

baptism ['bæptɪzm] *n.* Taufe, *die*

Baptist ['bæptɪst] *n.* Baptist, *der*/Baptistin, *die*

baptize [bæp'taɪz] *v.t.* taufen

bar [bɑː(r)] **1.** *n.* **a)** Stange, *die; (shorter, thinner also)* Stab, *der; (of cage, prison)* Gitterstab, *der;* **a ~ of soap** ein Stück Seife; **a ~ of chocolate** eine Tafel Schokolade; **b)** *(for refreshment)* Bar, *die; (counter)* Theke, *die.* **2.** *v.t., -rr-:* **a)** *(fasten)* verriegeln; **b)** ~ **sb.'s way** jmdm. den Weg versperren; **c)** *(prohibit, hinder)* verbieten; ~ **sb. from doing sth.** jmdn. daran hindern, etw. zu tun. **3.** *prep.* abgesehen von; ~ **none** ohne Einschränkung

barb [bɑːb] *n.* Widerhaken, *der*

barbarian [bɑː'beərɪən] *n.* Barbar, *der*

barbaric [bɑː'bærɪk] *adj.* barbarisch

barbarity [bɑː'bærɪtɪ] *n.* Grausamkeit, *die*

barbecue ['bɑːbɪkjuː] **1.** *n.* **a)** *(party)* Grillparty, *die;* **b)** *(food)* Grillgericht, *das.* **2.** *v.t.* grillen

barbed wire [bɑːbd 'waɪə(r)] *n.* Stacheldraht, *der*

barber ['bɑːbə(r)] *n.* [Herren]friseur, *der*

'bar code *n.* Strichcode, *der*

bare [beə(r)] **1.** *adj.* nackt; *(leafless, unfurnished)* kahl; *(empty)* leer; äußerst ⟨*Notwendige*⟩; **do sth. with one's ~ hands** etw. mit den bloßen Händen tun. **2.** *v.t.* entblößen ⟨*Kopf, Arm, Bein*⟩; blecken ⟨*Zähne*⟩. **'barefaced** *adj. (fig.)* unverhüllt. **'barefoot 1.** *adj.* barfüßig. **2.** *adv.* barfuß

barely ['beəlɪ] *adv.* kaum; knapp ⟨*vermeiden, entkommen*⟩

bargain ['bɑːgɪn] **1.** *n.* **a)** *(agreement)* Abmachung, *die;* **into the ~:** darüber hinaus; **b)** *(thing offered cheap)* günstiges Angebot; *(thing acquired cheaply)* guter Kauf. **2.** *v.i.* **a)** *(discuss)* handeln; **b)** ~ **for or on sth.** *(expect sth.)* mit etw. rechnen

barge [bɑːdʒ] **1.** *n.* Kahn, *der.* **2.** *v.i.* ~ **into sb.** jmdn. anrempeln; ~ **in** *(intrude)* hineinplatzen/hereinplatzen *(ugs.)*

baritone ['bærɪtəʊn] **1.** *n.* Bariton, *der.* **2.** *adj.* Bariton-

'bark [bɑːk] *n. (of tree)* Rinde, *die*

'bark [bɑːk] **1.** *n. (of dog)* Bellen, *das.* **2.** *v.i.* bellen; **be ~ing up the wrong tree** auf dem Holzweg sein

barley ['bɑːlɪ] *n.* Gerste, *die*

bar: ~**maid** *n. (Brit.)* Bardame, *die;* ~**man** ['bɑːmən] *n., pl.* ~**men** ['bɑːmən] Barmann, *der*

barmy ['bɑːmɪ] *adj. (sl.: crazy)* bescheuert *(salopp)*

barn [bɑːn] *n. (Brit.: for grain etc.)* Scheune, *die; (Amer.: for animals)* Stall, *der*

barnacle ['bɑːnəkl] *n.* Rankenfüßer, *der*

barometer [bə'rɒmɪtə(r)] *n.* Barometer, *das*

baron ['bærn] *n.* Baron, *der;* Freiherr, *der;* **baroness** ['bærənɪs] *n.* Baronin, *die;* Freifrau, *die*

baroque [bə'rɒk, bə'rəʊk] **1.** *n.* Barock, *das.* **2.** *adj.* barock

barracks ['bærəks] *n. pl.* Kaserne, *die*

barrage ['bærɑːʒ] *n. (Mil.)* Sperrfeuer, *das;* **a ~ of questions** ein Bombardement von Fragen

barrel ['bærl] *n.* **a)** Faß, *das;* **b)** *(of gun)* Lauf, *der*

barren ['bærn] *adj.* unfruchtbar

barricade [bærɪ'keɪd] **1.** *n.* Barrikade, *die.* **2.** *v.t.* verbarrikadieren

barrier ['bærɪə(r)] *n.* Barriere, *die; (at level crossing etc.)* Schranke, *die*

barring ['bɑːrɪŋ] *prep.* außer im Falle (+ *Gen.*)

barrister ['bærɪstə(r)] *n. (Brit.)* ~[-**at-law**] Barrister, *der;* ≈ [Rechts]anwalt/ -anwältin vor höheren Gerichten

barrow ['bærəʊ] *n.* **a)** Karre, *die;* Karren, *der;* **b)** *see* wheelbarrow

barter ['bɑːtə(r)] **1.** *v.t.* [ein]tauschen; ~ **sth. for sth.** [else] etw. für *od.* gegen etw. [anderes] [ein]tauschen. **2.** *v.i.* Tauschhandel treiben. **3.** *n.* Tauschhandel, *der*

base [beɪs] **1.** *n.* **a)** *(of lamp, mountain)* Fuß, *der; (of cupboard, statue)* Sockel, *der; (fig.: support)* Basis, *die;* **b)** *(Mil.)* Basis, *die;* Stützpunkt, *der.* **2.** *v.t.* **a)** **be ~d on sth.** sich auf etw. *(Akk.)* gründen; ~ **sth. on sth.** etw. auf etw. *(Dat.)* aufbauen; **b)** *in pass.* **be ~d in Paris** *(permanently)* in Paris sitzen; *(temporarily)* in Paris sein

'baseball *n.* Baseball, *der*

basement ['beɪsmənt] *n.* Untergeschoß, *das;* **a ~ flat** eine Kellerwohnung

bash [bæʃ] *v.t. (heftig)* schlagen

bashful ['bæʃfl] *adj.* schüchtern

basic ['beɪsɪk] *adj.* grundlegend; Grund⟨*prinzip, -bestandteil, -lohn, -gehalt usw.*⟩; Haupt⟨*problem, -grund, -sache*⟩; **be ~ to sth.** wesentlich für etw. sein. **basically** ['beɪsɪkəlɪ] *adv.* im Grunde; grundsätzlich ⟨*übereinstimmen*⟩; *(mainly)* hauptsächlich

basil ['bæzɪl] *n.* Basilikum, *das*

basin ['beɪsn] n. a) Becken, das; (wash-~) Waschbecken, das; (bowl) Schüssel, die; b) (of river) Becken, das

basis ['beɪsɪs] n., pl. **bases** ['beɪsiːz] Basis, die; Grundlage, die

bask [bɑːsk] v. i. sich [wohlig] wärmen

basket ['bɑːskɪt] n. Korb, der. '**basketball** n. Basketball, der

Basle [bɑːl] pr. n. Basel (das)

bass [beɪs] 1. n. a) Baß, der; b) (coll.) (double-~) [Kontra]baß, der; (~ guitar) Baß, der. 2. adj. Baß-. **bass guitar** n. Baßgitarre, die

bassoon [bə'suːn] n. Fagott, das

bastard ['bɑːstəd] 1. adj. unehelich. 2. n. a) uneheliches Kind; b) (coll. derog.: person) Schweinehund, der (derb)

baste ['beɪst] v. t. [mit Fett] begießen

bastion ['bæstɪən] n. Bastei, die

¹bat [bæt] n. (Zool.) Fledermaus, die

²bat 1. n. (Sport) Schlagholz, das; (for table-tennis) Schläger, der; **do sth. off one's own ~** (fig.) etw. auf eigene Faust tun. 2. v. t., -tt- schlagen

³bat 1. **not ~ an eyelid** nicht mit der Wimper zucken

batch [bætʃ] n. a) (of loaves) Schub, der; b) (of people) Gruppe, die; (of books, papers) Stapel, der

bated ['beɪtɪd] v. t. **with ~ breath** mit angehaltenem Atem

bath [bɑːθ] 1. n., pl. **~s** [bɑːðz] a) Bad, das; **have or take a ~:** ein Bad nehmen; b) (tub) Badewanne, die; **room with ~:** Zimmer mit Bad; c) usu. in pl. (building) Bad, das. 2. v. t. & i. baden. '**bath cubes** n. pl. Badesalz, das

bathe [beɪð] v. t. & i. baden. **bather** ['beɪðə(r)] n. Badende, der/die. '**bathing** ['beɪðɪŋ] n. Baden, das. '**bathing-costume**, '**bathing-suit** ns. Badeanzug, der

bath: **~-mat** n. Badematte, die; **~-room** n. Badezimmer, das; **~ salts** n. pl. Badesalz, das; **~-towel** n. Badetuch, das; **~-tub** see bath 1 b

baton ['bætn] n. a) (truncheon) Schlagstock, der; b) (Mus.) Taktstock, der

batsman ['bætsmən] n., pl. **batsmen** ['bætsmən] Schlagmann, der

battalion [bə'tæljən] n. Bataillon, das

¹batter ['bætə(r)] v. t. (strike) einschlagen auf (+ Akk.)

²batter n. (Cookery) [Back]teig, der

battery ['bætərɪ] n. Batterie, die

battery: **~ charger** n. Batterieladegerät, das; **~ farming** n. Batteriehaltung, die; **~ 'hen** n. Batteriehuhn, das

battle ['bætl] 1. n. Schlacht, die; (fig.) Kampf, der. 2. v. i. kämpfen

battle: **~axe** n. (coll.: woman) Schreckschraube, die (ugs.); **~field**, **~ground** ns. Schlachtfeld, das

battlements ['bætlmənts] n. pl. Zinnen Pl.

'**battleship** n. Schlachtschiff, das

batty ['bætɪ] adj. (sl.) bekloppt (salopp)

bauble ['bɔːbl] n. Flitter, der

baulk see balk

Bavaria [bə'veərɪə] pr. n. Bayern (das). **Bavarian** [bə'veərɪən] 1. adj. bay[e]risch. 2. n. Bayer, der/Bayerin, die

bawdy ['bɔːdɪ] adj. zweideutig; (stronger) obszön

¹bay [beɪ] n. (of sea) Bucht, die

²bay n. a) (space in room) Erker, der; b) [parking-]~: Stellplatz, der

³bay n. **hold or keep sb./sth. at ~:** sich (Dat.) jmdn./etw. vom Leib halten

bayonet ['beɪənɪt] n. Bajonett, das

bay 'window n. Erkerfenster, das

bazaar [bə'zɑː(r)] n. Basar, der

BBC abbr. **British Broadcasting Corporation** BBC, die

BC abbr. **before Christ** v. Chr.

be [biː] v., pres. t. **I am** [əm, stressed æm], **he is** [ɪz], **we are** [ə(r), stressed ɑː(r)]; p. t. **I was** [wəz, stressed wɒz], **we were** [wə(r), stressed wɜː(r)]; pres. p. **being** ['biːɪŋ]; p. p. **been** [bɪn, stressed biːn] 1. copula a) sein; **she is a mother/an Italian/a teacher** sie ist Mutter/Italienerin/Lehrerin; **be sensible!** sei vernünftig!; **be ill/unwell** krank sein/sich nicht wohl fühlen; **I am well** es geht mir gut; **I am hot** mir ist heiß; **I am freezing** mich friert es; **how are you/is she?** wie geht's (ugs.)/geht es ihr?; **it is the 5th today** heute haben wir den Fünften; **who's that?** wer ist das?; **if I were you** an deiner Stelle; **it's hers** es ist ihrs; b) (cost) kosten; **how much are the eggs?** was kosten die Eier?; **two times three is six, two threes are six** zweimal drei ist od. sind sechs; (constitute) bilden. 2. v. i. a) (exist) [vorhanden] sein; **there is/are ...:** es gibt ...; **for the time being** vorläufig; **be that as it may** wie dem auch sei; b) (remain) bleiben; **I shan't be a moment** ich komme sofort; **let it be** laß es sein; **let him/her be** laß ihn/sie in Ruhe; c) (happen) stattfinden; sein; d) (go, come) **be off with you!** geh/geht!; **I'm off home** ich gehe jetzt nach Hause; **she's from Australia** sie stammt od. ist aus Australien; e) (go or come *on visit)* sein; **have you [ever] been to London?** bist du schon einmal in London gewesen?; **has anyone been?** ist jemand dagewesen? **3.** *v. aux.* **a)** *forming passive* werden; **the child was found** das Kind wurde gefunden; **German is spoken** hier wird Deutsch gesprochen; **b)** *forming continuous tenses, active* **he is reading** er liest [gerade]; **I am leaving tomorrow** ich reise morgen [ab]; **the train was departing when I got there** der Zug fuhr gerade ab, als ich ankam; **c)** *forming continuous tenses, passive* **the house is/was being built** das Haus wird/wurde [gerade] gebaut; **d)** *expr. arrangement, obligation* be to sollen; **I am to go/to inform you** ich soll gehen/Sie unterrichten; **e)** *expr. destiny* **they were never to meet again** sie sollten sich nie wieder treffen; **f)** *expr. condition* **if I were to tell you that ...:** wenn ich dir sagen würde, daß ... **4. bride-/husband-to-be** zukünftige Braut/zukünftiger Ehemann

beach [biːtʃ] *n.* Strand, *der;* **on the ~:** am Strand. **'beach wear** *n.* Strandkleidung, *die*

beacon ['biːkn] *n.* Leuchtfeuer, *das;* *(Naut.)* Leuchtbake, *die*

bead [biːd] *n.* Perle, *die;* **~s** Perlen *Pl.;* Perlenkette, *die;* **~s** of dew/sweat Tau-/Schweißtropfen

beak [biːk] *n.* Schnabel, *der*

beaker ['biːkə(r)] *n.* Becher, *der*

beam [biːm] **1.** *n.* **a)** *(timber etc.)* Balken, *der;* **b)** *(ray etc.)* [Licht]strahl, *der.* **2.** *v. i.* **a)** *(shine)* strahlen; glänzen; **b)** *(smile)* strahlen; **~ at sb.** jmdn. anstrahlen

bean [biːn] *n.* Bohne, *die;* **full of ~s** *(fig. coll.)* putzmunter *(ugs.)*

¹bear [beə(r)] *n.* Bär, *der*

²bear 1. *v. t.,* **bore** [bɔː(r)], **borne** [bɔːn] **a)** tragen; aufweisen *(Spuren, Ähnlichkeit);* tragen, führen *(Namen, Titel);* **~ some/little relation to sth.** einen gewissen/wenig Bezug zu etw. haben; **b)** *(endure, tolerate)* ertragen *(Schmerz, Kummer);* **with neg.** ertragen, aushalten *(Schmerz);* ausstehen *(Geruch, Lärm);* **c)** *(be fit for)* vertragen; **it will not ~ scrutiny** es hält einer Überprüfung nicht stand; **it does not ~ thinking about** daran darf man gar nicht denken; **d)** *(give birth to)* gebären *(Kind, Junges).* **2.** *v. i.,* **bore, borne: ~ left** *(Person.)* sich links halten; **the path ~s to the left** der Weg führt nach

links. **bear 'out** *v. t. (fig.)* bestätigen *(Bericht, Erklärung);* **~ sb. out** jmdm. recht geben. **'bear with** *v. t.* Nachsicht haben mit

bearable ['beərəbl] *adj.* erträglich

beard [bɪəd] *n.* Bart, *der.* **'bearded** *adj.* bärtig. **be ~:** einen Bart haben

'bearer *n. (carrier)* Träger, *der/*Trägerin, *die;* *(of message, cheque)* Überbringer, *der/*Überbringerin, *die*

'bearing *n.* **a)** *(behaviour)* Verhalten, *das;* **b)** *(relation)* Bezug, *der;* **have some/no ~ on sth.** relevant/irrelevant für etw. sein; **c)** *(Mech. Engin.)* Lager, *das;* **d)** *(compass ~)* Position, *die;* **take a compass ~:** den Kompaßkurs feststellen; **get one's ~s** sich orientieren; *(fig.)* sich zurechtfinden

beast [biːst] *n.* Tier, *das;* *(fig.: brutal person)* Bestie, *die.* **'beastly** *adj., adv. (coll.)* scheußlich

beat [biːt] **1.** *v. t.,* **beat, beaten** ['biːtn] schlagen; klopfen *(Teppich);* *(surpass)* brechen *(Rekord);* **hard to ~:** schwer zu schlagen; **it ~s me how/why ...:** es ist mir ein Rätsel wie/warum ...; **~ time** den Takt schlagen; **~ it!** *(sl.)* hau ab! *(ugs.);* see also **beaten 2.** *v. i.,* **beat, beaten** schlagen **(on** auf + *Akk.);* *(Regen, Hagel:)* prasseln **(against** gegen). **3.** *n.* **a)** *(stroke, throbbing)* Schlagen, *das;* *(Mus.) (rhythm)* Takt, *der;* *(single ~)* Schlag, *der;* **b)** *(of policeman)* Runde, *die.* **beat 'off** *v. t.* abwehren *(Angriff).* **beat 'up** *v. t.* zusammenschlagen *(Person)*

beaten ['biːtn] **1.** *see* beat 1, 2. **2.** *adj.* **a)** **off the ~ track** weit abgelegen; **b)** gehämmert *(Silber, Gold)*

'beating *n.* **a)** *(punishment)* **a ~:** Schläge *Pl.;* Prügel *Pl.;* **b)** *(defeat)* Niederlage, *die;* **c)** **take some/a lot of ~:** nicht leicht zu übertreffen sein

'beat-up *adj. (sl.)* ramponiert *(ugs.)*

beautiful ['bjuːtɪfl] *adj.* schön; wunderschön *(Augen, Aussicht, Morgen)*. **beautify** ['bjuːtɪfaɪ] *v. t.* verschönen

beauty ['bjuːtɪ] *n.* Schönheit, *die;* *(beautiful feature)* Schöne, *das;* **the ~ of it** das Schöne daran

beauty: ~ parlour *see* **~ salon; ~ queen** *n.* Schönheitskönigin, *die;* **~ salon** *n.* Kosmetiksalon, *der;* **~ spot** *n.* Schönheitsfleck, *der;* *(place)* schönes Fleckchen [Erde]

beaver ['biːvə(r)] *n.* Biber, *der*

became *see* become

because [bɪˈkɒz] **1.** *conj.* weil. **2.** *adv.* **~ of** wegen (+ *Gen.)*

beckon ['bekn] *v. t. & i.* winken (**to** sb. jmdm.); *(fig.)* locken

become [bɪ'kʌm] **1.** *copula, became* [bɪ'keɪm], become werden; ~ **a politician** Politiker werden; ~ **a nuisance/ rule** zu einer Plage/zur Regel werden. **2.** *v. i.,* **became, become** werden; **what has** ~ **of him?** was ist aus ihm geworden? **3.** *v. t.,* **became, become** (*suit*) ~ **sb.** jmdm. stehen

becoming [bɪ'kʌmɪŋ] *adj.* **a)** *(fitting)* schicklich *(geh.);* **b)** *(flattering)* vorteilhaft ⟨*Hut, Kleid, Frisur*⟩

bed [bed] *n.* **a)** Bett, *das; (without bedstead)* Lager, *das;* **in** ~: im Bett; ~ **and breakfast** Zimmer mit Frühstück; **get out of/into** ~: aufstehen/ins Bett gehen; **go to** ~: ins Bett gehen; **put** sb. **to** ~: jmdn. ins Bett bringen; **b)** *(flat base)* Unterlage, *die;* **c)** *(of machine)* Bett, *das;* **c)** *(in garden)* Beet, *das;* **d)** *(of sea, lake)* Grund, *der; (of river)* Bett, *das.* '**bedclothes** *n. pl.* Bettzeug, *das.* **bedding** ['bedɪŋ] *n.* Matratze und Bettzeug

bedlam ['bedləm] *n., no indef. art.* Tumult, *der*

'**bedpan** *n.* Bettpfanne, *die*

bedraggled [bɪ'dræɡld] *adj. (soaked)* durchnäßt; *(with mud)* verdreckt

bed: ~**ridden** *adj.* bettlägerig; ~**room** *n.* Schlafzimmer, *das;* ~**side** *n.* Seite des Bettes, *die;* ~**side table/ lamp** Nachttisch, *der*/Nachttischlampe, *die;* ~**sit,** ~'**sitter** *ns. (coll.)* Wohnschlafzimmer, *das;* ~**spread** *n.* Tagesdecke, *die;* ~**stead** *n.* Bettgestell, *das;* ~**time** *n.* Schlafenszeit, *die;* **at** ~**time** vor dem Zubettgehen; **a** ~**time story** eine Gutenachtgeschichte

bee [biː] *n.* Biene, *die*

beech [biːtʃ] *n.* Buche, *die*

beef [biːf] **1.** *n.* **a)** Rindfleisch, *das;* **b)** *(coll.: muscles)* Muskeln. **2.** *v. t.* ~ **up** stärken. **beefburger** ['biːfbɜːɡə(r)] *n.* Beefburger, *der*

bee: ~**hive** *n.* Bienenstock, *der;* ~**keeper** *n.* Imker, *der*/Imkerin, *die;* ~**keeping** *n.* Imkerei, *die;* ~**line** *n.* **make a** ~**line for** sth./sb. schnurstracks auf etw./jmdn. zustürzen

been *see* **be**

beer [bɪə(r)] *n.* Bier, *das*

beet [biːt] *n.* Rübe, *die*

beetle ['biːtl] *n.* Käfer, *der*

'**beetroot** *n.* rote Beete *od.* Rübe

before [bɪ'fɔː(r)] **1.** *adv.* **a)** *(of time)* vorher; *(already)* schon; **the day** ~:

am Tag zuvor; **never** ~: noch nie; **b)** *(ahead in position)* vor[aus]. **2.** *prep. (of time; position)* vor (+ *Dat.*); *(direction)* vor (+ *Akk.*); **the day** ~ **yesterday** vorgestern; ~ **now/then** früher/vorher; ~ **Christ** vor Christus; ~ **leaving, he phoned** bevor er wegging, rief er an. **3.** *conj.* bevor. **be'forehand** *adv.* vorher; *(in anticipation)* im voraus

beg [beɡ] **1.** *v. t.,* **-gg-:** **a)** betteln um; **b)** *(ask earnestly for)* ~ sth. um etw. bitten. **2.** *v. i.,* **-gg-** betteln (**for** um)

began *see* **begin**

beggar ['beɡə(r)] *n.* **a)** Bettler, *der*/Bettlerin, *die;* **b)** *(coll.)* **poor** ~: armer Teufel

begin [bɪ'ɡɪn] **1.** *v. t.,* **-nn-,** began [bɪ-'ɡæn], begun [bɪ'ɡʌn] ~ sth. [mit] etw. beginnen; ~ **doing** *or* **to do** sth. anfangen *od.* beginnen, etw. zu tun. **2.** *v. i.,* **-nn-,** began, begun anfangen; ~ [up]on sth. etw. anfangen. **be'ginner** *n.* Anfänger, *der*/Anfängerin, *die.* **be'ginning** *n.* Anfang, *der;* **at** *or* **in the** ~: am Anfang; **at the** ~ **of February/the month** Anfang Februar/des Monats; **from the** ~: von Anfang an

begrudge [bɪ'ɡrʌdʒ] *v. t.* ~ sb. sth. jmdm. etw. mißgönnen; ~ **doing** sth. etw. ungern tun

begun *see* **begin**

behalf [bɪ'hɑːf] *n.* **on** *or* *(Amer.)* **in** ~ **of** sb./sth. für jmdn./etw.; *(more formally)* im Namen von jmdm./etw.

behave [bɪ'heɪv] **1.** *v. i.* sich verhalten; sich benehmen; **well-/ill-** *or* **badly** ~**d** brav/ungezogen. **2.** *v. refl.* ~ **oneself** sich benehmen. **behaviour** [bɪ'heɪvjə(r)] *n.* Verhalten, *das*

behead [bɪ'hed] *v. t.* enthaupten

behind [bɪ'haɪnd] **1.** *adv.* hinten; *(further back)* **be miles** ~: kilometerweit zurückliegen; **stay** ~: dableiben; **leave** sb./sth. ~: jmdn./etw. zurücklassen; **fall** ~: zurückbleiben; *(fig.)* in Rückstand geraten; **be/get** ~ **with one's payments/rent** mit seinen Zahlungen/der Miete im Rückstand sein/in Rückstand geraten. **2.** *prep.* **a)** hinter (+ *Dat.*); **one** ~ **the other** hintereinander; **b)** *(towards rear of)* hinter (+ *Akk.*)

being ['biːɪŋ] *n.* **a)** *(existence)* Dasein, *das;* **in** ~: bestehend; **come into** ~: entstehen; **b)** *(person etc.)* Wesen, *das*

belated [bɪ'leɪtɪd] *adj.,* **be'latedly** *adv.* verspätet

belch [beltʃ] **1.** *v. i.* heftig aufstoßen; rülpsen *(ugs.).* **2.** *n.* Rülpser, *der (ugs.)*

belfry ['belfrɪ] n. Glockenturm, der

Belgian ['beldʒən] 1. n. Belgier, der/Belgierin, die. 2. adj. belgisch

Belgium ['beldʒəm] pr. n. Belgien (das)

belie [bɪ'laɪ] v. t., **belying** [bɪ'laɪɪŋ] hinwegtäuschen über ⟨Tatsachen, wahren Zustand⟩; nicht erfüllen ⟨Versprechen⟩; nicht entsprechen ⟨Vorstellung (Dat.)⟩

belief [bɪ'li:f] n. a) Glaube, der (in an + Akk.); **in the ~ that** ...: in der Überzeugung, daß ...; b) (Relig.) Glaube[n], der

believable [bɪ'li:vəbl] adj. glaubhaft

believe [bɪ'li:v] 1. v. i. glauben (in an + Dat.); (have faith) glauben (in an + Akk.) ⟨Gott, Himmel usw.⟩; **I ~ so/not** ich glaube schon/nicht. 2. v. t. glauben; **~ sb.** jmdm. glauben; **I don't ~ you** das glaube ich dir nicht; **make ~ that** ...: so tun, als ob ...

Belisha beacon [bəli:ʃə 'bi:kn] n. (Brit.) gelbes Blinklicht an Zebrastreifen

belittle [bɪ'lɪtl] v. t. herabsetzen

bell [bel] n. Glocke, die; (door~) Klingel, die

belligerent [bɪ'lɪdʒərənt] adj. kriegführend ⟨Nation⟩; streitlustig ⟨Person⟩

bellow ['beləʊ] 1. v. i. brüllen. 2. v. t. ~ [out] brüllen ⟨Befehl⟩

bellows ['beləʊz] n. pl. Blasebalg, der

belly ['belɪ] n. Bauch, der. **bellyache** n. Bauchschmerzen Pl.

belong [bɪ'lɒŋ] v. i. ~ **to sb./sth.** jmdm./zu etw. gehören; ~ **to a club** einem Verein angehören; **where does this ~?** wo gehört das hin? **be'longings** n. pl. Habe, die; Sachen Pl.

beloved [bɪ'lʌvɪd] 1. adj. geliebt. 2. n. Geliebte, der/die

below [bɪ'ləʊ] 1. adv. a) (position) unten; (lower down) darunter; **from ~:** von unten [herauf]; b) (direction) nach unten; hinunter. 2. prep. unter (position: + Dat.; direction: + Akk.)

belt [belt] n. Gürtel, der; (for tools, weapons, ammunition) Gurt, der; (of trees) Streifen, der. **belt 'up** v. i. (Brit. sl.) die Klappe halten (salopp)

bemused [bɪ'mju:zd] adj. verwirrt

bench [bentʃ] n. Bank, die; (worktable) Werkbank, die

bend [bend] 1. n. Beuge, die; (in road) Kurve, die. 2. v. t., **bent** [bent] biegen; beugen ⟨Arm, Knie⟩; anwinkeln ⟨Bein⟩. 3. v. i., **bent** sich biegen; (bow) sich bücken. **bend 'down** v. i. sich

bücken. **bend 'over** v. i. sich nach vorn beugen

beneath [bɪ'ni:θ] prep. a) (unworthy of) ~ **sb.**, ~ **sb.'s dignity** unter jmds. Würde (Dat.); b) (arch./literary: under) unter (+ Dat.)

benefactor ['benɪfæktə(r)] n. Wohltäter, der; (patron) Gönner, der

beneficial [benɪ'fɪʃl] adj. nützlich; vorteilhaft ⟨Einfluß⟩

benefit ['benɪfɪt] 1. n. a) Vorteil, der; **be of ~ to sb./sth.** jmdm./einer Sache von Nutzen sein; **have the ~ of** den Vorteil (+ Gen.) haben; **with the ~ of** mit Hilfe (+ Gen.); **for sb.'s ~:** in jmds. Interesse (Dat.); b) (allowance) Beihilfe, die; **unemployment ~:** Arbeitslosenunterstützung, die. 2. v. t. nützen (+ Dat.). 3. v. i. ~ **by/from sth.** von etw. profitieren

benevolent [bɪ'nevələnt] adj. a) gütig; b) wohltätig ⟨Institution, Verein⟩

benign [bɪ'naɪn] adj. gütig; (Med.) gutartig

bent [bent] 1. see **bend** 2, 3. 2. n. (liking) Neigung, die (for zu). 3. a) adj. krumm; b) (Brit. sl.: corrupt) link (salopp)

bequeath [bɪ'kwi:ð] v. t. ~ **sth. to sb.** jmdm. etw. hinterlassen. **bequest** [bɪ'kwest] n. Legat, das (+ Akk.)

bereaved [bɪ'ri:vd] n. **the ~:** der/die Hinterbliebene/die Hinterbliebenen

beret ['bereɪ] n. Baskenmütze, die

Berlin [bɜ:'lɪn] pr. n. Berlin (das)

Berne [bɜ:n] pr. n. Bern (das)

berry ['berɪ] n. Beere, die

berserk [bə'sɜ:k] adj. rasend; **go ~:** durchdrehen (ugs.)

berth [bɜ:θ] n. (for ship) Liegeplatz, der; (sleeping-place) (in ship) Koje, die; (in train) Schlafwagenbett, das

beside [bɪ'saɪd] prep. a) neben (+ Dat.); ~ **the sea/lake** am Meer/See; b) **be ~ the point** nichts damit zu tun haben; c) ~ **oneself** außer sich

besides [bɪ'saɪdz] 1. adv. außerdem. 2. prep. außer

besiege [bɪ'si:dʒ] v. t. belagern

best [best] 1. adj. best...; **the ~ part of an hour** fast eine ganze Stunde. 2. adv. am besten. 3. n. **the ~:** der/die/das Beste; **do one's ~:** sein bestes tun; **make the ~ of it** das Beste daraus machen; **at ~:** bestenfalls. **best 'man** n. Trauzeuge, der (des Bräutigams). **best 'seller** n. Bestseller, der

bet [bet] 1. v. t. & i., **-tt-**, ~ **or ~ted** wetten; **I ~ him £10** ich habe mit ihm um

10 Pfund gewettet; ~ **on** sth. auf etw. *(Akk.)* setzen. **2.** *n.* Wette, *die; (fig. coll.)* Tip, *der*

betray [bɪ'treɪ] *v.t.* verraten (**to** an + *Akk.*). **betrayal** [bɪ'treɪəl] *n.* Verrat, *der*

better ['betə(r)] **1.** *adj.* besser; **~ and ~:** immer besser; **be much ~** *(recovered)* sich viel besser fühlen; **get ~** *(recover)* auf dem Wege der Besserung sein; **the ~ part of sth.** der größte Teil einer Sache *(Gen.).* **2.** *adv.* besser; **~ 'off** *(financially)* besser gestellt; **be ~ off without sb./sth.** ohne jmdn./etw. besser dran sein; **I'd ~ be off now** ich gehe jetzt besser. **3.** *n.* **get the ~ of sb./sth.** jmdn./etw. unterkriegen *(ugs.).* **a change for the ~:** eine vorteilhafte Veränderung. **4.** *v.t.* übertreffen

'betting shop *n.* Wettbüro, *das*

between [bɪ'twiːn] **1.** *prep.* **a) [in] ~:** zwischen *(position:* + *Dat.; direction:* + *Akk.*); **b)** *(amongst)* unter (+ *Dat.*); **~ ourselves, ~ you and me** unter uns *(Dat.)* gesagt; **c) ~ them/us** *(by joint action of)* gemeinsam; **~ us we had 40p** wir hatten zusammen 40 Pence. **2.** *adv.* **[in] ~:** dazwischen; *(in time)* zwischendurch

beverage ['bevərɪdʒ] *n.* Getränk, *das*

beware [bɪ'weə(r)] *v.t. & i.; only in imper. and inf.* **~ [of] sb./sth.** sich vor jmdm./etw. in acht nehmen; **~ of doing sth.** sich davor hüten, etw. zu tun; **'~ of the dog''** „Vorsicht, bissiger Hund!"

bewilder [bɪ'wɪldə(r)] *v.t.* verwirren. **be'wilderment** *n.* Verwirrung, *die*

bewitch [bɪ'wɪtʃ] *v.t.* verzaubern; *(fig.)* bezaubern

beyond [bɪ'jɒnd] **1.** *adv.* **a)** *(in space)* jenseits; *(on other side of wall, mountain range, etc.)* dahinter; **b)** *(in time)* darüber hinaus; **c)** *(in addition)* außerdem. **2.** *prep.* **a)** *(at far side of)* jenseits (+ *Gen.*); **b)** *(later than)* nach; **c)** *(out of reach or comprehension or range)* über ... (+ *Akk.*) hinaus

bias ['baɪəs] **1.** *n.* Voreingenommenheit, *die.* **2.** *v.t., -s- or -ss-* beeinflussen; **be ~ed in favour of/against sth./ sb.** für etw./jmdn. eingestellt sein/gegen etw./jmdn. voreingenommen sein

bib [bɪb] *n.* Lätzchen, *das*

Bible ['baɪbl] *n.* Bibel, *die.* **biblical** ['bɪblɪkl] *adj.* biblisch

bibliography [bɪblɪ'ɒgrəfɪ] *n.* Bibliographie, *die*

biceps ['baɪseps] *n.* Bizeps, *der*

bicker ['bɪkə(r)] *v.i.* sich zanken

bicycle ['baɪsɪkl] **1.** *n.* Fahrrad, *das; attrib.* Fahrrad-; **~ clip** Hosenklammer, *die.* **2.** *v.i.* radfahren

bid [bɪd] **1.** *v.t.* **a) -dd-, bid** *(at auction)* bieten; **b) -dd-, bade** [bæd, beɪd] *or* **bid, bidden** ['bɪdn] *or* **bid: ~ sb. welcome/goodbye** jmdn. willkommen heißen/sich von jmdm. verabschieden. **2.** *v.i., -dd-, bid* **a)** werben (**for** um); **b)** *(at auction)* bieten. **3.** *n.* **a)** *(attempt)* Gebot, *das;* **b)** *(attempt)* Versuch, *der*

bidden see bid 1

'bidder *n.* Bieter, *der*/Bieterin, *die*

bide ['baɪd] *v.t.* **~ one's time** den richtigen Augenblick abwarten

bifocal [baɪ'fəʊkl] **1.** *adj.* Bifokal-. **2.** *n. in pl.* Bifokalgläser *Pl.*

big [bɪg] *adj.* groß

bigamy ['bɪgəmɪ] *n.* Bigamie, *die*

big-'headed *adj.* *(coll.)* eingebildet

bigoted ['bɪgətɪd] *adj.* eifernd

big: ~ 'toe *n.* große Zehe; **~ 'top** *n.* Zirkuszelt, *das;* **~ 'wheel** *n.* *(at fair)* Riesenrad, *das*

bike [baɪk] *(coll.)* **1.** *n.* *(bicycle)* Rad, *das; (motor cycle)* Maschine, *die.* **2.** *v.i.* radfahren/[mit dem] Motorrad fahren

bikini [bɪ'kiːnɪ] *n.* Bikini, *der*

bilingual [baɪ'lɪŋgwəl] *adj.* zweisprachig

bilious ['bɪljəs] *adj.* *(Med.)* Gallen-; **~ attack** Gallenanfall, *der*

'bill [bɪl] *n.* *(of bird)* Schnabel, *der*

'bill *n.* **a)** *(Parl.)* Gesetzentwurf, *der;* **b)** *(note of charges)* Rechnung, *die;* **could we have the ~ please?** wir möchten zahlen; **c)** *(poster)* **'[stick] no ~s''** „[Plakate] ankleben verboten"

'billboard *n.* Reklametafel, *die*

billet ['bɪlɪt] **1.** *n.* Quartier, *das.* **2.** *v.t.* einquartieren (**with,** on bei)

'billfold *n.* *(Amer.)* Brieftasche, *die*

billiards ['bɪljədz] *n.* Billard[spiel], *das*

billion ['bɪljən] *n.* **a)** *(thousand million)* Milliarde, *die;* **b)** *(Brit.: million million)* Billion, *die*

billy-goat ['bɪlɪgəʊt] *n.* Ziegenbock, *der*

bin [bɪn] *n.* Behälter, *der; (for bread)* Brotkasten, *der; (for rubbish)* Mülleimer, *der*

binary ['baɪnərɪ] *adj.* binär

bind [baɪnd] *v.t., bound* [baʊnd] **a)** fesseln ⟨Person, Tier⟩; *(bandage)* wickeln ⟨Glied, Baum⟩; verbinden ⟨Wunde⟩ (**with** mit); **b)** *(fasten together)* zusammenbinden; **c)** binden ⟨Buch⟩; **d)** be

bound up with sth. *(fig.)* eng mit etw. verbunden sein; **e) be bound to do sth.** *(required)* verpflichtet sein, etw. zu tun; *(certain)* etw. ganz bestimmt tun; **it is bound to rain** es wird bestimmt regnen. **'binder** *n. (for papers)* Hefter, *der; (for magazines)* Mappe, *die.*

'binding 1. *adj.* bindend ⟨*Vertrag, Abkommen*⟩ **(on** für**). 2.** *n. (of book)* Einband, *der*

bingo ['bɪŋɡəʊ] *n.* Bingo, *das*

binoculars [bɪ'nɒkjʊləz] *n. pl.* |**a pair of**| ~: Fernglas, *das*

biodegradable [baɪəʊdɪ'ɡreɪdəbl] *adj.* biologisch abbaubar

biographer [baɪ'ɒɡrəfə(r)] *n.* Biograph, *der*/Biographin, *die*

biographical [baɪə'ɡræfɪkl] *adj.* biographisch

biography [baɪ'ɒɡrəfɪ] *n.* Biographie, *die*

biological [baɪə'lɒdʒɪkl] *adj.* biologisch

biologist [baɪ'ɒlədʒɪst] *n.* Biologe, *der*/Biologin, *die*

biology [baɪ'ɒlədʒɪ] *n.* Biologie, *die*

biotechnology [baɪəʊtek'nɒlədʒɪ] *n.* Biotechnologie, *die*

birch [bɜːtʃ] *n.* Birke, *die*

bird [bɜːd] *n.* Vogel, *der*

bird: ~ **cage** *n.* Vogelkäfig, *der;* ~**'s-eye 'view** *n.* Vogelperspektive, *die;* ~**'s nest** *n.* Vogelnest, *das*

Biro, (P) ['baɪrəʊ] *n., pl.* ~**s** Kugelschreiber, *der;* Kuli, *der* *(ugs.)*

birth [bɜːθ] *n.* **a)** Geburt, *die;* **give** ~ ⟨*Frau:*⟩ entbinden; ⟨*Tier:*⟩ jungen; werfen; **give** ~ **to a child** ein Kind zur Welt bringen; **b)** *(of movement, fashion, etc.)* Aufkommen, *das*

birth: ~ **certificate** *n.* Geburtsurkunde, *die;* ~ **control** *n.* Geburtenkontrolle, *die;* ~**day** *n.* Geburtstag, *der; attrib.* Geburtstags-; ~**place** *n.* Geburtsort, *der*

biscuit ['bɪskɪt] *n. (Brit.)* Keks, *der*

bisect [baɪ'sekt] *v.t.* halbieren

bishop ['bɪʃəp] *n.* **a)** *(Eccl.)* Bischof, *der;* **b)** *(Chess)* Läufer, *der*

¹bit [bɪt] *n.* **a)** *(for horse)* Gebiß, *das;* **b)** *(of drill)* [Bohr]einsatz, *der*

²bit *n.* **a)** *(piece)* Stück, *das;* **not a** or **one** ~ *(not at all)* überhaupt nicht; **a** ~ **tired/too early** ein bißchen müde/zu früh; **be a** ~ **of a coward/bully** ein ziemlicher Feigling sein/den starken Mann markieren *(ugs.)*

³bit *n. (Computing)* Bit, *das*

⁴bit see **bite** 1, 2

bitch [bɪtʃ] *n.* **a)** *(dog)* Hündin, *die;* **b)** *(sl. derog.: woman)* Miststück, *das* *(derb)*

bite [baɪt] **1.** *v.t.,* **bit** [bɪt], **bitten** ['bɪtn] beißen; ⟨*Moskito usw.:*⟩ stechen. **2.** *v.i.,* **bit, bitten** beißen/stechen; *(take bait)* anbeißen. **3.** *n.* Biß, *der; (piece)* Bissen, *der; (wound)* Bißwunde, *die; (by mosquito etc.)* Stich, *der.* **bite 'off** *v.t.* abbeißen

biting ['baɪtɪŋ] *adj.* beißend

bitten see **bite** 1, 2

bitter ['bɪtə(r)] *adj.* bitter. **'bitterly** *adv.* bitterlich ⟨*weinen, sich beschweren*⟩; ~ **cold** bitterkalt. **'bitterness** *n.* Bitterkeit, *die*

bizarre [bɪ'zɑː(r)] *adj.* bizarr

black [blæk] **1.** *adj.* **a)** schwarz; ~ **and blue** *(fig.)* grün und blau; **in** ~ **and white** *(fig.)* schwarz auf weiß; **in the** ~ *(in credit)* in den schwarzen Zahlen; **b) B~** *(dark-skinned)* schwarz. **2.** *n.* **a)** Schwarz, *das;* **b) B~** *(person)* Schwarze, *der/die.* **3.** *v.t.* bestreiken ⟨*Betrieb*⟩; boykottieren ⟨*Arbeit*⟩. **black 'out 1.** *v.t.* verdunkeln. **2.** *v.i.* das Bewußtsein verlieren

black: ~**berry** ['blækbərɪ] *n.* Brombeere, *die;* ~**bird** *n.* Amsel, *die;* ~**board** *n.* [Wand]tafel, *die;* ~**'currant** *n.* schwarze Johannisbeere

blacken ['blækn] *v.t.* schwärzen; verfinstern ⟨*Himmel*⟩

black: ~ **'eye** *n.* blaues Auge; **B~ 'Forest** *pr. n.* Schwarzwald, *der;* ~**'ice** *n.* Glatteis, *das;* ~**leg** *n. (Brit.)* Streikbrecher, *der/*brecherin, *die;* ~**list** *n.* schwarze Liste; ~**list** *v.t.* auf die schwarze Liste setzen; ~**mail 1.** *v.t.* erpressen; **2.** *n.* Erpressung, *die;* ~ **market** *n.* schwarzer Markt

'blackness *n.* Schwärze, *die; (darkness)* Finsternis, *die*

black: ~**-out** *n.* **a)** Verdunkelung, *die; (Theatre, Radio)* Blackout, *der;* **b)** *(Med.)* **have a** ~**out** das Bewußtsein verlieren; **B~ 'Sea** *pr. n.* Schwarze Meer, *das;* ~**smith** ['blæksmɪθ] *n.* Schmied, *der;* ~ **spot** *n.* Gefahrenstelle, *die*

bladder ['blædə(r)] *n.* Blase, *die*

blade [bleɪd] *n.* **a)** *(of sword, knife, razor, etc.)* Klinge, *die; (of saw, oar, propeller)* Blatt, *das;* **b)** *(of grass)* Spreite, *die*

blame [bleɪm] **1.** *v.t.* ~ **sb.** |**for sth.**| jmdm. die Schuld |an etw. *(Dat.)*| geben; **be to** ~ |**for sth.**| an etw. *(Dat.)* schuld sein; ~ **sth.** |**for sth.**| etw. |für etw.] verantwortlich machen. 2. *n.* Schuld, *die.* '**blameless** *adj.* untadelig

blancmange [blə'mɒnʒ] *n.* Flammeri, *der*

bland [blænd] *adj.* mild; *(suave)* verbindlich

blank [blæŋk] 1. *adj.* a) leer; kahl ⟨*Wand, Fläche*⟩; b) *(empty)* frei. 2. *n.* a) *(space)* Lücke, *die;* b) *(cartridge)* Platzpatrone, *die;* c) **draw a ~:** kein Glück haben. **blank 'cheque** *n.* Blankoscheck, *der;* *(fig.)* Blankovollmacht, *die*

blanket ['blæŋkɪt] *n.* Decke, *die;* **wet '~** *(fig.)* Trauerkloß, *der (ugs.)*

blare ['bleə(r)] 1. *v. i.* ⟨*Lautsprecher:*⟩ plärren; ⟨*Trompete:*⟩ schmettern. 2. *v. t.* **~ |out|** [hinaus]plärren ⟨*Worte*⟩; [hinaus]schmettern ⟨*Melodie*⟩

blasé ['blɑ:zeɪ] *adj.* blasiert

blasphemous ['blæsfəməs] *adj.* lästerlich

blasphemy ['blæsfəmɪ] *n.* Blasphemie, *die*

blast [blɑ:st] 1. *n.* a) **a ~ |of wind|** ein Windstoß; b) *(of horn)* Tuten, *das.* 2. *v. t. (blow up)* sprengen. **blast 'off** *v. i.* abheben

'**blasted** *adj. (damned)* verdammt *(salopp)*

'**blast-off** *n.* Abheben, *das*

blatant ['bleɪtənt] *adj.* a) *(flagrant)* eklatant; b) *(unashamed)* unverhohlen; unverfroren ⟨*Lüge*⟩

blaze [bleɪz] 1. *n.* Feuer, *das.* 2. *v.i.* brennen; lodern *(geh.)*

blazer ['bleɪzə(r)] *n.* Blazer, *der*

bleach [bli:tʃ] 1. *v. t.* bleichen. 2. *n.* Bleichmittel, *das*

bleak ['bli:k] *adj.* a) öde ⟨*Landschaft usw.*⟩; b) *(unpromising)* düster

bleat [bli:t] *v. i.* ⟨*Schaf:*⟩ blöken; ⟨*Ziege:*⟩ meckern

bled *see* **bleed**

bleed [bli:d] *v. i.,* **bled** [bled] bluten

bleeper ['bli:pə(r)] *n.* Kleinempfänger, *der*

blemish ['blemɪʃ] *n.* Fleck, *der*

blend [blend] 1. *v. t.* mischen. 2. *v. i.* sich mischen lassen. 3. *n.* Mischung, *die.* '**blender** *n.* Mixer, *der*

bless [bles] *v. t.* segnen; **~ you!** *(after sb. sneezes)* Gesundheit! **blessed** ['blesɪd] *adj.* a) *(revered)* heilig; b) *(cursed)* verdammt *(salopp).* '**blessing** *n.* Segen, *der*

blew *see* ¹**blow**

blight [blaɪt] *n. (fig.)* Fluch, *der*

blind [blaɪnd] 1. *adj.* blind; **~ in one eye** auf einem Auge blind. 2. *adv.* blindlings. 3. *n.* Jalousie, *die;* *(made of cloth)* Rouleau, *das;* *(of shop)* Markise, *die.* 4. *v. t.* blenden. '**blindfold** 1. *v. t.* die Augen verbinden (+ *Dat.*). 2. *adj.* mit verbundenen Augen *nachgestellt.* '**blinding** *adj.* blendend. '**blindly** *adv.* [wie] blind; *(fig.)* blindlings. '**blindness** *n.* Blindheit, *die*

blink [blɪŋk] *v. i.* a) blinzeln; b) *(shine intermittently)* blinken

'**blinkers** *n. pl.* Scheuklappen *Pl.*

bliss [blɪs] *n.* [Glück]seligkeit, *die.* '**blissful** ['blɪsfl] *adj.* [glück]selig

blister ['blɪstə(r)] 1. *n.* Blase, *die.* 2. *v.i.* ⟨*Haut:*⟩ Blasen bekommen; ⟨*Anstrich:*⟩ Blasen werfen

blizzard ['blɪzəd] *n.* Schneesturm, *der*

blob [blɒb] *n. (drop)* Tropfen, *der;* *(small mass)* Klacks, *der (ugs.)*

block [blɒk] 1. *n.* a) Klotz, *der; (for chopping on)* Hackklotz, *der; (of concrete or stone, building-stone)* Block, *der;* b) *(building)* [Häuser]block, *der;* **~ of flats/offices** Wohnblock, *der*/Bürohaus, *das.* 2. *v.t.* versperren ⟨*Tür, Straße, Durchgang, Sicht*⟩; verstopfen ⟨*Pfeife, Abfluß*⟩; verhindern ⟨*Fortschritt*⟩. **block 'up** *v.t.* verstopfen; versperren ⟨*Eingang*⟩

blockade [blɒ'keɪd] 1. *n.* Blockade, *die.* 2. *v.t.* blockieren

blockage ['blɒkɪdʒ] *n.* Block, *der; (of pipe, gutter)* Verstopfung, *die*

block: ~ 'booking *n.* Gruppenbuchung, *die; ~* '**capital** *n.* Blockbuchstabe, *der; ~* **head** *n.* Dummkopf, *der; ~* '**letters** *n. pl.* Blockschrift, *die*

bloke [bləʊk] *n. (Brit. coll.)* Typ, *der (ugs.)*

blonde [blɒnd] 1. *adj.* blond. 2. *n.* Blondine, *die*

blood [blʌd] *n.* Blut, *das*

blood: ~ 'donor *n.* Blutspender, *der*/-spenderin, *die; ~* **group** *n.* Blutgruppe, *die; ~***hound** *n.* Bluthund, *der; ~* **pressure** *n.* Blutdruck, *der; ~***shed** *n.* Blutvergießen, *das; ~***shot** *adj.* blutunterlaufen; ~**stained** *adj.* blutbefleckt; ~**stream** *n.* Blutstrom, *der; ~* **test** *n.* Blutprobe, *die; ~***thirsty** *adj.* blutrünstig; ~ **transfusion** *n.* Bluttransfusion, *die; ~***vessel** *n.* Blutgefäß, *das*

'**bloody** 1. *adj.* a) blutig; *(running with blood)* blutend; b) *(sl.: damned)* verdammt *(salopp).* 2. *adv. (sl.: damned)* verdammt *(salopp)*

bloom [bluːm] 1. *n.* Blüte, *die;* **be in ~:** in Blüte stehen. 2. *v.i.* blühen

blossom ['blɒsəm] 1. *n. (flower)* Blüte, *die; (mass)* Blütenmeer, *das (geh.).* 2. *v.i.* blühen; *〈Mensch:〉* aufblühen

blot [blɒt] 1. *n. (of ink)* Tintenklecks, *der; (stain)* Fleck, *der.* 2. *v.t.,* **-tt-** ablöschen *〈Tinte, Papier〉.* **blot 'out** *v.t. (fig.)* auslöschen

blotchy ['blɒtʃɪ] *adj.* fleckig

'blotting-paper *n.* Löschpapier, *das*

blouse [blaʊz] *n.* Bluse, *die*

¹blow [bləʊ] 1. *v.i.,* blew [bluː], blown [bləʊn] *〈Wind:〉* wehen; *〈Sturm:〉* blasen. 2. *v.t.,* blew, blown: a) blasen; *〈Wind:〉* wehen; machen *〈Seifenblase〉;* ~ **sb. a kiss** jmdm. eine Kußhand zuwerfen; b) ~ **one's nose** sich *(Dat.)* die Nase putzen; c) ~ **sth. to pieces** etw. in die Luft sprengen. **blow 'out** 1. *v.t.* ausblasen. 2. *v.i.* ausgeblasen werden. **blow 'over** 1. *v.i.* umgeblasen werden; *〈Streit, Sturm:〉* sich legen. 2. *v.t.* umblasen. **blow 'up** 1. *v.t.* a) *(shatter)* [in die Luft] sprengen; b) aufblasen *〈Ballon〉;* aufpumpen *〈Reifen〉;* c) *(coll.: exaggerate)* hochspielen. 2. *v.i. (explode)* explodieren

²blow *n.* a) Schlag, *der; (with axe)* Hieb, *der;* **come to ~s** handgreiflich werden; b) *(disaster)* [schwerer] Schlag. **'blow-dry** *v.t.* fönen. **'blowlamp** *n.* Lötlampe, *die*

blown see **¹blow**

blubber ['blʌbə(r)] *n.* Walspeck, *der*

blue [bluː] 1. *adj.* blau. 2. *n.* a) Blau, *das;* b) **have the ~s** deprimiert sein; c) *(Mus.)* **the ~s** der Blues; d) **out of the ~:** aus heiterem Himmel

blue: ~**bell** *n.* Glockenblume, *die;* ~**bottle** *n.* Schmeißfliege, *die;* ~**collar** *adj.* ~**collar worker** Arbeiter, *der/*Arbeiterin, *die;* ~ **jeans** *n. pl.* Blue jeans *Pl.;* ~**print** *n. (fig.)* Entwurf, *der*

bluff [blʌf] 1. *n.* Bluff, *der (ugs.);* **call sb.'s ~:** es darauf ankommen lassen *(ugs.).* 2. *v.i. & t.* bluffen *(ugs.)*

blunder ['blʌndə(r)] 1. *n.* [schwerer] Fehler. 2. *v.i.* a) *(make mistake)* einen [schweren] Fehler machen; b) *(move blindly)* tappen

blunt [blʌnt] 1. *adj.* a) stumpf; b) *(outspoken)* direkt; barsch *(ugs.) 〈Ablehnung〉.* 2. *v.t.* ~ **[the edge of]** stumpf machen. **'bluntly** *adv.* direkt; glatt *〈ablehnen〉*

blur [blɜː(r)] 1. *v.t.,* **-rr-:** a) verwischen;

b) *(become indistinct)* verschwimmen; **his vision was ~red** er sah alles verschwommen. 2. *n. (smear)* Fleck, *der; (dim image)* verschwommener Fleck

blurt [blɜːt] *v.t.* ~ **out** herausplatzen mit *(ugs.)*

blush [blʌʃ] 1. *v.i.* rot werden. 2. *n.* Rotwerden, *das*

bluster ['blʌstə(r)] *v.i.* sich aufplustern *(ugs.)*

blustery ['blʌstərɪ] *adj.* stürmisch

boar [bɔː(r)] *n. 〈wild〉* ~: Keiler, *der*

board [bɔːd] 1. *n.* a) Brett, *das; (black~)* Tafel, *die; (notice-~)* Schwarzes Brett; **above** ~ *(fig.)* korrekt; b) *(Commerc.)* ~ **[of directors]** Vorstand, *der; (supervisory* ~*)* Aufsichtsrat, *der;* c) *(Naut., Aeronaut.)* **on** ~: an Bord; d) ~ **and lodging** Unterkunft und Verpflegung; **full** ~: Vollpension, *die.* 2. *v.t.* ~ **the ship/plane** an Bord des Schiffes/Flugzeuges gehen; ~ **the train/bus** in den Zug/Bus einsteigen

'boarder *n. (Sch.)* Internatsschüler, *der/*-schülerin, *die*

'board game *n.* Brettspiel, *das*

boarding: ~**house** *n.* Pension, *die;* ~ **pass** *n.* Bordkarte, *die;* ~**school** *n.* Internat, *das*

board: ~ **meeting** *n.* Vorstandssitzung, *die;* ~**room** *n.* Sitzungssaal, *der*

boast [bəʊst] *v.i.* prahlen. **boastful** ['bəʊstfl] *adj.* prahlerisch

boat [bəʊt] *n.* Boot, *das*

¹bob [bɒb] *v.i.,* **-bb-:** ~ **[up and down]** sich auf und nieder bewegen

²bob *n. (~sled)* Bob, *der*

bobbin ['bɒbɪn] *n.* Spule, *die*

bob: ~**sled,** ~**sleigh** *ns.* Bobschlitten, *der*

bodice ['bɒdɪs] *n.* Mieder, *das; (part of dress)* Oberteil, *das*

bodily ['bɒdɪlɪ] *adj.* körperlich; ~ **needs** leibliche Bedürfnisse

body ['bɒdɪ] *n.* a) Körper, *der;* b) *(corpse)* Leiche, *die;* c) *(group)* Gruppe, *die; (with particular function)* Organ, *das.* **'bodyguard** *n. (single)* Leibwächter, *der; (group)* Leibwache, *die.* **'bodywork** *n.* Karosserie, *die*

bog [bɒg] 1. *n.* Moor, *das; (marsh, swamp)* Sumpf, *der.* 2. *v.t.,* **-gg-:** **be/get ~ged down** *(fig.)* sich verzettelt haben/sich verzetteln

boggle ['bɒgl] *v.i. (coll.)* **the mind ~s** da kann man nur [noch] staunen

bogus ['bəʊgəs] *adj.* falsch

¹boil [bɔɪl] 1. *v.i. & t.* kochen. 2. *n.*

come to/go off the ~: zu kochen anfangen/aufhören; **bring to the ~:** zum Kochen bringen. **boil 'down** *v. i.* ~ **down to sth.** *(fig.)* auf etw. hinauslaufen. **boil 'over** *v. i.* überkochen

²**boil** *n. (Med.)* Furunkel, *der*

'**boiler** *n.* Kessel, *der*

'**boiling-point** *n.* Siedepunkt, *der*

boisterous ['bɔɪstərəs] *adj.* ausgelassen

bold [bəʊld] *adj.* a) *(courageous)* mutig; *(daring)* kühn; b) *(auffallend* ⟨*Farbe, Muster*⟩. '**boldly** *adv. (courageously)* mutig; *(daringly)* kühn

Bolivia [bə'lɪvɪə] *pr. n.* Bolivien *(das)*

bollard ['bɒlɑːd] *n. (Brit.)* Poller, *der*

bolster ['bəʊlstə(r)] **1.** *n. (pillow)* Nackenrolle, *die.* **2.** *v. t. (fig.)* stärken

bolt [bəʊlt] **1.** *n.* a) *(on door or window)* Riegel, *der;* *(on gun)* Kammerverschluß, *der;* b) *(metal pin)* Schraube, *die;* *(without thread)* Bolzen, *der.* **2.** *v. i.* davonlaufen; *(Pferd:)* durchgehen; *(Fuchs, Kaninchen:)* flüchten. **3.** *v. t.* a) verriegeln ⟨*Tür, Fenster*⟩; b) *(fasten with ~s)* verschrauben/mit Bolzen verbinden; c) ~ [**down**] hinunterschlingen ⟨*Essen*⟩. **4.** *adv.* ~ **upright** kerzengerade

bomb [bɒm] **1.** *n.* Bombe, *die.* **2.** *v. t.* bombardieren

bombard [bɒm'bɑːd] *v. t.* beschießen. **bom'bardment** *n.* Beschuß, *der*

bombastic [bɒm'bæstɪk] *adj.* bombastisch

bomber ['bɒmə(r)] *n. (Air Force)* Bomber, *der (ugs.)*

'**bomb-shell** *n.* Bombe, *die;* *(fig.)* Sensation, *die*

bond [bɒnd] *n.* a) Band, *das;* in *pl. (shackles)* Fesseln; b) *(adhesion)* Verbindung, *die;* c) *(Commerc.)* Anleihe, *die*

bone [bəʊn] **1.** *n.* Knochen, *der;* *(of fish)* Gräte, *die.* **2.** *v. t.* den/die Knochen herauslösen aus; entgräten ⟨*Fisch*⟩. **bone 'dry** *adj.* knochentrocken *(ugs.).* **bone 'idle** *adj.* stinkfaul *(salopp)*

bonfire ['bɒnfaɪə(r)] *n.* Freudenfeuer, *das;* *(for rubbish)* Feuer, *das*

bonnet ['bɒnɪt] *n.* a) *(woman's)* Haube, *die;* *(child's)* Häubchen, *das;* b) *(Brit. Motor Veh.)* Motorhaube, *die*

bonus ['bəʊnəs] *n.* zusätzliche Leistung; *(to shareholders)* Bonus, *der;* **Christmas ~:** Weihnachtsgratifikation, *die*

bony ['bəʊnɪ] *adj.* a) Knochen-; *(like*

bone) knochenartig; b) *(skinny)* knochendürr *(ugs.);* spindeldürr

boo [buː] **1.** *int.* to surprise sb. huh; *expr. disapproval, contempt* buh. **2.** *n.* Buh, *das (ugs.).* **3.** *v. t.* ausbuhen *(ugs.).* **4.** *v. i.* buhen *(ugs.)*

booby ['buːbɪ] *n.* Trottel, *der (ugs.).* '**booby prize** *n.* Preis für den schlechtesten Teilnehmer an einem Wettbewerb. '**booby trap** *n.* a) Falle, mit der man jmdm. einen Streich spielen will; b) *(Mil.)* versteckte Sprengladung

book [bʊk] **1.** *n.* a) Buch, *das;* *(for accounts)* Rechnungsbuch, *das;* *(for exercises)* [Schreib]heft, *das.* **2.** *v. t.* buchen ⟨*Reise, Flug, Platz [im Flugzeug]*⟩; [vor]bestellen ⟨*Eintrittskarte, Tisch, Zimmer, Platz [im Theater]*⟩. **3.** *v. i.* buchen. **book 'in 1.** *v. i.* sich eintragen. **2.** *v. t.* eintragen. **book 'up** *v. i. & t.* buchen; **be ~ed up** ⟨*Hotel usw.*⟩: ausgebucht sein

book: ~case *n.* Bücherschrank, *der;* **~ends** *n. pl.* Buchstützen

'**booking office** *n.* [Fahrkarten]schalter, *der*

book: ~keeper *n.* Buchhalter, *der/*-halterin, *die;* **~keeping** *n.* Buchführung, *die;* Buchhaltung, *die*

booklet ['bʊklɪt] *n.* Broschüre, *die*

book: ~maker *n. (in betting)* Buchmacher, *der;* **~mark** *n.* Lesezeichen, *das;* **~seller** *n.* Buchhändler, *der/*-händlerin, *die;* **~shelf** *n.* Bücherbord, *das;* **~shop** *n.* Buchhandlung, *die;* **~stall** *n.* Bücherstand, *der;* **~store** *n. (Amer.)* Buchhandlung, *die;* **~ token** *n.* Büchergutschein, *der;* **~worm** *n.* Bücherwurm, *der*

¹**boom** [buːm] *n.* a) *(for camera or microphone)* Ausleger, *der;* b) *(Naut.)* Baum, *der*

²**boom 1.** *v. i.* a) dröhnen; b) ⟨*Geschäft, Verkauf, Gebiet:*⟩ sich sprunghaft entwickeln. **2.** *n.* a) Dröhnen, *das;* b) *(in business or economy)* Boom, *der*

boomerang ['buːməræŋ] *n.* Bumerang, *der*

boon [buːn] *n.* Segen, *der* **(to** für)

boorish ['bʊərɪʃ] *adj.* rüpelhaft

boost [buːst] **1.** *v. t.* in die Höhe treiben ⟨*Preis, Wert*⟩; stärken ⟨*Selbstvertrauen, Moral*⟩. **2.** *n.* Auftrieb, *der*

boot [buːt] **1.** *n.* a) Stiefel, *der;* **give sb. the ~** *(fig. coll.)* jmdn. rausschmeißen *(ugs.);* b) *(Brit.: of car)* Kofferraum, *der.* **2.** *v. t. (coll.: kick)* kicken *(ugs.)*

booth [buːð] *n.* a) Bude, *die;* b) *(telephone ~)* Zelle, *die*

'bootleg adj. schwarz verkauft/gebrannt

booze [buːz] (coll.) 1. v. i. saufen (derb). 2. n. Alkohol, der

border ['bɔːdə(r)] 1. n. a) Rand, der; (of table-cloth, handkerchief) Bordüre, die; b) (of country) Grenze, die; c) (flower-bed) Rabatte, die. 2. attrib. adj. Grenz(stadt, -streit). 3. v. t. a) (adjoin) [an]grenzen an (+ Akk.); b) (put a ~ to, act as ~ to) umranden; einfassen. 4. v. i. ~ on a) see 3 a; b) (resemble) grenzen an (+ Akk.). **'borderline** 1. n. Grenzlinie, die. 2. adj. be ~: auf der Grenze liegen; **a ~ case/candidate** ein Grenzfall

'bore [bɔː(r)] 1. v. t. bohren. 2. n. (of firearm) Kaliber, das

'bore [bɔː(r)] 1. n. a) it's a real ~: es ist wirklich ärgerlich; **what a ~!** wie ärgerlich!; b) (person) Langweiler, der (ugs.). 2. v. t. langweilen; **be ~d sich langweilen**

'bore see **'bear**

boredom ['bɔːdəm] n. Langeweile, die

'borehole n. Bohrloch, das

boring ['bɔːrɪŋ] adj. langweilig

born [bɔːn] 1. **be ~:** geboren werden. 2. adj. geboren; **be a ~ orator** der geborene Redner sein

borne see **'bear**

borough ['bʌrə] n. (town) Stadt, die; (village) Gemeinde, die

borrow ['bɒrəʊ] v. t. leihen (from von, bei); (from library) entleihen. **'borrower** n. (from bank) Kreditnehmer, der; (from library) Entleiher, der

bosom ['bʊzəm] n. Brust, die

boss [bɒs] 1. n. (coll.) Boß, der (ugs.); Chef, der. 2. v. t. ~ [about or around] herumkommandieren (ugs.). **'bossy** adj. (coll.) herrisch

botanical [bə'tænɪkl] adj. botanisch

botanist ['bɒtənɪst] n. Botaniker, der/Botanikerin, die

botany ['bɒtənɪ] n. Botanik, die

botch [bɒtʃ] 1. v. t. pfuschen bei (ugs.). 2. n. pfuschen (ugs.). **botch up** v. t. (bungle) verpfuschen (ugs.)

both [bəʊθ] 1. adj. beide; ~ [the] brothers die Brüder. 2. pron. beide; ~ [of them] are dead beide sind tot; ~ of you/them are ...: ihr seid/sie sind beide ... 3. adv. ~ A and B sowohl A als [auch] B; **he and I were** ~ there er und ich waren beide da

bother ['bɒðə(r)] 1. v. t. a) I can't be ~ed ich habe keine Lust; b) (annoy) lästig sein (+ Dat.); ⟨Lärm, Licht:⟩

stören; ⟨Schmerz, Zahn:⟩ zu schaffen machen (+ Dat.); **I'm sorry to ~ you, but ...:** es tut mir leid, wenn ich Sie störe, aber ...; c) (worry) Sorgen machen (+ Dat.); ⟨Problem, Frage:⟩ beschäftigen. 2. v. i. **don't ~ to do it** du brauchen es nicht zu tun; **you needn't/shouldn't have ~ed** das wäre nicht nötig gewesen; **don't ~!** nicht nötig! 3. n. a) (trouble) Ärger, der; b) (effort) Mühe, die. 4. int. (coll.) wie ärgerlich!

bottle ['bɒtl] 1. n. Flasche, die; **a ~ of beer** eine Flasche Bier. 2. v. t. a) (put into ~s) in Flaschen [ab]füllen; b) (preserve in jars) einmachen. **bottle up** v. t. a) (conceal) in sich (Dat.) aufstauen; b) (trap) einschließen

bottle: ~ bank n. Altglasbehälter, der; **~-neck** n. (fig.) Flaschenhals, der (ugs.); **~-opener** n. Flaschenöffner, der; **~-top** n. Flaschenverschluß, der

bottom ['bɒtəm] 1. n. a) unteres Ende; (of cup, glass, box) Boden, der; (of valley, well, shaft) Sohle, die; (of hill, cliff, stairs) Fuß, der; b) (buttocks) Hinterteil, das (ugs.); c) (of sea, lake) Grund, der; d) (farthest point) **at the ~ of the garden/street** hinten im Garten/am Ende der Straße; e) (underside) Unterseite, die; f) (fig.) **start at the ~:** ganz unten anfangen; **be ~ of the class** der/die Letzte in der Klasse sein. 2. adj. a) (lowest) unterst...; (lower) unter...; b) (fig.: last) letzt... **'bottomless** adj. bodenlos; unendlich tief ⟨Meer, Ozean⟩

bough [baʊ] n. Ast, der

bought see **buy** 1

boulder ['bəʊldə(r)] n. Felsbrocken, der

boulevard ['buːləvɑːd] n. Boulevard, der

bounce [baʊns] 1. v. i. a) springen; b) (coll.) ⟨Scheck:⟩ platzen (ugs.). 2. v. t. aufspringen lassen ⟨Ball⟩. 3. n. Aufprall, der. **'bouncer** n. (coll.) Rausschmeißer, der (ugs.). **bouncing** ['baʊnsɪŋ] adj. stramm ⟨Baby⟩. **bouncy** ['baʊnsɪ] adj. gut springend ⟨Ball⟩; (fig.: lively) munter

'bound [baʊnd] 1. n., usu. in pl. (limit) Grenze, die; **within the ~s of possibility** im Bereich des Möglichen; **sth. is out of ~s [to sb.]** der Zutritt zu etw. ist [für jmdn.] verboten. 2. v. t. **be ~ed by sth.** durch etw. begrenzt werden

'bound 1. v. i. hüpfen. 2. n. Satz, der

³bound *pred. adj.* be ~ for home/ Frankfurt auf dem Heimweg/nach Frankfurt unterwegs sein; **homeward** ~: auf dem Weg nach Hause

⁴bound *see* bind

boundary ['baʊndərɪ] *n.* Grenze, *die*

boundless *adj.* grenzenlos

bounty ['baʊntɪ] *n.* Kopfgeld, *das*

bouquet [bʊ'keɪ] *n.* [Blumen]strauß, *der*

bourgeois ['bʊəʒwɑː] **1.** *n., pl. same* Bürger, *der/*Bürgerin, *die.* **2.** *adj.* bürgerlich

bout [baʊt] *n.* a) *(contest)* Wettkampf, *der;* b) *(fit)* Anfall, *der*

boutique [buː'tiːk] *n.* Boutique, *die*

¹bow [bəʊ] a) *(curve, weapon, Mus.)* Bogen, *der;* b) *(knot, ribbon)* Schleife, *die*

²bow [baʊ] **1.** *v. i.* a) ~ [to sb.] sich [vor jmdm.] verbeugen; b) *(submit)* sich beugen (to *Dat.*). **2.** *n.* Verbeugung, *die*

³bow [baʊ] *n.* *(Naut.)* Bug, *der*

bowel ['baʊəl] *n.* *(Anat.)* ~s *pl., (Med.)* ~: Darm, *der*

¹bowl [bəʊl] *n.* *(basin)* Schüssel, *die; (shallower)* Schale, *die; (of spoon)* Schöpfteil, *der; (of pipe)* Kopf, *der*

²bowl 1. *n.* a) *(ball)* Kugel, *die;* b) *in pl. (game)* Bowls, *das.* **2.** *v. i.* a) *(play ~s)* Bowls spielen; b) *(Cricket)* werfen

bow-legged ['bəʊlegɪd] *adj.* O-beinig *(ugs.)*

¹bowler ['bəʊlə(r)] *n.* *(Cricket)* Werfer, *der*

²bowler *n.* ~ [hat] Bowler, *der*

bowling *n.* [ten-pin] ~: Bowling, *das;* go ~: bowlen gehen. **bowling-alley** *n.* Bowlingbahn, *die.* **bowling-green** *n.* Rasenfläche für Bowls

bow [bəʊ]: ~**-tie** *n.* Fliege, *die;* ~**-window** *n.* Erkerfenster, *das*

¹box [bɒks] *n.* Kasten, *der; (bigger)* Kiste, *die; (of cardboard)* Schachtel, *die*

²box 1. *n.* he gave him a ~ on the ear[s] er gab ihm eine Ohrfeige. **2.** *v. t.* a) he ~ed his ears *or* him round the ears ohrfeigte ihn; b) *(Sport)* ~ sb. gegen jmdn. boxen. **3.** *v. i.* boxen. **boxer** *n.* Boxer, *der.* **boxing** *n.* Boxen, *das*

boxing: B~ Day *n.* zweiter Weihnachtsfeiertag; ~**-glove** *n.* Boxhandschuh, *der;* ~**-match** *n.* Boxkampf, *der;* ~**-ring** *n.* Boxring, *der*

box: ~ **number** *n.* *(at newspaper office)* Chiffre, *die; (at post office)* Postfach, *das;* ~**-office** *n.* Kasse, *die;* ~**-room** *n.* *(Brit.)* Abstellraum, *der*

boy [bɔɪ] *n.* Junge, *der*

boycott ['bɔɪkɒt] **1.** *v. t.* boykottieren. **2.** *n.* Boykott, *der*

¹boy-friend *n.* Freund, *der*

boyish *adj.* jungenhaft

bra [brɑː] *n.* BH, *der* *(ugs.)*

brace [breɪs] **1.** *n.* a) *(connecting piece)* Klammer, *die;* b) *(strut)* Strebe, *die; (Dent.)* [Zahn]spange, *die;* b) *in pl. (trouser-straps)* Hosenträger. **2.** *v. refl.* ~ oneself for sth. sich auf etw. *(Akk.)* vorbereiten

bracelet ['breɪslɪt] *n.* Armband, *das*

bracing ['breɪsɪŋ] *adj.* belebend

bracken ['brækn] *n.* [Adler]farn, *der*

bracket ['brækɪt] **1.** *n.* a) *(support)* Konsole, *die;* b) *(mark)* Klammer, *die.* **2.** *v. t.* einklammern

brag [bræg] *v. i. & t.,* -gg- prahlen *(about* mit)

braid [breɪd] **1.** *n.* a) *(plait)* Flechte, *die (geh.);* Zopf, *der;* b) *(woven band)* Borte, *die; (on uniform)* Litze, *die.* **2.** *v. t.* flechten

Braille [breɪl] *n.* Blindenschrift, *die*

brain [breɪn] *n.* Gehirn, *das*

brain: ~**-child** *n.* *(coll.)* Geistesprodukt, *das;* ~**less** *adj.* hirnlos; ~**wash** *v. t.* einer Gehirnwäsche unterziehen; ~**wave** *n.* *(coll.: inspiration)* genialer Einfall

brainy *adj.* intelligent

brake [breɪk] **1.** *n.* Bremse, *die.* **2.** *v. t. & i.* bremsen; **braking distance** Bremsweg, *der.* **brake light** *n.* Bremslicht, *das*

bramble ['bræmbl] *n.* Dornenstrauch, *der*

bran [bræn] *n.* Kleie, *die*

branch [brɑːntʃ] **1.** *n.* a) *(bough)* Ast, *der; (twig)* Zweig, *der;* b) *(of artery, antlers)* Ast, *der;* c) *(office)* Zweigstelle, *die; (shop)* Filiale, *die.* **2.** *v. i.* sich verzweigen. **branch 'off** *v. i.* abzweigen. **branch 'out** *v. i. (fig.)* ~ out into sth. sich auch mit etw. befassen

branch line *n.* Nebenstrecke, *die*

brand [brænd] *n.* a) *(trade mark)* Markenzeichen, *das; (goods of particular make)* Marke, *die;* b) *(mark)* Brandmal, *das*

brandish ['brændɪʃ] *v. t.* schwenken; schwingen ⟨Waffe⟩

brand: ~ **name** *n.* Markenname, *der;* ~**-new** *adj.* nagelneu *(ugs.)*

brandy ['brændɪ] *n.* Weinbrand, *der*

brash [bræʃ] *adj.* dreist

brass [brɑːs] *n.* Messing, *das; attrib.* Messing-; **the** ~ *(Mus.)* das Blech; ~

player *(Mus.)* Blechbläser, *der;* **get down to ~ tacks** zur Sache kommen.
brass band *n.* Blaskapelle, *die*
brassière ['bræzjə(r)] *n.* Büstenhalter, *der*
brat [bræt] *n.* Balg, *das od. der (ugs.)*
bravado [brə'vɑːdəʊ] *n.* **do sth. out of ~:** so waghalsig sein, etw. zu tun
brave [breɪv] **1.** *adj.* tapfer. **2.** *n.* [indianischer] Krieger. **3.** *v.t.* trotzen (+ *Dat.*). **'bravely** *adv.* tapfer.
bravery ['breɪvərɪ] *n.* Tapferkeit, *die*
bravo ['brɑː'vəʊ] *int.* bravo
brawl [brɔːl] **1.** *v.i.* sich schlagen. **2.** *n.* Schlägerei, *die*
brawny ['brɔːnɪ] *adj.* muskulös
bray [breɪ] **1.** Iah, *das.* **2.** *v.i.* ⟨*Esel:*⟩ iahen
brazen ['breɪzn] **1.** *adj.* dreist; *(shameless)* schamlos. **2.** *v.t.* **~ |out|** trotzen (+ *Dat.*); **~ it out** *(deny guilt)* es abstreiten; *(not admit guilt)* es nicht zugeben
brazier ['breɪzɪə(r)] *n.* Kohlenbecken, *das*
Brazil [brə'zɪl] *pr. n.* Brasilien *(das).*
Bra'zil nut *n.* Paranuß, *die*
breach [briːtʃ] **1.** *n.* **a)** *(violation)* Verstoß, *der* (of gegen); **~ of faith/duty** Vertrauensbruch, *der*/Pflichtverletzung, *die;* **b)** *(of relations)* Bruch, *der;* **c)** *(gap)* Bresche, *die;* (fig.) Riß, *der.* **2.** *v.t.* durchbrechen
bread [bred] *n.* Brot, *das;* **a piece of ~ and butter** ein Butterbrot
bread: **~-bin** *n.* Brotkasten, *der;* **~-board** *n.* [Brot]brett, *das;* **~-crumb** *n.* Brotkrume, *die;* **~-crumbs** *(coating)* Paniermehl, *das;* **~-knife** *n.* Brotmesser, *das;* **~-line** *n.* **be** *or* **live on/below the ~line** gerade noch/nicht einmal mehr das Notwendigste zum Leben haben
breadth [bredθ] *n.* Breite, *die*
'bread-winner *n.* Ernährer, *der*/Ernährerin, *die*
break [breɪk] **1.** *v.t.,* **broke** [brəʊk], **broken** ['brəʊkn] **a)** brechen; *(so as to damage)* zerbrechen; kaputtmachen *(ugs.);* zerreißen ⟨*Seil*⟩; (fig.: interrupt) unterbrechen; brechen ⟨*Bann, Zauber, Schweigen*⟩; **the TV/my watch is broken** der Fernseher/meine Uhr ist kaputt *(ugs.);* **~ the habit** es sich *(Dat.)* abgewöhnen; **b)** *(fracture)* sich *(Dat.)* brechen ⟨*Arm, Bein usw.*⟩; **c)** brechen ⟨*Vertrag, Versprechen*⟩; verstoßen gegen ⟨*Regel, Gesetz*⟩; **d)** *(surpass)* brechen ⟨*Rekord*⟩; **e)** *(cushion)*

auffangen ⟨*Schlag, jmds. Fall*⟩. **2.** *v.i.* **broke, broken a)** kaputtgehen *(ugs.);* ⟨*Faden, Seil:*⟩ [zer]reißen; ⟨*Glas, Tasse, Teller:*⟩ zerbrechen; ⟨*Eis:*⟩ brechen; **~ in two/in pieces** zerbrechen/zerbrechen; **b)** **~ into** einbrechen in (+ *Akk.*) ⟨*Haus*⟩; aufbrechen ⟨*Auto, Safe*⟩; **~ into laughter/tears** in Gelächter/Tränen ausbrechen; **~ into a trot/run** zu traben/laufen anfangen; **c)** *(escape)* **~ out of prison** aus dem Gefängnis ausbrechen; **~ free** *or* **loose** sich losreißen; **d)** ⟨*Welle:*⟩ sich brechen **(on/against an + *Dat.*); e)** ⟨*Tag:*⟩ anbrechen; ⟨*Sturm:*⟩ losbrechen; **f) sb's voice is ~ing** jmd. kommt in den Stimmbruch. **3.** *n.* **a)** *(gap)* Bruch, *der;* *(of rope)* Reißen, *das;* **a ~ with sb./sth.** ein Bruch mit jmdm./etw.; **b)** *(gap)* Lücke, *die;* *(broken place)* Sprung, *der;* **c)** *(dash)* **they made a sudden ~:** sie stürmten plötzlich davon; **d)** *(interruption)* Unterbrechung, *die;* *(pause, holiday)* Pause, *die;* **take** *or* **have a ~:** Pause machen; **e)** *(coll.: chance)* Chance, *die.* **break 'down 1.** *v.i.* zusammenbrechen; ⟨*Verhandlungen:*⟩ scheitern; ⟨*Auto:*⟩ eine Panne haben. **2.** *v.t.* **a)** aufbrechen ⟨*Tür*⟩; brechen ⟨*Widerstand*⟩; niederreißen ⟨*Barriere, Schranke*⟩; **b)** *(analyse)* aufgliedern. **break 'in 1.** *v.i.* *(into building etc.)* einbrechen. **2.** *v.t.* **a)** zureiten ⟨*Pferd*⟩; **b)** einlaufen ⟨*Schuhe*⟩; **c) ~ the door in** die Tür aufbrechen. **'break into** *see* **~ 2 b. break 'off 1.** *v.t.* abbrechen; abreißen ⟨*Faden*⟩; auflösen ⟨*Verlobung*⟩. **2.** *v.i.* **a)** abbrechen; **b)** *(cease)* aufhören. **break 'out** *v.i.* ausbrechen; **~ out in spots/a rash** Pickel/einen Ausschlag bekommen. **break 'up 1.** *v.t.* **a)** *(~ into pieces)* zerkleinern; ausschlachten ⟨*Auto*⟩; aufbrechen ⟨*Erde*⟩; **b)** *(disband)* auflösen. **2.** *v.i.* **a)** *(~ into pieces, lit. or fig.)* zerbrechen; **b)** *(disband)* sich auflösen; ⟨*Schule:*⟩ schließen; ⟨*Schüler, Lehrer:*⟩ in die Ferien gehen; **c) ~ up |with sb.|** sich [von jmdm.] trennen
breakable ['breɪkəbl] **1.** *adj.* zerbrechlich. **2.** *n.* **~s** zerbrechliche Dinge
breakage ['breɪkɪdʒ] *n.* Zerbrechen, *das;* **~s must be paid for** zerbrochene Ware muß bezahlt werden
'breakdown *n.* **a)** *(of vehicle)* Panne, *die;* *(in machine)* Störung, *die;* **~ truck/van** Abschleppwagen, *der;* **b)** *(Med.)* Zusammenbruch, *der;* **c)** *(analysis)* Aufschlüsselung, *die*

'**breaker** n. a) (wave) Brecher, der; b) ~'s [yard] Autoverwertung, die
breakfast ['brekfəst] 1. n. Frühstück, das; for ~: zum Frühstück. 2. v.i. frühstücken. **breakfast cereal** n. ≈ Frühstücksflocken Pl. **breakfast television** n. Frühstücksfernsehen, das
'**break-in** n. Einbruch, der
'**breaking** n. ~ and entering (Law) Einbruch, der
break: ~**neck** adj. halsbrecherisch; ~**through** n. Durchbruch, der; ~**up** n. Auflösung, die; (of relationship) Bruch, der; ~**water** n. Wellenbrecher, der
breast [brest] n. Brust, die
breast: ~**bone** n. Brustbein, das; ~**feed** v.t. & i. stillen; ~**stroke** n. Brustschwimmen, das
breath [breθ] n. a) Atem, der; get one's ~ back wieder zu Atem kommen; hold one's ~: den Atem anhalten; be out of ~: außer Atem sein; say sth. under one's ~: etw. vor sich (Akk.) hin murmeln; b) (one respiration) Atemzug, der. **Breathalyser** (Brit.), **Breathalyzer** (P) ['breθəlaɪzə(r)] n. Alcotest-Röhrchen ℗, das; ~ test Alcotest ℗, der
breathe [bri:ð] 1. v.i. atmen; ~ in einatmen; ~ out ausatmen. 2. v.t. a) ~ [in/out] ein-/ausatmen; b) (utter) hauchen. '**breather** ['bri:ðə(r)] n. Verschnaufpause, die
'**breathless** adj. atemlos (with vor + Dat.)
'**breath-taking** adj. atemberaubend
bred see breed 1, 2
breeches ['brɪtʃɪz] n. pl. [pair of] ~: [Knie]bundhose, die; [riding-]~: Reithose, die
breed [bri:d] 1. v.t., bred [bred] a) (cause) erzeugen; b) züchten (Tiere, Pflanzen). 2. v.i., bred sich vermehren. 3. n. (of animals) Rasse, die. '**breeding** n. [good] ~: gute Erziehung
breeze [bri:z] n. Brise, die. **breezy** ['bri:zɪ] adj. windig
brevity ['brevɪtɪ] n. Kürze, die
brew [bru:] 1. v.t. a) brauen (Bier); ~ [up] kochen (Kaffee, Tee usw.). 2. v.i. a) (Bier:) gären (Kaffee, Tee:) ziehen; b) (Unwetter:) sich zusammenbrauen. 3. n. (brewed beer/tea) Bier, das/Tee, der. '**brewer** n. Brauer, der; (firm) Brauerei, die. **brewery** ['bru:ərɪ] n. Brauerei, die

bribe [braɪb] 1. n. Bestechung, die. 2. v.t. bestechen; ~ sb. to do/into doing sth. jmdn. bestechen, damit er etw. tut. **bribery** ['braɪbərɪ] n. Bestechung, die
brick [brɪk] 1. n. a) Ziegelstein, der; (toy) Bauklötzchen, das. 2. adj. Ziegelstein-. '**bricklayer** n. Maurer, der. '**bricklaying** n. Mauern, das
bridal ['braɪdl] adj. Braut-
bride [braɪd] n. Braut, die. '**bridegroom** n. Bräutigam, der. **bridesmaid** ['braɪdzmeɪd] n. Brautjungfer, die
¹**bridge** [brɪdʒ] 1. n. a) Brücke, die; b) (Naut.) [Kommando]brücke, die; c) (of nose) Nasenbein, das; d) (of spectacles) Steg, der. 2. v.t. eine Brücke bauen über (+ Akk.)
²**bridge** n. (Cards) Bridge, das
bridle ['braɪdl] n. Zaum, der. '**bridle path** n. Reitweg, der
¹**brief** [bri:f] adj. a) kurz; gering (Verspätung); b) (concise) knapp; in ~, to be ~: kurz gesagt
²**brief** 1. n. (instructions) Instruktionen Pl.; (Law: case) Mandat, das. 2. v.t. Instruktionen geben (+ Dat.); (inform) unterrichten. '**briefcase** n. Aktentasche, die. '**briefing** n. Briefing, das; (of reporters) Unterrichtung, die
'**briefly** adv. a) kurz; b) (concisely) knapp; kurz
briefs [bri:fs] n. pl. [pair of] ~: Slip, der
brigade [brɪ'geɪd] n. (Mil.) Brigade, die. **brigadier** [brɪgə'dɪə(r)] n. Brigadegeneral, der
bright [braɪt] adj. a) hell; grell (Scheinwerfer[licht], Sonnenlicht); strahlend (Sonnenschein, Augen, Tag); leuchtend (Farbe, Blume); ~ intervals/periods Aufheiterungen; b) (cheerful) fröhlich; c) (clever) intelligent.
brighten ['braɪtn] 1. v.t. ~ [up] aufhellen. 2. v.i. the weather or it is ~ing [up] es klärt sich auf. '**brightly** adv. a) hell; b) (cheerfully) fröhlich. '**brightness** n. see bright: a) Helligkeit, die; Grelle, die; Strahlen, das; Leuchtkraft, die; b) Fröhlichkeit, die; c) Intelligenz, die
brilliance ['brɪlɪəns] n. see brilliant: a) Helligkeit, die; Leuchten, das; b) Genialität, die; Glanz, der
brilliant ['brɪljənt] adj. a) hell (Licht); leuchtend (Farbe); b) genial (Mensch, Gedanke, Leistung); glänzend (Verstand, Aufführung, Idee)
brim [brɪm] 1. n. a) Rand, der; (of hat) [Hut]krempe, die. 2. v.i., -mm-: be

~**ming with sth.** randvoll mit etw. sein.
brim-'full *pred. adj.* randvoll (**with** mit)

brine [braɪn] *n.* Salzwasser, *das*

bring [brɪŋ] *v. t.,* **brought** [brɔːt] **a)** bringen; *(as a present or favour)* mitbringen; ~ **sth. with one** etw. mitbringen; **b)** ~ **sb. to do sth.** jmdn. dazu bringen, etw. zu tun; **I could not ~ myself to do it** ich konnte es nicht über mich bringen, es zu tun. **bring a'bout** *v. t.* verursachen. **bring 'back** *v. t.* **a)** *(return)* zurückbringen; *(from a journey)* mitbringen; **b)** *(recall)* in Erinnerung bringen; **c)** *(restore, reintroduce)* wieder einführen. **bring 'down** *v. t.* **a)** herunterbringen; **b)** *(kill, wound)* zur Strecke bringen; **c)** senken *(Preise, Inflationsrate, Fieber)*. **bring 'forward** *v. t.* **a)** nach vorne bringen; **b)** vorbringen *(Argument)*; zur Sprache bringen *(Fall, Angelegenheit)*; **c)** vorverlegen *(Termin)* (**to** auf + *Akk.*). **bring 'in** *v. t.* hereinbringen; einbringen *(Gesetzesvorlage, Verdienst, Summe)*. **bring 'off** *v. t. (conduct successfully)* zustande bringen. **bring 'on** *v. t.* **a)** *(cause)* verursachen; **b)** *(Sport)* einsetzen. **bring 'out** *v. t.* **a)** herausbringen; **b)** hervorheben *(Unterschied)*; **c)** einführen *(Produkt)*; herausbringen *(Buch, Zeitschrift)*. **bring 'up** *v. t.* **a)** heraufbringen; **b)** *(educate)* erziehen; *(rear)* aufziehen; **c)** zur Sprache bringen *(Angelegenheit, Thema, Problem)*

brink ['brɪŋk] *n.* Rand, *der;* **be on the ~ of doing sth.** nahe daran sein, etw. zu tun

brisk [brɪsk] *adj.* flott *(Gang)*; forsch *(Person, Art)*; frisch *(Wind)*; *(fig.)* rege *(Handel, Nachfrage)*; lebhaft *(Geschäft)*. **'briskly** *adv.* flott

bristle ['brɪsl] **1.** *n.* Borste, *die.* **2.** *v. i.* **a)** ~ |up| *(Haare:)* sich sträuben; **b)** ~ **with** *(fig.)* starren vor (+ *Dat.*). **'bristly** [brɪslɪ] *adj.* borstig

Britain ['brɪtn] *pr. n.* Großbritannien *(das)*

British ['brɪtɪʃ] **1.** *adj.* britisch; **he/she is ~:** er ist Brite/sie ist Britin. **2.** *n. pl.* **the ~:** die Briten. **British 'Isles** *pr. n. pl.* Britische Inseln

Briton ['brɪtn] *n.* Brite, *der*/Britin, *die*

Brittany ['brɪtənɪ] *pr. n.* Bretagne, *die*

brittle ['brɪtl] *adj.* spröde *(Material)*

broach [brəʊtʃ] *v. t.* anschneiden *(Thema)*

broad [brɔːd] *adj.* **a)** breit; *(extensive)* weit *(Ebene, Land)*; ausgedehnt

(Fläche); **b)** *(explicit)* klar *(Hinweis)*; breit *(Lächeln)*; **c)** *(main)* grob; *(generalized)* allgemein; **d)** stark *(Akzent)*.

broad 'bean *n.* Saubohne, *die*

broadcast ['brɔːdkɑːst] **1.** *n.* Sendung, *die; (live)* Übertragung, *die.* **2.** *v. t.,* **broadcast** senden; übertragen *(Livesendung)*. **3.** *v. i.,* **broadcast** senden. **'broadcasting** *n.* Senden, *das; (live)* Übertragen, *das;* **work in ~:** beim Funk arbeiten

broaden ['brɔːdn] **1.** *v. t.* **a)** verbreitern; **b)** ausweiten *(Diskussion)*. **2.** *v. i.* sich verbreitern; *(fig.)* sich erweitern

'broadly *adv.* **a)** deutlich *(hinweisen)*; breit *(grinsen, lächeln)*; **b)** *(in general)* allgemein *(beschreiben)*; ~ **speaking** allgemein gesagt

broad: ~-'**minded** *adj.* tolerant; ~**side** *n.* Breitseite, *die*

brocade [brə'keɪd] *n.* Brokat, *der*

broccoli ['brɒkəlɪ] *n.* Brokkoli, *der*

brochure ['brəʊʃə(r)] *n.* Broschüre, *die;* Prospekt, *der*

broil [brɔɪl] *v. t. (esp. Amer.)* grillen

broke [brəʊk] **1.** *see* **break 1, 2. 2.** *pred. adj. (coll.)* pleite *(ugs.)*

broken ['brəʊkn] **1.** *see* **break 1, 2. 2.** *adj.* **a)** zerbrochen; gebrochen *(Bein, Hals)*; verletzt *(Haut)*; abgebrochen *(Zahn)*; gerissen *(Seil)*; kaputt *(ugs.) (Uhr, Fernsehen, Fenster)*; ~ **glass** Glasscherben; **b)** *(imperfect)* gebrochen; **in ~ English** in gebrochenem Englisch; **c)** *(fig.)* ruiniert *(Ehe)*; gebrochen *(Mensch, Herz)*. **'broken-down** *adj.* baufällig *(Gebäude)*; kaputt *(ugs.) (Wagen)*. **broken-'hearted** *adj.* untröstlich

broker ['brəʊkə(r)] *n.* Makler, *der*

brolly ['brɒlɪ] *n. (Brit. coll.)* [Regen]schirm, *der*

bronchitis [brɒŋ'kaɪtɪs] *n.* Bronchitis, *die*

bronze [brɒnz] **1.** *n.* Bronze, *die.* **2.** *attrib. adj.* Bronze-; *(coloured like ~)* bronzefarben

brooch [brəʊtʃ] *n.* Brosche, *die*

brood [bruːd] **1.** *n.* Brut, *die.* **2.** *v. i.* [vor sich *(Akk.)* hin] brüten

brook [brʊk] *n.* Bach, *der*

broom [bruːm] *n.* **a)** Besen, *der;* **b)** *(Bot.)* Ginster, *der.* **'broomcupboard** *n.* Besenschrank, *der.* **'broomstick** *n.* Besenstiel, *der*

broth [brɒθ] *n.* Brühe, *die*

brothel ['brɒθl] *n.* Bordell, *das*

brother ['brʌðə(r)] *n.* Bruder, *der;* **my ~s and sisters** meine Geschwister.

'**brotherhood** *n. (organization)* Bruderschaft, *die.* '**brother-in-law** *n., pl.* brothers-in-law Schwager, *der*

brought *see* bring

brow [brau] *n.* a) *(eye~)* Braue, *die;* b) *(forehead)* Stirn, *die;* c) *(of hill)* Kuppe, *die*

'**browbeat** *v.t.,* forms as beat 1 einschüchtern

brown [braun] 1. *adj.* braun. 2. *n.* Braun, *das.* **brown 'bread** *n.* ≈ Mischbrot, *das*

Brownie ['brauni] *n.* Wichtel, *die*

brown 'paper *n.* Packpapier, *das*

browse [brauz] *v.i.* *(in shop)* sich umsehen; *(read)* blättern **(through** in + *Dat.)*

bruise [bru:z] 1. *n.* a) *(Med.)* blauer Fleck; b) *(on fruit)* Druckstelle, *die.* 2. *v.t.* quetschen ⟨Obst, Pflanzen⟩; ~ oneself/one's leg sich stoßen/sich am Bein stoßen

brunette [bru:'net] 1. *n.* Brünette, *die.* 2. *adj.* brünett

brunt [brʌnt] *n.* bear the ~ of the attack/financial cuts von dem Angriff/von den Einsparungen am meisten betroffen sein

brush [brʌʃ] 1. *n.* a) Bürste, *die;* *(for sweeping)* Besen, *der;* *(with short handle)* Handfeger, *der;* *(for painting or writing)* Pinsel, *der;* b) *(skirmish)* Zusammenstoß, *der;* c) *(light touch)* flüchtige Berührung. 2. *v.t.* a) kehren; fegen; abbürsten ⟨Kleidung⟩; ~ one's teeth/hair sich *(Dat.)* die Zähne putzen/die Haare bürsten; b) *(touch in passing)* streifen. 3. *v.i.* ~ past sb./sth. jmdn./etw. streifen. **brush 'up** *v.t. & i.* ~ **up** [on] auffrischen ⟨Kenntnisse usw.⟩

brusque [brʌsk] *adj.,* '**brusquely** *adv.* schroff

Brussels ['brʌslz] *pr. n.* Brüssel *(das).* **Brussels 'sprouts** *n. pl.* Rosenkohl, *der*

brutal ['bru:tl] *adj.* brutal. **brutality** [bru:'tælɪtɪ] *n.* Brutalität, *die.* **brutally** ['bru:təlɪ] *adv.* brutal

brute [bru:t] 1. *n.* a) *(animal)* Bestie, *die;* b) *(person)* Rohling, *der.* 2. *attrib. adj.* by ~ force mit roher Gewalt

B.Sc. *abbr.* Bachelor of Science

BST *abbr.* British Summer Time Britische Sommerzeit

bubble ['bʌbl] 1. *n.* Blase, *die;* *(small)* Perle, *die.* 2. *v.i.* ⟨Wasser, Schlamm, Lava:⟩ Blasen bilden. '**bubble bath** *n.* Schaumbad, *das*

¹**buck** [bʌk] *n. (deer, chamois)* Bock, *der;* *(rabbit, hare)* Rammler, *der*

²**buck** *n.* pass the ~ to sb. jmdm. die Verantwortung aufhalsen

³**buck** *(coll.)* 1. *v.i.* ~ 'up *(make haste)* sich ranhalten *(ugs.);* b) *(cheer up)* ~ up! Kopf hoch! 2. *v.t.* ~ one's ideas up *(coll.)* sich zusammenreißen

⁴**buck** *n. (Amer. sl.)* Dollar, *der*

bucket ['bʌkɪt] *n.* Eimer, *der*

buckle ['bʌkl] 1. *n.* Schnalle, *die.* 2. *v.t.* a) zuschnallen; ~ sth. on/up etw. anschnallen/festschnallen; b) verbiegen ⟨Stoßstange, Rad⟩. 3. *v.i.* ⟨Rad, Metallplatte:⟩ [sich] verbiegen

bud [bʌd] 1. *n.* Knospe, *die;* come into /be in ~: Knospen treiben. 2. *v.i.,* -dd- Knospen treiben

Buddhism ['budɪzm] *n.* Buddhismus, *der.* **Buddhist** ['budɪst] 1. *n.* Buddhist, *der*/Buddhistin, *die.* 2. *adj.* buddhistisch

budge [bʌdʒ] 1. *v.i.* sich rühren; ⟨Gegenstand:⟩ sich bewegen. 2. *v.t.* bewegen

budgerigar ['bʌdʒərɪgɑ:(r)] *n.* Wellensittich, *der*

budget ['bʌdʒɪt] 1. *n.* Etat, *der;* Haushalt[splan], *der.* 2. *v.i.* ~ for sth. etw. [im Etat] einplanen

budgie ['bʌdʒɪ] *n. (coll.)* Wellensittich, *der*

buff [bʌf] 1. *adj.* gelbbraun. 2. *n. (coll.: enthusiast)* Fan, *der (ugs.)*

buffalo ['bʌfələu] *n., pl.* ~es or same Büffel, *der*

buffer ['bʌfə(r)] *n.* Prellbock, *der;* *(on vehicle; also fig.)* Puffer, *der*

buffet ['bufeɪ] *n.* Büfett, *das.* '**buffet car** *n.* Büfettwagen, *der*

bug [bʌg] *n. (also coll.: microphone)* Wanze, *die*

buggy ['bʌgɪ] *n. (pushchair)* Sportwagen, *der*

bugle ['bju:gl] *n.* Bügelhorn, *das*

build [bɪld] 1. *v.t.,* built [bɪlt] bauen; *(fig.)* aufbauen ⟨System, Gesellschaft, Zukunft⟩. 2. *v.i.,* built bauen. 3. *n.* Körperbau, *der.* **build 'in** *v.t.* einbauen. **build 'on** *v.t.* aufbauen auf (+ *Dat.)*; bebauen ⟨Gebiet⟩. **build 'up** 1. *v.t.* aufhäufen ⟨Reserven, Mittel⟩; kräftigen ⟨Personen, Körper⟩; steigern ⟨Produktion, Kapazität⟩; stärken ⟨[Selbst]vertrauen⟩; aufbauen ⟨Firma, Geschäft⟩. 2. *v.i.* ⟨Spannung, Druck:⟩ zunehmen; ⟨Schlange, Rückstau:⟩ sich bilden; ⟨Verkehr:⟩ sich verdichten

'**builder** *n.* Bauunternehmer, *der*

'**building** n. **a)** Bau, der; **b)** (structure) Gebäude, das. '**building-site** n. Baustelle, die. '**building society** n. (Brit.) Bausparkasse, die

built see **build 1, 2**

built: ~-**in** adj. **a)** eingebaut; Einbau-(schrank, küche usw.); **b)** (fig.: instinctive) angeboren; ~-**up** adj. bebaut; ~-**up area** Wohngebiet, das; (Motor Veh.) geschlossene Ortschaft

bulb [bʌlb] n. **a)** (Bot., Hort.) Zwiebel, die; **b)** (of lamp) [Glüh]birne, die

Bulgaria [bʌl'geərɪə] pr. n. Bulgarien (das). **Bulgarian** [bʌl'geərɪən] **1.** adj. bulgarisch. **2.** n. **a)** (person) Bulgare, der/Bulgarin, die; **b)** (language) Bulgarisch, das; see also **English 2 a**

bulge [bʌldʒ] **1.** n. Ausbeulung, die; ausgebeulte Stelle. **2.** v. i. sich wölben

bulk [bʌlk] n. **a)** (large quantity) **in** ~: in großen Mengen; **b)** (large shape) massige Gestalt; **c)** (size) Größe, die; **d)** (greater part) der größte Teil; (of population, votes) Mehrheit, die. **bulky** adj. sperrig (Gegenstand); massig (Gestalt, Körper)

bull [bʊl] n. Bulle, der; (esp. for bullfight) Stier, der

'**bulldog** n. Bulldogge, die

bulldozer ['bʊldəʊzə(r)] n. Planierraupe, die

bullet ['bʊlɪt] n. Kugel, die

bulletin ['bʊlɪtɪn] n. Bulletin, das

'**bulletproof** adj. kugelsicher

'**bullfight** n. Stierkampf, der

bullion ['bʊljən] n. **gold** ~: Goldbarren Pl.

bullock ['bʊlək] n. Ochse, der

bull: ~**ring** n. Stierkampfarena, die; ~'**s-eye** n. (of target) Schwarze, das

bully ['bʊlɪ] **1.** n. (schoolboy etc.) ≈ Rabauke, der; (boss) Tyrann, der. **2.** v. t. schikanieren; (frighten) einschüchtern

'**bum** [bʌm] n. (Brit. sl.) Hintern, der (ugs.)

²**bum** n. (Amer. sl.: tramp) Penner, der (salopp)

bumble-bee ['bʌmblbi:] n. Hummel, die

bump [bʌmp] **1.** n. **a)** (sound) Bums, der; (impact) Stoß, der; **b)** (swelling) Beule, die; **c)** (hump) Buckel, der (ugs.). **2.** adv. bums. **3.** v. t. anstoßen. '**bump into** v. t. **a)** stoßen an (+ Akk.); **b)** (meet by chance) zufällig [wieder]treffen

'**bumper 1.** n. Stoßstange, die. **2.** attrib. adj. Rekord(ernte, -jahr)

'**bumpy** adj. holp[e]rig (Straße, Fahrt, Fahrzeug); uneben (Fläche); unruhig (Flug)

bun [bʌn] n. süßes Brötchen; (currant ~) Korinthenbrötchen, das

bunch [bʌntʃ] n. **a)** (of flowers) Strauß, der; (of grapes, bananas) Traube, die; (of parsley, radishes) Bund, das; ~ **of flowers/grapes** Blumenstrauß, der/Traube, die; **a** ~ **of keys** ein Schlüsselbund; **b)** (lot) Anzahl, die; **the best or pick of the** ~: der/die/das Beste [von allen]; **c)** (of people) Haufen, der (ugs.)

bundle ['bʌndl] n. Bündel, das; (of papers) Packen, der

bung [bʌŋ] **1.** n. Spund, der. **2.** v. t. (sl.) schmeißen (ugs.). **bung up** v. i. be/get ~ed up verstopft sein/verstopfen

bungalow ['bʌŋgələʊ] n. Bungalow, der

bungle ['bʌŋgl] v. t. stümpern bei

bunk [bʌŋk] n. (in ship, lorry) Koje, die; (in sleeping-car) Bett, das; (~-bed) Etagenbett, das

bunker ['bʌŋkə(r)] n. Bunker, der

bunny ['bʌnɪ] n. Häschen, das

buoy [bɔɪ] n. Boje, die

buoyancy ['bɔɪənsɪ] n. Auftrieb, der. **buoyant** ['bɔɪənt] adj. schwimmend; **be** ~: schwimmen

burden ['bɜ:dn] **1.** n. Last, die; **become a** ~ (fig.) zur Last werden. **2.** v. t. belasten (with)

bureau ['bjʊərəʊ, bjʊə'rəʊ] n. **a)** (Brit.: writing-desk) Sekretär, der; **b)** (office) Büro, das

bureaucracy [bjʊə'rɒkrəsɪ] n. Bürokratie, die. **bureaucrat** ['bjʊərəkræt] n. Bürokrat, der/Bürokratin, die. **bureaucratic** [bjʊərə'krætɪk] adj. bürokratisch

burglar ['bɜ:glə(r)] n. Einbrecher, der. '**burglar alarm** n. Alarmanlage, die. **burglary** ['bɜ:glərɪ] n. Einbruch, der. **burgle** ['bɜ:gl] v. t. einbrechen in (+ Akk.); **the shop/he was** ~d in dem Laden/bei ihm wurde eingebrochen

burial ['berɪəl] n. Begräbnis, das

burly ['bɜ:lɪ] adj. stämmig

Burma ['bɜ:mə] pr. n. Birma (das)

burn [bɜ:n] **1.** n. (on the skin) Verbrennung, die; (on material) Brandfleck, der. **2.** v. t., ~**t** [bɜ:nt] or ~**ed** a) verbrennen; ~ **oneself/one's hand** sich verbrennen/sich (Dat.) die Hand verbrennen; ~ **a hole in sth.** ein Loch in etw. (Akk.) brennen; **b)** als Brennstoff verwenden (Gas, Öl usw.); heizen mit (Kohle, Holz, Torf); **c)** (spoil) anbrennen lassen ⟨Fleisch, Kuchen⟩; be ~t angebrannt sein. **3.** v.i., ~t or ~ed brennen; ~ **to death** verbrennen; **she** ~s **easily** sie bekommt leicht einen Sonnenbrand. **burn 'down** v.t.&i. niederbrennen

'**burner** n. Brenner, der

'**burning** adj. glühend ⟨Leidenschaft, Haß, Wunsch⟩; brennend ⟨Wunsch, Frage, Problem⟩

burnt see **burn 2, 3**

burp [bɜːp] (coll.) **1.** n. Rülpser, der (ugs.). **2.** v.i. rülpsen (ugs.)

burrow ['bʌrəʊ] **1.** n. Bau, der. **2.** v.i. [sich (Dat.)] einen Gang graben

burst [bɜːst] **1.** n. **a)** (split) Bruch, der; **b)** (of firing) Salve, die; **c)** (fig.) **a** ~ **of applause/cheering** ein Beifallsausbruch/Beifallsrufe Pl. **2.** v.t., burst zum Platzen bringen; platzen lassen ⟨Luftballon⟩; ~ **pipe** Rohrbruch, der. **3.** v.i., burst **a)** platzen; ⟨Bombe:⟩ explodieren; ⟨Damm:⟩ brechen; ⟨Flußufer:⟩ überschwemmt werden; ⟨Furunkel, Geschwür:⟩ aufgehen; **be** ~**ing with sth.** zum Bersten voll sein mit etw.; **be** ~**ing with pride/impatience/excitement** vor Stolz/Ungeduld platzen/vor Aufregung außer sich sein. '**burst into** v.t. **a)** eindringen in; **b)** ~ **into tears/laughter** in Tränen/Gelächter ausbrechen; ~ **into flames** in Brand geraten. **burst 'out** v.i. **a)** herausstürzen; **b)** (exclaim) losplatzen; **c)** ~ **out laughing/crying** in Lachen/Tränen ausbrechen

bury ['berɪ] v.t. **a)** begraben; **b)** (hide) vergraben; ~ **one's face in one's hands** das Gesicht in den Händen vergraben; **c)** ~ **one's teeth in sth.** seine Zähne in etw. (Akk.) graben

bus [bʌs] n. Bus, der

bus: ~**-conductor** n. Busschaffner, der; ~**-driver** n. Busfahrer, der; ~ **fare** n. [Bus]fahrpreis, der

bush [bʊʃ] n. **a)** Busch, der; **b)** (shrubs) Gebüsch, das. '**bushy** adj. buschig

busily ['bɪzɪlɪ] adj. eifrig

business ['bɪznɪs] n. **a)** (trading operation) Geschäft, das; (company, firm) Betrieb, der; (large) Unternehmen, das; **b)** (buying and selling) Geschäfte Pl.; **c)** (task, province) Aufgabe, die; **mind your own** ~! kümmere dich um deine [eigenen] Angelegenheiten!; **d)** (difficult matter) Problem, das

business: ~ **letter** n. Geschäftsbrief, der; ~**-like** adj. geschäftsmäßig ⟨Art⟩; geschäftstüchtig ⟨Person⟩;

~**man** n. Geschäftsmann, der; ~ **school** n. kaufmännische Fachschule; ~**woman** n. Geschäftsfrau, die

busker ['bʌskə(r)] n. Straßenmusikant, der

bus: ~**-route** n. Buslinie, die; ~ **shelter** n. Wartehäuschen, das; ~**-station** n. Omnibusbahnhof, der; ~**-stop** n. Bushaltestelle, die

¹**bust** [bʌst] n. **a)** (sculpture) Büste, die; **b)** ~ [measurement] Oberweite, die

²**bust** (coll.) **1.** adj. kaputt (ugs.). **2.** v.t., ~**ed** or bust (break) kaputtmachen (ugs.); ~ **sth. open** etw. aufbrechen. **3.** v.i., ~**ed** or bust kaputtgehen (ugs.)

'**bus-ticket** n. Busfahrkarte, die

bustle ['bʌsl] v.i. ~ **about** geschäftig hin und her eilen. ~ n. Betrieb, der.

bustling ['bʌslɪŋ] adj. belebt ⟨Straße, Stadt, Markt usw.⟩; rege ⟨Tätigkeit⟩

busy ['bɪzɪ] **1.** adj. **a)** beschäftigt (**at, with** mit); arbeitsreich ⟨Leben⟩; ziemlich hektisch ⟨Zeit⟩; **I'm** ~ **now** ich habe jetzt zu tun; **he was** ~ **packing** er war mit Packen beschäftigt; **b)** (Amer. Teleph.) besetzt. **2.** v.refl. ~ **oneself** sich beschäftigen (**with** mit). '**busybody** n. G[e]schaftlhuber, der

but 1. [bət, stressed bʌt] conj. aber; correcting after a negative sondern; **not that book** ~ **this** nicht das Buch, sondern dieses. **2.** [bət] prep. außer (+ Dat.); **the next/last** ~ **one** der/die/das übernächste/vorletzte

butcher ['bʊtʃə(r)] **1.** n. Fleischer, der. **2.** v.t. (murder) niedermetzeln

butler ['bʌtlə(r)] n. Butler, der

¹**butt** [bʌt] n. **a)** (of rifle) Kolben, der; **b)** (of cigarette, cigar) Stummel, der

²**butt** n. (object of teasing or ridicule) Zielscheibe, die

³**butt 1.** n. (push) (by person) [Kopf]stoß, der; (by animal) Stoß (mit den Hörnern), der. **2.** v.t.&i. mit dem Kopf/den Hörnern stoßen. **butt 'in** v.i. dazwischenreden

butter ['bʌtə(r)] **1.** n. Butter, die. **2.** v.t. buttern

butter: ~**-bean** n. Mondbohne, die; ~**cup** n. Butterblume, die; ~**fly** n. **a)** Schmetterling, der; **b)** ~ [stroke] Delphinstil, der

buttock ['bʌtək] n. Hinterbacke, die; Gesäßhälfte, die; ~**s** Gesäß, das

button ['bʌtn] **1.** n. Knopf, der. **2.** v.t. ~ [up] zuknöpfen. '**buttonhole 1.** n. **a)** Knopfloch, das; **b)** (flower) Knopflochblume, die. **2.** v.t. zu fassen kriegen (ugs.)

buttress ['bʌtrɪs] *n. (Archit.)* Mauer-stütze, *die*

buxom ['bʌksəm] *adj.* drall

buy [baɪ] 1. *v. t.,* **bought** [bɔːt] kaufen; ~ **sb./oneself sth.** jmdm./sich etw. kaufen. 2. *n.* [Ein]kauf, *der;* **be a good ~:** preiswert sein. **buy 'up** *v. t.* aufkaufen

'**buyer** *n.* Käufer, *der*/Käuferin, *die*

buzz [bʌz] 1. *n.* Summen, *das.* 2. *v. i.* summen. **buzz 'off** *v. i. (sl.)* abhauen *(salopp)*

'**buzzer** *n.* Summer, *der*

by [baɪ] 1. *prep.* **a)** *(near, beside)* an (+ *Dat.*); bei; *(next to)* neben; ~ **the window/river** am Fenster/Fluß; **b)** *(to position beside)* zu; **c)** *(about, in the possession of)* bei; **d)** [**all**] **by herself/ himself** *etc.* [ganz] allein[e]; **e)** *(along)* entlang; *(via)* über (+ *Akk.*); **f)** *(passing)* vorbei an (+ *Dat.*); **g)** *(during)* bei; **by day/night** bei Tag/Nacht; **h)** *(through the agency of)* von; **written by ...:** geschrieben von ...; **i)** *(through the means of)* durch; **by bus/ship** *etc.* mit dem Bus/Schiff *usw.;* **by air/sea** mit dem Flugzeug/Schiff; **j)** *(not later than)* bis; **by now/this time** inzwischen; **k)** *indicating unit* pro; **by the minute/hour** pro Minute/Stunde; **day by day/month by month** Tag für Tag/ Monat für Monat; **10 ft. by 20 ft.** 10 [Fuß] mal 20 Fuß; **l)** *indicating amount* one by one einzeln; **two by two/three by three** zu zweit/dritt; **m)** *indicating factor* durch; **8 divided by 2 is** 4 8 geteilt durch 2 ist 4; **n)** *indicating extent* um; **wider by a foot** um einen Fuß breiter; **o)** *(according to)* nach. 2. *adv.* **a)** *(past)* vorbei; **b)** *(near)* **close/ near by** in der Nähe; **c)** **by and large** im großen und ganzen

bye[-bye] ['baɪ(baɪ)] *int. (coll.)* tschüs *(ugs.)*

bye-law *see* **by-law**

'**by-election** *n.* Nachwahl, *die*

bygone ['baɪgɒn] *adj.* vergangen

'**by-law** *n. (esp. Brit.)* Verordnung, *die*

'**bypass** 1. *n.* Umgehungsstraße, *die.* 2. *v. t.* **a)** the road ~es the town die Straße führt um die Stadt herum; **b)** *(fig.)* übergehen

'**by-product** *n.* Nebenprodukt, *das*

'**by-road** *n.* Nebenstraße, *die*

bystander ['baɪstændə(r)] *n.* Zuschauer, *der*/Zuschauerin, *die*

byte ['baɪt] *n. (Computing)* Byte, *das*

'**byway** *n.* Seitenweg, *die*

'**byword** *n.* Inbegriff, *der* (for *Gen.*)

C

C, c [siː] *n.* C, c, *das*

C. *abbr.* **a)** Celsius C; **b)** Centigrade C

cab [kæb] *n.* **a)** *(taxi)* Taxi, *das;* **b)** *(of lorry, truck)* Fahrerhaus, *das;* *(of train)* Führerstand, *der*

cabaret ['kæbəreɪ] *n.* Varieté, *das;* *(satirical)* Kabarett, *das*

cabbage ['kæbɪdʒ] *n.* Kohl, *der;* **red/ white ~:** Rot-/Weißkohl, *der*

cabin ['kæbɪn] *n.* **a)** *(in ship) (for passengers)* Kabine, *die;* *(for crew)* Kajüte, *die; (in aircraft)* Kabine, *die*

cabinet ['kæbɪnɪt] *n.* **a)** Schrank, *der; (in bathroom, for medicines)* Schränkchen, *das;* [**display**] **~:** Vitrine, *die;* **b)** **the C~** *(Polit.)* das Kabinett; **C~ Minister** Minister, *der*

cable ['keɪbl] 1. *n.* **a)** *(rope)* Kabel, *das; (of ~-car etc.)* Seil, *das;* **b)** *(Electr., Teleph.)* Kabel, *das;* **c)** *(message)* Kabel, *das.* 2. *v. t.* kabeln ⟨*Mitteilung, Nachricht*⟩. '**cable-car** *n.* Drahtseilbahn, *die.* **cable 'television** *n.* Kabelfernsehen, *das*

cache [kæʃ] *n.* geheimes [Waffen-/ Proviant-]lager

cackle ['kækl] 1. *n.* **a)** *(of hen)* Gackern, *das;* **b)** *(laughter)* [meckerndes] Gelächter. 2. *v. i.* **a)** ⟨*Henne:*⟩ gackern; **b)** *(laugh)* meckernd lachen

cactus ['kæktəs] *n., pl.* **cacti** ['kæktaɪ] *or* ~**es** Kaktus, *der*

caddie ['kædɪ] *n. (Golf)* Caddie, *der*

caddy ['kædɪ] *n.* Dose, *die*

cadet [kə'det] *n.* Offiziersschüler, *der;* **naval/police ~:** Marinekadett/Anwärter für den Polizeidienst

cadge [kædʒ] *v. t.* [sich *(Dat.)*] erbetteln

café, cafe ['kæfeɪ] *n.* Lokal, *das; (tearoom)* Café, *das*

cafeteria [kæfɪ'tɪərɪə] *n.* Cafeteria, *die*

caffeine ['kæfiːn] *n.* Koffein, *das*

cage [keɪdʒ] 1. *n.* **a)** Käfig, *der;* **b)** *(of lift)* Fahrkabine, *die.* 2. *v. t.* einsperren

cagey ['keɪdʒɪ] *adj. (coll.)* zugeknöpft

(ugs.); be ~ about sth. mit etw. hinterm Berg halten *(ugs.)*

Cairo ['kaɪərəʊ] *pr. n.* Kairo *(das)*

cajole [kə'dʒəʊl] *v. t.* ~ sb. into sth./doing sth. jmdm. etw. einreden/jmdm. einreden, etw. zu tun

cake [keɪk] **1.** *n.* Kuchen, *der;* a ~ of soap ein Riegel *od.* Stück Seife. **2.** *v. t.* verkrusten; ~d with dirt/blood schmutz-/blutverkrustet

calamity [kə'læmɪtɪ] *n.* Unheil, *das*

calcium ['kælsɪəm] *n.* Kalzium, *das*

calculate ['kælkjʊleɪt] **1.** *v. t.* a) berechnen; *(by estimating)* ausrechnen; b) be ~d to do sth. darauf abzielen, etw. zu tun. **2.** *v. i.* ~ on doing sth. damit rechnen, etw. zu tun. **'calculated** *adj.* kalkuliert ⟨Risiko⟩; vorsätzlich ⟨Handlung⟩. **calculation** [kælkjʊ-'leɪʃn] *n.* a) *(result)* Rechnung, *die;* he is out in his ~s er hat sich verrechnet; b) *(calculating)* Berechnung, *die.* **calculator** ['kælkjʊleɪtə(r)] *n.* Rechner, *der*

calculus ['kælkjuːləs] *n.* differential/integral ~: Differential-/Integralrechnung, *die*

calendar ['kælɪndə(r)] *n.* Kalender, *der; attrib.* Kalender-

¹calf [kɑːf] *n., pl.* calves Kalb, *das*

²calf *n., pl.* calves *(Anat.)* Wade, *die*

calibre *(Brit.; Amer.:* caliber*)* ['kælɪbə(r)] *n.* Kaliber, *das*

calico ['kælɪkəʊ] *n.* Kattun, *der*

California [kælɪ'fɔːnɪə] *pr. n.* Kalifornien *(das)*

caliper *see* calliper

call [kɔːl] **1.** *v. i.* a) rufen; ~ to sb. jmdm. etwas zurufen; ~ |out| for help um Hilfe rufen; b) *(pay brief visit)* [kurz] besuchen (at Akk.); ~ on sb. jmdn. besuchen; ~ round vorbeikommen *(ugs.);* ~ at a port/station einen Hafen anlaufen/an einem Bahnhof halten; c) *(Teleph.)* who is ~ing, please? wer spricht da, bitte?; thank you for ~ing vielen Dank für Ihren Anruf! **2.** *v. t.* a) rufen; aufrufen ⟨Namen, Nummer⟩; b) *(cry to, summon)* rufen; *(to a duty, to do sth.)* aufrufen; c) *(by radio/telephone)* rufen/anrufen; d) *(initially)* Kontakt aufnehmen mit; d) *(rouse)* wecken; e) einberufen ⟨Konferenz⟩; ausrufen ⟨Streik⟩; f) *(name)* nennen; he is ~ed Bob er heißt Bob; what is it ~ed in English? wie heißt das auf englisch? **3.** *n.* a) Ruf, *der;* a ~ for help ein Hilferuf; be on ~: Bereitschaftsdienst haben; b)

(visit) Besuch, *der;* make *or* pay a ~ on sb., make *or* pay sb. a ~: jmdn. besuchen; c) *(telephone ~)* Anruf, *der;* give sb. a ~: jmdn. anrufen; make a ~: telephonieren; d) *(invitation, summons)* Aufruf, *der;* e) *(need, occasion)* Anlaß, *der.* **call 'back 1.** *v. t.* zurückrufen. **2.** *v. i.* zurückrufen; *(come back)* zurückkommen. **'call for** *v. t.* a) *(send for, order)* bestellen; b) *(collect)* abholen; c) *(require, demand)* erfordern; this ~s for a celebration das muß gefeiert werden. **call 'in 1.** *v. i.* vorbeikommen *(ugs.)* (on bei). **2.** *v. t.* zu Rate ziehen ⟨Fachmann usw.⟩. **call 'off** *v. t.* absagen ⟨Treffen, Verabredung⟩; rückgängig machen ⟨Geschäft⟩; lösen ⟨Verlobung⟩; *(end)* abbrechen ⟨Streik⟩. **'call on** *v. t.* a) *see* ~ **1b;** b) *see* ~ |up|on. **call 'out 1.** *v. t.* alarmieren ⟨Truppen⟩; zum Streik aufrufen ⟨Arbeitnehmer⟩. **2.** *v. i. see* ~ **1a. call 'up** *v. t.* a) *(by telephone)* anrufen; b) *(Mil.)* einberufen. **'call [up]on** *v. t.* ~ upon sb.'s generosity an jmds. Großzügigkeit *(Akk.)* appellieren; ~ |up|on sb. to do sth. jmdn. auffordern, etw. zu tun

'call-box *n.* Telefonzelle, *die*

'caller *n.* *(visitor)* Besucher, *der*/Besucherin, *die;* *(on telephone)* Anrufer, *der*/Anruferin, *die*

'call-girl *n.* Callgirl, *das*

'calling *n.* Beruf, *der*

calliper ['kælɪpə(r)] *n.* a) |a pair of| ~s Tasterzirkel; b) *(Med.)* Beinschiene, *die*

callous ['kæləs] *adj.* gefühllos; herzlos ⟨Handlung, Verhalten⟩

'call-up *n. (Mil.)* Einberufung, *die*

calm [kɑːm] **1.** *n. (stillness)* Stille, *die;* *(serenity)* Ruhe, *die.* **2.** *adj.* ruhig. **3.** *v. t.* ~ sb. |down| jmdn. beruhigen. **4.** *v. i.* ~ |down| sich beruhigen. **'calmly** *adv.* ruhig; gelassen. **'calmness** *n.* Ruhe, *die;* *(of water)* Stille, *die*

Calor gas, (P) ['kælə gæs] *n.* Butangas, *das*

calorie ['kælərɪ] *n.* Kalorie, *die*

calves *pl. of* ¹,²calf

camber ['kæmbə(r)] *n.* Wölbung, *die*

came *see* come

camel ['kæml] *n.* Kamel, *das*

camera ['kæmərə] *n.* Kamera, *die.* **'cameraman** *n.* Kameramann, *der*

camouflage ['kæməflɑːʒ] **1.** *n.* Tarnung, *die.* **2.** *v. t.* tarnen

camp [kæmp] **1.** *n.* Lager, *das.* **2.** *v. i.* ~ |out| campen; *(in tent)* zelten; go ~ing Campen/Zelten fahren/gehen

campaign [kæm'peɪn] **1.** *n.* **a)** *(Mil.)* Feldzug, *der;* **b)** *(organized action)* Kampagne, *die; publicity* ~: Werbekampagne, *die.* **2.** *v. i.* ~ **for/against** *sth.* sich für etw. einsetzen/gegen etw. etwas unternehmen; **be** ~**ing** ⟨*Politiker:*⟩ im Wahlkampf stehen

camp-bed *n.* Campingliege, *die*

camper *n. (person)* Camper, *der/* Camperin, *die*

camping *n.* Camping, *das; (in tent)* Zelten, *das.* **'camping-ground** *(Amer.),* **'camping site** *ns.* Campingplatz, *der*

campsite *n.* Campingplatz, *der*

campus ['kæmpəs] *n.* Campus, *der*

¹can [kæn] **1.** *n.* **a)** *(milk-, watering-~)* Kanne, *die; (for oil, petrol)* Kanister, *der; (Amer.: for refuse)* Eimer, *der;* **b)** *(for preserving)* [Konserven]dose, *die;* **a** ~ **of tomatoes/beer** eine Dose Tomaten/Bier. **2.** *v. t.,* **-nn-** konservieren

²can [kən, *stressed* kæn] *v. aux., only in pres.* **can,** *neg.* **cannot** ['kænət], *(coll.)* **can't** [kɑːnt], *past* **could** [kʊd], *neg. (coll.)* **couldn't** ['kʊdnt] können; *(have right, be permitted)* dürfen; können; **I can't do that** das kann ich nicht; *(it would be wrong)* das kann ich nicht tun; **you can't smoke here** hier dürfen Sie nicht rauchen; **could you ring me tomorrow?** könnten Sie mich morgen anrufen?; **I could have killed him** ich hätte ihn umbringen können; **[that] could be [so]** das könnte od. kann sein

Canada ['kænədə] *pr. n.* Kanada *(das).* **Canadian** [kə'neɪdɪən] **1.** *adj.* kanadisch. **2.** *n.* Kanadier, *der/*Kanadierin, *die*

canal [kə'næl] *n.* Kanal, *der*

canary [kə'neərɪ] *n.* Kanarienvogel, *der*

Ca'nary Islands *pr. n. pl.* Kanarische Inseln *Pl.*

cancel ['kænsl] **1.** *v. t.,* *(Brit.)* **-ll-** absagen ⟨*Besuch, Urlaub, Reise, Sportveranstaltung*⟩; ausfallen lassen ⟨*Veranstaltung, Vorlesung, Zug, Bus*⟩; fallenlassen ⟨*Pläne*⟩; rückgängig machen ⟨*Einladung, Vertrag*⟩; zurücknehmen ⟨*Befehl*⟩; stornieren ⟨*Bestellung, Auftrag*⟩; kündigen ⟨*Abonnement*⟩; abbestellen ⟨*Zeitung*⟩. **2.** *v. i.,* *(Brit.)* **-ll-:** ~ [out] sich [gegenseitig] aufheben. **cancellation** [kænsə'leɪʃn] *n. see* **cancel 1:** Absage, *die;* Ausfall, *der;* Fallenlassen, *das;* Rückgängigmachen, *das;* Zurücknahme, *die;* Stornierung, *die;* Kündigung, *die;* Abbestellung, *die*

cancer ['kænsə(r)] *n.* **a)** *(Med.)* Krebs, *der;* **b) C~** *(Astrol., Astron.)* der Krebs

candelabra [kændɪ'lɑːbrə] *n.* Leuchter, *der*

candid ['kændɪd] *adj.* offen; ehrlich ⟨*Ansicht, Bericht*⟩

candidate ['kændɪdət, 'kændɪdeɪt] *n.* Kandidat, *der/*Kandidatin, *die*

candle ['kændl] *n.* Kerze, *die*

candle: ~**-light** *n.* Kerzenlicht, *das;* ~**stick** *n.* Kerzenhalter, *der; (elaborate)* Leuchter, *der;* ~**wick** *n. (material)* Frottierplüsch, *der*

candour *(Brit., Amer.:* **candor)** ['kændə(r)] *n. see* **candid:** Offenheit, *die;* Ehrlichkeit, *die*

candy ['kændɪ] *n. (Amer.) (sweets)* Süßigkeiten *Pl.; (sweet)* Bonbon, *das od. der.* **'candyfloss** ['kændɪflɒs] *n.* Zuckerwatte, *die*

cane [keɪn] **1.** *n.* **a)** *(stem)* Rohr, *das; (of raspberry, blackberry)* Sproß, *der;* **b)** *(material)* Rohr, *das;* **c)** *(stick)* [Rohr]stock, *der.* **2.** *v. t.* [mit dem Stock] schlagen

canine ['keɪnaɪn] *adj.* **a)** *(of dog[s])* Hunde-; **b)** ~ **tooth** Eckzahn, *der*

canister ['kænɪstə(r)] *n.* Büchse, *die; (for petrol, oil, etc.)* Kanister, *der*

cannabis ['kænəbɪs] *n. (hashish)* Haschisch, *das; (marijuana)* Marihuana, *das*

canned [kænd] *adj.* Dosen-; in Dosen nachgestellt; ~ **meat/fruit** Fleisch-/Obstkonserven *Pl.;* ~ **beer** Dosenbier; ~ **food** [Lebensmittel]konserven *Pl.;* ~ **music** Musikkonserve, *die*

cannibal ['kænɪbl] *n.* Kannibale, *der/*Kannibalin, *die.* **cannibalism** ['kænɪbəlɪzm] *n.* Kannibalismus, *der*

cannon ['kænən] **1.** *n.* Kanone, *die.* **2.** *v. i. (Brit.)* ~ **into sb./sth.** mit etw./jmdm. zusammenprallen. **'cannonball** *n.* Kanonenkugel, *die*

cannot *see* **²can**

canny ['kænɪ] *adj. (shrewd)* schlau

canoe [kə'nuː] *n.* Paddelboot, *das; (Indian* ~, *Sport)* Kanu, *das.* **canoeist** [kə'nuːɪst] *n.* Paddelbootfahrer, *der/*-fahrerin, *die*

canon ['kænən] *n.* **a)** *(general law, criterion)* Grundregel, *die;* **b)** *(Eccl.: person)* Kanoniker, *der*

canonize ['kænənaɪz] *v. t.* kanonisieren ⟨*Heiligen*⟩; heiligsprechen ⟨*Märtyrer*⟩

'can-opener *n.* Dosenöffner, *der*

canopy ['kænəpɪ] *n.* Baldachin, *der; (over entrance)* Vordach, *das*

can't [kɑːnt] *(coll.)* = **cannot;** *see* ²**can**

cantankerous [kæn'tæŋkərəs] *adj.* streitsüchtig

canteen [kæn'tiːn] *n.* Kantine, *die*

canter ['kæntə(r)] **1.** *n.* Handgalopp, *der.* **2.** *v. i.* leicht galoppieren

canvas ['kænvəs] *n.* Leinwand, *die*

canvass ['kænvəs] **1.** *v. t.* Wahlwerbung treiben in ⟨*einem Wahlkreis, Gebiet*⟩; Wahlwerbung treiben bei ⟨*Wählern, Bürgern*⟩. **2.** *v. i.* werben (**on behalf of** für); ~ **for votes** um Stimmen werben. **canvasser** *n. (for votes)* Wahlhelfer, *der/*-helferin, *die*

canyon ['kænjən] *n.* Cañon, *der*

cap [kæp] **1.** *n.* a) Mütze, *die; (nurse's, servant's)* Haube, *die; (with peak)* Schirmmütze, *die; (skull-~)* Kappe, *die;* b) *(of bottle, jar)* [Verschluß]kappe, *die; (petrol ~, radiator-~)* Deckel, *der.* **2.** *v. t.,* **-pp-:** a) verschließen ⟨*Flasche*⟩; zudecken ⟨*Bohrloch*⟩; mit einer Schutzkappe versehen ⟨*Zahn*⟩; b) *(fig.)* überbieten; **to ~ it all** obendrein

capability [keɪpə'bɪlɪtɪ] *n.* Fähigkeit, *die*

capable ['keɪpəbl] *adj.* a) **be ~ of sth.** ⟨*Person:*⟩ zu etw. imstande sein; b) *(gifted, able)* fähig

capacity [kə'pæsɪtɪ] *n.* a) Fassungsvermögen, *das;* **the machine is working to ~:** die Maschine ist voll ausgelastet; **a seating ~ of 300** 300 Sitzplätze; b) *(measure)* Rauminhalt, *der;* Volumen, *das;* **measure of ~:** Hohlmaß, *das;* c) *(position)* Eigenschaft, *die;* **in his ~ as ...:** in seiner Eigenschaft als ...

¹**cape** [keɪp] *n. (garment)* Umhang, *der;* Cape, *das*

²**cape** *n. (Geog.)* Kap, *das;* **the C~ [of Good Hope]** das Kap der guten Hoffnung; **C~ Town** Kapstadt *(das)*

caper ['keɪpə(r)] *v. i.* ~ [**about**] [herum]tollen

capital ['kæpɪtl] **1.** *attrib. adj.* a) To-des⟨*strafe, -urteil*⟩; Kapital⟨*verbrechen*⟩; b) groß, Groß⟨*buchstabe*⟩; c) *(principal)* Haupt⟨*stadt*⟩. **2.** *n.* a) *(letter)* Großbuchstabe, *der;* b) *(city, town)* Hauptstadt, *die;* c) *(stock, wealth)* Kapital, *das*

capitalism ['kæpɪtəlɪzm] *n.* Kapitalismus, *der.* **capitalist** ['kæpɪtəlɪst] **1.** *n.* Kapitalist, *der/*Kapitalistin, *die.* **2.** *adj.* kapitalistisch

capitalize ['kæpɪtəlaɪz] **1.** *v. t.* groß schreiben ⟨*Buchstaben, Wort*⟩. **2.** *v. i.* ~ **on sth.** aus etw. Kapital schlagen *(ugs.)*

capital 'punishment *n.* Todesstrafe, *die*

capitulate [kə'pɪtjʊleɪt] *v. i.* kapitulieren. **capitulation** [kəpɪtjʊ'leɪʃn] *n.* Kapitulation, *die*

capricious [kə'prɪʃəs] *adj.* launisch

Capricorn ['kæprɪkɔːn] *n.* der Steinbock

capsize [kæp'saɪz] **1.** *v. t.* zum Kentern bringen. **2.** *v. i.* kentern

capsule ['kæpsjuːl] *n.* Kapsel, *die*

captain ['kæptɪn] **1.** *n.* Kapitän, *der; (Army)* Hauptmann, *der.* **2.** *v. t.* ~ **a team** Kapitän einer Mannschaft sein

caption ['kæpʃn] *n. (heading)* Überschrift, *die; (under photograph, drawing)* Bildunterschrift, *die; (Cinemat., Telev.)* Untertitel, *der*

captivate ['kæptɪveɪt] *v. t.* fesseln. **captivating** ['kæptɪveɪtɪŋ] *adj.* bezaubernd; einnehmend ⟨*Lächeln*⟩

captive ['kæptɪv] **1.** *adj.* gefangen; **be taken ~:** gefangengenommen werden. **2.** *n.* Gefangener, *der/*Gefangene, *die.* **captivity** [kæp'tɪvɪtɪ] *n.* Gefangenschaft, *die;* **be held in ~:** gefangengehalten werden

captor ['kæptə(r)] *n.* **his ~:** der, der/ die, die ihn gefangennahm

capture ['kæptʃə(r)] **1.** *n.* a) *(of thief etc.)* Festnahme, *die; (of town)* Einnahme, *die;* b) *(thing, person)* Fang, *der.* **2.** *v. t.* festnehmen ⟨*Person*⟩; [ein]-fangen ⟨*Tier*⟩; einnehmen ⟨*Stadt*⟩; gefangennehmen ⟨*Phantasie*⟩

car [kɑː(r)] *n.* Auto, *das;* Wagen, *der;* **by ~:** mit dem Auto

carafe [kə'ræf] *n.* Karaffe, *die*

caramel ['kærəməl] *n.* Karamel, *der; (toffee)* Karamelbonbon, *das*

carat ['kærət] *n.* Karat, *das;* **a 22-~ gold ring** ein 22karätiger Goldring

caravan ['kærəvæn] *n. (Brit.)* Wohnwagen, *der.* **'caravan site** *n.* Campingplatz für Wohnwagen

carbohydrate [kɑːbəʊ'haɪdreɪt] *n.* Kohlenhydrat, *das*

carbon ['kɑːbən] *n.* Kohlenstoff, *der*

carbon: ~ **'copy** *n.* Durchschlag, *der;* ~ **dioxide** [~ daɪ'ɒksaɪd] *n.* Kohlendioxid, *das;* ~ **paper** *n.* Kohlepapier, *das*

carburettor *(Amer.:* **carburetor)** [kɑːbə'retə(r)] *n.* Vergaser, *der*

carcass *(Brit. also:* **carcase)** ['kɑːkəs] *n.* Kadaver, *der*

'car crash *n.* Autounfall, *der*

card [kɑːd] *n.* Karte, *die;* **play ~s** Karten spielen

card: ~**board** *n.* Pappe, *die;* ~**board 'box** *n.* [Papp]karton, *der; (smaller)* [Papp]schachtel, *die;* ~ **game** *n.* Kartenspiel, *das*

cardigan ['kɑːdɪgən] *n.* Strickjacke, *die*

cardinal ['kɑːdɪnl] **1.** *adj.* grundlegend ⟨*Frage, Doktrin, Pflicht*⟩; Kardinal- ⟨*fehler, -problem*⟩; Haupt⟨*punkt, -merkmal*⟩. **2.** *n. (Eccl.)* Kardinal, *der.* **cardinal 'number** *n.* Kardinalzahl, *die.* **cardinal 'sin** *n.* Todsünde, *die*

care [keə(r)] **1.** *n.* **a)** *(anxiety)* Sorge, *die;* **b)** *(pains)* Sorgfalt, *die;* **c)** *(caution)* Vorsicht, *die;* **take** ~: aufpassen; **d)** *medical* ~: ärztliche Betreuung; **e)** *(charge)* Obhut, *die (geh.);* **put sb. in** ~/**take sb. into** ~: jmdn. in Pflege geben/nehmen; ~ **of** *(on letter)* bei; **take** ~ **of sb./sth.** *(ensure safety of)* auf jmdn./etw. aufpassen; *(attend to)* sich um jmdn./etw. kümmern. **2.** *v. i.* ~ **for sb./sth.** *(look after)* sich um jmdn./ etw. kümmern; *(like)* jmdn./etw. mögen; ~ **to do sth.** etw. tun mögen; **I don't** ~ [**whether/how/what** *etc.*] es ist mir gleich[, ob/wie/was *usw.*]

career [kə'rɪə(r)] **1.** *n.* Beruf, *der.* **2.** *v. i.* rasen; ⟨*Pferd, Reiter:*⟩ galoppieren

'carefree *adj.* sorgenfrei

careful ['keəfl] *adj. (thorough)* sorgfältig; *(cautious)* vorsichtig; [**be**] ~! Vorsicht!; **be** ~ **of sb./sth.** *(be cautious of)* sich vor jmdm./etw. in acht nehmen; **be** ~ **with sb./sth.** vorsichtig mit jmdm./etw. umgehen. **carefully** *adv. (thoroughly)* sorgfältig; *(attentively)* aufmerksam; *(cautiously)* vorsichtig

careless ['keəlɪs] *adj.* **a)** *(inattentive)* unaufmerksam; *(thoughtless)* gedankenlos; leichtsinnig ⟨*Fahrer*⟩; nachlässig ⟨*Arbeiter, Arbeit*⟩; gedankenlos ⟨*Bemerkung, Handlung*⟩; unachtsam ⟨*Fahren*⟩; **b)** *(nonchalant)* ungezwungen. **carelessly** *adv. (without care)* nachlässig; *(thoughtlessly)* gedankenlos. **carelessness** *n. (lack of care)* Nachlässigkeit, *die; (thoughtlessness)* Gedankenlosigkeit, *die*

caress [kə'res] **1.** *n.* Liebkosung, *die.* **2.** *v. t.* liebkosen

'caretaker *n.* Hausmeister, *der/*-meisterin, *die*

'car ferry *n.* Autofähre, *die*

cargo ['kɑːgəʊ] *n.* Fracht, *die.* **cargo boat, 'cargo ship** *ns.* Frachter, *der*

Caribbean [kærɪ'biːən] **1.** *n.* **the** ~: die Karibik. **2.** *adj.* karibisch

caricature ['kærɪkətjʊə(r)] **1.** *n.* Karikatur, *die.* **2.** *v. t.* karikieren

carnage ['kɑːnɪdʒ] *n.* Gemetzel, *das*

carnal ['kɑːnl] *adj.* sinnlich

carnation [kɑː'neɪʃn] *n.* [Garten]nelke, *die*

carnet ['kɑːneɪ] *n. (of motorist)* Triptyk, *das;* |**camping**| ~: Ausweis für Camper

carnival ['kɑːnɪvl] *n.* Volksfest, *das*

carnivorous [kɑː'nɪvərəs] *adj.* fleischfressend

carol ['kærl] *n.* |**Christmas**| ~: Weihnachtslied, *das*

carp [kɑːp] *n., pl. same* Karpfen, *der*

'car-park *n.* Parkplatz, *der; (building)* Parkhaus, *das*

carpenter ['kɑːpɪntə(r)] *n.* Zimmermann, *der; (for furniture)* Tischler, *der/*Tischlerin, *die.* **carpentry** ['kɑːpɪntrɪ] *n.* Zimmerhandwerk, *das; (in furniture)* Tischlerhandwerk, *das*

carpet ['kɑːpɪt] *n.* Teppich, *der.* **'carpet-slipper** *n.* Hausschuh, *der.* **'carpet-sweeper** *n.* Teppichkehrer, *der*

'car-port *n.* Einstellplatz, *der*

carriage ['kærɪdʒ] *n.* **a)** *(horse-drawn)* Kutsche, *die;* **b)** *(Railw.)* Wagen, *der.* **'carriageway** *n.* Fahrbahn, *die*

carrier ['kærɪə(r)] *n.* **a)** *(bearer)* Träger, *der;* **b)** *(firm)* Transportunternehmen, *das.* **'carrier-bag** *n.* Tragetasche, *die.* **carrier pigeon** *n.* Brieftaube, *die*

carrot ['kærət] *n.* Möhre, *die*

carry ['kærɪ] *v. t.* **a)** tragen; *(emphasizing destination)* bringen; **b)** *(possess)* besitzen ⟨*Autorität, Gewicht*⟩. **carry a'way** *v. t.* forttragen; **be or get carried away** sich hinreißen lassen. **carry 'on 1.** *v. t.* fortführen; ~ **on** |**doing sth.**| weiterhin etw. tun. **2.** *v. i.* weitermachen. **carry 'out** *v. t.* durchführen; ausführen ⟨*Anweisung, Auftrag*⟩; vornehmen ⟨*Verbesserungen*⟩

'carry-cot *n.* Babytragetasche, *die*

cart [kɑːt] **1.** *n.* Wagen, *der.* **2.** *v. t. (sl.)* schleppen

cartilage ['kɑːtɪlɪdʒ] *n.* Knorpel, *der*

carton ['kɑːtn] *n.* [Papp]karton, *der; (of drink)* Tüte, *die; (of cream, yoghurt)* Becher, *der*

cartoon [kɑː'tuːn] *n.* humoristische Zeichnung; *(satirical)* Karikatur, *die; (film)* Zeichentrickfilm, *der*

cartridge ['kɑːtrɪdʒ] *n.* **a)** *(for gun)* Patrone, *die;* **b)** *(of film; cassette)* Kassette, *die* '**cart-wheel** *n.* *(Gymnastics)* Rad, *das;* **turn** *or* **do ~s** radschlagen

carve [kɑːv] 1. *v. t.* a) tranchieren ⟨Fleisch, Braten, Hähnchen⟩; b) *(from wood)* schnitzen; *(from stone)* meißeln. 2. *v. i.* **~ in wood/stone** in Holz schnitzen/in Stein meißeln. **carving** ['kɑːvɪŋ] *n. (in or from wood)* Schnitzerei, *die; (in or from stone)* Skulptur, *die.* '**carving-knife** *n.* Tranchiermesser, *das*

'**car wash** *n.* Waschanlage, *die*

cascade [kæs'keɪd] *n.* Kaskade, *die*

¹**case** [keɪs] *n.* a) *(instance, matter, set of arguments)* Fall, *der;* **it is |not| the ~ that ...:** es trifft [nicht] zu, daß ...; **in ~ ...:** falls ...; **|just| in ~:** für alle Fälle; **in ~ of emergency** im Notfall; **in any ~:** jedenfalls; **in that ~:** in diesem Fall; b) *(Med., Police, Soc. Serv., etc.)* Fall, *der;* c) *(Law)* Fall, *der; (action)* Verfahren, *das;* d) *(Ling.)* Fall, *der;* Kasus, *der (fachspr.)*

²**case** *n.* a) Koffer, *der; (brief-~)* |Akten|tasche, *die;* b) *(for spectacles, cigarettes)* Etui, *das;* c) *(crate)* Kiste, *die;* d) **|display-|~:** Schaukasten, *der*

cash [kæʃ] 1. *n.* Bargeld, *das;* **pay |in| ~, pay ~ down** bar zahlen. 2. *v. t.* einlösen ⟨Scheck⟩

cash: **~ and carry** *n.* cash and carry; *(store)* Cash-and-carry-Laden, *der;* **~card** *n.* Geldautomatenkarte, *die;* **~ desk** *n. (Brit.)* Kasse, *die;* **~ dispenser** *n.* Geldautomat, *der*

cashier [kæ'ʃɪə(r)] *n.* Kassierer, *der/*Kassiererin, *die*

cash: **~point** *n.* Geldautomat, *der;* **~register** *n.* |Registrier|kasse, *die*

casino [kə'siːnəʊ] *n.* Kasino, *das*

cask [kɑːsk] *n.* Faß, *das*

casket ['kɑːskɪt] *n.* a) Kästchen, *das;* b) *(Amer.: coffin)* Sarg, *der*

casserole ['kæsərəʊl] *n.* Schmortopf, *der*

cassette [kə'set, kæ'set] *n.* Kassette, *die.* **cas'sette-deck** *n.* Kassettendeck, *das.* **cas'sette recorder** *n.* Kassettenrecorder, *der*

cast [kɑːst] 1. *v. t.,* **cast** a) werfen; b) *(shape, form)* gießen; c) abgeben ⟨Stimme⟩. 2. *n.* a) *(Med.)* Gipsverband, *der;* b) *(actors)* Besetzung, *die.* **cast a'side** *v. t.* beiseite schieben ⟨Vorschlag⟩; vergessen ⟨Sorgen⟩; fallenlassen ⟨Hemmungen⟩. **cast 'off** *v. i. & t. (Naut.)* losmachen

castanets [kæstə'nets] *n. pl.* Kastagnetten Pl.

'**castaway** *n.* Schiffbrüchige, *der/die*

caste [kɑːst] *n.* Kaste, *die*

cast 'iron *n.* Gußeisen, *das*

castle ['kɑːsl] *n.* Burg, *die; (mansion)* Schloß, *das*

'**cast-offs** *n. pl.* abgelegte Sachen

castor ['kɑːstə(r)] *n. (wheel)* Rolle, *die*

castor: **~ oil** *n.* Rizinusöl, *das;* **~ sugar** *n.* Raffinade, *die*

castrate [kæ'streɪt] *v. t.* kastrieren.

castration [kæ'streɪʃn] *n.* Kastration, *die*

casual ['kæʒʊəl] *adj.* ungezwungen; leger ⟨Kleidung⟩; beiläufig ⟨Bemerkung⟩; flüchtig ⟨Bekannter, Bekanntschaft, Blick⟩; unbekümmert ⟨Haltung, Einstellung⟩. **casually** *adv.* ungezwungen; beiläufig ⟨bemerken⟩; flüchtig ⟨anschauen⟩; leger ⟨sich kleiden⟩

casualty ['kæʒʊəltɪ] *n.* a) *(injured person)* Verletzte, *der/die; (in battle)* Verwundete, *der/die; (dead person)* Tote, *der/die;* b) *(hospital department)* Unfallstation, *die*

cat [kæt] *n.* Katze, *die*

catalogue *(Amer.:* **catalog)** ['kætəlɒg] 1. *n.* Katalog, *der.* 2. *v. t.* katalogisieren

catalyst ['kætəlɪst] *n.* Katalysator, *der.* **catalytic** [kætə'lɪtɪk] *adj.* **~ converter** Katalysator, *der*

catapult ['kætəpʌlt] 1. *n.* Katapult, *das.* 2. *v. t.* katapultieren

cataract ['kætərækt] *n.* a) Katarakt, *der;* b) *(Med.)* grauer Star

catarrh [kə'tɑː(r)] *n.* Katarrh, *der*

catastrophe [kə'tæstrəfɪ] *n.* Katastrophe, *die.* **catastrophic** [kætə'strɒfɪk] *adj.* katastrophal

catch [kætʃ] 1. *v. t.,* **caught** [kɔːt] a) fangen; **~ hold of sb./sth.** jmdn./etw. festhalten; *(to stop oneself falling)* sich an jmdm./etw. festhalten; **get sth. caught** *or* **~ sth. on/in sth.** mit etw. an/in etw. *(Dat.)* hängenbleiben; **~ sb.'s finger in the door** sich *(Dat.)* den Finger in der Tür einklemmen; b) *(travel by)* nehmen; *(be in time for)* [noch] erreichen; c) *(surprise)* **~ sb. doing sth.** jmdn. [dabei] erwischen, wie er etw. tut *(ugs.);* d) *(become infected with)* sich *(Dat.)* zuziehen; **~ sth. from sb.** sich bei jmdm. mit etw. anstecken; **~ a cold** sich erkälten; **~ it** *(fig. coll.)* etwas kriegen *(ugs.);* e) **~ sb.'s attention/interest** jmds. Aufmerksamkeit erregen/jmds. Interesse wecken. 2. *v. i.,* **caught** a) *(begin to burn)* [anfangen zu] brennen; b) *(become hooked up)* hängenbleiben; ⟨*Haar, Faden:*⟩ sich verfangen. **3.** *n.* **a)** *(of ball)* make a ~: fangen; **b)** *(amount caught, lit. or fig.)* Fang, *der;* **c)** *(difficulty)* Haken, *der* (in an + *Dat.*); **d)** *(of door)* Schnapper, *der.* **catch 'on** *v.i. (coll.)* **a)** *(become popular)* [gut] ankommen *(ugs.);* **b)** *(understand)* kapieren *(ugs.).* **catch 'up 1.** *v.t.* ~ **sb. up** jmdn. einholen. **2.** *v.i.* ~ **up** gleichziehen; ~ **up on sth.** etw. nachholen

'**catching** *adj.* ansteckend

'**catchy** *adj.* eingängig

categorical [kæt'gorikl] *adj.* kategorisch

category ['kætıgərı] *n.* Kategorie, *die*

cater ['keıtə(r)] *v.i.* ~ **for sb./sth.** für jmdn./etw. [die] Speisen und Getränke liefern; *(fig.)* auf jmdn./etw. eingestellt sein. '**caterer** *n.* Lieferant von Speisen und Getränken. '**catering** *n.* **a)** *(trade)* Gastronomie, *die;* **b)** *(service)* Lieferung von Speisen und Getränken

caterpillar ['kætəpılə(r)] *n.* Raupe, *die*

cathedral [kə'θi:drl] *n.* Dom, *der*

Catherine wheel ['kæθrın wi:l] *n.* Feuerrad, *das*

Catholic ['kæθlık] **1.** *adj.* katholisch. **2.** *n.* Katholik, *der*/Katholikin, *die.* **Catholicism** [kə'θolısızm] *n.* Katholizismus, *der*

catkin ['kætkın] *n. (Bot.)* Kätzchen, *das*

'**Cat's-eye, (P)** *n. (Brit.: on road)* Bodenrückstrahler, *der*

cattle ['kætl] *n. pl.* Rinder *Pl.*

caught *see* **catch 1, 2**

cauldron ['kɔːldrən] *n.* Kessel, *der*

cauliflower ['kolıflaʊə(r)] *n.* Blumenkohl, *der*

cause [kɔːz] **1.** *n.* **a)** Ursache, *die* (of für *od. Gen.*); *(person)* Verursacher, *der*/Verursacherin, *die;* **be the** ~ **of sth.** etw. verursachen; **b)** *(reason)* Grund, *der;* ~ **for sth.** Grund zu etw.; **c)** *(object of support)* Sache, *die;* [in] a good ~: [für] eine gute Sache. **2.** *v.t.* verursachen; erregen ⟨*Aufsehen, Ärgernis*⟩; hervorrufen ⟨*Unruhe, Verwirrung*⟩; ~ **sb. worry/pain** jmdm. Sorge/Schmerzen bereiten; ~ **sb. to do sth.** jmdn. veranlassen, etw. zu tun

causeway ['kɔːzweı] *n.* Damm, *der*

caustic ['kɔːstık] *adj.* ätzend; *(fig.)* bissig; beißend ⟨*Spott*⟩

caution ['kɔːʃn] **1.** *n.* **a)** Vorsicht, *die;* **b)** *(warning)* Warnung, *die.* **2.** *v.t.*

(warn) warnen; *(warn and reprove)* verwarnen (**for** wegen)

cautious ['kɔːʃəs] *adj.,* '**cautiously** *adv.* vorsichtig

cavalry ['kævəlrı] *n.* Kavallerie, *die*

cave [keıv] *n.* Höhle, *die.* **cave 'in** *v.i.* einbrechen

'**caveman** *n.* Höhlenbewohner, *der*

cavern ['kævən] *n.* Höhle, *die.* **cavernous** ['kævənəs] *adj.* höhlenartig

caviar[e] ['kævıɑː(r)] *n.* Kaviar, *der*

cavity ['kævıtı] *n.* Hohlraum, *der; (in tooth)* Loch, *das*

CB *abbr.* **citizen's band** CB

cc [siː'siː] *abbr.* **cubic centimetre(s)** cm^3

CD *abbr.* **compact disc** CD

cease [siːs] **1.** *v.i.* aufhören. **2.** *v.t.* **a)** *(stop)* aufhören; **b)** *(end)* aufhören mit; einstellen ⟨*Bemühungen*⟩. '**cease-fire** *n.* Waffenruhe, *die*

cedar ['siːdə(r)] *n.* Zeder, *die*

ceiling ['siːlıŋ] *n.* **a)** Decke, *die;* **b)** *(upper limit)* Maximum, *das*

celebrate ['selıbreıt] *v.t.&i.* feiern. '**celebrated** *adj.* berühmt. **celebration** [selı'breıʃn] *n.* Feier, *die.* **celebrity** [sı'lebrıtı] *n.* Berühmtheit, *die*

celery ['selərı] *n.* Sellerie, *der od. die*

celibate ['selıbət] *adj.* zölibatär *(Rel.);* ehelos

cell [sel] *n.* Zelle, *die*

cellar ['selə(r)] *n.* Keller, *der*

cellist ['tʃelıst] *n.* Cellist, *der*/Cellistin, *die*

cello ['tʃeləʊ] *n., pl.* ~**s** Cello, *das*

Cellophane, (P) ['seləfeın] *n.* Cellophan Ⓦ, *das*

Celsius ['selsıəs] *adj.* Celsius

cement [sı'ment] **1.** *n.* Zement, *der.* **2.** *v.t.* zementieren; *(stick together)* zusammenkleben. **ce'ment-mixer** *n.* Betonmischmaschine, *die*

cemetery ['semıtərı] *n.* Friedhof, *der*

censor ['sensə(r)] **1.** *n.* Zensor, *der.* **2.** *v.t.* zensieren. '**censorship** *n.* Zensur, *die*

censure ['senʃə(r)] *v.t.* tadeln

census ['sensəs] *n.* Volkszählung, *die*

cent [sent] *n.* Cent, *der*

centenary [sen'tiːnərı] *adj. & n.* ~ [celebrations] Hundertjahrfeier, *die*

center *(Amer.) see* **centre**

centigrade ['sentıgreıd] *see* **Celsius**

centimetre *(Brit.; Amer.:* **centimeter)** ['sentımiːtə(r)] *n.* Zentimeter, *der*

centipede ['sentıpiːd] *n.* Tausendfüßler, *der*

central ['sentrl] *adj.* zentral

Central: ~ **A'merica** *pr. n.* Mittel-
amerika *(das);* ~ **'Europe** *pr. n.* Mit-
teleuropa *(das);* ~ **Euro'pean** *adj.*
mitteleuropäisch; **c~** '**heating** *n.*
Zentralheizung, *die*

centralize ['sentrəlaɪz] *v. t.* zentrali-
sieren

central reser'vation *n. (Brit.)* Mittelstreifen, *der*

centre ['sentə(r)] *(Brit.)* **1.** *n.* **a)** Mitte,
die; (of circle) Mittelpunkt, *der;* **b)** *(of
area, city)* Zentrum, *das.* **2.** *adj.* mittler... **3.** *v. i.* ~ **on** sth. sich auf etw.
(Akk.) konzentrieren; ~ |a|round sth.
sich um etw. drehen. **4.** *v. t.* **a)** in der
Mitte anbringen; **b)** *(concentrate)* be
~d |a|round sth. etw. zum Mittelpunkt
haben; ~ sth. on sth. etw. auf etw.
(Akk.) konzentrieren. **centre-'forward** *n.* Mittelstürmer, *der*

centrifugal [sentrɪ'fjuːgl] *adj.* ~ **force**
Zentrifugalkraft, *die;* Fliehkraft, *die*

century ['sentʃəri] *n. (hundred-year
period from a year ..00)* Jahrhundert,
das; (hundred years) hundert Jahre

ceramic [sɪ'ræmɪk] *adj.* keramisch

cereal ['sɪərɪəl] *n.* Getreide, *das;
(breakfast dish)* Getreideflocken *Pl.*

ceremonial [serɪ'məʊnɪəl] **1.** *adj.* feierlich; *(prescribed for ceremony)* zeremoniell. **2.** *n.* Zeremoniell, *das*

ceremony ['serɪmənɪ] *n.* Feier, *die;
(formal act)* Zeremonie, *die*

certain ['sɜːtn, 'sɜːtɪn] *adj.* **a)** *(settled,
definite)* bestimmt; **b)** be ~ **to do** sth.
etw. bestimmt tun; **c)** *(confident, sure
to happen)* sicher; **d)** *(indisputable)* unbestreitbar; **e)** **a** ~ **Mr Smith** ein gewisser Herr Smith; **to a** ~ **extent** in gewisser Weise. **certainly** *adv.* **a)** *(ad-
mittedly)* sicher|lich|; **b)** *(definitely)* be-
stimmt; **b)** *(in answer)* [aber] sicher;
|most| ~ '**not**! auf [gar] keinen Fall!
certainty ['sɜːtntɪ, 'sɜːtɪntɪ] *n.* **a)** be a
~: sicher sein; **b)** *(absolute conviction)*
Gewißheit, *die*

certificate [sə'tɪfɪkət] *n.* Urkunde,
die; (of action performed) Schein, *der*

certify ['sɜːtɪfaɪ] *v. t.* bescheinigen; bestätigen; **this is to** ~ **that** ...: hiermit
wird bescheinigt *od.* bestätigt, daß ...
cf. *abbr.* **compare** vgl.

chafe [tʃeɪf] *v. t.* wund scheuern

chaff [tʃɑːf] *n.* Spreu, *die*

chaffinch ['tʃæfɪntʃ] *n.* Buchfink, *der*

chagrin ['ʃægrɪn] *n.* Kummer, *der*

chain [tʃeɪn] **1.** *n.* Kette, *die;* ~ **of
shops/hotels** Laden-/Hotelkette, *die.*
2. *v. t.* [an]ketten (**to** an + *Akk.*)

chain: ~ **re'action** *n.* Kettenreakti-
on, *der;* ~**saw** *n.* Kettensäge, *die;*
~**-smoker** *n.* Kettenraucher, *der/
-raucherin, die;* ~ **store** Kettenladen,
der

chair [tʃeə(r)] **1.** *n.* **a)** Stuhl, *der;
(arm~, easy ~)* Sessel, *der;* **b)** *(profes-
sorship)* Lehrstuhl, *der;* **c)** *(at meeting)*
Vorsitz, *der.* **2.** *v. t.* den Vorsitz haben
bei

chair: ~**-back** *n.* Rückenlehne, *die;*
~**-lift** *n.* Sessellift, *der;* ~**man** ['tʃeə-
mən] *n., pl.* ~**men** ['tʃeəmən] Vorsitzende, *der/die*

chalet ['ʃæleɪ] *n.* Chalet, *das*

chalk [tʃɔːk] **1.** *n.* Kreide, *die.* **2.** *v. t.*
mit Kreide schreiben/malen auf

challenge ['tʃælɪndʒ] **1.** *n.* Herausforderung, *die.* **2.** *v. t.* **a)** *(to contest etc.)*
herausfordern; **b)** *(fig.)* auffordern;
(question) in Frage stellen. '**chal-
lenger** *n.* Herausforderer, *der/*Heraus-
forderin, *die.* **challenging** ['tʃæ-
lɪndʒɪŋ] *adj.* herausfordernd; fesselnd
⟨*Problem*⟩; anspruchsvoll ⟨*Arbeit*⟩

chamber ['tʃeɪmbə(r)] *n.* Kammer, *die*

chamber: ~**maid** *n.* Zimmermädchen, *das;* ~ **music** *n.* Kammermu-
sik, *die;* ~**-pot** *n.* Nachttopf, *der*

chameleon [kə'miːlɪən] *n.* Chamäle-
on

chamois ['ʃæmwɑː] *n.* **a)** Gemse, *die;*
b) ['ʃæmɪ] ~|**-leather**| Chamois[leder],
das

champagne [ʃæm'peɪn] *n.* Sekt, *der;
(from Champagne)* Champagner, *der*

champion ['tʃæmpɪən] **1.** *n.* **a)** *(defender)* Verfechter, *der/*Verfechterin,
die; **b)** *(Sport)* Meister, *der/*Meisterin,
die. **2.** *v. t.* verfechten ⟨*Sache*⟩; sich
einsetzen für ⟨*Person*⟩. '**championship** *n.* Meisterschaft, *die*

chance [tʃɑːns] **1.** *n.* **a)** *(fortune, trick
of fate)* Zufall, *der; attrib.* zufällig; ~
encounter Zufallsbegegnung, *die;
game of* ~: Glücksspiel, *das;* **by** ~: zufällig; **take a** ~: es riskieren; **the** ~**s
are that** ...: es ist wahrscheinlich,
daß ...; **by** |any| ~, **by some** ~ **or other**
zufällig; **b)** *(opportunity, possibility)*
Chance, *die;* **get a/the** ~ **to do** sth. ei-
ne/die Gelegenheit haben, etw. zu
tun. **2.** *v. t.* riskieren

chancellor ['tʃɑːnsələ(r)] *n.* Kanzler,
der; **C~ of the Exchequer** *(Brit.)*
Schatzkanzler, *der*

chandelier [ʃændə'lɪə(r)] *n.* Kron-
leuchter, *der*

change [tʃeɪndʒ] **1.** *n.* **a)** *(from Champagne)* Verändrung, *die;* Änderung, *die; (of job, surroundings, government, etc.)* Wechsel, *der;* **b)** *(for the sake of variety)* Abwechslung, *die;* **for a ~:** zur Abwechslung; **c)** *(money)* Wechselgeld, *das;* [**loose** or **small**] **~:** Kleingeld, *das;* [**here is**] **15 marks ~:** 15 Mark zurück; **keep the ~:** [es] stimmt so. **2.** *v. t.* **a)** *(switch)* wechseln; auswechseln ⟨Glühbirne, Batterie⟩; **~ one's clothes** sich umziehen; **~ one's address/name** seine Anschrift/seinen Namen ändern; **~ trains/buses** umsteigen; **b)** *(transform)* verwandeln (**into** + *Akk.*); *(alter)* ändern; **c)** *(exchange)* eintauschen (**for** für); wechseln ⟨Geld⟩. **3.** *v. i.* **a)** *(alter)* sich ändern; ⟨Person, Land:⟩ sich verändern; **b)** *(into something else)* sich verwandeln; **c)** *(put on other clothes)* sich umziehen.

change 'over *v. i.* **~ over from sth. to sth.** von etw. zu etw. übergehen

changeable ['tʃeɪndʒəbl] *adj.* veränderlich

'changing room *n. (Brit.)* Umkleideraum, *der*

channel ['tʃænl] **1.** *n. (also Telev., Radio)* Kanal, *der;* **the C~** *(Brit.)* der [Ärmel]kanal. **2.** *v. t. (fig.)* lenken.

'Channel Islands *pr. n. pl.* Kanalinseln *Pl.*

chant [tʃɑːnt] **1.** *v. t.* skandieren; *(Eccl.)* singen. **2.** *v. i.* Sprechchöre anstimmen; *(Eccl.)* singen. **3.** *n.* Sprechchor, *der; (Eccl.)* Gesang, *der*

chaos ['keɪɒs] *n.* Chaos, *das.* **chaotic** [keɪˈɒtɪk] *adj.* chaotisch

¹chap [tʃæp] *n. (Brit. coll.)* Bursche, *der;* Kerl, *der*

²chap *v. t.,* **-pp-** aufplatzen lassen

chapel ['tʃæpl] *n.* Kapelle, *die*

chaperon ['ʃæpərəʊn] **1.** *n.* Anstandsdame, *die.* **2.** *v. t.* beaufsichtigen

chaplain ['tʃæplɪn] *n.* Kaplan, *der*

chapter ['tʃæptə(r)] *n.* Kapitel, *das*

char [tʃɑː(r)] *v. t. & i.,* **-rr-** verkohlen

character ['kærɪktə(r)] *n.* **a)** Charakter, *der;* **b)** *(in novel etc.)* Figur, *die;* **c)** *(coll.: extraordinary person)* Original, *das;* **d)** *(symbol)* Zeichen, *das.* **characteristic** [kærɪktəˈrɪstɪk] **1.** *adj.* charakteristisch (**of** für). **2.** *n.* charakteristisches Merkmal. **characterize** ['kærɪktəraɪz] *v. t.* charakterisieren

charade [ʃəˈrɑːd] *n.* Scharade, *die; (fig.)* Farce, *die*

charcoal ['tʃɑːkəʊl] *n.* Holzkohle, *die*

charge [tʃɑːdʒ] **1.** *n.* **a)** *(price)* Preis, *der; (for services)* Gebühr, *die;* **b)** **be in**

~ of sth. für etw. die Verantwortung haben; **take ~:** die Verantwortung übernehmen; **c)** *(Law: accusation)* Anklage, *die;* **d)** *(attack)* Angriff, *der;* **e)** *(of explosives, electricity)* Ladung, *die.* **2.** *v. t.* **a)** **~ sb. sth., ~ sth. to sb.** jmdm. etw. berechnen; **b)** *(Law: accuse)* anklagen (**with** wegen); **c)** *(Electr.)* [auf]laden ⟨Batterie⟩; **d)** *(rush at)* angreifen. **3.** *v. i.* **a)** *(attack)* angreifen; **b)** *(coll.: hurry)* sausen

charitable ['tʃærɪtəbl] *adj.* **a)** wohltätig; **b)** *(lenient)* großzügig

charity ['tʃærɪtɪ] *n.* **a)** Wohltätigkeit, *die;* **b)** *(organization)* wohltätige Organisation

charlady ['tʃɑːleɪdɪ] *n. (Brit.)* Putzfrau, *die*

charlatan ['ʃɑːlətən] *n.* Scharlatan, *der*

charm [tʃɑːm] **1.** *n.* **a)** *(act)* Zauber, *der;* **b)** *(talisman)* Talisman, *der;* **c)** *(attractiveness)* Reiz, *der; (of person)* Charme, *der.* **2.** *v. t.* bezaubern.

'charming *adj.* bezaubernd

chart [tʃɑːt] **1.** *n.* **a)** *(map)* Karte, *die;* **b)** *(graph etc.)* Schaubild, *das;* **c)** **the ~s** die Hitliste. **2.** *v. t. (fig.: describe)* schildern

charter ['tʃɑːtə(r)] **1.** *n.* **a)** Charta, *die;* **b)** **on ~** gechartert. **2.** *v. t.* chartern ⟨Schiff, Flugzeug⟩. **chartered ac'countant** *n. (Brit.)* Wirtschaftsprüfer, *der/*-prüferin, *die*

'charter flight *n.* Charterflug, *der*

charwoman ['tʃɑːwʊmən] *n.* Putzfrau, *die*

chase [tʃeɪs] **1.** *n.* Verfolgungsjagd, *die.* **2.** *v. t. (pursue)* jagen; **~ sth.** *(fig.)* einer Sache *(Dat.)* nachjagen. **3.** *v. i.* **~ after sb./sth.** hinter jmdm./etw. herjagen. **chase 'up** *v. t. (coll.)* ausfindig machen

chasm ['kæzm] *n.* Kluft, *die*

chassis ['ʃæsɪ] *n., pl. same* ['ʃæsɪz] Chassis, *das;* Fahrgestell, *das*

chaste [tʃeɪst] *adj.* keusch

chastening ['tʃeɪsənɪŋ] *adj.* ernüchternd

chastise [tʃæˈstaɪz] *v. t.* züchtigen

chastity ['tʃæstɪtɪ] *n.* Keuschheit, *die*

chat [tʃæt] **1.** *n.* Schwätzchen, *das.* **2.** *v. i.,* **-tt-** plaudern; **~ with** or **to sb. about sth.** mit jmdm. von etw. plaudern. **chat 'up** *v. t. (Brit. coll.)* anmachen *(ugs.)*

'chat show *n.* Talk-Show, *die*

chattels ['tʃætlz] *n. pl.* bewegliche Habe *(geh.)*

chatter ['tʃætə(r)] 1. *v. i.* a) schwatzen; b) ⟨Zähne⟩ klappern. 2. *n.* Schwatzen, *das.* '**chatterbox** *n.* Quasselstrippe, *die (ugs.)*

chatty ['tʃætɪ] *adj.* gesprächig

chauffeur ['ʃəʊfə(r)] 1. *n.* Fahrer, *der;* Chauffeur, *der.* 2. *v. t.* fahren

chauvinist ['ʃəʊvɪnɪst] *n.* Chauvinist, *der*/Chauvinistin, *die.* **chauvinistic** [ʃəʊvɪ'nɪstɪk] *adj.* chauvinistisch

cheap [tʃiːp] *adj., adv.* billig. **cheapen** ['tʃiːpn] *v. t. (fig.)* herabsetzen. '**cheaply** *adv.* billig

cheat [tʃiːt] 1. *n.* Schwindler, *der*/ Schwindlerin, *die.* 2. *v. t. & i.* betrügen

¹**check** [tʃek] 1. *n.* a) Kontrolle, *die;* **make/keep a ~ on** kontrollieren; b) *(Amer.: bill)* Rechnung, *die.* 2. *v. t.* a) *(restrain)* unter Kontrolle halten; b) *(examine)* nachprüfen; kontrollieren ⟨Fahrkarte⟩; c) *(stop)* aufhalten. 3. *v. i.* **~ on sth.** etw. überprüfen; **~ with sb.** bei jmdm. nachfragen. **check 'in** *v. t. & i. (at airport)* einchecken. **check 'out** *v. t.* überprüfen. 2. *v. i.* abreisen. **check 'up** *v. i.* **~ up [on]** überprüfen

²**check** *n. (pattern)* Karo, *das*

checkers ['tʃekəz] *(Amer.)* see **draughts**

check: ~-in *n.* Abfertigung, *die;* **~-list** *n.* Checkliste, *die;* **~-mate** 1. *n.* [Schach]matt, *das;* 2. *int.* [schach]matt; **~-out [desk]** *n.* Kasse, *die;* **~-point** *n.* Kontrollpunkt, *der;* **~-up** *n. (Med.)* Untersuchung, *die*

cheek [tʃiːk] *n.* a) Backe, *die;* Wange, *die (geh.);* b) *(impertinence)* Frechheit, *die.* '**cheekily** *adv.,* '**cheeky** *adj.* frech

cheep [tʃiːp] 1. *v. i.* piep[s]en. 2. *n.* Piep[s]en, *das*

cheer [tʃɪə(r)] 1. *n.* a) *(applause)* Beifallsruf, *der;* b) *in pl. (Brit. coll.)* prost! 2. *v. t.* a) *(applaud)* ~ **sth./sb.** etw. bejubeln/jmdm. zujubeln; b) *(gladden)* aufmuntern. 3. *v. i.* jubeln. **cheer 'on** *v. t.* anfeuern ⟨Sportler⟩. **cheer 'up** 1. *v. t.* aufheitern. 2. *v. i.* bessere Laune bekommen; ~ **up!** Kopf hoch!

cheerful [['tʃɪəfl] *adj. (in good spirits)* fröhlich; *(bright, pleasant)* heiter. '**cheerfully** *adv.* vergnügt

'**cheering** 1. *adj.* fröhlich stimmend. 2. *n.* Jubeln, *das*

cheerio [tʃɪərɪ'əʊ] *int. (Brit. coll.)* tschüs *(ugs.)*

'**cheery** *adj.* fröhlich

cheese [tʃiːz] *n.* Käse, *der.* '**cheeseboard** *n.* Käseplatte, *die.* '**cheesecake** *n.* Käsetorte, *die*

cheetah ['tʃiːtə] *n.* Gepard, *der*

chef [ʃef] *n.* Küchenchef, *der; (as profession)* Koch, *der*

chemical ['kemɪkl] 1. *adj.* chemisch. 2. *n.* Chemikalie, *die*

chemist ['kemɪst] *n.* a) *(scientist)* Chemiker, *der*/Chemikerin, *die;* b) *(Brit.: pharmacist)* Drogist, *der*/Drogistin, *die;* ~'s [**shop**]Drogerie, *die.* **chemistry** ['kemɪstrɪ] *n.* Chemie, *die*

cheque [tʃek] *n.* Scheck, *der;* **pay by ~:** mit [einem] Scheck bezahlen. '**cheque-book** *n.* Scheckbuch, *das.* '**cheque card** *n.* Scheckkarte, *die*

cherish ['tʃerɪʃ] *v. t.* hegen ⟨Hoffnung, Gefühl⟩; in Ehren halten ⟨[Erinnerungs]gegenstand⟩

cherry ['tʃerɪ] *n.* Kirsche, *die*

chess [tʃes] *n., no art.* das Schach[spiel]

chess: ~-board *n.* Schachbrett, *das;* **~-man** *n.* Schachfigur, *die;* **~-player** *n.* Schachspieler, *der*/-spielerin, *die*

chest [tʃest] *n.* a) Kiste, *die;* b) *(Anat.)* Brust, *die;* **get sth. off one's ~** *(fig. coll.)* sich *(Dat.)* etw. von der Seele reden; c) ~ |**measurement**| Brustumfang, *der*

chestnut ['tʃesnʌt] 1. *n.* a) Kastanie, *die;* b) *(colour)* Kastanienbraun, *das.* 2. *adj. (colour)* ~[**-brown**] kastanienbraun. '**chestnut-tree** *n.* Kastanie, *die*

chest of 'drawers *n.* Kommode, *die*

chew [tʃuː] *v. t. & i.* kauen. '**chewinggum** *n.* Kaugummi, *der od. das*

chic [ʃiːk] *adj.* schick; elegant

chick [tʃɪk] *n.* a) Küken, *das;* b) *(sl.: young woman)* Biene, *die (ugs.)*

chicken ['tʃɪkɪn] 1. *n.* a) Huhn, *das;* *(grilled, roasted)* Hähnchen, *das;* b) *(coll.: coward)* Angsthase, *der.* 2. *adj. (coll.)* feig[e]. 3. *v. i.* ~ **out** *(sl.)* kneifen

'**chicken-pox** [~pɒks] *n.* Windpocken *Pl.*

chicory ['tʃɪkərɪ] *n. (plant)* Chicorée, *der od. die; (for coffee)* Zichorie, *die*

chief [tʃiːf] 1. *n.* a) Oberhaupt, *das; (of tribe)* Häuptling, *der;* b) *(of department)* Leiter, *der;* ~ **of police** Polizeipräsident, *der.* 2. *adj., usu. attrib.* a) Haupt-; b) *(leading)* führend. '**chiefly** *adv.* hauptsächlich

chieftain ['tʃiːftən] *n.* Stammesführer, *der*

chilblain ['tʃɪlbleɪn] n. Frostbeule, die

child [tʃaɪld] n., pl. ~ren ['tʃɪldrən] Kind, das. 'childbirth n. Geburt, die. 'childhood n. Kindheit, die

childish ['tʃaɪldɪʃ] adj.; **'childishly** adv. kindisch. '**childishness** n. (behaviour) kindisches Benehmen

child: ~less adj. kinderlos; ~like adj. kindlich; ~~minder ['~maɪndə(r)] n. (Brit.) Tagesmutter, die

children pl. of **child**

'**child's play** n. (fig.) ein Kinderspiel

Chile ['tʃɪlɪ] n. Chile (das)

chill [tʃɪl] 1. n. Kühle, die; (illness) Erkältung, die. 2. v.t. kühlen

chilli ['tʃɪlɪ] n., pl. ~es Chili, der

'**chilly** adj. kühl; **I am rather** ~: mir ist ziemlich kühl

chime [tʃaɪm] 1. n. Geläute, das. 2. v.i. läuten; ⟨Turmuhr:⟩ schlagen

chimney ['tʃɪmnɪ] n. Schornstein, der. '**chimney-sweep** n. Schornsteinfeger, der

chimpanzee [tʃɪmpən'ziː] n. Schimpanse, der

chin [tʃɪn] n. Kinn, das

China ['tʃaɪnə] pr. n. China (das)

china n. Porzellan, das; (crockery) Geschirr, das

Chinese [tʃaɪ'niːz] 1. adj. chinesisch. 2. n. a) pl. same (person) Chinese, der/Chinesin, die; b) (language) Chinesisch, das; see also **English 2 a**

chink [tʃɪŋk] n. (gap) Spalt, der

chip [tʃɪp] 1. n. a) Splitter, der; b) in pl. (Brit.: potato ~s) Pommes frites Pl.; c) (Gambling) Chip, der. 2. v.t., -pp- anschlagen. **chip 'in** (coll.) 1. v.i. a) (interrupt) sich einmischen; b) (contribute money) etwas beisteuern. 2. v.t (contribute) beisteuern

'**chipboard** n. Spanplatte, die

chipmunk ['tʃɪpmʌŋk] n. Chipmunk, das

chiropodist [kɪ'rɒpədɪst] n. Fußpfleger, der/-pflegerin, die

chiropody [kɪ'rɒpədɪ] n. Fußpflege, die

chirp [tʃɜːp] 1. v.i. zwitschern; ⟨Grille:⟩ zirpen. 2. n. Zwitschern, das; Zirpen, das

chisel ['tʃɪzl] 1. n. Meißel, der; (for wood) Stemmeisen, das. 2. v.t., (Brit.) -ll- meißeln; (in wood) hauen

chit [tʃɪt] n. Notiz, die

chit-chat ['tʃɪttʃæt] n. Plauderei, die

chivalrous ['ʃɪvlrəs] adj. ritterlich. '**chivalry** ['ʃɪvlrɪ] n. Ritterlichkeit, die

chives [tʃaɪvz] n. Schnittlauch, der

chloride ['klɔːraɪd] n. Chlorid, das

chlorine ['klɔːriːn] n. Chlor, das

chock [tʃɒk] n. Bremsklotz, der. '**chock-a-block** pred adj. vollgepfropft

chocolate ['tʃɒklət] n. Schokolade, die

choice [tʃɔɪs] 1. n. a) Wahl, die; from ~: freiwillig; b) (variety) Auswahl, die. 2. adj. ausgewählt

choir [kwaɪə(r)] n. Chor, der. '**choirboy** n. Chorknabe, der

choke [tʃəʊk] 1. v.t. a) ersticken; b) (block up) verstopfen. 2. v.i. (temporarily) keine Luft [mehr] bekommen; (permanently) ersticken (**on an** + Dat.). 3. n. (Motor Veh.) Choke, der

cholera ['kɒlərə] n. Cholera, die

cholesterol [kə'lestərɒl] n. Cholesterin, das

choose [tʃuːz] 1. v.t., **chose** [tʃəʊz], **chosen** ['tʃəʊzn] a) (decide) ~/~ **not to do sth.** sich dafür/dagegen entscheiden, etw. zu tun. 2. v.i., **chose**, **chosen** wählen (between zwischen); ~ **from sth.** aus etw./(from several) unter etw. (Dat.) [aus]wählen. **choos[e]y** ['tʃuːzɪ] adj. wählerisch

chop [tʃɒp] 1. n. a) Hieb, der; b) (of meat) Kotelett, das; c) **get the** ~ (coll.: be dismissed) rausgeworfen werden (ugs.). 2. v.t., -pp- hacken ⟨Holz⟩; kleinschneiden ⟨Fleisch, Gemüse⟩. '**chopper** n. (axe) Beil, das; (cleaver) Hackbeil, das

'**choppy** adj. bewegt

choral ['kɔːrl] adj. Chor-

chord [kɔːd] n. (Mus.) Akkord, der

chore [tʃɔː(r)] n. [lästige] Routinearbeit

chortle ['tʃɔːtl] 1. v.i. vor Lachen glucksen. 2. n. Glucksen, das

chorus ['kɔːrəs] n. a) (Mus.) Chor, der; b) (of song) Chorus, der

chose, chosen see **choose**

chow [tʃaʊ] n. (Amer. sl.: food) Futter, das (salopp)

Christ [kraɪst] n. Christus (der)

christen ['krɪsn] v.t. taufen. '**christening** n. Taufe, die

Christian ['krɪstjən] 1. adj. christlich. 2. n. Christ, der/Christin, die. **Christianity** [krɪst'ænɪtɪ] n. das Christentum

'**Christian name** n. Vorname, der

Christmas ['krɪsməs] n. Weihnachten, das od. Pl.; **merry or happy** ~: frohe od. fröhliche Weihnachten; **at** ~: [zu] Weihnachten

Christmas: ~ '**Day** n. erster Weihnachtsfeiertag; ~ '**Eve** n. Heiligabend, der; ~ **tree** n. Weihnachtsbaum, der

chrome [krəʊm], **chromium** ['krəʊmɪəm] ns. Chrom, das. '**chromium-plated** adj. verchromt

chronic ['krɒnɪk] adj. chronisch

chronicle ['krɒnɪkl] n. Chronik, die

chronological [krɒnə'lɒdʒɪkl] adj. chronologisch

chrysalis ['krɪsəlɪs] n., pl. ~es Puppe, die

chrysanthemum [krɪ'sænθɪməm] n. Chrysantheme, die

chubby ['tʃʌbɪ] adj. pummelig

chuck [tʃʌk] v. t. (coll.) schmeißen (ugs.). **chuck 'away**, **chuck 'out** v. t. (coll.) wegschmeißen (ugs.)

chuckle ['tʃʌkl] 1. v. i. leise [vor sich hin] lachen (at über + Akk.). 2. n. leises, glucksendes Lachen

chug [tʃʌg] v. i., -gg- tuckern

chum [tʃʌm] n. (coll.) Kumpel, der (salopp)

chunk [tʃʌŋk] n. dickes Stück. '**chunky** adj. a) (small and sturdy) stämmig; b) dick (Pullover)

church [tʃɜːtʃ] n. Kirche, die; go to ~: in die Kirche gehen; **the C~ of England** die Kirche von England. '**churchyard** n. Friedhof, der (bei einer Kirche)

churlish ['tʃɜːlɪʃ] adj. (ill-bred) ungehobelt; (surly) griesgrämig

churn [tʃɜːn] n. (Brit.) Butterfaß, das. **churn 'out** v. t. massenweise produzieren (ugs.)

chute [ʃuːt] n. Schütte, die; (for persons) Rutsche, die

CIA abbr. (Amer.) **Central Intelligence Agency** CIA, der od. die

CID abbr. (Brit.) **Criminal Investigation Department** C.I.D.; **the** ~: die Kripo

cider ['saɪdə(r)] n. ≈ Apfelwein, der

cigar [sɪ'gɑː(r)] n. Zigarre, die

cigarette [sɪgə'ret] n. Zigarette, die

cigarette: ~-**end** n. Zigarettenstummel, der; ~-**lighter** n. Feuerzeug, das; ~-**packet** n. Zigarettenschachtel, die

cinders ['sɪndəz] n. pl. Asche, die

cine ['sɪnɪ]: ~ **camera** n. Filmkamera, die; ~ **film** n. Schmalfilm, der

cinema ['sɪnɪmə] n. Kino, das; go to the ~: ins Kino gehen

cinnamon ['sɪnəmən] n. Zimt, der

cipher ['saɪfə(r)] n. Geheimschrift, die; in ~: chiffriert

circle ['sɜːkl] 1. n. Kreis, der. 2. v. i. kreisen. 3. v. t. umkreisen

circuit ['sɜːkɪt] n. a) (Electr.) Schaltung, die; b) (Motor-racing) Rundkurs, der

circular ['sɜːkjʊlə(r)] 1. adj. (round) kreisförmig. 2. n. Rundschreiben, das

circulate ['sɜːkjʊleɪt] 1. v. i. zirkulieren; ⟨Personen, Wein usw.:⟩ herumgehen (ugs.). 2. v. t. in Umlauf setzen; herumgehen lassen ⟨Buch, Bericht⟩ (**around** in + Dat.). **circulation** [sɜːkjʊ'leɪʃn] n. a) (Physiol.) Kreislauf, der; **poor** ~: Kreislaufstörungen Pl.; b) (copies sold) verkaufte Auflage

circumcise ['sɜːkəmsaɪz] v. t. beschneiden

circumference [sə'kʌmfərəns] n. Umfang, der

circumstances ['sɜːkəmstənsɪz] n. pl. Umstände; **in** or **under the** ~: unter diesen Umständen; **under no** ~: unter keinen Umständen

circus ['sɜːkəs] n. Zirkus, der

CIS abbr. **Commonwealth of Independent States** GUS

cissy ['sɪsɪ] see **sissy**

cistern ['sɪstən] n. Wasserkasten; (in roof) Wasserbehälter, der

citation [saɪ'teɪʃn] n. Zitat, das

cite [saɪt] v. t. (quote) zitieren; anführen (Beispiel)

citizen ['sɪtɪzən] n. a) (of town, city) Bürger, der/Bürgerin, die; b) (of state) [Staats]bürger, der/-bürgerin, die. '**citizenship** n. Staatsbürgerschaft, die

citrus ['sɪtrəs] n. ~ [**fruit**] Zitrusfrucht, die

city ['sɪtɪ] n. [Groß]stadt, die. **city 'centre** n. Stadtzentrum, das

civic ['sɪvɪk] adj. (staats)bürgerlich; ~ **centre** Verwaltungszentrum der Stadt

civil ['sɪvl] adj. a) (not military) zivil; b) (polite, obliging) höflich; c) (Law) Zivil-. **civil engi'neer** n. Bauingenieur, der/-ingenieurin, die. **civil engi'neering** n. Hoch- und Tiefbau, der

civilian [sɪ'vɪljən] 1. n. Zivilist, der. 2. adj. Zivil-

civility [sɪ'vɪlɪtɪ] n. Höflichkeit, die

civilization [sɪvɪlaɪ'zeɪʃn] n. Zivilisation, die

civilized ['sɪvɪlaɪzd] adj. zivilisiert

civil: ~ **law** n. Zivilrecht, das; ~ **rights** n. pl. Bürgerrechte; ~ '**servant** n. ≈ Staatsbeamte, der/-beamtin, die; **C~ 'Service** n. öffentlicher Dienst; ~ **war** n. Bürgerkrieg, der

clad [klæd] *adj. (arch./literary)* gekleidet ⟨in in + *Akk.*⟩

claim [kleɪm] **1.** *v. t.* **a)** beanspruchen
⟨*Thron, Gebiete*⟩; fordern ⟨*Lohnerhöhung, Schadensersatz*⟩; beantragen
⟨*Sozialhilfe usw.*⟩; **b)** *(assert)* behaupten. **2.** *v. i.* (Insurance) Ansprüche geltend machen. **3.** *n.* Anspruch, der ⟨to
auf + *Akk.*⟩; **lay ~ to sth.** auf etw.
(Akk.) Anspruch erheben. **claimant**
['kleɪmənt] *n.* Antragsteller, der/-stel-
lerin, die

clairvoyant [kleə'vɔɪənt] **1.** *n.* Hellse-
her, der/Hellseherin, die. **2.** *adj.* hell-
seherisch

clam [klæm] **1.** *n.* Klaffmuschel, die.
2. *v. i.,* **-mm-: ~ up** *(coll.)* den Mund
nicht [mehr] aufmachen

clamber ['klæmbə(r)] *v. i.* klettern

clammy ['klæmɪ] *adj.* feucht; kalt und
schweißig ⟨*Haut*⟩; klamm ⟨*Kleidung*⟩

clamour *(Brit.)*, *(Amer.)* **clamor** ['klæ-
mə(r)] **1.** *n. (noise, shouting)* Lärm,
der; lautes Geschrei. **2.** *v. i.* **~ for sth.**
nach etw. schreien

clamp [klæmp] **1.** *n.* Klammer, die
(for holding) Schraubzwinge, die. **2.**
v. t. klammern; einspannen ⟨*Werk-
stück*⟩. **3.** *v. i. (fig.)* **~ down on sb./sth.**
gegen jmdn./etw. rigoros vorgehen

clan [klæn] *n.* Sippe, die; *(of Scottish
Highlanders)* Clan, der

clandestine [klæn'destɪn] *adj.* heimlich

clang [klæŋ] **1.** *n. (of bell)* Läuten, das;
(of hammer) Klingen, das. **2.** *v. i.*
⟨*Glocke:*⟩ läuten; ⟨*Hammer:*⟩ klingen

clap [klæp] **1.** *n.* **a)** Klatschen, das; **b)**
~ of thunder Donnerschlag, der. **2.**
v. i., **-pp-** klatschen. **3.** *v. t.,* **-pp-: ~**
one's hands in die Hände klatschen; **~**
sth. etw. beklatschen; **~ sb.** jmdm.
Beifall klatschen. **'clapping** *n.* Applaus, der

claret ['klærət] **1.** *n.* roter Bordeaux-
wein. **2.** *adj.* weinrot

clarification [klærɪfɪ'keɪʃn] *n.* Klar-
stellung, die

clarify ['klærɪfaɪ] *v. t.* klären ⟨*Situation
usw.*⟩; *(by explanation)* klarstellen; erläutern ⟨*Bedeutung, Aussage*⟩

clarinet [klærɪ'net] *n.* Klarinette, die

clarity ['klærɪtɪ] *n.* Klarheit, die

clash [klæʃ] **1.** *n.,* *v. i.* **a)** scheppern
(ugs.); **b)** *(meet in conflict)* zusammenstoßen; **c)** *(disagree)* sich streiten; **d)**
⟨*Interesse, Ereignis:*⟩ kollidieren,
⟨*Farbe:*⟩ sich beißen *(ugs.)* (with mit).
2. *v. t.* gegeneinanderschlagen. **3.** *n.* **a)**

(of cymbals) Dröhnen, *das;* **b)** *(meeting in conflict)* Zusammenstoß, *der;* **c)**
(disagreement) Auseinandersetzung,
die; **d)** *(of personalities, colours)* Un-
verträglichkeit, *die;* *(of events)* Überschneiden, *das*

clasp [klɑːsp] **1.** *n.* Verschluß, der. **2.**
v. t. umklammern

class [klɑːs] **1.** *n.* Klasse, die; *(in society)* Gesellschaftsschicht, die; *(Sch.:
lesson)* Stunde, die. **2.** *v. t.* einstufen
(as als). **'class-conscious** *adj.* klas-
senbewußt

classic ['klæsɪk] **1.** *adj.* klassisch. **2.** *n.*
Klassiker, der; **~s** Altphilologie, die

classical ['klæsɪkl] *adj.* klassisch

classification [klæsɪfɪ'keɪʃn] *n.* Klas-
sifikation, *die*

classified ['klæsɪfaɪd] *adj.* **a)** *(secret)*
geheim; **b) ~ advertisement** Kleinanzeige, *die*

classify ['klæsɪfaɪ] *v. t.* klassifizieren

class: ~-mate *n.* Klassenkamerad,
der/-kameradin, *die;* **~-room** *n.*
Klassenzimmer, *das*

'classy *adj. (coll.)* klasse

clatter ['klætə(r)] **1.** *n.* Klappern, *das.*
2. *v. i.* **a)** klappern; **b)** *(move or fall
with a ~)* poltern

clause [klɔːz] *n.* **a)** Klausel, die; **b)**
(Ling.) Teilsatz, der; ⟨subordinate⟩ **~:**
Nebensatz, *der*

claustrophobia [klɒstrə'fəʊbɪə] *n.*
Klaustrophobie, *die.* **claustro-
phobic** [klɒstrə'fəʊbɪk] *adj.* beeng-
end ⟨*Ort*⟩

claw [klɔː] **1.** *n.* Kralle, die; *(of crab
etc.)* Schere, die. **2.** *v. t.* kratzen

clay [kleɪ] *n.* Lehm, der; *(for pottery)*
Ton, der

clean [kliːn] **1.** *adj.* sauber; frisch ⟨*Wäsche, Hemd*⟩. **2.** *adv.* glatt. **3.** *v. t.* saubermachen; putzen ⟨*Zimmer, Schuh*⟩;
reinigen ⟨*Teppich, Kleidung, Wunde*⟩;
~ one's teeth sich *(Dat.)* die Zähne
putzen. **4.** *n.* **give sth. a ~:** etw. putzen.
clean 'out *v. t.* **a)** saubermachen; **b)**
(sl.) **~ sb. out** *(take all sb.'s money)*
jmdn. [total] schröpfen *(ugs.).* **clean
'up 1.** *v. t.* **a)** aufräumen; **b)** *(fig.)* säubern. **2.** *v. i.* aufräumen

'cleaner *n.* **a)** Raumpfleger, der/-pfle-
gerin, die; *(woman also)* Putzfrau, die;
b) *usu. in pl. (dry-~)* Reinigung, die;
take sth. to the ~'s etw. in die Reinigung bringen

cleanliness ['klenlɪnɪs] *n.* Reinlichkeit, die

cleanly ['kliːnlɪ] *adv.* sauber

cleanse [klenz] v. t. [gründlich] reinigen. '**cleanser** n. Reinigungsmittel, das

'**clean-shaven** adj. glattrasiert

clear [klɪə(r)] 1. adj. a) klar; scharf ⟨Bild⟩; **make oneself ~:** sich deutlich [genug] ausdrücken; **make it ~ |to sb.| that ...:** [jmdm.] klar und deutlich sagen, daß ...; b) (complete) **three ~ days** volle drei Tage; c) (unobstructed) frei; **keep sth. ~** (not block) etw. frei halten. 2. adv. **keep ~ of sth./sb.** etw./jmdn. meiden; **please stand or keep ~ of the door** bitte von der Tür zurücktreten. 3. v. t. a) räumen ⟨Straße⟩; abräumen ⟨Schreibtisch⟩; freimachen ⟨Abfluß, Kanal⟩; **~ a space for sb./sth.** für jmdn./etw. Platz machen; b) (empty) räumen, leeren ⟨Briefkasten⟩; c) (remove) wegräumen; beheben ⟨Verstopfung⟩; d) (show to be innocent) freisprechen; e) (get permission for) **~ sth. with sb.** etw. von jmdm. genehmigen lassen. 4. v. i. a) ⟨Wetter, Himmel:⟩ sich aufheitern; b) (disperse) sich verziehen. 5. n. **we're in the ~** (free of suspicion) auf uns fällt kein Verdacht; (free of trouble) wir haben es geschafft. **clear 'off** v. i. abhauen (salopp). **clear 'out** 1. v. t. ausräumen. 2. v. i. (coll.) verschwinden. **clear 'up** 1. v. t. a) wegräumen ⟨Abfall⟩; aufräumen ⟨Platz, Sachen⟩; b) (explain) klären. 2. v. i. a) aufräumen; b) ⟨Wetter:⟩ sich aufhellen

clearance ['klɪərəns] n. a) (of obstruction) Beseitigung, die; b) (clear space) Spielraum, der

'**clear cut** adj. klar umrissen; klar ⟨Abgrenzung, Ergebnis⟩

'**clearing** n. Lichtung, die

'**clearly** adv. a) (distinctly) klar; deutlich ⟨sprechen⟩; b) (manifestly, unambiguously) eindeutig; klar ⟨denken⟩

'**clearway** n. (Brit.) Straße mit Halteverbot

cleaver ['kliːvə(r)] n. Hackbeil, das

clef [klef] n. Notenschlüssel, der

cleft [kleft] n. Spalte, die

clench [klentʃ] v. t. zusammenpressen; **~ one's fist or fingers** die Faust ballen; **~ one's teeth** die Zähne zusammenbeißen

clergy ['klɜːdʒɪ] n. pl. Geistlichkeit, die; Klerus, der. **clergyman** ['klɜːdʒɪmən] n., pl. **~men** ['klɜːdʒɪmən] Geistliche, der

clerical ['klerɪkl] adj. Büro⟨arbeit, -personal⟩; **~ error** Schreibfehler, der

clerk [klɑːk] n. (in bank) Bankangestellte, der/die; (in office) Büroangestellte, der/die

clever ['klevə(r)] adj. a) klug; b) (skilful) geschickt; c) (ingenious) geistreich ⟨Idee, Argument⟩; d) (smart, cunning) clever. '**cleverly** adv. a) klug; b) (skilfully) geschickt

cliché ['kliːʃeɪ] n. Klischee, das

click [klɪk] 1. n. Klicken, das. 2. v. i. klicken

client ['klaɪənt] n. a) Klient, der/Klientin, die; b) (customer) Kunde, der/Kundin, die

clientele [kliːɒn'tel] n. (of shop) Kundschaft, die

cliff [klɪf] n. Kliff, das. '**cliff-hanger** n. Thriller, der

climate ['klaɪmət] n. Klima, das

climax ['klaɪmæks] n. Höhepunkt, der

climb [klaɪm] 1. v. t. hinaufsteigen; klettern auf ⟨Baum⟩; ⟨Auto:⟩ hinaufkommen ⟨Hügel⟩. 2. v. i. a) klettern (**up** 'auf + Akk.); b) ⟨Flugzeug, Sonne:⟩ aufsteigen. 3. n. Aufstieg, der. **climb 'down** v. i. a) hinunterklettern; b) (fig.) nachgeben

'**climb-down** n. Rückzieher, der (ugs.)

climber ['klaɪmə(r)] n. Bergsteiger, der

clinch [klɪntʃ] 1. v. t. zum Abschluß bringen; perfekt machen (ugs.) ⟨Geschäft⟩. 2. n. (Boxing) Clinch, der

cling [klɪŋ] v. i., **clung** [klʌŋ] sich klammern (**to** an + Akk.). '**cling film** n. Klarsichtfolie, die

clinic ['klɪnɪk] n. Klinik, die. **clinical** ['klɪnɪkl] adj. a) (Med.) klinisch; b) (dispassionate) nüchtern

clink [klɪŋk] 1. n. (of glasses) Klirren, das; (of coins) Klimpern, das. 2. v. i. ⟨Flaschen:⟩ klirren; ⟨Münzen:⟩ klimpern. 3. v. t. klirren mit ⟨Glas⟩; klimpern mit ⟨Kleingeld⟩

¹**clip** [klɪp] 1. n. Klammer, die; (for paper) Büroklammer, die. 2. v. t., **-pp-** klammern (**|on|** to an + Akk.)

²**clip** v. t., **-pp-** (cut) schneiden ⟨Fingernägel, Haar, Hecke⟩; stutzen ⟨Flügel⟩

clique [kliːk] n. Clique, die

cloak [kləʊk] 1. n. Umhang, der. 2. v. t. [ein]hüllen. '**cloakroom** n. Garderobe, die; (Brit. euphem.: lavatory) Toilette, die

clock [klɒk] 1. n. a) Uhr, die; [**work**] **against the ~:** gegen die Zeit [arbeiten]; **round the ~:** rund um die Uhr; b) (coll.) (speedometer) Tacho, der (ugs.); (milometer) ≈ Kilometerzähler, der. 2. v. t. **~ |up|** zu verzeichnen haben

⟨*Erfolg*⟩; erreichen ⟨*Geschwindigkeit*⟩.
clock 'in, clock 'on *v.i.* [bei Arbeitsantritt] stechen. **clock 'off, clock 'out** *v.i.* [bei Arbeitsschluß] stechen

'clockwise *adv., adj.* im Uhrzeigersinn

'clockwork *n.* Uhrwerk, *das;* **a ~ car** ein Aufziehauto; **as regular as ~** *(fig.)* absolut regelmäßig

clog [klɒg] **1.** *n.* Clog, *der; (traditional)* Holzschuh, *der.* **2.** *v.t.,* **-gg-:** **~** [up] verstopfen

cloister ['klɔɪstə(r)] *n.* Kreuzgang, *der*

clone [kləʊn] **1.** *n.* Klon, *der.* **2.** *v.t.* klonen

close 1. [kləʊs] *adj.* **a)** *(in space)* dicht; nahe; **be ~ to sth.** nahe bei *od.* an etw. *(Dat.)* sein; **at ~ quarters** aus der Nähe betrachtet; **b)** *(in time)* nahe (**to** an + *Dat.*); **c)** eng ⟨*Freund, Zusammenarbeit*⟩; nahe ⟨*Verwandte, Bekanntschaft*⟩; **d)** eingehend ⟨*Untersuchung, Prüfung usw.*⟩; **e)** hart ⟨*Wett[kampf], Spiel*⟩; knapp ⟨*Ergebnis*⟩; **that was a ~ call or shave** *(coll.)* das war knapp! **2.** [kləʊs] *adv.* nah[e]; **~ by** in der Nähe; **~ to sb./sth.** nahe bei jmdm./etw. **3.** [kləʊz] *v.t.* **a)** *(shut)* schließen; zuziehen ⟨*Vorhang*⟩; schließen ⟨*Laden, Fabrik*⟩; sperren ⟨*Straße*⟩; **b)** *(conclude)* schließen ⟨*Diskussion, Versammlung*⟩. **4.** [kləʊz] *v.i.* **a)** *(shut)* sich schließen; **b)** ⟨*Laden, Fabrik:*⟩ schließen, *(ugs.)* zumachen. **5.** [kləʊz] *n.* Ende, *das;* Schluß, *der;* **come or draw to a ~:** zu Ende gehen; **bring or draw sth. to a ~:** etw. zu Ende bringen.
close [kləʊz] **'down 1.** *v.t.* schließen; stillegen ⟨*Werk*⟩. **2.** *v.i.* geschlossen werden ⟨*Werk:*⟩ stillgelegt werden. **close 'in** *v.i.* ⟨*Nacht, Dunkelheit:*⟩ hereinbrechen; ⟨*Tage:*⟩ kürzer werden; **~ in on** umzingeln. **close 'off** *v.t.* [ab]sperren

closed [kləʊzd] *adj.* geschlossen; **we're ~:** wir haben geschlossen.
'closed-circuit *adj.* **~ television** interne Fernsehanlage

close-down ['kləʊzdaʊn] *n. (Radio, Telev.)* Sendeschluß, *der*

closed '**shop** *n.* Closed Shop, *der*

closely ['kləʊslɪ] *adv.* **a)** dicht; **b)** *(intimately)* eng; **c)** genau ⟨*befragen, prüfen*⟩; streng ⟨*bewachen*⟩

closet ['klɒzɪt] *n. (Amer.: cupboard)* Schrank, *der*

close-up ['kləʊsʌp] *n.* **~** [picture/shot] Nahaufnahme, *die*

closing ['kləʊzɪŋ]: **~ date** *n. (for competition)* Einsendeschluß, *der; (to take part)* Meldefrist, *die;* **~-time** *n. (of pub)* Polizeistunde, *die*

closure ['kləʊʒə(r)] *n.* Schließung, *die; (of road)* Sperrung, *die*

clot [klɒt] **1.** *n.* **a)** *(blood)* Gerinnsel, *das;* **b)** *(Brit. sl.: stupid person)* Trottel, *der.* **2.** *v.i.,* **-tt-** ⟨*Blut:*⟩ gerinnen

cloth [klɒθ] *n., pl.* **~s** [klɒθs] **a)** Stoff, *der;* Tuch, *das;* **b)** *(dish~)* Spültuch, *das; (table-~)* [Tisch]decke, *die*

clothe [kləʊð] *v.t.* kleiden

clothes [kləʊðz] *n. pl.* Kleider *Pl.;* **put one's ~ on** sich anziehen; **take one's ~ off** sich ausziehen

'clothes: **~-brush** *n.* Kleiderbürste, *die;* **~-line** *n.* Wäscheleine, *die;* **~-peg** *(Brit.),* **~-pin** *(Amer.)* ns. Wäscheklammer, *die*

clothing ['kləʊðɪŋ] *n.* Kleidung, *die*

clotted cream [klɒtɪd 'kri:m] *n.* sehr fetter Rahm

cloud [klaʊd] *n.* **a)** Wolke, *die;* **every ~ has a silver lining** *(prov.)* es hat alles sein Gutes; **b)** **~ of dust/smoke** Staub-/Rauchwolke, *die.* **cloud 'over** *v.i.* sich bewölken

'cloudburst *n.* Wolkenbruch, *der*

'cloudless *adj.* wolkenlos

'cloudy *adj.* bewölkt ⟨*Himmel*⟩; trübe ⟨*Wetter, Flüssigkeit, Glas*⟩

clout [klaʊt] *(coll.)* **1.** *n.* Schlag, *der.* **2.** *v.t.* hauen *(ugs.)*

'clove [kləʊv] *n.* **~** [of garlic] [Knoblauch]zehe, *die*

²clove *n. (spice)* [Gewürz]nelke, *die*

clover ['kləʊvə(r)] *n.* Klee, *der.*
'cloverleaf *n.* Kleeblatt, *das*

clown [klaʊn] **1.** *n.* Clown, *der.* **2.** *v.i.* **~** [about or around] den Clown spielen

cloying ['klɔɪɪŋ] *adj.* süßlich

club [klʌb] **1.** *n.* **a)** *(weapon)* Keule, *die; (golf-~)* Schläger, *der;* **b)** *(association)* Klub, *der;* Verein, *der;* **c)** *(Cards)* Kreuz, *das;* **~s are trumps** Kreuz ist Trumpf; **the ace/seven of ~s** das Kreuzas/die Kreuzsieben. **2.** *v.t.,* **-bb- (beat)** prügeln; *(with ~)* knüppeln. **3.** *v.i.,* **-bb-:** **~ together** *(to buy something)* zusammenlegen

cluck [klʌk] **1.** *n.* Gackern, *das.* **2.** *v.i.* gackern

clue [klu:] *n.* Anhaltspunkt, *der; (in criminal investigation)* Spur, *die;* **not have a ~:** keine Ahnung haben. **'clueless** *adj. (coll.)* unbedarft *(ugs.)*

clump [klʌmp] *n.* Gruppe, *die; (of grass)* Büschel, *das*

clumsy ['klʌmzɪ] *adj.* schwerfällig, unbeholfen 〈*Person, Bewegung*〉; plump 〈*Form, Figur, Nachahmung*〉

clung *see* **cling**

cluster ['klʌstə(r)] **1.** *n.* *(of grapes, berries)* Traube, *die;* *(of fruit, flowers)* Büschel, *das;* *(of stars, huts)* Haufen, *der.* **2.** *v. i.* ~ |a|round **sb./sth.** sich um jmdn./etw. scharen *od.* drängen

clutch [klʌtʃ] **1.** *v. t.* umklammern. **2.** *v. i.* ~ **at sth.** nach etw. greifen; *(fig.)* sich an etw. *(Akk.)* klammern. **3.** *n.* **a)** *in pl. (fig.: control)* Klauen; **b)** *(Motor Veh.)* Kupplung, *die*

clutter ['klʌtə(r)] **1.** *n.* Durcheinander, *das.* **2.** *v. t.* ~ |up| **the table/room** überall auf dem Tisch/im Zimmer herumliegen

cm. *abbr.* **centimetre|s|** *cm*

Co. *abbr.* **a) company** Co.; **b) county**

c/o *abbr.* **care of** bei; c/o

coach [kəʊtʃ] **1.** *n.* **a)** *(horse-drawn)* Kutsche, *die;* **b)** *(Railw.)* Wagen, *der;* **c)** *(bus)* [Reise]bus, *der;* **by** ~: mit dem Bus; **d)** *(Sport)* Trainer, *der/* Trainerin, *die.* **2.** *v. t.* trainieren. '**coach station** *n.* Busbahnhof, *der.* '**coach tour** *n.* Rundreise [im Omnibus]

coagulate [kəʊ'æɡjʊleɪt] **1.** *v. t.* gerinnen lassen. **2.** *v. i.* gerinnen

coal [kəʊl] *n.* Kohle, *die.* '**coalfield** *n.* Kohlenrevier, *das*

coalition [kəʊə'lɪʃn] *n.* *(Polit.)* Koalition, *die*

coal: ~**-mine** *n.* [Kohlen]bergwerk, *das;* ~**-miner** *n.* [im Kohlenbergbau tätiger] Grubenarbeiter; ~**-mining** *n.* Kohlenbergbau, *der*

coarse [kɔːs] *adj.* **a)** *(in texture)* grob; **b)** *(unrefined, obscene)* derb

coast [kəʊst] **1.** *n.* Küste, *die.* **2.** *v. i.* im Freilauf fahren. **coastal** ['kəʊstl] *adj.* Küsten-. '**coaster** *n.* **a)** *(mat)* Untersetzer, *der;* **b)** *(ship)* Küstenmotorschiff, *der*

coast: ~**-guard** *n.* Küstenwache, -wacht, *die;* ~**-line** *n.* Küste, *die*

coat [kəʊt] **1.** *n.* **a)** Mantel, *der;* **b)** *(layer)* Schicht, *die;* *(of paint)* Anstrich, *der;* **c)** *(animal's hair, fur, etc.)* Fell, *das.* **2.** *v. t.* überziehen; *(with paint)* streichen

'**coat-hanger** *n.* Kleiderbügel, *der*

'**coating** *n.* Schicht, *die*

coat of arms *n.* Wappen, *das*

coax [kəʊks] *v. t.* überreden

cobble ['kɒbl] *n.* Pflasterstein, *der*

cobbler ['kɒblə(r)] *n.* Schuster, *der*

'**cobble-stone** *see* **cobble**

cobra ['kəʊbrə] *n.* Kobra, *die*

cobweb ['kɒbweb] *n.* Spinnengewebe, *das;* Spinnennetz, *das*

cocaine [kə'keɪn] *n.* Kokain, *das*

cock [kɒk] **1.** *n.* Hahn, *der.* **2.** *v. t.* spitzen 〈*Ohren*〉; ~ **a/the gun** den Hahn spannen. **cock-a-hoop** [kɒkə'huːp] *adj.* überschwenglich

cockatoo [kɒkə'tuː] *n.* Kakadu, *der*

cockerel ['kɒkərəl] *n.* junger Hahn

cock-eyed ['kɒkaɪd] *adj.* **a)** *(crooked)* schief; **b)** *(absurd)* verrückt

cockle ['kɒkl] *n.* Herzmuschel, *die*

cockney ['kɒknɪ] **1.** *adj.* Cockney-. **2.** *n.* Cockney, *der*

'**cockpit** *n.* Cockpit, *das*

cockroach ['kɒkrəʊtʃ] *n.* [Küchen-, Haus-]schabe, *die*

cocktail ['kɒkteɪl] *n.* Cocktail, *der.* '**cocktail cabinet** *n.* Hausbar, *die.* '**cocktail party** *n.* Cocktailparty, *die*

cocoa ['kəʊkəʊ] *n.* Kakao, *der*

coconut ['kəʊkənʌt] *n.* Kokosnuß, *die*

cocoon [kə'kuːn] *n.* *(Zool.)* Kokon, *der*

cod [kɒd] *n., pl. same* Kabeljau, *der*

COD *abbr.* **cash on delivery,** *(Amer.)* **collect on delivery** p. Nachn.

code [kəʊd] **1.** *n.* **a)** *(statutes etc.)* Gesetzbuch, *das;* ~**s of behaviour** Verhaltensnormen; **b)** *(system of signals)* Code, *der;* **be in** ~: verschlüsselt sein. **2.** *v. t.* chiffrieren; verschlüsseln

'**code-name** *n.* Deckname, *der.* '**code-word** *n.* Kennwort, *das*

cod-liver 'oil *n.* Lebertran, *der*

co-driver ['kəʊdraɪvə(r)] *n.* Beifahrer, *der/*-fahrerin, *die*

coed ['kəʊed] *(esp. Amer. coll.)* **1.** *n.* Studentin, *die.* **2.** *adj.* ~ **school** gemischte Schule

coeducational [kəʊedjʊ'keɪʃənl] *adj.* koedukativ; Koedukations-

coerce [kəʊ'ɜːs] *v. t.* zwingen; ~ **sb. into sth.** jmdn. zu etw. zwingen. **coercion** [kəʊ'ɜːʃn] *n.* Zwang, *der*

coexist [kəʊɪg'zɪst] *v. i.* koexistieren. **coexistence** [kəʊɪg'zɪstəns] *n.* Koexistenz, *die*

C. of E. [siː əv'iː] *abbr.* **Church of England**

coffee ['kɒfɪ] *n.* Kaffee, *der;* **three black/white** ~**s** drei [Tassen] Kaffee ohne/mit Milch

coffee: ~ **bar** *n.* Café, *das;* ~**-bean** *n.* Kaffeebohne, *die;* ~**-break** *n.* Kaffeepause, *die;* ~**-cup** *n.* Kaffeetasse, *die;* ~**-pot** *n.* Kaffeekanne, *die;* ~ **shop** *n.* Kaffeestube, *die;* ~**-table** *n.* Couchtisch, *der*

coffin ['kɒfɪn] n. Sarg, der

cog [kɒg] n. (Mech.) Zahn, der

cogent ['kəʊdʒənt] adj. überzeugend ⟨Argument⟩; zwingend ⟨Grund⟩

cognac ['kɒnjæk] n. Cognac, der ⓦ

cog: ~-**railway** n. Zahnradbahn, die; ~-**wheel** n. Zahnrad, das

cohere [kəʊ'hɪə(r)] v.i. zusammenhalten. **coherent** [kəʊ'hɪərənt] adj. zusammenhängend

coil [kɔɪl] 1. v.t. aufwickeln; (twist) aufdrehen. 2. v.i. ~ round sth. etw. umschlingen. 3. n. a) ~s of rope/wire aufgerollte Seile Pl./aufgerollter Draht; b) (single turn) Windung, die; c) (Electr.) Spule, die

coin [kɔɪn] 1. n. Münze, die. 2. v.t. prägen ⟨Wort, Redewendung⟩

coincide [kəʊɪn'saɪd] v.i. a) (in time) zusammenfallen; b) (agree) übereinstimmen (with mit). **coincidence** [kəʊ'ɪnsɪdəns] n. Zufall, der. **coincidental** [kəʊɪnsɪ'dentl] adj. zufällig

coke [kəʊk] n. Koks, der

colander ['kʌləndə(r)] n. Sieb, das

cold [kəʊld] 1. adj. a) kalt; **I feel ~:** mir ist kalt; b) (fig.) [betont] kühl ⟨Person, Aufnahme, Begrüßung⟩. 2. adv. kalt. 3. n. a) Kälte, die; b) (illness) Erkältung, die; ~ [in the head] Schnupfen, der. **cold-blooded** ['kəʊldblʌdɪd] adj. a) wechselwarm ⟨Tier⟩; b) kaltblütig ⟨Person, Mord⟩

coldly adv. [betont] kühl

coleslaw ['kəʊlslɔː] n. Krautsalat, der

collaborate [kə'læbəreɪt] v.i. a) zusammenarbeiten; ~ [with sb.] on sth. zusammen [mit jmdm.] an etw. (Dat.) arbeiten; b) (with enemy) kollaborieren. **collaboration** [kəlæbə'reɪʃn] n. Zusammenarbeit, die; (with enemy) Kollaboration, die. **collaborator** [kə'læbəreɪtə(r)] n. Mitarbeiter, der/-arbeiterin, die; (with enemy) Kollaborateur, der/Kollaborateurin, die

collage ['kɒlɑːʒ] n. Collage, die

collapse [kə'læps] 1. n. a) (of person) Zusammenbruch, der; b) (of structure) Einsturz, der; c) (of negotiations) Scheitern, das; (of company) Zusammenbruch, der. 2. v.i. a) (of person) zusammenbrechen; b) ⟨Stuhl:⟩ zusammenbrechen; ⟨Gebäude:⟩ einstürzen; c) ⟨Verhandlungen:⟩ scheitern, ⟨Unternehmen:⟩ zusammenbrechen; d) (fold down) ⟨Regenschirm, Fahrrad, Tisch:⟩ sich zusammenklappen lassen. **collapsible** [kə'læpsɪbl] adj. Klapp- ⟨stuhl, -tisch, -fahrrad⟩

collar ['kɒlə(r)] 1. n. a) Kragen, der; b) (for dog) [Hunde]halsband, das. 2. v.t. schnappen (ugs.). **collar-bone** n. Schlüsselbein, das

colleague ['kɒliːg] n. Kollege, der/Kollegin, die

collect [kə'lekt] 1. v.i. sich versammeln; ⟨Staub, Müll usw.:⟩ sich ansammeln. 2. v.t. sammeln; aufsammeln ⟨Müll, leere Flaschen usw.⟩; (coll.: fetch) abholen ⟨Menschen, Dinge⟩; ~ one's wits/thoughts seine Gedanken sammeln. **collected** adj. a) (gathered) gesammelt; b) (calm) gesammelt; gelassen. **collection** [kə'lekʃn] n. a) (collecting) Sammeln, das; (coll.: of goods, persons) Abholen, das; b) (amount of money collected) Sammlung, die; (in church) Kollekte, die; (from post-box) Leerung, die; d) (of stamps etc.) Sammlung, die. **collective** [kə'lektɪv] adj. kollektiv nicht präd. **collective bargaining** n. Tarifverhandlungen Pl.

collector [kə'lektə(r)] n. a) (of stamps etc.) Sammler, der/Sammlerin, die; b) (of taxes) Einnehmer, der/Einnehmerin, die. **collector's item, collector's piece** ns. Sammlerstück, das

college ['kɒlɪdʒ] n. a) (esp. Brit. Univ.) College, das; b) (place of further education) Fach[hoch]schule, die; **go to ~** (esp. Amer.) studieren

collide [kə'laɪd] v.i. zusammenstoßen (with mit)

collie ['kɒlɪ] n. Collie, der

colliery ['kɒljərɪ] n. Kohlengrube, die

collision [kə'lɪʒn] n. Zusammenstoß, der; **on a ~ course** (lit. or fig.) auf Kollisionskurs

colloquial [kə'ləʊkwɪəl] adj. umgangssprachlich

collusion [kə'luːʒn] n. geheime Absprache

Cologne [kə'ləʊn] 1. pr. n. Köln (das). 2. attrib. adj. Kölner

cologne see eau-de-Cologne

Colombia [kə'lɒmbɪə] pr. n. Kolumbien (das)

colon ['kəʊlən] n. Doppelpunkt, der

colonel ['kɜːnl] n. Oberst, der

colonial [kə'ləʊnɪəl] adj. Kolonial-; kolonial

colonize ['kɒlənaɪz] v.t. kolonisieren

colony ['kɒlənɪ] n. Kolonie, die

color etc. (Amer.) see colour etc.

colossal [kə'lɒsl] adj. ungeheuer; gewaltig ⟨Bauwerk⟩

colour ['kʌlə(r)] (Brit.) 1. n. Farbe,

die; **what ~ is it?** welche Farbe hat es?; **change ~:** die Farbe ändern; **he is off ~:** ihm ist nicht gut. 2. *v. t.* a) *(give ~ to)* Farbe geben (+ *Dat.*); b) *(paint)* malen; c) *(stain, dye)* färben. 3. *v. i.* |up| erröten. '**colour-blind** *adj.* farbenblind

coloured ['kʌləd] *(Brit.)* 1. *adj.* a) farbig; b) *(of non-white descent)* farbig; ~ **people** Farbige *Pl.* 2. *n.* Farbige, *der/ die*

'**colour film** *n.* Farbfilm, *der*

'**colourful** ['kʌləfl] *adj. (Brit.)* bunt; anschaulich ⟨*Sprache, Stil, Bericht*⟩

'**colouring** *n. (Brit.)* a) *(colours)* Farben *Pl.;* b) ~ |matter| *(in food etc.)* Farbstoff, *der*

'**colourless** *adj. (Brit.)* farblos

colour: ~ **photograph** *n.* Farbaufnahme, *die;* ~ **scheme** *n.* Farb[en]zusammenstellung, *die;* ~ **supplement** *n.* Farbbeilage, *die;* ~ **television** *n.* Farbfernsehen, *das; (set)* Farbfernsehgerät, *das;* ~ **transparency** *n.* Farbdia, *das*

colt [kəʊlt] *n.* [Hengst]fohlen, *das*

column ['kɒləm] *n.* a) Säule, *die;* b) *(of page)* Spalte, *die;* **sports** ~: Sportteil, *der.* **columnist** ['kɒləmɪst] *n.* Kolumnist, *der/*Kolumnistin, *die*

coma ['kəʊmə] *n.* Koma, *das;* **in a ~:** im Koma

comb [kəʊm] 1. *n.* Kamm, *der.* 2. *v. t.* a) kämmen; ~ **sb.'s/one's hair** jmdm./ sich die Haare kämmen; b) *(search)* durchkämmen

combat ['kɒmbæt] 1. *n.* Kampf, *der.* 2. *v. t.* bekämpfen. **combatant** ['kɒmbətənt] *n.* Kombattant, *der*

combination [kɒmbɪ'neɪʃn] *n.* Kombination, *die.* **combi'nation lock** *n.* Kombinationsschloß, *das*

combine 1. [kəm'baɪn] *v. t.* zusammenfügen (**into** zu); verbinden ⟨*Substanzen*⟩. 2. *v. i.* a) *(join together)* ⟨*Stoffe*⟩ sich verbinden. 3. ['kɒmbaɪn] *n.* ~ |harvester| Mähdrescher, *der*

combustion [kəm'bʌstʃn] *n.* Verbrennung, *die*

come [kʌm] *v. i.,* **came** [keɪm], **come** [kʌm] kommen; ~ **here!** komm [mal] her!; **[I'm] coming!** [ich] komme schon!; **the train came into the station** der Zug fuhr in den Bahnhof ein; **Christmas is coming** bald ist Weihnachten; **the handle has ~ loose** der Griff ist lose; **nothing came of it** es ist nichts daraus geworden. **come a'bout** *v. i.* passieren. **come across**

1. [--'-] *v. i. (be understood)* verstanden werden. 2. ['---'] kommen (+ *Dat.*). **come a'long** *v. i. (coll.)* a) *(hurry up)* ~ **along!** komm/kommt!; b) *(make progress)* nice going gute Fortschritte machen; c) *(to place)* mitkommen (**with** mit). **come 'back** *v. i.* zurückkommen. **come by** 1. ['--] *v. t. (obtain)* bekommen. 2. [-'-] *v. i.* vorbeikommen. **come 'down** *v. i.* a) *(fall)* ⟨*Schnee, Regen, Preis:*⟩ fallen; b) *(lower)* herunterkommen; c) *(land)* [not]landen; *(crash)* abstürzen. **come 'in** *v. i. (enter)* hereinkommen; ~ **in!** herein! '**come into** *v. t.* a) *(enter)* hereinkommen in (+ *Akk.*); b) *(inherit)* erben. **come off** 1. [-'-] *v. i.* a) ⟨*Griff, Knopf:*⟩ abgehen; *(be removable)* sich abnehmen lassen; b) *(succeed)* ⟨*Pläne, Versuche:*⟩ Erfolg haben; c) *(take place)* stattfinden. 2. ['--] *v. t.* ~ **off a horse/bike** vom Pferd/Fahrrad fallen; ~ **'off it!** *(coll.)* nun mach mal halblang! *(ugs.).* **come on** 1. [-'-] *v. i.* a) *(continue coming, follow)* kommen; ~ **on!** komm, komm/kommt, kommt!; *(encouraging)* na, komm; b) *(make progress)* ~ **on very well** gute Fortschritte machen. 2. ['--] *v. t. see* ~ **upon. come 'out** *v. i.* a) herauskommen; b) *(fig.)* ⟨*Sonne, Wahrheit, Buch:*⟩ herauskommen; c) ~ **out with** herausrücken mit *(ugs.).* **come 'over** 1. *v. i.* herüberkommen. 2. *v. t. (coll.)* kommen über (+ *Akk.*). **come 'round** *v. i.* a) *(visit)* vorbeischauen; b) *(recover)* wieder zu sich kommen. **come 'through** 1. *v. i.* durchkommen. 2. *v. t. (survive)* überleben. **come to** 1. ['--] *v. t. (amount to)* ⟨*Rechnung, Kosten:*⟩ sich belaufen auf (+ *Akk.*). 2. [-'-] *v. i.* wieder zu sich kommen. '**come under** *v. t.* a) *(be classed as or among)* kommen unter (+ *Akk.*); b) *(be subject to)* kommen unter (+ *Akk.*). **come 'up** *v. i.* a) *(~ higher)* hochkommen; b) ~ **up to sb.** *(approach for talk)* auf jmdn. zukommen; c) *(present itself)* sich ergeben; d) ~ **up to** *(reach)* reichen bis an (+ *Akk.*); entsprechen (+ *Dat.*) ⟨*Erwartungen*⟩; e) ~ **up against sth.** *(fig.)* auf etw. *(Akk.)* stoßen; f) ~ **up with** vorbringen ⟨*Vorschlag*⟩; wissen ⟨*Lösung, Antwort*⟩. '**come upon** *v. t. (meet by chance)* begegnen (+ *Dat.*)

'**come-back** *n. (to profession etc.)* Comeback, *das*

comedian [kə'miːdɪən] *n.* Komiker,

der. **comedienne** [kəmi:dɪ'en] *n.* Komikerin, *die*

'**come-down** *n.* Abstieg, *der*

comedy ['kɒmɪdɪ] **a)** *n.* Lustspiel, *das;* Komödie, *die;* **b)** *(humour)* Witz, *der;* Witzigkeit, *die*

comet ['kɒmɪt] *n.* Komet, *der*

comeuppance [kʌm'ʌpəns] *n.* get one's ~: die Quittung kriegen *(fig.)*

comfort ['kʌmfət] **1.** *n.* **a)** *(consolation)* Trost, *der;* **b)** *(physical wellbeing)* Behaglichkeit, *die;* **c)** *in pl.* Komfort, *der.* **2.** *v.t.* trösten. **comfortable** ['kʌmfətəbl] *adj.* **a)** bequem ⟨Bett, Schuhe⟩; komfortabel ⟨Haus, Zimmer⟩; **a** ~ **victory** ein leichter Sieg; **b)** *(at ease)* **be/feel** ~: sich wohl fühlen. **comfortably** ['kʌmfətəblɪ] *adv.* bequem; leicht ⟨gewinnen⟩

'**comfort station** *n. (Amer.)* öffentliche Toilette

comfy ['kʌmfɪ] *adj. (coll.)* bequem; gemütlich ⟨Haus, Zimmer⟩

comic ['kɒmɪk] **1.** *adj.* komisch. **2.** *n.* **a)** *(comedian)* Komiker, *der;* Komikerin, *die;* **b)** *(periodical)* Comic-Heft, *das.* **comical** ['kɒmɪkl] *adj.* komisch

coming ['kʌmɪŋ] **1.** *adj.* in the ~ week kommende Woche. **2.** *n.* ~s **and goings** das Kommen und Gehen

comma ['kɒmə] *n.* Komma, *das*

command [kə'mɑ:nd] **1.** *v.t.* **a)** *(order)* befehlen ⟨sb. jmdm.⟩; **b)** *(be in* ~ *of)* befehligen ⟨Schiff, Armee⟩; **c)** verfügen über *(+ Akk.)* ⟨Gelder, Wortschatz⟩. **2.** *n.* **a)** Kommando, *das; (in writing)* Befehl, *der;* **have/take** ~ **of** das Kommando über *(+ Akk.)* … haben/übernehmen; **b)** *(mastery, possession)* Beherrschung, *die*

commandeer [kɒmən'dɪə(r)] *v.t.* requirieren

com'mander *n.* Führer, *der*

com'manding *adj.* **a)** gebieterisch ⟨Erscheinung, Stimme⟩; imposant ⟨Gestalt⟩; **b)** beherrschend ⟨Ausblick, Lage⟩. **commanding 'officer** *n.* Befehlshaber, *der*/Befehlshaberin, *die*

com'mandment *n.* Gebot, *das*

commemorate [kə'meməreɪt] *v.t.* gedenken *(+ Gen.)*. **commemoration** [kəmemə'reɪʃn] *n.* Gedenken, *das;* **in** ~ **of** zum Gedenken an *(+ Akk.)*

commence [kə'mens] *v.t. & i.* beginnen. **com'mencement** *n.* Beginn, *der*

commend [kə'mend] *v.t. (praise)* loben. **commendable** [kə'mendəbl] *adj.* lobenswert; löblich. **commen-**

dation [kɒmen'deɪʃn] *n. (praise)* Lob, *das; (official)* Belobigung, *die; (award)* Auszeichnung, *die*

comment ['kɒment] **1.** *n.* Bemerkung, *die* (on über + *Akk.*); *(note)* Anmerkung, *die* (on über + *Akk.*); **no** ~! *(coll.)* kein Kommentar! **2.** *v.i.* ~ **on** sth. über etw. *(Akk.)* Bemerkungen machen; **he** ~**ed that** …: er bemerkte, daß … **commentary** ['kɒməntərɪ] *n.* **a)** Kommentar, *der* (on zu); **b)** *(Radio, Telev.)* **|live or running|** ~: Live-Reportage, *die.* **commentator** ['kɒmənteɪtə(r)] *n.* Kommentator, *der*/Kommentatorin, *die; (Sport)* Reporter, *der*/Reporterin, *die*

commerce ['kɒmɜ:s] *n.* Handel, *der.* **commercial** [kə'mɜ:ʃl] **1.** *adj.* Handels-; kaufmännisch ⟨Ausbildung⟩. **2.** *n.* Werbespot, *der.* **commercialism** [kə'mɜ:ʃəlɪzm] *n.* Kommerzialismus, *der.* **commercialize** [kə'mɜ:ʃəlaɪz] *v.t.* kommerzialisieren

commercial: ~ '**television** *n.* Werbefernsehen, *das;* ~ '**vehicle** *n.* Nutzfahrzeug, *das*

commiserate [kə'mɪzəreɪt] *v.i.* ~ **with** sb. jmdm. sein Mitgefühl aussprechen (on zu)

commission [kə'mɪʃn] **1.** *n.* **a)** *(official body)* Kommission, *die;* **b)** *(instruction, piece of work)* Auftrag, *der;* **c)** *(Mil.)* Ernennungsurkunde, *die;* **d)** *(pay of agent)* Provision, *die;* **e) in/out of** ~ ⟨Auto, Maschine⟩ in/außer Betrieb. **2.** *v.t.* beauftragen ⟨Künstler⟩; in Auftrag geben ⟨Gemälde usw.⟩. **commissionaire** [kəmɪʃə'neə(r)] *n. (esp. Brit.)* Portier, *der*

commissioner [kə'mɪʃənə(r)] *n. (of police)* Präsident, *der*

commit [kə'mɪt] *v.t.,* **-tt-: a)** begehen ⟨Verbrechen, Fehler, Ehebruch⟩; **b)** *(pledge, bind)* ~ **oneself/sb. to doing** sth. sich/jmdn. verpflichten, etw. zu tun; **c)** *(entrust)* anvertrauen (to *Dat.*); **d)** ~ **sb. for trial** jmdm. dem Gericht überstellen. **com'mitment** *n.* Verpflichtung (to gegenüber). **com-'mitted** *adj.* engagiert

committee [kə'mɪtɪ] *n.* Ausschuß, *der*

commodity [kə'mɒdɪtɪ] *n.* **a)** *household* ~: Haushaltsartikel, *der;* **b)** *(St. Exch.)* |vertretbare| Ware; *(raw material)* Rohstoff, *der*

common ['kɒmən] **1.** *adj.* **a)** *(belonging to all)* gemeinsam; **b)** *(public)* öffentlich; **c)** *(usual)* gewöhnlich; *(frequent)* häufig; allgemein verbreitet

⟨*Sitte, Redensart*⟩; **d)** *(vulgar)* ordinär.
2. *n.* **a)** *(land)* Gemeindeland, *das;* **b)**
have sth./nothing/a lot in ~ [with sb.]
etw./nichts/viel [mit jmdm.]
gemein[sam] haben. **'commoner** *n.*
Bürgerliche *der/die*

'common-law *adj.* she's his ~ wife sie
lebt mit ihm in eheähnlicher Gemeinschaft

'commonly *adv.* im allgemeinen

common: C~ 'Market *n.* gemeinsamer Markt; **~place 1.** *n.* Gemeinplatz, *der;* **2.** *adj.* alltäglich

Commons ['komənz] *n. pl.* **the** [House
of] ~: das Unterhaus

common: ~ 'sense *n.* gesunder
Menschenverstand; **~wealth** *n.* **the**
[**British**] **C~wealth** das Commonwealth

commotion [kə'məʊʃn] *n.* Tumult,
der

communal ['komjʊnl] *adj.* **a)** *(of or for
the community)* gemeindlich; **b)** *(for
common use)* gemeinsam

commune [kə'mju:n] *n.* Kommune,
die

communicate [kə'mju:nɪkeɪt] **1.** *v. t.*
übertragen ⟨*Krankheit*⟩; übermitteln
⟨*Informationen*⟩; vermitteln ⟨*Gefühle,
Ideen*⟩. **2.** *v. i.* **~ with sb.** mit jmdm.
kommunizieren. **communication**
[kəmju:nɪ'keɪʃn] *n.* **a)** *(of information)*
Übermittlung, *die;* **b)** *(message)* Mitteilung, *die* (to an + *Akk.*). **communi'cation-cord** *n.* Notbremse.
die. **communi'cations satellite** *n.*
Nachrichtensatellit, *der*

communicative [kə'mju:nɪkətɪv] *adj.*
gesprächig

Communion [kə'mju:nɪən] *n.* [Holy] ~
(Protestant Ch.) [das heilige] Abendmahl; *(RC Ch.)* [die heilige] Kommunion

communiqué [kə'mju:nɪkeɪ] *n.* Kommuniqué, *das*

communism ['komjʊnɪzm] *n.* Kommunismus, *der;* **C~:** der Kommunismus. **Communist, communist**
['komjʊnɪst] **1.** *n.* Kommunist,
*der/*Kommunistin, *die.* **2.** *adj.* kommunistisch

community [kə'mju:nɪtɪ] *n.* **a)** *(organized body)* Gemeinwesen, *das;* **the
Jewish ~:** die jüdische Gemeinde; **b)**
no pl. (public) Öffentlichkeit, *die.*
com'munity centre *n.* Gemeindezentrum, *das*

commute [kə'mju:t] **1.** *v. t.* umwandeln ⟨*Strafe*⟩ (to in + *Akk.*). **2.** *v. i.*

pendeln. com'muter *n.* Pendler,
*der/*Pendlerin, *die*

'compact [kəm'pækt] *adj.* kompakt

²compact ['kompækt] *n.* Puderdose
[mit Puder(stein)]

compact 'disc *n.* Compact Disc, *die*

companion [kəm'pænjən] *n.* Begleiter, *der/*Begleiterin, *die.* **com'panionship** *n.* Gesellschaft, *die*

company ['kʌmpənɪ] *n.* **a)** *(persons assembled, companionship)* Gesellschaft, *die;* **expect ~:** Besuch *od.* Gäste erwarten; **keep sb. ~:** jmdm. Gesellschaft leisten; **b)** *(firm)* Gesellschaft, *die;* **~ car** Firmenwagen, *der;*
c) *(of actors)* Truppe, *die;* Ensemble,
das; **d)** *(Mil.)* Kompanie, *die*

comparable ['kompərəbl] *adj.* vergleichbar (to, with mit)

comparative [kəm'pærətɪv] **1.** *adj.* **a)**
(relative) relativ; **in ~ comfort** relativ
komfortabel; **b)** *(Ling.)* komparativ
(fachspr.); **a ~ adjective/adverb** ein
Adjektiv/Adverb im Komparativ. **2.**
n. *(Ling.)* Komparativ, *der.* **com
'paratively** *adv.* verhältnismäßig

compare [kəm'peə(r)] **1.** *v. t.* verglichen (to, with mit); **~d with** *or* **to sb./
sth.** verglichen mit *od.* im Vergleich
zu jmdm./etw. **2.** *v. i.* sich vergleichen
lassen. **comparison** [kəm'pærɪsn] *n.*
Vergleich, *der;* **in** *or* **by ~** [with sb./
sth.] im Vergleich [zu jmdm./etw.]

compartment [kəm'pɑ:tmənt] *n.* *(in
drawer, desk, etc.)* Fach, *das;* *(of railway carriage)* Abteil, *das*

compass ['kʌmpəs] *n.* **a)** in *pl.* [a pair
of] ~es ein Zirkel; **b)** *(for navigating)*
Kompaß, *der*

compassion [kəm'pæʃn] *n.* Mitgefühl, *das* (for mit). **compassionate**
[kəm'pæʃənət] *adj.* mitfühlend; **on ~
grounds** aus persönlichen Gründen;
(for family reasons) aus familiären
Gründen

compatible [kəm'pætɪbl] *adj.* vereinbar; zueinander passend ⟨*Personen*⟩;
(Computing) kompatibel

compel [kəm'pel] *v. t.,* **-ll-** zwingen

compendium [kəm'pendɪəm] *n.*
Kompendium, *das*

compensate ['kompenseɪt] **1.** *v. i.* **~
for sth.** etw. ersetzen. **2.** *v. t.* **~ sb. for
sth.** jmdn. für etw. entschädigen.
compensation [kompen'seɪʃn] *n.*
Ersatz, *der;* *(for damages, injuries,
etc.)* Schaden[s]ersatz, *der*

compère ['kompeə(r)] *n.* *(Brit.)* Conférencier, *der*

compete [kəm'pi:t] v. i. konkurrieren (for um); (Sport) kämpfen

competence ['kɒmpɪtəns] n. Fähigkeiten Pl.

competent ['kɒmpɪtənt] adj. fähig; **not ~ to do sth.** nicht kompetent, etw. zu tun. **'competently** adv. kompetent

competition [kɒmpɪ'tɪʃn] n. **a)** (contest) Wettbewerb, der; (in magazine etc.) Preisausschreiben, das; **b)** (those competing) Konkurrenz, die

competitive [kəm'petɪtɪv] adj. wettbewerbsfähig ⟨Preis, Unternehmen⟩; ~ **sports** Leistungssport, der

competitor [kəm'petɪtə(r)] n. Konkurrent, der/Konkurrentin, die; (in contest, race) Teilnehmer, der/-nehmerin, die

compile [kəm'paɪl] v. t. zusammenstellen

complacency [kəm'pleɪsənsɪ] n. Selbstzufriedenheit, die

complacent [kəm'pleɪsənt] adj. selbstzufrieden

complain [kəm'pleɪn] v. i. sich beklagen (**about, at** über + Akk.); ~ **of sth.** über etw. klagen. **complaint** [kəm'pleɪnt] n. **a)** Beschwerde, die; **b)** (ailment) Leiden, das

complement 1. ['kɒmplɪmənt] n. **a)** (what completes) Vervollständigung, die; **b)** (full number) **a [full] ~:** die volle Zahl; (of people) die volle Stärke; **2.** ['kɒmplɪment] v. t. ergänzen. **complementary** [kɒmplɪ'mentərɪ] adj. **a)** (completing) ergänzend; **b)** (completing each other) einander ergänzend

complete [kəm'pli:t] **1.** adj. **a)** vollständig; (in number) vollzählig; **b)** (finished) fertig; **c)** (absolute) völlig ⟨Idiot⟩; absolut ⟨Katastrophe⟩; total, (ugs.) blutig ⟨Anfänger⟩. **2.** v. t. **a)** (finish) beenden; fertigstellen ⟨Gebäude, Arbeit⟩; **b)** ausfüllen ⟨Formular⟩. **com'pletely** adv. völlig; absolut ⟨erfolgreich⟩. **completion** [kəm'pli:ʃn] n. Beendigung, die; (of building, work) Fertigstellung, die

complex ['kɒmpleks] **1.** adj. kompliziert. **2.** n. Komplex, der

complexion [kəm'plekʃn] n. Gesichtsfarbe, die; (fig.) Gesicht, das

complexity [kəm'pleksɪtɪ] n. Kompliziertheit, die

complicate ['kɒmplɪkeɪt] v. t. komplizieren. **'complicated** adj. kompliziert. **complication** [kɒmplɪ'keɪʃn] n. Komplikation, die

complicity [kəm'plɪsɪtɪ] n. Mittäterschaft, die (**in** bei)

compliment 1. ['kɒmplɪmənt] n. Kompliment, das; in pl. (formal greetings) Grüße Pl.; **pay sb. a ~:** jmdn. ein Kompliment machen. **2.** ['kɒmplɪment] v. t. ~ **sb. on sth.** jmdm. Komplimente wegen etw. machen. **complimentary** [kɒmplɪ'mentərɪ] adj. **a)** schmeichelhaft; **b)** (free) Frei-

comply [kəm'plaɪ] v. i. ~ **with sth.** sich nach etw. richten; **he refused to ~:** er wollte sich nicht danach richten

component [kəm'pəʊnənt] **1.** n. Bestandteil, der. **2.** adj. **a** ~ **part** ein Bestandteil

compose [kəm'pəʊz] v. t. **a)** bilden; **be ~d of** sich zusammensetzen aus; **b)** verfassen ⟨Rede, Gedicht⟩; abfassen ⟨Brief⟩; **c)** (Mus.) komponieren. **com'poser** n. Komponist, der/Komponistin, die. **composition** [kɒmpə'zɪʃn] n. **a)** (constitution) (of soil etc.) Zusammensetzung, die; (of picture) Aufbau, der; **b)** (essay) Aufsatz, der; (Mus.) Komposition, die

compost ['kɒmpɒst] n. Kompost, der. **'compost heap** n. Komposthaufen, der

composure [kəm'pəʊʒə(r)] n. Gleichmut, der

¹compound 1. ['kɒmpaʊnd] adj. **a)** zusammengesetzt; **b)** (Med.) ~ **fracture** komplizierter Bruch. **2.** ['kɒmpaʊnd] n. **a)** (mixture) Mischung, die; **b)** (Ling.) Kompositum, das; **c)** (Chem.) Verbindung, die. **3.** ['kəm'paʊnd] v. t. verschlimmern ⟨Schwierigkeiten, Verletzung usw.⟩

²compound ['kɒmpaʊnd] n. umzäuntes Gelände

compound 'interest n. Zinseszinsen Pl.

comprehend [kɒmprɪ'hend] v. t. verstehen. **comprehensible** [kɒmprɪ'hensɪbl] adj. verständlich. **comprehension** [kɒmprɪ'henʃn] n. Verständnis, das

comprehensive [kɒmprɪ'hensɪv] **1.** adj. **a)** umfassend; **b)** ~ **school** Gesamtschule, die; **c)** (insurance) Vollkasko-. **2.** n. Gesamtschule, die

compress 1. [kəm'pres] v. t. **a)** (squeeze) zusammenpressen (**into** zu); **b)** komprimieren ⟨Luft, Gas, Bericht⟩. **2.** ['kɒmpres] n. Kompresse, die. **compression** [kəm'preʃn] n. Kompression, die. **compressor** [kəm'presə(r)] n. Kompressor, der

comprise [kəm'praɪz] *v.t. (include)* umfassen; *(consist of)* bestehen aus
compromise ['kɒmprəmaɪz] 1. *n.* Kompromiß, *der.* 2. *v.i.* Kompromisse/einen Kompromiß schließen. 3. *v.t.* kompromittieren
compulsion [kəm'pʌlʃn] *n.* Zwang, *der;* **be under no ~ to** do sth. keineswegs etw. tun müssen. **compulsive** [kəm'pʌlsɪv] *adj.* a) zwanghaft; **he is a ~** gambler im Spiel verfallen; b) **this book is ~ reading** von diesem Buch kann man sich nicht losreißen. **compulsory** [kəm'pʌlsəri] *adj.* obligatorisch
compunction [kəm'pʌŋkʃn] *n.* Schuldgefühle
computer [kəm'pju:tə(r)] *n.* Computer, *der*
computer: ~-aided, ~-assisted *adjs.* computergestützt; **~ program** *n.* Programm, *das;* **~ programmer** *n.* Programmierer, *der*/Programmiererin, *die;* **~ programming** *n.* Programmieren, *das;* **~ terminal** *n.* Terminal, *das*
computing [kəm'pju:tɪŋ] *n.* EDV, *die;* elektronische Datenverarbeitung
comrade ['kɒmreɪd, 'kɒmrɪd] *n.* Kamerad, *der*/Kameradin, *die.* '**comradeship** *n.* Kameradschaft, *die*
con [kɒn] *(coll.)* 1. *n.* Schwindel, *der.* 2. *v.t., -nn-* reinlegen *(ugs.);* **~ sb. into** sth. jmdm. etw. aufschwatzen *(ugs.)*
concave ['kɒnkeɪv] *adj.* konkav
conceal [kən'si:l] *v.t.* verbergen (**from** vor + *Dat.*). **con'cealment** *n.* Verbergen, *das*
concede [kən'si:d] *v.t.* zugeben
conceit [kən'si:t] *n.* Einbildung, *die.* **con'ceited** *adj.* eingebildet
conceivable [kən'si:vəbl] *adj.* vorstellbar; **it is scarcely ~ that ...**: man kann sich *(Dat.)* kaum vorstellen, daß ... **conceivably** [kən'si:vəblɪ] *adj.* möglicherweise; **he cannot ~ have done it** er kann es unmöglich getan haben
conceive [kən'si:v] 1. *v.t.* a) empfangen ⟨Kind⟩; b) *(form in mind)* sich *(Dat.)* vorstellen; haben ⟨Idee, Plan⟩. 2. *v.i.* a) *(become pregnant)* empfangen; b) **~ of** sth. sich *(Dat.)* etw. vorstellen
concentrate ['kɒnsəntreɪt] 1. *v.t.* konzentrieren. 2. *v.i.* sich konzentrieren (**on** auf + *Akk.*). '**concentrated** *adj.* konzentriert. **concentration** [kɒnsən'treɪʃn] *n.* Konzentration, *die*

concentric [kən'sentrɪk] *adj.* konzentrisch
concept ['kɒnsept] *n.* Begriff, *der; (idea)* Vorstellung, *die.* **conception** [kən'sepʃn] a) Vorstellung, *die* (**of** von); b) *(of child)* Empfängnis, *die*
concern [kən'sɜ:n] 1. *v.t.* a) *(affect)* betreffen; **so far as ... is ~ed** was ... betrifft; **'to whom it may ~'** ≈ „Bestätigung"; *(on certificate, testimonial)* ≈ „Zeugnis"; b) *(interest)* ~ **oneself with** or **about** sth. sich mit etw. befassen; c) *(trouble)* beunruhigen. 2. *n.* a) *(anxiety)* Besorgnis, *die; (interest)* Interesse, *das;* b) *(matter)* Angelegenheit, *die;* d) *(firm)* Unternehmen, *das.* **con'cerned** [kən'sɜ:nd] *adj.* a) *(involved)* betroffen; *(interested)* interessiert; **as** or **so far as I'm ~**: was mich betrifft; b) *(troubled)* besorgt. **con'cerning** *prep.* bezüglich
concert ['kɒnsət] *n.* Konzert, *das*
concerted [kən'sɜ:tɪd] *adj.* vereint
concert: ~-goer *n.* Konzertbesucher, *der*/-besucherin, *die;* **~-hall** *n.* Konzertsaal, *der*
concertina [kɒnsə'ti:nə] *n.* Konzertina, *die*
concerto [kən'tʃeətəʊ] *n.* Konzert, *das*
concession [kən'seʃn] *n.* Konzession, *die.* **concessionary** [kən'seʃənərɪ] *adj.* Konzessions-; **~ rate/fare** ermäßigter Tarif
conciliatory [kən'sɪljətərɪ] *adj.* versöhnlich
concise [kən'saɪs] *adj.* kurz und prägnant; knapp, konzis ⟨Stil⟩
conclude [kən'klu:d] 1. *v.t.* a) *(end)* beschließen; b) *(infer)* schließen (**from** aus); c) *(reach decision)* beschließen. 2. *v.i. (end)* schließen. **concluding** [kən'klu:dɪŋ] *adj.* abschließend. **conclusion** [kən'klu:ʒn] *n.* a) *(end)* Abschluß, *der;* **in ~**: zum Abschluß; b) *(result)* Ausgang, *der;* c) *(inference)* Schluß, *der;* **draw** or **reach a ~**: zu einem Schluß kommen. **conclusive** [kən'klu:sɪv] *adj.,* **con'clusively** *adv.* schlüssig
concoct [kən'kɒkt] *v.t.* zubereiten; zusammenbrauen ⟨Trank⟩. **concoction** [kən'kɒkʃn] *n.* Gebräu, *das*
concourse ['kɒnkɔ:s] *n.* Halle, *die;* **station ~**: Bahnhofshalle, *die*
concrete ['kɒnkri:t] 1. *adj.* konkret. 2. *n.* Beton, *der; attrib.* Beton-; **aus** Beton *präd.* '**concrete-mixer** *n.* Betonmischer, *der*

concur [kən'kɜ:(r)] *v. i.,* -rr-: ~ |with sb.| |in sth.| [jmdm.] [in etw. *(Dat.)*] zustimmen. **concurrent** [kən'kʌrənt] *adj.,* con'**currently** *adv.* gleichzeitig

concussion [kən'kʌʃn] *n.* Gehirnerschütterung, *die*

condemn [kən'dem] *v. t.* a) *(censure)* verdammen; b) *(Law: sentence)* verurteilen (**to** zu); c) für unbewohnbar erklären ⟨*Gebäude*⟩. **condemnation** [kɒndem'neɪʃn] *n.* Verdammung, *die*

condensation [kɒnden'seɪʃn] *n.* a) *(condensing)* Kondensation, *die*; b) *(water)* Kondenswasser, *das*

condense [kən'dens] 1. *v. t.* a) komprimieren; ~**d milk** Kondensmilch, *die*; b) *(Phys., Chem.)* kondensieren. 2. *v. i.* kondensieren

condescend [kɒndɪ'send] *v. i.* ~ **to do sth.** sich dazu herablassen, etw. zu tun. **conde'scending** *adj.* herablassend

condition [kən'dɪʃn] *n.* a) *(stipulation)* [Vor]bedingung, *die*; **on |the| ~ that ...:** unter der Voraussetzung, daß ...; **in** *pl. (circumstances)* Umstände *Pl.*; **weather/living ~s** Witterungs-/Wohnverhältnisse; **working ~s** Arbeitsbedingungen; b) *(of athlete etc.)* Form, *die*; *(of thing)* Zustand, *der*; *(of patient)* Verfassung, *die*; d) *Med.)* Leiden, *das*. **conditional** [kən'dɪʃnl] *adj.* a) bedingt; **be ~ |up|on sth.** von etw. abhängen; b) *(Ling.)* Konditional-

con'**ditioner** *n.* Frisiermittel, *das*

condolence [kən'dəʊləns] *n.* Anteilnahme, *die*; **letter of ~:** Beileidsbrief, *der*

condom ['kɒndɒm] *n.* Kondom, *das od. der*

condominium ['kɒndə'mɪnɪəm] *n. (Amer.)* Appartementhaus [mit Eigentumswohnungen]

condone [kən'dəʊn] *v. t.* hinwegsehen über (+ *Akk.); (approve)* billigen

conducive [kən'dju:sɪv] *adj.* **be ~ to sth.** einer Sache *(Dat.)* förderlich sein

conduct 1. ['kɒndʌkt] *n.* a) *(behaviour)* Verhalten, *das*; b) *(way of ~ing)* Führung, *die.* 2. [kən'dʌkt] *v. t.* a) führen; b) *(Mus.)* dirigieren; c) *(Phys.)* leiten; d) **~ed tour** Führung, *die.* con'**duction** [kən'dʌkʃn] *n. (Phys.)* Leitung, *die.* con'**ductor** [kən'dʌktə(r)] *n.* a) *(Mus.)* Dirigent, *der*/Dirigentin, *die*; b) *(of bus, tram)* Schaffner, *der.* con'**ductress** [kən'dʌktrɪs] *n.* Schaffnerin, *die*

cone [kəʊn] *n.* a) Kegel, *der; (traffic ~)* Leitkegel, *der;* b) *(Bot.)* Zapfen, *der;* c) **ice-cream ~:** Eistüte, *die*

confectioner [kən'fekʃənə(r)] *n.* ~**'s |shop|** Süßwarengeschäft, *das.* con'**fectionery** *n.* Süßwaren *Pl.*

confederate [kən'fedərət] *adj.* verbündet. **confederation** [kənfedə'reɪʃn] *n.* [Staaten]bund, *der*

confer [kən'fɜ:(r)] 1. *v. t.,* -rr-: ~ **sth.** |up|on sb. jmdm. etw. verleihen. 2. *v. i.,* -rr-: ~ **with sb.** sich mit jmdm. beraten

conference ['kɒnfərəns] *n.* a) Konferenz, *die;* b) **be in ~:** in einer Besprechung sein. '**conference-room** *n.* Konferenzraum, *der.* '**conference-table** *n.* Konferenztisch, *der*

confess [kən'fes] 1. *v. t.* a) gestehen; b) *(Eccl.)* beichten. 2. *v. i.* a) ~ **to sth.** etw. gestehen; b) *(Eccl.)* beichten (**to sb.** jmdm.). **confession** [kən'feʃn] *n.* a) Geständnis, *das;* b) *(Eccl.: of sins etc.)* Beichte, *die*

confetti [kən'fetɪ] *n.* Konfetti, *das*

confide [kən'faɪd] 1. *v. i.* ~ **in sb.** jmdm. anvertrauen. 2. *v. t.* ~ **sth. to sb.** jmdm. etw. anvertrauen

confidence ['kɒnfɪdəns] *n.* a) *(firm trust)* Vertrauen, *das;* **have ~ in sb./ sth.** Vertrauen zu jmdm./etw. haben; **have |absolute| ~ that ...:** [absolut] sicher sein, daß ...; b) *(assured expectation)* Gewißheit, *die;* c) *(self-reliance)* Selbstvertrauen, *das;* d) **in ~:** vertraulich; **this is in |strict| ~:** das ist [streng] vertraulich. '**confidence trick** *n. (Brit.)* Trickbetrug, *der*

confident ['kɒnfɪdənt] *adj.* zuversichtlich (**about** in bezug auf + *Akk.*)

confidential [kɒnfɪ'denʃl] *adj.* vertraulich. **confidentiality** [kɒnfɪdenʃɪ'ælɪtɪ] *n.* Vertraulichkeit, *die.* con'**fidentially** *adv.* vertraulich

'**confidently** *adv.* zuversichtlich

confine [kən'faɪn] *v. t.* a) einsperren; **be ~d to bed/the house** ans Bett/Haus gefesselt sein; b) *(fig.)* ~ **oneself to doing sth.** sich darauf beschränken, etw. zu tun. con'**fined** *adj.* begrenzt. con'**finement** *n. (imprisonment)* Einsperrung, *die.* **confines** ['kɒnfaɪnz] *n. pl.* Grenzen

confirm [kən'fɜ:m] *v. t.* bestätigen. **confirmation** [kɒnfə'meɪʃn] *n.* a) Bestätigung, *die;* b) *(Protestant Ch.)* Konfirmation, *die;(RC Ch.)* Firmung, *die.* con'**firmed** *adj.* eingefleischt ⟨*Junggeselle*⟩; überzeugt ⟨*Vegetarier*⟩

confiscate ['kɒnfɪskeɪt] *v. t.* beschlagnahmen. **confiscation** [kɒnfɪs'keɪʃn] *n.* Beschlagnahme, *die*

conflict 1. ['kɒnflɪkt] *n.* **a)** *(fight)* Kampf, *der;* **b)** *(clashing)* Konflikt, *der.* 2. [kən'flɪkt] *v. i. (be incompatible)* sich *(Dat.)* widersprechen; ~ **with sth.** einer Sache *(Dat.)* widersprechen. **con'flicting** *adj.* widersprüchlich

conform [kən'fɔːm] *v. i.* **a)** entsprechen (**to** *Dat.*); **b)** *(comply)* sich einfügen; ~ **to** *or* **with sth./with sb.** sich nach etw./jmdm. richten. **conformist** [kən'fɔːmɪst] *n.* Konformist, *der/*Konformistin, *die.* **conformity** [kən'fɔːmɪtɪ] *n.* Übereinstimmung, *die* (**with, to** mit)

confound [kən'faʊnd] *v. t.* **a)** *(defeat)* vereiteln; **b)** *(confuse)* verwirren. **con'founded** *adj. (coll. derog.)* verdammt

confront [kən'frʌnt] *v. t.* **a)** gegenüberstellen; ~ **sb. with sth./sb.** jmdn. mit etw./[mit] jmdm. konfrontieren; **b)** *(stand facing)* gegenüberstehen (+ *Dat.*). **confrontation** [kɒnfrən'teɪʃn] *n.* Konfrontation, *die*

confuse [kən'fjuːz] *v. t.* **a)** *(disorder)* durcheinanderbringen; **b)** *(mix up mentally)* verwechseln; **c)** *(perplex)* verwirren. **con'fused** *adj.* konfus; wirr ⟨Gedanken, Gerüchte⟩; verworren ⟨Lage, Situation⟩. **confusing** [kən'fjuːzɪŋ] *adj.* verwirrend. **confusion** [kən'fjuːʒn] *n.* **a)** Verwirrung, *die;* *(mixing up)* Verwechslung, *die;* **b)** *(embarrassment)* Verlegenheit, *die*

congeal [kən'dʒiːl] *v. i.* gerinnen

conger ['kɒŋgə(r)] *n.* ~ **leel** Seeaal, *der*

congested [kən'dʒestɪd] *adj.* verstopft ⟨Straße, Nase⟩. **congestion** [kən'dʒestʃn] *n. (of traffic)* Stauung, *die;* **nasal** ~: verstopfte Nase

conglomerate [kən'lɒmərət] *n. (Commerc.)* Großkonzern, *der.* **conglomeration** [kənɡlɒmə'reɪʃn] *n.* Anhäufung, *die*

congratulate [kən'ɡrætjʊleɪt] *v. t.* gratulieren (+ *Dat.*); ~ **sb./oneself on sth.** jmdm./sich zu etw. gratulieren. **congratulations** [kənɡrætjʊ'leɪʃnz] 1. *int.* ~! herzlichen Glückwunsch! (**on** zu). 2. *n. pl.* Glückwünsche *Pl.*

congregate ['kɒŋɡrɪɡeɪt] *v. i.* sich versammeln. **congregation** [kɒŋɡrɪ'ɡeɪʃn] *n. (Eccl.)* Gemeinde, *die*

congress ['kɒŋɡres] *n.* Kongreß, *der;* **C~** *(Amer.)* der Kongreß. **congressional** [kən'ɡreʃənl] *adj.* Kongreß-

conical ['kɒnɪkl] *adj.* kegelförmig

conifer ['kɒnɪfə(r)] *n.* Nadelbaum, *der*

conjecture [kən'dʒektʃə(r)] 1. *n.* Vermutung, *die.* 2. *v. t.* vermuten. 3. *v. i.* Vermutungen anstellen

conjugate ['kɒndʒʊɡeɪt] *v. t. (Ling.)* konjugieren. **conjugation** [kɒndʒʊ'ɡeɪʃn] *n. (Ling.)* Konjugation, *die*

conjunction [kən'dʒʌŋkʃn] *n.* **a)** Verbindung, *die;* **in** ~ **with** in Verbindung mit; **b)** *(Ling.)* Konjunktion, *die*

conjure ['kʌndʒə(r)] *v. i.* zaubern; **conjuring trick** Zaubertrick, *der.* **con'jure 'up** *v. t.* heraufbeschwören

conjurer, conjuror ['kʌndʒərə(r)] *n.* Zauberkünstler, *der/*-künstlerin, *die*

connect [kə'nekt] 1. *v. t.* verbinden (**to,** with mit). 2. *v. i.* ~ **with sth.** mit etw. zusammenhängen. **con'nected** *adj.* zusammenhängend. **connection,** *(Brit.)* **connexion** [kə'nekʃn] *n.* **a)** *(act, state)* Verbindung, *die;* **b)** *(fig.: of ideas)* Zusammenhang, *der;* **in** ~ **with** im Zusammenhang mit; **c)** *(train, bus, etc.)* Anschluß, *der*

connoisseur [kɒnə'sɜː(r)] *n.* Kenner, *der*

connotation [kɒnə'teɪʃn] *n.* Assoziation, *die*

conquer ['kɒŋkə(r)] *v. t.* besiegen; erobern ⟨Land⟩. **conqueror** ['kɒŋkərə(r)] *n. (of a country)* Eroberer, *der*

conquest ['kɒŋkwest] *n.* Eroberung, *die*

conscience ['kɒnʃəns] *n.* Gewissen, *das;* **have a clear/guilty** ~: ein gutes/ schlechtes Gewissen haben

conscientious [kɒnʃɪ'enʃəs] *adj.* pflichtbewußt; *(meticulous)* gewissenhaft; ~ **objector** Wehrdienstverweigerer [aus Gewissensgründen]. **consci'entiously** *adv.* pflichtbewußt; *(meticulously)* gewissenhaft

conscious ['kɒnʃəs] *adj.* **a)** he is not ~ **of** it es ist ihm nicht bewußt; **b)** *pred. (awake)* bei Bewußtsein *präd.;* **c)** *(realized by doer)* bewußt ⟨Versuch, Bemühung⟩. **consciousness** ['kɒnʃəsnɪs] *n.* Bewußtsein, *das*

conscript 1. [kən'skrɪpt] *v. t.* einberufen. 2. ['kɒnskrɪpt] *n.* Einberufene, *der/die.* **conscription** [kən'skrɪpʃn] *n.* Wehrpflicht, *die*

consecrate ['kɒnsɪkreɪt] *v. t.* weihen

consecutive [kən'sekjʊtɪv] *adj.* aufeinanderfolgend ⟨Monate, Jahre⟩; fortlaufend ⟨Zahlen⟩. **con'secutively** *adj.* hintereinander

consensus [kən'sensəs] *n.* Einigkeit, *die*

consent [kən'sent] 1. *v.i.* zustimmen. 2. *n. (agreement)* Zustimmung, *die* (to zu); **by common** *or* **general ~:** nach allgemeiner Auffassung

consequence ['kɒnsɪkwəns] *n.* **a)** *(result)* Folge, *die;* **in ~:** folglich; **as a ~:** infolgedessen; **b)** *(importance)* Bedeutung, *die.* **consequent** ['kɒnsɪkwənt] *adj.* daraus folgend. **'consequently** *adv.* infolgedessen

conservation [kɒnsə'veɪʃn] *n.* Erhaltung, *die;* **wildlife ~:** Schutz wildlebender Tierarten. **conservationist** [kɒnsə'veɪʃənɪst] *n.* Naturschützer, *der/*-schützerin, *die*

conservative [kən'sɜːvətɪv] 1. *adj.* **a)** konservativ; **b)** vorsichtig ⟨*Schätzung*⟩; **c)** C~ *(Brit. Polit.)* konservativ; **the C~ Party** die Konservative Partei. 2. *n.* C~ *(Brit. Polit.)* Konservative, *der/die.* **con'servatively** *adv.* vorsichtig ⟨*geschätzt*⟩

conservatory [kən'sɜːvətəri] *n.* Wintergarten, *der*

conserve [kən'sɜːv] *v.t.* erhalten; schonen ⟨*Kräfte*⟩

consider [kən'sɪdə(r)] *v.t.* **a)** *(think about)* ~ sth. an etw. *(Akk.)* denken; **he's ~ing emigrating** er denkt daran, auszuwandern; **b)** *(reflect on)* sich *(Dat.)* überlegen; **c)** *(regard as)* halten für; **all things ~ed** alles in allem. **considerable** [kən'sɪdərəbl] *adj.,* **con'siderably** *adv.* erheblich. **considerate** [kən'sɪdərət] *adj.* rücksichtsvoll; *(thoughtfully kind)* entgegenkommend. **consideration** [kənsɪdə'reɪʃn] *n.* **a)** Überlegung, *die;* **take sth. into ~:** etw. berücksichtigen; **the matter is under ~:** die Angelegenheit wird geprüft; **b)** *(thoughtfulness)* Rücksichtnahme, *die.* **con'sidering** *prep.* ~ **sth.** wenn man etw. bedenkt; ~ |that| ...: wenn man bedenkt, daß ...

consign [kən'saɪn] *v.t.* anvertrauen (to *Dat.*). **con'signment** *n. (Commerc.)* Sendung, *die; (large)* Ladung, *die*

consist [kən'sɪst] *v.i.* ~ **of** bestehen aus. **consistency** [kən'sɪstənsi] *n.* **a)** *(density)* Konsistenz, *die;* **b)** *(being consistent)* Konsequenz, *die*

consistent [kən'sɪstənt] *adj.* **a)** *(compatible)* [miteinander] vereinbar; **b)** *(uniform)* gleichbleibend ⟨*Qualität*⟩; **c)** *(unchanging)* konsequent

consolation [kɒnsə'leɪʃn] *n.* Trost, *der.* **conso'lation prize** *n.* Trostpreis, *der*

console [kən'səʊl] *v.t.* trösten

consolidate [kən'sɒlɪdeɪt] *v.t.* festigen

consonant ['kɒnsənənt] *n.* Konsonant, *der*

consort [kən'sɔːt] *v.i.* verkehren (**with** mit)

consortium [kən'sɔːtɪəm] *n., pl.* **consortia** [kən'sɔːtɪə] Konsortium, *das*

conspicuous [kən'spɪkjʊəs] *adj.* **a)** *(visible)* unübersehbar; **b)** *(obvious)* auffallend

conspiracy [kən'spɪrəsɪ] *n. (conspiring)* Verschwörung, *die; (plot)* Komplott, *das*

conspire [kən'spaɪə(r)] *v.i.* sich verschwören

constable ['kʌnstəbl, 'kɒnstəbl] *n. (Brit.)* Polizist, *der/*Polizistin, *die.* **constabulary** [kən'stæbjʊlərɪ] *n.* Polizei, *die*

constant ['kɒnstənt] *adj.* **a)** *(unceasing)* ständig; **b)** *(unchanging)* gleichbleibend. **'constantly** *adv.* **a)** *(unceasingly)* ständig; **b)** *(unchangingly)* konstant

constellation [kɒnstə'leɪʃn] *n.* Sternbild, *das*

consternation [kɒnstə'neɪʃn] *n.* Bestürzung, *die*

constipated ['kɒnstɪpeɪtɪd] *adj.* **be ~:** an Verstopfung leiden. **constipation** [kɒnstɪ'peɪʃn] *n.* Verstopfung, *die*

constituency [kən'stɪtjʊənsɪ] *n.* Wahlkreis, *der*

constituent [kən'stɪtjʊənt] *n.* **a)** *(part)* Bestandteil, *der;* **b)** *(Polit.)* Wähler, *der/*Wählerin, *die*

constitute ['kɒnstɪtjuːt] *v.t.* **a)** *(form, be)* sein; ~ **a threat** to eine Gefahr sein für; **b)** *(make up)* bilden. **constitution** [kɒnstɪ'tjuːʃn] *n.* **a)** *(of person)* Konstitution, *die;* **b)** *(of state)* Verfassung, *die.* **constitutional** [kɒnstɪ'tjuːʃənl] *adj. (of constitution)* der Verfassung *nachgestellt; (in harmony with constitution)* verfassungsmäßig

constrain [kən'streɪn] *v.t.* zwingen. **constraint** [kən'streɪnt] *n. (limitation)* Einschränkung, *die*

constrict [kən'strɪkt] *v.t.* verengen. **constriction** [kən'strɪkʃn] *n.* Verengung, *die*

construct [kən'strʌkt] *v.t.* bauen; *(fig.)* erstellen ⟨*Plan*⟩. **construction** [kən'strʌkʃn] *n.* **a)** *(constructing)* Bau, *der;* **be under ~:** im Bau sein; **b)** *(thing constructed)* Bauwerk, *das.* **con-**

structive [kən'strʌktɪv] *adj.* konstruktiv

consul ['kɒnsl] *n.* Konsul, *der.* **consulate** ['kɒnsjʊlət] *n.* Konsulat, *das*

consult [kən'sʌlt] *v.t.* konsultieren ⟨*Arzt, Fachmann*⟩; ~ **a book** in einem Buch nachsehen. **consultant** [kən'sʌltənt] *n.* Berater, *der*/Beraterin, *die*; *(Med.)* Chefarzt, *der*/-ärztin, *die.* **consultation** [kɒnsəl'teɪʃn] *n.* Beratung, *die*

consume [kən'sjuːm] *v.t.* verbrauchen; *(eat, drink)* konsumieren. **consumer** *n.* Verbraucher, *der*/Verbraucherin, *die.* **consumer goods** *n. pl.* Konsumgüter

consumption [kən'sʌmpʃn] *n.* Verbrauch, *der* (of an + *Dat.*); *(eating or drinking)* Verzehr, *der* (of von)

cont. *abbr.* continued Forts.

contact 1. ['kɒntækt] *n.* Berührung, *die*; *(fig.)* Kontakt, *der*; **be in ~ with sth.** etw. berühren; **be in ~ with sb.** *(fig.)* mit jmdm. Kontakt haben. 2. ['kɒntækt, kən'tækt] *v.t.* sich in Verbindung setzen mit. **contact lens** *n.* Kontaktlinse, *die*

contagious [kən'teɪdʒəs] *adj.* ansteckend

contain [kən'teɪn] *v.t.* **a)** *(hold, include)* enthalten; **b)** *(prevent from spreading)* aufhalten. **container** *n.* Behälter, *der*; *(cargo ~)* Container, *der*; **cardboard/wooden ~:** Pappkarton, *der*/Holzkiste, *die*

contaminate [kən'tæmɪneɪt] *v.t.* verunreinigen; *(with radioactivity)* verseuchen. **contamination** [kəntæmɪ'neɪʃn] *n.* Verunreinigung, *die*; *(with radioactivity)* Verseuchung, *die*

contemplate ['kɒntəmpleɪt] *v.t.* **a)** betrachten; *(mentally)* nachdenken über (+ *Akk.*); **b)** *(expect)* rechnen mit; *(consider)* ~ **sth./doing sth.** an etw. *(Akk.)* denken/daran denken, etw. zu tun. **contemplation** [kɒntəm'pleɪʃn] *n.* Betrachtung, *die*; *(mental)* Nachdenken, *das* (of über + *Akk.*)

contemporary [kən'tempərərɪ] 1. *adj.* zeitgenössisch. 2. *n.* Zeitgenosse, *der*/-genossin, *die*

contempt [kən'tempt] *n.* Verachtung, *die* (of, for für). **contemptible** [kən'temptɪbl] *adj.* verachtenswert. **contemptuous** [kən'temptjʊəs] *adj.* verächtlich

contend [kən'tend] *v.i.* **be able/have to ~ with** fertigwerden können/müssen mit. **contender** *n.* Bewerber, *der*/Bewerberin, *die*

¹content ['kɒntent] *n.* **a)** *in pl.* Inhalt, *der*; **⟨table of⟩ ~s** Inhaltsverzeichnis, *das*; **b)** *(amount contained)* Gehalt, *der* (of an + *Dat.*)

²content [kən'tent] 1. *pred. adj.* zufrieden. 2. *v.t.* zufriedenstellen; ~ **oneself with sth./sb.** sich mit etw./jmdm. zufriedengeben. **contented** *adj.*, **contentedly** *adv.* zufrieden

contention [kən'tenʃn] *n.* **a)** Streit, *der*; **b)** *(point asserted)* Behauptung, *die.* **contentious** [kən'tenʃəs] *adj.* strittig *(Punkt, Thema)*

contentment *n.* Zufriedenheit, *die*

contest 1. ['kɒntest] *n.* Wettbewerb, *der.* 2. [kən'test] *v.i.* **a)** bestreiten; in Frage stellen *(Behauptung)*; **b)** *(Brit.: compete for)* kandidieren für. **contestant** [kən'testənt] *n.* *(competitor)* Teilnehmer, *der*/Teilnehmerin, *die*

context ['kɒntekst] *n.* Kontext, *der*; **in/out of ~:** im/ohne Kontext; **in this ~:** in diesem Zusammenhang

continent ['kɒntɪnənt] *n.* Kontinent, *der*; **the C~:** das europäische Festland. **continental** [kɒntɪ'nentl] *adj.* **a)** kontinental; **b)** C~ *(mainland European)* kontinental[europäisch]. **continental breakfast** *n.* kontinentales Frühstück. **continental 'quilt** *n.* *(Brit.)* [Stepp]federbett, *das*

contingent [kən'tɪndʒənt] *n.* Kontingent, *das*

continual [kən'tɪnjʊəl] *adj.*, **continually** *adv.* *(frequent[ly])* ständig; *(without stopping)* unaufhörlich

continuation [kəntɪnjʊ'eɪʃn] *n.* Fortsetzung, *die*

continue [kən'tɪnjuː] 1. *v.t.* fortsetzen; **'~d on page 2'** „Fortsetzung auf S. 2"; ~ **doing or to do sth.** etw. weiter tun; **it ~d to rain** es regnete weiter. 2. *v.i.* *(persist)* *(Wetter, Zustand, Krise usw.:)* andauern; *(persist in doing sth.)* nicht aufhören; ~ **with sth.** mit etw. fortfahren. **continuity** [kɒntɪ'njuːɪtɪ] *n.* Kontinuität, *die.* **continuous** [kən'tɪnjʊəs] *adj.* **a)** ununterbrochen; anhaltend *(Regen, Sonnenschein)*; ständig *(Kritik, Streit)*; durchgezogen *(Linie)*; **b)** *(Ling.)* ~ **[form]** Verlaufsform, *die.* **continuously** *adv.* ununterbrochen; ständig *(sich ändern)*

contort [kən'tɔːt] *v.t.* verdrehen. **contortion** [kən'tɔːʃn] *n.* Verdrehung, *die*

contour ['kɒntʊə(r)] *n.* Kontur, *die*; ~ **map** Höhenlinienkarte, *die*

contraband ['kɒntrəbænd] n. Schmuggelware, die

contraception [kɒntrə'sepʃn] n. Empfängnisverhütung, die. **contraceptive** [kɒntrə'septɪv] 1. adj. empfängnisverhütend. 2. n. Verhütungsmittel, das

contract 1. ['kɒntrækt] n. Vertrag, der; ~ of employment Arbeitsvertrag, der; be under ~ to do sth. vertraglich verpflichtet sein, etw. zu tun. 2. [kən'trækt] v.t. (Med.) sich (Dat.) zuziehen. 3. v.i. a) ~ to do sth. sich vertraglich verpflichten, etw. zu tun; b) (become smaller, be drawn together) sich zusammenziehen. **contraction** [kən'trækʃn] n. Kontraktion, die. **contractor** [kən'træktə(r)] n. Auftragnehmer, der/-nehmerin, die

contradict [kɒntrə'dɪkt] v.t. widersprechen (+ Dat.). **contradiction** [kɒntrə'dɪkʃn] n. Widerspruch, der; in ~ to sb./sth. im Widerspruch zu jmdm./etw. **contradictory** [kɒntrə'dɪktərɪ] adj. widersprüchlich

contralto [kən'træltəʊ] n., pl. ~s Alt, der

contraption [kən'træpʃn] n. (coll.) [komisches] Gerät

contrary ['kɒntrərɪ] 1. adj. a) entgegengesetzt; be ~ to sth. im Gegensatz zu etw. stehen; b) [kən'treərɪ] (coll.: perverse) widerspenstig. 2. n. the ~: das Gegenteil, on the ~: im Gegenteil. 3. adv. ~ to sth. entgegen einer Sache

contrast 1. [kən'trɑːst] v.t. gegenüberstellen. 2. ['kɒntrɑːst] n. Kontrast, der (with zu); in ~, ...: im Gegensatz dazu, ...; [be] in ~ with sth. im Gegensatz zu etw. [stehen]. **con'trasting** adj. gegensätzlich

contravene [kɒntrə'viːn] v.t. verstoßen gegen. **contravention** [kɒntrə'venʃn] n. Verstoß, der (of gegen)

contribute [kən'trɪbjuːt] 1. v.t. ~ sth. [to or towards sth.] etw. [zu etw.] beitragen. 2. v.i. ~ to charity für karitative Zwecke spenden; ~ to the success of sth. zum Erfolg einer Sache (Gen.) beitragen. **contribution** [kɒntrɪ'bjuːʃn] n. Beitrag, der; (for charity) Spende, die (to für); make a ~: einen Beitrag leisten; (to charity) etwas spenden. **contributor** [kən'trɪbjʊtə(r)] n. (to encyclopaedia etc.) Mitarbeiter, der/Mitarbeiterin, die

contrite ['kɒntraɪt] adj. zerknirscht

contrive [kən'traɪv] v.t. ~ to do sth. es fertigbringen, etw. zu tun

control [kən'trəʊl] 1. n. a) Kontrolle, die (of über + Akk.); keep ~ of sth. etw. unter Kontrolle halten; be in ~ [of sth.] die Kontrolle [über etw. (Akk.)] haben; [go or get] out of ~: außer Kontrolle [geraten]; [get sth.] under ~: [etw.] unter Kontrolle [bringen]; b) (device) Regler, der; ~s Schalttafel, die. 2. v.t., -ll- kontrollieren; lenken ⟨Auto⟩; zügeln ⟨Zorn⟩; regeln ⟨Verkehr⟩. con'trol centre n. Kontrollzentrum, das. con'trol desk n. Schaltpult, das

con'troller n. (director) Leiter, der/Leiterin, die

control: ~ panel n. Schalttafel, die; ~ room n. Kontrollraum, der; ~ tower n. Kontrollturm, der

controversial [kɒntrə'vɜːʃl] adj. umstritten

controversy ['kɒntrəvɜːsɪ, kən'trɒvəsɪ] n. Auseinandersetzung, die

convalesce [kɒnvə'les] v.i. genesen. **convalescence** [kɒnvə'lesəns] n. Genesung, die

convection [kən'vekʃn] n. (Phys., Meteorol.) Konvektion, die

convector [kən'vektə(r)] n. Konvektor, der

convene [kən'viːn] 1. v.t. einberufen. 2. v.i. zusammenkommen

convenience [kən'viːnɪəns] n. a) for sb.'s ~ zu jmds. Bequemlichkeit; at your ~: wann es Ihnen paßt; b) (toilet) [public] ~: [öffentliche] Toilette. con'venience food n. Fertignahrung, die

convenient [kən'viːnɪənt] adj. günstig; (useful) praktisch; would it be ~ to or for you? würde es Ihnen passen? **con'veniently** adv. a) günstig ⟨gelegen, angebracht⟩; b) (opportunely) angenehmerweise

convent ['kɒnvənt] n. Kloster, das

convention [kən'venʃn] n. a) Brauch, der; b) (assembly) Konferenz, die; c) (agreement) Konvention, die. **conventional** [kən'venʃənl] adj. konventionell

converge [kən'vɜːdʒ] v.i. ~ [on each other] aufeinander zulaufen

conversant [kən'vɜːsənt] pred. adj. vertraut (with mit)

conversation [kɒnvə'seɪʃn] n. Unterhaltung, die; have a ~: ein Gespräch führen. **conversational** [kɒnvə'seɪʃənl] adj. ~ English gesprochenes Englisch

¹**converse** [kən'vɜːs] v.i. (formal) ~

|with sb.| |about or on sth.| sich [mit jmdm.] über etw. *(Akk.)*| unterhalten

²**converse** ['kɒnvɜːs] **1.** *adj.* entgegengesetzt; umgekehrt ⟨*Fall, Situation*⟩. **2.** *n.* Gegenteil, *das.* **conversely** [kɒn'vɜːslɪ] *adj.* umgekehrt

conversion [kən'vɜːʃn] *n.* **a)** Umwandlung, *die* (into in + *Akk.*); **b)** *(adaptation)* Umbau, *der;* **c)** *(of person)* Bekehrung, *die* (to zu)

convert [kən'vɜːt] **1.** *v.t.* umwandeln (into in + *Akk.*); ~ **sb.** [to sth.] jmdn. [zu etw.] bekehren. **2.** [kən'vɜːt] *v.i.* ~ **into sth.** sich in etw. *(Akk.)* umwandeln lassen. **3.** ['kɒnvɜːt] *n.* Konvertit, *der*/Konvertitin, *die.* **convertible** [kən'vɜːtɪbl] **1.** *adj.* be ~ into sth. sich in etw. *(Akk.)* umwandeln lassen. **2.** *n.* Kabrio[lett], *das*

convex ['kɒnveks] *adj.* konvex

convey [kən'veɪ] *v.t.* befördern. **conveyance** [kən'veɪəns] *n.* **a)** *(transportation)* Beförderung, *die;* **b)** *(formal: vehicle)* Beförderungsmittel, *das.* **con'veyancing** *n.* *(Law)* ~ |of property| [Eigentums]übertragung, *die.* **conveyor** [kən'veɪə(r)] *n.* ~ |belt| Fließband, *das*

convict 1. ['kɒnvɪkt] *n.* Strafgefangene, *der/die.* **2.** [kən'vɪkt] *v.t.* verurteilen. **conviction** [kən'vɪkʃn] *n.* **a)** *(Law)* Verurteilung, *die* (for wegen); **b)** *(belief)* Überzeugung, *die*

convince [kən'vɪns] *v.t.* überzeugen; ~ **sb. that** ...: jmdn. davon überzeugen, daß ...; be ~d that ...: davon überzeugt sein, daß ... **convincing** [kən'vɪnsɪŋ] *adj.* **con'vincingly** *adv.* überzeugend

convivial [kən'vɪvɪəl] *adj.* fröhlich

convoluted ['kɒnvəluːtɪd] *adj.* *(complex)* kompliziert

convoy ['kɒnvɔɪ] *n.* Konvoi, *der;* in~: im Konvoi

convulse [kən'vʌls] *v.t.* be ~d with sich krümmen vor (+ *Dat.*). **convulsions** [kən'vʌlʃnz] *n. pl.* Krämpfe

coo [kuː] *v.i.* gurren

cook [kʊk] **1.** *n.* Koch, *der*/Köchin, *die.* **2.** *v.t.* kochen ⟨*Mahlzeit*⟩; *(fry, roast)* braten; *(boil)* kochen. **3.** *v.i.* kochen. **cook 'up** *v.t.* erfinden ⟨*Geschichte*⟩

'cookbook *n.* *(Amer.)* Kochbuch, *das*

'cooker *n.* *(Brit.)* Herd, *der*

cookery ['kʊkərɪ] *n.* Kochen, *das.* **'cookery book** *n.* *(Brit.)* Kochbuch, *das*

cookie ['kʊkɪ] *n.* *(Amer.)* Keks, *der*

'cooking *n.* Kochen, *das.* **'cooking apple** *n.* Kochapfel, *der.* **'cooking utensil** *n.* Küchengerät, *das*

cool [kuːl] **1.** *adj.* a) kühl; store in a ~ place kühl aufbewahren; **b)** *(unemotional, unfriendly)* kühl; *(calm)* ruhig. **2.** *n.* Kühle, *die.* **3.** *v.i.* abkühlen. **4.** *v.t.* kühlen; *(from high temperature)* abkühlen. **cool 'down, cool 'off** *v.i. & t.* abkühlen

coolly ['kuːllɪ] *adv.* *(calmly)* ruhig; *(unemotionally)* kühl

coop [kuːp] **1.** *n.* *(for poultry)* Hühnerstall, *der.* **2.** *v.t.* ~ **up** einpferchen

co-operate [kəʊ'ɒpəreɪt] *v.i.* mitarbeiten (in bei); *(with each other)* zusammenarbeiten (in bei). **co-operation** [kəʊɒpə'reɪʃn] *n.* Zusammenarbeit, *die.* **co-operative** [kəʊ'ɒpərətɪv] **1.** *adj.* kooperativ; *(helpful)* hilfsbereit. **2.** *n.* Genossenschaft, *die*

co-ordinate [kəʊ'ɔːdɪneɪt] *v.t.* koordinieren. **co-ordination** [kəʊɔːdɪ'neɪʃn] *n.* Koordination, *die*

cop [kɒp] *n.* *(sl.: police officer)* Bulle, *der (salopp)*

cope [kəʊp] *v.i.* ~ **with** sb./sth. mit jmdm./etw. fertig werden

Copenhagen [kəʊpn'heɪgn] *pr. n.* Kopenhagen *(das)*

copier ['kɒpɪə(r)] *n.* *(machine)* Kopiergerät, *das*

co-pilot ['kəʊpaɪlət] *n.* Kopilot, *der*/Kopilotin, *die*

copious ['kəʊpɪəs] *adj.* reichhaltig

¹**copper** ['kɒpə(r)] *n.* Kupfer, *das*

²**copper** *(Brit. sl.)* see cop

coppice ['kɒpɪs], **copse** [kɒps] *ns.* Wäldchen, *das*

copulate ['kɒpjʊleɪt] *v.i.* kopulieren

copy ['kɒpɪ] **1.** *n.* **a)** *(reproduction)* Kopie, *die;* **b)** *(specimen)* Exemplar, *das.* **2.** *v.t. & i.* kopieren; *(transcribe)* abschreiben. **'copyright** *n.* Urheberrecht, *das*

coral ['kɒrl] *n.* Koralle, *die*

cord [kɔːd] *n.* **a)** Kordel, *die;* **b)** *(cloth)* Cord, *der;* **c)** in pl. *(trousers)* |pair of| ~s Cordhose, *die*

cordial ['kɔːdɪəl] **1.** *adj.* herzlich. **2.** *n.* *(drink)* Sirup, *der.* **'cordially** *adv.* herzlich

cordon ['kɔːdn] **1.** *n.* Kordon, *der.* **2.** *v.t.* ~ |off| absperren

corduroy ['kɔːdərɔɪ, 'kɔːdjʊrɔɪ] *n.* Cordsamt, *der*

core [kɔː(r)] **1.** *n.* *(of fruit)* Kerngehäuse, *das.* **2.** *v.t.* entkernen

cork [kɔːk] **1.** *n.* **a)** *(bark)* Kork, *der;* **b)**

(bottle-stopper) Korken, *der.* **2.** *v. t.* zukorken. '**corkscrew** *n.* Korkenzieher, *der*

¹**corn** [kɔ:n] *n.* Getreide, *das*

²**corn** *n.* *(on foot)* Hühnerauge, *das*

corned beef [kɔ:nd 'bi:f] *n.* Corned beef, *das*

corner ['kɔ:nə(r)] **1.** *n.* **a)** Ecke, *die; (curve)* Kurve, *die;* **on the ~:** an der Ecke/in der Kurve; **b)** *(of mouth, eye)* Winkel, *der.* **2.** *v. t. (fig.)* in die Enge treiben. **3.** *v. i.* die Kurve nehmen. '**corner kick** *n. (Footb.)* Eckball, *der.* '**cornerstone** *n. (fig.)* Eckpfeiler, *der*

cornet ['kɔ:nɪt] *n.* **a)** *(Brit.: for ice-cream)* [Eis]tüte, *die;* **b)** *(Mus.)* Kornett, *das*

corn: **~flakes** *n. pl.* Corn-flakes *Pl.;* **~flour** *(Brit.),* **~starch** *(Amer.) ns.* Maismehl, *das*

'**corny** *adj. (coll.: trite)* abgedroschen

coronation [kɒrə'neɪʃn] *n.* Krönung, *die*

coroner ['kɒrənə(r)] *n.* Coroner, *der; Beamter, der gewaltsame od. unnatürliche Todesfälle untersucht*

coronet [kɒrə'net] *n.* Krone, *die*

¹**corporal** ['kɔ:pərl] *adj.* körperlich

²**corporal** *n.* ≈ Hauptgefreite, *der*

corporation [kɔ:pə'reɪʃn] *n.* Stadtverwaltung, *die*

corps [kɔ:(r)] *n., pl. same* [kɔ:z] Korps, *das*

corpse [kɔ:ps] *n.* Leiche, *die*

corpulent ['kɔ:pjʊlənt] *adj.* korpulent

correct [kə'rekt] **1.** *v. t.* korrigieren. **2.** *adj.* korrekt; **that is ~:** das stimmt. **correction** [kə'rekʃn] *n.* Korrektur, *die.* **cor'rectly** *adv.* korrekt

correspond [kɒrɪ'spɒnd] *v. i.* **a)** [to each other] einander entsprechen; **~ to sth.** einer Sache *(Dat.)* entsprechen; **b)** *(communicate)* **~ with sb.** mit jmdm. korrespondieren. **correspondence** [kɒrɪ'spɒndəns] *n.* **a)** Übereinstimmung, *die* (with, to mit); **b)** *(communication)* Briefwechsel, *der.* **correspondent** [kɒrɪ'spɒndənt] *n. (reporter)* Korrespondent, *der/*Korrespondentin, *die.* **corre'sponding** *adj.* entsprechend (to *Dat.).* **corre'spondingly** *adv.* entsprechend

corridor ['kɒrɪdɔ:(r)] *n.* **a)** Flur, *der;* **b)** *(Railw.)* [Seiten]gang, *der*

corroborate [kə'rɒbəreɪt] *v. t.* bestätigen

corrode [kə'rəʊd] **1.** *v. t.* zerfressen. **2.** *v. i.* zerfressen werden. **corrosion** [kə'rəʊʒn] *n.* Korrosion, *die*

corrugated ['kɒrəgeɪtɪd] *adj.* **~ cardboard** Wellpappe, *die;* **~ iron** Wellblech, *das*

corrupt [kə'rʌpt] **1.** *adj. (depraved)* verdorben *(geh.); (influenced by bribery)* korrupt. **2.** *v. t. (deprave)* verderben *(geh.); (bribe)* bestechen. **corruption** [kə'rʌpʃn] *n. (moral deterioration)* Verdorbenheit, *die (geh.); (corrupt practices)* Korruption, *die*

corset ['kɔ:sɪt] *n.* Korsett, *das*

Corsica ['kɔ:sɪkə] *pr. n.* Korsika *(das)*

cortège [kɔ:'teɪʒ] *n.* Trauerzug, *der*

cosh [kɒʃ] *(Brit. coll.)* **1.** *n.* Totschläger, *der.* **2.** *v. t.* niederknüppeln

cosmetic [kɒz'metɪk] **1.** *adj.* kosmetisch. **2.** *n.* Kosmetikum, *das*

cosmic ['kɒzmɪk] *adj.* kosmisch

cosmonaut ['kɒzmənɔ:t] *n.* Kosmonaut, *der/*Kosmonautin, *die*

cosmopolitan [kɒzmə'pɒlɪtən] *adj.* kosmopolitisch

cosmos ['kɒzmɒs] *n.* Kosmos, *der*

cosset ['kɒsɪt] *v. t.* [ver]hätscheln

cost [kɒst] **1.** *n.* **a)** Kosten *Pl.;* **b)** *(fig.)* Preis, *der;* **at all ~s, at any ~:** um jeden Preis. **2.** *v. t.* **a)** *p. t., p. p.* **cost** *(lit. or fig.)* kosten; **how much does it ~?** was kostet es?; **b)** *p. t., p. p.* **costed** *(Commerc.: fix price of)* **~ sth.** den Preis für etw. kalkulieren. '**cost-effective** *adj.* rentabel

'**costly** *adj.* teuer

'**cost:** **~ of living** *n.* Lebenshaltungskosten *Pl.;* **~ price** *n.* Selbstkostenpreis, *der*

costume ['kɒstju:m] *n.* Kleidermode, *die; (theatrical ~)* Kostüm, *das*

cosy ['kəʊzɪ] *adj.* gemütlich

cot [kɒt] *n.* Kinderbett, *das*

cottage ['kɒtɪdʒ] *n.* Cottage, *das.* **cottage:** **~ cheese** *n.* Hüttenkäse, *der;* **~ industry** *n.* Heimarbeit, *die;* **~ pie** *n.* mit Kartoffelbrei überbackenes Hackfleisch

cotton ['kɒtən] **1.** *n.* Baumwolle, *die; (thread)* Baumwollgarn, *das.* **2.** *attrib. adj.* Baumwoll-. **3.** *v. i.* **~ 'on** *(coll.)* kapieren *(ugs.).* **cotton 'wool** *n.* Watte, *die*

couch [kaʊtʃ] *n.* Couch, *die*

couchette [ku:'ʃet] *n. (Railw.)* Liegesitz, *der*

cough [kɒf] **1.** *n.* Husten, *der.* **2.** *v. i.* husten. '**cough mixture** *n.* Hustensaft, *der*

could *see* ²**can**

couldn't ['kʊdnt] *(coll.)* = **could not;** *see* ²**can**

council ['kaʊnsl] *n.* Rat, *der;* local ~: Gemeinderat, *der;* city/town ~: Stadtrat, *der.* '**council flat** *n.* Sozialwohnung, *die.* '**council house** *n.* Haus des sozialen Wohnungsbaus

councillor ['kaʊnsələ(r)] *n.* Ratsmitglied, *das*

'**council tax** *n.* (Brit.) Gemeindesteuer, *die*

counsel ['kaʊnsl] 1. *n.* a) Rat[schlag], *der;* b) *pl. same* (Law) Rechtsanwalt, *der*/-anwältin, *die.* 2. *v.t.,* (Brit.) -ll-beraten. **counsellor,** (Amer.) **counselor** ['kaʊnsələ(r)] *n.* Berater, *der*/Beraterin, *die*

'**count** [kaʊnt] 1. *n.* Zählen, *das;* keep ~ [of sth.] [etw.] zählen; lose ~: sich verzählen. 2. *v.t.* a) zählen; b) *(include)* mitzählen; not ~ing abgesehen von; c) *(consider)* halten für; ~ oneself lucky sich glücklich schätzen können. 3. *v.i.* a) zählen; ~ [up] to ten bis zehn zählen; b) *(be included)* zählen. '**count on** *v.t.* ~ on sb./sth. sich auf jmdn./etw. verlassen. **count 'up** *v.t.* zusammenzählen

²**count** *n.* *(nobleman)* Graf, *der*

'**countdown** *n.* Countdown, *der od. das*

countenance ['kaʊntɪnəns] 1. *n.* *(literary: face)* Antlitz, *das.* 2. *v.t.* *(formal: approve)* gutheißen

'**counter** ['kaʊntə(r)] *n.* a) *(of shop, plane)* Ladentisch, *der;* *(in cafeteria)* Büfett, *das;* *(in bank)* Schalter, *der;* b) *(for games)* Spielmarke, *die*

²**counter** 1. *adj.* Gegen-. 2. *v.t.* a) *(oppose)* begegnen (+ Dat.); b) *(act against)* kontern. 3. *adv.* go ~ to zuwiderlaufen (+ Dat.)

counter: ~'**act** *v.t.* entgegenwirken (+ Dat.); ~'**attack** *n.* Gegenangriff, *der;* ~'**balance** *v.t.* *(fig.)* ausgleichen; ~'**espionage** *n.* Spionageabwehr, *die*

counterfeit ['kaʊntəfɪt] 1. *adj.* gefälscht; ~ money Falschgeld, *das.* 2. *v.t.* fälschen. '**counterfeiter** *n.* Fälscher, *der*/Fälscherin, *die*

counter: ~'**foil** *n.* Kontrollabschnitt, *der;* ~'**part** *n.* Gegenstück, *das* (of zu); ~'**pro'ductive** *adj.* sth. is ~-productive etw. bewirkt das Gegenteil des Gewünschten; ~'**sign** *v.t.* gegenzeichnen

countess ['kaʊntɪs] *n.* Gräfin, *die*

'**countless** *adj.* zahllos

country ['kʌntrɪ] *n.* a) Land, *das;* sb's [home] ~: jmds. Heimat; b) *(~ side)*

Landschaft, *die;* in the ~: auf dem Land. **countryman** ['kʌntrɪmən] *n.,* *pl.* **countrymen** ['kʌntrɪmən] Landsmann, *der.* '**countryside** *n.* a) *(rural areas)* Land, *das;* b) *(rural scenery)* Landschaft, *die*

county ['kaʊntɪ] *n.* (Brit.) Grafschaft, *die*

coup [ku:] *n.* a) Coup, *der;* b) *see* coup d'état. **coup d'état** [ku: deɪ'ta:] *n.* Staatsstreich, *der*

coupé ['ku:peɪ] *n.* Coupé, *das*

couple [kʌpl] 1. *n.* a) *(pair)* Paar, *das;* *(married)* [Ehe]paar, *das;* a ~ [of] *(a few)* ein paar; *(two)* zwei. 2. *v.t.* koppeln

coupon ['ku:pɒn] *n.* a) *(for rations)* Marke, *die;* b) *(in advertisement)* Coupon, *der*

courage ['kʌrɪdʒ] *n.* Mut, *der.* **courageous** [kə'reɪdʒəs] *adj.,* **cou'rageously** *adv.* mutig

courgette [kʊə'ʒet] *n.* (Brit.) Zucchino, *der*

courier ['kʊrɪə(r)] *n.* a) *(Tourism)* Reiseleiter, *der*/-leiterin, *die;* b) *(messenger)* Kurier, *der*

'**course** [kɔ:s] *n.* a) *(of ship, plane)* Kurs, *der;* ~ [of action] Vorgehensweise, *die;* b) of ~: natürlich; c) in due ~: zu gegebener Zeit; in the ~ of the day/his life im Lauf[e] des Tages/seines Lebens; d) *(of meal)* Gang, *der;* e) *(Sport)* Kurs, *der;* [Golf]platz, *der;* f) *(Educ.)* Kurs[us], *der;* g) *(Med.)* a ~ of treatment eine Kur

court [kɔ:t] 1. *n.* a) Hof, *der;* b) *(Tennis, Squash)* Platz, *der;* c) *(Law)* Gericht, *das.* 2. *v.t.* ~ sb. jmdn. umwerben

courteous ['kɜ:tɪəs] *adj.* höflich. **courtesy** ['kɜ:təsɪ] *n.* Höflichkeit, *die*

court: ~'**house** *n.* (Law) Gerichtsgebäude, *das;* ~'**martial** *n.,* *pl.* ~s martial *(Mil.)* Kriegsgericht, *das;* ~'**yard** *n.* Hof, *der*

cousin ['kʌzn] *n.* [first] ~: Cousin, *der*/Cousine, *die*

cove [kəʊv] *n.* (Geog.) [kleine] Bucht

covenant ['kʌvənənt] *n.* formelle Übereinkunft

cover ['kʌvə(r)] 1. *n.* a) *(piece of cloth)* Decke, *die;* *(of cushion, bed)* Bezug, *der;* *(lid)* Deckel, *der;* *(of hole, engine, typewriter, etc.)* Abdeckung, *die;* b) *(of book)* Einband, *der;* *(of magazine)* Umschlag, *der;* c) [send sb.] under separate ~: [etw.] mit getrennter Post [schicken]; d) take ~ [from sth.] Schutz [vor etw. *(Dat.)*] suchen; **under ~** *(from rain)* überdacht. **2.** *v. t.* **a)** bedecken; beziehen ⟨*Sessel, Kisses*⟩; zudecken ⟨*Pfanne*⟩; **the roses are ~ed with** greenfly die Rosen sind voller Blattläuse; **b)** *(include)* abdecken; **c)** *(Journ.)* berichten über (+ *Akk.*); **d)** decken ⟨*Kosten*⟩. **cover 'up** *v. t.* **1.** zudecken; *(fig.)* vertuschen. **2.** *v. i.* **~ up for sb.** jmdn. decken

coverage ['kʌvərɪdʒ] *n.* *(Journ.)* Berichterstattung, *die*

'cover charge *n.* [Preis für das] Gedeck

'covering *n.* Decke, *die*; *(of chair, bed)* Bezug, *der.* **'covering letter** *n.* Begleitbrief, *der*

covert ['kʌvət] *adj.* versteckt

'cover-up *n.* Verschleierung, *die*

covet ['kʌvɪt] *v. t.* begehren *(geh.)*. **covetous** ['kʌvɪtəs] *adj.* begehrlich *(geh.)*.

cow [kaʊ] *n.* Kuh, *die*

coward ['kaʊəd] *n.* Feigling, *der.* **cowardice** ['kaʊədɪs] *n.* Feigheit, *die.* **cowardly** *adj.* feig[e]

'cowboy *n.* Cowboy, *der*

cower ['kaʊə(r)] *v. i.* sich ducken

cow: ~-shed *n.* Kuhstall, *der*; **~slip** *n.* Schlüsselblume, *die*

coy [kɔɪ] *adj.* gespielt schüchtern

cozy *(Amer.) see* cosy

crab [kræb] *n.* Krabbe, *die.* **'crab-apple** *n.* Holzapfel, *der*

crack [kræk] **1.** *n.* **a)** *(noise)* Krachen, *das*; **b)** *(in china etc.)* Sprung, *der*; *(in rock)* Spalte, *die*; *(chink)* Spalt, *der*; **c)** *(coll.: try)* **have a ~ at sth./doing sth.** versuchen, etw. zu tun. **2.** *attrib. adj.* *(coll.)* erstklassig. **3.** *v. t.* **a)** knacken ⟨*Nuß, Problem, Kode*⟩; **b)** *(make a ~ in)* anschlagen ⟨*Porzellan usw.*⟩; **c)** ~ **a joke** einen Witz machen; **d)** ~ **a whip** mit einer Peitsche knallen. **4.** *v. i.* ⟨*Porzellan usw.*⟩: einen Sprung/Sprünge bekommen. **crack 'down** *v. i.* *(coll.)* ~ **down** [on sb./sth.] [gegen jmdn./etw.] [hart] vorgehen. **crack 'up** *v. i.* *(coll.)* ⟨*Person*⟩: zusammenbrechen

cracked [krækt] *adj.* gesprungen ⟨*Porzellan usw.*⟩; rissig ⟨*Verputz*⟩

cracker ['krækə(r)] *n.* **a)** [Christmas] ~ ≈ Knallbonbon, *der od. das*; **b)** *(biscuit)* Cracker, *der.* **'crackers** *pred. adj.* *(Brit. coll.)* übergeschnappt *(ugs.)*

crackle ['krækl] **1.** *v. i.* knistern; ⟨*Feuer*⟩: prasseln. **2.** *n.* Knistern, *das*

cradle ['kreɪdl] **1.** *n.* Wiege, *die.* **2.** *v. t.* wiegen

craft [krɑːft] *n.* **a)** *(trade)* Handwerk, *das*; *(art)* Kunsthandwerk, *das*; **b)** *pl. same* *(boat)* Boot, *das.* **craftsman** ['krɑːftsmən] *n.*, *pl.* **craftsmen** ['krɑːftsmən] Handwerker, *der*

'crafty *adj.* listig

crag [kræg] *n.* Felsspitze, *die.* **'craggy** *adj.* **a)** felsig; **b)** zerfurcht ⟨*Gesicht*⟩

cram [kræm] **1.** *v. t.*, **-mm-** *(overfill)* vollstopfen *(ugs.)*; *(force)* stopfen. **2.** *v. i.*, **-mm-** *(for exam)* büffeln *(ugs.)*

cramp [kræmp] **1.** *n.* *(Med.)* Krampf, *der.* **2.** *v. t.* einengen

cranberry ['krænbəri] *n.* Preiselbeere, *die*

crane [kreɪn] **1.** *n.* Kran, *der.* **2.** *v. t.* ~ **one's neck** den Hals recken

'crank [kræŋk] *n.* *(Mech. Engin.)* [Hand]kurbel, *die*

²crank *n.* Irre, *der/die (salopp)*

'crankshaft *n.* *(Mech. Engin.)* Kurbelwelle, *die*

'cranky *adj.* *(eccentric)* schrullig

cranny ['kræni] *n.* Ritze, *die*

crash [kræʃ] **1.** *n.* **a)** *(noise)* Krachen, *das*; **b)** *(collision)* Zusammenstoß, *der*; **have a ~:** einen Unfall haben. **2.** *v. i.* **a)** *(make a noise, go noisily)* krachen; **b)** *(have a collision)* einen Unfall haben; ⟨*Flugzeug, Flieger*⟩: abstürzen; **~ into sth.** gegen etw. krachen. **3.** *v. t.* **a)** *(smash)* schmettern; **b)** *(cause to have collision)* einen Unfall haben mit

crash: ~ barrier *n.* Leitplanke, *die*; **~ course** *n.* Intensivkurs, *der*; **~-helmet** *n.* Sturzhelm, *der*

crass [kræs] *adj.* kraß

crate [kreɪt] *n.* Kiste, *die*

crater ['kreɪtə(r)] *n.* Krater, *der*

cravat [krə'væt] *n.* Krawatte, *die*

crave [kreɪv] *v. t.* **a)** *(beg)* erbitten; **b)** *(long for)* sich sehnen nach. **'craving** *n.* Verlangen, *das (for nach)*

crawl [krɔːl] **1.** *v. i.* **a)** kriechen; ⟨*Baby, Insekt*⟩: krabbeln; **b)** *(coll.)* ~ **to sb.** vor jmdm. kriechen. **2.** *n.* **a)** **go at a ~:** im Schneckentempo fahren; **b)** *(swimming-stroke)* Kraulen, *das.*

'crawler lane *n.* Kriechspur, *die*

crayfish ['kreɪfɪʃ] *n.*, *pl. same* Flußkrebs, *der*

crayon ['kreɪən] *n.* [coloured] ~: Buntstift, *der*; *(wax)* Wachsmalstift, *der*

craze [kreɪz] *n.* Begeisterung, *die*

crazy ['kreɪzi] *adj.* verrückt; **be ~ about sb./sth.** *(coll.)* nach jmdm./etw. verrückt sein *(ugs.)*

creak [kriːk] **1.** *n.* Knarren, *das.* **2.** *v. i.* knarren

cream [kri:m] 1. *n.* **a)** Sahne, *die;* **b)** *(dessert, cosmetic)* Creme, *die.* 2. *adj.* ~[-coloured] creme[farben]. **cream 'cheese** *n.* ≈ Frischkäse, *der*

'**creamy** *adj.* *(with cream)* sahnig; *(like cream)* cremig

crease [kri:s] 1. *n.* *(pressed)* Bügelfalte, *die; (accidental)* Falte, *die.* 2. *v.t.* *(press)* eine Falte bügeln in (+ *Akk.);* *(accidentally)* zerknittern. 3. *v.i.* Falten bekommen; knittern. '**crease-resistant** *adj.* knitterfrei

create [kri:'eɪt] *v.t.* schaffen; verursachen ⟨*Verwirrung⟩;* machen ⟨*Eindruck⟩.* **creation** [kri:'eɪʃn] *n.* Schaffung, *die; (of the world)* Schöpfung, *die (geh.).* **creative** [kri:'eɪtɪv] *adj.* kreativ. **creator** [kri:'eɪtə(r)] *n.* Schöpfer, *der/*Schöpferin, *die*

creature ['kri:tʃə(r)] *n.* Geschöpf, *das*

crèche [kreʃ] *n.* [Kinder]krippe, *die*

credentials [krɪ'denʃlz] *n. pl.* Zeugnis, *das*

credibility [kredɪ'bɪlɪti] *n.* Glaubwürdigkeit, *die*

credible ['kredɪbl] *adj.* glaubwürdig

credit ['kredɪt] 1. *n.* **a)** *(honour)* Ehre, *die;* **take the** ~ **for** sth. die Anerkennung für etw. einstecken; **b)** *(Commerc.)* Kredit, *der.* 2. *v.t.* **a)** glauben; **b)** *(Finance)* gutschreiben. **creditable** ['kredɪtəbl] *adj.* anerkennenswert

'**credit card** *n.* Kreditkarte, *die*

creditor ['kredɪtə(r)] *n.* Gläubiger, *der/*Gläubigerin, *die*

creed [kri:d] *n.* Glaubensbekenntnis, *das*

creek [kri:k] *n.* **a)** *(Brit.: of coast)* [kleine] Bucht; **b)** *(of river)* [kurzer] Flußarm

creep [kri:p] 1. *v.i.,* **crept** [krept] kriechen; *(move timidly, slowly, stealthily)* schleichen. 2. *n.* **a)** *(sl.: person)* Fiesling, *der (salopp);* **b)** *(coll.)* **give sb. the** ~**s** jmdn. nicht [ganz] geheuer sein. '**creeper** *n.* Kletterpflanze, *die.* '**creepy** *adj.* unheimlich

cremate [krɪ'meɪt] *v.t.* einäschern. **cremation** [krɪ'meɪʃn] *n.* Einäscherung, *die.* **crematorium** [kremə-'tɔ:rɪəm] *n.* Krematorium, *das*

creosote ['kri:əsəʊt] *n.* Kreosot, *das*

crept *see* **creep** 1

crescent ['kresənt] *n.* Mondsichel, *die*

cress [kres] *n.* Kresse, *die*

crest [krest] *n.* Kamm, *der.* '**crestfallen** *adj.* niedergeschlagen

Crete [kri:t] *pr. n.* Kreta *(das)*

cretin ['kretɪn] *n. (coll.)* Trottel, *der*

crevasse [krɪ'væs] *n.* Gletscherspalte, *die*

crevice ['krevɪs] *n.* Spalt, *der*

crew [kru:] *n.* Besatzung, *die.* '**crew-cut** *n.* Bürstenschnitt, *der*

crib [krɪb] 1. *n.* Krippe, *die.* 2. *v.t.,* -bb- *(coll.)* abkupfern *(salopp)*

crick [krɪk] *n.* **a** ~ **[in one's neck/back]** ein steifer Hals/Rücken

¹**cricket** ['krɪkɪt] *n.* Kricket, *das*

²**cricket** *n. (Zool.)* Grille, *die*

'**cricket bat** *n.* Schlagholz, *das*

'**cricketer** *n.* Kricketspieler, *der/*-spielerin, *die*

cried *see* **cry**

crime [kraɪm] *n.* **a)** Verbrechen, *das;* **b)** *collect.* **a wave of** ~: eine Welle von Straftaten; ~ **doesn't pay** Verbrechen lohnen sich nicht

criminal ['krɪmɪnl] 1. *adj.* kriminell; strafbar; ~ **act** *or* **deed/offence** Straftat, *die.* 2. *n.* Kriminelle, *der/die*

crimson ['krɪmzn] 1. *adj.* purpurrot. 2. *n.* Purpurrot, *das*

cringe [krɪndʒ] *v.i.* zusammenzucken

crinkle ['krɪŋkl] 1. *n.* Knitterfalte, *die.* 2. *v.t.* zerknittern. 3. *v.i.* knittern

cripple ['krɪpl] 1. *n.* Krüppel, *der.* 2. *v.t.* zum Krüppel machen; *(fig.)* lähmen. **crippled** ['krɪpld] *adj.* verkrüppelt

crisis ['kraɪsɪs] *n., pl.* **crises** ['kraɪsi:z] Krise, *die*

crisp [krɪsp] 1. *adj.* knusprig. 2. **a)** *n. usu. in pl. (Brit.: potato* ~] [Kartoffel]chip, *der;* **b)** **be burned to a** ~: verbrannt sein. '**crispbread** *n.* Knäckebrot, *das*

'**crispy** *adj.* knusprig

criss-cross ['krɪskrɒs] 1. *adj.* ~ **pattern** Muster aus gekreuzten Linien. 2. *adv.* kreuz und quer. 3. *v.t.* wiederholt schneiden

criterion [kraɪ'tɪərɪən] *n., pl.* **criteria** [kraɪ'tɪərɪə] Kriterium, *das*

critic ['krɪtɪk] *n.* Kritiker, *der/*Kritikerin, *die.* **critical** ['krɪtɪkl] *adj.* kritisch; **be** ~ **of** sb./sth. jmdn./etw. kritisieren. **critically** ['krɪtɪkəli] *adv.* kritisch; ~ **ill** ernstlich krank

criticism ['krɪtɪsɪzm] *n.* Kritik, *die* (of an + *Dat.)*

criticize ['krɪtɪsaɪz] *v.t.* kritisieren (for wegen)

croak [krəʊk] 1. *n. (of frog)* Quaken, *das; (of person)* Krächzen, *das.* 2. *v.i.* ⟨*Frosch:⟩* quaken; ⟨*Person:⟩* krächzen. 3. *v.t.* krächzen

crochet [ˈkrəʊʃeɪ] **1.** *n.* Häkelarbeit, *die;* ~ **hook** Häkelhaken, *der.* **2.** *v.t.* häkeln

crock [krɒk] *n. (coll.)* [old] ~ *(person)* altes Wrack, *das (fig.); (vehicle)* [alte] Klapperkiste *(ugs.)*

crockery [ˈkrɒkərɪ] *n.* Geschirr, *das*

crocodile [ˈkrɒkədaɪl] *n.* Krokodil, *das*

crocus [ˈkrəʊkəs] *n.* Krokus, *der*

crony [ˈkrəʊnɪ] *n.* Kumpel, *der (ugs.)*

crook [krʊk] *n.* **a)** *(coll.: rogue)* Gauner, *der;* **b)** *(shepherd's)* Hirtenstab, *der*

crooked [ˈkrʊkɪd] *adj.* krumm; *(fig.: dishonest)* betrügerisch

crop [krɒp] *n.* **1.** [Feld]frucht, *die; (season's yield)* Ernte, *die.* **2.** *v.t.* stutzen ⟨*Haare usw.*⟩. **crop** **up** *v.i.* auftauchen

ˈcropper *n. (coll.)* **come a** ~: einen Sturz bauen *(ugs.)*

croquet [ˈkrəʊkeɪ] *n.* Krocket[spiel], *das*

croquette [krəˈket] *n.* Krokette, *die*

cross [krɒs] **1.** *n.* **a)** Kreuz, *das;* **b)** *(mixture)* Mischung, *die (between* aus*).* **2.** *v.t.* **a)** [über]kreuzen; ~ **one's arms/legs** die Arme verschränken/die Beine übereinanderschlagen; **keep one's fingers ~ed** [**for sb.**] *(fig.)* [jmdm.] die od. den Daumen drücken; **b)** *(go across)* kreuzen; überqueren ⟨*Straße, Gebirge*⟩; durchqueren ⟨*Land, Zimmer*⟩; ~ **sb.'s mind** *(fig.)* jmdm. einfallen; **c)** *(Brit.)* **a ~ed cheque** ein Verrechnungsscheck; **d)** ~ **oneself** sich bekreuzigen. **3.** *v.i.* aneinander vorbeigehen; ~ [**in the post**] ⟨*Briefe:*⟩ sich kreuzen. **4.** *adj.* verärgert; **sb. will be** ~: jmd. wird ärgerlich od. böse werden; **be** ~ **with sb.** böse auf jmdn. sein. **cross** **out** *v.t.* ausstreichen. **cross** **over** *v.t.* überqueren; *abs.* hinübergehen

cross: ~**bar** *n.* **a)** [Fahrrad]stange, *die;* **b)** *(Sport)* Querlatte, *die;* ~**check 1.** *n.* Gegenprobe, *die;* **2.** *v.t.* [nochmals] nachprüfen; nachkontrollieren; ~**country 1.** *adj.* Querfeldein-; **2.** *adv.* querfeldein; ~**examination** *n.* Kreuzverhör, *das;* ~**examine** *v.t.* ins Kreuzverhör nehmen; ~**eyed** [ˈkrɒsaɪd] *adj.* [nach innen] schielend; **be ~eyed** schielen; ~**fire** *n.* Kreuzfeuer, *das*

ˈcrossing *n.* **a)** *(act)* Überquerung, *die;* **b)** *(pedestrian ~)* Überweg, *der*

ˈcrossly *adv.* verärgert

cross: ~ **purposes** *n. pl.* **talk at** ~

purposes aneinander vorbeireden; ~**reference** *n.* Querverweis, *der;* ~**roads** *n. sing.* Kreuzung, *die; (fig.)* Wendepunkt, *der;* ~**section** *n.* Querschnitt, *der;* ~**word** *n.* ~**word** [**puzzle**] Kreuzworträtsel, *das*

crotchet [ˈkrɒtʃɪt] *n. (Brit. Mus.)* Viertelnote, *die*

crouch [kraʊtʃ] *v.i.* [sich zusammen]kauern

crow [krəʊ] *n.* Krähe, *die;* **as the** ~ **flies** Luftlinie

ˈcrowbar *n.* Brechstange, *die*

crowd [kraʊd] **1.** *n.* [Menschen]menge, *die.* **2.** *vt.* füllen. **3.** *v.i.* sich sammeln. **ˈcrowded** *adj.* überfüllt

crown [kraʊn] **1.** *n.* Krone, *die.* **2.** *v.t.* **a)** krönen; **b)** überkronen ⟨*Zahn*⟩

crucial [ˈkruːʃl] *adj.* entscheidend (**to** für)

crucifix [ˈkruːsɪfɪks] *n.* Kruzifix, *das*

crucifixion [kruːsɪˈfɪkʃn] *n.* Kreuzigung, *die*

crucify [ˈkruːsɪfaɪ] *v.t.* kreuzigen

crude [kruːd] *adj.* **a)** roh; ~ **oil** Rohöl, *das;* **b)** *(fig.)* grob ⟨*Entwurf, Worte*⟩

cruel [ˈkruːəl] *adj.* grausam. **cruelty** [ˈkruːəltɪ] *n.* Grausamkeit, *die*

cruise [kruːz] **1.** *v.i.* **a)** *(at random)* ⟨*Fahrzeug, Fahrer:*⟩ herumfahren. **2.** *n.* Kreuzfahrt, *die.* **ˈcruise missile** *n.* Marschflugkörper, *der.* **ˈcruiser** *n.* Kreuzer, *der*

crumb [krʌm] *n.* Krümel, *der*

crumble [ˈkrʌmbl] **1.** *v.t.* zerkrümeln ⟨*Keks, Kuchen*⟩. **2.** *v.i.* ⟨*Mauer:*⟩ zusammenfallen. **crumbly** [ˈkrʌmblɪ] *adj.* krümelig ⟨*Keks, Kuchen*⟩; bröckelig ⟨*Gestein*⟩

crumpet [ˈkrʌmpɪt] *n.* weiches Hefeküchlein zum Toasten

crumple [ˈkrʌmpl] **1.** *v.t.* **a)** *(crush)* zerdrücken; **b)** *(wrinkle)* zerknittern. **2.** *v.i.* knittern

crunch [krʌntʃ] **1.** *v.t.* [geräuschvoll] knabbern ⟨*Keks*⟩. **2.** *v.i.* ⟨*Schnee, Kies:*⟩ knirschen. **3.** *n.* Knirschen, *das;* **when it comes to the** ~: wenn es hart auf hart geht. **ˈcrunchy** *adj.* knusprig

crusade [kruːˈseɪd] **1.** *n. (Hist.; also fig.)* Kreuzzug, *der.* **2.** *v.i. (fig.)* zu Felde gehen. **cruˈsader** *n. (Hist.)* Kreuzfahrer, *der*

crush [krʌʃ] **1.** *v.t.* **a)** quetschen; **b)** *(powder)* zerstampfen; **c)** *(fig.)* niederschlagen. **2.** *n. (crowd)* Gedränge, *das*

crust [krʌst] *n.* Kruste, *die.* **ˈcrusty** *adj.* knusprig

crutch [krʌtʃ] n. Krücke, die; **go about on ~es** an Krücken gehen

crux [krʌks] n. **the ~ of the matter** der springende Punkt bei der Sache

cry [kraɪ] 1. n. (of grief) Schrei, der; (of words) Schreien, das; **a far ~ from ...** (fig.) etwas ganz anderes als ... 2. v.i. a) rufen; (loudly) schreien; b) (weep) weinen (over wegen). **cry 'off** v.i. absagen. **cry 'out** v.i. aufschreien

'**crying** adj. it's a ~ **shame** es ist eine wahre Schande

crypt [krɪpt] n. Krypta, die

cryptic ['krɪptɪk] adj. geheimnisvoll

crystal ['krɪstl] 1. n. a) Kristall, der; b) (glass) Bleikristall, das. 2. adj. (made of ~ glass) kristallen. **crystallize** ['krɪstəlaɪz] v.i. kristallisieren; (fig.) feste Form annehmen

cub [kʌb] n. a) Junge, das; (of wolf, fox, dog) Welpe, der; b) **Cub** see Cub Scout

Cuba ['kjuːbə] n. Kuba (das)

cubby[-hole] ['kʌbɪ(həʊl)] n. Kämmerchen, das

cube [kjuːb] n. Würfel, der. **cubic** ['kjuːbɪk] adj. a) würfelförmig; b) Kubik(meter usw.)

cubicle ['kjuːbɪkl] n. Kabine, die

'**Cub Scout** n. Wölfling, der

cuckoo ['kʊkuː] n. Kuckuck, der. '**cuckoo clock** n. Kuckucksuhr, die

cucumber ['kjuːkʌmbə(r)] n. [Salat]gurke, die

cuddle ['kʌdl] 1. n. enge Umarmung. 2. v.t. schmusen mit; hätscheln (kleines Kind). 3. v.i. schmusen

cuddly ['kʌdlɪ] adj. zum Schmusen nachgestellt. **cuddly 'toy** n. Plüschtier, das

cudgel ['kʌdʒl] n. Knüppel, der

¹**cue** [kjuː] n. (Billiards etc.) Queue, das

²**cue** n. (Theatre) Stichwort, das

¹**cuff** [kʌf] n. a) Manschette, die; **off the ~** (fig.) aus dem Stegreif; b) (Amer.: trouser turn-up) [Hosen]aufschlag, der

²**cuff** 1. v.t. ~ **sb.** jmdm. einen Klaps geben. 2. n. Klaps, der

'**cuff-link** n. Manschettenknopf, der

cul-de-sac ['kʌldəsæk] n. Sackgasse, die

culinary ['kʌlɪnərɪ] adj. kulinarisch

culminate ['kʌlmɪneɪt] v.i. gipfeln; ~ **in sth.** in etw. (Dat.) seinen Höchststand erreichen. **culmination** [kʌlmɪ'neɪʃn] n. Höhepunkt, der

culottes [kjuː'lɒts] n. pl. Hosenrock, der

culprit ['kʌlprɪt] n. Täter, der/Täterin, die

cult [kʌlt] n. Kult, der

cultivate ['kʌltɪveɪt] v.t. kultivieren (auch fig.); bestellen (Acker, Land); anbauen (Pflanzen). **cultivation** [kʌltɪ'veɪʃn] n. see cultivate: Kultivierung, die; Bestellen das; Anbau, der

culture ['kʌltʃə(r)] n. Kultur, die. '**cultured** adj. kultiviert

cumbersome ['kʌmbəsəm] adj. hinderlich (Kleider); sperrig (Pakete); schwerfällig (Arbeitsweise)

cunning ['kʌnɪŋ] 1. n. Schläue, die. 2. adj. schlau

cup [kʌp] n. a) Tasse, die; b) (prize, competition) Pokal, der; c) (~ful) Tasse, die; **a ~ of coffee/tea** eine Tasse Kaffee/Tee

cupboard ['kʌbəd] n. Schrank, der

'**Cup Final** n. Pokalendspiel, das

cupful ['kʌpfl] n. Tasse, die; **a ~ of water** eine Tasse Wasser

curable ['kjʊərəbl] adj. heilbar

curate ['kjʊərət] n. Kurat, der

curator [kjʊə'reɪtə(r)] n. (of museum) Direktor, der/Direktorin, die

curb [kɜːb] v.t. zügeln

curdle ['kɜːdl] v.i. gerinnen

cure [kjʊə(r)] 1. n. [Heil]mittel, das (for gegen); (fig.) Mittel, das. 2. v.t. a) heilen; b) [ein]pökeln (Fleisch)

curfew ['kɜːfjuː] n. Ausgangssperre, die

curiosity [kjʊərɪ'ɒsɪtɪ] n. a) Neugier[de], die; b) (object) Wunderding, das

curious ['kjʊərɪəs] adj. a) (inquisitive) neugierig; b) (strange, odd) seltsam

curl [kɜːl] 1. n. Locke, die. 2. v.t. locken. 3. v.i. a) sich locken; b) (Straße, Fluß): sich winden. '**curler** n. Lockenwickler, der. '**curly** adj. lockig

currant ['kʌrənt] n. Korinthe, die

currency ['kʌrənsɪ] n. (money) Währung, die; **foreign currencies** Devisen

current ['kʌrənt] 1. adj. a) verbreitet (Meinung); gebräuchlich (Wort); b) laufend (Jahr, Monat); c) (the present) aktuell (Ereignis, Mode); Tages-(politik, -preis); ~ **affairs** Tagespolitik, die. 2. n. a) (of water, air) Strömung, die; b) (Electr.) Strom, der. '**current account** n. Girokonto, das

'**currently** adv. zur Zeit

curriculum [kə'rɪkjʊləm] n. Lehrplan, der. **curriculum vitae** [~ 'viːtaɪ] n. Lebenslauf, der

¹**curry** [ˈkʌrɪ] *n.* Curry[gericht], *das*

²**curry** *v. t.* ~ **favour [with sb.]** sich [bei jmdm.] einschmeicheln

curse [kɜːs] **1.** *n.* Fluch, *der.* **2.** *v. t.* verfluchen. **3.** *v. i.* fluchen

cursory [ˈkɜːsərɪ] *adj.* flüchtig

curt [kɜːt] *adj.* kurz angebunden; kurz und schroff ⟨*Brief*⟩

curtain [ˈkɜːtən] *n.* Vorhang, *der;* **draw** *or* **pull the ~s** *(open)* die Vorhänge aufziehen; *(close)* die Vorhänge zuziehen

curtsy [ˈkɜːtsɪ] **1.** *n.* Knicks, *der.* **2.** *v. i.* einen Knicks machen (**to** vor + *Dat.*)

curve [kɜːv] **1.** *v. t.* krümmen. **2.** *v. i.* ⟨*Straße, Fluß:*⟩ eine Biegung machen. **3.** *n.* Kurve, *die*

cushion [ˈkʊʃn] **1.** *n.* Kissen, *das.* **2.** *v. t.* dämpfen ⟨*Aufprall, Stoß*⟩

cushy [ˈkʊʃɪ] *adj. (coll.)* bequem

custard [ˈkʌstəd] *n.* ≈ Vanillesoße, *die*

custodian [kʌˈstəʊdɪən] *n. (of museum)* Wächter, *der*/Wächterin, *die; (of valuables)* Hüter, *der*/Hüterin, *die*

custody [ˈkʌstədɪ] *n.* **a)** *(care)* Obhut, *die;* **b)** *(imprisonment)* **[be] in ~:** in Haft [sein]

custom [ˈkʌstəm] *n.* **a)** Brauch, *der;* **b)** *in pl. (duty on imports)* Zoll, *der.* '**customs officer** *n.* Zollbeamter, *der*/-beamtin, *die.* **customary** [ˈkʌstəmərɪ] *adj.* üblich

customer [ˈkʌstəmə(r)] *n.* Kunde, *der*/Kundin, *die*

cut [kʌt] **1.** *v. t.,* -**tt**-, **cut a)** schneiden; durchschneiden ⟨*Seil*⟩; ~ **one's way** sich *(Dat. od. Akk.)* ins Bein schneiden; **b)** abschneiden ⟨*Scheibe*⟩; schneiden ⟨*Hecke*⟩; mähen ⟨*Getreide, Gras*⟩; ~ **one's nails** sich *(Dat.)* die Nägel schneiden; **c)** *(reduce)* senken ⟨*Preise*⟩; kürzen ⟨*Lohn*⟩; **d)** ~ **sth. short** *(interrupt)* etw. abbrechen. **2.** *v. i.,* -**tt**-, **cut a)** ⟨*Messer:*⟩ schneiden; **b)** ~ **through** *or* **across the field/park** [quer] über das Feld/durch den Park gehen. **3.** *n.* **a)** *(act of cutting)* Schnitt, *der;* **b)** *(stroke, blow) (with knife)* Schnitt, *der; (with sword, whip)* Hieb, *der;* **c)** *(reduction)* Kürzung, *die; (in prices)* Senkung, *die; (in services)* Verringerung, *die;* **d)** *(of meat)* Stück, *das.* **cut a'way** *v. t.* abschneiden. **cut 'back** *v. t.* **a)** *(reduce)* einschränken; **b)** *(prune)* stutzen. **cut 'down 1.** *v. t.* **a)** fällen ⟨*Baum*⟩; **b)** *(reduce)* einschränken. **2.** *v. i.* ~ **down on sth.** etw. einschränken. **cut 'off** *v. t.* abschnei-

den; unterbrechen ⟨*Telefongespräch, Sprecher*⟩. **cut 'out 1.** *v. t.* **a)** ausschneiden **(of** aus); **b)** **be ~ out for** geeignet sein zu. **2.** *v. i.* ⟨*Motor:*⟩ aussetzen. **cut 'up** *v. t.* zerschneiden.

cut 'glass *n.* Kristall[glas], *das*

cutlery [ˈkʌtlərɪ] *n.* Besteck, *das*

cutlet [ˈkʌtlɪt] *n.* Kotelett, *das*

'**cut-price** *adj.* herabgesetzt

'**cutting 1.** *adj.* beißend ⟨*Bemerkung, Antwort*⟩. **2.** *n. (from newspaper)* Ausschnitt, *der*

c. v. *abbr.* **curriculum vitae**

cycle [ˈsaɪkl] **1.** *n.* **a)** *(recurrent period)* Zyklus, *der;* **b)** *(bicycle)* Rad, *das.* **2.** *v. i.* radfahren. **cyclist** [ˈsaɪklɪst] *n.* Radfahrer, *der*/-fahrerin, *die*

cylinder [ˈsɪlɪndə(r)] *n.* Zylinder, *der.* **cylindrical** [sɪˈlɪndrɪkl] *adj.* zylindrisch

cymbals [ˈsɪmblz] *n. pl.* Becken *Pl.*

cynic [ˈsɪnɪk] *n.* Zyniker, *der.* **cynical** [ˈsɪnɪkl] *adj.* zynisch; bissig ⟨*Bemerkung, Worte*⟩. **cynicism** [ˈsɪnɪsɪzm] *n.* Zynismus, *der*

Cyprus [ˈsaɪprəs] *pr. n.* Zypern *(das)*

Czech [tʃek] **1.** *adj.* tschechisch. **2.** *n.* **a)** *(language)* Tschechisch, *das;* **b)** *(person)* Tscheche, *der*/Tschechin, *die*

Czechoslovakia [tʃekəʊsləˈvækɪə] *n.* die Tschechoslowakei. **Czechoslovakian** [tʃekəʊsləˈvækɪən] **1.** *adj.* tschechoslowakisch. **2.** *pr. n.* Tschechoslowake, *der*/Tschechoslowakin, *die*

D

D, d [diː] *n.* D, d, *das*

dab [dæb] **1.** *n.* Tupfer, *der.* **2.** *v. t.,* -**bb**- abtupfen; ~ **sth. on** *or* **against sth.** etw. auf etw. *(Akk.)* tupfen

dabble [ˈdæbl] *v. i.* ~ **in sth.** sich in etw. *(Dat.)* versuchen

dachshund [ˈdækshʊnd] *n.* Dackel, *der*

dad [dæd] *n. (coll.)* Vater, *der*

daddy [ˈdædɪ] *n. (coll.)* Vati, *der (fam.).* **daddy-'long-legs** *n.* Schnake, *die*

daffodil [ˈdæfədɪl] *n.* Osterglocke, *die*

daft [dɑːft] *adj.* doof *(ugs.)*

dagger ['dægə(r)] *n.* Dolch, *der*

daily ['deɪlɪ] **1.** *adj.* täglich; ~ |news|-paper Tageszeitung, *die.* **2.** *adv.* täglich. **3.** *n.* Tageszeitung, *die*

dainty ['deɪntɪ] *adj.* zierlich; anmutig ⟨Bewegung, Person⟩; zart ⟨Gesichtszüge⟩

dairy ['deərɪ] *n.* **a)** Molkerei, *die;* **b)** *(shop)* Milchladen, *der*

dais ['deɪɪs] *n.* Podium, *das*

daisy ['deɪzɪ] *n.* Gänseblümchen, *das*

dam [dæm] **1.** *n.* [Stau]damm, *der.* **2.** *v. t.,* -mm-: **a)** ~ |up| sth. etw. ab-blocken; **b)** aufstauen ⟨Fluß⟩

damage ['dæmɪdʒ] **1.** *n.* Schaden, *der.* **2.** *v. t.* beschädigen. **damaging** ['dæmɪdʒɪŋ] *adj.* schädlich (to für)

damn [dæm] **1.** *v. t.* verdammen. **2.** *adj., adv., int. (coll.)* verdammt *(ugs.).* **3.** *n.* he doesn't give or care a ~: ihm ist es völlig wurscht *(ugs.)*

damp [dæmp] **1.** *adj.* feucht. **2.** *v. t. see* **dampen. 3.** *n.* Feuchtigkeit, *die*

dampen ['dæmpn] *v. t.* befeuchten; *(fig.)* dämpfen ⟨Begeisterung, Eifer⟩

dampness *n.* Feuchtigkeit, *die*

dance [dɑːns] **1.** *v. i. & t.* tanzen. **2.** *n.* **a)** Tanz, *der;* **b)** *(party)* Tanzveranstaltung, *die; (private)* Tanzparty, *die.*

'dance-hall *n.* Tanzsaal, *der*

'dancer *n.* Tänzer, *der*/Tänzerin, *die*

dandelion ['dændɪlaɪən] *n.* Löwenzahn, *der*

dandruff ['dændrʌf] *n.* [Kopf]schuppen *Pl.*

Dane [deɪn] *n.* Däne, *der*/Dänin, *die*

danger ['deɪndʒə(r)] *n.* Gefahr, *die;* in/out of ~: in/außer Gefahr. **dangerous** ['deɪndʒərəs] *adj.,* **dangerously** *adv.* gefährlich

dangle ['dæŋgl] **1.** *v. i.* baumeln (from an + *Dat.*). **2.** *v. t.* baumeln lassen

Danish ['deɪnɪʃ] **1.** *adj.* dänisch; sb. is ~: jmd. ist Däne/Dänin. **2.** *n.* Dänisch, *das; see also* **English 2 a**

dank [dæŋk] *adj.* feucht

Danube ['dænjuːb] *pr. n.* Donau, *die*

dare [deə(r)] **1.** *v. t.* **a)** [es] wagen; ~ to do sth. [es] wagen, etw. zu tun; **b)** *(challenge)* ~ sb. to do sth. jmdn. aufstacheln, etw. zu tun; I ~ you! trau dich! **2.** *n.* Mutprobe, *die.* **daring** ['deərɪŋ] *adj.* kühn

dark [dɑːk] **1.** *adj.* dunkel; *(dark-haired)* dunkelhaarig; ~blue/-brown dunkelblau/-braun; ~ glasses dunkle Brille. **2.** *n.* **a)** Dunkel, *das;* in the ~: im Dunkeln; keep sb. in the ~ *(fig.)*

jmdn. im dunkeln lassen; **b)** *no art. (nightfall)* Einbruch der Dunkelheit.

darken ['dɑːkn] *v. t.* verdunkeln.

'darkness *n.* Dunkelheit, *die*

'dark-room *n.* Dunkelkammer, *die*

darling ['dɑːlɪŋ] *n.* Liebling, *der*

darn [dɑːn] *v. t.* stopfen

dart [dɑːt] **1.** *n.* **a)** *(missile)* Pfeil, *der;* **b)** *(Sport)* Wurfpfeil, *der;* ~s *sing. (game)* Darts, *das.* **2.** *v. i.* sausen.

'dartboard *n.* Dartscheibe, *die*

dash [dæʃ] **1.** *v. i.* sausen. **2.** *v. t. (fling)* schleudern. **3.** *n.* **a)** make a ~: rasen *(ugs.)* (for zu); **b)** *(horizontal stroke)* Gedankenstrich, *der;* **c)** *(small amount)* Schuß, *der*

'dashboard *n.* Armaturenbrett, *das*

data ['deɪtə, 'dɑːtə] *n.* Daten *Pl.* **data 'processing** *n.* Datenverarbeitung, *die*

¹date [deɪt] *n. (Bot.)* Dattel, *die*

²date 1. *n.* **a)** Datum, *die; (on coin etc.)* Jahreszahl, *die;* ~ of birth Geburtsdatum, *das;* be out of ~: altmodisch sein; to ~: bis heute; **b)** *(coll.: appointment)* Verabredung, *die;* have/make a ~ with sb. mit jmdm. verabredet sein/sich mit jmdm. verabreden. **2.** *v. t.* **a)** datieren; **b)** *(coll.: make seem old)* alt machen. **3.** *v. i.* ~ back to/~ from stammen aus. **dated** ['deɪtɪd] *adj.* altmodisch. **'date-line** *n.* Datumsgrenze, *die*

dative ['deɪtɪv] *adj. & n.* ~ |case| Dativ, *der*

daub [dɔːb] *v. t. (smear)* beschmieren; *(put crudely)* schmieren

daughter ['dɔːtə(r)] *n.* Tochter, *die.* **'daughter-in-law** *n., pl.* **daughters-in-law** Schwiegertochter, *die*

daunt [dɔːnt] *v. t.* entmutigen

dawdle ['dɔːdl] *v. i.* bummeln *(ugs.)*

dawn [dɔːn] **1.** *v. i.* dämmern; sth. ~s |up|on sb. etw. dämmert jmdm. **2.** *n.* [Morgen]dämmerung, *die;* at ~: im Morgengrauen

day [deɪ] *n.* Tag, *der;* all ~ |long| den ganzen Tag [lang]; for two ~s zwei Tage [lang]; the ~ before yesterday/after tomorrow vorgestern/übermorgen; ~ after ~: Tag für Tag; ~ in ~ out tagaus, tagein; in the ~s when ...: zu der Zeit, als ...; these ~s heutzutage; in those ~s damals

day: ~break *n.* Tagesanbruch, *der;* ~dream **1.** *n.* Tagtraum, *der;* **2.** *v. i.* träumen; ~light *n.* Tageslicht, *das;* in broad ~light am hellichten Tag[e]; ~re'turn *n.* Tagesrückfahrkarte, *die;* ~**time** *n.* Tag, *der;* ~-**to**-~ *adj.* [tag]täglich; ~ **trip** *n.* Tagesausflug, *der*

daze ['deɪz] *v. t.* benommen machen. **dazed** ['deɪzd] *adj.* benommen

dazzle ['dæzl] *v. t.* blenden

DC *abbr.* direct current GS

dead [ded] **1.** *adj.* **a)** tot; **b)** plötzlich ⟨Halt⟩: genau ⟨Mitte⟩; **c)** *(numb)* taub. **2.** *adv.* völlig; ~ **straight** schnurgerade; ~ **easy/slow** kinderleicht/ganz langsam; ~ **on time** auf die Minute; ~ **tired** todmüde

deaden ['dedn] *v. t.* dämpfen; betäuben ⟨Schmerz⟩

dead: ~ **end** *n.* Sackgasse, *die;* ~**'heat** *n.* totes Rennen; ~**line** *n.* [letzter] Termin; ~**lock** *n.* völliger Stillstand

deadly ['dedlɪ] *adj.* tödlich; *(fig. coll.: boring)* todlangweilig

Dead 'Sea *pr. n.* Tote Meer, *das*

deaf [def] *adj.* taub; ~ **and dumb** taubstumm. **deafen** ['defn] *v. t.* ~ **sb.** bei jmdm. zur Taubheit führen; **I was** ~**ed by the noise** *(fig.)* ich war von dem Lärm wie betäubt. **'deafening** *adj.* ohrenbetäubend. **'deafness** *n.* Taubheit, *die*

¹deal [di:l] **1.** *v. t.,* **dealt** [delt] **a)** *(Cards)* austeilen; **b)** ~ **sb. a blow** jmdm. einen Schlag versetzen. **2.** *v. i.,* **dealt a) *(do business)* ~ **in sth.** mit etw. handeln; **b)** ~ **with sth.** *(occupy oneself)* mit etw. befassen; *(manage)* mit etw. fertig werden; *(be about)* von etw. handeln; ~ **with sb.** mit jmdm. fertig werden. **3.** *n. (coll.: arrangement)* Geschäft, *das.* **deal 'out** *v. t.* verteilen

²deal *n.* **a great** *or* **good** ~: viel; *(often)* ziemlich viel; **a great** *or* **good** ~ **of** viel

'dealer *n.* **a)** Händler, *der;* **b)** *(Cards)* Geber, *der;* **he's the** ~: er gibt

'dealings *n. pl.* **have** ~ **with sb.** mit jmdm. zu tun haben

dealt *see* ¹deal 1, 2

dean [di:n] *n. (Eccl.)* Dechant, *der*

dear [dɪə(r)] **1.** *adj.* **a)** lieb; **sb./sth. is** ~ **to sb.['s heart]** jmd. liebt jmdn./etw.; *(beginning letter)* **D**~ **Sir/Madam** Sehr geehrter Herr/Sehr verehrte gnädige Frau; **D**~ **Mr Jones/Mrs Jones** Sehr geehrter Herr Jones/Sehr verehrte Frau Jones; **D**~ **Malcolm/Emily** Lieber Malcolm/Liebe Emily; **b)** *(expensive)* teuer. **2.** *int.* ~, ~!, ~ **me!**, **oh** ~! [ach] du liebe od. meine Güte! **'dearly** *adv.* **a)** von ganzem Herzen; **b)** *(at high price)* teuer

dearth [dɜ:θ] *n.* Mangel, *der* **(of** an + *Dat.)*

death [deθ] *n.* **a)** Tod, *der;* ... **to** ~: zu Tode ...; **bleed to** ~: verbluten; **b)** *(instance)* Todesfall, *der*

death: ~ **penalty** *n.* Todesstrafe, *die;* ~ **sentence** *n.* Todesurteil, *das;* ~-**trap** *n.* lebensgefährliche Sache

debatable [dɪ'beɪtəbl] *adj. (questionable)* fraglich

debate [dɪ'beɪt] *n.* Debatte, *die*

debit ['debɪt] **1.** *n.* Soll, *das.* **2.** *v. t.* belasten ⟨Konto⟩

debris ['debri:] *n.* Trümmer *Pl.*

debt [det] *n.* Schuld, *die;* **be in** ~: Schulden haben; **get into** ~: in Schulden geraten. **debtor** ['detə(r)] *n.* Schuldner, *der/*Schuldnerin, *die*

début *(Amer.: debut)* ['deɪbu:, 'deɪbju:] *n.* Debüt, *das*

Dec. *abbr.* December Dez.

decade ['dekeɪd] *n.* Jahrzehnt, *das*

decadent ['dekədənt] *adj.* dekadent

decanter [dɪ'kæntə(r)] *n.* Karaffe, *die*

decay [dɪ'keɪ] **1.** *v. i.* verrotten; ⟨Gebäude:⟩ zerfallen; ⟨Zahn:⟩ faul werden. **2.** *n.* Verrotten, *das;* ⟨of building⟩ Zerfall, *der;* ⟨of tooth⟩ Fäule, *die*

deceased [dɪ'si:st] **1.** *adj* verstorben. **2.** *n.* Verstorbene, *der/die*

deceit [dɪ'si:t] *n.* Täuschung, *die.* **deceitful** [dɪ'si:tfl] *adj.* falsch ⟨Person, Art⟩; hinterlistig ⟨Trick⟩

deceive [dɪ'si:v] *v. t.* täuschen; *(be unfaithful to)* betrügen

December [dɪ'sembə(r)] *n.* Dezember, *der; see also* August

decency ['di:sənsɪ] *n.* Anstand, *der*

decent ['di:sənt] *adj.* anständig

deception [dɪ'sepʃn] *n.* Betrug, *der;* *(being deceived)* Täuschung, *die.* **deceptive** [dɪ'septɪv] *adj.* trügerisch

decibel ['desɪbel] *n.* Dezibel, *das*

decide [dɪ'saɪd] **1.** *v. t.* **a)** *(settle, judge)* entscheiden (**+** *Akk.*); **b)** *(resolve)* ~ **that ...:** beschließen, daß ...; ~ **to do sth.** sich entschließen, etw. zu tun. **2.** *v. i.* sich entscheiden *(in favour of* zugunsten von, **against** gegen). **de-'cided** *adj.,* **de'cidedly** *adv.* entschieden

deciduous [dɪ'sɪdjʊəs] *adj.* ~ **tree** ≈ Laubbaum, *der*

decimal ['desɪml] **1.** *n.* Dezimalbruch, *der.* **2.** *adj.* Dezimal-; ~ **'point** Komma, *das*

decimate ['desɪmeɪt] *v. t.* dezimieren

decipher [dɪ'saɪfə(r)] *v. t.* entziffern

decision [dɪ'sɪʒn] *n.* Entscheidung,

die. **decisive** [dɪˈsaɪsɪv] *adj.* entscheidend

deck [dek] *n.* Deck, *das; on ~:* an Deck; **below ~ls** unter Deck. **'deckchair** *n.* Liegestuhl, *der*

declaration [dekləˈreɪʃn] *n.* Erklärung, *die*

declare [dɪˈkleə(r)] *v.t.* erklären; kundtun *(geh.)* ⟨Wunsch, Absicht⟩; *~ sth./sb.* [to be] sth. etw./jmdn. für etw. erklären

declension [dɪˈklenʃn] *n.* Deklination, *die*

decline [dɪˈklaɪn] 1. *v.i.* nachlassen; ⟨Anzahl:⟩ sinken. 2. *v.t.* a) ablehnen; b) *(Ling.)* deklinieren. 3. *n. see* 1: Nachlassen, *das/Sinken, das (in Gen.);* *be on the ~:* nachlassen/sinken

decode [diːˈkəʊd] *v.t.* entziffern

decompose [diːkəmˈpəʊz] *v.i.* sich zersetzen

décor [ˈdeɪkɔː(r)] *n.* Ausstattung, *die*

decorate [ˈdekəreɪt] *v.t.* a) schmücken ⟨Raum, Straße, Baum⟩; verzieren ⟨Kuchen, Kleid⟩; (paint) streichen; (wallpaper) tapezieren; b) (award medal etc. to) auszeichnen. **decoration** [dekəˈreɪʃn] *n.* a) Schmücken, *das;* (with paint) Streichen, *das;* (with wallpaper) Tapezieren, *das;* (of cake, dress) Verzieren, *das;* b) (adornment) Schmuck, *der;* c) (medal etc.) Auszeichnung, *die.* **decorative** [ˈdekərətɪv] *adj.* dekorativ. **decorator** [ˈdekəreɪtə(r)] *n.* Maler, *der;* (paper-hanger) Tapezierer, *der*

decorum [dɪˈkɔːrəm] *n.* Schicklichkeit, *die (geh.)*

decoy [ˈdiːkɔɪ] *n.* Lockvogel, *der*

decrease 1. [dɪˈkriːs] *v.i.* abnehmen; ⟨Stärke:⟩ nachlassen. 2. [dɪˈkriːs] *v.t.* [ver]mindern ⟨Wert, Lärm⟩; schmälern ⟨Popularität, Macht⟩. 3. [ˈdiːkriːs] *n.* Rückgang, *der;* (in weight) Abnahme, *die;* (in strength) Nachlassen, *das;* (in value, noise) Minderung, *die*

decree [dɪˈkriː] 1. *n.* Dekret, *das;* Erlaß, *der.* 2. *v.t.* verfügen

decrepit [dɪˈkrepɪt] *adj.* altersschwach; (dilapidated) heruntergekommen

dedicate [ˈdedɪkeɪt] *v.t. ~ sth. to sb.* jmdm. etw. widmen. **'dedicated** *adj.* a) (devoted) *be ~ to sth./sb.* nur für etw./jmdn. leben; b) (to vocation) hingebungsvoll; *a ~ teacher* ein Lehrer mit Leib und Seele. **dedication** [dedɪˈkeɪʃn] *n.* a) (to Dat.); b) (devotion) Hingabe, *die*

deduce [dɪˈdjuːs] *v.t. ~ sth.* [from sth.] etw. [aus etw.] schließen

deduct [dɪˈdʌkt] *v.t. ~ sth.* [from sth.] etw. [von etw.] abziehen. **deduction** [dɪˈdʌkʃn] *n.* a) (deducting) Abzug, *der;* b) (deducing, thing deduced) Ableitung, *die;* c) (amount) Abzüge *Pl.*

deed [diːd] *n.* a) Tat, *die;* b) (Law) Urkunde, *die*

deem [diːm] *v.t.* erachten für

deep [diːp] 1. *adj.* (lit. or fig.) tief; tiefgründig ⟨Bemerkung⟩; *water ten feet ~:* drei Meter tiefes Wasser; *take a ~ breath* tief Atem holen; *be ~ in thought* in Gedanken versunken sein. 2. *adv.* tief. **'deepen** 1. *v.t.* vertiefen. 2. *v.i.* sich vertiefen. **deep-'freeze** *v.t.* tiefgefrieren. **'deeply** *adv.* (lit. or fig.) tief; äußerst ⟨interessiert, dankbar⟩

deer [dɪə(r)] *n., pl. same* Hirsch, *der;* (roe~) Reh, *das*

deface [dɪˈfeɪs] *v.t.* verunstalten

defamation [defəˈmeɪʃn] *n.* Diffamierung, *die.* **defamatory** [dɪˈfæmətərɪ] *adj.* diffamierend

default [dɪˈfɔːlt; dɪˈfɒlt] 1. *n.* lose/go by *~:* durch Abwesenheit verlieren/nicht zur Geltung kommen; *win by ~:* durch Nichterscheinen des Gegners gewinnen. 2. *v.i. ~ on one's payments/debts* seinen Zahlungsverpflichtungen nicht nachkommen

defeat [dɪˈfiːt] 1. *v.t.* besiegen. 2. *n.* (being ~ed) Niederlage, *die;* (~ing) Sieg, *der* (of über + Akk.). **de'featist** *adj.* defätistisch

defect 1. [ˈdiːfekt] *n.* a) (lack) Mangel, *der;* b) (shortcoming) Fehler, *der.* 2. [dɪˈfekt] *v.i.* überlaufen (to zu). **de'fection** [dɪˈfekʃn] *n.* Flucht, *die.* **defective** [dɪˈfektɪv] *adj.* defekt ⟨Maschine⟩; fehlerhaft ⟨Material, Arbeiten, Methode⟩. **defector** [dɪˈfektə(r)] *n.* Überläufer, *der/*-läuferin, *die*

defence [dɪˈfens] *n.* (Brit.) Verteidigung, *die;* (means of ~) Schutz, *der.* **de'fenceless** *adj.* wehrlos

defend [dɪˈfend] *v.t.* verteidigen. **de'fendant** [dɪˈfendənt] *n.* (Law) (accused) Angeklagte, *der/die;* (sued) Beklagte, *der/die.* **de'fender** *n.* Verteidiger, *der*

defense *etc.* (Amer.) *see* defence *etc.*

defensive [dɪˈfensɪv] 1. *adj.* defensiv. 2. *n. be on the ~:* in der Defensive sein

¹defer [dɪˈfɜː(r)] *v.t., -rr-:* aufschieben

²defer *v.i., -rr- ~:* [to sb.] sich [jmdm.] beugen. **deference** [ˈdefərəns] *n.* Respekt, *der;* **in** ~ **to sb./sth.** aus Achtung vor jmdm./etw. **deferential** [defə'renʃl] *adj.* respektvoll

defiance [dɪ'faɪəns] *n.* Trotz, *der;* **in** ~ **of sb./sth.** jmdm./einer Sache zum Trotz

defiant [dɪ'faɪənt] *adj.,* **de'fiantly** *adv.* trotzig

deficiency [dɪ'fɪʃənsɪ] *n.* Mangel, *der*

deficient [dɪ'fɪʃənt] *adj.* unzulänglich; **sb./sth. is** ~ **in sth.** jmdm./einer Sache mangelt es an etw. *(Dat.)*

deficit ['defɪsɪt] *n.* Defizit, *das* (of an + *Dat.*)

defile [dɪ'faɪl] *v. t.* verpesten ⟨*Luft*⟩; beflecken ⟨*Reinheit, Unschuld*⟩

define [dɪ'faɪn] *v. t.* definieren

definite ['defɪnɪt] *adj.* bestimmt; eindeutig ⟨*Antwort, Entscheidung, die Beschluß, Verbesserung*⟩; klar umrissen ⟨*Ziel, Plan*⟩; klar ⟨*Vorstellung*⟩; genau ⟨*Zeitpunkt*⟩. **'definitely** 1. *adv.* bestimmt; eindeutig ⟨*festlegen, größer sein, verbessert*⟩; endgültig ⟨*entscheiden*⟩. 2. *int. (coll.)* na, klar *(ugs.)*

definition [defɪ'nɪʃn] *n.* Definition, *die;* *(Telev., Phot.)* Schärfe, *die*

definitive [dɪ'fɪnɪtɪv] *adj.* endgültig ⟨*Beschluß, Antwort, Urteil*⟩; *(authoritative)* maßgeblich

deflate [dɪ'fleɪt] *v. t.* die Luft ablassen aus; *(fig.)* ernüchtern. **deflation** [dɪ'fleɪʃn] *n. (Econ.)* Deflation, *die*

deflect [dɪ'flekt] *v. t.* brechen ⟨*Licht*⟩; ~ **sb./sth. [from sb./sth.]** jmdm./etw. [von jmdm./etwas] ablenken

deform [dɪ'fɔːm] *v. t.* deformieren. **deformed** [dɪ'fɔːmd] *adj.* entstellt ⟨*Gesicht*⟩; verunstaltet ⟨*Person, Körperteil*⟩. **deformity** [dɪ'fɔːmɪtɪ] *n. (malformation)* Verunstaltung, *die*

defraud [dɪ'frɔːd] *v. t.* ~ **sb. [of sth.]** jmdn. [um etw.] betrügen

defray [dɪ'freɪ] *v. t.* bestreiten

defrost [diː'frɒst] *v. t.* auftauen ⟨*Speisen*⟩; abtauen ⟨*Kühlschrank*⟩

deft [deft] *adj.,* **'deftly** *adv.* sicher und geschickt

defunct [dɪ'fʌŋkt] *adj.* defekt ⟨*Maschine*⟩; veraltet ⟨*Gesetz*⟩

defuse [diː'fjuːz] *v. t.* entschärfen

defy [dɪ'faɪ] *v. t.* a) *(resist openly)* ~ **sb.** jmdm. trotzen; b) *(refuse to obey)* ~ **sb./sth.** sich jmdm./einer Sache widersetzen

degenerate [dɪ'dʒenəreɪt] *v. i.* ~ **[into sth.]** zu etw. ⟨*übel*⟩ verkommen

degradation [degrə'deɪʃn] *n.* Erniedrigung, *die*

degrade [dɪ'greɪd] *v. t.* erniedrigen

degree [dɪ'griː] *n.* a) Grad, *der;* **20** ~**s** 20 Grad; b) *(academic rank)* [akademischer] Grad

de-ice [diː'aɪs] *v. t.* enteisen

deign [deɪn] *v. t.* ~ **to do sth.** sich [dazu] herablassen, etw. zu tun

deity ['diːɪtɪ] *n.* Gottheit, *die*

dejected [dɪ'dʒektɪd] *adj.* niedergeschlagen. **dejection** [dɪ'dʒekʃn] *n.* Niedergeschlagenheit, *die*

delay [dɪ'leɪ] 1. *v. t. (make late)* aufhalten; verzögern ⟨*Ankunft, Abfahrt*⟩; **the train has been** ~**ed** der Zug hat Verspätung. 2. *v. i.* warten. 3. *n.* a) *(Transport)* Verzögerung, *die* (to bei); b) *(Transport)* Verspätung, *die*

delectable [dɪ'lektəbl] *adj.* köstlich

delegate 1. ['delɪgət] *n.* Delegierte, *der/die.* 2. ['delɪgeɪt] *v. t.* delegieren (**to** an + *Akk.*). **delegation** [delɪ'geɪʃn] *n.* Delegation, *die*

delete [dɪ'liːt] *v. t.* streichen (**from** in + *Dat.*); *(Computing)* löschen. **deletion** [dɪ'liːʃn] *n.* Streichung, *die;* *(Computing)* Löschung, *die*

deliberate [dɪ'lɪbərət] *adj.* a) *(intentional)* absichtlich; bewußt ⟨*Lüge, Irreführung*⟩; b) *(fully considered)* wohlüberlegt. **de'liberately** *adv.* absichtlich. **deliberation** [dɪlɪbə'reɪʃn] *n.* Überlegung, *die;* *(discussion)* Beratung, *die*

delicacy ['delɪkəsɪ] *n.* a) *(tactfulness and care)* Feingefühl, *das;* b) *(food)* Delikatesse, *die*

delicate ['delɪkət] *adj.* zart; *(requiring careful handling)* empfindlich; delikat ⟨*Frage, Angelegenheit*⟩

delicatessen [delɪkə'tesən] *n.* Feinkostgeschäft, *das*

delicious [dɪ'lɪʃəs] *adj.* köstlich

delight [dɪ'laɪt] 1. *v. t.* erfreuen. 2. *v. i.* **sb.** ~**s in doing sth.** es macht jmdm. Freude, etw. zu tun. 3. *n.* Freude, *die* (**at** über + *Akk.;* **in** an + *Dat.*). **de'lighted** *adj.* **be** ~ ⟨*Person:*⟩ hocherfreut sein; **be** ~ **by or with sth.** sich über etw. *(Akk.)* freuen. **delightful** [dɪ'laɪtfl] *adj.* wunderbar; köstlich ⟨*Geschmack*⟩; reizend ⟨*Person, Landschaft*⟩. **de'lightfully** *adv.* wunderbar

delinquent [dɪ'lɪŋkwənt] 1. *n.* Randalierer, *der.* 2. *adj.* kriminell

delirious [dɪ'lɪrɪəs] *adj.* **be** ~: im Delirium sein; **be** ~ **[with sth.]** *(fig.)* außer sich [vor etw. *(Dat.)*] sein

delirium [dɪ'lɪrɪəm] *n.* Delirium, *das*

deliver [dɪˈlɪvə(r)] v. t. **a)** bringen; liefern ⟨Ware⟩; zustellen ⟨Post, Telegramm⟩; überbringen ⟨Botschaft⟩; **b)** halten ⟨Rede⟩. **delivery** [dɪˈlɪvərɪ] n. Lieferung, die; (of letters, parcels) Zustellung, die. **deˈlivery van** n. Lieferwagen, der

delta [ˈdeltə] n. Delta, das

delude [dɪˈljuːd] v. t. täuschen

deluge [ˈdeljuːdʒ] **1.** n. sintflutartiger Regen. **2.** v. t. überschwemmen

delusion [dɪˈljuːʒn] n. Illusion, die

de luxe [dəˈlʌks] adj. Luxus-

demand [dɪˈmɑːnd] **1.** n. Forderung, die (for nach); (for commodity) Nachfrage, die; **sth. is in ~**: etw. ist gefragt/jmd. ist begehrt. **2.** v. t. verlangen (of, from von); fordern ⟨Recht⟩. **deˈmanding** adj. anspruchsvoll

demented [dɪˈmentɪd] adj. wahnsinnig

deˈmobilize v. t. demobilisieren ⟨Armee, Kriegsschiff⟩; aus dem Kriegsdienst entlassen ⟨Soldat⟩

democracy [dɪˈmɒkrəsɪ] n. Demokratie, die. **Democrat** [ˈdeməkræt] n. (Amer. Polit.) Demokrat, der/Demokratin, die. **democratic** [deməˈkrætɪk] adj., **democratically** [deməˈkrætɪkəlɪ] adv. demokratisch

demolish [dɪˈmɒlɪʃ] v. t. abreißen. **demolition** [deməˈlɪʃn] n. Abriß, der; ~**work** Abbrucharbeit, die

demon [ˈdiːmən] n. Dämon, der

demonstrate [ˈdemənstreɪt] **1.** v. t. zeigen; (be proof of) zeigen; beweisen. **2.** v. i. demonstrieren. **demonstration** [demənˈstreɪʃn] n. (also Pol. etc.) Demonstration, die; (proof) Beweis, der. **demonstrative** [dəˈmɒnstrətɪv] adj. **a)** offen ⟨Person⟩; **b)** (Ling.) Demonstrativ-. **demonstrator** [ˈdemənstreɪtə(r)] n. (Pol. etc.) Demonstrant, der/Demonstrantin, die

demoralize [dɪˈmɒrəlaɪz] v. t. demoralisieren

demote [diːˈməʊt] v. t. degradieren (to zu). **demotion** [diːˈməʊʃn] n. Degradierung, die (to zu)

demur [dɪˈmɜː(r)] v. i., -rr- Einwände erheben

demure [dɪˈmjʊə(r)] adj. betont zurückhaltend

den [den] n. Höhle, die

denial [dɪˈnaɪəl] n. (refusal) Verweigerung, die; (of request) Ablehnung, die

denim [ˈdenɪm] n. Denim ⓌＺ, der; Jeansstoff, der; ~ **jacket** Jeansjacke, die; ~**s** Bluejeans Pl.

Denmark [ˈdenmɑːk] pr. n. Dänemark (das)

denomination [dɪnɒmɪˈneɪʃn] n. (Relig.) Konfession, die

denote [dɪˈnəʊt] v. t. bezeichnen

denounce [dɪˈnaʊns] v. t. denunzieren; (accuse publicly) beschuldigen

dense [dens] adj. **a)** dicht; massiv ⟨Körper⟩; **b)** (stupid) dumm. **ˈdensely** adv. dicht; ~ **packed** dichtgedrängt. **density** [ˈdensɪtɪ] n. Dichte, die

dent [dent] **1.** n. Beule, die. **2.** v. t. einbeulen

dental [ˈdentl] adj. Zahn-. **dental floss** [ˈdentl flɒs] n. Zahnseide, die

dentist [ˈdentɪst] n. Zahnarzt, der/-ärztin, die. **dentistry** [ˈdentɪstrɪ] n. Zahnheilkunde, die

denture [ˈdentʃə(r)] n. ~|**s**| Zahnprothese, die

denunciation [dɪnʌnsɪˈeɪʃn] n. Denunziation, die; (public accusation) Beschuldigung, die

deny [dɪˈnaɪ] v. t. (declare untrue) bestreiten; (refuse) ~ **sb. sth.** jmdm. etw. verweigern; ~ **sb.'s request** jmdm. seine Bitte abschlagen

deodorant [diːˈəʊdərənt] **1.** adj. deodorierend. **2.** n. Deodorant, das

depart [dɪˈpɑːt] v. i. **a)** (go away) weggehen; **b)** (set out, leave) abfahren; (on one's journey) abreisen; **c)** (fig.: deviate) abweichen (**from** von)

department [dɪˈpɑːtmənt] n. Abteilung, die; (government ~) Ministerium, das; (of university) Seminar, das. **deˈpartment store** n. Kaufhaus, das

departure [dɪˈpɑːtʃə(r)] n. **a)** Abreise, die; (of train, bus, ship) Abfahrt, die; (of aircraft) Abflug, der; **b)** (deviation) ~ **from sth.** Abweichen von etw. **deˈparture lounge** n. Abflughalle, die

depend [dɪˈpend] v. i. **a)** ~ |**up**|**on** abhängen von; **it/that ~s** es kommt drauf an; **b)** (rely, trust) ~ |**up**|**on** sich verlassen auf (+ Akk.); (have to rely on) angewiesen sein auf (+ Akk.). **dependable** [dɪˈpendəbl] adj. zuverlässig. **dependant** [dɪˈpendənt] n. Abhängige, der/die. **dependence** [dɪˈpendəns] n. Abhängigkeit, die. **dependent** [dɪˈpendənt] **1.** n. see **dependant. 2.** adj. abhängig

depict [dɪˈpɪkt] v. t. darstellen

deplete [dɪˈpliːt] v. t. erheblich verringern

deplorable [dɪˈplɔːrəbl] adj. beklagenswert

deplore [dɪ'plɔ:(r)] *v. t.* **a)** *(disapprove of)* verurteilen; **b)** *(regret)* beklagen

deploy [dɪ'plɔɪ] *v. t.* einsetzen

deport [dɪ'pɔ:t] *v. t.* ausweisen. **deportation** [di:pɔ:'teɪʃn] *n.* Ausweisung, *die*

depose [dɪ'pəʊz] *v. t.* absetzen

deposit [dɪ'pɒzɪt] **1.** *n.* **a)** *(in bank)* Depot, *das; (credit)* Guthaben, *das; (Brit.: at interest)* Sparguthaben, *das;* **b)** *(first instalment)* Anzahlung, *die;* **put down a ~ on sth.** eine Anzahlung für etw. leisten; **c)** *(on bottle)* Pfand, *das.* **2.** *v. t.* **a)** *(lay down)* ablegen; abstellen ⟨*etw. Senkrechtes*⟩; **b)** *(in bank)* deponieren. **de'posit account** *n.* *(Brit.)* Sparkonto, *das*

depot ['depəʊ] *n.* Depot, *das*

depraved [dɪ'preɪvd] *adj.* verdorben. **depravity** [dɪ'prævɪtɪ] *n.* Verdorbenheit, *die*

depreciate [dɪ'pri:ʃɪeɪt] *v. i.* an Wert verlieren. **depreciation** [dɪpri:ʃɪ'eɪʃn] *n.* Wertverlust, *der*

depress [dɪ'pres] *v. t.* **a)** *(deject)* deprimieren; **b)** *(push down)* herunterdrücken. **depressed** [dɪ'prest] *adj.* deprimiert. **de'pressing** *adj.*, **de'pressingly** *adv.* deprimierend. **depression** [dɪ'preʃn] *n.* **a)** Depression, *die;* **b)** *(sunk place)* Vertiefung, *die;* **c)** *(Meteorol.)* Tiefdruckgebiet, *das;* **d)** *(Econ.)* Wirtschaftskrise, *die*

deprivation [deprɪ'veɪʃn] *n.* Entbehrung, *die*

deprive [dɪ'praɪv] *v. t.* **~ sb. of sth.** jmdm. etw. nehmen; *(prevent from having)* jmdm. etw. vorenthalten. **deprived** [dɪ'praɪvd] *adj.* benachteiligt ⟨*Kind, Familie usw.*⟩

depth [depθ] *n.* **a)** Tiefe, *die;* **in ~:** gründlich; **in the ~s of winter** im tiefsten Winter. **'depth-charge** *n.* Wasserbombe, *die*

deputation [depjʊ'teɪʃn] *n.* Abordnung, *die*

deputize ['depjʊtaɪz] *v. i.* **~ for sb.** jmdn. vertreten

deputy ['depjʊtɪ] *n.* [Stell]vertreter, *der/*-vertreterin, *die; attrib.* stellvertretend

derail [dɪ'reɪl] *v. t.* **be ~ed** entgleisen. **de'railment** *n.* Entgleisung, *die*

deranged [dɪ'reɪndʒd] *adj.* **[mentally] ~:** geistesgestört

derelict ['derɪlɪkt] **1.** *adj.* verlassen und verfallen. **2.** *n.* Ausgestoßene, *der/die*

deride [dɪ'raɪd] *v. t.* sich lustig machen

über (+ *Akk.*). **derision** [dɪ'rɪʒn] *n.* Spott, *der.* **derisive** [dɪ'raɪsɪv] *adj. (ironical)* spöttisch; *(scoffing)* verächtlich. **derisory** [dɪ'raɪzərɪ] *adj. (ridiculously inadequate)* lächerlich

derivation [derɪ'veɪʃn] *n.* Ableitung, *die*

derivative [dɪ'rɪvətɪv] **1.** *adj.* abgeleitet; *(lacking originality)* nachahmend. **2.** *n.* Ableitung, *die*

derive [dɪ'raɪv] **1.** *v. t.* **~ sth. from sth.** etw. aus etw. gewinnen; **~ pleasure from sth.** Freude an etw. *(Dat.)* haben. **2.** *v. i.* **~ from** beruhen auf (+ *Dat.*)

derogatory [dɪ'rɒgətərɪ] *adj.* abfällig

derrick ['derɪk] *n.* [Derrick]kran, *der*

derv [dɜ:v] *n.* Diesel[kraftstoff], *der*

descend [dɪ'send] **1.** *v. i.* **a)** *(go down)* hinuntergehen / -steigen / -klettern / -fahren; *(come down)* herunterkommen; ⟨*Fallschirm, Flugzeug:*⟩ niedergehen; **b)** *(slope downwards)* abfallen; **c)** **~ on sb.** jmdn. überfallen. **2.** *v. t. (go/come down)* hinunter- / heruntergehen / -steigen / -klettern / -fahren. **descendant** [dɪ'sendənt] *n.* Nachkomme, *der.* **de'scended** *adj.* **be ~ from sb.** von jmdm. abstammen. **descent** [dɪ'sent] *n.* **a)** Abstieg, *der; (of parachute, plane)* Niedergehen, *das;* **b)** *(lineage)* Herkunft, *die*

describe [dɪ'skraɪb] *v. t.* beschreiben. **description** [dɪ'skrɪpʃn] *n.* **a)** Beschreibung, *die;* **b)** *(sort, class)* Art, *die.* **descriptive** [dɪ'skrɪptɪv] *adj.* beschreibend; *(vivid)* anschaulich; **a purely ~ report** ein reiner Tatsachenbericht

desecrate ['desɪkreɪt] *v. t.* entweihen

¹desert ['dezət] *n.* Wüste, *die*

²desert [dɪ'zɜ:t] **1.** *v. t.* verlassen. **2.** *v. i.* ⟨*Soldat:*⟩ desertieren. **de'serted** *adj.* verlassen. **de'serter** *n.* Deserteur, *der.* **desertion** [dɪ'zɜ:ʃn] *n.* Desertion, *die*

desert 'island [dezət 'aɪlənd] *n.* einsame Insel

deserts [dɪ'zɜ:ts] *n. pl.* **get one's [just] ~:** das bekommen, was man verdient hat

deserve [dɪ'zɜ:v] *v. t.* verdienen. **deserving** [dɪ'zɜ:vɪŋ] *adj.* verdienstvoll; **a ~ cause** ein guter Zweck

design [dɪ'zaɪn] **1.** *n.* Entwurf, *der; (pattern)* Muster, *das; (established form of machine, engine, etc.)* Bauweise, *die; (general idea, construction)* Konstruktion, *die.* **2.** *v. t.* entwerfen; **be ~ed to do sth.** etw. tun sollen

designate ['dezıgneıt] v. t. **a)** bezeichnen; **b)** (appoint) designieren (geh.). **designation** [dezıg'neıʃn] n. Bezeichnung, die

'**designer** n. Designer, der/ Designerin, die; (of machines) Konstrukteur, der/Konstrukteurin, die; attrib. Modell(-kleidung, -jeans)

desirability [dızaıərə'bılıtı] n. Wunschbarkeit, die

desirable [dı'zaıərəbl] adj. wünschenswert

desire [dı'zaıə(r)] **1.** n. Wunsch, der (for nach); (longing) Sehnsucht, die (for nach). **2.** v. t. sich (Dat.) wünschen; (long for) sich sehnen nach

desist [dı'zıst] v. i. (literary) einhalten (geh.); ~ from sth. von etw. ablassen (geh.)

desk [desk] n. **a)** Schreibtisch, der; (in school) Tisch, der; (cash ~) Kasse, die; (reception ~) Rezeption, die

desolate ['desələt] adj. trostlos. **desolation** [desə'leıʃn] n. Trostlosigkeit, die

despair [dı'speə(r)] **1.** n. Verzweiflung, die; be the ~ of sb. jmdn. zur Verzweiflung bringen. **2.** v. i. verzweifeln. **desperate** ['despərət] adj. verzweifelt; extrem (Maßnahmen); be ~ for sth. etw. dringend brauchen. **desperation** [despə'reıʃn] n. Verzweiflung, die

despicable [dı'spıkəbl] adj. verabscheuungswürdig

despise [dı'spaız] v. t. verachten

despite [dı'spaıt] prep. trotz

despondent [dı'spɒndənt] adj. bedrückt

despot ['despɒt] n. Despot, der

dessert [dı'zɜːt] n. Nachtisch, der. **des'sert spoon** n. Dessertlöffel, der

destination [destı'neıʃn] n. Reiseziel, das; (of goods) Bestimmungsort, der; (of train, bus) Zielort, der

destine ['destın] v. t. bestimmen; ~d to do sth. dazu bestimmt sein, etw. zu tun

destiny ['destını] n. Schicksal, das

destitute ['destıtjuːt] adj. mittellos

destroy [dı'strɔı] v. t. zerstören. **de'stroyer** n. (also Naut.) Zerstörer, der. **destruction** [dı'strʌkʃn] n. Zerstörung, die. **destructive** [dı'strʌktıv] adj. zerstörerisch; verheerend (Sturm, Feuer)

detach [dı'tætʃ] v. t. entfernen; abnehmen (wieder zu Befestigendes); herausnehmen (innen Befindliches).

detachable [dı'tætʃəbl] adj. abnehmbar. **detached** [dı'tætʃt] adj. **a)** (impartial) unvoreingenommen; (unemotional) unbeteiligt; **b)** a ~ house ein Einzelhaus. **de'tachment** n. see detach: Entfernen, das; Abnehmen, das; Herausnehmen, das; **b)** (Mil.) Abteilung, die

detail ['diːteıl] **1.** n. Einzelheit, die; Detail, das; **in** ~: Punkt für Punkt; go **into** ~|s| ins Detail gehen. **2.** v. t. **a)** einzeln ausführen; **b)** (Mil.) abkommandieren. **detailed** [dı'teıld] adj. detailliert; eingehend (Studie)

detain [dı'teın] v. t. **a)** festhalten; (take into confinement) verhaften; **b)** (delay) aufhalten. **detainee** [diːteı'niː] n. Verhaftete, der/die

detect [dı'tekt] v. t. entdecken; wahrnehmen (Bewegung); aufdecken (Irrtum, Verbrechen). **detection** [dı'tekʃn] n. Entdeckung, die; (of error, crime) Aufdeckung, die. **detective** [dı'tektıv] n. Detektiv, der; private ~: Privatdetektiv, der; ~ work Ermittlungsarbeit, die; ~ story Detektivgeschichte, die. **detector** [dı'tektə(r)] n. Detektor, der

detention [dı'tenʃn] n. **a)** Festnahme, die; (confinement) Haft, die; **b)** (Sch.) Nachsitzen, das

deter [dı'tɜː(r)] v. t., **-rr-** abschrecken

detergent [dı'tɜːdʒənt] n. Waschmittel, das

deteriorate [dı'tıərıəreıt] v. i. sich verschlechtern; (Haus:) verfallen. **deterioration** [dıtıərıə'reıʃn] n. see deteriorate: Verschlechterung, die; Verfall, der

determination [dıtɜːmı'neıʃn] n. Entschlossenheit, die

determine [dı'tɜːmın] v. t. **a)** (decide) beschließen; **b)** (be a decisive factor for) bestimmen; **c)** (ascertain) feststellen. **determined** [dı'tɜːmınd] adj. **a)** be ~ to do sth. etw. unbedingt tun wollen; **b)** (resolute) entschlossen

deterrent [dı'terənt] n. Abschreckungsmittel, das (to für)

detest [dı'test] v. t. verabscheuen. **detestable** [dı'testəbl] adj. verabscheuenswert

detonate ['detəneıt] **1.** v. t. zünden. **2.** v. i. detonieren. **detonation** [detə'neıʃn] n. Detonation, die. **detonator** ['detəneıtə(r)] n. Sprengkapsel, die

detour ['diːtʊə(r)] n. Umweg, der; (diversion) Umleitung, die

detract [dɪ'trækt] v. i. ~ **from sth.** etw. beeinträchtigen

detriment ['detrɪmənt] n. **to the ~ of sth.** zum Nachteil einer Sache (Gen.). **detrimental** [detrɪ'mentl] adj. schädlich; **be ~ to sth.** einer Sache (Dat.) schaden

deuce [dju:s] n. (Tennis) Einstand, der

devaluation [di:vælju:'eɪʃn] n. Abwertung, die

devalue [di:'vælju:] v. t. abwerten

devastate ['devəsteɪt] v. t. verwüsten; (fig.) niederschmettern. **devastating** ['devəsteɪtɪŋ] adj. verheerend; (fig.) niederschmetternd. **devastation** [devə'steɪʃn] n. Verwüstung, die

develop [dɪ'veləp] 1. v. t. entwickeln; erschließen ⟨natürliche Ressourcen⟩; bekommen ⟨Krankheit, Fieber, Lust⟩; ~ **a taste for sth.** Geschmack an etw. (Akk.) finden. 2. v. i. sich entwickeln (from aus; into zu). **de'veloper** n. a) (Photog.) Entwickler, der; b) (of land) Bauunternehmer, der

de'veloping country n. Entwicklungsland, das

de'velopment n. Entwicklung, die (from aus; into zu); (of natural resources etc.) Erschließung, die

deviant ['di:vɪənt] adj. abweichend

deviate ['di:vɪeɪt] v. i. abweichen. **deviation** [di:vɪ'eɪʃn] n. Abweichung, die

device [dɪ'vaɪs] n. Gerät, das; (as part of sth.) Vorrichtung, die; **leave sb. to his own ~s** jmdn. sich (Dat.) selbst überlassen

devil ['devl] n. Teufel, der; **the D~:** der Teufel. **'devilish** adj. teuflisch

devious ['di:vɪəs] adj. a) (winding) verschlungen; ~ **route** Umweg, der; b) (unscrupulous, insincere) hinterhältig

devise [dɪ'vaɪz] v. t. entwerfen; schmieden ⟨Pläne⟩

devoid [dɪ'vɔɪd] adj. ~ **of sth.** (lacking) ohne etw.; (free from) frei von etw.

devolution [di:və'lu:ʃn] n. (Polit.) Dezentralisierung, die

devote [dɪ'vəʊt] v. t. widmen (to Dat.). **de'voted** adj. treu; aufrichtig ⟨Freundschaft, Liebe, Verehrung⟩; **be ~ to sb.** jmdn. innig lieben. **devotion** [dɪ'vəʊʃn] n. ~ **to sb./sth.** Hingabe an jmdn./etw.

devour [dɪ'vaʊə(r)] v. t. verschlingen

devout [dɪ'vaʊt] adj. fromm

dew [dju:] n. Tau, der

dexterity [dek'sterɪtɪ] n. Geschicklichkeit, die

dextrous ['dekstrəs] adj. geschickt

diabetes [daɪə'bi:ti:z] n. Zuckerkrankheit, die. **diabetic** [daɪə'betɪk] 1. adj. zuckerkrank ⟨Person⟩. 2. n. Diabetiker, der/Diabetikerin, die

diabolical [daɪə'bɒlɪkl] adj. teuflisch

diagnose ['daɪəgnəʊz] v. t. diagnostizieren; feststellen ⟨Fehler⟩. **diagnosis** [daɪəg'nəʊsɪs] n., pl. **diagnoses** [daɪəg'nəʊsi:z] Diagnose, die; **make a ~:** eine Diagnose stellen

diagonal [daɪ'ægənl] 1. adj. diagonal. 2. n. Diagonale, die. **di'agonally** adv. diagonal

diagram ['daɪəgræm] n. Diagramm, das

dial ['daɪəl] 1. n. (of clock or watch) Zifferblatt, das; (of gauge, meter, etc.) Skala, die; (Teleph.) Wählscheibe, die. 2. v. t. & i., (Brit.) -ll- (Teleph.) wählen; ~ **direct** selbst wählen; (dial extension) durchwählen

dialect ['daɪəlekt] n. Dialekt, der

dialling (Amer.: dialing): ~ **code** n. Vorwahl, die; ~ **tone** Wählton, der

dialogue ['daɪəlɒg] n. Dialog, der

'dial tone n. (Amer.) Wählton, der

diameter [daɪ'æmɪtə(r)] n. Durchmesser, der. **diametrical** [daɪə'metrɪkl] adj. **dia'metrically** adv. diametral

diamond ['daɪəmənd] n. a) Diamant, der; b) (figure) Raute, die; c) (Cards) Karo, das; see also **club** 1 c

diaper ['daɪəpə(r)] n. (Amer.) Windel, die

diaphragm ['daɪəfræm] n. Diaphragma, das

diarrhoea (Amer.: **diarrhea**) [daɪə'rɪə] n. Durchfall, der

diary ['daɪərɪ] n. a) Tagebuch, das; b) (for appointments) Terminkalender, der

dice [daɪs] 1. n. Würfel, der. 2. v. t. (Cooking) würfeln

dicey ['daɪsɪ] adj. (sl.) riskant

dictate [dɪk'teɪt] v. t. & i. diktieren; (prescribe) vorschreiben; ~ **to** Vorschriften machen (+ Dat.). **dictation** [dɪk'teɪʃn] n. Diktat, das. **dictator** [dɪk'teɪtə(r)] n. Diktator, der. **dictatorial** [dɪktə'tɔ:rɪəl] adj. diktatorisch. **dic'tatorship** n. Diktatur, die

dictionary ['dɪkʃənərɪ] n. Wörterbuch, das

did see **do**

diddle ['dɪdl] v. t. (sl.) übers Ohr hauen (ugs.)

didn't ['dɪdnt] (coll.) = **did not**; see **do**

die [daɪ] v. i., **dying** ['daɪɪŋ] sterben (of,

from an + *Dat.*); ⟨*Tier, Pflanze:*⟩ eingehen; **be dying to do sth.** darauf brennen, etw. zu tun; **be dying for sth.** etw. unbedingt brauchen. **die 'down** *v. i.* ⟨*Sturm, Wind, Protest:*⟩ sich legen; ⟨*Flammen:*⟩ kleiner werden; ⟨*Feuer:*⟩ herunterbrennen; ⟨*Lärm:*⟩ leiser werden. **die 'out** *v. i.* aussterben

'die-hard *n.* Ewiggestrige, *der/die*

diesel ['di:zl] *n.* ~ [**engine**] Diesel[motor], *der;* ~ [**fuel**] Diesel[kraftstoff], *der*

diet ['daɪət] **1.** *n.* Diät, *die;* **be/go on a** ~: eine Schlankheitskur machen. **2.** *v. i.* eine Schlankheitskur machen

differ ['dɪfə(r)] *v. i.* (be different) sich unterscheiden

difference ['dɪfərəns] *n.* **a)** Unterschied, *der;* **make no** ~ [**to sb.**] [jmdm.] nichts ausmachen; **it makes a** ~: es ist ein *od.* (ugs.) macht einen Unterschied; **b)** (disagreement) Meinungsverschiedenheit, *die*

different ['dɪfərənt] *adj.* verschieden; (pred. also) anders; (attrib. also) ander...; **be** ~ **from** *or* (esp. Brit.) *to* or (Amer.) **than** ...: anders sein als ...

differentiate [dɪfə'renʃɪeɪt] *v. t. & i.* unterscheiden (**between** zwischen + *Dat.*)

'differently *adv.* anders (**from,** *esp. Brit.* **to** als)

difficult ['dɪfɪkəlt] *adj.* schwierig. **'difficulty** *n.* Schwierigkeit, die mit [**great**] ~: [sehr] mühsam; **get into difficulties in** Schwierigkeiten kommen

diffident ['dɪfɪdənt] *adj.* zaghaft; (modest) zurückhaltend

diffuse 1. [dɪ'fju:z] *v. t.* verbreiten. **2.** *v. i.* sich ausbreiten (**through** in + *Dat.*). **3.** [dɪ'fju:s] *adj.* diffus

dig [dɪg] **1.** *v. i.,* -gg-, **dug** [dʌg] graben (**for** nach). **2.** *v. t.,* -gg-, **dug** graben; umgraben ⟨*Erde, Garten*⟩. **dig 'out** *v. t.* ausgraben. **dig 'up** *v. t.* ausgraben; umgraben ⟨*Garten*⟩; aufreißen ⟨*Straße*⟩

digest [dɪ'dʒest, daɪ'dʒest] *v. t.* verdauen. **digestion** [dɪ'dʒestʃn, daɪ'dʒestʃn] *n.* Verdauung, *die*

'digger *n.* Bagger, *der*

digit ['dɪdʒɪt] *n.* Ziffer, *die*

digital ['dɪdʒɪtl] *adj.* Digital-

dignified ['dɪgnɪfaɪd] *adj.* würdig; (stately) würdevoll

dignify ['dɪgnɪfaɪ] *v. t.* Würde verleihen (+ *Dat.*)

dignitary ['dɪgnɪtərɪ] *n.* Würdenträger, *der;* **dignitaries** (prominent people) Honoratioren

dignity ['dɪgnɪtɪ] *n.* Würde, *die*

digress [daɪ'gres] *v. i.* abschweifen. **digression** [daɪ'greʃn] *n.* Abschweifung, *die*

dike [daɪk] *n.* Deich, *der*

dilapidated [dɪ'læpɪdeɪtɪd] *adj.* verfallen ⟨*Gebäude*⟩; verwahrlost ⟨*Erscheinung*⟩

dilate [daɪ'leɪt] **1.** *v. i.* sich weiten. **2.** *v. t.* ausdehnen

dilemma [dɪ'lemə, daɪ'lemə] *n.* Dilemma, *das*

diligence ['dɪlɪdʒəns] *n.* Fleiß, *der*

diligent ['dɪlɪdʒənt] *adj.,* **'diligently** *adv.* fleißig

dilute 1. [daɪ'lju:t, 'daɪlju:t] *adj.* verdünnt. **2.** [daɪ'lju:t] *v. t.* verdünnen

dim [dɪm] **1.** *adj.* **a)** schwach ⟨*Licht, Flackern*⟩; dunkel ⟨*Zimmer*⟩; verschwommen ⟨*Gestalt*⟩; **b)** (vague) verschwommen; **c)** (coll.: stupid) beschränkt. **2.** *v. i.* schwächer werden

dime [daɪm] *n.* (Amer. coll.) Zehncentstück, *das*

dimension [dɪ'menʃn, daɪ'menʃn] *n.* Dimension, *die;* ~**s** (measurements) Abmessungen; Maße

diminish [dɪ'mɪnɪʃ] **1.** *v. i.* nachlassen; ⟨*Vorräte, Einfluß:*⟩ abnehmen; ⟨*Wert, Ansehen:*⟩ geringer werden. **2.** *v. t.* verringern; schmälern ⟨*Ansehen, Ruf*⟩

dimple ['dɪmpl] *n.* Grübchen, *das*

dim: ~-**wit** *n.* (coll.) Dummkopf, *der* (ugs.); ~-**witted** ['dɪmwɪtɪd] *adj.* (coll.) dusselig (salopp)

din [dɪn] *n.* Lärm, *der*

dine [daɪn] *v. i.* [zu Mittag/zu Abend] essen. **'diner** *n.* Gast, *der*

dinghy ['dɪŋɪ, 'dɪŋgɪ] *n.* Ding[h]i, *das;* (inflatable) Schlauchboot, *das*

dingy ['dɪndʒɪ] *adj.* schmuddelig

dining ['daɪnɪŋ]: ~-**car** *n.* Speisewagen, *der;* ~-**room** *n.* Eßzimmer, *das;* (in hotel etc.) Speisesaal, *der*

dinner ['dɪnə(r)] *n.* (at midday) Mittagessen, *das;* (in the evening) Abendessen, *das;* (formal) Diner, *das.* **'dinner-table** *n.* Eßtisch, *der.* **'dinner-time** *n.* Essenszeit, *die;* **at** ~-**time** zur Essenszeit; (12–2 p. m.) mittags

dinosaur ['daɪnəsɔ:(r)] *n.* Dinosaurier, *der*

dint [dɪnt] *n.* **by** ~ **of** durch; **by** ~ **of doing sth.** indem jmd. etw. tut

dip [dɪp] **1.** *v. t.,* -pp-: **a)** [ein]tauchen (**in** in + *Akk.*); **b)** ~ **one's headlights** abblenden. **2.** *v. i.* sinken; ⟨*incline*⟩ abfallen. **3.** *n.* **a)** (in road) Senke, *die;* **b)** (coll.: bathe) [kurzes] Bad

diphtheria [dɪfˈθɪərɪə] *n.* Diphtherie, *die*

diphthong [ˈdɪfθɒŋ] *n.* Diphthong, *der*

diploma [dɪˈpləʊmə] *n.* Diplom, *das*

diplomacy [dɪˈpləʊməsɪ] *n.* Diplomatie, *die*

diplomat [ˈdɪpləmæt] *n.* Diplomat, *der*/Diplomatin, *die*

diplomatic [dɪpləˈmætɪk] *adj.*, **diplo'matically** *adv.* diplomatisch

dire [ˈdaɪə(r)] *adj.* furchtbar

direct [dɪˈrekt, daɪˈrekt] **1.** *v. t.* **a)** *(turn)* richten (to{wards} auf + *Akk.*); ~ sb. to a place jmdn. den Weg zu einem Ort weisen; **b)** *(control)* leiten; ~ at ⟨*Verkehr*⟩; **c)** *(order)* anweisen; **d)** *(Theatre, Cinemat., etc.)* Regie führen bei. **2.** *adj.* direkt; durchgehend ⟨*Zug*⟩; unmittelbar ⟨*Ursache, Auswirkung, Erfahrung, Verantwortung*⟩; genau ⟨*Gegenteil*⟩; direkt ⟨*Widerspruch*⟩; diametral ⟨*Gegensatz*⟩; ~ speech direkte Rede. **3.** *adv.* direkt.
direct current *n.* Gleichstrom, *der.*
direct 'hit *n.* Volltreffer, *der*
direction [daɪˈrekʃn] *n.* **a)** Richtung, *die;* in the ~ of London in Richtung London; **b)** *(guidance)* Führung, *die;* **c)** *usu. in pl. (order)* Anordnung, *die;* ~s [for use] Gebrauchsanweisung, *die*
di'rectly *adv.* **a)** direkt; unmittelbar ⟨*folgen, verantwortlich sein*⟩; **b)** *(exactly)* genau; **c)** *(at once)* umgehend; **d)** *(shortly)* gleich
di'rect object *n.* direktes Objekt
director [daɪˈrektə(r)] *n.* **a)** *(Commerc.)* Direktor, *der*/Direktorin, *die;* board of ~s Aufsichtsrat, *der;* **b)** *(Theatre, Cinemat., etc.)* Regisseur, *der*/Regisseurin, *die*
directory [daɪˈrektərɪ] *n.* *(telephone ~)* Telefonbuch, *das;* *(of tradesmen etc.)* Branchenverzeichnis, *das;* ~ enquiries *(Brit.),* ~ information *(Amer.)* [Fernsprech]auskunft, *die*
dirt [dɜːt] *n.* Schmutz, *der;* ~ cheap spottbillig. **'dirty 1.** *adj.* schmutzig; get sth. ~: etw. schmutzig machen. **2.** *v. t.* schmutzig machen
disa'bility *n.* Behinderung, *die*
disabled [dɪsˈeɪbld] *adj.* behindert
disad'vantage *n.* Nachteil, *der;* at a ~: im Nachteil
disa'gree *v. i.* anderer Meinung sein; ~ with sb./sth. mit jmdm./etw. nicht übereinstimmen; ~ [with sb.] about or over sth. sich [mit jmdm.] über etw. *(Akk.)* nicht einig sein. **dis-**

a'greeable *adj.* unangenehm. **disa'greement** *n.* **a)** *(difference of opinion)* Uneinigkeit, *die;* be in ~ with sb./sth. mit jmdm./etw. nicht übereinstimmen; **b)** *(quarrel)* Meinungsverschiedenheit, *die;* **c)** *(discrepancy)* Diskrepanz, *die*
disal'low *v. t.* verbieten; *(Sport)* nicht geben ⟨*Tor*⟩
disap'pear *v. i.* verschwinden; ⟨*Brauch, Tierart:*⟩ aussterben. **disap'pearance** *n.* Verschwinden, *das*
disap'point *v. t.* enttäuschen. **disap'pointed** *adj.* enttäuscht. **disap'pointing** *adj.* enttäuschend. **disap'pointment** *n.* Enttäuschung, *die*
disap'proval *n.* Mißbilligung, *die*
disap'prove *v. i.* dagegen sein; ~ of sb./sth. jmdn. ablehnen/etw. mißbilligen
dis'arm *v. t.* entwaffnen. **disarmament** [dɪsˈɑːməmənt] *n.* Abrüstung, *die*
disarray [dɪsəˈreɪ] *n.* Unordnung, *die;* in ~: in Unordnung
disaster [dɪˈzɑːstə(r)] *n.* Katastrophe, *die;* ~ area Katastrophengebiet, *das*
disastrous [dɪˈzɑːstrəs] *adj.* katastrophal; verhängnisvoll ⟨*Irrtum, Entscheidung, Politik*⟩
dis'band 1. *v. t.* auflösen. **2.** *v. i.* sich auflösen
disbe'lief *n.* Unglaube, *der;* in ~: ungläubig
disbe'lieve *v. t.* ~ sb./sth. jmdm./etw. nicht glauben
disc [dɪsk] *n.* Scheibe, *die;* *(record)* Platte, *die;* floppy ~: Floppy disk, *die;* hard ~ *(fixed)* Festplatte, *die*
discard [dɪsˈkɑːd] *v. t.* wegwerfen; fallenlassen ⟨*Vorschlag, Idee*⟩
discern [dɪˈsɜːn] *v. t.* wahrnehmen. **discernible** [dɪˈsɜːnɪbl] *adj.* erkennbar. **di'scerning** *adj.* kritisch
discharge 1. [dɪsˈtʃɑːdʒ] *v. t.* **a)** entlassen *(from* aus); freisprechen ⟨*Angeklagte*⟩; **b)** ablassen ⟨*Flüssigkeit, Gas*⟩. **2.** [ˈdɪstʃɑːdʒ] *n.* **a)** Entlassung, *die (from* aus); *(of defendant)* Freispruch, *der;* **b)** *(emission)* Ausfluß, *der*
disciple [dɪˈsaɪpl] *n.* **a)** *(Relig.)* Jünger, *der;* **b)** *(follower)* Anhänger, *der*/Anhängerin, *die*
disciplinary [dɪsɪˈplɪnərɪ] *adj.* disziplinarisch; ~ action Disziplinarmaßnahmen
discipline [ˈdɪsɪplɪn] **1.** *n.* Disziplin, *die.* **2.** *v. t.* disziplinieren; *(punish)* bestrafen

'disc jockey n. Diskjockey, der

dis'claim v. t. abstreiten

disclose [dɪsˈkləʊz] v. t. enthüllen; bekanntgeben ⟨Information, Nachricht⟩.
dis'closure n. Enthüllung, die; (of information, news) Bekanntgabe, die

disco ['dɪskəʊ] n., pl. ~s (coll.) Disko, die

dis'colour (Brit.; Amer.: **discolor**) v. t. verfärben

dis'comfort n. a) no pl. (slight pain) Beschwerden Pl.; b) (hardship) Unannehmlichkeit, die

disconcert [dɪskənˈsɜːt] v. t. irritieren

discon'nect v. t. abtrennen; abstellen ⟨Telefon⟩

disconsolate [dɪsˈkɒnsələt] adj. a) (unhappy) unglücklich; b) (inconsolable) untröstlich

discon'tent n. Unzufriedenheit, die. **discon'tented** adj. unzufrieden

discon'tinue v. t. einstellen

discord ['dɪskɔːd] n. a) Zwietracht, die; b) (Mus.) Dissonanz, die. **discordant** [dɪsˈkɔːdənt] adj. a) (conflicting) gegensätzlich; b) a ~ note ein Mißton

discothèque ['dɪskətek] n. Diskothek, die

discount 1. ['dɪskaʊnt] n. (Commerc.) Rabatt, der (on auf + Akk.). 2. [dɪˈskaʊnt] v. t. (disbelieve) unberücksichtigt lassen

discourage [dɪsˈkʌrɪdʒ] v. t. a) entmutigen; b) (advise against) abraten. **dis'couragement** n. a) Entmutigung, die; b) (depression) Mutlosigkeit, die. **discouraging** [dɪsˈkʌrɪdʒɪŋ] adj. entmutigend

dis'courteous adj. unhöflich. **dis'courtesy** n. Unhöflichkeit, die

discover [dɪsˈkʌvə(r)] v. t. a) entdecken; b) (by search) herausfinden. **dis'covery** n. Entdeckung, die

dis'credit 1. n. Mißkredit, der; bring ~ on sb./sth., bring sb./sth. into ~: jmdn./etw. in Mißkredit bringen. 2. v. t. in Mißkredit bringen

discreet [dɪsˈkriːt] adj., **dis'creetly** adv. diskret

discrepancy [dɪsˈkrepənsɪ] n. Diskrepanz, die

discretion [dɪsˈkreʃn] n. (prudence) Umsicht, die

discriminate [dɪsˈkrɪmɪneɪt] v. i. a) unterscheiden; b) ~ against/in favour of sb. jmdn. diskriminieren/bevorzugen. **discrimination** [dɪskrɪmɪˈneɪʃn] n. a) Unterscheidung, die; b) Diskri-

minierung, die (against Gen.); ~ in favour of Bevorzugung (+ Gen.)

discus ['dɪskəs] n. Diskus, der

discuss [dɪsˈkʌs] v. t. besprechen; (debate) diskutieren über (+ Akk.). **dis'cussion** [dɪsˈkʌʃn] n. Gespräch, das; (debate) Diskussion, die

disdain [dɪsˈdeɪn] 1. n. Verachtung, die. 2. v. t. verachten; ~ to do sth. zu stolz sein, etw. zu tun. **disdainful** [dɪsˈdeɪnfl] adj. verächtlich

disease [dɪˈziːz] n. Krankheit, die. **diseased** [dɪˈziːzd] adj. krank

disem'bark v. i. von Bord gehen

disen'chant v. t. ernüchtern; **he became ~ed with her/it** sie/es hat ihn desillusioniert

disen'gage v. t. lösen (from aus, von); ~ the clutch auskuppeln

disen'tangle v. t. entwirren; (extricate) befreien (from aus)

dis'figure v. t. entstellen

disgrace [dɪsˈgreɪs] n. 1. Schande, die (to für). 2. v. t. Schande machen (+ Dat.); ~ oneself sich blamieren. **dis'graceful** [dɪsˈgreɪsfl] adj. skandalös; it's ~: es ist ein Skandal

disgruntled [dɪsˈgrʌntld] adj. verstimmt

disguise [dɪsˈgaɪz] 1. v. t. verkleiden ⟨Person⟩; verstellen ⟨Stimme⟩; tarnen ⟨Gegenstand⟩. 2. n. Verkleidung, die

disgust [dɪsˈgʌst] 1. n. (nausea) Ekel, der (at vor + Dat.); (revulsion) Abscheu, der (at vor + Dat.); (indignation) Empörung, die (at über + Akk.). 2. v. t. anwidern; (fill with nausea) ekeln; (fill with indignation) empören. **dis'gusted** adj. angewidert; (nauseated) angeekelt; (indignant) empört. **dis'gusting** adj. widerlich

dish [dɪʃ] n. a) Schale, die; (deeper) Schüssel, die; ~s (crockery) Geschirr, das; **wash** or (coll.) **do the ~s** Geschirr spülen; b) (type of food) Gericht, das. **dish 'out** v. t. austeilen ⟨Essen⟩; b) (coll.: distribute) verteilen. **dish 'up** v. t. auftragen

'dishcloth n. Spültuch, das

dis'hearten v. t. entmutigen

dishevelled (Amer.: **disheveled**) [dɪˈʃevld] adj. zerzaust ⟨Haar⟩; ungepflegt ⟨Erscheinung⟩

dis'honest adj., **dis'honestly** adv. unehrlich. **dis'honesty** n. Unehrlichkeit, die

dis'honour 1. n. Unehre, die. 2. v. t. beleidigen. **dishonourable** [dɪsˈɒnərəbl] adj. unehrenhaft

'dishwasher n. Geschirrspülmaschine, *die*

disil'lusion 1. v.t. ernüchtern. **2.** n. Desillusion, *die* (with über + Akk.).

disil'lusionment n. Desillusionierung, *die*

disin'fect v.t. desinfizieren. **disinfectant** [dɪsɪn'fektənt] **1.** adj. desinfizierend. **2.** n. Desinfektionsmittel, *das*

dis'integrate v.i. zerfallen. **disintegration** [dɪsɪntɪ'greɪʃn] n. Zerfall, *der*

dis'interested adj. **a)** (impartial) unvoreingenommen; **b)** (coll.: uninterested) desinteressiert

disjointed [dɪs'dʒɔɪntɪd] adj. unzusammenhängend

disk see disc

diskette [dɪ'sket] n. Diskette, *die*

dis'like 1. v.t. nicht mögen; ~ doing sth. etw. ungern tun. **2.** n. Abneigung, *die* (of, for gegen); **take a ~ to** sb./sth. eine Abneigung gegen jmdn./etw. empfinden

dislocate ['dɪsləkeɪt] v.t. ausrenken; auskugeln ⟨Schulter, Hüfte⟩

dis'lodge v.t. entfernen (**from** aus)

dis'loyal adj. illoyal (**to** gegenüber). **dis'loyalty** n. Illoyalität, *die* (**to** gegenüber)

dismal ['dɪzməl] adj. trist

dismantle [dɪs'mæntl] v.t. demontieren; abbauen ⟨Schuppen, Gerüst⟩

dismay [dɪs'meɪ] **1.** v.t. bestürzen. **2.** n. Bestürzung, *die* (**at** über + Akk.).

dismiss [dɪs'mɪs] v.t. entlassen; (reject) ablehnen. **dismissal** [dɪs'mɪsl] n. Entlassung, *die*

dis'mount v.i. absteigen

diso'bedience n. Ungehorsam, *der*

diso'bedient adj. ungehorsam

diso'bey v.t. nicht gehorchen (+ Dat.); nicht befolgen ⟨Befehl⟩

dis'order n. **a)** Durcheinander, *das*; **b)** (Med.) Störung, *die.* **dis'orderly** adj. (untidy) unordentlich; ~ conduct ungebührliches Benehmen

dis'organized adj. chaotisch

dis'orientated, dis'oriented adj. desorientiert

dis'own v.t. verleugnen

disparage [dɪ'spærɪdʒ] v.t. herabsetzen. **disparaging** [dɪ'spærɪdʒɪn] adj. abschätzig

disparity [dɪ'spærɪtɪ] n. Ungleichheit, *die*

dispatch [dɪ'spætʃ] **1.** v.t. **a)** schicken; **b)** (kill) töten. **2.** n. Bericht, *der*

dispel [dɪ'spel] v.t., **-ll-** vertreiben; zerstreuen ⟨Besorgnis, Befürchtung⟩

dispensable [dɪ'spensəbl] adj. entbehrlich

dispensary [dɪ'spensərɪ] n. Apotheke, *die*

dispense [dɪ'spens] v.i. ~ with verzichten auf (+ Akk.)

dispersal [dɪ'spɜːsl] n. Zerstreuung, *die*

disperse [dɪ'spɜːs] **1.** v.t. zerstreuen. **2.** v.i. sich zerstreuen

dispirited [dɪ'spɪrɪtɪd] adj. entmutigt

dis'place v.t. verschieben; (supplant) ersetzen

display [dɪ'spleɪ] **1.** v.t. zeigen; ausstellen ⟨Waren⟩. **2.** n. Ausstellung, *die*; (of goods) Auslage, *die*; (ostentatious show) Zurschaustellung, *die*

dis'please v.t. jmds. Mißfallen erregen. **dis'pleasure** n. Mißfallen, *das*

disposable [dɪ'spəʊzəbl] adj. Wegwerf-

disposal [dɪ'spəʊzl] n. Beseitigung, *die*; **have sth./sb. at one's ~:** etw./jmdn. zur Verfügung haben; **be at sb.'s ~:** jmdm. zur Verfügung stehen

dispose [dɪ'spəʊz] v.t. ~ with sb. to sth. jmdn. zu etw. veranlassen; ~ sb. to do sth. jmdn. dazu veranlassen, etw. zu tun. **dis'pose of** v.t. beseitigen; (settle) erledigen

disposed [dɪ'spəʊzd] adj. **be ~ to do** sth. dazu neigen, etw. zu tun; **be well ~ towards** sb./sth. jmdm. wohl gesinnt sein/einer Sache (Dat.) positiv gegenüberstehen. **disposition** [dɪspə'zɪʃn] n. Veranlagung, *die*; (nature) Art, *die*

dis'prove v.t. widerlegen

dispute [dɪ'spjuːt] **1.** n. Streit, *der* (over um). **2.** v.t. **a)** (discuss) sich streiten über (+ Akk.); **b)** (oppose) bestreiten

disqualifi'cation n. Ausschluß, *der*; (Sport) Disqualifikation, *die*

dis'qualify v.t. ausschließen (**from** von); (Sport) disqualifizieren

disre'gard 1. v.t. ignorieren. **2.** n. Mißachtung, *die* (of, for Gen.); (of wishes, feelings) Gleichgültigkeit, *die* (for, of gegenüber)

dis'reputable adj. verrufen

disrepute [dɪsrɪ'pjuːt] n. Verruf, *der*; **bring** sb./sth. **into ~:** jmdn./etw. in Verruf bringen

disre'spect n. Mißachtung, *die*; **show ~ for** sb./sth. keine Achtung vor jmdm./etw. haben. **disre'spectful** adj. respektlos

diver

disrupt [dɪsˈrʌpt] v.t. stören. **disruption** [dɪsˈrʌpʃn] n. Störung, die. **disruptive** [dɪsˈrʌptɪv] adj. störend

dissatis'faction n. Unzufriedenheit, die

dis'satisfied adj. unzufrieden

dissect [dɪˈsekt] v.t. sezieren

dissent [dɪˈsent] 1. v.i. a) (refuse to assent) nicht zustimmen; ~ from sth. mit etw. nicht übereinstimmen; b) (disagree) ~ from sth. von etw. abweichen. 2. n. Ablehnung, die; (from majority) Abweichung, die

dissertation [dɪsəˈteɪʃn] n. Dissertation, die

dis'service n. do sb. a ~: jmdm. einen schlechten Dienst erweisen

dissident [ˈdɪsɪdənt] n. Dissident, der/Dissidentin, die

dis'similar adj. unähnlich (to Dat.)

dissociate [dɪˈsəʊʃɪeɪt] v.t. trennen; ~ oneself sich distanzieren (from von)

dissolve [dɪˈzɒlv] 1. v.t. auflösen. 2. v.i. sich auflösen

dissuade [dɪˈsweɪd] v.t. abbringen (from von)

distance [ˈdɪstəns] n. a) Entfernung, die (from zu); b) (way to cover) Strecke, die; from a ~: von weitem; in/into the ~: in der/die Ferne

distant [ˈdɪstənt] adj. a) fern; entfernt ⟨Ähnlichkeit, Verwandtschaft, Verwandte⟩; b) (reserved) distanziert

dis'taste n. Abneigung, die (for gegen). **dis'tasteful** adj. unangenehm

distend [dɪˈstend] v.t. erweitern

distil, (Amer.) **distill** [dɪˈstɪl] v.t. destillieren; brennen ⟨Branntwein⟩. **distillation** [dɪstɪˈleɪʃn] n. Destillation, die. **distillery** [dɪˈstɪləri] n. Brennerei, die

distinct [dɪˈstɪŋkt] adj. deutlich; (different) verschieden. **distinction** [dɪˈstɪŋkʃn] n. Unterschied, der. **distinctive** [dɪˈstɪŋktɪv] adj. unverwechselbar. **dis'tinctly** adv. deutlich

distinguish [dɪˈstɪŋgwɪʃ] 1. v.t. a) (make out) erkennen; b) (differentiate) unterscheiden; c) (characterize) kennzeichnen; d) ~ oneself [by sth.] sich [durch etw.] hervortun. 2. v.i. unterscheiden; ~ between auseinanderhalten. **distinguished** [dɪˈstɪŋgwɪʃt] adj. angesehen; glänzend ⟨Laufbahn⟩; vornehm ⟨Aussehen⟩

distort [dɪˈstɔːt] v.t. verzerren; (fig.) verdrehen. **distortion** [dɪˈstɔːʃn] n. Verzerrung, die; (fig.) Verdrehung, die

distract [dɪˈstrækt] v.t. ablenken; ~ sb.|'s attention from sth.| jmdn. [von etw.] ablenken. **di'stracted** adj. von Sinnen nachgestellt; (mentally far away) abwesend. **distraction** [dɪˈstrækʃn] n. a) (diversion) Ablenkung, die; (interruption) Störung, die; b) **drive sb. to ~:** jmdn. zum Wahnsinn treiben

distraught [dɪˈstrɔːt] adj. aufgelöst (with vor + Dat.); verstört ⟨Blick⟩

distress [dɪˈstres] 1. n. a) Kummer, der (at über + Akk.); b) (pain) Qualen Pl.; c) **an aircraft/ship in ~:** ein Flugzeug in Not/ein Schiff in Seenot. 2. v.t. nahegehen (+ Dat.). **di'stressing** adj. erschütternd. **di'stress signal** n. Notsignal, das

distribute [dɪˈstrɪbjuːt] v.t. verteilen (to an + Akk.; among unter + Akk.); (Commerc.) vertreiben. **distribution** [dɪstrɪˈbjuːʃn] n. Verteilung, die; (Commerc.) Vertrieb, der. **distributor** [dɪˈstrɪbjʊtə(r)] n. Verteiler, der/Verteilerin, die; (Commerc.) Vertreiber, der

district [ˈdɪstrɪkt] n. Gegend, die; (Admin.) Bezirk, der. **district 'nurse** n. (Brit.) Gemeindeschwester, die

dis'trust [dɪsˈtrʌst] 1. n. Mißtrauen, das (of gegen). 2. v.t. mißtrauen (+ Dat.)

disturb [dɪˈstɜːb] v.t. a) stören; 'do not ~!', 'bitte nicht stören!'; b) (worry) beunruhigen. **disturbance** [dɪˈstɜːbəns] n. Störung, die; **political ~s** politische Unruhen. **disturbed** [dɪˈstɜːbd] adj. besorgt; |mentally| ~: geistig gestört

disuse [dɪsˈjuːs] n. **fall into ~:** außer Gebrauch kommen

disused [dɪsˈjuːzd] adj. stillgelegt; leerstehend ⟨Gebäude⟩

ditch [dɪtʃ] 1. n. Graben, der. 2. v.t. (sl.) sausenlassen ⟨Plan⟩; sitzenlassen ⟨Familie, Freund⟩

dither [ˈdɪðə(r)] v.i. schwanken

ditto [ˈdɪtəʊ] n., pl. ~s ebenso; ditto; ~ **marks** Unterführungszeichen, das

divan [dɪˈvæn] n. [Polster]liege, die

dive [daɪv] 1. v.i., dived or (Amer.) dove [dəʊv] a) einen Kopfsprung machen; (when already in water) tauchen; b) ⟨Vogel, Flugzeug usw.:⟩ einen Sturzflug machen. 2. n. a) Kopfsprung, der; (of bird, aircraft, etc.) Sturzflug, der; b) (coll.: place) Spelunke, die

'diver n. a) (Sport) Kunstspringer, der/-springerin, die; b) (as profession) Taucher, der/Taucherin, die

diverge [daɪ'vɜːdʒ] v. i. auseinandergehen. **divergent** [daɪ'vɜːdʒənt] adj. auseinandergehend

diverse [daɪ'vɜːs] adj. verschieden

diversion [daɪ'vɜːʃn] n. a) Ablenkung, die; **create a ~** : ein Ablenkungsmanöver durchführen; b) (Brit.: alternative route) Umleitung, die

diversity [daɪ'vɜːsɪtɪ] n. Vielfalt, die

divert [daɪ'vɜːt] v. t. umleiten 〈Verkehr, Fluß〉; ablenken 〈Aufmerksamkeit〉

divide [dɪ'vaɪd] 1. v. t. a) teilen; **~ sth. in two** etw. [in zwei Teile] zerteilen; b) (distribute) aufteilen 〈among/between unter + Akk. od. Dat.〉; c) (Math.) dividieren (fachspr.), teilen (by durch). 2. v. i. sich teilen; **~ [from sth.]** von etw. abzweigen. **divide 'out** v. t. aufteilen 〈among/between unter + Akk. od. Dat.〉; (distribute) verteilen (+ Akk.). **divide 'up** v. t. aufteilen

dividend ['dɪvɪdend] n. Dividende, die

dividers [dɪ'vaɪdəz] n. pl. Stechzirkel, der

divine [dɪ'vaɪn] adj. göttlich

diving ['daɪvɪŋ] n. Kunstspringen, das. **'diving-board** n. Sprungbrett, das. **'diving-suit** n. Taucheranzug, der

divinity [dɪ'vɪnɪtɪ] n. a) Göttlichkeit, die; b) (god) Gottheit, die

divisible [dɪ'vɪzɪbl] adj. teilbar (by durch)

division [dɪ'vɪʒn] n. a) Teilung, die; b) (Math.) Dividieren, das; c) (section, part) Abteilung, die; d) (group) Gruppe, die; e) (Mil. etc.) Division, die; f) (Footb. etc.) Liga, die; Spielklasse, die; (in British football) Division, die

divorce [dɪ'vɔːs] 1. n. [Ehe]scheidung, die. 2. v. t. **~ one's husband/wife** sich von seinem Mann/seiner Frau scheiden lassen. **divorced** [dɪ'vɔːst] adj. geschieden; **get ~** : sich scheiden lassen

divulge [daɪ'vʌldʒ] v. t. preisgeben

DIY abbr. **do-it-yourself**

dizzy ['dɪzɪ] adj. schwind[e]lig; **I feel ~** : mir ist schwindlig

do [də, stressed duː] 1. v. t., neg. coll. **don't** [dəʊnt], pres. t. **he does** [dʌz], neg. (coll.) **doesn't** ['dʌznt], p. t. **did** [dɪd], neg. (coll.) **didn't** ['dɪdnt], pres. p. **doing** ['duːɪŋ], p. p. **done** [dʌn] a) machen 〈Hausaufgaben, Hausarbeit, Examen, Handstand〉; erfüllen 〈Pflicht〉; verrichten 〈Arbeit〉; vorführen 〈Trick, Nummer, Tanz〉; durchführen 〈Test〉; machen 〈Übersetzung, Kopie, Bett〉; schaffen 〈Pensum〉; (clean) putzen

(arrange) [zurecht]machen 〈Haare〉; schminken 〈Lippen, Augen, Gesicht〉; machen (ugs.) 〈Nägel〉; (cut) schneiden 〈Nägel〉; (paint) machen (ugs.) 〈Zimmer〉; streichen 〈Haus, Möbel〉; (repair) in Ordnung bringen; **do the shopping / washing-up / cleaning** einkaufen [gehen]/abwaschen/saubermachen; **what can I do for you?** (in shop) was darf's sein?; **do sth. about sth./sb.** etw. gegen etw./jmdn. unternehmen; b) (cook) braten; **well done** durch[gebraten]; c) (solve) lösen 〈Problem, Rätsel〉; machen 〈Puzzle, Kreuzworträtsel〉; d) (sl.: swindle) reinlegen (ugs.); **do sb. out of sth.** jmdn. um etw. bringen; e) (satisfy) zusagen (+ Dat.). 2. v. i., forms as 1: a) (act) tun; **do as they do** mach es wie sie; b) (fare) **how are you doing?** wie geht's dir?; c) (get on) vorankommen; (in exams) abschneiden; **do well/badly at school** gut/schlecht in der Schule sein; d) **how do you do?** (formal) guten Tag/Morgen/Abend!; e) (serve purpose) es tun; (suffice) [aus]reichen; (be suitable) gehen; **that won't do** das geht nicht; **that will do!** jetzt aber genug! 3. v. substitute, forms as 1: **you mustn't act as he does** du darfst nicht so wie er handeln; **You went to Paris, didn't you? – Yes, I did** Du warst doch in Paris, nicht wahr? – Ja[, stimmt]; **come in, do!** komm doch herein! 4. v. aux. forms as 1: **I do love Greece** Griechenland gefällt mir wirklich gut; **little did he know that …**: er hatte keine Ahnung, daß …; **do you know him?** kennst du ihn?; **what does he want?** was will er?; **I don't** or **do not wish to take part** ich möchte nicht teilnehmen; **don't be so noisy!** seid [doch] nicht so laut! 5. n. [duː], pl. **do's** or **dos** [duːz] (Brit. coll.) Feier, die; Fete, die (ugs.). **do a'way with** v. t. abschaffen. **'do for** v. t. (coll.) **do for sb.** jmdn. fertigmachen (ugs.); **be done for** erledigt sein. **do 'in** v. t. (sl.) kaltmachen (salopp). **do 'up** v. t. a) (fasten) zumachen; binden 〈Schnürsenkel, Fliege〉; b) (wrap) einpacken. **'do with** v. t. **I could do with …**: ich brauche … **'do without** v. t. **do without sth.** auf etw. (Akk.) verzichten

docile ['dəʊsaɪl] adj. sanft; (submissive) unterwürfig

¹dock [dɒk] 1. n. a) Dock, das; b) usu. in pl. (area) Hafen, der. 2. v. t. [ein]docken. 3. v. i. anlegen

²**dock** n. (in lawcourt) Anklagebank, die; **stand/be in the ~**: ≈ auf der Anklagebank sitzen

'**docker** n. Hafenarbeiter, der

'**dockyard** n. Schiffswerft, die

doctor ['dɒktə(r)] 1. n. **a)** Arzt, der/Ärztin, die; as address Herr/Frau Doktor; **b)** (holder of degree) Doktor, der. 2. v. t. (coll.) verfälschen

doctrine ['dɒktrɪn] n. Lehre, die

document ['dɒkjʊmənt] n. Dokument, das; Urkunde, die

documentary [dɒkjʊ'mentərɪ] 1. adj. dokumentarisch. 2. n. (film) Dokumentarfilm, der

dodge [dɒdʒ] 1. v. i. ausweichen. 2. v. t. ausweichen (+ Dat.) ⟨Schlag, Hindernis usw.⟩; entkommen (+ Dat.) ⟨Polizei, Verfolger⟩. 3. n. (trick) Trick, der

dodgems ['dɒdʒəmz] n. pl. [Auto]skooterbahn, die; **have a ride/go on the ~**: Autoskooter fahren

dodgy ['dɒdʒɪ] adj. (Brit. coll.) (unreliable) unsicher; (risky) gewagt

doe [dəʊ] n. (deer) Damtier, das; (rabbit) [Kaninchen]weibchen, das

does [dʌz] see do

doesn't ['dʌznt] (coll.) = does not; see do

dog [dɒg] 1. n. Hund, der. 2. v. t., -gg- verfolgen; (fig.) heimsuchen

dog: **~-biscuit** n. Hundekuchen, der; **~-collar** n. [Hunde]halsband, das; (joc.: clerical collar) Kollar, das; **~-eared** adj. **a ~-eared book** ein Buch mit Eselsohren

dogged ['dɒgɪd] adj. hartnäckig ⟨Weigerung, Verurteilung⟩; zäh ⟨Durchhaltevermögen, Ausdauer⟩

dogma ['dɒgmə] n. Dogma, das. **dogmatic** [dɒg'mætɪk] adj. dogmatisch

doing ['du:ɪŋ] n. Tun, das

do-it-yourself [du:ɪtjə'self] 1. adj. Do-it-yourself-. 2. n. Heimwerken, das

doldrums ['dɒldrəmz] n. pl. **in the ~** (in low spirits) niedergeschlagen; (Econ.) in einer Flaute

dole [dəʊl] 1. n. (coll.) **the ~**: Stempelgeld, das (ugs.); **be/go on the ~**: stempeln gehen (ugs.). 2. v. i. **~ out** [in kleinen Mengen] verteilen

doll [dɒl] n. Puppe, die

dollar ['dɒlə(r)] n. Dollar, der

dollop ['dɒləp] n. (coll.) Klacks, der (ugs.)

'**doll's house** n. Puppenhaus, das

dolphin ['dɒlfɪn] n. Delphin, der

domain [də'meɪn] n. Gebiet, das

dome [dəʊm] n. Kuppel, die

domestic [də'mestɪk] adj. **a)** (household) häuslich; (family) familiär ⟨Angelegenheit, Reibereien⟩; **b)** (Econ.) inländisch; Binnen-; **c)** **~ animal/cat** Haustier, das/-katze, die

domesticated [də'mestɪkeɪtɪd] adj. gezähmt ⟨Tier⟩; (fig.) häuslich

dominant ['dɒmɪnənt] adj. vorherrschend

dominate ['dɒmɪneɪt] v. t. beherrschen. **domination** [dɒmɪ'neɪʃn] n. [Vor]herrschaft, die (**over** über + Akk.)

domineering [dɒmɪ'nɪərɪŋ] adj. herrisch

domino ['dɒmɪnəʊ] n. Domino[stein], der; **~es** sing. (game) Domino[spiel], das; **play ~es** Domino spielen

'**don** [dɒn] v. t. (Liter.) anlegen (geh.)

²**don** n. (Univ.) Dozent, der

donate [dəʊ'neɪt] v. t. spenden; (on large scale) stiften. **donation** [də'neɪʃn] n. Spende, die (**to** für); (large-scale) Stiftung, die

done [dʌn] see do

donkey ['dɒŋkɪ] n. Esel, der

donor ['dəʊnə(r)] n. Spender, der/ Spenderin, die

don't [dəʊnt] v. i. = do not; see do

doodle ['du:dl] v. i. [herum]kritzeln

doom [du:m] 1. n. Verhängnis, das. 2. v. t. verurteilen; **be ~ed** verloren sein; **be ~ed to fail** or **failure** zum Scheitern verurteilt sein

door [dɔ:(r)] n. Tür, die; (of castle, barn) Tor, das; **out of ~s** im Freien; **go out of ~s** nach draußen gehen

door: **~-bell** n. Türklingel, die; **~-handle** n. Türklinke, die; **~-mat** n. Fußmatte, die; **~-step** n. Türstufe, die; **on one's/the ~-step** (fig.) vor jmds. Tür; **~-way** n. Eingang, der

dope [dəʊp] 1. n. **a)** (sl.: narcotic) Stoff, der (salopp); **b)** (coll.: fool) Dussel, der. 2. v. t. dopen ⟨Pferd, Athleten⟩

dormant ['dɔ:mənt] adj. ruhend ⟨Tier, Pflanze⟩; untätig ⟨Vulkan⟩

dormitory ['dɔ:mɪtərɪ] n. Schlafsaal, der

dormouse ['dɔ:maʊs] n., pl. **dormice** ['dɔ:maɪs] Haselmaus, die

dose [dəʊs] 1. n. Dosis, die. 2. v. t. **~ sb. with sth.** jmdm. etw. geben

dot [dɒt] n. Punkt, der; **on the ~**: auf den Punkt genau

dote [dəʊt] v. i. **~ on sb./sth.** jmdn./ etw. abgöttisch lieben

dotted ['dɒtɪd] *adj.* gepunktet

dotty ['dɒtɪ] *adj.* (coll.) (silly) dümmlich; (feeble-minded) vertrottelt (ugs.); (absurd) blödsinnig (ugs.)

double ['dʌbl] **1.** *adj.* doppelt; ~ **bed/room** Doppelbett, *das*/-zimmer, *das*; **be** ~ **the height/width/length** doppelt so hoch/breit/lang sein. **2.** *adv.* doppelt. **3.** *n.* **a)** Doppelte, *das*; **b)** (twice as much) doppelt soviel; (twice as many) doppelt so viele; **c)** (person) Doppelgänger, *der*/-gängerin, *die*; **d)** *in pl.* (Tennis etc.) Doppel, *das*; **e) at the** ~ (Mil.) im Laufschritt; (fig.) ganz schnell. **4.** *v.t.* verdoppeln. **5.** *v.i.* sich verdoppeln. **double 'back** *v.i.* kehrtmachen. **double 'up** krümmen (**with** vor + *Dat.*)

double: ~-'**bass** *n.* Kontrabaß, *der*; ~-'**check** *v.t.* (verify twice) zweimal kontrollieren; (verify in two ways) zweifach überprüfen; ~ '**chin** *n.* Doppelkinn, *das*; ~-'**cross** *v.t.* ein Doppelspiel treiben mit; ~-'**decker** *n.* [dʌbl'dekə(r)] *n.* Doppeldeckerbus, *der*; ~ '**glazing** *n.* Doppelverglasung, *die*; ~-'**jointed** *n.* sehr gelenkig

doubly ['dʌblɪ] *adv.* doppelt

doubt [daʊt] **1.** *n.* Zweifel, *der* (about, as to, of an + *Dat.*); ~|s| |about or as to sth./as to future] Ungewißheit, (as to fact) Unsicherheit [über etw. (Akk.)/darüber, ob ...]; **there's no** ~ **that ...**: es besteht kein Zweifel daran, daß ...; ~|s| (hesitations) Bedenken *Pl.* (about gegen); **no** ~ (certainly) gewiß; (probably) sicherlich. **2.** *v.i.* zweifeln. **3.** *v.t.* zweifeln an (+ *Dat.*); **I don't** ~ **that** or **it** ich bezweifle das nicht; **I** ~ **whether** or **if** or **that ...**: ich bezweifle, daß ... **doubtful** ['daʊtfl] *adj.* skeptisch (Wesen); ungläubig (Blick)

dough [daʊ] *n.* **a)** Teig, *der*; **b)** (sl.: money) Knete, *die* (salopp). '**doughnut** *n.* [Berliner] Pfannkuchen, *der*

douse [daʊs] *v.t.* übergießen; (extinguish) ausmachen

¹**dove** [dʌv] *n.* Taube, *die*

²**dove** [dəʊv] see **dive 1**

dowdy ['daʊdɪ] *adj.* unansehnlich; (shabby) schäbig

¹**down** [daʊn] *n.* (feathers) Daunen *Pl.*

²**down 1.** *adv.* **a)** (to lower place) herunter/hinunter; (in lift) abwärts; **b)** (in lower place, downstairs) unten; ~ **there/here** da/hier unten; **the next floor** ~: ein Stockwerk tiefer; **be** ~ **with an illness** eine Krankheit haben;

be three points/games ~: mit drei Punkten/Spielen zurückliegen. **2.** *prep.* herunter/hinunter; **lower** ~ **the river** weiter unten am Fluß; **walk** ~ **the hill/road** den Berg/die Straße heruntergehen; **fall** ~ **the stairs/steps** die Treppe/Stufen herunterstürzen; **fall** ~ **a hole/ditch** in ein Loch/ einen Graben fallen; **go** ~ **the pub** in die Kneipe gehen; **live just** ~ **the road** ein Stück weiter unten in der Straße wohnen; **be** ~ **the pub/town** in der Kneipe/Stadt sein; **I've got coffee [all]** ~ **my skirt** mein ganzer Rock ist voll Kaffee. **3.** *v.t.* (coll.) schlucken (ugs.) (Getränk); ~ **tools** die Arbeit niederlegen

down: ~-**and-'out** *n.* Stadtstreicher, *der*/-streicherin, *die*; ~-'**cast** *adj.* niedergeschlagen; ~'**fall** *n.* Untergang, *der*; ~-'**hearted** *adj.* niedergeschlagen; ~'**hill** *adv.* bergab; ~ '**payment** *n.* Anzahlung, *die*; ~'**pour** *n.* Regenguß, *der*; ~-'**right** *adj.* ausgemacht; glatt ⟨Lüge⟩; ~'**stairs 1.** [-'-] *adv.* die Treppe hinunter ⟨gehen, fallen, kommen⟩; unten ⟨wohnen, sein⟩; **2.** ['--] *adj.* im Erdgeschoß *nachgestellt*; ~'**stream** *adv.* flußabwärts; ~-**to-'earth** *adj.* sachlich; ~'**town** *adv.* im/ (direction) ins Stadtzentrum; ~-'**trodden** *adj.* unterdrückt; ~'**under** *adv.* (coll.) in/(to) nach Australien/Neuseeland

downward ['daʊnwəd] **1.** *adj.* nach unten gerichtet. **2.** *adv.* abwärts ⟨sich bewegen⟩; nach unten ⟨sehen, gehen⟩.

downwards ['daʊnwədz] see **downward 2**

dowry ['daʊrɪ] *n.* Aussteuer, *die*

doze [dəʊz] **1.** *v.i.* dösen (ugs.). **2.** *n.* Nickerchen, *das* (ugs.). **doze 'off** *v.i.* eindösen (ugs.)

dozen ['dʌzn] *n.* **a)** Dutzend, *das*; **half a** ~: sechs; **b)** *in pl.* (coll.: many) Dutzende *Pl.*

Dr *abbr.* doctor Dr.

drab [dræb] *adj.* langweilig; trostlos ⟨Landschaft⟩; eintönig ⟨Leben⟩

draft [drɑːft] **1.** *n.* **a)** (of speech) Konzept, *das*; (of treaty, bill) Entwurf, *der*; **b)** (Amer.) see **draught. 2.** *v.t.* entwerfen. **drafty** (Amer.) see **draughty**

drag [dræg] **1.** *v.t.*, **-gg-** schleppen. **2.** *v.i.*, **-gg-** schleifen; (fig.: pass slowly) sich [hin]schleppen. **3.** *n.* (sl.) **in** ~: in Frauenkleidung. **drag 'on** *v.i.* sich [da]hin schleppen

dragon ['drægn] *n.* Drache, *der*. '**dragonfly** *n.* Libelle, *die*

drain [dreɪn] **1.** *n.* Abflußrohr, *das;* *(underground)* Kanalisationsrohr, *das;* *(grating at roadside)* Gully, *der;* go down the ~ *(fig. coll.)* für die Katz sein *(ugs.).* **2.** *v. t.* **a)** trockenlegen ⟨*Teich*⟩; entwässern ⟨*Land*⟩; ableiten ⟨*Wasser*⟩; **b)** *(Cookery)* abgießen ⟨*Wasser, Gemüse*⟩; **c)** austrinken ⟨*Glas*⟩. **3.** *v. i.* ⟨*Flüssigkeit:*⟩ ablaufen; ⟨*Geschirr, Gemüse:*⟩ abtropfen. **drainage** ['dreɪnɪdʒ] *n.* Kanalisation, *die.* **'draining-board** (*Brit.; Amer.:* **'drainboard**) *n.* Abtropfbrett, *das.* **'drainpipe** *n.* Regen[abfall]rohr, *das*

drake [dreɪk] *n.* Enterich, *der*

drama ['drɑːmə] *n.* Drama, *das.* **dramatic** [drə'mætɪk] *adj.* dramatisch. **dramatist** ['dræmətɪst] *n.* Dramatiker, *der*/Dramatikerin, *die.* **dramatize** ['dræmətaɪz] *v. t.* dramatisieren

drank *see* **drink 2**

drape [dreɪp] **1.** *v. t.* drapieren. **2.** *n.* *(Amer.:* curtain) Vorhang, *der.* **'draper** *n.* *(Brit.)* Textilkaufmann, *der;* ~'s [shop] Textilgeschäft, *das*

drastic ['dræstɪk] *adj.* drastisch

draught [drɑːft] *n.* [Luft]zug, *der;* there's a ~: es zieht

'draughtboard *n.* *(Brit.)* Damebrett, *das*

'draughts *n.* *(Brit.)* Damespiel, *das* **'draughtsman** [~mən] *n., pl.* **draughtsmen** [~mən] Zeichner, *der*/Zeichnerin, *die.* **'draughty** *adj.* zugig

draw [drɔː] **1.** *v. t.,* **drew** [druː], **drawn** [drɔːn] **a)** *(pull)* ziehen; ~ the curtains/blinds *(close)* die Vorhänge zuziehen/die Jalousien herunterlassen; ~ sth. towards one etw. zu sich heranziehen; **b)** *(attract)* anlocken; be ~n to sb. von jmdm. angezogen werden; **c)** *(take out)* herausziehen; schöpfen ⟨*Wasser*⟩; ~ money from the bank Geld bei der Bank holen/abheben; **d)** beziehen ⟨*Gehalt, Rente, Arbeitslosenunterstützung*⟩; **e)** ziehen ⟨*Strich*⟩; zeichnen ⟨*geometrische Figur, Bild*⟩; **f)** ziehen ⟨*Parallele, Vergleich*⟩; herausstellen ⟨*Unterschied*⟩. **2.** *v. i.* **drew, drawn:** ~ to an end zu Ende gehen. **3.** *n.* **a)** *(raffle)* Tombola, *die;* **b)** *(result of)* drawn game) Unentschieden, *das.* **draw 'back** **1.** *v. t.* zurückziehen. **2.** *v. i.* zurückweichen. **draw 'in** *v. i.* einfahren; ⟨*Tage:*⟩ kürzer werden. **draw 'out** *v. i.* abfahren; ⟨*Tage:*⟩ länger werden. **draw 'up 1.** *v. t.* **a)** aufsetzen

⟨*Vertrag*⟩; aufstellen ⟨*Liste*⟩; **b)** *(pull closer)* heranziehen. **2.** *v. i.* [an]halten

draw: ~**back** *n.* Nachteil, *der;* ~**bridge** *n.* Zugbrücke, *die*

drawer [drɔː(r), 'drɔːə(r)] *n.* Schublade, *die*

'drawing *n.* *(sketch)* Zeichnung, *die*

drawing: ~**-board** *n.* Zeichenbrett, *das;* ~**-pin** *n.* *(Brit.)* Reißzwecke, *die;* ~**-room** *n.* Salon, *der*

drawl [drɔːl] **1.** *v. i.* gedehnt sprechen. **2.** *n.* gedehntes Sprechen

drawn *see* **draw 1, 2**

dread [dred] **1.** *v. t.* sich sehr fürchten vor (+ *Dat.*); the ~ed day/moment der gefürchtete Tag/Augenblick. **2.** *n.* Angst, *die.* **dreadful** *adj.* schrecklich; *(coll.: very bad)* fürchterlich; I feel ~ *(unwell)* ich fühle mich scheußlich *(ugs.).* **'dreadfully** *adv.* schrecklich; *(coll.: very badly)* fürchterlich

dream [driːm] **1.** *n.* Traum, *der;* have a ~ about sb./sth. von jmdm./etw. träumen. **2.** *v. i. & t.* **dreamt** [dremt] *or* **dreamed** träumen

dreary ['drɪərɪ] *adj.* trostlos

dredge [dredʒ] *v. t.* ausbaggern. **'dredger** *n.* Bagger, *der*

dregs [dregz] *n. pl.* [Boden]satz, *der*

drench [drentʃ] *v. t.* durchnässen

dress [dres] **1.** *n.* Kleid, *das;* *(clothing)* Kleidung, *die.* **2.** *v. t.* **a)** anziehen; be well ~ed gut gekleidet sein; get ~ed sich anziehen; **b)** verbinden ⟨*Wunde*⟩. **3.** *v. i.* sich anziehen. **dress 'up** *v. i.* sich feinmachen

'dresser *n.* **a)** Anrichte, *die;* **b)** *(Amer.)* *see* **dressing-table**

'dressing *n.* **a)** *no pl.* Anziehen, *das;* **b)** *(Cookery)* Dressing, *das;* **c)** *(Med.)* Verband, *der*

dressing: ~**-gown** *n.* Bademantel, *der;* ~**-room** *n.* *(Sport)* Umkleideraum, *der;* *(for actor)* Garderobe, *die;* ~**-table** *n.* Frisierkommode, *die*

dress: ~**maker** *n.* Damenschneider, *der*/-schneiderin, *die;* ~**-making** *n.* Damenschneiderei, *die;* ~ **rehearsal** *n.* Generalprobe, *die*

drew *see* **draw 1, 2**

dribble ['drɪbl] *v. i.* **a)** *(slobber)* sabbern; **b)** *(Sport)* dribbeln

dried [draɪd] *adj.* getrocknet; ~ fruit[s] Dörrobst, *das;* ~ milk Trockenmilch, *die*

drier ['draɪə(r)] *n.* *(for hair)* Trockenhaube, *die;* *(hand-held)* Fön ⓦ, *der;* *(for laundry)* [Wäsche]trockner, *der*

drift [drɪft] 1. *n.* a) *(of snow or sand)* Verwehung, *die;* b) *(gist)* get or catch the ~ of sth. etw im wesentlichen verstehen. 2. *v. i.* a) treiben; ⟨Wolke:⟩ ziehen; b) ⟨Sand, Schnee:⟩ zusammengeweht werden. **'driftwood** *n.* Treibholz, *das*

drill [drɪl] 1. *n.* a) *(tool)* Bohrer, *der;* b) *(Mil.: training)* Drill, *der.* 2. *v. t. & i.* bohren (for nach)

drink [drɪŋk] 1. *n.* Getränk, *das; (alcoholic)* Glas, *das; (not with food)* Drink, *der;* have a ~: [etwas] trinken; *(alcoholic)* ein Glas trinken. 2. *v. t. & i.* **drank** [dræŋk], **drunk** [drʌŋk] trinken. **drinkable** ['drɪŋkəbl] *adj.* trinkbar. **'drinking-water** *n.* Trinkwasser, *das*

drip [drɪp] 1. *n.* a) Tropfen, *das;* b) *(coll.: feeble person)* Schlappschwanz, *der (salopp).* 2. *v. i.* **-pp-** tropfen; be ~ping with water/moisture triefend naß sein. **'drip-dry** *adj.* bügelfrei

'dripping *n. (Cookery)* Schmalz, *das*

drive [draɪv] 1. *n.* a) Fahrt, *die;* b) *(private road)* Zufahrt, *die; (entrance) (to small building)* Einfahrt, *die; (to large building)* Auffahrt, *die;* c) *(energy)* Tatkraft, *die;* d) *(Psych.)* Trieb, *der;* e) *(Motor Veh.)* left-hand/right-hand ~: Links-/Rechtssteuerung, *die.* 2. *v. t.,* **drove** [drəʊv], **driven** ['drɪvn] a) fahren; b) treiben ⟨Tier;⟩ c) *(compel to move)* vertreiben (out of, from aus); d) *(fig.)* ~ sb. to sth. jmdn. zu etw. treiben; ~ sb. to do sth. or into doing sth. jmdn. dazu treiben, etw. zu tun; e) *(power)* antreiben. 3. *v. i.,* **drove, driven** a) fahren; can you ~? kannst du Auto fahren?; b) *(go by car)* mit dem [eigenen] Auto fahren. **'drive at** *v. t. (fig.)* hinauswollen auf (+ *Akk.*); what are you driving at? worauf wollen Sie hinaus? **drive a'way** 1. *v. i.* wegfahren. 2. *v. t.* a) wegfahren; b) *(chase away)* vertreiben. **drive 'off** *see* drive away. **drive 'on** *v. i.* weiterfahren. **drive 'up** *v. i.* vorfahren (to vor + *Dat.*)

'drive-in *adj.* Drive-in-; ~ cinema or *(Amer.)* movie |theater| Autokino, *das*

drivel ['drɪvl] *n.* Gefasel, *das (ugs.);* talk ~: faseln *(ugs.)*

driven *see* drive 2, 3

driver ['draɪvə(r)] *n.* Fahrer, *der/*Fahrerin, *die; (of locomotive)* Führer, *der/*Führerin, *die;* ~s license *(Amer.)* Führerschein, *der*

driving ['draɪvɪŋ] 1. *n.* Fahren, *das.* 2. *adj.* peitschend ⟨Regen⟩

driving: ~-**instructor** *n.* Fahrlehrer, *der/*-lehrerin, *die;* ~-**lesson** *n.* Fahrstunde, *die;* ~-**licence** *n.* Führerschein, *der;* ~-**school** *n.* Fahrschule, *die;* ~-**test** *n.* Fahrprüfung, *die*

drizzle ['drɪzl] 1. *n.* Nieseln, *das.* 2. *v. i.* it's drizzling es nieselt

drone [drəʊn] 1. *v. i.* a) ⟨Biene:⟩ summen; ⟨Maschine:⟩ brummen; b) ⟨Rezitator:⟩ leiern. 2. *n.* see 1: Summen, *das;* Brummen, *das;* Geleier, *das*

drool [dru:l] *v. i.* ~ over eine kindische Freude haben an (+ *Dat.*)

droop [dru:p] *v. i.* herunterhängen; ⟨Blume:⟩ den Kopf hängen lassen

drop [drɒp] 1. *n.* a) Tropfen, *der;* in ~s tropfenweise; b) *(decrease)* Rückgang, *der.* 2. *v. i.,* **-pp-:** a) *(fall) (accidentally)* [herunter]fallen; *(deliberately)* sich [hinunter]fallen lassen; b) *(in amount etc.)* sinken; ⟨Preis, Wert:⟩ sinken, fallen; ⟨Wind:⟩ sich legen; ⟨Stimme:⟩ sich senken. 3. *v. t.,* **-pp-:** a) fallen lassen; abwerfen ⟨Bomben, Nachschub⟩; b) *(discontinue, abandon)* fallenlassen; c) *(omit)* auslassen. **drop 'by, drop 'in** *v. i.* vorbeikommen. **drop 'off** 1. *v. i.* a) *(fall off)* abfallen; b) *(fall asleep)* einnicken. 2. *v. t.* absetzen ⟨Fahrgast⟩. **drop 'out** *v. i.* a) herausfallen (of aus); b) *(withdraw)* aussteigen *(ugs.)* (of aus); c) *(beforehand)* seine Teilnahme absagen

'drop-out *n.* Aussteiger, *der/*Aussteigerin, *die*

drought [draʊt] *n.* Dürre, *die*

drove *see* drive 2, 3

drown [draʊn] 1. *v. i.* ertrinken. 2. *v. t.* ertränken; be ~ed ertrinken

drowsy ['draʊzɪ] *adj.* schläfrig; *(on just waking)* verschlafen

drudgery ['drʌdʒərɪ] *n.* Schufterei, *die*

drug [drʌg] 1. *n.* a) *(Med.)* [Arznei]mittel, *das;* b) *(narcotic)* Droge, *die;* be on ~s Rauschgift nehmen. 2. *v. t.,* **-gg-** betäuben ⟨Person⟩; ~ sb.'s food/drink jmds. Essen/Getränk *(Dat.)* ein Betäubungsmittel beimischen

drug: ~ **addict** *n.* Drogensüchtige, *der/die;* ~ **addiction** *n.* Drogensucht, *die;* ~-**store** *n. (Amer.)* Drugstore, *der*

drum [drʌm] 1. *n.* a) Trommel, *die;* b) in pl. *(in jazz or pop)* Schlagzeug, *das;* c) *(container)* Faß, *das.* 2. *v. i.* trommeln. **drum 'up** *v. i.* auftreiben

'drummer *n.* Schlagzeuger, *der*

'drumstick *n.* a) Trommelschlegel, *der;* b) *(Cookery)* Keule, *die*

drunk [drʌŋk] **1.** *adj.* be ~: betrunken sein; get ~: betrunken werden (on von); *(intentionally)* sich betrinken (on mit). **2.** *n.* Betrunkene, *der/die*

drunkard ['drʌŋkəd] *n.* Trinker, *der/* Trinkerin, *die*

drunken ['drʌŋkn] *attrib. adj.* betrunken; *(habitually)* ständig betrunken; ~ **driving** Trunkenheit am Steuer.

'**drunkenness** *n.* Betrunkenheit, *die; (habitual)* Trunksucht, *die*

dry [draɪ] **1.** *adj.* trocken; trocken, *(very ~)* herb ⟨Wein⟩; ausgetrocknet ⟨Flußbett⟩; run or become ~: trocknen. **2.** *v.t.* **a)** trocknen ⟨Haare, Wäsche⟩; abtrocknen ⟨Geschirr, Baby⟩; ~ one-self sich abtrocknen; ~ one's eyes or tears/hands sich (Dat.) die Tränen abwischen/die Hände abtrocknen; **b)** *(preserve)* trocknen, dörren ⟨Obst, Fleisch⟩. **3.** *v.i.* trocknen. **dry 'out** *v.t. & i.* trocknen. **dry 'up 1.** *v.t.* abtrocknen. **2.** *v.i.* **a)** ⟨~ the dishes⟩ abtrocknen; **b)** ⟨Brunnen, Quelle:⟩ versiegen; ⟨Fluß, Teich:⟩ austrocknen

dry: ~'**clean** *v.t.* chemisch reinigen; ~'**cleaner's** *n.* chemische Reinigung; ~'**cleaning** *n.* chemische Reinigung

'**dryer** *see* **drier**

'**dryness** *n.* Trockenheit, *die*

dual ['dju:əl] *adj.* doppelt. **dual 'carriageway** *n. (Brit.)* Straße mit Mittelstreifen. **dual-'purpose** *adj.* zweifach verwendbar

dubious ['dju:bɪəs] *adj. (doubting)* unschlüssig; *(suspicious)* zweifelhaft

duchess ['dʌtʃɪs] *n.* Herzogin, *die*

duck [dʌk] **1.** *n.* Ente, *die.* **2.** *v.i.* sich *(schnell)* ducken. **3.** *v.t.* ~ **one's head** den Kopf einziehen

duckling ['dʌklɪŋ] *n.* Entenküken, *das*

duct [dʌkt] *n.* Rohr, *das; (for air)* Ventil, *das*

dud [dʌd] **1.** *n. (useless thing)* Niete, die *(ugs.); (counterfeit)* Fälschung, *die.* **2.** *adj.* mies *(ugs.)*; schlecht; *(fake)* gefälscht; geplatzt ⟨Scheck⟩

due [dju:] **1.** *adj.* **a)** *(owed)* geschuldet; zustehend ⟨Eigentum, Recht usw.⟩; **there's sth. ~ to me, I've got sth. ~:** mir steht etw. zu; **b)** *(immediately payable)* fällig; **c)** *(that it is proper to give or use)* gebührend; angemessen ⟨Belohnung⟩; **be ~ to sb.** jmdm. gebühren; **with all ~ respect** bei allem gebotenen Respekt; **d)** *(attributable)* **the mistake was ~ to negligence** der Fehler war durch Nachlässigkeit verursacht; **it's ~ to**

her that we missed the train ihretwegen verpaßten wir den Zug; **e)** *(scheduled, expected);* **be ~ to do sth.** etw. tun sollen; **be ~ |to arrive|** ankommen sollen; **f)** *(likely to get, deserving)* **be ~ for sth.** etw. verdienen. **2.** *adv.* **a)** ~ **north** genau nach Norden; **b)** ~ **to** auf Grund (+ Gen.); aufgrund (+ Gen.). **3.** *n.* **a)** **give sb. his ~:** jmdm. Gerechtigkeit widerfahren lassen; **b)** ~**s** *(fees)* Gebühren *Pl.*

duel ['dju:əl] *n.* Duell, *das*

duet [dju:'et] *n. (for voices)* Duett, *das; (instrumental)* Duo, *das*

duffle ['dʌfl]: ~ **bag** *n.* Matchbeutel, *der;* ~ **coat** *n.* Dufflecoat, *der*

dug *see* **dig**

duke [dju:k] *n.* Herzog, *der*

dull [dʌl] **1.** *adj.* **a)** *(stupid)* beschränkt; *(slow to understand)* begriffsstutzig; **b)** *(boring)* langweilig; **c)** *(gloomy)* trübe ⟨Wetter, Tag⟩. **2.** *v.t.* abstumpfen ⟨Geist, Sinne, Verstand⟩

duly ['dju:lɪ] *adv.* ordnungsgemäß

dumb [dʌm] *adj.* **a)** stumm; **b)** *(coll.: stupid)* doof *(ugs.)*

dumbfounded [dʌm'faʊndɪd] *adj.* sprachlos

dummy ['dʌmɪ] *n.* **a)** *(of tailor)* Schneiderpuppe, *die; (in shop)* Schaufensterpuppe, *die; (of ventriloquist)* Puppe, *die; (stupid person)* Dummkopf, *der (ugs.)*; **like a stuffed ~:** wie ein Ölgötze *(ugs.)*; **b)** *(imitation)* Attrappe, *die;* **c)** *(esp. Brit.: for baby)* Schnuller, *der*

dump [dʌmp] **1.** *n.* **a)** *(place)* Müllkippe, *die; (heap)* Müllhaufen, *der; (permanent)* Müllhalde, *die;* **b)** *(Mil.)* Depot, *das;* **c)** *(coll.: town)* Kaff, *das (ugs.).* **2.** *v.t.* *(dispose of)* werfen; *(deposit)* abladen ⟨Sand, Müll usw.⟩; *(leave)* lassen; *(place)* abstellen

dumpling ['dʌmplɪŋ] *n.* Kloß, *der*

dumps *n. pl.* **be or feel down in the ~:** ganz down sein *(ugs.)*

dunce [dʌns] *n.* Null, *die (ugs.)*

dune [dju:n] *n.* Düne, *die*

dung [dʌŋ] *n.* Dung, *der*

dungarees [dʌŋgə'ri:z] *n. pl.* Latzhose, *die*

dungeon ['dʌndʒən] *n.* Kerker, *der*

dunk [dʌŋk] *v.t.* tunken

dupe [dju:p] **1.** *v.t.* übertölpeln. **2.** *n.* Dumme, *der/die*

duplex ['dju:pleks] *adj. (esp. Amer.) (two-storey)* zweistöckig ⟨Wohnung⟩; *(two-family)* Zweifamilien⟨haus⟩

duplicate 1. ['dju:plɪkət] *adj.* **a)** *(identical)* Zweit-; **b)** *(twofold)* doppelt. **2.** *n.*

Kopie, die; (second copy of letter/document/key) Duplikat, das; **in** ~: in doppelter Ausfertigung. **3.** ['dju:plɪkeɪt] v. t. **a)** (make a copy of, make in ~) ~ sth. eine zweite Anfertigung von etw. machen; **b)** (on machine) vervielfältigen; **c)** (do twice) noch einmal tun

durable ['djʊərəbl] adj. haltbar; dauerhaft ⟨Friede, Freundschaft usw.⟩

duration [djʊə'reɪ∫n] n. Dauer, die

duress [djʊə'res] n. Zwang, der

during ['djʊərɪŋ] prep. während; (at a point in) in (+ Dat.)

dusk [dʌsk] n. Einbruch der Dunkelheit

dust [dʌst] **1.** n. Staub, der. **2.** v. t. abstauben ⟨Möbel⟩; ~ **a room/ house** in einem Zimmer/Haus Staub wischen. **3.** v. i. Staub wischen. '**dustbin** n. (Brit.) Mülltonne, die. '**dustcart** (Brit.) Müllwagen, der

'**duster** n. Staubtuch, das

dust: ~**jacket** n. Schutzumschlag, der; ~**man** [~mən] n., pl. ~**men** [~mən] (Brit.) Müllmann, der; ~**pan** n. Kehrschaufel, die

'**dusty** adj. staubig; verstaubt ⟨Bücher, Möbel⟩

Dutch [dʌt∫] **1.** adj. holländisch; **sb. is** ~: jmd. ist Holländer/Holländerin. **2.** n. **a)** (language) Holländisch, das; see also **English 2a; b) the** ~ pl. die Holländer

Dutch: ~ '**courage** n. angetrunkener Mut; ~**man** [~mən] n., pl. ~**men** [~mən] Holländer, der; ~**woman** n. Holländerin, die

dutiful ['dju:tɪfl] adj. pflichtbewußt

duty ['dju:tɪ] n. Pflicht, die; (task) Aufgabe, die; **be on** ~: Dienst haben; **off** ~: nicht im Dienst; **be off** ~: keinen Dienst haben; ⟨ab ... Uhr⟩ dienstfrei sein; **b)** (tax) Zoll, der; **pay** ~ **on sth.** Zoll für etw. bezahlen. '**duty-free** adj. zollfrei

duvet ['du:veɪ] n. Federbett, das

dwarf [dwɔ:f] n., pl. ~**s** or **dwarves** ['dwɔ:vz] Zwerg, der/Zwergin, die

dwell [dwel] v. i., **dwelt** [dwelt] (literary) wohnen. '**dwell [up]on** v. t. (in discussion) sich ausführlich befassen mit; (in thought) in Gedanken verweilen bei

'**dwelling** n. Wohnung, die

dwelt see **dwell**

dwindle ['dwɪndl] v. i. ~ **[away]** abnehmen; ⟨Unterstützung, Interesse:⟩ nachlassen; ⟨Vorräte:⟩ schrumpfen

dye [daɪ] **1.** n. Färbemittel, das. **2.** v. t., ~**ing** ['daɪɪŋ] färben

dying ['daɪɪŋ] adj. sterbend; absterbend ⟨Baum⟩

dyke see **dike**

dynamic [daɪ'næmɪk] adj. dynamisch. **dynamism** ['daɪnəmɪzm] n. Dynamik, die

dynamite ['daɪnəmaɪt] n. Dynamit, das

dynamo ['daɪnəməʊ] n. Dynamo, der; (in car) Lichtmaschine, die

dynasty ['dɪnəstɪ] n. Dynastie, die

dysentry ['dɪsəntrɪ] n. Ruhr, die

E

E, e [i:] n. E, e, das

E. abbr. **a)** east O; **b)** eastern ö.

each [i:t∫] **1.** adj. jeder/jede/jedes; **they cost** or **are a pound** ~: sie kosten ein Pfund pro Stück. **2.** pron. **a)** jeder/jede/jedes; **b)** ~ **other** sich

eager ['i:gə(r)] adj. eifrig; **be** ~ **to do sth.** etw. unbedingt tun wollen. '**eagerly** adv. eifrig; gespannt ⟨warten⟩

eagle ['i:gl] n. Adler, der

¹**ear** [ɪə(r)] n. Ohr, das

²**ear** n. (Bot.) Ähre, die

ear: ~**ache** n. Ohrenschmerzen Pl.; ~**drum** n. Trommelfell, das

earl [ɜ:l] n. Graf, der

'**ear lobe** n. Ohrläppchen, das

early ['ɜ:lɪ] **1.** adj. früh. **2.** adv. früh; **I am a bit** ~: ich bin etwas zu früh gekommen; ~ **next week** Anfang der nächsten Woche; ~ **in June** Anfang Juni; **from** ~ **in the morning till late at night** von früh [morgens] bis spät [nachts]; ~ **on** schon früh

ear: ~**mark** v. t. vorsehen; ~**muffs** n. pl. Ohrenschützer, Pl.

earn [ɜ:n] v. t. verdienen; (bring in as income or interest) einbringen

earnest ['ɜ:nɪst] **1.** adj. ernsthaft. **2.** n. **in** ~: mit vollem Ernst

earnings ['ɜ:nɪŋz] n. pl. Verdienst, der; (of business etc.) Ertrag, der

ear: ~**phones** n. pl. Kopfhörer, der;

~-plug n. Ohropax, das ⓌⓅ; **~-ring** n. Ohrring, der; **~-shot** n. out of/within ~ shot außer/in Hörweite

earth [ɜːθ] 1. n. (also Brit. Electr.) Erde, die; how/what etc. on ~ ...? wie/was usw. in aller Welt ...? 2. v. t. (Brit. Electr.) erden

earthenware ['ɜːθnweə(r)] 1. n. Tonwaren Pl. 2. adj. Ton-

earth: **~quake** n. Erdbeben, das; **~worm** n. Regenwurm, der

'earthy adj. a) erdig; b) (coarse) derb

earwig ['ɪəwɪg] n. Ohrwurm, der

ease [iːz] 1. n. a) set sb. at ~: jmdn. beruhigen; at [one's] ~: entspannt; be or feel at [one's] ~: sich wohl fühlen; [stand] at ~! (Mil.) rührt euch!; b) with ~ (without difficulty) mit Leichtigkeit. 2. v. t. lindern ⟨Schmerz, Kummer⟩; entspannen ⟨Lage⟩; verringern ⟨Belastung, Druck, Spannung⟩. 3. v. i. nachlassen

easel ['iːzl] n. Staffelei, die

easily ['iːzɪlɪ] adv. leicht

easiness ['iːzɪnɪs] n. Leichtigkeit, die

east [iːst] 1. n. a) Osten, der; in/to-[wards]/from the ~: im/nach/von Osten; to the ~ of östlich von; b) usu. E~ (Geog., Polit.) Osten, der. 2. adj. östlich; Ost⟨küste, -wind, -grenze⟩. 3. adv. nach Osten; ~ of östlich von.

'East Ber'lin pr. n. (Hist.) Ostberlin, das. **'eastbound** adj. ⟨Zug, Verkehr usw.⟩ in Richtung Osten

Easter ['iːstə(r)] n. Ostern, das od. Pl.

'Easter egg n. Osterei, das

easterly ['iːstəlɪ] adj. östlich; ⟨Wind⟩ aus östlichen Richtungen

eastern ['iːstən] adj. östlich; Ost⟨grenze, -hälfte, -seite⟩; ~ Germany Ostdeutschland, das. **Eastern 'Europe** pr. n. Osteuropa, das

Easter 'Sunday n. Ostersonntag, der

East: ~ 'German (Hist.) 1. adj. ostdeutsch; 2. n. Ostdeutsche, der/die; ~ 'Germany pr. n. (Hist.) Ostdeutschland (das)

eastward(s) [iːstwəd(z)] adv. ostwärts

easy ['iːzɪ] 1. adj. a) leicht; on ~ terms auf Raten ⟨kaufen⟩; b) sorglos ⟨Leben, Zeit⟩; c) (free from constraint) ungezwungen. 2. adv. leicht; easier said than done leichter gesagt als getan; take it ~! (calm down!) beruhige dich!

'easy chair n. Sessel, der. **easy-'going** adj. gelassen; (lax) nachlässig

eat [iːt] v. t. & i., **ate** [et, eɪt], **eaten** ['iːtn] essen; ⟨Tier:⟩ fressen. **eat a'way** v. t.

⟨Rost, Säure:⟩ zerfressen. **eat 'out** v. i. essen gehen. **eat 'up** v. t. aufessen; ⟨Tier:⟩ auffressen

eaten see eat

eau-de-Cologne [əʊdəkə'ləʊn] n. Kölnisch Wasser, das

eaves [iːvz] n. pl. Dachgesims, das. **'eavesdrop** v. i. lauschen; ~ on belauschen. **'eavesdropper** n. Lauscher, der/Lauscherin, die

ebb [eb] 1. n. Ebbe, die; be at a low ~ (fig.) ⟨Person, Stimmung, Moral:⟩ auf dem Nullpunkt sein. 2. v. i. zurückgehen; ~ away (fig.) dahinschwinden. **'ebb-tide** n. Ebbe, die

ebony ['ebənɪ] n. Ebenholz, das

EC abbr. **European Community** EG

eccentric [ik'sentrɪk] 1. adj. exzentrisch. 2. n. Exzentriker, der/Exzentrikerin, die. **eccentricity** [eksen'trɪsɪtɪ] n. Exzentrizität, die

ecclesiastical [ɪkliːzɪ'æstɪkl] adj. kirchlich; geistlich ⟨Musik⟩

echo ['ekəʊ] 1. n. Echo, das. 2. v. t. zurückwerfen; (fig.: repeat) wiederholen

éclair [eɪ'kleə(r)] n. Eclair, das

eclipse [ɪ'klɪps] n. (Astron.) Finsternis, die; ~ of the sun Sonnenfinsternis, die

ecological [ɪkə'lɒdʒɪkl] adj. ökologisch

ecology [ɪ'kɒlədʒɪ] n. Ökologie, die

economic [iːkə'nɒmɪk] adj. a) Wirtschafts⟨politik, -abkommen, -system⟩; wirtschaftlich ⟨Entwicklung, Zusammenbruch⟩; b) (giving adequate return) wirtschaftlich

economical [iːkə'nɒmɪkl] adj. wirtschaftlich; sparsam ⟨Person⟩; be ~ with sth. mit etw. haushalten. **eco'nomically** adv. wirtschaftlich; (not wastefully) sparsam

economics [iːkə'nɒmɪks] n. Wirtschaftswissenschaft, die (meist Pl.)

economist [ɪ'kɒnəmɪst] n. Wirtschaftswissenschaftler, der/-wissenschaftlerin, die

economize [ɪ'kɒnəmaɪz] v. i. sparen; ~ on sth. etw. sparen

economy [ɪ'kɒnəmɪ] n. a) (frugality) Sparsamkeit, die; b) (instance) Einsparung, die; make economies zu Sparmaßnahmen greifen; c) (of country etc.) Wirtschaft, die. **e'conomy size** n. Haushaltspackung, die

ecstasy ['ekstəsɪ] n. Ekstase, die. **ec'static** [ɪk'stætɪk] adj. ekstatisch

ECU, ecu ['eɪkjuː] abbr. **European currency unit** Ecu, der od. die

eddy ['edɪ] n. Strudel, der

edge [edʒ] **1.** *n.* **a)** *(of knife, razor, weapon)* Schneide, *die;* **on** ~ *(fig.)* nervös *od.* gereizt **(about wegen); b)** *(of solid, bed, table)* Kante, *die; (of sheet of paper, road, forest, cliff)* Rand, *der.* **2.** *v. i.* sich schieben

edgy ['edʒɪ] *adj.* nervös

edible ['edɪbl] *adj.* eßbar

edict ['iːdɪkt] *n.* Erlaß, *der*

edit ['edɪt] *v. t.* herausgeben ⟨*Zeitung*⟩; redigieren ⟨*Buch, Artikel, Manuskript*⟩. **edition** [ɪ'dɪʃn] *n.* Ausgabe, *die.* **editor** ['edɪtə(r)] *n.* Redakteur, *der*/Redakteurin, *die; (of particular work)* Bearbeiter, *der*/Bearbeiterin, *die; (of newspaper)* Herausgeber, *der*/-geberin, *die.* **editorial** [edɪ-'tɔːrɪəl] **1.** *n.* Leitartikel, *der.* **2.** *adj.* redaktionell

educate ['edjʊkeɪt] *v. t.* **a)** *(bring up)* erziehen; *(train mind and character of)* bilden; **b)** *(provide schooling for)* **he was ~d at ...:** er hat seine Ausbildung in ... erhalten. **educated** ['edjʊkeɪtɪd] *adj.* gebildet. **education** [edjʊ'keɪʃn] *n.* Erziehung, *die; (system)* Erziehungswesen, *das.* **educational** [edjʊ'keɪʃnl] *adj.* pädagogisch; Lehr⟨*film, -spiele, -anstalt*⟩; Erziehungs⟨*methoden, -arbeit*⟩

EEC *abbr.* **European Economic Community** EWG

eerie ['ɪrɪ] *adj.* unheimlich

eel [iːl] *n.* Aal, *der*

effect [ɪ'fekt] *n.* **a)** Wirkung, *die* **(on** auf + *Akk.*); **the ~s of sth. on sth.** die Auswirkungen einer Sache *(Gen.)* auf etw. *(Akk.);* **take ~:** die erwünschte Wirkung erzielen; **in ~:** in Wirklichkeit; **b) come into ~:** gültig werden; ⟨*Gesetz:*⟩ in Kraft treten; **put into ~:** in Kraft setzen ⟨*Gesetz*⟩; verwirklichen ⟨*Plan*⟩; **with ~ from 2 November/Monday** mit Wirkung vom 2. November/ von Montag

effective [ɪ'fektɪv] *adj.* **a)** wirksam ⟨*Mittel, Maßnahmen*⟩; **be ~** ⟨*Arzneimittel:*⟩ wirken; **b)** *(in operation)* gültig; **~ from/as of** mit Wirkung vom. **effectively** *adv. (in fact)* effektiv; *(with effect)* wirkungsvoll

effectual [ɪ'fektjʊəl] *adj.* wirksam

effeminate [ɪ'femɪnət] *adj.* unmännlich

effervescent [efə'vesənt] *adj.* sprudelnd; *(fig.)* übersprudelnd

efficiency [ɪ'fɪʃənsɪ] *n. (of person)* Fähigkeit, *die;* Tüchtigkeit, *die; (of machine, factory, engine)* Leistungsfähig-

keit, *die; (of organization, method)* gutes Funktionieren

efficient [ɪ'fɪʃənt] *adj.* fähig ⟨*Person*⟩; tüchtig ⟨*Arbeiter, Sekretärin*⟩; leistungsfähig ⟨*Maschine, Motor, Fabrik*⟩; gut funktionierend ⟨*Methode, Organisation*⟩. **efficiently** *adj.* gut

effigy ['efɪdʒɪ] *n.* Bildnis, *das*

effluent ['eflʊənt] Abwässer *Pl.*

effort ['efət] *n.* **a)** Anstrengung, *die,* Mühe, *die;* **make an/every ~** *(physically)* sich anstrengen; *(mentally)* sich bemühen; **b)** *(attempt)* Versuch, *der.* **effortless** *adj.* mühelos

effrontery [ɪ'frʌntərɪ] *n.* Dreistigkeit, *die;* **have the ~ to do sth.** die Stirn besitzen, etw. zu tun

effusive [ɪ'fjuːsɪv] *adj.* überschwenglich; exaltiert *(geh.)* ⟨*Person*⟩

e.g. [iː'dʒiː] *abbr.* **for example** z. B.

egg [eg] *n.* Ei, *das.* **egg 'on** *v. t.* anstacheln

egg: **~-cup** *n.* Eierbecher, *der;* **~shell** *n.* Eierschale, *die;* **~-timer** *n.* Eieruhr, *die;* **~-white** *n.* Eiweiß, *das;* **~ yolk** *n.* Eigelb, *das*

ego ['egəʊ, 'iːgəʊ] *n., pl.* **~s** *(Psych.)* Ego, *das;* **b)** *(self-esteem)* Selbstbewußtsein, *das*

Egypt ['iːdʒɪpt] *pr. n.* Ägypten *(das).* **Egyptian** [ɪ'dʒɪpʃn] **1.** *adj.* ägyptisch. **2.** *n. (person)* Ägypter, *der*/Ägypterin, *die*

eiderdown ['aɪdədaʊn] *n.* Federbett, *das*

eight [eɪt] **1.** *adj.* acht; **at ~:** um acht; **half past ~:** halb neun; **~ thirty** acht Uhr dreißig; **~ ten/fifty** zehn nach acht/vor neun; *(esp. in timetable)* acht Uhr zehn/fünfzig; **~-year-old boy** achtjähriger Junge; **an ~-year-old** ein Achtjähriger/eine Achtjährige; **at [the age of] ~, aged ~:** mit acht Jahren; **~ times** achtmal. **2.** *n.* Acht, *die;* **the first/last ~:** die ersten/letzten acht; **there were ~ of us present** wir waren [zu] acht

eighteen [eɪ'tiːn] **1.** *adj.* achtzehn. **2.** *n.* Achtzehn, *die; See also* **eight.** **eighteenth** [eɪ'tiːnθ] **1.** *adj.* achtzehnt... **2.** *n. (fraction)* Achtzehntel, *das. See also* **eighth**

eighth [eɪtθ] **1.** *adj.* acht...; **be/come ~:** achter sein/als achter ankommen; **~largest** achtgrößt... **2.** *n. (in sequence)* achte, *der/die/das; (in rank)* Achte, *der/die/das; (fraction)* Achtel, *das;* **the ~ of May** der achte Mai

eightieth ['eɪtɪθ] *adj.* achtzigst...

eighty ['eɪtɪ] 1. *adj.* achtzig. 2. *n.* Acht-zig, *die;* **the eighties** *(years)* die achtziger Jahre; **be in one's eighties** in den Achtzigern sein. *See also* **eight**

Eire ['eərə] *pr. n.* Irland, *das;* Eire, *das*

either ['aɪðə(r), 'i:ðə(r)] 1. *adj.* **a)** *(each)* **at ~ end of the table** an beiden Enden des Tisches; **b)** *(one or other)* [irgend]ein ... [von beiden]; **take ~ one** nimm einen/eine/eins von [den] bei-den. 2. *pron.* **a)** *(each)* beide *Pl.;* **I can't cope with ~:** ich kann mit kei-nem von beiden fertig werden; **b)** *(one or other)* einer/eine/ein[e]s von [den beiden]. 3. *adv.* auch [nicht]; **'I don't like that ~:** ich mag es auch nicht. 4. *conj.* **~ ... or ...:** entweder ... oder ...; *(after negation)* weder ... noch ...

eject ['ɪdʒekt] 1. *v. t.* **a)** *(from hall, meeting)* hinauswerfen (**from** aus); **b)** ⟨*Gerät:*⟩ auswerfen; ⟨*Person:*⟩ heraus-holen *⟨Kassette⟩.* 2. *v. i.* sich hinaus-katapultieren. **ejector seat** ['ɪdʒektə si:t] *n.* Schleudersitz, *der*

eke out ['i:k 'aʊt] *v. t.* strecken

elaborate 1. [ɪ'læbərət] *adj.* kompli-ziert; kunstvoll [gearbeitet] ⟨*Arrange-ment, Verzierung*⟩. 2. [ɪ'læbəreɪt] *v. i.* mehr ins Detail gehen; **~ on** näher ausführen

elapse [ɪ'læps] *v. i.* ⟨*Zeit:*⟩ vergehen

elastic [ɪ'læstɪk] 1. *adj.* elastisch. 2. *n.* (**~ band**) Gummiband, *das.* **elastic 'band** *n.* Gummiband, *das*

elated [ɪ'leɪtɪd] *adj.* freudig erregt; **be or feel ~:** in Hochstimmung sein. **elation** [ɪ'leɪʃn] *n.* freudige Erregung

elbow ['elbəʊ] 1. *n.* Ell[en]bogen, *der.* 2. *v. t.* **~ sb. aside** jmdn. mit dem El-lenbogen zur Seite stoßen. **'elbow room** *n.* Ell[en]bogenfreiheit, *die*

¹elder ['eldə(r)] 1. *attrib. adj.* älter... 2. *n.* **a)** *(senior)* Ältere, *der/die;* **b)** *(vil-lage ~, church ~)* Älteste, *der/die*

²elder *n.* *(Bot.)* Holunder, *der.* **'elder-berry** *n.* Holunderbeere, *die*

elderly ['eldəlɪ] 1. *adj.* älter. 2. *n. pl.* **the ~:** ältere Menschen

eldest ['eldɪst] *adj.* ältest...

elect [ɪ'lekt] 1. *adj. postpos.* gewählt; **the President ~:** der designierte Präsi-dent. 2. *v. t.* wählen; **~ sb. chairman** jmdn. zum Vorsitzenden wählen. **election** [ɪ'lekʃn] *n.* Wahl, *die;* **general ~:** allgemeine Wahlen. **e'lec-tion campaign** *n.* Wahlkampagne, *die*

electioneer [ɪlekʃə'nɪə(r)] *v. i.* be/go **~ing** Wahlkampf machen

elector [ɪ'lektə(r)] *n.* Wähler, *der/* Wählerin, *die.* **electoral** [ɪ'lektərl] *adj.* Wahl-. **electorate** [ɪ'lektərət] *n.* Wähler *Pl.*

electric [ɪ'lektrɪk] *adj.* elektrisch; Elektro⟨*kabel, -motor, -herd, -kessel*⟩; Strom⟨*versorgung*⟩; *(fig.)* spannungs-geladen ⟨*Atmosphäre*⟩. **electrical** [ɪ'lektrɪkl] *adj.* elektrisch; Elektro⟨*ab-teilung, -handel, -geräte*⟩

electric: **~ 'blanket** *n.* Heizdecke, *die;* **~ 'fire** *n.* [elektrischer] Heizofen

electrician [ɪlek'trɪʃn] *n.* Elektriker, *der/*Elektrikerin, *die*

electricity [ɪlek'trɪsɪtɪ] *n.* Elektrizität, *die*

electric 'shock *n.* Stromschlag, *der*

electrify [ɪ'lektrɪfaɪ] *v. t.* elektrifizie-ren; *(fig.)* elektrisieren

electrocute [ɪ'lektrəkju:t] *v. t.* durch Stromschlag töten

electrode [ɪ'lektrəʊd] *n.* Elektrode, *die*

electron [ɪ'lektrɒn] *n.* Elektron, *das*

electronic [ɪlek'trɒnɪk] *adj.* elektro-nisch. **electronics** [ɪlek'trɒnɪks] *n.* Elektronik, *die*

elegance ['elɪgəns] *n.* Eleganz, *die*

elegant ['elɪgənt] *adj.* elegant

element ['elɪmənt] *n.* **a)** Element, *das;* **b)** *(Electr.)* Heizelement, *das;* **c) ~s** *(rudiments)* Grundlagen *Pl.* **elemen-tary** [elɪ'mentərɪ] *adj.* elementar; grundlegend ⟨*Fakten, Wissen*⟩; Grundschul⟨*bildung*⟩; Grund⟨*kurs, -ausbildung, -kenntnisse*⟩

elephant ['elɪfənt] *n.* Elefant, *der*

elevate ['elɪveɪt] *v. t.* [empor]heben. **elevation** [elɪ'veɪʃn] *n.* **a)** *(height)* Höhe, *die;* **b)** *(Archit.)* Aufriß, *der*

elevator ['elɪveɪtə(r)] *n.* *(Amer.)* Auf-zug, *der;* Fahrstuhl, *der*

eleven [ɪ'levn] 1. *adj.* elf. 2. *n.* *(also Sport)* Elf, *die. See also* **eight**

elevenses [ɪ'levnzɪz] *n. sing. or pl.* *(Brit. coll.)* ≈ zweites Frühstück [ge-gen elf Uhr]

eleventh [ɪ'levnθ] 1. *adj.* elft...; **at the ~ hour** in letzter Minute. 2. *n.* *(frac-tion)* Elftel, *das. See also* **eighth**

elf [elf] *n., pl.* **elves** [elvz] Elf, *der/* Elfe, *die*

elicit [ɪ'lɪsɪt] *v. t.* entlocken (**from** *Dat.*) gewinnen ⟨*Unterstützung*⟩

eligible ['elɪdʒɪbl] *adj.* **be ~ for sth.** *(fit)* für etw. geeignet sein; *(entitled)* zu etw. berechtigt sein

eliminate [ɪ'lɪmɪneɪt] *v. t.* **a)** *(remove)* beseitigen; ausschließen ⟨*Möglich-*

keit; b) *(exclude)* ausschließen; **be ~d** *(Sport)* ausscheiden. **elimination** [ɪlɪmɪ'neɪʃn] *n.* **a)** *(removal)* Beseitigung, *die;* **process of ~:** Ausleseverfahren, *das;* b) *(exclusion)* Ausschluß, *der;* *(Sport)* Ausscheiden, *das*

élite [eɪ'liːt] *n.* Elite, *die*

ellipse [ɪ'lɪps] *n.* Ellipse, *die.* **elliptical** [ɪ'lɪptɪkl] *adj.* elliptisch

elm [elm] *n.* Ulme, *die*

elongated ['iːlɒŋgeɪtɪd] *adj.* langgestreckt

elope [ɪ'ləʊp] *v.i.* durchbrennen *(ugs.)*

eloquence ['eləkwəns] *n.* Beredtheit, *die.* **eloquent** ['eləkwənt] *adj.* beredt ⟨*Person*⟩; gewandt ⟨*Stil, Redner*⟩

else [els] *adv.* **a)** *(besides)* sonst [noch]; **somebody/something ~:** [noch] jemand anders/noch etwas; **everybody/everything ~:** alle anderen/alles andere; **who/what/when/how ~?** wer/was/wann/wie sonst noch?; **why ~?** warum sonst?; **b)** *(instead)* ander...; *sb.* **~'s hat** der Hut von jmd. anders; **anybody/anything ~?** [irgend] jemand anders/etwas anderes; **somebody/something ~:** jemand anders/etwas anderes; **everybody/everything ~:** alle anderen/alles andere; **c)** *(otherwise)* sonst; **or ~:** oder aber; **do it or ~ ...!** tun Sie es, sonst ...! **elsewhere** *adv.* woanders

elude [ɪ'ljuːd] *v.t.* *(avoid)* ausweichen (+ *Dat.*); *(escape from)* entkommen (+ *Dat.*). **elusive** [ɪ'ljuːsɪv] *adj.* schwer zu erreichen ⟨*Person*⟩; schwer zu fassen ⟨*Straftäter*⟩; schwer definierbar ⟨*Begriff, Sinn*⟩

elves *pl. of* **elf**

emaciated [ɪ'meɪsɪeɪtɪd] *adj.* abgezehrt

emancipated [ɪ'mænsɪpeɪtɪd] *adj.* emanzipiert; **become ~:** sich emanzipieren

emancipation [ɪmænsɪ'peɪʃn] *n.* Emanzipation, *die*

embalm [ɪm'bɑːm] *v.t.* einbalsamieren

embankment [ɪm'bæŋkmənt] *n.* Damm, *der*

embargo [em'bɑːgəʊ] *n., pl.* **~es** Embargo, *das*

embark [ɪm'bɑːk] *v.i.* **a)** sich einschiffen (**for** nach); **b) ~ [up]on sth.** etw. in Angriff nehmen. **embarkation** [embɑː'keɪʃn] *n.* Einschiffung, *die*

embarrass [ɪm'bærəs] *v.t.* in Verlegenheit bringen. **embarrassed** [ɪm'bærəst] *adj.* verlegen; **feel ~:** verlegen

sein. **embarrassing** *adj.* peinlich. **embarrassment** *n.* Verlegenheit, *die*

embassy ['embəsɪ] *n.* Botschaft, *die*

embellish [em'belɪʃ] *v.t.* beschönigen ⟨*Wahrheit*⟩; ausschmücken ⟨*Geschichte, Bericht*⟩

embers ['embəz] *n. pl.* Glut, *die*

embezzle ['ɪmbezl] *v.t.* unterschlagen

embitter [ɪm'bɪtə(r)] *v.t.* verbittern

emblem ['embləm] *n.* Emblem, *das*

embody [ɪm'bɒdɪ] *v.t.* verkörpern

embrace [ɪm'breɪs] **1.** *v.t.* umarmen; *(fig.: accept, adopt)* annehmen. **2.** *v.i.* sich umarmen. **3.** *n.* Umarmung, *die*

embroider [ɪm'brɔɪdə(r)] *v.t.* sticken ⟨*Muster*⟩; besticken ⟨*Tuch, Kleid*⟩; *(fig.)* ausschmücken. **embroidery** [ɪm'brɔɪdərɪ] *n.* Stickerei, *die*

embroil [ɪm'brɔɪl] *v.t.* **become/be ~ed in sth.** in etw. (*Akk.*) verwickelt werden/sein

embryo ['embrɪəʊ] *n.* Embryo, *der*

emerald ['emərəld] **1.** *n.* Smaragd, *der.* **2.** *adj.* smaragdgrün

emerge [ɪ'mɜːdʒ] *v.i.* auftauchen (**from** aus, **from behind** hinter + *Dat.*); ⟨*Wahrheit:*⟩ an den Tag kommen; **it ~s that ...:** es stellt sich heraus, daß ...

emergency [ɪ'mɜːdʒənsɪ] **1.** *n.* Notfall, *der;* **in an** *or* **in case of ~:** im Notfall. **2.** *adj.* Not-

emigrant ['emɪgrənt] *n.* Auswanderer, *der*/Auswanderin, *die*

emigrate ['emɪgreɪt] *v.i.* auswandern (**to** nach, **from** aus). **emigration** [emɪ'greɪʃn] *n.* Auswanderung (**to** nach, **from** aus)

eminence ['emɪnəns] *n.* hohes Ansehen

eminent ['emɪnənt] *adj.* bedeutend; herausragend

emission [ɪ'mɪʃn] *n.* Emission, *die* (*fachspr.*); *(process also)* Abgabe, *die*

emit [ɪ'mɪt] *v.t.,* **-tt-** abgeben, emittieren *(fachspr.)* ⟨*Wärme, Strahlung usw.*⟩; ausstoßen ⟨*Rauch*⟩

emotion [ɪ'məʊʃn] *n.* Gefühl, *das.* **emotional** [ɪ'məʊʃənl] *adj.* emotional; Gemüts⟨*zustand, -störung*⟩; gefühlvoll ⟨*Stimme*⟩. **e'motionally** *adv.* emotional; gefühlvoll ⟨*sprechen*⟩; **~ disturbed** seelisch gestört

emotive [ɪ'məʊtɪv] *adj.* emotional

emperor ['empərə(r)] *n.* Kaiser, *der*

emphasis ['emfəsɪs] *n., pl.* **emphases** ['emfəsiːz] Betonung, *die;* **lay** *or* **place** *or* **put ~ on sth.** etw. betonen

emphasize ['emfəsaɪz] v. t. betonen

emphatic [ɪm'fætɪk] adj. nachdrücklich; demonstrativ ⟨Ablehnung⟩; **be ~ that ...**: darauf bestehen, daß ... **em'phatically** adv. nachdrücklich

empire ['empaɪə(r)] n. Reich, das

employ [ɪm'plɔɪ] v. t. a) (take on) einstellen; (have working for one) beschäftigen; **be ~ed by a company** bei einer Firma arbeiten; **be** b) (use) einsetzen (for, in, on für); anwenden ⟨Methode, List⟩ (for, in, on bei). **employee** (Amer.: **employe**) [emplɔɪ'iː, em'plɔɪi] n. Angestellte, der/die. **employer** [ɪm'plɔɪə(r)] n. Arbeitgeber, der/-geberin, die. **employment** [ɪm'plɔɪmənt] n. a) (work) Arbeit, die; b) (regular trade or profession) Beschäftigung, die. **em'ployment agency** n. Stellenvermittlung, die

empower [ɪm'paʊə(r)] v. t. (authorize) ermächtigen; (enable) befähigen

empress ['emprɪs] n. Kaiserin, die

emptiness ['emptɪnɪs] n. Leere, die

empty ['emptɪ] 1. adj. leer; frei ⟨Sitz, Parkplatz⟩. 2. v. t. leeren; (pour) schütten (over über + Akk.). 3. v. i. sich leeren. **'empty-handed** adj. mit leeren Händen

EMS abbr. **European Monetary System** EWS

emulate ['emjʊleɪt] v. t. nacheifern (+ Dat.)

emulsion [ɪ'mʌlʃn] n. Emulsion, die

enable [ɪ'neɪbl] v. t. **~ sb. to do sth.** es jmdm. ermöglichen, etw. zu tun

enamel [ɪ'næml] 1. n. Email, das. 2. v. t., (Brit.) **-ll-** emaillieren

enchant [ɪn'tʃɑːnt] v. t. verzaubern; (delight) entzücken. **en'chanted** adj. verzaubert. **en'chanting** adj. entzückend. **en'chantment** n. Verzauberung, die; (fig.) Zauber, der

encircle [ɪn'sɜːkl] v. t. umgeben

encl. abbr. **enclosed, enclosure(s)** Anl.

enclave ['enkleɪv] n. Enklave, die

enclose [ɪn'kləʊz] v. t. a) (surround) umgeben; (shut up or in) einschließen; b) (with letter) beilegen (with, in Dat.); **please find ~d** anbei erhalten Sie. **enclosure** [ɪn'kləʊʒə(r)] n. a) (in zoo) Gehege, das; b) (with letter) Anlage, die

encore ['ɒŋkɔː(r)] 1. int. Zugabe. 2. n. Zugabe, die

encounter [ɪn'kaʊntə(r)] 1. v. t. (as adversary) treffen auf (+ Akk.); (by chance) begegnen (+ Dat.); stoßen auf (+ Akk.) ⟨Problem, Widerstand

usw.⟩. 2. n. (chance meeting) Begegnung, die

encourage [ɪn'kʌrɪdʒ] v. t. ermutigen; (promote) fördern. **encouragement** n. Ermutigung, die (from durch)

encroach [ɪn'krəʊtʃ] v. i. **~ on** eindringen in (+ Akk.); in Anspruch nehmen ⟨Zeit⟩

encumber [ɪn'kʌmbə(r)] v. t. belasten. **encumbrance** [ɪn'kʌmbrəns] n. Belastung, die

encyclopaedia [ɪnsaɪklə'piːdɪə] n. Lexikon, das; Enzyklopädie, die. **encyclopaedic** [ɪnsaɪklə'piːdɪk] adj. enzyklopädisch

end [end] 1. n. a) Ende, das; (of nose, hair, finger) Spitze, die; **from ~ to ~**: von einem Ende zum anderen; **at the ~ of 1987/March** Ende 1987/März; **in the ~**: schließlich; **come to an ~**: ein Ende nehmen; **be at an ~**: zu Ende sein; b) (of box, packet, etc.) Schmalseite, die; (top/bottom surface) Ober-/Unterseite, die; **on ~**: hochkant; **make ~s meet** (fig.) zurechtkommen; **no ~ of** (coll.) unendlich viel/viele; c) (remnant) Rest, der; (of cigarette) Stummel, der; d) (purpose, object) Ziel, das; **~ in itself** Selbstzweck, der. 2. v. t. beenden. 3. v. i. enden. **end 'up** v. i. enden; **~ up in** (coll.) landen in (+ Dat.); **~ up [as] a teacher** (coll.) schließlich Lehrer werden

endanger [ɪn'deɪndʒə(r)] v. t. gefährden

endear [ɪn'dɪə(r)] v. t. **~ sb./sth./oneself to sb.** jmdn./etw./sich bei jmdm. beliebt machen. **en'dearing** adj. reizend; gewinnend ⟨Lächeln, Art⟩

endeavour (Brit.; Amer.: **endeavor**) [ɪn'devə(r)] 1. v. i. **~ to do sth.** sich bemühen, etw. zu tun. 2. n. Bemühung, die; (attempt) Versuch, der

'ending n. Schluß, der; (of word) Endung, die

endive ['endaɪv] n. Endivie, die

'endless adj. endlos. **'endlessly** adv. unaufhörlich ⟨streiten, schwatzen⟩

endorse [ɪn'dɔːs] v. t. a) indossieren ⟨Scheck⟩; b) beipflichten (+ Dat.) ⟨Meinung⟩; billigen ⟨Entscheidung, Handlung⟩; unterstützen ⟨Vorschlag⟩; c) (Brit. Law) einen Strafvermerk machen auf (+ Akk. od. Dat.). **en'dorsement** n. a) (of cheque) Indossament, das; b) (support) Billigung, die; (of proposal) Unterstützung, die; c) (Brit. Law) Strafvermerk, der

endow [ɪn'daʊ] v. t. [über Stiftungen/

eine Stiftung] finanzieren; **stiften** ⟨*Preis, Lehrstuhl*⟩; **be ~ed with charm/a talent for music** Charme/musikalisches Talent besitzen

endurable [ɪn'djʊərəbl] *adj.* erträglich

endurance [ɪn'djʊərəns] *n.* Ausdauer, *die*

endure [ɪn'djʊə(r)] *v.t.* ertragen

enema ['enəmə] *n.* Einlauf, *der*

enemy ['enəmɪ] **1.** *n.* Feind, *der* ⟨**of, to** *Gen.*⟩. **2.** *adj.* feindlich

energetic [enə'dʒetɪk] *adj.* energiegeladen; *(active)* tatkräftig

energy ['enədʒɪ] *n.* Energie, *die*

enforce [ɪn'fɔːs] *v.t.* durchsetzen; sorgen für ⟨*Disziplin*⟩; **~d** erzwungen ⟨*Schweigen*⟩; unfreiwillig ⟨*Untätigkeit*⟩

engage [ɪn'geɪdʒ] **1.** *v.t.* **a)** *(hire)* einstellen ⟨*Arbeiter*⟩; engagieren ⟨*Sänger*⟩; **b)** wecken ⟨*Interesse*⟩; auf sich *(Akk.)* ziehen ⟨*Aufmerksamkeit*⟩; **c)** ~ **the clutch/first gear** einkuppeln/ den ersten Gang einlegen. **2.** *v.i.* ~ **in sth.** sich an etw. *(Dat.)* beteiligen; ~ **in politics** sich politisch engagieren. **engaged** [ɪn'geɪdʒd] *adj.* **a) be ~** [to be married] [to sb.] [mit jmdm.] verlobt sein; **get ~** [to be married] [to sb.] sich [mit jmdm.] verloben; **b) be ~ in sth./in doing sth.** mit etw. beschäftigt sein/ damit beschäftigt sein, etw. zu tun; **be otherwise ~:** etwas anderes vorhaben; **c)** besetzt ⟨*Toilette, [Telefon]anschluß, Nummer*⟩; ~ **signal** *or* **tone** *(Brit.)* Besetztzeichen, *das.* **en'gagement** *n.* **a)** *(to be married)* Verlobung, *die* ⟨**to** mit⟩; **b)** *(appointment)* Verabredung, *die.* **en'gagement ring** *n.* Verlobungsring, *der*

engaging [ɪn'geɪdʒɪŋ] *adj.* bezaubernd; einnehmend ⟨*Persönlichkeit, Art*⟩

engine ['endʒɪn] *n.* **a)** Motor, *der; (rocket/jet ~)* Triebwerk, *das;* **b)** *(locomotive)* Lok[omotive], *die.* **'engine driver** *n.* Lok[omotiv]führer, *der*

engineer [endʒɪ'nɪə(r)] **1.** *n.* **a)** Ingenieur, *der*/Ingenieurin, *die; (service ~, installation ~)* Techniker, *der*/Technikerin, *die;* **b)** *(Amer.: engine-driver)* Lok[omotiv]führer, *der.* **2.** *v.t.* arrangieren. **engi'neering** *n.* Technik, *die*

England ['ɪŋglənd] *pr. n.* England *(das)*

English ['ɪŋglɪʃ] **1.** *adj.* englisch; **he/ she is ~:** er ist Engländer/sie ist Engländerin. **2.** *n.* **a)** Englisch, *das;* **say sth. in ~:** etw. auf englisch sagen; **I**

cannot *or* **do not speak ~:** ich spreche kein Englisch; **translate into/from** [the] **~:** ins Englische/aus dem Englischen übersetzen; **b)** *pl.* **the ~:** die Engländer

English: ~ '**Channel** *pr. n.* **the ~ Channel** der [Ärmel]kanal; **~man** [~mən] *n., pl.* **~men** [~mən] Engländer, *der;* **~woman** *n.* Engländerin, *die*

engrave [ɪn'greɪv] *v.t.* gravieren; eingravieren ⟨*Namen, Figur usw.*⟩. **engraving** [ɪn'greɪvɪŋ] *n.* Stich, *der; (from wood)* Holzschnitt, *der*

engross [ɪn'grəʊs] *v.t.* fesseln; **be ~ed in sth.** in etw. *(Akk.)* vertieft sein; **become** *or* **get ~ed in sth.** sich in etw. *(Akk.)* vertiefen

engulf [ɪn'gʌlf] *v.t.* verschlingen

enhance [ɪn'hɑːns] *v.t.* erhöhen ⟨*Wert, Aussichten, Schönheit*⟩; verstärken ⟨*Wirkung*⟩; heben ⟨*Aussehen*⟩

enigma [ɪ'nɪgmə] *n.* Rätsel, *das.* **enigmatic** [enɪg'mætɪk] *adj.* rätselhaft

enjoy [ɪn'dʒɔɪ] *v.t.* **a) I ~ed the book/work** das Buch/die Arbeit hat mir gefallen; **he ~s reading/travelling** er liest/reist gern; **b)** genießen ⟨*Rechte, Privilegien, Vorteile*⟩. **2.** *v. refl.* sich amüsieren. **enjoyable** [ɪn'dʒɔɪəbl] *adj.* schön; angenehm ⟨*Empfindung, Arbeit*⟩; unterhaltsam ⟨*Buch, Film, Stück*⟩. **en'joyment** *n.* Vergnügen, *das* ⟨**of** an + *Dat.*⟩

enlarge [ɪn'lɑːdʒ] **1.** *v.t.* vergrößern; verbreitern ⟨*Straße, Durchgang*⟩. **2.** *v.i.* ~ [**up]on sth.** etw. weiter ausführen. **en'largement** *n.* Vergrößerung, *die; (making wider)* Verbreiterung, *die*

enlighten [ɪn'laɪtn] *v.t.* aufklären ⟨**on, as to** über + *Akk.*⟩. **en'lightenment** *n.* Aufklärung, *die*

enlist [ɪn'lɪst] **1.** *v.t. (obtain)* gewinnen. **2.** *v.i.* ~ [for the army/navy] in die Armee/Marine eintreten; ~ [**as a soldier**] Soldat werden

enliven [ɪn'laɪvn] *v.t.* beleben

enmity ['enmɪtɪ] *n.* Feindschaft, *die*

enormous [ɪ'nɔːməs] *adj.* enorm; riesig, gewaltig ⟨*Figur, Tier, Menge*⟩. **e'normously** *adv.* enorm

enough [ɪ'nʌf] **1.** *adj.* genug; **there's ~ room** es ist Platz genug. **2.** *n.* genug; **be ~ to do sth.** genügen, etw. zu tun; **have had ~** [of sb./sth.] genug [von jmdm./etw.] haben; **I've had ~!** jetzt reicht's mir aber! **3.** *adv.* genug; **oddly/funnily ~:** merkwürdiger-/ *(ugs.)* komischerweise

enquire, enquiry *see* inquir-

enrage [ɪn'reɪdʒ] *v. t.* wütend machen; **be ~d by sth.** über etw. *(Akk.)* wütend werden

enrich [ɪn'rɪtʃ] *v. t.* reich machen; *(fig.)* bereichern

enrol *(Amer.:* **enroll)** [ɪn'rəʊl] **1.** *v. i.,* **-ll-** sich einschreiben; **~ for a course** sich zu einem Kurs anmelden. **2.** *v. t.* einschreiben. **en'rolment** *(Amer.:* **en'rollment)** *n.* Einschreibung, *die*

en route [ã 'ru:t] *adv.* unterwegs; **~ to Scotland/for Edinburgh** auf dem Weg nach Schottland/Edinburgh

ensign ['ensaɪn, 'ensn] *n.* Hoheitszeichen, *das*

enslave [ɪn'sleɪv] *v. t.* versklaven

ensue [ɪn'sju:] *v. i.* folgen **(from,** *or* **aus);** the discussion which **~d** die anschließende Diskussion

ensure [ɪn'ʃʊə(r)] *v. t.* **~ that ...** *(see to it that)* gewährleisten, daß ...; **~ sth.** etw. gewährleisten

entail [ɪn'teɪl] *v. t.* mit sich bringen; **sth. ~s doing sth.** etw. bedeutet, daß man etw. tun muß

entangle [ɪn'tæŋgl] *v. t.* sich verfangen lassen; **get** *or* **become ~d in** *or* **with sth.** sich in etw. *(Dat.)* verfangen

enter ['entə(r)] **1.** *v. i.* **a)** hineingehen; ⟨*Fahrzeug:*⟩ hineinfahren; *(come in)* hereinkommen; *(into room)* eintreten; **b)** *(register as competitor)* sich zur Teilnahme anmelden **(for an** *of* **Akk.). 2.** *v. t.* **a)** [hinein]gehen in *(+ Akk.);* ⟨*Fahrzeug:*⟩ [hinein]fahren in *(+ Akk.);* betreten ⟨*Gebäude, Zimmer:*⟩; einlaufen in *(+ Akk.)* ⟨*Hafen:*⟩; einreisen in *(+ Akk.)* ⟨*Land:*⟩; *(come into)* [herein]kommen in *(+ Akk.);* **b)** teilnehmen an *(+ Dat.)* ⟨*Rennen, Wettbewerb:*⟩; **c)** *(in book etc.)* eintragen (**in** *in* **+ Akk.).** **'enter into** *v. t.* aufnehmen ⟨*Verhandlungen:*⟩; eingehen ⟨*Verpflichtung:*⟩; schließen ⟨*Vertrag:*⟩. **'enter [up]on** *v. t.* beginnen

enterprise ['entəpraɪz] *n.* **a)** *(undertaking)* Unternehmen, *das;* **free/private ~:** freies/privates Unternehmertum; **b)** *(enterprising spirit)* Unternehmungsgeist, *der.* **enterprising** ['entəpraɪzɪŋ] *adj.* unternehmungslustig

entertain [entə'teɪn] *v. t.* **a)** *(amuse)* unterhalten; **b)** *(receive as guest)* bewirten; **c)** haben ⟨*Vorstellung:*⟩; hegen *(geh.)* ⟨*Gefühl, Verdacht, Zweifel:*⟩; *(consider)* in Erwägung ziehen. **enter'tainer** *n.* Unterhalter, *der/* Unterhalterin, *die.* **enter'taining** *adj.*

unterhaltsam. **enter'tainment** *n.* **a)** *(amusement)* Unterhaltung, *die;* **b)** *(performance, show)* Veranstaltung, *die*

enthral *(Amer.:* **enthrall)** [ɪn'θrɔ:l] *v. t.,* **-ll-** gefangennehmen *(fig.)*

enthuse [ɪn'θju:z] *(coll.)* **1.** *v. i.* in Begeisterung ausbrechen **(about** über *+ Akk.).* **2.** *v. t.* begeistern

enthusiasm [ɪn'θju:zɪæzm] *n.* Begeisterung, *die.* **enthusiast** [ɪn'θju:zɪæst] *n.* Enthusiast, *der; (for sports)* Fan, *der;* **a great DIY ~:** ein begeisterter Heimwerker. **enthusiastic** [ɪnθju:zɪ'æstɪk] *adj.* begeistert; **not be very ~ about doing sth.** keine große Lust haben, etw. zu tun

entice [ɪn'taɪs] *v. t.* locken **(into** in *+ Akk.);* **~ sb. into doing** *or* **to do sth.** jmdn. dazu verleiten, etw. zu tun

entire [ɪn'taɪə(r)] *adj.* **a)** *(whole)* ganz; **b)** *(intact)* vollständig. **en'tirely** *adv.* **a)** *(wholly)* völlig; **b)** *(solely)* ganz ⟨*für sich behalten:*⟩; voll ⟨*verantwortlich sein:*⟩; **it's up to you —** es liegt ganz bei dir. **entirety** [ɪn'taɪərəti] *n.* **in its ~:** in seiner/ihrer Gesamtheit

entitle [ɪn'taɪtl] *v. t.* berechtigen **(to** zu); **~ sb. to do sth.** jmdm. das Recht geben, etw. zu tun; **be ~d to [claim] sth.** Anspruch auf etw. *(Akk.)* haben; **be ~d to do sth.** das Recht haben, etw. zu tun

entourage [ɒntʊ'rɑ:ʒ] *n.* Gefolge, *das*

entrails ['entreɪlz] *n. pl.* Eingeweide *Pl.*

¹entrance [ɪn'trɑ:ns] *v. t.* hinreißen

²entrance ['entrəns] *n.* **a)** *(way in)* Eingang, *der* **(to** *Gen. od.* zu); *(for vehicles)* Einfahrt, *die.* **en'trance fee** *n.* Eintrittsgeld, *das*

entrant ['entrənt] *n. (for competition, race, etc.)* Teilnehmer, *der/*Teilnehmerin, *die* **(for** *Gen.,* an *+ Dat.)*

entreat [ɪn'tri:t] *v. t.* anflehen. **en-'treaty** *n.* flehentliche Bitte

entrepreneur [ɒntrəprə'nɜ:(r)] *n.* Unternehmer, *der/*Unternehmerin, *die*

entrust [ɪn'trʌst] *v. t.* **~ sb. with sth.** jmdm. etw. anvertrauen; **~ sth. to sb./sth.** jmdn./etw. jmdm./einer Sache anvertrauen; **~ a task to sb.** jmdn. mit einer Aufgabe betrauen

entry ['entrɪ] *n.* Eintritt, *der* **(into** in *+ Akk.); (into country)* Einreise, *die;* **'no ~'** *(for people)* „Zutritt verboten"; *(for vehicles)* „Einfahrt verboten"; **b)** *(way in)* Eingang, *der; (for vehicle)* Einfahrt, *die;* **c)** *(registration, item)*

Eintragung, die (in, into in + *Akk. od. Dat.*); (*in dictionary, encyclopaedia*) Eintrag, *der*

entry: ~ **fee** *n.* Eintrittsgeld, *das;* ~ **form** *n.* Anmeldeformular, *das;* ~ **visa** *n.* Einreisevisum, *das*

envelop [ɪn'veləp] *v. t.* [ein]hüllen (**in** in + *Akk.*); **be ~ed in flames** ganz von Flammen umgeben sein

envelope ['envələʊp, 'ɒnvələʊp] *n.* [Brief]umschlag, *der*

enviable ['enviəbl] *adj.* beneidenswert

envious ['enviəs] *adj.* neidisch (**of** auf + *Akk.*)

environment [ɪn'vaɪərənmənt] *n.* Umwelt, *die;* (*surrounding objects, region*) Umgebung, *die.* **environmental** [ɪnvaɪərən'mentl] *adj.* Umwelt-. **environ'mentalist** *n.* Umweltschützer, *der/*-schützerin, *die.* **environ'mentally** *adv.* ~ **friendly** umweltfreundlich

envisage [ɪn'vɪzɪdʒ] *v. t.* sich (*Dat.*) vorstellen

envoy ['envɔɪ] *n.* Gesandte, *der/*Gesandtin, *die*

envy ['envɪ] **1.** *n.* Neid, *der;* **you'll be the ~ of all your friends** alle deine Freunde werden dich beneiden. **2.** *v. t.* beneiden; ~ **sb. sth.** jmdn. um etw. beneiden

enzyme ['enzaɪm] *n.* Enzym, *das*

ephemeral [ɪ'femərl] *adj.* kurzlebig

epic ['epɪk] **1.** *adj.* episch. **2.** *n.* Epos, *das*

epidemic [epɪ'demɪk] **1.** *adj.* epidemisch. **2.** *n.* Epidemie, *die*

epilepsy ['epɪlepsɪ] *n.* Epilepsie, *die.* **epileptic** [epɪ'leptɪk] **1.** *adj.* epileptisch; **epileptic fit** epileptischer Anfall. **2.** *n.* Epileptiker, *der/*Epileptikerin, *die*

episode ['epɪsəʊd] *n.* **a)** Episode, *die;* **b)** (*of serial*) Folge, *die*

epitaph ['epɪtɑːf] *n.* Grab[in]schrift, *die*

epitome [ɪ'pɪtəmɪ] *n.* Inbegriff, *der.* **epitomize** [ɪ'pɪtəmaɪz] *v. t.* ~ **sth.** der Inbegriff einer Sache (*Gen.*) sein

epoch ['iːpɒk] *n.* Epoche, *die.* **'epoch-making** *adj.* epochemachend

equal ['iːkwl] **1.** *adj.* **a)** gleich; ~ **in** or **of** ~ **height/size/importance** etc. gleich hoch/groß/wichtig *usw.;* **b)** **be ~ to sth./sb.** (*strong, clever, etc. enough*) einer Sache/jmdm. gewachsen sein. **2.** *n.* Gleichgestellte, *der/die;* **have no ~:** nicht seines-/ihresgleichen haben. **3.** *v. t.,* (*Brit.*) -**ll**-: ~ **sb.** es

jmdm. gleich tun; **three times four ~s twelve** drei mal vier ist [gleich] zwölf.

equality [ɪ'kwɒlɪtɪ] *n.* Gleichheit, *die;* (*equal rights*) Gleichberechtigung, *die.* **equalize** ['iːkwəlaɪz] *v. i.* (*Sport*) den Ausgleich[streffer] erzielen. **'equalizer** *n.* (*Sport*) Ausgleich[streffer], *der.* **'equally** *adv.* gleich; (*just as*) ebenso; **in gleiche Teile** (*aufteilen*); gleichmäßig (*verteilen*). **equal oppor'tunity** *n.* Chancengleichheit, *die.* **'equals sign** *n.* (*Math.*) Gleichheitszeichen, *das*

equanimity [ekwə'nɪmɪtɪ] *n.* Gelassenheit, *die*

equate [ɪ'kweɪt] *v. t.* gleichsetzen (**with** mit). **equation** [ɪ'kweɪʒn] *n.* (*Math.*) Gleichung, *die*

equator [ɪ'kweɪtə(r)] *n.* Äquator, *der*

equilibrium [iːkwɪ'lɪbrɪəm] *n., pl.* **equilibria** [iːkwɪ'lɪbrɪə] *or* ~**s** Gleichgewicht, *das*

equinox ['ekwɪnɒks] *n.* Tagundnachtgleiche, *die*

equip [ɪ'kwɪp] *v. t.,* -**pp**- ausrüsten (*Fahrzeug, Armee*); ausstatten (*Küche*); **fully ~ped** komplett ausgerüstet/ausgestattet; ~ **sb./oneself** [**with sth.**] jmdn./sich [mit etw.] ausrüsten. **e'quipment** *n.* Ausrüstung, *die;* (*of kitchen, laboratory*) Ausstattung, *die;* (*needed for activity*) Geräte

equivalent [ɪ'kwɪvələnt] **1.** *adj.* gleichwertig; **be ~ to sth.** einer Sache (*Dat.*) entsprechen. **2.** *n.* **a)** (*thing, person*) Pendant, *das;* Gegenstück, *das* (**of** zu); **b)** **be the ~ of sth.** (*have same result*) einer Sache (*Dat.*) entsprechen

equivocal [ɪ'kwɪvəkl] *adj.* zweideutig

era ['ɪərə] *n.* Ära, *die*

eradicate [ɪ'rædɪkeɪt] *v. t.* ausrotten

erase [ɪ'reɪz] *v. t.* auslöschen; (*with rubber, knife*) ausradieren; (*from tape, also Computing*) löschen. **e'raser** *n.* [**pencil**] ~: Radiergummi, *der*

erect [ɪ'rekt] **1.** *adj.* aufrecht. **2.** *v. t.* errichten; aufstellen (*Standbild, Mast, Verkehrsschild, Gerüst, Zelt*). **erection** [ɪ'rekʃn] *n.* **a)** *see* erect 2: Errichtung, *die;* Aufstellen, *das;* **b)** (*Physiol.*) Erektion, *die*

ermine ['ɜːmɪn] *n.* Hermelin, *der*

erode [ɪ'rəʊd] *v. t.* **a)** (*Säure, Rost:*) angreifen; (*Wasser:*) auswaschen; (*Wind:*) verwittern lassen; **b)** (*fig.*) unterminieren. **erosion** [ɪ'rəʊʒn] *n.* **a)** *see* erode a: Angreifen, *das;* Auswaschung, *die;* Verwitterung, *die;* **b)** (*fig.*) Unterminierung, *die*

erotic [ɪ'rɒtɪk] *adj.* erotisch

err [ɜː(r)] *v.i.* sich irren

errand ['erənd] *n.* Botengang, *der;* *(shopping)* Besorgung, *die;* **go on** or **run an ~** : einen Botengang/eine Besorgung machen. **'errand boy** *n.* Laufbursche, *der*

erratic [ɪ'rætɪk] *adj.* unregelmäßig; sprunghaft ‹*Wesen, Person, Art*›; launenhaft ‹*Verhalten*›

erroneous [ɪ'rəʊnɪəs] *adj.* falsch; irrig ‹*Schlußfolgerung, Annahme*›

error ['erə(r)] *n.* *(mistake)* Fehler, *der;* *(wrong opinion)* Irrtum, *der;* **in ~** : irrtümlich[erweise]

erudite ['eruː'daɪt] *adj.* gelehrt

erupt [ɪ'rʌpt] *v.i.* ausbrechen. **eruption** [ɪ'rʌp/n] *n.* Ausbruch, *der*

escalate ['eskəleɪt] *v.i.* sich ausweiten (**into** zu); ‹*Preise, Kosten:*› [ständig] steigen. **escalator** ['eskəleɪtə(r)] *n.* Rolltreppe, *die*

escapade [eskə'peɪd] *n.* Eskapade, *die (geh.)*

escape [ɪ'skeɪp] **1.** *n.* Flucht, *die (from* aus); **have a narrow ~** : gerade noch einmal davonkommen. **2.** *v.i.* **a)** fliehen (from aus); *(successfully)* entkommen (from *Dat.*); **b)** ‹*Gas:*› ausströmen; ‹*Flüssigkeit:*› auslaufen. **3.** *v.t.* **a)** entkommen (+ *Dat.*) ‹*Verfolger, Feind*›; entgehen (+ *Dat.*) ‹*Bestrafung, Gefangennahme, Tod*›; verschont bleiben von ‹*Zerstörung, Auswirkungen*›; **b)** *(not be remembered by)* entfallen sein (+ *Dat.*). **e'scape route** *n.* Fluchtweg, *der*

escapism [ɪ'skeɪpɪzm] *n.* Realitätsflucht, *die*

escort **1.** ['eskɔːt] *n.* **a)** Begleitung, *die; (Mil.)* Eskorte, *die;* **b)** *(hired companion)* Begleiter, *der*/Begleiterin, *die.* **2.** [ɪ'skɔːt] *v.t.* begleiten; *(lead)* führen; *(Mil.)* eskortieren

Eskimo ['eskɪməʊ] **1.** *adj.* Eskimo-. **2.** *n., pl.* **~s** or same Eskimo, *der*/Eskimofrau, *die;* **the ~[s]** die Eskimos

esoteric [esəʊ'terɪk] *adj.* esoterisch

especial [ɪ'speʃl] *attrib. adj.* [ganz] besonder... **especially** [ɪ'speʃəlɪ] *adv.* besonders

espionage ['espɪənɑːʒ] *n.* Spionage, *die*

espresso [e'spresəʊ] *n., pl.* **~s** *(coffee)* Espresso, *der.* **e'spresso bar** *n.* Espressobar, *die*

Esq. [ɪ'skwaɪə(r)] *abbr.* Esquire ≈ Hr.; *(on letter)* ≈ Hrn.; Jim Smith, ~ : Hr./Hrn. Jim Smith

essay ['eseɪ] *n.* Essay, *der;* Aufsatz, *der (bes. Schulw.)*

essence ['esəns] *n.* **a)** Wesen, *das; (gist)* Wesentliche, *das;* **in ~** : im Wesentlichen; **b)** *(Cookery)* Essenz, *die*

essential [ɪ'senʃl] **1.** *adj.* **a)** *(fundamental)* wesentlich; **b)** *(indispensable)* unentbehrlich; lebensnotwendig ‹*Versorgungseinrichtungen, Güter*›; unabdingbar ‹*Qualifikation, Voraussetzung*›; **it is ~ that ...** : es ist unbedingt notwendig, daß ... **2.** *n. pl.* **the ~s** *(fundamentals)* das Wesentliche; *(items)* das Notwendigste. **es'sentially** *adv.* im Grunde

establish [ɪ'stæblɪʃ] *v.t.* **a)** schaffen ‹*Einrichtung, Präzedenzfall*›; gründen ‹*Organisation, Institut*›; errichten ‹*Geschäft, System*›; **b)** *(secure acceptance for)* etablieren; **become ~ed** sich einbürgern; **c)** *(prove)* beweisen; **d)** *(discover)* feststellen. **established** [ɪ'stæblɪʃt] *adj.* bestehend ‹*Ordnung*›; etabliert ‹*Schriftsteller*›; *(accepted)* üblich; fest ‹*Brauch*›; feststehend ‹*Tatsache*›; **become ~** : sich durchsetzen. **e'stablishment** *n.* **a)** *(setting up, foundation)* Gründung, *die;* **b)** [business] **~** : Unternehmen, *das*

estate [ɪ'steɪt] *n.* **a)** *(landed property)* Gut, *das;* **b)** *(Brit.: housing ~)* [Wohn]siedlung, *die;* **c)** *(of deceased person)* Erbmasse, *die.* **e'state agent** *n. (Brit.)* Grundstücksmakler, *der;* **e'state car** *n. (Brit.)* Kombiwagen, *der*

esteem [ɪ'stiːm] **1.** *n.* Wertschätzung, *die (geh.) (for Gen.,* für). **2.** *v.t.* schätzen; **highly ~ed** hochgeschätzt

estimate **1.** ['estɪmət] *n.* **a)** Schätzung, *die;* **at a rough ~** : grob geschätzt; **b)** *(Commerc.)* Kostenvoranschlag, *der.* **2.** ['estɪmeɪt] *v.t.* schätzen (**at** auf + *Akk.*). **estimation** [estɪ'meɪʃn] *n.* Schätzung, *die;* **in sb.'s ~** : nach jmds. Schätzung

estuary ['estjʊərɪ] *n.* [Trichter]mündung, *die*

etc. *abbr.* et cetera usw.

etch [etʃ] *v.t.* ätzen (**on** auf + *Akk.*); *(on metal also)* radieren; *(bes. Künstler:)* radieren; *(fig.)* einprägen (**in, on** *Dat.*). **'etching** *n. (Art)* Radierung, *die*

eternal [ɪ'tɜːnl] *adj.,* **e'ternally** *adv.* ewig

eternity [ɪ'tɜːnɪtɪ] *n.* Ewigkeit, *die*

ether [ɪ'θə(r)] *n.* Äther, *der.* **ethereal** [ɪ'θɪərɪəl] *adj.* ätherisch

ethical ['eθɪkl] *adj.* ethisch

ethics ['eθɪks] *n.* **a)** Moral, *die; (moral philosophy)* Ethik, *die;* **b)** *usu. constr. as pl. (moral code)* Ethik, *die (geh.)*
Ethiopia [i:θɪˈəʊpɪə] *pr. n.* Äthiopien *(das)*
ethnic ['eθnɪk] *adj.* ethnisch
etiquette ['etɪket] *n.* Etikette, *die*
etymology [etɪˈmɒlədʒɪ] *n.* Etymologie, *die*
eulogy ['ju:lədʒɪ] *n.* Lobrede, *die*
euphemism ['ju:fəmɪzm] *n.* Euphemismus, *der.* **euphemistic** [ju:fəˈmɪstɪk] *adj.* verhüllend
euphoria [ju:ˈfɔ:rɪə] *n.* Euphorie, *die (geh.)*
Euro- ['jʊərəʊ] *in comb.* euro-/Euro-. **'Eurocheque** *n.* Euroscheck, *der*
Europe ['jʊərəp] *pr. n.* Europa *(das).* **European** [jʊərəˈpi:ən] **1.** *adj.* europäisch; ~ |**Economic**| **Community** Europäische [Wirtschafts]gemeinschaft. **2.** *n.* Europäer, *der*/Europäerin, *die*
euthanasia [ju:θəˈneɪzɪə] *n.* Euthanasie, *die*
evacuate [ɪˈvækjʊeɪt] *v. t.* evakuieren (**from** aus). **evacuation** [ɪvækjʊˈeɪʃn] *n.* Evakuierung, *die* (**from** aus)
evade [ɪˈveɪd] *v. t.* ausweichen (+ *Dat.*) ⟨*Angriff, Angreifer, Schlag, Problem, Frage*⟩; sich entziehen (+ *Dat.*) ⟨*Verhaftung, Verantwortung*⟩; entkommen (+ *Dat.*) ⟨*Verfolger, Verfolgung*⟩; hinterziehen ⟨*Steuern*⟩; ~ **doing sth.** vermeiden, etw. zu tun
evaluate [ɪˈvæljʊeɪt] *v. t.* einschätzen; bewerten ⟨*Daten*⟩
evangelical [i:vænˈdʒelɪkl] *adj.* missionarisch *(fig.); (Protestant)* evangelikal. **evangelist** [ɪˈvændʒəlɪst] *n.* Evangelist, *der*
evaporate [ɪˈvæpəreɪt] **1.** *v. i.* verdunsten. **2.** *v. t.* verdunsten lassen. **evaporated 'milk** *n.* Kondensmilch, *die.* **evaporation** [ɪvæpəˈreɪʃn] *n.* Verdunstung, *die*
evasion [ɪˈveɪʒn] *n.* Umgehung, *die; (of responsibility, question)* Ausweichen, *das* (**of** vor + *Dat.*); **tax** ~: Steuerhinterziehung, *die.* **evasive** [ɪˈveɪsɪv] *adj.* **a) be/become** ~: ausweichen; **b)** ausweichend ⟨*Antwort*⟩
eve [i:v] *n.* Vorabend, *der* (**of** *Gen.*); *(day)* Vortag, *der* (**of** *Gen.*)
even ['i:vn] **1.** *adj.* **a)** eben ⟨*Boden, Fläche*⟩; gleich hoch ⟨*Stapel, Stuhl-, Tischbein*⟩; **be of** ~ **height/length** gleich hoch/lang sein; **b)** gerade ⟨*Zahl, Seite, Hausnummer*⟩; **c) be or**

get ~ **with sb.** *(quits)* es jmdm. heimzahlen; **break** ~: die Kosten decken. **2.** *adv.* sogar; selbst; sogar noch ⟨*weniger, schlimmer usw.*⟩; ~ **if** selbst wenn; ~ **so** |aber| trotzdem; **not or never** ~ ...: |noch| nicht einmal ...
even 'up *v. t.* ausgleichen
evening ['i:vnɪŋ] *n.* Abend, *der;* **this/tomorrow** ~: heute/morgen abend; **in the** ~: am Abend; *(regularly)* abends. **'evening class** *n.* Abendkurs, *der.* **'evening dress** *n.* Abendkleidung, *die*
'evenly *adv.* gleichmäßig
'even-numbered *adj.* gerade
event [ɪˈvent] *n.* **a) in the** ~ **of sb.'s death** im Falle seines Todes; **in the** ~: letzten Endes; **in the** ~ **of rain** bei Regenwetter; **b)** *(occurrence)* Ereignis, *das.* **e'ventful** *adj.* ereignisreich
eventual [ɪˈventjʊəl] *adj.* **predict sb.'s** ~ **downfall** vorhersagen, daß jmd. schließlich zu Fall kommen wird; **the career of Napoleon and his** ~ **defeat** der Aufstieg Napoleons und schließlich seine Niederlage. **eventuality** [ɪventjʊˈælɪtɪ] *n.* Eventualität, *die.* **e'ventually** *adv.* schließlich
ever ['evə(r)] *adv.* **a)** *(always)* immer; **for** ~: für immer; ewig ⟨*lieben, dasein, leben*⟩; ~ **since** |then| seit |dieser Zeit|; **b)** *(at any time)* je|mals|; **hardly** ~: so gut wie nie; **c)** *in comb. with compar. adj. or adv.* noch; ~**increasing** ständig zunehmend; **d)** *(coll.)* **what** ~ **does he want?** was will er nur?; **why** ~ **not?** warum denn nicht? **'evergreen 1.** *adj.* immergrün. **2.** *n.* immergrüne Pflanze. **ever'lasting** *adj.* **a)** *(eternal)* immerwährend; ewig ⟨*Leben*⟩; unvergänglich ⟨*Ruhm, Ehre*⟩; **b)** *(incessant)* endlos
every ['evrɪ] *adj.* **a)** jeder/jede/jedes; ~ **one** jeder/jede/jedes |einzelne|; **your** ~ **wish** all|e| Ihre Wünsche; **she comes** ~ **day** sie kommt jeden Tag; ~ **three/few days** alle drei/paar Tage; ~ **other** (~ *second, almost* ~) jeder/jede/jedes zweite; **b)** *(the greatest possible)* all ⟨*Respekt, Aussicht*⟩
every: ~**body** *n. & pron.* jeder; ~**body else** alle anderen; ~**day** *attrib. adj.* alltäglich; Alltags⟨*kleidung, -sprache*⟩; **in** ~**day life** im Alltag; ~**one** *see* ~**body;** ~**place** *(Amer.) see* ~**where;** ~**thing** *n. & pron.* alles; ~**where** *adv.* überall; **where you go/look** wohin man auch geht/sieht
evict [ɪˈvɪkt] *v. t.* ~ **sb.** |**from his home**|

jmdn. zur Räumung [seiner Wohnung] zwingen. **eviction** [ɪ'vɪkʃn] n. Zwangsräumung, die; the ~ of the tenant die zwangsweise Vertreibung des Mieters

evidence ['evɪdəns] n. a) Beweis, der; (indication) Anzeichen, das; be ~ of sth. etw. beweisen; b) (Law) Beweismaterial, das; give ~: aussagen

evident ['evɪdənt] adj. offensichtlich; be ~ to sb. jmdm. klar sein; it soon became ~ that ...: es stellte sich bald heraus, daß ... **evidently** adv. offensichtlich

evil ['iːvl, 'iːvɪl] 1. adj. böse; schlecht ⟨Charakter, Einfluß, System⟩. 2. n. a) Böse, das; b) (bad thing) Übel, das

evocative [ɪ'vɒkətɪv] adj. be ~ of sth. etw. heraufbeschwören

evoke [ɪ'vəʊk] v.t. heraufbeschwören; hervorrufen ⟨Bewunderung, Überraschung⟩; erregen ⟨Interesse⟩

evolution [iːvə'luːʃn] n. Entwicklung, die; (Biol.) Evolution, die

evolve [ɪ'vɒlv] 1. v.i. sich entwickeln (from aus, into zu). 2. v.t. entwickeln

ewe [juː] n. Mutterschaf, das

ex- pref. Ex-⟨Freundin, Präsident, Champion⟩; Alt-⟨[bundes]kanzler⟩

exacerbate [ek'sæsəbeɪt] v.t. verschärfen ⟨Lage⟩; verschlechtern ⟨Zustand⟩

exact [ɪg'zækt] 1. adj. genau. 2. v.t. fordern; erheben ⟨Gebühr⟩. **exacting** [ɪg'zæktɪŋ] adj. anspruchsvoll; hoch ⟨Anforderung⟩. **exactitude** [ɪg'zæktɪtjuːd] Genauigkeit, die. **exactly** [ɪg'zæktlɪ] adv. genau; not ~ (coll. iron.) nicht gerade. **exactness** [ɪg'zæktnɪs] n. Genauigkeit, die

exaggerate [ɪg'zædʒəreɪt] v.t. übertreiben. **exaggeration** [ɪgzædʒə'reɪʃn] n. Übertreibung, die

exam [ɪg'zæm] (coll.) see **examination**

examination [ɪgzæmɪ'neɪʃn] n. a) (inspection, Med.) Untersuchung, die; b) (Sch. etc.) Prüfung, die; (final ~ at university) Examen, das

examine [ɪg'zæmɪn] v.t. a) (inspect, Med.) untersuchen (for auf + Akk.); prüfen ⟨Dokument, Gewissen⟩; kontrollieren ⟨Ausweis, Gepäck⟩; b) (Sch. etc.) prüfen (in in + Dat.); c) (Law) verhören. **examiner** [ɪg'zæmɪnə(r)] n. Prüfer, der/Prüferin, die

example [ɪg'zɑːmpl] n. Beispiel, das; for ~ zum Beispiel; make a ~ of sb. ein Exempel an jmdm. statuieren

exasperate [ɪg'zæspəreɪt] v.t. (irritate) verärgern; (infuriate) zur Verzweiflung bringen. **exasperation** [ɪg'zæspəreɪʃn] n. see **exasperate**: Ärger, der/Verzweiflung, die (with über + Akk.); in ~: verärgert/verzweifelt

excavate ['ekskəveɪt] v.t. a) ausschachten; (with machine) ausbaggern; b) (Archaeol.) ausgraben. **excavation** [ekskə'veɪʃn] n. a) Ausschachtung, die; (with machine) Ausbaggerung, die; b) (Archaeol.) Ausgrabung, die. **excavator** ['ekskəveɪtə(r)] n. Bagger, der

exceed [ɪk'siːd] v.t. a) (be greater than) übertreffen (in an + Dat.); ⟨Kosten, Summe, Anzahl:⟩ übersteigen (by um); b) (go beyond) überschreiten; hinausgehen über (+ Akk.) ⟨Auftrag, Befehl⟩. **ex'ceedingly** adv. äußerst; ausgesprochen ⟨häßlich, dumm⟩

excel [ɪk'sel] 1. v.t., -ll- übertreffen; ~ oneself (lit. or iron.) sich selbst übertreffen. 2. v.i., -ll- sich hervortun (at, in in + Dat.)

excellence ['eksələns] n. hervorragende Qualität. **excellent** ['eksələnt] adj. hervorragend

except [ɪk'sept] 1. prep. ~ (for) [(coll.) for] außer (+ Dat.); ~ for (in all respects other than) abgesehen von. 2. v.t. ausnehmen (from bei); ~ed ausgenommen. **ex'cepting** prep. außer (+ Dat.). **exception** [ɪk'sepʃn] n. Ausnahme, die; take ~ to Anstoß nehmen an (+ Dat.). **exceptional** [ɪk'sepʃənl] adj. außergewöhnlich. **ex'ceptionally** adv. a) (as an exception) ausnahmsweise; b) (remarkably) ungewöhnlich

excerpt ['eksɜːpt] n. Auszug, der (from aus)

excess [ɪk'ses] n. a) Übermaß, das (of an + Dat.); eat/drink to ~: übermäßig essen/trinken; b) esp. in pl. (over-indulgence) Exzeß, der; c) be in ~ of sth. etw. übersteigen; d) (surplus) Überschuß, der

excess ['ekses]: ~ 'baggage n. Mehrgepäck, das; ~ 'fare n. Mehrpreis, der; pay the ~ fare nachlösen

excessive [ɪk'sesɪv] adj. übermäßig; übertrieben ⟨Forderung, Lob, Ansprüche⟩; unmäßig ⟨Esser, Trinker⟩. **ex'cessively** adv. übertrieben; unmäßig ⟨essen, trinken⟩

exchange [ɪks'tʃeɪndʒ] 1. v.t. a) tauschen ⟨Plätze, Ringe, Küsse⟩; umtauschen ⟨Geld⟩; wechseln ⟨Blicke, Worte⟩; ~ insults sich beleidigen; b) *(give in place of another)* eintauschen (for für, gegen); umtauschen *([gekaufte] Ware)* (for gegen). **2.** *n.* a) Tausch, *der;* in ~: dafür; in ~ for sth. für etw.; b) *(of money)* Umtausch, *der;* ~ rate, rate of ~: Wechselkurs, *der;* c) *(Teleph.)* Fernmeldeamt, *das*

exchequer [ɪksˈtʃekə(r)] *n.* (Brit.) Schatzamt, *das*

excise [ˈeksaɪz] *n.* Verbrauchsteuer, *die;* Customs and E~ (Brit.) Amt für Zölle und Verbrauchsteuer

excitable [ekˈsaɪtəbl] *adj.* leicht erregbar

excite [ɪkˈsaɪt] *v.t.* a) *(thrill)* begeistern; b) *(agitate)* aufregen. **ex'cited** *adj.* aufgeregt (at über + *Akk.*); get ~: sich aufregen. **ex'citement** *n.* Aufregung, *die;* *(enthusiasm)* Begeisterung, *die.* **exciting** [ɪkˈsaɪtɪŋ] *adj.* aufregend; *(full of suspense)* spannend

exclaim [ɪkˈskleɪm] **1.** *v.t.* ausrufen. **2.** *v.i.* aufschreien. **exclamation** [eksklə'meɪʃn] *n.* Ausruf, *der.* **exclaˈmation mark**, (Amer.) **exclaˈmation point** *ns.* Ausrufezeichen, *das*

exclude [ɪkˈskluːd] *v.t.* ausschließen. **excluding** [ɪkˈskluːdɪŋ] *prep.* ~ drinks/VAT Getränke ausgenommen/ ohne Mehrwertsteuer. **exclusion** [ɪk'skluːʒn] *n.* Ausschluß, *der.* **exclusive** [ɪkˈskluːsɪv] *adj.* a) alleinig *(Besitzer, Kontrolle);* Allein*(besitz, -recht);* *(Journ.)* Exklusiv*(bericht, -interview);* b) *(select)* exklusiv; c) ~ of ohne. **ex'clusively** *adv.* ausschließlich

excrement [ˈekskrɪmənt] *n.* Kot, *der (geh.)*

excrete [ɪkˈskriːt] *v.t.* ausscheiden

excruciating [ɪkˈskruːˈʃieɪtɪŋ] *adj.* unerträglich

excursion [ɪkˈskɜːʃn] *n.* Ausflug, *der*

excusable [ɪkˈskjuːzəbl] *adj.* entschuldbar; verzeihlich

excuse 1. [ɪkˈskjuːz] *v.t.* a) entschuldigen; ~ oneself sich entschuldigen; ~ me Entschuldigung; b) *(release, exempt)* befreien (from von). **2.** [ɪkˈskjuːs] *n.* Entschuldigung, *die*

ex-di'rectory *adj.* (Brit. Teleph.) Geheim*(nummer, -anschluß);* be ~: nicht im Telefonbuch stehen

execute [ˈeksɪkjuːt] *v.t.* a) hinrichten; b) *(put into effect)* ausführen. **execution** [eksɪˈkjuːʃn] *n.* a) Hinrichtung, *die;* b) *(putting into effect)* Ausführung, *die.* **exeˈcutioner** *n.* Scharfrichter, *der*

executive [ɪgˈzekjʊtɪv] **1.** *n.* leitender Angestellter/leitende Angestellte. **2.** *adj.* leitend *(Stellung, Funktion)*

executor [ɪgˈzekjʊtə(r)] *n.* (Law) Testamentsvollstrecker, *der*

exemplary [ɪgˈzemplərɪ] *adj.* a) *(model)* vorbildlich; b) *(deterrent)* exemplarisch

exemplify [ɪgˈzemplɪfaɪ] *v.t.* veranschaulichen

exempt [ɪgˈzempt] **1.** *adj.* |be| ~ |from sth.| |von etw.| befreit |sein|. **2.** *v.t.* befreien. **exemption** [ɪgˈzempʃn] *n.* Befreiung, *die*

exercise [ˈeksəsaɪz] **1.** *n.* a) Übung, *die;* b) *no pl. (physical exertion)* Bewegung, *die;* **take** ~: sich *(Dat.)* Bewegung schaffen. **2.** *v.t.* ausüben *(Recht, Macht, Einfluß);* walten lassen *(Vorsicht).* **3.** *v.i.* sich *(Dat.)* Bewegung schaffen. **'exercise book** *n.* [Schul]heft, *das*

exert [ɪgˈzɜːt] **1.** *v.t.* aufbieten *(Kraft);* ausüben *(Einfluß, Druck).* **2.** *v. refl.* sich anstrengen. **exertion** [ɪgˈzɜːʃn] *n.* a) *(of strength, force)* Aufwendung, *die;* *(of influence, pressure)* Ausübung, *die;* b) *(effort)* Anstrengung, *die*

exhale [eksˈheɪl] *v.t. & i.* ausatmen

exhaust [ɪgˈzɔːst] **1.** *v.t.* erschöpfen; erschöpfend behandeln *(Thema).* **2.** *n.* (Motor Veh.) Auspuff, *der;* *(gases)* Auspuffgase Pl. **ex'hausted** *adj.* erschöpft. **ex'hausting** *adj.* anstrengend. **exhaustion** [ɪgˈzɔːstʃn] *n.* Erschöpfung, *die.* **exhaustive** [ɪgˈzɔːstɪv] *adj.* umfassend. **ex'haustpipe** *n.* Auspuffrohr, *das*

exhibit [ɪgˈzɪbɪt] **1.** *v.t.* ausstellen; zeigen *(Mut, Symptome, Angst usw.).* **2.** *n.* Ausstellungsstück, *das.* **exhibition** [eksɪˈbɪʃn] *n.* Ausstellung, *die;* **make an** ~ of oneself sich unmöglich aufführen. **exhibitor** [ɪgˈzɪbɪtə(r)] *n.* Aussteller, *der*/Ausstellerin, *die*

exhilarated [ɪgˈzɪləreɪtɪd] *adj.* belebt. **exhilarating** [ɪgˈzɪləreɪtɪŋ] *adj.* belebend. **exhilaration** [ɪgzɪləˈreɪʃn] *n.* |feeling of| ~: Hochgefühl, *das*

exhort [ɪgˈzɔːt] *v.t.* ermahnen

exile [ˈeksaɪl] **1.** *n.* a) Exil, *das;* in/into ~: im/ins Exil; b) *(person)* Verbannte, *der/die.* **2.** *v.t.* verbannen

exist [ɪgˈzɪst] *v.i.* existieren; *(Zweifel, Gefahr, Problem, Situation:)* bestehen; ~ on sth. von etw. leben. **existence** [ɪgˈzɪstəns] *n.* Existenz, *die;* *(mode of living)* Dasein, *das;* **be in/ come into** ~: existieren/entstehen

exit ['eksɪt] n. *(way out)* Ausgang, der *(from aus)*; *(for vehicle)* Ausfahrt, die. **'exit visa** n. Ausreisevisum, das

exonerate [ɪg'zɒnəreɪt] v. t. entlasten

exorbitant [ɪg'zɔːbɪtənt] adj. [maßlos] überhöht

exorcize ['eksɔːsaɪz] v. t. austreiben

exotic [ɪg'zɒtɪk] adj. exotisch

expand [ɪk'spænd] **1.** v. i. a) sich ausdehnen; *(Commerc.)* expandieren; b) ~ **on** weiter ausführen. **2.** v. t. ausdehnen; *(Commerc.)* erweitern

expanse [ɪk'spæns] n. [weite] Fläche

expansion [ɪk'spænʃn] n. Ausdehnung, die; *(Commerc.)* Expansion, die

expect [ɪk'spekt] v. t. a) erwarten; ~ **to do sth.** damit rechnen, etw. zu tun; ~ **sb. to do sth.** damit rechnen, daß jmd. etw. tut; *(require)* von jmdm. erwarten, daß er etw. tut; b) *(coll.: think, suppose)* glauben; **I** ~ **so** ich glaube schon. **expectancy** [ɪk'spektənsɪ] n. Erwartung, die. **expectant** [ɪk'spektənt] adj. erwartungsvoll; ~ **mother** werdende Mutter. **ex'pectantly** adv. erwartungsvoll; gespannt 〈warten〉

expectation [ekspek'teɪʃn] n. Erwartung, die

expedient [ɪk'spiːdɪənt] **1.** adj. angebracht. **2.** n. Mittel, das

expedition [ekspɪ'dɪʃn] n. Expedition, die

expel [ɪk'spel] v. t., **-ll-** ausweisen *(from aus)*; ~ **sb. from school** jmdn. von der Schule verweisen

expend [ɪk'spend] v. t. a) aufwenden (|up|on für); b) *(use up)* aufbrauchen (|up|on für). **expendable** [ɪk'spendəbl] adj. entbehrlich; **be** ~: geopfert werden können

expenditure [ɪk'spendɪtʃə(r)] n. a) *(amount spent)* Ausgaben Pl. (on für); b) *(spending)* Ausgabe, die

expense [ɪk'spens] n. a) Kosten Pl.; **at sb.'s** ~: auf jmds. Kosten *(Akk.)*; **at one's own** ~: auf eigene Kosten; b) *usu. in pl. (Commerc. etc.; amount spent [and repaid])* Spesen Pl.; c) *(fig.)* [be] **at the** ~ **of sth.** auf Kosten von etw. [gehen]. **ex'pense account** n. Spesenabrechnung, die; **put sth. on one's** ~: etw. als Spesen abrechnen. **expensive** [ɪk'spensɪv] adj., **ex'pensively** adv. teuer

experience [ɪk'spɪərɪəns] **1.** n. Erfahrung, die; *(incident)* Erlebnis, das. **2.** v. t. erleben; haben 〈Schwierigkeiten〉; verspüren 〈Kälte, Schmerz, Gefühl〉. **ex'perienced** adj. erfahren

experiment 1. [ɪk'sperɪmənt] n. a) Experiment, das, Versuch, der (on an + Dat.); b) *(fig.)* Experiment, das. **2.** [ɪk'sperɪment] v. i. Versuche anstellen (on an + Dat.). **experimental** [ɪksperɪ'mentl] adj. experimentell; Experimentier〈theater, -kino〉

expert ['ekspɜːt] **1.** adj. ausgezeichnet; **be** ~ **in** or at **sth.** Fachmann od. Experte für etw. sein; **be** ~ **in** or at **doing sth.** etw. ausgezeichnet können. **2.** n. Fachmann, der; Experte, der/Expertin, die; **be an** ~ **in** or at/on **sth.** Fachmann od. Experte in etw. *(Dat.)*/für etw. sein. **expertise** [ekspɜː'tiːz] n. Fachkenntnisse; *(skill)* Können, das

expire [ɪk'spaɪə(r)] v. i. ablaufen. **expiry** [ɪk'spaɪərɪ] n. Ablauf, der

explain [ɪk'spleɪn] **1.** v. t., *also abs.* erklären. **2.** v. refl., *often abs.* **please** ~ |**yourself**| bitte erklären Sie mir das. **explain a'way** v. t. eine [plausible] Erklärung finden für

explanation [eksplə'neɪʃn] n. Erklärung, die; **need** ~: einer Erklärung bedürfen

explanatory [ɪk'splænətərɪ] adj. erklärend; erläuternd 〈Bemerkung〉

explicable [ɪk'splɪkəbl] adj. erklärbar

explicit [ɪk'splɪsɪt] adj. klar; ausdrücklich 〈Zustimmung, Erwähnung〉. **ex'plicitly** adv. ausdrücklich; deutlich 〈beschreiben, ausdrücken〉

explode [ɪk'spləʊd] **1.** v. i. explodieren. **2.** v. t. zur Explosion bringen

exploit 1. ['eksplɔɪt] n. Heldentat, die. **2.** [ɪk'splɔɪt] v. t. ausbeuten 〈Arbeiter usw.〉; ausnutzen 〈Gutmütigkeit, Freund, Unwissenheit〉. **exploitation** [eksplɔɪ'teɪʃn] n. *see* exploit 2: Ausbeutung, die; Ausnutzung, die

exploration [eksplə'reɪʃn] n. Erforschung, die; *(fig.)* Untersuchung, die

exploratory [ɪk'splɒrətərɪ] adj. Forschungs-

explore [ɪk'splɔː(r)] v. t. erforschen; *(fig.)* untersuchen. **ex'plorer** n. Entdeckungsreisende, der

explosion [ɪk'spləʊʒn] n. Explosion, die. **explosive** [ɪk'spləʊzɪv] **1.** adj. explosiv; n. Sprengstoff, der

export 1. [ɪk'spɔːt, 'ekspɔːt] v. t. exportieren; ausführen. **2.** ['ekspɔːt] n. Export, der. **ex'porter** n. Exporteur, der

expose [ɪk'spəʊz] v. t. a) *(uncover)* freilegen; entblößen 〈Haut, Körper〉; b) offenbaren 〈Schwäche〉; aufdecken 〈Mißstände, Verbrechen〉; entlarven 〈Täter, Spion〉; c) *(subject)* ~ **to sth.** einer Sache *(Dat.)* aussetzen; **d)** *(Photog.)* belichten. **exposed** [ɪk-'spəʊzd] *adj. (unprotected)* unge- schützt; ~ **position** exponierte Stel- lung. **exposure** [ɪk'spəʊʒə(r)] *n.* **a)** *(to cold etc.)* die of/suffer from ~: an Un- terkühlung *(Dat.)* sterben/leiden; **b)** *(Photog.) (exposing time)* Belichtung, die; *(picture)* Aufnahme, die. **ex- 'posure meter** *n.* Belichtungsmes- ser, der

expound [ɪk'spaʊnd] *v. t.* darlegen

express [ɪk'spres] **1.** *v. t.* ausdrücken; äußern *(Meinung, Wunsch, Dank, Be- dauern)*; ~ **oneself** sich ausdrücken. **2.** *attrib. adj.* **a)** Eil*(brief, -bote usw.)*; Schnell*(paket, -sendung)*; **b)** aus- drücklich *(Wunsch, Absicht)*. **3.** *adv.* als Eilsache *(senden)*. **4.** *n. (train)* Schnellzug, der. **expression** [ɪk- 'spreʃn] *n.* Ausdruck, der. **ex- pressive** [ɪk'spresɪv] *adj.* ausdrucks- voll

express: ~ **'train** *n.* D-Zug, der; ~**way** *n. (Amer.)* Schnellstraße, die **ex'pressly** *adv.* ausdrücklich

expulsion [ɪk'spʌlʃn] *n.* Ausweisung, die *(from aus)*; *(from school)* Verwei- sung, die *(from von)*

exquisite ['ekskwɪzɪt, ɪk'skwɪzɪt] *adj.* erlesen. **ex'quisitely** *adv.* vorzüg- lich; kunstvoll *(verziert, geschnitzt)*

extend [ɪk'stend] **1.** *v. t.* verlängern; ausstrecken *(Arm, Bein, Hand)*; aus- ziehen *(Leiter, Teleskop)*; verlängern lassen *(Leihbuch, Visum)*; ausdehnen *(Einfluß, Macht)*; vergrößern *(Haus, Geschäft, Fabrik)*; gewähren *([Gast]freundschaft, Hilfe, Kredit)* (to *Dat.*); ~ **the time limit** den Termin hinausschieben. **2.** *v. i.* sich er- strecken; **the season ~s from Novem- ber to March** die Saison geht von No- vember bis März

extension [ɪk'stenʃn] *n.* **a)** Verlänge- rung, die; **b)** *(part of house)* Anbau, der; **c)** *(telephone)* Nebenanschluß, der; *(number)* Apparat, der. **exten- sive** [ɪk'stensɪv] *adj.* ausgedehnt; um- fangreich *(Reparatur, Wissen, Nach- forschungen)*; beträchtlich *(Schäden)*; weitreichend *(Änderungen)*. **ex'tens- ively** *adv.* beträchtlich *(ändern, be- schädigen)*; ausführlich *(berichten, schreiben)*

extent [ɪk'stent] *n.* Ausdehnung, die; *(scope)* Umfang, der; *(of damage)* Ausmaß, das; **to what ~?** inwieweit? **exterior** [ɪk'stɪərɪə(r)] **1.** *adj.* äußer...;

Außen*(fläche, -wand)*. **2.** *n.* Äußere, das; *(of house)* Außenwände *Pl.*

exterminate [ɪk'stɜːmɪneɪt] *v. t.* aus- rotten; vertilgen *(Ungeziefer)*. **ex- termination** [ɪkstɜːmɪ'neɪʃn] *n.* Aus- rottung, die; *(of pests)* Vertilgung, die

external [ɪk'stɜːnl] *adj.* äußer...; Außen*(fläche, -abmessungen)*; purely ~: rein äußerlich; **for ~ use only** nur äußerlich anzuwenden

extinct [ɪk'stɪŋkt] *adj.* erloschen *(Vul- kan)*; ausgestorben *(Art, Rasse, Gat- tung)*. **extinction** [ɪk'stɪŋkʃn] *n.* Aus- sterben, das

extinguish [ɪk'stɪŋgwɪʃ] *v. t.* löschen. **ex'tinguisher** *n.* Feuerlöscher, der

extol [ɪk'stɒl] *v. t.*, **-ll-** rühmen; preisen

extort [ɪk'stɔːt] *v. t.* erpressen **(out of** von)**. **extortion** [ɪk'stɔːʃn] *n.* Erpres- sung, die. **extortionate** [ɪk'stɔːʃənət] *adj.* Wucher*(preis, -zinsen usw.)*; maßlos überzogen *(Forderung)*

extra ['ekstrə] **1.** *adj.* zusätzlich; Mehr*(arbeit, -kosten, -ausgaben)*; Sonder*(bus, -zug)*. **2.** *adv.* **a)** *(more than usually)* besonders; extra *(lang, stark, fein)*; **b)** *(additionally)* extra; **packing and postage ~:** zuzüglich Ver- packung und Porto. **3.** *n.* **a)** *(added to services, salary, etc.)* zusätzliche Lei- stung; **b)** *(in play, film, etc.)* Statist, der/Statistin, die

extract 1. ['ekstrækt] *n.* **a)** Extrakt, der *(fachspr. auch: das)*; **b)** *(from book, music, etc.)* Auszug, der. **2.** [ɪk'strækt] *v. t.* ziehen *(Zahn)*; herausziehen *(Dorn, Splitter usw.)*. **extraction** [ɪk- 'strækʃn] *n. (of tooth)* Extraktion, die; *(of thorn, splinter, etc.)* Herausziehen, das. **ex'tractor fan** *n.* Entlüfter, der

extradite ['ekstrədaɪt] *v. t.* ausliefern. **extradition** [ekstrə'dɪʃn] *n.* Ausliefe- rung, die

extraordinary [ɪk'strɔːdɪnərɪ] *adj.* au- ßergewöhnlich; merkwürdig *(Beneh- men)*; **how ~!** wie seltsam!

extravagance [ɪk'strævəgəns] *n.* **a)** Extravaganz, die; **b)** *(extravagant thing)* Luxus, der

extravagant [ɪk'strævəgənt] *adj.* ver- schwenderisch; aufwendig *(Lebens- stil)*; teuer *(Geschmack)*

extreme [ɪk'striːm] **1.** *adj.* **a)** äußerst... *(Spitze, Rand, Ende)*; extrem *(Gegen- sätze, Hitze, Kälte)*; höchst... *(Ge- fahr)*; äußerst... *(Notfall, Höflichkeit, Bescheidenheit)*; stärkst... *(Schmer- zen)*; größt... *(Wichtigkeit)*; **at the ~ edge/left** ganz am Rand/ganz links; **b)**

(not moderate) extrem; drastisch ⟨*Maßnahme*⟩. **2.** *n.* Extrem, *das;* go to ~s vor nichts zurückschrecken; go from one ~ to the other von einem Extrem ins andere fallen. **extremely** *adv.* äußerst. **extremist** [ɪkˈstriːmɪst] *n.* Extremist, *der*/Extremistin, *die; attrib.* extremistisch. **extremity** [ɪkˈstremɪtɪ] *n.* äußerstes Ende

extricate [ˈekstrɪkeɪt] *v.t.* ~ sth. from sth. etw. aus etw. herausziehen; ~ oneself/sb. from sth. sich/jmdn. aus etw. befreien

extrovert [ˈekstrəvɜːt] **1.** *n.* extrovertierter Mensch; be an ~: extrovertiert sein. **2.** *adj.* extrovertiert

exuberant [ɪgˈzjuːbərənt] *adj.* be ~: sich überschwenglich freuen

exude [ɪgˈzjuːd] *v.t.* absondern; *(fig.)* ausstrahlen

exult [ɪgˈzʌlt] *v.i.* jubeln (in, at, over über + *Akk.*)

eye [aɪ] **1.** *n.* **a)** Auge, *das;* keep an ~ on sb./sth. auf jmdn./etw. aufpassen; see ~ to ~: einer Meinung sein; with one's ~s shut *(fig.)* blind; *(easily)* im Schlaf; be up to one's ~s in work/debt bis über beide Ohren in Arbeit/Schulden stecken *(ugs.);* **b)** *(of needle)* Öhr, *das; (metal loop)* Öse, *die.* **2.** *v.t.,* beäugen; ~ sb. up and down jmdn. von oben bis unten mustern

eye: ~ball *n.* Augapfel, *der;* ~brow *n.* Augenbraue, *die;* ~lash *n.* Augenwimper, *die;* ~-level *n.* Augenhöhe, *die; attrib.* in Augenhöhe *nachgestellt;* at ~-level in Augenhöhe; ~lid *n.* Augenlid, *das;* ~-shadow *n.* Lidschatten, *der;* ~sight *n.* Sehkraft, *die;* have good ~sight gute Augen haben; his ~sight is poor er hat schlechte Augen; ~sore *n.* Schandfleck, *der;* ~witness *n.* Augenzeuge, *der*/-zeugin, *die*

F

F, f [ef] *n.* F, f, *das*

fable [ˈfeɪbl] *n.* Fabel, *die; (myth, lie)* Märchen, *das*

fabric [ˈfæbrɪk] *n.* Gewebe, *das*

fabricate [ˈfæbrɪkeɪt] *v.t. (invent)* erfinden. **fabrication** [fæbrɪˈkeɪʃn] *n.* Erfindung, *die*

fabulous [ˈfæbjʊləs] *adj.* **a)** sagenhaft; **b)** *(coll.: marvellous)* fabelhaft *(ugs.)*

face [feɪs] **1.** *n.* **a)** Gesicht, *das;* lie ~down|ward ⟨*Person/Buch:*⟩ auf dem Bauch/Gesicht liegen; make or pull a ~/~s Grimassen schneiden; on the ~ of it dem Anschein nach; in the ~ of sth. trotz etw. *(Gen.);* **b)** *(of mountain, cliff)* Wand, *die; (of clock, watch)* Zifferblatt, *das; (of dice)* Seite, *die; (of coin, playing-card)* Vorderseite, *die.* **2.** *v.t.* **a)** sich wenden zu; |stand| facing one another sich *(Dat.)* gegenüber |stehen|; **b)** *(fig.)* ins Auge sehen (+ *Dat.*) ⟨*Tod, Vorstellung:*⟩ stehen vor (+ *Dat.*) ⟨*Ruin, Entscheidung:*⟩; ~ the facts den Tatsachen ins Gesicht sehen; be ~d with sth. sich einer Sache *(Dat.)* gegenübersehen; **c)** *(coll.: bear)* verkraften. **3.** *v.i. (in train etc.)* ~ forwards/backwards ⟨*Person:*⟩ in/entgegen Fahrtrichtung sitzen. **face 'up to** *v.t.* ins Auge sehen (+ *Dat.*); sich abfinden mit ⟨*Möglichkeit*⟩

face: ~-cream *n.* Gesichtscreme, *die;* ~-flannel *n. (Brit.)* Waschlappen, *der;* ~-lift *n.* **a)** Facelifting, *das;* have or get a ~-lift sich liften lassen; **b)** *(fig.)* Verschönerung, *die*

facet [ˈfæsɪt] *n.* Facette, *die; (fig.)* Aspekt, *der*

facetious [fəˈsiːʃəs] *adj.* |gewollt| witzig

face: ~-to-~: persönlich ⟨*Gespräch, Treffen*⟩; ~ value *n.* Nennwert, *der;* accept sth. at |its| ~ value *(fig.)* etw. für bare Münze nehmen

facial [ˈfeɪʃl] *adj.* Gesichts-

facile [ˈfæsaɪl] *adj.* nichtssagend

facilities [fəˈsɪlɪtɪz] *n. pl.* Einrichtungen; cooking/washing ~: Koch-/Waschgelegenheit, *die;* sports ~: Sportanlagen; shopping ~: Einkaufsmöglichkeiten

facsimile [fækˈsɪmɪlɪ] *n.* **a)** Faksimile, *das;* **b)** see fax 1

fact [fækt] *n.* Tatsache, *die;* ~s and figures Fakten und Zahlen; the ~ remains that ...: Tatsache bleibt: ...; the true ~s of the case or matter der wahre Sachverhalt; know for a ~ that ...: genau wissen, daß ...; in ~: tatsächlich

faction [ˈfækʃn] *n.* Splittergruppe, *die*

factor [ˈfæktə(r)] *n.* Faktor, *der*

factory [ˈfæktərɪ] *n.* Fabrik, *die.* **'factory farm** *n.* Agrarfabrik, *die*

factual ['fæktjʋəl] *adj.* sachlich

faculty ['fækəltɪ] *n.* a) Fähigkeit, *die;* **mental ~:** geistige Kraft; b) *(Univ.)* Fakultät, *die*

fad [fæd] *n.* Marotte, *die*

fade [feɪd] *v. i.* a) ⟨Blätter, Blumen:⟩ [ver]welken; b) **~ [in colour]** [ver]bleichen; **the light ~d** es dunkelte; c) ⟨Laut:⟩ verklingen; d) *(fig.)* verblassen; ⟨Schönheit:⟩ verblühen; ⟨Hoffnung:⟩ schwinden; e) *(blend)* übergehen (**into** in + *Akk.*). **fade away** *v. i.* schwinden; ⟨Laut:⟩ verklingen (**into** in + *Dat.*)

faded ['feɪdɪd] *adj.* welk ⟨Blume, Blatt, Laub⟩; verblichen ⟨Stoff, Farbe⟩

fag [fæg] *n.* a) *(Brit. coll.)* Schinderei, *die (ugs.);* b) *(sl.: cigarette)* Stäbchen, *das (ugs.)*

fail [feɪl] **1.** *v. i.* a) scheitern; *(in examination)* nicht bestehen (**in** in + *Dat.*); b) *(become weaker)* ⟨Augenlicht, Gehör, Stärke:⟩ nachlassen; c) *(break down, stop)* ⟨Versorgung:⟩ zusammenbrechen; ⟨Motor:⟩ aussetzen; ⟨Batterie, Pumpe:⟩ ausfallen; ⟨Bremse:⟩ versagen. **2.** *v. t.* a) **~ to do sth.** *(not succeed in doing)* etw. nicht tun [können]; **~ to achieve one's purpose/aim** seine Absicht/sein Ziel verfehlen; b) *(be unsuccessful in)* nicht bestehen ⟨Prüfung⟩; c) *(reject)* durchfallen lassen *(ugs.)* ⟨Prüfling⟩; d) **~ to do sth.** *(not do)* etw. nicht tun; *(neglect to do)* [es] versäumen, etw. zu tun; **not ~ to do sth.** etw. tun; e) **words ~ me** mir fehlen die Worte; **his courage ~ed him** ihn verließ der Mut. **3.** *n.* **without ~:** auf jeden Fall. **failing 1.** *n.* Schwäche, *die.* **2.** *prep.* **~ that** andernfalls. **failure** ['feɪljə(r)] *n.* a) *(omission, neglect)* Versäumnis, *das;* b) *(lack of success)* Scheitern, *das;* **end in ~:** scheitern; c) *(person or thing)* Versager, *der;* **our plan/attempt was a ~:** unser Plan/Versuch war fehlgeschlagen

faint [feɪnt] **1.** *adj.* a) matt ⟨Licht, Farbe, Stimme, Lächeln⟩; schwach ⟨Geruch, Duft⟩; leise ⟨Flüstern, Geräusch, Stimme⟩; entfernt ⟨Ähnlichkeit⟩; undeutlich ⟨Umriß, Linie, Spur, Fotokopie⟩; b) *(giddy, weak)* matt; **she felt ~:** ihr war schwindelig. **2.** *v. i.* ohnmächtig werden (**from** vor + *Dat.*). **3.** *n.* Ohnmacht, *die.* **faintly** *adv.* schwach; entfernt ⟨sich ähneln⟩

¹fair [feə(r)] *n.* *(fun-~)* Jahrmarkt, *der; (exhibition)* Messe, *die;* **book-/trade ~:** Buch-/Handelsmesse, *die*

²fair 1. *adj.* a) *(just)* gerecht; begründet ⟨Beschwerde, Annahme⟩; fair ⟨Spiel, Kampf, Prozeß, Preis, Beurteilung, Handel⟩; **~ play** Fairneß, *die;* b) *(not bad, pretty good)* ganz gut ⟨Bilanz, Anzahl, Chance⟩; ziemlich ⟨Maß, Geschwindigkeit⟩; c) *(blond)* blond ⟨Haar, Person⟩; *(light)* hell ⟨Haut⟩; **(~-skinned)** hellhäutig ⟨Person⟩; d) schön ⟨Wetter, Tag⟩. **'fair-haired 1.** *adj.* blond. **2.** *adv.* fair ⟨kämpfen, spielen⟩. **'fairly** *adv.* a) fair ⟨kämpfen, spielen⟩; gerecht ⟨bestrafen, beurteilen, behandeln⟩; b) *(rather)* ziemlich. **'fairness** *n.* Gerechtigkeit, *die;* **in all ~** [to sb.] um fair [gegen jmdn.] zu sein

fairy ['feərɪ] *n.* Fee, *die*

fairy: ~ 'godmother *n.* gute Fee; **~ story, ~-tale** *ns.* Märchen, *das*

faith [feɪθ] *n.* a) *(reliance, trust)* Vertrauen, *das* (**in** zu); **have ~ in oneself** Selbstvertrauen haben; **in good ~:** in gutem Glauben; b) *(religious belief)* Glaube, *der.* **faithful** ['feɪθfl] *adj.* a) treu (**to** *Dat.*); b) *(conscientious)* pflichtbewußt; [ge]treu ⟨Diener⟩; c) *(accurate)* [wahrheits]getreu; originalgetreu ⟨Wiedergabe, Kopie⟩. **'faithfully** *adv.* a) treu ⟨dienen⟩; pflichtbewußt ⟨überbringen, zustellen⟩; hoch und heilig ⟨versprechen⟩; b) *(accurately)* wahrheitsgetreu ⟨erzählen⟩; originalgetreu ⟨wiedergeben⟩; genau ⟨befolgen⟩; c) **yours ~:** hochachtungsvoll

fake [feɪk] **1.** *adj.* unecht; gefälscht ⟨Dokument, Banknote, Münze⟩. **2.** *n.* a) Imitation, *die; (painting)* Fälschung, *die;* b) *(person)* Schwindler, *der*/Schwindlerin, *die.* **3.** *v. t.* fälschen ⟨Unterschrift⟩; vortäuschen ⟨Krankheit, Unfall⟩

falcon ['fɔːlkn] *n.* Falke, *der*

fall [fɔːl] **1.** *n.* a) Fallen, *das; (of person)* Sturz, *der;* **~ of snow/rain** Schnee-/Regenfall, *der;* **have a ~:** stürzen; b) *(collapse, defeat)* Fall, *der; (of dynasty, empire)* Untergang, *der;* c) *(decrease)* Rückgang, *der;* d) *(Amer.: autumn)* Herbst, *der.* **2.** *v. i.,* **fell** [fel], **~en** ['fɔːln] a) fallen ⟨Baum:⟩ umstürzen; ⟨Pferd:⟩ stürzen; **~ off sth., ~ down from sth.** von etw. [herunter]fallen; **~ down** [**into**] **sth.** in etw. *(Akk.)* [hinein]fallen; **~ to the ground** auf den Boden fallen; **~ down the stairs** *or* **downstairs** die Treppe herunter-/hinunterfallen; b) ⟨Nacht, Dunkelheit:⟩ hereinbrechen; ⟨Abend:⟩ anbrechen; c) ⟨Blätter:⟩ [ab]fallen; d) *(sink)* sinken;

⟨*Barometer:*⟩ fallen; ⟨*Absatz, Verkauf:*⟩ zurückgehen; **~ by 10 per cent/from 10[°C] to 0[°C]** um 10%/von 10[°C] auf 0[°C] sinken; **e)** *(be killed)* ⟨*Soldat:*⟩ fallen; **f)** *(collapse)* einstürzen; **~ to pieces, ~ apart** auseinanderfallen; **g)** *(occur)* fallen **(on** auf + *Akk.*). **fall 'back** *v.i.* zurückweichen. **fall 'back on** *v.t.* zurückgreifen auf (+ *Akk.*). **fall 'down** *v.i.* **a)** *see* **fall** 2 a; **b)** ⟨*Brücke, Gebäude:*⟩ einstürzen. **'fall for** *v.t.* *(coll.)* **~ for sb.** sich in jmdn. verknallen *(ugs.):* **~ for sth.** auf etw. *(Akk.)* hereinfallen *(ugs.).* **fall 'in** *v.i.* **a)** hineinfallen; **b)** *(Mil.)* antreten; **~ in!** angetreten!; **c)** ⟨*Gebäude, Wand usw.:*⟩ einstürzen. **fall 'off** *v.i.* **a)** herunterfallen; **b)** *(diminish)* nachlassen. **fall 'out** *v.i.* **a)** herausfallen; ⟨*Haare, Federn*⟩ ausfallen; **b)** *(quarrel)* **~ out [with sb.]** sich [mit jmdm.] streiten. **fall 'over** *v.i.* umfallen; ⟨*Person:*⟩ [hin]fallen. **fall 'through** *v.i.* *(fig.)* ins Wasser fallen *(ugs.)*

fallacy ['fæləsɪ] *n.* Irrtum, *der*
fallen *see* **fall** 2
fallible ['fælɪbl] *adj.* nicht unfehlbar; fehlbar ⟨*Person*⟩
'fall-out *n.* radioaktiver Niederschlag
fallow ['fæləʊ] *adj.* brachliegend; **~ ground/land** Brache, *die*/Brachland, *das;* **lie ~:** brachliegen
false [fɔːls, fɒls] *adj.* falsch; gefälscht ⟨*Urkunde, Dokument*⟩; künstlich ⟨*Wimpern*⟩; **under a ~ name** unter falschem Namen. **'falsely** *adv.* falsch; fälschlich[erweise] ⟨*annehmen, glauben, behaupten, beschuldigen*⟩
false: ~ a'larm *n.* blinder Alarm; **~ 'start** *n.* Fehlstart, *der;* **~ 'teeth** *n. pl.* [künstliches] Gebiß
falsify ['fɔːlsɪfaɪ] *v.t. (alter)* fälschen; *(misrepresent)* verfälschen ⟨*Tatsachen, Wahrheit*⟩
falter ['fɔːltə(r)] *v.i.* stocken
fame [feɪm] *n.* Ruhm, *der*
familiar [fə'mɪljə(r)] *adj.* **a)** vertraut; bekannt ⟨*Gesicht, Name, Lied*⟩; **he looks ~:** er kommt mir bekannt vor; **b)** *(informal)* ungezwungen ⟨*Sprache, Art*⟩. **familiarity** [fəmɪlɪ'ærɪtɪ] *n.* Vertrautheit, *die.* **familiarize** [fə'mɪljəraɪz] *v.t.* vertraut machen **(with** mit)
family ['fæmɪlɪ] *n.* Familie, *die*
family: ~ 'name *n.* Familienname, *der;* **~ 'planning** *n.* Familienplanung, *die;* **~ 'tree** *n.* Stammbaum, *der*
famine ['fæmɪn] *n.* Hungersnot, *die*

famished ['fæmɪʃt] *adj.* ausgehungert; **I'm absolutely ~** *(coll.)* ich sterbe vor Hunger *(ugs.)*
famous ['feɪməs] *adj.* berühmt
¹fan [fæn] **1.** *n.* Fächer, *der;* ⟨*apparatus*⟩ Ventilator, *der.* **2.** *v.t.,* **-nn-** fächeln ⟨*Gesicht*⟩; anfachen ⟨*Feuer*⟩; **~ oneself/sb.** sich/jmdm. Luft zufächeln. **fan 'out** *v.i.* fächern; ⟨*Soldaten:*⟩ ausfächern
²fan *n. (devotee)* Fan, *der*
fanatic [fə'nætɪk] *n.* Fanatiker, *der*/Fanatikerin, *die.* **fanatical** [fə'nætɪkl] *adj.* fanatisch. **fanaticism** [fə'nætɪsɪzm] *n.* Fanatismus, *der*
'fan belt *n.* Keilriemen, *der*
fanciful ['fænsɪfl] *adj.* überspannt ⟨*Vorstellung, Gedanke*⟩; phantastisch ⟨*Gemälde, Design*⟩
'fan club *n.* Fanklub, *der*
fancy ['fænsɪ] **1.** *n.* **a)** *(taste, inclination)* **he has taken a ~ to a new car/her** ein neues Auto/sie hat es ihm angetan; **take** *or* **catch sb.'s ~:** jmdm. gefallen; **b)** *(whim)* Laune, *die;* **tickle sb.'s ~:** jmdm. reizen. **2.** *attrib. adj.* kunstvoll ⟨*Arbeit, Muster*⟩; fein[st] ⟨*Kuchen, Spitzen*⟩. **3.** *v.t.* **a)** *(imagine)* sich ⟨*Dat.*⟩ einbilden; **~ that!** *(coll.)* sieh mal einer an!; **b)** *(suppose)* glauben; **c)** *(wish to have)* mögen; **what do you ~ for dinner?** was hättest du gern zum Abendessen? **fancy 'dress** *n.* [Masken]kostüm, *das;* **in ~:** kostümiert; **fancy-dress party** Kostümfest, *das;* **fancy-dress ball** Maskenball, *der*
fanfare ['fænfeə(r)] *n.* Fanfare, *die*
fang [fæŋ] *n.* Reißzahn, *der;* ⟨*of snake*⟩ Giftzahn, *der*
fan: ~ heater *n.* Heizlüfter, *der;* **~light** *n.* Oberlicht, *das;* **~ mail** *n.* Fanpost, *die*
fantastic [fæn'tæstɪk] *adj.* **a)** *(grotesque, quaint)* bizarr; **b)** *(coll.: excellent)* phantastisch *(ugs.)*
fantasy ['fæntəzɪ] *n.* Phantasie, *die;* *(mental image)* Phantasiegebilde, *das*
far [fɑː(r)] **1.** *adv.* weit; **~ above/below** hoch über/tief unter (+ *Dat.*); hoch oben/tief unten; **as ~ as Munich/the church** bis [nach] München/bis zur Kirche; **~ and wide** weit und breit; **from ~ and wide** von fern und nah; **~ too** viel zu; **~ longer/better** weit[aus] länger/besser; **as ~ as I remember/know** soweit ich mich erinnere/weiß; **go so ~ as to do sth.** so weit gehen und etw. tun; **so ~** *(until now)* bisher; **so ~ so good** so weit, so gut; **by ~:** bei wei-

tem; ~ **from easy/good** alles andere als leicht/gut. **2.** *adj.* **a)** *(remote)* weit entfernt; *(in time)* fern; **in the ~ distance** in weiter Ferne; **b)** *(more remote)* weiter entfernt; **the ~ bank of the river/side of the road** das andere Flußufer/die andere Straßenseite; **the ~ door/wall** *etc.* die hintere Tür/Wand *usw.*

farce [faːs] *n.* Farce, *die.* **farcical** [ˈfaːsɪkl] *adj. (absurd)* farcenhaft

fare [feə(r)] *n.* **a)** *(price)* Fahrpreis, *der; (money)* Fahrgeld, *das;* **what** or **how much is the ~?** was kostet die Fahrt?; **b)** *(food)* Kost, *die*

Far: ~ **'East** *n.* the ~ East der Ferne Osten; ~ **'Eastern** *adj.* fernöstlich; des Fernen Ostens *nachgestellt*

farewell [feəˈwel] **1.** *int.* leb[e] wohl *(veralt.).* **2.** *n. attrib.* ~ **speech/gift** Abschiedsrede, *die/*-geschenk, *das*

far-'fetched *adj.* weit hergeholt

farm [faːm] **1.** *n.* [Bauern]hof, *der; (larger)* Gut, *das;* ~ **animals** Nutzvieh, *das.* **2.** *v.t.* bebauen *⟨Land⟩.* **3.** *v.i.* Landwirtschaft treiben. **'farmer** *n.* Landwirt, *der/*-wirtin, *die*

'farmhouse *n.* Bauernhaus, *das; (larger)* Gutshaus, *das*

'farming *n.* Landwirtschaft, *die*

farm: ~**land** *n.* Acker- und Weideland, *das;* ~**yard** *n.* Hof, *der*

far: ~-'**reaching** *adj.* weitreichend; ~-'**sighted** *adj.* **a)** *(fig.)* weitblickend; **b)** *(Amer.: long-sighted)* weitsichtig

fart [faːt] *(coarse)* **1.** *v.i.* furzen *(derb).* **2.** *n.* Furz, *der (derb)*

farther [ˈfaːðə(r)] *see* **further 1 a, 2**

farthest [ˈfaːðɪst] *see* **furthest**

fascinate [ˈfæsɪneɪt] *v.t.* fesseln; bezaubern. **fascination** [fæsɪˈneɪʃn] *n.* Zauber, *der;* **have a ~ for sb.** einen besonderen Reiz auf jmdn. ausüben

Fascism [ˈfæʃɪzm] *n.* Faschismus, *der.* **Fascist** [ˈfæʃɪst] **1.** *n.* Faschist, *der/*Faschistin, *die.* **2.** *adj.* faschistisch

fashion [ˈfæʃn] **1.** *n.* **a)** Mode, *die;* **b)** *(manner)* Art [und Weise]; **talk/behave in a peculiar ~:** merkwürdig sprechen/sich merkwürdig verhalten. **2.** *v.t.* formen **(out of, from** aus; [in]to zu). **fashionable** [ˈfæʃənəbl] *adj.* modisch; vornehm *⟨Hotel, Restaurant⟩;* Mode*⟨farbe, -autor⟩.* **fashionably** [ˈfæʃənəblɪ] *adv.* modisch

¹fast [faːst] **1.** *v.i.* fasten. **2.** *n.* Fasten, *das*

²fast 1. *adj.* **a)** *(fixed, attached)* fest; **make [the boat] ~:** das Boot festmachen; **hard** and ~: fest; bindend *⟨Regel⟩;* klar *⟨Entscheidung⟩;* **b)** *(rapid)* schnell; ~ **train** Schnellzug, *der;* D-Zug, *der;* **c) be [ten minutes] ~** *⟨Uhr:⟩* [zehn Minuten] vorgehen. **2.** *adv.* **a) be ~ asleep** fest schlafen; *(when one should be awake)* fest eingeschlafen sein; **b)** *(quickly)* schnell

fasten [ˈfaːsn] *v.t.* befestigen **(on, to** an + *Dat.*); zumachen *⟨Kleid, Spange, Jacke⟩;* [ab]schließen *⟨Tür⟩;* anstecken *⟨Brosche⟩* **(to** an + *Akk.*); ~ **one's seat-belt** sich anschnallen. **'fastener, 'fastening** *ns.* Verschluß, *der*

fastidious [fæˈstɪdɪəs] *adj.* wählerisch; *(hard to please)* heikel

'fast lane *n.* Überholspur, *die;* **life in the ~** *(fig.)* Leben auf vollen Touren *(ugs.)*

fat [fæt] **1.** *adj.* dick; rund *⟨Wangen, Gesicht⟩.* **2.** *n.* Fett, *das*

fatal [ˈfeɪtl] *adj.* **a)** *(disastrous)* verheerend **(to** für); **it would be ~:** das wäre das Ende; **b)** *(deadly)* tödlich *⟨Unfall, Verletzung⟩.* **fatality** [fəˈtælɪtɪ] *n.* Todesopfer, *das.* **'fatally** *adv.* tödlich; **be ~ ill** todkrank sein

fate [feɪt] *n.* Schicksal, *das*

'fat-head *n.* Dummkopf, *der (ugs.)*

father [ˈfaːðə(r)] *n.* Vater, *der.* **Father 'Christmas** *n.* der Weihnachtsmann. **father-in-law** *n., pl.* ~**s-in-law** Schwiegervater, *der.* **'fatherly** *adj.* väterlich

fathom [ˈfæðəm] **1.** *n. (Naut.)* Faden, *der.* **2.** *v.t. (comprehend)* verstehen; ~ **sb./sth. out** jmdn./etw. ergründen

fatigue [fəˈtiːg] **1.** *n.* Ermüdung, *die.* **2.** *v.t.* ermüden

'fatness *n.* Dicke, *die*

fatten [ˈfætn] *v.t.* herausfüttern *⟨Person⟩;* mästen *⟨Tier⟩.* **'fattening** *adj.* **be ~:** dick machen

fatty [ˈfætɪ] *adj.* fett *⟨Fleisch, Soße⟩;* fetthaltig *⟨Speise, Nahrungsmittel⟩*

faucet [ˈfɔːsɪt] *n. (Amer.)* Wasserhahn, *der*

fault [fɔːlt, fɒlt] *n.* **a)** Fehler, *der;* **b)** *(responsibility)* Schuld, *die;* **it's your ~:** du bist schuld; **it isn't my ~:** ich habe keine Schuld; **be at ~:** im Unrecht sein; **c)** *(in machinery; also Electr.)* Defekt, *der.* **'faultless** *adj.* einwandfrei. **'faulty** *adj.* fehlerhaft; defekt *⟨Gerät, usw.⟩*

fauna [ˈfɔːnə] *n., pl.* ~**e** [ˈfɔːniː] or ~**s** Fauna, *die*

favor etc. *(Amer.) see* **favour** etc.

favour ['feɪvə(r)] **1.** *n.* **a)** Gunst, *die;* **b)** *(kindness)* Gefallen, *der;* **ask sb. a ~, ask ~ of sb.** jmdn. um einen Gefallen bitten; **do sb. a ~, do a ~ for sb.** jmdm. einen Gefallen tun; **as a ~:** aus Gefälligkeit; **c) be in ~ of sth.** für etw. sein. **2.** *v. t.* bevorzugen

favourable ['feɪvərəbl] *adj. (Brit.)* **a)** günstig ⟨Eindruck, Licht⟩; gewogen ⟨Haltung, Einstellung⟩; freundlich ⟨Erwähnung⟩; positiv ⟨Bericht/erstattung⟩, Bemerkung⟩; **b)** *(helpful)* günstig **(to** für) ⟨Wetter, Wind, Umstand⟩.

favourably ['feɪvərəblɪ] *adv. (Brit.)* wohlwollend; **be ~ disposed towards sb./sth.** jmdm./einer Sache positiv gegenüberstehen

favourite ['feɪvərɪt] *(Brit.)* **1.** *adj.* Lieblings-. **2.** *n.* **a)** Liebling, *der;* *(food/country etc.)* Lieblingsessen, *das/-land, das usw.;* **this/he is my ~:** das/ihn mag ich am liebsten; **b)** *(Sport)* Favorit, *der/*Favoritin, *die.*

favouritism ['feɪvərɪtɪzm] *n. (Brit.)* Begünstigung, *die; (when selecting sb. for a post etc.)* Günstlingswirtschaft, *die*

fawn [fɔːn] **1.** *n.* **a)** *(colour)* Rehbraun, *das;* **b)** *(young deer)* [Dam]kitz, *das.* **2.** *adj.* rehfarben

fax [fæks] **1.** *n.* [Tele]fax, *das.* **2.** *v. t.* faxen. **'fax machine** *n.* Faxgerät, *das*

FBI *abbr. (Amer.)* **Federal Bureau of Investigation** FBI, *das*

fear [fɪə(r)] **1.** *n.* Angst, *die* **(of** vor + *Dat.);* *(instance)* Befürchtung, *die;* **~ of death** *or* **dying/heights** Todes-/Höhenangst, *die;* **~ of doing sth.** Angst davor, etw. zu tun; **in ~:** angstvoll; **no ~!** *(coll.)* keine Bange! *(ugs.).* **2.** *v. t.* **a)** **~ sb./sth.** vor jmdm./etw. Angst haben; **~ to do** *or* **doing sth.** Angst haben, etw. zu tun; **b)** *(be worried about)* befürchten; **|that ...|** fürchten[, daß ...]. **fearful** ['fɪəfl] *adj.* **a)** *(terrible)* furchtbar; **b)** *(frightened)* ängstlich; **be ~ of sth./sb.** vor etw./jmdm. Angst haben. **'fearless** *adj.,* **'fearlessly** *adv.* furchtlos

feasibility [fiːzɪ'bɪlɪtɪ] *n.* Durchführbarkeit, *die*

feasible ['fiːzɪbl] *adj.* durchführbar

feast [fiːst] **1.** *n.* **a)** *(Relig.)* Fest, *das;* **b)** *(banquet)* Festessen, *das.* **2.** *v. i.* schlemmen; **~ on sth.** sich an etw. *(Dat.)* gütlich tun

feat [fiːt] *n.* Meisterleistung, *die*

feather ['feðə(r)] *n.* Feder, *die.*

'featherweight *n. (Boxing)* Federgewicht, *das*

feature ['fiːtʃə(r)] **1.** *n.* **a)** *usu. in pl. (of face)* Gesichtszug, *der;* **b)** *(characteristic)* [charakteristisches] Merkmal; **be a ~ of sth.** charakteristisch für etw. sein; **c)** *(Journ.)* Feature, *das;* **d)** *(Cinemat.)* **~ |film|** Hauptfilm, *der.* **2.** *v. t.* vorrangig vorstellen; *(in film)* in der Hauptrolle zeigen. **3.** *v. i.* vorkommen; **~ in** *(be important)* eine bedeutende Rolle haben bei

Feb. *abbr.* **February** Febr.

February ['febrʊərɪ] *n.* Februar, *der*

fed [fed] **1.** *see* **feed 1, 2. 2.** *pred. adj. (sl.)* **be/get ~ up with sb./sth.** jmdn./ etw. satt haben/kriegen *(ugs.);* **I'm ~ up** Ich hab' die Nase voll *(ugs.)*

federal ['fedərl] *adj.* Bundes-; föderativ ⟨System⟩. **federation** [fedə'reɪʃn] *n.* Föderation, *die*

fee [fiː] *n.* Gebühr, *die; (of doctor, lawyer, etc.)* Honorar, *das*

feeble ['fiːbl] *adj.* schwach; wenig überzeugend ⟨Entschuldigung⟩; zaghaft ⟨Versuch⟩; lahm ⟨Witz⟩

feed [fiːd] **1.** *v. t.,* **fed** [fed] **a)** füttern; **~ sb./an animal with sth.** jmdm. etw. zu essen/einem Tier [etw.] zu fressen geben; **b)** *(provide food for)* ernähren **(on,** with mit). **2.** *v. i.,* **fed** ⟨Tier:⟩ fressen **(from** aus); ⟨Person:⟩ essen **(off** von); **~ on sth.** ⟨Tier:⟩ etw. fressen. **3.** *n.* **a)** *(for baby)* Mahlzeit, *die;* **b)** *(fodder)* Futter, *das.* **'feedback** *n.* Reaktion, *die*

feel [fiːl] **1.** *v. t.,* **felt** [felt] **a)** *(explore by touch)* befühlen; **b)** *(perceive by touch)* fühlen; *(become aware of)* bemerken; *(have sensation of)* spüren; **c)** *(experience)* empfinden; verspüren ⟨Drang⟩; **~ the cold/heat** unter der Kälte/Hitze leiden; **~ |that| ...:** das Gefühl haben, daß ...; *(think)* glauben, daß ... **2.** *v. i.,* **felt a) ~ |about| in sth. |for sth.|** in etw. *(Dat.)* [nach etw.] [herum]suchen; **b)** *(be conscious that one is)* sich ... fühlen; **~ angry/sure/disappointed** böse/ sicher/enttäuscht sein; **~ like sth./ doing sth.** auf etw. *(Akk.)* Lust haben/ Lust haben, etw. zu tun; **c)** *(be consciously perceived as)* sich ... anfühlen. **'feel for** *v. t.* **~ for sb.** mit jmdm. Mitleid haben

'feeler *n.* Fühler, *der.* **'feeling** *n.* **a)** Gefühl, *das; (sense of touch)* |sense of| **~:** Tastsinn, *der;* **hurt sb.'s ~s** jmdn. verletzen; **b)** *(opinion)* Ansicht, *die*

feet *pl. of* **foot**

feign [feɪn] *v.t.* vortäuschen; ~ **to do sth.** vorgeben, etw. zu tun

¹fell *see* **fall 2**

²fell [fel] *v.t.* fällen ⟨Baum⟩

³fell *adj.* **in one ~ swoop** auf einen Schlag

fellow ['feləʊ] **1.** *n.* **a)** *(comrade)* Kamerad, *der;* **b)** *(Brit. Univ.)* Fellow, *der;* **c)** *(of academy or society)* Mitglied, *das;* **d)** *(coll.: man, boy)* Kerl, *der (ugs.).* **2.** *attrib. adj.* Mit-; ~ **man or human being** Mitmensch, *der*

¹felt [felt] *n.* Filz, *der*

²felt *see* **feel**

felt[-tipped] 'pen *n.* Filzstift, *der*

female ['fiːmeɪl] **1.** *adj.* weiblich; Frauen⟨*stimme, -chor, -verein*⟩. **2.** *n.* Frau, *die; (foetus, child)* Mädchen, *das; (animal)* Weibchen, *das*

feminine ['femɪnɪn] *adj.* weiblich; Frauen⟨*angelegenheit, -leiden*⟩; *(womanly)* feminin. **feminist** ['femɪnɪst] **1.** *adj.* feministisch; Feministen⟨*bewegung, -gruppe*⟩. **2.** *n.* Feministin, *die*/Feminist, *der*

fence [fens] **1.** *n.* Zaun, *der.* **2.** *v.i. (Sport)* fechten. **3.** *v.t.* ~ |**in**| einzäunen. '**fencer** *n.* Fechter, *der*/Fechterin, *die.* **fencing** ['fensɪŋ] *n. (Sport)* Fechten, *das*

fend [fend] *v.i.* ~ **for oneself** für sich selbst sorgen; *(in hostile surroundings)* sich allein durchschlagen. **fend 'off** *v.t.* abwehren

fender ['fendə(r)] *n.* **a)** *(for fire)* Kaminschutz, *der;* **b)** *(Amer.) (car bumper)* Stoßstange, *die; (car mudguard)* Kotflügel, *der*

ferment [fə'ment] **1.** *v.i.* gären. **2.** *v.t.* zur Gärung bringen. **fermentation** [fɜːmen'teɪʃn] *n.* Gärung, *die*

fern [fɜːn] *n.* Farnkraut, *das*

ferocious [fə'rəʊʃəs] *adj.* wild. **ferocity** [fə'rɒsɪtɪ] *n.* Wildheit, *die*

ferret ['ferɪt] *n.* Frettchen, *das*

ferry ['ferɪ] **1.** *n.* Fähre, *die; (service)* Fährverbindung, *die.* **2.** *v.t. (in boat)* ~ |**across** *or* **over**| übersetzen

fertile ['fɜːtaɪl] *adj. (fruitful)* fruchtbar; *(capable of developing)* befruchtet. **fertility** [fɜː'tɪlɪtɪ] *n.* Fruchtbarkeit, *die.* **fertilize** ['fɜːtɪlaɪz] *v.t.* befruchten. '**fertilizer** *n.* Dünger, *der*

fervent ['fɜːvənt] *adj.* leidenschaftlich; inbrünstig ⟨*Gebet, Wunsch, Hoffnung*⟩. **fervour** *(Brit.; Amer.:* **fervor**) ['fɜːvə(r)] *n.* Leidenschaftlichkeit, *die*

fester ['festə(r)] *v.i.* eitern

festival ['festɪvl] *n.* **a)** *(feast day)* Fest, *das;* **b)** *(of music etc.)* Festival, *das*

festive ['festɪv] *adj.* festlich; fröhlich; **the ~ season** die Weihnachtszeit.

festivity [fe'stɪvɪtɪ] *n.* **a)** *(gaiety)* Feststimmung, *die;* **b)** *(celebration)* Feier, *die;* **festivities** Feierlichkeiten *Pl.*

festoon [fe'stuːn] **1.** *n.* Girlande, *die.* **2.** *v.t.* schmücken (**with** mit)

fetch [fetʃ] *v.t.* **a)** holen; *(collect)* abholen (**from** von); ~ **sb. sth.,** ~ **sth. for sb.** jmdm. etw. holen; **b)** *(be sold for)* erzielen ⟨*Preis*⟩. '**fetching** *adj.* einnehmend

fête [feɪt] *n.* [Wohltätigkeits]basar, *der*

fetish ['fetɪʃ] *n.* Fetisch, *der.* **fetishism** ['fetɪʃɪzm] *n.* Fetischismus, *der.* **fetishist** ['fetɪʃɪst] *n.* Fetischist, *der*/Fetischistin, *die*

fetter ['fetə(r)] *v.t.* fesseln

feud [fjuːd] *n.* Fehde, *die*

feudal ['fjuːdl] *adj.* Feudal-; feudalistisch; ~ **system** Feudalsystem, *das*

fever ['fiːvə(r)] *n.* **a)** *(high temperature)* Fieber, *das;* **have a** |**high**| ~: [hohes] Fieber haben; **b)** *(disease)* Fieberkrankheit, *die.* '**feverish** *adj.* **a)** *(Med.)* fiebrig; **be ~:** Fieber haben; **b)** *(excited)* fiebrig

few [fjuː] **1.** *adj.* **a)** *(not many)* wenige; *abs.* nur wenige; **with very ~ exceptions** mit ganz wenigen Ausnahmen; **his ~ belongings** seine paar Habseligkeiten; **a ~ ...:** wenige ...; **b)** *(some)* wenige; **a ~ ...:** ein paar ...; **a ~ more ...:** noch ein paar ... **2.** *n.* **a)** *(not many)* wenige; **a ~:** wenige; **just a ~ of you/her friends** nur ein paar von euch/ihrer Freunde; **b)** *(some)* **with a ~ of our friends** mit einigen unserer Freunde; **quite a ~:** ziemlich viele

fiancé [fɪ'ɒseɪ] *n.* Verlobte, *der*

fiancée [fɪ'ɒseɪ] *n.* Verlobte, *die*

fiasco [fɪ'æskəʊ] *n., pl.* ~**s** Fiasko, *das*

fib [fɪb] **1.** *n.* Flunkerei, *die (ugs.);* **tell ~s** flunkern *(ugs.).* **2.** *v.i.,* -**bb-** flunkern *(ugs.)*

fibre *(Brit.; Amer.:* **fiber**) ['faɪbə(r)] *n.* **a)** Faser, *die;* **b)** *(material)* [Faser]gewebe, *das.* '**fibreglass** *n. (plastic)* glasfaserverstärkter Kunststoff

fiche [fiːʃ] *n., pl.* same *or* ~**s** Mikrofiche, *das od. der*

fickle ['fɪkl] *adj.* unberechenbar

fiction ['fɪkʃn] *n.* erzählende Literatur; **a ~/~s** eine Erfindung. **fictional** ['fɪkʃənl] *adj.* erfunden ⟨*Geschichte*⟩; fiktiv ⟨*Figur*⟩

fictitious [fɪk'tɪʃəs] *adj.* fingiert; falsch ⟨*Name, Identität*⟩

fiddle ['fɪdl] **1.** *n.* **a)** (*Mus.*) (*coll./derog.*) Fiedel, *die;* (*violin for traditional music*) Geige, *die;* |**as**| **fit as a ~:** kerngesund; **b)** (*sl.: swindle*) Gaunerei, *die.* **2.** *v. t.* (*sl.*) frisieren (*ugs.*) ⟨*Bücher, Rechnungen*⟩. **3.** *v. i.* herumspielen (**with** mit). **fiddler** ['fɪdlə(r)] *n.* Geiger, *der/*Geigerin, *die*

fiddly ['fɪdlɪ] *adj.* (*coll.*) knifflig

fidelity [fɪ'delɪtɪ] *n.* Treue, *die* (**to** zu)

fidget ['fɪdʒɪt] **1.** *v. i.* ~ |**about**| herumrutschen. **2.** *n.* (*person*) Zappelphilipp, *der* (*ugs.*). '**fidgety** *adj.* unruhig; zappelig ⟨*Kind*⟩

field [fiːld] *n.* **a)** Feld, *das;* **b)** (*for game*) Platz, *der;* [Spiel]feld, *das;* **c)** (*subject area*) [Fach]gebiet, *das;* **in the ~ of medicine** auf dem Gebiet der Medizin; **that is outside my ~:** das fällt nicht in mein Fach

field: ~**-day** *n.* **have a ~day** seinen großen Tag haben; ~ **events** *n. pl.* technische Disziplinen; ~**-glasses** *n. pl.* Feldstecher, *der;* **F~ 'Marshal** *n.* (*Brit. Mil.*) Feldmarschall, *der;* ~ **mouse** *n.* Brandmaus, *die*

fiend [fiːnd] *n.* **a)** (*wicked person*) Scheusal, *das;* **b)** (*evil spirit*) böser Geist. '**fiendish** *adj.* **a)** teuflisch; **b)** (*very awkward*) höllisch

fierce [fɪəs] *adj.* wild; erbittert ⟨*Widerstand, Kampf*⟩; scharf ⟨*Kritik*⟩. '**fiercely** *adv.* heftig ⟨*angreifen, Widerstand leisten*⟩; wütend ⟨*brüllen*⟩; aufs heftigste ⟨*kritisieren, bekämpfen*⟩

fiery ['faɪərɪ] *adj.* glühend; (*looking like fire*) feurig; (*blazing red*) feuerrot

fifteen [fɪf'tiːn] **1.** *adj.* fünfzehn. **2.** *n.* Fünfzehn, *die. See also* **eight**. **fifteenth** [fɪf'tiːnθ] **1.** *adj.* fünfzehnt... **2.** *n.* (*fraction*) Fünfzehntel, *das. See also* **eighth**

fifth [fɪfθ] **1.** *adj.* fünft... **2.** *n.* (*in sequence*) fünfte, *der/die/das;* (*in rank*) Fünfte, *der/die/das;* (*fraction*) Fünftel, *das. See also* **eighth**

fiftieth ['fɪftɪθ] *adj.* fünfzigst...

fifty ['fɪftɪ] **1.** *adj.* fünfzig. **2.** *n.* Fünfzig, *die. See also* **eight; eighty 2**

fig [fɪg] *n.* Feige, *die*

fig. *abbr.* **figure** Abb.

fight [faɪt] **1.** *v. i.,* **fought** [fɔːt] **a)** kämpfen; (*with fists*) sich schlagen; **b)** (*squabble*) [sich] streiten (**about** wegen). **2.** *v. t.,* **fought a)** ~ **sb./sth.** gegen jmdn./etw. kämpfen; (*using fists*) ~ **sb.** sich mit jmdm. schlagen; **b)** (*seek*

---

to overcome) bekämpfen; (*resis* sb./sth. gegen jmdn./etw. ankämpfen; **c)** ~ **a battle** einen Kampf austragen; **d)** kandidieren bei ⟨*Wahl*⟩. **3.** *v. t.* Kampf, *der* (**for** um). **fight against** *v. t.* kämpfen gegen; ankämpfen gegen ⟨*Wellen, Wind*⟩. **fight 'back 1.** *v. i.* zurückschlagen. **2.** *v. t.* (*suppress*) zurückhalten. **fight 'off** *v. t.* abwehren. '**fight with** *v. t.* **a)** kämpfen mit; **b)** (*squabble with*) [sich] streiten mit

'**fighter** *n.* Kämpfer, *der/*Kämpferin, *die;* (*aircraft*) Kampfflugzeug, *das*

'**fighting** *n.* Kämpfe

figment ['fɪgmənt] *n.* **a** ~ **of one's or the imagination** pure Einbildung

'**fig-tree** *n.* Feigenbaum, *der*

figurative ['fɪgərətɪv] *adj.* übertragen

figure ['fɪgə(r)] **1.** *n.* **a)** (*shape*) Form, *die;* **b)** (*carving, sculpture, one's bodily shape*) Figur, *die;* **c)** (*illustration*) Abbildung, *die;* **d)** (*person as seen*) Gestalt, *die;* (*literary*) Figur, *die;* **e)** (*numerical symbol*) Ziffer, *die;* (*number*) Zahl, *die;* (*amount of money*) Betrag, *der;* **f)** ~ **of speech** Redewendung, *die.* **2.** *v. i.* **a)** vorkommen; **b)** **that** ~**s** (*coll.*) das kann gut sein. **figure 'out** *v. t.* **a)** (*by arithmetic*) ausrechnen; **b)** (*understand*) verstehen

filament ['fɪləmənt] *n.* **a)** Faden, *der;* **b)** (*Electr.*) Glühfaden, *der*

filch ['fɪltʃ] *v. t.* stibitzen (*ugs.*)

¹**file** [faɪl] **1.** *n.* Feile, *die.* **2.** *v. t.* feilen ⟨*Fingernägel*⟩; mit der Feile bearbeiten ⟨*Holz, Eisen*⟩

²**file 1.** *n.* **a)** (*holder*) Ordner, *der;* (*box*) Kassette, *die;* **b)** (*papers*) Ablage, *die;* (*cards*) Kartei, *die.* **2.** *v. t.* **a)** [in die Kartei] einordnen/[in die Akten] aufnehmen; **b)** einreichen ⟨*Antrag*⟩

³**file 1.** *n.* (*Mil. etc.*) Reihe, *die;* |**in**| **single** *or* **Indian** ~: [im] Gänsemarsch. **2.** *v. i.* ~ |**in/out**| in einer Reihe [hinein-/hinaus]gehen

filigree ['fɪlɪgriː] *n.* Filigran, *das*

'**filing-cabinet** *n.* Aktenschrank, *der*

filings ['faɪlɪŋz] *n. pl.* Späne

fill [fɪl] **1.** *v. t.* **a)** füllen; besetzen ⟨*Sitzplätze*⟩; (*fig.*) ausfüllen ⟨*Gedanken, Zeit*⟩; (*pervade*) erfüllen; ~**ed with** voller ⟨*Reue, Bewunderung, Neid usw.*⟩; **b)** (*appoint sb. to*) besetzen ⟨*Posten*⟩. **2.** *v. i.* ~ |**with sth.**| sich [mit etw.] füllen. **3.** *n.* **eat/drink one's** ~: sich satt essen/trinken. **fill 'in** *v. t.* **a)** füllen; zuschütten ⟨*Erdloch*⟩; **b)** (*complete*) ausfüllen; **c)** ~ **sb. in** |**on sth.**| (*coll.*) jmdn. [über etw. (*Akk.*)] ins

Bild setzen. 2. *v. i.* ~ **in for** sb. für jmdn. einspringen. **fill 'out** *v. t.* ausfüllen. **fill 'up** *v. t.* a) füllen ‹with mit›; b) *(put petrol into)* tanken

fillet ['fɪlɪt] 1. *n.* Filet, *das.* 2. *v. t.* entgräten ‹Fisch›

'**filling** *n.* a) *(for teeth)* Füllung, *die;* b) *(for pancakes etc.)* Füllung, *die; (for sandwiches etc.)* Belag, *der; (for spreading)* Aufstrich, *der.* '**filling station** *n.* Tankstelle, *die*

filly ['fɪlɪ] *n.* junge Stute

film [fɪlm] 1. *n.* a) Film, *der;* b) *(thin layer)* Schicht, *die.* 2. *v. t.* filmen; drehen ‹Kinofilm, Szene›. '**film script** *n.* Drehbuch, *das.* '**film star** *n.* Filmstar, *der*

Filofax, (P) ['faɪləʊfæks] *n.* ≈ Terminplaner, *der*

filter ['fɪltə(r)] 1. *n.* Filter, *der.* 2. *v. t.* filtern. **filter 'through** *v. t.* durchsickern

'**filter-tip** *n.* a) Filter, *der;* b) ~ |ci-garette| Filterzigarette, *die*

filth [fɪlθ] *n.* Dreck, *der.* '**filthy** *adj.* schmutzig

fin [fɪn] *n.* Flosse, *die*

final ['faɪnl] 1. *adj.* letzt...; End‹spiel, -stadium, -stufe, -ergebnis›; endgültig ‹Entscheidung›. 2. *n.* a) *(Sport etc.)* Finale, *das;* b) ~s *pl. (university examination)* Examen, *das*

finale [fɪ'nɑːlɪ] *n.* Finale, *das*

finalist ['faɪnəlɪst] *n.* Teilnehmer/Teilnehmerin in der Endausscheidung; *(Sport)* Finalist, *der*/Finalistin, *die*

finalize ['faɪnəlaɪz] *v. t.* [endgültig] beschließen; *(complete)* zum Abschluß bringen

finally ['faɪnəlɪ] *adv.* a) *(in the end)* schließlich; b) *(expressing impatience etc.)* endlich; c) *(in conclusion)* abschließend; c) *(conclusively)* entschieden ‹sagen›

finance [faɪ'næns, 'faɪnæns] 1. *n.* a) *in pl. (resources)* Finanzen *Pl.;* b) *(management of money)* Geldwesen, *das;* c) *(support)* Geldmittel *Pl.* 2. *v. t.* finanzieren. **financial** [faɪ'nænʃl] *adj.* finanziell; Finanz‹mittel, -experte, -lage›; ~ **year** Geschäftsjahr, *das.* fi'**nancially** *adv.* finanziell. **financier** [faɪ'nænsɪə(r)] *n.* Finanzexperte, *der/-*expertin, *die*

finch [fɪntʃ] *n.* Fink[envogel], *der*

find [faɪnd] 1. *v. t.,* **found** [faʊnd] finden; *(come across unexpectedly)* entdecken; auftreiben ‹Geld, Gegenstand›; aufbringen ‹Kraft, Energie›;

want to ~: suchen; ~ **that** ...: herausfinden, daß ...; ~ sth. **necessary** etw. für nötig erachten; ~ sth./sb. **to be** ...: herausfinden, daß etw./jmd. ... ist/war; **you will** ~ |that| ...: Sie werden sehen, daß ... 2. *n.* Fund, *der.* **find 'out** *v. t.* herausfinden

'**finder** *n.* Finder, *der*/Finderin, *die*

'**findings** *n. pl.* Ergebnisse

¹**fine** [faɪn] 1. *n.* Geldstrafe, *die.* 2. *v. t.* mit einer Geldstrafe belegen

²**fine** *adj.* a) hochwertig ‹Qualität, Lebensmittel›; fein ‹Gewebe, Spitze›; edel ‹Holz, Wein›; b) *(delicate)* fein; zart ‹Porzellan›; *(thin)* hauchdünn; **cut** *or* **run it** ~: knapp kalkulieren; c) *(in small particles)* [hauch]fein ‹Sand, Staub›; ~ **rain** Nieselregen, *der;* d) *(sharp)* scharf ‹Spitze, Klinge›; spitz ‹Nadel, Schreibfeder›; e) *(excellent)* ausgezeichnet ‹Sänger, Schauspieler›; f) *(satisfactory)* schön; **that's** ~ **by** *or* **with me** ja, ist mir recht; g) *(in good health or state)* gut; **feel** ~: sich wohl fühlen; h) schön ‹Wetter›. **fine 'arts** *n. pl.* schöne Künste

finery ['faɪnərɪ] *n.* Pracht, *die; (garments etc.)* Staat, *der*

finger ['fɪŋgə(r)] 1. *n.* Finger, *der.* 2. *v. t.* berühren; *(meddle with)* befingern

finger: ~**mark** *n.* Fingerabdruck, *der;* ~**nail** *n.* Fingernagel, *der;* ~**print** *n.* Fingerabdruck, *der;* ~**tip** *n.* Fingerspitze, *die;* **have sth. at one's** ~**tips** *(fig.)* etw. im kleinen Finger haben *(ugs.)*

finish ['fɪnɪʃ] 1. *v. t.* a) beenden ‹Unterhaltung›; erledigen ‹Arbeit›; abschließen ‹Kurs, Ausbildung›; **have** ~**ed sth.** etw. fertig haben; ~ **writing/reading sth.** etw. zu Ende schreiben/lesen; b) aufessen ‹Mahlzeit›; auslesen ‹Buch, Zeitung›; austrinken ‹Flasche, Glas›. 2. *v. i.* a) aufhören; **have you** ~**ed?** sind Sie fertig?; **when does the concert** ~? wann ist das Konzert aus?; b) *(in race)* das Ziel erreichen. 3. *n.* a) Ende, *das;* b) *(~ing line)* Ziel, *das.* **finish 'off** *v. t.* abschließen

'**finishing post** *n.* Zielpfosten, *der*

finite ['faɪnaɪt] *adj.* begrenzt

Finland ['fɪnlənd] *pr. n.* Finnland *(das)*

Finn [fɪn] *n.* Finne, *der*/Finnin, *die*

Finnish ['fɪnɪʃ] 1. *adj.* finnisch. 2. *n.* Finnisch, *das; see also* **English 2 a**

fiord [fɪ'ɔːd] *n.* Fjord, *der*

fir [fɜː(r)] *n.* Tanne, *die*

fire ['faɪə(r)] 1. *n.* a) Feuer, *das;* **be on**

~: brennen; **catch** ~: Feuer fangen; ⟨*Wald, Gebäude:*⟩ in Brand geraten; **set** ~ **to** sth. etw. anzünden; b) *(in grate)* [offenes] Feuer; *(electric or gas* ~*)* Heizofen, *der;* **light the** ~: den Ofen anstecken; *(in grate)* das [Kamin]feuer anmachen; c) *(destructive burning)* Brand, *der;* d) *(of guns)* **come/be under** ~: unter Beschuß geraten/beschossen werden. 2. *v.t.* a) abschießen ⟨*Gewehr*⟩; abfeuern ⟨*Kanone*⟩; abgeben ⟨*Schuß*⟩; ~ **one's gun/ pistol/rifle at** sb. auf jmdn. schießen; **two shots were** ~**d** es fielen zwei Schüsse; ~ **questions at** sb. jmdn. mit Fragen bombardieren; b) *(coll.: dismiss)* feuern *(ugs.).* 3. *v.i.* feuern; ~ **at/on** schießen auf (+ *Akk.*); ~! Feuer!
fire: ~**-alarm** *n.* Feuermelder, *der;* ~**arm** *n.* Schußwaffe, *die;* ~ **brigade** *(Brit.),* ~ **department** *(Amer.)* ns. Feuerwehr, *die;* ~**-drill** *n.* Probe[feuer]alarm, *der;* ~**-engine** *n.* Löschfahrzeug, *das;* ~**-escape** *n. (staircase)* Feuertreppe, *die;* ~ **extinguisher** *n.* Feuerlöscher, *der;* ~ **hazard** *n.* Brandrisiko, *das;* ~**man** ['faɪəmən] *n., pl.* ~**men** [~mən] Feuerwehrmann, *der;* ~**-place** *n.* Kamin, *der;* ~**side** *n.* **at** *or* **by the** ~**side** am Kamin; ~ **station** *n.* Feuerwache, *die;* ~**wood** *n.* Brennholz, *das;* ~**work** *n.* Feuerwerkskörper, *der;* ~**works** *(display)* Feuerwerk, *das*
¹**firm** [fɜ:m] *n.* Firma, *die*
²**firm** *adj.* a) fest; stabil ⟨*Konstruktion, Stuhl*⟩; b) *(resolute, strict)* bestimmt.
firmly *adv.* a) fest; b) *(resolutely, strictly)* bestimmt
first [fɜ:st] 1. *adj.* erst...; **he was** ~ **to arrive** er kam als erster an. 2. *adv.* a) *(before anyone else)* zuerst; als erster/erste ⟨*sprechen, ankommen*⟩; *(before anything else)* an erster Stelle ⟨*stehen, kommen*⟩; ~ **come** ~ **served** wer zuerst kommt, mahlt zuerst *(Spr.);* b) *(beforehand)* vorher; c) *(for the* ~ *time)* zum ersten Mal; ~ **of all** zuerst; *(in importance)* vor allem. 3. *n.* a) **the** ~ *(in sequence)* der/die/das erste; *(in rank)* der/die/das Erste; b) **at** ~: zuerst; **from the** ~: von Anfang an
first: ~ **aid** *n.* erste Hilfe; ~**-aid box/ kit** Verbandkasten, *der/*Erste-Hilfe-Ausrüstung, *die;* ~**-class** 1. ['-'] *adj.* a) erster Klasse *nachgestellt;* Erste[r]-Klasse-⟨*Fahrkarte, Abteil, Post, Brief usw.*⟩; b) *(excellent)* erstklassig; 2. [-'-] *adv.* erster Klasse ⟨*reisen*⟩

firstly *adv.* zunächst [einmal]; *(followed by 'secondly')* erstens
first: ~ **name** *n.* Vorname, *der;* ~**-rate** *adj.* erstklassig; ~ **school** *n. (Brit.)* ≈ Grundschule, *die*
fir tree *n.* Tanne, *die*
fish [fɪʃ] 1. *n.* Fisch, *der.* 2. *v.i.* fischen; *(with rod)* angeln; **go** ~**ing** fischen/angeln gehen. **fish 'out** *v.t. (coll.)* herausfischen *(ugs.).*
fisherman ['fɪʃəmən] *n., pl.* **fishermen** ['fɪʃəmən] Fischer, *der; (angler)* Angler, *der*
fish: ~ **'finger** *n.* Fischstäbchen, *das;* ~**-hook** *n.* Angelhaken, *der*
fishing *n.* Fischen, *das; (with rod)* Angeln, *das*
fishing: ~ **boat** *n.* Fischerboot, *das;* ~**-net** *n.* Fischernetz, *das;* ~**-rod** *n.* Angelrute, *die*
fish: ~**monger** ['fɪʃmʌŋgə(r)] *n. (Brit.)* Fischhändler, *der/*-händlerin, *die;* ~ **shop** *n.* Fischgeschäft, *das*
fishy *adj.* a) fischartig; Fisch⟨*geschmack, -geruch*⟩; b) *(coll.: suspicious)* verdächtig
fist [fɪst] *n.* Faust, *die*
¹**fit** [fɪt] *n.* Anfall, *der; (fig.)* [plötzliche] Anwandlung; **be in** ~**s of** laughter sich vor Lachen biegen; **in a** ~ **of ...**: in einem Anfall von ...
²**fit** 1. *adj.* a) *(suitable)* geeignet; ~ **to eat** eßbar; b) *(worthy)* würdig; wert; c) *(proper)* richtig; **see** *or* **think** ~ [**to do** sth.] es für richtig halten[, etw. zu tun]; d) *(healthy)* fit *(ugs.);* **keep** ~: sich fit halten. 2. *n.* Paßform, *die;* **it is a good/ bad** ~: es sitzt *od.* paßt gut/nicht gut. 3. *v.t.* **-tt-:** a) ⟨*Kleider:*⟩ passen (+ *Dat.*); ⟨*Deckel, Bezug:*⟩ passen (+ *Akk.*); b) *(put into place)* anbringen (**to** an + *Dat. od. Akk.*); einbauen ⟨*Motor, Ersatzteil*⟩. 4. *v.i.,* **-tt-** passen.
fit 'in 1. *v.t.* unterbringen. 2. *v.i.* a) ⟨*Person:*⟩ sich anpassen (**with** an + *Akk.*); b) *(be in accordance with)* ~ **in with** sth. mit etw. übereinstimmen
fitful ['fɪtfl] *adj.* unbeständig; unruhig ⟨*Schlaf*⟩; launisch ⟨*Brise*⟩
fitment *n.* Einrichtung, *die*
fitness *n.* a) *(physical)* Fitneß, *die;* b) *(suitability)* Eignung, *die*
fitted *adj.* a) *(suited)* geeignet (**for** für, zu); b) *(shaped)* tailliert ⟨*Kleider*⟩; Einbau⟨*küche, schrank*⟩; ~ **carpet** Teppichboden, *der*
fitter *n.* Monteur, *der; (of pipes)* Installateur, *der; (of machines)* Maschinenschlosser, *der*

'fitting 1. *adj. (appropriate)* passend; *(becoming)* schicklich *(geh.)* ⟨*Benehmen*⟩. **2.** *n.* **a)** *usu. in pl. (fixture)* Anschluß, *der;* ~s *(furniture)* Ausstattung, *die;* **b)** *(Brit.: size)* Größe, *die*

five [faɪv] **1.** *adj.* fünf. **2.** *n.* Fünf, *die. See also* **eight. fiver** ['faɪvə(r)] *n. (Brit. coll.)* Fünfpfundschein, *der*

fix [fɪks] **1.** *v. t.* **a)** befestigen; **b)** festsetzen ⟨*Termin, Preis, Grenze*⟩; *(agree on)* ausmachen; **c)** *(repair)* reparieren; **d)** *(arrange)* arrangieren. **2.** *n. (coll.: predicament)* Klemme, *die (ugs.);* **be in a** ~**:** in der Klemme sitzen. **fix 'up** *v. t.* **a)** *(arrange)* arrangieren; festsetzen ⟨*Termin, Treffpunkt*⟩; **b)** *(provide)* versorgen; ~ **sb. up with sth.** jmdm. etw. verschaffen. **fixture** ['fɪkstʃə(r)] *n.* **a)** *(furnishing)* eingebautes Teil; **b)** *(Sport)* Veranstaltung, *die*

fizz [fɪz] *v. i.* (zischend) sprudeln

fizzle ['fɪzl] *v. i.* zischen. **fizzle 'out** *v. i.* ⟨*Kampagne:*⟩ im Sande verlaufen

fizzy ['fɪzɪ] *adj.* sprudelnd; ~ **lemonade** Brause[limonade], *die*

flabbergast ['flæbəgɑːst] *v. t.* umhauen *(ugs.)*

flabby ['flæbɪ] *adj.* schlaff

¹flag [flæg] *n.* Fahne, *die; (national* ~*, on ship)* Flagge, *die*

²flag *v. i.,* **-gg-** ⟨*Person:*⟩ abbauen; ⟨*Kraft, Begeisterung usw.:*⟩ nachlassen

flagon ['flægn] *n.* Kanne, *die*

'flag-pole *n.* Flaggenmast, *der*

flagrant ['fleɪgrənt] *adj.* eklatant; flagrant ⟨*Verstoß*⟩

'flagstone *n.* Steinplatte, *die*

flair [fleə(r)] *n.* Gespür, *das; (special ability)* Talent, *das*

flake [fleɪk] **1.** *n.* Flocke, *die; (of dry skin)* Schuppe, *die.* **2.** *v. i.* abblättern. **flaky** ['fleɪkɪ] *adj.* blättrig ⟨*Kruste*⟩; ~ **pastry** Blätterteig, *der*

flamboyant [flæm'bɔɪənt] *adj.* extravagant

flame [fleɪm] *n.* Flamme, *die;* **be in** ~**s** in Flammen stehen

flan [flæn] *n.* |**fruit|** ~**:** [Obst]torte, *die*

flank [flæŋk] *n.* Seite, *die; (of animal; also Mil.)* Flanke, *die*

flannel ['flænl] *n.* **a)** *(fabric)* Flanell, *der;* **b)** *(Brit.: for washing)* Waschlappen, *der*

flap [flæp] **1.** *v. t.,* **-pp-:** ~ **its wings** mit den Flügeln schlagen. **2.** *v. i.,* **-pp-** ⟨*Flügel:*⟩ schlagen; ⟨*Segel, Fahne, Vorhang:*⟩ flattern. **3.** *n.* **a)** Klappe, *die; (envelope-seal, of shoe)* Lasche, *die;* **b)** *(fig. coll.)* **in a** ~**:** furchtbar aufgeregt

flare [fleə(r)] **1.** *v. i.* flackern; *(fig.)* ausbrechen; **tempers ~d** die Gemüter erhitzten sich. **2.** *n.* Leuchtsignal, *das.* **flare 'up** *v. i.* **a)** aufflackern; **b)** *(break out)* [wieder] ausbrechen

flash [flæʃ] **1.** *n.* Aufleuchten, *das; (as signal)* Lichtsignal, *das;* ~ **of lightning** Blitz, *der;* **in a** ~**:** *(quickly)* im Nu. **2.** *v. t.* **a)** aufleuchten lassen; ~ **one's headlights** die Lichthupe betätigen; ~ **sb. a smile/glance** jmdm. ein Lächeln/ einen Blick zuwerfen; **b)** *(display briefly)* kurz zeigen. **3.** *v. i.* aufleuchten; ~ **by** *or* **past** ⟨*Zeit, Ferien:*⟩ wie im Fluge vergehen

flash: ~**back** *n.* Rückblende, *die* **(to auf** + *Akk.*)**;** ~**bulb** *n.* Blitzbirnchen, *das;* ~**cube** *n.* Blitzwürfel, *der;* ~**gun** *n.* Blitzgerät, *das;* ~**light** *n.* **a)** *(for signals)* Blinklicht, *das;* **b)** *(Amer.: torch)* Taschenlampe, *die*

'flashy *adj.* auffällig

flask [flɑːsk] *n.* **a)** *see* **Thermos; b)** *(for wine, oil)* [bauchige] Flasche; **c)** *(Chem.)* Kolben, *der*

¹flat [flæt] *n. (Brit.)* Wohnung, *die*

²flat 1. *adj.* **a)** flach; eben ⟨*Fläche*⟩; platt ⟨*Nase, Reifen*⟩; **b)** *(downright)* glatt *(ugs.)* ⟨*Absage, Weigerung, Widerspruch*⟩; **c)** *(Mus.)* [um einen Halbton] erniedrigt ⟨*Note*⟩; **d)** schal, abgestanden ⟨*Bier, Sekt*⟩; **e)** leer ⟨*Batterie*⟩. **2.** *adv. (Mus.)* zu tief

flat: ~ **'feet** *n. pl.* Plattfüße; ~**'fish** *n.* Plattfisch, *der;* ~**'footed** *adj.* plattfüßig

'flatly *adv.* rundweg

flatten ['flætn] **1.** *v. t.* flach drücken ⟨*Schachtel*⟩; dem Erdboden gleichmachen ⟨*Stadt, Gebäude*⟩. **2.** *v. refl.* ~ **oneself against sth.** sich flach gegen etw. drücken

flatter ['flætə(r)] *v. t.* schmeicheln (+ *Dat.*). **'flattering** *adj.* schmeichelhaft. **'flattery** *n.* Schmeichelei, *die*

flat 'tyre *n.* Reifenpanne, *die*

flaunt [flɔːnt] *v. t.* zur Schau stellen

flavor *etc. (Amer.) see* **flavour** *etc.*

flavour ['fleɪvə(r)] *(Brit.)* **1.** *n.* **a)** Geschmack, *der;* **b)** *(fig.)* Anflug, *der.* **2.** *v. t.* abschmecken. **'flavouring** *n. (Brit.)* Aroma, *das*

flaw [flɔː] *n.* Fehler, *der; (imperfection)* Makel, *der; (in workmanship or goods)* Mangel, *der*

flax [flæks] *n.* Flachs, *der*

flea [fliː] *n.* Floh, *der.* **flea market** *n. (coll.)* Flohmarkt, *der*

fled *see* **flee**

flee [fliː] **1.** *v.i.*, **fled** [fled] fliehen; ~ **from sth./sb.** aus etw./vor jmdm. flüchten. **2.** *v.t.*, **fled** fliehen aus

fleece [fliːs] **1.** *n.* [Schaf]fell, *das.* **2.** *v.t. (fig.)* ausplündern. **fleecy** ['fliːsɪ] *adj.* flauschig

fleet [fliːt] *n.* Flotte, *die*

fleeting ['fliːtɪŋ] *adj.* flüchtig

flesh [fleʃ] *n.* Fleisch, *das; (of fruit, plant)* [Frucht]fleisch, *das.* **fleshy** *adj.* fett; fleischig ⟨*Hände*⟩

flew see ²**fly** 1, 2

¹**flex** [fleks] *n.* (*Brit. Electr.*) Kabel, *das*

²**flex** *v.t.* beugen ⟨*Arm, Knie*⟩; ~ **one's muscles** seine Muskeln spielen lassen

flexible ['fleksɪbl] *adj.* **a)** biegsam; elastisch; **b)** *(fig.)* flexibel

flick [flɪk] *v.t.* schnippen; anknipsen ⟨*Schalter*⟩; verspritzen ⟨*Tinte*⟩. **flick through** *v.t.* durchblättern

flicker ['flɪkə(r)] **1.** *v.i.* flackern; ⟨*Fernsehapparat:*⟩ flimmern. **2.** *n.* Flackern, *das; (of TV)* Flimmern, *das*

¹**flight** [flaɪt] *n.* **a)** Flug, *der;* **b)** ~ |of stairs *or* steps| Treppe, *die*

²**flight** *n. (fleeing)* Flucht, *die;* **take** ~: die Flucht ergreifen; **put to** ~: in die Flucht schlagen

flight attendant *n.* Flugbegleiter, *der/*-begleiterin, *die*

flimsy ['flɪmzɪ] *adj.* **a)** dünn; nicht sehr haltbar ⟨*Verpackung*⟩; **b)** *(fig.)* fadenscheinig ⟨*Entschuldigung, Argument*⟩

flinch [flɪntʃ] *v.i.* zurückschrecken (**from** vor + *Dat.*); *(wince)* zusammenzucken

fling [flɪŋ] **1.** *n.* **have a** *or* **one's** ~: sich ausleben. **2.** *v.t.*, **flung** [flʌŋ] werfen; ~ **oneself into sth.** *(fig.)* sich in etw. *(Akk.)* stürzen

flint [flɪnt] *n.* Feuerstein, *der*

flip [flɪp] *v.t.*, **-pp-** schnipsen; ~ |over| *(turn over)* umdrehen. **'flip through** *v.t.* durchblättern

flippant ['flɪpənt] *adj.* leichtfertig

flipper ['flɪpə(r)] *n.* Flosse, *die*

flirt [flɜːt] *v.i.* flirten. **flirtation** [flɜːˈteɪʃn] *n.* Flirt, *der*

flit [flɪt] *v.i.* huschen

float [fləʊt] **1.** *v.i.* treiben; *(in air)* schweben. **2.** *n. (for carnival)* Festwagen, *der.* **3.** *v.t. (set afloat)* flott machen; *(fig.)* lancieren ⟨*Plan, Idee*⟩. **floating 'voter** *n.* Wechselwähler, *der/*-wählerin, *die*

flock [flɒk] **1.** *n.* **a)** Herde, *die; (of birds)* Schwarm, *der;* **b)** *(of people)* Schar, *die.* **2.** *v.i.* strömen; ~ **round sb.** sich um jmdn. scharen

flog [flɒg] *v.t.*, **-gg-:** **a)** auspeitschen; **b)** *(Brit. sl.: sell)* verscheuern *(salopp)*

flood [flʌd] **1.** *n.* Überschwemmung, *die;* **the F~** *(Bibl.)* die Sintflut. **2.** *v.i.* ⟨*Fluß:*⟩ über die Ufer treten; *(fig.)* strömen. **3.** *v.t.* überschwemmen. **'floodlight 1.** *n.* Scheinwerfer, *der.* **2.** *v.t.*, **floodlit** ['flʌdlɪt] anstrahlen

floor [flɔː(r)] **1.** *n.* **a)** Boden, *der;* **b)** *(storey)* Stockwerk, *das;* **first** ~ (*Amer.*) Erdgeschoß, *das;* **first** ~ (*Brit.*), **second** ~ (*Amer.*) erster Stock; **ground** ~: Erdgeschoß, *das;* Parterre, *das.* **2.** *v.t.* **a)** *(confound)* überfordern; **b)** *(knock down)* zu Boden schlagen

floor: ~**board** *n.* Dielenbrett, *das;* ~**-cloth** *n.* (*Brit.*) Scheuertuch, *das;* ~**-polish** *n.* Bohnerwachs, *das;* ~ **show** *n.* ≈ Unterhaltungsprogramm, *das*

flop [flɒp] **1.** *v.i.*, **-pp-:** **a)** plumpsen; **b)** *(coll.: fail)* fehlschlagen; ⟨*Theaterstück, Show:*⟩ durchfallen. **2.** *n. (coll.: failure)* Reinfall, *der (ugs.)*

floppy ['flɒpɪ] *adj.* weich und biegsam

flora ['flɔːrə] *n.* Flora, *die*

floral ['flɔːrl, 'flɒrl] *adj.* geblümt ⟨*Kleid, Stoff*⟩; Blumen⟨*muster*⟩

Florence ['florəns] *pr. n.* Florenz *(das)*

florid ['florɪd] *adj.* blumig ⟨*Stil, Redeweise*⟩; gerötet ⟨*Teint*⟩

florist ['florɪst] *n.* Florist, *der/*Floristin, *die*

flotsam ['flotsəm] *n.* ~ |and jetsam| Treibgut, *das*

flounder ['flaʊndə(r)] *v.i.* taumeln

flour ['flaʊə(r)] *n.* Mehl, *das*

flourish ['flʌrɪʃ] **1.** *v.i.* gedeihen; ⟨*Geschäft:*⟩ florieren, gutgehen. **2.** *v.t.* schwingen. **3.** *v.* **do sth. with a** ~: etw. schwungvoll tun

flout [flaʊt] *v.t.* mißachten

flow [fləʊ] **1.** *v.i.* fließen; ⟨*Körner, Sand:*⟩ rinnen, rieseln; ⟨*Gas:*⟩ strömen. **2.** *n.* **a)** Fließen, *das;* ~ **of water/people** Wasser-/Menschenstrom, *der;* ~ **of information** Informationsfluß, *der;* **b)** *(of tide, river)* Flut, *die*

flower ['flaʊə(r)] **1.** *n. (blossom)* Blüte, *die; (plant)* Blume, *die;* **come into** ~: zu blühen beginnen. **2.** *v.i.* blühen. **'flower-bed** *n.* Blumenbeet, *das.* **'flower-pot** *n.* Blumentopf, *der.* **'flowery** *adj.* geblümt ⟨*Stoff, Muster*⟩; *(fig.)* blumig ⟨*Sprache*⟩

flowing *adj.* fließend; wallend ⟨*Haar*⟩

flown see ²**fly** 1, 2

flu [fluː] *n. (coll.)* Grippe, *die*

fluctuate ['flʌktjʊeɪt] v.i. schwanken. **fluctuation** [flʌktjʊ'eɪʃn] n. Schwankung, die

fluency ['fluːənsɪ] n. Gewandtheit, die; (spoken) Redegewandtheit, die

fluent ['fluːənt] adj. gewandt ⟨Stil, Redeweise, Redner, Schreiber⟩; **be ~ in Russian, speak ~ Russian** fließend Russisch sprechen

fluff [flʌf] n. Flusen; Fusseln

fluffy ['flʌfɪ] adj. [flaum]weich ⟨Kissen, Küken⟩; flauschig ⟨Spielzeug, Decke⟩

fluid ['fluːɪd] 1. n. Flüssigkeit, die. 2. adj. flüssig

fluke [fluːk] n. (piece of luck) Glücksfall, der

flung see **fling 2**

fluorescent [fluə'resənt] adj. fluoreszierend. **fluorescent 'light** n. Leuchtstofflampe, die

fluoride ['fluːəraɪd] n. Fluorid, das; **fluoride toothpaste** fluorhaltige Zahnpasta

flurry ['flʌrɪ] n. **a)** Aufregung, die; **b)** (of rain/snow) [Regen-/Schnee]schauer, der

¹flush [flʌʃ] 1. v.i. rot werden. 2. v.t. ausspülen ⟨Becken⟩; **~ the toilet or lavatory** spülen. 3. n. Rotwerden, das

²flush adj. (level) bündig; **be ~ with sth.** mit etw. bündig abschließen

fluster ['flʌstə(r)] v.t. aus der Fassung bringen. **flustered** ['flʌstəd] adj. nervös

flute [fluːt] n. Flöte, die

flutter ['flʌtə(r)] 1. v.i. flattern. 2. v.t. flattern mit ⟨Flügel⟩

flux [flʌks] n. **in a state of ~:** im Fluß

¹fly [flaɪ] n. Fliege, die

²fly 1. v.i., flew [fluː], flown [fləʊn] **a)** fliegen; **~ away or off** wegfliegen; **b)** (fig.) **~** [by or past] wie im Fluge vergehen; **c)** ⟨Fahne⟩ gehißt sein. 2. v.t., flew, flown fliegen ⟨Flugzeug, Fracht, Einsatz usw.⟩; fliegen über (+ Akk.) ⟨Strecke⟩. 3. n. in sing. or pl. (on trousers) Hosenschlitz, der. **fly 'in** v.i. [mit dem Flugzeug] eintreffen (from aus). **fly 'out** v.i. abfliegen (of von)

flying ['flaɪɪŋ]: **~ 'saucer** n. fliegende Untertasse, die; **~ 'start** n. (Sport) fliegender Start; **~ 'visit** n. Stippvisite, die (ugs.)

fly: **~leaf** n. Vorsatzblatt, das; **~over** n. (Brit.) [Straßen]überführung, die

foal [fəʊl] n. Fohlen, das

foam [fəʊm] 1. n. Schaum, der. 2. v.i. schäumen. **foam 'rubber** n. Schaumgummi, der

fob [fob] v.t., **-bb-: ~ sb. off with sth.** jmdn. mit etw. abspeisen (ugs.)

focus ['fəʊkəs] 1. n., pl. **-es** or **foci** ['fəʊsaɪ] Brennpunkt, der; **out of/in ~:** unscharf/scharf eingestellt; unscharf/scharf ⟨Foto, Film usw.⟩; (fig.) **be the ~ of attention** im Brennpunkt des Interesses stehen. 2. v.t., **-s-** or **-ss-** einstellen (on auf + Akk.); bündeln ⟨Licht, Strahlen⟩. 3. v.i., **-s-** or **-ss-** (fig.) sich konzentrieren (on auf + Akk.)

fodder ['fodə(r)] n. [Vieh]futter, das

foe [fəʊ] n. (poet./rhet.) Feind, der

foetus ['fiːtəs] n. Fötus, der

fog [fog] n. Nebel, der. **'fog-light** n. (Motor Veh.) Nebelscheinwerfer, der

foggy ['fogɪ] adj. neblig

fogy ['fəʊgɪ] n. **[old] ~:** [alter] Opa (salopp)/[alte] Oma (salopp)

foible ['fɔɪbl] n. Eigenheit, die

¹foil [fɔɪl] n. Folie, die

²foil v.t. vereiteln

foist [fɔɪst] v.t. **~** [off] on to sb. jmdn. andrehen (ugs.); auf jmdn. abwälzen ⟨Probleme, Verantwortung⟩

fold [fəʊld] 1. v.t. [zusammen]falten; **~ one's arms** die Arme verschränken. 2. v.i. **a)** (become ~ed) sich zusammenfalten; **b)** (be able to be ~ed) sich falten lassen. 3. n. Falte, die; (line made by ~ing) Kniff, der. **fold 'up** v.t. zusammenfalten ⟨Laken⟩; zusammenklappen ⟨Stuhl⟩

'folder n. Mappe, die

foliage ['fəʊlɪɪdʒ] n. Blätter Pl.; (of tree also) Laub, das

folk [fəʊk] n. **a)** Volk, das; **b)** in pl. **~[s]** (people) Leute Pl.

folk: **~-dance** n. Volkstanz, der; **~lore** [~lɔː(r)] n. Folklore, die; **~-music** n. Volksmusik, die; **~-song** Volkslied, das; (modern) Folksong, der

follow ['foləʊ] 1. v.t. **a)** folgen (+ Dat.); **b)** entlanggehen/-fahren ⟨Straße usw.⟩; **c)** (come after) folgen auf (+ Akk.); **d)** (result from) die Folge sein von; **e)** (treat or take as guide) sich orientieren an (+ Akk.); **f)** folgen (+ Dat.) ⟨Prinzip, Instinkt, Trend⟩; verfolgen ⟨Politik⟩; befolgen ⟨Regel, Vorschrift, Rat, Warnung⟩; sich halten an (+ Akk.) ⟨Konventionen, Diät⟩; **g)** (grasp meaning of) folgen (+ Dat.); **do you ~ me?** verstehst du, was ich meine? 2. v.i. **a)** (go, come) **~ after sb./sth.** jmdm./einer Sache folgen; **b)** (come next in order or time) folgen; **as ~s** wie folgt; **c)** **~ from sth.**

(result) die Folge von etw. sein; *(be deducible)* aus etw. folgen. **follow 'on** *v. i. (continue)* ~ **on from** sth. die Fortsetzung von etw. sein. **follow 'up** *v. t.* a) ausbauen ⟨*Erfolg, Sieg*⟩; b) nachgehen (+ *Dat.*) ⟨*Hinweis*⟩

'**follower** *n.* Anhänger, *der*/Anhängerin, *die*

'**following** 1. *adj.* folgend; **the** ~: folgendes. 2. *prep.* nach. 3. *n.* Anhängerschaft, *die*

folly ['fɒlɪ] *n.* Torheit, *die (geh.)*

fond [fɒnd] *adj.* liebevoll; lieb ⟨*Erinnerung*⟩; **be** ~ **of** sb. jmdn. mögen; **be** ~ **of doing** sth. etw. gern tun

fondle ['fɒndl] *v. t.* streicheln

'**fondness** *n.* Liebe, *die;* ~ **for** sth. Vorliebe für etw.

font [fɒnt] *n.* Taufstein, *der*

food [fu:d] *n.* a) Nahrung, *die; (for animals)* Futter, *das;* b) *(as commodity)* Lebensmittel *Pl.;* c) *(in solid form)* Essen, *das;* d) *(particular kind)* Nahrungsmittel, *das;* Kost, *die.* '**food poisoning** *n.* Lebensmittelvergiftung, *die.* '**food processor** *n.* Küchenmaschine, *die*

fool [fu:l] 1. *n.* Dummkopf, *der (ugs.).* 2. *v. t.* ~ sb. **into doing** sth. jmdn. [durch Tricks] dazu bringen, etw. zu tun. **fool a'bout,** ~ **a'round** *v. i.* Unsinn machen

foolhardy ['fu:lhɑ:dɪ] *adj.* tollkühn

'**foolish** *adj.* töricht; verrückt *(ugs.)* ⟨*Idee, Vorschlag*⟩

'**foolproof** *adj. (infallible)* absolut sicher

foot [fʊt] 1. *n., pl.* **feet** [fi:t] a) Fuß, *der;* **on** ~: zu Fuß; **put one's** ~ **in it** *(fig. coll.)* ins Fettnäpfchen treten *(ugs.);* b) *(far end)* unteres Ende; *(of bed)* Fußende, *das;* c) *(measure)* Fuß, *der (30,48 cm).* 2. *v. t.* ~ **the bill** die Rechnung bezahlen

football ['fʊtbɔ:l] *n. (game, ball)* Fußball, *der.* '**football boot** *n.* Fußballschuh, *der.* '**footballer** *n.* Fußballspieler, *der*/-spielerin, *die.* '**football pools** *n. pl.* **the** ~: das Fußballtoto

foot: ~-**brake** *n.* Fußbremse, *die;* ~-**bridge** *n.* Fußgängerbrücke, *die;* ~**hold** *n.* Halt, *der*

'**footing** *n.* a) *(fig.)* **be on an equal** ~ [**with** sb.] [jmdm.] gleichgestellt sein; b) *(foothold)* Halt, *der*

foot: ~**note** *n.* Fußnote, *die;* ~**path** *n.* Fußweg, *der;* ~**print** *n.* Fußabdruck, *der;* ~**step** *n.* Schritt, *der;* **follow in** sb.'s ~**steps** *(fig.)* in jmds. Fuß-

stapfen *(Akk.)* treten; ~**wear** *n.* Schuhe *Pl.*

for [fə(r), *stressed* fɔ:(r)] 1. *prep.* a) für; **what is it** ~? wofür ist das?; **reason** ~ **living** Grund zu leben; **a request** ~ **help** eine Bitte um Hilfe; **study** ~ **a university degree** auf einen Hochschulabschluß hin studieren; **take** sb. ~ **a walk** mit jmdm. einen Spaziergang machen; **be** '~ **doing** sth. *(in favour)* dafür sein, etw. zu tun; **cheque/bill** ~ **£5** Scheck/Rechnung über 5 Pfund; b) *(on account of, as penalty of)* wegen; **were it not** ~ **you/ your help** ohne dich/deine Hilfe; ~ **fear of** aus Angst vor (+ *Dat.*); c) *(in spite of)* ~ **all** ...: trotz ...; ~ **all that,** ...: trotzdem ...; d) ~ **all I know/care** ...: möglicherweise/ was mich betrifft, ...; ~ **one thing,** ...: zunächst einmal ...; e) *(during)* **stay** ~ **a week** eine Woche bleiben; **we've/we haven't been here** ~ **three years** wir sind seit drei Jahren hier/nicht mehr hier gewesen; f) **walk** ~ **20 miles** 20 Meilen gehen. 2. *conj.* denn

forage ['fɒrɪdʒ] 1. *n.* Futter, *das.* 2. *v. i.* ~ **for** sth. auf der Suche nach etw. sein

forbad, forbade *see* forbid

forbid [fə'bɪd] *v. t.,* -**dd**-, **forbad** [fə'bæd] *or* **forbade** [fə'bæd, fə'beɪd], **forbidden** [fə'bɪdn] ~ sb. **to do** sth. jmdm. verbieten, etw. zu tun; ~ [sb.] sth. [jmdm.] etw. verbieten; **it is** ~**den** [**to do** sth.] es ist verboten[, etw. zu tun]. **forbidden** *see* forbid. **for'bidding** *adj.* furchteinflößend

force [fɔ:s] 1. *n.* a) *(strength, power)* Stärke, *die; (of explosion, storm)* Wucht, *die; (Phys.: physical strength)* Kraft, *die;* **in** ~: mit einem großen Aufgebot; b) *(validity)* Kraft, *die;* **in** ~: in Kraft; **come into** ~ ⟨*Gesetz usw.:*⟩ in Kraft treten; c) *(violence)* Gewalt, *die;* **by** ~: gewaltsam; d) *(group) (of workers)* Kolonne, *die;* Trupp, *der; (of police)* Einheit, *die; (Mil.)* Armee, *die;* **the** ~**s** die Armee; **be in the** ~**s** beim Militär sein. 2. *v. t.* a) zwingen; ~ sb. [**up]on** sb. jmdm. etw. aufzwingen; b) ~ [**open**] aufbrechen; ~ **one's way in** sich *(Dat.)* mit Gewalt Zutritt verschaffen. **forced** [fɔ:st] *adj.* a) *(contrived, unnatural)* gezwungen; b) *(compelled by force)* erzwungen; Zwangs⟨*arbeit*⟩. **forced 'landing** *n.* Notlandung, *die.* '**force-feed** *v. t.* zwangsernähren. **forceful** ['fɔ:sfl] *adj.* stark ⟨*Persönlichkeit, Charakter*⟩;

energisch ⟨Person, Art⟩; eindrucksvoll ⟨Sprache⟩

forceps ['fɔːseps] n., pl. same [**pair of**] ~: Zange, die

forcible ['fɔːsɪbl] adj., **forcibly** ['fɔːsɪblɪ] adv. gewaltsam

ford [fɔːd] 1. n. Furt, die. 2. v. t. durchqueren; (wade through) durchwaten

fore [fɔː(r)] 1. adj., esp. in comb. vorder...; Vorder⟨teil, -front usw.⟩. 2. n. to the ~: im Vordergrund

'forearm n. Unterarm, der

foreboding [fɔː'bəʊdɪŋ] n. Vorahnung, die

'forecast 1. v. t., forecast or forecasted vorhersagen. 2. n. Voraussage, die

'forecourt n. Vorhof, der

'forefather n., usu. in pl. Vorfahr, der

'forefinger n. Zeigefinger, der

'forefront n. [be] **in the ~ of** in vorderster Linie (+ Gen.) [stehen]

'foregone adj. **be a ~ conclusion** von vornherein feststehen; (be certain) so gut wie sicher sein

'foreground n. Vordergrund, der

'forehead ['fɒrɪd, 'fɔːhed] n. Stirn, die

foreign ['fɒrɪn] adj. a) (from abroad) ausländisch; Fremd⟨kapital, -sprache⟩; **he is ~:** er ist Ausländer; b) (abroad) fremd; ~ **country** Ausland, das; Außen⟨politik, -handel⟩; c) (from outside) fremd; ~ **body or substance** Fremdkörper, der. **'foreigner** n. Ausländer, der/Ausländerin, die

foreign: ~ **ex'change** n. Devisen Pl.; **F~ Office** n. (Brit. Hist./coll.) Außenministerium, das; **F~ 'Secretary** n. (Brit.) Außenminister, der

foreman ['fɔːmən] n., pl. **foremen** ['fɔːmən] Vorarbeiter, der

foremost ['fɔːməʊst, 'fɔːməst] 1. adj. a) vorderst...; b) (fig.) führend. 2. adv. **first and ~:** zunächst einmal

'forename n. Vorname, der

'forerunner n. Vorläufer, der/Vorläuferin, die

foresaw see foresee

foresee [fɔː'siː] v. t., forms as see voraussehen. **foreseeable** [fɔː'siːəbl] adj. vorhersehbar; **in the ~ future** in nächster Zukunft

foreseen see foresee

'foresight n. Weitblick, der

foreskin n. (Anat.) Vorhaut, die

forest ['fɒrɪst] n. Wald, der; (commercially exploited) Forst, der

fore'stall v. t. zuvorkommen (+ Dat.)

forestry ['fɒrɪstrɪ] n. Forstwirtschaft, die

'foretaste n. Vorgeschmack, der

fore'tell v. t., **fore'told** voraussagen

forever [fə'revə(r)] adv. (constantly) ständig

fore'warn v. t. vorwarnen

'foreword n. Vorwort, das

forfeit ['fɔːfɪt] 1. v. t. verlieren; verwirken (geh.) ⟨Recht, jmds. Gunst⟩. 2. n. Strafe, die; (games) Pfand, das

forgave see forgive

'forge [fɔːdʒ] 1. n. a) (workshop) Schmiede, die; b) (blacksmith's hearth) Esse, die. 2. v. t. a) schmieden (into zu); b) (fig.) schmieden ⟨Plan⟩; schließen ⟨Vereinbarung, Freundschaft⟩; c) (counterfeit) fälschen

²forge v. i. ~ **ahead** [das Tempo] beschleunigen; (fig.) Fortschritte machen

'forger n. Fälscher, der/Fälscherin, die

forgery ['fɔːdʒərɪ] n. Fälschung, die

forget [fə'get] 1. v. t., **-tt-**, forgot [fə'gɒt], forgotten [fə'gɒtn] vergessen; (~ learned ability) verlernen. 2. v. i., **-tt-**, forgot, forgotten es vergessen; ~ **about sth.** etw. vergessen; ~ **about it!** (coll.) schon gut! **forgetful** [fə'getfl] adj. vergeßlich. **for'getfulness** n. Vergeßlichkeit, die. **for'get-me-not** n. (Bot.) Vergißmeinnicht, das

forgive [fə'gɪv] v. t., forgave [fə'geɪv], forgiven [fə'gɪvn] verzeihen; vergeben ⟨Sünden⟩; ~ **sb.** [**sth.** or for **sth.**] jmdm. [etw.] verzeihen. **for'giveness** n. Verzeihung, die; (of sins) Vergebung, die

forgo [fɔː'gəʊ] v. t., forms as go verzichten auf (+ Akk.)

forgone see forgo

forgot, forgotten see forget

fork [fɔːk] 1. n. a) Gabel, die; **knives and ~s** Besteck, das; b) (in road) Abzweigung, die; (one branch) Abzweigung, die. 2. v. i. (divide) sich gabeln; (turn) abbiegen; ~ **left** links abbiegen. **fork 'out** v. i. (sl.) blechen (ugs.)

'fork-lift truck n. Gabelstapler, der

forlorn [fə'lɔːn] adj. a) (desperate) verzweifelt; b) (forsaken) verlassen

form [fɔːm] 1. n. a) (shape, type, style) Form, die; **take ~:** Gestalt annehmen; b) (printed sheet) Formular, das; c) (Brit. Sch.) Klasse, die; d) (bench) Bank, die; e) (Sport: physical condition) Form, die; (fig.) **true to ~:** wie üblich. 2. v. t. a) bilden; b) (shape) formen, gestalten (into zu); c) sich (Dat.) bilden ⟨Meinung, Urteil⟩; gewinnen ⟨*Eindruck*⟩; fassen ⟨*Plan*⟩; entwickeln ⟨*Vorliebe, Gewohnheit*⟩; schließen ⟨*Freundschaft*⟩; **d)** *(set up)* bilden ⟨*Regierung*⟩; gründen ⟨*Bund, Firma, Partei*⟩. **3.** *v. i.* sich bilden; ⟨*Idee:*⟩ Gestalt annehmen

formal ['fɔːml] *adj.* formell; förmlich ⟨*Person, Art, Einladung, Begrüßung*⟩; *(official)* offiziell; **a ~ 'yes'/'no'** eine bindende Zusage/endgültige Absage.

formality [fɔː'mælɪtɪ] *n.* **a)** *(requirement)* Formalität, *die*; **b)** *(being formal)* Förmlichkeit, *die*

format ['fɔːmæt] *n.* Format, *das*

formation [fɔː'meɪʃn] *n.* **a)** see **form** 2 a, d: Bildung, *die*; Gründung, *die*; **b)** *(Mil., Aeronaut.)* Formation, *die*

former ['fɔːmə(r)] *attrib. adj.* ehemalig; **in ~ times** früher; **the ~ :** der/die/das erstere; *pl.* die ersteren. **'formerly** *adv.* früher

formidable ['fɔːmɪdəbl] *adj.* gewaltig; gefährlich ⟨*Herausforderung, Gegner*⟩

formula ['fɔːmjʊlə] *n.* Formel, *die*

formulate ['fɔːmjʊleɪt] *v. t.* formulieren; *(devise)* entwickeln

forsake [fə'seɪk] *v. t.*, **forsook** [fə'sʊk], **~n** [fə'seɪkn] **a)** *(give up)* verzichten auf (+ *Akk.*); **b)** *(desert)* verlassen. **for'saken** *adj.* verlassen

fort [fɔːt] *n. (Mil.)* Fort, *das*

forte ['fɔːteɪ] *n.* Stärke, *die*

forth [fɔːθ] *adv.* **and so ~:** und so weiter; *see also* **back** 3

forthcoming ['---, -'--] *adj.* **a)** *(approaching)* bevorstehend; in Kürze erscheinend ⟨*Buch usw.*⟩; **b)** *pred.* **be ~** ⟨*Geld, Antwort:*⟩ kommen; ⟨*Hilfe:*⟩ geleistet werden; **not be ~ :** ausbleiben; **c)** *(responsive)* mitteilsam ⟨*Person*⟩

'forthright *adj.* direkt

forth'with *adv.* unverzüglich

fortieth ['fɔːtɪɪθ] *adj.* vierzigst ...

fortify ['fɔːtɪfaɪ] *v. t.* **a)** *(Mil.)* befestigen; **b)** *(strengthen)* stärken

fortitude ['fɔːtɪtjuːd] *n.* innere Stärke

fortnight ['fɔːtnaɪt] *n.* vierzehn Tage

fortress ['fɔːtrɪs] *n.* Festung, *die*

fortuitous [fɔː'tjuːɪtəs] *adj.*, **for'tuitously** *adv.* zufällig

fortunate ['fɔːtʃənət] *adj.* glücklich. **'fortunately** *adv.* glücklicherweise

fortune ['fɔːtʃən, 'fɔːtʃuːn] *n.* **a)** *(wealth)* Vermögen, *das*; **b)** *(luck)* Schicksal, *das*; **bad/good ~ :** Pech/Glück, *das*. **'fortune-teller** *n.* Wahrsager, *der*/Wahrsagerin, *die*

forty ['fɔːtɪ] **1.** *adj.* vierzig; **have ~ 'winks** ein Nickerchen machen *(ugs.)*.

2. *n.* Vierzig, *die. See also* **eight**; **eighty** 2

forum ['fɔːrəm] *n.* Forum, *das*

forward ['fɔːwəd] **1.** *adv.* **a)** *(in direction faced)* vorwärts; **b)** *(to the front)* nach vorn; vor⟨*laufen, -rücken, -schieben*⟩; **c)** *(closer)* heran; **he came ~ to greet me** er kam auf mich zu, um mich zu begrüßen; **d) come ~** ⟨*Zeuge, Helfer:*⟩ sich melden. **2.** *adj.* **a)** *(directed ahead)* vorwärts gerichtet; **b)** *(at or to the front)* Vorder-; vorder... **3.** *n. (Sport)* Stürmer, *der*/Stürmerin, *die*. **4.** *v. t. (send on)* nachschicken ⟨*Post*⟩ (**to an +** *Akk.*)

forwards ['fɔːwədz] *see* **forward** 1 a, b

forwent *see* **forgo**

fossil ['fɒsɪl] *n.* Fossil, *das*

foster ['fɒstə(r)] **1.** *v. t.* **a)** fördern; pflegen ⟨*Freundschaft*⟩; **b)** in Pflege haben ⟨*Kind*⟩. **2.** *adj.* **~ -:** Pflege⟨*kind, -eltern, -sohn usw.*⟩

fought *see* **fight** 1, 2

foul [faʊl] **1.** *adj.* **a)** abscheulich ⟨*Geruch, Geschmack*⟩; **b)** *(polluted)* verschmutzt ⟨*Wasser, Luft*⟩; *(putrid)* faulig ⟨*Wasser*⟩; stickig ⟨*Luft*⟩; **c)** *(sl.: awful)* scheußlich *(ugs.)*; anstößig ⟨*Sprache*⟩. **2.** *n. (Sport)* Foul, *das*. **3.** *v. t.* **a)** beschmutzen; verpesten ⟨*Luft*⟩; **b)** *(Sport)* foulen. **'foulsmelling** *adj.* übelriechend

¹found [faʊnd] *v. t.* **a)** *(establish)* gründen; stiften ⟨*Krankenhaus, Kloster*⟩; begründen ⟨*Wissenschaft, Religion*⟩; **b)** *(fig.: base)* begründen; **be ~ed** [up]**on sth.** [sich] auf etw. (*Akk.*) gründen

²found *see* **find** 1

foundation [faʊn'deɪʃn] *n.* **a)** Gründung, *die*; *(of hospital, monastery)* Stiftung, *die*; **b)** *usu. in pl.* **-s|** *(lit. or fig.)* Fundament, *das*; **be without ~** *(fig.)* unbegründet sein. **foun'dation stone** *n.* Grundstein, *der*

¹founder *n.* Gründer, *der*/Gründerin, *die*; *(of hospital)* Stifter, *der*/Stifterin, *die*

²founder *v. i.* **a)** ⟨*Schiff:*⟩ sinken; **b)** *(fig.: fail)* sich zerschlagen

fountain ['faʊntɪn] *n.* Fontäne, *die*; *(structure)* Springbrunnen, *der*; *(fig.)* Quelle, *die*. **'fountain-pen** *n.* Füllfederhalter, *der*

four [fɔː(r)] **1.** *adj.* vier. **2.** *n.* Vier, *die*; **on all ~s** auf allen vieren *(ugs.). See also* **eight**. **'four-poster** *n.* **~** [**bed**] Himmelbett, *das*. **foursome** ['fɔːsəm] *n.* Quartett, *das*; **go in** *or* **as a ~ :** zu viert gehen

fourteen [fɔː'tiːn] 1. *adj.* vierzehn. 2. *n.* Vierzehn, *die. See also* **eight.**

fourteenth [fɔː'tiːnθ] 1. *adj.* vierzehnt... 2. *n. (fraction)* Vierzehntel, *das. See also* **eighth**

fourth [fɔːθ] 1. *adj.* viert... 2. *n. (in sequence)* vierte, *der/die/das; (in rank)* Vierte, *der/die/das; (fraction)* Viertel, *das. See also* **eighth.** '**fourthly** *adv.* viertens

fowl [faʊl] *n.* Haushuhn, *das; (collectively)* Geflügel, *das*

fox [fɒks] 1. *n.* Fuchs, *der.* 2. *v.t.* verwirren

foyer ['fɔɪeɪ] *n.* Foyer, *das*

fraction ['frækʃn] *n.* a) *(Math.)* Bruch, *der;* b) *(small part)* Bruchteil, *der*

fracture ['fræktʃə(r)] 1. *n.* Bruch, *der.* 2. *v.t.* brechen

fragile ['frædʒaɪl] *adj.* zerbrechlich

fragment ['frægmənt] *n.* Bruchstück, *das.* **fragmentary** ['frægməntərɪ] *adj.* bruchstückhaft

fragrance ['freɪgrəns] *n.* Duft, *der.* **fragrant** ['freɪgrənt] *adj.* duftend

frail [freɪl] *adj.* zerbrechlich; gebrechlich ⟨Greis, Greisin⟩

frame [freɪm] 1. *n.* a) *(of vehicle)* Rahmen, *der; (of bed)* Gestell, *das;* b) *(border)* Rahmen, *der;* |**spectacle**| ~s [Brillen]gestell, *das.* 2. *v.t.* a) rahmen; b) formulieren ⟨Frage, Antwort⟩; c) *(sl.: incriminate)* ~ *sb.* jmdm. etwas anhängen *(ugs.).* '**frame-up** *n. (coll.)* abgekartetes Spiel *(ugs.).* '**framework** *n.* Gerüst, *das*

franc [fræŋk] *n.* Franc, *der; (Swiss)* Franken, *der*

France [frɑːns] *pr. n.* Frankreich *(das)*

franchise ['fræntʃaɪz] *n.* a) Stimmrecht, *das;* b) *(Commerc.)* Lizenz, *die*

¹**frank** *adj.* offen; freimütig ⟨Geständnis, Äußerung⟩; **be** ~ **with sb.** zu jmdm. offen sein

²**frank** *v.t. (Post)* frankieren

frankfurter ['fræŋkfɜːtə(r)] *(Amer.:* **frankfurt** ['fræŋkfɜːt]) *n.* Frankfurter [Würstchen]

frankly *adv.* offen; *(honestly)* offen gesagt

frantic ['fræntɪk] *adj.* a) verzweifelt ⟨Hilferufe, Gestikulieren⟩; **be** ~ **with fear/rage** *etc.* außer sich *(Dat.)* sein vor Angst/Wut *usw.;* b) hektisch ⟨Aktivität, Suche⟩. **frantically** ['fræntɪkəlɪ], '**franticly** *adv.* verzweifelt

fraternize ['frætənaɪz] *v.i.* ~ |**with sb.**| sich verbrüdern [mit jmdm.]

fraud [frɔːd] *n.* a) *no pl.* Betrug, *der;* b)

(trick) Schwindel, *der;* c) *(person)* Betrüger, *der/*Betrügerin, *die.* **fraudulent** ['frɔːdjʊlənt] *adj.* betrügerisch

fraught [frɔːt] *adj.* **be** ~ **with danger** voller Gefahren sein

¹**fray** [freɪ] *n.* [Kampf]getümmel, *das;* **enter** *or* **join the** ~: sich in den Kampf stürzen

²**fray** *v.i.* [sich] durchscheuern; ⟨Hosenbein, Teppich, Seilende:⟩ ausfransen; **our nerves/tempers began to** ~ *(fig.)* wir verloren langsam die Nerven/unsere Gemüter erhitzten sich

freak [friːk] *n.* a) Mißgeburt, *die; attrib.* ungewöhnlich ⟨Wetter, Ereignis⟩; b) *(sl.: fanatic)* Freak, *der*

freckle ['frekl] *n.* Sommersprosse, *die.* '**freckled** *adj.* sommersprossig

free [friː] 1. *adj.,* **freer** ['friːə(r)], **freest** ['friːɪst] a) frei; **get** ~: freikommen; **set** ~: freilassen; ~ **of charge/cost** gebührenfrei/kostenlos; **sb. is** ~ **to do sth.** es steht jmdm. frei, etw. zu tun; ~ **time** Freizeit, *die;* **he's** ~ **in the mornings** er hat morgens Zeit; b) *(without payment)* kostenlos, frei ⟨Unterkunft, Verpflegung⟩; Frei⟨karte, -exemplar⟩; Gratis⟨probe⟩; '**admission** ~', [Eintritt frei''; **for** ~ *(coll.)* umsonst. 2. *adv.* gratis; umsonst. 3. *v.t. (set at liberty)* freilassen; *(disentangle)* befreien ⟨of, from von⟩; ~ **sb./oneself from** jmdn./ sich befreien aus ⟨Gefängnis, Sklaverei⟩. **freedom** ['friːdəm] *n.* Freiheit, *die*

free: ~ '**gift** *n.* Gratisgabe, *die;* ~**hold** 1. *n.* Besitzrecht, *das.* 2. *adj.* Eigentums-; ~**lance** 1. *n.* freier Mitarbeiter/freie Mitarbeiterin; 2. *adj.* freiberuflich

'**freely** *adv. (willingly)* großzügig; freimütig ⟨eingestehen⟩; *(without restriction)* frei; *(frankly)* offen

free: **F**~**mason** *n.* Freimaurer, *der;* ~**-range** *adj.* freilaufend ⟨Huhn⟩; ~**-range eggs** Eier von freilaufenden Hühnern; ~ '**speech** *n.* Redefreiheit; ~**way** *n. (Amer.)* Autobahn, *die;* ~**-wheel** *v.i.* im Freilauf fahren

freeze [friːz] 1. *v.i.,* **froze** [frəʊz], **frozen** ['frəʊzn] a) frieren; *(become covered with ice)* zufrieren; ⟨Straße:⟩ vereisen; ⟨Flüssigkeit:⟩ gefrieren; ⟨Rohr, Schloß:⟩ einfrieren; b) *(become rigid)* steif frieren. 2. *v.t.,* **froze**, **frozen** a) *(preserve)* tiefkühlen; b) einfrieren ⟨Kredit, Löhne, Preise usw.⟩. '**freezer** *n.* Tiefkühltruhe, *die;* |upright| ~: Tiefkühlschrank, *der;* ~ **com-**

partment Tiefkühlfach, *das.* **freezing** ['fri:zɪŋ] **1.** *adj. (lit. or fig.)* frostig; **it's ~:** es ist eiskalt. **2.** *n.* **above/below ~:** über/unter dem/den Gefrierpunkt

freight [freɪt] *n.* Fracht, *die.* '**freighter** *n.* Frachter, *der*

French [frentʃ] **1.** *adj.* französisch; **he/she is ~:** er ist Franzose/sie ist Französin. **2.** *n.* **a)** *(language)* Französisch, *das; see also* **English 2 a;** **b) the ~** *pl.* die Franzosen

French: **~ 'bean** *n. (Brit.)* Gartenbohne, *die;* **~ 'dressing** *n.* Vinaigrette, *die;* **~'fries** *sg.* Pommes frites *Pl.* **~man** ['frentʃmən] *n., pl.* **~men** ['frentʃmən] Franzose, *der;* **~ 'window** *n.* französisches Fenster; **~woman** *n.* Französin, *die*

frenzied ['frenzɪd] *adj.* rasend **frenzy** ['frenzɪ] *n.* **a)** Wahnsinn, *der; (fury)* Raserei, *die*

frequency ['fri:kwənsɪ] *n.* **a)** Häufigkeit, *die;* **b)** *(Phys.)* Frequenz, *die* **frequent** **1.** ['fri:kwənt] *adj.* **a)** häufig; **become less ~:** seltener werden; **b)** *(habitual)* eifrig. **2.** [frɪ'kwent] *v.t.* häufig besuchen *⟨Café, Klub, usw.⟩.* **frequently** ['fri:kwəntlɪ] *adv.* häufig

fresco *n. pl.* **~es** *or* **~s** Fresko, *das* **fresh** [freʃ] *adj.* frisch; neu *⟨Beweise, Anstrich, Mut, Energie⟩;* **~ supplies** Nachschub, *der* (of an + *Dat.*); **make a ~ start** noch einmal von vorne anfangen; *(fig.)* neu beginnen

freshen ['freʃn] *v.i.* auffrischen. **freshen 'up** *v.i.* sich auffrischen **freshly** *adv.* frisch

freshness *n.* Frische, *die* **fresh 'water** *n.* Süßwasser, *das* **fret** [fret] *v.i., -tt-* sich *(Dat.)* Sorgen machen. **fretful** ['fretfl] *adj.* verdrießlich; quengelig *(ugs.)*

fretsaw *n.* Laubsäge, *die*

Fri. *abbr.* Friday Fr.

friar ['fraɪə(r)] *n.* Ordensbruder, *der* **friction** ['frɪkʃn] *n.* Reibung, *die*

Friday ['fraɪdeɪ, 'fraɪdɪ] *n.* Freitag, *der;* **on ~:** [am] Freitag; **on a ~,** **on ~s** freitags; **~ 13 August** Freitag, der 13. August; *(at top of letter etc.)* Freitag, den 13. August; **next/last ~:** [am] nächsten/letzten Freitag; **Good ~:** Karfreitag, *der*

fridge [frɪdʒ] *n. (Brit. coll.)* Kühlschrank, *die*

fried *see* ¹**fry**

friend [frend] *n.* **a)** Freund, *der*/Freundin, *die;* **be ~s** with sb.: mit jmdm. befreundet sein; **make ~s** [with

sb.] [mit jmdm.] Freundschaft schließen. **friendliness** ['frendlɪnɪs] *n.* Freundlichkeit, *die.* '**friendly 1.** *adj.* freundlich (**to** zu); freundschaftlich *⟨Rat, Beziehungen, Wettkampf⟩.* **2.** *n. (Sport)* Freundschaftsspiel, *das.* '**friendship** *n.* Freundschaft, *die*

frigate ['frɪɡət] *n. (Naut.)* Fregatte, *die* **fright** [fraɪt] *n.* Schreck. *der;* **take ~:** erschrecken. **frighten** ['fraɪtn] *v.t.* ⟨*Explosion, Schuß:⟩* erschrecken; *⟨Gedanke, Drohung:⟩* angst machen (+ *Dat.*); **be ~ed** at or by sth. vor etw. *(Dat.)* erschrecken. '**frightful** *adj.,* '**frightfully** *adv.* furchtbar

frigid ['frɪdʒɪd] *adj.* frostig; *(sexually)* frigid[e]

frill [frɪl] *n.* **a)** Rüsche, *die;* **b)** *in pl. (embellishments)* Beiwerk, *das.* '**frilly** *adj.* mit Rüschen besetzt; Rüschen⟨*kleid, -bluse⟩*

fringe [frɪndʒ] *n.* **a)** Fransenkante, *die* (**on** an + *Dat.*); **b)** *(hair)* [Pony]fransen *(ugs.);* **c)** *(edge)* Rand, *der*

frisk [frɪsk] **1.** *v.i.* **~ [about]** [herum]springen. **2.** *v.t. (coll.)* filzen *(ugs.).* '**frisky** *adj.* munter

¹**fritter** ['frɪtə(r)] *n.* **apple** *etc.* **~s** Apfelstücke *usw.* in Pfannkuchenteig

²**fritter** *v.t.* **~ away** vergeuden

frivolity [frɪ'vɒlɪtɪ] *n.* Oberflächlichkeit, *die*

frivolous ['frɪvələs] *adj.* **a)** frivol; **b)** *(trifling)* belanglos

frizzy ['frɪzɪ] *adj.* kraus

fro [frəʊ] *adv. see* **to 2**

frock [frɒk] *n.* Kleid, *das*

frog [frɒɡ] *n.* Frosch, *der.* **frogman** ['frɒɡmən] *n., pl.* **~men** ['frɒɡmən] Froschmann, *der.* '**frog-spawn** *n.* Froschlaich, *der*

frolic ['frɒlɪk] *v.i., -ck-:* **~ [about** *or* **around]** [herum]springen

from [frəm, *stressed* frɒm] *prep.* von; *(~ within; expr. origin)* aus; **~ Paris** aus Paris; **~ Paris to Munich** von Paris nach München; **be a mile ~ sth.** eine Meile von etw. entfernt sein; **where do you come ~? where are you ~?** woher kommen Sie?; **painted ~ life** nach dem Leben gemalt; **weak ~ hunger** schwach vor Hunger; **~ the year 1972** seit 1972; **~ [the age of] 18** ab 18 Jahre; **~ 4 to 6 eggs** 4 bis 6 Eier

front [frʌnt] **1.** *n.* **a)** Vorderseite, *die; (of house)* Vorderfront, *die;* **in** or **at the ~** [of sth.] vorn [in etw. *position:* **Dat., movement: Akk.*]; **to the ~:** nach vorn; **in ~:** vorn[e]; **be in ~ of sth./sb.**

vor etw./jmdm. sein; **b)** *(Mil.)* Front, *die;* **c)** *(at seaside)* Strandpromenade, *die;* **d)** *(Metereol.)* Front, *die;* **e)** *(bluff)* Fassade, *die.* **2.** *adj.* vorder...; Vorder-⟨*rad, -zimmer, -zahn*⟩; ~ **garden** Vorgarten, *der;* ~ **row** erste Reihe.

frontal ['frʌntl] *adj.* Frontal-. **front 'door** *n. (of flat)* Wohnungstür, *die; (of house)* Haustür, *die*

frontier ['frʌntɪə(r)] *n.* Grenze, *die*

front 'page *n.* Titelseite, *die*

frost [frɒst] **1.** *n.* Frost, *der;* **ten degrees of** ~ *(Brit.)* zehn Grad minus. **2.** *v.t.* ~**ed glass** Mattglas, *das.* **'frostbite** *n.* Erfrierung, *die.* **'frosting** *n. (esp. Amer.)* Glasur, *die.* **'frosty** *adj.* frostig

froth [frɒθ] **1.** *n.* Schaum, *der.* **2.** *v.i.* schäumen. **'frothy** *adj.* schaumig

frown [fraʊn] **1.** *v.i.* die Stirn runzeln (**[up]on** über + *Akk.*). **2.** *n.* Stirnrunzeln, *das*

froze *see* **freeze**

frozen ['frəʊzn] **1.** *see* **freeze. 2.** *adj.* **a)** zugefroren ⟨*Fluß, See*⟩; eingefroren ⟨*Wasserleitung*⟩; **I'm** ~ *(fig.)* ich bin eiskalt; **b)** *(to preserve)* tiefgekühlt; ~ **food** Tiefkühlkost, *die*

frugal ['fru:gl] *adj.* genügsam ⟨*Lebensweise, Mensch*⟩; frugal ⟨*Mahl*⟩

fruit [fru:t] *n.* Frucht, *die;* collect. Obst, *das*

fruitful ['fru:tfl] *adj.* fruchtbar

'fruit juice *n.* Obstsaft, *der*

fruitless *adj.* nutzlos ⟨*Versuch, Gespräch*⟩; fruchtlos ⟨*Verhandlung, Suche*⟩

fruit: ~ **machine** *n. (Brit.)* Spielautomat, *der;* ~ **'salad** *n.* Obstsalat, *der*

'fruity *adj.* fruchtig ⟨*Geschmack, Wein*⟩

frustrate [frʌ'streɪt] *v.t.* vereiteln ⟨*Plan, Versuch*⟩; zunichte machen ⟨*Hoffnung, Bemühungen*⟩. **'frustrated** *adj.* frustriert. **frustration** [frʌ'streɪʃn] *n.* Frustration, *die*

¹fry [fraɪ] *v.t. & i.* braten; **fried egg** Spiegelei, *das*

²fry *n. (fishes)* Brut, *die;* **small** ~ *(fig.)* unbedeutende Leute

'frying-pan *n.* Bratpfanne, *die*

ft. *abbr.* **feet, foot** ft.

fuck [fʌk] *(coarse)* **1.** *v.t. & i.* ficken *(vulg.).* **2.** *n.* Fick, *der (vulg.)*

fuddy-duddy ['fʌdɪdʌdɪ] *(sl.)* **1.** *adj.* verkalkt *(ugs.).* **2.** *n.* Fossil, *das (fig.)*

fudge [fʌdʒ] *n.* Karamelbonbon, *der od. das*

fuel ['fju:əl] *n.* Brennstoff, *der; (for vehicle)* Kraftstoff, *der; (for ship, aircraft)* Treibstoff, *der*

fugitive ['fju:dʒɪtɪv] *n.* Flüchtige, *der/die*

fugue [fju:g] *n. (Mus.)* Fuge, *die*

fulfil *(Amer.:* **fulfill)** [fʊl'fɪl] *v.t.,* **-ll-** erfüllen; halten ⟨*Versprechen*⟩. **ful'filment** *(Amer.:* **ful'fillment**) *n.* Erfüllung, *die*

full [fʊl] **1.** *adj.* **a)** voll; satt ⟨*Person*⟩; ~ **of** voller; **be** ~ **up** *(coll.)* voll [besetzt] sein; ⟨*Behälter:*⟩ randvoll sein; ⟨*Flug:*⟩ völlig ausgebucht sein; **I'm** ~ **[up]** *(coll.)* ich bin voll [bis obenhin] *(ugs.);* **be** ~ **of oneself** sehr von sich eingenommen sein; **b)** ausführlich ⟨*Bericht, Beschreibung*⟩; erfüllt ⟨*Leben*⟩; ganz ⟨*Stunde, Jahr, Monat, Seite*⟩; voll ⟨*Name, Bezahlung, Verständnis*⟩; ~ **details** alle Einzelheiten; **at** ~ **speed** mit Höchstgeschwindigkeit; **c)** voll ⟨*Gesicht*⟩; füllig ⟨*Figur*⟩; weit ⟨*Rock*⟩. **2.** *n.* **in** ~: vollständig. **3.** *adv. (exactly)* genau

full: ~ **back** *n.* Verteidiger, *der/*Verteidigerin, *die;* ~-**length** *adj.* lang ⟨*Kleid*⟩; ~ **'moon** *n.* Vollmond, *der;* ~-**scale** *adj.* **a)** in Originalgröße; **b)** großangelegt ⟨*Untersuchung, Suchaktion*⟩; ~ **'stop** *n.* Punkt, *der;* ~-**time** *adj.* ganztägig; ganztags⟨*arbeit*⟩

fully ['fʊlɪ] *adv.* voll [und ganz]; reich ⟨*belohnt*⟩; ausführlich ⟨*erklären*⟩

fulsome ['fʊlsəm] *adj.* übertrieben

fumble ['fʌmbl] *v.i.* ~ **at or with** [herum]fingern an (+ *Dat.*); ~ **in one's pockets for sth.** in seinen Taschen nach etw. kramen *(ugs.)*

fume [fju:m] **1.** *n. in pl.* ~**s** Dämpfe. **2.** *v.i.* vor Wut schäumen

fumigate ['fju:mɪgeɪt] *v.t.* ausräuchern

fun [fʌn] *n.* Spaß, *der;* **have** ~! viel Spaß!; **make** ~ **of sb.** sich über jmdn. lustig machen; **for** ~, **for the** ~ **of it** zum Spaß

function ['fʌŋkʃn] **1.** *n.* Aufgabe, *die;* Funktion, *die; (formal event)* Veranstaltung, *die.* **2.** *v.i.* ⟨*Maschine, System:*⟩ funktionieren; ~ **as** fungieren als; *(serve as)* dienen als. **functional** ['fʌŋkʃənl] *adj.* **a)** *(useful)* funktionell; **b)** *(working)* funktionsfähig

fund [fʌnd] **1.** *n.* **a)** *(money)* Fonds, *der;* **b)** *(fig.: stock)* Fundus, *der* (**of** von, an + *Dat.*). **2.** *v.t.* finanzieren

fundamental [fʌndə'mentl] *adj.* grundlegend (**to** für); elementar ⟨*Bedürfnisse*⟩. **fundamentally** [fʌndə-

'mentəli] *adv.* grundlegend; von Grund auf ⟨*verschieden, ehrlich*⟩

funeral ['fju:nərl] *n.* Beerdigung, *die.* ~ **director** Bestattungsunternehmer, *der;* ~ **service** Trauerfeier, *die*

'fun-fair *n.* (*Brit.*) Jahrmarkt, *der*

fungus ['fʌŋgəs] *n., pl.* **fungi** ['fʌŋgaɪ, 'fʌndʒaɪ] *or* ~**es** Pilz, *der*

funicular [fju:'nɪkjʊlə(r)] *adj. & n.* |railway| [Stand]seilbahn, *die*

funnel ['fʌnl] *n.* Trichter, *der; (of ship etc.)* Schornstein, *der*

funnily ['fʌnɪli] *adv.* komisch; ~ **enough** komischerweise

funny ['fʌni] *adj.* a) komisch; lustig; witzig ⟨*Mensch, Einfall*⟩; b) *(strange)* komisch. **'funny-bone** *n.* Musikantenknochen, *der*

fur [fɜ:(r)] *n.* a) Fell, *das; (garment)* Pelz, *der;* ~ **coat** Pelzmantel, *der;* b) *(in kettle)* Kesselstein, *der*

furious ['fjʊərɪəs] *adj.* wütend; heftig ⟨*Streit*⟩; wild ⟨*Tanz, Tempo, Kampf*⟩; **be** ~ **with sb.** wütend auf jmdn. sein. **'furiously** *adv.* wütend; wild ⟨*kämpfen*⟩: wie wild (*ugs.*) arbeiten

furl [fɜ:l] *v.t.* einrollen ⟨*Segel, Flagge*⟩

furnace ['fɜ:nɪs] *n.* Ofen, *der*

furnish ['fɜ:nɪʃ] *v.t.* a) möblieren; b) *(supply)* liefern; ~ **sb. with sth.** jmdm. etw. liefern. **'furnishings** *n. pl.* Einrichtungsgegenstände

furniture ['fɜ:nɪtʃə(r)] *n.* Möbel *Pl.;* **piece of** ~ Möbel[stück], *das*

furrow ['fʌrəʊ] *n.* Furche, *die*

furry ['fɜ:ri] *adj.* haarig; ~ **animal** *(toy)* Plüschtier, *das*

further ['fɜ:ðə(r)] 1. *adj.* a) *(in space)* weiter entfernt; b) *(additional)* weiter... 2. *adv.* weiter. 3. *v.t.* fördern. **further'more** *adv.* außerdem. **'furthermost** *adj.* äußerst ...

furthest ['fɜ:ðɪst] 1. *adj.* am weitesten entfernt. 2. *adv.* am weitesten ⟨*springen, laufen*⟩; am weitesten entfernt ⟨*sein, wohnen*⟩

furtive ['fɜ:tɪv] *adj.,* **furtively** *adv.* verstohlen

fury ['fjʊəri] *n.* Wut, *die; (of sea, battle)* Wüten, *das*

¹fuse [fju:z] 1. *v.t. (blend)* verschmelzen (**into** zu). 2. *v.i.* ~ **together** miteinander verschmelzen

²fuse *n.* |time-|~: |Zeit]zünder, *der; (cord)* Zündschnur, *die*

³fuse *(Electr.)* 1. *n.* Sicherung, *die.* 2. *v.i.* **the lights have** ~**d** die Sicherung ist durchgebrannt. **'fuse box** *n.* Sicherungskasten, *der*

fuselage ['fju:zəlɑ:ʒ] *n.* [Flugzeug]rumpf, *der*

fusion ['fju:ʒn] *n.* a) Verschmelzung, *die;* b) *(Phys.)* Fusion, *die*

fuss [fʌs] 1. *n.* Theater, *das (ugs.);* **make a** ~ |**about sth.**| einen Wirbel |um etw.| machen. 2. *v.i.* Wirbel machen; *(get agitated)* sich [unnötig] aufregen

fussy *adj. (fastidious)* eigen; penibel; **I'm not** ~ *(I don't mind)* ich bin nicht wählerisch

futile ['fju:taɪl] *adj.* vergeblich

future ['fju:tʃə(r)] 1. *adj.* [zu]künftig; **at some** ~ **date** zu einem späteren Zeitpunkt. 2. *n.* a) Zukunft, *die;* **in** ~: in Zukunft; künftig; b) *(Ling.)* Futur, *das;* Zukunft, *die.* **futuristic** [fju:tʃə-'rɪstɪk] *adj.* futuristisch

fuze [fju:z] *see* ²**fuse**

fuzzy ['fʌzi] *adj.* a) *(frizzy)* kraus; b) *(blurred)* verschwommen

G

G, g [dʒi:] *n.* G, g, *das*

gab [gæb] *n. (coll.)* **have the gift of the** ~: reden können

gabble ['gæbl] *v.i.* brabbeln (*ugs.*)

gable ['geɪbl] *n.* Giebel, *der*

gad [gæd] *v.i.,* -**dd**- *(coll.)* ~ **about** herumziehen

gadget ['gædʒɪt] *n.* Gerät, *das*

Gaelic ['geɪlɪk, 'gælɪk] 1. *adj.* gälisch. 2. *n.* Gälisch, *das*

gaffe [gæf] *n.* Fauxpas, *der*

gag [gæg] 1. *n.* a) Knebel, *der;* b) *(joke)* Gag, *der.* 2. *v.t.,* -**gg**- knebeln

gaiety ['geɪəti] *n.* Fröhlichkeit, *die*

gaily ['geɪli] *adv.* fröhlich; in leuchtenden Farben ⟨*bemalt, geschmückt*⟩

gain [geɪn] 1. *n.* a) Gewinn, *der;* b) *(increase)* Zunahme, *die* (**in** an + *Dat.*). 2. *v.t.* a) gewinnen; finden ⟨*Zugang, Zutritt*⟩; erwerben ⟨*Wissen, Ruf*⟩; erlangen ⟨*Freiheit*⟩; erzielen ⟨*Vorteil, Punkte*⟩; verdienen ⟨*Lebensunterhalt, Geldsumme*⟩; ~ **weight/five pounds** |**in weight**| zunehmen/fünf Pfund zunehmen; ~ **speed** schneller werden; b) ⟨*Uhr:*⟩ vorgehen um. 3. *v.i.* a) ~ **by**

sth. von etw. profitieren; **b)** ⟨*Uhr:*⟩ vorgehen

gait [geɪt] *n.* Gang, *der*

gala ['gɑːlə, 'geɪlə] *n.* Festveranstaltung, *die; attrib.* Gala⟨*abend, -vorstellung*⟩; **swimming ~:** Schwimmfest, *das*

galaxy ['gæləksɪ] *n.* Galaxie, *die*

gale [geɪl] *n.* Sturm, *der*

gall [gɔːl] *n. (sl.)* Unverschämtheit, *die*

gallant ['gælənt] *adj. (brave)* tapfer; ⟨*chivalrous*⟩ ritterlich. **gallantry** ['gæləntrɪ] *n. (bravery)* Tapferkeit, *die*

'**gall-bladder** *n.* Gallenblase, *die*

gallery ['gælərɪ] *n.* **a)** Galerie, *die;* **b)** *(Theatre)* dritter Rang

galley ['gælɪ] *n.* **a)** *(ship's kitchen)* Kombüse, *die;* **b)** *(Hist.)* Galeere, *die*

gallivant ['gælɪvænt] *v.i. (coll.)* herumziehen *(ugs.)*

gallon ['gælən] *n.* Gallone, *die*

gallop ['gæləp] **1.** *n.* Galopp, *der.* **2.** *v.i.* ⟨*Pferd, Reiter:*⟩ galoppieren

gallows ['gæləʊz] *n. sing.* Galgen, *der*

galore [gə'lɔː(r)] *adv.* im Überfluß; in Hülle und Fülle

galvanize ['gælvənaɪz] *v.t.* wachrütteln; **~ sb. into action** jmdn. veranlassen, sofort aktiv zu werden

gambit ['gæmbɪt] *n.* Gambit, *das*

gamble ['gæmbl] *v.i.* **a)** [um Geld] spielen; **b)** *(fig.)* spekulieren; **~ on sth.** sich auf etw. *(Akk.)* verlassen. **gambler** ['gæmblə(r)] *n.* Glücksspieler, *der*

'**game** [geɪm] *n.* **a)** Spiel, *das; (of [table-]tennis, chess, cards, cricket)* Partie, *die;* **b)** *(fig.: scheme)* Vorhaben, *das;* **c)** *in pl. (athletic contests)* Spiele; *(in school) (sports)* Sport, *der; (athletics)* Leichtathletik, *die;* **d)** *(Hunting, Cookery)* Wild, *das*

²**game** *adj.* mutig; **be ~ to do sth.** bereit sein, etw. zu tun

'**gamekeeper** *n.* Wildheger, *der*

gammon ['gæmən] *n.* Räucherschinken, *der*

gamut ['gæmət] *n.* Skala, *die*

gander ['gændə(r)] *n.* Gänserich, *der*

gang [gæŋ] **1.** *n.* Bande, *die; (of workmen, prisoners)* Trupp, *der.* **2.** *v.i.* **~ up against** *or* **on** *(coll.)* sich verbünden gegen

gangling ['gæŋglɪŋ] schlaksig *(ugs.)*

gangster ['gæŋstə(r)] *n.* Gangster, *der*

'**gangway** *n.* Gangway, *die; (Brit.: between seats)* Gang, *der*

gaol [dʒeɪl] *see* **jail**

gap [gæp] *n.* **a)** Lücke, *die;* **b)** *(in time)* Pause, *die;* **c)** *(divergence)* Kluft, *die*

gape [geɪp] *v.i.* **a)** den Mund aufsperren; ⟨*Loch, Abgrund, Wunde:*⟩ klaffen; **b)** *(stare)* Mund und Nase aufsperren *(ugs.);* **~ at sb./sth.** jmdn./ etw. mit offenem Mund anstarren

garage ['gærɑːdʒ] *n.* Garage, *die; (selling petrol)* Tankstelle, *die; (for repairing cars)* [Kfz-]Werkstatt, *die*

garb [gɑːb] *n.* Tracht, *die*

garbage ['gɑːbɪdʒ] *n.* **a)** Abfall, *der;* Müll, *der;* **b)** *(coll.: nonsense)* Quatsch, *der (salopp).* '**garbage can** *n. (Amer.)* Mülltonne, *die*

garble ['gɑːbl] *v.t.* verstümmeln

garden ['gɑːdn] *n.* Garten, *der.* '**garden centre** *n.* Gartencenter, *das.* **gardener** ['gɑːdnə(r)] *n.* Gärtner, *der/*Gärtnerin, *die.* **gardening** ['gɑːdnɪŋ] *n.* Gartenarbeit, *die*

gargle ['gɑːgl] *v.i.* gurgeln

garish ['geərɪʃ] *adj.* grell ⟨*Farbe, Licht*⟩; knallbunt ⟨*Kleidung*⟩

garland ['gɑːlənd] *n.* Girlande, *die*

garlic ['gɑːlɪk] *n.* Knoblauch, *der*

garment ['gɑːmənt] *n.* Kleidungsstück, *das;* **~s** *pl. (clothes)* Kleidung, *die;* Kleider

garnish ['gɑːnɪʃ] **1.** *v.t.* garnieren. **2.** *n.* Garnierung, *die*

garret ['gærɪt] *n.* Dachkammer, *die*

garrison ['gærɪsn] *n.* Garnison, *die*

garter ['gɑːtə(r)] *n.* Strumpfband, *das*

gas [gæs] **1.** *n.* **a)** *pl.* **~es** ['gæsɪz] Gas, *das;* **b)** *(Amer. coll.: petrol)* Benzin, *das.* **2.** *v.i.,* **-ss-** mit Gas vergiften. **gas 'cooker** *n. (Brit.)* Gasherd, *der.* **gas 'fire** *n.* Gasofen, *der*

gash [gæʃ] **1.** *n.* Schnittwunde, *die.* **2.** *v.t.* aufritzen ⟨*Haut*⟩; **~ one's finger** sich *(Dat. od. Akk.)* in den Finger schneiden

gas: **~ mask** *n.* Gasmaske, *die;* **~ meter** *n.* Gaszähler, *der*

gasoline (gasolene) ['gæsəliːn] *n. (Amer.)* Benzin, *das*

gasometer [gæ'sɒmɪtə(r)] *n.* Gasometer, *der*

gasp [gɑːsp] **1.** *v.i.* nach Luft schnappen (**with** *vor*); **he was ~ing for air** rang nach Luft. **2.** *v.t.* **~ out** hervorstoßen. **3.** *n.* Keuchen, *das*

'**gas station** *n. (Amer.)* Tankstelle, *die*

gastronomy [gæ'strɒnəmɪ] *n.* Gastronomie, *die*

'**gasworks** *n. sing.* Gaswerk, *das*

gate [geɪt] *n.* Tor, *das; (barrier)* Sperre, *die; (to field etc.)* Gatter, *das; (of level crossing)* [Bahn]schranke, *die; (in airport)* Flugsteig, *der*

gateau ['gætəʊ] *n., pl.* ~s *or* ~x ['gætəʊz] Torte, *die*

gate: ~**crasher** ['geɪtkræʃə(r)] *n.* ungeladener Gast; ~**way** *n.* Tor, *das*

gather ['gæðə(r)] 1. *v.t.* a) sammeln; zusammentragen ⟨*Informationen*⟩; pflücken ⟨*Obst, Blumen*⟩; b) ⟨*infer, deduce*⟩ schließen (**from** aus); c) ~ **speed/force** schneller/stärker werden. 2. *v.i.* sich versammeln ⟨*Wolken:*⟩ sich zusammenziehen. '**gathering** *n.* Versammlung, *die*

gaudy ['gɔːdɪ] *adj.* protzig; grell ⟨*Farben*⟩

gauge [geɪdʒ] *n.* 1. a) ⟨*measure*⟩ Maß, *das*; b) ⟨*instrument*⟩ Meßgerät, *das*. 2. *v.t.* messen; ⟨*fig.*⟩ beurteilen

gaunt [gɔːnt] *adj.* hager

gauntlet ['gɔːntlɪt] *n.* Stulpenhandschuh, *der*

gauze [gɔːz] *n.* Gaze, *die*

gave *see* **give** 1, 2

gay [geɪ] 1. *adj.* a) fröhlich; ⟨*brightcoloured*⟩ farbenfroh; b) ⟨*coll.: homosexual*⟩ schwul ⟨*ugs.*⟩; Schwulen⟨*lokal*⟩. 2. *n.* ⟨*coll.*⟩ Schwule, *der* ⟨*ugs.*⟩

gaze [geɪz] *v.i.* blicken; ⟨*fixedly*⟩ starren; ~ **at sb./sth.** jmdn./etw. anstarren

GB *abbr.* **Great Britain** GB

GCSE *abbr.* ⟨*Brit.*⟩ **General Certificate of Secondary Education**

gear [gɪə(r)] 1. *n.* a) ⟨*Motor Veh.*⟩ Gang, *der*; **top/bottom** ~ ⟨*Brit.*⟩ der höchste/erste Gang; **change** *or* **shift** ~: schalten; **put the car into** ~: einen Gang einlegen; **out of** ~: im Leerlauf; b) ⟨*coll.: clothes*⟩ Aufmachung, *die*; c) ⟨*equipment*⟩ Gerät, *das*; Ausrüstung, *die*. 2. *v.t.* ausrichten (**to** auf + *Akk.*). '**gearbox** *n.* Getriebekasten, *der*. '**gear-lever**, ⟨*Amer.*⟩ '**gear-shift** *ns.* Schalthebel, *der*

geese *pl. of* **goose**

geezer ['giːzə(r)] *n.* ⟨*sl.: old man*⟩ Opa, *der* ⟨*ugs.*⟩

gel [dʒel] *n.* Gel, *das*

gelatin ['dʒelətɪn], ⟨*Brit.*⟩ **gelatine** ['dʒelətiːn] *n.* Gelatine, *die*

gelignite ['dʒelɪgnaɪt] *n.* Gelatinedynamit, *das*

gem [dʒem] *n.* Edelstein, *der*

Gemini ['dʒemɪnaɪ, 'dʒemɪnɪ] *n.* Zwillinge *Pl.*

gender ['dʒendə(r)] *n.* ⟨*Ling.*⟩ [grammatisches] Geschlecht

gene [dʒiːn] *n.* ⟨*Biol.*⟩ Gen, *das*

general ['dʒenrl] 1. *adj.* allgemein; weitverbreitet ⟨*Ansicht*⟩; ⟨*true of [nearly] all cases*⟩ allgemeingültig; un-

gefähr ⟨*Vorstellung, Beschreibung usw.*⟩; **the** ~ **public** weite Kreise der Bevölkerung; **in** ~ **use** allgemein verbreitet; **as a** ~ **rule**, **in** ~: im allgemeinen. 2. *n.* ⟨*Mil.*⟩ General, *der*. **general e'lection** *see* **election**

generalization [dʒenrəlaɪˈzeɪʃn] *n.* Verallgemeinerung, *die*

generalize ['dʒenrəlaɪz] 1. *v.t.* verallgemeinern. 2. *v.i.* ~ **about sth.** [etw.] verallgemeinern

generally ['dʒenrəlɪ] *adv.* a) allgemein; ~ **available** überall erhältlich; ~ **speaking** im allgemeinen; b) ⟨*usually*⟩ im allgemeinen

general prac'titioner *n.* ⟨*Med.*⟩ Arzt/Ärztin für Allgemeinmedizin

generate ['dʒenəreɪt] *v.t.* erzeugen (**from** aus); ⟨*result in*⟩ führen zu.

generation [dʒenəˈreɪʃn] *n.* a) Generation, *die*; b) ⟨*production*⟩ Erzeugung, *die*. **generator** ['dʒenəreɪtə(r)] *n.* Generator, *der*

generosity [dʒenəˈrɒsɪtɪ] *n.* Großzügigkeit, *die*

generous ['dʒenərəs] *adj.* großzügig; reichlich ⟨*Vorrat, Portion*⟩. '**generously** *adv.* großzügig

genetic [dʒɪˈnetɪk] *adj.* genetisch. **genetics** [dʒɪˈnetɪks] *n.* Genetik, *die*

Geneva [dʒɪˈniːvə] 1. *pr. n.* Genf ⟨*das*⟩. 2. *attrib. adj.* Genfer

genial ['dʒiːnɪəl] *adj.* freundlich

genitals ['dʒenɪtlz] *n. pl.* Geschlechtsorgane

genitive ['dʒenɪtɪv] *adj. & n.* [**case**] Genitiv, *der*

genius ['dʒiːnɪəs] *n.* a) ⟨*person*⟩ Genie, *das*; b) ⟨*ability*⟩ Talent, *das*

genre ['ʒɑ̃rə] *n.* Genre, *das*

gent [dʒent] *n.* a) ⟨*coll./joc.*⟩ Gent, *der* ⟨*iron.*⟩; b) **the G~s** ⟨*Brit. coll.*⟩ die Herrentoilette

genteel [dʒenˈtiːl] *adj.* vornehm

gentle ['dʒentl] *adj.*, ~**r** ['dʒentlə(r)], ~**st** ['dʒentlɪst] sanft; liebenswürdig ⟨*Person, Verhalten*⟩; leicht, schwach ⟨*Brise*⟩; leise ⟨*Geräusch*⟩; gemächlich ⟨*Spaziergang, Tempo*⟩; mäßig ⟨*Hitze*⟩

gentleman ['dʒentlmən] *n., pl.* **gentlemen** ['dʒentlmən] Herr, *der*; ⟨*well-mannered*⟩ Gentleman, *der*; **Ladies and Gentlemen!** meine Damen und Herren!

'**gentleness** *n.* Sanftheit, *die*; ⟨*of nature*⟩ Sanftmütigkeit, *die*

gently ['dʒentlɪ] *adv.* ⟨*tenderly*⟩ zart; zärtlich; ⟨*mildly*⟩ sanft; ⟨*carefully*⟩ behutsam; ⟨*quietly, softly*⟩ leise

genuine ['dʒenjʊɪn] *adj.* **a)** *(real)* echt; **b)** *(true)* aufrichtig; wahr ⟨Grund, Not⟩. **'genuinely** *adv.* wirklich

genus ['dʒiːnəs, 'dʒenəs] *n., pl.* **genera** ['dʒenərə] *(Biol.)* Gattung, *die*

geographical [dʒiːə'græfɪkl] *adj.* geographisch

geography [dʒɪ'ɒɡrəfɪ] *n.* Geographie, *die;* Erdkunde, *die (Schulw.)*

geological [dʒiːə'lɒdʒɪkl] *adj.* geologisch

geologist [dʒɪ'ɒlədʒɪst] *n.* Geologe, *der*/Geologin, *die*

geology [dʒɪ'ɒlədʒɪ] *n.* Geologie, *die*

geometric [dʒiːə'metrɪk], **geometrical** [dʒiːə'metrɪkl] *adj.* geometrisch

geometry [dʒɪ'ɒmɪtrɪ] *n.* Geometrie, *die*

geranium [dʒə'reɪnɪəm] *n.* Geranie, *die;* Pelargonie, *die*

geriatric [dʒerɪ'ætrɪk] *adj.* geriatrisch

germ [dʒɜːm] *n.* Keim, *der*

German ['dʒɜːmən] **1.** *adj.* deutsch; he/she is ~: er ist Deutscher/sie ist Deutsche. **2.** *n.* **a)** *(person)* Deutsche, *der/die;* **b)** *(language)* Deutsch, *das; see also* English 2 a

German Democratic Re'public *pr. n. (Hist.)* Deutsche Demokratische Republik

Germanic [dʒɜː'mænɪk] *adj.* germanisch

German 'measles *n.* Röteln *Pl.*

Germany ['dʒɜːmənɪ] *pr. n.* Deutschland *(das);* **Federal Republic of ~:** Bundesrepublik Deutschland, *die*

germinate ['dʒɜːmɪneɪt] *v. i.* keimen

gesticulate [dʒe'stɪkjʊleɪt] *v. i.* gestikulieren. **gesticulation** [dʒestɪkjʊ'leɪʃn] *n.* Gesten *Pl.*

gesture ['dʒestʃə(r)] *n.* Geste, *die*

get [get] **1.** *v. t.,* -tt-, got [gɒt], got *or (Amer.)* gotten ['gɒtn] **a)** *(obtain, receive)* bekommen; kriegen *(ugs.);* sich *(Dat.)* besorgen ⟨Visum, Genehmigung⟩; sich *(Dat.)* beschaffen ⟨Geld⟩; *(find)* finden ⟨Zeit⟩; *(fetch)* holen; *(buy)* kaufen; **where did you ~ that?** wo hast du das her?; ~ **sb. a job/taxi,** ~ **a job/taxi for sb.** jmdm. einen Job verschaffen/ein Taxi besorgen; ~ **oneself sth.** sich *(Dat.)* etw. zulegen; **b)** ~ **the bus** *etc. (be in time for, catch)* den Bus *usw.* erreichen *od. (ugs.)* nehmen; *(travel by)* den Bus *usw.* nehmen; **c)** *(prepare)* machen *(ugs.),* zubereiten ⟨Essen⟩; **d)** *(win)* bekommen; finden ⟨Anerkennung⟩; erzielen ⟨Tor, Punkt, Treffer⟩; gewinnen ⟨Spiel, Preis, Be-

lohnung⟩; ~ **permission** die Erlaubnis erhalten; **e)** finden ⟨Schlaf, Ruhe⟩; bekommen ⟨Einfall, Vorstellung, Gefühl, Kopfschmerzen, Grippe⟩; gewinnen ⟨Eindruck⟩; **f) have got** *(coll.: have)* haben; **have got a cold** eine Erkältung haben; **have got to do sth.** etw. tun müssen; **g)** *(succeed in placing, bringing, etc.)* bringen; kriegen *(ugs.);* ~ **a message to sb.** jmdm. eine Nachricht zukommen lassen; ~ **things going** *or* **started** die Dinge in Gang bringen; **h)** ~ **everything packed/prepared** alles [ein]packen/vorbereiten; ~ **sth. ready/done** etw. fertig machen; ~ **one's feet wet** nasse Füße kriegen; ~ **one's hands dirty** *(Dat.)* die Hände schmutzig machen; ~ **one's hair cut** sich die Haare schneiden lassen; ~ **sb. to do sth.** *(induce)* jmdn. dazu bringen, etw. zu tun; **i)** ~ **sb. [on the telephone]** jmdn. [telefonisch] erreichen; **j)** *(coll.) (understand)* kapieren *(ugs.); (hear)* mitkriegen *(ugs.). 2. v. i.,* -tt-, got, got *or (Amer.)* gotten **a)** *(succeed in coming or going)* kommen; ~ **to London before dark** London vor Einbruch der Dunkelheit erreichen; ~ **to be** *(coll.)* ~ **working** sich an die Arbeit machen; ~ **going** *or* **started** *(leave)* losgehen; *(become lively or operative)* in Schwung kommen; ~ **going on** *or* **with sth.** mit etw. anfangen; **c)** ~ **to know sb.** jmdn. kennenlernen; **d)** *(become)* werden; ~ **ready/washed** sich fertigmachen/waschen; ~ **frightened/hungry** Angst/Hunger kriegen. **get a'bout** *v. i.* **a)** *(travel)* herumkommen; **b)** ⟨Gerücht:⟩ sich verbreiten. **'get at** *v. t.* **a)** herankommen an (+ Akk.); **b)** *(find out)* [he]rausfinden ⟨Wahrheit usw.⟩; **what are you getting at?** worauf wollen Sie hinaus? **get a'way** *v. i.* **a)** *(leave)* wegkommen; **b)** *(escape)* entkommen. **get 'back 1.** *v. i.* zurückkommen; ~ **back home** nach Hause kommen. **2.** *v. t. (recover)* zurückkommen; ~ **one's own back** *(sl.)* sich rächen. **get 'by** *v. i.* **a)** vorbeikommen; **b)** *(coll.: manage)* über die Runden kommen *(ugs.).* **get 'down 1.** *v. i.* hinunter-/heruntersteigen; ~ **down to sth.** *(start)* sich an etw. *(Akk.)* machen. **2.** *v. t.* **a)** ~ **sb./sth. down** jmdn./etw. hinunter-/herunterbringen; **b)** *(coll.: depress)* fertigmachen *(ugs.).* **get in 1.** *v. i. (into bus etc.)* einsteigen; *(arrive)* ankommen. **2.** *v. t. (fetch)* reinholen. **get 'off 1.** *v. i.* **a)** *(alight)* aussteigen; *(dismount)* absteigen; b) *(leave)* [weg]gehen; c) *(escape punishment)* davonkommen. 2. *v. t.* a) *(remove)* ausziehen ⟨Kleidung usw.⟩; entfernen ⟨Fleck usw.⟩; abbekommen ⟨Deckel usw.⟩; b) aussteigen aus; absteigen von ⟨Fahrrad⟩; ~ **off** the subject vom Thema abkommen. **get 'on** *v. i.* a) *(mount)* aufsteigen; *(enter vehicle)* einsteigen; b) *(make progress)* vorankommen; **he's ~ting on well** es geht ihm gut; c) *(manage)* zurechtkommen. **get 'on with** a) b) ~ **on** [well] with sb. mit jmdm. [gut] auskommen. **get 'out 1.** *v. i.* a) rausgehen/rausfahren (of aus); b) *(alight)* aussteigen; c) *(escape)* ausbrechen (of aus); *(fig.)* herauskommen; ~ **out of** *(avoid)* herumkommen um *(ugs.)*. 2. *v. t.* a) *(cause to leave)* rausbringen; b) *(withdraw)* abheben ⟨Geld⟩ (of von). **get 'over** *v. t.* a) *(cross)* gehen über (+ Akk.); *(climb)* klettern über (+ Akk.); b) *(recover from)* überwinden; hinwegkommen über (+ Akk.). **get 'round** *v. i.* ~ **round to doing sth.** dazu kommen, etw. zu tun. **get 'through** *v. i.* durchkommen. **get 'up** *v. i.* aufstehen. **get 'up to** *v. t.* ~ **up to mischief** etwas anstellen

get: ~**away** *n.* Flucht, *die; attrib.* Flucht⟨plan, -wagen⟩ **make one's ~away** entkommen; ~**-up** *n. (coll.)* Aufmachung, *die*

geyser ['giːzə(r)] *n.* a) *(spring)* Geysir, *der;* b) *(Brit.)* Durchlauferhitzer, *der*

ghastly ['gɑːstlɪ] *adj.* grauenvoll; entsetzlich ⟨Verletzungen⟩; schrecklich ⟨Fehler⟩

gherkin ['gɜːkɪn] *n.* Essiggurke, *die*

ghetto ['getəʊ] *n., pl.* ~**s** Getto, *das*

ghost [gəʊst] *n.* Geist, *der;* Gespenst, *das.* **'ghostly** *adj.* gespenstisch

giant ['dʒaɪənt] **1.** *n.* Riese, *der.* **2.** *attrib. adj.* riesig

gibberish ['dʒɪbərɪʃ] *n.* Kauderwelsch, *das*

gibe [dʒaɪb] *n.* Stichelei, *die*

giblets ['dʒɪblɪts] *n. pl.* [Geflügel]klein, *das*

giddiness ['gɪdɪnɪs] *n.* Schwindel, *der*

giddy ['gɪdɪ] *adj.* schwind[e]lig

gift [gɪft] *n.* a) Geschenk, *das;* **make sb. a ~ of sth., make a ~ of sth. to sb.** jmdm. etw. schenken; **a ~ box/pack** eine Geschenkpackung; b) *(talent)* Begabung, *die;* **have a ~ for languages/ mathematics** sprachbegabt/mathema-

tisch begabt sein. **'gifted** *adj.* begabt (**in, at** für). **'gift-wrap** *v. t.* als Geschenk einpacken

gigantic [dʒaɪˈgæntɪk] *adj.* gigantisch; riesig; enorm ⟨Verbesserung, Appetit⟩

giggle ['gɪgl] **1.** *n.* Kichern, *das.* **2.** *v. i.* kichern

gild [gɪld] *v. t.* vergolden

gill [gɪl] *n.* Kieme, *die*

gilt [gɪlt] **1.** *n.* Goldauflage, *die; (paint)* Goldfarbe, *die.* **2.** *adj.* vergoldet

gimmick ['gɪmɪk] *n. (coll.)* Gag, *der*

gin [dʒɪn] *n.* Gin, *der*

ginger ['dʒɪndʒə(r)] *n.* a) Ingwer, *der;* b) *(colour)* Rötlichgelb, *das.* **ginger 'beer** *n.* Ingwerbier, *das.* **'ginger-bread** *n.* Pfefferkuchen, *der*

gingerly ['dʒɪndʒəlɪ] *adv.* vorsichtig

gipsy *see* gypsy

giraffe [dʒɪˈrɑːf] *n.* Giraffe, *die*

girder ['gɜːdə(r)] *n.* Träger, *der*

girdle ['gɜːdl] *n.* Hüfthalter, *der*

girl [gɜːl] *n.* Mädchen, *das; (teenager)* junges Mädchen. **'girl-friend** *n.* Freundin, *die.* **'girlish** *adj.* mädchenhaft

giro ['dʒaɪərəʊ] *n.* a) Giro, *das; attrib.* Giro-; **bank ~:** Giroverkehr, *der;* b) *(coll.: cheque)* Scheck, *der*

girth [gɜːθ] *n.* a) Umfang, *der;* b) *(for horse)* Bauchgurt, *der*

gismo ['gɪzməʊ] *n. (sl.)* Ding, *das (ugs.)*

gist [dʒɪst] *n.* Wesentliche, *das; (of tale, question, etc.)* Kern, *der*

give [gɪv] **1.** *v. t.,* gave [geɪv], given ['gɪvn] a) geben (**to** *Dat.*); b) *(as gift)* schenken; ~ **sb. sth.,** ~ **sth. to sb.** jmdm. etw. schenken; ~ **and take** *(fig.)* Kompromisse eingehen; c) *(assign)* aufgeben ⟨Hausaufgaben usw.⟩; *(grant, award, offer, allow to have)* geben; verleihen ⟨Preis, Titel usw.⟩; lassen ⟨Wahl, Zeit⟩; verleihen ⟨Gewicht, Nachdruck⟩; bereiten, machen ⟨Freude, Mühe, Kummer⟩; bieten ⟨Schutz⟩; leisten ⟨Hilfe⟩; gewähren ⟨Unterstützung⟩; be ~ **n sth.** etw. bekommen; ~**n that** *(because)* da; *(if)* wenn; ~ **sb. hope** jmdm. Hoffnung machen; d) *(tell)* angeben ⟨Namen, Anschrift, Alter, Grund⟩; nennen ⟨Einzelheiten⟩; geben ⟨Rat, Befehl, Anweisung, Antwort⟩; fällen ⟨Urteil, Entscheidung⟩; sagen ⟨Meinung⟩; bekanntgeben ⟨Nachricht⟩; ~ **him my best wishes** richte ihm meine besten Wünsche aus; e) *(perform, sing, etc.)* geben ⟨Vorstellung, Konzert⟩; halten

⟨Vortrag, Seminar⟩; **f)** (produce) geben ⟨Licht, Milch⟩; ergeben ⟨Zahlen, Resultat⟩; **g)** (make, show) geben ⟨Zeichen, Stoß, Tritt⟩; machen ⟨Satz, Ruck⟩; ausstoßen ⟨Schrei, Seufzer, Pfiff⟩; ~ sb. **a** [friendly] look jmdm. einen [freundlichen] Blick zuwerfen; **h)** (inflict) versetzen ⟨Schlag, Stoß⟩; **sth. ~s me a headache** von etw. bekomme ich Kopfschmerzen; **i)** geben ⟨Party, Essen usw.⟩. **2.** v.i. **gave, given** (yield) nachgeben ⟨Knie:⟩ weich werden; ⟨Bett:⟩ federn. **3.** n. Nachgiebigkeit, die; (elasticity) Elastizität, die. **give a'way** v.t. **a)** verschenken; **b)** (in marriage) dem Bräutigam zuführen; **c)** (betray) verraten. **give 'back** v.t. zurückgeben. **give in 1.** [--] v.t. abgeben. **2.** [-'-] v.i. nachgeben (**to** Dat.). **give 'off** v.t. ausströmen ⟨Geruch⟩; aussenden ⟨Strahlen⟩. **give 'up 1.** v.t. aufgeben. **2.** v.t. aufgeben; widmen ⟨Zeit⟩; ~ **sth. up** (abandon habit) sich ⟨Dat.⟩ etw. abgewöhnen; ~ **oneself up** sich stellen. **give 'way** v.i. **a)** (yield) nachgeben; **b)** (in traffic) ~ **way** [to traffic from the right] [dem Rechtsverkehr] die Vorfahrt lassen; **'G~ Way** „Vorfahrt beachten"; **c)** (collapse) einstürzen

given see **give** 1, 2
gizmo see **gismo**
glacier ['glæsɪə(r)] n. Gletscher, der
glad [glæd] adj. froh; **be ~ of sth.** über etw. (Akk.) froh sein; für etw. dankbar sein. **gladden** ['glædn] v.t. erfreuen
glade [gleɪd] n. Lichtung, die
'gladly adv. gern
glamor (Amer.) see **glamour**
glamorous ['glæmərəs] adj. glanzvoll; glamourös ⟨Filmstar⟩
glamour ['glæmə(r)] n. Glanz, der; (of person) Ausstrahlung, die
glance [glɑːns] **1.** n. Blick, der. **2.** v.i. blicken; ~ **at sb./sth.** jmdn./etw. anblicken; ~ **at one's watch** auf seine Uhr blicken; ~ **at the newspaper** etc. einen Blick in die Zeitung usw. werfen; ~ **round** [the room] sich [im Zimmer] umsehen
gland [glænd] n. Drüse, die. **glandular** ['glændjʊlə(r)] adj. Drüsen-
glare [gleə(r)] **1.** n. **a)** grelles Licht; **b)** (hostile look) feindseliger Blick; **with a** ~: feindselig. **2.** v.i. (glower) [finster] starren; ~ **at sb./sth.** jmdn./etw. anstarren. **glaring** ['gleərɪŋ] adj. grell; (fig.: conspicuous) schreiend; grob ⟨Fehler⟩; kraß ⟨Gegensatz⟩

glass [glɑːs] n. **a)** (substance) Glas, das; **pieces of/broken** ~: Glasscherben Pl.; (smaller) Glassplitter Pl.; **b)** (drinking ~) Glas, das; **a ~ of milk** ein Glas Milch; **c)** (pane) [Glas]scheibe, die; **d)** in pl. (spectacles) [a pair of] ~es eine Brille. **'glassy** adj. gläsern
glaze [gleɪz] **1.** n. Glasur, die. **2.** v.t. **a)** glasieren; **b)** (fit with glass) verglasen. **glazier** ['gleɪzɪə(r)] n. Glaser, der
gleam [gliːm] **1.** n. Schein, der; (fainter) Schimmer, der; ~ **of hope** Hoffnungsschimmer, der. **2.** v.i. ⟨Licht:⟩ scheinen; ⟨Fußboden, Stiefel:⟩ glänzen; ⟨Zähne:⟩ blitzen; ⟨Augen:⟩ leuchten. **'gleaming** adj. glänzend
glean [gliːn] v.t. zusammentragen ⟨Informationen usw.⟩; ~ **sth. from sth.** einer Sache (Dat.) etw. entnehmen
glee [gliː] n. Freude, die; (gloating joy) Schadenfreude, die. **gleeful** ['gliːfl] adj. freudig; (gloating) schadenfroh
glen [glen] n. [schmales] Tal
glib [glɪb] adj. aalglatt ⟨Person⟩; leicht dahingesagt ⟨Antwort⟩
glide [glaɪd] v.i. gleiten; (through the air) schweben. **'glider** n. Segelflugzeug, das
glimmer ['glɪmə(r)] **1.** n. Schimmer, der (**of** von); (of fire) Glimmen, das. **2.** v.i. glimmen
glimpse [glɪmps] **1.** n. [kurzer] Blick; **catch** or **have** or **get a ~ of sb./sth.** jmdn./etw. [kurz] zu sehen bekommen. **2.** v.t. flüchtig sehen
glint [glɪnt] **1.** n. Schimmer, der. **2.** v.i. blinken; glitzern
glisten ['glɪsn] v.i. glitzern
glitter ['glɪtə(r)] **1.** v.i. glitzern; ⟨Juwelen, Sterne:⟩ funkeln. **2.** n. Glitzern, das; (of diamonds) Funkeln, das
gloat [gləʊt] v.i. ~ **over sth.** sich hämisch über etw. (Akk.) freuen
global ['gləʊbl] adj. weltweit; ~ **warming** globaler Temperaturanstieg
globe [gləʊb] n. **a)** Kugel, die; **b)** (Globus, der; **c)** (world) **the** ~: der Globus; der Erdball
gloom [gluːm] n. **a)** (darkness) Dunkel, das (geh.); **b)** (despondency) düstere Stimmung. **'gloomy** adj. **a)** düster; finster; **b)** (depressing) düster; (depressed) trübsinnig ⟨Person⟩
glorify ['glɔːrɪfaɪ] v.t. verherrlichen; **a glorified messenger-boy** ein besserer Botenjunge
glorious ['glɔːrɪəs] adj. **a)** (illustrious) ruhmreich ⟨Held, Sieg⟩; **b)** (delightful) wunderschön; herrlich

glory ['glɔːrɪ] **1.** *n.* **a)** *(splendour)* Schönheit, *die; (majesty)* Herrlichkeit, *die;* **b)** *(fame)* Ruhm, *der.* **2.** *v.i.* ~ **in** sth. *(be proud of)* sich einer Sache *(Gen.)* rühmen

gloss [glɒs] *n.* Glanz, *der;* ~ **paint** Lackfarbe, *die.* '**gloss over** *v.t.* bemänteln; beschönigen ⟨*Fehler*⟩

glossary ['glɒsərɪ] *n.* Glossar, *das*

'**glossy** *adj.* glänzend

glove [glʌv] *n.* Handschuh, *der.* '**glove compartment** *n.* Handschuhfach, *das*

glow [gləʊ] *v.i.* **a)** glühen; ⟨*Lampe, Leuchtfarbe:*⟩ schimmern, leuchten; **b)** *(fig.) (with warmth or pride)* ⟨*Gesicht, Wangen:*⟩ glühen (with vor + *Dat.*); *(with health or vigour)* strotzen (with vor + *Dat.*)

glower ['glaʊə(r)] *v.i.* finster dreinblicken; ~ **at sb.** jmdn. finster anstarren

'**glowing** *adj.* glühend; begeistert ⟨*Bericht*⟩

'**glow-worm** *n.* Glühwürmchen, *das*

glucose ['gluːkəʊz] *n.* Glucose, *die*

glue [gluː] **1.** *n.* Klebstoff, *der.* **2.** *v.t.* kleben; ~ **sth. to sth.** etw. an etw. *(Dat.)* an- od. festkleben

glum [glʌm] *adj.* verdrießlich

glut [glʌt] *n.* Überangebot, *das* (of an, von + *Dat.*)

glutton ['glʌtən] *n.* Vielfraß, *der (ugs.);* **a** ~ **for punishment** *(iron.)* ein Masochist *(fig.).* '**gluttony** ['glʌtənɪ] *n.* Gefräßigkeit, *die*

glycerine ['glɪsəriːn] *(Amer.:* **glycerin** ['glɪsərɪn]) *n.* Glyzerin, *die*

GMT *abbr.* Greenwich Mean Time GMT; WEZ

gnarled [nɑːld] *adj.* knorrig; knotig ⟨*Hand*⟩

gnash [næʃ] *v.t.* ~ **one's teeth** mit den Zähnen knirschen

gnat [næt] *n.* [Stech]mücke, *die*

gnaw [nɔː] **1.** *v.i.* ~ [**away**] **at sth.** an etw. *(Dat.)* nagen. **2.** *v.t.* nagen an (+ *Dat.*); abnagen ⟨*Knochen*⟩

gnome [nəʊm] *n.* Gnom, *der*

go [gəʊ] **1.** *v.i., pres.* **he goes** [gəʊz], *p.t.* **went** [went], *pres. p.* **going** ['gəʊɪŋ], *p.p.* **gone** [gɒn] **a)** *(gen.) (Fahrzeug:)* fahren; ⟨*Flugzeug:*⟩ fliegen; ⟨*Vierfüßler:*⟩ laufen; *(on horseback etc.)* reiten; *(in lift)* fahren; *(on outward journey)* weg-, abfahren; *(travel regularly:) (Verkehrsmittel:)* verkehren (**from ... to** zwischen + *Dat.* ... und); **go by** bicycle/car/bus/train or rail/boat or sea

or ship mit dem [Fahr]rad/Auto/Bus/Zug/Schiff fahren; **go by plane** *or* **air** fliegen; **go on foot** zu Fuß gehen; laufen *(ugs.);* **go on a journey** verreisen; **have far to go** es weit haben; **go to the toilet/cinema/a museum** auf die Toilette/ins Kino/ins Museum gehen; **go to the doctor's|** *etc.* zum Arzt *usw.* gehen; **go bathing** baden gehen; **go cycling** radfahren; **go to see sb.** jmdn. aufsuchen; **go and see whether ...:** nachsehen [gehen], ob ...; **I'll go!** ich geh schon!; *(answer phone)* ich geh ran *od.* nehme ab; *(answer door)* ich mache auf; **b)** *(start)* losgehen; *(in vehicle)* losfahren; **c)** *(pass, circulate)* gehen; **a shiver went up** *or* **down my spine** ein Schauer lief mir über den Rücken; **go to** *(be given to)* ⟨*Preis, Gelder, Job:*⟩ gehen an (+ *Akk.*); ⟨*Titel, Besitz:*⟩ übergehen auf (+ *Akk.*); **go towards** *(be of benefit to)* zugute kommen (+ *Dat.*); **d)** *(act, function effectively)* gehen; ⟨*Mechanismus, Maschine:*⟩ laufen; **keep going** *(in movement)* weitergehen/-fahren; *(in activity)* weitermachen; *(not fail)* sich aufrecht halten; **keep sth. going** etw. in Gang halten; **make sth. go, get/set sth. going** etw. in Gang bringen; **e)** *(go to work)* zur Arbeit gehen; **go to school** in die Schule gehen; **go to a comprehensive school** auf eine Gesamtschule gehen; **f)** *(depart)* gehen; ⟨*Bus, Zug:*⟩ [ab]fahren; ⟨*Post:*⟩ rausgehen *(ugs.);* **g)** *(cease to function)* kaputtgehen; ⟨*Sicherung:*⟩ durchbrennen; *(break)* brechen; ⟨*Seil usw.:*⟩ reißen; **h)** *(disappear)* weggehen; ⟨*Mantel, Hut, Fleck:*⟩ verschwinden; ⟨*Geruch, Rauch:*⟩ sich verziehen; ⟨*Geld, Zeit:*⟩ draufgehen *(ugs.)* (**in, on** für); **i) to go** *(still remaining)* **have sth.** [**still**] **to go** [noch] etw. übrig haben; **one week** *etc.* **to go to ...:** noch eine Woche *usw.* bis ...; **there's hours to go** es dauert noch Stunden; **j)** *(be sold)* weggehen *(ugs.);* verkauft werden; **going! going! gone!** zum ersten! zum zweiten! zum dritten!; **go to sb.** an jmdn. gehen; **k)** *(run)* ⟨*Grenze, Straße usw.:*⟩ verlaufen, gehen; *(lead)* ⟨*Weg:*⟩ führen; *(extend)* reichen; **as** *or* **so far as he/it goes** soweit es; **l)** *(turn out, progress)* ⟨*Projekt, Interview, Abend:*⟩ verlaufen; **how did your holiday go?** wie war Ihr Urlaub?; **things have been going well/badly** in der letzten Zeit läuft alles gut/schief; **m)** *(be, have form or nature)* sein;

⟨*Sprichwort, Gedicht, Titel:*⟩ lauten; **that's the way it goes** so ist es nun mal; **go hungry** hungern; **go without food/water** es ohne Essen/Wasser aushalten; **n)** *(become)* werden; **the tyre has gone flat** der Reifen ist platt; **o)** *(have usual place)* kommen; *(belong)* gehören; **where does the box go?** wo kommt *od.* gehört die Kiste hin?; **p)** *(fit)* passen; **go in|to| sth.** in etw. *(Akk.)* gehen *od.* [hinein]passen; **go through sth.** durch etw. [hindurch]gehen; **q)** *(match)* passen (**with** zu); **r)** ⟨*Turmuhr, Gong:*⟩ schlagen; ⟨*Glocke:*⟩ läuten; **s)** *(coll.: be acceptable or permitted)* erlaubt sein; **it/that goes without saying** es/das ist doch selbstverständlich. See also **going** 2. **2.** *n., pl.* **goes** [gəʊz] *(coll.)* **a)** *(attempt, try)* Versuch, *der;* *(chance)* Gelegenheit, *die;* **have a go** es versuchen; **let me have a go/can I have a go?** laß mich [auch ein]mal/kann ich [auch ein]mal?; *(ugs.);* **it's 'my** go ich bin an der Reihe *od.* dran; **at one** go auf einmal; **at the first** go auf Anhieb; **b)** *(vigorous activity)* **it's all** go es ist alles eine einzige Hetzerei *(ugs.);* **be on the** go auf Trab sein *(ugs.);* **c)** *(success)* **make a** go **of sth.** mit etw. Erfolg haben. **go a'head** *v. i.* **a)** *(in advance)* vorausgehen (**of** *Dat.*); **b)** *(proceed)* weitermachen; *(make progress)* ⟨*Arbeit:*⟩ fortschreiten, vorangehen. **go a'way** *v. i.* weggehen; *(on holiday or business)* verreisen. **go 'back** *v. i.* zurückgehen/-fahren; *(restart)* ⟨*Schule, Fabrik:*⟩ wieder anfangen; *(fig.)* zurückgehen; **go back to the beginning** noch mal von vorne anfangen. **go by** **1.** [-'-] *v. t.* **go by sth.** sich nach etw. richten; *(adhere to)* sich an etw. *(Akk.)* halten. **2.** [-'-] *v. i.* ⟨*Zeit:*⟩ vergehen. **go 'down** *v. i.* hinuntergehen/-fahren; ⟨*Sonne:*⟩ untergehen; ⟨*Schiff:*⟩ untergehen; *(fall to ground)* ⟨*Flugzeug usw.:*⟩ abstürzen. **2.** *v. t.* **go for** *v. t.* **go for sb./sth.** *(go to fetch)* jmdn./etw. holen; *(apply to)* für jmdn./etw. gelten; *(like)* jmdn./etw. gut finden. **go in** *v. i.* hineingehen; reingehen *(ugs.).* **go 'off 1.** *v. i.* **a) go off with sb./sth.** sich mit jmdn./etw. auf- und davonmachen *(ugs.);* **b)** ⟨*Alarm, Schußwaffe:*⟩ losgehen; ⟨*Wecker:*⟩ klingeln; ⟨*Bombe:*⟩ hochgehen; **c)** *(turn bad)* schlecht werden; **d)** ⟨*Strom:*⟩ ausfallen. **2.** *v. t.* *(begin to dislike)* **go off sth.** von etw. abkommen. **go 'on** *v. i.* **a)** weitergehen/-fahren; **b)** *(continue)* weiterma-

chen; **c)** *(happen)* passieren. **go 'out** *v. i.* ausgehen; **go out to work/for a meal** arbeiten/essen gehen. **go over 1.** [-'--] *v. i.* hinübergehen. **2.** ['---, -'--] *v. t.* *(re-examine)* durchgehen. **go 'round** *v. i.* **a)** *(coll.)* **go round and** or **to see sb.** bei jmdm. vorbeigehen *(ugs.);* **b)** *(look round)* sich umschauen; **c)** *(suffice)* reichen; langen *(ugs.);* **d)** *(spin)* sich drehen. **go through 1.** [-'-] *v. i.* ⟨*Ernennung:*⟩ durchkommen; ⟨*Antrag:*⟩ durchgehen. **2.** [-'--] **a)** *(rehearse)* durchgehen; **b)** *(examine)* durchsehen; **c)** *(endure)* durchmachen. **go 'under** *v. i.* untergehen; *(fig.: fail)* eingehen. **go 'up** *v. i.* **a)** hinaufgehen/-fahren; ⟨*Ballon:*⟩ aufsteigen; *(Theatre)* ⟨*Vorhang:*⟩ aufgehen; ⟨*Lichter:*⟩ angehen; **b)** *(increase)* ⟨*Zahl:*⟩ wachsen; ⟨*Preis, Wert, Niveau:*⟩ steigen; *(in price)* ⟨*Ware:*⟩ teurer werden. **go without 1.** ['---] *v. t.* verzichten auf (+ *Akk.*). **2.** [--'-] *v. i.* verzichten

goad [gəʊd] *v. t.* ~ **sb. into sth./doing sth.** jmdn. zu etw. anstacheln/dazu anstacheln, etw. zu tun

'go-ahead 1. *adj.* unternehmungslustig; *(progressive)* fortschrittlich. **2.** *n.* **give sb./sth. the ~:** jmdn./einer Sache grünes Licht geben

goal [gəʊl] *n.* **a)** *(aim)* Ziel, *das;* **b)** *(Footb., Hockey)* Tor, *das;* **score/kick a ~:** einen Treffer erzielen. **'goalkeeper** *n.* Torwart, *der*

goat [gəʊt] *n.* Ziege, *die*

gobble ['gɒbl] **1.** *v. t.* ~ **[down** or **up]** hinunterschlingen. **2.** *v. i.* schlingen

'go-between *n.* Vermittler, *der*/Vermittlerin, *die*

goblet ['gɒblɪt] *n.* Kelchglas, *das*

goblin ['gɒblɪn] *n.* Kobold, *der*

god [gɒd] *n.* **a)** Gott, *der;* **b)** God *(Theol.)* Gott. **'godchild** *n.* Patenkind, *das.* **'god-daughter** *n.* Patentochter, *die*

goddess ['gɒdɪs] *n.* Göttin, *die*

god: ~father *n.* Pate, *der;* **G~forsaken** *adj.* gottverlassen; **~mother** *n.* Patentante, *die;* **~send** *n.* Gottesgabe, *die;* **a ~send to sb.** für jmdn. ein Geschenk des Himmels sein; **~son** *n.* Patensohn, *der*

goggles ['gɒglz] *n. pl.* Schutzbrille, *die*

going ['gəʊɪŋ] **1.** *n.* **a)** *(progress)* Vorankommen, *das;* **while the ~ is good** solange es noch geht. **2.** *adj.* **a)** *(available)* erhältlich; **there is sth. ~:** es gibt etw.; **b)** **be ~ to do sth.** etw. tun [werden/wollen; **I was ~ to say** ich wollte sagen; **it's ~ to snow** es wird schneien; **a ~ concern** eine gesunde Firma

goings-'on *n. pl.* Ereignisse

gold [gəʊld] **1.** *n.* Gold, *das.* **2.** *attrib. adj.* golden; Gold(münze, -kette usw.)

golden ['gəʊldn] *adj.* golden. **golden 'wedding** *n.* goldene Hochzeit

gold: **~fish** *n.* Goldfisch, *der;* **~ 'medal** *n.* Goldmedaille, *die;* **~mine** *n.* Goldmine, *die;* (*fig.*) Goldgrube, *die;* **~-'plated** *adj.* vergoldet; **~smith** *n.* Goldschmied, *der/*-schmiede, *die*

golf [gɒlf] *n.* Golf, *das*

golf: **~ ball** *n.* Golfball, *der;* **~-club** *n.* a) (*implement*) Golfschläger, *der;* b) (*association*) Golfclub, *der;* **~-course** *n.* Golfplatz, *der*

'golfer *n.* Golfer, *der/*Golferin, *die*

gondola ['gɒndələ] *n.* Gondel, *die*

gone [gɒn] **1.** *see* **go 2. 2.** *pred. adj.* a) (*away*) weg; **it's time you were ~** es ist *od.* wird Zeit, daß du gehst; b) (*of time: after*) nach; **it's ~ ten o'clock** es ist zehn Uhr vorbei

gong [gɒŋ] *n.* Gong, *der*

good [gʊd] **1.** *adj.,* **better** ['betə(r)], **best** [best] a) gut; günstig ⟨Gelegenheit, Angebot⟩; ausreichend ⟨Vorrat⟩; ausgiebig ⟨Mahl⟩; **as ~ as** so gut wie; **his ~ eye/leg** sein gesundes Auge/Bein; **in ~ time** frühzeitig; **all in ~ time** alles zu seiner Zeit; **be ~ at sth.** in etw. (*Dat.*) gut sein; **too ~ to be true** zu schön, um wahr zu sein; **apples are ~ for you** Äpfel sind gesund; **be too much of a ~ thing** zuviel des Guten sein; **~ times** eine schöne Zeit; **feel ~:** sich wohl fühlen; **take a ~ look round** sich gründlich umsehen; **give sb. a ~ beating/scolding** jmdm. tüchtig verprügeln/ausschimpfen; **~ afternoon/day** guten Tag!; **~ evening/morning** guten Abend/Morgen!; **~ night** gute Nacht!; b) (*enjoyable*) schön ⟨Leben, Urlaub, Wochenende⟩; **the ~ life** das angenehme[, sorglose] Leben; **have a ~ time!** viel Spaß!; **have a ~ journey!** gute Reise!; c) (*well-behaved*) gut; brav; **be ~!** sei brav *od.* lieb!; [**as**] **~ as gold** ganz artig *od.* brav; d) (*virtuous*) rechtschaffen; (*kind*) nett; gut ⟨Absicht, Wünsche, Benehmen, Tat⟩; **be ~ to sb.** zu jmdm. gut sein; **would you be so ~ as to** *or* **~ enough to do that?** wären Sie so freundlich *od.* nett, das zu tun?; **that/ it is ~ of you** das/es ist nett *od.* lieb

von dir; e) (*commendable*) gut; **~ for 'you** *etc.* (*coll.*) bravo!; f) (*attractive*) schön; gut ⟨Figur⟩; **look ~:** gut aussehen; g) (*considerable*) [recht] ansehnlich ⟨Menschenmenge⟩; ganz schön, ziemlich (*ugs.*) ⟨Entfernung, Strecke⟩; gut ⟨Preis, Erlös⟩; h) **make ~** (*succeed*) erfolgreich sein; (*compensate for*) wiedergutmachen; (*indemnify*) ersetzen. **2.** *n. a)* (*use*) Nutzen, *der;* **be some ~ to sb./sth.** jmdm./einer Sache nützen; **be no ~ to sb./sth.** für jmdn./etw. nicht zu gebrauchen sein; **it is no/not much ~ doing sth.** es hat keinen/kaum einen Sinn, etw. zu tun; **what's the ~ of ...?, what ~ is ...?** was nützt ...?; b) (*benefit*) **for your/his** *etc.* **own ~:** zu deinem/seinem *usw.* Besten; **do no/little ~:** nichts/wenig helfen *od.* nützen; **do sb./sth. ~:** jmdm./einer Sache nützen; ⟨Ruhe, Erholung:⟩ jmdm./einer Sache guttun; ⟨Arznei:⟩ jmdm./einer Sache helfen; c) (*goodness*) Gute, *das;* **be up to no ~:** nichts Gutes im Sinn haben; d) **for ~** (*finally*) ein für allemal; (*permanently*) für immer; e) *in pl.* (*wares etc.*) Waren; (*belongings*) Habe, *die;* (*Brit. Railw.*) Fracht, *die; attrib.* Güter⟨wagen, -zug⟩

good: **~'bye** (*Amer.:* **~'by**) *int.* auf Wiedersehen!; (*on telephone*) auf Wiederhören!; **~-for-nothing 1.** *adj.* nichtsnutzig; **2.** *n.* Taugenichts, *der;* **~-'looking** *adj.* gutaussehend

'goodness 1. *n.* Güte, *die.* **2.** *int.* [**my**] **~!** meine Güte! (*ugs.*)

good'will *n.* guter Wille; *attrib.* Goodwill(botschaft, -reise usw.)

'goody *n.* (*coll.: hero*) Gute, *der/die*

gooey ['gu:ɪ] *adj.,* **gooier** ['gu:ɪə(r)], **gooiest** ['gu:ɪɪst] (*coll.*) klebrig

goose [gu:s] *n., pl.* **geese** [gi:s] Gans, *die*

gooseberry ['gʊzbərɪ] *n.* Stachelbeere, *die*

'goose: **~-pimples** *n. pl.* **have ~-pimples** eine Gänsehaut haben

'gore [gɔ:(r)] *v.t.* [mit den Hörnern] aufspießen *od.* durchbohren

²gore *n.* Blut, *das*

gorge [gɔ:dʒ] **1.** *n.* Schlucht, *die.* **2.** *v.i. & refl.* **~ [oneself]** sich vollstopfen (*ugs.*) (**on** mit)

gorgeous ['gɔ:dʒəs] *adj.* prächtig; hinreißend ⟨Frau, Mann, Lächeln⟩

gorilla [gə'rɪlə] *n.* Gorilla, *der*

gormless ['gɔ:mlɪs] *adj.* (*Brit. coll.*) dämlich (*ugs.*)

gorse [gɔ:s] *n.* Stechginster, *der*

gory ['gɔ:rɪ] *adj. (fig.)* blutrünstig

gosh [gɒʃ] *int. (coll.)* Gott!

'go-slow *n. (Brit.)* Bummelstreik, *der*

gospel ['gɒspl] *n.* Evangelium, *das*

gossamer ['gɒsəmə(r)] *n.* Altweibersommer, *der; attrib.* hauchdünn

gossip ['gɒsɪp] 1. *n.* **a)** *(talk)* Klatsch, *der (ugs.);* **b)** *(person)* Klatschbase, *die (ugs.).* 2. *v.i.* klatschen *(ugs.)*

got *see* get

Gothic ['gɒθɪk] *adj.* gotisch

gotten *see* get

gouge [gaʊdʒ] *v.t.* aushöhlen

goulash ['gu:læʃ] *n.* Gulasch, *das od. der*

gourmet ['gʊəmeɪ] *n.* Gourmet, *der*

gout [gaʊt] *n.* Gicht, *die*

govern ['gʌvn] 1. *v.t.* **a)** regieren ⟨*Land, Volk*⟩; verwalten ⟨*Provinz*⟩; **b)** *(dictate)* bestimmen. 2. *v.i.* regieren

governess ['gʌvənɪs] *n.* Gouvernante, *die (veraltet);* Hauslehrerin, *die*

government ['gʌvnmənt] *n.* Regierung, *die; attrib.* Regierungs-

governor ['gʌvənə(r)] *n.* **a)** *(of province etc.)* Gouverneur, *der;* **b)** *(of institution)* Direktor, *der/*Direktorin, *die;* **[board of]** ~s Vorstand, *der;* **c)** *(sl.: employer)* Boß, *der (ugs.)*

gown [gaʊn] *n.* **a)** [elegantes] Kleid; **b)** *(official or uniform robe)* Talar, *der*

GP *abbr.* general practitioner

grab [græb] 1. *v.t.,* -**bb**- greifen nach; *(seize)* packen; ~ **the chance** die Gelegenheit ergreifen; ~ **hold of sb./sth.** sich ⟨*Dat.*⟩ jmdn./etw. schnappen *(ugs.).* 2. *v.i.,* -**bb**-: ~ **at sth.** nach etw. greifen. 3. *n.* **make a** ~ **at** *or* **for sb./ sth.** nach jmdm./etw. greifen

grace [greɪs] *n.* **a)** *(charm)* Anmut, *die (geh.);* **b)** *(decency)* **have the** ~ **to do sth.** so anständig sein und etw. tun; **c)** *(delay)* Frist, *die;* **give sb. a day's** ~: jmdm. einen Tag Aufschub gewähren; **d)** *(prayers)* **say** ~: das Tischgebet sprechen. **graceful** ['greɪsfl] *adj.* elegant; graziös ⟨*Bewegung, Eleganz*⟩

gracious ['greɪʃəs] 1. *adj.* **a)** liebenswürdig; **b)** *(merciful)* gnädig. 2. *int.* **good** ~! [ach] du meine Güte!

grade [greɪd] 1. *n.* **a)** Rang, *der; (Mil.)* Dienstgrad, *der;* **b)** *(position)* Stufe, *die;* **c)** *(Amer. Sch.: class)* Klasse, *die;* **d)** *(Sch., Univ.: mark)* Note, *die;* Zensur, *die.* 2. *v.t.* **a)** einstufen ⟨*Schüler*⟩; [nach Größe/Qualität] sortieren ⟨*Eier, Kartoffeln*⟩; **b)** *(mark)* benoten

gradient ['greɪdɪənt] *n. (ascent)* Steigung, *die; (descent)* Gefälle, *das*

gradual ['grædʒʊəl] *adj.,* '**gradually** *adv.* allmählich

graduate 1. ['grædʒʊət] *n.* Graduierte, *der/die; (who has left university)* Akademiker, *der/*Akademikerin, *die;* **university** ~: Hochschulabsolvent, *der/*-absolventin, *die.* 2. ['grædʒʊeɪt] *v.i.* einen akademischen Grad/Titel erwerben; *(Amer. Sch.)* die [Schul]abschlußprüfung bestehen (**from** an + *Dat.*)

graffiti [grə'fi:ti:] *n. sing. or pl.* Graffiti *Pl.*

graft [grɑ:ft] 1. *n.* **a)** *(Bot.)* Edelreis, *das;* **b)** *(Med.) (operation)* Transplantation, *die; (thing ~ed)* Transplantat, *das;* **c)** *(Brit. sl.: work)* Plackerei, *die (ugs.).* 2. *v.t.* **a)** *(Bot.)* pfropfen; **b)** *(Med.)* transplantieren. 3. *v.i. (Brit. sl.)* schuften *(ugs.)*

grain [greɪn] *n.* **a)** Korn, *das; collect.* Getreide, *das;* **b)** *(particle)* Korn, *das;* **c)** *(in wood)* Maserung, *die; (in paper)* Faser, *die; (in leather)* Narbung, *die;* **go against the** ~ **[for sb.]** *(fig.)* jmdm. gegen den Strich gehen *(ugs.).* '**grainy** *adj.* körnig; gemasert ⟨*Holz*⟩; genarbt ⟨*Leder*⟩

gram [græm] *n.* Gramm, *das*

grammar ['græmə(r)] *n.* Grammatik, *die.* '**grammar book** *n.* Grammatik, *die.* '**grammar school** *n. (Brit.)* ≈ Gymnasium, *das*

grammatical [grə'mætɪkl] *adj.* **a)** grammat[ikal]isch richtig *od.* korrekt; **b)** *(of grammar)* grammatisch. **grammatically** [grə'mætɪkəlɪ] *adv.* grammati[kal]isch ⟨*richtig, falsch*⟩

gramme *see* gram

gramophone ['græməfəʊn] *n.* Plattenspieler, *der*

granary ['grænərɪ] *n.* Getreidesilo, *der od. das;* Kornspeicher, *der*

grand [grænd] *adj.* **a)** *(most or very important)* groß; ~ **finale** großes Finale; **b)** *(splendid)* grandios; **c)** *(coll.: excellent)* großartig

grand: ~**child** *n.* Enkel, *der/*Enkelin, *die;* Enkelkind, *das;* ~~-**dad[dy]** ['grændæd(ɪ)] *n. (coll./child lang.);* Opa, *der (Kinderspr./ugs.);* ~~**daughter** *n.* Enkelin, *die*

grandeur ['grændʒə(r), 'grændjə(r)] *n.* Erhabenheit, *die*

'**grandfather** *n.* Großvater, *der;* ~ **clock** *n.* Standuhr, *die*

grandiose ['grændɪəʊs] *adj.* grandios; *(pompous)* bombastisch

grand: ~**ma** *n. (coll./child lang.)* Oma,

die (Kinderspr./ugs.); ~**mother** *n.* Großmutter, *die;* ~**pa** *n. (coll./child lang.)* Opa, *der (Kinderspr./ugs.);* ~**parent** *n. (male)* Großvater, *der; (female)* Großmutter, *die;* ~**parents** Großeltern *Pl.;* ~ **pi'ano** *n.* [Konzert]flügel, *der;* ~**son** *n.* Enkel, *der;* ~**stand** *n.* [Haupt]tribüne, *die*

granite ['grænɪt] *n.* Granit, *der*

granny ['grænɪ] *n. (coll./child lang.)* Oma, *die (Kinderspr./ugs.)*

grant [grɑ:nt] **1.** *v. t.* **a)** erfüllen *⟨Wunsch⟩;* stattgeben (+ *Dat.*) *⟨Gesuch⟩;* **b)** *(concede, give)* gewähren; geben *⟨Zeit⟩;* bewilligen *⟨Geldmittel⟩;* zugestehen *⟨Recht⟩;* erteilen *⟨Erlaubnis⟩;* **c)** *(in argument)* zugeben; **take sb./sth. for** ~**ed** sich *(Dat.)* jmds. sicher sein/etw. für selbstverständlich halten. **2.** *n.* Zuschuß, *der; (financial aid [to student])* [Studien]beihilfe, *die; (scholarship)* Stipendium, *das*

granulated sugar [grænjʊleɪtɪd ˈʃʊgə(r)] *n.* Kristallzucker, *der*

granule ['grænju:l] *n.* Körnchen, *das*

grape [greɪp] *n.* Weintraube, *die;* **a bunch of** ~**s** eine Traube

'grapefruit *n., pl. same* Grapefruit, *die*

graph [grɑ:f] *n.* graphische Darstellung; ~ **paper** Diagrammpapier, *das*

graphic ['græfɪk] *adj.* **a)** graphisch; **b)** *(vivid)* plastisch; anschaulich. **graphically** ['græfɪkəlɪ] *adv.* **a)** *(vividly)* plastisch; **b)** *(using graphics)* graphisch.

graphics ['græfɪks] *n. (use of diagrams)* graphische Darstellung; **computer** ~: Computergraphik, *die*

grapple ['græpl] *v. i.* handgemein werden; ~ **with** *(fig.)* sich auseinandersetzen mit

grasp [grɑ:sp] **1.** *v. i.* ~ **at** ergreifen; sich stürzen auf (+ *Akk.*) *⟨Angebot⟩.* **2.** *v. t.* **a)** *(seize)* ergreifen; **b)** *(hold firmly)* festhalten; **c)** *(understand)* verstehen; erfassen *⟨Bedeutung⟩.* **3.** *n.* **a)** *(firm hold)* Griff, *der;* **b)** *(mental ~)* **have a good** ~ **of sth.** etw. gut beherrschen. **grasping** *adj.* habgierig

grass [grɑ:s] *n.* **a)** Gras, *das;* **b)** *(lawn)* Rasen, *der;* **c)** *(Brit. sl.: police informer)* Spitzel, *der.* **'grasshopper** *n.* Grashüpfer, *der.* **'grass-root[s]** *attrib. adj. (Polit.)* Basis-

¹grate [greɪt] *n.* Rost, *der; (recess)* Kamin, *der*

²grate *v. t.* **a)** reiben; *(less finely)* raspeln; **b)** *(grind)* ~ **one's teeth** mit den Zähnen knirschen

grateful ['greɪtfl] *adj.* dankbar (**to** *Dat.*). **'gratefully** *adv.* dankbar

'grater *n.* Reibe, *die;* Raspel, *die*

gratify ['grætɪfaɪ] *v. t.* freuen; **be gratified by or with or at sth.** über etw. *(Akk.)* erfreut sein. **'gratifying** *adj.* erfreulich

grating ['greɪtɪŋ] *n.* Gitter, *das*

gratitude ['grætɪtju:d] *n.* Dankbarkeit, *die* (**to** gegenüber)

gratuitous [grə'tju:ɪtəs] *adj. (motiveless)* grundlos

gratuity [grə'tju:ɪtɪ] *n.* Trinkgeld, *das*

¹grave [greɪv] *n.* Grab, *das*

²grave *adj.* **a)** *(important, solemn)* ernst; **b)** *(serious)* schwer *⟨Fehler, Irrtum⟩;* ernst *⟨Situation, Lage⟩;* groß *⟨Gefahr⟩;* schlimm *⟨Nachricht⟩*

'grave-digger *n.* Totengräber, *der*

gravel ['grævl] *n.* Kies, *der*

grave: ~**stone** *n.* Grabstein, *der;* ~**yard** *n.* Friedhof, *der*

gravity ['grævɪtɪ] *n.* **a)** *(of mistake, offence)* Schwere, *die; (of situation)* Ernst, *der;* **b)** *(Phys., Astron.)* Gravitation, *die;* Schwerkraft, *die*

gravy ['greɪvɪ] *n.* **a)** *(juices)* Bratensaft, *der;* **b)** *(dressing)* [Braten]soße, *die*

gray *etc. (Amer.) see* grey *etc.*

'graze [greɪz] *v. i.* grasen; weiden

²graze *n.* Schürfwunde, *die.* **2.** *v. t.* **a)** *(touch lightly)* streifen; **b)** *(scrape)* abschürfen *⟨Haut⟩;* zerkratzen *⟨Oberfläche⟩*

grease [gri:s] **1.** *n.* Fett, *das; (lubricant)* Schmierfett, *das.* **2.** *v. t.* einfetten; *(lubricate)* schmieren. **grease-proof** *adj.* fettdicht; ~ **paper** Pergament- *od.* Butterbrotpapier, *das*

greasy ['gri:sɪ] *adj.* fettig; fett *⟨Essen⟩; (lubricated)* geschmiert; *(dirty with lubricant)* schmierig

great [greɪt] *adj.* **a)** groß; **a** ~ **many** sehr viele; sehr gut *⟨Freund⟩; (impressive; coll.: splendid)* großartig; **be a** ~ **one for sth.** etw. sehr gern tun; **b)** Groß⟨onkel, -tante, -neffe, -nichte⟩; Ur⟨großmutter, -großvater, -enkel, -enkelin⟩. **Great 'Britain** *pr. n.* Großbritannien *(das).* **'greatly** *adv.* sehr; höchst *⟨verärgert⟩;* stark *⟨beeinflußt⟩;* bedeutend *⟨verbessert⟩.* **'greatness** *n.* Größe, *die*

Greece [gri:s] *pr. n.* Griechenland *(das)*

greed [gri:d] *n.* Gier, *die* (**for** nach); *(gluttony)* Gefräßigkeit, *die.* **'greedy** *adj.* gierig; *(gluttonous)* gefräßig

Greek [gri:k] **1.** *adj.* griechisch; **sb. is**

~: jmd. ist Grieche/Griechin. 2. *n.* **a)**
(person) Grieche, *der/*Griechin, *die;*
b) *(language)* Griechisch, *das; see also*
English 2 a

green [griːn] **1.** *adj.* **a)** grün; *(en-
vironmentally safe)* ökologisch; *c)*
(gullible) naiv; *(inexperienced)* grün;
d) *(Polit.)* G~: grün; **the G~s** die Grünen. **2.** *n.* **a)** *(colour)* Grün, *das;* **b)**
(piece of land) Grünfläche, *die;* **village
~:** Dorfanger, *der;* **c)** *in pl.* (~ *vegetables)* Grüngemüse, *das.* '**green belt**
n. Grüngürtel, *der.* **green ʼcard** *n.*
(Motor Veh.) grüne Karte

greenery [ˈgriːnərɪ] *n.* Grün, *das*

green: **~fly** *n. (Brit.)* grüne Blattlaus;
~gage [ˈgriːngeɪdʒ] *n.* Reineclaude,
die; **~grocer** *n. (Brit.)* Obst- und Ge-
müsehändler, *der/*-händlerin, *die;*
~house *n.* Gewächshaus, *das;* **~-
house effect** Treibhauseffekt, *der*

Greenland [ˈgriːnlənd] *pr. n.* Grönland *(das)*

'**Green Party** *n. (Polit.)* die Grünen

greet [griːt] *v. t.* begrüßen; *(in passing)*
grüßen; *(receive)* empfangen. '**greeting** *n.* Begrüßung, *die; (in passing)*
Gruß, *der; (words)* Grußformel, *die.*
'**greetings card** *n.* Grußkarte, *die;
(for birthday)* Glückwunschkarte, *die*

gregarious [grɪˈgeərɪəs] *adj.* gesellig

grenade [grɪˈneɪd] *n.* Granate, *die*

grew *see* **grow**

grey [greɪ] **1.** *adj.* grau. **2.** *n.* Grau,
das. '**greyhound** *n.* Windhund, *der*

grid [grɪd] *n.* **a)** *(grating)* Rost, *der;* **b)**
(of lines) Gitter[netz], *das;* **c)** *(for supply)* Versorgungsnetz, *das*

grief [griːf] *n.* Kummer, *der* (**over, at**
über + *Akk.,* um); *(at loss of sb.)*
Trauer, *die* (for um); **come to ~** *(fail)*
scheitern

grievance [ˈgriːvəns] *n. (complaint)*
Beschwerde, *die; (grudge)* Groll, *der*

grieve [griːv] **1.** *v. t.* betrüben; bekümmern. **2.** *v. i.* trauern (for um)

grievous [ˈgriːvəs] *adj.* schwer *(Verwundung, Krankheit)*

'**grill** [grɪl] **1.** *v. t. (cook)* grillen; *(fig.:
question)* in die Mangel nehmen
(ugs.). **2.** *n.* **a)** **mixed ~:** gemischte
Grillplatte; **b)** *(on cooker)* Grill, *der*

grille (²**grill**) *n.* Gitter, *das;* **b)**
(Motor Veh.) [Kühler]grill, *der*

grim [grɪm] *adj.* *(stern)* streng; grimmig *(Lächeln, Schweigen); (unrelent-
ing)* erbittert *(Widerstand, Kampf);
(ghastly)* grauenvoll *(Aufgabe, Nachricht);* trostlos *(Aussichten)*

grimace [grɪˈmeɪs] **1.** *n.* Grimasse, *die.*
2. *v. i.* Grimassen schneiden; **~ with
pain** vor Schmerz das Gesicht verziehen

grime [graɪm] *n.* Schmutz, *der.* **grimy**
[ˈgraɪmɪ] *adj.* schmutzig

grin [grɪn] **1.** *n.* Grinsen, *das.* **2.** *v. i.,
-nn-* grinsen; **~ at sb.** jmdn. angrinsen

grind [graɪnd] **1.** *v. t.,* **ground** [graʊnd]
a) ~ [up] zermahlen; mahlen *(Kaffee,
Pfeffer, Getreide);* **b)** *(sharpen)* schleifen *(Schere, Messer);* schärfen
(Klinge); **c)** *(rub harshly)* zerquetschen; **~ one's teeth** mit den Zähnen
knirschen. **2.** *v. i.,* **ground:** **~ to a halt**
(Fahrzeug:) quietschend zum Stehen
kommen; *(fig.) (Verkehr:)* zum Erliegen kommen. **3.** *n. (coll.)* Plackerei,
die (ugs.). '**grinder** *n.* Schleifmaschi-
ne, *die; (coffee~ etc.)* Mühle, *die.*
'**grindstone** *n.* Schleifstein, *der*

grip [grɪp] **1.** *n.* **a)** *(firm hold)* Halt, *der;
(fig.: power)* Umklammerung, *die;*
have a ~ on sth. etw. festhalten; *(fig.)*
etwas im Griff haben; **loosen one's ~:**
loslassen; **lose one's ~** *(fig.)* nachlassen; **b)** *(strength or way of ~ping)*
Griff, *der.* **2.** *v. t.,* **-pp-** *(fest)* halten;
(Reifen:) greifen; *(fig.)* fesseln *(Publikum, Aufmerksamkeit).* **3.** *v. i.,* **-pp-**
(Räder, Bremsen usw.:) greifen

gripe [graɪp] *v. i. (sl.)* meckern *(ugs.)*
(**about** über + *Akk.*)

gripping [ˈgrɪpɪŋ] *adj. (fig.)* packend

grisly [ˈgrɪzlɪ] *adj.* grausig

gristle [ˈgrɪsl] *n.* Knorpel, *der*

grit [grɪt] **1.** *n.* **a)** Sand, *der;* **b)** *(coll.:
courage)* Schneid, *der (ugs.).* **2.** *v. t.,
-tt-:* **a)** streuen *(Straßen);* **b)** **~ one's
teeth** die Zähne zusammenbeißen
(ugs.)

groan [grəʊn] **1.** *n.* Stöhnen, *das; (of
thing)* Ächzen, *das.* **2.** *v. i.* [auf]stöh-
nen (**at** bei); *(Tisch, Planken:)* ächzen.
3. *v. i.* stöhnen

grocer [ˈgrəʊsə(r)] *n.* Lebensmittel-
händler, *der/*-händlerin, *die.* **gro-
cery** [ˈgrəʊsərɪ] *n.* **a)** *in pl. (goods)* Lebensmittel *Pl.;* **b)** **~[store]** Lebensmittelgeschäft, *das*

groggy [ˈgrɒgɪ] *adj.* groggy *präd. (ugs.)*

groin [grɔɪn] *n.* Leistengegend, *die*

groom [gruːm, grʊm] **1.** *n.* **a)** *(stable-
boy)* Stallbursche, *der;* **b)** *(bride~)*
Bräutigam, *der.* **2.** *v. t.* striegeln
(Pferd); (fig.) vorbereiten (**for** auf
+ *Akk.*)

groove [gruːv] *n.* Rille, *die*

grope [grəʊp] *v. i.* tasten (**for** nach)

¹gross [grəʊs] *adj.* **a)** *(flagrant)* grob ⟨*Fahrlässigkeit, Fehler*⟩; **b)** *(obese)* fett; **c)** *(total)* Brutto-

²gross *n., pl. same* Gros, *das*

grossly *adj. (flagrantly)* äußerst; grob ⟨*übertreiben*⟩

grotesque [grəʊˈtesk] *adj.* grotesk

grotto [ˈgrɒtəʊ] *n., pl.* ~es *or* ~s Grotte, *die*

grotty [ˈgrɒtɪ] *adj. (Brit. sl.)* mies *(ugs.)*

¹ground [graʊnd] **1.** *n.* **a)** Boden, *der*; **get off the** ~ *(coll.)* konkrete Gestalt annehmen; **[sports]** ~: Sportplatz, *der*; **c)** *in pl. (attached to house)* Anlage, *die*; **d)** *(reason)* Grund, *der*; **on the** ~[s] **of** auf Grund (+ *Gen.*); **on the** ~[s] **that** ...: unter Berufung auf die Tatsache, daß ...; **e)** *in pl. (sediment)* Satz, *der.* **2.** *v. t. (Aeronaut.)* am Boden festhalten

²ground 1. *see* grind 1, 2. **2.** *adj.* gemahlen ⟨*Kaffee, Getreide*⟩

ground ˈfloor *see* floor 1 b

ˈgrounding *n.* Grundkenntnisse *Pl.*

ˈgroundless *adj.* unbegründet

ground: ~**sheet** *n.* Bodenplane, *die*; ~**sman** [ˈgraʊndzmən] *n., pl.* -**smen** [ˈgraʊndzmən] *(Sport)* Platzwart, *der*; ~**work** *n.* Vorarbeiten *Pl.*

group [gruːp] **1.** *n.* Gruppe, *die.* **2.** *v. t.* gruppieren

¹grouse [graʊs] *n., pl. same* Rauhfußhuhn, *das*; **[red]** ~ *(Brit.)* Schottisches Moorschneehuhn

²grouse *v. i. (coll.)* meckern *(ugs.)*

grove [grəʊv] *n.* Wäldchen, *das*

grovel [ˈgrɒvl] *v. i., (Brit.)* -**ll**- *(fig.)* katzbuckeln

grow [grəʊ] **1.** *v. i.,* grew [gruː], grown [grəʊn] **a)** wachsen; ~ **out of** *or* **from sth.** sich aus etw. entwickeln; *(from sth. abstract)* von etw. herrühren; ~ **in** gewinnen an (+ *Dat.*) ⟨*Größe, Bedeutung*⟩; **b)** *(become)* werden; ~ **apart** *(fig.)* sich auseinanderleben; ~ **to love/hate sb./sth.** jmdn./etw. liebenlernen/hassenlernen; ~ **to like sb./sth.** nach und nach Gefallen an jmdm./ etw. finden. **2.** *v. t.,* grew, grown ziehen; *(on a large scale)* anpflanzen; züchten ⟨*Blumen*⟩. **grow ˈup** *v. i.* **a)** aufwachsen; *(become mature)* erwachsen werden; ⟨*Legende:*⟩ entstehen

growl [graʊl] **1.** *n.* Knurren, *das*; *(of bear)* Brummen, *das.* **2.** *v. i.* knurren ⟨*Bär:*⟩ [böse] brummen

grown [grəʊn] **1.** *see* grow. **2.** *adj.* erwachsen. **ˈgrown-up 1.** *n.* Erwachsene, *der/die.* **2.** *adj.* erwachsen

growth [grəʊθ] *n.* **a)** Wachstum, *das* (of, in *Gen.*); *(increase)* Zunahme, *die* (of, in *Gen.*); **b)** *(Med.)* Gewächs, *das*

grub [grʌb] *n.* **a)** Larve, *die; (maggot)* Made, *die; (sl.: food)* Fressen, *das (salopp)*

grubby [ˈgrʌbɪ] *adj.* schmudd[e]lig *(ugs.)*

grudge [grʌdʒ] **1.** *v. t.* ~ **sb. sth.** jmdm. etw. mißgönnen; ~ **doing sth.** etw. ungern tun. **2.** *n.* Groll, *der*; **bear sb. a.** ~ *or* **a** ~ **against sb.** jmdm. gegenüber nachtragend sein. **grudging** [ˈgrʌdʒɪŋ] *adj.* widerwillig; widerwillig gewährt ⟨*Zuschuß*⟩. **ˈgrudgingly** *adv.* widerwillig

gruelling *(Amer.:* **grueling**) [ˈgruːəlɪŋ] *adj.* aufreibend; strapaziös ⟨*Reise*⟩

gruesome [ˈgruːsəm] *adj.* grausig

gruff [grʌf] *adj.* barsch; rauh ⟨*Stimme*⟩

grumble [ˈgrʌmbl] *v. i.* murren; ~ **about** *or* **over sth.** sich über etw. (*Akk.*) beklagen

grumpy [ˈgrʌmpɪ] *adj.* unleidlich

grunt [grʌnt] **1.** *n.* Grunzen, *das.* **2.** *v. i.* grunzen

guarantee [gærənˈtiː] **1.** *v. t.* **a)** garantieren für; **[eine] Garantie geben auf** (+ *Akk.*); **the clock is** ~**d for a year** die Uhr hat ein Jahr Garantie; **b)** *(promise)* garantieren *(ugs.); (ensure)* bürgen für ⟨*Qualität*⟩. **2.** *n.* **a)** *(Commerc. etc.)* Garantie, *die; (document)* Garantieschein, *der*; **b)** *(coll.: promise)* Garantie, *die (ugs.);* **give sb. a** ~ **that** ...: jmdm. garantieren, daß ...

guard [gɑːd] **1.** *n.* **a)** *(guardsman)* Wachtposten, *der*; *(group of soldiers)* Wache, *die;* **be on** ~: Wache haben; **be on [one's]** ~ *(lit. or fig.)* sich hüten; **b)** *(Brit. Railw.)* [Zug]schaffner, *der/*-schaffnerin, *die;* **c)** *(Amer.: prison warder)* [Gefängnis]wärter, *der/*-wärterin, *die;* **d)** *(safety device)* Schutz, *der.* **2.** *v. t.* bewachen; hüten ⟨*Geheimnis*⟩; schützen ⟨*Leben*⟩; beschützen ⟨*Prominenten*⟩. **ˈguard against** *v. t.* sich hüten vor (+ *Dat.*); vorbeugen (+ *Dat.*) ⟨*Krankheit, Irrtum*⟩

ˈguarded *adj.* zurückhaltend

guardian [ˈgɑːdɪən] *n.* **a)** Hüter, *der*; Wächter, *der*; **b)** *(Law)* Vormund, *der*

guerrilla [gəˈrɪlə] *n.* Guerillakämpfer, *der/*-kämpferin, *die; attrib.* Guerilla-

guess [ges] **1.** *v. t.* **a)** *(estimate)* schätzen; *(surmise)* raten; *(surmise correctly)* erraten; raten ⟨*Rätsel*⟩; ~ **what!** *(coll.)* stell dir vor!; **b)** *(esp. Amer.:*

suppose) I ~: ich glaube. **2.** *v. i. (estimate)* schätzen; *(make assumption)* vermuten; *(surmise correctly)* es erraten; ~ **at sth.** etw. schätzen; **keep sb.** ~**ing** *(coll.)* jmdn. im unklaren lassen. **3.** *n.* Schätzung, *die;* **make** *or* **have a** ~: schätzen. **'guesswork** *n.* **be** ~: eine Vermutung sein

guest [gest] *n.* Gast, *der.* **'guesthouse** *n.* Pension, *die*

guffaw [gʌ'fɔ:] **1.** *n.* brüllendes Gelächter. **2.** *v. i.* brüllend lachen

guidance ['gaɪdns] *n.* **a)** *(leadership)* Führung, *die; (by teacher etc.)* [An]leitung, *die;* **b)** *(advice)* Rat, *der*

guide [gaɪd] **1.** *n.* **a)** Führer, *der/*Führerin, *die; (Tourism)* [Fremden]führer, *der/*-führerin, *die;* **b)** *(indicator)* **be a** [good] ~ **to sth.** ein [guter] Anhaltspunkt für etw. sein; **be no** ~ **to sth.** keine Rückschlüsse auf etw. *(Akk.)* zulassen; **c)** *(Brit.)* |**Girl**| **G** ~: Pfadfinderin, *die;* **d)** *(handbook)* Handbuch, *das;* **e)** *(for tourists)* [Reise]führer, *der.* **2.** *v. t. (fig.)* bestimmen *(Handeln, Urteil);* **be** ~**d by sth./sb.** sich von etw./jmdm. leiten lassen. **'guidebook** *n.* [Reise]führer, *der.* **guided 'missile** *n.* Lenkflugkörper, *der.* **'guide-dog** *n.* Blinden[führ]hund, *der.* **guided 'tour** *n.* Führung, *die* (of durch). **'guideline** *n.* Richtlinie, *die*

guild [gɪld] *n.* **a)** Verein, *der;* **b)** *(Hist.)* Gilde, *die;* Zunft, *die*

guile [gaɪl] *n.* Hinterlist, *die*

guillotine ['gɪlətiːn] *n.* **a)** Guillotine, *die;* **b)** *(guilty feeling)* Schuldgefühle *Pl.* **'guilty** *adj.* **a)** schuldig; **be** ~ **of murder** des Mordes schuldig sein; **find sb.** ~/**not** ~ |**of sth.**| jmdn. [an etw. *(Dat.)*] schuldig sprechen/[von etw.] freisprechen; **feel** ~ *(coll.)* ein schlechtes Gewissen haben; **b)** schuldbewußt *(Miene, Blick, Verhalten);* schlecht *(Gewissen)*

guinea-pig ['gɪnɪpɪg] *n.* Meerschweinchen, *das; (fig.)* Versuchskaninchen, *das (ugs.)*

guise [gaɪz] *n.* Gestalt, *die;* **in the** ~ **of** in Gestalt (+ *Gen.*)

guitar [gɪ'tɑ:(r)] *n.* Gitarre, *die.* **guitarist** [gɪ'tɑ:rɪst] *n.* Gitarrist, *der/*Gitarristin, *die*

gulf [gʌlf] *n.* **a)** *(Geog.)* Golf, *der;* **b)** *(wide gap)* Kluft, *die*

gull [gʌl] *n.* Möwe, *die*

gullet ['gʌlɪt] *n.* **a)** Speiseröhre, *die;* **b)** *(throat)* Kehle, *die*

gullible ['gʌlɪbl] *adj.* leichtgläubig

gully ['gʌlɪ] *n. (artificial channel)* Abzugsrinne, *die; (drain)* Gully, *der*

gulp [gʌlp] **1.** *v. t.* hinunterschlingen; hinuntergießen *(Getränk).* **2.** *n.* **a)** Schlucken, *das;* **b)** *(large mouthful of drink)* kräftiger Schluck. **gulp 'down** *v. t.* hinunterschlingen; hinuntergießen *(Getränk)*

¹gum [gʌm] *n. (Anat.)* ~|**s**| Zahnfleisch, *das*

²gum 1. *n.* **a)** Gummi, *das; (glue)* Klebstoff, *der;* **b)** *(Amer.) see* chewing-gum. **2.** *v. t.,* -**mm**-: **a)** *(smear with* ~) mit Klebstoff bestreichen; gummieren *(Briefmarken, Etiketten usw.);* **b)** *(fasten with* ~) kleben. **'gumboot** *n.* Gummistiefel, *der*

gumption ['gʌmpʃn] *n. (coll.)* Grips, *der*

gun [gʌn] *n.* Schußwaffe, *die; (rifle)* Gewehr, *das; (pistol)* Pistole, *die; (revolver)* Revolver, *der.* **gun 'down** *v. t.* niederschießen

gun: ~-**fire** *n.* Geschützfeuer, *das;* ~**man** ['gʌnmən] *n., pl.* ~**men** ['gʌnmən] bewaffneter Mann

gun: ~-**powder** *n.* Schießpulver, *das;* ~**shot** *n.* Schuß, *der*

gurgle ['gɜːgl] **1.** *n.* Gluckern, *das; (of brook)* Plätschern, *das.* **2.** *v. i.* gluckern *(Bach:)* plätschern, *(Baby:)* lallen; *(with delight)* glucksen

gush [gʌʃ] **1.** *n.* Schwall, *der.* **2.** *v. i.* **a)** strömen; ~ **out** herausströmen; **b)** *(fig.: enthuse)* schwärmen

gust [gʌst] *n.* ~ |**of wind**| Bö[e], *die*

gusto ['gʌstəʊ] *n.* Genuß, *der; (vitality)* Schwung, *der*

'gusty *adj.* böig

gut [gʌt] **1.** *n.* **a)** *(material)* Darm, *der;* **b)** *in pl. (bowels)* Eingeweide *Pl.;* Gedärme *Pl.;* **c)** *in pl. (coll.: courage)* Schneid, *der (ugs.).* **2.** *v. t.,* -**tt**-: **a)** *(remove* ~*s of)* ausnehmen; **b)** *(remove fittings from)* ausräumen; **the house was** ~**ted** |**by fire**| das Haus brannte aus

gutter ['gʌtə(r)] *n. (below edge of roof)* Dachrinne, *die; (at side of street)* Rinnstein, *der;* Gosse, *die*

guttural ['gʌtərl] *adj.* guttural; kehlig

guy [gaɪ] *n.* **a)** *(sl.: man)* Typ, *der (ugs.);* **b)** *in pl. (Amer.: everyone)* |**listen,**| **you** ~**s!** |hört mal,| Kinder! *(ugs.)*

guzzle ['gʌzl] **1.** *v. t. (eat)* hinunterschlingen; *(drink)* hinuntergießen. **2.** *v. i.* schlingen

gym [dʒɪm] *n. (coll.)* **a)** *(gymnasium)* Turnhalle, *die;* **b)** *(gymnastics)* Turnen, *das*

gymnasium *n.* [dʒɪm'neɪzɪəm] *n., pl.* ~**s** *or* **gymnasia** [dʒɪm'neɪzɪə] Turnhalle, *die*

gymnast ['dʒɪmnæst] *n.* Turner, *der*/Turnerin, *die*

gymnastic [dʒɪm'næstɪk] *adj.* turnerisch ⟨*Können*⟩; ~ **equipment** Turngeräte. **gymnastics** [dʒɪm'næstɪks] *n.* Gymnastik, *die; (esp. with apparatus)* Turnen, *das*

'gym-slip *n.* Trägerrock, *der*

gynaecologist [gaɪnɪ'kɒlədʒɪst] *n.* Frauenarzt, *der*/Frauenärztin, *die*

gynaecology [gaɪnɪ'kɒlədʒɪ] *n.* Gynäkologie, *die*

gypsy, Gypsy ['dʒɪpsɪ] *n.* Zigeuner, *der*/Zigeunerin, *die*

gyrate [dʒaɪə'reɪt] *v. i.* sich drehen

H

¹H, h [eɪtʃ] *n.* H, h, *das*

haberdashery ['hæbədæʃərɪ] *n. (goods)* Kurzwaren *Pl.; (Amer.: menswear)* Herrenmoden *Pl.*

habit ['hæbɪt] *n.* **a)** Gewohnheit, *die;* **good/bad** ~: gute/schlechte [An]gewohnheit; **get** *or* **fall into a** *or* **the** ~ **of doing sth.** [es] sich *(Dat.)* angewöhnen, etw. zu tun; **b)** *(coll.: addiction)* Süchtigkeit, *die*

habitable ['hæbɪtəbl] *adj.* bewohnbar

habitat ['hæbɪtæt] *n.* Habitat, *das*

habitation [hæbɪ'teɪʃn] *n.* **fit/unfit for human** ~: bewohnbar/unbewohnbar

habitual [hə'bɪtjʊəl] *adj.* **a)** gewohnt; **b)** *(given to habit)* gewohnheitsmäßig; Gewohnheits⟨*trinker*⟩. **ha'bitually** *adv. (regularly)* regelmäßig

¹hack [hæk] *v. t.* hacken ⟨*Holz*⟩; ~ **sth. to bits** *or* **pieces** etw. in Stücke hacken. **hack 'off** *v. t.* abhacken. **hack 'out** *v. t.* heraushauen **(from** aus)

²hack *n. (derog.: writer)* Schreiberling, *der*

hackneyed ['hæknɪd] *adj.* abgegriffen; abgedroschen *(ugs.)*

'hack-saw *n.* [Metall]bügelsäge, *die*

had *see* **have**

haddock ['hædək] *n., pl. same* Schellfisch, *der*

hadn't ['hædnt] *(coll.)* = **had not;** *see* **have**

haemorrhage ['hemərɪdʒ] *n.* Blutung, *die*

haemorrhoid ['hemərɔɪd] *n.* Hämorrhoide, *die*

hag [hæg] *n.* [alte] Hexe

haggard ['hægəd] *adj.* ausgezehrt; *(with worry)* abgehärmt

haggle ['hægl] *v. i.* sich zanken **(over, about** wegen); *(over price)* feilschen **(over, about** um)

Hague [heɪg] *pr. n.* **The** ~: Den Haag *(das)*

¹hail [heɪl] **1.** *n.* Hagel, *der.* **2.** *v. i.* **it** ~**s** *or* **is** ~**ing** es hagelt; ~ **down** *(fig.)* niederprasseln **(on** auf + *Akk.)*

²hail *v. t.* **a)** *(call out to)* anrufen; *(signal to)* anhalten ⟨*Taxi*⟩; **b)** *(acclaim)* zujubeln (+ *Dat.);* bejubeln **(as** als)

'hailstone *n.* Hagelkorn, *das*

hair [heə(r)] *n.* **a)** *(one strand)* Haar, *das;* **b)** collect. Haar, *das;* Haare *Pl.; attrib.* Haar-; **have** *or* **get one's** ~ **done** sich *(Dat.)* das Haar *od.* die Haare machen lassen *(ugs.)*

hair: ~**brush** *n.* Haarbürste, *die;* ~**conditioner** *n.* Frisiermittel, *das;* ~**cut** *n.* **a)** *(act)* Haareschneiden, *das;* **go for/need a** ~**cut** zum Friseur gehen/müssen; **get/have a** ~**cut** sich *(Dat.)* die Haare schneiden lassen; **b)** *(style)* Haarschnitt, *der;* ~**do** *n. (style)* Frisur, *die;* ~**dresser** *n.* Friseur, *der*/Friseuse, *die;* **go to the** ~**dresser's** zum Friseur gehen; ~**pin** *n.* Haarnadel, *die;* ~**pin 'bend** *n.* Haarnadelkurve, *die;* ~**-raising** ['heəreɪzɪŋ] *adj.* haarsträubend; ~**-style** *n.* Frisur, *die*

hairy ['heərɪ] *adj.* **a)** behaart; flauschig ⟨*Pullover, Teppich*⟩; **b)** *(sl.: difficult)* haarig

hale [heɪl] *adj.* ~ **and hearty** gesund und munter

half [hɑːf] **1.** *n., pl.* **halves** [hɑːvz] **a)** Hälfte, *die;* ~ **[of sth.]** die Hälfte [von etw.]; ~ **of Europe** halb Europa; **one and a** ~ **hours, one hour and a** ~: anderthalb *od.* eineinhalb Stunden; **divide sth. in** ~ *or* **into halves** etw. halbieren; **she is three and a** ~: sie ist dreieinhalb; **b)** *(Footb. etc.: period)* Halbzeit, *die.* **2.** *adj.* halb; ~ **the house/books/time** die Hälfte des Hauses/der Bücher/der Zeit; ~ **an hour** eine halbe Stunde. **3.** *adv.* **a)** zur Hälfte; halb ⟨*schließen, aufessen, fertig, voll, geöffnet*⟩; *(almost)* fast ⟨*ersticken, tot sein*⟩; ~ **as much/many** halb so viel/viele; **only** ~ **hear what** ...: nur zum Teil hören, was ...; **b)** ~ **past** *or* *(coll.)* ~ **one/two/three** *etc.* halb zwei/drei/vier *usw.*; ~ **past twelve** halb eins

half: ~**-caste** *n.* Mischling, *der*; ~**'hearted** *adj.* halbherzig; ~**'hour** *n.* halbe Stunde; ~**'mast** *n.* **be** [**flown**] **at** ~**-mast** auf Halbmast stehen; ~**-note** *n.* *(Amer. Mus.)* halbe Note; ~**-'price 1.** *n.* halber Preis; **2.** *adj.* zum halben Preis *nachgestellt*; **3.** *adv.* zum halben Preis; ~**'term** *n.* *(Brit.)* *(holiday)* ~**-term** [**holiday/ break**] Ferien in der Mitte des Trimesters; ~**'time** *n.* *(Sport)* Halbzeit, *die*; ~**'way 1.** *adj.* ~**-way point** Mitte, *die*; **2.** *adv.* die Hälfte des Weges ⟨*begleiten, fahren*⟩

hall [hɔ:l] *n.* **a)** Saal, *der*; *(building)* Halle, *die*; **b)** *(entrance* ~*)* Flur, *der*

'hallmark *n.* [Feingehalts]stempel, *der*; *(fig.)* Kennzeichen, *das*

hallo [hə'ləʊ] *int.* **a)** *(to call attention)* hallo; **b)** *(Brit.) see* hello

Hallowe'en [hæləʊ'i:n] *n.* Halloween, *das*; Abend vor Allerheiligen

hallucination [həlu:sɪ'neɪʃn] *n.* Halluzination, *die*

'hallway *n.* Flur, *der*

halo ['heɪləʊ] *n., pl.* ~**es** Heiligenschein, *der*

halt [hɒlt, hɔ:lt] **1.** *n.* **a)** Pause, *die*; *(interruption)* Unterbrechung, *die*; **call a** ~ **to sth.** mit etw. Schluß machen; **b)** *(Brit. Railw.)* Haltepunkt, *der*. **2.** *v. i.* **a)** stehenbleiben; ⟨*Fahrer:*⟩ anhalten; *(for a rest)* eine Pause machen; *(esp. Mil.)* haltmachen; ~**, who goes there?** *(Mil.)* halt, wer da?; **b)** *(end)* eingestellt werden. **3.** *v. t.* anhalten; einstellen ⟨*Projekt*⟩. **'halting** *adj.* schleppend; zögernd ⟨*Antwort*⟩

halve [hɑ:v] *v. t.* halbieren

halves *pl. of* **half**

ham [hæm] *n.* Schinken, *der*

hamburger ['hæmbɜ:gə(r)] *n.* Hacksteak, *das*; *(in roll)* Hamburger, *der*

hamlet ['hæmlɪt] *n.* Weiler, *der*

hammer ['hæmə(r)] **1.** *n.* Hammer, *der.* **2.** *v. t.* hämmern. **3.** *v. i.* hämmern (**at** an + *Dat.*). **hammer 'out** *v. t.* ausklopfen ⟨*Delle, Beule*⟩; *(fig.: devise)* ausarbeiten

hammock ['hæmək] *n.* Hängematte, *die*

'hamper ['hæmpə(r)] *n.* [Deckel]korb, *der*

²hamper *v. t.* behindern

hamster ['hæmstə(r)] *n.* Hamster, *der*

hand [hænd] **1.** *n.* **a)** Hand, *die*; **by** ~ *(manually)* mit der *od.* von Hand; **give** *or* **lend** [**sb.**] **a** ~ [**with** *or* **in sth.**] [jmdm.] [bei etw.] helfen; **b)** *(share)* **have a** ~ **in sth.** bei etw. seine Hände im Spiel haben; **c)** *(worker)* Arbeiter, *der*; *(Naut.: seaman)* Matrose, *der*; **d)** *(of clock or watch)* Zeiger, *der*; **e)** **at** ~: in der Nähe; **on the one** ~ ..., [**but**] **on the other** [~] ...: einerseits ..., andererseits ...; **f)** *(Cards)* Karte, *die.* **2.** *v. t.* geben; ⟨*Überbringer:*⟩ übergeben ⟨*Sendung, Lieferung*⟩. **hand 'in** *v. t.* abgeben (**to, at** bei); einreichen ⟨*Petition*⟩. **hand 'out** *v. t.* austeilen. **hand 'over** *v. t.* übergeben (**to** *Dat.*)

hand: ~**-bag** *n.* Handtasche, *die*; ~**-baggage** *n.* Handgepäck, *das*; ~**book** *n.* Handbuch, *das*; ~**-brake** *n.* Handbremse, *die*; ~**cuff 1.** *n.* *usu. in pl.* Handschelle, *die*; **2.** *v. t.* ~**cuff sb.** jmdm. Handschellen anlegen

handful ['hændfʊl] *n.* Handvoll, *die*; **be a** ~ *(fig. coll.)* einen ständig auf Trab halten *(ugs.)*

handicap ['hændɪkæp] **1.** *n.* **a)** *(Sport, also fig.)* Handikap, *das*; **b)** *(physical)* Behinderung, *die.* **2.** *v. t.,* **-pp-** benachteiligen. **handicapped** ['hændɪkæpt] *adj.* [**mentally/physically**] ~: [geistig/körperlich] behindert

handicraft ['hændɪkrɑ:ft] *n.* [Kunst]-handwerk, *das*; *(needlework, knitting, etc.)* Handarbeit, *die*

handiwork ['hændɪwɜ:k] *n.* handwerkliche Arbeit; **it's all his own** ~: das hat er selbst gemacht

handkerchief ['hæŋkətʃɪf] *n., pl.* ~**s** *or* **handkerchieves** ['hæŋkətʃi:vz] Taschentuch, *das*

handle ['hændl] **1.** *n.* Griff, *der*; *(of door)* Klinke, *die*; *(of axe, brush, comb, broom, saucepan)* Stiel, *der*; *(of cup, jug)* Henkel, *der.* **2.** *v. t.* **a)** *(touch, feel)* anfassen; **b)** *(control)* handhaben ⟨*Fahrzeug, Flugzeug*⟩; **c)** *(deal/cope with)* umgehen/fertigwerden mit. **'handlebars** *n. pl.* Lenkstange, *die*

hand: ~**-luggage** *n.* Handgepäck, *das*; ~**-made** *adj.* handgearbeitet; ~**shake** *n.* Händedruck, *der*

handsome ['hænsəm] *adj.* gutaussehend

hand: ~**-stand** *n.* Handstand, *der*; ~**writing** *n.* [Hand]schrift, *die*

handy ['hændɪ] *adj.* greifbar; keep/ have sth. ~: etw. greifbar haben.
'**handyman** *n.* Handwerker, *der;* |home| ~: Heimwerker, *der*

hang [hæŋ] **1.** *v. t.* a) *p. t., p. p.* **hung** [hʌŋ] hängen; aufhängen ⟨*Bild, Gardinen*⟩; ankleben ⟨*Tapete*⟩; b) *p. t., p. p.* **hanged** (*execute*) hängen (**for** we- gen); ~ **oneself** sich erhängen. **2.** *v. i.,* **hung** a) hängen; ⟨*Kleid usw.*⟩ fallen; b) (*be executed*) hängen. **3.** *n.* **get the** ~ **of** sth. (*coll.*) mit etw. klarkommen (*ugs.*). **hang a'bout, hang a'round** *v. i.* a) (*loiter*) herumlungern (*salopp*); b) (*coll.: wait*) warten. **hang 'on** *v. i.* a) sich festhalten (**to** an + *Dat.*); b) (*sl.: wait*) warten; c) ~ **on to** (*coll.: keep*) behalten. **hang 'out 1.** *v. t.* auf- hängen ⟨*Wäsche*⟩. **2.** *v. i.* a) heraus- hängen; b) (*sl.: live*) wohnen; (*be often present*) sich herumtreiben (*ugs.*). **hang 'up** *v. t.* **1.** aufhängen. **2.** *v. i.* (*Teleph.*) auflegen

hangar ['hæŋə(r)] *n.* Hangar, *der*
'**hanger** *n.* Bügel, *der*
'**hang-glider** *n.* Drachen, *der*
'**hanging** *n.* (*execution*) Hinrichtung [durch den Strang]
hang: ~**man** [hæŋmən] *n., pl.* ~**men** [hæŋmən] Henker, *der;* ~**over** *n.* Ka- ter, *der* (*ugs.*); ~**-up** *n.* (*sl.*) Macke, *die* (*ugs.*)

hanker ['hæŋkə(r)] *v. i.* ~ **after** ein hef- tiges Verlangen haben nach
hanky ['hæŋkɪ] *n.* (*coll.*) Taschentuch, *das*
Hanover ['hænəʊvə(r)] *pr. n.* Hanno- ver (*das*)

haphazard [hæp'hæzəd] *adj.,* **hap- 'hazardly** *adv.* willkürlich
happen ['hæpn] *v. i.* geschehen; ⟨*Vor- hergesagtes:*⟩ eintreffen; ~ **to** sb. jmdm. passieren; ~ **to do** sth./**be** sb. zufällig etw. tun/jmd. sein; **as it** ~**s** *or* **it so** ~**s I have** ...: zufällig habe ich ...
'**happening** *n.* Ereignis, *das*
happily ['hæpɪlɪ] *adv.* a) glücklich ⟨*lä- cheln*⟩; vergnügt ⟨*spielen, lachen*⟩; b) (*gladly*) mit Vergnügen
happiness ['hæpɪnɪs] *n. see* **happy** a: Glück, *das;* Heiterkeit, *die;* Zufrie- denheit, *die*
happy ['hæpɪ] *adj.* a) (*joyful*) glück- lich; heiter ⟨*Bild, Veranlagung*⟩; er- freulich ⟨*Erinnerung, Szene*⟩; froh ⟨*Ereignis*⟩; (*contented*) zufrieden; b) **be** ~ **to do** sth. (*glad*) etw. gern tun.
happy-go-'lucky *adj.* sorglos
harass ['hærəs] *v. t.* schikanieren.

'**harassment** *n.* Schikanierung, *die;* **sexual** ~: [sexuelle] Belästigung
harbour (*Brit.; Amer.:* **harbor**) ['hɑːbə(r)] **1.** *n.* Hafen, *der;* **in** ~: im Hafen. **2.** *v. t.* Unterschlupf gewähren (+ *Dat.*) ⟨*Verbrecher, Flüchtling*⟩; he- gen ⟨*Groll, Verdacht*⟩
hard [hɑːd] **1.** *adj.* a) hart; fest ⟨*Gelee*⟩; stark ⟨*Regen*⟩; streng ⟨*Frost, Winter*⟩; gesichert ⟨*Beweis, Daten*⟩; b) (*diffi- cult*) schwer; **this is** ~ **to believe** das ist kaum zu glauben; **do** sth. **the** ~ **way** es sich (*Dat.*) bei etw. unnötig schwer- machen; c) (*strenuous*) hart; d) (*vigor- ous*) kräftig ⟨*Schlag, Stoß, Tritt*⟩; e) (*harsh*) hart. **2.** *adv.* a) (*strenuously*) hart ⟨*arbeiten, trainieren*⟩; fleißig ⟨*stu- dieren, üben*⟩; genau ⟨*überlegen*⟩; gut ⟨*aufpassen, zuhören*⟩; **try** ~: sich sehr bemühen; b) (*vigorously*) heftig; fest ⟨*schlagen, drücken, klopfen*⟩; c) (*se- verely*) hart; **be** ~ **up** knapp bei Kasse sein (*ugs.*); **feel** ~ **done by** sich schlecht behandelt fühlen
hard: ~**back** *n.* gebundene Ausgabe; ~**board** *n.* Hartfaserplatte, *die;* ~**-boiled** *adj.* a) hartgekocht ⟨*Ei*⟩; b) (*tough*) hartgesotten
harden ['hɑːdn] **1.** *v. t.* härten; (*fig.*) abhärten ⟨**to** gegen⟩. **2.** *v. i.* hart wer- den; (*become confirmed*) sich verhär- ten. **hardened** ['hɑːdnd] *adj.* abge- härtet ⟨**to** gegen⟩; hartgesotten ⟨*Ver- brecher*⟩
hard: ~**-headed** *adj.* nüchtern; ~**-hearted** *adj.* hartherzig (**towards** gegenüber)
hardly ['hɑːdlɪ] *adv.* kaum; ~ **anyone** *or* **anybody/anything** fast niemand/ nichts; ~ **ever** so gut wie nie; ~ **at all** fast überhaupt nicht
'**hardness** *n.* Härte, *die*
'**hardship** *n.* a) Not, *die;* Elend, *die;* b) (*instance*) Notlage, *die*
hard: ~'**shoulder** *n.* (*Brit.*) Stand- spur, *die;* ~**ware** *n.* a) (*goods*) Eisen- waren *Pl.; attrib.* Eisenwaren(ge- schäft); b) (*Computing*) Hardware, *die;* ~**-wearing** *adj.* strapazierfähig; ~**-working** *adj.* fleißig
hardy ['hɑːdɪ] *adj.* abgehärtet; zäh ⟨*Rasse*⟩; winterhart ⟨*Pflanze*⟩
hare [heə(r)] *n.* Hase, *der*
hark [hɑːk] *v. i.* |*just*| ~ **at him** hör ihn dir/hört ihn euch nur an!; ~ **back to** zurückkommen auf (+ *Akk.*)
harm [hɑːm] **1.** *n.* Schaden, *der;* **do** sb. ~, **do** ~ **to** sb. jmdm. schaden. **2.** *v. t.* etwas [zuleide] tun (+ *Dat.*); schaden

(+ *Dat.*) ⟨*Beziehungen, Land, Ruf*⟩.
harmful ['hɑːmfl] *adj.* schädlich (**to**
für). '**harmless** *adj.* harmlos
harmonica [hɑː'mɒnɪkə] *n.* Mundharmonika, *die*
harmonious [hɑː'məʊnɪəs] *adj.* harmonisch
harmonize ['hɑːmənaɪz] 1. *v. t.* aufeinander abstimmen. 2. *v. i.* harmonieren (**with** mit)
harmony ['hɑːmənɪ] *n.* Harmonie,
die; **be in ~:** harmonieren
harness ['hɑːnɪs] 1. *n.* Geschirr, *das.*
2. *v. t.* anschirren; *(fig.)* nutzen
harp [hɑːp] 1. *n.* Harfe, *die.* 2. *v. i.* **~ on**
[**about**] sth. immer wieder von etw. re-
den; *(critically)* auf etw. *(Dat.)* herum-
reiten *(salopp)*
harpoon [hɑː'puːn] *n.* Harpune, *die*
harrowing ['hærəʊɪŋ] *adj.* entsetzlich; grauenhaft ⟨*Anblick, Geschichte*⟩
harsh [hɑːʃ] *adj.* **a)** rauh ⟨*Gewebe,
Klima*⟩; schrill ⟨*Ton, Stimme*⟩; grell
⟨*Licht*⟩; hart ⟨*Bedingungen, Leben*⟩; **b)**
(excessively severe) streng ⟨*äu-
ßerst⟩* streng ⟨*Disziplin*⟩; rücksichtslos
⟨*Tyrann, Herrscher, Politik*⟩. '**harshly**
adv. [sehr] hart
harvest ['hɑːvɪst] 1. *n.* Ernte, *die.* 2.
v. t. ernten
has *see* **have**
hash [hæʃ] *n.* **a)** *(Cookery)* Haschee,
das; **b) make a ~ of** sth. *(coll.)* etw.
verpfuschen *(ugs.)*
hasn't ['hæznt] = **has not;** *see* **have**
hassle ['hæsl] *(coll.)* 1. *n.* Ärger, *der.* 2.
v. t. schikanieren
haste [heɪst] *n.* Eile, *die; (rush)* Hast,
die; **make ~:** sich beeilen
hasten ['heɪsn] 1. *v. t.* beschleunigen.
2. *v. i.* eilen
hastily ['heɪstɪlɪ] *adv. (hurriedly)* eilig;
(rashly) übereilt
hasty ['heɪstɪ] *adj.* eilig; flüchtig
⟨*Skizze, Blick*⟩; *(rash)* übereilt
hat [hæt] *n.* Hut, *der*
¹**hatch** [hætʃ] *n.* Luke, *die; (serving-~)*
Durchreiche, *die*
²**hatch** 1. *v. t.* ausbrüten. 2. *v. i.*
[aus]schlüpfen. **hatch 'out** 1. *v. i.*
ausschlüpfen. 2. *v. t.* ausbrüten
'**hatchback** *n. (car)* Schrägheckli-
mousine, *die*
hatchet ['hætʃɪt] *n.* Beil, *das;* **bury the
~** *(fig.)* das Kriegsbeil begraben
hate [heɪt] 1. *n.* Haß, *der.* 2. *v. t.* hassen; **I ~ to say this** *(coll.)* ich sage das
nicht gern. **hateful** ['heɪtfl] *adj.* abscheulich

hatred ['heɪtrɪd] *n.* Haß, *der*
haughty ['hɔːtɪ] *adj.* hochmütig
haul [hɔːl] 1. *v. i. & t.* ziehen. 2. *n.* **a)**
Ziehen, *das;* **b)** *(catch)* Fang, *der;*
(fig.) Beute, *die.* **haulage** ['hɔːlɪdʒ] *n.*
Transport, *der*
haunch [hɔːntʃ] *n.* **~es** auf seinem Hinterteil sitzen
auf seinem Hinterteil sitzen
haunt [hɔːnt] *v. t.* **~ a house/castle** in
einem Haus/Schloß spuken; **a ~ed
house** ein Haus, in dem es spukt.
'**haunting** *adj.* sehnsüchtig
have [hæv] *v. t., pres.* **he has** [hæz],
p. t. & p. p. **had** [hæd] haben; *(obtain)*
bekommen; *(take)* nehmen; bekom-
men ⟨*Kind*⟩; **~ breakfast/dinner/lunch**
frühstücken/zu Abend/zu Mittag essen; **~ a cup of tea** eine Tasse Tee trinken; **~ sb. to stay** jmdn. zu Besuch haben; **you've had it now** *(coll.)* jetzt ist es
aus *(ugs.)*; **~ a game of football** Fußball spielen. 2. *v. aux.* **he has** [hæz],
stressed hæz],
had [həd], əd, *stressed* hæd] **I ~/I had
read** ich habe/hatte gelesen; **I ~/I had
gone** ich bin/war gegangen; **if I had
known** …: wenn ich gewußt hätte …; **~ to**
sth. **made** etw. machen lassen; **~ to**
müssen. **have 'on** *v. t.* **a)** *(wear)* tragen; **b)** *(Brit. coll.: deceive)* **~ sb.** **on**
jmdn. auf den Arm nehmen *(ugs.)*.
have 'out *v. t.* **a)** **~ a tooth/one's tonsils out** sich *(Dat.)* einen Zahn ziehen
lassen/sich *(Dat.)* die Mandeln herausnehmen lassen; **b)** **~ it out with sb.**
mit jmdm. offen sprechen
haven ['heɪvn] *n.* geschützte Anlegestelle, *die; (fig.)* Zufluchtsort, *der*
haven't ['hævnt] = **have not;** *see* **have**
haversack ['hævəsæk] *n.* Brotbeutel,
der
havoc ['hævək] *n.* **a)** *(devastation)* Verwüstungen; **cause** *or* **wreak ~:** Verwüstungen anrichten; **b)** *(confusion)*
Chaos; **play ~ with** sth. etw. völlig
durcheinanderbringen
¹**hawk** [hɔːk] *n.* Falke, *der*
²**hawk** *v. t.* hausieren mit. '**hawker** *n.*
Hausierer, *der*/Hausiererin, *die*
hay [heɪ] *n.* Heu, *das*
hay: **~ fever** *n.* Heuschnupfen, *der;*
~stack *n.* Heuschober, *der (südd.);*
Heudieme, *die (nordd.);* **~wire** *adj.*
(coll.) **go ~wire** ⟨*Instrument:*⟩ verrückt
spielen *(ugs.)*
hazard ['hæzəd] 1. *n.* Gefahr, *die.* 2.
v. t. **~ a guess** mit Raten probieren.
hazardous ['hæzədəs] *adj.* gefährlich

haze [heɪz] *n.* Dunst[schleier], *der*

hazelnut ['heɪzlnʌt] *n.* Haselnuß, *die*

hazy ['heɪzɪ] *adj.* dunstig; *(fig.)* vage

he [hɪ, *stressed* hiː] *pron.* er

head [hed] **1.** *n.* **a)** Kopf, *der;* ~ **first** mit dem Kopf voran; ~ **over heels** kopfüber; **keep/lose one's** ~: einen klaren Kopf behalten/den Kopf verlieren; **in one's** ~: im Kopf; **enter sb.'s** ~: jmdm. in den Sinn kommen; **use your** ~: gebrauch deinen Verstand; **a** *or* **per** ~: pro Kopf; **b)** *in pl. (on coin)* ~**s** Kopf; ~**s or tails?** Kopf oder Zahl?; **c)** *(leader)* Leiter, *der*/Leiterin, *die;* **d)** *(on beer)* Blume, *die.* **2.** *attrib. adj.* ~ **waiter** Oberkellner, *der;* ~ **office** Hauptverwaltung, *die.* **3.** *v.t.* **a)** *(stand at top of)* anführen ⟨Liste⟩; *(lead)* leiten; führen ⟨Bewegung⟩; **b)** *(Football)* köpfen. **4.** *v.i.* steuern; ~ **for London** ⟨Flugzeug, Schiff:⟩ Kurs auf London nehmen; ⟨Auto:⟩ in Richtung London fahren; **you're** ~**ing for trouble** du wirst Ärger bekommen.

'**headache** *n.* Kopfschmerzen *Pl.*

'**header** *n. (Footb.)* Kopfball, *der*

'**headgear** *n.* Kopfbedeckung, *die*

'**heading** *n.* Überschrift, *die*

head: ~**lamp** *n.* Scheinwerfer, *der;* ~**land** *n.* Landspitze, *die;* ~**light** *n.* Scheinwerfer, *der;* ~**line** *n.* Schlagzeile, *die;* ~**long** *adv.* kopfüber; ~'**master** *n.* Schulleiter, *der;* ~'**mistress** *n.* Schulleiterin, *die;* ~**on 1.** ['--] *adj.* frontal; Frontal⟨zusammenstoß⟩; **2.** ['--] *adv.* frontal; ~'**phones** *n. pl.* Kopfhörer, *der;* ~'**quarters** *n. sing. or pl.* Hauptquartier, *das;* ~**rest** *n.* Kopfstütze, *die;* ~**room** *n.* [lichte] Höhe, *die;* ~**strong** *adj.* eigensinnig; ~**way** *n.* **make** ~**way** Fortschritte machen; ~ **wind** *n.* Gegenwind, *der*

heady ['hedɪ] *adj.* berauschend

heal [hiːl] **1.** *v.t.* heilen. **2.** *v.i.* ~ [**up**] [ver]heilen

health [helθ] *n.* Gesundheit, *die;* **in good/very good** ~: bei guter/bester Gesundheit; **good** *or* **your** ~! auf deine Gesundheit!

health: ~ **centre** *n.* Poliklinik, *die;* ~ **food** *n.* Reformhauskost, *die;* ~-**food shop** *n.* Reformhaus, *das;* ~ **service** *n.* Gesundheitsdienst, *der*

healthy ['helθɪ] *adj.* gesund

heap [hiːp] **1.** *n.* Haufen, *der;* ~**s of** *(coll.)* jede Menge *(ugs.).* **2.** *v.t.* aufhäufen

hear [hɪə(r)] **1.** *v.t.,* **heard** [hɜːd] **a)** hö-

ren; **b)** *(understand)* verstehen. **2.** *v.i.,* **heard:** ~ **about sb./sth.**/ etw. [etwas] hören; **he wouldn't** ~ **of it** er wollte nichts davon hören. **3.** *int.* H~! H~! bravo!; richtig! **hear 'out** *v.t.* ausreden lassen

heard *see* **hear 1, 2**

'**hearing** *n.* Gehör, *das;* **be hard of** ~: schwerhörig sein. '**hearing-aid** *n.* Hörgerät, *das*

hearsay ['hɪəseɪ] *n.* Gerücht, *das;* **it's only** ~: es ist nur ein Gerücht

hearse [hɜːs] *n.* Leichenwagen, *der*

heart [hɑːt] *n. (also Cards)* Herz, *das;* **by** ~: auswendig; **at** ~: im Grunde seines/ihres Herzens; **take/lose** ~: Mut schöpfen/verlieren; **my** ~ **sank** mein Mut sank; **the** ~ **of the matter** der wahre Kern der Sache; *see also* **club 1 c**

heart: ~ **attack** *n.* Herzanfall, *der;* *(fatal)* Herzschlag, *der;* ~**beat** *n.* Herzschlag, *der;* ~~-**breaking** *adj.* herzzerreißend; ~~-**broken** *adj.* **she was** ~~-**broken** ihr Herz war gebrochen; ~**burn** *n.* Sodbrennen, *das*

hearten ['hɑːtn] *v.t.* ermutigen.

'**heartening** *adj.* ermutigend

heart: ~ **failure** *n.* Herzversagen, *das;* ~**felt** *adj.* tiefempfunden ⟨Beileid⟩; aufrichtig ⟨Dankbarkeit⟩

hearth [hɑːθ] *n.* Platz vor dem Kamin.

'**hearth-rug** *n.* Kaminvorleger, *der*

heartily ['hɑːtɪlɪ] *adv.* von Herzen; **eat** ~: tüchtig essen

heartless *adj.* herzlos

hearty ['hɑːtɪ] *adj.* herzlich; ungeteilt ⟨Zustimmung⟩; herzhaft ⟨Mahlzeit⟩

heat [hiːt] **1.** *n.* **a)** *(hotness)* Hitze, *die;* **b)** *(Phys.)* Wärme, *die;* **c)** *(Sport)* Vorlauf, *der.* **2.** *v.t.* heizen. **heat 'up** *v.t.* heiß machen

'**heated** *adj. (angry)* hitzig

'**heater** *n.* Ofen, *der; (for water)* Boiler, *der*

heath [hiːθ] *n.* Heide, *die*

heathen ['hiːðn] **1.** *adj.* heidnisch. **2.** *n.* Heide, *der*/Heidin, *die*

heather ['heðə(r)] *n.* Heidekraut, *das*

'**heating** *n.* Heizung, *die*

heat: ~~-**stroke** *n.* Hitzschlag, *der;* ~**wave** *n.* Hitzewelle, *die*

heave [hiːv] **1.** *v.t.* **a)** heben; **b)** *(coll.: throw)* schmeißen *(ugs.);* **c)** ~ **a sigh** aufseufzen. **2.** *v.i. (pull)* ziehen. **3.** *n.* Zug, *der*

heaven ['hevn] *n.* Himmel, *der;* **in** ~: im Himmel; **for H~'s sake!** um Gottes willen! '**heavenly** *adj.* himmlisch

heavily ['hevılı] *adj.* schwer; *(to a great extent)* stark; schwer *(bewaffnet)*; tief *(schlafen)*; dicht *(bevölkert)*; **smoke/drink** ~: ein starker Raucher/Trinker sein; **it rained/snowed** ~: es regnete/schneite stark

heavy ['hevı] *adj.* schwer; unmäßig *(Trinken, Rauchen)*; **a** ~ **smoker/drinker** ein starker Raucher/Trinker; **be a** ~ **sleeper** sehr fest schlafen

heavy-: **~duty** *adj.* strapazierfähig *(Kleidung, Material)*; schwer *(Werkzeug, Maschine)*; ~ **'goods vehicle** *n. (Brit.)* Schwerlastwagen, *der;* **~weight** *n.* Schwergewicht, *das*

Hebrew ['hi:bru:] 1. *adj.* hebräisch. 2. *n. (language)* Hebräisch, *das*

heckle ['hekl] *v.t.* Zwischenrufe unterbrechen. **heckler** ['heklə(r)] *n.* Zwischenrufer, *der*

hectic ['hektık] *adj.* hektisch

he'd [hid, *stressed* hi:d] a) = **he had;** b) = **he would**

hedge [hedʒ] 1. *n.* Hecke, *die.* 2. *v.t.* ~ **one's bets** *(fig.)* nicht alles auf eine Karte setzen. 3. *v.i.* sich nicht festlegen

hedgehog ['hedʒhog] *n.* Igel, *der*

'hedgerow *n.* Hecke, *die* [als Feldbegrenzung]

heed [hi:d] 1. *v.t.* beachten; beherzigen *(Rat, Lektion)*; ~ **the danger/risk** sich *(Dat.)* der Gefahr/des Risikos bewußt sein. 2. *n.* **give** *or* **pay** ~ **to, take** ~ **of** Beachtung schenken (+ *Dat.*). **'heedless** *adj.* unachtsam; **be** ~ **of** sth. auf etw. *(Akk.)* nicht achten

heel [hi:l] *n.* Ferse, *die; (of shoe)* Absatz, *der;* **Achilles'** ~ *(fig.)* Achillesferse, *die;* **down at** ~ *(fig.)* heruntergekommen; **take to one's** ~**s** Fersengeld geben *(ugs.)*

hefty ['heftı] *adj.* kräftig; *(heavy)* schwer

height [haıt] *n.* **a)** Höhe, *die; (of person, animal, building)* Größe, *die;* **b)** *(fig.: highest point)* Höhepunkt, *der.* **heighten** ['haıtn] *v.t.* aufstocken; *(fig.)* verstärken

heir [eə(r)] *n.* Erbe, *der/*Erbin, *die.* **heiress** ['eərıs] *n.* Erbin, *die*

heirloom ['eəlu:m] *n.* Erbstück, *das*

held *see* ²**hold 1, 2**

helicopter ['helıkoptə(r)] *n.* Hubschrauber, *der*

heliport ['helıpɔ:t] *n.* Heliport, *der*

helium ['hi:lıəm] *n.* Helium, *das*

hell [hel] *n.* **a)** Hölle, *die;* **b)** *(coll.)* [oh] ~! verdammter Mist! *(ugs.);* **what the**

~! ach, zum Teufel! *(ugs.);* **run like** ~: wie der Teufel rennen *(ugs.)*

he'll [hıl, *stressed* hi:l] = **he will**

hello [hə'ləʊ, he'ləʊ] *int. (greeting)* hallo; *(surprise)* holla

hell's 'angel *n.* Rocker, *der*

helm [helm] *n. (Naut.)* Ruder, *das*

helmet ['helmıt] *n.* Helm, *der*

help [help] 1. *v.t.* **a)** ~ sb. [to do sth.] jmdm. helfen[, etw. zu tun]; **can I** ~ **you?** *(in shop)* was möchten Sie bitte?; **b)** *(serve)* ~ **oneself** sich bedienen; ~ **oneself to sth.** sich *(Dat.)* etw. nehmen; *(coll.: steal)* etw. mitgehen lassen *(ugs.);* **c)** *(avoid)* **if I/you can** ~ **it** wenn es irgend zu vermeiden ist; *(remedy)* **I can't** ~ **it** ich kann nichts dafür *(ugs.);* **it can't be** ~**ed** es läßt sich nicht ändern; **d)** *(refrain from)* **I can't** ~ **thinking** *or* **can't** ~ **but think that ...**: ich kann mir nicht helfen, ich glaube, ...; **I can't** ~ **laughing** ich kann einfach nicht lachen. 2. *n.* Hilfe, *die;* **with the** ~ **of ...**: mit Hilfe ... (+ *Gen.*); **be of** [**some**|**no**|**much**] ~ **to sb.** jmdm. eine gewisse/keine/eine große Hilfe sein.

help 'out 1. *v.i.* aushelfen. 2. *v.t.* ~ **sb. out** jmdm. helfen

'helper *n.* Helfer, *der/*Helferin, *die*

helpful ['helpfl] *adj. (willing)* hilfsbereit; *(useful)* hilfreich; nützlich

'helping 1. *adj.* **lend** [sb.] **a** ~ **hand** [**with sth.**] *(fig.)* [jmdm.] [bei etw.] helfen. 2. *n.* Portion, *die*

'helpless *adj.,* **'helplessly** *adv.* hilflos

helter-skelter [heltə'skeltə(r)] *n.* [spiralförmige] Rutschbahn

hem [hem] 1. *n.* Saum, *der.* 2. *v.t.,* **-mm-** säumen. **hem 'in** *v.t.* einschließen; **feel** ~**med in** sich eingeengt fühlen

hemisphere ['hemısfıə(r)] *n.* Halbkugel, *die*

'hem-line *n.* Saum, *der*

hemp [hemp] *n.* Hanf, *der*

hen [hen] *n.* Huhn, *das;* Henne, *die*

hence [hens] *adv. (therefore)* daher.

hence'forth *adv.* von nun an

henchman ['hentʃmən] *n., pl.* **henchmen** ['hentʃmən] Handlanger, *der*

henpecked ['henpekt] *adj.* **a** ~ **husband** ein Pantoffelheld, *der (ugs.);* **be** ~: unter dem Pantoffel stehen *(ugs.)*

¹her [hə(r), *stressed* hɜ:(r)] *pron.* sie; *as indirect object* ihr; **it was** ~: sie war's

²her *poss. pron. attr.* ihr

herald ['herəld] 1. *n.* Herold, *der.* 2. *v.t.* ankündigen. **heraldic** [he'rældık] *adj.* heraldisch. **heraldry** ['herəldrɪ] *n.* Heraldik, *die*

herb [hɜ:b] *n.* Kraut, *das*. **herbaceous** [hɜ:'beɪʃəs] *adj.* krautartig; ~ **border** Staudenrabatte, *die*. **herbal** ['hɜ:bl] *attrib. adj.* Kräuter

herd [hɜ:d] **1.** *n.* Herde, *die; (of wild animals)* Rudel, *das.* **2.** *v. t.* a) treiben; ~ **people together** Menschen zusammenpferchen; b) *(tend)* hüten

here [hɪə(r)] **1.** *adv.* a) *(in or at this place)* hier; **down/in/up** ~ : hier unten/drin/oben; ~ **you are** *(coll.: giving sth.)* hier; b) *(to this place)* hierher; **in|to** ~ : hierherein; **come/bring** ~ : [hier]herkommen/-bringen. **2.** *int. (attracting attention)* he. **here'by** *adv. (formal)* hiermit

hereditary [hɪ'redɪtərɪ] *adj.* a) erblich ⟨*Titel, Amt*⟩; b) *(Biol.)* angeboren

heresy ['herɪsɪ] *n.* Ketzerei, *die*

heretic ['herɪtɪk] *n.* Ketzer, *der*/Ketzerin, *die*

here'with *adv.* in der Anlage

heritage ['herɪtɪdʒ] *n.* Erbe, *das*

hermetic [hɜ:'metɪk] *adj.* luftdicht. **hermetically** [hɜ:'metɪkəlɪ] *adv.* hermetisch

hermit ['hɜ:mɪt] *n.* Einsiedler, *der*/Einsiedlerin, *die*

hernia ['hɜ:nɪə] *n.* Bruch, *der*

hero ['hɪərəʊ] *n., pl.* ~**es** Held, *der*. **heroic** [hɪ'rəʊɪk] *adj.* heldenhaft

heroin ['herəʊɪn] *n.* Heroin, *das*

heroine ['herəʊɪn] *n.* Heldin, *die*

heroism ['herəʊɪzm] *n.* Heldentum, *das*

heron ['hern] *n.* Reiher, *der*

herring ['herɪŋ] *n.* Hering, *der*

hers [hɜ:z] *poss. pron. pred.* ihrer/ihre/ihres; **the book is** ~: das Buch gehört ihr

her'self *pron.* a) *emphat.* selbst; **[all] by** ~: [ganz] allein[e]; b) *refl.* sich; allein[e] ⟨*tun, wählen*⟩; **younger than/as heavy as** ~: jünger als/so schwer wie sie selbst

he's [hɪz, *stressed* hi:z] a) = **he is;** b) = **he has**

hesitant ['hezɪtənt] *adj.* zögernd ⟨*Reaktion*⟩; stockend ⟨*Rede*⟩

hesitate ['hezɪteɪt] *v. i.* zögern; *(falter)* ins Stocken geraten; ~ **to do sth.** Bedenken haben, etw. zu tun. **hesitation** [hezɪ'teɪʃn] *n.* a) *(indecision)* Unentschlossenheit, *die; without* ~: ohne zu zögern; b) *(instance of faltering)* Unsicherheit, *die;* c) *(reluctance)* Bedenken *Pl.*

heterosexual [hetərəʊ'seksjʊəl] **1.** *adj.* heterosexuell. **2.** *n.* Heterosexuelle, *der/die*

het up [het 'ʌp] *adj.* aufgeregt

hew [hju:] *v. t., p. p.* **hewn** [hju:n] *or* **hewed** [hju:d] hacken ⟨*Holz*⟩; losschlagen ⟨*Kohle, Gestein*⟩

hewn *see* **hew**

hexagon ['heksəgən] *n.* Sechseck, *das*

hey [heɪ] *int.* he; ~ **presto!** simsalabim!

heyday ['heɪdeɪ] *n.* Blütezeit, *die*

HGV *abbr. (Brit.)* heavy goods vehicle

hi [haɪ] *int.* hallo *(ugs.)*

hiatus [haɪ'eɪtəs] *n.* Unterbrechung, *die*

hibernate ['haɪbəneɪt] *v. i.* Winterschlaf halten. **hibernation** [haɪbə'neɪʃn] *n.* Winterschlaf, *der*

hiccup ['hɪkʌp] **1.** *n.* a) Schluckauf, *der;* **have/get [the]** ~**s** den Schluckauf haben/bekommen; b) *(fig.: stoppage)* Störung, *die.* **2.** *v. i.* schlucksen *(ugs.)*

hid *see* ¹**hide**

hidden *see* ¹**hide**

¹**hide** [haɪd] **1.** *v. t.,* **hid** [hɪd], **hidden** ['hɪdn] a) verstecken ⟨*Gegenstand, Person usw.*⟩ **(from** vor + *Dat.*); verbergen ⟨*Gefühle, Sinn usw.*⟩ **(from** vor + *Dat.*); verheimlichen ⟨*Tatsache, Absicht usw.*⟩ **(from** *Dat.*); b) *(obscure)* verdecken. **2.** *v. i.,* **hid, hidden** sich verstecken **(from** vor + *Dat.*)

²**hide** *n.* Haut, *die; (of furry animal)* Fell, *das; (dressed)* Leder, *das*

hide-and-'seek *n.* Versteckspiel, *das;* **play** ~: Verstecken spielen

hideous ['hɪdɪəs] *adj.* scheußlich

'hide-out *n.* Versteck, *das*

'hiding ['haɪdɪŋ] *n.* **go into** ~: sich verstecken; *(to avoid police, public attention)* untertauchen; **be in** ~: sich versteckt halten; *(to avoid police, public attention)* untergetaucht sein

²**hiding** *n. (coll.: beating)* Tracht Prügel; **give sb. a [good]** ~: jmdm. eine [ordentliche] Tracht Prügel verpassen *(ugs.)*

'hiding-place *n.* Versteck, *das*

hierarchy ['haɪərɑ:kɪ] *n.* Hierarchie, *die*

hi-fi ['haɪfaɪ] *(coll.)* **1.** *adj.* Hi-Fi-. **2.** *n.* Hi-Fi-Anlage, *die*

high [haɪ] **1.** *adj.* a) hoch; groß ⟨*Höhe*⟩; stark ⟨*Wind*⟩; *(coll.: on a drug)* high *(ugs.);* c) **it's** ~ **time you left** es ist höchste Zeit, daß du gehst. **2.** *adv.* hoch; **search** *or* **look** ~ **and low** überall suchen. **3.** *n.* a) *(~est level/ figure)* Höchststand, *der;* b) *(Met-*

eorol.) Hoch, *das.* '**highbrow** *(coll.)* **1.** *n.* Intellektuelle, *der/die.* **2.** *adj.* intellektuell *(Person, Gerede usw.);* hochgestochen *(abwertend) (Person, Musik, Literatur usw.).* '**high chair** *n.* Hochstuhl, *der*

higher edu·cation *n.* Hochschulbildung, *die*

high: ~-'**handed** *adj.* selbstherrlich; ~-**heeled** [haɪ'hiːld] *adj.* ⟨Schuhe⟩ mit hohen Absätzen; ~ **jump** *n.* Hochsprung, *der;* ~**land** ['haɪlənd] *n.* Hochland, *das;* ~**light 1.** *n.* a) Höhepunkt, *der;* b) *(bright area)* Licht, *das;* **2.** *v. t.,* ~**lighted** ein Schlaglicht werfen auf (+ *Akk.*) ⟨*Probleme usw.*⟩

'**highly** *adv.* sehr; hoch⟨*interessant, -angesehen, -bezahlt, -gebildet*⟩; leicht ⟨*entzündlich*⟩; stark ⟨*gewürzt*⟩; **think** ~ **of sb./sth.** eine hohe Meinung von jmdm./etw. haben; **speak** ~ **of sb./sth.** jmdn./etw. sehr loben. **highlystrung** ['haɪlstrʌŋ] *adj.* übererregbar

Highness ['haɪnɪs] *n.* His/her *etc.* ~: Seine/Ihre *usw.* Hoheit

high: ~-'**pitched** ['haɪpɪtʃt] *adj.* hoch ⟨*Ton, Stimme*⟩; ~ '**pressure** *n.* a) *(Meteorol.)* Hochdruck, *der;* b) *(Mech. Engin.)* Überdruck, *der;* ~-'**rise** *adj.* ~-**rise building** Hochhaus, *das;* ~-**rise block of flats/office block** Wohn-/Bürohochhaus, *das;* ~ **school** *n.* ≈ Oberschule, *die;* ~ **season** *n.* Hochsaison, *die;* ~**way** *n.* öffentliche Straße

hijack ['haɪdʒæk] *v. t.* entführen. '**hijacker** *n.* Entführer, *der;* /*(of aircraft)* Hijacker, *der*

hike [haɪk] *n.* Wanderung, *die.* '**hiker** *n.* Wanderer, *der*/Wanderin, *die*

hilarious [hɪ'leərɪəs] *adj.* urkomisch

hill [hɪl] *n.* Hügel, *der;* *(higher)* Berg, *der;* *(slope)* Hang, *der*

hill: ~-**billy** ['hɪlbɪlɪ] *n. (Amer.)* Hinterwäldler, *der*/Hinterwäldlerin, *die;* ~**side** *n.* Hang, *der;* ~**top** *n.* [Berg]gipfel, *der*

'**hilly** *adj.* hüg[e]lig

hilt [hɪlt] *n.* Griff, *der;* |up| to the ~ *(fig.)* voll und ganz

him [ɪm, *stressed* hɪm] *pron.* ihn; *as indirect object* ihm; **it was** ~: er war's

Himalayas [hɪmə'leɪəz] *pr. n. pl.* Himalaya, *der*

him·self *pron.* a) *emphat.* selbst; b) *refl.* sich. See *also* **herself**

hind [haɪnd] *adj.* hinter...; ~ **legs** Hinterbeine

hinder ['hɪndə(r)] *v. t. (impede)* behin-

dern; *(delay)* verzögern ⟨*Vollendung einer Arbeit, Vorgang*⟩; aufhalten *(Person);* ~ **sb. from doing sth.** jmdn. daran hindern, etw. zu tun

'**hindquarters** *n. pl.* Hinterteil, *das*

hindrance ['hɪndrəns] *n.* Hindernis, *das* (**to** für)

'**hindsight** *n.* **with |the benefit of|** ~: im nachhinein

Hindu ['hɪnduː, hɪn'duː] **1.** *n.* Hindu, *der.* **2.** *adj.* hinduistisch; Hindu⟨*gott, -tempel*⟩

hinge [hɪndʒ] **1.** *n.* Scharnier, *das.* **2.** *v. t.* mit Scharnieren versehen. **3.** *v. i.* *(depend)* abhängen (**|up|on** von)

hint [hɪnt] **1.** *n.* a) *(suggestion)* Wink, *der;* b) *(slight trace)* Spur, *die* (**of** von); **the** ~/**no** ~ **of a smile** der Anflug/nicht die Spur eines Lächelns; c) *(information)* Tip, *der* (**on** für). **2.** *v. i.* ~ **at** andeuten

hip [hɪp] *n.* Hüfte, *die*

hippie ['hɪpɪ] *n. (coll.)* Hippie, *der*

hippopotamus [hɪpə'pɒtəməs] *n.* Nilpferd, *das*

hippy *see* **hippie**

hire [haɪə(r)] **1.** *n.* Mieten, *das;* **be on** ~ |**to sb.**| |**an jmdn.**| vermietet sein; **for** ~: zu vermieten. **2.** *v. t.* a) *(employ)* anwerben; engagieren ⟨*Anwalt, Berater usw.*⟩; b) *(obtain use of)* mieten; ~ **sth. from sb.** etw. bei jmdm. mieten; c) *(grant use of)* ~ |**out**| vermieten; ~ **sth.** |**out**| **to sb.** etw. jmdm. *od.* an jmdn. vermieten. '**hire-car** *n.* Mietwagen, *der.* **hire-'purchase** *n. (Brit.)* Ratenkauf, *der; attrib.* Raten-; **pay for/buy sth. on** ~: etw. in Raten bezahlen/auf Raten kaufen

his [ɪz, *stressed* hɪz] *poss. pron.* a) *attrib.* sein; b) *pred.* seiner/seine/sein[e]s; *see also* **hers**

hiss [hɪs] **1.** *n.* Zischen, *das.* **2.** *v. i.* zischen

historian [hɪ'stɔːrɪən] *n.* Historiker, *der*/Historikerin, *die*

historic [hɪ'stɒrɪk] *adj.* historisch. **historical** [hɪ'stɒrɪkl] *adj.* historisch; geschichtlich ⟨*Belege, Hintergrund*⟩

history ['hɪstərɪ] *n.* Geschichte, *die*

hit [hɪt] **1.** *v. t.,* -**tt-,** hit schlagen; *(with missile)* treffen ⟨*Geschoß, Ball usw.*⟩; treffen ⟨*Fahrzeug:*⟩ prallen gegen; ⟨*Schiff:*⟩ laufen gegen; ~ **one's head on sth.** mit dem Kopf gegen etw. stoßen; ~ **it off with sb.** gut mit jmdm. auskommen. **2.** *v. i.,* -**tt-,** hit schlagen. **3.** *n.* a) *(blow)* Schlag, *der;* *(shot or bomb striking target)* Treffer, *der;* b) *(suc-*

cess) Erfolg, *der; (in entertainment)* Schlager, *der;* Hit, *der (ugs.).* 'hit 'back *v. t. & i.* zurückschlagen. 'hit [up]on *v. t.* kommen auf (+ *Akk.*) ⟨*Idee*⟩; finden ⟨*richtige Antwort, Methode*⟩

hitch [hɪtʃ] 1. *v. t.* a) binden ⟨*Seil*⟩ (round um + *Akk.*); [an]koppeln ⟨*Anhänger usw.*⟩ (to an + *Akk.*); spannen ⟨*Zugtier usw.*⟩ (to vor + *Akk.*); b) ~ a lift *or* ride *(coll.)* per Anhalter fahren. 2. *n. (problem)* Problem, *das.* hitch 'up *v. t.* hochheben ⟨*Rock*⟩

'hitch-hike *v. i.* per Anhalter fahren. 'hitch-hiker *n.* Anhalter, *der/*Anhalterin, *die*

'hit parade *n.* Hitparade, *die*

HIV *abbr.* human immuno-deficiency virus HIV

hive [haɪv] *n.* [Bienen]stock, *der*

HMS *abbr.* (Brit.) Her/His Majesty's Ship H.M.S.

hoard [hɔːd] 1. *n.* Vorrat, *der.* 2. *v. t.* ~ [up] horten; hamstern ⟨*Lebensmittel*⟩

hoarding [hɔːdɪŋ] *n. (fence)* Bauzaun, *der; (Brit.: for advertisements)* Reklamewand, *die*

hoar-frost [hɔːfrɒst] *n.* [Rauh]reif, *der*

hoarse [hɔːs] *adj.* heiser

hoax [həʊks] 1. *v. t.* anführen *(ugs.);* foppen. 2. *n. (deception)* Schwindel, *der; (practical joke)* Streich, *der; (false alarm)* blinder Alarm

hob [hɒb] *n.* [Koch]platte, *die*

hobble [hɒbl] *v. i.* ~ [about] [herum]humpeln

hobby [hɒbɪ] *n.* Hobby, *das.* 'hobby-horse *n.* Steckenpferd, *das*

hobnailed [hɒbneɪld] *adj.* Nagel- ⟨*schuh, -stiefel*⟩

hobo [həʊbəʊ] *n., pl.* -es (Amer.) Landstreicher, *der/*-streicherin, *die*

hockey [hɒkɪ] *n.* Hockey, *das.* 'hockey-stick *n.* Hockeyschläger, *der*

hoe [həʊ] 1. *n.* Hacke, *die.* 2. *v. t. & i.* hacken

hog [hɒg] 1. *n.* [Mast]schwein. 2. *v. t.,* -gg- *(coll.)* mit Beschlag belegen

hoist [hɔɪst] 1. *v. t.* hochziehen, hissen ⟨*Flagge usw.*⟩; hieven ⟨*Last*⟩; setzen ⟨*Segel*⟩. 2. *n.* [Lasten]aufzug, *der*

¹hold [həʊld] *n. (of ship)* Laderaum, *der; (of aircraft)* Frachtraum, *der*

²hold 1. *v. t.,* held [held] a) halten; *(carry)* tragen; *(keep fast)* festhalten; ~ the door open for sb. jmdm. die Tür aufhalten; ~ sth. in place etw. halten;

b) *(contain)* enthalten; *(be able to contain)* fassen ⟨*Liter, Personen usw.*⟩; c) *(possess)* besitzen; haben; d) *(keep possession of)* halten ⟨*Stützpunkt, Stadt, Stellung⟩;* ~ the line *(Teleph.)* am Apparat bleiben; ~ one's own sich behaupten; e) *(cause to take place)* stattfinden lassen; abhalten ⟨*Veranstaltung, Konferenz, Gottesdienst, Sitzung⟩;* veranstalten ⟨*Festival, Auktion⟩;* austragen ⟨*Meisterschaften⟩;* führen ⟨*Unterhaltung, Gespräch⟩;* durchführen ⟨*Untersuchung⟩;* halten ⟨*Vortrag, Rede⟩;* f) *(think, believe)* ~ a view *or* an opinion eine Ansicht haben (on über + *Akk.*); ~ that ...: der Ansicht sein, daß ...; ~ oneself responsible for sth. sich für etw. verantwortlich fühlen; ~ sth. against sb. jmdm. etw. vorwerfen. 2. *v. i.,* held halten; ⟨*Wetter:*⟩ sich halten. 3. *n.* a) *(grasp)* Griff, *der; grab or* seize ~ of sth. etw. ergreifen; get *or* lay *or* take ~ of sth. etw. fassen *od.* packen; keep ~ of sth. etw. festhalten; get ~ of sth. *(fig.)* etw. auftreiben; get ~ of sb. *(fig.)* jmdn. erreichen; b) *(influence)* Einfluß, *der* (on, over auf + *Akk.*); c) *(Sport)* Griff, *der.* hold 'back 1. *v. t.* zurückhalten. 2. *v. i.* zögern. hold 'on 1. *v. t.* [fest]halten. 2. *v. i.* a) sich festhalten; ~ on to sich festhalten an (+ *Dat.*); *(keep)* behalten; b) *(coll.: wait)* warten. hold 'out 1. *v. t.* ausstrecken ⟨*Hand, Arm usw.⟩;* hinhalten ⟨*Tasse, Teller⟩.* 2. *v. i. (resist)* sich halten. hold 'up *v. t.* a) *(raise)* hochhalten; heben ⟨*Hand, Kopf⟩;* b) *(delay)* aufhalten; c) *(rob)* überfallen. 'hold with *v. t.* not ~ with sth. etw. ablehnen

'holdall *n.* Reisetasche, *die*

'holder *n.* a) *(of post, title)* Inhaber, *der/*Inhaberin, *die;* b) ⟨*Zigaretten*⟩-spitze, *die;* ⟨*Papier-, Zahnputzglas*⟩-halter, *der*

'hold-up *n.* a) *(robbery)* [Raub]überfall, *der;* b) *(delay)* Verzögerung, *die*

hole [həʊl] *n.* Loch, *das; (of fox, badger, rabbit)* Bau, *der;* pick ~s in *(fig.)* zerpflücken *(ugs.)*

holiday [hɒlɪdeɪ] *n.* a) [arbeits]freier Tag; *(public ~)* Feiertag, *der;* b) in *sing. or pl. (Brit.: vacation)* Urlaub, *der; (Sch.)* [Schul]ferien *Pl.* 'holiday-maker *n.* Urlauber, *der/*Urlauberin, *die*

Holland [hɒlənd] *pr. n.* Holland *(das)*

hollow [hɒləʊ] 1. *adj.* hohl; eingefallen ⟨Wangen, Schläfen⟩; (fig.) leer ⟨Versprechen⟩. 2. n. [Boden]senke, die. 3. v. t. ~ **out** aushöhlen

holly ['hɒlɪ] n. Stechpalme, die

hologram ['hɒləgræm] n. Hologramm, der

holster ['həʊlstə(r)] n. [Pistolen]halfter, die od. das

holy ['həʊlɪ] adj. heilig

Holy: ~ '**Ghost** see ~ **Spirit;** ~ **Land** n. **the** ~ **Land** das Heilige Land; ~ '**Spirit** n. Heiliger Geist

homage ['hɒmɪdʒ] n. Huldigung, die (to an + Akk.); **pay or do** to **sb./sth.** jmdm./einer Sache huldigen

home [həʊm] 1. n. a) Heim, das; (flat) Wohnung, die; (house) Haus, das; (household) [Eltern]haus, das; (native country) Heimat, die; **at** ~: zu Hause; **be/feel at** ~ (fig.) zu Hause fühlen; **make yourself at** ~: fühl dich wie zu Hause; b) (institution) Heim, das. 2. adj. a) Haus-; b) (Sport) Heim-. 3. adv. nach Hause

home: ~ **address** n. Privatanschrift, die; ~**com'puter** n. Heimcomputer, der; ~**grown** adj. selbstgezogen; ~**land** n. Heimat, die

'**homeless** 1. adj. obdachlos. 2. n. **the** ~: die Obdachlosen. '**homelessness** n. Obdachlosigkeit, die

homely ['həʊmlɪ] adj. wohnlich ⟨Zimmer usw.⟩; behaglich ⟨Atmosphäre⟩

home: ~**made** adj. selbstgemacht; selbstgebacken ⟨Brot⟩; hausgemacht ⟨Lebensmittel⟩; **H**~ **Office** n. (Brit.) Innenministerium, das; **H**~ '**Secretary** n. (Brit.) Innenminister, der; ~**sick** adj. heimwehkrank; **become/be** ~**sick** Heimweh bekommen/haben; ~'**town** n. Heimatstadt, die; ~**work** n. (Sch.) Hausaufgaben Pl.; **piece of** ~**work** Hausaufgabe, die

homicide ['hɒmɪsaɪd] n. Tötung, die; (manslaughter) Totschlag, der

homosexual [hɒsəməʊ'seksjʊəl] 1. adj. homosexuell. 2. n. Homosexuelle, der/die

hone [həʊn] v. t. wetzen

honest ['ɒnɪst] adj. ehrlich. '**honestly** adv. ehrlich; redlich ⟨handeln⟩; ~! ehrlich!; (annoyed) also wirklich! '**honesty** ['ɒnɪstɪ] n. Ehrlichkeit, die

honey ['hʌnɪ] n. Honig, der. '**honeycomb** n. Honigwabe, die. '**honeymoon** n. Flitterwochen Pl.; (journey) Hochzeitsreise, die

honk [hɒŋk] 1. v. i. ⟨Fahrzeug, Fahrer:⟩ hupen. 2. n. Hupen, das

honor, honorable (Amer.) see **honour, honourable**

honorary ['ɒnərərɪ] adj. Ehren⟨mitglied, -präsident, -doktor, -bürger⟩

honour ['ɒnə(r)] (Brit.) 1. n. a) Ehre, die; b) (distinction) Auszeichnung, die. 2. v. t. ehren; (Commerc.) honorieren. '**honourable** ['ɒnərəbl] adj. (Brit.) ehrenwert (geh.)

hood [hʊd] n. a) Kapuze, die; b) (Amer. Motor Veh.) Motorhaube, die; c) (of pram) Verdeck, das

hoodlum ['huːdləm] n. Rowdy, der

hoodwink ['hʊdwɪŋk] v. t. hinters Licht führen

hoof [huːf] n., pl. ~s or **hooves** [huːvz] Huf, der

hook [hʊk] 1. n. Haken, der; **by** ~ **or by crook** mit allen Mitteln. 2. v. t. a) (grasp) mit Haken/mit einem Haken greifen; b) (fasten) mit Haken/mit einem Haken befestigen (**to** an + Dat.); c) **be** ~**ed** [**on sth.**] (addicted) [von etw.] abhängig sein; (harmlessly) auf etw. stehen (ugs.). **hook 'up** v. t. festhaken (**to** an + Akk.)

hooligan ['huːlɪgən] n. Rowdy, der. **hooliganism** ['huːlɪgənɪzm] n. Rowdytum, das

hoop [huːp] n. Reifen, der

hooray [hʊ'reɪ] int. hurra

hoot [huːt] 1. v. i. a) (call out) johlen; b) ⟨Eule:⟩ schreien; c) ⟨Fahrzeug, Fahrer:⟩ hupen. 2. n. a) (shout) ~ **of derision** verächtliches Gejohle; b) (of owl) Schrei, der; c) (of vehicle) Hupen, das. '**hooter** n. (Brit.: siren) Sirene, die

hoover ['huːvə(r)] (Brit.) 1. n. a) **H**~ (**P**) [Hoover]staubsauger, der; b) (made by any company) Staubsauger, der. 2. v. t. staubsaugen

hooves pl. of **hoof**

[^1]**hop** [hɒp] n. a) (plant) Hopfen, der; b) in pl. (Brewing) Hopfen, der

[^2]**hop** 1. v. i., -**pp**-: a) hüpfen; ⟨Hase:⟩ hoppeln; b) (fig. coll.) ~ **out of bed** aus dem Bett springen; ~ **into the car/on** [**to**] **the bus/train** sich ins Auto/in den Bus/Zug schwingen (ugs.). 2. v. t., -**pp**- (Brit. sl.) ~ **it** sich verziehen (ugs.). 3. n. a) Hüpfer, der; b) (Brit. coll.) **catch sb. on the** ~: jmdn. überraschen

hope [həʊp] 1. n. Hoffnung, die; **sb.'s** ~[**s**] **of sth.** jmds. Hoffnung auf etw. (Akk.); **raise sb.'s** ~**s** jmdm. Hoffnung machen. 2. v. i. & t. hoffen (**for** auf + Akk.); **I** ~ **so/not** hoffentlich/hoffentlich nicht; ~ **for the best** das Beste hoffen. **hopeful** ['həʊpfl] *adj.* **a)** (*promising*) vielversprechend. '**hopefully** *adv.* **a)** (*expectantly*) voller Hoffnung; **b)** (*coll.: it is hoped that*) hoffentlich. '**hopeless** *adj.* **a)** hoffnungslos; **b)** (*inadequate*) miserabel. '**hopelessly** *adv.* **a)** hoffnungslos; **b)** (*inadequately*) miserabel

hopscotch ['hɒpskɒtʃ] *n.* Himmel-und-Hölle-Spiel, *das*

horde [hɔːd] *n.* Horde, *die*

horizon [hə'raɪzn] *n.* Horizont, *der*; **on the ~:** am Horizont

horizontal [hɒrɪ'zɒntl] *adj.* horizontal; waagerecht. **hori'zontally** *adv.* horizontal; (*flat*) waagerecht

hormone ['hɔːməʊn] *n.* Hormon, *das*

horn [hɔːn] *n.* Horn, *das*; (*of vehicle*) Hupe, *die*

hornet ['hɔːnɪt] *n.* Hornisse, *die*

'**horny** *adj.* (*hard*) hornig

horoscope ['hɒrəskəʊp] *n.* Horoskop, *das*

horrible ['hɒrɪbl] *adj.* grauenhaft; grausig (*Monster*); grauenvoll (*Verbrechen, Alptraum*)

horrid ['hɒrɪd] *adj.* scheußlich

horrific [hə'rɪfɪk] *adj.* schrecklich

horrify ['hɒrɪfaɪ] *v. t.* mit Schrecken erfüllen; **be horrified** (*shocked, scandalized*) entsetzt sein (**at, by** über + *Akk.*). '**horrifying** *adj.* grauenhaft

horror ['hɒrə(r)] **1.** *n.* Entsetzen, *das* (**at** über + *Akk.*); (*repugnance*) Grausen, *das*; (*horrifying thing*) Greuel, *der.* **2.** *attrib. adj.* Horror-. '**horror-stricken**, '**horror-struck** *adjs.* von Entsetzen gepackt

hors-d'œuvre [ɔː'dɜːvr] *n.* Hors-d'œuvre, *das*; ≈ Vorspeise, *die*

horse [hɔːs] *n.* Pferd, *das*

horse: ~**back:** **on** ~**back** zu Pferd; ~**man** ['hɔːsmən] *n., pl.* ~**men** ['hɔːsmən] (*[skilled] rider*) [guter] Reiter; ~**play** *n.* Balgerei, *die*; ~**power** *n., pl. same* (*Mech.*) Pferdestärke, *die*; ~**racing** *n.* Pferderennsport, *der*; ~**radish** *n.* Meerrettich, *der*; ~**shoe** *n.* Hufeisen, *das*

horticulture ['hɔːtɪkʌltʃə(r)] *n.* Gartenbau, *der*

hose [həʊz], '**hose-pipe** *ns.* Schlauch, *der*

hospice ['hɒspɪs] *n.* (*Brit.: for the terminally ill*) Sterbeklinik, *die*

hospitable [hɒ'spɪtəbl] *adj.* gastfreundlich (*Person, Wesensart*); **be ~ to sb.** jmdn. gastfreundlich aufnehmen

hospital ['hɒspɪtl] *n.* Krankenhaus, *das*; **in ~** (*Brit.*), **in the ~** (*Amer.*) im Krankenhaus

hospitality [hɒspɪ'tælɪtɪ] *n.* Gastfreundschaft, *die*

¹**host** [həʊst] *n.* (*large number*) Menge, *die*; **a ~ of people/children** eine Menge Leute/eine Schar von Kindern

²**host** *n.* Gastgeber, *der*/-geberin, *die*

hostage ['hɒstɪdʒ] *n.* Geisel, *die*

hostel ['hɒstl] *n.* (*Brit.*) Wohnheim, *das*

hostess ['həʊstɪs] *n.* Gastgeberin, *die*; (*in night-club*) Animierdame, *die*

hostile ['hɒstaɪl] *adj.* **a)** feindlich; **b)** (*unfriendly*) feindselig (**to|wards**); **be ~ to sth.** etw. ablehnen

hostility [hɒ'stɪlɪtɪ] *n.* Feindseligkeit, *die*

hot [hɒt] *adj.* **a)** heiß; warm (*Mahlzeit, Essen*); **I am/feel ~:** mir ist heiß; **b)** (*pungent*) scharf (*Gewürz, Senf usw.*); scharf gewürzt (*Essen*); **c)** (*recent*) noch warm (*Nachrichten*); **d)** (*sl.: illegally obtained*) heiß (*Ware, Geld*)

hot 'air *n.* (*sl.*) leeres Gerede (*ugs.*).

'**hotbed** *n.* (*Hort.*) Mistbeet, *das*; (*fig.: of vice, corruption*) Brutstätte, *die* (**of** für)

'**hot dog** *n.* (*coll.*) Hot dog, *der od. das*

hotel [həʊ'tel] *n.* Hotel, *das.* **ho'tel room** *n.* Hotelzimmer, *das*

hot: ~**house** *n.* Treibhaus, *das*; ~**line** *n.* (*Polit.*) heißer Draht

'**hotly** *adv.* heftig

hot: ~**plate** *n.* Kochplatte, *die*; (*to keep food* ~) Warmhalteplatte, *die*; ~-**water bottle** *n.* Wärmflasche, *die*

hound [haʊnd] **1.** *n.* Jagdhund, *der.* **2.** *v. t.* verfolgen

hour ['aʊə(r)] *n.* **a)** Stunde, *die*; **half an** ~: eine halbe Stunde; **an** ~ **and a half** anderthalb Stunden; **be paid by the** ~: stundenweise bezahlt werden; **the 24-~ clock** die Vierundzwanzigstundenuhr; **b)** (*time o'clock*) Zeit, *die*; **the small** ~**s** (**of the morning**) die frühen Morgenstunden; **0100/0200/1700/ 1800** ~**s** (**on** 24-~ **clock**) 1.00/2.00/ 17.00/18.00 Uhr. '**hourly** *adj., adv.* stündlich; **be paid** ~: stundenweise bezahlt werden

house 1. [haʊs] *n., pl.* ~**s** ['haʊzɪz] Haus, *das*; **to/at my** ~: zu mir [nach Hause]/bei mir [zu Hause]. **2.** [haʊz] *v. t.* **a)** ein Heim geben (+ *Dat.*); **b)** *(keep, store)* unterbringen. **house-boat** ['haʊsbəʊt] *n.* Hausboot, *das*

household ['haʊshəʊld] *n.* Haushalt, *der; attrib.* Haushalts-. '**house-holder** *n.* Wohnungsinhaber, *der/* -inhaberin, *die*

house [haʊs]: **~keeper** *n.* Haushälterin, *die; ~keeping* *n.* Hauswirtschaft, *die; ~plant* *n.* Zimmerpflanze, *die; ~trained* *adj. (Brit.)* stubenrein ⟨Hund, Katze⟩; **~warming** *n.* **~warming [party]** Einzugsfeier, *die;* **~wife** *n.* Hausfrau, *die; ~work* *n.* Hausarbeit, *die*

housing ['haʊzɪŋ] *n. (dwellings)* Wohnungen; *(provision of dwellings)* Wohnungsbeschaffung, *die.* '**housing estate** *n. (Brit.)* Wohnsiedlung, *die*

hovel ['hɒvl] *n.* [armselige] Hütte

hover ['hɒvə(r)] *v. i.* **a)** schweben; **b)** *(linger)* sich herumdrücken *(ugs.).* '**hovercraft** *n., pl. same* Hovercraft, *das;* Luftkissenfahrzeug, *das.* '**hover mower** *n.* Luftkissenmäher, *der*

how [haʊ] *adv.* wie; **~ to ride a bike/swim** radfahren/schwimmen lernen; **~ 'are you?** wie geht es dir?; *(greeting)* guten Morgen/Tag/ Abend!; **~ do you 'do?** *(formal)* guten Morgen/Tag/Abend!; **~ much?** wieviel?; **~ many?** wieviel?; wie viele?

however [haʊ'evə(r)] *adv.* **a)** wie ... auch; **b)** *(nevertheless)* jedoch; aber

howl [haʊl] **1.** *n. (of animal)* Heulen, *das; (of distress)* Schrei, *der; ~s of laughter* brüllendes Gelächter. **2.** *v. i.* ⟨Tier, Wind:⟩ heulen; *(with distress)* schreien. **3.** *v. t.* [hinaus]schreien

howler ['haʊlə(r)] *n. (coll.: blunder)* Schnitzer, *der (ugs.)*

HP *abbr. (Brit.)* hire-purchase

HQ *abbr.* headquarters HQ

hub [hʌb] *n.* [Rad]nabe, *die; (fig.)* Mittelpunkt, *der*

hubbub ['hʌbʌb] *n.* Lärm, *der;* **a ~ of voices** ein Stimmengewirr

'**hub-cap** *n.* Radkappe, *die*

huddle ['hʌdl] *v. i.* sich drängen; **~ together** sich zusammendrängen. **huddle 'up** *v. i. (nestle up)* sich zusammenkauern; *(crowd together)* sich [zusammen]drängen

¹**hue** [hju:] *n.* Farbton, *der*

²**hue** *n.* **~ and cry** lautes Geschrei; *(protest)* Gezeter, *das*

huff [hʌf] **1.** *v. i.* **~ and puff** schnaufen und keuchen. **2.** *n.* **in a ~:** beleidigt

hug [hʌg] **1.** *n.* Umarmung, *die;* **give**

sb. a ~: jmdn. umarmen. **2.** *v. t., -gg-* umarmen

huge [hju:dʒ] *adj.* riesig; gewaltig ⟨Unterschied, Verbesserung, Interesse⟩

hulking ['hʌlkɪŋ] *adj. (coll.)* **~ great** klobig

hull [hʌl] *n. (Naut.)* Schiffskörper, *der*

hum [hʌm] **1.** *v. i., -mm-:* **a)** summen; ⟨Maschine:⟩ brummen; **b)** **~ and haw** *(coll.)* herumdrucksen *(ugs.).* **2.** *v. t., -mm-* summen. **3.** *n.* **a)** Summen, *das; (of machinery)* Brummen, *das;* **b)** *(of voices, conversation)* Gemurmel, *das; (of traffic)* Brausen, *das*

human ['hju:mən] **1.** *adj.* menschlich; **the ~ race** die menschliche Rasse. **2.** *n.* Mensch, *der.* **human 'being** *n.* Mensch, *der*

humane [hju:'meɪn] *adj.* human

humanitarian [hju:mænɪ'teərɪən] *adj.* humanitär

humanity [hju:'mænɪtɪ] *n.* **a)** *(mankind)* Menschheit, *die; (people collectively)* Menschen; **b)** *(being humane)* Humanität, *die*

humble ['hʌmbl] **1.** *adj.* **a)** demütig; **b)** *(modest)* bescheiden; **c)** *(low-ranking)* einfach; niedrig ⟨Status, Rang usw.⟩. **2.** *v. t.* **a)** demütigen; **~ oneself** sich demütigen *od.* erniedrigen; **b)** *(defeat decisively)* [vernichtend] schlagen

humbly ['hʌmblɪ] *adv.* demütig

humdrum ['hʌmdrʌm] *adj.* alltäglich; eintönig ⟨Leben⟩

humid ['hju:mɪd] *adj.* feucht. **humidity** [hju:'mɪdɪtɪ] *n.* Feuchtigkeit, *die*

humiliate [hju:'mɪlɪeɪt] *v. t.* demütigen. **humiliation** [hju:mɪlɪ'eɪʃn] *n.* Demütigung, *die*

humility [hju:'mɪlɪtɪ] *n.* Demut, *die*

humor *(Amer.) see* humour

humorous ['hju:mərəs] *adj.* lustig, komisch ⟨Geschichte, Name, Situation⟩; witzig ⟨Bemerkung⟩

humour ['hju:mə(r)] *(Brit.)* **1.** *n.* **a)** Humor, *der;* **sense of ~:** Sinn für Humor; **b)** *(mood)* Laune, *die.* **2.** *v. t.* **~ sb.** jmdm. seinen Willen lassen

hump [hʌmp] **1.** *n.* **a)** *(of person)* Buckel, *der; (of animal)* Höcker, *der;* **b)** *(mound)* Hügel, *der.* **2.** *v. t. (Brit. sl.: carry)* schleppen. **humpback 'bridge** *n.* gewölbte Brücke

¹**hunch** [hʌntʃ] *v. t.* **~ [up]** hochziehen

²**hunch** *n. (feeling)* Gefühl, *das*

'**hunchback** *n. (back)* Buckel, *der; (person)* Bucklige, *der/die;* **be a ~:** einen Buckel haben

hundred ['hʌndrəd] **1.** adj. hundert; **a or one ~:** [ein]hundert; **two/several ~:** zweihundert/mehrere hundert; **a or one ~ and one** [ein]hundert[und]eins. **2.** n. **a)** (number) hundert; **a or one/ two ~:** [ein]hundert/zweihundert; **b)** (written figure; group) Hundert, das; **c)** (indefinite amount) ~s Hunderte. See also **eight. hundredth** ['hʌndrədθ] **1.** adj. hundertst...; **a ~ part** ein Hundertstel. **2.** n. (fraction) Hundertstel, das; (in sequence) hundertste, der/die/das; (in rank) Hundertste, der/ die/das. **'hundredweight** n., pl. same (Brit.) 50,8 kg; ≈ Zentner, der

hung see **hang 1, 2**

Hungarian [hʌŋ'geərɪən] **1.** adj. ungarisch; **sb. is ~:** jmd. ist Ungar/Ungarin. **2.** n. **a)** (person) Ungar, der/Ungarin, die; **b)** (language) Ungarisch, das; see also **English 2 a**

Hungary ['hʌŋgərɪ] pr. n. Ungarn (das)

hunger ['hʌŋgə(r)] **1.** n. Hunger, der. **2.** v. i. ~ **after** or **for sb./sth.** [heftiges] Verlangen nach jmdm./etw. haben. **'hunger-strike** n. Hungerstreik, der; **go on ~:** in den Hungerstreik treten

hungry ['hʌŋgrɪ] adj. hungrig; **be ~:** Hunger haben; **go ~:** hungern

hunk [hʌŋk] n. [großes] Stück

hunt [hʌnt] **1.** n. Jagd, die; (search) Suche, die. **2.** v. t. jagen; (search for) Jagd machen auf (+ Akk.); (Mörder usw.). **3.** v. i. jagen; **go ~ing** auf die Jagd gehen; **~ after** or **for** Jagd machen auf (+ Akk.); (seek) suchen **'hunter** n. Jäger, der

'hunting n. die Jagd (**of** auf + Akk.); (searching) Suche, die (**for** nach)

hurdle ['hɜːdl] n. Hürde, die

hurl [hɜːl] v. t. werfen; (violently) schleudern; **~ insults at sb.** jmdm. Beleidigungen ins Gesicht schleudern

hurrah [hʊ'rɑː], **hurray** [hʊ'reɪ] int. hurra

hurricane ['hʌrɪkən] n. Orkan, der

hurried ['hʌrɪd] adj. eilig; überstürzt ⟨Abreise⟩; in Eile ausgeführt ⟨Arbeit⟩

hurry ['hʌrɪ] **1.** n. Eile, die; **in a ~:** eilig; **be in a ~:** es eilig haben; **there's no ~:** es eilt nicht. **2.** v. t. antreiben ⟨Person⟩; hinunterschlingen ⟨Essen⟩; **~ one's work** seine Arbeit in zu großer Eile erledigen. **3.** v. i. sich beeilen; (to or from place) eilen. **hurry 'up 1.** v. i. sich beeilen. **2.** v. t. antreiben

hurt [hɜːt] **1.** v. t., **hurt a)** wen tun (+ Dat.); (injure) verletzen; **~ oneself** sich (Dat.) weh tun; (injure oneself) sich verletzen; **~ one's arm/back** sich (Dat.) am Arm/Rücken weh tun; (injure) sich (Dat.) den Arm/am Rücken verletzen; **b)** (damage, be detrimental to) schaden (+ Dat.); **c)** (upset) verletzen ⟨Person, Stolz⟩. **2.** v. i., **hurt a)** weh tun; **b)** (cause damage, be detrimental) schaden. **3.** adj. gekränkt ⟨Tonfall, Miene⟩. **4.** n. (emotional pain) Schmerz, der. **hurtful** ['hɜːtfl] adj. verletzend

hurtle ['hɜːtl] v. i. rasen (ugs.)

husband ['hʌzbənd] n. Ehemann, der; **my/your/her ~:** mein/dein/ihr Mann; **~ and wife** Mann und Frau

hush [hʌʃ] **1.** n. (silence) Schweigen, das; (stillness) Stille, die. **2.** v. t. (silence) zum Schweigen bringen; (still) beruhigen. **3.** v. i. still sein; **~!** still! **hush 'up** v. t. vertuschen

husk [hʌsk] n. Spelze, die

'husky ['hʌskɪ] adj. heiser

²husky n. Eskimohund, der

hustle ['hʌsl] **1.** v. t. drängen (**into** zu). **2.** n. **~ and bustle** geschäftiges Treiben

hut [hʌt] n. Hütte, die

hutch [hʌtʃ] n. Stall, der

hyacinth ['haɪəsɪnθ] n. Hyazinthe, die

hybrid ['haɪbrɪd] **1.** n. Hybride, die od. der (between aus); (fig.: mixture) Mischung, die. **2.** adj. hybrid ⟨Züchtung⟩

hydrangea [haɪ'dreɪndʒə] n. Hortensie, die

hydrant ['haɪdrənt] n. Hydrant, der

hydraulic [haɪ'drɔːlɪk] adj. hydraulisch

hydrochloric acid [haɪdrəkləʊrɪk 'æsɪd] n. Salzsäure, die

hydroelectric [haɪdrəʊɪ'lektrɪk] adj. hydroelektrisch; **~ power station** Wasserkraftwerk, das

hydrofoil ['haɪdrəfɔɪl] n. Tragflächenboot, das

hydrogen ['haɪdrədʒən] n. Wasserstoff, der. **'hydrogen bomb** n. Wasserstoffbombe, die

hyena [haɪ'iːnə] n. Hyäne, die

hygiene ['haɪdʒiːn] n. Hygiene, die.

hygienic [haɪ'dʒiːnɪk] adj. hygienisch

hymn [hɪm] n. Hymne, die; (sung in service) Kirchenlied, das. **'hymnbook** n. Gesangbuch, das

hypermarket ['haɪpəmɑːkɪt] n. (Brit.) Verbrauchermarkt, der

hyphen ['haɪfn] **1.** n. Bindestrich, der. **2.** v. t. mit Bindestrich schreiben

hyphenate ['haɪfəneɪt] *see* **hyphen** 2
hypnosis [hɪp'nəʊsɪs] *n., pl.* **hypnoses** [hɪp'nəʊsi:z] Hypnose, *die;* (*act, process*) Hypnotisierung, *die;* **under ~:** in Hypnose (*Dat.*). **hypnotic** [hɪp-'nɒtɪk] *adj.* hypnotisch. **hypnotism** ['hɪpnətɪzm] *n.* Hypnotik, *die;* (*act*) Hypnotisieren, *das.* **hypnotist** ['hɪp-nətɪst] *n.* Hypnotiseur, *der*/Hypnotiseuse, *die.* **hypnotize** ['hɪpnətaɪz] *v.t.* hypnotisieren
hypochondria [haɪpə'kɒndrɪə] *n.* Hypochondrie, *die.* **hypochondriac** [haɪpə'kɒndrɪæk] *n.* Hypochonder, *der*
hypocrisy [hɪ'pɒkrɪsɪ] *n.* Heuchelei, *die.* **hypocrite** ['hɪpəkrɪt] *n.* Heuchler, *der*/Heuchlerin, *die.* **hypocritical** [hɪpə'krɪtɪkl] *adj.* heuchlerisch
hypodermic [haɪpə'dɜ:mɪk] *adj. & n.* **~ |syringe|** Injektionsspritze, *die*
hypotenuse [haɪ'pɒtənju:z] *n.* Hypotenuse, *die*
hypothesis [haɪ'pɒθɪsɪs] *n., pl.* **hypotheses** [haɪ'pɒθɪsi:z] Hypothese, *die.* **hypothetical** [haɪpə'θetɪkl] *adj.* hypothetisch
hysteria [hɪ'stɪərɪə] *n.* Hysterie, *die.* **hysterical** [hɪ'sterɪkl] *adj.* hysterisch. **hysterics** [hɪ'sterɪks] *n. pl.* (*laughter*) hysterischer Lachanfall; (*crying*) hysterischer Weinkrampf; **have ~:** hysterisch lachen/weinen

I

¹I, i [aɪ] *n.* I, i, *das*
²I *pron.* ich
ice [aɪs] **1.** *n.* **a)** Eis, *das;* **feel/be like ~** (*be very cold*) eiskalt sein; **b)** (*~ cream*) [Speise]eis, *das;* **an ~/two ~s** ein/zwei Eis. **2.** *v.t.* glasieren ⟨*Kuchen*⟩. **ice** ˈover, **ice** ˈup *v.i.* ⟨*Gewässer:*⟩ zufrieren
ˈice age *n.* Eiszeit, *die*
iceberg ['aɪsbɜ:g] *n.* Eisberg, *der*
ice: ~box *n.* (*Amer.*) Kühlschrank, *der;* **~-ˈcold** *adj.* eiskalt; **~ˈcream** *n.* Eis, *das;* Eiscreme, *die;* **one ~-cream/two/too many ~-creams** ein/

zwei/zuviel Eis; **~-cube** *n.* Eiswürfel, *die;* **~ hockey** *n.* Eishockey, *das*
Iceland ['aɪslənd] *pr. n.* Island (*das*).
Icelandic [aɪs'lændɪk] **1.** *adj.* isländisch. **2.** *n.* Isländisch, *das; see also* **English** 2 a
ice: ~ ˈlolly *n.* Eis am Stiel; **~-rink** *n.* Eisbahn, *die;* **~-skate 1.** *n.* Schlittschuh, *der;* **2.** *v.i.* Schlittschuh laufen; **~-skating** *n.* Schlittschuhlaufen, *das*
icicle ['aɪsɪkl] *n.* Eiszapfen, *der*
icing ['aɪsɪŋ] *n.* Zuckerguß, *der.* **ˈicing sugar** *n.* (*Brit.*) Puderzucker, *der*
icon ['aɪkɒn] *n.* Ikone, *die*
icy ['aɪsɪ] *adj.* **a)** ⟨*Berge, Landschaft, Straße*⟩; eisreich ⟨*Region, Land*⟩; **in ~ conditions** bei Eis; **b)** (*very cold*) eiskalt; eisig; (*fig.*) frostig
I'd [aɪd] **a)** = **I had; b)** = **I would**
idea [aɪ'dɪə] *n.* Idee, *die;* Gedanke, *der;* (*mental picture*) Vorstellung, *die;* (*vague notion*) Ahnung, *die;* **have you any ~ |of| how ...?** weißt du ungefähr, wie ...?; **have no ~ |of| where ...:** keine Ahnung haben, wo ...; **not have the slightest** *or* **faintest ~:** nicht die leiseste Ahnung haben
ideal [aɪ'dɪəl] **1.** *adj.* ideal; vollendet ⟨*Ehemann, Gastgeber*⟩; vollkommen ⟨*Welt*⟩. **2.** *n.* Ideal, *das.* **idealism** [aɪ-'dɪəlɪzm] *n.* Idealismus, *der.* **idealist** [aɪ'dɪəlɪst] *n.* Idealist, *der*/Idealistin, *die.* **idealistic** [aɪdɪə'lɪstɪk] *adj.* idealistisch. **idealize** [aɪ'dɪəlaɪz] *v.t.* idealisieren. **ideally** [aɪ'dɪəlɪ] *adv.* ideal; **~, ...:** idealerweise *od.* im Idealfall ...
identical [aɪ'dentɪkl] *adj.* identisch; **be ~:** sich (*Dat.*) völlig gleichen; **~ twins** eineiige Zwillinge
identification [aɪdentɪfɪ'keɪʃn] *n.* Identifizierung, *die;* (*of plants, animals*) Bestimmung, *die*
identify [aɪ'dentɪfaɪ] *v.t.* identifizieren; bestimmen ⟨*Pflanze, Tier*⟩
identity [aɪ'dentɪtɪ] *n.* Identität, *die;* **proof of ~:** Identitätsnachweis, *der;* |**case of**| **mistaken ~** |Personen|verwechslung, *die.* **iˈdentity card** *n.* |Personal|ausweis, *der*
idiocy ['ɪdɪəsɪ] *n.* Idiotie, *die*
idiom ['ɪdɪəm] *n.* [Rede]wendung, *die.* **idiomatic** [ɪdɪə'mætɪk] *adj.* idiomatisch
idiosyncrasy [ɪdɪə'sɪŋkrəsɪ] *n.* Eigentümlichkeit, *die.* **idiosyncratic** [ɪdɪə-sɪŋ'krætɪk] *adj.* eigenwillig
idiot ['ɪdɪət] *n.* Idiot, *der* (*ugs.*).
idiotic [ɪdɪ'ɒtɪk] *adj.* idiotisch (*ugs.*)

idle ['aɪdl] **1.** *adj.* **a)** *(lazy)* faul; **b)** *(not in use)* außer Betrieb *nachgestellt*; **be ~** ⟨*Maschinen, Fabrik:*⟩ stillstehen; **c)** bloß ⟨*Neugier, Spekulation:*⟩; leer ⟨*Geschwätz:*⟩. **2.** *v. i.* ⟨*Motor:*⟩ leerlaufen. **idle a'way** *v. t.* vertun
'idleness *n.* Faulheit, *die*
idol ['aɪdl] *n.* Idol, *das.* **idolize** ['aɪdəlaɪz] *v. t.* vergöttern
idyllic [ɪ'dɪlɪk] *adj.* idyllisch
i.e. [aɪ'i:] *abbr.* that is d. h.; i. e.
if [ɪf] *conj.* **a)** wenn; **if anyone should ask ...:** falls jemand fragt, ...; **if I knew what to do ...:** wenn ich wüßte, was ich tun soll ...; **if I were you** an deiner Stelle; **if so/not** wenn ja/nein od. nicht; **if then/that/at all** wenn überhaupt; **as if** als ob; **if I only knew, if only I knew!** wenn ich das nur wüßte!; **if it isn't Ronnie!** das ist doch Ronnie!; **b)** *(whenever)* ⟨*immer*⟩ wenn; **c)** *(whether)* ob; **d)** *(though)* auch od. selbst wenn; **e)** *(despite being)* wenn auch
igloo ['ɪglu:] *n.* Iglu, *der od.* das
ignite [ɪg'naɪt] **1.** *v. t.* anzünden. **2.** *v. i.* sich entzünden. **ignition** [ɪg'nɪʃn] *n.* **a)** *(igniting)* Zünden, *das*; ⟨*Motor Veh.*⟩ Zündung, *die*; **~ key** Zündschlüssel, *der*
ignorance ['ɪgnərəns] *n.* Unwissenheit, *die*; **keep sb. in ~ of sth.** jmdn. in Unkenntnis über etw. (*Akk.*) lassen
ignorant ['ɪgnərənt] *adj.* unwissend; **be ~ of sth.** *(uninformed)* über etw. (*Akk.*) nicht informiert sein
ignore [ɪg'nɔ:(r)] *v. t.* ignorieren; nicht befolgen ⟨*Befehl, Rat*⟩; übergehen ⟨*Frage, Bemerkung*⟩
ill [ɪl] **1.** *adj.* **a)** *(sick)* krank; **fall ~:** krank werden. **2.** *adv.* **be ~ at ease** sich unwohl fühlen. **3.** *n.* Übel, *das*
I'll [aɪl] **a)** = I shall; **b)** = I will
'ill-advised *adj.* unklug
illegal [ɪ'li:gl] *adj.*, **il'legally** *adv.* illegal
illegible [ɪ'ledʒɪbl] *adj.* unleserlich
illegitimate [ɪlɪ'dʒɪtɪmət] *adj.* unehelich ⟨*Kind*⟩
ill health *n.* schwache Gesundheit
illicit [ɪ'lɪsɪt] *adj.* unerlaubt ⟨*Beziehung, [Geschlechts]verkehr*⟩; Schwarz-⟨*handel, -verkauf, -arbeit*⟩
'ill-informed *adj.* schlecht informiert; auf Unkenntnis beruhend ⟨*Bemerkung, Urteil*⟩
illiteracy [ɪ'lɪtərəsɪ] *n.* Analphabetentum, *das*
illiterate [ɪ'lɪtərət] *adj.* des Lesens und

Schreibens unkundig; analphabetisch ⟨*Bevölkerung*⟩
illness ['ɪlnɪs] *n.* Krankheit, *die*
illogical [ɪ'lɒdʒɪkl] *adj.* unlogisch
ill-'treat *v. t.* mißhandeln. **ill-'treatment** *n.* Mißhandlung, *die*
illuminate [ɪ'lu:mɪneɪt] *v. t.* beleuchten. **illuminating** [ɪ'lu:mɪneɪtɪŋ] *adj.* aufschlußreich. **illumination** [ɪlu:mɪ'neɪʃn] *n.* Beleuchtung, *die*
illusion [ɪ'lu:ʒn] *n.* Illusion, *die*; **be under the ~ that ...:** sich (*Dat.*) einbilden, daß ... **illusory** [ɪ'lu:sərɪ] *adj.* illusorisch
illustrate ['ɪləstreɪt] *v. t.* **a)** *(serve as example of)* veranschaulichen; **b)** illustrieren ⟨*Buch, Erklärung*⟩. **illustration** [ɪlə'streɪʃn] *n.* **a)** *(example)* Beispiel, *das* (**of** für); **b)** *(picture)* Abbildung, *die*
ill 'will *n.* Böswilligkeit, *die*
I'm [aɪm] = I am
image ['ɪmɪdʒ] *n.* **a)** Bildnis, *das (geh.)*; **b)** *(Optics)* Bild, *das*; **c)** ⟨*public*⟩ ~: Image, *das*
imaginable [ɪ'mædʒɪnəbl] *adj.* **the best solution ~:** die denkbar beste Lösung
imaginary [ɪ'mædʒɪnərɪ] *adj.* imaginär *(geh.)*; eingebildet ⟨*Krankheit*⟩
imagination [ɪmædʒɪ'neɪʃn] *n.* **a)** Phantasie, *die*; **b)** *(fancy)* Einbildung, *die*
imaginative [ɪ'mædʒɪnətɪv] *adj.* phantasievoll; *(showing imagination)* einfallsreich
imagine [ɪ'mædʒɪn] *v. t.* **a)** sich (*Dat.*) vorstellen; **b)** *(coll.: suppose)* glauben; **c)** *(get the impression)* ~ **that ...:** sich (*Dat.*) einbilden[, daß ...]
imbalance [ɪm'bæləns] *n.* Unausgeglichenheit, *die*
imbecile ['ɪmbɪsi:l] *n.* Idiot, *der (ugs.)*
imitate ['ɪmɪteɪt] *v. t.* nachahmen. **imitation** [ɪmɪ'teɪʃn] *n.* **a)** Nachahmung, *die*; **b)** *(counterfeit)* Imitation, *die*
immaculate [ɪ'mækjʊlət] *adj.* *(spotless)* makellos; *(faultless)* tadellos
immaterial [ɪmə'tɪərɪəl] *adj.* unerheblich
immature [ɪmə'tjʊə(r)] *adj.* unreif; noch nicht voll entwickelt ⟨*Lebewesen*⟩. **immaturity** [ɪmə'tjʊərɪtɪ] *n.* Unreife, *die*
immediate [ɪ'mi:djət] *adj.* **a)** unmittelbar; *(nearest)* nächst... ⟨*Nachbar[schaft], Umgebung, Zukunft*⟩; engst... ⟨*Familie*⟩; **b)** *(occurring at once)* prompt; unverzüglich ⟨*Han-*

deln, *Maßnahmen*⟩; umgehend ⟨*Antwort*⟩. **im'mediately 1.** *adv.* **a)** unmittelbar; **b)** *(without delay)* sofort. **2.** *conj. (coll.)* sobald

immemorial [ɪmɪ'mɔːrɪəl] *adj.* from time ~: seit undenklichen Zeiten

immense [ɪ'mens] *adj.* **a)** ungeheuer; **b)** *(coll.: great)* enorm. **im'mensely** *adv.* **a)** ungeheuer; **b)** *(coll.: very much)* unheimlich *(ugs.)*

immerse [ɪ'mɜːs] *v. t.* [ein]tauchen; be ~d in thought/one's work in Gedanken versunken/in seine Arbeit vertieft sein. **immersion** [ɪ'mɜːʃn] *n.* Eintauchen, *das*. **im'mersion heater** *n.* Heißwasserbereiter, *der*

immigrant ['ɪmɪɡrənt] **1.** *n.* Einwanderer, *der*/Einwanderin, *die*. **2.** *adj.* Einwanderer-; ~ **workers** ausländische Arbeitnehmer

immigration [ɪmɪ'ɡreɪʃn] *n.* Einwanderung *die* (into nach, from aus); *attrib.* Einwanderungs⟨*kontrolle, -gesetz*⟩; ~ **officer** Beamter/Beamtin der Einwanderungsbehörde

imminent ['ɪmɪnənt] *adj.* unmittelbar bevorstehend; drohend ⟨*Gefahr*⟩; be ~: unmittelbar bevorstehen/drohen

immobile [ɪ'məʊbaɪl] *adj.* (*immovable*) unbeweglich. **immobilize** [ɪ'məʊbəlaɪz] *v. t.* verankern; *(fig.)* lähmen

immodest [ɪ'mɒdɪst] *adj.* unbescheiden; *(improper)* unanständig

immoral [ɪ'mɒrəl] *adj.* unmoralisch; *(in sexual matters)* sittenlos. **immorality** [ɪmə'rælɪtɪ] *n.* Unmoral, *die*; *(in sexual matters)* Sittenlosigkeit, *die*

immortal [ɪ'mɔːtl] *adj.* unsterblich. **immortality** [ɪmɔː'tælɪtɪ] *n.* Unsterblichkeit, *die*. **immortalize** [ɪ'mɔːtəlaɪz] *v. t.* unsterblich machen

immovable [ɪ'muːvəbl] *adj.* unbeweglich; be ~: sich nicht bewegen lassen

immune [ɪ'mjuːn] *adj.* **a)** *(exempt)* sicher (from vor + *Dat.*); **b)** *(not susceptible)* unempfindlich (to gegen); **c)** *(Med.)* immun (to gegen). **immunity** [ɪ'mjuːnɪtɪ] *n.* **a)** diplomatic ~: diplomatische Immunität; **b)** *(Med.)* Immunität, *die*. **immunize** ['ɪmjʊnaɪz] *v. t.* immunisieren

imp [ɪmp] *n.* **a)** Kobold, *der*; **b)** *(coll.: child)* Racker, *der (fam.)*

impact ['ɪmpækt] *n.* **a)** Aufprall, *der* (on, against auf + *Akk.*); *(collision)* Zusammenprall, *der*; **b)** *(fig.)* Wirkung, *die*

impair [ɪm'peə(r)] *v. t.* beeinträchtigen; schaden (+ *Dat.*) ⟨*Gesundheit*⟩

impale [ɪm'peɪl] *v. t.* aufspießen

impart [ɪm'pɑːt] *v. t.* **a)** *(give)* [ab]geben (to an + *Akk.*); **b)** *(communicate)* kundtun *(geh.)* (to *Dat.*); vermitteln ⟨*Kenntnisse*⟩ (to *Dat.*)

impartial [ɪm'pɑːʃl] *adj.* unparteiisch; gerecht ⟨*Entscheidung, Urteil*⟩

impassable [ɪm'pɑːsəbl] *adj.* unpassierbar (to für); *(to vehicles)* unbefahrbar (to für)

impasse ['æmpɑːs] *n.* Sackgasse, *die*

impassive [ɪm'pæsɪv] *adj.* ausdruckslos

impatience [ɪm'peɪʃəns] *n.* Ungeduld, *die* (at über + *Akk.*)

impatient [ɪm'peɪʃənt] *adj.* ungeduldig; ~ at sth./with sb. ungeduldig über etw. *(Akk.)*/mit jmdm. **im'patiently** *adv.* ungeduldig

impeccable [ɪm'pekəbl] *adj.* makellos; tadellos ⟨*Manieren*⟩

impede [ɪm'piːd] *v. t.* behindern. **impediment** [ɪm'pedɪmənt] *n.* **a)** Hindernis, *das* (to für); **b)** *(speech defect)* Sprachfehler, *der*

impel [ɪm'pel] *v. t.*, **-ll-** treiben; feel ~led to do sth. sich genötigt *od.* gezwungen fühlen, etw. zu tun

impending [ɪm'pendɪŋ] *adj.* bevorstehend

impenetrable [ɪm'penɪtrəbl] *adj.* undurchdringlich (by, to für)

imperative [ɪm'perətɪv] **1.** *adj.* dringend erforderlich. **2.** *n.* *(Ling.)* Imperativ, *der*

imperceptible [ɪmpə'septɪbl] *adj.* nicht wahrnehmbar; *(very slight or gradual)* unmerklich

imperfect [ɪm'pɜːfɪkt] **1.** *adj.* **a)** *(incomplete)* unvollständig; **b)** *(faulty)* mangelhaft. **2.** *n.* *(Ling.)* Imperfekt, *das*. **imperfection** [ɪmpə'fekʃn] *n.* **a)** *(incompleteness)* Unvollständigkeit, *die*; **b)** *(fault)* Mangel, *der*. **im'perfectly** *adv.* **a)** *(incompletely)* unvollständig; **b)** *(faultily)* fehlerhaft

imperial [ɪm'pɪərɪəl] *adj.* kaiserlich. **imperialism** [ɪm'pɪərɪəlɪzm] *n.* Imperialismus, *der*

imperil [ɪm'perɪl] *v. t.*, *(Brit.)* **-ll-** gefährden

imperious [ɪm'pɪərɪəs] *adj.* herrisch

impersonal [ɪm'pɜːsənl] *adj.* unpersönlich

impersonate [ɪm'pɜːsəneɪt] *v. t.* sich ausgeben als; *(to entertain)* imitieren; nachahmen. **impersonator** [ɪm'pɜːsəneɪtə(r)] *n.* *(entertainer)* Imitator, *der*/Imitatorin, *die*

impertinence [ɪm'pɜːtɪnəns] *n.* Unverschämtheit, *die*

impertinent [ɪm'pɜːtɪnənt] *adj.* unverschämt

imperturbable [ɪmpə'tɜːbəbl] *adj.* gelassen; **be completely ~**: durch nichts zu erschüttern sein

impervious [ɪm'pɜːvɪəs] *adj.* undurchlässig; **be ~ to sth.** *(fig.)* unempfänglich für etw. sein

impetuous [ɪm'petjʊəs] *adj.* unüberlegt; impulsiv ⟨*Person*⟩

impetus ['ɪmpɪtəs] *n.* **a)** Kraft, *die;* **b)** *(fig.)* Motivation, *die*

impinge [ɪm'pɪndʒ] *v. i.* **~ on sth.** auf etw. *(Akk.)* Einfluß nehmen

impish *adj.* lausbübisch

implacable [ɪm'plækəbl] *adj.* unversöhnlich; erbittert ⟨*Gegner*⟩

implausible [ɪm'plɔːzɪbl] *adj.* unglaubwürdig

implement 1. ['ɪmplɪmənt] *n.* Gerät, *das.* 2. ['ɪmplɪment] *v. t.* [in die Tat] umsetzen ⟨*Politik, Plan usw.*⟩

implicate ['ɪmplɪkeɪt] *v. t.* belasten; **be ~d in a scandal** in einen Skandal verwickelt sein. **implication** [ɪmplɪ'keɪʃn] *n.* Implikation, *die;* **by ~**: implizit

implicit [ɪm'plɪsɪt] *adj.* **a)** *(implied)* implizit *(geh.);* unausgesprochen ⟨*Drohung, Zweifel*⟩; **b)** *(resting on authority)* unbedingt; blind ⟨*Vertrauen*⟩

implore [ɪm'plɔː(r)] *v. t.* anflehen (**for** um)

imply [ɪm'plaɪ] *v. t.* **a)** implizieren *(geh.);* *(say indirectly)* hindeuten auf (+ *Akk.*); **b)** *(insinuate)* unterstellen

impolite [ɪmpə'laɪt] *adj.* unhöflich

import 1. [ɪm'pɔːt] *v. t.* importieren, einführen ⟨*Waren*⟩ (**from** aus, **into** nach). 2. ['ɪmpɔːt] *n.* **a)** *(process)* Import, *der;* **b)** *(article)* Importgut, *das*

importance [ɪm'pɔːtəns] *n.* Wichtigkeit, *die* (**to** für); *(significance)* Bedeutung, *die;* **be of ~**: wichtig sein; **full of one's own ~**: von seiner eigenen Wichtigkeit überzeugt

important [ɪm'pɔːtənt] *adj.* wichtig (**to** für); *(significant)* bedeutend

im'porter *n.* Importeur, *der*

impose [ɪm'pəʊz] *v. t.* auferlegen *(geh.)* ⟨*Bürde, Verpflichtung*⟩ (**[up]on** *Dat.*); erheben ⟨*Steuer*⟩ (**on** auf + *Akk.*); verhängen ⟨*Kriegsrecht*⟩; anordnen ⟨*Rationierung*⟩. **im'pose on** *v. t.* ausnutzen ⟨*Gutmütigkeit, Toleranz usw.*⟩; **~ on sb.** sich jmdm. aufdrängen

imposing [ɪm'pəʊzɪŋ] *adj.* imposant

imposition [ɪmpə'zɪʃn] *n.* **a)** Auferlegung, *die; (of tax)* Erhebung, *die;* **b)** *(unreasonable demand)* Zumutung, *die*

impossibility [ɪmpɒsɪ'bɪlɪtɪ] *n.* Unmöglichkeit, *die*

impossible [ɪm'pɒsɪbl] *adj.,* **impossibly** [ɪm'pɒsɪblɪ] *adv.* unmöglich

impostor [ɪm'pɒstə(r)] *n.* Hochstapler, *der*/-staplerin, *die; (swindler)* Betrüger, *der*/Betrügerin, *die*

impound [ɪm'paʊnd] *v. t.* beschlagnahmen

impoverished [ɪm'pɒvərɪʃt] *adj.* **be/ become ~**: verarmt sein/verarmen

impracticable [ɪm'præktɪkəbl] *adj.* undurchführbar

impractical [ɪm'præktɪkl] *adj.* **a)** *(unpractical)* unpraktisch; **b)** *see* **impracticable**

imprecise [ɪmprɪ'saɪs] *adj.* ungenau

impregnable [ɪm'pregnəbl] *adj.* uneinnehmbar ⟨*Festung, Bollwerk*⟩; *(fig.)* unanfechtbar ⟨*Ruf, Stellung*⟩

impregnate ['ɪmpregneɪt] *v. t.* imprägnieren

impress [ɪm'pres] *v. t.* beeindrucken; *abs.* Eindruck machen; **be ~ed by** *or* **with sth.** von etw. beeindruckt sein. **im'press [up]on** *v. t.* einschärfen (+ *Dat.*); **~ sth. [up]on sb.'s memory** jmdm. etw. einschärfen. **impression** [ɪm'preʃn] *n.* **a)** Eindruck, *der;* **form an ~ of sb.** sich *(Dat.)* ein Bild von jmdm. machen; **b)** *(impersonation)* **do an ~ of sb.** jmdn. imitieren; **do ~s an** andere Leute imitieren. **impressionist** [ɪm'preʃənɪst] *n.* Impressionist, *der*/Impressionistin, *die*

impressive [ɪm'presɪv] *adj.* beeindruckend; imponierend

imprint 1. ['ɪmprɪnt] *n.* Abdruck, *der; (fig.)* Stempel, *der.* 2. [ɪm'prɪnt] *v. t.* aufdrucken; *(fig.)* einprägen (**on** *Dat.*)

imprison [ɪm'prɪzn] *v. t.* in Haft nehmen; **be ~ed** sich in Haft befinden. **im'prisonment** *n.* Haft, *die;* **a long term of ~**: eine lange Haftstrafe

improbable [ɪm'prɒbəbl] *adj.* unwahrscheinlich

impromptu [ɪm'prɒmptjuː] 1. *adj.* improvisiert; **an ~ speech** eine Stegreifrede. 2. *adv.* aus dem Stegreif

improper [ɪm'prɒpə(r)] *adj.* **a)** *(wrong)* unrichtig; **b)** *(unseemly)* unpassend; *(indecent)* unanständig. **im'properly** *adv. see* **improper:** unrichtig; unpassend; unanständig

improvable [ɪmˈpruːvəbl] adj. verbesserungsfähig

improve [ɪmˈpruːv] 1. v. i. besser werden; ⟨Person, Wetter:⟩ sich bessern. 2. v. t. verbessern. 3. v. refl. ~ oneself sich weiterbilden. im'prove [up]on v. t. überbieten ⟨Rekord, Angebot⟩; verbessern ⟨Leistung⟩. **improvement** [ɪmˈpruːvmənt] n. Verbesserung, die (on, over gegenüber); make ~s to sth. Verbesserungen an etw. (Dat.) vornehmen

improvise [ˈɪmprəvaɪz] v. t. improvisieren

impudence [ˈɪmpjʊdəns] n. Unverschämtheit, die; (brazenness) Dreistigkeit, die

impudent [ˈɪmpjʊdənt] adj., 'impud-ently adv. unverschämt; (brazen[ly]) dreist

impulse [ˈɪmpʌls] n. Impuls, der; on [an] ~; spontan. **impulsive** [ɪmˈpʌlsɪv] adj. impulsiv

impunity [ɪmˈpjuːnɪti] v. t. with ~: ungestraft

impure [ɪmˈpjʊə(r)] adj. unrein. im-purity [ɪmˈpjʊərɪti] n. Unreinheit, die; (foreign body) Fremdstoff, der

impute [ɪmˈpjuːt] v. t. zuschreiben (to Dat.)

in [ɪn] 1. prep. (position; also fig.) in (+ Dat.); (into) in (+ Akk.); in this heat bei dieser Hitze; two feet in diameter mit einem Durchmesser von zwei Fuß; there are three feet in a yard ein Yard hat drei Fuß; draw in crayon/ink mit Kreide/Tinte zeichnen; pay in pounds/dollars in Pfund/Dollars bezahlen; in fog/rain etc. bei Nebel/Regen usw.; in the 20th century im 20. Jahrhundert; 4 o'clock in the morning/afternoon 4 Uhr morgens/abends; in 1990 [im Jahre] 1990; in three minutes/years in drei Minuten/Jahren; in doing this, he ...; indem er das tut! dat, er ...; in that ...; insofern als. 2. adv. a) (inside) hinein⟨gehen usw.⟩; herein-⟨kommen usw.⟩; b) (at home, work, etc.) be in dasein; c) have it in for sb. es auf jmdn. abgesehen haben (ugs.); sb. is in for sth. ⟨about to undergo⟩ jmdm. steht etw. bevor. 3. adj. (coll.: in fashion) in (ugs.). 4. n. know the ins and outs of sth. sich in einer Sache genau auskennen

ina'bility n. Unfähigkeit, die

inaccessible [ɪnəkˈsesɪbl] adj. unzugänglich

in'accuracy n. a) (incorrectness) Un-

richtigkeit, die; b) (imprecision) Ungenauigkeit, die

in'accurate adj. a) (incorrect) unrichtig; b) (imprecise) ungenau

in'active adj. untätig. **inac'tivity** n. Untätigkeit, die

in'adequate adj. unzulänglich; (incompetent) ungeeignet; feel ~: sich überfordert fühlen

inadvertent [ɪnədˈvɜːtənt] adj., inad-'vertently adv. versehentlich

inad'visable adj. nicht ratsam

inane [ɪˈneɪn] adj. dümmlich

in'animate adj. unbelebt

inap'plicable adj. nicht zutreffend

inap'propriate adj. unpassend

in'apt adj. unpassend

inar'ticulate adj. a) she's rather/very ~: sie kann sich ziemlich/sehr schlecht ausdrücken; b) (indistinct) unverständlich

inat'tentive adj. unaufmerksam (to gegenüber)

in'audible adj. unhörbar

inau'spicious adj. (ominous) unheilvoll; (unlucky) unglücklich

'inborn adj. angeboren (in Dat.)

in-'built adj. jmdm./einer Sache eigen

incalculable [ɪnˈkælkjʊləbl] adj. (very great) unermeßlich

in'capable adj. a) be ~ of doing sth. außerstande sein, etw. zu tun; be ~ of sth. zu etw. unfähig sein; b) be ~ of nicht zulassen ⟨Beweis, Messung usw.⟩

incapacitate [ɪnkəˈpæsɪteɪt] v. t. unfähig machen

incarcerate [ɪnˈkɑːsəreɪt] v. t. einkerkern (geh.)

incendiary [ɪnˈsendɪərɪ] adj. & n. ~ device Brandsatz, der; ~ [bomb] Brandbombe, die

¹incense [ˈɪnsens] n. Weihrauch, der

²incense [ɪnˈsens] v. t. erzürnen

incentive [ɪnˈsentɪv] n. Anreiz, der

incessant [ɪnˈsesənt] adj., in'cess-antly adv. unablässig

incest [ˈɪnsest] n. Inzest, der. **inces-tuous** [ɪnˈsestjʊəs] adj. inzestuös

inch [ɪntʃ] 1. n. Inch, der; Zoll, der (veralt.). 2. v. t. & i. ~ [one's way] for-ward sich Zoll für Zoll vorwärtsbewegen

incident [ˈɪnsɪdənt] n. a) (notable event) Vorfall, der; b) (clash) Zwischenfall, der

incidental [ɪnsɪˈdentl] adj. beiläufig ⟨Bemerkung⟩; Neben⟨ausgaben, -einnahmen⟩. **incidentally** [ɪnsɪˈdentəlɪ] adv. nebenbei [bemerkt]

incinerate [ɪnˈsɪnəreɪt] v. t. verbrennen. **incinerator** [ɪnˈsɪnəreɪtə(r)] n. Verbrennungsofen, der

incision [ɪnˈsɪʒn] n. Einschnitt, der

incisive [ɪnˈsaɪsɪv] adj. schneidend ⟨Ton⟩; scharf ⟨Verstand⟩; scharfsinnig ⟨Kritik, Frage, Bemerkung, Argument⟩

incite [ɪnˈsaɪt] v. t. anstiften; aufstacheln ⟨Massen, Volk⟩. **inˈcitement** n. Anstiftung, die/Aufstachelung, die

inclination [ɪnklɪˈneɪʃn] n. Neigung, die

incline 1. [ɪnˈklaɪn] v. t. a) (bend) neigen; b) (dispose) veranlassen. **2.** v. i. (be disposed) neigen (to|wards| zu). **3.** [ˈɪnklaɪn] n. Steigung, die. **inclined** [ɪnˈklaɪnd] adj. geneigt; **they are ~ to be slow** sie neigen zur Langsamkeit; **if you feel |so| ~:** wenn Sie Lust dazu haben

include [ɪnˈkluːd] v. t. einschließen; (contain) enthalten; **~d in the price** im Preis inbegriffen. **including** [ɪnˈkluːdɪŋ] prep. einschließlich (+ Gen.); **~ VAT** inklusive Mehrwertsteuer. **inclusion** [ɪnˈkluːʒn] n. Aufnahme, die. **inclusive** [ɪnˈkluːsɪv] adj. einschließlich; **be ~ of sth.** etw. einschließen; **from 2 to 6 January ~:** vom 2. bis einschließlich 6. Januar; **cost £50 ~:** 50 Pfund kosten, alles inbegriffen

incognito [ɪnkɒgˈniːtəʊ] adj., adv. inkognito

incoherent adj. zusammenhanglos

income [ˈɪnkʌm] n. Einkommen, das. **ˈincome tax** n. Einkommensteuer, die; (on wages, salary) Lohnsteuer, die

incoming [ˈɪnkʌmɪŋ] adj. ankommend; landend ⟨Flugzeug⟩; einfahrend ⟨Zug⟩; eingehend ⟨Telefongespräch, Auftrag⟩

inˈcomparable adj. unvergleichlich

incomˈpatible adj. unvereinbar; **be ~** ⟨Menschen:⟩ nicht zueinander passen

inˈcompetence [ɪnˈkɒmpɪtəns] n. Unfähigkeit, die; Unvermögen, das

inˈcompetent adj. unfähig

incomˈplete adj. unvollständig

incompreˈhensible adj. unbegreiflich; unverständlich ⟨Rede, Argument⟩

inconˈceivable adj. unvorstellbar

inconˈclusive adj. ergebnislos; nicht schlüssig ⟨Beweis, Argument⟩

incongruous [ɪnˈkɒŋgrʊəs] adj. unpassend

inconsequential [ɪnkɒnsɪˈkwenʃl] adj. belanglos

inconˈsiderate adj. rücksichtslos

inconˈsistency n. see **inconsistent:** Widersprüchlichkeit, die; Inkonsequenz, die; Unbeständigkeit, die

inconˈsistent adj. widersprüchlich; (illogical) inkonsequent; (irregular) unbeständig

inconsolable [ɪnkənˈsəʊləbl] adj. untröstlich

inconˈspicuous adj. unauffällig

incontinence [ɪnˈkɒntɪnəns] n. (Med.) Inkontinenz, die

incontinent [ɪnˈkɒntɪnənt] adj. (Med.) inkontinent; **be ~:** an Inkontinenz leiden

incontrovertible [ɪnkɒntrəˈvɜːtəbl] adj. unbestreitbar; unwiderlegbar ⟨Beweis⟩

inconˈvenience 1. n. Unannehmlichkeit (to für); **put sb. to a lot of ~:** jmdm. große Unannehmlichkeiten bereiten. **2.** v. t. Unannehmlichkeiten bereiten (+ Dat.); (disturb) stören

inconˈvenient adj. unbequem; ungünstig ⟨Lage, Standort⟩; **come at an ~ time** zu ungelegener Zeit kommen; **be ~ for sb.** jmdm. nicht passen

incorporate [ɪnˈkɔːpəreɪt] v. t. aufnehmen (in|to|, with in + Akk.)

incorrect adj. a) unrichtig; **be ~:** nicht stimmen; **it is ~ to say that ...:** es stimmt nicht, daß ...; b) (improper) inkorrekt. **incorrectly** adv. a) unrichtigerweise; falsch ⟨beantworten, aussprechen⟩; b) (improperly) inkorrekt

increase 1. [ɪnˈkriːs] v. i. zunehmen; ⟨Lärm:⟩ größer werden; ⟨Preise, Nachfrage:⟩ steigen; **~ in weight/size/price** schwerer/größer/teurer werden. **2.** v. t. a) (make greater) erhöhen; b) (intensify) verstärken. **3.** [ˈɪnkriːs] n. Zunahme, die (in Gen.); **be on the ~:** ständig zunehmen. **increasing** [ɪnˈkriːsɪŋ] adj. steigend; **an ~ number of people** mehr und mehr Menschen. **inˈcreasingly** adv. in zunehmendem Maße; **become ~ apparent** immer deutlicher werden

inˈcredible adj. (also coll.: remarkable) unglaublich. **inˈcredibly** adv. (also coll.: remarkably) unglaublich

incredulous [ɪnˈkredjʊləs] adj. ungläubig

incriminate [ɪnˈkrɪmɪneɪt] v. t. belasten

incubate [ˈɪŋkjʊbeɪt] v. t. bebrüten; (to hatching) ausbrüten. **incubation** [ɪŋkjʊˈbeɪʃn] n. Bebrütung, die. **incubator** [ˈɪŋkjʊbeɪtə(r)] n. Inkubator, der; (for babies also) Brutkasten, der

incur [ɪn'kɜː(r)] *v. t.*, **-rr-** sich (*Dat.*) zuziehen ⟨*Unwillen, Ärger*⟩; ~ **debts/expenses/risks** Schulden machen/Ausgaben machen/Risiken eingehen

in'curable *adj.* unheilbar

incursion [ɪn'kɜː.ʃn] *n.* Eindringen, *das*; (*by sudden attack*) Einfall, *der*

indebted [ɪn'detɪd] *pred. adj.* **be |much| ~ to sb. for sth.** jmdm. für etw. [sehr] zu Dank verpflichtet sein

in'decency *n.* Unanständigkeit, *die*

in'decent *adj.*, **in'decently** *adv.* unanständig

inde'cision *n.* Unentschlossenheit, *die*

inde'cisive *adj.* a) ergebnislos ⟨*Streit, Diskussion*⟩; nichtssagend ⟨*Ergebnis*⟩; b) (*hesitating*) unentschlossen

indeed [ɪn'diːd] *adv.* a) in der Tat; **thank you very much ~**: haben Sie vielen herzlichen Dank; **~ it is** in der Tat; b) (*in fact*) ja sogar; **~, he can ...**: ja, er kann sogar ...; c) (*admittedly*) zugegebenermaßen

in'definite *adj.* a) (*vague*) unbestimmt; b) (*unlimited*) unbegrenzt. **in'definitely** *adv.* a) (*vaguely*) unbestimmt; b) (*unlimitedly*) unbegrenzt; auf unbestimmte Zeit ⟨*verschieben*⟩

indelible [ɪn'delɪbl] *adj.* unauslöschlich; **~ ink** Wäschetinte, *die*

indemnify [ɪn'demnɪfaɪ] *v. t.* absichern (**against** gegen); (*compensate*) entschädigen. **indemnity** [ɪn'demnɪtɪ] *n.* Absicherung, *die*; (*compensation*) Entschädigung, *die*

inde'pendence *n.* Unabhängigkeit, *die*

inde'pendent *adj.*, **inde'pendently** *adv.* unabhängig (**of** von)

indescribable [ɪndɪ'skraɪbəbl] *adj.* unbeschreiblich

indestructible [ɪndɪ'strʌktɪbl] *adj.* unzerstörbar

indeterminate [ɪndɪ'tɜːmɪnət] *adj.* unbestimmt; unklar ⟨*Konzept*⟩

index ['ɪndeks] 1. *n.* Register, *das.* 2. *v. t.* mit einem Register versehen. **'index finger** *n.* Zeigefinger, *der*

India ['ɪndɪə] *n.* Indien (*das*). **Indian** ['ɪndɪən] 1. *adj.* a) indisch; b) |American| ~: indianisch. 2. *n.* a) Inder, *der*/Inderin, *die*; b) |American| ~: Indianer, *der*/Indianerin, *die*. **Indian 'Ocean** *pr. n.* Indischer Ozean

indicate ['ɪndɪkeɪt] 1. *v. t.* a) (*be a sign of*) erkennen lassen; b) (*state briefly*) andeuten; c) (*mark, point out*) anzeigen; d) (*suggest, make evident*) zum Ausdruck bringen (**to** gegenüber). 2.

v. i. (*Motor Veh.*) blinken. **indication** [ɪndɪ'keɪʃn] *n.* [An]zeichen, *das* (**of** *Gen.*, **für**). **indicative** [ɪn'dɪkətɪv] 1. *adj.* **a) be ~ of sth.** auf etw. (*Akk.*) schließen lassen; b) (*Ling.*) indikativisch. 2. *n.* (*Ling.*) Indikativ, *der.* **indicator** ['ɪndɪkeɪtə(r)] *n.* (*on vehicle*) Blinker, *der*

indict [ɪn'daɪt] *v. t.* anklagen (**for, on a charge of** *Gen.*)

in'difference *n.* Gleichgültigkeit, *die* (**to|wards|** gegenüber)

in'different *adj.* a) gleichgültig; b) (*not good*) mittelmäßig

indi'gestion *n.* Magenverstimmung, *die*; (*chronic*) Verdauungsstörungen

indignant [ɪn'dɪgnənt] *adj.* entrüstet (**at, over, about** über + *Akk.*); indigniert ⟨*Blick, Geste*⟩. **in'dignantly** *adv.* entrüstet; indigniert. **indignation** [ɪndɪg'neɪʃn] *n.* Entrüstung, *die* (**about, at, against, over** über + *Akk.*)

in'dignity *n.* Demütigung, *die*

indigo ['ɪndɪgəʊ] 1. *adj.* ~ |**blue**| indigoblau. 2. *n.* ~ |**blue**| Indigoblau, *das*

indi'rect *adj.* indirekt; ~ **speech** indirekte Rede. **indi'rectly** *adv.* indirekt. **indirect 'object** *n.* indirektes Objekt; (*in German*) Dativobjekt, *das*

indi'screet *adj.* indiskret. **indi'scretion** *n.* Indiskretion, *die*

indiscriminate [ɪndɪ'skrɪmɪnət] *adj.* unkritisch

indi'spensable *adj.* unentbehrlich (**to** für); unabdingbar ⟨*Voraussetzung*⟩

indisputable [ɪndɪ'spjuːtəbl] *adj.*, **indisputably** [ɪndɪ'spjuːtəblɪ] *adv.* unbestreitbar

indi'stinct *adj.*, **indi'stinctly** *adv.* undeutlich

indi'stinguishable *adj.* nicht unterscheidbar

individual [ɪndɪ'vɪdjʊəl] 1. *adj.* a) einzeln; b) (*distinctive, characteristic*) individuell. 2. *n.* einzelne, *der/die.* **indi'vidually** *adv.* einzeln

indi'visible *adj.* unteilbar

indoctrinate [ɪn'dɒktrɪneɪt] *v. t.* indoktrinieren

indolence ['ɪndələns] *n.* Trägheit, *die*

indolent ['ɪndələnt] *adj.* träge

indomitable [ɪn'dɒmɪtəbl] *adj.* unbeugsam

Indonesia [ɪndə'niːʃə] *pr. n.* Indonesien (*das*)

'indoor *adj.* ~ **swimming-pool/sports** Hallenbad, *das*/-sport, *der*; ~ **plants** Zimmerpflanzen; ~ **games** Spiele im Haus; (*Sport*) Hallenspiele

indoors [ɪn'dɔːz] adv. drinnen; im Haus; go/come ~: nach drinnen gehen/kommen

induce [ɪn'djuːs] v. t. ~ sb. to do sth. jmdn. dazu bringen, etw. zu tun. **in'ducement** n. (incentive) Anreiz, der

indulge [ɪn'dʌldʒ] **1.** v. t. **a)** nachgeben (+ Dat.) ⟨Wunsch, Verlangen, Verlockung⟩; frönen (geh.) (+ Dat.) ⟨Leidenschaft⟩; **b)** (please) verwöhnen. **2.** v. i. ~ in frönen (geh.) (+ Dat.) ⟨Leidenschaft⟩. **indulgence** [ɪn'dʌldʒəns] n. **a)** Nachsicht, die; (humouring) Nachgiebigkeit, die (with gegenüber); (thing indulged in) Luxus, der

indulgent [ɪn'dʌldʒənt] adj. nachsichtig (with, to[wards] gegenüber)

industrial [ɪn'dʌstrɪəl] adj. industriell; Arbeits(unfall, -medizin, -psychologie)

industrial: ~ **'action** n. Arbeitskampfmaßnahmen; **take** ~ **action**: in den Ausstand treten; ~ **dispute** n. Arbeitskonflikt, der; ~ **estate** n. Industriegebiet, das

industrialize [ɪn'dʌstrɪəlaɪz] v. t. industrialisieren

industrious [ɪn'dʌstrɪəs] adj. fleißig; (busy) emsig

industry ['ɪndəstrɪ] n. **a)** Industrie, die; **b)** see **industrious**: Fleiß, der; Emsigkeit, die

in'edible adj. ungenießbar

ineffective adj. unwirksam; fruchtlos ⟨Anstrengung, Versuch⟩

ineffectual [ɪnɪ'fektjʊəl] adj. unwirksam; fruchtlos ⟨Versuch, Bemühung⟩; ineffizient ⟨Methode, Person⟩

inefficiency n. Leistungsschwäche, die; (of organization, method) schlechtes Funktionieren

inefficient adj. leistungsschwach; schlecht funktionierend ⟨Organisation, Methode⟩

in'elegant adj. unelegant

in'eligible adj. ungeeignet; **be** ~ **for** nicht in Frage kommen für ⟨Beförderung, Position⟩; nicht berechtigt sein zu ⟨Leistungen des Staats usw.⟩

inept [ɪ'nept] adj. unbeholfen

ine'quality n. Ungleichheit, die

inert [ɪ'nɜːt] adj. **a)** reglos; (sluggish) träge; **b)** (Chem.) inert; ~ **gas** Edelgas, das. **inertia** [ɪ'nɜːʃə] n. Trägheit, die

inescapable [ɪnɪ'skeɪpəbl] adj. unausweichlich

ines'sential n. unwesentlich; (dispensable) entbehrlich

inevitable [ɪn'evɪtəbl] adj. unvermeidlich; unabwendbar ⟨Ereignis, Krieg,

Schicksal⟩; zwangsläufig ⟨Ergebnis, Folge⟩. **inevitably** [ɪn'evɪtəblɪ] adv. zwangsläufig

ine'xact adj. ungenau

inex'cusable adj. unverzeihlich

inexhaustible [ɪnɪg'zɔːstɪbl] adj. unerschöpflich; unverwüstlich ⟨Person⟩

inexorable [ɪn'eksərəbl] adj. unerbittlich

inex'pensive adj. preisgünstig

inex'perience n. Unerfahrenheit, die. **inex'perienced** adj. unerfahren; ~ **in sth.** wenig vertraut mit etw.

inex'plicable adj. unerklärlich

in'fallible adj. unfehlbar

infamous ['ɪnfəməs] adj. berüchtigt

infancy ['ɪnfənsɪ] n. frühe Kindheit; **be in its** ~ (fig.) noch in den Anfängen stecken

infant ['ɪnfənt] n. kleines Kind. **infantile** ['ɪnfəntaɪl] adj. kindlich; (childish) kindisch

infantry ['ɪnfəntrɪ] n. Infanterie, die

'infant school n. (Brit.) ≈ Vorschule, die

infatuated [ɪn'fætjʊeɪtɪd] adj. **be** ~ **with sb.** in jmdn. vernarrt sein

infect [ɪn'fekt] v. t. anstecken; infizieren; **the wound became** ~**ed** die Wunde entzündete sich. **infection** [ɪn'fekʃn] n. Infektion, die; **throat/ear/eye** ~: Hals-/Ohren-/Augenentzündung, die. **infectious** [ɪn'fekʃəs] adj. ansteckend; **be** ~ ⟨Person:⟩ eine ansteckende Krankheit haben

infer [ɪn'fɜː(r)] v. t., **-rr-** schließen (from aus); ziehen ⟨Schlußfolgerung⟩. **inference** ['ɪnfərəns] n. [Schluß]folgerung, die

inferior [ɪn'fɪərɪə(r)] **1.** adj. (of lower quality) minderwertig ⟨Ware⟩; minder... ⟨Qualität⟩; unterlegen ⟨Gegner⟩; ~ **to sth.** schlechter als etw.; **feel** ~: Minderwertigkeitsgefühle haben. **2.** n. Untergebene, der/die. **inferiority** [ɪnfɪərɪ'ɒrɪtɪ] n. Minderwertigkeit, die/ Unterlegenheit, die. **inferi'ority complex** n. Minderwertigkeitskomplex, der

infernal [ɪn'fɜːnl] adj. **a)** (of hell) höllisch; **b)** (coll.) verdammt (salopp)

inferno [ɪn'fɜːnəʊ] n. Inferno, das

in'fertile adj. unfruchtbar. **infer'tility** n. Unfruchtbarkeit, die

infest [ɪn'fest] v. t. ⟨Ungeziefer:⟩ befallen; ⟨Unkraut:⟩ überwuchern; ~**ed with** befallen/überwuchert von

infidelity [ɪnfɪ'delɪtɪ] n. Untreue, die (to gegenüber)

infiltrate ['ınfıltreıt] *v. t.* a) infiltrieren; unterwandern ⟨*Partei, Organisation*⟩; b) einschleusen ⟨*Agenten*⟩

infinite ['ınfınıt] *adj.* a) *(endless)* unendlich; b) *(very great)* ungeheuer

infinitive [ın'fınıtıv] *n. (Ling.)* Infinitiv, *der*

infinity [ın'fınıtı] *n.* Unendlichkeit, *die*

infirm [ın'fɜːm] *adj.* gebrechlich. **infirmity** [ın'fɜːmıtı] *n.* Gebrechlichkeit, *die; (malady)* Gebrechen, *das*

inflamed [ın'fleımd] *adj. (Med.)* **be/become** ~: entzündet sein/sich entzünden

inflammable [ın'flæməbl] *adj.* feuergefährlich

inflammation [ınflə'meıʃn] *n. (Med.)* Entzündung, *die*

inflammatory [ın'flæmətərı] *adj.* aufrührerisch; **an** ~ **speech** eine Hetzrede

inflatable [ın'fleıtəbl] *adj.* aufblasbar; ~ **dinghy** Schlauchboot, *das*

inflate [ın'fleıt] *v. t.* aufblasen; *(with pump)* aufpumpen

inflation [ın'fleıʃn] *n. (Econ.)* Inflation, *die*

in'flexible *adj.* a) *(stiff)* unbiegsam; b) *(obstinate)* ⟨geistig⟩ unbeweglich

inflict [ın'flıkt] *v. t.* zufügen ⟨*Leid, Schmerzen*⟩, beibringen ⟨*Wunde*⟩, versetzen ⟨*Schlag*⟩ (**on** *Dat.*)

influence ['ınfluəns] **1.** *n.* Einfluß, *der;* **be a good/bad** ~ **[on** sb.**]** einen guten/schlechten Einfluß [auf jmdn.] ausüben. **2.** *v. t.* beeinflussen. **influential** [ınflu'enʃl] *adj.* einflußreich

influenza [ınflu'enzə] *n.* Grippe, *die*

influx ['ınflʌks] *n.* Zustrom, *der*

inform [ın'fɔːm] **1.** *n.* informieren (**of, about** über + *Akk.*); **keep** sb. ~**ed** jmdn. auf dem laufenden halten. **2.** *v. i.* ~ **against** *or* **on** sb. jmdn. denunzieren (**to** bei)

in'formal *adj.* a) zwanglos; b) *(unofficial)* informell. **infor'mality** *n.* Zwanglosigkeit, *die*

informant [ın'fɔːmənt] *n.* Informant, *der/*Informantin, *die*

information [ınfə'meıʃn] *n.* Informationen *Pl.;* **give** ~ **on** sth. Auskunft über etw. *(Akk.)* erteilen; **piece** *or* **bit of** ~ : Information, *die;* ~ **centre** Auskunftsbüro, *das*

informative [ın'fɔːmətıv] *adj.* informativ; **not very** ~ : nicht sehr aufschlußreich ⟨*Dokument, Schriftstück*⟩

informed [ın'fɔːmd] *adj.* informiert

in'former *n.* Denunziant, *der/*Denunziantin, *die*

infra-red [ınfrə'red] *adj.* infrarot

in'frequent *adj.,* **in'frequently** *adv.* selten

infringe [ın'frındʒ] *v. t. & i.* ~ **[on]** verstoßen gegen. **in'fringement** *n.* Verstoß, *der* (**of** gegen)

infuriate [ın'fjuərıeıt] *v. t.* wütend machen; **be** ~**d** wütend sein (**by** über + *Akk.*). **infuriating** [ın'fjuərıeıtıŋ] *adj.* ärgerlich

ingenious [ın'dʒiːnıəs] *adj.* einfallsreich; genial ⟨*Methode, Idee*⟩; raffiniert ⟨*Spielzeug, Maschine*⟩. **ingenuity** [ındʒı'njuːıtı] *n.* Genialität, *die*

ingot ['ıŋgət] *n.* Ingot, *der*

ingratiate [ın'greıʃıeıt] *v. refl.* ~ **oneself with** sb. sich bei jmdm. einschmeicheln

in'gratitude *n.* Undankbarkeit, *die* (**to/wards**) gegenüber

ingredient [ın'griːdıənt] *n.* Zutat, *die*

ingrowing ['ıngrəuıŋ] *adj.* eingewachsen ⟨*Zehennagel usw.*⟩

inhabit [ın'hæbıt] *v. t.* bewohnen. **inhabitable** [ın'hæbıtəbl] *adj.* bewohnbar. **inhabitant** [ın'hæbıtənt] *n.* Bewohner, *der/*Bewohnerin, *die*

inhale [ın'heıl] *v. t. & i.* einatmen; inhalieren *(ugs.)* ⟨*Zigarettenrauch usw.*⟩

inherit [ın'herıt] *v. t.* erben. **inheritance** [ın'herıtəns] *n.* Erbe, *das; (inheriting)* Erbschaft, *die*

inhibit [ın'hıbıt] *v. t.* hemmen. **in'hibited** *adj.* gehemmt. **inhibition** [ınhı'bıʃn] *n.* Hemmung, *die*

inho'spitable *adj.* ungastlich ⟨*Person, Verhalten*⟩; unwirtlich ⟨*Gegend, Klima*⟩

in'human *adj.* unmenschlich

initial [ı'nıʃl] **1.** *adj.* anfänglich; Anfangs⟨*stadium, -schwierigkeiten*⟩. **2.** *n. esp.* **in** *pl.* Initiale, *die.* **3.** *v. t. (Brit.)* -**ll**- abzeichnen ⟨*Scheck, Quittung*⟩; paraphieren ⟨*Vertrag, Abkommen usw.*⟩. **i'nitially** *adv.* anfangs; am Anfang

initiate [ı'nıʃıeıt] *v. t.* a) *(introduce)* einführen (**into** in + *Akk.*); *(into knowledge, mystery)* einweihen (**into** in + *Akk.*); b) *(begin)* einleiten. **tiation** [ınıʃı'eıʃn] *n.* a) *(introduction)* Einführung, *die; (into knowledge, mystery)* Einweihung, *die*

initiative [ı'nıʃıətıv] *n.* Initiative, *die;* **lack** ~ : keine Initiative haben

inject [ın'dʒekt] *v. t.* [ein]spritzen; injizieren *(Med.).* **injection** [ın'dʒekʃn] *n.* Spritze, *die;* Injektion, *die*

injure ['ındʒə(r)] *v. t.* a) verletzen; **his**

leg was ~d er wurde/(state) war am Bein verletzt; **b)** (impair) schaden (+ Dat.). **injured** ['ɪndʒəd] adj. verletzt; verwundet (Soldat). **injury** ['ɪndʒərɪ] n. Verletzung, die (to Gen.)

in'justice n. Ungerechtigkeit, die

ink [ɪŋk] n. Tinte, die

inkling ['ɪŋklɪŋ] n. Ahnung, die; **have an ~ of sth.** etw. ahnen

inland ['ɪnlənd, 'ɪnlænd] adj. Binnen-; binnenländisch. **Inland 'Revenue** n. (Brit.) ≈ Finanzamt, das

'in-laws n. pl. (coll.) Schwiegereltern

inlet ['ɪnlət] n. [schmale] Bucht

'inmate n. Insasse, der/Insassin, die

inn [ɪn] n. (hotel) Gasthof, der; (pub) Wirtshaus, das

innate ['ɪ'neɪt] adj. angeboren

inner ['ɪnə(r)] adj. inner...; Innen(hof, -tür, -fläche, -seite usw.); **~ tube** Schlauch, der. **innermost** ['ɪnə-məʊst] adj. innerst...

innocence ['ɪnəsns] n. **a)** Unschuld, die; **b)** (naivity) Naivität, die

innocent ['ɪnəsnt] adj. **a)** unschuldig (of an + Dat.); **b)** (naive) naiv

innocuous [ɪ'nɒkjʊəs] adj. harmlos

innovation [ɪnə'veɪʃn] n. Innovation, die; (thing, change) Neuerung, die

innumerable [ɪ'njuːmərəbl] adj. unzählig

inoculate [ɪ'nɒkjʊleɪt] v.t. impfen. **inoculation** [ɪnɒkjʊ'leɪʃn] n. Impfung, die

inoffensive adj. harmlos

in'opportune adj. unpassend; unangebracht (Bemerkung)

inordinate [ɪ'nɔːdɪnət] adj. unmäßig; ungeheuer (Menge)

inor'ganic adj. anorganisch

'in-patient n. stationär behandelter Patient/behandelte Patientin

'input n. Input, der od. das

inquest ['ɪŋkwest] n. gerichtliche Untersuchung der Todesursache

inquire [ɪn'kwaɪə(r)] **1.** v.i. sich erkundigen (about, after nach, of bei); **~ into** untersuchen. **2.** v.t. sich erkundigen nach (Weg, Namen). **inquiry** [ɪn-'kwaɪərɪ] n. **a)** (question) Erkundigung, die (into über + Akk.); **make inquiries** Erkundigungen einziehen; **b)** (investigation) Untersuchung, die

inquisitive [ɪn'kwɪzɪtɪv] adj. neugierig

'inroad n. Eingriff, der (on, into in + Akk.); **make ~s into sb.'s savings** jmds. Ersparnisse angreifen

in'sane adj. geisteskrank

in'sanitary adj. unhygienisch

in'sanity n. Geisteskrankheit, die

insatiable [ɪn'seɪʃəbl] adj. unersättlich; unstillbar (Verlangen)

inscribe [ɪn'skraɪb] v.t. schreiben; (on stone, rock) einmeißeln; (with) mit einer Inschrift versehen (Denkmal, Grabstein). **inscription** [ɪn'skrɪpʃn] n. Inschrift, die; (on coin) Aufschrift, die

inscrutable [ɪn'skruːtəbl] adj. unergründlich; undurchdringlich (Miene)

insect ['ɪnsekt] n. Insekt, das. **insecticide** [ɪn'sektɪsaɪd] n. Insektizid, das. **'insect repellent** n. Insektenschutzmittel, das

inse'cure adj. unsicher. **inse'curity** n. Unsicherheit, die

in'sensitive adj. **a)** gefühllos (Person, Art); (unappreciative) unempfänglich (to für); **b)** (physically) unempfindlich (to gegen)

in'separable adj. untrennbar; (fig.) unzertrennlich

insert [ɪn'sɜːt] v.t. einlegen (Film); einwerfen (Münze); hineinstecken (Schlüssel); einstecken (Nadel). **insertion** [ɪn'sɜːʃn] n. see **insert**: Einlegen, das; Einwerfen, das; Hineinstecken, das; Einstecken, das

inside 1. [-'-, '--] n. **a)** (internal side) Innenseite, die; **on the ~:** innen; **to/from the ~:** nach/von innen; **b)** (inner part) Innere, das. **2.** [--] adj. inner...; Innen(wand, -einrichtung, -ansicht); (fig.) intern. **3.** [-'-] adv. (on or in the ~) innen; (to the ~) nach innen hinein/herein; (indoors) drinnen; **come ~:** hereinkommen; **take a look ~:** hineinsehen; **go ~:** [ins Haus] hineingehen; **turn a jacket ~ out** eine Jacke nach links wenden; **know sth. ~ out** etw. in- und auswendig kennen. **4.** [-'-] prep. (position) in (+ Dat.); (direction) in (+ Akk.) hinein

insidious [ɪn'sɪdɪəs] adj. heimtückisch

'insight n. (discernment) Verständnis, das; **gain an ~ into sth.** Einblick in etw. (Akk.) gewinnen

insig'nificant adj. unbedeutend; geringfügig (Summe)

insin'cere adj. unaufrichtig. **insin'cerity** n. Unaufrichtigkeit, die

insinuate [ɪn'sɪnjʊeɪt] v.t. andeuten (to sb. jmdm. gegenüber). **insinuation** [ɪnsɪnjʊ'eɪʃn] n. Anspielung, die (about auf + Akk.)

insipid [ɪn'sɪpɪd] adj. fade

insist [ɪn'sɪst] v.i. bestehen (lupion auf + Dat.); **~ on doing sth./on sb.'s doing sth.** darauf bestehen, etw. zu tun/daß jmd. etw. tut; **if you ~:** wenn du darauf bestehst. **insistence** [ɪn-'sɪstəns] n. Bestehen, das (on auf + Dat.). **insistent** [ɪn'sɪstənt] adj. be ~ that ...: darauf bestehen, daß ...

insolence ['ɪnsələns] n. Unverschämtheit, die; Frechheit, die

insolent ['ɪnsələnt] adj., **insolently** adv. unverschämt; frech

in'soluble adj. **a)** (esp. Chem.) unlöslich; **b)** (not solvable) unlösbar

in'solvent adj. zahlungsunfähig

insomnia [ɪn'sɒmnɪə] n. Schlaflosigkeit, die. **insomniac** [ɪn'sɒmnɪæk] n. be an ~: an Schlaflosigkeit leiden

inspect [ɪn'spekt] v. t. prüfend betrachten; (examine officially) überprüfen; kontrollieren ⟨Räumlichkeiten⟩. **inspection** [ɪn'spekʃn] n. Überprüfung, die; (of premises) Kontrolle, die; Inspektion, die; on ⟨closer⟩ ~: bei näherer Betrachtung. **inspector** [ɪn'spektə(r)] n. **a)** (on bus, train, etc.) Kontrolleur, der/Kontrolleurin, die; **b)** (Brit.) ≈ Polizeiinspektor, der

inspiration [ɪnspə'reɪʃn] n. Inspiration, die (geh.)

inspire [ɪn'spaɪə(r)] v. t. **a)** inspirieren (geh.)⟨Person⟩; **b)** (instil) einflößen (in Dat.). **inspiring** [ɪn'spaɪərɪŋ] adj. inspirierend (geh.)

insta'bility n. Instabilität, die; (of person) Labilität, die

install [ɪn'stɔːl] v. t. installieren; einbauen ⟨Badezimmer⟩; anschließen ⟨Telefon, Herd⟩; ~ oneself sich installieren. **installation** [ɪnstə'leɪʃn] n. **a)** Installation, die; (of bathroom) Einbau, der; (of telephone, cooker) Anschluß, der; **b)** (apparatus etc. installed) Anlage, die

instalment (Amer.: **installment**) [ɪn'stɔːlmənt] n. **a)** (part-payment) Rate, die; pay by or in ~s in Raten zahlen; **b)** (of serial, novel) Fortsetzung, die; (Radio, Telev.) Folge, die

instance ['ɪnstəns] n. (example) Beispiel, das (of für); **for ~:** zum Beispiel; **in many ~s** (cases) in vielen Fällen; **in the first ~:** zunächst einmal

instant ['ɪnstənt] **1.** adj. unmittelbar; sofortig ⟨Wirkung, Linderung, Ergebnis⟩; ~ coffee/tea Pulverkaffee/Instanttee, der; ~ potatoes fertiger Kartoffelbrei. **2.** n. Augenblick, der; **at that very ~:** genau in dem Augenblick; **come here this ~:** komm sofort her; **in an ~:** augenblicklich. **instantaneous** [ɪnstən'teɪnɪəs] adj. unmittel-

bar; **his reaction was ~:** er reagierte sofort. **instantly** adv. sofort

instead [ɪn'sted] adv. statt dessen; ~ of doing sth. [an]statt etw. zu tun; ~ of sth. anstelle einer Sache (Gen.); **I will go ~ of you** ich gehe an deiner Stelle

instep n. (of foot) Spann, der; Fußrücken, der; (of shoe) Blatt, das

instigate ['ɪnstɪgeɪt] v. t. anstiften (to zu); initiieren (geh.) ⟨Reformen, Projekt usw.⟩. **instigation** [ɪnstɪ'geɪʃn] n. Anstiftung, die; (of reforms, project, etc.) Initiierung, die; at sb.'s ~: auf jmds. Betreiben (Akk.)

instil (Amer.: **instill**) [ɪn'stɪl] v. t., -ll-einflößen (in Dat.); beibringen ⟨gutes Benehmen, Wissen⟩ (in Dat.)

instinct ['ɪnstɪŋkt] n. Instinkt, der. **instinctive** [ɪn'stɪŋktɪv] adj., **instinctively** adv. instinktiv

institute ['ɪnstɪtjuːt] **1.** n. Institut, das. **2.** v. t. einführen; einleiten ⟨Suche, Verfahren⟩; anstrengen ⟨Prozeß⟩

institution [ɪnstɪ'tjuːʃn] n. Institution, die; (home) Heim, das; Anstalt, die

instruct [ɪn'strʌkt] v. t. **a)** (teach) unterrichten ⟨Klasse, Fach⟩; **b)** (direct, command) anweisen. **instruction** [ɪn'strʌkʃn] n. **a)** (teaching) Unterricht, der; **b)** esp. in pl. (direction, order) Anweisung, die; ~ manual/~s for use Gebrauchsanleitung, die. **instructive** [ɪn'strʌktɪv] adj. aufschlußreich; lehrreich ⟨Erfahrung, Buch⟩. **instructor** [ɪn'strʌktə(r)] n. Lehrer, der/Lehrerin, die; (Mil.) Ausbilder, der

instrument ['ɪnstrəmənt] n. Instrument, das. **instrumental** [ɪnstrə'mentl] adj. **a)** (Mus.) Instrumental-; **b)** (helpful) dienlich (to Dat.); **he was ~ in finding me a job** er hat zu einer Stelle verholfen

insufferable [ɪn'sʌfərəbl] adj. (unbearably arrogant) unausstehlich

insufficient adj. nicht genügend; unzulänglich ⟨Beweise⟩; unzureichend ⟨Versorgung, Beleuchtung⟩. **insufficiently** adv. ungenügend

insulate ['ɪnsjʊleɪt] v. t. isolieren (against, from gegen); **insulating tape** Isolierband, das. **insulation** [ɪnsjʊ-'leɪʃn] n. Isolierung, die

insulin ['ɪnsjʊlɪn] n. Insulin, das

insult 1. ['ɪnsʌlt] n. Beleidigung, die (to Gen.). **2.** [ɪn'sʌlt] v. t. beleidigen. **insulting** [ɪn'sʌltɪŋ] adj. beleidigend

insuperable [ɪn'suːpərəbl] adj. unüberwindlich

insurance [ɪnˈʃʊərəns] *n.* Versicherung, *die;* *(fig.)* Sicherheit, *die;* **take out ~ against/on sth.** eine Versicherung gegen etw. abschließen/etw. versichern lassen; **travel ~:** Reisegepäck- und -unfallversicherung, *die.* **inˈsurance policy** *n.* Versicherungspolice, *die*

insure [ɪnˈʃʊə(r)] *v. t.* versichern ⟨Person⟩; versichern lassen ⟨Gepäck, Gemälde usw.⟩; **~ [oneself] against sth.** [sich] gegen etw. versichern

insurmountable [ɪnsəˈmaʊntəbl] *adj.* unüberwindlich

intact [ɪnˈtækt] *adj.* a) *(entire)* unbeschädigt; intakt ⟨Uhr, Maschine usw.⟩; b) *(unimpaired)* unversehrt

'**intake** *n.* a) *(action)* Aufnahme, *die;* b) *(persons, things)* Neuzugänge; *(amount)* aufgenommene Menge

inˈtangible *adj.* nicht greifbar; *(mentally)* unbestimmbar

integral [ˈɪntɪgrl] *adj.* a) *(essential)* wesentlich ⟨Bestandteil⟩; b) *(whole)* vollständig

integrate [ˈɪntɪgreɪt] *v. t.* integrieren ⟨into in + Akk.⟩. **integration** [ɪntɪˈgreɪʃn] *n.* Integration, *die* ⟨into in + Akk.⟩

integrity [ɪnˈtegrɪtɪ] *n.* Redlichkeit, *die*

intellect [ˈɪntəlekt] *n.* Verstand, *der;* Intellekt, *der.* **intellectual** [ɪntəˈlektjʊəl] **1.** *adj.* intellektuell; geistig anspruchsvoll ⟨Person, Publikum⟩. **2.** *n.* Intellektuelle, *der/die*

intelligence [ɪnˈtelɪdʒəns] *n.* a) Intelligenz, *die;* b) *(information)* Informationen *Pl.;* c) **military ~** *(organization)* militärischer Geheimdienst. **intelligent** [ɪnˈtelɪdʒənt] *adj.* intelligent

intelligible [ɪnˈtelɪdʒɪbl] *adj.* verständlich (to für)

intend [ɪnˈtend] *v. t.* beabsichtigen; **it was ~ed as a joke** das sollte ein Witz sein. **inˈtended** *adj.* beabsichtigt ⟨Wirkung⟩; **be ~ for sb./sth.** für jmdn./etw. gedacht sein

intense [ɪnˈtens] *adj.* a) intensiv; groß ⟨Hitze, Belastung, Interesse⟩; stark ⟨Schmerzen⟩; b) *(earnest)* ernst. **inˈtensely** *adv.* äußerst; intensiv ⟨studieren, fühlen⟩

intensify [ɪnˈtensɪfaɪ] **1.** *v. t.* intensivieren. **2.** *v. i.* zunehmen

intensity [ɪnˈtensɪtɪ] *n. see* **intense a:** Intensität, *die;* Größe, *die;* Stärke, *die*

intensive [ɪnˈtensɪv] *adj.* intensiv; Intensiv⟨kurs⟩; **be in ~** auf der Intensivstation sein. **inˈtensively** *adv.* intensiv

intent [ɪnˈtent] **1.** *n.* Absicht, *die;* **to all ~s and purposes** im Grunde. **2.** *adj.* **be ~ on achieving sth.** etw. unbedingt erreichen wollen

intention [ɪnˈtenʃn] *n.* Absicht, *die.* **intentional** [ɪnˈtenʃənl] *adj.,* **inˈtentionally** *adv.* absichtlich

inˈtently *adv.* aufmerksam

interact [ɪntərˈækt] *v. i.* interagieren. **interaction** [ɪntərˈækʃn] *n.* Interaktion, *die*

intercede [ɪntəˈsiːd] *v. i.* sich einsetzen (**with** bei; **on behalf of** für)

intercept [ɪntəˈsept] *v. t.* abfangen

interchange 1. [ˈɪntətʃeɪndʒ] *n.* a) Austausch, *der;* b) *(road junction)* [Autobahn]kreuz, *das.* **2.** [ɪntəˈtʃeɪndʒ] *v. t.* austauschen. **interchangeable** [ɪntəˈtʃeɪndʒəbl] *adj.* austauschbar

inter-city [ɪntəˈsɪtɪ] *adj.* Intercity-; **~ train** Intercity[-Zug], *der*

intercom [ˈɪntəkɒm] *n. (coll.)* Gegensprechanlage, *die*

interconnect [ɪntəkəˈnekt] **1.** *v. t.* miteinander verbinden. **2.** *v. i.* miteinander in Zusammenhang stehen

intercourse [ˈɪntəkɔːs] *n. (sexual)* [Geschlechts]verkehr, *der*

interest [ˈɪntrəst] **1.** *n.* a) Interesse, *das;* **take** *or* **have an ~ in sb./sth.** sich für jmdn./etw. interessieren; **[just] for** *or* **out of ~:** [nur] interessehalber; **with ~:** interessiert; **act in one's own/sb.'s ~|s|** im eigenen/in jmds. Interesse handeln; **be of ~:** interessant sein (**to** für); b) *(Finance)* Zinsen *Pl.* **2.** *v. t.* interessieren; **be ~ed** sich interessieren (**in** für). **ˈinteresting** *adj.* interessant

interfere [ɪntəˈfɪə(r)] *v. i.* sich einmischen (**in** in + Akk.); **~ with sth.** sich ⟨Dat.⟩ an etw. ⟨Dat.⟩ zu schaffen machen. **interference** [ɪntəˈfɪərəns] *n.* a) *(interfering)* Einmischung, *die;* b) *(Radio, Telev.)* Störung, *die*

interim [ˈɪntərɪm] **1.** *n.* **in the ~:** in der Zwischenzeit. **2.** *adj.* vorläufig

interior [ɪnˈtɪərɪə(r)] **1.** *adj.* inner...; Innen⟨fläche, -wand⟩. **2.** *n.* Innere, *das*

interject [ɪntəˈdʒekt] *v. t.* einwerfen. **interjection** [ɪntəˈdʒekʃn] *n.* Ausruf, *der*

interloper [ˈɪntələʊpə(r)] *n.* Eindringling, *der*

interlude [ˈɪntəluːd] *n.* Pause, *die;* *(music)* Zwischenspiel, *das*

intermediate [ɪntəˈmiːdjət] *adj.* Zwischen-

interminable [ɪnˈtɜːmɪnəbl] *adj.* endlos

intermission [ɪntə'mɪʃn] n. Pause, die
intermittent [ɪntə'mɪtnt] adj. in Abständen auftretend. **inter'mittently** adv. in Abständen
intern [ɪn'tɜːn] v.t. gefangenhalten
internal [ɪn'tɜːnl] adj. inner...; Innen-⟨fläche, -abmessungen⟩. **internally** [ɪn'tɜːnəlɪ] adv. innerlich
international [ɪntə'næʃənl] 1. adj. international. 2. n. a) (Sport) (contest) Länderspiel, das; (participant) Nationalspieler, der/-spielerin, die. **inter'nationally** adv. international
in'ternment n. Internierung, die
interplay ['ɪntəpleɪ] n. Zusammenspiel, das
interpret [ɪn'tɜːprɪt] 1. v.t. a) interpretieren; deuten ⟨Traum, Zeichen⟩; b) (between languages) dolmetschen. 2. v.i. dolmetschen. **interpretation** [ɪntɜːprɪ'teɪʃn] n. Interpretation, die; (of dream, symptoms) Deutung, die. **in'terpreter** n. Dolmetscher, der/Dolmetscherin, die
interrogate [ɪn'terəgeɪt] v.t. verhören; ausfragen ⟨Freund, Kind usw.⟩. **interrogation** [ɪnterə'geɪʃn] n. Verhör, das
interrogative [ɪntə'rɒgətɪv] adj. (Ling.) Interrogativ-
interrupt [ɪntə'rʌpt] 1. v.t. unterbrechen; **don't ~ me when I'm busy** stör mich nicht, wenn ich zu tun habe. 2. v.i. unterbrechen; stören. **interruption** [ɪntə'rʌpʃn] n. Unterbrechung, die; Störung, die
intersect [ɪntə'sekt] v.i. a) ⟨Straßen:⟩ sich kreuzen; b) (Geom.) sich schneiden. **intersection** [ɪntə'sekʃn] n. a) (road junction) Kreuzung, die; b) (Geom.) Schnittpunkt, der
intersperse [ɪntə'spɜːs] v.t. **be ~d with** durchsetzt sein mit
interval ['ɪntəvl] n. a) [Zeit]abstand, der; **at ~s** in Abständen; b) (break; also Brit. Theatre etc.) Pause, die; **sunny ~s** Aufheiterungen Pl.
intervene [ɪntə'viːn] v.i. a) [vermittelnd] eingreifen (**in** in + Akk.); b) **the intervening years** die dazwischenliegenden Jahre. **intervention** [ɪntə'venʃn] n. Eingreifen, das
interview ['ɪntəvjuː] 1. n. a) (for job) Vorstellungsgespräch, das; b) (Journ., Radio, Telev.) Interview, das. 2. v.t. ein Vorstellungsgespräch führen mit; interviewen ⟨Politiker, Filmstar usw.⟩. **'interviewer** n. Interviewer, der/Interviewerin, die

intestine [ɪn'testɪn] n. Darm, der
intimacy ['ɪntɪməsɪ] n. a) Vertrautheit, die; b) (sexual) Intimität, die
intimate 1. ['ɪntɪmət] adj. a) eng ⟨Freund, Verhältnis⟩; genau, (geh.) intim ⟨Kenntnis⟩; b) (sexually) intim. 2. ['ɪntɪmeɪt] v.t. (imply) andeuten. **intimately** ['ɪntɪmətlɪ] adv. genau[estens] ⟨kennen⟩; eng ⟨verbinden⟩
intimidate [ɪn'tɪmɪdeɪt] v.t. einschüchtern. **intimidation** [ɪntɪmɪ'deɪʃn] n. Einschüchterung, die
into [before vowel 'ɪntʊ, before consonant 'ɪntə] prep. in (+ Akk.); (against) gegen; **I went out ~ the street** ich ging auf die Straße hinaus; **translate sth. ~ English** etw. ins Englische übersetzen
in'tolerable adj. unerträglich
in'tolerance n. Intoleranz, die
in'tolerant adj. intolerant (**of** gegenüber)
intonation [ɪntə'neɪʃn] n. Intonation, die
intoxicate [ɪn'tɒksɪkeɪt] v.t. betrunken machen. **intoxication** [ɪntɒksɪ'keɪʃn] n. Rausch, der
intractable [ɪn'træktəbl] adj. hartnäckig ⟨Problem⟩
intransigent [ɪn'trænsɪdʒənt] adj. unnachgiebig
in'transitive adj. (Ling.) intransitiv
'in-tray n. Eingangskorb, der
intrepid [ɪn'trepɪd] adj. unerschrocken
intricacy ['ɪntrɪkəsɪ] n. Kompliziertheit, die
intricate ['ɪntrɪkət] adj. kompliziert
intrigue [ɪn'triːg] v.t. faszinieren. **intriguing** [ɪn'triːgɪŋ] adj. faszinierend
intrinsic [ɪn'trɪnsɪk] adj. innewohnend; inner...; **~ value** innerer Wert
introduce [ɪntrə'djuːs] v.t. einführen; **~ oneself/sb.** [**to sb.**] sich/jmdn. [jmdm.] vorstellen. **introduction** [ɪntrə'dʌkʃn] n. Einführen, das; Einführung, die; (to person) Vorstellung, die; (to book) Einleitung, die. **introductory** [ɪntrə'dʌktərɪ] adj. einleitend; Einführungs⟨kurs, -vortrag⟩
introspective [ɪntrə'spektɪv] adj. in sich (Akk.) gerichtet
introvert ['ɪntrəvɜːt] 1. n. Introvertierte, der/die; **be an ~:** introvertiert sein. 2. adj. introvertiert
intrude [ɪn'truːd] v.i. stören. **in'truder** n. Eindringling, der. **intrusion** [ɪn'truːʒn] n. Störung, die. **intrusive** [ɪn'truːsɪv] adj. aufdringlich
intuition [ɪntjuː'ɪʃn] n. Intuition, die

intuitive [ɪn'tjuːɪtɪv] *adj.*, **in'tuitively** *adv.* intuitiv

inundate ['ɪnʌndeɪt] *v. t.* überschwemmen

inure [ɪ'njʊə(r)] *v. t.* gewöhnen (to an + *Akk.*)

invade [ɪn'veɪd] *v. t.* einfallen in (+ *Akk.*). **in'vader** *n.* Angreifer, *der*

¹invalid ['ɪnvəlɪd] *(Brit.)* **1.** *n.* Kranke, *der/die; (disabled)* Körperbehinderte, *der/die.* **2.** *adj.* körperbehindert

²invalid [ɪn'vælɪd] *adj.* nicht schlüssig 〈*Argument, Theorie*〉; ungültig 〈*Fahrkarte, Garantie, Vertrag*〉. **invalidate** [ɪn'vælɪdeɪt] *v. t.* aufheben; widerlegen 〈*Theorie, These*〉

in'valuable *adj.* unersetzlich 〈*Person*〉; unschätzbar 〈*Dienst, Hilfe*〉; außerordentlich wichtig 〈*Rolle*〉

in'variable *adj.* unveränderlich. **in'variably** [ɪn'veərɪəblɪ] *adv.* immer; ausnahmslos 〈*falsch, richtig*〉

invasion [ɪn'veɪʒn] *n.* Invasion, *die*

invective [ɪn'vektɪv] *n.* Beschimpfungen *Pl.*

invent [ɪn'vent] *v. t.* erfinden. **invention** [ɪn'venʃn] *n.* Erfindung, *die.* **inventive** [ɪn'ventɪv] *adj.* **a)** schöpferisch 〈*Person, Begabung*〉; **b)** *(original)* originell. **inventor** [ɪn'ventə(r)] *n.* Erfinder, *der/* Erfinderin, *die*

inventory ['ɪnvəntərɪ] *n.* Bestandsliste, *die;* **make** *or* **take an ~ of sth.** von etw. ein Inventar aufstellen

inverse ['ɪnvɜːs] *adj.* umgekehrt

invert [ɪn'vɜːt] *v. t.* umstülpen

in'vertebrate *n.* wirbelloses Tier

inverted 'commas *n. pl. (Brit.)* Anführungszeichen *Pl.*

invest [ɪn'vest] *v. t.* **a)** *(Finance)* anlegen (**in** in + *Dat.*); investieren (**in** in + *Dat. od. Akk.*); **b)** *(fig.)* investieren; ~ **sb. with sth.** jmdm. etw. übertragen; ~ **sth. with sth.** einer Sache *(Dat.)* etw. verleihen

investigate [ɪn'vestɪgeɪt] *v. t.* untersuchen. **investigation** [ɪnvestɪ'geɪʃn] *n.* Untersuchung, *die.* **investigator** [ɪn'vestɪgeɪtə(r)] *n.:* [**private**] ~: [Privat]detektiv, *der/-*detektivin, *die*

in'vestment *n.* Investition, *die; (money invested)* angelegtes Geld; **be a good** ~ *(fig.)* sich bezahlt machen. **investor** [ɪn'vestə(r)] *n.* [Kapital]anleger, *der/-*anlegerin, *die*

inveterate [ɪn'vetərət] *adj.* eingefleischt 〈*Trinker, Raucher*〉; unverbesserlich 〈*Lügner*〉

invigorate [ɪn'vɪgəreɪt] *v. t.* stärken;

(physically) kräftigen. **invigorating** [ɪn'vɪgəreɪtɪŋ] *adj.* kräftigend 〈*Getränk, Klima*〉

invincible [ɪn'vɪnsɪbl] *adj.* unbesiegbar

in'visible *adj.* unsichtbar

invitation [ɪnvɪ'teɪʃn] *n.* Einladung, *die;* **at sb.'s** ~: auf jmds. Einladung *(Akk.)*

invite [ɪn'vaɪt] *v. t.* **a)** *(request to come)* einladen; **b)** *(request to do sth.)* auffordern; **c)** *(bring on)* herausfordern 〈*Kritik, Verhängnis*〉. **inviting** [ɪn'vaɪtɪŋ] *adj.* einladend; verlockend 〈*Gedanke, Vorstellung*〉

invoice ['ɪnvɔɪs] **1.** *n. (bill)* Rechnung, *die.* **2.** *v. t.* ~ **sb.** eine Rechnung schicken; ~ **sb. for sth.** jmdm. etw. in Rechnung stellen

invoke [ɪn'vəʊk] *v. t.* anrufen

in'voluntarily *adv.*, **in'voluntary** *adj.* unwillkürlich

involve [ɪn'vɒlv] *v. t.* **a)** *(implicate)* verwickeln; **b) become** *or* **get** ~**d in a fight** in eine Schlägerei verwickelt werden; **get** ~**d with sb.** sich mit jmdm. einlassen; **c)** *(entail)* mit sich bringen. **involved** [ɪn'vɒlvd] *adj.* verwickelt; *(complicated)* kompliziert

invulnerable [ɪn'vʌlnərəbl] *adj.* unverwundbar; *(fig.)* unantastbar

inward ['ɪnwəd] **1.** *adj.* inner... **2.** *adv.* einwärts 〈*gerichtet, gebogen*〉; **open** ~: nach innen öffnen. **inwardly** *adv.* im Inneren; innerlich. **inwards** ['ɪnwədz] *see* **inward 2**

iodine ['aɪədiːn] *n.* Jod, *das*

ion ['aɪən] *n.* Ion, *das*

iota [aɪ'əʊtə] *n.* **not one** *or* **an** ~: nicht ein Jota *(geh.)*

IOU [aɪəʊ'juː] *n.* Schuldschein, *der*

Iran [ɪ'rɑːn] *pr. n.* Iran, *der od. (das)*

Iraq [ɪ'rɑːk] *pr. n.* Irak, *der od. (das)*

irate [aɪ'reɪt] *adj.* wütend

Ireland ['aɪələnd] *pr. n.* Irland *(das)*

iris ['aɪərɪs] *n. (Bot., Anat.)* Iris, *die*

Irish ['aɪərɪʃ] **1.** *adj.* irisch; **sb. is** ~: jmd. ist Ire/Irin. **2.** *n.* **a)** *(language)* Irisch, *das; see also* **English 2 a;** **b)** *constr. as pl.* **the** ~: die Iren

Irish: ~**man** ['aɪərɪʃmən] *n., pl.* ~**men** ['aɪərɪʃmən] Ire, *der;* ~ **Re'public** *pr. n.* Irische Republik; ~ **'Sea** *pr. n.* Irische See; ~**woman** *n.* Irin, *die*

irk [ɜːk] *v. t.* ärgern. **irksome** ['ɜːksəm] *adj.* lästig

iron ['aɪən] **1.** *n.* **a)** *(metal)* Eisen, *das;* **b)** *(for smoothing)* Bügeleisen, *das.* **2.** *attrib. adj.* eisern; Eisen〈*platte usw.*〉.

3. *v. t. & i.* bügeln. **iron 'out** *v. t.* herausbügeln; *(fig.)* aus dem Weg räumen

Iron 'Curtain *n. (Hist.)* Eiserner Vorhang

ironic [aɪˈrɒnɪk], **ironical** [aɪˈrɒnɪkl] *adj.* ironisch

ironing [ˈaɪənɪŋ] *n.* Bügeln, *das; (items)* Bügelwäsche, *die;* **do the ~:** bügeln. **'ironing-board** *n.* Bügelbrett, *das*

ironmonger [ˈaɪənmʌŋgə(r)] *n. (Brit.)* Eisenwarenhändler, *der/*-händlerin, *die*

irony [ˈaɪrənɪ] *n.* Ironie, *die;* **the ~ was that ...:** die Ironie lag darin, daß ...

irradiate [ɪˈreɪdɪeɪt] *v. t.* bestrahlen

irrational [ɪˈræʃənl] *adj.* irrational

irreconcilable [ɪˈrekənsaɪləbl] *adj. (incompatible)* unvereinbar

irrefutable [ɪrɪˈfjuːtəbl] *adj.* unwiderlegbar

irregular [ɪˈregjʊlə(r)] *adj.* unregelmäßig; unkorrekt ⟨*Verhalten, Handlung usw.*⟩. **irregularity** [ɪregjʊˈlærɪtɪ] *n. see* **irregular:** Unregelmäßigkeit, *die;* Unkorrektheit, *die*

irrelevant [ɪˈrelɪvənt] *adj.* belanglos; irrelevant *(geh.)*

irreparable [ɪˈrepərəbl] *adj.* nicht wiedergutzumachend *nicht präd.;* irreparabel *(geh., Med.)*

irreplaceable [ɪrɪˈpleɪsəbl] *adj.* unersetzlich

irrepressible [ɪrɪˈpresɪbl] *adj.* nicht zu unterdrückend *nicht präd.;* **she is ~:** sie ist nicht unterzukriegen *(ugs.)*

irreproachable [ɪrɪˈprəʊtʃəbl] *adj.* untadelig

irresistible [ɪrɪˈzɪstɪbl] *adj.* unwiderstehlich; bestechend ⟨*Argument*⟩

irresolute [ɪˈrezəluːt] *adj.* unentschlossen

irrespective [ɪrɪˈspektɪv] *adj.* **~ of** ungeachtet (+ *Gen.*)

irresponsible [ɪrɪˈspɒnsɪbl] *adj.* verantwortungslos ⟨*Person*⟩; unverantwortlich ⟨*Benehmen*⟩

irretrievable [ɪrɪˈtriːvəbl] *adj.* nicht mehr wiederzubekommen *nicht attr.*

irreverent [ɪˈrevərənt] *adj.* respektlos

irreversible [ɪrɪˈvɜːsɪbl], **irrevocable** [ɪˈrevəkəbl] *adjs.* unwiderruflich

irrigate [ˈɪrɪgeɪt] *v. t.* bewässern. **irrigation** [ɪrɪˈgeɪʃn] *n.* Bewässerung, *die*

irritable [ˈɪrɪtəbl] *adj. (quick to anger)* reizbar; *(temporarily)* gereizt

irritant [ˈɪrɪtənt] *n.* Reizstoff, *der*

irritate [ˈɪrɪteɪt] *v. t.* **a)** ärgern; **get ~d**

ärgerlich werden; **be ~d by sth.** sich über etw. *(Akk.)* ärgern; **b)** *(Med.)* reizen. **irritating** [ˈɪrɪteɪtɪŋ] *adj.* lästig.

irritation [ɪrɪˈteɪʃn] *n.* **a)** Ärger, *der;* **b)** *(Med.)* Reizung, *die*

is *see* **be**

Islam [ˈɪzlɑːm] *n.* Islam, *der*

island [ˈaɪlənd] *n.* Insel, *die.* **'islander** *n.* Inselbewohner, *der/*-bewohnerin, *die*

isle [aɪl] *n.* Insel, *die*

isn't [ˈɪznt] *(coll.)* = **is not;** *see* **be**

isolate [ˈaɪsəleɪt] *v. t.* isolieren. **isolated** [ˈaɪsəleɪtɪd] *adj.* **a)** *(single)* einzeln; **~ cases/instances** Einzelfälle; **b)** *(remote)* abgelegen. **isolation** [aɪsəˈleɪʃn] *n.* **a)** *(act)* Isolierung, *die;* **b)** *(state)* Isolation, *die*

Israel [ˈɪzreɪl] *pr. n.* Israel *(das).* **Israeli** [ɪzˈreɪlɪ] **1.** *adj.* israelisch. **2.** *n.* Israeli, *der/die*

issue [ˈɪʃuː, ˈɪsjuː] **1.** *n.* **a)** *(point in question)* Frage, *die;* **make an ~ of sth.** etw. aufbauschen; **evade** *or* **dodge the ~:** ausweichen; **b)** *(of magazine etc.)* Ausgabe, *die;* **c)** *(result, outcome)* Ergebnis, *das.* **2.** *v. t.* **a)** *(give out)* ausgeben; ausstellen ⟨*Paß*⟩; erteilen ⟨*Lizenz, Befehl*⟩; **~ sb. with sth.** etw. an jmdn. austeilen; **b)** *(publish)* herausgeben ⟨*Publikation*⟩

it [ɪt] *pron.* **a)** es; **I can't cope with it any more** ich halte das nicht mehr länger aus; **what is it?** was ist los?; **b)** *(the thing, animal, young child previously mentioned)* er/sie/es; *as direct obj.* ihn/sie/es; *as indirect obj.* ihm/ihr/ihm; **c)** *(the person in question)* **who is it?** wer ist da?; **it was the children** es waren die Kinder; **is it you, Dad?** bist du es, Vater?

Italian [ɪˈtæljən] **1.** *adj.* italienisch; *sb.* **is ~:** jmd. ist Italiener/Italienerin. **2.** *n.* **a)** *(person)* Italiener, *der/*Italienerin, *die;* **b)** *(language)* Italienisch, *das; see also* **English 2 a**

italic [ɪˈtælɪk] **1.** *adj.* kursiv. **2.** *n. in pl.* Kursivschrift, *die;* **in ~s** kursiv

Italy [ˈɪtəlɪ] *pr. n.* Italien *(das)*

itch [ɪtʃ] **1.** *n.* Juckreiz, *der;* **I have an ~:** es juckt mich. **2.** *v. i.* **a)** einen Juckreiz haben; **it ~es** es juckt; **b)** *or* **be ~ing to do sth.** darauf brennen, etw. zu tun. **'itchy** *adj.* kratzig; **be ~:** ⟨*Körperteil:*⟩ jucken

it'd [ˈɪtəd] *(coll.)* **a)** = **it had; b)** = **it would**

item [ˈaɪtəm] *n.* **a)** Ding, *das;* Sache, *die; (in shop, catalogue)* Artikel, *der;*

(on radio, TV) Nummer, *die; ~* **of**
clothing Kleidungsstück, *das;* **b) ~** *[of*
news] Nachricht, *die.* **itemize** ['aɪtə-
maɪz] *v.t.* einzeln aufführen
itinerary [aɪ'tɪnərəri] *n.* Reiseroute,
die
it'll [ɪtl] *(coll.)* = it will
its [ɪts] *poss. pron. attrib.* sein/ihr/sein
it's [ɪts] **a)** = it is; **b)** = it has
itself [ɪt'self] *pron.* **a)** *emphat.* selbst;
b) *refl.* sich
I've [aɪv] = **I have**
ivory ['aɪvəri] *n.* Elfenbein, *das; attrib.*
elfenbeinern; Elfenbein-
ivy ['aɪvɪ] *n.* Efeu, *der*

J

J, j [dʒeɪ] *n.* J, j, *das*
jab [dʒæb] **1.** *v.t.,* -bb- stoßen. **2.** *n.* **a)**
Stoß, *der; (with needle)* Stich, *der;* **b)**
(Brit. coll.: injection) Spritze, *die*
jabber ['dʒæbə(r)] *v.i.* plappern *(ugs.)*
jack [dʒæk] *n.* **a)** *(for car)* Wagenhe-
ber, *der;* **b)** *(Cards)* Bube, *der*
jackal ['dʒækl] *n.* Schakal, *der*
jackdaw ['dʒækdɔ:] *n.* Dohle, *die*
jacket ['dʒækɪt] *n.* **a)** Jacke, *die; (of*
suit) Jackett, *das;* sports ~: Sakko,
der; **b)** *(of book)* Schutzumschlag, *der;*
c) ~ potatoes in der Schale gebackene
Kartoffeln
'jackpot *n.* Jackpot, *der;* **hit the ~**
(fig.) das große Los ziehen
jaded ['dʒeɪdɪd] *adj.* abgespannt
jagged ['dʒægɪd] *adj.* gezackt
jaguar ['dʒægjʊə(r)] *n.* Jaguar, *der*
jail [dʒeɪl] **1.** *n.* Gefängnis, *das.* **2.** *v.t.*
ins Gefängnis bringen. **'jailbreak** *n.*
Gefängnisausbruch, *der.* **jailer,**
jailor ['dʒeɪlə(r)] *n.* Gefängniswärter,
der/-wärterin, die
'jam [dʒæm] **1.** *v.t.,* -mm-: **a)** *(between*
two surfaces) einklemmen; **b)** *(make*
immovable) blockieren; *(fig.)* lähmen.
2. *v.i.,* -mm-: **a)** *(become wedged)* sich
verklemmen; **b)** ⟨*Maschine:*⟩ klemmen. **3.** *n.* **a)** *(crush, stoppage)*
Blockierung, *die;* **b)** *(coll.: dilemma)*
be in a ~: in der Klemme stecken

(ugs.). **jam 'on** *v.t.* ~ **the brakes |full|**
on [voll] auf die Bremse steigen *(ugs.)*
²jam *n.* Marmelade, *die*
Jamaica [dʒə'meɪkə] *pr. n.* Jamaika
(das)
Jan. *abbr.* **January** Jan.
jangle ['dʒæŋgl] **1.** *v.i.* klimpern;
⟨*Klingel:*⟩ bimmeln. **2.** *v.t.* rasseln mit
janitor ['dʒænɪtə(r)] *n.* Hausmeister,
der
January ['dʒænjʊəri] *n.* Januar, *der;*
see also **August**
Japan [dʒə'pæn] *n.* Japan *(das).* **Jap-**
anese [dʒæpə'ni:z] **1.** *adj.* japanisch.
2. *n., pl. same* **a)** *(person)* Japaner,
*der/*Japanerin, *die;* **b)** *(language)* Japanisch, *das; see also* **English 2a**
¹jar [dʒɑ:(r)] **1.** *v.i.,* -rr- quietschen;
(fig.) ~ **on sb./sb.'s nerves** jmdm. auf
die Nerven gehen. **2.** *v.t.,* -rr- erschüttern
²jar *n.* Topf, *der; (glass ~)* Glas, *das*
jargon ['dʒɑ:gən] *n.* Jargon, *der*
jasmin[e] ['dʒæsmɪn] *n.* Jasmin, *der*
jaundice ['dʒɔ:ndɪs] *n. (Med.)* Gelb-
sucht, *die.* **jaundiced** ['dʒɔ:ndɪst] *adj.*
(fig.) verbittert
jaunt [dʒɔ:nt] *n.* Ausflug, *der*
javelin ['dʒævlɪn] *n.* **a)** Speer, *der;* **b)**
(Sport: event) Speerwerfen, *das*
jaw [dʒɔ:] *n.* Kiefer, *der.* **'jawbone** *n.*
Kieferknochen, *der*
jay [dʒeɪ] *n.* Eichelhäher, *der*
jazz [dʒæz] **1.** *n.* Jazz, *der; attrib.* Jazz-.
2. *v.t.* ~ **up** aufpeppen *(ugs.)*
jealous ['dʒeləs] *adj.* eifersüchtig (of
auf + *Akk.*). **'jealousy** *n.* Eifersucht,
die
jeans [dʒi:nz] *n. pl.* Jeans *Pl.*
jeer [dʒɪə(r)] *v.i.* höhnen *(geh.); ~* **at**
sb. jmdn. verhöhnen
jelly ['dʒelɪ] *n.* Gelee, *das; (dessert)*
Götterspeise, *die.* **'jellyfish** *n.* Qualle, *die*
jeopardize ['dʒepədaɪz] *v.t.* gefährden
jeopardy ['dʒepədɪ] *n.* **in ~:** in Gefahr;
gefährdet
jerk [dʒɜ:k] **1.** *n.* Ruck, *der.* **2.** *v.t.* reißen an (+ *Dat.*). **3.** *v.i.* zucken
jersey ['dʒɜ:zɪ] *n.* Pullover, *der;*
(Sport) Trikot, *das*
jest [dʒest] **1.** *n.* Scherz, *der;* **in ~:** im
Scherz. **2.** *v.i.* scherzen
Jesus ['dʒi:zəs] *pr. n.* Jesus *(der)*
jet [dʒet] *n.* **a)** *(stream)* Strahl, *der;* **b)**
(nozzle) Düse, *die;* **c)** *(aircraft)* Düsen-
flugzeug, *das;* Jet, *der*
jet: **~-black** *adj.* pechschwarz; **~ en-**

gine n. Düsentriebwerk, das; **~ lag** n. Jet-travel-Syndrom, das; **~-propelled** adj. düsengetrieben
jetsam ['dʒetsəm] n. see **flotsam**
'**jet-set** n. Jet-set, der
jettison ['dʒetɪsən] v. t. über Bord werfen; (discard) wegwerfen
jetty ['dʒetɪ] n. Landungsbrücke, die
Jew [dʒuː] n. Jude, der/Jüdin, die
jewel ['dʒuːəl] n. Juwel, das od. der. **jeweller** (Amer.: **jeweler**) ['dʒuːələ(r)] n. Juwelier, der. **jewellery** (Brit.), **jewelry** ['dʒuːəlrɪ] n. Schmuck, der
Jewish ['dʒuːɪʃ] adj. jüdisch
jib [dʒɪb] v. i., **-bb-** sich sträuben (**at** gegen)
jibe see **gibe**
jiffy ['dʒɪfɪ] n. (coll.) **in a ~:** sofort
jig [dʒɪg] n. Jig, die
'**jigsaw** n. ~ **|puzzle|** Puzzle, das
jilt [dʒɪlt] v. t. sitzenlassen (ugs.)
jingle ['dʒɪŋgl] 1. n. (Commerc.) Werbespruch, der. 2. v. i. klimpern; ⟨Glöckchen:⟩ bimmeln. 3. v. t. klimpern mit ⟨Münzen, Schlüsseln⟩
jinx [dʒɪŋks] (coll.) 1. n. Fluch, der. 2. v. t. verhexen
jitters ['dʒɪtəz] n. pl. (coll.) großes Zittern. **jittery** ['dʒɪtərɪ] adj. (coll.) (nervous) nervös; (frightened) verängstigt
job [dʒɒb] n. **a)** (piece of work) Arbeit, die; **I have a ~ for you** ich habe eine Aufgabe für dich; **b)** (employment) Stelle, die; Job, der (ugs.). '**job-centre** n. (Brit.) Arbeitsvermittlungsstelle, die. '**jobless** adj. arbeitslos
jockey ['dʒɒkɪ] n. Jockei, der
jocular ['dʒɒkjʊlə(r)] adj. lustig
jodhpurs ['dʒɒdpəz] n. pl. Reithose, die
jog [dʒɒg] 1. v. t., **-gg-: a)** (shake) rütteln; **b)** (nudge) |an|stoßen; **~ sb.'s memory** jmds. Gedächtnis (Dat.) auf die Sprünge helfen. 2. v. i., **-gg-: a)** (up and down) auf und ab hüpfen; **b)** (trot) ⟨Pferd:⟩ |dahin|trotten; **c)** (Sport) joggen. 3. n. **go for a ~:** joggen gehen. '**jogging** n. Jogging, das
join [dʒɔɪn] 1. v. t. **a)** (connect) verbinden (**to** mit); **b)** (come into company of) sich gesellen zu; **c)** eintreten in (+ Akk.) ⟨Armee, Firma, Verein, Partei⟩. 2. v. i. ⟨Straßen:⟩ zusammenlaufen. **join in** 1. [-'-] v. t. mitmachen (**with** bei). 2. ['--] v. t. mitmachen bei. **join 'up** 1. v. i. (Mil.) einrücken. 2. v. t. miteinander verbinden
'**joiner** n. Tischler, der/Tischlerin, die

joint [dʒɔɪnt] 1. n. **a)** (Building) Fuge, die; **b)** (Anat.) Gelenk, das; **c)** **a ~ |of meat|** ein Stück Fleisch; (for roasting) ein Braten; **d)** (sl.: place) Laden, der. 2. adj. **a)** (of two or more) gemeinsam; **b)** Mit⟨autor, -erbe, -besitzer⟩. '**jointly** adv. gemeinsam
joist [dʒɔɪst] n. (Building) Deckenbalken, der; (steel) |Decken|träger, der
joke [dʒəʊk] 1. n. Witz, der; Scherz, der. 2. v. i. scherzen, Witze machen (**about** über + Akk.); **joking apart** Scherz beiseite! '**joker** n. **a)** Spaßvogel, der; **b)** (Cards) Joker, der
jollity ['dʒɒlɪtɪ] n. Fröhlichkeit, die; (merry-making) Festlichkeit, die
jolly ['dʒɒlɪ] 1. adj. fröhlich. 2. adv. (Brit. coll.) ganz schön (ugs.); **~ good!** ausgezeichnet!
jolt [dʒəʊlt] 1. v. t. ⟨Fahrzeug:⟩ durchrütteln. 2. v. i. ⟨Fahrzeug:⟩ holpern. 3. n. **a)** (jerk) Stoß, der; Ruck, der; **b)** (fig.: shock) Schock, der
Jordan ['dʒɔːdn] pr. n. Jordanien (das)
jostle ['dʒɒsl] 1. v. i. ~ |**against each other**| aneinanderstoßen. 2. v. t. stoßen
jot [dʒɒt] n. |**not**| **a ~:** |k|ein bißchen. **jot 'down** v. t. [rasch] aufschreiben. '**jotter** n. Notizblock, der
journal ['dʒɜːnl] n. Zeitschrift, die. '**journalism** n. Journalismus, der. '**journalist** ['dʒɜːnəlɪst] n. Journalist, der/Journalistin, die
journey ['dʒɜːnɪ] n. **a)** Reise, die; **b)** (of vehicle) Fahrt, die
jovial ['dʒəʊvɪəl] adj. herzlich ⟨Gruß⟩; fröhlich ⟨Person⟩
joy [dʒɔɪ] n. Freude, die. **joyful** ['dʒɔɪfl] adj. froh|gestimmt| ⟨Person⟩; freudig ⟨Blick, Ereignis, Gesang⟩. '**joyride** n. (coll.) Spritztour, die
JP abbr. Justice of the Peace
jubilant ['dʒuːbɪlənt] adj. jubelnd; **be ~** ⟨Person:⟩ frohlocken. **jubilation** [dʒuːbɪ'leɪʃn] n. Jubel, der
jubilee ['dʒuːbɪliː] n. Jubiläum, das
judge [dʒʌdʒ] 1. n. **a)** Richter, der/Richterin, die; **b)** (in contest) Preisrichter, der/-richterin, die; **c)** (fig.: critic) Kenner, der/Kennerin, die. 2. v. t. **a)** (sentence) richten (geh.); **b)** (form opinion about) |be|urteilen. '**judg[e]ment** n. **a)** Urteil, das; **b)** (critical faculty) Urteilsvermögen, das
judicial [dʒuː'dɪʃl] adj. gerichtlich
judicious [dʒuː'dɪʃəs] adj. klarblickend
judo ['dʒuːdəʊ] n. Judo, das

jug [dʒʌg] n. Krug, der; (with lid, water-~) Kanne, die

juggernaut ['dʒʌgənɔːt] n. (Brit.: lorry) schwerer Brummer (ugs.)

juggle ['dʒʌgl] v. i. jonglieren. **juggler** ['dʒʌglə(r)] n. Jongleur, der/Jongleuse, die

juice [dʒuːs] n. Saft, der. **juicy** ['dʒuː-sɪ] adj. saftig

juke-box ['dʒuːkbɒks] n. Jukebox, die; Musikbox, die

Jul. abbr. July Jul.

July [dʒʊ'laɪ] n. Juli, der; see also August

jumble ['dʒʌmbl] 1. v. t. ~ up durcheinanderbringen. 2. n. Durcheinander, das. '**jumble sale** n. (Brit.) Trödelmarkt, der

jumbo jet [dʒʌmbəʊ 'dʒet] n. Jumbo-Jet, der

jump [dʒʌmp] 1. n. a) Sprung, der; b) (in prices) sprunghafter Anstieg. 2. v. i. a) springen; ~ for joy einen Freudensprung machen; b) ~ to conclusions voreilige Schlüsse ziehen. 3. v. t. a) überspringen; b) ~ the queue (Brit.) sich vordrängeln. **jump a'bout, jump a'round** v. i. herumspringen (ugs.). '**jump at** v. t. (fig.) sofort zugreifen bei ⟨Angebot, Gelegenheit⟩

'**jumper** n. Pullover, der.

jumpy ['dʒʌmpɪ] adj. nervös

Jun. abbr. June Jun.

junction ['dʒʌŋkʃn] n. a) (of railway lines, roads) ≈ Einmündung, die; b) (crossroads) Kreuzung, die

juncture ['dʒʌŋktʃə(r)] n. at this ~: zu diesem Zeitpunkt

June [dʒuːn] n. Juni, der; see also August

jungle ['dʒʌŋgl] n. Dschungel, der

junior ['dʒuːnɪə(r)] adj. a) (in age) jünger; ~ team (Sport) Juniorenmannschaft, die; b) (in rank) rangniedriger ⟨Person⟩; niedriger ⟨Rang⟩. '**junior school** n. (Brit.) Grundschule, die

junk [dʒʌŋk] n. Trödel, der (ugs.); (trash) Ramsch, der (ugs.). '**junk food** n. minderwertige Kost. '**junk shop** n. Trödelladen, der (ugs.)

Jupiter ['dʒuːpɪtə(r)] pr. n. (Astron.) Jupiter, der

jurisdiction [dʒʊərɪs'dɪkʃn] n. Gerichtsbarkeit, die

juror ['dʒʊərə(r)] n. Geschworene, der/die

jury ['dʒʊərɪ] n. a) (in court) the ~: die Geschworenen; b) (in competition) Jury, die

just [dʒʌst] 1. adj. (morally right) gerecht. 2. adv. a) (exactly) genau; ~ then/enough gerade da/genug; ~ as (exactly as) genauso wie; (when) gerade, als; ~ as you like or please ganz wie Sie wünschen/du magst; ~ as good etc. genauso gut usw.; b) (barely) gerade [eben]; (with little time to spare) gerade noch; (no more than) nur; ~ under £10 nicht ganz zehn Pfund; c) (at this moment) gerade; not ~ now im Moment nicht; d) (coll.) (simply) einfach; (only) nur; esp. with imper. mal [eben]; ~ look at that! guck dir das mal an!; ~ a moment einen Moment mal; ~ in case für alle Fälle

justice ['dʒʌstɪs] n. a) Gerechtigkeit, die; b) (magistrate) Schiedsrichter, der/-richterin, die; J~ of the Peace Friedensrichter, der/-richterin, die

justifiable [dʒʌstɪ'faɪəbl] adj. berechtigt. **justifiably** [dʒʌstɪ'faɪəblɪ] adv. zu Recht

justification [dʒʌstɪfɪ'keɪʃn] n. Rechtfertigung, die

justify ['dʒʌstɪfaɪ] v. t. rechtfertigen; **be justified in doing sth.** etw. zu Recht tun

jut [dʒʌt] v. i., **-tt-**: ~ [out] [her]vorragen; herausragen

juvenile ['dʒuːvənaɪl] 1. adj. a) jugendlich; b) (immature) kindisch. 2. n. Jugendliche, der/die. **juvenile delinquency** [~ dɪ'lɪŋkwənsɪ] n. Jugendkriminalität, die. **juvenile delinquent** [~ dɪ'lɪŋkwənt] n. jugendlicher Straftäter/jugendliche Straftäterin

juxtapose [dʒʌkstə'pəʊz] v. t. nebeneinanderstellen (with, to und). **juxtaposition** [dʒʌkstəpə'zɪʃn] n. Nebeneinanderstellung, die

K

K, k [keɪ] n. K, k, das

kaleidoscope [kə'laɪdəskəʊp] n. Kaleidoskop, das

kangaroo [kæŋgə'ruː] n. Känguruh, das

karate [kəˈrɑːtɪ] n. Karate, das

keel [kiːl] n. (Naut.) Kiel, der

keen [kiːn] adj. a) (sharp) scharf; b) (cold) schneidend ⟨Wind, Kälte⟩; c) (eager) begeistert ⟨Fußballfan, Sportler⟩; lebhaft ⟨Interesse⟩; be ~ to do sth. darauf erpicht sein, etw. zu tun; d) (sensitive) scharf ⟨Augen⟩; fein ⟨Sinne⟩. **'keenly** adv. a) (sharply) scharf; b) (eagerly) eifrig; brennend ⟨interessiert sein⟩; c) (acutely) be ~ aware of sth. sich (Dat.) einer Sache (Gen.) voll bewußt sein

keep [kiːp] 1. v.t., kept [kept] a) halten ⟨Versprechen, Schwur, Sabbat, Fasten⟩; einhalten ⟨Verabredung, Vereinbarung⟩; begehen, feiern ⟨Fest⟩; b) (have charge of) aufbewahren; c) (retain) behalten; (not lose or destroy) aufheben ⟨Quittung, Rechnung⟩; d) halten ⟨Bienen, Hund usw.⟩; e) führen ⟨Tagebuch, Geschäft, Ware⟩; f) (support) versorgen ⟨Familie⟩; g) (detain) festhalten; ~ sb. waiting jmdn. warten lassen; **what kept you?** wo bleibst du denn?; k) (reserve) aufheben. 2. v.i., kept a) (remain) bleiben; **are you ~ing well?** geht's dir gut?; b) ~ |to the| left/right sich links/rechts halten; ~ doing sth. (repeatedly) etw. immer wieder tun; ~ talking/working etc. until ...: weiterreden/-arbeiten usw., bis ...; c) (remain good) ⟨Lebensmittel:⟩ sich halten. 3. n. a) (maintenance) Unterhalt, der; b) for ~s (coll.) auf Dauer; c) (Hist.: tower) Bergfried, der. **keep 'back** 1. v.i. zurückbleiben. 2. v.t. a) (restrain) zurückhalten ⟨Menschenmenge, Tränen⟩; b) (withhold) verschweigen ⟨Informationen, Tatsachen⟩ (from Dat.). **keep 'down** 1. v.i. unten bleiben. 2. v.t. a) niedrig halten ⟨Steuern, Preise usw.⟩; keep one's weight down nicht zunehmen; b) **keep your voice down!** rede nicht so laut! **keep 'off** 1. v.i. ⟨Person:⟩ wegbleiben. 2. v.t. fernhalten; **'keep off the grass'** „Betreten des Rasens verboten". **keep 'out** 1. v.i. **'keep out'** „Zutritt verboten". 2. v.t. nicht hereinlassen. **keep 'up** 1. v.i. **keep up with sb./ sth.** mit jmdm./etw. Schritt halten. 2. v.t. aufrechterhalten ⟨Freundschaft, jmds. Moral⟩; **keep one's strength up** sich bei Kräften halten; **keep it up!** weiter so!

keep-'fit n. Fitneßtraining, das

'keeping n. be in ~ with sth. einer Sache (Dat.) entsprechen

'keepsake n. Andenken, das

keg [keg] n. [kleines] Faß

kennel [ˈkenl] n. Hundehütte, die

Kenya [ˈkenjə] pr. n. Kenia (das)

kept see keep 1, 2

kerb [kɜːb], **'kerbstone** ns. (Brit.) Bordstein, der

kernel [ˈkɜːnl] n. Kern, der

ketchup [ˈketʃʌp] n. Ketchup, der od. das

kettle [ˈketl] n. [Wasser]kessel, der

key [kiː] n. a) Schlüssel, der; b) (on piano, typewriter, etc.) Taste, die; c) (Mus.) Tonart, die

key: **~board** n. (of piano etc.) Klaviatur, die; (of typewriter etc.) Tastatur, die; **~hole** n. Schlüsselloch, das; **~ring** n. Schlüsselring, der

kg. abbr. **kilogram|s|** kg

khaki [ˈkɑːkɪ] 1. adj. khakifarben. 2. n. (cloth) Khaki, der

kick [kɪk] 1. n. a) [Fuß]tritt, der; (Footb.) Schuß, der; **give sb. a ~:** jmdm. einen Tritt geben; b) (coll.: thrill) **do sth. for ~s** etw. zum Spaß tun; **he gets a ~ out of it** er hat Spaß daran. 2. v.i. treten; ⟨Pferd:⟩ ausschlagen. 3. v.t. einen Tritt geben (+ Dat.) ⟨Person, Hund⟩; treten gegen ⟨Gegenstand⟩; kicken (ugs.); schießen ⟨Ball⟩. **kick a'bout, kick a'round** v.t. [in der Gegend] herumkicken (ugs.). **kick 'off** v.i. (Footb.) anstoßen. **kick 'up** v.t. (coll.) ~ up a fuss/row Krach schlagen/anfangen (ugs.)

kid [kɪd] 1. n. a) (young goat) Kitz, das; b) (coll.: child) Kind, das. 2. v.t., -dd- (coll.) auf den Arm nehmen (ugs.); ~ oneself sich (Dat.) was vormachen

kidnap [ˈkɪdnæp] v.t., (Brit.) -pp- entführen. **'kidnapper** n. Entführer, der/Entführerin, die

kidney [ˈkɪdnɪ] n. Niere, die. **'kidney machine** n. künstliche Niere

kill [kɪl] v.t. a) töten; (deliberately) umbringen; **be ~ed in action** im Kampf fallen; **be ~ed in a car crash** bei einem Autounfall ums Leben kommen; b) ~ **time** die Zeit totschlagen. **'killer** n. Mörder, der/Mörderin, die. **'killing** n. a) Töten, das; b) **make a** ~ (coll.: great profit) einen [Mords]reibach machen (ugs.). **'killjoy** n. Spielverderber, der/-verderberin, die

kiln [kɪln] n. Brennofen, der

kilo [ˈkiːləʊ] n., pl. ~s Kilo, das

kilogram, kilogramme [ˈkɪləgræm] n. Kilogramm, das

kilometre (*Brit.; Amer.:* **kilometer**) ['kɪləmiːtə(r) (*Brit.*), kɪ'lɒmɪtə(r)] *n.* Kilometer, *der*

kilowatt *n.* ['kɪləwɒt] Kilowatt, *das*

kilt [kɪlt] *n.* Kilt, *der*

kin [kɪn] *n.* Verwandte

¹kind [kaɪnd] *n.* **a)** (*class, sort*) Art, *die;* **several ~s of apples** mehrere Sorten Äpfel; **all ~s of things/excuses** alles mögliche/alle möglichen Ausreden; **no ... of any ~:** keinerlei ...; **what ~ is it?** was für einer/eine/eins ist es?; **what ~ of [a] tree is this?** was für ein Baum ist das?; **b)** (*implying vagueness*) **a ~ of ...:** [so] eine Art ...; **~ of cute** (*coll.*) irgendwie niedlich (*ugs.*)

²kind *adj.* liebenswürdig; (*showing friendliness*) freundlich; **be ~ to animals** gut zu Tieren sein; **how ~!** wie nett [von ihm/Ihnen *usw.*]!

kindergarten ['kɪndəgɑːtn] *n.* Kindergarten, *der*

kindle ['kɪndl] (*fig.*) wecken

kindly ['kaɪndlɪ] **1.** *adv.* **a)** freundlich; nett; **b)** *in polite request* netterweise; **thank you ~:** herzlichen Dank. **2.** *adj.* freundlich; nett; (*kindhearted*) gütig

¹kindness *n.* **a)** *no pl.* (*kind nature*) Freundlichkeit, *die;* **b) do sb. a ~** (*kind act*) jmdm. eine Gefälligkeit erweisen

kindred ['kɪndrɪd] *adj.* verwandt; **~ 'spirit** Gleichgesinnte, *der/die*

king [kɪŋ] *n.* König, *der.* **kingdom** ['kɪŋdəm] *n.* Königreich, *das*

kingfisher *n.* Eisvogel, *der*

king-size[d] *adj.* extragroß; King-size-⟨Zigaretten⟩

kink [kɪŋk] *n.* (*in pipe, wire, etc.*) Knick, *der;* (*in hair, wool*) Welle, *die*

kinky *adj.* (*coll.*) spleenig; (*sexually*) abartig

kiosk ['kiːɒsk] *n.* **a)** Kiosk, *der;* **b)** (*telephone booth*) [Telefon]zelle, *die*

kip [kɪp] *n.* (*Brit. sl.: sleep*) **have a/get some ~:** eine Runde pennen (*salopp*)

kipper ['kɪpə(r)] *n.* Kipper, *der*

kiss [kɪs] **1.** *n.* Kuß, *der.* **2.** *v. t.* küssen; **~ sb. good night/goodbye** jmdm. einen Gutenacht-/Abschiedskuß geben. **3.** *v. i.* **they ~ed** sie küßten sich

kit [kɪt] *n.* **a)** (*Brit.: set of items*) Set, *das;* **b)** (*Brit.: clothing etc.*) **sports ~:** Sportzeug, *das;* **riding-/skiing-~:** Reit-/Skiausrüstung, *die.* **'kitbag** *n.* Tornister, *der*

kitchen ['kɪtʃn] *n.* Küche, *die; attrib.* Küchen-. **kitchen 'sink** *n.* [Küchen]ausguß, *der*

kite [kaɪt] *n.* Drachen, *der*

kith [kɪθ] *n.* **~ and kin** Freunde und Verwandte

kitten ['kɪtn] *n.* Kätzchen, *das*

kitty ['kɪtɪ] *n.* (*money*) Kasse, *die*

kleptomania [kleptə'meɪnɪə] *n.* Kleptomanie, *die.* **kleptomaniac** [kleptə-'meɪniæk] *n.* Kleptomane, *der*/Kleptomanin, *die*

km. *abbr.* **kilometre[s]** km

knack [næk] *n.* Talent, *das;* **get the ~ [of doing sth.]** den Bogen rauskriegen [, wie man etw. macht] (*ugs.*); **have lost the ~:** es nicht mehr zustande bringen

knapsack ['næpsæk] *n.* Rucksack, *der;* (*Mil.*) Tornister, *der*

knead [niːd] *v. t.* kneten

knee [niː] *n.* Knie, *das*

knee-: ~cap *n.* Kniescheibe, *die;* **~-deep** *adj.* knietief; **~-high** *adj.* kniehoch; **~-jerk reaction** *n.* (*fig.*) automatische Reaktion; **~-joint** *n.* Kniegelenk, *das*

kneel [niːl] *v. i.,* **knelt** [nelt] *or* (*esp. Amer.*) **kneeled** knien; **~ down** niederknien

knelt *see* **kneel**

knew *see* **know**

knickers ['nɪkəz] *n. pl.* (*Brit.*) [Damen]schlüpfer, *der*

knife [naɪf] **1.** *n., pl.* **knives** [naɪvz] Messer, *das.* **2.** *v. t.* (*stab*) einstechen auf (+ *Akk.*); (*kill*) erstechen

knight [naɪt] *n.* **a)** (*Hist.*) Ritter, *der;* **b)** (*Chess*) Springer, *der.* **'knighthood** *n.* Ritterwürde, *die*

knit [nɪt] *v. t.,* **-tt-** stricken; **~ one's brow** die Stirn runzeln. **'knitting** *n.* Stricken, *das;* (*work being knitted*) Strickarbeit, *die.* **'knitting needle** *n.* Stricknadel, *die.* **'knitwear** *n.* Strickwaren *Pl.*

knives *pl. of* **knife** 1

knob [nɒb] *n.* **a)** (*on door, walking-stick, etc.*) Knauf, *der;* **b)** (*control on radio etc.*) Knopf, *der;* **c)** (*of butter*) Klümpchen, *das*

knock [nɒk] **1.** *v. t.* **a)** (*strike*) (*lightly*) klopfen an (+ *Akk.*); (*forcefully*) schlagen gegen *od.* an (+ *Akk.*); **~ a hole in sth.** ein Loch in etw. (+ *Akk.*) schlagen; **b)** (*sl.: criticize*) herziehen über (+ *Akk.*) (*ugs.*). **2.** *v. i.* klopfen (**at an** + *Akk.*). **3.** *n.* Klopfen, *das.* **knock 'down** *v. t.* **a)** (*in car*) umfahren; **b)** (*demolish*) abreißen. **knock 'off 1.** *v. t.* **a)** (*coll.: leave*) Feierabend machen; **b)** (*deduct*) **~ five pounds off the price** es fünf Pfund billiger machen; **c)** *(coll.: do quickly)* aus dem Ärmel schütteln *(ugs.)*; **d)** *(sl.: steal)* klauen *(salopp)*. **2.** *v. i. (coll.)* Feierabend machen. **knock 'out** *v. t.* **a)** *(make unconscious)* bewußtlos umfallen lassen; **b)** *(Boxing)* k. o. schlagen; **c)** *(sl.: exhaust)* kaputtmachen *(ugs.)*. **knock 'over** *v. t.* umstoßen; ⟨Fahrer, Fahrzeug:⟩ umfahren ⟨Person⟩

'knock-down *adj.* ~ prices Schleuderpreise

'knocker *n.* [Tür]klopfer, *der*

knock: ~-kneed ['nɒkniːd] *adj.* X-beinig ⟨Person⟩; ~-out *n. (Boxing)* K.-o.-Schlag, *der*

knot [nɒt] **1.** *n.* Knoten, *der.* **2.** *v. t.* **-tt-** knoten ⟨Seil, Faden usw.⟩

'knotty *adj. (fig.: puzzling)* verwickelt

know [nəʊ] *v. t.,* knew [njuː], known [nəʊn] **a)** *(recognize)* erkennen (by an + *Dat.,* for als + *Akk.*); **b)** *(be able to distinguish)* ~ sth. from sth. etw. von etw. unterscheiden können; **c)** *(be aware of)* wissen; **d)** *(have understanding of)* können ⟨ABC, Einmaleins, Deutsch usw.⟩; ~ how to mend fuses wissen, wie man Sicherungen repariert; ~ how to drive a car Auto fahren können; **e)** kennen ⟨Person⟩. **'know-all** *n.* Neunmalkluge, *der/die.* **'know-how** *n.* praktisches Wissen

'knowing *adj.* **a)** wissend ⟨Blick, Lächeln⟩; **b)** *(cunning)* verschlagen. **'knowingly** *adv.* **a)** *(intentionally)* wissentlich; **b)** vielsagend ⟨lächeln, anblicken⟩

knowledge ['nɒlɪdʒ] *n.* **a)** *(familiarity)* Kenntnisse (of in + *Dat.*); **b)** *(awareness)* Wissen, *das;* have no ~ of sth. nichts von etw. wissen; keine Kenntnis von etw. haben *(geh.)*; **c)** **[a]** ~ of languages/French Sprach-/Französischkenntnisse *Pl.* **knowledgeable** ['nɒlɪdʒəbl] *adj.* be ~ about or on sth. viel über etw. *(Akk.)* wissen

known [nəʊn] **1.** *see* know. **2.** *adj.* bekannt

knuckle ['nʌkl] *n.* [Finger]knöchel, *der*

Korea [kə'rɪə] *pr. n.* Korea *(das)*

kosher ['kəʊʃə(r)] *adj.* koscher

kudos ['kjuːdɒs] *n. (coll.)* Prestige, *das*

kW *abbr.* **kilowatt[s]** kW

L

L, l [el] *n.* L, l, *das*

£ *abbr.* **pound[s]** £; cost £5 5 £ *od.* Pfund kosten

l. *abbr.* **litre[s]** l

lab [læb] *n. (coll.)* Labor, *das*

label ['leɪbl] **1.** *n.* Schildchen, *das; (on bottles, in clothes)* Etikett, *das; (tied/ stuck to an object)* Anhänger/Aufkleber, *der.* **2.** *v. t., (Brit.)* **-ll-: a)** etikettieren; auszeichnen ⟨Waren⟩; *(write on)* beschriften; **b)** *(fig.)* ~ sb./sth. **[as]** sth. jmdn./etw. als etw. etikettieren

labor *(Amer.) see* labour

laboratory [lə'bɒrətəri] *n.* Labor[atorium], *das*

labored, laborer *(Amer.) see* labour. **laborious** [lə'bɔːrɪəs] *adj.* mühsam. **la'boriously** *adv.* mühevoll

labour ['leɪbə(r)] *(Brit.)* **1.** *n.* **a)** Arbeit, *die;* **b)** *(workers)* Arbeiterschaft, *die;* **immigrant** ~: ausländische Arbeitskräfte; **c)** **L~,** the ~ Party *(Polit.)* die Labour Party; **d)** *(childbirth)* Wehen *Pl.;* be in ~: in den Wehen liegen. **2.** *v. i.* hart arbeiten (**at,** on an + *Dat.*). **3.** *v. t.* ~ the point sich lange darüber verbreiten

laboured ['leɪbəd] *adj. (Brit.)* mühsam; schwerfällig ⟨Stil⟩; his breathing was ~: er atmete schwer

'labourer *n. (Brit.)* Arbeiter, *der*/Arbeiterin, *die*

'labour-saving *adj.* arbeit[s]sparend

labyrinth ['læbərɪnθ] *n.* Labyrinth, *das*

lace [leɪs] **1.** *n.* **a)** *(for shoe)* Schnürsenkel, *der;* **b)** *(fabric)* Spitze, *die; attrib.* Spitzen-. **2.** *v. t.* ~ **[up]** [zu]schnüren

lacerate ['læsəreɪt] *v. t.* aufreißen

'lace-up 1. *attrib. adj.* Schnür-. **2.** *n.* Schnürschuh/-stiefel, *der*

lack [læk] **1.** *n.* Mangel, *der* (of an + *Dat.*). **2.** *v. t.* sb./sth. ~s sth. jmdm./ einer Sache fehlt es an etw. *(Dat.)*

lackey ['lækɪ] *n.* Lakai, *der*

'lacking *adj.* be ~: fehlen

laconic [lə'kɒnɪk] *adj.* lakonisch

lacquer ['lækə(r)] n. Lack, der
lacrosse [lə'krɒs] n. Lacrosse, das
lacy ['leɪsɪ] adj. Spitzen-
lad [læd] n. Junge, der
ladder ['lædə(r)] **1.** n. **a)** Leiter, die; **b)** (Brit.: in tights etc.) Laufmasche, die. **2.** v. i. (Brit.) Laufmaschen/eine Laufmasche bekommen. **3.** v. t. (Brit.) Laufmaschen/eine Laufmasche machen in (+ Akk.)
laden ['leɪdn] beladen (with mit)
ladle ['leɪdl] n. Schöpfkelle, die
lady ['leɪdɪ] n. **a)** Dame, die; **~-in-waiting** (Brit.) Hofdame, die; **b)** 'Ladies' (WC) „Damen"; **c)** as form of address **Ladies** meine Damen; **d)** (Brit.) as title **L~:** Lady
lady: ~bird, (Amer.) **~bug** ns. Marienkäfer, der; **~like** adj. damenhaft
¹lag [læg] v. i., **-gg-:** ~ [behind] zurückbleiben; (fig.) im Rückstand sein
²lag v. t., **-gg-** (insulate) isolieren
lager ['lɑ:gə(r)] n. Lagerbier, das
lagging n. Isolierung, die
lagoon [lə'gu:n] n. Lagune, die
laid see **²lay**
laid-back adj. (coll.) gelassen
lain see **²lie**
lair [leə] n. (of wild animal) Unterschlupf, der; (of pirates, bandits) Schlupfwinkel, der
lake [leɪk] n. See, der
lamb [læm] n. **a)** Lamm, das; **b)** (meat) Lamm[fleisch], das. **lamb 'chop** n. Lammkotelett, das. **lamb's-wool** n. Lambswool, die
lame [leɪm] adj., **lamely** adv. lahm
lament [lə'ment] **1.** n. Klage, die (for um). **2.** v. t. ~ that ...: beklagen, daß ... **3.** v. i. klagen (geh.); ~ over sth. etw. beklagen (geh.). **lamentable** ['læməntəbl] adj. beklagenswert
laminated ['læmɪneɪtɪd] adj. lamelliert; ~ glass Verbundglas, das
lamp [læmp] n. Lampe, die; (in street) [Straßen]laterne, die. **lamppost** n. Laternenpfahl, der. **'lampshade** n. Lampenschirm, der
lance [lɑ:ns] **1.** n. Lanze, die. **2.** v. t. (Med.) mit der Lanzette öffnen
lance-corporal n. Obergefreite, der
land [lænd] n. Land, das; **have** or **own** ~: Grundbesitz haben. **2.** v. t. **a)** (set ashore) [an]landen; **b)** (Aeronaut.) landen; **c)** ~ **oneself in trouble** sich in Schwierigkeiten bringen; ~ **sb. with sth., ~ sth. on sb.** jmdm. etw. aufhalsen (ugs.). **3.** v. i. **a)** (Boot usw.:) anlegen, landen; (Passagier:) aussteigen

(from aus); **we ~ed at Dieppe** wir gingen in Dieppe an Land; **b)** (Aeronaut.) landen; **c)** ~ **on one's feet** (fig.) [wieder] auf die Füße fallen. **'landed** adj. ~ **gentry/aristrocracy** Landadel, der.
'landing n. **a)** (of ship, aircraft) Landung, die; **b)** (on stairs) Treppenabsatz, der; (passage) Treppenflur, der.
'landing-card n. Landekarte, die.
'landing-stage n. Landesteg, der.
land: ~lady n. **a)** (of rented property) Vermieterin, die; **b)** (of public house) [Gast]wirtin, die; **~-locked** adj. vom Land eingeschlossen ⟨Bucht, Hafen⟩; ⟨Staat⟩ ohne Zugang zum Meer; **~lord** n. **a)** (of rented property) Vermieter, der; **b)** (of public house) [Gast]wirt, der; **~mark** n. **a)** Orientierungspunkt, der; **b)** (fig.) Markstein, der; **~owner** n. Grundbesitzer, der/-besitzerin, die; **~scape** ['lændskeɪp] n. Landschaft, die; **~slide** n. Erdrutsch, der
lane [leɪn] n. **a)** (in the country) Landsträßchen, das; Weg, der; **b)** (in town) Gasse, die; **c)** (part of road) [Fahr]spur, die; **'get in ~'** „bitte einordnen"; **d)** (Sport) Bahn, die
language ['læŋgwɪdʒ] n. Sprache, die; (style) Ausdrucksweise, die
languid ['læŋgwɪd] adj. träge
languish ['læŋgwɪʃ] v. i. **a)** (lose vitality) ermatten (geh.); **b)** ~ **under sth.** unter etw. (Dat.) schmachten (geh.)
lank [læŋk] adj. **a)** hager; **b)** glatt herabhängend ⟨Haar⟩
lanky ['læŋkɪ] adj. schlaksig (ugs.)
lantern ['læntən] n. Laterne, die
¹lap [læp] n. (part of body) Schoß, der
²lap n. (Sport) Runde, die
³lap 1. v. i., **-pp-** schlecken. **2.** v. t., **-pp-:** ~ [up] [auf]schlecken. **lap 'up** v. t. (fig.) schlucken
lapel [lə'pel] n. Revers, das
Lapland ['læplænd] pr. n. Lappland (das)
lapse [læps] **1.** n. **a)** (interval) **a/the ~ of ...:** eine/die Zeitspanne von ...; **b)** (mistake) Fehler, der; ~ **of memory** Gedächtnislücke, die. **2.** v. i. **a)** ⟨Vertrag, usw.:⟩ ungültig werden; **b)** ~ **into** verfallen in (+ Akk.)
larceny ['lɑ:sənɪ] n. Diebstahl, der
lard [lɑ:d] n. Schweineschmalz, das
larder ['lɑ:də(r)] n. Speisekammer, die
large [lɑ:dʒ] **1.** adj. groß. **2.** n. **at ~** (not in prison etc.) auf freiem Fuß. **3.** adv. see **by 2d. 'largely** adv. weitgehend
'large-size[d] adj. groß

¹lark [lɑ:k] *n. (Ornith.)* Lerche, *die*

²lark *(coll.)* 1. *n.* Jux, *der (ugs.).* 2. *v.i.* ~ |about *or* around| herumalbern *(ugs.)*

larva ['lɑ:və] *n., pl.* ~e ['lɑ:vi:] Larve, *die*

laryngitis [lærɪn'dʒaɪtɪs] *n.* Kehlkopfentzündung, *die*

larynx ['lærɪŋks] *n.* Kehlkopf, *der*

lascivious [lə'sɪvɪəs] *adj.* lüstern *(geh.)*

laser ['leɪzə(r)] *n.* Laser, *der.* '**laser beam** *n.* Laserstrahl, *der*

lash [læʃ] 1. *n.* a) *(stroke)* [Peitschen]hieb, *der;* b) *(on eyelid)* Wimper, *die.* 2. *v.i.* ⟨*Welle, Regen:*⟩ peitschen (**against** gegen, **on** auf + *Akk.*). 3. *v.t.* a) *(fasten)* festbinden (**to** an + *Dat.*); b) *(as punishment)* auspeitschen. **lash 'down** 1. *v.t.* festbinden. 2. *v.i.* ⟨*Regen:*⟩ niederprasseln. **lash 'out** *v.i.* a) *(hit out)* um sich schlagen; ~ out **at sb.** nach jmdm. schlagen; b) ~ out **on sth.** *(coll.: spend freely)* sich *(Dat.)* etw. leisten

lashings ['læʃɪŋz] *n. pl.* ~ **of sth.** Unmengen von etw.

lass [læs] *n.* Mädchen, *das*

lasso [lə'su:] Lasso, *das*

¹last [lɑ:st] 1. *adj.* letzt...; **be ~ to arrive** als letzter/letzte ankommen; ~ **night** gestern nacht. 2. *adv.* a) [ganz] zuletzt; als letzter/letzte ⟨*sprechen, ankommen*⟩; b) *(on ~ previous occasion)* das letzte Mal; zuletzt. 3. *n.* a) *(person or thing)* letzte...; b) **at** |**long**| ~: endlich

²last *v.i.* a) *(continue)* dauern; ⟨*Wetter, Ärger:*⟩ anhalten; b) *(suffice)* reichen

last-ditch *adj.* ~ **attempt** letzter verzweifelter Versuch

lasting *adj.* bleibend; dauerhaft ⟨*Beziehung*⟩; nachhaltig ⟨*Eindruck, Wirkung*⟩

lastly *adv.* schließlich

latch [lætʃ] *n.* Riegel, *der;* **on the ~:** nur eingeklinkt. **latch 'on to** *v.t.* *(coll.: understand)* kapieren *(ugs.)*

late [leɪt] 1. *adj.* a) spät; **am I ~?** komme ich zu spät?; **be ~ for the train** den Zug verpassen; **the train is |an hour| ~:** der Zug hat [eine Stunde] Verspätung; ~ **shift** Spätschicht, *die;* ~ **summer** Spätsommer, *der;* b) *(dead)* verstorben; c) *(former)* ehemalig. *See also* **later** 1; **latest.** 2. *adv.* a) *(after proper time)* verspätet; b) *(at/till a ~ hour)* spät; **be up ~:** bis spät in die Nacht aufbleiben; **work ~ at the office** [abends] lange im Büro arbeiten; |**a bit**| ~ **in the day** *(fig. coll.)* reichlich

spät. 3. *n. of* ~: in letzter Zeit.

latecomer ['leɪtkʌmə(r)] *n.* Zuspätkommende, *der/die.* '**lately** *adv.* in letzter Zeit. '**lateness** *n.* a) *(delay)* Verspätung, *die;* b) **the ~ of the performance** der späte Beginn der Vorstellung

latent ['leɪtənt] *adj.* latent

later ['leɪtə(r)] 1. *adv.* ~ |**on**| später. 2. *adj.* später; *(more recent)* neuer

lateral ['lætərl] *adj.* seitlich (**to** von); ~ **thinking** Querdenken, *das*

latest ['leɪtɪst] *adj.* a) *(modern)* neu[e]st...; b) *(most recent)* letzt...; c) **at** |**the**| ~/**the very** ~: spätestens/allerspätestens

lathe [leɪð] *n.* Drehbank, *die*

lather ['lɑːðə(r)] 1. *n.* [Seifen]schaum, *der.* 2. *v.t.* einschäumen

Latin ['lætɪn] 1. *adj.* lateinisch. 2. *n.* Latein, *das; see also* **English 2 a.** **Latin A'merica** *n.* Lateinamerika *(das).* **Latin-A'merican** *adj.* lateinamerikanisch

latitude ['lætɪtjuːd] *n.* a) *(freedom)* Freiheit, *die;* b) *(Geog.)* Breite, *die*

latrine [lə'triːn] *n.* Latrine, *die*

latter ['lætə(r)] *attrib. adj.* letzter...; **the ~:** der/die/das letztere; *pl.* die letzteren. '**latterly** *adv.* in letzter Zeit

lattice ['lætɪs] *n.* Gitter, *das*

laudable ['lɔːdəbl] *adj.* lobenswert

laugh [lɑːf] 1. *n.* Lachen, *das; (continuous)* Gelächter, *das.* 2. *v.i.* lachen; ~ **out loud** laut auflachen; ~ **at sb./sth.** über jmdn./etw. lachen; *(jeer)* jmdn. auslachen/etw. verlachen. **laugh 'off** *v.t.* mit einem Lachen abtun

laughable ['lɑːfəbl] *adj.* lachhaft; lächerlich

'**laughing** *n.* **be no ~ matter** nicht zum Lachen sein. '**laughing-gas** *n.* Lachgas, *das.* '**laughing-stock** *n.* **make sb. a ~, make a ~ of sb.** jmdn. zum Gespött machen

laughter ['lɑːftə(r)] *n.* Lachen, *das; (continuous)* Gelächter, *das*

launch [lɔːntʃ] *v.t.* a) zu Wasser lassen ⟨*Boot*⟩; vom Stapel lassen ⟨*neues Schiff*⟩; abschießen ⟨*Harpune, Torpedo*⟩; schleudern ⟨*Speer*⟩; b) *(fig.)* auf den Markt bringen ⟨*Produkt*⟩; vorstellen ⟨*Buch, Schallplatte, Sänger*⟩; ~ **an attack** einen Angriff durchführen. '**launching pad**, **launch pad** *ns.* [Raketen]abschußrampe, *die*

launder ['lɔːndə(r)] *v.t.* waschen und bügeln. **launderette** [lɔːndə'ret],

laundrette [lɔːnˈdret], *(Amer.)*
laundromat [ˈlɔːndrəmæt] *ns.*
Waschsalon, *der.* **laundry** [ˈlɔːndrɪ]
n. **a)** *(place)* Wäscherei, *die;* **b)** *(clothes etc.)* Wäsche, *die*
lava [ˈlɑːvə] *n.* Lava, *die*
lavatory [ˈlævətərɪ] *n.* Toilette, *die*
lavender [ˈlævɪndə(r)] *n.* Lavendel, *der*
lavish [ˈlævɪʃ] **1.** *adj.* großzügig. **2.** *v. t.*
~ sth. on sb. jmdn. mit etw. überhäufen
law [lɔː] *n.* **a)** Gesetz, *das;* **break the** ~:
gegen das Gesetz verstoßen; **take the**
~ **into one's own hands** sich *(Dat.)*
selbst Recht verschaffen; ~ **and order**
Ruhe und Ordnung; **b)** *(of game)* Regel, *die;* **c)** *(as subject)* Jura *o.* Art.
law: ~**abiding** [ˈlɔːəbaɪdɪŋ] *adj.* gesetzestreu; ~**court** *n.* Gerichtsgebäude, *das; (room)* Gerichtssaal, *der;* ~**ful** [ˈlɔːfl] *adj.* rechtmäßig *(Besitzer, Erbe)*; legal, gesetzmäßig *(Vorgehen, Maßnahme)*; ~**less** *adj.* gesetzlos
lawn [lɔːn] *n.* Rasen, *die.* **lawn-mower** *n.* Rasenmäher, *der*
law suit *n.* Prozeß, *der*
lawyer [ˈlɔːjə(r)] *n.* Rechtsanwalt, *der*/Rechtsanwältin, *die*
lax [læks] *adj.* lax
laxative [ˈlæksətɪv] *n.* Abführmittel, *das*
laxity [ˈlæksɪtɪ], **laxness** *ns.* Laxheit, *die*
¹**lay** [leɪ] *adj.* Laien-
²**lay** *v. t.,* **laid** [leɪd] **a)** legen *(Teppichboden, Rohr, Kabel)*; **b)** *(impose)* auferlegen *(Verantwortung, Verpflichtung)* (on *Dat.*); verhängen *(Strafe)* (on über + *Akk.*); **c)** ~ **the table** den Tisch decken; **d)** *(Biol.)* legen *(Ei)*.
lay a'side *v. t.* beiseite legen. **lay 'by** *v. t.* beiseite legen. **lay 'down** *v. t.* **a)** hinlegen; **b)** festlegen *(Regeln, Bedingungen)*. **lay 'off** **1.** *v. t. (from work)* vorübergehend entlassen. **2.** *v. i. (coll.: stop)* aufhören. **lay 'out** *v. t.* **a)** *(spread out)* ausbreiten; **b)** anlegen *(Garten)*. **lay 'up** *v. t.* **a)** *(store)* lagern; **b)** **I was laid up in bed for a week** ich mußte eine Woche mein Bett hüten
³**lay** *see* ²**lie**
lay: ~**about** *n. (Brit.)* Gammler, *der (ugs.)*; ~**by** *n., pl.* ~**bys** *(Brit.)* Parkbucht, *die;* Haltebucht, *die*
layer [ˈleɪə(r)] *n.* Schicht, *die*
layette [leɪˈet] *n.* **baby's** ~: Babyausstattung, *die*
lay: ~**man** [ˈleɪmən] *n., pl.* ~**men** [ˈleɪ-**

mən] Laie, *der;* ~**out** *n. (of garden, park)* Anlage, *die; (of book, advertisement, etc.)* Layout, *das*
laze [leɪz] *v. i.* faulenzen; ~ **around** or **about** herumfaulenzen *(ugs.)*
lazily [ˈleɪzɪlɪ] *adv.* faul
laziness [ˈleɪzɪnɪs] *n.* Faulheit, *die*
lazy [ˈleɪzɪ] *adj.* faul. **lazy-bones** *n. sing.* Faulpelz, *der*
lb. *abbr.* **pound[s]** ≈ Pfd.
¹**lead** [led] *n.* **a)** *(metal)* Blei, *das;* **b)** *(in pencil)* [Bleistift]mine, *die.* **2.** *attrib. adj.* Blei-
²**lead** [liːd] **1.** *v. t.,* **led** [led] **a)** führen; ~ **sb. to do sth.** *(fig.)* jmdn. dazu bringen, etw. zu tun; **b)** *(fig.: influence)* ~ **sb. to do sth.** jmdn. veranlassen, etw. zu tun; **be easily led** sich leicht beeinflussen lassen; **he led me to believe that ...:** er machte mich glauben, daß ...; **c)** *(be first in)* anführen; **d)** *(direct)* anführen *(Bewegung, Abordnung)*; leiten *(Diskussion, Orchester)*. **2.** *v. i.,* **led a)** *(Straße usw., Tür:)* führen; **b)** *(be first)* führen; *(go in front)* vorangehen. **3.** *n.* **a)** *(precedent)* Beispiel, *das; (clue)* Anhaltspunkt, *der;* **follow sb.'s** ~: jmds. Beispiel *(Dat.)* folgen; **b)** *(first place)* Führung, *die;* **be in the** ~: in Führung liegen; **c)** *(distance ahead)* Vorsprung, *der;* **d)** *(leash)* Leine, *die;* **on a** ~: an der Leine; **e)** *(Electr.)* Kabel, *das;* **f)** *(Theatre)* Hauptrolle, *die.* **lead a'way** *v. t.* abführen *(Gefangenen, Verbrecher)*. **lead 'off 1.** *v. t.* abführen. **2.** *v. i.* beginnen. **lead 'on 1.** *v. t.* ~ **sb. on** *(entice)* jmdn. auf den Leim führen. **2.** *v. i.* ~ **on to the next topic** *etc.* zum nächsten Thema usw. führen. **lead 'up to** *v. t.* schließlich führen zu
'**leader** *n.* **a)** Führer, *der*/Führerin, *die; (of political party)* Vorsitzende, *der/die; (of expedition)* Leiter, *der*/Leiterin, *die;* **b)** *(Brit. Journ.)* Leitartikel, *der.* '**leadership** *n.* Führung, *die*
lead-free [ˈledfriː] *adj.* bleifrei
leading [ˈliːdɪŋ] *adj.* führend
leading: ~ '**lady** *n.* Hauptdarstellerin, *die;* ~ '**man** *n.* Hauptdarsteller, *der;* ~ '**question** *n.* Suggestivfrage, *die;* ~ '**role** *n.* Hauptrolle, *die; (fig.)* führende Rolle
lead [led] *n.:* ~'**pencil** *n.* Bleistift, *der;* ~**poisoning** *n.* Bleivergiftung, *die*
leaf [liːf] *n., pl.* **leaves** [liːvz] Blatt, *das; (of table)* Platte, *die.* **leaf 'through** *v. t.* durchblättern

leaflet ['liːflɪt] *n.* [Hand]zettel, *der;* *(advertising)* Reklamezettel, *der;* *(political)* Flugblatt, *das*

'**leafy** *adj.* belaubt

league [liːg] *n.* a) *(agreement)* Bündnis, *das;* be in ~ with sb. mit jmdm. im Bunde sein; b) *(Sport)* Liga, *die*

leak [liːk] 1. *n.* a) *(hole)* Leck, *das; (in roof, tent; also fig.)* undichte Stelle; b) *(escaping gas)* durch ein Leck austretendes Gas. 2. *v. i.* a) *(escape)* austreten **(from** aus); b) 〈*Faß, Tank, Schiff:*〉 lecken; 〈*Rohr, Leitung, Dach:*〉 undicht sein; 〈*Gefäß, Füller:*〉 auslaufen; c) *(fig.)* ~ |out| durchsickern. 3. *v. t.* ~ sth. to sb. jmdm. etw. zuspielen. **leakage** ['liːkɪdʒ] *n.* Auslaufen, *das;* *(of fluid, gas)* Ausströmen, *das; (fig.: of information)* Durchsickern, *das.*
'**leaky** *adj.* undicht; leck 〈*Boot*〉

¹**lean** [liːn] 1. *adj.* mager. 2. *n. (meat)* Magere, *das*

²**lean** 1. *v. i.,* **leaned** [liːnd, lent] *or (Brit.)* **leant** [lent] a) sich beugen; ~ **against the door** sich gegen die Tür lehnen; ~ **down/forward** sich herab-/vorbeugen; ~ **back** sich zurücklehnen; b) *(support oneself)* ~ **against/on** sth. sich gegen/an etw. *(Akk.)* lehnen; c) *(be supported)* lehnen **(against** an + *Dat.*); d) *(fig.)* ~ |up|on sb. *(rely)* auf jmdn. bauen; ~ to|wards| sth. *(tend)* zu etw. neigen. 2. *v. t.,* **leaned** *or (Brit.)* **leant** lehnen **(against** gegen *od.* an + *Akk.*). **lean** '**over** *v. i.* sich hinüberbeugen

'**leaning** *n.* Neigung, *die*

leant *see* ²**lean**

leap [liːp] 1. *v. i.,* **leaped** [liːpt, lept] *or* **leapt** [lept] a) springen; 〈*Herz:*〉 hüpfen; b) *(fig.)* ~ **at the chance** die Gelegenheit beim Schopf packen. 2. *v. t.,* **leaped** *or* **leapt** überspringen. 3. *n.* Sprung, *der;* **with** *or* **in one** ~: mit einem Satz; **by** ~**s and bounds** *(fig.)* mit Riesenschritten. '**leap-frog** 1. *n.* Bockspringen, *das.* 2. *v. i.,* **-gg-** Bockspringen machen
'**leap year** *n.* Schaltjahr, *das*

learn [lɜːn] 1. *v. t.,* **learned** [lɜːnd, lɜːnt] *or* **learnt** [lɜːnt] a) lernen; ~ **to swim** schwimmen lernen; b) *(find out)* erfahren. 2. *v. i.,* **learned** *or* **learnt** a) lernen; ~ **about** sth. etwas über etw. *(Akk.)* lernen; b) *(get to know)* erfahren **(of** von). **learned** ['lɜːnɪd] *adj.* gelehrt. '**learner** *n. (beginner)* Anfänger, *der/*Anfängerin, *die;* ~ |**driver**|

Fahrschüler, *der/-*schülerin, *die.* '**learning** *n. (of person)* Gelehrsamkeit, *die*

learnt *see* **learn**

lease [liːs] 1. *n. (of land, business premises)* Pachtvertrag, *der; (of house, flat, office)* Mietvertrag, *der.* 2. *v. t.* a) *(grant* ~ *on)* verpachten 〈*Grundstück, Geschäft, Rechte*〉; vermieten 〈*Haus, Wohnung, Büro*〉; b) *(take* ~ *on)* pachten 〈*Grundstück, Geschäft*〉; mieten 〈*Haus, Wohnung, Büro*〉. '**leasehold** *n. see* **lease** 2: **have the** ~ **of** *or* **on sth.** etw. gepachtet/gemietet haben

leash [liːʃ] *n.* Leine, *die*

least [liːst] 1. *adj. (smallest)* kleinst...; *(in quantity)* wenigst...; *(in status)* geringst... 2. *n.* Geringste, *das;* **the** ~ **I can do** das mindeste, was ich tun kann; **at** ~: mindestens; *(anyway)* wenigstens; **at the** |**very**| ~: |aller|mindestens; **not** |**in**| **the** ~: nicht im geringsten. 3. *adv.* am wenigsten

leather ['leðə(r)] 1. *n.* Leder, *das.* 2. *adj.* ledern; Leder|jacke, *-mantel*|. '**leather goods** *n.* Lederwaren *Pl.*
'**leathery** *adj.* ledern

¹**leave** [liːv] *n.* a) *(permission)* Erlaubnis, *die;* b) *(from duty or work)* Urlaub, *der;* ~ |**of absence**| Urlaub, *der;* c) **take one's** ~ sich verabschieden

²**leave** *v. t.,* **left** [left] a) *(make or let remain)* hinterlassen; ~ **sb. to do sth.** es jmdm. überlassen, etw. zu tun; *(in will)* ~ **sb. sth.,** ~ **sth. to sb.** jmdm. etw. hinterlassen; b) *(refrain from doing, using, etc.)* stehenlassen 〈*Abwasch, Essen*〉; c) *(in given state)* lassen; ~ **sb. alone** *(allow to be alone)* jmdn. allein lassen; *(stop bothering)* jmdn. in Ruhe lassen; d) *(refer, entrust)* ~ **sth. to sb./ sth.** etw. jmdm./einer Sache überlassen; e) *(go away from, quit, desert)* verlassen; ~ **home at 6 a.m.** um 6 Uhr früh von zu Hause weggehen/-fahren; ~ **Bonn at 6 p.m.** *(by car, in train)* um 18 Uhr von Bonn abfahren; *(by plane)* um 18 Uhr in Bonn abfliegen; *abs.* **the train** ~**s at 8.30 a.m.** der Zug fährt *od.* geht um 8.30 Uhr; ~ **on the 8 a.m. train/flight** mit dem Acht-Uhr-Zug fahren/der Acht-Uhr-Maschine fliegen. **leave** **a**'**side** *v. t.* beiseite lassen. **leave** **be**'**hind** *v. t.* zurücklassen; *(by mistake)* vergessen; liegenlassen. **leave** '**off** *v. t. (stop)* aufhören mit; *abs.* aufhören. **leave** '**out** *v. t.* auslassen. **leave** '**over** *v. t.* **be left over** übrig [geblieben] sein

leaves *pl. of* **leaf**

Lebanon ['lebənən] *pr. n.* [the] ~ : [der] Libanon

lecherous ['letʃərəs] *adj.* lüstern (geh.)

lecture ['lektʃə(r)] **1. a)** *n.* Vortrag, *der;* (Univ.) Vorlesung, *die;* **b)** *(reprimand)* Strafpredigt, *die (ugs.)*. **2.** *v. i.* ~ [to sb.] [on sth.] [vor jmdm.] einen Vortrag/(Univ.) eine Vorlesung [über etw. (Akk.)] halten. **3.** *v. t. (scold)* ~ sb. jmdm. eine Strafpredigt halten. '**lecturer** *n.* Vortragende, *der/die;* **senior** ~ : Dozent, *der/*Dozentin, *die*

led *see* ²**lead 1, 2**

ledge [ledʒ] *n.* Sims, *der od. das;* (of rock) Vorsprung, *der*

ledger ['ledʒə(r)] *n. (Commerc.)* Hauptbuch, *das*

lee [liː] *n.* **a)** *(shelter)* Schutz, *der;* **b)** ~ [side] *(Naut.)* Leeseite, *die*

leech [liːtʃ] *n.* [Blut]egel, *der*

leek [liːk] *n.* Stange Porree *od.* Lauch; ~s Porree, *der;* Lauch, *der*

leer [lɪə(r)] **1.** *n.* anzüglicher/spöttischer Blick. **2.** *v. i.* ~ at sb. jmdm. einen anzüglichen/spöttischen [Seiten]blick zuwerfen

leeward ['liːwəd] **1.** *adj.* to/on the ~ side of the ship nach/in Lee. **2.** *n.* Leeseite, *die;* to ~ : leewärts

'**leeway** *n.* **a)** *(Naut.)* Leeweg, *der;* Abdrift, *die;* **b)** *(fig.)* Spielraum, *der*

¹**left** *see* ²**leave**

²**left** [left] **1.** *adj.* **a)** link...; on the ~ side auf der linken Seite; links; **b)** L~ *(Polit.)* link... **2.** *adv.* nach links. **3.** *n.* **a)** *(~-hand side)* linke Seite; on *or* to the ~ [of sb./sth.] links [von jmdm./ etw.]; **b)** *(Polit.)* the L~: die Linke

left: ~-hand *adj.* link...; ~'handed **1.** *adj.* linkshändig; ⟨Werkzeug⟩ für Linkshänder; be ~-handed Linkshänder/Linkshänderin sein; **2.** *adv.* linkshändig; ~'luggage [office] *n.* *(Brit. Railw.)* Gepäckaufbewahrung, *die;* ~-overs *n. pl.* Reste; ~ 'wing *n.* linker Flügel; ~-wing *adj. (Polit.)* linksgerichtet; Links⟨extremist, -intellektueller⟩; ~'winger *n.* **a)** *(Sport)* Linksaußen, *der;* **b)** *(Polit.)* Angehöriger/Angehörige des linken Flügels

leg [leg] *n.* **a)** Bein, *das;* pull sb.'s ~ *(fig.)* jmdn. auf den Arm nehmen *(ugs.);* stretch one's ~s sich *(Dat.)* die Beine vertreten; **b)** ~ of lamb Lammkeule, *die;* **c)** *(of journey)* Etappe, *die*

legacy ['legəsɪ] *n.* Vermächtnis, *das (Rechtsspr.);* Erbschaft, *die*

legal ['liːgl] *adj.* **a)** *(concerning the law)* juristisch; Rechts⟨beratung, -streit, -experte, -schutz⟩; gesetzlich ⟨Vertreter⟩; rechtlich ⟨Gründe, Stellung⟩; Gerichts⟨kosten⟩; **b)** *(required by law)* gesetzlich ⟨Verpflichtung⟩; gesetzlich verankert ⟨Recht⟩; **c)** *(lawful)* legal; rechtsgültig ⟨Vertrag, Testament⟩.

legality [lɪˈgælɪtɪ] *n.* Legalität, *die*

legalize ['liːgəlaɪz] *v. t.* legalisieren

legend ['ledʒənd] *n.* Sage, *die;* (unfounded belief) Legende, *die.* **legendary** ['ledʒəndərɪ] *adj.* legendär

legibility [ledʒɪˈbɪlɪtɪ] *n.* Leserlichkeit, *die*

legible ['ledʒɪbl] *adj.* leserlich; easily/ scarcely ~ : leicht/kaum lesbar

legion ['liːdʒn] *n.* Legion, *die*

legislate ['ledʒɪsleɪt] *v. i.* Gesetze verabschieden. **legislation** [ledʒɪsˈleɪʃn] *n.* **a)** *(laws)* Gesetze; **b)** *(legislating)* Gesetzgebung, *die.* **legislative** ['ledʒɪslətɪv] *adj.* gesetzgebend. **legislator** ['ledʒɪsleɪtə(r)] *n.* Gesetzgeber, *der.* **legislature** ['ledʒɪsleɪtʃə(r)] *n.* Legislative, *die*

legitimate [lɪˈdʒɪtɪmət] *adj.* **a)** *(lawful)* legitim; rechtmäßig ⟨Besitzer, Regierung⟩; **b)** *(valid)* berechtigt; **c)** ehelich ⟨Kind⟩

leisure ['leʒə(r)] *n.* Freizeit, *die; attrib.* Freizeit-. '**leisurely** *adj.* gemächlich

lemon ['lemən] *n.* Zitrone, *die.* **lemonade** [lemə'neɪd] *n.* [Zitronen]limonade, *die*

lend [lend] *v. t.,* **lent** [lent] leihen; ~ sth. to sb. jmdm. etw. leihen. '**lender** *n.* Verleiher, *der/*Verleiherin, *die*

length [leŋθ, leŋkθ] *n.* **a)** *(also of time)* Länge, *die;* be six feet in ~ : sechs Fuß lang sein; a short ~ of time kurze Zeit; **b)** at ~ *(for a long time)* lange; (eventually) schließlich; at [great] ~ (in great detail) lang und breit; at some ~ : ziemlich ausführlich; **c)** go to any/ great ~s alles nur/alles Erdenkliche tun; **d)** *(piece of material)* Länge, *die;* Stück, *das.* **lengthen** ['leŋθən] **1.** *v. i.* länger werden. **2.** *v. t.* verlängern; länger machen ⟨Kleid⟩. **lengthways** ['leŋθweɪz] *adv.* der Länge nach; längs. '**lengthy** *adj.* überlang

lenient ['liːnɪənt] *adj.* nachsichtig

lens [lenz] *n.* Linse, *die*

Lent [lent] *n.* Fastenzeit, *die*

lent *see* **lend**

lentil ['lentl] *n.* Linse, *die*

Leo ['liːəʊ] *n., pl.* ~s der Löwe

leopard ['lepəd] *n.* Leopard, *der*

leotard ['li:ətɑ:d] *n.* Turnanzug, *der*
leper ['lepə(r)] *n.* Leprakranke, *der/die*
leprosy ['leprəsɪ] *n.* Lepra, *die*
lesbian ['lezbɪən] **1.** *n.* Lesbierin, *die.*
2. *adj.* lesbisch
less [les] **1.** *adj.* weniger; of **~ value/**
importance weniger wertvoll/wichtig.
2. *adv.* weniger; **~ and ~:** immer we-
niger; **~ and ~ |often|** immer seltener.
3. *n.* weniger. **4.** *prep. (deducting)* ten
~ three zehn weniger drei. **lessen**
['lesn] **1.** *v. t.* verringern. **2.** *v. i.* sich
verringern. **lesser** ['lesə(r)] *attrib.*
adj. geringer.
lesson ['lesn] *n.* **a)** *(class)* [Unter-
richts]stunde, *die;* **b)** *(example, warn-*
ing) Lehre, *die;* **c)** *(Eccl.)* Lesung, *die*
let [let] **1.** *v. t.,* **-tt-,** let **a)** *(allow to)* lassen; **~ sb. do sth.** jmdn. etw. tun las-
sen; **~ alone** *(far less)* geschweige
denn; **b)** *(cause to)* **~ sb. know** jmdn.
wissen lassen; **c)** *(Brit.: rent out)* vermieten. **2.** *v. aux.,* **-tt-,** let lassen; Let's
go to the cinema. – Yes, **~'s/No, ~'s**
not Komm/Kommt, wir gehen ins Kino. – Ja, gut/Nein, lieber nicht; **~**
them come in sie sollen hereinkommen. **let 'down** *v. t.* **a)** *(lower)* herun-
ter-/hinunterlassen; **b)** *(Dressm.)* auslassen; **c)** *(disappoint, fail)* im Stich
lassen. **let 'in** *v. t.* **a)** *(admit)* herein-/
hineinlassen; **b)** **~ oneself in for sth.**
sich auf etw. *(Akk.)* einlassen; **c)** **~ sb.**
in on a secret/plan *etc.* jmdn. in ein
Geheimnis/einen Plan *usw.* einwei-
hen. **'let into** *v. t.* **a)** *(admit into)* lassen in (+ *Akk.*); **b)** *(fig.: acquaint*
with) **~ sb. into a secret** jmdn. in ein
Geheimnis einweihen. **let 'off** *v. t.* **a)**
(excuse) laufenlassen *(ugs.);* **~ sb. off**
sth. jmdm. etw. erlassen; **b)** *(allow to*
alight) aussteigen lassen; **c)** abbren-
nen *(Feuerwerk).* **let 'on** *(sl.)* **1.** *v. i.*
don't ~ on! nichts verraten! **2.** *v. t.* sb.
~ on to me that ...: man hat mir ge-
steckt, daß ... *(ugs.).* **let 'out** *v. t.* **a)** **~**
sb./an animal out jmdn./ein Tier her-
aus-/hinauslassen; **b)** ausstoßen
(Schrei); **~ out a groan** aufstöhnen
(Schrei); **c)** *(Dressm.)* auslassen; **d)** *(Dressm.)*
auslassen; **e)** *(Brit.: rent out)* vermie-
ten. **let 'through** *v. t.* durchlassen.
let 'up *v. i. (coll.)* nachlassen
'let-down *n.* Enttäuschung, *die*
lethal ['li:θl] *adj.* tödlich
lethargic [lɪ'θɑ:dʒɪk] *adj.* träge; *(apa-*
thetic) lethargisch
lethargy ['leθədʒɪ] *n.* Trägheit, *die;*
(apathy) Lethargie, *die*

letter ['letə(r)] **a)** Brief, *der* (to an
+ *Akk.*); **b)** *(of alphabet)* Buchstabe,
der. **'letter bomb** *n.* Briefbombe,
die. **'letter-box** *n.* Briefkasten, *der*
'lettering *n.* Typographie, *die*
lettuce ['letɪs] *n.* [Kopf]salat, *der*
leukaemia, *(Amer.)* **leukemia**
[lu:'ki:mɪə] *n.* Leukämie, *die*
level ['levl] **1.** *n.* **a)** Höhe, *die; (storey)*
Etage, *die;* **b)** *(fig.: steady state)* Ni-
veau, *das;* **be on a ~ |with sb./sth.|** auf
dem gleichen Niveau sein |wie jmd./
etw.]. **2.** *adj.* **a)** waagerecht; eben
⟨Boden, Land⟩; **b)** *(on a ~)* be **~ |with**
sth./sb.| auf gleicher Höhe [mit etw./
jmdm.] sein; **c)** *(fig.)* **keep a ~ head** einen kühlen Kopf bewahren; **do one's**
~ best *(coll.)* sein möglichstes tun. **3.**
v. t., (Brit.) **-ll-: a)** *(make ~)* ebnen; **b)**
(aim) richten ⟨Blick, Gewehr⟩ (at auf
+ *Akk.*); *(fig.)* richten ⟨Kritik *usw.*⟩
(at gegen). **level 'crossing** *n. (Brit.*
Railw.) [schienengleicher] Bahnüber-
gang. **level-'headed** *adj.* besonnen
lever ['li:və(r)] **1.** *n.* Hebel, *der.* **2.** *v. t.*
~ sth. open etw. aufhebeln. **leverage**
['li:vərɪdʒ] *n.* Hebelwirkung, *die*
levity ['levɪtɪ] *n. (frivolity)* Unernst, *der*
levy ['levɪ] **1.** *n. (tax)* Steuer, *die.* **2.** *v. t.*
erheben
lewd [lju:d] geil; anzüglich ⟨Geste⟩;
schlüpfrig ⟨Witz⟩
liability [laɪə'bɪlɪtɪ] *n.* **a)** Haftung, *die;*
b) *(handicap)* Belastung, *die* (to für)
liable ['laɪəbl] *pred. adj.* **a)** *(legally*
bound) be **~ for sth.** für etw. haftbar
sein od. haften; **b)** *(prone)* be **~ to sth.**
⟨Person:⟩ zu etw. neigen; be **~ to do**
sth. ⟨Sache:⟩ leicht etw. tun; ⟨Person:⟩
dazu neigen, etw. zu tun
liaise [lɪ'eɪz] *v. i. (coll.)* eine Verbindung herstellen; **~ on a project** bei einem Projekt zusammenarbeiten. **li-**
aison [lɪ'eɪzɒn] *n. (co-operation)* Zusammenarbeit, *die*
liar ['laɪə(r)] *n.* Lügner, *der*/Lügnerin,
die
libel ['laɪbl] **1.** *n.* Verleumdung, *die.* **2.**
v. t., (Brit.) **-ll-** verleumden. **libellous**
(Amer.: **libelous)** ['laɪbələs] *adj.* verleumderisch
liberal ['lɪbərl] **1.** *adj.* **a)** großzügig; **b)**
(Polit.) liberal; **the L~ Democrats**
(Brit.) die Liberaldemokraten. **2.** *n.*
L~ *(Polit.)* Liberale, *die*
liberate ['lɪbəreɪt] *v. t.* befreien **(from**
aus). **liberation** [lɪbə'reɪʃn] *n.* Befreiung, *die.* **liberator** ['lɪbəreɪtə(r)] *n.*
Befreier, *der*/Befreierin, *die*

liberty ['lɪbətɪ] n. Freiheit, *die;* **take the ~ of doing sth.** sich *(Dat.)* die Freiheit nehmen, etw. zu tun; **take liberties with sb.** sich *(Dat.)* Freiheiten gegen jmdn. herausnehmen *(ugs.)*

Libra ['liːbrə] n. Waage, *die*

librarian [laɪ'breərɪən] n. Bibliothekar, *der*/Bibliothekarin, *die*

library ['laɪbrərɪ] n. Bibliothek, *die;* **public ~:** öffentliche Bücherei. **'library book** n. Buch aus der Bibliothek

Libya ['lɪbɪə] pr. n. Libyen *(das)*

lice pl. of louse

licence ['laɪsəns] **1.** n. [behördliche] Genehmigung; Lizenz, *die;* |driving-| **~:** Führerschein, *der.* **2.** v.t. see **license 1**

license ['laɪsəns] **1.** v.t. ermächtigen; **get a car ~d** ≈ die Kfz-Steuer für ein Auto bezahlen. **2.** n. *(Amer.)* see **licence 1**

licentious [laɪ'senʃəs] adj. zügellos ⟨*Person*⟩; unzüchtig ⟨*Benehmen*⟩

lichen ['laɪkn, 'lɪtʃn] n. Flechte, *die*

lick [lɪk] **1.** v.t. a) lecken; b) *(sl.: beat)* verdreschen *(ugs.).* **2.** n. Lecken, *das.* **lick 'off** v.t. ablecken

lid [lɪd] n. a) Deckel, *der;* b) *(eyelid)* Lid, *das*

lido ['liːdəʊ] n., pl. **~s** Freibad, *das*

¹**lie** [laɪ] **1.** n. Lüge, *die;* **tell ~s/a ~:** lügen. **2.** v.i., **lying** ['laɪɪŋ] lügen; **~ to sb.** jmdn. be- od. anlügen

²**lie** v.i., **lying** ['laɪɪŋ], **lay** [leɪ], **lain** [leɪn] **a)** liegen; *(assume horizontal position)* sich legen; b) **~ idle** ⟨*Maschine, Fabrik:*⟩ stillstehen. **lie a'bout, lie a'round** v.i. herumliegen *(ugs.).* **lie 'back** v.i. sich zurücklegen; *(sitting)* sich zurücklehnen. **lie 'down** v.i. sich hinlegen

lie-detector ['laɪdɪtektə(r)] n. Lügendetektor, *der*

'lie-in n. *(coll.)* **have a ~:** [sich] ausschlafen

lieu [ljuː] n. **in ~ of sth.** anstelle einer Sache *(Gen.);* **get holiday in ~:** statt dessen Urlaub bekommen

lieutenant [lef'tenənt] n. *(Army)* Oberleutnant, *der*

life [laɪf] n., pl. **lives** [laɪvz] Leben, *das;* **for ~:** lebenslänglich ⟨*inhaftiert*⟩; **true to ~:** wahrheitsgetreu

life: ~belt n. Rettungsring, *der;* **~boat** n. Rettungsboot, *das;* **~buoy** n. Rettungsring, *der;* **~cycle** n. Lebenszyklus, *der;* **~guard** n. Rettungsschwimmer, *der*/-schwimmerin,

die; **~insurance** n. Lebensversicherung, *die;* **~jacket** n. Schwimmweste, *die;* **~less** adj. leblos, *(fig.)* farblos; **~like** adj. lebensecht; **~line** n. Rettungsleine; *die; (fig.)* Rettungsanker, *der;* **~long** adj. lebenslang; **~saving** n. Rettungsschwimmen, *das; attrib.* Rettungs-; **~ sentence** n. lebenslängliche Freiheitsstrafe; **~size, ~sized** adj. lebensgroß; **in Lebensgröße** *nachgestellt;* **~style** n. Lebensstil, *der;* **~time** n. Lebenszeit, *die;* **during my ~time** während meines Lebens; **the chance of a ~time** einmalige Gelegenheit

lift [lɪft] **1.** v.t. heben; *(fig.)* erheben ⟨*Gemüt, Geist*⟩. **2.** n. **a)** *(in vehicle)* **get a ~:** mitgenommen werden; **give sb. a ~:** jmdn. mitnehmen; b) *(Brit.: elevator)* Aufzug, *der.* **3.** v.i ⟨*Nebel:*⟩ sich auflösen. **'lift off** v.t. & i. abheben. **lift 'up** v.t. hochheben; heben ⟨*Kopf*⟩

'lift-off n. Abheben, *das*

ligament ['lɪgəmənt] n. Band, *das*

light [laɪt] **1.** n. **a)** Licht, *das;* **~ of day** Tageslicht, *das;* b) *(lamp)* Licht, *das;* *(fitting)* Lampe, *die;* c) *(signal to traffic)* Ampel, *die;* d) *(to ignite)* **have you got a ~?** haben Sie Feuer? **set ~ to sth.** etw. anzünden; e) **bring sth. to ~:** etw. ans [Tages]licht bringen; **throw od. shed ~** |**up|on sth.** Licht in etw. *(Akk.)* bringen; f) *(aspect)* **in that ~:** aus dieser Sicht; **seen in this ~:** so gesehen; **in the ~ of** angesichts (+ *Gen.);* **show sb. in a bad ~:** ein schlechtes Licht auf jmdn. werfen. **2.** adj. hell; **~-blue/~-brown etc.** hellblau/-braun usw. **3.** v.t., **lit** [lɪt] or **lighted a)** *(ignite)* anzünden; b) *(illuminate)* erhellen. **light 'up 1.** v.i. a) *(become lit)* erleuchtet werden; b) *(become bright)* aufleuchten ⟨*with vor:*⟩. **2.** v.t. a) *(illuminate)* erleuchten; b) anzünden ⟨*Zigarette*⟩

²**light 1.** adj. leicht; *(mild)* mild ⟨*Strafe*⟩. **2.** adv. **travel ~:** mit wenig od. leichtem Gepäck reisen

'light-bulb n. Glühbirne, *die*

'lighted adj. brennend ⟨*Kerze, Zigarette*⟩; angezündet ⟨*Streichholz*⟩

lighten ['laɪtn] v.t. *(make less heavy, difficult)* leichter machen

²**lighten 1.** v.t. *(make brighter)* aufhellen; heller machen ⟨*Raum*⟩. **2.** v.i. sich aufhellen

'lighter n. Feuerzeug, *das*

light: ~headed adj. leicht benommen; **~'hearted** adj. a) *(humorous)* unbeschwert; b) *(optimistic)* unbekümmert; **~house** n. Leuchtturm, der

'lighting n. Beleuchtung, die

'lightly adv. **a)** leicht; **b)** (without serious consideration) leichtfertig; **c)** (cheerfully) leichthin; **not treat sth. ~:** etw. nicht auf die leichte Schulter nehmen; **d) get off ~:** glimpflich davonkommen

¹lightness n. (of weight; also fig.) Leichtigkeit, die

²lightness n. (of colour) Helligkeit, die

lightning ['laɪtnɪŋ] n. Blitz, der; **flash of ~:** Blitz, der. **'lightning-conductor** n. Blitzableiter, der

lightweight 1. adj. leicht. **2.** n. Leichtgewicht, das

¹like [laɪk] **1.** adj. **a)** (resembling) wie; **your dress is ~ mine** deine Kleid ist so ähnlich wie meins; **in a case ~ that** in so einem Fall; **what is sb./sth. ~?** wie ist jmd./etw.?; **b)** (characteristic of) typisch für ⟨dich, ihn usw.⟩; **c)** (similar) ähnlich. **2.** prep. (in the manner of) wie; **[just] ~ that** [einfach] so. 3. n. **a)** (equal) his/her ~: seines-/ihresgleichen; **b)** (similar things) **the ~:** so etwas; **and the ~:** und dergleichen

²like 1. v.t. (be fond of, wish for) mögen; **~ vegetables** Gemüse mögen; gern Gemüse essen; **like sth. better** etw. gern tun; **would you ~ a drink?** möchtest du etwas trinken?; **would you ~ me to do it?** möchtest du, daß ich es tue?; **how do you ~ it?** wie gefällt es dir?; **if you ~** expr. assent wenn du willst. **2.** n., pl. **likes and dislikes** Vorlieben und Abneigungen. **likeable** ['laɪkəbl] adj. nett; sympathisch

likelihood ['laɪklɪhʊd] n. Wahrscheinlichkeit, die

likely ['laɪklɪ] **1.** adj. wahrscheinlich; **there are ~ to be [traffic] hold-ups** man muß mit [Verkehrs]staus rechnen; **they are [not] ~ to come** sie werden wahrscheinlich [nicht] kommen; **is it ~ to rain tomorrow?** wird es morgen wohl regnen?; **this is not ~ to happen** es ist unwahrscheinlich, daß das geschieht. **2.** adv. wahrscheinlich; **as ~ as not** höchstwahrscheinlich; **not ~!** (coll.) auf keinen Fall!

'like-minded adj. gleichgesinnt

liken ['laɪkn] v.t. **~ sth./sb. to sth./sb.** etw./jmdn. mit etw./jmdm. vergleichen

'likeness n. Ähnlichkeit, die (to mit)

likewise ['laɪkwaɪz] adv. ebenso

liking ['laɪkɪŋ] n. Vorliebe, die; **take a**

~ to sb./sth. an jmdm./etw. Gefallen finden; **sth. is [not] to sb.'s ~:** etw. ist [nicht] nach jmds. Geschmack

lilac ['laɪlək] n. **a)** (Bot.) Flieder, der; **b)** (colour) Zartlila, das

lily ['lɪlɪ] n. Lilie, die

limb [lɪm] n. **a)** (Anat.) Glied, das; **b)** **be out on a ~** (fig.) exponiert sein

limber up [lɪmbər ʌp] v.i. (loosen up) die Muskeln lockern

¹lime [laɪm] n. **|quick|** [ungelöschter] Kalk

²lime n. (fruit) Limone, die

³lime see **lime-tree**

'limelight n. **be in the ~:** im Rampenlicht [der Öffentlichkeit] stehen

limerick ['lɪmərɪk] n. Limerick, der

'lime-tree n. Linde, die

limit ['lɪmɪt] n. **a)** (boundary) Grenze, die; **set or put a ~ on sth.** etw. begrenzen; **be over the ~** ⟨Autofahrer:⟩ zu viele Promille haben; **lower/upper ~:** Untergrenze/Höchstgrenze, die; **without ~:** unbegrenzt; **within ~s** inerhalb gewisser Grenzen; **b)** (coll.) **this is the ~!** das ist [doch] die Höhe!; **he/she is just [the |very|] ~:** er/sie ist [einfach] unmöglich. **2.** v.t. begrenzen (**to** auf + Akk.); einschränken ⟨Freiheit⟩. **limitation** [lɪmɪ'teɪʃn] n. Beschränkung, die

'limited adj. **a)** (restricted) begrenzt; **b)** (intellectually narrow) beschränkt.

'limitless adj. grenzenlos

limousine ['lɪmʊziːn] n. Limousine, die

¹limp [lɪmp] **1.** v.i. hinken. **2.** n. Hinken, das

²limp adj. schlaff. **'limply** adv. schlaff; (weakly) schwach

limpet ['lɪmpɪt] n. (Zool.) Napfschnecke, die

limpid ['lɪmpɪd] adj. klar

linctus ['lɪŋktəs] n. Hustensaft, der

line [laɪn] **1.** n. **a)** (string, cord, rope, etc.) Leine, die; **b)** (telephone cable) Leitung, die; **c)** (long mark; also Math., Phys.) Linie, die; **d)** (row, series) Reihe, die; (Amer.: queue) Schlange, die; **bring sb. into ~:** dafür sorgen, daß jmd. nicht aus der Reihe tanzt (ugs.); **e)** (row of words on a page) Zeile, die; **f)** (wrinkle) Falte, die; **g)** (direction, course) Richtung, die; **on the ~s of** nach Art (+ Gen.); **be on the right/wrong ~s** in die richtige/falsche Richtung gehen; **along or on the same ~s** in der gleichen Richtung; **h)** (Railw.) Bahnlinie, die; (track) Gleis, das; **i)** (field of activity)

Branche, *die;* **j)** *(Commerc.: product)* Artikel, *der;* Linie, *die (fachspr.).* **2.** *v.t.* **a)** linieren ⟨*Papier*⟩; **a ~d face** ein faltiges Gesicht; **b)** säumen *(geh.)* ⟨*Straße, Strecke*⟩. **line 'up 1.** *v.t.* antreten lassen ⟨*Gefangene, Soldaten usw.*⟩; [in einer Reihe] aufstellen ⟨*Gegenstände*⟩. **2.** *v.i.* ⟨*Gefangene, Soldaten:*⟩ antreten; *(queue up)* sich anstellen

²**line** *v.t.* füttern ⟨*Kleidungsstück*⟩; ausschlagen ⟨*Schublade usw.*⟩

lineage ['lɪnɪɪdʒ] *n.* Abstammung, *die*

linear ['lɪnɪə(r)] *adj.* linear

linen ['lɪnɪn] **1.** *n.* **a)** Leinen, *das;* **b)** *(shirts, sheets, etc.)* Wäsche, *die.* **2.** *adj.* Leinen⟨*faden, -bluse*⟩; Lein⟨*tuch*⟩

liner ['laɪnə(r)] *n.* Linienschiff, *das*

line-up *n.* Aufstellung, *die*

linger ['lɪŋgə(r)] *v.i.* verweilen *(geh.);* bleiben

lingerie ['læʒərɪ] *n.* |women's| ~: Damenunterwäsche, *die*

lingo ['lɪŋgəʊ] *n. (coll.)* Sprache, *die*

linguist ['lɪŋgwɪst] *n.* Sprachkundige, *der/die*

linguistic [lɪŋ'gwɪstɪk] *adj. (of ~s)* linguistisch; *(of language)* sprachlich. **linguistics** [lɪŋ'gwɪstɪks] *n.* Linguistik, *die*

lining ['laɪnɪŋ] *n. (of clothes)* Futter, *das; (of objects, machines, etc.)* Auskleidung, *die*

link [lɪŋk] **1.** *n.* **a)** *(of chain)* Glied, *das;* **b)** *(connection)* Verbindung, *die.* **2.** *v.t.* verbinden; ~ **arms** sich unterhaken. **link 'up** *v.t.* miteinander verbinden

links [lɪŋks] *n.* |golf| ~: Golfplatz, *der*

lino ['laɪnəʊ] *n., pl.* ~**s** Linoleum, *das*

linseed ['lɪnsɪːd] *n.* Leinsamen, *der.* **linseed 'oil** *n.* Leinöl, *das*

lint [lɪnt] *n.* Mull, *der*

lintel ['lɪntl] *n. (Archit.)* Sturz, *der*

lion ['laɪən] *n.* Löwe, *der.* **lioness** ['laɪənɪs] *n.* Löwin, *die*

lip [lɪp] *n.* **a)** Lippe, *die;* **lower/upper ~:** Unter-/Oberlippe, *die;* **b)** *(of cup)* [Gieß]rand, *der; (of jug)* Schnabel, *der*

lip: ~**-read** *v.i.* von den Lippen lesen; ~**-reading** *n.* Lippenlesen, *das;* ~**-service** *n.* **pay** ~**-service to sth.** ein Lippenbekenntnis zu etw. ablegen; ~**stick** *n.* Lippenstift, *der*

liquefy ['lɪkwɪfaɪ] **1.** *v.t.* verflüssigen. **2.** *v.i.* sich verflüssigen

liqueur [lɪ'kjʊə(r)] *n.* Likör, *der*

liquid ['lɪkwɪd] **1.** *adj.* flüssig. **2.** *n.* Flüssigkeit, *die*

liquidate ['lɪkwɪdeɪt] *v.t. (Commerc.)* liquidieren. **liquidation** [lɪkwɪ'deɪʃn] *n. (Commerc.)* Liquidation, *die*

liquidize ['lɪkwɪdaɪz] *v.t.* auflösen; *(Cookery)* [im Mixer] pürieren. **liquidizer** *n.* Mixer, *der*

liquor ['lɪkə(r)] *n. (drink)* Alkohol, *der*

liquorice ['lɪkərɪs] *n.* Lakritze, *die*

Lisbon ['lɪzbən] *pr. n.* Lissabon *(das)*

lisp [lɪsp] **1.** *v.i. & t.* lispeln. **2.** *n.* Lispeln, *das*

¹**list** [lɪst] **1.** *n.* Liste, *die.* **2.** *v.t.* aufführen; auflisten; *(verbally)* aufzählen

²**list** *v.i. (Naut.)* Schlagseite haben

listen ['lɪsn] *v.i.* zuhören; ~ **to music/ the radio** Musik/Radio hören; **they ~ed to his words** sie hörten ihm zu.

listener ['lɪsnə(r)] *n.* Zuhörer, *der*/Zuhörerin, *die; (to radio)* Hörer, *der*/Hörerin, *die*

listless ['lɪstlɪs] *adj.* lustlos

lit *see* ¹**light 3**

litany ['lɪtənɪ] *n.* Litanei, *die*

liter *(Amer.) see* **litre**

literacy ['lɪtərəsɪ] *n.* Lese- und Schreibfertigkeit, *die*

literal ['lɪtərl] *adj.* **a)** wörtlich; **b)** *(not exaggerated)* buchstäblich. **literally** ['lɪtərəlɪ] *adv.* **a)** wörtlich; **b)** *(actually)* buchstäblich; **c)** *(coll.: with some exaggeration)* geradezu

literary ['lɪtərərɪ] *adj.* literarisch

literate ['lɪtərət] *adj.* des Lesens und Schreibens kundig; *(educated)* gebildet

literature ['lɪtrətʃə(r)] *n.* Literatur, *die*

lithe [laɪð] *adj.* geschmeidig

litigation [lɪtɪ'geɪʃn] *n.* Rechtsstreit, *der*

litre ['liːtə(r)] *n. (Brit.)* Liter, *der od. das*

litter ['lɪtə(r)] **1.** *n.* **a)** *(rubbish)* Abfall, *der;* **b)** *(of animals)* Wurf, *der.* **2.** *v.t.* verstreuen. **'litter-basket** *n.* Abfallkorb, *der.* **'litter-bin** Abfalleimer, *der*

little ['lɪtl] **1.** *adj.,* ~**r** ['lɪtlə(r)], ~**st** ['lɪtlɪst] *(Note: it is more common to use the compar. and superl. forms* **smaller, smallest**) **a)** klein; **a** ~ **way** nach kurzes Stück; **after a** ~ **while** nach kurzer Zeit; **b)** *(not much)* wenig; **there is very** ~ **tea left** es ist kaum noch Tee da; **a** ~ ... *(a small quantity of)* etwas ...; ein bißchen ... **2.** *n.* wenig; **a** ~ *(a small quantity)* etwas; *(somewhat)* ein wenig; ~ **by** ~: nach und nach

liturgy ['lɪtədʒɪ] *n.* Liturgie, *die*

¹**live** [laɪv] **1.** *adj.* **a)** *attrib.* lebend; **b)** *(Radio, Telev.)* ~ **performance** Live-Aufführung, *die;* ~ **broad-**

cast Live-Sendung, *die;* c) *(Electr.)* stromführend. **2.** *adv. (Radio, Telev.)* live ⟨*übertragen usw.*⟩

²**live** [lɪv] **1.** *v. i.* a) leben; b) *(make permanent home)* wohnen; leben. **2.** *v. t.* leben. **live 'down** *v. t.* Gras wachsen lassen über (+ *Akk.*); **he will never be able to ~ it down** das wird ihm ewig anhängen. **live on 1.** ['--] *v. t.* leben von. **2.** [-'-] *v. i.* weiterleben. **live 'up to** *v. t.* gerecht werden (+ *Dat.*)

livelihood ['laɪvlɪhʊd] *n.* Lebensunterhalt, *der*

liveliness ['laɪvlɪnɪs] *n.* Lebhaftigkeit, *die*

lively ['laɪvlɪ] *adj.* lebhaft; lebendig ⟨*Schilderung;*⟩ rege ⟨*Handel*⟩

liven up [laɪvn 'ʌp] **1.** *v. t.* Leben bringen in (+ *Akk.*). **2.** *v. i. ⟨Person:⟩* aufleben

liver ['lɪvə(r)] *n.* Leber, *die*

livery ['lɪvərɪ] *n.* Livree, *die*

lives *pl. of* **life**

livestock ['laɪvstɒk] *n. pl.* Vieh, *das*

livid ['lɪvɪd] *adj. (Brit. coll.)* fuchtig *(ugs.)*

living ['lɪvɪŋ] **1.** *n.* a) Leben, *das;* b) **make a ~:** seinen Lebensunterhalt verdienen; c) **the ~:** die Lebenden. **2.** *adj.* lebend; **within ~ memory** seit Menschengedenken. **'living-room** *n.* Wohnzimmer, *das*

lizard ['lɪzəd] *n.* Eidechse, *die*

llama ['lɑːmə] *n.* Lama, *das*

load [ləʊd] **1.** *n. (burden, weight; also fig.)* Last, *die; (amount carried)* Ladung, *die.* **2.** *v. t.* a) *(put — on)* beladen; *(put as load)* ~ **sb. with work** *(fig.)* jmdm. Arbeit auftragen; b) laden ⟨*Gewehr*⟩; ~ **a camera** einen Film [in einen Fotoapparat] einlegen. **load 'up** *v. i.* laden (with *Akk.*)

loaded *adj.* **a ~ question** eine suggestive Frage; **be ~** *(sl.: rich)* [schwer] Kohle haben *(salopp)*

¹**loaf** [ləʊf] *n., pl.* **loaves** [ləʊvz] Brot, *das;* [Brot]laib, *der;* **a ~ of bread** ein Laib Brot

²**loaf** *v. i.* ~ **round town/the house** in der Stadt/zu Hause herumlungern *(ugs.)*

loan [ləʊn] **1.** *n.* a) *(thing lent)* Leihgabe, *die;* **be out on ~:** ausgeliehen sein; **have sth. on ~** [from sb.] etw. [von jmdm.] geliehen haben; b) *(money lent)* Darlehen, *das.* **2.** *v. t.* ~ **sth. to sb.** jmdm. etw. leihen

loath [ləʊθ] *pred. adj.* **be ~ to do sth.** etw. ungern tun

loathe [ləʊð] *v. t.* verabscheuen

loathing ['ləʊðɪŋ] *n.* Abscheu, *der* (of, for vor + *Dat.*). **loathsome** ['ləʊðsəm] *adj.* abscheulich; widerlich

loaves *pl. of* '**loaf**

lobby ['lɒbɪ] *n.* a) *(pressure group)* Lobby, *die;* b) *(of hotel)* Eingangshalle, *die; (of theatre)* Foyer, *das*

lobe [ləʊb] *n. (ear~)* Ohrläppchen, *das*

lobster ['lɒbstə(r)] *n.* Hummer, *der*

local ['ləʊkl] **1.** *adj.* lokal *(bes. Zeitungsw.);* Kommunal⟨*wahl, -abgaben*⟩; *(of this area)* hiesig; *(of that area)* dortig; ortsansässig ⟨*Firma, Familie;*⟩ ⟨*Wein, Produkt, Spezialität*⟩ [aus] der Gegend; **she's a ~ girl** sie ist von hier/dort. **2.** *n.* a) *(person)* Einheimische, *der/die;* b) *(Brit. coll.: pub)* [Stamm]kneipe, *die*

local: ~ **anaes'thetic** *n.* Lokalanästhetikum, *das;* ~ **au'thority** *n. (Brit.)* Kommunalverwaltung, *die;* ~ **call** *n. (Teleph.)* Ortsgespräch, *das;* ~ **'government** *n.* Kommunalverwaltung, *die*

locality [ləʊ'kælɪtɪ] *n.* Ort, *der*

'locally *adv.* im/am Ort

locate [ləʊ'keɪt] *v. t.* a) **be ~d** liegen; b) *(determine position of)* ausfindig machen. **location** [ləʊ'keɪʃn] *n.* a) Lage, *die;* b) *(Cinemat.)* **be on ~:** bei Außenaufnahmen sein

loch [lɒx, lɒk] *n. (Scot.)* See, *der*

¹**lock** [lɒk] *n. (of hair)* [Haar]strähne, *die*

²**lock 1.** *n.* a) *(of door etc.)* Schloß, *das;* b) *(on canal etc.)* Schleuse, *die.* **2.** *v. t.* zuschließen. **3.** *v. i.* ⟨*Tür, Kasten usw.:*⟩ sich zuschließen lassen. **lock a'way** *v. t.* einschließen; einsperren ⟨*Person*⟩. **lock 'in** *v. t.* einschließen; *(deliberately)* einsperren. **lock 'out** *v. t.* aussperren (of aus); ~ **oneself out** sich aussperren. **lock 'up 1.** *v. i.* abschließen. **2.** *v. t.* a) abschließen ⟨*Haus, Tür*⟩; b) *(imprison)* einsperren

locker [ləʊkə(r)] *n.* Schließfach, *das*

locket ['lɒkɪt] *n.* Medaillon, *das*

lock: ~**jaw** *n. (Med.)* Kieferklemme, *die;* ~**out** *n.* Aussperrung, *die;* ~**smith** *n.* Schlosser, *der*

locomotive [ləʊkə'məʊtɪv] *n.* Lokomotive, *die*

locust ['ləʊkəst] *n.* Heuschrecke, *die*

lodge [lɒdʒ] **1.** *n.* a) *(cottage)* Pförtner-/Gärtnerhaus, *das;* b) *(porter's room)* [Pförtner]loge, *die.* **2.** *v. t.* a) einlegen ⟨*Beschwerde, Protest usw.*⟩; b) einreichen ⟨*Klage*⟩. **3.** *v. i.* [zur Miete] wohnen. **'lodger** *n.* Untermieter, *der/*Untermieterin, *die.* **lodging** ['lɒdʒɪŋ] *n.* [möbliertes] Zimmer

loft [lɒft] *n. (attic)* [Dach]boden, *der*

lofty ['lɒftɪ] *adj.* **a)** *(exalted)* hoch; **b)** *(haughty)* hochmütig

log [lɒg] *n.* **a)** *(timber)* [geschlagener] Baumstamm; *(as firewood)* [Holz]scheit, *das;* **b)** ~[-book] *(Naut.)* Logbuch, *das.* **log 'cabin** *n.* Blockhütte, *die.* **log·fire** *n.* Holzfeuer, *das*

loggerheads ['lɒgəhedz] *n. pl.* be at ~ **with sb.** mit jmdm. im Clinch liegen

logic ['lɒdʒɪk] *n.* Logik, *die.* **logical** ['lɒdʒɪkl] *adj.* logisch; **she has a** ~ **mind** sie denkt logisch. **logically** ['lɒdʒɪkəlɪ] *adv.* logisch

logo ['ləʊgəʊ] *n., pl.* ~s Signet, *das*

loin [lɔɪn] *n.* Lende, *die.* 'loincloth *n.* Lendenschurz, *der*

loiter ['lɔɪtə(r)] *v. i.* trödeln; *(linger suspiciously)* herumlungern

loll [lɒl] *v. i.* sich lümmeln *(ugs.)*

lollipop ['lɒlɪpɒp] *n.* Lutscher, *der*

London ['lʌndən] **1.** *pr. n.* London *(das).* **2.** *attrib. adj.* Londoner. 'London·er *pr. n.* Londoner, *der/*Londonerin, *die*

lone [ləʊn] *attrib. adj.* einsam. **loneliness** ['ləʊnlɪnɪs] *n.* Einsamkeit, *die*

lonely ['ləʊnlɪ] *adj.* einsam

loner ['ləʊnə(r)] *n.* Einzelgänger, *der/*-gängerin, *die*

lonesome ['ləʊnsəm] *adj.* einsam

¹**long** [lɒŋ] **1.** *adj.,* ~**er** ['lɒŋgə(r)], ~**est** ['lɒŋgɪst] **a)** lang; weit *(Reise, Weg);* **b)** *(elongated)* länglich; schmal; **c) in the** ~ **run** auf die Dauer. **2.** *n.* *(~ interval)* **take** ~: lange dauern; **for** ~: lange; *(since ~ ago)* seit langem; **before** ~: bald. **3.** *adv.,* ~**er,** ~**est a)** lang[e]; **as or so** ~ **as** solange; **you should have finished** ~ **before now** du hättest schon längst fertig sein sollen; **much** ~**er** viel länger; **b) as or so** ~ **as** *(provided that)* solange; wenn

²**long** *v. i.* ~ **for sb./sth.** sich nach jmdm./etw. sehnen; ~ **to do sth.** sich danach sehnen, etw. zu tun

long-distance 1. ['---] *adj.* Fern*(gespräch, -verkehr usw.);* Langstrecken*(läufer, -flug usw.).* **2.** ['-'-] *adv.* **phone** ~: ein Ferngespräch führen

longevity [lɒn'dʒevɪtɪ] *n.* Langlebigkeit, *die*

'**longhand** *n.* Langschrift, *die*

'**longing 1.** *n.* Sehnsucht, *die.* **2.** *adj.* sehnsüchtig. '**longingly** *adv.* sehnsüchtig

longitude ['lɒŋgɪtju:d] *n.* Länge, *die*

long: ~ **jump** *n. (Brit. Sport)* Weitsprung, *der;* ~**lived** ['lɒŋlɪvd] *adj.* langlebig; ~**playing 'record** *n.* Langspielplatte, *die;* ~**range** *adj.* **a)** Langstrecken*(flugzeug, -rakete usw.);* **b)** *(relating to time)* langfristig; ~**sighted** [lɒŋ'saɪtd] *adj.* weitsichtig; *(fig.)* weitblickend; ~**sleeved** ['lɒŋsli:vd] *adj.* langärmelig; ~**standing** *attrib. adj.* seit langem bestehend; alt *(Schulden, Streit);* ~**suffering** *adj.* schwer geprüft; ~**term** *adj.* langfristig; ~ **wave** *n. (Radio)* Langwelle, *die;* ~**winded** [lɒŋ'wɪndɪd] *adj.* langatmig

loo [lu:] *n. (Brit. coll.)* Klo, *das (ugs.)*

look [lʊk] **1.** *v. i.* **a)** sehen; gucken *(ugs.);* **b)** *(search)* nachsehen; **c)** *(face)* zugewandt sein (**to**[wards] *Dat.);* **d)** *(appear)* aussehen; ~ **well/ill** gut/ schlecht aussehen. **2.** *n.* **a)** Blick, *der;* **have or take a** ~ **at sb./sth.** sich *(Dat.)* jmdn./etw. ansehen; **b)** *(appearance)* Aussehen, *das.* **look 'after** *v. t. (care for)* sorgen für. **look a'head** *v. i. (fig.)* an die Zukunft denken. '**look at** *v. t.* **a)** *(regard)* ansehen; **b)** *(consider)* betrachten. **look 'back** *v. i.* **a)** sich umsehen; **b)** ~ **back on or to sth.** an etw. *(Akk.)* zurückdenken. '**look 'down** [**up**]**on** *v. t.* **a)** herunter-/hinuntersehen auf (+ *Akk.);* **b)** *(fig.: despise)* herabsehen auf (+ *Akk.).* '**look for** *v. t.* **a)** *(seek)* suchen nach; **b)** *(expect)* erwarten. **look 'out** *v. i.* **a)** hinaus-/ heraussehen (**of** aus); **b)** *(take care)* aufpassen; **c)** ~ **out on sth.** *(Zimmer, Wohnung usw.)* zu etw. hin liegen. **look 'out for** *v. t. (be prepared for)* achten auf (+ *Akk.);* *(keep watching for)* Ausschau halten nach *(Arbeit, Gelegenheit, Sammelobjekt usw.).* **look 'over** *v. t.* **a)** sehen über (+ *Akk.);* **b)** *(survey)* sich *(Dat.)* ansehen *(Haus).* **look 'round** *v. i.* sich umsehen. '**look through** *v. t.* **a)** ~ **through sth.** durch etw. [hindurch] sehen; **b)** *(inspect)* durchsehen *(Papiere).* '**look to** *v. t. (rely on)* ~ **to sb./sth. for sth.** etw. von jmdm./etw. erwarten. **look 'up 1.** *v. i.* **a)** aufblicken; **b)** *(improve)* besser werden. **2.** *v. t.* nachschlagen *(Wort);* heraussuchen *(Telefonnummer, Zugverbindung usw.).* **look 'up to** *v. t.* ~ **up to sb.** zu jmdm. aufsehen

'**look-alike** *n.* Doppelgänger, *der/*-gängerin, *die*

looker-'on *n.* Zuschauer, *der/*Zuschauerin, *die*

'**looking-glass** n. Spiegel, *der*

'**look-out** n., *pl.* ~s a) *(observation post)* Ausguck, *der;* b) *(person)* Wache, *die;* c) *(Brit. fig.)* **that's a bad ~:** das sind schlechte Aussichten; **that's his ~:** das ist sein Problem; d) **keep a ~ [for sb./sth.]** [nach etw./jmdm.] Ausschau halten

'**loom** [lu:m] n. *(Weaving)* Webstuhl, *der*

²**loom** v. i. auftauchen

loop [lu:p] 1. n. a) Schleife, *die;* b) *(cord)* Schlaufe, *die.* 2. v. t. zu einer Schlaufe formen. '**loophole** n. *(fig.)* Lücke, *die*

loose [lu:s] adj. a) *(not firm)* locker ⟨Zahn, Schraube, Knopf⟩; b) *(not fixed)* lose ⟨Knopf, Buchseite, Brett, Stein⟩; offen ⟨Haar⟩; c) **be at a ~ end** *(fig.)* nichts zu tun haben; d) *(inexact)* ungenau. '**loose-fitting** adj. bequem geschnitten. '**loose-leaf** adj. Loseblatt-; ~ **file** Ringbuch, *das*

'**loosely** adv. locker; lose ⟨zusammenhängen⟩; frei ⟨übersetzen⟩

loosen ['lu:sn] v. t. lockern. **loosen 'up** v. i. sich auflockern; *(relax)* auftauen

'**looseness** n. Lockerheit, *die*

loot [lu:t] 1. v. t. plündern. 2. n. Beute, *die.* '**looter** n. Plünderer, *der*

lop [lɒp] v. t. ~ **sth.** [**off** or **away**] etw. abbauen *od.* abhacken

lopsided [lɒp'saɪdɪd] adj. schief

lord [lɔ:d] 1. n. a) *(master)* Herr, *der;* b) **L~** *(Relig.)* Herr, *der;* c) *(Brit.: as title)* Lord, *der;* **the House of L~s** *(Brit.)* das Oberhaus. 2. *int. (coll.)* Gott; **oh/good L~!** du lieber Himmel! '**lordship** n. Lordschaft, *die*

lore [lɔ:(r)] n. Überlieferung, *die*

lorry ['lɒrɪ] n. *(Brit.)* Lastwagen, *der;* Lkw, *der.* '**lorry-driver** n. *(Brit.)* Lastwagenfahrer, *der;* Lkw-Fahrer, *der*

lose [lu:z] 1. v. t., **lost** [lɒst] a) verlieren; ~ **one's way** sich verlaufen/verfahren; b) ⟨Uhr:⟩ nachgehen; c) *(waste)* vertun ⟨Zeit⟩; *(miss)* versäumen ⟨Gelegenheit⟩; d) ~ **weight** abnehmen. 2. v. i., **lost a)** *(in match, contest)* verlieren; b) ⟨Uhr:⟩ nachgehen. '**loser** n. Verlierer, *der*/Verliererin, *die*

loss [lɒs] n. a) Verlust, *der* (**of** Gen.); **sell at a ~:** mit Verlust verkaufen; **be at a ~:** nicht [mehr] weiterwissen; **be at a ~ for words** um Worte verlegen sein; **be at a ~ what to do** nicht wissen, was zu tun ist

lost [lɒst] 1. *see* **lose.** 2. adj. a) verloren; **get ~** ⟨*Person:*⟩ sich verlaufen/verfahren; **get ~!** *(sl.)* verdufte! *(salopp);* ~ **cause** aussichtslose Sache; b) *(wasted)* vertan ⟨Zeit⟩; *(missed)* versäumt ⟨Gelegenheit⟩

lot [lɒt] n. a) *(destiny)* Los, *das;* b) *(set of persons)* Haufen, *der;* **the ~:** [sie] alle; c) *(set of things)* Menge, *die;* **the ~:** alle/alles; d) *(coll.: large quantity)* ~s or **a** ~ **of money** *etc.* viel *od.* eine Menge Geld *usw.;* **sing** *etc.* **a ~:** viel singen *usw.;* **like sth. a** ~: etw. sehr mögen; **have ~s to do** viel zu tun haben; e) *(for choosing)* Los, *das;* **draw/cast/throw ~s [for sth.]** um etw. losen

lotion ['ləʊʃn] n. Lotion, *die*

lottery ['lɒtərɪ] n. Lotterie, *die*

loud [laʊd] 1. adj. a) laut; lautstark ⟨Protest, Kritik⟩; b) *(flashy, conspicuous)* aufdringlich; grell ⟨Farbe⟩. 2. adv. laut; **laugh out ~:** laut auflachen; **say sth. out ~:** etw. aussprechen. **loud 'hailer** n. Megaphon, *das*

'**loudly** adv. laut

'**loudness** n. Lautstärke, *die*

loud'speaker n. Lautsprecher, *der*

lounge [laʊndʒ] 1. v. i. ~ **[about** or **around]** [faul] herumliegen/-sitzen/-stehen. 2. n. a) *(in hotel)* [Hotel]halle, *die;* *(at airport)* Wartehalle, *die;* b) *(sitting-room)* Wohnzimmer, *das*

louse [laʊs] n., *pl.* **lice** [laɪs] Laus, *die*

lousy ['laʊzɪ] adj. a) *(disgusting)* ekelhaft; b) *(very poor)* lausig *(ugs.);* **feel ~:** sich mies *(ugs.)* fühlen

lout [laʊt] n. Rüpel, *der;* Flegel, *der*

louver, louvre ['lu:və(r)] n. ~ **window** Jalousiefenster, *das;* ~ **door** Jalousietür, *die*

lovable ['lʌvəbl] adj. liebenswert

love [lʌv] 1. n. a) Liebe, *die* (**of, for** zu); **in ~ [with]** verliebt [in (+ *Akk.*)]; **fall in ~ [with]** sich verlieben [in (+ *Akk.*)]; **for ~:** aus Liebe; ~ **from Beth** *(in letter)* herzliche Grüße von Beth; **send one's ~ to sb.** jmdn. grüßen lassen; b) *(sweetheart)* Geliebte, *der/ die;* **[my]** ~ *(coll.: form of address)* [mein] Liebling *od.* Schatz; c) *(Tennis)* **fifteen/thirty** ~: fünfzehn/dreißig null. 2. v. t. a) lieben; **our/their** ~d **ones** unsere/ihre Lieben; b) *(like)* **I'd** ~ **a cigarette** ich hätte sehr gerne eine Zigarette; ~ **to do** *or* ~ **doing sth.** etw. gern tun

love: ~ **affair** n. Liebesverhältnis, *das;* ~-**letter** n. Liebesbrief, *der;* ~-**life** n. Liebesleben, *das*

loveliness ['lʌvlɪnɪs] *n.* Schönheit, *die*

lovely ['lʌvlɪ] *adj.* [wunder]schön; herrlich ⟨*Tag, Essen*⟩

lover ['lʌvə(r)] *n.* **a)** Liebhaber, *der;* Geliebte, *der; (woman)* Geliebte, *die;* **be ~s** ein Liebespaar sein; **b)** *(person who likes sth.)* Freund, *der*/Freundin, *die*

love: **~sick** *adj.* an Liebeskummer leidend; liebeskrank *(geh.);* **~-song** *n.* Liebeslied, *das;* **~-story** *n.* Liebesgeschichte, *die*

loving ['lʌvɪŋ] *adj.* **a)** *(affectionate)* liebend; **b)** *(expressing love)* liebevoll. **'lovingly** *adv.* liebevoll

low [ləʊ] **1.** *adj.* **a)** niedrig; tief ausgeschnitten ⟨*Kleid*⟩; tief ⟨*Ausschnitt*⟩; tiefliegend ⟨*Grund*⟩; **b)** *(of humble rank)* nieder...; niedrig; **c)** *(inferior)* niedrig; gering ⟨*Intelligenz, Bildung*⟩; **d)** *(in pitch)* tief; *(in loudness)* leise. **2.** *adv.* **a)** *(to a ~ position)* tief; **b)** *(not loudly)* leise; **c) lie ~** *(hide)* untertauchen. **'lowbrow** *adj. (coll.)* schlicht ⟨*Person*⟩; [geistig] anspruchslos ⟨*Buch, Programm*⟩. **'low-cut** *adj.* [tief] ausgeschnitten ⟨*Kleid*⟩

¹lower ['ləʊə(r)] *v.t.* **a)** herab-/hinablassen; **b)** senken ⟨*Blick*⟩; auslassen ⟨*Saum*⟩; senken ⟨*Preis, Miete, Zins usw.*⟩; **~ one's voice** leiser sprechen

²lower 1. *compar. adj.* unter...; Unter⟨*grenze-, arm, -lippe usw.*⟩. **2.** *compar. adv.* tiefer

low: **~-fat** *adj.* fettarm; **~-grade** *adj.* minderwertig; **~land** ['ləʊlənd] *n.* Tiefland, *das*

lowly ['ləʊlɪ] *adj. (modest)* bescheiden

low: **~-lying** *adj.* tiefliegend; **~ point** *n.* Tiefpunkt, *der;* **~ pressure** *n. (Meteorol.)* Tiefdruck, *der*

loyal ['lɔɪəl] *adj.* treu. **loyalty** ['lɔɪəltɪ] *n.* Treue, *die*

lozenge ['lɒzɪndʒ] *n.* Pastille, *die*

LP *abbr.* **long-playing record** LP, *die*

Ltd. *abbr.* **Limited** GmbH

lubricant ['lu:brɪkənt] *n.* Schmiermittel, *das*

lubricate ['lu:brɪkeɪt] *v.t.* schmieren. **lubrication** [lu:brɪ'keɪʃn] *n.* Schmierung, *die;* attrib. Schmier⟨*system, -vorrichtung*⟩

lucid ['lu:sɪd] *adj.* klar. **lucidity** [lu:-'sɪdɪtɪ] *n.* Klarheit, *die*

luck [lʌk] *n.* Glück, *das;* **good ~:** Glück, *das;* **bad** *or* **hard ~:** Pech, *das;* **good ~!** viel Glück!; **be in/out of ~:** Glück/kein Glück haben; **no such ~:** schön wär's. **luckily** ['lʌkɪlɪ] *adv.*

glücklicherweise. **lucky** ['lʌkɪ] *adj.* **a)** glücklich; **be ~:** Glück haben; **b)** *(bringing good luck)* Glücks⟨*zahl, -tag usw.*⟩; **~ charm** Glücksbringer, *der*

lucrative ['lu:krətɪv] *adj.* einträglich; lukrativ

ludicrous ['lu:dɪkrəs] *adj.* lächerlich; lachhaft ⟨*Angebot, Ausrede*⟩

lug [lʌg] *v.t.,* -gg- *(drag)* schleppen

luggage ['lʌgɪdʒ] *n.* Gepäck, *das.* **'luggage-locker** *n.* [Gepäck]schließfach, *das.* **'luggage-rack** *n.* Gepäckablage, *die*

lugubrious [lu:'gu:brɪəs] *adj. (mournful)* kummervoll; *(dismal)* düster

lukewarm ['lu:kwɔ:m] *adj.* lauwarm

lull [lʌl] **1.** *v.t.* **a)** *(soothe)* lullen; **b)** *(fig.)* einlullen; **~ sb. into a false sense of security** jmdn. in einer trügerischen Sicherheit wiegen. **2.** *n.* Pause, *die*

lullaby ['lʌləbaɪ] *n.* Schlaflied, *das*

lumbago [lʌm'beɪgəʊ] *n., pl.* **~s** *(Med.)* Hexenschuß, *der*

lumber ['lʌmbə(r)] **1.** *n.* **a)** *(furniture)* Gerümpel, *das;* **b)** *(useless material)* Kram, *der (ugs.);* **c)** *(Amer.: timber)* [Bau]holz, *das.* **2.** *v.t.* **~ sb. with sth./ sb.** jmdm. etw./jmdn. aufhalsen *(ugs.)*

lumbering *adj.* schwerfällig

lumberjack ['lʌmbədʒæk] *n. (Amer.)* Holzfäller, *der*

luminous ['lu:mɪnəs] *adj.* [hell] leuchtend; Leucht⟨*anzeige, -zeiger usw.*⟩

lump [lʌmp] **1.** *n.* **a)** Klumpen, *der; (of sugar, butter, etc.)* Stück, *das; (of wood)* Klotz, *der; (of dough)* Kloß, *der; (of bread)* Brocken, *der;* **b)** *(swelling)* Beule, *die.* **2.** *v.t.* **~ sth. with sth.** etw. und etw. zusammentun. **lump 'sum** *n.* Pauschalsumme, *die*

lumpy *adj.* klumpig ⟨*Brei*⟩; ⟨*Kissen, Matratze*⟩ mit klumpiger Füllung

lunacy ['lu:nəsɪ] *n.* Wahnsinn, *der*

lunar ['lu:nə(r)] *adj.* Mond-

lunatic ['lu:nətɪk] **1.** *adj.* wahnsinnig. **2.** *n.* Wahnsinnige, *der/die;* Irre, *der/ die.* **'lunatic asylum** *n. (Hist.)* Irrenanstalt, *die (veralt., ugs.)*

lunch [lʌntʃ] **1.** *n.* Mittagessen, *das;* **have** *or* **eat [one's] ~:** zu Mittag essen. **2.** *v.i.* zu Mittag essen

luncheon voucher ['lʌntʃn vaʊtʃə(r)] *n. (Brit.)* Essenmarke, *die*

lunch: **~-hour** *n.* Mittagspause, *die;* **~-time** *n.* Mittagszeit, *die;* **at ~-time** mittags

lung [lʌŋ] *n. (right or left)* Lungenflügel, *der;* **~s** Lunge, *die.* **'lung cancer** *n.* Lungenkrebs, *der*

lunge [lʌndʒ] 1. *n.* Sprung nach vorn. 2. *v. i.* ~ **at sb. with a knife** jmdn. mit einem Messer angreifen

¹**lurch** [lɜːtʃ] *n.* **leave sb. in the** ~: jmdn. im Stich lassen

²**lurch** 1. *n.* Rucken, *das.* 2. *v. i.* rucken; ⟨*Betrunkener:*⟩ torkeln

lure [ljʊə(r), lʊə(r)] 1. *v. t.* locken. 2. *n.* Lockmittel, *das*

lurid ['ljʊərɪd, 'lʊərɪd] *adj.* a) *(in colour)* grell; b) *(sensational)* reißerisch

lurk [lɜːk] *v. i.* lauern

luscious ['lʌʃəs] *adj.* köstlich [süß]; saftig [süß] ⟨*Obst*⟩

lush [lʌʃ] *adj.* saftig ⟨*Wiese*⟩; grün ⟨*Tal*⟩; üppig ⟨*Vegetation*⟩

lust [lʌst] 1. *n.* a) *(sexual)* Sinnenlust, *die;* b) *(strong desire)* Gier, *die* **(for** nach). 2. *v. i.* ~ **after** [lustvoll] begehren *(geh.).* **lustful** ['lʌstfl] *adj.* lüstern *(geh.).*

lustily ['lʌstɪlɪ] *adv.* kräftig; aus voller Kehle ⟨*rufen, singen*⟩

lustre ['lʌstə(r)] *n. (Brit.)* a) Schimmer, *der;* b) *(fig.: splendour)* Glanz, *der*

lusty ['lʌstɪ] *adj.* kräftig

Luxembourg, Luxemburg ['lʌksəmbɜːg] *pr. n.* Luxemburg *(das)*

luxuriant [lʌgˈzjʊərɪənt] *adj.* üppig

luxuriate [lʌgˈzjʊərɪeɪt] *v. i.* ~ **in** sich aalen in (+ *Dat.*)

luxurious [lʌgˈzjʊərɪəs] *adj.* luxuriös

luxury ['lʌkʃərɪ] *n.* a) Luxus, *der;* b) *(article)* Luxusgegenstand, *der;* **luxuries** Luxus, *der*

LW *abbr. (Radio)* **long wave** LW

lying ['laɪɪŋ] *adj.* verlogen ⟨*Person*⟩. See also ²**lie 2**

lynch [lɪntʃ] *v. t.* lynchen

lyric ['lɪrɪk] 1. *adj.* lyrisch; ~ **poetry** Lyrik, *die.* 2. *n.* **in** *pl. (of song)* Text, *der.* **lyrical** ['lɪrɪkl] *adj.* a) lyrisch; b) *(coll.: enthusiastic)* gefühlvoll

M

M, m [em] *n.* M, m, *das*

m. *abbr.* a) **masculine** m.; b) **metre[s]** m; c) **million[s]** Mill.; d) **minute[s]** Min.

MA *abbr.* **Master of Arts** M. A.

mac [mæk] *n. (Brit. coll.)* Regenmantel, *der*

macaroni [mækəˈrəʊnɪ] *n.* Makkaroni *Pl.*

machine [məˈʃiːn] *n.* Maschine, *die.* **ma·chine-gun** *n.* Maschinengewehr, *das*

machinery [məˈʃiːnərɪ] *n.* a) *(machines)* Maschinen *Pl.;* b) *(mechanism)* Mechanismus, *der*

machine- ~ **tool** *n.* Werkzeugmaschine, *die;* ~**-washable** *adj.* waschmaschinenfest

machinist [məˈʃiːnɪst] *n.* Maschinist, *der/*Maschinistin, *die;* **[sewing-]**~: [Maschinen]näherin, *die/*-näher, *der*

macho ['mætʃəʊ] *adj.* Macho-; **he is** ~: er ist ein Macho

mackerel ['mækərl] *n., pl. same or* ~**s** Makrele, *die*

mackintosh ['mækɪntɒʃ] *n.* Regenmantel, *der*

mad [mæd] *adj.* a) *(insane)* geisteskrank; b) *(frenzied)* wahnsinnig; **drive sb. mad** jmdn. um den Verstand bringen; c) *(foolish)* verrückt *(ugs.);* d) *(very enthusiastic)* **be** ~ **about or on sb./sth.** auf jmdn./etw. wild sein *(ugs.);* e) *(coll.: annoyed)* ~ **[with or at sb.]** sauer [auf jmdn.] *(ugs.);* f) *(with rabies)* toll[wütig]; **[run etc.] like** ~: wie wild [laufen *usw.*]

madam ['mædəm] *n.* gnädige Frau; **Dear M~** *(in letter)* Sehr verehrte gnädige Frau

madden ['mædn] *v. t. (irritate)* [ver]ärgern. **maddening** ['mædnɪŋ] *adj. (irritating)* [äußerst] ärgerlich

made *see* **make 1**

¹**madly** *adv. (coll.)* wahnsinnig *(ugs.)*

madman ['mædmən] *n., pl.* **madmen** ['mædmən] *n.* Wahnsinnige, *der*

madness *n.* Wahnsinn, *der*

magazine [mægəˈziːn] *n.* a) Zeitschrift, *die;* b) *(of firearm)* Magazin, *das*

maggot ['mægət] *n.* Made, *die*

magic ['mædʒɪk] 1. *n.* a) Magie, *die;* **work like** ~: wie ein Wunder wirken; b) *(conjuring)* Zauberei, *die.* 2. *adj.* a) *(magisch;* Zauber⟨*trank, -baum*⟩; b) *(fig.)* wunderbar. **magical** ['mædʒɪkl] *adj.* zauberhaft. **magician** [məˈdʒɪʃn] *n.* Magier, *der/*Magierin, *die; (conjurer)* Zauberer, *der/*Zauberin, *die*

magistrate ['mædʒɪstreɪt] *n.* Friedensrichter, *der/*-richterin, *die*

magnanimity [mægnəˈnɪmɪtɪ] *n.* Großmut, *die*

magnanimous [mæg'nænıməs] *adj.*
groẞmütig (**towards** gegen)

magnate ['mægneıt] *n.* Magnat,
der/Magnatin, *die*

magnesium [mæg'ni:zıəm] *n.* Magnesium, *das*

magnet ['mægnıt] *n.* Magnet, *der.*
magnetic [mæg'netık] *adj.* magnetisch. **magnetic 'tape** *n.* Magnet-
band, *das*

magnetism ['mægnıtızm] *n.* a) *(force,
lit. or fig.)* Magnetismus, *der*; b) *(fig.:
charm)* Anziehungskraft, *die*

magnetize ['mægnıtaız] *v. t.* magneti-
sieren

magnification [mægnıfı'keıʃn] *n.*
Vergröẞerung, *die*

magnificence [mæg'nıfısəns] *n.*
Pracht, *die*; *(beauty)* Herrlichkeit, *die*;
(lavishness) Üppigkeit, *die*

magnificent [mæg'nıfısənt] *adj.* a)
prächtig; herrlich ⟨*Garten, Kunstwerk,
Wetter*⟩; *(lavish)* üppig ⟨*Mahl*⟩; b)
(coll.: excellent) fabelhaft *(ugs.)*

magnify ['mægnıfaı] *v. t.* a) vergrö-
ẞern; b) *(exaggerate)* aufbauschen.
'magnifying glass *n.* Lupe, *die*

magnitude ['mægnıtju:d] *n.* a) *(size)*
Gröẞe, *die*; b) *(importance)* Wichtigkeit, *die*

magpie ['mægpaı] *n.* Elster, *die*

mahogany [mə'hɒgənı] *n.* Mahagoni[holz], *das*; *attrib.* Mahagoni-

maid [meıd] *n.* Dienstmädchen, *das*

maiden ['meıdn] 1. *n.* Jungfrau, *die.* 2.
adj. a) *(unmarried)* unverheiratet; b)
(first) ~ **voyage/speech** Jungfernfahrt/
-rede, *die.* **'maiden name** *n.* Mäd-
chenname, *der*

mail [meıl] 1. *n. see* ²**post** 1. 2. *v. t.* ab-
schicken

mail: ~**bag** *n.* Postsack, *der*; ~**box** *n.*
(Amer.) Briefkasten, *der*; ~**ing list** *n.*
Adressenliste, *die*; ~**man** *n. (Amer.)*
Briefträger, *der*; ~ **order** *n.* Bestel-
lung per Post

maim [meım] *v. t.* verstümmeln

main [meın] 1. *n.* a) *(channel, pipe)*
Hauptleitung, *die*; ~**s** *(Electr.)* Strom-
netz, *das*; b) **in the** ~: im groẞen und
ganzen. 2. *attrib. adj.* Haupt-; **the** ~
thing is that ...: die Hauptsache ist,
daẞ ... **mainland** ['meınlənd] *n.* Festland, *das*

'mainly *adv.* hauptsächlich

main: ~**stay** *n.* [wichtigste] Stütze; ~
street [*Brit.* '-'-, *Amer.* '--'] *n.* Haupt-
straẞe, *die*

maintain [meın'teın] *v. t.* a) *(keep up)*

aufrechterhalten; b) *(provide for)* ~ **sb.**
für jmds. Unterhalt aufkommen; c)
(preserve) instand halten; warten ⟨*Maschine*⟩; d) ~ **that** ...: behaupten,
daẞ ... **maintenance** ['meıntənəns]
n. a) *(keeping up)* Aufrechterhaltung,
die; b) *(preservation)* Instandhaltung,
die; *(of machinery)* Wartung, *die*; c)
(Law: money paid to support sb.) Unterhalt, *der*

maison[n]ette [meızə'net] *n.* [zwei-
stöckige] Wohnung

maize [meız] *n.* Mais, *der*

majestic [mə'dʒestık] *adj.*, **majestically** [mə'dʒestıkəlı] *adv.* majestätisch

majesty ['mædʒıstı] *n.* Majestät, *die*
(geh.); **Your/Her** *etc.* **M~**: Eure/Seine
usw. Majestät

major ['meıdʒə(r)] 1. *adj.* a) *attrib.
(greater)* gröẞer...; b) *attrib. (important)* bedeutend...; *(serious)* schwer; ~
road Hauptverkehrsstraẞe, *die*; c)
(Mus.) Dur-; **C** ~: C-Dur. 2. *n. (Mil.)*
Major, *der.* 3. *v. i. (Amer. Univ.)* ~ **in**
sth. etw. als Hauptfach haben

Majorca [mə'jɔ:kə] *pr. n.* Mallorca
(das)

majority [mə'dʒɒrıtı] *n.* Mehrheit,
die; **be in the** ~: in der Mehrzahl sein

make [meık] 1. *v. t.*, **made** [meıd] a)
machen (**of** aus); bauen ⟨*Straẞe,
Flugzeug*⟩; anlegen ⟨*Teich, Weg usw.*⟩;
zimmern ⟨*Tisch, Regal*⟩; basteln
⟨*Spielzeug, Vogelhäuschen usw.*⟩; nähen ⟨*Kleider*⟩; *(manufacture)* herstellen; *(prepare)* zubereiten ⟨*Mahlzeit*⟩;
machen, kochen ⟨*Kaffee, Tee*⟩;
backen ⟨*Brot, Kuchen*⟩; b) *(establish,
enact)* treffen ⟨*Unterscheidung, Über-
einkommen*⟩; ziehen ⟨*Vergleich*⟩; erlassen ⟨*Gesetz*⟩; aufstellen ⟨*Regeln,
Behauptung*⟩; stellen ⟨*Forderung*⟩; geben ⟨*Bericht*⟩; vornehmen ⟨*Zahlung*⟩;
erheben ⟨*Protest, Beschwerde*⟩; c)
(cause to be or become) **happy/
known** *etc.* glücklich/bekannt *usw.*
machen; ~ **sb. captain** jmdn. zum Kapitän machen; d) ~ **sb. do sth.** *(cause)*
jmdn. dazu bringen, etw. zu tun;
(compel) jmdn. zwingen, etw. zu tun;
be made to do sth. etw. tun müssen; e)
(earn) machen ⟨*Profit, Verlust*⟩; verdienen ⟨*Lebensunterhalt*⟩; f) **what do
you** ~ **of him?** was hältst du von ihm?;
g) *(arrive at)* erreichen; **make it** *(succeed in arriving)* es schaffen; h) ~ '**do
with/without sth.** mit/ohne etw. auskommen. 2. *n.*

(brand) Marke, *die*. '**make for** *v.t.* zusteuern auf (+ *Akk.*). **make 'off** *v.i.* sich davonmachen. **make 'off with** *v.t.* ~ off with sb./sth. sich mit jmdm./etw. [auf und] davonmachen. **make 'out** 1. *v.t.* a) *(write)* ausstellen; b) *(claim)* behaupten; c) *(manage to see or hear)* ausmachen; *(manage to read)* entziffern; d) *(pretend)* vorgeben. 2. *v.i.* *(coll.)* zurechtkommen (**at** bei). **make 'over** *v.t.* überschreiben. **make 'up** 1. *v.t.* a) *(assemble)* zusammenstellen; b) *(invent)* erfinden; c) *(constitute)* bilden; **be made up of ...**: bestehen aus ...; d) *(apply cosmetics to)* schminken; ~ **up one's face** sich schminken. 2. *v.i.* *(be reconciled)* sich wieder vertragen. **make 'up for** *v.t.* wiedergutmachen; ~ **up for lost time** Versäumtes nachholen

'**make-believe** 1. *n.* it's only ~: das ist bloß Phantasie. 2. *adj.* nicht echt

'**maker** *n.* *(manufacturer)* Hersteller, *der*

make: ~**shift** *adj.* behelfsmäßig; ~~**up** *n.* *(Cosmetics)* Make-up, *das*

making ['meɪkɪŋ] *n.* **in the** ~: im Entstehen; **have the** ~**s of a leader** das Zeug zum Führer haben *(ugs.)*

maladjusted [mælə'dʒʌstɪd] *adj.* verhaltensgestört

malady ['mælədɪ] *n.* Leiden, *das*

malaise [mə'leɪz] *n.* Unbehagen, *das*

malaria [mə'leərɪə] *n.* Malaria, *die*

Malaysia [mə'leɪzɪə] *pr. n.* Malaysia *(das)*

male [meɪl] 1. *adj.* männlich; Männer-⟨stimme, -chor, -verein⟩; ~ **doctor/nurse** Arzt, *der*/Krankenpfleger, *der*. 2. *n.* *(person)* Mann, *der*; *(animal)* Männchen, *das*

malevolence [mə'levələns] *n.* Boshaftigkeit, *die*

malevolent [mə'levələnt] *adj.* boshaft

malfunction [mæl'fʌŋkʃn] 1. *n.* Störung, *die*; *(Med.)* Funktionsstörung, *die*. 2. *v.i.* nicht richtig funktionieren

malice ['mælɪs] *n.* Bosheit, *die*. **malicious** [mə'lɪʃəs] *adj.* böse

malign [mə'laɪn] *v.t.* verleumden

malignant [mə'lɪgnənt] *adj.* bösartig

malinger [mə'lɪŋgə(r)] *v.i.* simulieren. **ma'lingerer** *n.* Simulant, *der*/Simulantin, *die*

malleable ['mælɪəbl] *adj.* formbar

mallet ['mælɪt] *n.* Holzhammer, *der*

malnutrition [mælnju:'trɪʃn] *n.* Unterernährung, *die*

malt [mɔːlt] *n.* Malz, *das*

Malta ['mɔːltə] *pr. n.* Malta *(das)*

maltreat [mæl'tri:t] *v.t.* mißhandeln. **mal'treatment** *n.* Mißhandlung, *die*

mammal ['mæml] *n.* Säugetier, *das*

mammoth ['mæməθ] 1. *n.* Mammut, *das*. 2. *adj.* Mammut-; gigantisch ⟨Vorhaben⟩

man [mæn] 1. *n.* a) *pl.* **men** [men] Mann, *der*; b) *(human race)* der Mensch. 2. *v.t.*, **-nn-** bemannen ⟨Schiff⟩; besetzen ⟨Büro, Stelle usw.⟩; bedienen ⟨Telefon, Geschütz⟩

manacle ['mænəkl] 1. *n.*, *usu. in pl.* [Hand]fessel, *die*. 2. *v.t.* Handfesseln anlegen (+ *Dat.*)

manage ['mænɪdʒ] 1. *v.t.* a) leiten ⟨Geschäft⟩; b) *(supervise)* betreuen ⟨Mannschaft⟩; c) *(cope with)* schaffen; d) ~ **to do sth.** es fertigbringen, etw. zu tun; **he** ~**d to do it** es gelang ihm, es zu tun. 2. *v.i.* zurechtkommen; ~ **without sth.** ohne etw. auskommen; **I can** ~: es geht. **'manageable** ['mænɪdʒəbl] *adj.* leicht frisierbar ⟨Haar⟩; fügsam ⟨Person, Tier⟩; überschaubar ⟨Größe, Menge⟩. '**management** *n.* a) *(of a business)* Leitung, *die*; b) *(managers)* **the** ~: die Geschäftsleitung. '**manager** *n.* *(of shop or bank)* Filialleiter, *der*/-leiterin, *die*; *(of football team)* [Chef]trainer, *der*/-trainerin, *die*; *(of restaurant, shop, hotel)* Geschäftsführer, *der*/-führerin, *die*. **manageress** [mænɪdʒə'res] *n.* Geschäftsführerin, *die*. **managing** ['mænɪdʒɪŋ] *adj.* ~ **director** Geschäftsführer, *der*/-führerin, *die*

¹**mandarin** ['mændərɪn] *n.* ~ [orange] Mandarine, *die*

²**mandarin** *n.* *(bureaucrat)* Bürokrat, *der*/Bürokratin, *die*

mandarine ['mændərɪn] *see* ¹**mandarin**

mandate ['mændeɪt] *n.* Mandat, *das*

mandatory ['mændətərɪ] *adj.* obligatorisch

mandolin[e] [mændə'lɪn] *n.* Mandoline, *die*

mane [meɪn] *n.* Mähne, *die*

maneuver[able] *(Amer.)* *see* **manœuvr-**

manful ['mænfl] *adj.*, **manfully** ['mænfəlɪ] *adv.* mannhaft

manger ['meɪndʒə(r)] *n.* Krippe, *die*

mangle ['mæŋgl] *v.t.* verstümmeln ⟨Person⟩; demolieren ⟨Sache⟩

mangy ['meɪndʒɪ] *adj.* a) *(Vet. Med.)* räudig; b) *(shabby)* schäbig

man: ~**handle** *v.t.* a) von Hand bewegen ⟨*Gegenstand*⟩; **b)** grob behandeln ⟨*Person*⟩; **~hole** *n.* Mannloch, *das*

'**manhood** *n.* Mannesalter, *das*

man: ~-hour *n.* Arbeitsstunde, *die;* **~-hunt** *n.* Verbrecherjagd, *die*

mania ['meɪnɪə] *n.* Manie, *die*

manicure ['mænɪkjʊə(r)] **1.** *n.* Maniküre, *die.* **2.** *v. t.* maniküren

manifest ['mænɪfest] **1.** *adj.* offenkundig. **2.** *v. t. (reveal)* offenbaren.

'**manifestly** *adv.* offenkundig

manifesto [mænɪ'festəʊ] *n., pl.* **~s** Manifest, *das*

manifold ['mænɪfəʊld] *adj. (literary)* mannigfaltig *(geh.)*

manipulate [mə'nɪpjʊleɪt] *v. t.* **a)** manipulieren; **b)** *(handle)* handhaben.

manipulation [mənɪpjʊ'leɪʃn] *n.* **a)** Manipulation, *die;* **b)** *(handling)* Handhabung, *die*

mankind [mæn'kaɪnd] *n.* Menschheit, *die*

manly ['mænlɪ] *adj.* männlich

'**man-made** *adj.* künstlich; *(synthetic)* Kunst⟨*faser, -stoff*⟩

manned [mænd] *adj.* bemannt

manner ['mænə(r)] *n.* **a)** Art, *die;* Weise, *die;* **in this ~:** auf diese Art und Weise; **b)** *(general behaviour)* Art, *die;* **c)** *in pl.* Manieren *Pl.* **mannerism** ['mænərɪzm] *n.* Eigenart, *die*

manœuvrable [mə'nu:vrəbl] *adj. (Brit.)* manövrierfähig

manœuvre [mə'nu:və(r)] *(Brit.)* **1.** *n.* Manöver, *das.* **2.** *v. t. & i.* manövrieren

manor ['mænə(r)] *n.* **a)** *(land)* [Land]gut, *das;* **b)** *see* **manor-house.**

'**manor-house** *n.* Herrenhaus, *das*

'**manpower** *n.* Arbeitskräfte *Pl.*

mansion ['mænʃn] *n.* Herrenhaus, *das*

manslaughter ['mænslɔ:tə(r)] *n.* Totschlag, *der*

mantelpiece ['mæntlpi:s] *n.* Kaminsims, *der od. das*

mantle ['mæntl] *n.* Umhang, *der*

manual ['mænjʊəl] **1.** *adj.* **a)** manuell; **~ work** Handarbeit; **b)** *(not automatic)* handbetrieben; ⟨*Bedienung, Schaltung*⟩ von Hand. **2.** *n.* Handbuch, *das*

manufacture [mænjʊ'fæktʃ(ə)(r)] **1.** *n.* Herstellung, *die.* **2.** *v. t.* herstellen.

manu'facturer *n.* Hersteller, *der*

manure [mə'njʊə(r)] **1.** *n.* Dung, *der.* **2.** *v. t.* düngen

manuscript ['mænjʊskrɪpt] *n.* Manuskript, *das*

many ['menɪ] **1.** *adj.* viele; **how ~**

people/books? wie viele *od.* wieviel Leute/Bücher? **2.** *n.* viele [Leute]; **~ of us** viele von uns; **a good/great ~:** eine Menge

map [mæp] **1.** *n.* [Land]karte, *die; (street plan)* Stadtplan, *der.* **2.** *v. t.,* **-pp-** kartographieren. **~ 'out** *v. t.* im einzelnen festlegen

maple ['meɪpl] *n.* Ahorn, *der*

mar [mɑ:(r)] *v. t.* verderben

marathon ['mærəθən] *n.* **a)** Marathon[lauf], *der;* **b)** *(fig.)* Marathon, *das*

marauder [mə'rɔ:də(r)] *n.* Plünderer, *der*

marble ['mɑ:bl] *n.* **a)** *(stone)* Marmor, *der;* **b)** *(toy)* Murmel, *die;* [**game of**] **~s** Murmelspiel, *das*

March [mɑ:tʃ] *n.* März, *der; see also* **August**

march 1. *n.* Marsch, *der;* |**protest**| **~:** Protestmarsch, *der.* **2.** *v. i.* marschieren. **march 'off** *v. i.* losmarschieren. **2.** *v. i.* abführen. **march 'past** *v. i.* vorbeimarschieren

'**marcher** *n.* |**protest**| **~:** Demonstrant, *der*/Demonstrantin, *die*

mare [meə(r)] *n.* Stute, *die*

margarine [mɑ:dʒə'ri:n], *(coll.)* **marge** [mɑ:dʒ] *ns.* Margarine, *die*

margin ['mɑ:dʒɪn] *n.* **a)** *(of page)* Rand, *der;* **b)** *(extra amount)* Spielraum, *der;* |**profit**| **~:** [Gewinn]spanne, *die;* **by a narrow ~:** knapp. **marginal** ['mɑ:dʒɪnl] *adj.,* '**marginally** *adv.* unwesentlich

marigold ['mærɪɡəʊld] *n.* Ringelblume, *die*

marijuana [mærɪjʊ'ɑ:nə] *n.* Marihuana, *das*

marina [mə'ri:nə] *n.* Jachthafen, *der*

marinade [mærɪ'neɪd] **1.** *n.* Marinade, *die.* **2.** *v. t.* marinieren

marine [mə'ri:n] **1.** *adj.* Meeres-; See⟨*versicherung, -recht usw.*⟩; Schiffs⟨*ausrüstung, -turbine usw.*⟩. **2.** *n. (person)* Marineinfanterist, *der.*

mariner ['mærɪnə(r)] *n.* Seemann, *der*

marionette [mærɪə'net] *n.* Marionette, *die*

marital ['mærɪtl] *adj.* ehelich; **~ status** Familienstand, *der*

maritime ['mærɪtaɪm] *adj.* See-

'**mark** [mɑ:k] **1.** *n.* **a)** *(trace)* Spur, *die; (stain etc.)* Fleck, *der; (scratch)* Kratzer, *der;* **b)** *(sign)* Zeichen, *das;* **c)** *(Sch.)* Note, *die;* **d)** *(target)* Ziel, *das.* **2.** *v. t.* **a)** *(dirty)* schmutzig machen; *(scratch)* zerkratzen; **b)** *(put distinguishing ~ on)* kennzeichnen, markieren (with mit); c) *(Sch.) (correct)* korrigieren; *(grade)* benoten; **d)** ~ **time** auf der Stelle treten. **mark 'off** *v. t.* abgrenzen (**from** von, gegen). **mark 'out** *v. t.* markieren

²**mark** *n. (monetary unit)* Mark, *die*

marked ['mɑ:kt] *adj.*, **markedly** ['mɑ:kɪdlɪ] *adv.* deutlich

'**marker** *n.* Markierung, *die.* '**marker pen** *n.* Markierstift, *der*

market ['mɑ:kɪt] 1. *n.* Markt, *der.* 2. *v. t.* vermarkten. '**marketing** *n.* Marketing, *das.* '**market-place** *n.* Marktplatz, *der; (fig.)* Markt, *der*

'**marking** *n.* **a)** Markierung, *die;* **b)** *(on animal)* Zeichnung, *die*

marksman ['mɑ:ksmən] *n., pl.* **marksmen** ['mɑ:ksmən] Scharfschütze, *der*

marmalade ['mɑ:məleɪd] *n.* [orange] ~ : Orangenmarmelade, *die*

¹**maroon** [mə'ru:n] 1. *adj.* kastanienbraun. 2. *n.* Kastanienbraun, *das*

²**maroon** *v. t.* **a)** *(Naut.: put ashore)* aussetzen; ⟨*Flut, Hochwasser:*⟩ von der Außenwelt abschneiden

marquee [mɑ:'ki:] *n.* Festzelt, *das*

marquess, marquis ['mɑ:kwɪs] *n.* Marquis, *der*

marriage ['mærɪdʒ] *n.* **a)** Ehe, *die* (**to** mit); **b)** *(wedding)* Hochzeit, *die*

married ['mærɪd] *adj.* **a)** verheiratet; ~ **couple** Ehepaar, *das;* **b)** *(marital)* Ehe⟨*leben, -name*⟩

marrow ['mærəʊ] *n.* **a)** [vegetable] ~ : Speisekürbis, *der;* **b)** *(Anat.)* [Knochen]mark, *das*

marry ['mærɪ] 1. *v. t.* **a)** heiraten; **b)** *(join)* trauen; **they were** *or* **got/have got married** sie haben geheiratet. 2. *v. i.* heiraten

Mars [mɑ:z] *pr. n. (Astron.)* Mars, *der*

marsh [mɑ:ʃ] *n.* Sumpf, *der*

marshal ['mɑ:ʃl] 1. *n.* **a)** *(officer in army)* Marschall, *der;* **b)** *(Sport)* Ordner, *der.* 2. *v. t., (Brit.)* -**ll**- aufstellen ⟨*Truppen*⟩; ordnen ⟨*Fakten*⟩. '**marshalling yard** *n.* Rangierbahnhof, *der*

marshmallow [mɑ:'ʃmæləʊ] *n.* *(sweet)* ≈ Mohrenkopf, *der*

'**marshy** *adj.* sumpfig

marsupial [mɑ:'sju:pɪəl] *n.* Beuteltier, *das*

martial ['mɑ:ʃl] *adj.* kriegerisch. **martial 'law** *n.* Kriegsrecht, *das*

martyr ['mɑ:tə(r)] 1. *n.* Märtyrer, *der/*Märtyrerin, *die.* 2. *v. t.* **be** ~**ed** den Märtyrertod sterben

marvel ['mɑ:vl] 1. *n.* Wunder, *das.* 2.

v. i., (Brit.) -**ll**- *(literary)* ~ **at sth.** über etw. *(Akk.)* staunen. **marvellous** ['mɑ:vələs] *adj.*, '**marvellously** *adv.* wunderbar

marvelous[ly] *(Amer.)* see **marvellous[ly]**

Marxism ['mɑ:ksɪzm] *n.* Marxismus, *der.* **Marxist** ['mɑ:ksɪst] 1. *n.* Marxist, *der/*Marxistin, *die.* 2. *adj.* marxistisch

marzipan ['mɑ:zɪpæn] *n.* Marzipan, *das*

mascara [mæ'skɑ:rə] *n.* Mascara, *das*

mascot ['mæskɒt] *n.* Maskottchen, *das*

masculine ['mæskjʊlɪn] *adj.* männlich. **masculinity** [mæskju'lɪnɪtɪ] *n.* Männlichkeit, *die*

mash [mæʃ] 1. *n.* **a)** Brei, *der;* **b)** *(Brit. coll.: ~ed potatoes)* Kartoffelbrei, *der.* 2. *v. t.* zerdrücken; ~**ed potatoes** Kartoffelbrei, *der*

mask [mɑ:sk] 1. *n.* Maske, *die.* 2. *v. t.* maskieren

masochism ['mæsəkɪzm] *n.* Masochismus, *der.* **masochist** ['mæsəkɪst] *n.* Masochist, *der/*Masochistin, *die.* **masochistic** [mæsə'kɪstɪk] *adj.* masochistisch

mason ['meɪsn] *n.* **a)** Steinmetz, *der;* **b)** M~ *(Free~)* [Frei]maurer, *der.* **Masonic** [mə'sɒnɪk] *adj.* [frei]maurerisch; ~ **lodge** [Frei]maurerloge, *die.* **masonry** ['meɪsnrɪ] *n.* Mauerwerk, *das*

masquerade [mæskə'reɪd, mɑ:skə'reɪd] 1. *n.* Maskerade, *die.* 2. *v. i.* ~ **as sb./sth.** sich als jmd./etw. ausgeben

¹**mass** [mæs] *n. (Eccl.)* Messe, *die*

²**mass** [mæs] 1. *n.* **a)** Masse, *die;* **b) a** ~ **of ...**: eine Unmenge von ... 2. *v. t.* anhäufen. 3. *v. i.* sich ansammeln; ⟨*Truppen:*⟩ sich massieren

massacre ['mæsəkə(r)] 1. *n.* Massaker, *das.* 2. *v. t.* massakrieren

massage ['mæsɑ:ʒ] 1. *n.* Massage, *die.* 2. *v. t.* massieren

massive ['mæsɪv] *adj.* massiv; gewaltig ⟨*Aufgabe*⟩; enorm ⟨*Schulden*⟩

mass: ~ '**media** *n. pl.* Massenmedien *Pl.*; ~~-**pro'duced** *adj.* serienmäßig produziert; ~ **pro'duction** *n.* Massenproduktion, *die*

mast [mɑ:st] *n.* Mast, *der*

master ['mɑ:stə(r)] 1. *n.* **a)** Herr, *der;* **b)** *(of dog)* Herrchen, *das; (of ship)* Kapitän, *der;* **c)** *(Sch.: teacher)* Lehrer, *der;* **d)** *(expert, great artist)* Meister, *der* (**at** in + *Dat.*); **e)** M~ **of**

Arts/Science Magister Artium/rerum naturalium. 2. *adj.* Haupt-. 3. *v. t.* *(learn)* erlernen; **have ~ed a language** eine Sprache beherrschen. **masterful** ['mɑ:stəfl] *adj. (masterly)* meisterhaft

'**master-key** *n.* Hauptschlüssel, *der*
'**masterly** ['mɑ:stəlɪ] *adj.* meisterhaft
master: **~mind** 1. *n.* führender Kopf; 2. *v. t.* **~mind the plot** der Kopf des Komplotts sein; **~piece** *n. (work of art)* Meisterwerk, *das;* **~-stroke** *n.* Meisterstück, *das;* **~ switch** *n.* Hauptschalter, *der*
mastery ['mɑ:stərɪ] *n.* **a)** *(skill)* Meisterschaft, *die;* **b)** *(knowledge)* Beherrschung, *die* (of *Gen.*)
masturbate ['mæstəbeɪt] *v. i. & t.* masturbieren. **masturbation** [mæstə-'beɪʃn] *n.* Masturbation, *die*
mat [mæt] *n.* **a)** Matte, *die;* **b)** *(to protect table etc.)* Untersetzer, *der*
'**match** [mætʃ] 1. *n.* **a) be no ~ for sb.** sich mit jmdm. nicht messen können; **meet one's ~:** seinen Meister finden; **b) be a** *[good etc.]* **~ for sth.** [gut *usw.*] zu etw. passen; **c)** *(Sport)* Spiel, *das;* *(Boxing)* Kampf, *der.* 2. *v. t.* **a)** *(equal)* **~ sb. at chess** es mit jmdm. im Schach aufnehmen [können]; **b)** *(harmonize with)* passen zu; **a handbag and ~ing shoes** eine Handtasche und [dazu] passende Schuhe; **~ each other** zueinander passen. 3. *v. i.* zusammenpassen
²**match** *n. (~stick)* Streichholz, *das*
'**matchless** *adj.* unvergleichlich
'**matchstick** *n.* Streichholz, *das*
'**mate** [meɪt] 1. *n.* **a)** Kumpel, *der (ugs.);* **b)** *(Naut.)* ≈ Kapitänleutnant, *der;* **c)** *(workman's assistant)* Gehilfe, *der;* **d)** *(Zool.) (male)* Männchen, *das; (female)* Weibchen, *das.* 2. *v. i.* sich paaren. 3. *v. t.* paaren ⟨*Tiere*⟩
²**mate** *(Chess) see* **checkmate**
material [mə'tɪərɪəl] 1. *adj.* **a)** materiell; **b)** *(relevant)* wesentlich. 2. *n.* **a)** **~[s]** Material, *das;* **building/writing ~s** Bau-/Schreibmaterial, *das;* **b)** *(cloth)* Stoff, *der.* **materialism** [mə'tɪərɪə-lɪzm] *n.* Materialismus, *der.* **materialistic** [mətɪərɪə'lɪstɪk] *adj.* materialistisch. **materialize** [mə'tɪərɪəlaɪz] *v. i.* ⟨*Plan, Idee:*⟩ sich verwirklichen; ⟨*Treffen:*⟩ zustande kommen
maternal [mə'tɜ:nl] *adj.* mütterlich; Mutter⟨*instinkt*⟩
maternity [mə'tɜ:nɪtɪ] *n.* Mutterschaft, *die.* **ma'ternity dress** *n.*

Umstandskleid, *das.* **ma'ternity hospital** *n.* Entbindungsheim, *das*
matey ['meɪtɪ] *adj.,* **matier** ['meɪtɪə(r)], **matiest** ['meɪtɪɪst] *(Brit. coll.)* kameradschaftlich
math [mæθ] *(Amer. coll.) see* **maths**
mathematical [mæθɪ'mætɪkl] *adj.,* **mathematically** [mæθɪ'mætɪkəlɪ] *adv.* mathematisch
mathematician [mæθɪmə'tɪʃn] *n.* Mathematiker, *der/*Mathematikerin, *die*
mathematics [mæθɪ'mætɪks] *n.* Mathematik, *die*
maths [mæθs] *n. (Brit. coll.)* Mathe, *die (Schülerspr.)*
matinée ['mætɪneɪ] *n.* Nachmittagsvorstellung, *die*
matrices *pl. of* **matrix**
matriculate [mə'trɪkjʊleɪt] 1. *v. t.* immatrikulieren (**in** an + *Dat.*). 2. *v. i.* sich immatrikulieren. **matriculation** [mətrɪkjʊ'leɪʃn] *n.* Immatrikulation, *die*
matrimonial [mætrɪ'məʊnɪəl] *adj.* Ehe-
matrimony ['mætrɪmənɪ] *n.* Ehestand, *der*
matrix ['meɪtrɪks] *n., pl.* **matrices** ['meɪtrɪsi:z] *or* **~es** Matrix, *die*
matron ['meɪtrən] *n. (in school)* ≈ Hausmutter, *die; (in hospital)* Oberschwester, *die*
matt [mæt] *adj.* matt
'**matted** *adj.* verfilzt
matter ['mætə(r)] 1. *n.* **a)** *(affair)* Angelegenheit, *die;* **~s** die Dinge; **money ~s** Geldangelegenheiten; **b) it's a ~ of taste** das ist Geschmackssache; **[only] a ~ of time** [nur noch] eine Frage der Zeit; **c) what's the ~?** was ist [los]?; **d)** *(physical material)* Materie, *die.* 2. *v. i.* etwas ausmachen; **what does it ~?** was macht das schon?; **[it] doesn't ~:** [das] macht nichts *(ugs.).* '**matter-of-fact** *adj.* sachlich
mattress ['mætrɪs] *n.* Matratze, *die*
mature [mə'tjʊə(r)] 1. *adj.* reif; ausgereift ⟨*Stil, Käse, Portwein, Sherry*⟩. 2. *v. t.* reifen lassen. 3. *v. i.* reifen. **maturity** [mə'tjʊərɪtɪ] *n.* Reife, *die*
Maundy Thursday [mɔ:ndɪ 'θɜ:zdɪ] *n.* Gründonnerstag, *der*
mausoleum [mɔ:sə'lɪəm] *n.* Mausoleum, *das*
mauve [məʊv] *adj.* mauve
mawkish ['mɔ:kɪʃ] *adj.* rührselig
max. *abbr.* **maximum** *(adj.)* max., *(n.)* Max.

maxim ['mæksɪm] *n.* Maxime, *die*
maximum ['mæksɪməm] **1.** *n., pl.*
maxima ['mæksɪmə] Maximum, *das.*
2. *adj.* maximal; Maximal-; ~ **speed/**
temperature Höchstgeschwindigkeit,
die/-temperatur, *die*

May [meɪ] *n.* Mai, *der; see also* **August**
may *v. aux., only in pres.* **may**, *neg.*
(coll.) **mayn't** [meɪnt], *past* **might**
[maɪt], *neg. (coll.)* **mightn't** ['maɪtnt] **a)**
expr. possibility können; **it** ~ **be**
true das kann stimmen; **I** ~ **be wrong** vielleicht irre ich mich; **it** ~ **not be**
possible das wird vielleicht nicht möglich sein; **he** ~ **have missed his train**
vielleicht hat er seinen Zug verpaßt; **it**
~ **or might rain** es könnte regnen; **we**
~ **or might as well go** wir könnten eigentlich ebensogut [auch] gehen; **b)**
expr. permission dürfen; **c)** *expr. wish*
mögen; ~ **the best man win!** auf daß
der Beste gewinnt!

maybe ['meɪbiː, ˌmeɪbɪ] *adv.* vielleicht
mayn't [meɪnt] *(coll.)* = **may not;** *see*
may

mayonnaise [meɪə'neɪz] *n.* Mayonnaise, *die*

mayor [meə(r)] *n.* Bürgermeister, *der*
mayoress ['meərɪs] *n.* (woman mayor)
Bürgermeisterin, *die; (mayor's wife)*
[Ehe]frau des Bürgermeisters

maze [meɪz] *n.* Labyrinth, *das*
me [mɪ, *stressed* miː] *pron.* mich; *as indirect object* mir; **who, me?** wer, ich?;
not me ich nicht; **it's me** ich bin's

meadow ['medəʊ] *n.* Wiese, *die*
meagre ['miːgə(r)] *adj.* dürftig
meal [miːl] *n.* Mahlzeit, *die;* **go out for**
a ~: essen gehen. **mealtime** *n.* Essenszeit, *die*

¹mean [miːn] *n.* **a)** Mittelweg, *der;* **b)**
(Math.) Mittelwert, *der*

²mean *adj.* **a)** *(miserly)* geizig; **b)** *(unkind)* gemein; **b)** *(shabby)* schäbig

³mean *v. t.,* **meant** [ment] **a)** *(intend)*
beabsichtigen; ~ **to do sth.** etw. tun
wollen; **b)** *(design, destine)* **be** ~**t to do**
sth. etw. tun sollen; **c)** *(intend to convey)* meinen; **I [really]** ~ **it** ich meine
das ernst; **what do you** ~ **by that?** was
hast du damit gemeint?; **d)** *(signify)*
bedeuten

meander [mɪ'ændə(r)] *v. i.* **a)** *(Fluß:)*
sich winden; **b)** *(Person:)* schlendern

'meaning *n.* Bedeutung, *die; (of text
etc., life)* Sinn, *der.* **meaningful**
['miːnɪŋfl] *adj.* bedeutungsvoll *(Blick,
Ergebnis);* sinnvoll *(Aufgabe, Gespräch).* **'meaningless** *adj.* *(Wort,*

means [miːnz] *n.* **a)** Möglichkeit, *die;*
[Art und] Weise; **by this** ~: hierdurch;
~ **of transport** Transportmittel, *das;* **b)**
pl. (resources) Mittel *Pl.;* **live within/**
beyond one's ~: seinen Verhältnissen
entsprechend/über seine Verhältnisse
leben; **c) by all** ~! selbstverständlich!;
by no [manner of] ~: ganz und gar
nicht; **by** ~ **of** durch; mit [Hilfe von]
'means test *n.* Überprüfung der Be-
dürftigkeit

meant *see* **³mean**
mean: ~ **time** *n.* **in the** ~ **time** inzwischen; ~**time,** ~**while** *advs.* inzwischen

measles ['miːzlz] *n.* Masern *Pl.*
measly ['miːzlɪ] *adj.* *(coll.)* pop[e]lig
(ugs.)

measurable ['meʒərəbl] *adj.* meßbar
measure ['meʒə(r)] **1.** *n.* **a)** Maß, *das;*
for good ~: sicherheitshalber, als
extra) zusätzlich; **made to** ~: maßgeschneidert; **b)** *(degree)* **in some/large**
~: in gewisser Hinsicht/ in hohem
Maße; **c)** *(for measuring)* Maß, *das;* **d)**
(step) Maßnahme, *die;* **take** ~**s** Maßnahmen treffen. **2.** *v. t.* messen
⟨Größe, Menge usw.⟩; ausmessen
⟨Raum⟩. **3.** *v. i.* messen. **measure 'up**
to *v. t.* entsprechen (+ *Dat.*)

'measured ['meʒəd] *adj.* gemessen
⟨Schritt, Worte⟩

'measurement *n.* **a)** Messung, *die;* **b)**
(dimension) Maß, *das*

meat [miːt] *n.* Fleisch, *das.* **'meaty**
adj. **a)** fleischig; **b)** *(fig.)* gehaltvoll
mechanic [mɪ'kænɪk] *n.* Mechaniker,
*der/*Mechanikerin, *die*

mechanical [mɪ'kænɪkl] *adj.,*
me'chanically *adv.* mechanisch.
mechanical 'pencil *n.* *(Amer.)*
Drehbleistift, *der*

me'chanics *n.* **a)** Mechanik, *die;* **b)**
pl. (mechanism) Mechanismus, *der*

mechanism ['mekənɪzm] *n.* Mechanismus, *der*

mechanization [mekənaɪ'zeɪʃn] *n.*
Mechanisierung, *die*

mechanize ['mekənaɪz] *v. t.* mechani-
sieren

medal ['medl] *n.* Medaille, *die; (decoration)* Orden, *der*

medallion [mɪ'dæljən] *n.* [große] Medaille

medallist ['medəlɪst] *n.* Medaillenge-
winner, *der/*-gewinnerin, *die*

meddle ['medl] *v. i.* ~ **with sth.** sich

(Dat.) an etw. *(Dat.)* zu schaffen machen; ~ **in sth.** sich in etw. *(Akk.)* einmischen

media ['mi:dɪə] *see* **mass media; medium 1**

mediaeval *see* **medieval**

mediate ['mi:dɪeɪt] *v.i.* vermitteln. **mediator** ['mi:dɪeɪtə(r)] *n.* Vermittler, *der*/Vermittlerin, *die*

medical ['medɪkl] *adj.* medizinisch; ärztlich ⟨*Behandlung, Untersuchung*⟩

medical: ~ **certificate** *n.* Attest, *das;* ~ **school** *n.* medizinische Hochschule; ~ **student** *n.* Medizinstudent, *der*/-studentin *die*

medicated ['medɪkeɪtɪd] *adj.* medizinisch

medication [medɪ'keɪʃn] *n. (medicine)* Medikament, *das*

medicinal [mɪ'dɪsɪnl] *adj.* medizinisch

medicine ['medsən, 'medɪsɪn] *n.* **a)** *(science)* Medizin, *die;* **b)** *(preparation)* Medikament, *das*

medieval [medɪ'i:vl] *adj.* mittelalterlich

mediocre [mi:dɪ'əʊkə(r)] *adj.* mittelmäßig. **mediocrity** [mi:dɪ'ɒkrɪtɪ] *n.* Mittelmäßigkeit, *die*

meditate ['medɪteɪt] *v.i.* nachdenken, *(esp. Relig.)* meditieren (**up**|**on** über + *Akk.*). **meditation** [medɪ'teɪʃn] *n.* **a)** *(act)* Nachdenken, *das;* **b)** *(Relig.)* Meditation, *die*

Mediterranean [medɪtə'reɪnɪən] *pr. n.* **the ~:** das Mittelmeer

medium ['mi:dɪəm] **1.** *n., pl.* **media** ['mi:dɪə] *or* **~s** *adj.* *(substance)* Medium, *das;* **b)** *(means)* Mittel, *das;* **by** *or* **through the ~ of** durch; **c)** *pl.* **~s** *(Spiritualism)* Medium, *das;* **d)** *in pl.* **media** *(mass media)* Medien *Pl.* **2.** *adj.* mittler ...; medium *nur präd.* ⟨*Steak*⟩. **'medium-size[d]** *adj.* mittelgroß

medley ['medlɪ] *n.* **a)** buntes Gemisch; **b)** *(Mus.)* Potpourri, *das*

meek [mi:k] *adj.* **a)** *(humble)* sanftmütig; **b)** *(submissive)* zu nachgiebig

meet [mi:t] **1.** *v.t.,* **met** [met] **a)** treffen; *(collect)* abholen; **b)** *(make the acquaintance of)* kennenlernen; **pleased to ~ you** [sehr] angenehm; **c)** *(experience)* stoßen auf (+ *Akk.*) ⟨*Widerstand, Problem*⟩; **d)** *(satisfy)* entsprechen (+ *Dat.*) ⟨*Wunsch, Bedürfnis, Kritik*⟩; **e)** *(pay)* decken ⟨*Kosten*⟩; bezahlen ⟨*Rechnung*⟩. **2.** *v.i.,* **met a)** *(by chance)* sich *(Dat.)* begegnen; **b)** *(by arrangement)* sich treffen; **we've met before** wir kennen uns bereits; **b)** ⟨*Komi-*

tee, Ausschuß usw.:⟩ tagen. **meet 'up** *v.i.* sich treffen; ~ **up with sb.** *(coll.)* sich treffen. **'meet with** *v.t.* **a)** begegnen (+ *Dat.*); **b)** *(experience)* haben ⟨*Erfolg, Unfall*⟩; stoßen auf (+ *Akk.*) ⟨*Widerstand*⟩

'meeting *n.* **a)** Begegnung, *die; (by arrangement)* Treffen, *das;* **b)** *(assembly)* Versammlung, *die; (of committee etc.)* Sitzung, *die*

megalomania [megələ'meɪnɪə] *n.* Größenwahn, *der*

megaphone ['megəfəʊn] *n.* Megaphon, *das*

melancholic [melən'kɒlɪk] *adj.* melancholisch

melancholy ['melənkəlɪ] **1.** *n.* Melancholie, *die.* **2.** *adj.* melancholisch

mellow ['meləʊ] **1.** *adj.* **a)** *(softened by age or experience)* abgeklärt; **b)** *(ripe, well-matured)* reif. **2.** *v.i.* reifen

melodic [mɪ'lɒdɪk], **melodious** [mɪ-'ləʊdɪəs] *adjs.,* **me'lodiously** *adv.* melodisch

melodrama ['melədrɑ:mə] *n.* Melodrama, *das.* **melodramatic** [melədrə'mætɪk] *adj.* melodramatisch

melody ['melədɪ] *n.* Melodie, *die*

melon ['melən] *n.* Melone, *die*

melt [melt] **1.** *v.i.* schmelzen. **2.** *v.t.* schmelzen; zerlassen ⟨*Butter*⟩. **melt a'way** *v.i.* [weg]schmelzen. **melt 'down 1.** *v.i.* schmelzen. **2.** *v.t.* einschmelzen

melting: ~-**point** *n.* Schmelzpunkt, *der;* ~-**pot** *n. (fig.)* Schmelztiegel, *der*

member ['membə(r)] *n.* Mitglied, *das;* **be a ~:** Mitglied sein; ~ **of a/the family** Familienangehörige, *der/die;* **b)** **M~ |of Parliament|** *(Brit.)* Abgeordnete [des Unterhauses], *der/die.* **'membership** *n.* **a)** Mitgliedschaft, *die* (of **in** + *Dat.*); **b)** *(number of members)* Mitgliederzahl, *die;* **c)** *(members)* Mitglieder *Pl.*

membrane ['membreɪn] *n. (Biol.)* Membran, *die*

memento [mɪ'mentəʊ] *n., pl.* ~**es** *or* ~**s** Andenken, *das* (of **an** + *Akk.*)

memo ['meməʊ] *n., pl.* ~**s** *(coll.)* *see* **memorandum**

memoirs ['memwɑ:z] *n. pl.* Memoiren *Pl.*

memorable ['memərəbl] *adj.* denkwürdig ⟨*Ereignis, Tag*⟩; unvergeßlich ⟨*Film, Buch, Aufführung*⟩

memorandum [memə'rændəm] *n., pl.* **memoranda** [memə'rændə] *or* ~**s** Mitteilung, *die*

memorial [mɪ'mɔːrɪəl] **1.** *adj.* Gedenk-. **2.** *n.* Denkmal, *das* (**to** für)

memorize ['meməraɪz] *v.t.* sich (*Dat.*) merken *od.* einprägen; *(learn by heart)* auswendig lernen

memory ['memərɪ] *n.* **a)** Gedächtnis, *das;* **b)** *(thing remembered, act of remembering)* Erinnerung, *die* (**of** an + *Akk.*); **from ~:** aus dem Gedächtnis; **in ~ of** zur Erinnerung an (+ *Akk.*); **c)** *(Computing)* Speicher, *der*

men *pl. of* **man**

menace ['menɪs] **1.** *v.t.* bedrohen. **2.** *n.* Plage, *die.* **'menacing** ['menəsɪŋ] *adj.* drohend

mend [mend] **1.** *v.t.* reparieren; ausbessern *⟨Kleidung⟩*; kleben *⟨Glas, Porzellan⟩*. **2.** *v.i.* *⟨Knochen, Bein usw.:⟩* heilen. **3.** *n.* **be on the ~:** auf dem Wege der Besserung sein

'menfolk *n. pl.* Männer

menial ['miːnɪəl] *adj.* niedrig; untergeordnet *⟨Aufgabe⟩*

meningitis [menɪn'dʒaɪtɪs] *n.* Hirnhautentzündung, *die* (**to** für)

menopause ['menəpɔːz] *n.* Wechseljahre *Pl.*

menstruate ['menstrʊeɪt] *v.i.* menstruieren. **menstruation** [menstrʊ'eɪʃn] *n.* Menstruation, *die*

menswear ['menzweə(r)] *n.* Herrenbekleidung, *die*

mental ['mentl] *adj.* **a)** *(of the mind)* geistig; Geistes*⟨zustand, -störung⟩*; **b)** *(Brit. coll.: mad)* verrückt *(salopp)*

mental: ~ a'rithmetic *n.* Kopfrechnen, *das;* **~ 'hospital** *n.* Nervenklinik, *die (ugs.);* **~ 'illness** *n.* Geisteskrankheit, *die*

mentality [men'tælɪtɪ] *n.* Mentalität, *die*

'mentally *adv.* geistig

mention ['menʃn] **1.** *n.* Erwähnung, *die.* **2.** *v.t.* erwähnen (**to** gegenüber); **don't ~ it** keine Ursache

menu ['menjuː] *n.* [Speise]karte, *die*

mercenary ['mɜːsɪnərɪ] **1.** *adj.* gewinnsüchtig. **2.** *n.* Söldner, *der*

merchandise ['mɜːtʃəndaɪz] *n.* [Handels]ware, *die*

merchant ['mɜːtʃənt] *n.* Kaufmann, *der.* **merchant 'bank** *n.* Handelsbank, *die.* **merchant 'navy** *n.* *(Brit.)* Handelsmarine, *die*

merciful ['mɜːsɪfl] *adj.* gnädig. **mercifully** ['mɜːsɪfəlɪ] *adv.* *(fortunately)* glücklicherweise

merciless ['mɜːsɪlɪs] *adj.* **'mercilessly** *adv.* gnadenlos

mercury ['mɜːkjʊrɪ] **1.** *n.* Quecksilber, *das.* **2.** *pr. n.* **M~** *(Astron.)* Merkur, *der*

mercy ['mɜːsɪ] *n.* Erbarmen, *das* (**on** mit); **show sb.** [**no**] **~:** mit jmdm. [kein] Erbarmen haben; **be at the ~ of sb./ sth.** jmdm./einer Sache [auf Gedeih und Verderb] ausgeliefert sein

mere [mɪə(r)] *adj.* **'merely** *adv.* bloß

merge [mɜːdʒ] **1.** *v.t.* **a)** *(combine)* zusammenschließen; **b)** *(blend gradually)* verschmelzen (**with** mit). **2.** *v.i.* **a)** *(combine)* fusionieren (**with** mit); **b)** *⟨Straße:⟩* zusammenlaufen (**with** mit).

merger ['mɜːdʒə(r)] *n.* Fusion, *die*

meringue [mə'ræŋ] *n.* Meringe, *die;* Baiser, *das*

merit ['merɪt] **1.** *n.* **a)** *(worth)* Verdienst, *das;* **b)** *(good feature)* Vorzug, *der.* **2.** *v.t.* verdienen

mermaid ['mɜːmeɪd] *n.* Nixe, *die*

merrily ['merɪlɪ] *adv.* munter

merriment ['merɪmənt] *n.* Fröhlichkeit, *die*

merry ['merɪ] *adj.* fröhlich; **~ Christmas!** frohe *od.* fröhliche Weihnachten! **'merry-go-round** *n.* Karussell, *das.* **'merry-making** *n.* Feiern, *das*

mesh [meʃ] *n.* **a)** Masche, *die;* **b)** *(netting; also fig.: network)* Geflecht, *das;* **wire ~** Maschendraht, *der*

mesmerize ['mezməraɪz] *v.t.* faszinieren

mess [mes] *n.* **a)** *(dirty/untidy state)* **[be] a ~ or in a ~:** schmutzig/unaufgeräumt [sein]; **what a ~!** was für ein Dreck *(ugs.)*/Durcheinander!; **b)** *(bad state)* **be [in] a ~:** sich in einem schlimmen Zustand befinden; *⟨Person:⟩* schlimm dran sein; **get into a ~:** in Schwierigkeiten geraten; **make a ~ of** verpfuschen *(ugs.)* *⟨Arbeit, Leben⟩;* **c)** *(Mil.)* Kasino, *das.* **mess a'bout,** **mess a'round 1.** *v.i.* *(potter)* herumwerken; *(fool about)* herumalbern. **2.** *v.t.* **~ sb. about** *or* **around** mit jmdm. nach Belieben umspringen. **mess 'up** *v.t.* **a)** *(make dirty)* schmutzig machen; *(make untidy)* in Unordnung bringen; **b)** *(bungle)* **~ it/things up** Mist bauen *(ugs.)*

message ['mesɪdʒ] *n.* Nachricht, *die;* **give sb. a ~:** jmdm. etwas ausrichten

messenger ['mesɪndʒə(r)] *n.* Bote, *der/*Botin, *die*

Messiah [mɪ'saɪə] *n.* Messias, *der*

Messrs ['mesəz] *n. pl.* **a)** *(in name of firm)* ≈ Fa.; **b)** *pl. of* **Mr;** *(in list of names)* **~ A and B** die Herren A und B

'**messy** adj. (dirty) schmutzig; (untidy) unordentlich

met see **meet**

metabolism [mɪ'tæbəlɪzm] n. Stoffwechsel, der

metal ['metl] 1. n. Metall, das. 2. adj. Metall-. **metallic** [mɪ'tælɪk] adj. metallisch; **have a ~ taste** nach Metall schmecken. **metallurgy** [mɪ'tælədʒɪ] n. Metallurgie, die

metamorphosis [metə'mɔ:fəsɪs] n., pl. **metamorphoses** [metə'mɔ:fəsi:z] Metamorphose, die

metaphor ['metəfə(r)] n. Metapher, die. **metaphorical** [metə'fɒrɪkl] adj., **metaphorically** [metə'fɒrɪkəlɪ] adv. metaphorisch

meteor ['mi:tɪə(r)] n. Meteor, der. **meteoric** [mi:tɪ'ɒrɪk] adj. (fig.) kometenhaft

meteorological [mi:tɪərə'lɒdʒɪkl] adj. meteorologisch ⟨Instrument⟩; Wetter⟨ballon, -bericht⟩

meteorologist [mi:tɪə'rɒlədʒɪst] n. Meteorologe, der/Meteorologin, die. **meteorology** [mi:tɪə'rɒlədʒɪ] n. Meteorologie, die

'**meter** ['mi:tə(r)] n. a) Zähler, der; (for coins) Münzzähler, der; b) (parking-~) Parkuhr, die

²**meter** (Amer.) see ¹, ²**metre**

method ['meθəd] n. Methode, die. **methodical** [mɪ'θɒdɪkl] adj., **methodically** adv. systematisch

Methodist ['meθədɪst] n. Methodist, der/Methodistin, die

meths [meθs] n. (Brit. coll.) [Brenn]-spiritus, der

methylated spirit[s] [meθɪleɪtɪd 'spɪrɪt(s)] n. [pl.] Brennspiritus, der

meticulous [mɪ'tɪkjʊləs] adj., **meticulously** adv. (scrupulous[ly]) sorgfältig; (over-scrupulous[ly]) übergenau

'**metre** ['mi:tə] n. (Brit.: poetic rhythm) Metrum, das

²**metre** n. (Brit.: unit) Meter, der od. das. **metric** ['metrɪk] adj. metrisch; ~ **system** metrisches System. **metrication** [metrɪ'keɪʃn] n. Umstellung auf das metrische System

metronome ['metrənəʊm] n. Metronom, das

metropolis [mɪ'trɒpəlɪs] n. Metropole, die. **metropolitan** [metrə'pɒlɪtən] adj. ~ **New York** der Großraum New York; ~ **London** Großlondon (das)

Mexican ['meksɪkən] 1. adj. mexikanisch. 2. n. Mexikaner, der/Mexikanerin, die

Mexico ['meksɪkəʊ] pr. n. Mexiko (das)

miaow [mɪ'aʊ] 1. v. i. miauen. 2. n. Miauen, das

mice pl. of **mouse**

microbe ['maɪkrəʊb] n. Mikrobe, die

micro ['maɪkrəʊ]: ~**chip** n. Mikrochip, der; ~**computer** n. Mikrocomputer, der; ~**fiche** n. Mikrofiche, das od. der; ~**film** 1. n. Mikrofilm, der; 2. v. t. auf Mikrofilm aufnehmen

microphone ['maɪkrəfəʊn] n. Mikrophon, das

microprocessor [maɪkrəʊ'prəʊsesə(r)] n. Mikroprozessor, der

microscope ['maɪkrəskəʊp] n. Mikroskop, das. **microscopic** [maɪkrə'skɒpɪk] adj. mikroskopisch; (fig.: very small) winzig

'**microwave** n. Mikrowelle, die; ~ [**oven**] Mikrowellenherd, der

mid- [mɪd] in comb. in ~**air** in der Luft; in ~**sentence** mitten im Satz; ~**July** Mitte Juli; **the ~-60s** die Mitte der sechziger Jahre; **a man in his ~-fifties** ein Mittfünfziger; **be in one's ~-thirties** Mitte Dreißig sein

midday ['mɪddeɪ, mɪd'deɪ] n. a) (noon) zwölf Uhr; b) (middle of day) Mittag, der; attrib. Mittags-

middle ['mɪdl] 1. attrib. adj. mittler... 2. n. a) Mitte, die; **in the ~ of the forest/night** mitten im Wald/in der Nacht; b) (waist) Taille, die

middle: ~ **'age** n. mittleres [Lebens]alter; ~**-aged** ['mɪdleɪdʒd] adj. mittleren Alters nachgestellt; **M~ 'Ages** n. pl. **the M~ Ages** das Mittelalter; ~ **class** n. Mittelstand, der; ~**-class** adj. bürgerlich; **M~ 'East** pr. n. **the M~ East** der Nahe [und Mittlere] Osten; **M~ 'Eastern** adj. nahöstlich

middling ['mɪdlɪŋ] adj. mittelmäßig

midge [mɪdʒ] n. Stechmücke, die

midget ['mɪdʒɪt] 1. n. Liliputaner, der/Liliputanerin, die. 2. adj. winzig

Midlands ['mɪdləndz] n. pl. **the ~** (Brit.) Mittelengland

'**midnight** n. Mitternacht, die

'**midpoint** n. Mitte, die

midriff ['mɪdrɪf] n. Bauch, der

midst [mɪdst] n. **in the ~ of sth.** mitten in einer Sache; **in our/their/your ~:** in unserer/ihrer/eurer Mitte

midsummer ['---, -'--] n. die [Zeit der] Sommersonnenwende

midway ['--, -'-] adv. auf halbem Weg[e] ⟨sich treffen, sich befinden⟩

'**midwife** *n., pl.* '**midwives** Hebamme, *die*

mid·winter *n.* die [Zeit der] Wintersonnenwende

'**might** *see* **may**

²**might** [maɪt] *n.* **a)** *(force)* Gewalt, *die;* **b)** *(power)* Macht, *die*

mightn't ['maɪtnt] *(coll.)* = might not; *see* **may**

mighty ['maɪtɪ] **1.** *adj.* mächtig. **2.** *adv. (coll.)* verdammt *(ugs.)*

migraine ['miːɡreɪn] *n.* Migräne, *die*

migrant ['maɪɡrənt] *n.* **a)** Auswanderer, *der*/Auswanderin, *die;* **b)** *(bird)* Zugvogel, *der*

migrate [maɪˈɡreɪt] *v. i.* **a)** *(to a town)* abwandern; *(to another country)* auswandern; **b)** ⟨Vogel:⟩ fortziehen. **migration** [maɪˈɡreɪʃn] *n.* **a)** *(to a town)* Abwandern, *das; (to another country)* Auswandern, *das;* **b)** *(of birds)* Zug, *der*

mike [maɪk] *n. (coll.)* Mikro, *das*

Milan [mɪˈlæn] *pr. n.* Mailand *(das)*

mild [maɪld] *adj.* mild; sanft ⟨Person⟩

mildew ['mɪldjuː] *n.* **a)** Schimmel, *der;* **b)** *(on plant)* Mehltau, *der*

mildly *adv.* **a)** *(gently)* mild[e]; **b)** *(slightly)* ein bißchen; **c)** **to put it ~:** gelinde gesagt

mile [maɪl] *n.* **a)** Meile, *die;* **b)** *(fig. coll.)* ~s better/too big tausendmal besser/viel zu groß; **be ~s ahead of sb.** jmdm. weit voraus sein. **mileage** ['maɪlɪdʒ] *n.* [Anzahl der] Meilen; **a low ~:** ein niedriger Meilenstand.

'**milestone** *n.* Meilenstein, *der*

militant ['mɪlɪtənt] **1.** *adj.* militant. **2.** *n.* Militante, *der/die*

military ['mɪlɪtərɪ] **1.** *adj.* militärisch; Militär⟨regierung, -akademie, -uniform, -parade⟩; ~ **service** Militärdienst, *der.* **2.** *n.* **the ~:** das Militär

militate ['mɪlɪteɪt] *v. i.* ~ **against/in favour of sth.** [deutlich] gegen/für etw. sprechen

militia [mɪˈlɪʃə] *n.* Miliz, *die*

milk [mɪlk] **1.** *n.* Milch, *die.* **2.** *v. t.* melken

milk: ~ '**chocolate** *n.* Milchschokolade, *die;* ~ **jug** *n.* Milchkännchen, *das;* ~**man** ['mɪlkmən] *n., pl.* ~**men** ['mɪlkmən] Milchmann, *der;* ~ **shake** *n.* Milchshake, *der;* ~**tooth** *n.* Milchzahn, *der*

'**milky** *adj.* milchig. **Milky 'Way** *n.* Milchstraße, *die*

mill [mɪl] **1.** *n.* **a)** Mühle, *die;* **b)** *(factory)* Fabrik, *die.* **2.** *v. t.* **a)** mahlen ⟨Ge-

treide⟩; **b)** fräsen ⟨Metallgegenstand⟩.

mill a·bout *(Brit.),* **mill a·round** *v. i.* durcheinanderlaufen

'**miller** *n.* Müller, *der*

millet ['mɪlɪt] *n.* Hirse, *die*

milligram ['mɪlɪɡræm] *n.* Milligramm, *das*

millilitre *(Brit.; Amer.:* **milliliter)** ['mɪlɪliːtə(r)] *n.* Milliliter, *der od. das*

millimetre *(Brit.; Amer.:* **millimeter)** ['mɪlɪmiːtə(r)] *n.* Millimeter, *der*

milliner ['mɪlɪnə(r)] *n.* Modist, *der*/Modistin, *die.* '**millinery** *n.* Hutmacherei, *die*

million ['mɪljən] **1.** *adj.* **a** *or* one/two ~: eine Million/zwei Millionen; **half a ~:** eine halbe Million. **2.** *n.* **a)** Million, *die;* **b)** *(indefinite amount)* ~s of people eine Unmenge Leute. **millionaire** [mɪljəˈneə(r)] *n.* Millionär, *der*/Millionärin, *die.* **millionth** ['mɪljənθ] **1.** *adj.* millionst... **2.** *n. (fraction)* Millionstel, *das*

'**millstone** *n.* Mühlstein, *der*

mime [maɪm] **1.** *n.* **a)** *(performance)* Pantomime, *die;* **b)** *(art)* Pantomimik, *die.* **2.** *v. i.* pantomimisch agieren. **3.** *v. t.* pantomimisch darstellen

mimic ['mɪmɪk] **1.** *n.* Imitator, *der.* **2.** *v. t.,* -**ck**- nachahmen

min. *abbr.* **a)** minute[s] Min.; **b)** minimum *(adj.)* mind., *(n.)* Min.

mince [mɪns] **1.** *n.* Hackfleisch, *das.* **2.** *v. t.* durch den [Fleisch]wolf drehen ⟨Fleisch⟩. '**mincemeat** *n.* **a)** Hackfleisch, *das;* **b)** *(sweet)* süße Pastetenfüllung aus Obst, Rosinen, Gewürzen, Nierenfett usw. **mince 'pie** *n.* mit „mincemeat b" gefüllte Pastete

'**mincer** *n.* Fleischwolf, *der*

mind [maɪnd] **1.** *n.* **a)** Geist, *der;* **b)** *(remembrance)* bear *or* keep sth. in ~: an etw. *(Akk.)* denken; have [got] sb./sth. in ~: an jmdn./etw. denken; **c)** *(opinion)* give sb. a piece of one's ~: jmdm. gründlich die Meinung sagen; **to my ~:** meiner Meinung *od.* Ansicht nach; **change one's ~:** seine Meinung ändern; **I have a good ~ to** do that ich hätte große Lust, das zu tun; **make up one's ~, make one's ~ up** sich entscheiden; **d)** *([normal] mental powers)* Verstand, *der;* **be out of one's ~:** den Verstand verloren haben; **e)** *(frame of ~:)* [seelische] Verfassung. **2.** *v. t.* **a)** I can't afford a bicycle, never ~ a car ich kann mir kein Fahrrad leisten, geschweige denn ein Auto; **b)** *usu. neg.*

or interrog. (object to) **would you ~ opening the door?** würdest du bitte die Tür öffnen?; **I wouldn't ~ a walk** ich hätte nichts gegen einen Spaziergang; **c)** *(take care)* **~ you don't go too near the cliff-edge!** paß auf, daß du nicht zu nah an den Klippenrand gehst!; **~ how you go!** paß auf! **d)** *(have charge of)* aufpassen auf (+ *Akk.*). **3.** *v. i.* **a)** **~!** Vorsicht!; Achtung!; **b)** *(care, object)* **do you ~ if I smoke?** stört es Sie, wenn ich rauche?; **c)** **never ~** *(it's not important)* macht nichts. **mind 'out** *v. i.* aufpassen **(for** auf + *Akk.*); **~ out!** Vorsicht!

'**minded** *adj.* **mechanically ~:** technisch veranlagt; **not politically ~:** unpolitisch

mindful ['maɪndfl] *adj.* **be ~ of** sth. etw. berücksichtigen

'**mindless** *adj.* geistlos ⟨*Person*⟩; sinnlos ⟨*Gewalt*⟩

¹**mine** [maɪn] *n.* **a)** Bergwerk, *das;* **b)** *(explosive)* Mine, *die*

²**mine** *poss. pron. pred.* meiner/meine/mein[e]s; *see also* **hers**

'**minefield** *n.* Minenfeld, *das*

'**miner** *n.* Bergmann, *der*

mineral ['mɪnərl] **1.** *adj.* mineralisch; Mineral⟨*salz, -quelle*⟩. **2.** *n.* **a)** Mineral, *das;* **b)** *(Brit.: soft drink)* Erfrischungsgetränk, *das.* '**mineral water** *n.* Mineralwasser, *das*

minesweeper ['maɪnswiːpə(r)] *n.* Minensuchboot, *das*

mingle ['mɪŋgl] **1.** *v. t.* [ver]mischen. **2.** *v. i.* sich [ver]mischen **(with** mit)

mini ['mɪnɪ] *n.* *(coll.)* **a)** *(car)* M~, (P) Mini, *der;* **b)** *(skirt)* Mini, *der (ugs.)*

mini- ['mɪnɪ] *in comb.* Mini-; Klein⟨*bus, -wagen, -taxi*⟩

miniature ['mɪnɪtʃə(r)] **1.** *n.* *(picture)* Miniatur, *die.* **2.** *adj.* Miniatur-

mini: **~bus** *n.* Kleinbus, *der;* **~cab** *n.* Minicar, *das*

minim ['mɪnɪm] *n.* *(Brit. Mus.)* halbe Note

minimal ['mɪnɪml] *adj.* minimal

minimize ['mɪnɪmaɪz] *v. t.* **a)** *(reduce)* auf ein Mindestmaß reduzieren; **b)** *(understate)* bagatellisieren

minimum ['mɪnɪməm] **1.** *n., pl.* **minima** ['mɪnɪmə] Minimum, *das* **(of** an + *Dat.*). **2.** *attrib. adj.* Mindest-

mining ['maɪnɪŋ] *n.* Bergbau, *der; attrib.* Bergbau-. '**mining industry** *n.* Bergbau, *der.* '**mining town** *n.* Bergbaustadt, *die*

minion ['mɪnjən] *n.* Lakai, *der*

minister ['mɪnɪstə(r)] **1.** *n.* **a)** *(Polit.)* Minister, *der*/Ministerin, *die;* **b)** *(Eccl.)* Geistliche, *der/die;* Pfarrer, *der*/Pfarrerin, *die.* **2.** *v. i.* **~ to sb.** sich um jmdn. kümmern. **ministerial** [mɪnɪ'stɪərɪəl] *adj.* *(Polit.)* Minister-; ministeriell. **ministry** ['mɪnɪstrɪ] *n.* **a)** *(Polit.)* Ministerium, *das;* **b)** *(Eccl.)* geistliches Amt

mink [mɪŋk] *n.* Nerz, *der*

minnow ['mɪnəʊ] *n.* Elritze, *die*

minor ['maɪnə(r)] **1.** *adj.* **a)** *(lesser)* kleiner...; **b)** *(unimportant)* weniger bedeutend; *(not serious)* leicht; **~ road** kleine Straße; **c)** *(Mus.)* Moll-; **A ~:** a-Moll. **2.** *n.* Minderjährige, *der/die.* **minority** [maɪ'nɒrɪtɪ, mɪ'nɒrɪtɪ] *n.* Minderheit, *die;* **in the ~:** in der Minderheit

minstrel ['mɪnstrl] *n.* fahrender Sänger

¹**mint** [mɪnt] **1.** *n.* *(place)* Münzanstalt, *die.* **2.** *adj.* funkelnagelneu *(ugs.);* **in ~ condition** in tadellosem Zustand. **3.** *v. t.* prägen

²**mint** *n.* **a)** *(plant)* Minze, *die;* **b)** *(peppermint)* Pfefferminz, *das; attrib.* Pfefferminz-

minuet [mɪnjʊ'et] *n.* Menuett, *das*

minus ['maɪnəs] *prep.* minus; weniger; *(without)* abzüglich (+ *Gen.*)

minuscule ['mɪnəskjuːl] *adj.* winzig

¹**minute** ['mɪnɪt] *n.* **a)** Minute, *die; (moment)* Moment, *der;* **b)** **~s** *(of meeting)* Protokoll, *das;* **take the ~s of a meeting** bei einer Sitzung [das] Protokoll führen

²**minute** [maɪ'njuːt] *adj.* *(tiny)* winzig

miracle ['mɪrəkl] *n.* Wunder, *das.* **miraculous** [mɪ'rækjʊləs] *adj.* wunderbar

mirage ['mɪrɑːʒ] *n.* Fata Morgana, *die*

mirror ['mɪrə(r)] **1.** *n.* Spiegel, *der.* **2.** *v. t.* [wider]spiegeln

misadventure [mɪsəd'ventʃə(r)] *n.* Mißgeschick, *das*

misapprehension [mɪsæprɪ'henʃn] *n.* Mißverständnis, *das;* **be under a ~:** einem Irrtum unterliegen

misbehave [mɪsbɪ'heɪv] *v. i. & refl.* sich schlecht benehmen. **misbehaviour** *(Amer.:* **misbehavior)** [mɪsbɪ'heɪvjə(r)] *n.* schlechtes Benehmen

miscalculate [mɪs'kælkjʊleɪt] **1.** *v. t.* falsch berechnen; *(misjudge)* falsch einschätzen. **2.** *v. i.* sich verrechnen. **miscalculation** [mɪskælkjʊ'leɪʃn] *n.* Rechenfehler, *der; (misjudgement)* Fehleinschätzung, *die*

miscarriage [mɪsˈkærɪdʒ] *n.* a) Fehlgeburt, *die;* b) ~ **of justice** Justizirrtum, *das*

miscellaneous [mɪsəˈleɪnɪəs] *adj.* a) [kunter]bunt; b) *with pl. n.* verschieden. **miscellany** [mɪˈselənɪ] *n.* [bunte] Sammlung; [buntes] Gemisch

mischief [ˈmɪstʃɪf] *n.* a) Unfug, *der;* **get up to ~:** etwas anstellen; b) *(harm)* Schaden, *der.* **mischievous** [ˈmɪstʃɪvəs] *adj.* spitzbübisch; schelmisch

misconception [mɪskənˈsepʃn] *n.* falsche Vorstellung (**about** von); **be** [**labouring**] **under a ~ about sth.** *(Dat.)* eine falsche Vorstellung von etw. machen

misconduct [mɪsˈkɒndʌkt] *n.* unkorrektes Verhalten

misconstrue [mɪskənˈstruː] *v. t.* mißverstehen

miscount [mɪsˈkaʊnt] **1.** *v. i.* sich verzählen. **2.** *v. t.* falsch zählen

misdeed [mɪsˈdiːd] *n.* Missetat, *die (veralt., scherzh.)*

misdemeanour *(Amer.:* **misdemeanor** [mɪsdɪˈmiːnə(r)] *n.* Missetat, *die (veralt., scherzh.)*

misdirect [mɪsdɪˈrekt, mɪsdaɪˈrekt] *v. t.* falsch adressieren ⟨*Brief*⟩; in die falsche Richtung schicken ⟨*Person*⟩

miser [ˈmaɪzə(r)] *n.* Geizhals, *der*

miserable [ˈmɪzərəbl] *adj.* a) unglücklich; **feel ~:** sich elend fühlen; b) trist ⟨*Wetter, Urlaub*⟩. **miserably** [ˈmɪzərəblɪ] *adv.* unglücklich; jämmerlich ⟨*versagen*⟩; ~ **poor** bettelarm

miserly [ˈmaɪzəlɪ] *adj.* geizig

misery [ˈmɪzərɪ] *n.* a) Elend, *das;* b) *(coll.: discontented person)* ~[-**guts**] Miesepeter, *der (ugs.)*

misfire [mɪsˈfaɪə(r)] *v. i.* a) ⟨*Motor:*⟩ Fehlzündungen haben; b) ⟨*Plan, Versuch:*⟩ fehlschlagen; ⟨*Streich, Witz:*⟩ danebengehen

misfit [ˈmɪsfɪt] *n.* Außenseiter, *der/* Außenseiterin, *die*

misfortune [mɪsˈfɔːtʃuːn] *n.* Mißgeschick, *das*

misgiving [mɪsˈgɪvɪŋ] *n.* ~[s] Bedenken *Pl.*

misguided [mɪsˈgaɪdɪd] *adj.* töricht

mishandle [mɪsˈhændl] *v. t.* falsch behandeln

mishap [ˈmɪshæp] *n.* Mißgeschick, *das*

mishear [mɪsˈhɪə(r)] **1.** *v. i.,* **misheard** [mɪsˈhɜːd] sich verhören. **2.** *v. t.,* **misheard** falsch verstehen

mishit 1. [ˈmɪshɪt] *n.* Fehlschlag, *der.*

2. [mɪsˈhɪt] *v. t.,* -**tt**-, **mishit** verschlagen

mishmash [ˈmɪʃmæʃ] *n.* Mischmasch, *der (ugs.)* (**of** aus)

misinform [mɪsɪnˈfɔːm] *v. t.* falsch informieren

misinterpret [mɪsɪnˈtɜːprɪt] *v. t. (make wrong inference from)* falsch deuten; mißdeuten. **misinterpretation** [mɪsɪntɜːprɪˈteɪʃn] *n.* **be open to ~:** leicht mißdeutet werden können

misjudge [mɪsˈdʒʌdʒ] *v. t.* falsch einschätzen; falsch beurteilen ⟨*Person*⟩. **misjudgement, misjudgment** [mɪsˈdʒʌdʒmənt] *n.* Fehleinschätzung, *die; (of person)* falsche Beurteilung

mislay [mɪsˈleɪ] *v. t.,* **mislaid** [mɪsˈleɪd] verlegen

mislead [mɪsˈliːd] *v. t.,* **misled** [mɪsˈled] irreführen. **mis'leading** *adj.* irreführend

mismanage [mɪsˈmænɪdʒ] *v. t.* schlecht abwickeln ⟨*Geschäft, Projekt*⟩. **mismanagement** [mɪsˈmænɪdʒmənt] *n.* schlechte Abwicklung

misnomer [mɪsˈnəʊmə(r)] *n.* unzutreffende Bezeichnung

misplace [mɪsˈpleɪs] *v. t.* an den falschen Platz stellen/legen/setzen *usw.*

misprint 1. [ˈmɪsprɪnt] *n.* Druckfehler, *der.* **2.** [mɪsˈprɪnt] *v. t.* verdrucken

mispronounce [mɪsprəˈnaʊns] *v. t.* falsch aussprechen

misread [mɪsˈriːd] *v. t.,* **misread** [mɪsˈred] falsch lesen

misrepresent [mɪsreprɪˈzent] *v. t.* falsch darstellen. **misrepresentation** [mɪsreprɪzenˈteɪʃn] *n.* falsche Darstellung

Miss [mɪs] *n. (unmarried woman)* Frau; Fräulein *(veralt.); (girl)* Fräulein

miss 1. *n.* Fehlschlag, *der; (shot)* Fehlschuß, *der; (throw)* Fehlwurf, *der.* **2.** *v. t.* a) *(fail to hit)* verfehlen; b) *(let slip)* verpassen; ~ **an opportunity** sich *(Dat.)* eine Gelegenheit entgehen lassen; c) *(fail to catch)* verpassen ⟨*Zug*⟩; d) *(fail to take part in)* versäumen; ~ **school** in der Schule fehlen; e) *(fail to see)* übersehen; *(fail to hear)* nicht mitbekommen; f) *(feel the absence of)* vermissen; **she ~es him** er fehlt ihr. **3.** *v. i. (not hit sth.)* nicht treffen. **miss 'out 1.** *v. t.* weglassen. **2.** *v. i.* ~ **out on sth.** *(coll.)* sich *(Dat.)* etw. entgehen lassen

misshapen [mɪsˈʃeɪpn] *adj.* mißgebildet

missile ['mɪsaɪl] *n.* **a)** *(thrown)* [Wurf]geschoß, *das;* **b)** *(Mil.)* Rakete, *die.* '**missile base**, '**missile site** *ns.* Raketenbasis, *die*

missing *adj.* fehlend; **be ~:** fehlen; ⟨Person:⟩ *(Mil. etc.)* vermißt werden; *(not present)* fehlen; **~ person** Vermißte, *der/die*

mission ['mɪʃn] *n.* **a)** Mission, *die;* **b)** *(planned operation)* Einsatz, *der.* **missionary** ['mɪʃənərɪ] *n.* Missionar, *der/*Missionarin, *die*

misspell ['mɪs'spel] *v. t., forms as* ¹**spell** falsch schreiben

mist [mɪst] *n.* *(fog)* Nebel, *der; (haze)* Dunst, *der; (on windscreen etc.)* Beschlag, *der.* **mist 'up** *v. i.* [sich] beschlagen

mistake [mɪ'steɪk] **1.** *n.* Fehler, *der;* **by ~:** versehentlich. **2.** *v. t., forms as* **take 1: a)** falsch verstehen; **b)** **~ x for y** x mit y verwechseln. **mistaken** [mɪ'steɪkn] *adj.* **be ~:** sich täuschen; **a case of ~ identity** eine Verwechslung. **mi'stakenly** *adv.* irrtümlicherweise

mistletoe ['mɪsltəʊ] *n.* Mistel, *die*

mistook *see* **mistake 2**

mistress ['mɪstrɪs] *n.* **a)** *(Brit. Sch.: teacher)* Lehrerin, *die;* **b)** *(lover)* Geliebte, *die*

mistrust [mɪs'trʌst] **1.** *v. t.* mißtrauen (+ *Dat.*). **2.** *n.* Mißtrauen, *das* (of gegenüber + *Dat.*). **mistrustful** [mɪs'trʌstfl] *adj.* mißtrauisch (of gegenüber)

'**misty** *adj.* dunstig

misunderstand [mɪsʌndə'stænd] *v. t., forms as* **understand** mißverstehen. **misunder'standing** *n.* Mißverständnis, *das*

misuse 1. [mɪs'ju:z] *v. t.* mißbrauchen. **2.** [mɪs'ju:s] *n.* Mißbrauch, *der*

mite [maɪt] *n.* **a)** *(Zool.)* Milbe, *die;* **b)** *(small child)* Würmchen, *das (fam.);* **poor little ~:** armes Kleines

miter *(Amer.) see* **mitre**

mitigate ['mɪtɪgeɪt] *v. t.* **a)** *(reduce)* lindern; **b)** *(make less severe)* mildern; **mitigating circumstances** mildernde Umstände

mitre ['maɪtə(r)] *n. (Brit. Eccl.)* Mitra, *die*

mitten ['mɪtn] *n.* Fausthandschuh, *der*

mix [mɪks] **1.** *v. t.* [ver]mischen; verrühren *(Zutaten).* **2.** *v. i.* **a)** *(become ~ed)* sich vermischen; **b)** *(be sociable, participate)* Umgang mit anderen [Menschen] haben; **~ with** Umgang haben mit; **~ well** kontaktfreudig sein. **3.** *n.*

(coll.) Mischung, *die;* |cake-|**~:** Backmischung, *die.* **mix 'up** *v. t.* **a)** vermischen; **b)** *(muddle)* durcheinanderbringen; *(confuse)* verwechseln; **c) be/ get ~ed up in sth.** in etw. *(Akk.)* verwickelt sein/werden

mixed [mɪkst] *adj.* **a)** gemischt; **b)** *(diverse)* unterschiedlich. **mixed 'grill** *n.* Mixed grill, *der.* **mixed 'up** *adj.* *(coll.)* verwirrt ⟨Person⟩; **be/feel very ~:** völlig durcheinander sein

'**mixer** *n. (for food)* Mixer, *der*

mixture ['mɪkstʃə(r)] *n.* **a)** Mischung, *die* (of aus); **b)** *(Med.)* Mixtur, *die*

'**mix-up** *n.* Durcheinander, *das; (misunderstanding)* Mißverständnis, *das*

mm. *abbr.* **millimetre[s]** mm

moan [məʊn] **1.** *n.* **a)** Stöhnen, *das;* **b)** **have a ~** *(complain)* jammern. **2.** *v. i.* **a)** stöhnen (with vor + *Dat.*); **b)** *(complain)* jammern (**about** über + *Akk.*). **3.** *v. t.* stöhnen

moat [məʊt] *n.* |castle| **~:** Burggraben, *der*

mob [mɒb] **1.** *n.* **a)** *(rabble)* Mob, *der;* **b)** *(sl.: group)* **Peter and his ~:** Peter und seine ganze Blase *(salopp).* **2.** *v. t.,* **-bb-** belagern *(coll.) ⟨Star⟩*

mobile ['məʊbaɪl] **1.** *adj.* beweglich; *(on wheels)* fahrbar. **2.** *n.* Mobile, *die.* **mobile 'home** *n.* transportable Wohneinheit. **mobile 'phone** *n.* Mobiltelefon, *das*

mobility [mə'bɪlɪtɪ] *n.* Beweglichkeit, *die*

mobilization [məʊbɪlaɪ'zeɪʃn] *n.* Mobilisierung, *die*

mobilize ['məʊbɪlaɪz] *v. t.* mobilisieren

moccasin ['mɒkəsɪn] *n.* Mokassin, *der*

mocha ['mɒkə] *n.* Mokka, *der*

mock [mɒk] **1.** *v. t.* sich lustig machen über (+ *Akk.*). **2.** *v. i.* sich lustig machen (at über + *Akk.*). **3.** *adj.* Schein⟨kampf, -angriff, -ehe⟩. **mockery** ['mɒkərɪ] *n.* Spott, *der;* **make a ~ of sth.** etw. zur Farce machen

'**mock-up** *n.* Modell |in Originalgröße|

mode [məʊd] *n.* **a)** Art [und Weise], *die;* **b)** *(fashion)* Mode, *die*

model ['mɒdl] **1.** *n.* **a)** Modell, *das;* **b)** *(example to be imitated)* Vorbild, *das;* **c)** *(Art)* Modell, *das; (Fashion)* Mannequin, *das; (male)* Dressman *der.* **2.** *adj.* **a)** *(exemplary)* Muster-; **b)** *(miniature)* Modell-. **3.** *v. t.,* **(Brit.)** **-ll-: a)** modellieren; **~ sth. after** *or* |up|on **sth.** etw. einer Sache *(Dat.)* nachbilden; **b)**

(Fashion) vorführen. **4.** *v. i. (Fashion)* als Mannequin/Dressman arbeiten; *(Art)* Modell stehen/sitzen

modem ['məʊdem *n.* Modem, *der*

moderate 1. ['mɒdərət] *adj.* **a)** gemäßigt 〈*Ansichten*〉; maßvoll 〈*Trinker, Forderungen*〉; **b)** mittler... 〈*Größe, Menge, Wert*〉; *(reasonable)* angemessen 〈*Preis, Summe*〉. **2.** ['mɒdərət] *n.* Gemäßigte, *der/die.* **3.** ['mɒdəreɪt] *v. t.* mäßigen. **4.** *v. i.* nachlassen. **moderately** ['mɒdərətlɪ] *adv.* einigermaßen; mäßig 〈*begeistert, groß, begabt*〉. **moderation** [mɒdə'reɪʃn] *n.* Mäßigkeit, *die;* in ~: mit Maßen

modern ['mɒdn] *adj.* modern; heutig 〈*Zeit[alter], Welt, Mensch*〉; ~ **languages** neuere Sprachen. **modernize** ['mɒdənaɪz] *v. t.* modernisieren

modest ['mɒdɪst] *adj.* bescheiden; einfach 〈*Haus, Kleidung*〉. '**modestly** *adv.* bescheiden. '**modesty** *n.* Bescheidenheit, *die*

modification [mɒdɪfɪ'keɪʃn] *n.* [Ab]änderung, *die*

modify ['mɒdɪfaɪ] *v. t.* [ab]ändern

modulate ['mɒdjʊleɪt] *v. t. & i.* modulieren. **modulation** [mɒdjʊ'leɪʃn] *n.* Modulation, *die*

module ['mɒdjuːl] *n.* **a)** Bauelement, *das;* **b)** *(Astronaut.)* **command ~:** Kommandoeinheit, *die*

mohair ['məʊheə(r)] *n.* Mohair, *der*

moist [mɔɪst] *adj.* feucht (with von).

moisten ['mɔɪsn] *v. t.* anfeuchten.

moisture ['mɔɪstʃə(r)] *n.* Feuchtigkeit, *die.* **moisturizer** ['mɔɪstʃəraɪzə(r)], **moisturizing cream** ['mɔɪstʃəraɪzɪŋ kriːm] *ns.* Feuchtigkeitscreme, *die*

molar ['məʊlə(r)] *n.* Backenzahn, *der*

molasses [mə'læsɪz] *n.* Melasse, *die*

mold *(Amer.)* see [1,2]**mould**

molder, molding, moldy *(Amer.)* see **mould-**

[1]**mole** [məʊl] *n. (on skin)* Leberfleck, *der*

[2]**mole** *n. (animal)* Maulwurf, *der*

molecular [mə'lekjʊlə(r)] *adj.* molekular

molecule ['mɒlɪkjuːl] *n.* Molekül, *das*

'**molehill** *n.* Maulwurfshügel, *der*

molest [mə'lest] *v. t.* belästigen

mollify ['mɒlɪfaɪ] *v. t.* besänftigen

mollusc, *(Amer.)* **mollusk** ['mɒləsk] *n.* Weichtier, *das*

mollycoddle ['mɒlɪkɒdl] *v. t.* [ver]hätscheln

molt *(Amer.)* see **moult**

molten ['məʊltn] *adj.* geschmolzen

mom [mɒm] *(Amer. coll.)* see [2]**mum**

moment ['məʊmənt] *n.* Augenblick, *der;* **at any ~,** *(coll.)* **any ~:** jeden Augenblick; **one** *or* **just a** *or* **wait a ~!** einen Augenblick!; **in a ~** *(very soon)* sofort; **at the ~:** im Augenblick; **the ~ of truth** die Stunde der Wahrheit.

momentarily ['məʊməntərɪlɪ] *adv.* einen Augenblick lang. **momentary** ['məʊməntərɪ] *adj.* kurz

momentous [mə'mentəs] *adj. (important)* bedeutsam; *(of consequence)* folgenschwer

momentum [mə'mentəm] *n.* Schwung, *der*

Mon. *abbr.* **Monday** Mo.

monarch ['mɒnək] *n.* Monarch, *der*/Monarchin, *die.* '**monarchy** *n.* Monarchie, *die*

monastery ['mɒnəstrɪ] *n.* Kloster, *das.* **monastic** [mə'næstɪk] *adj.* mönchisch

Monday ['mʌndeɪ, 'mʌndɪ] *n.* Montag, *der; see also* **Friday**

monetary ['mʌnɪtərɪ] *adj.* **a)** *(of currency)* monetär; Währungs〈*politik, -system*〉; **b)** *(of money)* finanziell

money ['mʌnɪ] *n.* Geld, *das;* **make ~** 〈*Person:*〉 [viel] Geld verdienen; 〈*Geschäft:*〉 etwas einbringen; **for 'my ~:** wenn man mich fragt

money: ~bag *n.* Geldsack, *der;* **~box** *n.* Sparbüchse, *die;* **~making** *adj.* gewinnbringend; **~order** *n.* Postanweisung, *die*

Mongolia [mɒŋ'gəʊlɪə] *pr. n.* Mongolei, *die.* **Mongolian** [mɒŋ'gəʊlɪən] **1.** *adj.* mongolisch. **2.** *n. (person)* Mongole, *der*/Mongolin, *die*

mongrel ['mʌŋgrəl] *n.* ~ [**dog**] Promenadenmischung, *die*

monitor ['mɒnɪtə(r)] **1.** *n.* **a)** *(Sch.)* Aufsichtsschüler, *der*/-schülerin, *die;* **b)** *(Med., Telev., etc.)* Monitor, *der.* **2.** *v. t.* beobachten 〈*Wetter, Flugzeug*〉; abhören 〈*Sendung, Telefongespräch*〉

monk [mʌŋk] *n.* Mönch, *der*

monkey ['mʌŋkɪ] *n.* Affe, *der.*

monkey: ~ business *n. (coll.: mischief)* Schabernack, *der;* **~nut** *n.* Erdnuß, *die;* **~wrench** *n.* Universalschraubenschlüssel, *der*

mono ['mɒnəʊ] *adj.* Mono〈*platte[nspieler], -wiedergabe*〉

monocle ['mɒnəkl] *n.* Monokel, *das*

monologue *(Amer.:* **monolog)** ['mɒnəlɒg] *n.* Monolog, *der*

monopolize [mə'nɒpəlaɪz] *v. t.*

(Econ.) monopolisieren; *(fig.)* mit Beschlag belegen; ~ **the conversation** den/die anderen nicht zu Wort kommen lassen

monopoly [mə'nɒpəlɪ] *n.* a) *(Econ.)* Monopol, *das* (of auf + *Dat.*); b) *(exclusive possession)* alleiniger Besitz

monotone ['mɒnətəʊn] *n.* gleichbleibender Ton. **monotonous** [mə'nɒtənəs] *adj.,* **mo'notonously** *adv.* eintönig. **monotony** [mə'nɒtənɪ] *n.* Eintönigkeit, *die*

monsoon [mɒn'su:n] *n.* Monsun, *der*

monster ['mɒnstə(r)] *n.* a) *(creature)* Ungeheuer, *das*; *(huge thing)* Ungetüm, *das*; b) *(inhuman person)* Unmensch, *der*. **monstrosity** [mɒn-'strɒsɪtɪ] *n.* a) *(outrageous thing)* Ungeheuerlichkeit, *die*; b) *(hideous building etc.)* Ungetüm, *das*. **monstrous** ['mɒnstrəs] *adj.* a) *(huge)* riesig; b) *(outrageous)* ungeheuerlich; c) *(atrocious)* scheußlich

month [mʌnθ] *n.* Monat, *der*; **for a ~/~s** einen Monat [lang]/monatelang. **'monthly 1.** *adj.* monatlich; Monats‹einkommen, -gehalt›. **2.** *adv.* einmal im Monat. **3.** *n.* Monatsschrift, *die*

monument ['mɒnjʊmənt] *n.* Denkmal, *das*. **monumental** [mɒnjʊ-'mentl] *adj.* a) *(massive)* monumental; b) gewaltig ‹Mißerfolg, Irrtum›

moo [mu:] **1.** *n.* Muhen, *das*. **2.** *v.i.* muhen

mooch [mu:tʃ] *v.i. (sl.)* ~ **about** or **around/along** herumschleichen *(ugs.)*/ zockeln *(ugs.)*

mood [mu:d] *n.* a) Stimmung, *die*; **be in a good/bad ~:** [bei] guter/schlechter Laune sein; **I'm not in the ~:** ich habe keine Lust dazu; b) *(bad ~)* Verstimmung, *die*. **'moody** *adj.* a) *(sullen)* mißmutig; b) *(subject to moods)* launenhaft

moon [mu:n] *n.* Mond, *der*

moon: **~beam** *n.* Mondstrahl, *der*; **~light 1.** *n.* Mondlicht, *das*; Mondschein, *der*; **2.** *v.i. (coll.)* nebenberuflich abends arbeiten; **~lit** *adj.* mondbeschienen *(geh.)*

¹moor [mʊə(r), mɔ:(r)] *n. (Geog.)* [Hoch]moor, *das*

²moor *v.t. & i.* festmachen; vertäuen. **'mooring** *n.* ~[s] Anlegestelle, *die*

moose [mu:s] *n., pl. same* Amerikanischer Elch

moot [mu:t] **1.** *adj.* umstritten; offen ‹Frage›; strittig ‹Punkt›. **2.** *v.t.* erörtern ‹Frage, Punkt›

mop [mɒp] **1.** *n.* a) Mop, *der*; b) ~ [of hair] Wuschelkopf, *der*. **2.** *v.t.,* -**pp**- moppen ‹Fußboden›; *(wipe)* abwischen ‹Träne, Schweiß, Stirn›. **mop 'up** *v.t.* aufwischen

mope [məʊp] *v.i.* Trübsal blasen

moped ['məʊped] *n.* Moped, *das*

moral ['mɒrl] **1.** *adj.* a) moralisch; sittlich ‹Wert›; Moral‹begriff, -prinzip›; b) *(virtuous)* moralisch ‹Leben, Person›. **2.** *n.* a) Moral, *die*; b) in *pl.* *(habits)* Moral, *die*

morale [mə'rɑ:l] *n.* Moral, *die*; **low/high ~:** schlechte/gute Moral

morality [mə'rælɪtɪ] *n.* Moral, *die*

morbid ['mɔ:bɪd] *adj.* krankhaft; morbid *(geh.)* ‹Faszination, Neigung›

more [mɔ:(r)] **1.** *adj.* mehr; **any** or **some** ~ ‹apples, books, etc.› noch welche; **any** or **some** ~ ‹tea, paper, etc.› noch etwas; **any** or **some** ~ **apples/tea** noch Äpfel/Tee; **I haven't any ~ [apples/tea]** ich habe keine [Äpfel]/keinen [Tee] mehr; ~ **and** ~: immer mehr. **2.** *n.* mehr; ~ **and** ~: immer mehr; **six or** ~: mindestens sechs. **3.** *adv.* a) mehr; ~ **interesting** interessanter; b) *(nearer, rather)* eher; c) *(again)* wieder; **no ~, not any** ~: nicht mehr; **once** ~: noch einmal; d) ~ **and** ~: immer mehr; ~ **absurd** immer absurder; e) ~ **or less** *(fairly)* mehr oder weniger; *(approximately)* annähernd. **more'over** *adv.* außerdem

morgue [mɔ:g] *see* mortuary

morning ['mɔ:nɪŋ] *n.* Morgen, *der*; *(not afternoon)* Vormittag, *der*; *attrib.* morgendlich; Morgen-; **this ~:** heute morgen; **tomorrow ~,** *(coll.)* **in the ~:** morgen früh; **[early] in the ~:** am [frühen] Morgen; *(regularly)* [früh] morgens

Moroccan [mə'rɒkən] **1.** *adj.* marokkanisch. **2.** *n.* Marokkaner, *der*/Marokkanerin, *die*

Morocco [mə'rɒkəʊ] *pr. n.* Marokko *(das)*

moron ['mɔ:rɒn] *n. (coll.)* Schwachkopf, *der (ugs.)*

Morse [code] [mɔ:s ('kəʊd)] *n.* Morsealphabet, *das*

mortal ['mɔ:tl] **1.** *adj.* a) sterblich; b) *(fatal)* tödlich (to für). **2.** *n.* Sterbliche, *der/die*. **mortality** [mɔ:'tælɪtɪ] *n.* a) Sterblichkeit, *die*; b) ~ [rate] Sterblichkeitsrate, *die*. **'mortally** *adv.* tödlich

mortar ['mɔ:tə(r)] *n.* Mörtel, *der*

mortgage ['mɔ:gɪdʒ] **1.** *n.* Hypothek,

die. **2.** *v.t.* mit einer Hypothek belasten

mortuary ['mɔːtjʊərɪ] *n.* Leichenschauhaus, *das*

mosaic [məʊ'zeɪk] *n.* Mosaik, *das*

Moscow ['mɒskəʊ] *pr. n.* Moskau *(das)*

Moselle [məʊ'zel] *pr. n.* Mosel, *die*

Moslem ['mɒzləm] *see* **Muslim**

mosque [mɒsk] *n.* Moschee, *die*

mosquito [mɒs'kiːtəʊ] *n., pl.* ~es Stechmücke, *die; (in tropics)* Moskito, *der*

moss [mɒs] *n.* Moos, *das.* **'mossy** *adj.* moosig

most [məʊst] **1.** *adj. (in number, majority of)* die meisten; *(in amount)* meist...; **make the ~ mistakes/the ~ noise** die meisten Fehler/den größten Lärm machen; **for the ~ part** größtenteils. **2.** *n.* **a)** *(greatest amount)* **the ~ it will cost is £10** es wird höchstens zehn Pfund kosten; **pay the ~:** am meisten bezahlen; **b)** *(greater part)* **~ of the girls** die meisten Mädchen; **~ of his friends** die meisten seiner Freunde; **~ of the poem** der größte Teil des Gedichts; **~ of the time** die meiste Zeit; **c)** *(on ~ occasions)* meistens. **3.** *adv.* **a)** am meisten; **the ~ interesting book** das interessanteste Buch; **~ often** am häufigsten; **b)** *(exceedingly)* äußerst. **'mostly** *adv. (most of the time)* meistens; *(mainly)* größtenteils

MOT *see* **MOT test**

motel [məʊ'tel] *n.* Motel, *das*

moth [mɒθ] *n.* Nachtfalter, *der; (in clothes)* Motte, *die.* **'mothball** *n.* Mottenkugel, *die.* **'moth-eaten** *adj.* von Motten zerfressen

mother ['mʌðə(r)] **1.** *n.* Mutter, *die.* **2.** *v.t. (over-protect)* bemuttern. **'motherhood** *n.* Mutterschaft, *die*

mother: ~-in-law *n., pl.* **~s-in-law** Schwiegermutter, *die;* **~land** *n.* Vaterland, *das*

motherly ['mʌðəlɪ] *adj.* mütterlich; **~ love** Mutterliebe, *die*

mother: ~-of-'pearl *n.* Perlmutt, *das;* **M~'s Day** *n.* Muttertag, *der;* **~'tongue** *n.* Muttersprache, *die*

'moth-proof *adj.* mottenfest

motif [məʊ'tiːf] *n.* Motiv, *das*

motion ['məʊʃn] **1.** *n.* **a)** Bewegung, *die;* **b)** *(proposal)* Antrag, *der.* **2.** *v.t. & i.* ~ **[to]** sb. **to do** sth. jmdm. bedeuten *(geh.)*, etw. zu tun. **'motionless** *adj.* bewegungslos

motivate ['məʊtɪveɪt] *v.t.* motivieren.

motivation [məʊtɪ'veɪʃn] *n.* Motivation, *die*

motive ['məʊtɪv] *n.* Beweggrund, *der;* **the ~ for the crime** das Tatmotiv

motley ['mɒtlɪ] *adj.* buntgemischt

motor ['məʊtə(r)] **1.** *n.* **a)** Motor, *der;* **b)** *(Brit.:* ~ **car)** Auto, *das.* **2.** *adj.* Motor*(mäher, -jacht usw.).* **3.** *v.i. (Brit.)* [mit dem Auto] fahren

motor: ~bike *n. (coll.)* Motorrad, *das;* **~ boat** *n.* Motorboot, *das;* **~ car** *n. (Brit.)* Kraftfahrzeug, *das;* **~cycle** *n.* Motorrad, *das*

'motoring *n. (Brit.)* Autofahren, *das*

'motorist *n.* Autofahrer, *der*/-fahrerin, *die*

motorize ['məʊtəraɪz] *v.t.* motorisieren

motor: ~-racing *n.* Autorennsport, *der;* **~ vehicle** *n.* Kraftfahrzeug, *das;* **~way** *n. (Brit.)* Autobahn, *die*

MOT test *n. (Brit.)* ≈ TÜV, *der*

mottled ['mɒtld] *adj.* gesprenkelt

motto ['mɒtəʊ] *n., pl.* ~es Motto, *das*

¹mould [məʊld] **1.** *n. (hollow container)* Form, *die.* **2.** *v.t.* formen **(out of, from** aus)

²mould *n. (Bot.)* Schimmel, *der*

moulder ['məʊldə(r)] *v.i.* ~ **[away]** [ver]modern

'moulding *n.* **a)** Formteil, *das* **(of, in** aus); *(Archit.)* Zierleiste, *die;* **b)** *(wooden)* Leiste, *die*

'mouldy *adj.* schimmlig; **go ~:** schimmeln

moult [məʊlt] *v.i.* ⟨*Vogel:*⟩ sich mausern; ⟨*Hund, Katze:*⟩ sich haaren

mound [maʊnd] *n.* **a)** *(of earth)* Hügel, *der;* **b)** *(heap)* Haufen, *der*

mount [maʊnt] **1.** *n.* **a)** M~ Vesuvius/Everest der Vesuv/der Mount Everest; **b)** *(animal)* Reittier, *das; (horse)* Pferd, *das;* **c)** *(of picture, photograph)* Passepartout, *das;* **d)** *(for gem)* Fassung, *die.* **2.** *v.t.* **a)** hinaufsteigen ⟨*Treppe*⟩; steigen auf (+ *Akk.*) ⟨*Plattform, Reittier, Fahrzeug*⟩; **b)** aufziehen ⟨*Bild*⟩; einfassen ⟨*Edelstein usw.*⟩; **c)** inszenieren ⟨*Stück, Oper*⟩; organisieren ⟨*Ausstellung*⟩; durchführen ⟨*Angriff, Operation*⟩. **3.** *v.i.* ~ **[up]** *(increase)* steigen (to auf + *Akk.*)

mountain ['maʊntɪn] *n.* Berg, *der;* **in the ~s** im Gebirge. **mountaineer** [maʊntɪ'nɪə(r)] *n.* Bergsteiger, *der*/Bergsteigerin, *die.* **mountai'neering** *n.* Bergsteigen, *das.* **mountainous** ['maʊntɪnəs] *adj.* **a)** gebirgig; **b)** *(huge)* riesig

mourn [mɔːn] 1. *v. i.* trauern; ~ **for** *or* **over** trauern um ⟨*Toten*⟩. 2. *v. t.* betrauern. **'mourner** *n.* Trauernde, *der/die*. **mournful** ['mɔːnfl] *adj.* klagend ⟨*Stimme, Ton, Schrei*⟩; trauervoll ⟨*geh.*⟩⟨*Person*⟩. **'mourning** *n.* Trauer, *die;* **be in/go into** ~: Trauer tragen/anlegen

mouse [maʊs] *n., pl.* **mice** [maɪs] Maus, *die*. **'mouse trap** *n.* Mausefalle, *die*

mousse [muːs] *n.* Mousse, *die*

moustache [mə'stɑːʃ] *n.* Schnurrbart, *der*

mousy ['maʊsɪ] *adj.* a) mattbraun ⟨*Haar*⟩; b) ⟨*timid*⟩ scheu

mouth 1. [maʊθ] *n.* a) ⟨*of person*⟩ Mund, *der;* b) ⟨*of animal*⟩ Maul, *das;* **with one's** ~ **open/full** mit offenem/vollem Mund; b) ⟨*harbour entrance*⟩ [Hafen]einfahrt, *die;* ⟨*of tunnel, cave*⟩ Eingang, *der;* ⟨*of river*⟩ Mündung, *die*. 2. [maʊð] *v. t.* mit Lippenbewegungen sagen. **mouthful** ['maʊθfʊl] *n.* Mundvoll, *der*

mouth: **~-organ** *n.* Mundharmonika, *die;* **~piece** *n.* a) Mundstück, *das;* b) ⟨*fig.*⟩ Sprachrohr, *das*

movable ['muːvəbl] *adj.* beweglich

move [muːv] 1. *n.* a) ⟨*change of home*⟩ Umzug, *der;* b) ⟨*action taken*⟩ Schritt, *der;* ⟨*Footb. etc.*⟩ Spielzug, *der;* c) ⟨*turn in game*⟩ Zug, *der;* **make a** ~: ziehen; **it's your** ~: du bist am Zug; b) **on the** ~ ⟨*Person:*⟩ unterwegs sein; c) **make a** ~ ⟨*do sth.*⟩ etwas tun; ⟨*coll.: leave*⟩ losziehen ⟨*ugs.*⟩; **get a** ~ **on** ⟨*coll.*⟩ einen Zahn zulegen ⟨*ugs.*⟩; **get a** ~ **on!** ⟨*coll.*⟩ [mach] Tempo! ⟨*ugs.*⟩. 2. *v. t.* a) ⟨*change position of*⟩ bewegen; wegräumen ⟨*Hindernis, Schutt*⟩; ⟨*transport*⟩ befördern; ~ **sth. to a new position** etw. an einen neuen Platz bringen; ~ **house** umziehen; b) ⟨*in game*⟩ ziehen; c) ⟨*affect*⟩ bewegen; ~ **sb. to tears** jmdn. zu Tränen rühren; **be** ~**d by sth.** über etw. *(Akk.)* gerührt sein; d) ⟨*prompt*⟩ ~ **sb. to do sth.** jmdn. dazu bewegen, etw. zu tun; e) ⟨*propose*⟩ beantragen. 3. *v. i.* a) sich bewegen; ⟨*in vehicle*⟩ fahren; b) ⟨*in games*⟩ ziehen; c) ⟨*do sth.*⟩ handeln; d) ⟨*change home*⟩ umziehen ⟨*to nach*⟩; ~ **into a flat** in eine Wohnung einziehen; ~ **out of a flat** aus einer Wohnung ausziehen; ~ **to London** nach London ziehen; e) ⟨*change posture or state*⟩ sich bewegen; **don't** ~! keine Bewegung! **move a'bout** 1. *v. i.* zu-

gange sein; ⟨*travel*⟩ unterwegs sein. 2. *v. t.* herumräumen. **move a'long** 1. *v. i.* a) gehen/fahren; b) ~ **along, please!** gehen/fahren Sie bitte weiter! 2. *v. t.* zum Weitergehen/-fahren auffordern. **move 'in** 1. *v. i.* a) ⟨*to home etc.*⟩ einziehen; b) ~ **in on** ⟨*Truppen, Polizeikräfte:*⟩ vorrücken gegen. 2. *v. t.* hineinbringen. **move 'off** *v. i.* sich in Bewegung setzen. **move 'on** 1. *v. i.* weitergehen/-fahren; ~ **on to another question** ⟨*fig.*⟩ zu einer anderen Frage übergehen. 2. *v. t.* zum Weitergehen/-fahren auffordern. **move 'out** *v. t.* ausziehen ⟨*of aus*⟩. **move 'over** *v. i.* rücken. **move 'up** *v. i.* a) rücken; b) ⟨*in queue, hierarchy*⟩ aufrücken

'movement *n.* a) Bewegung, *die;* ⟨*trend, tendency*⟩ Tendenz, *die* ⟨*towards* zu⟩; b) *in pl.* Aktivitäten *Pl.;* c) ⟨*Mus.*⟩ Satz, *der*

movie ['muːvɪ] *n.* ⟨*Amer. coll.*⟩ Film, *der;* **the** ~**s** der Film; **go to the** ~**s** ins Kino gehen

moving ['muːvɪŋ] *adj.* a) beweglich; b) ⟨*affecting*⟩ ergreifend

mow [məʊ] *v. t., p.p.* **mown** [məʊn] *or* **mowed** [məʊd] mähen. **mow 'down** *v. t.* ⟨*shoot*⟩ niedermähen ⟨*Menschen*⟩

'mower *n.* Rasenmäher, *der*

mown *see* **mow**

MP *abbr.* **Member of Parliament**

m.p.g. *abbr.* **miles per gallon**

m.p.h. *abbr.* **miles per hour**

Mr ['mɪstə(r)] *n.* Herr; ⟨*in an address*⟩ Herrn

Mrs ['mɪsɪz] *n.* Frau

Ms [mɪz] *n.* Frau

Mt. *abbr.* **Mount**

much [mʌtʃ] 1. *adj.*, **more** [mɔː(r)], **most** [məʊst] viel; **too** ~: zuviel *indekl.* 2. *n.* vieles; ~ **of the day** der Großteil des Tages; **not be** ~ **to look at** nicht sehr ansehnlich sein. 3. *adv.*, **more, most** a) viel ⟨*besser, schöner usw.*⟩; ~ **more lively/attractive** viel lebhafter/attraktiver; b) mit Abstand ⟨*der/die/das beste, klügste usw.*⟩; c) ⟨*greatly*⟩ sehr ⟨*lieben, genießen usw.*⟩; ⟨*for* ~ *of the time*⟩ viel ⟨*lesen, spielen usw.*⟩; ⟨*often*⟩ oft ⟨*sehen, besuchen usw.*⟩; **[pretty** *or* **very]** ~ **the same** fast [genau] der-/die-/dasselbe

muck [mʌk] *n.* a) ⟨*coll.: something disgusting*⟩ Dreck, *der* ⟨*ugs.*⟩; b) ⟨*coll.: nonsense*⟩ Mist, *der* ⟨*ugs.*⟩. **muck a'bout, muck a'round** ⟨*Brit. sl.*⟩ *v. i.* a) herumalbern ⟨*ugs.*⟩; b) ⟨*tinker*⟩ her-

umfummeln (**with** an + *Dat.*). **muck
'in** *v. i. (coll.)* mit anpacken (**with** bei).
muck 'up *v. t.* **a)** *(Brit. sl.: bungle)*
vermurksen *(ugs.);* **b)** *(make dirty)*
dreckig machen *(ugs.);* **c)** *(coll.: spoil)*
vermasseln *(salopp)*

'**mucky** *adj.* dreckig *(ugs.)*

mucus ['mju:kəs] *n.* Schleim, *der*

mud [mʌd] *n.* Schlamm, *der*

muddle ['mʌdl] **1.** *n.* Durcheinander,
das. **2.** *v. t.* ~ |**up**| durcheinanderbrin-
gen; ~ **up** *(mix up)* verwechseln (**with**
mit). **muddle a'long, muddle 'on**
v. i. vor sich *(Akk.)* hin wursteln
(ugs.). **muddle 'through** *v. i.* sich
durchwursteln *(ugs.)*

muddy ['mʌdɪ] *adj.* schlammig; **get** *or*
become ~: verschlammen

'**mudguard** *n.* Schutzblech, *das; (of
car)* Kotflügel, *der*

¹**muff** [mʌf] *n.* Muff, *der*

²**muff** *v. t.* verpatzen *(ugs.)*

muffle ['mʌfl] *v. t.* **a)** *(envelop)* ~ |**up**|
einhüllen; **b)** dämpfen ⟨*Geräusch*⟩.

'**muffler** *n.* **a)** *(wrap, scarf)* Schal,
der; **b)** *(Amer. Motor Veh.)* Schalldämpfer, *der*

mug [mʌg] **1.** *n.* **a)** Becher, *der (meist
mit Henkel); (for beer etc.)* Krug, *der;*
b) *(sl.: face, mouth)* Visage, *die (salopp).* **c)** *(Brit. sl.: gullible person)* Trottel, *der (ugs.).* **2.** *v. t.* **-gg-** *(rob)* überfallen und berauben. '**mugger** *n.*
Straßenräuber, *der/*-räuberin, *die.*
'**mugging** *n.* Straßenraub, *der*

'**muggy** ['mʌgɪ] *adj.* schwül

mule [mju:l] *n.* Maultier, *das*

multicoloured *(Brit., Amer.:* **multi-
colored)** ['mʌltɪkʌləd] *adj.* mehrfar-
big; bunt ⟨*Stoff, Kleid*⟩

multinational [mʌltɪ'næʃənl] **1.** *adj.*
multinational. **2.** *n.* multinationaler
Konzern, *der;* Multi, *der (ugs.)*

multiple ['mʌltɪpl] *adj.* mehrfach.
multiple-'choice *adj.* Multiple-
choice-⟨*Test, Frage*⟩. **multiple 'store**
n. (Brit.: shop) Kettenladen, *der*

multiplication [mʌltɪplɪ'keɪʃn] *n.*
Multiplikation, *die*

multiply ['mʌltɪplaɪ] **1.** *v. t.* multiplizieren, malnehmen (**by** mit). **2.** *v. i.*
sich vermehren

multi-storey ['mʌltɪstɔːrɪ] *adj.* mehr-
stöckig; ~ **car park/block of flats**
Parkhaus/Wohnhochhaus, *das*

multitude ['mʌltɪtjuːd] *n. (crowd)*
Menge, *die; (great number)* Vielzahl,
die

¹**mum** [mʌm] *(coll.)* **1.** *int.* ~'**s the word**

nicht weitersagen! **2.** *adj.* **keep** ~: den
Mund halten *(ugs.)*

²**mum** *n. (Brit. coll.: mother)* Mama, *die
(fam.)*

mumble ['mʌmbl] *v. i. & t.* nuscheln
(ugs.)

mumps [mʌmps] *n.* Mumps, *der*

munch [mʌntʃ] *v. t. & i.* ~ |**one's food**|
mampfen *(salopp)*

mundane [mʌn'deɪn] *adj.* **a)** *(dull)* banal; **b)** *(worldly)* weltlich

Munich ['mju:nɪk] *pr. n.* München
(das)

municipal [mjʊ'nɪsɪpl] *adj.* kommunal; Kommunal⟨*politik, -verwaltung*⟩

mural ['mjʊərl] *n.* Wandbild, *das*

murder ['mɜːdə(r)] **1.** *n.* Mord, *der (of*
an + *Dat.*). **2.** *v. t.* ermorden. '**murderer** *n.* Mörder, *der/*Mörderin, *die.*
'**murderess** *n.* Mörderin, *die.* **murderous** ['mɜːdərəs] *adj.* tödlich; Mord⟨*absicht, -drohung*⟩; mör-
derisch *(ugs.)* ⟨*Kampf*⟩

murk [mɜːk] *n.* Dunkelheit, *die.*
'**murky** *adj.* **a)** *(dark)* düster; **b)**
(dirty) schmutzig-trüb ⟨*Wasser*⟩

murmur ['mɜːmə(r)] **1.** *n.* **a)** *(subdued
sound)* Rauschen, *das;* **b)** *(expression
of discontent)* Murren, *das;* **c)** *(soft
speech)* Murmeln, *das.* **2.** *v. t.* murmeln. **3.** *v. i.* ⟨*Person:*⟩ murmeln; *(complain)* murren

muscle ['mʌsl] *n.* Muskel, *der.* **muscular** ['mʌskjʊlə(r)] *adj.* **a)** *(Anat.)*
Muskel-; **b)** *(strong)* muskulös

muse [mju:z] *(literary) v. i.* [nach]sin-
nen *(geh.)* (**on, over** über + *Akk.*)

museum [mjuː'ziːəm] *n.* Museum, *das*

mush [mʌʃ] *n.* Brei, *der*

mushroom ['mʌʃrʊm, 'mʌʃruːm] **1.** *n.*
Pilz, *der; (cultivated)* Champignon,
der. **2.** *v. i.* wie Pilze aus dem Boden
schießen

'**mushy** *adj.* breiig

music ['mju:zɪk] *n.* **a)** Musik, *die;*
piece of ~: Musikstück, *das;* **set sth. to**
~: etw. vertonen; **b)** *(score)* Noten *Pl.*
musical ['mju:zɪkl] **1.** *adj.* musikalisch; Musik⟨*instrument, -verständnis,
-notation, -abend*⟩. **2.** *n.* Musical, *das*

Muslim ['mɒslɪm, 'mʌzlɪm] **1.** *adj.*
moslemisch. **2.** *n.* Moslem, *der/*Mos-
lime, *die*

muslin ['mʌzlɪn] *n.* Musselin, *der*

mussel ['mʌsl] *n.* Muschel, *die*

must [məst, *stressed* mʌst] **1.** *v. aux.,
only in pres., neg. (coll.)* **mustn't**
['mʌsnt] müssen; *with neg.* dürfen. **2.**
n. (coll.) Muß, *das*

mustache *see* **moustache**
mustard ['mʌstəd] *n.* Senf, *der*
muster ['mʌstə(r)] 1. *n.* pass ~: akzeptabel sein. 2. *v. t.* versammeln; *(Mil., Naut.)* [zum Appell] antreten lassen; *(fig.)* zusammennehmen ⟨*Kraft, Mut, Verstand*⟩. 3. *v. i.* sich [ver]sammeln.
muster 'up *v. t.* aufbringen
mustn't ['mʌsnt] *(coll.)* = **must not**; *see* **must 1**
musty ['mʌstɪ] *adj.* muffig
mutant ['mju:tənt] 1. *adj.* mutiert. 2. *n.* Mutante, *die*
mutation [mju:'teɪʃn] *n.* Mutation, *die*
mute [mju:t] 1. *adj.* stumm. 2. *n.* Stumme, *der/die.* '**muted** *adj.* gedämpft
mutilate ['mju:tɪleɪt] *v. t.* verstümmeln. **mutilation** [mju:tɪ'leɪʃn] *n.* Verstümmelung, *die*
mutinous ['mju:tɪnəs] *adj.* meuternd
mutiny ['mju:tɪnɪ] 1. *n.* Meuterei, *die.* 2. *v. i.* meutern
mutter ['mʌtə(r)] *v. i. & t.* murmeln. '**muttering** *n.* Gemurmel, *das*
mutton ['mʌtn] *n.* Hammelfleisch, *das*
mutual ['mju:tjʊəl] *adj.* a) gegenseitig; b) *(coll.: shared)* gemeinsam. '**mutually** *adv.* a) gegenseitig; be ~ exclusive sich [gegenseitig] ausschließen; b) *(in common)* gemeinsam
muzzle ['mʌzl] 1. *n.* a) *(of dog)* Schnauze, *die; (of horse, cattle)* Maul, *das; (of gun)* Mündung, *die;* c) *(put over animal's mouth)* Maulkorb, *der.* 2. *v. t.* a) einen Maulkorb anlegen (+ *Dat.*) ⟨*Hund*⟩; b) *(fig.)* mundtot machen *(ugs.)* (+ *Dat.*)
MW *abbr. (Radio)* **medium wave** MW
my [maɪ] *poss. pron. attrib.* mein; my!, myl!, |my oh my! [ach du] meine Güte! *(ugs.)*
myself [maɪ'self] *pron.* a) *emphat.* selbst; I thought so ~: das habe ich auch gedacht; b) *refl.* mich/mir. *See also* **herself**
mysterious [mɪ'stɪərɪəs] *adj.* rätselhaft; geheimnisvoll ⟨*Fremder, Orient*⟩. **my'steriously** *adv.* auf rätselhafte Weise; geheimnisvoll ⟨*lächeln usw.*⟩
mystery ['mɪstərɪ] *n.* a) Rätsel, *das;* b) *(secrecy)* Geheimnis, *das.* '**mystery tour** *n.* Fahrt ins Blaue *(ugs.)*
mystic ['mɪstɪk] 1. *adj.* mystisch. 2. *n.* Mystiker, *der/*Mystikerin, *die.* **mystical** ['mɪstɪkl] *adj.* mystisch
mystify ['mɪstɪfaɪ] *v. t.* verwirren
myth [mɪθ] *n.* Mythos, *der.* **mythical** ['mɪθɪkl] *adj.* a) *(based on myth)* mythisch; b) *(invented)* fiktiv. **mythological** [mɪθə'lɒdʒɪkl] *adj.* mythologisch. **mythology** [mɪ'θɒlədʒɪ] *n.* Mythologie, *die*

N

N, n [en] *n.* N, n, *das*
N. *abbr.* a) north N; b) northern n.
NAAFI ['næfɪ] *abbr. (Brit.)* Navy, Army and Air Force Institutes *Kaufhaus für Angehörige der britischen Truppen*
nab [næb] *v. t.* a) *(arrest)* schnappen *(ugs.);* b) *(seize)* sich *(Dat.)* schnappen
nag [næg] *v. i. & t.* -gg-: ~ |at| sb. an jmdm. herumnörgeln; ~ |at| sb. to do sth. jmdm. zusetzen *(ugs.),* daß er etw. tut. '**nagging** *n.* 1. *adj. (persistent)* quälend; bohrend ⟨*Schmerz*⟩. 2. *n.* Genörgel, *das*
nail [neɪl] 1. *n.* Nagel, *der;* hit the ~ on the head *(fig.)* den Nagel auf den Kopf treffen *(ugs.).* 2. *v. t.* nageln (to an + *Akk.*). **nail 'down** *v. t.* festnageln; zunageln ⟨*Kiste*⟩
nail: ~**-brush** *n.* Nagelbürste, *die;* ~**-clippers** *n. pl.* |pair of| ~**-clippers** Nagelknipser, *der;* ~**-file** *n.* Nagelfeile, *die;* ~ **polish** *n.* Nagellack, *der;* ~**-polish remover** *n.* Nagellackentferner, *der;* ~**-scissors** *n. pl.* |pair of| ~**-scissors** Nagelschere, *die;* ~ **varnish** *(Brit.) see* ~ **polish**
naïve, naive [naɪ'i:v] *adj.,* **na'ively, na'ively** *adv.* naiv
naked ['neɪkɪd] *adj.* nackt; visible to or with the ~ eye mit bloßem Auge zu erkennen. '**nakedness** *n.* Nacktheit, *die*
name [neɪm] 1. *n.* a) Name, *der;* what's your ~/the ~ of this place? wie heißt du/dieser Ort?; my ~ is Jack ich heiße Jack; last ~: Nachname, *der;* by ~: namentlich ⟨*erwähnen, aufrufen usw.*⟩; know sb. by ~: jmdn. mit Namen kennen; b) *(reputation)* Ruf, *der;* make a ~ for oneself sich *(Dat.)* einen Namen machen; c) call sb. ~s jmdn. beschimpfen. 2. *v. t.* a) *(give ~ to)* ei-

nen Namen geben (+ *Dat.*); ~ **sb. John** jmdn. John nennen; ~ **sb. after** *or* (*Amer.*) **for sb.** jmdn./etw. nach jmdm. benennen; **be ~d John** John heißen; **a man ~d Smith** ein Mann namens Smith; b) *(call by right ~)* benennen; c) *(nominate)* ~ **sb.** [**as**] **sth.** jmdn. zu etw. ernennen. **'nameless** *adj.* namenlos. **'namely** *adv.* nämlich. **'namesake** *n.* Namensvetter, *der*/-schwester, *die*

nanny ['nænɪ] *n. (Brit.)* Kindermädchen, *das.* **'nanny-goat** *n.* Ziege, *die*

nap [næp] **1.** *n.* Nickerchen, *das (fam.);* **have a ~:** ein Nickerchen halten. **2.** *v. i.,* **-pp-** dösen *(ugs.);* **catch sb. ~ping** *(fig.)* jmdn. überrumpeln

nape [neɪp] *n.* ~ [**of the neck**] Nacken, *der;* Genick, *das*

napkin ['næpkɪn] *n.* Serviette, *die*

Naples ['neɪplz] *pr. n.* Neapel *(das)*

nappy ['næpɪ] *n. (Brit.)* Windel, *die*

narcissus [nɑːˈsɪsəs] *n., pl.* **narcissi** [nɑːˈsɪsaɪ] *or* ~**es** Narzisse, *die*

narcotic [nɑːˈkɒtɪk] **1.** *n.* **a)** *(drug)* Rauschgift, *das;* b) *(active ingredient)* Betäubungsmittel, *das.* **2.** *adj.* **a)** narkotisch; ~ **drug** Rauschgift, *das;* b) *(causing drowsiness)* einschläfernd

narrate [nəˈreɪt] *v. t.* erzählen; kommentieren *(Film).* **narration** [nəˈreɪʃn] *n.* Erzählung, *die.* **narrative** ['nærətɪv] **1.** *n.* Erzählung, *die.* **2.** *adj.* erzählend. **narrator** [nəˈreɪtə(r)] *n.* Erzähler, *der*/Erzählerin, *die*

narrow ['nærəʊ] **1.** *adj.* **a)** schmal; schmal geschnitten *(Rock, Hose, Ärmel usw.);* eng *(Tal, Gasse);* b) *(limited)* eng; begrenzt *(Auswahl);* c) knapp *(Sieg, Mehrheit);* **have a ~ escape** mit knapper Not entkommen (**from** *Dat.*); d) *(not tolerant)* engstirnig. **2.** *v. i.* sich verschmälern *(Tal:)* sich verengen. **3.** *v. t.* verschmälern; *(fig.)* einengen. **narrow 'down** *v. t.* einengen (**to** auf + *Akk.*)

narrow-'minded *adj.* engstirnig

nasal ['neɪzl] *adj.* **a)** *(Anat.)* Nasen-; b) näselnd; **speak in a ~ voice** näseln

nastily ['nɑːstɪlɪ] *adv.* **a)** *(unpleasantly)* scheußlich; b) *(ill-naturedly)* gemein; **behave ~:** häßlich sein

nasty ['nɑːstɪ] *adj.* **a)** *(unpleasant)* scheußlich *(Geruch, Geschmack);* gemein *(Trick, Person);* häßlich *(Angewohnheit);* **that was a ~ thing to say/do das war gemein;** b) *(ill-natured)* böse; **be ~ to sb.** häßlich zu jmdm. sein; c) *(serious)* übel; schlimm *(Krankheit,*

Husten, Verletzung); **she had a ~ fall** sie ist übel gefallen

nation ['neɪʃn] *n.* Nation, *die; (people)* Volk, *das.* **national** ['næʃənl] **1.** *adj.* national; National*(flagge, -held, -theater, -gericht, -charakter);* Staats*(sicherheit, -religion);* überregional *(Rundfunkstation, Zeitung);* landesweit *(Streik).* **2.** *n. (citizen)* Staatsbürger, *der*/-bürgerin, *die;* **foreign ~:** Ausländer, *der*/Ausländerin, *die*

national: ~ '**anthem** *n.* Nationalhymne, *die;* ~ '**costume** *n.* Nationaltracht, *die;* N~ '**Health [Service]** *n. (Brit.)* staatlicher Gesundheitsdienst; N~ **Health doctor/patient/spectacles** ≈ Kassenarzt, *der*/-patient, *der*/-brille, *die;* N~ **In'surance** *n. (Brit.)* Sozialversicherung, *die*

nationalism ['næʃənəlɪzm] *n.* Nationalismus, *der.* **nationalist** ['næʃənəlɪst] **1.** *n.* Nationalist, *der*/Nationalistin, *die.* **2.** *adj.* nationalistisch

nationality [næʃəˈnælɪtɪ] *n.* Staatsangehörigkeit, *die;* **what's his ~?** welche Staatsangehörigkeit hat er?

nationalization [næʃənəlaɪˈzeɪʃn] *n.* Verstaatlichung, *die*

nationalize ['næʃənəlaɪz] *v. t.* verstaatlichen

'nationally *adv.* landesweit

native ['neɪtɪv] **1.** *n.* **a)** *(of specified place)* **a ~ of Britain** ein gebürtiger Brite/eine gebürtige Britin; b) *(person born in a place)* Eingeborene, *der/die;* c) *(local inhabitant)* Einheimische, *der/die.* **2.** *adj.* eingeboren; einheimisch *(Pflanze, Tier);* ~ **inhabitant** Eingeborene/Einheimische, *der/die;* ~ **land** Geburts- *od.* Heimatland, *das;* ~ **language** Muttersprache, *die*

nativity [nəˈtɪvɪtɪ] *n.* **the N~** [**of Christ**] die Geburt Christi. **na'tivity play** *n.* Krippenspiel, *das*

NATO, Nato ['neɪtəʊ] *abbr.* **N**orth **At**lantic **T**reaty **O**rganization NATO, *die*

natter ['nætə(r)] *(Brit. coll.)* **1.** *v. i.* quatschen *(ugs.).* **2.** *n.* **have a ~:** quatschen *(ugs.)*

natural ['nætʃrəl] *adj.* natürlich; Natur*(zustand, -seide, -gewalt).* **natural 'gas** *n.* Erdgas, *das.* **natural 'history** *n.* Naturkunde, *die*

naturalism ['nætʃrəlɪzm] *n.* Naturalismus, *der*

naturalist ['nætʃrəlɪst] *n.* Naturforscher, *der*/-forscherin, *die*

naturalization [nætʃrəlaɪˈzeɪʃn] *n.* Einbürgerung, *die*

naturalize ['nætʃrəlaɪz] *v. t.* einbürgern

'**naturally** *adv.* **a)** *(by nature)* von Natur aus ⟨*blaß, fleißig usw.*⟩; *(in a true-to-life way)* naturgetreu; **b)** *(of course)* natürlich

'**naturalness** Natürlichkeit, *die*

nature ['neɪtʃə(r)] *n.* **a)** Natur, *die;* **b)** *(essential qualities)* Beschaffenheit, *die;* **in the ~ of things** naturgemäß; **c)** *(kind)* Art, *die;* **things of this ~:** derartiges; **d)** *(character)* Wesen, *das;* **be proud/friendly** *etc.* **by ~:** ein stolzes/freundliches *usw.* Wesen haben. '**nature reserve** *n.* Naturschutzgebiet, *das.* '**nature study** *n.* Naturkunde, *die.* '**nature trail** *n.* Naturlehrpfad, *der*

naught [nɔːt] *n.* *(arch./dial.)* **come to ~:** zunichte werden

naughtily ['nɔːtɪlɪ] *adv.* ungezogen

naughtiness ['nɔːtɪnɪs] *n.* Ungezogenheit, *die*

naughty ['nɔːtɪ] *adj.* ungezogen; **you ~ boy/dog** du böser Junge/Hund

nausea ['nɔːzɪə] *n.* Übelkeit, *die.* **nauseate** ['nɔːzɪeɪt] *v. t.* *(disgust)* anwidern. '**nauseating** *adj.* *(disgusting)* widerlich. **nauseous** ['nɔːzɪəs] *adj.* **sb. is** *or* **feels ~:** jmdm. ist übel

nautical ['nɔːtɪkl] *adj.* nautisch. **nautical 'mile** *n.* Seemeile, *die*

naval ['neɪvl] *adj.* Marine-; See⟨*-schlacht, -macht, -streitkräfte*⟩; **~ ship** Kriegsschiff, *das*

nave [neɪv] *n.* [Mittel]schiff, *das*

navel ['neɪvl] *n.* Nabel, *der*

navigate ['nævɪgeɪt] *v. t.* **a)** navigieren ⟨*Schiff, Flugzeug*⟩; **b)** befahren ⟨*Fluß usw.*⟩. **navigation** [nævɪ'geɪʃn] *n.* Navigation, *die.* **navigator** ['nævɪgeɪtə(r)] *n.* Navigator, *der*/Navigatorin, *die*

navy ['neɪvɪ] *n.* **a)** [Kriegs]marine, *die;* **b)** *see* **navy blue. navy 'blue** *n.* Marineblau, *das.* '**navy-blue** *adj.* marineblau

Nazi ['nɑːtsɪ] **1.** *n.* Nazi, *der.* **2.** *adj.* nazistisch; Nazi-

NB *abbr.* **nota bene** NB

NCO *abbr.* **non-commissioned officer** Uffz.

NE *abbr.* **north-east** NO

near [nɪə(r)] **1.** *adv.* nah[e]; **stand/live |quite| ~:** [ganz] in der Nähe stehen/wohnen; **come** *or* **draw ~/~er** ⟨*Tag, Zeitpunkt:*⟩ näher/näherrücken; **get ~er together** näher zusammenrücken; **~ at hand** in Reichweite *(Dat.);* ⟨*Ort*

ganz in der Nähe; **~ to** = 2. 2. *prep.* **a)** *(position)* nahe an/bei (+ *Dat.*); *(fig.)* in der Nähe (+ *Gen.*); **keep ~ me** halte dich in meiner Nähe; **it's ~ here** es ist hier in der Nähe; **b)** *(motion)* nahe an (+ *Akk.*); *(fig.)* in der Nähe (+ *Gen.*); **don't come ~ me** komm mir nicht zu nahe. **3.** *adj.* **a)** *(in space or time)* nahe; **in the ~ future** in nächster Zukunft; **the ~est man** der am nächsten stehende Mann; **b)** *(in nature)* **£30 or ~/~est offer** 30 Pfund oder nächstbestes Angebot; **~ escape** Entkommen mit knapper Not; **that was a ~ miss/thing!** das war knapp! **4.** *v. t.* sich nähern (+ *Dat.*); **the building is ~ing completion** das Gebäude steht kurz vor seiner Vollendung. **5.** *v. i.* ⟨*Zeitpunkt:*⟩ näherrücken. '**nearby** *adj.* nahe gelegen

'**nearly** *adv.* fast; **be ~ in tears** den Tränen nahe sein; **it is ~ six o'clock** es ist kurz vor sechs Uhr; **are you ~ ready?** bist du bald fertig?

'**nearness** *n.* Nähe, *die*

near-sighted *adj.* *(Amer.)* kurzsichtig

neat [niːt] *adj.* **a)** *(tidy)* ordentlich; **b)** *(undiluted)* pur; **c)** *(smart)* gepflegt ⟨*Erscheinung, Kleidung*⟩; **d)** *(deft)* geschickt. '**neatly** *adv. see* **neat a, c, d:** ordentlich; gepflegt; geschickt. '**neatness** *n. see* **neat a, c, d:** Ordentlichkeit, *die;* Gepflegtheit, *die;* Geschicktheit, *die*

necessarily [nesɪ'serɪlɪ] *adv.* zwangsläufig; **it is not ~ true** es muß nicht [unbedingt] stimmen

necessary ['nesɪsərɪ] **1.** *adj.* nötig; notwendig; **do everything ~:** das Nötige *od.* Notwendige tun. **2.** *n.* **the necessaries of life** das Lebensnotwendige

necessitate [nɪ'sesɪteɪt] *v. t.* erforderlich machen

necessity [nɪ'sesɪtɪ] *n.* **a)** *(need, necessary thing)* Notwendigkeit, *die;* **do sth. out of** *or* **from ~:** etw. notgedrungen tun; **of ~:** notwendigerweise; **b)** *(want)* Not, *der*

neck [nek] *n.* **a)** Hals, *der;* **be a pain in the ~** *(coll.)* jmdm. auf die Nerven gehen *(ugs.);* **break one's ~** *(fig. coll.)* sich den Hals brechen; **~ and ~** Kopf an Kopf; **b)** *(of garment)* Kragen, *der*

neck: ~lace ['neklɪs] *n.* [Hals]kette, *die;* *(with jewels)* Kollier, *das;* **~line** *n.* [Hals]ausschnitt, *der;* **~tie** *n.* Krawatte, *die*

nectar ['nektə(r)] *n.* Nektar, *der*
née (*Amer.: nee*) [neɪ] *adj.* geborene
need [niːd] 1. *n.* a) Notwendigkeit, *die* (for, of *Gen.*); (demand) Bedarf, *der* (for, of an + *Dat.*); as the ~ arises nach Bedarf; if ~ be nötigenfalls; there's no ~ for that [das ist] nicht nötig; there's no ~ to do sth. es ist nicht nötig, etw. zu tun; be in ~ of sth. etw. brauchen; there's no ~ for you to come du brauchst nicht zu kommen; b) *no pl.* (emergency) Not, *die*; in case of ~: im Notfall; c) (thing) Bedürfnis, *das.* 2. *v. t.* a) (require) brauchen; sth. that urgently ~s doing etw., was dringend gemacht werden muß; it ~s a coat of paint es muß gestrichen werden; b) expr. necessity müssen; I ~ to do it ich muß es tun; it ~s/doesn't ~ to be done es muß getan werden/es braucht nicht getan zu werden; c) pres. he ~, neg. ~ not *or* (coll.) ~n't ['niːdnt] expr. desirability müssen; with neg. brauchen zu
needle [niːdl] 1. *n.* Nadel, *die.* 2. *v. t.* (coll.) nerven (ugs.)
needless ['niːdlɪs] *adj.* unnötig; ~ to add *or* say, ...: überflüssig zu sagen, daß ... '**needlessly** *adv.* unnötig
'**needlework** *n.* Handarbeit, *die;* do ~: handarbeiten
needn't ['niːdnt] (coll.) = need not; *see* need 2 c
'**needy** *adj.* notleidend; bedürftig
negation [nɪ'geɪʃn] *n.* Verneinung, *die*
negative ['negətɪv] 1. *adj.* negativ. 2. *n.* a) (Photog.) Negativ, *das;* b) (~ statement) negative Aussage; (answer) Nein, *das.* '**negatively** *adv.* negativ
neglect [nɪ'glekt] 1. *v. t.* vernachlässigen; she ~ed to write sie hat es versäumt zu schreiben. 2. *n.* Vernachlässigung, *die;* be in a state of ~ (Gebäude:) verwahrlost sein. **neglectful** [nɪ'glektfl] *adj.* gleichgültig (of gegenüber); be ~ of sich nicht kümmern um
negligence ['neglɪdʒəns] *n.* Nachlässigkeit, *die;* (Law, Insurance, etc.) Fahrlässigkeit, *die*
negligent ['neglɪdʒənt] *adj.* nachlässig; be ~ about sth. sich um etw. nicht kümmern
negligible ['neglɪdʒɪbl] *adj.* unerheblich
negotiable [nɪ'gəʊʃəbl] *adj.* a) verhandlungsfähig (Forderung, Bedingungen); b) passierbar (Straße, Fluß)
negotiate [nɪ'gəʊʃɪeɪt] 1. *v. i.* verhandeln (for, on, about über + *Akk.*). 2.

v. t. a) (arrange) aushandeln; b) überwinden (Hindernis); passieren (Straße, Fluß); nehmen (Kurve).
negotiation [nɪgəʊʃɪ'eɪʃn] *n.* Verhandlung, *die.* **negotiator** [nɪ'gəʊʃɪeɪtə(r)] *n.* Unterhändler, *der/-händlerin, die*
Negress ['niːgrɪs] *n.* Negerin, *die*
Negro ['niːgrəʊ] 1. *n., pl.* ~es Neger, *der.* 2. *adj.* Neger-
neigh [neɪ] 1. *v. i.* wiehern. 2. *n.* Wiehern, *das*
neighbor etc. (Amer.) see **neighbour** etc.
neighbour ['neɪbə(r)] 1. *n.* Nachbar, *der/*Nachbarin, *die;* my next-door ~s meine Nachbarn von nebenan. 2. *v. t. & i.* ~ [upon] grenzen an (+ *Akk.*). '**neighbourhood** *n.* (district) Gegend, *die;* (neighbours) Nachbarschaft, *die;* [somewhere] in the ~ of £100 [so] um [die] 100 Pfund. '**neighbouring** *adj.* Nachbar-; angrenzend (Felder)
neither ['naɪðə(r), niː'ðə(r)] 1. *adj.* keiner/keine/keins der beiden. 2. *pron.* keiner/keine/keins von *od.* der beiden. 3. *adv.* (also not) auch nicht; ~ am I, (sl.) me ~: ich auch nicht. 4. *conj.* (not either) weder; ~ ... nor ...: weder ... noch ...
neon ['niːɒn] *n.* Neon, *das*
neon: ~ 'light *n.* Neonlampe, *die;* ~ 'sign *n.* Neonreklame, *die*
nephew ['nevjuː, 'nefjuː] *n.* Neffe, *der*
nepotism ['nepətɪzm] *n.* Vetternwirtschaft, *die*
Neptune ['neptjuːn] *pr. n.* (Astron.) Neptun, *der*
nerve [nɜːv] *n.* Nerv, *der;* get on sb.'s ~s jmdm. auf die Nerven gehen (ugs.); lose one's ~: die Nerven verlieren; what [a] ~! [so eine] Frechheit! '**nerve gas** *n.* Nervengas, *das.* '**nerve-racking** *adj.* nervenaufreibend
nervous ['nɜːvəs] *adj.* a) (Anat., Med.) Nerven-; ~ breakdown Nervenzusammenbruch, *der;* b) (having delicate nerves) nervös; be a ~ wreck mit den Nerven völlig am Ende sein; c) (Brit.: timid) be ~ of *or* about Angst haben vor (+ *Dat.*); be a ~ person ängstlich sein. '**nervously** *adv.* nervös. '**nervousness** *n.* Ängstlichkeit, *die*
nervy ['nɜːvɪ] *adj.* a) nervös; b) (Amer. coll.: impudent) unverschämt
nest 1. *n.* Nest, *das.* 2. *v. i.* nisten. '**nest-egg** *n.* (fig.) Notgroschen, *der*

nestle ['nesl] v. i. **a)** sich schmiegen (to, up against an + Akk.); **b)** (lie half hidden) eingebettet sein

¹net [net] **1.** n. Netz, das. **2.** v. t., -tt- [mit einem Netz] fangen

²net adj. **a)** netto; Netto⟨einkommen, -[verkaufs]preis usw.⟩; ~ **weight** Nettogewicht, das; **b)** (ultimate) End⟨ergebnis, -effekt⟩

net: ~**ball** n. Netzball, der. ~ '**curtain** n. Store, der

Netherlands ['neðələndz] pr. n. sing. or pl. Niederlande Pl.

nett see ²**net a**

'**netting** n. ([piece of] net) Netz, das; **wire** ~: Maschendraht, der

nettle ['netl] n. Nessel, die

'**network** n. Netz, das

neuralgia [njʊə'rældʒə] n. Neuralgie, die

neurosis [njʊə'rəʊsɪs] n., pl. **neuroses** [njʊə'rəʊsiːz] Neurose, die. **neurotic** [njʊə'rɒtɪk] adj. **a)** nervenkrank; **b)** (coll.) neurotisch

neuter ['njuːtə(r)] adj. sächlich

neutral ['njuːtrl] **1.** adj. neutral. **2.** n. (~ gear) Leerlauf, der. **neutrality** [njuː'trælɪtɪ] n. Neutralität, die

neutralize ['njuːtrəlaɪz] v. t. neutralisieren

neutron ['njuːtrɒn] n. Neutron, das

never ['nevə(r)] adv. **a)** nie; ~-**ending** endlos; **b)** (coll.) you ~ believed that, did you? hast du das doch wohl nicht geglaubt?; **well, I ~ [did]!** [na] so was!

never the'less adv. trotzdem

new [njuː] adj. neu

new: ~-**born** adj. neugeboren; ~**comer** ['njuːkʌmə(r)] n. Neuankömmling, der; ~**fangled** ['njuːfæŋgld] adj. neumodisch; ~**found** adj. neu; ~**laid** adj. frisch [gelegt] '**newly** adv. (recently) neu; ~ **married** seit kurzem verheiratet. '**newly-wed** n. Jungverheiratete, der/die

new 'moon n. Neumond, der

'**newness** n. Neuheit, die

news [njuːz] n., no pl. **a)** Nachricht, die; **be in the** ~ : Schlagzeilen machen; **good/bad** ~ : schlechte/gute Nachrichten; **b)** (Radio, Telev.) Nachrichten Pl.

news: ~**agent** n. Zeitungshändler, der/-händlerin, die; ~ **bulletin** n. Nachrichten Pl.; ~**flash** n. Kurzmeldung, die; ~**caster** n. Nachrichtensprecher, der/-sprecherin, die; ~ '**headline** n. Schlagzeile, die; ~-**letter** n. Rundschreiben, das;

~**paper** ['njuːspeɪpə(r)] n. **a)** Zeitung, die; **b)** (material) Zeitungspapier, das; ~**reader** n. Nachrichtensprecher, der/-sprecherin, die; ~**reel** n. Wochenschau, die; ~**sheet** n. Informationsblatt, das; ~ **summary** n. Kurznachrichten Pl.; ~**worthy** adj. [für die Medien] interessant

newt [njuːt] n. [Wasser]molch, der

New: **new 'year** n. Neujahr, das; **over the new year** silvestern; **a Happy** ~ **Year** ein glückliches od. gutes neues Jahr. ~ '**Year's** (Amer.), ~ **Year's Day** ns. Neujahrstag, der; ~ **Year's 'Eve** n. Silvester, der od. das; ~ **Zealand** [~ 'ziːlənd] pr. n. Neuseeland (das); ~ '**Zealander** n. Neuseeländer, der/-länderin, die

next [nekst] **1.** adj. nächst...; **the** ~ **but one** der/die/das übernächste; ~ **to** (fig.: almost) fast; nahezu; [**the**] ~ **time** das nächste Mal; **the** ~ **best** der/die/das nächstbeste; **am I** ~ **?** komme ich jetzt dran? **2.** adv. (in the ~ place) als nächstes; (on the ~ occasion) das nächste Mal; **it's my turn** ~ : ich komme als nächster dran; **sit/stand** ~ **to sb.** neben jmdm. stehen/sitzen; **place sth.** ~ **to sb./sth.** etw. neben jmdn./ etw. stellen. **3.** n. **a)** the week after ~ : [die] übernächste Woche; **b)** (person) ~ **of kin** nächster/nächste Angehörige; ~, **please!** der nächste, bitte! '**next-door** adj. gleich nebenan nachgestellt

NHS abbr. (Brit.) National Health Service

nib [nɪb] n. Feder, die

nibble ['nɪbl] v. t. & i. knabbern (at, on an + Dat.)

nice [naɪs] adj. nett; angenehm ⟨Stimme⟩; schön ⟨Wetter⟩; (iron.: disgraceful, difficult) schön; ~ **[and] warm/fast** schön warm/schnell; ~-**looking** hübsch. '**nicely** adv. (coll.) **a)** (well) nett; gut ⟨arbeiten, sich benehmen, plaziert sein⟩; **b)** (all right) gut; **that will do** ~ : das reicht völlig. **niceties** ['naɪsɪtɪz] n. pl. Feinheiten

niche [nɪtʃ, niːʃ] n. **a)** (in wall) Nische, die; **b)** (fig.: suitable place) Platz, der

nick n. **a)** (notch) Kerbe, die; **b)** (sl. prison) Knast, der (salopp); **c)** (Brit.: police station) Wache, die; **d)** in good/poor ~ (coll.) gut/nicht gut im Schuß (ugs.); **e)** in the ~ of time gerade noch rechtzeitig. **2.** v. t. **a)** einkerben; **b)** (Brit. sl.: arrest) einlochen (salopp); **c)** (Brit. sl.: steal) klauen (salopp)

nickel ['nɪkl] *n.* **a)** Nickel, *das;* **b)** *(Amer. coll.: coin)* Fünfcentstück, *das*

nickname ['nɪkneɪm] *n.* Spitzname, *der; (affectionate)* Koseform, *die*

nicotine ['nɪkəti:n] *n.* Nikotin, *das*

niece [ni:s] *n.* Nichte, *die*

Nigeria [naɪ'dʒɪərɪə] *pr. n.* Nigeria *(das)*

niggardly ['nɪgədlɪ] *adj.* knaus[e]rig *(ugs.)*

niggling ['nɪglɪŋ] *adj.* **a)** *(petty)* belanglos; **b)** *(trivial)* nichtssagend; **c)** *(nagging)* nagend

night [naɪt] *n.* Nacht, *die; (evening)* Abend, *der;* **the following ~:** die Nacht/der Abend darauf; **the previous ~:** die vorausgegangene Nacht/der vorausgegangene Abend; **on Sunday ~:** Sonntag nacht/[am] Sonntag abend; **for the ~:** über Nacht; **at ~:** nachts/abends; **late at ~:** spätabends

night: ~cap *n. (drink)* Schlaftrunk, *der;* **~club** *n.* Nachtklub, *der;* **~-dress** *n.* Nachthemd, *das;* **~fall** *n.* Einbruch der Dunkelheit

nightie ['naɪtɪ] *n. (coll.)* Nachthemd, *das*

nightingale ['naɪtɪŋgeɪl] *n.* Nachtigall, *die*

'night-life *n.* Nachtleben, *das*

nightly ['naɪtlɪ] **1.** *adj. (happening every night/evening)* allnächtlich/allabendlich. **2.** *adv. (every night)* jede Nacht; *(every evening)* jeden Abend

night: ~mare *n.* Alptraum, *der;* **~ school** *n.* Abendschule, *die;* **~ shift** *n.* Nachtschicht, *die;* **~-time** *n.* Nacht, *die;* **in the** *or* **at ~-time** nachts; **~-'watchman** *n.* Nachtwächter, *der*

nil [nɪl] *n.* null

Nile [naɪl] *pr. n.* Nil, *der*

nimble ['nɪmbl] *adj.,* **nimbly** ['nɪmblɪ] *adv.* flink

nine [naɪn] **1.** *adj.* neun. **2.** *n.* Neun, *die. See also* **eight**

nineteen [naɪn'ti:n] **1.** *adj.* neunzehn. **2.** *n.* Neunzehn, *die. See also* **eight.**

nineteenth [naɪn'ti:nθ] **1.** *adj.* neunzehnt... **2.** *n. (fraction)* Neunzehntel, *das. See also* **eighth**

ninetieth ['naɪntɪθ] *adj.* neunzigst...

ninety ['naɪntɪ] **1.** *adj.* neunzig. **2.** *n.* Neunzig, *die. See also* **eight; eighty 2**

ninth [naɪnθ] **1.** *adj.* neunt... **2.** *n. (in sequence)* neunte, *der/die/das; (in rank)* Neunte, *der/die/das; (fraction)* Neuntel, *das. See also* **eighth**

nip 1. *v. t.,* **-pp-** zwicken. **2.** *v. i.,* **-pp-** *(Brit. sl.)* **~ in** hinein-/hereinflitzen *(ugs.);* **~ out** hinaus-/herausflitzen *(ugs.).* **3.** *n. (pinch, squeeze)* Kniff, *der; (bite)* Biß, *der.* **'nipper** *n. (Brit. coll.: child)* Balg, *das (ugs.)*

nipple ['nɪpl] *n.* **a)** Brustwarze, *die;* **b)** *(of feeding-bottle)* Sauger, *der*

nitric acid ['naɪtrɪk æsɪd] *n.* Salpetersäure, *die*

nitrogen ['naɪtrədʒən] *n.* Stickstoff, *der*

nitwit ['nɪtwɪt] *n. (coll.)* Trottel, *der (ugs.)*

no [nəʊ] **1.** *adj.* kein. **2.** *adv.* **a)** *(by no amount)* nicht; **no less [than]** nicht weniger [als]; **no more wine?** keinen Wein mehr?; **b)** *(as answer)* nein. **3.** *n., pl.* **noes** [nəʊz] Nein, *das*

No. *abbr.* number Nr.

Noah's ark [nəʊəz 'ɑ:k] *n.* die Arche Noah

nobility [nə'bɪlɪtɪ] *n.* Adel, *der;* **many of the ~:** viele Adlige

noble ['nəʊbl] **1.** *adj.* ad[e]lig; edel *⟨Gedanken, Gefühle⟩.* **2.** *n.* Adlige, *der/die.* **nobleman** ['nəʊblmən] *n., pl.* **noblemen** ['nəʊblmən] Adlige, *der*

nobly ['nəʊblɪ] *adv.* **a)** edel[gesinnt]; **b)** *(generously)* edelmütig *(geh.)*

nobody ['nəʊbədɪ] **1.** *n. & pron.* niemand; keiner; *(person of no importance)* Niemand, *der*

nocturnal [nɒk'tɜ:nl] *adj.* nächtlich; **~ animal/bird** Nachttier, *das/*-vogel, *der*

nod [nɒd] **1.** *v. i.,* **-dd-** nicken. **2.** *v. t.,* **-dd-: ~ one's head [in greeting]** [zum Gruß] mit dem Kopf nicken. **3.** *n.* [Kopf]nicken, *das.* **nod 'off** *v. i.* einnicken *(ugs.)*

noise [nɔɪz] *n.* Geräusch, *das; (loud, harsh, unwanted)* Lärm, *der.* **'noiseless** *adj.* **'noiselessly** *adv.* lautlos.

noisily ['nɔɪzɪlɪ] *adv.,* **noisy** ['nɔɪzɪ] *adj.* laut

nomad ['nəʊmæd] *n.* Nomade, *der.* **nomadic** [nəʊ'mædɪk] *adj.* nomadisch; **~ tribe** Nomadenstamm, *der*

'no man's land *n.* Niemandsland, *das*

nominal ['nɒmɪnl] *adj.* nominell; äußerst niedrig *⟨Preis, Miete⟩*

nominate ['nɒmɪneɪt] *v. t.* **a)** *(propose)* nominieren; **b)** *(appoint)* ernennen. **nomination** [nɒmɪ'neɪʃn] *n. see* **nominate:** Nominierung, *die;* Ernennung, *die*

nominative ['nɒmɪnətɪv] *adj. & n.* **~ [case]** Nominativ, *der*

nominee [nɒmɪ'ni:] *n. (candidate)* Kandidat, *der/*Kandidatin, *die*

non- [nɒn] *pref.* nicht-

nonchalant ['nɒnʃələnt] *adj.* unbekümmert

non-commissioned 'officer *n.* Unteroffizier, *der*

non-com'mittal [nɒnkə'mɪtl] *adj.* unverbindlich; **he was ~:** er hat sich nicht klar geäußert

nondescript ['nɒndɪskrɪpt] *adj.* unscheinbar; undefinierbar ‹Farbe›

none [nʌn] **1.** *pron.* kein...; **~ of them** keiner/keine/keines von ihnen; **~ of this** nichts davon. **2.** *adv.* keineswegs; **I'm ~ the wiser** now jetzt bin ich um nichts klüger; **~ the less** nichtsdestoweniger

nonentity [nɒ'nentɪtɪ] *n.* Nichts, *das*

non-existent [nɒnɪg'zɪstənt] *adj.* nicht vorhanden

non-'fiction *n.* Sachliteratur, *die*

non-'iron *adj.* bügelfrei

non-'member *n.* Nichtmitglied, *das*

nonplus [nɒn'plʌs] *v. t.,* **-ss-** verblüffen

nonsense ['nɒnsəns] **1.** *n.* Unsinn, *der.* **2.** *int.* Unsinn. **nonsensical** [nɒn'sensɪkl] *adj.* unsinnig

non-'smoker *n.* **a)** *(person)* Nichtraucher, *der/*-raucherin, *die;* **b)** *(train compartment)* Nichtraucherabteil, *das*

non-'stick *adj.* **~ frying-pan** *etc.* Bratpfanne *usw.* mit Antihaftbeschichtung

non-stop 1. ['--] *adj.* durchgehend ‹Zug, Busverbindung›; Nonstop‹flug, -revue›. **2.** [-'-] *adv.* ohne Unterbrechung ‹tanzen, reden, reisen, senden›; nonstop ‹fliegen, tanzen, fahren›

noodle ['nu:dl] *n., usu. pl.* Nudel, *die*

nook [nʊk] *n.* Winkel, *der;* Ecke, *die*

noon [nu:n] *n.* Mittag, *der;* zwölf Uhr [mittags]; **at/before ~:** um/vor zwölf [Uhr mittags]

'no one *pron. see* **nobody**

noose [nu:s] *n.* Schlinge, *die*

nor [nɔ(r), *stressed* nɔː(r)] *conj.* noch; **neither/not ... ~ ...:** weder ... noch ...

norm [nɔːm] *n.* Norm, *die*

normal ['nɔːml] **1.** *adj.* normal. **2.** *n.* **a)** *(~ value)* Normalwert, *der;* **b)** *(usual state)* normaler Stand; **everything is back to** *or* **has returned to ~:** es hat sich wieder alles normalisiert. **normality** [nɔː'mælɪtɪ] Normalität, *die.* **'normally** *adv.* **a)** *(in normal way)* normal; **b)** *(ordinarily)* normalerweise

north [nɔːθ] **1.** *n.* **a)** Norden, *der;* **in/** **to⟨wards⟩/from the ~:** im/nach/von Norden; **to the ~ of** nördlich von; **b)** *usu.* **N~** *(Geog., Polit.)* Norden, *der.* **2.** *adj.* nördlich; Nord‹wind, -küste, -grenze›. **3.** *adv.* nach Norden; **~ of** nördlich von

north: **N~ 'Africa** *pr. n.* Nordafrika *(das);* **N~ A'merica** *pr. n.* Nordamerika *(das);* **N~ A'merican 1.** *adj.* nordamerikanisch; **2.** *n.* Nordamerikaner, *der/*-amerikanerin, *die;* **~bound** *adj.* ‹Zug, Verkehr *usw.*› in Richtung Norden; **~-'east 1.** *n.* Nordosten, *der;* **2.** *adj.* nordöstlich; Nordost‹wind, -küste›; **3.** *adv.* nordostwärts; nach Nordosten; **~-'eastern** *adj.* nordöstlich

northerly ['nɔːðəlɪ] *adj.* nördlich; ‹Wind› aus nördlichen Richtungen

northern ['nɔːðən] *adj.* nördlich; Nord‹grenze, -hälfte, -seite›. **Northern 'Ireland** *pr. n.* Nordirland *(das)*

North: **~ 'Germany** *pr. n.* Norddeutschland *(das);* **~ 'Pole** *n.* Nordpol, *der;* **~ 'Sea** *pr. n.* Nordsee, *die*

northward[s] ['nɔːθwəd(z)] *adv.* nordwärts

north: **~-'west 1.** *n.* Nordwesten, *der;* **2.** *adj.* nordwestlich; Nordwest‹wind, -küste›; **3.** *adv.* nordwestwärts; nach Nordwesten; **~-'western** *adj.* nordwestlich

Norway ['nɔːweɪ] *pr. n.* Norwegen *(das).* **Norwegian** [nɔː'wiːdʒn] **1.** *adj.* norwegisch; **sb. is ~:** jmd. ist Norweger/Norwegerin. **2.** *n.* **a)** *(person)* Norweger, *der/*Norwegerin, *die;* **b)** *(language)* Norwegisch, *das; see also* **English 2 a**

Nos. *abbr.* **numbers** Nrn.

nose [nəʊz] **1.** *n.* Nase, *die.* **2.** *v. t.* **~ one's way** sich *(Dat.)* vorsichtig seinen Weg bahnen. **3.** *v. i.* sich vorsichtig bewegen. **nose a'bout, nose a'round** *v. i. (coll.)* herumschnüffeln *(ugs.)*

nose: **~-bleed** *n.* Nasenbluten, *das;* **~-dive 1.** *n.* Sturzflug, *der;* **2.** *v. i.* im Sturzflug hinuntergehen

nosey *see* **nosy**

nostalgia [nɒ'stældʒə] *n.* Nostalgie, *die;* **~ for sth.** Sehnsucht nach etw. **nostalgic** [nɒ'stældʒɪk] *adj.* nostalgisch

nostril ['nɒstrɪl] *n.* Nasenloch, *das; (of horse)* Nüster, *die*

nosy ['nəʊzɪ] *adj. (sl.)* neugierig

not [nɒt] *adv.* nicht; **he is ~ a doctor** er ist kein Arzt; **~ at all** überhaupt nicht; **~ ... but ...:** nicht ..., sondern ...; **~ a thing** gar nichts

notable ['nəʊtəbl] *adj.* bemerkenswert; **be ~ for** sth. für etw. bekannt sein. **notably** ['nəʊtəblɪ] *adv.* besonders

notation [nəʊ'teɪʃn] *n.* Notierung, *die*

notch [nɒtʃ] **1.** *n.* Kerbe, *die.* **2.** *v. t.* kerben. **notch up** *v. t.* erreichen

note [nəʊt] **1.** *n.* **a)** *(Mus.) (sign)* Note, *die; (key of piano)* Taste, *die; (sound)* Ton, *der;* **b)** *(jotting)* Notiz, *die;* **take** *or* **make ~s** sich *(Dat.)* Notizen machen; **take** *or* **make a ~ of** sth. *(Dat.)* etw. notieren; **c)** *(comment, footnote)* Anmerkung, *die;* **d)** *(short letter)* [kurzer] Brief; **e)** *(importance)* **a person/something of ~:** eine bedeutende Persönlichkeit/etwas Bedeutendes; **be of ~:** bedeutend sein. **2.** *v. t.* **a)** *(pay attention to)* beachten; **b)** *(notice)* bemerken; **c)** *(write)* **~** |**down**| [sich *(Dat.)*] notieren. **notebook** *n.* Notizbuch, *das*

'noted *adj.* bekannt (**for** für, wegen)

note: **~pad** *n.* Notizblock, *der;* **~paper** *n.* Briefpapier, *das;* **~worthy** *adj.* bemerkenswert

nothing ['nʌθɪŋ] *n.* nichts; **~ interesting** nichts Interessantes; **~ much** nichts Besonderes; **~ more than** nur; **~ more, ~ less** nicht mehr, nicht weniger; **next to ~** so gut wie nichts; **have |got| or be ~ to do with** sth. *(not concern)* nichts zu tun haben mit jmdm./etw.; **have ~ to do with** sb. *(avoid)* jmdm. aus dem Weg gehen

notice ['nəʊtɪs] **1.** *n.* **a)** Anschlag, *der; (in newspaper)* Anzeige, *die;* **b)** *(warning)* **at short/a moment's ~:** kurzfristig/von einem Augenblick zum andern; **c)** *(formal notification)* Ankündigung, *die;* **until further ~:** bis auf weiteres; **d)** *(ending an agreement)* Kündigung, *die;* **give** sb. **a month's ~:** jmdm. mit einer Frist von einem Monat kündigen; **hand in one's ~, give ~** *(Brit.),* **give ~** *(Amer.)* kündigen; **e)** *(attention)* **bring** sb./sth. **to** sb.'s **~:** jmdn. auf jmdn./etw. aufmerksam machen; **take no ~ of** sb./sth. *(disregard)* keine Notiz von jmdm./etw. nehmen; **take no ~:** sich nicht darum kümmern. **2.** *v. t.* bemerken. **noticeable** ['nəʊtɪsəbl] *adj.* wahrnehmbar *(Fleck, Schaden, Geruch);* merklich *(Verbesserung);* spürbar *(Mangel).* **'notice-board** *n. (Brit.)* Anschlagbrett, *das;* Schwarzes Brett

notification [nəʊtɪfɪ'keɪʃn] *n.* Mitteilung, *die* (**of** sth. über etw. *[Akk.]*)

notify ['nəʊtɪfaɪ] *v. t.* **a)** *(make known)* ankündigen; **b)** *(inform)* benachrichtigen (**of** über + *Akk.*)

notion ['nəʊʃn] *n.* Vorstellung, *die;* **not have the faintest/least ~ of how/what** etc. nicht die blasseste/geringste Ahnung haben, wie/was *usw.*

notoriety [nəʊtə'raɪətɪ] *n.* traurige Berühmtheit

notorious [nə'tɔːrɪəs] *adj.* berüchtigt (**for** wegen); notorisch *(Lügner)*

nougat ['nuːgɑː] *n.* Nougat, *das od. der*

nought [nɔːt] *n.* Null, *die*

noun [naʊn] *n. (Ling.)* Substantiv, *das*

nourish ['nʌrɪʃ] *v. t.* ernähren (**on** mit). **'nourishing** *adj.* nahrhaft. **'nourishment** *n.* Nahrung, *die*

Nov. *abbr.* November Nov.

novel ['nɒvl] **1.** *n.* Roman, *der.* **2.** *adj.* neuartig. **novelist** ['nɒvəlɪst] *n.* Romanautor, *der/*-autorin, *die*

novelty ['nɒvltɪ] *n.* **a) be a/no ~:** etwas/nichts Neues sein; **b)** *(newness)* Neuheit, *die;* **c)** *(gadget)* Überraschung, *die*

November [nə'vembə(r)] *n.* November, *der; see also* **August**

novice ['nɒvɪs] *n.* Anfänger, *der/*Anfängerin, *die*

now [naʊ] **1.** *adv.* jetzt; *(nowadays)* heutzutage; *(immediately)* [jetzt] sofort; **just ~** *(very recently)* gerade eben; |**every**| **~ and again** hin und wieder; **well ~:** also; **~, ~:** na, na; **~ then** na *(ugs.).* **2.** *conj.* |**that**|...: jetzt, wo... **3.** *n.* **before ~:** früher; **by ~:** inzwischen; **a week from ~:** [heute] in einer Woche. **nowadays** ['naʊədeɪz] *adv.* heutzutage

nowhere ['nəʊweə(r)] *adv.* nirgends; nirgendwo; *(to no place)* nirgendwohin

nozzle ['nɒzl] *n.* Düse, *die*

nuance ['njuːɑ̃s] *n.* Nuance, *die*

nuclear ['njuːklɪə(r)] *adj.* Atom-; Kern*(explosion);* atomar *(Antrieb, Gefechtskopf, Wettrüsten, Abrüstung);* nuklear *(Abschreckung, Sprengkörper);* atomgetrieben *(Unterseeboot)*

nucleus ['njuːklɪəs] *n., pl.* **nuclei** ['njuːklɪaɪ] Kern, *der*

nude [njuːd] **1.** *adj.* nackt. **2.** *n.* **a)** *(figure)* Akt, *der;* **b) in the ~:** nackt

nudge [nʌdʒ] **1.** *v. t.* anstoßen. **2.** *n.* Stoß, *der*

nudism ['njuːdɪzm] *n.* Nudismus, *der;* Freikörperkultur, *die.* **nudist** ['njuːdɪst] *n.* Nudist, *der/*Nudistin, *die; at-*

trib. Nudisten-. **nudity** ['nju:dɪtɪ] *n.* Nacktheit, *die*

nugget ['nʌgɪt] *n.* Klumpen, *der; (of gold)* Goldklumpen, *der; (fig.)* ~s of wisdom goldene Weisheiten

nuisance ['nju:səns] *n.* Ärgernis, *das*; what a ~! so etwas Dummes!

null [nʌl] *adj.* ~ and void null und nichtig

numb [nʌm] **1.** *adj.* gefühllos, taub (with vor + *Dat.*); *(without emotion)* benommen. **2.** *v. t.* betäuben

number ['nʌmbə(r)] **1.** *n.* **a)** *(in series)* Nummer, *die; you've got the wrong ~ (Teleph.)* Sie sind falsch verbunden; **dial a wrong ~**: sich verwählen *(ugs.)*; **b)** *(esp. Math.: numeral)* Zahl, *die;* **c)** *(sum, total, quantity)* [An]zahl, *die;* a ~ of people/things einige Leute/Dinge; a ~ of times mehrmals. **2.** *v. t.* **a)** *(assign ~ to)* numerieren; **b)** *(amount to, comprise)* zählen; **c)** *(include)* zählen (among, with zu); **d)** sb.'s days are ~ed jmds. Tage sind gezählt. **'number-plate** *n.* Nummernschild, *das*

numeral ['nju:mərl] *n.* Ziffer, *die*

numerate [nju:mərət] *adj.* be ~: rechnen können

numerical [nju:'merɪkl] *adj.* numerisch; Zahlen⟨*wert, -folge*⟩; zahlenmäßig ⟨*Stärke, Überlegenheit*⟩

numerous ['nju:mərəs] *adj.* zahlreich

nun [nʌn] *n.* Nonne, *die*

nurse [nɜːs] **1.** *n.* **a)** Krankenschwester, *die;* ⟨**male**⟩ ~: Krankenpfleger, *der.* **2.** *v. t.* **a)** pflegen ⟨*Kranke*⟩; **b)** *(fig.)* hegen *(geh.)* ⟨*Gefühl, Groll*⟩

nursery ['nɜːsərɪ] *n.* **a)** *(room)* Kinderzimmer, *das;* **b)** *(crèche)* Kindertagesstätte, *die;* **c)** *see* **nursery school; d)** *(for plants)* Gärtnerei, *die.* **nursery rhyme** *n.* Kinderreim, *der.* **'nursery school** *n.* Kindergarten, *der*

nursing ['nɜːsɪŋ] *n.* Krankenpflege, *die; attrib.* Pflege⟨*personal, -beruf*⟩. **'nursing home** *n.* Pflegeheim, *das*

nurture ['nɜːtʃə(r)] *v. t. (rear)* aufziehen; *(fig.)* nähren

nut [nʌt] *n.* **a)** Nuß, *die;* **b)** *(Mech. Engin.)* [Schrauben]mutter, *die;* **c)** *(crazy person)* Verrückte, *der/die (ugs.).* **'nut-case** *n. (sl.)* Verrückte, *der/die (ugs.).* **'nutcrackers** *n. pl.* Nußknacker, *der*

nutmeg ['nʌtmeg] *n.* Muskat, *der*

nutrient ['nju:trɪənt] *n.* Nährstoff, *der*

nutrition [nju:'trɪʃn] *n.* Ernährung, *die; (food)* Nahrung, *die.* **nutritious** [nju:'trɪʃəs] *adj.* nahrhaft

'nutshell *n.* Nußschale, *die;* **in a ~** *(fig.)* in aller Kürze

nutty ['nʌtɪ] *adj.* **a)** *(in taste)* nussig; **b)** *(sl.: crazy)* verrückt *(ugs.)*

nuzzle ['nʌzl] *v. i.* sich kuscheln (**up to, against** an + *Akk.*)

NW *abbr.* north-west NW

nylon ['naɪlɒn] *n.* **a)** Nylon, *das; attrib.* Nylon-; **b)** *in pl. (stockings)* Nylonstrümpfe

nymph [nɪmf] *n.* Nymphe, *die*

O

O, o [əʊ] *n.* O, o, *das*

oaf [əʊf] *n.* Stoffel, *der (ugs.)*

oak [əʊk] *n.* Eiche, *die*

OAP *abbr. (Brit.)* old-age pensioner Rentner, *der*/Rentnerin, *die*

oar [ɔː(r)] *n.* Ruder, *das*

oasis [əʊ'eɪsɪs] *n., pl.* **oases** [əʊ'eɪsi:z] Oase, *die*

oat [əʊt] *n.* ~s Hafer, *der*

oath [əʊθ] *n.* **a)** Eid, *der;* Schwur, *der;* **b)** *(swear-word)* Fluch, *der*

obedience [ə'bi:dɪəns] *n.* Gehorsam, *der*

obedient [ə'bi:dɪənt] *adj.* gehorsam; be ~ to sb./sth. jmdm./einer Sache gehorchen. **o'bediently** *adv.* gehorsam

obelisk ['ɒbəlɪsk] *n.* Obelisk, *der*

obese [əʊ'bi:s] *adj.* fettleibig. **obesity** [əʊ'bi:sɪtɪ] *n.* Fettleibigkeit, *die*

obey [əʊ'beɪ] **1.** *v. t.* gehorchen (+ *Dat.*); sich halten an (+ *Akk.*) ⟨*Vorschrift, Regel*⟩; befolgen ⟨*Befehl*⟩. **2.** *v. i.* gehorchen

obituary [ə'bɪtjʊərɪ] *n.* Nachruf, *der* (to, of auf + *Akk.*)

object 1. ['ɒbdʒɪkt] *n.* **a)** *(thing)* Gegenstand, *der;* **b)** *(purpose)* Ziel, *das;* **c)** *(obstacle)* money/time *etc.* is no ~: Geld/Zeit *usw.* spielt keine Rolle; **d)** *(Ling.)* Objekt, *das.* **2.** [əb'dʒekt] *v. i.* **a)** Einwände/einen Einwand erheben (**to** gegen); **b)** *(have objection or dislike)* etwas dagegen haben; ~ to sb./sth. etwas gegen jmdn./etw. haben. **3.** *v. t.* einwenden. **objection** [əb-

'dʒekʃn] n. a) Einwand, der; raise or make an ~ [to sth.] einen Einwand [gegen etw.] erheben; b) (dislike) Abneigung, die; have an/no ~ to sb./sth. etw./nichts gegen jmdn./etw. haben; have no ~s nichts dagegen haben. **objectionable** [əb'dʒek ʃənəbl] adj. unangenehm ⟨Anblick, Geruch⟩; anstößig ⟨Bemerkung, Wort, Benehmen⟩

objective [əb'dʒektɪv] 1. adj. objektiv. 2. n. (goal) Ziel, das. **ob'jectively** adv. objektiv. **objectivity** [ɒbdʒek-'tɪvɪtɪ] n. Objektivität, die

obligation [ɒblɪ'geɪʃn] n. Verpflichtung, die; be under an ~ to sb. jmdm. verpflichtet sein; without ~: unverbindlich

obligatory [ə'blɪɡətərɪ] adj. obligatorisch; it has become ~ to ...: es ist jetzt Pflicht, zu ...

oblige [ə'blaɪdʒ] v. t. a) (be binding on) ~ sb. to do sth. jmdm. vorschreiben, etw. zu tun; b) (compel) zwingen; be ~d to do sth. gezwungen sein, etw. zu tun; feel ~d to do sth. sich verpflichtet fühlen, etw. zu tun; c) (be kind to) ~ sb. by doing sth. jmdm. den Gefallen tun und etw. tun; d) (grateful) be much/greatly ~d to sb. [for sth.] jmdm. [für etw.] sehr verbunden sein; much ~d! besten Dank! **obliging** [ə'blaɪdʒɪŋ] adj. entgegenkommend

oblique [ə'bliːk] adj. schief ⟨Gerade, Winkel⟩; (fig.) indirekt

obliterate [ə'blɪtəreɪt] v. t. auslöschen

oblivion [ə'blɪvɪən] n. Vergessenheit, die; sink or fall into ~: in Vergessenheit geraten

oblivious [ə'blɪvɪəs] adj. be ~ to or of sth. sich ⟨Dat.⟩ einer Sache ⟨Gen.⟩ nicht bewußt sein

oblong ['ɒblɒŋ] 1. adj. rechteckig. 2. n. Rechteck, das

obnoxious [əb'nɒkʃəs] adj. widerlich

oboe ['əʊbəʊ] n. Oboe, die

obscene [əb'siːn] adj. obszön. **obscenity** [əb'senɪtɪ] n. Obszönität, die

obscure [əb'skjʊə(r)] 1. adj. a) (unexplained) dunkel; b) (hard to understand) schwer verständlich ⟨Argument, Dichtung, Autor, Stil⟩; c) (unknown) unbekannt. 2. v. t. a) (make indistinct) verdunkeln; versperren ⟨Aussicht⟩; b) (make unintelligible) unverständlich machen

obsequious [əb'siːkwɪəs] adj. unterwürfig

observance [əb'zɜːvəns] n. Einhaltung, die

observant [əb'zɜːvənt] adj. aufmerksam

observation [ɒbzə'veɪʃn] n. a) Beobachtung, die; be [kept] under ~: beobachtet werden; (by police) überwacht werden; b) (remark) Bemerkung, die (on über + Akk.)

observatory [əb'zɜːvətərɪ] n. (Astron.) Sternwarte, die

observe [əb'zɜːv] v. t. a) (watch) beobachten; (perceive) bemerken; b) (abide by, keep) einhalten; c) (say) bemerken. **ob'server** n. Beobachter, der/Beobachterin, die

obsess [əb'ses] v. t. ~ sb. von jmdm. Besitz ergreifen (fig.); be/become ~ed with or by sb./sth. von jmdm./etw. besessen sein/werden. **obsession** [əb-'seʃn] n. Zwangsvorstellung, die. **obsessive** [əb'sesɪv] adj. zwanghaft; be ~ about sth. von etw. besessen sein

obsolete ['ɒbsəliːt] adj. veraltet

obstacle ['ɒbstəkl] n. Hindernis, das (to für)

obstinacy ['ɒbstɪnəsɪ] n. see obstinate: Starrsinn, der; Hartnäckigkeit, die

obstinate ['ɒbstɪnət] adj. starrsinnig; (adhering to particular course of action) hartnäckig

obstruct [əb'strʌkt] v. t. a) (block) blockieren; behindern ⟨Verkehr⟩; ~ sb.'s view jmdm. die Sicht versperren; b) (fig.: impede; also Sport) behindern. **obstruction** [əb'strʌkʃn] n. Blockierung, die; (of progress; also Sport) Behinderung, die. **obstructive** [əb-'strʌktɪv] adj. hinderlich; obstruktiv ⟨Politik, Taktik⟩; be ~ ⟨Person:⟩ sich querlegen (ugs.)

obtain [əb'teɪn] v. t. bekommen; erzielen ⟨Resultat, Wirkung⟩. **obtainable** [əb'teɪnəbl] adj. erhältlich

obtrusive [əb'truːsɪv] adj. aufdringlich; (conspicuous) auffällig

obtuse [əb'tjuːs] adj. a) stumpf ⟨Winkel⟩; b) (stupid) begriffsstutzig

obvious ['ɒbvɪəs] adj. offenkundig; (easily seen) augenfällig; be ~ [to sb.] that ...: [jmdm.] klar sein, daß ... 'obviously adv. offenkundig; sichtlich ⟨enttäuschen, überraschen usw.⟩

occasion [ə'keɪʒn] 1. n. a) Gelegenheit, die; rise to the ~: sich der Situation gewachsen zeigen; on several ~s bei mehreren Gelegenheiten; on ~[s] gelegentlich; b) (special occurrence) Anlaß, der; it was quite an ~: es war ein Ereignis; c) (reason) Grund, der (for zu). **2.** *v.t.* verursachen. **occa-sional** [ə'keɪʒənl] *adj.* gelegentlich; vereinzelt ⟨Regenschauer⟩. **oc'ca-sionally** *adv.* gelegentlich; [only] very ~: gelegentlich einmal

occult [ɒ'kʌlt, 'ɒkʌlt] *adj.* okkult; the ~: das Okkulte

occupant ['ɒkjʊpənt] *n.* Bewohner, der/Bewohnerin, die; (of car, bus, etc.) Insasse, der/Insassin, die

occupation [ɒkjʊ'peɪʃn] *n.* **a)** (Mil.) Besetzung, die; (period) Besatzungs-zeit, die; **b)** (activity) Beschäftigung, die; **c)** (profession) Beruf, der. **occu-pational** [ɒkjʊ'peɪʃənl] *adj.* Berufs-⟨beratung, -risiko⟩; ~ **therapy** Beschäf-tigungstherapie, die

occupier ['ɒkjʊpaɪə(r)] *n.* (Brit.) Besit-zer, der/Besitzerin, die; (tenant) Bewohner, der/Bewohnerin, die

occupy ['ɒkjʊpaɪ] *v.t.* **a)** (Mil.; as demonstration) besetzen; **b)** (live in) bewohnen; **c)** (take up, fill) einneh-men; belegen ⟨Zimmer⟩; in Anspruch nehmen ⟨Zeit, Aufmerksamkeit⟩; **d)** (busy, employ) beschäftigen

occur [ə'kɜː(r)] *v.i.*, **-rr-:** **a)** (be met with) vorkommen; ⟨Gelegenheit:⟩ sich bieten; ⟨Problem:⟩ auftreten; **b)** (hap-pen) ⟨Veränderung:⟩ eintreten; ⟨Un-fall, Vorfall:⟩ sich ereignen; **c)** ~ **to sb.** (be thought of) jmdm. in den Sinn kommen; ⟨Idee:⟩ jmdm. kommen.

occurrence [ə'kʌrəns] *n.* **a)** (incid-ent) Ereignis, das; Begebenheit, die; **b)** (occurring) Vorkommen, das

ocean ['əʊʃn] *n.* Ozean, der; Meer, das

o'clock [ə'klɒk] *adv.* **it is two/six ~:** es ist zwei/sechs Uhr; **at two/six ~:** um zwei/sechs Uhr; **six ~** *attrib.* Sechs-Uhr-⟨Zug, Maschine, Nachrichten⟩

Oct. *abbr.* October Okt.

octagon ['ɒktəgən] *n.* Achteck, das

octane ['ɒkteɪn] *n.* Oktan, das

octave ['ɒktɪv] *n.* Oktave, die

October [ɒk'təʊbə(r)] *n.* Oktober, der; *see also* **August**

octopus ['ɒktəpəs] *n.* Tintenfisch, der

odd [ɒd] *adj.* **a)** (surplus, spare) übrig ⟨Stück, Silbergeld⟩; **£25 and a few ~ pence** 25 Pfund und ein paar Pence; **b)** (occasional) gelegentlich; ~ **job/~~job man** Gelegenheitsarbeit, die/-arbeiter, der; **c)** (one of pair or group) einzeln; ~ **socks** nicht zusam-mengehörende Socken; **be the ~ man out** ⟨Gegenstand:⟩ nicht dazu passen; **d)** (uneven) ungerade ⟨Zahl, Seite, Hausnummer⟩; **e)** (plus something)

forty ~: über vierzig; **twelve pounds ~:** etwas mehr als zwölf Pfund; **f)** (strange, eccentric) seltsam. **oddity** ['ɒdɪtɪ] *n.* (object, event) Kuriosität, die. **'oddly** *adv.* seltsam; ~ **enough** seltsamerweise. **'odd-numbered** *adj.* ungerade

odds [ɒdz] *n. pl.* **a)** (Betting) Odds *Pl.;* **b)** [the] ~ **are that she did it** wahr-scheinlich hat sie es getan; **the ~ are against/in favour of sb./sth.** jmds. Aussichten/die Aussichten für etw. sind gering/gut; **c)** ~ **and ends** Klei-nigkeiten; (of food) Reste; **d) be at ~ with sb. over sth.** mit jmdm. in etw. (Dat.) uneinig sein; **e) it makes no/ little ~** [whether ...] es ist völlig/ziem-lich gleichgültig; ob ...]

odious ['əʊdɪəs] *adj.* widerwärtig

odor *etc.* (Amer.) *see* **odour** *etc.*

odour ['əʊdə(r)] *n.* Geruch, der. **'odourless** *adj.* geruchlos

of [əv, *stressed* ɒv] *prep.* von; *indicating material, substance* aus; **articles of clothing** Kleidungsstücke; **a friend of mine** ein Freund von mir; **where's that pencil of mine?** wo ist mein Bleistift?; **it was clever of you to do that** es war klug von dir, das zu tun; **the approval of sb.** jmds. Zustimmung; **the works of Shakespeare** Shakespeares Werke; **be made of ...:** aus ... [hergestellt] sein; **the fifth of January** der fünfte Januar; **his love of his father** seine Liebe zu sei-nem Vater; **person of extreme views** Mensch mit extremen Ansichten; **a boy of 14 years** ein vierzehnjähriger Junge; **the five of us** wir fünf

off [ɒf] **1.** *adv.* **a)** (away) **be a few miles ~:** wenige Meilen entfernt sein; **the lake is not far ~:** der See ist nicht weit [weg]; **I'm ~ now** ich gehe jetzt; ~ **we go!** los geht's!; **b)** (not on or attached or supported) ab; **get the lid ~:** den Deckel abbekommen; **c)** be ~ (switched or turned ~) ⟨Wasser, Gas, Strom:⟩ abgestellt sein; **the light/radio** *etc.* **is ~:** das Licht/Radio *usw.* ist aus; **d)** the meat *etc.* **is ~:** das Fleisch *usw.* ist schlecht [geworden]; **e)** be ~ (cancelled) abgesagt sein; ⟨Verlo-bung:⟩ [auf]gelöst sein; ~ **and on** im-mer und wieder (ugs.); **f)** (not at work) frei; **on my day ~:** an meinem freien Tag; **have a week ~:** eine Woche Ur-laub bekommen; **g)** (no longer avail-able) [the] **soup** *etc.* **is ~:** es gibt keine Suppe *usw.* mehr; **h)** (situated as re-gards money etc.) **he is badly** *etc.* **~:** er ist schlecht *usw.* gestellt. **2.** *prep.* von; **be ~ school/work** in der Schule/am Arbeitsplatz fehlen; **be ~ one's food** keinen Appetit haben; **just ~ the square** ganz in der Nähe des Platzes

offal ['ɒfl] *n.* Innereien *Pl.*

offence [ə'fens] *n.* (*Brit.*) **a)** (*hurting of sb.'s feelings*) Kränkung, *die;* **I meant no ~:** ich wollte Sie/ihn *usw.* nicht kränken; **b)** (*annoyance*) **give ~:** Mißfallen erregen; **take ~:** verärgert sein; **c)** (*crime*) Straftat, *die;* **criminal ~:** strafbare Handlung

offend [ə'fend] **1.** *v.i.* verstoßen (**against** gegen). **2.** *v.t.* **~ sb.** bei jmdm. Anstoß erregen; (*hurt feelings of*) jmdn. kränken. **offender** *n.* Straffällige, *der/die*

offense (*Amer.*) *see* offence

offensive [ə'fensɪv] **1.** *adj.* **a)** (*aggressive*) offensiv; Angriffs⟨*waffe*⟩; **b)** (*giving offence*) ungehörig; (*indecent*) anstößig. **2.** *n.* Offensive, *die;* **take the** *or* **go on the ~:** in die *od.* zur Offensive übergehen

offer ['ɒfə(r)] **1.** *v.t.* anbieten; vorbringen ⟨*Entschuldigung*⟩; bieten ⟨*Chance*⟩; aussprechen ⟨*Beileid*⟩; **~ to help** seine Hilfe anbieten; **~ resistance** Widerstand leisten. **2.** *n.* Angebot, *das;* **[have/be] on ~:** im Angebot [haben/sein]

offhand 1. *adv.* **a)** (*without preparation*) auf Anhieb ⟨*sagen, wissen*⟩; spontan ⟨*beschließen, entscheiden*⟩; **b)** (*casually*) leichthin. **2.** *adj.* **a)** (*without preparation*) spontan; **b)** (*casual*) beiläufig; **be ~ with sb.** zu jmdm. kurz angebunden sein

office ['ɒfɪs] *n.* **a)** Büro, *das;* **b)** (*branch*) Zweigstelle, *die;* **c)** (*position*) Amt, *das;* **hold ~:** amtieren. **'office hours** *n. pl.* Dienststunden *Pl.*

officer ['ɒfɪsə(r)] *n.* **a)** (*Army etc.*) Offizier, *der;* **b)** (*official*) Beamte, *der*/Beamtin, *die;* **c)** (*constable*) Polizeibeamte, *der*/-beamtin, *die*

official [ə'fɪʃl] **1.** *adj.* offiziell; amtlich ⟨*Verlautbarung*⟩; regulär ⟨*Streik*⟩. **2.** *n.* Beamte, *der*/Beamtin, *die;* (*party, union, or sports ~*) Funktionär, *der*/Funktionärin, *die.* **officially** *adv.* offiziell

officious [ə'fɪʃəs] *adj.* übereifrig

offing ['ɒfɪŋ] *n.* **be in the ~:** bevorstehen; ⟨*Gewitter:*⟩ aufziehen

off: **~licence** *n.* (*Brit.*) ≈ Wein- und Spirituosenladen, *der;* **~load** *v.t.* abladen; **~putting** ['ɒfpʊtɪŋ] *adj.*

(*Brit. coll.*) abstoßend; **~set** ['--, -'-] *v.t., forms as* set: ausgleichen; **~shore** *adj.* küstennah; **~side** *adj.* Abseits-; **be ~side** abseits sein; **~spring** *n., pl. same* Nachkommenschaft, *die;* (*of animal*) Junge *Pl.*

often ['ɒfn, 'ɒftn] *adv.* oft; **every so ~:** gelegentlich

oh [əʊ] *int.* oh; *expr. pain* au

oil [ɔɪl] **1.** *n.* Öl, *das.* **2.** *v.t.* ölen

oil: **~field** *n.* Ölfeld, *das;* **~painting** *n.* Ölgemälde, *das;* **~ refinery** *n.* [Erd]ölraffinerie, *die;* **~ rig** *see* 'rig 1; **~skins** *n. pl.* Ölzeug, *das;* **~slick** *n.* Ölteppich, *der;* **~tanker** *n.* Öltanker, *der;* **~ well** *n.* Ölquelle, *die*

oily ['ɔɪlɪ] *adj.* ölig; ölverschmiert ⟨*Gesicht, Hände*⟩

ointment ['ɔɪntmənt] *n.* Salbe, *die*

OK [əʊ'keɪ] (*coll.*) **1.** *adj.* in Ordnung; okay (*ugs.*). **2.** *adv.* gut. **3.** *int.* okay (*ugs.*). **4.** *v.t.* (*approve*) zustimmen (+ *Dat.*); **be OK'd by sb.** von jmdm. das Okay bekommen (*ugs.*)

okay [əʊ'keɪ] *see* OK

old [əʊld] *adj.* alt; **be [more than] 30 years ~:** [über] 30 Jahre alt sein

old: **~ 'age** *n.* [fortgeschrittenes] Alter; **~-age** *attrib. adj.* Alters⟨*rente, -ruhegeld*⟩; **~-age pensioner** Rentner, *der*/Rentnerin, *die;* **~-fashioned** [əʊld'fæʃnd] *adj.* altmodisch

olive ['ɒlɪv] *n.* Olive, *die.* **olive 'oil** *n.* Olivenöl, *das*

Olympic [ə'lɪmpɪk] *adj.* olympisch; **~ Games** Olympische Spiele

omelette (**omelet**) ['ɒmlɪt] *n.* Omelett, *das*

omen ['əʊmən] *n.* Vorzeichen, *das*

ominous ['ɒmɪnəs] *adj.* (*of evil omen*) ominös; (*worrying*) beunruhigend

omission [ə'mɪʃn] *n.* Auslassung, *die;* (*failure to act*) Unterlassung, *die*

omit [ə'mɪt] *v.t.,* -tt- weglassen; **~ to do sth.** es versäumen, etw. zu tun

on [ɒn] **1.** *prep.* auf (*position:* + *Dat.; direction:* + *Akk.*); (*attached to*) an (+ *Dat./Akk.*); (*concerning, about*) über (+ *Akk.*); *in expressions of time* an (*einem Abend, Tag usw.*); **write sth. on the wall** etw. an die Wand schreiben; **be hanging on the wall** an der Wand hängen; **have sth. on one** etw. bei sich haben; **on the bus/train** in Bus/Zug; (*by bus/train*) mit dem Bus/Zug; **on Oxford 56767** unter der Nummer Oxford 56767; **on Sundays** sonntags; **on [his] arrival** bei seiner

Ankunft; **on entering the room ...:** beim Betreten des Zimmers ...; **it's just on 9** es ist fast 9 Uhr; **the drinks are on me** *(coll.)* die Getränke gehen auf mich. **2.** *adv.* **with/without a hat/coat on** mit/ohne Hut/Mantel; **have a hat on** einen Hut aufhaben; **on and on** immer weiter; **speak/wait/work** *etc.* **on** weiterreden/-warten/-arbeiten *usw.;* **from now on** von jetzt an; **the light/radio** *etc.* **is on** das Licht/Radio *usw.* ist an; **is Sunday's picnic on?** findet das Picknick am Sonntag statt?; **what's on at the cinema?** was läuft im Kino?; **on and off** immer mal wieder *(ugs.);* **on to, onto auf** (+ *Akk.)*

once [wʌns] **1.** *adv.* **a)** einmal; **~ a week/month/year** einmal die Woche/ im Monat/im Jahr; **~ again** *or* **more** noch einmal; **~** [**and**] **for all** ein für allemal; **never/not ~:** nicht ein einziges Mal; **b)** *(multiplied by one)* ein mal; **c)** *(formerly)* früher einmal; **~ upon a time there lived a king** es war einmal ein König; **d) at ~ a)** *(immediately)* sofort; **(at the same time)** gleichzeitig; **all at ~** *(suddenly)* plötzlich; *(simultaneously)* alle[s] zugleich. **2.** *conj.* wenn; *(with past tense)* als. **3.** *n.* [just *or* only] **this ~:** [nur] dieses eine Mal

'oncoming *adj.* entgegenkommend ⟨Fahrzeug, Verkehr⟩

one [wʌn] **1.** *adj.* **a)** see also **eight 1;** *(single, only)* einzig; **no/not ~:** kein; **the ~ thing** das einzige; **at ~ time** einmal; **~ morning/night** eines Morgens/ Nachts. **2.** *n. a)* eins; **b)** *(number, symbol)* Eins, *die;* **c)** *(unit)* **in ~s** einzeln. **3.** *pron. a)* ein... (of + *Gen.)*; **big ~s and little ~s** große und kleine; **the older/younger ~:** der/die/das ältere/ jüngere; **this ~:** dieser/diese/dieses [da]; **that ~:** der/die/das [da]; **which ~?** welcher/welche/welches?; **which ~s?** welche?; **~ by ~:** einzeln; **love/ hate ~ another** sich lieben/hassen; **be kind to ~ another** nett zueinander sein; **b)** *(people in general; coll.: I, we)* man; *as indirect object* einem; *as direct object* einen; **~'s** sein

one-: **~'self** *pron.* **a)** *emphat.* selbst; **be ~self** man selbst sein; **b)** *refl.* sich; *see also* **herself;** **~-sided** *adj.* einseitig; **~-way** *adj.* **a)** in einer Richtung *nachgestellt;* Einbahn⟨straße, -verkehr⟩; **b)** einfach ⟨Fahrpreis, Flug⟩

onion ['ʌnjən] *n.* Zwiebel, *die*

'onlooker *n.* Zuschauer, *der/*Zuschauerin, *die*

only ['əʊnlɪ] **1.** *attrib. adj.* einzig...; **the ~ person** der/die einzige; **an ~ child** ein Einzelkind. **2.** *adv.* nur; **we had been waiting ~ 5 minutes when ...:** wir hatten erst 5 Minuten gewartet, als ...; **it's ~/~ just 6 o'clock** es ist erst 6 Uhr/ gerade erst 6 Uhr vorbei; **he ~ just made it** er hat es gerade noch geschafft; **~ if** nur [dann]..., wenn; **~ the other day/week** erst neulich

'onset *n. (of winter)* Einbruch, *der; (of disease)* Ausbruch, *der*

onslaught ['ɒnslɔːt] *n.* [heftige] Attacke *(fig.)*

onus ['əʊnəs] *n.* **the ~ is on him to do it** es ist seine Sache, es zu tun

onward[s] ['ɒnwədz] *adv. (in space)* vorwärts; **from X ~:** von X an; **from that day ~:** von diesem Tag an

ooze [uːz] **1.** *v.i.* sickern (from aus). **2.** *v.t.* triefen von *od.* vor (+ *Dat.);* *(fig.)* ausstrahlen

opaque [əʊˈpeɪk] *adj.* lichtundurchlässig; opak *(fachspr.)*

open ['əʊpn] **1.** *adj.* **a)** offen; *(not blocked or obstructed)* frei; *(available)* frei ⟨Stelle⟩; **in the ~ air** im Freien; **be ~** ⟨Laden, Museum, Bank usw.:⟩ geöffnet sein; **have an ~ mind about** *or* **on sth.** einer Sache gegenüber aufgeschlossen sein; **b)** unverhohlen ⟨Bewunderung, Haß, Verachtung⟩; **c)** *(frank, communicative)* offen ⟨Wesen, Streit, Abstimmung, Regierungsstil⟩; *(not secret)* öffentlich ⟨Wahl⟩; **d)** geöffnet ⟨Regenschirm⟩; aufgeblüht ⟨Blume, Knospe⟩; aufgeschlagen ⟨Zeitung, Landkarte⟩. **2.** *n.* **in the ~** *(outdoors)* unter freiem Himmel; [out] **the ~** *(fig.)* öffentlich bekannt. **3.** *v.t.* **a)** öffnen; **b)** eröffnen ⟨Konferenz, Diskussion, Laden⟩; beginnen ⟨Verhandlungen, Spiel⟩; **(unfold, spread out)** aufschlagen ⟨Zeitung, Landkarte⟩; öffnen ⟨Schirm⟩. **4.** *v.i.* **a)** sich öffnen; **into/on to sth.** zu etw. führen; **b)** *(become ~ to customers)* öffnen; *(start trading etc.)* eröffnet werden; **c)** *(start)* beginnen; *(Ausstellung:)* eröffnet werden; ⟨Theaterstück:⟩ Premiere haben. **open 'up 1.** *v.t.* öffnen; *(establish)* eröffnen. **2.** *v.i.* sich öffnen; ⟨Filiale:⟩ eröffnet werden; ⟨Firma:⟩ sich niederlassen

'open-air *attrib. adj.* Openair⟨konzert⟩; **~** [**swimming-**]**pool** Freibad, *das*

'opener *n.* Öffner, *der*

'opening 1. *n.* **a)** Öffnen, *das; (becoming open)* Sichöffnen, *das; (of exhibi-*

tion, new centre) Eröffnen, *das;* b) *(establishment, ceremony)* Eröffnung, *die;* c) *(initial part)* Anfang, *der;* d) *(gap, aperture)* Öffnung, *die;* e) *(opportunity)* Möglichkeit, *die; (vacancy)* freie Stelle. **2.** *adj.* einleitend. **'opening hours** n. pl. Öffnungszeiten *Pl.*

openly *adv.* a) *(publicly)* in der Öffentlichkeit; öffentlich *(zugeben, verurteilen)*; b) *(frankly)* offen

open: ~-**minded** *adj.* aufgeschlossen; ~-**plan** *adj.* ~-**plan office** Großraumbüro, *das;* ~ '**sandwich** *n.* belegtes Brot

opera ['ɒpərə] *n.* Oper, *die*

opera: ~-**glasses** *n. pl.* Opernglas, *das;* ~-**house** *n.* Opernhaus, *das;* ~-**singer** *n.* Opernsänger, *der/*-sängerin, *die*

operate ['ɒpəreɪt] **1.** *v.i.* a) *(be in action)* in Betrieb sein; *(Bus, Zug usw.:)* verkehren; b) *(function)* arbeiten; **the torch ~s on batteries** die Taschenlampe arbeitet mit Batterien; c) ~ **|on sb.|** *(Med.)* |jmdn.| operieren. **2.** *v.t.* bedienen *(Maschine)*; unterhalten *(Busverbindung, Telefondienst)*; betätigen *(Hebel, Bremse)*. **'operating-theatre** *n. (Brit. Med.)* Operationssaal, *der*

operation [ɒpə'reɪʃn] *n.* a) *(causing to work) (of machine)* Bedienung, *die; (of bus service, telephone service, etc.)* Unterhaltung, *die; (of lever, brake)* Betätigung, *die;* b) **come into** ~ *(Gesetz, Gebühr usw.:)* in Kraft treten; **be in/out of** ~ *(Maschine, Gerät usw.:)* in/außer Betrieb sein; c) *(Med.)* Operation, *die;* **have an** ~: operiert werden

operational [ɒpə'reɪʃənl] *adj. (esp. Mil.: ready to function)* einsatzbereit

operative ['ɒpərətɪv] *adj.* **become** ~ *(Gesetz:)* in Kraft treten; **the scheme is** ~: das Programm läuft

operator ['ɒpəreɪtə(r)] *n.* [Maschinen]bediener, *der/*-bedienerin, *die; (Teleph.) (at exchange)* Vermittlung, *die; (at switchboard)* Telefonist, *der/*Telefonistin, *die*

opinion [ə'pɪnjən] *n.* Meinung, *die* **(on** über + *Akk.,* zu); **have a high/low** ~ **of sb.** eine/keine hohe Meinung von jmdm. haben; **in my** ~: meiner Meinung nach. **opinionated** [ə'pɪnjəneɪtɪd] *adj.* rechthaberisch

opium ['əʊpɪəm] *n.* Opium, *das*

opponent [ə'pəʊnənt] *n.* Gegner, *der/* Gegnerin, *die*

opportune ['ɒpətjuːn] *adj.* a) *(favour-*

able) günstig; b) *(well-timed)* zur rechten Zeit *nachgestellt.* **opportunism** [ɒpə'tjuːnɪzm] *n.* Opportunismus, *der*

opportunist [ɒpə'tjuːnɪst] *n.* Opportunist, *der/*Opportunistin, *die*

opportunity [ɒpə'tjuːnɪtɪ] *n.* Gelegenheit, *die*

oppose [ə'pəʊz] **1.** *v.t.* sich wenden gegen. **2.** *v.i.* **the opposing team** die gegnerische Mannschaft. **opposed** [ə'pəʊzd] *adj.* **as** ~ **to** im Gegensatz zu; **be** ~ **to sth.** *(Personen:)* gegen etw. sein

opposite ['ɒpəzɪt] **1.** *adj.* gegenüberliegend *(Straßenseite, Ufer)*; entgegengesetzt *(Ende, Weg, Richtung)*; **the** ~ **sex** das andere Geschlecht. **2.** *n.* Gegenteil, *das* (**of** von). **3.** *adv.* gegenüber. **4.** *prep.* gegenüber

opposition [ɒpə'zɪʃn] *n.* a) Opposition, *die; (resistance)* Widerstand, *der* **(to** gegen); **in** ~ **to entgegen;** b) *(Brit. Polit.)* **the O**~: die Opposition

oppress [ə'pres] *v.t.* unterdrücken; *(fig.) (Gefühl:)* bedrücken. **oppression** [ə'preʃn] *n.* Unterdrückung, *die*

oppressive [ə'presɪv] *adj.* repressiv; *(fig.)* bedrückend *(Ängste, Atmosphäre)*; *(hot and close)* drückend *(Wetter, Klima, Tag)*

opt [ɒpt] *v.i.* sich entscheiden (**for** für); ~ **to do sth.** sich dafür entscheiden, etw. zu tun; ~ **out** nicht mitmachen/*(stop taking part)* nicht länger mitmachen (**of** bei)

optical ['ɒptɪkl] *adj.* optisch

optician [ɒp'tɪʃn] *n.* Optiker, *der/*Optikerin, *die*

optima *pl. of* **optimum**

optimism ['ɒptɪmɪzm] *n.* Optimismus, *der.* **optimist** ['ɒptɪmɪst] *n.* Optimist, *der/*Optimistin, *die.* **optimistic** [ɒptɪ'mɪstɪk] *adj.* optimistisch

optimum ['ɒptɪməm] **1.** *n., pl.* **optima** ['ɒptɪmə] Optimum, *das.* **2.** *adj.* optimal

option ['ɒpʃn] *n. (choice)* Wahl, *die; (thing)* Wahlmöglichkeit, *die.* **optional** ['ɒpʃənl] *adj.* nicht zwingend; ~ **subject** Wahlfach, *das*

opulence ['ɒpjʊləns] *n.* Wohlstand, *der*

opulent ['ɒpjʊlənt] *adj.* wohlhabend; feudal *(Auto, Haus usw.)*

or [ə(r), *stressed* ɔː(r)] *conj.* a) oder; **he cannot read or write** er kann weder lesen noch schreiben; **without food or water** ohne Essen und Wasser; **15 or 20 minutes** 15 bis 20 Minuten; **in a day**

or two in ein, zwei Tagen; b) *introducing explanation* das heißt; **or rather** beziehungsweise

oracle ['ɒrəkl] *n.* Orakel, *das*

oral ['ɔːrl] *adj.* mündlich; *(Med.)* oral

orange ['ɒrɪndʒ] 1. *n.* a) *(fruit)* Orange, *die;* Apfelsine, *die;* b) *(colour)* Orange, *das.* 2. *adj.* orange[farben]

orator ['ɒrətə(r)] *n.* Redner, *der*/Rednerin, *die*

oratory ['ɒrətərɪ] *n.* Redekunst, *die*

orbit ['ɔːbɪt] 1. *n. (Astron.)* [Umlauf]bahn, *die.* 2. *v. i.* kreisen. 3. *v. t.* umkreisen. **orbital** ['ɔːbɪtl] *adj.* ~ **road** Ringstraße, *die*

orchard ['ɔːtʃəd] *n.* Obstgarten, *der; (commercial)* Obstplantage, *die*

orchestra ['ɔːkɪstrə] *n.* Orchester, *das.* **orchestral** [ɔːˈkestrl] *adj.* Orchester-

orchid ['ɔːkɪd] *n.* Orchidee, *die*

ordain [ɔːˈdeɪn] *v. t.* a) *(Eccl.)* ordinieren; b) *(decree)* verfügen

ordeal [ɔːˈdiːl] *n.* Qual, *die*

order ['ɔːdə(r)] 1. *n.* a) *(sequence)* Reihenfolge, *die;* **out of** ~ : durcheinander; b) *(regular arrangement, normal state)* Ordnung, *die;* **be/not be in** ~ : in Ordnung/nicht in Ordnung sein *(ugs.);* **be out of/in** ~ *(not in/in working condition)* nicht funktionieren/funktionieren; **'out of** ~' „außer Betrieb"; **in good/bad** ~ : in gutem/schlechtem Zustand; c) *(command)* Anweisung, *die; (Mil.)* Befehl, *der;* d) **in** ~ **to do sth.** um etw. zu tun; e) *(Commerc.)* Auftrag, *der* (for für + Akk.); *(to waiter,* ~ed *goods)* Bestellung, *die;* f) **keep** ~ : Ordnung [be]wahren; *see also* **law & order;** g) *(religious* ~ *)* Orden, *der.* 2. *v. t.* a) *(command)* befehlen; *(Richter:)* verfügen; ~ **sb. to do sth.** jmdn. anweisen/ *(Milit.)* jmdm. befehlen, etw. zu tun; b) *(Commerc.)* bestellen **(from** bei); c) *(arrange)* ordnen

orderly ['ɔːdəlɪ] 1. *adj.* friedlich; diszipliniert *(Menge); (methodical)* methodisch; *(tidy)* ordentlich. 2. *n.* a) *(Mil.)* [Offiziers]bursche, *der;* b) **medical** ~ : ≈ Krankenpflegehelfer, *der*

ordinal ['ɔːdɪnl] *adj. & n.* ~ **[number]** Ordinalzahl, *die*

ordinary ['ɔːdɪnərɪ] *adj. (normal)* normal *(Gebrauch); (usual)* üblich *(Verfahren); (not exceptional)* gewöhnlich

ordination [ɔːdɪˈneɪʃn] *n. (Eccl.)* Ordination, *die;* Ordinierung, *die*

ore [ɔː(r)] *n.* Erz, *das*

organ ['ɔːgən] *n.* a) *(Mus.)* Orgel, *die;* b) *(Biol.)* Organ, *das*

organic [ɔːˈgænɪk] *adj.* organisch; biologisch-dynamisch *(Ackerbau);* biodynamisch *(Nahrungsmittel)*

organism ['ɔːgənɪzm] *n.* Organismus, *der*

organist ['ɔːgənɪst] *n.* Organist, *der*/Organistin, *die*

organization [ɔːgənaɪˈzeɪʃn] *n.* Organisation, *die;* ~ **of time/work** Zeit-/Arbeitseinteilung, *die*

organize ['ɔːgənaɪz] *v. t.* organisieren; einteilen *(Arbeit, Zeit);* veranstalten *(Konferenz, Festival);* ~ **into groups** in Gruppen einteilen. '**organizer** *n.* Organisator, *der*/Organisatorin, *die; (of event, festival)* Veranstalter, *der*/Veranstalterin, *die*

orgasm ['ɔːgæzm] *n.* Orgasmus, *der*

orgy ['ɔːdʒɪ] *n.* Orgie, *die*

orient 1. ['ɔːrɪənt] *n.* **the O**~: der Orient. 2. ['ɔːrɪent] *v. t.* ausrichten **(towards** nach); ~ **oneself** sich orientieren

oriental [ɔːrɪˈentl] 1. *adj.* orientalisch. 2. *n.* Asiat, *der*/Asiatin, *die*

orientate ['ɔːrɪənteɪt] *see* **orient** 2.

orientation [ɔːrɪənˈteɪʃn] *n.* Orientierung, *die*

orienteering [ɔːrɪənˈtɪərɪŋ] *n. (Brit.)* Orientierungsrennen, *das*

orifice ['ɒrɪfɪs] *n.* Öffnung, *die*

origin ['ɒrɪdʒɪn] *n. (derivation)* Herkunft, *die; (beginnings)* Anfänge *Pl.; (source)* Ursprung, *der;* **country of** ~ : Herkunftsland, *das;* **have its** ~ **in sth.** seinen Ursprung in etw. *(Dat.)* haben.

original [əˈrɪdʒɪnl] 1. *adj.* ursprünglich; Ur*(text, -fassung);* eigenständig *(Forschung); (inventive)* originell; **an** ~ **painting** ein Original. 2. *n.* Original, *das.* **originality** [ərɪdʒɪˈnælɪtɪ] *n.* Originalität, *die.* **originally** [əˈrɪdʒɪnəlɪ] *adv.* a) ursprünglich; b) originell *(schreiben usw.).* **originate** [əˈrɪdʒɪneɪt] *v. i.* ~ **from** entstehen aus; ~ **in** seinen Ursprung haben in (+ *Dat.)*

ornament ['ɔːnəmənt] *n.* Ziergegenstand, *der.* **ornamental** [ɔːnəˈmentl] *adj.* dekorativ; Zier*(pflanze, -naht usw.)*

ornate [ɔːˈneɪt] *adj.* reich verziert; prunkvoll *(Dekoration)*

ornithology [ɔːnɪˈθɒlədʒɪ] *n.* Ornithologie, *die*

orphan ['ɔːfn] 1. *n.* Waise, *die.* 2. *v. t.* **be** ~**ed** [zur] Waise werden. **orphanage** ['ɔːfənɪdʒ] *n.* Waisenhaus, *das*

orthodox ['ɔ:θədɒks] *adj.* orthodox

oscillate ['ɒsɪleɪt] *v. i.* schwingen. **oscillation** [ɒsɪ'leɪʃn] *n.* Schwingen, *das*; *(single ~)* Schwingung, *die*

ostensible [ɒ'stensɪbl] *adj.* vorgeschoben. **ostensibly** [ɒ'stensɪblɪ] *adv.* vorgeblich

ostentatious [ɒsten'teɪʃəs] *adj.* prunkhaft 〈Kleidung, Schmuck〉; prahlerisch 〈Art〉

osteopath ['ɒstɪəpæθ] *n.* Spezialist für Knochenleiden

ostrich ['ɒstrɪtʃ] *n.* Strauß, *der*

other ['ʌðə(r)] **1.** *adj.* **a)** *(not the same)* ander...; the ~ **two/three** etc. *(the remaining)* die beiden/drei usw. anderen; the ~ **one** der/die/das andere; **some** ~ **time** ein andermal; **b)** *(further)* **one** ~ **thing** noch eins; **some/six** ~ **people** noch ein paar/noch sechs [andere *od.* weitere] Leute; **no** ~ **questions** keine weiteren Fragen; **c)** ~ **than** *(different from)* anders als; *(except)* außer; **d)** the ~ **day/evening** neulich/neulich abends. **2.** *n.* anderer/andere/anderes; **there are six** ~s es sind noch sechs andere da; **any** ~: irgendein anderer/-eine andere/-ein anderes; **not any** ~: kein anderer/keine andere/kein anderes; **one after the** ~: einer/eine/eins nach dem/der/dem anderen. **3.** *adv.* anders; ~ **than that,** ...: abgesehen davon, ...

otherwise ['ʌðəwaɪz] **1.** *adv.* **a)** *(in a different way)* anders; **b)** *(or else)* anderenfalls; **c)** *(in other respects)* im übrigen. **2.** *pred. adj.* anders

otter ['ɒtə(r)] *n.* [Fisch]otter, *der*

ouch [aʊtʃ] *int.* autsch

ought [ɔ:t] *v. aux. only in pres. and past tense, neg. (coll.)* **oughtn't** ['ɔ:tnt] **I** ~ **to do/have done it** *expr. moral duty* ich müßte es tun/hätte es tun müssen; *expr. desirability* ich sollte es tun/hätte es tun sollen; ~ **not** *or* ~**n't you to have left by now?** müßtest du nicht schon weg sein?; **one** ~ **not to do it** man sollte es nicht tun; **he** ~ **to be hanged/in hospital** er gehört an den Galgen/ins Krankenhaus; **that** ~ **to be enough** das dürfte reichen; **he** ~ **to win** er müßte [eigentlich] gewinnen

oughtn't ['ɔ:tnt] *(coll.)* = **ought not**

ounce [aʊns] *n. (measure)* Unze, *die*

our ['aʊə(r)] *poss. pron. attrib.* unser

ours ['aʊəz] *poss. pron. pred.* unserer/unsere/unseres; *see also* **hers**

ourselves [aʊə'selvz] *pron.* **a)** *emphat.* selbst; **b)** *refl.* uns. *See also* **herself**

oust [aʊst] *v. t.* verdrängen; ~ **sb. from his job/from power** jmdn. von seinem Arbeitsplatz vertreiben/jmdn. entmachten

out [aʊt] *adv.* **a)** *(away from place)* ~ **here/there** hier/da draußen; **be** ~ **in the garden** draußen im Garten sein; **what's it like** ~? wie ist es draußen?; **go** ~ **shopping** etc. einkaufen usw. gehen; **be** ~ *(not at home, not in one's office, etc.)* nicht dasein; **she was** ~ **all night** sie war eine/die ganze Nacht weg; **have a day** ~ **in London** einen Tag in London verbringen; **row** ~ **to** ...: hinaus-/herausrudern zu ...; **be** ~ **at sea** auf See sein; **b)** *(Sport, Games)* **be** ~ 〈Ball:〉 aus *od.* im Aus sein; 〈Mitspieler:〉 ausscheiden; 〈Schlagmann:〉 aus[geschlagen] sein; **not** ~: nicht aus; **c)** *be* ~ *(asleep)* weg sein *(ugs.)*; *(unconscious)* bewußtlos sein; **d)** *(no longer burning)* aus[gegangen]; **e)** *(in error)* **be 3 %** ~ **in one's calculations** sich um 3 % verrechnet haben; **this is £5** ~: das stimmt um 5 Pfund nicht; **f)** *(not in fashion)* passé *(ugs.)*; **out** *(ugs.)*; **g)** **say it** ~ **loud** es laut sagen; ~ **with it!** heraus mit der Sprache; **their secret is** ~: ihr Geheimnis ist bekannt geworden; [**the**] **truth will** ~: die Wahrheit wird an den Tag kommen; **the sun/moon is** ~: die Sonne/der Mond scheint; **the third volume is just** ~: der dritte Band ist soeben erschienen; **the roses are** ~: die Rosen blühen; **h)** **be** ~ **for sth./to do sth.** auf etw. *(Akk.)* aussein, etw. zu tun; **be** ~ **for trouble** Streit suchen; **i)** *(to or at an end)* **before the day/month was** ~: am selben Tag/vor Ende des Monats. *See also* **out of**

out: ~**bid** *v. t.,* ~**bid** überbieten; ~**board** *adj.* ~**board motor** Außenbordmotor, *der;* **at the** ~**break of war** bei Kriegsausbruch; **an** ~**break of flu** eine Grippeepidemie; ~**building** *n.* Nebengebäude, *das;* ~**burst** *n.* Ausbruch, *der;* **an** ~**burst of weeping/laughter** ein Weinkrampf/Lachanfall; **an** ~**burst of temper** ein Wutanfall; ~**cast** *n.* Ausgestoßene, *der/die;* **a social** ~**cast** ein Geächteter/eine Geächtete; ~**come** *n.* Ergebnis, *das;* Resultat, *das;* ~**cry** *n.* [Aufschrei der] Empörung; ~**dated** *adj.* überholt; ~**do** *v. t.* überbieten (**in** an + *Dat.*); ~**door** *adj.* ~**door shoes/things** Straßenschuhe/-kleidung, *die;* ~**door games/pursuits** Spiele/Beschäftigungen im Freien; ~**door swimming-pool** Freibad, *das;* ~'**doors 1.** *adv.* draußen; **go** ~**doors** nach draußen gehen; **2.** *n.* **the [great]** ~**doors** die freie Natur

outer ['aʊtə(r)] *adj.* äußer...; Außen‹fläche, -seite, -wand, -tür›. **outer** '**space** *n.* Weltraum, *der*

out: ~**fit** *n.* **a)** *(clothes)* Kleider *Pl.;* **b)** *(equipment)* Ausrüstung, *die;* **c)** *(coll.: organization)* Laden, *der (ugs.);* ~**going 1.** *adj.* **a)** [aus dem Amt] scheidend ‹Regierung, Präsident›; **b)** *(friendly)* kontaktfreudig ‹Person›; **2.** *n., in pl.* ~**s** *(expenditure)* Ausgaben *Pl.;* ~'**grow** *v.i., forms as* grow *herauswachsen aus* ‹Kleider›; *(leave behind)* entwachsen (+ *Dat.*); ~**house** *n.* Nebengebäude, *das*

'**outing** *n.* Ausflug, *der*

out: ~**landish** [aʊt'lændɪʃ] *adj.* ausgefallen; ~**law 1.** *n.* Bandit, *der*/Banditin, *die;* **2.** *v.t.* verbieten; ~**lay** *n.* Ausgaben *Pl.* (on für); ~**let** ['aʊtlet, 'aʊtlɪt] *n.* **a)** Ablauf, -fluß, *der;* **b)** *(fig.)* Ventil, *das;* ~**line 1.** *n.* **a)** *in sing. or pl.* Umriß, *der;* **b)** *(short account)* Grundriß, *der;* *(of topic)* Übersicht, *die* (of über + *Akk.*); **2.** *v.t. (describe)* umreißen; ~**live** [aʊt'lɪv] *v.t.* überleben; ~**look** *n.* **a)** *(view)* Aussicht, *die* (over über + *Akk.*, on to auf + *Akk.*); *(fig.; Meteorol.)* Aussichten *Pl.;* **b)** *(mental attitude)* Einstellung, *die* (on zu); ~**lying** *adj.* entlegen; ~**moded** [aʊt'məʊdɪd] *adj.* antiquiert; ~**number** *v.t.* zahlenmäßig überlegen sein (+ *Dat.*)

'**out of** *prep.* **a)** *(from within)* aus; **go** ~ **the door** zur Tür hinausgehen; **b)** *(not within)* be ~ **the country** im Ausland sein; **be** ~ **town/the room** nicht in der Stadt/im Zimmer sein; **feel** ~ **it** *or* **things** sich ausgeschlossen fühlen; **c)** *(from among)* **one** ~ **every three smokers** jeder dritte Raucher; **58** ~ **every 100** 58 von hundert; **d)** *(beyond range of)* außer ‹Reich-/Hörweite, Sicht, Kontrolle›; **e)** *(from)* aus; **get money** ~ **sb.** Geld aus jmdm. herausholen; **do well** ~ **sb./sth.** von jmdm./ etw. profitieren; **f)** aus ‹Mitleid, Furcht, Neugier usw.›; **g)** *(without)* ~ **money** ohne Geld; **we're** ~ **tea** wir haben keinen Tee mehr; **h)** *(away from)* von ... entfernt; **ten miles** ~ **London** 10 Meilen außerhalb von London

out: ~-**of**-'**date** *attrib. adj.* veraltet;

(expired) ungültig ‹Karte›; ~-**patient** *n.* ambulanter Patient/ambulante Patientin; ~-**patients[' department]** Poliklinik, *die;* ~'**play** *v.t. (Sport)* besser spielen als; ~**post** *n.* Außenposten, *der; (of civilization etc.; also Mil.)* Vorposten, *der;* ~**put** *n.* Produktion, *die; (of liquid, electricity, etc.)* Leistung, *die; (Computing)* Ausgabe, *die*

outrage 1. ['aʊtreɪdʒ] *n.* **a)** *(deed)* Verbrechen, *das; (during war)* Greueltat, *die; (against decency)* grober Verstoß; **b)** *(strong resentment)* Empörung, *die* (at gegen). **2.** [aʊt'reɪdʒ] *v.t.* empören.

outrageous [aʊt'reɪdʒəs] *adj.* unverschämt; unverschämt hoch ‹Preis›; unerhört ‹Frechheit, Skandal›

out: ~**right 1.** [-'-] *adv.* **a)** ganz, komplett ‹kaufen, verkaufen›; **b)** *(openly)* freiheraus ‹erzählen, sagen, lachen›; **2.** ['--] *adj.* ausgemacht ‹Unehrlichkeit›; glatt *(ugs.)* ‹Ablehnung, Absage, Lüge›; klar ‹Sieg, Niederlage, Sieger›; ~**set** *n.* Anfang, *der;* **at the** ~**set** zu Anfang; **from the** ~**set** von Anfang an

outside 1. [-'-, '--] *n.* **a)** Außenseite, *die;* **on the** ~: außen; **to/from the** ~: nach/von außen; **b)** *(external appearance)* Äußere, *das;* **c)** **at the [very]** ~ *(coll.)* äußerstenfalls; höchstens. **2.** ['--] *adj.* **a)** äußer...; Außen‹wand, -antenne, -kajüte, -toilette, -durchmesser›; ~ **lane** Überholspur, *die;* **b)** **have only an** ~ **chance** nur eine sehr geringe Chance haben. **3.** [-'-] *adv. (on the* ~) draußen; *(to the* ~) nach draußen. **4.** [-'-] *prep.* **a)** *(position)* außerhalb (+ *Gen.*); ~ **the door** vor der Tür; **b)** *(to the* ~ *of)* aus ... hinaus; **go** ~ **the house** nach draußen gehen. **out-'sider** *n. (Sport; also fig.)* Außenseiter, *der*

out: ~**size** *adj.* überdimensional; ~**size clothes** Kleidung in Übergröße; ~**skirts** *n. pl.* Stadtrand, *der;* **the** ~**skirts of the town** die Außenbezirke der Stadt; ~'**spoken** *adj.* freimütig; **be** ~ **about sth.** sich freimütig über etw. äußern; ~-'**standing** *adj.* **a)** *(exceptional)* hervorragend; überragend ‹Bedeutung›; außergewöhnlich ‹Person, Mut, Fähigkeit›; **b)** *(not yet settled)* ausstehend ‹Schuld, Geldsumme›; unbezahlt ‹Rechnung›; ungelöst ‹Problem›; ~'**standingly** *adv.* außergewöhnlich; ~**stretched** *adj.* ausgestreckt; *(spread out)* ausgebreitet; ~'**strip** *v.t. (pass in running)* überholen; *(in competition)* überflügeln;

~-tray n. Ablage für Ausgänge; **~vote** v.t. überstimmen

outward ['aʊtwəd] **1.** adj. a) (external, apparent) [rein] äußerlich; äußere ⟨Erscheinung, Bedingung⟩; b) Hin⟨reise, -fracht⟩. **2.** adv. nach außen ⟨aufgehen, richten⟩. '**outwardly** adv. nach außen hin ⟨Gefühle zeigen⟩; öffentlich ⟨Loyalität erklären⟩. '**outwards** see outward 2

out: ~**weigh** v.t. schwerer wiegen als; überwiegen ⟨Nachteile⟩; ~'**wit** v.t., **-tt-** überlisten

oval ['əʊvl] **1.** adj. oval. n. Oval, das

ovation [əʊ'veɪʃn] n. Ovation, die; a **standing ~:** stehende Ovationen

oven ['ʌvn] n. [Back]ofen, der

oven: ~**-glove** n. Topfhandschuh, der; ~**-proof** adj. feuerfest; ~**-ready** adj. backfertig ⟨Pommes frites, Pastete⟩; bratfertig ⟨Geflügel⟩

over ['əʊvə(r)] **1.** adv. a) (outward and downward) hinüber; **climb/look/jump ~:** hinüber- od. (ugs.) rüberklettern/ -sehen/-springen; b) (so as to cover surface) **board/cover ~:** zunageln/ -decken; c) (across a space) hinüber; (towards speaker) herüber; **he swam ~ to us/the other side** er schwamm zu uns herüber/hinüber zur anderen Seite; ~ **here/there** (direction) hier herüber/dort hinüber; (location) hier/ dort; |**come in, please,**| ~ (Radio) übernehmen Sie bitte; ~ **and out** (Radio) Ende; d) (in excess etc.) **children of 12 and ~:** Kinder im Alter von zwölf Jahren und darüber; **be** |**left**| ~: übrig[ge]blieben] sein; e) (from beginning to end) von Anfang bis Ende; **say sth. twice ~:** etw. zweimal sagen; |**all**| ~ **again,** (Amer.) ~: noch einmal [von vorn]; ~ **and** ~ |**again**| immer wieder; f) (at an end) vorbei; vorüber; **be ~:** vorbei sein; ⟨Aufführung:⟩ zu Ende sein; **get sth. ~ with** etw. hinter sich (Akk.) bringen; **be ~ and done with** erledigt sein; g) **all ~** (completely finished) aus [und vorbei]; **I ache all ~:** mir tut alles weh; **be shaking all ~:** am ganzen Körper zittern. **2.** prep. a) (above, on, round about) über (position: + Dat.; direction: + Akk.); (across) über (+ Akk.); **look ~ a wall** über eine Mauer sehen; **fall ~ a cliff** von einem Felsen stürzen; **the pub ~ the road** die Wirtschaft gegenüber; **hit sb. ~ the head** jmdm. auf den Kopf schlagen; ~ **the page** auf der nächsten Seite; b) (in or across every part of)

[überall] in (+ Dat.); (to and fro upon) über (+ Akk.); (all through) durch; **all ~** (in or on all parts of) überall in (+ Dat.); **travel all ~ the country** das ganze Land bereisen; **all ~ Spain** in ganz Spanien; **all ~ the world** in der ganzen Welt; c) (on account of) wegen; d) (engaged with) bei; **take trouble ~ sth.** sich (Dat.) mit etw. Mühe geben; **be a long time ~ sth.** lange für etw. brauchen; ~ **work/dinner** bei der Arbeit/beim Essen; e) (superior to, in charge of) über (+ Akk.); **have command/authority ~ sb.** Befehlsgewalt über jmdn./Weisungsbefugnis gegenüber jmdm. haben; **be ~ sb.** (in rank) über jmdm. stehen; f) (beyond, more than) über (+ Akk.); ~ **and above** zusätzlich zu; g) (throughout, during) über (+ Akk.); ~ **the weekend/summer** übers Wochenende/den Sommer über; ~ **the past years** in den letzten Jahren

over: ~**all 1.** n. (Brit.: garment) Arbeitskittel, der; **2.** adj. a) Gesamt- ⟨breite, -einsparung, -abmessung⟩; **have an ~all majority** die absolute Mehrheit haben; b) (general) allgemein; **3.** ['---, --'] adv. a) (in all parts) insgesamt; b) (taken as a whole) im großen und ganzen; ~**awe** v.t. Ehrfurcht einflößen (+ Dat.); ~**balance** v.i. das Gleichgewicht verlieren; ~**bearing** adj. herrisch; ~**board** adv. über Bord; **fall ~board** über Bord gehen; ~**cast** adj. trübe; bewölkt ⟨Himmel⟩; ~**charge** v.t. a) (beyond reasonable price) zuviel abverlangen (+ Dat.); b) (beyond right price) zuviel berechnen (+ Dat.); ~**coat** n. Mantel, der; ~**come** v.t., forms as **come:** a) überwinden; bezwingen ⟨Feind⟩; ⟨Dämpfe:⟩ betäuben; b) **he was ~come by grief/with emotion** Kummer/Rührung überwältigte ihn; ~**-cooked** adj. verkocht; ~**crowded** adj. überfüllt; ~**do** v.t. (carry to excess) übertreiben; ~**do it** or **things** (work too hard) sich übernehmen; ~**done** adj. a) (exaggerated) übertrieben; b) (~cooked) verkocht; verbraten ⟨Fleisch⟩; ~**dose** n. Überdosis, die; ~**draft** n. Kontoüberziehung, die; **have an ~draft of £50** sein Konto um 50 Pfund überzogen haben; ~**draw** v.t., forms as **draw 1** überziehen ⟨Konto⟩; ~**drawn** adj. überzogen ⟨Konto⟩; **I am ~drawn** |**at the bank**| mein Konto ist überzogen;

~**drive** n. Schongang, der; ~'**due** adj. überfällig; **the train is 15 minutes** ~**due** der Zug hat schon 15 Minuten Verspätung; ~'**eat** v. i., forms as eat zuviel essen; ~**estimate** 1. [~'estɪmeɪt] v. t. überschätzen; 2. [~'estɪmət] n. zu hohe Schätzung; ~'**fill** v. t. zu voll machen; ~'**flow** 1. [--'-] v. i. laufen über (+ Akk.) ⟨Rand⟩; (flow over brim of) überlaufen aus; ~'**flow its banks** ⟨Fluß:⟩ über die Ufer treten; 2. [--'-] v. i. überlaufen; 3. ['---] n. ~**flow** [pipe] Überlauf, der; ~'**full** adj. zu voll; übervoll; ~**grown** adj. überwachsen (with von); ~'**hang** 1. [--'-] v. t., ~**hung** [əʊvə'hʌŋ] ⟨Felsen, Stockwerk:⟩ hinausragen über (+ Akk.); 2. ['---] n. Überhang, der; ~'**hanging** adj. überhängend; ~'**haul** 1. [--'-] v. t. überholen; überprüfen ⟨System⟩; 2. ['---] n. Überholung, die; ~**head** 1. [--'-] adv. über mir/ihm/uns usw.; 2. ['---] adj. ~**head wires** Oberleitung, die; 3. ['---] n. ~**heads**, (Amer.) ~**head** (Commerc.) Gemeinkosten Pl.; ~'**hear** v. t., forms as hear 1 (accidentally) zufällig [mit]hören; (intentionally) belauschen; ~'**heat** v. i. zu heiß werden; ⟨Maschine, Lager:⟩ heißlaufen

overjoyed [əʊvə'dʒɔɪd] adj. überglücklich (**at** über + Akk.)

over: ~**lap** 1. [--'-] v. t. überlappen; 2. [--'-] v. i. ⟨Flächen, Dachziegel:⟩ sich überlappen ⟨Aufgaben:⟩ sich überschneiden; 3. n. Überlappung, die; ~'**leaf** adv. auf der Rückseite; ~'**load** v. t. überladen; ~'**look** v. t. a) ⟨Hotel, Zimmer, Haus:⟩ Aussicht bieten auf (+ Akk.); b) (ignore, not see) übersehen; (allow to go unpunished) hinwegsehen über (+ Akk.)

'**overly** adv. allzu

over: ~**night** 1. [--'-] adv. (also fig.: suddenly) über Nacht; **stay** ~ **night** übernachten; 2. ['---] adj. ~**night stay** Übernachtung, die; **be an** ~**night success** (fig.) über Nacht Erfolg haben; ~'**pay** v. t., forms as pay 2 überbezahlen; ~'**power** v. t. überwältigen; ~'**powering** adj. überwältigend; durchdringend ⟨Geruch:⟩; ~'**priced** adj. zu teuer; ~'**rate** v. t. überschätzen; ~**re'act** v. i. unangemessen heftig reagieren (**to** auf + Akk.); ~**re'action** n. Überreaktion, die (**to** auf + Akk.); ~'**ride** v. t. forms as ride 3 sich hinwegsetzen über (+ Akk.); ~'**ripe** adj. überreif; ~'**rule** v. t. auf-

heben ⟨Entscheidung⟩; zurückweisen ⟨Einwand, Argument⟩; ~**rule** sb. jmds. Vorschlag ablehnen; ~'**run** v. t., forms as run 3: **be** ~**run with** überlaufen sein von ⟨Touristen⟩; überwuchert sein von ⟨Unkraut⟩; ~**seas** 1. [--'-] adv. in Übersee ⟨leben, sein⟩; nach Übersee ⟨gehen⟩; 2. ['---] adj. Übersee-; ~'**see** v. t., forms as see 1 überwachen; (manage) leiten ⟨Abteilung⟩; ~'**shadow** v. t. überschatten; ~'**shoot** v. t., forms as shoot 1 hinausschießen über (+ Akk.); ~'**shoot [the runway]** ⟨Pilot, Flugzeug:⟩ zu weit kommen; ~'**sight** n. Versehen, das; ~'**sleep**, forms as sleep 2 verschlafen; ~'**spend** v. i., forms as spend zuviel [Geld] ausgeben; ~'**statement** n. Übertreibung, die; ~'**step** v. t. überschreiten

overt [əʊ'vɜːt] adj. unverhohlen

over: ~'**take** v. t. überholen; '**no** ~**taking**' (Brit.) „Überholen verboten"; ~'**throw** 1. [--'-] v. t. forms as throw 1 stürzen; 2. ['---] n. Sturz, der; ~**time** 1. n. Überstunden; 2. adv. **work** ~**time** Überstunden machen; ~**tone** n. (fig.) Unterton, der

overture ['əʊvətjʊə(r)] n. (Mus.) Ouvertüre, die

over: ~'**turn** 1. v. t. umstoßen; 2. v. i. ⟨Auto, Boot:⟩ umkippen; ⟨Boot:⟩ kentern; ~**use** [əʊvə'juːz] v. t. zu oft verwenden; ~**weight** [əʊvə'weɪt] adj. übergewichtig ⟨Person⟩; **be** ~**weight** Übergewicht haben

overwhelm [əʊvə'welm] v. t. überwältigen. **over'whelming** adj. überwältigend

over: ~'**work** 1. v. t. mit Arbeit überlasten; 2. v. i. sich überarbeiten; ~'**wrought** adj. überreizt

owe [əʊ] v. t., **owing** ['əʊɪŋ] schulden; ~ **sb. sth.**, ~ **sth. to sb.** jmdm. etw. schulden; (fig.) jmdm. etw. verdanken. **owing** ['əʊɪŋ] pred. adj. ausstehend; **be** ~: ausstehen. '**owing to** prep. wegen

owl [aʊl] n. Eule, die

own [əʊn] 1. adj. eigen; **be sb.'s** ~ [property] jmdm. selbst gehören; **a house/ideas of one's** ~: ein eigenes Haus/eigene Ideen; **on one's/its** ~: allein. 2. v. t. besitzen; **be** ~**ed by sb.** jmdm. gehören. **own 'up** v. i. gestehen; ~ **up to sth.** etw. zugeben

'**owner** n. Besitzer, der/Besitzerin, die; (of shop, hotel, firm, etc.) Inhaber, der/Inhaberin, die. '**ownership** n. Besitz, der

ox [ɒks] *n., pl.* **oxen** ['ɒksn] Ochse, *der*
oxygen ['ɒksɪdʒən] *n.* Sauerstoff, *der*
oyster ['ɔɪstə(r)] *n.* Auster, *die*
oz. *abbr.* ounce|s|
ozone ['əʊzəʊn] *n.* Ozon, *das.*
'**ozone-friendly** *adj.* ozonsicher;
(not using (CFCs) FCKW-frei. '**ozone
layer** *n.* Ozonschicht, *die*

P

P, p [piː] *n.* P, p, *das*
p. *abbr.* a) page S.; b) *(Brit.)* penny/
pence p
pace [peɪs] 1. *n.* a) *(step)* Schritt, *der;*
b) *(speed)* Tempo, *das;* **keep ~ with**
Schritt halten mit. 2. *v. i.* **~ up and
down** auf und ab gehen. 3. *v. t.* auf-
und abgehen in (+ *Dat.*)
'**pacemaker** *n. (Sport, Med.)* Schritt-
macher, *der*
Pacific [pə'sɪfɪk] 1. *adj. (Geog.)* **~
Ocean** Pazifischer *od.* Stiller Ozean.
2. *n.* **the ~:** der Pazifik
pacifier ['pæsɪfaɪə(r)] *n. (Amer.:
dummy)* Schnuller, *der*
pacifism ['pæsɪfɪzm] *n.* Pazifismus,
der. **pacifist** ['pæsɪfɪst] 1. *n.* Pazifist,
der/Pazifistin, *die.* 2. *adj.* pazifistisch
pacify ['pæsɪfaɪ] *v. t.* besänftigen
pack [pæk] 1. *n.* a) *(bundle)* Bündel,
das; (Mil.) Tornister, *der; (rucksack)*
Rucksack, *der;* b) *(derog.: lot) (people)*
Bande, *die;* **a ~ of lies/nonsense** ein
Sack voll Lügen/eine Menge Unsinn;
c) *(Brit.)* **~ |of cards|** [Karten]spiel,
das; d) *(wolves, wild dogs)* Rudel, *das;*
(hounds) Meute, *die;* e) *(packet)*
Packung, *die.* 2. *v. t.* a) einpacken;
(fill) packen; **~ one's bags** seine Koffer packen; b) *(cram)* vollstopfen
(ugs.); c) *(wrap)* verpacken (in in +
Dat. od. Akk.). 3. *v. i* packen; **send sb.
~ing** *(fig.)* jmdn. rausschmeißen
(ugs.). **pack 'up** 1. *v. t.* zusammen-
packen *(Sachen, Werkzeug);* packen
(Paket). 2. *v. i. (coll.: stop)* aufhören
package ['pækɪdʒ] 1. *n.* Paket, *das.* 2.
v. t. verpacken
package: ~ deal *n.* Paket, *das;* **~**

holiday, ~ tour *ns.* Pauschalreise,
die
packed [pækt] *adj.* a) gepackt; **~
lunch** Lunchpaket, *das;* b) *(crowded)*
[über]voll; **~ out** gerammelt voll *(ugs.)*
packet ['pækɪt] *n.* Päckchen, *das;
(box)* Schachtel, *die;* **a ~ of cigarettes**
ein Päckchen/eine Schachtel Zigaretten
'**packing** *n. (material)* Verpackungs-
material, *das; postage and* **~:** Porto
und Verpackung. '**packing-case** *n.*
[Pack]kiste, *die*
pact [pækt] *n.* Pakt, *der*
'**pad** [pæd] 1. *n.* Polster, *das; (block of
paper)* Block, *der.* 2. *v. t.,* **-dd-** polstern *(Jacke, Schulter).* **pad 'out** *v. t.
(fig.)* auswalzen
²**pad** *v. i.,* **-dd-** tappen
padding ['pædɪŋ] *n.* Polsterung, *die;
(fig.)* Füllsel, *das*
'**paddle** ['pædl] 1. *n.* [Stech]paddel,
das. 2. *v. t. & i.* paddeln
²**paddle** 1. *v. i. (with feet)* planschen.
2. *n.* **have a/go for a ~:** ein bißchen planschen/planschen gehen.
paddling-pool ['pædlɪŋpuːl] *n.*
Planschbecken, *das*
paddock ['pædək] *n.* Koppel, *die*
'**padlock** 1. *n.* Vorhängeschloß, *das.*
2. *v. t.* [mit einem Vorhängeschloß]
verschließen
pagan ['peɪgən] 1. *n.* Heide, *der/*Hei-
din, *die.* 2. *adj.* heidnisch
'**page** [peɪdʒ] *n. (boy)* Page, *der*
²**page** *n. (of book etc.)* Seite, *die*
pageant ['pædʒənt] *n. (spectacle)*
Schauspiel, *das.* **pageantry** ['pæ-
dʒəntrɪ] *n.* Prunk, *der*
paid [peɪd] 1. *see* **pay** 2, 3. 2. *adj.* a) bezahlt *(Urlaub, Arbeit);* b) **put ~ to**
(Brit. coll.) zunichte machen; kurzen
Prozeß machen mit *(ugs.) (Person)*
pail [peɪl] *n.* Eimer, *der*
pain [peɪn] *n.* a) *(suffering)* Schmerzen; *(mental* ~) Qualen; **be in ~:**
Schmerzen haben; b) *(instance)*
Schmerz, *der;* **I have a ~ in my knee/
stomach** mein Knie/Magen tut weh; c)
in pl. (trouble taken) Mühe, *die;* **take
~s** *sich (Dat.)* Mühe geben (over mit,
bei). **painful** ['peɪnfl] *adj.* a) schmerzhaft; **be ~** *(Körperteil:)* weh tun; b)
(distressing) schmerzlich *(Gedanke,
Erinnerung);* traurig *(Pflicht).* '**pain-
killer** *n.* schmerzstillendes Mittel.
'**painless** *adj.* schmerzlos; *(fig.)* un-
problematisch. **painstaking** ['peɪnz-
teɪkɪŋ] *adj.* gewissenhaft

paint [peɪnt] 1. *n.* Farbe, *die; (on car)* Lack, *der.* 2. *v.t. (cover, colour)* [an]streichen; *(make picture of, make by ~ing)* malen; bemalen ⟨*Wand, Vase, Decke*⟩. **'paintbox** *n.* Malkasten, *der;* **~brush** *n.* Pinsel, *der*

'painter *n.* Maler, *der*/Malerin, *die*

'painting *n. (art)* Malerei, *die; (picture)* Gemälde, *das;* Bild, *das*

pair [peə(r)] 1. *n.* Paar, *das;* **a ~ of** gloves/socks/shoes *etc.* ein Paar Handschuhe/Socken/Schuhe *usw.;* in ~s paarweise; **a ~ of** trousers/jeans eine Hose/Jeans. 2. *v.t.* paaren. **pair 'off** *v.i.* Zweiergruppen bilden

pajamas [pə'dʒɑːməz] *(Amer.) see* **pyjamas**

Pakistan [pɑːkɪ'stɑːn] *pr. n.* Pakistan *(das).* **Pakistani** [pɑːkɪ'stɑːnɪ] 1. *adj.* pakistanisch. 2. *n.* Pakistani, *der/die*

pal [pæl] *n. (coll.)* Kumpel, *der (ugs.)*

palace ['pælɪs] *n.* Palast, *der*

palate ['pælət] *n.* Gaumen, *der*

palatial [pə'leɪʃl] *adj.* palastartig

¹pale [peɪl] *adj.* blaß, *(nearly white)* bleich ⟨*Gesichtsfarbe, Haut, Gesicht*⟩; blaß ⟨*Farbe*⟩; fahl ⟨*Licht*⟩; **go ~:** blaß/bleich werden; *(fig.)* **~ imitation** schlechte Nachahmung

²pale *n.* **beyond the ~:** unmöglich

Palestine ['pælɪstaɪn] *pr. n.* Palästina *(das).* **Palestinian** [pælɪ'stɪnɪən] 1. *adj.* palästinensisch. 2. *n.* Palästinenser, *der/*Palästinenserin, *die*

palette ['pælɪt] *n.* Palette, *die*

¹pall [pɔːl] *n.* **a)** *(over coffin)* Sargtuch, *das;* **b)** *(fig.)* Schleier, *der*

²pall *v.i.* ~ [**on sb.**] [jmdm.] langweilig werden

pallor ['pælə(r)] *n.* Blässe, *die*

¹palm [pɑːm] *n. (tree)* Palme, *die*

²palm *n.* Handteller, *der.* **palm 'off** *v.t.* ~ **sth. off on sb.,** ~ **sb. off with sth.** jmdm. etw. andrehen *(ugs.)*

palmistry ['pɑːmɪstrɪ] *n.* Handlesekunst, *die*

palm: **P~ 'Sunday** *n.* Palmsonntag, *der;* **~-tree** *n.* Palme, *die*

paltry ['pɔːltrɪ, 'pɒltrɪ] *adj.* schäbig

pamper ['pæmpə(r)] *v.t.* verhätscheln; ~ **oneself** sich verwöhnen

pamphlet ['pæmflɪt] *n. (leaflet)* Prospekt, *der; (booklet)* Broschüre, *die*

pan [pæn] *n.* [Koch]topf, *der; (for frying)* Pfanne, *die*

panacea [pænə'sɪə] *n.* Allheilmittel, *das*

Panama [pænə'mɑː] *pr. n.* Panama *(das);* ~ **Ca'nal** Panamakanal, *der*

'pancake *n.* Pfannkuchen, *der*

panda ['pændə] *n.* Panda, *der*

pandemonium [pændɪ'məʊnɪəm] *n.* Chaos, *das; (uproar)* Tumult, *der*

pander ['pændə(r)] *v.i.* ~ **to** allzu sehr entgegenkommen (+ *Dat.*)

pane [peɪn] *n.* Scheibe, *die*

panel ['pænl] *n.* **a)** Paneel, *das;* **b)** *(esp. Telev., Radio, etc.) (quiz team)* Rateteam, *das; (in public discussion)* Podium, *das*

pang [pæŋ] *n. (of pain)* Stich, *der;* **feel ~s of conscience/guilt** Gewissensbisse haben; **~|s| of hunger** quälender Hunger

panic ['pænɪk] 1. *n.* Panik, *die;* **hit the ~ button** *(fig. coll.)* Alarm schlagen; *(~)* durchdrehen *(ugs.).* 2. *v.i.,* **-ck-** in Panik *(Akk.)* geraten; **don't ~!** nur keine Panik! **'panic-stricken,** **'panic-struck** *adjs.* von Panik erfaßt

panorama [pænə'rɑːmə] *n.* Panorama, *das*

pansy ['pænzɪ] *n.* Stiefmütterchen, *das*

pant [pænt] *v.i.* keuchen; ⟨*Hund:*⟩ hecheln

panther ['pænθə(r)] *n.* Panther, *der*

panties ['pæntɪz] *n. pl. (coll.)* |**pair of**| ~: Schlüpfer, *der*

pantomime ['pæntəmaɪm] *n. (Brit.)* Märchenspiel im Varietéstil, *das um Weihnachten aufgeführt wird*

pantry ['pæntrɪ] *n.* Speisekammer, *die*

pants [pænts] *n. pl.* **a)** *(esp. Amer. coll.: trousers)* |**pair of**| ~: Hose, *die;* **b)** *(Brit. coll.: underpants)* Unterhose, *die*

paper ['peɪpə(r)] 1. *n.* **a)** *(material)* Papier, *das;* **b)** *in pl. (documents)* Unterlagen *Pl.; (to prove identity etc.)* Papiere *Pl.;* **c)** *(in examination) (Univ.)* Klausur, *die; (Sch.)* Arbeit, *die;* **d)** *(newspaper)* Zeitung, *die;* **e)** *(learned article)* Referat, *das.* 2. *adj.* aus Papier *nachgestellt;* Papier⟨*mütze, -taschentuch*⟩. 3. *v.t.* tapezieren

paper: **~back** 1. *n.* Paperback, *das;* 2. *adj.* **~back book** Paperback, *das;* **~'bag** *n.* Papiertüte, *die;* **~-clip** *n.* Büroklammer, *die; (larger)* Aktenklammer, *die;* **~weight** *n.* Briefbeschwerer, *der;* **~work** *n.* Schreibarbeit, *die*

par [pɑː(r)] *n.* **feel below ~:** nicht ganz auf dem Posten sein *(ugs.);* **be on a ~ with sb./sth.** jmdm./einer Sache gleichkommen

parable ['pærəbl] *n.* Gleichnis, *das*

parachute ['pærəʃuːt] 1. *n.* Fallschirm, *der.* 2. *v.i.* ⟨*Truppen:*⟩ abspringen (**into** über + *Dat.*)

parade [pə'reɪd] 1. *n.* a) *(display)* Zurschaustellung, *die;* b) *(Mil.)* Appell, *der;* c) *(procession)* Umzug, *der; (of troops)* Parade, *die.* 2. *v. t.* zur Schau stellen. 3. *v. i.* paradieren

paradise ['pærədaɪs] *n.* Paradies, *das*

paradox ['pærədɒks] *n.* Paradox[on], *das.* **paradoxical** [pærə'dɒksɪkl] *adj.* paradox

paraffin ['pærəfɪn] *n.* Paraffin, *das; (Brit.: fuel)* Petroleum, *das*

paragon ['pærəgən] Muster, *das (of* an + *Dat.);* ~ **of virtue** Tugendheld, *der*

paragraph ['pærəgrɑːf] *n.* Absatz, *der*

parallel ['pærəlel] 1. *adj.* parallel; *(fig.: similar)* vergleichbar; ~ **bars** Barren, *der.* 2. *n.* Parallele, *die;* ~ [of latitude] Breitenkreis, *der*

paralyse ['pærəlaɪz] *v. t.* lähmen; *(fig.)* lahmlegen (*Verkehr, Industrie*). **paralysis** [pə'rælɪsɪs] *n.* Lähmung, *die*

paralyze *(Amer.) see* **paralyse**

paramount ['pærəmaʊnt] *adj.* größt... (*Wichtigkeit*); Haupt(*überlegung*); **be** ~: Vorrang haben

paranoia [pærə'nɔɪə] *n.* Paranoia, *die (Med.); (tendency)* Verfolgungswahn, *der.* **paranoid** ['pærənɔɪd] *adj.* **be** ~ (*Person:*) an Verfolgungswahn leiden

parapet ['pærəpɪt] *n.* Brüstung, *die*

paraphernalia [pærəfə'neɪlɪə] *n. sing.* Apparat, *der*

paraphrase ['pærəfreɪz] 1. *n.* Umschreibung, *die.* 2. *v. t.* umschreiben

parasite ['pærəsaɪt] *n.* Schmarotzer, *der.* **parasitic** [pærə'sɪtɪk] *adj.* a) *(Biol.)* parasitisch; b) *(fig.)* schmarotzerhaft

parasol ['pærəsɒl] *n.* Sonnenschirm, *der*

paratroops ['pærətruːps] *n. pl.* Fallschirmjäger *Pl.*

parcel ['pɑːsl] *n.* Paket, *das*

parched [pɑːtʃt] *adj.* ausgedörrt; trocken (*Lippen*)

parchment ['pɑːtʃmənt] *n.* Pergament, *das*

pardon ['pɑːdn] 1. *n.* Verzeihung, *die;* **beg sb.'s** ~: jmdn. um Entschuldigung bitten; **I beg your** ~: entschuldigen Sie bitte. 2. *v. t.* a) ~ **sb. [for] sth.** jmdm. etw. verzeihen; b) *(excuse)* entschuldigen. **pardonable** ['pɑːdənəbl] *adj.* verzeihlich

pare [peə(r)] *v. t. (trim)* schneiden; *(peel)* schälen

parent ['peərənt] *n.* Elternteil, *der;* ~**s** Eltern *Pl.*

parenthesis [pə'renθɪsɪs] *n., pl.* **parentheses** [pə'renθɪsiːz] *(bracket)* runde Klammer

Paris ['pærɪs] *pr. n.* Paris *(das)*

parish ['pærɪʃ] *n.* Gemeinde, *die.* **parishioner** [pə'rɪʃənə(r)] *n.* Gemeinde[mit]glied, *das*

park [pɑːk] 1. *n.* Park, *der.* 2. *v. i.* parken. 3. *v. t.* abstellen; parken (*Kfz*); **a** ~**ed car** ein parkendes Auto. '**parking** *n.* Parken, *das;* 'No ~' „Parken verboten"

parking: ~**-light** *n.* Parkleuchte, *die;* ~**-lot** *n. (Amer.)* Parkplatz, *der;* ~**-meter** *n.* Parkuhr, *die;* ~**-space** *n.* a) *no pl.* Parkraum, *der;* b) *(single space)* Parkplatz, *der;* ~**-ticket** *n.* Strafzettel [für falsches Parken]

parliament ['pɑːləmənt] *n.* Parlament, *das;* [**Houses of] P**~ *(Brit.)* Parlament, *das.* **parliamentary** [pɑːlə'mentərɪ] *adj.* parlamentarisch; Parlaments(*geschäfte, -wahlen, -reform*)

parlour *(Brit.; Amer.: parlor)* ['pɑːlə(r)] *n. (dated)* Wohnzimmer, *das*

parochial [pə'rəʊkɪəl] *adj.* krähwinklig

parody ['pærədɪ] 1. *n.* Parodie, *die (of* auf + *Akk.).* 2. *v. t.* parodieren

parole [pə'rəʊl] *n.* bedingter Straferlaß *(Rechtsw.);* **on** ~: auf Bewährung

parquet ['pɑːkɪ, 'pɑːkeɪ] *n.* ~ [**floor/ flooring**] Parkett, *das*

parrot ['pærət] *n.* Papagei, *der*

parry ['pærɪ] *v. t.* abwehren (*Faustschlag*); *(Fencing; also fig.)* parieren

parsley ['pɑːslɪ] *n.* Petersilie, *die*

parsnip ['pɑːsnɪp] *n.* Gemeiner Pastinak, *der*

parson ['pɑːsn] *n.* Pfarrer, *der*

part [pɑːt] 1. *n.* a) Teil, *der;* **the greater** ~: der größte Teil; der Großteil; **for the most** ~: größtenteils; **in** ~: teilweise; **in large** ~: groß[en]teils; **in** ~**s** zum Teil; b) *(of machine)* [Einzel]teil, *das;* c) *(share)* Anteil, *der;* d) *(Theatre)* Rolle, *die;* e) *(Mus.)* Part, *der;* Stimme, *die;* f) *usu. in pl. (region)* Gegend, *die; (of continent, world)* Teil, *der;* g) *(side)* Partei, *die;* **take sb.'s** ~: jmds. od. für jmdn. Partei ergreifen; h) **take [no]** ~ [**in sth.**] [nicht] (an etw. *Dat.*]) [nicht] beteiligen; i) **take sth. in good** ~: etw. nicht übelnehmen. 2. *adv.* teils. 3. *v. t.* a) *(divide into* ~*s)* teilen; scheiteln (*Haar*); b) *(separate)* trennen. 4. *v. i.* (*Seil, Tau, Kette:*) reißen; (*Wege, Personen:*) sich trennen; ~ **with** sich trennen von (*Besitz, Geld*)

partial ['pɑːʃl] *adj.* a) *(biased)* voreingenommen; b) **be/not be ~ to sth.** eine Schwäche/keine besondere Vorliebe für etw. haben; c) partiell ⟨*Lähmung, Sonnenfinsternis*⟩; **a ~ success** ein Teilerfolg. **partially** *adv.* teilweise

participant [pɑːˈtɪsɪpənt] *n.* Beteiligte, *der/die* (in an + *Dat.*)

participate [pɑːˈtɪsɪpeɪt] *v.i.* sich beteiligen (in an + *Dat.*); *(in arranged event)* teilnehmen (in an + *Dat.*).

participation [pɑːtɪsɪˈpeɪʃn] *n.* Beteiligung, *die* (in an + *Dat.*); *(in arranged event)* Teilnahme, *die* (in bei, an + *Dat.*)

participle ['pɑːtɪsɪpl] *n.* Partizip, *das*

particle ['pɑːtɪkl] *n.* Teilchen, *das*

particular [pəˈtɪkjʊlə(r)] 1. *adj.* a) besonder...; **here in ~:** besonders hier; **nothing/anything** [in] **~:** nichts/irgend etwas Besonderes; b) *(fastidious)* genau; **I am not ~:** es ist mir gleich; **be ~ about sth.** es mit etw. genau nehmen. 2. *n., in pl.* Einzelheiten; Details; *(of person)* Personalien *Pl.* **particularly** *adv.* besonders

'**parting** 1. *n.* a) [final] **~:** Abschied, *der*; b) *(Brit.: in hair)* Scheitel, *der.* 2. *attrib. adj.* Abschieds-

partisan ['pɑːtɪzæn] *n.* Partisan, *der/*Partisanin, *die*

partition [pɑːˈtɪʃn] 1. *n.* a) *(Polit.)* Teilung, *die*; b) *(room-divider)* Trennwand, *die.* 2. *v.t.* a) *(divide)* aufteilen ⟨*Land, Zimmer*⟩; b) *(Polit.)* teilen ⟨*Land*⟩. **partition off** *v.t.* abteilen

'**partly** *adv.* zum Teil; teilweise

partner ['pɑːtnə(r)] *n.* Partner, *der/*Partnerin, *die.* '**partnership** *n.* Partnerschaft, *die*; **business ~:** [Personen]gesellschaft, *die*

partridge ['pɑːtrɪdʒ] *n., pl. same or* **~s** Rebhuhn, *das*

part-time 1. ['--] *adj.* Teilzeit⟨*arbeit, -arbeiter*⟩. 2. [-'-] *adv.* stundenweise, halbtags ⟨*arbeiten, studieren*⟩

party ['pɑːtɪ] *n.* a) *(Polit., Law)* Partei, *die*; *attrib.* Partei-; b) *(group)* Gruppe, *die*; c) *(social gathering)* Party, *die*

pass [pɑːs] 1. *n.* a) *(passing of an examination)* bestandene Prüfung; **'~'** *(mark)* Ausreichend, *das*; **get a ~** in maths die Mathematikprüfung bestehen; b) *(written permission)* Ausweis, *der*; c) *(Footb.)* Paß, *der* *(fachspr.)*; Ballabgabe, *die*; d) *(in mountains)* Paß, *der.* 2. *v.i.* a) *(go by)* ⟨*Fußgänger:*⟩ vorbeigehen; ⟨*Fahrer, Fahrzeug:*⟩ vorbeifahren; ⟨*Zeit, Se-*

kunde:⟩ vergehen; *(by chance)* ⟨*Person, Fahrzeug:*⟩ vorbeikommen; b) *(come to an end)* vorbeigehen; ⟨*Gewitter, Unwetter:*⟩ vorüberziehen; c) *(be accepted)* durchgehen (as als, for für); d) *(in exam)* bestehen. 3. *v.t.* a) ⟨*Fußgänger:*⟩ vorbeigehen an (+ *Dat.*); ⟨*Fahrer, Fahrzeug:*⟩ vorbeifahren an (+ *Dat.*); *(by chance)* ⟨*Person, Fahrzeug:*⟩ vorbeikommen an (+ *Dat.*); b) *(overtake)* vorbeifahren an (+ *Dat.*); c) bestehen ⟨*Prüfung*⟩; d) *(approve)* verabschieden ⟨*Gesetzentwurf*⟩; annehmen ⟨*Vorschlag*⟩; bestehen lassen ⟨*Prüfungskandidaten*⟩; e) *(Footb. etc.)* abgeben (to an + *Akk.*); f) *(spend)* verbringen ⟨*Leben, Zeit, Tag*⟩; g) *(hand)* **~ sb.** sth. jmdm. etw. reichen *od.* geben; h) fällen ⟨*Urteil*⟩; machen ⟨*Bemerkung*⟩; i) **~ water** Wasser lassen. **pass a'way** *v.i. (euphem.)* die Augen schließen *(verhüll.).* **pass 'off** *v.t.* **~ sth. off as sth.** etw. als etw. ausgeben. **pass 'on** *v.t.* weitergeben (to an + *Akk.*). **pass 'out** *v.i.* ohnmächtig werden. **pass 'up** *v.t.* entgehen lassen ⟨*Gelegenheit*⟩; ablehnen ⟨*Angebot*⟩

passable ['pɑːsəbl] *adj.* a) *(acceptable)* passabel; b) befahrbar ⟨*Straße*⟩

passage ['pæsɪdʒ] *n.* a) *(voyage)* Überfahrt, *die*; b) *(way)* Durchgang, *der*; *(corridor)* Korridor, *der*; c) *(part of book etc.)* Textstelle, *die*; *(Mus.)* Stelle, *die*

passenger ['pæsɪndʒə(r)] *n.* Passagier, *der*; *(on train)* Reisende, *der*; *(on bus, in taxi)* Fahrgast, *der*; *(in car, on motor cycle)* Mitfahrer, *der/*Mitfahrerin, *die*; *(in front seat of car)* Beifahrer, *der/*Beifahrerin, *die.* '**passenger seat** *n.* Beifahrersitz, *der*

passer-by [pɑːsəˈbaɪ] *n.* Passant, *der/* Passantin, *die*

'**passing** 1. *n. (of time, years)* Lauf, *der*; **in ~:** beiläufig ⟨*bemerken usw.*⟩. 2. *adj.* a) vorbeifahrend ⟨*Zug, Auto*⟩; vorbeikommend ⟨*Person*⟩; b) flüchtig ⟨*Blick*⟩; vorübergehend ⟨*Mode, Interesse*⟩; flüchtig ⟨*Bekanntschaft*⟩

passion ['pæʃn] *n.* Leidenschaft, *die*; *(enthusiasm)* leidenschaftliche Begeisterung; **he has a ~ for steam engines** Dampfloks sind seine Leidenschaft. **passionate** ['pæʃənət] *adj.* leidenschaftlich; heftig ⟨*Verlangen*⟩

passive ['pæsɪv] 1. *adj.* a) passiv; b) *(Ling.)* Passiv-. 2. *n. (Ling.)* Passiv, *das*

pass: ~**port** n. a) [Reise]paß, der; attrib. Paß-; b) (fig.) Schlüssel, der (**to** zu); ~**word** n. a) Parole, die; Losung, die; b) (Computing) Paßwort, das

past [pɑːst] 1. adj. a) pred. (over) vorbei; b) attrib. (previous) früher; vergangen; ehemalig ⟨Präsident, Vorsitzende usw.⟩; c) attrib. (just gone by) letzt...; vergangen; **in the** ~ **few days** während der letzten Tage; d) (Ling.) ~ **tense** Vergangenheit, die. 2. n. Vergangenheit, die; **in the** ~: früher; in der Vergangenheit ⟨leben⟩; **be a thing of the** ~: der Vergangenheit angehören. 3. prep. (in time) nach; (in place) hinter (+ Dat.); **half** ~ **three** halb vier; **five** |**minutes**| ~ **two** fünf [Minuten] nach zwei; **gaze/walk** ~ **sb./sth.** an jmdm./etw. vorbeiblicken/vorbeigehen; ~ **repair** nicht mehr zu reparieren. 4. adv. vorbei; **hurry** ~: vorübereilen

pasta ['pæstə] n. Nudeln Pl.

paste [peɪst] 1. n. a) Brei, der; b) (glue) Kleister, der; c) (of meat, fish, etc.) Paste, die. 2. v.t. kleben; ~ **sth. into sb.** etw. in etw. (Akk.) einkleben

pastel ['pæstl] 1. n. (crayon) Pastellstift, der. 2. adj. pastellfarben; Pastell⟨farben, -töne, -zeichnung⟩

pasteurize ['pɑːstʃəraɪz] v.t. pasteurisieren

pastille ['pæstɪl] n. Pastille, die

pastime ['pɑːstaɪm] n. Zeitvertreib, der; (person's specific ~) Hobby, das

pastor ['pɑːstə(r)] n. Pfarrer, der/Pfarrerin, die; Pastor, der/Pastorin, die

pastoral ['pɑːstərl] adj. Weide-; ländlich ⟨Reiz, Idylle, Umgebung⟩

pastry ['peɪstrɪ] n. Teig, der; (article of food) Gebäckstück, das; **pastries** collect. [Fein]gebäck, das

pasture ['pɑːstʃə(r)] n. Weide, die

pasty ['pæstɪ] n. Pastete, die

¹**pat** [pæt] 1. n. a) (tap) Klaps, der; b) (of butter) Stückchen, das. 2. v.t., **-tt-** leicht klopfen auf (+ Akk.); tätscheln, (once) einen Klaps geben (+ Dat.) ⟨Person, Hund, Pferd⟩; ~ **sb. on the arm/head** jmdm. den Arm/Kopf tätscheln

²**pat** [pæt] **have sth. off** ~: etw. parat haben

patch [pætʃ] 1. n. a) Stelle, die; **fog** ~**es** Nebelfelder; b) (on worn garment) Flicken, der; **be not a** ~ **on sth.** (fig. coll.) nichts gegen etw. sein. 2. v.t. flicken. **patch 'up** v.t. reparieren; (fig.) beilegen ⟨Streit⟩

patchy ['pætʃɪ] adj. uneinheitlich ⟨Qualität⟩; ungleichmäßig ⟨Arbeit⟩; sehr lückenhaft ⟨Wissen⟩

pâté ['pæteɪ] n. Pastete, die

patent ['peɪtənt, 'pætənt] 1. adj. (obvious) offenkundig. 2. n. Patent, das. 3. v.t. patentieren lassen. **patent 'leather** n. Lackleder, das; ~ **shoes** Lackschuhe. '**patently** adv. offenkundig; ~ **obvious** ganz offenkundig

paternal [pə'tɜːnl] adj. väterlich

path [pɑːθ] n. Weg, der; (line of motion) Bahn, die

pathetic [pə'θetɪk] adj. a) (pitiful) mitleiderregend; b) (contemptible) armselig ⟨Entschuldigung⟩; erbärmlich ⟨Person, Leistung⟩

'**pathway** n. Weg, der

patience ['peɪʃəns] n. Geduld, die

patient ['peɪʃənt] 1. adj. geduldig. 2. n. Patient, der/Patientin, die. '**patiently** adv. geduldig

patio ['pætɪəʊ] n., pl. ~**s** Veranda, die; Terrasse, die

patriot ['peɪtrɪət] n. Patriot, der/Patriotin, die. **patriotic** [peɪtrɪ'ɒtɪk] adj. patriotisch. **patriotism** ['peɪtrɪətɪzm] n. Patriotismus, der

patrol [pə'trəʊl] 1. n. (Police) Streife, die; (Mil.) Patrouille, die; **be on** ~: patrouillieren; **on** ~: patrouillieren; ⟨Polizei:⟩ Streife laufen/fahren. 3. v.t., **-ll-** patrouillieren durch (+ Akk.); abpatrouillieren ⟨Straßen, Gegend, Lager⟩; patrouillieren vor (+ Dat.) ⟨Küste, Grenze⟩; ⟨Polizei:⟩ Streife laufen/fahren in (+ Dat.) ⟨Straßen, Stadtteil⟩. **pa'trol boat** n. Patrouillenboot, das. **pa'trol car** n. Streifenwagen, der

patron ['peɪtrən] n. a) Gönner, der/Gönnerin, die; (of institution, campaign) Schirmherr, der/Schirmherrin, die; b) (customer) (of shop) Kunde, der/Kundin, die; (of restaurant, hotel) Gast, der; (of theatre, cinema) Besucher, der/Besucherin, die; c) ~ |**saint**| Schutzheilige, der/die. **patronage** ['pætrənɪdʒ] n. Gönnerschaft, die; (for campaign, institution) Schirmherrschaft, die

patronize ['pætrənaɪz] v.t. a) (frequent) besuchen; b) (condescend to) ~ **sb.** jmdn. herablassend behandeln. **patronizing** ['pætrənaɪzɪŋ] adj. gönnerhaft; herablassend

patter ['pætə(r)] 1. n. (of rain) Prasseln, das; (of feet) Trappeln, das. 2. v.i. ⟨Regen:⟩ prasseln

pattern ['pætən] *n.* Muster, *das;* *(model)* Vorlage, *die;* *(for sewing)* Schnittmuster, *das;* *(for knitting)* Strickmuster, *das*

paunch [pɔːntʃ] *n.* Bauch, *der*

pauper ['pɔːpə(r)] *n.* Arme, *der/die*

pause [pɔːz] 1. *n.* Pause, *die.* 2. *v. i.* eine Pause machen; ⟨*Redner:*⟩ innehalten; *(hesitate)* zögern

pave [peɪv] *v. t.* befestigen; *(with stones)* pflastern; ~ the way for sth. *(fig.)* einer Sache *(Dat.)* den Weg ebnen. '**pavement** *n.* a) *(Brit.: footway)* Bürgersteig, *der;* b) *(Amer.: roadway)* Fahrbahn, *die*

pavilion [pə'vɪljən] *n.* Pavillon, *der;* *(Brit. Sport)* Klubhaus, *das*

paw [pɔː] *n.* Pfote, *die;* *(of bear, lion, tiger)* Pranke, *die*

¹**pawn** [pɔːn] *n. (Chess)* Bauer, *der;* *(fig.)* Schachfigur, *die*

²**pawn** 1. *n.* Pfand, *das;* in ~: verpfändet. 2. *v. t.* verpfänden. '**pawnbroker** *n.* Pfandleiher, *der/*-leiherin, *die.* '**pawnshop** *n.* Leihhaus, *das*

pay [peɪ] 1. *n. (wages)* Lohn, *der;* *(salary)* Gehalt, *das;* be in the ~ of sb./ sth. für jmdn./etw. arbeiten. 2. *v. t.,* paid [peɪd] bezahlen; zahlen ⟨*Geld*⟩; ~ sb. to do sth. jmdn. dafür bezahlen, daß er etw. tut; ~ sb. £10 jmdm. 10 Pfund zahlen. 3. *v. i.,* paid a) zahlen; ~ for sth./sb. etw./für jmdn. bezahlen; sth. ~s for itself etw. macht sich bezahlt; b) *(be profitable)* sich lohnen; ⟨*Geschäft:*⟩ rentabel sein; it ~s to be careful es lohnt sich, vorsichtig zu sein. *See also* **paid.** **pay 'back** *v. t.* zurückzahlen; I'll ~ you back later ich gebe dir das Geld später zurück. **pay 'in** *v. t.* einzahlen. **pay 'off** *v. t.* auszahlen ⟨*Arbeiter*⟩; abbezahlen ⟨*Schulden*⟩; ablösen ⟨*Hypothek*⟩; befriedigen ⟨*Gläubiger*⟩. **pay 'out** *v. t.* auszahlen; *(spend)* ausgeben. **pay 'up** *v. i.* zahlen

payable ['peɪəbl] *adj.* zahlbar; be ~ to sb. an jmdn. zu zahlen sein; make a cheque ~ to the Post Office/to sb. einen Scheck auf die Post/auf jmds. Namen ausstellen

payee [peɪ'iː] *n.* Zahlungsempfänger, *der/*-empfängerin, *die*

'**payment** *n.* a) *(of sum, bill, debt, fine)* Bezahlung, *die;* *(of interest, instalment, tax, fee)* Zahlung, *die;* in ~ |for sth.| als Bezahlung [für etw.]; b) *(amount)* Zahlung, *die*

pay: ~-**packet** *n. (Brit.)* Lohntüte,

die; ~ **phone** *n.* Münzfernsprecher, *der;* ~-**rise** *n.* Lohn-/Gehaltserhöhung, *die;* ~-**roll** *n.* Lohnliste, *die;* be on sb.'s ~-**roll** für jmdn. arbeiten; ~-**slip** *n.* Lohnstreifen, *der/*Gehaltszettel, *der;* ~ **station** *n. (Amer.) see* ~ **phone**

PC *abbr.* a) *(Brit.)* **police constable** Wachtm.; b) **personal computer** PC

PE *abbr.* **physical education**

pea [piː] *n.* Erbse, *die*

peace [piːs] *n.* Frieden, *der;* *(tranquillity)* Ruhe, *die;* ~ of mind Seelenfrieden, *der.* **peaceable** ['piːsəbl] *adj.* friedfertig; *(calm)* friedlich. **peaceful** ['piːsfl] *adj.* friedlich; friedfertig ⟨*Person, Volk*⟩. '**peacefully** *adv.* friedlich; **die** ~: sanft entschlafen

'**peacetime** *n.* Friedenszeiten *Pl.*

peach [piːtʃ] *n.* Pfirsich, *der*

'**peacock** *n.* Pfau, *der*

peak [piːk] 1. *n.* a) *(of cap)* Schirm, *der;* b) *(of mountain)* Gipfel, *der;* *(fig.)* Höhepunkt, *der.* 2. *attrib. adj.* Höchst-, Spitzen⟨*preise, -werte*⟩; ~-**hour traffic** Stoßverkehr, *der.* **peaked** [piːkt] *adj.* ~ **cap** Schirmmütze, *die*

peal [piːl] *n.* Läuten, *das;* ~ of bells Glockenläuten, *das;* a ~/~s of laughter schallendes Gelächter

peanut ['piːnʌt] *n.* Erdnuß, *die;* ~ butter Erdnußbutter, *die;* ~s *(coll.: little money)* ein paar Kröten *(salopp)*

pear [peə(r)] *n.* Birne, *die*

pearl [pɜːl] *n.* Perle, *die*

'**pear-tree** *n.* Birnbaum, *der*

peasant ['pezənt] *n.* [armer] Bauer, *der;* Landarbeiter, *der*

peat [piːt] *n.* Torf, *der*

pebble ['pebl] *n.* Kiesel[stein], *der*

peck [pek] 1. *v. t.* hacken; picken ⟨*Körner*⟩. 2. *v. i.* picken (at nach); ~ at one's food in seinem Essen herumstochern. 3. *n. (kiss)* flüchtiger Kuß. '**pecking order** *n.* Hackordnung, *die*

peckish ['pekɪʃ] *adj. (coll.)* feel/get ~: Hunger haben/bekommen

peculiar [pɪ'kjuːlɪə(r)] *adj.* a) *(strange)* seltsam; I feel |slightly| ~: mir ist [etwas] komisch; b) *(especial)* besonder...; c) *(belonging exclusively)* eigentümlich (to *Dat.*). **peculiarity** [pɪkjuːlɪ'ærɪtɪ] *n.* a) *(odd trait)* Eigentümlichkeit, *die;* b) *(distinguishing characteristic)* [charakteristisches] Merkmal. **pe'culiarly** *adv.* a) *(strangely)* seltsam; b) *(especially)* besonders

pedal ['pedl] 1. *n.* Pedal, *das.* 2. *v. i.,*

(Brit.) -ll- in die Pedale treten. **'pedal-bin** n. Treteimer, *der*

pedant ['pednt] n. Pedant, *der*/Pedantin, *die*. **pedantic** [pɪ'dæntɪk] *adj.* pedantisch

peddle ['pedl] v.t. auf der Straße verkaufen; *(door to door)* hausieren mit

pedestal ['pedɪstl] n. Sockel, *der*

pedestrian [pɪ'destrɪən] **1.** *adj. (uninspired)* trocken; langweilig. **2.** n. Fußgänger, *der*/-gängerin, *die*. **pedestrian 'crossing** n. Fußgängerüberweg, *der*

pedigree ['pedɪgriː] **1.** n. Stammbaum, *der*. **2.** *adj.* mit Stammbaum *nachgestellt*

pedlar ['pedlə(r)] n. Straßenhändler, *der*/-händlerin, *die*; *(door to door)* Hausierer, *der*/Hausiererin, *die*

pee *(coll.)* **1.** v.i. pinkeln *(salopp);* Pipi machen *(Kinderspr.).* **2.** n. **a)** have **a** ~: pinkeln *(salopp);* **b)** *(urine)* Pipi, *das (Kinderspr.)*

peek [piːk] *see* ²**peep**

peel [piːl] **1.** v.t. schälen. **2.** v.i. ⟨Person, Haut:⟩ sich schälen; ⟨Farbe:⟩ abblättern. **3.** n. Schale, *die*. **'peelings** n. pl. Schalen

¹**peep** [piːp] **1.** v.i. ⟨Maus, Vogel:⟩ piep[s]en. **2.** n. Piepsen, *das;* *(coll.: remark etc.)* Piep[s], *der*

²**peep** **1.** v.i. gucken *(ugs.);* *(furtively)* verstohlen gucken *(ugs.).* **2.** n. kurzer/ verstohlener Blick. **'peep-hole** n. Guckloch, *das.* **peeping 'Tom** n. Spanner, *der (ugs.)*

¹**peer** [pɪə(r)] n. Peer, *der;* *(equal)* Gleichgestellte, *der/die*

²**peer** v.i. forschend schauen; *(with difficulty)* angestrengt schauen; ~ at sth./sb. [sich *(Dat.)*] etw. genau ansehen/jmdn. forschend ansehen; *(with difficulty)* [sich *(Dat.)*] etw./jmdn. angestrengt ansehen

peerage ['pɪərɪdʒ] n. Peerswürde, *die*

peevish ['piːvɪʃ] *adj.* nörgelig

peg [peg] n. *(for holding together)* Stift, *der;* *(for tying things to)* Pflock, *der;* *(for hanging things on)* Haken, *der;* *(clothes-~)* Wäscheklammer, *die;* *(tent-~)* Hering, *der;* off the ~ *(Brit.: ready-made)* von der Stange *(ugs.)*

pejorative [pɪ'dʒɒrətɪv] *adj.* **pe'joratively** *adv.* abwertend

pelican ['pelɪkən] n. Pelikan, *der.* **'pelican crossing** n. *(Brit.)* Ampelübergang, *der*

pellet ['pelɪt] n. Kügelchen, *das*

pelmet ['pelmɪt] n. Blende, *die*

¹**pelt** [pelt] n. Fell, *das*

²**pelt** **1.** v.t. ~ sb. with sth. jmdn. mit etw. bewerfen. **2.** v.i. **a)** it was ~ing down [with rain] es goß wie aus Kübeln *(ugs.);* **b)** *(run fast)* rasen *(ugs.)*

pelvis ['pelvɪs] n., pl. **pelves** ['pelviːz] or ~**es** *(Anat.)* Becken, *das*

¹**pen** [pen] n. *(enclosure)* Pferch, *der.* **2.** v.t., -nn-: ~ sb. in a corner jmdn. in eine Ecke drängen. **pen 'in** v.t. einpferchen

²**pen** **1.** n. Federhalter, *der;* *(fountain-~)* Füller, *der;* *(ball-~)* Kugelschreiber, *der;* *(felt-tip ~)* Filzstift, *der.* **2.** v.t., -nn- schreiben

penal ['piːnl] *adj.* Straf-

penalize ['piːnəlaɪz] v.t. bestrafen; *(Sport)* eine Strafe verhängen gegen

penalty ['penltɪ] n. **a)** Strafe, *die;* pay the ~/the ~ for or of sth. dafür/für etw. büßen [müssen]; **b)** *(Footb.)* Elfmeter, *der*

penance ['penəns] n. Buße, *die;* act of ~: Bußwerk, *das;* do ~: Buße tun

pence *see* **penny**

pencil ['pensl] **1.** n. Bleistift, *der;* red/ coloured ~: Rot-/Buntstift, *der.* **2.** v.t., *(Brit.)* -ll- mit einem Bleistift/ Farbstift schreiben. **'pencil-case** n. Griffelkasten, *der;* *(of soft material)* Federmäppchen, *das.* **'pencil-sharpener** n. Bleistiftspitzer, *der*

pendant ['pendənt] n. Anhänger, *der*

pending ['pendɪŋ] **1.** *adj.* unentschieden ⟨Angelegenheit, Sache⟩; schwebend ⟨Verfahren⟩. **2.** *prep.* ~ his return bis zu seiner Rückkehr

pendulum ['pendjʊləm] n. Pendel, *das*

penetrate ['penɪtreɪt] v.t. eindringen in (+ Akk.); *(pass through)* durchdringen. **penetrating** ['penɪtreɪtɪŋ] *adj.* durchdringend. **penetration** [penɪ'treɪʃn] n. Eindringen, *das (of in* + *Akk.);* *(passing through)* Durchdringen, *das*

'pen-friend n. Brieffreund, *der/* -freundin, *die*

penguin ['peŋgwɪn] n. Pinguin, *der*

penicillin [penɪ'sɪlɪn] n. Penizillin, *das*

peninsula [pɪ'nɪnsjʊlə] n. Halbinsel, *die*

penis ['piːnɪs] n. Penis, *der*

penitence ['penɪtəns] n. Reue, *die*

penitent ['penɪtənt] *adj.* reuevoll *(geh.);* reuig *(geh.)* ⟨Sünder⟩

penitentiary [penɪ'tenʃərɪ] n. *(Amer.)* Straf[vollzugs]anstalt, *die*

'penknife n. Taschenmesser, *das*

pennant ['penənt] n. Wimpel, der; (on official car etc.) Ständer, der

penniless ['penɪlɪs] adj. mittellos

penny ['penɪ] n., pl. usu. **pennies** ['penɪz] (for separate coins), **pence** [pens] (for sum of money) Penny, der; **fifty pence** fünfzig Pence; **two/fifty pence |piece|** Zwei-/Fünfzigpencestück, das

pension [pen∫n] n. Rente, die; (payment to retired civil servant also) Pension, die; **be on a ~:** eine Rente beziehen; **widow's ~:** Witwenrente, die. **pension 'off** v.t. berenten (Amtsspr.); auf Rente setzen (ugs.); pensionieren (Lehrer, Beamten)

'pensioner n. Rentner, der/Rentnerin, die; (retired civil servant) Pensionär, der/Pensionärin, die

pensive ['pensɪv] adj. nachdenklich

pentagon ['pentəgən] n. Fünfeck, das

pent: ~**house** n. Penthouse, das; ~**up** adj. angestaut (Ärger, Wut); unterdrückt (Sehnsucht, Gefühle)

penultimate [pe'nʌltɪmət] adj. vorletzt...

people ['pi:pl] n. a) constr. as pl. Leute Pl.; Menschen; (as opposed to animals) Menschen Pl.; **city/country ~** (inhabitants) Stadt-/Landbewohner; **local ~:** Einheimische, der; **working ~:** arbeitende Menschen; **coloured/white ~:** Farbige/Weiße; ~ **say ...:** man sagt ...; **a crowd of ~:** eine Menschenmenge; b) (nation) Volk, das

pepper ['pepə(r)] 1. n. a) Pfeffer, der; b) (vegetable) Paprikaschote, die; **red/green ~:** roter/grüner Paprika. 2. v.t. a) pfeffern; b) (pelt) bombardieren (ugs.)

pepper: ~**corn** n. Pfefferkorn, das; ~**mint** n. (sweet) Pfefferminz, das; ~**pot** n. Pfefferstreuer, der

per [pə(r), stressed pɜ:(r)] prep. pro

perceive [pə'si:v] v.t. wahrnehmen; (with the mind) spüren; ~**d** vermeintlich (Bedrohung, Gefahr, Wert)

per cent (Brit.: Amer.: **percent**) [pə'sent] 1. adv. **ninety ~ effective** zu 90 Prozent wirksam. 2. adj. **a 5 ~ increase** ein Zuwachs von 5 Prozent. 3. n. a) Prozent, das; b) see percentage

percentage [pə'sentɪdʒ] n. Prozentsatz, der

perceptible [pə'septɪbl] adj. wahrnehmbar

perception [pə'sep∫n] n. (act) Wahrnehmung, die; (result) Erkenntnis, die; (faculty) Wahrnehmungsvermögen, das

perceptive [pə'septɪv] adj. einfühlsam (Person, Bemerkung)

perch [pɜ:t∫] 1. n. Sitzstange, die. 2. v.i. a) sich niederlassen; b) (be supported) sitzen. 3. v.t. setzen/stellen/legen

percolate ['pɜ:kəleɪt] v.i. [durch]sickern. **percolator** ['pɜ:kəleɪtə(r)] n. Kaffeemaschine, die

percussion [pə'kʌ∫n] n. (Mus.) Schlagzeug, das; ~ **instrument** Schlaginstrument, das

perennial [pə'renjəl] 1. adj. a) (Bot.) ausdauernd; b) immer wieder auftretend (Problem). 2. n. (Bot.) ausdauernde Pflanze

perfect 1. ['pɜ:fɪkt] adj. vollkommen; perfekt (Englisch, Timing); tadellos (Zustand); (coll.: unmitigated) absolut; **a ~ stranger** ein völlig Fremder. 2. [pə'fekt] v.t. vervollkommnen. **perfection** [pə'fek∫n] n. Perfektion, die; **to ~:** perfekt. **perfectionism** [pə'fek∫ənɪzm] n. Perfektionismus, der. **perfectionist** [pə'fek∫ənɪst] n. Perfektionist, der/Perfektionistin, die. **'perfectly** adv. a) (completely) vollkommen; **be ~ entitled to do sth.** durchaus berechtigt sein, etw. zu tun; b) (faultlessly) perfekt; tadellos (sich verhalten)

perforate ['pɜ:fəreɪt] v.t. perforieren; (make opening into) durchlöchern. **perforation** [pɜ:fə'reɪ∫n] n. a) (hole) Loch, das; b) in pl. ~s Perforation, die; (in sheets of stamps) Zähnung, die

perform [pə'fɔ:m] 1. v.t. ausführen (Arbeit, Operation); erfüllen (Pflicht, Aufgabe); vollbringen (Helden|tat, Leistung); ausfüllen (Funktion); vollbringen (Wunder); anstellen (Berechnungen); durchführen (Experiment, Sektion); vorführen (Trick); aufführen (Theaterstück, Scharade); vortragen (Lied, Sonate usw.). 2. v.i. a) eine Vorführung geben; (sing) singen; (play) spielen. **performance** [pə'fɔ:məns] n. a) (of duty, task) Erfüllung, die; b) [notable] achievement; Motor Veh.) Leistung, die; c) (at theatre, cinema, etc.) Vorstellung, die; **her ~ as Desdemona** ihre Darstellung der Desdemona; **the ~ of a play/opera** die Aufführung eines Theaterstücks/einer Oper. **per'former** n. Künstler, der/Künstlerin, die. **per'forming** attrib. adj. dressiert (Tier)

perfume ['pɜ:fju:m] n. Duft, der; (fluid) Parfüm, das

perfunctory [pə'fʌŋktərɪ] *adj.* ober-flächlich ⟨*Arbeit, Überprüfung*⟩; flüchtig ⟨*Erkundigung, Bemerkung*⟩

perhaps [pə'hæps] *adv.* vielleicht

peril ['perl] *n.* Gefahr, *die.* **perilous** ['perələs] *adj.* gefahrvoll; **be** ~: gefährlich sein

perimeter [pə'rɪmɪtə(r)] *n.* [äußere] Begrenzung; Grenze, *die*

period ['pɪərɪəd] **1.** *n.* **a)** *(of history or life)* Periode, *die*; Zeit, *die*; *(any portion of time)* Zeitraum, *der*; **the Classical/Romantic** ~: die Klassik/Romantik; **b)** *(Sch.)* Stunde, *die*; **chemistry/English** ~: Chemie-/Englischstunde, *die*; **c)** *(menstruation)* Periode, *die*; **d)** *(punctuation mark)* Punkt, *der*. **2.** *adj.* zeitgenössisch ⟨*Tracht, Kostüm*⟩; antik ⟨*Möbel*⟩. **periodic** [pɪərɪ'ɒdɪk] *adj.* regelmäßig; *(intermittent)* gelegentlich. **periodical** [pɪərɪ'ɒdɪkl] **1.** *adj. see* **periodic. 2.** *n.* Zeitschrift, *die*; **weekly/monthly** ~: Wochenzeitschrift/Monatsschrift, *die.* **periodically** *adv.* regelmäßig; *(intermittently)* gelegentlich

peripheral [pə'rɪfərl] *adj.* peripher *(geh.)*; Rand⟨*problem, -erscheinung*⟩

periphery [pə'rɪfərɪ] *n.* Peripherie, *die*

periscope ['perɪskəʊp] *n.* Periskop, *das*

perish ['perɪʃ] *v.i.* **a)** *(die)* umkommen; **b)** *(rot)* verderben; ⟨*Gummi:*⟩ altern. **perishable** ['perɪʃəbl] *adj.* [leicht] verderblich

'**perishing** *(coll.)* **1.** *adj.* mörderisch ⟨*Kälte*⟩; **it's/I'm** ~: es ist bitterkalt/ich komme um vor Kälte *(ugs.).* **2.** *adv.* mörderisch ⟨*kalt*⟩

perjury ['pɜ:dʒərɪ] *n.* Meineid, *der*; **commit** ~: einen Meineid leisten

'**perk** [pɜ:k] *(coll.)* **1.** *v.i.* ~ **up** munter werden. **2.** *v.t.* ~ **up** aufmuntern

²**perk** *n.* *(Brit. coll.)* [Sonder]vergünstigung, *die*

perky ['pɜ:kɪ] *adj.* lebhaft; munter

perm [pɜ:m] **1.** *n.* Dauerwelle, *die.* **2.** *v.t.* **have one's hair** ~**ed** sich *(Dat.)* eine Dauerwelle machen lassen

permanence ['pɜ:mənəns] *n.* Dauerhaftigkeit, *die*

permanent ['pɜ:mənənt] *adj.* fest ⟨*Sitz, Bestandteil, Mitglied*⟩; ständig ⟨*Wohnsitz, Adresse, Kampf*⟩; Dauer⟨*stellung, -visum*⟩; bleibend ⟨*Schaden*⟩. '**permanently** *adv.* dauernd; auf Dauer ⟨*verhindern, bleiben*⟩

permeable ['pɜ:mɪəbl] *adj.* durchlässig; **be** ~ **to** sth. etw. durchlassen

permeate ['pɜ:mɪeɪt] **1.** *v.t.* dringen durch; **be** ~**d with** *or* **by** sth. *(fig.)* von etw. durchdrungen sein. **2.** *v.i.* ~ **through** sth. etw. durchdringen

permissible [pə'mɪsɪbl] *adj.* zulässig; **be** ~ **to** *or* **for** sb. jmdm. erlaubt sein

permission [pə'mɪʃn] *n.* Erlaubnis, *die*; *(given by official body)* Genehmigung, *die*; **give** sb. ~ **to do** sth. jmdm. erlauben, etw. zu tun

permissive [pə'mɪsɪv] *adj.* **the** ~ **society** die permissive Gesellschaft

permit **1.** [pə'mɪt] *v.t.*, **-tt-** zulassen ⟨*Berufung, Einspruch usw.*⟩; ~ **sb.** sth. jmdm. etw. erlauben; **sb. is** ~**ted to do** sth. es ist jmdm. erlaubt, etw. zu tun. **2.** *v.i.*, **-tt-** es zulassen. **3.** ['pɜ:mɪt] *n.* Genehmigung, *die*

pernicious [pə'nɪʃəs] *adj.* verderblich; bösartig ⟨*Krankheit*⟩

perpendicular [pɜ:pən'dɪkjʊlə(r)] *adj.* senkrecht

perpetrate ['pɜ:pɪtreɪt] *v.t.* begehen; verüben ⟨*Greuel*⟩

perpetual [pə'petjʊəl] *adj.* **a)** *(eternal)* ewig; **b)** *(continuous; coll.: repeated)* ständig. **per'petually** *adv.* **a)** *(eternally)* ewig; **b)** *(continuously; coll.: repeatedly)* ständig

perpetuate [pə'petjʊeɪt] *v.t.* aufrechterhalten

perplex [pə'pleks] *v.t.* verwirren. **perplexed** [pə'plekst] *adj.* verwirrt; *(puzzled)* ratlos. **perplexity** [pə'pleksɪtɪ] *n.* Verwirrung, *die*; *(puzzlement)* Ratlosigkeit, *die*

persecute ['pɜ:sɪkju:t] *v.t.* verfolgen. **persecution** [pɜ:sɪ'kju:ʃn] *n.* Verfolgung, *die*

perseverance [pɜ:sɪ'vɪərəns] *n.* Beharrlichkeit, *die*; Ausdauer, *die*

persevere [pɜ:sɪ'vɪə(r)] *v.i.* ausharren; ~ **with** *or* **at** *or* **in** sth. bei etw. dabeibleiben

Persian ['pɜ:ʃn] *adj.* persisch; Perser⟨*katze, -teppich*⟩

persist [pə'sɪst] *v.i.* **a)** nicht nachgeben; ~ **in doing** sth. etw. weiterhin [beharrlich] tun; **b)** *(continue to exist)* anhalten. **persistence** [pə'sɪstəns] *n.* Hartnäckigkeit, *die*. **persistent** [pə'sɪstənt] *adj.* **a)** hartnäckig; **b)** *(constantly repeated)* dauernd; hartnäckig ⟨*Gerüchte*⟩. **per'sistently** *adv.* hartnäckig

person ['pɜ:sn] *n.* Mensch, *der*; **in** ~: persönlich; selbst

personal ['pɜ:sənl] *adj.* persönlich; Privat⟨*angelegenheit, -leben*⟩; ~ **com-**

puter Personalcomputer, *der;* ~ **stereo** Walkman, *der;* ~ **hygiene** Körperpflege, *die.* **personal as'sistant** *n.* persönlicher Referent/persönliche Referentin

personality [pɜːsə'nælɪtɪ] *n.* Persönlichkeit, *die*

'**personally** *adv.* persönlich

personification [pəsɒnɪfɪ'keɪʃn] *n.* Verkörperung, *die*

personify [pə'sɒnɪfaɪ] *v. t.* verkörpern; **be kindness personified** die Freundlichkeit in Person sein

personnel [pɜːsə'nel] *n.* Belegschaft, *die; (of shop, restaurant, etc.)* Personal, *das; attrib.* Personal-

perspective [pə'spektɪv] *n.* Perspektive, *die; (fig.)* Blickwinkel, *der*

perspiration [pɜːspɪ'reɪʃn] *n.* Schweiß, *der*

perspire [pə'spaɪə(r)] *v. i.* schwitzen

persuade [pə'sweɪd] *v. t.* **a)** *(convince)* überzeugen **(of** von); ~ **oneself [that] ...:** sich *(Dat.)* einreden, daß ...; **b)** *(induce)* überreden. **persuasion** [pə'sweɪʒn] *n.* Überzeugung, *die;* **it didn't take much** ~: es brauchte nicht viel Überredungskunst. **persuasive** [pə'sweɪsɪv] *adj.,* **per'suasively** *adv.* überzeugend

pert [pɜːt] *adj.* keck

pertinent ['pɜːtɪnənt] *adj.* relevant **(to** für**)**

perturb [pə'tɜːb] *v. t.* beunruhigen

Peru [pə'ruː] *pr. n.* Peru *(das).* **Peruvian** [pə'ruːvɪən] **1.** *adj.* peruanisch. **2.** *n.* Peruaner, *der*/Peruanerin, *die*

pervade [pə'veɪd] *v. t.* durchdringen.

pervasive [pə'veɪsɪv] *adj.* durchdringend 〈*Geruch, Kälte*〉; weit verbreitet 〈*Ansicht*〉; sich ausbreitend 〈*Gefühl*〉

perverse [pə'vɜːs] *adj.* starrköpfig

perversion [pə'vɜːʃn] *n.* **a)** *(sexual)* Perversion, *die;* **b)** ~ **of justice** Rechtsbeugung, *die.* **pervert 1.** [pə'vɜːt] *v. t. (morally)* verderben. **2.** ['pɜːvɜːt] *n.* perverser Mensch. **perverted** [pə-'vɜːtɪd] *adj. (sexually)* pervers

pessimism ['pesɪmɪzm] *n.* Pessimismus, *der.* **pessimist** ['pesɪmɪst] *n.* Pessimist, *der*/Pessimistin, *die.* **pessimistic** [pesɪ'mɪstɪk] *adj.* pessimistisch

pest [pest] *n. (thing)* Ärgernis, *das; (person)* Nervensäge, *die (ugs.); (animal)* Schädling, *der*

pester ['pestə(r)] *v. t.* belästigen; nerven *(ugs.);* ~ **sb. for sth.** jmdm. wegen etw. in den Ohren liegen

pesticide ['pestɪsaɪd] *n.* Pestizid, *das*

pet [pet] **1.** *n.* **a)** *(animal)* Haustier, *das;* **b)** *(as term of endearment)* Schatz, *der.* **2.** *adj. (favourite)* Lieblings-. **3.** *v. i.,* **-tt-** knutschen *(ugs.)*

petal ['petl] *n.* Blütenblatt, *das*

peter ['piːtə(r)] *v. i.* ~ **out** [allmählich] zu Ende gehen; 〈*Weg:*〉 sich verlieren

petite [pə'tiːt] *adj.* zierlich

petition [pə'tɪʃn] **1.** *n.* Petition, *die;* Eingabe, *die.* **2.** *v. t.* eine Eingabe richten an (+ *Akk.*)

petrify ['petrɪfaɪ] *v. t.* **be petrified with fear/shock** starr vor Angst/Schrecken sein

petrol ['petrl] *n. (Brit.)* Benzin, *das*

petroleum [pɪ'trəʊlɪəm] *n.* Erdöl, *das*

petrol: ~-**pump** *n. (Brit.)* Zapfsäule, *die;* ~-**station** *n. (Brit.)* Tankstelle, *die;* ~-**tank** *n. (Brit.)* Benzintank, *der;* ~-**tanker** *n. (Brit.)* Benzintankwagen, *der*

'**pet shop** *n.* Tierhandlung, *die*

petticoat ['petɪkəʊt] *n.* Unterrock, *der*

petty ['petɪ] *adj.* kleinlich 〈*Vorschrift, Einwand*〉; belanglos 〈*Detail, Sorgen*〉

petulant ['petjʊlənt] *adj.* bockig

pew [pjuː] *n. (Eccl.)* Kirchenbank, *die*

pewter ['pjuːtə(r)] *n.* Pewter, *der*

phantom ['fæntəm] *n.* Phantom, *das*

pharmacist ['fɑːməsɪst] *n.* Apotheker, *der*/Apothekerin, *die*

pharmacy ['fɑːməsɪ] *n. (dispensary)* Apotheke, *die*

phase [feɪz] *n.* Phase, *die.* **phase 'in** *v. t.* stufenweise einführen. **phase 'out** *v. t.* allmählich abschaffen 〈*Verfahrensweise, Methode*〉; *(stop producing)* 〈langsam〉 auslaufen lassen

Ph.D. [piːeɪtʃ'diː] *abbr.* **Doctor of Philosophy** Dr. phil.

pheasant ['fezənt] *n.* Fasan, *der*

phenomenal [fɪ'nɒmɪnl] *adj.* phänomenal

phenomenon [fɪ'nɒmɪnən] *n., pl.* **phenomena** [fɪ'nɒmɪnə] Phänomen, *das*

phew [fjuː] *int.* puh

Philippines ['fɪlɪpiːnz] *pr. n. pl.* Philippinen *Pl.*

philistine ['fɪlɪstaɪn] *n.* Banause, *der*/Banausin, *die*

philosopher [fɪ'lɒsəfə(r)] *n.* Philosoph, *der*/Philosophin, *die*

philosophical [fɪlə'sɒfɪkl] *adj.* **a)** philosophisch; **b)** *(resigned)* abgeklärt

philosophy [fɪ'lɒsəfɪ] *n.* Philosophie, *die*

phlegm [flem] *n.* Schleim, *der*

phobia ['fəʊbɪə] *n.* Phobie, *die*

phone [fəʊn] *(coll.)* **1.** *n.* Telefon, *das;* by ~: telefonisch; **be on the** ~: Telefon haben; *(be phoning)* telefonieren. **2.** *v. t. & i.* anrufen. **phone 'back** *v. t. & i.* zurückrufen; *(make further call)* wieder anrufen. **phone 'up** *v. t. & i.* anrufen

phone: ~ **book** *n.* Telefonbuch, *das;* ~ **box** *n.* Telefonzelle, *die;* ~ **call** *n.* Anruf, *der;* ~ **card** *n.* Telefonkarte, *die;* ~ **number** *n.* Telefonnummer, *die*

phonetic [fə'netɪk] *adj.* phonetisch. **phonetics** [fə'netɪks] *n.* Phonetik, *die*

phoney ['fəʊnɪ] *adj. (coll.)* (sham) falsch; gefälscht ⟨Brief, Dokument⟩

phonograph ['fəʊnəgrɑːf] *n. (Amer.)* Plattenspieler, *der*

phony see **phoney**

phosphorus ['fɒsfərəs] *n.* Phosphor, *der*

photo ['fəʊtəʊ] *n., pl.* ~s Foto, *das*

photo: ~**copier** *n.* Fotokopiergerät, *das;* ~**copy** **1.** *n.* Fotokopie, *die;* **2.** *v. t.* fotokopieren

photogenic [fəʊtə'dʒiːnɪk] *adj.* fotogen

photograph ['fəʊtəgrɑːf] **1.** *n.* Fotografie, *die;* Foto, *das;* **take a** ~ [**of sb./ sth.**] fotografieren. **2.** *v. t. & i.* fotografieren. **photographer** [fə'tɒgrəfə(r)] *n.* Fotograf, *der/*Fotografin, *die.* **photographic** [fəʊtə-'græfɪk] *adj.* fotografisch; Foto⟨ausrüstung, -apparat, -ausstellung⟩. **photography** [fə'tɒgrəfɪ] *n.* Fotografie, *die*

phrase [freɪz] **1.** *n.* [Rede]wendung, *die.* **2.** *v. t.* formulieren. **'phrasebook** *n.* Sprachführer, *der*

physical ['fɪzɪkl] *adj.* **a)** physisch ⟨Gewalt⟩; dinglich ⟨Welt, Universum⟩; **b)** *(of physics)* physikalisch; **c)** *(bodily)* körperlich. **physical edu'cation** *n. (Sch.)* Sport, *der.* **'physically** *adv. (relating to the body)* körperlich

physician [fɪ'zɪʃn] *n.* Arzt, *der/*Ärztin, *die*

physicist ['fɪzɪsɪst] *n.* Physiker, *der/* Physikerin, *die*

physics ['fɪzɪks] *n.* Physik, *die*

physiology [fɪzɪ'ɒlədʒɪ] *n.* Physiologie, *die*

physiotherapy [fɪzɪəʊ'θerəpɪ] *n.* Physiotherapie, *die*

physique [fɪ'ziːk] *n.* Körperbau, *der*

pianist ['piːənɪst] *n.* Pianist, *der/*Pianistin, *die*

piano [pɪ'ænəʊ] *n., pl.* ~s *(upright)* Klavier, *das; (grand)* Flügel, *der.* **piano-ac'cordion** *n.* Akkordeon, *das*

¹pick [pɪk] *n. (tool)* Spitzhacke, *die*

²pick 1. *n.* **a)** *(choice)* Wahl, *die;* **take your** ~: du hast die Wahl; **b)** *(best part)* Elite, *die;* **the** ~ **of the fruit** die besten Früchte. **2.** *v. t.* **a)** pflücken ⟨Blumen, Äpfel usw.⟩; lesen ⟨Trauben⟩; **b)** *(select)* auswählen; ~ **one's way** sich *(Dat.)* vorsichtig s[einen Weg suchen; **c)** ~ **one's nose** in der Nase bohren; **d)** ~ **sb.'s pocket** jmdn. bestehlen; **he had his pocket** ~**ed** er wurde von einem Taschendieb bestohlen; **e)** ~ **a lock** ein Schloß knacken *(salopp).* **3.** *v. i.* ~ **and choose** wählerisch sein. **'pick at** *v. t.* herumstochern in (+ *Dat.*) ⟨Essen⟩. **'pick on** *v. t. (victimize)* es abgesehen haben auf (+ *Akk.*). **pick 'out** *v. t.* **a)** *(choose)* auswählen; *(for oneself)* sich *(Dat.)* aussuchen; **b)** *(distinguish)* entdecken ⟨Detail, jmds. Gesicht in der Menge⟩. **pick up 1.** ['--] *v. t.* **a)** [in die Hand] nehmen; hochnehmen ⟨Baby⟩; *(after dropping)* aufheben; aufnehmen ⟨Masche⟩; ~ **up the telephone** den [Telefon]hörer abnehmen; **b)** *(collect)* mitnehmen; *(by arrangement)* abholen ⟨at, from von⟩; *(obtain)* holen ⟨c⟩ *(become infected by)* sich *(Dat.)* holen *(ugs.)* ⟨Virus, Grippe⟩; **d)** ⟨Bus, Autofahrer:⟩ mitnehmen; **e)** *(rescue from the sea)* [aus Seenot] bergen; **f)** empfangen ⟨Signal, Funkspruch usw.⟩; **g)** *(coll.: make acquaintance of)* aufreißen *(ugs.).* **2.** [-'-] *v. i.* **a)** sich bessern; **b)** ⟨Wind:⟩ auffrischen

'pickaxe *(Amer.:* **'pickax)** *see* **¹pick**

picket ['pɪkɪt] **1.** *n.* Streikposten, *der.* **2.** *v. i.* Streikposten stehen. **3.** *v. t.* Streikposten stellen vor (+ *Dat.*). **'picket-line** *n.* Streikpostenkette, *die*

pickle ['pɪkl] **1.** *n., usu. in pl. (food)* [Mixed] Pickles *Pl.* **2.** *v. t.* einlegen ⟨Gurken, Zwiebeln, Eier⟩; marinieren ⟨Hering⟩

pick: ~-**me-up** *n.* Stärkungsmittel, *das;* ~**pocket** *n.* Taschendieb, *der/*-diebin, *die;* ~**up** *n.* **a)** ~ [truck] Kleinlastwagen, *der;* **b)** *(of record-player, guitar)* Tonabnehmer, *der*

picnic ['pɪknɪk] **1.** *n.* Picknick, *das;* **go for** *or* **on/have a** ~: ein Picknick machen. **2.** *v. i.,* -**ck**- picknicken; Picknick machen. **'picnic site** *n.* Picknickplatz, *der*

pictorial [pɪk'tɔːrɪəl] *adj.* illustriert ⟨*Bericht, Zeitschrift*⟩; bildlich ⟨*Darstellung*⟩

picture ['pɪktʃə(r)] 1. *n.* a) Bild, *das;* **get the ~** ⟨*coll.*⟩ verstehen[, worum es geht]; **put sb. in the ~:** jmdn. ins Bild setzen; b) *(film)* Film, *der;* c) *in pl. (Brit.: cinema)* Kino, *das;* **go to the ~s** ins Kino gehen; **what's on at the ~s?** was läuft im Kino? 2. *v.t.* **~** [**to oneself**] sich *(Dat.)* vorstellen. **'picture-book** *n.* Bilderbuch, *das.* **picture postcard** *n.* Ansichtskarte, *die*

picturesque [pɪktʃə'resk] *adj.* malerisch

pidgin ['pɪdʒɪn] *n.* Pidgin, *das.* **pidgin English** *n.* Pidgin-Englisch, *das*

pie [paɪ] *n. (of meat, fish, etc.)* Pastete, *die; (of fruit etc.)* ≈ Obstkuchen, *der*

piece [piːs] 1. *n.* a) Stück, *das; (of broken glass or pottery)* Scherbe, *die; (of jigsaw puzzle, crashed aircraft, etc.)* Teil, *der; (Amer.: distance)* [kleines] Stück; **a ~ of meat/cake** ein Stück Fleisch/Kuchen; **~ of furniture/luggage** Möbel-/Gepäckstück, *das;* **a three-~ suite** eine dreiteilige Sitzgarnitur; **~ of luck** Glücksfall, *der; **~ of news/gossip/information** Nachricht, *die*/Klatsch, *der*/Information, *die;* b) *(Chess)* Figur, *die; (coin) gold* **~:** Goldstück, *das;* **a 10p ~:** ein 10-Pence-Stück, *das;* d) *(literary or musical composition)* Stück, *das;* **~ of music** Musikstück, *das.* 2. *v.t.* **~ to'gether** zusammenfügen **(from** aus)

piece: **~meal** *adv., adj.* stückweise; **~work** *n.* Akkordarbeit, *die*

pier [pɪə(r)] *n. (at seaside)* Pier, *der*

pierce [pɪəs] *v.t. (prick)* durchstechen; *(penetrate)* [ein]dringen in (+ *Akk.*) ⟨*Körper, Fleisch, Herz*⟩; **~ a hole in sth.** ein Loch in etw. *(Akk.)* stechen.

piercing ['pɪəsɪŋ] *adj.* durchdringend ⟨*Stimme, Schrei, Blick*⟩

piety ['paɪətɪ] *n.* Frömmigkeit, *die*

pig [pɪg] *n.* a) Schwein, *das; **~s might fly** *(iron.)* da müßte schon ein Wunder geschehen; b) *(coll.: greedy person)* Vielfraß, *der* (ugs.)

pigeon ['pɪdʒɪn] *n.* Taube, *die.* **'pigeon-hole** *n.* [Ablage]fach, *das; (for letters)* Postfach, *das*

piggy ['pɪgɪ]: **~back** *n.* **give sb. a ~back** jmdn. huckepack nehmen; **~ bank** *n.* Sparschwein[chen], *das*

pig'headed *adj.* dickschädelig (ugs.)

pigment ['pɪgmənt] *n.* Pigment, *das*

pig: **~sty** *n. (lit. or fig.)* Schweinestall, *der;* **~tail** *n. (plaited)* Zopf, *der;* **~tails** *(at either side of head)* Rattenschwänzchen *Pl.* (ugs.)

pike [paɪk] *n., pl. same* Hecht, *der*

pilchard ['pɪltʃəd] *n.* Sardine, *die*

'pile [paɪl] 1. *n.* a) *(of dishes, plates)* Stapel, *der; (of paper, books, letters)* Stoß, *der; (of clothes)* Haufen, *der;* b) *(coll.: large quantity)* Haufen, *der* (ugs.). 2. *v.t.* a) *(load)* [voll] beladen; b) *(heap up)* aufstapeln ⟨*Holz, Steine*⟩; aufhäufen ⟨*Abfall, Schnee*⟩. **pile 'in** *v.i. (seen from outside)* hineindrängen; *(seen from inside)* hereindrängen. **pile into** *v.t.* sich zwängen in (+ *Akk.*) ⟨*Auto, Zimmer, Zugabteil*⟩. **pile on 1.** *v.i. see pile in.* 2. *v.t. (fig.)* **~ on the pressure** Druck machen. **pile on to** *v.t.* drängen in (+ *Akk.*) ⟨*Bus usw.*⟩. **pile 'out** *v.i.* nach draußen drängen. **pile 'up** 1. *v.i.* a) ⟨*Waren, Post, Arbeit, Schnee:*⟩ sich auftürmen; ⟨*Verkehr:*⟩ sich stauen; b) *(crash)* aufeinander auffahren. 2. *v.t.* aufstapeln ⟨*Steine, Bücher usw.*⟩; aufhäufen ⟨*Abfall, Schnee*⟩

²pile *n. (of fabric etc.)* Flor, *der*

³pile *n. (stake)* Pfahl, *der.* **'pile-driver** *n.* [Pfahl]ramme, *die.*

piles [paɪlz] *n. pl. (Med.)* Hämorrhoiden *Pl.*

'pile-up *n.* Massenkarambolage, *die*

pilfer ['pɪlfə(r)] *v.t.* stehlen

pilgrim ['pɪlgrɪm] *n.* Pilger, *der*/Pilgerin, *die.* **pilgrimage** ['pɪlgrɪmɪdʒ] *n.* Pilgerfahrt, *die*

pill [pɪl] *n.* a) Tablette, *die;* Pille, *die* (ugs.); b) *(coll.: contraceptive)* **the ~** *or* **P~:** die Pille (ugs.); **be on the ~:** die Pille nehmen (ugs.)

pillage ['pɪlɪdʒ] *v.t.* [aus]plündern

pillar ['pɪlə(r)] *n.* Säule, *die.* **'pillar-box** *n. (Brit.)* Briefkasten, *der*

pillion ['pɪljən] *n.* Beifahrersitz, *der;* **ride ~:** als Beifahrer/Beifahrerin mitfahren

pillow ['pɪləʊ] *n.* [Kopf]kissen, *das.* **'pillowcase,** **'pillowslip** *ns.* [Kopf]kissenbezug, *der*

pilot ['paɪlət] 1. *n.* a) *(Aeronaut.)* Pilot, *der*/Pilotin, *die;* b) *(Naut.)* Lotse, *der.* 2. *adj.* Pilot⟨*programm, -studie, -projekt usw.*⟩. 3. *v.t.* a) *(Aeronaut.)* fliegen; b) *(Naut.: fig.)* lotsen

'pilot-light *n.* Zündflamme, *die*

pimp [pɪmp] *n.* Zuhälter, *der*

pimple ['pɪmpl] *n.* Pickel, *der*

pin 1. *n.* a) Stecknadel, *die;* **~s and needles** *(fig.)* Kribbeln, *das;* b) *(peg)*

Stift, *der;* c) *(Electr.)* **a two-/three-~~
plug** ein zwei-/dreipoliger Stecker. **2.
v. t., -nn-: a)** nageln ⟨*Knochen, Bein*⟩;
~ a badge to one's lapel sich *(Dat.)* ein
Abzeichen ans Revers stecken; **b)**
(fig.) **~ one's hopes on sb./sth.** seine
[ganze] Hoffnung auf jmdn./etw. setzen; **~ the blame for sth. on sb.** jmdm.
die Schuld an etw. *(Dat.)* zuschieben;
c) ~ sb. against the wall jmdn. an die
Wand drängen. **pin 'down** *v. t.* **a)**
(fig.) festnageln **(to** *or* **on** auf +
Akk.); **b)** *(trap)* festhalten. **pin 'up**
v. t. aufhängen ⟨*Bild, Foto*⟩: anschlagen ⟨*Bekanntmachung, Liste*⟩; auf-
stecken ⟨*Haar*⟩: heften ⟨*Saum*⟩

pinafore ['pɪnəfɔ:(r)] *n.* Schürze *die
(mit Oberteil)*

pincers ['pɪnsəz] *n. pl.* **a)** [**pair of**] **~:**
Beißzange, *die;* **b)** *(of crab etc.)* Schere, *die*

pinch [pɪntʃ] **1.** *n.* **a)** *(squeezing)* Kniff,
der; **give sb. a ~ on the arm/cheek**
jmdn. *od.* jmdm. in den Arm/die
Backe kneifen; **b)** *(fig.)* **feel the ~:**
knapp bei Kasse sein *(ugs.);* **at a ~:**
zur Not; **c)** *(small amount)* Prise, *die.*
2. *v. t.* **a)** kneifen; **~ sb.'s cheek/bot-
tom** jmdn. in die Wange/den Hintern
(ugs.) kneifen; **b)** *(coll.: steal)* klauen
(salopp)

'pincushion *n.* Nadelkissen, *das*

'pine [paɪn] *n. (tree)* Kiefer, *die*

²pine *v. i.* kümmern [vor Kummer] verzehren *(geh.)*. **pine a'way** *v. i.* dahin-
kümmern

pineapple ['paɪnæpl] *n.* Ananas, *die*

'pine-tree *n.* Kiefer, *die*

ping-pong *(Amer.:* **Ping-Pong,** P)
['pɪŋpɒŋ] *n.* Tischtennis, *das*

pink [pɪŋk] **1.** *n.* Pink, *das;* Rosa, *das.*
2. *adj.* pinkfarben; rosa

pinkie ['pɪŋkɪ] *n. (Amer., Scot.)* kleiner
Finger

'pin-money *n.* Taschengeld, *das*

pinnacle ['pɪnəkl] *n.* Gipfel, *der; (fig.)*
Höhepunkt, *der*

'pin-point *v. t.* genau festlegen

pint [paɪnt] *n.* Pint, *das;* ≈ halber Liter

'pin-up *(coll.) n.* Pin-up-Girl, *das; (picture) (of beautiful girl)* Pin-up-[-Foto],
das; (of sports, film or pop star) Starfo-
to, *das*

pioneer [paɪə'nɪə(r)] **1.** *n.* Pionier, *der.*
2. *v. t.* Pionierarbeit leisten für

pious ['paɪəs] *adj.* fromm

pip [pɪp] *n. (seed)* Kern, *der*

pipe [paɪp] **1.** *n.* **a)** *(tube)* Rohr, *das;* **b)**

(Mus.) Pfeife, *die;* **c)** [**tobacco-**]**~:** [Ta-
baks]pfeife, *die.* **2.** *v. t.* [durch ein
Rohr/durch Rohre] leiten. **pipe
'down** *v. i. (coll.)* ruhig sein. **pipe 'up**
v. i. (coll.) etwas sagen

'pipeline *n.* Pipeline, *die;* **in the ~**
(fig.) in Vorbereitung

piper ['paɪpə(r)] *n.* Pfeifer, *der*/Pfeife-
rin, *die; (bagpiper)* Dudelsackspieler,
der/-spielerin, *die*

piping hot ['paɪpɪŋ hɒt] *adj.* kochend-
heiß

piquant ['pi:kənt] *adj.* pikant

pique [pi:k] *n.* **in a** [**fit of**] **~:** verstimmt

piracy ['paɪrəsɪ] *n.* Seeräuberei, *die*

pirate ['paɪrət] *n.* **a)** Pirat, *der;* Seeräu-
ber, *der;* **b)** *(Radio)* **~ radio station** Pi-
ratensender, *der*

Pisces ['paɪsi:z] *n.* Fische *Pl.*

piss [pɪs] *(coarse)* **1.** *n.* **a)** *(urine)* Pisse,
die (derb); **b)** **have a/go for a ~:** pis-
sen/pissen gehen *(derb).* **2.** *v. i.* pissen
(derb)

pistol ['pɪstl] *n.* Pistole, *die*

piston ['pɪstən] *n.* Kolben, *der*

pit [pɪt] **1.** *n. (hole, mine)* Grube, *die;
(natural)* Vertiefung, *die.* **2.** *v. t.*, -tt-:
~ one's wits/skill *etc.* **against sth.** seinen Verstand/sein Können *usw.* an
etw. *(Dat.)* messen

¹pitch [pɪtʃ] **1.** *n.* **a)** *(Brit.: usual place)*
[Stand]platz, *der; (Sport: playing-area)*
Feld, *das;* Platz, *der;* **b)** *(Mus.)* Ton-
höhe, *die;* **c)** *(slope)* Neigung, *die.* **2.**
v. t. **a)** *(erect)* aufschlagen; **~ camp**
ein/das Lager aufschlagen; **b)** *(throw)*
werfen. **3.** *v. i.* stürzen; ⟨*Schiff:*⟩
stampfen; **~ forward** vornüberstürzen

²pitch *n. (substance)* Pech, *das.* **pitch-
'black** *adj.* pechschwarz; stockdunkel *(ugs.)* ⟨*Nacht*⟩. **pitch-'dark** *adj.*
stockdunkel *(ugs.)*

pitcher ['pɪtʃə(r)] *n.* [Henkel]krug, *der*

'pitchfork *n.* Heugabel, *die*

'pitfall *n.* Fallstrick, *der*

pith [pɪθ] *n.* **a)** *(of orange etc.)* weiße
Haut; **b)** *(fig.)* Kern, *der.* **'pithy** *adj.*
(fig.) prägnant

pitiable ['pɪtɪəbl], **pitiful** ['pɪtɪfl] *adjs.*
a) mitleiderregend; **b)** *(contemptible)*
jämmerlich

'pitiless *adj.* unbarmherzig

pittance ['pɪtəns] *n.* Hungerlohn, *der*

pity ['pɪtɪ] **1.** *n.* Mitleid, *das;* **feel ~ for
sb.** Mitgefühl für jmdn. empfinden;
have/take ~ on sb. Erbarmen mit
jmdm. haben; [**what a**] **~!** [wie] schade! **2.** *v. t.* bemitleiden; **I ~ you** du tust
mir leid

pivot ['pɪvət] 1. *n.* [Dreh]zapfen, *der.* 2. *v. i.* sich drehen

pixie ['pɪksɪ] *n.* Kobold, *der*

pizza ['piːtsə] *n.* Pizza, *die*

placard ['plækɑːd] *n.* Plakat, *das*

placate [plə'keɪt] *v. t.* beschwichtigen

place [pleɪs] 1. *n.* a) *(spot)* Stelle, *die;* a [good] ~ to park/to stop ein [guter] Platz zum Parken/eine [gute] Stelle zum Halten; **do you know a good/cheap ~ to eat?** weißt du, wo man gut/billig essen kann?; ~ of worship Andachtsort, *der;* all over the ~: überall; *(coll.: in a mess)* ganz durcheinander *(ugs.);* b) *(rank, position)* Stellung, *die;* put sb. in his ~: jmdn. in seine Schranken weisen; c) *(country, town)* Ort, *der;* ~ of birth Geburtsort, *der;* 'go ~s *(coll.: fig.)* es [im Leben] zu was bringen *(ugs.);* d) *(coll.: premises)* Bude, *die (ugs.);* **she is at his ~:** sie ist bei ihm; *at* this ~, *in* his ~: hier; **change ~s [with sb.]** [mit jmdm.] die Plätze tauschen; *(fig.)* [mit jmdm.] tauschen; *(step, stage)* in the first ~: zuerst; **why didn't you say so in the first ~?** warum hast du das nicht gleich gesagt?; g) *(proper ~)* Platz, *der;* **everything fell into ~** *(fig.)* alles wurde klar; **out of ~:** nicht am richtigen Platz; *(several things)* in Unordnung; **in ~** *(position in competition)* Platz, *der.* 2. *v. t.* a) *(vertically)* stellen; *(horizontally)* legen; b) *in p.p. (situated)* gelegen; c) *(find situation or home for)* unterbringen (with bei); d) *(class)* einordnen; einstufen; **be ~d second in the race** im Rennen den zweiten Platz belegen

placid ['plæsɪd] *adj.* ruhig

plagiarism ['pleɪdʒərɪzm] *n.* Plagiat, *das.* **plagiarize** ['pleɪdʒəraɪz] *v. t.* plagiieren

plague [pleɪg] 1. *n.* a) *(esp. Hist.: epidemic)* Seuche, *die;* the ~ *(bubonic)* die Pest; b) *(infestation)* ~ of rats Rattenplage, *die.* 2. *v. t.* plagen; **~d with** or **by sth.** von etw. geplagt

plaice [pleɪs] *n., pl. same* Scholle, *die*

plain [pleɪn] 1. *adj.* a) *(clear)* klar; *(obvious)* offensichtlich; b) *(frank)* offen; schlicht *〈Wahrheit〉;* **be ~ sailing** *(fig.)* [ganz] einfach sein; c) *(unsophisticated)* einfach; schlicht *〈Kleidung〉;* unliniert *〈Papier〉;* ohne Muster; d) wenig attraktiv *〈Mädchen〉.* 2. *adv.* a) *(clearly)* deutlich; b) *(simply)* einfach. 3. *n.* Ebene, *die.* **plain 'chocolate** *n.* halbbittere Schokolade. **plain 'clothes** *n. pl.* **in ~:** in Zivil

plainly *adv.* a) *(clearly)* deutlich; b) *(obviously)* offensichtlich; *(undoubtedly)* eindeutig; c) *(frankly)* offen; d) *(simply)* schlicht

plaintiff ['pleɪntɪf] *n.* Kläger, *der/*Klägerin, *die*

plaintive ['pleɪntɪv] *adj.* klagend

plait [plæt] 1. *n.* Zopf, *der.* 2. *v. t.* flechten

plan [plæn] 1. *n.* Plan, *der;* [go] **according to ~:** nach Plan [verlaufen], planmäßig [verlaufen]. 2. *v. t.,* -nn- planen; *(design)* entwerfen. 3. *v. i.,* -nn- planen

¹**plane** [pleɪn] *n.* ~|-tree] Platane, *die*

²**plane** 1. *n. (tool)* Hobel, *der.* 2. *v. t.* hobeln

³**plane** *n.* a) *(Geom.: fig.)* Ebene, *die;* b) *(aircraft)* Flugzeug, *das;* Maschine, *die (ugs.)*

planet ['plænɪt] *n.* Planet, *der*

plank [plæŋk] *n.* Brett, *das; (thicker)* Bohle, *die; (on ship)* Planke, *die*

plankton ['plæŋktən] *n.* Plankton, *das*

planner *n.* Planer, *der/*Planerin, *die*

planning *n.* Planen, *das;* Planung, *die*

plant [plɑːnt] 1. *n.* a) *(Bot.)* Pflanze, *die;* b) *no indef. art. (machinery)* Maschinen; c) *(factory)* Fabrik, *die;* Werk, *das.* 2. *v. t.* a) pflanzen; b) *(sl.: conceal)* anbringen *〈Wanze〉;* legen *〈Bombe〉;* ~ **sth. on sb.** jmdm. etw. unterschieben. **plantation** [plɑːn'teɪʃn] *n.* Plantage, *die*

plaque [plɑːk, plæk] *n.* a) Platte, *die; (commemorating sb.)* [Gedenk]tafel, *die;* b) *(Dent.)* Plaque, *die*

plaster ['plɑːstə(r)] 1. *n.* a) *(for walls etc.)* [Ver]putz, *der;* b) ~ [of Paris] Gips, *der;* c) *see* **sticking-plaster.** 2. *v. t.* a) verputzen *〈Wand〉;* b) *(daub)* ~ **sth. on sth.** etw. dick auf etw. *(Akk.)* auftragen. **plastered** ['plɑːstəd] *adj. (sl.: drunk)* voll *(salopp).* **plasterer** *n.* Gipser, *der*

plastic ['plæstɪk] 1. *n.* Plastik, *das;* Kunststoff, *der.* 2. *adj.* aus Plastik *od.* Kunststoff *nachgestellt;* ~ **bag** Plastiktüte, *die;* ~ **surgery** plastische Chirurgie

Plasticine, (P) ['plæstɪsiːn] *n.* Plastilin, *das*

plate [pleɪt] 1. *n.* a) Teller, *der; (serving ~)* Platte, *die;* b) *(metal ~ with name etc.)* Schild, *das;* c) *(for printing)* Platte, *die; (illustration)* [Bild]tafel, *die.* 2. *v. t.* ~ **sth. [with gold/silver]** etw. vergolden/versilbern

plateau ['plætəʊ] *n., pl.* ~x ['plætəʊz] *or* ~s Hochebene, *die;* Plateau, *das*

plate 'glass n. Flachglas, das
platform ['plætfɔːm] n. **a)** (Brit. Railw.) Bahnsteig, der; ~ 4 Gleis 4; **b)** (stage) Podium, das
platinum ['plætɪnəm] n. Platin, das
platitude ['plætɪtjuːd] n. Platitüde, die (geh.); Gemeinplatz, der
platoon [plə'tuːn] n. (Mil.) Zug, der
plausible ['plɔːzɪbl] adj. plausibel; einleuchtend
play [pleɪ] **1.** n. **a)** (Theatre) [Theater]stück, das; television ~: Fernsehspiel, das; **b)** (recreation) Spielen, das; Spiel, das; ~ on words Wortspiel, das; **c)** (Sport) Spiel, das; **d)** come into ~, be brought or called into ~: ins Spiel kommen. **2.** v. i. **a)** spielen; ~ safe sichergehen; ~ for time Zeit gewinnen wollen; **b)** (Mus.) spielen (on auf + Dat.). **3.** v. t. (also Sport, Theatre, Cards, Mus.) spielen; abspielen ⟨Schallplatte, Tonband⟩; schlagen ⟨Ball⟩; spielen gegen ⟨Mannschaft, Gegner⟩; ~ the violin etc. Geige usw. spielen; ~ a trick/joke on sb. jmdn. hereinlegen (ugs.)/jmdm. einen Streich spielen (fig.); ~ one's cards right (fig.) es richtig anfassen (fig.). **play a'bout, play a'round** v. i. spielen; stop ~ing about or around hör doch auf mit dem Unsinn! **play a'long** v. i. mitspielen. **play 'back** v. t. abspielen ⟨Tonband⟩. **play 'down** v. t. herunterspielen. **play 'up** v. i. (coll.) ⟨Kinder:⟩ nichts als Ärger machen. **2.** v. t. (coll.: annoy) ärgern
'playboy n. Playboy, der
'player n. Spieler, der/Spielerin, die
playful ['pleɪfl] adj. spielerisch; (frolicsome) verspielt
play: ~**ground** n. Spielplatz, der; (Sch.) Schulhof, der; ~ **group** n. Spielgruppe, die
playing: ~-**card** n. Spielkarte, die; ~-**field** n. Sportplatz, der
play: ~**mate** n. Spielkamerad, der/ Spielkameradin, die; ~-**off** n. Entscheidungsspiel, das; ~-**pen** Laufgitter, das; ~**thing** n. Spielzeug, das; ~**wright** ['pleɪraɪt] n. Dramatiker, der/Dramatikerin, die
PLC, plc abbr. (Brit.) public limited company ≈ GmbH
plea [pliː] n. Appell, der (for zu)
plead [pliːd] **1.** v. i. **a)** inständig bitten (for um); (imploringly) flehen (for um); ~ with sb. for sth. jmdn. inständig um etw. bitten; **b)** (Law; also fig.) plädieren. **2.** v. t. **a)** inständig bitten;

(imploringly) flehen; **b)** (Law) ~ guilty/not guilty sich schuldig/nicht schuldig bekennen. **'pleading** adj. flehend
pleasant ['plezənt] adj. angenehm
please [pliːz] **1.** v. t. gefallen (+ Dat.); ~ oneself tun, was man will; ~ yourself ganz wie du willst. **2.** v. i. I come and go as I ~: ich komme und gehe, wie es mir gefällt; if you ~: bitte schön. **3.** int. bitte; ~ do! aber bitte od. gern! **pleased** [pliːzd] adj. (satisfied) zufrieden (by mit); (happy) erfreut (by über + Akk.); be ~ at or about sth. sich über etw. (Akk.) freuen. **pleasing** ['pliːzɪŋ] adj. gefällig
pleasure ['pleʒə(r)] n. (joy) Freude, die; (enjoyment) Vergnügen, das; have the ~ of doing sth. das Vergnügen haben, etw. zu tun; with ~: mit Vergnügen
pleat [pliːt] n. Falte, die. **'pleated** adj. gefältelt; Falten⟨rock⟩
pledge [pledʒ] **1.** n. Versprechen, das. **2.** v. t. versprechen; geloben ⟨Treue⟩
plentiful ['plentɪfl] adj. reichlich; be ~: reichlich vorhanden sein
plenty ['plentɪ] n. ~ of viel; eine Menge; (coll.: enough) genug
pleurisy ['plʊərɪsɪ] n. Pleuritis, die; Brustfellentzündung, die
pliable ['plaɪəbl] adj. biegsam
plied see **ply**
pliers ['plaɪəz] n. pl. |pair of| ~: Zange, die
plight [plaɪt] n. Notlage, die
plimsoll ['plɪmsl] n. (Brit.) Turnschuh, der
plinth [plɪnθ] n. Sockel, der
plod [plɒd] v. i., -**dd**- trotten. **plod 'on** v. i. (fig.) sich weiterkämpfen
plonk [plɒŋk] n. (sl.) [billiger] Wein
plot [plɒt] **1.** n. **a)** (conspiracy) Verschwörung, die; **b)** (of play, novel) Handlung, die; **c)** (of ground) Stück Land. **2.** v. t., -**tt**-: **a)** [heimlich] planen; **b)** (mark on map) einzeichnen. **3.** v. i., -**tt**-: ~ against sb. sich gegen jmdn. verschwören. **'plotter** n. Verschwörer, der/Verschwörerin, die
plough [plaʊ] **1.** n. Pflug, der. **2.** v. t. pflügen. **plough 'back** v. t. (Finance) reinvestieren
plow (Amer./arch.) see **plough**
ploy [plɔɪ] n. Trick, der
pluck [plʌk] **1.** v. t. **a)** pflücken ⟨Obst⟩; ~ |out| auszupfen ⟨Federn, Haare⟩; **b)** (pull at) zupfen an (+ Dat.); **c)** (strip of feathers) rupfen. **2.** v. i. ~ at sth. an

etw. *(Dat.)* zupfen. 3. *n*. Mut, *der*.
pluck 'up *v. t.* ~ **up |one's| courage** all
seinen Mut zusammennehmen

pluckily ['plʌkɪlɪ] *adv.*, **'plucky** *adj*.
tapfer

plug [plʌg] 1. *n*. a) *(filling hole)* Pfropfen, *der*; *(in cask)* Spund, *der*; *(for
basin etc.)* Stöpsel, *der*; b) *(Electr.)*
Stecker, *der*. 2. *v. t.* **-gg-**: a) ~ |up| zu-
stopfen *(Loch usw.)*; b) *(coll.: advertise)* Schleichwerbung machen für.
plug 'in *v. t.* anschließen

plug-hole *n*. Abfluß, *der*

plum [plʌm] *n*. a) Pflaume, *die*; b)
(fig.) Leckerbissen, *der*; **a ~ job** ein
Traumjob *(ugs.)*

plumage ['plu:mɪdʒ] *n*. Gefieder, *das*

¹plumb [plʌm] 1. *v. t.* [aus]loten. 2.
adv. a) lotrecht; b) *(fig.)* genau

²plumb *v. t.* ~ **in** fest anschließen.
plumber ['plʌmə(r)] *n*. Klempner,
der. **plumbing** ['plʌmɪŋ] *n*. a)
Klempnerarbeiten *Pl.*; b) *(waterpipes)*
Wasserleitungen *Pl.*

plumb-line *n*. Lot, *das*

plume [plu:m] *n*. Feder, *die*; *(ornamental bunch)* Federbusch, *der*

plummet ['plʌmɪt] *v. i.* stürzen

plump [plʌmp] *adj.* mollig; rundlich.
plump for *v. t.* sich entscheiden für

plunder ['plʌndə(r)] 1. *v. t.* [aus]plün-
dern *(Gebäude, Gebiet)*. 2. *n*. Plünde-
rung, *die*; *(booty)* Beute, *die*

plunge [plʌndʒ] 1. *v. t.* stecken; *(into
liquid)* tauchen. 2. *v. i.* a) ~ **into sth.** in
etw. *(Akk.)* stürzen; b) *(Straße usw.:)*
steil abfallen. 3. *n*. Sprung, *der*; **take
the ~** *(fig. coll.)* den Sprung wagen

plural ['plʊərl] 1. *adj.* pluralisch; Plu-
ral-; ~ **noun** Substantiv im Plural. 2.
n. Mehrzahl, *die*; Plural, *der*

plus [plʌs] 1. *prep.* plus *(+ Dat.)*. 2. *n*.
(advantage) Pluspunkt, *der*

plush [plʌʃ] 1. *n*. Plüsch, *der*. 2. *adj.*
(coll.) feudal *(ugs.)*

Pluto ['plu:təʊ] *pr. n. (Astron.)* Pluto,
der

ply [plaɪ] 1. *v. t.* a) *(use)* gebrauchen; b)
nachgehen *(+ Dat.)* *(Handwerk, Ar-
beit)*; c) *(supply)* ~ **sb. with sth.** jmdn.
mit etw. versorgen; d) *(assail)* überhäufen. 2. *v. i.* ~ **between** zwischen
(Orten) [hin- und her]pendeln

plywood *n*. Sperrholz, *das*

p.m. [pi:'em] *adv.* nachmittags; **one** ~:
ein Uhr mittags

pneumatic [nju:'mætɪk] *adj.* pneuma-
tisch. **pneumatic 'drill** *n*. Preßluft-
bohrer, *der*

pneumonia [nju:'məʊnɪə] *n*. Lungen-
entzündung, *die*

PO *abbr.* a) **postal order** PA; b) **Post
Office** PA

¹poach [pəʊtʃ] *v. t.* a) *(catch illegally)*
wildern; illegal fangen *(Fische)*; b)
stehlen, *(ugs.)* klauen *(Idee)*

²poach *v. t. (Cookery)* pochieren *(Ei)*;
dünsten *(Fisch, Fleisch, Gemüse)*

poacher *n*. Wilderer, *der*

pocket ['pɒkɪt] 1. *n*. a) Tasche, *die*; b)
(fig.) **be in ~**: Geld verdient haben; **be
out of ~**: draufgelegt haben. 2. *adj.*
Taschen*(rechner, -uhr, -ausgabe)*. 3.
v. t. a) einstecken; b) *(steal)* in die
eigene Tasche stecken *(ugs.)*. **'pocket-
book** *n*. *(wallet)* Brieftasche, *die*;
(notebook) Notizbuch, *das*. **'pocket-
money** *n*. Taschengeld, *das*

'pock-marked *adj.* a) pockennarbig
(Gesicht, Haut); b) **a wall ~ with bul-
lets** eine mit Einschüssen übersäte
Wand

pod [pɒd] *n*. Hülse, *die*; *(of pea)* Schote, *die*

podgy ['pɒdʒɪ] *adj.* dicklich

poem ['pəʊɪm] *n*. Gedicht, *das*

poet ['pəʊɪt] *n*. Dichter, *der*. **poetic**
[pəʊ'etɪk] *adj.* dichterisch

poetry ['pəʊɪtrɪ] *n*. [Vers]dichtung,
die; Lyrik, *die*

poignant ['pɔɪnjənt] *adj.* tief *(Bedauern, Trauer)*; ergreifend *(Anblick)*

point [pɔɪnt] 1. *n*. a) *(tiny mark, dot)*
Punkt, *der*; b) *(of tool, pencil, etc.)*
Spitze, *die*; c) *(single item; unit of scor-
ing)* Punkt, *der*; d) *(stage, degree)* up
to a ~: bis zu einem gewissen Grad;
he gave up at this ~: an diesem Punkt
gab er auf; e) *(moment)* Zeitpunkt,
der; **be on the ~ of doing sth.** etw. gerade tun wollen; f) *(distinctive trait)* Seite, *die*; **best/strong ~**: starke Seite;
Stärke, *die*; g) *(thing to be discussed)*
come to or **get to the ~**: zum Thema
kommen; **be beside the ~**: keine Rolle
spielen; **make a ~ of doing sth.** [gro-
ßen] Wert darauf legen, etw. zu tun;
h) *(of story, joke, remark)* Pointe, *die*;
i) *(purpose)* Zweck, *der*; Sinn, *der*; j)
(precise place, matter) Punkt, *der*; Stelle,
die; ~ **of view** *(fig.)* Standpunkt, *der*;
k) *(Brit.)* |**power** or **electric| ~**: Steck-
dose, *der*; l) **usu in pl.** *(Brit. Railw.)*
Weiche, *die*. 2. *v. i.* a) zeigen, weisen
(to, at auf *+ Akk.)*; b) ~ **towards** or **to**
(fig.) [hin]deuten auf *(+ Akk.)*. 3. *v. t.*
richten *(Waffe, Kamera)* **(at** auf *+
Akk.)*; ~ **one's finger at sth./sb.** mit

dem Finger auf etw./jmdn. zeigen. **point 'out** *v.t.* hinweisen auf (+ *Akk.*); ~ **sth./sb. out to sb.** jmdn. auf etw./jmdn. hinweisen

point-'blank 1. *adj. (lit. or fig.)* direkt; glatt ⟨*Weigerung*⟩; ~ **range** kürzeste Entfernung. 2. *adv. (at very close range)* aus kürzester Entfernung

'pointed *adj.* a) spitz; b) *(fig.)* unmißverständlich

'pointer *n.* a) Zeiger, *der;* *(rod)* Zeigestock, *der;* b) *(coll.: indication)* Hinweis, *der* (to auf + *Akk.*)

'pointless *adj.* sinnlos; belanglos ⟨*Bemerkung, Geschichte*⟩

poise [pɔɪz] *n. (composure)* Haltung, *die; (self-confidence)* Selbstvertrauen, *das.* **poised** [pɔɪzd] *adj.* selbstsicher

poison ['pɔɪzn] 1. *n.* Gift, *das.* 2. *v.t.* vergiften. **'poisoning** *n.* Vergiftung, *die.* **poisonous** ['pɔɪzənəs] *adj.* giftig

poke 1. *v.t.* a) ~ **sth. [with sth.]** [mit etw.] gegen etw. stoßen; ~ **sth. into sth.** etw. in etw. *(Akk.)* stoßen; ~ **the fire** das Feuer schüren; b) stecken ⟨*Kopf*⟩. 2. *v.i.* a) [herum]stochern (at, in, among in + *Dat.*); b) *(pry)* schnüffeln *(ugs.).* 3. *n.* a) *(thrust)* Stoß, *der;* **give sb. a ~ [in the ribs]** jmdm. einen [Rippen]stoß versetzen; **give the fire a ~:** das Feuer [an]schüren. **poke a'bout, poke a'round** *v.i.* herumschnüffeln *(ugs.)*

'poker *n.* Schüreisen, *das*

²poker *n. (Cards)* Poker, *das od. der*

'poker-faced *adj.* mit unbewegter Miene *nachgestellt*

poky ['pəʊkɪ] *adj.* winzig

Poland ['pəʊlənd] *pr. n.* Polen *(das)*

polar ['pəʊlə(r)] *adj.* polar ⟨*Kaltluft, Gewässer*⟩; Polar⟨*eis, -gebiet, -fuchs*⟩. **polar 'bear** *n.* Eisbär, *der*

Pole [pəʊl] *n.* Pole, *der*/Polin, *die*

'pole *n. (support)* Stange, *die;* **drive sb. up the ~** *(Brit. sl.)* jmdn. zum Wahnsinn treiben *(ugs.)*

²pole *n. (Astron., Geog., Magn., Electr., fig.)* Pol, *der.* **'pole-star** *n.* Polarstern, *der*

'pole-vault *n.* Stabhochsprung, *der*

police [pə'liːs] 1. *n. pl.* Polizei, *die; (members)* Polizisten *Pl.; attrib.* Polizei-. 2. *v.t.* [polizeilich] überwachen ⟨*Fußballspiel*⟩; kontrollieren ⟨*Gebiet*⟩. **police:** ~ **force** *n.* the ~ force die Polizei; ~**man** [pə'liːsmən] *n., pl.* -**men** [pə'liːsmən] Polizist, *der;* ~ **station** *n.* Polizeirevier, *das;* ~**woman** *n.* Polizistin, *die*

'policy ['pɒlɪsɪ] *n.* Politik, *die*

'policy *n. (Insurance)* Police, *die*

polio ['pəʊlɪəʊ] *n., no art.* Polio, *die;* [spinale] Kinderlähmung

Polish ['pəʊlɪʃ] 1. *adj.* polnisch; **sb. is ~:** jmd. ist Pole/Polin. 2. *n.* Polnisch, *das; see also* **English 2 a**

polish ['pɒlɪʃ] 1. *v.t.* a) polieren; bohnern ⟨*Fußboden*⟩; putzen ⟨*Schuhe*⟩; b) *(fig.)* ausfeilen ⟨*Text, Theorie, Stil*⟩. 2. *n.* a) *(smoothness)* Glanz, *der;* b) *(substance)* Politur, *die;* c) *(fig.)* Schliff, *der.* **polish 'off** *v.t. (coll.)* a) *(consume)* verdrücken *(ugs.);* b) *(complete quickly)* durchziehen *(ugs.).* **polish 'up** *v.t.* a) polieren; b) ausfeilen ⟨*Stil*⟩; aufpolieren ⟨*Kenntnisse*⟩

polite [pə'laɪt] *adj.,* ~**r** [pə'laɪtə(r)], ~**st** [pə'laɪtɪst] höflich. **po'liteness** *n.* Höflichkeit, *die*

political [pə'lɪtɪkl] *adj.* politisch

politician [pɒlɪ'tɪʃn] *n.* Politiker, *der*/Politikerin, *die*

politics ['pɒlɪtɪks] *n.* Politik, *die; (of individual)* politische Einstellung

polka ['pɒlkə, 'pəʊlkə] *n.* Polka, *die.* **'polka dot** *n.* [großer] Tupfen

poll [pəʊl] 1. *n.* a) *(voting)* Abstimmung, *die; (to elect sb.)* Wahl, *die;* **go to the ~s** zur Wahl gehen; b) *(opinion ~)* Umfrage, *die.* 2. *v.t.* a) *(take vote[s] of)* abstimmen/wählen lassen; b) *(take opinion of)* befragen

pollen ['pɒlən] *n.* Pollen, *der;* Blütenstaub, *der.* **'pollen count** *n.* Pollenmenge, *die*

'polling-booth *n.* Wahlkabine, *die*

'poll-tax *n.* Kopfsteuer, *die*

pollutant [pə'luːtənt] *n.* [Umwelt]schadstoff, *der*

pollute [pə'luːt] *v.t.* verschmutzen ⟨*Luft, Boden, Wasser*⟩. **pollution** [pə'luːʃn] *n.* [Umwelt]verschmutzung, *die*

polo ['pəʊləʊ] *n.* Polo, *das.* **'polo-neck** *n.* Rollkragen, *der*

polyester [pɒlɪ'estə(r)] *n.* Polyester, *der*

polystyrene [pɒlɪ'staɪriːn] *n.* Polystyrol, *das;* ~ **foam** Styropor ⟨Ⓦ⟩, *das*

polytechnic [pɒlɪ'teknɪk] *n. (Brit.)* ≈ technische Hochschule

polythene ['pɒlɪθiːn] *n.* Polyäthylen, *das;* ~ **bag** Plastikbeutel, *der*

pomegranate ['pɒmɪgrænɪt] *n.* Granatapfel, *der*

'pommel-horse *n.* Seitpferd, *das*

pomp [pɒmp] *n.* Pomp, *der*

pom-pom ['pɒmpɒm] *n.* Pompon, *der;* ~ **hat** Pudelmütze, *die*

pompous ['pɒmpəs] *adj.* großspurig; gespreizt ‹*Sprache*›

pond [pɒnd] *n.* Teich, *der*

ponder ['pɒndə(r)] **1.** *v. t.* nachdenken über (+ *Akk.*) ‹*Frage, Ereignis*›; abwägen ‹*Vorteile, Worte*›. **2.** *v. i.* nachdenken (over, on über + *Akk.*)

ponderous ['pɒndərəs] *adj.* schwer

pong [pɒŋ] (*Brit. coll.*) **1.** *n.* Mief, *der* (*ugs.*). **2.** *v. i.* miefen (*ugs.*)

pony ['pəʊnɪ] *n.* Pony, *das*. **'ponytail** *n.* Pferdeschwanz, *der*. **ponytrekking** ['pəʊnɪtrekɪŋ] *n.* (*Brit.*) Ponyreiten, *das*

poodle ['puːdl] *n.* Pudel, *der*

¹pool [puːl] *n.* **a)** Tümpel, *der*; **b)** (*temporary*) Lache, *die*; ~ **of blood** Blutlache, *die*; **c)** (*swimming~~*) Schwimmbecken, *das*; (*public*) Schwimmbad, *das*; (*in house or garden*) Pool, *der*

²pool 1. *n.* **a)** (*Gambling*) [gemeinsame Spiel]kasse; **the ~s** (*Brit.*) das Toto; **b)** (*common supply*) Topf, *der*; **a ~ of experience** ein Erfahrungsschatz; **c)** (*game*) Pool[billard], *das*. **2.** *v. t.* zusammenlegen ‹*Geld, Ersparnisse*›; bündeln ‹*Anstrengungen*›

poor [pʊə(r)] **1.** *adj.* **a)** arm; **b)** (*inadequate*) schlecht; schwach ‹*Spiel, Gesundheit, Leistung, Rede*›; dürftig ‹*Kleidung, Essen, Unterkunft*›; **of ~ quality** minderer Qualität; **c)** (*paltry*) schwach ‹*Trost*›; schlecht ‹*Aussichten*›; **d)** (*unfortunate*) arm (*auch iron.*); **e)** karg ‹*Boden*›; **f)** (*deficient*) arm (**in** an + *Dat.*); ~ **in vitamins** vitaminarm. **2.** *n. pl.* the ~: die Armen. **poorly** ['pʊəlɪ] *adv., pred. adj.* schlecht

¹pop [pɒp] **1.** *v. i.* **-pp-:** **a)** (*make sound*) knallen; **b)** (*coll.: go quickly*) let's ~ **round to Fred's** komm, wir gehen kurz bei Fred vorbei (*ugs.*). **2.** *v. t.* **-pp-:** **a)** (*coll.: put*) ~ **the meat in the fridge** das Fleisch in den Kühlschrank tun; **b)** platzen ‹*Luftballon*›. **3.** *n.* **a)** Knall, *der*; Knallen, *das*; **b)** (*coll.: drink*) Brause, *die* (*ugs.*). **4.** *adv.* **go ~:** knallen. **pop 'out** *v. i.* hervorschießen; ~ **out to the shops** schnell einkaufen gehen

²pop (*coll.*) **1.** *n.* Popmusik, *die*; Pop, *der*. **2.** *adj.* Pop‹*star, -musik usw.*›

'popcorn *n.* Popcorn, *das*

pope [pəʊp] *n.* Papst, *der*/Päpstin, *die*

poplar ['pɒplə(r)] *n.* Pappel, *die*

popper ['pɒpə(r)] *n.* (*Brit. coll.*) Druckknopf, *der*

poppy ['pɒpɪ] *n.* Mohn, *der*

popular ['pɒpjʊlə(r)] *adj.* **a)** (*well liked*) beliebt; populär ‹*Entscheidung, Maßnahme*›; **b)** verbreitet ‹*Aberglaube, Irrtum, Meinung*›; allgemein ‹*Wahl, Unterstützung*›. **popularity** [pɒpjʊ'lærɪtɪ] *n.* Beliebtheit, *die*; (*of decision, measure*) Popularität, *die*. **popularize** ['pɒpjʊləraɪz] *v. t.* **a)** (*make popular*) populär machen; **b)** (*make understandable*) breiteren Kreisen zugänglich machen. **'popularly** *adv.* allgemein

populate ['pɒpjʊleɪt] *v. t.* bevölkern; bewohnen ‹*Insel*›. **population** [pɒpjʊ'leɪʃn] *n.* Bevölkerung, *die*; **Britain has a ~ of 56 million** Großbritannien hat 56 Millionen Einwohner

porcelain ['pɔːslɪn] *n.* Porzellan, *das*

porch [pɔːtʃ] *n.* Vordach, *das*; (*with side walls*) Vorbau, *der*; (*enclosed*) Windfang, *der*

porcupine ['pɔːkjʊpaɪn] *n.* Stachelschwein, *das*

¹pore [pɔː(r)] *n.* Pore, *die*

²pore *v. i.* ~ **over sth.** etw. [genau] studieren

pork [pɔːk] *n.* Schweinefleisch, *das*; *attrib.* Schweine-. **pork 'chop** *n.* Schweinekotelett, *das*. **pork 'pie** *n.* Schweinepastete, *die*

porn [pɔːn] *n.* (*coll.*) Pornographie, *die*; Pornos (*ugs.*)

pornographic [pɔːnə'græfɪk] *adj.* pornographisch; Porno- (*ugs.*)

pornography [pɔː'nɒgrəfɪ] *n.* Pornographie, *die*

porous ['pɔːrəs] *adj.* porös

porridge ['pɒrɪdʒ] *n.* [Hafer]brei, *der*

¹port [pɔːt] **1.** *n.* **a)** Hafen, *der*; **b)** (*Naut., Aeronaut.: left side*) Backbord, *das*. **2.** *adj.* (*Naut., Aeronaut.: left*) Backbord-; backbordseitig

²port *n.* (*wine*) Portwein, *der*

portable ['pɔːtəbl] *adj.* tragbar

¹porter ['pɔːtə(r)] *n.* (*Brit.: doorman*) Pförtner, *der*; (*of hotel*) Portier, *der*

²porter *n.* [Gepäck]träger, *der*/-trägerin, *die*; (*in hotel*) Hausdiener, *der*

portfolio [pɔːt'fəʊlɪəʊ] *n. pl.* ~**s a)** (*Polit.*) Geschäftsbereich, *der*; **b)** (*case, contents*) Mappe, *die*

porthole ['pɔːthəʊl] *n.* (*Naut.*) Seitenfenster, *das*; (*round*) Bullauge, *das*

portion ['pɔːʃn] *n.* **a)** (*part*) Teil, *der*; (*of ticket*) Abschnitt, *der*; **b)** (*of food*) Portion, *die*

portly ['pɔːtlɪ] *adj.* beleibt

portrait ['pɔːtrɪt] *n.* Porträt, *das*

portray [pɔː'treɪ] *v. t.* darstellen; (*make likeness of*) porträtieren

Portugal ['pɔːtjʊgl] *pr. n.* Portugal *(das).* **Portuguese** [pɔːtjʊ'giːz] **1.** *adj.* portugiesisch; *sb.* **is ~:** ist Portuguese/Portugiesin. **2.** *n., pl. same* **a)** *(person)* Portugiese, *der/*Portugiesin, *die;* **b)** *(language)* Portugiesisch, *das; see also* **English 2 a**

pose [pəʊz] **1.** *v. t.* aufwerfen ⟨*Frage, Problem*⟩; darstellen ⟨*Bedrohung*⟩; mit sich bringen ⟨*Schwierigkeiten*⟩. **2.** *v. i.* **a)** *(assume attitude)* posieren; *(fig.)* sich geziert benehmen; **b) ~ as** sich geben als. **3.** *n.* Pose, *die;* **strike a ~:** eine Pose einnehmen. **poser** ['pəʊzə(r)] *n. (question)* knifflige Frage

posh [pɔʃ] *adj. (coll.)* vornehm; nobel *(spött.);* stinkvornehm *(salopp)*

position [pə'zɪʃn] **1.** *n.* **a)** *(place occupied)* Platz, *der; (of player in team, of plane, ship, etc.)* Position, *die; (of hands of clock, words, stars)* Stellung, *die; (of building)* Lage, *die;* **be in/out of ~:** an seinem Platz/nicht an seinem Platz sein; **b)** *(Mil.)* Stellung, *die;* **c)** *(fig.: mental attitude)* Standpunkt, *der;* **d)** *(fig.: situation)* **be in a good ~** |**financially|** [finanziell] gut gestellt sein; **be in a ~ of strength** eine starke Position haben; **e)** *(rank)* Stellung, *die;* **f)** *(job)* Stelle, *die;* **g)** *(posture)* Haltung, *die.* **2.** *v. t.* plazieren; postieren ⟨*Polizisten, Wachen*⟩; **~ oneself** sich stellen/*(sit)* setzen

positive ['pɔzɪtɪv] *adj.* **a)** *(also Math.)* positiv; konstruktiv ⟨*Vorschlag*⟩; *(definite)* eindeutig; *(convinced)* sicher; **I'm ~ of it** ich bin [mir] [dessen] ganz sicher; **b)** *(Electr.)* positiv ⟨*Elektrode, Ladung*⟩; Plus⟨*platte, -leiter*⟩; **c)** *as intensifier (coll.)* echt

possess [pə'zes] *v. t.* besitzen; *(as faculty or quality)* haben; ⟨*Furcht usw.:*⟩ ergreifen; **what ~ed you?** *(coll.)* was ist in dich gefahren? **possessed** [pə'zest] *adj.* besessen. **possession** [pə'zeʃn] *n.* **a)** *(thing possessed)* Besitz, *der;* **some of my ~s** einige meiner Sachen; **b)** *in pl. (property)* Besitz, *der;* **c)** *(possessing)* Besitz, *der;* **be in ~ of sth.** im Besitz einer Sache *(Gen.)* sein; **take ~ of** in Besitz nehmen; beziehen ⟨*Haus, Wohnung*⟩. **possessive** [pə'zesɪv] *adj.* **a)** besitzergreifend; **be ~ about sth./sb.** etw. eifersüchtig hüten/ an jmdn. Besitzansprüche stellen; **b)** *(Ling.)* possessiv. **possessor** [pə'zesə(r)] *n.* Besitzer, *der/*Besitzerin, *die* **possibility** [pɔsɪ'bɪlɪtɪ] *n.* Möglichkeit, *die*

possible ['pɔsɪbl] *adj.* möglich; *(likely)* [gut] möglich; **if ~:** wenn möglich; **as ... as ~:** so ... wie möglich; möglichst ... **possibly** ['pɔsɪblɪ] *adv.* **a) as often as I ~ can** so oft ich irgend kann; **I cannot ~ commit myself** ich kann mich unmöglich festlegen; **b)** *(perhaps)* möglicherweise

¹**post** [pəʊst] *n.* **a)** *(as support)* Pfosten, *der;* **b)** *(stake)* Pfahl, *der;* **c)** *(starting/ finishing ~)* Start-/Zielpfosten, *der*

²**post 1.** *n.* **a)** *(Brit.: one dispatch/delivery of letters)* Postausgang, *der/* Post|zustellung|, *die;* **by return of ~:** postwendend; **b)** *no indef. art. (Brit.: official conveying)* Post, *die;* **by ~:** mit der Post; per Post; **c)** *(~ office)* Post, *die.* **2.** *v. t.* **a)** abschicken; **b)** *(fig. coll.)* **keep sb. ~ed** jmdn. auf dem laufenden halten

³**post 1.** *n.* **a)** *(job)* Stelle, *die;* Posten, *der;* **b)** *(Mil.: also fig.)* Posten, *der.* **2.** *v. t.* postieren; plazieren

postage ['pəʊstɪdʒ] *n.* Porto, *das*

postal ['pəʊstl] *adj.* Post-; postalisch ⟨*Aufgabe, Einrichtung*⟩; *(by post)* per Post *nachgestellt.* **'postal order** *n.* ≈ Postanweisung, *die*

post: ~-box *n. (Brit.)* Briefkasten, *der;* **~card** *n.* Postkarte, *die;* **~code** *n. (Brit.)* Postleitzahl, *die;* **~-'date** *v. t. (give later date to)* vordatieren

poster ['pəʊstə(r)] *n.* Plakat, *das*

posterior [pɔ'stɪərɪə(r)] *n. (joc.)* Hinterteil, *das (ugs.)*

posterity [pɔ'sterɪtɪ] *n., no art.* Nachwelt, *die*

posthumous ['pɔstjʊməs] *adj.* postum

post: ~man ['pəʊstmən], *pl.* **~men** ['pəʊstmən] *n.* Briefträger, *der;* **~mark 1.** *n.* Poststempel, *der;* **2.** *v. t.* abstempeln

post-mortem [pəʊst'mɔːtəm] *n.* Obduktion, *die*

post office *n.* **a)** *(organization)* Post, *der;* **the P~ Office** die Post; **b)** *(place)* Postamt, *das;* Post, *die*

postpone [pə'spəʊn] *v. t.* verschieben; *(for an indefinite period)* aufschieben. **post'ponement** *n.* Verschiebung, *die/*Aufschub, *der*

postscript ['pəʊskrɪpt] *n.* Nachschrift, *die; (fig.)* Nachtrag, *der*

posture ['pɔstʃə(r)] *n.* [Körper]haltung, *die*

'**post-war** *adj.* Nachkriegs-; der Nachkriegszeit *nachgestellt*

posy ['pəʊzɪ] *n.* Sträußchen, *das*

pot [pɒt] 1. *n.* a) [Koch]topf, *der;* go to ~ *(coll.)* den Bach runtergehen *(ugs.);* b) *(container, contents)* Topf, *der; (tea-pot, coffee-pot)* Kanne, *die;* c) *(coll.: large sum)* **a** ~ **of/~s of** massenweise. 2. *v.t.* ~ |up| eintopfen *(Pflanze)*

potassium [pəˈtæsɪəm] *n.* Kalium, *das*

potato [pəˈteɪtəʊ] *n., pl.* ~es Kartoffel, *die*

potent [ˈpəʊtənt] *adj.* [hoch]wirksam *(Droge);* stark *(Schnaps usw.);* schlagkräftig *(Waffe)*

potential [pəˈtenʃl] 1. *adj.* potentiell *(geh.);* möglich. 2. *n.* Potential, *das (geh.);* Möglichkeiten

'pot-hole *n.* a) Schlagloch, *das;* b) *(cave)* [tiefe] Höhle. **'pot-holer** *n.* Höhlenforscher, *der/-forscherin, die*

'pot-shot *n.* take a ~ |at sb./sth.| aufs Geratewohl [auf jmdn./etw.] schießen

'potted *adj.* a) *(planted)* Topf-; b) *(abridged)* kurzgefaßt

¹'potter *n.* Töpfer, *der/Töpferin, die*

²'potter *v.i.* ~ |about| [he]rumwerkeln *(ugs.)*

pottery [ˈpɒtərɪ] *n.* a) Töpferware, *die;* b) *(workshop, craft)* Töpferei, *die*

¹'potty [ˈpɒtɪ] *adj.* *(Brit. sl.)* verrückt *(ugs.)* *(about, on* nach)

²'potty *n.* *(Brit. coll.)* Töpfchen, *das*

pouch [paʊtʃ] *n.* Beutel, *der*

pouffe [puːf] *n.* Sitzpolster, *das*

poultry [ˈpəʊltrɪ] *n.* Geflügel, *das*

pounce [paʊns] *v.i.* a) sich auf sein Opfer stürzen; *(Raubvogel:)* herabstoßen auf (+ *Akk.*); b) *(fig.)* ~ |up|on/at sich stürzen auf (+ *Akk.*).

¹'pound [paʊnd] *n.* a) *(unit of weight)* [britisches] Pfund *(453,6 Gramm);* two ~|s| of apples 2 Pfund Äpfel; b) *(unit of currency)* Pfund, *das*

²'pound *n.* *(enclosure)* Pferch, *der; (for stray dogs)* Zwinger, *der; (for cars)* Abstellplatz, *der*

³'pound 1. *v.t.* *(crush)* zerstoßen. 2. *v.i.* a) *(make one's way heavily)* stampfen; b) *(Herz:)* heftig schlagen

pour [pɔː(r)] 1. *v.t.* gießen; *(into cup, glass)* einschenken. 2. *v.i.* a) *(flow)* strömen; *(Rauch:)* hervorquellen *(from* aus); ~ |with rain| in Strömen regnen; b) *(fig.)* strömen; ~ in herein-/hineinströmen; ~ out heraus-/hinausströmen. **pour 'down** *v.i.* it's ~ing down es gießt [in Strömen] *(ugs.)*

pout [paʊt] 1. *v.i.* einen Schmollmund machen. 2. *v.t.* aufwerfen *(Lippen)*

poverty [ˈpɒvətɪ] *n.* Armut, *die*

powder [ˈpaʊdə(r)] 1. *n.* a) Pulver, *das;* b) *(cosmetic)* Puder, *der.* 2. *v.t.* a) pudern; b) *(reduce to* ~) pulverisieren; ~ed milk Milchpulver, *das.* **'powdery** *adj.* pul|v[e]rig

power [ˈpaʊə(r)] 1. *n.* a) *(ability)* Kraft, *die;* do all in one's ~ to help sb. alles in seiner Macht Stehende tun, um jmdm. zu helfen; b) *(faculty)* Fähigkeit, *die;* c) *(strength, intensity)* Kraft, *die; (of blow)* Wucht, *die;* d) *(authority, political* ~) Macht, *die* (over über + *Akk.*); come into ~: an die Macht kommen; e) *(authorization)* Vollmacht, *die;* f) *(State)* Macht, *die;* g) *(Math.)* Potenz, *die;* h) *(Mech., Electr.)* Kraft, *die; (electric current)* Strom, *der.* 2. *v.t.* *(Triebstoff, Strom:)* antreiben; *(Batterie:)* mit Energie versorgen. **powerful** [ˈpaʊəfl] *adj.* a) *(strong)* stark; kräftig *(Tritt, Schlag, Tier);* heftig *(Gefühl, Empfindung);* hell, strahlend *(Licht);* b) *(mighty)* *(Clique, Person, Herrscher).* **powerless** *adj.* machtlos. **power station** *n.* Kraftwerk, *das*

p.p. [piːˈpiː] *abbr.* by proxy pp[a].

pp. *abbr.* pages

practicable [ˈpræktɪkəbl] *adj.* durchführbar *(Projekt, Plan)*

practical [ˈpræktɪkl] *adj.* a) praktisch; praktisch veranlagt *(Person);* b) *(virtual)* tatsächlich; c) *(feasible)* möglich. **practical 'joke** *n.* Streich, *der.* **practically** *adv.* praktisch; *(almost)* so gut wie; praktisch *(ugs.)*

¹'practice [ˈpræktɪs] *n.* a) *(repeated exercise)* Übung, *die;* be out of ~: außer Übung sein; b) *(session)* Übungen *Pl.;* **piano** ~: Klavierüben, *das;* c) *(of doctor, lawyer, etc.)* Praxis, *die;* d) *(action)* put sth. into ~: etw. in die Praxis umsetzen; e) *(custom)* Gewohnheit, *die;* **regular** ~: Brauch, *der*

²'practice, practiced, practicing *(Amer.)* see practis-

practise [ˈpræktɪs] 1. *v.t.* a) *(apply)* anwenden; praktizieren; b) ausüben *(Beruf, Religion);* c) trainieren in (+ *Dat.*) *(Sportart);* ~ the piano/flute Klavier/Flöte üben. 2. *v.i.* üben.

practised [ˈpræktɪst] *adj.* geübt.

practising [ˈpræktɪsɪŋ] *adj.* praktizierend *(Arzt, Katholik usw.)*

pragmatic [prægˈmætɪk] *adj.* pragmatisch

Prague [prɑːg] *pr. n.* Prag *(das)*

prairie [ˈpreərɪ] *n.* Grassteppe, *die; (in North America)* Prärie, *die*

praise [preɪz] 1. *v. t.* loben; *(more strongly)* rühmen. 2. *n.* Lob, *das.* '**praiseworthy** *adj.* lobenswert

pram [præm] *n. (Brit.)* Kinderwagen, *der*

prance [prɑːns] *v. i.* **a)** ⟨*Pferd:*⟩ tänzeln; **b)** *(fig.)* stolzieren; ~ **about** *or* **around** herumhüpfen

prank [præŋk] *n.* Streich, *der*

prattle ['prætl] 1. *v. i.* plappern *(ugs.).* 2. *n.* Geplapper, *das (ugs.)*

prawn [prɔːn] *n.* Garnele, *die*

pray [preɪ] *v. i.* beten (**for** um). **prayer** [preə(r)] *n.* **a)** ⟨*Gebet, das;* **b)** *no art. (praying)* Beten, *das*

preach [priːtʃ] 1. *v. i.* predigen (**to** zu, vor + *Dat.;* **on** über + *Akk.*). 2. *v. t.* halten ⟨*Predigt*⟩; predigen ⟨*Evangelium, Botschaft*⟩. '**preacher** *n.* Prediger, *der*/Predigerin, *die*

precarious [prɪˈkeərɪəs] *adj.* **a)** *(uncertain)* labil; prekär; **make a ~ living** eine unsichere Existenz haben; **b)** *(insecure, dangerous)* gefährlich

precaution [prɪˈkɔːʃn] *n.* Vorsichts-, Schutzmaßnahme, *die;* **as a ~:** vorsichtshalber

precede [prɪˈsiːd] *v. t. (in order or time)* vorangehen (+ *Dat.*). **precedence** ['presɪdəns] *n.* Priorität, *die (geh.),* Vorrang, *der* (**over** vor + *Dat.*). **precedent** ['presɪdənt] *n.* Präzedenzfall, *der*

precinct ['priːsɪŋkt] *n.* **a)** [**pedestrian**] ~**:** Fußgängerzone, *die;* **b)** *(Amer.: district)* Bezirk, *der*

precious ['preʃəs] 1. *adj.* **a)** kostbar ⟨*Schmuckstück, Zeit*⟩; **b)** *(beloved)* lieb; **c)** *(affected)* affektiert. 2. *adv. (coll.)* herzlich ⟨*wenig, wenige*⟩

precipice ['presɪpɪs] *n.* Abgrund, *der*

precipitate 1. [prɪˈsɪpɪtət] *adj.* eilig ⟨*Flucht*⟩; übereilt ⟨*Entschluß*⟩. 2. [prɪˈsɪpɪteɪt] *v. t. (hasten)* beschleunigen; *(trigger)* auslösen

precipitation [prɪsɪpɪˈteɪʃn] *n. (Meteorol.)* Niederschlag, *der*

precipitous [prɪˈsɪpɪtəs] *adj.* **a)** *(steep)* sehr steil; **b)** *see* **precipitate** 1

précis ['preɪsiː] *n., pl. same* [preɪsiːz] Zusammenfassung, *die*

precise [prɪˈsaɪs] *adj.* genau; präzise; fein ⟨*Instrument*⟩; förmlich ⟨*Art*⟩; **be** [**more**] ~**:** sich präzise[r] ausdrücken. **preˈcisely** *adv.* genau. **precision** [prɪˈsɪʒn] *n.* Genauigkeit, *die*

preclude [prɪˈkluːd] *v. t.* ausschließen

precocious [prɪˈkəʊʃəs] *adj.* frühreif ⟨*Kind*⟩; altklug ⟨*Äußerung*⟩

preconceived [priːkənˈsiːvd] *adj.* vorgefaßt ⟨*Ansicht, Vorstellung*⟩. **preconception** [priːkənˈsepʃn] *n.* vorgefaßte Meinung (**of** über + *Akk.*)

precondition [priːkənˈdɪʃn] *n.* Vorbedingung, *die* (**of** für)

precursor [priːˈkɜːsə(r)] *n.* Wegbereiter, *der*/-bereiterin, *die*

predator ['predətə(r)] *n.* Raubtier, *das; (fish)* Raubfisch, *der.* '**predatory** *adj.* räuberisch; ~ **animal** Raubtier, *das*

predecessor ['priːdɪsesə(r)] *n.* Vorgänger, *der*/-gängerin, *die*

predestine [priːˈdestɪn] *v. t.* von vornherein bestimmen (**to** zu)

predicament [prɪˈdɪkəmənt] *n.* Dilemma, *das*

predicate ['predɪkət] *n. (Ling.)* Prädikat, *das.* **predicative** [prɪˈdɪkətɪv] *adj. (Ling.)* prädikativ

predict [prɪˈdɪkt] *v. t.* voraus-, vorhersagen; vorhersehen ⟨*Folgen*⟩. **predictable** [prɪˈdɪktəbl] *adj.* voraussagbar; vorhersehbar ⟨*Ereignis, Reaktion*⟩; berechenbar ⟨*Person*⟩. **prediction** [prɪˈdɪkʃn] *n.* Vorhersage, *die*

predominance [prɪˈdɒmɪnəns] *n.* **a)** *(control)* Vorherrschaft, *die* (**over** über + *Akk.*); **b)** *(majority)* Überzahl, *die* (**of** von)

predominant [prɪˈdɒmɪnənt] *adj. (having more power)* dominierend; *(prevailing)* vorherrschend

predominate [prɪˈdɒmɪneɪt] *v. i. (be more powerful)* dominierend sein; *(be more important)* vorherrschen

pre-eminent [priːˈemɪnənt] *adj.* herausragend

pre-empt [priːˈempt] *v. t.* zuvorkommen (+ *Dat.*)

preen [priːn] *v. t.* putzen ⟨*Federn*⟩

prefab ['priːfæb] *n. (coll.)* Fertighaus, *das.* **prefabricated** [priːˈfæbrɪkeɪtɪd] *adj.* vorgefertigt

preface ['prefəs] 1. *n.* Vorwort, *das* (**to** Gen.). 2. *v. t. (introduce)* einleiten

prefect ['priːfekt] *n. (Sch.)* die Aufsicht führender älterer Schüler/führende ältere Schülerin

prefer [prɪˈfɜː(r)] *v. t.,* **-rr-** vorziehen; ~ **to do sth.** etw. lieber tun; ~ **sth. to sth.** etw. einer Sache *(Dat.)* vorziehen. **preferable** ['prefərəbl] *adj.* vorzuziehen *präd.;* vorzuziehend *attr.;* besser (**to** als). **preferably** ['prefərəblɪ] *adv.* am besten; *(as best liked)* am liebsten; **Wine or beer? – Wine, ~!** Wein oder Bier? – Lieber Wein! **preference**

['prefərəns] *n.* **a)** *(greater liking)* Vorliebe, *die;* for ~ see **preferably; have a ~ for sth. [over sth.]** etw. [einer Sache *(Dat.)*] vorziehen; **do sth. in ~ to sth. else** etw. lieber als etw. anderes tun; **b)** *(thing preferred)* **what are your ~s?** was wäre dir am liebsten?; **c) give ~ to sb.** jmdn. bevorzugen. **preferential** [prefə'renʃl] *adj.* bevorzugt *(Behandlung)*

prefix ['pri:fɪks] *n.* Präfix, *das*

pregnancy ['pregnənsɪ] *n.* *(of woman)* Schwangerschaft, *die;* *(of animal)* Trächtigkeit, *die*

pregnant ['pregnənt] *adj.* schwanger *(Frau);* trächtig *(Tier)*

prehistoric [pri:hɪ'stɒrɪk] *adj.* prähistorisch. **prehistory** [pri:'hɪstərɪ] *n.* Vorgeschichte, *die*

prejudge [pri:'dʒʌdʒ] *v. t.* vorschnell urteilen über (+ *Akk.*)

prejudice ['predʒʊdɪs] 1. *n.* Vorurteil, *das.* 2. *v. t.* beeinflussen. **prejudiced** ['predʒʊdɪst] *adj.* voreingenommen *(about* gegenüber, **against** gegen*)*

preliminary [prɪ'lɪmɪnərɪ] 1. *adj.* Vor-; vorbereitend *(Forschung, Maßnahme).* 2. *n., usu. in pl.* **preliminaries** Präliminarien *Pl.;* **as a ~ to sth.** als Vorbereitung auf etw. *(Akk.)*

prelude ['prelju:d] *n.* **a)** *(introduction)* Anfang, *der* (**to** *Gen.);* **b)** *(Theatre, Mus.)* Vorspiel, *das*

premature ['premətjʊə(r)] *adj.* **a)** *(hasty)* übereilt; **b)** *(early)* vorzeitig *(Altern, Ankunft);* verfrüht *(Bericht, Eile);* ~ **baby** Frühgeburt, *die.* **prematurely** *adv.* *(early)* vorzeitig; zu früh *(geboren werden);* *(hastily)* übereilt

premeditated [pri:'medɪteɪtɪd] *adj.* vorsätzlich

premier ['premɪə(r)] *n.* Premier[minister], *der*/Premierministerin, *die*

première ['premɪeə(r)] *n.* Premiere, *die;* Erstaufführung, *die*

premise ['premɪs] *n.* **a)** ~**s** *pl.* *(building)* Gebäude, *das;* *(buildings and land)* Gelände, *das;* *(rooms)* Räumlichkeiten *Pl.;* **b)** see **premiss**

premiss ['premɪs] *n.* Prämisse, *die*

premium ['pri:mɪəm] *n.* Prämie, *die;* **be at a ~** *(fig.)* sehr gefragt sein. **'Premium Bond** *n.* *(Brit.)* Prämienanleihe, *die;* Losanleihe, *die*

premonition [premə'nɪʃn] *n.* Vorahnung, *die*

preoccupation [prɒkjʊ'peɪʃn] *n.* Sorge, *die* **(with** um*)*

preoccupied [prɪ'ɒkjʊpaɪd] *adj.* *(lost in thought)* gedankenverloren; *(concerned)* besorgt **(with** um*)*

pre-'packed *adj.* abgepackt

preparation [prepə'reɪʃn] *n.* Vorbereitung, *die;* ~**s** *pl.* Vorbereitungen *Pl.* **(for** für*)*. **preparatory** [prɪ'pærətərɪ] 1. *adj.* vorbereitend *(Maßnahme, Schritt);* ~ **work** Vorarbeiten *Pl.* 2. *adv.* ~ **to sth.** vor etw. *(Dat.)*

prepare [prɪ'peə(r)] 1. *v. t.* **a)** vorbereiten; ausarbeiten *(Plan, Rede);* vorbereiten *(Person)* **(for** auf + *Akk.*); **be ~d to do sth.** *(be willing)* bereit sein, etw. zu tun; **b)** herstellen *(Chemikalie usw.);* zubereiten *(Essen).* 2. *v. i.* sich vorbereiten **(for** auf + *Akk.*)

prepaid [pri:'peɪd] *adj.* ~ **envelope** frankierter Umschlag

preponderance [prɪ'pɒndərəns] *n.* Überlegenheit, *die* (**over** über + *Akk.*)

preposition [prepə'zɪʃn] *n.* *(Ling.)* Präposition, *die*

prepossessing [pri:pə'zesɪŋ] *adj.* einnehmend

preposterous [prɪ'pɒstərəs] *adj.* absurd; grotesk *(Äußeres, Kleidung)*

prerequisite [pri:'rekwɪzɪt] 1. *n.* [Grund]voraussetzung, *die.* 2. *adj.* unbedingt erforderlich

prerogative [prɪ'rɒgətɪv] *n.* Privileg, *das;* Vorrecht, *das*

Presbyterian [prezbɪ'tɪərɪən] 1. *adj.* presbyterianisch. 2. *n.* Presbyterianer, *der*/Presbyterianerin, *die*

prescribe [prɪ'skraɪb] *v. t.* **a)** *(impose)* vorschreiben; **b)** *(Med.: also fig.)* verschreiben. **prescription** [prɪ'skrɪpʃn] *n.* **a)** Vorschreiben, *das;* **b)** *(Med.)* Rezept, *das*

presence ['prezəns] *n.* **a)** *(of person)* Anwesenheit, *die;* *(of things)* Vorhandensein, *das;* **in the ~ of** in Anwesenheit (+ *Gen.*); **b)** ~ **of mind** Geistesgegenwart, *die*

¹**present** ['prezənt] 1. *adj.* **a)** anwesend **(at** bei*);* **all those ~:** alle Anwesenden; **b)** *(existing now)* gegenwärtig; jetzig *(Bischof, Chef usw.);* **c)** *(Ling.)* ~ **tense** Präsens, *das;* Gegenwart, *die.* 2. *n.* **a)** the ~: die Gegenwart; **at ~:** zur Zeit; **for the ~:** vorläufig; **b)** *(Ling.)* Präsens, *das;* Gegenwart, *die*

²**present** 1. ['prezənt] *n.* *(gift)* Geschenk, *das.* 2. [prɪ'zent] *v. t.* **a)** schenken; überreichen *(Preis, Medaille, Geschenk);* ~ **sth. to sb. or sb. with sth.** jmdm. etw. schenken/überreichen; ~

sb. with difficulties/a problem jmdn. vor Schwierigkeiten/ein Problem stellen; b) überreichen ⟨Gesuch⟩ (to bei); vorlegen ⟨Scheck, Bericht, Rechnung⟩ (to Dat.); c) ~ one's case seinen Fall darlegen; c) (exhibit) zeigen; bereiten ⟨Schwierigkeit⟩; d) (introduce) vorstellen (to Dat.); vorlegen ⟨Abhandlung⟩; moderieren ⟨Sendung⟩. 3. v. refl. ⟨Problem:⟩ auftreten; ⟨Möglichkeit:⟩ sich ergeben; ~ oneself for an interview zu einem Gespräch erscheinen.

presentable [prɪ'zentəbl] adj. ansehnlich; I'm not ~: ich kann mich nicht so zeigen. **presentation** [prezən'teɪʃn] n. a) (giving) Schenkung, die; (of prize, medal) Überreichung, die; b) (ceremony) Verleihung, die; c) (of petition) Überreichung, die; (of cheque, report, account) Vorlage, die; (of case) Darlegung, die

present-day adj. heutig

presenter [prɪ'zentə(r)] n. (Radio, Telev.) Moderator, der/Moderatorin, die

presentiment [prɪ'zentɪmənt] n. Vorahnung, die

presently ['prezntlɪ] adv. bald; (Amer., Scot.: now) zur Zeit

preservation [prezə'veɪʃn] n. Erhaltung, die; (of leather, wood, etc.) Konservierung, die. **preservative** [prɪ'zɜːvətɪv] n. Konservierungsmittel, das. **preserve** [prɪ'zɜːv] 1. n. a) in sing. or pl. (fruit) Eingemachte, das; b) (fig.: special sphere) Domäne, die (geh.); c) wildlife/game ~: Tierschutzgebiet, das/Wildpark, der. 2. v. t. a) (keep safe) schützen (from vor + Dat.); b) bewahren ⟨Brauch⟩; wahren ⟨Anschein, Reputation⟩; c) (keep from decay) konservieren; einmachen ⟨Obst, Gemüse⟩; d) (protect) hegen ⟨Tierart, Wald⟩

preside [prɪ'zaɪd] v. i. präsidieren, vorsitzen (over Dat.); (at meeting etc.) den Vorsitz haben (at bei)

presidency ['prezɪdənsɪ] n. a) Präsidentschaft, die; b) (of society) Vorsitz, der

president ['prezɪdənt] n. a) Präsident, der/Präsidentin, die; b) (of society) Vorsitzende, der/die. **presidential** [prezɪ'denʃl] adj. Präsidenten-

¹press [pres] 1. n. a) (newspapers etc.) Presse, die; attrib. Presse-; b) see printing-press; c) (for flattening, compressing, etc.) Presse, die. 2. v. t. a) drücken; drücken auf (+ Akk.) ⟨Klin-

gel, Knopf⟩; treten auf (+ Akk.) ⟨Gas-, Brems-, Kupplungspedal usw.⟩; b) (urge) drängen ⟨Person⟩; (force) aufdrängen (lupJon Dat.); nachdrücklich vorbringen ⟨Forderung, Argument⟩; he did not ~ the point er ließ die Sache auf sich beruhen; c) (compress) pressen; auspressen ⟨Orangen, Saft⟩; keltern ⟨Trauben, Äpfel⟩; d) (iron) bügeln; e) be ~ed for time/money zu wenig Zeit/Geld haben. 3. v. i. a) (exert pressure) drücken; b) (be urgent) drängen; c) (make demand) ~ for sth. auf etw. (Akk.) drängen.

press a'head, press 'on v. i. (continue) [zügig] weitermachen; (continue travelling) [zügig] weitergehen/-fahren; ~ on with one's work sich mit der Arbeit ranhalten (ugs.)

²press v. t. ~ into service/use in Dienst nehmen; einsetzen

'press conference n. Pressekonferenz, die

pressing adj. (urgent) dringend

press: ~ release n. Presseinformation, die; ~-up n. Liegestütz, der

pressure ['preʃə(r)] 1. n. Druck, der; put ~ on sb. jmdn. unter Druck setzen; atmospheric ~: Luftdruck, der. 2. v. t. unter Druck setzen ⟨Person⟩; ~ sb. into doing sth. jmdn. [dazu] drängen, etw. zu tun. **'pressure-cooker** n. Schnellkochtopf, der. **'pressure group** n. Pressure-group, die

pressurize ['preʃəraɪz] v. t. a) see pressure 2; b) ~d cabin Druckkabine, die

prestige [pre'stiːʒ] n. Prestige, das. **prestigious** [pre'stɪdʒəs] adj. angesehen

presumably [prɪ'zjuːməblɪ] adv. vermutlich

presume [prɪ'zjuːm] 1. v. t. a) ~ to do sth. sich (Dat.) anmaßen, etw. zu tun; (take the liberty) sich (Dat.) erlauben, etw. zu tun; b) (suppose) annehmen. 2. v. i. lupJon sth. etw. ausnützen. **presumption** [prɪ'zʌmpʃn] n. a) (arrogance) Anmaßung, die; b) (assumption) Annahme, die. **presumptuous** [prɪ'zʌmptjʊəs] adj. anmaßend

presuppose [priːsə'pəʊz] v. t. voraussetzen

pretence [prɪ'tens] n. (Brit.) a) (pretext) Vorwand, der; b) no art. (make-believe, insincere behaviour) Verstellung, die; it is all or just a ~: das ist alles nicht echt

pretend [prɪ'tend] 1. v. t. a) vorgeben;

she ~ed to be asleep sie tat, als ob sie schlief[e]; b) *(imagine in play)* ~ to be sth. so tun, als ob man etw. sei. 2. *v. i.* sich verstellen; **she's only** ~**ing** sie tut nur so

pretense *(Amer.) see* **pretence**

pretension [prɪ'tenʃn] *n.* **a)** Anspruch, *der* (to auf + *Akk.*); b) *(pretentiousness)* Überheblichkeit, *die.* **pretentious** [prɪ'tenʃəs] *adj.* hochgestochen; wichtigtuerisch *⟨Person⟩;* *(ostentatious)* großspurig

pretext [pri:tekst] *n.* Vorwand, *der;* |up|on *or* under the ~ of doing sth. unter dem Vorwand, etw. tun zu wollen

prettily ['prɪtɪlɪ] *adv.* hübsch; sehr schön *⟨singen, tanzen⟩*

pretty ['prɪtɪ] 1. *adj.* *(also iron.)* hübsch. 2. *adv.* ziemlich; **I am** ~ **well** es geht mir ganz gut

prevail [prɪ'veɪl] *v. i.* a) die Oberhand gewinnen **(against,** over über + *Akk.*); b) |up|on sb. to do sth. jmdn. dazu bewegen, etw. zu tun; b) *(predominate)* *⟨Zustand, Bedingung:⟩* vorherrschen; c) *(be current)* herrschen

prevalence ['prevələns] *n.* Vorherrschen, *das*

prevalent ['prevələnt] *adj.* a) *(existing)* herrschend; weit verbreitet *⟨Krankheit⟩;* b) *(predominant)* vorherrschend

prevent [prɪ'vent] *v. t.* *(hinder)* verhindern; *(forestall)* vorbeugen; ~ **sb. from doing sth.,** ~ **sb.'s doing sth.,** *(coll.)* ~ **sb. doing sth.** jmdn. daran hindern, etw. zu tun. **prevention** [prɪ'venʃn] *n.* Verhinderung, *die;* *(forestalling)* Vorbeugung, *die.* **preventive** [prɪ'ventɪv] *adj.* vorbeugend; Präventiv*⟨maßnahme⟩*

preview ['pri:vju:] *n.* *(of film, play)* Voraufführung, *die;* *(of exhibition)* Vernissage, *die* (geh.)

previous ['pri:vɪəs] 1. *adj.* a) früher *⟨Anstellung, Gelegenheit⟩;* vorherig *⟨Abend⟩;* vorig *⟨Besitzer, Wohnsitz⟩;* **the ~ page** die Seite davor; b) *(prior)* ~ **to** vor (+ *Dat.*). 2. *adv.* ~ **to** vor (+ *Dat.*). **'previously** *adv.* vorher

pre-war ['pri:wɔː(r)] *adj.* Vorkriegs-

prey [preɪ] 1. *n., pl. same* a) *(animal[s])* Beute, *die;* **beast/bird of** ~: Raubtier, *das/*-vogel, *der;* b) *(victim)* Opfer, *das.* 2. *v. i.* ~ |up|on *⟨Raubtier, Raubvogel:⟩* schlagen; *(plunder)* ausplündern *⟨Person⟩;* Jagd machen auf (+ *Akk.*); ~ |up|on sb.'s mind jmdm. keine Ruhe lassen

price [praɪs] *n.* *(lit. or fig.)* Preis, *der;* **at a** ~ of zum Preis von; **what is the** ~ of **this?** was kostet das?; **at/not at any** ~: um jeden/keinen Preis. **'priceless** *adj.* a) *(invaluable)* unbezahlbar; b) *(coll.: amusing)* köstlich

price: ~-**list** *n.* Preisliste, *die;* ~-**rise** *n.* Preisanstieg, *der;* ~-**tag** *n.* Preisschild, *das*

prick [prɪk] 1. *v. t.* stechen; stechen in *⟨Ballon⟩;* aufstechen *⟨Blase⟩.* 2. *v. i.* stechen. 3. *n.* Stich, *der.* **'prick up** *v. t.* aufrichten *⟨Ohren⟩;* ~ **up one's/its ears** die Ohren spitzen

prickle ['prɪkl] 1. *n.* a) Dorn, *der;* b) *(Zool., Bot.)* Stachel, *der.* 2. *v. i.* kratzen. **prickly** ['prɪklɪ] *adj.* dornig; stachelig; *(fig.)* empfindlich

pride [praɪd] 1. *n.* a) Stolz, *der;* *(arrogance)* Hochmut, *der;* **take** |a| ~ **in** sth. auf jmdn./etw. stolz sein; **sb.'s** ~ **and joy** jmds. ganzer Stolz; b) *(of lions)* Rudel, *das.* 2. *v. refl.* ~ **oneself** |up|on sth. auf etw. *(Akk.)* stolz sein

pried *see* **pry**

priest [pri:st] *n.* Priester, *der.* **'priesthood** *n.* geistliches Amt

prim [prɪm] *adj.* spröde; *(prudish)* zimperlich

primarily ['praɪmərɪlɪ] *adv.* in erster Linie

primary ['praɪmərɪ] 1. *adj.* a) *(first)* primär *(geh.);* grundlegend; b) *(chief)* Haupt*⟨rolle, -ziel, -zweck⟩.* 2. *n.* *(Amer.: election)* Vorwahl, *die.* **'primary school** *n.* Grundschule, *die*

primate ['praɪmeɪt] *n.* a) *(Eccl.)* Primas, *der;* b) *(Zool.)* Primat, *der*

¹prime [praɪm] 1. *n.* Höhepunkt, *der;* **be in one's** ~ : in den besten Jahren sein. 2. *adj.* a) Haupt-; hauptsächlich; b) *(excellent)* erstklassig; vortrefflich *⟨Beispiel⟩*

²prime *v. t.* a) *(equip)* vorbereiten; ~ **sb. with information/advice** jmdn. instruieren/jmdm. Ratschläge erteilen; b) grundieren *⟨Wand, Decke⟩;* c) schärfen *⟨Sprengkörper⟩*

prime: ~ **'minister** *n.* Premierminister, *der/*-ministerin, *die;* ~ **'number** *n.* *(Math.)* Primzahl, *die*

¹primer *n.* a) *(explosive)* Zündvorrichtung, *die;* b) *(paint)* Grundierlack, *der*

primeval [praɪ'mi:vl] *adj.* urzeitlich; Ur*⟨zeiten, -wälder⟩*

primitive ['prɪmɪtɪv] *adj.* primitiv; *(prehistoric)* urzeitlich *⟨Mensch⟩*

primrose ['prɪmrəʊz] *n.* gelbe Schlüsselblume

Primus, (P) ['praɪməs] n. ~ |stove| Primuskocher, der

prince [prɪns] n. Prinz, der. **'princely** adj. fürstlich

princess [prɪn'ses] n. Prinzessin, die; (wife of prince) Fürstin, die

principal ['prɪnsɪpl] 1. adj. Haupt-; (most important) wichtigst... 2. n. (of college) Rektor, der/Rektorin, die

principality [prɪnsɪ'pælɪtɪ] n. Fürstentum, das

'principally adv. in erster Linie

principle ['prɪnsɪpl] n. Prinzip, das; **on the ~ that** ...: nach dem Grundsatz, daß ...; **in ~**: im Prinzip; **do sth. on ~** or **as a matter of ~**: etw. prinzipiell od. aus Prinzip tun

print [prɪnt] 1. n. a) (impression) Abdruck, der; (finger~) Fingerabdruck, der; b) (~ed lettering) Gedruckte, das; (type-face) Druck, der; c) **be in/out of ~** ⟨Buch:⟩ erhältlich/vergriffen sein; d) (~ed picture or design) Druck, der; e) (Photog.) Abzug, der. 2. v. t. a) drucken ⟨Buch, Zeitschrift usw.⟩; b) (write) in Druckschrift schreiben.

print 'out v. t. (Computing) ausdrucken

'printed adj. a) gedruckt; b) (published) veröffentlicht. **'printed matter** n. (Post) Drucksachen Pl.

'printer n. a) (worker) Drucker, der/Druckerin, die; (firm) Druckerei, die; b) (Computing) Drucker, der

'printing n. a) Drucken, das; b) (writing like print) Druckschrift, die; c) (edition) Auflage, die. **'printing-press** n. Druckerpresse, die

'printout n. (Computing) Ausdruck, der

prior ['praɪə(r)] 1. adj. vorherig ⟨Warnung, Zustimmung usw.⟩; früher ⟨Verabredung⟩; Vor⟨geschichte, -kenntnis⟩. 2. adv. **~ to** vor (+ Dat.); **~ to doing sth.** bevor man etw. tut/tat; **~ to that** vorher. **priority** [praɪ'ɒrɪtɪ] n. a) (precedence) Vorrang, der; attrib. vorrangig; **have** or **take ~**: Vorrang haben (over or + Dat.); **have ~** (on road) Vorfahrt haben; **give ~ to sb./sth.** jmdm./einer Sache den Vorrang geben; **give top ~ to sth.** einer Sache (Dat.) höchste Priorität einräumen; b) (matter) vordringliche Angelegenheit

prism ['prɪzm] n. Prisma, das

prison ['prɪzn] n. a) Gefängnis, das; attrib. Gefängnis-; b) (custody) Haft, die; **in ~**: im Gefängnis; **go to ~**: ins Gefängnis gehen. **'prisoner** n. Ge-

fangene, der/die; **take sb. ~**: jmdn. gefangennehmen

pristine ['prɪstiːn] adj. unberührt; **in ~ condition** in tadellosem Zustand

privacy ['prɪvəsɪ] n. Privatsphäre, die; (being undisturbed) Ungestörtheit, die; **invasion of ~** Eindringen in die Privatsphäre; **in the strictest ~**: unter strengster Geheimhaltung

private ['praɪvət] 1. adj. a) (outside State system) privat; Privat⟨schule, -industrie, -klinik usw.⟩; b) persönlich ⟨Dinge, Meinung, Interesse⟩; nichtöffentlich ⟨Versammlung, Sitzung⟩; privat ⟨Telefongespräch, Vereinbarung⟩; Privat⟨strand, -parkplatz, -leben⟩; geheim ⟨Verhandlung, Geschäft⟩; persönlich ⟨Gründe⟩; (confidential) vertraulich. 2. n. a) (Brit. Mil.) einfacher Soldat; b) **in ~**: privat; in kleinem Kreis ⟨feiern⟩; (confidentially) ganz im Vertrauen. **'privately** adv. privat ⟨erziehen, zugeben⟩; vertraulich ⟨jmdn. sprechen⟩; insgeheim ⟨denken, glauben⟩; **~ owned** in Privatbesitz

privation [praɪ'veɪʃn] n. Not, die; **suffer many ~s** viele Entbehrungen erleiden

privatize ['praɪvətaɪz] v. t. privatisieren

privet ['prɪvɪt] n. Liguster, der

privilege ['prɪvɪlɪdʒ] n. (right, immunity) Privileg, das; (special benefit) Sonderrecht, das; (honour) Ehre, die. **'privileged** adj. privilegiert

privy ['prɪvɪ] adj. **be ~ to sth.** in etw. (Akk.) eingeweiht sein

'prize [praɪz] 1. n. a) (reward, money) Preis, der; **win** or **take first ~**: den ersten Preis gewinnen; b) (in lottery) Gewinn, der. 2. v. t. **~ sth. |highly|** etw. hoch schätzen

²prize v. t. ~ |open| aufstemmen

prize: **~-giving** n. Preisverleihung, die; **~-money** n. Geldpreis, der; (Sport) Preisgeld, das; **~-winner** n. Preisträger, der/-trägerin, die; (in lottery) Gewinner, der/Gewinnerin, die

pro [prəʊ] n. in pl. the **~s and cons** das Pro und Kontra

probability [prɒbə'bɪlɪtɪ] n. Wahrscheinlichkeit, die; **in all ~**: aller Wahrscheinlichkeit nach

probable ['prɒbəbl] adj. wahrscheinlich; **highly ~**: höchstwahrscheinlich. **probably** ['prɒbəblɪ] adv. wahrscheinlich

probation [prə'beɪʃn] n. a) Probezeit, die; b) (Law) Bewährung, die; **on ~**:

auf Bewährung. **probationary** [prə'beɪʃənərɪ] *adj.* Probe-; ~ **period** Probezeit, *die*

probe [prəʊb] 1. *n.* a) Untersuchung, *die* (**into** *Gen.*); b) *(Med., Astron.)* Sonde, *die*. 2. *v. t.* untersuchen

problem ['prɒbləm] *n.* Problem, *das;* *(puzzle)* Rätsel, *das;* **what's the ~?** *(coll.)* wo fehlt's denn?; **the ~ about** *or* **with sb./sth.** das Problem mit jmdm./ bei etw. **problematic** [prɒblə'mætɪk], **problematical** [prɒblə'mætɪkl] *adj.* problematisch

procedure [prə'si:dʒə(r)] *n.* Verfahren, *das*

proceed [prə'si:d] *v. i. (formal)* a) *(on foot)* gehen; *(as or by vehicle)* fahren; *(after interruption)* weitergehen/-fahren; b) *(begin and carry on)* beginnen; *(after interruption)* fortfahren; ~ **in** *or* **with sth.** *(begin)* [mit] etw. beginnen; *(continue)* etw. fortsetzen; c) *(be under way) (Verfahren:)* laufen; *(be continued after interruption)* fortgesetzt werden. **pro'ceedings** *n. pl.* a) *(events)* Vorgänge, *Pl.* b) *(Law)* Verfahren, *das;* **legal ~:** Gerichtsverfahren, *das;* **start/take** [**legal**] **~:** gerichtlich vorgehen (**against** gegen)

proceeds ['prəʊsi:dz] *n. pl.* Erlös, *der* (**from** aus)

¹process ['prəʊses] 1. *n.* a) *(of time or history)* Lauf, *der;* **he learnt a lot in the ~:** er lernte eine Menge dabei; **be in the ~ of doing sth.** gerade etw. tun; b) *(proceeding, natural operation)* Vorgang, *der;* c) *(method)* Verfahren, *das*. 2. *v. t.* verarbeiten ⟨*Rohstoff, Signal*⟩; bearbeiten ⟨*Antrag, Akte*⟩; *(Photog.)* entwickeln ⟨*Film*⟩

²process [prə'ses] *v. i.* ziehen. **cession** [prə'seʃn] *n.* Zug, *der; (religious)* Prozession, *die; (festive)* Umzug, *der;* **go/march in ~:** ziehen

proclaim [prə'kleɪm] *v. t.* erklären ⟨*Absicht*⟩; geltend machen ⟨*Recht, Anspruch*⟩; verkünden ⟨*Amnestie*⟩; ausrufen ⟨*Republik*⟩. **proclamation** [prɒklə'meɪʃn] *n.* a) *(proclaiming)* Verkündung, *die;* b) *(notice)* Bekanntmachung, *die; (decree)* Erlaß, *der*

procure [prə'kjʊə(r)] *v. t.* beschaffen

prod 1. *v. t.,* **-dd-** *(poke)* stupsen *(ugs.);* stoßen mit ⟨*Stock, Finger usw.*⟩; ~ **sb.** gently jmdn. anstupsen. 2. *n.* Stupser, *der;* **give sb. a ~:** jmdm. einen Stupser geben

prodigal ['prɒdɪgl] *adj.* verschwenderisch; ~ **son** verlorener Sohn

prodigious [prə'dɪdʒəs] *adj.* ungeheuer

prodigy ['prɒdɪdʒɪ] *n.* [außergewöhnliches] Talent; **child ~:** Wunderkind, *das*

produce 1. ['prɒdju:s] *n.* Produkte *Pl.;* Erzeugnisse *Pl.* 2. [prə'dju:s] *v. t.* a) vorzeigen ⟨*Paß, Fahrkarte*⟩; b) produzieren ⟨*Show, Film*⟩; inszenieren ⟨*Theaterstück, Hörspiel*⟩; herausgeben ⟨*Schallplatte, Buch*⟩; c) *(manufacture)* herstellen; *(in nature; Agric.)* produzieren; d) *(cause)* hervorrufen; bewirken ⟨*Änderung*⟩; e) *(bring into being)* erzeugen; führen zu ⟨*Situation*⟩; f) *(yield)* geben ⟨*Milch*⟩; legen ⟨*Eier*⟩; g) ⟨*Baum, Blume:*⟩ tragen ⟨*Früchte, Blüten*⟩; entwickeln ⟨*Triebe*⟩; bilden ⟨*Keime*⟩. **producer** [prə'dju:sə(r)] *n.* a) *(Cinemat., Theatre, Radio, Telev.)* Produzent, *der/*Produzentin, *die;* b) *(Brit. Theatre/Radio/Telev.)* Regisseur, *der/*Regisseurin, *die*

product ['prɒdʌkt] *n.* a) Produkt, *das; (of industrial process)* Erzeugnis, *das; (of art or intellect)* Werk, *das;* b) *(result)* Folge, *die;* c) *(Math.)* Produkt, *das* (**of** aus)

production [prə'dʌkʃn] *n.* a) *(Cinemat.)* Produktion, *die; (Theatre)* Inszenierung, *die; (of record, book)* Herausgabe, *die;* b) *(making)* Produktion, *die; (manufacturing)* Herstellung, *die; (thing produced)* Produkt, *das; (thing created)* Werk, *das;* c) *(yielding)* Produktion, *die; (yield)* Ertrag, *der*. **pro'duction line** *n.* Fertigungsstraße, *die*

productive [prə'dʌktɪv] *adj.* leistungsfähig ⟨*Betrieb, Bauernhof*⟩; fruchtbar ⟨*Gespräch, Verhandlungen*⟩. **productivity** [prɒdʌk'tɪvɪtɪ] *n.* Produktivität, *die*

Prof. [prɒf] *abbr.* Professor Prof.

profane [prə'feɪn] *adj.* a) *(irreligious)* gotteslästerlich; b) *(secular)* weltlich; c) *(irreverent)* respektlos ⟨*Bemerkung*⟩; profan ⟨*Sprache*⟩

profess [prə'fes] *v. t.* a) *(declare openly)* bekunden ⟨*Vorliebe, Abneigung*⟩; ~ **to be/do sth.** erklären, etw. zu sein/tun; b) *(claim)* vorgeben; ~ **to be/do sth.** behaupten, etw. zu sein/tun

profession [prə'feʃn] *n.* a) Beruf, *der;* **be a pilot by ~:** von Beruf Pilot sein; b) *(body of people)* Berufsstand, *der.* **professional** [prə'feʃənl] 1. *adj.* a) Berufs⟨*ausbildung, -leben*⟩; beruflich ⟨*Qualifikation*⟩; b) *(worthy of or of profes-*

sion) (in technical expertise) fachmännisch; *(in attitude)* professionell; *(in experience)* routiniert; **c) ~ people** Angehörige hochqualifizierter Berufe; **d)** *(by profession)* gelernt; *(not amateur)* Berufs⟨*musiker, -sportler*⟩; Profi-⟨*sportler*⟩; **e)** *(paid)* Profi⟨*sport, -boxen*⟩. **2.** *n. (trained person)* Fachmann, *der*/Fachfrau, *die;* *(non-amateur; also Sport)* Profi, *der*

professor [prəˈfesə(r)] *n.* **a)** *(Univ.)* Professor, *der*/Professorin, *die* (of für); **b)** *(Amer.: teacher at university)* Dozent, *der*/Dozentin, *die*

proficiency [prəˈfɪʃənsɪ] *n.* Können, *das*

proficient [prəˈfɪʃənt] *adj.* fähig; gut ⟨*Pianist, Reiter usw.*⟩; geschickt ⟨*Radfahrer, Handwerker*⟩; **be ~ at** or **in maths** viel von Mathematik verstehen

profile [ˈprəʊfaɪl] *n.* **a)** *(side aspect)* Profil, *das;* **b)** *(biographical sketch)* Porträt, *das;* **c)** *(fig.)* **keep a low ~:** sich zurückhalten

profit [ˈprɒfɪt] *n.* Gewinn, *der;* Profit, *der;* **make a ~ from** or **out of sth.** mit etw. Geld verdienen; **make [a few pence] ~ on sth.** [ein paar Pfennige] an etw. *(Dat.)* verdienen. **profit by** *v. t.* profitieren von; Nutzen ziehen aus ⟨*Fehler, Erfahrung*⟩. **profit from** *v. t.* profitieren von

profitable [ˈprɒfɪtəbl] *adj.* rentabel; einträglich; *(fruitful)* nützlich

profiteer [prɒfɪˈtɪə(r)] **1.** *n.* Profitmacher, *der*/-macherin, *die.* **2.** *v. i.* bereichern. **profiteering** *n.* Wucher, *der*

profligate [ˈprɒflɪɡət] *adj.* verschwenderisch; **be ~ of** or **with sth.** verschwenderisch umgehen mit etw.

profound [prəˈfaʊnd] *adj.* tief; nachhaltig ⟨*Wirkung, Einfluß*⟩; tiefgreifend ⟨*Wandel, Veränderung*⟩; tiefempfunden ⟨*Beileid, Mitgefühl*⟩; tiefsitzend ⟨*Mißtrauen*⟩

program [ˈprəʊɡræm] **1.** *n.* **a)** *(Amer.)* see **programme** 1; **b)** *(Computing)* Programm, *das.* **2.** *v. t.,* **-mm-** *(Computing)* programmieren

programme [ˈprəʊɡræm] *n.* **a)** *[notice of] events)* Programm, *das;* **b)** *(Radio, Telev.)* Sendung, *die;* **c)** *(plan, instructions for machine)* Programm, *das*

progress [ˈprəʊɡres] **1.** *n.* **a)** *no pl., no indef. art. (onward movement)* [Vorwärts]bewegung, *die;* *(advance)* Fortschritt, *der;* **make ~:** vorankommen; ⟨*Student, Patient:*⟩ Fortschritte ma-

chen; **in ~:** im Gange. **2.** [prəˈɡres] *v. i.* **a)** *(move forward)* vorankommen; **b)** *(be carried on, develop)* Fortschritte machen. **progression** [prəˈɡreʃn] *n.* **a)** *(development)* Fortschritt, *der;* **b)** *(succession)* Folge, *die.* **progressive** [prəˈɡresɪv] *adj.* **a)** fortschreitend ⟨*Verbesserung, Verschlechterung*⟩; schrittweise ⟨*Reform*⟩; allmählich ⟨*Veränderung*⟩; **b)** *(favouring reform; in culture)* fortschrittlich; progressiv. **pro'gressively** *adv.* immer ⟨*schlechter, weiter*⟩

prohibit [prəˈhɪbɪt] *v. t. (forbid)* verbieten; **~ sb.'s doing sth., ~ sb. from doing sth.** jmdm. verbieten, etw. zu tun. **prohibition** [prəʊhɪˈbɪʃn, prəʊɪˈbɪʃn] *n.* Verbot, *das.* **prohibitive** [prəˈhɪbɪtɪv] *adj.* unerschwinglich ⟨*Preis, Miete*⟩; untragbar ⟨*Kosten*⟩

project 1. [ˈprɒdʒekt] *v. t.* werfen ⟨*Schein*⟩; senden ⟨*Strahl*⟩; *(Cinemat.)* projizieren. **2.** [prəˈdʒekt] *v. i. (jut out)* ⟨*Felsen:*⟩ vorspringen; ⟨*Zähne, Brauen:*⟩ vorstehen. **3.** [ˈprɒdʒekt] *n.* Projekt, *das*

projectile [prəˈdʒektaɪl] *n.* Geschoß, *das*

projection [prəˈdʒekʃn] *n.* **a)** *(protruding thing)* Vorsprung, *der;* **b)** *(estimate)* Hochrechnung, *die;* *(forecast)* Voraussage, *die*

projector [prəˈdʒektə(r)] *n.* Projektor, *der*

proliferate [prəˈlɪfəreɪt] *v. i. (increase)* sich ausbreiten. **proliferation** [prəlɪfəˈreɪʃn] *n.* starke Zunahme

prolific [prəˈlɪfɪk] *adj.* **a)** *(fertile)* fruchtbar; **b)** *(productive)* produktiv

prologue *(Amer.:* **prolog)** [ˈprəʊlɒɡ] *n.* Prolog, *der* (to zu)

prolong [prəˈlɒŋ] *v. t.* verlängern. **prolonged** [prəˈlɒŋd] *adj.* lang; lang anhaltend ⟨*Beifall*⟩

promenade [prɒməˈnɑːd] *n.* Promenade, *die*

prominence [ˈprɒmɪnəns] *n.* **a)** *(conspicuousness)* Auffälligkeit, *die;* **b)** *(distinction)* Bekanntheit, *die*

prominent [ˈprɒmɪnənt] *adj.* **a)** *(conspicuous)* auffallend; **b)** *(foremost)* herausragend; **he was ~ in politics** er war ein prominenter Politiker; **c)** *(projecting)* vorspringend; vorstehend ⟨*Backenknochen, Brauen*⟩

promiscuity [prɒmɪˈskjuːɪtɪ] *n.* Promiskuität, *die (geh.)*

promiscuous [prəˈmɪskjʊəs] *adj.* promiskuitiv *(geh.);* **a ~ man** ein Mann, der häufig die Partnerin wechselt

promise ['prɒmɪs] **1.** *n.* **a)** Versprechen, *das;* **sb.'s ~s** jmds. Versprechungen; **give** *or* **make a ~ [to sb.]** [jmdm.] ein Versprechen geben; **give** *or* **make a ~ [to sb.] to do sth.** [jmdm.] versprechen, etw. zu tun; **b)** *(fig.: reason for expectation)* Hoffnung, *die;* **a painter of** *or* **with ~:** ein vielversprechender Maler. **2.** *v.t.* **a)** versprechen; **~ sth. to sb., ~ sb. sth.** jmdm. etw. versprechen; **b)** *(fig.: give reason for expectation of)* verheißen *(geh.);* **~ sb. sth.** jmdm. etw. in Aussicht stellen. **3.** *v.i.* **~ well** *or* **favourably** vielversprechend sein; **I can't ~:** ich kann es nicht versprechen. **promising** ['prɒmɪsɪŋ] *adj.* vielversprechend

promote [prə'məʊt] *v.t.* **a)** *(to more senior job)* befördern; **b)** *(encourage)* fördern; **c)** *(publicize)* Werbung machen für; **d)** *(Footb.)* **be ~d** aufsteigen. **pro'moter** *n.* Veranstalter, *der/* Veranstalterin, *die.* **promotion** [prə'məʊʃn] *n.* **a)** Beförderung, *die;* **win** *or* **gain ~:** befördert werden; **b)** *(furtherance)* Förderung, *die;* **c)** *(publicization)* Werbung, *die;* *(instance)* Werbekampagne, *die;* **d)** *(Footb.)* Aufstieg, *der.* **promotional** [prə'məʊʃənl] *adj.* Werbe⟨kampagne, -broschüre usw.⟩

prompt [prɒmpt] **1.** *adj.* **a)** *(ready to act)* bereitwillig; **be ~ in doing sth.** *or* **to do sth.** etw. unverzüglich tun; **b)** *(done readily)* sofortig; **her ~ answer** ihre prompte Antwort; **take ~ action** sofort handeln; **c)** *(punctual)* pünktlich. **2.** *adv.* pünktlich; **at 6 o'clock ~:** Punkt 6 Uhr. **3.** *v.t.* **a)** *(incite)* veranlassen; **b)** *(supply with words)* soufflieren (+ *Dat.);* *(give suggestion to)* weiterhelfen (+ *Dat.);* **c)** hervorrufen ⟨*Kritik*⟩; provozieren ⟨*Antwort*⟩. **'promptly** *adv.* **a)** *(quickly)* prompt; **b)** *(punctually)* pünktlich

prone [prəʊn] *adj.* *(liable)* **be ~ to** anfällig sein für ⟨*Krankheiten*⟩; **be ~ to do sth.** dazu neigen, etw. zu tun

prong [prɒŋ] *n.* *(of fork)* Zinke, *die*

pronoun ['prəʊnaʊn] *n.* *(Ling.)* Pronomen, *das;* Fürwort, *das*

pronounce [prə'naʊns] **1.** *v.t.* **a)** *(declare)* verkünden; **~ sb./sth. [to be] sth.** jmdn./etw. für etw. erklären; **~ sb. fit for work** jmdn. für arbeitsfähig erklären; **b)** aussprechen ⟨*Wort, Buchstaben usw.*⟩. **2.** *v.i.* **~ on sth.** zu etw. Stellung nehmen; **~ for** *or* **in favour of/against sth.** sich für/gegen etw. aussprechen. **pronounced** [prə-

'naʊnst] *adj.* *(marked)* ausgeprägt. **pro'nouncement** *n.* Erklärung, *die;* **make a ~ [about sth.]** eine Erklärung [zu etw.] abgeben

pronunciation [prənʌnsɪ'eɪʃn] *n.* Aussprache, *die;* **what is the ~ of this word?** wie wird dieses Wort ausgesprochen?

proof [pru:f] **1.** *n.* **a)** *(fact, evidence)* Beweis, *der;* **b)** *no indef. art. (Law)* Beweismaterial, *das;* **c)** *(proving)* **in ~ of** zum Beweis (+ *Gen.);* **d)** *no art. (standard of strength)* Proof *o. Art.;* **100° ~ (Brit.). 128° ~ (Amer.)** 64 Vol.-% Alkohol; **e)** *(Printing)* Abzug, *der.* **2.** *adj.* **be ~ against sth.** unempfindlich gegen etw. sein; *(fig.)* gegen etw. immun sein; **b)** *in comb.* ⟨kugel-, einbruch-, idioten⟩sicher; ⟨schall-, wasser⟩dicht; **flame-~:** nicht brennbar

'proof-read *v.t.* Korrektur lesen. **'proof-reader** *n.* Korrektor, *der/* Korrektorin, *die*

prop [prɒp] **1.** *n.* Stütze, *die;* *(Mining)* Strebe, *die.* **2.** *v.t.,* **-pp-** stützen; **the ladder was ~ped against the house** die Leiter war gegen das Haus gelehnt. **prop 'up** *v.t.* stützen; *(fig.)* vor dem Konkurs bewahren ⟨*Firma*⟩; stützen ⟨*Regierung*⟩

propaganda [prɒpə'gændə] *n.* Propaganda, *die*

propagate ['prɒpəgeɪt] **1.** *v.t.* **a)** *(Hort., Agric.)* vermehren **(from, by** durch); **b)** *(spread)* verbreiten. **2.** *v.i.* **a)** *(Bot.)* sich vermehren; **b)** *(spread)* sich ausbreiten. **propagation** [prɒpə'geɪʃn] *n.* **a)** *(Hort., Agric.)* Züchtung, *die;* **b)** *(Bot.)* Vermehrung, *die;* **c)** *(spreading)* Verbreitung, *die*

propel [prə'pel] *v.t.,* **-ll-** antreiben. **pro'peller** *n.* Propeller, *der.* **pro'pelling 'pencil** *n.* *(Brit.)* Drehbleistift, *der*

propensity [prə'pensɪtɪ] *n.* **have a ~ to do sth.** *or* **for doing sth.** dazu neigen, etw. zu tun

proper ['prɒpə(r)] *adj.* **a)** *(accurate)* richtig; zutreffend ⟨*Beschreibung*⟩; eigentlich ⟨*Wortbedeutung*⟩; **b)** *postpos. (strictly so called)* im engeren Sinn nachgestellt; **in London ~:** in London selbst; **c)** *(genuine)* echt; richtig ⟨*Wirbelsturm, Schauspieler*⟩; **d)** *(satisfactory)* richtig; zufriedenstellend ⟨*Antwort*⟩; **e)** *(suitable)* angemessen; *(morally fitting)* gebührend; **do sth. the ~ way** etw. richtig machen; **f)** *attrib.*

(coll.: thorough) richtig. **'properly** *adv.* richtig; *(rightly)* zu Recht; ~ **speaking** genaugenommen

proper: ~ **'name,** ~ **'noun** *ns. (Ling.)* Eigenname, *der*

property ['prɒpətɪ] *n.* **a)** *(possession[s])* Eigentum, *das;* **b)** *(estate)* Besitz, *der;* Immobilie, *die (fachspr.);* **c)** *(attribute)* Eigenschaft, *die; (effect, special power)* Wirkung, *die*

prophecy ['prɒfɪsɪ] *n. (prediction)* Vorhersage, *die; (prophetic utterance)* Prophezeiung, *die*

prophesy ['prɒfɪsaɪ] *v. t. (predict)* vorhersagen; *(fig.)* prophezeien ⟨*Unglück*⟩*; (as fortune-teller)* weissagen

prophet ['prɒfɪt] *n.* Prophet, *der.* **pro-phetic** [prə'fetɪk] *adj.* prophetisch

proportion [prə'pɔ:ʃn] **1.** *n.* **a)** *(portion)* Teil, *der;* **b)** *(ratio)* Verhältnis, *das;* **the** ~ **of sth. to sth.** das Verhältnis von etw. zu etw.; **c)** *(correct relation; Math.)* Proportion, *die;* **be in** ~ **[to** *or* **with sth.]** im richtigen Verhältnis [zu *od.* mit etw.] stehen; **keep things in** ~ *(fig.)* die Dinge im richtigen Licht sehen; **be out of** ~**/all** *or* **any** ~ **[to** *or* **with sth.]** in keinem/keinerlei Verhältnis zu etw. stehen; **d)** *in pl. (size)* Dimension, *die.* **2.** *v. t.* proportionieren.

proportional [prə'pɔ:ʃənl] *adj.* **a)** *(in proportion)* entsprechend; **be** ~ **to sth.** einer Sache *(Dat.)* entsprechen; **b)** *(Math.)* **be directly/indirectly** ~ **to sth.** einer Sache *(Dat.)* direkt/umgekehrt proportional sein. **proportionate** [prə'pɔ:ʃənət] *adj. see* **proportional a**

proposal [prə'pəʊzl] *n.* Vorschlag, *der; (offer)* Angebot, *das;* ~ **[of marriage]** [Heirats]antrag, *der*

propose [prə'pəʊz] **1.** *v. t.* **a)** vorschlagen; ~ **sth. to sb.** jmdm. etw. vorschlagen; ~ **marriage [to sb.]** [jmdm.] einen Heiratsantrag machen; **b)** *(nominate)* ~ **sb. as/for sth.** jmdn. als/für etw. vorschlagen; **c)** *(intend)* ~ **doing** *or* **to do sth.** beabsichtige, etw. zu tun. **2.** *v. i. (offer marriage)* ~ **[to sb.]** jmdm. einen Heiratsantrag machen. **pro-position** [prɒpə'zɪʃn] *n.* **a)** *(proposal)* Vorschlag, *der;* **make** *or* **put a** ~ **to sb.** jmdm. einen Vorschlag machen; **b)** *(statement; Logic)* Aussage, *die*

propound [prə'paʊnd] *v. t.* darlegen

proprietary [prə'praɪətərɪ] *adj.* ~ **name** *or* **term** Markenname, *der*

proprietor [prə'praɪətə(r)] *n.* Inhaber, *der*/Inhaberin, *die*

propriety [prə'praɪətɪ] *n.* Anstand,

der; **breach of** ~**:** Verstoß gegen die guten Sitten

propulsion [prə'pʌlʃn] *n.* Antrieb, *der*

prosaic [prə'zeɪɪk] *adj.* prosaisch *(geh.);* nüchtern

proscribe [prə'skraɪb] *v. t.* verbieten

prose [prəʊz] *n.* Prosa, *die; attrib.* Prosa⟨*werk, -stil*⟩

prosecute ['prɒsɪkju:t] **1.** *v. t.* strafrechtlich verfolgen; ~ **sb. for sth./doing sth.** jmdn. wegen etw. strafrechtlich verfolgen/jmdn. strafrechtlich verfolgen, weil *or* etw. tut/getan hat. **2.** *v. i.* Anzeige erstatten. **pro-secution** [prɒsɪ'kju:ʃn] *n. (bringing to trial)* [strafrechtliche] Verfolgung; *(court procedure)* Anklage, *die; (prosecuting party)* Anklage[vertretung], *die;* **the** ~**:** die Anklage. **prosecutor** ['prɒsɪkju:tə(r)] *n.* Ankläger, *der*/Anklägerin, *die;* **public** ~ ≈ Generalstaatsanwalt, *der*/-anwältin, *die*

prospect 1. ['prɒspekt] *n.* **a)** *(expectation)* Erwartung, *die* (of hinsichtlich); **[at the]** ~ **of sth./doing sth.** [bei der] Aussicht auf etw.*(Akk.)*/[darauf], etw. zu tun; **b)** *in pl. (hope of success)* Zukunftsaussichten; **a man with [good]** ~**s** ein Mann mit Zukunft; **sb.'s** ~**s of sth./doing sth.** jmds. Chancen auf etw. *(Akk.)*/darauf, etw. zu tun; **the** ~**s for sb./sth.** die Aussichten für jmdn./etw. **2.** [prə'spekt] *v. i.* nach Bodenschätzen suchen. **prospective** [prə'spektɪv] *adj.* voraussichtlich; zukünftig *(Erbe, Braut)*; potentiell *(Käufer, Kandidat)*. **prospector** [prə'spektə(r)] *n.* Prospektor, *der; (for gold)* Goldsucher, *der*

prospectus [prə'spektəs] *n.* Prospekt, *der; (Brit. Univ.)* Studienführer, *der*

prosper ['prɒspə(r)] *v. i.* gedeihen; *(Geschäft:)* florieren; *(Berufstätiger:)* Erfolg haben. **prosperity** [prɒ'sperɪtɪ] *n.* Wohlstand, *der.* **prosperous** ['prɒspərəs] *adj.* wohlhabend; florierend ⟨*Unternehmen*⟩

prostitute ['prɒstɪtju:t] *n.* Prostituierte, *die.* **prostitution** [prɒstɪ'tju:ʃn] *n.* Prostitution, *die*

prostrate 1. ['prɒstreɪt] *adj.* [auf dem Bauch] ausgestreckt. **2.** [prə'streɪt] *v. refl.* ~ **oneself [at sth./before sb.]** sich [vor etw./jmdm.] niederwerfen

protagonist [prəʊ'tægənɪst] *n. (Lit.)* Protagonist, *der*/Protagonistin, *die*

protect [prə'tekt] *v. t.* **a)** schützen *(from vor* + *Dat., against gegen);* **b)** *(preserve)* unter [Natur]schutz stellen

⟨Pflanze, Tier⟩. **protection** [prə-'tekʃn] n. Schutz, der (from vor + Dat., **against** gegen). **protective** [prə'tektɪv] adj. schützend; Schutz-⟨hülle, -anstrich, -vorrichtung, -maske⟩; be ~ **towards sb.** fürsorglich gegenüber jmdm. sein

protein ['prəʊti:n] n. Protein, das (fachspr.); Eiweiß, das

protest 1. ['prəʊtest] n. **a)** Beschwerde, die; **make** or **lodge a** ~ [**against sb.**/ **sth.**] eine Beschwerde [gegen jmdn./ etw.] einreichen; **b)** (gesture of disapproval) ~[s] Protest, der; **under** ~: unter Protest; **in** ~ [**against sth.**] aus Protest [gegen etw.]; **c)** no art. (dissent) Protest, der. 2. [prə'test] v.t. (affirm) beteuern. 3. [prə'test] v.i. protestieren (**about** gegen); (make written or formal ~) Protest einlegen (**to** bei)

Protestant ['prɒtɪstənt] 1. n. Protestant, der/Protestantin, die. 2. adj. protestantisch; evangelisch

pro·tester n. Protestierende, der/die; (at demonstration) Demonstrant, der/ Demonstrantin, die

protocol ['prəʊtəkɒl] n. Protokoll, das

proton ['prəʊtɒn] n. Proton, das

prototype ['prəʊtətaɪp] n. Prototyp, der

protract [prə'trækt] v.t. verlängern. **protractor** [prə'træktə(r)] n. (Geom.) Winkelmesser, der

protrude [prə'tru:d] v.i. herausragen (**from** aus); ⟨Zähne⟩ vorstehen

proud [praʊd] 1. adj. **a)** stolz; ~ **to do sth.** or **to be doing sth.** stolz darauf, etw. zu tun; ~ **of sb.**/**sth.**/**doing sth.** stolz auf/darauf/davon, etw. zu tun; **b)** (arrogant) hochmütig. 2. adv. (Brit. coll.) **do sb.** ~: jmdn. verwöhnen. **proudly** adv. **a)** stolz; **b)** (arrogantly) hochmütig

prove [pru:v] 1. v.t., p.p. ~**d** or **proven** ['pru:vn] beweisen; nachweisen ⟨Identität⟩; ~ **one's ability** sein Können unter Beweis stellen; ~ **sb. right**/ **wrong** ⟨Ereignis:⟩ jmdm. recht/unrecht geben; **be** ~**d wrong** or **to be false** ⟨Theorie:⟩ widerlegt werden; ~ **one's/sb.'s case** or **point** beweisen, daß man recht hat/jmdm. recht geben. 2. v. refl., p.p. **proved** or **proven:** ~ **oneself** sich bewähren. 3. v.i., p.p. **proved** or **proven:** ~ [**to be**] sich erweisen als

proven see **prove**

proverb ['prɒvɜ:b] n. Sprichwort, das. **proverbial** [prə'vɜ:bɪəl] adj. sprichwörtlich

provide [prə'vaɪd] v.t. **a)** besorgen; liefern ⟨Beweis⟩; bereitstellen ⟨Dienst, Geld⟩; ~ **a home**/**a car for sb.** jmdm. Unterkunft/ein Auto [zur Verfügung] stellen; **b)** ⟨Vertrag, Gesetz:⟩ vorsehen. **pro·vide for** v.t. **a)** (make provision for) vorsorgen für ⟨Plan, Gesetz:⟩ vorsehen; **b)** (maintain) sorgen für, versorgen ⟨Familie, Kind⟩. **pro·vided** conj. ~ [**that**] ...: vorausgesetzt, [daß] ...

providence ['prɒvɪdəns] n. **a)** [divine] ~: die [göttliche] Vorsehung; **b)** P~ (God) der Himmel

province ['prɒvɪns] n. **a)** Provinz, die; **b)** the ~s (regions outside capital) die Provinz; **c)** (sphere of action) [Tätigkeits]bereich, der; (area of responsibility) Zuständigkeitsbereich, der. **provincial** [prə'vɪnʃl] adj. Provinz-

provision [prə'vɪʒn] n. **a)** (providing) Bereitstellung, die; **make** ~ **for** vorsorgen od. Vorsorge treffen für ⟨Notfall⟩; **b)** ~**s** pl. (food) Lebensmittel

provisional [prə'vɪʒənl] adj., **provisionally** [prə'vɪʒənəlɪ] adv. vorläufig; provisorisch

proviso [prə'vaɪzəʊ] n., pl. ~**s** Vorbehalt, der

provocation [prɒvə'keɪʃn] n. Provokation, die

provocative [prə'vɒkətɪv] adj. provozierend; (sexually) aufreizend

provoke [prə'vəʊk] v.t. **a)** provozieren ⟨Person⟩; reizen ⟨Person, Tier⟩; ~ **sb. into doing sth.** jmdn. so sehr provozieren, daß er etw. tut; **b)** (give rise to) hervorrufen; erregen

prow [praʊ] n. (Naut.) Bug, der

prowl [praʊl] 1. v.i. streifen. 2. v.t. durchstreifen. 3. n. **be on the** ~: auf einem Streifzug sein

proximity [prɒk'sɪmɪtɪ] n. Nähe, die

proxy ['prɒksɪ] n. **by** ~: durch einen Bevollmächtigten/eine Bevollmächtigte

prude [pru:d] n. prüder Mensch

prudence ['pru:dəns] n. Besonnenheit, die

prudent ['pru:dənt] adj. **a)** (careful) besonnen; **b)** (circumspect) vorsichtig

prudish ['pru:dɪʃ] adj. prüde

¹**prune** [pru:n] n. Backpflaume, die

²**prune** v.t. **a)** (trim) [be]schneiden; **b)** (fig.) reduzieren

pry [praɪ] v.i. neugierig sein. **'pry into** v.t. seine Nase stecken in (+ Akk.) (ugs.) ⟨Angelegenheit⟩

PS abbr. postscript PS

psalm [sɑ:m] n. Psalm, der

pseudonym ['sju:dənɪm] n. Pseudonym, das

psychiatric [saɪkɪ'ætrɪk] adj. psychiatrisch

psychiatrist [saɪ'kaɪətrɪst] n. Psychiater, der/Psychiaterin, die

psychiatry [saɪ'kaɪətrɪ] n. Psychiatrie, die

psychic ['saɪkɪk] adj. be ~: übernatürliche Fähigkeiten haben

psychoanalyse [saɪkəʊænəlaɪz] v.t. psychoanalysieren. **psychoa'nalysis** n. Psychoanalyse, die. **psycho'analyst** n. Psychoanalytiker, der/-analytikerin, die

psychological [saɪkə'lɒdʒɪkl] adj. psychologisch; psychisch ⟨Problem⟩

psychologist [saɪ'kɒlədʒɪst] n. Psychologe, der/Psychologin, die

psychology [saɪ'kɒlədʒɪ] n. Psychologie, die

psychopath ['saɪkəpæθ] n. Psychopath, der/Psychopathin, die

PTO abbr. please turn over b. w.

pub [pʌb] n. (Brit. coll.) Kneipe, die (ugs.)

puberty ['pju:bətɪ] n., no art. Pubertät, die

public ['pʌblɪk] **1.** adj. öffentlich; **make sth. ~:** etw. bekannt machen. **2.** n., sing. or pl. **a)** (the people) Öffentlichkeit, die; **b)** (section of community) Publikum, das; **c) in ~:** öffentlich

publican ['pʌblɪkən] n. (Brit.) [Gast]wirt, der/-wirtin, die

publication [pʌblɪ'keɪʃn] n. Veröffentlichung, die

public: ~ con'venience n. öffentliche Toilette; ~ 'holiday n. gesetzlicher Feiertag; ~ 'house n. (Brit.) Gastwirtschaft, die; Gaststätte, die

publicity [pʌb'lɪsɪtɪ] n. Publicity, die; (advertising) Werbung, die; ~ campaign Werbekampagne, die

publicize ['pʌblɪsaɪz] v.t. publik machen ⟨Ungerechtigkeit⟩; werben für, Reklame machen für ⟨Produkt⟩

public 'library n. öffentliche Bücherei

'publicly adv. öffentlich; ~ owned staatseigen

public: ~ re'lations n., sing. or pl. Public Relations Pl.; ~ **school** n. **a)** (Brit.) Privatschule, die; **b)** (Scot., Amer.) staatliche od. öffentliche Schule; ~ **transport** n. öffentlicher Personenverkehr

publish ['pʌblɪʃ] v.t. (Verlag:) verlegen ⟨Buch, Zeitschrift, Musik usw.⟩;

⟨Autor:⟩ veröffentlichen ⟨Text⟩. **'publisher** n. Verleger, der/Verlegerin, die; ~|s| (company) Verlag, der. **'publishing** n., no art. Verlagswesen, das

puck [pʌk] n. (Ice Hockey) Puck, der

pucker ['pʌkə(r)] **1.** v.t. ~ |up| runzeln ⟨Brauen, Stirn⟩; kräuseln ⟨Lippen⟩. **2.** v.i. ~ |up| ⟨Stoff:⟩ sich kräuseln

pudding ['pʊdɪŋ] n. **a)** Pudding, der; **b)** (dessert) süße Nachspeise

puddle ['pʌdl] n. Pfütze, die

puerile ['pjʊəraɪl] adj. kindisch

puff [pʌf] **1.** n. **a)** Stoß, der; ~ of breath/wind Atem-/Windstoß, der; **b)** ~ of smoke Rauchstoß, der; **c)** (pastry) Blätterteigteilchen, das. **2.** v.i. **a)** ~ |and blow| schnaufen [und keuchen]; **b)** (~ cigarette smoke etc.) paffen (ugs.) (at an + Dat.); **c)** ⟨Person:⟩ keuchen; ⟨Zug, Lokomotive:⟩ schnaufend fahren. **3.** v.t. blasen ⟨Rauch⟩; stäuben ⟨Puder⟩. **puff 'out** v.t. **a)** bauschen ⟨Segel⟩; **b)** (put out of breath) außer Atem bringen ⟨Person⟩; **be ~ed |out|** außer Atem sein

puff 'pastry n. Blätterteig, der

puffy ['pʌfɪ] adj. verschwollen

pugnacious [pʌg'neɪʃəs] adj. kampflustig

pull [pʊl] **1.** v.t. **a)** (draw, tug) ziehen an (+ Dat.); ziehen ⟨Hebel⟩; ~ sb.'s or sb. by the hair/ears/sleeve jmdn. an den Haaren/Ohren/am Ärmel ziehen; ~ sth. over one's ears/head sich ⟨Dat.⟩ etw. über die Ohren/den Kopf ziehen; ~ to pieces in Stücke reißen; (fig.) zerpflücken ⟨Argument usw.⟩; **b)** (extract) [her]ausziehen; [heraus]ziehen ⟨Zahn⟩; **c)** (strain) sich ⟨Dat.⟩ zerren ⟨Muskel⟩. **2.** v.i. **a)** ziehen; 'P~' „Ziehen"; **b)** ~ |to the left/right| ⟨Auto, Boot:⟩ [nach links/rechts] ziehen; **c)** (pluck) ~ **at** ziehen an (+ Dat.); ~ **at sb.'s sleeve** jmdn. am Ärmel ziehen. **3.** n. **a)** Zug, der; **b)** (influence) Einfluß, der (with auf + Akk., bei). **pull a'part** v.t. **a)** (take to pieces) auseinandernehmen; **b)** (fig.: criticize) zerpflücken; verreißen ⟨Buch, [literarisches] Werk⟩. **pull 'down** v.t. **a)** herunterziehen; **b)** (demolish) abreißen. **pull 'in 1.** v.t. hereinziehen. **2.** v.i. ⟨Zug:⟩ einfahren; **b)** (move to side of road) an die Seite fahren; (stop) anhalten. **pull 'off** v.t. **a)** (remove) abziehen; (violently) abreißen; **b)** (accomplish) an Land ziehen (ugs.). **pull 'out 1.** v.t. herausziehen. **2.** v.i. **a)** (depart) abfahren; **b)**

(away from roadside) ausscheren. **pull 'through** *v. i.* ⟨*Patient:*⟩ durchkommen. **pull to'gether** *v. refl.* sich zusammennehmen. **pull 'up 1.** *v. t.* **a)** hochziehen; **b)** [he]rausziehen ⟨*Unkraut, Pflanze*⟩; **c)** *(reprimand)* zurechtweisen. **2.** *v. i. (stop)* anhalten.

pulley ['pʊlɪ] *n.* Rolle, *die*

pullover ['pʊləʊvə(r)] *n.* Pullover, *der*

pulp [pʌlp] **1.** *n.* Brei, *der.* **2.** *v. t.* zerdrücken ⟨*Rübe*⟩; einstampfen ⟨*Druckerzeugnis*⟩

pulpit ['pʊlpɪt] *n.* Kanzel, *die*

pulsate [pʌl'seɪt] *v. i.* pulsieren

¹**pulse** [pʌls] *n.* Puls, *der*; *(single beat)* Pulsschlag, *der*

²**pulse** *n. (Cookery)* Hülsenfrucht, *die*

pulverize ['pʌlvəraɪz] *v. t.* pulverisieren

puma ['pju:mə] *n.* Puma, *der*

pumice ['pʌmɪs] *n.* ~[-stone] Bimstein, *der*

pummel ['pʌml] *v. t., (Brit)* -ll- einschlagen auf (+ *Akk.*)

pump [pʌmp] **1.** *n.* Pumpe, *die.* **2.** *v. i.* pumpen. **3.** *v. t.* pumpen; ~ sth. dry etw. leerpumpen; ~ sb. for information Auskünfte aus jmdm. herausholen; ~ up aufpumpen

pumpkin ['pʌmpkɪn] *n.* Kürbis, *der*

pun [pʌn] *n.* Wortspiel, *das*

¹**punch 1.** *v. t.* **a)** *(with fist)* boxen; **b)** *(pierce)* lochen; ~ a hole ein Loch stanzen; ~ a hole/holes in sth. etw. lochen. **2.** *n.* **a)** *(blow)* Faustschlag, *der*; **b)** *(for making holes) (in leather, tickets)* Lochzange, *die; (in paper)* Locher, *der*

²**punch** *n. (drink)* Punsch, *der*

punch: ~ **line** ~ Pointe, *die*; ~**-up** *n. (Brit. coll.)* Prügelei, *die*

punctual ['pʌŋktjʊəl] *adj.* pünktlich. **punctuality** [pʌŋktjʊ'ælɪtɪ] *n.* Pünktlichkeit, *die.* **punctually** *adv.* pünktlich

punctuate [pʌŋktjʊət] *v. t.* mit Satzzeichen versehen. **punctuation** [pʌŋktjʊ'eɪʃn] *n.* Zeichensetzung, *die.* **punctu'ation mark** *n.* Satzzeichen, *das*

puncture ['pʌŋktʃə(r)] **1.** *n.* **a)** *(flat tyre)* Reifenpanne, *die;* **b)** *(hole)* Loch, *das.* **2.** *v. t.* durchstechen; **be** ~**d** ⟨*Reifen:*⟩ platt sein

pundit ['pʌndɪt] *n.* Experte, *der*/Expertin, *die*

pungent ['pʌndʒənt] *adj.* beißend, ätzend ⟨*Rauch*⟩; scharf ⟨*Soße*⟩; stechend riechend ⟨*Gas*⟩

punish ['pʌnɪʃ] *v. t.* bestrafen. **punishable** ['pʌnɪʃəbl] *adj.* strafbar. '**punishment** *n.* **a)** *(punishing)* Bestrafung, *die;* **b)** *(penalty)* Strafe, *die*

punitive ['pju:nɪtɪv] *adj.* **a)** *(penal)* Straf-; **b)** *(severe)* [allzu] rigoros

punk [pʌŋk] *n.* **a)** *(Amer. sl.: worthless person)* Dreckskerl, *der (salopp);* **b)** *(admirer of ~ rock)* Punk, *der; (performer)* Punk[rock]er, *der/*-[rock]erin, *die;* **c)** *(music)* Punkrock, *der*

punt [pʌnt] *n.* Stechkahn, *der*

puny ['pju:nɪ] *adj.* **a)** *(undersized)* zu klein ⟨*Baby, Junge*⟩; **b)** *(feeble)* gering ⟨*Kraft*⟩; schwach ⟨*Waffe, Person*⟩

pup [pʌp] *n.* Welpe, *der*

pupa ['pju:pə] *n., pl.* ~e ['pju:pi:] Puppe, *die.* **pupate** [pju:'peɪt] *v. i.* sich verpuppen

pupil ['pju:pɪl] *n.* **a)** Schüler, *der/* Schülerin, *die;* **b)** *(Anat.)* Pupille, *die*

puppet ['pʌpɪt] *n.* Puppe, *die; (marionette; also fig.)* Marionette, *die*

puppy ['pʌpɪ] *n.* Hundejunge, *das;* Welpe, *der*

purchase ['pɜ:tʃəs] **1.** *n.* **a)** Kauf, *der;* **make a** ~: etwas kaufen; **b)** *(hold)* Halt, *der; (leverage)* Hebelwirkung, *die.* **2.** *v. t.* kaufen. '**purchaser** *n.* Käufer, *der/*Käuferin, *die*

pure [pjʊə(r)] *adj.* rein

purée ['pjʊəreɪ] *n.* Püree, *das*

'**purely** *adv.* **a)** *(solely)* rein; **b)** *(merely)* lediglich

purgatory ['pɜ:gətərɪ] *n.* **it was** ~ *(fig.)* es war eine Strafe

purge [pɜ:dʒ] **1.** *v. t.* **a)** *(cleanse)* reinigen *(of* von); **b)** *(remove)* entfernen; **c)** *(rid)* säubern ⟨*Partei*⟩ *(of* von). **2.** *n.* Säuberung[saktion], *die*

purification [pjʊərɪfɪ'keɪʃn] *n.* Reinigung, *die*

purify ['pjʊərɪfaɪ] *v. t.* reinigen

purist ['pjʊərɪst] *n.* Purist, *der/*Puristin, *die*

puritan, *(Hist.)* **Puritan** ['pjʊərɪtn] *n.* Puritaner, *der/*Puritanerin, *die.* **puritanical** [pjʊərɪ'tænɪkl] *adj.* puritanisch

purity ['pjʊərɪtɪ] *n.* Reinheit, *die*

purl [pɜ:l] **1.** *n.* linke Masche. **2.** *v. t.* ~ **three [stitches]** drei linke Maschen stricken

purple ['pɜ:pl] **1.** *adj.* lila; violett. **2.** *n.* Lila, *das;* Violett, *das*

purport [pə'pɔ:t] *v. t.* ~ **to do sth.** *(profess)* [von sich] behaupten, etw. zu tun; *(be intended to seem)* den Anschein erwecken sollen, etw. zu tun

purpose ['pɜːpəs] n. a) (object) Zweck, der; (intention) Absicht, die; **what is the ~ of doing that?** was hat es für einen Zweck, das zu tun?; **on ~:** mit Absicht; absichtlich; b) (effect) **to no ~:** ohne Erfolg; **to some/good ~:** mit einigem/gutem Erfolg; c) (determination) Entschlossenheit, die. **purposeful** ['pɜːpəsfl] adj. zielstrebig; (with specific aim) entschlossen. **'purposely** adv. absichtlich

purr [pɜː(r)] 1. v. i. schnurren. 2. n. Schnurren, das

purse [pɜːs] 1. n. Portemonnaie, das. 2. v. t. kräuseln ⟨Lippen⟩

purser ['pɜːsə(r)] n. Zahlmeister, der/ -meisterin, die

pursue [pə'sjuː] v. t. a) (chase) verfolgen; b) (look into) nachgehen (+ Dat.); c) (engage in) betreiben. **pursuer** [pə'sjuːə(r)] n. Verfolger, der/Verfolgerin, die. **pursuit** [pə'sjuːt] n. a) Verfolgung, die; (of knowledge, truth, etc.) Streben, das (of nach); **in ~ of** auf der Jagd nach ⟨Wild, Dieb usw.⟩; in Ausführung (+ Gen.) ⟨Beschäftigung⟩; **with the police in [full] ~:** mit der Polizei [dicht] auf den Fersen; b) (pastime) Beschäftigung, die

pus [pʌs] n. Eiter, der.

push [pʊʃ] 1. v. t. a) schieben; (make fall) stoßen; drücken gegen ⟨Tür⟩; **~ one's way through/into/on to** etc. sich (Dat.) einen Weg durch/in/auf usw. etw. (Akk.) bahnen; b) (fig.: impel) drängen; (tax) ~ sb. [hard] jmdn. [stark] fordern; **be ~ed for sth.** (coll.: find it difficult to provide sth.) mit etw. knapp sein; **be ~ed for money or cash** knapp bei Kasse sein (ugs.); d) (sell illegally, esp. drugs) pushen ⟨Drogenjargon⟩. 2. v. i. a) schieben; (in queue) drängeln; (at door) drücken; **~ and shove** schubsen und drängeln; b) (make demands) **~ for sth.** etw. fordern; c) (make one's way) **he ~ed between us** er drängte sich zwischen uns; **~ through the crowd** sich durch die Menge drängeln. 3. n. a) Stoß, der; **give sth. a ~:** etw. schieben; b) (effort) Anstrengungen Pl.; (Mil.: attack) Vorstoß, der; c) (crisis) **when it comes to the ~,** (Amer. coll.) **when ~ comes to shove** wenn es ernst wird; d) (Brit. sl.: dismissal) **get the ~:** rausfliegen (ugs.). **push a'head** v. i. ~ **ahead with** sth. etw. vorantreiben. **push 'in** v. i. sich hineindrängen. **push 'off** v. i. a)

(Boating) abstoßen; b) (sl.: leave) abhauen (salopp). **push 'on** 1. v. i. (with plans etc.) weitermachen. 2. v. t. draufdrücken ⟨Deckel usw.⟩. **push 'up** v. t. hochschieben; (fig.) hochtreiben

push: **~-button** n. [Druck]knopf, der; Drucktaste; **~-chair** n. (Brit.) Sportwagen, der; **~-over** n. (coll.) Kinderspiel, das

pushy ['pʊʃɪ] adj. (coll.) [übermäßig] ehrgeizig ⟨Person⟩

pussy ['pʊsɪ] n. (child lang.: cat) Miezekatze, die (fam.)

put [pʊt] 1. v. t., -tt-, put a) (place) tun; (vertically) stellen; (horizontally) legen; **~ plates on the table** Teller auf den Tisch stellen; **~ a stamp on the letter** eine Briefmarke auf den Brief kleben; **~ the letter in an envelope/the letter-box** den Brief in einen Umschlag/in den Briefkasten stecken; **~ sth. in one's pocket** etw. in die Tasche stecken; **~ petrol in the tank** Benzin in den Tank füllen; **~ the car in[to] the garage** das Auto in die Garage stellen; **~ the plug in the socket** den Stecker in die Steckdose stecken; **~ one's hands over one's eyes** sich (Dat.) die Hände auf die Augen legen; **where shall I ~ it?** wo soll ich es hintun (ugs.)/-stellen/-legen usw.?; (fig.) **be ~ in a difficult position** in eine schwierige Lage geraten; **~ sb. on to sth.** jmdn. auf etw. (Akk.) hinweisen; **~ sb. to work** jmdn. arbeiten lassen; **~ sb. on antibiotics** jmdn. auf Antibiotika setzen; **~ oneself in sb.'s place or situation** sich in jmds. Lage (Akk.) versetzen; b) (submit) unterbreiten ⟨Vorschlag, Plan⟩ (to Dat.); c) (express) ausdrücken; **let's ~ it like this: ...:** sagen wir so: ...; **~ sth. into English** etc. etw. ins Englische usw. übertragen; **~ sth. into words** etw. in Worte fassen; d) (write) schreiben; **~ one's name on the list** seinen Namen auf die Liste setzen; **~ sth. on the bill** etw. auf die Rechnung setzen; e) (stake) setzen (on auf + Akk.); f) (estimate) **~ sb./sth. at** jmdn./etw. schätzen auf (+ Akk.). 2. v. i., -tt-, put (Naut.) ~ [out] to sea in See stechen. **put a'cross** v. t. a) (communicate) vermitteln (to Dat.); b) (make acceptable) ankommen mit. **put a'way** v. t. a) wegräumen; reinstellen ⟨Auto⟩; (in file) abheften; b) (save) beiseite legen; c) (coll.) (eat) verdrücken (ugs.); (drink) runterkippen (ugs.); d) (coll.:

confine) einsperren (*ugs.*). **put 'back**
v. t. a) ~ **the book** das Buch zu-
rücktun; b) ~ **the clock back** die Uhr
zurückstellen; c) (*postpone*) verschieben. **put 'down** *v. t.* a) (*set down*) (*vertically*) hinstellen; (*horizontally*) hinlegen; auflegen (*Hörer*); b) (*suppress*)
niederwerfen; c) (*humiliate*) herabsetzen; d) (*kill*) töten; e) (*write*) notieren;
f) (*attribute*) ~ **sth. down to sth.** etw.
auf etw. (*Akk.*) zurückführen. **put
'forward** *v. t.* a) (*propose*) aufwarten
mit; b) (*nominate*) vorschlagen; c) ~
the clock forward die Uhr vorstellen.
put 'in 1. *v. t.* a) (*install*) einbauen; b)
(*submit*) stellen (*Forderung*); einreichen (*Bewerbung*); c) (*devote*) aufwenden (*Mühe*); (*perform*) einlegen
(*Sonderschicht, Überstunden*). **2.** *v. i.* ~
in for sich bewerben um (*Stellung*);
beantragen (*Urlaub*). **put 'off** *v. t.* a)
(*postpone*) verschieben (**until** auf +
Akk.); (*postpone engagement with*)
vertrösten (**until** auf + *Akk.*); b)
(*switch off*) ausmachen; c) (*repel*) abstoßen; ~ **sb. off sth.** jmdm. etw. ver-
leiden; d) (*distract*) stören; e) (*dissuade*) ~ **sb. off doing sth.** jmdn. davon abbringen, etw. zu tun. **put 'on**
v. t. a) anziehen (*Kleidung, Hose
usw.*); aufsetzen (*Hut, Brille*); drauf-
setzen (*Deckel*); ~ **it on** (*coll.*) [nur]
Schau machen (*ugs.*); b) anmachen
(*Radio, Licht*); aufsetzen (*Wasser,
Kessel*); c) (*gain*) ~ **on weight** zunehmen; d) (*stage*) spielen (*Stück*); zeigen (*Film*). **put 'out** *v. t.* a) rausbringen; b) ausmachen (*Licht*); löschen
(*Feuer*); c) (*inconvenience*) in Verlegenheit bringen. **put 'through** *v. t.* a)
(*carry out*) durchführen (*Plan, Programm*); b) (*Teleph.*) verbinden (**to**
mit). **put 'up 1.** *v. t.* a) heben (*Hand*);
errichten (*Gebäude, Denkmal*); aufstellen (*Gerüst*); b) (*display*) aushän-
gen; c) hochnehmen (*Fäuste*); leisten
(*Widerstand, Gegenwehr*); d) (*propose*)
vorschlagen; (*nominate*) aufstellen; e)
(*incite*) ~ **sb. up to sth.** jmdn. zu etw.
anstiften; f) (*accommodate*) unterbringen; g) (*increase*) [he]raufsetzen
(*Preis, Miete*). **2.** *v. i.* (*lodge*) übernachten. **put 'up with** *v. t.* sich (*Dat.*)
bieten lassen (*Beleidigung, Beneh-
men*); sich abfinden mit (*Lärm,
Elend*); sich abgeben mit (*Person*)
putrefy ['pju:trɪfaɪ] *v. i.* sich zersetzen
putrid ['pju:trɪd] *adj.* (*rotten*) faul; ~
smell Fäulnisgeruch, *der*

putt [pʌt] (*Golf*) **1.** *v. i. & t.* putten. **2.** *n.*
Putt, *der*. **'putter** *n.* Putter, *der*
putty ['pʌtɪ] *n.* Kitt, *der*
'put-up *adj.* **a** ~ **job** ein abgekartetes
Spiel (*ugs.*)
puzzle ['pʌzl] **1.** *n.* (*problem, enigma*)
Rätsel, *das*; (*toy*) Geduldspiel, *das*.
2. *v. t.* rätselhaft *od.* ein Rätsel sein
(+ *Dat.*). **3.** *v. i.* ~ **over** *or* **about sth.**
sich (*Dat.*) über etw. den Kopf zerbre-
chen. **puzzled** ['pʌzld] *adj.* ratlos.
puzzling ['pʌzlɪŋ] *adj.* rätselhaft
PVC *abbr.* **polyvinyl chloride** PVC, *das*
pygmy ['pɪgmɪ] *n.* Pygmäe, *der*
pyjamas [pɪ'dʒɑ:məz] *n. pl.* [**pair of**] ~:
Schlafanzug, *der*
pylon ['paɪlən] *n.* Mast, *der*
pyramid ['pɪrəmɪd] *n.* Pyramide, *die*
Pyrenees [pɪrə'ni:z] *pr. n. pl.* **the** ~:
die Pyrenäen
python ['paɪθən] *n.* Python, *die*

Q

Q, q [kju:] *n.* Q, q, *das*
quack [kwæk] **1.** *v. i.* (*Ente:*) quaken.
2. *n.* Quaken, *das*
quadrangle ['kwɒdræŋgl] *n.* [vier-
eckiger] Innenhof
quadruped ['kwɒdrʊped] *n.* Vierfüßler, *der*
quadruple ['kwɒdrʊpl] **1.** *adj.* vier-
fach. **2.** *v. t.* vervierfachen. **3.** *v. i.* sich
vervierfachen
quagmire ['kwægmaɪə(r)] *n.* Sumpf,
der; Morast, *der*
¹quail [kweɪl] *n.* (*Ornith.*) Wachtel, *die*
²quail *v. i.* (*Person:*) [ver]zagen
quaint [kweɪnt] *adj.* drollig (*Häuschen, Einrichtung*); malerisch (*Ort*);
(*odd*) kurios (*Bräuche, Anblick*)
quake [kweɪk] **1.** *n.* (*coll.*) [Erd]beben,
das. **2.** *v. i.* beben; ~ **with fear** vor
Angst zittern
Quaker ['kweɪkə(r)] *n.* Quäker, *der*/
Quäkerin, *die*
qualification [kwɒlɪfɪ'keɪʃn] *n.* a)
Qualifikation, *die*; (*condition*) Voraussetzung, *die*; b) (*limitation*) Vorbehalt,
der; **without** ~: vorbehaltlos

qualified ['kwɒlɪfaɪd] *adj.* **a)** qualifiziert; *(by training)* ausgebildet; **b)** *(restricted)* nicht uneingeschränkt; **a ~ success** kein voller Erfolg; **~ acceptance** bedingte Annahme

qualify ['kwɒlɪfaɪ] **1.** *v.t.* **a)** *(make competent)* berechtigen (for zu); **b)** *(modify)* einschränken. **2.** *v.i.* **a)** **~ in law/medicine** seinen [Studien]abschluß in Jura/Medizin machen; **~ as a doctor/lawyer** sein Examen als Arzt/Anwalt machen; **b)** *(fulfil a condition)* in Frage kommen (for für); **c)** *(Sport)* sich qualifizieren

quality ['kwɒlɪtɪ] **1.** *n.* **a)** Qualität, *die;* **b)** *(characteristic)* Eigenschaft, *die.* **2.** *adj.* Qualitäts-

qualm [kwɑːm] *n.* Bedenken, *das* (over, about gegen)

quandary ['kwɒndərɪ] *n.* Dilemma, *das*

quantity ['kwɒntɪtɪ] *n.* **a)** Quantität, *die;* **b)** *(amount, sum)* Menge, *die*

quarantine ['kwɒrəntiːn] *n.* Quarantäne, *die;* **be in ~:** unter Quarantäne stehen

quarrel ['kwɒrl] **1.** *n.* **a)** Streit, *der;* **have/pick a ~ with sb.** [about/over sth.] sich mit jmdm. [über etw. *(Akk.)*] streiten/Streit anfangen; **b)** *(cause of complaint)* Einwand, *der* (with gegen). **2.** *v.i.,* *(Brit.)* **-ll-** [sich] streiten (over um, about über + *Akk.*); **~ with each other** [sich] [miteinander] streiten; *(fall out)* sich [zer]streiten (over um, about über + *Akk.*). **quarrelsome** ['kwɒrlsəm] *adj.* streitsüchtig

¹quarry ['kwɒrɪ] *n.* Steinbruch, *der*

²quarry *n.* *(prey)* Beute, *die*

quart [kwɔːt] *n.* Quart, *das*

quarter ['kwɔːtə(r)] **1.** *n.* **a)** Viertel, *das;* **a** *or* **one ~ of** ein Viertel (+ *Gen.*); **a ~ of a mile/an hour** eine Viertelmeile/-stunde; **b)** *(of year)* Quartal, *das;* Vierteljahr, *das;* **c)** **a ~ to/past six** Viertel vor/nach sechs; **d)** *(direction)* Richtung, *die;* **e)** *(area of town)* [Stadt]viertel, *das;* **f)** **~s** *pl.* *(lodgings)* Quartier, *das* *(bes. Milit.);* Unterkunft, *die;* **g)** *(Amer. coin)* Vierteldollar, *der.* **2.** *v.t.* **a)** *(divide)* vierteln; **b)** *(lodge)* einquartieren *(Soldaten).* **quarter-final** *n.* Viertelfinale, *das.* **quarterly 1.** *adj.* vierteljährlich. **2.** *n.* Vierteljah[r]esschrift, *die*

quartet [kwɔː'tet] *n.* Quartett, *das*

quartz [kwɔːts] *n.* Quarz, *der*

quash [kwɒʃ] *v.t.* **a)** *(annul)* aufheben; **b)** *(suppress)* niederschlagen

quaver ['kweɪvə(r)] **1.** *n.* *(Brit. Mus.)* Achtelnote, *die.* **2.** *v.i.* *(vibrate)* zittern

quay [kiː], **quayside** *ns.* Kai, *der*

queasy ['kwiːzɪ] *adj.* unwohl

queen [kwiːn] *n.* **a)** Königin, *die;* **b)** *(Chess, Cards)* Dame, *die.* **queen 'mother** *n.* Königinmutter, *die*

queer [kwɪə(r)] **1.** *adj.* **a)** *(strange)* sonderbar; *(eccentric)* verschroben; **b)** *(shady)* merkwürdig; **c)** *(out of sorts)* unwohl; **d)** *(sl. derog.: homosexual)* schwul *(ugs.).* **2.** *n.* *(sl. derog.: homosexual)* Schwule, *der (ugs.)*

quell [kwel] *v.t.* *(literary)* niederschlagen *(Aufstand);* zügeln *(Furcht)*

quench [kwentʃ] *v.t.* löschen

query ['kwɪərɪ] **1.** *n.* Frage, *die.* **2.** *v.t.* in Frage stellen ⟨Anweisung, Glaubwürdigkeit⟩; beanstanden ⟨Rechnung⟩

quest [kwest] *n.* Suche, *die* (for nach)

question ['kwestʃn] **1.** *n.* **a)** Frage, *die;* **ask sb. a ~:** jmdm. eine Frage stellen; **b)** *(doubt, objection)* Zweifel, *der* (about an + *Dat.*); **there is no ~ about sth.** es besteht kein Zweifel an etw. *(Dat.);* **beyond all** *or* **without ~:** ohne Frage; **c)** *(problem, concern)* Frage, *die;* **sth./it is only a ~ of time** etw./es ist [nur] eine Frage der Zeit; **it is [only] a ~ of doing sth.** es geht [nur] darum, etw. zu tun; **the person/thing in ~:** die fragliche Person/Sache; **sth./it is out of the ~:** etw./es ist ausgeschlossen. **2.** *v.t.* **a)** befragen; ⟨Polizei, Gericht usw.:⟩ vernehmen; **b)** *(throw doubt upon, raise objections to)* bezweifeln. **questionable** ['kwestʃənəbl] *adj.* fragwürdig. **'question mark** *n.* Fragezeichen, *das*

questionnaire [kwestʃə'neə(r)] *n.* Fragebogen, *der*

queue [kjuː] **1.** *n.* Schlange, *die.* **join the ~:** sich anstellen. **2.** *v.i.* **~ [up]** Schlange stehen

quibble ['kwɪbl] **1.** *n.* Spitzfindigkeit, *die.* **2.** *v.i.* streiten

quiche [kiːʃ] *n.* Quiche, *die*

quick [kwɪk] **1.** *adj.* schnell; kurz ⟨Rede, Pause⟩; flüchtig ⟨Kuß, Blick⟩; **be ~!** mach schnell! *(ugs.);* **be ~ to do sth.** etw. schnell tun; **a ~ temper** ein aufbrausendes Wesen. **2.** *adv.* schnell. **3.** *n.* empfindliches Fleisch; **be cut to the ~** *(fig.)* tief getroffen sein. **quicken** ['kwɪkn] **1.** *v.t.* beschleunigen. **2.** *v.i.* sich beschleunigen. **'quickly** *adv.* schnell. **'quickness** *n.* **a)** *(speed)* Schnelligkeit, *die;* **b)** *(~ of perception)* Schärfe, *die*

racist

quick: ~**sand** n. Treibsand, der; ~-**tempered** [~'tempəd] adj. hitzig; be ~-**tempered** leicht aufbrausen; ~-**witted** adj. geistesgegenwärtig

quid [kwɪd] n., pl. same (Brit. sl.) Pfund, das

quiet ['kwaɪət] 1. adj., ~er ['kwaɪətə(r)], ~est ['kwaɪətɪst] a) (silent) still; (not loud) leise; keep ~ about sth. (fig.) etw. geheimhalten; b) (peaceful, not busy) ruhig; c) (not overt) versteckt; on the ~: still und heimlich. 2. n. Ruhe, die; (silence, stillness) Stille, die.

quieten ['kwaɪətn] v. t. beruhigen. **quieten 'down** v. i. sich beruhigen.

'**quietly** adv. a) (silently) still; (not loudly) leise; b) (peacefully) ruhig

'**quietness** n. (absence of noise) Stille, die; (peacefulness) Ruhe, die

quill [kwɪl] n. (feather) Kielfeder, die; (of porcupine) Stachel, der

quilt [kwɪlt] 1. n. Schlafdecke, die. 2. v. t. wattieren

quince [kwɪns] n. Quitte, die

quintet [kwɪn'tet] n. Quintett, das

quip [kwɪp] 1. n. Witzelei, die. 2. v. i., -pp- witzeln (at über + Akk.)

quirk [kwɜ:k] n. Marotte, die; a ~ of fate eine Laune des Schicksals

quit [kwɪt] v. t., -tt-, (Amer.) quit (give up) aufgeben; (stop) aufhören mit; ~ doing sth. aufhören, etw. zu tun; they were given notice to ~ [the flat] ihnen wurde [die Wohnung] gekündigt

quite [kwaɪt] adv. a) (entirely) ganz; völlig; fest (entschlossen); ~ [so]! [ja], genau!; b) (to some extent) ziemlich; ganz (gern); ~ a few ziemlich viele

quits [kwɪts] pred. adj. be ~ [with sb.] [mit jmdm.] quitt sein (ugs.)

¹**quiver** ['kwɪvə(r)] v. i. zittern (with vor + Dat.); (Stimme, Lippen:) beben (geh.); (Lid:) zucken

²**quiver** n. (for arrows) Köcher, der

quiz [kwɪz] 1. n., pl. -zes Quiz, das. 2. v. t., -zz- ausfragen (about sth. nach etw., about sb. über jmdn.). **quizzical** ['kwɪzɪkl] adj. fragend

quoit [kɔɪt] n. [Gummi]ring, der

quorum ['kwɔ:rəm] n. Quorum, das

quota ['kwəʊtə] n. a) (share) Anteil, der; b) (goods to be produced) Produktionsmindestquote, die; c) (maximum number) Höchstquote, die

quotation [kwəʊ'teɪʃn] n. a) Zitieren, das; (passage) Zitat, das; b) (estimate) Kosten[vor]anschlag, der. **quo'tation-marks** n. pl. Anführungszeichen Pl.

quote [kwəʊt] 1. v. t. also abs. zitieren (from aus); zitieren aus (Buch, Text); (mention) anführen; nennen (Preis). 2. n. (coll.) a) (passage) Zitat, das; b) (estimate) Kosten[vor]anschlag, der; c) usu. in pl. (quotation-mark) Anführungszeichen, das

R

R, r [ɑ:(r)] n. R, r, das

R. abbr. River Fl.

rabbi ['ræbaɪ] n. Rabbi[ner], der; (as title) Rabbi, der

rabbit ['ræbɪt] n. Kaninchen, das

rabbit: ~-**burrow** n. Kaninchenbau, der; ~-**hutch** n. (also fig.) Kaninchenstall, der; ~-**warren** n. Kaninchengehege, das; (fig.) Labyrinth, das

rabble ['ræbl] n. Mob, der

rabid ['ræbɪd] adj. a) tollwütig; b) (extreme) fanatisch

rabies ['reɪbi:z] n. Tollwut, die

¹**race** [reɪs] 1. n. Rennen, das; (fig.) a ~ against time ein Wettlauf mit der Zeit. 2. v. i. a) (in swimming, running, etc.) um die Wette schwimmen/laufen usw. (with, against mit); b) (Motor:) durchdrehen; (Puls:) jagen; c) (rush) sich sehr beeilen; ~ after sb. jmdn. hinterherhetzen. 3. v. t. um die Wette schwimmen/laufen usw. mit

²**race** n. (Anthrop., Biol.) Rasse, die; the human ~: die Menschheit

race: ~**course** n. Rennbahn, die; ~-**horse** n. Rennpferd, das; ~-**track** n. Rennbahn, die

racial ['reɪʃl] adj. Rassen(diskriminierung, -konflikt, -gleichheit); rassisch (Gruppe, Minderheit). **racialism** ['reɪʃəlɪzm] n. Rassismus, der. **racialist** ['reɪʃəlɪst] 1. n. Rassist, der/Rassistin, die. 2. adj. rassistisch

racing ['reɪsɪŋ] n. Rennsport, der; (with horses) Pferdesport, der. '**racing-car** n. Rennwagen, der. '**racing driver** n. Rennfahrer, der/-fahrerin, die

racism ['reɪsɪzm] n. Rassismus, der.

racist ['reɪsɪst] 1. n. Rassist, der/Rassistin, die. 2. adj. rassistisch

rack [ræk] 1. *n.* *(for luggage)* Ablage, *die;* *(for toast, plates)* Ständer, *der;* *(on bicycle, motor cycle)* Gepäckträger, *der.* 2. *v. t.* ~ one's **brain[s]** *(fig.)* sich *(Dat.)* den Kopf zerbrechen *(ugs.)*

¹**racket** ['rækɪt] *n.* Schläger, *der*

²**racket** *n.* a) *(disturbance)* Lärm, *der;* Krach, *der;* b) *(scheme)* Schwindelgeschäft, *das (ugs.).* **racketeer** [rækɪ-'tɪə(r)] *n.* Ganove, *der;* *(profiteer)* Wucherer, *der*

racoon [rə'ku:n] *n.* Waschbär, *der*

racy ['reɪsɪ] *adj.* flott *(ugs.)* ⟨*Stil*⟩

radar ['reɪdɑː(r)] *n.* Radar, *das od. der*

radiant ['reɪdɪənt] *adj.* strahlend; fröhlich ⟨*Stimmung*⟩; be ~: strahlen (with vor + *Dat.*)

radiate ['reɪdɪeɪt] 1. *v. i.* a) ⟨*Hitze, Wärme:*⟩ ausstrahlen; ⟨*Schein, Wellen:*⟩ ausgehen (from von); b) *(from central point)* strahlenförmig ausgehen (from von). 2. *v. t.* ausstrahlen ⟨*Licht, Wärme; Glück, Liebe*⟩; aussenden ⟨*Strahlen, Wellen*⟩. **radiation** [reɪdɪ'eɪʃn] *n.* *(of energy)* Emission, *die;* *(of signals)* Ausstrahlung, *die;* *(energy transmitted)* Strahlung, *die.* **radiator** ['reɪdɪeɪtə(r)] *n.* a) *(for heating)* Heizkörper, *der;* b) *(Motor Veh.)* Kühler, *der*

radical ['rædɪkl] *adj.* 1. a) *(thorough; also Polit.)* radikal; drastisch ⟨*Maßnahme*⟩; b) *(progressive)* radikal; c) *(fundamental)* grundlegend. 2. *n.* *(Polit.)* Radikale, *der/die*

radio ['reɪdɪəʊ] 1. *n., pl.* ~s a) *no indef. art.* Funk, *der;* *(for private communication)* Sprechfunk, *der;* b) *no indef. art.* *(Broadcasting)* Rundfunk, *der;* on the ~: im Radio; c) *(apparatus)* Radio, *das.* 2. *attrib. adj.* *(Broadcasting)* Rundfunk-; Radio⟨*welle, -teleskop*⟩; Funk⟨*mast, -turm, -taxi*⟩. 3. *v. t.* funken

radio: ~**active** *adj.* radioaktiv; ~**ac'tivity** *n.* Radioaktivität, *die;* ~**con'trolled** *adj.* funkgesteuert

radish ['rædɪʃ] *n.* Rettich, *der;* *(small, red)* Radieschen, *das*

radius ['reɪdɪəs] *n., pl.* **radii** ['reɪdɪaɪ] *or* ~**es** *(Math.)* Radius, *der;* *(fig.)* Umkreis, *der*

RAF [ɑːreɪ'ef, *(coll.)* ræf] *abbr.* **Royal Air Force**

raffle ['ræfl] 1. *n.* Tombola, *die;* ~ **ticket** Los, *das.* 2. *v. t.* ~ [off] verlosen

raft [rɑːft] *n.* Floß, *das*

rafter ['rɑːftə(r)] *n.* Sparren, *der*

¹**rag** [ræg] *n.* a) [Stoff]fetzen, *der;* b)

(old and torn clothes) Lumpen *Pl.;* c) *(derog.: newspaper)* Käseblatt, *das (salopp)*

²**rag** *v. t.,* -gg- *(tease)* aufziehen

rag: ~**bag** *n.* *(fig.)* Sammelsurium, *das;* ~ **doll** *n.* Stoffpuppe, *die*

rage [reɪdʒ] 1. *n.* a) *(violent anger)* Wut, *der;* *(fit of anger)* Wutausbruch, *der;* b) sth. is [all] the ~: etw. ist [ganz] groß in Mode. 2. *v. i.* a) *(rave)* toben; ~ at *or* against sth./sb. gegen etw./ jmdn. wüten; b) *(be violent, unchecked)* toben; ⟨*Krankheit:*⟩ wüten

ragged ['rægɪd] *adj.* zerrissen

raid [reɪd] 1. *n.* Einfall, *der;* Überfall, *der;* *(Mil.)* Überraschungsangriff, *der;* *(by police)* Razzia, *die* (on in + *Dat.*). 2. *v. t.* ⟨*Polizei:*⟩ eine Razzia machen auf (+ *Akk.*); ⟨*Räuber, Soldaten:*⟩ überfallen. ¹**raider** *n.* Räuber, *der/* Räuberin, *die*

rail [reɪl] *n.* a) Stange, *die;* *(on ship)* Reling, *die;* *(as protection against contact)* Barriere, *die;* b) *(Railw.: of track)* Schiene, *die;* c) *(~way)* [Eisen]bahn, *die; attrib.* Bahn-; by ~: mit der Bahn

railing ['reɪlɪŋ] *n.* *(round park)* Zaun, *der;* *(on staircase)* Geländer, *das*

'**railroad** *(Amer.),* '**railway** *ns.* a) *(track)* Bahnlinie, *die;* Bahnstrecke, *die;* b) *(system)* [Eisen]bahn, *die*

railway: ~ **carriage** *n.* Eisenbahnwagen, *der;* ~ **engine** *n.* Lokomotive, *die;* ~ **line** *n.* [Eisen]bahnlinie, *die;* ~ **station** *n.* Bahnhof, *der*

rain [reɪn] 1. *n.* a) Regen, *der;* b) *(fig.: of arrows, blows, etc.)* Hagel, *der.* 2. *v. i. impers.* it is ~ing es regnet. 3. *v. t.* hageln lassen ⟨*Schläge, Hiebe*⟩

rain: ~**bow** ['reɪnbəʊ] *n.* Regenbogen, *der;* ~**-check** *n.* *(Amer. fig.)* take a ~-check on sth. auf etw. *(Akk.)* später wieder zurückkommen; ~**coat** *n.* Regenmantel, *der;* ~**fall** *n.* Niederschlag, *der;* ~**proof** *adj.* regendicht; ~**water** *n.* Regenwasser, *das*

rainy *adj.* regnerisch ⟨*Tag, Wetter*⟩; regenreich ⟨*Gebiet, Sommer*⟩; ~ **season** Regenzeit, *die;* keep sth. for a ~ **day** *(fig.)* sich *(Dat.)* etw. für schlechte Zeiten aufheben

raise [reɪz] *v. t.* a) *(lift up)* heben; erhöhen ⟨*Temperatur, Miete, Gehalt*⟩; hochziehen ⟨*Fahne*⟩; aufziehen ⟨*Vorhang*⟩; hochheben ⟨*Arm*⟩; ~ one's **glass** to sb. das Glas auf jmdn. erheben; b) *(set upright)* aufrichten; erheben ⟨*Banner*⟩; ~ **sb.'s spirits** jmds. Stimmung heben; c) erheben ⟨*Forde-*

rungen, Einwände); aufwerfen ⟨*Frage*⟩; zur Sprache bringen ⟨*Thema, Problem*⟩; **d)** aufziehen ⟨*Vieh, [Haus]tiere*⟩; großziehen ⟨*Familie, Kinder*⟩; **e)** aufbringen ⟨*Geld, Betrag*⟩; **f)** aufheben ⟨*Belagerung, Blockade, Embargo, Verbot*⟩

raisin ['reɪzn] *n*. Rosine, *die*

rake [reɪk] **1.** *n*. Rechen, *der*; Harke, *die*. **2.** *v. t.* **a)** harken; **b)** ~ **the fire** die Asche entfernen; **c)** *(with eyes, shots)* bestreichen. **rake in** *v. t.* *(coll.)* scheffeln *(ugs.)*. **rake up** *v. t.* zusammenharken; *(fig.)* wieder ausgraben

'**rake-off** *n*. *(coll.)* [Gewinn]anteil, *der*

rakish ['reɪkɪʃ] *adj*. flott; keß

rally ['rælɪ] **1.** *v. i. (regain health)* sich wieder [ein wenig] erholen. **2.** *v. t.* **a)** *(reassemble)* wieder zusammenrufen; **b)** einigen ⟨*Partei, Kräfte*⟩; sammeln ⟨*Anhänger*⟩. **3.** *n*. **a)** *(mass meeting)* Versammlung, *die*; **b)** |**motor**| ~: Rallye, *die*; **c)** *(Tennis)* Ballwechsel, *der*

ram [ræm] **1.** *n*. *(Zool.)* Schafbock, *der*; Widder, *der*. **2.** *v. t.*, **-mm-**: **a)** *(force)* stopfen; ~ **a post into the ground** einen Pfosten in die Erde rammen; ~ **sth. home to sb.** jmdm. etw. deutlich vor Augen führen; **b)** *(collide with)* rammen

ramble ['ræmbl] **1.** *n*. |**nature**| ~: Wanderung, *die*. **2.** *v. i.* **a)** *(walk)* umherstreifen **(through,** in **in** + *Dat.*); **b)** *(in talk)* zusammenhangloses Zeug reden; **keep rambling on about sth.** sich endlos über etw. *(Akk.)* auslassen.

rambler ['ræmblə(r)] *n*. Wanderer, *der*/Wanderin, *die*. **rambling** ['ræmblɪŋ] **1.** *n*. Wandern, *das*. **2.** *adj*. **a)** *(irregularly arranged)* verschachtelt; verwinkelt ⟨*Straßen*⟩; **b)** *(incoherent)* unzusammenhängend ⟨*Erklärung*⟩; **c)** ~ **rose** Kletterrose, *die*

ramp [ræmp] *n*. Rampe, *die*

rampage 1. ['ræmpeɪdʒ] *n*. Randale, *die (ugs.)*; **be/go on the** ~ *(coll.)* randalieren. **2.** [ræm'peɪdʒ] *v. i.* randalieren

rampant ['ræmpənt] *adj*. zügellos ⟨*Gewalt, Rassismus*⟩; steil ansteigend ⟨*Inflation*⟩; üppig ⟨*Wachstum*⟩

rampart ['ræmpɑːt] *n*. Wehrgang, *der*

'**ramshackle** *adj*. klapprig ⟨*Auto*⟩; verkommen ⟨*Gebäude*⟩

ran *see* **run** 2, 3

ranch [rɑːntʃ] *n*. Ranch, *die*

rancid ['rænsɪd] *adj*. ranzig

rancour *(Brit.: Amer.:* **rancor)** ['ræŋkə(r)] *n*. [tiefe] Verbitterung

random ['rændəm] **1.** *n*. **at** ~: wahllos;

willkürlich; *(aimlessly)* ziellos; **choose at** ~: aufs Geratewohl wählen. **2.** *adj*. willkürlich

randy ['rændɪ] *adj*. geil; scharf *(ugs.)*

rang *see* ²**ring** 2, 3

range [reɪndʒ] **1.** *n*. **a)** ~ **of mountains** Bergkette, *die*; **b)** *(of subjects)* Palette, *die*; *(of knowledge, voice)* Umfang, *der*; **c)** *(of missile etc.)* Reichweite, *die*; **at a** ~ **of 200 metres** auf eine Entfernung von 200 Metern; **d)** *(series, selection)* Kollektion, *die*; **e)** *(stove)* Herd, *der*. **2.** *v. i.* ⟨*Preise, Temperaturen:*⟩ schwanken, sich bewegen **(from ... to** zwischen [+ *Dat.*] ... und)

'**ranger** *n*. Förster, *der*/Försterin, *die*

¹**rank** [ræŋk] **1.** *n*. **a)** *(position in hierarchy)* Rang, *der*; *(Mil. also)* Dienstgrad, *der*; **b)** *(social position)* [soziale] Stellung; **c)** *(row)* Reihe, *die*; **the** ~ **and file** *(fig.)* die breite Masse; **the** ~**s** *(enlisted men)* die Mannschaften und Unteroffiziere. **2.** *v. i.* ~ **among** zählen zu. **3.** *v. i.* ~ **among** zählen zu

²**rank** *adj*. **a)** kraß ⟨*Außenseiter*⟩; **b)** ~ **weeds** [wild]wucherndes Unkraut

ransack ['rænsæk] *v. t.* **a)** *(search)* durchsuchen **(for** nach); **b)** *(pillage)* plündern

ransom ['rænsəm] *n*. ~ |**money**| Lösegeld, *das;* **hold to** ~: als Geisel festhalten

rant [rænt] *v. i.* ~ |**and rave**| wettern *(ugs.)* **(about** über + *Akk.*)

rap [ræp] **1.** *n*. [energisches] Klopfen. **2.** *v. t.*, **-pp-** klopfen. **3.** *v. i.*, **-pp-** klopfen **(on an** + *Akk.*)

¹**rape** [reɪp] **1.** *n*. Vergewaltigung, *die*. **2.** *v. t.* vergewaltigen

²**rape** *n*. *(Bot., Agric.)* Raps, *der*

rapid ['ræpɪd] **1.** *adj*. schnell ⟨*Bewegung, Wachstum, Puls*⟩; rasch ⟨*Fortschritt, Ausbreitung*⟩. **2.** *n. in pl.* Stromschnellen, *die*. **rapidity** [rə'pɪdɪtɪ] *n*. Schnelligkeit, *die*. '**rapidly** *adv*. schnell

rapist ['reɪpɪst] *n*. Vergewaltiger, *der*

rapport [ræ'pɔː(r)] *n*. [harmonisches] Verhältnis

rapt [ræpt] *adj*. gespannt ⟨*Miene*⟩

rapture ['ræptʃə(r)] *n*. |**state of**| ~: Verzückung, *die*. **rapturous** ['ræptʃərəs] *adj*. begeistert

¹**rare** [reə(r)] *adj*., '**rarely** *adv*. selten

²**rare** *adj*. *(Cookery)* englisch gebraten

rarity ['reərɪtɪ] *n*. Seltenheit, *die*

¹**rash** [ræʃ] *n*. [Haut]ausschlag, *der*

²**rash** *adj*. voreilig ⟨*Urteil, Entscheidung*⟩; überstürzt ⟨*Versprechung*⟩

rasher ['ræʃə(r)] *n.* Speckscheibe, *die*
'**rashly** *adv.* voreilig
rasp [rɑːsp] *n. (tool)* Raspel, *die*
raspberry ['rɑːzbərɪ] *n.* Himbeere, *die*
rat [ræt] *n.* **a)** Ratte, *die;* **smell a ~** *(fig.)* Lunte riechen *(ugs.);* **b)** *(coll. derog.: person)* Ratte, *die (derb)*
rate [reɪt] **1.** *n.* **a)** *(proportion)* Rate, *die;* **b)** *(tariff)* Satz, *der;* **~ |of pay|** Lohnsatz, *der;* **c)** *(speed)* Geschwindigkeit, *die;* Tempo, *das;* **d)** *(Brit.: levy)* **|local or council|**~**s** Gemeindeabgaben; **e)** *(coll.)* **at any ~** *(at least)* zumindest; wenigstens; *(whatever happens)* auf jeden Fall; **at this ~ we won't get any work done** so kriegen wir gar nichts fertig *(ugs.).* **2.** *v. t.* **a)** einschätzen *(Intelligenz, Leistung);* **b)** *(consider)* betrachten; rechnen **(among** *gen.).* **3.** *v. i.* **~ as** gelten als
rather ['rɑːðə(r)] *adv.* **a)** *(by preference)* lieber; **b)** *(somewhat)* ziemlich; **I ~ think that …:** ich bin ziemlich sicher, daß …; **c)** *(more truly)* vielmehr; **or ~:** beziehungsweise
ratification [rætɪfɪ'keɪʃn] *n.* Ratifizierung, *die*
ratify ['rætɪfaɪ] *v. t.* ratifizieren
rating ['reɪtɪŋ] *n.* **a)** *(estimated standing)* Einschätzung, *die;* **b)** *(Radio, Telev.)* **|popularity|** ~: Einschaltquote, *die;* **c)** *(Brit. Navy)* Matrose, *der*
ratio ['reɪʃɪəʊ] *n., pl.* ~**s** Verhältnis, *das*
ration ['ræʃn] **1.** *n.* ~**|s|** Ration, *die* (**of** an + *Dat.*). **2.** *v. t.* rationieren *(Benzin, Zucker usw.)*
rational ['ræʃənl] *adj. (having reason)* rational *(Wesen); (sensible)* vernünftig *(Person, Art usw.)*
rationalize ['ræʃənəlaɪz] *v. t.* rationalisieren
'**rat race** *n.* erbarmungsloser Konkurrenzkampf
rattle ['rætl] **1.** *v. i.* a) *(Fenster:)* klappern; *(Flaschen:)* klirren; *(Kette:)* rasseln; **b)** *(Zug, Bus:)* rattern. **2.** *v. t.* **a)** klappern mit *(Würfel, Geschirr);* klirren lassen *(Fenster|scheiben|);* rasseln mit *(Kette);* **b)** *(sl.: disconcert)* ~ **sb., get sb.** ~**d** jmdn. durcheinanderbringen. **3.** *n.* **a)** *(of baby)* Rassel, *die;* **b)** *(sound)* Klappern, *das.* **rattle 'off** *v. t. (coll.)* herunterrasseln *(ugs.)*
'**rattlesnake** *n.* Klapperschlange, *die*
raucous ['rɔːkəs] *adj.* rauh
ravage ['rævɪdʒ] **1.** *v. t.* heimsuchen *(Gebiet, Stadt).* **2.** *n. in pl.* verheerende Wirkung
rave [reɪv] **1.** *v. i.* **a)** *(talk wildly)* irrere-

den; **b)** *(speak admiringly)* schwärmen **(about** von). **2.** *attrib. adj. (coll.)* begeistert *(Kritik)*
raven ['reɪvn] *n.* Rabe, *der*
ravenous ['rævənəs] *adj.* **I'm ~:** ich habe einen Bärenhunger *(ugs.)*
ravine [rə'viːn] *n.* Schlucht, *die*
raving ['reɪvɪŋ] **1.** *adj.* irreredend *(Idiot).* **2.** *adv.* **be ~ mad** völlig verrückt sein *(ugs.)*
ravish ['rævɪʃ] *v. t. (charm)* entzücken. '**ravishing** *adj.* bildschön *(Anblick, Person);* hinreißend *(Schönheit)*
raw [rɔː] *adj.* **a)** *(uncooked)* roh; **b)** *(inexperienced)* unerfahren; **c)** *(stripped of skin)* blutig *(Fleisch);* offen *(Wunde);* **d)** *(chilly)* naßkalt. **raw ma'terial** *n.* Rohstoff, *der*
ray [reɪ] *n.* Strahl, *der;* **~ of sunshine/ light** Sonnen-/Lichtstrahl, *der*
raze [reɪz] *v. t.* **~ to the ground** dem Erdboden gleichmachen
razor ['reɪzə(r)] *n.* Rasiermesser, *das;* **|electric|** ~: [elektrischer] Rasierapparat. '**razor-blade** *n.* Rasierklinge, *die*
RC *abbr.* **Roman Catholic** r.-k.; röm.-kath.
Rd. *abbr.* **road** Str.
RE *abbr. (Brit.)* **Religious Education** Religionslehre, *die*
re [riː] *prep. (Commerc.)* betreffs
reach [riːtʃ] **1.** *v. t.* **a)** *(arrive at)* erreichen; ankommen in (+ *Dat.*) *(Stadt, Land);* erzielen *(Übereinstimmung);* kommen zu *(Entscheidung; Ausgang, Eingang);* **you can ~ her at this number** du kannst sie unter dieser Nummer erreichen; **b)** *(extend to) (Straße:)* führen bis zu; *(Leiter, Haar:)* reichen bis zu. **2.** *v. i.* **a)** *(stretch out hand)* ~ **for sth.** nach etw. greifen; **~ across the table** über den Tisch langen; **b)** *(be long/tall enough)* **sth. will/won't** ~: etw. ist/ist nicht lang genug; **I can't ~:** ich komme nicht daran; **c)** *(go as far as) (Wasser, Gebäude, Besitz:)* reichen **|up|** bis [hinauf] zu). **3.** *n.* Reichweite, *die;* **be within easy ~:** leicht erreichbar sein; **be out of ~:** nicht erreichbar sein. **reach 'out** *v. i.* die Hand ausstrecken **(for** nach)
react [rɪ'ækt] *v. i.* reagieren **(to** auf + *Akk.*). **reaction** [rɪ'ækʃn] *n.* Reaktion, *die* **(to** auf + *Akk.*)
reactionary [rɪ'ækʃənrɪ] *(Polit.)* **1.** *adj.* reaktionär. **2.** *n.* Reaktionär, *der/*Reaktionärin, *die*
reactor [rɪ'æktə(r)] *n.* **|nuclear|** ~: Kernreaktor, *der*

read [ri:d] 1. *v. t.*, **read** [red] a) lesen; ~ sb. sth., ~ sth. to sb. jmdm. etwas vorlesen; ~ **the gas meter** das Gas ablesen; b) *(interpret)* deuten; ~ **between the lines** zwischen den Zeilen lesen; c) *(study)* studieren. 2. *v. i.*, **read a)** lesen; ~ **to sb.** jmdm. vorlesen; b) *(convey meaning)* lauten; **the contract ~s as follows** der Vertrag hat folgenden Wortlaut. **read 'out** *v. t.* laut vorlesen. **read 'over, read 'through** *v. t.* durchlesen. **read 'up** *v. t.* sich informieren (on über + Akk.)

readable ['ri:dəbl] *adj.* a) *(pleasant to read)* lesenswert; b) *(legible)* leserlich

'reader *n.* a) Leser, der/Leserin, die; b) *(book)* Lesebuch, das

'readership *n.* Leserschaft, die

readily ['redɪlɪ] *adv.* a) *(willingly)* bereitwillig; b) *(easily)* ohne weiteres

readiness ['redɪnɪs] *n.* Bereitschaft, die; **be in ~** bereit sein (for für)

'reading *n.* a) Lesen, das; b) *(figure shown)* Anzeige, die; c) *(recital)* Lesung, die (from aus); d) *(Parl.)* Lesung, die. **reading-lamp, 'reading-light** *ns.* Leselampe, die. **'reading-matter** *n.* Lesestoff, der; Lektüre, die

ready ['redɪ] 1. *adj.* a) *(prepared)* fertig; **be ~ to do sth.** bereit sein, etw. zu tun; **get ~** : sich fertigmachen; b) *(willing)* bereit; c) *(within reach)* griffbereit. 2. *adv.* fertig. 3. *n.* **at the ~** (Schußwaffe) im Anschlag

ready: ~ 'cash see ~ **money**; ~-'**made** *adj.* a) Konfektions(anzug, -kleidung); b) *(fig.)* vorgefertigt; ~ '**money** *n.* Bargeld, das

real [rɪəl] *adj.* a) *(actually existing)* real (Ereignis, Lebewesen); wirklich (Macht); b) *(genuine)* echt (Interesse, Gold, Seide); c) *(complete)* total (ugs.) (Desaster, Enttäuschung); d) *(true)* wahr (Grund, Name, Glück); echt (Mitleid, Sieg); **the ~ thing** der/die/das Echte; e) **be for ~** *(sl.)* echt sein.

'real estate *n.* Immobilien *Pl.*

realism ['rɪəlɪzm] *n.* Realismus, der

'realist *n.* Realist, der/Realistin, die

realistic [rɪə'lɪstɪk] *adj.* realistisch

reality [rɪ'ælɪtɪ] *n.* Realität, die

realization [rɪəlaɪ'zeɪʃn] *n.* Erkenntnis, die

realize ['rɪəlaɪz] *v. t.* a) *(be aware of)* bemerken; erkennen (Fehler); **I didn't ~** *(abs.)* ich habe es nicht gewußt; ~ [that]...: merken, daß ...; b) *(make happen)* verwirklichen; c) *(erbringen* (Summe, Preis)

really ['rɪəlɪ] *adv.* wirklich; **not ~** : eigentlich nicht; |**well,**| ~! |also| so was!

realm [relm] *n.* Königreich, das

realtor ['rɪəltə(r)] *(Amer.)* Grundstücksmakler, der

reap [ri:p] *v. t.* *(cut)* schneiden (Getreide); *(gather in)* einfahren (Getreide, Ernte)

reappear [ri:ə'pɪə(r)] *v. i.* wieder auftauchen; *(come back)* [wieder] zurückkommen

¹**rear** [rɪə(r)] 1. *n.* a) *(back part)* hinterer Teil; b) *(back)* Rückseite, die; c) *(Mil.)* Rücken, der. 2. *adj.* hinter...; ~ **axle** Hinterachse, die

²**rear** 1. *v. t.* großziehen (Kind, Familie); halten (Vieh). 2. *v. i.* (Pferd:) sich aufbäumen

rear: ~-**guard** *n.* *(Mil.)* Nachhut, die; ~-**light** *n.* Rücklicht, das

rearm [ri:'ɑ:m] *v. i. & t.* wiederaufrüsten

rearrange [ri:ə'reɪndʒ] *v. t.* umräumen (Möbel); verlegen (Spiel) (for auf + Akk.); ändern (Programm)

rear-view 'mirror *n.* Rückspiegel, der

reason ['ri:zn] 1. *n.* a) *(cause)* Grund, der; **have no ~ to complain** sich nicht beklagen können; **for that |very| ~** : aus [eben] diesem Grund; b) *(power to understand; sense)* Vernunft, die; *(power to think)* Verstand, der; **in or within ~** : innerhalb eines vernünftigen Rahmens. 2. *v. i.* a) schlußfolgern (from aus); b) ~ **with** diskutieren mit (about, on über + Akk.); **you can't ~ with her** mit ihr kann man nicht vernünftig reden. 3. *v. t.* schlußfolgern

reasonable ['ri:zənəbl] *adj.* a) vernünftig; b) *(inexpensive)* günstig

reasonably ['ri:zənəblɪ] *adv.* a) *(within reason)* vernünftig; b) *(fairly)* ganz (gut); ziemlich (gesund)

reassurance [ri:ə'ʃʊərəns] *n.* a) *(calming)* give sb. ~ : jmdn. beruhigen; b) *(confirmation)* Bestätigung, die

reassure [ri:ə'ʃʊə(r)] *v. t.* beruhigen; ~ **sb. about his health** jmdm. versichern, daß er gesund ist. **reassuring** [ri:ə'ʃʊərɪŋ] *adj.* beruhigend

rebate ['ri:beɪt] *n.* a) *(refund)* Rückzahlung, die; b) *(discount)* Preisnachlaß, der (on auf + Akk.)

rebel 1. ['rebl] *n.* Rebell, der/Rebellin, die. 2. *attrib. adj.* Rebellen-. 3. [rɪ'bel] *v. i.*, **-ll-** rebellieren. **rebellion** [rɪ'beljən] *n.* Rebellion, die. **rebellious** [rɪ'beljəs] *adj.* rebellisch

rebound 1. [rɪ'baʊnd] *v.i.* **a)** *(spring back)* abprallen **(from** von); **b)** *(fig.)* zurückfallen **(upon** auf + *Akk.).* **2.** ['riːbaʊnd] *n.* Abprall, *der*

rebuff [rɪ'bʌf] **1.** *n.* [schroffe] Abweisung. **2.** *v.t.* [schroff] zurückweisen

rebuild [riː'bɪld] *v.t.,* **rebuilt** [riː'bɪlt] wieder aufbauen

rebuke [rɪ'bjuːk] **1.** *v.t.* tadeln, rügen **(for** wegen). **2.** *n.* Rüge, *die*

recall 1. [rɪ'kɔːl] *v.t.* **a)** *(remember)* sich erinnern an (+ *Akk.*); **b)** *(serve as reminder of)* erinnern an (+ *Akk.*); **c)** abberufen *(Botschafter).* **2.** [rɪ'kɔːl, 'riːkɔːl] *n.* **a)** [powers of] ~: Gedächtnis, *das*; **b)** beyond ~: unwiderruflich

recant [rɪ'kænt] *v.i.* [öffentlich] widerrufen

recap ['riːkæp] *v.t. & i.,* **-pp-** *(coll.)* rekapitulieren

recapitulate [riːkə'pɪtjʊleɪt] *v.t. & i.* rekapitulieren

recapture [rɪː'kæptʃə(r)] *v.t.* wieder ergreifen *(Gefangenen);* wieder einfangen *(Tier)*

recede [rɪ'siːd] *v.i.* ⟨*Hochwasser, Flut:*⟩ zurückgehen; ~ **into the distance]** in der Ferne verschwinden. **receding** [rɪ'siːdɪŋ] *adj.* fliehend ⟨*Kinn, Stirn*⟩

receipt [rɪ'siːt] *n.* **a)** *(receiving)* Empfang, *der*; **b)** *(written acknowledgement)* Quittung, *die*; **c)** in pl. *(amount received)* Einnahmen **(from** aus)

receive [rɪ'siːv] *v.t.* **a)** *(get)* erhalten; beziehen *(Gehalt, Rente);* **b)** *(accept)* entgegennehmen *(Bukett, Lieferung);* **c)** *(entertain)* empfangen *(Gast).* **re'ceiver** *n.* **a)** Empfänger, *der/*Empfängerin, *die*; **b)** *(Teleph.)* [Telefon]hörer, *der*; **c)** *(of stolen goods)* Hehler, *der/*Hehlerin, *die*

recent ['riːsənt] *adj.* jüngst ⟨*Ereignisse, Vergangenheit usw.*⟩*;* the ~ **closure of the factory** die kürzlich erfolgte Schließung der Fabrik. **'recently** *adv.* *(a short time ago)* vor kurzem; *(in the recent past)* in der letzten Zeit

receptacle [rɪː'septəkl] *n.* Behälter, *der*; Gefäß, *das*

reception [rɪ'sepʃn] *n.* **a)** *(welcome)* Aufnahme, *die*; **b)** *(party)* Empfang, *der*; **c)** *(Brit.: foyer)* die Rezeption. **re'ceptionist** *n.* *(in hotel)* Empfangschef, *der/*-dame, *die*; *(at doctor's)* Sprechstundenhilfe, *die*. **re'ception desk** *n.* Rezeption, *die*

receptive [rɪ'septɪv] *adj.* aufgeschlossen, empfänglich (to für)

recess [rɪ'ses, 'riːses] *n.* **a)** *(alcove)* Nische, *die*; **b)** *(Brit. Parl.; Amer.: short vacation)* Ferien *Pl.; (Amer. Sch.; between classes)* Pause, *die*

recharge [riː'tʃɑːdʒ] *v.t.* aufladen ⟨*Batterie*⟩

recipe ['resɪpɪ] *n.* Rezept, *das*

recipient [rɪ'sɪpɪənt] *n.* Empfänger, *der/*Empfängerin, *die*

reciprocal [rɪ'sɪprəkl] *adj.* gegenseitig ⟨*Abkommen, Zuneigung*⟩

reciprocate [rɪ'sɪprəkeɪt] *v.t.* erwidern

recital [rɪ'saɪtl] *n. (performance)* [Solisten]konzert, *das; (of literature also)* Rezitation, *die*

recitation [resɪ'teɪʃn] *n.* Rezitation, *die*

recite [rɪ'saɪt] *v.t.* **a)** rezitieren ⟨*Gedicht*⟩; **b)** *(list)* aufzählen

reckless ['reklɪs] *adj.* unbesonnen; rücksichtslos *(Fahrweise);* ~ **of the dangers/consequences** ungeachtet der Gefahren/Folgen

reckon ['rekn] *v.t.* **a)** *(work out)* ausrechnen *(Kosten);* bestimmen *(Position);* **b)** *(consider)* halten **(as** für); **c)** *(estimate)* schätzen. **'reckon on** *v.t.* **a)** *(rely on)* zählen auf (+ *Akk.*); **b)** *(expect)* rechnen mit. **'reckon with** *v.i.* rechnen mit

'reckoning *n.* Berechnung, *die*; by my ~: nach meiner Rechnung

reclaim [rɪ'kleɪm] *v.t.* **a)** zurückbekommen ⟨*Steuern*⟩; **b)** urbar machen ⟨*Land*⟩

recline [rɪ'klaɪn] *v.i.* liegen; **reclining seat** Liegesitz, *der*

recluse [rɪ'kluːs] *n.* Einsiedler, *der/*Einsiedlerin, *die*

recognition [rekəg'nɪʃn] *n.* **a)** Wiedererkennen, *das*; **be beyond all ~:** nicht wiederzuerkennen sein; **b)** *(acknowledgement)* Anerkennung, *die*; **in ~ of** als Anerkennung für

recognize ['rekəgnaɪz] *v.t.* **a)** *(know again)* wiedererkennen **(by** an + *Dat.,* **from** durch); **b)** *(acknowledge)* erkennen; anerkennen ⟨*Gültigkeit, Land*⟩; **be ~d as** gelten als

recoil 1. [rɪ'kɔɪl] *v.i.* zurückfahren. **2.** ['riːkɔɪl, rɪ'kɔɪl] *n.* Rückstoß, *der*

recollect [rekə'lekt] **1.** *v.t.* sich erinnern an (+ *Akk.*). **2.** *v.i.* sich erinnern. **recollection** [rekə'lekʃn] *n.* Erinnerung, *die*

recommend [rekə'mend] *v.t.* empfehlen. **recommendation** [rekəmen'deɪʃn] *n.* Empfehlung, *die*; **on sb.'s ~:** auf jmds. Empfehlung *(Akk.)*

recompense ['rekəmpens] 1. *v.t.* entschädigen. 2. *n.* Entschädigung, *die*

reconcile ['rekənsaɪl] *v.t.* a) *(restore to friendship)* versöhnen; b) ~ oneself to sth. sich mit etw. versöhnen

reconnaissance [rɪ'kɒnɪsəns] *n.* (Mil.) Aufklärung, *die*

reconnoitre (Brit.; Amer.: **reconnoiter**) [rekə'nɔɪtə(r)] *v.i.* auf Erkundung [aus]gehen

reconsider [ri:kən'sɪdə(r)] *v.t.* [noch einmal] überdenken

reconstruct [ri:kən'strʌkt] *v.t.* wieder aufbauen; *(fig.)* rekonstruieren. **reconstruction** [ri:kən'strʌkʃn] *n.* Wiederaufbau, *der;* (thing reconstructed) Rekonstruktion, *die*

record 1. [rɪ'kɔ:d] *v.t.* a) aufzeichnen; ~ a new LP eine neue LP aufnehmen; b) (register officially) dokumentieren; protokollieren (Verhandlung). 2. ['rekɔ:d] *n.* a) be on ~ (Prozeß, Verhandlung, Besprechung:) protokolliert sein; have sth. on ~: etw. dokumentiert haben; b) (report) Protokoll, das; c) (document) Dokument, das; [strictly] off the ~: [ganz] inoffiziell; d) (for ~-player) Schallplatte, die; e) have a [criminal/police] ~: vorbestraft sein; f) (Sport) Rekord, der

recorded [rɪ'kɔ:dɪd] *adj.* aufgezeichnet (Konzert, Rede); ~ music Musikaufnahmen. **recorded de'livery** *n.* (Brit. Post.) eingeschriebene Sendung (ohne Versicherung)

recorder [rɪ'kɔ:də(r)] *n.* (Mus.) Blockflöte, *die*

recording [rɪ'kɔ:dɪŋ] *n.* a) (process) Aufzeichnung, die; b) (what is recorded) Aufnahme, die. **re'cording studio** *n.* Tonstudio, das

record ['rekɔ:d]: **~-player** *n.* Plattenspieler, der; **~ token** *n.* [Schall]plattengutschein, der

re-count 1. [ri:'kaʊnt] *v.t.* [noch einmal] nachzählen. 2. ['ri:kaʊnt] *n.* Nachzählung, *die*

recoup [rɪ'ku:p] *v.t.* [wieder] hereinbekommen (/Geld/einsatz)

recourse [rɪ'kɔ:s] *n.* have ~ to sb./sth. bei jmdm./zu etw. Zuflucht nehmen

recover [rɪ'kʌvə(r)] 1. *v.t.* zurückbekommen. 2. *v.i.* ~ from sth. sich von etw. [wieder] erholen; be [fully] ~ed [völlig] wiederhergestellt sein. **recovery** [rɪ'kʌvərɪ] *n.* Erholung, die; make a quick/good ~: sich schnell/gut erholen

recreation [rekrɪ'eɪʃn] *n.* Freizeitbe-

schäftigung, die; Hobby, das. **recreational** [rekrɪ'eɪʃənl] *adj.* Freizeit-

recruit [rɪ'kru:t] 1. *n.* a) (Mil.) Rekrut, der; b) (new member) neues Mitglied. 2. *v.t.* (Mil.: enlist) anwerben; (into party etc.) werben (Mitglied); einstellen (neuen Mitarbeiter). **re'cruitment** *n.* (Mil.) Anwerbung, die; (of new staff) Neueinstellung, die; ~ of members Mitgliederwerbung, die

rectangle ['rektæŋgl] *n.* Rechteck, das. **rectangular** [rek'tæŋgjʊlə(r)] *adj.* rechteckig

rector ['rektə(r)] *n.* a) Pfarrer, der; b) (Univ.) Rektor, der/Rektorin, die. **rectory** ['rektərɪ] *n.* Pfarrhaus, das

recuperate [rɪ'kju:pəreɪt] *v.i.* sich erholen. **recuperation** [rɪkju:pə'reɪʃn] *n.* Erholung, die

recur [rɪ'kɜ:(r)] *v.i.*, -rr- sich wiederholen; (Krankheit:) wiederkehren; (Symptom:) wieder auftreten. **recurrence** [rɪ'kʌrəns] *n.* Wiederholung, die; (of illness, thought, feeling) Wiederkehr, die; (of symptom) Wiederauftreten, das. **recurrent** [rɪ'kʌrənt] *adj.* immer wiederkehrend

recycle [ri:'saɪkl] *v.t.* wiederverwerten. **recycling** [ri:'saɪklɪŋ] *n.* Recycling, das

red [red] 1. *adj.* rot. 2. *n.* Rot, das. **Red 'Cross** *n.* Rotes Kreuz. **red'currant** *n.* [rote] Johannisbeere

redden ['redn] *v.i.* (Gesicht, Himmel:) sich röten; (Person:) rot werden

reddish ['redɪʃ] *adj.* rötlich

redecorate [ri:'dekəreɪt] *v.t.* renovieren; (with wallpaper) neu tapezieren; (with paint) neu streichen

redeem [rɪ'di:m] *v.t.* a) [wieder] einlösen (Pfand); einlösen (Gutschein, Coupon); b) (save) retten. **redemption** [rɪ'dempʃn] *n.* (from sin) Erlösung, die

redeploy [ri:dɪ'plɔɪ] *v.t.* woanders einsetzen (Arbeitskräfte)

red: **~-'handed** *adj.* catch sb. ~-handed jmdn. auf frischer Tat ertappen; **~ 'herring** *n.* (fig.) Ablenkungsmanöver, das; **~-hot** *adj.* [rot]glühend; **Red 'Indian** (Brit.) 1. *n.* Indianer, der/Indianerin, die. 2. *adj.* Indianer-

redirect [ri:dɪ'rekt] *v.t.* nachsenden (Post, Brief usw.); umleiten (Verkehr)

rediscover [ri:dɪ'skʌvə(r)] *v.t.* wiederentdecken

red: **~-'letter day** *n.* großer Tag; **~ 'light** *n.* rotes Warnlicht; (traffic-

light) rote Ampel; **drive through a ~ light** bei rot über die Ampel fahren; **~-'light district** *n.* Strich, *der* (*salopp*)

redo [riːˈduː] *v. t. forms as* **do** noch einmal machen ⟨*Bett, Hausaufgabe*⟩; neu frisieren ⟨*Haare*⟩

redouble [riːˈdʌbl] *v. t.* verdoppeln

redress [rɪˈdres] **1.** *n.* Entschädigung, *die.* **2.** *v. t.* wiedergutmachen; **~ the balance** das Gleichgewicht wiederherstellen

red 'tape *n.* (*fig.*) (unnötige) Bürokratie

reduce [rɪˈdjuːs] *v. t.* a) senken ⟨*Preis, Gebühr, Fieber, Aufwendungen, Blutdruck usw.*⟩; reduzieren ⟨*Geschwindigkeit, Gewicht*⟩; **at ~d prices** zu herabgesetzten Preisen; b) **~ to silence/tears** verstummen lassen/zum Weinen bringen. **reduction** [rɪˈdʌkʃn] *n.* (*in price, costs, speed, etc.*) Senkung, *die* (*in Gen.*); **~ in wages/weight** Lohnsenkung, *die*/Gewichtsabnahme, *die*

redundancy [rɪˈdʌndənsɪ] *n.* (*Brit.*) Arbeitslosigkeit, *die;* **redundancies** Entlassungen

redundant [rɪˈdʌndənt] *adj.* (*Brit.*) arbeitslos; **be made ~:** den Arbeitsplatz verlieren; **make ~:** entlassen

red 'wine *n.* Rotwein, *der*

reed [riːd] *n.* Schilf(rohr), *das*

reef [riːf] *n.* Riff, *das*

'reef-knot *n.* Kreuzknoten, *der*

reek [riːk] *v. i.* stinken (**of** nach)

reel [riːl] **1.** *n.* ⟨*Garn-, Angel*⟩rolle, *die;* ⟨*Film-, Tonband*⟩spule, *die.* **2.** *v. i.* a) (*be in a whirl*) sich drehen; b) (*sway*) torkeln

refectory [rɪˈfektərɪ] *n.* Mensa, *die*

refer [rɪˈfɜː(r)] **1.** *v. i.,* -rr-: a) **~ to** (*allude to*) sich beziehen auf (+ *Akk.*) ⟨*Buch, Person usw.*⟩; (*speak of*) sprechen von ⟨*Person, Problem usw.*⟩; b) **~ to** (*apply to, relate to*) betreffen; c) **~ to** (*consult, cite as proof*) nachsehen in (+ *Dat.*). **2.** *v. t.,* -rr-: **~ sb./sth. to sb./ sth.** jmdn./etw. an jmdn./auf etw. (*Akk.*) verweisen

referee [refəˈriː] *n.* (*Sport*) **1.** *n.* (*umpire*) Schiedsrichter, *der*/-richterin, *die;* (*Boxing*) Ringrichter, *der.* **2.** *v. t.* als Schiedsrichter/-richterin leiten

reference [ˈrefrəns] *n.* a) (*allusion*) Hinweis, *der* (**to** auf + *Akk.*); **make no ~ to sth.** etw. nicht ansprechen; b) (*testimonial*) Zeugnis, *das*

referendum [refəˈrendəm] *n.* Volksentscheid, *der*

refill 1. [riːˈfɪl] *v. t.* nachfüllen; **~ the glasses** nachschenken. **2.** [ˈriːfɪl] *n.* (*for ball-pen*) Ersatzmine, *die*

refine [rɪˈfaɪn] *v. t.* a) (*purify*) raffinieren; b) (*make cultured*) kultivieren; c) (*improve*) verbessern; verfeinern ⟨*Stil, Technik*⟩. **refined** [rɪˈfaɪnd] *adj.* kultiviert. **re'finement** *n.* Kultiviertheit, *die;* (*improvement*) Verbesserung, *die*

refinery [rɪˈfaɪnərɪ] *n.* Raffinerie, *die*

reflect [rɪˈflekt] *v. t.* a) reflektieren; b) (*fig.*) widerspiegeln ⟨*Ansichten*⟩; c) (*contemplate*) nachdenken über (+ *Akk.*); **~ what/how ...:** überlegen, was/wie ... **re'flect [up]on** *v. i.* a) (*consider*) nachdenken über (+ *Akk.*); b) **~ badly [up]on sb./sth.** auf jmdn./ etw. ein schlechtes Licht werfen. **reflection** [rɪˈflekʃn] *n.* a) Reflektieren, *die;* (*by surface of water*) Spiegelung, *die;* b) (*image*) Spiegelbild, *das;* c) (*consideration*) Nachdenken, *das* (**upon** über + *Akk.*); **on ~:** bei weiterem Nachdenken. **reflective** [rɪˈflektɪv] *adj.* a) reflektierend; b) (*thoughtful*) nachdenklich. **reflector** [rɪˈflektə(r)] *n.* Rückstrahler, *der*

reflex [ˈriːfleks] **1.** *n.* Reflex, *der.* **2.** *adj.* **~ action** Reflexhandlung, *die*

reflexive [rɪˈfleksɪv] *adj.* (*Ling.*) reflexiv

reform [rɪˈfɔːm] **1.** *v. t.* (*make better*) bessern ⟨*Person*⟩; reformieren ⟨*Institution*⟩. **2.** *n.* Reform, *die* (**in** Gen.). **reformation** [refəˈmeɪʃn] *n.* (*of character*) Wandlung, *die;* **the R~** (*Hist.*) die Reformation. **re'former** *n.* |**political**| **~:** Reformpolitiker, *der*/Reformpolitikerin, *die*

refract [rɪˈfrækt] *v. t.* (*Phys.*) brechen

¹refrain [rɪˈfreɪn] *n.* Refrain, *der*

²refrain *v. i.* **~ from doing sth.** es unterlassen, etw. zu tun

refresh [rɪˈfreʃ] *v. t.* erfrischen. **re'freshing** *adj.* erfrischend; wohltuend ⟨*Abwechslung*⟩. **re'freshment** *n.* Erfrischung, *die*

refrigerate [rɪˈfrɪdʒəreɪt] *v. t.* a) kühl lagern ⟨*Lebensmittel*⟩; b) (*chill*) kühlen; (*freeze*) einfrieren. **refrigeration** [rɪfrɪdʒəˈreɪʃn] *n.* kühle Lagerung; (*chilling*) Kühlung, *die;* (*freezing*) Einfrieren, *das.* **refrigerator** [rɪˈfrɪdʒəreɪtə(r)] *n.* Kühlschrank, *der*

refuel [riːˈfjuːəl], (*Brit.*) -ll- **1.** *v. t.* auftanken. **2.** *v. i.* [auf]tanken

refuge [ˈrefjuːdʒ] *n.* Zuflucht, *die;* **take ~ in** Schutz *od.* Zuflucht suchen in (+ *Dat.*) (**from** vor + *Dat.*)

refugee [refjʊˈdʒi:] n. Flüchtling, der
refund 1. [ri:ˈfʌnd] v.t. (pay back) zurückzahlen ⟨Geld⟩; erstatten ⟨Kosten⟩. **2.** [ˈri:fʌnd] n. Rückzahlung, die; (of expenses) [Rück]erstattung, die
refusal [rɪˈfju:zl] n. Ablehnung, die; (after a period of time) Absage, die; ~ to do sth. Weigerung, etw. zu tun
¹refuse [rɪˈfju:z] **1.** v.t. ablehnen; verweigern ⟨Zutritt, Einreise, Erlaubnis⟩; ~ sb. admittance/entry/permission jmdm. den Zutritt/die Einreise/die Erlaubnis verweigern; ~ to do sth. sich weigern, etw. zu tun. **2.** v.i. ablehnen; (after request) sich weigern
²refuse [ˈrefju:s] n. Abfall, der
refuse [ˈrefju:s]: ~ collection n. Müllabfuhr, die; ~ collector n. Müllwerker, der; ~ disposal n. Abfallbeseitigung, die
refute [rɪˈfju:t] v.t. widerlegen
regain [rɪˈgeɪn] v.t. zurückgewinnen ⟨Zuversicht, Vertrauen, Augenlicht⟩; ~ one's strength wieder zu Kräften kommen
regal [ˈri:gl] adj. majestätisch
regalia [rɪˈgeɪlɪə] n. pl. (of royalty) Krönungsinsignien
regard [rɪˈgɑ:d] **1.** v.t. a) (look at) betrachten; b) (give heed to) beachten; c) (fig.: look upon, contemplate) betrachten; ~ sb. as a friend/fool/genius jmdn. als Freund/Dummkopf/ein Genie halten; be ~ed as gelten als; d) (concern, have relation to) betreffen; as ~s sb./sth., ~ing sb./sth. was jmdn./etw. angeht od. betrifft. **2.** n. a) (attention) pay or have ~ to sb./sth. jmdm./etw. Beachtung schenken; without ~ to ohne Rücksicht auf (+ Akk.); b) (esteem) Achtung, die; hold sb./sth. in high ~: jmdn./etw. sehr schätzen; c) in pl. Grüße; give her my ~s grüße sie von mir; with kind[est] ~s mit herzlich[st]en Grüßen. **re'gardless** adj. ohne Rücksicht (of auf + Akk.)
regatta [rɪˈgætə] n. Regatta, die
regenerate [rɪˈdʒenəreɪt] v.t. erneuern
regime, régime [reɪˈʒi:m] n. [Regierungs]system, das
regiment [ˈredʒɪmənt, ˈredʒmənt] n. Regiment, das. **regimental** [redʒɪˈmentl] adj. Regiments-
region [ˈri:dʒn] n. a) (area) Gebiet, das; b) (administrative division) Bezirk, der; in the ~ of (fig.) ungefähr. **regional** [ˈri:dʒənl] adj. regional

register [ˈredʒɪstə(r)] **1.** n. Register, das; (at school) Klassenbuch, das. **2.** v.t. a) (enter) registrieren; (cause to be entered) registrieren lassen; anmelden ⟨Auto, Patent⟩; (at airport) einchecken ⟨Gepäck⟩; abs. (at hotel) sich ins Fremdenbuch eintragen; ~ with the police sich polizeilich anmelden; b) (enrol) anmelden; (Univ.) sich einschreiben; c) zum Ausdruck bringen ⟨Überraschung⟩; ~ a protest Protest anmelden. **registered** [ˈredʒɪstəd] adj. eingetragen ⟨Firma⟩; eingeschrieben ⟨Student, Brief⟩; ~ trade mark eingetragenes Warenzeichen; by ~ post per Einschreiben
registrar [ˈredʒɪstrɑ:(r), redʒɪˈstrɑ:(r)] n. Standesbeamte, der/-beamtin, die
registration [redʒɪˈstreɪʃn] n. Registrierung, die; (enrolment) Anmeldung, die; (of students) Einschreibung, die. **regi'stration document** n. (Brit.) Kraftfahrzeugbrief, der. **regi'stration number** n. amtliches Kennzeichen
registry [ˈredʒɪstrɪ] n. ~ [office] Standesamt, das
regret [rɪˈgret] **1.** v.t., -tt- bedauern; I ~ to say that ...: ich muß leider sagen, daß ... **2.** n. Bedauern, das; have no ~s nichts bereuen. **regretfully** [rɪˈgretfəlɪ] adv. mit Bedauern. **regrettable** [rɪˈgretəbl] adj. bedauerlich. **regrettably** [rɪˈgretəblɪ] adv. bedauerlicherweise
regroup [ri:ˈgru:p] **1.** v.t. umgruppieren. **2.** v.i. a) (form new group) sich neu gruppieren; b) (Mil.) sich neu formieren
regular [ˈregjʊlə(r)] **1.** adj. regelmäßig; geregelt ⟨Arbeit⟩; fest ⟨Anstellung⟩; ~ customer Stammkunde, der/-kundin, die; ~ army reguläre Armee. **2.** n. (coll.: ~ customer) Stammkunde, der/-kundin, die; (in pub) Stammgast, der. **regularity** [regjʊˈlærɪtɪ] n. Regelmäßigkeit, die. **'regularly** adv. regelmäßig
regulate [ˈregjʊleɪt] v.t. (control) regeln; (restrict) begrenzen; (adjust) regulieren. **regulation** [regjʊˈleɪʃn] n. a) see regulate: Regelung, die; Begrenzung, die; Regulierung, die; b) (rule) Vorschrift, die
rehabilitate [ri:həˈbɪlɪteɪt] v.t. rehabilitieren; ~ [back into society] wieder [in die Gesellschaft] eingliedern
rehash 1. [ri:ˈhæʃ] v.t. aufwärmen. **2.** [ˈri:hæʃ] n. Aufguß, der

rehearsal [rɪˈhɜːsl] n. Probe, *die*. **rehearse** [rɪˈhɜːs] v. t. proben
reign [reɪn] 1. n. Herrschaft, *die*. 2. v. i.
herrschen (over über + *Akk.*)
rein [reɪn] n. Zügel, *der*
reincarnation [ˌriːɪnkɑːˈneɪʃn] n.
(Relig.) Reinkarnation, *die*
reindeer [ˈreɪndɪə(r)] n., pl. same
Ren[tier], *das*
reinforce [ˌriːɪnˈfɔːs] v. t. verstärken;
~d concrete Stahlbeton, *der*. **rein-
'forcement** n. Verstärkung, *die;* ~[s]
(additional men etc.) Verstärkung, *die*
reinstate [ˌriːɪnˈsteɪt] v. t. *(in job)* wieder einstellen
reinvigorate [ˌriːɪnˈvɪɡəreɪt] v. t. neu
beleben; **feel** ~d sich gestärkt fühlen
reiterate [riːˈɪtəreɪt] v. t. wiederholen
reject 1. [rɪˈdʒekt] v. t. ablehnen; zurückweisen *(Bitte, Annäherungsversuch)*. 2. [ˈriːdʒekt] *(thing)* Ausschuß,
der. **rejection** [rɪˈdʒekʃn] n. Ablehnung, *die/*Zurückweisung, *die*
rejoice [rɪˈdʒɔɪs] v. i. sich freuen (over,
at über + *Akk.*)
¹rejoin [rɪˈdʒɔɪn] v. t. *(reply)* erwidern
(to auf + *Akk.*)
²rejoin [ˌriːˈdʒɔɪn] v. t. wieder eintreten
in (+ *Akk.*) *(Partei, Verein)*
rejoinder [rɪˈdʒɔɪndə(r)] n. Erwiderung, *die* (to auf + *Akk.*)
rejuvenate [rɪˈdʒuːvəneɪt] v. t. verjüngen
rekindle [ˌriːˈkɪndl] v. t. wieder anfachen; wieder aufleben lassen *(Verlangen, Hoffnungen)*
relapse [rɪˈlæps] 1. v. i. *(Kranker:)* einen Rückfall bekommen. 2. n. Rück-
fall, *der*
relate [rɪˈleɪt] 1. v. t. a) erzählen *(Geschichte)*; erzählen von *(Abenteuer)*;
b) *(bring into relation)* in Zusammenhang bringen (to, with mit). 2. v. i. a) ~
to *(have reference to)* in Zusammenhang
stehen mit; betreffen *(Person)*; b) ~ to
(feel involved with) eine Beziehung haben zu. **re'lated** adj. verwandt (to
mit). **relation** [rɪˈleɪʃn] n. a) *(connection)* Beziehung, *die*, Zusammenhang,
der (of ... and zwischen ... und); **in or
with** ~ **to** in bezug auf (+ *Akk.*); b) in
pl. *(dealings)* Verhältnis, *das* (with
zu); c) *(relative)* Verwandte, *der/die*.
re'lationship n. a) *(mutual tie)* Beziehung, *die* (with zu); b) *(kinship)*
Verwandtschaftsverhältnis, *das;* c)
(connection) Beziehung, *die; (between
cause and effect)* Zusammenhang,
der; d) *(sexual)* Verhältnis, *das*

relative [ˈrelətɪv] 1. n. Verwandte, *der/
die*. 2. adj. relativ. **'relatively** adv.
relativ; verhältnismäßig. **relative
'pronoun** n. *(Ling.)* Relativprono-
men, *das*
relax [rɪˈlæks] 1. v. t. a) entspannen
(Muskel, Körper[teil]); lockern
(Griff); b) *(make less strict)* lockern
(Gesetz, Disziplin). 2. v. i. sich entspannen. **relaxation** [ˌriːlækˈseɪʃn] n.
Entspannung, *die;* **for** ~: zur Entspannung. **relaxed** [rɪˈlækst] adj. entspannt, gelöst *(Atmosphäre, Person)*.
re'laxing adj. entspannend
relay 1. [ˈriːleɪ] n. a) *(race)* Staffel, *die;*
b) *(gang)* Schicht, *die;* **work in** ~s
schichtweise arbeiten; c) *(Electr.)* Re-
lais, *das*. 2. [riːˈleɪ] v. t. a) weiterleiten;
b) *(Radio, Telev.)* übertragen. **'relay
race** n. Staffellauf, *der; (Swimming)*
Staffelschwimmen, *das*
release [rɪˈliːs] 1. v. t. a) *(free)* freilassen *(Tier, Häftling, Sklaven)*; *(from
jail)* entlassen (**from** aus); b) *(let go)*
loslassen; lösen *(Handbremse)*; c)
(make known) veröffentlichen *(Erklärung, Nachricht)*; *(issue)* herausbringen *(Film, Schallplatte)*. 2. n. a) *see*
1 a: Freilassung, *die;* Entlassung, *die;*
b) *(of published item)* Veröffentlichung, *die;* c) *(handle, lever, button)*
Auslöser, *der*
relegate [ˈrelɪɡeɪt] v. t. a) ~ **sb. to the
position of ...:** jmdn. zu ... degradieren; b) *(Sport)* absteigen lassen; **be** ~**d**
absteigen (to in + *Akk.*). **relegation**
[ˌrelɪˈɡeɪʃn] n. *(Sport)* Abstieg, *der*
relent [rɪˈlent] v. i. nachgeben. **re-
'lentless** adj., **re'lentlessly** adv.
unerbittlich
relevance [ˈrelɪvəns] n. Relevanz, *die*
(to für)
relevant [ˈrelɪvənt] adj. relevant (to
für); wichtig *(Information)*
reliability [rɪˌlaɪəˈbɪlɪti] n. Zuverlässigkeit, *die*
reliable [rɪˈlaɪəbl] adj., **reliably** [rɪ-
ˈlaɪəblɪ] adv. zuverlässig
reliance [rɪˈlaɪəns] n. Abhängigkeit,
die (on von)
reliant [rɪˈlaɪənt] adj. **be** ~ **on sb./sth.**
auf jmdn./etw. angewiesen sein
¹relief [rɪˈliːf] n. a) Erleichterung, *die;*
give [sb.] ~ [from pain] [jmdm.]
[Schmerz]linderung verschaffen; **what
a** ~!, **that's a** ~! da bin ich aber erleichtert!; b) *(assistance)* Hilfe, *die*
²relief n. *(Art)* Relief, *das*
relief: ~ **bus** n. Entlastungsbus, *der;*

(as replacement) Ersatzbus, *der;* ~ **map** *n.* Reliefkarte, *die;* ~ **road** *n.* Entlastungsstraße, *die*

relieve [rɪ'liːv] *v. t.* **a)** erleichtern; unterbrechen *(Eintönigkeit);* abbauen *(Anspannung);* stillen *(Schmerzen);* I **am** *or* **feel** ~**d to hear that ...:** es erleichtert mich zu hören, daß ...; **b)** ablösen *(Wache, Truppen)*

religion [rɪ'lɪdʒn] *n.* Religion, *die*

religious [rɪ'lɪdʒəs] *adj.* religiös; Religions(*freiheit, -unterricht*). **re'ligiously** *adv. (conscientiously)* gewissenhaft

relinquish [rɪ'lɪŋkwɪʃ] *v. t.* **a)** *(give up)* aufgeben; **b)** ~ **one's hold** *or* **grip on sb./sth.** jmdn./etw. loslassen

relish ['relɪʃ] **1.** *n.* **a)** *(liking)* Vorliebe, *die;* **do sth. with |great| ~:** etw. mit |großem| Genuß tun; **b)** *(condiment)* Relish, *das.* **2.** *v. t.* genießen

relive [riː'lɪv] *n.* noch einmal durchleben

reload [riː'ləʊd] *v. t.* nachladen *(Schußwaffe)*

reluctance [rɪ'lʌktəns] *n.* Widerwille, *der;* **have a |great| ~ to do sth.** etw. nur mit Widerwillen tun

reluctant [rɪ'lʌktənt] *adj.* unwillig; **be ~ to do sth.** etw. nur ungern tun. **re'luctantly** *adv.* nur ungern

rely [rɪ'laɪ] *v. i. (have trust)* sich verlassen/*(be dependent)* angewiesen sein (**|up|on** *or* **upon** *Akk.*)

remain [rɪ'meɪn] *v. i.* **a)** *(be left over)* übrigbleiben; **b)** *(stay)* bleiben; ~ **behind** noch bleiben; **c)** *(continue to be)* bleiben; **it ~s to be seen** es wird sich zeigen. **remainder** [rɪ'meɪndə(r)] *n.* Rest, *der.* **re'maining** *adj.* restlich. **re'mains** *n. pl.* **a)** Reste; **b)** *(human)* sterbliche [Über]reste *(verhüll.)*

remand [rɪ'mɑːnd] **1.** *v. t.* ~ **sb. |in custody|** jmdn. in Untersuchungshaft behalten. **2.** *n.* **on** ~: in Untersuchungshaft

remark [rɪ'mɑːk] **1.** *v. t.* bemerken (**to** gegenüber). **2.** *v. i.* eine Bemerkung machen (**|up|on** zu, **über** + *Akk.*). **3.** *n.* Bemerkung, *die* (**on** über + *Akk.*).

remarkable [rɪ'mɑːkəbl] *adj.* **a)** *(notable)* bemerkenswert; **b)** *(extraordinary)* außergewöhnlich. **remarkably** [rɪ'mɑːkəblɪ] *adv.* **a)** *(notably)* bemerkenswert; **b)** *(exceptionally)* außergewöhnlich

remarry [riː'mærɪ] *v. i. & t.* wieder heiraten

remedy ['remɪdɪ] **1.** *n.* [Heil]mittel,

das (**for gegen**). **2.** *v. t.* beheben *(Problem);* retten *(Situation)*

remember [rɪ'membə(r)] *v. t.* **a)** sich erinnern an (+ *Akk.*); **I ~ed to bring the book** ich habe daran gedacht, das Buch mitzubringen; **an evening to ~:** ein unvergeßlicher Abend; **b)** *(convey greetings)* ~ **me to them** grüße sie von mir. **remembrance** [rɪ'membrəns] *n.* Gedenken, *das;* **in ~ of sb.** zu jmds. Gedächtnis

remind [rɪ'maɪnd] *v. t.* erinnern (**of** an + *Akk.*); ~ **sb. to do sth.** jmdn. daran erinnern, etw. zu tun; **that ~s me, ...:** dabei fällt mir ein, ... **re'minder** *n.* Erinnerung, *die* (**of** an + *Akk.*); *(letter)* Mahnung, *die;* Mahnbrief, *der*

reminisce [remɪ'nɪs] *v. i.* sich in Erinnerungen *(Dat.)* ergehen (**about** an + *Akk.*). **reminiscences** [remɪ'nɪsənsɪz] *n. pl.* Erinnerungen; *(memoirs)* [Lebens]erinnerungen *Pl.* **reminiscent** [remɪ'nɪsənt] *adj.* **be ~ of sth.** an etw. *(Akk.)* erinnern

remiss [rɪ'mɪs] *adj.* nachlässig (**of von**)

remission [rɪ'mɪʃn] *n.* **a)** *(of debt, punishment)* Erlaß, *der;* **b)** *(of prison sentence)* Straferlaß, *der*

remit [rɪ'mɪt] *v. t.,* **-tt-** *(send)* überweisen *(Geld).* **remittance** [rɪ'mɪtəns] *n.* Überweisung, *die*

remnant ['remnənt] *n.* Rest, *der*

remonstrate ['remənstreɪt] *v. i.* protestieren (**against** gegen); ~ **with sb.** jmdm. Vorenthaltungen machen (**about, on wegen**)

remorse [rɪ'mɔːs] *n.* Reue, *die* (**for, about** über + *Akk.*). **re'morseful** [rɪ'mɔːsfl] *adj.* reumütig. **re'morseless** *adj.* unerbittlich

remote [rɪ'məʊt] *adj.,* ~**r** [rɪ'məʊtə(r)], ~**st** [rɪ'məʊtɪst] **a)** fern *(Vergangenheit, Zukunft, Zeit);* abgelegen *(Ort, Gebiet);* ~ **from** weit entfernt von; **b)** *(slight)* gering *(Chance).* **remote con'trol** *n. (of vehicle)* Fernlenkung, *die; (for TV set)* Fernbedienung, *die.* **remote-con'trol[led]** *adj.* ferngelenkt; fernbedient *(Anlage)*

re'motely *adv.* entfernt *(verwandt);* **they are not ~ alike** sie haben nicht die entfernteste Ähnlichkeit

removable [rɪ'muːvəbl] *adj.* abnehmbar; entfernbar *(Trennwand);* herausnehmbar *(Futter)*

removal [rɪ'muːvl] *n.* **a)** Entfernung, *die; (of obstacle, problem)* Beseitigung, *die;* **b)** *(transfer of furniture)* Umzug, *der*

removal: ~ **firm** n. Spedition, die; ~ **man** n. Möbelpacker, der; ~ **van** n. Möbelwagen, der

remove [rɪˈmuːv] v. t. entfernen; beseitigen ⟨Spur, Hindernis⟩; (take off) abnehmen; ausziehen ⟨Kleidungsstück⟩; ~ **a book from the shelf** ein Buch vom Regal nehmen. **reˈmover** n. **a)** (of paint/varnish/hair/rust) Farb- / Lack- / Haar- / Rostentferner, der; **b)** (man) Möbelpacker, der; |firm of| ~s Spedition[sfirma], die

remunerate [rɪˈmjuːnəreit] v. t. bezahlen. **remuneration** [rɪmjuːnəˈreɪʃn] n. Bezahlung, die

Renaissance [rəˈneɪsɑ̃s, rɪˈneɪsəns] n. (Hist.) Renaissance, die

rename [riːˈneɪm] v. t. umbenennen

render [ˈrendə(r)] v. t. **a)** (make) machen; **b)** erweisen ⟨Dienst⟩; **c)** (translate) übersetzen (by mit). **ˈrendering** n. (translation) Übersetzung, die

rendezvous [ˈrɒndeɪvuː] n., pl. same [ˈrɒndeɪvuːz] **a)** (meeting-place) Treffpunkt, der; **b)** (meeting) Verabredung, die

renegade [ˈrenɪɡeɪd] **1.** n. Abtrünnige, der/die. **2.** adj. abtrünnig

renew [rɪˈnjuː] v. t. erneuern; fortsetzen ⟨Angriff, Bemühungen⟩; (extend) erneuern ⟨Vertrag, Ausweis usw.⟩; ~ **a library book** ⟨Bibliothekar/Benutzer:⟩ ein Buch [aus der Bücherei] verlängern/verlängern lassen. **renewal** [rɪˈnjuːəl] n. Erneuerung, die

renounce [rɪˈnaʊns] v. t. verzichten auf (+ Akk.); verstoßen ⟨Person⟩; ~ **the devil/one's faith** dem Teufel/seinem Glauben abschwören

renovate [ˈrenəveɪt] v. t. renovieren ⟨Gebäude⟩; restaurieren ⟨Möbel usw.⟩. **renovation** [renəˈveɪʃn] n. Renovierung, die/Restaurierung, die

renown [rɪˈnaʊn] n. Renommee, das. **renowned** [rɪˈnaʊnd] adj. berühmt (for wegen, für)

rent [rent] **1.** n. (for house etc.) Miete, die; (for land) Pacht, die. **2.** v. t. **a)** (use) mieten ⟨Haus, Wohnung usw.⟩; pachten ⟨Land⟩; mieten ⟨Auto⟩; **b)** (let) vermieten ⟨Haus, Auto usw.⟩ (to Dat., an + Akk.); verpachten ⟨Land⟩ (to Dat., an + Akk.). **rent ˈout** v. t. see **rent 2 b**

rental [ˈrentl] n. Miete, die

renunciation [rɪnʌnsɪˈeɪʃn] n. see **renounce:** Verzicht, der; Verstoßung, die

reopen [riːˈəʊpn] **1.** v. t. wieder öffnen; wiedereröffnen

⟨Geschäft, Lokal usw.⟩; wiederaufnehmen ⟨Diskussion, Verhandlung⟩. **2.** v. i. ⟨Geschäft, Lokal usw.:⟩ wieder öffnen

reorder [riːˈɔːdə(r)] v. t. **a)** (Commerc.) nachbestellen ⟨Ware⟩; **b)** (rearrange) umordnen

reorganization [riːɔːɡənaɪˈzeɪʃn] n. Umorganisation, die; (of time, work) Neueinteilung, die

reorganize [riːˈɔːɡənaɪz] v. t. umorganisieren; neu einteilen ⟨Zeit, Arbeit⟩

rep [rep] n. (coll.: representative) Vertreter, der/Vertreterin, die

repaid see **repay**

repair [rɪˈpeə(r)] **1.** v. t. (mend) reparieren; ausbessern ⟨Kleidung, Straße⟩. **2.** n. Reparatur, die; **be in good/bad** ~: in gutem/schlechtem Zustand sein. **reˈpair man** n. Mechaniker, der; (in house) Handwerker, der. **reˈpair shop** n. Reparaturwerkstatt, die

repatriate [riːˈpætrieɪt] v. t. repatriieren. **repatriation** [riːpætriˈeɪʃn] n. Repatriierung, die

repay [riːˈpeɪ] v. t., repaid [riːˈpeɪd] zurückzahlen ⟨Schulden usw.⟩; erwidern ⟨Besuch, Gruß, Freundlichkeit⟩; ~ **sb. for sth.** jmdm. etw. vergelten. **reˈpayment** n. Rückzahlung, die

repeal [rɪˈpiːl] **1.** v. t. aufheben ⟨Gesetz, Erlaß usw.⟩. **2.** n. Aufhebung, die

repeat [rɪˈpiːt] **1.** n. Wiederholung, die. **2.** v. t. wiederholen; **please** ~ **after me:** ...: sprich/sprecht/sprechen Sie mir bitte nach: ... **reˈpeated** adj. wiederholt; (several) mehrere; make ~ **efforts to** ...: wiederholt od. mehrfach versuchen, ...zu... **reˈpeatedly** adv. mehrmals

repel [rɪˈpel] v. t., -ll-: **a)** (drive back) abwehren; **b)** (be repulsive to) abstoßen. **repellent** [rɪˈpelənt] adj. abstoßend

repent [rɪˈpent] v. i. bereuen (of Akk.). **repentance** [rɪˈpentəns] n. Reue, die. **repentant** [rɪˈpentənt] adj. reuig

repercussion [riːpəˈkʌʃn] n., usu. in pl. Auswirkung, die (|up|on auf + Akk.)

repertoire [ˈrepətwɑː(r)] n. Repertoire, das

repertory [ˈrepətəri] n. (Theatre) Repertoiretheater, das. **ˈrepertory company** n. Repertoiretheater, das

repetition [repɪˈtɪʃn] n. Wiederholung, die

repetitious [repɪˈtɪʃəs] adj. sich immer wiederholend attr.

repetitive [rɪ'petɪtɪv] *adj.* eintönig

rephrase [ri:'freɪz] *v. t.* umformulieren; **I'll ~ that** ich will es anders ausdrücken

replace [rɪ'pleɪs] *v. t.* **a)** *(vertically)* zurückstellen; *(horizontally)* zurücklegen; **b)** *(take place of)* ersetzen; **~ A with** *or* **by B** A durch B ersetzen; **c)** *(exchange)* austauschen, auswechseln ⟨*Maschinen[teile] usw.*⟩. **re'placement** *n.* **a)** *see* **replace a**: Zurückstellen, *das;* Zurücklegen, *das;* **b)** *(provision of substitute for)* Ersatz, *der; attrib.* Ersatz-; **c)** *(substitute)* Ersatz, *der;* **~ [part]** Ersatzteil, *das*

replay 1. [ri:'pleɪ] *v. t.* wiederholen ⟨*Spiel*⟩; nochmals abspielen ⟨*Tonband usw.*⟩. **2.** ['ri:pleɪ] *n.* Wiederholung, *die;* *(match)* Wiederholungsspiel, *das*

replenish [rɪ'plenɪʃ] *v. t.* auffüllen

replica ['replɪkə] *n.* Nachbildung, *die*

reply [rɪ'plaɪ] **1.** *v. i.* **~ [to sb./sth.]** [jmdm./auf etw. *(Akk.)*] antworten. **2.** *v. t.* **~ that** ...: antworten, daß ... **3.** *n.* Antwort, *die* (**to** auf + *Akk.*)

report [rɪ'pɔ:t] **1.** *v. t.* **a)** *(relate)* berichten/*(in writing)* einen Bericht schreiben über (+ *Akk.*); *(state formally also)* melden; **b)** *(name to authorities)* melden (**to** *Dat.*); *(for prosecution)* anzeigen (**to** bei). **2.** *v. i.* **a)** Bericht erstatten (**on** über + *Akk.*); berichten (**on** über + *Akk.*); **b)** *(present oneself)* sich melden (**to** bei). **3.** *n.* **a)** *(account)* Bericht, *der* (**on, about** über + *Akk.*); **b)** *(Sch.)* Zeugnis, *das;* **c)** *(of gun)* Knall, *der.* **reportedly** [rɪ'pɔ:tɪdlɪ] *adv.* wie verlautet. **reported 'speech** *n.* indirekte Rede. **re'porter** *n.* Reporter, *der*/Reporterin, *die*

repossess [ri:pə'zes] *v. t.* wieder in Besitz nehmen

reprehensible [reprɪ'hensɪbl] *adj.* tadelnswert

represent [reprɪ'zent] *v. t.* **a)** darstellen (**as** als); **b)** *(act for)* vertreten. **representation** [reprɪzen'teɪʃn] *n.* **a)** *(depicting, image)* Darstellung, *die;* **b)** *(acting for sb.)* Vertretung, *die;* **c)** **make ~s to sb.** bei jmdm. Protest einlegen. **representative** [reprɪ'zentətɪv] **1.** *n.* **a)** *(Commerc.)* Vertreter, *der*/Vertreterin, *die;* **b)** **R~** *(Amer. Polit.)* Abgeordneter/Abgeordnete. **2.** *adj.* *(typical)* repräsentativ (**of** für)

repress [rɪ'pres] *v. t.* unterdrücken. **repression** [rɪ'preʃn] *n.* Unterdrückung, *die.* **repressive** [rɪ'presɪv] *adj.* repressiv

reprieve [rɪ'pri:v] **1.** *v. t.* **~ sb.** *(postpone execution)* jmdm. Strafaufschub gewähren; *(remit execution)* jmdn. begnadigen. **2.** *n.* Strafaufschub, *der* (**of** für)/Begnadigung, *die;* *(fig.)* Gnadenfrist, *der*

reprimand ['reprɪmɑ:nd] **1.** *n.* Tadel, *der.* **2.** *v. t.* tadeln

reprint 1. [ri:'prɪnt] *v. t.* wieder abdrucken. **2.** ['ri:prɪnt] *n.* Nachdruck, *der*

reprisal [rɪ'praɪzl] *n.* Vergeltungsakt, *der* (**for** gegen)

reproach [rɪ'prəʊtʃ] **1.** *v. t.* **~ sb.** jmdm. Vorwürfe machen. **2.** *n.* Vorwurf, *der.* **reproachful** [rɪ'prəʊtʃfl] *adv.* vorwurfsvoll

reproduce [ri:prə'dju:s] **1.** *v. t.* wiedergeben. **2.** *v. i.* *(multiply)* sich fortpflanzen. **reproduction** [ri:prə'dʌkʃn] *n.* **a)** Wiedergabe, *die;* **b)** *(producing offspring)* Fortpflanzung, *die;* **c)** *(copy)* Reproduktion, *die*

reprove [rɪ'pru:v] *v. t.* tadeln

reptile ['reptaɪl] *n.* Reptil, *das*

republic [rɪ'pʌblɪk] *n.* Republik, *die.* **republican** [rɪ'pʌblɪkən] **1.** *adj.* republikanisch. **2.** *n.* **R~** *(Amer. Polit.)* Republikaner, *der*/Republikanerin, *die*

repudiate [rɪ'pju:dɪeɪt] *v. t.* zurückweisen

repugnance [rɪ'pʌgnəns] *n.* Abscheu, *der* (**to[wards]** vor + *Dat.*)

repugnant [rɪ'pʌgnənt] *adj.* widerlich (**to** *Dat.*)

repulse [rɪ'pʌls] *v. t.* abwehren

repulsion [rɪ'pʌlʃn] *n.* *(disgust)* Widerwille, *der* (**towards** gegen)

repulsive [rɪ'pʌlsɪv] *adj.* abstoßend

reputable ['repjʊtəbl] *adj.* angesehen ⟨*Person, Beruf, Zeitung usw.*⟩; anständig ⟨*Verhalten*⟩; seriös ⟨*Firma*⟩

reputation [repjʊ'teɪʃn] *n.* **a)** Ruf, *der;* **have a ~ for** *or* **of doing/being sth.** in dem Ruf stehen, etw. zu tun/sein; **b)** *(good name)* Name, *der*

repute [rɪ'pju:t] **1.** *v. t. in pass.* **be ~d [to be] sth.** als etw. gelten; **she is ~d to have/make ...:** man sagt, daß sie ... hat/macht. **2.** *n.* Ruf, *der.* **reputed** [rɪ'pju:tɪd] *adj.,* **re'putedly** *adv.* angeblich

request [rɪ'kwest] **1.** *v. t.* bitten; **~ sth. of** *or* **from sb.** jmdn. um etw. bitten. **2.** *n.* Bitte, *die* (**for** um); **at sb.'s ~** auf jmds. Bitte *(Akk.)* [hin]. **re'quest stop** *n.* *(Brit.)* Bedarfshaltestelle, *die*

require [rɪ'kwaɪə(r)] *v. t.* **a)** *(need)* brauchen; **b)** *(order, demand)* verlangen (of von); **be ~d to do sth.** etw. tun müssen. **re'quirement** *n.* **a)** *(need)* Bedarf, *der;* **b)** *(condition)* Erfordernis, *das*

requisite ['rekwɪzɪt] **1.** *adj.* notwendig (to, for für). **2.** *n. in pl.* **toilet/travel ~s** Toiletten-/Reiseartikel *Pl.*

requisition [rekwɪ'zɪʃn] **1.** *n. (order for sth.)* Anforderung, *die* (for Gen.). **2.** *v. t.* anfordern

rescind [rɪ'sɪnd] *v. t.* für ungültig erklären

rescue ['reskjuː] **1.** *v. t.* retten (**from** aus). **2.** *n.* Rettung, *die; attrib.* Rettungs‹*dienst, -mannschaft*›; **go/come to the/sb.'s ~:** jmdm. zu Hilfe kommen. **rescuer** ['reskjuːə(r)] *n.* Retter, *der*/Retterin, *die*

research [rɪ'sɜːtʃ, 'riːsɜːtʃ] **1.** *n.* Forschung, *die* (**into, on** über + *Akk.*); **~ work** Recherchen *Pl.* **2.** *v. i.* forschen; **~ into sth.** etw. erforschen. **researcher** [-'--, '---] *n.* Forscher, *der*/ Forscherin, *die*

resell [riː'sel] *v. t., resold* [riː'səʊld] weiterverkaufen (to an + *Akk.*)

resemblance [rɪ'zembləns] *n.* Ähnlichkeit, *die* (to mit)

resemble [rɪ'zembl] *v. t.* ähneln, gleichen (+ *Dat.*)

resent [rɪ'zent] *v. t.* übelnehmen. **resentful** [rɪ'zentfl] *adj.* übelnehmerisch, nachtragend ‹*Person, Art*›; **be ~ of** *or* **feel ~ about sth.** etw. übelnehmen. **re'sentment** *n.* Groll, *der* (geh.); **feel ~ towards** *or* **against sb.** einen Groll auf jmdn. haben

reservation [rezə'veɪʃn] *n.* **a)** Reservierung, *die;* **have a ~ [for a room]** ein Zimmer reserviert haben; **b)** *(doubt)* Vorbehalt, *der* (about gegen); Bedenken (about bezüglich + *Gen.*); **without ~:** ohne Vorbehalt

reserve [rɪ'zɜːv] **1.** *v. t.* reservieren lassen ‹*Zimmer, Tisch, Platz*›; *(set aside)* reservieren; **~ the right to do sth.** sich (*Dat.*) [das Recht] vorbehalten, etw. zu tun. **2.** *n.* **a)** *(extra amount)* Reserve, *die* (of an + *Dat.*) **have/hold** *or* **keep sth. in ~:** etw. in Reserve haben/ halten; **b)** *(place set apart)* Reservat, *das;* **c)** *(Sport)* Reservespieler, *der*/-spielerin, *die;* **the R~s** die Reserve; **d)** *(reticence)* Zurückhaltung, *die.* **reserved** [rɪ'zɜːvd] *adj. (reticent)* reserviert

reservoir ['rezəvwɑː(r)] *n. [(artificial) lake)* Reservoir, *das*

reshape [riː'ʃeɪp] *v. t.* umgestalten

reshuffle [riː'ʃʌfl] **1.** *v. t.* **a)** umbilden ‹*Kabinett*›; **b)** *(Cards)* neu mischen. **2.** *n.* Umbildung, *die*

reside [rɪ'zaɪd] *v. i. (formal)* wohnen; wohnhaft sein *(Amtsspr.).* **residence** ['rezɪdəns] *n.* **a)** *(abode)* Wohnsitz, *der; (of ambassador etc.)* Residenz, *die;* **b)** *(stay)* Aufenthalt, *der.* **'residence permit** *n.* Aufenthaltsgenehmigung, *die.* **resident** ['rezɪdənt] **1.** *adj.* wohnhaft; **be ~ in England** sein Wohnsitz in England haben. **2.** *n. (inhabitant)* Bewohner, *der*/Bewohnerin, *die; (at hotel)* Hotelgast, *der.* **residential** [rezɪ'denʃl] *adj.* Wohn‹*gebiet, -siedlung, -straße*›; **~ hotel** Hotel für Dauergäste

residue ['rezɪdjuː] *n.* **a)** Rest, *der;* **b)** *(Chem.)* Rückstand, *der*

resign [rɪ'zaɪn] **1.** *v. t.* zurücktreten von ‹*Amt*›. **2.** *v. refl.* **~ oneself to sth./to doing sth.** sich mit etw. abfinden/sich damit abfinden, etw. zu tun. **3.** *v. i. (Arbeitnehmer:)* kündigen; *(Regierungsbeamter:)* zurücktreten (**from** von). **resignation** [rezɪg'neɪʃn] *n.* **a)** *see* **resign 3:** Kündigung, *die;* Rücktritt, *der;* **tender one's ~:** seine Kündigung/seinen Rücktritt einreichen; **b)** *(being resigned)* Resignation, *die;* **with ~:** resigniert. **resigned** [rɪ'zaɪnd] *adj.* resigniert; **be ~ to sth.** sich mit etw. abgefunden haben

resilience [rɪ'zɪlɪəns] *n.* **a)** Elastizität, *die;* **b)** *(fig.)* Unverwüstlichkeit, *die*

resilient [rɪ'zɪlɪənt] *adj.* elastisch; *(fig.)* unverwüstlich

resin ['rezɪn] *n.* Harz, *das*

resist [rɪ'zɪst] **1.** *v. t.* **a)** standhalten (+ *Dat.*) ‹*Frost, Hitze, Feuchtigkeit usw.*›; **b)** *(oppose)* sich widersetzen (+ *Dat.*); widerstehen (+ *Dat.*) ‹*Versuchung*›. **2.** *v. i. see* **1 b:** sich widersetzen; widerstehen. **resistance** [rɪ'zɪstəns] *n.* Widerstand, *der* (to gegen). **resistant** [rɪ'zɪstənt] *adj.* **a)** *(opposed)* **be ~ to** sich widersetzen (+ *Dat.*); **b)** *(having power to resist)* widerstandsfähig (to gegen)

resold *see* **resell**

resolute ['rezəluːt] *adj.* resolut, energisch ‹*Person*›; entschlossen ‹*Tat*›

resolution [rezə'luːʃn] *n.* **a)** *(firmness)* Entschlossenheit, *die;* **b)** *(decision)* Entschließung, *die; (Polit. also)* Resolution, *die;* **c)** *(resolve)* Vorsatz, *der;* **make a ~:** einen Vorsatz fassen

resolve [rɪ'zɒlv] **1.** *v. t.* **a)** lösen ‹*Problem, Rätsel*›; ausräumen ‹*Schwierig-*

keit⟩; b) *(decide)* beschließen; c) *(settle)* beilegen ⟨*Streit*⟩; regeln ⟨*Angelegenheit*⟩. **2.** *n.* a) *(resoluteness)* Entschlossenheit, *die.*

resolved [rɪ'zɒlvd] *adj.* ~ [to do sth.] entschlossen[, etw. zu tun]

resonant ['rezənənt] *adj.* hallend ⟨*Ton, Klang*⟩

resort [rɪ'zɔːt] **1.** *n.* a) *(place)* Aufenthalt[sort], *der;* |**holiday**| ~: Ferienort, *der;* **ski** ~: Skiurlaubsort, *der;* **seaside** ~: Seebad, *das;* b) *(recourse)* **as a last** ~: als letzter Ausweg. **2.** *v. i.* ~ **to sth./ sb.** zu etw. greifen/sich an jmdn. wenden **(for** um**)**

resound [rɪ'zaʊnd] *v. i.* widerhallen. **re'sounding** *adj.* hallend ⟨*Lärm*⟩; überwältigend ⟨*Sieg, Erfolg*⟩

resource [rɪ'sɔːs, rɪ'zɔːs] *n. usu. in pl. (stock)* Mittel *Pl.;* Ressource, *die.* **resourceful** [rɪ'sɔːsfl, rɪ'zɔːsfl] *adj.* findig ⟨*Person*⟩

respect [rɪ'spekt] **1.** *n.* a) *(esteem)* Respekt, *der,* Achtung, *die* **(for** vor + *Dat.*⟩; **show** ~ **for sb./sth.** Respekt vor jmdm./etw. zeigen; b) *(aspect)* Hinsicht, *die;* **in some** ~s in mancher Hinsicht; c) **with** ~ **to** ...: in bezug auf ... *(Akk.);* **was** ... **[an]**betrifft. **2.** *v. t.* respektieren; achten. **respectable** [rɪ'spektəbl] *adj.* angesehen ⟨*Bürger usw.*⟩; ehrenwert ⟨*Motive*⟩; *(decent)* ehrbar *(geh.)* ⟨*Leute, Kaufmann*⟩; anständig, respektabel ⟨*Beschäftigung usw.*⟩. **respectful** [rɪ'spektfl] *adj.* respektvoll (to|wards) gegenüber). **re'spectfully** *adv.* respektvoll

respective [rɪ'spektɪv] *adj.* jeweilig. **re'spectively** *adv.* beziehungsweise

respiration [respɪ'reɪʃn] *n.* Atmung, *die*

respite ['respaɪt] *n.* Ruhepause, *die; (delay)* Aufschub, *der;* **without** ~: ohne Pause

resplendent [rɪ'splendənt] *adj.* prächtig

respond [rɪ'spɒnd] **1.** *v. i.* a) *(answer)* antworten **(to** auf + *Akk.*⟩; b) *(react)* reagieren **(to** auf + *Akk.*⟩; ⟨*Patient, Bremsen:*⟩ ansprechen **(to** auf + *Akk.*⟩. **2.** *v. t.* antworten; erwidern

response [rɪ'spɒns] *n.* a) *(answer)* Antwort, *die* **(to** auf + *Akk.*⟩; **in** ~ |**to**| als Antwort [auf **(** + *Akk.*⟩]; b) *(reaction)* Reaktion, *die*

responsibility [rɪspɒnsɪ'bɪlɪtɪ] *n.* a) *(being responsible)* Verantwortung, *die;* b) *(duty)* Verpflichtung, *die*

responsible [rɪ'spɒnsɪbl] *adj.* a) ver-

antwortlich; **be** ~ **to sb.** jmdm. gegenüber verantwortlich sein **(for** für); b) *(trustworthy)* verantwortungsvoll. **responsibly** [rɪ'spɒnsɪblɪ] *adv.* verantwortungsbewußt

responsive [rɪ'spɒnsɪv] *adj.* aufgeschlossen ⟨*Person*⟩; **be** ~ **to sth.** auf etw. *(Akk.)* reagieren

¹**rest** [rest] **1.** *v. i.* ruhen; ~ **on** ruhen auf **(** + *Dat.*⟩; ~ **from sth.** sich von etw. ausruhen; ~ **assured that** ...: seien Sie versichert, daß ...; ~ **with sb.** ⟨*Verantwortung:*⟩ bei jmdm. liegen. **2.** *v. t.* a) ~ **sth. against** etw. an etw. *(Akk.)* lehnen; b) ausruhen ⟨*Augen*⟩. **3.** *n.* a) *(repose)* Ruhe, *die;* b) *(break, relaxation)* Ruhe[pause], *die;* Erholung, *die* **(from** von); **take a** ~: sich ausruhen **(from** von); c) *(pause)* **have a** ~: [eine] Pause machen; ~ **period** [Ruhe]pause, *die*

²**rest** *n.* **the** ~: der Rest; **we'll do the** ~: alles Übrige erledigen wir

restaurant ['restər̄o, 'restərɒnt] *n.* Restaurant, *das*

rested ['restɪd] *adj.* ausgeruht

restful ['restfl] *adj.* ruhig ⟨*Tag, Woche*⟩

restive ['restɪv] *adj.* unruhig

'**restless** *adj.* unruhig ⟨*Nacht, Schlaf, Bewegung*⟩; ruhelos ⟨*Person*⟩

restoration [restə'reɪʃn] *n.* a) *(of peace, health)* Wiederherstellung, *die; (of work of art, building)* Restaurierung, *die;* b) **the R~** *(Brit. Hist.)* die Restauration

restore [rɪ'stɔː(r)] *v. t.* a) *(give back)* zurückgeben; b) restaurieren ⟨*Bauwerk, Kunstwerk usw.*⟩; ~ **sb. to health** jmdn. wiederherstellen; c) wiederherstellen ⟨*Ordnung, Ruhe*⟩

restrain [rɪ'streɪn] *v. t.* zurückhalten ⟨*Gefühl, Lachen, Person*⟩; bändigen ⟨*unartiges Kind, Tier*⟩; ~ **sb./oneself from doing sth.** jmdn. davon abhalten/ sich zurückhalten, etw. zu tun. **restrained** [rɪ'streɪnd] *adj.* zurückhaltend ⟨*Wesen, Kritik*⟩; beherrscht ⟨*Reaktion, Worte*⟩. **restraint** [rɪ'streɪnt] *n.* a) *(restriction)* Einschränkung, *die;* b) *(reserve)* Zurückhaltung, *die;* c) *(self-control)* Selbstbeherrschung, *die*

restrict [rɪ'strɪkt] *v. t.* beschränken **(to** auf + *Akk.*⟩. **re'stricted** *adj.* beschränkt. **restriction** [rɪ'strɪkʃn] *n.* Beschränkung, *die* **(on** *Gen.*⟩. **restrictive** [rɪ'strɪktɪv] *adj.* restriktiv

'**rest room** *n. (esp. Amer.)* Toilette, *die*

result [rɪ'zʌlt] **1.** *v. i.* a) *(follow)* ~ **from sth.** die Folge einer Sache *(Gen.)* sein;

b) *(end)* ~ **in sth.** in etw. *(Dat.)* resultieren. **2.** *n.* Ergebnis, *das;* **be the ~ of sth.** die Folge einer Sache *(Gen.)* sein; **as a ~ |of this|** infolgedessen. **re'sultant** [rɪ'zʌltənt] *attrib. adj.* daraus resultierend

resume [rɪ'zju:m] *v. t.* wiederaufnehmen; fortsetzen *(Reise)*

résumé ['rezʊmeɪ] *n.* Zusammenfassung, *die*

resumption [rɪ'zʌmpʃn] *n.* Wiederaufnahme, *die*

resurrection [rezə'rekʃn] *n. (Relig.)* Auferstehung, *die*

resuscitate [rɪ'sʌsɪteɪt] *v. t.* wiederbeleben

retail ['riːteɪl] **1.** *adj.* Einzel⟨handel⟩; Einzelhandels⟨geschäft, -preis⟩. **2.** *adv.* **buy/sell ~:** en détail kaufen/verkaufen. **'retailer** *n.* Einzelhändler, *der/*-händlerin, *die.* **retail 'price index** *n. (Brit.)* Preisindex des Einzelhandels

retain [rɪ'teɪn] *v. t.* behalten; ein-, zurückbehalten ~⟨Gelder⟩

retaliate [rɪ'tælɪeɪt] *v. i.* Vergeltung üben **(against** an + *Dat.).* **retaliation** [rɪtælɪ'eɪʃn] *n.* Vergeltung, *die;* **in ~ for** als Vergeltung für

retarded [rɪ'tɑːdɪd] *adj.* |mentally| ~: |geistig| zurückgeblieben

retch [retʃ] *v. i.* würgen

retentive [rɪ'tentɪv] *adj.* gut ⟨Gedächtnis⟩

rethink [riː'θɪŋk] *v. t.,* **rethought** [riː'θɔːt] noch einmal überdenken

reticence ['retɪsəns] *n.* Zurückhaltung, *die*

reticent ['retɪsənt] *adj.* zurückhaltend **(on, about** in bezug auf + *Akk.*)

retina ['retɪnə] *n.* Netzhaut, *die*

retinue ['retɪnju:] *n.* Gefolge, *das*

retire [rɪ'taɪə/] *v. i.* **a)** ⟨*Angestellter, Arbeiter:*⟩ in Rente *(Akk.)* gehen; ⟨*Beamter, Militär:*⟩ in Pension od. den Ruhestand gehen; **b)** *(withdraw)* sich zurückziehen **(to** in + *Akk.*). **retired** [rɪ'taɪəd] *adj.* aus dem Berufsleben ausgeschieden; ⟨*Beamter, Soldat*⟩ im Ruhestand, pensioniert. **re'tirement** *n.* Ruhestand, *der*

retiring [rɪ'taɪərɪŋ] *adj. (shy)* zurückhaltend

retort [rɪ'tɔːt] **1.** *n.* Entgegnung, *die* **(to** auf + *Akk.*). **2.** *v. t.* entgegnen

retrace [rɪ'treɪs] *v. t.* zurückverfolgen; **~ one's steps** denselben Weg noch einmal zurückgehen

retract [rɪ'trækt] *v. t.* zurücknehmen

retrain [riː'treɪn] **1.** *v. i.* [sich] umschulen [lassen]. **2.** *v. t.* umschulen

retreat [rɪ'triːt] **1.** *n.* **a)** *(withdrawal)* Rückzug, *der;* **beat a ~** *(fig.)* das Feld räumen; **b)** *(place)* Zufluchtsort, *der.* **2.** *v. i.* sich zurückziehen

retribution [retrɪ'bju:ʃn] *n.* Vergeltung, *die*

retrieval [rɪ'triːvl] *n.* **a)** *(of situation)* Rettung, *die;* **beyond** *or* **past ~:** hoffnungslos; **b)** *(rescue)* Rettung, *die; (from wreckage)* Bergung, *die*

retrieve [rɪ'triːv] *v. t.* **a)** *(rescue)* retten **(from** aus); *(from wreckage)* bergen **(from** aus); **b)** *(recover)* zurückholen ⟨*Brief*⟩; wiederholen ⟨*Ball*⟩; wiederbekommen ⟨*Geld*⟩; **c)** *(Computing)* wiederauffinden ⟨*Informationen*⟩; **d)** ⟨*Hund:*⟩ apportieren; **e)** retten ⟨*Situation*⟩. **re'triever** *n.* Apportierhund, *der; (breed)* Retriever, *der*

return [rɪ'tɜːn] **1.** *v. i. (come back)* zurückkommen; *(go back)* zurückgehen; *(by vehicle)* zurückfahren. **2.** *v. t.* **a)** *(bring back)* zurückbringen; zurückgeben ⟨*geliehenen/gestohlenen Gegenstand*⟩; **~ed with thanks** mit Dank zurück; **b)** *(reward)* ⟨*Besuch, Gruß, Liebe,*⟩ sich revanchieren für *(ugs.)* ⟨*Freundlichkeit, Gefallen*⟩; **c)** *(elect)* wählen ⟨*Kandidaten*⟩; **d) ~ a verdict of guilty/not guilty** ⟨*Geschworene:*⟩ auf „schuldig"/„nicht schuldig" erkennen. **3.** *n.* **a)** Rückkehr, *die;* **many happy ~s |of the day|!** herzlichen Glückwunsch [zum Geburtstag]!; **b) by ~ |of post|** postwendend; **c)** *(ticket)* Rückfahrkarte, *die; (for flight)* Rückflugschein, *der;* **d) ~|s| *(proceeds)*** Gewinn, *der* **(on, from** aus); **e)** *(bringing back)* Zurückbringen, *das; (of property, goods, book)* Rückgabe, *die* **(to** an + *Akk.*); **receive/get sth. in ~ |for sth.|** etw. [für etw.] bekommen

return: **~ 'fare** *n.* Preis für eine Rückfahrkarte/*(for flight)* einen Rückflugschein; **~ 'flight** *n.* Rückflug, *der;* **~ 'journey** *n.* Rückreise, *die;* Rückfahrt, *die;* **~ 'match** *n.* Rückspiel, *das;* **~ 'ticket** *n. (Brit.)* Rückfahrkarte, *die; (for flight)* Rückflugschein, *der*

retype [riː'taɪp] *v. t.* neu tippen

reunion [riː'ju:nJən] *n. (gathering)* Treffen, *das*

reunite [riːjʊ'naɪt] *v. t.* wieder zusammenführen

reuse 1. [riː'ju:z] *v. t.* wiederverwenden. **2.** [riː'ju:s] *n.* Wiederverwendung, *die*

rev [rev] *(coll.)* **1.** *n., usu. in pl.* Umdrehung, *die.* **2.** *v. i.,* -vv- hochtourig laufen. **3.** *v. t.,* -vv- aufheulen lassen. **rev 'up** *v. t.* aufheulen lassen

Rev. ['revərənd, *(coll.)* rev] *abbr.* Reverend Rev.

reveal [rɪ'viːl] *v. t.* enthüllen *(geh.);* be ~ed *(Wahrheit:)* ans Licht kommen. **re'vealing** *adj.* aufschlußreich

revel ['revl] *v. i., (Brit.)* -ll- genießen (in *Akk.);* ~ in doing sth. es [richtig] genießen, etw. zu tun

revelation [revə'leɪʃn] *n.* **a)** Enthüllung, *die (geh.);* be a ~: einem die Augen öffnen; **b)** *(Relig.)* Offenbarung, *die*

revelry ['revlrɪ] *n.* Feiern, *das*

revenge [rɪ'vendʒ] **1.** *v. t.* rächen *(Person, Tat).* **2.** *n. (action)* Rache, *die;* take ~ *or* have one's ~ [on sb.] [for sth.] Rache [an jmdm.] [für etw.] nehmen; **in** ~ **for sth.** als Rache für etw.

revenue ['revənjuː] *n.* ~[s] Einnahmen

revere [rɪ'vɪə(r)] *v. t.* verehren. **reverence** ['revərəns] *n.* Ehrfurcht, *die*

Reverend ['revərənd] *adj.* the ~ John Wilson Hochwürden John Wilson

reverent ['revərənt] *adj.* ehrfürchtig

reverie ['revərɪ] *n.* Träumerei, *die*

reversal [rɪ'vɜːsl] *n.* Umkehrung, *die*

reverse [rɪ'vɜːs] **1.** *adj.* entgegengesetzt *(Richtung);* Rück(seite); umgekehrt *(Reihenfolge).* **2.** *n.* **a)** *(contrary)* Gegenteil, *das;* **b)** *(Motor Veh.)* Rückwärtsgang, *der;* **put the car into** ~, **go into** ~: den Rückwärtsgang einlegen. **3.** *v. t.* umkehren *(Reihenfolge);* ~ **the charge[s]** *(Brit.)* ein R-Gespräch anmelden; **b)** zurücksetzen *(Fahrzeug).* **4.** *v. i.* zurücksetzen; rückwärts fahren. **reverse 'gear** *n. (Motor Veh.)* Rückwärtsgang, *der; see also* **gear 1 a**

reversible [rɪ'vɜːsɪbl] *adj.* beidseitig tragbar *(Kleidungsstück);* Wende(mantel, -jacke)

re'versing light *n.* Rückfahrscheinwerfer, *der*

revert [rɪ'vɜːt] *v. i.* ~ **to** zurückkommen auf (+ *Akk.) (Thema, Frage);* ~ **to savagery** in den Zustand der Wildheit zurückfallen

review [rɪ'vjuː] **1.** *n.* **a)** *(survey)* Überblick, *der* (of über + *Akk.);* **b)** *(reexamination)* [nochmalige] Überprüfung; **c)** *(of book, play, etc.)* Kritik, *die;* Rezension, *die.* **2.** *v. t.* **a)** *(survey)* untersuchen; prüfen; **b)** *(re-examine)* überprüfen; **c)** *(Mil.)* inspizieren; **d)**

(write a criticism of) rezensieren. **re'viewer** *n.* Rezensent, *der/*Rezensentin, *die*

revile [rɪ'vaɪl] *v. t.* schmähen *(geh.)*

revise [rɪ'vaɪz] *v. t.* **a)** *(check over)* durchsehen *(Manuskript);* **b)** *(for exam)* wiederholen; *abs.* lernen. **re'vision** [rɪ'vɪʒn] *n.* **a)** *(checking over)* Durchsicht, *die;* **b)** *(amended version)* revidierte Fassung; **c)** *(for exam)* Wiederholung, *die*

revisit [riː'vɪzɪt] *v. t.* wieder besuchen

revitalize [riː'vaɪtəlaɪz] *v. t.* neu beleben

revival [rɪ'vaɪvl] *n.* Neubelebung, *die*

revive [rɪ'vaɪv] **1.** *v. i. (come back to consciousness)* wieder zu sich kommen; *(be reinvigorated)* zu neuem Leben erwachen. **2.** *v. t.* **a)** *(restore to consciousness)* wiederbeleben; *(reinvigorate)* wieder zu Kräften kommen lassen; **b)** wieder wecken *(Lebensgeister, Interesse)*

revoke [rɪ'vəʊk] *v. t.* aufheben *(Entscheidung);* widerrufen *(Befehl);* widerrufen *(Erlaubnis, Genehmigung)*

revolt [rɪ'vəʊlt] **1.** *v. i.* revoltieren (**against** gegen). **2.** *v. t.* mit Abscheu erfüllen. **3.** *n.* Revolte, *die (auch fig.);* Aufstand, *der.* **re'volting** *adj.* abscheulich; *(coll.: unpleasant)* widerlich

revolution [revə'luːʃn] *n.* Revolution, *die.* **revolutionary** [revə'luːʃənərɪ] **1.** *adj.* revolutionär. **2.** *n.* Revolutionär, *der/*Revolutionärin, *die*

revolve [rɪ'vɒlv] **1.** *v. t.* drehen. **2.** *v. i.* sich drehen (**round, about, on** um)

revolver [rɪ'vɒlvə(r)] *n.* [Trommel]revolver, *der*

revolving [rɪ'vɒlvɪŋ] *attrib. adj.* Dreh(bühne, -tür)

revue [rɪ'vjuː] *n.* Kabarett, *das; (musical show)* Revue, *die*

revulsion [rɪ'vʌlʃn] *n.* Abscheu, *der* (**at** vor + *Dat.,* gegen)

reward [rɪ'wɔːd] **1.** *n.* Belohnung, *die.* **2.** *v. t.* belohnen. **re'warding** *adj.* lohnend; **be ~/financially ~:** sich lohnen/einträglich sein

rewind [riː'waɪnd] *v. t.,* rewound [riː'waʊnd] **a)** wieder aufziehen *(Uhr);* **b)** zurückspulen *(Film, Band)*

reword [riː'wɜːd] *v. t.* umformulieren

rewrite [riː'raɪt] *v. t.,* rewrote [riː'rəʊt], rewritten [riː'rɪtn] noch einmal [neu] schreiben; *(write differently)* umschreiben

rhetoric ['retərɪk] *n.* [art of] ~: Redekunst, *die;* Rhetorik, *die.* **rhetorical** [rɪ'tɒrɪkl] *adj.* rhetorisch

rheumatic [ruː'mætɪk] *adj.* rheumatisch

rheumatism ['ruːmətɪzm] *n.* Rheumatismus, *der;* Rheuma, *das (ugs.)*

Rhine [raɪn] *pr. n.* Rhein, *der*

rhino ['raɪnəʊ] *n., pl. same or* ~s *(coll.),* **rhinoceros** [raɪ'nɒsərəs] *n., pl. same or* ~es Nashorn, *das;* Rhinozeros, *das*

rhododendron [rəʊdə'dendrən] *n.* Rhododendron, *der*

rhubarb ['ruːbɑːb] *n.* Rhabarber, *der*

rhyme [raɪm] **1.** *n.* Reim, *der;* without ~ or reason ohne Sinn und Verstand. **2.** *v. i.* sich reimen (with auf + *Akk.*)

rhythm ['rɪðm] *n.* Rhythmus, *der.* **rhythmic** ['rɪðmɪk], **rhythmical** ['rɪðmɪkl] *adj.* rhythmisch

rib [rɪb] **1.** *n.* Rippe, *die.* **2.** *v. t.,* -bb- *(coll.)* aufziehen *(ugs.)*

ribald ['rɪbəld] *adj.* zotig

ribbon ['rɪbn] *n.* Band, *das; (on typewriter)* [Farb]band, *das*

rice [raɪs] *n.* Reis, *der.* **rice 'pudding** *n.* Milchreis, *der.* **'rice wine** *n.* Reiswein, *der*

rich [rɪtʃ] **1.** *adj.* **a)** reich ⟨an + *Dat.*⟩; *(fertile)* fruchtbar ⟨*Land, Boden*⟩; **b)** *(splendid)* prachtvoll; **c)** *(containing much fat, oil, eggs, etc.)* gehaltvoll; **d)** *(deep, full)* voll[tönend] ⟨*Stimme*⟩; voll ⟨*Ton*⟩; satt ⟨*Farbe, Farbton*⟩. **2.** *n. pl.* the ~: die Reichen; ~ and poor Arm und Reich. **riches** ['rɪtʃɪz] *n. pl.* Reichtum, *der.* **'richly** *adv.* **a)** *(splendidly)* reich; üppig ⟨*ausgestattet*⟩; prächtig ⟨*gekleidet*⟩; **b)** *(fully)* voll und ganz; ~ deserved wohlverdient. **'richness** *n.* **a)** *(of food)* Reichhaltigkeit, *die;* **b)** *(of voice)* voller Klang; *(of colour)* Sattheit, *die*

rickets ['rɪkɪts] *n.* Rachitis, *die*

rickety ['rɪkɪtɪ] *adj.* wack[e]lig

ricochet ['rɪkəʃeɪ] **1.** *n.* **a)** Abprallen, *das;* **b)** *(hit)* Abpraller, *der.* **2.** *v. i.,* ~ed ['rɪkəʃeɪd] abprallen (off von)

rid [rɪd] *v. t.,* -dd-, rid: ~ sth. of sth. etw. von etw. befreien; ~ oneself of sb./sth. sich von jmdm./etw. befreien; be ~ of sb./sth. jmdn./etw. los sein *(ugs.);* get ~ of sb./sth. jmdn./etw. loswerden

riddance ['rɪdəns] *n.* good ~! Gott sei Dank ist er/es *usw.* weg!

ridden *see* ride 2, 3

¹riddle ['rɪdl] *n.* Rätsel, *das*

²riddle *v. t.* durchlöchern; ~d with bullets von Kugeln durchsiebt

ride [raɪd] **1.** *n. (on horseback)* [Aus]ritt,

der; (in vehicle, at fair) Fahrt, *die;* ~ in a train/coach Zug-/Busfahrt, *die;* go for a ~: ausreiten; go for a [bi]cycle ~: radfahren; go for a ~ [in the car] [mit dem Auto] wegfahren; take sb. for a ~ *(fig. sl.: deceive)* jmdn. reinlegen *(ugs.).* **2.** *v. i.,* rode [rəʊd], ridden ['rɪdn] *(on horse)* reiten; *(on bicycle, in vehicle)* fahren; ~ to town on one's bike/in one's car/on the train mit dem Rad/Auto/Zug in die Stadt fahren. **3.** *v. t.,* rode, ridden reiten ⟨*Pferd usw.*⟩; fahren mit ⟨*Fahrrad*⟩. **ride a'way, ride 'off** *v. i.* wegreiten/-fahren

'rider *n.* **a)** Reiter, *der*/Reiterin, *die; (of cycle)* Fahrer, *der*/Fahrerin, *die;* **b)** *(addition)* Zusatz, *der*

ridge [rɪdʒ] *n.* **a)** *(of roof)* First, *der;* **b)** *(long hilltop)* Grat, *der;* Kamm, *der;* **c)** *(Meteorol.)* ~ [of high pressure] langgestrecktes Hoch

ridicule ['rɪdɪkjuːl] **1.** *n.* Spott, *der.* **2.** *v. t.* verspotten

ridiculous [rɪ'dɪkjʊləs] *adj.* lächerlich

riding ['raɪdɪŋ] *n.* Reiten, *das.* **'riding lesson** *n.* Reitstunde, *die.* **'riding-school** *n.* Reitschule, *die*

rife [raɪf] *pred. adj.* weit verbreitet

riff-raff ['rɪfræf] *n.* Gesindel, *das*

rifle ['raɪfl] **1.** *n.* Gewehr, *das.* **2.** *v. t.* durchwühlen. **3.** *v. i.* ~ through sth. etw. durchwühlen

rift [rɪft] *n.* Unstimmigkeit, *die*

¹rig [rɪg] *n. (for oil-well)* [Öl]förderturm, *der; (off shore)* Förderinsel, *die.* **rig 'out** *v. t.* ausstaffieren. **rig 'up** *v. t.* aufbauen

²rig *v. t.,* -gg- manipulieren ⟨*[Wahl]ergebnis*⟩; fälschen ⟨*Wahl*⟩

rigging ['rɪgɪŋ] *n.* Takelung, *die*

right [raɪt] **1.** *adj.* **a)** *(just, morally good, sound)* richtig; **b)** *(correct, true)* richtig; you're [quite] ~: du hast [völlig] recht; be ~ in sth. recht mit etw. haben; is that clock ~? geht die Uhr da richtig?; put or set ~: richtigstellen ⟨*Irrtum, Behauptung*⟩; wiedergutmachen ⟨*Unrecht*⟩; berichtigen ⟨*Fehler*⟩; richtig stellen ⟨*Uhr*⟩; put or set sb. ~: jmdn. berichtigen; that's ~: ja[wohl]; so ist es; is that ~? stimmt das?; *(indeed?)* aha!; [am I] ~? nicht [wahr]?; **c)** *(preferable, most suitable)* richtig; recht; do sth. the ~ way etw. richtig machen; **d)** *(opposite of left)* recht...; on the ~ side rechts; **e)** R~ *(Polit.)* recht... **2.** *v. t.* aus der Welt schaffen ⟨*Unrecht*⟩. **3.** *n.* **a)** *(fair claim, authority)* Recht, *das;* have a/no ~ to sth.

ein/kein Anrecht *od.* Recht auf etw. *(Akk.)* haben; **in one's own ~:** aus eigenem Recht; **~ of way** Vorfahrtsrecht, *das;* **have ~ of way** Vorfahrt haben; **b)** *(what is just)* Recht, *das;* **by ~|s|** von Rechts wegen; **in the ~:** im Recht; **c)** *(~-hand side)* rechte Seite; **on or to the ~ |of sb./sth.|** rechts |von jmdm./etw.|; **d)** *(Polit.)* **the R~:** die Rechte. **4.** *adv.* **a)** *(correctly)* richtig; **b)** *(to the ~-hand side)* nach rechts; **c)** *(completely)* ganz; **d)** *(exactly)* genau; **~ 'now** im Moment; jetzt sofort ⟨*handeln*⟩; **e)** *(straight)* direkt

'right angle *n.* rechter Winkel; **at ~s to sth.** rechtwinklig zu etw.

righteous ['raɪtʃəs] *adj.* rechtschaffen

rightful ['raɪtfl] *adj.* rechtmäßig ⟨*Besitzer, Herrscher*⟩

right: **~-hand** *adj.* recht...; **~-'handed 1.** *adj.* rechtshändig ⟨*Werkzeug*⟩ für Rechtshänder; **be ~-handed** ⟨*Person:*⟩ Rechtshänder/Rechtshänderin sein; **2.** *adv.* rechtshändig; **~-hand 'man** *n.* rechte Hand

'rightly *adv.* zu Recht

right: **~-'minded** *adj.* gerecht denkend; **~ 'wing** *n.* rechter Flügel; **~-wing** *adj.* *(Polit.)* rechtsgerichtet; Rechts⟨*extremist, -intellektueller*⟩; **~-winger** *n.* **a)** *(Sport)* Rechtsaußen, *der;* **b)** *(Polit.)* Rechte, *der/die*

rigid ['rɪdʒɪd] *adj.* **a)** starr; *(stiff)* steif; **b)** *(strict)* streng; unbeugsam ⟨*System*⟩. **rigidity** [rɪ'dʒɪtɪ] *n. see* **rigid:** Starrheit, *die;* Steifheit, *die;* Strenge, *die*

rigmarole ['rɪgmərəʊl] *n.* **a)** *(talk)* langatmiges Geschwafel *(ugs.);* **b)** *(procedure)* Zirkus, *der*

rigor ['rɪgə(r)] *(Amer.) see* **rigour**

rigor mortis [rɪgə 'mɔːtɪs] *n.* Totenstarre, *die*

rigorous ['rɪgərəs] *adj.* streng

rigour ['rɪgə(r)] *n. (Brit.)* Strenge, *die*

rile [raɪl] *v.t. (coll.)* ärgern

rim [rɪm] *n.* Rand, *der;* *(of wheel)* Felge, *die*

rind [raɪnd] *n.* *(of fruit)* Schale, *die;* *(of cheese)* Rinde, *die;* *(of bacon)* Schwarte, *die*

¹ring [rɪŋ] **1.** *n.* **a)** Ring, *der;* **b)** *(Boxing)* Ring, *der;* *(in circus)* Manege, *die.* **2.** *v.t. (surround)* umringen; einkreisen ⟨*Wort usw.*⟩

²ring 1. *n.* **a)** *(act of sounding bell)* Läuten, *das;* Klingeln, *das;* **b)** *(Brit. coll.: telephone call)* Anruf, *der;* **give sb. a**

~: jmdn. anrufen; **c)** *(fig.: impression)* **have the ~ of truth |about it|** glaubhaft klingen. **2.** *v.i.,* rang [ræŋ], rung [rʌŋ] **a)** *(sound clearly)* [er]schallen; ⟨*Hammer:*⟩ [er]dröhnen; **b)** *(be sounded)* ⟨*Glocke,, Klingel, Telefon:*⟩ läuten; ⟨*Wecker, Telefon, Kasse:*⟩ klingeln; **the doorbell rang** es klingelte; **c)** *(~ bell)* läuten **(for nach);** **d)** *(Brit.: make telephone call)* anrufen. **3.** *v.t.,* rang, rung **a)** läuten ⟨*Glocke:*⟩; **~ the |door|bell** läuten; klingeln; **it ~s a bell** *(fig. coll.)* es kommt mir |irgendwie| bekannt vor; **b)** *(Brit.: telephone)* anrufen. **ring 'back** *(Brit.) v.t. & i.* **a)** *(again)* wieder anrufen; **b)** *(in return)* zurückrufen. **ring 'off** *v.i. (Brit.)* auflegen. **ring 'out** *v.i.* ertönen

ring: **~ binder** *n.* Ringbuch, *das;* **~-finger** *n.* Ringfinger, *der*

ringing ['rɪŋɪŋ] *n.* Läuten, *das;* *(Brit. Teleph.)* **~ tone** Freiton, *der*

'ringleader *n.* Anführer, *der/*Anführerin, *die*

ringlet ['rɪŋlɪt] *n.* [Ringel]löckchen, *das*

'ring road *n.* Ringstraße, *die*

rink [rɪŋk] *n.* *(for ice-skating)* Eisbahn, *die;* *(for roller-skating)* Rollschuhbahn, *die*

rinse [rɪns] **1.** *v.t.* **a)** *(wash out)* ausspülen ⟨*Mund, Gefäß usw.*⟩; **b)** [aus]spülen ⟨*Wäsche usw.*⟩; abspülen ⟨*Hände, Geschirr*⟩. **2.** *n.* Spülen, *das;* **give sth. a |good/quick| ~:** etw. |gut/schnell| ausspülen/abspülen/spülen. **rinse 'out** *v.t.* ausspülen

riot ['raɪət] **1.** *n.* Aufruhr, *der;* **~s** Unruhen *Pl.;* **run ~:** randalieren. **2.** *v.i.* randalieren. **'rioter** *n.* Randalierer, *der.* **riotous** ['raɪətəs] *adj.* **a)** gewalttätig; **b)** *(unrestrained)* wild

rip [rɪp] **1.** *n.* Riß, *der.* **2.** *v.t.,* **-pp-** zerreißen; **~ open** aufreißen. **rip 'off** *v.t.* **a)** *(remove from)* reißen von; *(remove)* abreißen; **b)** *(sl.: defraud)* übers Ohr hauen *(ugs.).* **rip 'out** *v.t.* herausreißen **(of aus)**

RIP *abbr.* rest in peace R.I.P.

'rip-cord *n.* Reißleine, *die*

ripe [raɪp] *adj.* reif **(for zu).** **ripen** ['raɪpn] **1.** *v.t.* zur Reife bringen. **2.** *v.i.* reifen. **'ripeness** *n.* Reife, *die*

'rip-off *n. (sl.)* Nepp, *der (ugs.)*

riposte [rɪ'pɒst] **1.** *n.* *(retort)* [rasche] Entgegnung. **2.** *v.i.* [rasch] antworten

ripple ['rɪpl] **1.** *n.* kleine Welle. **2.** *v.i.* ⟨*See:*⟩ sich kräuseln; ⟨*Welle:*⟩ plätschern. **3.** *v.t.* kräuseln

rise [raɪz] 1. *n.* a) *(advancement)* Aufstieg, *der;* b) *(in value, price, cost)* Steigerung, *die; (in population, temperature)* Zunahme, *die;* c) *(Brit.)* |payl ~ *(in wages)* Lohnerhöhung, *die; (in salary)* Gehaltserhöhung, *die;* d) *(hill)* Anhöhe, *die;* e) give ~ to führen zu; Anlaß geben zu *(Spekulation).* 2. *v.i.* rose [rəʊz], risen ['rɪzn] a) *(go up)* aufsteigen; b) *(Sonne, Mond:)* aufgehen; c) *(increase, reach higher level)* steigen; d) *(advance) (Person:)* aufsteigen; e) *(Teig, Kuchen:)* aufgehen; f) *(Theatre) (Vorhang:)* aufgehen; *(Fluß:)* entspringen. **rise 'up** *v.i.* a) ~ **up** |in revolt| aufbegehren *(geh.);* b) *(Berg:)* aufragen

risen *see* rise 2

'riser *n.* early ~: Frühaufsteher, *der*/Frühaufsteherin, *die*

rising ['raɪzɪŋ] 1. *n. (of sun, moon, etc.)* Aufgang, *der.* 2. *adj.* a) aufgehend *(Sonne, Mond usw.);* b) steigend *(Kosten, Temperatur, Wasser, Flut);* c) *(sloping upwards)* ansteigend

risk [rɪsk] 1. *n.* Gefahr, *die; (chance taken)* Risiko, *das;* at one's own ~: auf eigene Gefahr *od.* eigenes Risiko; take the ~ of doing sth. es riskieren, etw. zu tun; be at ~ *(Zukunft, Plan:)* gefährdet sein. 2. *v.t.* riskieren; I'll ~ it ich lasse es darauf ankommen. **'risky** *adj.* gefährlich; gewagt *(Experiment, Projekt)*

risqué ['rɪskeɪ] *adj.* gewagt

rissole ['rɪsəʊl] *n.* Rissole, *die*

rite [raɪt] *n.* Ritus, *der*

ritual ['rɪtʃʊəl] 1. *adj.* rituell; Ritual-*(mord, -tötung).* 2. *n.* Ritual, *das*

rival ['raɪvl] 1. *n. (competitor)* Rivale, *der*/Rivalin, *die;* business ~s Konkurrenten. 2. *v.t., (Brit.)* -ll- nicht nachstehen *(+ Dat.).* **'rivalry** ['raɪvlrɪ] *n.* Rivalität, *die (geh.)*

river ['rɪvə(r)] *n.* Fluß, *der.* **'river-bed** *n.* Flußbett, *das.* **'riverside** 1. *n.* Flußufer, *das.* 2. *attrib. adj.* am Fluß gelegen; am Fluß *nachgestellt*

rivet ['rɪvɪt] 1. *n.* Niete, *die.* 2. *v.t.* a) |ver|nieten; b) *(fig.)* fesseln. **'riveting** *adj.* fesselnd

RN *abbr. (Brit.)* Royal Navy Königl. Mar.

road [rəʊd] *n.* Straße, *die;* across *or* over the ~ |from us| [bei uns] gegenüber; by ~ *(by car/bus/lorry)* per Auto/Bus/Lkw; be on the ~: auf Reisen *od.* unterwegs sein; *(Theaterensemble usw.:)* auf Tournee *od.* Tour sein

road: ~ **accident** *n.* Verkehrsunfall, *der;* ~**block** *n.* Straßensperre, *die;* ~**hog** *n.* Verkehrsrowdy, *der;* ~**map** *n.* Straßenkarte, *die;* ~ **safety** *n.* Verkehrssicherheit, *die;* ~ **sense** *n.* Gespür für Verkehrssituationen; ~**side** *n.* Straßenrand, *der;* at *or* by/along the ~**side** am Straßenrand; ~ **sign** *n.* Verkehrszeichen, *das;* Straßenschild, *das (ugs.);* ~**sweeper** *n.* Straßenkehrer, *der*/-kehrerin, *die;* ~**user** *n.* Verkehrsteilnehmer, *der*/-teilnehmerin, *die;* ~**way** *n.* Fahrbahn, *die;* ~**works** *n. pl.* Straßenbauarbeiten *Pl.;* ~**worthy** *adj.* fahrtüchtig

roam [rəʊm] 1. *v.i.* umherstreifen. 2. *v.t.* streifen durch

roar [rɔː(r)] 1. *n. (of wild beast)* Gebrüll, *das; (of applause)* Tosen, *das; (of engine, traffic)* Dröhnen, *das;* ~s/a ~ |of laughter| dröhnendes Gelächter. 2. *v.i.* brüllen (with vor + *Dat.*); *(Motor:)* dröhnen. **'roaring** *adj.* a) bullernd *(ugs.) (Feuer);* b) a ~ success ein Bombenerfolg; do a ~ trade ein Bombengeschäft machen

roast [rəʊst] 1. *v.t.* braten; rösten *(Kaffeebohnen, Kastanien).* 2. *attrib. adj.* gebraten *(Fleisch, Ente usw.);* Brat*(hähnchen, -kartoffeln);* Röst*(kastanien);* ~ **beef** *(sirloin)* Roastbeef, *das.* 3. *n.* Braten, *der*

rob [rɒb] *v.t.,* -bb- ausrauben *(Bank, Safe, Kasse);* berauben *(Person).* **robber** ['rɒbə(r)] *n.* Räuber, *der*/Räuberin, *die.* **robbery** ['rɒbərɪ] *n.* Raub, *der;* robberies Raubüberfälle

robe [rəʊb] *n.* Gewand, *das (geh.); (of judge, vicar)* Talar, *der*

robin ['rɒbɪn] *n.* ~ |redbreast| Rotkehlchen, *das*

robot ['rəʊbɒt] *n.* Roboter, *der*

robust [rəʊ'bʌst] *adj.* robust

¹rock [rɒk] *n.* a) *(piece of ~)* Fels, *der;* b) *(large ~, hill)* Felsen, *der;* c) *(substance)* Fels, *der; (esp. Geol.)* Gestein, *das;* d) *(boulder)* Felsbrocken, *der; (Amer.: stone)* Stein, *der;* e) stick of ~: Zuckerstange, *die;* f) be on the ~s *(fig. coll.) (Ehe, Firma:)* kaputt sein *(ugs.)*

²rock 1. *v.t.* wiegen; *(in cradle)* schaukeln. 2. *v.i.* a) schaukeln; b) *(sway)* schwanken. 3. *n. (Mus.)* Rock, *der; attrib.* Rock-; ~ **and** *or* **'n' roll** |music| Rock and Roll, *der*

rock: ~**-'bottom** *(coll.)* 1. *adj.* ~-bottom prices Schleuderpreise *(ugs.);* 2. *n.* reach *or* touch ~-bottom *(Handel,*

Preis:) in den Keller fallen *(ugs.);* her spirits reached **~bottom** ihre Stimmung war auf dem Tiefpunkt; **~climbing** n. [Fels]klettern, *das*
rockery ['rɔkərɪ] n. Steingarten, *der*
rocket ['rɔkɪt] 1. n. Rakete, *die.* 2. v.i. *(Preise:)* in die Höhe schnellen
rocking: **~chair** n. Schaukelstuhl, *der;* **~horse** n. Schaukelpferd, *das*
rocky *adj.* felsig; **b)** *(coll.: unsteady)* wackelig *(ugs.)*
rod [rɔd] n. Stange, *die; (for punishing)* Rute, *die; (for fishing)* [Angel]rute, *die*
rode see ride 2, 3
rodent ['rəʊdənt] n. Nagetier, *das*
¹roe [rəʊ] n. *(of fish)* [hard] ~: Rogen, *der;* [soft] ~: Milch, *die*
²roe n. ~ [deer] Reh, *das*
rogue [rəʊg] n. Schurke, *der*
role, rôle [rəʊl] n. Rolle, *die*
¹roll [rəʊl] n. **a)** Rolle, *die; (of cloth etc.)* Ballen, *der;* ~ of film Rolle Film; **b)** [bread] ~: Brötchen, *das*
²roll 1. n. *(of drum)* Wirbel, *der.* 2. v.t. **a)** rollen; *(between surfaces)* drehen; **b)** *(shape by ~ing)* rollen; drehen *(Zigarette);* **c)** walzen *(Rasen, Metall usw.);* ausrollen *(Teig).* 3. v.i. **a)** rollen; **b)** *(Maschine:)* laufen; **get sth. ~ing** *(fig.)* etw. ins Rollen bringen; **be ~ing in money** *or* in it *(coll.)* im Geld schwimmen *(ugs.).* **roll a'bout** v.i. herumrollen; *(Schiff:)* schlingern; *(Kind, Hund:)* sich wälzen. **roll 'back** v.t. zurückrollen. **roll 'by** v.i. *(Zeit:)* vergehen. **roll 'in** v.i. *(coll.) (Briefe, Geldbeträge:)* eingehen. **roll 'out** v.t. ausrollen *(Teig, Teppich).* **roll 'over** v.i. *(Person:)* sich umdrehen, *(to make room)* sich zur Seite rollen. **roll 'up** 1. v.t. aufrollen *(Teppich);* zusammenrollen *(Landkarte, Dokument usw.);* hochkrempeln *(Ärmel).* 2. v.i. *(coll.: arrive)* aufkreuzen *(salopp)*
'roll-call n. Ausrufen aller Namen; *(Mil.)* Zählappell, *der*
'roller n. **a)** Rolle, *die; (for lawn, road, etc.)* Walze, *die;* **b)** *(for hair)* Lockenwickler, *der*
roller: **~blind** n. Rouleau, *das;* **~coaster** n. Achterbahn, *die;* **~skate** 1. n. Rollschuh, *der;* 2. v.i. Rollschuh laufen; **~skating** n. Rollschuhlaufen, *das*
'rolling adj. wellig *(Gelände);* ~ hills sanfte Hügel
rolling: **~pin** n. Teigrolle, *die;* **~stock** n. *(Brit. Railw.)* Fahrzeugbestand, *der*

ROM [rɔm] abbr. *(Computing)* read only memory ROM
Roman ['rəʊmən] 1. n. Römer, *der/* Römerin, *die.* 2. adj. römisch.
Roman 'Catholic 1. adj. römisch-katholisch. 2. n. Katholik, *der/*Katholikin, *die;* **sb. is a** ~: jmd. ist römisch-katholisch
romance [rə'mæns] n. **a)** *(love affair)* Romanze, *die;* **b)** *(love-story)* [romantische] Liebesgeschichte
Romania [rəʊ'meɪnɪə] pr. n. Rumänien *(das).* **Romanian** [rəʊ'meɪnɪən] 1. adj. rumänisch. 2. n. **a)** *(person)* Rumäne, *der/*Rumänin, *die;* **b)** *(language)* Rumänisch, *das; see also* English 2 a
Roman 'numeral n. römische Ziffer
romantic [rəʊ'mæntɪk] adj. romantisch
romanticism [rəʊ'mæntɪsɪzm] n. *(Lit., Art., Mus.)* Romantik, *die*
Romany ['rəʊmənɪ] 1. **a)** *(person)* Rom, *der;* **b)** *(language)* Romani, *das.* 2. adj. Roma~; *(Ling.)* Romani~
Rome [rəʊm] pr. n. Rom *(das)*
romp [rɔmp] 1. v.i. **a)** [herum]tollen; **b)** ~ home *or* in *(coll.: win easily)* spielend gewinnen. 2. n. Tollerei, *die*
rompers ['rɔmpəz] n. pl. Spielhöschen, *das*
roof [ru:f] 1. n. **a)** Dach, *das;* ~ of the mouth Gaumen, *der.* 2. v.t. bedachen. **'roofing** n. *(material)* Deckung, *die*
roof: **~rack** n. Dachgepäckträger, *der;* **~top** n. Dach, *das*
¹rook [rʊk] n. *(Ornith.)* Saatkrähe, *die*
²rook n. *(Chess)* Turm, *der*
room [ru:m, rʊm] n. **a)** *(in building)* Zimmer, *das; (for function)* Saal, *der;* **b)** *(space)* Platz, *der;* **make ~ [for sb./ sth.]** [jmdm./einer Sache] Platz machen; **there is still ~ for improvement in his work** seine Arbeit ist noch verbesserungsfähig
room: **~mate** n. Zimmergenosse, *der/*-genossin, *die;* **~service** n. Zimmerservice, *der;* **~temperature** n. Zimmertemperatur, *die*
roomy [ru:mɪ] adj. geräumig
roost [ru:st] 1. n. [Sitz]stange, *die.* 2. v.i. *(Vogel:)* sich [zum Schlafen] niederlassen
¹root [ru:t] 1. n. Wurzel, *die;* put down ~s/take ~: Wurzeln schlagen. 2. v.i. *(Pflanze:)* wurzeln. 3. v.i. **stand ~ed to the spot** wie angewurzelt dastehen. **root 'out** v.t. ausrotten

²**root** *v.i* **a)** *(turn up ground)* wühlen (for nach); **b)** *(coll.)* ~ **for** *(cheer)* anfeuern

rope [rəʊp] **1.** *n.* **a)** *(cord)* Seil, *das*; **b)** **know the ~s** sich auskennen. **2.** *v.t.* festbinden. **rope 'in** *v.t.* *(fig.)* einspannen *(ugs.)*

rope-'ladder *n.* Strickleiter, *die*

rosary ['rəʊzərɪ] *n.* Rosenkranz, *der*

¹**rose** [rəʊz] *n.* **a)** *(plant, flower)* Rose, *die*; **b)** *(colour)* Rosa, *das*

²**rose** *see* **rise 2**

rosé [rəʊ'zeɪ, 'rəʊzeɪ] *n.* Rosé, *der*

rose: **~bed** *n.* Rosenbeet, *das*; **~bud** *n.* Rosenknospe, *die*; **~bush** *n.* Rosenstrauch, *der*

rosemary ['rəʊzmərɪ] *n.* Rosmarin, *der*

'**rose petal** *n.* Rosen[blüten]blatt, *das*

rosette [rəʊ'zet] *n.* Rosette, *die*

roster ['rɒstə(r)] *n.* Dienstplan, *der*

rostrum ['rɒstrəm] *n.,* *pl.* **rostra** ['rɒstrə] *or* **~s** Podium, *das*

rosy ['rəʊzɪ] *adj.* rosig

rot [rɒt] **1.** *n.* **a)** *see* **2:** Verrottung, *die*; Fäulnis, *die*; *(fig.: deterioration)* Verfall, *der*; **stop the ~** *(fig.)* dem Verfall Einhalt gebieten; **b)** *(sl.: nonsense)* Quark, *der (salopp)*. **2.** *v.i.,* **-tt-** verrotten; *⟨Fleisch, Gemüse, Obst:⟩* verfaulen. **3.** *v.t.,* **-tt-** verrotten lassen; verfaulen lassen *⟨Fleisch, Gemüse, Obst⟩*; zerstören *⟨Zähne⟩*

rota ['rəʊtə] *n.* **a)** *(Brit.) (order of rotation)* Turnus, *der*; *(list)* Arbeitsplan, *der*

rotary ['rəʊtərɪ] *adj.* rotierend

rotate [rəʊ'teɪt] **1.** *v.i. (revolve)* rotieren; sich drehen. **2.** *v.t.* in Rotation versetzen. **rotation** [rəʊ'teɪʃn] *n.* **a)** Rotation, *die,* Drehung, *die (about* um); **b)** *(succession)* turnusmäßiger Wechsel; **in** *or* **by ~:** im Turnus

rote [rəʊt] *n.* **by ~:** auswendig

rotten ['rɒtn] *adj.,* **~er** ['rɒtnə(r)], **~est** ['rɒtnɪst] **a)** *(decayed)* verrottet; verfault *⟨Obst, Gemüse⟩*; faul *⟨Ei, Holz, Zähne⟩*; **~ to the core** *(fig.)* verdorben bis ins Mark; **b)** *(corrupt)* verdorben; **c)** *(sl.: bad)* mies *(ugs.)*

rotund [rəʊ'tʌnd] *adj.* **a)** *(round)* rund; **b)** *(plump)* rundlich

rouble ['ruːbl] *n.* Rubel, *der*

rouge [ruːʒ] *n.* Rouge, *das*

rough [rʌf] **1.** *adj.* **a)** *(coarse, uneven)* rauh; holp[e]rig *⟨Straße usw.⟩*; uneben *⟨Gelände⟩*; unruhig *⟨Überfahrt⟩*; **b)** *(violent)* grob *⟨Person, Worte, Behandlung⟩*; **c)** *(trying)* hart; **this is ~ on him** das ist hart für ihn; **sth. is ~ going**

etw. ist nicht einfach; **d)** *(approximate)* grob *⟨Skizze, Schätzung⟩*; vag *⟨Vorstellung⟩*; **~ paper/notebook** Konzeptpapier, *das/*Kladde, *die*; **e)** *(coll.: ill)* angeschlagen *(ugs.)*. **2.** *n.* **[be] in ~:** [sich] im Rohzustand [befinden]. **3.** *adv.* rauh ⟨spielen⟩; **sleep ~:** im Freien schlafen. **4.** *v.t.* **~ it** primitiv leben. **rough 'out** *v.t.* grob entwerfen. **rough 'up** *v.t. (sl.)* anrempeln *(ugs.)*

roughage ['rʌfɪdʒ] *n.* Ballaststoffe *Pl.*

rough: **~-and-'ready** *adj.* provisorisch; **~-and-'tumble** *n.* [milde] Rauferei; **~ copy, ~ draft** *ns.* grobe Skizze; grober Entwurf

roughen ['rʌfn] *v.t.* aufrauhen

'**roughly** *adv.* **a)** *(violently)* roh; grob; **b)** *(crudely)* leidlich; grob ⟨skizzieren, bearbeiten, bauen⟩; **c)** *(approximately)* ungefähr; grob *⟨geschätzt⟩*

'**roughness** *n.* **a)** Rauheit, *die*; *(unevenness)* Unebenheit, *die*; **b)** *(violence)* Roheit, *die*

'**roughshod** *adj.* **ride ~ over sb./sth.** jmdn./etw. mit Füßen treten

roulette [ruː'let] *n.* Roulette, *das*

round [raʊnd] **1.** *adj.* rund; **in ~ figures** rund gerechnet. **2.** *n.* **a)** *(recurring series)* Serie, *die*; **~ of talks/negotiations** Gesprächs-/Verhandlungsrunde, *die*; **the daily ~:** der Alltag; **b)** *(of ammunition)* Ladung, *die*; **50 ~s [of ammunition]** 50 Schuß Munition; **c)** *(of game or contest)* Runde, *die*; **d)** *(burst)* **~ of applause** Beifallssturm, *der*; **e)** *⟨of drinks⟩* Runde, *die*; **f)** *(regular calls)* Runde, *die*; Tour, *die*; **go [on]** *or* **make one's ~s** seine Runden machen; **g) a ~ of toast/sandwiches** eine Scheibe Toast/eine Portion Sandwiches. **3.** *adv.* **a) all the year ~:** das ganze Jahr hindurch; **the third time ~:** beim dritten Mal; **have a look ~:** sich umsehen; **ask sb. ~ [for a drink]** jmdn. zu einem Gläschen zu sich einladen; **b)** *(by indirect way)* herum; **walk ~:** außen herum gehen; **c)** *(here)* hier; *(there)* dort; **I'll go ~ tomorrow** ich gehe morgen hin. **4.** *prep.* **a)** um [... herum]; **travel ~ England** durch England reisen; **run ~ the streets** durch die Straßen rennen; **walk ~ and ~ sth.** immer wieder um etw. herumgehen; **b)** *(in various directions from)* um [... herum]; rund um *⟨einen Ort⟩*. **5.** *v.t.* **~ a bend** um eine Kurve fahren/kommen *usw.* **round 'off** *v.t.* abrunden. **round 'up** *v.t.* verhaften *⟨Verdächtige⟩*; zusammentreiben *⟨Vieh⟩*

round: ~ **a'bout** adv. (on all sides) ringsum; ~**about 1.** n. **a)** (Brit.: merry-go-round) Karussell, das; **b)** (Brit.: road junction) Kreisverkehr, der. **2.** adj. umständlich

rounders ['raʊndəz] n. sing. (Brit.) Rounders, das

round: ~ **'number** n. runde Zahl; ~**shouldered** [raʊnd'ʃəʊldəd] adj. ⟨Person⟩ mit einem Rundrücken; ~ **'trip** n. Rundreise, die

rouse [raʊz] v.t. wecken (**from** aus)

rousing ['raʊzɪŋ] adj. mitreißend ⟨Lied⟩; leidenschaftlich ⟨Rede⟩

rout [raʊt] **1.** n. [wilde] Flucht; (defeat) verheerende Niederlage. **2.** v.t. aufreiben ⟨Feind, Truppen⟩; vernichtend schlagen ⟨Gegner⟩

route [ruːt] n. Route, die; Weg, der

routine [ruː'tiːn] **1.** n. **a)** Routine, die; **b)** (coll.: set speech) Platte, die (ugs.); **c)** (Theatre) Nummer, die; (Dancing, Skating) Figur, die. **2.** adj. routinemäßig; Routine⟨arbeit⟩

roux [ruː] n. Mehlschwitze, die

¹row [raʊ] **1.** (coll.) n. **a)** (noise) Krach, der; **make a** ~: Krach machen; **b)** (quarrel) Krach, der (ugs.); **have/start a** ~: Krach haben/anfangen (ugs.). **2.** v.i sich streiten

²row [rəʊ] n. Reihe, die; **in a** ~: in einer Reihe

³row [rəʊ] v.i. & t. (with oars) rudern

rowan ['raʊən] n. ~[-**tree**] Eberesche, die

row-boat ['rəʊbəʊt] n. (Amer.) Ruderboot, das

rowdy ['raʊdɪ] **1.** adj. rowdyhaft; **the party was** ~: auf der Party ging es laut zu. **2.** n. Krawallmacher, der

rowing-boat ['rəʊɪŋbəʊt] n. (Brit.) Ruderboot, das

royal ['rɔɪəl] adj. königlich

royal: R~ **'Air Force** n. (Brit.) Königliche Luftwaffe; ~ **'blue** n. (Brit.) Königsblau, das; ~ **'family** n. königliche Familie; R~ **'Navy** n. (Brit.) Königliche Kriegsmarine

royalty ['rɔɪəltɪ] n. **a)** (payment) Tantieme, die (**on** für); **b)** collect. (royal persons) Mitglieder des Königshauses

RSPCA abbr. (Brit.) Royal Society for the Prevention of Cruelty to Animals britischer Tierschutzverein

rub [rʌb] **1.** v.t., -**bb**- reiben (**on, against** an + Dat.); (to remove dirt etc.) abreiben; (to dry) trockenreiben; ~ **sth. off sth.** etw. von etw. reiben. **2.** v.i., -**bb**- reiben (**[up]on, against** an +

Dat.). **3.** n. **give it a** ~: reib es ab; **there's the** ~ (fig.) da liegt der Haken [dabei] (ugs.). **rub 'down** v.t. abreiben. **rub 'in** v.t. einreiben; **there's no need to or don't** ~ **it in** (fig.) reib es mir nicht [dauernd] unter die Nase. **rub 'off** v.t. wegreiben; wegwischen. **rub 'out** v.t. ausreiben; (using eraser) ausradieren. **2.** v.i. sich ausreiben/sich ausradieren lassen

rubber ['rʌbə(r)] n. **a)** Gummi, das od. der; **b)** (eraser) Radiergummi, der

rubber: ~ **'band** n. Gummiband, das; ~ **plant** n. Gummibaum, der; ~ **'stamp** n. Gummistempel, der; ~-**stamp** v.t. (fig.) absegnen (ugs.)

rubbish ['rʌbɪʃ] **1.** n. **a)** (refuse) Abfall, der; (to be collected and dumped) Müll, der; **b)** (worthless material) Plunder, der (ugs.); **be** ~: nichts taugen; (nonsense) Quatsch, der (ugs.). **2.** int. Quatsch (ugs.). **'rubbish-bin** n. Abfall-/Mülleimer, der. **'rubbish dump** n. Müllkippe, die

rubble ['rʌbl] n. Trümmer Pl.

ruby ['ruːbɪ] n. Rubin, der

rucksack ['rʌksæk, 'rʊksæk] n. Rucksack, der

rudder ['rʌdə(r)] n. Ruder, das

ruddy ['rʌdɪ] adj. **a)** (reddish) rötlich; **b)** (Brit. sl.: bloody) verdammt (salopp)

rude [ruːd] adj. **a)** unhöflich; (stronger) rüde; **be** ~ **to sb.** zu jmdm. grob unhöflich sein/jmdn. rüde behandeln; **b)** (abrupt) unsanft; ~ **awakening** böses Erwachen. **'rudely** adv. **a)** (impolitely) unhöflich; rüde; **b)** (abruptly) jäh (geh.). **'rudeness** n. (bad manners) ungehöriges Benehmen

rudimentary [ruːdɪ'mentərɪ] elementar; primitiv ⟨Gebäude⟩

rudiments ['ruːdɪmənts] n. pl. Grundlagen Pl.

rueful ['ruːfl] adj. reumütig

ruffian ['rʌfɪən] n. Rohling, der

ruffle ['rʌfl] v.t. **a)** kräuseln; ~ **sb.'s hair** jmdm. durch die Haare fahren; **b)** (upset) aus der Fassung bringen

rug [rʌg] n. [kleiner, dicker] Teppich

Rugby ['rʌgbɪ] n. Rugby, das

rugged ['rʌgɪd] adj. **a)** (uneven) zerklüftet; unwegsam ⟨Land⟩; zerfurcht ⟨Gesicht⟩; **b)** (sturdy) robust

ruin ['ruːɪn] **1.** n. **a)** in sing. or pl. (remains) Ruine, die; **in ~s** in Trümmern; **b)** (downfall) Ruin, der. **2.** v.t. ruinieren; verderben ⟨Urlaub, Abend⟩; ~**ed** (reduced to ruins) verfal-

len; **a ~ed castle/church** eine Burg-/
Kirchenruine. **ruinous** ['ruːɪnəs] *adj.*
ruinös

rule [ruːl] **1.** *n.* **a)** Regel, *die; the ~s of
the game* die Spielregeln; **be against
the ~s** regelwidrig sein; *(fig.)* gegen
die Spielregeln verstoßen; **as a ~:** in
der Regel; **~ of thumb** Faustregel, *die;*
b) *no pl. (government)* Herrschaft, *die*
(over über + *Akk.*). **2.** *v. t.* **a)** *(control)*
beherrschen; **b)** *(be the ruler of)* regieren; ⟨*Monarch, Diktator usw.:*⟩ herrschen über (+ *Akk.*). **3.** *v. i.* **a)** *(govern)* herrschen; **b)** *(decide)* entscheiden (**against** gegen; **in favour of** für).
rule 'out *v. t.* ausschließen; *(prevent)*
unmöglich machen

ruled [ruːld] *adj.* liniert ⟨*Papier*⟩
ruler ['ruːlə(r)] *n.* **a)** *(person)* Herrscher, *der*/Herrscherin, *die;* **b)** *(for
measuring)* Lineal, *das*

ruling ['ruːlɪŋ] **1.** *adj.* herrschend
⟨*Klasse*⟩; regierend ⟨*Partei*⟩. **2.** *n.* Entscheidung, *die*

rum [rʌm] *n.* Rum, *der*

Rumania *etc.* [ruːˈmeɪnɪə] *see* **Romania** *etc.*

rumble ['rʌmbl] **1.** *n.* Grollen, *das.* **2.**
v. i. **a)** grollen; ⟨*Magen:*⟩ knurren; **b)**
⟨*Fahrzeug:*⟩ rumpeln *(ugs.)*

ruminate ['ruːmɪneɪt] *v. i.* **~ on** *or* **over**
sth. über etw. *(Akk.)* grübeln

rummage ['rʌmɪdʒ] *v. i.* wühlen; **~
through sth.** in etw. durchwühlen *(ugs.)*

rummy ['rʌmɪ] *n.* Rommé, *das*

rumour *(Brit.; Amer.:* **rumor**)
['ruːmə(r)] *n.* **a)** Gerücht, *das;* **there is
a ~ that ...:** es geht das Gerücht, daß ...
2. *v. t.* **it is ~ed that ...:** es geht das Gerücht, daß ...

rump [rʌmp] *n.* **a)** *(buttocks)* Hinterteil, *das (ugs.);* **b)** *(remnant)* Rest, *der*
rumple ['rʌmpl] *v. t.* **a)** *(crease)* zerknittern; **b)** *(tousle)* zerzausen
'rump steak *n.* Rumpsteak, *das*

rumpus ['rʌmpəs] *n. (coll.)* Krach, *der
(ugs.);* **kick up** *or* **make a ~:** einen
Spektakel veranstalten *(ugs.)*

run [rʌn] **1.** *n.* **a)** Lauf, *der;* **on the ~:**
auf der Flucht; **b)** *(trip in vehicle)*
Fahrt, *die; (for pleasure)* Ausflug, *der;*
c) *(continuous stretch)* Länge, *die;* **d)**
(spell) **she has had a long ~ of success**
sie war lange [Zeit] erfolgreich; **have a
long ~** ⟨*Stück, Show:*⟩ viele Aufführungen erleben; **e)** *(succession)* Serie,
die; (Cards) Sequenz, *die;* **a ~ of victories** eine Siegesserie; **f)** *(use)* **have
the ~ of sth.** etw. zu seiner freien Ver-

fügung haben; **g)** *(enclosure)* Auslauf,
der; **h)** *(in stocking etc.)* Laufmasche,
die. **2.** *v. i.,* **-nn-, ran** [ræn], **run a)** laufen; **~ for the bus** laufen, um den Bus
zu kriegen *(ugs.);* **~ to help sb.** jmdm.
zu Hilfe eilen; **b)** *(roll, slide)* laufen;
⟨*Ball, Kugel:*⟩ rollen, laufen; ⟨*Schlitten, [Schiebe]tür:*⟩ gleiten; **c)** ⟨*Rad,
Maschine:*⟩ laufen; **d)** *(operate on a
schedule)* fahren; **~ between two places**
⟨*Zug, Bus:*⟩ zwischen zwei Orten verkehren; **e)** *(flow)* laufen; ⟨*Fluß:*⟩ fließen; ⟨*Augen:*⟩ tränen; **his nose was
~ning** ihm lief die Nase; **f)** ⟨*Vertrag,
Theaterstück:*⟩ laufen; **g)** *(have wording)* lauten; ⟨*Geschichte:*⟩ gehen *(fig.);*
h) ⟨*Butter, Eis:*⟩ zerlaufen; ⟨*Farben:*⟩
auslaufen; **i)** *(in election)* kandidieren.
3. *v. t.,* **-nn-, ran, run a)** laufen lassen;
(drive) fahren; **~ one's hand/fingers
through/along** *or* **over sth.** mit der
Hand/den Fingern durch etw. fahren/
über etw. *(Akk.)* streichen; **~ an** *or*
one's eye along *or* **down** *or* **over sth.**
(fig.) etw. überfliegen; **b)** *(cause to
flow)* laufen lassen; **~ a bath** ein
Bad einlaufen lassen; **c)** *(organize,
manage)* führen, leiten ⟨*Geschäft
usw.*⟩; veranstalten ⟨*Wettbewerb*⟩; **d)**
(operate) bedienen ⟨*Maschine*⟩; verkehren lassen ⟨*Verkehrsmittel*⟩; einsetzen ⟨*Sonderbus, -zug*⟩; laufen lassen ⟨*Motor*⟩; **e)** *(own and use)* sich
(Dat.) halten ⟨*Auto*⟩; **f)** **~ sb. into town**
etc. jmdn. in die Stadt *usw.* fahren.
run a'cross *v. t.* **~ across sb./sth.**
jmdn. treffen/auf etw. *(Akk.)* stoßen.
run a'way *v. i.* **a)** *(flee)* weglaufen;
fortlaufen; **b)** *(abscond)* **~ away [from
home]** (von zu Hause) weglaufen. **run
'down 1.** *v. t.* **a)** *(collide with)* überfahren; **b)** *(criticize)* heruntermachen
(ugs.); **c)** *(reduce)* abbauen. **2.** *v. i.* **a)**
hin-/herunterlaufen; **b)** *(decline)* sich
verringern; **c)** ⟨*Uhr, Spielzeug:*⟩ ablaufen; ⟨*Batterie*⟩ leer werden. **'run into**
v. t. **a)** **~ into a tree** gegen einen Baum
fahren; **b)** *(meet)* **~ into sb.** jmdm. in
die Arme laufen *(ugs.);* **c)** stoßen auf
(+ *Akk.*) ⟨*Schwierigkeiten, Widerstand
usw.*⟩; **d)** *(amount to)* **~ into thousands**
in die Tausende gehen. **run 'off 1.** *v. i.*
weglaufen. **2.** *v. t.* abziehen ⟨*Kopien*⟩.
run 'out *v. i.* **a)** hin-/herauslaufen; **b)**
⟨*Vorräte, Bestände:*⟩ zu Ende gehen.
run 'out of *v. t.* **sb. ~s out of sth.**
jmdm. geht etw. aus; **I'm ~ning out of
patience** meine Geduld geht zu Ende.
run 'over 1. ['---] *v. t. (knock down)*

überfahren. 2. [´--] *v.i.* überlaufen.
'run **through** *v.t.* durchspielen ⟨*Theaterstück*⟩. 'run **to** *v.t.* a) *(amount to)* sich belaufen auf ⟨*Akk.*⟩; b) *(be sufficient for)* sth. will ~ to sth. etw. reicht für etw. run 'up 1. *v.i.* hinlaufen; come ~ning up hingelaufen kommen. 2. *v.t.* a) rasch nähen ⟨*Kleidungsstück*⟩; b) zusammenkommen lassen ⟨*Schulden, Rechnung*⟩. run 'up **against** *v.t.* stoßen auf ⟨+ *Akk.*⟩ ⟨*Probleme, Widerstand usw.*⟩

run: **~away** 1. *n.* Ausreißer, *der*/Ausreißerin, *die* (ugs.); 2. *attrib. adj.* durchgegangen ⟨*Pferd*⟩; außer Kontrolle geraten ⟨*Fahrzeug, Preise*⟩; galoppierend ⟨*Inflation*⟩; **~down** 1. [´--] *n.* (coll.: *briefing*) Übersicht, *die* (on über + *Akk.*⟩; 2. [-´-] *adj.* (*tired*) mitgenommen

¹**rung** [rʌŋ] *n.* Sprosse, *die*
²**rung** *see* ²**ring** 2, 3
'**runner** *n.* a) Läufer, *der*/Läuferin, *die*; b) (*Bot.*) Ausläufer, *der*; c) (*on sledge*) Kufe, *die*. **runner bean** *n.* (*Brit.*) Stangenbohne, *die*. **runner-'up** *n.* Zweite, *der/die*; **the runners-up** die Plazierten

'**running** 1. *n.* a) (*management*) Leitung, *die*; b) (*action*) Laufen, *das*; in/ out of the ~: im/aus dem Rennen. 2. *adj.* (*in succession*) hintereinander; win for the third year ~: schon drei Jahre hintereinander gewinnen. **running 'commentary** *n.* (*Broadcasting; also fig.*) Live-Kommentar, *der*

runny ['rʌni] *adj.* a) laufend ⟨*Nase*⟩; b) zu dünn ⟨*Farbe, Marmelade*⟩

run: **-of-the-'mill** *adj.* ganz gewöhnlich; **~-up** *n.* a) during *or* in the **~-up** to an event im Vorfeld eines Ereignisses; b) (*Sport*) Anlauf, *der;* **~way** *n.* (*for take-off*) Startbahn, *die;* (*for landing*) Landebahn, *die*

rupture ['rʌptʃə(r)] 1. *n.* Bruch, *der.* 2. *v.t.* ~ oneself sich (*Dat.*) einen Bruch zuziehen

rural ['rʊərl] *adj.* ländlich
ruse [ruːz] *n.* List, *die*
¹**rush** [rʌʃ] *n.* (*Bot.*) Binse, *die*
²**rush** 1. *n.* a) (*hurry*) Eile, *die;* what's all the ~? wozu diese Hast?; be in a [great] ~: in [großer] Eile sein; b) (*period of great activity*) Hochbetrieb, *der;* (~-hour) Stoßzeit, *die;* c) make a ~ for sth. sich auf etw. ⟨*Akk.*⟩ stürzen. 2. *v.t.* a) ~ sb./sth. somewhere jmdn./ etw. auf schnellstem Wege irgendwohin bringen; be ~ed (*have to hurry*) in

Eile sein; ~ sb. into doing sth. jmdn. dazu drängen, etw. zu tun; b) (*perform quickly*) auf die Schnelle erledigen; ~ it zu schnell machen. 3. *v.i.* a) (*move quickly*) eilen; ⟨*Hund, Pferd:*⟩ laufen; ~ to help sb. jmdm. zu Hilfe eilen; b) (*hurry unduly*) sich zu sehr beeilen; don't ~! nur keine Eile! rush a'bout, rush a'round *v.i.* herumhetzen
'**rush-hour** *n.* Stoßzeit, *die*
rusk [rʌsk] *n.* Zwieback, *der*
Russia ['rʌʃə] *pr. n.* Rußland ⟨*das*⟩
Russian ['rʌʃn] 1. *adj.* russisch; sb. is ~: jmd. ist Russe/Russin. 2. *n.* a) (*person*) Russe, *der*/Russin, *die*; b) (*language*) Russisch, *das; see also* **English** 2a
rust [rʌst] 1. *n.* Rost, *der.* 2. *v.i.* rosten
rustic ['rʌstɪk] *adj.* a) ländlich; b) rustikal ⟨*Mobiliar*⟩
rustle ['rʌsl] 1. *n.* Rascheln, *das.* 2. *v.i.* rascheln. 3. *v.t.* a) rascheln lassen; b) (*Amer.: steal*) stehlen. **rustle 'up** *v.t.* zusammenzaubern ⟨*Mahlzeit*⟩
'**rust-proof** *adj.* rostfrei
rusty *adj.* rostig
rut [rʌt] *n.* Spurrille, *die;* be in a ~ (*fig.*) aus dem [Alltags]trott nicht mehr herauskommen
ruthless ['ruːθlɪs] *adj.* rücksichtslos
rye [raɪ] *n.* Roggen, *der*

S

S, s [es] *n.* S, s, *das*
S. *abbr.* a) south S; b) southern s.
sabbath ['sæbəθ] *n.* Sabbath, *der*
sabbatical [sə'bætɪkl] 1. *adj.* ~ term/ year Forschungssemester/-jahr, *das.* 2. *n.* Forschungsurlaub, *der*
sabotage ['sæbətɑːʒ] 1. *n.* Sabotage, *die.* 2. *v.t.* einen Sabotageakt verüben auf ⟨+ *Akk.*⟩; (*fig.*) sabotieren
saccharin ['sækərɪn] *n.* Saccharin, *das*
sachet ['sæʃeɪ] *n.* Beutel, *der;* (*cushion-shaped*) Kissen, *das*
sack [sæk] 1. *n.* a) Sack, *der;* b) (*coll.: dismissal*) Rausschmiß, *der* (ugs.); **get the** ~: rausgeschmissen werden (ugs.); **give sb. the** ~: jmdn. raus-

schmeißen *(ugs.).* 2. *v. t. (coll.)* rausschmeißen *(ugs.)* **(for wegen)**

sacrament ['sækrəmənt] *n.* Sakrament, *das*

sacred ['seɪkrɪd] *adj.* heilig

sacrifice ['sækrɪfaɪs] 1. *n.* Opfer, *das.* 2. *v. t.* opfern

sacrilege ['sækrɪlɪdʒ] *n.* **[act of]** ~: Sakrileg, *das*

sad [sæd] *adj.* traurig **(at, about** über + *Akk.);* schmerzlich ⟨*Tod, Verlust*⟩; **feel ~:** traurig sein. **sadden** ['sædn] *v. t.* traurig stimmen

saddle ['sædl] 1. *n.* Sattel, *der.* 2. *v. t.* a) satteln ⟨*Pferd usw.*⟩; b) *(fig.)* ~ **sb. with sth.** jmdm. etw. aufbürden *(geh.).* **'saddle-bag** *n.* Satteltasche, *die*

sadism ['seɪdɪzm] *n.* Sadismus, *der.* **sadist** ['seɪdɪst] *n.* Sadist, *der*/Sadistin, *die.* **sadistic** [sə'dɪstɪk] *adj.,* **sa'distically** *adv.* sadistisch

'sadly *adv.* a) *(with sorrow)* traurig; b) *(unfortunately)* leider

'sadness *n.* Traurigkeit, *die*

safari [sə'fɑːrɪ] *n.* Safari, *die;* **on ~:** auf Safari

safe [seɪf] 1. *n.* Safe, *der;* Geldschrank, *der.* 2. *adj.* a) *(out of danger)* sicher **(from** vor + *Dat.);* **he's ~:** er ist in Sicherheit; ~ **and sound** sicher und wohlbehalten; b) *(free from danger)* ungefährlich; sicher ⟨*Ort, Hafen*⟩; **wish sb. a ~ journey** jmdm. eine gute Reise wünschen; **to be on the ~ side** zur Sicherheit; c) *(reliable)* sicher ⟨*Methode, Investition*⟩. **'safeguard** 1. *n.* Schutz, *der.* 2. *v. t.* schützen. **'safely** *adv.* sicher; **did the parcel arrive ~?** ist das Paket heil angekommen? **safety** ['seɪftɪ] *n.* Sicherheit, *die.* **safety: ~-belt** *n.* Sicherheitsgurt, *der;* ~ **helmet** *n.* Schutzhelm, *der;* ~ **margin** *n.* Spielraum, *der;* ~**-pin** *n.* Sicherheitsnadel, *die;* ~**-valve** *n.* Sicherheitsventil, *das; (fig.)* Ventil, *das*

sag [sæg] *v. i.,* **-gg-** durchhängen; *(sink)* sich senken

saga ['sɑːgə] *n.* a) *(story of adventure)* Heldenepos, *das; (medieval narrative)* Saga, *die;* b) *(coll.: long involved story)* [ganzer] Roman *(fig.)*

'sage [seɪdʒ] *n. (Bot.)* Salbei, *der od. die*

²sage 1. *adj.* weis. 2. *n.* Weise, *der*

Sagittarius [sædʒɪ'teərɪəs] *n.* der Schütze

Sahara [sə'hɑːrə] *pr. n.* **the ~** [Desert] die [Wüste] Sahara

said *see* **say** 1

sail [seɪl] 1. *n.* a) Segelfahrt, *die;* b) *(piece of canvas)* Segel, *das.* 2. *v. i.* a) *(travel on water)* fahren; *(in sailing boat)* segeln; b) *(start voyage)* auslaufen **(for** nach). 3. *v. t.* a) steuern ⟨*Boot, Schiff*⟩; segeln mit ⟨*Segeljacht, -schiff*⟩; b) durchfahren/⟨*Segelschiff:*⟩ durchsegeln ⟨*Meer*⟩

sail: ~board *n.* Surfbrett, *das* **(zum Windsurfen);** ~**boarding** *n.* Windsurfen, *das;* ~**boat** *n. (Amer.)* Segelboot, *das*

'sailing *n.* Segeln, *das.* **'sailing boat** *n.* Segelboot, *das.* **'sailing ship** *n.* Segelschiff, *das*

sailor ['seɪlə(r)] *n.* Seemann, *der; (in navy)* Matrose, *der*

saint 1. [sənt] *adj.* **S~ Michael** der heilige Michael / Sankt Michael. 2. [seɪnt] *n.* Heilige, *der/die.* **'saintly** ['seɪntlɪ] *adj.* heilig

sake [seɪk] *n.* **for the ~ of** um ... *(Gen.)* willen; **for my** *etc.* ~: um meinetwillen *usw.;* mir *usw.* zuliebe

salad ['sæləd] *n.* Salat, *der.* **'salad cream** *n.* ≈ Mayonnaise, *die.* **'salad dressing** *n.* Salatsoße, *die*

salary ['sælərɪ] *n.* Gehalt, *das*

sale [seɪl] *n.* a) Verkauf, *der; (at reduced prices)* Ausverkauf, *der;* **[up] for ~:** zu verkaufen; b) ~**s** *(amount sold)* Verkaufszahlen *Pl.* **(of** für); Absatz, *der;* c) **[jumble** *or* **rummage]** ~: [Wohltätigkeits]basar, *der*

salesman ['seɪlzmən] *n., pl.* ~**men** ['seɪlzmən] Verkäufer, *der.* **'salesmanship** *n.* Kunst des Verkaufens

'saleswoman *n.* Verkäuferin, *die*

salient ['seɪlɪənt] *adj.* auffallend

saliva [sə'laɪvə] *n.* Speichel, *der*

sallow ['sæləʊ] *adj.* blaßgelb

salmon ['sæmən] *n.* Lachs, *der*

saloon [sə'luːn] *n.* a) *(Brit.)* ~ **[bar]** separater Teil eines Pubs mit mehr Komfort; b) *(Brit.)* ~ **[car]** Limousine, *die*

salt [sɔːlt, sɒlt] 1. *n.* **[common]** ~: [Koch]salz, *das.* 2. *adj. (containing or tasting of* ~) salzig; *(preserved with* ~) gepökelt ⟨*Fleisch*⟩; gesalzen ⟨*Butter*⟩. 3. *v. t.* a) salzen; b) *(cure)* [ein]pökeln; c) ~ **the roads** Salz auf die Straßen streuen. **'salt-cellar** *n.* Salzstreuer, *der.* **salt 'water** *n.* Salzwasser, *das*

'salty *adj.* salzig

salute [sə'luːt] 1. *v. t.* grüßen. 2. *v. i.* *(Mil., Navy)* [militärisch] grüßen. 3. *n.* Salut, *der;* militärischer Gruß

salvage ['sælvɪdʒ] 1. *n.* Bergung, *die.* 2. *v. t.* bergen

salvation [sæl'veɪʃn] n. Erlösung, die.
Salvation 'Army n. Heilsarmee, die
salvo ['sælvəʊ] n. Salve, die
Samaritan [sə'mærɪtən] n. good ~:
[barmherziger] Samariter; **the ~s** (organization) ≈ die Telefonseelsorge
same [seɪm] **1.** adj. the ~: der/die/das
gleiche; **the ~ [thing]** (identical) der-/
die-/dasselbe. **2.** adv. **all** or **just the ~:**
trotzdem
sample ['sɑːmpl] **1.** n. (example) [Muster]beispiel, das; (specimen) Probe,
die; [commercial] ~: Muster, das. **2.**
v. t. probieren
sanctify ['sæŋktɪfaɪ] v. t. heiligen
sanctimonious [sæŋktɪ'məʊnɪəs] adj.
scheinheilig
sanction ['sæŋkʃn] **1.** n. Sanktion,
die. **2.** v. t. sanktionieren
sanctity ['sæŋktɪtɪ] n. Heiligkeit, die
sanctuary ['sæŋktʃʊərɪ] n. **a)** (holy place) Heiligtum, das; **b)** (refuge) Zufluchtsort, der; **c)** (for animals) Naturschutzgebiet, das
sand [sænd] **1.** n. Sand, der. **2.** v. t. ~
sth. [down] etw. [ab]schmirgeln
sandal ['sændl] n. Sandale, die
sand: ~**bag 1.** n. Sandsack, der; **2.**
v. t. mit Sandsäcken schützen;
~**bank** n. Sandbank, die; ~**castle**
n. Sandburg, die; ~**paper 1.** n. Sandpapier, das; **2.** v. t. [mit Sandpapier]
[ab]schmirgeln; ~**pit** n. Sandkasten,
der; ~**stone** n. Sandstein, der
sandwich ['sænwɪdʒ] **1.** n. Sandwich,
der od. das; ≈ [zusammengeklapptes]
belegtes Brot; **cheese** ~: Käsebrot,
das. **2.** v. t. einschieben (**between** zwischen + Akk.; **into** in + Akk.)
'sandy adj. **a)** sandig; Sand(boden,
-strand); **b)** rotblond (Haar)
sane [seɪn] adj. **a)** geistig gesund; **b)**
(sensible) vernünftig
sang see **sing**
sanitary ['sænɪtərɪ] adj. sanitär (Verhältnisse, Anlagen). **'sanitary napkin** (Amer.), **'sanitary towel** (Brit.)
ns. Damenbinde, die
sanitation [sænɪ'teɪʃn] n. Kanalisation und Abfallbeseitigung
sanity ['sænɪtɪ] n. geistige Gesundheit; **lose one's** ~: den Verstand verlieren
sank see **sink** 2, 3
Santa Claus ['sæntə klɔːz] n. der
Weihnachtsmann
sap [sæp] **1.** n. Saft, der. **2.** v. t., -**pp**-
zehren an (+ Dat.)
sapling ['sæplɪŋ] n. junger Baum

sarcasm ['sɑːkæzm] n. Sarkasmus,
der. **sarcastic** [sɑː'kæstɪk] adj. sarkastisch
sardine [sɑː'diːn] n. Sardine, die
Sardinia [sɑː'dɪnɪə] pr. n. Sardinien
(das)
sardonic [sɑː'dɒnɪk] adj. höhnisch;
sardonisch (Lächeln)
sash [sæʃ] n. Schärpe, die
sat see **sit**
Sat. abbr. Saturday Sa.
Satan ['seɪtən] pr. n. Satan, der. **satanic** [sə'tænɪk] adj. satanisch
satchel ['sætʃl] n. [Schul]ranzen, der
satellite ['sætəlaɪt] n. Satellit, der
satellite: ~ **'broadcasting** n. Satellitenfunk, der; ~**dish** n. Satellitenschüssel, die; ~ **'television** n. Satellitenfernsehen, das
satin ['sætɪn] n. Satin, der
satire ['sætaɪə(r)] n. Satire, die (**on** auf
+ Akk.). **satirical** [sə'tɪrɪkl] adj. satirisch
satisfaction [sætɪs'fækʃn] n. Befriedigung, die (**at**, with über + Akk.);
meet with sb.'s [complete] ~: jmdn. [in
jeder Weise] zufriedenstellen
satisfactory [sætɪs'fæktərɪ] adj. zufriedenstellend
satisfy ['sætɪsfaɪ] v. t. **a)** befriedigen;
zufriedenstellen (Kunden); stillen
(Hunger, Durst); **b)** (convince) ~ **sb.**
[**of sth.**] jmdn. [von etw.] überzeugen.
'satisfying adj. befriedigend; sättigend (Gericht, Speise)
saturate ['sætʃəreɪt] v. t. durchnässen;
[mit Feuchtigkeit durch]tränken
(Boden, Erde). **saturated** ['sætʃəreɪtɪd] adj. durchnäßt. **saturation** [sætʃə'reɪʃn] n. Durchnässung, die
Saturday ['sætədeɪ, 'sætədɪ] n. Sonnabend, der; Samstag, der; see also **Friday**
Saturn ['sætən] pr. n. (Astron.) Saturn,
der
sauce [sɔːs] n. **a)** Soße, die; **b)** (impudence) Frechheit, die. **saucepan**
['sɔːspən] n. Kochtopf, der; (with straight handle) Kasserolle, die
saucer ['sɔːsə(r)] n. Untertasse, die
saucy ['sɔːsɪ] adj. **a)** (rude) frech; **b)**
(pert, jaunty) keck
Saudi Arabia [saʊdɪ ə'reɪbɪə] pr. n.
Saudi-Arabien (das)
sauna ['sɔːnə, 'saʊnə] n. Sauna, die
saunter ['sɔːntə(r)] v. i. schlendern
sausage ['sɒsɪdʒ] n. Wurst, die. **sausage 'roll** n. Blätterteig mit Wurstfüllung

savage ['sævɪdʒ] 1. *adj.* a) *(uncivilized)* primitiv; wild *(Volksstamm)*; unzivilisiert *(Land)*; b) *(fierce)* brutal; wild *(Tier)*. 2. *n.* Wilde, *der/die (veralt.)*.

savagery ['sævɪdʒrɪ] *n.* Brutalität, *die*

save [seɪv] 1. *v. t.* a) *(rescue)* retten (from vor + *Dat.)*; ~ oneself from falling sich [beim Hinfallen] fangen; b) *(put aside)* aufheben; sparen *(Geld)*; sammeln *(Briefmarken usw.)*; *(conserve)* sparsam umgehen mit; c) *(make unnecessary)* sparen *(Geld, Zeit, Energie)*; ~ sb./oneself sth. jmdm./sich etw. ersparen; d) *(Sport)* abwehren *(Schuß, Ball)*. 2. *v. i.* sparen (on *Akk.)*. 3. *n.* *(Sport)* Abwehr, *die.*

save 'up 1. *v. t.* sparen. 2. *v. i.* sparen (for für, auf + *Akk.)*

'saver *n.* Sparer, *der/*Sparerin, *die*

saving ['seɪvɪŋ] 1. *n.* in pl. Ersparnisse *Pl.* 2. *adj.* *(kosten-, benzin-)*sparend

savings: ~ **account** *n.* Sparkonto, *das;* ~ **bank** *n.* Sparkasse, *die*

saviour ['seɪvjə(r)] *n.* a) Retter, *der/*Retterin, *die;* b) *(Relig.)* the S~: der Heiland

savor etc. *(Amer.) see* savour etc.

savour ['seɪvə(r)] *(Brit.)* 1. *n.* *(flavour)* Geschmack, *der.* 2. *v. t.* genießen

savoury ['seɪvərɪ] *(Brit.)* 1. *adj.* a) pikant; salzig; b) *(appetizing)* appetitanregend. 2. *n.* [pikantes] Häppchen

'saw [sɔ:] 1. *n.* Säge, *die.* 2. *v. t., p.p.* **sawn** [sɔ:n] *or* **sawed** [zɛ:]sägen; ~ in half in der Mitte durchsägen. 3. *v. i., p.p.* **sawn** *or* **sawed** sägen; ~ **through** sth. etw. durchsägen

²saw *see* see

'sawdust *n.* Sägemehl, *das*

sawn *see* **¹saw 2, 3**

saxophone ['sæksəfəʊn] *n.* Saxophon, *das*

say [seɪ] 1. *v. t. pres. t.* **he says** [sez], *p.t. & p.p.* **said** [sed] a) sagen; **that is to ~:** das heißt; **do as** *or* **what I ~:** tun Sie, was ich sage; **when all is said and done** letzten Endes; **go without ~ing** sich von selbst verstehen; **she is said to be clever/to have done it** man sagt, sie sei klug/habe es getan; b) *(recite)* sprechen *(Gebet, Text)*; c) *(have specified wording or reading)* sagen; *(Zeitung:)* schreiben; *(Uhr:)* zeigen *(Uhrzeit)*; **what does it ~ here?** was steht hier? 2. *n.* **have a** *or* **some ~:** ein Mitspracherecht haben **(in** bei); **have no ~:** nichts zu sagen haben; **have one's ~:** seine Meinung sagen. **'saying** *n.* Redensart, *die*

scab [skæb] *n.* [Wund]schorf, *der*

scaffold ['skæfəld] *n.* Schafott, *das*

'scaffolding *n.* Gerüst, *das*

scald [skɔ:ld, skɒld] 1. *n.* Verbrühung, *die.* 2. *v. t.* verbrühen

'scale [skeɪl] *n.* a) *(of fish, reptile, etc.)* Schuppe, *die;* b) *(in kettle etc.)* Kesselstein, *der;* *(on teeth)* Zahnstein, *der*

²scale *n.* a) in *sing. or pl. (weighing-instrument)* ~[s] Waage, *die;* b) *(dish of balance)* Waagschale, *die*

³scale 1. *n.* a) *(series of degrees)* Skala, *die;* b) *(Mus.)* Tonleiter, *die;* c) *(dimensions)* Ausmaß, *das;* **be on a small ~:** bescheidenen Umfang haben; d) *(ratio of reduction)* Maßstab, *der;* **what is the ~ of the map?** welchen Maßstab hat diese Karte?; e) *(indication) (on map)* Maßstab, *der;* *(on thermometer)* [Anzeige]skala, *die.* 2. *v. t.* ersteigen *(Mauer, Leiter, Gipfel)*.

scale 'down *v. t.* [entsprechend] drosseln *(Produktion)*; Abstriche machen bei *(Planungen)*

scalp [skælp] *n.* Kopfhaut, *die*

scalpel ['skælp] *n.* Skalpell, *das*

scam [skæm] *n.* *(Amer. sl.)* Masche, *die (ugs.)*

scamper ['skæmpə(r)] *v. i.* *(Person:)* flitzen; *(Tier:)* huschen

scampi ['skæmpɪ] *n. pl.* Scampi *Pl.*

scan [skæn] 1. *v. t., -nn-* a) *(search thoroughly)* absuchen (for nach); b) *(look over cursorily)* flüchtig ansehen; überfliegen *(Zeitung, Liste usw.)* (for auf der Suche nach); c) *(Med.)* szintigraphisch untersuchen. 2. *v. i., -nn-* *(Vers[zeile]:)* das richtige Versmaß haben. 3. *n. (Med.)* szintigraphische Untersuchung, *die*

scandal ['skændl] *n.* a) Skandal, *der* **(about/of** um); *(story)* Skandalgeschichte, *die;* b) *(outrage)* Empörung, *die;* c) *(gossip)* Klatsch, *der (ugs.)*.

scandalize ['skændəlaɪz] *v. t.* schockieren. **scandalous** ['skændələs] *adj.* skandalös; schockierend *(Bemerkung)*

Scandinavia [skændɪ'neɪvɪə] *pr. n.* Skandinavien *(das)*

scant [skænt] *adj.* wenig. **scanty** ['skæntɪ] *adj.* spärlich; knapp *(Bikini)*

scapegoat ['skeɪpgəʊt] *n.* Sündenbock, *der;* **make sb. a ~:** jmdn. zum Sündenbock machen

scar [skɑ:(r)] 1. *n.* Narbe, *die.* 2. *v. t., -rr-:* ~ **sb./sb.'s face** bei jmdm./in jmds. Gesicht *(Dat.)* Narben hinterlassen

scarce [skeəs] *adj.* **a)** *(insufficient)* knapp; **b)** *(rare)* selten; **make oneself ~** *(coll.)* sich aus dem Staub machen *(ugs.)*. **'scarcely** *adv.* kaum. **scarcity** ['skeəsıtı] *n.* Knappheit, *die* (of an + *Dat.*)

scare [skeə(r)] **1.** *n.* **a)** *(sensation of fear)* Schreck[en], *der;* **give sb. a ~:** jmdm. einen Schreck[en] einjagen; **b)** *(general alarm)* [allgemeine] Hysterie; **bomb ~:** Bombendrohung, *die.* **2.** *v. t.* *(frighten)* Angst machen (+ *Dat.*); *(startle)* erschrecken. **scare a'way, scare 'off** *v. t.* verscheuchen

'scarecrow *n.* Vogelscheuche, *die*

scared [skeəd] *adj.* **be ~ of sb./sth.** vor jmdm./etw. Angst haben; **be ~ of doing/to do sth.** sich nicht [ge]trauen, etw. zu tun

scarf [skɑːf] *n., pl.* **~s or scarves** [skɑːvz] Schal, *der; (square)* Halstuch, *das; (worn over hair)* Kopftuch, *das*

scarlet ['skɑːlıt] **1.** *n.* Scharlach, *der.* **2.** *adj.* scharlachrot. **scarlet 'fever** *n.* Scharlach, *der*

scarves *see* **scarf**

scary ['skeərı] *adj.* furchterregend ⟨Anblick⟩; schaurig ⟨Film, Geschichte⟩

scatter ['skætə(r)] **1.** *v. t.* **a)** vertreiben; auseinandertreiben ⟨Menge⟩; **b)** *(distribute irregularly)* verstreuen. **2.** *v. i.* sich auflösen ⟨Menge⟩; sich zerstreuen; *(in fear)* auseinanderstieben. **scattered** ['skætəd] *adj.* verstreut; vereinzelt ⟨Regenschauer⟩

scavenge ['skævındʒ] *v. i.* **~ for sth.** nach etw. suchen. **'scavenger** *n.* *(animal)* Aasfresser, *der; (fig. derog.: person)* Aasgeier, *der (ugs.)*

scene [siːn] *n.* **a)** *(place of event)* Schauplatz, *der; ~* **of the crime** Tatort, *der;* **b)** *(division of act)* Auftritt, *der;* **c)** *(view)* Anblick, *der;* **d)** **behind the ~s** hinter den Kulissen. **scenery** ['siːnərı] *n.* **a)** Landschaft, *die;* **b)** *(Theatre)* Bühnenbild, *das.* **scenic** ['siːnık] *adj.* landschaftlich schön

scent [sent] **1.** *n.* **a)** *(smell)* Duft, *der;* **b)** *(Hunting; also fig.: trail)* Fährte, *die;* **be on the ~ of sb./sth.** *(fig.)* jmdm./einer Sache auf der Spur sein; **c)** *(Brit.: perfume)* Parfüm, *das.* **2.** *v. t.* wittern

sceptic ['skeptık] *n.* Skeptiker, *der*/Skeptikerin, *die.* **sceptical** ['skeptıkl] *adj.* skeptisch; **be ~ about or of sb./sth.** jmdm./einer Sache skeptisch gegenüberstehen. **scepticism** ['skeptısızm] *n.* Skepsis, *die*

schedule ['ʃedjuːl] **1.** *n.* **a)** *(list)* Tabelle, *die; (for event)* Programm, *das;* **b)** *(of work)* Zeitplan, *der;* **c)** **on ~:** plangemäß. **2.** *v. t.* zeitlich planen. **'scheduled flight** *n.* Linienflug, *der*

scheme [skiːm] *n.* **a)** *(arrangement)* Anordnung, *die;* **b)** *(plan)* Programm, *das; (project)* Projekt, *das;* **c)** *(dishonest plan)* Intrige, *die*

schizophrenia [skıtsə'friːnıə] *n.* Schizophrenie, *die.* **schizophrenic** [skıtsə'frenık, skıtsə'friːnık] *adj.* schizophren

scholar ['skɒlə(r)] *n.* Gelehrte, *der/die.* **'scholarly** *adj.* wissenschaftlich; gelehrt ⟨Person⟩. **'scholarship** *n.* **a)** *(award)* Stipendium, *das;* **b)** *(scholarly work)* Gelehrsamkeit, *die*

school [skuːl] *n.* Schule, *die; (Amer.: college)* Hochschule, *die;* **be at or in ~:** in der Schule sein; *(attend ~)* zur Schule gehen; **go to ~:** zur Schule gehen; **~ holidays/exchange** Schulferien *Pl.*/Schüleraustausch, *der*

school: **~boy** *n.* Schüler, *der;* **~girl** *n.* Schülerin, *die;* **~master** *n.* Lehrer, *der;* **~mistress** *n.* Lehrerin, *die;* **~teacher** *n.* Lehrer, *der*/Lehrerin, *die*

sciatica [saı'ætıkə] *n.* Ischias, *die*

science ['saıəns] *n.* Wissenschaft, *die.* **science 'fiction** *n.* Science-fiction, *die.* **scientific** [saıən'tıfık] *adj.* wissenschaftlich. **scientist** ['saıəntıst] *n.* Wissenschaftler, *der*/Wissenschaftlerin, *die*

scintillating ['sıntıleıtıŋ] *adj.* *(fig.)* geistsprühend

scissors ['sızəz] *n. pl.* **[pair of] ~:** Schere, *die*

¹scoff [skɒf] *v. i.* *(mock)* spotten; **~ at** sich lustig machen über (+ *Akk.*)

²scoff *v. t.* *(sl.: eat greedily)* verschlingen

scold [skəʊld] *v. t.* ausschimpfen (for wegen); **she ~ed him for being late too** schimpfte ihn aus, weil er zu spät kam

scone [skɒn, skəʊn] *n.* weicher, oft zum Tee gegessener kleiner Kuchen

scoop [skuːp] **1.** *n.* **a)** Schaufel, *die; (for ice-cream etc.)* Portionierer, *der;* **b)** *(Journ.)* Knüller, *der (ugs.).* **2.** *v. t.* schaufeln ⟨Kohlen, Zucker⟩; schöpfen ⟨Flüssigkeit⟩. **scoop 'out** *v. t.* **a)** *(hollow out)* aushöhlen; schaufeln ⟨Loch, Graben⟩; **b)** [her]ausschöpfen ⟨Flüssigkeit⟩; auslöffeln ⟨Fruchtfleisch⟩; *(with a knife)* herausschneiden ⟨Gehäuse, Fruchtfleisch⟩. **scoop 'up** *v. t.*

schöpfen ⟨*Flüssigkeit, Suppe*⟩; schaufeln ⟨*Erde*⟩

scooter ['sku:tə(r)] *n.* **a)** *(toy)* Roller, *der;* **b)** |motor| ~: [Motor]roller, *der*

scope [skəʊp] *n.* **a)** Bereich, *der; (of discussion etc.)* Rahmen, *der;* **b)** *(opportunity)* Entfaltungsmöglichkeiten *Pl.*

scorch [skɔ:tʃ] *v.t.* versengen.
'**scorching** *adj.* glühend heiß

score [skɔ:(r)] **1.** *n.* **a)** *(points)* [Spiel]stand, *der; (made by one player)* Punktzahl, *die;* **keep |the| ~:** zählen; **b)** *(Mus.)* Partitur, *die; (Cinemat.)* [Film]musik, *die;* **c)** *pl. same or* ~**s** *(group of 20)* zwanzig; **d)** *in pl. (great numbers)* ~**s** |and ~**s|** of zig *(ugs.);* Dutzende [von]; **e) on that** ~: was das betrifft; **f) pay off or settle an old** ~ *(fig.)* eine alte Rechnung begleichen. **2.** *v.t.* erzielen ⟨*Erfolg, Punkt usw.*⟩; ~ **a goal** ein Tor schießen. **3.** *v.i.* **a)** *(make ~)* Punkte/einen Punkt erzielen; *(~ goal/goals)* ein Tor/Tore schießen/werfen; **b)** *(keep ~)* aufschreiben. '**score-board** *n.* Anzeigetafel, *die.* '**scorer** *n.* **a)** *(recorder)* Anschreiber, *der/*Anschreiberin, *die;* **b)** *(Footb.)* Torschütze, *der/*-schützin, *die*

scorn [skɔ:n] **1.** *n.* Verachtung, *die.* **2.** *v.t.* verachten; in den Wind schlagen ⟨*Rat*⟩; ausschlagen ⟨*Angebot*⟩.
scornful ['skɔ:nfl] *adj.* verächtlich ⟨*Lächeln, Blick*⟩; **be ~ of sth.** für etw. nur Verachtung haben

Scorpio ['skɔ:pɪəʊ] *n.* der Skorpion
scorpion ['skɔ:pɪən] *n.* Skorpion, *der*
Scot [skɒt] *n.* Schotte, *der/*Schottin, *die*

Scotch [skɒtʃ] **1.** *adj. see* **Scottish. 2.** *n.* Scotch, *der;* schottischer Whisky
scotch *v.t.* den Boden entziehen (+ *Dat.*) ⟨*Gerücht*⟩; zunichte machen ⟨*Plan*⟩

Scotch: ~ **egg** *n.* hartgekochtes Ei in Wurstbrät; ~ **whisky** *n.* schottischer Whisky

scot-'free *adj.* |get off/go| ~: ungeschoren [davonkommen *od.* bleiben]
Scotland ['skɒtlənd] *pr. n.* Schottland (*das*)

Scots [skɒts] **1.** *adj. (esp. Scot.)* schottisch; **sb. is** ~: jmd. ist Schotte/Schottin. **2.** *n. (dialect)* Schottisch, *das.* **Scotsman** ['skɒtsmən] *n., pl.* **Scotsmen** ['skɒtsmən] Schotte, *der.* '**Scotswoman** *n.* Schottin, *die*
Scottish ['skɒtɪʃ] *adj.* schottisch; **sb. is** ~: jmd. ist Schotte/Schottin

scoundrel ['skaʊndrl] *n.* Schuft, *der*
¹**scour** [skaʊə(r)] *v.t. (search)* durchkämmen (for nach)
²**scour** *v.t.* scheuern ⟨*Topf, Metall*⟩.
'**scourer** *n.* Topfreiniger, *der*
scourge [skɜ:dʒ] *n.* Geißel, *die*

scout [skaʊt] **1.** *n.* **a)** |Boy| S~: Pfadfinder, *der;* **b)** *(Mil.)* Späher, *der.* **2.** *v.i.* ~ **for** Ausschau halten nach

scowl [skaʊl] **1.** *v.i.* ein mürrisches Gesicht machen. **2.** *n.* mürrischer [Gesichts]ausdruck

scram [skræm] *v.i.,* **-mm-** *(sl.)* abhauen *(salopp)*

scramble ['skræmbl] **1.** *v.i.* **a)** *(clamber)* klettern; ~ **through a hedge** sich durch eine Hecke zwängen; **b)** *(move hastily)* rennen *(ugs.);* ~ **for sth.** um etw. rangeln. **2.** *v.t. (Teleph., Radio)* verschlüsseln. **scrambled 'egg** *n.* Rührei, *das*

¹**scrap** [skræp] **1.** *n.* **a)** *(of paper)* Fetzen, *der; (of food)* Bissen, *der;* **b)** *in pl. (odds and ends) (of food)* Reste *Pl.;* **c)** *(smallest amount)* **not a** ~ of kein bißchen; *(of sympathy, truth also)* nicht ein Fünkchen; **not a** ~ **of evidence** nicht die Spur eines Beweises; **d)** ~ |metal| Schrott, *der;* ~ **iron** Alteisen, *das.* **2.** *v.t.,* **-pp-** wegwerfen; *(send for ~)* verschrotten; *(fig.)* aufgeben
²**scrap** *(coll.)* **1.** *n. (fight)* Rauferei, *die.* **2.** *v.i.,* **-pp-** sich raufen

'**scrap-book** *n.* [Sammel]album, *das*
scrape [skreɪp] **1.** *v.t.* **a)** *(make smooth)* schaben ⟨*Häute, Möhren, Kartoffeln usw.*⟩; abziehen ⟨*Holz*⟩; *(damage)* verschrammen ⟨*Fußboden, Auto*⟩; **b)** *(remove)* [ab]kratzen ⟨*Farbe, Schmutz, Rost*⟩ (off, from von); **c)** *(draw along)* schleifen; **d)** ~ **together** *(raise)* zusammenkratzen *(ugs.); (save up)* zusammensparen. **2.** *v.i.* **a)** *(move with sound)* schleifen; **b)** *(emit scraping noise)* ein schabendes Geräusch machen; **c)** *(rub)* streifen (against, over *Akk.*). **3.** *n.* **a)** *(act, sound)* Kratzen, *das* (against an + *Akk.*); **b)** *(predicament)* Schwulitäten *Pl. (ugs.).*
scrape 'by *v.i. (fig.)* sich über Wasser halten (on mit). **scrape 'out** *v.t.* **a)** *(excavate)* buddeln *(ugs.);* scharren; **b)** *(clean)* auskratzen. **scrape through** **1.** ['--] *v.t.* sich zwängen durch; *(fig.)* mit Hängen und Würgen kommen durch ⟨*Prüfung*⟩. **2.** [-'-] *v.i.* sich durchzwängen; *(fig.: in examination)* mit Hängen und Würgen durchkommen

'scraper *n. (for shoes)* Kratzeisen, *das;* (grid) Abtreter, *der;* (tool, kitchen utensil) Schaber, *der;* (for removing ice from car windows) [Eis]kratzer, *der*

scrap: ~-heap *n.* Schutthaufen, *der;* ~ 'paper *n.* Schmierpapier, *das*

scrappy ['skræpɪ] *adj.* lückenhaft

'scrap-yard *n.* Schrottplatz, *der*

scratch [skrætʃ] 1. *v.t.* a) *(score surface of)* zerkratzen; *(score skin of)* kratzen; b) *(get scratch[es] on)* ~ oneself/one's hands *etc.* sich schrammen/ sich *(Dat.)* die Hände *usw.* zerkratzen; c) *(scrape without marking)* kratzen; kratzen an (+ *Dat.*) ⟨*Insektenstich usw.*⟩; ~ oneself/one's arm sich kratzen/sich *(Dat.)* den Arm *od.* am Arm kratzen. 2. *v.i.* kratzen; ⟨~ oneself⟩ sich kratzen. 3. *n.* a) *(mark, wound)* Kratzer, *der (ugs.);* Schramme, *die;* b) *(sound)* Kratzen, *das;* c) have a [good] ~: sich [ordentlich] kratzen; d) *start from* ~: bei Null anfangen *(ugs.);* *be up to* ~ ⟨*Arbeit, Leistung:*⟩ nichts zu wünschen übriglassen; ⟨*Person:*⟩ den Anforderungen genügen. scratch a'bout, scratch a'round *v.i.* scharren; *(fig.: search)* suchen (for nach). scratch 'out *v.t.* auskratzen ⟨*Auge*⟩

scrawl [skrɔːl] 1. *v.t.* hinkritzeln. 2. *v.i.* kritzeln. 3. *n.* Gekritzel, *das; (handwriting)* Klaue, *die (salopp)*

scrawny ['skrɔːnɪ] *adj.* mager; dürr

scream [skriːm] 1. *v.i.* schreien (with vor + *Dat.*). 2. *v.t.* schreien. 3. *n.* Schrei, *der; (of jet engine)* Heulen, *das; ~s of pain* Schmerzensschreie

screech [skriːtʃ] 1. *v.i. & t.* kreischen. 2. *n.* Kreischen, *das*

screen [skriːn] 1. *n.* a) *(partition)* Trennwand, *die; (piece of furniture)* Wandschirm, *der;* b) *(of trees, persons, fog)* Wand, *die;* c) *(Cinemat.)* Leinwand, *die;* [TV] ~: Bildschirm, *der.* 2. *v.t.* a) *(shelter)* schützen (from vor + *Dat.*); *(conceal)* verdecken; b) vorführen ⟨*Film*⟩; c) *(for disease)* untersuchen. 'screenplay *n.* Drehbuch, *das*

screw [skruː] 1. *n.* Schraube, *die.* 2. *v.t.* schrauben (to an + *Akk.*); ~ together zusammenschrauben; ~ down festschrauben. screw 'up *v.t.* a) *(crumple up)* zusammenknüllen ⟨*Blatt Papier*⟩; b) verziehen ⟨*Gesicht*⟩; zusammenkneifen ⟨*Augen, Mund*⟩; c) *(sl.: bungle)* vermurksen *(salopp);* ~ it/ things up Mist bauen *(salopp)*

screw: ~-cap *n.* Schraubverschluß,

der; ~-driver *n.* Schraubenzieher, *der;* ~-top *see* ~-cap

screwy ['skruːɪ] *adj. (sl.)* spinnig *(ugs.)*

scribble ['skrɪbl] 1. *v.t.* hinkritzeln. 2. *v.i.* kritzeln. 3. *n.* Gekritzel, *das*

script [skrɪpt] *n.* a) *(handwriting)* Handschrift, *die;* b) *(of play)* Regiebuch, *das; (of film)* [Dreh]buch, *das;* c) *(for broadcaster)* Manuskript, *das*

scripture ['skrɪptʃə(r)] *n.* a) [Holy] S~, the [Holy] S~s die [Heilige] Schrift; b) *(Sch.)* Religion, *die*

'script-writer *n. (of film)* Drehbuchautor, *der/*-autorin, *die*

scroll [skrəʊl] *n. (roll)* Rolle, *die*

scrounge ['skraʊndʒ] *(coll.)* 1. *v.t.* schnorren *(ugs.);* ~ off, from von). 2. *v.i.* schnorren *(ugs.)* (from bei). 'scrounger *n. (coll.)* Schnorrer, *der/* Schnorrerin, *die (ugs.)*

'scrub [skrʌb] 1. *v.t., -bb-:* a) schrubben *(ugs.);* scheuern; b) *(coll.: cancel)* zurücknehmen ⟨*Befehl*⟩; sausenlassen *(ugs.)* ⟨*Plan*⟩. 2. *v.i., -bb-* schrubben *(ugs.);* scheuern. 3. *n.* give sth. a ~: etw. schrubben *(ugs.) od.* scheuern

²scrub *n. (brushwood)* Buschwerk, *das; (area)* Buschland, *das*

'scruff [skrʌf] *n.* by the ~ of the neck beim Genick

²scruff *n. (Brit. coll.) (man)* vergammelter Typ *(ugs.); (woman, girl)* Schlampe, *die.* 'scruffy *adj.* vergammelt *(ugs.)*

scrum [skrʌm] *n.* Gedränge, *das*

scruple ['skruːpl] *n.* Skrupel, *der;* have no ~s about doing sth. keine Skrupel haben, etw. zu tun

scrupulous ['skruːpjʊləs] *adj.* gewissenhaft ⟨*Person*⟩; unbedingt ⟨*Ehrlichkeit*⟩; peinlich ⟨*Sorgfalt*⟩

scrutinize ['skruːtɪnaɪz] *v.t.* [genau] untersuchen ⟨*Forschungs]gegenstand*⟩; [über]prüfen ⟨*Rechnung, Paß, Fahrkarte*⟩; mustern ⟨*Person*⟩

scrutiny ['skruːtɪnɪ] *n.* a) *(critical gaze)* musternder Blick; b) *(examination) (of recruit)* Musterung, *die; (of bill, passport, ticket)* [Über]prüfung, *die*

scuff [skʌf] 1. *v.t.* streifen; verschrammen ⟨*Schuhe, Fußboden*⟩. 2. *n.* Schramme, *die*

scuffle ['skʌfl] 1. *n.* Handgreiflichkeiten *Pl.* 2. *v.i.* handgreiflich werden (with gegen)

scullery ['skʌlərɪ] *n.* Spülküche, *die*

sculptor ['skʌlptə(r)] *n.* Bildhauer, *der/*-hauerin, *die*

sculpture ['skʌlptʃə(r)] *n.* a) *(art)*

Bildhauerei, *die;* **b)** *(piece of work)* Skulptur, *die;* Plastik, *die; (pieces collectively)* Skulpturen

scum [skʌm] *n.* **a)** Schmutzschicht, *die; (film)* Schmutzfilm, *der;* **b)** *(fig. derog.)* Abschaum, *der*

scurry ['skʌrɪ] *v.i.* huschen

¹scuttle ['skʌtl] *n.* Kohlenfüller, *der*

²scuttle *(Naut.) v.t.* versenken

³scuttle *v.i.* rennen; flitzen *(ugs.);* ⟨*Maus, Krabbe:*⟩ huschen

scythe [saɪð] *n.* Sense, *die*

SE *abbr. south-east* SO

sea [siː] *n.* **a)** Meer, *das; the* ~: das Meer; die See; **by** ~: mit dem Schiff; **by the** ~: am Meer; **at** ~: auf See *(Dat.);* **be all at** ~ *(fig.)* nicht mehr weiter wissen; **put [out] to** ~: in See *(Akk.)* gehen; **b)** *(specific tract of water)* Meer, *das*

sea: ~ **'air** *n.* Seeluft, *die;* ~**'bed** *n.* Meeresboden, *der;* ~**gull** *n.* [See]möwe, *die*

¹seal [siːl] *n. (Zool.)* Robbe, *die;* [common] ~: [Gemeiner] Seehund

²seal 1. *n. (wax etc., stamp, impression)* Siegel, *das.* **2.** *v.t.* **a)** *(stamp, affix* ~ *to)* siegeln ⟨*Dokument*⟩; *(fasten with* ~*)* verplomben ⟨*Tür, Stromzähler:*⟩ **b)** *(close securely)* abdichten ⟨*Behälter, Rohr usw.*⟩; zukleben ⟨*Umschlag, Paket*⟩; **c)** *(stop up)* verschließen; abdichten ⟨*Leck*⟩; verschmieren ⟨*Riß*⟩. **seal 'off** *v.t.* abriegeln

sea: ~**legs** *n. pl.* Seebeine *Pl. (Seemannsspr.);* **get** *or* **find one's** ~**legs** sich *(Dat.)* Seebeine wachsen lassen; ~**level** *n.* Meeresspiegel, *der*

'sealing-wax *n.* Siegellack, *der*

'sea-lion *n.* Seelöwe, *der*

seam [siːm] *n.* **a)** Naht, *die;* **b)** *(of coal)* Flöz, *das*

seaman ['siːmən] *n., pl.* **seamen** ['siː-mən] Matrose, *der*

'sea mist *n.* Küstennebel, *der*

'seamless *adj.* nahtlos

'seamy *adj.* **the** ~ **side** [of life etc.] *(fig.)* die Schattenseite[n] [des Lebens *usw.*]

seance ['seɪɒns], **séance** ['seɪãs] *n.* Séance, *die*

sea: ~**plane** *n.* Wasserflugzeug, *das;* ~**port** *n.* Seehafen, *der*

sear ['sɪə(r)] *v.t.* versengen

search [sɜːtʃ] **1.** *v.t.* durchsuchen (for nach); absuchen ⟨*Gebiet, Fläche*⟩ (for nach); *(fig.: probe)* erforschen ⟨*Herz, Gewissen*⟩; suchen in (+ *Dat.*) ⟨*Gedächtnis*⟩ (for nach). **2.** *v.i.* suchen (for nach). **3.** *n.* Suche, *die* (for nach);

(of building, room, etc.) Durchsuchung, *die;* **in** ~ **of** sb./sth. auf der Suche nach jmdm./etw. **'searching** *adj.* prüfend, forschend ⟨*Blick*⟩; bohrend ⟨*Frage*⟩

search: ~**light** *n.* Suchscheinwerfer, *der;* ~**party** *n.* Suchtrupp, *der;* ~**warrant** *n.* Durchsuchungsbefehl, *der*

sea: ~**shore** *n.* [Meeres]küste, *die; (beach)* Strand, *der;* ~**sick** *adj.* seekrank; ~**sickness** *n.* Seekrankheit, *die;* ~**side** *n.* [Meeres]küste, *die;* **by/to/at the** ~**side** am/ans/am Meer; ~**side town** Seestadt, *die*

season ['siːzn] **1.** *n.* **a)** Jahreszeit, *die; nesting* ~: Nistzeit, *die;* **b)** *(period of social activity)* [opera/football] ~: [Opern-/Fußball]saison, *die;* **holiday** *or (Amer.)* **vacation** ~: Urlaubszeit, *die; tourist* ~: Reisezeit, *die;* **c)** *raspberries are* **in/out of** *or* **not in** ~: jetzt ist die/nicht die Saison *od.* Zeit für Himbeeren; **be in** ~ *(on heat)* brünstig sein; **d)** *see* **season-ticket. 2.** *v.t.* würzen ⟨*Fleisch, Rede*⟩. **seasonable** ['siːzənəbl] *adj.* der Jahreszeit gemäß. **'seasoned** *adj. (fig.)* erfahren. **'seasoning** *n.* Gewürze *Pl.;* Würze, *die.* **'season-ticket** *n.* Dauerkarte, *die*

seat [siːt] **1.** *n.* **a)** Sitzgelegenheit, *die; (in vehicle, cinema, etc.)* Sitz, *der; (of toilet)* [Klosett]brille, *die (ugs.);* **b)** *(place)* Platz, *der; (in vehicle)* [Sitz]platz, *der;* **have** *or* **take a** ~: sich [hin]setzen; **c)** *(part of chair)* Sitzfläche, *die;* **d)** *(buttocks)* Gesäß, *das; (part of clothing)* Gesäßpartie, *die; (of trousers)* Sitz, *der.* **2.** *v.t.* **a)** *(cause to sit)* setzen ⟨*Platzanweiser:*⟩ einen Platz anweisen (+ *Dat.*); ~ **oneself** sich setzen; **b)** *(have* ~*s for)* Sitzplätze bieten (+ *Dat.*); ~ **500 people** 500 Sitzplätze haben. **'seat-belt** *n.* Sicherheitsgurt, *der.* **'seated** *adj.* sitzend; **remain** ~: sitzen bleiben. **'seating** *n.* Sitzplätze *Pl.; attrib.* Sitz⟨*ordnung, -plan*⟩

sea: ~**urchin** *n.* Seeigel, *der;* ~**wall** *n.* Strandmauer, *die;* ~**water** *n.* Meerwasser, *das;* ~**weed** *n.* [See]tang, *der;* ~**worthy** *adj.* seetüchtig

secluded [sɪ'kluːdɪd] *adj. (hidden)* versteckt; *(isolated)* abgelegen; zurückgezogen ⟨*Leben*⟩. **seclusion** [sɪ'kluːʒn] *n. (remoteness)* Abgelegenheit, *die; (privacy)* Zurückgezogenheit, *die*

'second ['sekənd] **1.** *adj.* zweit...; ~

largest/highest *etc.* zweitgrößt.../ -höchst... *usw.;* **come/be ~:** zweiter/ zweite werden/sein. **2.** *n.* **a)** *(unit of time or angle)* Sekunde, *die;* **b)** *(coll.: moment)* Sekunde, *die (ugs.);* **wait a few ~s** einen Moment warten; **in a ~** *(immediately)* sofort *(ugs.);* *(very quickly)* im Nu *(ugs.);* **just a ~!** *(coll.)* einen Moment!; **c) the ~** *(in sequence)* der/die/das Zweite; **d)** *in pl. (helping of food)* zweite Portion. **3.** *v.t. (support)* unterstützen

²second [sɪˈkɒnd] *v.t. (transfer)* vor- übergehend versetzen

secondary [ˈsekəndərɪ] *adj. (of less importance)* zweitrangig; *Neben- ⟨sache⟩;* **be ~ to sth.** einer Sache *(Dat.)* untergeordnet sein. **'secondary school** *n.* höhere Schule

second: ~-best 1. [ˈ---] *adj.* zweit- best...; **2.** [-ˈ-ˈ-] *n.* Zweitbeste, *der/die/ das;* **~-class 1.** [ˈ---] *adj. (of lower class)* zweiter Klasse *nachgestellt;* Zweite[r]-Klasse-⟨*Fahrkarte, Abteil, Post, Brief usw.⟩;* **~-class stamp** Brief- marke für einen *Zweiter-Klasse-Brief;* **2.** [-ˈ-ˈ-] *adv.* zweiter Klasse *⟨fahren⟩;* **~ 'floor** *see* **floor 1 b;** **~-hand** *n.* Sekun- denzeiger, *der;* **~-hand 1.** [ˈ---] *adj.* **a)** gebraucht ⟨*Kleidung, Auto usw.⟩;* anti- quarisch ⟨*Buch⟩;* **b)** *(selling used goods)* Gebrauchtwaren-; Second- hand⟨*laden⟩;* **c)** ⟨*Nachrichten, Bericht⟩* aus zweiter Hand; **2.** [-ˈ-ˈ-] *adv.* aus zweiter Hand

'secondly *adv.* zweitens

second: ~ name *n.* Nachname, *der;* **~-'rate** *adj.* zweitklassig; **~ 'thoughts** *n. pl.* **have ~ thoughts** es sich *(Dat.)* anders überlegen (**about** mit); **we've had ~ thoughts about buy- ing it** wir wollen es nun doch nicht kaufen; **but on ~ thoughts ...:** wenn ich's mir [noch mal] überlege, ...

secrecy [ˈsiːkrɪsɪ] *n.* **a)** *(keeping of se- cret)* Geheimhaltung, *die;* **b)** *(secret- iveness)* Heimlichtuerei, *die;* **c) in ~:** im geheimen

secret [ˈsiːkrɪt] **1.** *adj.* geheim; Ge- heim⟨*fach, -tür, -abkommen, -kode⟩;* heimlich ⟨*Trinker, Liebhaber⟩;* **keep sth. ~:** etw. geheimhalten (**from** vor + *Dat.*). **2.** *n.* **a)** Geheimnis, *das;* **make no ~ of sth.** kein Geheimnis aus etw. machen; *(fig.)* keinen Hehl aus etw. machen; **keep ~s/ a ~:** schwei- gen *(fig.);* **b) in ~:** im geheimen. **se- cret 'agent** *n.* Geheimagent, *der/* -agentin, *die*

secretarial [sekrəˈteərɪəl] *adj.* Sekre- tärinnen⟨*kursus, -tätigkeit⟩;* ⟨*Arbeit⟩* als Sekretärin

secretary [ˈsekrətərɪ] *n.* Sekretär, *der/*Sekretärin, *die*

secretive [ˈsiːkrɪtɪv] *adj.* verschlossen ⟨*Person⟩:* **be ~:** geheimnisvoll tun (**about** mit)

'secretly *adv.* heimlich; insgeheim ⟨*etw. glauben⟩*

sect [sekt] *n.* Sekte, *die*

section [ˈsekʃn] *n.* **a)** *(part cut off)* Ab- schnitt, *der;* Stück, *das; (part of divided whole)* Teil, *der;* **b)** *(of firm)* Abteilung, *die; (of organization)* Sekti- on, *die;* **c)** *(of chapter, book)* Ab- schnitt, *der; (of statute etc.)* Para- graph, *der*

sector [ˈsektə(r)] *n.* Sektor, *der*

secular [ˈsekjʊlə(r)] *adj.* weltlich

secure [sɪˈkjʊə(r)] **1.** *adj.* sicher; *(firmly fastened)* fest; **~ against burg- lars** gegen Einbruch geschützt. **2.** *v.t.* **a)** sichern (**for** *Dat.*); beschaffen ⟨*Auf- trag⟩* (**for** *Dat.*); *(for oneself)* sich *(Dat.)* sichern; **b)** *(fasten)* sichern. **se- 'curely** *adv. (firmly)* fest ⟨*verriegeln, zumachen⟩;* sicher ⟨*befestigen, unter- gebracht sein⟩.* **security** [sɪˈkjʊərɪtɪ] *n.* **a)** Sicherheit, *die;* **~ [measures]** Si- cherheitsmaßnahmen, **b)** *(Finance)* securities *pl.* Wertpapiere

security: ~ forces *n. pl.* Sicherheits- kräfte *Pl.;* **~ guard** *n.* Wächter, *der/* Wächterin, *die;* **~ risk** *n.* Sicherheits- risiko, *das*

sedan [sɪˈdæn] *n. (Amer. Motor Veh.)* Limousine, *die*

sedate [sɪˈdeɪt] **1.** *adj.* bedächtig; ge- setzt ⟨*alte Dame⟩;* gemächlich ⟨*Tem- po, Leben⟩.* **2.** *v.t.* sedieren **sedation** [sɪˈdeɪʃn] *n.* Sedation, *die;* **be under ~:** sediert sein. **sedative** [ˈsedətɪv] **1.** *n.* Beruhigungsmittel, *das.* **2.** *adj.* seda- tiv

sedentary [ˈsedəntərɪ] *adj.* sitzend

sediment [ˈsedɪmənt] *n.* Ablagerung, *die; (of tea, coffee, etc.)* Bodensatz, *der*

seduce [sɪˈdjuːs] *v.t.* verführen. **se- duction** [sɪˈdʌkʃn] *n.* Verführung, *die.* **seductive** [sɪˈdʌktɪv] *adj.* ver- führerisch; verlockend ⟨*Angebot⟩*

see [siː] **1.** *v.t.,* **saw** [sɔː], **seen** [siːn] **a)** sehen; **I can ~ it's hard for you** ich ver- stehe, daß es nicht leicht für dich ist; **I ~ what you mean** ich verstehe[, was du meinst]; **b)** *(meet [with])* sehen; tref- fen; *(meet socially)* sich treffen mit; **I'll ~ you there/at five** wir sehen uns dort/um fünf; ~ you!, [I'll] be ~ing you! *(coll.)* bis bald! *(ugs.)*; c) *(speak to)* sprechen ⟨Person⟩ *(about wegen)*; *(visit)* gehen zu ⟨Arzt, Anwalt usw.⟩; *(receive)* empfangen; d) *(find out)* feststellen; *(by looking)* nachsehen; e) *(make sure)* ~ [that]...: darauf achten, daß...; f) *(imagine)* sich *(Dat.)* vorstellen; g) *(escort)* begleiten. **2.** *v. i.,* saw, seen **a)** sehen; **b)** *(make sure)* nachsehen; **c)** I ~ : ich verstehe; you ~ : weißt du/wißt ihr/wissen Sie. **'see about** *v. t.* sich kümmern um. **see 'off** *v. t.* **a)** *(say goodbye to)* verabschieden; **b)** *(chase away)* vertreiben. **see 'out** *v. t.* **a)** *(escort)* hinausbegleiten (of aus); **b)** ~ **oneself out** allein hinausfinden. **see through** *v. t.* **a)** [--] hindurchsehen durch; *(fig.)* durchschauen; **b)** [--] *(not abandon)* zu Ende bringen. **'see to** *v. t.* sich kümmern um

seed [siːd] **1.** *n.* **a)** Samen, der; *(of grape etc.)* Kern, der; **b)** *no pl., no indef. art.* ⟨~s collectively⟩ Samen[körner] *Pl.;* *(as collected for sowing)* Saatgut, das; *(for birds)* Körner *Pl.;* **go or run to ~**: Samen bilden; *(fig.)* herunterkommen *(ugs.);* **c)** *(Sport)* gesetzter Spieler/gesetzte Spielerin. **2.** *v. t.* **a)** *(place ~s in)* besäen; **b)** *(Sport)* setzen ⟨Spieler⟩; **be ~ed number one** als Nummer eins gesetzt werden/sein. **'seedless** *adj.* kernlos

seedling ['siːdlɪŋ] *n.* Sämling, der

'seedy *adj.* **a)** *(coll.: unwell)* **feel ~**: sich [leicht] angeschlagen fühlen; **b)** *(shabby)* schäbig, *(ugs.)* vergammelt ⟨Aussehen⟩; heruntergekommen ⟨Stadtteil⟩; **c)** *(disreputable)* zweifelhaft

'seeing *conj.* ~ [that]...: in Anbetracht dessen, daß ...

seek [siːk] *v. t.,* sought [sɔːt] suchen; anstreben ⟨Posten, Amt⟩; sich bemühen um ⟨Anerkennung, Interview, Einstellung⟩; *(try to reach)* aufsuchen

seem [siːm] *v. i.* scheinen; **you ~ tired** du wirkst müde; **she ~ s nice** sie scheint nett zu sein. **'seeming** *adj.* scheinbar. **'seemingly** *adv.* **a)** *(evidently)* offensichtlich; **b)** *(to outward appearance)* scheinbar

seemly ['siːmlɪ] *adj.* schicklich

seen *see* **see**

seep [siːp] *v. i.* ~ [away] [ab]sickern

'see-saw *n.* Wippe, *die*

seethe [siːð] *v. i.* **a)** ~ [with anger/inwardly] vor Wut/innerlich schäumen; **b)** ⟨Straßen usw.:⟩ wimmeln (**with** von)

'see-through *adj.* durchsichtig

segment ['segmənt] *n.* *(of orange, pineapple, etc.)* Scheibe, *die*

segregate ['segrɪgeɪt] *v. t.* trennen; *(racially)* absondern. **segregation** [segrɪ'geɪʃn] *n.* Trennung, *die;* [racial] ~: Rassentrennung, *die*

seismic ['saɪzmɪk] *adj.* seismisch

seize [siːz] **1.** *v. t.* **a)** ergreifen; ~ **power** die Macht ergreifen; ~ **sb. by the arm/collar** jmdn. am Arm/Kragen packen; ~ **the opportunity** [to do sth.] die Gelegenheit ergreifen [und etw. tun]; ~ **any/a** *or* **the chance** [to do sth.] jede/die Gelegenheit nutzen[, um etw. zu tun]; **be ~d with remorse/panic** vor Gewissensbissen geplagt/von Panik ergriffen werden; **b)** *(capture)* gefangennehmen ⟨Person⟩; kapern ⟨Schiff⟩; mit Gewalt übernehmen ⟨Flugzeug, Gebäude⟩; einnehmen ⟨Festung, Brücke⟩; **c)** *(confiscate)* beschlagnahmen. **2.** *v. i. see* ~ **up. 'seize on** *v. t.* sich *(Dat.)* vornehmen ⟨Einzelheit, Aspekt, Schwachpunkt⟩; aufgreifen ⟨Idee, Vorschlag⟩. **seize 'up** *v. i.* sich festfressen

seizure ['siːʒə(r)] *n.* **a)** *see* **seize** 1 b, c: Gefangennahme, *die;* Kapern, *das;* Übernahme, *die;* Einnahme, *die;* Beschlagnahme, *die;* **b)** *(Med.)* Anfall, *der*

seldom ['seldəm] *adv.* selten

select [sɪ'lekt] **1.** *adj.* ausgewählt. **2.** *v. t.* auswählen. **selection** [sɪ'lekʃn] *n.* **a)** *(what is selected [from])* Auswahl, *die* (**of** an + *Dat.,* **from** aus); **b)** *(act of choosing)* [Aus]wahl, *die.* **selective** [sɪ'lektɪv] *adj.* *(using selection)* selektiv; *(careful in one's choice)* wählerisch

self [self] *n., pl.* selves [selvz] Selbst, *das (geh.);* Ich, *das*

self- *pref.* selbst-/Selbst-

self: **~-ad'dressed** *adj.* **~-addressed envelope** adressierter Rückumschlag; **~-ad'hesive** *adj.* selbstklebend; **~-ap'pointed** *adj.* selbsternannt; **~-as'surance** *n.* Selbstsicherheit, *die;* **~-as'sured** *adj.* selbstsicher; **~-'catering 1.** *adj.* mit Selbstversorgung *nachgestellt;* **2.** *n.* Selbstversorgung, *die;* **~-'centred** *adj.* egozentrisch; **~-'confidence** *n.* Selbstbewußtsein, *das;* **~-'confident** *adj.* selbstbewußt; **~-'conscious** *adj.* unsicher; **~-'consciousness** *n.* Unsicherheit, *die;* **~-con'tained** *adj.* abgeschlossen ⟨Wohnung⟩; **~-con'trol** *n.* Selbstbeherrschung, *die;* **~-**

con'trolled *adj.* voller Selbstbeherrschung *nachgestellt;* ~de'ception *n.* Selbsttäuschung, *die;* ~de'fence *n.* Notwehr, *die;* in ~defence aus Notwehr; ~drive *adj.* ~drive hire |company| Autovermietung, *die;* ~drive vehicle Mietwagen, *der;* ~employed *adj.* selbständig; ~'evident *adj.* offenkundig; ~ex'planatory *adj.* ohne weiteres verständlich; be ~explanatory für sich selbst sprechen; ~'help *n.* Selbsthilfe, *die;* ~im'portant *adj.* eingebildet; ~in'dulgent *adj.* maßlos; ~'interest *n.* Eigeninteresse, *das*

'selfish *adj.,* 'selfishly *adv.* selbstsüchtig. 'selfishness *n.* Selbstsucht, *die*

self: ~'pity *n.* Selbstmitleid, *das;* ~'portrait *n.* Selbstporträt, *das;* ~pos'sessed *adj.* selbstbeherrscht; ~'raising flour *n. (Brit.)* mit Backpulver versetztes Mehl; ~re'spect *n.* Selbstachtung, *die;* ~re'specting *adj.* no ~respecting person ...: niemand, der etwas auf sich hält; ~'righteous *adj.* selbstgerecht; ~'sacrifice *n.* Selbstaufopferung, *die;* ~'satisfied *adj.* selbstzufrieden; *(smug)* selbstgefällig; ~'service *n.* Selbstbedienung, *die; attrib.* Selbstbedienungs-; ~'sufficient *adj.* unabhängig; selbständig ⟨*Person⟩;* ~'willed *adj.* eigenwillig

sell [sel] 1. *v. t.,* sold [sǝʊld] ~ sth. to sb., ~ sb. sth. jmdm. etw. verkaufen; be sold out ausverkauft sein. 2. *v. i.,* sold sich verkaufen; ⟨*Person:⟩* verkaufen. sell 'off *v. t.* verkaufen. sell 'out 1. *v. t.* a) ausverkaufen; b) *(coll.: betray)* verpfeifen *(ugs.).* 2. *v. i.* we have or are sold out wir sind ausverkauft

'sell-by date *n.* ≈ Mindesthaltbarkeitsdatum, *das*

'seller *n.* a) Verkäufer, *der/*Verkäuferin, *die;* b) *(product)* be a good/slow ~: sich gut/nur langsam verkaufen

Sellotape, (P) ['selǝteɪp] *n.* ≈ Tesafilm, *der* ⓦ

'sellotape *v. t.* mit Tesafilm kleben

'sell-out *n.* be a ~: ausverkauft sein; *(coll.: betrayal)* Verrat sein

selves *pl. of* self

semaphore ['semǝfɔ:(r)] 1. *n. (system)* Winken, *das.* 2. *v. i.* ~ to sb. jmdm. im Winksignal übermitteln

semblance ['semblǝns] *n.* Anschein, *der*

semen ['si:mǝn] *n.* Samen, *der*

semi- [semɪ] *pref.* halb-/Halb-

semi: ~breve *n. (Brit. Mus.)* ganze Note; ~circle *n.* Halbkreis, *der;* ~'circular *adj.* halbkreisförmig; ~'colon *n.* Semikolon, *das;* ~de'tached *adj. & n.* ~detached |house| Doppelhaushälfte, *die;* ~'final *n.* Halbfinale, *das*

seminar ['semɪnɑ:(r)] *n.* Seminar, *das*

'semitone *n. (Mus.)* Halbton, *der*

semolina [semǝ'li:nǝ] *n.* Grieß, *der*

senate ['senǝt] *n.* Senat, *der.* senator ['senǝtǝ(r)] *n.* Senator, *der*

send [send] *v. t.,* sent [sent] schicken; senden *(geh.).* send a'way 1. *v. t.* wegschicken. 2. *v. i.* ~ away |to sb.| for sth. etw. [bei jmdm.] anfordern. send 'back *v. t.* zurückschicken. 'send for *v. t.* a) *(tell to come)* holen lassen; rufen ⟨*Polizei, Arzt usw.⟩;* b) *(order from elsewhere)* anfordern. send 'off *v. t.* 1. a) *(dispatch)* abschicken ⟨*Sache⟩;* b) *(Sport)* vom Platz stellen. 2. *v. i. see* send away 2. send 'up *v. t. (Brit. coll.: parody)* parodieren

'sender *n.* Absender, *der*

'send-off *n.* Verabschiedung, *die*

senile ['si:naɪl] *adj.* senil. senility [sɪ'nɪlɪtɪ] *n.* Senilität, *die*

senior ['si:nɪǝ(r)] 1. *adj.* a) *(older)* älter; b) höher ⟨*Rang, Beamter, Stellung⟩;* leitend ⟨*Angestellter, Stellung⟩.* 2. *n. (older)* Ältere, *der/die; (of higher rank)* Vorgesetzte, *der/die.* senior 'citizen *n.* Senior, *der/*Seniorin, *die.* seniority [si:nɪ'ɒrɪtɪ] *n. (greater length of service)* höheres Dienstalter; *(higher rank)* höherer Rang

sensation [sen'seɪʃn] *n.* a) *(feeling)* Gefühl, *das;* b) *(person, event, etc.)* Sensation, *die.* sensational [sen'seɪʃǝnl] *adj.* sensationell

sense [sens] 1. *n.* a) *(faculty)* Sinn, *der;* ~ of smell/touch/taste Geruchs-/Tast-/Geschmackssinn; come to one's ~s das Bewußtsein wiedererlangen; b) *in pl. (normal state of mind)* Verstand, *der;* have taken leave of one's ~s den Verstand verloren haben; c) *(consciousness)* Gefühl, *das;* ~ of responsibility/guilt Verantwortungs-/Schuldgefühl, *das;* d) *(practical wisdom)* Verstand, *der;* sound or good ~: [gesunder Menschen]verstand; not have the ~ to do sth. nicht so schlau sein, etw. zu tun; there is no ~ in doing that es hat keinen Sinn, das zu tun; e) *(meaning)* Sinn, *der; (of word)* Bedeutung, *die;* make ~: einen

Sinn ergeben; **in a** or **one ~**: in gewisser Hinsicht; **make ~ of** etw. verstehen. **2.** v. t. spüren. **'senseless** adj. **a)** (unconscious) bewußtlos; **b)** (purposeless) sinnlos

sensible ['sensɪbl] adj. **a)** (reasonable) vernünftig; **b)** (practical) zweckmäßig

sensibly ['sensɪblɪ] adv. **a)** (reasonably) vernünftig; **b)** (practically) zweckmäßig

sensitive ['sensɪtɪv] adj. empfindlich; **be ~ to sth.** empfindlich auf etw. (Akk.) reagieren. **sensitivity** [sensɪ'tɪvɪtɪ] n. Empfindlichkeit, die

sensory ['sensərɪ] adj. Sinnes-

sensual ['sensjʊəl] adj. sinnlich

sensuous ['sensjʊəs] adj. sinnlich

sent see **send**

sentence ['sentəns] **1.** n. **a)** (Law) [Straf]urteil, das; **b)** (Ling.) Satz, der. **2.** v. t. verurteilen (**to** zu)

sentiment ['sentɪmənt] n. **a)** Gefühl, das; **b)** (sentimentality) Sentimentalität, die; **c)** (opinion) Gedanke, der. **sentimental** [sentɪ'mentl] adj. sentimental. **sentimentality** [sentɪmen-'tælɪtɪ] n. Sentimentalität, die

sentry ['sentrɪ] n. Wache, die

separable ['sepərəbl] adj. trennbar

separate 1. ['sepərət] adj. verschieden ⟨Fragen, Probleme, Gelegenheiten⟩; gesondert ⟨Teil⟩; separat ⟨Eingang, Toilette, Blatt Papier, Abteil⟩; (one's own, individual) eigen ⟨Zimmer, Identität, Organisation⟩; **keep two things ~**: zwei Dinge auseinanderhalten. **2.** ['sepəreɪt] v. t. trennen; **they are ~d** (no longer live together) sie leben getrennt. **3.** v. i. **a)** (disperse) sich trennen; **b)** ⟨Ehepaar:⟩ sich trennen. **separately** ['sepərətlɪ] adv. getrennt. **separation** [sepə'reɪʃn] n. Trennung, die

Sept. abbr. September Sept.

September [sep'tembə(r)] n. September, der; see also **August**

septic ['septɪk] adj. septisch; **go ~**: eitrig werden

sequel ['siːkwl] n. **a)** (consequence, result) Folge, die (**to** von); **b)** (continuation) Fortsetzung, die

sequence ['siːkwəns] n. **a)** Reihenfolge, die; **b)** (part of film) Sequenz, die

sequin ['siːkwɪn] n. Paillette, die

serenade [serə'neɪd] **1.** n. Ständchen, das. **2.** v. t. **~ sb.** jmdm. ein Ständchen bringen

serene [sɪ'riːn] adj. gelassen. **serenity** [sɪ'renɪtɪ] n. Gelassenheit, die

sergeant ['sɑːdʒənt] n. (Mil.) Unterof-

fizier, der; (police officer) ≈ Polizeimeister, der. **sergeant-'major** n. ≈ [Ober]stabsfeldwebel, der

serial ['sɪərɪəl] n. Fortsetzungsgeschichte, die; (Radio, Telev.) Serie, die. **serialize** ['sɪərɪəlaɪz] v. t. in Fortsetzungen veröffentlichen; (Radio, Telev.) in Fortsetzungen senden

series ['sɪəriːz, 'sɪərɪz] n., pl. same **a)** (sequence) Reihe, die; (of events, misfortunes) Folge, die; **b)** (set of successive issues) Serie, die; **radio/TV ~**: Hörfunkreihe/Fernsehserie, die; **c)** (set of books) Reihe, die

serious ['sɪərɪəs] adj. **a)** (earnest) ernst; **b)** (important, grave) ernst ⟨Angelegenheit, Lage, Problem, Zustand⟩; ernsthaft ⟨Frage, Einwand, Kandidat⟩; schwer ⟨Krankheit, Unfall, Fehler, Niederlage⟩; ernstzunehmend ⟨Rivale⟩; ernstlich ⟨Gefahr, Bedrohung⟩; bedenklich ⟨Mangel⟩. **'seriously** adv. **a)** (earnestly) ernst; **take sth./sb. ~**: etw./jmdn. ernst nehmen; **b)** (severely) ernstlich; schwer ⟨verletzt⟩. **'seriousness** n. Ernst, der; **in all ~**: ganz im Ernst

sermon ['sɜːmən] n. Predigt, die

serrated [se'reɪtɪd] adj. gezackt; **~ knife** Sägemesser, das

serum ['sɪərəm] n. Serum, das

servant ['sɜːvənt] n. Diener, der/Dienerin, die

serve [sɜːv] **1.** v. t. **a)** (work for) dienen (+ Dat.); **b)** (be useful to) dienlich sein (+ Dat.); **c)** (meet needs of) nutzen (+ Dat.); **~ a/no purpose** einen Zweck erfüllen/keinen Zweck haben; **d)** durchlaufen ⟨Lehre⟩; verbüßen ⟨Haftstrafe⟩; **e)** (dish up) servieren; (pour out) einschenken (**to** Dat.); **f)** **~[s]** or **it ~s him right!** (coll.) [das] geschieht ihm recht! **2.** v. i. **a)** dienen; **~ as chairman** das Amt des Vorsitzenden innehaben; **~ as a Member of Parliament** Mitglied des Parlaments sein; **~ on a jury** Geschworener/Geschworene sein; **b)** (be of use) **~ to do sth.** dazu dienen, etw. zu tun; **~ to show sth.** etw. zeigen; **~ for** or **as** dienen als; **c)** (Sport) aufschlagen. **3.** n. see **service 1 g. serve 'up** v. t. **a)** servieren; **b)** (offer for consideration) auftischen (ugs.)

service ['sɜːvɪs] **1.** n. **a)** Dienst, der; **do sb. a ~**: jmdm. einen guten Dienst erweisen; **b)** (Eccl.) Gottesdienst, der; **c)** (attending to customer) Service, der; (in shop, garage, etc.) Bedienung, die,

d) *(system of transport)* Verbindung, *die;* **there is no |bus| ~ on Sundays** Sonntags verkehren keine Busse; **e)** *(provision of maintenance)* |**after-sale**| **~:** Kundendienst, *der;* **take one's car in for a ~:** sein Auto zur Inspektion bringen; **f)** *(operation)* Betrieb, *der;* **out of ~:** außer Betrieb; **g)** *(Sport)* Aufschlag, *der;* **whose ~ is it?** wer hat Aufschlag?; **h)** *(crockery set)* Service, *das;* **i)** *(assistance)* **can I be of ~ |to you|?** kann ich Ihnen behilflich sein?; **I'm at your ~:** ich stehe zu Ihren Diensten; **j)** *(Mil.)* **the |armed or fighting|** ~s die Streitkräfte; **in the ~** beim Militär; **k)** |**motorway**| ~s [Autobahn]-raststätte, *die*. **2.** *v. t.* warten ⟨*Wagen, Waschmaschine, Heizung*⟩. **serviceable** ['sɜːvɪsəbl] *adj.* **a)** *(useful)* nützlich; **b)** *(durable)* haltbar

service: ~ area *n.* Raststätte, *die;* **~ charge** *n.* Bedienungsgeld, *das;* **~ industry** *n.* Dienstleistungsbetrieb, *der;* **~man** *n.* ['sɜːvɪsmən], *pl.* **~men** ['sɜːvɪsmən] Militärangehörige, *der;* **~ station** *n.* Tankstelle, *die*

serviette [sɜːvɪ'et] *n.* *(Brit.)* Serviette, *die*

servile ['sɜːvaɪl] *adj.* unterwürfig

serving ['sɜːvɪŋ] *n.* Portion, *die*. **'serving spoon** *n.* Vorlegelöffel, *der*

session ['seʃn] *n.* *(meeting)* Sitzung, *die;* **be in ~:** tagen

set [set] **1.** *v. t.,* **-tt-, set a)** *(put) (horizontally)* legen; *(vertically)* stellen; **~ sb. ashore** jmdn. an Land setzen; **~ sth./things right or in order** etw./die Dinge in Ordnung bringen; **b)** *(apply)* setzen; **~ a match to sth.** ein Streichholz an etw. ⟨*Akk.*⟩ halten; *see also* **fire 1 a; 'light 1 d; c)** *(adjust)* einstellen **(at** auf + *Akk.*⟩; aufstellen ⟨*Falle*⟩; stellen ⟨*Uhr*⟩; **~ the alarm for 5.30 a.m.** den Wecker auf 5.30 Uhr stellen; **d)** **be ~** ⟨*Buch, Film:*⟩ spielen; **e)** *(specify)* festlegen ⟨*Bedingungen*⟩; festsetzen ⟨*Termin, Ort usw.*⟩ **(for** auf + *Akk.*⟩; **~ limits** Grenzen setzen; **f)** **~ sb. thinking that ...:** jmdn. auf den Gedanken bringen, daß ...; **g)** *(put forward)* stellen ⟨*Frage, Aufgabe*⟩; aufgeben ⟨*Hausaufgabe*⟩; aufstellen ⟨*Rekord*⟩; *(compose)* zusammenstellen ⟨*Rätsel, Fragen*⟩; **~ sb. an example, ~ an example to sb.** jmdm. ein Beispiel geben; **~ sb. a task/problem** jmdm. eine Aufgabe stellen/jmdn. vor ein Problem stellen; **~ |sb./oneself| a target** [jmdm./sich] ein Ziel setzen; **h)** *(Med.:*

put into place) [ein]richten; einrenken ⟨*verrenktes Gelenk*⟩; **i)** legen ⟨*Haare*⟩; **j)** decken ⟨*Tisch*⟩; auflegen ⟨*Gedeck*⟩; **k)** fassen ⟨*Edelstein*⟩. **2.** *v. i.,* **-tt-, set a)** *(solidify)* fest werden; **b)** *(go down)* ⟨*Sonne, Mond:*⟩ untergehen. **3.** *n.* **a)** *(group)* Satz, *der;* ~ |**of two**| Paar, *das;* **a ~ of chairs** eine Sitzgruppe; **b)** *(radio, TV)* Gerät, *das;* **c)** *(Tennis)* Satz, *der;* **d)** *(of hair)* Legen, *das;* **e)** *(Theatre: scenery)* Bühnenbild, *das;* *(area of performance) (of film)* Drehort, *der;* *(of play)* Bühne, *die;* **f)** *(of people)* Kreis, *der;* **g)** *(Math.)* Menge, *die*. **4.** *adj.* **a)** *(fixed)* ⟨*Absichten, Zielvorstellungen, Zeitpunkt*⟩; **be ~ in one's ways or habits** in seinen Gewohnheiten festgefahren sein; **~ meal or menu** Menü, *das;* **b)** vorgeschrieben ⟨*Buch, Lektüre*⟩; **c)** *(ready)* **be |all| ~ for sth.** zu etw. bereit sein; **be |all| ~ to do sth.** bereit sein, etw. zu tun; **d)** *(determined)* **be ~ on sth./doing sth.** zu etw. entschlossen sein/entschlossen sein, etw. zu tun. **'set about** *v. t.* **~ about sth.** sich an etw. ⟨*Akk.*⟩ machen; **~ about doing sth.** sich daranmachen, etw. zu tun. **set a'side** *v. t.* **a)** beiseite legen; **b)** aufheben ⟨*Urteil, Entscheidung*⟩. **set 'back** *v. t.* **a)** aufhalten ⟨*Entwicklung*⟩; zurückwerfen ⟨*Projekt, Programm*⟩; **b)** *(coll.: cost)* kosten ⟨*Person*⟩; **c)** *(place at a distance)* zurücksetzen. **set 'down** *v. t.* **a)** absetzen ⟨*Fahrgast*⟩; **b)** *(record)* niederschreiben. **set 'off 1.** *v. i.* *(begin journey)* aufbrechen; *(start to move)* loslaufen; ⟨*Fahrzeug:*⟩ losfahren. **2.** *v. t.* **a)** *(cause to explode)* explodieren lassen; abbrennen ⟨*Feuerwerk*⟩; **b)** auslösen ⟨*Reaktion, Alarmanlage*⟩. **set 'out 1.** *v. i.* **a)** *(begin journey)* aufbrechen **(for** nach/zu); **b)** ~ **out to do sth.** sich ⟨*Dat.*⟩ vornehmen, etw. zu tun. **2.** *v. t.* darlegen. **set 'up 1.** *v. t.* **a)** errichten ⟨*Straßensperre, Denkmal*⟩; aufbauen ⟨*Zelt, Klapptisch*⟩; **b)** *(establish)* gründen ⟨*Firma, Organisation*⟩; einrichten ⟨*Büro*⟩. **2.** *v. i.* **~ up in business** ein Geschäft aufmachen

'set-back *n.* Rückschlag, *der*

settee [se'tiː] *n.* Sofa, *das*

'setting *n.* **a)** *(Mus.)* Vertonung, *die;* **b)** *(surroundings)* Rahmen, *der;* *(of novel etc.)* Schauplatz, *der*

settle ['setl] **1.** *v. t.* **a)** *(horizontally)* [sorgfältig] legen; *(vertically)* [sorgfältig] stellen; *(at an angle)* [sorgfältig] lehnen; **b)** *(determine, resolve)* sich einigen auf ⟨*Preis*⟩; beilegen ⟨*Streit, Konflikt, Meinungsverschiedenheit*⟩; ausräumen ⟨*Zweifel*⟩; entscheiden ⟨*Frage, Spiel*⟩; **c)** bezahlen ⟨*Rechnung, Betrag*⟩; erfüllen ⟨*Forderung, Anspruch*⟩; ausgleichen ⟨*Konto*⟩. **2.** *v.i.* **a)** *(become established)* sich niederlassen; *(as colonist)* sich ansiedeln; **b)** *(pay)* abrechnen; **c)** *(in chair, in front of fire, etc.)* sich niederlassen; *(to work etc.)* sich konzentrieren **(to** auf + *Akk.*); *(into way of life, retirement, etc.)* sich gewöhnen **(into** an + *Akk.*); **d)** *(subside)* ⟨*Haus, Fundament, Boden:*⟩ sich senken; **e)** ⟨*Schnee:*⟩ liegenbleiben. **settle 'down 1.** *v.i.* **a)** *(make oneself comfortable)* sich niederlassen **(in** in + *Dat.*); **b)** *(in town or house)* heimisch werden. **2.** *v.t.* **a)** ~ **oneself down** sich [gemütlich] hinsetzen; **b)** *(calm down)* beruhigen. **'settle for** *v.t.* *(agree to)* sich zufriedengeben mit. **settle 'in** *v.i.* *(in new home)* sich einleben. **'settle on** *v.t.* *(decide on)* sich entscheiden für. **settle 'up** *v.i.* abrechnen; ~ **up with the waiter** beim Kellner bezahlen **'settlement** *n.* **a)** *(of argument, conflict, dispute, differences)* Beilegung, *die; (of question)* Klärung, *die; (of bill, account)* Bezahlung, *die; (of court case)* Vergleich, *der;* **b)** *(colony)* Siedlung, *die*

settler ['setlə(r)] *n.* Siedler, *der/*Siedlerin, *die*

set: ~**-to** *n., pl.* ~**-tos:** have a ~**-to** Streit haben; *(with fists)* sich prügeln; ~**-up** *n.* System, *das*

seven ['sevn] **1.** *adj.* sieben. **2.** *n.* Sieben, *die. See also* **eight**

seventeen [sevn'ti:n] **1.** *adj.* siebzehn. **2.** *n.* Siebzehn, *die. See also* **eight**.

seventeenth [sevn'ti:nθ] **1.** *adj.* siebzehnt... **2.** *n.* *(fraction)* Siebzehntel, *das. See also* **eighth**

seventh ['sevnθ] **1.** *adj.* sieb[en]t... **2.** *n. (in sequence)* sieb[en]te, *der/die/das; (in rank)* Sieb[en]te, *der/die/das; (fraction)* Sieb[en]tel, *das. See also* **eighth**

seventieth ['sevntɪɪθ] *adj.* siebzigst...

seventy ['sevntɪ] **1.** *adj.* siebzig. **2.** *n.* Siebzig, *die. See also* **eight; eighty 2**

sever ['sevə(r)] *v.t.* **a)** *(cut)* durchtrennen; *(fig.)* abbrechen ⟨*Beziehungen*⟩; **b)** *(separate)* abtrennen; *(with axe etc.)* abhacken

several ['sevrl] **1.** *adv.* mehrere; einige; ~ **times** mehrmals. **2.** *pron.* einige;

~ **of us** einige von uns; ~ **of the buildings** einige *od.* mehrere [der] Gebäude

severe [sɪ'vɪə(r)] *adj.,* ~**r** [sɪ'vɪərə(r)], ~**st** [sɪ'vɪərɪst] hart ⟨*Urteil, Strafe, Kritik, Test, Prüfung*⟩; streng ⟨*Frost, Stil, Schönheit*⟩; schwer ⟨*Dürre, Verlust, Behinderung, Verletzung, Krankheit*⟩; rauh ⟨*Wetter*⟩; heftig ⟨*Anfall, Schmerz*⟩; bedrohlich ⟨*Mangel, Knappheit*⟩; stark ⟨*Blutung*⟩. **se'verely** *adv.* hart; schwer ⟨*verletzt, behindert*⟩. **severity** [sɪ'verɪtɪ] *n.* Strenge, *die; (of drought, shortage)* großes Ausmaß; *(of criticism)* Schärfe, *die*

sew [səʊ] *v.t. & i., p.p.* **sewn** [səʊn] *or* **sewed** [səʊd] nähen. **sew 'on** *v.t.* annähen ⟨*Knopf*⟩; aufnähen ⟨*Abzeichen, Band*⟩. **sew 'up** *v.t.* nähen ⟨*Saum, Naht, Wunde*⟩

sewer ['sju:ə(r), 'su:ə(r)] *n. (tunnel)* Abwasserkanal, *der; (pipe)* Abwasserleitung, *die*

sewing *n.* Näharbeit, *die.* **'sewingmachine** *n.* Nähmaschine, *die*

sewn *see* **sew**

sex [seks] *n.* **a)** Geschlecht, *das;* **b)** *(sexuality; coll.: intercourse)* Sex, *der (ugs.);* have ~ **with sb.** *(coll.)* mit jmdm. schlafen

sexism ['seksɪzm] *n.* Sexismus, *der*

sexist ['seksɪst] *adj.* sexistisch

'sex maniac *n.* Triebverbrecher, *der*

sexual ['sekʃʊəl] *adj.* sexuell. **sexual 'intercourse** *n.* Geschlechtsverkehr, *der.* **sexuality** [sekʃʊ'ælɪtɪ] *n.* Sexualität, *die*

'sexy *adj.* sexy *(ugs.)*

shabbily ['ʃæbɪlɪ] *adv.,* **shabby** ['ʃæbɪ] *adj.* schäbig

shack [ʃæk] *n.* [armselige] Hütte

shackle ['ʃækl] **1.** *n., usu. in pl.* Fessel, *die.* **2.** *v.t.* anketten **(to** an + *Akk.*)

shade [ʃeɪd] **1.** *n.* **a)** Schatten, *der;* **b)** *(colour)* Ton, *der; (fig.)* Schattierung, *die;* **c)** *(lamp~)* [Lampen]schirm, *der.* **2.** *v.t.* **a)** *(screen)* beschatten; **b)** *(darken with lines)* ~ **[in]** [ab]schattieren. **3.** *v.i.* übergehen **(into** in + *Akk.*)

shadow ['ʃædəʊ] **1.** *n.* Schatten, *der.* **2.** *v.t. (follow)* beschatten. **'shadowy** *adj. (indistinct)* schattenhaft

shady ['ʃeɪdɪ] *adj.* **a)** schattig; **b)** *(disreputable)* zwielichtig

shaft [ʃɑːft] *n.* **a)** *(of tool, golf club)* Schaft, *der;* **b)** *(Mech. Engin.)* Welle, *die;* **c)** *(of mine, lift)* Schacht, *der;* **d)** *(of light, lightning)* Strahl, *der*

shaggy ['ʃægɪ] *adj.* zottelig

shake [ʃeɪk] **1.** *n.* Schütteln, *das;* give

sb./sth. a ~: jmdn./etw. schütteln. 2. *v. t.*, shook [ʃʊk], shaken ['ʃeɪkn] *(move violently)* schütteln; ~ one's fist/a stick at sb. jmdm. mit der Faust/ einem Stock drohen; ~ hands sich *(Dat.)* die Hand geben; b) *(cause to tremble)* erschüttern 〈Gebäude usw.〉; ~ one's head den Kopf schütteln; c) *(shock)* erschüttern. 3. *v. i.*, shook, shaken wackeln 〈Boden, Stimme:〉 beben; 〈Hand:〉 zittern. shake 'off *v. t.* abschütteln. shake 'up *v. t.* a) *(upset, shock)* einen Schrecken einjagen (+ *Dat.*); b) *(coll.: reorganize)* umkrempeln *(ugs.)*

shaken *see* shake 2, 3

shaky ['ʃeɪkɪ] *adj.* wack[e]lig 〈Möbelstück, Leiter〉; zittrig 〈Hand, Stimme, Greis〉; feel ~: sich zittrig fühlen

shall [ʃl, *stressed* ʃæl] *v. aux. only in pres.* shall, *neg. (coll.)* shan't [ʃɑːnt], *past* should [ʃəd, *stressed* ʃʊd], *neg. (coll.)* shouldn't ['ʃʊdnt] a) *expr. simple future* werden; b) *should expr. conditional* würde/würdest/würden/würdet; I should have been killed if I had let go sich ich wäre getötet worden, wenn ich losgelassen hätte; if we should be defeated falls wir unterliegen [sollten]; c) *expr. will or intention* what ~ we do? was sollen wir tun?; let's go in, ~ we? gehen wir doch hinein, oder?; we should be safe by now jetzt dürften wir in Sicherheit sein; he shouldn't do things like that! er sollte so etwas nicht tun!

shallot [ʃə'lɒt] *n.* Schalotte, *die*

shallow ['ʃæləʊ] *adj.* seicht 〈Wasser, Fluß〉; flach 〈Schüssel, Teller, Wasser〉; *(fig.)* flach 〈Person〉

sham [ʃæm] 1. *adj.* unecht; imitiert 〈Leder, Holz, Pelz〉. 2. *n. (pretence)* Heuchelei, *die*; *(person)* Heuchler, *der*/Heuchlerin, *die*. 3. *v. t.*, -mm- vortäuschen. 4. *v. i.*, -mm- simulieren

shambles ['ʃæmblz] *n. (coll.)* Chaos, *das*; the room was a ~: das Zimmer glich einem Schlachtfeld

shame [ʃeɪm] *n.* a) Scham, *die*; b) *(state of disgrace)* Schande, *die*; put sb./sth. to ~: jmdn. beschämen/etw. in den Schatten stellen; c) what a ~! wie schade! 'shamefaced *adj.* betreten. shameful ['ʃeɪmfl] *adj.* beschämend. 'shameless *adj.* schamlos

shampoo [ʃæm'puː] 1. *v. t.* schamponieren. 2. *n.* Shampoo[n], *das*

shamrock ['ʃæmrɒk] *n.* Klee, *der*

shandy ['ʃændɪ] *n.* Bier mit Limonade

shan't [ʃɑːnt] *(coll.)* = shall not

¹shanty ['ʃæntɪ] *n. (hut)* [armselige] Hütte

²shanty *n. (song)* Shanty, *das*

'shanty town *n.* Elendsviertel, *das*

shape [ʃeɪp] 1. *v. t.* formen; bearbeiten 〈Holz, Stein〉 (into zu). 2. *n.* Form, *die*; take ~: Gestalt annehmen. shape 'up *v. i.* sich entwickeln

'shapeless *adj.* formlos; unförmig 〈Kleid, Person〉

shapely ['ʃeɪplɪ] *adj.* wohlgeformt 〈Beine, Busen〉; gut 〈Figur〉

share [ʃeə(r)] 1. *n.* a) *(portion)* Teil, *der od. das*; [fair] ~: Anteil, *der*; fair ~s gerechte Teile; do more than one's [fair] ~ of the work mehr als seinen Teil zur Arbeit beitragen. b) *(Commerc.)* Aktie, *die*. 2. *v. t.* teilen; gemeinsam tragen 〈Verantwortung〉. 3. *v. i.* ~ in teilnehmen an (+ *Dat.*); beteiligt sein an (+ *Dat.*) 〈Gewinn〉; teilen 〈Freude, Erfahrung〉. share 'out *v. t.* aufteilen (among unter + *Akk.*)

share: ~holder *n.* Aktionär, *der*/ Aktionärin, *die*; ~-out *n.* Aufteilung, *die*

shark [ʃɑːk] *n.* Hai[fisch], *der*

sharp [ʃɑːp] 1. *adj.* a) scharf; spitz 〈Nadel, Bleistift, Gipfel, Winkel〉; deutlich 〈Unterscheidung〉; sauer 〈Apfel〉; herb 〈Wein〉; *(shrill, piercing)* schrill 〈Schrei, Pfiff〉; heftig 〈Schmerz, Krampf, Kampf〉; begabt 〈Schüler, Student〉; b) *(derog.: dishonest)* gerissen; *(Mus.)* [um einen Halbton] erhöht 〈Note〉. 2. *adv.* a) *(punctually)* at six o'clock ~: Punkt sechs Uhr; b) turn ~ right/left scharf nach rechts/ links abbiegen; c) look ~! halt dich ran! *(ugs.)*; d) *(Mus.)* zu hoch 〈singen, spielen〉. sharpen ['ʃɑːpn] *v. t.* schärfen; [an]spitzen 〈Bleistift〉. 'sharpener *n. (for pencils)* Spitzer, *der (ugs.)*. 'sharp-eyed *adj.* scharfäugig; be ~ scharfe Augen haben. 'sharply *adv.* scharf; in scharfem Ton 〈antworten〉. 'sharpness *n.* Schärfe, *die*; *(fineness of point)* Spitzheit, *die*

shatter ['ʃætə(r)] 1. *v. t.* zertrümmern; zerbrechen 〈Glas, Fenster〉; zerschlagen 〈Hoffnungen〉. 2. *v. i.* zerbrechen

shattered ['ʃætəd] *adj.* a) zerbrochen 〈Glas, Fenster〉; *(fig.)* zerstört 〈Hoffnungen〉; zerrüttet 〈Nerven〉; b) *(coll.: greatly upset)* she was ~ by the news die Nachricht hat sie schwer mitgenommen; I'm ~! ich bin ganz erschüttert!; *(Brit. coll.: exhausted)* ich bin kaputt! *(ugs.)*. **'shattering** *adj.* verheerend 〈Wirkung〉; vernichtend 〈Schlag, Niederlage〉

shave [ʃeɪv] **1.** *v.t.* rasieren; abrasieren 〈Haare〉. **2.** *v.i.* sich rasieren. **3.** *n.* Rasur, *die;* **have a ~:** sich rasieren. **shave 'off** *v.t.* abrasieren

'shaven ['ʃeɪvn] *adj.* rasiert; [kahl]geschoren 〈Kopf〉

'shaver *n.* Rasierapparat, *der.* **'shaver point** *n.* Anschluß für den Rasierapparat

shaving ['ʃeɪvɪŋ] *n.* **a)** Rasieren, *das;* **b)** *in pl. (of wood, metal, etc.)* Späne

shaving: **~-brush** *n.* Rasierpinsel, *der;* **~-cream** *n.* Rasiercreme, *die;* **~-foam** *n.* Rasierschaum, *der*

shawl [ʃɔːl] *n.* Schultertuch, *das*

she [ʃi, *stressed* ʃiː] *pron.* sie

sheaf [ʃiːf] *n., pl.* **sheaves** [ʃiːvz] *(of corn etc.)* Garbe, *die; (of paper, arrows, etc.)* Bündel, *das*

shear [ʃɪə(r)] *v.t., p.p.* **shorn** [ʃɔːn] *or* **sheared** *(clip)* scheren. **shears** [ʃɪəz] *n. pl.* |pair of| ~: Schere, *die;* **garden** ~: Gartenschere, *die*

sheath [ʃiːθ] *n., pl.* ~**s** [ʃiːðz, ʃiːθs] **a)** *(for knife, sword, etc.)* Scheide, *die;* **b)** *(condom)* Gummischutz, *der*

sheaves *pl. of* **sheaf**

¹shed [ʃed] *v.t.,* -**dd**-, **shed a)** verlieren; abwerfen 〈Laub, Geweih〉; **b)** vergießen 〈Blut, Tränen〉; **c)** verbreiten 〈Licht〉

²shed *n.* Schuppen, *der*

she'd [ʃiːd, *stressed* ʃiːd] **a)** = **she had; b)** = **she would**

sheen [ʃiːn] *n.* Glanz, *der*

sheep [ʃiːp] *n., pl. same* Schaf, *das.* **'sheep-dog** *n.* Hütehund, *der*

sheepish ['ʃiːpɪʃ] *adj.* verlegen

sheepskin *n.* Schaffell, *das*

sheer [ʃɪə(r)] *adj.* **a)** rein; blank 〈Unsinn, Gewalt〉; **by chance** rein zufällig; **b)** schroff 〈Felsen, Abfall〉

sheet [ʃiːt] *n.* **a)** Laken, *das;* **b)** *(of thin metal or plastic)* Folie, *die; (of iron, tin)* Blech, *das; (of glass)* Platte, *die; (of paper)* Bogen, *der;* Blatt, *das;* **c)** 〈Eis-, Nebel〉decke, *die*

sheik[h] [ʃeɪk, ʃiːk] *n.* Scheich, *der*

shelf [ʃelf] *n., pl.* **shelves** [ʃelvz] Brett, *das;* **shelves** *(set)* Regal, *das.* **'shelf-life** *n.* Lagerfähigkeit, *die*

shell [ʃel] **1.** *n.* **a)** Schale, *die; (of snail)* Haus, *das; (of turtle, tortoise)* Panzer, *der; (on beach)* Muschel, *die; (Mil.) (bomb)* Granate, *die.* **2.** *v.t.* **a)** *(take* out of ~*)* schälen; **b)** *(Mil.)* |mit Artillerie| beschießen. **shell 'out** *v.t. & i. (sl.)* blechen *(ugs.)* **(on** für)

she'll [ʃɪl, *stressed* ʃiːl] = **she will**

'shellfish *n., pl. same* **a)** Schal[en]tier, *das; (oyster, clam)* Muschel, *die; (crustacean)* Krebstier, *das;* **b)** *in pl. (Gastr.)* Meeresfrüchte *Pl.*

shelter ['ʃeltə(r)] **1.** *n.* **a)** *(shield)* Schutz, *der* **(against** vor + *Dat.,* gegen); **bomb** *or* **air-raid** ~: Luftschutzraum, *der;* **get under** ~: sich unterstellen; **b)** *no pl. (place of safety)* Zuflucht, *die.* **2.** *v.t.* schützen **(from** vor + *Dat.)*; Unterschlupf gewähren (+ *Dat.*) 〈Flüchtling〉. **3.** *v.i.* Schutz suchen **(from** vor + *Dat.)*. **'sheltered** *adj.* geschützt; behütet 〈Leben〉

shelve [ʃelv] **1.** *v.t. (defer)* auf Eis legen *(ugs.)*. **2.** *v.i. (slope)* abfallen

shelves *pl. of* **shelf**

shelving *n.* Regale *Pl.*

shepherd ['ʃepəd] **1.** *n.* Schäfer, *der.* **2.** *v.t.* führen. **'shepherdess** *n.* Schäferin, *die*

shepherd: ~**'s 'crook** *n.* Schäferstock, *der;* ~**'s 'pie** *n.* Auflauf aus Hackfleisch mit einer Schicht Kartoffelbrei darüber

sherry ['ʃerɪ] *n.* Sherry, *der*

she's [ʃɪz, *stressed* ʃiːz] **a)** = **she is; b)** = **she has**

shield [ʃiːld] **1.** *n.* Schild, *der.* **2.** *v.t.* schützen **(from** vor + *Dat.)*

shift [ʃɪft] **1.** *v.t.* **a)** *(move)* umstellen 〈Möbel〉; wegnehmen 〈Arm, Hand, Fuß〉; wegräumen 〈Schutt〉; entfernen 〈Schmutz, Fleck〉; ~ **the responsibility/ blame on to sb.** die Verantwortung/ Schuld auf jmdn. schieben; **b)** *(Amer. Motor Veh.)* ~ **gears** schalten. **2.** *v.i.* **a)** 〈Wind:〉 drehen **(to** nach); 〈Ladung:〉 verrutschen; **b)** *(sl.: move quickly)* rasen. **3.** *n.* **a)** **a ~ in emphasis** eine Verlagerung des Akzents; **a ~ in public opinion** ein Umschwung der öffentlichen Meinung; **b)** *(for work)* Schicht, *die;* **eight-hour/late ~:** Achtstunden-/ Spätschicht, *die;* **do** *or* **work the late** ~: Spätschicht haben. **'shift work** *n.* Schichtarbeit, *die*

shifty ['ʃɪftɪ] *adj.* verschlagen

shilling ['ʃɪlɪŋ] *n. (Hist.)* Shilling, *der*

shilly-shally ['ʃɪlɪʃælɪ] *v.i.* zaudern; **stop** ~**ing!** entschließ dich endlich!

shimmer ['ʃɪmə(r)] **1.** *v.i.* schimmern. **2.** *n.* Schimmer, *der*

shin [ʃɪn] **1.** *n.* Schienbein, *das.* **2.** *v.i.,* -**nn**-: ~ **up/down a tree** *etc.* einen

Baum *usw.* hinauf-/hinunterklettern.

'**shin-bone** *n.* Schienbein, *das*

shine [ʃaɪn] **1.** *v.i.,* **shone** [ʃɒn] ⟨*Lampe, Licht, Stern:*⟩ leuchten; ⟨*Sonne, Mond:*⟩ scheinen; *(reflect light)* glänzen. **2.** *v.t.,* **shone:** ~ **a light on sth./in sb.'s eyes** etw. anleuchten/ jmdm. in die Augen leuchten. **3.** *n.* Glanz, *der*

shingle ['ʃɪŋgl] *n. (pebbles)* Kies, *der*

'**shingles** *n. (Med.)* Gürtelrose, *die*

shin: ~-**guard,** ~-**pad** *ns.* Schienbeinschutz, *der*

shiny ['ʃaɪnɪ] *adj.* glänzend

ship [ʃɪp] **1.** *n.* Schiff, *das.* **2.** *v.t.,* -**pp**- *(transport by sea)* verschiffen; *(send by road, train, or air)* verschicken ⟨*Waren*⟩. '**shipbuilding** *n.* Schiffbau, *der*

'**shipment** *n.* **a)** Versand, *der; (by sea)* Verschiffung, *die;* **b)** *(amount)* Sendung, *die*

'**shipowner** *n.* Schiffseigentümer, *der*/-eigentümerin, *die; (of several ships)* Reeder, *der*/Reederin, *die*

'**shipper** *n.* Spediteur, *der*/Spediteurin, *die; (company)* Spedition, *die*

'**shipping** *n.* **a)** *(ships)* Schiffe; *(traffic)* Schiffahrt, *die;* **b)** *(transporting)* Versand, *der*

ship: ~-**shape** *adj.* in bester Ordnung; ~-**wreck 1.** *n.* Schiffbruch, *der.* **2.** *v.t.* **be** ~**wrecked** Schiffbruch erleiden; ~**yard** *n.* [Schiffs]werft, *die*

shirk [ʃɜːk] *v.t.* sich drücken vor (+ *Dat.*). '**shirker** *n.* Drückeberger, *der (ugs.)*

shirt [ʃɜːt] *n.* ⟨**man's**⟩ ~: [Herren- od. Ober]hemd, *das;* ⟨**woman's**⟩ ~: Hemdbluse, *die.* '**shirt-sleeve** *n.* Hemdsärmel, *der;* **in** ~**s** in Hemdsärmeln

shit [ʃɪt] *(coarse)* **1.** *v.i.,* -**tt**-, **shitted** *or* **shit** scheißen *(derb).* **2.** *n.* **a)** Scheiße, *die (derb);* **have** ⟨*Brit.*⟩ *or* ⟨*Amer.*⟩ **take a** ~: scheißen *(derb);* **b)** *(person)* Scheißkerl, *der (derb);* **c)** *(nonsense)* Scheiß, *der (salopp)*

shiver ['ʃɪvə(r)] **1.** *v.i.* zittern (**with** vor + *Dat.*). **2.** *n.* Schau[d]er, *der (geh.)*

shoal [ʃəʊl] *n. (of fish)* Schwarm, *der*

shock [ʃɒk] **1.** *n.* **a)** Schock, *der;* **give sb. a** ~: jmdm. einen Schock versetzen; **b)** *(violent impact)* Erschütterung, *die (of durch);* **c)** *(Electr.)* Schlag, *der;* **d)** *(Med.)* Schock, *der.* **2.** *v.t.* ~ **sb.** [**deeply**] ein [schwerer] Schock für jmdn. sein; *(scandalize)* jmdn. schockieren. '**shock absorber** *n.* Stoßdämpfer, *der*

'**shocking** *adj.* **a)** schockierend; **b)** *(coll.: very bad)* fürchterlich *(ugs.)*

'**shock-proof** *adj.* stoßfest

shod *see* **shoe 2**

shoddy ['ʃɒdɪ] *adj.* schäbig; minderwertig ⟨*Arbeit, Stoff, Artikel*⟩

shoe [ʃuː] **1.** *n.* Schuh, *der; (of horse)* [Huf]eisen, *das;* **put oneself into sb.'s** ~**s** *(fig.)* sich in jmds. Lage *(Akk.)* versetzen. **2.** *v.t.,* ~**ing,** **shod** [ʃɒd] beschlagen ⟨*Pferd*⟩

shoe: ~-**horn** *n.* Schuhlöffel, *der;* ~-**lace** *n.* Schnürsenkel, *der;* ~-**maker** *n.* Schuhmacher, *der;* ~-**polish** *n.* Schuhcreme, *die;* ~-**shop** *n.* Schuhgeschäft, *das;* ~-**string** *n.* **on a** ~**string** *(coll.)* mit ganz wenig Geld

shone *see* **shine 1, 2**

shoo [ʃuː] **1.** *int.* sch. **2.** *v.t.* scheuchen; ~ **away** fortscheuchen

shook *see* **shake 2, 3**

shoot [ʃuːt] **1.** *v.i.,* **shot** [ʃɒt] **a)** schießen (**at** auf + *Akk.*); **b)** *(move rapidly)* schießen *(ugs.).* **2.** *v.t.,* **shot a)** *(wound)* anschießen; *(kill)* erschießen; *(hunt)* schießen; ~ **sb. dead** jmdn. erschießen; **b)** schießen mit ⟨*Bogen, Munition, Pistole*⟩; abschießen ⟨*Pfeil, Kugel*⟩ (**at** auf + *Akk.*); **c)** *(Cinemat.)* drehen ⟨*Film, Szene*⟩. **3.** *n.* *(Bot.)* Trieb, *der.* **shoot 'down** *v.t.* niederschießen ⟨*Person*⟩; abschießen ⟨*Flugzeug*⟩. **shoot 'out** *v.i.* hervorschießen. **shoot 'up** *v.i.* in die Höhe schießen; ⟨*Preise, Kosten, Temperatur:*⟩ in die Höhe schnellen

'**shooting:** ~-**range** *n.* Schießstand, *der;* ~ -**star** *n.* Sternschnuppe, *die*

'**shoot-out** *n.* Schießerei, *die*

shop [ʃɒp] **1.** *n.* Laden, *der;* Geschäft, *das;* **go to the** ~**s** einkaufen gehen; **talk** ~: fachsimpeln *(ugs.).* **2.** *v.i.,* -**pp**- einkaufen; **go** ~**ping** einkaufen gehen. **shop a'round** *v.i.* sich umsehen (**for** nach)

shop: ~ **assistant** *n.* ⟨*Brit.*⟩ Verkäufer, *der*/Verkäuferin, *die;* ~-**keeper** *n.* Ladenbesitzer, *der*/-besitzerin, *die;* ~-**lifter** *n.* Ladendieb, *der*/-diebin, *die;* ~-**lifting** *n.* Ladendiebstahl, *der;* ~-**owner** *see* ~-**keeper**

'**shopper** *n.* Käufer, *der*/Käuferin, *die*

'**shopping** *n.* **a)** Einkaufen, *das;* **do the/one's** ~: einkaufen/[seine] Einkäufe machen; **b)** *(items bought)* Einkäufe *Pl.*

shopping: ~-**bag** *n.* Einkaufstasche, *die;* ~-**basket** *n.* Einkaufskorb, *der;*

~ **centre** n. Einkaufszentrum, das; ~**list** n. Einkaufszettel, der; ~ **mall** [~ mæl] n. Einkaufszentrum, das; ~ **street** n. Geschäftsstraße, die; ~ **trolley** n. Einkaufswagen, der

shop: ~**soiled** adj. (Brit.) (slightly damaged) leicht beschädigt; (slightly dirty) angeschmutzt; ~ '**window** n. Schaufenster, das

shore [ʃɔː(r)] n. Ufer, das; (beach) Strand, der. **shore 'up** v. t. abstützen ⟨Mauer, Haus⟩; (fig.) stützen

shorn see shear

short [ʃɔːt] 1. adj. a) kurz; **in a ~ time** or while (soon) bald; in Kürze; **a ~ time** or while ago/later vor kurzem/ kurze Zeit später; **in ~,** ...: kurz, ...; b) klein ⟨Person, Wuchs⟩; c) (deficient, scanty) knapp; **go ~** [of sth.] [an etw. ⟨Dat.⟩] Mangel leiden; **be ~ of sth.** jmdm. fehlt es an etw. ⟨Dat.⟩; **time is getting/iʃ ~:** die Zeit wird/ist knapp; **be in ~ supply** knapp sein; **be ~** [of cash] knapp [bei Kasse] sein (ugs.). 2. adv. a) (abruptly) plötzlich; **stop ~:** plötzlich abbrechen; **stop sb. ~:** jmdm. ins Wort fallen; b) **stop ~ of doing sth.** davor zurückschrecken, etw. zu tun. **shortage** [ˈʃɔːtɪdʒ] n. Mangel, der ⟨of an + Dat.⟩; ~ of fruit/teachers Obstknappheit, die/ Lehrermangel, der

short: ~**bread** n. Shortbread, das; Keks aus Butterteig; ~ '**circuit** n. (Electr.) Kurzschluß, der; ~**coming** n., usu. in pl. Unzulänglichkeit, die; ~ '**cut** n. Abkürzung, die; **take a ~ cut** den Weg abkürzen

shorten [ˈʃɔːtn] 1. v. i. kürzer werden. 2. v. t. kürzen; verkürzen ⟨Besuch, Wartezeit⟩

short: ~**hand** n. Stenographie, die; ~**hand typist** Stenotypist, der/-typistin, die; ~ **list** n. (Brit.) engere Auswahl; **be on/put sb. on the ~ list** in der engeren Auswahl sein/jmdn. in die engere Auswahl nehmen; ~**list** v. t. in die engere Auswahl nehmen; ~**lived** adj. kurzlebig

'**shortly** adv. in Kürze; gleich (ugs.); ~ **before/after sth.** kurz vor/nach etw.

'**short-range** adj. a) Kurzstrecken-⟨flugzeug, -rakete usw.⟩; b) (relating to time) kurzfristig

shorts [ʃɔːts] n. pl. a) (trousers) kurze Hose[n]; Shorts Pl.; b) (Amer.: underpants) Unterhose, die

short: ~ '**sighted** adj. kurzsichtig; ~**sleeved** [ˈ~sliːvd] adj. kurzärm[e]-

lig; ~**staffed** [~ˈstaːft] adj. be [very] ~**staffed** [viel] zu wenig Personal haben; ~ '**story** n. Kurzgeschichte, die; ~**term** adj. kurzfristig; (provisional) vorläufig ⟨Lösung⟩; ~ **wave** n. (Radio) Kurzwelle, die

shot [ʃɒt] 1. n. a) Schuß, der; **fire a ~:** einen Schuß abgeben ⟨at auf + Akk.⟩; **like a ~** (fig.) wie der Blitz (ugs.); **I'd do it like a ~:** ich würde es auf der Stelle tun; b) (Athletics) **put the ~:** die Kugel stoßen; [**putting] the ~:** Kugelstoßen, das; c) (Sport: stroke, kick, throw) Schuß, der; d) (Photog.) Aufnahme, die; (Cinemat.) Einstellung, die. 2. see shoot 1, 2. 3. adj. **be/get ~ of** (sl.) los sein/loswerden. '**shotgun** n. Schrotflinte, die

should see shall

shoulder [ˈʃəʊldə(r)] 1. n. Schulter, die. 2. v. t. schultern; (fig.) übernehmen

shoulder: ~**bag** n. Umhängetasche, die; ~**blade** n. Schulterblatt, das; ~**strap** n. (on garment) Schulterklappe, die; (on bag) Trageriemen, der

shouldn't [ˈʃʊdnt] (coll.) = should not; see shall

shout [ʃaʊt] 1. n. Ruf, der; (inarticulate) Schrei, der. 2. v. i. & t. schreien. **shout 'down** v. t. niederschreien. **shout 'out** 1. v. i. aufschreien. 2. v. t. [laut] rufen

'**shouting** n. Geschrei, das

shove [ʃʌv] 1. n. Stoß, der. 2. v. t. stoßen; schubsen (ugs.); (coll.: put) tun. **shove a'way** v. t. (coll.) wegschubsen (ugs.). **shove 'off** v. i. (sl.: leave) abschieben (ugs.)

shovel [ˈʃʌvl] 1. n. Schaufel, die. 2. v. t., (Brit.) -ll- schaufeln

show [ʃəʊ] 1. n. a) (entertainment, performance) Show, die; (Theatre) Vorstellung, die; (Radio, Telev.) [Unterhaltungs]sendung, die; b) (exhibition) Ausstellung, die; Schau, die; **put sth. on ~:** etw. ausstellen; **be on ~:** ausgestellt sein; c) (appearance) Anschein, der; **be for ~:** reine Angeberei sein (ugs.). 2. v. t., p. p. shown [ʃəʊn] a) zeigen; vorzeigen ⟨Paß, Fahrschein usw.⟩; ~ **sb. sth.,** ~ **sth. to sb.** jmdm. etw. zeigen; b) beweisen ⟨Mut, Urteilsvermögen usw.⟩; ~ **sb. that ...:** jmdm. beweisen, daß ...; ~ [**sb.] kindness/ mercy** freundlich [zu jmdm.] sein/Erbarmen [mit jmdm.] haben; c) ⟨Thermometer, Uhr usw.:⟩ anzeigen; d) (exhibit in a show) ausstellen; zeigen

⟨*Film*⟩. **3.** *v. i., p. p.* **shown a)** *(be visible)* sichtbar *od.* zu sehen sein; *(come into sight)* sich zeigen; **b)** *(be ~n)* ⟨*Film:*⟩ laufen. **show 'in** *v. t.* hinein-/herein-führen. **show 'off** *v. i.* angeben *(ugs.)*; prahlen. **show 'out** *v. t.* hinausführen. **show 'round** *v. t.* herum-führen. **show 'through** *v. i.* durch-scheinen. **show 'up 1.** *v. t.* **a)** *(make visible)* [deutlich] sichtbar machen; **b)** *(coll.: embarrass)* blamieren. **2.** *v. i.* **a)** *(be visible)* [deutlich] zu sehen sein; **b)** *(coll.: arrive)* sich blicken lassen *(ugs.)*

'**show-down** *n. (fig.)* Kraftprobe, *die*; **have a ~ [with sb.]** sich [mit jmdm.] auseinandersetzen

shower ['ʃaʊə(r)] **1.** *n.* **a)** Schauer, *der*; **~ of rain/hail** Regen-/Hagel-schauer, *der*; **b)** *(for washing)* Dusche, *die*; **have *or* take a [cold/quick] ~:** [kalt/schnell] duschen. **2.** *v. t. (lavish)* **~ sth. [up]on sb., ~ sb. with sth.** jmdn. mit etw. überhäufen. **3.** *v. i. (have a ~)* duschen

shower: **~-curtain** *n.* Duschvor-hang, *der*; **~ gel** *n.* Duschgel, *das*; **~-proof** *adj.* [bedingt] regendicht

'**showery** *adj.* **it is ~:** es gibt immer wieder kurze Schauer; **a ~ day** ein Tag mit Schauerwetter

'**show-jumping** *n.* Springreiten, *das*

shown *see* show 2, 3

show: **~-off** *n. (coll.)* Angeber, *der/* Angeberin, *die*; **~-piece** *n. (of exhibition, collection)* Schaustück, *das*; *(highlight)* Paradestück, *das*; **~room** *n.* Ausstellungsraum, *der*

'**showy** *adj.* protzig *(ugs.)*

shrank *see* shrink

shred [ʃred] **1.** *n.* Fetzen, *der*; *(fig.)* Spur, *die*; **tear sth. to ~s** etw. zerfet-zen; *(fig.)* etw. zerpflücken. **2.** *v. t.,* **-dd-** [im Reißwolf] zerkleinern

shrew [ʃruː] *n. (Zool.)* Spitzmaus, *die*

shrewd [ʃruːd] *adj.* klug; genau ⟨*[Ein]schätzung*⟩

shriek [ʃriːk] **1.** *n.* [Auf]schrei, *der.* **2.** *v. i.* [auf]schreien. **3.** *v. t.* schreien

shrift [ʃrɪft] *n.* **give sb. short ~:** jmdn. kurz abfertigen *(ugs.)*; **get short ~:** kurz abgefertigt werden *(ugs.)*

shrill [ʃrɪl] *adj.* schrill

shrimp [ʃrɪmp] *n.* Garnele, *die*

shrine [ʃraɪn] *n. (tomb)* Grab, *das*

shrink [ʃrɪŋk] **1.** *v. i.,* **shrank** [ʃræŋk], **shrunk** [ʃrʌŋk] **a)** schrumpfen ⟨*Kleidung, Stoff:*⟩ einlaufen; ⟨*Metall, Holz:*⟩ sich zusammenziehen; **b)** *(recoil)* **~ from sb./sth.** vor jmdm. zu-

rückweichen/vor etw. *(Dat.)* zurück-schrecken; **~ from doing sth.** sich scheuen, etw. zu tun. **2.** *v. t.,* **shrank, shrunk** einlaufen lassen ⟨*Textilien*⟩

shrivel ['ʃrɪvl] *v. i., (Brit.)* **-ll-:** ~ [up] verschrumpeln; ⟨*Pflanze, Blume:*⟩ welk werden

shroud [ʃraʊd] **1.** *n.* Leichentuch, *das.* **2.** *v. t.* **~ sth. in sth.** etw. in etw. *(Akk.)* hüllen

Shrove [ʃrəʊv] '**Tuesday** *n.* Fast-nachtsdienstag, *der*

shrub [ʃrʌb] *n.* Strauch, *der*

shrug [ʃrʌg] **1.** *v. t. & i.,* **-gg-:** ~ [one's shoulders] die Achseln zucken. **2.** *n.* ~ [of one's *or* the shoulders] Achsel-zucken, *das.* **shrug 'off** *v. t.* in den Wind schlagen

shrunk *see* shrink

shrunken ['ʃrʌŋkn] *adj.* verhutzelt *(ugs.)* ⟨*Person*⟩; schrump[e]lig ⟨*Apfel*⟩

shudder ['ʃʌdə(r)] **1.** *v. i.* zittern (with vor + *Dat.*). **2.** *n.* Zittern, *das*

shuffle ['ʃʌfl] **1.** *n.* **a)** Schlurfen, *das*; **walk with a ~:** schlurfen; **b)** *(Cards)* Mischen, *das*; **give the cards a [good] ~:** die Karten [gut] mischen. **2.** *v. t.* **a)** *(Cards)* mischen; **b)** ~ **one's feet** von einem Fuß auf den anderen treten

shun [ʃʌn] *v. t.,* **-nn-** meiden

shunt [ʃʌnt] *v. t. (Railw.)* rangieren

shush [ʃʊʃ] *int.* still

shut [ʃʌt] **1.** *v. t.,* **-tt-, shut** zumachen; schließen; zusammenklappen ⟨*Klapp-messer, Fächer*⟩; ~ **one's finger in the door** sich *(Dat.)* den Finger in der Tür einklemmen. **2.** *v. i.,* **-tt-, shut** schlie-ßen; ⟨*Blüte:*⟩ sich schließen. **shut 'down 1.** *v. t.* **a)** schließen, zumachen ⟨*Deckel*⟩; **b)** stillegen ⟨*Fabrik*⟩; ab-schalten ⟨*Kernreaktor*⟩. **2.** *v. i.* ⟨*Laden, Fabrik:*⟩ geschlossen werden. **shut 'out** *v. t.* aussperren. **shut 'up 1.** *v. t.* abschließen; einsperren ⟨*Tier, Per-son*⟩. **2.** *v. i. (coll.: be quiet)* den Mund halten

shutter ['ʃʌtə(r)] *n.* **a)** [Fenster]laden, *der*; **b)** *(Photog.)* Verschluß, *der*; ~ **release** Auslöser, *der*; ~ **speed** Ver-schlußzeit, *die*

shuttle ['ʃʌtl] **1.** *n. (in loom)* Schiff-chen, *das.* **2.** *v. i.* pendeln. '**shuttle-cock** *n.* Federball, *der.* '**shuttle service** *n.* Pendelverkehr, *der*

shy [ʃaɪ] *adj.,* **~er** *or* **shier** ['ʃaɪə(r)], **~est** *or* **shiest** ['ʃaɪst] scheu; *(diffident)* schüchtern. **shy a'way** *v. i.* ~ **away from sth./doing sth.** etw. scheuen/sich scheuen, etw. zu tun

'**shyness** n. Scheuheit, die; (diffidence) Schüchternheit, die
Siamese [saɪə'miːz]: ~ '**cat** n. Siamkatze, die; ~ '**twins** n. pl. siamesische Zwillinge
Siberia [saɪ'bɪərɪə] pr. n. Sibirien (das)
Sicily ['sɪsɪlɪ] pr. n. Sizilien (das)
sick [sɪk] adj. **a)** (ill) krank; **be off** ~: krank [gemeldet] sein; **b)** (Brit.: vomiting or about to vomit) **be** ~: sich erbrechen; **I'm going to be** ~: ich muß mich erbrechen; **sb. gets/feels** ~: jmdm. wird/ist [es] übel od. schlecht; **be/get** ~ **of sb./sth.** (fig.) jmdn./etw. satt haben/allmählich satt haben; **make sb.** ~ (disgust) jmdn. anekeln. '**sicken** ['sɪkn] **1.** v. i. **be** ~**ing for sth.** (Brit.) krank werden; etw. ausbrüten (ugs.). **2.** v. t. (disgust) anwidern. '**sickening** adj. ekelerregend, widerlich ‹Anblick, Geruch›
sickle ['sɪkl] n. Sichel, die
'**sick-leave** n. Urlaub wegen Krankheit; **be on** ~ ≈ krank geschrieben sein
sickly ['sɪklɪ] adj. kränklich
'**sickness** n. Krankheit, die; (nausea) Übelkeit, die
sick: ~**-pay** n. Entgeltfortzahlung im Krankheitsfalle; (paid by insurance) Krankengeld, das; ~**-room** n. Krankenzimmer, das
side [saɪd] **1.** n. **a)** Seite, die; ~ **of beef** Rinderhälfte, die; ~ **of bacon** Speckseite, die; **walk/stand** ~ **by** ~: nebeneinander gehen/stehen; **work/fight** ~ **by** ~ [with sb.] Seite an Seite [mit jmdm.] arbeiten/kämpfen; **live** ~ **by** ~ [with sb.] in [jmds.] unmittelbarer Nachbarschaft leben; **to one** ~: zur Seite; **on one** ~: an der Seite; **on the** ~ (as ~line) nebenbei; **take** ~**s** [with/against sb.] [für/gegen] jmdn. Partei ergreifen; **b)** (Sport: team) Mannschaft, die. **2.** v. i. ~ **with sb.** sich auf jmds. Seite (Akk.) stellen. **3.** adj. Seiten-
side: ~**board** n. Anrichte, die; ~**-car** n. Beiwagen, der; ~**-dish** n. Beilage, die; ~**-door** n. Seitentür, die; ~**-effect** n. Nebenwirkung, die; ~**-entrance** n. Seiteneingang, der; ~**-exit** n. Seitenausgang, der; ~**light** n. Begrenzungsleuchte, die; **drive on** ~**lights** mit Standlicht fahren; ~**line** n. (occupation) Nebenbeschäftigung, die; ~**-road** n. Seitenstraße, die; ~**-show** n. Nebenattraktion, die; ~**-step 1.** n. Schritt zur Seite; **2.** v. t.

ausweichen (+ Dat.); ~**-street** n. Seitenstraße, die; ~**-track** v. t. **get** ~**tracked** abgelenkt werden; ~**walk** n. (Amer.) Bürgersteig, der; ~**ways** ['saɪdweɪz] **1.** adv. **look at sb./sth.** ~**ways** jmdn./etw. von der Seite ansehen; **2.** adj. seitlich
siding ['saɪdɪŋ] n. Abstellgleis, das
sidle ['saɪdl] v. i. schleichen [up to zu]
siege [siːdʒ] n. Belagerung, die; (by police) Umstellung, die; **lay** ~ **to sth.** etw. belagern
sieve [sɪv] **1.** n. Sieb, das. **2.** v. t. sieben
sift [sɪft] v. t. sieben; ~ **sth. from sth.** etw. von etw. trennen. **sift 'out** v. t. aussieben
sigh [saɪ] **1.** n. Seufzer, der; **breathe** or **give** or **heave a** ~: einen Seufzer ausstoßen; ~ **of relief/contentment** Seufzer der Erleichterung/Zufriedenheit. **2.** v. i. seufzen; ~ **with relief/despair** erleichtert/verzweifelt seufzen
sight [saɪt] **1.** n. **a)** (faculty) Sehvermögen, das; **know sb. by** ~: jmdn. vom Sehen kennen; **b)** (act of seeing; spectacle) Anblick, der; **catch/lose** ~ **of sb./sth.** jmdn./etw. erblicken/aus dem Auge verlieren; **at first** ~: auf den ersten Blick; **c)** in pl. ~**s** (places of interest) Sehenswürdigkeiten; **see the** ~**s** die Sehenswürdigkeiten ansehen; **d)** (range) Sichtweite, die; **in** ~: in Sicht; **within** or **in** ~ **of sb./sth.** (able to see) in jmds. Sichtweite (Dat.)/in Sichtweite einer Sache; **out of** ~: außer Sicht; **e)** (of gun) Visier, das; **set/have** [set] **one's** ~**s on sth.** (fig.) etw. anpeilen. **2.** v. t. sichten ‹Land, Schiff, Flugzeug›; sehen ‹Entflohenen, Vermißten›. '**sightseeing** n. **go** ~: Besichtigungen machen. **sightseer** ['saɪtsiːə(r)] n. Tourist (der die Sehenswürdigkeiten besichtigt)
sign [saɪn] **1.** n. **a)** (symbol, signal, indication) Zeichen, das; (of future event) Anzeichen, das; **as a** ~ **of** als Zeichen (+ Gen.); **b)** (Astrol.) ~ [of the zodiac] Sternzeichen, das; **c)** (notice; on shop etc.) Schild, das. **2.** v. t. & i. unterschreiben; ~ **one's name** [mit seinem Namen] unterschreiben. **sign 'on** v. i. (as unemployed) sich arbeitslos melden. **sign 'up** v. i. sich [vertraglich] verpflichten (**with** bei); (for course) sich einschreiben
signal ['sɪgnl] **1.** n. Signal, das; **a** ~ **for sth./to sb.** ein Zeichen zu etw./für jmdn. **2.** v. i., (Brit.) -**ll**- signalisieren; Signale geben; ‹Kraftfahrer:› blinken;

(with hand) anzeigen; ~ **to sb. [to do sth.]** jmdm. ein Zeichen geben[, etw. zu tun]. **'signal-box** n. Stellwerk, *das*

signature ['sɪɡnətʃə(r)] n. Unterschrift, *die; (on painting)* Signatur, *die.* **'signature tune** n. Erkennungsmelodie, *die*

'signboard n. Schild, *das*

signet-ring ['sɪɡnɪt rɪŋ] n. Siegelring, *der*

significance [sɪɡ'nɪfɪkəns] n. Bedeutung, *die;* **be of [no]** ~: [nicht] von Bedeutung sein

significant [sɪɡ'nɪfɪkənt] adj. a) *(noteworthy, important)* bedeutend; b) *(full of meaning)* bedeutsam. **sig'nificantly** adv. a) *(meaningfully)* bedeutungsvoll; ~ **[enough]** bedeutsamerweise; b) *(notably)* bedeutend

signify ['sɪɡnɪfaɪ] v. t. bedeuten

'signpost n. Wegweiser, *der*

silence ['saɪləns] 1. n. Schweigen, *das; (keeping a secret)* Verschwiegenheit, *die; (stillness)* Stille, *die;* **there was** ~: es herrschte Schweigen/Stille; **in** ~: schweigend. 2. v. t. zum Schweigen bringen; *(fig.)* ersticken *⟨Proteste⟩;* mundtot machen *⟨Gegner⟩.* **'silencer** n. *(Arms; Brit. Motor Veh.)* Schalldämpfer, *der*

silent ['saɪlənt] adj. stumm; *(noiseless)* unhörbar; *(still)* still; **be** ~ *(say nothing)* schweigen; ~ **film** Stummfilm, *der.* **'silently** adv. schweigend; stumm *⟨weinen, beten⟩; (noiselessly)* lautlos

silhouette [sɪlʊ'et] 1. n. a) *(picture)* Schattenriß, *der;* b) *(appearance against the light)* Silhouette, *die.* 2. v. t. **be** ~**d against sth.** sich als Silhouette gegen etw. abheben

silicon ['sɪlɪkən] n. Silicium, *das;* ~ **chip** Siliciumchip, *der*

silk [sɪlk] 1. n. Seide, *die.* 2. attrib. adj. seiden; Seiden-. **'silkworm** n. Seidenraupe, *die.* **'silky** adj. seidig

sill [sɪl] n. *(of door)* [Tür]schwelle, *die; (of window)* Fensterbank, *die*

silly ['sɪlɪ] adj. dumm; *(imprudent, unwise)* töricht; *(childish)* albern

silo ['saɪləʊ] n., pl. ~**s** Silo, *der*

silt [sɪlt] n. Schlamm, *der;* Schlick, *der*

silver ['sɪlvə(r)] 1. n. Silber, *das.* 2. attrib. adj. silbern; Silber*(pokal, -münze)*

silver-: ~ **'medal** n. Silbermedaille, *die;* ~ **'paper** n. Silberpapier, *das;* ~**-plated** adj. versilbert; ~ **'wedding** n. Silberhochzeit, *die*

similar ['sɪmɪlə(r)] adj. ähnlich (**to** *Dat.*). **similarity** [sɪmɪ'lærɪtɪ] n. Ähnlichkeit, *die* (**to** mit). **'similarly** adv. ähnlich; *(in exactly the same way)* ebenso

simile ['sɪmɪlɪ] n. Vergleich, *der*

simmer ['sɪmə(r)] 1. v. i. *⟨Flüssigkeit:⟩* sieden. 2. v. t. köcheln lassen. **simmer 'down** v. i. sich abregen *(ugs.)*

simple ['sɪmpl] adj. einfach; *(unsophisticated, not elaborate)* schlicht *⟨Mobiliar, Schönheit, Kunstwerk, Kleidung⟩;* **it was a** ~ **misunderstanding** es war [ganz] einfach ein Mißverständnis. **'simple-minded** adj. a) *(unsophisticated)* schlicht; b) *(unintelligent)* beschränkt. **simpleton** ['sɪmpltən] n. Einfaltspinsel, *der (ugs.).* **simplicity** [sɪm'plɪsɪtɪ] n. Einfachheit, *die; (unpretentiousness, lack of sophistication)* Schlichtheit, *die.* **simplification** [sɪmplɪfɪ'keɪʃn] n. Vereinfachung, *die.* **simplify** ['sɪmplɪfaɪ] v. t. vereinfachen. **simplistic** [sɪm'plɪstɪk] adj. *[all]zu* simpel. **simply** ['sɪmplɪ] adv. einfach; *(in an unsophisticated manner)* schlicht; *(merely)* nur; **it** ~ **isn't true** es ist einfach nicht wahr; **I was** ~ **trying to help** ich wollte nur helfen

simulate ['sɪmjʊleɪt] v. t. a) *(feign)* vortäuschen; b) simulieren *⟨Bedingungen, Wetter usw.⟩*

simultaneous [sɪml'teɪnɪəs] adj., **simul'taneously** adv. gleichzeitig

sin [sɪn] 1. n. Sünde, *die.* 2. v. i., -**nn**- sündigen

since [sɪns] 1. adv. seitdem. 2. prep. seit; ~ **seeing you** ...: seit ich dich gesehen habe; ~ **then/that time** inzwischen. 3. conj. a) *(seit)* seit; **it a long time/ so long/not so long** ~ ...: es ist lange/so lange/gar nicht lange her, daß ...; b) *(seeing that, as)* da

sincere [sɪn'sɪə(r)] adj., ~**r** [sɪn'sɪərə(r)], ~**st** [sɪn'sɪərɪst] aufrichtig; herzlich *⟨Grüße, Glückwünsche usw.⟩.* **sin'cerely** adv. aufrichtig; **yours** ~: mit freundlichen Grüßen. **sincerity** [sɪn'serɪtɪ] n. Aufrichtigkeit, *die*

sinew ['sɪnjuː] n. Sehne, *die*

sinful ['sɪnfl] adj. sündig; *(reprehensible)* sündhaft; **it is** ~ **to** ...: es ist eine Sünde, ... zu ...

sing [sɪŋ] v. i. & t., **sang** [sæŋ], **sung** [sʌŋ] singen. **sing 'up** v. i. lauter singen

singe [sɪndʒ] v. t. & i., ~**ing** versengen

singer ['sɪŋə(r)] n. Sänger, *der*/Sängerin, *die*

single ['sɪŋgl] 1. *adj.* **a)** einfach; *(sole)* einzig; *(separate, individual, isolated)* einzeln; **not a ~ one** kein einziger/keine einzige/kein einziges; **every ~ one** jeder/jede/jedes einzelne; **every ~ day** jeden Tag; **~ ticket** *(Brit.)* einfache Fahrkarte; **b)** *(for one person)* Einzel- *(bett, -zimmer)*; **c)** *(unmarried)* ledig; **a ~ man/woman** ein Lediger/eine Ledige; **~ people** Ledige. 2. *n.* **a)** *(Brit.: ticket)* einfache Fahrkarte; **[a] ~/two ~s to Manchester, please** einmal/zweimal einfach nach Manchester, bitte; **b)** *(record)* Single, *die;* **c)** in pl. *(Tennis etc.)* Einzel, *das.* **single 'out** *v. t.* **~ sb./sth. out as/for sth.** jmdn./etw. als/für etw. auswählen

single: **~-decker** 1. *n.* **be a ~-decker** 〈*Bus, Straßenbahn:*〉 nur ein Deck haben; 2. *adj.* **~-decker bus/tram** Bus/Straßenbahn mit [nur] einem Deck; **~ [European] market** *n.* [europäischer] Binnenmarkt; **~-'handed** *adv.* allein; **~-minded** *adj.* zielstrebig

singlet ['sɪŋglɪt] *n.* *(Brit.)* *(vest)* Unterhemd, *das;* *(Sport)* Trikot, *das*

singly ['sɪŋglɪ] *adv.* einzeln

singular ['sɪŋgjʊlə(r)] 1. *adj.* **a)** *(Ling.)* singularisch; Singular-; **~ noun** Substantiv im Singular; **b)** *(extraordinary)* einmalig. 2. *n.* *(Ling.)* Einzahl, *die;* Singular, *der.* **'singularly** *adv.* *(extraordinarily)* außerordentlich

sinister ['sɪnɪstə(r)] *adj.* finster; *(of evil omen)* unheilverkündend

sink [sɪŋk] 1. *n.* Spülbecken, *das.* 2. *v. i.,* **sank** [sæŋk] *or* **sunk** [sʌŋk], **sunk** sinken. 3. *v. t.,* **sank** *or* **sunk, sunk a)** versenken 〈*Schiff:*〉; **b)** niederbringen 〈*Schacht:*〉. **sink 'in** *v. i.* *(fig.)* jmdm. ins Bewußtsein dringen; 〈*Warnung, Lektion:*〉 verstanden werden

'sinner *n.* Sünder, *der/*Sünderin, *die*

sinus ['saɪnəs] *n.* Nebenhöhle, *die*

sip [sɪp] 1. *v. t.,* **-pp-: ~ [up]** schlürfen. 2. *v. i.,* **-pp-: ~ at/from sth.** an etw. *(Dat.)* nippen. 3. *n.* Schlückchen, *das*

siphon ['saɪfn] 1. *n.* Siphon, *der.* 2. *v. t.* [durch einen Saugheber] laufen lassen

sir [sɜː(r)] *n.* **a)** *(formal address)* der Herr; *(to teacher)* Herr Meier/ Schmidt *usw.;* **b)** *(in letter)* **Dear Sir** Sehr geehrter Herr; **Dear Sirs** Sehr geehrte [Damen und] Herren; **Dear Sir or Madam** Sehr geehrte Dame/Sehr geehrter Herr; **c)** **Sir** [sə(r)] *(title of knight etc.)* Sir

siren ['saɪərən] *n.* Sirene, *die*

sirloin ['sɜːlɔɪn] *n.* **a)** *(Brit.)* Roastbeef, *das;* **~ steak** Rumpsteak, *das;* **b)** *(Amer.)* Rumpsteak, *das*

sissy ['sɪsɪ] 1. *n.* Waschlappen, *der.* 2. *adj.* feige

sister ['sɪstə(r)] *n.* **a)** Schwester, *die;* **b)** *(Brit.: nurse)* Oberschwester, *die.* **'sister-in-law** *n., pl.* **sisters-in-law** Schwägerin, *die*

sit [sɪt] 1. *v. i.,* **-tt-, sat** [sæt] **a)** *(become seated)* sich setzen; **~ on** *or* **in a chair/ in an armchair** sich auf einen Stuhl/in einen Sessel setzen; **b)** *(be seated)* sitzen. 2. *v. t.,* **-tt-, sat a)** setzen; **b)** *(Brit.)* machen 〈*Prüfung*〉. **sit 'back** *v. i.* sich zurücklehnen; *(fig.)* sich im Sessel zurücklehnen. **sit 'down** *v. i.* **a)** *(become seated)* sich setzen **(on/in** auf/in + Akk.); **b)** *(be seated)* sitzen. **sit 'up** 1. *v. i.* **a)** *(rise)* sich aufsetzen; **b)** *(be sitting erect)* [aufrecht] sitzen; **c)** *(stay up)* aufbleiben. 2. *v. t.* aufsetzen

site [saɪt] 1. *n.* **a)** *(land)* Grundstück, *das;* **b)** *(location)* Sitz, *der;* *(of new factory etc.)* Standort, *der.* 2. *v. t.* stationieren 〈*Raketen*〉; **~ a factory in London** London als Standort einer Fabrik wählen; **be ~d** gelegen sein

'sitting *n.* Sitzung, *die;* **the first ~ [for lunch]** der erste Schub [zum Mittagessen]

situate ['sɪtjʊeɪt] *v. t.* legen. **'situated** *adj.* gelegen; **be ~:** liegen. **situation** [sɪtjʊ'eɪʃn] *n.* **a)** *(location)* Lage, *die;* **b)** *(circumstances)* Situation, *die;* **c)** *(job)* Stelle, *die*

six [sɪks] 1. *adj.* sechs. 2. *n.* Sechs, *die. See also* **eight**

sixteen [sɪks'tiːn] 1. *adj.* sechzehn. 2. *n.* Sechzehn, *die. See also* **eight**. **sixteenth** [sɪks'tiːnθ] 1. *adj.* sechzehnt... 2. *n.* *(fraction)* Sechzehntel, *das. See also* **eighth**

sixth [sɪksθ] 1. *adj.* sechst... 2. *n.* *(in sequence)* sechste, *der/die/das;* *(in rank)* Sechste, *der/die/das;* *(fraction)* Sechstel, *das. See also* **eighth**

sixtieth ['sɪkstɪɪθ] *adj.* sechzigst...

sixty ['sɪkstɪ] 1. *adj.* sechzig. 2. *n.* Sechzig, *die. See also* **eight; eighty 2**

size [saɪz] *n.* Größe, *die;* *(of paper)* Format, *das;* **be twice the ~ of** etw. zweimal so groß wie etw. sein; **a ~ 8 dress** ein Kleid [in] Größe 8; **be ~ 8** 〈*Person:*〉 Größe 8 haben. **size 'up** *v. t.* taxieren 〈*Lage*〉

sizeable ['saɪzəbl] *adj.* ziemlich groß; beträchtlich 〈*Summe, Einfluß*〉

sizzle ['sɪzl] *v. i.* zischen

skate 1. *n. (ice-~)* Schlittschuh, *der; (roller-~)* Rollschuh, *der.* **2.** *v.i. (ice-~)* Schlittschuh laufen; *(roller-~)* Rollschuh laufen. **'skateboard 1.** *n.* Skateboard, *das;* Rollerbrett, *das.* **2.** *v.i.* Skateboard fahren. **'skater** *n. (ice-~)* Eisläufer, *der/*Eisläuferin, *die; (roller-~)* Rollschuhläufer, *der/*-läuferin, *die.* **'skating** ['skeitiŋ] *n. (ice-~)* Schlittschuhlaufen, *das; (roller-~)* Rollschuhlaufen, *das.* **'skating rink** *n. (ice)* Eisbahn, *die; (for roller-skating)* Rollschuhbahn, *die*

skeleton ['skelitn] *n.* Skelett, *das.* **'skeleton key** *n.* Dietrich, *der.* **'skeleton staff** *n.* Minimalbesetzung, *die*

skeptic etc. *(Amer.) see* **sceptic** etc.

sketch [sketʃ] **1.** *n.* **a)** *(drawing)* Skizze, *die.* **b)** *(play)* Sketch, *der.* **2.** *v.t.* skizzieren. **'sketch-book** *n.* Skizzenbuch, *das.* **'sketch map** *n.* Faustskizze, *die*

'sketchy *adj.* skizzenhaft; lückenhaft ⟨*Informationen, Bericht*⟩

skew [skju:] **1.** *adj.* schräg. **2.** *n.* **on the ~:** schief

skewer ['skju:ə(r)] **1.** *n.* Bratspieß, *der.* **2.** *v.t.* aufspießen

ski [ski:] **1.** *n.* **a)** Ski, *der;* **b)** *(on vehicle)* Kufe, *die.* **2.** *v.i.* Ski laufen *od.* fahren. **'ski boot** *n.* Skistiefel, *der;* **'ski-lift** *n.* Skilift, *der*

skid [skid] **1.** *v.i.,* **-dd-** schlittern; *(from one side to the other; spinning round)* schleudern. **2.** *n.* Schlittern/Schleudern, *das.* **'skid marks** *n. pl.* Schleuderspur, *die*

skier ['ski:ə(r)] *n.* Skiläufer, *der/*-läuferin, *die*

skiing ['ski:iŋ] *n.* Skilaufen, *das; (Sport)* Skisport, *der*

skilful ['skilfl] *adj.* geschickt; gewandt ⟨*Redner*⟩; gut ⟨*Beobachter, Lehrer*⟩

skill [skil] *n.* **a)** *(expertness)* Geschick, *das; (of artist)* Können, *das;* **b)** *(technique)* Fertigkeit, *die; (of weaving, bricklaying)* Technik, *die.* **skilled** ['skild] *adj.* **a)** *see* **skilful;** **b)** qualifiziert ⟨*Arbeit, Tätigkeit*⟩; **~ trade** Ausbildungsberuf, *der;* **c)** *(trained)* ausgebildet. **skillful** *(Amer.) see* **skilful**

skim [skim] *v.t.,* **-mm-: a)** *(remove)* abschöpfen; **b)** abrahmen ⟨*Milch*⟩; **c)** *see* **~ through. skim 'off** *v.t.* abschöpfen. **'skim through** *v.t.* überfliegen ⟨*Buch, Zeitung*⟩

skimmed 'milk *n.* entrahmte Milch

skimp [skimp] **1.** *v.t.* sparen an

(+ Dat.). **2.** *v.i.* sparen **(with, on** an *+ Dat.).* **'skimpy** *adj.* winzig ⟨*Badeanzug*⟩; spärlich ⟨*Wissen*⟩

skin [skin] **1.** *n.* **a)** Haut, *die;* **b)** *(fur)* Fell, *die;* **c)** *(peel)* Schale, *die.* **2.** *v.t.,* **-nn-** häuten; schälen ⟨*Frucht*⟩

skin: ~ cream *n.* Hautcreme, *die;* **~-deep** *adj. (fig.)* oberflächlich; **~-diver** *n.* Taucher, *der/*Taucherin, *die;* **~flint** *n.* Geizhals, *der;* **~head** *n. (Brit.)* Skinhead, *der*

skinny ['skini] *adj.* mager

'skin-tight *adj.* hauteng

¹skip [skip] **1.** *v.i.,* **-pp-: a)** hüpfen; **b)** *(with skipping-rope)* seilspringen. **2.** *v.t.,* **-pp-** *(omit)* überspringen; **~ breakfast/lunch** das Frühstück/Mittagessen auslassen. **3.** *n.* Hüpfer, *der*

²skip *n. (Building)* Container, *der*

ski: ~ pass *n.* Skipaß, *der;* **~ pole** *n.* Skistock, *der*

skipper ['skipə(r)] *n.* Kapitän, *der*

'skipping-rope *(Brit.),* **'skip-rope** *(Amer.) ns.* Sprungseil, *das*

'ski-resort *n.* Skiurlaubsort, *der*

skirmish ['skɜ:miʃ] *n. (Mil.)* **a)** Gefecht, *das;* **b)** *(argument)* Auseinandersetzung, *die*

skirt [skɜ:t] **1.** *n.* Rock, *der.* **2.** *v.t.* herumgehen um. **skirt 'round** *v.t.* herumgehen um; *(fig.)* umgehen

'skirting *n.* **~|-board|** *(Brit.)* Fußleiste, *die*

ski: ~-run *n.* Skihang, *der; (prepared)* [Ski]piste, *die;* **~-stick** *n.* Skistock, *der*

skittle ['skitl] *n.* **a)** Kegel, *der;* **b)** **~s** *sing. (game)* Kegeln, *das*

skive [skaiv] *v.i. (Brit. sl.)* sich drücken *(ugs.).* **skive 'off** *(Brit. sl.)* **1.** *v.i.* sich verdrücken *(ugs.).* **2.** *v.t.* schwänzen *(ugs.)*

skulk [skʌlk] *v.i.* lauern

skull [skʌl] *n.* Schädel, *der*

skunk [skʌŋk] *n.* Stinktier, *das*

sky [skai] *n.* Himmel, *der;* **in the ~:** am Himmel

sky: ~-high 1. *adj.* himmelhoch; astronomisch *(ugs.)* ⟨*Preise usw.*⟩; **2.** *adv.* **go ~-high** ⟨*Preise usw.:*⟩ in astronomische Höhen klettern *(ugs.);* **~light** *n.* Dachfenster, *das;* **~scraper** *n.* Wolkenkratzer, *der*

slab [slæb] *n.* **a)** *(flat stone etc.)* Platte, *die;* **b)** *(thick slice)* dicke Scheibe; *(of cake)* [dickes] Stück; *(of chocolate, toffee)* Tafel, *die*

slack [slæk] **1.** *adj.* **a)** *(lax)* nachlässig; schlampig *(ugs.);* **b)** *(loose)* schlaff;

locker ⟨*Verband*⟩. **2.** *n.* **take in** *or* **up the ~**: das Seil/die Schnur *usw.* straffen. **3.** *v. i. (coll.)* bummeln *(ugs.)*

slacken ['slækn] **1.** *v. i.* **a)** *(loosen)* sich lockern; **b)** *(diminish)* nachlassen; ⟨*Geschwindigkeit:*⟩ sich verringern. **2.** *v. t.* **a)** *(loosen)* lockern; **b)** *(diminish)* verringern

slacks [slæks] *n. pl.* **[pair of] ~**: lange Hose; Slacks *Pl. (Mode)*

slag [slæg] *n.* Schlacke, *die*

slain *see* **slay**

slake [sleɪk] *v. t.* stillen

slam [slæm] **1.** *v. t.,* **-mm-: a)** *(shut)* zuschlagen; **b)** *(put violently)* knallen *(ugs.)*. **2.** *v. i.,* **-mm-** zuschlagen

slander ['slɑ:ndə(r)] **1.** *n.* Verleumdung, *die* (**on** *Gen.*). **2.** *v. t.* verleumden. **slanderous** ['slɑ:ndərəs] *adj.* verleumderisch

slang [slæŋ] *n.* Slang, *der;* ⟨*Theater-, Soldaten-, Juristen*⟩jargon, *der; attrib.* Slang⟨*wort, -ausdruck*⟩

slant [slɑ:nt] **1.** *v. i.* ⟨*Fläche:*⟩ sich neigen; ⟨*Linie:*⟩ schräg verlaufen. **2.** *v. t.* **a)** *(slope)* schräg legen; **b)** *(fig.: bias)* [so] hinbiegen *(ugs.)* ⟨*Meldung, Bemerkung*⟩. **3.** *n.* Schräge, *die;* **on the** *or* **a ~:** schräg

slap [slæp] **1.** *v. t.,* **-pp-: a)** schlagen; **b)** *(put)* knallen *(ugs.)*. **2.** *v. i.,* **-pp-** schlagen; klatschen. **3.** *n.* Schlag, *der.* **4.** *adv.* voll; **~ in the middle** genau in der Mitte. **'slapdash** *adj.* schludrig *(ugs.)*. **'slap-up** *attrib. adj. (sl.)* ⟨*Essen*⟩ mit allen Schikanen *(ugs.)*

slash [slæʃ] **1.** *v. t.* **a)** aufschlitzen; **b)** *(fig.)* [drastisch] reduzieren; [drastisch] kürzen ⟨*Gehalt, Umfang*⟩. **2.** *n.* **a)** *(slit)* Schlitz, *der;* **b)** *(~ing stroke)* Hieb, *der*

slat [slæt] *n.* Latte, *die*

slate [sleɪt] **1.** *n.* **a)** *(Geol.)* Schiefer, *der;* **b)** *(Building)* Schieferplatte, *die.* **2.** *v. t. (Brit. coll.: criticize)* in der Luft zerreißen *(ugs.)*

slaughter ['slɔ:tə(r)] **1.** *n.* Schlachten, *das; (massacre)* Gemetzel, *das.* **2.** *v. t.* schlachten; *(massacre)* abschlachten

slave [sleɪv] **1.** *n.* Sklave, *der*/Sklavin, *die.* **2.** *v. i.* **~ [away]** schuften *(ugs.);* sich abplagen (at mit). **'slave-driver** *n. (fig.)* Sklaventreiber, *der*/-treiberin, *die.* **slavery** ['sleɪvərɪ] *n.* Sklaverei, *die.* **slavish** ['sleɪvɪʃ] *adj.* sklavisch

slay [sleɪ] *v. t.,* **slew** [slu:], **slain** [sleɪn] *(literary)* ermorden

sleazy ['sli:zɪ] *adj.* schäbig; *(disreputable)* anrüchig.

sled [sled], **sledge** [sledʒ] *ns.* Schlitten, *der.* **'sledge-hammer** *n.* Vorschlaghammer, *der*

sleek [sli:k] *adj. (glossy)* seidig

sleep [sli:p] **1.** *n.* Schlaf, *der;* **get/go to ~**: einschlafen; **put to ~**: einschläfern ⟨*Tier*⟩. **2.** *v. i.,* **slept** [slept] schlafen. **3.** *v. t.* **slept: the hotel ~s 80** das Hotel hat 80 Betten. **'sleeper** *n.* **a) be a heavy/light ~**: einen tiefen/leichten Schlaf haben; **b)** *(Brit. Railw.: support)* Schwelle, *die;* **c)** *(Railw.) (coach)* Schlafwagen, *der; (train)* **[night] ~**: Nachtzug mit Schlafwagen

sleeping: ~-bag *n.* Schlafsack, *der;* **~-car** *n.* Schlafwagen, *der;* **~-pill, ~-tablet** *ns.* Schlaftablette, *die*

sleep: ~less *adj.* schlaflos; **~walk** *v. i.* schlafwandeln; **~walker** *n.* Schlafwandler, *der*/-wandlerin, *die*

'sleepy *adj.* schläfrig

sleet [sli:t] **1.** *n.* Schneeregen, *der.* **2.** *v. i. impers.* **it is ~ing** es gibt Schneeregen

sleeve [sli:v] *n.* **a)** Ärmel, *der; (fig.)* **have sth. up one's ~**: etw. in petto haben *(ugs.)*; **roll up one's ~s** die Ärmel hochkrempeln *(ugs.);* **b)** *(for record)* Hülle, *die.* **'sleeveless** *adj.* ärmellos

sleigh [sleɪ] *n.* Schlitten, *der*

sleight [slaɪt] **of 'hand** *n.* Fingerfertigkeit, *die*

slender ['slendə(r)] *adj.* **a)** *(slim)* schlank; schmal ⟨*Buch, Band*⟩; **b)** gering ⟨*Chance, Mittel, Hoffnung*⟩

slept *see* **sleep** 2, 3

sleuth [slu:θ] *n.* Detektiv, *der*

¹slew [slu:] *v. i. & t.* schwenken

²slew *see* **slay**

slice [slaɪs] **1.** *n.* Scheibe, *die; (of apple, melon, peach, cake, pie)* Stück, *das;* **a ~ of cake** ein Stück Kuchen. **2.** *v. t.* in Scheiben schneiden; in Stücke schneiden ⟨*Bohnen, Apfel, Kuchen usw.*⟩; **~d bread** Schnittbrot, *das*

slick [slɪk] **1.** *adj. (coll.)* **a)** *(dexterous)* professionell; **b)** *(pretentiously dexterous)* clever *(ugs.)*. **2.** *n.* **[oil-]~**: Ölteppich, *der*

slid *see* **slide** 1, 2

slide [slaɪd] **1.** *v. i.,* **slid** [slɪd] rutschen; ⟨*Kolben, Schublade, Feder:*⟩ gleiten. **2.** *v. t.,* **slid** schieben. **3.** *n.* **a)** *(children's ~)* Rutschbahn, *die;* **b)** *(Photog.)* Dia[positiv], *das.* **sliding** ['slaɪdɪŋ] **door** *n.* Schiebetür, *die*

slight [slaɪt] **1.** *adj.* leicht; schwach ⟨*Hoffnung, Aussichten, Wirkung*⟩; **not in the ~est** nicht im geringsten. **2.** *n.*

Verunglimpfung, die (on Gen.); (lack of courtesy) Affront, der (on gegen).

'slightly adv. ein bißchen; leicht ⟨verletzen, riechen nach, gewürzt sein, ansteigen⟩; flüchtig ⟨jmdn. kennen⟩; oberflächlich ⟨etw. kennen⟩

slim [slɪm] 1. adj. schlank; schmal ⟨Band, Buch⟩; schwach ⟨Aussicht, Hoffnung⟩; gering ⟨Gewinn, Chancen⟩. 2. v. i., -mm- abnehmen

slime [slaɪm] n. Schleim, der. **slimy** ['slaɪmɪ] adj. schleimig

sling [slɪŋ] 1. n. (Med.) Schlinge, die. 2. v. i., slung [slʌŋ] (coll.: throw) schmeißen (ugs.). **sling 'out** v. t. (coll.) wegschmeißen (ugs.); ~ sb. out jmdn. rausschmeißen (ugs.).

slink [slɪŋk] v. i., slunk [slʌŋk] schleichen. **slink a'way, slink 'off** v. i. davonschleichen

slip [slɪp] 1. v. i., -pp-: a) (slide) rutschen; ⟨Messer:⟩ abrutschen; (and fall) ausrutschen; b) (escape) schlüpfen; c) (go) ~ to the butcher's etc. [rasch] zum Fleischer usw. rüberspringen (ugs.). 2. v. t., -pp-: a) stecken; ~ the dress over one's head das Kleid über den Kopf streifen; b) ~ sb.'s mind or memory jmdm. entfallen. 3. n. a) (fall) after his ~: nachdem er ausgerutscht [und gestürzt] war; b) (mistake) Versehen, das; ~ of the tongue Versprecher, der; c) (underwear) Unterrock, der; d) (piece of paper) Zettel, der; e) give sb. the ~: jmdm. entwischen (ugs.). **slip a'way** v. i. a) ⟨Person:⟩ sich fortschleichen; b) ⟨Zeit:⟩ verfliegen. **slip 'down** v. i. runterrutschen (ugs.). **slip 'in** v. i. ⟨Person:⟩ sich hineinschleichen. '**slip into** v. t. schlüpfen in (+ Akk.) ⟨Kleidungsstück⟩. **slip 'off** 1. v. i. a) runterrutschen (ugs.); b) see slip away a. 2. v. t. abstreifen ⟨Schmuck, Handschuh⟩; schlüpfen aus ⟨Kleid, Schuh⟩. **slip 'on** v. t. überstreifen ⟨Handschuh, Ring⟩; schlüpfen in (+ Akk.) ⟨Kleid, Schuh⟩. **slip 'out** v. i. ⟨Person:⟩ sich hinausschleichen. **slip 'over** v. i. (fall) ausrutschen. **slip 'up** v. i. (coll.) einen Schnitzer machen (ugs.).

slipped [slɪpt] **'disc** n. Bandscheibenvorfall, der

'slipper n. Hausschuh, der

slippery ['slɪpərɪ] adj. schlüpfrig

slip: ~road n. (Brit.) (to motorway) Auffahrt, die; (from motorway) Ausfahrt, die; ~shod adj. schludrig (ugs.); ~up n. (coll.) Schnitzer, der

slit [slɪt] 1. n. Schlitz, der. 2. v. t., -tt-, slit aufschlitzen; ~ sb.'s throat jmdm. die Kehle durchschneiden

slither ['slɪðə(r)] v. i. rutschen

sliver ['slɪvə(r)] n. Splitter, der

slobber ['slɒbə(r)] v. i. sabbern (ugs.)

slog [slɒg] 1. v. t., -gg- (in boxing, fight) voll treffen. 2. v. i., -gg- (work) schuften (ugs.). 3. n. a) (hit) wuchtiger Schlag; b) (work) Plackerei, die (ugs.)

slogan ['sləʊgən] n. Slogan, der; (advertising ~) Werbeslogan, der

slop [slɒp] 1. v. i. schwappen (out of, from aus). 2. v. t. (intentionally) kippen. **slop 'over** v. i. überschwappen

slope [sləʊp] 1. n. a) (slant) Neigung, die; b) (slanting ground) Hang, der. 2. v. i. (slant) sich neigen; ⟨Boden, Garten:⟩ abschüssig sein; ~ downwards/upwards ⟨Straße:⟩ abfallen/ansteigen. **slope a'way** v. i. (sl.) sich verdrücken (ugs.)

sloppy ['slɒpɪ] adj. schludrig (ugs.)

slosh [slɒʃ] 1. v. i. platschen (ugs.); ⟨Flüssigkeit:⟩ schwappen. 2. v. t. (coll.: pour clumsily) schwappen

slot [slɒt] 1. n. a) (hole) Schlitz, der; b) (groove) Nut, die. 2. v. t., -tt-: ~ sth. into place/sth. etw. einfügen/in etw. (Akk.) einfügen. **slot in** 1. v. t. einfügen. 2. v. i. sich einfügen

sloth [sləʊθ] n. a) (lethargy) Trägheit, die; b) (Zool.) Faultier, das

slot-machine n. Automat, der; (for gambling) Spielautomat, der

slouch [slaʊtʃ] v. i. sich schlecht halten

slovenly ['slʌvnlɪ] adj. schlampig (ugs.)

slow [sləʊ] 1. adj. langsam; langwierig ⟨Arbeit⟩; be [ten minutes] ~ ⟨Uhr:⟩ [zehn Minuten] nachgehen. 2. adv. langsam. 3. v. i. langsamer werden; ~ to a halt anhalten. **slow 'down, slow 'up** v. i. langsamer werden

'slowcoach n. Trödler, der/Trödlerin, die (ugs.)

'slowly adv. langsam

slow 'motion n. in ~: in Zeitlupe

slowness n. Langsamkeit, die

sludge [slʌdʒ] n. Schlamm, der

slug [slʌg] n. Nacktschnecke, die

sluggish ['slʌgɪʃ] adj. träge; schleppend ⟨Nachfrage⟩

sluice [sluːs] 1. n. Schütz, das. 2. v. t. ~ [down] abspritzen

slum [slʌm] n. Slum, der; (single house or apartment) Elendsquartier, das

slumber ['slʌmbə(r)] *(poet./rhet.)* 1. *n.* ~|s| Schlummer, *der (geh.).* 2. *v.i.* schlummern *(geh.)*

slump [slʌmp] 1. *n.* Sturz, *der (fig.); (in demand, investment, sales)* starker Rückgang (**in** *Gen.*); *(economic depression)* Depression, *die.* 2. *v.i.* a) *(Commerc.)* stark zurückgehen; *(Preise, Kurse:)* stürzen; b) *(collapse)* ⟨*Person:*⟩ fallen; ~ed **in a chair** in einem Sessel zusammengesunken

slung *see* **sling** 2

slunk *see* **slink**

slur [slɜː(r)] 1. *v.t.,* -rr-: ~ **one's words/ speech** undeutlich sprechen. 2. *n.* Beleidigung, *die* (on für)

slurp [slɜːp] *(coll.)* 1. *v.t.* ~ |up| schlürfen. 2. *n.* Schlürfen, *das*

slush [slʌʃ] *n.* Schneematsch, *der.* **'slushy** *adj.* a) matschig; b) *(sloppy)* sentimental

slut [slʌt] *n.* Schlampe, *die (ugs.)*

sly [slaɪ] 1. *adj.* schlau; gerissen *(ugs.)* ⟨*Geschäftsmann, Trick*⟩; verschlagen ⟨*Blick*⟩. 2. *n.* **on the** ~: heimlich

¹smack [smæk] 1. *n.* a) *(sound)* Klatsch, *der;* b) *(blow)* Schlag, *der; (on child's bottom)* Klaps, *der (ugs.).* 2. *v.t.* a) [mit der flachen Hand] schlagen; b) ~ **one's lips** [mit den Lippen] schmatzen. 3. *adv. (coll.)* direkt

²smack *v.i.* ~ **of** schmecken nach; *(fig.)* riechen nach *(ugs.)*

small [smɔːl] 1. *adj.* klein; gering ⟨*Wirkung, Appetit, Fähigkeit*⟩; schmal ⟨*Taille*⟩; dünn ⟨*Stimme*⟩; **make sb. feel** ~: jmdn. beschämen. 2. *n.* ~ **of the back** Kreuz, *das.* 3. *adv.* klein

small: ~ **ad** *n. (coll.)* Kleinanzeige, *die;* ~ **'change** *n.* Kleingeld, *das;* ~**holding** *n.* landwirtschaftlicher Kleinbetrieb; ~-'**minded** *adj.* kleinlich; ~**pox** *n.* Pocken *Pl.;* ~ **talk** *n.* leichte Unterhaltung; *(at parties)* Smalltalk, *der;* **make** ~ **talk** [**with sb.**] [mit jmdm.] Konversation machen

smarmy ['smɑːmɪ] *adj. (coll.)* kriecherisch

smart [smɑːt] 1. *adj.* a) *(clever)* clever; *(ingenious)* raffiniert; b) *(neat)* schick; schön ⟨*Haus, Garten, Auto*⟩; c) *attrib. (fashionable)* elegant; smart. 2. *v.i.* schmerzen. **smart alec[k]** [smɑːt ˈælɪk] *n. (coll.)* Besserwisser, *der.* **smarten** ['smɑːtn] *v.t.* herrichten; ~ **oneself** |up| auf sein Äußeres achten. **'smartly** *adv.* a) *(cleverly)* clever; b) *(neatly)* schmuck ⟨*[an]gestrichen*⟩; smart, flott ⟨*gekleidet, geschnitten*⟩

smash [smæʃ] 1. *v.t.* a) zerschlagen; b) ~ **sb. in the face/mouth** jmdm. *[hart]* ins Gesicht/auf den Mund schlagen; c) *(Tennis etc.)* schmettern. 2. *v.i.* a) zerbrechen; b) *(crash)* krachen (**into** gegen). 3. *n.* a) *(sound)* Krachen, *das;* b) *see* **smash-up**; c) *(Tennis)* Schmetterball, *der.* **smash 'in** *v.t.* zerschmettern; einschlagen ⟨*Tür, Schädel*⟩. **smash 'up** *v.t.* zertrümmern

smash-and-'grab [raid] *n. (coll.)* Schaufenstereinbruch, *der*

'smashing *adj. (coll.)* toll *(ugs.)*

'smash-up *n.* schwerer Zusammenstoß

smattering ['smætərɪŋ] *n.* |have| **a** ~ **of** German *etc.* ein paar Brocken Deutsch *usw.* [können]

smear [smɪə(r)] 1. *v.t.* a) *(daub)* beschmieren; *(put on or over)* schmieren; b) *(smudge)* verwischen; c) *(fig.)* in den Schmutz ziehen. 2. *n.* a) *(blotch)* ⟨*Schmutz*⟩fleck, *der;* b) *(fig.)* Beschmutzung, *die* (on *Gen.*)

smell [smel] 1. *n.* a) **have a good/bad sense of** ~: einen guten/schlechten Geruchssinn haben; b) *(odour)* Geruch, *der* (of nach); *(pleasant also)* Duft, *der* (of nach); **a** ~ **of burning/ gas** ein Brand-/Gasgeruch; c) *(stink)* Gestank, *der.* 2. *v.t.,* **smelt** [smelt] *or* **smelled** [smeld] a) *(perceive)* riechen; b) *(inhale ~ of)* riechen an (+ *Dat.*). 3. *v.i.,* **smelt** *or* **smelled** a) *(emit* ~*)* riechen; *(pleasantly also)* duften; b) ~ **of sth.** *(lit. or fig.)* nach etw. riechen; c) *(stink)* riechen. **'smelly** *adj.* stinkend; **be** ~: stinken

smelt *see* **smell** 2, 3

smile [smaɪl] 1. *n.* Lächeln, *das;* **give sb. a** ~: jmdn. anlächeln. 2. *v.i.* lächeln; ~ **at sb./sth.** jmdn. anlächeln/ über etw. *(Akk.)* lächeln

smirk [smɜːk] 1. *v.i.* grinsen. 2. *n.* Grinsen, *das*

smith [smɪθ] *n.* Schmied, *der*

smithereens [smɪðəˈriːnz] *n. pl.* **blow/ smash sth. to** ~: etw. in tausend Stücke sprengen/schlagen

smock [smɒk] *n.* Kittel, *der*

smog [smɒg] *n.* Smog, *der*

smoke [sməʊk] 1. *n.* Rauch, *der.* 2. *v.i. & t.* rauchen. **smoked** [sməʊkt] *adj. (Cookery)* geräuchert

smoke: ~ **detector** *n.* Rauchmelder, *der;* ~**less** *adj.* rauchlos; rauchfrei ⟨*Zone*⟩

'smoker *n.* a) Raucher, *der*/Raucherin, *die;* b) *(Railw.)* Raucherabteil, *das*

'smoke-screen n. [künstliche] Nebelwand; *(fig.)* Vernebelung *die (for Gen.)*

smoking ['sməʊkɪŋ] n. **a)** Rauchen, *das;* 'no ~' „Rauchen verboten"; **b)** *(seating area)* [do you want to sit in] ~ or non-~? möchten Sie für Raucher oder Nichtraucher?

smoky ['sməʊkɪ] adj. *(emitting smoke)* rauchend; *(smoke-filled)* verräuchert

smooth [smu:ð] **1.** adj. **a)** *(even)* glatt; eben ⟨Straße, Weg⟩; **b)** *(mild)* weich; **c)** *(not jerky)* geschmeidig ⟨Bewegung⟩; ruhig ⟨Fahrt, Flug⟩; weich ⟨Landung⟩; **d)** *(without problems)* reibungslos. **2.** v.t. glätten. **'smoothly** adv. **a)** *(evenly)* glatt; **b)** *(not jerkily)* geschmeidig ⟨sich bewegen⟩; weich ⟨landen⟩; reibungslos ⟨funktionieren⟩

smother ['smʌðə(r)] v.t. ersticken; *(fig.)* unterdrücken ⟨Gähnen⟩; ersticken ⟨Gelächter, Schreie⟩

smoulder ['sməʊldə(r)] v.i. schwelen; she was ~ing with rage Zorn schwelte in ihr

smudge [smʌdʒ] **1.** v.t. verwischen. **2.** v.i. schmieren. **3.** n. Fleck, *der*

smug [smʌg] adj. selbstgefällig

smuggle ['smʌgl] v.t. schmuggeln. **smuggle 'in** v.t. einschmuggeln; hinein-/hereinschmuggeln ⟨Person⟩. **smuggle 'out** v.t. hinaus-/herausschmuggeln

smuggler ['smʌglə(r)] n. Schmuggler, *der*/Schmugglerin, *die*

smuggling ['smʌglɪŋ] n. Schmuggel, *der*

smutty ['smʌtɪ] adj. *(lewd)* schmutzig

snack [snæk] n. Imbiß, *der.* **'snack-bar** n. Schnellimbiß, *der*

snag [snæg] n. *(problem)* Haken, *der;* what's the ~? wo klemmt es? *(ugs.)*

snail [sneɪl] n. Schnecke, *die;* at [a] ~'s pace im Schneckentempo *(ugs.)*

snake [sneɪk] n. Schlange, *die*

snap [snæp] **1.** v.t., **-pp- a)** *(break)* zerbrechen; ~ **sth. in two** or **in half** etw. in zwei Stücke brechen; **b)** ~ one's fingers mit den Fingern schnalzen; **c)** ~ **sth. home** or **into place** etw. einschnappen lassen; ~ **shut** zuschnappen lassen ⟨Portemonnaie, Schloß⟩; zuklappen ⟨Buch, Etui⟩; ~ **sth. open** etw. aufschnappen lassen; **d)** *(take photograph of)* knipsen; **e)** *(say sharply)* fauchen; *(speak crisply or curtly)* bellen. **2.** v.i., **-pp- a)** *(break)* brechen; **b)** *(fig.: give way under strain)* ausrasten *(ugs.);* my patience

has finally ~ped nun ist mir der Geduldsfaden aber gerissen. **3.** n. *(Photog.)* Schnappschuß, *der.* **'snap at** v.t. *(speak sharply to)* anfauchen *(ugs.).* **snap 'off** v.t. & i. abbrechen. **snap 'up** v.t. *(fig. coll.)* [sich *(Dat.)*] schnappen *(ugs.)*

'snapshot n. Schnappschuß, *der*

snare [sneə(r)] **1.** n. Schlinge, *die.* **2.** v.t. [mit einer Schlinge] fangen

'snarl [snɑ:l] **1.** v.i. knurren. **2.** n. Knurren, *das*

²snarl n. *(tangle)* Knoten, *der.* **snarl 'up** v.t. *(bring to a halt)* zum Erliegen bringen; **get ~ed up in the traffic** im Verkehr steckenbleiben

'snarl-up n. Stau, *der*

snatch [snætʃ] **1.** v.t. **a)** *(grab)* schnappen; ~ **sth. from sb.** jmdm. etw. wegreißen; ~ **some sleep** ein bißchen schlafen; **b)** *(steal)* klauen *(ugs.).* **2.** v.i. einfach zugreifen. **3.** n. **~es of** talk/conversation Gesprächsfetzen *Pl.*

sneak [sni:k] **1.** v.t. schmuggeln; ~ **a look** at schielen nach. **2.** v.i. **a)** schleichen; **b)** *(Brit. Sch. sl.: tell tales)* petzen *(Schülerspr.).* **3.** n. *(Brit. Sch. sl.)* Petzer, *der (Schülerspr.)*

sneer [snɪə(r)] **1.** v.i. höhnisch lächeln/grinsen. **'sneer at** v.t. höhnisch anlächeln/angrinsen; *(scorn)* verhöhnen

sneeze [sni:z] **1.** v.i. niesen. **2.** n. Niesen, *das*

sniff [snɪf] **1.** n. Schnuppern, *das; (with running nose, while crying)* Schniefen, *das.* **2.** v.i. schniefen; *(to detect a smell)* schnuppern. **3.** v.t. riechen od. schnuppern an (+ *Dat.*). **'sniff at** v.t. **a)** *see* sniff 3; **b)** *(show contempt for)* die Nase rümpfen über

snigger ['snɪgə(r)] **1.** v.i. [boshaft] kichern. **2.** n. [boshaftes] Kichern

snip [snɪp] **1.** v.t., **-pp-** schnippeln *(ugs.),* schneiden ⟨Loch⟩; schnippeln *(ugs.)* od. schneiden an (+ *Dat.*) ⟨Tuch, Haaren, Hecke⟩; *(cut off)* abschnippeln *(ugs.);* abschneiden. **2.** n. *(cut)* Schnitt, *der;* Schnipser, *der (ugs.)*

snipe [snaɪp] v.i. ~ **at** aus dem Hinterhalt beschießen. **'sniper** n. Heckenschütze, *der*

snippet ['snɪpɪt] n. *(of information in newspaper)* Notiz, *die; (of conversation)* Gesprächsfetzen, *der;* useful **~s of information** nützliche Hinweise

snivel ['snɪvl] v.i., *(Brit.)* **-ll-** schniefen

snob [snɒb] n. Snob, *der.* **snobbery** ['snɒbərɪ] n. Snobismus, *der.* **snobbish** ['snɒbɪʃ] adj. snobistisch

snooker ['snu:kə(r)] n. Snooker, das
snoop [snu:p] v. i. schnüffeln (ugs.)
snooty ['snu:tɪ] adj. (coll.) hochnäsig (ugs.)
snooze [snu:z] (coll.) 1. v. i. dösen (ugs.). 2. n. Nickerchen, das (fam.)
snore [snɔ:(r)] 1. v. i. schnarchen. 2. n. Schnarcher, der (ugs.); ~s Schnarchen, das
snorkel ['snɔ:kl] n. Schnorchel, der
snort [snɔ:t] v. i. schnauben (with, in vor + Dat.)
snot [snɒt] n. (sl.) Rotz, der (derb).
snotty adj. rotznäsig (salopp); ~child/nose Rotznase, die (salopp)
snout [snaʊt] n. Schnauze, die; (of pig) Rüssel, der
snow [snəʊ] 1. n. Schnee, der. 2. v. i. impers. it ~s/is ~ing es schneit. **snow 'in** v. t. they are ~ed in sie sind eingeschneit. **snow 'under** v. t. be ~ed under (with work) erdrückt werden; (with gifts, mail) überschüttet werden
snow: ~**ball** 1. n. Schneeball, der; 2. v. i. (fig.) lawinenartig zunehmen; ~**bound** adj. eingeschneit; ~**drift** n. Schneewehe, die; ~**drop** n. Schneeglöckchen, das; ~**fall** n. Schneefall, der; ~**flake** n. Schneeflocke, die; ~**man** n. Schneemann, der; ~**plough** n. Schneepflug, der; ~**storm** n. Schneesturm, der
'snowy adj. schneereich (Gegend); schneebedeckt (Berge)
snub [snʌb] 1. v. t., -**bb**-: a) (rebuff) brüskieren; b) (reject) ablehnen. 2. n. Abfuhr, die
snub-'nosed adj. stupsnasig
'snuff [snʌf] n. Schnupftabak, der; take a pinch of ~: eine Prise schnupfen
²snuff v. t. ~ [out] löschen (Kerze)
snuffle ['snʌfl] v. i. schnüffeln
snug [snʌg] adj. gemütlich; behaglich; be a ~ fit genau passen
snuggle ['snʌgl] v. i. ~ up to sb. sich an jmdn. kuscheln; ~ together sich aneinanderkuscheln; ~ up or down in bed sich ins Bett kuscheln
so [səʊ] 1. adv. so; as winter draws near, so it gets darker je näher der Winter rückt, desto dunkler wird es; so ... as so ... wie; so far bis hierher; (until now) bisher; (to such a distance) so weit; so much the better um so besser; so long! bis dann! (ugs.); and so on [and so forth] und so weiter [und so fort]; so as to um ... zu; so [that] damit; I'm so glad/tired! ich bin ja so froh/

müde!; It's a rainbow! – So it is! Es ist ein Regenbogen! – Ja, wirklich!; 'You suggested it. – So I did Du hast es vorgeschlagen. – Das stimmt; is that so? so? (ugs.); wirklich?; so am/have/would/could/will/do I uch ich auch. 2. pron. he suggested that I take the train, and if I had done so, ... : er riet mir, den Zug zu nehmen, und wenn ich es getan hätte, ...; I'm afraid so leider ja; I told you so ich habe es dir [doch] gesagt; a week or so etwa eine Woche; very much so in der Tat. 3. conj. (therefore) daher; so there you 'are! ich habe also recht!; so 'there! [und] fertig!; so? na und?; so you see ...: du siehst also ...; so where have you been? wo warst du denn?

soak [səʊk] 1. v. t. a) einweichen (Wäsche in Lauge); eintauchen (Brot in Milch); b) (wet) naß machen. 2. v. i. a) (steep) put sth. in sth. to ~: etw. in etw. (Dat.) einweichen; b) (drain) (Feuchtigkeit, Nässe:) sickern. **'soaking** adj. & adv. ~ [wet] völlig durchnäßt
'so-and-so n., pl. ~'s a) (person not named) [Herr/Frau] Soundso; b) (coll.: disliked person) Biest, das (ugs.)
soap [səʊp] n. Seife, die; ~ with and water mit Wasser und Seife
soap: ~ **opera** n. Seifenoper, die (ugs.); ~ **powder** n. Seifenpulver, das; ~**suds** n. pl. Seifenschaum, der
'soapy adj. seifig; ~ **water** Seifenlauge, die
soar [sɔ:(r)] v. i. aufsteigen; (fig.) (Preise, Kosten usw.:) in die Höhe schießen (ugs.)
sob [sɒb] 1. v. i., -**bb**- schluchzen (with vor + Dat.). 2. n. Schluchzer, der
sober ['səʊbə(r)] adj. a) (not drunk) nüchtern; b) (serious) ernst. **sober 'up** 1. v. i. nüchtern werden. 2. v. t. ausnüchtern
'sobering adj. ernüchternd
so-called ['səʊkɔ:ld] adj. sogenannt; (alleged) angeblich
soccer ['sɒkə(r)] n. Fußball, der
sociable ['səʊʃəbl] adj. gesellig
social ['səʊʃl] adj. a) sozial; gesellschaftlich; b) (of ~ life) gesellschaftlich; gesellig (Abend, Beisammensein)
socialism ['səʊʃəlɪzm] n. Sozialismus, der. **socialist** ['səʊʃəlɪst] 1. n. Sozialist, der/Sozialistin, die. 2. adj. sozialistisch
socialize ['səʊʃəlaɪz] v. i. geselligen Umgang pflegen; ~ with sb. (chat) sich mit jmdm. unterhalten

'**socially** *adv.* meet ~: sich privat treffen; ~ deprived sozial benachteiligt

social: ~ se'**curity** *n.* a) *(Brit.: benefit)* Sozialhilfe, *die;* b) *(system)* soziale Sicherheit; ~ '**service** *n.* staatliche Sozialleistung; ~ **work** *n.* Sozialarbeit, *die;* ~ **worker** *n.* Sozialarbeiter, *der/-*arbeiterin, *die*

society [sə'saɪətɪ] *n.* a) Gesellschaft, *die;* b) **high** ~: High-Society, *die;* b) *(club, association)* Verein, *der*

sociologist [səʊsɪ'ɒlədʒɪst] *n.* Soziologe, *der/*Soziologin, *die*

sociology [səʊsɪ'ɒlədʒɪ] *n.* Soziologie, *die*

'**sock** [sɒk] *n.* Socke, *die*

²**sock** *y. t. (coll.: hit)* hauen (ugs.)

socket ['sɒkɪt] *n.* a) *(Anat.) (of eye)* Höhle, *die;* *(of joint)* Pfanne, *die;* b) *(Electr.)* Steckdose, *die*

soda ['səʊdə] *n.* Soda, *das.* '**soda water** *n.* Soda[wasser], *das*

sodden ['sɒdn] *adj.* durchnäßt (with von)

sodium ['səʊdɪəm] *n.* Natrium, *das*

sofa ['səʊfə] *n.* Sofa, *das*

soft [sɒft] *adj.* weich; *(quiet)* leise; *(gentle)* sanft; **have a** ~ **spot for sb.** eine Vorliebe für jmdn. haben. '**soft-boiled** *adj.* weichgekocht ⟨Ei⟩. '**soft drink** *n.* alkoholfreies Getränk

soften ['sɒfn] 1. *v. i.* weicher werden. 2. *v. t.* aufweichen ⟨Boden⟩; enthärten ⟨Wasser⟩; mildern ⟨Farbe⟩

'**softly** *adv. (quietly)* leise; *(gently)* sanft

soft: ~ **toy** *n.* Stofftier, *das;* ~**ware** *n. (Computing)* Software, *die*

soggy ['sɒgɪ] *adj.* aufgeweicht

'**soil** [sɔɪl] *n.* Erde, *die;* Boden, *der*

²**soil** *v. t.* beschmutzen

solace ['sɒləs] *n.* Trost, *der;* **take or find** ~ **in sth.** Trost in etw. *(Dat.)* finden

solar ['səʊlə(r)] *adj.* Sonnen-

sold *see* **sell**

solder ['səʊldə(r)] 1. *n.* Lot, *das.* 2. *v. t.* löten

soldier ['səʊldʒə(r)] *n.* Soldat, *der*

'**sole** [səʊl] *n. (of foot/shoe)* Sohle, *die*

²**sole** *adj.* einzig; alleinig ⟨Verantwortung, Recht⟩; Allein⟨erbe, -eigentümer⟩. '**solely** *adv.* einzig und allein

solemn ['sɒləm] *adj.* feierlich; ernst ⟨Anlaß, Gespräch⟩

solicitor [sə'lɪsɪtə(r)] *n. (Brit.: lawyer)* Rechtsanwalt, *der/-*anwältin, *die*

solid ['sɒlɪd] 1. *adj.* a) *(rigid)* fest; b) *(of the same substance all through)*

massiv; c) *(well-built)* stabil; solide gebaut ⟨Haus, Mauer usw.⟩; d) *(complete)* ganz; **a good** ~ **meal** eine kräftige Mahlzeit. 2. *n.* fester Körper

solidarity [sɒlɪ'dærɪtɪ] *n.* Solidarität, *die*

solidify [sə'lɪdɪfaɪ] *v. i* fest werden

solitary ['sɒlɪtərɪ] *adj.* a) einsam; ~ **confinement** Einzelhaft, *die;* b) *(sole)* einzig

solitude ['sɒlɪtjuːd] *n.* Einsamkeit, *die*

solo ['səʊləʊ] 1. *n., pl.* ~**s** *(Mus.)* Solo, *das.* 2. *adj.* a) *(Mus.)* Solo-; b) ~ **flight** Alleinflug, *der.* 3. *adv.* a) *(Mus.)* solo; b) **go/fly** ~ *(Aeronaut.)* einen Alleinflug machen. **soloist** ['səʊləʊɪst] *n. (Mus.)* Solist, *der/*Solistin, *die*

solstice ['sɒlstɪs] *n.* Sonnenwende, *die*

soluble ['sɒljʊbl] *adj.* a) *(esp. Chem.)* löslich; b) *(solvable)* lösbar

solution [sə'luːʃn] *n.* a) *(esp. Chem.)* Lösung, *die;* b) *(result of solving)* Lösung, *die* (to Gen.); **find a** ~ **to sth.** eine Lösung für etw. finden; etw. lösen

solvable ['sɒlvəbl] *adj.* lösbar

solve [sɒlv] *v. t.* lösen

solvent ['sɒlvənt] 1. *adj.* a) *(esp. Chem.)* lösend; b) *(Finance)* solvent. 2. *n. (esp. Chem.)* Lösungsmittel, *das*

sombre *(Amer.:* **somber)** ['sɒmbə(r)] *adj.* dunkel; düster ⟨Stimmung, Atmosphäre⟩

some [səm, *stressed* sʌm] 1. *adj.* a) *(one or other)* [irgend]ein; ~ **day** eines Tages; b) *(a considerable quantity of)* einig...; c) *(a small quantity of)* ein bißchen; would you like ~ wine/cherries? möchten Sie [etwas] Wein/[ein paar] Kirschen?; **do** ~ **shopping/reading** einkaufen/lesen; d) *(to a certain extent)* ~ **guide** eine gewisse Orientierungshilfe. 2. *pron.* einig...; **would you like** ~? möchtest du etwas/*(plural)* welche?; ~ ..., **others** ...: manche ...,... andere ...

somebody ['sʌmbədɪ] *n. & pron.* jemand; ~ **or other** irgend jemand

'**somehow** *adv.* ~ [or other] irgendwie

someone ['sʌmwʌn] *see* **somebody**

somersault ['sʌməsɔːlt] *n.* Purzelbaum, *der (ugs.);* Salto, *der (Sport);* **turn a** ~: einen Purzelbaum schlagen *(ugs.)/*einen Salto springen

something *n. & pron.* etwas; ~ **new** etwas Neues; ~ **or other** irgend etwas; **see** ~ **of sb.** jmdn. sehen

'**sometime** 1. *adj.* ehemalig. 2. *adv.* irgendwann

'**sometimes** *adv.* manchmal

'**somewhat** *adv.* ziemlich

'**somewhere 1.** *adv.* **a)** *(in a place)* irgendwo; **b)** *(to a place)* irgendwohin. **2.** *n.* look for ~ to stay sich nach einer Unterkunft umsehen

son [sʌn] *n.* Sohn, *der*

sonata [sə'nɑːtə] *n.* Sonate, *die*

song [sɒŋ] *n.* **a)** Lied, *das;* **b)** *(bird cry)* Gesang, *der*

'**son-in-law** *n., pl.* **sons-in-law** Schwiegersohn, *der*

soon [suːn] *adv.* **a)** bald; *(quickly)* schnell; **b)** *(early)* früh; **none too** ~: keinen Augenblick zu früh; ~er or later früher oder später; **c) we'll set off as** ~ **as he arrives** sobald er ankommt, machen wir uns auf den Weg; **as** ~ **as possible** so bald wie möglich; **d)** *(willingly)* just **as** ~ [as ...] genauso gern [wie ...]; **she would** ~er **die than** ...: sie würde lieber sterben, als ...

soot [sʊt] *n.* Ruß, *der*

soothe [suːð] *v.t.* **a)** *(calm)* beruhigen; **b)** lindern *⟨Schmerz⟩*

'**sooty** *adj.* verrußt; rußig

sophisticated [sə'fɪstɪkeɪtɪd] *adj.* **a)** *(cultured)* kultiviert; **b)** *(elaborate, complex)* hochentwickelt; subtil *⟨Argument, System⟩*

soporific [sɒpə'rɪfɪk] *adj.* einschläfernd

sopping ['sɒpɪŋ] *adj. & adv.* ~ [wet] völlig durchnäßt

soppy ['sɒpɪ] *adj. (Brit. coll.)* rührselig; sentimental *⟨Person⟩*

soprano [sə'prɑːnəʊ] *n.* Sopran, *der;* *(female also)* Sopranistin, *die*

sordid ['sɔːdɪd] *adj.* dreckig; unerfreulich *⟨Detail, Geschichte⟩*

sore [sɔː(r)] **1.** *adj.* weh; *(inflamed or injured)* wund; **a** ~ **throat** Halsschmerzen *Pl.;* **sb. has a** ~ **back/foot** *etc.* jmdm. tut der Rücken/Fuß *usw.* weh. **2.** *n.* wunde Stelle. '**sorely** *adv.* sehr; dringend *⟨nötig⟩;* ~ **tempted** stark versucht

sorrow ['sɒrəʊ] *n.* Kummer, *der*

sorry ['sɒrɪ] *adj.* **a) sb. is** ~ **that** ...: es tut jmdm. leid, daß ...; ~ **about** or **for sth.** jmdm. tut etwas leid; **I am** or **feel** ~ **for him** er tut mir leid; **sb. is** or **feels** ~ **for sth.** jmd. bedauert etw.; ~! Entschuldigung!; ~? wie bitte?; **I'm** ~ **to say leider; you'll be** ~! das wird dir noch leid tun; **b)** *(wretched)* traurig

sort [sɔːt] **1.** *n.* **a)** Art, *die;* *(type)* Sorte, *die;* **a new** ~ **of bicycle** ein neuartiges Fahrrad; **all** ~s **of** ...: alle möglichen ...; **there are all** ~s **of things to do**

es gibt alles mögliche *od.* allerlei zu tun; ~ **of** *(coll.: more or less)* mehr oder weniger; **nothing of the** ~: nichts dergleichen; **b) be out of** ~s nicht in Form sein. **2.** *v.t.* sortieren. **sort 'out** *v.t.* **a)** *(settle)* klären; schlichten *⟨Streit⟩;* beenden *⟨Verwirrung⟩;* **b)** *(select)* aussuchen

'**sort code** *n.* Bankleitzahl, *die*

sortie ['sɔːtɪ] *n.* Ausfall, *der;* *(flight)* Einsatz, *der*

SOS *n.* SOS, *das*

'**so so, 'so-so** *adj., adv.* so lala *(ugs.)*

soufflé ['suːfleɪ] *n.* Soufflé, *das*

sought *see* **seek**

soul [səʊl] *n.* Seele, *die;* **not a** ~: keine Menschenseele

'**soul-destroying** *adj.* **a)** *(boring)* nervtötend; **b)** *(depressing)* deprimierend

soulful ['səʊlfl] *adj.* gefühlvoll; *(sad)* schwermütig

soul: ~ **mate** *n.* Seelenverwandte, *der/die;* ~**-searching** *n.* Gewissenskampf, *der*

'**sound** [saʊnd] **1.** *adj.* **a)** *(healthy)* gesund; intakt *⟨Gebäude, Mauerwerk⟩;* **of** ~ **mind** im Vollbesitz der geistigen Kräfte; **b)** *(well-founded)* vernünftig *⟨Argument, Rat⟩;* klug *⟨Wahl⟩;* **it makes** ~ **sense** es ist sehr vernünftig; **c)** *(Finance: secure)* gesund, solide *⟨Basis⟩;* klug *⟨Investition⟩.* **2.** *adv.* fest, tief *⟨schlafen⟩*

'**sound 1.** *n.* **a)** *(Phys.)* Schall, der; **b)** *(noise)* Laut, *der;* *(of wind, sea, car, footsteps, breaking glass or twigs)* Geräusch, *das;* *(of voices, laughter, bell)* Klang, *der;* **do sth. without a** ~: etw. lautlos tun; **c)** *(Radio, Telev., Cinemat.)* Ton, *der;* **b)** *(fig.: impression)* **I like the** ~ **of your plan** ich finde, Ihr Plan hört sich gut an; **I don't like the** ~ **of this** das hört sich nicht gut an. **2.** *v.i.* klingen; **it** ~s **as if** .../**like** ...: es klingt, als .../wie ...; **that** ~s **a good idea to me** ich finde, die Idee hört sich an; **that** ~s **odd to me** das hört sich seltsam an, finde ich; ~s **good to me!** klingt gut! *(ugs.).* **3.** *v.t.* **a)** ertönen lassen; **b)** *(utter)* ~ **a note of caution** zur Vorsicht mahnen. **sound 'off** *v.i.* tönen *(ugs.),* schwadronieren **(on, about,** von). **sound 'out** *v.i.* ausfragen *⟨Person⟩;* ~ **sb. out on sth.** bei jmdm. wegen etw. vorfühlen

sound: ~ **barrier** *n.* Schallmauer, *die;* ~ **effect** *n.* Geräuscheffekt, *der*

'**sounding-board** *n.* **a)** *(Mus.)* Decke,

die; b) (fig.: trial audience) ≈ Testgruppe, *die*

'**soundless** *adj.* lautlos

'**soundly** *adv.* **a)** *(solidly)* stabil, solide *(bauen);* **b)** *(deeply)* tief, fest *(schlafen);* **c)** *(thoroughly)* ordentlich *(ugs.)* *(verhauen);* vernichtend *(schlagen, besiegen)*

sound: ~-**proof** 1. *adj.* schalldicht; 2. *v.t.* schalldicht machen; ~-**track** *n.* Soundtrack, *der;* ~-**wave** *n.* Schallwelle, *die*

soup [su:p] *n.* Suppe, *die;* **be/land in the** ~ *(fig. sl.)* in der Patsche sitzen/landen *(ugs.)*

soup: ~-**plate** *n.* Suppenteller, *der;* ~-**spoon** *n.* Suppenlöffel, *der*

sour ['saʊə(r)] *adj.* **a)** sauer; **b)** *(morose)* griesgrämig; säuerlich *(Blick);* **c)** *(unpleasant)* bitter

source [sɔ:s] *n.* Quelle, *die;* ~ **of income/infection** Einkommensquelle, *die*/Infektionsherd, *der;* **at** ~: an der Quelle

south [saʊθ] 1. *n.* **a)** Süden, *der;* **in/to|wards/from the** ~: im/nach/von Süden; **to the** ~ **of** südlich von; **b)** *usu.* S~ *(Geog., Polit.)* Süden, *der.* 2. *adj.* südlich; Süd*(küste, -wind, -grenze).* 3. *adv.* nach Süden; ~ **of** südlich von

South: ~ '**Africa** *pr. n.* Südafrika *(das);* ~ '**African** *adj.* südafrikanisch; ~ A'**merica** *pr. n.* Südamerika *(das);* ~ A'**merican** *adj.* südamerikanisch; **s**~-**bound** *adj.* *(Zug, Verkehr usw.)* in Richtung Süden; **s**~-'**east** 1. *n.* Südosten, *der.* 2. *adj.* südöstlich; Südost*(wind, -küste).* 3. *adv.* südostwärts; nach Südosten; **s**~-'**eastern** *adj.* südöstlich

southerly ['sʌðəlɪ] *adj.* südlich; *(Wind)* aus südlichen Richtungen

southern ['sʌðən] *adj.* südlich; Süd*(grenze, -hälfte, -seite)*

South: ~ '**Germany** *pr. n.* Süddeutschland *(das);* ~ '**Pole** *pr. n.* Südpol, *der*

southward[s] ['saʊθwəd(s)] *adv.* südwärts

south: ~-'**west** 1. *n.* Südwesten, *der;* 2. *adj.* südwestlich; Südwest*(wind, -küste);* 3. *adv.* südwestwärts; nach Südwesten; ~-'**western** *adj.* südwestlich

souvenir [su:və'nɪə(r)] *n.* Souvenir, *das (of aus)*

sovereign ['sɒvrɪn] *n. (ruler)* Souverän, *der.* **sovereignty** ['sɒvrɪntɪ] *n.* Souveränität, *die*

Soviet ['səʊvɪət, 'sɒvɪət] *adj. (Hist.)* sowjetisch; Sowjet*(bürger, -literatur)*

Soviet '**Union** *pr. n.* *(Hist.)* Sowjetunion, *die*

¹**sow** [səʊ] *v.t., p.p.* **sown** [səʊn] *or* **sowed** [səʊd] **a)** *(plant)* [aus]säen; **b)** einsäen *(Feld, Boden)*

²**sow** [saʊ] *n. (female pig)* Sau, *die*

sown *see* ¹**sow**

soya [bean] ['sɔɪə (bi:n)] *n.* Sojabohne, *die*

spa [spɑ:] *n.* **a)** *(place)* Bad, *das;* Badeort, *der;* **b)** *(spring)* Mineralquelle, *die*

space [speɪs] *n.* **a)** Raum, *der;* **b)** *(interval between points)* Platz, *der;* **clear a** ~: Platz schaffen; **c) the wide open** ~**s** das weite, flache Land; **d)** *(Astron.)* Weltraum, *der;* **e)** *(blank between words)* Zwischenraum, *der;* **f)** *(interval of time)* Zeitraum, *der;* **in the** ~ **of a minute/an hour** innerhalb einer Minute/Stunde; **in a short** ~ **of time he was back** nach kurzer Zeit war er zurück.

space 'out *v.t.* verteilen

space: ~ **age** *n.* [Welt]raumzeitalter, *das;* ~-**bar** *n.* Leertaste, *die;* ~-**craft** *n.* Raumfahrzeug, *das;* ~-**saving** *adj.* platzsparend; ~-**ship** *n.* Raumschiff, *das;* ~-**suit** *n.* Raumanzug, *der;* ~ **travel** *n.* Raumfahrt, *die*

spacious ['speɪʃəs] *adj.* geräumig

spade [speɪd] *n.* **a)** Spaten, *der;* **b)** *(Cards)* Pik, *das; see also* **club 1c**

spaghetti [spə'getɪ] *n.* Spaghetti *Pl.*

Spain [speɪn] *pr. n.* Spanien *(das)*

span [spæn] 1. *n.* **a)** Spanne, *die;* Zeitspanne, *die;* **b)** *(of bridge)* Spannweite, *die.* 2. *v.t., -nn-* überspannen *(Fluß);* umfassen *(Zeitraum)*

Spaniard ['spænjəd] *n.* Spanier, *der/* Spanierin, *die*

Spanish ['spænɪʃ] 1. *adj.* spanisch; *sb.* **is** ~: jmd. ist Spanier/Spanierin. 2. *n.* **a)** *(language)* Spanisch, *das; see also* **English 2a;** **b) the** ~ *pl.* die Spanier

spank [spæŋk] 1. *n.* ≈ Klaps, *der (ugs.).* 2. *v.t.* ~ *sb.* jmdm. den Hintern versohlen *(ugs.)*

spanner ['spænə(r)] *n. (Brit.)* Schraubenschlüssel, *der*

spar [spɑ:(r)] *v.i., -rr-:* **a)** *(Boxing)* sparren; **b)** *(fig.: argue)* [sich] zanken

spare [speə(r)] 1. *adj.* **a)** *(not in use)* übrig; ~ **time/moment** Freizeit, *die*/freier Augenblick; **there is one** ~ **seat** ein Platz ist noch frei; **b)** *(for use when needed)* zusätzlich, Extra*(bett, -tasse);* ~ **room** Gästezimmer, *das.* 2. *n.* Ersatzteil, *das/-reifen, der usw.* 3.

v. t. **a)** entbehren; **we arrived with ten minutes to** ~: wir kamen zehn Minuten früher an; **b)** *(not inflict on)* ~ **sb. sth.** jmdm. etw. ersparen; **c)** *(not hurt)* [ver]schonen; **d)** *(fail to use)* **not** ~ **any expense/pains** *or* **efforts** keine Kosten/Mühe scheuen; **no expense ~d** an nichts gespart

spare: ~ **'part** *n.* Ersatzteil, *das;* ~ **'tyre** *n.* Reserve-, Ersatzreifen, *der;* ~ **'wheel** *n.* Ersatzrad, *das*

sparing ['speərɪŋ] *adj.* sparsam

spark [spɑːk] **1.** *n.* **a)** Funke, *der; (fig.)* **a** ~ **of generosity/decency** ein Funke[n] Großzügigkeit/Anstand; **b) a bright** ~ *(person, also iron.)* ein schlauer Kopf. **2.** *v. i.* ~ **[off]** zünden; *(fig.)* auslösen

sparkle ['spɑːkl] **1.** *v. i.* **a)** *(Diamant:)* glitzern; *(Augen:)* funkeln; **b)** *(be lively)* sprühen *(with* vor + *Dat.)*. **2.** *n.* Funkeln, *das.* **sparkling** ['spɑːklɪŋ] *adj.* glitzernd *(Diamant);* funkelnd *(Augen).* **sparkling 'wine** *n.* Schaumwein, *der*

spark-plug *n.* Zündkerze, *die*

sparrow ['spærəʊ] *n.* Spatz, *der*

sparse [spɑːs] *adj.* spärlich; dünn *(Besiedlung)*

spasm ['spæzm] *n.* Krampf, *der*

spasmodic [spæz'mɒdɪk] *adj.* **a)** *(marked by spasms)* krampfartig; **b)** *(intermittent)* sporadisch

spastic ['spæstɪk] **1.** *n.* Spastiker, *der/* Spastikerin, *die.* **2.** *adj.* spastisch

spat *see* **spit 1, 2**

spate [speɪt] *n.* **a) the river is in [full]** ~: der Fluß führt Hochwasser; **b)** *(fig.)* **a** ~ **of sth.** eine Flut von etw.; **a** ~ **of burglaries** eine Einbruchsserie

spatial ['speɪʃl] *adj.* räumlich

spatter ['spætə(r)] *v. t.* spritzen; ~ **sb./sth. with sth.** jmdn./etw. mit etw. bespritzen

spatula ['spætjʊlə] *n.* Spachtel, *die*

spawn [spɔːn] **1.** *v. t. (fig.)* hervorbringen. **2.** *v. i. (Zool.)* laichen. **3.** *n. (Zool.)* Laich, *der*

speak [spiːk] **1.** *v. i.,* spoke [spəʊk], spoken ['spəʊkn] **a)** sprechen; ~ [**with sb.**] **on** *or* **about sth.** [mit jmdm.] über etw. *(Akk.)* sprechen; ~ **for/against sth.** sich für/gegen etw. aussprechen; **b)** *(on telephone)* **Is Mr Grant there?** – S~**ing!** Ist Mister Grant da? – Am Apparat!; **who is** ~**ing, please?** wer ist am Apparat, bitte? **2.** *v. t.,* spoke, spoken sprechen *(Satz, Wort, Sprache);* sagen *(Wahrheit);* ~ **one's mind** sagen, was man denkt. **'speak**

for *v. t.* sprechen für; **sth. is spoken for** *(reserved)* etw. ist schon vergeben. **'speak of** *v. t.* sprechen von; ~**ing of Mary** da wir gerade von Mary sprechen; **nothing to** ~ **of** nichts Besonderes. **'speak to** *v. t.* sprechen *od.* reden mit. **speak 'up** *v. i.* lauter sprechen

'speaker *n.* **a)** *(in public)* Redner, *der/*Rednerin, *die;* **b)** *(of a language)* Sprecher *der/*Sprecherin, *die;* **be a 'French** ~: Französisch sprechen; **c)** *(loudspeaker)* Lautsprecher, *der*

'speaking 1. *n.* Sprechen, *das;* ~ **clock** *(Brit.)* telefonische Zeitansage. **2.** *adv.* **strictly/generally** ~: genaugenommen/im allgemeinen

spear [spɪə(r)] *n.* Speer, *der.* **'spearhead 1.** *n. (fig.)* Speerspitze, *die.* **2.** *v. t. (fig.)* anführen. **'spearmint** *n. (Bot.)* Grüne Minze; ~ **chewing-gum** Pfefferminzkaugummi, *der od. das*

special ['speʃl] *adj.* speziell; besonder...; **nobody** ~: niemand Besonderer. **special de'livery** *n. (Post)* Eilzustellung, *die*

specialist ['speʃəlɪst] *n.* **a)** Spezialist, *der/*Spezialistin, *die* (**in** für); **b)** *(Med.)* Facharzt, *der/*-ärztin, *die*

speciality [speʃɪ'ælɪtɪ] *n.* Spezialität, *die*

specialize ['speʃəlaɪz] *v. i.* sich spezialisieren (**in** auf + *Akk.*)

'specially *adv.* **a)** speziell; **make sth.** ~: etw. speziell *od.* extra anfertigen; **b)** *(especially)* besonders

special 'offer *n.* Sonderangebot, *das;* **on** ~: im Sonderangebot

specialty ['speʃltɪ] *(esp. Amer.) see* **speciality**

species ['spiːʃiːz] *n., pl. same* Art, *die*

specific [spɪ'sɪfɪk] *adj.* bestimmt; **could you be more** ~? kannst du dich genauer ausdrücken? **specifically** [spɪ'sɪfɪkəlɪ] *adv.* ausdrücklich; eigens; extra *(ugs.)*

specification [spesɪfɪ'keɪʃn] *n., often pl. (details)* technische Daten; *(for building)* Baubeschreibung, *die*

specify ['spesɪfaɪ] *v. t.* ausdrücklich sagen; **unless otherwise specified** wenn nicht anders angegeben

specimen ['spesɪmən] *n.* **a)** *(example)* Exemplar, *das;* **b)** *(sample)* Probe, *die*

speck [spek] *n.* **a)** *(spot)* Fleck, *der;* **b)** *(particle)* Teilchen, *das;* ~ **of soot/dust** Rußflocke, *die/*Staubkörnchen, *das*

specs [speks] *n. pl. (coll.: spectacles)* Brille, *die*

spectacle ['spektəkl] n. a) in pl. [pair of] ~s Brille, die; b) (public show) Spektakel, das; c) (object of attention) Anblick, der. '**spectacle case** n. Brillenetui, das

spectacular [spek'tækjʊlə(r)] adj. spektakulär

spectator [spek'teɪtə(r)] n. Zuschauer, der/Zuschauerin, die

specter (Amer.) see **spectre**

spectra pl. of **spectrum**

spectre ['spektə(r)] n. (Brit.) a) (ghost) Gespenst, das; b) (fig.) Schreckgespenst, das

spectrum ['spektrəm] n., pl. **spectra** ['spektrə] Spektrum, das

speculate ['spekjʊleɪt] v. i. spekulieren (about, on über + Akk.). **speculation** [spekjʊ'leɪʃn] n. Spekulation, die (over über + Akk.). **speculative** ['spekjʊlətɪv] adj. spekulativ. **speculator** ['spekjʊleɪtə(r)] n. Spekulant, der/Spekulantin, die

sped see **speed** 2

speech [spiːtʃ] n. a) (public address) Rede, die; make or deliver or give a ~: eine Rede halten; b) (faculty or manner of speaking) Sprache, die. '**speechless** adj. sprachlos (with vor + Dat.)

speed [spiːd] 1. n. Geschwindigkeit, die; Schnelligkeit, die; at a ~ of ...: mit einer Geschwindigkeit von ... 2. v. i. a) p. t. & p. p. **sped** [sped] or **speeded** schnell fahren; rasen (ugs.); b) p. t. & p. p. **speeded** (go too fast) zu schnell fahren; rasen (ugs.). '**speedboat** n. Rennboot, das

'**speeding** n. Geschwindigkeitsüberschreitung, die

'**speed limit** n. Geschwindigkeitsbeschränkung, die

speedometer [spiː'dɒmɪtə(r)] n. Tachometer, der od. das

'**speedy** adj. schnell; umgehend, prompt (Antwort)

¹**spell** [spel] 1. v. t., **spelt** [spelt] (Brit.) or **spelled** a) schreiben; (aloud) buchstabieren; b) (fig.: mean) bedeuten. 2. v. i., **spelt** (Brit.) or **spelled** (say) buchstabieren; (write) richtig schreiben

²**spell** n. (period) Weile, die; a cold ~: eine Kälteperiode

³**spell** n. a) (magic charm) Zauberspruch, der; cast a ~ on sb. jmdn. verzaubern; b) (fascination) Zauber, der; break the ~: den Bann brechen. '**spellbound** adj. verzaubert

'**spelling** n. Rechtschreibung, die

spelt see ¹**spell**

spend [spend] v. t., **spent** [spent] a) (pay out) ausgeben; ~ a penny (fig. coll.) mal verschwinden (ugs.); b) verbringen (Zeit). '**spendthrift** n. Verschwender, der/Verschwenderin, die

spent 1. see **spend**. 2. adj. a) (used up) verbraucht; b) (drained of energy) erschöpft

sperm [spɜːm] n. pl ~s or same (Biol.) Sperma, das

spew [spjuː] v. t. spucken

sphere [sfɪə(r)] n. a) (field of action) Bereich, der; Sphäre, die (geh.); b) (Geom.) Kugel, die. **spherical** ['sferɪkl] adj. kugelförmig

spice [spaɪs] 1. n. Gewürz, das; (fig.) Würze, die. 2. v. t. würzen. **spicy** ['spaɪsɪ] adj. pikant; würzig

spider ['spaɪdə(r)] n. Spinne, die

spike [spaɪk] n. Stachel, der. **spiky** ['spaɪkɪ] adj. stachelig

spill [spɪl] 1. v. t., **spilt** [spɪlt] or **spilled** verschütten (Flüssigkeit); ~ sth. on sth. etw. auf etw. (Akk.) schütten; ~ the beans aus der Schule plaudern. 2. v. i., **spilt** or **spilled** überlaufen

spilt see **spill**

spin [spɪn] 1. v. t., -nn-, **spun** [spʌn] a) spinnen; ~ yarn Garn spinnen; b) (in washing-machine etc.) schleudern. 2. v. i., -nn-, **spun** sich drehen; my head is ~ning (fig.) mir schwirrt der Kopf.

spin 'out v. t. (prolong) in die Länge ziehen

spinach ['spɪnɪdʒ] n. Spinat, der

spinal ['spaɪnl] adj. Wirbelsäulen-; Rückgrat[s]-. **spinal 'column** n. Wirbelsäule, die. **spinal 'cord** n. Rückenmark, das

spindle ['spɪndl] n. Spindel, die. **spindly** ['spɪndlɪ] adj. spindeldürr

spin-'drier n. Wäscheschleuder, die

spin-'dry v. t. schleudern

spine [spaɪn] n. a) (backbone) Wirbelsäule, die; b) (Bot., Zool.) Stachel, der. '**spineless** adj. (fig.) rückgratlos

'**spin-off** n. Nebenprodukt, das

spinster ['spɪnstə(r)] n. ledige Frau

spiny ['spaɪnɪ] adj. stachelig

spiral ['spaɪrl] 1. adj. spiralförmig. 2. n. Spirale, die. 3. v. i., (Brit.) -ll- (Weg:) sich hochwinden; (Kosten:) in die Höhe klettern; (Rauch:) in einer Spirale aufsteigen. **spiral 'staircase** n. Wendeltreppe, die

spire ['spaɪə(r)] n. Turmspitze, die

spirit ['spɪrɪt] n. a) in pl. (distilled liquor) Spirituosen Pl.; b) (mental atti-

tude) Geisteshaltung, *die;* **in the right/ wrong ~:** mit der richtigen/falschen Einstellung; **take sth. in the wrong ~:** etw. falsch auffassen; c) *(courage)* Mut, *der;* **d)** *(mental tendency)* Geist, *der;* **high ~s** gehobene Stimmung; **in poor** or **low ~s** niedergedrückt. **'spirited** *adj.* beherzt

'**spirit-level** *n.* Wasserwaage, *die*

spiritual ['spɪrɪtʃʊəl] *adj.* spirituell *(geh.)*

spit [spɪt] 1. *v.i.,* -tt-, spat [spæt] or spit spucken. 2. *v.t.,* -tt-, spat or spit spucken. 3. *n.* Spucke, *die.* **spit out** *v.t.* ausspucken

spite [spaɪt] 1. *n.* a) Boshaftigkeit, *die;* **b) in ~ of** trotz; **in ~ of oneself** obwohl man es eigentlich nicht will. 2. *v.t.* ärgern. **spiteful** ['spaɪtfl] *adj.* gehässig

spittle ['spɪtl] *n.* Spucke, *die*

splash [splæʃ] 1. *v.t.* spritzen; **~ sth. on** |to| etw. |auf| jmdn./etw. mit etw. bespritzen. 2. *v.i.* a) spritzen; b) *(in water)* platschen *(ugs.).* 3. *n.* a) *(liquid)* Spritzer, *der;* b) *(noise)* Plätschern, *das*

splendid ['splendɪd] *adj.* *(excellent)* großartig; *(magnificent)* prächtig

splendour *(Brit.; Amer.:* **splendor)** ['splendə(r)] *n.* Pracht, *die*

splint [splɪnt] *n.* Schiene, *die*

splinter ['splɪntə(r)] *n.* Splitter, *der*

split [splɪt] 1. *n.* a) *(tear)* Riß, *der;* b) *(division into parts)* [Auf]teilung, *die;* *(fig.)* Spaltung, *die.* 2. *adj.* gespalten; **be ~ on** a question [sich *(Dat.)*] in einer Frage uneins sein. 3. *v.t.,* -tt-, split a) *(tear)* zerreißen; b) *(divide)* teilen. 4. *v.i.,* -tt-, split a) ⟨*Holz:*⟩ splittern; ⟨*Stoff, Seil:*⟩ reißen; **~ apart** zersplittern; b) *(divide into parts)* sich teilen. **split up** *v.t.* aufteilen. 2. *v.i.* *(coll.)* sich trennen; **~ up with sb.** sich von jmdm. trennen

splutter ['splʌtə(r)] *v.i.* ⟨*Person:*⟩ prusten; ⟨*Motor:*⟩ stottern

spoil [spɔɪl] 1. *v.t.,* spoilt [spɔɪlt] or spoiled a) *(impair)* verderben; b) *(pamper)* verwöhnen; **be ~t for choice** die Qual der Wahl haben. 2. *v.i.,* spoilt or spoiled a) verderben; b) **be ~ing for a fight** Streit suchen. 3. *n.* **~s** *pl.*] Beute, *die.* '**spoilsport** *n.* Spielverderber, *der/*-verderberin, *die*

spoilt *see* **spoil** 1, 2

'**spoke** [spəʊk] *n.* Speiche, *die*

²**spoke, spoken** *see* **speak**

spokesman ['spəʊksmən] *n., pl.* **spokesmen** ['spəʊksmən] Sprecher, *der*

sponge [spʌndʒ] 1. *n.* Schwamm, *der.* 2. *v.t.* mit einem Schwamm waschen. '**sponge on** *v.t.* **~ on sb.** bei od. von jmdm. schnorren *(ugs.)*

sponge: ~bag *n.* *(Brit.)* Kulturbeutel, *der;* **~cake** *n.* Biskuitkuchen, *der*

sponger ['spʌndʒə(r)] *n.* Schmarotzer, *der/*Schmarotzerin, *die*

spongy ['spʌndʒɪ] *adj.* schwammig

sponsor ['spɒnsə(r)] 1. *n.* Sponsor, *der.* 2. *v.t.* a) sponsern; b) *(Polit.)* sb. jmds. Kandidatur unterstützen

spontaneous [spɒn'teɪnɪəs] *adj.* spontan

spooky ['spuːkɪ] *adj.* gespenstisch

spool [spuːl] *n.* Spule, *die*

spoon [spuːn] *n.* a) Löffel, *der;* b) *(amount)* *see* **spoonful.** **spoonful** ['spuːnfʊl] *n.* **a ~ of sugar** ein Löffel [voll] Zucker

sporadic [spə'rædɪk] *adj.* sporadisch

spore [spɔː(r)] *n.* Spore, *die*

sport [spɔːt] 1. *n.* a) Sport, *der;* **~s** Sportarten; **water/indoor ~:** Wasser-/ Hallensport, *der;* b) *(fun)* Spaß, *der;* c) **be a [real] ~** *(coll.)* ein prima Kerl sein *(ugs.);* **be a ~!** sei kein Spielverderber! 2. *v.t.* stolz tragen. '**sporting** *adj.* a) sportlich; b) **give sb. a ~ chance** jmdm. eine [faire] Chance geben

sports: ~car *n.* Sportwagen, *der;* **~jacket** *n.* sportlicher Sakko, *der;* **~man** ['spɔːtsmən] *n., pl.* **~men** ['spɔːtsmən] Sportler, *der;* **~manship** ['spɔːtsmənʃɪp] *n.* *(fairness)* [sportliche] Fairneß; **~wear** *n.* Sport[be]kleidung, *die;* **~woman** *n.* Sportlerin, *die*

sporty *adj.* sportlich

spot [spɒt] 1. *n.* a) *(precise place)* Stelle, *die;* **on this ~:** an dieser Stelle; **be in a tight ~** *(fig. coll.)* in der Klemme sitzen *(ugs.);* **put sb. on the ~** *(fig. coll.)* jmdn. in Verlegenheit bringen; b) *(suitable area)* Platz, *der;* c) *(dot)* Tupfen, *der;* d) *(stain)* **~** |of blood/grease/ ink| [Blut-/Fett-/Tinten]fleck, *der;* e) *(Brit. coll.: small amount)* **do a ~ of** work/sewing ein bißchen arbeiten/nähen; f) *(drop)* **a ~** or **a few ~s of** rain ein paar Regentropfen; g) *(Med.)* Pickel, *der.* 2. *v.t.,* -tt- *(detect)* entdecken; erkennen ⟨*Gefahr*⟩

spot: ~check *n.* Stichprobe, *die;* **~less** *adj.* fleckenlos; **her house is absolutely ~** *(fig.)* ihr Haus ist makellos sauber; **~light** *n.* Scheinwerfer, *der;* **be in the ~light** *(fig.)* im Rampenlicht stehen

spotted ['spɒtɪd] *adj.* gepunktet

spotty *adj.* (pimply) picklig

spouse [spaʊs] *n.* [Ehe]gatte, *der/*-gattin, *die*

spout [spaʊt] 1. *n.* Schnabel, *der; (of tap)* Ausflußrohr, *das.* 2. *v.i. (gush)* schießen (**from** aus)

sprain [spreɪn] 1. *v.t.* verstauchen. 2. *n.* Verstauchung, *die*

sprang *see* **spring** 2, 3

sprawl [sprɔːl] *v.i.* **a)** sich ausstrecken; *(fall)* der Länge nach hinfallen; **b)** *(straggle)* sich ausbreiten

¹**spray** [spreɪ] *n.* (bouquet) Strauß, *der*

²**spray** 1. *v.t.* spritzen; sprühen *(Parfüm)*; besprühen ⟨Haar, Pflanze⟩. 2. *n.* **a)** *(drops)* Sprühnebel, *der;* **b)** *(liquid)* Spray, *der od. das*

spread [spred] 1. *v.t.,* **spread a)** ausbreiten ⟨Tuch, Landkarte⟩ (**on auf** + *Dat.*); streichen ⟨Butter, Farbe, Marmelade⟩; **b)** *(extend range of)* verbreiten; **c)** *(distribute)* verteilen. 2. *v.i.,* **spread** sich ausbreiten. 3. *n.* **a)** Verbreitung, *die; (of city, poverty)* Ausbreitung, *die;* **b)** *(coll.: meal)* Festessen, *das;* **c)** *(paste)* Brotaufstrich, *der.*

spread 'out 1. *v.t.* ausbreiten. 2. *v.i.* sich verteilen

spree [spriː] *n.* **go on a shopping ~:** ganz groß einkaufen gehen

sprig [sprɪɡ] *n.* Zweig, *der*

sprightly ['spraɪtlɪ] *adj.* munter

spring [sprɪŋ] 1. *n.* **a)** *(season)* Frühling, *der;* **in** [**the**] **~:** im Frühling *od.* Frühjahr; **b)** *(water)* Quelle, *die;* **c)** *(Mech.)* Feder, *die;* **d)** *(jump)* Sprung, *der.* 2. *v.i.,* **sprang** [spræŋ] *or (Amer.)* **sprung** [sprʌŋ], **sprung a)** *(jump)* springen; ~ **to life** *(fig.)* [plötzlich] zum Leben erwachen; **b)** *(arise)* entspringen (**from** *Dat.*). 3. *v.t.,* **sprang** *or (Amer.)* **sprung, sprung:** ~ **sth. on sb.** jmdm. mit etw. überfallen

spring: **~board** *n.* Sprungbrett, *das;* ~-'**clean** 1. *n.* Frühjahrsputz, *der;* 2. *v.t.* Frühjahrsputz machen; ~ '**onion** *n.* Frühlingszwiebel, *die;* **~time** *n.* Frühling, *der*

sprinkle ['sprɪŋkl] *v.t.* streuen; sprengen ⟨Flüssigkeit⟩. **sprinkler** ['sprɪŋklə(r)] *n. (Hort.)* Sprinkler, *der*

sprint [sprɪnt] 1. *v.t. & i.* rennen; sprinten (bes. *Sport*). 2. *n.* Sprint, *der*

sprout [spraʊt] 1. *n.* **a) Brussels ~s** Rosenkohl, *der;* **b)** *(Bot.)* Trieb, *der.* 2. *v.i.* sprießen *(geh.)*

spruce [spruːs] 1. *adj.* gepflegt. 2. *n.* Fichte, *die*

sprung [sprʌŋ] 1. *see* **spring** 2, 3. 2. *attrib. adj.* gefedert

spud [spʌd] *n. (sl.)* Kartoffel, *die*

spun *see* **spin**

spur [spɜː(r)] 1. *n.* Sporn, *der; (fig.)* Ansporn, *der;* **on the ~ of the moment** ganz spontan. 2. *v.t.,* **-rr-** *(fig.)* anspornen

spurious ['spjʊərɪəs] *adj.* gespielt ⟨Interesse⟩; zweifelhaft ⟨Anspruch⟩

spurn [spɜːn] *v.t.* zurückweisen

¹**spurt** [spɜːt] *n.* Spurt, *der;* **put on a ~:** einen Spurt einlegen

²**spurt** 1. *v.i.* ~ **out** [**from** *or* **of**] herausspritzen [aus]. 2. *n.* Strahl, *der*

spy [spaɪ] 1. *n.* Spion, *der/*Spionin, *die.* 2. *v.i.* spionieren; ~ **on sb.** jmdm. nachspionieren

squabble ['skwɒbl] 1. *n.* Streit, *der.* 2. *v.i.* sich zanken (**over, about** wegen)

squad [skwɒd] *n.* **a)** *(Mil.)* Gruppe, *die;* **b)** *(group)* Mannschaft, *die*

squadron ['skwɒdrən] *n.* **a)** *(Navy)* Geschwader, *das;* **b)** *(Air Force)* Staffel, *die*

squalid ['skwɒlɪd] *adj.* **a)** *(dirty)* schmutzig; **b)** *(poor)* schäbig

squall [skwɔːl] *n. (gust)* Bö, *die*

squalor ['skwɒlə(r)] *n.* Schmutz, *der*

squander ['skwɒndə(r)] *v.t.* vergeuden

square [skweə(r)] 1. *n.* **a)** *(Geom.)* Quadrat, *das;* **b)** *(open area)* Platz, *der.* 2. *adj.* **a)** quadratisch; **b) a ~ foot/mile** ein Quadratfuß/eine Quadratmeile. 3. *v.t.* **a)** *(Math.)* quadrieren; **b)** ~ **it with sb.** es mit jmdm. klären. 4. *v.i.* *(agree)* übereinstimmen.

square 'up *v.i.* (settle up) abrechnen

square 'root *n.* Quadratwurzel, *die*

squash [skwɒʃ] 1. *v.t.* *(crush)* zerquetschen; ~ **sth. flat** etw. platt drücken. 2. *n.* **a)** Fruchtsaftgetränk, *das;* **b)** *(Sport)* Squash, *das*

squat [skwɒt] *v.i.,* **-tt-:** **a)** *(crouch)* hocken; **b)** ~ **in a house** ein Haus besetzen. '**squatter** *n.* Hausbesetzer, *der/*-besetzerin, *die*

squawk [skwɔːk] *v.i.* ⟨Krähe:⟩ krähen; ⟨Huhn:⟩ kreischen

squeak [skwiːk] 1. *n.* **a)** *(of animal)* Quieken, *das;* **b)** *(of brakes, hinge, etc.)* Quietschen, *das.* 2. *v.i.* **a)** ⟨Tier:⟩ quieken; **b)** ⟨Scharnier, Tür, Bremse, Schuh usw.:⟩ quietschen

squeal [skwiːl] 1. *v.i.* **a)** ~ **with pain/in fear** ⟨Person:⟩ vor Schmerz/Angst aufschreien; ⟨Tier:⟩ vor Schmerz/Angst laut quieken; **b)** ⟨Bremsen: Räder:⟩

kreischen; ⟨*Reifen:*⟩ quietschen. **2.** *n.*
Kreischen, *das; (of tyres)* Quietschen,
das; (of animal) Quieken, *das*

squeamish ['skwi:mɪʃ] *adj.* be ~:
zartbesaitet sein

squeeze [skwi:z] **1.** *n.* Druck, *der; give
sth. a small* ~: etw. [leicht] drücken. **2.**
v. t. **a)** *(press)* drücken; drücken auf
(+ Akk.) ⟨*Tube, Plastikflasche*⟩; *(to get
juice)* auspressen; **b)** *(extract)* drücken
(out of aus); ~ out sth. etw. heraus-
drücken; **c)** *(force)* zwängen

squelch [skweltʃ] *v. i.* quatschen *(ugs.)*

squid [skwɪd] *n.* Kalmar, *der*

squiggle ['skwɪgl] *n.* Schnörkel, *der*

squint [skwɪnt] **1.** *n.* Schielen, *das.* **2.**
v. i. **a)** *(Med.)* schielen; **b)** *(with half-
closed eyes)* blinzeln

squire ['skwaɪə(r)] *n.* ≈ Gutsherr, *der*

squirm [skwɜːm] *v. i.* sich winden
(with vor + *Dat.*)

squirrel ['skwɪrl] *n.* Eichhörnchen, *das*

squirt [skwɜːt] **1.** *v. t.* spritzen; sprühen ⟨*Spray, Puder*⟩; ~ sth. at sb. jmdm.
mit etw. bespritzen/besprühen. **2.** *v. i.*
spritzen. **3.** *n.* Spritzer, *der*

St *abbr.* Saint St.

St. *abbr.* Street Str.

st. *abbr. (Brit.: unit of weight)* stone

stab [stæb] **1.** *v. t.,* -bb- stechen; ~ sb.
in the chest jmdm. in die Brust ste-
chen. **2.** *v. i.,* -bb- stechen. **3.** *n.* **a)**
Stich, *der;* **b)** *(coll.: attempt)* make or
have a ~ [at it] [es] versuchen

stability [stə'bɪlɪtɪ] *n.* Stabilität, *die*

stabilize ['steɪbɪlaɪz] **1.** *v. t.* stabilisieren. **2.** *v. i.* sich stabilisieren

¹stable ['steɪbl] *adj.* stabil; gefestigt
⟨*Person*⟩

²stable *n.* Stall, *der*

stack [stæk] **1.** *n.* **a)** *(pile)* Stoß, *der;*
Stapel, *der;* **b)** *(coll.: large amount)*
Haufen, *der (ugs.);* **c)** [chimney-]~:
Schornstein, *der.* **2.** *v. t.* ~ [up]
[auf]stapeln

stadium ['steɪdɪəm] *n.* Stadion, *das*

staff [stɑːf] **1.** *n.* **a)** *(stick)* Stock, *der;*
b) *(personnel)* Personal, *das; (of
school)* Lehrkollegium, *das.* **2.** *v. t.* mit
Personal ausstatten. **'staff-room** *n.*
(Sch.) Lehrerzimmer, *das*

stag [stæg] *n.* Hirsch, *der*

stage [steɪdʒ] **1.** *n.* **a)** *(Theatre)* Bühne,
die; **b)** *(part of process)* Stadium, *das;*
at this ~: in diesem Stadium; do sth.
by ~s etw. abschnittsweise tun; in the
final ~s in der Schlußphase; **c)** *(distance)* Etappe, *die.* **2.** *v. t.* **a)** *(present)*
inszenieren; **b)** *(arrange)* veranstalten

stage: ~-**coach** *n.* Postkutsche, *die;*
~ **door** *n.* Bühneneingang, *der;* ~
fright *n.* Lampenfieber, *das;*
~-**manage** *v. t. (fig.)* veranstalten

stagger ['stægə(r)] **1.** *v. i.* schwanken.
2. *v. t. (astonish)* die Sprache verschlagen (+ *Dat.*)

stagnant ['stægnənt] *adj.* **a)** stehend
⟨*Gewässer*⟩; **b)** *(Econ.)* stagnierend

stagnate [stæg'neɪt] *v. i.* **a)** ⟨*Wasser:*⟩
abstehen; **b)** ⟨*Wirtschaft, Geschäft:*⟩
stagnieren; ⟨*Person:*⟩ abstumpfen.
stagnation [stæg'neɪʃn] *n.* **a)** *(of
water)* Stehen, *das;* **b)** *(Econ.)* Stagnation, *die*

staid [steɪd] *adj.* gesetzt

stain [steɪn] **1.** *v. t.* **a)** verfärben; *(make
~s on)* Flecken hinterlassen auf
(+ *Dat.*); **b)** *(colour)* beizen ⟨*Holz*⟩. **2.**
n. Fleck, *der.* **stained 'glass** *n.* far-
biges Glas; ~ '**window** Fenster mit
Glasmalerei

'stainless *adj.* fleckenlos. **stainless
'steel** *n.* Edelstahl, *der*

stair [steə(r)] *n. (step)* [Treppen]stufe,
die; ~s Treppe, *die.* '**staircase** *n.*
Treppenhaus, *das*

stake [steɪk] *n.* **a)** *(pointed stick)* Pfahl,
der; **b)** *(wager)* Einsatz, *der;* be at ~:
auf dem Spiel stehen

stale [steɪl] *adj.* alt; muffig; abgestanden ⟨*Luft*⟩; alt[backen] ⟨*Brot*⟩; schal
⟨*Bier, Wein usw.*⟩

'stalemate *n.* Patt, *das*

¹stalk [stɔːk] *v. t.* sich heranpirschen
an (+ *Akk.*)

²stalk *n. (Bot.) (main stem)* Stengel,
der; (of leaf, flower, fruit) Stiel, *der*

stall [stɔːl] **1.** *n.* **a)** Stand, *der;* **b)** *(Brit.
Theatre)* ~s Parkett, *das.* **2.** *v. t.* ab-
würgen *(ugs.)* ⟨*Motor*⟩. **3.** *v. i.* ⟨*Motor:*⟩
stehenbleiben

stallion ['stæljən] *n.* Hengst, *der*

stalwart ['stɔːlwət] *adj. (determined)*
entschieden; *(loyal)* treu

stamina ['stæmɪnə] *n.* Ausdauer, *die*

stammer ['stæmə(r)] **1.** *v. i.* stottern. **2.**
v. t. stammeln. **3.** *n.* Stottern, *das*

stamp [stæmp] **1.** *v. t.* **a)** *(impress, imprint sth. on)* [ab]stempeln; **b)** ~ one's
foot mit dem Fuß aufstampfen; **c)** *(put
postage ~ on)* frankieren; ~ed ad-
dressed envelope frankierter Rückumschlag; **d)** become or be ~ed on sb.'s
memory or mind sich jmdm. fest ein-
prägen. **2.** *v. i.* aufstampfen. **3.** *n.* Marke, *die; (postage ~)* Briefmarke, *die;
(instrument for ~ing)* Stempel, *der.*
'stamp on *v. t.* **a)** zertreten ⟨*Insekt*⟩;

~ **on sb's foot** jmdm. auf den Fuß treten; b) *(suppress)* durchgreifen gegen. **stamp 'out** v. t. [aus]stanzen; *(fig.)* ausmerzen

stamp: ~ **album** n. Briefmarkenalbum, *das;* ~-**collecting** n. Briefmarkensammeln, *das*

stampede [stæm'pi:d] n. Stampede, *die*

stand [stænd] **1.** v. i., **stood** [stʊd] a) stehen; b) **my offer/promise still ~s** mein Angebot/Versprechen gilt nach wie vor; **as it ~s, as things ~:** wie die Dinge [jetzt] liegen; **I'd like to know where I ~** *(fig.)* ich möchte wissen, wo ich dran bin; c) *(be candidate)* kandidieren; d) |not| ~ **in sb.'s way** *(fig.)* jmdm. [keine] Steine in den Weg legen; e) *(be likely)* ~ **to win or gain/lose sth.** etw. gewinnen/verlieren können. **2.** v. t., **stood** a) *(set in position)* stellen; b) *(endure)* ertragen; **I cannot ~** |**the sight of**| **him/her** ich kann ihn/sie nicht ausstehen; **he can't ~ the pressure/strain** er ist dem Druck/den Strapazen nicht gewachsen; **I can't ~ it any longer!** ich halte es nicht mehr aus!; c) *(buy)* ~ **sb. sth.** jmdm. etw. ausgeben. **3.** n. a) *(support)* Ständer, *der;* b) *(stall; at exhibition)* Stand, *der;* c) *(raised structure)* Tribüne, *die.* **stand a'bout, stand a'round** v. i. herumstehen. **stand a'side** v. i. zur Seite treten. **'stand between** v. t. sth. ~s **between sb. and sth.** *(fig.)* etw. steht jmdm. bei etw. im Wege. **stand by 1.** [-'-] v. i. a) *(be near)* daneben stehen; b) *(be ready)* sich zur Verfügung halten. **2.** ['--] v. t. a) *(support)* ~ **by sb./one another** jmdm./sich [gegenseitig] beistehen; b) *(adhere to)* ~ **by sth.** zu etw. stehen. **'stand for** v. t. a) *(signify)* bedeuten; b) *(coll.: tolerate)* sich *(Dat.)* bieten lassen. **stand 'in** v. i. aushelfen; ~ **in for sb.** für jmdn. einspringen. **stand 'out** v. i. *(be prominent)* herausragen; ~ **out a mile** *(fig.)* nicht zu übersehen sein. **'stand over** v. t. beaufsichtigen. **stand 'up** v. i. a) aufstehen; ~ **up straight** sich aufrecht hinstellen; b) *(cause)* standhalten; ~ **up well** |**in comparison with sb./sth.**| [im Vergleich zu jmdm./ etw.] gut abschneiden; ~ **up for sb./ sth.** für jmdn./etw. Partei ergreifen; ~ **up to sb.** sich jmdm. entgegenstellen. **standard** ['stændəd] **1.** n. a) Maßstab, *der; safety* ~ Sicherheitsnormen; **above/below/up to** ~: überdurchschnittlich [gut]/unter dem Durch-

schnitt/der Norm entsprechend; b) *(degree)* Niveau, *das;* ~ **of living** Lebensstandard, *der;* c) ~s *(morals)* Prinzipien; d) *(flag)* Standarte, *die.* **2.** *adj.* Standard-; **be ~ practice** allgemein üblich sein. **standardize** ['stændədaɪz] v. t. standardisieren

'standard lamp n. Stehlampe, *die*

stand: ~-**by 1.** n. **be on** ~-**by** einsatzbereit sein; **2.** *adj.* Ersatz-; ~-**in 1.** n. Ersatz, *der;* **2.** *adj.* Ersatz-.

'standing 1. n. a) *(repute)* Ansehen, *das;* b) *(duration)* **of long/short** ~: von langer/kurzer Dauer. **2.** *adj.* a) *(erect)* stehend; b) fest ⟨*Regel, Brauch*⟩. **standing:** ~**'order** n. Dauerauftrag, *der;* ~ **o'vation** n. stürmischer Beifall; ~-**room** n. Stehplätze

stand: ~-**pipe** n. Standrohr, *das;* ~**point** n. *(fig.)* Standpunkt, *der;* ~**still** n. Stillstand, *der;* **be at a ~still** stillstehen; **come to a ~still** zum Stehen kommen

stank see **stink 1**

staple ['steɪpl] **1.** n. [Heft]klammer, *die.* **2.** v. t. heften (**on to** an + Akk.). **stapler** ['steɪplə(r)] n. [Draht]hefter, *der*

star [stɑː(r)] **1.** n. a) [Stern]stern, *der;* b) *(prominent person)* Star, *der.* **2.** v. i. ~ **in a film** in einem Film die Hauptrolle spielen

starboard ['stɑːbəd] n. Steuerbord, *das*

starch [stɑːtʃ] n. Stärke, *die*

stardom ['stɑːdəm] n. Starruhm, *der*

stare [steə(r)] v. i. starren; ~ **at sb./sth.** jmdn./etw. anstarren

starfish n. Seestern, *der*

stark [stɑːk] **1.** *adj.* scharf ⟨*Kontrast, Umriß*⟩. **2.** *adv.* völlig; ~ **naked** splitternackt *(ugs.)*

starling ['stɑːlɪŋ] n. Star, *der*

starry ['stɑːrɪ] *adj.* sternklar

start [stɑːt] **1.** v. i. a) *(begin)* anfangen; ~ **on sth.** etw. beginnen; b) *(set out)* aufbrechen; c) *(begin to function)* anlaufen; ⟨*Auto, Motor usw.*:⟩ anspringen. **2.** v. t. a) *(begin)* beginnen [mit]; ~ **doing** or **to do sth.** [damit] anfangen, etw. zu tun; b) *(cause)* auslösen; anfangen ⟨*Streit, Schlägerei*⟩; legen/*(accidentally)* verursachen ⟨*Brand*⟩; c) *(set up)* ins Leben rufen ⟨*Organisation, Projekt*⟩; d) *(switch on)* einschalten; anlassen ⟨*Motor, Auto*⟩. **3.** n. a) Anfang, *der;* Beginn, *der;* *(of race)* Start, *der;* **from the ~:** von Anfang an; **from ~ to finish** von Anfang bis Ende;

make a ~: anfangen (**on** mit); (on journey) aufbrechen; **b)** (Sport: ~ing-place) Start, der. '**starter** n. **a)** (food) Vorspeise, die; **b)** (Sport) Starter, der
startle ['stɑ:tl] v.t. erschrecken; **be ~d by** sth. über etw. (Akk.) erschrecken.
startling ['stɑ:tlɪŋ] adj. erstaunlich
starvation [stɑ:'veɪʃn] n. Verhungern, das
starve [stɑ:v] v.i. **~ [to death]** verhungern
state [steɪt] **1.** n. **a)** (condition) Zustand, der; **b)** (nation) Staat, der; **be in a ~:** aufgeregt sein; **d) lie in ~:** aufgebahrt sein. **2.** v.t. (express) erklären; angeben ⟨Alter usw.⟩
stately ['steɪtlɪ] adj. majestätisch; stattlich ⟨Körperbau, Gebäude⟩. **stately 'home** n. Herrensitz, der
'**statement** n. **a)** (stating, account) Aussage, die; (declaration) Erklärung, die; **b)** |bank| ~: Kontoauszug, der
statesman ['steɪtsmən] n., pl. **statesmen** ['steɪtsmən] Staatsmann, der
static ['stætɪk] adj. statisch
station ['steɪʃn] **1.** n. **a)** see **railway-station; b)** (status) Rang, der. **2.** v.t. aufstellen ⟨Wache⟩
stationary ['steɪʃənərɪ] adj. stehend; **be ~:** stehen
stationer ['steɪʃənə(r)] n. **~'s |shop|** Schreibwarengeschäft, das. **stationery** ['steɪʃənərɪ] n. **a)** (writing materials) Schreibwaren Pl.; **b)** (writing-paper) Briefpapier, das
'**station-wagon** n. (Amer.) Kombiwagen, der
statistical [stə'tɪstɪkl] attrib. adj., **statistically** [stə'tɪstɪkəlɪ] adv. statistisch
statistics [stə'tɪstɪks] n. Statistik, die
statue ['stætju:] n. Statue, die
stature ['stætʃə(r)] n. Statur (fig.); (fig.) Format, das
status ['steɪtəs] n. Rang, der; **social ~:** [gesellschaftlicher] Status. '**status symbol** n. Statussymbol, das
statute ['stætju:t] n. Gesetz, das. **statutory** ['stætjʊtərɪ] adj. gesetzlich
staunch [stɔ:ntʃ] adj. treu ⟨Freund⟩; überzeugt ⟨Katholik usw.⟩
stave [steɪv] v.t. **~ 'off** abwenden; stillen ⟨Hunger⟩
stay [steɪ] **1.** n. Aufenthalt, der; (visit) Besuch, der; **come/go for a short ~ with** sb. jmdn. kurz besuchen. **2.** v.i. bleiben; **~ put** (coll.) ⟨Person:⟩ bleiben|, wo man ist|; **~ the night in a** hotel die Nacht in einem Hotel ver-

bringen. **3.** v.t. **~ the course** (fig.) durchhalten. **stay a'way** v.i. wegbleiben. **stay be'hind** v.i. zurückbleiben. **stay 'in** v.i. zu Hause bleiben. **stay 'out** v.i. **a)** (not go home) wegbleiben (ugs.); **b)** (remain outside) draußen bleiben. **stay 'up** v.i. aufbleiben
stead [sted] n. **a) in** sb.'s **~:** an jmds. Stelle (Dat.); **b) stand** sb. **in good ~:** jmdm. zustatten kommen
steadfast ['stedfɑ:st] adj. standhaft; zuverlässig ⟨Freund⟩
steadily ['stedɪlɪ] adv. **a)** (stably) fest; **b)** (continuously) stetig
steady ['stedɪ] **1.** adj. **a)** (stable) stabil; (not wobbling) standfest; **b)** (still) ruhig; **c)** (regular, constant) stetig; gleichmäßig ⟨Arbeit, Tempo⟩; stabil ⟨Preis, Lohn⟩; gleichbleibend ⟨Temperatur⟩; **we had ~ rain/drizzle** wir hatten Dauerregen/es nieselte [bei uns] ständig; **d) a ~ job** eine feste Stelle; **a ~ boy-friend** ein fester Freund. **2.** v.t. festhalten ⟨Leiter⟩; beruhigen ⟨Nerven⟩
steak [steɪk] n. Steak, das
steal [sti:l] **1.** v.t., **stole** [stəʊl], **stolen** ['stəʊln] stehlen (**from** Dat.). **2.** v.i., **stole, stolen a)** stehlen; **~ from** sb. jmdn. bestehlen; **b) ~ in/out** sich hinein-/hinausstehlen
stealth [stelθ] n. Heimlichkeit, die; **by ~:** heimlich. **stealthy** ['stelθɪ] adj. heimlich
steam [sti:m] **1.** n. Dampf, der; **let off ~** (fig.) Dampf ablassen (ugs.); **run out of ~** (fig.) den Schwung verlieren; **under one's own ~** (fig.) aus eigener Kraft. **2.** v.t. (Cookery) dämpfen; dünsten. **3.** v.i. dämpfen; **~ing hot** dampfend heiß. **steam 'up** v.i. beschlagen
'**steam engine** n. Dampflok[omotive], die
'**steamer** n. Dämpfer, der
'**steamroller** n. Dampfwalze, die
'**steam train** n. Dampfzug, der
'**steamy** adj. dunstig; beschlagen ⟨Glas⟩
steel [sti:l] **1.** n. Stahl, der. **2.** attrib. adj. stählern; Stahl⟨helm, -block, -platte⟩. **3.** v.t. **~ oneself for/against** sth. sich für/gegen etw. wappnen (geh.); **~ oneself to do** sth. allen Mut zusammennehmen, um etw. zu tun. '**steelworks** n. sing. or pl. Stahlwerk, das
'**steep** [sti:p] adj. **a)** steil; **b)** (coll.: ex-

cessive) happig *(ugs.);* **the bill is | a bit]** ~: die Rechnung ist [ziemlich] gesalzen *(ugs.)*

²**steep** *v. t. (soak)* einweichen

steeple ['sti:pl] *n.* Kirchturm, *der*

steer [stɪə(r)] 1. *v. t.* steuern; lenken. 2. *v. i.* steuern; ~ **clear of sb./sth.** *(fig. coll.)* jmdm./einer Sache aus dem Weg[e] gehen. **steering** *n. (Motor Veh.)* Lenkung, *die.* **steering-wheel** *n.* Lenkrad, *das*

¹**stem** [stem] 1. *n.* a) *(Bot.)* Stiel, *der;* b) *(Ling.)* Stamm, *der.* 2. *v. i.* -mm-: ~ **from sth.** auf etw. *(Akk.)* zurückzuführen sein

²**stem** *v. t.,* -mm- *(check, dam up)* aufhalten; eindämmen *(Flut);* stillen *(Blutung)*

stench [stentʃ] *n.* Gestank, *der*

stencil ['stensl] *n.* Schablone, *die; (for duplicating)* Matrize, *die*

step [step] 1. *n.* a) Schritt, *der;* **take a ~ back/forwards** einen Schritt zurücktreten/nach vorn treten; b) *(stair)* Stufe, *die;* **a flight of ~s** eine Treppe; **[pair of] ~s** *(ladder)* Stehleiter, *die;* ~s **be in ~:** im Schritt sein; *(with music)* im Takt sein; d) **take ~s to do sth.** Schritte unternehmen, um etw. zu tun; e) *(stage)* ~ **by ~:** Schritt für Schritt; **what is the next ~?** wie geht es weiter?; f) *(grade)* Stufe, *die.* 2. *v. i.* -pp- treten; ~ **inside** eintreten; ~ **into** sb's shoes *(fig.)* an jmds. Stelle treten; ~ **over sb./sth.** über jmdn./etw. steigen. **step 'back** *v. i.* zurücktreten. **step 'in** *v. i.* a) eintreten; b) *(fig.) (take sb.'s place)* einspringen; *(intervene)* eingreifen. **step 'up** 1. *v. i. (ascend)* hinaufsteigen. 2. *v. t.* erhöhen; verstärken *(Anstrengungen)*

step: ~**child** *n.* Stiefkind, *das;* ~**daughter** *n.* Stieftochter, *die;* ~**father** *n.* Stiefvater, *der;* ~**ladder** *n.* Stehleiter, *die;* ~**mother** *n.* Stiefmutter, *die*

'**stepping-stone** *n.* Trittstein, *der; (fig.)* Sprungbrett, *das* **(to** für)

stereo ['steriəʊ] 1. *n.* Stereo, *das; (equipment)* Stereoanlage, *die.* 2. *adj.* stereo; Stereo⟨*aufnahme, -platte*⟩

stereophonic [steriə'fɒnɪk] *adj.* stereophonic

stereotype ['steriətaip] 1. *n.* Stereotyp, *das.* 2. *v. t.* in ein Klischee zwängen; ~**d** stereotyp

sterile ['sterail] *adj.* steril

sterilize ['sterilaiz] *v. t.* sterilisieren

sterling ['stɜ:lɪŋ] 1. *n.* Sterling, *der;* in

~: in Pfund [Sterling]. 2. *attrib. adj.* a) ~ **silver** Sterlingsilber, *das;* b) *(fig.)* gediegen

¹**stern** [stɜ:n] *adj.* streng; ernst ⟨*Warnung*⟩

²**stern** *n. (Naut.)* Heck, *das*

'**sternly** *adv.* streng

steroid ['steroid] *n.* Steroid, *das*

stethoscope ['steθəskəʊp] *n.* Stethoskop, *das*

stew [stju:] 1. *n.* Eintopf, *der.* 2. *v. t.* schmoren [lassen]

steward ['stju:əd] *n.* a) *(on ship, plane)* Steward, *der;* b) *(at public meeting etc.)* Ordner, *der.* **stewardess** *n.* Stewardeß, *die*

stick [stɪk] 1. *v. t.,* stuck [stʌk] a) *(thrust point of)* stecken; ~ **sth. in[to] sth.** mit etw. in etw. *(Akk.)* stechen; b) *(coll.: put)* stecken; ~ **a picture on the wall/a vase on the shelf** ein Bild an die Wand hängen/eine Vase aufs Regal stellen; ~ **sth. in the kitchen** etw. in die Küche tun *(ugs.);* c) *(with glue etc.)* kleben; d) **the car is stuck in the mud** das Auto ist im Schlamm steckengeblieben; **the door is stuck** die Tür klemmt [fest]. 2. *v. i.,* stuck a) *(be fixed by point)* stecken; b) *(adhere)* kleben; ~ **to sth.** an etw. *(Dat.)* kleben; c) *(become immobile)* ⟨*Auto, Räder:*⟩ steckenbleiben; ⟨*Schublade, Tür, Griff, Bremse:*⟩ klemmen; ⟨*Schlüssel:*⟩ feststecken. 3. *n.* Stock, *der;* **a ~ of chalk** ein Stück Kreide; **a ~ of celery/rhubarb** eine Stange Sellerie/Rhabarber. **stick a'bout, stick a'round** *v. i. (coll.)* dableiben; *(wait)* warten. '**stick by** *v. t. (fig.)* stehen zu. **stick 'on** *v. t. (glue on)* aufkleben. **stick 'out** 1. *v. t.* herausstrecken ⟨*Zunge*⟩; b)~ **it out** *(coll.)* durchhalten. 2. *v. i.* a) ⟨*Bauch:*⟩ vorstehen; **his ears** ~ **out** er hat abstehende Ohren; b) *(fig.: be obvious)* sich abheben; ~ **out a mile** *(sl.)* [klar] auf der Hand liegen; ~ **out like a sore thumb** *(coll.)* ins Auge springen. '**stick to** *v. t.* a) *(be faithful to)* halten ⟨*Versprechen*⟩; bleiben bei ⟨*Entscheidung*⟩; b) ~ **to the point** beim Thema bleiben. **stick 'up** 1. *v. t.* a) *(coll.)* anschlagen ⟨*Poster*⟩; ~ **up one's hand** die Hand heben; b) *(seal)* zukleben. 2. *v. i.* ~ **up for sb./sth.** für jmdn./etw. eintreten; ~ **up for yourself!** setz dich zur Wehr!

'**sticker** *n.* Aufkleber, *der*

'**sticking-plaster** *n.* Heftpflaster, *das*

'**sticky** *adj.* a) klebrig; ~ **label** Aufkleber, *der*; **b)** *(humid)* schwül ‹*Klima, Luft*›

stiff [stɪf] *adj.* **a)** *(rigid)* steif; hart ‹*Bürste, Stock*›; **be ˹rozen ~**: steif vor Kälte sein; **b)** *(intense, severe)* hartnäckig; **c)** *(formal)* steif; **d)** *(difficult)* hart ‹*Test*›; schwer ‹*Frage, Prüfung*›; **e)** *(coll.)* **be bored/scared ~**: sich zu Tode langweilen/eine wahnsinnige Angst haben *(ugs.)*. **stiffen** ['stɪfn] **1.** *v. t.* steif machen. **2.** *v. i.* steifer werden; ‹*Person:*› erstarren. **'stiffness** *n.* Steifheit, *die*

stifle ['staɪfl] **1.** *v. t.* ersticken; *(fig.)* unterdrücken. **2.** *v. i.* ersticken. **stifling** ['staɪflɪŋ] *adj.* stickig; drückend ‹*Hitze*›

stigma ['stɪɡmə] *n.* Stigma, *das (geh.)*

stile [staɪl] *n.* Zauntritt, *der*

stiletto [stɪ'letəʊ] *n.* ~ **[heel]** Stöckelabsatz, *der*

¹still [stɪl] **1.** *pred. adj.* still; **be ~**: [still] stehen; **hold sth. ~**: etw. ruhig halten; **keep** *or* **stay ~**: stillhalten; **stand ~**: stillstehen. **2.** *adv.* **a)** *(without change)* noch; *expr. surprise or annoyance* immer noch; **b)** *(nevertheless)* trotzdem; **c)** *with comparative (even)* noch

²still *n.* Destillierapparat, *der*

still: **~born** *adj.* totgeboren; **~ 'life** *n.* *(Art)* Stilleben, *das*

stilt [stɪlt] *n.* Stelze, *die.* **'stilted** *adj.* gestelzt

stimulant ['stɪmjʊlənt] *n.* Stimulans, *das*

stimulate ['stɪmjʊleɪt] *v. t.* anregen. **stimulation** [stɪmjʊ'leɪʃn] *n.* Anregung, *die*

stimulus ['stɪmjʊləs] *n., pl.* **stimuli** ['stɪmjʊlaɪ] Ansporn, *der*

sting [stɪŋ] **1.** *n.* **a)** *(wounding)* Stich, *der*; *(by jellyfish, nettles)* Verbrennung, *die*; **b)** *(from ointment, wind)* Brennen, *das.* **2.** *v. t., stung* [stʌŋ] stechen. **3.** *v. i., stung* Brennen. **'stinging-nettle** *n.* Brennessel, *die*

stingy ['stɪndʒɪ] *adj.* geizig; knaus[e]rig *(ugs.)*

stink [stɪŋk] **1.** *v. i., stank* [stæŋk] *or* **stunk** [stʌŋk], **stunk** stinken (**of** nach). **2.** *n.* Gestank, *der*

stint [stɪnt] **1.** *v. i.* **~ on sth.** an etw. *(Dat.)* sparen. **2.** *n.* [Arbeits]pensum, *das*

stipulate ['stɪpjʊleɪt] *v. t.* *(demand)* fordern; *(lay down)* festlegen. **stipulation** [stɪpjʊ'leɪʃn] *n.* *(condition)* Bedingung, *die*

stir [stɜː(r)] **1.** *v. t., -rr-:* **a)** *(mix)* rühren; umrühren ‹*Tee, Kaffee*›; **b)** *(move)* bewegen. **2.** *v. i., -rr- (move)* sich rühren. **3.** *n.* Aufregung, *die.* **stir 'in** *v. t.* einrühren. **stir 'up** *v. t.* **a)** *(disturb)* aufrühren; **b)** *(fig.: arouse)* wecken ‹*Interesse, Leidenschaft*›

stirring ['stɜːrɪŋ] *adj.* bewegend ‹*Musik, Poesie*›; mitreißend ‹*Rede*›

stirrup ['stɪrəp] *n.* Steigbügel, *der*

stitch [stɪtʃ] **1.** *n.* **a)** *(Sewing)* Stich, *der*; *(Knitting)* Masche, *die*; **b)** *(pain)* **have a ~**: Seitenstechen haben. **2.** *v. t.* nähen

stoat [stəʊt] *n.* Hermelin, *das*

stock [stɒk] **1.** *n.* **a)** *(origin, family, breed)* Abstammung, *die*; **b)** *(supply, store)* Vorrat, *der*; *(in shop etc.)* Warenbestand, *der*; **be in/out of ~** ‹*Ware:*› vorrätig/nicht vorrätig sein; **have sth. in ~**: etw. auf Lager haben; **take ~ of sth.** *(fig.)* über etw. *(Akk.)* Bilanz ziehen; **c)** *(Cookery)* Brühe, *die.* **2.** *v. t.* **a)** *(supply with ~)* beliefern; **b)** *(Commerc.: keep in ~)* auf Lager haben. **3.** *attrib. adj.* Standard-.

stock: **~broker** Effektenmakler, *der*/-maklerin, *die*; **~ cube** *n.* Brühwürfel, *der*; **~ exchange** *n.* Börse, *die*

stocking ['stɒkɪŋ] *n.* Strumpf, *der*

'stockist *n.* Fachhändler, *der*/-händlerin, *die*

stock: **~market** *n.* **a)** Börse, *die*; **b)** *(trading)* Börsengeschäft, *das*; **~pile** **1.** *n.* Vorrat, *der*; *(weapons)* Arsenal, *das*; **2.** *v. t.* horten; anhäufen ‹*Waffen*›; **~'still** *pred. adj.* bewegungslos; **~taking** *n.* Inventur, *die*

stocky ['stɒkɪ] *adj.* stämmig

stodgy ['stɒdʒɪ] *adj.* pappig

stoical ['stəʊɪkl] *adj.* stoisch

stoke [stəʊk] *v. t.* heizen ‹*Ofen, Kessel*›; unterhalten ‹*Feuer*›

stole *see* **steal**

stolen ['stəʊln] **1.** *see* **steal.** **2.** *attrib. adj.* heimlich ‹*Vergnügen, Kuß*›

stolid ['stɒlɪd] *adj.* stur *(ugs.)*

stomach ['stʌmək] **1.** *n.* **a)** Magen, *der*; **b)** *(abdomen)* Bauch, *der*. **2.** *v. t.* *(fig.: tolerate)* ausstehen. **'stomach-ache** *n.* Magenschmerzen *Pl.*

'stomach upset *n.* Magenverstimmung, *die*

stone [stəʊn] **1.** *n.* **a)** Stein, *der*; **a ~'s throw [away]** *(fig.)* nur einen Steinwurf weit entfernt; **b)** *(Brit.: weight unit)* Gewicht von 6,35 kg. **2.** *adj.* steinern; Stein‹*mauer, -brücke*›. **3.** *v. t.* mit Steinen bewerfen

stone: S~ Age n. Steinzeit, die;
~-cold adj. eiskalt; **~-ˈdeaf** adj.
stocktaub (ugs.)

stony [ˈstəʊnɪ] adj. steinig

stood see stand 1, 2

stool [stuːl] n. Hocker, der

stoop [stuːp] 1. v. i. ~ **[down]** sich
bücken. 2. n. **walk with a ~**: gebeugt
gehen

stop [stɒp] 1. v. t., -pp-: a) anhalten
⟨Person, Fahrzeug⟩; aufhalten ⟨Fort-
schritt, Verkehr, Feind⟩; b) (not let continue) unterbrechen ⟨Redner, Spiel,
Gespräch⟩; beenden ⟨Krieg, Arbeit⟩;
stoppen ⟨Produktion, Uhr⟩; einstellen
⟨Zahlung, Lieferung⟩; ~ **that!** hör damit auf; **~ smoking/crying** aufhören
zu rauchen/weinen; c) (not let happen)
verhindern ⟨Verbrechen, Unfall⟩; ~
sth. [from] happening verhindern, daß
etw. geschieht; d) (switch off) abstellen ⟨Maschine⟩; e) (block up) zustopfen ⟨Loch⟩; verschließen ⟨Wasser-
hahn, Flasche⟩; f) **~ a cheque** einen
Scheck sperren lassen. 2. v. i., -pp-: a)
(not extend further) aufhören
⟨Zahlungen, Lieferungen:⟩ eingestellt
werden; b) (not move further) halten
⟨Fahrzeug, Fahrer:⟩ halten; ⟨Ma-
schine, Motor:⟩ stillstehen; ⟨Uhr, Fußgänger, Herz:⟩ stehenbleiben. 3. n. a)
(halt) Halt, der; **bring to a ~**: zum Stehen bringen ⟨Fahrzeug⟩; zum Erliegen
bringen ⟨Verkehr⟩; unterbrechen ⟨Ar-
beit⟩; **come to a ~**: stehenbleiben
⟨Fahrzeug:⟩ zum Stehen kommen;
⟨Arbeit, Verkehr:⟩ zum Erliegen kommen; **put a ~ to** abstellen ⟨Mißstände,
Unsinn⟩; b) (place) Haltestelle, die.
stop ˈby v. i. (Amer.) vorbeischauen
(ugs.). **stop ˈout** v. i. (coll.) draußen
bleiben. **stop ˈover** v. i. übernachten
(at bei). **stop ˈup** 1. v. t. zustopfen
⟨Loch, Öffnung⟩. 2. v. i. (coll.) see stay
up

stop: ~gap n. Notlösung, die;
~-light n. (traffic-light) rotes Licht;
~over n. Stopover, der

stoppage [ˈstɒpɪdʒ] n. a) (halt) Stillstand, der; (strike) Streik, der; b) (deduction) Abzug, der

stopper [ˈstɒpə(r)] n. Stöpsel, der

stop: ~-press n. letzte Meldung/
Meldungen; **~ sign** n. Stoppschild,
das; **~watch** n. Stoppuhr, die

storage [ˈstɔːrɪdʒ] n. Lagerung, die;
(of films, books, documents) Aufbewahrung, die; (of data, water, electricity) Speicherung, die. **ˈstorage**

heater n. [Nacht]speicherofen, der.
ˈstorage tank n. Sammelbehälter,
der

store [stɔː(r)] 1. n. a) (Amer.: shop) Laden, der; b) (Brit.: large general shop)
Kaufhaus, das; c) (warehouse) Lager,
das; **put sth. in ~**: etw. einlagern; d)
(stock) Vorrat, der ⟨of an + Dat.⟩; **be**
or lie in ~ for sb. jmdn. erwarten; e)
set [great] ~ by or on sth. [großen] Wert
auf etw. (Akk.) legen. 2. v. t. einlagern; speichern ⟨Getreide, Energie,
Wissen, Daten⟩. **store ˈup** v. t. speichern; **~ up provisions** sich (Dat.) Vorräte anlegen

store: ~house n. Lager[haus], das;
~-room n. Lagerraum, der

storey [ˈstɔːrɪ] n. Stockwerk, das

stork [stɔːk] n. Storch, der

storm [stɔːm] 1. n. Unwetter, das;
(thunder~) Gewitter, das. 2. v. t. & i.
stürmen. **ˈstormy** adj. stürmisch

¹story [ˈstɔːrɪ] n. a) Geschichte, die; b)
(news item) Bericht, der; c) (coll.: lie)
Märchen, das

²story (Amer.) see storey

stout [staʊt] adj. a) (strong) fest; b)
(fat) beleibt

stove [stəʊv] n. Ofen, der; (for cooking) Herd, der

stow [stəʊ] v. t. verstauen (into in +
Dat.). **stow aˈway** 1. v. t. verwahren.
2. v. i. als blinder Passagier reisen

straddle [ˈstrædl] v. t. ~ **a fence/chair**
rittlings auf einem Zaun/Stuhl sitzen

straggle [ˈstrægl] v. i. ~ **[along] behind**
the others den anderen hinterher-
zockeln (ugs.). **straggler** [ˈstræglə(r)]
n. Nachzügler, der

straight [streɪt] 1. adj. a) gerade; glatt
⟨Haar⟩; **in a ~ line** in gerader Linie; b)
(undiluted) **drink whisky ~**: Whisky
pur trinken; c) (direct) direkt ⟨Blick,
Schuß, Weg⟩; **be ~ with sb.** zu jmdm.
offen sein; **get sth. ~** (fig.) etw. genau
verstehen; **put or set the record ~** die
Sache richtigstellen. 2. adv. a) gerade;
b) (directly) geradewegs; **~ after** sofort nach; **come ~ to the point** direkt
zur Sache kommen; **look sb. ~ in the**
eye jmdn. direkt in die Augen
blicken; **~ ahead** or on immer geradeaus; c) (frankly) aufrichtig; d) (clearly)
klar ⟨sehen, denken⟩. **straight aˈway**
adv. (coll.) sofort

straighten [ˈstreɪtn] 1. v. t. a) gerade-
ziehen ⟨Teppich⟩; glätten ⟨Kleidung,
Haare⟩; b) (put in order) aufräumen.
2. v. i. gerade werden. **straighten**

'**out 1.** *v. t.* **a)** geradebiegen; glätten ⟨*Decke, Teppich*⟩; **b)** *(clear up)* klären. **2.** *v. i.* gerade werden. **straighten** '**up 1.** *v. t. see* tidy up. **2.** *v. i.* sich aufrichten

straight'forward *adj.* **a)** *(frank)* freimütig; schlicht ⟨*Stil, Sprache, Bericht*⟩; klar ⟨*Anweisung, Vorstellungen*⟩; **b)** *(simple)* einfach

strain [streɪn] **1.** *n.* **a)** *(pull)* Belastung, *die;* *(on rope)* Spannung, *die;* *(tension)* Streß, *der;* **be under |a great deal of]** ~: unter großem Streß stehen; **c)** *(person, thing)* **be a** ~ **on sb./sth.** jmdn./etw. belasten; **d)** *(muscular injury)* Zerrung, *die.* **2.** *v. t.* **a)** *(overexert)* überanstrengen; zerren ⟨*Muskel*⟩; **b)** *(stretch tightly)* [fest] spannen; **c)** *(filter)* durchseihen; seihen *(through durch).* **3.** *v. i. (strive intensely)* sich anstrengen. **strained** [streɪnd] *adj.* gezwungen ⟨*Lächeln*⟩; ~ **relations** gespannte Beziehungen

'**strainer** *n.* Sieb, *das*

strait [streɪt] *n.* **a)** *in sing. or pl. (Geog.)* Meerenge, *die;* **b)** *usu. in pl. (distress, difficulty)* Schwierigkeiten. '**straitjacket** *n.* Zwangsjacke, *die.* **strait'laced** [streɪt'leɪst] *adj.* puritanisch

[1]**strand** [strænd] *n. (thread)* Faden, *der;* *(of beads)* Kette, *die;* *(of hair)* Strähne, *die;* *(of rope)* Strang, *der*

[2]**strand** *v. t. (leave behind)* trocken setzen; **be [left]** ~**ed** *(fig.)* seinem Schicksal überlassen sein

strange [streɪndʒ] *adj. (peculiar)* seltsam; sonderbar; ~ **to say** seltsamerweise; **feel** ~: sich komisch fühlen. **stranger** ['streɪndʒə(r)] *n.* Fremde, *der/die;* **he is a** ~ **here/to the town** er ist hier/in der Stadt fremd

strangle ['stræŋgl] *v. t.* erwürgen. '**stranglehold** *n.* Würgegriff, *der.* **strangulation** [stræŋgjʊ'leɪʃn] *n.* Erwürgen, *das*

strap [stræp] **1.** *n.* **a)** *(leather)* Riemen, *der;* *(textile)* Band, *das;* *(shoulder-~)* Träger, *der;* *(for watch)* Armband, *das;* **b)** *(to grasp in vehicle)* Halteriemen, *der.* **2.** *v. t.,* **-pp-:** ~ **[into position/down** festschnallen; ~ **oneself in** sich anschnallen. '**strapless** *adj.* trägerlos

'**strapping** ['stræpɪŋ] *adj.* stramm

strata *pl. of* stratum

strategic [strə'tiːdʒɪk] *adj.* strategisch

strategist ['strætɪdʒɪst] *n.* Stratege, *der/*Strategin, *die*

strategy ['strætɪdʒɪ] *n.* Strategie, *die*

stratosphere ['strætəsfɪə(r)] *n.* Stratosphäre, *die*

stratum ['strɑːtəm] *n.,* *pl.* **strata** ['strɑːtə] Schicht, *die*

straw [strɔː] *n.* **a)** *no pl.* Stroh, *das;* **b)** *(single stalk)* Strohhalm, *der;* **that's the last** *or* **final** ~: jetzt reicht's aber; **c)** **|drinking-|~:** Strohhalm, *der*

strawberry ['strɔːbərɪ] *n.* Erdbeere, *die*

stray [streɪ] **1.** *v. i.* **a)** *(wander)* streunen; **b)** *(deviate)* abweichen **(from** von). **2.** *n. (animal)* streunendes Tier. **3.** *adj.* **a)** *(straying)* streunend; **b)** *(occasional)* vereinzelt

streak [striːk] *n.* Streifen, *der;* *(in hair)* Strähne, *die;* **have a jealous/cruel** ~: zur Eifersucht/Grausamkeit neigen. '**streaky** *adj.* streifig; ~ **bacon** durchwachsener Speck

stream [striːm] **1.** *n. (of water)* Wasserlauf, *der;* *(brook)* Bach, *der.* **2.** *v. i.* strömen; ⟨*Sonnenlicht:*⟩ fluten. '**streamline** *v. t.* [eine] Stromlinienform geben **(+** *Dat.*); **be** ~**lined** eine Stromlinienform haben

street [striːt] *n.* Straße, *die;* **in the** ~: auf der Straße; **in** *(Brit.)* **or on ... Street** in der ...straße

street: ~**car** *n. (Amer.)* Straßenbahn, *die;* ~**lamp** *n.* Straßenlaterne, *die;* ~**lighting** *n.* Straßenbeleuchtung, *die;* ~**map** *n.* Stadtplan, *der;* ~**market** *n.* Markt, *der;* ~**plan** *n.* Stadtplan, *der;* ~**wise** *adj. (coll.)* **be** ~**wise** wissen, wo es langgeht

strength [streŋθ] *n. (power)* Kraft, *die;* *(strong point, force, intensity, amount of ingredient)* Stärke, *die;* *(of poison, medicine)* Wirksamkeit, *die;* **not know one's own** ~: nicht wissen, wie stark man ist; **give sb.** ~: jmdn. stärken; **go from** ~ **to** ~: immer erfolgreicher werden; **on the** ~ **of sth./that** auf Grund einer Sache *(Gen.)*/dessen; **in full** ~: in voller Stärke; **the police were there in** ~: ein starkes Polizeiaufgebot war da. **strengthen** ['streŋθən] *v. t.* stärken; *(reinforce, intensify)* verstärken

strenuous ['strenjʊəs] *adj.* **a)** *(energetic)* energisch; gewaltig ⟨*Anstrengung*⟩; **b)** *(requiring exertion)* anstrengend

stress [stres] **1.** *n.* **a)** *(strain)* Streß, *der;* **be under** ~: unter Streß *(Dat.)* stehen; **b)** *(emphasis)* Betonung, *die.* **2.** *v. t. (emphasize)* betonen

stretch [stretʃ] **1.** *v. t.* **a)** *(lengthen)* strecken ⟨*Arm, Hand*⟩; recken ⟨*Hals*⟩;

nen (*Gummiband*); (*tighten*) spannen; b) (*widen*) dehnen. **2. a)** *v. i.* (*extend in length*) sich dehnen; b) ~ (*to sth.* (*be sufficient for*) für etw. reichen. **3.** *v. refl.* sich strecken. **4.** *n.* a) have a ~: sich strecken; b) at a ~ (*fig.*) wenn es sein muß; c) (*expanse*) Abschnitt, *der;* a ~ of road ein Stück Straße; d) (*period*) a four-hour ~: eine [Zeit]spanne von vier Stunden; at a ~: ohne Unterbrechung. **5.** *adj.* Stretch- ⟨hose, -gewebe⟩

stretcher ['stretʃə(r)] *n.* [Trag]bahre, *die*

strew [struː] *v. t., p. p.* strewed [struːd] *or* strewn [struːn] streuen

stricken ['strɪkn] *adj.* (*afflicted*) heimgesucht; havariert ⟨*Schiff*⟩; be ~ with fear/grief angsterfüllt/gramgebeugt

strict [strɪkt] *adj.* a) (*firm*) streng; in ~ confidence streng vertraulich; b) (*precise*) streng. **strictly** *adv.* streng; ~ |speaking] strenggenommen

stride [straɪd] **1.** *n.* Schritt, *der;* put sb. off his ~ (*fig.*) jmdn. aus dem Konzept bringen; take sth. in one's ~ (*fig.*) mit etw. gut fertig werden. **2.** *v. i.,* strode [strəʊd], stridden ['strɪdn] [mit großen Schritten] gehen

strident ['straɪdənt] *adj.* schrill

strife [straɪf] *n.* Streit, *der*

strike [straɪk] **1.** *n.* (*Industry*) Streik, *der;* Ausstand, *der;* be on/go |out] or come out on ~: in den Streik getreten sein/in den Streik treten. **2.** *v. t.,* struck [strʌk] a) (*hit*) schlagen; ⟨*Schlag, Geschoß:*⟩ treffen; (*Blitz:*) [ein]schlagen in (+ *Akk.*); b) (*delete*) streichen (from, off aus); c) (*ignite*) anzünden ⟨*Streichholz*⟩; d) (*chime*) schlagen; e) (*impress*) beeindrucken; ~ sb. as [being] silly jmdm. dumm erscheinen; it ~s sb. that ...: es scheint jmdm., daß ...; f) (*occur to*) einfallen (+ *Dat.*). **3.** *v. i.,* struck a) (*deliver a blow*) zuschlagen; ⟨*Blitz:*⟩ einschlagen; ⟨*Unheil, Katastrophe:*⟩ hereinbrechen (geh.); (*hit*) schlagen (against gegen, |up|on auf + *Akk.*); b) (*ignite*) zünden; c) (*chime*) schlagen; d) (*Industry*) streiken. **strike 'back** *v. i.* zurückschlagen. **strike 'off** *v. t.* (~ off list) streichen ⟨*Namen*⟩; (from professional body) die Zulassung entziehen (+ *Dat.*). **'strike up** *v. t.* beginnen ⟨*Unterhaltung*⟩; schließen ⟨*Freundschaft*⟩

'strike pay *n.* Streikgeld, *das*

'striker *n.* Streikende, *der/die*

striking ['straɪkɪŋ] *adj.* auffallend; erstaunlich (*Ähnlichkeit*); schlagend ⟨*Beispiel*⟩

string [strɪŋ] **1.** *n.* a) (*thin cord*) Schnur, *die;* (to tie up parcels etc. also) Bindfaden, *der;* pull |a few or some] ~s (*fig.*) seine Beziehungen spielen lassen; with no ~s attached ohne Bedingung[en]; b) (*of bow*) Sehne, *die;* (of racket, musical instrument) Saite, *die.* **2.** *v. t.,* strung [strʌŋ] (*thread*) auffädeln. **string a'long** *v. t.* (*deceive*) an der Nase herumführen (ugs.). **string to'gether** *v. t.* auffädeln; miteinander verknüpfen ⟨*Wörter*⟩. **string 'up** *v. t.* aufhängen

string 'bag *n.* [Einkaufs]netz, *das*

stringent ['strɪndʒənt] *adj.* streng

¹strip [strɪp] **1.** *v. t.,* -pp- ausziehen (*Person*). **2.** *v. i.,* -pp- sich ausziehen

²strip *n.* (*narrow piece*) Streifen, *der*

stripe [straɪp] *n.* Streifen, *der.* **striped** [straɪpt] *adj.* gestreift

strip: ~ light *n.* Neonröhre, *die;* ~ lighting *n.* Neonbeleuchtung, *die*

stripper ['strɪpə(r)] *n.* Stripper, *der*/ Stripperin, *die* (ugs.)

stripy ['straɪpɪ] *adj.* gestreift; Streifen- ⟨*muster*⟩

strive [straɪv] *v. i.,* strove [strəʊv], striven ['strɪvn] sich bemühen; ~ after or for sth. nach etw. streben

strode *see* stride 2

¹stroke [strəʊk] *n.* a) (*act of striking*) Schlag, *der;* b) (*Med.*) Schlaganfall, *der;* c) (*sudden impact*) ~ of lightning Blitzschlag, *der;* ~ of |good] luck Glücksfall, *der;* d) at a or one ~: auf einen Schlag; not do a ~ |of work] keinen [Hand]schlag tun; ~ of genius genialer Einfall, *der;* e) (*in swimming*) Zug, *der;* f) (*of clock*) Schlag, *der;* on the ~ of nine Punkt neun [Uhr]

²stroke 1. *v. t.* streicheln. **2.** *n.* give sb./sth. a ~: jmdm./etw. streicheln

stroll [strəʊl] **1.** *v. i.* spazierengehen. **2.** *n.* go for a ~: einen Spaziergang machen

strong [strɒŋ] *adj.,* ~er ['strɒŋə(r)], ~est ['strɒŋɪst] stark; fest ⟨*Fundament, Schuhe*⟩; robust ⟨*Konstitution, Magen*⟩; kräftig ⟨*Arme, Muskeln, Tritt, Zähne*⟩; leistungsfähig ⟨*Wirtschaft*⟩; gut, handfest ⟨*Grund, Beispiel, Argument*⟩; glühend ⟨*Anhänger*⟩; kräftig ⟨*Geruch, Geschmack, Stimme*⟩; there is a ~ possibility that ...: es ist sehr wahrscheinlich, daß ...; take ~ measures/action energisch vorgehen.

'**stronghold** n. Festung, die; (fig.) Hochburg, die. **strong language** n. derbe Ausdrucksweise

'**strongly** adv. stark; solide ⟨gearbeitet⟩; energisch ⟨protestieren, bestreiten⟩; nachdrücklich ⟨unterstützen⟩; dringend ⟨raten⟩; fest ⟨glauben⟩

strong: ~**man** n. Muskelmann, der (ugs.); ~-**minded** adj. willensstark; ~-**room** n. Tresorraum, der

strove see **strive**

struck see **strike** 2, 3

structural ['strʌktʃərl] adj. baulich

structure ['strʌktʃə(r)] n. a) Struktur, die; b) (something constructed) Konstruktion, die; (building) Bauwerk, das

struggle ['strʌgl] 1. v. i. kämpfen; ~ to do sth. sich abmühen, etw. zu tun; ~ against or with sb./sth. mit jmdm./ etw. od. gegen jmdn./etw. kämpfen; ~ with sth. (try to cope) mit etw. kämpfen. 2. n. Kampf, der

strum [strʌm] 1. v. i., -mm- klimpern (ugs.) (on auf + Dat.). 2. v. t., -mm- klimpern (ugs.) auf (+ Dat.)

strung see **string** 2

¹**strut** [strʌt] 1. v. i., -tt- stolzieren. 2. n. stolzierender Gang

²**strut** n. (support) Strebe, die

stub [stʌb] 1. n. a) (remaining portion) Stummel, der; (of cigarette) Kippe, die; b) (counterfoil) Abschnitt, der. 2. v. t., -bb-: a) ~ one's toe ⌊against or on sth.⌋ sich ⌊Dat.⌋ den Zeh ⌊an etw. (Dat.)⌋ stoßen; b) ausdrücken ⟨Zigarette⟩. **stub 'out** v. t. ausdrücken

stubble ['stʌbl] n. Stoppeln Pl.

stubborn ['stʌbən] adj. a) (obstinate) starrköpfig; störrisch ⟨Tier, Gesicht, Haltung⟩; b) (resolute) hartnäckig. '**stubbornness** n. see **stubborn**: Starrköpfigkeit, die; Hartnäckigkeit, die

stuck see **stick** 1, 2

'**stuck up** adj. (conceited) eingebildet

student ['stju:dənt] n. Student, der/ Studentin, die; (in school or training establishment) Schüler, der/Schülerin, die; **be a ~ of** sth. etw. studieren

studio ['stju:dɪəʊ] n., pl. ~s a) (workroom) Atelier, das; b) (Cinemat., Radio, Telev.) Studio, das

studious ['stju:dɪəs] adj. lerneifrig

study ['stʌdɪ] 1. n. a) Studium, das; b) (room) Arbeitszimmer, das. 2. v. t. studieren; sich (Dat.) ⌊sorgfältig⌋ durchlesen ⟨Prüfungsfragen, Bericht⟩

stuff [stʌf] 1. n. (material[s]) Zeug, das (ugs.). 2. v. t. a) stopfen; zustopfen ⟨Loch, Ohren⟩; (Cookery) füllen; ~ sth. with or full of sth. etw. mit etw. vollstopfen (ugs.); b) (sl.) ~ **him!** zum Teufel mit ihm! '**stuffing** n. a) (material) Füllmaterial, das; b) (Cookery) Füllung, die

stuffy ['stʌfɪ] adj. stickig

stumble ['stʌmbl] v. i. stolpern (over über + Akk.). **stumbling-block** ['stʌmblɪŋblɒk] n. Stolperstein, der

stump [stʌmp] 1. n. (of tree, branch, tooth) Stumpf, der; (of cigar, pencil) Stummel, der. 2. v. t. verwirren; be ~ed ratlos sein. '**stumpy** adj. gedrungen; ~ **tail** Stummelschwanz, der

stun [stʌn] v. t., -nn- (knock senseless) betäuben; be ~ned at or by sth. (fig.) von etw. wie betäubt sein

stung see **sting** 2, 3

stunk see **stink** 1

¹**stunt** [stʌnt] v. t. hemmen

²**stunt** n. halsbrecherisches Kunststück; (Cinemat.) Stunt, der

stupendous [stju:'pendəs] adj. gewaltig

stupid ['stju:pɪd] adj. dumm; (ridiculous) lächerlich; **it would be ~ to do** sth. es wäre töricht, etw. zu tun. **stupidity** [stu:'pɪdɪtɪ] n. Dummheit, die. '**stupidly** adv. dumm

stupor ['stju:pə(r)] n. Benommenheit, die; **in a drunken ~:** sinnlos betrunken

sturdy ['stɜ:dɪ] adj. kräftig; stämmig ⟨Beine, Arme⟩

stutter ['stʌtə(r)] 1. v. i. stottern. 2. n. Stottern, das

'**sty** [staɪ] see **pigsty**

sty, stye [staɪ] n. (Med.) Gerstenkorn, das

style [staɪl] n. Stil, der; **dress in the latest ~:** sich nach der neuesten Mode kleiden; ⌊hair-⌋~: Frisur, die

stylish ['staɪlɪʃ] adj. stilvoll; elegant ⟨Kleidung, Auto, Person⟩

stylist ['staɪlɪst] n. (hair-~) Haarstilist, der/-stilistin, die

stylus ['staɪləs] n., pl. **styli** ['staɪlaɪ] or ~**es** [Abtast]nadel, die

suave [swɑ:v] adj. gewandt

sub- [sʌb] pref. unter-; sub-

sub'conscious (Psych.) 1. adj. unterbewußt. 2. n. Unterbewußtsein, das

'**subcontract** v. t. an einen Subunternehmer vergeben

subdivide ['---, ,--'-] v. t. unterteilen

subdue [səb'dju:] v. t. bändigen ⟨Kind, Tier⟩; dämpfen ⟨Zorn, Lärm, Licht⟩. **subdued** [səb'dju:d] adj. gedämpft

subject 1. ['sʌbdʒɪkt] *n.* **a)** Staatsbürger, *der*/-bürgerin, *die*; *(to monarch)* Untertan, *der*/Untertanin, *die*; **b)** *(topic)* Thema, *das*; *(of study)* Fach, *das*; change the ~: das Thema wechseln. **2.** ['sʌbdʒɪkt] *adj.* be ~ to sth. von etw. abhängen. **3.** [səb'dʒekt] *v. t.* unterwerfen (to *Dat.*); *(expose)* ~ sb./sth. to sth. jmdn./etw. einer Sache (*Dat.*) aussetzen

subjective [səb'dʒektɪv] *adj.* subjektiv

subjugate ['sʌbdʒʊgeɪt] *v. t.* unterjochen (to unter + *Akk.*)

subjunctive [səb'dʒʌŋktɪv] (*Ling.*) *n.* Konjunktiv, *der*

sub'let *v. t.*, **-tt-, sublet** untervermieten

sublime [sə'blaɪm] *adj.* erhaben

submarine ['sʌbmə'ri:n] *n.* Unterseeboot, *das*; U-Boot, *das*

submerge [səb'mɜːdʒ] *v. t.* **a)** ~ sth. [in the water] etw. eintauchen; **b)** *(flood)* ⟨*Wasser:*⟩ überschwemmen; be ~d in water unter Wasser stehen

submission [səb'mɪʃn] *n.* **a)** *(surrender, meekness)* Unterwerfung, *die*; **b)** *(presentation)* Einreichung, *die* (to bei)

submissive [səb'mɪsɪv] *adj.* gehorsam

submit [səb'mɪt] *v. t.*, **-tt-** *(present)* einreichen; vorbringen ⟨*Vorschlag*⟩; ~ sth. to sb. jmdm. etw. vorlegen

subordinate 1. [sə'bɔːdɪnət] *adj.* untergeordnet. **2.** [sə'bɔːdɪnət] *n.* Untergebene, *der/die.* **3.** [sə'bɔːdɪneɪt] *v. t.* unterordnen (to *Dat.*)

subscribe [səb'skraɪb] *v. i.* **a)** *(support)* ~ to sth. sich einer Sache anschließen; **b)** *(make contribution)* ~ to sth. eine Spende für etw. zusichern. **sub'scriber** *n.* *(to newspaper etc.)* Abonnent, *der*/Abonnentin, *die* (to *Gen.*).

subscription [səb'skrɪpʃn] *n.* *(membership fee)* Mitgliedsbeitrag, *der* (to für); *(to newspaper etc.)* Abonnement, *das*

subsequent ['sʌbsɪkwənt] *adj.* folgend; später ⟨*Gelegenheit*⟩

subservient [səb'sɜːvɪənt] *adj.* untergeordnet (to *Dat.*); *(servile)* unterwürfig

subside [səb'saɪd] *v. i.* **a)** *(sink lower)* ⟨*Flut, Fluß:*⟩ sinken; ⟨*Boden, Haus:*⟩ sich senken; **b)** *(abate)* nachlassen

subsidiary [səb'sɪdɪərɪ] **1.** *adj.* untergeordnet ⟨*Funktion, Stellung*⟩; Neben⟨*fach, -aspekt*⟩. **2.** *n.* (*Commerc.*) Tochtergesellschaft, *die*

subsidize ['sʌbsɪdaɪz] *v. t.* subventio-

nieren. **subsidy** ['sʌbsɪdɪ] *n.* Subvention, *die*

subsist [səb'sɪst] *v. i.* ~ on sth. von etw. leben. **subsistence** [səb'sɪstəns] *n.* [Über]leben, *das*

substance ['sʌbstəns] *n.* **a)** Stoff, *der*; **b)** *(solidity)* Substanz, *die*; **c)** *(content)* Inhalt, *der*

sub'standard *adj.* unzulänglich

substantial [səb'stænʃl] *adj.* **a)** *(considerable)* beträchtlich; **b)** gehaltvoll ⟨*Essen*⟩; **c)** *(solid)* solide ⟨*Möbel, Haus*⟩; wesentlich ⟨*Unterschied*⟩. **sub'stantially** *adv.* **a)** *(considerably)* wesentlich; **b)** *(solidly)* solide; **c)** *(essentially)* im wesentlichen

substitute ['sʌbstɪtjuːt] **1.** *n.* ~ [s *pl.*] Ersatz, *der.* **2.** *v. t.* ~ A for B B durch A ersetzen. **substitution** [sʌbstɪ'tjuːʃn] *n.* Ersetzung, *die*

'subtitle *n.* Untertitel, *der*

subtle ['sʌtl] *adj.* subtil (geh.); zart ⟨*Duft, Parfüm, Hinweis*⟩; fein ⟨*Geschmack, Unterschied, Humor*⟩

subtract [səb'trækt] *v. t.* abziehen. **subtraction** [səb'trækʃn] *n.* Subtraktion, *die*

suburb ['sʌbɜːb] *n.* Vorort, *der.* **sub'urban** [sə'bɜːbən] *adj.* Vorort-; ⟨*Leben, Haus*⟩ am Stadtrand

subversive [səb'vɜːsɪv] *adj.* subversiv

'subway *n.* **a)** *(passage)* Unterführung, *die*; **b)** *(Amer.: railway)* Untergrundbahn, *die*; U-Bahn, *die*

succeed [sək'siːd] *v. i.* **a)** Erfolg haben; sb. ~s in sth. jmdm. gelingt etw.; jmd. schafft etw.; sb. ~s in doing sth. es gelingt jmdm., etw. zu tun; jmd. schafft es, etw. zu tun; ~ in business/college geschäftlich/im Studium erfolgreich sein; I did not ~ in doing it ich habe es nicht geschafft; **b)** *(come next)* die Nachfolge antreten

success [sək'ses] *n.* Erfolg, *der*; make a ~ of sth. bei etw. Erfolg haben. **successful** [sək'sesfl] *adj.* erfolgreich; be ~ in sth./doing sth. Erfolg bei etw. haben/dabei haben, etw. zu tun. **suc'cessfully** *adv.* erfolgreich

succession [sək'seʃn] *n.* **a)** Folge, *die*; in ~: hintereinander; **b)** *(series)* Serie, *die*; **c)** *(to throne)* Erbfolge, *die*

successive [sək'sesɪv] *adj.* aufeinanderfolgend. **suc'cessively** *adv.* hintereinander

successor [sək'sesə(r)] *n.* Nachfolger, *der*/Nachfolgerin, *die*

succinct [sək'sɪŋkt] *adj.* **a)** *(terse)* knapp; **b)** *(clear)* prägnant

succulent ['sʌkjʊlənt] *adj.* saftig

succumb [sə'kʌm] *v. i.* unterliegen; ~ **to sth.** einer Sache *(Dat.)* erliegen

such [sʌtʃ] **1.** *adj.* **a)** *(of that kind)* solch...; ~ **a person** ein solcher Mensch; ~ **a book** ein solches Buch; ~ **people** solche Leute; ~ **things** so etwas; **I said no** ~ **thing** ich habe nichts dergleichen gesagt; **there is no** ~ **bird** einen solchen Vogel gibt es nicht; **or some** ~ **thing** oder so etwas; **you'll do no** ~ **thing** das wirst du nicht tun; **experiences** ~ **as these** solche Erfahrungen; **b)** *(so great)* solch...; **derartig;** **I got** ~ **a fright that ...:** ich bekam einen derartigen *(ugs.)* so einen Schrecken, daß ...; ~ **was the force of the explosion that ...:** die Explosion war so stark, daß ...; **to** ~ **an extent** dermaßen; **c)** *with adj.* so; ~ **a big house** ein so großes Haus; **as** ~ **a long time** so lange. **2.** *pron.* **as** ~: als solcher/solche/solches; *(strictly speaking)* im Grunde genommen; **an sich;** ~ **as we live** [zum Beispiel]; ~ **is life** so ist das Leben. **such-and-such** ['sʌtʃən-sʌtʃ] *adj.* **at** ~ **a time** um die und die Zeit. **'suchlike** *pron.* derlei

suck [sʌk] *v. t.* saugen *(out of* aus*)*; lutschen ⟨*Bonbon*⟩. **suck 'up 1.** *v. t.* aufsaugen. **2.** *v. i.* ~ **up to sb.** *(sl.)* jmdm. in den Hintern kriechen *(salopp)*

'sucker *n.* **a)** *(suction pad)* Saugfuß, *der;* *(Zool.)* Saugnapf, *der;* **b)** *(sl.: dupe)* Dumme, *der/die*

suckle ['sʌkl] *v. t.* säugen

suction ['sʌkʃn] *n.* Saugwirkung, *die*

Sudan [su:'dɑ:n] *pr. n.* [**the**] ~: [der] Sudan

sudden ['sʌdn] **1.** *adj.* **a)** *(unexpected)* plötzlich; **b)** *(abrupt)* jäh ⟨*Abgrund, Übergang, Ruck*⟩; **there was a** ~ **bend in the road** plötzlich machte die Straße eine Biegung. **2.** *n.* **all of a** ~: plötzlich. **'suddenly** *adv.* plötzlich. **'suddenness** *n.* Plötzlichkeit, *die*

suds [sʌdz] *n.* |**soap-|~:** [Seifen]lauge, *die;* *(froth)* Schaum, *der*

sue [su:] **1.** *v. t.* verklagen *(for* auf + *Akk.)*. **2.** *v. i.* klagen *(for* auf + *Akk.)*

suede [sweɪd] *n.* Wildleder, *das*

suet ['su:ɪt] *n.* Talg, *der*

Suez ['su:ɪz, 'sju:ɪz] *pr. n.* Suez *(das);* ~ **Canal** Suez-Kanal, *der*

suffer ['sʌfə(r)] **1.** *v. t.* erleiden; durchmachen ⟨*Schweres, Kummer*⟩; dulden ⟨*Unverschämtheit*⟩. **2.** *v. i.* leiden. **'suffer from** *v. t.* leiden unter *(+ Dat.)*; leiden an *(+ Dat.)* ⟨*Krankheit*⟩

sufferance ['sʌfərəns] *n.* Duldung, *die;* **he remains here on** ~ **only** er ist hier bloß geduldet

'suffering *n.* Leiden, *das*

suffice [sə'faɪs] **1.** *v. i.* genügen; ~ **it to say ...:** nur soviel sei gesagt: ... **2.** *v. t.* genügen *(+ Dat.)*

sufficiency [sə'fɪʃənsɪ] *n.* Zulänglichkeit, *die*

sufficient [sə'fɪʃənt] *adj.* genug; ~ **money/food** genug Geld/genug zu essen; **be** ~: genügen; ~ **reason** Grund genug; **have you had** ~? *(food, drink)* haben Sie schon genug? **suffi-ciently** *adv.* genug; *(adequately)* ausreichend; ~ **large** groß genug; **a** ~ **large number** eine genügend große Zahl

suffix ['sʌfɪks] *n.* Nachsilbe, *die*

suffocate ['sʌfəkeɪt] **1.** *v. t.* ersticken; **he was** ~**d by the smoke** der Rauch erstickte ihn. **2.** *v. i.* ersticken. **suffoca-tion** [sʌfə'keɪʃn] *n.* Erstickung, *die;* **a feeling of** ~: das Gefühl, zu ersticken

sugar ['ʃʊgə(r)] *n.* Zucker, *der;* **two** ~**s, please** *(lumps)* zwei Stück Zucker, bitte; *(spoonfuls)* zwei Löffel Zucker, bitte. **2.** *v. t.* zuckern

sugar: ~ **basin** *see* ~**bowl;** ~**beet** *n.* Zuckerrübe, *die;* ~**bowl** *n.* Zuckerschale, *der;* *(covered)* Zuckerdose, *die;* ~**cane** *n.* Zuckerrohr, *das;* ~**coated** *adj.* gezuckert; mit Zucker überzogen ⟨*Dragee usw.*⟩; ~**lump** *n.* Zuckerstück, *das;* *(when counted)* Stück Zucker

'sugary *adj.* süß; *(fig.)* süßlich

suggest [sə'dʒest] *v. t.* **a)** *(propose)* vorschlagen; ~ **sth. to sb.** jmdm. etw. vorschlagen; **he** ~**ed going to the cinema** er schlug vor, ins Kino zu gehen; **b)** *(assert)* **are you trying to** ~ **that he is lying** wollen Sie damit sagen, daß er lügt?; **c)** *(make one think of)* suggerieren; ⟨*Symptome, Tatsachen:*⟩ schließen lassen auf *(+ Akk.)*. **sug-gestion** [sə'dʒestʃn] *n.* **a)** Vorschlag, *der;* **at** *or* **on sb.'s** ~: auf jmds. Vorschlag *(Akk.);* **b)** *(insinuation)* Andeutungen *Pl.;* **c)** *(fig.: trace)* Spur, *die.* **suggestive** [sə'dʒestɪv] *adj.* **a)** **be** ~ **of sth.** auf etw. *(Akk.)* schließen lassen; **b)** *(indecent)* anzüglich

suicidal [su:ɪ'saɪdl] *adj.* selbstmörderisch; **I felt** *or* **was quite** ~: ich hätte mich am liebsten gleich umgebracht

suicide ['su:ɪsaɪd] *n.* Selbstmord, *der.* **'suicide attempt** *n.* Selbstmordversuch, *der*

suit [su:t] 1. *n.* a) *(for men)* Anzug, *der;* *(for women))* Kostüm, *das;* b) *(law)* ~ [at law] Prozeß, *der;* c) *(Cards)* Farbe, *die;* **follow** ~ *(fig.)* das Gleiche tun. 2. *v. t.* a) anpassen (to *Dat.*); b) be ~ed [to sth./one another] [zu etw./zueinander] passen; c) *(satisfy needs of)* passen (+ *Dat.*); **will Monday ~ you? paßt Ihnen Montag?; does the climate ~ you?** bekommt Ihnen das Klima?; d) *(go well with)* passen zu; **does this hat ~ me?** steht mir dieser Hut?; **black ~s her** Schwarz steht ihr gut. 3. *v. refl.* ~ **oneself** tun, was man will; ~ **yourself!** [ganz] wie du willst!

suitability [su:tə'bɪlɪtɪ] *n.* Eignung, *die* (for für)

suitable ['su:təbl] *adj.* geeignet; angemessen ⟨*Kleidung*⟩; *(convenient)* passend; **Monday is the most ~ day** [for me] Montag paßt [mir] am besten.

suitably ['su:təblɪ] *adv.* angemessen; entsprechend ⟨*gekleidet*⟩

suitcase *n.* Koffer, *der*

suite [swi:t] *n.* a) *(of furniture)* Garnitur, *die;* **three-piece ~:** Polstergarnitur, *die;* b) *(of rooms)* Suite, *die*

suitor ['su:tə(r)] *n.* Freier, *der*

sulfur, sulfuric (Amer.) see sulph-

sulk [sʌlk] *v. i.* schmollen. **sulky** *adj.* schmollend; eingeschnappt (ugs.)

sullen ['sʌlən] *adj.* mürrisch

sulphur ['sʌlfə(r)] *n.* Schwefel, *der.* **sulphuric** [sʌl'fjʊərɪk] *adj.* ~ **acid** Schwefelsäure, *die*

sultan ['sʌltən] *n.* Sultan, *der*

sultana [sʌl'tɑːnə] *n.* Sultanine, *die*

sultry ['sʌltrɪ] *adj.* schwül

sum [sʌm] *n.* a) Summe, *die* (of aus); [total] Ergebnis, *das;* b) *(Arithmetic)* Rechenaufgabe, *die;* **do ~s** (coll.) rechnen; **she is good at ~s** (coll.) sie kann gut rechnen. **sum 'up** 1. *v. t.* a) zusammenfassen; b) *(Brit.: assess)* einschätzen. 2. *v. i.* ein Fazit ziehen

summarily ['sʌmərɪlɪ] *adv.* summarisch; ~ **dismissed** fristlos entlassen

summarize ['sʌməraɪz] *v. t.* zusammenfassen

summary ['sʌmərɪ] 1. *adj.* summarisch; fristlos ⟨*Entlassung*⟩. 2. *n.* Zusammenfassung, *die*

summer ['sʌmə(r)] *n.* Sommer, *der;* **in** [the] ~: im Sommer. **'summerhouse** *n.* [Garten]laube, *die.* **'summertime** *n.* Sommer, *der.* **'summery** *adj.* sommerlich

summing 'up *n.* Zusammenfassung, *die*

summit ['sʌmɪt] *n.* Gipfel, *der*

summon ['sʌmən] *v. t.* a) rufen (to zu); holen ⟨*Hilfe*⟩; b) *(Law)* vorladen. **summon 'up** *v. t.* aufbringen

summons ['sʌmənz] *n.* Vorladung, *die*

sump [sʌmp] *n.* Ölwanne, *die*

sumptuous ['sʌmptjʊəs] *adj.* üppig; luxuriös ⟨*Möbel, Kleidung*⟩

sun [sʌn] 1. *n.* Sonne, *die;* **catch the ~** *(be in sunny position)* viel Sonne abbekommen; *(get ~burnt)* einen Sonnenbrand bekommen. 2. *v. refl.,* -**nn**- sich sonnen

Sun. *abbr.* Sunday So.

sun: ~**bathe** *v. i.* sonnenbaden; ~**bathing** *n.* Sonnenbaden, *das;* ~**beam** *n.* Sonnenstrahl, *der;* ~**bed** *n.* *(with UV lamp)* Sonnenbank, *die;* *(in garden)* Gartenliege, *die;* ~**burn** *n.* Sonnenbrand, *der;* ~**burnt** *adj.* **be/get ~burnt** einen Sonnenbrand haben/bekommen

sundae ['sʌndeɪ] *n.* **[ice-cream] ~:** Eisbecher, *der*

Sunday ['sʌndeɪ, 'sʌndɪ] *n.* Sonntag, *der;* see also **Friday**

'sundial *n.* Sonnenuhr, *die*

sundry ['sʌndrɪ] 1. *adj.* verschieden. 2. *n. in pl.* Verschiedenes

'sunflower *n.* Sonnenblume, *die*

sung see **sing**

sun: ~**glasses** *n. pl.* Sonnenbrille, *die;* ~**hat** *n.* Sonnenhut, *der*

sunk see **sink** 2, 3

sun: ~**lamp** *n.* Höhensonne, *die;* ~**lit** *adj.* sonnenbeschienen; ~**light** *n.* Sonnenlicht, *das*

sunny ['sʌnɪ] *adj.* sonnig; ~ **intervals** Aufheiterungen

sun: ~**rise** *n.* Sonnenaufgang, *der;* ~**roof** *n.* *(Motor Veh.)* Schiebedach, *das;* ~**set** *n.* Sonnenuntergang, *der;* ~**shade** *n.* Sonnenschirm, *der;* ~**shine** *n.* Sonnenschein, *der;* ~**stroke** *n.* Sonnenstich, *der;* ~**tan** *n.* [Sonnen]bräune, *die;* **get a ~-tan** braun werden; ~**tan lotion** *n.* Sonnencreme, *die;* ~**-tanned** *adj.* braun[gebrannt]; ~**tan oil** *n.* Sonnenöl, *das*

super ['su:pə(r)] *adj.* *(coll.)* super *(ugs.)*

superb [su:'pɜ:b] *adj.* einzigartig; erstklassig ⟨*Essen*⟩

supercilious [su:pə'sɪlɪəs] *adj.* hochnäsig

superficial [su:pə'fɪʃl] *adj.* oberflächlich

superfluous [sʊ'pɜ:flʊəs] *adj.* überflüssig

super: ~**glue** *n.* Sekundenkleber, *der;* ~**human** *adj.* übermenschlich

superintendent [su:pərɪn'tendənt] *n. (Brit. Police)* Kommissar, *der/*Kommissarin, *die*

superior [su:'pɪərɪə(r)] 1. *adj.* a) *(of higher quality)* besonders gut ⟨*Restaurant, Qualität, Stoff⟩;* überlegen ⟨*Technik, Intelligenz⟩;* **he thinks he is ~ to us** er hält sich für besser als wir; b) *(having higher rank)* höher...; **be ~ to sb.** jmdm. einen höheren Rang als jmd. haben. 2. *n.* Vorgesetzte, *der/die.* **superiority** [su:pɪərɪ'ɒrɪtɪ] *n.* Überlegenheit, *die* **(to** über + *Akk.)*

superlative [su:'pɜ:lətɪv] 1. *adj.* a) unübertrefflich; b) *(Ling.)* **a ~ adjective/adverb** ein Adjektiv/Adverb im Superlativ. 2. *n. (Ling.)* Superlativ, *der*

super: ~**market** *n.* Supermarkt, *der;* ~**natural** *adj.* übernatürlich; ~**power** *n. (Polit.)* Supermacht, *die*

supersede [su:pə'si:d] *v. t.* ablösen (by durch)

supersonic [su:pə'sɒnɪk] *adj.* Überschall-

superstition [su:pə'stɪʃn] *n.* Aberglaube, *der.* **superstitious** [su:pə'stɪʃəs] *adj.* abergläubisch

supervise ['su:pəvaɪz] *v. t.* beaufsichtigen. **supervision** [su:pə'vɪʒn] *n.* Aufsicht, *die.* **supervisor** ['su:pəvaɪzə(r)] *n.* Aufseher, *der/*Aufseherin, *die*

supper ['sʌpə(r)] *n.* Abendessen, *das;* **have** ⟨one's⟩ ~: zu Abend essen. '**supper-time** *n.* Abendbrotzeit, *die;* **it's** ~: es ist Zeit zum Abendessen

supplant [sə'plɑ:nt] *v. t.* ablösen, ersetzen **(by** durch)

supple ['sʌpl] *adj.* geschmeidig

supplement ['sʌplɪmənt] 1. *n.* a) Ergänzung, *die* **(to** + *Gen.);* *(addition)* Zusatz, *der;* b) *(of book)* Nachtrag, *der;* c) *(to fare)* Zuschlag, *der.* 2. *v. t.* ergänzen. **supplementary** [sʌplɪ'mentərɪ] *adj.* zusätzlich; ~ **fare/charge** Zuschlag, *der*

supplier [sə'plaɪə(r)] *n. (Commerc.)* Lieferant, *der/*Lieferantin, *die*

supply [sə'plaɪ] 1. *v. t.* liefern ⟨*Waren usw.⟩;* beliefern ⟨*Kunden, Geschäft⟩;* ~ **sth. to sb.,** ~ **sb. with sth.** jmdn. mit etw. versorgen/*(Commerc.)* beliefern. 2. *n.* Vorräte *Pl.;* **military/medical supplies** militärischer/medizinischer Nachschub; ~ **and demand** *(Econ.)* Angebot und Nachfrage

support [sə'pɔ:t] 1. *v. t.* a) *(hold up)* stützen ⟨*Mauer, Verletzten⟩; (bear*

weight of) tragen; b) unterstützen ⟨*Politik, Verein⟩; (Footb.)* ~ **Spurs** Spurs-Fan sein; c) *(provide for)* ernähren ⟨*Familie, sich selbst⟩;* d) *(speak in favour of)* befürworten. 2. *n.* a) Unterstützung, *die;* **in** ~: zur Unterstützung; **speak in** ~ **of sb./sth.** jmdn. unterstützen/etw. befürworten; b) *(money)* Unterhalt, *der;* c) *(sb./sth. that* ~s) Stütze, *die.* **sup'porter** *n.* Anhänger, *der/*Anhängerin, *die;* **football** ~: Fußballfan, *der.* **sup'porting** *adj. (Cinemat., Theatre)* ~ **role** Nebenrolle, *die;* ~ **actor/actress** Schauspieler/-spielerin in einer Nebenrolle; ~ **film** Vorfilm, *der.* **supportive** [sə'pɔ:tɪv] *adj.* hilfreich; **be very** ~ **to** [jmdm.] eine große Hilfe *od.* Stütze sein

suppose [sə'pəʊz] *v. t.* a) *(assume)* annehmen; ~ **or supposing** [that] **he ...:** angenommen, [daß] er ...; b) *(presume)* vermuten; **I** ~ **so** *(doubtfully)* ja, vermutlich; *(more confidently)* ich glaube schon; c) **be** ~**d to do/be sth.** *(be generally believed to do/be sth.)* etw. tun/sein sollen; d) *(allow)* **you are not** ~**d to do that** das darfst du nicht; **I'm not** ~**d to be here** ich dürfte eigentlich gar nicht hier sein. **supposedly** [sə'pəʊzɪdlɪ] *adv.* angeblich

supposition [sʌpə'zɪʃn] *n.* Annahme, *die;* Vermutung, *die*

suppress [sə'pres] *v. t.* unterdrücken. **suppression** [sə'preʃn] *n.* Unterdrückung, *die*

supremacy [su:'preməsɪ] *n.* a) *(supreme authority)* Souveränität, *die;* b) *(superiority)* Überlegenheit, *die*

supreme [su:'pri:m] *adj.* höchst...

surcharge ['sɜ:tʃɑ:dʒ] *n.* Zuschlag, *der*

sure [ʃʊə(r)] 1. *adj.* sicher; **be** ~ **of sth.** sich ⟨*Dat.⟩* einer Sache ⟨*Gen.⟩* sicher sein; ~ **of oneself** selbstsicher; **don't be too** ~: da wäre ich mir nicht so sicher; **there is** ~ **to be a garage** es gibt bestimmt eine Tankstelle; **don't worry, it's** ~ **to turn out well** keine Sorge, es wird schon alles gutgehen; **for** ~ *(coll.)* auf jeden Fall; **make** ~ [of sth.] sich [einer Sache] vergewissern; **make** *or* **be** ~ **you do it, be** ~ **to do it** *(do not fail to do it)* sieh zu, daß du es tust; *(do not forget)* vergiß nicht, es zu tun; **a** ~ **winner** ein todsicherer Tip *(ugs.).* 2. *adv.* ~ **enough** tatsächlich. 3. *int.* ~!, ~ **thing!** *(Amer.)* na klar! *(ugs.).* **sure-footed** ['ʃʊəfʊtɪd] *adj.* trittsicher. **'surely** 1. *adv.* **a)** *as sentence-modifier* doch; ~ **we've met before?** wir kennen uns doch, oder?; **b)** *(steadily)* sicher; **slowly but ~:** langsam, aber sicher; **c)** *(certainly)* sicherlich. **2.** *int. (Amer.)* natürlich

surf [sɜːf] *n.* Brandung, *die*

surface ['sɜːfɪs] 1. *n.* Oberfläche, *die;* **outer ~:** Außenfläche, *die;* **the earth's ~:** die Erdoberfläche; **on the ~:** an der Oberfläche; *(fig.)* oberflächlich betrachtet. 2. *v. i.* auftauchen; *(fig.)* hochkommen. **'surface area** *n.* Oberfläche, *die.* **'surface mail** *n.* gewöhnliche Post

'surfboard *n.* Surfbrett, *das*

surfeit ['sɜːfɪt] *n.* Übermaß, *das*

'surfer *n.* Surfer, *der*/Surferin, *die*

'surfing *n.* Surfen, *das*

surge [sɜːdʒ] *v. i.* ⟨Wellen:⟩ branden; **the crowd ~d forward** die Menschenmenge drängte sich nach vorn

surgeon ['sɜːdʒən] *n.* Chirurg, *der*/Chirurgin, *die*

surgery ['sɜːdʒərɪ] *n.* **a)** Chirurgie, *die;* **undergo ~:** sich einer Operation *(Dat.)* unterziehen; **b)** *(Brit.: place)* Praxis, *die;* **doctor's/dental ~:** Arzt-/Zahnarztpraxis, *die;* **c)** *(Brit.: time)* Sprechstunde, *die*

surgical ['sɜːdʒɪkl] *adj.* chirurgisch; ~ **treatment** Operation, *die*/Operationen

surly ['sɜːlɪ] *adj.* mürrisch

surmise [sə'maɪz] 1. *n.* Vermutung, *die.* 2. *v. t.* mutmaßen

surmount [sə'maʊnt] *v. t.* überwinden

surname ['sɜːneɪm] *n.* Nachname, *der;* Zuname, *der*

surpass [sə'pɑːs] *v. t.* übertreffen; ~ **oneself** sich selbst übertreffen

surplus ['sɜːpləs] 1. *n.* Überschuß, *der* (of an + *Dat.*). 2. *adj.* überschüssig; **be ~ to sb.'s requirements** von jmdm. nicht benötigt werden

surprise [sə'praɪz] 1. *n.* **a)** Überraschung, *die;* **take sb. by ~:** jmdn. überrumpeln; **to my great ~, much to my ~:** zu meiner großen Überraschung; **it came as a ~ to us** es war für uns eine Überraschung; **b)** *attrib.* überraschend, unerwartet *(Besuch);* **a ~ attack** ein Überraschungsangriff. 2. *v. t.* überraschen; überrumpeln ⟨*Feind*⟩; **I shouldn't be ~d if ...:** es würde mich nicht wundern, wenn ...; **be ~d at sb./sth.** sich über jmdn./etw. wundern. **surprising** [sə'praɪzɪŋ] *adj.* überraschend

surreal [sə'rɪəl] *adj.* surrealistisch

surrealism [sə'rɪəlɪzm] *n.* Surrealismus, *der*

surreptitious [sʌrəp'tɪʃəs] *adj.* heimlich; verstohlen ⟨*Blick*⟩

surrogate ['sʌrəgət] *n.* Ersatz, *der*

surround [sə'raʊnd] 1. *v. t.* **a)** *(come or be all round)* umringen; ⟨*Truppen, Heer:*⟩ umzingeln ⟨*Stadt, Feind*⟩; **b)** *(encircle)* umgeben; **be ~ed by or with sth.** von etw. umgeben sein. **sur'rounding** *adj.* umliegend; **the ~ countryside** die [Landschaft in der] Umgebung. **sur'roundings** *n. pl.* Umgebung, *die*

surveillance [sə'veɪləns] *n.* Überwachung, *die;* **be under ~:** überwacht werden

survey 1. [sə'veɪ] *v. t.* betrachten; überblicken ⟨*Landschaft*⟩; inspizieren ⟨*Gebäude*⟩; bewerten ⟨*Situation*⟩. 2. ['sɜːveɪ] *n.* Überblick, *der* (of über + *Akk.*); *(poll)* Umfrage, *die; (Surv.)* Vermessung, *die.* **surveyor** [sə'veɪə(r)] *n.* *(of building)* Gutachter, *der*/Gutachterin, *die; (of land)* Landvermesser, *der*/-vermesserin, *die*

survival [sə'vaɪvl] *n.* Überleben, *das;* **fight for ~:** Existenzkampf, *der*

survive [sə'vaɪv] 1. *v. t.* überleben. 2. *v. i.* ⟨*Person:*⟩ überleben; ⟨*Schriften, Traditionen:*⟩ erhalten bleiben. **survivor** [sə'vaɪvə(r)] *n.* Überlebende, *der/die*

susceptible [sə'septɪbl] *adj.* empfänglich (to für); *(to illness)* anfällig (to für)

suspect 1. [sə'spekt] *v. t.* **a)** *(imagine to be likely)* vermuten; ~ **the worst** das Schlimmste befürchten; ~ **sb. to be sth.,** ~ **that sb. is sth.** glauben *od.* vermuten, daß jmd. etw. ist; **b)** *(mentally accuse)* verdächtigen; ~ **sb. of sth./of doing sth.** jmdn. einer Sache verdächtigen/jmdn. verdächtigen, etw. zu tun. 2. ['sʌspekt] *adj.* fragwürdig; verdächtig ⟨*Stoff, Paket*⟩. 3. ['sʌspekt] *n.* Verdächtige, *der/die*

suspend [sə'spend] *v. t.* **a)** *(hang up)* [auf]hängen; **b)** *(stop)* suspendieren; **c)** *(from work)* ausschließen (from von); sperren ⟨*Sportler*⟩. **suspended 'sentence** *n.* *(Law)* Strafe mit Bewährung

suspender belt [sə'spendə belt] *n.* *(Brit.)* Strumpfbandgürtel, *der*

suspenders [sə'spendəz] *n. pl.* **a)** (Brit.: for stockings) Strumpfbänder; **b)** (Amer.: for trousers) Hosenträger

suspense [sə'spens] *n.* Spannung, die; keep sb. in ~: jmdn. auf die Folter spannen. **suspension** [sə'spen∫n] *n.* (Motor Veh.) Federung, die. **su'spension bridge** *n.* Hängebrücke, die

suspicion [sə'spɪ∫n] *n.* **a)** (uneasy feeling) Mißtrauen, das (of gegenüber); (unconfirmed belief) Verdacht, der; have a ~ that ...: den Verdacht haben, daß ...; **b)** (suspecting) Verdacht, der (of auf + Akk.); on ~ of murder wegen Mordverdachts; be under ~: verdächtig werden

suspicious [sə'spɪʃəs] *adj.* **a)** (tending to suspect) mißtrauisch (of gegenüber); be ~ of sb./sth. jmdm./einer Sache mißtrauen; **b)** (arousing suspicion) verdächtig

sustain [sə'steɪn] *v. t.* **a)** (support) tragen ⟨Gewicht⟩; (fig.) aufrechterhalten; **b)** erleiden ⟨Verlust, Verletzung⟩

sustenance ['sʌstɪnəns] *n.* Nahrung, die

SW *abbr.* **a)** south-west SW; **b)** (Radio) short wave KW

swab [swɒb] *n.* (Med.: pad) Tupfer, der

swagger ['swægə(r)] *v. i.* großspurig stolzieren

¹swallow ['swɒləʊ] **1.** *v. t.* schlucken; (by mistake) verschlucken. **2.** *v. i.* schlucken. **3.** *n.* Schluck, der. **swallow 'up** *v. t.* verschlucken

²swallow *n.* Schwalbe, die

swam *see* **swim 1**

swamp [swɒmp] **1.** *n.* Sumpf, der. **2.** *v. t.* überschwemmen. **'swampy** *adj.* sumpfig

swan [swɒn] *n.* Schwan, der

swap [swɒp] **1.** *v. t.,* -pp- tauschen (for gegen). **2.** *v. i.,* -pp- tauschen. **3.** *n.* Tausch, der

swarm [swɔ:m] **1.** *n.* Schwarm, der. **2.** *v. i.* schwärmen; (teem) wimmeln (with von)

swarthy ['swɔ:ðɪ] *adj.* dunkel

swastika ['swɒstɪkə] *n.* Hakenkreuz, das

swat [swɒt] *v. t.,* -tt- totschlagen

sway [sweɪ] **1.** *v. i.* [hin und her] schwanken; (gently) sich wiegen. **2.** *v. t.* **a)** wiegen; **b)** (influence) beeinflussen. **3.** *n.* (fig.) Herrschaft, die; hold ~ over sb. über jmdn. herrschen

swear [sweə(r)] **1.** *v. t.,* swore [swɔ:(r)], sworn [swɔ:n] schwören ⟨Eid usw.⟩. **2.**

v. i., swore, sworn **a)** fluchen; **b)** ~ to sth. etw. beschwören. **'swear at** *v. t.* beschimpfen. **'swear by** *v. t.* (coll.) schwören auf (+ Akk.)

'swear-word *n.* Kraftausdruck, der

sweat [swet] **1.** *n.* Schweiß, der. **2.** *v. i.* schwitzen

sweater ['swetə(r)] *n.* Pullover, der

'sweaty *adj.* schweißig

Swede [swi:d] *n.* Schwede, der/ Schwedin, die

swede *n.* Kohlrübe, die

Sweden ['swi:dn] *pr. n.* Schweden (das)

Swedish ['swi:dɪʃ] **1.** *adj.* schwedisch; sb. is ~: jmd. ist Schwede/ Schwedin. **2.** *n.* Schwedisch, das; see also **English 2 a**

sweep [swi:p] **1.** *v. t.,* swept [swept] **a)** fegen; kehren; **b)** ~ the country ⟨Epidemie, Mode:⟩ das Land überrollen. **2.** *v. i.,* swept **a)** fegen; kehren; **b)** (go fast) ⟨Person, Auto:⟩ rauschen; ⟨Wind usw.:⟩ fegen. **3.** *n.* **a)** give sth. a ~: etw. fegen od. kehren; **b)** (curve) Bogen, der. **sweep 'up** *v. t.* zusammenfegen; zusammenkehren

'sweeping *adj.* pauschal; weitreichend ⟨Einsparung⟩; umwälzend ⟨Veränderung⟩

sweet [swi:t] **1.** *adj.* süß; reizend ⟨Wesen, Gesicht, Mädchen⟩; have a ~ tooth gern Süßes mögen; how ~ of you! wie nett od. lieb von dir! **2.** *n.* (Brit.) **a)** (candy) Bonbon, das od. der; **b)** (dessert) Nachtisch, der. **sweet-and-'sour** *attrib. adj.* süßsauer. **'sweet corn** *n.* Zuckermais, der

sweeten ['swi:tn] *v. t.* süßen. **'sweetener** *n.* Süßstoff, der

'sweetheart *n.* Schatz, der

'sweetness *n.* Süße, die

sweet: ~ **'pea** *n.* Wicke, die; ~-**shop** *n.* (Brit.) Süßwarengeschäft, das

swell [swel] **1.** *v. t.,* swelled, swollen ['swəʊlən] or swelled anschwellen lassen. **2.** *v. i.,* swelled, swollen or swelled **a)** (expand) ⟨Körperteil:⟩ anschwellen; ⟨Segel:⟩ sich blähen; ⟨Material:⟩ aufquellen; **b)** (Anzahl:) zunehmen. **'swelling** *n.* Schwellung, die

swelter ['sweltə(r)] *v. i.* ~ing glühend heiß ⟨Tag, Wetter⟩; ~ing heat Bruthitze, die

swept *see* **sweep 1, 2**

swerve [swɜ:v] **1.** *v. i.* einen Bogen machen; ~ to the right/left nach rechts/links [aus]schwenken. **2.** *n.* Bogen, der

swift [swɪft] 1. *adj.* schnell. 2. *n.* Mauersegler, *der.* **'swiftly** *adv.* schnell

swig [swɪg] *(coll.)* Schluck, *der*

swill [swɪl] *v. t.* ~ loutl lauslspülen

swim [swɪm] 1. *v. i.*, **-mm-**, **swam** [swæm], **swum** [swʌm] schwimmen; **my head was** ~**ming** mir war schwindelig. 2. *n.* **have a/go for a** ~: schwimmen/schwimmen gehen. **'swimmer** *n.* Schwimmer, *der*/Schwimmerin, *die*; **be a good/poor** ~: gut/schlecht schwimmen können. **'swimming** *n.* Schwimmen, *das*

swimming: ~**-baths** *n. pl.* Schwimmbad, *das*; ~**-costume** *n.* Badeanzug, *der*; ~**-pool** *n.* Schwimmbecken, *das*; *(building)* Schwimmbad, *das*; ~**-trunks** *n. pl.* Badehose, *die*

'swim-suit *n.* Badeanzug, *der*

swindle ['swɪndl] 1. *v. t.* betrügen; ~ **sb. out of sth.** jmdn. um etw. betrügen. 2. *n.* Schwindel, *der*; Betrug, *der.* **swindler** ['swɪndlə(r)] *n.* Schwindler, *der*/Schwindlerin, *die*

swine [swaɪn] *n.* Schwein, *das*

swing [swɪŋ] 1. *n.* a) Schaukel, *die*; b) *(~ing)* Schaukeln, *das*; **in full** ~ *(fig.)* in vollem Gang[e]. 2. *v. i.*, **swung** [swʌŋ] a) schwingen; *(in wind)* schaukeln; b) *(go in sweeping curve)* schwenken. 3. *v. t.*, **swung** schwingen. **swing-'door** *n.* Pendeltür, *die*

swipe [swaɪp] *(coll.)* 1. *v. t.* a) *(hit)* knallen *(ugs.)*; b) *(sl.: steal)* klauen *(ugs.)*

swirl [swɜːl] 1. *v. i.* wirbeln. 2. *v. t.* umherwirbeln. 3. *n.* Spirale, *die*

swish [swɪʃ] 1. *v. i.* zischen. 2. *n.* Zischen, *das.* 3. *adj. (coll.)* schick *(ugs.)*

Swiss [swɪs] 1. *adj.* Schweizer; schweizerisch; **sb. is** ~: jmd. ist Schweizer/Schweizerin. 2. *n.* Schweizer, *der*/Schweizerin, *die*; **the** ~ *pl.* die Schweizer. **Swiss 'roll** *n.* Biskuitrolle, *die*

switch [swɪtʃ] 1. *n.* a) *(esp. Electr.)* Schalter, *der*; b) *(change)* Wechsel, *der.* 2. *v. t.* a) *(change)* ~ **sth.** loverl **to sth.** etw. auf etw. *(Akk.)* umstellen od. *(Electr.)* umschalten; b) *(exchange)* tauschen. 3. *v. i.* wechseln; ~ loverl **to sth.** auf etw. *(Akk.)* umstellen od. *(Electr.)* umschalten. **switch 'off** *v. t. & i.* ausschalten; *(also fig. coll.)* abschalten. **switch 'on** 1. *v. t.* einschalten; anschalten. 2. *v. i.* sich anschalten

switch: ~**back** *n.* Achterbahn, *die*; ~**board** *n.* lTelefonlzentrale, *die*

Switzerland ['swɪtsələnd] *pr. n.* die Schweiz

swivel ['swɪvl] 1. *v. i.*, **-ll-** sich drehen. 2. *v. t.*, **-ll-** drehen. **'swivel chair** *n.* Drehstuhl, *der*

swollen ['swəʊlən] 1. *see* swell. 2. *adj.* geschwollen; angeschwollen ⟨Fluß⟩

swoon [swuːn] *(literary)* *v. i.* ohnmächtig werden

swoop [swuːp] 1. *n.* a) Sturzflug, *der*; b) *(coll.: raid)* Razzia, *die.* 2. *v. i.* herabstoßen; ~ **on sb.** sich auf jmdn. stürzen

sword [sɔːd] *n.* Schwert, *das.* **'swordfish** *n.* Schwertfisch, *der*

swore, sworn *see* swear

swot [swɒt] *(Brit. coll.)* 1. *n.* Streber, *der*/Streberin, *die.* 2. *v. i.*, **-tt-** büffeln *(ugs.)*

swum *see* swim 1

swung *see* swing 2, 3

sycamore ['sɪkəmɔː(r)] *n.* Bergahorn, *der*

sycophant ['sɪkəfænt] *n.* Kriecher, *der*

syllable ['sɪləbl] *n.* Silbe, *die*

syllabus ['sɪləbəs] *n.* Lehrplan, *der*; *(for exam)* Studienplan, *der*

symbol ['sɪmbl] *n.* Symbol, *das (of* für)

symbolic [sɪm'bɒlɪk], **symbolical** [sɪm'bɒlɪkl] *adj.* symbolisch. **symbolism** ['sɪmbəlɪzm] *n.* Symbolik, *die.* **symbolize** ['sɪmbəlaɪz] *v. t.* symbolisieren

symmetrical [sɪ'metrɪkl] *adj.* symmetrisch

symmetry ['sɪmɪtrɪ] *n.* Symmetrie, *die*

sympathetic [sɪmpə'θetɪk] *adj.* mitfühlend

sympathize ['sɪmpəθaɪz] *v. i.* a) ~ **with sb.** mit jmdm. lmitlfühlen; b) ~ **with** *(understand)* Verständnis haben für

sympathy ['sɪmpəθɪ] *n.* Mitgefühl, *das*; **in deepest** ~: mit aufrichtigem Beileid

symphonic [sɪm'fɒnɪk] *adj.* sinfonisch

symphony ['sɪmfənɪ] *n.* Sinfonie, *die*

symptom ['sɪmptəm] *n.* Symptom, *das.* **symptomatic** [sɪmptə'mætɪk] *adj.* symptomatisch **(of** für)

synagogue *(Amer.:* **synagog)** ['sɪnəgɒg] *n.* Synagoge, *die*

synchromesh ['sɪŋkrəmeʃ] *n. (Motor Veh.)* Synchrongetriebe, *das*

synchronize ['sɪŋkrənaɪz] *v. t.* synchronisieren; gleichstellen ⟨Uhren⟩

syndicate ['sɪndɪkət] *n.* Syndikat, *das*

syndrome ['sɪndrəʊm] *n.* Syndrom, *das*

synonym ['sɪnənɪm] *n.* Synonym, *das.* **synonymous** [sɪ'nɒnɪməs] *adj.* **a)** *(Ling.)* synonym (with mit); **b)** ~ with *(fig.)* gleichbedeutend mit

synopsis [sɪ'nɒpsɪs] *n., pl.* **synopses** [sɪ'nɒpsiːz] Inhaltsangabe, *die*

syntactic [sɪn'tæktɪk] *adj.* syntaktisch

syntax ['sɪntæks] *n.* Syntax, *die*

synthesis ['sɪnθɪsɪs] *n., pl.* **syntheses** ['sɪnθɪsiːz] Synthese, *die*

synthesize ['sɪnθɪsaɪz] *v. t.* zur Synthese bringen; *(Chem.)* synthetisieren. **synthesizer** ['sɪnθɪsaɪzə(r)] *n. (Mus.)* Synthesizer, *der*

synthetic [sɪn'θetɪk] *adj.* synthetisch

syphilis ['sɪfɪlɪs] *n.* Syphilis, *die*

syphon *see* siphon

Syria ['sɪrɪə] *pr. n.* Syrien *(das)*

syringe [sɪ'rɪndʒ] **1.** *n.* Spritze, *die.* **2.** *v. t.* spritzen; ausspritzen ⟨Ohr⟩

syrup ['sɪrəp] *n.* Sirup, *der*

system ['sɪstəm] *n.* System, *das.* **systematic** [sɪstə'mætɪk] *adj.,* **systematically** [sɪstə'mætɪkəlɪ] *adv.* systematisch. **systematize** ['sɪstəmə-taɪz] *v. t.* systematisieren. '**systems analyst** *n.* Systemanalytiker, *der/*-analytikerin, *die*

T

T, t [tiː] *n.* T, t, *das;* **to a T** ganz genau; **T-junction** Einmündung, *die;* **T-bone steak** T-bone-Steak, *das;* **T-shirt** T-shirt, *das*

ta [tɑː] *int. (Brit. coll.)* danke

tab [tæb] *n.* **a)** *(projecting flap)* Zunge, *die; (on clothing)* Etikett, *das; (with name)* Namensschild, *das;* **b) pick up the ~** *(Amer. coll.)* die Zeche bezahlen; **c) keep ~s** or **a ~ on** *(watch)* [genau] beobachten

tabby ['tæbɪ] *n.* ~ [cat] Tigerkatze, *die*

table ['teɪbl] **1.** *n.* **a)** Tisch, *der;* **b)** *(list)* Tabelle, *die;* ~ **of contents** Inhaltsverzeichnis, *das.* **2.** *v. t.* einbringen

tableau ['tæbləʊ] *n., pl.* ~x ['tæbləʊz] Tableau, *das*

table: ~**-cloth** *n.* Tischdecke, *die;* ~ **manners** *n. pl.* Tischmanieren *Pl.;* ~**-mat** *n.* Set, *das;* ~ **salt** *n.* Tafelsalz, *das;* ~**spoon** *n.* Servierlöffel, *der;* ~**spoonful** *n.* ≈ Eßlöffel[voll], *der*

tablet ['tæblɪt] *n.* **a)** Tablette, *die;* **b)** *(of soap)* Stück, *das*

table: ~ **tennis** *n.* Tischtennis, *das;* ~ **tennis bat** Tischtennisschläger, *der;* ~ **wine** *n.* Tischwein, *der*

tabloid ['tæblɔɪd] *n.* Boulevardzeitung, *die*

taboo, tabu [tə'buː] **1.** *n.* Tabu, *das.* **2.** *adj.* Tabu⟨wort⟩; **be ~:** tabu sein

tabulate ['tæbjʊleɪt] *v. t.* tabellarisch darstellen. **tabulator** ['tæbjʊleɪtə(r)] *n.* Tabulator, *der*

tacit ['tæsɪt] *adj.,* **tacitly** *adv.* stillschweigend

taciturn ['tæsɪtɜːn] *adj.* schweigsam; wortkarg

tack [tæk] **1.** *n.* **a)** *(nail)* kleiner Nagel; **b)** *(stitch)* Heftstich, *der;* **c)** *(Naut., also fig.)* Kurs, *der.* **2.** *v. t.* **a)** *(nail)* festnageln; **b)** *(stitch)* heften. **3.** *v. i. (Naut.)* kreuzen

tackle ['tækl] **1.** *v. t.* **a)** angehen ⟨Problem usw.⟩; ~ **sb. about/on/over sth.** jmdn. auf etw. *(Akk.)* ansprechen; *(ask for sth.)* jmdn. um etw. angehen; **b)** *(Sport)* angreifen ⟨Spieler⟩; *(Amer. Footb.; Rugby)* fassen. **2.** *n.* **a)** *(equipment)* Ausrüstung, *die;* **b)** *(Sport)* Angriff, *der; (sliding ~)* Tackling, *das; (Amer. Footb.; Rugby)* Fassen und Halten

tacky ['tækɪ] *adj.* klebrig

tact [tækt] *n.* Takt, *der;* **he has no ~:** er hat kein Taktgefühl. **tactful** ['tæktfl] *adj.,* **tactfully** *adv.* taktvoll

tactical ['tæktɪkl] *adj.* taktisch

tactics ['tæktɪks] *n. pl.* Taktik, *die*

tactless *adj.,* **tactlessly** *adv.* taktlos

tadpole ['tædpəʊl] *n.* Kaulquappe, *die*

tag [tæg] *n.* Schild, *das.* **tag along** *v. i.* mitkommen

²tag *n. (game)* Fangen, *das*

tail [teɪl] **1.** *n.* **a)** Schwanz, *der;* **b)** *in pl. (on coin)* ~**s** [it is] Zahl. **2.** *v. t. (sl.: follow)* beschatten. **tail 'back** *v. i.* sich stauen. **tail 'off** *v. i.* **a)** zurückgehen; **b)** *(into silence)* verstummen

tail: ~**-back** *n. (Brit.)* Rückstau, *der;* ~**-end** *n.* Ende, *das;* ~**-gate** *n. (Motor Veh.)* Heckklappe, *die;* ~**-light** *n.* Rücklicht, *das*

tailor ['teɪlə(r)] *n.* Schneider, *der/*

Schneiderin, *die*. **'tailor-made** *adj*. maßgeschneidert

'tail wind *n*. Rückenwind, *der*

taint [teɪnt] *v. t*. verderben; **be ~ed with sth**. mit etw. behaftet sein *(geh.)*

Taiwan [taɪ'wɑːn] *pr. n*. Taiwan *(das)*

take [teɪk] **1.** *v. t*., **took** [tʊk], **taken** ['teɪkn] **a)** *(get hold of, grasp, seize)* nehmen; **b)** *(capture)* einnehmen ⟨*Stadt, Festung*⟩; machen ⟨*Gefangenen*⟩; **c)** *(gain, earn)* ⟨*Laden:*⟩ einbringen; ⟨*Person:*⟩ einnehmen ⟨*Film, Stück:*⟩ einnehmen; *(win)* gewinnen ⟨*Satz, Spiel, Preis, Titel*⟩; **d)** *(~ away with one)* mitnehmen; *(steal)* mitnehmen *(verhüll.)*; **~ place** stattfinden; *(spontaneously)* sich ereignen; ⟨*Wandlung:*⟩ sich vollziehen; **e)** *(avail oneself of, use)* nehmen; machen ⟨*Pause, Ferien, Nickerchen*⟩; **~ the opportunity to do/of doing sth**. die Gelegenheit dazu benutzen, etw. zu tun; **f)** *(carry, guide, convey)* bringen; **~ sb. to visit sb**. jmdn. zu Besuch bei jmdm. mitnehmen; **~ home** mit nach Hause nehmen; *(earn)* nach Hause bringen ⟨*Geld*⟩; *(accompany)* nach Hause bringen; **g)** *(remove)* nehmen; *(deduct)* abziehen; **~ sth./sb. from sb**. jmdm. etw./jmdm. wegnehmen; **h)** *(make)* machen ⟨*Foto, Kopie*⟩; *(photograph)* aufnehmen; aufnehmen ⟨*Brief, Diktat*⟩; machen ⟨*Prüfung, Sprung, Spaziergang, Reise*⟩; ablegen ⟨*Gelübde, Eid*⟩; treffen ⟨*Entscheidung*⟩; **i)** *(conduct)* halten ⟨*Gottesdienst, Unterricht*⟩; **Ms X ~us for maths** in Mathe haben wir Frau X; **j)** *(eat, drink)* nehmen ⟨*Zucker, Milch, Tabletten, Überdosis*⟩; trinken ⟨*Tee, Kaffee, Kognak usw.*⟩; **k)** *(need, require)* brauchen ⟨*Platz, Zeit*⟩; haben ⟨*Objekt, Plural-s*⟩; gebraucht werden mit ⟨*Kasus*⟩; **sth. ~s an hour/a year/all day** etw. dauert eine Stunde/ein Jahr/einen ganzen Tag; **l)** *(ascertain and record)* notieren ⟨*Namen, Adresse, Autonummer usw.*⟩; fühlen ⟨*Puls*⟩; messen ⟨*Temperatur, Größe usw.*⟩; **m)** *(assume)* **~ it [that]**...: annehmen, daß ...; **~ sb./sth. for/to be sth**. jmdn./etw. für etw. halten; **n)** *(react to)* aufnehmen; **~ sth. well/ badly** etw. gut/nur schwer verkraften; **~ sth. calmly** *or* **coolly** etw. gelassen [auf]nehmen; **o)** *(accept)* annehmen; **p)** *(adopt, choose)* ergreifen ⟨*Maßnahmen*⟩; unternehmen ⟨*Schritte*⟩; **~ the wrong road** die falsche Straße nehmen; **q)** **be ~n ill** krank werden; **r)** **~**

sth. to bits *or* **pieces** etw. auseinandernehmen. **2.** *v. i*., **took, taken a)** ⟨*Transplantat:*⟩ vom Körper angenommen werden; ⟨*Sämling, Pflanze:*⟩ angehen; **b)** *(detract)* **~ from sth**. etw. schmälern. **'take after** *v. t*. *(resemble)* jmdm. ähnlich sein; **~ as one's example** es jmdm. gleichtun. **take a'way** *v. t*. **a)** *(remove)* wegnehmen; *(to a distance)* mitnehmen; **~ sth. away from sb**. jmdm. etw. abnehmen; **to ~ away** ⟨*Pizza, Snack usw.*⟩ zum Mitnehmen; **b)** *(Math.: deduct)* abziehen. **take a'way from** *v. t*. schmälern. **take 'back** *v. t*. zurücknehmen; *(return)* zurückbringen. **take 'down** *v. t*. **a)** *(carry or lead down)* hinunterbringen; **b)** abnehmen ⟨*Bild, Ankündigung, Weihnachtsschmuck*⟩; herunterziehen ⟨*Hose*⟩; **~ sth. down from a shelf** etw. von einem Regal herunternehmen; **c)** *(write down)* aufnehmen. **take 'in** *v. t*. **a)** hineinbringen; *(bring indoors)* hereinholen; **b)** enger machen ⟨*Kleidungsstück*⟩; **c)** *(understand)* begreifen; **d)** *(cheat)* hereinlegen *(ugs.)*; *(deceive)* täuschen. **take 'off 1.** *v. t*. **a)** abnehmen ⟨*Deckel, Hut, Tischtuch, Verband*⟩; abziehen ⟨*Kissenbezug*⟩; ausziehen ⟨*Schuhe, Handschuhe*⟩; ablegen ⟨*Mantel, Schmuck*⟩; **b)** *(deduct)* abziehen; **~ sth. off sth**. etw. von etw. abziehen; **c)** **~ a day** *etc*. **off** sich *(Dat.)* einen Tag *usw*. frei nehmen *(ugs.)*; **d)** *(mimic)* nachahmen. **2.** *v. i*. *(Aeronaut.)* starten. **take 'on** *v. t*. **a)** *(undertake)* übernehmen; auf sich *(Akk.)* nehmen ⟨*Bürde*⟩; **b)** *(employ)* einstellen; **c)** *(as opponent)* es aufnehmen mit; *(Sport: meet)* antreten gegen. **take 'out** *v. t*. **a)** *(remove)* herausnehmen; ziehen ⟨*Zahn*⟩; **~ sth. out of sth**. etw. aus etw. [heraus]nehmen; **b)** *(withdraw)* abheben ⟨*Geld*⟩; **c)** *(go out with)* **~ sb. out** mit jmdm. ausgehen; **~ sb. out to** *or* **for lunch** jmdn. zum Mittagessen einladen; **d)** *(get issued)* abschließen ⟨*Versicherung*⟩; ausleihen ⟨*Bücher*⟩; **~ out a subscription to sth**. etw. abonnieren; **e)** **~ it out on sb**. seine Wut an jmdm. auslassen. **take 'over 1.** *v. t*. übernehmen. **2.** *v. i*. übernehmen; ⟨*Manager, Firmenleiter:*⟩ die Geschäfte übernehmen; ⟨*Regierung, Präsident:*⟩ die Amtsgeschäfte übernehmen; **~ over from sb**. jmdn. ersetzen; *(temporarily)* jmdn. vertreten. **'take to** *v. t*. **a)** *(get into habit of)* **~ to doing sth**. es sich *(Dat.)* angewöhnen, etw. zu tun; b) *(like)* sich hingezogen fühlen zu ‹Person›; sich erwärmen für ‹Sache›. **take 'up** 1. *v. t.* a) *(lift up)* hochheben; *(pick up)* aufheben; herausreißen ‹Dielen›; aufreißen ‹Straße›; b) *(carry or lead up)* hinaufbringen; c) in Anspruch nehmen ‹Zeit›; brauchen/*(undesirably)* wegnehmen ‹Platz›; d) *(start)* ergreifen ‹Beruf›; anfangen ‹Tennis, Schach, Gitarre usw.›; aufnehmen ‹Arbeit, Kampf›; antreten ‹Stelle›; ~ **up a hobby** sich *(Dat.)* ein Hobby zulegen; e) *(pursue further)* ~ **sth. up with sb.** sich in einer Sache an jmdn. wenden. 2. *v. i.* ~ **up with sb.** *(coll.)* sich mit jmdm. einlassen

'**take-away** *n.* *(meal)* Essen zum Mitnehmen; *(restaurant)* Restaurant mit Straßenverkauf

taken *see* **take**

take: ~**-off** *n.* a) *(Aeronaut.)* Start, *der;* b) *(coll.: caricature)* Parodie, *die;* ~**-over** *n.* Übernahme, *die*

takings ['teɪkɪŋz] *n. pl.* Einnahmen

talcum ['tælkəm] *n.* ~ [**powder**] Körperpuder, *der*

tale [teɪl] *n.* Erzählung, *die;* Geschichte, *die* (of von, about über + *Akk.*)

talent ['tælənt] *n.* Talent, *das;* **have [great/no etc.] ~ [for sth.]** [viel/kein usw.] Talent [zu *od.* für etw.] haben.

'**talented** *adj.* talentiert

talk [tɔːk] 1. *n.* a) *(discussion)* Gespräch, *das;* **have a ~ [with sb.] [about sth.]** [mit jmdm.] [über etw. *(Akk.)*] sprechen; **have *or* hold ~s [with sb.]** [mit jmdm.] Gespräche führen; b) *(speech, lecture)* Vortrag, *der.* 2. *v. i.* sprechen (**with,** *to* mit); *(lecture)* sprechen; *(converse)* sich unterhalten; *(have ~s)* Gespräche führen; *(gossip)* reden; ~ **on the phone** telefonieren. 3. *v. t.* reden; ~ **sb. into/out of sth.** jmdn. zu etw. überreden/jmdm. etw. ausreden. **talk 'over** *v. t.* besprechen. **talk 'round** *v. t.* ~ **sb. round** jmdn. überreden

talkative ['tɔːkətɪv] *adj.* gesprächig

talking: ~ **point** *n.* Gesprächsthema, *das;* ~**-to** *n.* *(coll.)* Standpauke, *die* *(ugs.)*

tall [tɔːl] *adj.* hoch; groß ‹Person, Tier›; **that's a ~ order** das ist ziemlich viel verlangt; ~ **story** unglaubliche Geschichte

tally ['tælɪ] 1. *n.* **keep a ~ of sth.** über etw. *(Akk.)* Buch führen. 2. *v. i.* übereinstimmen

talon ['tælən] *n.* Klaue, *die*

tambourine [tæmbə'riːn] *n.* Tamburin, *das*

tame [teɪm] 1. *adj.* zahm; *(fig.: spiritless)* lahm *(ugs.)*. 2. *v. t.* zähmen

tamper ['tæmpə(r)] *v. i.* ~ **with** sich *(Dat.)* zu schaffen machen an (+ *Dat.*)

tampon ['tæmpɒn] *n.* Tampon, *der*

tan [tæn] 1. *v. t.,* -**nn**- gerben ‹Tierhaut, Fell›. 2. *v. i.,* -**nn**- braun werden. 3. *n.* a) *(colour)* Gelbbraun, *das;* b) *(sun-~)* Bräune, *die;* **have/get a ~:** braun sein/werden. 4. *adj.* gelbbraun

tandem ['tændəm] *n.* ~ [**bicycle**] Tandem, *das*

tang [tæŋ] *n.* *(taste)* Geschmack, *der;* *(smell)* Geruch, *der*

tangent ['tændʒənt] *n.* Tangente, *die;* **go off at a ~** *(fig.)* plötzlich vom Thema abschweifen

tangible ['tændʒɪbl] *adj.* greifbar; spürbar ‹Unterschied, Verbesserung›; handfest ‹Beweis›

tangle ['tæŋgl] 1. *n.* Gewirr, *das;* *(in hair)* Verfilzung, *die.* 2. *v. t.* verheddern *(ugs.);* verfilzen ‹Haar›. **tangle 'up** *v. t.* verheddern *(ugs.)*

tango ['tæŋgəʊ] *n., pl.* ~**s** Tango, *der*

tank [tæŋk] *n.* a) Tank, *der;* b) *(Mil.)* Panzer, *der*

tankard ['tæŋkəd] *n.* Krug, *der*

tanker ['tæŋkə(r)] *n.* *(ship)* Tanker, *der;* *(vehicle)* Tank[last]wagen, *der*

tanned [tænd] *adj.* braungebrannt

tantalize ['tæntəlaɪz] *v. t.* reizen. **tantalizing** ['tæntəlaɪzɪŋ] *adj.* verlockend

tantamount ['tæntəmaʊnt] *adj.* **be ~ to sth.** gleichbedeutend mit etw. sein

tantrum ['tæntrəm] *n.* Wutanfall, *der;* *(of child)* Trotzanfall, *der;* **throw a ~:** einen Wutanfall/Trotzanfall bekommen

'**tap** [tæp] *n.* Hahn, *der;* **hot/cold[-water] ~:** Warm-/Kaltwasserhahn, *der;* **be on ~** *(fig.)* zur Verfügung stehen. 2. *v. t.,* -**pp**-: a) anzapfen ‹Reserven, Markt›; b) *(Teleph.)* abhören; anzapfen *(ugs.)*

²**tap** 1. *v. t.,* -**pp**- klopfen an (+ *Akk.*); *(on upper surface)* klopfen auf (+ *Akk.*). 2. *v. i.,* -**pp**-: ~ **at/on sth.** an etw. *(Akk.)* klopfen; *(on upper surface)* auf etw. *(Akk.)* klopfen. 3. *n.* Klopfen, *das.* '**tap-dance** 1. *n.* Step[tanz], *der.* 2. *v. i.* steptanzen; steppen

tape [teɪp] 1. *n.* a) Band, *das;* **adhesive *or* (coll.) sticky ~:** Klebeband, *das;* b) *(for recording)* [Ton]band, *das (of mit)*; **make a ~ of sth.** etw. auf Band aufnehmen. 2. *v. t.* a) *(record on ~)* [auf Band] aufnehmen; b) *(bind with ~)* [mit Klebeband] zukleben; c) **have got sb./sth.~d** *(sl.)* jmdn. durchschaut haben/etw. im Griff haben

tape: ~ **cassette** *n.* Tonbandkassette, *die;* ~ **deck** *n.* Tapedeck, *das;* ~**measure** *n.* Bandmaß, *das*

taper ['teɪpə(r)] 1. *v. i.* sich verjüngen; ~ **[to a point]** spitz zulaufen. 2. *n.* [wax] ~: Wachsstock, *der*

tape: ~ **recorder** *n.* Tonbandgerät, *das;* ~ **recording** *n.* Tonbandaufnahme, *die*

tapestry ['tæpɪstrɪ] *n.* Gobelingewebe, *das; (wall-hanging)* Bildteppich, *der*

tapeworm *n.* Bandwurm, *der*

tap-water *n.* Leitungswasser, *das*

tar [tɑː(r)] 1. *n.* Teer, *der.* 2. *v. t.,* -rr- teeren

target ['tɑːgɪt] *n.* a) Ziel, *das; hit/miss the/its ~:* [das Ziel] treffen/das Ziel verfehlen; b) *(Sport)* Zielscheibe, *die*

tariff ['tærɪf] *n.* a) *(tax)* Zoll, *der;* b) *(list of charges)* Tarif, *der*

tarnish ['tɑːnɪʃ] 1. *v. t.* stumpf werden lassen *(Metall); (fig.)* beflecken *(Ruf).* 2. *v. i.* stumpf werden

tarpaulin [tɑːˈpɔːlɪn] *n.* Persenning, *die*

tart [tɑːt] *adj.* herb; sauer *(Obst); (fig.)* scharfzüngig

²**tart** *n.* a) *(Brit.) (filled pie)* ≈ Obstkuchen, *der; (small pastry)* Obsttörtchen, *das;* b) *(sl.: prostitute)* Nutte, *die (salopp).* **tart up** *v. t. (Brit. coll.)* ~ **oneself up, get ~ed up** sich auftakeln *(ugs.)*

tartan ['tɑːtən] 1. *n.* Schotten[stoff], *der.* 2. *adj.* Schotten(rock, -jacke)

tartar ['tɑːtə(r)] *n.* Zahnstein, *der*

tartar sauce ['tɑːtə 'sɔːs] *n.* Remoulade[nsoße], *die*

task [tɑːsk] *n.* Aufgabe, *die;* **take sb. to** ~: jmdm. eine Lektion erteilen. **task force** *n.* Sonderkommando, *das*

tassel ['tæsl] *n.* Quaste, *die*

taste [teɪst] 1. *v. t.* a) schmecken; *(try a little)* probieren; b) *(recognize flavour of)* [heraus]schmecken. 2. *v. i.* schmecken (**of** nach); **not ~ of anything** schmecken nach nichts. 3. *n.* a) *(flavour)* Geschmack, *der; (sense of)* ~: Geschmack[ssinn], *der;* b) *(discernment)* Geschmack, *der;* c) *(sample)* Kostprobe, *die.* **tasteful** ['teɪstfl]

adj., **tastefully** *adv.* geschmackvoll. **tasteless** *adj.* geschmacklos. **tasty** ['teɪstɪ] *adj.* lecker

tat [tæt] *n. see* ²**tit**

tattered ['tætəd] *adj.* zerlumpt *(Kleidung);* zerfleddert *(Buch).* **tatters** ['tætəz] *n. pl.* be in ~: in Fetzen sein; *(fig.)* ruiniert sein

tattoo [təˈtuː] 1. *v. t.* tätowieren. 2. *n.* Tätowierung, *die*

tatty ['tætɪ] *adj. (coll.)* schäbig

taught *see* **teach**

taunt [tɔːnt] 1. *v. t.* verspotten (**about** wegen). 2. *n.* spöttische Bemerkung

Taurus ['tɔːrəs] *n.* der Stier

taut [tɔːt] *adj.* straff *(Seil, Kabel);* gespannt *(Muskel)*

tavern ['tævən] *n.* Schenke, *die*

tawny ['tɔːnɪ] *adj.* gelbbraun

tax [tæks] 1. *n.* Steuer, *die.* 2. *v. t.* a) besteuern; versteuern *(Einkommen);* b) *(fig.)* strapazieren *(Kräfte, Geduld).* **taxable** ['tæksəbl] *adj.* steuerpflichtig. **taxation** [tækˈseɪʃn] *n.* Besteuerung, *die; (taxes payable)* Steuern, *die.* **tax-free** *adj.* steuerfrei

taxi ['tæksɪ] 1. *n.* Taxi, *das.* 2. *v. i.,* ~**ing** *or* **taxying** *(Flugzeug:)* rollen. **taxi-driver** *n.* Taxifahrer, *der/*-fahrerin, *die*

tax inspector *n.* Steuerinspektor, *der/*-inspektorin, *die*

taxi: ~**-rank** *(Brit.),* ~ **stand** *(Amer.) ns.* Taxistand, *der*

tax: ~**payer** *n.* Steuerzahler, *der/*-zahlerin, *die;* ~ **return** *n.* Steuererklärung, *die*

tea [tiː] *n.* a) Tee, *der;* b) *(meal)* [high] ~: Abendessen, *das.* **tea-bag** *n.* Teebeutel, *der.* **tea-break** *n. (Brit.)* Teepause, *die*

teach [tiːtʃ] 1. *v. t.,* **taught** [tɔːt] unterrichten; *(at university)* lehren; ~ **sb./ oneself/an animal sth.** jmdm./sich/einem Tier etw. beibringen; ~ **sb. to ride** jmdm. das Reiten beibringen. 2. *v. i.,* **taught** unterrichten. **teacher** *n.* Lehrer, *der/*Lehrerin, *die*

tea: ~**cloth** *n.* Geschirrtuch, *das;* ~**cup** *n.* Teetasse, *die*

teak [tiːk] *n.* Teak[holz], *das*

tea-leaf *n.* Teeblatt, *das*

team [tiːm] *n.* Team, *das; (Sport also)* Mannschaft, *die.* **team up** *v. i.* sich zusammentun *(ugs.)*

team-work *n.* Teamarbeit, *die*

teapot *n.* Teekanne, *die*

¹**tear** [teə(r)] 1. *n.* Riß, *der.* 2. *v. t.,* **tore** [tɔː(r)], **torn** [tɔːn] a) *(rip)* zerreißen;

(pull apart) auseinanderreißen; *(damage)* aufreißen; ~ **open** aufreißen ⟨Brief, Paket⟩; **b)** ~ **sth. out of sb.'s hands** jmdm. etw. aus der Hand reißen. **3.** *v. i.* ⟨tore, torn **a)** *(rip)* [zer]reißen; **b)** *(move hurriedly)* rasen *(ugs.)*.

tear a'way *v. t.* wegreißen; ~ **oneself away** *(fig.)* sich losreißen. **tear 'up** *v. t.* zerreißen

²**tear** [tɪə(r)] *n.* Träne, *die.* **tearful** ['tɪəfl] *adj.* weinend

tear [tɪə(r)]: ~**-drop** *n.* Träne, *die;* ~**-gas** *n.* Tränengas, *das*

tease [tiːz] **1.** *v. t.* necken *(about* wegen*)*; aufziehen *(ugs.)* *(about* mit*)*. **2.** *v. i.* seine Späße machen

tea: ~**-shop** *n. (Brit.)* ≈ Café, *das;* ~**-spoon** *n.* Teelöffel, *der;* ~**-strainer** *n.* Teesieb, *das*

teat [tiːt] *n.* **a)** Zitze, *die;* **b)** *(of rubber or plastic)* Sauger, *der*

tea: ~**-time** *n.* Teezeit, *die;* ~**-towel** *n.* Geschirrtuch, *das*

technical ['teknɪkl] *adj.* technisch ⟨Problem, Daten, Fortschritt⟩; Fach-⟨kenntnis, -sprache, -griff, -wörterbuch⟩; ~ **term** Fachbegriff, *der.* Fachausdruck, *der.* **technicality** [teknɪ'kælɪtɪ] *n.* technisches Detail

technician [tek'nɪʃn] *n.* Techniker, *der*/Technikerin, *die*

technique [tek'niːk] *n.* Technik, *die; (procedure)* Methode, *die*

technological [teknə'lɒdʒɪkl] *adj.* technisch; technologisch

technology [tek'nɒlədʒɪ] *n.* Technik, *die; (application of science)* Technologie, *die*

teddy ['tedɪ] *n.* ~ [**bear**] Teddy[bär], *der*

tedious ['tiːdɪəs] *adj.* langwierig ⟨Reise, Arbeit⟩; *(uninteresting)* langweilig

tee [tiː] *(Golf)* Tee, *das*

teem [tiːm] *v. i.* wimmeln *(with* von*)*

teenage[d] ['tiːneɪdʒ(d)] *attrib. adj.* im Teenageralter *nachgestellt.* **teenager** ['tiːneɪdʒə(r)] *n.* Teenager, *der; (loosely)* Jugendliche, *der/die*

teens [tiːnz] *n. pl.* Teenagerjahre

teeter ['tiːtə(r)] *v. i.* wanken; ~ **on the edge of sth.** schwankend am Rande einer Sache *(Gen.)* stehen

teeth *pl. of* **tooth**

teething troubles ['tiːðɪŋ trʌblz] *n. pl.* **have** ~ *(fig.)* Anfangsschwierigkeiten haben

teetotal [tiː'təʊtl] *adj.* abstinent lebend. **teetotaller** [tiː'təʊtələ(r)] *n.* Abstinenzler, *der*/Abstinenzlerin, *die*

telecommunications [telɪkəmjuːnɪ-'keɪʃnz] *n. pl.* Fernmelde- *od.* Nachrichtentechnik, *die*

telegram ['telɪɡræm] *n.* Telegramm, *das*

telegraph ['telɪɡrɑːf] *n.* Telegraf, *der;* ~ **pole** Telegrafenmast, *der*

telepathy [tɪ'lepəθɪ] *n.* Telepathie, *die*

telephone ['telɪfəʊn] **1.** *n.* Telefon, *das; attrib.* Telefon-; **answer the** ~: Anrufe entgegennehmen; *(on one occasion)* ans Telefon gehen; *(speak)* sich melden; **be on the** ~: Telefon haben; *(be speaking)* telefonieren *(to* mit*)*. **2.** *v. t.* anrufen. **3.** *v. i.* anrufen; ~ **for a taxi** nach einem Taxi telefonieren

telephone: ~ **book** *n.* Telefonbuch, *das;* ~ **booth,** *(Brit.)* ~**-box** *ns.* Telefonzelle, *die;* ~ **call** *n.* Telefongespräch, *das;* ~ **directory** *n.* Telefonverzeichnis, *das;* ~ **exchange** *n.* Fernmeldeamt, *das;* ~ **number** *n.* Telefonnummer, *die;* ~ **operator** *n.* Telegrafist, *der*/Telegrafistin, *die*

telephoto [telɪ'fəʊtəʊ] *adj. (Photog.)* ~ **lens** Teleobjektiv, *das*

teleprinter ['telɪprɪntə(r)] *n.* Fernschreiber, *der*

telescope ['telɪskəʊp] *n.* Teleskop, *das;* Fernrohr, *das.* **telescopic** [telɪ-'skɒpɪk] *adj. (collapsible)* ausziehbar; Teleskop⟨antenne⟩

televise ['telɪvaɪz] *v. t.* im Fernsehen senden *od.* übertragen

television ['telɪvɪʒn, telɪ'vɪʒn] *n.* **a)** *no art.* das Fernsehen; **on** ~: im Fernsehen; **watch** ~: fernsehen; **b)** *(~ set)* Fernsehapparat, *der;* Fernseher, *der (ugs.)*

television: ~ **channel** *n.* [Fernseh]kanal, *der;* ~ **programme** *n.* Fernsehsendung, *die;* ~ **set** *n.* Fernsehgerät, *das*

Telex, telex ['teleks] **1.** *n.* Telex, *das.* **2.** *v. t.* ein Telex schicken (+ *Dat.*); telexen ⟨Nachricht⟩

tell [tel] **1.** *v. t.,* told [təʊld] **a)** *(relate)* erzählen; *(make known)* sagen ⟨Name, Adresse⟩; anvertrauen ⟨Geheimnis⟩; ~ **sb. sth.** *or* **sth. to sb.** jmdm. etw. erzählen/sagen/anvertrauen; ~ **sb. the way to the station** jmdm. den Weg zum Bahnhof beschreiben; ~ **sb. the time** jmdm. die Uhrzeit sagen; ~ **tales** *(lie)* Lügengeschichten erzählen; *(gossip)* tratschen *(ugs.)*; **b)** *(instruct)* sagen; ~ **sb.** [**not**] **to do sth.** jmdm. sagen, er soll[e] etw. [nicht] tun; **c)** *(determine)* feststellen; *(see, recognize)* erkennen (by an + *Dat.*); *(with reference to the future)* [vorher]sagen; **d)** *(distinguish)* unterscheiden; **e) all told** insgesamt. **2.** *v. i.*, told **a)** *(determine)* how can you ~? wie kann man das feststellen *od.* wissen?; **you never can ~:** man kann nie wissen; **b)** *(give information)* erzählen **(of, about** von); **c)** *(reveal secret)* es verraten; **time will ~:** das wird sich zeigen; **d)** *(produce an effect)* sich auswirken. **tell a'part** *v. t.* auseinanderhalten. **tell 'off** *v. t. (coll.)* ~ **sb. off [for sth.]** jmdn. [für *od.* wegen etw.] ausschimpfen

teller ['telə(r)] *n.* **a)** *(in bank)* see **cashier; b)** *(counting votes)* Stimmenzähler, *der*/-zählerin, *die*

telly ['telɪ] *n. (Brit. coll.)* Fernseher, *der (ugs.)*

temp [temp] *n. (Brit. coll.)* Zeitarbeitskraft, *die*

temper ['tempə(r)] **1.** *n.* **a)** *(nature)* Naturell, *das;* **be in a good/bad ~:** gute/schlechte Laune haben; **keep/lose one's ~:** sich beherrschen/die Beherrschung verlieren; **b)** *(anger)* fit of ~: Wutanfall, *der;* **have a ~:** jähzornig sein. **2.** *v. t.* mäßigen; mildern ⟨*Kritik*⟩

temperament ['tempɾəmənt] *n. (nature)* Veranlagung, *die;* Natur, *die; (disposition)* Temperament, *das;* **temperamental** [tempɾə'mentl] *adj.* launenhaft

temperate ['tempɾət] *adj.* gemäßigt

temperature ['tempɾɪtʃə(r)] *n.* Temperatur, *die;* **have or run a ~** *(coll.)* Temperatur *od.* Fieber haben

template ['templɪt] *n.* Schablone, *die*

¹**temple** ['templ] *n.* Tempel, *der*

²**temple** *n. (Anat.)* Schläfe, *die*

tempo ['tempəʊ] *n., pl.* **~s** or **tempi** ['tempɪ:] Tempo, *das*

temporary ['tempɾəɾɪ] *adj.* vorübergehend; provisorisch ⟨*Gebäude, Büro*⟩

tempt [tempt] *v. t.* **a)** ~ **sb. to do sth.** jmdn. geneigt machen, etw. zu tun; **be ~ed to do sth.** versucht sein, etw. zu tun; ~ **sb. out** jmdn. hinauslocken; **b)** *(provoke)* herausfordern; ~ **fate** das Schicksal herausfordern. **temptation** [temp'teɪʃn] *n.* **a)** no pl. *(attracting)* Verlockung, *die; (being attracted)* Versuchung, *die;* **b)** *(thing)* Verlokkung, *die.* **'tempting** *adj.* verlockend

ten [ten] **1.** *adj.* zehn. **2.** *n.* Zehn, *die. See also* **eight**

tenable ['tenəbl] *adj.* haltbar ⟨*Theorie*⟩; vertretbar ⟨*Standpunkt*⟩

tenacious [tɪ'neɪʃəs] *adj.* hartnäckig.
tenacity [tɪ'næsɪtɪ] *n.* Hartnäckigkeit, *die*

tenant ['tenənt] *n. (of flat, residential building)* Mieter, *der*/Mieterin, *die; (of farm, shop)* Pächter, *der*/Pächterin, *die*

¹**tend** [tend] *v. i.* ~ **to do sth.** dazu neigen *od.* tendieren, etw. zu tun; ~ **to sth.** zu etw. neigen; **he ~s to get upset if ...:** er regt sich leicht auf, wenn ...

²**tend** *v. t.* sich kümmern um; hüten ⟨*Schafe*⟩; bedienen ⟨*Maschine*⟩

tendency ['tendənsɪ] *n. (inclination)* Tendenz, *die;* **have a ~ to do sth.** dazu neigen, etw. zu tun

¹**tender** ['tendə(r)] *adj.* **a)** *(not tough)* zart; **b)** *(loving)* zärtlich; **c)** *(sensitive)* empfindlich

²**tender 1.** *v. t.* **a)** *(present)* einreichen ⟨*Rücktritt*⟩; vorbringen ⟨*Entschuldigung*⟩; **b)** *(offer as payment)* anbieten. **2.** *n.* Angebot, *das*

'tenderly *adv. (gently)* behutsam; *(lovingly)* zärtlich

'tenderness *n. see* ¹**tender:** Zartheit, *die;* Zärtlichkeit, *die;* Empfindlichkeit, *die*

tendon ['tendən] *n. (Anat.)* Sehne, *die*

tenement ['tenɪmənt] *n.* Mietshaus, *das*

tenet ['tenɪt] *n.* Grundsatz, *der*

tenner ['tenə(r)] *n. (Brit. coll.)* Zehnpfundschein, *der*

tennis ['tenɪs] *n.* Tennis, *das*

tennis: **~-ball** *n.* Tennisball, *der;* **~-court** *n. (for lawn ~)* Tennisplatz, *der; (indoor)* Tennishalle, *die;* **~-racket** *n.* Tennisschläger, *der*

tenor ['tenə(r)] *n. (Mus.)* Tenor, *der*

¹**tense** [tens] *n. (Ling.)* Zeit, *die*

²**tense 1.** *adj.* gespannt. **2.** *v. i.* **sb. ~s** jmds. Muskeln spannen sich an. **3.** *v. t.* anspannen. **tension** ['tenʃn] *n.* **a)** Spannung, *die;* **b)** *(mental strain)* Anspannung, *die*

tent [tent] *n.* Zelt, *das*

tentacle ['tentəkl] *n.* Tentakel, *der od. das*

tentative ['tentətɪv] *adj.* **a)** *(not definite)* vorläufig; **b)** *(hesitant)* zaghaft

tenterhooks ['tentəhʊks] *n. pl.* **be on ~:** [wie] auf glühenden Kohlen sitzen

tenth [tenθ] **1.** *adj.* zehnte... **2.** *n. (in sequence)* zehnte, *der/die/das; (in rank)* Zehnte, *der/die/das; (fraction)* Zehntel, *das. See also* **eighth**

'tent-peg *n.* Zeltpflock, *der*

tenuous ['tenjʊəs] *adj.* dünn ⟨*Atmo*

sphäre⟩; dürftig ⟨*Argument*⟩; unbegründet ⟨*Anspruch*⟩

tepid ['tepɪd] *adj.* lauwarm

term [tɜːm] **1.** *n.* **a)** [Fach]begriff, *der;*
b) *in pl. (conditions)* Bedingungen;
come to ~s with sth. mit etw. zurechtkommen; *(resign oneself to sth.)* sich
mit etw. abfinden; **c)** *in pl. (charges)*
Konditionen; **d) in the short/long/me-
dium ~:** kurz-/lang-/mittelfristig; **e)**
(Sch.) Halbjahr, *das;* *(Univ.: one of
two/three divisions per year)* Semester,
das/Trimester, *das;* **f)** *(limited period)*
Zeitraum, *der;* ~ **[of office]** Amtszeit,
die; **g)** *in pl. (mode of expression)* Worte; **h)** *in pl. (relations)* **be on good/bad
~s with sb.** jit jmdm. auf gutem/
schlechtem Fuß stehen. **2.** *v. t.* nennen

terminal ['tɜːmɪnl] **1.** *n.* **a)** *(for train or
bus)* Bahnhof, *der;* *(for airline passengers)* Terminal, *der od. das;* **b)**
(Teleph.; Computing) Terminal, *das.* **2.**
adj. (Med.) unheilbar

terminate ['tɜːmɪneɪt] *v. t.* **a)** beenden;
lösen ⟨*Vertrag*⟩; **b)** *(Med.)* unterbrechen ⟨*Schwangerschaft*⟩. **termina-
tion** [tɜːmɪ'neɪʃn] *n.* **a)** *no pl.* Beendigung, *die;* *(of lease)* Ablauf, *der;* **b)**
(Med.) Schwangerschaftsabbruch, *der*

termini *pl. of* **terminus**

terminology [tɜːmɪ'nɒlədʒɪ] *n.* Termi-
nologie, *die*

terminus ['tɜːmɪnəs] *n., pl.* ~**es** *or* ter-
mini ['tɜːmɪnaɪ] Endstation, *die*

terrace ['terəs, 'terɪs] *n.* Häuserreihe,
die. **terraced house** ['terəst haʊs,
'terɪst haʊs] *n.* Reihenhaus, *das*

terrain [te'reɪn] *n.* Gelände, *das*

terrible ['terɪbl] *adj.* **a)** *(coll.: very great
or bad)* schrecklich *(ugs.)*; **b)** *(coll.: incompetent)* schlecht; **c)** *(causing terror)* furchtbar. **terribly** ['terɪblɪ] *adv.*
a) *(coll.: very)* unheimlich *(ugs.)*; **b)**
(coll.: appallingly) furchtbar *(ugs.)*; **c)**
(coll.: incompetently) schlecht; **d)**
(fearfully) auf erschreckende Weise

terrier ['terɪə(r)] *n.* Terrier, *der*

terrific [tə'rɪfɪk] *adj. (coll.)* **a)** *(great,
intense)* irrsinnig *(ugs.)*; **b)** *(magnificent)* sagenhaft *(ugs.)*; **c)** *(highly expert)* klasse *(ugs.)*

terrify ['terɪfaɪ] *v. t.* **a)** angst machen
(+ *Dat.*); **be terrified that ...:** Angst
haben, daß ...; **b)** *(scare)* Angst einjagen (+ *Dat.*). **terrifying** *adj.* entsetzlich ⟨*Erlebnis, Buch*⟩; furchterregend ⟨*Anblick*⟩; beängstigend ⟨*Geschwindigkeit*⟩

territorial [terɪ'tɔːrɪəl] *adj.* territorial;

Gebiets⟨*anspruch usw.*⟩. **territory**
['terɪtrɪ] *n.* Gebiet, *das*

terror ['terə(r)] *n.* [panische] Angst;
Schrecken, *der.* **terrorism** ['terərɪzm]
n. Terrorismus, *der;* *(terrorist acts)*
Terror, *der.* '**terrorist** *n.* Terrorist,
der/Terroristin, *die.* **terrorize** ['terə-
raɪz] *v. t.* **a)** *(frighten)* in [Angst und]
Schrecken versetzen; **b)** *(coerce)* terrorisieren

terse [tɜːs] *adj.* **a)** *(concise)* kurz und
bündig; **b)** *(curt)* knapp

test [test] **1.** *n.* **a)** *(Sch.)* Klassenarbeit,
die; *(Univ.)* Klausur, *die;* **put sb./sth.
to the ~:** jmdn./etw. erproben; **b)**
(analysis) Test, *der.* **2.** *v. t.* untersuchen ⟨*Wasser, Augen*⟩; testen ⟨*Gehör,
Augen*⟩; prüfen ⟨*Schüler*⟩; ~ **sb. for
Aids** jmdn. auf Aids untersuchen.
'**test out** *v. t.* ausprobieren ⟨*Produkte*⟩ (**on** an + *Dat.*); erproben ⟨*Theorie, Idee*⟩

Testament ['testəmənt] *n.* **Old/New ~**
(Bibl.) Altes/Neues Testament

testicle ['testɪkl] *n.* Testikel, *der
(fachspr.)*; Hoden, *der*

testify ['testɪfaɪ] **1.** *v. i.* **a)** ~ **to sth.** etw.
bezeugen; **b)** *(Law)* ~ **against sb.** ge-
gen jmdn. aussagen. **2.** *v. t.* bestätigen

testimonial [testɪ'məʊnɪəl] Zeugnis,
das; Referenz, *die*

testimony ['testɪmənɪ] *n.* Aussage, *die*

'**test-tube** *n.* Reagenzglas, *das*

testy ['testɪ] *adj.* leicht reizbar ⟨*Person*⟩; gereizt ⟨*Antwort*⟩

tetanus ['tetənəs] *n.* Tetanus, *der*

tetchy ['tetʃɪ] *adj.* leicht reizbar; gereizt

tether ['teðə(r)] **1.** *n.* **be at the end of
one's ~:** am Ende [seiner Kraft] sein.
2. *v. t.* anbinden (**to** an + *Dat. od.
Akk.*)

text [tekst] *n.* Text, *der.* '**textbook** *n.*
Lehrbuch, *das*

textile ['tekstaɪl] *n.* Stoff, *der;* ~**s** Textilien *Pl.*

texture ['tekstʃə(r)] *n.* Beschaffenheit,
die; *(of fabric)* Struktur, *die*

Thai [taɪ] **1.** *adj.* thailändisch. **2.** *n.* **a)**
pl. same or ~**s** Thai, *der/die;* **b)** *(language)* Thai, *das.* **Thailand** ['taɪlænd]
pr. n. Thailand *(das)*

Thames [temz] *pr. n.* Themse, *die*

than [ðæn, *stressed* ðæn] *conj.* als; **I
know you better ~ [I do] him** ich kenne
dich besser als ihn

thank [θæŋk] *v. t.* ~ **sb. [for sth.]** jmdm.
[für etw.] danken; ~ **God** *or* **goodness**
or **heaven[s]** Gott sei Dank; **[I] ~ you**

danke; **no**, ~ **you** nein, danke; **yes**, ~ **you** ja, bitte; ~ **you very much** vielen herzlichen Dank. **thankful** ['θæŋkfl] *adj.* dankbar. '**thankless** *adj.* un- dankbar. **thanks** [θæŋks] *n.pl.* **a)** *(gratitude)* Dank, *der;* ~ **to** *(with the help of)* dank; *(on account of the bad influence of)* wegen; **b)** *(formula expr. gratitude)* danke; **no**, ~: nein, danke; **yes**, ~: ja, bitte; **many** ~ *(coll.)* vielen Dank. '**thank-you** *n. (coll.)* Danke- schön, *das*

that 1. [ðæt] *adj., pl.* **those** [ðəʊz] **a)** dieser/diese/dieses; **b)** *(coupled or contrasted with 'this')* der/die/das. **2.** [ðæt] *pron., pl.* **those a)** der/die/das; **what bird is** ~? was für ein Vogel ist das?; **like** ~: so; **[just] like** ~ *(without effort, thought)* einfach so; ~'**s right!** gut *od.* recht so; *(iron.)* nur so weiter!; ~ **will do** das reicht; **b)** *(Brit.)* **who is** ~? wer ist das?; *(on telephone)* wer ist am Apparat? **3.** [ðət] *rel. pron., pl.* **same** der/die/das; **everyone** ~ **I know** jeder, den ich kenne; **this is all [the money]** ~ **I have** das ist alles [Geld], was ich habe. **4.** [ðæt] *adv. (coll.)* so. **5.** [ðət] *rel. adv.* der/die/das; **the day** ~ **I** first met her der Tag, an dem ich sie zum ersten Mal sah. **6.** [ðət, *stressed* ðæt] *conj.* daß; **[in order]** ~: damit

thatch [θætʃ] *n. (of straw)* Strohdach, *das; (of reeds)* Schilfdach, *das; (roof- ing)* Dachbedeckung, *die.* '**thatched** [θætʃt] *adj.* stroh-/schilfgedeckt

thaw [θɔː] **1.** *v.i.* **a)** tauen; **b)** *(melt)* auftauen. **2.** *v.t.* auftauen. **thaw 'out** *see* **thaw 2, 3**

the [*before vowel* ðɪ, *before consonant* ðə, *when stressed* ðiː] **1.** *def. art.* der/ die/das. **2.** *adv.* ~ **more I practise** better I play je mehr ich übe, desto *od.* um so besser spiele ich; **so much** ~ **worse for sb./sth.** um so schlimmer für jmdn./etw.

theatre *(Amer.:* **theater)** ['θɪətə(r)] *n.* **a)** Theater, *das;* **b)** *(lecture* ~*)* Hör- saal, *der;* **c)** *(Brit. Med.) see* **operating theatre**. **theatrical** [θɪ'ætrɪkl] *adj.* **a)** schauspielerisch; **b)** *(showy)* theatra- lisch

theft [θeft] *n.* Diebstahl, *der*

their [ðeə(r)] *poss. pron. attrib.* ihr

theirs [ðeəz] *poss. pron. pred.* ihrer/ih- re/ihres

them [ðəm, *stressed* ðem] *pron.* sie; *(as indirect object)* ihnen; *see also* '**her**

theme [θiːm] *n.* Thema, *das*

themselves [ðəm'selvz] *pron.* **a)** em-

phat. selbst; **b)** *refl.* sich ⟨*waschen usw.*⟩; sich selbst ⟨*die Schuld geben, regieren*⟩. *See also* **herself**

then [ðen] **1.** *adv.* **a)** *(at that time)* da- mals; ~ **and there** *auf* der Stelle; **b)** *(after that)* dann; ~ **[again]** *(and also)* außerdem; **but** ~ *(after all)* aber schließlich; **c)** *(in that case)* dann; **but** ~ **again** aber andererseits. **2.** *n.* **before** ~: vorher; davor; **since** ~: seitdem. **3.** *adj.* damalig

theological [θiːə'lɒdʒɪkl] *adj.* theolo- gisch; Theologie⟨*student*⟩

theology [θɪ'ɒlədʒɪ] *n.* Theologie, *die*

theoretical [θɪə'retɪkl] *adj.* theore- tisch

theory ['θɪərɪ] *n.* Theorie, *die;* **in** ~: theoretisch

therapeutic [θerə'pjuːtɪk] *adj.* thera- peutisch

therapist ['θerəpɪst] *n.* Therapeut, *der/*Therapeutin, *die*

therapy ['θerəpɪ] *n.* Therapie, *die*

there [ðeə(r)] **1.** *adv.* **a)** *(in/at that place)* da; dort; *(fairly close)* da; **be down/in/up** ~: da unten/drin/oben sein; **b)** *(calling attention)* **hello** *or* **hi** ~! hallo!; **you** ~! Sie da!; **c)** *(in that re- spect)* **as so** ~: und damit basta *(ugs.)*; **d)** *(to that place)* dahin, dorthin ⟨*gehen, fahren, rücken*⟩; **down/up** ~: dort hinunter/hinauf; **e)** [ðə(r), *stressed* ðeə(r)] **was** ~ **anything in it?** war da irgendwas drin?; ~ **was once es** war einmal; ~ **is enough food** es gibt genug zu essen. **2.** *int.* ~, ~: na, na *(ugs.)*; ~ **[you are]!** da, siehst du! **3.** *n.* da; dort; **near** ~: da *od.* dort in der Nähe. **thereabouts** ['ðeərəbaʊts] *adv.* **a)** da [in der Nähe]; **b)** *(near that number)* ungefähr. **therefore** ['ðeə- fɔː(r)] *adv.* deshalb; also

thermal ['θɜːml] *adj.* thermisch; ~ **underwear** kälteisolierende Unterwä- sche

thermometer [θə'mɒmɪtə(r)] *n.* Ther- mometer, *das*

Thermos, thermos, (P) ['θɜːməs] *n.* ~ **[flask/jug/bottle]** Thermosflasche, *die* ⓦ

thermostat ['θɜːməstæt] *n.* Thermo- stat, *der*

these *pl. of* **this**

thesis ['θiːsɪs] *n., pl.* **theses** ['θiːsiːz] **a)** *(proposition)* These, *die;* **b)** *(disserta- tion)* Dissertation, *die* **(on über** **+ Akk.)**

they [ðeɪ] *pron.* **a)** sie; **b)** *(people in general)* man

they'd [ðeɪd] **a)** = they would; **b)** = they had

they'll [ðeɪl] = they will

they're [ðeə(r)] = they are

they've [ðeɪv] = they have

thick [θɪk] **1.** *adj.* **a)** dick; **a rope two inches ~, a two-inch ~ rope** ein zwei Zoll starkes *od.* dickes Seil; **b)** *(dense)* dicht ⟨*Haar, Nebel, Wolken usw.*⟩; **c)** *(filled)* **~ with** voll von; **d)** dickflüssig ⟨*Sahne*⟩; dick ⟨*Suppe, Schlamm, Kleister*⟩; **e)** *(stupid)* dumm. **2.** *n.* **in the ~ of** mitten in (+ *Dat.*). **thick 'ear** *n.* **give sb. a ~** *(Brit. sl.)* jmdm. ein paar hinter die Ohren geben *(ugs.)*

thicken [ˈθɪkn] **1.** *v. t.* dicker machen; eindicken ⟨*Sauce*⟩. **2.** *v. i.* **a)** dicker werden; **b)** ⟨*Nebel:*⟩ dichter werden; **c)** **the plot ~s** die Sache wird kompliziert

thickly *adv.* **a)** *(in a thick layer)* dick; **b)** *(densely)* dicht

thickness *n.* **a)** Dicke, *die;* **be two metres in ~** zwei Meter dick sein; **b)** *(denseness)* Dichte, *die*

thick: **~-set** *adj.* gedrungen; **~skinned** *adj. (fig.)* dickfellig *(ugs.)*

thief [θiːf] *n., pl.* **thieves** [θiːvz] Dieb, *der/*Diebin, *die*

thieve [θiːv] *v. i.* stehlen

thieves *pl. of* **thief**

thigh [θaɪ] *n.* Oberschenkel, *der*

thimble [ˈθɪmbl] *n.* Fingerhut, *der*

thin [θɪn] **1.** *adj.* **a)** dünn; **a tall, ~ man** ein großer, hagerer Mann; **b)** *(sparse)* dünn, schütter ⟨*Haar*⟩. **2.** *adv.* dünn. **3.** *v. t.,* **-nn-: a)** dünner machen; **b)** *(dilute)* verdünnen. **thin 'out** *v. i.* ⟨*Menschenmenge:*⟩ sich verlaufen; ⟨*Verkehr:*⟩ abnehmen

thing [θɪŋ] *n.* **a)** Sache, *die;* Ding, *das;* **what's that ~ in your hand?** was hast du da in der Hand?; **be a rare ~:** etwas Seltenes sein; **b)** *(action)* **it was the right ~ to do** es war das einzig Richtige; **that was a foolish/friendly ~ to do** das war eine große Dummheit/ das war sehr freundlich; **c)** *(fact)* [Tat]sache, *die;* **the best/worst ~ about her** das Beste/Schlimmste an ihr; **d)** *(idea)* **say the first ~ that comes into one's head** das sagen, was einem gerade so einfällt; **what a ~ to say!** wie kann man nur so etwas sagen!; **e)** *(task)* **she has a reputation for getting ~s done** sie ist für ihre Tatkraft bekannt; **a big ~ to undertake** ein großes Unterfangen; **f)** *(affair)* Sache, *die;* Angelegenheit, *die;* **g)** *(circumstance)*

take ~s too seriously alles zu ernst nehmen; **how are ~s?** wie geht's [dir]?; **h)** *(individual, creature)* Ding, *das;* **i)** *in pl. (personal belongings, clothes)* Sachen; **j)** *(product of work)* Sache, *die;* **the latest ~:** der letzte Schrei; **k)** *(what is important or proper)* das Richtige; **the ~ is ...** *(question)* die Frage ist ...

think [θɪŋk] **1.** *v. t.,* **thought** [θɔːt] **a)** *(consider)* meinen; **we ~ [that] he will come** wir denken *od.* glauben, daß er kommt; **what do you ~?** was meinst du? **do you really ~ so?** findest du wirklich?; **what do you ~ of him/it?** was hältst du von ihm/davon?; ..., **don't you ~?** ... , findest *od.* meinst du nicht auch?; **I ~ so/not** ich glaube schon/nicht; **I ~ I'll try** ich glaube, ich werde es versuchen; **b)** *(imagine)* sich (*Dat.*) vorstellen. **2.** *v. i.,* **thought** [nach]denken; **I need time to ~:** ich muß es mir erst überlegen; **I've been ~ing** ich habe nachgedacht; **~ twice** es sich (*Dat.*) zweimal überlegen. **'think of** *v. t.* **a)** denken an (+ *Akk.*); **he ~s of everything** er denkt einfach an alles; **b)** *(have as idea)* **we'll ~ of something** wir werden uns etwas einfallen lassen; **can you ~ of anyone who ...?** fällt dir jemand ein, der ...?; **c)** *(remember)* sich erinnern an (+ *Akk.*); **I just can't ~ of her name** ich komme einfach nicht auf ihren Namen; **d)** **~ little/nothing of sb./sth.** *(consider contemptible)* wenig/nichts von jmdm./ etw. halten. **think 'over** *v. t.* sich (*Dat.*) überlegen. **think 'through** *v. t.* [gründlich] durchdenken. **think 'up** *v. t. (coll.)* sich (*Dat.*) ausdenken

'thinker *n.* Denker, *der/*Denkerin, *die*

third [θɜːd] **1.** *adj.* dritt... **2.** *n. (in sequence)* dritte, *der/die/das;* **(in rank)** Dritte, *der/die/das;* **(fraction)** Drittel, *das. See also* **eighth**. **'thirdly** *adv.* drittens

third-rate *adj.* drittklassig

Third 'World *n.* dritte Welt

thirst [θɜːst] **1.** *n.* Durst, *der;* **die of ~:** verdursten. **2.** *v. i.* **~ for revenge/ knowledge** nach Rache/Wissen dürsten *(geh.)*. **'thirsty** *adj.* durstig; **be ~:** Durst haben

thirteen [θɜːˈtiːn] **1.** *adj.* dreizehn. **2.** *n.* Dreizehn, *die. See also* **eight**. **thirteenth** [θɜːˈtiːnθ] *adj.* dreizehnt... *See also* **eighth**

thirtieth [ˈθɜːtɪɪθ] **1.** *adj.* dreißigst... **2.** *n. (fraction)* Dreißigstel, *das. See also* **eighth**

thirty ['θɜːtɪ] 1. *adj.* dreißig. 2. *n.* Dreißig, *die. See also* eight; eighty 2

this [ðɪs] 1. *adj., pl.* these [ðiːz] dieser/diese/dieses; *(with less emphasis)* der/die/das; **at ~ time** zu dieser Zeit; **by ~ time** inzwischen; mittlerweile; **these days** heut[zut]age; **before ~ time** vorher; zuvor; **all ~ week** die[se] ganze Woche; **~ morning/evening** *etc.* heute morgen/abend *usw.;* **these last three weeks** die letzten drei Wochen; **~ Monday** *(to come)* nächsten Montag. 2. *pron., pl.* **these a) what's ~?** was ist [denn] das?; **fold it like ~!** falte es so!; b) *(the present)* **before ~:** bis jetzt; c) *(Brit. Teleph.: person speaking)* **~ is Andy** hier [spricht *od.* ist] Andy; *(Amer. Teleph.)* **who did you say ~ was?** wer ist am apparat?; d) **~ and that** dies und das

thistle ['θɪsl] *n.* Distel, *die*

thorn [θɔːn] *n.* a) *(part of plant)* Dorn, *der;* b) *(plant)* Dornenstrauch, *der.* **'thorny** *adj.* a) dornig; b) *(fig.)* heikel

thorough ['θʌrə] *adj.* gründlich

thorough: **~bred** *n.* reinrassiges Tier; *(horse)* Rassepferd, *das;* **~fare** *n.* Durchfahrtsstraße, *die;* **'no ~fare'** „Durchfahrt verboten"; *(on foot)* „kein Durchgang"

'thoroughly *adv.* gründlich *(untersuchen);* gehörig *(erschöpft);* so richtig *(genießen);* zutiefst *(beschämt);* total *(verdorben, verwöhnt);* **be ~ fed up with sth.** *(sl.)* von etw. die Nase gestrichen voll haben *(ugs.).* **'thoroughness** *n.* Gründlichkeit, *die*

those *see* that 1, 2

though [ðəʊ] 1. *(conj.)* a) *(despite the fact that)* obwohl; **late ~ it was** obwohl es so spät war; **the car, ~ powerful, is also economical** der Wagen ist zwar stark, aber [zugleich] auch wirtschaftlich; b) *(but nevertheless)* aber; **a slow ~ certain method** eine langsame, aber *od.* wenn auch sichere Methode; c) *(even if)* [even] **~:** auch wenn; d) *(and yet)* **~ you never know** obwohl man nie weiß. 2. *adv.* *(coll.)* trotzdem

thought [θɔːt] 1. *see* think. 2. *n.* a) no pl. Denken, *das;* b) no pl., no art. *(reflection)* Überlegung, *die;* Nachdenken, *das;* c) *(consideration)* Rücksicht, *die* (**for** auf + *Akk.);* d) *(idea, conception)* Gedanke, *der;* **it's the ~ that counts** der gute Wille zählt; **give up all ~[s] of sth.** sich *(Dat.)* etw. aus dem Kopf schlagen. **thoughtful** ['θɔːtfl] *adj.* a) nachdenklich; b) *(considerate)*

rücksichtsvoll; *(helpful)* aufmerksam. **'thoughtfully** *adv.* a) nachdenklich; b) *(considerately)* rücksichtsvollerweise. **'thoughtless** *adj.* a) gedankenlos; b) *(inconsiderate)* rücksichtslos. **'thoughtlessly** *adv.* a) gedankenlos; b) *(inconsiderately)* aus Rücksichtslosigkeit

thousand ['θaʊznd] 1. *adj.* a) tausend; **a or one ~:** eintausend; **two/several ~:** zweitausend/mehrere tausend; **a or one ~ and one** [ein]tausend[und]eins; b) **a ~ [and one]** *(fig.: innumerable)* tausend *(ugs.).* 2. *n.* a) *(number)* tausend; **a or one/two ~:** ein-/zweitausend; b) *(written figure, group)* Tausend, *das;* c) *(indefinite amount)* **~s** Tausende. **thousandth** ['θaʊzndθ] 1. *adj.* tausendst... 2. *n.* *(fraction)* Tausendstel, *das;* *(in sequence)* Tausendste, *der/die/das*

thrash [θræʃ] *v.t.* a) verprügeln; b) *(defeat)* vernichtend schlagen. **thrash 'out** *v.t.* ausdiskutieren

thread [θred] 1. *n.* a) Faden, *der;* b) *(of screw)* Gewinde, *das.* 2. *v.t.* a) einfädeln; auffädeln *(Perlen);* b) **~ one's way through sth.** sich durch etw. schlängeln. **'threadbare** *adj.* abgenutzt; abgetragen *(Kleidung);* *(fig.)* abgedroschen *(Argument)*

threat [θret] *n.* Drohung, *die.* **threaten** ['θretn] *v.t.* a) bedrohen; **~ sb. with sth.** jmdm. etw. androhen; **~ to do sth.** damit drohen, etw. zu tun; c) drohen mit *(Gewalt, Rache usw.).* **threatening** ['θretnɪŋ] *adj.* drohend

three [θriː] 1. *adj.* drei. 2. *n.* Drei, *die. See also* eight

three: **~-dimensional** [θriːdɪ'menʃnl] *adj.* dreidimensional; **~fold** *adj., adv.* dreifach; **a ~fold increase** ein Anstieg auf das Dreifache; **~-quarters** 1. *n.* a) drei Viertel *pl.* (**of** + *Gen.);* b) **~-quarters of an hour** eine Dreiviertelstunde; 2. *adv.* dreiviertel *(voll);* **~some** ['θriːsəm] *n.* Dreigespann, *der;* Trio, *das*

thresh [θreʃ] *v.t.* dreschen

threshold ['θreʃəʊld] *n.* Schwelle, *die*

threw *see* throw 1

thrift [θrɪft] *n.* Sparsamkeit, *die.* **'thrifty** *adj.* sparsam

thrill [θrɪl] 1. *v.t.* a) *(excite)* faszinieren; b) *(delight)* begeistern. 2. *n.* a) Erregung, *die;* b) *(exciting experience)* aufregendes Erlebnis. **'thriller** *n.* Thriller, *der.* **'thrilling** *adj.* aufregend; spannend *(Buch, Film)*

thrive [θraɪv] *v. i.,* **thrived** *or* **throve** [θrəʊv], **thrived** *or* **thriven** ['θrɪvn] **a)** *(Pflanze:)* wachsen und gedeihen; **b)** *(prosper)* aufblühen (on bei)

throat [θrəʊt] *n.* Hals, *der;* (esp. inside) Kehle, *die;* **a** [sore] ~: Halsschmerzen

throb [θrɒb] **1.** *v. i.,* -**bb**- pochen; ⟨Motor:⟩ dröhnen. **2.** *n.* Pochen, *das;* (of engine) Dröhnen, *das*

throes [θrəʊz] *n. pl.* Qual, *die;* be in the ~ of sth. *(fig.)* mitten in etw. *(Dat.)* stecken *(ugs.)*

thrombosis [θrɒm'bəʊsɪs] *n., pl.* **thromboses** [θrɒm'bəʊsiːz] Thrombose, *die*

throne [θrəʊn] *n.* Thron, *der*

throng [θrɒŋ] *n.* [Menschen]menge, *die*

throttle ['θrɒtl] *v. t.* erdrosseln

through [θruː] **1.** *prep.* **a)** durch; **b)** (Amer.: up to and including) bis [einschließlich]; **c)** (by reason of) durch; infolge von ⟨Vernachlässigung, Einflüssen⟩. **2.** *adv.* **a)** let sb. ~: jmdn. durchlassen; **b)** (Teleph.) be ~: durch sein *(ugs.);* be ~ to sb. mit jmdm. verbunden sein. **3.** *attrib. adj.* durchgehend ⟨Zug⟩. **through'out 1.** *prep.* ~ **the war/period** den ganzen Krieg/die ganze Zeit hindurch; ~ **the country** im ganzen Land. **2.** *adv.* (entirely) ganz; (always) stets; die ganze Zeit [hindurch]

throve *see* **thrive**

throw [θrəʊ] **1.** *v. t.,* **threw** [θruː], **thrown** [θrəʊn] **a)** werfen; ~ **sth. to sb.** jmdm. etw. zuwerfen; ~ **sth. at sb.** etw. nach jmdm. werfen; **b)** (bring to the ground) zu Boden werfen; abwerfen ⟨Reiter⟩; **c)** (coll.: disconcert) ⟨Frage:⟩ aus der Fassung bringen. **2.** *n.* Wurf, *der.* **throw a'way** *v. t.* **a)** wegwerfen; **b)** (lose by neglect) verschenken ⟨Vorteil, Spiel usw.⟩. **throw 'up 1.** *v. t.* **a)** hochwerfen ⟨Arme, Hände⟩; **b)** (produce) hervorbringen ⟨Ideen usw.⟩. **2.** *v. i.* (coll.) brechen *(ugs.)*

'throw-away *adj.* **a)** Wegwerf-; Einweg-; **b)** beiläufig ⟨Bemerkung⟩

thrown *see* **throw 1**

thrush [θrʌʃ] *n.* (Ornith.) Drossel, *die*

thrust [θrʌst] **1.** *v. t.,* **thrust** stoßen; ~ **aside** *(fig.)* beiseite schieben. **2.** *n.* Stoß, *der*

thud [θʌd] *n.* dumpfer Schlag

thug [θʌg] *n.* Schläger, *der*

thumb [θʌm] **1.** *n.* Daumen, *der;* get the ~s up ⟨Person, Projekt:⟩ akzeptiert

werden; be under sb.'s ~: unter jmds. Fuchtel stehen. **2.** *v. t.* ~ **a lift** per Anhalter fahren. **'thumb through** *v. t.* durchblättern

thumb: ~ **index** *n.* Daumenregister, *das;* ~**tack** *n.* (Amer.) Reißzwecke, *die*

thump [θʌmp] **1.** *v. t.* [mit Wucht] schlagen. **2.** *v. i.* **a)** hämmern (at, on gegen); **b)** ⟨Herz:⟩ heftig pochen. **3.** *n.* (blow) Schlag, *der;* (sound) Bums, *der (ugs.);* dumpfer Schlag

thunder ['θʌndə(r)] **1.** *n.* Donner, *der.* **2.** *v. i.* donnern. **'thunderclap** *n.* Donnerschlag, *der.* **'thunderstorm** *n.* Gewitter, *das.* **'thundery** *adj.* gewittrig

Thurs. *abbr.* **Thursday** Do.

Thursday ['θɜːzdeɪ, 'θɜːzdɪ] *n.* Donnerstag, *der; see also* **Friday**

thus [ðʌs] *adv.* so

thwart [θwɔːt] *v. t.* durchkreuzen ⟨Pläne⟩; vereiteln ⟨Versuch⟩; ~ **sb.** jmdm. einen Strich durch die Rechnung machen

thyme [taɪm] *n.* Thymian, *der*

thyroid ['θaɪrɔɪd] *n.* Schilddrüse, *die*

tiara [tɪ'ɑːrə] *n.* Diadem, *das*

tick [tɪk] **1.** *v. i.* ticken. **2.** *v. t.* **a)** mit einem Häkchen versehen; **b)** *see* ~ **off a. 3.** *n.* **a)** (of clock etc.) Ticken, *das;* **b)** (mark) Häkchen, *das.* **tick 'off** *v. t.* **a)** (cross off) abhaken; **b)** (coll.: reprimand) rüffeln *(ugs.)*

ticket ['tɪkɪt] *n.* Karte, *die;* (for bus, train) Fahrschein, *der;* (for aeroplane) Flugschein, *der;* (for lottery, raffle) Los, *das;* (for library) Ausweis, *der;* **price** ~: Preisschild, *das.* **'ticket-collector** *n.* (on train) Schaffner, *der*/Schaffnerin, *die;* (on station) Fahrkartenkontrolleur, *der*/-kontrolleurin, *die.* **'ticket-office** *n.* Fahrkartenschalter, *der;* (for advance booking) Kartenvorverkaufsstelle, *die*

tickle ['tɪkl] **1.** *v. t.* kitzeln. **2.** *v. i.* kitzeln. **ticklish** ['tɪklɪʃ] *adj.* kitzlig

tidal ['taɪdl] *adj.* Gezeiten-. **'tidal wave** *n.* Flutwelle, *die*

tiddly-winks ['tɪdlɪwɪŋks] *n. sing.* (game) Flohhüpfen, *das*

tide [taɪd] **1.** *n.* Tide, *die (nordd.);* **high** ~: Flut, *die;* **low** ~: Ebbe, *die;* **the ~s** die Gezeiten; **the ~ is in/out** es ist Flut/Ebbe. **2.** *v. t.* ~ **sb. over** jmdm. über die Runden helfen *(ugs.)*

tidiness ['taɪdɪnɪs] *n.* Ordentlichkeit, *die*

tidy ['taɪdɪ] **1.** *adj.* ordentlich; aufgeräumt ⟨Zimmer, Schreibtisch⟩. **2.** v.t. aufräumen; ~ **oneself** sich zurechtmachen. **tidy 'up** v.i. aufräumen

tie [taɪ] **1.** v.t., **tying** ['taɪɪŋ] binden (**to** an + Akk., **into** zu); ~ **a knot** einen Knoten machen; (Sport) ~ **the match** unentschieden spielen. **2.** v.i., **tying a)** (be fastened) **it** ~**s at the back** es wird hinten gebunden; **b)** (have equal scores) ~ **for second place** mit gleicher Punktzahl den zweiten Platz erreichen. **3.** n. **a)** Krawatte, die; **b)** (bond) Band, das; (restriction) Bindung, die; **c)** (equality of scores) Punktgleichheit, die; **d)** (Sport: match) Begegnung, die. **tie 'in** v.i. ~ **in with sth.** zu etw. passen. **tie 'up** v.t. **a)** festbinden; ~ **up a parcel** ein Paket verschnüren; **b)** (keep busy) beschäftigen

tier [tɪə(r)] n. **a)** Rang, der; **b)** (unit) Stufe, die

tiger ['taɪgə(r)] n. Tiger, der

tight [taɪt] **1.** adj. **a)** (firm) fest; fest angezogen ⟨Schraube, Mutter⟩; festsitzend ⟨Deckel⟩; **b)** (close-fitting) eng ⟨Kleid, Schuh usw.⟩; **c)** (impermeable) ~ **seal/joint** dichter Verschluß/dichte Fuge; **d)** (taut) straff; **e)** (difficult to negotiate) **a** ~ **corner** eine enge Kurve; **be in a** ~ **corner** (fig.) in der Klemme sein (ugs.); **f)** (strict) streng ⟨Kontrolle, Disziplin⟩; **g)** (coll.: stingy) knauserig (ugs.); **h)** (coll.: drunk) voll (salopp). **2.** adv. fest; **hold** ~! halt dich fest! **3.** n. in pl. **a)** (Brit.) |**pair of**| ~s Strumpfhose, die; **b)** (of dancer etc.) Trikothose, die. **tighten** ['taɪtn] **1.** v.t. **a)** |fest| anziehen ⟨Knoten, Schraube⟩; straffziehen ⟨Seil⟩; **b)** verschärfen ⟨Kontrolle⟩. **2.** v.i. sich spannen. **tight-fisted** [taɪt'fɪstɪd] adj. geizig. **'tightrope** n. Drahtseil, das

tile [taɪl] **1.** n. (on roof) Ziegel, der; (on floor, wall) Fliese, die; Kachel, die. **2.** v.t. [mit Ziegeln] decken ⟨Dach⟩; fliesen ⟨Wand, Fußboden⟩; kacheln ⟨Wand⟩

¹till [tɪl] **1.** prep. bis; (followed by article + noun) bis zu; **not** [...] ~: erst. **2.** conj. bis

²till n. Kasse, die

tilt [tɪlt] **1.** v.i. kippen. **2.** v.t. kippen; neigen ⟨Kopf⟩. **3.** n. **a)** Schräglage, die; **a** 45° ~: eine Neigung von 45°; **b)** |**at**| **full** ~: mit voller Wucht

timber ['tɪmbə(r)] n. [Bau]holz, das

time [taɪm] **1.** n. **a)** Zeit, die; **in** [**the course of**] ~, **as** ~ **goes on/went on** mit der Zeit; **im Laufe der Zeit; in** ~, **with** ~ (sooner or later) mit der Zeit; **in** |**good**| ~ (not late) rechtzeitig; **all the** **or this** ~: die ganze Zeit; (without ceasing) ständig; **a short** ~ **ago** vor kurzem; ~ **off or out** freie Zeit; **in** 'no ~: im Handumdrehen; **in a week's/year's** ~: in einer Woche/in einem Jahr; **harvest/Christmas** ~: Ernte-/Weihnachtszeit, die; **on** ~ (punctually) pünktlich; **ahead of** ~: zu früh ⟨ankommen⟩; vorzeitig ⟨fertig werden⟩; **have a good** ~: sich amüsieren; Spaß haben (ugs.); **b)** (occasion) Mal, das; **for the first** ~: zum ersten Mal; **at** ~**s** gelegentlich; ~ **and again,** ~ **after** ~: immer [und immer] wieder; **at one** ~, **at** |**one and**| **the same** ~ (simultaneously) gleichzeitig; **one at a** ~: einzeln; **two at a** ~: jeweils zwei; **c)** (point in day etc.) [Uhr]zeit, die; **tell the** ~: die Uhr lesen; **what** ~ **is it?**, **what is the** ~? wie spät ist es?; **by this/that** ~: inzwischen; **by the** ~ |**that**| **we arrived** bis wir hinkamen; **d)** (multiplication) mal; **three** ~**s four** drei mal vier; **e)** (Mus.) Takt, der; **in** ~: im Takt. **2.** v.t. **a)** zeitlich abstimmen; **be well** ~**d** zur richtigen Zeit kommen; **b)** (set to operate at correct ~) einstellen; **c)** (measure ~ taken by) stoppen

time: ~ **bomb** n. Zeitbombe, die; ~**-lag** n. zeitliche Verzögerung; ~**-limit** n. Frist, die

timely ['taɪmlɪ] adj. rechtzeitig

time: ~**-scale** n. Zeitskala, die; ~**-switch** n. Zeitschalter, der; ~**-table** n. **a)** (scheme of work) Zeitplan, der; (Educ.) Stundenplan, der; **b)** (Transport) Fahrplan, der; ~**-zone** n. Zeitzone, die

timid ['tɪmɪd] adj. **a)** scheu ⟨Tier⟩; **b)** zaghaft ⟨Mensch⟩; (shy) schüchtern

timing ['taɪmɪŋ] n. **a)** **that was perfect** ~! du kommst gerade im richtigen Augenblick!; **b)** (Theatre, Sport) Timing, das

tin [tɪn] **1.** n. **a)** (metal) Zinn, das; ~-|**plate**| Weißblech, das; **b)** (Brit.: for preserving) |Konserven|dose, die. **2.** v.t., **-nn-** (Brit.) zu Konserven verarbeiten. **tin 'foil** n. Stanniol, das; Alufolie, die

tinge [tɪndʒ] **1.** v.t., ~**ing** ['tɪndʒɪŋ] tönen. **2.** n. [leichte] Färbung; (fig.) Hauch, der

tingle ['tɪŋgl] v.i. kribbeln

tinker ['tɪŋkə(r)] **1.** n. Kesselflicker, der. **2.** v.i. ~ **with sth.** an etw. (Dat.) herumbasteln (ugs.)

tinkle ['tɪŋkl] **1.** *n.* Klingeln, *das.* **2.** *v. i.* klingeln

tinned [tɪnd] *adj. (Brit.)* Dosen-

tin: ~**opener** *n. (Brit.)* Dosenöffner, *der.* ~**pot** *attrib. adj. (derog.)* schäbig

tinsel ['tɪnsl] *n.* Lametta, *das*

tint [tɪnt] **1.** *n.* Farbton, *der.* **2.** *v. t.* tönen; kolorieren ‹*Zeichnung*›

tiny ['taɪnɪ] *adj.* winzig

¹tip [tɪp] *n.* (end, point) Spitze, *die*

²tip [tɪp] **1.** *v. i.*, **-pp-** *(lean, fall)* kippen; ~ **over** umkippen. **2.** *v. t.*, **-pp-: a)** *(make tilt)* kippen; **b)** *(make overturn)* umkippen; *(fig.: discharge)* kippen; **c)** voraussagen ‹*Sieger*›; ~ **sb. to win** auf jmds. Sieg tippen; **d)** *(reward)* ~ **sb.** jmdm. Trinkgeld geben. **3.** *n.* **a)** *(money)* Trinkgeld, *das;* **b)** *(special information)* Hinweis, *der;* Tip, *der (ugs.);* **c)** *(Brit.)* Müllkippe, *die.* **tip 'off** *v. t.* ~ **sb. off** jmdm. einen Hinweis *od. (ugs.)* Tip geben

'tip-off *n.* Hinweis, *der*

tipsy ['tɪpsɪ] *adj. (coll.)* angeheitert; beschwipst *(ugs.)*

tip: ~**toe 1.** *v. i.* auf Zehenspitzen gehen; **2.** *n.* **on** ~**toe|s|** auf Zehenspitzen; ~**top** *adj.* tipptopp *(ugs.)*

¹tire ['taɪə(r)] *(Amer.) see* **tyre**

²tire 1. *v. t.* ermüden. **2.** *v. i.* müde werden; ermüden; ~ **of sth./doing sth.** einer Sache *(Gen.)* überdrüssig werden. **tire 'out** *v. t.* erschöpfen; ~ **oneself out doing sth.** etw. bis zur Erschöpfung tun

tired ['taɪəd] *adj.* **a)** *(weary)* müde; **b)** *(fed up)* **be** ~ **of sth./doing sth.** etw. satt haben/es satt haben etw. zu tun.
'tireless *adj.* unermüdlich. **tiresome** ['taɪəsəm] *adj.* **a)** *(wearisome)* mühsam; **b)** *(annoying)* lästig. **tiring** ['taɪərɪŋ] *adj.* ermüdend

tissue ['tɪʃuː, 'tɪsjuː] *n.* **a)** *(paper)* Papiertuch, *das;* ~: Papiertuch, *das; (handkerchief)* Papiertaschentuch, *das;* **c)** |**paper**| Seidenpapier, *das*

¹tit [tɪt] *n. (Ornith.)* Meise, *die*

²tit *n.* **it's** ~ **for tat** wie du mir, so ich dir

'titbit *n.* **a)** *(food)* Häppchen, *das (ugs.);* **b)** *(piece of news)* Neuigkeit, *die*

title ['taɪtl] *n.* Titel, *der.* **'title-role** *n.* Titelrolle, *die*

tittle-tattle ['tɪtltætl] *n.* Klatsch, *der (ugs.)*

to 1. [*before vowel* tʊ, *before consonant* tə, *stressed* tuː] *prep.* **a)** *(in the direction of and reaching)* zu; *(with name of place)* nach; **go to work/to the theatre** zur Arbeit/ins Theater gehen; **to France** nach Frankreich; **b)** *(as far as)* bis zu; **from London to Edinburgh** von London [bis] nach Edinburgh; **increase from 10 % to 20 %** von 10 % auf 20 % steigen; **c)** *introducing relationship or indirect object* **to sb./sth.** jmdm./einer Sache *(Dat.);* **lend/explain** *etc.* **sth. to sb.** jmdm. etw. leihen/erklären *usw.;* **speak to sb.** mit jmdm. sprechen; **that's all there is to it** mehr ist nicht dazu zu sagen; **what's that to you?** was geht das dich an?; **to me** *(in my opinion)* meiner Meinung nach; **14 miles to the gallon** 14 Meilen auf eine Gallone; **d)** *(until)* bis; **to the end** bis zum Ende; **to this day** bis heute; **five |minutes| to eight** fünf [Minuten] vor acht; **e)** *with infinitive of a verb* zu; *expr. purpose, or after* too um [...] zu; **want to know** wissen wollen; **do sth. to annoy sb.** etw. tun, um jmdn. zu ärgern; **too hot to drink** zu heiß zum Trinken; **he would have phoned but forgot to** er hätte angerufen, aber er vergaß es. **2.** *adv.* [tuː] **to and fro** hin und her

toad [təʊd] *n. (also fig. derog.)* Kröte, *die*

'toadstool *n.* Giftpilz, *der*

toast [təʊst] **1.** *n.* **a)** *no pl.* Toast, *der;* **a piece of** ~: eine Scheibe Toast; **b)** *(call to drink)* Toast, *der;* **drink a** ~ **to sb./sth.** auf jmdn./etw. trinken. **2.** *v. t.* **a)** rösten; toasten ‹*Brot*›; **b)** *(drink to)* trinken auf (+ *Akk.*). **'toaster** *n.* Toaster, *der*

tobacco [tə'bækəʊ] *n., pl.* ~**s** Tabak, *der.* **tobacconist** [tə'bækənɪst] *n.* Tabak[waren]händler, *der/*-händlerin, *die*

toboggan [tə'bɒgən] **1.** *n.* Schlitten, *der.* **2.** *v. i.* Schlitten fahren

today [tə'deɪ] **1.** *n.* heute; ~**'s newspaper** die Zeitung von heute. **2.** *adv.* heute

toddler ['tɒdlə(r)] *n.* ≈ Kleinkind, *das*

to-do [tə'duː] *n.* Getue, *das (ugs.)*

toe [təʊ] **1.** *n.* Zeh, *der;* Zehe, *die; (of footwear)* Spitze, *die.* **2.** *v. t.,* ~**ing** *(fig.)* ~ **the line** *or (Amer.)* **mark** sich einordnen. **'toe-nail** *n.* Zeh[en]nagel, *der*

toffee ['tɒfɪ] *n.* Karamel, *der; (Brit.: piece)* Toffee, *das;* Sahnebonbon, *das*

together [tə'geðə(r)] *adv.* **a)** *(in or into company)* zusammen; **b)** *(simultaneously)* gleichzeitig; **c)** *(one with another)* miteinander

toil [tɔɪl] **1.** *v. i.* schwer arbeiten. **2.** *n.* [harte] Arbeit

toilet ['tɔɪlɪt] *n.* Toilette, *die.* 'toilet-bag *n.* Kulturbeutel, *der.* 'toilet-paper *n.* Toilettenpapier, *das*

toiletries ['tɔɪlɪtrɪz] *n. pl.* Körperpflegemittel; Toilettenartikel

toilet: ~-roll *n.* Rolle Toilettenpapier; ~ water *n.* Toilettenwasser, *das;* Eau de Toilette, *das*

token ['təʊkn] *n.* a) *(voucher)* Gutschein, *der;* b) *(counter, disc)* Marke, *die;* c) *(sign)* Zeichen, *das.* **2.** *attrib. adj.* symbolisch ⟨*Preis*⟩

Tokyo ['təʊkjəʊ] *pr. n.* Tokio *(das)*

told *see* **tell**

tolerable ['tɒlərəbl] *adj.* a) *(endurable)* erträglich (to, for für); b) *(fairly good)* leidlich; annehmbar. **tolerance** ['tɒlərəns] *n.* Toleranz, *die.* **tolerant** ['tɒlərənt] *adj.* tolerant (of, towards gegen[über]). **tolerate** ['tɒləreɪt] *v. t.* dulden; *(bear)* ertragen ⟨*Schmerzen*⟩. **toleration** [tɒlə'reɪʃn] *n.* Tolerierung, *die (geh.)*

¹toll [təʊl] *n.* a) Gebühr, *die;* b) *(damage etc.)* Aufwand, *der;* take its ~ of sth. einen Tribut an etw. *(Dat.)* fordern *(fig.)*

²toll *v. i.* ⟨*Glocke:*⟩ läuten

'toll-bridge *n.* gebührenpflichtige Brücke

tom [tɒm] *n.* *(cat)* Kater, *der*

tomato [tə'mɑːtəʊ] *n., pl.* ~es Tomate, *die.* **to'mato juice** *n.* Tomatensaft, *der.* **tomato 'purée** *n.* Tomatenmark, *das*

tomb [tuːm] *n.* Grab, *das;* *(monument)* Grabmal, *das*

'tomboy *n.* Wildfang, *der*

'tombstone *n.* Grabstein, *der*

'tom-cat *n.* Kater, *der*

tome [təʊm] *n.* dicker Band; Wälzer, *der (ugs.)*

tomfoolery [tɒm'fuːlərɪ] *n.* Blödsinn, *der (ugs.)*

tomorrow [tə'mɒrəʊ] **1.** *n.* morgen; ~ morning/afternoon/evening/night morgen früh od. vormittag/nachmittag/abend/nacht; ~'s newspaper die morgige Zeitung. **2.** *adv.* morgen; see you ~! *(coll.)* bis morgen!; the day after ~: übermorgen

ton [tʌn] *n.* Tonne, *die*

tone [təʊn] **1.** *n.* a) *(sound)* Klang, *der;* *(Teleph.)* Ton, *der;* b) *(style of speaking)* Ton, *der;* c) *(tint, shade)* [Farb]ton, *der;* d) *(fig.: character)* lower/raise the ~ of sth. das Niveau einer Sache *(Gen.)* senken/erhöhen; set the ~: den Ton angeben. **2.** *v. t.* tönen; abtönen ⟨*Farbe*⟩. **tone 'down** *v. t.* [ab]dämpfen ⟨*Farbe*⟩; *(fig.)* mäßigen ⟨*Sprache*⟩

tongs [tɒŋz] *n. pl.* |pair of| ~: Zange, *die*

tongue [tʌŋ] *n.* Zunge, *die; bite one's* ~ *(lit. or fig.)* sich auf die Zunge beißen; **find one's** ~: seine Sprache wiederfinden; **hold one's** ~: stillschweigen; **he made the remark ~ in cheek** *(fig.)* er meinte die Bemerkung nicht ernst. **'tongue-twister** *n.* Zungenbrecher, *der (ugs.)*

tonic ['tɒnɪk] **1.** *n.* a) *(Med.)* Tonikum, *das;* b) *(fig.: invigorating influence)* Wohltat, *die (geh.);* c) *(~ water)* Tonic, *das.* **2.** *attrib. adj.* kräftigend; *(fig.)* wohltuend ⟨*Wirkung*⟩. **'tonic water** *n.* Tonic[wasser], *das*

tonight [tə'naɪt] **1.** *n.* a) *(this evening)* heute abend; ~'s performance die heutige [Abend]vorstellung; b) *(this or the coming night)* heute nacht. **2.** *adv.* a) *(this evening)* heute abend; b) *(during this or the coming night)* heute nacht; **|I'll see you ~!** bis heute abend!

tonne [tʌn] *n.* [metrische] Tonne

tonsil ['tɒnsl] *n.* [Gaumen]mandel, *die;* **have one's ~s out** sich *(Dat.)* die Mandeln herausnehmen lassen. **tonsillitis** [tɒnsə'laɪtɪs] *n.* Mandelentzündung, *die*

too [tuː] *adv.* a) *(excessively)* zu; ~ difficult a task eine zu schwierige Aufgabe; b) *(also)* auch; c) *(coll.: very)* besonders; **not ~ pleased** nicht gerade erfreut

took *see* **take**

tool [tuːl] *n.* Werkzeug, *das;* *(garden ~)* Gerät, *das;* |set of| ~s Werkzeug, *das.* **'tool box** *n.* Werkzeugkasten, *der.* **'tool kit** *n.* Werkzeug, *das*

toot [tuːt] **1.** *v. i.* *(on car etc. horn)* hupen. **2.** *n.* Tuten, *das*

tooth [tuːθ] *n., pl.* **teeth** [tiːθ] a) Zahn, *der;* b) *(of rake, fork, comb)* Zinke, *die;* *(of cog-wheel, saw)* Zahn, *der*

tooth: ~ache *n.* Zahnschmerzen *Pl.;* ~-brush *n.* Zahnbürste, *die;* ~paste *n.* Zahnpasta, *die;* ~pick *n.* Zahnstocher, *der*

¹top [tɒp] **1.** *n.* a) *(highest part)* Spitze, *die;* *(of table)* Platte, *die;* *(~ end)* oberes Ende; *(of tree)* Wipfel, *der;* *(~ floor)* oberstes Stockwerk, *das;* *(rim of glass)* Rand, *der;* **on ~ of one another**

aufeinander; **on ~ of sth.** *(fig.: in addition)* zusätzlich zu etw.; **from ~ to bottom** von oben bis unten; **at the ~:** oben; **at the ~ of the building/hill/ pile/stairs** oben im Gebäude/[oben] auf dem Hügel/[oben] auf dem Stapel/oben an der Treppe; b) *(highest rank)* Spitze, *die;* **~ of the table** *(Sport)* Tabellenspitze, *die;* **be [at the] ~ of the class** der/die Klassenbeste sein; c) *(upper surface)* Oberfläche, *die; (of cupboard, chest)* Oberseite, *die;* **on ~ of sth.** [oben] auf etw. *(position: Dat.; direction: Akk.);* d) *(folding roof)* Verdeck, *das;* e) *(upper deck of bus)* Oberdeck, *das;* f) *(cap of pen)* [Verschluß]kappe, *die;* g) *(upper garment)* Oberteil, *das;* h) *(lid)* Deckel, *der; (of bottle)* Stöpsel, *der.* 2. *adj.* oberst...; höchst... ⟨*Ton, Preis*⟩; **~ end** oberes Ende; **the ~ pupil** der beste Schüler; **~ speed** Spitzen- *od.* Höchstgeschwindigkeit, *die.* 3. *v. t.* a) *(be taller than)* überragen; b) *(surpass)* übertreffen. **top 'up** *(Brit. coll.) v. t.* auffüllen ⟨*Tank, Flasche, Glas*⟩

²**top** *n. (toy)* Kreisel, *der*

top-: ~**'hat** *n.* Zylinder[hut], *der;* ~**-heavy** *adj.* oberlastig

topic ['tɒpɪk] *n.* Thema, *das.* **topical** ['tɒpɪkl] *adj.* aktuell

topless *adj.* **a ~ dress/swimsuit** ein busenfreies Kleid/ein Oben-ohne-Badeanzug

topmost ['tɒpməʊst, 'tɒpməst] *adj.* oberst...; höchst... ⟨*Gipfel, Note*⟩

topple ['tɒpl] 1. *v. i.* fallen. 2. *v. t.* stürzen. **topple 'down** *v. i.* hinab-/herabfallen. **topple 'over** *v. i.* umfallen

top 'secret *adj.* streng geheim

topsy-turvy ['tɒpsɪ'tɜːvɪ] *adv.* verkehrtrum *(ugs.);* **turn sth. ~:** etw. auf den Kopf stellen *(ugs.)*

torch [tɔːtʃ] *n. (Brit.)* Taschenlampe, *die*

tore, torn *see* ¹**tear 2, 3**

tornado [tɔː'neɪdəʊ] *n., pl.* ~**es** Wirbelsturm, *der; (in North America)* Tornado, *der*

torpedo [tɔː'piːdəʊ] 1. *n., pl.* ~**es** Torpedo, *der.* 2. *v. t.* torpedieren

torrent ['tɒrənt] *n.* reißender Bach; *(fig.)* Flut, *die.* **torrential** [tə'renʃl] *adj.* wolkenbruchartig ⟨*Regen*⟩

torso ['tɔːsəʊ] *n., pl.* ~**s** Rumpf, *der;* **bare ~:** nackter Oberkörper

tortoise ['tɔːtəs] *n.* Schildkröte, *die.* **tortoiseshell** ['tɔːtəʃel] *n.* Schildpatt, *das*

tortuous ['tɔːtjʊəs] *adj.* verschlungen; *(fig.)* umständlich

torture ['tɔːtʃə(r)] 1. *n.* Folter, *die.* 2. *v. t.* foltern; *(fig.)* quälen

toss [tɒs] 1. *v. t.* a) *(throw upwards)* hochwerfen; **~ a pancake** einen Pfannkuchen [durch Hochwerfen] wenden; b) *(throw casually)* werfen; schmeißen *(ugs.);* c) **~ a coin** eine Münze werfen; d) *(Cookery: mix)* wenden; mischen ⟨*Salat*⟩. 2. *v. i.* a) **~ and turn** sich [schlaflos] im Bett wälzen; b) ⟨*Schiff:*⟩ hin und her geworfen werden; c) *(~ coin)* eine Münze werfen; **~ for sth.** mit einer Münze um etw. losen. 3. *n.* a) **~ of a coin** Hochwerfen einer Münze; b) *(throw)* Wurf, *der.* **toss 'up** *v. i.* eine Münze werfen; **~ up for sth.** mit einer Münze um etw. losen

¹**tot** [tɒt] *n. (coll.)* a) kleines Kind; b) *(of liquor)* Gläschen, *das*

²**tot** *(coll.) v. t.,* ~**tt-: ~ 'up** zusammenziehen *(ugs.)*

total ['təʊtl] 1. *adj.* a) gesamt; Gesamt⟨*gewicht, -wert, usw.*⟩; b) *(absolute)* völlig *nicht präd.;* **a ~ beginner** ein absoluter Anfänger. 2. *n. (number)* Gesamtzahl, *die; (amount)* Gesamtbetrag, *der; (result of addition)* Summe, *die;* **a ~ of 200** insgesamt 200; **in ~:** insgesamt. 3. *v. t., (Brit.)* -**ll-:** a) addieren, zusammenzählen ⟨*Zahlen*⟩; b) *(amount to)* [insgesamt] betragen

totalitarian [təʊtælɪ'teərɪən] *adj.* totalitär

'totally *adv.* völlig

totter ['tɒtə(r)] *v. i.* wanken; taumeln

touch [tʌtʃ] 1. *v. t.* a) berühren; b) *(harm)* anrühren; *(fig.: rival)* ~ **sth.** an etw. *(Akk.)* heranreichen; d) *(affect emotionally)* rühren. 2. *v. i.* sich berühren; **don't ~ !** nicht anfassen! 3. *n.* a) Berührung, *die;* b) *no art. (faculty)* [**sense of**] ~**:** Tastsinn, *der;* c) *(small amount)* **a ~ of salt/pepper** *etc.* eine Spur Salz/Pfeffer *usw.;* **a ~ of irony** *etc.* ein Anflug von Ironie *usw.;* d) *(fig.)* Detail, *das;* e) *(communication)* **be in/out of ~ [with sb.]** [in] Kontakt haben; **get in ~:** mit jmdm. Kontakt aufnehmen. **touch 'down** *v. i.* ⟨*Flugzeug:*⟩ landen. **touch on** *v. t. (mention)* ansprechen. **touch 'up** *v. t. (improve)* ausbessern

'touch: ~-and-go *adj.* **it is ~-and-go [whether...]** es steht auf des Messers Schneide [, ob...]; ~**down** *n. (Aeronaut.)* Landung, *die*

'touching *adj.* rührend. **touchy** ['tʌt∫ɪ] *adj.* empfindlich; heikel ⟨*Thema*⟩

tough [tʌf] *adj.* **a)** fest ⟨*Material, Stoff*⟩; zäh ⟨*Fleisch; fachspr.: Werkstoff, Metall*⟩; widerstandsfähig ⟨*Belag, Glas, Haut*⟩; strapazierfähig ⟨*Kleidung*⟩; **b)** *(hardy)* zäh ⟨*Person*⟩; **c)** *(difficult)* schwierig; **d)** *(severe; harsh)* hart; **e)** *(coll.)* ~ **luck** Pech, *das*. **toughen** ['tʌfn] *v. t.* ~ [**up**] abhärten ⟨*Person*⟩; verschärfen ⟨*Gesetz*⟩

tour [tʊə(r)] **1.** *n.* **a)** ⟨*Rund*⟩reise, *die*; Tour, *die (ugs.)*; **b)** *(Theatre, Sport)* Tournee, *die*; **c)** *(of house etc.)* Besichtigung, *die*; **d)** ~ [**of duty**] Dienstzeit, *die.* **2.** *v. i.* **a)** ~/**go** ~**ing in** *or* **through a country** eine Reise *od. (ugs.)* Tour durch ein Land machen; **b)** *(Theatre, Sport)* eine Tournee machen. **3.** *v. t.* **a)** besichtigen ⟨*Stadt, Gebäude*⟩; ~ **a country/region** eine Reise *od. (ugs.)* Tour durch ein Land/Gebiet machen; **b)** *(Theatre, Sport)* ~ **a country/the provinces** eine Tournee durch das Land/die Provinz machen

tourism ['tʊərɪzm] *n.* **a)** Tourismus, *der;* **b)** *(operation of tours)* Touristik, *die.* **tourist** ['tʊərɪst] **1.** *n.* Tourist, *der/*Touristin, *die.* **2.** *attrib. adj.* Touristen-. '**tourist infor'mation centre**, '**tourist office** *ns.* Fremdenverkehrsbüro, *das*

tournament ['tʊənəmənt] *n.* *(Hist.; Sport)* Turnier, *das*

'**tour operator** *n.* Reiseveranstalter, *der/*-veranstalterin, *die*

tousle ['taʊzl] *v. t.* zerzausen

tout [taʊt] **1.** *v. i.* ~ **for customers** Kunden anreißen *(ugs.) od.* werben. **2.** *n.* Anreißer, *der/*Anreißerin, *die (ugs.);* **ticket** ~: Kartenschwarzhändler, *der/*-händlerin, *die*

tow [təʊ] **1.** *v. t.* schleppen; ziehen ⟨*Anhänger, Wasserskiläufer*⟩. **2.** *n.* Schleppen, *das;* **give a car a** ~: einen Wagen schleppen; **on** ~: im Schlepp[tau]. **tow a'way** *v. t.* abschleppen

toward [tə'wɔːd], **towards** [tə'wɔːdz] *prep.* **a)** *(in direction of)* ~ **sb./sth.** auf jmdn./etw. zu; **turn** ~ **sb.** sich zu jmdm. umdrehen; **feel sth.** ~ **sb.** jmdm. gegenüber etw. empfinden; **c)** *(for)* **a contribution** ~ **sth.** ein Beitrag zu etw.; **proposals** ~ **solving a problem** Vorschläge zur Lösung eines Problems; **d)** *(near)* gegen; ~ **the end of May** [gegen] Ende Mai

towel ['taʊəl] *n.* Handtuch, *das*

tower ['taʊə(r)] **1.** *n.* Turm, *der.* **2.** *v. i.* in die Höhe ragen. '**tower above** *v. t.* ~ **above sb./sth.** jmdn./etw. überragen

'**tower block** *n.* Hochhaus, *das*

'**towering** *attrib. adj.* hoch aufragend; *(fig.)* herausragend ⟨*Leistung*⟩

town [taʊn] *n.* Stadt, *die;* **the** ~ **of Cambridge** die Stadt Cambridge; **in** [**the**] ~: in der Stadt; **the** ~ *(people)* die Stadt; **be in/out of** ~: in der Stadt/nicht in der Stadt sein

town: ~ '**centre** *n.* Stadtmitte, *die;* Stadtzentrum, *das;* ~ '**hall** *n.* Rathaus, *das;* ~ '**planning** *n.* Stadtplanung, *die*

tow: ~**-path** *n.* Leinpfad, *der;* ~**-rope** *n.* Abschleppseil, *das*

toxic ['tɒksɪk] *adj.* giftig

toy [tɔɪ] **1.** *n.* Spielzeug, *das;* ~**s** Spielzeug, *das.* **2.** *adj.* Spielzeug-. **3.** *v. i.* ~ **with the idea of doing sth.** mit dem Gedanken spielen, etw. zu tun. '**toyshop** *n.* Spielwarengeschäft, *das*

trace [treɪs] **1.** *v. t.* **a)** *(copy)* durchpausen; abpausen; **b)** zeichnen ⟨*Linie*⟩; **c)** *(follow track of)* folgen (+ *Dat.*); verfolgen; **d)** *(find)* finden. **2.** *n.* Spur, *die.* '**tracing paper** ['treɪsɪŋ peɪpə(r)] *n.* Pauspapier, *das*

track [træk] **1.** *n.* **a)** Spur, *die;* *(of wild animal)* Fährte, *die;* ~**s** *(footprints)* [Fuß]spuren; *(of animal also)* Fährte, *die;* **keep** ~ **of sb./sth.** jmdn./etw. im Auge behalten; **b)** *(path)* Weg, *der;* *(footpath)* Pfad, *der;* **c)** *(Sport)* Bahn, *die; cycling/greyhound* ~: Radrennbahn, *die/*Windhundrennbahn, *die;* **d)** *(Railw.)* Gleis, *das;* **e)** *(course taken)* Route, *die;* *(of rocket, satellite)* Bahn, *die.* **2.** *v. t.* ~ **an animal** die Spur/Fährte eines Tieres verfolgen; **the police** ~**ed him** [**to Paris**] die Polizei folgte seiner Spur [bis nach Paris]. **track 'down** *v. t.* aufspüren

track: ~ **events** *n. pl.* Laufwettbewerbe; ~ **suit** *n.* Trainingsanzug, *der*

¹**tract** [trækt] *n. (area)* Gebiet, *das*

²**tract** *n. (pamphlet)* [Flug]schrift, *die*

tractor ['træktə(r)] *n.* Traktor, *der*

trade [treɪd] **1.** *n.* **a)** *(line of business)* Gewerbe, *das; he's a butcher/lawyer etc.* **by** ~: er ist von Beruf Metzger/Rechtsanwalt *usw.;* **b)** *no indef. art (commerce)* Handel, *der;* **c)** *(craft)* Handwerk, *das.* **2.** *v. i. (buy and sell)* Handel treiben. **3.** *v. t.* tauschen; austauschen ⟨*Waren, Grüße*⟩; sich *(Dat.)*

sagen ⟨Beleidigungen⟩; ~ **sth. for sth.** etw. gegen etw. tauschen. **trade 'in** v. t. in Zahlung geben

'**trade mark** n. Warenzeichen, das; **leave one's ~ on sth.** (fig.) einer Sache (Dat.) seinen Stempel aufdrücken

'**trader** n. Händler, der/Händlerin, die

trade: ~ '**union** n. Gewerkschaft, die; attrib. Gewerkschafts-; ~-'**unionist** n. Gewerkschaft[l]er, der/Gewerkschaft[l]erin, die

trading ['treɪdɪŋ] n. Handel, der. '**trading estate** n. (Brit.) Gewerbegebiet, das. '**trading stamp** n. Rabattmarke, die

tradition [trə'dɪʃn] n. Tradition, die. **traditional** [trə'dɪʃənl] adj. traditionell; herkömmlich ⟨Erziehung, Methode⟩. **tra'ditionally** adv. traditionell

traffic ['træfɪk] **1.** n. **a)** no indef. art. Verkehr, der; **b)** (trade) Handel, der. **2.** v. i., -ck-: ~ **in** etw. mit etw. handeln

traffic: ~ **circle** n. (Amer.) Kreisverkehr, der; ~ **jam** n. [Verkehrs]stau, der; ~ **lights** n. pl. [Verkehrs]ampel, die; ~ **sign** n. Verkehrszeichen, das; ~ **signals** see ~ **lights;** ~ **warden** n. (Brit.) Hilfspolizist, der; (woman) Hilfspolizistin, die; Politesse, die

tragedy ['trædʒɪdɪ] n. Tragödie, die. **tragic** ['trædʒɪk] adj. tragisch

trail [treɪl] **1.** n. **a)** Spur, die; ~ **of smoke/dust** Rauch-/Staubfahne, die; **b)** (Hunting) Spur, die; Fährte, die; **c)** (path) Pfad, der; Weg, der. **2.** v. t. **a)** (pursue) verfolgen; **b)** (drag) ~ **sth.** [after or behind one] etw. hinter sich (Dat.) herziehen. **3.** v. i. **a)** (be dragged) schleifen; **b)** (lag) hinterhertrotten; **c)** ⟨Pflanze:⟩ kriechen

trailer ['treɪlə(r)] n. **a)** Anhänger, der; (Amer.: caravan) Wohnanhänger, der; **b)** (Cinemat., Telev.) Trailer, der

train [treɪn] **1.** v. t. **a)** ausbilden (**in in** + Dat.); erziehen ⟨Kind⟩; abrichten ⟨Hund⟩; dressieren ⟨Tier⟩; **b)** (Sport) trainieren; **c)** (Hort.) ziehen. **2.** v. i. **a)** eine Ausbildung machen; **he is ~ing as or to be a doctor/engineer** er macht eine Arzt-/Ingenieurausbildung; **b)** (Sport) trainieren. **3.** n. **a)** (Railw.) Zug, der; **on the ~:** im Zug; **b)** (of skirt etc.) Schleppe, die; **c)** ~ **of thought** Gedankengang, der. '**train-driver** n. Lokomotivführer, der/-führerin, die

trained [treɪnd] adj. ausgebildet ⟨Arbeiter, Lehrer, Arzt, Stimme⟩; abgerichtet ⟨Hund⟩; dressiert ⟨Tier⟩; geschult ⟨Geist, Auge, Ohr⟩

trainee [treɪ'niː] n. Auszubildende, der/die

'**trainer** n. [Konditions]trainer, der/-trainerin, die

'**train fare** n. Fahrpreis, der

'**training** n. **a)** Ausbildung, die; **b)** (Sport) Training, das

train: ~ **journey** n. Bahnfahrt, die; (long) Bahnreise, die; ~ **set** n. [Modell]eisenbahn, die; ~ **station** n. (Amer.) Bahnhof, der

trait [treɪt] n. Eigenschaft, die

traitor ['treɪtə(r)] n. Verräter, der/Verräterin, die

tram [træm] n. (Brit.) Straßenbahn, die; ~**lines** Straßenbahnschienen

tramp [træmp] **1.** n. Landstreicher, der/-streicherin, die; (in city) Stadtstreicher, der/-streicherin, die. **2.** v. i. **a)** (tread heavily) trampeln; **b)** (walk) marschieren

trample ['træmpl] **1.** v. t. zertrampeln. **2.** v. i. trampeln. '**trample on** v. t. herumtrampeln auf (+ Dat.)

trampoline ['træmpəliːn] n. Trampolin, das

trance [trɑːns] n. Trance, die; **be in a ~:** in Trance sein

tranquil ['træŋkwɪl] adj. ruhig. **tranquillity** [træŋ'kwɪlɪtɪ] Ruhe, die. **tranquillizer** ['træŋkwɪlaɪzə(r)] n. Beruhigungsmittel, das

transact [træn'zækt] v. t. ~ **business** Geschäfte tätigen. **transaction** [træn'zækʃn] n. Geschäft, das; (financial) Transaktion, die

transcend [træn'send] v. t. übersteigen

transcript ['trænskrɪpt] n. Abschrift, die; (of trial) Protokoll, das

transfer 1. [træns'fɜː(r)] v. t., -rr-: **a)** (move) verlegen (**to nach**); überweisen ⟨Geld⟩ (**to auf** + Akk.); übertragen ⟨Befugnis, Macht⟩ (**to** Dat.); **b)** übereignen ⟨Gegenstand, Grundbesitz⟩ (**to** Dat.); **c)** versetzen ⟨Arbeiter, Angestellte⟩; (Footb.) transferieren. **2.** [træns'fɜː(r)] v. i., -rr-: **a)** (when travelling) umsteigen; **b)** (change job etc.) wechseln. **3.** ['trænsfɜː(r)] n. **a)** (moving) Verlegung, die; (of powers) Übertragung, die (**to an** + Akk.); (of money) Überweisung, die; **b)** (of employee etc.) Versetzung, die; (Footb.) Transfer, der; **c)** (picture) Abziehbild, das. **transferable** ['trænsfɜːrəbl] adj. übertragbar

transform [træns'fɔːm] v. t. verwandeln. **transformation** [trænsfə-

'mei∫n] n. Verwandlung, die. **trans-**
'former n. (Electr.) Transformator, der
transfusion [træns'fju:ʒn] n. (Med.)
Transfusion, die
transient ['trænziənt] adj. kurzlebig;
vergänglich
transistor [træn'zistə(r)] n. Transistor, der
transit ['trænsit] n. **in ~:** auf der
Durchreise; ⟨Waren⟩ auf dem Transport; **passengers in ~:** Transitreisende
transition [træn'siʒn, træn'ziʃn] n.
Übergang, der; Wechsel, der
transitive ['trænsitiv] adj. (Ling.)
transitiv
transitory ['trænsitəri] adj. vergänglich; (fleeting) flüchtig
translate [træns'leit] v.t. übersetzen.
translation [træns'leiʃn] n. Übersetzung, die. **translator** [træns'leitə(r)]
n. Übersetzer, der/Übersetzerin, die
translucent [træns'lu:sənt] adj.
durchscheinend
transmission [træns'miʃn] n. a)
Übertragung, die; b) (Motor Veh.) Antrieb, der; (gearbox) Getriebe, das
transmit [træns'mit] v.t., -tt-: a) (pass
on) übersenden; übertragen; b)
durchlassen ⟨Licht⟩; leiten ⟨Wärme⟩.
trans'mitter n. Sender, der
transparency [træns'pærənsi] n. a)
Durchsichtigkeit, die; b) (Photog.)
Transparent, das; (slide) Dia, das
transparent [træns'pærənt] adj.
durchsichtig
transpire [træn'spaiə(r)] v.i. sich herausstellen; (coll.: happen) passieren
transplant 1. [træns'plɑ:nt] v.t.
verpflanzen ⟨Organ⟩; b) (plant in another place) umpflanzen. 2. ['trænsplɑ:nt] n. (Med.) Transplantation, die;
Verpflanzung, die
transport 1. [træns'pɔ:t] v.t. transportieren; befördern. 2. ['trænspɔ:t] n. a)
Transport, der; Beförderung, die; attrib. Beförderungs-; b) (means of conveyance) Verkehrsmittel, das; **be without ~:** kein ⟨eigenes⟩ Fahrzeug haben
transpose [træns'pəʊz] v.t. vertauschen; umstellen
transvestite [træns'vestait] n. Transvestit, der
trap [træp] n. a) Falle, die; **set** od. **lay
a ~ for an animal** eine Falle für ein
Tier legen od. aufstellen; **set** or **lay a
~ for sb.** (fig.) jmdm. eine Falle stellen; **fall into a/sb.'s ~** (fig.) in die
jmdm. in die Falle gehen; b) (sl.:
mouth) Klappe, die (salopp). 2. v.t.,

-pp-: a) [in od. mit einer Falle] fangen
⟨Tier⟩; (fig.) in eine Falle locken ⟨Person⟩; **be ~ped** (fig.) in eine Falle gehen/in der Falle sitzen; **be ~ped in a
cave/by the tide** in einer Höhle festsitzen/von der Flut abgeschnitten sein;
b) (confine) einschließen; einklemmen ⟨Körperteil⟩. **trap'door** n. Falltür, die
trapeze [trə'pi:z] n. Trapez, das
trash [træʃ] n., no indef. art. a) (rubbish) Abfall, der; b) (badly made
thing) Mist, der (ugs.); (bad literature)
Schund, der (ugs.)
trauma ['trɔ:mə] n., pl. **-ta** ['trɔ:mətə]
or **-s** Trauma, das. **traumatic**
[trɔ:'mætik] adj. traumatisch
travel ['trævl] 1. n. Reisen, das; attrib.
Reise-. 2. v.i., (Brit.) -ll- reisen; (go in
vehicle) fahren. 3. v.t., (Brit.) -ll- zurücklegen ⟨Strecke, Entfernung⟩; benutzen ⟨Weg, Straße⟩; **we had ~led 10
miles** wir waren 10 Meilen gefahren
'travel agency n. Reisebüro, das
'travel agent n. Reisebürokaufmann, der/-kauffrau, die
traveler, traveling (Amer.) see
travell-
traveller ['trævlə(r)] n. (Brit.) a) Reisende, der/die; b) in pl. (gypsies etc.)
fahrendes Volk. **'traveller's
cheque** n. Reisescheck, der
travelling ['trævliŋ] attrib. adj. (Brit.)
Wander⟨zirkus, -ausstellung⟩
trawler ['trɔ:lə(r)] n. (Fisch)trawler, der
tray [trei] n. Tablett, das; (for correspondence) Ablageschachtel; (for correspondence) Ablageschachtel, die
treacherous ['tretʃərəs] adj. a) treulos ⟨Person⟩; b) (deceptive) tückisch.
treachery ['tretʃəri] n. Verrat, der
treacle ['tri:kl] n. (Brit.) Sirup, der
tread [tred] 1. n. a) (of tyre, boot, etc.)
Lauffläche, die; **2 millimetres of ~ on
a tyre** 2 Millimeter Profil auf einem
Reifen; b) (sound of walking) Schritt,
der. 2. v.i., **trod** [trɒd], **trodden** ['trɒdn]
or **trod** treten (in/on in/auf + Akk.);
(walk) gehen. 3. v.t. **trod**, **trodden** or
trod treten auf (+ Akk.); stampfen
⟨Weintrauben⟩
treason ['tri:zn] n. **[high]** ~: Hochverrat, der
treasure ['treʒə(r)] 1. n. Schatz, der;
Kostbarkeit, die; ~**s** ⟨of art⟩ Kunstschätze.
2. v.t. in Ehren halten. **'treasure-
hunt** n. Schatzsuche, die
treasurer ['treʒərə(r)] n. Kassenwart,
der/-wartin, die. **treasury** ['treʒəri] n.
the T~: das Finanzministerium

treat [triːt] **1.** *n.* **a)** [besonderes] Vergnügen; **b)** *(entertainment)* Vergnügen, *für dessen Kosten jmd. anderes aufkommt;* **lay on a special ~ for sb.** jmdm. etwas Besonderes bieten. **2.** *v. t.* **a)** behandeln; **~ sth. as a joke** etw. als Witz nehmen; **~ sth. with contempt** für etw. nur Verachtung haben; **b)** *(Med.)* behandeln; **~ sb. for sth.** jmdn. wegen etw. behandeln; *(before confirmation of diagnosis)* jmdn. auf etw. *(Akk.)* behandeln; **c)** klären *(Abwässer)*; **d)** *(provide with at own expense)* einladen; **~ sb. to sth.** jmdm. etw. spendieren; **~ oneself to a new hat** sich *(Dat.)* einen neuen Hut leisten

treatise [ˈtriːtɪs, ˈtriːtɪz] *n.* Abhandlung, *die*

'treatment *n.* Behandlung, *die*

treaty [ˈtriːtɪ] *n.* [Staats]vertrag, *der*

treble [ˈtrebl] **1.** *adj.* **a)** dreifach; **b)** *(Brit. Mus.)* **~ voice** Sopranstimme, *die.* **2.** *n.* **a)** *(~ quantity)* Dreifache, *das;* **b)** *(Mus.)* **he is a ~:** er singt Sopran. **3.** *v. t.* verdreifachen. **4.** *v. i.* sich verdreifachen. **'treble clef** *n. (Mus.)* Violinschlüssel, *der*

tree [triː] *n.* Baum, *der*

trek [trek] **1.** *v. i.,* **-kk-** ziehen **(across** durch). **2.** *n.* [schwierige] Reise

trellis [ˈtrelɪs] *n.* Gitter, *das; (for plants)* Spalier, *das*

tremble [ˈtrembl] *v. i.* zittern **(with** vor **+** *Dat.)*

tremendous [trɪˈmendəs] *adj.* gewaltig; *(coll.: wonderful)* großartig

tremor [ˈtremə(r)] *n.* **a)** Zittern, *das;* **b)** [earth] ~ leichtes Erdbeben

trench [trentʃ] *n.* Graben, *der; (Mil.)* Schützengraben, *der*

trend [trend] *n.* **a)** Trend, *der;* **upward** ~: steigende Tendenz; **b)** *(fashion)* Mode, *die;* [Mode]trend, *der.* **'trendy** *adj. (Brit. coll.)* modisch; Schickimicki*(kneipe) (ugs.)*

trepidation [trepɪˈdeɪʃn] *n.* Beklommenheit, *die*

trespass [ˈtrespəs] *v. i.* **~ on** unerlaubt betreten *(Grundstück).* **'trespasser** *n.* Unbefugte, *der/die*

trial [ˈtraɪəl] *n.* **a)** *(Law)* [Gerichts]verfahren, *das;* **be on ~** [for murder] [wegen Mordes] angeklagt sein; **b)** *(testing)* Test; Test; **on ~:** jmdn. probeweise einstellen; [by] **~ and error** [durch] Ausprobieren; **c)** *(trouble)* Problem, *das; (for child)* Prüfung, *die; (Sport) (competition)* Testspiel, *das*

triangle [ˈtraɪæŋgl] *n.* **a)** Dreieck, *das;* **b)** *(Mus.)* Triangel, *das od. der.* **triangular** [traɪˈæŋgjələ(r)] *adj.* dreieckig

tribe [traɪb] *n.* Stamm, *der*

tribulation [trɪbjʊˈleɪʃn] *n.* Kummer, *der*

tribunal [traɪˈbjuːnl] *n.* Schiedsgericht, *das*

tributary [ˈtrɪbjʊtərɪ] *n.* Nebenfluß, *der*

tribute [ˈtrɪbjuːt] *n.* Tribut, *der* **(to** an **+** *Akk.);* **pay ~ to sb./sth.** jmdm./einer Sache den schuldigen Tribut zollen *(geh.)*

trice [traɪs] *n.* **in a ~:** im Handumdrehen

trick [trɪk] **1.** *n.* **a)** Trick, *der;* **it was all a ~:** das war [alles] nur Bluff; **b)** *(feat of skill etc.)* Kunststück, *das;* **that should do the ~** *(coll.)* damit dürfte es klappen *(ugs.);* **c)** *(knack)* **get** or **find the ~** [of doing sth.] den Dreh finden[, wie man etw. tut]; **d)** *(prank)* Streich, *der;* **play a ~ on sb.** jmdm. einen Streich spielen; **e)** *(Cards)* Stich, *der.* **2.** *v. t.* täuschen; hereinlegen; **~ sb. out of/into sth.** jmdm. etw. ablisten. **3.** *adj.* **~ photograph** Trickaufnahme, *die;* **~ question** Fangfrage, *die.*

trickery [ˈtrɪkərɪ] *n.* [Hinter]list, *die*

trickle [ˈtrɪkl] *v. i.* rinnen; *(in drops)* tröpfeln

trickster [ˈtrɪkstə(r)] *n.* Schwindler, *der/*Schwindlerin, *die*

'tricky *adj.* verzwickt *(ugs.)*

tricycle [ˈtraɪsɪkl] *n.* Dreirad, *das*

tried *see* **try** 2, 3

trifle [ˈtraɪfl] *n.* **a)** *(Brit. Gastron.)* Trifle, *das;* **b)** *(thing of slight value)* Kleinigkeit, *die.* **trifling** [ˈtraɪflɪŋ] *adj.* unbedeutend *(Angelegenheit);* gering *(Wert)*

trigger [ˈtrɪgə(r)] **1.** *n.* **a)** *(of gun)* Abzug, *der; (of machine)* Drücker, *der;* **b)** *(fig.)* Auslöser, *der.* **2.** *v. t.* **~ [off]** auslösen

trigonometry [trɪgəˈnɒmɪtrɪ] *n.* Trigonometrie, *die*

trim [trɪm] **1.** *v. t.,* **-mm-: a)** schneiden *(Hecke);* [nach]schneiden *(Haar);* beschneiden *(Papier, Hecke, Budget);* **b)** *(ornament)* besetzen **(with** mit). **2.** *adj.* proper; gepflegt *(Garten).* **3.** *n.* **a) be in ~** *(healthy)* in Form od. fit sein; **b)** *(cut)* Nachschneiden, *das.* **'trimming** *n.* **a)** *(decorations)* Verzierung, *die;* **b)** *in pl. (coll.: accompaniments)* Beilagen; **with all the ~s** mit allem Drum und Dran *(ugs.)*

Trinity ['trɪnɪtɪ] *n. (Theol.)* the [Holy] ~: die Heilige Dreieinigkeit

trinket ['trɪŋkɪt] *n.* kleines, billiges Schmuckstück

trio ['tri:əʊ] *n., pl.* ~s Trio, *das*

trip [trɪp] 1. *n.* a) Reise, *die; (shorter)* Ausflug, *der;* b) *(coll.: drug-induced hallucinations)* Trip, *der.* 2. *v. i.,* -pp- stolpern (on über + *Akk.*). **trip 'up** 1. *v. i.* a) stolpern; b) *(fig.)* einen Fehler machen. 2. *v. t.* a) stolpern lassen; b) *(fig.)* aufs Glatteis führen *(fig.)*

tripe [traɪp] *n.* a) Kaldaunen *Pl.;* b) *(sl.: rubbish)* Quatsch, *der (ugs.)*

triple ['trɪpl] 1. *adj.* a) *(threefold)* dreifach; b) *(three times greater than)* ~ the ...: der/die/das dreifache ... 2. *n.* Dreifache, *das.* 3. *v. i.* sich verdreifachen. 4. *v. t.* verdreifachen

triplet ['trɪplɪt] *n.* Drilling, *der*

triplicate ['trɪplɪkət] *n.* **in ~:** in dreifacher Ausfertigung

tripod ['traɪpɒd] *n.* Dreibein, *das*

'**tripper** *n. (Brit.)* Ausflügler, *der*/Ausflüglerin, *die*

trite [traɪt] *adj.* banal

triumph ['traɪəmf, 'traɪʌmf] 1. *n.* Triumph, *der (over über + Akk.).* 2. *v. i.* triumphieren (over über + *Akk.*). **triumphant** [traɪ'ʌmfənt] *adj.* a) siegreich; b) triumphierend ⟨*Blick*⟩

trivial ['trɪvɪəl] *adj.* belanglos. **triviality** [trɪvɪ'ælɪtɪ] *n.* Belanglosigkeit, *die*

trod, trodden *see* tread 2, 3

trolley ['trɒlɪ] *n.* a) *(for serving food)* Servierwagen, *der;* b) **[supermarket]** ~: Einkaufswagen, *der*

trombone [trɒm'bəʊn] *n.* Posaune, *die*

troop [tru:p] 1. *n.* a) in *pl.* Truppen; b) *(fig.)* Schar, *die.* 2. *v. i.* ~ **in/out** hinein-/hinausströmen

trophy ['trəʊfɪ] *n.* Trophäe, *die*

tropic ['trɒpɪk] *n.* the T~s *(Geog.)* die Tropen; the ~ of Cancer/Capricorn *(Astron., Geog.)* der Wendekreis des Krebses./Steinbocks. **tropical** ['trɒpɪk] *adj.* tropisch; Tropen⟨*krankheit, -kleidung*⟩

trot [trɒt] 1. *n. (coll.)* on the ~: hintereinander; be on the ~: auf Trab sein *(ugs.).* 2. *v. i.,* -tt- traben

trouble ['trʌbl] 1. *n.* a) Ärger, *der;* Schwierigkeiten *Pl.;* there'll be ~ [if ...] es wird Ärger geben, [wenn ...]; what's the ~? was ist denn?; b) **engine/brake** ~: Probleme mit dem Motor/der Bremse; **suffer from heart/liver** ~:

Probleme mit dem Herz/der Leber haben; c) *(inconvenience)* Mühe, *die;* **take a lot of** ~: sich *(Dat.)* sehr viel Mühe geben; **it's more** ~ **than it's worth** es lohnt sich nicht; d) in *sing.* or *pl. (unrest)* Unruhen. 2. *v. t.* a) *(agitate)* beunruhigen; **don't let it** ~ **you** mach dir deswegen keine Sorgen; b) *(inconvenience)* stören. 3. *v. i. (make an effort)* sich bemühen. **troubled** ['trʌbld] *adj.* a) *(worried)* besorgt; b) *(restless)* unruhig. '**trouble-maker** *n.* Unruhestifter *der*/-stifterin, *die.* **troublesome** ['trʌblsəm] *adj.* schwierig; lästig ⟨*Krankheit*⟩

trough [trɒf] *n.* Trog, *der*

troupe [tru:p] *n.* Truppe, *die*

trousers ['traʊzəz] *n. pl.* **[pair of]** ~: Hose, *die*

'**trouser suit** *n. (Brit.)* Hosenanzug, *der*

trousseau ['tru:səʊ] *n., pl.* ~s or ~x ['tru:səʊz] Aussteuer, *die*

trout [traʊt] *n., pl.* same Forelle, *die*

trowel ['traʊəl] *n.* Kelle, *die; (Hort.)* Pflanzkelle, *die*

truant ['tru:ənt] *n.* **play ~:** [die Schule] schwänzen *(ugs.)*

truce [tru:s] *n.* Waffenstillstand, *der*

truck [trʌk] *n.* a) Last[kraft]wagen, *der;* Lkw, *der;* b) *(Brit. Railw.)* offener Güterwagen

truculent ['trʌkjʊlənt] *adj.* aufsässig

trudge [trʌdʒ] *v. i.* trotten; *(through snow etc.)* stapfen

true [tru:] *adj.,* ~r ['tru:ə(r)], ~st ['tru:ɪst] a) wahr; wahrheitsgetreu ⟨*Bericht*⟩; richtig ⟨*Vorteil*⟩; *(rightly so called)* eigentlich; echt, wahr ⟨*Freund*⟩; **is it ~ that ...?** stimmt es, daß ...?; ~ **to life** lebensecht; b) *(loyal)* treu

truffle ['trʌfl] *n.* Trüffel, *die od. (ugs.) der*

truism ['tru:ɪzm] *n.* Binsenweisheit, *die*

truly ['tru:lɪ] *adv.* a) wirklich; b) *(accurately)* zutreffend; **yours ~:** mit freundlichen Grüßen

trump [trʌmp] *(Cards)* 1. *n.* Trumpf, *der.* 2. *v. t.* übertrumpfen. '**trump up** *v. t. (coll.)* konstruieren

trumpet ['trʌmpɪt] *n.* Trompete, *die.* '**trumpeter** *n.* Trompeter, *der*/Trompeterin, *die*

truncheon ['trʌntʃn] *n.* Schlagstock, *der*

trundle ['trʌndl] *v. t. & i.* rollen

trunk [trʌŋk] *n.* a) *(of elephant etc.)*

Rüssel, *der;* b) *(large box)* Schrank-koffer, *der;* c) *(of tree)* Stamm, *der;* d) *(of body)* Rumpf, *der;* e) *(Amer.: of car)* Kofferraum, *der;* f) *in pl. (Brit.)* |swimming| ~s Badehose, *die*

truss [trʌs] *n. (Med.)* Bruchband, *das*
trust [trʌst] 1. *n.* a) Vertrauen, *das;* **place** *or* **put one's ~ in sb./sth.** sein Vertrauen auf *od.* in jmdn./etw. set-zen; **take sth. on ~:** etw. einfach glau-ben; b) *(organization managed by trustees)* Treuhandgesellschaft, *die;* |charitable| ~: Stiftung, *die;* *(association of companies)* Trust, *der;* c) *(Law)* **hold in ~:** treuhänderisch ver-walten. 2. *v.t. (rely on)* trauen (+ *Dat.*); vertrauen (+ *Dat.*) *(Per-son);* ~ **sb. with sth.** jmdm. etw. anver-trauen. 3. *v.i.* a) ~ **to** sich verlassen auf (+ *Akk.*); b) *(believe)* ~ **in sb./sth.** auf jmdn./etw. vertrauen. **trustee** [trʌˈstiː] *n.* Treuhänder, *der/*Treuhän-derin, *die.* **trustful** [ˈtrʌstfl], **'trust-ing** *adjs.* vertrauensvoll. **'trust-worthy** *adj.* vertrauenswürdig
truth [truːθ] *n., pl.* ~s [truːðz, truːθs] Wahrheit, *die;* **tell the |whole| ~:** die |ganze| Wahrheit sagen. **truthful** [ˈtruːθfl] *adj.* ehrlich
try [traɪ] 1. *n.* Versuch, *der;* **have a ~ at sth./doing sth.** etw. versuchen/ver-suchen, etw. zu tun; **give it a ~, have a ~:** es versuchen. 2. *v.t.* a) *(attempt)* ver-suchen; b) *(test usefulness of)* proba-bieren; c) *(test)* auf die Probe stellen ⟨Fä-higkeit, Kraft, Geduld⟩; d) *(Law.: take to trial)* ~ **a case** einen Fall verhan-deln; ~ **sb. |for sth.|** jmdn. |wegen ei-ner Sache| vor Gericht stellen. 3. *v.i.* es versuchen; ~ **hard/harder** sich (*Dat.*) viel/mehr Mühe geben. **try 'on** *v.t.* anprobieren ⟨Kleidungsstück⟩.
try 'out *v.t.* ausprobieren
'trying *adj.* a) *(testing)* schwierig; b) *(difficult to endure)* anstrengend
T-shirt [ˈtiːʃɜːt] *n.* T-Shirt, *das*
tub [tʌb] *n.* Kübel, *der;* *(for ice-cream etc.)* Becher, *der*
tuba [ˈtjuːbə] *n. (Mus.)* Tuba, *die*
tubby [ˈtʌbɪ] *adj.* rundlich
tube [tjuːb] *n.* a) *(for conveying liquids etc.)* Rohr, *das;* b) *(small cylinder)* Tu-be, *die;* *(for sweets, tablets)* Röhrchen, *das;* c) *(Anat., Zool.)* Röhre, *die;* d) *(of TV etc.)* Röhre, *die;* e) *(Brit. coll.: underground railway)* U-Bahn, *die*
tuber [ˈtjuːbə(r)] *n. (Bot.)* Knolle, *die*
tuberculosis [tjuːbɜːkjʊˈləʊsɪs] *n.* Tu-berkulose, *die*

tube: ~ **station** *n. (Brit. coll.)* U-Bahnhof, *der;* ~ **train** *n. (Brit. coll.)* U-bahn-Zug, *der*
tubing [ˈtjuːbɪŋ] *n.* Rohre *Pl.*
tubular [ˈtjuːbjʊlə(r)] *adj.* rohrförmig
tuck [tʌk] 1. *v.t.* stecken. 2. *n. (in fab-ric) (for decoration)* Biese, *die;* *(to tighten)* Abnäher, *der.* **tuck 'in** 1. *v.t.* hineinstecken. 2. *v.i. (coll.)* zulangen *(ugs.).* **tuck 'up** *v.t.* a) hochkrempeln ⟨Armel, Hose⟩; hochnehmen ⟨Rock⟩; b) *(cover snugly)* zudecken
Tue., Tues. *abbrs.* **Tuesday** Di.
Tuesday [ˈtjuːzdeɪ, ˈtjuːzdɪ] *n.* Diens-tag, *der; see also* **Friday**
tuft [tʌft] *n.* Büschel, *das*
tug [tʌg] 1. *n.* a) Ruck, *der;* ~ **of war** Tauziehen, *das;* b) ~ |boat| Schlepper, *der.* 2. *v.t.,* -**gg-** ziehen. 3. *v.i.,* -**gg-** zerren (**at** an + *Dat.*)
tuition [tjuːˈɪʃn] *n.* Unterricht, *der*
tulip [ˈtjuːlɪp] *n.* Tulpe, *die*
tumble [ˈtʌmbl] 1. *v.i.* stürzen; fallen. 2. *n.* Sturz, *der.* **'tumble-drier** *n.* Wäschetrockner, *der.* **'tumble-dry** *v.t.* im Automaten trocknen
tumbler [ˈtʌmblə(r)] *n. (short)* Whisky-glas, *das; (long)* Wasserglas, *das*
tummy [ˈtʌmɪ] *n. (child lang./coll.)* Bäuchlein, *das.* **'tummy-ache** *n. (child lang./coll.)* Bauchweh, *das*
tumour *(Brit.:* *Amer.:* **tumor)** [ˈtjuːmə(r)] *n.* Tumor, *der*
tumult [ˈtjuːmʌlt] *n.* Tumult, *der*
tuna [ˈtjuːnə] *n., pl. same or* ~**s** Thun-fisch, *der*
tune [tjuːn] 1. *n.* a) *(melody)* Melodie, *die;* **change one's ~** *(fig.)* sein Verhal-ten ändern; **call the ~:** den Ton ange-ben; b) *(correct pitch)* **sing in/out of ~:** richtig/falsch singen; **be in/out of ~** ⟨Instrument:⟩ richtig gestimmt/ver-stimmt sein. 2. *v.t.* a) *(Mus.: put in ~)* stimmen; b) *(Radio, Telev.)* einstellen (**to** auf + *Akk.*); c) einstellen ⟨Motor, Vergaser⟩. **tune 'in** *v.t. (Radio, Telev.)* ~ **to a station** einen Sender einstellen
tuneful [ˈtjuːnfl] *adj.* melodisch
tunic [ˈtjuːnɪk] *n. (of soldier)* Uniform-jacke, *die; (of schoolgirl)* Kittel, *der*
'tuning-fork [ˈtjuːnɪŋfɔːk] *n.* Stimm-gabel, *die*
Tunisia [tjuːˈnɪzɪə] *pr. n.* Tunesien *(das)*
tunnel [ˈtʌnl] 1. *n.* Tunnel, *der; (dug by animal)* Gang, *der.* 2. *v.i., (Brit.)* -**ll-** einen Tunnel graben
turban [ˈtɜːbən] *n.* Turban, *der*
turbine [ˈtɜːbaɪn] *n.* Turbine, *die*

turbulence ['tɜːbjʊləns] *n.* a) Aufgewühltheit, *die*; (fig.) Aufruhr, *der*; b) (Phys.) Turbulenz, *die*

turbulent ['tɜːbjʊlənt] *adj.* a) aufgewühlt; b) (Phys.) turbulent

tureen [tjʊəˈriːn] *n.* Terrine, *die*

turf [tɜːf] *n., pl. ~s or* turves [tɜːvz] a) *no pl.* Rasen, *der*; b) (segment) Rasenstück, *das.* **turf 'out** *v.t.* (sl.) rausschmeißen (ugs.)

Turk [tɜːk] *n.* Türke, *der*/Türkin, *die*

Turkey ['tɜːkɪ] *pr. n.* die Türkei

turkey *n.* Truthahn, *der*/Truthenne, *die*; (esp. as food) Puter, *der*/Pute, *die*

Turkish ['tɜːkɪʃ] 1. *adj.* türkisch; *sb.* is *~*: ist Türke/Türkin. 2. *n.* Türkisch, *das; see also* English 2 a

turmoil ['tɜːmɔɪl] *n.* Aufruhr, *der*

turn [tɜːn] 1. *n.* a) it's his/her/my ~ to do sth. jmd. ist an der Reihe, etw. zu tun; **it's your ~ |next|** du bist als nächster/nächste dran (ugs.) *od.* an der Reihe; **out of ~**: außer der Reihe; (fig.) an der falschen Stelle ⟨lachen⟩; **take |it in| ~** sich abwechseln (ugs.) b) (rotary motion) Drehung, *die*; c) (change of direction) Wende, *die*; **take a ~ to the right/left, do or take a right/left ~**: nach rechts/links abbiegen; (fig.) **take a favourable ~** sich zum Guten wenden; **the ~ of the year/century** die Jahres-/Jahrhundertwende; d) (bend) Kurve, *die*; (corner) Ecke, *die*; e) (short performance) Nummer, *die*; f) (service) do sb. **a good ~**: jmdm. einen guten Dienst erweisen; g) (coll.: fright) give sb. quite **a ~**: jmdm. einen gehörigen Schrekken einjagen (ugs.). 2. *v.t.* a) (make revolve) drehen; b) (reverse) umdrehen; wenden ⟨Pfannkuchen, Auto, Heu⟩; **~ sth. upside down or on its head** (lit. or fig.) etw. auf den Kopf stellen; **~ the page** umblättern; c) (give new direction to) drehen, wenden ⟨Kopf⟩; **~ a hose/gun on sb.** ein Schlauch/ein Gewehr auf jmdn./etw. richten; **~ one's attention/mind to sth.** sich/seine Gedanken einer Sache (Dat.) zuwenden; d) **~ sb. loose on sb./sth.** jmdn. auf jmdn./etw. loslassen; e) (cause to become) verwandeln; **~ the lights |down| low** das Licht dämpfen; **~ a play/book into a film** ein Theaterstück/Buch verfilmen; f) (shape in lathe) drechseln ⟨Holz⟩; drehen ⟨Metall⟩; g) drehen ⟨Pirouette⟩; schlagen ⟨Purzelbaum⟩. 3. *v.i.* a) (revolve) sich drehen; b) (reverse direction) ⟨Person:⟩ sich herumdrehen; ⟨Auto:⟩ wenden;

c) (take new direction) sich wenden; (~ round) sich umdrehen; **~ to the left/right** nach links/rechts abbiegen; d) (become) werden; **~ |in|to sth.** zu etw. werden; (be transformed) sich in etw. (Akk.) verwandeln; e) (become sour) ⟨Milch:⟩ sauer werden. **turn a'way** 1. *v.i.* sich abwenden. 2. *v.t.* a) (avert) abwenden; b) (send away) wegschikken. **turn 'down** *v.t.* a) herunterschlagen ⟨Kragen⟩; b) niedriger stellen ⟨Heizung⟩; herunterdrehen ⟨Gas⟩; leiser stellen ⟨Ton, Radio, Fernseher⟩; c) (reject) ablehnen; abweisen ⟨Kandidaten usw.⟩. **turn 'in 1.** *v.t.* a) nach innen drehen; b) (hand in) abgeben. 2. *v.i.* a) (enter) einbiegen; b) (coll.: go to bed) in die Falle gehen (salopp). **turn 'off 1.** *v.t.* abschalten; abstellen ⟨Wasser, Gas⟩; zudrehen ⟨Wasserhahn⟩. 2. *v.i.* abbiegen. **turn on** *v.t.* a) [-ˈ-] anschalten; aufdrehen ⟨Wasserhahn, Gas⟩; b) [ˈ--] (attack) angreifen. **turn 'out 1.** *v.t.* a) (expel) hinauswerfen (ugs.)*; b) (switch off) ausschalten; abdrehen ⟨Gas⟩; c) (produce) produzieren; d) (Brit.) (empty) ausräumen; leeren; (get rid of) wegwerfen. 2. *v.i.* a) (prove to be) sb./sth. **~s out to be sth.** jmd./etw. stellt sich als jmd./etw. heraus; **everything ~ed out well/all right in the end** alles endete gut; b) (appear) ⟨Fans usw.:⟩ erscheinen. **turn 'over 1.** *v.t.* a) umdrehen. 2. *v.i.* a) (tip over) umkippen; ⟨Boot:⟩ kentern; ⟨Auto, Flugzeug:⟩ sich überschlagen; b) (from one side to the other) sich umdrehen; c) (~ a page) weiterblättern. **turn 'round** *v.i.* sich umdrehen. **'turn to** *v.i.* (fig.) **~ to sb.** sich an jmdn. wenden; **~ to sb. for help/advice** bei jmdm. Hilfe/Rat suchen; **~ to drink** sich in den Alkohol flüchten. **turn 'up 1.** *v.i.* a) ⟨Person:⟩ erscheinen; b) (present itself) auftauchen; ⟨Gelegenheit:⟩ sich bieten. 2. *v.t.* a) hochschlagen ⟨Kragen⟩; b) lauter stellen ⟨Ton, Radio, Fernseher⟩; aufdrehen ⟨Heizung, Gas⟩; heller machen ⟨Licht⟩

'turning *n.* Abzweigung, *die.* **'turning-point** *n.* Wendepunkt, *der*

turnip ['tɜːnɪp] *n.* Kohlrübe, *die*

turn-: **~out** *n.* (of people) Beteiligung, *die* (for an + Dat.); **~over** *n.* a) (Commerc.) Umsatz, *der*; (of stock) Umschlag, *die*; b) (of staff) Fluktuation, *die*; **~pike** *n.* (Amer.) gebührenpflichtige Autobahn; **~stile** *n.* Drehkreuz, *das;* ~**table** *n.* Plattenteller, *der;* ~-**up** *n.* (*Brit. Fashion*) Aufschlag, *der*

turpentine ['tɜːpntaɪn] *n.* Terpentin, *das*

turquoise ['tɜːkwɔɪz] **1.** *n.* **a)** Türkis, *der;* **b)** (*colour*) Türkis, *das.* **2.** *adj.* türkis[farben]

turret ['tʌrɪt] *n.* Türmchen, *das*

turtle ['tɜːtl] *n.* **a)** Meeresschildkröte, *die;* **b)** (*Amer.: freshwater reptile*) Wasserschildkröte, *die*

turves *see* **turf b**

tusk [tʌsk] *n.* Stoßzahn, *der*

tussle ['tʌsl] **1.** *n.* Gerangel, *das* (*ugs.*). **2.** *v. i.* sich balgen

tutor ['tjuːtə(r)] *n.* [private] ~: [Privat]lehrer, *der/*-lehrerin, *die*

tuxedo [tʌk'siːdəʊ] *n., pl.* ~s *or* ~es (*Amer.*) Smoking, *der*

TV [tiː'viː] *n.* **a)** Fernsehen, *das;* **b)** (*television set*) Fernseher, *der* (*ugs.*)

twaddle ['twɒdl] *n.* Gewäsch, *das* (*ugs.*)

twang [twæŋ] **1.** *v. t.* zupfen ⟨*Saite*⟩. **2.** *n.* [nasal] ~: Näseln, *das*

tweed [twiːd] *n.* Tweed, *der*

tweezers ['twiːzəz] *n. pl.* [pair of] ~: Pinzette, *die*

twelfth [twelfθ] **1.** *adj.* zwölft... **2.** *n.* (*fraction*) Zwölftel, *das. See also* **eighth**

twelve [twelv] **1.** *adj.* zwölf. **2.** *n.* Zwölf, *die. See also* **eight**

twentieth ['twentɪɪθ] **1.** *adj.* zwanzigst... **2.** *n.* (*fraction*) Zwanzigstel, *das. See also* **eighth**

twenty ['twentɪ] **1.** *adj.* zwanzig. **2.** *n.* Zwanzig, *die. See also* **eight**; **eighty 2**

twice [twaɪs] *adv.* **a)** zweimal; **b)** (*doubly*) doppelt

twiddle ['twɪdl] *v. t.* herumdrehen an (+ *Dat.*) (*ugs.*)

¹**twig** [twɪg] *n.* Zweig, *der*

²**twig** (*coll.*) **1.** *v. t.,* -**gg-** kapieren (*ugs.*). **2.** *v. i.,* -**gg-** es kapieren (*ugs.*)

twilight ['twaɪlaɪt] *n.* **a)** (*evening light*) Dämmerlicht, *das;* **b)** (*period of half-light*) Dämmerung, *die*

twin [twɪn] **1.** *attrib. adj.* **a)** Zwillings-; **b)** (*forming a pair*) Doppel-. **2.** *n.* Zwilling, *der.* **twin 'beds** *n. pl.* zwei Einzelbetten

twine [twaɪn] **1.** *n.* Bindfaden, *der.* **2.** *v. i.* sich winden (*about, around* um)

twinge [twɪndʒ] *n.* Stechen, *das;* ~[s] **of conscience** (*fig.*) Gewissensbisse

twinkle ['twɪŋkl] **1.** *v. i.* funkeln (*with* vor + *Dat.*). **2.** *n.* Funkeln, *das*

twinkling ['twɪŋklɪŋ] *n.* **in a** ~, **in the** ~ **of an eye** im Handumdrehen

'**twin town** *n.* (*Brit.*) Partnerstadt, *die*

twirl [twɜːl] **1.** *v. t.* [schnell] drehen. **2.** *v. i.* wirbeln (*around* über + *Akk.*)

twist [twɪst] **1.** *v. t.* **a)** verdrehen ⟨*Worte, Bedeutung*⟩; ~ **one's ankle** sich (*Dat.*) den Knöchel verrenken; ~ **sb.'s arm** jmdm. den Arm umdrehen; (*fig.*) jmdm. [die] Daumenschrauben anlegen; **b)** (*rotate*) drehen. **2.** *v. i.* sich winden. **3.** *n.* **a)** (*motion*) Drehung, *die;* **b)** (*unexpected occurrence*) überraschende Wendung

twit [twɪt] *n.* (*Brit. sl.*) Trottel, *der* (*ugs.*)

twitch [twɪtʃ] **1.** *v. i.* ⟨*Mund, Lippe:*⟩ zucken. **2.** *n.* Zucken, *das*

twitter ['twɪtə(r)] **1.** *n.* Zwitschern, *das.* **2.** *v. i.* zwitschern

two [tuː] **1.** *adj.* zwei. **2.** *n.* Zwei, *die. See also* **eight**

two: ~-**faced** ['tuːfeɪst] *adj.* (*fig.*) falsch; ~-**fold** *adj., adv.* zweifach; **a** ~**fold increase** ein Anstieg auf das Doppelte; ~-**piece** **1.** *n.* Zweiteiler, *der;* **2.** *adj.* zweiteilig; ~-**some** ['tuːsəm] *n.* Paar, *das;* ~-**way** *adj.* **a)** zweibahnig (*Verkehrsw.*); '~-**way traffic ahead**' „Achtung Gegenverkehr"; **b)** ~-**way mirror** Einwegspiegel, *der*

tycoon [taɪ'kuːn] *n.* Magnat, *der*

tying *see* **tie 1, 2**

type [taɪp] **1.** *n.* **a)** Art, *die;* (*person*) Typ, *der;* **what** ~ **of car** ...? was für ein Auto ...?; **b)** (*Printing*) Drucktype, *die.* **2.** *v. t.* [mit der Maschine] schreiben; tippen (*ugs.*). **3.** *v. i.* maschinenschreiben. **type 'out** *v. t.* [mit der Schreibmaschine] abschreiben; abtippen (*ugs.*)

'**typewriter** *n.* Schreibmaschine, *die.* '**typewritten** *adj.* maschine[n]geschrieben

typhoid ['taɪfɔɪd] *n.* ~ **Typhus**, *der*

typhoon [taɪ'fuːn] *n.* Taifun, *der*

typical ['tɪpɪkl] *adj.* typisch (*of* für)

typify ['tɪpɪfaɪ] *v. t.* ~ **sth.** als typisches Beispiel für etw. dienen

typing ['taɪpɪŋ] *n.* Maschinenschreiben, *das*

typist ['taɪpɪst] *n.* Schreibkraft, *die*

tyrannical [tɪ'rænɪkl] *adj.* tyrannisch

tyranny ['tɪrənɪ] *n.* Tyrannei, *die*

tyrant ['taɪərənt] *n.* Tyrann, *der*

tyre ['taɪə(r)] *n.* Reifen, *der*

U

___

U, u [ju:] *n.* U, u, *das*

ubiquitous [ju:'bɪkwɪtəs] *adj.* allgegenwärtig

udder ['ʌdə(r)] *n.* Euter, *das*

ugliness ['ʌglɪnɪs] *n.* Häßlichkeit, *die*

ugly ['ʌglɪ] *adj.* a) häßlich; b) *(nasty)* übel ⟨*Wunde, Laune usw.*⟩

UK *abbr.* United Kingdom

Ukraine [ju:'kreɪn] *pr. n.* Ukraine, *die*

ulcer ['ʌlsə(r)] *n.* Geschwür, *das*

ulterior [ʌl'tɪərɪə(r)] *adj.* hintergründig; ~ **motive** Hintergedanke, *der*

ultimate ['ʌltɪmət] **1.** *attrib. adj.* **a)** *(final)* letzt...; *(eventual)* endgültig ⟨*Sieg*⟩; **b)** *(fundamental)* tiefst... **2.** *n.* the ~ **in comfort/luxury** der Gipfel an Bequemlichkeit/Luxus. **'ultimately** *adv.* **a)** *(in the end)* schließlich; **b)** *(in the last analysis)* letzten Endes

ultimatum [ʌltɪ'meɪtəm] *n., pl.* ~s *or* **ultimata** [ʌltɪ'meɪtə] Ultimatum, *das*

ultra'violet *adj.* (Phys.) ultraviolett; UV-⟨*Lampe, Filter*⟩

umbilical cord [ʌm'bɪlɪkl kɔ:d] *n.* Nabelschnur, *die*

umbrage ['ʌmbrɪdʒ] *n.* take ~ [at sth.] [an etw. (+ *Dat.*)] Anstoß nehmen

umbrella [ʌm'brelə] *n.* [Regen]schirm, *der*

umpire ['ʌmpaɪə(r)] *n.* Schiedsrichter, *der*/-richterin, *die*

umpteen [ʌmp'ti:n] *adj. (coll.)* zig *(ugs.)*; x *(ugs.)*

unabashed [ʌnə'bæʃt] *adj.* ungeniert

unable [ʌn'eɪbl] *pred. adj.* be ~ to do sth. etw. nicht tun können

unabridged [ʌnə'brɪdʒd] *adj.* ungekürzt

unac'ceptable *adj.* unannehmbar

unac'countable *adj.* unerklärlich. **unaccountably** [ʌnə'kaʊntəblɪ] *adv.* unerklärlicherweise

unac'customed *adj.* ungewohnt; be ~ to sth. etw. *(Akk.)* nicht gewöhnt sein

unadulterated [ʌnə'dʌltəreɪtɪd] *adj.* **a)** *(pure)* unverfälscht; **b)** *(utter)* völlig

unaided [ʌn'eɪdɪd] *adj.* ohne fremde Hilfe

unanimity [ju:nə'nɪmɪtɪ] *n.* Einmütigkeit, *die*

unanimous [ju:'nænɪməs] *adj.* einstimmig; be ~ **in doing sth.** etw. einmütig tun

unarmed [ʌn'ɑ:md] *adj.* unbewaffnet; ~ **combat** Kampf ohne Waffen

unassuming [ʌnə'sju:mɪŋ] *adj.* bescheiden

unattached [ʌnə'tætʃt] *adj.* **a)** nicht befestigt; **b)** *(without a partner)* ungebunden

unat'tended *adj.* **a)** ~ **to** *(not dealt with)* unerledigt; nicht bedient ⟨*Kunde*⟩; nicht behandelt ⟨*Patient*⟩; **b)** *(not supervised)* unbewacht ⟨*Parkplatz, Gepäck*⟩

unat'tractive *adj.* unattraktiv

unauthorized [ʌn'ɔ:θəraɪzd] *adj.* unbefugt; **no entry for ~ persons** Zutritt für Unbefugte verboten

una'vailable *adj.* nicht erhältlich ⟨*Ware*⟩; be ~ **for comment** zur Stellungnahme nicht zur Verfügung stehen

una'voidable *adj.* unvermeidlich

unaware [ʌnə'weə(r)] *adj.* be ~ **of sth.** sich *(Dat.)* einer Sache *(Gen.)* nicht bewußt sein. **unawares** [ʌnə'weəz] *adv.* **catch sb. ~:** jmdn. überraschen

unbalanced [ʌn'bælənst] *adj.* **a)** unausgewogen; **b)** *(mentally ~)* unausgeglichen

un'bearable *adj.*, **unbearably** [ʌn'beərəblɪ] *adv.* unerträglich

unbeatable [ʌn'bi:təbl] *adj.* unschlagbar *(ugs.)*

un'beaten *adj.* **a)** ungeschlagen; **b)** *(not surpassed)* unerreicht; ungebrochen ⟨*Rekord*⟩

unbe'lievable *adj.* **a)** unglaublich; **b)** *(tremendous)* unwahrscheinlich

unbiased, unbiassed [ʌn'baɪəst] *adj.* unvoreingenommen

unblemished [ʌn'blemɪʃt] *adj.* makellos ⟨*Haut, Ruf*⟩

un'block *v. t.* frei machen

un'bolt *v. t.* aufriegeln ⟨*Tür*⟩

unborn [ʌn'bɔ:n, *attrib.* 'ʌnbɔ:n] *adj.* ungeboren

un'breakable *adj.* unzerbrechlich

unburden [ʌn'bɜ:dn] *v. t.* ~ **oneself** sein Herz ausschütten

un'button *v. t.* aufknöpfen

uncalled-for [ʌn'kɔ:ldfɔ:(r)] *adj.* unangebracht

uncanny [ʌn'kænɪ] *adj.* unheimlich

uncaring [ʌn'keərɪŋ] *adj.* gleichgültig

unceasing [ʌn'siːsɪŋ] *adj.* unaufhörlich

unceremonious [ˌʌnserɪ'məʊnɪəs] *adj.* **a)** *(informal)* formlos; **b)** *(abrupt)* brüsk. **unceremoniously** *adv.* ohne Umschweife

un'certain *adj.* **a)** *(not sure)* **be ~ |whether ...|** sich *(Dat.)* nicht sicher sein|, ob ...|; **b)** *(not clear)* ungewiß ⟨*Ergebnis, Zukunft*⟩; **of ~ age/origin** unbestimmten Alters/unbestimmter Herkunft; **c)** *(ambiguous)* vage; **in no ~ terms** ganz eindeutig. **uncertainty** [ʌn'sɜːtntɪ] *n.* **a)** Ungewißheit, *die;* **b)** *(hesitation)* Unsicherheit, *die*

unchanged [ʌn'tʃeɪndʒd] *adj.* unverändert

un'charitable *adj.* **uncharitably** [ʌn'tʃærɪtəblɪ] *adv.* lieblos

un'civil *adj.* unhöflich

uncle [ʌŋkl] *n.* Onkel, *der*

un'comfortable *adj.* **a)** unbequem; **b)** *(feeling discomfort)* **be ~:** sich unbehaglich fühlen; **c)** *(uneasy, disconcerting)* unangenehm; peinlich ⟨*Stille*⟩. **un'comfortably** *adv.* unbequem; **be ~ aware of sth.** sich *(Dat.)* einer Sache peinlich bewußt sein

un'common *adj.* ungewöhnlich

uncompli'mentary *adj.* wenig schmeichelhaft

uncompromising [ʌn'kɒmprəmaɪzɪŋ] *adj.* kompromißlos

uncon'ditional *adj.* bedingungslos ⟨*Kapitulation*⟩; kategorisch ⟨*Ablehnung*⟩; ⟨*Versprechen*⟩ ohne Vorbehalte

un'conscious 1. *adj.* **a)** *(Med.)* bewußtlos; **b)** *(unaware)* **be ~ of sth.** sich einer Sache *(Gen.)* nicht bewußt sein; **c)** *(not intended; Psych.)* unbewußt. **2.** *n.* Unbewußte, *das.* **un'consciously** *adv.* unbewußt

uncon'ventional *adj.*, **uncon'ventionally** *adv.* unkonventionell

unco'operative *adj.* unkooperativ; *(unhelpful)* wenig hilfsbereit

un'cork *v. t.* entkorken

uncouth [ʌn'kuːθ] *adj.* ungehobelt ⟨*Person, Benehmen*⟩; grob ⟨*Bemerkung*⟩

un'cover *v. t.* aufdecken

undaunted [ʌn'dɔːntɪd] *adj.* unverzagt

undecided [ʌndɪ'saɪdɪd] *adj.* **a)** *(not settled)* nicht entschieden; **b)** *(hesitant)* unentschlossen

undeniably [ʌndɪ'naɪəblɪ] *adv.* unbestreitbar

under ['ʌndə(r)] **1.** *prep.* **a)** *(underneath, below)* unter *(position: + Dat.; motion: + Akk.); from ~ the table/bed* unter dem Tisch/Bett hervor; **b)** *(undergoing)* **~ treatment** in Behandlung; **~ repair** in Reparatur; **~ construction** im Bau; **c)** *(in conditions of)* bei ⟨*Streß, hohen Temperaturen usw.*⟩; **d)** *(subject to)* unter *(+ Dat.);* **~ the terms of the contract** nach den Bestimmungen des Vertrags; **e)** *(with the use of)* unter *(+ Dat.);* **~ an assumed name** unter falschem Namen; **f)** *(less than)* unter *(+ Dat.).* **2.** *adv.* **a)** *(in or to a lower or subordinate position)* darunter; **b)** *(in/into a state of unconsciousness)* **be ~/put sb. ~:** in Narkose liegen/jmdn. in Narkose versetzen

under: ~carriage *n.* Fahrwerk, *das;* **~clothes** *n. pl.,* **~clothing** *see* **underwear; ~cover** *adj.* **(disguised)** getarnt; *(secret)* verdeckt; **~cover agent** Geheimagent, *der;* **~current** *n.* Unterströmung, *die; (fig.)* Unterton, *der;* **~'cut** *v. t.,* **~cut** unterbieten; **~dog** *n.* **a)** *(in fight)* Unterlegene, *der/die;* **b)** *(fig.)* Benachteiligte, *der/die;* **~'done** *adj.* halbgar; **~estimate** [ʌndər'estɪmət] **1.** *v. t.* unterschätzen; **2.** [ʌndər'estɪmət] *n.* Unterschätzung, *die;* **~'fed** *adj.* unterernährt; **~'foot** *adv.* am Boden; **be trampled ~foot** mit Füßen zertrampelt werden; **~'go** *v. t.,* forms as **go 1** durchmachen; **~go treatment** sich einer Behandlung unterziehen; **~go a change** sich verändern; **~'graduate** *n.* **~graduate |student|** Student/Studentin vor der ersten Prüfung; **~ground 1.** |--'-| *adv.* **a)** unter der Erde; *(Mining)* unter Tage; **b)** *(fig.) (in hiding)* im Untergrund; *(into hiding)* in den Untergrund; **2.** ['---] *adj.* unterirdisch ⟨*Höhle, See*⟩; **~ground railway** Untergrundbahn, *die;* U-Bahn, *die;* **~ground car-park** Tiefgarage, *die;* **3.** *n. (railway)* U-Bahn, *die;* **~ station/train** U-Bahnhof, *der/*U-Bahn-Zug, *der;* **~'growth** *n.* Unterholz, *das;* **~hand, ~handed** *adj.* **a)** *(secret)* heimlich; **b)** *(crafty)* hinterhältig; **~lay** *n.* Unterlage, *die;* **~'lie** *v. t.,* forms as ²**lie: ~lie sth.** *(fig.)* einer Sache *(Dat.)* zugrundeliegen; **~lying cause** eigentliche Ursache; **~'line** *v. t.* unterstreichen

underling ['ʌndəlɪŋ] *n.* Untergebene, *der/die*

under: ~'lying *see* **underline; ~mine**

v. t. **a)** unterhöhlen; **b)** *(fig.)* untergraben; unterminieren ⟨*Autorität*⟩

underneath [ʌndəˈniːθ] **1.** *prep.* unter (*position:* + *Dat.; motion:* + *Akk.*). **2.** *adv.* darunter

under: ~**paid** *adj.* unterbezahlt; ~**pants** *n. pl.* Unterhose, *die;* ~**pass** *n.* Unterführung, *die;* ~**play** *v. t.* herunterspielen; ~**privileged** *adj.* unterprivilegiert; ~**rate** *v. t.* unterschätzen; ~**seal** *n.* Unterbodenschutz, *der*

understand [ʌndəˈstænd] **1.** *v. t.,* understood [ʌndəˈstʊd] **a)** verstehen; **make oneself understood** sich verständlich machen; **b)** *(have heard)* gehört haben; **c)** *(take as implied)* it was understood that ...: es wurde allgemein angenommen, daß ... **2.** *v. i.,* understood **a)** verstehen; **b)** *(gather, hear)* if I ~ correctly wenn ich mich nicht irre; he is, I ~, no longer here er ist, wie ich höre, nicht mehr hier. **understandably** [ʌndəˈstændəblɪ] *adv.* verständlicherweise. **understanding 1.** *adj.* verständnisvoll. **2.** *n.* **a)** *(agreement)* Verständigung, *die;* **reach an ~ with sb.** sich mit jmdm. verständigen; **on the ~ that ...:** unter der Voraussetzung, daß ...; **b)** *(intelligence)* Verstand, *der;* **c)** *(insight)* Verständnis, *das* (of, for für)

under: ~**statement** *n.* Untertreibung, *die;* ~**study** *n.* Ersatzspieler, *der/*-spielerin, *die;* ~**take** *v. t.,* forms as take 1 unternehmen; ~**take a task** eine Aufgabe übernehmen; ~**take to do sth.** sich verpflichten, etw. zu tun; ~**taker** *n.* Leichenbestatter, *der/*-bestatterin, *die;* ~**taking** *n.* **a)** *(task)* Aufgabe, *die;* **b)** *(pledge)* Versprechen, *das;* ~**tone** *n.* in ~tones or an ~tone mit gedämpfter Stimme; ~**tone of criticism** kritischer Unterton; ~**tow** *n.* Unterströmung, *die;* ~**value** *v. t.* unterbewerten; ~**water 1.** [ˈ----] *attrib. adj.* Unterwasser-. **2.** [--ˈ--] *adv.* unter Wasser; ~**wear** *n.* Unterwäsche, *die;* ~**weight** *adj.* untergewichtig; ~**world** *n.* Unterwelt, *die.* **unde'sirable** *adj.* unerwünscht; **it is ~ that ...:** es ist nicht wünschenswert, daß ...

undeveloped [ʌndɪˈveləpt] *adj.* **a)** *(immature)* nicht voll ausgebildet; **b)** *(not built on)* nicht bebaut

undies [ˈʌndɪz] *n. pl.* (coll.) Unterwäsche, *die*

un'dignified *adj.* blamabel

undo [ʌnˈduː] *v. t.,* undoes [ʌnˈdʌz], un-

doing [ʌnˈduːɪŋ], undid [ʌnˈdɪd], undone [ʌnˈdʌn] *(unfasten)* aufmachen

un'done *adj.* **a)** *(not accomplished)* unerledigt; **b)** *(not fastened)* offen

undoubted [ʌnˈdaʊtɪd] *adj.* unzweifelhaft. **un'doubtedly** *adv.* zweifellos

un'dress 1. *v. t.* ausziehen; **get ~ed** sich ausziehen **2.** *v. i.* sich ausziehen

un'due *attrib. adj.* übertrieben; übermäßig

undulating [ˈʌndjʊleɪtɪŋ] *adj.* Wellen⟨*linie*⟩; **~ country** sanfte Hügellandschaft

unduly [ʌnˈdjuːlɪ] *adv.* übermäßig

undying [ʌnˈdaɪɪŋ] *adj.* ewig; unsterblich ⟨*Ruhm*⟩

unearth [ʌnˈɜːθ] *v. t.* **a)** ausgraben; **b)** *(fig.: discover)* aufdecken

unearthly [ʌnˈɜːθlɪ] *adj.* unheimlich; **at an ~ hour** in aller Herrgottsfrühe

un'easy *adj.* **a)** *(anxious)* besorgt; **he felt ~:** ihm war unbehaglich zumute; **b)** *(restless)* unruhig

uneatable [ʌnˈiːtəbl] *adj.* ungenießbar

uneco'nomic *adj.* unrentabel. **uneco'nomical** *adj.* **~ [to run]** unwirtschaftlich

unemployed [ʌnɪmˈplɔɪd] **1.** *adj.* arbeitslos. **2.** *n. pl.* the ~: die Arbeitslosen. **unem'ployment** *n.* Arbeitslosigkeit, *die.* **unem'ployment benefit** *n.* Arbeitslosengeld, *das*

un'ending *adj.* endlos

un'equal *adj.* unterschiedlich; ungleich ⟨*Kampf*⟩; **~ to sth.** einer Sache *(Dat.)* nicht gewachsen sein. **un'equalled** *(Amer.:* **unequaled)** [ʌnˈiːkwld] *adj.* unerreicht

une'quivocal *adj.* eindeutig

unerring [ʌnˈɜːrɪŋ] *adj.* unfehlbar

un'ethical *adj.* unmoralisch

un'even *adj.* **a)** *(not smooth)* uneben; **b)** *(not uniform)* ungleichmäßig; **c)** *(odd)* ungerade ⟨*Zahl*⟩. **un'evenly** *adv.* ungleichmäßig

unex'pected *adj.* unerwartet

un'fair *adj.* unfair; ungerecht. **un'fairly** *adv.* **a)** *(unjustly)* ungerecht; unfair ⟨*spielen*⟩; **b)** *(unreasonably)* zu Unrecht. **un'fairness** *n.* Ungerechtigkeit, *die*

un'faithful *adj.* untreu

unfa'miliar *adj.* **a)** *(strange)* unbekannt; ungewohnt ⟨*Arbeit*⟩; **b)** **be ~ with sth.** sich mit etw. nicht auskennen

un'fasten *v. t.* **a)** öffnen; **b)** *(detach)* lösen

un'favourable adj. ungünstig. **un'favourably** adv. ungünstig; **be ~ disposed towards sb./sth.** jmdm./etw. gegenüber ablehnend eingestellt sein

un'feeling adj. gefühllos

unfinished [ʌn'fɪnɪʃt] adj. unvollendet ⟨Werk⟩; unerledigt ⟨Arbeit⟩

un'fit adj. **a)** ungeeignet; **b)** (not physically fit) nicht fit (ugs.); **~ for military service** [wehrdienst]untauglich

un'flattering adj. wenig schmeichelhaft

un'flinching adj. unerschrocken

un'fold **1.** v. t. entfalten; ausbreiten ⟨Zeitung, Landkarte⟩. **2.** v. i. sich entfalten; (develop) sich entwickeln

unfore'seen adj. unvorhergesehen

unforgettable [ʌnfə'ɡetəbl] adj. unvergeßlich

un'fortunate adj. unglücklich. **un'fortunately** adv. leider

un'founded adj. (fig.) unbegründet

un'freeze v. t. & i., **unfroze** [ʌn'frəʊz], **unfrozen** [ʌn'frəʊzn] auftauen

un'friendly adj. unfreundlich; feindlich ⟨Staat⟩

un'furl **1.** v. t. aufrollen; losmachen ⟨Segel⟩. **2.** v. i. sich aufrollen

un'furnished adj. unmöbliert

ungainly [ʌn'ɡeɪnlɪ] adj. unbeholfen

ungram'matical adj. ungrammatisch

un'grateful adj. undankbar

un'happily adv. **a)** unglücklich; **b)** (unfortunately) leider

un'happiness n. Bekümmertheit, die

un'happy adj. unglücklich; (not content) unzufrieden (about with); **be** or **feel ~ about doing sth.** Bedenken haben, etw. zu tun

un'harmed adj. unbeschädigt; (uninjured) unverletzt

un'healthy adj. ungesund

un'helpful adj. wenig hilfsbereit ⟨Person⟩; ⟨Bemerkung, Kritik⟩ die einem nicht weiterhilft

un'hook v. t. vom Haken nehmen; aufhaken ⟨Kleid⟩

un'hurt adj. unverletzt

unhy'gienic adj. unhygienisch

unicorn ['juːnɪkɔːn] n. Einhorn, das

uni'dentified adj. nicht identifiziert; **~ flying object** unbekanntes Flugobjekt

unification [juːnɪfɪ'keɪʃn] n. Einigung, die

uniform ['juːnɪfɔːm] **1.** adj. einheitlich; **be ~ in shape/size** die gleiche Form/Größe haben. **2.** n. Uniform, die; **in/out of ~:** in/ohne Uniform.

uniformity [juːnɪ'fɔːmɪtɪ] n. Einheitlichkeit, die. **'uniformly** adv. einheitlich

unify ['juːnɪfaɪ] v. t. einigen

unilateral [juːnɪ'lætərl] adj. einseitig

uni'maginable adj. unvorstellbar

uni'maginative adj. phantasielos

unim'portant adj. unwichtig; bedeutungslos

unin'habitable adj. unbewohnbar

unin'habited adj. unbewohnt

unin'jured adj. unverletzt

uninspiring [ʌnɪn'spaɪərɪŋ] adj. langweilig

unin'telligent adj. nicht intelligent

unin'telligible adj. unverständlich

unin'tended adj. unbeabsichtigt

unin'tentional adj., **unin'tentionally** adv. unabsichtlich

unin'terested adj. desinteressiert (**in** an + Dat.)

union ['juːnɪən] n. **a)** (trade ~) Gewerkschaft, die; **b)** (Polit.) Union, die. **Union 'Jack** n. (Brit.) Union Jack, der

unique [juː'niːk] adj. einzigartig

unison ['juːnɪsn] n. Unisono, das; **in ~:** einstimmig; **act in ~** (fig.) vereint handeln

unit ['juːnɪt] n. **a)** (also Mil., Math.) Einheit, die; **~ of length/monetary ~:** Längen-/Währungseinheit, die; **b)** (piece of furniture) Element, das; **kitchen ~:** Küchenelement, das

unite [juː'naɪt] **1.** v. t. vereinigen; einen, einigen ⟨Partei, Mitglieder⟩. **2.** v. i. sich vereinigen. **u'nited** adj. **a)** (harmonious) einig; **b)** (combined) gemeinsam

United: ~ 'Kingdom pr. n. Vereinigtes Königreich [Großbritannien und Nordirland]; **~ 'Nations** pr. n. sing. Vereinte Nationen Pl.; **~ States [of A'merica]** pr. n. sing. Vereinigte Staaten [von Amerika]

unity ['juːnɪtɪ] n. Einheit, die

universal [juːnɪ'vɜːsl] adj., **universally** adv. allgemein

universe ['juːnɪvɜːs] n. Universum, das

university [juːnɪ'vɜːsɪtɪ] n. Universität, die; attrib. Universitäts-

un'just adj. ungerecht

unkempt [ʌn'kempt] adj. ungepflegt

un'kind adj., **un'kindly** adv. unfreundlich. **un'kindness** n. Unfreundlichkeit, die

un'known **1.** adj. unbekannt. **2.** adv. **~ to sb.** ohne daß jmd. davon weiß/wußte

un'lawful *adj.* ungesetzlich

unless [ən'les] *conj.* es sei denn; wenn ... nicht

un'like 1. *adj.* nicht ähnlich. **2.** *prep.* be ~ **sb./sth.** jmdm./einer Sache nicht ähnlich sein; ~ **him**, ...: im Gegensatz zu ihm ...

un'likely *adj.* unwahrscheinlich; **be ~ to do sth.** etw. wahrscheinlich nicht tun

un'limited *adj.* unbegrenzt

un'load *v.t.* entladen ⟨Lastwagen, Waggon⟩; löschen ⟨Schiff, Schiffsladung⟩; ausladen ⟨Gepäck⟩

un'lock *v.t.* aufschließen

un'lucky *adj.* a) unglücklich; *(not successful)* glücklos; **be |very| ~:** [großes] Pech haben; b) *(bringing bad luck)* an ~ **number** eine Unglückszahl; **be ~:** Unglück bringen

un'manned *adj.* unbemannt

un'married *adj.* unverheiratet; ledig

un'mask *v.t.* *(fig.)* entlarven

unmis'takable *adj.* deutlich; unverwechselbar ⟨Handschrift, Stimme⟩. **unmistakably** [ʌnmɪ'steɪkəblɪ] *adv.* unverkennbar

un'mitigated *adj.* vollkommen; **be an ~ disaster** *(coll.)* eine einzige Katastrophe sein

un'natural *adj.*, **un'naturally** *adv.* unnatürlich; *(abnormal)* nicht normal

un'necessarily *adv.*, **un'necessary** *adj.* unnötig

unof'ficial *adj.*, **unof'ficially** *adv.* inoffiziell

un'pack *v.t. & i.* auspacken

un'paid *adj.* unbezahlt; nicht bezahlt; ~ **for** nicht bezahlt

un'palatable [ʌn'pælətəbl] *adj.* ungenießbar

un'paralleled *adj.* beispiellos

un'pardonable *adj.* unverzeihlich

un'pleasant *adj.*, **un'pleasantly** *adv.* unangenehm. **un'pleasantness** *n. (bad feeling)* Verstimmung, die

un'plug *v.t.*, **-gg-:** ~ **a lamp** den Stecker einer Lampe herausziehen

un'popular *adj.* unbeliebt ⟨Lehrer, Regierung usw.⟩, unpopulär ⟨Maßnahme, Politik⟩ (with bei)

un'precedented *adj.* beispiellos

unpre'dictable *adj.* unberechenbar

unpre'pared *adj.* unvorbereitet

unprepos'sessing *adj.* wenig attraktiv

unpre'tentious *adj.* einfach ⟨Wein, Stil, Haus⟩; bescheiden ⟨Person⟩

unprincipled [ʌn'prɪnsɪpld] *adj.* skrupellos

unprintable [ʌn'prɪntəbl] *adj.* nicht druckreif

unpro'ductive *adj.* fruchtlos ⟨Diskussion, Nachforschung⟩; unproduktiv ⟨Zeit, Arbeit⟩

unpro'fessional *adj. (contrary to standards)* standeswidrig

un'profitable *adj.* unrentabel

un'promising *adj.* nicht sehr vielversprechend

un'qualified *adj.* a) unqualifiziert; b) *(absolute)* uneingeschränkt; voll ⟨Erfolg⟩

un'questionable *adj.* unbezweifelbar ⟨Tatsache⟩; unbestreitbar ⟨Recht, Ehrlichkeit⟩. **unquestionably** [ʌn'kwestʃənəblɪ] *adv.* ohne Frage

unravel [ʌn'rævl] **1.** *v.t., (Brit.)* **-ll-** entwirren; *(undo)* aufziehen; *(fig.)* ~ **a mystery/the truth** ein Geheimnis enträtseln/die Wahrheit aufdecken. **2.** *v.i., (Brit.)* **-ll-** sich aufziehen

un'real *adj.* unwirklich

unrea'listic *adj.* unrealistisch

un'reasonable *adj.* unvernünftig; übertrieben ⟨Ansprüche, Forderung, Preis, Kosten⟩

unrecognizable [ʌn'rekəgnaɪzəbl] *adj.* **be |absolutely or quite| ~:** [überhaupt] nicht wiederzuerkennen sein

unre'lated *adj.* **be ~:** nicht miteinander zusammenhängen; *(by family)* nicht verwandt sein

unre'liable *adj.* unzuverlässig

unrequited [ʌnrɪ'kwaɪtɪd] *adj.* unerwidert

unreservedly [ʌnrɪ'zɜːvɪdlɪ] *adv.* uneingeschränkt

un'rest *n.* Unruhen *Pl.*

un'ripe *adj.* unreif

un'rivalled *(Amer.:* **un'rivaled)** *adj.* unübertroffen

un'roll 1. *v.t.* aufrollen. **2.** *v.i.* sich aufrollen

unruly [ʌn'ruːlɪ] *adj.* ungebärdig

un'safe *adj.* nicht sicher; **feel ~:** sich unsicher fühlen

un'said *adj.* ungesagt

un'salted *adj.* ungesalzen

unsatis'factory *adj.* unbefriedigend

un'savoury *(Amer.:* **un'savory)** *adj.* unangenehm; zweifelhaft ⟨Angelegenheit⟩; unerfreulich ⟨Einzelheiten⟩

unscathed [ʌn'skeɪðd] *adj.* unversehrt

un'screw 1. *v.t.* abschrauben. **2.** *v.i.* sich abschrauben lassen

un'scrupulous *adj.* skrupellos
un'seemly *adj.* unschicklich
unself'conscious *adj.* unbefangen
un'selfish *adj.* selbstlos. **un'selfishness** *n.* Selbstlosigkeit, *die*
un'settled *adj. (changeable)* wechselhaft; *(fig.)* ruhelos ⟨*Leben*⟩; unruhig ⟨*Zeit, Land*⟩
un'settling *adj.* störend
unshak[e]able [ʌn'ʃeɪkəbl] *adj.* unerschütterlich
un'shaven *adj.* unrasiert
un'sightly *adj.* unschön
un'skilled *adj.* ungelernt ⟨*Arbeiter*⟩
un'sociable *adj.* ungesellig
unso'phisticated *adj.* einfach
un'sound *adj.* **a)** *(diseased)* nicht gesund; krank; **b)** baufällig ⟨*Gebäude*⟩; **c)** *(ill-founded)* wenig stichhaltig; nicht vertretbar ⟨*Ansicht, Methode*⟩; **d)** of ~ **mind** unzurechnungsfähig
unspeakable [ʌn'spiːkəbl] *adj.* unbeschreiblich; *(very bad)* unsäglich
un'stable *adj.* nicht stabil; [mentally/emotionally] ~: [psychisch] labil
un'steadily *adv.* unsicher
un'steady *adj.* unsicher; wackelig ⟨*Leiter, Tisch*⟩
un'stuck *adj.* come ~: sich lösen; *(fig. coll.: fail) (Person:)* baden gehen *(ugs.)* (over mit)
unsuc'cessful *adj.* erfolglos; be ~: keinen Erfolg haben. **unsuc'cessfully** *adv.* erfolglos
un'suitable *adj.* ungeeignet
unsu'specting *adj.* nichtsahnend
un'sweetened *adj.* ungesüßt
unsympa'thetic *adj.* wenig mitfühlend; be ~: kein Mitgefühl zeigen
unthinkable [ʌn'θɪŋkəbl] *adj.* unvorstellbar
un'tidily *adv.* unordentlich
un'tidiness *n. see* untidy: Ungepflegtheit, *die;* Unaufgeräumtheit, *die*
un'tidy *adj.* ungepflegt ⟨*Äußeres, Person, Garten*⟩; unaufgeräumt ⟨*Zimmer*⟩
un'tie *v. t.,* **un'tying** aufknüpfen ⟨*Seil, Paket*⟩; aufbinden ⟨*Knoten*⟩; losbinden ⟨*Pferd, Boot*⟩
until [ən'tɪl] **1.** *prep.* bis; ~ [the] **evening** bis zum Abend; ~ **then** bis dahin; **not** ~ [**Christmas/the summer**] erst [Weihnachten/im Sommer]. **2.** *conj.* bis
un'timely *adj.* **a)** ungelegen; **b)** *(premature)* vorzeitig
un'tiring *adj.* unermüdlich
un'told *adj.* unbeschreiblich; unermeßlich ⟨*Reichtümer, Anzahl*⟩
untoward [ʌntə'wɔːd, ʌn'təʊəd] *adj.*

ungünstig; **nothing** ~ **happened** es gab keine Schwierigkeiten
untranslatable [ʌntræns'leɪtəbl] *adj.* unübersetzbar
un'true *adj.* unwahr; **that's** ~: das ist nicht wahr
un'trustworthy *adj.* unzuverlässig
un'truth *n.* Unwahrheit, *die*
¹unused [ʌn'juːzd] *adj. (new, fresh)* unbenutzt; *(not utilized)* ungenutzt
²unused [ʌn'juːst] *adj. (unaccustomed)* be ~ **to sth./doing sth.** etw. *(Akk.)* nicht gewohnt sein/nicht gewohnt sein, etw. zu tun
un'usual *adj.,* **un'usually** *adv.* ungewöhnlich
un'veil *v. t.* enthüllen; *(fig.)* vorstellen ⟨*Produkt*⟩; enthüllen ⟨*Plan*⟩
un'versed *adj.* nicht bewandert (**in** in + *Dat.*)
un'wanted *adj.* unerwünscht
un'warranted *adj.* ungerechtfertigt
un'welcome *adj.* unwillkommen
un'well *adj.* unwohl; **look** ~: nicht wohl *od.* gut aussehen; **he feels** ~ *(poorly)* er fühlt sich nicht wohl
unwieldy [ʌn'wiːldɪ] *adj.* sperrig
un'willing *adj.* widerwillig; be ~ **to do sth.** etw. nicht tun wollen. **un'willingly** *adv.* widerwillig
unwind [ʌn'waɪnd] **1.** *v. t.,* unwound [ʌn'waʊnd] abwickeln. **2.** *v. i.,* unwound **a)** sich abwickeln; **b)** *(coll.: relax)* sich entspannen
un'wise *adj.* unklug
unwitting [ʌn'wɪtɪŋ] *adj.,* **un'wittingly** *adv.* unwissentlich
un'workable *adj.* undurchführbar ⟨*Plan*⟩
un'worthy *adj.* unwürdig; be ~ **of sth.** einer Sache *(Gen.)* nicht würdig sein; be ~ **of sb./sth.** ⟨*Verhalten:*⟩ einer Person/Sache *(Gen.)* unwürdig sein
un'wrap *v. t.,* **-pp-** auswickeln
un'written *adj.* ungeschrieben
un'zip *v. t.,* **-pp-:** ~ **a dress/bag** *etc.* den Reißverschluß eines Kleides/einer Tasche *usw.* öffnen
up [ʌp] **1.** *adv.* **a)** *(to higher place)* nach oben; *(in lift)* aufwärts; **the bird flew up to the roof** der Vogel flog aufs Dach [hinauf]; **up into the air** in die Luft [hinauf]; **up here/there** hier herauf/dort hinauf; **higher/a little way up** höher/ein kurzes Stück hinauf; **come on up!** komm [hier/weiter] herauf!; **b)** *(to upstairs)* herauf/hinauf; nach oben; **c)** *(in higher place, upstairs)* oben; **up here/there** hier/da oben; **the**

next floor up ein Stockwerk höher; **d)** *(out of bed)* be up aufsein; **e)** *(in price, value, amount)* prices have gone up/are up die Preise sind gestiegen; butter is up [by ...] Butter ist [...] teurer; **f)** *(as far as)* up to sth. bis zu etw.; up to here/ there bis hier[hin]/bis dorthin; **g)** [not] be/feel up to sth. *(capable of sth.)* einer Sache *(Dat.)* [nicht] gewachsen sein/ sich einer Sache *(Dat.)* [nicht] gewachsen fühlen; [not] be/feel up to doing sth. [nicht] in der Lage sein/sich [nicht] in der Lage fühlen, etw. zu tun; **h)** be up to sth. *(doing)* etw. anstellen *(ugs.)*; it is [not] up to sb. to do sth. *(sb.'s duty)* es ist [nicht] jmds. Sache, etw. zu tun; **i)** be three points/games up mit drei Punkten/Spielen vorn liegen; **j)** walk up and down auf und ab gehen; **k)** time is up die Zeit ist abgelaufen. **2.** *prep.* herauf/hinauf; walk up the hill/road den Berg/die Straße hinaufgehen; walk up and down the platform auf dem Bahnsteig auf und ab gehen; further up the ladder/coast weiter oben auf der Leiter/an der Küste; live just up the road ein Stück weiter oben in der Straße wohnen. **3.** *adj.* *(coll.: amiss)* what's up? was ist los? *(ugs.)*; something is up irgendwas ist los *(ugs.)*. **4.** *v. t.*, **-pp-** *(coll.: increase)* erhöhen

'upbringing *n.* Erziehung, *die*

up'date *v. t.* auf den aktuellen Stand bringen

up'grade *v. t.* **a)** aufwerten *(Stellung)*; **b)** *(improve)* verbessern

upheaval [ʌp'hiːvl] *n.* Aufruhr, *der;* *(disturbance)* Durcheinander, *das*

up'hill 1. *adj.* *(fig.)* an ~ task/struggle eine mühselige Aufgabe/ein harter Kampf. **2.** *adv.* bergauf

uphold *v. t.*, **upheld** unterstützen; wahren *(Tradition)*

upholster [ʌp'həʊlstə(r)] *v. t.* polstern. **up'holsterer** *n.* Polsterer, *der/*Polsterin, *die.* **up'holstery** *n.* **a)** *(craft)* Polster[er]handwerk, *das;* **b)** *(padding)* Polsterung, *die*

'upkeep *n.* Unterhalt, *der*

'up-market *adj.* exklusiv

upon [ə'pɒn] *prep.* auf *(direction:* + *Akk.; position:* + *Dat.)*

upper ['ʌpə(r)] **1.** *compar. adj.* ober...; Ober*(grenze, -lippe, -arm usw.);* ~ circle oberer Rang; ~ class[es] Oberschicht, *die;* have/get/gain the ~ hand die Oberhand haben/gewinnen/erhalten. **2.** *n.* Oberteil, *das.* **upper 'deck**

n. Oberdeck, *das.* **'uppermost 1.** *adj.* oberst... **2.** *adv.* ganz oben

'upright 1. *adj.* aufrecht. **2.** *n.* seitliche Leiste

'uprising *n.* Aufstand, *der*

'uproar *n.* Aufruhr, *der*

up'root *v. t.* [her]ausreißen; *(Sturm:)* entwurzeln

upset 1. [ʌp'set] *v. t.*, **-tt-**, upset **a)** *(overturn)* umkippen; *(accidentally)* umstoßen *(Tasse, Milch usw.)*; **b)** *(distress)* erschüttern; *(make angry)* aufregen; don't let it ~ you nimm es nicht so schwer; **c)** *(make ill)* sth. ~s sb. etw. bekommt jmdm. nicht; **d)** durcheinanderbringen *(Plan)*. **2.** *v. i.*, **-tt-**, upset umkippen. **2.** *adj.* *(distressed)* bestürzt; *(agitated)* aufgeregt; get ~ [about/over sth.] sich [über etw. *(Akk.)*] aufregen. **4.** ['ʌpset] *n.* **a)** *(agitation)* Aufregung, *die; (annoyance)* Verärgerung, *die;* **b)** stomach ~: Magenverstimmung, *die;* **c)** *(upheaval)* Aufruhr, *der.* **up'setting** *adj.* erschütternd; *(sad)* traurig; *(annoying)* ärgerlich

'upshot *n.* Ergebnis, *das*

upside 'down 1. *adv.* verkehrt herum; turn sth. ~: etw. auf den Kopf stellen. **2.** *adj.* auf dem Kopf stehend *(Bild)*; be ~: auf dem Kopf stehen

upstairs 1. [-'-] *adv.* nach oben *(gehen, kommen)*; oben *(sein, wohnen)*. **2.** [--] *adj.* im Obergeschoß *nachgestellt*

'upstart *n.* Emporkömmling, *der*

up'stream *adv.* flußaufwärts

'uptake *n.* be quick/slow on the ~ *(coll.)* schnell begreifen/schwer von Begriff sein *(ugs.)*

uptight [-'-, '--] *adj.* *(coll.: tense)* nervös *(about wegen)*

up to 'date *adj.* be/keep ~: auf dem neusten Stand sein/bleiben; bring sth. ~: etw. auf den neusten Stand bringen. **up-to-'date** *attrib. adj.* *(current)* aktuell; *(modern)* modern

'upturn *n.* Aufschwung, *der* (in *Gen.*)

upward ['ʌpwəd] **1.** *adj.* nach oben gerichtet. **2.** *adv.* aufwärts *(sich bewegen)*; nach oben *(sehen, gehen)*. **up-wards** ['ʌpwədz] *adv.* **a)** *see* upward 2; **b)** ~ of über (+ *Akk.*)

uranium [jʊə'reɪnɪəm] *n.* Uran, *das*

Uranus ['jʊərənəs, jʊə'reɪnəs] *pr. n.* *(Astron.)* Uranus, *der*

urban ['ɜːbn] *adj.* städtisch; Stadt*(gebiet, -bevölkerung, -planung)*

urchin ['ɜːtʃɪn] *n.* Strolch, *der*

urge [ɜːdʒ] **1.** *v. t.* ~ sb. to do sth. jmdn. drängen, etw. zu tun. **2.** *n.* Trieb, *der.*

urge '**on** *v. t.* antreiben; *(encourage)* anfeuern

urgency ['ɜːdʒənsɪ] *n.* Dringlichkeit, *die*

urgent ['ɜːdʒənt] *adj.* dringend; *(to be dealt with immediately)* eilig; **be in ~ need of sth.** etw. dringend brauchen.

'**urgently** *adv.* dringend; *(immediately)* eilig

urinate ['jʊərɪneɪt] *v. i.* urinieren

urine ['jʊərɪn] *n.* Urin, *der;* Harn, *der*

urn [ɜːn] *n.* **a)** tea/coffee ~: Tee-/Kaffeemaschine, *die;* **b)** *(vessel)* Urne, *die*

Uruguay ['jʊərəgwaɪ] *pr. n.* Uruguay *(das)*

US *abbr.* United States USA

us [əs, *stressed* ʌs] *pron.* uns; **it's us** wir sind's *(ugs.)*

USA *abbr.* United States of America USA

usage ['juːzɪdʒ, 'juːsɪdʒ] *n.* **a)** Brauch, *der;* **b)** *(Ling.)* Sprachgebrauch, *der*

use 1. [juːs] *n.* **a)** Gebrauch, *der; (of dictionary, calculator, room)* Benutzung, *die; (of word, pesticide, spice)* Verwendung, *die;* [not] **be in ~:** [nicht] in Gebrauch sein; **be no longer in ~:** nicht mehr verwendet werden; **make ~ of sb./sth.** jmdn./etw. gebrauchen/ *(exploit)* ausnutzen; **make good ~ of, turn** *or* **put to good ~:** gut nutzen ‹Zeit, Talent, Geld›; **put sth. to ~:** etw. verwenden; **b)** *(usefulness)* Nutzen, *der;* **is it of [any] ~?** ist das [irgendwie] von Nutzen?; **be [of] no ~ |to sb.|** [jmdm.] nicht nützen; **it's no ~ |doing that|** es hat keinen Sinn[, das zu tun]; **c)** *(purpose)* Verwendung, *die;* **have/find a ~ for sth./sb.** für etw./jmdn. Verwendung haben/finden; **have no/not much ~ for sth./sb.** etw./jmdn. nicht/kaum brauchen. **2.** [juːz] *v. t.* **a)** benutzen; nutzen ‹Gelegenheit›; anwenden ‹Gewalt›; in Anspruch nehmen ‹Firma, Dienstleistung›; nutzen ‹Zeit, Gelegenheit›; verwenden ‹Kraftstoff, Butter, Wort›; **b)** ~**d to** ['juːst tə]: **I** ~**d to live in London** früher habe ich in London gelebt. **use up** *v. t.* aufbrauchen; verbrauchen ‹Geld, Energie›

used 1. *adj.* **a)** [juːzd] gebraucht; gestempelt ‹Briefmarke›; ~ **car** Gebrauchtwagen, *der;* **b)** [juːst] ~ **to sth.** [an] etw. *(Akk.)* gewöhnt. **2.** [juːst] *see* **use 2 b**

useful ['juːsfl] *adj.* nützlich; praktisch ‹Werkzeug›; hilfreich ‹Rat, Idee›.

'**usefulness** *n.* Nützlichkeit, *die*

'**useless** *adj.* unbrauchbar ‹Werkzeug,

Rat, Idee›; nutzlos ‹Wissen, Information, Protest, Anstrengung, Kampf›; zwecklos ‹Widerstand, Protest›

'**user** *n.* Benutzer, *der*/Benutzerin, *die.*

'**user-friendly** *adj.* benutzerfreundlich

usher ['ʌʃə(r)] **1.** *n. (in court)* Gerichtsdiener, *der; (at cinema, church)* Platzanweiser, *der.* **2.** *v. t.* führen. **usher in** *v. t.* hineinführen; *(fig.)* einläuten

usherette [ʌʃə'ret] *n.* Platzanweiserin, *die*

USSR *abbr. (Hist.)* Union of Soviet Socialist Republics UdSSR, *die*

usual ['juːʒʊəl] *adj.* üblich. **usually** ['juːʒʊəlɪ] *adv.* gewöhnlich

usurp [juː'zɜːp] *v. t.* sich *(Dat.)* widerrechtlich aneignen

utensil [juː'tensɪl] *n.* Utensil, *das;* writing ~s Schreibutensilien; kitchen ~s Küchengeräte

uterus ['juːtərəs] *n.* Gebärmutter, *die*

utility [juː'tɪlɪtɪ] *n.* **a)** Nutzen, *der;* **b)** |public| ~: öffentlicher Versorgungsbetrieb. **u'tility room** *n.* Raum, in den |größeren| Haushaltsgeräte *(z. B. Waschmaschine)* installiert sind

utilize ['juːtɪlaɪz] *v. t.* nutzen

utmost ['ʌtməʊst] **1.** *adj.* äußerst...; größt... ‹Höflichkeit, Eleganz, Einfachheit, Geschwindigkeit›. **2.** *n.* Äußerste, *das;* **do** *or* **try one's ~ to do sth.** mit allen Mitteln versuchen, etw. zu tun

¹**utter** ['ʌtə(r)] *adj.* völlig; vollkommen; ~ **fool** Vollidiot, *der (ugs.)*

²**utter** *v. t.* **a)** von sich geben ‹Schrei, Seufzer›; **b)** *(say)* sagen. **utterance** ['ʌtərəns] *n.* Worte *Pl.*

'**utterly** *adv.* völlig; vollkommen; äußerst ‹dumm, lächerlich›

'**U-turn** *n.* Wende [um 180°]; *(fig.)* Kehrtwendung, *die;* **make a ~:** wenden; 'No ~s' „Wenden verboten"

V

¹**V, v** [viː] *n.* V, v, *das*

²**V** *abbr.* volt|s| V

v. *abbr.* versus gg.

vacancy ['veɪkənsɪ] *n.* **a)** *(job)* freie

Stelle; b) *(room)* freies Zimmer; **'vacancies** „Zimmer frei"; **'no vacancies'** „belegt"

vacant ['veɪkənt] *adj.* **a)** frei; **'situations ~'** „Stellenangebote"; **b)** *(mentally)* leer

vacate [vəˈkeɪt] *v. t.* räumen

vacation [vəˈkeɪʃn] *n.* **a)** *(Brit. Univ.)* Ferien *Pl.;* **b)** *(Amer.) see* **holiday b**

vaccinate ['væksɪneɪt] *v. t.* impfen. **vaccination** [væksɪˈneɪʃn] *n.* Impfung, *die;* **have a ~:** geimpft werden

vaccine ['væksi:n] *n.* Impfstoff, *der*

vacuum ['vækjʊəm] **1.** *n.* **a)** Vakuum, *das;* **live in a ~:** im luftleeren Raum leben; **b)** *(coll.: ~ cleaner)* Sauger, *der (ugs.).* **2.** *v. t. & i.* [staub]saugen

vacuum: ~ cleaner *n.* Staubsauger, *der;* **~ flask** *n. (Brit.)* Thermosflasche, *die;* **~-packed** *adj.* vakuumverpackt

vagaries ['veɪgərɪz] *n. pl.* Launen *Pl.*

vagina [vəˈdʒaɪnə] *n.* Scheide, *die*

vagrant ['veɪgrənt] *n.* Landstreicher, *der*/Landstreicherin, *die;* *(in cities)* Stadtstreicher, *der*/Stadtstreicherin, *die*

vague [veɪg] *adj.* vage; verschwommen ⟨*Form, Umriß*⟩; *(absent-minded)* geistesabwesend; **not have the ~st idea** *or* **notion** nicht die blasseste *od.* leiseste Ahnung haben. **'vaguely** *adv.* vage; entfernt ⟨*bekannt sein, erinnern an*⟩; schwach ⟨*sich erinnern*⟩

vain [veɪn] *adj.* **a)** *(conceited)* eitel; **b)** *(useless)* leer; vergeblich ⟨*Hoffnung, Versuch*⟩; **in ~:** vergeblich. **'vainly** *adv.* vergebens

vale [veɪl] *n. (arch./poet.)* Tal, *das*

valentine ['væləntaɪn] *n.* **~ [card]** Grußkarte zum Valentinstag

valet ['væleɪ] *n.* Kammerdiener, *der*

valiant ['vælɪənt] *adj.,* **'valiantly** *adv.* tapfer

valid ['vælɪd] *adj.* **a)** *(legally acceptable)* gültig; berechtigt ⟨*Anspruch*⟩; **b)** *(justifiable)* stichhaltig ⟨*Argument*⟩; triftig ⟨*Grund*⟩; begründet ⟨*Einwand, Entschuldigung*⟩. **validate** ['vælɪdeɪt] *v. t.* rechtskräftig machen. **validity** [vəˈlɪdɪtɪ] *n.* Gültigkeit, *die*

valley ['vælɪ] *n.* Tal, *das*

valour *(Amer.:* **valor)** ['vælə(r)] *n.* Tapferkeit, *die*

valuable ['væljʊəbl] **1.** *adj.* wertvoll; **be ~ to sb.** für jmdn. wertvoll sein. **2.** *n.* **~s** Wertsachen

valuation [væljʊˈeɪʃn] *n.* Schätzung, *die*

value ['vælju:] **1.** *n.* Wert, *der;* **be of great/little/some/no ~ [to sb.]** [für jmdn.] von großem/geringem/einigem/keinerlei Nutzen sein; **know the ~ of sth.** wissen, was etw. wert ist; **something/nothing of ~:** etwas/nichts Wertvolles. **2.** *v. t.* schätzen. **value added 'tax** *n.* Mehrwertsteuer, *die*

valve [vælv] *n.* **a)** Ventil, *das;* **b)** *(Anat.)* Klappe, *die*

vampire ['væmpaɪə(r)] *n.* Vampir, *der*

van [væn] *n.* **[delivery] ~:** Lieferwagen, *der*

vandal ['vændl] *n.* Rowdy, *der.* **vandalism** ['vændəlɪzm] *n.* Wandalismus, *der.* **vandalize** ['vændəlaɪz] *v. t.* [mutwillig] beschädigen

vanilla [vəˈnɪlə] **1.** *n.* Vanille, *die.* **2.** *adj.* Vanille-

vanish ['vænɪʃ] *v. i.* verschwinden

vanity ['vænɪtɪ] *n.* Eitelkeit, *die.* **'vanity bag** *n.* Kosmetiktäschchen, *das*

vantage-point ['vɑ:ntɪdʒ pɔɪnt] *n.* Aussichtspunkt, *der*

vapour *(Brit.;* *Amer.:* **vapor)** ['veɪpə(r)] *n.* Dampf, *der*

variable ['veərɪəbl] *adj.* **a)** *(alterable)* veränderbar; **be ~:** verändert werden können; **b)** *(inconsistent)* unbeständig ⟨*Wetter, Wind, Leistung*⟩; wechselhaft ⟨*Wetter, Launen, Qualität*⟩

variance ['veərɪəns] *n.* **be at ~ [with sth.]** [mit etw.] nicht übereinstimmen

variant ['veərɪənt] *n.* Variante, *die*

variation [veərɪˈeɪʃn] *n.* **a)** *(varying)* Veränderung, *die;* *(difference)* Unterschied, *der;* **b)** *(variant)* Variante, *die* ⟨*of, on Gen.*⟩

varicose vein [værɪkəʊs 'veɪn] *n.* Krampfader, *die*

varied ['veərɪd] *adj.* unterschiedlich; abwechslungsreich ⟨*Diät, Leben*⟩

variety [vəˈraɪətɪ] *n.* **a)** *(diversity)* Vielfältigkeit, *die;* *(in diet, routine)* Abwechslung, *die;* **add** *or* **give ~ to sth.** etw. abwechslungsreicher gestalten; **b)** *(assortment)* Auswahl, *die* ⟨*of an + Dat.,* von⟩; **for a ~ of reasons** aus verschiedenen Gründen; **c)** *(Theatre)* Varieté, *das;* **d)** *(form)* Art, *die;* *(of fruit, vegetable)* Sorte, *die;* *(cultivated)* Züchtung, *die*

various ['veərɪəs] *adj.* **a)** pred. *(different)* verschieden; unterschiedlich; **b)** attrib. *(several)* verschiedene; **at ~ times** mehrere Male. **'variously** *adv.* unterschiedlich

varnish ['vɑ:nɪʃ] **1.** *n.* Lasur, *die.* **2.** *v. t.* lasieren

vary ['veərɪ] **1.** *v. t.* verändern; ändern ⟨*Bestimmungen, Programm, Methode, Route*⟩; *(add variety to)* abwechslungsreicher gestalten. **2.** *v. i. (become different)* sich ändern; ⟨*Preis, Qualität:*⟩ schwanken; *(be different)* unterschiedlich sein. **'varying** *adj.* wechselnd; *(different)* unterschiedlich

vase [vɑːz] *n.* Vase, *die*

vast [vɑːst] *adj.* **a)** *(huge)* riesig; weit ⟨*Fläche, Meer*⟩; **b)** *(coll.: great)* enorm; Riesen⟨*menge, -summe*⟩. **'vastly** *adv. (coll.)* enorm; weitaus *(besser)*; weit *(überlegen, unterlegen)*

VAT [viːeɪˈtiː, væt] *abbr.* **value added tax** MwSt.

vat [væt] *n.* Bottich, *der*

Vatican ['vætɪkən] *pr. n.* Vatikan, *der*

¹vault [vɔːlt, vɒlt] *n.* **a)** *(Archit.)* Gewölbe, *das;* **b)** *(in bank)* Tresorraum, *der;* **c)** *(tomb)* Gruft, *die*

²vault 1. *v. i.* sich schwingen. **2.** *v. t.* sich schwingen über (+ *Akk.*). **3.** *n.* Sprung, *der*

VD *n.* Geschlechtskrankheit, *die*

VDU *abbr.* **visual display unit**

veal [viːl] *n.* Kalb[fleisch], *das; attrib.* Kalbs-

veer [vɪə(r)] *v. i.* ⟨*Auto:*⟩ ausscheren. **veer a'way, veer 'off** *v. i.* ⟨*Auto:*⟩ ausscheren; ⟨*Fahrer, Straße:*⟩ abbiegen

veg [vedʒ] *n., pl. same (coll.)* Gemüse, *das*

vegetable ['vedʒɪtəbl] *n.* Gemüse, *das;* **fresh ~s** frisches Gemüse; *attrib.* Gemüse⟨*suppe, -extrakt, -garten*⟩. **'vegetable oil** *n.* Pflanzenöl, *das*

vegetarian [vedʒɪˈteərɪən] **1.** *n.* Vegetarier, *der*/Vegetarierin, *die.* **2.** *adj.* vegetarisch

vegetate ['vedʒɪteɪt] *v. i.* nur noch [dahin]vegetieren. **vegetation** [vedʒɪ-ˈteɪʃn] *n.* Vegetation, *die*

vehement ['viːəmənt] *adj.,* **'vehemently** *adv.* heftig

vehicle ['viːɪkl] *n.* **a)** Fahrzeug, *das;* **b)** *(fig.: medium)* Vehikel, *das*

veil [veɪl] **1.** *n.* Schleier, *der.* **2.** *v. t.* verschleiern

vein [veɪn] *n.* **a)** Vene, *die; (any bloodvessel)* Ader, *die;* **b)** *(fig.: mood)* Stimmung, *die;* **in a similar ~:** vergleichbarer Art

Velcro, (P) ['velkrəʊ] *n.* Klettverschluß, *der*Ⓦ

velocity [vɪˈlɒsɪtɪ] *n.* Geschwindigkeit, *die*

velvet ['velvɪt] **1.** *n.* Samt, *der.* **2.** *adj.*

aus Samt *nachgestellt;* Samt-. **'velvety** *adj.* samtig

vendetta [venˈdetə] *n.* Hetzkampagne, *die; (feud)* Fehde, *die*

vending-machine ['vendɪŋ məʃiːn] *n.* [Verkaufs]automat, *der*

vendor ['vendə(r)] *n.* Verkäufer, *der*/ Verkäuferin, *die*

veneer [vɪˈnɪə(r)] *n.* Furnier, *das*

venerable ['venərəbl] *adj.* ehrwürdig

ve'nereal disease *n. (Med.)* Geschlechtskrankheit, *die*

venetian blind [vɪˈniːʃn blaɪnd] *n.* Jalousie, *die*

Venezuela [venɪˈzweɪlə] *pr. n.* Venezuela *(das)*

vengeance ['vendʒəns] *n.* **a)** Rache, *die;* **take ~ [up]on sb. [for sth.]** sich an jmdm. [für etw.] rächen; **b)** **with a ~** *(coll.)* gewaltig *(ugs.)*

Venice ['venɪs] *pr. n.* Venedig *(das)*

venison ['venɪsn, 'venɪzn] *n.* Hirsch, *der;* Hirschfleisch, *das; (roe deer)* Reh[fleisch], *das*

venom ['venəm] *n.* Gift, *das.* **venomous** ['venəməs] *adj.* giftig

¹vent [vent] **1.** *n.* **a)** Öffnung, *die;* **b)** *(fig.)* Ventil, *das (fig.);* **give ~ to** Luft machen (+ *Dat.*). **2.** *v. t. (fig.)* Luft machen (+ *Dat.*)

²vent *n. (in garment)* Schlitz, *der*

ventilate ['ventɪleɪt] *v. t.* belüften. **ventilation** [ventɪˈleɪʃn] *n.* Belüftung, *die.* **'ventilator** ['ventɪleɪtə(r)] *n.* **a)** Ventilator, *der;* **b)** *(Med.)* Beatmungsgerät, *das*

ventriloquist [venˈtrɪləkwɪst] *n.* Bauchredner, *der*/-rednerin, *die*

venture ['ventʃə(r)] **1.** *n.* Unternehmung, *die.* **2.** *v. i.* **a)** *(dare)* wagen; **b)** *(dare to go)* sich wagen. **3.** *v. t.* wagen. **venture 'out** *v. i.* sich hinauswagen

venue ['venjuː] *n. (Sport)* [Austragungs]ort, *der; (Mus., Theatre)* [Veranstaltungs]ort, *der; (meeting-place)* Treffpunkt, *der*

Venus ['viːnəs] *pr. n. (Astron.)* Venus, *die*

veranda[h] [vəˈrændə] *n.* Veranda, *die*

verb [vɜːb] *n.* Verb, *das.* **verbal** ['vɜːbl] *adj.,* **verbally** ['vɜːbəlɪ] *adv.* **a)** *(relating to words)* sprachlich; **b)** *(orally)* mündlich

verbatim [vəˈbeɪtɪm] *adj., adv.* [wort]wörtlich

verbose [vəˈbəʊs] *adj.* weitschweifig ⟨*Roman, Autor*⟩; langatmig ⟨*Rede, Redner*⟩

verdict ['vɜːdɪkt] n. Urteil, das; ~ of guilty/not guilty Schuld-/Freispruch, der; **reach a** ~: zu einem Urteil kommen

verge [vɜːdʒ] n. **a)** Rasensaum, der; (on road) Bankette, die; **b)** (fig.) be on the ~ of war/tears am Rande des Krieges stehen/den Tränen nahe sein; **be on the** ~ **of doing sth.** kurz davor stehen, etw. zu tun. '**verge on** v.t. [an]grenzen an (+ Akk.)

verger ['vɜːdʒə(r)] n. Küster, der

verification [verɪfɪ'keɪʃn] n. **a)** (check) Überprüfung, die; **b)** (confirmation) Bestätigung, die

verify ['verɪfaɪ] v.t. **a)** (check) überprüfen; **b)** (confirm) bestätigen

vermin ['vɜːmɪn] n. Ungeziefer, das

vernacular [və'nækjʊlə(r)] n. Landessprache, die

versatile ['vɜːsətaɪl] adj. vielseitig; (having many uses) vielseitig verwendbar. **versatility** [vɜːsə'tɪlɪti] n. Vielseitigkeit, die

verse [vɜːs] n. **a)** (stanza) Strophe, die; **b)** (poetry) Lyrik, die; **write some** ~: einige Verse schreiben; **piece of** ~: Gedicht, das; **written in** ~: in Versform; **c)** (in Bible) Vers, der. **versed** [vɜːst] adj. **be [well]** ~ **in sth.** sich in etw. (Dat.) [gut] auskennen

version ['vɜːʃn] n. Version, die; (in another language) Übersetzung, die; (of vehicle, machine, tool) Modell, das

versus ['vɜːsəs] prep. gegen

vertebra ['vɜːtɪbrə] n., pl. ~e ['vɜːtɪbriː] Wirbel, der. **vertebrate** ['vɜːtɪbrət] n. Wirbeltier, das

vertical ['vɜːtɪkl] adj. senkrecht; **be** ~: senkrecht stehen. **vertically** ['vɜːtɪkəli] adv. senkrecht

vertigo ['vɜːtɪgəʊ] n. Schwindel, der

verve [vɜːv] n. Schwung, der

very ['veri] **1.** attrib. adj. **a)** (precise, exact) genau; **you're the** ~ **person I wanted to see** genau dich wollte ich sehen; **at the** ~ **moment when ...:** im selben Augenblick, als ...; **at the** ~ **centre** genau in der Mitte; **the** ~ **thing** genau das Richtige; **b)** (extreme) ganz; **at the** ~ **back/front** ganz hinten/vorn; **at the** ~ **end/beginning** ganz am Ende/Anfang; **from the** ~ **beginning** von Anfang an; **only a** ~ **little** nur ein ganz kleines bißchen; **c)** (mere) bloß ⟨Gedanke⟩; **d)** (absolute) absolut ⟨Minimum, Maximum⟩; **the** ~ **most I can offer is ...:** ich kann allerhöchstens .. anbieten; for **the** ~ **last time** zum allerletzten Mal;

e) emphat. before their ~ eyes vor ihren Augen. **2.** adv. **a)** (extremely) sehr; **it's** ~ **near** es ist ganz in der Nähe; **probably** höchstwahrscheinlich; **not** ~ **much** nicht sehr; ~ **little** [nur] sehr wenig ⟨verstehen, essen⟩; **thank you** [~,] ~ **much** [vielen,] vielen Dank; **b)** (absolutely) aller⟨best..., -letzt..., -leichtest...⟩; **at the** ~ **latest** allerspätestens; **c)** (precisely) **the** ~ **same one** genau der-/die-/dasselbe

vessel ['vesl] n. **a)** (receptacle) Gefäß, das; |drinking-|~: Trinkgefäß, das; **b)** (Naut.) Schiff, das

vest [vest] **1.** n. **a)** (Brit.) Unterhemd, das; **b)** (Amer.: waistcoat) Weste, die. **2.** v.t. ~ **sb. with sth.**, ~ **sth. in sb.** jmdm. etw. verleihen. **vested** adj. **have a** ~ **interest in sth.** ein persönliches Interesse an etw. (Dat.) haben

vestige ['vestɪdʒ] n. Spur, die; **not a** ~ **of truth** kein Fünkchen Wahrheit

vestment ['vestmənt] n. [Priester]gewand, das

vestry ['vestri] n. Sakristei, die

vet [vet] n. **1.** Tierarzt, der/-ärztin, die. **2.** v.t., **-tt-** überprüfen

veteran ['vetərən] n. Veteran, der/Veteranin, die. **veteran 'car** n. (Brit.) Veteran, der

veterinarian [vetərɪ'neərɪən] n. (Amer.) Tierarzt, der/-ärztin, die

veterinary ['vetərɪnəri] adj. tiermedizinisch. **veterinary 'surgeon** n. (Brit.) Tierarzt, der/-ärztin, die

veto ['viːtəʊ] **1.** n., pl. ~**es** Veto, das. **2.** v.t. sein Veto einlegen gegen

vex [veks] v.t. (ver]ärgern; (cause to worry) beunruhigen; **be ~ed with sb.** sich über jmdn. ärgern. **vexation** [vek'seɪʃn] n. Verärgerung, die. **vexed** [vekst] adj. **a)** verärgert; **b)** ~ **question** vieldiskutierte Frage

VHF abbr. Very High Frequency UKW

via ['vaɪə] prep. über (+ Akk.) ⟨Ort, Sender, Telefon⟩; durch ⟨Eingang, Schornstein, Person⟩; per ⟨Post⟩

viability [vaɪə'bɪlɪti] n. (feasibility) Realisierbarkeit, die

viable ['vaɪəbl] adj. (feasible) realisierbar

viaduct ['vaɪədʌkt] n. Viadukt, das od. der

vibrant ['vaɪbrənt] adj. lebensprühend ⟨Atmosphäre⟩; lebhaft ⟨Farbe⟩

vibrate [vaɪ'breɪt] **1.** v.i. vibrieren; (under strong impact) beben. **2.** v.t. vibrieren lassen. **vibration** [vaɪ'breɪʃn] n. Vibrieren/Beben, das

vicar ['vɪkə(r)] *n.* Pfarrer, *der.* **vicarage** ['vɪkərɪdʒ] *n.* Pfarrhaus, *das*
vicarious [vɪ'keərɪəs] *adj.* nachempfunden
¹vice [vaɪs] *n.* Laster, *das*
²vice *n. (Brit.: tool)* Schraubstock, *der*
vice: ~'**chairman** *n.* stellvertretender Vorsitzender; ~'**president** *n.* Vizepräsident, *der/-*präsidentin, *die*
vice versa [vaɪsɪ 'vɜ:sə] *adv.* umgekehrt
vicinity [vɪ'sɪnɪtɪ] *n.* Umgebung, *die;* **in the** ~ |of a place] in der Nähe [eines Ortes]
vicious ['vɪʃəs] *adj.* a) *(malicious)* böse; bösartig ⟨*Tier*⟩; b) *(violent)* brutal. **vicious 'circle** *n.* Teufelskreis, *der*
viciously *adv.* a) *(maliciously)* boshaft; b) *(violently)* brutal
victim ['vɪktɪm] *n.* Opfer, *das; (of sarcasm, abuse)* Zielscheibe, *die (fig.).* **victimization** [vɪktɪmaɪ'zeɪʃn] *n.* Schikanierung, *die.* **victimize** ['vɪktɪmaɪz] *v. t.* schikanieren
victor ['vɪktə(r)] *n.* Sieger, *der/*Siegerin, *die*
victorious [vɪk'tɔ:rɪəs] *adj.* siegreich
victory ['vɪktərɪ] *n.* Sieg, *der* (**over** über + *Akk.*); *attrib.* Sieges-
video ['vɪdɪəʊ] **1.** *adj.* Video-. **2.** *n., pl.* ~**s** (~ *recorder)* Videorecorder, *der;* (~*tape,* ~ *recording)* Video, *das (ugs.).* **3.** *v. t. see* **videotape 2**
video: ~ **camera** *n.* Videokamera, *die;* ~ **cas'sette** *n.* Videokassette, *die;* ~ **game** *n.* Videospiel, *das;* ~ '**nasty** *n.* Horrorvideo, *das;* ~ re**corder** *n.* Videorecorder, *der;* ~ **recording** *n.* Videoaufnahme, *die;* ~**tape 1.** *n.* Videoband, *das;* **2.** *v. t.* [auf Videoband *(Akk.)*] aufnehmen
vie [vaɪ] *v. i.,* vying ['vaɪɪŋ] ~ [with sb.] for sth. [mit jmdm.] um etw. wetteifern
Vienna [vɪ'enə] **1.** *pr. n.* Wien *(das).* **2.** *attrib. adj.* Wiener. **Viennese** [vɪə'ni:z] **1.** *adj.* Wiener. **2.** *n., pl. same* Wiener, *der/*Wienerin, *die*
Vietnam [vɪet'næm] *pr. n.* Vietnam *(das).* **Vietnamese** [vɪetnə'mi:z] **1.** *adj.* vietnamesisch. **2.** *n., pl. same* a) *(person)* Vietnamese, *der/*Vietnamesin, *die;* b) *(language)* Vietnamesisch, *das*
view [vju:] **1.** *n.* a) *(range of vision)* Sicht, *die;* **be out of/in** ~: nicht zu sehen/zu sehen sein; b) *(what is seen)* Aussicht, *die;* c) *(picture)* Ansicht, *die;* d) *(opinion)* Ansicht, *die;* **what is your** ~ **or are your** ~**s on this?** was meinst

du dazu?; **hold** *or* **take the** ~ **that ...:** der Ansicht sein, daß ...; **in my** ~: meiner Ansicht nach; **e) be on** ~: besichtigt werden können; **in** ~ **of sth.** *(fig.)* angesichts einer Sache; **with a** ~ **to doing sth.** in der Absicht, etw. zu tun. **2.** *v. t.* a) *(look at)* sich *(Dat.)* ansehen; b) *(consider)* betrachten; c) *(inspect)* besichtigen. **3.** *v. i. (Telev.)* fernsehen.
viewer *n.* a) *(Telev.)* [Fernseh]zuschauer, *der/-*zuschauerin, *die;* b) *(for slides)* Diabetrachter, *der*
view: ~**finder** *n.* Sucher, *der;* ~**point** *n.* Standpunkt, *der*
vigil ['vɪdʒɪl] *n.* Wachen, *das;* **keep** ~: wachen
vigilance ['vɪdʒɪləns] *n.* Wachsamkeit, *die*
vigilant ['vɪdʒɪlənt] *adj.* wachsam
vigor *(Amer.) see* **vigour**
vigorous ['vɪgərəs] *adj.* kräftig; heftig ⟨*Attacke, Protest*⟩; energisch ⟨*Versuch, Anstrengung, Leugnen, Maßnahme*⟩. **vigorously** *adv.* heftig; kräftig ⟨*schrubben, drücken*⟩
vigour ['vɪgə(r)] *n. (Brit.) (of person)* Vitalität, *die; (of body)* Kraft, *die; (of protest, attack)* Heftigkeit, *die*
vile [vaɪl] *adj.* gemein ⟨*Verleumdung*⟩; vulgär ⟨*Sprache*⟩; *(repulsive)* widerwärtig; *(coll.: very unpleasant)* scheußlich *(ugs.)*
villa ['vɪlə] *n.* a) |holiday] ~: Ferienhaus, *das;* b) |country] ~: Landhaus, *das*
village ['vɪlɪdʒ] *n.* Dorf, *das; attrib.* Dorf-. **villager** *n.* Dorfbewohner, *der/-*bewohnerin, *die*
villain ['vɪlən] *n.* a) Verbrecher, *der;* b) *(Theatre)* Bösewicht, *der.* **villainous** ['vɪlənəs] *adj.* gemein
vindicate ['vɪndɪkeɪt] *v. t.* a) *(justify)* rechtfertigen; b) *(clear)* rehabilitieren. **vindication** [vɪndɪ'keɪʃn] *n.* a) *(justification)* Rechtfertigung, *die;* b) *(clearing)* Rehabilitierung, *die*
vindictive [vɪn'dɪktɪv] *adj.* nachtragend
vine [vaɪn] *n.* Weinrebe, *die*
vinegar ['vɪnɪgə(r)] *n.* Essig, *der*
vineyard ['vɪnjɑ:d, 'vɪnjəd] *n.* Weinberg, *der*
vintage ['vɪntɪdʒ] **1.** *n.* Jahrgang, *der.* **2.** *adj.* erlesen ⟨*Wein*⟩. **vintage 'car** *n. (Brit.)* Oldtimer, *der*
vinyl ['vaɪnɪl] *n.* Vinyl, *das*
viola [vɪ'əʊlə] *n.* Bratsche, *die*
violate ['vaɪəleɪt] *v. t.* a) verletzen; brechen ⟨*Vertrag, Versprechen, Gesetz*⟩;

b) *(profane, rape)* schänden. **violation** [vaɪə'leɪʃn] *n. see* violate: Verletzung, *die;* Bruch, *der;* Schändung, *die*

violence ['vaɪələns] *n.* a) *(force)* Heftigkeit, *die;* (of blow) Wucht, *die;* b) *(brutality)* Gewalt, *die;* (at public event) Gewalttätigkeiten; **resort to** *or* **use ~:** Gewalt anwenden

violent ['vaɪələnt] *adj.* gewalttätig; *(fig.)* heftig; wuchtig *(Schlag, Stoß)*; Gewalt*(verbrecher, -tat)*. **'violently** *adv.* brutal; *(fig.)* heftig

violet ['vaɪələt] **1.** *n.* a) Veilchen, *das;* b) *(colour)* Violett, *das.* **2.** *adj.* violett

violin [vaɪə'lɪn] *n.* Violine, *die;* Geige, *die.* **vio'linist** *n.* Geiger, *der/*Geigerin, *die*

VIP [viːaɪ'piː] *n.* Prominente, *der/die;* **the ~s** die Prominenz

viper ['vaɪpə(r)] *n.* Viper, *die*

virgin ['vɜːdʒɪn] **1.** *n.* a) Jungfrau, *die;* b) **the [Blessed] V~ [Mary]** die [Heilige] Jungfrau [Maria]. **2.** *adj. (unspoiled)* unberührt. **virginity** [və'dʒɪnɪtɪ] *n.* Unschuld, *die*

Virgo ['vɜːgəʊ] *n., pl.* **~s** die Jungfrau

virile ['vɪraɪl] *adj.* männlich. **virility** [vɪ'rɪlɪtɪ] *n.* Männlichkeit, *die*

virtual ['vɜːtjʊəl] *adj.* a **~ ...:** so gut wie ein/eine ...; **the traffic came to a ~ standstill** der Verkehr kam praktisch zum Stillstand *(ugs.).* **'virtually** *adv.* so gut wie; praktisch *(ugs.)*

virtue ['vɜːtjuː] *n.* a) *(moral excellence)* Tugend, *die;* b) *(advantage)* Vorteil, *der;* c) **by ~ of** auf Grund (+ *Gen.*)

virtuoso [vɜːtjʊ'əʊzəʊ] *n., pl.* **virtuosi** [vɜːtjʊ'əʊziː] *or* **~s** Virtuose, *der/*Virtuosin, *die*

virtuous ['vɜːtjʊəs] *adj.* rechtschaffen *(Person);* tugendhaft *(Leben)*

virulent ['vɪrʊlənt] *adj.* a) *(Med.)* virulent; starkwirkend *(Gift);* b) *(fig.)* heftig; scharf *(Angriff)*

virus ['vaɪərəs] *n.* Virus, *das*

visa ['viːzə] *n.* Visum, *das*

vis-à-vis [viːzɑː'viː] *prep. (in relation to)* bezüglich (+ *Gen.*)

viscount ['vaɪkaʊnt] *n.* Viscount, *der*

viscous ['vɪskəs] *adj.* dickflüssig

visibility [vɪzɪ'bɪlɪtɪ] *n.* a) Sichtbarkeit, *die;* b) *(range of vision)* Sicht, *die; (Meteorol.)* Sichtweite, *die*

visible ['vɪzɪbl] *adj.* sichtbar. **'visibly** *adv.* sichtlich

vision ['vɪʒn] *n.* a) *(sight)* Sehkraft, *die;* b) *(dream)* Vision, *die;* c) *usu. pl. (imaginings)* Phantasien, *die;* d) *(insight, foresight)* Weitblick, *der*

visit ['vɪzɪt] **1.** *v.t.* besuchen; aufsuchen *(Arzt).* **2.** *v.i.* einen Besuch/Besuche machen. **3.** *n.* Besuch, *der;* **pay** *or* **make a ~ to sb.,** pay sb. a ~: jmdm. einen Besuch abstatten *(geh.)*

'visiting: ~ card *n.* Visitenkarte, *die;* **~ hours** *n. pl.* Besuchszeiten

visitor ['vɪzɪtə(r)] *n.* Besucher, *der/*Besucherin, *die; (to hotel)* Gast, *der;* **have ~s/a ~:** Besuch haben

visual ['vɪʒʊəl, 'vɪzjʊəl] *adj.* visuell; optisch *(Eindruck, Darstellung).* **visual 'aids** *n. pl.* Anschauungsmaterial, *das.* **visual dis'play unit** *n.* Bildschirmgerät, *das*

visualize ['vɪzjʊəlaɪz, 'vɪʒʊəlaɪz] *v.t.* a) *(imagine)* sich *(Dat.)* vorstellen; b) *(envisage)* voraussehen

'visually *adv.* bildlich

vital ['vaɪtl] *adj.* a) *(essential to life)* lebenswichtig; b) *(essential)* unbedingt notwendig; c) *(crucial)* entscheidend (to für); **it is ~ that you ...:** es ist von entscheidender Bedeutung, daß Sie ... **vitality** [vaɪ'tælɪtɪ] *n.* Vitalität, *die.* **'vitally** *adv.* ~ **important** von allergrößter Wichtigkeit; *(crucial)* von entscheidender Bedeutung

vitamin ['vɪtəmɪn, 'vaɪtəmɪn] *n.* Vitamin, *das*

vivacious [vɪ'veɪʃəs] *adj.* lebhaft. **vivacity** [vɪ'væsɪtɪ] *n.* Lebhaftigkeit, *die*

vivid ['vɪvɪd] *adj.* lebhaft *(Farbe, Erinnerung);* lebendig *(Schilderung).* **'vividly** *adv.* lebendig *(beschreiben);* **remember sth. ~:** sich lebhaft an etw. *(Akk.)* erinnern

vixen ['vɪksn] *n.* Füchsin, *die*

vocabulary [və'kæbjʊlərɪ] *n.* a) *(list)* Vokabelverzeichnis, *das;* **learn ~:** Vokabeln lernen; b) *(range of language)* Wortschatz, *der*

vocal ['vəʊkl] *adj.* a) *(concerned with voice)* stimmlich; b) lautstark *(Minderheit, Protest).* **vocal cords** *n. pl.* Stimmbänder

vocalist ['vəʊkəlɪst] *n.* Sänger, *der/*Sängerin, *die*

vocation [və'keɪʃn] *n.* Berufung, *die.* **vocational** [və'keɪʃənl] *adj.* berufsbezogen. **vocational 'guidance** *n.* Berufsberatung, *die.* **vocational 'training** *n.* berufliche Bildung

vociferous [və'sɪfərəs] *adj.* laut; lautstark *(Forderung, Protest)*

vodka ['vɒdkə] *n.* Wodka, *der*

vogue [vəʊg] *n.* Mode, *die;* **be in/come into ~:** in Mode sein/kommen

voice [vɔɪs] **1.** *n.* Stimme, *die;* **in a**

firm/loud/soft ~: mit fester/lauter/ sanfter Stimme. **2.** *v.t.* zum Ausdruck bringen

void [vɔɪd] **1.** *adj.* a) *(empty)* leer; b) *(invalid)* ungültig; **c)** ~ **of** ohne [jeden/ jedes/jede]. **2.** *n.* Nichts, *das*

volatile ['vɒlətaɪl] *adj.* a) *(Chem.)* flüchtig; b) *(fig.)* impulsiv; brisant ⟨*Lage*⟩

volcanic [vɒl'kænɪk] *adj.* vulkanisch

volcano [vɒl'keɪnəʊ] *n., pl.* ~**es** Vulkan, *der*

volition [və'lɪʃn] *n.* Wille, *der;* **of one's own** ~: aus eigenem Willen

volley ['vɒlɪ] *n.* a) *(of missiles)* Salve, *die;* **a** ~ **of arrows** ein Hagel von Pfeilen; b) *(Tennis)* Volley, *der.* **'volleyball** *n.* Volleyball, *der*

volt [vəʊlt] *n.* Volt, *das.* **voltage** ['vəʊltɪdʒ] *n.* Spannung, *die*

voluble ['vɒljʊbl] *adj.* redselig

volume ['vɒlju:m] *n.* a) *(book)* Band, *der;* b) *(loudness)* Lautstärke, *die; (of voice)* Volumen, *das;* c) *(space)* Rauminhalt, *der; (amount of substance)* Teil, *der.* **'volume control** *n.* Lautstärkeregler, *der*

voluntarily ['vɒləntərɪlɪ] *adv.,* **voluntary** ['vɒləntərɪ] *adj.* freiwillig

volunteer [vɒlən'tɪə(r)] **1.** *n.* Freiwillige, *der/die.* **2.** *v.t.* anbieten ⟨*Hilfe, Dienste*⟩; herausrücken mit ⟨*Informationen*⟩. **3.** *v.i.* sich [freiwillig] melden; ~ **to do** or ~ **for the shopping** sich zum Einkaufen bereiterklären

voluptuous [və'lʌptjʊəs] *adj.* üppig

vomit ['vɒmɪt] **1.** *v.t.* erbrechen. **2.** *v.i.* sich übergeben. **3.** *n.* Erbrochene, *das*

voracious [və'reɪʃəs] *adj.* gefräßig ⟨*Person*⟩; unbändig ⟨*Appetit*⟩

vote [vəʊt] **1.** *n.* a) *(individual ~)* Stimme, *die;* b) *(act of voting)* Abstimmung, *die;* **take a** ~ **on sth.** über etw. *(Akk.)* abstimmen; **c)** *(right to ~)* Stimmrecht, *das.* **2.** *v.i.* abstimmen; *(in election)* wählen; ~ **for/against** stimmen für/gegen; ~ **to do sth.** beschließen, etw. zu tun; ~ **Labour/Conservative** *etc.* Labour/die Konservativen *usw.* wählen. **3.** *v.t.* ~ **sb. Chairman/President** *etc.* jmdn. zum Vorsitzenden/Präsidenten *usw.* wählen. **'voter** *n.* Wähler, *der/*Wählerin, *die*

vouch [vaʊtʃ] **1.** *v.t.* ~ **that...:** sich dafür verbürgen, daß ... **2.** *v.i.* ~ **for sb./ sth.** sich für jmdn./etw. verbürgen

'voucher *n.* Gutschein, *der*

vow [vaʊ] **1.** *n.* Gelöbnis, *das; (Relig.)* Gelübde, *das.* **2.** *v.t.* geloben

vowel ['vaʊəl] *n.* Vokal, *der*

voyage ['vɔɪɪdʒ] **1.** *n.* Reise, *die; (sea* ~*)* Seereise, *die;* **outward/homeward** ~**, ~ out/home** Hin-/Rückreise, *die;* **a** ~ **to the moon** ein Mondflug. **2.** *v.i.* *(literary)* reisen

vulgar ['vʌlgə(r)] *adj.* vulgär; ordinär ⟨*Person, Benehmen, Witz*⟩. **vulgarity** [vʌl'gærɪtɪ] *n.* Vulgarität, *die*

vulnerable ['vʌlnərəbl] *adj.* a) *(exposed to danger)* angreifbar; **be** ~ **to sth.** für etw. anfällig sein; **be** ~ **to attack/in a** ~ **position** leicht angreifbar sein; b) *(without protection)* schutzlos

vulture ['vʌltʃə(r)] *n.* Geier, *der*

vying *see* **vie**

W

¹W, w ['dʌblju:] *n.* W, w, *das*

²W *abbr.* **watt[s]** W

W. *abbr.* a) **west** W.; b) **western** w.

wad [wɒd] *n.* a) Knäuel, *das; (smaller)* Pfropfen, *der;* b) *(of papers)* Bündel, *das.* **'wadding** *n.* Futter, *das*

waddle ['wɒdl] **1.** *v.i.* watscheln. **2.** *n.* watschelnder Gang

wade [weɪd] *v.i.* waten. **'wade through** *v.t. (fig. coll.)* durchackern *(ugs.)* ⟨*Buch*⟩

wafer ['weɪfə(r)] *n.* Waffel, *die.* **'wafer-thin** *adj.* hauchdünn

¹waffle ['wɒfl] *n. (Gastr.)* Waffel, *die*

²waffle *(Brit. coll.: talk)* **1.** *v.i.* schwafeln *(ugs.)*. **2.** *n.* Geschwafel, *das (ugs.)*

waft [wɒft, wɑ:ft] **1.** *v.t.* weben. **2.** *v.i.* ziehen

wag [wæg] **1.** *v.t.,* -**gg-** ⟨*Hund:*⟩ wedeln mit ⟨*Schwanz*⟩; ~ **one's finger at sb.** jmdm. mit dem Finger drohen. **2.** *v.i.,* -**gg-** ⟨*Schwanz:*⟩ wedeln

wage [weɪdʒ] **1.** *n. in sing.* or *pl.* Lohn, *der.* **2.** *v.t.* führen. **'wage increase** *n.* Lohnerhöhung, *die.* **'wage packet** *n.* Lohntüte, *die*

wager ['weɪdʒə(r)] *(dated/formal)* **1.** *n.* Wette, *die;* **lay a** ~ **on sth.** auf etw. *(Akk.)* wetten. **2.** *v.t. & i.* wetten

waggle ['wægl] *(coll.)* **1.** *v.t.* ~ **its tail**

⟨*Hund.:*⟩ mit dem Schwanz wedeln. 2. *v. i.* hin und her schlagen

waggon *(Brit.)*, **wagon** ['wægən] *n.* Wagen, *der*

wail [weɪl] 1. *v. i.* klagen *(geh.)* (for um); ⟨*Kind.:*⟩ heulen. 2. *n.* klagender Schrei; ~s Geheul, *das*

waist [weɪst] *n.* Taille, *die;* tight round the ~: eng in der Taille. **waistcoat** ['weɪskəʊt] *n. (Brit.)* Weste, *die.* **'waistline** *n.* Taille, *die;* be bad for the ~: schlecht für die schlanke Linie sein

wait [weɪt] 1. *v. i.* a) warten; ~ [for] an hour eine Stunde warten; ~ a moment Moment mal; keep sb. ~ing, make sb. ~: jmdn. warten lassen; b) ~ at table servieren. 2. *v. t. (await)* warten auf (+ *Akk.*); ~ one's turn warten, bis man drankommt. 3. *n.* a) after a long/ short ~: nach langer/kurzer Wartezeit; b) lie in ~ for sb./sth. jmdm./einer Sache auflauern. **wait be'hind** *v. i.* noch hier-/dableiben. **'wait for** *v. t.* warten auf (+ *Akk.*); ~ for sb. to do sth. darauf warten, daß jmd. etw. tut; ~ for the rain to stop warten, bis der Regen aufhört. **'wait on** *v. t. (serve)* bedienen. **wait 'up** *v. i.* aufbleiben (for wegen)

'waiter *n.* Kellner, *der;* ~! Herr Ober! **'waiting:** ~-list *n.* Warteliste, *die;* ~-room *n.* Wartezimmer, *das; (Railw.)* Warteraum, *der*

'waitress ['weɪtrɪs] *n.* Servorerin, *die;* ~! Fräulein! *(veralt.)*

waive [weɪv] *v. t.* verzichten auf (+ *Akk.*)

¹wake [weɪk] 1. *v. i.,* woke [wəʊk], woken ['wəʊkn] aufwachen. 2. *v. t.,* woke, woken wecken. 3. *n. (by corpse)* Totenwache, *die.* **wake 'up** 1. *v. i.* aufwachen; ~ up to sth. *(fig.: realize)* etw. erkennen. 2. *v. t.* a) wecken; b) *(fig.: enliven)* wachrütteln

²wake *n.* Kielwasser, *das;* in the ~ of sth. *(fig.)* im Gefolge von etw.

waken ['weɪkn] 1. *v. t.* wecken. 2. *v. i.* aufwachen

Wales [weɪlz] *pr. n.* Wales *(das)*

walk [wɔ:k] 1. *v. i.* a) laufen; *(not run)* gehen; *(not drive)* zu Fuß gehen; learn to ~: laufen lernen; b) *(exercise)* gehen. 2. *v. t.* a) *(lead)* führen; ausführen ⟨*Hund.*⟩; b) *(accompany)* bringen. 3. *n.* a) Spaziergang, *der;* go [out] for or take or have a ~: einen Spaziergang machen; ten minutes' ~ from here zehn Minuten zu Fuß von hier;

b) *(gait)* Gang, *der;* c) *(path)* [Spazier]weg, *der.* **walk a'way** with *v. t. (coll.: win easily)* spielend leicht gewinnen. **'walk into** *v. t. (hit by accident)* laufen gegen ⟨*Pfosten, Laternenpfahl⟩;* ~ into sb. mit jmdm. zusammenstoßen; ~ into a trap in eine Falle gehen. **walk 'off** with *v. t.* sich davonmachen mit. **walk 'out** *v. i.* a) *(leave in protest)* aus Protest den Saal verlassen; b) *(go on strike)* in den Streik treten. **walk 'out of** *v. t. (leave in protest)* aus Protest verlassen. **walk 'out on** *v. t. (coll.)* verlassen

'walker *n.* Spaziergänger, *der/-*gängerin, *die; (rambler)* Wanderer, *der/* Wanderin, *die*

walkie-talkie [wɔ:kɪ'tɔ:kɪ] *n.* Walkietalkie, *das*

'walking *n.* [Spazieren]gehen, *das;* at ~ pace im Schrittempo; be within ~ distance zu Fuß zu erreichen sein

'walking: ~ holiday *n.* Wanderurlaub, *der;* ~ shoe *n.* Wanderschuh, *der;* ~-stick *n.* Spazierstock, *der*

'walk: ~-out *n.* Arbeitsniederlegung, *die;* ~-over *n. (fig.: easy victory)* Spaziergang, *der (ugs.)*

wall [wɔ:l] *n.* Wand, *die; (freestanding)* Mauer, *die;* drive sb. up the ~ *(fig. coll.)* jmdn. auf die Palme bringen *(ugs.);* go to the ~ *(fig.)* an die Wand gedrückt werden. **wall 'up** *v. t.* zumauern

wallet ['wɒlɪt] *n.* Brieftasche, *die*

'wallflower *n.* Goldlack, *der*

wallop ['wɒləp] *(coll.)* 1. *v. t.* schlagen. 2. *n.* Schlag, *der*

wallow ['wɒləʊ] *v. i.* a) sich wälzen; b) *(fig.)* schwelgen (in in + *Dat.*)

wall: ~-painting *n.* Wandgemälde, *das;* ~paper 1. *n.* Tapete, *die;* 2. *v. t.* tapezieren; ~-to-~ adj. ~-to-~ carpeting Teppichboden, *der*

walnut ['wɔ:lnʌt] *n.* Walnuß, *die*

walrus ['wɔ:lrəs] *n.* Walroß, *das*

waltz [wɔ:lts, wɒ:ls] 1. *n.* Walzer, *der.* 2. *v. i.* Walzer tanzen

wan [wɒn] *adj.* bleich

wand [wɒnd] *n.* Stab, *der*

wander ['wɒndə(r)] 1. *v. i. (go aimlessly)* umherirren; *(walk slowly)* bummeln. 2. *v. t.* wandern durch. 3. *n. (coll.)* Spaziergang, *der.* **wander a'bout** *v. i.* sich herumtreiben. **wander 'off** *v. i. (stray)* weggehen

wane [weɪn] *v. i.* abnehmen

wangle ['wæŋgl] *v. t. (coll.)* organisieren *(ugs.)*

want [wɒnt] 1. *v. t.* a) *(desire)* wollen; ~ to do sth. etw. tun wollen; I ~ it done by tonight ich will, daß es bis heute abend fertig wird; b) *(require, need)* brauchen; 'W~ed – cook" „Koch/Köchin gesucht"; you're ~ed on the phone du wirst am Telefon verlangt; the windows ~ painting die Fenster müßten gestrichen werden; you ~ to be [more] careful du solltest vorsichtig[er] sein; c) ~ed [by the police] [polizeilich] gesucht. 2. *n.* a) *(lack)* Mangel, *der* (of an + *Dat.*); for ~ of sth. aus Mangel an etw. *(Dat.)*; b) *(need)* Not, *der*; c) *(desire)* Bedürfnis, *das*. 'want for *v. t.* sb. ~s for nothing *or* doesn't ~ for anything jmdm. fehlt es an nichts

'wanting *adj.* be ~: fehlen; sb./sth. is ~ in sth. jmdm./einer Sache fehlt es an etw. *(Dat.)*; be found ~: für unzureichend befunden werden

wanton ['wɒntən] *adj.*, 'wantonly *adv.* mutwillig

war [wɔː(r)] *n.* Krieg, *der*; between the ~s zwischen den Weltkriegen; declare ~: den Krieg erklären (on *Dat.*); be at ~: sich im Krieg befinden; make ~: Krieg führen (on gegen)

warble ['wɔːbl] *v. t. & i.* trällern

ward [wɔːd] *n.* a) *(in hospital)* Station, *die*; she's in W~ 3 sie liegt auf Station 3; b) *(child)* Mündel, *das od. die*; c) *(electoral division)* Wahlbezirk, *der*. ward 'off *v. t.* abwehren

warden ['wɔːdn] *n.* a) *(of hostel)* Heimleiter, *der/*-leiterin, *die; (of youth hostel)* Herbergsvater, *der/*-mutter, *die;* b) *(supervisor)* Aufseher, *der/*Aufseherin, *die*

'warder *n. (Brit.)* Wärter, *der*

wardrobe ['wɔːdrəʊb] *n.* a) Kleiderschrank, *der;* b) *(clothes)* Garderobe, *die*

warehouse ['weəhaʊs] *n.* Lagerhaus, *das; (part of building)* Lager, *das*

wares [weəz] *n. pl.* Ware, *die*

warfare ['wɔːfeə(r)] *n.* Krieg, *der*

'warhead *n.* Sprengkopf, *der*

warily ['weərɪlɪ] *adv.* vorsichtig; *(suspiciously)* mißtrauisch

'warlike *adj.* kriegerisch

warm [wɔːm] 1. *adj.* a) warm; I am [very] ~: mir ist [sehr] warm; b) *(enthusiastic)* herzlich *(Grüße, Dank)*. 2. *v. t.* wärmen; warm machen *(Flüssigkeit)*; ~ one's hands sich *(Dat.)* die Hände wärmen. 3. *v. i.* – to sb./sth. *(come to like)* sich für jmdn./etw. er-

wärmen. warm 'up 1. *v. i.* warm werden; *⟨Sportler:⟩* sich aufwärmen. 2. *v. t.* aufwärmen *⟨Speisen⟩;* erwärmen *⟨Raum, Zimmer⟩*

warm: ~-blooded ['wɔːmblʌdɪd] *adj.* warmblütig; ~-hearted ['wɔːmhɑːtɪd] *adj.* warmherzig *⟨Person⟩*

'warmly *adv.* a) warm; b) *(fig.)* herzlich *⟨willkommen heißen, gratulieren, begrüßen, grüßen, danken⟩*

warmonger ['wɔːmʌŋə(r)] *n.* Kriegshetzer, *der/*-hetzerin, *die*

warmth [wɔːmθ] *n.* a) Wärme, *die;* b) *(fig.)* Herzlichkeit, *die*

warn [wɔːn] *v. t.* a) *(inform, give notice)* warnen (against, of, about vor + *Dat.*); ~ sb. that ...: jmdn. darauf hinweisen, daß ...; ~ sb. not to do sth. jmdn. davor warnen, etw. zu tun; b) *(admonish)* ermahnen; *(officially)* abmahnen. 'warning 1. *n.* a) *(advance notice)* Vorwarnung, *die;* b) *(lesson)* let that be a ~ to you laß dir das eine Warnung sein; c) *(caution)* Verwarnung, *die; (less official)* Warnung, *die.* 2. *adj.* Warn*⟨schild, -signal usw.⟩*

warp [wɔːp] 1. *v. i.* sich verbiegen; *⟨Holz, Schallplatte:⟩* sich verziehen. 2. *v. t.* a) verbiegen; b) *(fig.)* a ~ed sense of humour ein abartiger Humor

war: ~-path *n.* be on the ~-path *(fig.)* in Rage sein; ~plane *n.* Kampfflugzeug, *das*

warrant ['wɒrənt] 1. *n. (for sb.'s arrest)* Haftbefehl, *der; [search]* ~: Durchsuchungsbefehl, *der.* 2. *v. t.* a) *(justify)* rechtfertigen; b) *(guarantee)* garantieren. 'warranty *n.* Garantie, *die*

warrior ['wɒrɪə(r)] *n. (esp. literary)* Krieger, *der* (geh.)

Warsaw ['wɔːsɔː] 1. *pr. n.* Warschau *(das).* 2. *attrib. adj.* Warschauer

'warship *n.* Kriegsschiff, *das*

wart [wɔːt] *n.* Warze, *die*

'wartime *n.* a) Kriegszeit, *die;* in *or* during ~: im Krieg; b) *attrib.* Kriegs*⟨rationierung, -evakuierung usw.⟩*

wary ['weərɪ] *adj.* vorsichtig; *(suspicious)* mißtrauisch (of gegenüber); be ~ of sb./sth. sich vor jmdn./etw. in acht nehmen

was *see* be

wash [wɒʃ] 1. *v. t.* a) waschen; ~ oneself sich waschen; ~ one's hands/face/hair sich *(Dat.)* die Hände/das Gesicht/die Haare waschen; ~ the clothes Wäsche waschen; ~ the dishes [Geschirr] spülen; ~ the floor den Fußboden aufwischen; b) *(remove)* waschen ⟨*Fleck*⟩ (out of aus); abwaschen ⟨*Schmutz*⟩ (off von); c) *(carry along)* spülen. 2. *v. i.* a) sich waschen; b) ⟨*Stoff, Kleidungsstück:*⟩ sich waschen lassen. 3. *n.* a) give sb./sth. a [good] ~: jmdn./etw. [gründlich] waschen; b) *(laundering)* Wäsche, *die;* c) *(of ship)* Sog, *der.* **wash 'down** *v. t.* abspritzen ⟨*Auto, Deck, Hof*⟩. **wash 'off** 1. *v. t.* ~ sth. off etw. abwaschen. 2. *v. i.* abgehen; *(from fabric etc.)* herausgehen. **wash 'out** *v. t.* ausscheuern ⟨*Topf*⟩; ausspülen ⟨*Mund*⟩; ~ **dirt/marks out of clothes** Schmutz/Flecken aus Kleidern [her]auswaschen. **wash 'up** 1. *v. t. (Brit.)* ~ **the dishes up** das Geschirr spülen. 2. *v. i.* spülen

washable ['wɒʃəbl] *adj.* waschbar

'wash-basin *n.* Waschbecken, *das*

'washing *n.* Wäsche, *die;* **do the ~:** waschen

washing: ~-**machine** *n.* Waschmaschine, *die;* ~-**powder** *n.* Waschpulver, *das;* ~-**'up** *n. (Brit.)* Abwasch, *der;* **do the ~-up** spülen; ~-**'up liquid** *n.* Spülmittel, *das*

wasn't ['wɒznt] *(coll.)* = **was not;** *see* **be**

wasp *n.* Wespe, *die*

waste [weɪst] 1. *n.* a) *(useless remains)* Abfall, *der;* ⟨*kitchen ~*⟩ Küchenabfälle *Pl.;* b) *(extravagant use)* Verschwendung, *die;* **it's a ~ of time/money/energy** das ist Zeit-/Geld-/Energieverschwendung. 2. *v. t. (squander)* verschwenden; **all his efforts were ~d** all seine Mühe war umsonst; **don't ~ my time!** stehlen Sie mir nicht die Zeit! 3. *adj.* a) ~ **material** Abfall, *der;* b) **lay sth. ~:** etw. verwüsten. **waste a'way** *v. i.* immer mehr abmagern

waste: ~ **disposal** *n.* Abfallbeseitigung, *die;* ~-**disposal unit** *n.* Müllzerkleinerer, *der*

wasteful ['weɪstfl] *adj.* a) *(extravagant)* verschwenderisch; b) *(causing waste)* unwirtschaftlich

waste: ~**land** *n.* Ödland, *das;* ~ **'paper** *n.* Papierabfall, *der;* ~-**'paper basket** *n.* Papierkorb, *der*

watch [wɒtʃ] 1. *n.* a) ⟨wrist-/pocket-⟩~: [Armband-/Taschen]uhr, *die;* **keep ~:** Wache halten; **keep [a] ~ for sb./sth.** auf jmdn./etw. achten; c) *(Naut.)* Wache, *die.* 2. *v. i.* a) ~ **for sb./sth.** auf jmdn./etw. warten. 3. *v. t.* a) *(observe)* sich *(Dat.)* ansehen ⟨*Sportveranstaltung, Fernsehsendung*⟩; ~ [the] **television** *or* **TV** fernsehen; ~ **sb. do** *or*

doing sth. zusehen, wie jmd. etw. tut; **we are being ~ed** wir werden beobachtet; b) *(be careful of, look after)* achten auf (+ *Akk.*). **watch 'out** *v. i.* a) *(be careful)* aufpassen; ~ **out!** Vorsicht!; b) *(look out)* ~ **out for sb./sth.** auf jmdn./etw. achten

'watch-dog *n.* Wachhund, *der; (fig.)* [public] ~: *[Leiter/Leiterin einer] Aufsichtsbehörde*

watchful ['wɒtʃfl] *adj.* wachsam

watch: ~-**maker** *n.* Uhrmacher, *der/* Uhrmacherin, *die;* ~-**man** ['wɒtʃmən] *n., pl.* ~-**men** ['wɒtʃmən] Wachmann, *der;* ~-**strap** *n.* [Uhr]armband, *das;* ~-**tower** *n.* Wachtturm, *der*

water ['wɔːtə(r)] 1. *n.* a) Wasser, *das;* b) *in pl. (part of the sea etc.)* Gewässer *Pl.* 2. *v. t.* a) bewässern ⟨*Land*⟩; wässern ⟨*Pflanzen*⟩; ~ **the flowers** die Blumen [be]gießen; b) verwässern ⟨*Bier usw.*⟩; c) tränken ⟨*Tier*⟩. 3. *v. i.* ⟨*Augen:*⟩ tränen; **my mouth was ~ing** mir lief das Wasser im Munde zusammen. **water 'down** *v. t.* verwässern

water: ~-**butt** *n.* Regentonne, *die;* ~-**colour** *n.* a) *(paint)* Wasserfarbe, *die;* b) *(picture)* Aquarell, *das;* ~-**cress** *n.* Brunnenkresse, *die;* ~-**fall** *n.* Wasserfall, *der*

'watering-can *n.* Gießkanne, *die*

water: ~-**lily** *n.* Seerose, *die;* ~-**line** *n. (Naut.)* Wasserlinie, *die;* ~-**logged** ['wɔːtəlɒgd] *adj.* naß ⟨*Boden*⟩; aufgeweicht ⟨*Sportplatz*⟩; ~-**main** *n.* Hauptwasserleitung, *die;* ~-**mark** *n.* Wasserzeichen, *das;* ~-**melon** *n.* Wassermelone, *die;* ~ **meter** *n.* Wasseruhr, *die;* ~ **polo** *n.* Wasserball, *der;* ~-**proof** 1. *adj.* wasserdicht; wasserfest ⟨*Farbe*⟩; 2. *v. t.* wasserdicht machen; imprägnieren ⟨*Stoff*⟩; ~-**shed** *n. (fig.)* Wendepunkt, *der;* ~-**ski** 1. *n.* Wasserski, *der;* 2. *v. i.* Wasserski laufen; ~-**skiing** *n.* Wasserskilaufen, *das;* ~-**tight** *adj.* wasserdicht; ~-**tower** *n.* Wasserturm, *der;* ~-**way** *n.* Wasserstraße, *die*

watery *adj.* wäßrig

watt [wɒt] *n.* Watt, *das*

wave [weɪv] 1. *n.* a) Welle, *die;* b) *(gesture)* give sb. **a ~:** jmdm. zuwinken; **with a ~ of one's hand** mit einem Winken. 2. *v. i.* a) ⟨*Fahne, Flagge, Wimpel:*⟩ wehen; ⟨*Baum, Gras, Korn:*⟩ sich wiegen; b) *(with hand)* winken; ~ **at** *or* **to sb.** jmdm. winken. 3. *v. t.* schwenken; schwingen ⟨*Schwert*⟩; ~ **one's hand at** *or* **to sb.** jmdm. winken;

~ **goodbye to sb.** jmdm. zum Abschied zuwinken. **wave a'side** v.t. **a)** abtun ⟨Zweifel, Einwand⟩; **b)** (signal to move) ~ **sb. aside** [jmdm.] abwinken

wave: ~**band** n. Wellenbereich, der; ~**length** n. Wellenlänge, die; **be on the same** ~**length [as sb.]** (fig.) die gleiche Wellenlänge [wie jmd.] haben

waver ['weɪvə(r)] v.i. schwanken

wavy ['weɪvɪ] adj. wellig; ~ **line** Schlangenlinie, die

¹**wax** [wæks] **1.** n. **a)** Wachs, das; **b)** (in ear) Schmalz, das. **2.** v.t. wachsen

²**wax** v.i. **a)** (Mond:) zunehmen; **b)** (become) werden

wax: ~**work** n. Wachsfigur, die; ~**works** n. sing./pl. same Wachsfigurenkabinett, das

waxy adj. wachsweich

way [weɪ] **1.** n. **a)** Weg, der; **ask the** or **one's** ~: nach dem Weg fragen; **'W In/Out'** „Ein-/Ausgang"; **by** ~ **of Switzerland** über die Schweiz; **lead the** ~: vorausgehen; **go out of one's** ~: einen Umweg machen; (fig.) keine Mühe scheuen; (fig.) Art und Weise, die; **do it this** ~: mach es so; **c)** (distance) Stück, das; **it's a long** ~ **off** or **a long** ~ **from here** es ist weit weg von hier; **all the** ~: den ganzen Weg; **d)** (direction) Richtung, die; **she went this/that/the other** ~: sie ist in diese/die/die andere Richtung gegangen; **stand sth. the right/wrong** ~ **up** etw. richtig/falsch herum stellen; **e)** (respect) **in [exactly] the same** ~: [ganz] genauso; **in some** ~**s** in gewisser Hinsicht; **in one** ~: auf eine Art; **in every** ~: in jeder Hinsicht; **in a** ~: auf eine Art; **f)** (custom) Art, die; **g) get** or **have one's [own]** ~, **have it one's [own]** ~: seinen Willen kriegen; **be in sb.'s** or **the** ~: [jmdm.] im Weg sein; **make** ~ **for sth.** für etw. Platz machen; (fig.) einer Sache (Dat.) Platz machen; **in a bad** ~: schlecht; **either** ~: so oder so; **by the** ~: übrigens. **2.** adv. weit; ~ **back** (coll.) vor langer Zeit. **way'lay** v.t., forms as ¹**lay 1: a)** (ambush) überfallen; **b)** (stop for conversation) abfangen. **way-'out** adj. (coll.) verrückt

WC abbr. **water-closet** WC, das

we [wɪ, stressed wiː] pl. pron. wir

weak [wiːk] adj. **a)** schwach; (easily led) labil ⟨Charakter, Person⟩; **b)** dünn ⟨Getränk⟩

weaken ['wiːkn] **1.** v.t. schwächen; beeinträchtigen ⟨Augen⟩. **2.** v.i. ⟨Entschlossenheit, Kraft:⟩ nachlassen

weakling ['wiːklɪŋ] n. Schwächling, der

weakly adv. schwach

weakness n. Schwäche, die

wealth [welθ] n. **a)** (abundance) Fülle, die; **b)** (riches, being rich) Reichtum, der. **wealthy 1.** adj. reich. **2.** n. pl. **the** ~: die Reichen

wean [wiːn] v.t. abstillen; ~ **sb. [away] from sth.** (fig.) jmdm. etw. abgewöhnen

weapon ['wepən] n. Waffe, die

wear [weə(r)] **1.** n. **a)** ~ **[and tear]** Abnutzung, die; **b)** (clothes) Kleidung, die. **2.** v.t., wore [wɔː(r)], worn [wɔːn] **a)** (have on) tragen ⟨Schmuck, Brille, Kleidung, Perücke⟩; **I haven't a thing to** ~: ich habe überhaupt nichts anzuziehen; **b)** (rub) abtragen ⟨Kleidungsstück⟩; abnutzen ⟨Teppich⟩; **a [badly] worn tyre** ein [stark] abgefahrener Reifen. **3.** v.i., wore, worn **a)** ⟨Kleider:⟩ sich durchscheuern; ⟨Absätze:⟩ sich ablaufen; ⟨Teppich:⟩ sich abnutzen; **b)** (endure rubbing) halten; ~ **well/badly** sich gut/schlecht tragen. **wear a'way 1.** v.t. abschleifen. **2.** v.i. sich abnutzen. **wear 'down** v.t. (fig.) zermürben. **wear 'off** v.i. ⟨Schicht:⟩ abgehen; ⟨Wirkung, Schmerz:⟩ nachlassen. **wear 'out 1.** v.t. **a)** aufbrauchen; auftragen ⟨Kleidungsstück⟩; **b)** (fig.: exhaust) kaputtmachen (ugs.); **be worn out** kaputt sein (ugs.). **2.** v.i. kaputtgehen (ugs.)

wearable ['weərəbl] adj. **sth. is [not]** ~: man kann etw. [nicht] anziehen

wearily ['wɪərɪlɪ] adv. müde

weary ['wɪərɪ] **1.** adj. **a)** (tired) müde; **b) be** ~ **of sth.** einer Sache (Gen.) überdrüssig sein. **2.** v.t. **be wearied by sth.** durch etw. erschöpft sein. **3.** v.i. ~ **of sth./sb.** einer Sache/jmds. überdrüssig werden

weasel ['wiːzl] n. Wiesel, das

weather ['weðə(r)] **1.** n. Wetter, das; **what's the** ~ **like? wie** ist das Wetter?; **in all** ~**s** bei jedem Wetter; **he is feeling under the** ~ (fig.) er ist [zur Zeit] nicht ganz auf dem Posten. **2.** v.t. abwettern ⟨Sturm⟩; (fig.) durchstehen ⟨schwere Zeit⟩

weather: ~**-beaten** adj. wettergegerbt ⟨Gesicht⟩; verwittert ⟨Felsen, Gebäude⟩; ~**cock** n. Wetterhahn, der; ~ **forecast** n. Wettervorhersage, die; ~**man** n. Meteorologe, der; ~**report** n. Wetterbericht, der; ~**-vane** n. Wetterfahne, die

¹weave [wi:v] **1.** *n.* Bindung, *die.* **2.** *v.t.,* wove [wəʊv], woven ['wəʊvn] **a)** weben; flechten ⟨*Korb, Kranz*⟩; **b)** *(fig.)* einflechten ⟨*Thema usw.*⟩ (into in + *Akk.*)

²weave *v.i.* *(take intricate course)* sich schlängeln

weaver *n.* Weber, *der*/Weberin, *die*

web [web] *n.* Netz, *das;* spider's ~: Spinnennetz, *das;* **webbed feet** [webd 'fi:t] *n. pl.* Schwimmfüße

we'd [wɪd, *stressed* wi:d] **a)** = we had; **b)** = we would

Wed. *abbr.* Wednesday Mi.

wedding ['wedɪŋ] *n.* Hochzeit, *die*

wedding: ~ **anniversary** *n.* Hochzeitstag, *der;* ~ **cake** *n.* Hochzeitskuchen, *der;* ~ **day** *n.* Hochzeitstag, *der;* ~ **dress** *n.* Brautkleid, *das;* ~ **present** *n.* Hochzeitsgeschenk, *das;* ~ **ring** *n.* Ehering, *der*

wedge [wedʒ] **1.** *n.* Keil, *der.* **2.** *v.t.* verkeilen; ~ **a door/window open** eine Tür/ein Fenster festklemmen, damit sie/es offen bleibt. **'wedge-shaped** *adj.* keilförmig

wedlock ['wedlɒk] *n.* **born in/out of** ~: ehelich/unehelich geboren

Wednesday ['wenzdeɪ, 'wenzdɪ] *n.* Mittwoch, *der; see also* Friday

¹wee [wi:] *adj. (child lang./Scot.)* klein

²wee *see* wee-wee

weed [wi:d] **1.** *n.* ~|s] Unkraut, *das.* **2.** *v.t.* jäten. **weed 'out** *v.t. (fig.)* aussieben

'weed-killer *n.* Unkrautvertilgungsmittel, *das*

weedy *adj.* spillerig *(ugs.)* ⟨*Person*⟩

week [wi:k] *n.* Woche, *die;* **for several** ~s mehrere Wochen lang; **once a** ~, **every** ~: einmal in der Woche; **three times a** ~: dreimal in der Woche; **a two**-~ **visit** ein zweiwöchiger Besuch; **a** ~ **today/tomorrow** heute/morgen in einer Woche; **a** ~ **on Monday, Monday** ~: Montag in einer Woche. **'weekday** *n.* Wochentag, *der.* **weekend** [-'-, '--] *n.* Wochenende, *das;* **at the** ~: am Wochenende; **go away for the** ~: übers Wochenende wegfahren

weekly ['wi:klɪ] **1.** *adj.* wöchentlich; Wochen⟨*zeitung, -zeitschrift, -lohn*⟩. **2.** *adv.* wöchentlich. **3.** *n. (newspaper)* Wochenzeitung, *die; (magazine)* Wochenzeitschrift, *die*

weep [wi:p] *v.i. & t.,* **wept** [wept] weinen. **weeping 'willow** *n.* Trauerweide, *die*

'wee-wee *(coll.)* **1.** *n.* Pipi, *das (ugs.);*

do a ~: Pipi machen *(ugs.).* **2.** *v.i.* Pipi machen *(ugs.)*

weigh [weɪ] *v.t. & i.* wiegen. **weigh 'down** *v.t. (fig.: depress)* niederdrücken. **weigh 'up** *v.t.* abwägen

weight [weɪt] *n.* Gewicht, *das;* **what is your** ~? wieviel wiegen Sie?; **be under/over** ~: zuwenig/zuviel wiegen. **'weighting** *n.* Zulage, *die.* **'weightlessness** *n.* Schwerelosigkeit, *die*

weight: ~**lifter** *n.* Gewichtheber, *der*/-heberin, *die;* ~**lifting** *n.* Gewichtheben, *das*

weighty *adj.* **a)** *(heavy)* schwer; **b)** *(important)* gewichtig

weir [wɪə(r)] *n.* Wehr, *das*

weird [wɪəd] *adj. (coll.: odd)* bizarr

welcome ['welkəm] **1.** *int.* willkommen; ~ **home/to England!** willkommen zu Hause/in England! **2.** *n.* **a)** Willkommen, *das;* **b)** *(reception)* Empfang, *der.* **3.** *v.t.* begrüßen. **4.** *adj.* **a)** willkommen; gefällig ⟨*Anblick*⟩; **b)** *pred.* **you are** ~ **to take it** du kannst es gern nehmen; **you're** ~: gern geschehen!

weld [weld] *v.t. (join)* verschweißen; *(repair, make, attach)* schweißen (**[on]** to an + *Akk.*). **'welder** *n.* Schweißer, *der*/Schweißerin, *die*

welfare ['welfeə(r)] *n.* Wohl, *das.* **Welfare 'State** *n.* Wohlfahrtsstaat, *der.* **'welfare work** *n.* Sozialarbeit, *die*

¹well [wel] *n.* **a)** Brunnen, *der;* **b)** *see* oil well; **c)** *(stair*~*)* Treppenloch, *das*

²well **1.** *int.* ~! meine Güte!; ~, **let's forget that** na ja, lassen wir das; ~, **who was it?** nun *od.* und, wer war's?; **oh** ~|, **never mind|** na ja|, macht nichts|; ~? na? **2.** *adv.,* **better** ['betə(r)], **best** [best] gut; gründlich ⟨*trocknen, schütteln*⟩; **the business/patient is doing** ~: das Geschäft geht gut/dem Patienten geht es gut; ~ **done!** großartig!; **he is** ~ **over forty** er ist weit über vierzig; **as** ~ *(in addition)* auch; **A as** ~ **as B:** B und auch [noch] A. **3.** *adj. (in good health)* **How are you feeling now?** – **Quite** ~, **thank you** Wie fühlen Sie sich jetzt? – Ganz gut, danke; **look** ~: gut aussehen; **feel** ~: sich wohl fühlen; **he isn't [very]** ~: es geht ihm nicht [sehr] gut; **get** ~ **soon!** gute Besserung!; **make sb.** ~: jmdn. gesund machen

we'll [wɪl, *stressed* wi:l] = we will

well: ~**-behaved** *see* behave 1a; ~**-being** *n.* Wohl, *das;* ~**-bred** *adj.*

anständig; **~built** adj. ⟨Person:⟩ mit guter Figur; **be ~built** eine gute Figur haben; **~ done** adj. ⟨Cookery⟩ durchgebraten; **~-dressed** adj. gutgekleidet; **~-educated** adj. gebildet; **~heeled** adj. (coll.) gutbetucht (ugs.)

wellington ['welɪŋtən] n. ~ **[boot]** Gummistiefel, der

well: **~-known** adj. bekannt; **~made** adj. gut [gearbeitet]; **~-mannered** adj. ⟨Person:⟩ mit guten Manieren; **be ~mannered** gute Manieren haben; **~-meaning** adj. wohlmeinend; **be ~-meaning** es gut meinen; **~-meant** adj. gutgemeint; **~ off** adj. wohlhabend; **sb. is ~ off** jmdm. geht es [finanziell] gut; **~-read** ['welred] adj. belesen; **~-timed** adj. zeitlich gut gewählt; **~-to-do** adj. wohlhabend; **~-wisher** n. Sympathisant, der/Sympathisantin, die

Welsh [welʃ] 1. adj. walisisch; **sb. is ~:** jmd. ist Waliser/Waliserin. 2. n. a) (language) Walisisch, das; see also **English 2 a**; b) pl. **the ~:** die Waliser. **Welshman** ['welʃmən] n., pl. **~men** ['welʃmən] Waliser, der. **~ 'rabbit**, **~ 'rarebit** ['reəbɪt] ns. Käsetoast, der

went see go 1

wept see weep

were see be

we're [wɪə(r)] = we are

weren't (coll.) = were not; see be

west [west] 1. n. a) Westen, der; **in/to[wards]/from the ~** im/nach/von Westen; **to the ~ of** westlich von; b) usu. W~ (Geog., Polit.) Westen, der. 2. adj. westlich; West⟨küste, -wind, -grenze, -tor⟩. 3. adv. nach Westen; **~ of** westlich von

West: **~ Ber'lin** pr. n. (Hist.) West-Berlin (das); **w~bound** adj. ⟨Zug, Verkehr usw.⟩ in Richtung Westen; **~ Country** n. (Brit.) Westengland, das; **~ 'End** n. (Brit.) Westend, das

westerly ['westəlɪ] adj. westlich; ⟨Wind⟩ aus westlichen Richtungen

western ['westən] 1. adj. westlich; West⟨grenze, -hälfte, -seite⟩; **~ Germany** Westdeutschland, das. 2. n. Western, der. **Western 'Europe** pr. n. Westeuropa (das)

West: **~ 'German** (Hist.) 1. adj. westdeutsch; 2. n. Westdeutsche, der/die; **~ 'Germany** pr. n. (Hist.) Westdeutschland (das); **~ 'Indian** 1. adj. westindisch; 2. n. Westinder, der/-inderin, die; **~ 'Indies** pr. n. pl. westindische Inseln

westward[s] ['westwəd(z)] adv. westwärts

wet [wet] 1. adj. a) naß; b) (rainy) regnerisch; feucht ⟨Klima;⟩ c) frisch ⟨Farbe⟩; **'~ paint**„ „frisch gestrichen"; d) (sl.: feeble) schlapp (ugs.). 2. v. t., wet or wetted befeuchten. 3. n. a) (moisture) Feuchtigkeit, die; b) **in the ~:** im Regen. **wetness** n. Nässe, die. **'wet suit** n. Tauchanzug, der

we've [wɪv, stressed wiːv] = we have

whack [wæk] (coll.) 1. v. t. hauen (ugs.). 2. n. Schlag, der

whale [weɪl] n. a) Wal, der; b) (coll.) **we had a ~ of a [good] time** wir haben uns bombig (ugs.) amüsiert

wharf [wɔːf] n., pl. **wharves** [wɔːvz] or **~s** Kai, der

what [wɒt] 1. adj. welch...; **~ book?** welches Buch?; **~ time** um wieviel Uhr fängt es an?; **~ kind of man is he?** was für ein Mensch ist er?; **~ a fool you are!** was für ein Dummkopf du doch bist!; **~ cheek/luck!** was für eine Frechheit/ein Glück!; **I will give you ~ help I can** ich werde dir helfen, so gut ich kann. 2. adv. **~ do I care?** was kümmert's mich?; **~ does it matter?** was macht's? 3. pron. was; **~?** wie?; was? (ugs.); **~ is your name?** wie heißt du/heißen Sie?; **~ about ...?** (~ will become of ...?) was ist mit ...?; **~ about a game of chess?** wie wär's mit einer Partie Schach?; **~'s-his/-her/-its-name** wie heißt er/sie/es noch; **~ for?** wozu?; **~ is it like?** wie ist es?; **so ~?** na und?; **do ~ I tell you**, was ich dir sage

whatever [wɒt'evə(r)] 1. adj. **~ problems you have** was für Probleme Sie auch haben; **nothing ~** absolut nichts. 2. pron. **do ~ you like** mach, was du willst; **~ happens, ...:** was auch geschieht, ...; **or ~:** oder was auch immer; **~ does he want?** (coll.) was will er nur?

wheat [wiːt] n. Weizen, der

wheedle ['wiːdl] v. t. **~ sb. into doing sth.** jmdm. so lange gut zureden, bis er etw. tut; **~ sth. out of sb.** jmdm. etw. abschwatzen (ugs.)

wheel [wiːl] 1. n. a) Rad, das; **[potter's] ~:** Töpferscheibe, die; b) (steering ~) Lenkrad, das; (ship's ~) Steuerrad, das; **at or behind the ~** (of car) am Steuer. 2. v. t. (push) schieben. 3. v. i. a) (turn round) kehrtmachen; b) (circle) kreisen

wheel: **~barrow** n. Schubkarre, die;

~**chair** n. Rollstuhl, der; ~-**clamp** n. Parkkralle, die

wheeze [wi:z] v.t. schnaufen

when [wen] 1. adv. wann; **the time ~** ...: die Zeit, zu der/(with past tense) als ...; **the day ~** ...: der Tag, an dem/(with past tense) als ... 2. conj. a) (at the time that) als; (with present or future tense) wenn; ~ **reading [a newspaper]** beim Lesen [einer Zeitung]; b) (whereas) why do you go abroad ~ it's cheaper here? warum fährst du ins Ausland, wo es doch hier billiger ist? 3. pron. **by/till ~** ...?; bis wann ...?; **since ~** ...? seit wann ...?

whence [wens] adv., conj. (arch./literary) woher

whenever [wen'evə(r)] 1. adv. wann immer; **or ~**: oder wann immer; ~ **did he do it?** (coll.) wann hat er es nur getan? 2. conj. jedesmal wenn

where [weə(r)] 1. adv. a) (position) wo; ~ **shall we sit?** wohin wollen wir uns setzen?; b) (to ~) wohin. 2. conj. wo. 3. pron. **near/not far from ~ it happened** nahe der Stelle/nicht weit von der Stelle, wo es passiert ist

whereabouts 1. [weərə'baʊts] adv. (where) wo; (to where) wohin. 2. ['weərəbaʊts] n., sing. or pl. (of thing) Verbleib, der; (of person) Aufenthalt[sort], der

where: ~**as** conj. während; **he is very quiet, ~as she is an extrovert** er ist sehr ruhig, sie dagegen ist eher extravertiert; ~**by** adv. mit dem/der/denen; ~**upon** [weərə'pɒn] adv. worauf

wherever [weər'evə(r)] 1. adv. a) (position) wo immer; **sit ~ you like** setz dich, wohin du magst; **or ~**: oder wo immer; b) (direction) wohin immer; **or ~**: oder wohin immer; c) ~ **have you been?** (coll.) wo hast du bloß gesteckt? 2. conj. a) (position) überall [da], wo; ~ **possible** wo od. wenn [irgend] möglich; b) (direction) wohin auch; ~ **he went** wohin er auch ging

whet [wet] v.t., -**tt**-: a) (sharpen) wetzen; b) (fig.) anregen ⟨Appetit⟩

whether ['weðə(r)] conj. ob; **I don't know ~ to go [or not]** ich weiß nicht, ob ich gehen soll [oder nicht]

which [wɪtʃ] 1. adj. welch...; ~ **one** welcher/welche/welches; ~ **ones** welche; ~ **way** (how) wie; (in ~ direction) wohin. 2. pron. a) interrog. welcher/welche/welches; ~ **of you?** wer von euch?; b) rel. der/die/das; **of ~**: dessen/deren; **after ~**: worauf[hin]

whichever [wɪtʃ'evə(r)] 1. adj. welcher/welche/welches ... auch. 2. pron. a) welcher/welche/welches ... auch; b) (coll.) ~ **could it be?** welcher/welche/welches könnte das nur sein?

whiff [wɪf] n. (puff; fig.: trace) Hauch, der; (smell) leichter Geruch

while [waɪl] 1. n. Weile, die; [for] **a** ~: eine Weile; **a long ~**: lange; **for a little or short ~**: eine kleine Weile; **be worth sb.'s ~**: sich [für jmdn.] lohnen. 2. conj. a) während; (as long as) solange; b) (although) obgleich; c) (whereas) während. **while a'way** v.t. ~ **away the time** sich (Dat.) die Zeit vertreiben (by, with mit)

whilst [waɪlst] (Brit.) see **while** 2

whim [wɪm] n. Laune, die

whimper ['wɪmpə(r)] 1. n. ~[s] Wimmern, das; (of dog etc.) Winseln, das. 2. v.i. wimmern; ⟨Hund:⟩ winseln

whimsical ['wɪmzɪkl] adj. launenhaft; (odd, fanciful) spleenig

whine [waɪn] 1. v.i. a) heulen; ⟨Hund:⟩ jaulen; b) (complain) jammern. 2. n. a) Heulen, das; (of dog) Jaulen, das; b) (complaint) ~[s] Gejammer, das

whip [wɪp] 1. n. a) Peitsche, die; b) (Brit. Parl.) Fraktionsgeschäftsführer, der/-führerin, die. 2. v.t., -**pp**-: a) peitschen; b) (Cookery) schlagen; c) (move quickly) reißen; d) (sl.: steal) klauen (ugs.). **whip 'out** v.t. [blitzschnell] herausziehen. **whip 'up** v.t. a) (arouse) anheizen (ugs.); b) (coll.: make quickly) schnell hinzaubern ⟨Gericht, Essen⟩

whipped 'cream n. Schlagsahne, die

whirl [wɜ:l] 1. v.t. [im Kreis] herumwirbeln. 2. v.i. wirbeln. 3. n. a) Wirbeln, das; **she was or her thoughts were in a** ~ (fig.) ihr schwirrte der Kopf; b) (bustle) Trubel, der. **whirl 'round** 1. v.t. [im Kreis] herumwirbeln. 2. v.i. [im Kreis] herumwirbeln; ⟨Rad, Rotor:⟩ wirbeln

whirl: ~**pool** n. Strudel, der; (bathing pool) Whirlpool, der; ~**wind** n. Wirbelwind, der

whirr [wɜ:(r)] 1. v.i. surren. 2. n. Surren, das

whisk [wɪsk] 1. n. (Cookery) Schneebesen, der; (part of mixer) Rührbesen, der. 2. v.t. a) (Cookery) schlagen [mit dem Schnee-/Rührbesen]; b) (convey rapidly) in Windeseile bringen. **whisk a'way** v.t. a) (remove suddenly) ~ **sth. away [from sb.]**

[jmdm.] etw. [plötzlich] wegreißen; b) *(convey rapidly)* in Windeseile wegbringen

whisker ['wɪskə(r)] *n.* a) ~s *(on man's cheek)* Backenbart, *der;* b) *(of cat, mouse, rat)* Schnurrhaar, *der*

whiskey *(Amer., Ir.)*, **whisky** ['wɪskɪ] *n.* Whisky, *der; (American or Irish)* Whiskey, *der*

whisper ['wɪspə(r)] 1. *v.i.* flüstern; ~ **to sb.** jmdm. etwas zuflüstern. 2. *v.t.* flüstern; ~ **sth. to sb.** jmdm. etw. zuflüstern. 3. *n.* a) Flüstern, *das;* **in a ~, in ~s** im Flüsterton; b) *(rumour)* Gerücht, *das*

whistle ['wɪsl] 1. *v.i.* pfeifen; ~ **at sb.** *(in disapproval)* jmdn. auspfeifen. 2. *v.t.* pfeifen. 3. *n.* a) *(sound)* Pfiff, *der; (whistling)* Pfeifen, *das;* b) *(instrument)* Pfeife, *die;* **blow a/one's ~:** pfeifen

white [waɪt] 1. *adj.* weiß. 2. *n.* a) *(colour)* Weiß, *das;* b) *(of egg)* Eiweiß, *das;* c) W~ *(person)* Weiße, *der/die*

white: ~ **bread** *n.* Weißbrot, *das;* ~ '**coffee** *n. (Brit.)* Kaffee mit Milch; ~-'**collar worker** *n.* Angestellte, *der/die;* **W~ House** *pr. n. (Amer. Polit.)* the W~ House das Weiße Haus

whiten ['waɪtn] 1. *v.t.* weiß machen; weißen ⟨*Wand, Schuhe*⟩. 2. *v.i.* weiß werden

'**whiteness** *n.* Weiß, *das*

white: W~ '**Paper** *n. (Brit.)* öffentliches Diskussionspapier über Vorhaben der Regierung; ~**wash** 1. *n.* [weiße] Tünche; *(fig.)* Schönfärberei, *die;* 2. *v.t.* [weiß] tünchen; ~ '**wine** *n.* Weißwein, *der*

Whit [wɪt] '**Monday** *n.* Pfingstmontag, *der*

Whitsun ['wɪtsn] *n.* Pfingsten, *das od. Pl.;* **at** ~: zu od. an Pfingsten

whittle ['wɪtl]: ~ **a'way** *v.t.* ~ **away sb.'s rights/power** jmdm. nach und nach alle Rechte/Macht nehmen; ~ '**down** *v.t.* allmählich reduzieren ⟨*Anzahl, Gewinn*⟩; verkürzen ⟨*Liste*⟩

whiz, whizz [wɪz] 1. *v.i., -zz-* zischen. 2. *n.* Zischen, *das.* '**whiz[z]-kid** *n. (coll.)* Senkrechtstarter, *der*

who [hu, *stressed* hu:] *pron.* a) *interrog.* wer; *(coll.: whom)* wen; *(coll.: to whom)* wem; b) *rel.* der/die/das; *pl.* die; *(coll.: whom)* den/die/das; *(coll.: to whom)* dem/der/denen; **anyone/ those** ~ ...: wer ...; **everybody** ~ ...: jeder, der ...

whoa [wəʊ] *int.* brr

who'd [hʊd, *stressed* hu:d] a) = **who had;** b) = **who would**

whoever [hu:'evə(r)] *pron.* a) wer [immer]; b) *(no matter who)* wer ... auch; c) *(coll.)* ~ **could it be?** wer könnte das nur sein?

whole [həʊl] 1. *adj.* ganz; **the** ~ **lot** [of them] [sie] alle. 2. *n.* Ganze, *das;* **the** ~: das Ganze; **the** ~ **of my money/the village/London** mein ganzes Geld/das ganze Dorf/ganz London; **as a** ~: als Ganzes; **on the** ~: im großen und ganzen

whole: ~-**hearted** [həʊl'hɑ:tɪd] *adj.* herzlich ⟨*Dank[barkeit]*⟩; rückhaltlos ⟨*Unterstützung*⟩; ~**meal** *adj.* Vollkorn-; ~ **note** *n. (Amer. Mus.)* ganze Note; ~ '**number** *n.* ganze Zahl; ~**sale** 1. *adj.* a) Großhandels-; b) *(fig.: on a large scale)* massenhaft; Massen-; 2. *adv.* a) en gros; b) *(fig.: on a large scale)* massenweise; ~**saler** ['həʊlseɪlə(r)] *n.* Großhändler, *der/*-**händlerin**, *die*

wholesome ['həʊlsəm] *adj.* gesund

who'll [hʊl, *stressed* hu:l] = **who will**

wholly ['həʊllɪ] *adv.* völlig

whom [hu:m] *pron.* a) *interrog.* wen; *as indirect object* wem; b) *rel.* den/der/das; *pl.* die; *as indirect object* dem/der/dem; *pl.* denen

whooping cough ['hu:pɪŋ kɒf] *n.* Keuchhusten, *der*

whopper ['wɒpə(r)] *n. (coll.)* a) Riese, *der;* b) *(lie)* faustdicke Lüge

whopping ['wɒpɪŋ] *adj. (coll.)* riesig; Riesen- *(ugs.);* faustdick ⟨*Lüge*⟩

whore [hɔ:(r)] *n.* Hure, *die*

who's [hu:z] a) = **who is;** b) = **who has**

whose [hu:z] *pron.* a) *interrog.* wessen; ~ [**book**] **is that?** wem gehört das [Buch]?; b) *rel.* dessen/deren/dessen; *pl.* deren

who've [hʊv, *stressed* hu:v] = **who have**

why [waɪ] 1. *adv.* a) *(for what reason)* warum; *(for what purpose)* wozu; ~ **is that?** warum das?; b) *(on account of which)* **the reason** ~ **he did it** der Grund, warum er es tat. 2. *int.* ~, **certainly/of course!** aber sicher!

wick [wɪk] *n.* Docht, *der*

wicked ['wɪkɪd] *adj.* böse. '**wickedness** *n.* Bosheit, *die*

wicker ['wɪkə(r)] *n.* Korbgeflecht, *das; attrib.* Korb⟨*waren, -stuhl*⟩. '**wickerwork** *n.* a) *(material)* Korbgeflecht, *das;* b) *(articles)* Korbwaren

wicket ['wɪkɪt] *n. (Cricket)* Tor, *das*

wide [waɪd] **1.** *adj.* **a)** *(broad)* breit; groß ‹Abstand, Winkel›; **three feet ~:** drei Fuß breit; **b)** *(extensive)* weit; umfassend ‹Lektüre, Wissen, Kenntnisse›; reichhaltig ‹Auswahl, Sortiment›; **c)** *(off target)* **be ~ of sth.** etw. verfehlen. **2.** *adv.* **a)** **~ awake** hellwach; **b)** *(off target)* **shoot ~:** danebenschießen; **go ~:** das Ziel verfehlen. **wide-angle 'lens** *n.* Weitwinkelobjektiv, *das*

'widely *adv.* **a)** *(over a wide area)* weit ‹verbreitet, gestreut›; **b)** *(by many people)* weithin ‹bekannt, akzeptiert›; **a ~ held view** eine weitverbreitete Ansicht; **c)** *(greatly)* erheblich ‹sich unterscheiden›

widen ['waɪdn] **1.** *v.t.* verbreitern. **2.** *v.i.* sich verbreitern

wide: **~open** *attrib. adj.*, **~ 'open** *pred. adj.* weit geöffnet ‹Fenster, Tür›; weit aufgerissen ‹Mund, Augen›; **be ~ open** ‹Fenster, Tür:› weit offenstehen; **~spread** *adj.* weitverbreitet *präd. getrennt geschr.*

widow ['wɪdəʊ] *n.* Witwe, *die.* **widowed** ['wɪdəʊd] *adj.* verwitwet. **widower** ['wɪdəʊə(r)] *n.* Witwer, *der*

width [wɪdθ] *n.* Breite, *die*; *(of garment)* Weite, *die*

wield [wiːld] *v.t.* schwingen; *(fig.)* ausüben ‹Macht, Einfluß›

wife [waɪf] *n., pl.* **wives** [waɪvz] Frau, *die*

wig [wɪg] *n.* Perücke, *die*

wiggle ['wɪgl] *(coll.)* **1.** *v.t.* hin und her bewegen. **2.** *v.i.* wackeln

wild [waɪld] **1.** *adj.* **a)** wildlebend ‹Tier›; wildwachsend ‹Pflanze›; **b)** wild ‹Landschaft›; *(unrestrained)* wild ‹Erregung›; **run ~** ‹Pferd, Hund:› frei herumlaufen; ‹Kind:› herumtoben; **send or drive sb. ~:** jmdn. rasend vor Erregung machen; **d)** *(coll.: very keen)* **be ~ about sb./sth.** wild auf jmdn./etw. sein. **2.** *n.* **the ~[s]** die Wildnis; **see an animal in the ~:** ein Tier in freier Wildbahn sehen

wilderness ['wɪldənɪs] *n.* Wildnis, *die*; *(desert)* Wüste, *die*

wild: **~·'goose chase** *n.* *(fig.)* aussichtslose Suche; **~life** *n.* die Tier- und Pflanzenwelt; **~life park/reserve/ sanctuary** Naturpark, *der/*-reservat, *das/*-schutzgebiet, *das*

'wildly *adv.* wild; **be ~ excited about sth.** über etw. *(Akk.)* ganz aus dem Häuschen sein *(ugs.)*; **~ inaccurate** völlig ungenau

wilful ['wɪlfl] *adj.*, **wilfully** ['wɪlfəlɪ] *adv.* **a)** *(deliberate[ly])* vorsätzlich; **b)** *(obstinate[ly])* starrsinnig

¹will [wɪl] *v. aux., only in: pres.* **will**, *neg. (coll.)* **won't** [wəʊnt], *past* **would** [wʊd], *neg. (coll.)* **wouldn't** ['wʊdnt] He **won't help me.** **W~/Would you?** He will mir nicht helfen. Bist du bereit?; **the car won't start** das Auto springt nicht an; **~/would you pass the salt, please?** gibst du bitte mal das Salz rüber?/würdest du bitte mal das Salz rübergeben?; **~ you be quiet!** willst du wohl ruhig sein!; **he ~ sit there hour after hour** er pflegt dort stundenlang zu sitzen; **he '~ insist on doing it** er besteht unbedingt darauf, es zu tun; **~ you have some more cake?** möchtest *od.* willst du noch etwas Kuchen?; **the box ~ hold 5 lb. of tea** in die Kiste gehen 5 Pfund Tee; **tomorrow he ~ be in Oxford** morgen ist er in Oxford; **I promise I won't do it again** ich verspreche, ich mach's nicht noch mal; **if he tried, he would succeed** wenn er es versuchen würde, würde er es erreichen; **~ you please tidy up** würdest du bitte aufräumen?

²will [wɪl] *n.* **a)** *(faculty)* Wille, *der*; **b)** *(Law: testament)* Testament, *das*; **c)** *(desire)* **at ~:** nach Belieben; **~ to live** Lebenswille, *der*; **against one's/sb.'s ~:** gegen seinen/jmds. Willen

'willing *adj.* willig; **ready and ~:** bereit; **be ~ to do sth.** bereit sein, etw. zu tun. **'willingly** *adv.* **a)** *(with pleasure)* gern[e]; **b)** *(voluntarily)* freiwillig. **'willingness** *n.* Bereitschaft, *die*

willow ['wɪləʊ] *n.* Weide, *die*

'will-power *n.* Willenskraft, *die*

willy-nilly [wɪlɪ'nɪlɪ] *adv.* wohl oder übel ‹etw. tun müssen›

wilt [wɪlt] *v.i.* ‹Pflanze, Blumen:› welk werden, welken

wily ['waɪlɪ] *adj.* listig; gewieft ‹Person›

wimp [wɪmp] *n.* *(coll.)* Schlappschwanz, *der (ugs.)*

win [wɪn] **1.** *v.t.*, **-nn-**, **won** [wʌn] gewinnen; bekommen ‹Stipendium, Vertrag, Recht›; **~ sb. sth.** jmdm. etw. einbringen. **2.** *v.i.*, **-nn-**, **won** gewinnen. **3.** *n.* Sieg, *der*; **have a ~ :** gewinnen. **win 'over, win 'round** *v.t.* bekehren; *(to one's side)* auf seine Seite bringen; *(convince)* überzeugen. **win 'through** *v.i.* Erfolg haben

wince [wɪns] *v.i.* zusammenzucken **(at** bei)

winch [wɪntʃ] **1.** n. Winde, die. **2.** v. t. winden; ~ **up** hochwinden

¹**wind** [wɪnd] **1.** n. Wind, der; (Med.) Blähungen; **get ~ of sth.** (fig.) Wind von etw. bekommen; **be in the ~** (fig.) in der Luft liegen; **get/have the ~ up** (sl.) Manschetten (ugs.) kriegen/haben. **2.** v. t. the blow ~ed him der Schlag nahm ihm den Atem

²**wind** [waɪnd] **1.** v. i., wound [waʊnd] **a)** (curve) sich winden; (move) sich schlängeln; **b)** (coil) sich wickeln. **2.** v. t., wound **a)** (coil) wickeln; ~ sth. on [to] sth. etw. auf etw. (Akk.) [auf]wickeln; **b)** aufziehen ⟨Uhr⟩. wind 'down v. t. **a)** herunterdrehen ⟨Autofenster⟩; **b)** (fig.: reduce gradually) einschränken. wind 'up **1.** v. t. **a)** hochdrehen ⟨Autofenster⟩; **b)** (coil) aufwickeln; **c)** aufziehen ⟨Uhr⟩; **d)** (coll.: annoy deliberately) auf die Palme bringen (ugs.); **e)** beschließen ⟨Debatte⟩; **f)** (Finance, Law) auflösen. **2.** v. i. **a)** (conclude) schließen; **b)** (coll.: end up) ~ up in prison/hospital [zum Schluß] im Gefängnis/Krankenhaus landen (ugs.)

wind [wɪnd]: ~**break** n. Windschutz, der; ~-**chill factor** n. Wind-chill-Index, der (Meteor.)

winder ['waɪndə(r)] n. (of watch) Krone, die; (of clock, toy) Aufziehschraube, die

wind [wɪnd]: ~**fall** n. **a)** (fruit) ~falls Fallobst, das; **b)** (fig.) warmer Regen (ugs.); ~ **farm** n. Windpark, der; Windfarm, die; ~ **instrument** n. (Mus.) Blasinstrument, das; ~**mill** n. Windmühle, die

window ['wɪndəʊ] n. Fenster, das; (shop~) [Schau]fenster, das; **break a** ~: eine Fensterscheibe zerbrechen

window: ~-**box** n. Blumenkasten, der; ~-**cleaner** n. Fensterputzer, der/-putzerin, die; ~-**dressing** n. (fig.) Schönfärberei, die; ~-**pane** n. Fensterscheibe, die; ~-**shopping** n. Schaufensterbummeln, das; **go** ~-**shopping** einen Schaufensterbummel machen; ~-**sill** n. (inside) Fensterbank, die; (outside) Fenstersims, der od. das

wind [wɪnd]: ~**pipe** n. (Anat.) Luftröhre, die; ~**screen**, (Amer.) ~**shield** ns. (Motor Veh.) Windschutzscheibe, die; ~**screen**/~**shield wiper** Scheibenwischer, der; ~**screen**/~**shield washer** Scheibenwaschanlage, die; ~**surfer** n. Windsurfer, der;

~**surfing** n. Windsurfen, das; ~**swept** adj. windgepeitscht; vom Wind zerzaust ⟨Person, Haare⟩; ~-**tunnel** n. Windkanal, der

windward ['wɪndwəd] adj. ~ **side** Windseite, die

windy adj. windig

wine [waɪn] n. Wein, der

wine: ~-**bar** n. Weinstube, die; ~-**cellar** n. [Wein]keller, das; ~-**glass** n. Weinglas, das; ~-**list** n. Weinkarte, die; ~-**tasting** n. ['waɪnteɪstɪŋ] n. Weinprobe, die

wing [wɪŋ] n. **a)** (Ornith., Archit., Sport) Flügel, der; **b)** (Aeronaut.) Tragfläche, die; **c)** (Brit. Motor. Veh.) Kotflügel, der

wink [wɪŋk] **1.** v. i. **a)** blinzeln; (as signal) zwinkern; ~ **at sb.** jmdm. zuzwinkern; **b)** (flash) blinken. **2.** n. **a)** Blinzeln, das; (signal) Zwinkern, das; **give sb. a** ~: jmdm. zuzwinkern; **b)** not sleep a ~: kein Auge zutun

winner n. Sieger, der/Siegerin, die; (of competition or prize) Gewinner, der/Gewinnerin, die

winning adj. **a)** attrib. siegreich; ~ **number** Gewinnzahl, die; **b)** (charming) einnehmend; gewinnend ⟨Lächeln⟩. **winning-post** n. Zielpfosten, der. **winnings** n. pl. Gewinn, der

winter ['wɪntə(r)] n. Winter, der; **in** [the] ~: im Winter. **winter 'sports** n. pl. Wintersport, der

wintry ['wɪntrɪ] adj. winterlich; ~ **shower** Schneegestöber, das

wipe [waɪp] **1.** v. t. **a)** abwischen; [auf]wischen ⟨Fußboden⟩; (dry) abtrocknen; ~ **one's mouth/eyes/nose** sich (Dat.) den Mund/die Tränen/die Nase abwischen; ~ **one's feet/shoes** [sich (Dat.)] die Füße/Schuhe abtreten; **b)** (get rid of) [ab]wischen; ~ **one's/sb.'s tears** sich/jmdm. die Tränen abwischen. **2.** n. **give sth. a** ~: etw. abwischen. wipe 'down v. t. abwischen; (dry) abtrocknen. wipe 'off v. t. **a)** (remove) wegwischen; löschen ⟨Bandaufnahme⟩; **b)** (pay off) zurückzahlen ⟨Schulden⟩. wipe 'out v. t. **a)** (remove) wegwischen; (erase) auslöschen; **b)** (cancel) tilgen; zunichte machen ⟨Vorteil, Gewinn usw.⟩; **c)** (destroy) ausrotten ⟨Rasse, Tierart, Feinde⟩; ausmerzen ⟨Seuche, Korruption⟩. wipe 'up v. t. **a)** aufwischen; **b)** (dry) abtrocknen

wiper n. (Motor Veh.) Wischer, der

wire ['waɪə(r)] 1. n. a) Draht, der; b) (Electr., Teleph.) Leitung, die; c) (coll.: telegram) Telegramm, das. 2. v. t. a) (fasten) ~ sth. together etw. mit Draht verbinden; b) (Electr.) ~ sth. to sth. etw. an etw. (Akk.) anschließen; ~ a house in einem Haus die Stromleitungen legen; c) (coll.: telegraph) ~ sb. jmdm. or an jmdn. telegrafieren.

'wireless n. (Brit.) Radio, das. **wire 'netting** n. Maschendraht, der

wiring ['waɪərɪŋ] n. [elektrische] Leitungen

wisdom ['wɪzdəm] n. a) Weisheit, die; b) (prudence) Klugheit, die. **'wisdom tooth** n. Weisheitszahn, der

wise [waɪz] adj. a) weise; vernünftig ⟨Meinung⟩; b) (prudent) klug; c) be none the ~r kein bißchen klüger als vorher sein. **'wisely** adv. weise; (prudently) klug

wish [wɪʃ] 1. v. t. wünschen; I ~ I was or were rich ich wollte, ich wäre reich; I ~ to go ich möchte gehen; ~ sb. luck/success etc. jmdm. Glück/Erfolg usw. wünschen; ~ sb. well jmdm. alles Gute wünschen. 2. v. i. wünschen; ~ for sth. sich ⟨Dat.⟩ etw. wünschen. 3. n. Wunsch, der; make a ~: sich ⟨Dat.⟩ etwas wünschen; get or have one's ~: seinen Wunsch erfüllt bekommen. **wishful thinking** [wɪʃfl 'θɪŋkɪŋ] n. Wunschdenken, das

wishy-washy ['wɪʃɪwɒʃɪ] adj. labberig (ugs.); (fig.) lasch

wisp [wɪsp] n. (of straw) Büschel, das; ~ of hair Haarsträhne, die; ~ of cloud/smoke Wolkenfetzen, der/ Rauchfahne, die

wistful ['wɪstfl] adj., **'wistfully** adv. wehmütig

wit [wɪt] n. a) (humour) Witz, der; b) (intelligence) Geist, der; be at one's ~s or ~s' end sich ⟨Dat.⟩ keinen Rat mehr wissen; be frightened or scared out of one's ~s Todesangst haben; have/keep one's ~s about one auf Draht (ugs.) sein/nicht den Kopf verlieren; c) (person) geistreicher Mensch

witch [wɪtʃ] n. Hexe, die

witch: ~craft n. Hexerei, die; ~-doctor n. Medizinmann, der; ~-hunt n. Hexenjagd, die (for auf + Akk.)

with [wɪð] prep. mit; put sth. ~ sth. etw. zu etw. stellen/legen; have nothing to write ~: nichts zum Schreiben haben; I'm not '~ you (coll.) ich kom-

me nicht mit; tremble ~ fear vor Angst zittern; I have no money ~ me ich habe kein Geld bei mir od. bei mir; sleep ~ the window open bei offenem Fenster schlafen

with'draw 1. v. t., forms as draw 1 zurückziehen; abziehen ⟨Truppen⟩; ~ sth. from an account etw. von einem Konto abheben. 2. v. i., forms as draw 1 sich zurückziehen. **withdrawal** [wɪð'drɔːəl] n. a) Zurücknahme, die; (of troops) Abzug, der; (of money) Abhebung, die; b) (from drugs) Entzug, der; ~ symptoms Entzugserscheinungen. **with'drawn** adj. (unsociable) verschlossen

wither ['wɪðə(r)] 1. v. t. verdorren lassen. 2. v. i. [ver]welken. **wither a'way** v. i. dahinwelken (geh.)

with'hold v. t., forms as ²hold: ~ sth. from sb. jmdm. etw. vorenthalten

within [wɪ'ðɪn] prep. innerhalb; stay/ be ~ the law den Boden des Gesetzes nicht verlassen; ~ eight miles of sth. acht Meilen im Umkreis von etw.

without [wɪ'ðaʊt] prep. ohne; ~ doing sth. ohne etw. zu tun; ~ his knowing ohne daß er davon weiß/wußte

with'stand v. t., withstood [wɪð'stʊd] standhalten (+ Dat.); aushalten ⟨Beanspruchung, hohe Temperaturen⟩

witness ['wɪtnɪs] 1. n. Zeuge, der/ Zeugin, die (of, to Gen.). 2. v. t. a) (see) ~ sth. Zeuge/Zeugin einer Sache (Gen.) sein; b) bestätigen ⟨Unterschrift⟩. **'witness-box** (Brit.), **'witness-stand** (Amer.) ns. Zeugenstand, der

witticism ['wɪtɪsɪzm] n. Witzelei, die **wittingly** ['wɪtɪŋlɪ] adv. wissentlich **witty** ['wɪtɪ] adj. witzig; geistreich ⟨Person⟩

wives pl. of **wife**

wizard ['wɪzəd] n. Zauberer, der. **wizardry** ['wɪzədrɪ] n. Zauberei, die

wizened ['wɪznd] adj. runz[e]lig

wobble ['wɒbl] v. i. wackeln. **wobbly** ['wɒblɪ] adj. wack[e]lig

woe [wəʊ] n. (arch./literary/joc.) ~[s] Jammer, der; ~ betide you! wehe dir!

woke, woken see ¹wake 1, 2

wolf [wʊlf] 1. n., pl. wolves [wʊlvz] Wolf, der. 2. v. t. ~ [down] verschlingen

woman ['wʊmən] n., pl. women ['wɪmɪn] Frau, die; ~ doctor Ärztin, die; ~ friend Freundin, die. **womanizer** ['wʊmənaɪzə(r)] n. Schürzenjäger, der.

'womanly adj. fraulich

womb [wu:m] *n.* Gebärmutter, *die*

women *pl. of* **woman**

women: ~**folk** *n. pl.* Frauen; **W~'s 'Lib** (*coll.*), **W~'s Libe'ration** *ns.* die Frauenbewegung; ~**'s 'rights** *n. pl.* die Rechte der Frau

won *see* **win 1, 2**

wonder ['wʌndə(r)] **1.** *n.* **a)** (*thing*) Wunder, *das;* **b)** (*feeling*) Staunen, *das.* **2.** *adj.* Wunder-. **3.** *v. i.* sich wundern; staunen (**at** über + *Akk.*). **4.** *v. t.* sich fragen; **I ~ what the time is** wie viel Uhr mag es wohl sein?; **I ~ whether I might open the window** dürfte ich vielleicht das Fenster öffnen?

wonderful ['wʌndəfl] *adj.,* **wonderfully** ['wʌndəfəlɪ] *adv.* wunderbar

won't [wəʊnt] (*coll.*) = **will not;** *see* ¹**will**

woo [wu:] *v. t.* **a)** (*literary: court*) ~ **sb.** um jmdn. werben (*geh.*); **b)** umwerben ⟨*Kunden, Wähler*⟩

wood [wʊd] *n.* **a)** Holz, *das;* **touch ~** (*Brit.*), **knock on ~** (*Amer.*) unberufen!; **b)** (*trees*) Wald, *der.* **'woodcut** *n.* Holzschnitt, *der.* **'woodcutter** *n.* Holzfäller, *der*

'wooded *adj.* bewaldet

'wooden *adj.* **a)** hölzern; Holz-; **b)** (*fig.: stiff*) hölzern

wood: ~**land** ['wʊdlənd] *n.* Waldland, *das;* ~**pecker** *n.* Specht, *der;* ~**wind** *n.* the ~**wind** [**section**] die Holzbläser; ~**wind instrument** Holzblasinstrument, *das;* ~**work** *n.* **a)** (*craft*) Arbeiten mit Holz; **b)** (*things*) Holzarbeit[en]; ~**worm** *n.* Holzwurm; **it's got ~worm** da ist der Holzwurm drin (*ugs.*)

'woody *adj.* **a)** (*wooded*) waldreich; **b)** (*consisting of wood*) holzig

wool [wʊl] *n.* Wolle, *die; attrib.* Woll-.

woollen (*Amer.:* **woolen**) ['wʊlən] **1.** *adj.* wollen. **2.** *n.* ~**s** Wollsachen *Pl.*

'woolly *adj.* **a)** wollig; Woll⟨*pullover, -mütze*⟩; **b)** (*confused*) verschwommen

word [wɜ:d] **1.** *n.* Wort, *das;* ~**s** (*of song or actor*) Text, *der;* **in other ~s** mit anderen Worten; ~ **for ~:** Wort für Wort; **too funny** *etc.* **for ~s** unsagbar komisch *usw.;* **have ~s** einen Wortwechsel haben; **have a ~** [**with sb.**] **about sth.** [mit jmdm.] über etw. (*Akk.*) sprechen; **could I have a ~** [**with you?**] kann ich dich mal sprechen?; **say a few ~s** ein paar Worte sprechen; **keep/break one's ~:** sein Wort halten/brechen; **by ~ of mouth** durch mündliche Mitteilung; **send ~ that ...:** Nach-

richt geben, daß ... **2.** *v. t.* formulieren. **'wording** *n.* Formulierung, *die*

word: ~ **order** *n.* Wortstellung, *die;* ~ **processing** *n.* Textverarbeitung, *die;* ~ **processor** *n.* Textverarbeitungssystem, *das*

wore *see* **wear 2, 3**

work [wɜ:k] **1.** *n.* **a)** Arbeit, *die;* **at ~** (*engaged in ~ing*) bei der Arbeit; (*fig.: operating*) am Werk; (*at job*) auf der Arbeit; **out of ~:** arbeitslos; **be in ~:** eine Stelle haben; **b)** ~**s** *sing. or pl.* (*factory*) Werk, *das;* **c)** ~**s** *pl.* (*~ing parts*) Werk, *das;* (*operations*) Arbeiten; **d)** (*thing made or achieved*) Werk, *das;* **a ~ of art/literature** ein Kunstwerk/literarisches Werk. **2.** *v. i.* **a)** arbeiten; **b)** (*function effectively*) funktionieren; **make the television ~:** den Fernsehapparat in Ordnung bringen; **c)** (*have an effect*) wirken (**on** auf + *Akk.*); **d)** ~ **loose** sich lockern. **3.** *v. t.* **a)** bedienen ⟨*Maschine*⟩; betätigen ⟨*Bremse*⟩; **b)** (*get labour from*) arbeiten lassen; **c)** ausbeuten ⟨*Steinbruch, Grube*⟩; **d)** (*cause to go gradually*) führen; ~ **one's way up/into sth.** sich hocharbeiten/in etw. hineinarbeiten. **work 'off** *v. t.* **a)** (*get rid of*) loswerden; abreagieren ⟨*Wut*⟩; **b)** abarbeiten ⟨*Schuld*⟩. **work on** *v. t.* **a)** ~ **on sth.** an etw. (*Dat.*) arbeiten; **b)** (*try to persuade*) ~ **on sb.** jmdn. bearbeiten (*ugs.*). **work 'out 1.** *v. t.* **a)** (*calculate*) ausrechnen; **b)** (*solve*) lösen; **c)** (*devise*) ausarbeiten. **2.** *v. i.* **a)** sth. ~**s out at £2** etw. ergibt 2 Pfund; **b)** (*have result*) laufen; **things ~ed out** [**well**] **in the end** es ist schließlich doch alles gutgegangen. **work 'up 1.** *v. t.* **a)** (*excite*) aufpeitschen ⟨*Menge*⟩; **get ~ed up** sich aufregen. **2.** *v. i.* ~ **up to sth.** ⟨*Musik:*⟩ sich zu etw. steigern; ⟨*Geschichte, Film:*⟩ auf etw. (*Akk.*) zusteuern

workable ['wɜ:kəbl] *adj.* (*feasible*) durchführbar

workaholic [wɜ:kə'hɒlɪk] *n.* (*coll.*) arbeitswütiger Mensch

'worker *n.* Arbeiter, *der/*Arbeiterin, *die*

'workforce *n.* Belegschaft, *die*

'working *adj.* **a)** (*in work*) werktätig; **b)** ~ **model** funktionsfähiges Modell

working: ~ **class** *n.* Arbeiterklasse, *die;* ~**-class** *adj.* der Arbeiterklasse *nachgestellt;* **sb. is ~-class** jmd. gehört zur Arbeiterklasse; ~ **clothes** *n. pl.* Arbeitskleidung, *die;* ~ **'day** *n.* **a)** (*portion of day*) Arbeitstag, *der;* **b)**

(day when work is done) Werktag, *der;* ~ '**order** *n.* be in |good| ~ order betriebsbereit sein; *(Auto:)* fahrbereit sein

workman ['wɜ:kmən] *n., pl.* ~**men** ['wɜ:kmən] Arbeiter, *der.* '**workmanship** *n. (quality)* Kunstfertigkeit, *die*

work: ~**-out** *n.* [Fitneß]training, *das;* ~**shop** *n.* a) *(room)* Werkstatt; *die,* b) *(building)* Werk, *das*

world [wɜ:ld] *n.* a) Welt, *die;* in the ~: auf der Welt; **the tallest building in the** ~: das höchste Gebäude der Welt; **all over the** ~: in *od.* auf der ganzen Welt; b) *(vast amount)* it will do him a *or* the ~ of good es wird ihm unendlich guttun; a ~ of difference ein weiter Unterschied. **world** '**champion** *n.* Weltmeister, *der/*-meisterin, *die.* **world-**'**famous** *adj.* weltberühmt

'**worldly** *adj.* weltlich; weltlich eingestellt *(Person)*

world-wide 1. ['--] *adj.* weltweit *nicht präd.* 2. [-'-] *adv.* weltweit

worm [wɜ:m] 1. *n.* Wurm, *der.* 2. *v.t.* a) ~ **oneself into sb.'s favour** sich in jmds. Gunst *(Akk.)* schleichen; b) ~ **sth. out of sb.** etw. aus jmdm. herausbringen *(ugs.)*. '**worm-eaten** *adj.* wurmstichig

worn *see* **wear** 2, 3

'**worn-out** *adj.* a) abgetragen *(Kleidungsstück);* abgenutzt *(Teppich);* b) erschöpft *(Person)*

worried ['wʌrɪd] *adj.* besorgt

worry ['wʌrɪ] 1. *v.t.* a) beunruhigen; b) *(bother)* stören. 2. *v.i.* sich *(Dat.)* Sorgen machen. '**worrying** *adj.* a) *(causing worry)* beunruhigend; b) *(full of worry)* sorgenvoll *(Zeit, Woche)*

worse [wɜ:s] 1. *adj.* schlechter; schlimmer *(Schmerz, Krankheit, Benehmen)*. 2. *adv.* schlechter/ schlimmer. 3. *n.* Schlimmeres. **worsen** ['wɜ:sn] 1. *v.t.* verschlechtern. 2. *v.i.* sich verschlechtern

worship ['wɜ:ʃɪp] 1. *v.t., (Brit.)* -pp-: a) anbeten; b) *(idolize)* abgöttisch verehren. 2. *v.i., (Brit.)* -pp- am Gottesdienst teilnehmen. 3. *n.* a) Anbetung, *die; (service)* Gottesdienst, *der;* b) **Your/His W~:** ≈ Euer/seine Ehren. '**worshipper** *(Amer.:* **worshiper)** *n.* Gottesdienstbesucher, *der/*-besucherin, *die*

worst [wɜ:st] 1. *adj.* schlechtest...; schlimmst... *(Schmerz, Krankheit, Benehmen)*. 2. *adv.* am schlechtesten/

schlimmsten. 3. *n.* a) **the** ~: der/die/ das Schlimmste; **get** *or* **have the** ~ **of it** *(suffer the most)* am meisten zu leiden haben; **if the** ~ **comes to the** ~: wenn es zum Schlimmsten kommt; b) *(poorest in quality)* Schlechteste, *der/ die/das*

worsted ['wʊstɪd] *n.* Kammgarn, *das*

worth [wɜ:θ] 1. *adj.* wert; it's ~ £80 es ist 80 Pfund wert; **is it** ~ **hearing/the effort?** ist es hörenswert/der Mühe wert?; **is it** ~ **doing?** lohnt es sich?; **it isn't** ~ **it** es lohnt sich nicht. 2. *n.* Wert, *der;* **ten pounds'** ~ **of petrol** Benzin für zehn Pfund. '**worthless** *adj.* a) *(valueless)* wertlos; b) *(having bad qualities)* nichtswürdig. '**worthwhile** *adj.* lohnend

worthy ['wɜ:ðɪ] *adj.* würdig

wouldn't ['wʊdnt] *(coll.)* = would not; *see* ¹**will**

¹**wound** [wu:nd] 1. *n.* Wunde, *die.* 2. *v.t.* verwunden; *(fig.)* verletzen

²**wound** *see* ²**wind**

wove, woven *see* ¹**weave** 2

wrangle ['ræŋgl] 1. *v.i.* [sich] streiten. 2. *n.* Streit, *der*

wrap [ræp] 1. *v.t., -pp-* a) *(enclose)* einwickeln; *(fig.)* hüllen; ~**ped** abgepackt *(Brot usw.);* b) ~ **sth. [a]round sth.** etw. um etw. wickeln. 2. *n.* Umschlag[e]tuch, *das.* **wrap 'up** *v.t.* a) *see* **wrap** 1; b) *(conclude)* abschließen; c) **be** ~**ped up in one's work** in seine Arbeit völlig versunken sein

'**wrapper** *n.* a) sweet-/toffee-~-[s] Bonbonpapier, *das;* b) *(of book)* Schutzumschlag, *der*

'**wrapping** *n.* Verpackung, *die.* '**wrapping-paper** *n. (strong)* Packpapier, *das; (decorative)* Geschenkpapier, *das*

wrath [rɒθ] *n.* Zorn, *der*

wreak [ri:k] *v.t.* a) *(cause)* anrichten; b) ~ **vengeance on sb.** an jmdm. Rache nehmen

wreath [ri:θ] *n., pl.* **wreaths** [ri:ðz, ri:θs] Kranz, *der*

wreck [rek] 1. *n.* a) Wrack, *das;* b) *(destruction of ship)* Schiffbruch, *der.* 2. *v.t.* a) *(destroy)* ruinieren; zu Schrott fahren *(Auto);* **be** ~**ed** *(shipwrecked)* Schiffbruch erleiden; b) *(fig.: ruin)* zerstören; ruinieren *(Gesundheit, Urlaub)*. **wreckage** ['rekɪdʒ] *n.* Wrackteile *Pl.; (fig.)* Trümmer *Pl.*

wren [ren] *n.* Zaunkönig, *der*

wrench [rentʃ] 1. *n.* a) *(tool)* verstellbarer Schraubenschlüssel; b) *(violent* *twist)* Verrenkung, *die;* c) *(fig.)* **be a great ~ |for sb.|** sehr schmerzhaft für jmdn. sein. 2. *v. t.* a) reißen; **~ sth. from sb.** jmdm. etw. entreißen; b) **~ one's ankle** sich *(Dat.)* den Knöchel verrenken

wrest [rest] *v. t.* **~ sth. from sb.** jmdm. etw. entreißen

wrestle ['resl] *v. i.* ringen. **wrestler** ['reslə(r)] *n.* Ringer, *der*/Ringerin, *die.* **wrestling** ['reslɪŋ] *n.* Ringen, *das*

wretch [retʃ] *n.* Kreatur, *die*

wretched ['retʃɪd] *adj.* a) *(miserable)* unglücklich; b) *(coll.: damned)* elend; c) *(very bad)* erbärmlich

wriggle ['rɪgl] 1. *v. i.* a) sich winden; ⟨*Fisch:*⟩ zappeln; b) *(move)* sich schlängeln. 2. *v. t.* **~ one's way** sich schlängeln. 3. *n.* Windung, *die*

wring [rɪŋ] *v. t.,* **wrung** [rʌŋ] a) wringen; **~ out** auswringen; b) **~ sb.'s hand** jmdm. fest die Hand drücken; **~ the neck of an animal** einem Tier den Hals umdrehen; c) **~ sth. from** *or* **out of sb.** *(fig.)* jmdm. etw. abpressen. **wringing 'wet** *adj.* tropfnaß

wrinkle ['rɪŋkl] 1. *n.* Falte, *die; (in paper)* Knick, *der.* 2. *v. t.* falten. 3. *v. i.* sich in Falten legen. **wrinkled** ['rɪŋkld], **wrinkly** ['rɪŋklɪ] *adjs.* runz[e]lig

wrist [rɪst] *n.* Handgelenk, *das.* **'wrist-watch** *n.* Armbanduhr, *die*

writ [rɪt] *n. (Law)* Verfügung, *die*

write [raɪt] 1. *v. i.,* **wrote** [rəʊt], **written** ['rɪtn] schreiben; **~ to sb./a firm** jmdm./an eine Firma schreiben. 2. *v. t.,* **wrote, written** schreiben; ausschreiben ⟨*Scheck*⟩; **the written language** die Schriftsprache; **written applications** schriftliche Anträge. **write 'back** *v. i.* zurückschreiben. **write 'down** *v. t.* aufschreiben. **write 'off** 1. *v. t.* a) abschreiben ⟨*Schulden, Verlust*⟩; b) *(destroy)* zu Schrott fahren. 2. *v. i.* **~ off for sth.** etw. [schriftlich] anfordern

'write-off *n.* Totalschaden, *der*

writer ['raɪtə(r)] *n.* Schriftsteller, *der*/Schriftstellerin, *die; (of letter, article)* Verfasser, *der*/Verfasserin, *die*

'write-up *n. (by critic)* Kritik, *die*

writhe [raɪð] *v. i.* sich winden

writing ['raɪtɪŋ] *n.* a) Schreiben, *das;* **put sth. in ~:** etw. schriftlich machen *(ugs.);* b) *(handwriting, something written)* Schrift, *die.* **'writing paper** *n.* Schreibpapier, *das*

written *see* write

wrong [rɒŋ] 1. *adj.* a) *(morally bad)* unrecht *(geh.); (unfair)* ungerecht; b) *(mistaken)* falsch; **be ~** ⟨*Person:*⟩ sich irren; **the clock is ~:** die Uhr geht falsch; c) *(not suitable)* falsch; **give the ~ answer** eine falsche Antwort geben; **|the| ~ way round** verkehrt herum; d) *(out of order)* nicht in Ordnung; **what's ~?** ist etwas nicht in Ordnung? 2. *adv.* falsch. 3. *n.* Unrecht, *das;* **do ~:** unrecht tun. 4. *v. t.* **~ sb.** jmdn. ungerecht behandeln. **wrongful** ['rɒŋfl] *adj.* a) *(unfair)* unrecht *(geh.);* b) *(unlawful)* rechtswidrig. **'wrongfully** *adv.* a) *(unfairly)* unrecht *(geh.)* ⟨*handeln*⟩; zu Unrecht ⟨*beschuldigen*⟩; b) *(unlawfully)* rechtswidrig. **wrongly** *adv.* a) falsch; b) *(mistakenly)* zu Unrecht; c) *see* wrongfully a

wrote *see* write

wrought iron [rɔːt 'aɪən] *n.* Schmiedeeisen, *das; attrib.* schmiedeeisern

wrung *see* wring

wry [raɪ] *adj.,* **~er** *or* **wrier** ['raɪə(r)], **~est** *or* **wriest** ['raɪɪst] ironisch ⟨*Blick*⟩; fein ⟨*Humor, Witz*⟩

X

X, x [eks] *n.* X, x, *das*

Xerox, (P), xerox ['zɪərɒks] 1. *n. (copy)* Xerokopie, *die.* 2. **xerox** *v. t.* xerokopieren

Xmas ['krɪsməs, 'eksməs] *n. (coll.)* Weihnachten, *das*

'X-ray 1. *n. (picture)* Röntgenaufnahme, *die.* 2. *v. t.* röntgen; durchleuchten ⟨*Gepäck*⟩

Y

Y, y [waɪ] *n.* Y, y, *das*

yacht [jɒt] *n.* a) *(for racing)* Segeljacht, *die;* b) *(for pleasure)* Jacht, *die.* **'yachting** *n.* Segeln, *das*

Yank [jæŋk] *n. (Brit. coll.: American)* Ami, *der (ugs.)*

yank *(coll.)* 1. *v. t.* reißen an (+ *Dat.*). 2. *n.* Reißen, *das*

yap [jæp] *v. i.*, -**pp**- kläffen

'yard [jɑːd] *n. (measure)* Yard, *das*

²yard *n.* a) *(attached to building)* Hof, *der;* in the ~: auf dem Hof; b) *(for storage)* Lager, *das*

'yardstick *n. (fig.)* Maßstab, *der*

yarn [jɑːn] *n.* a) *(thread)* Garn, *das;* b) *(coll.: story)* Geschichte, *die*

yawn [jɔːn] 1. *n.* Gähnen, *das.* 2. *v. i.* gähnen. **'yawning** *adj.* gähnend

year [jɪə(r)] *n.* a) Jahr, *das;* for [many] ~s jahrelang; once a ~, every ~: einmal im Jahr; a ten-~-old ein Zehnjähriger/eine Zehnjährige; b) *(group of students, vintage of wine)* Jahrgang, *der.* **'yearbook** *n.* Jahrbuch, *das.* **'yearly** 1. *adj.* jährlich; Einjahres-⟨*abonnement*⟩. 2. *adv.* jährlich

yearn [jɜːn] *v. i.* ~ for or after sth./for sb. sich nach etw./jmdm. sehnen; ~ to do sth. sich danach sehnen, etw. zu tun. **'yearning** *n.* Sehnsucht, *die*

yeast [jiːst] *n.* Hefe, *die*

yell [jel] 1. *n.* gellender Schrei. 2. *v. t. & i.* [gellend] schreien

yellow ['jeləʊ] 1. *adj.* gelb. 2. *n.* Gelb, *das.* **'yellowish** *adj.* gelblich

yelp [jelp] 1. *v. i.* jaulen. 2. *n.* Jaulen, *das*

yen [jen] *n. (coll.: longing)* sb. has a ~ to do sth. es drängt jmdn. danach, etw. zu tun

yes [jes] 1. *adv.* ja; *(in contradiction)* doch. 2. *n., pl.* ~es Ja, *das*

yesterday ['jestədeɪ, 'jestədɪ] 1. *n.* gestern; the day before ~: vorgestern; ~'s paper die gestrige Zeitung. 2. *adv.* gestern; the day before ~: vorgestern

yet [jet] 1. *adv.* a) *(still)* noch; ~ again noch einmal; b) *(hitherto)* bisher; his best ~: sein bisher bestes; c) *neg.* not [just] ~: [jetzt] noch nicht; d) *(before all is over)* doch noch; he could win ~: er könnte noch gewinnen; e) *with compar. (even)* noch; f) *(nevertheless)* doch. 2. *conj.* doch

yew [juː] *n.* ~[-tree] Eibe, *die*

Yiddish ['jɪdɪʃ] 1. *adj.* jiddisch. 2. *n.* Jiddisch, *das; see also* English 2 a

yield [jiːld] 1. *v. t. (give)* bringen; hervorbringen ⟨*Ernte*⟩; abwerfen ⟨*Gewinn*⟩. 2. *v. i.* a) sich unterwerfen; b) *(give right of way)* Vorfahrt gewähren. 3. *n.* Ertrag, *der*

yodel ['jəʊdl] *v. i. & t., (Brit.)* -ll- jodeln

yoga ['jəʊgə] *n.* Joga, *der od. das*

yoghurt, yogurt ['jɒgət] *n.* Joghurt, *der od. das*

yoke [jəʊk] *n.* Joch, *das*

yokel ['jəʊkl] *n.* [Bauern]tölpel, *der*

yolk [jəʊk] *n.* Dotter, *der;* Eigelb, *das*

yonder ['jɒndə(r)] *(literary)* 1. *adj.* ~ tree jener Baum dort *(geh.).* 2. *adv.* dort drüben

you [ju, *stressed* juː] *pron.* a) *sing./pl.* du/ihr; *(polite) sing. or pl.* Sie; *as direct object* dich/euch/Sie; *as indirect object* dir/euch/Ihnen; *refl.* dich/dir/euch; *(polite)* sich; it was ~: du warst/ihr wart/Sie waren es; b) *(one)* man

you'd [jʊd, *stressed* juːd] a) = you had; b) = you would

you'll [jʊl, *stressed* juːl] a) = you will; b) = you shall

young [jʌŋ] 1. *adj.*, ~er ['jʌŋgə(r)], ~est ['jʌŋgɪst] jung. 2. *n. pl. (of animals)* Junge; the ~ (~ *people*) die jungen Leute. **youngster** ['jʌŋstə(r)] *n.* a) *(child)* Kleine, *der/die/das;* b) *(young person)* Jugendliche, *der/die*

your [jɔː(r), *stressed* jʊə(r), jɔː(r)] *poss. pron. attrib.: sing.* dein; *pl.* euer; *(polite) sing. or pl.* Ihr

you're [jʊə(r), *stressed* jʊə(r), jɔː(r)] = you are

yours [jʊəz, jɔːz] *poss. pron. pred.: sing.* deiner/deine/dein[e]s; *pl.* euer/eure/eures; *(polite) sing. or pl.* Ihrer/Ihre/Ihr[e]s; *see also* hers

yourself [jəˈself, jʊəˈself, jɔːˈself] *pron.* a) *emphat.* selbst; b) *refl.* dich/dir/*(polite)* sich. *See also* herself

yourselves [jəˈselvz, jʊəˈselvz, jɔːˈselvz] *pron.* a) *emphat.* selbst; b) *refl.* euch/*(polite)* sich. *See also* herself

youth [juːθ] *n.* a) Jugend, *die;* b) *pl.* ~s [juːðz] *(young man)* Jugendliche, *der.* **'youth club** *n.* Jugendklub, *der*

youthful ['juːθfl] *adj.* jugendlich

'youth hostel *n.* Jugendherberge, *die*

you've [jʊv, *stressed* juːv] = you have

Yugoslav ['juːgəslɑːv] *see* Yugoslavian

Yugoslavia [juːgəˈslɑːvɪə] *pr. n.* Jugoslawien *(das).* **Yugoslavian** [juːgəˈslɑːvɪən] 1. *adj.* jugoslawisch. 2. *n.* Jugoslawe, *der*/Jugoslawin, *die*

Z

Z, z [zed, *(Amer.)* zi:] *n.* Z, z, *das*

Zaire [zɑː'ɪə(r)] *pr. n.* Zaire *(das)*

Zambia ['zæmbɪə] *pr. n.* Sambia *(das)*

zany ['zeɪnɪ] *adj.* irre komisch *(ugs.);* Wahnsinns⟨*humor, -komiker*⟩

zeal [ziːl] *n.* Eifer, *der.* **zealous** ['zeləs] *adj.* eifrig

zebra ['zebrə, 'ziːbrə] *n.* Zebra, *das.* **zebra 'crossing** *n. (Brit.)* Zebrastreifen, *der*

zenith ['zenɪθ] *n.* Zenit, *der*

zero ['zɪərəʊ] *n., pl.* ~s Null, *die*

zest [zest] *n. (enthusiasm)* Begeisterung, *die;* ~ **for living** Lebenslust, *die*

zigzag ['zɪgzæg] **1.** *adj.* zickzackförmig; Zickzack⟨*muster, -anordnung*⟩. **2.** *n.* Zickzacklinie, *die*

Zimbabwe [zɪm'bɑːbwɪ] *pr. n.* Simbabwe *(das)*

zinc [zɪŋk] *n.* Zink, *das*

zip [zɪp] **1.** *n.* Reißverschluß, *der.* **2.** *v. t.,* **-pp-:** ~ **|up| sth.** den Reißverschluß an etw. *(Dat.)* zuziehen

'Zip code *n. (Amer.)* Postleitzahl, *die*

zip-fastener *see* zip 1

zipper ['zɪpə(r)] *see* zip 1

zither ['zɪðə(r)] *n.* Zither, *die*

zodiac ['zəʊdɪæk] *n.* Tierkreis, *der;* **sign of the** ~: Tierkreiszeichen, *das*

zombie *(Amer.:* **zombi**) ['zɒmbɪ] *n.* Zombie, *der*

zone [zəʊn] *n.* Zone, *die*

zoo [zuː] *n.* Zoo, *der*

zoological [zəʊə'lɒdʒɪkl] *adj.* zoologisch

zoologist [zəʊ'ɒlədʒɪst] *n.* Zoologe, *der*/Zoologin, *die*

zoology [zəʊ'ɒlədʒɪ] *n.* Zoologie, *die*

zoom [zuːm] *v. i.* rauschen. **zoom 'in on** *v. t. (Cinemat., Telev.)* zoomen auf (+ *Akk.*)

'zoom lens *n.* Zoomobjektiv, *das*

A

a, A [a:] das; ~, ~ **a)** (Buchstabe) a/A; **das A und O** (fig.) the essential thing/ things (Gen. for); **von A bis Z** (fig. ugs.) from beginning to end; **b)** (Musik) [key of] A

a Abk. Ar, Are

à [a] Präp. mit Nom., Akk. (Kaufmannsspr.) **zehn Marken à 50 Pfennig** ten stamps at 50 pfennigs each

A Abk. Autobahn ≈ M

Aal der; ~[e]s, ~e eel; ~ **grün** (Kochk.) green eels; stewed eels; **aalen** refl. V. (ugs.) stretch out; **aal·glatt** (abwertend) **1.** Adj. slippery; ~ **sein** be as slippery as an eel; **2.** adv. smoothly

Aas das; ~es, ~e od. Äser **a)** o. Pl. carrion no art.; **b)** Pl. ~e (rotting) carcass; **c)** Pl. Äser (salopp) (abwertend) swine; (anerkennend) devil

ab 1. Präp. mit Dat. **a)** from; **ab 1980** as from 1980; **ab Werk** (Kaufmannsspr.) ex works; **ab Frankfurt fliegen** fly from Frankfurt; **b)** [(Rang)folge] from ... on[wards]; **ab 20 DM** from 20 DM [upwards]; **2.** Adv. **a)** (weg) off; away; **b)** (ugs.: Aufforderung) off; away; **ab nach Hause** get off home; **Gewehr ab!** (milit. Kommando) order arms!; **d)** **ab und zu** od. **an** now and then

ab|ändern tr. V. alter; amend (text); **Ab·änderung** die alteration; (eines Textes) amendment

ab|arbeiten tr. V. work for (meal); work off (debt, amount)

ab·artig Adj. deviant; abnormal

Abb. Abk. Abbildung Fig.

Ab·bau der **a)** dismantling; (von Zelten, Lagern) striking; (von **s. abbauen** c: cutback (Gen. in); pruning; reduction; **c)** (Bergbau) mining; (von Stein) quarrying

ab|bauen tr. V. **a)** dismantle; strike (tent, camp); **b)** (beseitigen) gradually remove; break down (prejudices, inhibitions); **c)** (verringern) cut back

(staff); prune (jobs); reduce (wages); **d)** (Bergbau) mine; quarry (stone)

ab|beißen 1) unr. tr. V. bite off; **2.** unr. itr. V. have a bite

ab|bekommen unr. tr. V. **a)** get; **b)** einen **Schlag/ein paar Kratzer** ~: get hit/get a few scratches; **etwas** ~ (getroffen werden) be hit; (verletzt werden) be hurt; **c)** (los-, herunterbekommen) get (paint, lid, chain) off

ab|berufen unr. tr. V. recall (ambassador, envoy) (aus, von from)

ab|bestellen tr. V. cancel

ab|bezahlen tr. V. pay off

ab|biegen unr. itr. V.; mit sein turn off; **links/rechts** ~: turn [off] left/right

Ab·bild das (eines Menschen) likeness; (eines Gegenstandes) copy; (fig.) portrayal; **ab|bilden** tr. V. copy; reproduce (object, picture); depict (person, landscape); (fig.) portray; **Abbildung** die illustration

ab|binden unr. tr. V. **a)** (losbinden) untie; undo; **b)** (abschnüren) put a tourniquet on (artery, arm, leg, etc.); tie (umbilical cord)

ab|blasen unr. tr. V. (ugs.) call off

ab|blättern itr. V.; mit sein flake off

ab|blenden itr. V. dip (Brit.) or (Amer.) dim one's headlight; **Abblend·licht** das dipped (Brit.) or (Amer.) dimmed beam

ab|blitzen itr. V.; mit sein (ugs.) **sie ließ alle Verehrer** ~: she gave all her admirers the brush-off

ab|brausen tr. V.: s. **abduschen**

ab|brechen 1. unr. tr. V. **a)** break off; break (needle, pencil); **b)** (zerlegen) strike (tent, camp); **c)** (abreißen) demolish, pull down (building); **d)** (beenden) break off (negotiations, [diplomatic] relations, discussion, activity); (vorzeitig) cut short (conversation, holiday, activity); **2.** unr. itr. V. **a)** mit sein break [off]; **b)** (aufhören) break off

ab|bremsen 1. *tr. V.* a) brake; b) retard ⟨*motion*⟩; 2. *itr. V.* brake

ab|brennen 1. *unr. itr. V.; mit sein* a) be burned down; **das Haus ist abgebrannt** the house has burned down; b) ⟨*fuse*⟩ burn away; ⟨*candle*⟩ burn down; 2. *unr. tr. V.* a) let off ⟨*firework*⟩; b) burn down ⟨*building*⟩

ab|bringen *unr. tr. V.* **jmdn. davon** ~, **etw. zu tun** dissuade sb. from doing sth. **jmdn. vom Kurs** ~: make sb. change course

ab|bröckeln *itr. V.; mit sein (auch fig.)* crumble away

Ab·bruch der a) *o. Pl.* demolition; pulling down; b) ⟨*Beendigung*⟩ breaking-off; c) **einer Sache** ⟨*Dat.*⟩ **[keinen]** ~ **tun** do [no] harm to sth.

ab|buchen *tr. V.* ⟨*bank*⟩ debit ⟨*von* to⟩; ⟨*creditor*⟩ claim by direct debit ⟨*von* to⟩

ab|bürsten *tr. V.* a) brush off; b) ⟨*säubern*⟩ brush ⟨*garment*⟩

ab|büßen *tr. V.* serve [out] ⟨*prison sentence*⟩

Abc [aː]be(ː)ˈtseː] **das;** ~ *(auch fig.)* ABC; **Abc-Schütze der** child just starting school

ab|dampfen *itr. V.; mit sein (ugs.: abfahren)* set off

ab|danken *itr. V.* ⟨*ruler*⟩ abdicate; ⟨*government, minister*⟩ resign; **Abdankung die;** ~, ~**en** *s.* **abdanken:** abdication; resignation

ab|decken 1. *tr. V.* a) open up; ⟨*gale*⟩ take the roof/roofs off ⟨*house*⟩, take the tiles off ⟨*roof*⟩; b) ⟨*herunternehmen, -reißen*⟩ take off; c) ⟨*abräumen*⟩ clear ⟨*table*⟩; clear away ⟨*dishes*⟩; d) ⟨*schützen*⟩ cover ⟨*person*⟩

ab|dichten *tr. V.* seal

ab|drängen *tr. V.* push away

ab|drehen 1. *tr. V.* a) ⟨*ausschalten*⟩ turn off; **den Hahn** ~ ⟨*fig.*⟩ turn off the supply; b) ⟨*abtrennen*⟩ twist off; 2. *itr. V.; meist mit sein* turn off

Ab·druck der; *Pl.* **Abdrücke** mark; ⟨*Fuß*~⟩ footprint; ⟨*Wachs*~⟩ impression; ⟨*Gips*~⟩ cast; **ab|drücken** 1. *itr. V.* pull the trigger; shoot; 2. *tr. V.* ⟨*zudrücken*⟩ constrict

ab|dunkeln *tr. V.* darken ⟨*room*⟩; dim ⟨*light*⟩

ab|duschen *tr. V.* **sich/jmdn. [warm]** ~: take/give sb. a [hot] shower

abend *Adv.* **heute/morgen/gestern** ~: this/tomorrow/yesterday evening; **Abend der;** ~**s,** ~**e** evening; **guten** ~! good evening; **am [frühen/späten]** ~: [early/late] in the evening; **zu** ~ **essen**

have dinner; *(allgemeiner)* have one's evening meal; **ein bunter** ~: a social [evening]

Abend-: ~**an·zug der** evening suit; ~**brot das** supper; ~**essen das** dinner; ~**kasse die** box-office *(open on the evening of the performance);* ~**kleid das** evening dress; ~**kurs[us] der** evening class; ~**land das;** *o. Pl.* West

abendlich *Adj.* evening; ⟨*quiet, coolness*⟩ of the evening

Abend-: ~**mahl das;** *o. Pl.* *(Rel.)* Communion; *(N.T.)* Last Supper; ~**programm das** evening programmes *pl.;* ~**rot das** red glow of the sunset sky

abends *Adv.* in the evenings; **um sechs Uhr** ~: at six o'clock in the evening

Abend-: ~**schule die** night school; ~**stern der** evening star; ~**stunde die** evening hour; ~**vorstellung die** evening performance

Abenteuer das; ~**s,** ~ a) *(auch fig.)* adventure; b) *(Unternehmen)* venture; c) *(Liebesaffäre)* affair; **abenteuerlich** *Adj.* a) *(riskant)* risky; b) *(bizarr)* bizarre; **Abenteuer·roman der** adventure novel; **Abenteurer der;** ~**s,** ~: adventurer

aber 1. *Konj.* but; 2. *Partikel* ~ **ja/ nein!** why, yes/no! ~ **natürlich!** but of course!; **du bist** ~ **groß!** aren't you tall!

Aber·glaube[n] der superstition; **aber·gläubisch** *Adj.* superstitious

abermals *Adv.* once again; once more

Abf. *Abk.* Abfahrt dep.

ab|fahren 1. *unr. itr. V.; mit sein* a) *(wegfahren)* leave; **wo fährt der Zug nach Paris ab?** where does the Paris train leave from?; b) *(hinunterfahren)* drive down; *(Skisport)* ski down; 2. *unr. tr. V.* a) *(abtransportieren)* take away; b) *(abnutzen)* wear out; **abgefahrene Reifen** worn tyres; **Ab·fahrt die** a) departure; b) *(Skisport)* descent; *(Strecke)* run; **Abfahrtslauf der** *(Skisport)* downhill [racing]; **Ab·fahrt[s]·zeit die** time of departure; departure time

Ab·fall der *(Küchen~ o. ä.)* rubbish, *(Amer.)* trash *no indef. art., no pl.;* *(Fleisch~)* offal *no indef. art., no pl.;* *(Industrie~)* waste *no indef. art.; (auf der Straße)* litter *no indef. art., no pl.;* **Abfall·eimer der** rubbish bin; trash can *(Amer.); (auf der Straße)* litter bin;

trash can *(Amer.)*; **ạb|fallen** *unr. itr.
V.; mit sein* **a)** fall off; **b)** *(abschüssig
sein)* *(land, road, etc.)* drop away,
slope; **c)** *(übrigbleiben)* be left [over];
für dich wird [dabei] auch etwas ~:
you'll get something out of it too; **d)**
von jmdm. ~: leave sb.; **vom Glauben
~:** desert the faith; **ạb · fällig 1.** *Adj.*
disparaging; **2.** *adv.* **sich ~ über jmdn.
äußern** make disparaging remarks
about sb.

ạb|fangen *unr. tr. V.* catch; intercept
⟨*agent, message, aircraft*⟩; **b)** repel
⟨*charge, assault*⟩; ward off ⟨*blow, attack*⟩

ạb|färben *itr. V.* **a)** ⟨*colour, garment,
etc.*⟩ run; **b) auf jmdn./etw. ~** *(fig.)* rub
off on sb./sth.

ạb|fassen *tr. V.* write ⟨*report, letter,
etc.*⟩; draw up ⟨*will*⟩

ạb|fegen *tr. V.* **a)** brush off; **etw. von
etw. ~:** brush sth. off sth.; **b)** *(säubern)*
etw. ~: brush sth. clean

ạb|fertigen *tr. V.* dispatch ⟨*mail*⟩;
deal with ⟨*applicant*⟩; handle ⟨*passengers*⟩; serve ⟨*customer*⟩; clear ⟨*ship*⟩
for sailing; clear ⟨*aircraft*⟩ for take-
off; clear ⟨*lorry*⟩ for departure

ạb|feuern *tr. V.* fire

ạb|finden 1. *unr. tr. V.* **a) jmdn. mit
etw. ~:** compensate sb. with sth.; **seine
Gläubiger ~:** settle with one's cred-
itors; **2.** *unr. refl. V.* **sich ~:** resign
oneself; **sich ~ mit** come to terms
with; learn to live with ⟨*noise, heat*⟩;
Ạbfindung die; **~,** **~en** settlement;
eine ~ in Höhe von ... zahlen make a
settlement of ...

ạb|flauen *itr. V.; mit sein* die down;
subside; ⟨*interest, conversation*⟩ flag;
⟨*business*⟩ become slack; ⟨*noise*⟩ abate

ạb|fliegen *unr. itr. V.; mit sein* leave

ạb|fließen *unr. itr. V.; mit sein* flow
off

Ạb · flug der departure

Ạb · fluß der drain; *(Rohr)* drain-pipe;
(für Abwasser) waste-pipe

ạb|fragen *tr. V.* test; **jmdm. od. jmdn.
die Vokabeln ~:** test sb. on his/her vocabulary

Ạbfuhr die; **~,** **~en a)** removal; **b)**
jmdm. eine ~ erteilen *(fig. ugs.)* rebuff
sb.; **ạb|führen 1.** *tr. V.* **a)** *(nach Fest-
nahme)* take away; **b)** *(zahlen)* pay
out; **c)** *(abbringen)* take away; **2.** *itr. V.*
(für Stuhlgang sorgen) be a laxative;
Ạbführ · mittel das laxative

ạb|füllen *tr. V.* *(in Flaschen)* bottle; *(in
Dosen)* can

Ạb · gabe die a) handing in; *(eines
Briefes, Pakets, Telegramms)* delivery;
(eines Gesuchs, Antrags) submission;
b) *(Steuer, Gebühr)* tax; *(auf Produkte)*
duty; **c)** *(Ausstrahlung)* release;
emission; **d)** *(Sport: Abspiel)* pass

Ạb · gang der a) leaving; departure;
(Abfahrt) departure; *(Theater)* exit; **b)**
(jmd., der ausscheidet) departure;
(Schule) leaver; **c)** *(bes. Amtsspr.: Todesfall)* death; **d)** *(Turnen)* dismount

Ạb · gas das exhaust

ạbgearbeitet *Adj.* work-worn
⟨*hands*⟩

ạb|geben 1. *unr. tr. V.* **a)** *(aushändi-
gen)* hand over; deliver ⟨*letter, parcel,
telegram*⟩; hand in, submit ⟨*application*⟩; hand in ⟨*school work*⟩; **den
Mantel in der Garderobe ~:** leave
one's coat in the cloakroom; **b)** hand
itr. **jmdm. [etwas] von etw. ~:** let sb.
have some of sth.; **c)** *(abfeuern)* fire;
2. *unr. refl. V.* **sich mit jmdm./etw. ~:**
spend time on sb./sth.; *(geringschät-
zig)* waste one's time on sb./sth

ạb · gebrannt *Adj. (ugs.)* broke *(coll.)*

ạbgebrüht *Adj. (ugs.)* hardened

ạb · gedroschen *Adj. (ugs.)* hackneyed

ạb · gegriffen *Adj.* battered

ạb|gehen *unr. itr. V.; mit sein* **a)** *(sich
entfernen)* leave; *(Theater)* exit; **b)**
(ausscheiden) leave; **c)** *(abfahren)*
⟨*train, ship, bus*⟩ leave, depart; **d)** *(ab-
geschickt werden)* ⟨*message, letter*⟩ be
sent [off]; **e)** *(abzweigen)* branch off; **f)**
(sich lösen) come off

ạbgehetzt *Adj.* exhausted

ạb · gelegen *Adj.* remote; *(einsam)*
isolated; out-of-the-way ⟨*district*⟩

ạb · geneigt *Adj.* averse *(Dat.* to);
[nicht] ~ sein, etw. zu tun [not] be averse
to doing sth.

Ạbgeordnete der/die; *adj. Dekl.*
member [of parliament]; *(z. B. in
Frankreich)* deputy

ạb · gerissen *Adj.* ragged

ạb · geschlagen *Adj. (Sport)* [well]
beaten

ạb · geschlossen *Adj.* secluded

ạb · gesehen *Adv.* **~ von** apart from; **~
davon, daß ...** apart from the fact that ...

ạb · gespannt *Adj.* weary; exhausted

ạb · gestanden *Adj.* flat

ạb · gestorben *Adj.* dead ⟨*branch,
tree*⟩; numb ⟨*fingers, legs, etc.*⟩

ạb · getreten *Adj.* worn down

ạbgewetzt *Adj.* well-worn; battered
⟨*case etc.*⟩

ab|gewöhnen tr. V.; jmdm. etw. ~: make sb. give up sth.; **sich** (Dat.) etw. ~: give up sth.

ab|gießen unr. tr. V. pour away ⟨liquid⟩; drain ⟨potatoes⟩

abgöttisch Adj. idolatrous

ab|grenzen tr. V. a) bound; etw. gegen od. von etw. ~: separate sth. from sth.; b) (unterscheiden) distinguish

Ab·grund der abyss; chasm; (Abhang) precipice

ab|hacken tr. V. chop off; **jmdm. die Hand** usw. ~: chop sb.'s hand etc. off

ab|haken tr. V. tick off; check off (Amer.)

ab|halten unr. tr. V. a) jmdn./etw. [von jmdm./etw.] ~: keep sb./sth. off [sb./sth.]; b) jmdn. davon ~, etw. zu tun stop sb. doing sth.; c) (durchführen) hold ⟨elections, meeting, referendum⟩

ab|handeln tr. V. a) jmdm. etw. ~: do a deal with sb. for sth.; b) (darstellen) deal with

abhanden Adv. ~ kommen get lost; go astray; **etw. kommt jmdm.** ~: sb. loses sth.

Ab·handlung die treatise (über + Akk. on)

Ab·hang der slope; incline; **¹ab|hängen** unr. itr. V. von jmdm./etw. ~: depend on sb./sth.; **²ab|hängen** 1. tr. V. a) take down; b) (abkuppeln) uncouple; c) (ugs.) shake off ⟨coll.⟩ ⟨pursuer, competitor⟩. 2. itr. V. ⟨den Hörer auflegen⟩ hang up; **abhängig** Adj. dependent (von on); (süchtig) addicted (von to); **von jmdm./etw.** ~ sein depend on sb./sth.; **Abhängigkeit** die ~, ~en dependence; (Sucht) addiction

ab|härten tr. V. harden

ab|hauen 1. unr. tr. V. a) Prät. haute ab knock off; b) Prät. hieb (geh.) od. haute ab (mit Schwert, Axt usw.) chop off; 2. unr. itr. V.; mit sein; Prät. haute ab (salopp) beat it (sl.)

ab|heben 1. unr. tr. V. a) lift off ⟨lid, cover, etc.⟩; [den Hörer] ~: answer [the telephone]; b) (von einem Konto) withdraw ⟨money⟩; 2. unr. itr. V. ⟨balloon⟩ rise; ⟨aircraft, bird⟩ take off; ⟨rocket⟩ lift off; 3. unr. refl. V. stand out (von against)

ab|heften tr. V. file

ab|hetzen refl. V. rush [around]; s. auch abgehetzt

Ab·hilfe die; o. Pl. action to improve matters; ~ schaffen put things right

ab|holen tr. V. collect, pick up ⟨parcel, book, tickets, etc.⟩; pick up ⟨person⟩

ab|hören tr. V. a) jmdm. od. jmdn. Vokabeln ~: test sb.'s vocabulary [orally]; **das Einmaleins** ~: ask questions on the multiplication table; b) tap ⟨telephone conversation, telephone⟩; bug ⟨coll.⟩ ⟨conversation, premises⟩; jmdn. ~: tap sb.'s telephone

Abi das; ~s, ~s (Schülerspr.), **Abitur** das; ~s, ~e Abitur (school-leaving examination at grammar school needed for entry to higher education); ≈ A levels (Brit.); **Abiturient** der; ~en, ~en sb. who is taking/has passed the 'Abitur'

ab|jagen tr. V. jmdm. etw. ~: finally get sth. away from sb.

Abk. Abk. Abkürzung abbr.

ab|kaufen tr. V. jmdm. etw. ~: buy sth. from sb.

ab|klopfen tr. V. a) knock off; b) (säubern) knock the dirt/snow/crumbs etc. off; c) (untersuchen) tap

ab|knicken 1. tr. V. snap off; 2. itr. V.; mit sein snap

ab|kochen tr. V. boil

ab|kommen unr. itr. V.; mit sein a) vom Weg ~: lose one's way; vom Kurs ~: go off course; von der Fahrbahn ~: leave the road; vom Thema ~: stray from the topic; b) von einem Plan ~: abandon a plan; **das Abkommen das;** ~s, ~: agreement; **abkömmlich** Adj. free; available

ab|kratzen 1. tr. V. a) (mit den Fingern) scratch off; (mit einem Werkzeug) scrape off; b) (säubern) scrape [clean]; 2. itr. V.; mit sein (derb) snuff it (sl.)

ab|kühlen 1. tr. V. cool down; 2. itr., refl. V.; itr. meist mit sein cool down; **Ab·kühlung** die cooling

ab|kürzen tr., itr. V. a) (räumlich) shorten; **den Weg** ~: take a shorter route; b) (zeitlich) cut short; c) (kürzer schreiben) abbreviate (mit to); **Abkürzung die** a) (Weg) short cut; b) (Wort) abbreviation

ab|laden unr. tr., itr. V. unload

ab|lagern tr. V. deposit

ab|lassen 1. unr. tr. V. let out (aus of); let off ⟨steam⟩; 2. unr. itr. V. a) von jmdm./etw. ~: leave sb./sth. alone; b) von etw. ~ (etw. aufgeben) give sth. up

Ab·lauf der a) (Verlauf) course; (einer Veranstaltung) passing off; b) o. Pl. (Ende) nach ~ eines Jahres after a year; **nach** ~ **einer Frist** at the end of a period of time; **ab|laufen** unr. itr. V.;

mit sein a) flow away; *(aus einem Behälter)* run out; b) *(verlaufen)* pass off; c) ⟨*alarm clock*⟩ run down; ⟨*parking meter*⟩ expire; d) ⟨*period, contract, passport*⟩ expire

ab|lecken *tr. V.* a) lick off; b) *(säubern)* lick clean

ab|legen 1. *tr. V.* a) lay *or* put down; b) *(Bürow.)* file; c) stop wearing ⟨*clothes*⟩; d) give up ⟨*habit*⟩; lose ⟨*shyness*⟩; e) swear ⟨*oath*⟩; sit ⟨*examination*⟩; make ⟨*confession*⟩; 2. *tr., itr. V.* take off; **möchten Sie ~?** would you like to take your coat off?; 3. *itr. V.* **|vom Kai|** ~: cast off; **Ableger der;** **~s, ~** *(Steckling)* cutting

ab|lehnen *tr. V.* a) decline; decline, turn down ⟨*money, invitation, position*⟩; reject ⟨*suggestion, applicant*⟩; b) *(mißbilligen)* disapprove of; **Ablehnung die; ~, ~en** a) rejection; b) *(Mißbilligung)* disapproval

ab|leiten *tr. V.* a) divert; b) *(herleiten)* **etw. aus/von etw. ~:** derive sth. from sth.; **Ab·leitung die** derivation

ab|lenken *tr. V.* a) deflect; b) **jmdn. von etw. ~:** distract sb. from sth.; c) *(zerstreuen)* **sich ~:** amuse oneself; **Ab·lenkung die** *s.* ablenken: deflection; distraction; diversion

ab|lesen *unr. tr. V.* a) read ⟨*speech, lecture*⟩; **werden Sie frei sprechen oder ~?** will you be talking from notes or reading your speech?; b) read ⟨*gas meter, thermometer, etc.*⟩; check ⟨*time, speed, temperature*⟩; c) *(erkennen)* see

ab|liefern *tr., itr. V.* hand in; deliver ⟨*goods*⟩

ab|lösen *tr. V.* a) **etw. |von etw.| ~:** get sth. off |sth.|; b) **jmdn. ~:** relieve sb.; **sich** *od.* **einander ~:** take turns; 2. *refl. V.* **sich |von etw.| ~:** come off |sth.|

Ab·lösung die *(eines Postens)* changing; **ich schicke Ihnen jemanden zur ~:** I'll send someone to relieve you

ab|machen *tr. V.* a) *(ugs.)* take off; take down ⟨*sign, rope*⟩; b) *(vereinbaren)* agree; **Abmachung die; ~, ~en** agreement

ab|magern *itr. V.; mit sein* become thin; *(absichtlich)* slim; **Abmagerungs·kur die** reducing diet

ab|marschieren *itr. V.; mit sein* depart; *(Milit.)* march off

ab|melden *tr. V.* a) **sich/jmdn. ~:** report that one/sb. is leaving; b) *(Umzug melden)* notify the authorities that one is moving from an address; c) **ein Auto ~:** cancel a car's registration; **Ab·mel-**

dung die a) *(beim Weggehen)* report that one is leaving; b) *(beim Umzug)* registration of a move with the authorities at one's old address; c) **~ eines Autos** cancellation of a car's registration

ab|montieren *tr. V.* take off ⟨*part*⟩; dismantle ⟨*machine, equipment*⟩

ab|mühen *refl. V.* toil; **sie mühte sich mit dem schweren Koffer ab** she struggled with the heavy suitcase

Abnahme die; ~, ~n a) *o. Pl. (das Entfernen)* removal; b) *(Verminderung)* decrease; **ab|nehmen** 1. *tr. u. itr. V.* a) *(entfernen)* take off; take down ⟨*picture, curtain, lamp*⟩; b) **jmdm. den Koffer ~:** take sb.'s suitcase; **jmdm. eine Arbeit ~:** save sb. a job; c) **jmdm. ein Versprechen/einen Eid ~:** make sb. give a promise/swear an oath; d) *(prüfen)* inspect and approve; test and pass ⟨*vehicle*⟩; e) **jmdm. etw. ~** *(wegnehmen)* take sth. off sb.; f) *(beim Telefon)* answer ⟨*telephone*⟩; pick up ⟨*receiver*⟩; g) *(Handarb.)* decrease; **das nehme ich dir/ihm** *usw.* **nicht ab** I won't buy that *(coll.)*; 2. *unr. itr. V.* a) *(Gewicht verlieren)* lose weight; b) *(sich verringern)* decrease; drop; ⟨*attention, interest*⟩ flag; ⟨*brightness*⟩ diminish; **wir haben ~den Mond** there is a waning moon; c) *(beim Telefon)* answer the telephone

Ab·neigung die dislike (gegen for)

ab|nutzen, *(landsch.:)* **ab|nützen** *tr., refl. V.* wear out; **abgenutzt worn**

Abonnement [abɔnə'mã:] **das; ~s, ~s** subscription (Gen. to); **abonnieren** *tr. V.* subscribe to

Ab·ordnung die delegation

ab|passen *tr. V.* a) *(abwarten)* wait for; b) *(aufhalten)* catch

ab|pausen *tr. V.* trace

ab|pfeifen *(Sport)* 1. *itr. V.* blow the whistle; 2. *tr. V.* [blow the whistle to] stop; **Ab·pfiff der** *(Sport)* final whistle; *(Halbzeit~)* half-time whistle

ab|pflücken *tr. V.* pick

ab|plagen *refl. V.* slave away

ab|prallen *itr. V.; mit sein* rebound; ⟨*bullet, missile*⟩ ricochet

ab|putzen *tr. V. (ugs.)* a) wipe off; b) *(säubern)* wipe; **jmdm./sich das Gesicht ~:** clean sb.'s/one's face

ab|quälen *refl. V.* **sich |mit etw.| ~:** struggle with sth.|

ab|rackern *refl. V. (ugs.)* flog oneself to death *(coll.)*

ab|rasieren *tr. V.* shave off

ab|raten *unr. itr. V.* jmdm. von etw. ~: advise sb. against sth.

ab|räumen *tr. V.* **a)** clear away; **b)** *(leer machen)* clear ⟨table⟩

ab|rechnen 1. *itr. V.* cash up; **mit jmdm. ~** *(fig.)* call sb. to account; **2.** *tr. V.* **die Kasse ~:** reckon up the till; **seine Spesen ~:** claim one's expenses; **Ab·rechnung die a)** cashing up *no art.;* *(Aufstellung)* statement; **b)** *(fig.: Vergeltung)* reckoning

ab|reiben *unr. tr. V.* **a)** rub off; **b)** *(säubern)* rub

Ab·reise die departure **(nach** for); **bei meiner ~:** when I left/leave; **ab|reisen** *itr. V.; mit sein* leave **(nach** for)

ab|reißen 1. *unr. tr. V.* **a)** tear off; tear down ⟨poster, notice⟩; pull off ⟨button⟩; **b)** *(niederreißen)* demolish, pull down ⟨building⟩; **2.** *unr. itr. V.; mit sein* **a)** fly off; ⟨shoe-lace⟩ break off; **b)** *(aufhören)* come to an end; ⟨connection, contact⟩ be broken off

ab|richten *tr. V.* train

Ab·riß der a) *o. Pl.:* abreißen 1 b: demolition; pulling down; **b)** *(knappe Darstellung)* outline

ab|rollen 1. *tr. V.* unwind; **2.** *itr. V.; mit sein* unwind [itself]

ab|rücken 1. *tr. V. (wegschieben)* move away; **2.** *tr. V.; mit sein* move away

Ab·ruf der: auf ~: on call; *(DV)* in retrievable form; **ab|rufen** *unr. tr. V.* summon; call

ab|runden *tr. V. (auch fig.)* round off; **b)** round ⟨figure⟩ up/down **(auf +** Akk. to); **etw. nach oben/unten ~:** round sth. up/down

abrupt [ap'rʊpt] **1.** *Adj.* abrupt; **2.** *adv.* abruptly

ab|rüsten *itr., tr. V.* disarm; **Ab·rüstung die; ~:** disarmament

ab|rutschen *itr. V.; mit sein* **a)** slip; **b)** *(nach unten rutschen)* slide down

Abs. *Abk.* **a)** Absender; **b)** Absatz

Ab·sage die *(auf eine Einladung)* refusal; *(auf eine Bewerbung)* rejection; **ab|sagen 1.** *tr. V.* cancel; ⟨participation⟩; **2.** *itr. V.* jmdm. ~: tell sb. one cannot come

ab|sägen *tr. V.* saw off

Ab·satz der a) *(am Schuh)* heel; **b)** *(Textunterbrechung)* break; **c)** *(Textabschnitt)* paragraph; **d)** *(Kaufmannsspr.)* sales *pl.*

ab|saufen *unr. itr. V.; mit sein (ugs.)* ⟨engine, car⟩ flood

ab|saugen *tr. V.* **a)** suck away; **b)** *(säubern)* hoover *(Brit. coll.)*

ab|schaben *tr. V.* **a)** scrape off; **b)** *(säubern)* scrape [clean]

ab|schaffen *tr. V.* **a)** *(beseitigen)* abolish ⟨capital punishment, regulation, customs duty, institution⟩; repeal ⟨law⟩; put an end to ⟨injustice, abuse⟩; **b)** *(weggeben)* get rid of; **Ab·schaffung die** abolition; *(von Gesetzen)* repeal; *(von Unrecht, Mißstand)* ending

ab|schalten *tr., itr. V.* switch off; shut down ⟨power-station⟩

abschätzig 1. *Adj.* derogatory; **2.** *adv.* derogatorily

Ab·scheu der; ~s detestation; abhorrence; **abscheulich 1.** *Adj.* **a)** disgusting ⟨smell, taste⟩; repulsive ⟨sight⟩; **b)** *(verwerflich)* disgraceful ⟨behaviour⟩; abominable ⟨crime⟩; **2.** *adv.* disgracefully

ab|schicken *tr. V.* send [off]

ab|schieben *unr. tr. V.* **a)** push away; **b)** *(abwälzen)* shift ⟨responsibility, blame⟩; **c)** *(außer Landes bringen)* deport

Abschied der; ~[e]s, ~e parting **(von** from); farewell **(von** to); **~ nehmen** take one's leave **(von** of)

Abschieds-: ~brief der farewell letter; ~geschenk das parting gift; ~gruß der goodbye; farewell

ab|schießen *unr. tr. V.* **a)** shoot down ⟨aeroplane⟩; **b)** fire ⟨arrow⟩; launch ⟨spacecraft⟩; **c)** *(töten)* take

ab|schirmen *tr. V.* **a)** *(schützen)* shield; **b)** *(fernhalten)* screen off ⟨light, radiation⟩

ab|schlachten *tr. V.* slaughter

Ab·schlag der a) *(Kaufmannsspr.)* discount; **b)** *(Teilzahlung)* interim payment; *(Vorschuß)* advance; **c)** *(Fußball)* goalkeeper's kick out; **ab|schlagen 1.** *unr. tr. V.* **a)** knock off; *(mit dem Beil, Schwert usw.)* chop off; **b)** *(ablehnen)* refuse; **c)** *(abwehren)* beat of; **2.** *unr. itr. V.* **c)** *(Fußball)* kick the ball out

ab|schleifen *unr. tr. V.* *(von Holz)* sand off; *(von Metall, Glas usw.)* grind off

Abschlepp·dienst der breakdown recovery service; tow[ing] service *(Amer.);* **ab|schleppen** *tr. V.* tow; take ⟨ship⟩ in tow; **ein Auto zur Werkstatt ~:** tow a car to the garage; **Ab·schlepp·seil das** tow-rope; *(aus Draht)* towing cable

ab|schließen 1. *unr. tr. V.* **a)** *auch itr.*

(zuschließen) lock *(door, gate, cupboard)*; lock [up] *(house, flat, room, park)*; b) *(verschließen)* seal; etw. **luftdicht ~**: seal sth. hermetically; c) *(begrenzen)* border; d) *(zum Abschluß bringen)* conclude; e) *(vereinbaren)* strike *(bargain, deal)*; make *(purchase)*; enter into *(agreement)*; 2. unr. itr. V. *(aufhören, enden)* end; **~d sagte er ...**: in conclusion he said ...; **Abschluß der** *(Beendigung)* conclusion; end

ab|schmecken tr. V. a) *(kosten)* taste; try; b) *(würzen)* season

ab|schmieren tr. V. *(Technik)* grease

ab|schminken tr. V. **jmdn./sich ~**: remove sb.'s/one's make-up

ab|schmirgeln tr. V. rub off with emery; *(mit Sandpapier)* sand off

ab|schnallen tr. V. unfasten

ab|schneiden 1. unr. tr. V. a) *(auch fig.: isolieren)* cut off; cut down *(sth. hanging)*; etw. von etw. ~: cut sth. off sth.; **sich** *(Dat.)* **eine Scheibe Brot ~**: cut oneself a slice of bread; b) *(kürzer schneiden)* cut; c) **jmdm. den Weg ~**: take a short cut to get ahead of sb.; 2. unr. itr. V. **bei etw. gut/schlecht ~**: do well/badly in sth.; **Ab · schnitt der** a) *(Kapitel)* section; b) *(Zeitspanne)* phase; d) *(Teil eines Formulars)* [detachable] portion

ab|schrauben tr. V. unscrew [and remove]

ab|schrecken tr. V. a) deter; b) *(fernhalten)* scare off; c) *(Kochk.)* pour cold water over; **Abschreckung die; ~, ~en** deterrence

ab|schreiben 1. unr. tr. V. a) copy out; etw. bei od. von jmdm. ~ *(in der Schule)* copy sth. off sb.; *(als Plagiator)* plagiarize sth. from sb.; b) *(Wirtsch.)* amortize; 2. unr. itr. V. **bei od. von jmdm. ~** *(in der Schule)* copy off sb.; *(als Plagiator)* copy from sb.; **Ab · schreibung die** *(Wirtsch.)* amortization; **Ab · schrift die** copy

ab|schürfen tr. V. graze

Ab · schuß der a) *(eines Flugzeugs)* shooting down; b) *(von Geschossen)* firing; *(eines Raumschiffs)* launching

abschüssig Adj. downward sloping *(land)*

ab|schütteln tr. V. shake off; *(herunterschütteln)* shake down

ab|schwächen 1. tr. V. a) *(mildern)* tone down *(statement, criticism)*; b) *(verringern)* lessen *(effect, impression)*; cushion *(blow, impact)*; 2. refl.

V. *(interest, demand)* wane; **Abschwächung die; ~, ~en** a) *(Milderung)* toning down; b) *(eines Aufpralls, Stoßes usw.)* cushioning

ab|schweifen itr. V.; mit sein digress; **Abschweifung die; ~, ~en** digression

ab|schwören unr. itr. V. **dem Teufel/seinem Glauben ~**: renounce the Devil/one's faith; **dem Alkohol/Laster ~**: forswear alcohol/vice

absehbar Adj. foreseeable; **in ~er Zeit** within the foreseeable future; **ab|sehen** 1. unr. tr. V. a) *(voraussehen)* predict; foresee *(event)*; b) **es auf etw.** *(Akk.)* **abgesehen haben** be after sth.; **er hat es darauf abgesehen, uns zu ärgern** he's out to annoy us; **der Chef hat es auf ihn abgesehen** the boss has got it in for him; 2. unr. itr. V. a) **von etw. ~** *(etw. nicht beachten)* leave aside sth.; *s. auch* abgesehen; b) **von etw. ~** *(auf etw. verzichten)* refrain from sth.

ab|seilen 1. tr. V. lower [with a rope]. 2. refl. V. *(Bergsteigen)* abseil

ab|sein unr. itr. V.; mit sein *(Zusschr. nur im Inf. u. Part.)* *(abgegangen sein)* have come off

abseits 1. Präp. mit Gen. away from; 2. Adv. a) far away; b) *(Ballspiele)* **~ sein od. stehen** be offside; **Abseits das; ~, ~**: **das war ein klares ~**: that was clearly offside

ab|senden unr. od. regelm. tr. V. dispatch; **Ab · sender der** sender; *(Anschrift)* sender's address

ab|setzen 1. tr. V. a) take off *(hat, glasses, etc.)*; b) *(hinstellen)* put down *(bag, suitcase)*; c) *(aussteigen lassen)* **jmdn. ~** *(im öffentlichen Verkehr)* put sb. down; let sb. out *(Amer.)*; *(im privaten Verkehr)* drop sb. [off]; d) remove *(chancellor, judge)* from office; depose *(king, emperor)*; 2. refl. V. a) *(sich ablagern)* be deposited; b) *(flüchten)* get away

Absetzung die; ~, ~en s. absetzen 1 d: removal; deposition

ab|sichern 1. tr. V. make safe; 2. refl. V. safeguard oneself

Ab · sicht die; ~, ~en intention; **etw. mit ~ tun** do sth. intentionally; **etw. ohne od. nicht mit ~ tun** do sth. unintentionally; **ab · sichtlich** 1. Adj. intentional; deliberate; 2. adv. intentionally; deliberately

ab|sinken unr. itr. V.; mit sein sink

absolut Adj. absolute; **Absolutismus der; ~** *(hist.)* absolutism no art.

Absolvent der; ~en, ~en *(einer Schu-le)* one who has taken the leaving *or (Amer.)* final examination; *(einer Aka-demie)* graduate; **absolvieren** tr. V. complete; **Absolvierung** die; ~: completion

ab·sonderlich Adj. strange; odd; **ab|sondern 1.** tr. V. exude; *(Physiol.)* secrete; **2.** refl. V. isolate oneself

absorbieren tr. V. absorb

ab|speisen tr. V. jmdn. mit etw. ~: fob sb. off with sth.

abspenstig Adj. jmdm. etw. ~ machen get sb. to part with sth.

ab|sperren tr. V. seal off; close off

Ab·spiel das *(Ballspiele)* passing; **ab|spielen 1.** tr. V. **a)** play ⟨record, tape⟩; **b)** vom Blatt ~: play (piece of music) at sight; **c)** *(Ballspiele)* pass; **2.** refl. V. take place

Ab·sprache die arrangement; **eine ~ treffen** make an arrangement; **ab|sprechen** tr. V. **a)** jmdm. etw. ~: deny that sb. has sth.; **b)** *(vereinbaren)* arrange

ab|springen unr. itr. V.; mit sein jump off; *(herunterspringen)* jump down; **vom Fahrrad ~:** jump off one's bicycle; **Ab·sprung** der take-off; *(das Herunterspringen)* jump

ab|spülen 1. tr. V. **a)** wash off; **b)** *(reinigen)* rinse off; **sich** *(Dat.)* **die Hände** usw. ~: rinse one's hands *etc.*; **das Geschirr ~** *(bes. südd.)* wash the dishes; **2.** itr. V. *(bes. südd.)* wash up

ab|stammen itr. V. be descended **(von** from); **Abstammung** die; ~, ~en descent

Ab·stand der **a)** distance; **in 20 Meter ~:** at a distance of 20 metres; **b)** *(Unterschied)* gap

ab|stauben tr., itr. V. dust

Abstecher der; ~s, ~ side-trip

ab|stehen unr. itr. V. ⟨hair⟩ stand up; ⟨pigtail[s]⟩ stick out; **~de Ohren** protruding ears

Ab·steige die; ~, ~n *(ugs. abwertend)* cheap and crummy hotel *(sl.)*; **ab|steigen** unr. itr. V.; mit sein **a)** vom Pferd/Fahrrad] ~: get off [one's horse/bicycle]; **b)** *(abwärts gehen)* go down

ab|stellen tr. V. **a)** put down; **b)** *(unterbringen)* put; *(parken)* park; **c)** *(ausschalten, abdrehen)* turn off; **d)** *(unterbinden)* put a stop to

Abstell-: ~**kammer** die, ~**raum** der lumber-room

ab|stempeln tr. V. **a)** frank ⟨letter⟩;

cancel ⟨stamp⟩; **b)** *(fig.)* label, brand **(zu, als** as)

ab|sterben unr. itr. V.; mit sein **a)** [gradually] die; **b)** *(gefühllos werden)* go numb

Abstieg der; ~[e]s, ~e **a)** descent; **b)** *(Niedergang)* decline

ab|stimmen 1. itr. V. vote **(über +** Akk. on); **2.** tr. V. etw. mit jmdm. ~: discuss and agree on sth. with sb.; **Ab·stimmung** die **a)** vote; während der ~; during the voting; **b)** *(Absprache)* agreement

abstinent [apsti'nɛnt] Adj. teetotal; **~ sein** be a teetotaller; **Abstinenz** die; ~: teetotalism; **Abstinenzler** der; ~s, ~: teetotaller

ab|stoppen 1. tr. V. halt; stop; check ⟨advance⟩; **2.** itr. V. come to a halt; ⟨person⟩ stop

Ab·stoß der *(Fußball)* goal-kick; **ab|stoßen** unr. tr. V. **a)** push off; **b)** *(beschädigen)* chip ⟨crockery, paintwork, plaster⟩; **c)** *(verkaufen)* sell off; **d)** *(anwidern)* repel; put off; **abstoßend** Adj. repulsive

abstrakt [ap'strakt] Adj. abstract

ab|streifen tr. V. pull off; strip off ⟨berries⟩; **die Asche [von der Zigarette/ Zigarre] ~:** remove the ash [from one's cigarette/cigar]

ab|streiten unr. tr. V. deny

Ab·strich der **a)** *(Med.)* swab; **einen ~ machen** take a swab; **b)** *(Streichung, Kürzung)* cut; **~e machen** make cuts **(an +** Dat. in)

ab|stumpfen itr. V.; mit sein jmd. stumpft ab *(wird unsensibel)* sb.'s mind becomes deadened

Ab·sturz der fall; *(eines Flugzeugs)* crash; **ab|stürzen** itr. V.; mit sein fall; ⟨aircraft, pilot, passenger⟩ crash

ab|stützen 1. refl. V. support oneself **(mit** on, **an +** Dat. against); **2.** tr. V. support

ab|suchen tr. V. search **(nach** for)

absurd Adj. absurd

Abszeß der; Abszesses, Abszesse **a)** *(Med.)* abscess; **b)** *(Geschwür)* ulcer

Abszisse die; ~, ~en *(Math.)* abscissa

Abt der; ~[e]s, Äbte abbot

Abt. Abk. Abteilung

ab|tasten tr. V. etw. ~: feel sth. all over

ab|tauen 1. itr. V.; mit sein *(eis-/schneefrei werden)* become clear of ice/snow; ⟨refrigerator⟩ defrost; **2.** tr. V. melt; thaw; defrost ⟨refrigerator⟩

Abtei die; ~, ~en abbey

Abteil das; ~[e]s, ~e compartment;
Ab·teilung die department; **Ab·teilungs·leiter** der head of department

ab|tippen tr. V. (ugs.) type out
Äbtissin die; ~, ~nen abbess
ab|tönen tr. V. tint
ab|töten tr. V. destroy ⟨parasites, germs⟩; deaden ⟨nerve, feeling⟩
ab|tragen unr. tr. V. (abnutzen) wear out; abgetragen well worn
abträglich Adj. (geh.) einer Sache (Dat.) ~ sein be detrimental to sth.
Ab·transport der s. abtransportieren: taking away; removal; **ab|transportieren** tr. V. take away; remove ⟨dead, injured⟩
ab|treiben 1. unr. tr. V. a) carry away; jmdn./ein Schiff vom Kurs ~ drive sb./a ship off course; b) abort ⟨foetus⟩; ein Kind ~ lassen have an abortion; 2. unr. itr. V.; mit sein be carried away; ⟨ship⟩ be drives off course; **Abtreibung** die; ~, ~en abortion
ab|trennen tr. V. detach
ab|treten 1. unr. tr. V. a) sich (Dat.) die Füße/Schuhe ~: wipe one's feet; b) jmdm. etw. ~: let sb. have sth.; 2. unr. itr. V.; mit sein a) ⟨Theater⟩ exit; (fig.) make one's exit; b) (zurücktreten) step down; ⟨monarch⟩ abdicate; **Abtreter** der; ~s, ~: doormat
ab|trocknen tr. V. dry; sich (Dat.) die Hände/die Tränen ~: dry one's hands/tears
ab|tropfen itr. V.; mit sein drip off
abtrünnig Adj. (einer Partei) renegade; (einer Religion, Sekte) apostate; der Kirche/dem Glauben ~ werden desert the Church/the faith
ab|tun unr. tr. V. dismiss
ab|wägen unr. od. regelm. tr., itr. V. weigh up; abgewogen carefully weighted; balanced ⟨judgement⟩
ab|wählen tr. V. vote out; drop ⟨school subject⟩
ab|wandeln tr. V. adapt
ab|wandern itr. V.; mit sein migrate; (in ein anderes Land) emigrate; **Ab·wanderung** die migration; (in ein anderes Land) emigration
Ab·wandlung die adaptation
ab|warten 1. itr. V. wait; sie warteten ab they awaited events; **warte ab!** wait and see; (als Drohung) just you wait!; 2. tr. V. wait for
abwärts Adv. downwards; (bergab) downhill; den Fluß ~: downstream

Abwasch der; ~[e]s washing-up (Brit.); washing dishes (Amer.); den ~ machen do the washing-up/wash the dishes; **abwaschbar** Adj. washable; **ab|waschen** 1. unr. tr. V. a) wash off; b) (reinigen) wash down; wash [up] ⟨dishes⟩; 2. unr. itr. V. wash up (Brit.); wash the dishes (Amer.)
Ab·wasser das; Pl. -wässer sewage
ab|wechseln refl., itr. V. alternate; wir wechselten ab we took turns; **abwechselnd** Adv. alternately; **Ab·wechslung** die; ~, ~en variety; (Wechsel) change; zur ~: for a change
Ab·weg der: auf ~e kommen od. geraten go astray; **abwegig** erroneous; false ⟨suspicion⟩
Ab·wehr die; ~ a) repulsion; (von Schlägen) fending off; (Sport) clearance; clearing (Amer.); b) (Sport: Hintermannschaft) defence; **ab|wehren** tr. V. a) repulse; fend off ⟨blow⟩; (Sport) clear ⟨ball, shot⟩; b) avert ⟨danger, consequences⟩
ab|weichen unr. itr. V.; mit sein a) deviate; b) (sich unterscheiden) differ; **Abweichung** die; ~, ~en a) deviation; b) (Unterschied) difference
ab|weisen unr. tr. V. turn away; turn down ⟨applicant, suitor⟩; **abweisend** Adj. cold ⟨look, tone of voice⟩; in ~em Ton coldly; **Ab·weisung** die; ~, ~en s. abweisen: turning away; turning down
ab|wenden 1. unr. od. regelm. tr. V. a) turn away; b) nur regelm. (verhindern) avert. 2. unr. od. regelm. refl. V. turn away
ab|werben unr. tr. V. lure away
ab|werfen 1. unr. tr. V. a) drop; throw off ⟨clothing⟩; jettison ⟨ballast⟩; throw ⟨rider⟩; b) (ins Spielfeld werfen) throw out ⟨ball⟩; c) (einbringen) bring in; 2. unr. itr. V. (Sport) throw the ball out
ab|werten tr., itr. V. devalue; **abwertend** Adj. derogatory ⟨term⟩; **Ab·wertung** die devaluation
abwesend Adj. absent; **Abwesenheit** die; ~ absence
ab|wickeln tr. V. a) unwind; b) (erledigen) deal with ⟨case⟩; do ⟨business⟩; **Abwicklung** die; ~, ~en s. abwickeln 1 b: dealing (Gen. with); doing
ab|wiegen unr. tr. V. weigh out; weigh ⟨single item⟩
ab|wimmeln tr. V. (ugs.) get rid of
ab|wischen tr. V. a) wipe away; b) (säubern) wipe

Ab·wurf der a) dropping; *(von Ballast)* jettisoning; b) **beim ~ stolperte der Torwart** the goalkeeper stumbled as he threw the ball out

ab|zahlen *tr. V.* pay off *(debt, loan)*

ab|zählen *tr. V.* count

Ab·zahlung die paying off; **etw. auf ~ kaufen/verkaufen** buy/sell sth. on easy terms

Ab·zeichen das emblem; *(Anstecknadel, Plakette)* badge

ab|zeichnen 1. *tr. V.* a) *(kopieren)* copy; b) *(signieren)* initial; 2. *refl. V.* stand out; *(fig.)* begin to emerge

Abzieh·bild das transfer; **ab|ziehen** 1. *unr. tr. V.* a) pull off; peel off ⟨skin⟩; strip ⟨bed⟩; b) *(Fot.)* make a print/prints of; c) *(Milit., auch fig.)* withdraw; d) *(subtrahieren)* subtract; take away; *(abrechnen)* deduct; 2. *unr. itr. V.; mit sein (sich verflüchtigen)* escape; b) *(Milit.)* withdraw; **Ab·zug** der a) *(an einer Schußwaffe)* trigger; b) *(Fot.)* print; c) *(Verminderung)* deduction; **abzüglich** *Präp. mit Gen. (Kaufmannsspr.)* less

ab|zweigen 1. *itr. V.; mit sein* branch off; 2. *tr. V.* put aside; **Abzweigung** die; ~, ~en turn-off; *(Gabelung)* fork

ach *Interj.* a) *(betroffen, mitleidig)* oh [dear]; b) *(bedauernd, unwirsch)* oh; c) *(klagend)* ah; d) *(erstaunt)* oh; ~, **wirklich?** no, really?; ~, **der!** oh, him!; e) ~ **so!** oh, I see; ~ **was** *od.* **wo!** of course not

Achat der; ~[e]s, ~e *(Min.)* agate

Achse die; ~, ~n a) *(Rad~)* axle; b) *(Dreh~, Math., Astron.)* axis

Achsel die; ~, ~n *(Schulter)* shoulder; *(~höhle)* armpit

Achsel-: **~haare** *Pl.* armpit hair *sing.*; **~höhle** die armpit

¹**acht** *Kardinalz.* eight; **um ~ [Uhr]** at eight [o'clock]; **um halb ~** at half past seven; **dreiviertel ~, Viertel vor ~:** [a] quarter to eight; **es steht ~ zu ~/~ zu 2** *(Sport)* the score is eight all/eight to two; ²**acht: sie waren zu ~:** there were eight of them

³**acht: etw. außer ~ lassen** disregard sth.; **sich in ~ nehmen** be careful; **sich vor jmdm./etw. in ~ nehmen** be wary of sb./sth.

acht... *Ordinalz.* eighth; **der ~e September** the eighth of September; **München, [den] 8. Mai 1984** Munich, 8 May 1984; **Acht** die; ~, ~en a) eight; b) *(Figur)* figure eight; c) *(Verbiegung)* buckle; **mein Rad hat eine ~:** my

wheel is buckled; **Achte** der/die; adj. *Dekl.* eighth

acht-, Acht-: **~eck** das; ~s, ~e octagon; **~eckig** *Adj.* octagonal; **~einhalb** *Bruchz.* eight and a half

achtel *Bruchz.* eighth; **Achtel** das *(schweiz. meist* der); ~s, ~ eighth; **Achtel·note** die *(Musik)* quaver

achten 1. *tr. V.* respect; 2. *itr. V.* **auf etw. (Akk.) ~:** pay heed to sth.

achtens *Adv.* eighthly; **Achterbahn** die roller-coaster; **acht·fach** *Vervielfältigungsz.* eightfold; **die ~fache Menge** eight times the quantity; **~fach vergrößert/verkleinert** magnified/reduced eight times; **das Achtfache kosten** cost eight times as much

acht|geben *unr. itr. V.* a) **auf jmdn./etw. ~:** take care of sb./sth.; b) *(vorsichtig sein)* be careful

acht-: **~hundert** *Kardinalz.* eight hundred; **~jährig** *Adj. (8 Jahre alt)* eight-year-old *attrib.;* eight years old *pred.; (8 Jahre dauernd)* eight-year *attrib.;* **~köpfig** *Adj. (family, committee)* of eight

acht·los 1. *Adj.* heedless; 2. *adv.* heedlessly

acht-: **~mal** *Adv.* eight times; **~spurig** *Adj.* eight-lane ⟨road⟩; eight-track ⟨cassette⟩; **~stellig** *Adj.* eight-figure *attrib.;* **~stellig** sein have eight figures; **~stimmig** 1. *Adj.* eight-part *attrib.;* 2. *adv.* in eight parts; **~stöckig** *Adj.* eight-storey *attrib.;* **~tägig** *Adj. (8 Tage alt)* eight-day-old *attrib.; (8 Tage dauernd)* eight-day[-long] *attrib.;* **~tausend** *Kardinalz.* eight thousand; **~teilig** *Adj.* eight-piece ⟨tea-service, tool-set, etc.⟩; eight-part ⟨series, serial⟩

Achtung die; ~ a) respect (vor + *Dat., Gen.* for); b) ~! watch out!; ~, **fertig, los!** on your marks, get set, go!

acht·zehn *Kardinalz.* eighteen; **18 Uhr 33** 6.33 p.m.; *(auf der 24-Stunden-Uhr)* 1833; **achtzehn·jährig** *Adj. (18 Jahre alt)* eighteen-year-old *attrib.;* eighteen years old *pred.; (18 Jahre dauernd)* eighteen-year *attrib*

achtzig *Kardinalz.* eighty; **mit ~ [km/h] fahren** drive at *or* (coll.) do eighty [k.p.h.]; **über/etwa ~ [Jahre alt]** sein be over/about eighty [years old]; **mit ~ [Jahren]** *od.* **Achtzig** at eighty [years of age]; **achtzig·jährig** *Adj. (80 Jahre alt)* eighty-year-old *attrib.;* eighty years old *pred.; (80 Jahre dauernd)* eighty-year *attrib.*

ächzen *itr. V.* groan

Acker der; ~s, **Äcker** field; **Ackerbau** der; *o. Pl.* arable farming *no indef. art.*

A.D. *Abk.* Anno Domini AD

ADAC [a:de:a:'tse:] der; ~ *Abk.* Allgemeiner Deutscher Automobilclub

Adams·apfel der *(ugs.)* Adam's apple

adäquat [atlɛ'kva:t] *Adj.* ap- propriate *(Dat. to)*; suitable *(Dat. for)*

addieren 1. *tr. V.* add [up]; 2. *itr. V.* add; **Addition** die; ~, ~en addition

ade *Interj. (veralt., landsch.)* farewell *(dated)*; bye *(coll.)*

Adel der; ~s nobility; **der niedere/hohe** ~: the lesser nobility/the aristocracy; **adelig** *s.* adlig; **Adelige** *s.* Adlige; **adeln** *tr. V.* jmdn. ~: give sb. a title; *(in den hohen Adel erheben)* raise sb. to the peerage

Adels-: ~**geschlecht** das noble family; ~**stand** der nobility; *(hoher Adel)* nobility; ~**titel** der title of nobility

Ader die; ~, ~n a) blood-vessel; b) *o. Pl. (Anlage, Begabung)* streak; c) *(Bot., Geol.)* vein; d) *(Elektrot.)* core

adieu [a'diø:] *Interj. (veralt.)* adieu

Adjektiv das; ~s, ~e *(Sprachw.)* adjective

Adjutant der; ~en, ~en adjutant

Adler der; ~s, ~: eagle

adlig *Adj.* noble; ~ **sein** be a noble [man/woman]; **Adlige** der/die *adj. Dekl.* noble [man/woman]

Admiral der; ~s, ~e *od.* **Admiräle** admiral

adoptieren *tr. V.* adopt; **Adoption** die; ~, ~en adoption

Adoptiv-: ~**eltern** *Pl.* adoptive parents; ~**kind** das adopted child

Adressat der; ~en, ~en, **Adressatin** die; ~, ~nen addressee; **Adreß-buch** das directory; **Adresse** die; ~, ~n address; **bei jmdm. an die falsche** ~ **kommen** *od.* **geraten** *(fig. ugs.)* come to the wrong address *(fig.)*; **adressieren** *tr. V.* address

adrett 1. *Adj.* smart. 2. *adv.* smartly

Advent [at'vɛnt] der; ~s a) Advent; b) *(Adventssonntag)* Sunday in Advent

Advents-: ~**kalender** der Advent calendar; ~**kranz** der garland of evergreens with four candles for the Sundays in Advent

Adverb [at'vɛrp] das; ~s, ~ien *(Sprachw.)* adverb; **adverbial** *(Sprachw.)* 1. *Adj.* adverbial; 2. *adv.* adverbially

Advokat [atvo'ka:t] der; ~en, ~en *(österr., schweiz., sonst veralt.)* lawyer; advocate *(arch.)*

Aero- [aero- *od.* ɛ:ro-]: ~**gramm** das air[-mail] letter; ~**sol** das; ~s, ~e aerosol

Affäre die; ~, ~n affair; **sich aus der** ~ **ziehen** *(ugs.)* get out of it

Affe der; ~n, ~n a) monkey; *(Menschen~)* ape; b) *(salopp) (dummer Kerl)* oaf; clot *(Brit. sl.)*; *(Geck)* dandy

Affekt der; ~[e]s, ~e emotion; **im** ~: in the heat of the moment; **affektiert** *(abwertend)* 1. *Adj.* affected; 2. *adv.* affectedly

Affen·theater das *(salopp)* farce

Afghane [af'ga:nə] der; ~n, ~n a) Afghan; b) *(Hund)* Afghan hound; **afghanisch** *Adj.* Afghan; **Afghanistan** [af'ga:nısta:n] *(das)*; ~s Afghanistan

Afrika *(das)*; ~s Africa; **Afrikaner** der; ~s, ~, ~African; **afrikanisch** *Adj.* African

After der; ~s, ~: anus

AG [a:'ge:] *Abk.* die; ~, ~s Aktiengesellschaft PLC *(Brit.)*; Ltd. *(private company) (Brit.)*; Inc. *(Amer.)*

Agent der; ~en, ~en; **Agentin** die; ~, ~nen agent; **Agentur** die; ~, ~en agency

Aggregat das; ~[e]s, ~e *(Technik)* unit; *(Elektrot.)* set; **Aggregat·zustand** der *(Chemie)* state

Aggression die; ~, ~en aggression; **aggressiv** 1. *Adj.* aggressive; 2. *adv.* aggressively; **Aggressivität** die; ~: aggressiveness; **Aggressor** der; ~s, ~en aggressor

Agitation die; ~: agitation; **agitieren** *itr. V.* agitate

Agrar·land das; *Pl.* ~länder agrarian country

Ägypten *(das)*; ~s Egypt; **Ägypter** der; ~s, ~Egyptian; **ägyptisch** *Adj.* Egyptian

ah *Interj. (verwundert)* oh; *(freudig, genießerisch)* ah; *(verstehend)* oh; ah

äh [ɛ(:)] *Interj.* a) *(angeekelt)* ugh; b) *(stotternd)* er; hum

aha [a'ha(:)] *Interj. (verstehend)* oh[, I see]; *(triumphierend)* aha

Ahn der; ~[e]s, *od.* ~en, ~en *(geh.)*, **Ahne** der; ~n, ~n forebear; ancestor

ähneln *itr. V.* jmdm. ~: resemble *or* be like sb.; jmdm. sehr/wenig ~: strongly resemble *or* be very like sb./bear little resemblance to sb.; **einer Sache** *(Dat.)* ~: be similar to sth.; be like sth.; **sich**

(Dat.) ~: resemble one another; be alike

ahnen *tr. V.* a) *(im voraus fühlen)* have a premonition of; b) *(vermuten)* suspect; **das konnte ich doch nicht ~!** I had no way of knowing that

ähnlich 1. *Adj.* similar; **jmdm. ~ sein** be like sb.; ~ **wie** like; 2. *adv.* similarly; *(answer, react)* in a similar way; 3. *Präp. mit Dat.* like; **Ähnlichkeit** die; ~, ~en similarity; **mit jmdm. ~ haben** be like sb.

Ahnung die; ~, ~en a) *(Vorgefühl)* premonition; b) *(ugs.: Kenntnisse)* knowledge; **von etw. [viel] ~ haben** know [a lot] about sth.; **keine ~!** [I've] no idea; **ahnungs·los** *Adj. (nichts ahnend)* unsuspecting; *(naiv, unwissend)* naïve

ahoi *Interj. (Seemannsspr.)* ahoy

Ahorn ['a:horn] der; ~s, ~e maple

Ähre [ɛːrə] die; ~, ~n ear

Aids [e:ts] das; ~: Aids

Aids-: **~kranke** der/die person suffering from Aids; **~test** der Aids test

Akademie die; ~, ~n academy; *(Bergbau, Forst~, Bau~)* school; college; **Akademiker** der; ~s, ~, **Akademikerin** die; ~, ~nen [university/college] graduate; **akademisch** 1. *Adj.* academic; 2. *adv.* academically

Akazie [a'ka:tsiə] die; ~, ~n acacia

akklimatisieren *refl. V.* become or get acclimatized

Akkord der; ~[e]s, ~e a) *(Musik)* chord; b) *(Wirtsch.) (~arbeit)* piece-work; *(~lohn)* piece-work pay no indef. art., no pl.; *(~satz)* piece-rate

Akkordeon das; ~s, ~s accordion

Akku der; ~s, ~s *(ugs.)*, **Akkumulator** der; ~s, ~en accumulator *(Brit.)*; storage battery

akkurat 1. *Adj.* meticulous; 2. *adv.* meticulously

Akkusativ der; ~s, ~e *(Sprachw.)* accusative [case]; **Akkusativ·objekt** das *(Sprachw.)* accusative or direct object

Akne die; ~, ~n *(Med.)* acne

Akrobat der; ~en, ~en acrobat; **Akrobatik** die; ~ acrobatics *pl.*; **akrobatisch** *Adj.* acrobatic

Akt der; ~[e]s, ~e a) *(auch Theater, Zirkus~, Varieté~)* act; b) *(Zeremonie)* ceremony; c) *(Geschlechts~)* sexual act; d) *(bild. Kunst)* nude; **Akt·bild** das nude [picture]

Akte die; ~, ~n file

Akten-: **~deckel** der folder; **~kof-**

fer der attaché case; **~mappe** die brief-case; **~ordner** der file; **~tasche** die brief-case; **~zeichen** das reference

Akteur [ak'tø:ɐ̯] der; ~s, ~e person involved

Akt·foto das nude photo

Aktie ['aktsiə] die; ~, ~n *(Wirtsch.)* share; ~**n** shares *(Brit.)*; stock *(Amer.)*; **die ~n fallen/steigen** share or stock prices are falling/rising; **Aktien·gesellschaft** die joint-stock company

Aktion die; ~, ~en a) action *no indef. art.*; *(militärisch)* operation; b) *(Kampagne)* campaign

Aktionär der; ~s, ~e shareholder

aktiv 1. *Adj.* a) active; b) *(Milit.)* serving *attrib. (officer, soldier)*; 2. *adv.* actively; **Aktiv** das; ~s, ~e *(Sprachw.)* active; **Aktive** der/die *adj. Dekl. (Sport)* participant; **aktivieren** *tr. V.* mobilize *(party members, group, class, etc.)*; **den Kreislauf ~:** stimulate the circulation; **Aktivität** die; ~, ~en activity

Akt·modell das nude model

Aktualität die; ~, ~en a) *(Gegenwartsbezug)* relevance [to the present]; b) *(von Nachrichten usw.)* topicality; **aktuell** *Adj.* topical; *(gegenwärtig)* current; *(neu)* up-to-the-minute; **eine ~e Sendung** *(Ferns., Rundf.)* a [news and] current affairs programme

Akupunktur die; ~, ~en *(Med.)* acupuncture

Akustik die; ~ a) *(Lehre vom Schall)* acoustics *sing., no art.*; b) *(Schallverhältnisse)* acoustics *pl.*; **akustisch** 1. *Adj.* acoustic. 2. *adv.* acoustically

akut *Adj. (auch Med.)* acute; pressing; urgent *(question, issue)*

Akzent der; ~[e]s, ~e a) *(Sprachw.) (Betonung)* stress; *(Betonungszeichen)* accent; b) *(Sprachmelodie, Aussprache)* accent

akzeptabel 1. *Adj.* acceptable; 2. *adv.* acceptably; **akzeptieren** *tr. V.* accept

à la [a la] *(Gastr., ugs.)* à la

Alabaster der; ~s, ~: alabaster

à la carte [ala'kart] *(Gastr.)* à la carte

Alarm der; ~[e]s, ~e alarm; *(Flieger~)* air-raid warning; ~ **geben** */(fig. ugs.)* **schlagen** raise the alarm; **blinder ~:** false alarm

alarm-, Alarm-: **~anlage** die alarm system; **~bereit** *Adj.* on alert *postpos.*; **~bereitschaft** die alert

alarmieren *tr. V.* a) alarm; b) *(zu Hilfe rufen)* call [out] ⟨*doctor, police, fire brigade, etc.*⟩

Alarm-: **~sirene** die warning siren; **~stufe** die alert stage

Albaner der; ~s, ~Albanian; **Albanien** [al'ba:niən] *(das)*; ~s Albania; **albanisch** *Adj.* Albanian

Albatros der; ~, ~se *(Zool.)* albatross

Alben *s.* Album

albern *Adj.* a) silly; **sich ~ benehmen** act silly; b) *(ugs.: nebensächlich)* silly; stupid; **Albernheit** die; ~, ~en silliness

Albino der; ~s, ~s albino

Album das; ~s, Alben album

Alge die; ~, ~n alga

Algebra [*österr.:* al'ge:bra] die; ~: algebra

Algerien [al'ge:riən] *(das)*; ~s Algeria; **Algerier** der; ~s, ~: Algerian; **algerisch** *Adj.* Algerian

alias *Adv.* alias

Alibi das; ~s, ~s alibi

Alkohol der; ~s, ~e alcohol; **alkohol·frei** *Adj.* non-alcoholic; **Alkoholiker** der; ~s, ~: alcoholic; **alkoholisch** *Adj.* alcoholic; **Alkoholismus** der; ~: alcoholism *no art.*

all *Indefinitpron. u. unbest. Zahlw.* 1. *attr. (ganz, gesamt...)* all; **~es andere/Weitere/übrige** everything else; **~es Schöne** everything *or* all that is beautiful; **~es Gute!** all the best!; **wir/ihr/sie ~e** all of us/you/them; **~e Anwesenden** all those present; **~e Bewohner der Stadt** all the inhabitants of the town; **~e Jahre wieder** every year; **~e fünf Minuten/Meter** every five minutes/metres; **Bücher ~er Art** all kinds of books; **in ~er Ruhe** in peace and quiet; 2. *alleinstehend* **~e all; ~e, die...:** all those who...; b) **~es** *(auf Sachen bezogen)* everything; *(auf Personen bezogen)* everybody; **das ~es** all that; **trotz ~em** in spite of everything; **~es in ~em** all in all; **vor ~em** above all; **das ist ~es** that's all *or (coll.)* it; **ist das ~es?** is that all *or (coll.)* it?; **~es mal herhören!** *(ugs.)* listen everybody!; **~es aussteigen!** *(ugs.)* everyone out!; *(vom Schaffner gesagt)* all change!

All das; ~s *s.* Weltall

alle *Adj.; nicht attr.:* **~ sein** be all gone; **~ werden** run out

alle·dem *Pron.* **trotz ~:** in spite of *or* despite all that

Allee die; ~, ~n avenue

allein [a'lain] 1. *Adj.; nicht attr.* a) *(für sich)* alone; on one's/its own; by oneself/itself; **ganz ~:** all on one's/its own; b) *(einsam)* alone; 2. *adv. (ohne Hilfe)* by oneself/itself; on one's/its own; **etw. ~ tun** do sth. oneself; **von ~** *(ugs.)* by oneself/itself; 3. *Adv.* a) *(geh.: ausschließlich)* alone; b) *(bloß)* **~ der Gedanke|schon|der Gedanke ~:** the mere thought [of it]; **alleine** *(ugs.) s.* allein 1a, 2, 3b; **alleinig** *Adj.; nicht präd.* sole

allein-, Allein-: **~gang** der *(fig.)* independent initiative; **im ~gang** of one's own bat; **~stehend** *Adj.* ⟨*person*⟩ living alone; *(ledig)* single ⟨*person*⟩; **~stehende** der/die; *adj. Dekl.* person living alone; *(Ledige[r])* single person

alle·mal *Adv.* a) *(ugs.)* any time *(coll.)*; **was der kann, das kann ich doch ~:** anything he can do, I can do too; b) **ein für ~:** once and for all; **allen·falls** *Adv.* a) *(höchstens)* at [the] most; b) *(bestenfalls)* at best

aller-: **~dings** *Adj.* a) *(einschränkend)* though; **es stimmt ~dings, daß...:** it's true though that...; b) *(zustimmend)* [yes,] certainly; **das war ~dings Pech** that was bad luck, to be sure; **~erst...** *Adj.; nicht präd.* very first; **der/die/das ~erste** the very first; b) *(best...)* very best

Allergie die; ~, ~n *(Med.)* allergy; **allergisch** 1. *Adj.* *(Med.)* allergic; 2. *adv.* **auf etw. (Akk.) ~ reagieren** have an allergic reaction to sth.

aller-, Aller-: **~größt...** *Adj.* utmost ⟨*trouble, care, etc.*⟩; biggest ⟨*car, house, town, etc.*⟩ of all; tallest ⟨*person*⟩ of all; **am ~größten sein** be [the] biggest/tallest of all; **~hand** *indekl. unbest. Gattungsz. (ugs.)* a) *attr.* all kinds *or* sorts of; b) *alleinstehend* all kinds *or* sorts of things; **das ist ~hand** *(viel)* that's a lot; **das ist ja ~hand!** that's just not on! *(Brit. coll.)*; **~heiligen das;** ~: *(bes. kath. Kirche)* All Saints' Day; **~herzlichst** 1. *Adj.* warmest ⟨*thanks, greetings, congratulations*⟩; most cordial ⟨*reception, welcome, invitation*⟩; 2. *adv.* most warmly; **~höchst...** *Adj.* highest ⟨*building, tree, etc.*⟩ of all; 2. *adv.* **am ~höchsten** ⟨*fly, jump, etc.*⟩ the highest of all; **~höchstens** *Adv.* at the very most

allerlei *indekl. unbest. Gattungsz.:* *attr.* all kinds *or* sorts of; *alleinstehend* all kinds *or* sorts of things; **Al-**

lerlei das; ~s, ~s *(Gemisch)* pot-pourri; *(Durcheinander)* jumble

aller-, Aller-: ~**letzt...** *Adj.; nicht präd.* **a)** very last; **b)** *(ugs. abwertend)* most dreadful *(coll.)*; **das ist das Aller-letzte** that is the absolute limit; ~**liebst...** 1) *Adj.* most favourite; **es wäre mir am ~liebsten** *od.* **das ~liebste, wenn...:** I should like it best of all if ...; 2. *adv.* **etw. am ~liebsten tun** like doing sth. best of all; ~**meist...** 1. *Indefinitpron. u. unbest. Zahlw.* by far the most *attrib.*; **das ~meiste/am ~meisten** most of all/by far the most; 2. *Adv.* **am ~meisten** most of all; ~**mindest...** *Adj.*slightest; least; **das ~mindeste** the very least; ~**nächst...** 1. *Adj.* very nearest *attrib.*; *(Reihenfolge ausdrückend)* very next *attrib.*; 2. *adv.* **am ~nächsten** nearest of all; ~**neu[e]st...** *Adj.* very latest *attrib.*; **das Allerneu[e]ste** the very latest; ~**schlimmst...** *Adj.* very worst *attrib.*; ~**schönst...** 1. *Adj.* most beautiful *attrib.*; loveliest *attrib.*; *(angenehmst...)* very nicest *attrib.*; 2. *adv.* **er singt am ~schönsten** his singing is the most beautiful of all; ~**seits** *Adv.* **guten Morgen ~seits!** good morning everyone

Allerwelts-: ~**gesicht** das nondescript face; ~**wort** das hackneyed word

allerwenigst... 1. *Adj.* lest ... of all; *Pl.* fewest ... of all; 2. *adv.* **am ~wenigsten** least of all

alle·samt *Indefinitpron. u. unbest. Zahlw. (ugs.)* all [of you/us/them]; **wir ~:** we all

Alles·kleber der all-purpose adhesive

all·gemein 1. *Adj.* general; universal *(conscription, suffrage)*; **im ~en Interesse** in the common interest; **im ~en** in general; 2. *adv.* **a)** generally; *(ausnahmslos)* universally; **es ist ~ bekannt, daß ...:** it is common knowledge that ...; **b)** *(unverbindlich)* *(write, talk, discuss)* in general terms

Allgemein-: ~**befinden** das *(Med.)* general state of health; ~**bildung** die; *o. Pl.* general education

Allgemeinheit die; ~ **a)** generality; **b) die ~:** the general public

Allgemein-: ~**medizin** die; *o. Pl.* general medicine; ~**wohl** das public good

All·heilmittel das *(auch fig.)* cureall; panacea

Alligator der; ~s, ~en alligator

Alliierte der; adj. Dekl. ally; **die ~n** the Allies

all-: ~**jährlich** 1. *Adj.* annual; yearly; 2. *adv.* annually; every year; ~**mächtig** *Adj.* all-powerful

all·mählich 1. *Adj.* gradual; 2. *adv.* gradually; 3. *adv.* **wir sollten ~ gehen** it's time we got going

all-, All-: ~**morgendlich** 1. *Adj.* regular morning; 2. *adv.* every morning; ~**seitig** 1. *Adj.* general; all-round, *(Amer.)* all-around *attrib.*; 2. *adv.* generally; ~**seits** *Adv.* on all sides; ~**tag** der **a)** *(Werktag)* weekday; **b)** *o. Pl. (Einerlei)* daily routine; **der graue ~** the dull routine of everyday life; ~**täglich** *Adj.* ordinary *(face, person, appearance, etc.)*; everyday *(topic, event, sight)*; commonplace *(remark)*; **ein nicht ~täglicher Anblick** a sight one doesn't see every day; ~**tags** *Adv.* [on] weekdays; ~**zu** *Adv.* all too; **nicht ~zu viele** not too many

allzu-: ~**früh** *Adv.* all too early; *(~bald)* all too soon; ~**lang[e]** *Adv.* too long; ~**oft** *Adv.* too often; ~**sehr** *Adv.* too much; **nicht ~sehr** not too much; ~**viel** *Adv.* too much

Alm die; ~, ~en mountain pasture; Alpine pasture; **Alm·hütte** die Alpine hut

Almosen das; ~s, ~ alms *pl.*

Alp die; ~, ~en *(bes. schweiz.) s.* Alm

Alpaka das; ~s, ~s alpaca

Alpen *Pl.* die ~: the Alps

Alpen-: ~**rose** die rhododendron; ~**veilchen** das cyclamen

Alpha das; ~[s], ~[s] alpha; **Alphabet** das; ~[e]s, ~e alphabet; **alphabetisch** 1. *Adj.* alphabetical; 2. *adv.* alphabetically

Alp·horn das alpenhorn; **alpin** *Adj.* Alpine; **Alpinist** der; ~en, ~en Alpinist

als *Konj.* **a)** *(zeitlich)* when; **damals, ~:** [in the days] when; **gerade ~:** just as; **b)** *(kausal)* **um so mehr, ~:** all the more since *or* in that; **c)** *Vergleichspartikel* **größer/älter/mehr/weniger ~:** bigger/older/more/less than; **anders ~ wir sein/leben** be different/live differently from us; **soviel/soweit ~ möglich** as much/as far as possible; **so bald/schnell ~ möglich** as soon/as quickly as possible; **~ [wenn od. ob]** *(+ Konjunktiv II)* as if; as though; ~ **ob ich das nicht wüßte!** as if I didn't know!; **d)**

~ **Rentner/Arzt** as a pensioner/a doctor sich ~ **wahr/Lüge erweisen** prove to be true/a lie

also 1. *Adv.* so; therefore; 2. *Partikel* a) *(das heißt)* that is; b) *(nach Unterbrechung)* well [then]; c) *(verstärkend)* **na** ~! there you are[, you see]; ~ **schön** well all right then

alt, älter, ältest... *Adj.* a) old; ~ **und jung** old and young; **seine** ~**en Eltern** his aged parents; **wie** ~ **bist du?** how old are you?; **mein älterer/ältester Bruder** my elder/eldest brother; b) *(nicht mehr frisch)* old; ~**es Brot** stale bread; c) *(vom letzten Jahr)* old; ~**e Äpfel/Kartoffeln** last year's apples/potatoes; d) *(langjährig)* long-standing *(acquaintance)*; e) *(antik, klassisch)* ancient; f) *(vertraut)* old familiar *(streets, sights, etc.)*; **ganz der/die** ~**e sein** be just the same

¹**Alt** *der;* ~s, ~e *(Musik)* alto; *(Frauenstimme)* contralto; *(im Chor)* contraltos *pl.*

²**Alt** *das;* ~[s], ~: *top fermented, dark beer*

Altar *der;* ~[e]s, **Altäre** altar

alt-, Alt-: ~**bau·wohnung die** flat *(Brit.)* or *(Amer.)* apartment in an old building; ~**bekannt** *Adj.* well-known; ~**bier das** s. ²**Alt**

Alte der/die; *adj. Dekl.* a) *(alter Mensch)* old man/woman; *Pl.* old people; b) *(salopp) (Vater, Ehemann)* old man *(coll.); (Mutter, Ehefrau)* old woman *(coll.); (Chef)* governor *(sl.); (Chefin)* boss *(coll.);* **die** ~**n** *(Eltern)* my/his *etc.* old man and old woman 4(coll.); c) *Pl. (Tiereltern)* parents

alt·ehrwürdig *Adj.* (geh.) venerable; time-honoured *(customs);* **Alt·englisch das** Old English

Alter das; ~s, ~: age; *(hohes* ~*)* old age; **im** ~: in one's old age; **im** ~ **von** at the age of; **älter** 1. *s.* **alt**; 2. *Adj.* *(nicht mehr jung)* elderly; **mit sein** *V.;* **altern** *itr. V.;* **mit sein** age

alters-, Alters-: ~**genosse der,** ~**genossin die** contemporary; ~**gruppe die** age-group; ~**schwach** *Adj.* old and infirm *(person);* old and weak *(animal);* ~**schwäche die;** *o. Pl. (bei Menschen)* [old] age and infirmity; *(bei Tieren)* [old] age and weakness; ~**stufe die** age; ~**unterschied der** age difference; ~**versorgung die** provision for one's old age; *(System)* pension scheme

Altertum das; ~s antiquity *no art.*

Älteste der/die; *adj. Dekl.* a) *(Dorf~, Vereins~, Kirchen~ usw.)* elder; b) *(Sohn, Tochter)* eldest

alt-, Alt-: ~**griechisch das** classical or ancient Greek; ~**hochdeutsch das** Old High German; ~**klug** ~ **klüger, ~klugst...** 1. *Adj.* precocious; 2. *adv.* precociously; ~**last die** *(Ökologie)* old, improperly disposed of harmful waste; *(fig.)* inherited problem

ältlich *Adj.* rather elderly

alt-, Alt-: ~**modisch** 1. *Adj.* old-fashioned; 2. *adv.* in a old-fashioned way; ~**rosa** *Adj.* old rose; ~**stadt die** old [part of the] town; ~**waren·händler der** second-hand dealer

Alu das; ~s *(ugs.)* aluminium; **Alu-folie die** aluminium foil; **Aluminium das;** ~s aluminium

am *Präp. + Art.* a) = **an dem;** b) **Frankfurt am Main** Frankfurt on [the] Main; **am Marktplatz** on the market square; **am Meer/Fluß** by the sea/on or by the river; **am Anfang/Ende** at the beginning/end; **am 19. November** on 19 November; **am schnellsten laufen** run [the] fastest; **am Verwelken sein** be wilting

Amateur [ama'tø:ɐ̯] *der;* ~s, ~e amateur

Amazonas der; ~: Amazon

Amboß der; ~**es, Ambosse, Ambosse** anvil

ambulant *(Med.)* 1. *Adj.* out-patient *attrib.;* 2. *adv.* **jmdn.** ~ **behandeln** give sb. out-patient treatment; **Ambulanz die;** ~, ~**en** a) *(in Kliniken)* out-patient[s'] department; b) *(Krankenwagen)* ambulance

Ameise die; ~, ~**n** ant

Ameisen-: ~**bär der** ant-eater; ~**haufen der** anthill

amen *Adv.* amen; **Amen das;** ~s, ~: Amen

Amerika (das); ~s America; **Amerikaner der;** ~s, ~ a) American; b) *(Gebäck) small, flat iced cake;* **Amerikanerin die;** ~, ~**nen** American; **amerikanisch** *Adj.* American

Amino·säure die *(Chemie)* amino acid

Ammann der; ~**[e]s, Ämänner** *(schweiz.) (Gemeinde~, Bezirks~)* ≈ mayor; *(Land~)* cantonal president

Amme die; ~, ~**n** wet-nurse

Amnestie [amnɛs'tiː] *die;* ~, ~**n** amnesty; **amnestieren** *tr. V.* grant an amnesty to

Amöbe die; ~, ~n (Biol.) amoeba
Amok der: ~ laufen run amok;
Amok·läufer der madman
Ampel die; ~, ~n a) (Verkehrs~) traffic lights pl.; b) (für Pflanzen) hanging
flowerpot
Amphibie [am'fi:biə] die; ~, ~n
(Zool.) amphibian; **Amphi-
bien·fahrzeug** das amphibious
vehicle
Amphi·theater das amphitheatre
Ampulle die; ~, ~n (Med.) ampoule
Amputation die; ~, ~en (Med.) amputation; **amputieren** tr. V. amputate
Amsel die; ~, ~n blackbird
Amt das; ~[e]s, Ämter a) (Stellung)
post; position; (hohes politisches od.
kirchliches ~) office; im ~ sein be in
office; b) (Aufgabe) task; job; c) (Behörde) office; d) (Fernsprechvermitt-
lung) exchange; **amtieren** itr. V. a)
hold office; b) (vorübergehend) act
(als as); **amtlich 1.** Adj. a) official;
(ugs.: sicher) definite; 2. adv. officially; **Amt·mann** der; Pl. ...männer
od. ...leute, **Amt·männin** die; ~,
~nen senior civil servant
Amts-: ~arzt der medical officer;
~gericht das local or district court;
~geschäfte Pl. official duties;
~leitung die (Fernspr.) exchange line
Amulett das; ~[e]s, ~e amulet; charm
amüsant 1. Adj. entertaining; 2. adv.
in an entertaining way; **amüsieren
1.** refl. V. a) (sich vergnügen) enjoy
oneself; sich mit jmdm. ~: have fun or
a good time with sb.; b) (belustigt sein)
be amused; sich über jmdn./etw. ~:
find sb./sth. funny; 2. tr. V. amuse
an 1. Präp. mit Dat. a) (räumlich) at;
(auf) on; Frankfurt an der Oder
Frankfurt on [the] Oder; Tür an Tür
next door to one another; an ... vorbei
past; b) (zeitlich) on; an jedem Sonntag every Sunday; an Ostern (bes.
südd.) at Easter; c) arm/reich an Vit-
aminen low/rich in vitamins; jmdn. an
etw. erkennen recognize sb. by sth.; an
etw. leiden suffer from sth.; an einer
Krankheit sterben die of a disease; d)
an [und für] sich actually; 2. Präp. mit
Akk. a) to; (auf, gegen) on; b) an etw./
jmdn. glauben believe in sth./sb.; an
etw. denken think of sth.; sich an etw.
erinnern remember sth.; 3. Adv. a)
(Verkehrsw.) Köln an: 9.15 arriving
Cologne 09.15; b) (ugs.: in Betrieb)
on; die Waschmaschine/der Fernseher

ist an the washing-machine/television
is on; s. auch ansein; c) (ugs.: ungefähr) around; about; an [die] 20000
DM around or about 20,000 DM
Analyse die; ~, ~n analysis; analy-
sieren tr. V. analyse; **analytisch 1.**
Adj. analytical; 2. adv. analytically
Ananas die; ~, ~ od. ~se pineapple
Anarchie die; ~, ~n anarchy; **Anarchist** der; ~en, ~en anarchist
Anatomie die; ~, ~n anatomy; **anatomisch** Adj. anatomical
an|bahnen 1. tr. V. initiate (negoti-
ations, talks, process, etc.); develop
(relationship, connection); 2. refl. V.
(development) be in the offing;
(friendship, relationship) start to develop
an|bändeln itr. V. mit jmdm. ~ (ugs.)
get off with sb. (Brit. coll.); pick sb. up
An·bau der; Pl. Anbauten a) o. Pl.
(Gebäude) extension; c)
o. Pl. (das Anpflanzen) growing
an|bauen 1. tr. V. a) build on; b) (an-
pflanzen) grow; 2. tr. V. (das Haus
vergrößern) build an extension
an·bei Adv. (Amtsspr.) herewith;
Rückporto ~: return postage enclosed
an|beißen 1. unr. tr. V. bite into; take
a bite of; 2. unr. itr. V. (auch fig. ugs.)
bite
an|belangen tr. V. was mich/dies usw.
anbelangt as far as I am/this matter is
etc. concerned
an|beten tr. V. (auch fig.) worship
An·betracht der: in ~ einer Sache
(Gen.) in view of sth.
an|betreffen unr. tr. V. s. anbelangen
an|betteln tr. V. jmdn. ~: beg from
sb.; jmdn. um etw. ~: beg sb. for sth.
Anbetung die; ~, ~en (auch fig.) worship
an|biedern refl. V. sich [bei jmdm.] ~:
curry favour [with sb.]
an|bieten 1. unr. tr. V. offer; jmdm.
etw. ~: offer sb. sth.; 2. unr. refl. V. a)
offer one's services; sich ~, etw. zu tun
offer to do sth.; b) (fig.) (possibility, solution) suggest itself
an|binden unr. tr. V. tie [up] (an +
Dat. od. Akk. to); tie up, moor (boat)
(an + Dat. od. Akk. to); tether (animal) (an + Dat. od. Akk. to)
an|blasen unr. tr. V. a) blow at; b)
(anfachen) blow on
An·blick der sight; **an|blicken** tr. V.
look at
an|blinzeln tr. V. a) blink at; b) (zu-
zwinkern) wink at

an|brechen 1. *unr. tr. V.* **a)** crack; **b)** (*öffnen*) open; **c)** (*zu verbrauchen beginnen*) break into ⟨*supplies, reserves*⟩; **2.** *unr. itr. V.; mit sein* (*geh.: beginnen*) ⟨*dawn, day*⟩ break; ⟨*age, epoch*⟩ dawn

an|brennen 1. *unr. tr. V.* (*anzünden*) light; **2.** *unr. itr. V.; mit sein* burn

an|bringen *unr. tr. V.* **a)** (*befestigen*) put up ⟨*sign, aerial, curtain, plaque*⟩ (**an** + *Dat.* on); **b)** (*äußern*) make ⟨*request, complaint, comment*⟩; **c)** (*zeigen*) demonstrate ⟨*knowledge, experience*⟩; **d)** (*ugs.: herbeibringen*) bring

An·bruch der *o. Pl.* (*geh.: Beginn*) dawn[ing]; **der ~ des Tages** daybreak

an|brüllen *tr. V.* (*ugs.*) bellow at

Andacht die; ~, ~en a) (*Sammlung*) rapt attention; (*im Gebet*) silent worship; **b)** (*Gottesdienst*) prayers *pl.*;

andächtig 1. *Adj.* (*ins Gebet versunken*) devout; **2.** *adv.* with rapt attention; (*ins Gebet versunken*) devoutly

an|dauern *itr. V.* ⟨*negotiations*⟩ continue, go on; ⟨*weather, rain*⟩ last

andauernd 1. *Adj.* continual; constant; **2.** *adv.* continually; constantly

Anden *die* ~: the Andes

An·denken das; ~s, ~ **a)** *o. Pl.* memory; **zum ~ an jmdn./etw.** to remind you/us *etc.* of sb./sth.; **b)** (*Erinnerungsstück*) memento; (*Reisesouvenir*) souvenir

ander... *Indefinitpron.* **1.** *attr.* **a)** other; **ein ~er/eine ~e/ein ~es** another; **das Kleid gefällt mir nicht, haben Sie noch ~e/~es?** I don't like that dress, do you have any others/another?; **jemand ~er** *od.* **~es** someone else; (*in Fragen*) anyone else; **niemand ~er** *od.* **~es** nobody else; **etwas ~es** something else; (*in Fragen*) anything else; **nichts ~es** nothing else; not anything else; **b)** (*verschieden*) different; **2.** *alleinstehend* **ein ~r/eine ~e:** another [one]; **nicht drängeln, einer nach dem ~n** don't push, one after the other; **ein ~er/eine ~e/ein ~es** another [one]; **ein[e]s nach dem ~[e]n** first things first; **ich will weder das eine noch das ~e** I don't want either; **anderen·falls** *Adv.* otherwise; **anderer·seits** *Adv.* on the other hand; **ander·mal** *Adv.*: **ein ~:** another time; **andern·falls** *Adv.* otherwise

ändern 1. *tr. V.* change; alter ⟨*garment*⟩; change ⟨*person*⟩; **2.** *refl. V.* change

anders *Adv.* **a)** (*verschieden*) ⟨*think,*

act, feel, do⟩ differently (**als** from *or esp. Brit.* to); ⟨*be, look, sound, taste*⟩ different (**als** from *or esp. Brit.* to); **es war alles ganz ~:** it was all quite different; **b)** (*sonst*) else; **niemand ~:** nobody else; **jemand ~:** someone else; (*in Fragen*) anyone else

anders-, Anders-: ~artig *Adj.* different; **~farbig** *Adj.* different-coloured *attrib.*; of a different colour *postpos.*; **~gläubige der/die** person of a different religion; **~herum** *Adv.* the other way round *or* (*Amer.*) around; **~herum gehen/fahren** go/drive round *or* (*Amer.*) around the other way; **~wo** *Adv.* (*ugs.*) elsewhere; **~woher** *Adv.* (*ugs.*) from somewhere else; **~wohin** *Adv.* (*ugs.*) somewhere else

andert·halb *Bruchz.* one and a half; **~ Stunden** an hour and a half

Änderung die; ~, ~en change (*Gen.* in); alteration (*Gen.* of)

anderweitig 1. *Adj.* other; **2.** *adv.* in another way

an|deuten 1. *tr. V.* **a)** (*zu verstehen geben*) hint; **b)** (*nicht vollständig ausführen*) outline; (*kurz erwähnen*) indicate; **2.** *refl. V.* be indicated; **An·deutung die** hint

An·drang der; *o. Pl.* crowd; (*Gedränge*) crush

andre... *s.* ander...

an|drehen *tr. V.* **a)** (*einschalten*) turn on; **b) jmdm. etw. ~** (*ugs.*) palm sb. off with sth.

andrer·seits *Adv.* on the other hand

an|drohen *tr. V.* **jmdm. etw. ~:** threaten sb. with sth.; **An·drohung die threat**

an|drücken *tr. V.* press down

an|ecken *itr. V.; mit sein* **bei jmdm. ~** (*fig. ugs.*) rub sb. [up *(Brit.)*] the wrong way

an|eignen *refl. V.* **a)** appropriate; **b)** (*lernen*) acquire; learn

an·einander *Adv.* **~ denken** think of each other *or* one another; **~ vorbeigehen** pass each other *or* one another

aneinander: ~binden *unr. tr. V.* tie together; **~|legen** *tr. V.* put *or* place next to each other *or* one another; **~|liegen** *unr. itr. V.* lie next to each other

Anekdote die; ~, ~n anecdote

an|ekeln *tr. V.* disgust

Anemone die; ~, ~n anemone

an|erkennen *unr. tr. V.* **a)** recognize ⟨*country, record, verdict, qualification,* *document*>; acknowledge <*debt*>; accept <*demand, bill, conditions, rules*>; allow <*claim, goal*>; **b)** *(nicht leugnen)* acknowledge; **c)** *(würdigen)* appreciate; respect <*viewpoint, opinion*>; **ein ~der Blick** an appreciative look; **a̱nerkennens·wert** *Adj.* commendable; **Anerkennung die**; ~, ~en *s.* **anerkennen: a)** recognition; acknowledgement; acceptance; allowance; **b)** acknowledgement; **c)** appreciation; respect *(Gen. for)*

a̱n|fachen *tr. V.* fan; *(fig.)* arouse <*anger, curiosity, enthusiasm*>; inflame <*passion*>; stir up <*hatred*>; inspire <*hope*>; ferment <*discord, war*>

a̱n|fahren 1. *unr. tr. V.* **a)** run into; hit; **b)** *(herbeifahren)* deliver; **c)** *(ansteuern)* stop at <*village etc.*>; <*ship*> put in at <*port*>; **d)** *(zurechtweisen)* shout at; **2.** *unr. itr. V.; mit sein* **a)** *(starten)* start off; **b) angefahren kommen** come driving/riding up; **A̱n·fahrt die a)** *(das Anfahren)* journey; **b)** *(Weg)* approach

A̱n·fall der attack; *(epileptischer ~, fig.)* fit; **einen ~ bekommen** *od. (ugs.)* **kriegen** have an attack/a fit; **a̱n·fallen 1.** *unr. tr. V.* attack; **2.** *unr. itr. V.; mit sein* <*costs*> be incurred; <*interest*> accrue; <*work*> come up; **a̱n·fällig** *Adj.* <*person*> with a delicate constitution; <*machine*> susceptible to faults; **gegen** *od.* **für etw. ~ sein** be susceptible to sth.

A̱n·fang der beginning; start; *(erster Abschnitt)* beginning; **am** *od.* **zu ~:** at first; **von ~ an** from the outset; **~ 1984/der Woche** *usw.* at the beginning of 1984/of the week *etc.;* **a̱n·fangen 1.** *unr. tr. V.* **a)** begin; start; **mit etw. ~:** start [on] sth.; **~, etw. zu tun** start to do sth.; **b)** *(zu sprechen ~)* begin; **von etw. ~:** start on about sth.; **c)** *(eine Stelle antreten)* start; **2.** *unr. tr. V.* **a)** begin; start; *(anbrechen)* start; **b)** *(machen)* do; **A̱n·fänger der;** ~s, ~: beginner; **a̱nfänglich** *Adj.* initial; **a̱nfangs** *Adv.* at first; initially

A̱nfangs-: ~**buchstabe der** initial [letter]; ~**stadium das** initial stage **a̱n|fassen 1.** *tr. V.* **a)** *(fassen, halten)* take hold of; **b)** *(berühren)* touch; **jmdn. ~** *(an der Hand nehmen)* take sb.'s hand; **d)** *(angehen)* tackle <*problem, task, etc.*>; **e)** *(behandeln)* treat <*person*>; **2.** *itr. V.* **|mit|** ~**:** lend a hand **a̱nfechtbar** *Adj.: s.* **anfechten a:** disputable; contestable; challengeable;

a̱n|fechten *unr. tr. V.* **a)** dispute <*statement, contract*>; contest <*will*>; challenge <*decision, law, opinion*>; **b)** *(beunruhigen)* trouble

a̱n|fertigen *tr. V.* make

a̱n|feuchten *tr. V.* moisten <*lips, stamp*>; dampen <*ironing, cloth, etc.*>

a̱n|feuern *tr. V.* spur on

a̱n|flehen *tr. V.* beseech; implore

a̱n|fliegen 1. *unr. itr. V.; mit sein* fly in; **angeflogen kommen** come flying in; **gegen den Wind ~:** fly into the wind; **2.** *unr. tr. V.* fly to <*city, country, airport*>; **A̱n·flug der a)** approach; **b)** *(Hauch)* hint; **c)** *(Anwandlung)* fit; **in einem ~ von Großzügigkeit** in a fit of generosity

a̱n|fordern *tr. V.* ask for; order <*goods, materials*>; send for <*ambulance*>; **A̱n·forderung die a)** *(das Anfordern)* request *(Gen. for);* **b)** *(Anspruch)* demand

A̱n·frage die inquiry; *(Parl.)* question; **a̱n|fragen** *itr. V.* inquire; ask

a̱n|freunden *refl. V.* become friends

a̱n|fügen *tr. V.* add

a̱n|fühlen *refl. V.* feel

a̱n|führen *tr. V.* **a)** lead; **b)** *(zitieren)* quote; **c)** *(nennen)* give <*example, reason, details, proof*>; **d)** *(ugs.: hereinlegen)* have on *(Brit. coll.)*; dupe; **A̱n·führer der** leader; *(Rädelsführer)* ringleader; **A̱n·führung die a)** *(das Zitieren, Zitat)* quotation; **b)** *(Nennung)* giving

A̱nführungs-: ~**strich der,** ~**zeichen das** quotation-mark

A̱n·gabe die a) *(das Mitteilen)* giving; **b)** *(Information)* piece of information; ~**n** information *sing.;* **c)** *(Ballspiele)* service; serve; **a̱n|geben 1.** *tr. V.* **a)** give <*reason*>; declare <*income, dutiable goods*>; name <*witness*>; **b)** *(bestimmen)* set <*course, direction*>; **den Takt ~:** keep time; **2.** *unr. itr. V.* **a)** *(prahlen)* boast; brag; *(sich angeberisch benehmen)* show off; **b)** *(Ballspiele)* serve; **A̱ngeber der;** ~s, ~: braggart; **A̱ngeberei die;** ~: showing-off; **a̱ngeblich 1.** *Adj.* alleged; **2.** *adv.* supposedly; allegedly

a̱n·geboren *Adj.* innate *(characteristic)*; congenital <*disease*>

A̱n·gebot das a) offer; **b)** *(Wirtsch.)* supply; *(Sortiment)* range

a̱n·gebracht *Adj.* appropriate

a̱n·gegriffen *Adj.* weakened <*health, stomach*>; strained <*nerves, voice*>

a̱ngeheitert *Adj.* tipsy

an|gehen 1. *unr. itr. V.; mit sein* **a)** ⟨*radio, light, heating*⟩ come on; ⟨*fire*⟩ catch; **b)** *(anwachsen, wachsen)*⟨*plant*⟩ take root; **e) es mag noch ~:** it's [just about] acceptable; **f) gegen etw./jmdn. ~:** fight sth./sb.; **2.** *unr. tr. V.* **a)** *(angreifen)* attack; **b)** *(in Angriff nehmen)* tackle ⟨*problem, difficulty*⟩; take ⟨*fence, hedge*⟩ (ask (**um** for); **d)** *(betreffen)* concern; **das geht dich nichts an** it's none of your business; **angehend** *Adj.* budding; *(zukünftig)* prospective

an|gehören *itr. V.* jmdm./einer Sache ~: belong to sb./sth.; **der Regierung/einer Familie ~:** be a member of the government/a family; **an·gehörig** *Adj.* belonging (*Dat.* to); **Angehörige der/die;** *adj. Dekl.* **a)** *(Verwandte)* relative; relation; **b)** *(Mitglied)* member

Angeklagte der/die; *adj. Dekl.* accused; defendant

Angel die; ~, ~n a) fishing-rod; **b)** *(Tür-, Fenster- usw.)* hinge; **etw. aus den ~n heben** *(fig.)* turn sth. upside down

An·gelegenheit die matter; *(Aufgabe, Problem)* affair

Angel·haken der fish-hook; **angeln 1.** *tr. V. (zu fangen suchen)* fish for; *(fangen)* catch. **2.** *itr. V.* angle; fish; **Angel·rute die** fishing-rod

Angel·sachse der Anglo-Saxon

Angel·schnur die fishing-line

an·gemessen *Adj.* appropriate; reasonable, fair ⟨*price, fee*⟩

an·genehm 1. *Adj.* pleasant; **~e Reise/Ruhe!** [have a] pleasant journey/have a good rest; |**sehr**| **~!** delighted to meet you; **2.** *adv.* pleasantly

an·gesehen *Adj.* respected

angesichts *Präp. mit Gen. (geh.)* **a)** in the face of; **b)** *(fig.: in Anbetracht)* in view of

angespannt *Adj.* **a)** close ⟨*attention*⟩; taut ⟨*nerves*⟩; **b)** tense ⟨*situation*⟩; tight ⟨*market, economic situation*⟩

angestellt *Adj.* **bei jmdm. ~ sein** be employed by sb.; work for sb.; **Angestellte der/die;** *adj. Dekl.* [salaried] employee

an·getan *Adj.* **von jmdm./etw. ~ sein** be taken with sb./sth.

an·getrunken *Adj.* [slightly] drunk

an·gewiesen *Adj.* **auf jmdn./etw. ~ sein** have to rely on sb./sth.

an|gewöhnen *tr. V.* **jmdm. etw. ~:** get sb. used to sth.; **jmdm. ~, etw. zu tun**

get sb. used to doing sth.; **sich** *(Dat.)* **etw. ~:** get into the habit of sth.; |**es**| **sich** *(Dat.)* **~, etw. zu tun** get into the habit of doing sth.; **An·gewohnheit die** habit

an|gleichen 1. *unr. tr. V.* **etw. einer Sache** *(Dat.)* **od. an etw.** *(Akk.)* **~:** bring sth. into line with sth.; **2.** *unr. refl. V.* **sich jmdm./einer Sache od. an jmdn./etw. ~:** become like sb./sth.; **An·gleichung die: die ~ der Löhne an die Preise** bringing wages into line with prices

Angler der; ~s, ~ angler

Anglistik die; ~: English studies *pl.*, *no art.*

Angola (das); ~s Angola

Angora-: ~katze die angora cat; **~wolle die** angora [wool]

an|greifen 1. *unr. tr. V.* **a)** *(auch fig.)* attack; **b)** *(schwächen)* affect ⟨*health, heart, stomach, intestine, voice*⟩; weaken ⟨*person*⟩; **2.** *unr. itr. V. (auch fig.)* attack; **An·greifer der** *(auch fig.)* attacker; **An·griff der a)** attack; **zum ~ blasen** *(auch fig.)* sound the attack; **b) etw. in ~ nehmen** tackle sth.

angst *Adj.* **jmdm. ist/wird |es| ~ |und bange|** sb. is/becomes frightened; **Angst die; ~, Ängste a)** *(Furcht)* fear; **~ bekommen** *od. (ugs.)* **kriegen** become frightened; **~ haben** be frightened **(vor** + *Dat.* of); **b)** *(Sorge)* anxiety; **~ haben** be anxious **(um** about); **keine ~, ich vergesse es schon nicht!** don't worry, I won't forget [it]!; **ängstigen 1.** *tr. V.* frighten; *(beunruhigen)* worry; **2.** *refl. V.* be frightened; *(sich sorgen)* worry; **ängstlich 1.** *Adj.* anxious; **2.** *adv.* anxiously; **Ängstlichkeit die; ~:** timidity

an|gucken *tr. V. (ugs.)* look at; **sich** *(Dat.)* **etw./jmdn. ~:** have a look at sth./ sb.

an|gurten *tr. V.* strap in; **sich ~:** put on one's seat-belt

an|haben *unr. tr. V.* **a)** *(ugs.: am Körper tragen)* have on; **b) jmdm./einer Sache etwas ~ können** be able to harm sb./sth.

an|halten 1. *unr. tr. V.* **a)** stop; **b)** *(auffordern)* urge; **2.** *unr. itr. V.* **a)** stop; **b)** *(andauern)* go on; last; **anhaltend 1.** *Adj.* constant; continuous; **2.** *adv.* constantly; continuously; **An·halter der** hitch-hiker; **per ~ fahren** hitch[-hike]; **An·halterin die** hitchhiker; **Anhalts·punkt der** clue (**für** to); *(für eine Vermutung)* grounds *pl.*

an·hand 1. *Präp. mit Gen.* with the help of; **2.** *Adv.* ~ **von** with the help of
An·hang der a) *(Buchw.)* appendix; **b)** *(Anhängerschaft)* following; **c)** *(Verwandtschaft)* family; **an|hängen 1.** *tr. V.* **a)** hang up (**an** + *Akk.* on); **b)** *(ankuppeln)* couple on (**an** + *Akk.* to); hitch up ⟨*trailer*⟩ (**an** + *Akk.* to); **c)** *(anfügen)* add (**an** + *Akk.* to); **2.** *refl. V.* **a)** hang on (**an** + *Akk.* to); **b)** *(ugs.: sich anschließen)* **sich |an jmdn.** *od.* **bei jmdn.|** ~: tag along [with sb.] *(coll.)*.
An·hänger der a) *(Mensch)* supporter; **b)** *(Wagen)* trailer; **c)** *(Schmuckstück)* pendant; **d)** *(Schildchen)* tag; **Anhängerschaft die** ~, ~**en** supporters *pl.*; **anhänglich** *Adj.* devoted ⟨*dog, friend*⟩; **Anhänglichkeit die** ~: devotion
an|hauchen *tr. V.* breathe on ⟨*mirror, glasses*⟩; blow on ⟨*fingers, hands*⟩
an|häufen *tr. V.* accumulate; **Anhäufung die** accumulation
an|heben *unr. tr. V.* **a)** lift [up]; **b)** *(erhöhen)* raise ⟨*prices, wages, etc.*⟩
an|heften *tr. V.* attach ⟨*label, list*⟩; put up ⟨*sign, notice*⟩
anheim|stellen *(geh.) tr. V.* **|es| jmdm.** ~, **etw. zu tun** leave it to sb. to do sth.
An·hieb der: auf ~ *(ugs.)* straight off
an|himmeln *tr. V.* worship
An·höhe die rise
an|hören 1. *tr. V.* listen to; **sich** *(Dat.)* **jmdn./etw.** ~: listen to sb./sth.; **2.** *refl. V.* sound
animieren *tr. V.* encourage
Anis der; ~**[es]** aniseed
Ank. *Abk.* **Ankunft** arr.
An·kauf der purchase; **an|kaufen** *tr. V.* purchase; buy
Anker der; ~**s,** ~ anchor; **vor** ~ **gehen/liegen** drop anchor/lie at anchor; ~ **werfen** drop anchor; **ankern** *itr. V.* **a)** anchor; **b)** *(vor Anker liegen)* be anchored; **Anker·platz der** anchorage
An·klage die a) charge; **unter** ~ **stehen** have been charged (**wegen** with); **b)** *(~vertretung)* prosecution; **Anklage·bank die** dock; **auf der** ~ **sitzen** *(auch fig.)* be in the dock; **an|klagen** *tr. V.* **a)** *(Rechtsw.)* charge ⟨*Gen.*, **wegen** with⟩; accuse; **b)** *(geh.: beschuldigen)* accuse; **An·kläger der** prosecutor
an|klammern 1. *tr. V.* peg *(Brit.)*, pin *(Amer.)* ⟨*clothes, washing*⟩ up; clip ⟨*sheet etc.*⟩; *(mit Heftklammern)* staple ⟨*sheet etc.*⟩; **2.** *refl. V.* **sich an jmdn./etw.** ~: cling to sb./sth.

An·klang der: |bei jmdm.| ~ **finden** meet with [sb.'s] approval
an|kleben 1. *tr. V.* stick up ⟨*poster, etc.*⟩; **2.** *itr. V.; mit sein* stick
an|kleiden *tr. V.* *(geh.)* dress; **sich** ~: dress
an|klopfen *itr. V.* knock
an|knüpfen 1. *tr. V.* **a)** tie on (**an** + *Akk.* to); **b)** *(beginnen)* start up ⟨*conversation*⟩; establish ⟨*relations, business links*⟩; form ⟨*relationship*⟩; **2.** *itr. V.* **an etw.** *(Akk.)* ~: take sth. up; **ich knüpfe dort an, wo ...** I'll pick up where ...
an|kommen *unr. itr. V.; mit sein* **a)** *(eintreffen)* arrive; **seid ihr gut angekommen?** did you arrive safely?; **b) |bei jmdm.| |gut|** ~ *(fig. ugs.)* go down [very] well [with sb.]; **c)** **gegen jmdn./etw.** ~: be able to deal with sb./fight sth.; **d)** *unpers.* **es kommt auf jmdn./etw. an** *(jmd./etw. ist ausschlaggebend)* it depends on sb./sth.; **es kommt auf etw.** *(Akk.)* **an** *(etw. ist wichtig)* sth. matters (*Dat.* to); **es kommt |ganz| darauf** *od.* **drauf an** *(ugs.)* it [all] depends; **e)** *unpers.* **es darauf** *od.* **drauf** ~ **lassen** *(ugs.)* chance it; **es auf etw.** *(Akk.)* ~ **lassen** [be prepared to] risk sth.
an|koppeln 1. *tr. V.* couple ⟨*carriage*⟩ up; hitch ⟨*trailer*⟩ up; dock ⟨*spacecraft*⟩; **2.** *itr. V.* ⟨*spacecraft*⟩ dock
an|kreuzen *tr. V.* mark with a cross
an|kündigen 1. *tr. V.* announce; **2.** *refl. V.* announce itself; **An·kündigung die** announcement
Ankunft die; ~, **Ankünfte** arrival; **„~"** 'arrivals'
Ankunfts-: ~**halle die** arrival[s] hall; ~**tafel die** arrivals board
an|kuppeln *tr. V. s.* **ankoppeln 1**
an|kurbeln *tr. V.* **a)** crank [up]; **b)** *(fig.)* boost ⟨*economy, production, etc.*⟩
Anl. *Abk.* **Anlage** encl.
an|lächeln *tr. V.* smile at; **an|lachen 1.** *tr. V.* smile at. **2.** *refl. V.* **sich** *(Dat.)* **jmdn.** ~ *(ugs.)* get off with sb. *(Brit. coll.)*; pick sb. up
An·lage die a) *o. Pl. (das Anlegen)* *(einer Kartei)* establishment; *(eines Parks, Gartens usw.)* laying out; *(eines Parkplatzes, Stausees)* construction; **b)** *(Grün~)* park; *(um ein Schloß usw. herum)* grounds *pl.*; **c)** *(Einrichtung)* facilities *pl.*; ⟨*militärische* ~⟩ military installations; **d)** *(Werk)* plant; **e)** *(Musik~, Lautsprecher~ usw.)* system; **f)** *(Geld~)* investment; **g)** *(Konzeption)* conception; *(Struktur)* structure; **h)**

(Veranlagung) aptitude; *(Neigung)* tendency; i) *(Beilage zu einem Brief)* enclosure

Anlaß der; Anlasses, Anlässe a) cause (zu for); etw. zum ~ nehmen, etw. zu tun take sth. as an opportunity to do sth.; aus aktuellem ~: because of current events; b) *(Gelegenheit)* occasion

an|lassen 1. *unr. tr. V.* a) leave *(light, radio, heating, etc.)* on; leave *(engine)* running; leave *(candle)* burning; b) keep *(coat, gloves, etc.)* on; c) *(in Gang setzen)* start [up]; 2. *unr. refl. V.* sich gut/schlecht ~: get off to a good/bad start; **Anlasser** der; ~s, ~ starter

an·läßlich *Präp. mit Gen.* on the occasion of

An·lauf der a) run-up; [mehr] ~ nehmen take [more of] a run-up; b) *(Versuch)* attempt; beim od. im ersten/dritten ~: at the first/third attempt; **an|laufen** 1. *unr. itr. V.; mit sein* a) angelaufen kommen come running along; *(auf einen zu)* come running up; b) gegen jmdn./etw. ~: run at sb./sth.; c) *(Anlauf nehmen)* take a run-up; d) *(zu laufen beginnen)* *(engine)* start [up]; *(fig.)* *(film)* open; *(production, campaign, search)* start; e) rot/dunkel *usw.* ~: go or turn red/dark *etc.*; f) *(beschlagen)* mist up; 2. *unr. tr. V.* put in at *(port)*

an|legen 1. *tr. V.* a) put or lay *(domino, card)* [down] (an + *Akk.* next to); place, position *(ruler, protractor)* (an + *Akk.* on); put *(ladder)* up (an + *Akk.* against); b) die Flügel/Ohren ~: close its wings/lay its ears back; die Arme ~: put one's arms to one's sides; c) *(geh.: anziehen, umlegen)* don; d) *(schaffen, erstellen)* lay out *(town, garden, plantation, street)*; start *(file, album)*; compile *(statistics, index)*; e) *(investieren)* invest; f) *(ausgeben)* spend (für on); g) es darauf ~, etw. zu tun be determined to do sth.; 2. *itr. V.* a) *(landen)* moor; b) *(Kartenspiele)* lay a card/cards; c) *(Domino)* play [a domino/dominoes]; d) *(das Gewehr~)* aim (auf + *Akk.* at); 3. *refl. V.* sich mit jmdm. ~: pick an argument with sb.

Anlege-: ~platz der berth; ~steg der jetty

an|lehnen 1. *tr. V.* a) lean (an + *Akk. od. Dat.* against); b) leave *(door, window)* slightly open; 2. *refl. V.* sich [an jmdn. od. jmdm./etw.] ~: lean [on sb./ against sth.]; **Anlehnung** die; ~,

~en: in ~an (+ *Akk.)* in imitation of; following

Anleihe die; ~, ~n loan

an|leiten *tr. V.* instruct; **An·leitung** die instructions *pl.*

an|lernen *tr. V.* train

an|liegen *unr. itr. V.* a) *(pullover etc.)* fit tightly; b) *(ugs.: vorliegen)* be on; **An·liegen** das; ~s, ~ *(Bitte)* request; *(Angelegenheit)* matter; **anliegend** *Adj.* a) *(angrenzend)* adjacent; b) *(beiliegend)* enclosed; **Anlieger** der; ~s, ~: resident; „~ frei" 'except for access'

an|locken *tr. V.* attract *(customers, tourists, etc.)*; lure *(bird, animal)*

an|lügen *tr. V.* lie to

an|machen *tr. V.* a) put *(light, radio, heating)* on; light *(fire)*; b) mix *(cement, plaster, paint, etc.)*; dress *(salad)*

an|malen *tr. V.* paint

an|maßen *refl. V.* sich *(Dat.)* etw. ~: claim sth. [for oneself]; **an·maßend** 1. *Adj.* presumptuous; *(arrogant)* arrogant; 2. *adv.* presumptuously; *(arrogant)* arrogantly; **Anmaßung** die; ~, ~en presumption; *(Arroganz)* arrogance

an|melden *tr. V.* a) *(als Teilnehmer)* enrol (zu for); sich ~: enrol (zu for); b) *(melden, anzeigen)* license *(radio, television)*; apply for *(patent)*; register *(domicile, car, trade mark)*; sich ~: register one's new address; c) *(ankündigen)* announce; sind Sie angemeldet? do you have an appointment?; sich beim Arzt ~: make an appointment to see the doctor; d) *(geltend machen)* express *(reservation, doubt, wish)*; put forward *(demand)*; **An·meldung** die a) *(zur Teilnahme)* enrolment; b) *s.* anmelden b: licensing; application *(Gen. for)*; registration; c) *(Ankündigung)* announcement; *(beim Arzt, Rechtsanwalt usw.)* making an appointment

an|merken *tr. V.* a) jmdm. seinen Ärger/seine Verlegenheit *usw.* ~: notice that sb. is annoyed/embarrassed *etc.*; man merkt ihm [nicht] an, daß er krank ist you can[not] tell that he is ill; sich nichts ~ lassen not let it show; b) *(geh.: bemerken)* note; **Anmerkung** die; ~, ~en a) *(Fußnote)* note; b) *(geh.: Bemerkung)* comment

An·mut die; ~ *(geh.)* grace; **an·mutig** *(geh.)* 1. *Adj.* graceful *(girl, movement, dance)*; charming, delightful

⟨girl, smile, picture, landscape⟩; **2.** adv. ⟨move, dance⟩ gracefully; ⟨smile, greet⟩ charmingly

an|nähen tr. V. sew on

an|nähern 1. refl. V. get closer (Dat. to sth); **2.** tr. V. bring closer (Dat. to); **annähernd 1.** Adv. almost; (ungefähr) approximately; **2.** adj. approximate

Annahme die; ~, ~n **a)** (das Annehmen) acceptance; **b)** (Vermutung) assumption; **in der** ~, **daß** ...: on the assumption that...; **annehmbar 1.** Adj. **a)** acceptable; **b)** (recht gut) reasonable; **2.** adv. reasonably [well]; **annehmen 1.** unr. tr. V. **a)** accept; take; accept ⟨alms, invitation, condition, help⟩; take ⟨food, telephone call⟩; accept, take up ⟨offer, challenge⟩; **b)** (Sport) take ⟨ball, pass, etc.⟩; **c)** (billigen) approve; **d)** (aufnehmen) take on ⟨worker, patient, pupil⟩; **e)** (hinnehmen) accept ⟨fate, verdict, punishment⟩; **f)** (adoptieren) adopt; **g)** (haften lassen) take ⟨dye, ink⟩; **h)** (sich aneignen) adopt ⟨habit, mannerism, name, attitude⟩; **i)** (bekommen) take on ⟨look, appearance, form, dimension⟩; **j)** (vermuten, voraussetzen) assume; **angenommen, [daß]** ...: assuming [that] ...; **2.** unr. refl. V. (geh.) sich jmds./einer Sache ~: look after sb./sth.; **Annehmlichkeit die;** ~, ~en comfort; (Vorteil) advantage

annektieren tr. V. annex

Annonce [a'nõːsə] **die;** ~, ~n advertisement; advert (Brit. coll.); **annoncieren** tr. V. advertise

annullieren tr. V. annul

anonym 1. Adj. anonymous; **2.** adv. anonymously; **Anonymität die;** ~: anonymity

Anorak der; ~s, ~s anorak

an|ordnen tr. V. **a)** (arrangieren) arrange; **b)** (befehlen) order; **An·ordnung die** s. anordnen: **a)** arrangement; **b)** order

an·organisch Adj. inorganic

an|packen 1. tr. V. **a)** (ugs.: anfassen) grab hold of; **b)** (angehen) tackle; **2.** itr. V. |mit| ~ (ugs.: mithelfen) lend a hand

an|passen 1. tr. V. **a)** (passend machen) fit; **b)** (abstimmen) suit (Dat. to); **2.** refl. V. adapt [oneself] (Dat. to); ⟨animal⟩ adapt; **Anpassung die;** ~, ~en adaptation (an + Akk. to); **anpassungs·fähig** Adj. adaptable

an|pfeifen 1. unr. tr. V. das Spiel/die zweite Halbzeit ~: blow the whistle to start the game/the second half; **2.** unr. itr. V. blow the whistle; **An·pfiff der a)** (Sport) whistle for the start of play; **b)** (salopp: Zurechtweisung) bawling-out (coll.)

an|pflanzen tr. V. **a)** plant; **b)** (anbauen) grow

an|pöbeln tr. V. (ugs.) abuse

an|prangern tr. V. denounce (als as)

an|preisen unr. tr. V. extol

An·probe die fitting; **an|probieren** tr. V. try on

an|rechnen tr. V. **a)** count; **b)** jmdm. etw. ~ (in Rechnung stellen) charge sb. for sth.

An·recht das right; **ein** ~ **auf etw.** (Akk.) **haben** be entitled to sth.

An·rede die form of address; **an|reden** tr. V. address

an|regen tr. V. **a)** stimulate ⟨imagination, digestion⟩; whet ⟨appetite⟩; **b)** (ermuntern) prompt; (vorschlagen) propose; **anregend** Adj. stimulating; **An·regung die a)** s. anregen: stimulation; whetting; **b)** (Denkanstoß) stimulus; **c)** (Vorschlag) proposal

an|reichern 1. tr. V. enrich; **2.** refl. V. accumulate

An·reise die journey [there/here]; **an|reisen** itr. V.; mit sein travel there/here; **mit der Bahn** ~: go/come by train

An·reiz der incentive

an|rempeln tr. V. barge into; (absichtlich) jostle

An·richte die; ~, ~n sideboard; **an|richten** tr. V. **a)** arrange ⟨food⟩; (servieren) serve; **b)** cause ⟨disaster, confusion, devastation, etc.⟩

anrüchig Adj. **a)** disreputable; **b)** (unanständig) indecent

an|rücken itr. V.; mit sein ⟨troops⟩ advance; ⟨firemen, police⟩ move in

An·ruf der call; **Anruf·beantworter der;** ~s, ~ : [telephone-]answering machine; **an|rufen** unr. tr. V. **a)** call or shout to ⟨friend, passer-by⟩; call ⟨sleeping person⟩; **b)** (geh.: angehen, bitten) appeal to ⟨person, court⟩ (um for); call upon ⟨God⟩; **c)** auch itr. (telefonisch ~) call; **Anrufer der;** ~s, ~ : caller

an|rühren tr. V. **a)** touch; **b)** (bereiten) mix

ans Präp. + Art. **a)** = an das; **b)** sich ~ Arbeiten machen set to work

An·sage die announcement; **an|sagen** tr. V. a) announce; b) *(Kartenspiele)* s. bid

an|sammeln 1. tr. V. accumulate; amass *(riches, treasure)*; **2.** refl. V. accumulate; *(fig.) (anger, excitement)* build up; **An·sammlung die** a) collection; b) *(Auflauf)* crowd

ansässig Adj. resident

An·satz der *(erstes Zeichen, Beginn)* beginnings pl.

an|schaffen tr. V. [sich *(Dat.)*] etw. ~ get [oneself] sth.; **An·schaffung die** purchase

an|schalten tr. V. switch on

an|schauen tr. V. *(bes. südd., österr., schweiz.)* s. ansehen; **anschaulich 1.** vivid; **2.** adv. vividly; **Anschauung die**; ~, ~en a) *(Wahrnehmung)* experience; b) *(Auffassung)* view

An·schein der appearance; **allem od. dem ~ nach** to all appearances; **an·scheinend** Adv. apparently

an|schieben unr. tr. V. push *(vehicle)*

an|schießen unr. tr. V. shoot and wound

An·schlag der a) *(Bekanntmachung)* notice; *(Plakat)* poster; b) *(Attentat)* assassination attempt; *(auf ein Gebäude, einen Zug o. ä.)* attack; c) *(Texterfassung)* keystroke; d) **mit dem Gewehr im ~**: with rifle/rifles levelled; **an|schlagen** unr. tr. V. put up, *(notice, announcement, message)* (an + Akk. on); b) *(beschädigen)* chip

an|schließen 1. unr. tr. V. a) connect (an + Akk. od. Dat. to); connect up *(electrical device)*; b) *(festschließen)* lock, secure (an + Dat. od. Akk. to); **2.** unr. refl. V. sich jmdm./einer Sache ~: join sb./sth.; **An·schluß der** connection; **Anschluß·zug der** connecting train

an|schnallen tr. V. put on *(skis, skates)*; **sich ~** *(im Auto)* put on one's seatbelt; *(im Flugzeug)* fasten one's seatbelt

an|schrauben tr. V. screw on (an + Akk. to)

an|schreien unr. tr. V. shout at

An·schrift die address

Anschuldigung die; ~, ~en accusation

an|schwellen unr. itr. V.; mit sein a) swell [up]; *(fig.)* swell; *(water, river)* rise; b) *(lauter werden)* grow louder; *(noise)* rise

an|schwemmen tr. V. wash ashore

an|sehen unr. tr. V. a) look at; watch *(television programme)*; see *(play, film)*; jmdn. groß/böse ~: stare at sb./give sb. an angry look; **hübsch usw. anzusehen sein** be pretty etc. to look at; **sieh [mal] [einer] an!** *(ugs.)* well, I never! *(coll.)*; b) *(erkennen)* man sieht ihm sein Alter nicht an he does not look his age; man sieht ihr die Strapazen an she's showing the strain; c) *(zusehen bei)* etw. [mit] ~: watch sth.; **das kann man doch nicht [mit] ~**: I/you can't just stand by and watch that; **Ansehen das**, ~s [high] standing; **an·sehnlich** Adj. a) *(beträchtlich)* considerable; b) *(gut aussehend, stattlich)* handsome

an|sein unr. itr. V.; mit sein *(ugs.)(light, gas, etc.)* be on

an|setzen tr. V. a) *(in die richtige Stellung bringen)* position *(ladder, jack, drill, saw)*; b) *(anfügen)* attach, put on (an + Akk. od. Dat. to); c) *(festlegen)* fix *(meeting etc.)* (für, auf + Akk. for); fix, set *(deadline, date, price)*; d) *(veranschlagen)* estimate; e) *(anrühren)* mix

An·sicht die a) *(Meinung)* opinion; view; **meiner ~ nach** in my opinion or view; b) *(Bild)* view; **Ansichts·karte die** picture postcard

an|spannen 1. tr. V. a) harness *(horse etc.)* (an + Akk. to); yoke up *(oxen)* (an + Akk. to); hitch up *(carriage, cart, etc.)* (an + Akk. to); b) *(anstrengen)* strain; **An·spannung die** strain

an|spielen itr. V. auf jmdn./etw. ~: allude to sb./sth.; **Anspielung die**; ~, ~en allusion (auf + Akk. to); *(verächtlich, böse)* insinuation (auf + Akk. about)

An·sporn der incentive; **an|spornen** tr. V. spur on

An·sprache die speech; address; **an|sprechen 1.** unr. tr. V. a) speak to; b) *(gefallen)* appeal to; **2.** unr. itr. V. *(reagieren)* respond (auf + Akk. to)

an|springen 1. unr. tr. V.; mit sein *(car, engine)* start; **2.** unr. itr. V. jump up at

An·spruch der a) claim; *(Forderung)* demand; **[keine] Ansprüche stellen** make [no] demands; **in ~ nehmen** take advantage of *(offer)*; exercise *(right)*; take up *(time)*; b) *(Anrecht)* right

an·spruchs-: ~los 1. Adj. a) *(genügsam)* undemanding; b) *(schlicht)* unpretentious; **2.** adv. a) *(genügsam)* undemandingly; *(live)* modestly; b) *(schlicht)* unpretentiously; **~voll 1.** Adj. discriminating *(reader, audience,* *gourmet); (schwierig)* demanding; ambitious *(subject)*

an|spucken *tr. V.* spit at

Anstalt die; ~, ~en institution

An·stand der *o. Pl.* decency; **anständig** 1. *Adj.* a) decent; *(ehrbar)* respectable; 2. *adv.* decently; *(ordentlich)* properly

an|starren *tr. V.* stare at

an·statt *Konj.* ~ zu arbeiten/~, daß er arbeitet instead of working

an|stecken 1. *tr. V.* a) pin on *(badge, brooch);* put on *(ring);* b) *(infizieren, auch fig.)* infect; 2. *itr. V.* be infectious; **ansteckend** *Adj.* infectious; *(durch Berührung)* contagious; **Ansteckung** die; ~, ~en infection; *(durch Berührung)* contagion

an|stehen *unr. itr. V. (Schlange stehen)* queue [up], *(Amer.)* stand in line *(nach for)*

an·stelle 1. *Präp. mit Gen.* instead of; 2. *Adv.* ~ **von** instead of

an|stellen 1. *refl. V.* queue [up], *(Amer.)* stand in line *(nach* for); 2. *tr. V.* a) *(aufdrehen)* turn on; b) *(einschalten)* switch on; c) *(einstellen)* employ; **An·stellung** die a) *o. Pl.* employment; b) *(Stellung)* job

Anstieg der; ~[e]s rise, increase *(+ Gen.* in)

an|stiften *tr. V.* incite; **An·stifter** der, **An·stifterin** die instigator; **An·stiftung** die incitement

an|stimmen *tr. V.* start singing *(song);* start playing *(piece of music);* ein Geschrei ~: start shouting

An·stoß der a) *o. Pl.* initiative (zu for); den |ersten| ~ zu etw. geben initiate sth.; b) ~ erregen cause offence (bei to); [kei-nen] ~ an etw. *(Dat.)* nehmen [not] object to sth.; **an|stoßen** 1. *unr. itr. V.* a) *mit sein* an etw. *(Akk.)* ~: bump into sth.; b) |mit den Gläsern| ~: clink glasses; **auf** jmdn./etw. ~: drink to sb./sth.; 2. *unr. tr. V.* jmdn./etw. ~: give sb./sth. a push; jmdn. aus Versehen ~: knock into sb. inadvertently; **anstößig** 1. *Adj.* offensive; 2. *adv.* offensively

an|strahlen *tr. V.* a) illuminate; *(mit Scheinwerfer)* floodlight; b) *(anblicken)* beam at

an|streben *tr. V. (geh.)* aspire to; *(mit großer Anstrengung)* strive for

an|streichen *unr. tr. V.* a) paint; b) *(markieren)* mark

an|strengen 1. *refl. V.* make an effort; sich mehr/sehr ~: make more of an ef-

fort/a great effort; 2. *tr. V.* strain *(eyes, ears, voice);* be a strain on *(person);* seine Phantasie ~: exercise one's imagination; **anstrengend** *Adj. (körperlich)* strenuous; *(geistig)* demanding; **Anstrengung** die; ~, ~en a) effort; große ~en machen, etw. zu tun make every effort to do sth.; b) *(Strapaze)* strain

An·strich der the paint

An·sturm der rush (auf + Akk. to); *(auf Banken, Waren)* run (auf + Akk. on)

Antarktika (das); ~s Antarctica; **Antarktis** die; ~: die ~: the Antarctic; **antarktisch** *Adj.* Antarctic

An·teil der share (an + Dat. of); ~ an etw. *(Dat.)* nehmen take an interest in sth.; **An·teilnahme** die a) interest (an + Dat. in); b) *(Mitgefühl)* sympathy (an + Dat. with)

Antenne die; ~, ~n aerial; antenna *(Amer.)*

anthrazit [antra'tsi:t] *Adj.; nicht attr.* anthracite[-grey]; **anthrazit·grau** *Adj.* anthracite-grey

anti-, Anti- anti-; **Anti·alkoholiker** der teetotaller; **Antibiotikum** das; ~s, Antibiotika *(Med.)* antibiotic

antik *Adj.* a) classical; b) *(aus vergangenen Zeiten)* antique *(furniture, fittings, etc.);* **Antike** die ~ classical antiquity *no art.*

Antilope die; ~, ~n antelope

Antipathie die; ~, ~n antipathy

Antiquariat antiquarian bookshop/department; *(mit neueren gebrauchten Büchern)* second-hand bookshop/department; **Antiquität** die; ~, ~en an antique

Antrag der; ~[e]s, Anträge a) application (auf + Akk. for); einen ~ stellen make an application; b) *(Formular)* application form

an|treffen *unr. tr. V.* find; *(zufällig)* come across

an|treiben *unr. tr. V.* a) drive *(animals, column of prisoners)* on or along; *(fig.)* urge; b) *(in Bewegung setzen)* drive; power *(ship, aircraft)*

an|treten 1. *unr. itr. V.; mit sein* a) form up; *(in Linie)* line up; *(Milit.)* fall in; b) *(sich stellen)* meet one's opponent; *(als Mannschaft)* line up; gegen jmdn. ~: meet sb./line up against sb.; 2. *unr. tr. V.* a) start *(job, apprenticeship);* take up *(position, appoint-*

ment⟩; set out on ⟨*journey*⟩; begin ⟨*prison sentence*⟩; come into ⟨*inheritance*⟩

An·trieb der drive

An·tritt der: vor ~ Ihres Urlaubs before you go on holiday *(Brit.)* or *(Amer.)* vacation; vor ~ der Reise before setting out on the journey

an|tun *unr. tr. V.* a) jmdm. ein Leid ~: hurt sb.; jmdm. etwas Böses/ein Unrecht ~: do sb. harm/an injustice; b) jmd./etw. hat es jmdm. angetan sb. was taken with sb./sth.; *s. auch* angetan

Antwort die; ~, ~en a) answer; reply; er gab mir keine ~: he didn't answer [me] *or* reply; b) *(Reaktion)* response; **antworten** *itr. V.* a) answer; reply; auf etw. *(Akk.)* ~: answer sth.; reply to sth.; jmdm. ~: answer sb.; reply to sb.; b) *(reagieren)* respond **(auf +** *Akk.* to)

an|vertrauen 1. *tr. V.* jmdm. etw. ~: entrust sth. with sth.; *(fig.: mitteilen)* confide sth. to sb.; 2. *refl. V.* sich jmdm./einer Sache ~: put one's trust in sb./sth.; sich jmdm. ~ *(fig.: sich jmdm. mitteilen)* confide in sb

an|wachsen *unr. itr. V.; mit sein* a) grow on; b) *(Wurzeln schlagen)* take root; c) *(zunehmen)* grow

Anwalt der; ~[e]s, **Anwälte, Anwältin** die; ~, ~nen a) *(Rechts~)* lawyer; solicitor *(Brit.)*; attorney *(Amer.)*; *(vor Gericht)* barrister *(Brit.)*; attorney[-at-law] *(Amer.)*; advocate *(Scot.)*; b) *(Fürsprecher)* advocate

An·wärter der candidate **(auf +** *Akk.* for); *(Sport)* contender **(auf +** *Akk.* for)

an|weisen *unr. tr. V.* instruct; *s. auch* angewiesen; **An·weisung** die instruction

an|wenden *unr. (auch regelm.) tr. V.* use, employ ⟨*process, trick, method, violence, force*⟩; use ⟨*medicine, money, time*⟩; apply ⟨*rule, paragraph, proverb, etc.*⟩ **(auf +** *Akk.* to); **An·wendung** die *s.* anwenden: use; employment; application

An·wesen das property

anwesend *Adj.* present **(bei** at); die Anwesenden those present; **Anwesenheit** die; ~: presence

an|widern *tr. V.* nauseate

An·zahl die; ~: number; eine ganze ~: a whole lot

an|zahlen *tr. V.* put down ⟨*sum*⟩ as a deposit **(auf +** *Akk.* on); *(bei Ratenzahlung)* make a down payment of

⟨*sum*⟩ **(auf +** *Akk.* on); **An·zahlung** die deposit; *(bei Ratenzahlung)* down payment

An·zeichen das sign; indication

Anzeige die; ~, ~n a) *(Straf~)* report; b) *(Inserat)* advertisement; c) *(eines Instruments)* display; **an|zeigen** *tr. V.* a) *(Strafanzeige erstatten)* jmdn./etw. ~: report sb./sth. to the police/the authorities; b) *(zeigen)* show; indicate; *(time, date)*; **Anzeigen·teil** der advertisement section or pages *pl.*

an|ziehen *unr. tr. V.* a) *(auch fig.)* attract; b) draw up ⟨*knees, feet, etc.*⟩; c) tighten ⟨*rope, wire, screw, knot, belt, etc.*⟩; put on ⟨*handbrake*⟩; d) *(ankleiden)* dress; **sich** ~: get dressed; e) *(anlegen)* put on ⟨*clothes*⟩; **anziehend** *Adj.* attractive; **An·zug** der a) suit; b) im ~ sein ⟨*storm*⟩ be approaching; ⟨*fever, illness*⟩ be coming on; ⟨*enemy*⟩ be advancing; **anzüglich** 1. *Adj.* insinuating ⟨*remark, question*⟩; 2. *adv.* in an insinuating way

an|zünden *tr. V.* light; set fire to ⟨*building etc.*⟩

an|zweifeln *tr. V.* doubt; question

apart 1. *Adj.* individual *attrib.*; 2. *adv.* in an individual style

Apartment das; ~s, ~s studio flat *(Brit.)*; studio apartment *(Amer.)*

Apathie die; ~, ~n apathy; **apathisch** 1. *Adj.* apathetic; 2. *adv.* apathetically

Aperitif [aperi'ti:f] der; ~s, ~s aperitif

Apfel der; ~s, Äpfel apple

Apfel-: ~**baum** der apple-tree; ~**kuchen** der apple-cake; *(mit Äpfeln belegt)* apple flan; ~**mus** das apple purée; ~**saft** der apple-juice

Apfelsine die; ~, ~n orange

Apfel-: ~**strudel** der apfelstrudel; ~**wein** der cider

Apostel der; ~s, ~: apostle

Apotheke die; ~, ~n a) chemist's [shop] *(Brit.)*; drugstore *(Amer.)*; b) *(Haus~)* medicine cabinet; *(Reise~, Bord~)* first-aid kit; **Apotheker** der; ~s, ~, **Apothekerin** die; ~, ~nen [dispensing] chemist *(Brit.)*; druggist

App. *Abk.* Apparat ext.

Apparat der; ~[e]s, ~e a) apparatus *no pl.*; *(Haushaltsgerät)* appliance; *(kleiner)* gadget; b) *(Radio~)* radio; *(Fernseh~)* television; *(Foto~)* camera; c) *(Telefon)* telephone; *(Nebenstelle)* extension; d) *(Personen und Hilfsmittel)* organization; *(Verwaltungs~)* system

Appartement [apartə'mãː, *schweiz. auch:* -'mɛnt] das; ~s, ~s (*schweiz. auch:* ~e) a) s. Apartment; b) (*Hotelsuite*) suite

Appell der; ~s, ~e a) appeal (**zu** for, **an** + Akk. to); b) (*Milit.*) muster; (*Anwesenheits~*) roll-call; **appellieren** itr. V. appeal (**an** + Akk. to)

Appetit der; ~[e]s, ~e appetite (**auf** + Akk. for); **guten ~!** enjoy your meal!; **appetitlich** Adj. a) appetizing; b) (*sauber, ansprechend*) attractive and hygienic; **Appetit·losigkeit** die; ~: lack of appetite

applaudieren itr. V. applaud; **Applaus** der; ~es, ~e applause

Aprikose die; ~, ~n apricot

April der; ~[s], ~e April; **der ~:** April

Aquädukt der od. das; ~[e]s, ~e aqueduct

Aquaplaning das; ~[s] aquaplaning

Aquarell das; ~s, ~e water-colour [painting]

Aquarium das; ~s, Aquarien aquarium

Äquator der; ~s equator

Ar das od. der; ~s, ~e are

Ära die; ~, Ären era

Araber der; ~s, ~ Arab; **Arabien** [a'raːbi̯ən] (das); ~s Arabia; **arabisch** Adj. Arabian; Arabic (*language, numeral, literature, etc.*)

Arbeit die; ~, ~en a) work no indef. art.; **vor/nach der ~** (*ugs.*) before/after work; b) (*Produkt, Werk*) work; c) (*Aufgabe* usw.) job; d) (*Klassen~*) test; **arbeiten** 1. itr. V. work; 2. tr. V. (*herstellen*) make; **Arbeiter** der; ~s, ~: worker; (*Bau~, Land~*) labourer; **Arbeiter·klasse** die working class[es pl.]; **Arbeiterschaft** die; ~: workers pl.; **Arbeit·geber** der; ~s, ~: employer; **Arbeitnehmer** der; ~s, ~: employee

arbeits-, Arbeits-: ~amt das job centre (*Brit.*); ~bedingungen Pl. working conditions; ~fähig Adj. fit for work postpos.; (*grundsätzlich*) able to work postpos.; ~gang der operation; ~kraft die a) capacity for work; b) (*Mensch*) worker; ~los Adj. unemployed; ~lose der/die; adj. Dekl. unemployed person/man/woman etc.; **die** ~n the unemployed; ~losigkeit die; ~: unemployment no indef. art.; ~markt der labour market; ~platz der a) work-place; b) (~stätte) place of work; c) (~verhältnis) job; ~scheu Adj. work-shy; ~tag der

working day; ~teilung die division of labour; ~unfähig Adj. unfit for work postpos.; (*grundsätzlich*) unable to work postpos.; ~zeit die working hours pl.; **die tägliche** ~zeit the working day

Archäologe der; ~n, ~n archaeologist; **Archäologie** die; ~: archaeology no art.; **archäologisch** Adj. archaeological

Arche die; ~, ~n ark; **die ~ Noah** Noah's Ark

Architekt der; ~en, ~en architect; **Architektur** die; ~ architecture

Archiv das; ~s, ~e archives pl.; archive

Ären s. Ära

Arena die; ~, Arenen arena; (*Stierkampf~, Manege*) ring

arg, ärger, ärgst... (*geh., landsch.*) 1. Adj. a) (*schlimm*) bad; **im** ~en liegen be in a sorry state; b) (*unangenehm groß, stark*) severe (pain, hunger, shock, disappointment); serious (error, dilemma); extreme (embarrassment); gross (exaggeration, injustice); 2. adv. (*äußerst, sehr*) extremely

Ärger der; ~s a) annoyance; b) (*Unannehmlichkeiten*) trouble; ~ **bekommen** get into trouble; **ärgerlich** 1. Adj. a) annoyed; b) (*Ärger erregend*) annoying; 2. adv. a) with annoyance; b) (*Ärger erregend*) annoyingly; **ärgern** 1. tr. V. a) annoy; b) (*reizen*) tease; 2. refl. V. sich [über jmdn./etw.] ~: be/get annoyed [at sb./about sth.]; **Ärgernis** das; ~ses, ~se annoyance; (*etw. Anstößiges*) nuisance

arg-, Arg-: ~listig Adj. deceitful; (*heimtückisch*) malicious; ~los 1. Adj. unsuspecting; 2. adv. unsuspectingly; ~losigkeit die; ~: unsuspecting nature

ärgst... s. arg

Argument das; ~[e]s, ~e argument a) **Argumentation** die; ~, ~en argumentation; **argumentieren** itr. V. argue

Argwohn der; ~[e]s suspicion; **argwöhnisch** (*geh.*) 1. Adj. suspicious; 2. adv. suspiciously

Arie ['aːri̯ə] die; ~, ~n aria

Aristokrat der; ~en, ~en aristocrat; **Aristokratin** die; ~, ~nen aristocrat; **Aristokratie** die; ~, ~n aristocracy; **aristokratisch** 1. Adj. aristocratic; 2. adv. aristocratically

arithmetisch 1. Adj. arithmetical; 2. adv. arithmetically

Ark̲a̲de die; ~, ~n arcade

Ar̲k̲tis die; ~: Arctic; **arktisch** Adj. Arctic; (fig.) arctic

arm, **ärmer**, **ärmst...** Adj. poor; ~ **und reich** (veralt.) rich and poor [alike]; ~ **an Nährstoffen** poor in nutrients; der/ die **Ärmste** od. **Arme** the poor man/ boy/woman/girl

Arm der; ~[e]s, ~e arm; jmdm. [mit etw.] **unter die ~e greifen** help sb. out [with sth.]; **ein Hemd mit halbem ~**: a short-sleeved shirt

Arm̲a̲turen·brett das instrument panel; (im Kfz) dashboard

Arm-: ~**band** das bracelet; (Uhr~) strap; ~**band·uhr** die wrist-watch

Arm̲e̲e die; ~, ~n (auch fig.) army

Ärmel der; ~s, ~: sleeve; [sich (Dat.)] etw. aus dem ~ **schütteln** (ugs.) produce sth. just like that

Ärmel·kanal der [English] Channel

ärmer s. **arm**; **ärmlich** 1. Adj. cheap ⟨clothing⟩; shabby ⟨flat, office⟩; meagre ⟨meal⟩. 2. adv. cheaply ⟨furnished, dressed⟩

Arm·reif der armlet

arm·selig Adj. a) miserable; pathetic ⟨result, figure⟩; meagre ⟨meal, food⟩; paltry ⟨return, salary, sum, fee⟩; b) (abwertend: erbärmlich) miserable; **ärmst...** s. **arm**, **Ar̲m̲ut** die; ~ poverty

Aroma das; ~s, **Aromen** (Duft) aroma; (Geschmack) flavour; **aromatisch** Adj. aromatic; distinctive ⟨taste⟩; ~ **duften** give off an aromatic fragrance

arrangieren [arãˈʒiːrən] 1. tr. V. (geh., Musik) arrange; 2. refl. V. sich ~: adapt; sich mit jmdm. ~: come to an accommodation with sb.

Arr̲e̲st der; ~[e]s, ~e detention

arrog̲a̲nt 1. Adj. arrogant; 2. adv. arrogantly; **Arrog̲a̲nz** die; ~ arrogance

Arsch der; ~[e]s, **Ärsche** (derb) arse (Brit. coarse); ass (Amer. sl.); **leck mich an ~!** (fig.) piss off (coarse); im ~ **sein** (fig.) be buggered (coarse); b) (widerlicher Mensch) arse-hole (Brit. coarse); ass-hole (Amer. sl.); **Ar̲s̲chloch** das (derb) s. **Arsch b**

Art die; ~, ~en a) kind; sort; **Bücher aller** ~: all kinds or sorts of books; [so] **eine ~ ...**: a sort of ...; **aus der ~ schlagen** not be true to type; (in einer Familie) be different from all the rest of the family; b) (Biol.) species; c) o. Pl. (Wesen) nature; (Verhaltensweise) way; (gutes Benehmen) behaviour; die **feine englische ~** (ugs.) the proper way

to behave; d) (Weise) way; **auf diese ~**: in this way; ~ **und Weise** way; (Kochk.) **nach** ~ **des Hauses** à la maison; **nach Schweizer ~**: Swiss style

Arterie [arˈteːriə] die; ~, ~n artery

artig Adj. well-behaved; **sei** ~: be a good boy/girl/dog etc.

Artikel der; ~s, ~ a) article; b) (Ware) item

Artiller̲i̲e die; ~, ~n artillery

Artisch̲o̲cke die; ~, ~n artichoke

Art̲i̲st der; ~en, ~en [variety/circus] performer

Arzn̲e̲i die; ~, ~en (veralt.), **Arz·nei·mittel** das medicine

Arzt der; ~es, **Ärzte**, **Ärztin** die; ~, ~nen doctor; **ärztlich** 1. Adj. medical; **auf** ~**e Verordnung** on doctor's orders; 2. adv. sich ~ **behandeln lassen** have medical treatment

As das; ~ses, ~se ace

Asbest der; ~[e]s, ~e asbestos

Asche die; ~, ~n ash[es pl.]; (sterbliche Reste) ashes pl.

Aschen-: ~**becher** der ashtray; ~**brödel** das; ~s, ~ (auch fig.) Cinderella

Ascher·mittwoch der Ash Wednesday

Äser s. **Aas**

Asi̲a̲t der; ~en, ~en, **Asiatin** die; ~, ~nen Asian; **asiatisch** Adj. Asian; **Asien** [ˈaːzi̯ən] (das); ~s Asia

Askese die; ~: asceticism; **Asket** der; ~en, ~en ascetic; **asketisch** 1. Adj. ascetic; 2. adv. ascetically

asozial 1. Adj. asocial; 2. adv. asocially

Aspekt der; ~[e]s, ~e aspect

Asphalt der; ~[e]s, ~e asphalt

Aspik der (österr. auch das); ~s, ~e aspic

aß 1. u. 3. Pers. Sg. Prät. v. **essen**

Assist̲e̲nt der; ~en, ~en, **Assistentin** die; ~, ~nen assistant

Ast der; ~[e]s, **Äste** branch; sich (Dat.) einen ~ **lachen** (ugs.) split one's sides [with laughter]

Aster die; ~, ~n aster; (Herbst~) Michaelmas daisy

ästhetisch 1. Adj. aesthetic; 2. adv. aesthetically

Asthma das; ~s asthma

Astrol̲o̲ge der; ~n, ~n astrologer; **Astrologie** die; ~: astrology no art.; **Astrol̲o̲gin** die; ~, ~nen astrologer

Astron̲a̲ut der; ~en, ~en; **Astronautin** die; ~, ~nen astronaut

Astron̲o̲m der; ~en, ~en astronomer;

Astronomie die; ~: astronomy *no art.;* **astronomisch** *Adj.* astronomical

Asyl das; ~s, ~e a) asylum; b) *(Obdachlosen~)* hostel; **Asylant** der; ~en, ~en, **Asylantin** die; ~, ~nen person granted [political] asylum; **Asyl·bewerber** der person seeking [political] asylum

Atelier [atə'lie:] das; ~s, ~s studio

Atem der; ~s breath; **außer ~ sein/geraten** be/get out of breath

atem-, Atem-: ~**beraubend** 1. *Adj.* breath-taking; 2. *adv.* breathtakingly; ~**los** 1. *Adj.* breathless; 2. *adv.* breathlessly; ~**pause** die breathing space; ~**zug** der breath

Atheismus der; ~: atheism *no art.;* **Atheist** der; ~en, ~en atheist; **atheistisch** 1. *Adj.* atheistic; 2. *adv.* atheistically

Athen (das); ~s Athens

Äther der; ~s, ~ ether

Äthiopien [ɛ'tio:piən] (das); ~s Ethiopia

Athlet der; ~en, ~en a) *(Sportler)* athlete; b) *(ugs.: kräftiger Mann)* muscleman; **athletisch** *Adj.* athletic

Atlanten s. ¹**Atlas**

Atlantik der; ~s Atlantic; **atlantisch** *Adj.* Atlantic; **der Atlantische Ozean** the Atlantic Ocean

Atlas der; ~ *od.* ~ses, **Atlanten** *od.* ~se atlas

atmen *itr., tr. V.* breathe

Atmosphäre [atmo'sfɛ:rə] die; ~, ~n *(auch fig.)* atmosphere

Atmung die; ~: breathing

Atom das; ~s, ~e atom; **atomar** *Adj.* atomic; *(Atomwaffen betreffend)* nuclear

Atom-: ~**bombe** die atom bomb; ~**energie** die; *o. Pl.* nuclear energy *no indef. art.;* ~**kern** der atomic nucleus; ~**kraft** die; *o. Pl.* nuclear power *no indef. art.;* ~**kraftwerk** das nuclear power-station; ~**krieg** der nuclear war; ~**müll** der nuclear waste; ~**physik** die nuclear physics *sing., no art.;* ~**pilz** der mushroom cloud; ~**reaktor** der nuclear reactor; ~**waffe** die nuclear weapon; ~**waffen·frei** *Adj.* nuclear-free; ~**zeitalter** das; *o. Pl.* nuclear age

Attacke die; ~, ~n *(auch Med.)* attack **(auf + Akk.** on)

Attentat das; ~[e]s, ~e assassination attempt; *(erfolgreich)* assassination; **Attentäter** der; ~s, ~, **Attentäterin** die; ~, ~nen would-be assassin; *(erfolgreich)* assassin

Attest das; ~[e]s, ~e medical certificate

Attraktion die; ~, ~en attraction; **attraktiv** 1. *Adj.* attractive; 2. *adv.* attractively; **Attraktivität** die; ~: attractiveness

Attrappe die; ~, ~n dummy

Attribut das; ~[e]s, ~e attribute

ätzen 1. *tr. V.* etch; 2. *itr. V.* corrode; **ätzend** 1. *Adj.* corrosive; *(fig.)* caustic ⟨*wit, remark, criticism*⟩; pungent ⟨*smell*⟩; 2. *adv.* caustically *(ironic, critical)*

au *Interj.* a) *(bei Schmerz)* ouch; b) *(bei Überraschung, Begeisterung)* oh

Aubergine [obɛr'ʒi:nə] die; ~, ~n aubergine *(Brit.);* egg-plant

auch 1. *Adv.* a) as well; too; also; **Klaus war ~ dabei** Klaus was there as well *or* too; **Klaus war also there; ich gehe jetzt. – Ich ~:** I'm going now – So am I; **Mir ist warm. – Mir ~:** I feel warm – So do I; **das weiß ich ~ nicht** I don't know either; b) *(sogar, selbst)* even; **~ wenn, wenn ~:** even if; 2. *Partikel* a) **etwas anderes habe ich ~ nicht** erwartet I never expected anything else; **nun hör aber ~ zu!** now listen!; b) **bist du dir ~ im klaren, was das bedeutet?** are you sure you understand what that means?; **bist du ~ glücklich?** are you truly happy?; **lügst du ~ nicht?** you're not lying, are you?; c) **wo .../wer .../was ... usw. ~:** wherever/ whoever/whatever etc. ...; **wie dem ~ sei** however that may be; d) **mag er ~ noch so klug sein** no matter how clever he is

Audienz die; ~, ~en audience

auf 1. *Präp. mit Dat.* a) on; ~ **See** at sea; ~ **dem Baum** in the tree; ~ **der Erde** on earth; ~ **der Welt** in the world; ~ **der Straße** in the street; b) at ⟨*post office, town, hall, police station*⟩; ~ **seinem Zimmer** *(ugs.)* in his room; **Geld ~ der Bank haben** have money in the bank; ~ **der Schule/Uni** at school/ university; c) at ⟨*party, wedding*⟩; on ⟨*course, trip, walk, holiday, tour*⟩; 2. *Präp. mit Akk.* a) on; ~ **einen Berg steigen** climb up a mountain; ~ **die Straße gehen** go [out] into the street; b) ~ **die Schule/Uni gehen** go to school/university; ~ **einen Lehrgang gehen** go on a course; c) ~ **10 km [Entfernung]** for [a distance of] 10 km; **wir näherten uns der Hütte [bis] ~ 30 m** we approached to within 30 m of the hut; **d)** ~ **Jahre |hinaus|** for years [to come]; **etw.** ~ **nächsten Mittwoch verschieben** postpone sth. until next Wednesday; **die Nacht von Sonntag** ~ **Montag** Sunday night; **das fällt** ~ **einen Montag** it falls on a Monday; **e)** ~ **diese Art und Weise** in this way; ~ **deutsch** in German; ~ **das sorgfältigste** *(geh.)* most carefully; **f)** ~ **Wunsch** on request; ~ **meine Bitte** at my request; ~ **Befehl** on command; **g) ein Teelöffel** ~ **einen Liter Wasser** one teaspoon to one litre of water; ~ **die Sekunde/den Millimeter |genau|** [precise] to the second/millimetre; ~ **deine Gesundheit!** your health; ~ **bald/morgen!** *(bes. südd.)* see you soon/tomorrow; **3.** *Adv.* **a)** ~ **!** *(steh/steht auf!)* up you get!; **b) sie waren längst** ~ **und davon** they had made off long before; **c)** ~ **!** *(bes. südd.: los)* come on; ~ **geht's** off we go; ~ **ins Schwimmbad!** come on, off to the swimming-pool!; **d)** ~ **und ab** *(hin und her)* up and down; to and fro; **e) Helm/Hut/Brille** ~ **!** helmet/hat/ glasses on!; **f) Fenster/Mund** ~ **!** open the window/your mouth!

auf|atmen *itr. V.* breathe a sigh of relief

auf|bahren *tr. V.* lay out; **aufgebahrt sein** lie in state

Auf·bau der; ~|e|s, ~ten a) *o. Pl.* building; **b)** *o. Pl. (Struktur)* structure; **c)** *Pl. (Schiffbau)* superstructure *sing.*

auf|bauen *tr. V.* **a)** erect ⟨*hut, kiosk, podium*⟩; set up ⟨*equipment, train set*⟩; build ⟨*house, bridge*⟩; put up ⟨*tent*⟩; **b)** *(hinstellen, arrangieren)* lay *or* set out ⟨*food, presents, etc.*⟩; **c)** *(fig.: schaffen)* build ⟨*state, economy, etc.*⟩; build up ⟨*business, organization, army, spy network*⟩; **d)** *(fig.: strukturieren)* structure

auf|bäumen *refl. V.* rear up; **sich gegen jmdn./etw.** ~ *(fig.)* rise up against sb./sth.

auf|bessern *tr. V.* improve; increase ⟨*pension, wages, etc.*⟩

auf|bewahren *tr. V.* keep; **etw. kühl** ~ **!** store sth. in a cool place; **Auf·bewahrung** die keeping

auf|bieten *unr. tr. V.* exert ⟨*strength, energy, will-power, influence, authority*⟩; call on ⟨*skill, wit, powers of persuasion or eloquence*⟩

auf|blasen *unr. tr. V.* blow up; inflate

auf|bleiben *unr. itr. V.; mit sein* **a)** *(geöffnet bleiben)* stay open; **b)** *(nicht zu Bett gehen)* stay up

auf|blenden *itr. V.* switch to full beam

auf|blicken *itr. V.* **a)** look up; *(kurz)* glance up; **b) zu jmdm.** ~ *(fig.)* look up to sb.

auf|blühen *itr. V.; mit sein* **a)** come into bloom; ⟨*bud*⟩ open; **b)** *(fig.: aufleben)* blossom [out]

auf|brauchen *tr. V.* use up

auf|brechen 1. *unr. tr. V.* break open ⟨*lock, safe, box, crate, etc.*⟩; break into ⟨*car*⟩; force [open] ⟨*door*⟩; **2.** *unr. itr. V.; mit sein* **a)** ⟨*bud*⟩ open; ⟨*ice [sheet], surface, ground*⟩ break up; ⟨*wound*⟩ open; **b)** *(losgehen, -fahren)* set off

auf|bringen *unr. tr. V.* **a)** find; raise ⟨*money*⟩; *(fig.)* summon [up] ⟨*strength, energy, courage*⟩; find ⟨*patience*⟩; **b)** *(kreieren)* start ⟨*fashion, custom, rumour*⟩; introduce ⟨*slogan, theory*⟩; **c) jmdn.** ~ **:** make sb. angry; **d) jmdn. gegen jmdn./etw.** ~ **:** set sb. against sb./ sth.

Auf·bruch der departure

auf|brühen *tr. V.* brew [up]

auf|decken *tr. V.* **a)** uncover; **b)** *(Kartenspiele)* show; **c)** *(fig.)* reveal; uncover; *(enthüllen)* expose

auf|drängen 1. *tr. V.* **jmdm. etw.** ~ **:** force sth. on sb.; **2.** *refl. V.* **sich jmdm.** ~ **:** force oneself on sb.

auf|drehen *tr. V.* unscrew ⟨*bottle-cap, nut*⟩; undo ⟨*screw*⟩; turn on ⟨*tap, gas, water*⟩; open ⟨*valve, bottle, vice*⟩; **b)** *(ugs.)* turn up ⟨*radio, record-player, etc.*⟩

auf·dringlich 1. *Adj.* pushy *(coll.)* ⟨*person*⟩; *(fig.)* insistent ⟨*music, advertisement*⟩; pungent ⟨*perfume, smell*⟩; loud ⟨*colour, wallpaper*⟩; **2.** *adv. (behave)* pushily, *(coll.)*; **Aufdringlichkeit** die; ~s. aufdringlich: pushiness *(coll.)*; insistent manner; pungency

auf·einander *Adv.* on top of one another

aufeinander-: ~**|folgen** *itr. V.; mit sein* follow one another; ~**folgend** successive; ~**|legen 1.** *tr. V.* lay ⟨*planks etc.*⟩ one on top of the other; **2.** *refl. V.* lie on top of one another; ~**|liegen** *unr. itr. V.* lie on top of each other *or* one another; ~**|prallen** *itr. V.; mit sein* crash into one another; collide; *(fig.)* ⟨*opinions*⟩ clash; ~**|treffen** *unr. itr. V.; mit sein* meet

Aufenthalt der; ~|e|s, ~e a) stay; **b)** *(Fahrtunterbrechung)* stop

Aufenthalts-: ~**erlaubnis** die residence permit; ~**raum** der *(in einer*

Schule o. ä.) common-room *(Brit.)*; *(in einer Jugendherberge)* day-room; *(in einem Betrieb o. ä.)* recreation-room

auf|essen *unr. tr. (auch itr.) V.* eat up

auf|fahren 1. *unr. itr. V.*; *mit sein* a) **auf ein anderes Fahrzeug ~** *(aufprallen)* drive into the back of another vehicle; b) **auf den Vordermann zu dicht ~**: drive too close to the car in front; c) *(vorfahren)* drive up; d) *(in Stellung gehen)* move up [into position]; 2. *unr. tr. V.* a) *(in Stellung bringen)* move up; b) *(ugs.: auftischen)* serve up; **Auf|fahrt die** a) drive up; b) *(Weg)* drive; c) *(Autobahn~)* slip-road *(Brit.)*; access road *(Amer.)*; d) *(schweiz.) s.* Himmelfahrt

auf|fallen *unr. itr. V.*; *mit sein* stand out; **jmdm. fällt etw. auf** sb. notices sth.; **auffallend** 1. *Adj.* conspicuous; *(eindrucksvoll, bemerkenswert)* striking; 2. *adv.* conspicuously; *(eindrucksvoll, bemerkenswert)* strikingly; **auf|fällig** 1. *Adj.* conspicuous; garish ⟨*colour*⟩; 2. *adv.* conspicuously

auf|fangen *unr. tr. V.* a) catch; b) *(aufnehmen, sammeln)* collect

auf|fassen *tr. V.* grasp; a) **etw. als etw. ~**: regard sth. as sth.; **etw. persönlich/falsch ~**: take sth. personally/misunderstand sth.; **Auf|fassung die** *(Ansicht)* view; *(Begriff)* conception; **der ~ sein, daß ...**: take the view that ...

auffindbar *Adj.* findable; **auf|finden** *unr. tr. V.* find

auf|fordern *tr. V.* **jmdn. ~, etw. zu tun** call upon sb. to do sth.; *(einladen, ermuntern)* ask sb. to do sth.; **jmdn. [zum Tanz] ~**: ask sb. to dance; **Auf|forderung die** request; *(nachdrücklicher)* demand; *(Einladung, Ermunterung)* invitation

auf|fressen *unr. tr. V. (auch fig.)* eat up

auf|führen 1. *tr. V.* a) put on ⟨*film*⟩; stage ⟨*play, ballet, opera*⟩; perform ⟨*piece of music*⟩; b) *(auflisten)* list; 2. *refl. V.* behave; **Auf|führung die** performance

Auf|gabe die a) task; b) *(fig.: Zweck, Funktion)* function; c) *(Schulw.: Übung)* exercise; *(Prüfungs~)* question; *(Haus~) s.* Haus~; d) *(Rechen-, Mathematik~)* problem; e) *(Kapitulation)* retirement; *(im Schach)* resignation; **jmdn. zur ~ zwingen** force sb. to retire/resign; f) *(das Aufgeben a)* giving up; g) *(einer Postsendung)* posting *(Brit.)*; mailing *(Amer.)*; *(eines Telegramms)* handing in; *(einer Bestellung, einer Annonce)* placing; h) *(von Gepäck)* checking in

Auf·gang der a) *(eines Gestirns)* rising; b) *(Treppe)* stairs *pl.*; staircase; stairway; *(in einem Bahnhof, zu einer Galerie, einer Tribüne)* steps *pl.*

auf|geben 1. *unr. tr. V.* a) give up; *(Sport)* retire from ⟨*race, competition*⟩; b) *(übergeben, übermitteln)* post *(Brit.)*, mail ⟨*letter, parcel*⟩; hand in, *(telefonisch)* phone in ⟨*telegram*⟩; place ⟨*advertisement, order*⟩; check ⟨*luggage, baggage*⟩ in; c) *(Schulw.: als Hausaufgabe)* set *(Brit.)*; assign *(Amer.)*; d) **jmdm. ein Rätsel ~**: set *(Brit.)* or *(Amer.)* assign sb. a puzzle; 2. *unr. itr. V.* a) give up; *(im Sport)* retire; *(im Schach)* resign

Auf·gebot das a) *(Menge)* contingent; **ein gewaltiges ~ an Polizisten/Fahrzeugen/Material** a huge force of police/array of vehicles/materials; b) *(zur Heirat)* notice of an/the intended marriage; *(kirchlich)* banns *pl.*

auf|gehen *unr. itr. V.*; *mit sein* a) rise; b) *(sich öffnen [lassen])* ⟨*door, parachute, wound*⟩ open; ⟨*stage curtain*⟩ go up; ⟨*knot, button, zip, bandage, shoelace, stitching*⟩ come undone; ⟨*boil, pimple, blister*⟩ burst; ⟨*flower, bud*⟩ open [up]; c) *(keimen)* come up; d) *(aufgetrieben werden)* ⟨*dough, cake*⟩ rise; e) *(Math.) ⟨calculation⟩* work out; ⟨*equation*⟩ come out; f) **etw. geht jmdm. auf** sb. realizes sth.

aufgeklärt *Adj.* enlightened; **~ sein** *(sexualkundlich)* know the facts of life

auf·gelegt *Adj.* **gut/schlecht usw. ~ sein** be in a good/bad *etc.* mood; **zu etw. ~ sein** be in the mood for sth.

aufgeregt 1. *Adj.* excited; *(nervös, beunruhigt)* agitated; 2. *adv.* excitedly; *(nervös, beunruhigt)* agitatedly

auf·geschlossen *Adj.* open-minded *(gegenüber as regards; about)*; *(interessiert, empfänglich)* receptive *(Dat. für to)*; *(zugänglich)* approachable; **Auf·geschlossenheit die** *s.* aufgeschlossen: open-mindedness; receptiveness; approachableness

aufgeweckt *Adj.* bright; **Aufgewecktheit die**; **~:** brightness

auf|gießen *unr. tr. V.* make ⟨*coffee, tea*⟩

auf|gliedern *tr. V.* subdivide, break down *(in + Akk.* into); **Auf·gliederung die** subdivision; breakdown

auf|greifen *unr. tr. V.* pick up
auf Grund, aufgrund *s.* Grund c
auf|haben *(ugs.)* 1. *unr. tr. V.* a) *(aufgesetzt haben)* have on; b) *(geöffnet haben)* have ⟨zip⟩ undone; have ⟨door, window, jacket, blouse⟩ open; 2. *unr. itr. V.* ⟨shop, office⟩ be open
auf|halten *unr. tr. V.* a) halt; b) *(stören)* hold up; c) *(ugs.: geöffnet halten)* hold ⟨sack, door, etc.⟩ open; **die Augen [und Ohren]** ~: keep one's eyes [and ears] open; 2. *unr. refl. V.* a) stay; b) **sich mit jmdm./etw.** ~: spend [a long] time on sth./sb.
auf|hängen 1. *tr. V.* a) hang up; hang ⟨picture, curtains⟩; b) *(erhängen)* hang; 2. *refl. V.* hang oneself; **Aufhänger der;** ~s, ~ loop
auf|heben *unr. tr. V.* a) pick up; b) *(aufbewahren)* keep; c) *(abschaffen)* abolish; repeal ⟨law⟩; rescind ⟨order, instruction⟩; cancel ⟨contract⟩; lift ⟨ban, prohibition⟩; d) *(ausgleichen)* cancel out; neutralize ⟨effect⟩.
Aufheben das; ~s: viel ~[s]/kein ~ von jmdm./etw. machen make a great fuss/not make any fuss about sb./sth.
auf|heitern 1. *tr. V.* cheer up; 2. *refl. V.* ⟨weather⟩ brighten up
auf|hetzen *tr. V.* incite
auf|holen 1. *tr. V.* make up ⟨time, delay⟩; pull back ⟨lead⟩; 2. *itr. V.* catch up; ⟨athlete, competitor⟩ make up ground
auf|horchen *itr. V.* prick up one's ears
auf|hören *itr. V.* stop; [damit] ~, etw. zu tun stop doing sth.
auf|kaufen *tr. V.* buy up
auf|klappen *tr. V.* open, fold open ⟨chair, table⟩; open [up] ⟨suitcase, trunk⟩; open ⟨book, knife⟩
auf|klären 1. *tr. V.* a) clear up ⟨matter, mystery, question, misunderstanding, error, confusion⟩; solve ⟨crime, problem⟩; explain ⟨event, incident, cause⟩; resolve ⟨contradiction, disagreement⟩; b) *(unterrichten)* enlighten; **ein Kind ~ *(sexualkundlich)*** tell a child the facts of life; 2. *refl. V.* a) ⟨misunderstanding, mystery⟩ be cleared up; b) ⟨weather⟩ brighten [up]; ⟨sky⟩ brighten; **Auf·klärung die** *s.* aufklären 1: a) clearing up; solution; explanation; resolution; b) enlightenment; **die ~ der Kinder** *(über Sexualität)* telling the children the facts of life
auf|kleben *tr. V.* stick on; *(mit Klei-*

ster) paste on; **Auf·kleber der** sticker
auf|knöpfen *tr. V.* unbutton; undo
auf|kochen 1. *tr. V.* bring to the boil; 2. *itr. V. mit sein* come to the boil
auf|kommen *unr. itr. V.; mit sein* a) ⟨wind⟩ spring up; ⟨storm, gale⟩ blow up; ⟨fog⟩ come down; ⟨rumour⟩ start; ⟨suspicion, doubt, feeling⟩ arise; ⟨fashion, style, invention⟩ come in; ⟨boredom⟩ set in; ⟨mood, atmosphere⟩ develop; b) ~ **für** *(bezahlen)* bear ⟨costs⟩; pay for ⟨damage⟩; pay ⟨expenses⟩; be liable for ⟨debts⟩; stand ⟨loss⟩; c) ~ **für** *(Verantwortung tragen für)* be responsible for
auf|krempeln *tr. V.* roll up
auf|laden 1. *unr. tr. V.* a) load (auf + Akk. on [to]); b) jmdm. etw. ~ *(ugs.)* load sb. with sth.; *(fig.)* saddle sb. with sth.; c) charge [up] ⟨battery⟩; 2. *unr. refl. V.* ⟨battery⟩ charge
Auf·lage die a) *(Buchw.)* edition; b) *(Verpflichtung)* condition
auf|lassen *unr. tr. V. (ugs.)* a) leave ⟨door, window, jacket, etc.⟩ open; b) keep on ⟨hat, glasses, etc.⟩
auf|lauern *itr. V.* jmdm. ~: lie in wait for sb.
Auf·lauf der a) *(Menschen~)* crowd; b) *(Speise)* soufflé
auf|leben *itr. V.; mit sein* revive; *(fig.: wieder munter werden)* come to life
auf|legen 1. *tr. V.* a) put on; den Hörer ~: put down the receiver; b) *(Buchw.)* publish; 2. *itr. V.* ⟨den Hörer ~⟩ hang up
auf|lehnen *refl. V.* rebel; **Auflehnung die;** ~, ~en rebellion
auf|leuchten *itr. V.; auch mit sein* light up; *(für kurze Zeit)* flash
auf|lockern *tr. V.* a) loosen; break up ⟨soil⟩; b) *(fig.)* introduce some variety into ⟨landscape, lesson, lecture⟩; relieve ⟨pattern, façade⟩; make ⟨mood, atmosphere, evening⟩ more relaxed; **Auf·lockerung die** a) *s.* auflockern a: loosening; breaking up; b) **zur ~ der Stimmung/des Abends** to make the mood/evening more relaxed
auf|lösen 1. *tr. V.* dissolve; resolve ⟨difficulty, contradiction⟩; solve ⟨puzzle, equation⟩; break off ⟨engagement⟩; cancel ⟨arrangement, contract, agreement⟩; dissolve ⟨organization⟩; 2. *refl. V.* dissolve (in + Akk. into); ⟨parliament⟩ dissolve itself; ⟨crowd, demonstration⟩ break up; ⟨fog, mist⟩ lift; *(fig.)* ⟨empire, social order⟩ dis-

integrate; **Auf·lösung die a)** *s.* **auf-lösen** 1: dissolving; resolution; solution; breaking off; cancellation; dissolution; **b)** *s.* **auflösen** 2: dissolving; breaking up lifting; disintegration

auf|machen 1. *tr. V.* **a)** open; undo ⟨*button, knot*⟩; **b)** *(ugs.: eröffnen)* open [up] ⟨*shop, business, etc.*⟩; 2. *itr. V.* **a)** ⟨*shop, office, etc.*⟩ open; **b)** *(ugs.: die Tür öffnen)* open the door; **jmdm. ~:** open the door to sb.; **c)** *(ugs.: eröffnet werden)* ⟨*shop, business*⟩ open [up]; **Aufmachung die;** ~, ~**en** presentation; *(Kleidung)* get-up

auf|marschieren *itr. V.;* **mit sein** assemble; *(heranmarschieren)* march up; **Truppen sind an der Grenze aufmarschiert** troops were deployed along the border

aufmerksam 1. *Adj.* **a)** attentive; sharp ⟨*eyes*⟩; **jmdn. auf jmdn./etw. ~ machen** draw sb.'s attention to sb./sth.; **auf jmdn./etw. ~ werden** become aware of sb./sth.; ~ **werden** notice; **b)** *(höflich)* attentive; 2. *adv.* attentively; **Aufmerksamkeit die;** ~, ~**en a)** *o. Pl.* attention; **b)** *(Höflichkeit)* attentiveness; **c)** *(Geschenk)* small gift

auf|muntern *tr. V.* **a)** cheer up; **b)** *(beleben)* liven up; **c)** *(ermutigen)* encourage; **Aufmunterung die;** ~, ~**s** auf-muntern: cheering up; livening up; encouragement

Aufnahme die; ~, ~**n a)** *s.* **aufnehmen** b: opening; establishment; taking up; **b)** *(Empfang)* reception; **c)** *s.* **aufnehmen d:** admission (**in** + *Akk.* into); **d)** *(Einschließung)* inclusion; **e)** *(Finanzw.)* raising; **f)** *(Aufzeichnung)* taking; *(von Personalien, eines Diktats)* taking [down]; **g)** *s.* **aufnehmen k:** taking: photographing; filming; **h)** *(Bild)* shot; **i)** *(das Aufnehmen auf Tonträger, das Aufgenommene)* recording; **j)** *(Anklang)* reception; response *(Gen.* to); **k)** *(Einverleibung, Absorption)* absorption

auf|nehmen *unr. tr. V.* **a)** *(aufheben)* pick up; *(fig.)* take up ⟨*idea, theme, etc.*⟩; **es mit jmdm./etw. ~/nicht ~ können** *(fig.)* be a/no match for sb./ sth.; **b)** *(beginnen mit)* open ⟨*negotiations, talks*⟩; establish ⟨*relations, contacts*⟩; take up ⟨*studies, activity, occupation*⟩; start ⟨*production, investigation*⟩; **c)** *(empfangen)* receive; *(beherbergen)* take in; **d)** *(beitreten lassen)* admit (**in** + *Akk.* to); **e)** *(einschließen, verzeichnen)* include; **f)** *(erfassen)*

take in ⟨*impressions, information, etc.*⟩; **g)** *(absorbieren)* absorb; **h)** *(Finanzw.)* raise ⟨*mortgage, money, loan*⟩; **i)** *(reagieren auf)* receive; **j)** *(aufschreiben)* take down; take [down] ⟨*dictation, particulars*⟩; **k)** *(fotografieren)* take ⟨*picture*⟩; photograph; take a photograph of ⟨*scene, subject*⟩; *(filmen)* film; **l)** *(auf Tonträger)* record

auf|opfern *refl. V.* devote oneself sacrificingly (**für** to); **aufopfernd** 1. *Adj.* self-sacrificing; 2. *adv.* self-sacrificingly

auf|passen *itr. V.* **a)** watch out; *(konzentriert sein)* pay attention; **paß mal auf!** *(ugs.: hör mal zu!)* now listen; **auf jmdn./etw. ~:** keep an eye on sb./ sth.

auf|platzen *itr. V.;* **mit sein** burst open; ⟨*seam, cushion*⟩ split open; ⟨*wound*⟩ open up

Auf·prall der; ~**[e]s,** ~**e** impact; **auf|prallen** *itr. V.; mit sein* **auf etw.** *(Akk.)* ~**:** hit sth.

Auf·preis der additional charge

auf|pumpen *tr. V.* pump up

auf|putschen *tr. V.* stimulate; arouse ⟨*passions, urge*⟩; **Aufputsch·mittel das** stimulant

auf|räumen *tr., itr. V.* clear up

auf·recht 1. *Adj.* *(auch fig.)* upright; 2. *adv.* ⟨*walk, sit, hold oneself*⟩ straight; **aufrecht|erhalten** *unr. tr. V.* maintain; keep up ⟨*deception, fiction, contact, custom*⟩

auf|regen 1. *tr. V.* excite; *(ärgern)* annoy; irritate; *(beunruhigen)* agitate; 2. *refl. V.* get worked up (**über** + *Akk.* about); **Auf·regung die** excitement *no Pl.; (Beunruhigung)* agitation *no pl.;* **jmdn. in ~ versetzen** make sb. excited/agitated

auf|reißen 1. *unr. tr. V.* **a)** *(öffnen)* tear open; wrench open ⟨*drawer*⟩; fling open ⟨*door, window*⟩; **die Augen/ den Mund ~:** open one's eyes/mouth wide; **b)** *(beschädigen)* tear open; tear ⟨*clothes*⟩; break up ⟨*road, soil*⟩; 2. *itr. V.; mit sein* ⟨*clothes*⟩ tear; ⟨*seam*⟩ split; ⟨*wound*⟩ open; ⟨*cloud*⟩ break up

auf|reizen *tr. V.* excite; **auf·reizend** 1. *Adj.* provocative; 2. *adv.* provocatively

auf|richten 1. *tr. V.* erect; put up; **den Oberkörper ~:** raise one's upper body; **jmdn. [wieder] ~** *(fig.)* give fresh heart to sb.; 2. *refl. V.* stand up [straight]; **sich an jmdm./etw. [wieder] ~** *(fig.)* take heart from sb./sth.

auf·richtig 1. *Adj.* sincere; 2. *adv.* sincerely; **Auf·richtigkeit** die sincerity

auf|rücken *itr. V.; mit sein* move up

Auf·ruf der a) call; b) *(Appell)* appeal *(an + Akk.* to); **auf|rufen** *unr. V.* a) call; b) jmdn. ~, etw. zu tun call upon sb. to do sth.; c) *(Rechtsspr.)* appeal for *(witnesses)*

Aufruhr der; ~s, ~e a) *(Widerstand)* rebellion; b) *o. Pl. (Erregung)* turmoil; **aufrührerisch** *Adj.* inflammatory

Auf·rüstung die armament

aufs *Präp. + Art.* = **auf das**

auf|sagen *tr. V.* recite

auf|sammeln *tr. V.* gather up

aufsässig 1. *Adj.* recalcitrant; 2. *adv.* recalcitrantly

Auf·satz der *(Text)* essay

auf|saugen *(auch regelm.) tr. V.* soak up; *(fig.)* absorb

auf|schieben *unr. V.* postpone

Auf·schlag der a) *(Aufprall)* impact; b) *(Preis~)* surcharge; c) *(Ärmel~)* cuff; *(Hosen~)* turn-up; *(Revers)* lapel; d) *(Tennis usw.)* serve

auf|schlagen 1. *unr. itr. V.* a) *mit sein* auf etw. *(Dat. od. Akk.)* ~: hit sth.; b) *(teurer werden)* ⟨price, rent, costs⟩ go up; c) *(Tennis usw.)* serve.; 2. *unr. tr. V.* a) *(öffnen)* crack ⟨nut, egg⟩ [open]; knock a hole in ⟨ice⟩; sich *(Dat.)* das Knie/den Kopf ~: cut one's knee/head; b) open ⟨book, newspaper, one's eyes⟩ schlagt S. 15 auf! turn to page 15; c) turn up ⟨collar, sleeve, trouserleg⟩; d) *(aufbauen)* set up ⟨camp⟩; pitch ⟨tent⟩; put up ⟨bed, hut, scaffolding⟩; e) 5% auf etw. *(Akk.)* ~: put 5% on sth.

auf|schließen 1. *unr. tr. V.* unlock; 2. *unr. itr. V.* [jmdm.] ~: unlock the door/gate *etc.* [for sb.]; **Auf·schluß** der information *no pl.*

auf|schneiden 1. *unr. tr. V.* a) cut open; b) *(zerteilen)* cut; 2. *unr. itr. V.* *(ugs.: prahlen)* boast *(mit* about); **Auf·schnitt** der; *o. Pl.* [assorted] cold meats *pl.*/cheeses *pl.*

auf|schnüren *tr. V.* undo

auf|schrauben *tr. V.* unscrew; unscrew the top of ⟨bottle, jar, etc.⟩

auf|schreiben *unr. V.* write down; [sich *(Dat.)*] etw. ~: make a note of sth.; **Auf·schrift** die inscription

Auf·schub der postponement; die Sache duldet keinen ~: the matter brooks no delay

Auf·schwung der upturn *(Gen.* in)

Aufsehen das; ~s stir; [großes] ~ erregen cause a [great] stir; **Auf·seher** der *(im Gefängnis)* warder *(Brit.)*; [prison] guard *(Amer.)*; *(im Park)* park-keeper; *(im Museum, auf dem Parkplatz)* attendant; *(auf einem Gut, Sklaven~)* overseer

auf|sein *unr. itr. V.; mit sein; nur im Inf. und Part. zusammengeschrieben (ugs.)* a) be open; b) *(nicht im Bett sein)* be up

auf|setzen 1. *tr. V.* a) put on; b) *(verfassen)* draw up ⟨text⟩; 2. *refl. V.* sit up

Auf·sicht die supervision; *(bei Prüfungen)* invigilation *(Brit.)*; proctoring *(Amer.)*

auf|springen *unr. itr. V.; mit sein* a) jump up; b) *(hinaufspringen)* jump on *(auf + Akk.* to); c) *(rissig werden)* crack

Auf·stand der rebellion; **auf·ständisch** *Adj.* rebellious

auf|stehen *unr. itr. V. mit sein* stand up; *(aus dem Liegen)* get up

auf|steigen *unr. itr. V.; mit sein* a) *(auf ein Fahrzeug)* get on; **auf etw.** *(Akk.)* ~: get on [to] sth.; b) *(bergan steigen)* climb; c) *(hochsteigen)* ⟨sap, smoke, mist⟩ rise; d) *(beruflich, gesellschaftlich)* rise *(zu* to); **zum Direktor** ~: rise to be manager

auf|stellen 1. *tr. V.* a) put up *(auf + Akk.* on); set up ⟨skittles⟩; *(postieren)* post; b) *(aufrecht hinstellen)* stand up; c) *(Sport)* select, pick ⟨team, player⟩; d) *(bilden)* put together ⟨team of experts⟩; raise ⟨army⟩; e) *(nominieren)* nominate; put up; 2. *refl. V.* position oneself; **Auf·stellung** die a) *s.* aufstellen 1a: putting up; setting up; posting; b) *s.* aufstellen b: standing up; c) *s.* aufstellen c: selection; picking; c) *s.* aufstellen d: putting together; raising; d) *(Nominierung)* nomination

Aufstieg der; ~[e]s, ~e a) climb; b) *s.* aufsteigen d: rise

auf|stoßen 1. *unr. tr. V.* push open; 2. *unr. itr. V.* belch; ⟨baby⟩ bring up wind

Auf·strich der spread

auf|stützen 1. *tr. V.* rest ⟨one's arms etc.⟩; 2. *refl. V.* support oneself; die Arme auf etw. *(Akk. od. Dat.)* ~: rest one's arms on sth.

auf|suchen *tr. V.* call on; go to ⟨doctor⟩

Auf·takt der *(fig.)* start

auf|tauchen itr. V.; mit sein a) surface; b) (sichtbar werden) appear

auf|tauen 1. tr. V. thaw; **2.** itr. V.; mit sein (auch fig.) thaw

auf|teilen tr. V. a) divide [up]; b) (verteilen) share out

Auftrag der; ~[e]s, **Aufträge** a) instructions pl.; in jmds. ~ (Dat.) on sb.'s instructions; auf jmds. ~ on behalf of sb; b) (Bestellung) order; (bei Künstlern, Architekten usw.) commission; c) (Mission) task; (Aufgabe) job; **auf|tragen** unr. tr. V. a) jmdm. ~, etw. zu tun instruct sb. to do sth.; b) (aufstreichen) put on 〈paint, make-up, etc.〉; **Auftrag·geber** der client

auf|treten unr. itr. V.; mit sein a) tread; b) (sich benehmen) behave; c) (eine Vorstellung geben) appear; als Zeuge/Kläger ~: appear as a witness/a plaintiff; d) (auftauchen) 〈problem, difficulty, difference of opinion〉 arise; 〈symptom, danger, pest〉 appear; **Auftreten** das; ~s (Benehmen) manner

Auf·trieb der a) (Physik) (statischer ~) buoyancy; (dynamischer ~) lift; b) (fig.) impetus; das hat ihm ~/neuen ~ gegeben that has given him a lift/given him new impetus

Auf·tritt der a) (Vorstellung) appearance; b) (Theater: das Auftreten) entrance; (Szene) scene

auf|tun unr. refl. V. (geh.) open; (fig.) open up

auf|wachen itr. V.; mit sein wake up, awaken (aus from); (aus Ohnmacht, Narkose) come round (aus from)

auf|wachsen unr. itr. V.; mit sein grow up

Auf·wand der; ~[e]s cost; expense

auf|wärmen 1. tr. V. heat or warm up 〈food〉; **2.** refl. V. warm oneself up

aufwärts Adv. upwards

auf|wecken tr. V. wake [up]; waken

auf|weichen 1. tr. V. soften; **2.** itr. V.; mit sein become soft; soften up

auf·wendig 1. Adj. lavish; (kostspielig) costly; expensive; **2.** adv. lavishly; (kostspielig) expensively

auf|wiegeln tr. V. incite; stir up

auf|wirbeln tr. V. swirl up

auf|wischen tr. V. a) wipe or mop up; b) (säubern) wipe 〈floor〉; (mit Wasser) wash 〈floor〉

auf|zählen tr. V. list; **Auf·zählung** die a) listing; b) (Liste) list

auf|zeichnen tr. V. a) record; b) (zeichnen) draw; **Auf·zeichnung**

die record; (Film~, Ton~) recording; ~en (Notizen) notes

auf|ziehen 1. unr. tr. V. a) pull open 〈drawer〉; open, draw [back] 〈curtains〉; undo 〈zip〉; b) wind up 〈clock, toy, etc.〉. **2.** unr. itr. V.; mit sein come up; 〈clouds, storm〉 gather

Auf·zucht die raising; rearing

Auf·zug der a) (Lift) lift (Brit.); elevator (Amer.); b) (abwertend: Aufmachung) get-up; c) (Theater: Akt) act

Aug·apfel der eyeball; **Auge** das; ~s, ~n eye; gute/schlechte ~n haben have good/poor eyesight; auf einem ~ blind blind in one eye; da wird er ~n machen (fig. ugs.) his eyes will pop out of his head; ich traute meinen ~n nicht I couldn't believe my eyes; ein ~ od. beide ~n zudrücken (fig.) turn a blind eye; jmdn./etw. nicht aus den ~n lassen not take one's eyes off sb./sth.; ins ~ gehen (fig. ugs.) end in disaster; unter vier ~n (fig.) in private

Augen-: ~arzt der eye specialist; ~blick [auch: '--'] der s. ¹Moment; ~blicklich [auch: --'--] **1.** Adj. a) (sofortig) immediate; b) (gegenwärtig) present; **2.** adv. a) (sofort) at once; b) (zur Zeit) at the moment; ~braue die eyebrow; ~lid das eyelid; ~zeuge der eyewitness

August der; ~[e]s od. ~, ~e August

Auktion die; ~, ~en auction

Aula die; ~, Aulen od. ~s hall

aus 1. Präp. mit Dat. a) (aus dem Inneren von) out of; b) (Herkunft, Quelle, Ausgangspunkt angebend, auch zeitlich) from; ~ Spanien/Köln usw. from Spain/Cologne etc.; c) ~ der Mode/Übung sein be out of fashion/training; d) (Grund, Ursache angebend) out of; etw. ~ Erfahrung wissen know sth. from experience; ~ Versehen by mistake; e) (bestehend ~ of; (hergestellt ~) made of; ~ etw. bestehen consist of sth.; f) ~ ihm ist ein guter Arzt geworden he made a good doctor; **2.** Adv. a) (ugs.: vorbei) ~ jetzt! that's enough; b) „~" (an Lichtschaltern) 'out'; (an Geräten) 'off'; c) vom Fenster/obersten Stockwerk ~: from the window/top storey; von mir ~ (ugs.) if you like; von sich (Dat.) ~: of one's own accord

aus|atmen itr., tr. V. breathe out

Aus·bau der; ~[e]s a) (Erweiterung) extension; b) (Ausgestaltung) conversion (zu into); **aus|bauen** tr. V. a) (demontieren) remove (aus from); b) (erweitern) extend

Aus·beute die yield; **aus|beuten** tr.
V. exploit

aus|bilden tr. V. **a)** train; **b)** (entwickeln) develop; **Aus·bildung** die **a)** training; **b)** (Entwicklung) development

Aus·blick der view (auf + Akk. of)

aus|brechen unr. itr. V.; mit sein **a)** break out (aus of); (fig.) break free (aus from); **b)** jmdm. bricht der Schweiß aus sb. breaks into a sweat; **c)** ⟨volcano⟩ erupt; **d)** (beginnen) break out; ⟨crisis⟩ break; **e)** in Gelächter/Weinen ~: burst out laughing/crying; in Beifall/Tränen ~: burst into applause/tears

aus|breiten 1. tr. V. spread [out] ⟨map, cloth, sheet, etc.⟩; open out ⟨fan, newspaper⟩; (nebeneinanderlegen) spread out; 2. refl. V. spread

Aus·bruch der **a)** (Flucht) escape (aus from); **b)** (Beginn) outbreak; **c)** (Gefühls~) outburst; **d)** (eines Vulkans) eruption

aus|brüten tr. V. hatch out; (im Brutkasten) incubate

Aus·dauer die stamina; **aus·dauernd** Adj. with stamina postpos.

aus|dehnen 1. tr. V. **a)** (fig.) extend (auf + Akk. to); (zeitlich) prolong; 2. refl. V. expand; (zeitlich) go on; **Aus·dehnung** die expansion; (fig.) extension; (zeitlich) prolongation

aus|denken unr. refl. V. sich (Dat.) etw. ~: think sth. up

Aus·druck der; ~[e]s, **Ausdrücke** expression; (Terminus) term; **etw. zum ~ bringen** express sth.; **aus|drücken** 1. tr. V. **a)** (auspressen) squeeze ⟨juice⟩ out; squeeze [out] ⟨lemon, grape, orange, etc.⟩; squeeze out ⟨sponge⟩; (boil, pimple); **b)** stub out ⟨cigarette⟩; **c)** (mitteilen) express; 2. refl. V. **a)** express oneself; **b)** (offenbar werden) be expressed; **ausdrücklich** [od. '--] 1. Adj. express attrib. ⟨command, wish, etc.⟩; explicit ⟨reservation⟩; 2. adv. expressly; (mention) explicitly; **ausdrucks·los** 1. Adj. expressionless; 2. adv. expressionlessly; **ausdrucks·voll** 1. Adj. expressive; 2. adv. expressively

aus·einander Adv. apart; etw. ~ schreiben write sth. as separate words **auseinander-, Auseinander-** ~|brechen 1. unr. itr. V.; mit sein (auch fig.) break up; 2. unr. tr. V. break ⟨sth.⟩ up; ~|gehen unr. itr. V.;

mit sein **a)** part; ⟨crowd⟩ disperse; **b)** (fig.) ⟨opinions, views⟩ differ; ~|halten unr. tr. V. tell ⟨things, people⟩ apart; ~|nehmen unr. tr. V. take ⟨sth.⟩ apart; ~|setzen 1. tr. V. jmdm. etw. ~setzen explain sth. to sb.; 2. refl. V. sich mit jmdm. ~setzen have it out with sb.; sich mit etw. ~setzen concern oneself with sth.; ~setzung die ~, ~en a) (Streit) argument; b) (Kampfhandlungen) clash

Aus·fahrt die exit

Aus·fall der a) (das Nichtstattfinden) cancellation; b) (Einbuße, Verlust) loss; c) (eines Motors) failure; (einer Maschine, eines Autos) breakdown; **aus|fallen** unr. itr. V.; mit sein a) fall out; b) (nicht stattfinden) be cancelled; etw. ~ lassen cancel sth.; c) (ausscheiden) drop out; d) (nicht mehr funktionieren) ⟨engine, brakes, signal⟩ fail; ⟨machine, car⟩ break down; e) (ein bestimmtes Ergebnis zeigen) turn out; **ausfallend** Adj. |gegen jmdn.| ~ sein/werden be/become abusive [towards sb.]; **Ausfall·straße** die main road out of the/a town/city

aus·findig Adv. jmdn./etw. ~ machen find sb./sth.

Aus·flug der outing; **Ausflügler** der; ~s, ~: day-tripper; excursionist (Amer.)

Ausflugs-: ~**dampfer** der pleasure steamer; ~**lokal** das restaurant/café catering for [day-]trippers

aus|fragen tr. V. jmdn. ~: question sb., ask sb. questions (nach, über + Akk. about)

aus|fransen itr. V.; mit sein fray

Aus·fuhr die ~, ~en s. Export; **aus|führen** tr. V. a) (ausgehen mit) take ⟨person⟩ out; b) (spazierenführen) take ⟨person, animal⟩ for a walk; c) (exportieren) export; d) (durchführen) carry out; (Sport) take ⟨penalty, free kick, corner⟩; **ausführlich** [auch: '--] 1. Adj. detailed; full; 2. adv. in detail; **Aus·führung** die (Durchführung) carrying out; (Sport) taking

aus|füllen tr. V. a) fill; fill in ⟨form, crossword puzzle⟩; b) (beanspruchen, einnehmen) take up ⟨space⟩

Aus·gabe die a) o. Pl. giving out; (von Essen) serving; b) (Geld~) item of expenditure; ~n expenditure sing. (für on); c) (Edition) edition

Aus·gang der a) o. Pl. (Erlaubnis zum Ausgehen) time off; (von Soldaten) leave; b) (Tür ins Freie) exit (Gen.

from); c) *(Anat.)* outlet; d) *(Ende)* end; *(eines Romans, Films usw.)* ending; e) o. Pl. *(Ergebnis)* outcome; *(eines Wettbewerbs)* result; **ein Unfall mit tödlichem ~**: an accident with fatal consequences; **Ausgangspunkt der** starting-point

aus|geben *unr. tr. V.* a) give out; serve *(food, drinks)*; b) *(verbrauchen)* spend *(money)* **(für on)**

ausgebucht *Adj.* booked up

aus·gefallen *Adj.* unusual

ausgeglichen *Adj.* balanced; well-balanced *(person)*; equable *(climate)*

aus|gehen *unr. itr. V.; mit sein* a) go out; b) *(fast aufgebraucht sein)* run out; c) *(enden)* end; **gut/schlecht ~**: turn out well/badly; *(story, film)* end happily/unhappily; d) **von jmdm./etw. ~**: come from sb./sth.; e) **von etw. ~** *(etw. zugrunde legen)* take sth. as one's starting-point; *(etw. annehmen)* assume sth.

aus·gelassen 1. *Adj.* exuberant *(mood, person)*; lively *(party, celebration)*; *(wild)* boisterous; 2. *adv.* exuberantly; *(wild)* boisterously

aus·genommen *Konj.* except

ausgeprägt *Adj.* marked

ausgerechnet *Adv.* *(ugs.)* ~ **heute/ morgen** today/tomorrow of all days; ~ **hier** here of all places; ~ **Sie** you of all people

aus·geschlossen *Adj.* **das ist ~**: that is out of the question

aus·geschnitten *Adj.* low-cut *(dress, blouse, etc.)*

aus·gestorben *Adj.* **[wie] ~**: deserted

ausgezeichnet *[od. '--'--']* 1. *Adj.* excellent; outstanding *(expert)*; 2. *adv.* excellently

ausgiebig 1. *Adj.* substantial *(meal)*; 2. *adv.* *(profit)* handsomely; *(read)* extensively; **von etw. ~ Gebrauch machen** make full use of sth.

aus|gießen *unr. tr. V.* a) pour out *(aus of)*; b) *(leeren)* empty

Ausgleich der; ~[e]s, ~e a) *s.* ausgleichen a: evening out; reconciliation; b) *(Schadensersatz)* compensation; **als** *od.* **zum ~ für etw.** to make up sth.; **aus|gleichen** *unr. tr. V.* a) even out; reconcile *(differences of opinions, contradictions)*; b) compensate for *(damage)*; make up for *(misfortune, lack)*; **etw. durch etw. ~**: make up for sth. with sth.; **sich ~**: balance out; *(sich gegenseitig aufheben)* cancel each other out

aus|graben *unr. tr. V.* dig up; *(Archäol.)* excavate; **Aus·grabung die** *(Archäol.)* excavation

aus|halten *unr. tr. V.* stand; bear; endure; withstand *(attack, load, pressure, test, wear and tear)*; **er konnte es zu Hause nicht mehr ~**: he couldn't stand it at home any more; **es ist nicht zum Aushalten** it is unbearable

aus|handeln *tr. V.* negotiate

aus|händigen *tr. V.* hand over

Aus·hang der notice

aus|heben *unr. tr. V.* dig out *(earth etc.)*; dig *(trench, grave, etc.)*

aus|helfen *unr. itr. V.* help out; **jmdm. ~**: help sb. out **(mit, bei with)**; **Aus·hilfe die** a) o. Pl. *(das Aushelfen)* help; b) *s.* Aushilfskraft; **Aushilfs·kraft die** temporary worker; *(in Läden, Gaststätten)* temporary assistant; *(Sekretärin)* temporary secretary; temp *(coll.)*

aus|holen *itr. V.* **[mit dem Arm] ~**: draw back one's arm; *(zum Schlag)* raise one's arm

aus|kennen *unr. refl. V. (an einem Ort usw.)* know one's way around; *(in einem Fach, einer Angelegenheit usw.)* know what's what; **sie kennt sich in dieser Stadt aus** she knows her way around the town; **sich [gut] mit/in etw.** *(Dat.)* ~: know [a lot] about sth.

Aus·klang der *(geh.)* end; **zum ~ des Festes** to end *or* close the festival

aus|kleiden *tr. V. (geh.)* undress; **sich ~**: undress

aus|klingen *unr. itr. V. mit sein* end

aus|klopfen *tr. V.* a) beat out *(aus + Dat.* of); b) *(säubern)* beat *(carpet)*; knock *(pipe)* out

aus|kochen *tr. V.* boil; *(keimfrei machen)* sterilize *(instruments etc.)* [in boiling water]

aus|kommen *unr. itr. V.; mit sein* a) manage **(mit on)**; b) **mit jmdm. [gut] ~**: get on [well] with sb.

Auskommen das; ~s livelihood

Auskunft die; ~, Auskünfte a) piece of information; **Auskünfte** information *sing.*; **[jmdm. über etw.** *(Akk.)]* ~ **geben** give [sb.] information [about sth.]; b) o. Pl. *(Stelle)* information desk/counter/office/centre *etc.*; *(Fernspr.)* directory enquiries *no art.* *(Brit.)*; directory information *no art.* *(Amer.)*

aus|lachen *tr. V.* laugh at

aus|laden *unr. tr. V.* unload *(goods etc.)*

Aus·lage die a) Pl. (Unkosten) expenses; b) (ausgestellte Ware) item on display; **~n** goods on display

Aus·land das; o. Pl. foreign countries pl.; im/ins ~: abroad; aus dem ~: from abroad; **Ausländer** der; **~s, ~**, **Ausländerin** die; **~, ~nen** foreigner; **ausländisch** Adj. foreign

Auslands-: ~aufenthalt der stay abroad; **~gespräch** das (Fernspr.) international call; **~korrespondent** der foreign correspondent; **~reise** die trip abroad

aus|lassen unr. tr. V. a) (weglassen) leave out; b) (versäumen) miss (opportunity, chance, etc.)

Auslauf der a) o. Pl. keinen/zuwenig ~ haben have no/too little chance to run around outside; b) (Raum) space to run around in; **aus|laufen** unr. itr. V.; mit sein a) run out (aus of); b) (leer laufen) empty; (egg) run out; c) (in See stechen) sail (nach for); d) (erlöschen) (contract, agreement, etc.) run out; **Aus·läufer** der a) (Geogr.) foothill usu. in pl.; b) (Met.) (eines Hochs) ridge; (eines Tiefs) trough

aus|legen tr. V. a) (hinlegen) lay out; display (goods, exhibits); b) etw. mit Fliesen/Teppichboden ~: tile/carpet sth.; c) (leihen) lend; d) (interpretieren) interpret; etw. falsch ~: misinterpret sth.; **Auslegung** die; **~, ~en** interpretation

aus|leihen unr. tr. V. s. leihen

aus|liefern tr. V. jmdm. etw. od. etw. an jmdn. ~: hand sth. over to sb.

aus|löschen tr. V. a) extinguish; b) (beseitigen) erase (drawing, writing)

aus|losen tr. V. etw. ~: draw lots for sth.

aus|lösen tr. V. a) trigger (mechanism, device, alarm, etc.); release (camera shutter); b) provoke (discussion, anger, laughter, reaction, outrage, heart attack); cause (sorrow, horror, surprise, disappointment, panic, war); excite, arouse (interest, enthusiasm); **Auslöser** der; **~s, ~** (Fot.) shutter release

aus|machen tr. V. a) (ugs.) put out (light, fire, cigarette, candle); switch off (television, radio, hi-fi); turn off (gas); b) (vereinbaren) agree [on]; ~, daß ...: agree that ...; c) (auszeichnen, kennzeichnen) make up; d) wenig/nichts/viel ~: make little/no/a great difference; e) das macht mir nichts aus I don't mind

Aus·maß das a) (Größe) size; b) (Grad) extent

aus|messen unr. tr. V. measure up

Aus·nahme die; **~, ~n** exception; mit ~ von with the exception of; bei jmdm. eine ~ machen make an exception in sb.'s case; **Ausnahme·zustand** der state of emergency; **ausnahms·weise** Adv. by way of an exception; Dürfen wir mitkommen? – Ausnahmsweise [ja] May we come too? – Yes, just this once

aus|nehmen unr. tr. V. a) gut (fish, rabbit, chicken); b) (ausschließen von) exclude; (gesondert behandeln) make an exception of

aus|nutzen, (bes. südd., österr.) **aus|nützen** tr. V. a) take advantage of; b) (ausbeuten) exploit

aus|packen tr., itr. V. unpack; (auswickeln) unwrap

aus|pressen tr. V. squeeze out (juice); squeeze (orange, lemon); (keltern) press (grapes etc.)

aus|probieren tr. V. try out

Aus·puff der exhaust

aus|radieren tr. V. rub out; erase

aus|rauben tr. V. rob

aus|räumen 1. tr. V. a) clear out (aus of); b) (fig.) clear up; dispel (prejudice, suspicion, misgivings); 2. itr. V. clear everything out

aus|rechnen tr. V. work out; das kannst du dir leicht ~ (ugs.) you can easily work that out [for yourself]

Aus·rede die excuse; **aus|reden** 1. itr. V. finish [speaking]; 2. tr. V. jmdm. etw. ~: talk sb. out of sth.

aus|reichen itr. V. be enough or sufficient (zu for); **ausreichend** 1. Adj. sufficient; enough; (als Note) fair. 2. adv. sufficiently

aus|reißen 1. unr. tr. V. tear out; pull out (plants, weeds); 2. unr. itr. V.; mit sein a) (sich lösen) come off; b) (ugs.: weglaufen) run away (Dat. from)

aus|renken tr. V. dislocate

aus|richten tr. V. a) jmdm. etw. ~: tell sb. sth.; b) (einheitlich anordnen) line up; c) (erreichen) achieve

aus|rollen tr. V. roll out

aus|rotten tr. V. eradicate

Aus·ruf der cry; **aus|rufen** unr. tr. V. a) call out; „Schön!" rief er aus 'Lovely', he exclaimed; b) (offiziell verkünden) proclaim; declare (state of emergency); c) (zum Kauf anbieten) cry; **Ausrufe·zeichen** das exclamation mark

aus|ruhen refl., itr. V. have a rest;
|sich| ein wenig/richtig ~: rest a little/
have a good rest; **ausgeruht sein** be
rested

aus|rüsten tr. V. equip; **Aus·rü-
stung die a)** o. Pl. equipping; **b)**
(~sgegenstände) equipment no pl.

aus|rutschen itr. V.; mit sein slip

Aus·sage die statement; **aus|sagen
1.** tr. V. **a)** say; **c)** (vor Gericht, vor der
Polizei) state; (unter Eid) testify; **2.**
itr. V. make a statement; (unter Eid)
testify

aus|schalten tr. V. **a)** switch or turn
off; **b)** (fig.) eliminate; exclude ⟨emo-
tion, influence⟩; dismiss ⟨doubt, objec-
tion⟩; shut out ⟨feeling, thought⟩

Aus·schank der; ~|e|s, serving

Aus·schau die: nach jmdm./etw. ~
halten keep a look-out for sb./sth.;
aus|schauen itr. V. nach jmdm./etw.
~ look out for sb./sth.

aus|scheiden 1. unr. itr. V.; mit sein
a) aus etw. ~: leave sth.; aus dem Amt
~: leave office; **b)** (Sport) be elimin-
ated; **c)** diese Möglichkeit/dieser Kandidat scheidet aus this possibility/candi-
date has to be ruled out; **2.** unr. tr.
V. (Physiol.) excrete ⟨waste⟩; eliminate, expel ⟨poison⟩; exude ⟨sweat⟩;
Aus·scheidung die a) (Physiol.) s.
ausscheiden 2: excretion; elimination;
expulsion; exudation; ~en (Ausge-
schiedenes) excreta; **b)** (Sport) quali-
fier

aus|schenken tr. V. serve

aus|schimpfen tr. V. jmdn. ~: tell sb.
off

aus|schlafen 1. unr. itr., refl. V. have
a good sleep; **2.** unr. tr. V. seinen
Rausch ~: sleep off the effects of alcohol

Aus·schlag der a) (Haut~) rash; **b)**
(eines Zeigers, einer Waage) deflec-
tion; (eines Pendels) swing; **den ~ geben** (fig.) tip the scales (fig.);
aus|schlagen 1. unr. tr. V. **a)** knock
out; **b)** (ablehnen) turn down; **2.** unr.
itr. V. **a)** ⟨horse⟩ kick; **b)** ⟨needle,
pointer⟩ be deflected, swing; **c)** (sprießen) come out [in bud]; **aus-
schlag·gebend** Adj. decisive

aus|schließen unr. tr. V. **a)** (aussto-
ßen) expel (aus from); **b)** (nicht teilnehmen lassen) exclude (aus from); **c)**
(fig.) rule out ⟨possibility⟩; **jeden Irrtum ~**: rule out all possibility of error;
e) (aussperren) lock out; **ausschließlich** [od. '·'--, -'--] **1.** Adj. ex-

clusive; **2.** Adv. exclusively; **3.** Präp.
mit Gen. excluding; **Aus·schluß der**
exclusion (von from); (aus einer Gemeinschaft) expulsion (aus from); **unter ~ der Öffentlichkeit** with the public excluded; (Rechtsw.) in camera

aus|schmücken tr. V. deck out

aus|schneiden unr. tr. V. cut out;
Aus·schnitt der a) (Zeitungs~) cutting; clipping; **b)** (Hals~) neck; **ein
tiefer ~**: a plunging neck-line; **c)**
(Teil) part; (eines Textes) excerpt; (eines Films) clip; (Bild~) detail

aus|schreiben unr. itr. V. **a)** (nicht ab-
gekürzt schreiben) etw. ~: write sth.
out in full; **b)** (ausstellen) make out
⟨cheque, invoice, receipt⟩; **c)** (bekanntgeben) call ⟨election, meeting⟩; advertise ⟨flat, job⟩; put ⟨supply order etc.⟩
out to tender; **Aus·schreibung die**
s. **ausschreiben c**: calling; advertisement; invitation to tender

Ausschreitungen Pl. acts of violence

Aus·schuß der committee

aus|schütten tr. V. tip out ⟨water,
sand, coal, etc.⟩; (ausleeren) empty
⟨bucket, bowl, container⟩

ausschweifend 1. Adj. wild ⟨ima-
gination, emotion, hope, desire, orgy⟩;
extravagant ⟨idea⟩; riotous, wild ⟨en-
joyment⟩; dissolute ⟨life, person⟩; **2.**
adv. ~ leben lead a dissolute life;
Ausschweifung die; ~, ~en (im Genießen) dissolution

aus|sehen unr. itr. V. look ⟨wie like⟩;
so siehst du aus! (ugs.) that's what you
think!; **Aussehen das**; ~s appearance

aus|sein unr. itr. V.; mit sein; nur im
Inf. und Part. zusammengeschrieben **a)**
⟨play, film, war⟩ be over; **wann ist die
Vorstellung aus?** what time does the
performance end?; **die Schule ist aus**
school is out; **b)** ⟨fire, candle, etc.⟩ be
out; **c)** ⟨radio, light, etc.⟩ be off

außen Adv. outside; **die Vase ist ~ bemalt** the vase is painted on the outside; **das Fenster geht nach ~ auf** the
window opens outwards; **von ~**: from
the outside

außen-, Außen-: ~handel der; o.
Pl. foreign trade no art.; ~minister
der Foreign Minister; ~ministerium
das Foreign Ministry; ~politik die
foreign politics sing.; ~politisch **1.**
Adj. ⟨question⟩ relating to foreign policy; **2.** adv. as regards foreign policy;
~seite die outside

Außenseiter der; ~s, ~, **Außenseiterin** die; ~, ~nen outsider

außer 1. *Präp. mit Dat.* **a)** *(abgesehen von)* apart from; aside from *(Amer.)*; **b)** *(außerhalb von)* out of; ~ **sich sein** be beside oneself (**vor** + *Dat.* with); **c)** *(zusätzlich zu)* in addition to; 2. *Präp. mit Akk.* ~ **sich geraten** become beside oneself (**vor** + *Dat.* with); 3. *Konj.* except; **äußer...** *Adj.* outer; outside *(pocket)*; outlying *(district, area)*; external *(injury, form, circumstances, cause, force)*; outward *(appearance, similarity, effect, etc.)*; foreign *(affairs)*

außer·dem *[auch: --'-] Adv.* as well; *(überdies)* besides

Äußere das; ~n [outward] appearance

außer-: ~**ehelich** 1. *Adj.* extramarital; illegitimate *(child, birth)*; 2. *adv.* outside marriage; ~**gewöhnlich** 1. *Adj.* **a)** unusual; **b)** *(das Gewohnte übertreffend)* exceptional; 2. *adv.* **a)** unusually; **b)** *(sehr)* exceptionally; ~**halb** *Präp. mit Gen.* outside

äußerlich 1. *Adj.* external *(use, injury)*; outward *(appearance, calm, similarity, etc.)*; 2. *adv.*: s. *Adj.*: externally; outwardly

äußern 1. *tr. V.* express, voice *(opinion, view, criticism, reservations, disapproval, doubt)*; express *(wish)*; voice *(suspicion)*; 2. *refl. V.* **a) sich über etw.** *(Akk.)* ~: give one's view on sth.; **b)** *(illness)* manifest itself (**in** + *Dat.*, **durch**)

außer·ordentlich 1. *Adj.* **a)** extraordinary; **b)** *(das Gewohnte übertreffend)* exceptional; 2. *adv. (sehr)* exceptionally; extremely *(pleased, relieved)*

äußerst *Adv.* extremely; **äußerst...** *Adj.* **a)** extreme; **b)** *(letztmöglich)* latest possible *(date, deadline)*; *(höchst...)* highest *(price)*; *(niedrigst...)* lowest *(price)*; **c)** *(schlimmst...)* worst

außerstande *Adv.* ~ **sein,** etw. **zu tun** *(nicht befähigt)* be unable to do sth.; *(nicht in der Lage)* not be in a position to do sth.

Äußerung die; ~, ~en comment

aus|setzen 1. *tr. V.* **a)** expose *(Dat.* to); **Belastungen ausgesetzt sein** be subject to strains; **b)** *(sich selbst überlassen)* abandon *(baby, animal)*; *(auf einer einsamen Insel)* maroon; **c) an jmdm./etw. etwas auszusetzen haben** find fault with sb./sth.; 2. *itr. V.* **a)** *(aufhören)* stop; *(engine, machine)* cut

out; **b)** *(pausieren)* *(player)* miss a turn; **mit der Arbeit/dem Training [ein paar Wochen]** ~: stop work/training [for a few weeks]

Aus·sicht die **a)** view (**auf** + *Akk.* of); **b)** *(fig.)* prospect; ~ **auf etw.** *(Akk.)* **haben,** etw. **in** ~ **haben** have the prospect of sth.

aussichts-, Aussichts-: ~**los** 1. *Adj.* hopeless. 2. *adv.* hopelessly; ~**reich** *Adj.* promising; ~**turm der** look-out tower

aus|sortieren *tr. V.* sort out

aus|spannen *itr. V.* take *or* have a break

aus|sperren 1. *tr. V.* lock out; shut *(animal)* out; 2. *tr. V.* lock the workforce out; **Aus·sperrung die** the lockout

aus|spielen *tr. V.* **a)** *auch itr.* *(Kartenspiel)* lead; **b) jmdn./etw. gegen jmdn./ etw.** ~: play sb./sth. off against sb./ sth.

Aus·sprache die **a)** pronunciation; **b)** *(Gespräch)* discussion

aus|sprechen 1. *unr. tr. V.* **a)** pronounce; **b)** *(ausdrücken)* express; voice *(suspicion, request)*; 2. *unr. refl. V.* **a) sich lobend/mißbilligend** *usw.* **über jmdn./etw.** ~: speak highly/disapprovingly of *etc.* sb./sth.; **c)** *(offen sprechen)* say what's on one's mind; **sich bei jmdm.** ~: have a heart-toheart talk with sb.; **d)** *(Strittiges klären)* talk things out (**mit** with); 3. *unr. itr. V.* *(zu Ende sprechen)* finish [speaking]; **Aus·spruch der** remark

aus|spucken 1. *itr. V.* spit. 2. *tr. V.* spit out

aus|spülen *tr. V.* rinse out

Aus·stand der the strike

aus|statten ['aʊsʃtatn] *tr. V.* provide (**mit** with); *(mit Gerät)* equip (**mit** with); *(mit Möbeln, Teppichen, Gardinen usw.)* furnish; **Ausstattung die;** ~, ~**en a)** s. **ausstatten** provision; equipping; furnishing; **b)** *(Ausrüstung)* equipment; *(Innen~ eines Autos)* trim; **c)** *(Einrichtung)* furnishings *pl.*

aus|stehen 1. *unr. itr. V.* ~ **noch** ~ *(debt)* be outstanding; *(decision)* be still to be taken; *(solution)* be still to be found; 2. *unr. tr. V.* **ich kann ihn/ das nicht** ~: I can't stand him/it

aus|steigen *unr. itr. V.; mit sein* get out; *(aus einem Zug, Bus)* get off

aus|stellen *tr. V.* **a)** put on display; display; *(im Museum, auf einer Messe)* exhibit; **b)** *(ausfertigen)* make out

⟨*cheque, prescription, receipt, bill*⟩; issue ⟨*visa, passport, certificate*⟩; **c)** ⟨ugs.: *ausschalten*⟩ switch off ⟨*cooker, radio, heating, engine*⟩; **Aus·stel·lung die a)** exhibition; **b)** *s.* **ausstellen b:** making out; issuing

aus|sterben *unr. itr. V.;* mit sein die out; ⟨*species*⟩ become extinct

Aus·steuer die trousseau (*consisting mainly of household linen*)

Ausstieg der: ~[e]s, ~e ⟨*Tür*⟩ exit

aus|stopfen *tr. V.* stuff

aus|stoßen *unr. tr. V.* **a)** expel; give off, emit ⟨*gas, fumes, smoke*⟩; **b)** give ⟨*cry, whistle, laugh, sigh, etc.*⟩; let out ⟨*cry, scream, yell*⟩; utter ⟨*curse, threat, etc.*⟩

aus|strahlen 1. *tr. V.* **a)** ⟨*auch fig.*⟩ radiate; ⟨*lamp*⟩ give out ⟨*light*⟩; **b)** ⟨*Rundf., Ferns.*⟩ broadcast; **2.** *itr. V.* **a)** radiate; ⟨*light*⟩ be given out; ⟨*fig.*⟩ ⟨*pain*⟩ spread; **b)** auf jmdn./etw. ~ ⟨*fig.*⟩ communicate itself to sb./influence sth.; **Aus·strahlung die** ⟨*fig.*⟩ charisma

aus|strecken 1. *tr. V.* stretch out; put out ⟨*feelers*⟩; **2.** *refl. V.* stretch out

aus|streichen *unr. tr. V.* cross out

aus|strömen *itr. V.;* mit sein pour out; ⟨*gas, steam*⟩ escape

aus|suchen *tr. V.* choose; pick

Aus·tausch der a) exchange; im ~ für od. gegen in exchange for; **b)** ⟨*das Ersetzen*⟩ replacement (**gegen** with); **aus|tauschen** *tr. V.* **a)** exchange (**gegen** for); **b)** ⟨*ersetzen*⟩ replace (**gegen** with); **Austausch·motor der** replacement engine

aus|teilen *tr. V.* distribute **an** + Akk. to); ⟨*aushändigen*⟩ hand out ⟨*books, post, etc.*⟩ (**an** + Akk. to); give ⟨*orders*⟩; deal [out] ⟨*cards*⟩; give out ⟨*marks, grades*⟩; serve ⟨*food etc.*⟩

Auster die: ~, ~n oyster

aus|tragen *unr. tr. V.* **a)** deliver ⟨*newspapers, post*⟩; **b)** ⟨*pregnant woman*⟩ carry ⟨*child*⟩ to full term; ⟨*nicht abtreiben*⟩ have ⟨*child*⟩; **c)** ⟨*ausfechten*⟩ settle ⟨*conflict, differences*⟩; fight out ⟨*battle*⟩

Australien [aus'traːli̯ən] (*das*); ~s Australia; **Australier der;** ~s, ~: Australian; **australisch** *Adj.* Australian

aus|treiben *unr. tr. V.* **a)** exorcize; cast out ⟨*evil spirit, demon*⟩; **b)** jmdm. etw. ~: cure sb. of sth.

aus|treten 1. *unr. tr. V.* **a)** tread out ⟨*spark, cigarette-end*⟩; trample out

⟨*fire*⟩; **b)** ⟨*bahnen*⟩ tread out ⟨*path*⟩; **c)** wear out ⟨*shoes*⟩; **2.** *unr. itr. V.;* mit sein **a)** ⟨ugs.: *zur Toilette gehen*⟩ pay a call (*coll.*); **b)** aus etw. ~ ⟨*ausscheiden*⟩ leave sth.

aus|trinken *tr. V.* drink up ⟨*drink*⟩; finish ⟨*glass, cup, etc.*⟩

Aus·tritt der leaving

aus|trocknen 1. *tr. V.* dry out; dry up ⟨*river bed, marsh*⟩; **2.** *itr. V.;* mit sein dry out; ⟨*river bed, pond, etc.*⟩ dry up; ⟨*skin, hair*⟩ become dry

aus|üben *tr. V.* practise ⟨*art, craft*⟩; follow ⟨*profession*⟩; carry on ⟨*trade*⟩; do ⟨*job*⟩; hold ⟨*office*⟩; wield ⟨*power, right, control*⟩

Aus·verkauf der sale; **ausverkauft** *Adj.* sold out

Aus·wahl die a) choice; **b)** ⟨*Sortiment*⟩ range; viel/wenig ~ haben have a wide/limited selection (**an** + Dat., **von** of); **aus|wählen** *tr. V.* choose (**aus** from)

Aus·wanderer der emigrant; **aus|wandern** *itr. V.;* mit sein emigrate; **Aus·wanderung die** emigration

auswärtig *Adj.* **a)** non-local; **b)** ⟨*das Ausland betreffend*⟩ foreign; **auswärts** *Adv.* **a)** ⟨*nach außen*⟩ outwards; **b)** ⟨*nicht zu Hause*⟩ ⟨*sleep*⟩ away from home; ~essen eat out; **c)** ⟨*nicht am Ort*⟩ in another town; (*Sport*) away; **Auswärts·spiel das** (*Sport*) away match

aus|waschen *unr. tr. V.* wash out

aus|wechseln *tr. V.* **a)** change (**gegen** + Akk. for); **b)** ⟨*ersetzen*⟩ replace (**gegen** with); (*Sport*) substitute ⟨*player*⟩

Aus·weg der way out (**aus** of); **ausweg·los 1.** *Adj.* hopeless. **2.** *adv.* hopelessly

aus|weichen *unr. itr. V.;* mit sein get out of the way (Dat. of); ⟨*Platz machen*⟩ make way (Dat. for); einem Schlag/Angriff ~: dodge a blow/evade an attack; dem Feind ~: avoid [contact with] the enemy; einer Frage ~: evade a question; eine ~de Antwort an evasive answer

Ausweis der; ~es, ~e card; ⟨*Personal*~⟩ identity card; **aus|weisen 1.** *unr. tr. V.* **a)** expel (**aus** from); **b)** jmdn. als etw. ~: show that sb. is/was sth.; **2.** *unr. refl. V.* prove or establish one's identity [by showing one's papers]; können Sie sich ~? do you have any means of identification?; **Aus·weisung die** expulsion (**aus** from)

aus|weiten *tr. V.* stretch

aus·wendig *Adv.* etw. ~ können/lernen know/learn sth. [off] by heart

aus|werten *tr. V.* analyse and evaluate; **Aus·wertung die** analysis and evaluation

aus|wirken *refl. V.* have an effect (**auf** + *Akk.* on); **sich günstig** ~: have a favourable effect; **Aus·wirkung die** effect (**auf** + *Akk.* on)

Aus·wuchs der a) *(Wucherung)* growth; excrescence *(Med., Bot.);* **b)** *(fig.)* unhealthy product; *(Exzeß)* excess

aus|zahlen 1. *tr. V.* **a)** pay out ⟨*money*⟩; **b)** pay off ⟨*employee, worker*⟩; buy out ⟨*business partner*⟩; **2.** *refl. V.* pay

aus|zählen *tr. V.* **a)** count [up] ⟨*votes etc.*⟩; **b)** *(Boxen)* count out

aus|zeichnen *tr. V.* **a)** *(mit einem Preisschild)* mark; **b)** *(ehren)* honour; **Aus·zeichnung die a)** *o. Pl. (von Waren)* marking; **b)** *(Ehrung)* honouring; *(Orden)* decoration; *(Preis)* award

aus|ziehen 1. *unr. tr. V.* **a)** pull out ⟨*couch*⟩; extend ⟨*table, tripod, etc.*⟩; **b)** *(ablegen)* take off ⟨*clothes*⟩; **c)** *(entkleiden)* undress; **sich** ~: get undressed; **2.** *unr. itr. V.; mit sein* move out (**aus** of); **Aus·zug der a)** *(das Ausziehen)* move; **b)** *(Bankw.)* statement; **c)** *(Textpassage)* extract

Auto das; ~s, ~s car; automobile *(Amer.);* ~ **fahren** drive; *(mitfahren)* go in the car

Auto-: ~**bahn die** motorway *(Brit.);* expressway *(Amer.);* ~**biographie** [-----'-] **die** autobiography; ~**bus der** *s.* Bus; ~**fähre die** car ferry; ~**fahren das** driving; motoring; ~**fahrer der** [car-]driver; ~**fahrt die** drive; ~**gramm** [---'] **das;** ~**s,** ~**e** autograph; ~**kino das** drive-in cinema

Automat der; ~**en,** ~**en a)** *(Verkaufs~)* [vending-] machine; *(Spiel~)* slot-machine; **b)** *(in der Produktion)* robot; **Automatik die;** ~, ~**en** automatic control mechanism; *(Getriebe~)* automatic transmission; **automatisch** *(auch fig.)* **1.** *Adj.* automatic; **2.** *adv.* automatically; **automatisieren** *tr. V.* automate; **Automatisierung die;** ~, ~**en** automation

auto-, Auto-: ~**mobil** [---'-] **das;** ~**s,** ~**e** *(geh.)* motor car; automobile *(Amer.);* ~**nom** [--'-] **1.** *Adj.* autonomous; **2.** *adv.* autonomously; ~**nomie**

[----'-] die; ~, ~**n** autonomy; ~**nummer die** [car] registration number

Autopsie [auto'psi:] **die;** ~, ~**n** post-mortem [examination]

Autor der; ~**s,** ~**en** author

Auto-: ~**radio das** car radio; ~**reifen der** car tyre; ~**reisezug der** Motorail train *(Brit.);* auto train *(Amer.)*

Autorin die; ~, ~**nen** authoress; author

autoritär *Adj.* authoritarian; **Autorität die;** ~, ~**en** authority

Auto-: ~**schlange die** queue of cars; ~**schlüssel der** car key; ~**stopp der** hitch-hiking; **per** ~**stopp fahren,** ~**stopp machen** hitch-hike; ~**unfall der** car accident; ~**vermietung die** car rental firm; ~**werkstatt die** garage

Avocado [avo'ka:do] **die;** ~, ~**s** avocado [pear]

Axt die; ~, **Äxte** axe

Azalee [atsa'le:ə] **die;** ~, ~**n** azalea

B

b, B [be:] **das;** ~, ~ **a)** *(Buchstabe)* b/B; **b)** *(Musik)* [key of] B flat

B *Abk.* **Bundesstraße** ≈ A *(Brit.)*

Baby ['be:bi] **das;** ~**s,** ~**s** baby; **Baby·sitter** [-sɪtɐ] **der;** ~**s,** ~: babysitter

Bach der; ~[**e**]**s, Bäche a)** stream; brook; **b)** *(Rinnsal)* stream [of water]

Back·blech das baking-sheet

Back·bord das *(Seew., Luftf.)* port [side]; **Backe die;** ~, ~**n** cheek

backen 1. *unr. itr. V.* bake; **2.** *unr. tr. V.* **a)** bake; **b)** *(bes. südd.) s.* braten

Backen·zahn der molar

Bäcker der; ~**s,** ~: baker; **er ist** ~: he is a baker; **zum/beim** ~: to the/at the baker's; **Bäckerei die;** ~, ~**en** baker's [shop]

Back-: ~**fisch der** fried fish *(in breadcrumbs);* ~**form die** baking-tin *(Brit.);* baking-pan *(Amer.);* ~**hähnchen das,** ~**hendl das** *(österr.),* ~**huhn das** fried chicken *(in breadcrumbs);* ~**ofen der** the oven; ~**pulver**

das baking-powder; **~stein** der brick; **~waren** Pl. bread, cakes, and pastries

Bad das; ~[e]s, Bäder a) bath; *(das Schwimmen)* swim; *(im Meer o. ä.)* bathe; **ein ~ nehmen** *(geh.)* take a bath; *(schwimmen)* go for a swim; *(im Meer o. ä.)* bathe; b) *(Badezimmer)* bathroom; **ein Zimmer mit ~:** a room with [private] bath; c) *(Schwimm~)* [swimming-]pool; d) *(Heil~)* spa; *(See~)* bathe *(seaside)* resort

Bade-: ~an·zug der bathing costume; **~hose** die bathing trunks pl; **~mantel** der dressing-gown; bathrobe; **~meister** der swimming-pool attendant; **~mütze** die bathing cap

baden 1. itr. V. a) have a bath; b) *(schwimmen)* bathe; ~ **gehen** go for a bathe; **2.** tr. V. bath *(child, patient, etc.)*; bathe *(wound, eye, etc.)*

Bäder s. Bad

Bade-: ~strand der bathing-beach; **~tuch** das bath towel; **~wanne** die bath[-tub]; **~wasser** das bath water; **~zimmer** das bathroom

Bagatelle die; ~, ~n trifle

Bagger der; ~s, ~: excavator; *(Schwimm~)* dredger; **Bagger·see** der flooded gravel-pit

Bahn die; ~, ~en a) *(Weg)* path; b) *(Route)* path; *(eines Geschosses)* trajectory; c) *(Sport)* track; *(für Pferderennen)* course *(Brit.)*; track *(Amer.)*; *(für einzelne Teilnehmer)* lane; *(Kegel~)* alley; *(Bowling~)* lane; d) *(Eisen~)* railways pl.; railroad *(Amer.)*; *(Zug)* train; jmdn. zur ~ bringen take sb. to the station; |mit der| ~ fahren go by train; f) *(Straßen~)* tram; streetcar *(Amer.)*

bahn-, Bahn-: ~brechend Adj. pioneering; **~bus** der railway bus; **~damm** der railway embankment

bahnen tr. V. clear *(way, path)*; jmdm./einer Sache einen Weg ~ *(fig.)* pave the way for sb./sth.

Bahn-: ~fahrt die train journey; **~hof** der [railway or *(Amer.)* railroad] station; **~reise** die train journey; **~schranke** die level-crossing *(Brit.)* or *(Amer.)* grade crossing barrier/gate; **~steig** der; ~[e]s, ~e [station] platform; **~übergang** der level-crossing *(Brit.)*; grade crossing *(Amer.)*; **~verbindung** die train connection

Bahre die; ~, ~n a) *(Kranken~)* stretcher; b) *(Toten~)* bier

Baiser [bε'ze:] das; ~s, ~s meringue

Bajonett das; ~[e]s, ~e bayonet

Bakterie [bak'te:riə] die; ~, ~n bacterium

Balance [ba'lanṣə] die; ~, ~n balance; **balancieren** itr., tr. V.; itr. mit sein balance

bald Adv. a) soon; *(leicht, rasch)* quickly; easily; **wird's ~?** get a move on, will you; **bis ~!** see you soon; b) *(ugs.: fast)* almost

Baldrian ['baldria:n] der; ~s, ~e valerian

Balkan ['balka:n] der; ~s: der ~: the Balkans pl.; *(Gebirge)* Balkan Mountains pl. **auf dem ~:** in the Balkans

Balken der; ~s, ~: beam

Balkon [bal'kɔn, bal'ko:n] der; ~s, ~s [bal'kɔns] od. ~e [bal'ko:nə] a) balcony; b) *(im Theater, Kino)* circle

Ball der; ~[e]s, Bälle a) ball; ~ **spielen** play ball; b) *(Fest)* ball

Ballade die; ~, ~n ballad

Ballast der; ~[e]s, ~e ballast

ballen 1. tr. V. clench *(fist)*; **2.** refl. V. *(fist)* clench; **Ballen** der; ~s, ~ a) *(Packen)* bale; b) *(Hand~, Fuß~)* ball

Ballett das; ~[e]s, ~e ballet

Ball-: ~junge der ballboy; **~kleid** das ball gown

Ballon [ba'lɔŋ] der; ~s, ~s balloon

Ball-: ~saal der ballroom; **~spiel** das ball game; **~spielen** das; ~s playing ball *no art.*

Ballungs·gebiet das conurbation

Balsam der; ~s, ~e balsam; *(fig.)* balm

Balte der; ~n, ~n, **Baltin** die; ~, ~nen Balt; **Baltikum** das; ~s Baltic States pl.; **baltisch** Adj. Baltic

Bambus der; ~ od. ~ses, ~se bamboo

banal Adj. a) banal; b) *(gewöhnlich)* commonplace

Banane die; ~, ~n banana

Banause der; ~n, ~n *(abwertend)* philistine

band 1. u. 3. Pers. Sg. Prät. v. binden

¹Band das; ~[e]s, Bänder a) ribbon; *(Haar~, Hut~)* band; *(Schürzen~)* string; b) *(Klebe~, Isolier~, Ton~ usw.)* tape; etw. auf ~ *(Akk.)* aufnehmen tape[-record] sth.; c) s. Förderband; d) s. Fließband; e) am laufenden ~ *(ugs.)* nonstop; f) *(Anat.)* ligament

²Band der; ~[e]s, Bände ['bɛndə] volume

³Band [bɛnt] die; ~, ~s band; *(Beat~, Rock~ usw.)* group

¹Bande die; ~, ~n a) gang; b) *(ugs.: Gruppe)* mob *(sl.)*

²Bande die; ~, ~n *(Sport)* [perimeter] barrier; *(mit Reklame)* billboards pl.; *(Billard)* cushion

Bänder s. ¹Band

bändigen tr. V. tame ⟨*animal*⟩; control ⟨*person, anger, urge*⟩

Bandit der; ~en, ~en bandit

Band·scheibe die [intervertebral] disc

bang, bange; banger, bangst... od. **bänger, bängst...:** 1. *Adj.* afraid; scared; *(besorgt)* anxious; **mir ist/wurde ~** |zumute| I am/became scared; 2. *adv.* anxiously; **bangen** itr. V. be anxious

¹Bank die; ~, Bänke bench; *(mit Lehne)* bench seat; *(Kirchen~)* pew; etw. **auf die lange ~ schieben** *(ugs.)* put sth. off

²Bank die; ~, ~en bank

¹Bankett das; ~|e|s, ~e banquet

²Bankett das; ~|e|s, ~e *(an Straßen)* shoulder; *(unbefestigt)* verge

Bankier [baŋˈkjeː] der; ~s, ~s banker

Bank-: ~**konto** das bank account; ~**leitzahl** die bank sorting code number; ~**note** die banknote; bill *(Amer.)*; ~**raub** der bank robbery; ~**räuber** der bank robber

bankrott *Adj.* bankrupt; ~ **gehen** go bankrupt; **Bankrott** der; ~|e|s, ~e bankruptcy; ~ **machen** go bankrupt

Bann der; ~|e|s *(fig. geh.)* spell

bar 1. *Adj.* cash; 2. *adv.* in cash

Bar die; ~, ~s bar

Bär der; ~en, ~en bear

Baracke die; ~, ~n hut

Barbar der; ~en, ~en barbarian; **Barbarei** die; ~, ~en *(Roheit)* barbarity; b) *(Kulturlosigkeit)* barbarism no indef. art.; **barbarisch** 1. *Adj.* a) *(roh)* barbarous; b) *(unzivilisiert)* barbaric; 2. *adv.* a) *(roh)* barbarously; b) *(unzivilisiert)* barbarically

Bar·dame die barmaid

Barett das; ~|e|s, ~e *(eines Geistlichen)* biretta; *(eines Richters, Professors)* cap; *(Baskenmütze)* beret

bar·fuß indekl. Adj.; nicht attr. barefooted; ~ **herumlaufen/gehen** run about/go barefoot

barg 1. u. 3. Pers. Sg. Prät. v. bergen

Bar-: ~**geld** das cash; ~**hocker** der bar stool

Bariton [ˈbaː)ritɔn] der; ~s, ~e baritone

Barkasse die; ~, ~n launch

barmherzig *(geh.)* 1. *Adj.* merciful; 2. *adv.* mercifully; **Barmherzigkeit** die; ~ *(geh.)* mercy

Barock das od. der; ~|s| a) baroque; b) *(Zeit)* baroque age

Baro·meter das barometer

Baron der; ~s, ~e baron; *(als Anrede)* [Herr] ~: ≈ my lord; **Baronin** die; ~, ~nen baroness; *(als Anrede)* [Frau] ~: ≈ my Lady

Barren der; ~s, ~ a) *(Gold~, Silber~ usw.)* bar; b) *(Turngerät)* parallel bars pl.

Barriere [baˈrjeːrə] die; ~, ~n *(auch fig.)* barrier

Barrikade die; ~, ~n barricade

barsch 1. *Adj.* curt; 2. *adv.* curtly

Barsch der; ~|e|s, ~e perch

barst 1. u. 3. Pers. Sg. Prät. v. bersten

Bart der; ~|e|s, Bärte a) beard; *(Oberlippen~, Schnurr~)* moustache; b) *(von Katzen, Mäusen, Robben)* whiskers pl.; c) *(am Schlüssel)* bit; **bärtig** *Adj.* bearded; **Bart·wuchs** der growth of beard

Bar·zahlung die cash payment

Basalt der; ~|e|s, ~e basalt

Basar der; ~s, ~e bazaar

Basis die; ~, Basen a) *(Grundlage)* basis; b) *(Math., Archit., Milit.)* base

Baske der; ~n, ~n, **Baskin** die; ~, ~nen Basque

Basken-: ~**land** das Basque region; ~**mütze** die beret

Basket·ball [ˈba(ː)skət-] der basketball

Baß der; Basses, Bässe *(Musik)* a) bass; b) *(Instrument)* double-bass

Bassin [baˈsɛ̃ː] das; ~s, ~s *(Schwimm~)* pool; *(im Garten)* pond

Bassist der; ~en, ~en *(Musik)* a) *(Sänger)* bass; b) *(Instrumentalist)* double-bass player; bassist; *(in einer Rockband)* bass guitarist

Bast der; ~|e|s, ~e bast; *(Raffia~)* raffia

basta *Interj.* *(ugs.)* that's enough; **und damit ~!** and that's that!

Bastelei die; ~, ~en; a) *(Gegenstand)* piece of handicraft work; b) *(ugs.: das Basteln)* handicraft work; **basteln** 1. tr. V. make; 2. itr. V. make things [with one's hands]

Bastion die; ~, ~en bastion

bat 1. u. 3. Pers. Sg. Prät. v. bitten

Bataillon [batalˈjoːn] das; ~s, ~e *(Milit.)* battalion

Batik der; ~s, ~en od. die; ~, ~en batik

Batist der; ~|e|s, ~e batiste
Batterie die; ~, ~n battery
Batzen der; ~s, ~ (ugs.) a) (Klumpen) lump; b) (Menge) pile (coll.)
¹Bau der; ~|e|s, ~ten a) o. Pl. (Errichtung) building; im ~ sein be under construction; b) (Gebäude) building; c) auf dem ~ arbeiten (Bauarbeiter sein) be in the building trade; d) o. Pl. (Struktur) structure
²Bau der; ~|e|s, ~e (Kaninchen~) burrow; hole; (Fuchs~) earth
Bau·arbeiten Pl. building work sing.
Bauch der; ~|e|s, Bäuche (auch fig.: von Schiffen, Flugzeugen) belly; **bauchig** Adj. bulbous
Bauch-: ~laden der vendor's tray; ~landung die belly-landing; ~nabel der (ugs.) belly-button (coll.); ~redner der ventriloquist; ~schmerzen Pl. stomach-ache sing.; ~speichel·drüse die pancreas; ~tanz der belly-dance; ~tänzerin die belly-dancer; ~weh das (ugs.) tummy-ache (coll.); stomach-ache
bauen 1. tr. V. build; 2. itr. V. a) build; wir wollen ~: we want to build a house; (bauen lassen) we want to have a house built; b) auf jmdn./etw. ~ (fig.) rely on sb./sth.
¹Bauer der; ~n, ~n (fig.) farmer; (mit niedrigem sozialem Status) peasant; b) (Schachfigur) pawn; c) (Kartenspiele) s. Bube
²Bauer das od. der; ~s, ~: [bird-]cage
Bäuerin die; ~, ~nen a) s. ¹Bauer a: [lady] farmer; peasant [woman]; b) (Frau eines Bauern) farmer's wife; **bäuerlich** Adj. farming attrib.; (ländlich) rural
Bauern-: ~haus das farmhouse; ~hof der farm
bau-, Bau-: ~fällig Adj. ramshackle; unsafe (roof, ceiling); ~jahr das year of construction; (bei Autos) year of manufacture; (mit Holzklötzen) box of bricks; ~klotz der building-brick
baulich Adj.; nicht präd. structural
Baum der; ~|e|s, Bäume tree; **Bäumchen** das; ~s, ~ small tree
Bau·meister der (hist.) [architect and] master builder
baumeln itr. V. (ugs.) dangle (an + Dat. from)
Baum-: ~schule die tree nursery; ~stamm der tree-trunk; ~stumpf der tree-stump; ~wolle die cotton

Bau·platz der site for building
bäurisch (abwertend) 1. Adj. boorish; 2. adv. boorishly
Bau·satz der the kit
Bausch der; ~|e|s, ~e od. Bäusche a) (Watte~) a wad; b) etw. in ~ und Bogen verwerfen/verdammen reject/condemn sth. wholesale; **bauschen** 1. tr. V. billow (sail, curtains, etc.); 2. refl. V. (dress, sleeve) puff out; (ungewollt) bunch up; (im Wind) (curtain, flag, etc.) billow [out]; **bauschig** Adj. puffed (dress); baggy (trousers)
bau-, Bau-: ~sparen itr. V.; nur Inf. gebr. save with a building society; ~spar·kasse die ≈ building society; ~stein der a) building stone; b) (Bestandteil) element; (Elektronik, DV) module; c) (~klotz) building-brick; ~stelle die building site; (beim Straßenbau) road-works pl.
Bauten Pl.: s. Bau
Bau-: ~unternehmer der building contractor; ~weise die the method of construction; ~werk das building; (Brücke, Staudamm) structure
Bayer der; ~n, ~n Bavarian; **bay[e]risch** Adj. Bavarian; **Bayern** (das); ~s Bavaria
Bazille die; ~, ~n (ugs.) s. Bazillus a; **Bazillus** der; ~, Bazillen a) bacillus; b) (fig.) cancer
Bd. Abk. Band Vol.
beabsichtigen tr. V. intend
beachten tr. V. a) follow (rule, regulations, instruction); heed, follow (advice); obey (traffic signs); observe (formalities); b) (berücksichtigen) take account of; (achten auf) pay attention to; **beachtlich** 1. Adj. considerable; 2. adv. considerably; **Beachtung** die a) s. beachten a: following; heeding; obeying; b) (Berücksichtigung) consideration; c) (Aufmerksamkeit) attention
Beamte der; adj. Dekl. official; (Staats~) [permanent] civil servant; (Kommunal~) [established] local government officer; (Polizei~) [police] officer; **Beamtin** die; ~, ~nen s. Beamte
beängstigend Adj. worrying
beanspruchen tr. V. a) claim; etw. ~ können be entitled to expect sth.; b) (ausnutzen) make use of (person, equipment); take advantage of (hospitality, services); c) (erfordern) demand (energy, attention, stamina); take up (time, space, etc.); **Bean-**

spruchung die; ~, ~en demands pl. (Gen. on); die ~ durch den Beruf the demands of his/her job

beanstanden tr. V. take exception to; (sich beklagen über) complain about; Beanstandung die; ~, ~en complaint

beantragen tr. V. apply for

beantworten tr. V. answer; reply to ⟨letter⟩; return ⟨greeting⟩

bearbeiten tr. V. a) deal with; handle ⟨case⟩; b) (adaptieren) adapt (für for); Bearbeitung die; ~, ~en a) die ~ eines Antrags/eines Falles usw. dealing with an application/handling a case etc.; b) (Adaption) adaptation

beaufsichtigen tr. V. supervise; look after ⟨child⟩

beauftragen tr. V. entrust

bebauen tr. V. build on; develop; Bebauung die; ~, ~en a) development; b) (Gebäude) buildings pl.

beben itr. V. shake; Beben das; ~s, ~ ⟨Erd~⟩ earthquake

bebildern tr. V. illustrate

Becher der; ~s, ~ ⟨Glas~, Porzellan~⟩ glass; tumbler; (Plastik~) beaker; cup; (Eis~) (aus Glas, Metall) sundae dish; (aus Pappe) tub; (Joghurt~) carton

Becken das; ~s, ~ a) (Wasch~) basin; (Abwasch~) sink; (Toiletten~) pan; b) (Anat.) pelvis; c) Pl. (Musik) cymbals

bedacht Adj. auf etw. (Akk.) ~ sein be intent on sth.; bedächtig 1. Adj. a) deliberate; measured ⟨steps, stride, speech⟩; b) (besonnen) thoughtful; well-considered ⟨words⟩; 2. adv. a) deliberately; b) (besonnen) thoughtfully

bedanken refl. V. say thank you; sich bei jmdm. [für etw.] ~: thank sb. [for sth.]

Bedarf der; ~[e]s need (an + Dat. of); requirement (an + Dat. for); (Bedarfsmenge) needs pl.; requirements pl.; bei ~: if required

bedauerlich Adj. regrettable; bedauerlicher·weise Adv. regrettably; bedauern tr., itr. V. a) feel sorry for; sie läßt sich gerne ~: she likes being pitied; b) (schade finden) regret; ich bedaure sehr, daß ...: I am very sorry that ...; Bedauern das; ~s regret; zu meinem ~: to my regret; bedauerns·wert Adj. (geh.) unfortunate ⟨person⟩

bedecken tr. V. cover; bedeckt Adj. overcast ⟨sky⟩

bedenken unr. tr. V. a) consider; b) (beachten) take into consideration; Bedenken das; ~s, ~ reservation (gegen about); ohne ~: without hesitation; bedenken·los 1. Adj. unhesitating; (skrupellos) unscrupulous; 2. adv. without hesitation; (skrupellos) unscrupulously; bedenklich 1. Adj. a) dubious ⟨methods, transactions, etc.⟩; b) (bedrohlich) alarming; 2. adv. alarmingly; Bedenk·zeit die; o. Pl. time for reflection

bedeuten tr. V. a) mean; was soll das ~? what does that mean?; b) (sein) represent; das bedeutet ein Wagnis that is being really daring; bedeutend 1. Adj. a) important; b) (groß) substantial; considerable ⟨success⟩; 2. adv. considerably; Bedeutung die; ~, ~en a) meaning; b) o. Pl. (Wichtigkeit) importance

bedeutungs-: ~los Adj. insignificant; ~voll 1. Adj. a) significant; b) (vielsagend) meaningful; meaning ⟨look⟩; 2. adv. meaningfully

bedienen 1. tr. V. a) serve; werden Sie schon bedient? are you being served?; b) (handhaben) operate ⟨machine⟩; 2. itr. V. serve; 3. refl. V. help oneself; sich selbst ~ (im Geschäft, Restaurant usw.) serve oneself; Bedienung die; ~, ~en a) o. Pl. (das Bedienen) service; ~ inbegriffen service included; b) o. Pl. (das Handhaben) operation; c) (Serviererfin]) waiter/waitress; Bedienungs·anleitung die operating instructions pl.

bedingen tr. V. cause; Bedingung die; ~, ~en condition; unter der ~, daß ...: on condition that ...; bedingungs·los Adj. unconditional

bedrängen tr. V. a) besiege ⟨town, fortress, person⟩; put ⟨opposing player⟩ under pressure; b) (belästigen) pester; bedrohen tr. V. threaten; bedrohlich 1. Adj. (unheilverkündend) ominous; (gefährlich) dangerous; 2. adv. (unheilverkündend) ominously; (gefährlich) dangerously; Bedrohung die threat (Gen. to)

bedrucken tr. V. print

bedrücken tr. V. depress

Beduine der; ~n, ~n Bed[o]uin

bedürfen unr. itr. V. jmds./einer Sache ~ (geh.) require or need sb./sth.; Bedürfnis das; ~ses, ~se need (nach for); das ~ haben, etw. zu tun feel a need to do sth.; bedürftig Adj. needy

Beef·steak ['bi:f-] **das** [beef]steak; **deutsches ~:** ≈ beefburger

beehren *tr. V. (geh.)* honour

beeiden *tr. V.* ~, **daß ...:** swear [on oath] that ...; **eine Aussage ~:** swear to the truth of a statement

beeilen *refl. V.* hurry [up *(coll.)*]

beeindrucken *tr. V.* impress; **beeindruckend** *Adj.* impressive

beeinflussen *tr. V.* influence; **Beeinflussung die;** ~, ~**en** influencing

beeinträchtigen *tr. V.* restrict ⟨*sights, freedom*⟩; detract from ⟨*pleasure, enjoyment, value*⟩; spoil ⟨*appetite, good humour*⟩; impair ⟨*quality, reactions, efficiency, vision, hearing*⟩; damage, harm ⟨*sales, reputation*⟩

beenden *tr. V.* end; finish ⟨*piece of work etc.*⟩; complete ⟨*studies*⟩

beengen *tr. V.* restrict

beerben *tr. V.* jmdn. ~: inherit sb's estate

beerdigen *tr. V.* bury; **Beerdigung die;** ~, ~**en** burial; *(Trauerfeier)* funeral; **Beerdigungs·institut das** [firm *sing.* of] undertakers *pl.*

Beere die; ~, ~**n** berry

Beet das; ~[e]s, ~e *(Blumen~)* bed; *(Gemüse~)* plot

befahrbar *Adj.* passable; **befahren** *unr. tr. V.* **a)** drive on ⟨*road*⟩; drive across ⟨*bridge*⟩; use ⟨*railway line*⟩; **die Straße ist stark/wenig ~:** the road is heavily/little used; **b)** sail ⟨*sea*⟩; navigate, sail up/down ⟨*river, canal*⟩

befallen *unr. tr. V.* **a)** overcome; ⟨*misfortune*⟩ befall; **von Panik/Angst ~ werden** be seized with panic/fear; **b)** ⟨*pests*⟩ attack

befangen 1. *Adj.* **a)** self-conscious ⟨*person*⟩; **b)** *(voreingenommen)* biased; **2.** *adv.* self-consciously; **Befangenheit die;** ~ **a)** self-consciousness; **b)** *(Voreingenommenheit)* bias

befassen *refl. V.* **sich mit etw. ~:** occupy oneself with sth.; ⟨*article, book*⟩ deal with sth.; *(etw. studieren)* study sth.

Befehl der; ~[e]s, ~e **a)** order; **b)** **den ~ über jmdn./etw. haben** be in command of sb./sth.; **befehlen 1.** *unr. tr., itr. V.* order; *(Milit.)* order; **man befahl ihm zu warten** he was told to wait; **2.** *unr. itr. V.* **über jmdn./etw. ~:** have command of *or* be in command of sb./sth.; **Befehls·haber der;** ~s, ~ *(Milit.)* commander

befestigen *tr. V.* **a)** fix; **etw. an der Wand ~:** fix sth. to the wall; **b)** *(haltbar machen)* stabilize ⟨*bank, embankment*⟩; make up ⟨*road, path, etc.*⟩; **c)** *(sichern)* fortify ⟨*town etc.*⟩; strengthen ⟨*border*⟩; **Befestigung die;** ~, ~**en a)** fixing; **b)** *(Milit.)* fortification

befeuchten *tr. V.* moisten; damp ⟨*hair, cloth*⟩

befiehlst, befiehlt 2., 3. *Pers. Sg. Präsens v.* befehlen

befinden *unr. refl. V.* be; **Befinden das;** ~**s** health; *(eines Patienten)* condition

beflecken *tr. V.* stain

befohlen 2. *Part. v.* befehlen

befolgen *tr. V.* follow, obey ⟨*instruction, grammatical rule*⟩; obey, comply with ⟨*law, regulation*⟩; follow ⟨*advice, suggestion*⟩

befördern *tr. V.* **a)** carry; transport; **b)** *(aufrücken lassen)* promote; **Beförderung die a)** *o. Pl.* carriage; transport; *(Personen)* transport; **b)** *(das Aufrückenlassen)* promotion

befragen *tr. V.* **a)** question ⟨*über + Akk.* about⟩; **b)** *(konsultieren)* ask; **Befragung die;** ~, ~**en a)** questioning; **b)** *(Konsultation)* consultation; **c)** *(Umfrage)* opinion poll

befreien 1. *tr. V.* **a)** free; liberate ⟨*country, people*⟩ ⟨*von* from⟩; **b)** *(freistellen)* exempt ⟨*von* from⟩; **c)** **jmdn. von Schmerzen ~:** free sb. of pain; **2.** *refl. V.* free oneself ⟨*von* from⟩; **Befreier der** liberator; **Befreiung die;** ~ **a)** *s.* befreien 1a: freeing; liberation; **b)** *(Freistellung)* exemption; **c)** **die ~ von Schmerzen** release from pain

befremden *tr. V.* jmdn. ~: put sb. off

befreunden *refl. V. s.* anfreunden; [**gut** *od.* **eng**] **befreundet sein** be [good *or* close] friends ⟨*mit* with⟩

befriedigen *tr. V.* satisfy; gratify ⟨*lust*⟩; **b)** *(ausfüllen)* ⟨*job, occupation, etc.*⟩ fulfil; **c)** *(sexuell)* satisfy; **sich** [**selbst**] **~:** masturbate; **befriedigend 1.** *Adj.* satisfactory; **2.** *adv.* satisfactorily; **Befriedigung die;** ~ **a)** *s.* befriedigen **a:** satisfaction; gratification; **b)** *(Genugtuung)* satisfaction

befristet *Adj.* temporary ⟨*visa*⟩; fixed-term ⟨*ban, contract*⟩

befruchten *tr. V.* fertilize ⟨*egg*⟩; pollinate ⟨*flower*⟩; impregnate ⟨*female*⟩; **Befruchtung die;** ~, ~**en** *s.* befruchten: fertilization; pollination; impregnation

Befugnis die; ~, ~se authority
befühlen tr. V. feel
Befund der (bes. Med.) result[s pl.]
befürchten tr. V. fear; **ich befürchte, daß ...**: I am afraid that ...
befürworten tr. V. support
begabt Adj. talented; **Begabung** die; ~, ~en talent
begann 1. u. 3. Pers. Sg. Prät. v. beginnen
begatten tr. V. mate with; ⟨man⟩ copulate with; **sich** ~: mate; ⟨persons⟩ copulate; **Begattung** die mating; (bei Menschen) copulation
begeben unr. refl. V. (geh.) proceed; make one's way; go; **sich zu Bett** ~: retire to bed; **sich an die Arbeit** ~: commence work
begegnen itr. V.; mit sein jmdm. ~: meet sb.; **sich** (Dat.) ~: meet [each other]; **Begegnung** die; ~, ~en a) meeting; b) (Sport) match
begehen unr. tr. V. a) commit ⟨crime, adultery, indiscretion, sin, suicide, faux-pas, etc.⟩; make ⟨mistake⟩; **eine [furchtbare] Dummheit** ~: do something [really] stupid; b) (geh.: feiern) celebrate
begehren tr. V. desire; **begehrens·wert** Adj. desirable; **begehrlich** 1. Adj. greedy; 2. adv. greedily; **begehrt** Adj. much sought-after
begeistern 1. tr. V. jmdn. [für etw.] ~: fire sb. with enthusiasm [for sth.]; 2. refl. V. get enthusiastic (für about); **begeistert** 1. Adj. enthusiastic (von about); 2. adv. enthusiastically; **Begeisterung** die; ~: enthusiasm
Begierde die; ~, ~n desire (nach for); **begierig** 1. Adj. eager; 2. adv. eagerly
begießen unr. tr. V. water ⟨plants⟩
Beginn der; ~[e]s beginning; [gleich] **zu** ~: [right] at the beginning; **beginnen** 1. unr. itr. V. start; begin; **mit dem Bau** ~: start or begin building; **dort beginnt der Wald** the forest starts there; 2. unr. tr. V. start; begin; start ⟨argument⟩; ~, etw. zu tun start to do sth.
beglaubigen tr. V. certify; **Beglaubigung** die; ~, ~en certification
begleichen unr. tr. V. settle ⟨bill, debt⟩; pay ⟨sum⟩
begleiten tr. V. accompany; **jmdn. nach Hause** ~: see sb. home; **Begleiter** der; ~s, ~, **Begleiterin** die; ~, ~nen companion; (zum Schutz) escort; (Führer[in]) guide; **Begleitung**

die; ~, ~en a) o. Pl. er bot uns seine ~ an he offered to accompany us; **in** ~ **eines Erwachsenen** accompanied by an adult; b) (Musik) accompaniment
beglückwünschen tr. V. congratulate (zu on)
begnadet Adj. (geh.) divinely gifted; **begnadigen** tr. V. pardon; reprieve; **Begnadigung** die; ~, ~en reprieving; (Straferlaß) pardon; reprieve
begnügen refl. V. content oneself
Begonie [be'go:niə] die; ~, ~n begonia
begonnen 2. Part. v. beginnen
begraben unr. tr. V. bury; **Begräbnis** das; ~ses, ~se burial; (~feier) funeral
begreifen 1. unr. tr. V. understand; **er konnte nicht** ~, **was geschehen war** he could not grasp what had happened; 2. itr. V. understand; **schnell** od. **leicht/langsam** od. **schwer** ~: be quick/ slow on the uptake; **begreiflich** Adj. understandable
begrenzen tr. V. limit, restrict (auf + Akk. to)
Begriff der a) concept; (Terminus) term; b) (Auffassung) idea; **sich** (Dat.) **keinen** ~ **von etw. machen können** not be able to imagine sth.; **ein/kein** ~ **sein** be/not be well known; c) **im** ~ **sein** od. **stehen, etw. zu tun** be about to do sth.; **begriffs·stutzig** Adj. (abwertend) obtuse
begründen tr. V. a) give reasons for; b) (gründen) found; establish ⟨fame, reputation⟩; **Begründer** der founder; **begründet** Adj. well-founded; reasonable ⟨demand, objection, complaint⟩; **Begründung** die; ~, ~en reason[s]; **mit der** ~, **daß ...**: on the grounds that ...
begrüßen tr. V. a) greet; ⟨hostess, host⟩ welcome; b) (fig.) welcome; **Begrüßung** die; ~, ~en greeting; (von Gästen) welcoming; (Zeremonie) welcome (Gen. for)
begünstigen tr. V. favour
begutachten tr. V. a) examine and report on; b) (ugs.) have a look at
begütert Adj. wealthy
begütigen tr. V. placate
behäbig 1. Adj. slow and ponderous; 2. adv. slowly and ponderously
behagen itr. V. etw. behagt jmdm. sb. likes sth.; **Behagen** das; ~s pleasure; **behaglich** 1. Adj. comfortable; 2. adv. comfortably; **Behaglichkeit** die; ~: comfortableness

behalten *unr. tr. V.* **a)** keep; etw. für sich ~: keep sth. to oneself; **b)** *(zurück~)* be left with *(scar, defect, etc.)*; **c)** *(sich merken)* remember

Behälter der; ~s, ~ container; *(für Abfälle)* receptacle

behandeln *tr. V. (auch Med.)* treat; handle *(matter, machine, device)*; deal with *(subject, question etc.)*

Behandlung die; ~, ~en treatment

behängen *tr. V.* hang

beharren *itr. V.* auf etw. *(Dat.)* ~ *(etw. nicht aufgeben)* persist in sth.; *(auf etw. bestehen)* insist on sth.; **beharr-lich 1.** *Adj.* dogged; **2.** *adv.* doggedly; **Beharrlichkeit** die; ~: doggedness

behauen *unr. tr. V.* hew

behaupten 1. *tr. V.* **a)** maintain; assert; ~, jmd. zu sein/etw. zu wissen claim to be sb./know sth.; **b)** *(verteidigen)* maintain *(position)*; retain *(record)*; **2.** *refl. V.* **a)** assert oneself; *(nicht untergehen)* hold one's ground; *(dableiben)* survive; **b)** *(Sport)* win through; **Behauptung** die; ~, ~en assertion

Behausung die; ~, ~en dwelling

beheben *unr. tr. V.* remove *(danger, difficulty)*; repair *(damage)*; remedy *(abuse, defect)*; **Behebung** die; ~, ~en s. beheben: removal; repair; remedying

beheimatet *Adj.* an einem Ort/in einem Land usw. ~ sein be native to a place/to a country etc.

beheizen *tr. V.* heat

behelfen *unr. refl. V.* make do

behelfs·mäßig 1. *Adj.* makeshift; **2.** *adv.* in a makeshift way

behelligen *tr. V.* bother; *(zudringlich werden gegen)* pester

behend, behende 1. *Adj. (geschickt)* deft; *(flink)* nimble; **2.** *adv.; s. Adj.:* deftly; nimbly

beherbergen *tr. V.* accommodate

beherrschen 1. *tr. V.* **a)** control; rule *(country, people)*; **b)** *(meistern)* control *(vehicle, animal)*; be in control of *(situation)*; **c)** *(bestimmen, dominieren)* dominate *(townscape, landscape, discussions)*; **d)** *(zügeln)* control *(feelings)*; control, curb *(impatience)*; **e)** *(gut können)* have mastered *(instrument, trade)*; have a good command of *(language)*; **2.** *refl. V.* control oneself; **beherrscht 1.** *Adj.* self-controlled; **2.** with self-control; **Beherr-schung** die; ~ **a)** control; *(eines

Volks, Landes usw.) rule; **b)** *(das Meistern)* control; **c)** *(Beherrschtheit)* self-control; **d)** *(das Können)* mastery

beherzigen *tr. V.* take *(sth.)* to heart

beherzt 1. *Adj.* spirited; **2.** *adv.* spiritedly

behilflich *Adj.* [jmdm.] ~ sein help [sb.] (bei with)

behindern *tr. V.* **a)** hinder; impede *(movement)*; hold up *(traffic)*; **b)** *(Sport, Verkehrsw.)* obstruct; **behin-dert** *Adj.* handicapped; **Behinderte** der/die; *adj. Dekl.* handicapped person; die ~n the handicapped; WC für ~: toilet for disabled persons; **Be-hinderung** die; ~, ~en **a)** hindrance; **b)** *(Sport, Verkehrsw.)* obstruction; **c)** *(Gebrechen)* handicap

Behörde die; ~, ~n authority; *(Amt, Abteilung)* department; **behördlich 1.** *Adj.* official; **2.** *adv.* officially

behüten *tr. V.* protect (vor + *Dat.* from); *(bewachen)* guard

behutsam 1. *Adj.* careful; **2.** *adv.* carefully

bei *Präp. mit Dat.* **a)** *(nahe)* near; *(dicht an, neben)* by; wer steht da ~ ihm? who is standing there with him?; etw. ~ sich haben have sth. with *or* on one; sich ~ jmdm. entschuldigen apologize to sb.; **b)** *(unter)* among; war heute ein Brief für mich ~ der Post? was there a letter for me in the post today?; **c)** *(an)* by; jmdn. ~ der Hand nehmen take sb. by the hand; **d)** *(im Wohn-/Lebens-/Arbeitsbereich von)*: uns tut man das nicht we don't do that; ~ mir [zu Hause] at my house; ~ uns um die Ecke/gegenüber round the corner from us/opposite us; ~ seinen El-tern leben live with one's parents; wir sind ~ ihr eingeladen we have been invited to her house; wir treffen uns ~ uns/Peter we'll meet at our/Peter's place; ~ uns in der Firma in our company; ~ Schmidt *(auf Briefen)* c/o Schmidt; ~ einer Firma sein be with a company; ~ jmdm./einem Verlag ar-beiten work for sb./a publishing house; **e)** *(im Bereich eines Vorgangs)* at; ~ einer Hochzeit/einem Empfang usw. be at a wedding/reception etc.; ~ einem Unfall in an accident; **f)** *(im Werk von)* ~ Goethe in Goethe; **g)** *(im Falle von)* in the case of; wie ~ den Rö-mern as with the Romans; ~ der Hauskatze in the domestic cat; **h)** *(modal)* ~ Tag/Nacht by day/night; ~ Tageslicht by daylight; ~ Nebel in fog; i) *(im Falle des Auftretens von)* „~ **Nässe Schleudergefahr”** 'slippery when wet'; j) *(angesichts)* with; ~ **dieser Hitze** in this heat; ~ **deinen guten Augen/ihrem Talent** with your good eyesight/her talent; k) *(trotz)* ~ **all seinem Engagement/seinen Bemühungen** in spite of *or* despite *or* for all his commitment/efforts

bei|behalten *unr. tr. V.* keep; retain; keep up ⟨custom, habit⟩; keep to ⟨course, method⟩; preserve, maintain ⟨way of life; attitude⟩

bei|bringen *unr. tr. V.* a) jmdm. etw. ~: teach sb. sth.; b) *(ugs.: mitteilen)* jmdm. ~, daß ...: break it to sb. that ...; c) *(zufügen)* jmdm./sich etw. ~: inflict sth. on sb./oneself

Beichte die; ~, ~n confession *no def. art.*; **beichten** 1. *itr. V.* confess; 2. *tr. V. (auch fig.)* confess

Beicht-: ~**stuhl** der confessional; ~**vater** der father confessor

beid... *Indefinitpron. u. Zahlw.* 1. *Pl.* ~e both; *(der/die/das eine oder der/die/das andere)* either *sing.*; **die** ~**en** the two; **die/seine** ~**en Brüder** the/his two brothers; **die** ~**en ersten Strophen** the first two verses; **kennst du die** ~**en?** do you know these two?; **alle** ~**e** both of us/you/them; **ihr/euch** ~**e** you two; **ihr/euch** ~**e nicht** neither of you; **wir/uns** ~**e** the two of us/both of us; **er hat** ~**e Eltern verloren** he has lost both [his] parents; **mit** ~**en Händen** with both hands; **ich habe** ~**e gekannt** I knew both of them; **einer/eins von** ~**en** one of the two; **keiner/keins von** ~**en** neither [of them]; 2. *Neutr. Sg.*; ~**es** both *pl.*; *(das eine oder das andere)* either; ~**es ist möglich** either is possible; **ich glaube** ~**es/**~**es nicht** I believe both things/neither thing; **das ist** ~**es nicht richtig** neither of those is correct; **beiderlei** *Gattungsz., indekl.* ~ **Geschlechts** of both sexes; **beider·seits** 1. *Präp. mit Gen.* on both sides of; 2. *Adv.* on both sides

bei·einander *Adv.* together; ~ **Trost suchen** seek comfort from each other

Bei·fahrer der, **Bei·fahrerin** die a) passenger; b) *(berufsmäßig)* co-driver; *(im LKW)* driver's mate; **Beifahrer·sitz** der the passenger seat; *(eines Motorrads)* pillion

Bei·fall der; *o. Pl.* a) applause; b) *(Zustimmung)* approval; **bei·fällig** 1. *Adj.* approving; 2. *adv.* approvingly

beige [beːʃ] *Adj.* beige; **Beige das**; ~, ~ *od. (ugs.)* ~s beige

Bei·geschmack der: einen bitteren *usw.* ~ **haben** have a slightly bitter *etc.* taste [to it]

Bei·hilfe die a) aid; *(Zuschuß)* allowance; b) *o. Pl. (Rechtsw.: Mithilfe)* aiding and abetting

Beil das; ~[e]s, ~e axe; *(kleiner)* hatchet

Bei·lage die a) *(Zeitungs~)* supplement; b) *(zu Speisen)* side-dish; *(Gemüse~)* vegetables *pl.*

bei·läufig 1. *Adj.* casual; 2. *adv.* casually

bei|legen *tr. V.* a) enclose; b) *(schlichten)* settle ⟨dispute etc.⟩

Bei·leid das sympathy; |**mein**| **herzliches** *od.* **aufrichtiges** ~! please accept my sincere condolences

bei|liegen *unr. tr. V.* **einem Brief** ~: be enclosed with a letter; **bei·liegend** *Adj.* enclosed; ~ **senden wir ...**: please find enclosed ...

beim *Präp. + Art.* a) = bei dem; b) ~ **Film sein** be in films; c) **er will** ~ **Arbeiten nicht gestört werden** he doesn't want to be disturbed when working; ~ **Duschen sein** be taking a shower

bei|messen *unr. tr. V.* attach

Bein das; ~[e]s, ~e leg; **jmdm. ein** ~ **stellen** trip sb.; *(fig.)* put *or* throw a spanner *or (Amer.)* a monkey-wrench in sb.'s works; **wieder auf den** ~**en sein** be back on one's feet again

bei·nah[e] *Adv.* almost

Bei·name der the epithet

Bein·bruch der: das ist |doch| kein ~ *(ugs.)* it's not the end of the world

bein·halten *tr. V. (Papierdt.)* involve

-beinig *adj.* -legged

bei|pflichten *itr. V.* agree ⟨Dat. with⟩

bei·irren *tr. V.* sich durch nichts/von niemandem ~ **lassen** not be deterred by anything/anybody

beisammen *Adv.* together; **beisammen|haben** *unr. tr. V.* a) have got together; b) **er hat** |**sie**| **nicht alle beisammen** *(ugs.)* he's not all there *(coll.)*; **Beisammen·sein das** get-together

Bei·schlaf der sexual intercourse

Bei·sein das: in jmds. ~: in the presence of sb. *or* in sb.'s presence

bei·seite *Adv.* aside

Beis[e]l das; ~s, ~ *od.* ~n *(österr.)* pub *(Brit. coll.)*; bar *(Amer.)*

bei|setzen *tr. V.* lay to rest; inter ⟨ashes⟩; **Bei·setzung die**; ~, ~en funeral; burial

Bei·spiel das example (für of); **zum ~:** for example; **mit gutem ~ vorangehen** set a good example; **beispielhaft** Adj. exemplary; **beispiel·los** Adj. unparalleled; **beispiels·weise** Adv. for example

beißen 1. unr. tr., itr. V. (auch fig.) bite; 2. unr. refl. V. (ugs.) ⟨colours, clothes⟩ clash; **beißend** Adj. biting ⟨cold⟩; acrid ⟨smoke, fumes⟩; sharp ⟨frost⟩; **Beiß·zange** die s. Kneifzange

Bei·stand der o. Pl. (geh.: Hilfe) aid; **bei|stehen** unr. itr. V. jmdm. ~: aid sb.

bei|steuern tr. V. contribute

Beitrag der; ~[e]s, Beiträge contribution; (Versicherungs~) premium; (Mitglieds~) subscription; **bei|tragen** unr. tr., itr. V. contribute (zu to)

bei|treten unr. itr. V.; mit sein join ⟨union, club, etc.⟩; **einem Abkommen/ Pakt accede to** ⟨pact, agreement⟩; **Bei·tritt** der joining

Bei·wagen der side-car

Bei·werk das; o. Pl. accessories pl.

bei|wohnen itr. V. einer Sache (Dat.) ~ (geh.) be present at sth.

Beize die; ~, ~n (Holzbearb.) [wood]stain

beizeiten Adv. in good time

beizen tr. V. (Holzbearb.) stain

bejahen [bəˈjaːən] tr. V. a) auch itr. answer ⟨sth.⟩ in the affirmative; b) (gutheißen) approve of; **das Leben ~:** have a positive or an affirmative attitude to life; **Bejahung** die; ~, ~en a) affirmative reply; b) (das Gutheißen) approval

bejammern tr. V. lament

bejubeln tr. V. cheer; acclaim

bekämpfen tr. V. a) fight against; b) combat ⟨disease, epidemic, pest, unemployment, crime, etc.⟩; **Bekämpfung** die; ~ a) fight (Gen. against); b) s. bekämpfen b: combating

bekannt Adj. well-known; b) jmd./ etw. ist jmdm. ~: sb. knows sb./sth.; **Darf ich ~ machen? Meine Eltern** may I introduce my parents?; **Bekannte** der/die; adj. Dekl. acquaintance

Bekannt·gabe die; ~ announcement; **bekannt|geben** unr. tr. V. announce

bekanntlich Adv. as is well known; **etw. ist ~ der Fall** sth. is known to be the case

bekannt|machen tr. V. announce; (der Öffentlichkeit) make public; **Bekannt·machung** die; ~, ~en announcement

Bekanntschaft die; ~, ~en acquaintance

bekannt|werden unr. itr. V.; mit sein (nur im Inf. und 2. Part. zusammengeschr.) become known

bekehren 1. tr. V. convert; 2. refl. V. become converted; **Bekehrung** die; ~, ~en (auch fig.) conversion (zu to)

bekennen 1. unr. tr. V. a) confess; **daß ...** admit that ...; b) (Rel.) profess; 2. refl. V. **sich zum Islam ~:** profess Islam; **sich zu Buddha ~:** profess one's faith in Buddha; **sich zu seiner Schuld ~:** confess one's guilt; **sich schuldig/nicht schuldig ~:** confess/not confess one's guilt; (vor Gericht) plead guilty/not guilty; **Bekenntnis** das; ~ses, ~se a) confession; b) (Eintreten) **ein ~ zum Frieden** a declaration for peace; c) (Konfession) denomination

beklagen 1. tr. V. (geh.) a) (betrauern) mourn; b) (bedauern) lament; 2. refl. V. complain

bekleckern tr. V. (ugs.) etw./sich [mit Soße usw.] ~: drop or spill sauce etc. down sth./oneself

bekleiden tr. V. a) clothe; **mit etw. bekleidet sein** be wearing sth.; b) (geh.: innehaben) occupy ⟨office, position⟩; **Bekleidung** die clothing; clothes pl.

beklemmend Adj. oppressive; **Beklemmung** die; ~, ~en oppressive feeling; **beklommen** Adj. uneasy; (stärker) apprehensive

bekloppt Adj. (salopp) barmy (Brit. sl.); loony (sl.)

beknien tr. V. (ugs.) beg

bekommen 1. unr. tr. V. a) get; get; receive ⟨money, letter, reply, news, orders⟩; (erreichen) catch ⟨train, bus, flight⟩; **was ~ Sie?** (im Geschäft) can I help you?; (im Lokal, Restaurant) what would you like?; **was ~ Sie [dafür]?** how much is that?; **Hunger/ Durst ~:** get hungry/thirsty; **Angst/ Mut ~:** become frightened/take heart; **er bekommt einen Bart** he's growing a beard; **sie bekommt eine Brust** her breasts are developing; **Zähne ~:** ⟨baby⟩ teethe; **sie bekommt ein Kind** she's expecting a baby; b) etw. durch die Tür/ins Auto ~: get sth. through the door/into the car; 2. unr. V.; in der Funktion eines Hilfsverbs zur Umschreibung des Passivs get; **etw. geschenkt ~:** get [given] sth. or be given

sth. as a present; **3.** *unr. itr. V.; mit
sein* jmdm. gut ~: do sb. good; **jmdm.
[gut] ~:** *(food, medicine)* agree with
sb.; **wohl bekomm's!** your [very good]
health!

bekömmlich *Adj.* easily digestible

beköstigen *tr. V.* cater for

bekräftigen *tr. V.* reinforce *(statement)*; reaffirm *(promise)*

bekreuzigen *refl. V. (kath. Kirche)*
cross oneself

bekriegen *tr. V.* wage war on; *(fig.)*
fight; **sich ~:** be at war; *(fig.)* fight

bekümmern *tr. V.* jmdn. ~: cause sb.
worry; **bekümmert** *Adj.* worried;
(stärker) distressed

bekunden *tr. V.* express

belächeln *tr. V.* smile [pityingly/
tolerantly *etc.*] at

beladen *unr. tr. V.* load *(ship)*; load
[up] *(car, wagon)*; load up *(horse, donkey)*

Belag der; ~[e]s, Beläge **a)** coating; **b)**
(Fußboden~) covering; *(Straßen~)*
surface; *(Brems~)* lining; **c)** *(von Kuchen, Scheibe Brot usw.)* topping; *(von
Sandwiches)* filling

belagern *tr. V. (auch fig.)* besiege;
Belagerung die; ~, ~en siege; *(fig.)*
besieging

Belang der; ~[e]s, ~e **a)** von/ohne ~
sein be of importance/of no importance; **b)** *Pl. (Interessen)* interests

belangen *tr. V. (Rechtsw.)* sue; *(strafrechtlich)* prosecute

belang·los *Adj. (trivial)* trivial; *(unerheblich)* of no importance (**für** for);
Belanglosigkeit die; ~, ~en unim-
portance; *(Trivialität)* triviality

belassen *unr. tr. V.* leave

belasten *tr. V.* **a)** etw. ~: put sth.
under strain; *(durch Gewicht)* put
weight on sth.; **b)** *(beeinträchtigen)*
pollute *(atmosphere)*; put pressure on
(environment); **c)** *(in Anspruch nehmen)* burden (**mit** with); **d)** jmdn. ~
(responsibility, guilt) weigh upon sb.;
(thought) weigh upon sb.'s mind; **e)**
(Rechtsw.) incriminate

belästigen *tr. V.* bother; *(sehr aufdringlich)* pester; *(sexuell)* molest

Belästigung die; ~, ~en **a)** strain; *(das
Belasten)* straining; *(durch Gewicht)*
loading; *(Last)* load; **b)** die ~ der At-
mosphäre/Umwelt durch Schadstoffe
the pollution of the atmosphere by
harmful substances/the pressure on
the environment caused by harmful
substances; **c)** *(Bürde, Sorge)* burden

belaufen *unr. refl. V.* sich auf ...*(Akk.)*
~: come to ...

belauschen *tr. V.* eavesdrop on

beleben 1. *tr. V.* enliven; stimulate
(economy); **2.** *refl. V. (market, economic activity)* revive, pick up; **belebend 1.** *Adj.* invigorating; **2.** *adv. ~*
wirken have an invigorating effect;
belebt *Adj.* busy *(street, crossing,
town, etc.)*

Beleg der; ~[e]s, ~e *(Beweisstück)*
piece of [supporting] documentary
evidence; *(Quittung)* receipt

belegen *tr. V.* **a)** *(Milit.: beschießen)*
bombard; *(mit Bomben)* attack; **b)**
(mit Belag versehen) cover *(floor)* (**mit**
with); fill *(flan base, sandwich)*; top
(open sandwich); **eine Scheibe Brot mit
Käse ~:** put some cheese on a slice of
bread; **c)** *(in Besitz nehmen)* occupy
(seat, room, etc.); **d)** *(Hochschulw.)*
enrol for *(seminar, lecture-course)*; **e)**
den ersten/letzten Platz ~ *(Sport)* take
first place/come last; **f)** *(nachweisen)*
prove; give a reference for *(quotation)*

Belegschaft die; ~, ~en staff

belegt *Adj.* **a)** ein ~es Brot an open *or
(Amer.)* openface sandwich; *(zugeklappt)* a sandwich; **ein ~es Brötchen**
a roll with topping; an open-face roll
(Amer.); *(zugeklappt)* a filled roll; a
sandwich roll *(Amer.)*; **b)** *(mit Belag
bedeckt)* furred *(tongue, tonsils)*; **c)**
(heiser) husky *(voice)*; **d)** *(nicht mehr
frei)* room, flat) occupied

belehren *tr. V.* teach; instruct; *(aufklären)* enlighten; *(informieren)* inform; **ich lasse mich gern ~:** I'm quite
willing to believe otherwise; **Beleh-
rung** die; ~, ~en instruction; *(Zu-
rechtweisung)* lecture

beleibt *Adj. (geh.)* portly

beleidigen *tr. V.* insult; **beleidigt**
Adj. insulted; *(gekränkt)* offended;
Beleidigung die; ~, ~en **a)** insult; **b)**
(Rechtsw.) (schriftlich) libel; *(münd-
lich)* slander

belesen *Adj.* well-read

beleuchten *tr. V.* light up; light
(stairs, room, street, etc.); **Beleuchtung** die; ~, ~en lighting;
(Anstrahlung) illumination

beleumdet *Adj.* übel/gut ~ sein have
a bad/good reputation

Belgien ['bɛlɡiən] *(das)*; ~s Belgium;
Belgier der; ~s, ~ Belgian; **belgisch** *Adj.* Belgian

belichten *tr. V. (Fot.)* expose; *itr.*
richtig/falsch/kurz ~: use the right/

wrong exposure/a short exposure time; **Belichtung die** *(Fot.)* exposure

Belieben das; ~s: nach ~: just as you/they *etc.* like

beliebig 1. *Adj.* any; **2.** *adv.* as you like/he likes *etc.; ~* **lange/viele** as long/many as you like/he likes *etc.*

beliebt *Adj.* popular; favourite *attrib.;* **Beliebtheit die; ~:** popularity

beliefern *tr. V.* supply

bellen *itr. V.* bark

belohnen *tr. V.* reward ⟨person, thing⟩; **Belohnung die; ~, ~en** reward

belügen *unr. tr. V.* lie to

belustigen *tr. V.* amuse; **Belustigung die; ~, ~en** amusement

bemächtigen *refl. V.* **sich jmds./einer Sache ~** *(geh.)* seize sb./sth.

bemalen *tr. V.* paint; *(verzieren)* decorate

bemängeln *tr. V.* find fault with

bemerkbar *Adj.* **sich ~ machen** attract attention [to oneself]; *(erkennbar werden)* become apparent; *(spürbar werden)* make itself felt; **bemerken** *tr. V. a) (wahrnehmen)* notice; **ich wurde nicht bemerkt** I was unobserved; **b)** *(äußern)* remark; **bemerkenswert 1.** *Adj.* remarkable; **2.** *adv.* remarkably; **Bemerkung die; ~, ~en a)** *(Äußerung)* remark; comment; **b)** *(Notiz)* note; *(Anmerkung)* comment

bemitleiden *tr. V.* pity; feel sorry for; **bemitleidens·wert** *Adj.* pitiable

bemogeln *tr. V. (ugs.)* cheat; diddle *(Brit. sl.)*

bemühen *refl. V.* make an effort; **sich ~, etw. zu tun** endeavour to do sth.; **sich um etw. ~:** try to obtain sth.; **sich um eine Stelle ~:** try to get a job; **sich um jmdn. ~** *(kümmern)* seek to help sb.; **Bemühung die; ~, ~en** effort

benachbart *Adj.* neighbouring *attrib.*

benachrichtigen *tr. V.* notify (von of); **Benachrichtigung die; ~, ~en** notification

benachteiligen *tr. V.* put at a disadvantage; *(diskriminieren)* discriminate against

benehmen *unr. refl. V.* behave; **Benehmen das; ~s** behaviour; **kein ~ haben** have no manners *pl.*

beneiden *tr. V.* envy; **jmdn. um etw. ~:** envy sb. sth.; **beneidens·wert** *Adj.* enviable

Benelux·länder *Pl.* Benelux countries

benennen *unr. tr. V.* name

Bengel der; ~s, ~ od. (nordd.) ~s a) *(abwertend: junger Bursche)* young rascal; **b)** *(fam.: kleiner Junge)* little lad

benommen *Adj.* dazed; *(durch Fieber, Alkohol)* muzzy

benoten *tr. V.* mark *(Brit.);* grade *(Amer.);* **einen Test mit ,,gut" ~:** mark a test 'good' *(Brit.);* assign a grade of 'good' to a test *(Amer.)*

benötigen *tr. V.* need; require

benutzen *tr. V.* use; **Benutzer der; ~s, ~:** user; **Benutzung die; ~:** use

Benzin das; ~s petrol *(Brit.);* gasoline *(Amer.);* gas *(Amer. coll.); (Wasch~)* benzine

Benzol das; ~s, ~e *(Chemie)* benzene

beobachten *tr. V.* observe; watch; **Beobachter der; ~s, ~:** observer; **Beobachtung die; ~, ~en** observation

bepacken *tr. V.* load

bepflanzen *tr. V.* plant

bequem 1. *Adj.* **a)** comfortable; **b)** *(abwertend: träge)* idle; **2.** *adv.* **a)** comfortably; **b)** *(leicht)* easily; **bequemen** *refl. V.* **sich dazu ~, etw. zu tun** *(geh.)* condescend to do sth.; **Bequemlichkeit die; ~ a)** comfort; **b)** *(Trägheit)* idleness

berappen *tr., itr. V. (ugs.)* s. **blechen**

beraten 1. *unr. tr. V.* **a)** advise; **jmdn. gut/schlecht ~:** give sb. good/bad advice; **b)** *(besprechen)* discuss ⟨plan, matter⟩; **2.** *unr. itr. V.* **über etw.** *(Akk.)* **~:** discuss sth. **3.** *unr. refl. V.* **sich mit jmdm. ~, ob ...:** discuss with sb. whether ...; **Berater der; ~s, ~:** adviser; **beratschlagen 1.** *tr. V.* discuss; **2.** *itr. V.* **über etw.** *(Akk.)* **~:** discuss sth.; **Beratung die; ~, ~en a)** advice *no indef. art.; (durch Arzt, Rechtsanwalt)* consultation; **b)** *(Besprechung)* discussion

berauben *tr. V. (auch fig.)* rob (Gen. of)

berauschen *(geh.)* **1.** *tr. V. (auch fig.)* intoxicate; **2.** *refl. V.* become intoxicated (**an** + *Dat.* with)

berechnen *tr. V. a) (auch fig.)* calculate; predict ⟨behaviour, consequences⟩; **b)** *(anrechnen)* charge; **jmdm. 10 Mark für etw. od. jmdm. etw. mit 10 Mark ~:** charge sb. 10 marks for sth.; **jmdm. zuviel ~:** overcharge sb.; **Berechnung die a)** calculation; **b)** *o. Pl. (Eigennutz)* [calculating] self-interest

berechtigen *tr. V.* entitle; *itr.* **die**

Karte berechtigt zum Eintritt the ticket entitles the bearer to admission; **berechtigt** *Adj.* a) *(gerechtfertigt)* justified; b) *(befugt)* authorized; **Berechtigung die;** ~, ~en a) *(Befugnis)* entitlement; *(Recht)* right; b) *(Rechtmäßigkeit)* legitimacy

bereden *tr. V.* a) *(besprechen)* discuss; b) **jmdn.** ~, **etw. zu tun** talk sb. into doing sth.

Bereich der; ~[e]s, ~e area; **im privaten/staatlichen** ~: in the private/public sector

bereichern *refl. V.* get rich; **Bereicherung die;** ~, ~en a) money-making; b) *(Nutzen)* valuable acquisition

bereifen *tr. V.* put tyres on ⟨*car*⟩; put a tyre on ⟨*wheel*⟩; **Bereifung die;** ~, ~en [set *sing.* of] tyres *pl.*

bereinigen *tr. V.* clear up *(misunderstanding)*; settle, resolve ⟨*dispute*⟩

bereit *Adj.* ready; ~ **sein, etw. zu tun** be ready *or* willing to do sth.

bereiten *tr. V.* a) prepare; make ⟨*tea, coffee*⟩; b) *(verursachen)* cause ⟨*trouble, sorrow, difficulty, etc.*⟩

bereit-: ~|**halten** *unr. tr. V.* have ready; ~|**legen** *tr. V.* lay out ready; ~|**liegen** *unr. itr. V.* be ready

bereits *Adv.* already

Bereitschaft die; ~, ~: readiness; willingness; **Bereitschafts·dienst der:** ~**dienst haben** ⟨*doctor, nurse*⟩ be on call; ⟨*policeman, fireman*⟩ be on stand-by duty; ⟨*chemist's*⟩ be on rota duty *(for dispensing outside normal hours)*

bereit-: ~|**stehen** *unr. itr. V.* be ready; ~|**stellen** *tr. V.* place ready; get ready ⟨*food, drinks*⟩; ready, make ⟨*money, funds*⟩ available; ~**willig 1.** *Adj.* willing. **2.** *adv.* readily

bereuen 1. *unr. tr. V.* regret; **2.** *itr. V.* be sorry; *(Rel.)* repent

Berg der; ~[e]s, ~e a) hill; *(im Hochgebirge)* mountain; b) *(Haufen)* huge pile; *(von Akten, Abfall auch)* mountain

berg-, Berg-: ~**ab** [-'-] *Adv.* downhill; ~**auf** [-'-] *Adv.* uphill; ~**bahn die** mountain railway; *(Seilbahn)* mountain cableway; ~**bau der;** *o. Pl.* mining

bergen *unr. tr. V.* a) rescue, save ⟨*person*⟩; salvage ⟨*ship, cargo, belongings*⟩; b) *(geh.: enthalten)* hold

Berg-: ~**führer der** mountain guide; ~**hütte die** mountain hut

bergig *Adj.* hilly; *(mit hohen Bergen)* mountainous

Berg-: ~**kristall der** rock crystal; ~**land das** hilly country *no indef. art; (mit hohen Bergen)* mountainous country *no indef. art.;* ~**mann der;** *Pl.* ~**leute** miner; ~**station die** top station; ~**steigen das;** ~s mountaineering *no art.;* ~**steiger der** mountaineer

Bergung die; ~, ~en a) rescue; b) *(von Schiffen, Gut)* salvaging

Berg-: ~**wacht die** mountain rescue service; ~**werk das** mine

Bericht der; ~[e]s, ~e report; **berichten** *tr., itr. V.* report

Bericht-: ~**erstatter der;** ~s, ~: reporter; ~**erstattung die** reporting *no indef. art.*

berichtigen *tr. V.* correct; **Berichtigung die;** ~, ~en correction

berieseln *tr. V.* a) *(bewässern)* irrigate; b) **sich ständig mit Musik** ~ **lassen** *(ugs. abwertend)* constantly have music on in the background

Berlin (das); ~s Berlin; **Berliner 1.** *Adj.; nicht präd.* Berlin; **2. der;** ~s, ~: a) Berliner; b) (~ *Pfannkuchen)* [jam *(Brit.)* or *(Amer.)* jelly] doughnut; **berlinisch** *Adj.* Berlin *attrib.*

Bern (das); ~s Bern[e]

Bernhardiner der; ~s, ~: St. Bernard [dog]

Bern·stein der; *o. Pl.* amber

bersten *unr. itr. V.; mit sein (geh.)* ⟨*ice*⟩ break up; ⟨*glass*⟩ shatter [into pieces]; ⟨*wall*⟩ crack up

berüchtigt *Adj.* notorious **(wegen** for); *(verrufen)* disreputable

berücksichtigen *tr. V.* take into account; consider ⟨*applicant, application, suggestion*⟩; **Berücksichtigung die;** ~: **bei** ~ **aller Umstände** taking all the circumstances into account

Beruf der; ~[e]s, ~e occupation; *(akademischer)* profession; *(handwerklicher)* trade; **was sind Sie von** ~? what do you do for a living?

¹**berufen 1.** *unr. tr. V.* a) *(einsetzen)* appoint; b) **berufe es nicht!** *(ugs.)* don't speak too soon!; **2.** *unr. refl. V.* **sich auf etw.** *(Akk.)* ~: refer to sth.; **sich auf jmdn.** ~: quote *or* mention sb.'s name

²**berufen** *Adj.* a) competent; **aus** ~**em Munde** from somebody qualified to speak; b) **sich dazu** ~ **fühlen, etw. zu tun** feel called to do sth.

beruflich 1. *Adj.; nicht präd.* vocational ⟨*training etc.*⟩; *(bei akademischen Berufen)* professional ⟨*training etc.*⟩; **2.** *adv.* ~ **erfolgreich sein** be successful in one's career; **sich** ~ **weiterbilden** undertake further job training

berufs-, Berufs-: ~**ausbildung** die vocational training; ~**beratung** die vocational guidance; ~**erfahrung** die; *o. Pl.* [professional] experience; ~**geheimnis das** professional secret; *(Schweigepflicht)* professional secrecy; ~**krankheit** die occupational disease; ~**leben das** working life; ~**schule** die vocational school; ~**soldat** der regular soldier; ~**sportler** der professional sportsman; ~**tätig** *Adj.* working *attrib.*; ~**tätige der/die;** *adj. Dekl.* working person; ~**tätige** *Pl.* working people; ~**verkehr** der rush-hour traffic

Berufung die; ~, ~en a) *(für ein Amt)* offer of an appointment **(auf, in, an +** *Akk.* to); b) *(innerer Auftrag)* vocation; c) *(das Sichberufen)* **unter** ~ *(Dat.)* **auf jmdn./etw.** referring or with reference to sb./sth.; d) *(Rechtsw.: Einspruch)* appeal; ~ **einlegen** lodge an appeal

beruhen *itr. V.* **auf etw.** *(Dat.)* ~**:** be based on sth.; **etw. auf sich** ~ **lassen** let sth. rest

beruhigen [bə'ru:ɪgn̩] **1.** *tr. V.* calm [down]; pacify ⟨*child, baby*⟩; salve ⟨*conscience*⟩; (trösten) soothe; *(von einer Sorge befreien)* reassure; **2.** *refl. V.* ⟨*person*⟩ calm down; ⟨*sea*⟩ become calm; **Beruhigung** die; ~ *s.* **beruhigen 1:** calming [down]; pacifying; salving; soothing; reassurance; **Beruhigungs·mittel das** tranquillizer

berühmt *Adj.* famous; **berühmtberüchtigt** *Adj.* notorious; **Berühmtheit** die; ~, ~en a) *o. Pl.* *(Ruhm)* fame; b) *(Mensch)* celebrity

berühren *tr. V.* a) touch; *(fig.)* touch on ⟨*topic, issue. etc.*⟩; **sich** ~**:** touch; b) *(beeindrucken)* affect; **das berührt mich nicht** it's a matter of indifference to me; **Berührung** die; ~, ~en touch; **mit jmdm./etw. in** ~ *(Akk.)* **kommen** *(auch fig.)* come into contact with sb./sth.

besagen *tr. V.* say; *(bedeuten)* mean

besänftigen *tr. V.* calm [down]; pacify; calm, soothe ⟨*temper*⟩

Besatz der *(Borte)* trimming *no indef. art.*

Besatzung die a) *(Mannschaft)* crew;

---

b) *(Milit.: Verteidigungstruppe)* garrison; c) *(Milit.: Okkupationstruppen)* occupying forces *pl.*

besaufen *unr. refl. V. (salopp)* get canned *(Brit. sl.)* or bombed *(Amer. sl.);* **Besäufnis das;** ~**ses,** ~**se** *(salopp)* booze-up *(Brit. sl.):* blast *(Amer. sl.)*

beschädigen *tr. V.* damage; **Beschädigung** die a) *o. Pl.* damaging; b) *(Schaden)* damage

¹**beschaffen** *tr. V.* obtain, get *(Dat.* for)

²**beschaffen** *Adj.* so ~ **sein, daß ...:** be such that ...; **Beschaffenheit** die; ~**:** properties *pl.*

Beschaffung die *s.* **beschaffen:** obtaining; getting

beschäftigen 1. *refl. V.* occupy oneself; **sich viel mit Musik/den Kindern** ~**:** devote a great deal of one's time to music/the children; **sehr beschäftigt sein** be very busy; **2.** *tr. V.* **a)** *(geistig in Anspruch nehmen)* **jmdn.** ~**:** preoccupy sb.) **b)** *(angestellt haben)* employ ⟨*workers, staff*⟩; c) *(zu tun geben)* occupy; **jmdn. mit etw.** ~**:** give sb. sth. to occupy him/her; **Beschäftigte der/die;** *adj. Dekl.* employee; **Beschäftigung** die; ~, ~en a) *(Tätigkeit)* activity; b) *(Anstellung, Stelle)* job; c) *(mit einer Frage, einem Problem)* consideration **(mit** of); *(Studium)* study **(mit** of); d) *o. Pl. (von Arbeitskräften)* employment

beschämen *tr. V.* shame; **beschämend 1.** *Adj.* a) *(schändlich)* shameful; b) *(demütigend)* humiliating; **2.** *adv.* shamefully; **beschämt** *Adj.* ashamed; **Beschämung** die; ~**:** shame

beschatten *tr. V.* a) *(geh.)* shade; b) *(überwachen)* shadow

beschaulich 1. *Adj.* peaceful ⟨*life, manner, etc.*⟩; **2.** *adv.* peacefully

Bescheid der; ~[e]s, ~e a) *(Auskunft)* information; *(Antwort)* answer; reply; **jmdm.** ~ **geben** *od.* **sagen[, ob ...]** let sb. know or tell sb. [whether ...]; **sage bitte im Hotel** ~**, daß ...:** please let the hotel know that ...; [**über etw.** *(Akk.)*] ~ **wissen** know [about sth.]; b) *(Entscheidung)* decision

¹**bescheiden 1.** *unr. tr. V.* **jmdn./etw. abschlägig** ~**:** turn sb./sth. down; **2.** *unr. refl. V. (geh.)* be content

²**bescheiden 1.** *Adj.* modest; **2.** *adv.* modestly; **Bescheidenheit** die; ~**:** modesty

bescheinigen tr. V. confirm ⟨sth.⟩ in writing; **Bescheinigung** die; ~, ~en written confirmation no indef. art.; (Schein, Attest) certificate

beschenken tr. V. give ⟨sb.⟩ a present/presents

bescheren tr. V. jmdn. [mit etw.] ~: give sb. [sth. as] a Christmas present/Christmas presents

Bescherung die; ~, ~en a) (zu Weihnachten) giving out of the Christmas presents; **b) das ist ja eine schöne** ~ (ugs.) this is a pretty kettle of fish

beschießen unr. tr. V. fire at; (mit Artillerie) bombard

beschimpfen tr. V. abuse; swear at; **Beschimpfung** die; ~, ~en insult; ~en abuse sing.; insults

Beschlag der a) fitting; b) jmdn./etw. mit ~ belegen od. in ~ nehmen monopolize sb./sth.; ¹**beschlagen** 1. unr. tr. V. shoe ⟨horse⟩; 2. unr. itr. V.; mit sein ⟨window⟩ mist up (Brit.), fog up (Amer.); (durch Dampf) steam up

²**beschlagen** Adj. knowledgeable

Beschlag·nahme die; ~, ~n confiscation; **beschlag·nahmen** tr. V. confiscate

beschleunigen 1. tr. V. accelerate; speed up ⟨work, delivery⟩; quicken ⟨pace, step[s], pulse⟩; 2. refl. V. ⟨heartrate⟩ increase; ⟨pulse⟩ quicken; 3. itr. V. ⟨driver, car, etc.⟩ accelerate; **Beschleunigung** die; ~, ~en s. beschleunigen 1: acceleration; speeding up; quickening

beschließen unr. tr. V. **a)** decide; pass ⟨law⟩; ~, etw. zu tun decide or resolve to do sth.; **b)** (beenden) end

Beschluß der decision; (gemeinsam gefaßt) resolution; **einen** ~ **fassen** come to a decision/pass a resolution; **beschluß·fähig** Adj. quorate; **Beschluß·fähigkeit** die; o. Pl. presence of a quorum

beschmieren tr. V. etw./sich ~: get sth./oneself in a mess

beschmutzen tr. V. make ⟨sth.⟩ dirty

beschneiden unr. tr. V. **a)** cut ⟨hedge⟩; prune ⟨bush⟩; cut back ⟨tree⟩; **einem Vogel die Flügel** ~: clip a bird's wings; **b)** (Med., Rel.) circumcise; **Beschneidung** die; ~, ~en a) s. beschneiden a: cutting; pruning; cutting back; b) (Med., Rel.) circumcision

beschönigen tr. V. gloss over

beschränken 1. tr. V. restrict (auf + Akk. to); 2. refl. V. sich auf etw. (Akk.)

~: restrict oneself to sth.; **beschränkt** 1. Adj. a) (dumm) dull-witted; b) (engstirnig) narrow-minded; 2. adv. narrow-mindedly; **Beschränktheit** die; ~: a) (Dummheit) lack of intelligence; b) (Engstirnigkeit) narrow-mindedness; **Beschränkung** die; ~, ~en restriction

beschreiben unr. tr. V. **a)** write on; (vollschreiben) write ⟨page, side, etc.⟩; **b)** (darstellen) describe; **Beschreibung** die; ~, ~en description

beschriften tr. V. label; inscribe ⟨stone⟩; letter ⟨sign, label, etc.⟩; (mit Adresse) address

beschuldigen tr. V. accuse (Gen. of); **Beschuldigte der/die; adj. Dekl.** accused; **Beschuldigung** die; ~, ~en accusation

beschummeln tr. V. (ugs.) cheat; diddle (Brit. coll.)

Beschuß der fire

beschützen tr. V. protect (vor + Dat. from); **Beschützer** der; ~s, ~, **Beschützerin** die; ~, ~nen protector

Beschwerde die; ~, ~n a) complaint (gegen, über + Akk. about); b) Pl. (Schmerz) pain sing.; (Leiden) trouble sing.

beschweren 1. refl. V. complain (über + Akk., wegen about); 2. tr. V. weight down; **beschwerlich** Adj. arduous; (ermüdend) exhausting

beschwichtigen tr. V. pacify; mollify ⟨anger etc.⟩; **Beschwichtigung** die; ~, ~en pacification; (des Zorns usw.) mollification

beschwingt Adj. lively

beschwipst Adj. (ugs.) tipsy

beschwören unr. tr. V. **a)** swear to; ~, daß ...: swear that ...; **eine Aussage** ~: swear a statement on oath; **b)** charm ⟨snake⟩; c) (erscheinen lassen) invoke ⟨spirit⟩; **d)** (bitten) implore; **Beschwörung** die; ~, ~en a) (Zauberspruch) spell; incantation; b) s. beschwören c: invoking; c) (Bitte) entreaty

beseitigen tr. V. remove; eliminate ⟨error, difficulty⟩; dispose of ⟨rubbish⟩; **Beseitigung** die; ~: s. beseitigen: removal; elimination; disposal

Besen der; ~s, ~ broom; **ich freß' einen** ~, **wenn das stimmt** (salopp) I'll eat my hat if that's right (coll.); **neue** ~ **kehren gut** (Spr.) a new broom sweeps clean (prov.)

besessen Adj. **a)** possessed; **b)** (fig.) obsessive ⟨gambler⟩; **von einer Idee** ~

sein be obsessed with an idea; **Be-sessenheit die; ~ a)** possession; **b)** obsessiveness

besetzen tr. V. **a)** (mit Pelz, Spitzen) edge; trim; (mit Perlen besetzt set with pearls); **b)** (belegen; auch Milit.: erobern) occupy; **c)** (vergeben) fill ⟨post, position, role, etc.⟩; **besetzt** Adj. occupied; ⟨table, seat⟩ taken pred.; (gefüllt) full; (Fernspr.) engaged; busy (Amer.); **Besetzung die; ~, ~en a)** (einer Stellung) filling; **b)** (Film, Theater usw.) cast; **c)** (Eroberung) occupation

besichtigen tr. V. see ⟨sights⟩; see the sights of ⟨town⟩; view ⟨house etc. for sale⟩; **Besichtigung die; ~, ~en zur ~ der Stadt/des Schlosses/der Wohnung** to see the sights of the town/to see the castle/to view the flat

besiedeln tr. V. settle

besiegen tr. V. defeat

besinnen unr. refl. V. **a)** think it over; **b) sich** [auf jmdn./etw.] **~:** remember [sb./sth.]; **Besinnung die; ~:** consciousness; **die ~ verlieren** faint; [wieder] **zur ~ kommen** regain consciousness; **besinnungs·los 1.** Adj. unconscious; **2.** adv. mindlessly

Besitz der a) property; **b)** (das Besitzen) possession; **im ~ einer Sache** (Gen.) **sein** be in possession of sth.; **besitzen** unr. tr. V. own; have ⟨quality, talent, etc.⟩; (nachdrücklicher) possess; **Besitzer der; ~s, ~, Besitzerin die; ~, ~nen** owner

besoffen Adj. (salopp) canned (Brit. sl.); bombed (Amer. sl.); **Besoffene der/die;** adj. Dekl. (salopp) drunk

besohlen tr. V. sole; **neu ~:** resole

besonder... Adj.; nicht präd. special; **ein ~es Ereignis** an unusual or a special event; **keine ~e Leistung** no great achievement; **Besonderheit die; ~, ~en** special feature; (Eigenart) peculiarity; **besonders 1.** Adv. particularly; **2.** Adj.; nicht attr.; nur verneint (ugs.) **nicht ~ sein** be nothing special

besonnen 1. Adj. prudent; **2.** adv. prudently; **Besonnenheit die; ~:** prudence

besorgen tr. V. **a)** get; (kaufen) buy; **b)** (erledigen) take care of; **Besorgnis die; ~, ~se** concern; **besorgt 1.** Adj. concerned (um about); **2.** adv. with concern; **Besorgung die; ~, ~en** purchase

bespitzeln tr. V. spy on

besprechen unr. tr. V. discuss; (re-

zensieren) review; **Besprechung die; ~, ~en** discussion; (Konferenz) meeting; (Rezension) review

bespritzen tr. V. **a)** splash; (mit einem Wasserstrahl) spray; **b)** (beschmutzen) bespatter

besprühen tr. V. spray

besser 1. Adj. **a)** better; **um so ~:** so much the better; **b)** (sozial höher gestellt) superior; **2.** adv. [immer] **alles ~ wissen** always know better; **es ~ haben** be better off; **~ gesagt** be [more] precise; **3.** Adv. (lieber) **das läßt du ~ sein** od. (ugs.) **bleiben** you'd better not do that

besser|gehen unr. itr. V.; mit sein **jmdm. geht es besser** sb. feels better

bessern 1. refl. V. improve; ⟨person⟩ mend one's ways; **2.** tr. V. improve; reform ⟨criminal⟩; **Besserung die; ~:** recovery; **gute ~!** get well soon

best... 1. Adj. **a)** best; **bei ~er Gesundheit/Laune sein** be in the best of health/spirits pl.; **im ~en Falle** at best; **in den ~en Jahren, im ~en Alter** in one's prime; **die ~en ... (Akk.)** best wishes to ...; **mit den ~en Grüßen** od. **Wünschen** with best wishes; (als Briefschluß) ≈ yours sincerely; **b)** es **ist** od. **wäre das ~e, wenn ...:** it would be best if ...; **der/die/das nächste ~e ...:** the first ... one comes across; **einen Witz zum ~en geben** entertain [those present] with a joke; **das Beste vom Besten** the very best; **sein Bestes tun** do one's best; **zu deinem Besten** for your benefit; **2.** adv. **am ~en** best; **3.** Adv. **am ~en fährst du mit dem Zug** it would be best for you to go by train

Bestand der a) o. Pl. existence, (Fort~) continued existence; **b)** (Vorrat) stock (an + Dat. of)

bestanden Adj. **von** od. **mit etw. ~ sein** have sth. growing on it; **mit Tannen ~e Hügel** fir-covered hills

beständig 1. Adj. **a)** nicht präd. constant; **b)** (gleichbleibend) constant; steadfast ⟨person⟩; settled ⟨weather⟩; **c)** (widerstandsfähig) resistant (gegen to); **2.** adv. constantly; **Beständigkeit die; ~ a)** steadfastness; **b)** (Widerstandsfähigkeit) resistance (gegen to)

Bestand·teil der component

bestärken tr. V. confirm

bestätigen 1. tr. V. confirm; endorse ⟨document⟩; acknowledge ⟨receipt⟩; **2.** refl. V. be confirmed; ⟨rumour⟩ prove to be true; **Bestätigung die; ~, ~en**

confirmation; *(des Empfangs)* acknowledgement; *(schriftlich)* letter of confirmation

bestatten *tr. V. (geh.)* inter *(formal)*; bury; **Bestattung die; ~, ~en** *(geh.)* interment *(formal)*; burial; *(Feierlichkeit)* funeral

bestäuben *tr. V.* **a)** dust; **b)** *(Biol.)* pollinate

bestaunen *tr. V.* marvel at

bestechen *unr. tr. V.* bribe; **bestechlich** *Adj.* corruptible; open to bribery *postpos.*; **Bestechung die; ~, ~en** bribery *no indef. art.*; **Bestechungs·geld** *das* bribe

Besteck *das; ~[e]s, ~e* cutlery setting; *(ugs.: Gesamtheit der Bestecke)* cutlery

bestehen 1. *unr. itr. V.* **a)** exist; es besteht [die] Aussicht/Gefahr, daß ...: there is a prospect/danger that ...; noch besteht die Hoffnung, daß ...: there is still hope that ...; **b)** *(fortdauern)* survive; last; **c)** aus etw. ~: consist of sth.; *(hergestellt sein)* be made of sth.; **d)** auf etw. *(Dat.)* ~: insist on sth.; **2.** *unr. tr. V.* pass *(test, examination)*; **Bestehen das; ~s** existence; die Firma feiert ihr 10jähriges ~: the firm is celebrating its tenth anniversary

bestehen|bleiben *unr. itr. V.; mit sein* remain; *(regulation)* remain in force

bestehend *Adj.* existing; current *(conditions)*

bestehlen *unr. tr. V.* rob

besteigen *unr. tr. V.* **a)** climb; mount *(horse, bicycle)*; ascend *(throne)*; **b)** board *(ship, aircraft)*; get on *(bus, train)*; **Besteigung die** ascent

bestellen *tr. V.* **a)** *auch itr.* order (bei from); würden Sie mir bitte ein Taxi ~? would you order me a taxi?; **b)** *(reservieren lassen)* reserve *(tickets, table)*; **c)** jmdn. [für 10 Uhr] zu sich ~: ask sb. to go/come to see one [at 10 o'clock]; **d)** *(ausrichten)* jmdm. etw. ~: tell sb. sth.; bestell deinem Mann schöne Grüße von mir give your husband my regards; **Bestellung die** **a)** order; **b)** *(Reservierung)* reservation

besten·falls *Adv.* at best; **bestens** *Adv.* extremely well

besteuern *tr. V.* tax

bestialisch 1. *Adj.* **a)** bestial; **b)** *nicht präd.* *(ugs.: schrecklich)* ghastly *(coll.)*; **2.** *adv.* **a)** in a bestial manner; **b)** *(ugs.: schrecklich)* awfully *(coll.)*; **Bestialität die; ~:** bestiality

besticken *tr. V.* embroider

Bestie [ˈbɛstiə] *die; ~, ~n* beast

bestimmen 1. *tr. V.* **a)** *(festsetzen)* decide on; fix *(price, time, etc.)*; **b)** *(vorsehen)* intend; das ist für dich bestimmt that is meant for you; **c)** *(identifizieren)* identify; determine *(age, position)*; define *(meaning)*; **d)** *(prägen)* determine the character of; **2.** *itr. V.* **a)** make the decisions; **b)** über jmdn. ~: tell sb. what to do; [frei] über etw. *(Akk.)* ~: do as one wishes with sth.; **bestimmend 1.** *Adj.* decisive; **2.** *adv.* decisively; **bestimmt 1.** *Adj.* **a)** *(speziell)* particular; *(gewiß)* certain; *(genau)* definite; **b)** *(festgelegt)* fixed; given *(quantity)*; **c)** *(Sprachw.)* definite *(article etc.)*; **d)** *(entschieden)* firm; **2.** *adv.* **a)** *(deutlich)* clearly; *(genau)* precisely; **b)** *(entschieden)* firmly **3.** *Adv.* for certain; du weißt es doch [ganz] ~ noch I'm sure you must remember it; ich habe das ~ liegengelassen I must have left it behind; **Bestimmtheit die; ~:** firmness; *(im Auftreten)* decisiveness; **Bestimmung die a)** *o. Pl. (das Festsetzen)* fixing; **b)** *(Vorschrift)* regulation; **c)** *o. Pl. (Zweck)* purpose; **d)** *s.* bestimmen 1 c: identification; determination; definition; **e)** *(Sprachw.)* modifier; **adverbiale ~:** adverbial qualification

best·möglich *Adj.* best possible

bestrafen *tr. V.* punish (für, wegen for); es wird mit Gefängnis bestraft it is punishable by imprisonment; **Bestrafung die; ~, ~en** punishment

bestrahlen *tr. V.* **a)** illuminate; floodlight *(building)*; **b)** *(Med.)* treat *(tumour, part of body)* using radiotherapy; **Bestrahlung die; ~, ~en** *(Med.)* radiation [treatment] *no indef. art.*

Bestreben *das* endeavour[s *pl.*]; **bestrebt** *Adj.:* ~ sein, etw. zu tun endeavour to do sth.; **Bestrebung die; ~, ~en** effort; *(Versuch)* attempt

bestreichen *unr. tr. V.* A mit B ~: spread B on A

bestreiten *unr. tr. V.* **a)** dispute; *(leugnen)* deny; **b)** *(finanzieren)* finance *(studies)*; pay for *(studies, sb.'s keep)*; meet *(costs, expenses)*; **c)** *(gestalten)* carry *(programme, conversation, etc.)*

bestreuen *tr. V.* sprinkle

Bestseller *der; ~s, ~:* best seller

bestürzt 1. *Adj.* dismayed; **2.** *adv.* with dismay

Besuch der; ~|e|s, ~e a) visit (Gen., bei to); **ein ~ bei jmdm.** a visit to sb.; (kurz) a call on sb.; b) (Teilnahme) attendance (Gen. at); c) (Gast) visitor; (Gäste) visitors pl.; **~ haben** have visitors/a visitor; **besuchen** tr. V. a) visit; (weniger formell) go to see (person); go to (exhibition, theatre, museum, etc.); (zur Besichtigung) go to see (church, exhibition, etc.); b) **die Schule/Universität ~:** go to school/university; **Besucher** der; ~s, ~, **Besucherin** die; ~, ~nen visitor; **besucht** Adj. **gut/schlecht ~:** well/poorly attended (lecture, performance, etc.); much/little frequented (restaurant etc.)

betagt Adj. (geh.) elderly

betasten tr. V. feel [with one's fingers]

betätigen 1. refl. V. occupy oneself; **sich politisch/körperlich ~:** engage in political/physical activity; **2.** tr. V. operate (lever, switch, flush, etc.); apply (brake); **Betätigung** die; ~, ~en: a) activity; b) o. Pl. s. **betätigen 2:** operation; application

betäuben tr. V. a) (Med.) anaesthetize; deaden (nerve); **jmdn. örtlich ~:** give sb. a local anaesthetic; b) (unterdrücken) deaden (pain); still (unease, fear); c) (benommen machen) daze; (mit einem Schlag) stun; **Betäubung** die; ~, ~en: a) (Med.) anaesthetization; (Narkose) anaesthesia; b) (Benommenheit) daze; **Betäubungsmittel** das narcotic; (Med.) anaesthetic

beteiligen 1. refl. V. take part (an + Dat. in); **2.** tr. V. **jmdn. |mit 10 %| an etw.** (Dat.) ~: give sb. a [10 %] share of sth.; **beteiligt** Adj. a) involved (an + Dat. in); b) (finanziell) **an einem Unternehmen/am Gewinn ~ sein** have a share in a business/in the profit; **Beteiligte** der/die; adj. Dekl. person involved; **Beteiligung** die; ~, ~en a) participation (an + Dat. in); b) (Anteil) share (an + Dat. in)

beten 1. itr. V. pray (für, um for); 2. tr. V. say (prayer)

beteuern tr. V. affirm; protest (one's innocence); **Beteuerung** die; ~, ~en s. **beteuern:** affirmation; protestation

Beton [be'tɔŋ, bes. österr.: be'to:n] der; ~s, ~s [-ɔŋs] od. (bes. österr.:) ~e [-o:nǝ] concrete

betonen tr. V. a) stress (word, syllable); b) (hervorheben) emphasize

betonieren tr. V. concrete; surface (road etc.) with concrete

betont 1. Adj. a) stressed; b) (bewußt) studied; **2.** adv. studiedly; **Betonung** die; ~, ~en a) stressing; b) (Akzent) stress; (Intonation) intonation; c) (Hervorhebung) emphasis

betören tr. V. (geh.) captivate

betr. Abk. betreffs, betrifft re; **Betr.** Abk. Betreff re

Betracht: jmdn./etw. in ~ ziehen consider sb./sth.; **jmdn./etw. außer ~ lassen** disregard sb./sth.; **betrachten** tr. V. a) look at; b) **jmdn./etw. als etw. ~:** regard sb./sth. as sth.; c) (beurteilen) consider; **Betrachter** der; ~s, ~: observer

beträchtlich 1. Adj. considerable; **2.** adv. considerably

Betrachtung die; ~, ~en a) contemplation; (Untersuchung) examination; b) (Überlegung) reflection

Betrag der; ~|e|s, **Beträge** amount; „~ dankend erhalten" 'received with thanks'; **betragen 1.** unr. itr. V. be; (bei Geldsummen) come to; **2.** unr. refl. V. behave; **Betragen** das; ~s behaviour

Betreff der; ~|e|s, ~e (im Brief) heading; **betreffen** unr. tr. V. concern; (new rule, change, etc.) affect; **betreffend** Adj. concerning; **der ~e Sachbearbeiter** the person dealing with this matter; **in dem ~en Fall** in the case in question; **betreffs** Präp. mit Gen. (Amtsspr., Kaufmannsspr.) concerning

betreiben unr. tr. V. a) proceed with, (energisch) press ahead with (task, case, etc.); pursue (policy, studies); carry on (trade); go in for (sport); b) run (business, shop); c) (in Betrieb halten) operate

¹**betreten** unr. tr. V. (hineintreten in) enter; (treten auf) step on to; (begehen) walk on (carpet, grass, etc.); „Betreten verboten" 'Keep off'; (kein Eintritt) 'Keep out'

²**betreten 1.** Adj. embarrassed; **2.** adv. with embarrassment

betreuen tr. V. look after; care for (invalid); supervise (youth group); see to the needs of (tourists, sportsmen); **Betreuung** die; ~ care no indef. art.

Betrieb der; ~|e|s, ~e a) business; (Firma) firm; b) o. Pl. (das In-Funktion-Sein) operation; **außer ~ sein** not operate; (wegen Störung) be out of order; **in/außer ~ setzen** start up/stop

⟨machine etc.⟩; **c)** o. Pl. (ugs.: Treiben) bustle; (Verkehr) traffic; **es herrscht großer ~, es ist viel ~:** it's very busy; **betrieblich** Adj. firm's; company

Betriebs-: ~angehörige der/die employee; **~anleitung die, ~anweisung die** operating instructions pl.; **~ausflug der** staff outing; **~ferien** Pl. firm's annual close-down sing.; „Wegen **~ferien geschlossen"** 'closed for annual holidays'; **~klima das** working atmosphere; **~rat der a)** works committee; **b)** (Person) member of a/the works committee; **~wirt der** graduate in business management; **~wirtschaft die;** o. Pl. business management

betrinken unr. refl. V. get drunk

betroffen 1. Adj. upset; (bestürzt) dismayed; **2.** adv. in dismay; **Betroffenheit die; ~:** dismay

betrüblich Adj. gloomy; **betrübt 1.** Adj. sad; gloomy ⟨face etc.⟩; **2.** sadly; (schwermütig) gloomily

Betrug der; ~[e]s deception; (Delikt) fraud; **betrügen 1.** unr. tr. V. deceive; be unfaithful to ⟨husband, wife⟩; (Rechtsw.) defraud; (beim Spielen) cheat; **jmdn. um 100 DM ~:** cheat or (coll.) do sb. out of 100 marks; (arglistig) swindle sb. out of 100 marks; **2.** unr. itr. V. cheat; (bei Geschäften) swindle people; **Betrüger der; ~s, ~:** swindler; (Hochstapler) con man (coll.); (beim Spielen) cheat; **Betrügerei die; ~, ~en** deception; (beim Spielen usw.) cheating; (bei Geschäften) swindling; **Betrügerin die; ~, ~nen** swindler; (beim Spielen) cheat

betrunken Adj. drunken attrib.; drunk pred.; **Betrunkene der/die;** adj. Dekl. drunk

Bett das; ~[e]s, ~en a) bed; **ins od. zu ~ gehen** go to bed; **die Kinder ins ~ bringen** put the children to bed; **b)** (Feder~) duvet

Bett-: ~bezug der duvet cover; **~decke die** blanket; (gesteppt) quilt

Bettelei die; ~, ~en begging no art.; **betteln** itr. V. beg (um for)

bettlägerig Adj. bedridden

Bettlaken das bed sheet

Bettler der; ~s, ~, Bettlerin die; ~, ~nen beggar

Bett-: ~ruhe die bed rest; **~wäsche die** bed-linen; **~zeug das;** o. Pl. (ugs.) bedclothes pl.

betucht Adj. (ugs.) well-heeled (coll.); well-off

betupfen tr. V. dab

Beuge die; ~, ~n (Turnen) bend; **beugen 1.** tr. V. **a)** bend; bow ⟨head⟩; **b)** (Sprachw.: flektieren) inflect ⟨word⟩; **2.** refl. V. **a)** bend over; **sich nach vorn/hinten ~:** bend forwards/bend over backwards; **sich aus dem Fenster ~:** lean out of the window; **b)** (sich fügen) give way; **Beugung die; ~, ~en** (Sprachw.) inflexion

Beule die; ~, ~n bump; (Vertiefung) dent; **beulen** itr. V. bulge

beunruhigen tr., refl. V. worry

beurlauben tr. V. **a)** jmdn. [für zwei Tage] ~: give sb. [two days'] leave of absence; **b)** (suspendieren) suspend

beurteilen tr. V. judge; assess ⟨situation etc.⟩; **Beurteilung die; ~, ~en a)** judgement; (einer Lage usw.) assessment; **b)** (Gutachten) assessment

Beute die; ~, ~n (Gestohlenes) haul; loot no indef. art.; **b)** (von Raubtieren) prey; (eines Jägers) bag

Beutel der; ~s, ~ bag; (kleiner, für Tabak usw.) pouch

bevölkern tr. V. populate; **Bevölkerung die; ~, ~en** population; (Volk) people

bevollmächtigen tr. V. authorize; **Bevollmächtigte der/die;** adj. Dekl. authorized representative

bevor Konj. before; ~ **du nicht unterschrieben hast** until you have signed; **bevorstehen** unr. itr. V. be near; **unmittelbar ~:** be imminent; **jmdm. steht etw. bevor** sth. is in store for sb.; **bevorstehend** Adj. forthcoming; **unmittelbar ~:** imminent

bevorzugen tr. V. **a)** (vorziehen) prefer (vor + Dat. to); **b)** (begünstigen) favour; give preference or preferential treatment to (vor + Dat. over); **bevorzugt 1.** Adj. favoured; (privilegiert) privileged; preferential ⟨treatment⟩; **2.** adv. jmdn. ~ behandeln give sb. preferential treatment; **Bevorzugung die; ~, ~en** (Begünstigung) preferential treatment

bewachen tr. V. guard; **bewachter Parkplatz** car park with an attendant; **Bewacher der; ~s, ~:** guard; **Bewachung die; ~, ~en** guarding

bewaffnen: 1. tr. V. arm; **2.** refl. V. (auch fig.) arm oneself (mit with); **Bewaffnung die; ~, ~en a)** arming; **b)** (Waffen) weapons pl.

bewahren tr. V. **a)** protect (vor + Dat. from); **b)** (erhalten) seine Fassung ~: retain one's composure; Stillschweigen ~: remain silent

bewähren *refl. V.* prove oneself/itself; **bewährt** *Adj.* proven 〈*method, design, etc.*〉; well-tried 〈*recipe, cure*〉; reliable 〈*worker*〉; **Bewährung die;** ~, ~en *(Rechtsw.)* probation

bewaldet *Adj.* wooded

bewältigen *tr. V.* cope with; overcome 〈*difficulty, problem*〉; cover 〈*dis­tance*〉; **Bewältigung die;** ~, ~en *s.* **bewältigen:** coping with; overcoming; covering

bewandert *Adj.* well-versed

Bewandtnis die; ~, ~se: **mit etw. hat es [s]eine eigene/besondere ~:** there's a [special] story behind sth.

bewässern *tr. V.* irrigate; **Bewässerung die;** ~, ~en irrigation

¹bewegen 1. *tr. V.* **a)** move; **b)** *(ergreifen)* move; **c)** *(innerlich beschäftigend)* preoccupy; 2. *refl. V.* move

²bewegen *unr. tr. V.* **jmdn. dazu ~, etw. zu tun** 〈*thing*〉 induce sb. to do sth.; 〈*person*〉 prevail upon sb. to do sth.; **Beweg·grund der** motive

beweglich *Adj.* **a)** movable; moving 〈*target*〉; **b)** *(rege)* agile 〈*mind*〉; **bewegt** *Adj.* eventful; *(unruhig)* turbulent; **Bewegung die;** ~, ~ movement; *(bes. Technik, Physik)* motion; **b)** *(körperliche ~)* exercise; **c)** *(Ergriffenheit)* emotion; **d)** *(Bestreben, Gruppe)* movement; **Bewegungs·freiheit die;** *o. Pl.* freedom of movement; **bewegungs·los** *Adj.* motionless

Beweis der; ~es, ~e proof *(Gen., für* of); **belastende** ~e incriminating evidence; **beweisbar** *Adj.* provable; **beweisen** *unr. tr. V.* prove; **Beweis·material das** evidence

bewenden *unr. V.* **es bei** *od.* **mit etw. ~ lassen** content oneself with sth.

bewerben *unr. refl. V.* apply **(bei** to, um for); **Bewerber der** applicant; **Bewerbung die** application

bewerfen *unr. tr. V.* **jmdn./etw. mit etw. ~:** throw sth. at sb./sth.

bewerten *tr. V.* assess; rate; *(dem Geldwert nach)* value **(mit** at); **Bewertung die** assessment; *(dem Geldwert nach)* valuation

bewilligen *tr. V.* grant; **Bewilligung die;** ~, ~en granting

bewirken *tr. V.* bring about; cause

bewirten *tr. V.* feed; **jmdn. mit etw. ~:** serve sb. sth.

bewirtschaften *tr. V.* **a)** manage

〈*estate, farm, restaurant, business, etc.*〉; **b)** farm 〈*fields, land*〉

Bewirtung die; ~, ~en provision of food and drink

bewog *l. u. 3. Pers. Sg. Prät. v.* **²bewegen**

bewohnbar *Adj.* habitable; **bewohnen** *tr. V.* inhabit, live in 〈*house, area*〉; live in 〈*room, flat*〉; **Bewohner der;** ~s, ~, **Bewohnerin die;** ~, ~nen *(eines Hauses, einer Wohnung)* occupant; *(einer Stadt, eines Gebietes)* inhabitant; **bewohnt** *Adj.* occupied 〈*house etc.*〉; inhabited 〈*area*〉

bewölken *refl. V.* cloud over; become overcast; **bewölkt** *Adj.* cloudy; overcast; **Bewölkung die;** ~, ~en cloud [cover]

Bewunderer der; ~s, ~, **Bewunderin die;** ~, ~nen admirer; **bewundern** *tr. V.* admire (wegen, für for); **bewunderns·wert** *Adj.* **a)** admirable; 2. *adv.* admirably; **Bewunderung die;** ~: admiration

bewußt 1. *Adj.* conscious 〈*reaction, behaviour, etc.*〉; *(absichtlich)* deliberate 〈*lie, deception, attack, etc.*〉; **etw. ist/wird jmdm. ~:** sb. is/becomes aware of sth.; sb. realizes sth.; **sich** *(Dat.)* **einer Sache** *(Gen.)* ~ **sein/werden** be/become aware of something; 2. *adv.* consciously; *(absichtlich)* deliberately; **bewußt·los** *Adj.* unconscious; **Bewußtlosigkeit die;** ~: unconsciousness; **Bewußt·sein das a)** consciousness; **das ~ verlieren/wiedererlangen** lose/regain consciousness; **bei vollem ~ sein** be fully conscious; **b)** *(deutliches Wissen)* awareness

bezahlbar *Adj.* affordable; **bezahlen** 1. *tr. V.* pay 〈*person, bill, taxes, rent, amount*〉; pay for 〈*goods etc.*〉; **das macht sich bezahlt** it pays off; 2. *itr. V.* pay; **Herr Ober, ich möchte ~** *od.* **bitte ~:** waiter, the bill *or (Amer.)* check please; **Bezahlung die** payment; *(Lohn, Gehalt)* pay

bezaubernd 1. *Adj.* enchanting; 2. *adv.* enchantingly

bezeichnen *tr. V.* **a)** jmdn./sich/etw. **als etw. ~:** call sb./oneself/sth. sth.; **b)** *(Name, Wort sein für)* denote; **bezeichnend** *Adj.* characteristic **(für** of); **Bezeichnung die** **a)** marking; *(Angabe durch Zeichen)* indication; **b)** *(Name)* name

bezeugen *tr. V.* testify to

bezichtigen *tr. V.* accuse

beziehen 1. *unr. tr. V.* **a)** cover ⟨*seat, cushion, etc.*⟩; **die Betten frisch ~:** put clean sheets on the beds; **b)** *(einziehen in)* move into ⟨*house, office*⟩; **c)** *(Milit.)* take up ⟨*position, post*⟩; **d)** *(erhalten)* obtain ⟨*goods*⟩; take ⟨*newspaper*⟩; draw ⟨*pension, salary*⟩; **e)** *(in Beziehung setzen)* apply **(auf** + *Akk.* to); **2.** *unr. refl. V.* **a)** **es/der Himmel bezieht sich** it/the sky is clouding over *or* becoming overcast; **b)** **sich auf jmdn./ etw.** ~ *(sich berufen auf)* ⟨*person, letter, etc.*⟩ refer to sb./sth.; *(betreffen)* ⟨*question, statement, etc.*⟩ relate to sb./sth.; **wir** ~ **uns auf Ihr Schreiben vom 28. 8.** with reference to your letter of 28 August; **Beziehung die a)** relation; *(Zusammenhang)* connection **(zu** with); **zwischen A und B besteht keine/eine ~:** there is no/a connection between A and B; **b)** *(Freundschaft, Liebes~)* relationship; **c)** *(Hinsicht)* respect; **in mancher** ~: in many respects; **beziehungs·weise** *Konj.* and ... respectively; *(oder)* or

Bezirk der; ~[e]s, ~e district

bezug: **in** ~ **auf jmdn./etw.** regarding sb./sth.

Bezug der a) *(für Kissen usw.)* cover; *(für Polstermöbel)* loose cover; slipcover *(Amer.)*; *(für Betten)* duvet cover; *(für Kopfkissen)* pillowcase; **b)** *o. Pl. (Erwerb)* obtaining; *(Kauf)* purchase; ~ **einer Zeitung** taking a newspaper; **c)** *Pl.* salary *sing.*; **d)** *(Papierdt.)* **mit od. unter ~ auf etw.** *(Akk.)* with reference to sth.; ~ **nehmend auf unser Telex** with reference to our telex; **bezüglich** *Präp. mit Gen.* regarding

bezwecken *tr. V.* aim to achieve

bezweifeln *tr. V.* doubt

bezwingen *unr. tr. V.* conquer ⟨*enemy, mountain, pain, etc.*⟩; defeat ⟨*opponent*⟩; capture ⟨*fortress*⟩

BH [beːˈhaː] *der*; ~[s], ~[s] *Abk.:* Büstenhalter bra

Bibel die; ~, ~n *(auch fig.)* Bible

Biber der; ~s, ~: beaver

Bibliothek die; ~, ~en library

biblisch *Adj.* biblical

Bidet [biˈdeː] *das*; ~s, ~s bidet

bieder *Adj.* unsophisticated; *(langweilig)* stolid; *(treuherzig)* trusting

biegen 1. *unr. tr. V.* bend; **2.** *unr. refl. V.* bend; *(nachgeben)* give; **3.** *unr. itr. V.; mit sein* turn; **biegsam** *Adj.* flexible; pliable ⟨*material*⟩; **Biegung die**; ~, ~en bend

Biene die; ~, ~n bee

Bienen-: ~**honig** der bees' honey; ~**königin die** queen bee; ~**korb** der straw hive; ~**stock** der beehive

Bier das; ~[e]s, ~e beer

Bier-: ~**deckel** der beer-mat; ~**dose die** beer can; ~**faß das** beer-barrel; ~**flasche die** beer-bottle; ~**garten** der beer garden; ~**glas das** beer-glass; ~**kasten** der beer-crate; ~**zelt das** beer tent

Biest das; ~[e]s, ~er *(ugs. abwertend)* **a)** *(Tier, Gegenstand)* wretched thing; **b)** *(Mensch)* wretch

bieten 1. *unr. tr. V.* **a)** offer; put on ⟨*programme etc.*⟩; provide ⟨*shelter, guarantee, etc.*⟩; **b)** **ein schreckliches Bild** ~: present a terrible picture; **einen prächtigen Anblick** ~: be a splendid sight; **2.** *unr. refl. V.* **sich jmdm.** ~: present itself to sb.; **3.** *unr. itr. V.* bid

Bigamie die; ~: bigamy *no def. art.*

Bikini der; ~s, ~s bikini

Bilanz die; ~, ~en **a)** balance sheet; **b)** *(Ergebnis)* outcome; ~ **ziehen** take stock

Bild das; ~[e]s, ~er **a)** picture; **b)** *(Anblick)* sight; **c)** *(Metapher)* image

bilden 1. *tr. V.* **a)** form ⟨*as from*⟩; *(modellieren)* mould **(aus** from); **eine Gasse** ~: make a path; **sich** *(Dat.)* **ein Urteil** ~: form an opinion; **b)** *(ansammeln)* build up ⟨*fund, capital*⟩; **c)** *(darstellen)* be ⟨*exception etc.*⟩; **d)** *(erziehen)* educate; **2.** *refl. V.* **a)** form; **b)** *(lernen)* educate oneself

Bilder·buch das picture-book *(for children)*

Bild·hauer der sculptor

bild·hübsch *Adj.* really lovely; stunningly beautiful ⟨*girl*⟩

bildlich 1. *Adj.* pictorial; *(übertragen)* figurative; **2.** *adv.* pictorially; *(übertragen)* figuratively; **Bildnis** [ˈbɪltnɪs] *das*; ~ses, ~se portrait

Bild·schirm der *(Ferns., Informationst.)* screen; **Bildschirm·gerät das** VDU; visual display unit

bild·schön *Adj.* really lovely; stunningly beautiful ⟨*girl, woman*⟩

Bildung die; ~, ~en **a)** *(Erziehung)* education; *(Kultur)* culture; **b)** *(das Formen)* formation; **Bildungs·lücke die** gap in one's education

Billard [ˈbɪljart, *österr.:* biˈjaːʁ] *das*; ~s, ~e billiards

Billard-: ~**kugel die** billiard-ball; ~**stock der** billiard-cue; ~**tisch der** billiard-table

Billett [bɪl'jet] *das;* ~[e]s, ~e *od.* ~s *(schweiz., veralt.)* ticket

Billiarde die; ~, ~n thousand million million; quadrillion *(Amer.)*

billig 1. *Adj.* a) cheap; b) *(abwertend: primitiv)* cheap ⟨trick⟩; feeble ⟨excuse⟩; **2.** *adv.* cheaply

billigen *tr. V.* approve; **Billigung die;** ~: approval

Billion die; ~, ~en million million; trillion *(Amer.)*

bimmeln *itr. V. (ugs.)* ring

bin *1. Pers. Sg. Präsens v.* ¹sein

Binde die; ~, ~n a) *(Verband)* bandage; *(Augen~)* blindfold; b) *(Arm~)* armband

Binde-: ~**gewebe das** *(Anat.)* connective tissue; ~**haut die** *(Anat.)* conjunctiva

binden 1. *unr. tr. V.* a) *(auch fig.)* tie; knot ⟨tie⟩; make up ⟨wreath, bouquet⟩; **jmdn. an sich** *(Akk.)* ~ *(fig.)* make sb. dependent on one; b) *(fesseln, festhalten, zusammenhalten, fig.: verpflichten, Buchw.)* bind; c) *(Kochk.: legieren)* thicken ⟨sauce⟩; **2.** *unr. refl. V.* tie oneself down; **Binder der;** ~s, ~ tie; **Bindestrich der** hyphen; **Bind·faden der** string

Bindung die; ~, ~en a) *(Beziehung)* relationship (**an** + *Akk.* to); b) *(Verbundenheit)* attachment (**an** + *Akk.* to); c) *(Ski~)* binding

binnen *Präp. mit Dat. od. (geh.) Gen.* within

Binsen·weisheit die truism

bio-, Bio: ~**chemie die** biochemistry; ~**graph der;** ~en, ~en biographer; ~**graphie die;** ~, ~n biography; ~**graphisch** *Adj.* biographical; ~**loge der;** ~n, ~n biologist; ~**logie die;** ~: biology *no art.;* ~**logisch** *Adj.* a) biological; b) *(natürlich)* natural ⟨medicine, cosmetic, etc.⟩; ~**top der** *od.* **das;** ~s, ~e *(Biol.)* biotope

Birke die; ~, ~n birch[-tree]; *(Holz)* birch[wood]

Birma (das); ~s Burma

Birn·baum der pear-tree; **Birne die;** ~, ~n a) pear; b) *(Glüh~)* [light-]bulb; c) *(salopp: Kopf)* nut *(sl.)*

bis 1. *Präp. mit Akk.* a) *(zeitlich)* until; till; *(die ganze Zeit über und bis zu einem bestimmten Zeitpunkt)* up until; *(nicht später als)* by; b) *(räumlich)* to; **dieser Zug fährt nur ~ Offenburg** this train only goes as far as Offenburg; ~ **5 000 Mark** up to 5,000

marks; c) ~ **auf** *(einschließlich)* down to; *(mit Ausnahme von)* except for; **2.** *Adv.* ~ **zu 6 Personen** up to six people. **3.** *Konj.* a) *(nebenordnend)* by; b) *(unterordnend)* until; till; *(österr.: sobald)* when

Bisam·ratte die musk-rat

Bischof der; ~s, **Bischöfe** bishop; **bischöflich** *Adj.* episcopal

bis·her *Adv.* up to now; *(aber jetzt nicht mehr)* until now; till now; **bisherig** *Adj. (vorherig)* previous; *(momentan)* present

Biskaya [bɪs'ka:ja] **die;** ~: the Bay of Biscay

Biskuit [bɪs'kvi:t] **das** *od.* **der;** ~[e]s, ~s *od.* ~e a) sponge biscuit; b) *(~teig)* sponge

bis·lang *Adv.; s.* **bisher**

Bison der; ~s, ~s bison

Biß der; Bisses, Bisse bite

bißchen *indekl. Indefinitpron.* a) *adj.* **ein** ~ **Geld/Wasser** a bit of *or* a little money/a drop of water; **ein/kein** ~ **Angst haben** be a bit/not a bit frightened; b) *adv.* **ein/kein** ~ a bit *or* a little/not a *or* one bit; c) *subst.* **ein** ~: a bit; a little; *(bei Flüssigkeiten)* a drop; a little; **das/kein** ~: the little [bit]/not a *or* one bit

Bissen der; ~s, ~: mouthful

bissig 1. *Adj.* a) ~ **sein** ⟨dog⟩ bite; **ein** ~**er Hund** a dog that bites; „**Vorsicht, ~er Hund**" 'beware of the dog'; b) *(schneidend)* cutting ⟨remark, tone, etc.⟩; **2.** *adv.* ⟨say⟩ cuttingly

Biß·wunde die bite

bist *2. Pers. Sg. Präsens v.* ¹sein

Bistum ['bɪstu:m] **das;** ~s, **Bistümer** bishopric; diocese

bis·weilen *Adv. (geh.)* from time to time

bitte 1. *Adv.* please; **2.** *Interj.* a) *(Bitte, Aufforderung)* please; **zwei Tassen Tee, ~:** two cups of tea, please; **~[, nehmen Sie doch Platz]!** do take a seat; **Noch eine Tasse Tee? –** |**Ja**| ~! Another cup of tea? – Yes, please; b) *(Aufforderung, etw. anzunehmen)* ~ |**schön** *od.* **sehr**|! there you are!; c) *(Ausdruck des Einverständnisses)* ~ |**gern**|! certainly; of course; **Entschuldigung! – Bitte!** [I'm] sorry! – That's all right!; d) ~ |**schön** *od.* **sehr**|! *(im Laden, Lokal)* yes, please?; e) |**wie**| ~? *(Nachfrage)* sorry; f) **Vielen Dank! – Bitte** |**schön** *od.* **sehr**| Many thanks! – Not at all *or* you're welcome

Bitte die; ~, ~n request; *(inständig)* plea; **bitten** *unr. tr. V.* **a)** *auch itr.* ask (um for); **darf ich Sie um Feuer/ein Glas Wasser ~?** could I ask you for a light/a glass of water, please?; **b)** *(einladen)* ask

bitter 1. *Adj.* **a)** bitter; plain ⟨*chocolate*⟩; **b)** *(fig.) (verbittert)* bitter; **c)** *(schmerzlich)* bitter, painful, hard ⟨*loss*⟩; hard ⟨*time, fate, etc.*⟩; dire ⟨*need*⟩; desperate ⟨*poverty*⟩; grievous ⟨*injustice, harm*⟩; 2. *adv. (sehr stark)* desperately; ⟨*regret*⟩ bitterly

bitter-: ~böse 1. *Adj.* furious; 2. *adv.* furiously; **~kalt** *Adj.; präd. getrennt geschr.* bitterly cold

bitterlich 1. *Adj.* slightly bitter ⟨*taste*⟩. 2. *adv. (heftig)* ⟨*cry, complain, etc.*⟩ bitterly; **bitter·süß** *Adj. (auch fig.)* bitter-sweet

Bitt·steller der; ~s, ~ petitioner

Biwak das; ~s, ~s *(bes. Milit., Bergsteigen)* bivouac

bizarr 1. *Adj.* bizarre; 2. *adv.* bizarrely

Bizeps der; ~⟨es⟩, ~e biceps

Blähung die; ~, ~en flatulence no art., no pl.

Blamage [bla'ma:ʒə] die; ~, ~n disgrace; **blamieren** 1. *tr. V.* disgrace; 2. *refl. V.* disgrace oneself; *(sich lächerlich machen)* make a fool of oneself

blank *Adj.* shiny

Blanko-: ~scheck der *(auch fig.)* blank cheque; **~vollmacht** die *(auch fig.)* carte blanche

Bläschen ['blɛːsçən] das; ~s, ~ a) [small] bubble; b) *(in der Haut)* [small] blister; **Blase** die; ~, ~n a) bubble; b) *(in der Haut)* blister; c) *(Harn~)* bladder; **Blase·balg** der bellows *pl.*; **blasen** 1. *unr. itr. V.* blow; 2. *unr. tr. V.* a) blow; b) *(spielen)* play ⟨*musical instrument, tune, melody, etc.*⟩; **Bläser** der; ~s, ~ *(Musik)* wind player

blasiert *(abwertend)* 1. *Adj.* blasé; 2. *adv.* in a blasé way

Blas-: ~instrument das wind instrument; **~kapelle** die brass band; **~musik** die brass-band music

Blasphemie [blasfe'mi:] die; ~, ~n blasphemy

Blas·rohr das blowpipe

blaß 1. *Adj.* pale; 2. *adv.* palely; **Blässe** die; ~: paleness

Blatt das; ~⟨e⟩s, **Blätter** a) *(von Pflanzen)* leaf; b) *(Papier)* sheet; c) *(Buchseite usw.)* page; etw. vom ~ spielen sight-read sth.; d) *(Zeitung)* paper; e)

(Spielkarten) hand; **f)** *(am Werkzeug, Ruder)* blade; **Blättchen** das; ~s, ~ a) *(von Pflanzen)* [small] leaf; b) *(Papier)* [small] sheet; **blättern** *itr. V.* in einem Buch ~: leaf through a book; **Blätter·teig** der puff pastry

Blatt-: ~gold das; *o. Pl.* gold leaf; **~laus** die aphid

blau *Adj.* blue; **ein ~er Fleck** a bruise; **~ sein** *(fig. ugs.)* be tight *(coll.)*; **das Blaue vom Himmel herunterlügen** *(ugs.)* lie like anything; **Blau** das; ~s, ~ *od. (ugs.:)* ~s blue

blau-, Blau-: ~äugig *Adj.* a) blue-eyed; b) *(naiv)* naive; **~beere** die bilberry; **~grau** *Adj.* blue-grey; **~grün** *Adj.* blue-green

bläulich *Adj.* bluish

blau-, Blau-: ~licht das flashing blue light; **~machen** *itr. V. (ugs.)* skip work; **~mann** der; *Pl.* **~männer** *(ugs.)* boiler suit; **~säure** die; *o. Pl. (Chemie)* prussic acid; **~stichig** *Adj. (Fot.)* with a blue cast *postpos., not pred.*; **~stichig sein** have a blue cast

Blazer ['ble:zɐ] der; ~s, ~: blazer

Blech das; ~⟨e⟩s, ~e a) sheet metal; *(Stück Blech)* metal sheet; b) *(Back~)* [baking] tray

Blech-: ~büchse die, **~dose** die tin

blechen *tr., itr. V. (ugs.)* cough up *(sl.)*

blechern *Adj.* 1. *(metallisch klingend)* tinny ⟨*sound, voice*⟩; 2. *adv.* tinnily

Blech-: ~musik die *(abwertend)* brass-band music; **~napf** der metal bowl

Blechner der; ~s, ~ *(südd.)* s. **Klempner**

Blech-: ~schaden der *(Kfz-W.)* damage no indef. art. to the bodywork; **~trommel** die tin drum

blecken *tr. V.* **die Zähne ~:** bare one's/its teeth

Blei das; ~⟨e⟩s, ~e lead

Bleibe die; ~, ~n place to stay; **bleiben** *unr. itr. V.; mit sein* a) stay; remain; **~ Sie bitte am Apparat** hold the line please; **wo bleibt er so lange?** where has he got to?; **auf dem Weg ~:** keep to the path; **sitzen ~:** stay or remain sitting down or seated; **bei etw. ~:** *(fig.: an etw. festhalten)* keep to sth.; b) *(übrigbleiben)* be left; remain; **bleibend** *Adj.* lasting; permanent ⟨*damage*⟩; **bleiben|lassen** *unr. tr. V.* **etw. ~:** give sth. a miss

bleich *Adj.* pale; **¹bleichen** *tr. V.* bleach; **²bleichen** *regelm., veralt. auch unr. itr. V.* become bleached

blei-, Blei-: ~frei *Adj.* unleaded ⟨*fuel*⟩; **~kristall das** lead crystal; **~kugel die** lead ball; *(Geschoß)* lead bullet; **~schwer** *Adj.* heavy as lead *postpos.*; **~stift der** pencil; **mit ~:** in pencil; **~stift·spitzer der** pencil-sharpener

Blende die ~, ~n **a)** *(Lichtschutz)* shade; *(am Fenster)* blind; **b)** *(Optik, Film, Fot.)* diaphragm; *(Blendenzahl)* aperture setting; **blenden** 1. *tr. V.* **a)** *(auch fig.)* dazzle; **b)** *(blind machen)* blind; 2. *itr. V.* ⟨*light*⟩ be dazzling; **blendend** 1. *Adj.* es geht mir ~: I feel wonderfully well; 2. *adv.* wir haben uns ~ amüsiert we had a marvellous time

blich *1. u. 3. Pers. Sg. Prät. v.* **²bleichen**

Blick der; ~[e]s, ~e a) look; *(flüchtig)* glance; **b)** *(Ausdruck)* look in one's eyes; **mit mißtrauischem ~:** with a suspicious look in one's eye; **c)** *(Aussicht)* view; **ein Zimmer mit ~ aufs Meer** a room with a sea view; **d)** *o. Pl. (Urteil[skraft])* eye; **blicken** 1. *itr. V.* look; *(flüchtig)* glance; 2. *tr. V.* **sich ~ lassen** put in an appearance

Blick-: ~feld das field of vision; **~punkt der** view; **~winkel der a)** angle of vision; **b)** *(fig.)* point of view; viewpoint

blieb *1. u. 3. Pers. Sg. Prät. v.* bleiben

blies *1. u. 3. Pers. Sg. Prät. v.* blasen

blind 1. *Adj.* **a)** *(auch fig.)* blind; **~ werden** go blind; **b)** *(trübe)* clouded ⟨*glass*⟩; **c) ein ~er Passagier** a stowaway; **d) ~er Alarm** a false alarm; 2. *adv.* **a)** *(ohne hinzusehen)* without looking; *(wahllos)* blindly; **b)** *(unkritisch)* ⟨*trust*⟩ implicitly; ⟨*obey*⟩ blindly; **Blind·darm der a)** caecum; **b)** *(volkst.: Wurmfortsatz)* appendix; **Blinde der/die;** *adj. Dekl.* blind person; blind man/woman; **die ~n** the blind; **Blinde·kuh** *o. Art.* blind man's buff

Blinden-: ~hund der guide-dog; **~schrift die** Braille

Blindheit die ~ *(auch fig.)* blindness; **blindlings** *Adv.* blindly; ⟨*trust*⟩ implicitly; **Blind·schleiche die; ~, ~n** slowworm; **blind·wütig** 1. *Adj.* raging ⟨*anger, hatred, fury, etc.*⟩; wild ⟨*rage*⟩; 2. *adv.* in a blind rage

blinken 1. *itr. V.* **a)** ⟨*light, glass, crystal*⟩ flash; ⟨*star*⟩ twinkle; ⟨*metal, fish*⟩ gleam; **b)** *(Verkehrsw.)* indicate; 2. *tr. V.* flash; **Blinker der; ~s, ~** indicator [light]

Blink-: ~licht das a) flashing light; **b)** *s.* **Blinker; ~zeichen das** flashlight signal

blinzeln *itr. V.* blink; *(mit einem Auge, um ein Zeichen zu geben)* wink

Blitz der; ~es, ~e a) lightning *no indef. art.*; **ein ~:** a flash of lightning; **[schnell] wie der ~:** like lightning; **b)** *(~licht)* flash

blitz-, Blitz-: ~ableiter der lightning-conductor; **~artig** 1. *Adj.* lightning; 2. *adv.* like lightning; *(disappear)* in a flash; **~blank** *Adj. (ugs.)* **~blank [geputzt]** sparkling clean; brightly polished ⟨*shoes*⟩

blitzeblank *s.* blitzblank; **blitzen** *itr. V.* **a)** *unpers.* **es blitzte** *(einmal)* there was a flash of lightning; *(mehrmals)* there was lightning; **b)** *(glänzen)* ⟨*light, glass, crystal*⟩ flash; ⟨*metal*⟩ gleam

blitz-, Blitz-: ~gerät das flash [unit]; **~licht das;** *Pl.* **~lichter** flash[light]; **~schnell** 1. *Adj.* lightning *attrib.;* **~schnell sein** be like lightning; 2. *adv.* like lightning; *(disappear)* in a flash; **~start der** the lightning start

Block der; ~[e]s, Blöcke *od.* **~s a)** *Pl. nur* **Blöcke** *(Brocken)* block; **b)** *(Wohn~)* block; **c)** *Pl. nur* **Blöcke** *(Gruppierung von politischen Kräften, Staaten)* bloc; **d)** *(Schreib~)* pad

Blockade die; ~, ~n blockade

Block-: ~flöte die recorder; **~haus das, ~hütte die** log cabin

blockieren *tr. V.* block; jam *(telephone line)*; halt *(traffic)*; lock ⟨*wheel, machine, etc.*⟩

Block·schrift die block capitals *pl.*

blöd[e] *(ugs.)* 1. *Adj.* **a)** *(dumm)* stupid; idiotic *(coll.);* **b)** *(unangenehm)* stupid; 2. *adv.* stupidly; idiotically *(coll.);* **Blödelei die; ~, ~en** silly joke; **blödeln** *itr. V.* make silly jokes; **Blödheit die; ~, ~en** stupidity

blöd-, Blöd-: ~mann der; *Pl.* **~männer** *(salopp)* stupid idiot *(coll.);* **~sinn der;** *o. Pl. (ugs.)* nonsense; **mach doch keinen ~sinn!** don't be stupid; **~sinnig** *(ugs.)* 1. *Adj.* idiotic *(coll.);* 2. *adv.* idiotically *(coll.)*

blöken *itr. V.* ⟨*sheep*⟩ bleat; ⟨*cattle*⟩ low

blond *Adj.* fair-haired, blond ⟨*man, race*⟩; blonde ⟨*woman*⟩; blond/blonde, fair ⟨*hair*⟩; **Blondine die; ~, ~n** blonde

bloß 1. *Adj.* **a)** *(nackt)* naked; **b)** *(nichts als)* mere ⟨*words, promises, tri-*

viality, suspicion, etc.); der ~e Gedanke daran the mere thought of it; **2.**
Adv. (ugs.: nur) only; **3. Partikel** was
hast du dir ~ dabei gedacht? what on
earth were you thinking of?; **Blöße**
die; ~: *sich (Dat.)* eine/keine ~ geben
show a/not show any weakness;
bloß|stellen *tr. V.* show up; expose
(swindler, criminal, etc.)

Blouson [blu'zõ:] das *od.* der; ~[s], ~s
blouson

blubbern *itr. V. (ugs.)* bubble

Bluejeans, Blue jeans ['blu:dʒi:ns]
Pl. od. die; ~, ~: [blue] jeans *pl.*

Blues [blu:s] der; ~, ~: blues *pl.*

Bluff der; ~s, ~s bluff; **bluffen** *tr., itr.
V.* bluff

blühen *itr. V.* a) *(plant)* flower, be in
flower *or* bloom; *(flower)* be in
bloom, be out; *(tree)* be in blossom;
~de Gärten gardens full of flowers; b)
(florieren) thrive; c) *(ugs.: bevorstehen)* jmdm. ~ be in store for sb.; das
kann dir auch noch ~: the same could
happen to you; **blühend** *Adj.* a)
(frisch, gesund) glowing *(colour, complexion, etc.)*; radiant *(health)*; b)
(übertrieben) vivid *(imagination)*

Blümchen das; ~s, ~: [little] flower;
Blume die; ~, ~n a) flower; b) *(des
Weines)* bouquet; c) *(des Biers)* head

blumen-, Blumen-: ~beet das
flower-bed; ~erde die potting compost; ~geschäft das florist's; ~ge-
schmückt *Adj.* flower-bedecked;
adorned with flowers *postpos.*; ~ka-
sten der flower-box; *(vor einem Fenster)* window box; ~kohl der cauliflower; ~strauß der bunch of
flowers; *(Bukett)* bouquet of flowers;
~topf der flowerpot; ~vase die
[flower] vase; ~zwiebel die bulb

Bluse die; ~, ~n blouse

Blut das; ~[e]s blood

blut-, Blut-: ~arm *Adj. (Med.)* anaemic; ~armut die *(Med.)* anaemia;
~bad das blood-bath; ~bahn die
bloodstream; ~befleckt *Adj.* blood-
stained; ~beschmiert *Adj.* smeared
with blood *postpos.*; ~buche die copper beech; ~druck der blood pressure

Blüte die; ~, ~n a) flower; bloom; *(eines Baums)* blossom; ~n treiben
flower; *(tree)* blossom; b) *(das Blühen)* flowering; *(Baum~)* blossoming

Blut·egel der leech; **bluten** *itr. V.*
bleed *(aus from)*

blüten-, Blüten-: ~blatt das petal;

~honig der blossom honey; ~staub
der pollen; ~weiß *Adj.* sparkling
white

Bluter der; ~s, ~ *(Med.)* haemophiliac

Blut-: ~erguß der haematoma; *(blauer Fleck)* bruise; ~fleck[en] der
blood-stain; ~gefäß das *(Anat.)*
blood-vessel; ~gerinnsel das blood-
clot; ~gruppe die blood group;
~hochdruck der high blood pressure; ~hund der bloodhound

blutig a) bloody; jmdn. ~ schlagen
beat sb. to a pulp; b) *(fig. ugs.: völlig)*
complete *(beginner, layman, etc.)*

blut-, Blut-: ~jung *Adj.* very young;
~konserve die container of stored
blood; ~konserven stored blood;
~körperchen das blood corpuscle;
rote/weiße ~körperchen red/white
corpuscles; ~krebs der leukaemia;
~kreislauf der blood circulation;
~lache die pool of blood; ~leer *Adj.*
bloodless; ~leere die restricted
blood supply; ~orange die blood
orange; ~probe die a) *(~entnahme,
~untersuchung)* blood test; b) *(kleine
~menge)* blood sample; ~rache die
blood revenge; ~rot *Adj.* blood-red;
~rünstig 1. *Adj.* bloodthirsty; 2.
adv. bloodthirstily; ~schande die
incest; ~spende die *(das Spenden)*
giving no indef. art. of blood; *(~men-
ge)* blood-donation; ~spender der
blood-donor; ~spur die trail of
blood; ~stillend *Adj.* styptic

bluts-, Bluts-: ~tropfen der drop of
blood; ~verwandt *Adj.* related by
blood *postpos.*; ~verwandtschaft
die blood relationship

Blut-: ~tat die *(geh.)* bloody deed;
~transfusion die blood-transfusion

Blutung die; ~, ~en a) bleeding *no indef. art., no pl.*; b) *(Regel~)* period

blut-, Blut-: ~unterlaufen *Adj.* suf-
fused with blood *postpos.*; bloodshot
(eyes); ~vergießen das; ~s blood-
shed; ~vergiftung die blood-
poisoning *no indef. art., no pl.*;
~wurst die black pudding

Bö die; ~, ~en gust [of wind]

Bob der; ~, ~s bob[-sleigh]

Bob-: ~bahn die bob[-sleigh] run;
~fahrer der bobber

¹**Bock** der; ~[e]s, Böcke a) *(Reh~, Ka-
ninchen~)* buck; *(Ziegen~)* billy-
goat; he-goat; *(Schafs~)* ram; b) *(Gestell)* trestle; c) *(Turngerät)* buck

²**Bock** das; ~s *(Bier)* bock [beer];
Bock·bier das bock [beer]

bocken itr. V. refuse to go on; (vor einer Hürde) refuse; (sich aufbäumen) buck; **bockig 1.** Adj. stubborn and awkward; (coll.). **2.** adv. stubbornly [and awkwardly]; **Bocks·horn das: sich ins ~horn jagen lassen** (ugs.) let oneself be browbeaten

Bock-: **~springen das** (Turnen) vaulting [over the buck]; **~wurst die** bockwurst

Boden der; ~s, Böden a) (Erd~) ground; (Fuß~) floor; **am ~ zerstört [sein]** (ugs.) [be] shattered (coll.); **bleiben wir doch auf dem ~ der Tatsachen** (fig.) let's stick to the facts; b) (unterste Fläche) bottom; (Torten~) base; c) (Dach~, Heu~) loft

boden-, Boden-: **~belag** der floor-covering; **~frost** der ground frost; **~kammer die** attic; **~los Adj. a)** bottomless; b) (ugs.: unerhört) incredible (foolishness, meanness, etc.); **~nebel** der ground fog/mist; **~satz** der sediment; **~schätze** Pl. mineral resources

Boden·see der; o. Pl. Lake Constance

boden-, Boden-: **~ständig** Adj. indigenous (culture, population, etc.); **~turnen** das floor exercises pl.; **~welle die** bump

Bodybuilding [bɔdibildiŋ] das; ~s body-building no art.

Böe die; ~, ~n s. Bö

bog 1. u. 3. Pers. Sg. Prät. v. biegen

Bogen der; ~s, ~, (südd., österr.:) Bögen a) curve; (Math.) arc; b) (Archit.) arch; c) (Waffe, Musik: Geigen~ usw.) bow; d) (Papier~) sheet

bogen-, Bogen-: **~fenster** das arched window; **~förmig** Adj. arched; **~schießen** das archery no art.

Boheme [boˈɛːm] die; ~: bohemian society; **Bohemien** [boeˈmjɛː] der; ~s, ~s bohemian

Bohle die; ~, ~n [thick] plank

Böhnchen das; ~s, ~: [small] bean; **Bohne die;** ~, ~n bean; **nicht die ~** (ugs.) not one little bit

Bohnen-: **~eintopf** der bean stew; **~kaffee** der real coffee; **~kraut** das savory; **~stange die** (auch ugs.: Mensch) beanpole; **~stroh das: dumm wie ~stroh** (ugs.) as thick as two short planks (coll.); **~suppe** die bean soup

bohnern tr., itr. V. polish; **Bohner·wachs** das floor-polish

bohren 1. tr. V. a) bore; (mit Bohrer, Bohrmaschine) drill, bore (hole); sink (well, shaft, pole, post etc.) (in + Akk. into); b) (bearbeiten) drill (wood, concrete, etc.); c) (drücken in) bore (in + Akk. in[to]); **2.** itr. V. a) drill; **in der Nase ~:** pick one's nose; **nach Öl/Wasser usw. ~:** drill for oil/water etc.; b) (ugs.: drängen, fragen) keep on; **3.** refl. V. bore its way; **bohrend** Adj. a) gnawing (pain, hunger, remorse); b) (hartnäckig) piercing (look etc.); probing (question); **Bohrer** der; ~s, ~ drill; **Bohr·turm** der derrick; **Bohrung die;** ~, ~en drill-hole

böig Adj. gusty

Boiler [ˈbɔylɐ] der; ~s, ~: water-heater

Boje die; ~, ~n buoy

Bolivien [boˈliːvjən] (das); ~s Bolivia

Böller·schuß der gun salute

Boll·werk das bulwark; (fig.) bulwark; bastion; stronghold

Bolschewik der; ~en, ~i, (abwertend:) ~en Bolshevik; **Bolschewismus** der; ~: Bolshevism no art.; **Bolschewist** der; ~en, ~en Bolshevist; **bolschewistisch** Adj. Bolshevik

bolzen (ugs.) itr. V. kick the ball about **Bolzen** der; ~s, ~ bolt

bombardieren tr. V. a) bomb; b) (fig. ugs.) bombard; **Bombardierung die;** ~, ~en a) (Milit.) bombing; b) (fig. ugs.) bombardment

bombastisch 1. Adj. bombastic; **2.** adv. bombastically

Bombe die; ~, ~n bomb

Bomben-: **~angriff** der bomb attack; **~anschlag** der bomb attack; **~drohung die** bomb threat; **~erfolg** der (ugs.) smash hit (sl.); **~form** der (ugs.) top form

Bomber der; ~s, ~: bomber

Bon [bɔŋ] der; ~s, ~s a) voucher; coupon; b) (Kassenzettel) receipt

Bonbon [bɔŋˈbɔŋ] der od. (österr. nur) das; ~s, ~s sweet (Brit.); candy (Amer.); (fig.) treat

bongen tr. V. (ugs.) ring up

Bongo der; ~[s], ~s od. die; ~, ~s bongo [drum]

Bonmot [bõˈmoː] das; ~s, ~s bon mot

Bonze der; ~n, ~n bigwig (coll.)

Boom [buːm] der; ~s, ~s boom

Boot das; ~[e]s, ~e boat

Boots-: **~fahrt die** boat trip; **~haus** das boathouse; **~steg** der landing-stage; **~verleih** der boat-hire

¹**Bord** das; ~[e]s, ~e shelf

²**Bord** der; ~[e]s, ~e (eines Schiffes)

side; **an ~**: on board; **über ~**: overboard
Bordell das; ~s, ~e brothel
Bord·stein der kerb
Bordüre die; ~, ~n edging
borgen tr. V.: s. leihen
Borke die; ~, ~n bark
borniert 1. Adj. bigoted; 2. adv. in a bigoted way
Börse die; ~, ~n stock market; (Gebäude) stock exchange
Börsen-: **~krach** der stock-market crash; **~makler** der stockbroker
Borste die; ~, ~n bristle; **borstig** Adj. bristly
Borte die; ~, ~n braiding no indef. art.; edging no indef. art.
bös s. böse; **bös·artig** 1. Adj. a) malicious ⟨person, remark, etc.⟩; vicious ⟨animal⟩; b) (Med.) malignant; 2. adv. maliciously; **Bös·artigkeit** die a) maliciousness; (von Tieren) viciousness; b) (Med.) malignancy
Böschung die; ~, ~en embankment
böse 1. Adj. a) wicked; evil; b) (übel) bad ⟨times, illness, dream, etc.⟩; nasty ⟨experience, affair, situation, trick, surprise, etc.⟩; c) (ugs.) ⟨wütend⟩ mad (coll.); (verärgert) cross (coll.); d) (fam.: ungezogen) naughty; f) (ugs.: arg) terrible (coll.) ⟨pain, fall, shock, disappointment, storm, etc.⟩; 2. adv. a) (übel) ⟨end⟩ badly; **es war doch nicht ~ gemeint** I didn't mean it nastily; b) (ugs.) ⟨wütend⟩ angrily; (verärgert) crossly (coll.); c) (ugs.: sehr) terribly (coll.); **boshaft** 1. Adj. malicious; 2. adv. maliciously; **Boshaftigkeit** die; ~, ~en a) o. Pl. maliciousness; b) (Bemerkung) malicious remark; **Bosheit** die; ~, ~en a) o. Pl. malice; b) (Bemerkung) malicious remark
Boß der; Bosses, Bosse (ugs.) boss (coll.)
bös·willig 1. Adj. malicious; wilful ⟨desertion⟩; 2. adv. maliciously; wilfully ⟨desert⟩; **Bös·willigkeit** die; ~: malice; maliciousness
bot 1. u. 3. Pers. Sg. Prät. v. bieten
Botanik die; ~ botany no art.; **botanisch** 1. Adj. botanical; 2. adv. botanically
Bötchen das; ~s, ~ little boat
Bote der; ~n, ~n a) messenger; b) (Laufbursche) errand-boy; **Botschaft** die; ~, ~en a) message; b) (diplomatische Vertretung) embassy; **Botschafter** der; ~s, ~: ambassador

Böttcher der; ~s, ~: cooper
Bottich der; ~s, ~e tub
Bouillon [bul'jɔŋ] die; ~, ~s bouillon
Boulevard [bulə'va:ɐ̯] der; ~s, ~s boulevard
Bourgeoisie [burʒoa'zi:] die; ~, ~n bourgeoisie
Boutique [bu'ti:k] die; ~, ~s od. ~n boutique
Bowle ['bo:lə] die; ~, ~n punch (made of wine, champagne, sugar, and fruit or spices)
bowlen ['boʊlən] itr. V. bowl; **Bowling** ['boʊlɪŋ] das; ~s, ~s [ten-pin] bowling; **Bowling·bahn** die bowling-alley
Box die; ~, ~en a) box; b) (Lautsprecher) speaker; c) (Pferde-) [loose] box; d) (Motorsport) pit
boxen 1. itr. V. box; **gegen jmdn. ~**: fight sb.; box [against] sb.; 2. tr. V. punch; **Boxer** der; ~s, ~ (Sportler, Hund) boxer
Box-: **~handschuh** der boxing glove; **~kampf** der boxing match; (im Streit) fist-fight; **~ring** der boxing ring; **~sport** der; o. Pl. boxing no art.
Boy [bɔy] der; ~s, ~s servant; (im Hotel) page-boy
Boykott [bɔy'kɔt] der; ~[e]s, ~s boycott; **boykottieren** tr. V. boycott
¹brach 1. u. 3. Pers. Sg. Prät. v. brechen
²brach Adj. fallow; (auf Dauer) uncultivated
Brachial·gewalt die; o. Pl. brute force
Brach·land das fallow [land]; (auf Dauer) uncultivated land; **brach|liegen** itr. V. (auch fig.) lie fallow; (auf Dauer) lie waste
brachte 1. u. 3. Pers. Sg. Prät. v. bringen
Branche ['brɑ̃:ʃə] die; ~, ~n [branch of] industry
Brand der; ~[e]s, Brände fire; **beim ~ der Scheune** when the barn caught fire; **etw. in ~ stecken** set fire to sth.
branden itr. V. (geh.) break
Brandenburg (das); ~s Brandenburg
brand-, Brand-: **~marken** tr. V. brand ⟨person⟩; denounce ⟨thing⟩; **~neu** Adj. (ugs.) brand-new; **~salbe** die ointment for burns; **~schaden** der fire damage no pl., no indef. art.; **~stelle** die burn; **~stifter** der arsonist; **~stiftung** die arson
Brandung die; ~, ~en surf

Brand·wunde die burn
brannte *1. u. 3. Pers. Sg. Prät. v.* bren‐
nen
Brannt·wein der spirits *pl.; (Sorte)*
spirit
Brasilianer der; ~s, ~, Brazilian;
brasilianisch *Adj.* Brazilian; **Brasi‐**
lien [bra'zi:ljən] (das); ~s Brazil
brät *3. Pers. Sg. Präsens v.* braten;
Brat·apfel der baked apple; **braten**
unr. tr., itr. V. fry; *(im Backofen)*
roast; **Braten** der; ~s, ~ a) joint; b) *o.*
Pl. roast [meat] *no indef. art.*
Braten-: ~saft der meat juice[s *pl.*];
~soße die gravy
Brat-: ~fett das [cooking] fat; ~fisch
der fried fish; ~hähnchen das,
(südd., österr.) ~hendl das roast
chicken; *(gegrillt)* broiled chicken;
~hering der fried herring; ~kartof‐
feln *Pl.* fried potatoes; home fries
(Amer.); ~pfanne die frying-pan;
~spieß der spit; ~wurst die [fried/
grilled] sausage
Brauch der; ~[e]s, Bräuche custom
brauchbar *Adj.* useful; *(benutzbar)*
usable; wearable ⟨clothes⟩;
brauchen 1. *tr. V.* a) *(benötigen)*
need; b) *(aufwenden müssen)* mit dem
Auto braucht er zehn Minuten it takes
him ten minutes by car; wie lange
brauchst du dafür? how long will it
take you?; *(im allgemeinen)* how long
does it take you?; c) *(benutzen, ge‐*
brauchen) use; ich könnte es gut ~: I
could do with it; 2. *mod. V.; 2. Part*~:
need; du brauchst nicht zu helfen there
is no need [for you] to help; du
brauchst doch nicht gleich zu weinen
there's no need to start crying
Brauchtum ['brauxtu:m] das; ~s,
Bräuchtümer custom
Braue die; ~, ~n [eye]brow
brauen *tr. V.* brew; **Brauerei** die; ~,
~en brewery
braun *Adj.* brown; ~ werden *(sonnen‐*
gebräunt) get a tan; **Braun** das; ~s,
~, *(ugs.)* ~s brown; **Braun·bär** der
brown bear; **Bräune** die; ~: [sun]‐
tan; **bräunen** *tr. V.* a) tan; sich ~: get
a tan; b) *(Kochk.)* brown; **braun·ge‐**
brannt *Adj.* [sun‐]tanned; **Braun‐**
kohle die brown coal; lignite;
bräunlich *Adj.* brownish; **Bräu‐**
nung die; ~, ~en browning
Braus *s.* Saus
Brause die; ~, ~n a) fizzy drink;
(~pulver) sherbet; b) *(veralt.: Dusche)*
shower; **brausen** 1. *itr. V.* a) ⟨wind,

water, etc.⟩ roar; b) *(sich schnell bewe‐*
gen) race; c) *auch refl.: s.* duschen 1; 2.
tr. V. s. duschen 2
Brause-: ~pulver das sherbet; ~ta‐
blette die effervescent tablet
Braut die; ~, Bräute bride
Bräutigam der; ~s, ~e [bride]groom
Braut-: ~jungfer die bridesmaid;
~kleid das wedding dress; ~paar
das bride and groom
brav 1. *Adj.* a) *(artig)* good; b) *(redlich)*
honest; 2. *adv.* nun **iß schön** ~ deine
Suppe be a good boy/girl and eat up
your soup
bravo ['bra:vo] *Interj.* bravo; **Bravo**
das; ~s, ~s cheer; **Bravo·ruf** der
cheer
BRD [be:|ɛr'de:] die; ~ *Abk.* Bundesre‐
publik Deutschland FRG
Brech-: ~bohne die green bean;
~eisen das crowbar
brechen 1. *unr. tr. V.* a) break; sich
(Dat.) den Arm/das Genick ~: break
one's arm/neck; b) *(ablenken)* break
⟨waves⟩; refract ⟨light⟩; c) *(bezwingen)*
overcome ⟨resistance⟩; break ⟨will, si‐
lence, record, blockade, etc.⟩; d) *(nicht*
einhalten) break ⟨agreement, contract,
promise, the law, etc.⟩; e) *(ugs.: erbre‐*
chen) bring up. 2. *unr. itr. V.* a) mit
sein break; **brechend voll sein** be full
to bursting; b) mit jmdm. ~: break
with sb.; c) *mit sein* durch etw. ~:
break through sth.; d) *(ugs.: sich erbre‐*
chen) throw up. 3. *unr. refl. V.* ⟨waves
etc.⟩ break; ⟨rays etc.⟩ be refracted;
Brecher der; ~s, ~: breaker
Brech-: ~mittel das emetic; ~reiz
der nausea; ~stange die crowbar
Brei der; ~[e]s, ~e *(Hafer~)* porridge
(Brit.), oatmeal *(Amer.) no indef. art.;*
(Reis~) rice pudding; *(Grieß~)* se‐
molina *no indef. art.;* **breiig** *Adj.*
mushy
breit 1. *Adj.* a) wide; broad, wide
⟨hips, face, shoulders, forehead, etc.⟩;
etw. ~er machen widen sth.; die Beine
~ machen open one's legs; ein 5 cm
~er Saum a hem 5 cm wide; b) *(groß)*
die ~e Masse the general public;
2. *adv.* ~ gebaut sturdily built;
breit·beinig 1. *Adj.* rolling ⟨gait⟩; 2.
adv. with one's legs apart; **Breite**
die; ~, ~n a) *s.* breit 1 a: width;
breadth; b) *(Geogr.)* latitude;
breiten *(geh.) tr., refl. V.* spread
Breiten-: ~grad der degree of latit‐
ude; parallel *(~kreis);* ~kreis der
parallel

breit-, Breit-: ~|**machen** refl. V. (ugs.) **a)** take up room; **b)** (sich ausbreiten) be spreading; ~**schult[e]rig** Adj. broad-shouldered; ~**seite die** long side; (eines Schiffes) side; ~|**treten** unr. tr. V. (ugs. abwertend) go on about; ~**wand die** (Kino) big screen

Brems-: ~**backe die** brake-shoe; ~**belag der** brake lining

¹Bremse die; ~, ~n brake

²Bremse die; ~, ~n (Insekt) horse-fly

bremsen tr. V. **a)** auch itr. brake; **b)** (fig.) slow down (rate, development, production, etc.); restrict (imports etc.)

Brems-: ~**klotz der** brake pad; ~**licht das;** Pl. ~**lichter** brake-light; ~**pedal das** brake-pedal; ~**spur die** skid-mark; ~**weg der** braking distance

brenn·bar Adj. combustible; **brennen** 1. unr. itr. V. **a)** burn; (house etc.) be on fire; schnell/leicht ~: catch fire quickly/easily; **es brennt!** fire!; **b)** (glühen) be alight; **c)** (leuchten) be on; **das Licht ~ lassen** leave the light on; **d) die Sonne brannte** the sun was burning down; **e)** (schmerzen) (wound etc.) sting; (feet etc.) be sore; **f) darauf ~, etw. zu tun** be dying to do sth.; 2. unr. tr. V. **a)** burn (hole, pattern, etc.); **einem Tier ein Zeichen ins Fell ~:** brand an animal; **b)** (mit Hitze behandeln) fire (porcelain etc.); **c)** (rösten) roast (coffee-beans, almonds, etc.); **brennend** 1. Adj. (auch fig.) burning; (cigarette) urgent (topic); 2. adv. **es interessiert mich ~, ob ...:** I'm dying to know whether ...; **Brennessel die;** ~, ~n stinging nettle

Brenn-: ~**glas das** burning-glass; ~**holz das;** o. Pl. firewood; ~**material das** fuel; ~**nessel die** s. Brennessel; ~**punkt der** focus; ~**spiritus der** methylated spirits; ~**stoff der** fuel

brenzlig Adj. **a)** (smell, taste, etc.) of burning not pred.; **b)** (ugs.: gefährlich) dicey (sl.)

Bresche die; ~, ~n gap; breach; [für jmdn.] in die ~ springen stand in [for sb.]

Brett das; ~[e]s, ~er **a)** board; (lang und dick) plank; (Diele) floorboard; Schwarzes ~: notice-board; **ein ~ vor dem Kopf haben** (fig. ugs.) be thick; **b)** Pl. (Ski) skis

Bretter-: ~**wand die** wooden partition; ~**zaun der** wooden fence

Brett·spiel das board game

Brezel die; ~, ~n pretzel

Bridge [brɪtʃ] **das;** ~: bridge

Brief der; ~[e]s, ~e letter

Brief-: ~**beschwerer der;** ~s, ~: paperweight; ~**block der;** Pl. ~**blocks** writing-pad; ~**bogen der** sheet of writing-paper; ~**freund der** pen-friend; pen-pal (coll.); ~**geheimnis das** privacy of the post; ~**karte die** correspondence card; ~**kasten der a)** post-box; **b)** (privat) letter-box; ~**kopf der a)** letter-heading; **b)** (aufgedruckt) letter-head; ~**kuvert das** (veralt.) s. ~**umschlag**

brieflich 1. Adj. written; 2. adv. by letter; **Brief·marke die** [postage] stamp

Briefmarken-: ~**album das** stamp-album; ~**sammler der** stamp-collector; ~**sammlung die** stamp-collection

Brief-: ~**öffner der** letter-opener; ~**papier das** writing-paper; ~**partner der,** ~**partnerin die** pen-friend; ~**schreiber der** [letter-]writer; ~**tasche die** wallet; ~**taube die** carrier pigeon; ~**träger der** postman; letter-carrier (Amer.); ~**trägerin die** postwoman; [female] letter-carrier (Amer.); ~**um·schlag der** envelope; ~**waage die** letter-scales pl.; ~**wahl die** postal vote; ~**wechsel der** correspondence

Bries das; ~es, ~e (Kochk.) sweetbreads pl.

briet 1 u. 3. Pers. Sg. Prät. v. braten

Brigade die; ~, ~n (Milit.) brigade

Brikett das; ~s, ~s briquette

brillant [brɪl'jant] 1. Adj. brilliant. 2. adv. brilliantly; **Brillant der;** ~en, ~en brilliant

Brillant-: ~**ring der** (brilliant-cut) diamond ring; ~**schmuck der;** o. Pl. (brilliant-cut) diamond jewellery

Brillanz die; ~ brilliance

Brille die; ~, ~n **a)** glasses pl.; spectacles pl.; **eine ~:** a pair of glasses or spectacles; **eine ~ tragen** wear glasses or spectacles; **b)** (ugs.: Klosett~) [lavatory] seat

Brillen-: ~**etui das,** ~**futteral das** glasses-case; spectacle-case; ~**glas das** [spectacle-]lens; ~**schlange die** spectacled cobra; ~**träger der** person who wears glasses; ~ **sein** wear glasses

Brimborium das; ~s (ugs. abwertend) hoo-ha (coll.)

bringen *unr. tr. V.* **a)** *(her~)* bring; *(hin~)* take; **jmdm. Glück/Unglück ~:** bring sb. [good] luck/bad luck; **jmdm. eine Nachricht ~:** bring sb. news; **b)** *(begleiten)* take; **jmdn. nach Hause/zum Bahnhof ~:** take sb. home/to the station; **c) es zu etwas/nichts ~:** get somewhere/get nowhere; **d) jmdn. ins Gefängnis ~** *(crime, misdeed)* land sb. in gaol; **jmdn. wieder auf den rechten Weg ~** *(fig.)* get sb. back on the straight and narrow; **jmdn. zum Lachen/zur Verzweiflung ~:** make sb. laugh/drive sb. to despair; **jmdn. dazu ~, etw. zu tun get** sb. to do sth.; **etw. hinter sich ~** *(ugs.)* get sth. over and done with; **e) jmdn. um seinen Besitz ~:** do sb. out of his property; **f)** *(präsentieren)* present; *(veröffentlichen)* publish; *(senden)* broadcast; **g) ein Opfer ~:** make a sacrifice; **h) einen großen Gewinn/hohe Zinsen ~:** make a large profit/earn high interest; **i) das bringt es mit sich, daß ...:** that means that ...; **j)** *(verursachen)* cause

brisant *Adj.* explosive; **Brisanz die; ~:** explosiveness

Brise die; ~, ~n breeze

Britannien (das); ~s Britain; *(hist.)* Britannia; **Brite der; ~n, ~n** Briton; **die ~n** the British; **er ist [kein] ~:** he is [not] British; **Britin die; ~, ~nen** Briton; British girl/woman; **britisch** *Adj.* British; **die Britischen Inseln** the British Isles

bröckelig *Adj.* crumbly; **bröckeln 1.** *itr. V.* **a)** crumble; **b)** *mit sein* **on der Wand ~:** crumble away from the wall; **2.** *tr. V.* crumble; **Brocken der; ~s, ~** *(von Brot)* hunk; *(von Fleisch)* chunk; *(von Lehm, Kohle, Erde)* lump; **ein paar ~ Englisch** *(fig.)* a smattering of English

brodeln *itr. V.* bubble

Broiler ['brɔylɐ] **der; ~s, ~** *(regional) s.* **Brathähnchen**

Brokat der; ~[e]s, ~e brocade

Brokkoli *Pl.* broccoli *sing.*

Brom·beere die blackberry

Bronchie ['brɔnçiə] **die; ~, ~n** bronchial tube; **Bronchitis die; ~,** bronchitis

Bronze ['brõːsə] **die; ~:** bronze; **Bronze·medaille die** bronze medal

Brosche die; ~, ~n brooch

Broschüre die; ~, ~n booklet

Brösel der; ~s, ~: breadcrumb; **bröselig** *Adj.* crumbly; **bröseln** *itr. V.* crumble

Brot das; ~[e]s, ~e bread *no pl., no indef. art.*; *(Laib ~)* loaf [of bread]; *(Scheibe ~)* slice [of bread]

Brot-: **~aufstrich der** spread; **~belag der** topping; *(im zusammengeklappten Brot)* filling

Brötchen das; ~s, ~: roll

Brot-: **~erwerb der** way to earn a living; **~korb der** the bread-basket; **~laib der** loaf [of bread]; **~messer das** bread-knife; **~rinde die** [bread] crust; **~zeit die** *(südd.)* **a)** *(Pause)* [tea-/coffee-/lunch-]break; **b)** *o. Pl. (Vesper)* snack; *(Vesperbrot)* sandwiches *pl.*

Bruch der; ~[e]s, Brüche a) break; **in die Brüche gehen** *(zerbrechen)* get broken; *(fig.)* break up; **b)** *(Med.: Knochen~)* fracture; break; **c)** *(Med.: Eingeweide~)* hernia; **d)** *(fig.) (eines Versprechens)* breaking; *(eines Abkommens, Gesetzes)* violation; **e)** *(Math.)* fraction; **brüchig** *Adj.* **a)** brittle *(rock, brickwork)*; **b)** *(fig.)* crumbling *(relationship, marriage, etc.)*

Bruch-: **~landung die** crash-landing; **~rechnen das** fractions *pl.*; **~strich der** fraction line; **~stück das** fragment; **~teil der** fraction; **im ~teil einer Sekunde** in a split second

Brücke die; ~, ~n a) *(auch: Kommando-, Zahnmed., Bodenturnen, Ringen)* bridge; **b)** *(Landungs~)* gangway; **c)** *(Teppich)* rug

Brücken-: **~bogen der** arch [of a/the bridge]; **~geländer das** parapet

Bruder der; ~s, Brüder brother; **Brüderchen das; ~s, ~:** little brother; **brüderlich 1.** *Adj.* brotherly; **2.** *adv.* in a brotherly way; **Brüderlichkeit die; ~:** brotherliness; **Bruderschaft die; ~: |mit jmdm.| ~ trinken** drink to close friendship [with sb.] *(agreeing to use the familiar 'du' form)*

Brühe die; ~, ~n a) stock; *(als Suppe)* clear soup; **b)** *(ugs. abwertend) (Getränk)* muck; *(verschmutztes Wasser)* filthy water; **brühen** *tr. V.* **a)** blanch; **b)** *(auf~)* brew, make *(tea)*; make *(coffee)*

brüh-, Brüh-: **~warm** *Adj.* etw. **~warm weitererzählen** *(ugs.)* pass sth. on straight away; **~würfel der** stock cube

brüllen 1. *itr. V.* **a)** *(bull, cow, etc.)* bellow; *(lion, tiger, etc.)* roar; **b)** *(ugs.) (schreien)* roar; *(weinen)* howl; **2.** *tr. V.* yell

brummen *tr., itr. V.* **a)** *(insect)* buzz; *(bear)* growl; *(engine etc.)* drone; **b)**

(unmelodisch singen) drone; c) *(mürrisch sprechen)* mumble; **Brummer** der; ~s, ~ *(ugs.)* a) *(Fliege)* bluebottle; b) *(Lkw)* heavy lorry *(Brit.)* or truck; **brummig** *Adj. (ugs.)* grumpy

Brumm-: ~**kreisel** der humming top; ~**schädel** der *(ugs.)* thick head

brünett *Adj.* dark-haired *(person)*; dark ⟨hair⟩; **Brünette** die; ~, ~n brunette

Brunnen der; ~s, ~ a) well; b) *(Spring~)* fountain; **Brunnen·kresse** die watercress

Brunst die; ~, **Brünste** *(von männlichen Tieren)* rut; *(von weiblichen Tieren)* heat; **Brunst·zeit** die *(bei männlichen Tieren)* rutting season; *(bei weiblichen Tieren)* [season of] heat

brüsk 1. *Adj.* brusque; 2. *adv.* brusquely; **brüskieren** *tr. V.* offend; *(stärker)* insult; *(schneiden)* snub

Brüssel *(das)* ~s Brussels

Brust die; ~, **Brüste** a) chest; b) *(der Frau)* breast; c) *(Hähnchen~)* breast; *(Rinder~)* brisket; d) *o. Pl. (~schwimmen)* breast-stroke

brüsten *refl. V.* sich mit etw. ~: boast about sth.

Brust-: ~**kasten** *(ugs.)* chest; ~**korb** der *(Anat.)* thorax *(Anat.)*; ~**krebs** der breast cancer; ~**schwimmen** *unr. itr. V.; nur im Inf.* do [the] breast-stroke; ~**schwimmen** das breast-stroke; ~**tasche** die breast pocket

Brüstung die; ~, ~en parapet; *(Balkon~)* balustrade

Brust·warze die nipple

Brut die; ~, ~en a) brooding; b) *(Jungtiere, auch fig. scherzh.: Kinder)* brood

brutal 1. *Adj.* brutal; violent ⟨attack, programme, etc.⟩; brute ⟨force, strength⟩; 2. *adv.* brutally; **Brutalität** die; ~, ~en a) *o. Pl.* brutality; b) *(Handlung)* act of brutality

brüten *itr. V.* a) brood; b) *(grübeln)* ponder (über + *Dat.* over); **brütend·heiß** *Adj. (ugs.)* boiling hot; **Brüter** der; ~s, ~ *(Kernphysik)* breeder

Brut-: ~**kasten** der incubator; ~**stätte** die *(auch fig.)* breeding-ground

brutto *Adv.* gross

Brutto-: ~**einkommen** das gross income; ~**gehalt** das gross salary; ~**sozialprodukt** das *(Wirtsch.)* gross national product

brutzeln 1. *itr. V.* sizzle. 2. *tr. V. (ugs.)* fry [up]

Bub der; ~en, ~en *(südd., österr., schweiz.)* boy; lad; **Bube** der; ~n, ~n *(Kartenspiele)* jack; knave; **Bubi** der; ~s, ~s a) [little] boy or lad; b) *(salopp: Schnösel)* young lad

Buch das; ~[e]s, **Bücher** book; *(Dreh~)* script; über etw. *(Akk.)* ~ führen keep a record of sth.

Buch-: ~**binder** der bookbinder; ~**druck** der; *o. Pl.* letterpress printing

Buche die; ~, ~n a) beech[-tree]; b) *o. Pl. (Holz)* beech[wood]

Buch·ecker die beech-nut

buchen *tr. V.* a) enter; b) *(vorbestellen)* book

Bücher·brett das bookshelf

Bücherei die; ~, ~en library

Bücher-: ~**regal** das bookshelves *pl.*; ~**schrank** der bookcase; ~**wurm** der *(scherzh.)* bookworm

Buch-: ~**fink** der chaffinch; ~**führung** die bookkeeping; ~**halter** der bookkeeper; ~**haltung** die a) accountancy; b) *(Abteilung)* accounts department; ~**händler** der bookseller; ~**handlung** die bookshop; ~**klub** der book club; ~**laden** der bookshop; ~**messe** die book fair; ~**rücken** der spine

Buchs·baum [ˈbʊks-] der box[-tree]

Buchse [ˈbʊksə] die; ~, ~n a) *(Elektrot.)* socket; b) *(Technik)* bush

Büchse [ˈbʏksə] die; ~, ~n a) tin; b) *(ugs.: Sammel~)* [collecting-]box; c) *(Gewehr)* rifle; *(Schrot~)* shotgun; **Büchsen-:** s. **Dosen-**

Buchstabe der; ~ns, ~n letter; *(Druckw.)* character; ein großer/kleiner ~: a capital [letter]/small letter; **buchstabieren** *tr. V.* spell; **buchstäblich** *Adv.* literally

Bucht die; ~, ~en bay

Buchung die; ~, ~en a) entry; b) *(Vorbestellung)* booking

Buckel der; ~s, ~ a) hump; einen ~ machen ⟨cat⟩ arch its back; ⟨person⟩ hunch one's shoulders; b) *(ugs.: Rücken)* back; rutsch mir den ~ runter! *(salopp)* get lost! *(sl.)*; **buckeln** *itr. V. (ugs.)* bow and scrape; vor jmdm. ~: kowtow to sb.

bücken *refl. V.* bend down

bucklig *Adj.* hunchbacked; **Bucklige** der/die; *adj. Dekl.* hunchback

¹**Bückling** der; ~s, ~e *(ugs. scherzh.: Verbeugung)* bow

²**Bückling** der; ~s, ~e *(Hering)* bloater

buddeln itr., tr. V. (ugs.) dig
Buddha ['bʊda] der; ~s, ~s Buddha; **Buddhismus** der; ~: Buddhism no art.; **Buddhist** der; ~en, ~en Buddhist; **buddhistisch** Adj. Buddhist attrib.
Bude die; ~, ~n a) kiosk; (Markt~) stall; (Jahrmarkts~) booth; b) (Bau~) hut; c) (ugs.) (Haus) dump (coll.); (Zimmer) room; digs pl. (Brit. coll.)
Budget [by'dʒe:] das; ~s, ~s budget
Büfett das; ~|e|s, ~s od. ~e a) sideboard; b) (Schanktisch) bar; c) (Verkaufstisch) counter; d) **kaltes ~**: cold buffet
Büffel der; ~s, ~: buffalo
büffeln (ugs.) 1. itr. V. swot (Brit. sl.); cram; 2. tr. V. swot up (Brit. sl.); cram
Buffet [by'fe:] das; ~s, ~s s. Büfett
Bug der; ~|e|s, ~e u. Büge bow
Bügel der; ~s, ~ a) (Kleider~) hanger; b) (Brillen~) ear-piece; c) (an einer Tasche, Geldbörse) frame
bügel-, Bügel-: ~**brett** das ironing-board; ~**eisen** das iron; ~**falte** die [trouser] crease; ~**frei** Adj. non-iron
bügeln tr., itr. V. iron
bugsieren [bʊ'ksi:rən] tr. V. (ugs.) shift; manœuvre; steer (person)
buh Interj. boo; **Buh** das; ~s, ~s (ugs.) boo; **buhen** itr. V. (ugs.) boo
buhlen itr. V. (ugs. abwertend) **um jmds. Gunst ~**: court sb.'s favour
Buh·mann der; Pl. Buhmänner (ugs.) whipping-boy
Bühne die; ~, ~n a) stage; b) (Theater) theatre
bühnen-, Bühnen-: ~**arbeiter** der stage-hand; ~**bildner** der; ~s, ~: stage designer; ~**reif** Adj. (play etc.) ready for the stage; (imitation etc.) worthy of the stage; dramatic (entrance etc.)
Buh·ruf der boo
buk 1. u. 3. Pers. Sg. Prät. v. backen
Bukett das; ~s, ~s od. ~e (geh.) bouquet
Bulette die; ~, ~n (bes. berl.) rissole
Bulgare der; ~n, ~n Bulgarian; **Bulgarien** [bʊl'ga:riən] (das); ~s Bulgaria; **bulgarisch** Adj. Bulgarian
Bull-: ~**auge** das circular porthole; ~**dogge** die bulldog; ~**dozer** [-do:zɐ] der; ~s, ~: bulldozer
Bulle der; ~n, ~n a) bull; b) (salopp: Polizist) cop (sl.); **Bullen·hitze** die (ugs.) sweltering or boiling heat
Bulletin [byl'tɛ̃:] das; ~s, ~s bulletin
bullig 1. Adj. a) beefy (person, appearance, etc.); chunky (car); b) (drückend) sweltering (heat); 2. adv. ~ **heiß** boiling hot

Bull·terrier der bull-terrier
bum Interj. bang
Bumerang der; ~s, ~e od. ~s boomerang
Bummel der; ~s, ~ a) stroll (durch around); b) (durch Lokale) pub-crawl (coll.); **Bummelei** die; ~, ~en (ugs.) a) dawdling; b) (Faulenzerei) loafing about; **bummelig** (ugs.) 1. Adj. a) slow; b) (nachlässig) slipshod; 2. adv. a) slowly; b) (nachlässig) in a slipshod way; **bummeln** itr. V. a) mit sein stroll (durch around); **durch die Kneipen ~**: go on a pub-crawl (Brit. coll.); b) (trödeln) dawdle; c) (faulenzen) laze about
bums Interj. bang; **Bums** der; ~es, ~e (ugs.) bang; (dumpfer) thud; **bumsen** itr. V. (ugs.) a) bang; (dumpfer) thump; unpers. es bumste ganz furchtbar there was a terrible bang/thud; b) mit sein (stoßen) bang
¹**Bund** der; ~|e|s, Bünde a) (Vereinigung) association; (Bündnis, Pakt) alliance; b) (föderativer Staat) federation; c) (an Röcken, Hosen) waistband
²**Bund** das; ~|e|s, ~e bunch; **Bündchen** das; ~s, ~ band; **Bündel** das; ~s, ~ bundle; **bündeln** tr. V. bundle up (newspapers, old clothes, rags, etc.); tie (banknotes etc.) into bundles/a bundle; tie (flowers, radishes, carrots, etc.) into bunches/a bunch; sheave (straw, hay, etc.)
Bundes- federal; (in Namen, Titeln) Federal
bundes-, Bundes-: ~**bürger** der (veralt.) West German citizen; ~**deutsch** Adj. (veralt.) West German; ~**land** das [federal] state; (österr.) province; ~**liga** die national division; ~**rat** der Bundesrat; ~**republik** die federal republic; die **~republik Deutschland** The Federal Republic of Germany; ~**straße** die federal highway; ≈ A road (Brit.); ~**tag** der Bundestag
Bundestags-: ~**abgeordnete** der/die member of parliament; member of the Bundestag; ~**wahl** die parliamentary or general election
bundes-, Bundes-: ~**trainer** der national team manager; ~**wehr** die [Federal] Armed Forces pl.; ~**weit** Adj., adv. nation-wide

Café

Bund-: ~**falten** *Pl.* pleats; ~**hose** die knee-breeches

bündig 1. *Adj.* a) succinct; b) *(schlüssig)* conclusive; 2. *adv.* a) succinctly; b) *(schlüssig)* conclusively

Bündnis das; ~ses, ~se alliance

Bungalow ['bʊŋgalo] der; ~s, ~s bungalow

Bunker der; ~s, ~ a) bunker; b) *(Luftschutz~)* air-raid shelter

bunt 1. *Adj.* a) colourful; *(farbig)* coloured; ~e **Farben/Kleidung** bright colours/brightly coloured clothes; b) *(fig.)* varied *(programme etc.)*; 2. *adv.* a) colourfully; b) *(fig.)* ein ~ gemischtes **Programm** a varied programme

bunt-, Bunt-: ~**bemalt** *Adj.* brightly painted; ~**papier** das coloured paper; ~**specht** der spotted woodpecker; ~**stift** der coloured pencil/crayon

Bürde die; ~, ~n *(geh.)* weight; load

Burg die; ~, ~en a) castle; b) *(Strand~)* wall of sand

Bürge der; ~n, ~n guarantor; **bürgen** *itr. V.* a) für jmdn./etw. ~: vouch for sb./sth.; b) *(fig.)* guarantee

Bürger der; ~s, ~, **Bürgerin** die; ~, ~nen citizen

Bürger-: ~**initiative** die citizens' action group; ~**krieg** der civil war

bürgerlich *Adj.* a) *nicht präd.* *(staats~)* civil *(rights, marriage, etc.)*; civic *(duties)*; b) *(dem Bürgertum zugehörig)* middle-class; die ~e **Küche** good plain cooking; c) *(Polit.)* nonsocialist; *(nicht marxistisch)* non-Marxist

bürger-, Bürger-: ~**meister** der mayor; ~**nah** *Adj.* which/who reflects the general public's interests *postpos., not pred.;* ~**pflicht** die duty as a citizen; ~**steig** der the pavement *(Brit.);* sidewalk *(Amer.)*

Bürgertum ['--tuːm] das; ~s a) middle class; b) *(Groß~)* bourgeoisie

Bürgin die; ~, ~nen s. **Bürge**; **Bürgschaft** die; ~, ~en a) guarantee; b) *(Betrag)* penalty

Büro das; ~s, ~s office

Büro-: ~**angestellte** der/die office-worker; ~**artikel** der item of office equipment; ~**haus** das office-block; ~**klammer** die paper-clip

Bürokrat der; ~en, ~en bureaucrat; **Bürokratie** die; ~, ~n bureaucracy; **bürokratisch** 1. *Adj.* bureaucratic; 2. *adv.* bureaucratically

Bürschchen ['byrʃən] das; ~, ~:

little fellow; **Bursche** der; ~n, ~n a) boy; lad; b) *(abwertend: Kerl)* guy *(sl.)*

burschikos 1. *Adj.* a) sporty *(look, clothes)*; [tom]boyish *(behaviour, girl, haircut)*; b) *(ungezwungen)* casual *(comment, behaviour, etc.)*; 2. *adv.* a) [tom]boyishly; b) *(ungezwungen)* in a colloquial way

Bürste die; ~, ~n brush; **bürsten** *tr. V.* brush

Bus der; ~ses, ~se bus; **Bus·bahnhof** der bus station

Busch der; ~[e]s, Büsche bush; **auf den ~ klopfen** *(fig. ugs.)* sound things out

Büschel das; ~s, ~: tuft; *(von Heu, Stroh)* handful

Busen der; ~s, ~ bust

Bus-: ~**fahrer** der bus-driver; ~**haltestelle** die bus-stop; ~**linie** die bus-route

Bussard der; ~s, ~e buzzard

Buße die; ~, ~n *(Rel.)* penance *no art.;* **büßen** 1. *tr. V.* a) atone for; b) *(fig.)* pay for; 2. *itr. V.* a) für etw. ~: atone for sth.; b) *(fig.)* pay; **Buß·geld** das *(Rechtsw.)* fine

Büsten·halter der bra; brassière *(formal)*

Butan·gas das butane gas

Butt der; ~[e]s, ~e flounder; butt

Bütten·papier das handmade paper *(with deckle-edge)*

Butter die; ~: butter; **es ist alles in ~** *(ugs.)* everything's fine

butter-, Butter-: ~**blume** die *(Sumpfdotterblume)* marsh marigold; *(Hahnenfuß)* buttercup; ~**brot** das slice of bread and butter; *(zugeklappt)* sandwich; ~**creme** die butter-cream; ~**milch** die buttermilk; ~**weich** *Adj.* beautifully soft

b.w. *Abk.* bitte wenden p.t.o.

bzw. *Abk.* beziehungsweise

C
---

c, C [tseː] das; ~, ~: a) *(Buchstabe)* c/C; b) *(Musik)* [key of] C

ca. *Abk.* cirka o.

Café das; ~s, ~s café

Cafeteria die; ~, ~s cafeteria
cal *Abk.* [Gramm]kalorie cal.
Callgirl ['kɔ:lgɜ:l] das; ~s, ~s call-girl
Camp [kemp] das; ~s, ~s camp; **campen** *itr. V.* camp; **Camping** das; ~s camping
Camping-: ~bus der motor caravan; camper; ~platz der campsite; campground *(Amer.)*
Canasta das; ~s canasta
Caravan ['ka(:)ravan] der; ~s, ~s *(Wohnwagen)* caravan; trailer *(Amer.)*
Cayenne·pfeffer [ka'jɛn-] der cayenne [pepper]
CD [tse:'de:] die; ~, ~s CD
CDU [tse:de:'|u:] die; ~ *Abk.* Christlich-Demokratische Union [Deutschlands] [German] Christian Democratic Party
C-Dur ['tse:-] das; ~: C major
Cello ['tʃɛlo] das; ~s, ~s *od.* **Celli** cello
Celsius *o. Art.* 20 Grad ~: 20 degrees Celsius *or* centigrade
Cembalo ['tʃɛmbalo] das; ~s, ~s *od.* **Cembali** harpsichord
Ceylon ['tsailɔn] (das); ~s *(hist.)* Ceylon *(Hist.)*
Champagner [ʃam'panjɐ] der; ~s, ~ champagne *(from Champagne)*
Champignon ['ʃampɪnjɔn] der; ~s, ~s mushroom
Chance ['ʃã:sə] die; ~, ~n a) chance; b) *Pl. (Aussichten)* prospects; [bei jmdm] ~n haben stand a chance [with sb.]
Chaos ['ka:ɔs] das; ~: chaos *no art.*
Charakter der; ~s, ~e [...'tɛːrə] character; **charakterisieren** *tr. V.* characterize; **charakteristisch** *Adj.* characteristic (für of); **charakterlich** 1. *Adj.* character *attrib.;* 2. *adv.* in [respect of] character; **charakter·los** *Adj.* unprincipled; *(niederträchtig)* despicable; *(labil)* spineless
charmant [ʃar'mant] 1. *Adj.* charming; 2. *adv.* charmingly; **Charme** [ʃarm] der; ~s charm
Charter- ['tʃartɐ-]: ~flug der charter flight; ~maschine die chartered aircraft
Chassis [ʃa'si:] das; ~ [ʃa'si:(s)], ~ [ʃa'si:s] chassis
Chauffeur [ʃɔ'fø:ɐ] der; ~s, ~e driver; *(privat angestellt)* chauffeur
Chef [ʃɛf] der; ~s, ~s, **Chefin** die; ~, ~nen *(Leiter[in])* head; *(der Polizei, des Generalstabs)* chief; *(einer Partei, Bande)* leader; *(Vorgesetzte[r])* superior; boss *(coll.)*

Chef-: ~koch der chef; head cook; ~sekretärin die director's secretary
Chemie die; ~ a) chemistry *no art.;* b) *(ugs.: Chemikalien)* chemicals *pl.;* **Chemiker** der; ~s, ~, **Chemikerin** die; ~, ~nen *(graduate)* chemist; **chemisch** 1. *Adj.* chemical; 2. *adv.* chemically
Chicorée ['ʃikore] der; ~s *od.* die; ~: chicory
Chiffon ['ʃɪfõ] der; ~s, ~s chiffon
Chiffre ['ʃɪfrə] die; ~, ~n a) *(Zeichen)* symbol; b) *(Geheimzeichen)* cipher; c) *(in Annoncen)* box number
Chile ['tʃi:le, 'ʃi:lə] (das); ~s Chile; **Chilene** [tʃi'le:nə, ʃi'le:nə] der; ~n, ~n, **Chilenin** die; ~, ~nen Chilean; **chilenisch** *Adj.* Chilean
Chili ['tʃi:li] der; ~s, ~es a) *Pl. (Schoten)* chillies; b) *o. Pl. (Gewürz)* chilli [powder]
China (das); ~s China; **Chinese** der; ~n, ~n, **Chinesin** die; ~, ~nen Chinese; **chinesisch** *Adj.* Chinese
Chip [tʃɪp] der; ~s, ~s a) *(Spielmarke)* chip; b) *(Kartoffel~)* [potato] crisp *(Brit.)* or *(Amer.)* chip; c) *(Elektronik)* [micro]chip
Chirurg der; ~en, ~en surgeon; **Chirurgie** die; ~, ~n a) *o. Pl.* surgery *no art.;* b) *(Abteilung)* surgical department; *(Station)* surgical ward; **chirurgisch** 1. *Adj.* surgical; 2. *adv.* surgically; by surgery
Chlor das; ~s chlorine; **Chloroform** das; ~s chloroform; **Chlorophyll** das; ~s chlorophyll
Cholera die; ~: cholera
cholerisch *Adj.* irascible; choleric *(temperament)*
Cholesterin das; ~s cholesterol
Chor der; ~[e]s, **Chöre** ['kø:rə] *(auch Archit.)* choir; *(in Oper, Sinfonie, Theater; Komposition)* chorus; **im ~ rufen** shout in chorus; **Choral** der; ~s, **Choräle** *(Kirchenlied)* chorale
Choreographie die; ~, ~n choreography
Chose ['ʃo:zə] die; ~, ~n *(ugs.)* stuff; **die ganze ~**: the whole lot *(coll.)* or *(sl.)* shoot
Chow-Chow [tʃau 'tʃau] der; ~s, ~s chow
Christ der; ~en, ~en Christian
Christ-: ~baum der *(bes. südd.)* Christmas tree; ~demokrat der *(Politik)* Christian Democrat
Christenheit die; ~ Christendom *no art.;* **Christentum** das; ~s Chris-

tianity *no art.; (Glaube)* Christian
faith

Christin die; ~, ~nen Christian;
Christ·kind das; *o. Pl.* Christ-child
(as bringer of Christmas gifts); **christlich** 1. *Adj.* Christian. 2. *adv.* in a
[truly] Christian spirit

Christ-: ~messe die *(kath. Rel.)*
Christmas Mass; ~mette die *(kath.
Rel.)* Christmas Mass; *(ev. Rel.)* midnight service [on Christmas Eve];
~rose die Christmas rose; ~stollen
der [German] Christmas loaf *(with
candied fruit, almonds, etc.)*

Christus (der); ~ *od.* **Christi** Christ

Chrom das; ~s chromium

Chromosom das; ~s, ~en *(Biol.)*
chromosome

Chronik die; ~, ~en chronicle; **chronisch** *Adj.* chronic

Chrysantheme die; ~, ~n chrysanthemum

City ['sɪti] die; ~, ~s city centre

clever ['klɛvɐ] 1. *Adj. (raffiniert)*
shrewd; *(intelligent, geschickt)* clever;
2. *adv.: s. Adj.:* shrewdly; cleverly

Clique ['klɪkə] die; ~, ~n a) *(abwertend)* clique; b) *(Freundeskreis)* set;
(größere Gruppe) crowd *(coll.)*

Clown [klaun] der; ~s, ~s clown

Club *s.* **Klub**

cm *Abk.:* Zentimeter cm.

Co. *Abk.:* Compagnie Co.

Cockpit das; ~s, ~s cockpit

Cocktail ['kɔkteɪl] der; ~s, ~s cocktail

Cognac ⓦ der; ~s, ~s Cognac

Color- *(Fot.)* colour *(film, slide, etc.)*

Colt ⓦ der; ~s, ~s Colt (P) [revolver]

Comic·heft das comic

Computer [kɔm'pju:tɐ] der; ~s, ~:
computer

Container [kɔn'te:nɐ] der; ~s, ~: container; *(für Müll)* [refuse] skip

cool [ku:l] *(ugs.)* 1. *Adj.* cool; ~ bleiben keep one's cool *(sl.);* 2. *adv.*
coolly *(coll.)*

Cord der; ~[e]s, ~e *od.* ~s cord;
(~samt) corduroy

Corned beef ['kɔ:nd 'bi:f] das; ~ ~:
corned beef

Couch [kautʃ] die, *(schweiz. auch:)*
der; ~, ~es sofa

Coup [ku:] der; ~s, ~s coup

Coupon [ku'põ:] der; ~s, ~s coupon,
voucher

Courage [ku'ra:ʒə] die; ~ *(ugs.)* courage

Cousin [ku'zɛ̃:] der; ~s, ~s, **Cousine**
die; ~, ~n cousin

Cowboy ['kaubɔy] der; ~s, ~s cowboy

Credo *s.* **Kredo**

Creme [kre:m] die; ~, ~s, *(schweiz.:)*
~n cream

ČSFR [tʃe:ɛsɛf'ɛr] die; ~ : die ~ : Czechoslovakia

CSU [tse:ɛs'u:] die; ~ *Abk.:* Christ-
lich-Soziale Union CSU

Curry ['kœri] das; ~s, ~s curry-powder

D

d, D [de:] das; ~, ~ a) *(Buchstabe)*
d/D; b) *(Musik)* [key of] D

D *Abk.* Damen

da 1. *Adv.* a) *(dort)* there; da draußen/
drinnen/drüben/unten out/in/over/
down there; **da,** wo where; b) *(hier)*
here; c) *(zeitlich)* then; *(in dem Augenblick)* at that moment; *(deshalb)* der
Zug war schon weg, da habe ich den
Bus genommen the train had already
gone, so I took the bus; e) *(ugs.: in diesem Fall)* da kann man nichts machen
there's nothing one can do about it; 2.
Konj. (weil) as; since

da·bei *Adv.* a) with it/him/her/them;
nahe ~: close by; b) *(währenddessen)*
at the same time; *(bei diesem Anlaß)*
then; on that occasion; **die ~ entste-
henden Kosten** the expense involved;
c) *(außerdem)* ~ [auch] what is more;
d) *(hinsichtlich dessen)* about it/them;
was hast du dir denn ~ gedacht? what
'were you thinking of?

dabei-: ~bleiben *unr. itr. V.; mit
sein* stay there; be there; ~haben
unr. tr. V. have with one; ~sein *unr.
itr. V.; mit sein (Zusschr. nur im Inf. u.
2. Part.)* a) *(anwesend sein)* be there;
be present *(bei at); (teilnehmen)* take
part *(bei in);* b) [gerade] ~sein, etw. zu
tun be just doing sth.; ~stehen *unr.
itr. V.* stand there

da|bleiben *unr. itr. V.; mit sein* stay
there; *(hier bleiben)* stay here

Dach das; ~[e]s, Dächer roof

Dach-: ~decker [~dɛkɐ] der; ~s, ~:
roofer; ~garten der roof-garden;
~kammer die attic [room]; ~luke

die skylight; **~pappe** die roofing-felt; **~rinne** die gutter

Dachs [daks] der; **~es**, **~e** badger

dachte *1. u. 3. Pers. Sg. Prät. v.* **denken**

Dach-: **~terrasse** die roof-terrace; **~ziegel** der roof-tile

Dackel der; **~s**, **~:** dachshund

da·durch *Adv.* a) through it/them; b) *(durch diesen Umstand)* as a result; *(durch dieses Mittel)* by this [means]

da·für *Adv.* a) for it/them; **~**, **daß** ...: *(wenn man berücksichtigt, daß)* considering that ...; *(damit)* so that ...; **~ sorgen [, daß ...]** see to it [that ...]; b) **~ sein** be in favour [of it]; **ein Beispiel ~ ist ...:** an example of this is ...; c) *(als Gegenleistung)* in return [for it]; *(beim Tausch)* in exchange; *(statt dessen)* instead

dafür|können *unr. tr. V.* **etwas/nichts ~:** be/not be responsible

dagegen *Adv.* a) against it/them; **etwas ~ haben** have sth. against it; **ich habe nichts ~:** I've no objection; **sein** be against it; b) *(im Vergleich dazu)* by or in comparison

da·heim *Adv.* *(bes. südd., österr., schweiz.)* a) *(zu Hause)* at home; *(nach Präp.)* home; b) *(in der Heimat)* [back] home

da·her *Adv.* a) from there; b) *(durch diesen Umstand)* hence; c) *(deshalb)* therefore; so

daher|kommen *unr. itr. V.* come along

da·hin a) there; b) *(fig.)* **~ mußte es kommen** it had to come to that; c) **bis ~:** to there; *(zeitlich)* until then; d) **~ sein** be or have gone; e) *(in diesem Sinne)* **~ [gehend], daß ...:** to the effect that ...

da·hinten *Adv.* over there

da·hinter *Adv.* behind it/them; *(folgend)* after it/them

Dahlie ['da:li̯ə] die; **~**, **~n** dahlia

da-: **~lassen** *unr. tr. V.* *(ugs.)* leave [there]; *(hier lassen)* leave here; **~liegen** *unr. itr. V.* lie there

dalli *Adv.* *(ugs.)* **[~] ~!** get a move on!

damalig *Adj.; nicht präd.* at that or the time *postpos;* **damals** *Adv.* at that time

Damast der; **~[e]s**, **~e** damask

Dame die; **~**, **~n** a) *(Frau)* lady; b) *(Schach, Kartenspiele)* queen; c) *o. Pl. (Spiel)* draughts *(Brit.);* checkers *(Amer.)*

Damen-: **~binde** die sanitary towel

(Brit.) or *(Amer.)* napkin; **~friseur** der ladies' hairdresser; **~rad** das lady's bicycle; **~toilette** die ladies' toilet

da·mit 1. *Adv.* a) with it/them; b) *(gleichzeitig)* with that; c) *(daher)* thus; 2. *Konj.* so that

dämlich *(ugs. abwertend)* 1. *Adj.* stupid; 2. *adv.* stupidly

Damm der; **~[e]s**, **Dämme** embankment; levee *(Amer.);* *(Deich)* dike; *(Stau~)* dam

dämmern *itr. V.* **es dämmert** *(morgens)* it is getting light; *(abends)* it is getting dark; **Dämmerung** die; **~**, **~en** a) *(Abend~)* twilight; dusk; b) *(Morgen~)* dawn

Dämon der; **~s**, **~en** [dɛ'moːnən] demon; **dämonisch** *Adj.* daemonic

Dampf der; **~[e]s**, **Dämpfe** steam *o. Pl., no indef. art.;* **dampfen** *itr. V.* steam *(vor + Dat.* with)

dämpfen *tr. V.* a) *(garen)* steam ⟨fish, vegetables, potatoes⟩; b) *(mildern)* muffle ⟨sound⟩; cushion, absorb ⟨blow, impact, shock⟩

Dampfer der; **~s**, **~:** steamer

Dampf-: **~maschine** die steam engine; **~nudel** die *(südd., Kochk.)* steamed yeast dumpling; **~walze** die steamroller

da·nach *Adv.* a) *(zeitlich)* after it/that; then; b) *(räumlich)* after it/them; c) *(entsprechend)* in accordance with it/them

Däne der; **~n**, **~n** Dane

da·neben *Adv.* a) beside him/her/it/them *etc.;* b) *(im Vergleich dazu)* in comparison

daneben-: **~benehmen** *unr. refl. V. (ugs.)* blot one's copybook *(coll.);* **~gehen** *unr. itr. V.;* **mit sein** miss [the target]; **~schießen** *unr. itr. V.* miss [the target]

Dänemark (das) **~s** Denmark; **Dänin** die; **~**, **~nen** Dane; Danish woman/girl; **dänisch** *Adj.* Danish; *s. auch* **deutsch, Deutsch**

dank *Präp. mit Dat. u. Gen.* thanks to; **Dank** der; **~[e]s** thanks *pl.;* **mit [vielem od. bestem] ~** zurück thanks for the loan; *(bes. geschrieben)* returned with thanks!; **vielen/besten/herzlichen ~!** thank you very much; **dankbar** 1. *Adj.* grateful; *(anerkennend)* appreciative ⟨child, audience, etc.⟩; **[jmdm.] für etw. ~ sein** be grateful [to sb.] for sth.; 2. *adv.* gratefully; **Dankbarkeit** die; **~:** gratitude; **danke** *Höflich-*

keitsformel thank you; *(ablehnend)* no, thank you; ~ **schön/sehr/vielmals** thank you very much; **danken 1.** *itr. V. (Dank aussprechen)* thank; **ich danke Ihnen vielmals** thank you very much; **na, ich danke!** *(ugs.)* no, 'thank you!; **2.** *tr. V.* |**aber bitte,**| **nichts zu ~:** don't mention it; **Danke·schön das;** ~**s** thank-you

dann *Adv.* **a)** then; **was ~?** what happens then?; **noch drei Tage, ~ ist** Ostern another three days and it will be Easter; **bis ~:** see you then; ~ **und wann** now and then; **b)** *(in diesem Falle)* then; in that case; ~ **will ich nicht weiter stören** in that case I won't disturb you any further; |**na,**| ~ **eben nicht!** in that case, forget it!; **nur ~, wenn ...:** only if ...

daran [da'ran] *Adv.* **a)** *(an dieser/diese Stelle, an diesem/diesen Gegenstand)* on it/them; **dicht ~:** close to it/them; **nahe ~ sein, etw. zu tun** be on the point of doing sth.; **b)** *(hinsichtlich dieser Sache)* about it/them; ~ **ist nichts zu machen** there's nothing one can do about it; **kein Wort ~ ist wahr** not a word of it is true; **mir liegt viel ~:** it means a lot to me; **c)** **ich wäre beinahe ~ erstickt** I almost choked on it; **er ist ~ gestorben** he died of it

daran|setzen *tr. V.* devote *(energy etc.)* to it; summon up *(ambition)* for it; *(aufs Spiel setzen)* risk *(one's life, one's honour)* for it

darauf *Adv.* **a)** on it/them; *(oben ~)* on top of it/them; **b)** **er hat ~ geschossen** he shot at it/them; **c)** *(danach)* after that; **ein Jahr ~ / kurz ~ starb er** he died a year later/shortly afterwards

darauf-: ~**folgend** *Adj.* following; ~**hin** [--'-] *Adv.* **a)** thereupon; **b)** *(unter diesem Gesichtspunkt)* with a view to this/that

daraus *Adv.* **a)** from it/them; out of it/them; **b)** **mach dir nichts ~** don't worry about it; **was ist ~ geworden?** what has become of it?

darf *1. u. 3. Pers. Sg. Präsens v.* **dürfen;**
darfst *2. Pers. Sg. Präsens v.* **dürfen**

darin *Adv.* **a)** in it/them; **b)** *(in dieser Hinsicht)* in that respect

dar|legen *tr. V.* explain; set forth *(reasons, facts)*

Darm der; ~|e|s, **Därme** intestines *pl.;* bowels *pl.*

dar|stellen *tr. V.* **a)** depict; portray; **etw. graphisch ~:** present sth. graphically; **b)** *(verkörpern)* play; act; **c)**

(schildern) describe *(person, incident, etc.);* present *(matter, argument);* **d)** *(sein, bedeuten)* represent

Darsteller der; ~**s,** ~ actor; **Darstellerin** die; ~, ~**nen** actress; **Darstellung** die **a)** representation; *(Schilderung)* portrayal **b)** *(Bild)* picture; graphische/schematische ~: diagram; *(Graph)* graph; **b)** *(Beschreibung, Bericht)* description; account

darüber *Adv.* **a)** over it/them; **b)** ~ **hinaus** in additon [to that]; *(noch obendrein)* what is more; **c)** *(über dieser/diese Angelegenheit)* about it/them; **d)** *(über diese Grenze, dieses Maß hinaus)* over [that]

darüber|stehen *unr. itr. V. (fig.)* be above such things

darum *Adv.* **a)** [a]round it/them; **b)** *(diesbezüglich)* **ich sorge mich ~:** I worry about it; **c)** ['--] *(deswegen)* for that reason

darunter *Adv.* **a)** *(unter dem Genannten/das Genannte)* under it/them; **b)** *(unter dieser Grenze, diesem Maß)* less; **Bewerber im Alter von 40 Jahren und ~:** applicants aged 40 and under

das 1. *best. Art. Nom. u. Akk.* the; **2.** *Demonstrativpron.* **a)** *attr.* **das Kind war es** it was 'that child; **b)** *alleinstehend* **das** |**da**| that one; **das** |**hier**| this one [here]; **3.** *Relativpron. (Mensch)* who; that; *(Sache, Tier)* which; that

da|sein *unr. itr. V.; mit sein; Zuschr. nur im Inf. u. Part.* **a)** be there; *(hier sein)* be here; **noch ~** *(übrig sein)* be left; **ist Herr X da?** is Mr X about *or* available?; **ich bin gleich wieder da** I'll be right back; **b)** *(fig.) (case)* occur; *(moment)* have arrived; *(situation)* have arisen

Da·sein das existence

da|sitzen *unr. itr. V.* sit there

dasjenige *s.* **derjenige**

daß *Konj.* **a)** that; **entschuldigen Sie bitte,** ~ **ich mich verspätet habe** please forgive me for being late; **ich verstehe nicht,** ~ **sie ihn geheiratet hat** I don't understand why she married him; **b)** *(nach Pronominaladverbien o. ä.)* [the fact] that; **das liegt daran,** ~ **du nicht aufgepaßt hast** that comes from your not paying attention; **c)** *(im Konsekutivsatz)* that; |**so**| ~: so that; **d)** *(im Finalsatz)* so that; **e)** *(im Ausruf)* ~ **mir das passieren mußte!** why did it have to [go and] happen to me!

dasselbe *s.* **derselbe**

da|stehen *unr. itr. V.* **a)** stand there;

b) *(fig.)* **gut ~:** be in a good position; **|ganz| allein ~:** be [all] alone in the world

Daten 1. *s.* **Datum; 2.** *Pl.* data

Daten-: **~schutz** der data protection; **~verarbeitung die** data processing *no def. art.*

datieren *tr. V.* date

Dativ der; ~, ~e *(Sprachw.)* dative [case]; **Dativ·objekt das** *(Sprachw.)* indirect object

Dattel die; ~, ~n date; **Dattel·palme die** date-palm

Datum das; ~s, Daten date

Dauer die; ~ a) length; **für die ~ eines Jahres** *od.* **von einem Jahr** for a period of one year; b) *(Fortbestehen)* **von ~ sein** last [long]; **auf die ~:** in the long run; **auf ~:** permanently

dauer-, Dauer-: **~auftrag der** *(Bankw.)* standing order; **~haft 1.** *Adj.* a) [long-]lasting *⟨peace, friendship, etc.⟩*; b) *(haltbar)* durable; **2.** *adv.* lastingly; **~karte die** season ticket; **~lauf der** jogging *no art.;* **ein ~lauf a** jog

¹dauern *itr. V.* last; *⟨job etc.⟩* take; **einen Moment, es dauert nicht lange** just a minute, it won't take long

dauernd 1. *Adj.* constant *⟨noise, interruptions, etc.⟩;* permanent *⟨institution⟩;* **2.** *adv.* constantly; **er kommt ~ zu spät** he keeps on arriving late

Dauer-: **~stellung die** permanent position; **~welle die** perm; **~wurst die** smoked sausage *(with good keeping properties, esp. salami)*

Daumen der; ~s, ~: thumb

Daune die; ~, ~n down [feather]; **~n** down *sing.*

davon *Adv.* a) *(von dieser Stelle entfernt, weg)* from it/them; *(von dort)* from there; *(mit Entfernungsangabe)* away [from it/them]; b) *(hinsichtlich dieser Sache)* about it/them; c) *(durch diese Angelegenheit verursacht)* by it/them; **das kommt ~!** *(ugs.)* [there you are,] that's what happens; d) **ich hätte gern ein halbes Pfund ~:** I would like half a pound of that/those; e) **~ kann man nicht leben** you can't live on that

davon-: **~fahren** *unr. itr. V.; mit sein* leave; *(mit dem Auto)* drive off; *(mit dem Fahrrad, Motorrad)* ride off; **~kommen** *unr. itr. V.; mit sein* get away; **~laufen** *unr. itr. V.; mit sein* run away; **~tragen** *unr. tr. V.* a) carry away; take away *⟨rubbish⟩;* b) *(geh.: erringen)* gain *⟨a victory, fame⟩;*

c) *(geh.: sich zuziehen)* receive *⟨injuries⟩*

da·vor *Adv.* a) in front of it/them; b) *(zeitlich)* before [it/them]

davor-: **~liegen** *unr. itr. V.* lie in front of it/them; **~schieben 1.** *unr. tr. V.* push in front of it/them; **2.** *unr. refl. V.* move in front of it/them; **~stehen** *unr. itr. V.* stand in front of it/them; **~stellen 1.** *tr. V.* put in front of it/them; **2.** *refl. V.* plant oneself in front of it/them

da·zu *Adv.* a) *(zusätzlich zu dieser Sache)* with it/them; *(gleichzeitig)* at the same time; *(außerdem)* what is more; b) *(diesbezüglich)* about it/them; c) *(zu diesem Zweck)* for it; d) *(zu diesem Ergebnis)* to it; **~ reicht unser Geld nicht** we haven't enough money for that

dazu-: **~geben** *unr. tr. V.* add; **~gehören** *tr. V.* belong to it/them; **~kommen** *unr. itr. V.; mit sein* a) *(hinkommen)* arrive; b) *(hinzukommen)* **kommt noch etwas dazu?** is there anything else [you would like]?; **~ kommt daß...** *(fig.)* what's more, ...; on top of that ...; **~rechnen** *tr. V.* add on; **~tun** *unr. tr. V.* *(ugs.)* add

da·zwischen *Adv.* in between; *(darunter)* among them

dazwischen-: **~kommen** *unr. itr. V.; mit sein* a) **mit dem Finger ~kommen** get one's finger caught [in it]; b) *(es verhindern)* prevent it; **es ist mir etwas ~gekommen** I had problems; **~reden** *itr. V.* interrupt

DDR [de:de:'|ɛr] **die;** ~ *Abk.* *(1949–1990)* Deutsche Demokratische Republik GDR; East Germany *(in popular use)*

Debatte die; ~, ~n debate (über + *Akk.* on); **zur ~ stehen** be under discussion

Debüt [de'by:] **das; ~s, ~s** debut

Deck das; ~|e|s, ~s deck

Deck·bett das *s.* **Oberbett; Decke die; ~, ~n** a) *(Tisch~)* tablecloth; b) *(Woll~, Pferde~, fig.)* blanket; *(Reise~)* rug; c) *(Zimmer~)* ceiling

Deckel der; ~s, ~ a) lid; *(auf Flaschen, Gläsern usw.)* top; *(Schacht~, Uhr~, Buch~ usw.)* cover; b) *(Bier~)* beer-mat

decken 1. *tr. V.* a) etw. über etw. *(Akk.)* ~: spread sth. over sth. b) roof *⟨house⟩;* cover *⟨roof⟩;* c) **den Tisch ~:** lay the table; d) *(schützen; Finanzw., Versicherungsw.)* cover; e) *(befriedigen)* meet *⟨need, demand⟩;* **2.** *itr. V.*

(den Tisch ~) lay the table; **Deckmantel** der; *o. Pl.* cover; **Deckung** die; ~, ~en a) *(Schutz; auch fig.)* cover *(esp. Mil.);* *(Boxen)* guard; *(bes. Fußball)* defence; **in ~ gehen** take cover; b) *(Befriedigung)* meeting; c) *(Finanzw., Versicherungsw.)* cover[ing]; **deckungs·gleich** *Adj.* *(Geom.)* congruent

defekt *Adj.* defective; faulty; **~ sein** have a defect; be faulty; *(nicht funktionieren)* not be working; **Defekt** der; ~[e]s, ~e defect, fault **(an** + *Dat.* in)

defensiv 1. *Adj.* defensive; 2. *adv.* defensively; **Defensive** die; ~, ~n defensive; **in der ~:** on the defensive; die ~ *(Sport)* defensive play

definieren *tr. V.* define; **Definition** die; ~, ~en definition

definitiv 1. *Adj.* definitive; 2. *adv.* finally

Defizit das; ~s, ~e a) deficit; b) *(Mangel)* deficiency

deformieren *tr. V.* a) *(verformen)* distort; b) *(entstellen)* deform *(also fig.)*

deftig *Adj. (ugs.)* a) [good] solid *attrib.* ⟨meal etc.⟩; [nice] big ⟨sausage etc.⟩; b) *(derb)* crude, coarse ⟨joke, speech, etc.⟩

Degen der; ~s, ~ a) *(Waffe)* [light] sword; b) *(Fechtsport)* épée

degradieren *tr. V.* demote

dehnbar *Adj.* a) *(elastisch)* ⟨material etc.⟩ that stretches *not pred.;* elastic ⟨waistband etc.⟩; **Dehnbarkeit** die; ~: elasticity; **dehnen** *tr., refl. V.* stretch

Deich der; ~[e]s, ~e dike

Deichsel ['daɪks(ə)l] die; ~, ~n shaft; **deichseln** *tr. V. (ugs.)* fix

dein *Possessivpron.* your; **viele Grüße von Deinem Emil** with best wishes, yours Emil; **das Buch dort, ist das ~[e]s?** that book over there, is it yours?; **du und die Deinen** *(geh.)* you and yours; **deiner** *Gen. des Personalpronomens* **du** *(geh.)* of you; **deinerseits** *Adv. (von deiner Seite)* on your part; *(auf deiner Seite)* for your part; **deinet·wegen** *Adv.* because of you; *(für dich)* on your behalf; *(dir zuliebe)* for your sake

dekadent *Adj.* decadent; **Dekadenz** die; ~: decadence

deklamieren *tr., itr. V.* recite

Deklination die; ~, ~en *(Sprachw.)* declension; **deklinieren** *tr. V. (Sprachw.)* decline

Dekolleté [dekɔl'te:] das; ~s, ~s low[-cut] neckline; décolletage

Dekor das; ~s, ~s od. ~e decoration; *(Muster)* pattern; **Dekorateur** [dekora'tø:ɐ̯] der; ~s, ~e, **Dekorateurin** die; ~, ~nen *(Schaufenster~)* window-dresser; *(von Innenräumen)* interior designer; **Dekoration** die; ~, ~en decorations *pl.;* *(Schaufenster~)* window display; **dekorativ** 1. *Adj.* decorative; 2. *adv.* decoratively; **dekorieren** *tr. V.* decorate ⟨room etc.⟩; dress ⟨shop-window⟩

Deko·stoff der furnishing fabric

Dekret das; ~[e]s, ~e decree

Delegation die; ~, ~en delegation; **delegieren** *tr. V.* a) send as a delegate/as delegates; b) delegate ⟨task etc.⟩ **(an** + *Akk.* to); **Delegierte** der/ die; *adj. Dekl.* delegate

delikat *Adj.* a) delicious; *(fein)* delicate ⟨bouquet, aroma⟩; b) *(heikel)* delicate; **Delikatesse** die; ~, ~n delicacy

Delikt das; ~[e]s, ~e offence

Delinquent der; ~en, ~en offender

Delirium das; ~s, Delirien delirium

Delle die; ~, ~n *(ugs.)* dent

Delphin der; ~s, ~e dolphin

dem 1. *best. Art., Dat. Sg. v.* ¹**der** 1 u. **das** 1 to the; *(nach Präp.)* the; 2. *Demonstrativpron., Dat. Sg. v.* ¹**der** 2 u. **das** 2: a) *attr.* that; **gib es dem Mann** give it to 'that man; b) *alleinstehend* **gib es nicht dem, sondern dem da!** don't give it to him, give it to that man/child *etc.;* 3. *Relativpron., Dat. Sg. v.* ¹**der** 3 u. **das** 3 *(Person)* that/ whom; *(Sache)* that/which; **der Mann/das Kind, dem ich das Geld gab** the man/the child I gave the money to

Demagoge der; ~n, ~n demagogue

demagogisch *Adj.* demagogic

Dementi das; ~s, ~s denial; **dementieren** 1. *tr. V.* deny; 2. *itr. V.* deny it

dem-: ~entsprechend 1. *Adj.* appropriate; 2. *adv.* accordingly; *(vor Adjektiven)* correspondingly; **~gemäß** *Adv.* a) *(infolgedessen)* consequently; b) *(entsprechend)* accordingly; **~jenigen** *s.* derjenige; **~nach** *Adv.* therefore; **~nächst** *Adv.* shortly

Demokrat der; ~en, ~en democrat; *(Parteimitglied)* Democrat; **Demokratie** die; ~, ~n democracy; **demokratisch** 1. *Adj.* democratic; 2. *adv.* democratically; **demokratisieren** *tr. V.* democratize

demolieren *tr. V.* wreck; smash up ⟨*furniture*⟩

Demonstrant der; ~en, ~en demonstrator; **Demonstrantin** die; ~, ~nen demonstrator; **Demonstration** die; ~, ~en demonstration (für in support of, gegen against); **demonstrativ** 1. *Adj.* a) pointed; b) *(Sprachw.)* demonstrative; 2. *adv.* pointedly; **Demonstrativ·pronomen** das *(Sprachw.)* demonstrative pronoun; **demonstrieren** 1. *itr. V.* demonstrate (für in support of, gegen against); 2. *tr. V.* demonstrate

dem·selben *s.* derselbe

Demut die; ~: humility; **demütig** 1. *Adj.* humble; 2. *adv.* humbly; **demütigen** 1. *tr. V.* humiliate; 2. *refl. V.* humble oneself; **Demütigung** die; ~, ~en humiliation

dem·selben *s.* derselbe

dem·zufolge *Adv.* consequently

¹**den** 1. *best. Art., Akk. Sg. v.* ¹der 1: the; 2. *Demonstrativpron., Akk. Sg. v.* ¹der 2: a) *attr.* that; ich meine den Mann I mean 'that man; b) *alleinstehend* ich meine den [da] I mean 'that one; 3. *Relativpron., Akk. Sg. v.* ¹der 3 *(Person)* that/whom; *(Sache)* that/ which; der Mann, den ich gesehen habe the man that I saw

²**den** 1. *best. Art., Dat. Pl. v.* ¹der 1, ¹die 1, das 1 the; 2. *Demonstrativpron. Dat. Pl. v.* ¹der 2a, ¹die 2a, das 2a those.

denen 1. *Demonstrativpron., Dat. Pl. v.* ¹der 2b, ¹die 2b, das 2b them; gib es ~, nicht den anderen give it to 'them, not to the others; 2. *Relativpron., Dat. Pl. v.* ¹der 3, ¹die 3, das 3 *(Personen)* that/whom; *(Sachen)* that/which; die Menschen, ~ wir Geld gegeben haben the people to whom we gave money; die Tiere, ~ er geholfen hat the animals that he helped

denjenigen *s.* derjenige

denkbar 1. *Adj.* conceivable; 2. *adv. (sehr, äußerst)* extremely; **denken** 1. *unr. itr. V.* think (an + *Akk.* of, über + *Akk.* about); wie denkst du darüber? what do you think about it?; what's your opinion of it?; schlecht von jmdm. ~: think badly of sb.; denk daran, daß .../zu ...: don't forget that .../to ...; ich denke nicht daran! no way!; not on your life!; ich denke nicht daran, das zu tun I've no intention of doing that; 2. *unr. tr. V.* think; wer hätte das gedacht? who would have thought it?; eine gedachte Linie an imaginary line; 3. *unr. refl. V.* a)

(sich vorstellen) imagine; b) sich *(Dat.)* bei etw. etwas ~: mean something by sth.; ich habe mir nichts [Böses] dabei gedacht I didn't mean any harm [by it]; **Denken** das; ~s thinking; *(Denkweise)* thought; **Denker** der; ~s, ~: thinker

denk-, Denk- ~faul *Adj.* mentally lazy; ~mal das; ~s, ~mals, ~mäler od. ~male monument; ~vermögen das ability to think [creatively]; ~würdig *Adj.* memorable; ~zettel der lesson

denn 1. *Konj. (kausal)* for; because; b) *(geh.: als)* than; 2. *Adv.* es sei ~, ...: unless ...; 3. *Partikel (in Fragesätzen)* wie geht es dir ~? tell me, how are you?; wie heißt du ~? tell me your name; warum ~ nicht? why ever not?

dennoch *Adv.* nevertheless

denselben *s.* derselbe

Denunziant der; ~en, ~en informer; grass *(sl.)*; **denunzieren** *tr. V.* denounce; *(bei der Polizei)* inform against; grass on *(sl.)* (bei to)

Deo das; ~s, ~s, **Deodorant** das; ~s, ~s *(auch.)* ~e deodorant

Deponie die; ~, ~n tip *(Brit.)*; dump; **deponieren** *tr. V.* put; *(im Safe o. ä.)* deposit

Deportation die; ~, ~en transportation; *(ins Ausland)* deportation; **deportieren** *tr. V.* transport; *(ins Ausland)* deport; **Deportierte** der/die; *adj. Dekl.* transportee; *(ins Ausland)* deportee

Depot [de'po:] das; ~s, ~s a) depot; *(Lagerhaus)* warehouse; *(für Möbel usw.)* depository; *(im Freien, für Munition o. ä.)* dump; *(in einer Bank)* strong-room; safe deposit; b) *(hinterlegte Wertgegenstände)* deposits *pl.*

Depp der; ~en *(auch.)* ~s, ~en *(auch.)* ~e *(bes. südd., österr., schweiz. abwertend)* s. **Dummkopf**

Depression die; ~, ~en depression; **depressiv** 1. *Adj.* depressive; 2. *adv.* ~ veranlagt sein have a tendency towards depression; **deprimieren** *tr. V.* depress; **deprimierend** *Adj.* depressing; **deprimiert** 1. *Adj.* depressed; 2. *adv.* dejectedly

¹**der** 1. *best. Art. Nom.* the; der Tod death; der „Faust" 'Faust'; der Bodensee/Mount Everest Lake Constance/Mount Everest; der Iran/Sudan Iran/the Sudan; der Mensch/ Mann ist ...: man is .../men are ...; 2. *Demonstrativpron.* a) *attr.* that; der Mann war es it was 'that man; b) *al-*

leinstehend he; der war es it was 'him;
der [da] (Person) that man/boy; (Sache) that one; der [hier] (Person) this
man/boy; (Sache) this one; 3. Relativpron. (Person) who/that; (Sache)
which/that; der Mann, der da drüben
entlanggeht the man walking along
over there; 4. Relativ- u. Demonstrativpron. the one who

²der 1. best. Art. a) Gen. Sg. v. ¹die 1:
der Hut der Frau the woman's hat; der
Henkel der Tasse the handle of the
cup; b) Dat. Sg. v. ¹die 1 to the; (nach
Präp.) the; c) Gen. Pl. v. ¹der 1, ¹die 1,
das 1: das Haus der Freunde our/their
etc. friends' house; das Bellen der
Hunde the barking of the dogs; 2. Demonstrativpron. a) Gen. Sg. v. ¹die 2:
of the; of that; b) Dat. Sg. v. ¹die 2
attr. der Frau [da/hier] gehört es it be-
longs to that woman there/this
woman here; c) Gen. Pl. v. ¹der 2,
¹die 2 a, das 2 a of those; 3. Relativpron.; Dat. Sg. v. ¹die 3: die Frau, der
ich es gegeben habe the woman I gave
it to; die Katze, der er einen Tritt gab
the cat [that] he kicked

der·art Adv. so; es hat lange nicht
mehr ~ geregnet it hasn't rained as
hard as that for a long time; sie hat ~
geschrien, daß ...: she screamed so
much that ...; der·artig 1. Adj. such;
2. adv. s. derart

derb 1. Adj. a) tough ⟨material⟩; stout,
⟨shoes⟩; b) ⟨kraftvoll, deftig⟩ earthy
⟨scenes, humour⟩; 2. adv. a) strongly
⟨made, woven, etc.⟩; b) ⟨kraftvoll, def-
tig⟩ earthily

deren 1. Relativpron. a) Gen. Sg. v.
¹die 3 (Personen) whose; (Sachen) of
which; b) Gen. Pl. v. ¹der 3, ¹die 3, das
3 (Personen) whose; (Sachen) Maßnahmen, ~ Folgen wir noch nicht ab-
sehen können measures, the consequences of which we cannot yet
foresee; 2. Demonstrativpron. a) Gen.
Sg. v. ¹die 2: meine Tante, ihre Freundin und ~ Hund my aunt, her friend
and 'her dog; b) Gen. Pl. v. ¹der 2, ¹die
2, das 2: meine Verwandten und ~ Kinder my relatives and their children

derent-: ~wegen Adv. 1. relativ (Personen) because of whom; (Sachen)
because of which; 2. demonstrativ because of them; ~willen Adv. um
~willen (Personen) for whose sake;
(Sachen) for the sake of which

derer Demonstrativpron.; Gen. Pl. v.
¹der 2, ¹die 2, das 2 of those

der·gleichen indekl. Demonstrativpron. a) attr. such; like that postpos.,
not pred.; b) alleinstehend that sort of
thing

der·jenige, die·jenige, das·jeni-
ge Demonstrativpron. a) attr. that; Pl.
those; b) alleinstehend that one; Pl.
those

derlei indekl. Demonstrativpron.: s.
dergleichen

der·maßen Adv. ~ schön usw.,
daß ...: so beautiful etc. that ...

derselbe, dieselbe, dasselbe Demonstrativpron. a) attr. the same; b)
alleinstehend the same one; Pl. the
same people; er sagt immer dasselbe
he always says the same thing; noch
einmal dasselbe, bitte (ugs.) [the] same
again please

der·zeit Adv. at present; der·zeitig
Adj. present; current

des 1. best. Art.; Gen. Sg. v. ¹der 1, das
1: die Mütze des Jungen the boy's cap;
das Klingeln des Telefons the ringing
of the telephone; 2. Demonstrativpron.; Gen. Sg. v. ¹der 2, das 2: er ist
der Sohn des Mannes, der ...: he's the
son of the man who ...

Deserteur [dezɛr'tøːɐ̯] der; ~s, ~e
deserter; desertieren itr. V.; mit
sein desert

des·gleichen Adv. likewise; er ist
Arzt, ~ sein Sohn he is a doctor, as is
his son

des·halb Adv. for that reason; ~ bin
ich zu dir gekommen that is why I
came to you

Des·infektion die disinfection;
Desinfektions·mittel das disinfectant; des·infizieren tr. V. disinf-
fect

Des·interesse das lack of interest

Despot [dɛs'poːt] der; ~en, ~en despot; (fig. abwertend) tyrant; despo-
tisch 1. Adj. despotic; 2. adv. des-
potically

des·selben s. derselbe

dessen 1. Relativpron.; Gen. Sg. v.
¹der 3, das 3 attr. (Person) whose; (Sache) of which; 2. Demonstrativpron.;
Gen. Sg. v. ¹der 2, das 2: mein Onkel,
sein Sohn und ~ Hund my uncle, his
son, and 'his dog

Dessert [dɛ'seːɐ̯] das; ~s, ~s dessert

destillieren tr. V. (Chemie) distil

desto Konj., vor Komp. je eher, ~ besser the sooner the better

des·wegen Adv. s. deshalb

Detail [de'tai] das; ~s, ~s detail; de-

tailliert 1. *Adj.* detailed; 2. *adv.* in detail; **sehr ~**: in great detail

Detektiv der; ~s, ~e [private] detective

Detonation die; ~, ~en detonation; explosion

Deut *in* **keinen ~**: not one bit

deuten 1. *itr. V.* point; |mit dem Finger| **auf jmdn./etw. ~**: point [one's finger] at sb./sth.; 2. *tr. V.* interpret

deutlich 1. *Adj.* clear; 2. *adv.* clearly; **Deutlichkeit** die; ~a) clarity; b) *(Eindeutigkeit)* clearness

deutsch 1. *Adj.* German; **Deutsche Mark** Deutschmark; German mark; **auf** *od.* **in ~**: in German; **auf |gut| ~** *(ugs.)* in plain English; 2. *adv.* **~ sprechen/schreiben** speak/write German; **Deutsch** das; ~|s| German; **gutes/ fließend ~ sprechen** speak good/fluent German; **¹Deutsche** der/die; *adj. Dekl.* German; **~|r| sein** be German; **²Deutsche** das; *adj. Dekl.* das ~: German; **aus dem ~n/ins ~ übersetzen** translate from/into German; **Deutschland (das)**; ~s Germany

deutsch-, Deutsch-: **~lehrer** der German teacher; **~sprachig** *Adj.* a) German-speaking; b) German-language *attrib.*; **~unterricht** der German teaching; *(Unterrichtsstunde)* German lesson

Deutung die; ~, ~en interpretation

Devise die; ~, ~n motto; **Devisen** *Pl.* foreign currency sing.

Dezember der; ~s, ~: December

dezent 1. *Adj.* quiet *(colour, pattern, suit)*; subdued *(lighting, music)*; 2. *adv.* discreetly; *(dress)* unostentatiously

dezimal *Adj.* decimal

Dezimal-: **~system** das decimal system; **~zahl** die decimal [number]

dezimieren *tr. V.* decimate

dgl. *Abk.* dergleichen, desgleichen

d. h. *Abk.* das heißt i. e.

Di. *Abk.* Dienstag Tue|s|.

Dia das; ~s, ~s slide

Diabetiker der; ~s, ~, **Diabetikerin, die**; ~, ~nen diabetic

Diagnose [dia'gno:zə] die; ~, ~n diagnosis

diagonal 1. *Adj.* diagonal; 2. *adv.* diagonally; **Diagonale** die; ~, ~n diagonal

Dialekt der; ~|e|s, ~e dialect

Dialog der; ~|e|s, ~e dialogue

Diamant der; ~en, ~en diamond

diät *adv.* **~ kochen** cook according to

a/one's diet; **~ essen** be on a diet; **Diät die**; ~, ~en diet; **eine ~ einhalten** keep to a diet; **Diäten** *Pl.* [parliamentary] allowance sing.

dich 1. *Akk. von* du you; 2. *Akk. des Reflexivpron. der 2. Pers. Sg.* yourself

dicht 1. *Adj.* a) thick; dense *(forest, hedge, crowd)*; heavy, dense *(traffic)*; b) *(undurchlässig) (für Luft)* airtight; *(für Wasser)* watertight; 2. *adv.* a) densely *(populated, wooded)*; b) *(undurchlässig)* tightly; c) *mit Präp. (nahe)* **~ neben** right next to

dicht-besiedelt *Adj. (präd. getrennt geschrieben)* densely populated

Dichte die; ~ *(Physik, fig.)* density

dichten 1. *itr. V.* write poetry; 2. *tr. V. (verfassen)* write; compose; **Dichter** der; ~s, ~: poet; *(Schriftsteller)* writer; author; **Dichterin** die; ~, ~nen poet|ess|; *(Schriftstellerin)* writer; author|ess|; **dichterisch** *Adj.* poetic; *(schriftstellerisch)* literary

dicht|machen *tr., itr. V. (ugs.)* shut; *(endgültig)* shut down

¹Dichtung die; ~, ~en seal; *(am Hahn usw.)* washer; *(am Vergaser, Zylinder usw.)* gasket

²Dichtung die; ~, ~en a) work of literature; *(in Versform)* poetic work; poem; b) *o. Pl. (Dichtkunst)* literature; *(in Versform)* poetry

dick 1. *Adj.* a) thick; stout *(tree)*; fat *(person, legs, etc.)*; swollen *(cheek, ankle, tonsils, etc.)*; ~ **werden** get fat; **5 cm ~ sein** be 5 cm thick; b) *(ugs.: groß)* big *(mistake)*; hefty, *(coll.)* fat *(salary)*; 2. *adv.* thickly; **etw. ~ unterstreichen** underline sth. heavily; **sich ~ anziehen** wrap up warm|ly|; **etw. 5 cm ~ schneiden** cut sth. 5 cm. thick; **~ geschwollen** *(ugs.)* badly swollen; **¹Dicke** die; ~: thickness; *(von Menschen, Körperteilen)* fatness; **²Dicke** der/die; *adj. Dekl. (ugs.)* fatty *(coll.)*; **dick-fellig** *(ugs.)* *Adj.* thick-skinned; **Dickicht** ['dɪkɪçt] das; ~|e|s, ~e thicket

dick-, Dick-: **~kopf** der *(ugs.)* mule *(coll.)*; **ein ~kopf sein** be stubborn as a mule; **einen ~kopf haben** be pigheaded; **~köpfig** *Adj. (ugs.)* pigheaded; **~milch** die sour milk

¹die 1. *best. Art. Nom.* the; **die Helga** *(ugs.)* Helga; **die Frau/Menschheit** women *pl.*/mankind; 2. *Demonstrativpron.* a) *attr.* **die Frau war es** it was 'that woman; b) *alleinstehend* she; **die war es** it was 'her; **die |da| *(Person)*** that woman/girl; *(Sache)* that one; **3.** *Relativpron. Nom. (Person)* who; that; *(Sache, Tier)* which; that; **4.** *Relativ- u. Demonstrativpron.* the one who

²die 1. *best. Art.* **a)** *Akk. Sg. v.* **¹die 1** the; **ich sah die Frau** I saw the women; **b)** *Nom. u. Akk. Pl. v.* **¹der 1, ¹die 1, das 1** the; **2.** *Demonstrativpron. Nom. u. Akk. Pl. v.* **¹der 1, ¹die 1, das 1:** *attr.* **ich meine die Männer, die ...** I mean those men who ...; *alleinstehend* **ich meine die [da]** I mean 'them; **3.** *Relativpron.* **a)** *Akk. Sg. v.* **¹die 3** *(Person)* who; *(Sache)* that; **b)** *Nom. u. Akk. Pl. v.* **¹der 3, ¹die 3, das 3** *(Personen)* whom; *(Sachen)* which; **die Männer, die ich gesehen habe** the men I saw

Dieb der; ~[e]s, ~e thief; **Diebin** die; ~, ~nen [woman] thief; **diebisch 1.** *Adj.* **a)** thieving; **b)** *(verstohlen)* mischievous; **2.** *adv.* mischievously; **Diebstahl** der; ~[e]s, Diebstähle theft

die·jenige *s.* derjenige

Diele die; ~, ~n hall[way]

dienen *itr. V.* serve; **womit kann ich ~?** what can I do for you?; **Diener** der; ~s, ~ servant; **einen ~ machen** *(ugs.)* bow; make a bow; **Dienerin** die; ~, ~nen maid; servant

dienlich *Adj.* helpful; **Dienst** der; ~[e]s, ~e **a)** *o. Pl. (Tätigkeit)* work; *(von Soldaten, Polizeibeamten, Krankenhauspersonal usw.)* duty; **seinen ~ antreten** start work/go on duty; **~ haben** be at work/on duty; *(doctor)* be on call; *(chemist)* be open; **b)** *(Arbeitsverhältnis)* post; **Major außer ~:** retired major; **c)** *o. Pl. (Tätigkeitsbereich)* service; *s. auch* öffentlich; **d)** *(Hilfe)* service

Diens·tag der Tuesday; **am ~:** on Tuesday; **~, der 1. Juni** Tuesday, 1 June; **er kommt am ~:** he is coming on Tuesday; **ab nächsten ~:** from next Tuesday [onwards]; **in einer Woche a week on Tuesday**; **~ vor einer Woche** a week last Tuesday; **diens·tags** *Adv.* on Tuesday[s]

dienst-, Dienst-: **~bereit** *Adj.* *(chemist)* open *pred.*; *(doctor)* on call; *(dentist)* on duty; **~bote** der servant; **~eifrig** *Adj.* zealous; **~frei** *Adj.* free *(time)*; **~geheimnis das a)** professional secret; *(im Staatsdienst)* official secret; **b)** *o. Pl.* professional secrecy; *(im Staatsdienst)* official secrecy; **~grad** der *(Milit.)* rank; **~leistung** die *(auch Wirtsch.)* service

dienstlich 1. *Adj.* business *(call)*; *(im Staatsdienst)* official *(letter, call, etc.)*; **2.** *adv.* on business; *(im Staatsdienst)* on official business

dienst-, Dienst-: **~reise** die business trip; **~stelle** die office; **~wagen** der official car; *(Geschäftswagen)* company car; **~weg** der official channels *pl.*; **~zeit** die **a)** period of service; **b)** *(tägliche Arbeitszeit)* working hours *pl.*

dies *s.* dieser

dies·bezüglich *adv.* regarding this

diese *s.* dieser

Diesel der; ~[s], ~: diesel

die·selbe *s.* derselbe

Diesel·motor der diesel engine

dieser, diese, dieses, dies *Demonstrativpron.* **a)** *attr.* this; *Pl.* these; **b)** *alleinstehend* this one; *Pl.* these; **dies alles** all this; **dies und das**, *(geh.)* **dieses und jenes** this and that

diesig *Adj.* hazy

dies-: **~mal** *Adv.* this time; **~seits 1.** *Präp. mit Gen.* on this side of; **2.** *Adv.* **~seits von** on this side of

Dietrich der; ~s, ~e picklock

diffamieren *tr. V.* defame; **Diffamierung** die; ~, ~en defamation

Differenz die; ~, ~en difference; *(Meinungsverschiedenheit)* difference [of opinion]; **differenziert** *Adj.* complex; subtly differentiated *(methods, colours)*; sophisticated *(taste)*

diffus *Adj. (Physik, Chemie)* diffuse; **b)** *(geh.)* vague; vague and confused *(idea, statement, etc.)*; **2.** *adv.* in a vague and confused way

Digital- digital *(clock, display, etc.)*

digitalisieren *tr. V. (DV)* digitalize

Diktat das; ~[e]s, ~e dictation

Diktator der; ~s, ~en dictator; **diktatorisch 1.** *Adj.* dictatorial; **2.** *adv.* dictatorially; **Diktatur** die; ~, ~en dictatorship

diktieren *tr. V.* dictate

Diktier·gerät das dictating machine

Dilemma das; ~s, ~s dilemma

Dilettant [dile'tant] der; ~en, ~en, **Dilettantin** die; ~, ~nen dilettante; **dilettantisch 1.** *Adj.* dilettante; amateurish; **2.** *adv.* amateurishly

Dill der; ~[e]s, ~e dill

Dimension die; ~, ~en *(Physik, fig.)* dimension

DIN [di:n] *Abk.* Deutsche Industrie-Norm[en] *German Industrial Standard[s]*; DIN; **DIN-A4-Format** A4

¹Ding das; ~|e|s, ~e a) thing; b) *meist Pl.* nach Lage der ~e the way things are; **persönliche/private** ~e personal/private matters; **ein** ~ **der Unmöglichkeit sein** be quite impossible; **vor allem** ~en above all; c) **guter** ~e **sein** (*geh.*) be in good spirits; **²Ding** das; ~|e|s, ~er (*ugs.*) thing; **das ist ja ein** ~! that's really something

Diözese die; ~, ~n diocese

Dipl.-Ing. *Abk.* Diplomingenieur *academically qualified engineer*

Diplom das; ~s, ~e ≈ |first| degree (*in a scientific or technical subject);* (*für einen Handwerksberuf*) diploma; **Diplom-:** qualified

Diplomat der; ~en, ~en, **Diplomatin** die; ~, ~nen diplomat; **diplomatisch** 1. *Adj.* diplomatic; 2. *adv.* diplomatically

dir 1. *Dat. von* du to you; (*nach Präp.*) you; **Freunde von** ~: friends of yours; 2. *Dat. des Reflexivpron. der 2. Pers. Sg.* yourself

direkt 1. *Adj.* direct; 2. *adv.* straight; directly; **etw.** ~ **übertragen** broadcast sth. live; **Direkt·flug** der direct flight

Direktion die; ~, ~en management; (*Büroräume*) managers' offices *pl.*; **Direktor** der; ~s, ~en, **Direktorin** die; ~, ~nen director; (*einer Schule*) headmaster/headmistress; (*einer Strafanstalt*) governor; (*einer Abteilung*) manager

Direkt·übertragung die live broadcast

Dirigent der; ~en, ~en conductor; **dirigieren** *tr. V.* a) *auch itr.* conduct; b) (*führen*) steer

Disco ['dɪsko:] die; ~, ~s disco

Diskette die; ~, ~n (*DV*) floppy disc

Diskont·satz der (*Finanzw.*) discount rate

Diskothek die; ~, ~en discothèque

Diskrepanz die; ~, ~en discrepancy

diskret 1. *Adj.* (*vertraulich*) confidential; (*taktvoll*) discreet; tactful; 2. *adv.* (*vertraulich*) confidentially; (*taktvoll*) discreetly; tactfully; **Diskretion** die; ~ a) (*Verschwiegenheit, Takt*) discretion; b) (*Unaufdringlichkeit*) discreetness

diskriminieren *tr. V.* discriminate against; **Diskriminierung** die; ~, ~en discrimination

Diskussion die; ~, ~en discussion; **zur** ~ **stehen** be under discussion

Diskussions-: ~beitrag der contribution to a/the discussion; **~leiter** der chairman [of the discussion]

diskutieren 1. *itr. V.* über etw. (*Akk.*) ~: discuss sth.; 2. *tr. V.* discuss

disqualifizieren *tr. V.* disqualify

Distanz die; ~, ~en (*auch fig.*) distance; **distanzieren** *refl. V.* sich von jmdm./etw. ~ (*fig.*) dissociate oneself from sb./sth.; **distanziert** *Adj.* reserved

Distel die; ~, ~n thistle

Distel·fink der the goldfinch

Disziplin die; ~, ~en discipline; (*Selbstbeherrschung*) [self-]discipline; **disziplinieren** 1. *tr. V.* discipline; 2. *refl. V.* discipline oneself; **diszipliniert** 1. *Adj.* well-disciplined; (*beherrscht*) disciplined; 2. *adv.* in a well-disciplined way; (*beherrscht*) in a disciplined way

divers... [di'vɛrs...] *Adj.; nicht präd.* various; (*mehrer...*) several

Dividende [divi'dɛndə] die; ~, ~n (*Wirtsch.*) dividend

dividieren *tr. V.* divide; **Division** die; ~, ~en (*auch Milit.*) division

DM *Abk.* Deutsche Mark DM

Do. *Abk.* Donnerstag Thur|s|.

doch 1. *Konj.* but; 2. *Adv.* a) (*jedoch*) but; b) (*dennoch*) all the same; still; c) (*geh.: nämlich*) wußte er ~, daß ...: because he knew that ...; d) (*entgegen allen gegenteiligen Behauptungen, Annahmen*) er war also ~ der Mörder! so he 'was the murderer!; e) (*ohnehin*) in any case; 3. *Interj.* Das stimmt nicht. – Doch! That's not right. – [Oh] yes it is!; Hast du keinen Hunger? – Doch! Aren't you hungry? – Yes [I am]!; 4. *Partikel* a) (*Ungeduld ausdrückend*) paß ~ auf! [oh] do be careful!; das ist ~ nicht zu glauben that's just incredible!; b) (*Zweifel ausdrückend*) du hast ~ meinen Brief erhalten? you did get my letter, didn't you?; c) (*Überraschung ausdrückend*) das ist ~ Karl! there's Karl! d) (*verstärkt Bejahung/Verneinung ausdrückend*) gewiß/sicher ~: [why] certainly; of course; ja ~: [yes,] all right; nicht ~! (*abwehrend*) [no,] don't!; e) (*Wunsch verstärkend*) wäre es ...: if only it were ...

Docht der; ~|e|s, ~ wick

Dock das; ~s, ~s dock

Dogge die; ~, ~n: |deutsche| ~: Great Dane

Dogma das; ~s, Dogmen (*auch fig.*) dogma; **dogmatisch** (*Theol., auch fig.*) *Adj.* dogmatic

Dohle die; ~, ~n jackdaw

Doktor der; ~s, ~en *(auch ugs. Arzt)* doctor; *(Titel)* Doctor; **Doktor·arbeit** die doctoral thesis

Doktrin die; ~, ~en doctrine

Dokument das; ~[e]s, ~e document

Dokumentar-: ~**bericht** der documentary report; ~**film** der documentary [film]

Dokumentation die; ~, ~en o. Pl. documentation; b) *(Bericht)* documentary report

dokumentieren tr. V. a) document; *(fig.)* demonstrate; b) *(festhalten)* record

Dolch der; ~[e]s, ~e dagger

Dolde die; ~, ~n *(Bot.)* umbel

doll *(bes. nordd., salopp)* 1. Adj. a) *(ungewöhnlich)* incredible; b) *(großartig)* great *(coll.)*; 2. adv. a) *(großartig)* fantastically [well] *(coll.)*; b) *(sehr)* ⟨hurt⟩ dreadfully *(coll.)*, like mad

Dollar der; ~[s], ~s dollar; **zwei** ~: two dollars

dolmetschen itr. V. act as interpreter; **Dolmetscher** der; ~s, ~, **Dolmetscherin** die; ~, ~nen interpreter

Dom der; ~[e]s, ~e cathedral

dominieren itr. V. dominate

dominikanisch Adj. Dominican; **die Dominikanische Republik** the Dominican Republic

Domizil das; ~s, ~e *(geh.)* domicile; residence

Dom·pfaff der; ~en od. ~s, ~en *(Zool.)* bullfinch

Dompteur [dɔmp'tøːɐ] der; ~s, ~e, **Dompteuse** [dɔmp'tøːzə] die; ~, ~n tamer

Donau die; ~: Danube

Donner der; ~s, ~: thunder; **donnern** itr. V. a) *(unpers.)* thunder; b) *(fig.)* thunder; ⟨engine⟩ roar

Donners·tag der Thursday; s. auch **Dienstag**; **donnerstags** Adv. on Thursday[s]; s. auch **dienstags**

Donner·wetter das *(ugs.)* a) *(Krach)* row; b) ['–'–'·–] **zum ~** [noch einmal]! damn it!; ~! my word

doof *(ugs.)* 1. Adj. stupid; dumb *(coll.)*; 2. adv. stupidly

Doppel das; ~s, ~ a) *(Kopie)* duplicate; copy; b) *(Sport)* doubles sing. or pl.

doppel-, Doppel-: ~**bett** das double bed; ~**bock** das extra-strong bock beer; ~**decker** der; ~s, ~: biplane; ~**deutig** [~dɔytɪç] 1. Adj. a)

ambiguous; b) *(anzüglich)* suggestive; 2. adv. a) ambiguously; b) *(anzüglich)* suggestively; ~**fenster** das double-glazed window; ~**gänger** der; ~s, ~, ~**gängerin** die; ~, ~nen double; ~**kinn** das double chin; ~**punkt** der colon

doppelt 1. Adj. double; **die ~e Menge** twice the quantity; **mit ~er Kraft arbeiten** work with twice as much energy; 2. adv. ~ **so groß/alt wie ...:** twice as large/old as ...; **sich ~ anstrengen** try twice as hard; **Doppelte** das; adj. Dekl. **das ~ bezahlen** pay twice as much; pay double

Doppel-: ~**tür** die double door; ~**zentner** der 100 kilograms; ~**zimmer** das double room

Dorf das; ~[e]s, Dörfer village; **auf dem ~** in the country; **Dorf·bewohner** der villager

Dorn der; ~[e]s, ~en thorn; **jmdm. ein ~ im Auge sein** annoy sb. intensely; **dornig** Adj. thorny; **Dorn·röschen (das)** the Sleeping Beauty

dörren tr. V. dry

Dörr-: ~**fleisch** das *(südd.)* lean bacon; ~**obst** das dried fruit

Dorsch der; ~[e]s, ~e cod

dort Adv. there; s. auch **da** 1 a

dort-: ~|**bleiben** unr. itr. V.; mit sein stay there; ~**her** Adv. [von] ~**her** from there; ~**hin** Adv. there

dortig Adj.; nicht präd. there

Dose die; ~, ~n a) *(Blech~)* tin; *(Pillen~)* box; *(Zucker~)* bowl; b) *(Konserven~)* can; tin *(Brit.)*; *(Bier~)* can

dösen itr. V. *(ugs.)* doze

Dosen-: ~**bier** das canned beer; ~**milch** die canned or *(Brit.)* tinned milk; ~**öffner** der can opener; tin-opener *(Brit.)*

dosieren tr. V. etw. ~: measure out the required dose of sth.; **Dosis** die; ~, **Dosen** dose

Dotter der od. das; ~s, ~: yolk

Dotter·blume die marsh marigold

Dozent der; ~en, ~en, **Dozentin** die; ~, ~nen lecturer (für in)

Dr. Abk.: **Doktor** Dr

Drache der; ~n, ~n *(Myth.)* dragon; **Drachen** der; ~s, ~ a) kite; b) *(Fluggerät)* hang-glider

Dragée, Dragee [dra'ʒeː] das; ~s, ~s dragée

Draht der; ~[e]s, Drähte a) wire; b) *(Leitung)* wire; *(Telefonleitung)* line; wire; c) *(Telefonverbindung)* line

draht-, Draht-: ~**los** *(Nachrichtenw.)*

1. *Adj.* wireless; 2. *adv.* etw. ~los telegrafieren/übermitteln radio sth.; ~seil das [steel] cable; ~seil·bahn die cable railway; ~zieher der ⟨fig.⟩ wire puller

drall *Adj.* strapping ⟨girl⟩; full, rounded ⟨cheeks, face, bottom⟩

Drama das; ~s, Dramen drama; ⟨fig., ugs.⟩ disaster; **dramatisch** 1. *Adj.* dramatic. 2. *adv.* dramatically; **dramatisieren** *tr. V.* dramatize

dran *Adv.* ⟨ugs.⟩ a) häng das Schild ~! put the sign up!; b) arm ~ sein be in a bad way; gut/schlecht ~ sein be well off/badly off; früh/spät ~ sein be early/late; ich bin ~: it's my turn; **dran·bleiben** *unr. itr. V.; mit sein* ⟨ugs.⟩ (am Telefon) hang on ⟨coll.⟩

drang *1. u. 3. Pers. Sg. Prät. v. dringen*

Drang der; ~[e]s, Dränge urge

dränge *1. u. 3. Pers. Sg. Konjunktiv II v. dringen*

drängeln ⟨ugs.⟩ 1. *itr. V.* a) push [and shove]; b) ⟨auf jmdn. einreden⟩ go on ⟨coll.⟩; 2. *tr. V.* a) push; shove; b) ⟨einreden auf⟩ go on at ⟨coll.⟩; 3. *refl. V.* sich nach vorn ~: push one's way to the front

drängen 1. *itr. V.* a) push; b) die Zeit drängt time is pressing; 2. *tr. V.* a) push; b) ⟨antreiben⟩ press; urge; 3. *refl. V.* crowd

drangsalieren *tr. V.* ⟨quälen⟩ torment; ⟨plagen⟩ plague

dran-: ~|halten *unr. refl. V.* ⟨ugs.⟩ get a move on ⟨coll.⟩; ~|kommen *unr. itr. V.; mit sein* ⟨ugs.⟩ have one's turn; ~nehmen *unr. tr. V.* ⟨ugs.⟩ (beim Friseur usw.) see to; (beim Arzt) see

drastisch 1. *Adj.* drastic ⟨measure, means⟩; 2. *adv.* drastically; ⟨punish⟩ severely

drauf *Adv.* ⟨ugs.⟩ on it

drauf-, Drauf-: ~gänger der daredevil; ~gängerisch *Adj.* daring; ~|gehen *unr. itr. V.; mit sein* ⟨ugs.⟩ (umkommen) kick the bucket ⟨sl.⟩; b) ⟨verbraucht werden⟩ go ⟨für on⟩; ~|zahlen ⟨ugs.⟩ a) *itr. V.* noch etwas/1 250 DM ~zahlen fork out ⟨sl.⟩ or pay a bit more/an extra 1,250 marks; 2. *itr. V.* ⟨Unkosten haben⟩ ich zahle dabei noch ~: it's costing me money

draußen *Adv.* outside; hier/da ~: out here/there; von/nach ~: from outside/outside

Dreck der; ~[e]s a) ⟨ugs.⟩ dirt; ⟨sehr viel⟩ filth; ⟨Schlamm⟩ mud; b) ⟨salopp abwertend: Angelegenheit⟩ mach dei-

nen ~ allein do it yourself; das geht dich einen |feuchten| ~ an ⟨salopp⟩ none of your damned business ⟨sl.⟩; c) ⟨salopp abwertend: Zeug⟩ junk no indef. art.; **Dreck·arbeit** die ⟨auch fig.⟩ dirty work no indef. art., no pl./dirty job; **dreckig** 1. *Adj.* a) ⟨ugs., auch fig.⟩ dirty; ⟨sehr schmutzig⟩ filthy; b) ⟨salopp: unverschämt⟩ cheeky; 2. *adv.* a) es geht ihm ~ ⟨ugs.⟩ he's in a bad way; b) ⟨salopp: unverschämt⟩ cheekily

Dreck-: ~sau die, ~schwein das ⟨derb⟩ filthy swine

Dreh der; ~s, ~s ⟨ugs.⟩ a) den ~ heraushaben have [got] the knack; b) |so| um den ~: about that

Dreh-: ~arbeiten Pl. ⟨Film⟩ shooting sing. ⟨zu of⟩; ~bank die lathe; ~buch das screenplay; [film] script

drehen 1. *tr. V.* a) turn; b) ⟨formen⟩ twist ⟨rope, thread⟩; roll ⟨cigarette⟩; ⟨Film⟩ shoot ⟨scene⟩; film ⟨report⟩; make; ⟨film⟩ 2. *itr. V.* ⟨car⟩ turn; ⟨wind⟩ change; b) an etw. ⟨Dat.⟩ ~: turn sth.; c) ⟨Film⟩ film; 3. *refl. V.* a) turn; b) ⟨ugs.: zum Gegenstand haben⟩ sich um etw. ~: be about sth.

Dreh-: ~orgel die barrel-organ; ~restaurant das revolving restaurant; ~stuhl der swivel chair; ~tür die revolving door

Drehung die; ~, ~en turn; ⟨um einen Mittelpunkt⟩ revolution

drei *Kardinalz.* three; **Drei** die; ~, ~en three; eine ~ schreiben ⟨Schulw.⟩ get a C

drei-, Drei-: ~eck das; ~s, ~e ⟨Geom.⟩ triangle; ~eckig *Adj.* triangular; ~ein·halb *Bruchz.* three and a half

Dreier der; ~s, ~ ⟨ugs.⟩ three; **dreierlei** *Gattungsz.; indekl.* a) *attr.* three kinds or sorts of; three different; b) *subst.* three [different] things

drei-, Drei-: ~fach *Vervielfältigungsz.* triple; die ~fache Menge three times the amount; ~fache das; *adj. Dekl.* das ~fache three times as much; das ~fache von 3 ist 9 three times three is nine; ~hundert *Kardinalz.* three hundred; ~jährig *Adj.* (3 Jahre alt) three-year-old *attrib.*; (3 Jahre dauernd) three-year *attrib.*; ~kampf der ⟨Sport⟩ triathlon; ~klang der triad; ~köpfig *Adj.* ⟨family, crew⟩ of three; ~mal *Adv.* three times; ~malig *Adj.* eine ~malige Wiederholung three repeats

drein *(ugs.) s.* darein

drein-: ~|**blicken**, ~|**schauen** *itr. V.* look

drei-, **Drei-:** ~**rad** *das* tricycle; ~**satz** *der;* rule of three; ~**seitig** *Adj.* three-sided *⟨figure⟩;* three-page *⟨letter, leaflet, etc.⟩*

dreißig *Kardinalz.* thirty; *s. auch* achtzig; **dreißigjährig** *Adj. ⟨30 Jahre alt⟩* thirty-year-old *attrib.; ⟨30 Jahre dauernd⟩* thirty-year *attrib.;* **dreißigst...** *Ordinalz.* thirtieth; **Dreißigstel** *das;* ~**s**, ~: thirtieth

dreist 1. *Adj.* brazen; barefaced *⟨lie⟩;* 2. *adv.* brazenly

drei·stellig *Adj.* three-figure *attrib.*

Dreistigkeit *die;* ~, ~**en** a) *o. Pl.* brazenness; b) *⟨Handlung⟩* brazen act

drei-, **Drei-:** ~**tausend** *Kardinalz.* three thousand; ~**teilig** *Adj.* three-part *attrib.;* three-piece *attrib. ⟨suit⟩;* ~**viertel** *Bruchz.* three-quarters; ~**viertel·stunde** [---'--] *die* three-quarters of an hour; ~**viertel·takt** [-'---] *der* three-four time; ~**zehn** *Kardinalz.* thirteen; *s. auch* achtzehn

Dresche *die;* ~ *(salopp)* walloping *(sl.);* thrashing; **dreschen** 1. *unr. tr. V.* a) thresh; b) *(salopp: schlagen)* wallop *(sl.);* thrash; 2. *unr. itr. V.* thresh

dressieren *tr. V.* train *⟨animal⟩;* **Dressur** *die;* ~, ~**en** training

Drill *der;* ~|**e**|**s** drilling; *(Milit.)* drill; **drillen** *tr. V. (auch Milit.)* drill

Drilling *der;* ~**s**, ~**e** triplet

drin *Adv. (ugs.)* a) in it; b) *s.* drinnen

dringen *unr. itr. V.* a) *mit sein durch/ in etw.* ~: penetrate sth.; b) *mit sein in* jmdn. ~ *(geh.)* press sb.; c) *auf etw. (Akk.)* ~: insist upon sth.; **dringend** 1. *Adj.* urgent; strong *⟨suspicion, advice⟩;* 2. *adv.* urgently *⟨advise, suspect⟩* strongly; ~ **erforderlich** essential; **dringlich** 1. *Adj.* urgent; 2. *adv.* urgently; **Dringlichkeit** *die;* ~: urgency

drinnen *Adv.* inside; *(im Haus)* indoors; inside

dritt *in* wir waren zu ~: there were three of us

dritt... *Ordinalz.* third; **Drittel** *das,* *(schweiz. meist* der); ~**s**, ~: third; **dritteln** *tr. V.* split or divide three ways; **drittens** *Adv.* thirdly

DRK [de:|ɛr'ka:] *das;* ~ *Abk.* Deutsches Rotes Kreuz German Red Cross

Dr. med. *Abk.* doctor medicinae MD

droben *Adv. (südd., österr., sonst geh.)* up there

Droge *die;* ~, ~**n** drug

drogen-: ~**abhängig**, ~**süchtig** *Adj.* addicted to drugs *postpos.*

Drogerie *die;* ~, ~**n** chemist's [shop] *(Brit.);* drugstore *(Amer.);* **Drogist** *der;* ~**en**, ~**en**, **Drogistin** *die;* ~, ~**nen** chemist *(Brit.);* druggist *(Amer.)*

drohen *itr., mod. V.* threaten; *(bevorstehen)* be threatening; **jmdm. droht** etw. sb. is threatened with sth.; **drohend** *Adj.* threatening; *(bevorstehend)* impending

Drohne *die;* ~, ~**n** drone

dröhnen *itr. V.* boom; *⟨machine⟩* roar

Drohung *die;* ~, ~**en** threat

drollig 1. *Adj.* funny; comical; *(niedlich)* sweet; cute *(Amer.);* 2. *adv.:* s. *Adj.:* comically; sweetly; cutely *(Amer.)*

Dromedar *das;* ~**s**, ~**e** dromedary

Drops *der od. das;* ~, ~: fruit *or (Brit.)* acid drop

drosch *1. u. 3. Pers. Sg. Prät. v.* dreschen

Drossel *die;* ~, ~**n** thrush

drosseln *tr. V.* a) turn down *⟨heating, air-conditioning⟩;* throttle back *⟨engine⟩;* b) *(herabsetzen)* reduce

Dr. phil. *Abk.* doctor philosophiae Dr

drüben *Adv.* dort *od.* da ~: over there; ~ **auf der anderen Seite** over on the other side

¹**Druck** *der;* ~|**e**|**s**, **Drücke** a) *(auch fig.)* pressure; b) *o. Pl.* ein ~ **auf den Knopf** a touch of the button; ²**Druck** *der;* ~|**e**|**s**, ~**e** a) *o. Pl.* printing; **in** ~ **gehen** go to press; b) *(Produkt)* print; **Druck·buchstabe** *der* printed letter; **drucken** *tr., itr. V.* print

drücken 1. *tr. V.* a) press; press, push *⟨button⟩;* squeeze *⟨juice, pus⟩* (aus out of); **jmdm. die Hand** ~: squeeze sb.'s hand; b) *(liebkosen)* jmdn. ~: hug [and squeeze] sb.; c) *⟨shoe etc.⟩* pinch; d) *(herabsetzen)* push down *⟨price, rate⟩;* depress *⟨sales⟩;* bring down *⟨standard⟩;* 2. *itr. V.* a) press; **auf den Knopf** ~: press *or* push the button; „**bitte** ~": 'push'; b) *(Druck verursachen) ⟨shoe etc.⟩* pinch; 3. *refl. V. (ugs.: sich entziehen)* shirk; **sich vor etw. (Dat.)** ~: get out of sth.; **drückend** *Adj.* heavy *⟨debt, taxes⟩;* serious *⟨worries⟩;* grinding *⟨poverty⟩;* b) *⟨schwül⟩* oppressive

Drucker *der;* ~**s**, ~: printer; **Druckerei** *die;* ~, ~**en** printing-works; *(Firma)* printing-house; printer's

druck-, Druck-: ~**fehler** der misprint; printer's error; ~**knopf** der press-stud *(Brit.);* snap-fastener; ~**luft** die compressed air; ~**mittel** das means of bringing pressure to bear *(gegenüber* on); ~**reif** 1. *Adj.* ready for publication; *(~fertig)* ready for press; 2. *adv.* ⟨speak⟩ in a polished manner; ~**sache** die *(Postw.)* printed matter; ~**schrift** die a) printed writing; b) *(Schriftart)* type[-face]; c) *(Schriftwerk)* pamphlet

drum *Adv.* *(ugs.)* a) *s.* darum; b) [a]round; alles *od.* das [ganze] Drum und Dran *(bei einer Mahlzeit)* all the trimmings; *(bei einer Feierlichkeit)* all the palaver that goes with it *(coll.);* **Drum·herum das;** ~**s** everything that goes/went with it

drunter *Adv. (ugs.)* underneath; es *od.* alles geht ~ und drüber everything is topsy-turvy

Drüse die; ~, ~**n** gland

Dschungel ['dʒʊŋl̩] der; ~**s**, ~ *(auch fig.)* jungle

dt. *Abk.* deutsch G.

Dtzd. *Abk.* Dutzend doz.

du *Personalpron.;* 2. *Pers. Sg. Nom.* you; *(in Briefen)* Du you; du zueinander sagen use the familiar form in addressing one another; *s. auch (Gen.)* deiner, *(Dat.)* dir, *(Akk.)* dich

Dübel der; ~**s**, ~: plug

ducken 1. *refl. V.* duck; 2. *itr. V. (fig. abwertend)* humble oneself (vor + *Dat.* before)

Dudel·sack der bagpipes *pl.*

Duell das; ~**s**, ~**e** duel; **duellieren** *refl. V.* fight a duel

Duett das; ~[**e**]**s**, ~**e** *(Musik)* duet; im ~ singen sing a duet

Duft der; ~[**e**]**s**, **Düfte** scent; *(von Parfüm, Blumen)* scent; fragrance; *(von Kaffee usw.)* aroma; **duften** *itr. V.* smell (**nach** of)

dulden *tr. V.* tolerate; put up with; **duldsam** 1. *Adj.* tolerant (**gegen** towards); 2. *adv.* tolerantly

dumm, dümmer, dümmst... 1. *Adj.* a) stupid; b) *(unvernünftig)* foolish; c) *(ugs.: töricht, albern)* idiotic; silly; d) *(ugs.: unangenehm)* nasty *(feeling);* annoying *(habit);* das wird mir jetzt zu ~ *(ugs.)* I've had enough of it; 2. *adv. (ugs.)* idiotically; **Dumme** der/die; *adj. Dekl.* fool; **der** ~ **sein** *(ugs.)* be the loser; **dummer·weise** *Adv.* a) unfortunately; *(ärgerlicherweise)* annoyingly; b) *(törichterweise)* foolishly;

Dummheit die; ~, ~**en** a) *o. Pl.* stupidity; b) *(unkluge Handlung)* stupid thing; **Dumm·kopf** der *(ugs.)* nitwit *(coll.)*

dumpf 1. *Adj.* a) dull ⟨thud, rumble of thunder⟩; muffled ⟨sound, thump⟩; b) *(muffig)* musty; c) *(stumpfsinnig)* dull; 2. *adv.* a) ⟨echo⟩ hollowly; b) *(stumpfsinnig)* apathetically

Düne die; ~, ~**n** dune

düngen 1. *tr. V.* fertilize ⟨soil, lawn⟩; spread fertilizer on ⟨field⟩; scatter fertilizer around ⟨plants⟩; 2. *itr. V.* **gut** ~ ⟨substance⟩ be a good fertilizer; **Dünger** der; ~**s**, ~: fertilizer

dunkel 1. *Adj. (auch fig.)* dark; *(tief)* deep ⟨voice, note⟩; *(undeutlich)* vague; 2. *adv. (tief)* ⟨speak⟩ in a deep voice; b) *(undeutlich)* vaguely

Dünkel der; ~**s** *(geh.)* arrogance; *(Einbildung)* conceit[edness]

dunkel-: ~**blond** *Adj.* light brown ⟨hair⟩; ⟨person⟩ with light brown hair; ~**häutig** *Adj.* dark-skinned

Dunkelheit die; ~: darkness; **Dunkel·kammer** die dark-room; **dunkeln** *itr. V. (unpers.)* es dunkelt *(geh.)* it is growing dark; **Dunkel·ziffer** die number of unrecorded cases

dünn 1. *Adj.* thin; slim ⟨book⟩; fine ⟨stocking⟩; watery ⟨coffee, tea, beer⟩; 2. *adv.* thinly ⟨sliced, populated⟩; lightly ⟨dressed⟩

Dunst der; ~[**e**]**s**, **Dünste** a) *o. Pl.* haze; *(Nebel)* mist; b) *(Geruch)* smell; **dünsten** *tr. V.* steam ⟨fish, vegetables⟩; braise ⟨meat⟩; stew ⟨fruit⟩; **dunstig** *Adj.* hazy

Duo das; ~**s**, ~**s** *(Musik)* duet; *(fig. scherzh.)* duo; pair

Duplikat das; ~[**e**]**s**, ~**e** duplicate

Dur das; ~ *(Musik)* major [key]

durch 1. *Präp. mit Akk.* a) *(räumlich)* through; b) *(modal)* by: ~ **Boten** by courier; zehn [geteilt] ~ zwei ten divided by two; 2. *Adv.* a) *(hin~)* das ganze Jahr ~: throughout the whole year; b) *(ugs.: vorbei)* es war 3 Uhr ~: it was gone 3 o'clock; c) ~ und ~ naß/überzeugt wet through [and through]/completely totally convinced

durch|arbeiten 1. *tr. V.* work through; 2. *itr. V.* work through; die Nacht ~: work through the night

durch·aus *Adv.* absolutely; perfectly; quite ⟨correct, possible, understandable⟩; das ist ~ richtig that is entirely right; ~ **nicht** by no means

durch|beißen *unr. tr. V.* bite through

durch|blättern *tr. V.* leaf through

Durch·blick der *(ugs.)* **den |absoluten|** ~ **haben** know [exactly] what's going on; **durch|blicken** *itr. V.* **a)** look through; durch etw. ~: look through sth.; **b)** ~ **lassen, daß …/wie …**: hint that …/at how …

Durch·blutung die; *o. Pl.* flow of blood (+ *Gen.* to); [blood-]circulation

¹**durch|bohren** *tr. V.* drill through ⟨*wall, plank*⟩; drill ⟨*hole*⟩; ²**durch-bohren** *tr. V.* pierce

¹**durch|brechen 1.** *unr. tr. V.* etw. ~: break sth. in two; **2.** *unr. itr. V.; mit sein* **a)** break in two; **b)** *(hervorkommen)* ⟨*sun*⟩ break through; **c)** *(einbrechen)* fall through ⟨*ice, floor, etc.*⟩; ²**durch·brechen** *unr. tr. V.* break through

durch|brennen *unr. itr. V.; mit sein* **a)** ⟨*heating coil, light bulb*⟩ burn out; ⟨*fuse*⟩ blow; **b)** *(ugs.: weglaufen) (von zu Hause)* run away; *(mit der Kasse, mit dem Geliebten/der Geliebten)* run off

durch|bringen *unr. tr. V.* get through; *(bei Wahlen)* jmdn. ~: get sb. elected; **seine Familie/sich** ~: support one's family/ oneself

Durch·bruch der *(fig.)* breakthrough

durch|drehen 1. *tr. V.* put ⟨*meat*⟩ through the mincer *or (Amer.)* grinder; **2.** *itr. V. auch mit sein (ugs.)* crack up *(coll.)*

¹**durch|dringen** *unr. tr. V.; mit sein* ⟨*rain, sun*⟩ come through; ²**durch-dringen** *unr. tr. V.* penetrate; jmdn. ~ ⟨*idea*⟩ take hold of sb. [completely]

durch·einander *Adv.* ~ **sein** ⟨*papers, desk, etc.*⟩ be in a muddle; *(verwirrt sein)* be confused; *(aufgeregt sein)* be flustered; **Durcheinander das;** ~**s a)** muddle; mess; **b)** *(Wirrwarr)* confusion

durcheinander|bringen *unr. tr. V.* **a)** get ⟨*room, flat*⟩ into a mess; get ⟨*papers, file*⟩ into a muddle; muddle up ⟨*papers, file*⟩; **b)** *(verwirren)* confuse; **c)** *(verwechseln)* confuse ⟨*names etc.*⟩; get ⟨*names etc.*⟩ mixed up

durch|fahren *unr. itr. V.; mit sein* **a)** |durch etw.| ~: drive through [sth.]; **b)** *(nicht anhalten)* go straight through; *(mit dem Auto)* drive straight through; **der Zug fährt |in H.| durch** the train doesn't stop [at H.]; **Durch·fahrt die a)** „~ **verboten"** 'no entry except for access'; **auf der** ~ **sein** be passing through; **b)** *(Weg)* thoroughfare; „**bit-te |die|** ~ **freihalten"** 'please do not obstruct'

Durch·fall der diarrhoea *no art.;* **durch|fallen** *unr. itr. V.; mit sein* **a)** fall through; **b)** *(ugs.: nicht bestehen)* fail

durch|finden *unr. refl. V.* find one's way through

durchführbar *Adj.* practicable; **durch|führen 1.** *tr. V.* carry out; put into effect ⟨*decision, programme*⟩; perform ⟨*operation*⟩; hold ⟨*meeting, election, examination*⟩; **2.** *itr. V.* **durch etw./unter etw.** *(Dat.)* ~ ⟨*track, road*⟩ go through/under sth.; **Durch·füh-rung die** carrying out; *(einer Operation)* performing; *(einer Versammlung, Wahl, Prüfung)* holding; *(eines Wettbewerbs)* staging

Durch·gang der a) passage[way]; „**kein** ~**", 2.** ~ **verboten"** 'no thoroughfare'; **b)** *(Phase)* stage; *(einer Versuchsreihe)* run; *(Sport, Wahlen)* round

Durchgangs-: ~straße die through road; **~verkehr der** through traffic

durch|geben *unr. tr. V.* announce ⟨*news*⟩; give ⟨*results, weather report*⟩; **eine Meldung im Radio/Fernsehen** ~: make an announcement on the radio/ on television

durch·gefroren *Adj.* frozen stiff; chilled to the bone

durch|gehen 1. *unr. itr. V.; mit sein* **a)** |durch etw.| ~: go *or* walk through [sth.]; **b)** *(hindurchdringen)* |durch etw.| ~: ⟨*rain, water*⟩ come through [sth.]; **c)** *(direkt zum Ziel führen)* ⟨*train etc.*⟩ go [right] through (bis to); *(flight)* go direct; **d)** *(andauern)* go on (bis zu until); **e)** *(hingenommen werden)* ⟨*discrepancy*⟩ be tolerated; *(mistake, discrepancy)* be allowed to pass; **jmdm. etw.** ~ **lassen** let sb. get away with sth. **f)** ⟨*horse*⟩ bolt; **2.** *unr. tr. V.; mit sein* go through ⟨*newspaper, text*⟩

durch·gehend 1. *Adj.* **a)** continuous ⟨*line, pattern, etc.*⟩; constantly recurring ⟨*motif*⟩; **b)** *(direkt)* through *attrib.* ⟨*train, carriage*⟩; direct ⟨*flight, connection*⟩; **2.** *adv.* ~ **geöffnet haben/blei-ben** be/stay open all day

durch|greifen *unr. itr. V.* |hart| ~: take drastic measures *or* steps

durch|halten 1. *unr. itr. V.* hold out; *(bei einer schwierigen Aufgabe)* see it through; **2.** *unr. tr. V.* stand

durch|hängen *unr. itr. V.* sag
durch|kämmen *tr. V.* a) comb ⟨hair⟩
through; b) *(durchsuchen)* comb ⟨area etc.⟩

durch|kommen *unr. itr. V.; mit sein*
a) come through; *(mit Mühe)* get through; b) *(ugs.: beim Telefonieren)* get through; c) *(durchgehen, -fahren usw.)* durch etw. ~: come through sth.; d) *(ugs.: überleben)* pull through

¹durch|kreuzen *tr. V.* cross out;
²durch|kreuzen *tr. V.* *(vereiteln)* frustrate

durch|lassen *unr. tr. V.* a) jmdn. [durch etw.] ~: let sb. through [sth.]; b) *(durchlässig sein)* let ⟨light, water, etc.⟩ through; **durchlässig** *Adj.* permeable; *(porös)* porous; *(undicht)* leaky; ⟨raincoat, shoe⟩ that lets in water

Durch·lauf der *(Sport, DV)* run;
¹durch|laufen 1. *unr. itr. V.; mit sein* a) [durch etw.] ~: run through [sth.]; *(durchrinnen)* trickle through [sth.]; b) *(passieren)* ⟨runners⟩ run or pass through; c) *(ohne Pause laufen)* run without stopping; 2. *unr. tr. V.* go through ⟨soles⟩; **²durch·laufen** *unr. tr. V.* go through ⟨phase, stage⟩;
durchlaufend 1. *Adj.* continuous; 2. *adv.* ⟨numbered, marked⟩ in sequence

durch|lesen *unr. tr. V.* etw. [ganz] ~: read sth. [all the way] through

durch·leuchten *tr. V.* x-ray; *(fig.)* investigate ⟨case, matter, problem, etc.⟩ thoroughly

durch·löchern *tr. V.* make holes in
durch|machen *(ugs.)* 1. *tr. V.* a) undergo ⟨change⟩; complete ⟨training course⟩; go through ⟨stage, phase⟩; serve ⟨apprenticeship⟩; b) *(erleiden)* go through; c) *(durcharbeiten)* work through ⟨lunch-break etc.⟩; 2. *itr. V.* a) *(durcharbeiten)* work [right] through; *(durchfeiern)* celebrate all night/day etc.; keep going all night/day etc.

Durchmesser der; ~s, ~: diameter
durch|nehmen *unr. tr. V.* *(Schulw.: behandeln)* do

durch|probieren *tr. V.* taste ⟨wines, cakes, etc.⟩ one after another

durch·queren *tr. V.* cross; travel across ⟨country⟩; ⟨train⟩ go through ⟨country⟩

durch|rechnen *tr. V.* calculate ⟨costs etc.⟩ [down to the last penny]; check ⟨bill⟩ thoroughly

Durch·reise die journey through;
durch|reisen *itr. V.; mit sein* travel

through; **Durchreise·visum** das transit visa

durch|reißen 1. *unr. tr. V.* etw. ~: tear sth. in two or in half; 2. *unr. tr. V.; mit sein* ⟨fabric, garment⟩ rip, tear; ⟨thread, rope⟩ snap [in two]

durch|rosten *itr. V.; mit sein* rust through

durchs *Präp.* + *Art.* = durch das
Durch·sage die announcement; *(an eine bestimmte Person)* message

durchschaubar *Adj.* transparent;
leicht ~ easy to see through; **durch·schauen** *tr. V.* a) see through ⟨person, plan, etc.⟩; see ⟨situation⟩ clearly

durch|schlafen *unr. itr. V.* sleep [right] through

Durch·schlag der a) *(Kopie)* carbon [copy]; b) *(Küchengerät)* strainer;
durch|schlagen *unr. tr. V.* etw. ~: chop sth. in two; **durchschlagend** *Adj.* resounding ⟨success⟩; decisive ⟨effect, measures⟩; conclusive ⟨evidence⟩

durch·schneiden *unr. tr. V.* cut through ⟨thread, cable⟩; cut ⟨ribbon, sheet of paper⟩ in two; cut ⟨throat, umbilical cord⟩; etw. in der Mitte ~: cut sth. in half; **Durch·schnitt** der average; im ~: on average; über/unter dem ~ liegen be above/below average; **durchschnittlich** 1. *Adj.* a) *nicht präd.* average ⟨growth, performance, output⟩; b) *(ugs.: nicht außergewöhnlich)* ordinary ⟨life, person, etc.⟩; c) *(mittelmäßig)* modest; ordinary ⟨appearance⟩; 2. *adv.* ⟨earn etc.⟩ on [an] average; ~ groß of average height

Durchschnitts-: ~alter das average age; ~geschwindigkeit die average speed

Durch·schrift die carbon [copy]
durch|sehen 1. *unr. itr. V.* [durch etw.] ~: look through [sth.]; 2. *unr. tr. V.* look through

durch|sein *unr. itr. V., mit sein; nur im Inf. u. Part.* zusammengeschrieben *(ugs.)* a) [durch etw.] ~: be through [sth.]; b) *(abgefahren sein)* ⟨train, bus, etc.⟩ have gone; c) *(fertig sein)* have finished; durch etw. ~: have got through sth.; d) ⟨cheese⟩ be ripe; ⟨meat⟩ be well done

durch|setzen 1. *tr. V.* carry through; achieve ⟨objective⟩; enforce ⟨demand, claim⟩; 2. *refl. V.* assert oneself; ⟨idea etc.⟩ find or gain acceptance

Durch·sicht die: nach ~ der Unterlagen after looking or checking through the documents; **dụrchsichtig** *Adj.* *(auch fig.)* transparent

dụrch|sprechen *unr. tr. V.* talk *(matter etc.)* over; discuss *(matter etc.)* thoroughly

dụrch|stehen *unr. tr. V.* stand *(pace, boring job)*; come through *(difficult situation)*; get over *(illness)*

dụrch|stellen *tr. V.* put *(call)* through (in + *Akk.*, **auf** + *Akk.* to)

dụrch|streichen *unr. tr. V.* cross out; *(in Formularen)* delete

durch·sụchen *tr. V.* search (**nach** for); search, scour *(area)* (**nach** for); **Durchsụchung** die; ~, ~en search

dụrch|treten *unr. tr. V.* press *(clutch-, brake-pedal)* right down

durchtrịeben *(abwertend)* **1.** *Adj.* crafty; sly; **2.** *adv.* craftily; slyly

durch·wạchsen *Adj.* ~er Speck streaky bacon

Dụrchwahl die; **a)** direct dialling; **mein Apparat hat keine ~:** I don't have an outside line; **b)** *s.* Durchwahlnummer; **dụrch|wählen** *itr. V.* **a)** dial direct; **b)** *(bei Nebenstellenanlagen)* dial straight through; **Dụrchwahl·nummer** die number of the/ one's direct line

dụrch|zählen *tr. V.* count; count up

dụrch|ziehen 1. *unr. tr. V.* jmdn./etw. |durch etw.| ~: pull sb./sth. through [sth.]; **ein Gummiband |durch etw.| ~:** draw an elastic through [sth.]; **2.** *unr. itr. V.; mit sein* pass through; *(soldiers)* march through

Dụrch·zug der *o. Pl.* draught

dụrfen 1. *unr. Modalverb;* 2. *Part.* ~ **a)** etw. tun ~: be allowed to do sth.; **darf ich rauchen?** may I smoke?; **was darf es sein?** can I help you?; **b)** *Konjunktiv II + Inf.* das dürfte der Grund sein that is probably the reason; **2.** *unr. tr., itr. V.* **er hat nicht gedurft** he was not allowed to; **dụrfte,** *1. u. 3. Pers. Sg. Prät. v. dürfen;* **dụrfte** *1. u. 3. Pers. Sg. Konjunktiv II v.* dürfen

dụrr *Adj.* **a)** withered; arid, barren *(ground, earth)*; **b)** *(mager)* scrawny; **Dụrre** die; ~, ~n drought

Dụrst der; ~|e|s thirst; ~ **haben** be thirsty; **ich habe ~ auf ein Bier** I could just drink a beer; **dụrstig** *Adj.* thirsty; **durst·stillend** *Adj.* thirstquenching

Dụsche die; ~, ~n shower; **dụschen** *itr., refl. V.* have a shower

Dụse die; ~, ~n *(Technik)* nozzle; *(eines Vergasers)* jet

Dụsen-: ~**flugzeug** das jet aircraft; ~**motor** der jet engine

dụster 1. *Adj.* **a)** dark; gloomy; dim *(light)*; **b)** *(fig.)* gloomy; sombre *(colour, music)*; **2.** *adv.* *(fig.)* gloomily

Dụtzend das; ~s, ~e dozen; **zwei ~:** two dozen; **dụtzend·weise** *Adv.* in [their] dozens *(coll.)*

dụzen *tr. V.* call *(sb.)* 'du' *(the familiar form of address)*

dynạmisch 1. *Adj.* **a)** *(auch fig.)* dynamic; **2.** *adv.* dynamically

Dynamịt das; ~s dynamite

Dynamo der; ~s, ~s dynamo

Dynastịe die; ~, ~n dynasty

D-Zug ['de:-] der express train

E

e, E [e:] das; ~, ~ **a)** *(Buchstabe)* e/E; **b)** *(Musik)* [key of] E

Ẹbbe die; ~, ~n ebb tide; *(Zustand)* low tide; **es ist ~:** the tide is out

ẹben 1. *Adj.* **a)** flat; **b)** *(glatt)* level; **2.** *adv.* **a)** *(gerade jetzt)* just; **b)** *(kurz)* [for] a moment; **Ẹbene die, ~, ~n a)** plain; **in der ~:** on the plain; **b)** *(Geom., Physik)* plane; **c)** *(fig.)* level

ẹben·falls *Adv.* likewise; as well; **danke, ~:** thank you, [and] [the] same to you

Ẹben·holz das ebony

ẹben·so *Adv.* **a)** *mit Adjektiven* just as; **b)** *mit Verben* in exactly the same way

ẹbenso-: ~**gern** *Adv.* ~**gern mag ich Erdbeeren |wie ...|** I like strawberries just as much [as ...]; ~**gern würde ich an den Strand gehen** I would just as soon go to the beach; ~**gut** *Adv.* just as well; ~**sehr** *Adv.* **a)** *mit Adjektiven* just as; **b)** *mit Verben* just as much

Ẹber der; ~s, ~: boar

Ẹber·esche die rowan; mountain ash

ẹbnen *tr. V.* level *(ground)*

Ẹcho das; ~s, ~s echo

ẹcht 1. *Adj.* **a)** genuine; real *(love, friendship)*; **b)** *nicht präd. (typisch)* real, typical; **gut** *Adv.* just as well; **2.** *adv.* **a)** *(ugs. verstärkend)* really; **b)** *(typisch)* typically

Eck-: ~**ball** der *(Sport)* corner[-kick/ -hit/-throw]; einen ~**ball** treten take a corner; ~**bank** die corner seat

Ecke die; ~, ~n corner; an der ~: on or at the corner; um die ~: round the corner; ~**ckig** Adj. square; angular

Eck·zahn der canine tooth

edel Adj. a) *nicht präd.* thoroughbred *(horse)*; species *(rose)*; b) *(großmütig)* noble[-minded], high-minded *(person)*; noble *(thought, gesture, feelings, deed)*; honourable *(motive)*

Edel-: ~**metall** das precious metal; ~**stahl** der stainless steel; ~**stein** der precious stone; gem[stone]

Edition die; ~, ~en edition

EDV Abk. elektronische Datenverarbeitung EDP

Efeu der; ~s ivy

Effekt der; ~[e]s, ~e effect; **effekt·voll** Adj. effective; dramatic *(pause, gesture, entrance)*

EG ['e:'ge:] die; ~ Abk. a) Europäische Gemeinschaft EC; b) Erdgeschoß

egal Adj. *nicht attr. (ugs.: einerlei)* es ist jmdm. ~: it's all the same to sb.; [ganz] ~, wie/wer usw. ...: no matter how/who etc. ...

Egge die; ~, ~n harrow

ehe Konj. before

Ehe die; ~, ~n marriage

Ehe-: ~**bett** das marriage-bed; *(Doppelbett)* double bed; ~**frau** die wife; *(verheiratete Frau)* married woman; ~**krach** der *(ugs.)* row; ~**leute** Pl. married couple

ehelich Adj. marital; matrimonial; conjugal *(rights, duties)*; legitimate *(child)*

ehemalig Adj. former

Ehe-: ~**mann** der; Pl. ~**männer** husband; *(verheirateter Mann)* married man; ~**paar** das married couple

eher Adv. a) *(früher)* earlier; sooner; b) *(lieber)* rather; sooner

Ehe-: ~**ring** der wedding-ring; ~**scheidung** die divorce

Ehre die; ~, ~n honour; jmdm. ~ antun pay tribute to sb.; **ehren** tr. V. a) honour; Sehr geehrter Herr Müller!/Sehr geehrte Frau Müller! Dear Herr Müller/Dear Frau Müller; b) *(Ehre machen)* deine Hilfsbereitschaft ehrt dich your willingness to help does you credit; **ehrenhaft** Adj. honourable

ehren-, Ehren-: ~**rührig** Adj. defamatory *(allegations)*; ~**sache** die: das ist ~sache that is a point of

honour; ~**sache!** you can count on me!; ~**voll** Adj. honourable; ~**wert** Adj. *(geh.)* worthy; ~**wort** das; pl. ~**worte:** ~**wort** [!/?] word of honour [!/?]

ehrerbietig Adj. *(geh.)* respectful

Ehr·furcht die reverence (vor + Dat. for); **ehrfürchtig** Adj. reverent

ehr-, Ehr-: ~**gefühl** das; o. Pl. sense of honour; ~**geiz** der ambition; ~**geizig** Adj. ambitious

ehrlich Adj. honest; genuine *(concern, desire, admiration)*; upright *(character)*; **Ehrlichkeit** die; ~ s. ehrlich: honesty; genuineness; uprightness

ehr·los Adj. dishonourable

Ehrung die; ~, ~en: die ~ der Preisträger the prize-giving *(Brit.)* or *(Amer.)* awards ceremony; bei der ~ der Sieger when the winners were awarded their medals/trophies

ehr·würdig Adj. venerable

Ei das; ~[e]s, ~er egg

Eiche die; ~, ~n oak[-tree]; *(Holz)* oak[-wood]

Eichel die; ~, ~n acorn

eichen tr. V. calibrate *(measuring instrument, thermometer)*; standardize *(weights, measures, containers, products)*; adjust *(weighing-scales)*

Eich·hörnchen das squirrel

Eid der; ~[e]s, ~e oath

Eidechse ['aidɛksə] die; ~, ~n lizard

eide·stattlich Adj. *(Rechtsw.)* eine ~e Erklärung a statutory declaration

Ei·dotter der od. das egg yolk

Eier-: ~**becher** der egg-cup; ~**kuchen** der pancake; *(Omelett)* omelette; ~**likör** der egg-liqueur; ~**stock** der *(Physiol., Zool.)* ovary; ~**uhr** die egg-timer

Eifer der; ~s eagerness

Eifer·sucht die jealousy (auf + Akk. of); **eifer·süchtig** Adj. jealous (auf + Akk. of)

eifrig Adj. eager

Ei·gelb das; ~[e]s, ~e egg yolk

eigen Adj. own; *(selbständig)* separate

eigen-, Eigen-: ~**art** die *(Wesensart)* particular nature; *(Zug)* peculiarity; eine ~art dieser Stadt one of the characteristic features of this city; ~**artig** Adj. peculiar; strange; odd; ~**händig** 1. Adj. personal *(signature)*; holographic *(will, document)*; ~e *(present, sign)* personally; ~**heim** das house of one's own

Eigenheit die; ~, ~en peculiarity

eigen-, Eigen-: ~**lob** das self-praise;

~mächtig *Adj.* unauthorized; **~name der** proper name; **~nützig** *Adj.* self-seeking; selfish *(motive)*

eigens *Adv.* specially

Eigenschaft die; ~, ~en quality; characteristic; *(von Sachen, Stoffen)* property

Eigenschafts·wort das adjective

eigen-, Eigen-: **~sinn der;** *o. Pl.* obstinacy; **~sinnig** *Adj.* obstinate; **~ständig** *Adj.* independent

eigentlich 1. *Adj.* *(wirklich)* actual; real; *(wahr)* true; *(ursprünglich)* original; **2.** *Adv.* actually; **3.** *Partikel* wie spät ist es ~? tell me, what time is it?; was willst du ~? what exactly do you want?

Eigen·tor das *(Ballspiele, fig.)* own goal

Eigentum das; ~s property; *(einschließlich Geld usw.)* assets *pl.*

Eigentümer der; ~s, ~: owner; *(Hotel~, Geschäfts~)* proprietor; **Eigentümerin die;** ~, ~nen owner; *(Hotel~, Geschäfts~)* proprietress; proprietor; **Eigentums·wohnung die** owner-occupied flat *(Brit.)*; condominium apartment *(Amer.)*

eigen·willig *Adj.* self-willed

eignen *refl. V.* be suitable; **Eignung die;** ~: suitability; seine ~ zum Fliegen his aptitude for flying

Eignungs-: **~prüfung die, ~test der** aptitude test

Eil-: **~bote der** special messenger; „durch *od.* per **~boten**" *(veralt.)* 'express'; **~brief der** express letter

Eile die; ~: hurry; in ~ sein be in a hurry; **eilen** *itr. V.* a) *mit sein* hurry; *(besonders schnell)* rush; b) *(dringend sein)* be urgent; „eilt!" 'urgent'; **eilig 1.** *Adj.* a) hurried; es ~ haben be in a hurry; b) *(dringend)* urgent; **2.** *adv.* hurriedly; **Eil·zug der** semi-fast train

Eimer der; ~s, ~: bucket; *(Milch~)* pail; *(Abfall~)* bin; ein ~ [voll] Wasser a bucket of water; im ~ sein *(salopp)* be up the spout *(sl.)*

¹ein 1. *Kardinalz.* one; **2.** *unbest. Art.* a/an; **3.** *Indefinitpron.; s.* irgendein a; *s. auch* einer

²ein *(elliptisch)* ~ – aus *(an Schaltern)* on – off

Einakter der; ~s, ~: one-act play

einander *reziprokes Pron.; Dat. u. Akk. (geh.)* each other; one another

ein|arbeiten *tr. V.* train *(employee)*

ein·armig *Adj.* one-armed

ein|äschern *tr. V.* cremate

ein|atmen *tr., itr. V.* breathe in

ein·äugig *Adj.* one-eyed

Ein·bahn·straße die one-way street

Ein·band der; *Pl.* -bände binding

Ein·bau der; ~s, ~ten fitting; *(eines Motors)* installation; **ein|bauen** *tr. V.* build in, fit; install *(engine, motor)*; **Einbau·küche die** fitted kitchen

ein·beinig *Adj.* one-legged

ein|berufen *unr. tr. V.* summon; call; **Ein·berufung die** a) *(das Einberufen)* calling; b) *(zur Wehrpflicht)* call-up; conscription; draft *(Amer.)*

Einbett·zimmer das single room

ein|beziehen *unr. tr. V.* include

ein|biegen *unr. itr. V.; mit sein* turn

ein|bilden *refl. V.* a) sich *(Dat.)* etw. ~: imagine sth.; b) *(ugs.)* sich *(Dat.)* etwas ~: be conceited *(auf + Akk.* about); **Ein·bildung die** a) *(Phantasie)* imagination; b) *(falsche Vorstellung)* fantasy; c) *(Hochmut)* conceitedness

ein|binden *unr. tr. V.* bind *(book)*; etw. neu ~: rebind sth.

ein|blenden *tr. V. (Rundf., Ferns., Film)* insert

Ein·blick der a) view; ~ in etw. *(Akk.)* haben be able to see into sth.; b) *(Durchsicht)* jmdm. ~ in etw. *(Akk.)* gewähren allow sb. to look at *or* examine sth.; c) *(Kenntnis)* insight

ein|brechen *unr. itr. V.* a) *mit haben od. sein* break in; in eine Bank ~: break into a bank; bei jmdm. ~: burgle sb.; b) *mit sein (einstürzen)* *(roof, ceiling)* cave in; c) *mit sein (durchbrechen)* fall through; **Einbrecher der;** ~s, ~: burglar

ein|bringen *unr. tr. V.* a) bring in *(harvest)*; b) *(verschaffen)* Gewinn/Zinsen ~: yield a profit/bring in interest; jmdm. Ruhm ~: bring sb. fame; c) *(Parl.: vorlegen)* introduce *(bill)*; d) invest *(capital, money)*

Ein·bruch der a) burglary; ein ~ in eine Bank a break-in at a bank; b) *(das Einstürzen)* collapse

ein|bürgern 1. *tr. V.* naturalize; **2.** *refl. V. (custom, practice)* become established; *(person, plant, animal)* become naturalized; **Einbürgerung die;** ~, ~en naturalization

Einbuße die loss; **ein|büßen** *tr. V.* lose; *(durch eigene Schuld)* forfeit

ein|checken *tr., itr. V. (Flugw.)* check in

ein|cremen *tr. V.* put cream on *(hands etc.)*; sich ~: put cream on

ein|dämmen *tr. V. (fig.)* check; stem

ein|decken 1. *refl. V.* stock up; 2. *tr. V.* (*ugs.: überhäufen*) jmdn. mit Arbeit ~: swamp sb. with work

eindeutig *Adj.* clear; **Eindeutigkeit** die; ~, ~en clarity

ein|dringen *unr. itr. V.; mit sein* in etw. *(Akk.)* ~: penetrate into sth.; *⟨bullet⟩* pierce sth.; *(allmählich)* *⟨water, sand, etc.⟩* seep into sth.; **ein·dringlich** *Adj.* urgent; impressive *⟨voice⟩*; forceful, powerful *⟨words⟩*; **Eindringling** der; ~s, ~e intruder

Ein·druck der; ~|e|s, **Eindrücke** impression; **ein|drücken** *tr. V.* smash in *⟨mudguard, bumper⟩*; stave in *⟨side of ship⟩*; smash *⟨pier, column, support⟩*; break *⟨window⟩*; crush *⟨ribs⟩*; flatten *⟨nose⟩*; **eindrucks·voll** 1. *Adj.* impressive; 2. *adv.* impressively

eine *s.* ¹**ein**

ein|ebnen *tr. V.* level

eineiig ['ain|aiiç] *Adj.* identical *⟨twins⟩*

ein·ein·halb *Bruchz.* one and a half; ~ Stunden an hour and a half

ein|engen *tr. V.* a) jmdn. ~: restrict sb.'s movement[s]; b) *(fig.)* restrict

einer, eine, eines, eins *Indefinitpron. (man)* one; *(jemand)* someone; somebody; *(fragend, verneint)* anyone; anybody; **kaum einer** hardly anybody; **ein|e|s ist sicher** one thing is for sure

Einer der; ~s, ~ a) *(Math.)* unit; b) *(Sport)* single sculler; **im ~:** in the single sculls

einerlei *Adj.* ~, ob/wo/wer *usw.* no matter whether/where/who *etc.;* **es ist ~:** it makes no difference

Einerlei das; ~s monotony

einerseits *Adv.* on the one hand

ein·fach 1. *Adj.* a) simple; b) *(nicht mehrfach)* single *⟨knot, ticket, journey⟩*; 2. *Partikel* simply; just; **Einfachheit** die; ~: simplicity

ein|fädeln 1. *tr. V.* thread (in + *Akk.* into); 2. *refl. V. (Verkehrsw.)* filter in

ein|fahren 1. *unr. itr. V.; mit sein* come in *⟨train⟩* pull in; **in den Bahnhof ~:** pull into the station; 2. *unr. tr. V.* a) bring in *⟨harvest⟩*; b) *(beschädigen)* knock down *⟨wall⟩*; smash in *⟨mudguard⟩*; **Ein·fahrt** die a) *(das Hineinfahren)* entry; **Vorsicht bei der ~ des Zuges!** stand clear [of the edge of the platform], the train is approaching; b) *(Zufahrt)* entrance; *(Autobahn~)* slip road; „**keine ~**" 'no entry'

Ein·fall der a) *(Idee)* idea; b) *o. Pl.*

(Licht~) incidence *(Optics);* **ein|fallen** *unr. itr. V.; mit sein* a) jmdm. ~: occur to sb.; **was fällt dir denn ein!** what do you think you're doing?; b) *(in Erinnerung kommen)* **ihr Name fällt mir nicht ein** I cannot think of her name; **plötzlich fiel ihr ein, daß ...:** suddenly she remembered that ...; c) *(von Licht)* come in

einfalls-: ~**los** *Adj.* unimaginative; lacking in ideas; ~**reich** *Adj.* imaginative; full of ideas

Einfalt die; ~: simpleness; simplemindedness; **einfältig** *Adj.* simple; naïve; naïve *⟨remarks⟩*

ein|fangen *unr. tr. V.* catch

ein|fassen *tr. V.* border; edge; frame *⟨picture⟩*; set *⟨gem⟩*; edge *⟨grave, lawn, etc.⟩*; **Ein·fassung** die *s.* einfassen: border; edging; frame; setting

ein|finden *unr. refl. V.* arrive; *(sich treffen)* meet; *⟨crowd⟩* gather

ein|fliegen *unr. tr. V.* fly in

ein|flößen *tr. V.* a) jmdm. Tee ~: pour tea into sb.'s mouth; b) *(fig.)* jmdm. Angst ~: put fear into sb.

Ein·fluß der influence; **Einfluß·bereich** der sphere of influence; **einfluß·reich** *Adj.* influential

ein·förmig *Adj.* monotonous

ein|frieren 1. *unr. itr. V.; mit sein* freeze; *⟨pipes⟩* freeze up; 2. *unr. tr. V.* a) deep-freeze *⟨food⟩*; b) *(fig.)* freeze

ein|fügen *tr. V.* fit in; fit in; etw. in etw. *(Akk.)* ~: fit sth. into sth.

ein|fühlen *refl. V.* sich in jmdn. ~: empathize with sb.; **einfühlsam** *Adj.* understanding; **Ein·fühlung** die; ~: empathy (in + *Akk.* with)

Ein·fuhr die; ~, ~en *s.* Import; **ein|führen** *tr. V.* a) *(als Neuerung)* introduce *⟨fashion, method, technology⟩*; b) *(importieren)* import; **Ein·führung** die introduction

Ein·gabe die petition; *(Beschwerde)* complaint

Ein·gang der entrance; „**kein ~**" 'no entry'; **ein·gängig** *Adj.* catchy; **eingangs** *Adv.* at the beginning; pedes

Eingangs-: ~**halle** die entrance hall; *(eines Hotels, Theaters)* foyer; ~**tür** die *(von Kaufhaus, Hotel usw.)* [entrance] door; *(von Wohnung, Haus usw.)* front door

ein·gebildet *Adj.* a) imaginary *⟨illness⟩*; b) *(arrogant)* conceited

Eingeborene der/die; *adj. Dekl. (veralt.)* native

ein|gehen 1. *unr. itr. V.; mit sein* **a)** arrive; **b)** *(fig.)* in die Geschichte ~: go down in history; **c)** *(schrumpfen)* shrink; **d)** auf eine Frage ~/nicht ~: go into *or* deal with/ignore a question; auf jmdn. ~: be responsive to sb.; auf jmdn. nicht ~: ignore sb.'s wishes; **2.** *unr. tr. V.* enter into ⟨contract, matrimony⟩; take ⟨risk⟩; accept ⟨obligation⟩

eingehend *Adj.* detailed

Ein·gemachte das; **~n** preserved fruit/vegetables

ein|gemeinden *tr. V.* incorporate ⟨village⟩ (in + Akk., nach into)

ein·geschnappt *Adj. (ugs.)* huffy

Ein·geständnis das confession; admission; **ein|gestehen** *unr. tr. V.* admit

Eingeweide das; **~s, ~;** *meist Pl.* entrails *pl.;* innards *pl*

ein·gewöhnen *refl. V.* get used to one's new surroundings

ein|gießen *unr. tr., itr. V.* pour in

ein|gliedern *tr. V.* integrate (in + Akk. into); incorporate ⟨village, company⟩ (in + Akk. into); *(einordnen)* include (in + Akk. in)

ein|graben *unr. tr. V.* bury (in + Akk. in); sink ⟨pile, pipe⟩ (in + Akk. into)

ein|gravieren *tr. V.* engrave (in + Akk. on)

ein|greifen *unr. itr. V.* intervene (in + Akk. in); **Ein·griff der a)** intervention (in + Akk. in); **b)** *(Med.)* operation

ein|haken 1. *tr. V.* **a)** *(mit Haken befestigen)* fasten; **b)** sich ~: link arms; **2.** *refl. V.* sich bei jmdm. ~: link arms with sb.

Ein·halt der: jmdm./einer Sache ~ gebieten *od.* tun *(geh.)* halt sb./sth.; **ein|halten 1.** *unr. tr. V.* keep ⟨appointment⟩; meet ⟨deadline, commitments⟩; keep to ⟨diet, speed-limit, agreement⟩; observe ⟨regulation⟩; **2.** *unr. itr. V. (geh.)* stop

ein·heimisch *Adj.* native; home *attrib.* ⟨team⟩; **Einheimische der/die;** *adj. Dekl.* local

Einheit die; ~, ~en unity; **einheitlich 1.** *Adj.* unified; *(unterschiedslos)* uniform ⟨dress⟩; standard ⟨procedure, practice⟩; **2.** *adv.* ~ gekleidet sein be dressed the same

einhellig 1. *Adj.* unanimous; **2.** *adv.* unanimously

ein|holen 1. *tr. V.* **a)** catch up with ⟨person, vehicle⟩; **b)** make up ⟨arrears, time⟩; **2.** *itr. V. (ugs.)* s. einkaufen 1

ein·hundert *Kardinalz. s.* hundert

einig *Adj.* sich *(Dat.)* ~ sein be agreed; sich *(Dat.)* ~ werden reach agreement

einig... *Indefinitpron. u. unbest. Zahlwort* some; ~e wenige a few; ~e hundert several hundred

einigen 1. *tr. V.* unite; **2.** *refl. V.* reach an agreement

einigermaßen *Adv.* somewhat

Einigkeit die; ~ a) unity; **b)** *(Übereinstimmung)* agreement

ein·jährig *Adj.* one-year-old *attrib.;* one year old *pred.;* *(ein Jahr dauernd)* one-year *attrib.*

Ein·kauf der a) Einkäufe machen do some shopping; **b)** *(eingekaufte Ware)* purchase; **c)** *o. Pl. (Abteilung)* purchasing department; **ein|kaufen 1.** *itr. V.* shop; ~ gehen go shopping; **2.** *tr. V.* buy; purchase; **Ein·käufer der** buyer; purchaser

Einkaufs-: ~bummel der [leisurely] shopping expedition; **~zentrum das** shopping centre

ein|kehren *itr. V.; mit sein* stop; in einem Wirtshaus ~: stop at an inn

ein|klammern *tr. V.* etw. ~: put sth. in brackets; bracket sth.

Ein·klang der harmony; in *od.* im ~ stehen accord

ein|kleben *tr. V.* stick in

ein|kleiden *tr. V.* clothe

ein|klemmen *tr. V.* **a)** *(quetschen)* catch; **b)** *(fest einfügen)* clamp

ein|kochen *tr. V.* preserve ⟨fruit etc.⟩

Einkommen das; **~s, ~:** income

ein|kreisen *tr. V.* **a)** etw. ~: put a circle round sth.; **b)** *(umzingeln)* surround

Einkünfte *Pl.* income *sing.;* feste ~: a regular income

¹ein|laden *unr. tr. V.* load ⟨goods⟩

²ein|laden *unr. tr. V.* invite ⟨person⟩ (zu for); **einladend** *Adj.* inviting; **Ein·ladung die** invitation

Ein·lage die a) *(in Brief)* enclosure; **b)** *(Kochk.)* vegetables, dumplings, *etc.* added to a clear soup; **c)** *(Schuh~)* arch-support; **d)** *(Programm~)* interlude

ein|lagern *tr. V.* store; lay in ⟨stores⟩

Einlaß der; Einlasses, Einlässe admission; **ein|lassen** *unr. tr. V.* **a)** *(hereinlassen)* admit; let in; **b)** *(einfüllen)* run ⟨water⟩

Ein·lauf der *(Med.)* enema; **ein|laufen 1.** *unr. itr. V.; mit sein* **a)** ⟨ship⟩ come in; **b)** *(kleiner werden)* shrink; **2.** *unr. tr. V.* wear in ⟨shoes⟩

ein|leben refl. V. settle down

ein|legen tr. V. a) load ⟨film⟩; engage ⟨gear⟩; b) (Kochk.) pickle

ein|leiten tr. V. a) introduce; b) induce ⟨birth⟩; c) lead in; etw. in etw. (Akk.) ~: lead sth. into sth. **Ein·leitung die** a) introduction; b) (einer Geburt) induction

ein|leuchten itr. V. jmdm. ~: be clear to sb.; **ein·leuchtend** Adj. plausible

ein|liefern tr. V. take ⟨letter, person⟩ (bei, in + Abk. to)

ein|lösen tr. V. cash ⟨cheque⟩

ein|machen tr. V. preserve ⟨fruit etc.⟩; (in Gläser) bottle

einmal 1. Adv. a) once; noch ~ so groß [wie] twice as big [as]; etw. noch ~ tun do sth. again; b) ['-'-] (später) one day; (früher) once; es war ~ ...: once upon a time there was ...; 2. Partikel nicht ~: not even; wieder ~: yet again; **Einmal·eins das**; ~: [multiplication] tables pl.; **einmalig** 1. Adj. a) unique; one-off ⟨payment, purchase⟩; b) (ugs.) fantastic (coll.); 2. adv. (ugs.) really fantastically (coll.)

Ein·marsch der a) entry; b) (Besetzung) invasion (in + Akk. of); **ein|marschieren** itr. V.; mit sein march in

ein|mischen refl. V. interfere (in + Akk. in)

einmütig 1. Adj. unanimous; 2. adv. unanimously

ein|nähen tr. V. sew in

Einnahme die; ~, ~en a) income; (Staats~) revenue; (Kassen~) takings pl.; b) (von Arzneimitteln) taking; c) (einer Stadt, Burg) taking; **ein|nehmen** unr. tr. V. a) take; (verdienen) earn; b) (ausfüllen) take up ⟨amount of room⟩; c) (beeinflussen) jmdn. für sich ~: win sb. over

Ein·öde die barren waste

ein|ordnen 1. tr. V. arrange; put in order; 2. refl. V. a) (Verkehrsw.) get into the correct lane; „~" 'get in lane'; b) (sich einfügen) fit in

ein|packen 1. tr. V. pack (in + Akk. in); (einwickeln) wrap [up]; 2. itr. V. (ugs.) er kann ~: he's had it (coll.)

ein|parken tr., itr. V. park

ein|pflanzen tr. V. a) plant; b) (Med., fig.) implant

ein|prägen tr. V. a) stamp (in + Akk. into, on); b) (fig.) sich ⟨Dat.⟩ etw. ~: memorize sth.; jmdm. etw. ~: impress sth. on sb.; **einprägsam** Adj. easily remembered

ein|rahmen tr. V. frame

ein|räumen tr. V. a) put away; b) (füllen) seinen Schrank ~: put one's things away in one's cupboard; ein Zimmer ~: put the furniture into a room; c) (zugestehen) admit

ein|reden 1. tr. V. jmdm. etw. ~: talk sb. into believing sth.; sich ⟨Dat.⟩ ~, daß ...: persuade oneself that ...; 2. itr. V. auf jmdn. ~: talk insistently to sb.

ein|regnen refl. V.; unpers. es hat sich eingeregnet it's begun to rain steadily.

ein|reiben unr. tr. V. rub ⟨substance⟩ in; etw. mit Öl ~: rub oil into sth.

ein|reichen tr. V. submit; lodge ⟨complaint⟩; tender ⟨resignation⟩

ein|reihen 1. refl. V. sich in etw. (Akk.) ~: join sth.; 2. tr. V. jmdn. in eine Kategorie ~: place sb. in a category **Einreiher der**; ~s, ~: single-breasted suit/jacket

Ein·reise die entry; **Einreise·erlaubnis die** entry permit; **ein|reisen** itr. V.; mit sein enter; nach Schweden ~: enter Sweden

ein|reißen 1. unr. tr. V. a) pull down ⟨building⟩; b) (einen Riß machen in) tear; rip; 2. unr. itr. V.; mit sein tear; rip

ein|renken tr. V. a) (Med.) set; b) (ugs.) bereinigen) sort out

ein|richten 1. refl. V. sich schön ~: furnish one's home beautifully; sich häuslich ~: make oneself at home; 2. tr. V. furnish ⟨flat, house⟩; fit out ⟨shop⟩; equip ⟨laboratory⟩; **Ein·richtung die** a) (einer Wohnung) furnishing; b) (Mobiliar) furnishings pl.

ein|rollen 1. tr. V. roll up ⟨carpet etc.⟩; put ⟨hair⟩ in curlers; 2. itr. V.; mit sein roll in

ein|rosten itr. V.; mit sein go rusty

ein|rücken 1. itr. V.; mit sein (einmarschieren) move in; 2. indent ⟨line, heading, etc.⟩

eins 1. Kardinalz. one; es ist ~: it is one o'clock; ~ zu null one-nil; ~ zu ~: one all; „~, zwei, drei!" 'ready, steady, go'; 2. Adj. mir ist alles ~: it's all the same to me; 3. Indefinitpron. s. irgendein; **Eins die**; ~, ~en a) one; b) (Schulnote) one; A

einsam Adj. a) lonely ⟨person, decision⟩; b) (einzeln) solitary ⟨tree, wanderer⟩; c) (abgelegen) isolated; d) (menschenleer) deserted; **Einsamkeit die**; ~ a) loneliness; b) (Alleinsein) solitude; c) (Abgeschiedenheit) isolation

ein|sammeln *tr. V.* a) *(auflesen)* pick up; gather up; b) *(sich aushändigen lassen)* collect in; collect *(tickets)*

Ein·satz *der* a) *(aus Stoff)* inset; *(in Kochtopf, Nähkasten usw.)* compartment; b) *(Betrag)* stake; c) *(Gebrauch)* use; *(von Truppen)* deployment

Einsatz-: ~**befehl** *der* order to go into action; **den** ~**befehl haben** have operational command; ~**leiter** *der* head of operations; ~**wagen** *der (der Polizei)* police car; *(der Feuerwehr)* fire-engine; *(Notarztwagen)* ambulance

ein|saugen *unr. (auch regelm.) tr. V.* suck in; breathe [in] *(fresh air)*

ein|schalten 1. *tr. V.* a) switch on *(radio, TV, electricity, etc.)*; b) *(fig.)* call in *(press, police, expert, etc.)*; 2. *refl. V.* a) switch [itself] on; b) *(eingreifen)* intervene *(in + Akk. in)*

ein|schärfen *tr. V.* **jmdm. etw.** ~: impress sth. [up]on sb.

ein|schätzen *tr. V.* judge *(person)*; assess *(situation, income, damages)*; *(schätzen)* estimate; **Ein·schätzung** *die s.* **einschätzen:** judging; assessment; estimation

ein|schenken *tr., itr. V.* a) *(eingießen)* pour [out]; **jmdm. etw.** ~: pour out sth. for sb.; b) *(füllen)* fill [up] *(glass, cup)*

ein|scheren *itr. V.; mit sein* **auf eine Fahrspur** ~: get *or* move into a lane

ein|schicken *tr. V.* send in

ein|schieben *unr. tr. V.* a) push in; b) *(einfügen)* insert; put on *(trains, buses)*

ein|schiffen *tr., refl. V.* embark

ein|schlafen *unr. itr. V.; mit sein* a) fall asleep; b) *(verhüll.: sterben)* pass away; c) *(gefühllos werden)* go to sleep; **ein|schläfern** *tr. V.* a) **jmdn.** ~: send sb. to sleep, *(betäuben)* put sb. to sleep; b) *(schmerzlos töten)* **ein Tier** ~: put an animal to sleep; **einschläfernd** *Adj.* soporific; 2. *adv.* ~ **wirken** have a soporific effect

ein|schlagen 1. *unr. tr. V.* a) knock in; b) *(zertrümmern)* smash [in]; c) *(einwickeln)* wrap up *(present)*; cover *(book)*; 2. *unr. itr. V.* a) *(bomb)* land; *(lightning)* strike; b) **auf jmdn./etw.** ~: rain blows on sb./sth.

einschlägig 1. *Adj.* specialist *(journal, shop)*; relevant *(literature, passage)*; 2. *adv.* **er ist** ~ **vorbestraft** he has previous convictions for a similar offence/similar offences

ein|schleichen *unr. refl. V.* steal in

ein|schließen *unr. tr. V.* a) **etw. in etw.** *(Dat.)* ~: lock sth. up [in sth.]; **jmdn./sich** ~: lock sb./oneself in; b) *(umgeben)* surround; **einschließlich** 1. *Präp. mit Gen.* including; ~ **der Unkosten** including expenses; 2. *adv.* **bis** ~ **30. Juni** up to and including 30 June

ein|schmeicheln *refl. V.* **sich bei jmdm.** ~: ingratiate oneself with sb.

ein|schmuggeln *tr. V.* smuggle in

ein|schneiden *unr. tr. V.* a) make a cut in; b) *(einritzen)* carve; **einschneidend** *Adj.* drastic

ein|schneien *itr. V.; mit sein* get snowed in

Ein·schnitt *der* cut

ein|schränken 1. *tr. V.* a) reduce, curb *(expenditure, consumption)*; b) *(eingrenzen)* limit; restrict; **jmdn. in seinen Rechten** ~: limit *or* restrict sb.'s rights; 2. *refl. V.* economize; **Einschränkung** *die;* ~, ~**en** restriction; limitation; *(Vorbehalt)* reservation

ein|schreiben *unr. tr. V.* a) *(Postw.)* register *(letter)*; b) *(eintragen)* **sich/ jmdn.** ~: enter one's/sb.'s name; **Ein·schreiben** *das (Postw.)* registered letter; **per** ~: by registered mail

ein|schreiten *unr. itr. V.* intervene

ein|schüchtern *tr. V.* intimidate

ein|schulen *tr. V.* **eingeschult werden** start school

ein|sehen *unr. tr. V.* a) *(überblicken)* see into; b) *(prüfend lesen)* look at; c) *(erkennen)* realize; d) *(begreifen)* see

ein|seifen *tr. V.* lather

ein·seitig 1. *Adj.* a) on one side *postpos.*; b) *(tendenziös)* one-sided; 2. *adv.* a) on one side; b) *(tendenziös)* one-sidedly

ein|senden *unr. tr. V. (auch regelm.) tr. V.* send [in]

ein|setzen 1. *tr. V.* a) *(hineinsetzen)* put in; b) put on *(special train etc.)*; c) *(ernennen)* appoint; d) *(in Aktion treten lassen)* use; e) *(aufs Spiel setzen)* stake *(money)*; f) *(riskieren)* risk; 2. *itr. V.* begin; *(storm)* break. 3. *refl. V. (sich engagieren)* **ich werde mich dafür** ~, **daß** ...: I shall do what I can to see that ...; **sich nicht genug** ~: *(pupil)* be lacking application; *(minister)* be lacking in commitment

Ein·sicht *die* a) view *(in + Akk. into)*; b) *(Einblick)* ~ **in die Akten nehmen** take *or* have a look at the files; c) *(Erkenntnis)* insight; **einsichtig** *Adj.* a)

(verständnisvoll) understanding; **b)** *(verständlich)* comprehensible

Ein·siedler der hermit

ein·silbig *Adj.* **a)** monosyllabic ⟨*word*⟩; **b)** *(fig.)* taciturn ⟨*person*⟩

ein|sinken *unr. itr. V.* sink in

Einsitzer der; ~s, ~: single-seater; **einsitzig** *Adj.* single-seater *attrib.*

ein|spannen *tr. V.* harness ⟨*horse*⟩; put in ⟨*paper*⟩: fix ⟨*fabric*⟩; clamp ⟨*work*⟩

ein|sparen *tr. V.* save

ein|sperren *tr. V.* lock up

einsprachig *Adj.* monolingual

ein|springen *unr. itr. V.; mit sein* stand in; *(aushelfen)* step in and help out

ein|spritzen *tr. V.* inject; **jmdm. etw. ~:** inject sb. with sth.; **Einspritz·motor der** fuel-injection engine

Ein·spruch der objection (**gegen** to)

einspurig 1. *Adj.* single-track ⟨*road*⟩; **2.** *adv.* **die Autobahn ist nur ~ befahrbar** only one lane of the motorway is open

einst *Adv. (geh.)* once

ein|stampfen *tr. V.* pulp ⟨*books*⟩

Ein·stand der: seinen ~ geben celebrate starting a new job

ein|stecken *tr. V.* **a)** put in; **b)** *(mitnehmen)* put ⟨*sth.*⟩ in one's pocket/bag *etc.*

ein|stehen *unr. itr. V.* **für jmdn. ~:** vouch for sb.; **für etw. ~:** take responsibility for sth.

ein|steigen *unr. itr. V.; mit sein* **a)** *(in ein Fahrzeug)* get in; **in ein Auto ~:** get into a car; **in den Bus ~:** get on the bus; **b)** *(eindringen)* climb in

einstellbar *Adj.* adjustable.

ein|stellen 1. *tr. V.* **a)** *(einordnen)* put away ⟨*books etc.*⟩; **b)** *(unterstellen)* put in ⟨*car, bicycle*⟩; **c)** *(beschäftigen)* take on ⟨*workers*⟩; **d)** *(regulieren)* adjust; **e)** *(beenden)* stop; call off ⟨*search, strike*⟩; **f)** *(Sport)* equal ⟨*record*⟩; **2.** *refl. V.* **a)** arrive; **b)** ⟨*pain, worry*⟩ begin; ⟨*success*⟩ come; ⟨*symptoms, consequences*⟩ appear; **c) sich auf etw.** *(Akk.)* **~:** prepare oneself for sth.; **sich schnell auf neue Situationen ~:** adjust quickly to new situations

ein·stellig *Adj.* single-figure *attrib.*

Ein·stellung die a) *(von Arbeitskräften)* employment; **b)** *(Regulierung)* adjustment; **c)** *(Beendigung)* stopping; **d)** *(Sport)* **die ~ eines Rekordes** the equalling of a record; **e)** *(Ansicht)*

attitude; **ihre politische/religiöse ~:** her political/religious views *pl.*; **f)** *(Film)* take

Ein·stich der a) insertion; **b)** *(~stelle)* puncture; prick

Ein·stieg der; ~|e|s, ~e *(Eingang)* entrance; *(Tür)* door/doors

ein|stimmen 1. *itr. V.* join in. **2.** *tr. V.* **jmdn. auf etw.** *(Akk.)* **~:** get sb. in the [right] mood for sth.

einstimmig 1. *Adj.* **a)** *(Musik)* for one voice; **b)** *(einmütig)* unanimous ⟨*decision, vote*⟩; **2.** *adv.* **a)** *(Musik)* in unison; **b)** *(einmütig)* unanimously

ein·stöckig *Adj.* single-storey *attrib.*

ein|studieren *tr. V.* rehearse

ein|stufen *tr. V.* classify; categorize

ein·stündig *Adj.* one-hour *attrib.*

ein|stürmen *itr. V.* **mit Fragen auf jmdn. ~:** besiege sb. with questions

Ein·sturz der collapse; **ein|stürzen** *itr. V.; mit sein* collapse

einst·weilen *Adv.* for the time being

eintägig *Adj.* one-day *attrib.;* **Eintags·fliege die** *(Zool.)* mayfly; *(fig.-ugs.)* seven-day wonder

ein|tauchen 1. *tr. V.* dip; *(untertauchen)* immerse; **2.** *itr. V.; mit sein* dive in; *(submarine)* dive

ein|tauschen *tr. V.* exchange (**gegen** for)

ein·tausend *Kardinalz.: s.* **tausend**

ein|teilen *tr. V.* **a)** divide up; classify ⟨*plants, species*⟩; **b)** *(disponieren, verplanen)* organize

einteilig *Adj.* one-piece

eintönig 1. *Adj.* monotonous; **2.** *adv.* monotonously; **Eintönigkeit die; ~:** monotony

Ein·topf der stew

Ein·tracht die; *o. Pl.* harmony; **ein·trächtig** *Adj.* harmonious

Eintrag der; ~|e|s, Einträge entry; **ein|tragen** *unr. tr. V.* **a)** enter; **b)** *(Amtsspr.)* register

einträglich *Adj.* lucrative

ein|treffen *unr. itr. V.; mit sein* **a)** arrive; **b)** *(verwirklicht werden)* come true

ein|treiben *unr. tr. V.* collect ⟨*taxes, debts*⟩; *(durch Gerichtsverfahren)* recover ⟨*debts, money*⟩

ein|treten 1. *unr. itr. V.; mit sein* **a)** enter; **bitte, treten Sie ein!** please come in; **b)** *(Mitglied werden)* **in einen Verein/einen Orden ~:** join a club/ enter a religious order; **c)** *(Raumfahrt)* enter; **2.** *unr. tr. V.* kick in ⟨*door, window, etc.*⟩

ein|trichtern *tr. V. (salopp)* jmdm. etw. ~: drum sth. into sb.

Ein·tritt der a) entry; entrance; vor dem ~ in die Verhandlungen *(fig.)* before entering into negotiations; b) *(Beitritt)* der ~ in einen Verein/einen Orden joining a club/entering a religious order; c) *(von Raketen)* entry; d) *(Zugang, Eintrittsgeld)* admission; e) *(Beginn)* onset; ~ der Dunkelheit nightfall

Eintritts-: ~**geld** das admission fee; ~**karte** die admission ticket; ~**preis** der admission charge

ein|trocknen *itr. V.; mit sein* dry; ⟨water, toothpaste⟩ dry up; ⟨leather⟩ dry out; ⟨berry, fruit⟩ shrivel

ein|üben *tr. V.* practise

einverstanden *Adj.* ~ sein agree; mit jmdm./etw. ~ sein approve of sb./sth.

Ein·verständnis das consent

ein|wachsen *unr. itr. V.; mit sein* grow into the flesh; **eingewachsen** ingrown ⟨toe-nail⟩

Einwand der; ~[e]s, **Einwände** objection ⟨gegen to⟩

Ein·wanderer der immigrant; **ein|wandern** *itr. V.; mit sein* immigrate ⟨in + Akk. into⟩; **Ein·wanderung** die immigration

einwand·frei 1. *Adj.* flawless; impeccable ⟨behaviour⟩; indisputable ⟨proof⟩; 2. *adv.* flawlessly; ⟨behave⟩ impeccably; ⟨prove⟩ beyond question

ein|wechseln *tr. V.* a) change ⟨money⟩; b) *(Sport)* substitute ⟨player⟩

ein|wecken *tr. V.* preserve; bottle

Ein·weg·flasche die non-returnable bottle

ein|weichen *tr. V.* soak

ein|weihen *tr. V.* open [officially] ⟨bridge, road⟩; dedicate ⟨monument⟩; **Einweihung** die; ~, ~en s. **einweihen**: [official] opening; dedication

ein|weisen *unr. tr. V.* a) *(in eine Tätigkeit)* introduce; b) *(in ein Amt)* install

ein|wenden *unr. (auch regelm.) tr. V.* dagegen läßt sich vieles ~: there is a lot to be said against that

ein|werfen *unr. tr. V.* a) mail ⟨letter⟩; insert ⟨coin⟩; b) smash ⟨window⟩; c) throw in ⟨ball⟩; d) *(bemerken, sagen)* throw in ⟨remark⟩

ein|wickeln *tr. V.* wrap [up]

ein|willigen *itr. V.* agree ⟨in + Akk. to⟩; **Einwilligung** die; ~, ~en agreement

ein|winken *tr. V. (Verkehrsw.)* guide in ⟨aircraft, car⟩

ein|wirken a) *(beeinflussen)* auf jmdn. ~: influence sb.; b) *(eine Wirkung ausüben)* have an effect ⟨auf + Akk. on⟩; **Ein·wirkung** die *(Einfluß)* influence; *(Wirkung)* effect

Einwohner der; ~s, ~, **Einwohnerin** die; ~, ~nen inhabitant

Ein·wurf der a) insertion; *(von Briefen)* mailing; b) *(Ballspiele)* throw-in; c) *(Bemerkung)* interjection

Ein·zahl die; o. Pl. singular

ein|zahlen *tr. V.* pay in; **Ein·zahlung** die payment

ein|zäunen *tr. V.* fence in; enclose; **Einzäunung** die; ~, ~en fencing-in

ein|zeichnen *tr. V.* draw or mark in

einzeilig *Adj.* one-line attrib.

Einzel das; ~s, ~ *(Sport)* singles pl.

Einzel-: ~**bett** das single bed; ~**fall** der a) particular case; b) *(Ausnahme)* isolated case; ~**gänger** [-gɛŋɐ] der; ~s, ~: loner; ~**haft** die solitary confinement; ~**handel** der retail trade; ~**händler** der retailer

Einzelheit die; ~, ~en a) detail; b) *(einzelner Umstand)* particular

Einzel·kind das only child

einzeln *Adj.* a) *(für sich allein)* individual; b) *(alleinstehend)* solitary ⟨building, tree⟩; single ⟨lady, gentleman⟩; c) ~e ⟨wenige⟩ a few; ⟨einige⟩ some; d) *substantivisch* der/jeder ~e the/each individual; ~es some things pl.; das Einzelne the particular

Einzel-: ~**teil** das individual part; ~**zelle** die single cell; ~**zimmer** das single room

ein|ziehen 1. *unr. tr. V.* a) put in; thread in ⟨tape, elastic⟩; b) *(einholen)* haul in ⟨net⟩; c) *(einatmen)* breathe in ⟨scent, fresh air⟩; inhale ⟨smoke⟩; d) *(einberufen)* call up ⟨recruits⟩; e) *(beitreiben)* collect; 2. *unr. itr. V.; mit sein* a) ⟨liquid⟩ soak in; b) *(einkehren)* enter; c) *(in eine Wohnung)* move in

einzig 1. *Adj.* only; **kein** ~es **Wort** not a single word; 2. *adv.* a) *intensivierend bei Adj.* extraordinarily; b) *(ausschließlich)* only; das ~ **Wahre** the only thing; be **einzig·artig** 1. *Adj.* unique; 2. *adv.* uniquely

Ein·zug der a) entry ⟨in + Akk. into⟩; b) *(in eine Wohnung)* move; **Ein·zugs·bereich** der catchment area

Eis das; ~es a) ice; b) *(Speise-)* ice-cream; **ein** ~ **am Stiel** an ice-lolly *(Brit.)* or *(Amer.)* ice pop

Eis-: ~**bahn** die ice-rink; ~**bär** der polar bear; ~**becher** der ice-cream sundae; **~bein** das *(Kochk.)* knuckle of pork; **~berg** der iceberg; **~beutel** der ice-bag; **~café** das ice-cream parlour

Ei·schnee der stiffly beaten eggwhite

Eisen das; **~s, ~**: iron

Eisen·bahn die a) railway; railroad *(Amer.)*; mit der **~ fahren** go by train; b) *(Bahnstrecke)* railway line; railroad track *(Amer.)*; **Eisenbahner** der; **~s, ~**: railwayman; railroader *(Amer.)*; **Eisenbahn·unglück** das train crash

Eisen-: ~erz das iron ore; **~kette** die iron chain; **~ring** der iron ring; **~stange** die iron bar; **~waren** *Pl.* ironmongery *sing.*; **~zeit** die Iron Age

eisern 1. *Adj. (auch fig.)* iron; 2. *adv.* resolutely; *(save, train)* with iron determination; **~ durchgreifen** take drastic measures

eis-, Eis-: ~fach das freezing compartment; **~frei** *Adj.* ice-free; **~gekühlt** *Adj.* iced; **~glatt** *Adj.* icy; **~glätte** die black ice; **~hockey** das ice hockey

eisig 1. *Adj.* a) icy *(wind, cold)*; icy [cold] *(water)*; b) *(fig.)* frosty; 2. *adv.* a) **~ kalt sein** be icy cold; b) *(fig.)* *(smile)* frostily; **eisig·kalt** *Adj. s.* eiskalt 1 a

eis-, Eis-: ~kaffee der iced coffee; **~kalt** 1. *Adj.* a) ice-cold *(drink)*; freezing cold *(weather)*; b) *(gefühllos)* icy; ice-cold *(look)*; 2. *adv.* es lief mir **~kalt über den Rücken** a cold shiver went down my spine; **~kunstlauf** der figure skating; **~kunst·läufer** der figure skater; **~lauf** der iceskating; **~|laufen** *unr. itr. V.; mit sein* ice-skate; **~laufen** das ice-skating; **~läufer** der ice-skater; **~schrank** der refrigerator; **~sport** der ice sports *pl.;* **~tanz** der *(Sport)* ice-dancing; **~waffel** die [ice-cream] wafer; **~wein** der wine made from grapes frozen on the vine; **~würfel** der ice cube; **~zapfen** der icicle; **~zeit** die ice age

eitel *Adj.* vain; **Eitelkeit** die; **~, ~en** vanity

Eiter der; **~s** pus; **eitern** *itr. V.* suppurate; **eitrig** *Adj.* suppurating

Ei·weiß das a) egg-white; b) *(Protein)* protein

¹Ekel der; **~s** revulsion; |**einen**| **~ vor etw.** *(Dat.)* **haben** have a revulsion for

sth.; **²Ekel** das; **~s, ~** *(ugs. abwertend)* horror; **er ist ein |altes| ~**: he is quite obnoxious; **ekelhaft** *Adj.* revolting *(sight)*; horrible *(weather, person)* **ekeln 1.** *refl. V.* be disgusted; **sich vor etw.** *(Dat.)* **~**: find sth. repulsive; 2. *tr. u. itr. V. (unpers.)* **es ekelt mich** *od.* **mir ekelt davor** I find it revolting; **eklig** *Adj.* a) s. ekelhaft; b) *(ugs.: gemein)* nasty

Ekstase [ɛkˈstaːzə] die; **~, ~n** ecstasy

Ekzem das; **~s, ~e** *(Med.)* eczema

Elan der; **~s** zest; vigour

elastisch *Adj.* elasticated *(material)*; springy *(surface)*; supple *(person, body)*; **Elastizität** die; **~**: elasticity; *(Federkraft)* springiness; *(Geschmeidigkeit)* suppleness

Elch der; **~|e|s, ~e** elk; *(in Nordamerika)* moose

Elefant der; **~en, ~en** elephant

elegant 1. *Adj.* elegant; 2. *adv.* elegantly; **Eleganz** die; **~**: elegance

elektrifizieren *tr. V.* electrify; **Elektrifizierung** die; **~, ~en** electrification

Elektriker der; **~s, ~**: electrician; **elektrisch 1.** *Adj.* electric; electrical *(resistance, wiring, system)*; 2. *adv.* **~ kochen** cook with electricity; **~ geladen sein** be electrically charged; **elektrisieren** 1. *tr. V. (Med.)* treat using electricity; 2. *refl. V.* get an electric shock; **Elektrizität** die; **~** electricity

Elektrizitäts·werk das power station

Elektro-: ~artikel der electrical appliance; **~auto** das electric car; **~gerät** das electrical appliance; **~geschäft** das electrical shop *or (Amer.)* store; **~herd** der electric cooker; **~mobil** das electric car; **~motor** der electric motor

Elektron das; **~s, ~en** [-ˈtroːnən] electron

Elektronen-: ~|ge|hirn das *(ugs.)* electronic brain *(coll.)*; **~rechner** der electronic computer

Elektronik die; **~** a) electronics *sing.,* no art.; b) *(Teile)* electronics *pl.;* **elektronisch 1.** *Adj.* electronic; 2. *adv.* electronically

Elektro-: ~rasierer der electric shaver; **~technik** die electrical engineering *no art.;* **~techniker** der a) electronics engineer; b) *(Elektriker)* electrician

Element das; **~|e|s, ~e** element; **ele-**

mentar *Adj.* **a)** *(grundlegend)* fundamental; **b)** *(einfach)* elementary ⟨*knowledge*⟩; **c)** *(naturhaft)* elemental ⟨*force*⟩; **Elementar·teilchen das** *(Physik)* elementary particle

elend *Adj.* wretched; miserable; **Elend das**; ~s misery

Elends-: **~quartier das** slum [dwelling]; **~viertel das** slum area

elf *Kardinalz.* eleven; **Elf die**; ~, ~en **a)** eleven; **b)** *(Sport)* team; side

Elfe die; ~, ~n fairy

Elfen·bein das ivory

Elfenbein-: **~schnitzerei die** *o. Pl.* ivory-carving; **~turm der** *(fig.)* ivory tower

Elf·meter der *(Fußball)* penalty; **einen ~ schießen** take a penalty; **Elfmeter·schießen das** *(Fußball)* durch **~schießen** by *or* on penalties

eliminieren *tr. V.* eliminate

Elite die; ~, ~n élite

Ell·bogen der; ~s, ~: elbow

Elle die; ~, ~n **a)** *(Anat.)* ulna; **b)** *(frühere Längeneinheit)* cubit; **c)** *(veralt.: Maßstock)* ≈ yardstick; **Ellen·bogen** *s.* Ellbogen

Ellipse die; ~, ~n ellipse

Elsaß das; ~ *od.* Elsasses Alsace

Elster die; ~, ~n magpie

elterlich *Adj.* parental; **Eltern** *Pl.* parents *pl.*

eltern-, **Eltern-:** **~abend der** *(Schulw.)* parents' evening; **~haus das** home; **~los** *Adj.* orphaned; **~teil der** parent

Email [e'maɪ] **das**; ~s, ~s, **Emaille** [e'maljə] **die**; ~, ~n enamel

Emanzipation die; ~, ~en emancipation; **emanzipieren** *refl. V.* emancipate; **emanzipiert** *Adj.* emancipated

Embargo das; ~s, ~s embargo

Emblem das; ~s, ~e emblem

Embryo der; ~s, ~nen [-y'oːnən] *od.* ~s embryo

Emigrant der; ~en, ~en emigrant; *(Flüchtling)* emigré; **Emigration die**; ~, ~en *(das Emigrieren)* emigration; **emigrieren** *itr. V.; mit sein* emigrate

Emotion die; ~, ~en emotion; **emotional 1.** *Adj.* emotional; emotive ⟨*topic, question*⟩; **2.** *adv.* emotionally

Empfang der; ~[e]s, Empfänge reception; *(Entgegennahme)* receipt; **empfangen** *unr. tr. V.* receive; **Empfänger der**; ~s, ~ **a)** recipient; *(eines Briefs)* addressee; **b)** *(Empfangsgerät)* receiver

empfänglich *Adj.* **a)** receptive (für to); **b)** *(beeinflußbar)* susceptible; **Empfängnis die**; ~: conception; **Empfängnis·verhütung die** contraception

empfangs-, **Empfangs-:** **~berechtigt** *Adj.* authorized to receive payment/goods *postpos.*; **~chef der** head receptionist; **~dame die** receptionist; **~halle die** reception lobby

empfehlen 1. *unr. tr. V.* recommend; **2.** *unr. refl. V.* **a)** take one's leave; **b)** *unpers.* **es empfiehlt sich, ... zu ...:** it's advisable to ...; **empfehlens·wert** *Adj.* **a)** to be recommended *postpos.*; recommendable; **b)** *(ratsam)* advisable; **Empfehlung die**; ~, ~en **a)** recommendation; **b)** *(Empfehlungsschreiben)* letter of recommendation; **empfiehl** *Imperativ Sg. v.* empfehlen; **empfiehlst** *2. Pers. Sg. Präsens v.* empfehlen; **empfiehlt** *3. Pers. Sg. Präsens v.* empfehlen

empfinden *unr. tr. V.* **a)** *(wahrnehmen)* feel; **b)** *(auffassen)* etw. **als Beleidigung ~:** feel sth. to be an insult; **Empfinden das**; ~s feeling; **für mein od. nach meinem ~:** to my mind; **empfindlich 1.** *Adj.* **a)** sensitive; fast ⟨*film*⟩; **b)** *(leicht beleidigt)* sensitive; **c)** *(anfällig)* **zart und ~:** delicate; **d)** *(spürbar)* severe ⟨*punishment, shortage*⟩; **2.** *adv.* **~ auf etw.** *(Akk.)* **reagieren** *(sensibel)* be susceptible to sth.; *(beleidigt)* react oversensitively to sth.; **Empfindlichkeit die**; ~, ~en *s.* empfindlich: sensitivity; severity; *(eines Films)* speed

empfindsam *Adj.* sensitive ⟨*nature*⟩; **Empfindung die**; ~, ~en *(Gefühl)* feeling

empfing *1. u. 3. Pers. Sg. Prät. v.* empfangen

empfohlen 1. *2. Part. v.* empfehlen; **2.** *Adj.* recommended

empirisch 1. *Adj.* empirical; **2.** *adv.* empirically

empor *Adv.* *(geh.)* upwards

Empore die; ~, ~n gallery

empören 1. *tr. V.* fill with indignation; outrage; **2.** *refl. V.* become indignant *or* outraged; **empörend** *Adj.* outrageous; **empört** *Adj.* outraged

emsig 1. *Adj.* industrious ⟨*person*⟩; bustling ⟨*activity*⟩; **2.** *adv.* industriously

Emu der; ~s, ~s *(Zool.)* emu

Ende das; ~s, ~n end; **am ~ der Stra-**

ße/Stadt at the end of the road/town; am/bis/gegen ~ des Monats at/by/towards the end of the month; ~ April at the end of April; zu ~ sein ⟨patience, war⟩ be at an end; ⟨school⟩ be over; ⟨film, game⟩ have finished; ~ gut, alles gut all's well that ends well (prov.); **enden** itr. V. a) end; ⟨programme⟩ finish; b) in der Gosse ~: end up in the gutter; ⟨dort sterben⟩ die in the gutter

end·gültig 1. Adj. final ⟨consent, decision⟩; conclusive ⟨evidence⟩; **2.** adv. das ist ~ vorbei that's all over and done with; **sich ~ trennen** separate for good

End-: ~**kampf** der (Sport) final; (Milit.) final battle; ~**lauf** der (Sport) final

endlich 1. Adv. a) ⟨nach langer Zeit⟩ at last; b) ⟨schließlich⟩ in the end; **2.** Adj. finite

end-, End-: ~**los 1.** Adj. a) ⟨ohne Ende⟩ infinite; ⟨ringförmig⟩ continuous; b) ⟨nicht enden wollend⟩ endless; interminable ⟨speech⟩; **2.** adv. ~los lange dauern be interminably long; ~**runde** die (Sport) final; ~**spiel** das (Sport) final; ~**spurt** der (bes. Leichtathletik) final spurt; ~**stadium** das final stage; (Med.) terminal stage; ~**station** die terminus

Endung die; ~, ~en (Sprachw.) ending

Energie die; ~, ~n energy

Energie-: ~**politik** die energy policy; ~**quelle** die energy source; ~**versorgung** die energy supply

energisch 1. Adj. a) energetic ⟨person⟩; firm ⟨action⟩; b) forceful ⟨voice, words⟩; **2.** adv. a) energetically; ~ **durchgreifen** take drastic action; b) ⟨reject, say⟩ forcefully; ⟨stress⟩ emphatically; ⟨deny⟩ strenuously

eng [ɛŋ] **1.** Adj. a) ⟨schmal⟩ narrow b) ⟨dicht⟩ close ⟨writing⟩; c) ⟨fest anliegend⟩ close-fitting; d) ⟨beschränkt⟩ narrow; e) ⟨nahe⟩ close ⟨friend⟩; **2.** adv. a) ⟨dicht⟩ ~ [zusammen] sitzen/stehen sit/stand close together; b) ⟨fest anliegend⟩ ~ **anliegen/sitzen** fit closely; c) ⟨beschränkt⟩ etw. zu ~ auslegen interpret sth. too narrowly; d) ⟨nahe⟩ closely; **Enge** die; ~, ~n confinement

Engel der; ~s, ~: angel

eng·herzig Adj. petty

England (das); ~s England; **Engländer** der; ~s, ~: Englishman/English boy; **er ist** ~: he is English; **die** ~: the

English; **Engländerin** die; ~, ~nen Englishwoman/English girl; **englisch 1.** Adj. English; **die** ~**e Sprache/Literatur** the English language/English literature; **2.** adv. ~ **sprechen** speak English; **Englisch** das; ~[s] English

englisch-, Englisch-: ~**lehrer** der 'English teacher; ~**sprachig** Adj. a) English-language ⟨book, magazine⟩; b) ⟨~ sprechend⟩ English-speaking ⟨population, country⟩; ~**unterricht** der English teaching; ⟨Unterrichtsstunde⟩ English lesson

Eng·paß (der a) defile; b) (fig.) bottleneck; **eng·stirnig** Adj. narrowminded

Enkel der; ~s, ~: grandson; **Enkelin** die; ~, ~nen granddaughter; **Enkel·kind** das grandchild

enorm 1. Adj. enormous ⟨sum, costs⟩; tremendous (coll.) ⟨effort⟩; immense ⟨strain⟩; **2.** adv. tremendously (coll.)

Ensemble [ã'sã:b]] das ensemble; ⟨Theater~⟩ company

entarten itr. V.; mit sein degenerate

entbehren tr. V. ⟨verzichten auf⟩ do without; **entbehrlich** Adj. dispensable; **Entbehrung** die; ~, ~en privation

entbinden 1. unr. tr. V. a) jmdn. von einem Versprechen ~: release sb. from a promise; **seines Amtes od. von seinem Amt entbunden werden** be relieved of [one's] office; b) jmdn. ~ (Med.) deliver sb.'s baby; **2.** unr. itr. V. give birth; **Entbindung** die (Med.) delivery

entblößen 1. refl. V. take one's clothes off; ⟨exhibitionist⟩ expose oneself; **2.** tr. V. uncover ⟨one's arm etc.⟩

entdecken tr. V. a) discover; b) ⟨ausfindig machen⟩ jmdn. ~: find sb.; etw. ~: find or discover sth.; **Entdecker** der; ~s, ~: discoverer; **Entdeckung** die; ~, ~en discovery

Ente die; ~, ~n duck

entehren tr. V. dishonour; ~d degrading

enteignen tr. V. expropriate; **Enteignung** die expropriation

enterben tr. V. disinherit

entern tr., itr. V. board ⟨ship⟩

entfachen tr. V. (geh.) a) kindle, light ⟨fire⟩; b) (fig.) provoke ⟨quarrel, argument⟩; arouse ⟨passion, enthusiasm⟩

entfallen unr. itr. V.; mit sein a) ⟨aus dem Gedächtnis⟩ es ist mir ~: it escapes me; **b)** *(zugeteilt werden)* **auf jmdn./etw. ~**: be allotted to sb./sth.; **c)** *(wegfallen)* lapse

entfalten 1. *tr. V.* **a)** open [up]; unfold ⟨*map etc.*⟩; **b)** *(fig.)* display ⟨*ability, talent*⟩; **2.** *refl. V.* **a)** open [up]; **b)** *(fig.)* ⟨*personality, talent, etc.*⟩ develop; **Entfaltung die**; **~, ~en** *(fig.)* **a)** *(Entwicklung)* development; **b)** *s.* **entfalten 1 b**: display

entfernen 1. *tr. V.* remove; take out ⟨*tonsils etc.*⟩; **2.** *refl. V.* go away; **entfernt 1.** *Adj.* **a)** *(fern)* remote; **das ist od. liegt weit ~ von der Stadt** it is a long way from the town; **10 km/zwei Stunden ~**: 10 km/two hours away; **b)** slight ⟨*acquaintance*⟩; distant ⟨*relation*⟩; slight ⟨*resemblance*⟩; **2.** *adv.* **a)** *(fern)* remotely; **b)** slightly ⟨*acquainted*⟩; distantly ⟨*related*⟩; **Entfernung die**; **~, ~en a)** *(Abstand)* distance; **b)** *(das Beseitigen)* removal

entfesseln *tr. V.* unleash

entflammen 1. *tr. V.* arouse ⟨*enthusiasm etc*⟩; **2.** *itr. V.; mit sein* flare up

entfliehen *unr. itr. V.; mit sein* escape; **jmdm. ~**: escape from sb.

entfremden 1. *tr. V.* **a)** etw. seinem Zweck ~: use sth. for a different purpose; **b)** *(Philos., Soziol.)* entfremdet alienated; **2.** *refl. V.* sich jmdm./einer Sache ~: become estranged from sb./unfamiliar with sth.; **Entfremdung die**; **~, ~en** alienation; estrangement

entführen *tr. V.* kidnap ⟨*child etc.*⟩; hijack ⟨*plane, lorry, etc.*⟩; **Entführer der** *s.* **entführen**: kidnapper; hijacker; **Entführung die** *s.* **entführen**: kidnapping; hijacking

entgegen 1. *Adv.* towards; **2.** *Präp. mit Dat.* **~ meinem Wunsch** against my wishes; **~ dem Befehl** contrary to orders

entgegen-, Entgegen-: **~|bringen** *unr. tr. V.* *(fig.)* show ⟨*love, understanding*⟩; **~|fahren** *unr. itr. V.; mit sein* **jmdm. ~fahren** come/go to meet sb.; **~|gehen** *unr. itr. V.; mit sein* **a)** **jmdm. ~gehen** go to meet sb.; **b)** *(fig.)* be heading for ⟨*catastrophe, hard times*⟩; **~gesetzt 1.** *Adj.* **a)** *(umgekehrt)* opposite ⟨*end, direction*⟩; **b)** *(gegensätzlich)* opposing; **2.** *adv.* genau **~gesetzt handeln/denken** do/think exactly the opposite; **~|kommen** *unr. itr. V.; mit sein* **jmdm. ~kommen** come to meet sb.; *(Zugeständnisse machen)* be accommodating towards sb.; **~kommen das** co-operation;

(Zugeständnis) concession; **~kommend** *Adj.* obliging; **~|nehmen** *unr. itr. V.* receive; **~|treten** *unr. itr. V.; mit sein* go/come up to; *(fig.)* stand up to ⟨*difficulties*⟩

entgegnen *tr. V.* retort; reply

entgehen *unr. itr. V.; mit sein* **a)** *(entkommen)* escape; **b)** **jmdm. entgeht etw.** sb. misses sth.

entgeistert *Adj.* dumbfounded

Entgelt das; **~[e]s, ~e** payment; fee

entgiften *tr. V.* decontaminate ⟨*substance etc.*⟩; detoxicate ⟨*body etc.*⟩

entgleisen *itr. V.; mit sein* **a)** be derailed; **b)** *(fig.)* make a/some faux pas

entgräten *tr. V.* fillet

enthaaren *tr. V.* remove hair from; **Enthaarungs·mittel das** hair remover

¹enthalten 1. *unr. tr. V.* contain; **2.** *unr. refl. V.* **sich einer Sache** *(Gen.)* **~**: abstain from sth.; **sich der Stimme ~**: abstain; **²enthalten** *Adj.* in etw. *(Dat.)* **~ sein** be contained in sth.; **das ist im Preis ~**: that is included in the price; **enthaltsam 1.** *Adj.* abstemious; *(sexuell)* abstinent; **2.** *adv.* **~ leben** live in abstinence; **Enthaltsamkeit die**; **~**: abstinence; **Enthaltung die** abstention

enthaupten *tr. V. (geh.)* behead

enthäuten *tr. V.* skin

entheben *unr. tr. V. (geh.)* relieve

enthemmt *Adj.* uninhibited

enthüllen *tr. V.* unveil ⟨*monument etc.*⟩; reveal ⟨*face, truth, secret*⟩; **Enthüllung die**; **~, ~en** *s.* **enthüllen**: unveiling; revelation

Enthusiasmus [ɛntu'zjasmʊs] **der**; **~**: enthusiasm; **enthusiastisch 1.** *Adj.* enthusiastic; **2.** *adv.* enthusiastically

entkalken *tr. V.* decalcify

entkleiden *tr. V. (geh.)* **a)** undress; **b)** *(berauben)* strip

entkommen *unr. itr. V.; mit sein* escape

entkorken *tr. V.* uncork ⟨*bottle*⟩

entkräften *tr. V.* **a)** weaken; völlig **~**: exhaust; **b)** *(fig.)* refute ⟨*argument etc.*⟩; **Entkräftung die**; **~, ~en** debility; völlige **~**: exhaustion; **b)** *(fig.)* refutation

entladen 1. *unr. tr. V.* unload; **2.** *unr. refl. V.* **a)** ⟨*storm*⟩ break; **b)** *(fig.)* ⟨*anger etc.*⟩ erupt; ⟨*aggression etc.*⟩ be released

entlang 1. *Präp. mit Akk. u. Dat.* along; **2.** *Adv.* along; **hier/dort ~, bitte!** this/that way please!

entlang-: ~|**fahren** unr. itr. V.; mit sein **a)** drive along; **b)** (streichen) go along; ~|**gehen** unr. itr. V.; mit sein (person) go or walk along; ~|**laufen** unr. itr. V.; mit sein **a)** walk/run along; **b)** (verlaufen) go or run along

entlarven tr. V. expose

entlassen unr. tr. V. **a)** (aus dem Gefängnis) release; (aus dem Krankenhaus, der Armee) discharge; **b)** (aus einem Arbeitsverhältnis) dismiss; (wegen Arbeitsmangels) make redundant (Brit.); lay off; **Entlassung die**; ~, ~en s. entlassen: release; discharge; dismissal; redundancy (Brit.); laying off

entlasten tr. V. **a)** relieve; **b)** (Rechtsw.) exonerate (defendant); **Entlastung die**; ~, ~en **a)** relief; **b)** (Rechtsw.) exoneration; defence

entlaufen unr. itr. V.; mit sein run away; ein ~er Sträfling/Sklave an escaped convict/a runaway slave

entlausen tr. V. delouse

entledigen refl. V. sich jmds./einer Sache (Gen.) ~ (geh.) rid oneself of sb./sth.

entleeren tr. V. empty; evacuate (bowels, bladder)

entlegen Adj. remote

entleihen unr. tr. V. borrow

entlocken tr. V. (geh.) jmdm. etw. ~: elicit sth. from sb.

entlohnen tr. V. pay; **Entlohnung die**; ~, ~en payment; (Lohn) pay

entlüften tr. V. ventilate; **Entlüfter der**; ~s, ~: ventilator

entmachten tr. V. deprive of power

entmilitarisieren tr. V. demilitarize

entmündigen tr. V. incapacitate; **Entmündigung die**; ~, ~en incapacitation

entmutigen tr. V. discourage

Entnahme die; ~, ~n (von Wasser) drawing; (von Blut) extraction

entnehmen unr. tr. V. **a)** [einer Sache (Dat.)] ~: take sth. [from sth.]; **b)** (ersehen aus) gather (Dat. from)

entnervend Adj. nerve-racking

entpuppen refl. V. sich als etw./jmd. ~: turn out to be sth./sb.

entrahmen tr. V. skim (milk)

entreißen unr. tr. V. jmdm. etw. ~: snatch sth. from sb.

entrichten tr. V. (Amtsspr.) pay (fee)

entrümpeln tr. V. clear out; **Entrümpelung die**; ~, ~en clear-out

entrüsten **1.** refl. V. sich [über etw. (Akk.)] ~: be indignant [at or about

sth.]; **2.** tr. V. (empören) jmdn. ~: make sb. indignant; **Entrüstung die** indignation (über + Akk. at, about)

Entsafter der; ~s, ~: juice-extractor

entsagen itr. V. einer Sache (Dat.) ~ (geh.) renounce sth.; **Entsagung die**; ~, ~en (geh.) renunciation

entschädigen tr. V. compensate (für for); jmdn. für etw. ~ (fig.) make up for sth.; **Entschädigung die** compensation

entschärfen tr. V. defuse; tone down (discussion, criticism)

entscheiden **1.** unr. refl. V. **a)** decide; **b)** (unpers.) morgen entscheidet es sich, ob ...: I/we/you will know tomorrow whether ...; **2.** unr. itr. V. über etw. (Akk.) ~: settle sth; **3.** unr. tr. V. decide on (dispute); decide (outcome, result); **entscheidend 1.** Adj. crucial; decisive (action); **2.** adv. jmdn./etw. ~ beeinflussen have a decisive influence on sb./sth.; **Entscheidung die** decision

entschieden 1. Adj. **a)** (entschlossen) determined; resolute; **b)** (eindeutig) definite; **2.** adv. resolutely; das geht ~ zu weit that is going much too far

entschlafen unr. itr. V.; mit sein pass away

entschließen unr. refl. V. decide; **Entschließung die** resolution; **entschlossen** Adj. determined; **Entschlossenheit die**; ~: determination; **Entschluß der** decision

entschlüsseln tr. V. decipher

entschuldigen 1. refl. V. apologize; **2.** tr. (auch itr.) V. excuse (person); sich ~ lassen ask to be excused; ~ Sie [bitte]! (bei Fragen, Bitten) excuse me; (bedauernd) I'm sorry; **Entschuldigung die**; ~, ~en **a)** apology; **b)** (Grund) excuse; **c)** (Höflichkeitsformel) ~! (bei Fragen, Bitten) excuse me; (bedauernd) [I'm] sorry

entschwinden unr. itr. V.; mit sein (geh.) disappear; vanish

entsetzen 1. refl. V. be horrified; **2.** tr. V. horrify; **Entsetzen das**; ~s horror; **entsetzlich 1.** Adj. **a)** horrible (accident, crime, etc.); **b)** nicht präd. (ugs.: stark) terrible (thirst, hunger); **2.** adv. terribly (coll.)

entsinnen unr. refl. V. sich jmds./einer Sache ~: remember sb./sth.

entspannen 1. tr. V. relax; **2.** refl. V. **a)** (person) relax; **b)** (fig.) (situation, tension) ease; **Entspannung die**; o. Pl. **a)** relaxation; **b)** (politisch) easing

of tension; détente; **Entspannungs·politik** die policy of détente
entsprechen unr. itr. V. a) (übereinstimmen mit) einer Sache (Dat.) ~: correspond to sth.; b) (nachkommen) einem Wunsch ~: comply with a request; den Anforderungen ~: meet the requirements; **entsprechend** 1. Adj. a) corresponding; (angemessen) appropriate; b) nicht attr. (dem~) in accordance postpos.; 2. adv. a) (angemessen) appropriately; b) (dem~) accordingly; 3. Präp. mit Dativ: ~ einer Sache in accordance with sth.
entspringen unr. itr. V.; mit sein a) (river) rise; b) (entstehen aus) einer Sache (Dat.) ~: spring from sth.
entstehen unr. itr. V.; mit sein a) originate; (quarrel, friendship, etc.) arise; b) (gebildet werden) be formed (aus from, durch by); c) (sich ergeben) occur; (als Folge) result; **Entstehung** die; ~: origin
entsteinen tr. V. stone
entstellen tr. V. a) disfigure; b) (verfälschen) distort (text, facts); **Entstellung** die a) disfigurement; b) (Verfälschung) distortion
entstören tr. V. (Elektrot.) suppress (engine, electrical appliance)
enttarnen tr. V. uncover
enttäuschen tr. V. disappoint; **enttäuscht** Adj. disappointed; dashed (hopes); **Enttäuschung** die disappointment
entwachsen unr. itr. V.; mit sein einer Sache (Dat.) ~: grow out of sth.
entwaffnen tr. V. (auch fig.) disarm; **entwaffnend** Adj. disarming
entwarnen itr. V. sound the all-clear; **Entwarnung** die all-clear
entwässern tr. V. drain; **Entwässerung** die; ~, ~en drainage
entweder Konj.: ~ ... oder either ... or
entweichen unr. itr. V.; mit sein escape
entwenden tr. V. (geh.) purloin
entwerfen unr. tr. V. design (furniture, dress); draft (novel etc.); draw up (plans etc.)
entwerten tr. V. a) cancel (ticket, postage stamp); b) devalue (currency)
entwickeln 1. refl. V. develop; 2. tr. V. produce (vapour, smell); display (ability, characteristic); develop (equipment, photograph, film); elaborate (theory, ideas); **Entwicklung** die; ~, ~en a) development; (von Dämpfen usw.) production; in der ~

sein (young person) be adolescent; b) (Darlegung) elaboration; c) (Fot.) developing
Entwicklungs-: **~helfer** der development aid worker; **~hilfe** die [development] aid; **~land** das; Pl. **~länder** developing country; **~politik** die development aid policy
entwirren tr. V. disentangle
entwischen itr. V.; mit sein (ugs.) get away
entwöhnen tr. V. wean
entwürdigend Adj. degrading
Entwurf der a) design; b) (Konzept) draft
entwurzeln tr. V. uproot
entziehen 1. unr. tr. V. a) take away; b) (nicht zugestehen) withdraw; 2. unr. refl. V. sich seinen Pflichten (Dat.) ~: evade one's duty; das entzieht sich meiner Kontrolle that is beyond my control; **Entziehung** die a) withdrawal; b) (Entziehungskur) withdrawal treatment no indef. art.
entziffern tr. V. decipher
entzückend Adj. delightful; **entzückt** Adj. delighted
Entzug der; ~[e]s withdrawal
entzündbar Adj. [in]flammable; **entzünden** 1. tr. V. light (fire); strike (match); 2. refl. V. a) ignite; b) (anschwellen) become inflamed; **entzündlich** Adj. a) [in]flammable (substance); b) (Med.) inflammatory; **Entzündung** die; ~, ~en inflammation
entzwei Adj. (geh.) in pieces; **entzweien** refl. V. fall out; **entzweigehen** unr. itr. V.; mit sein (geh.) break
Enzian ['ɛntsia:n] der; ~s, ~e gentian
Enzyklika die; ~, **Enzykliken** encyclical
Enzyklopädie die; ~, ~n encyclopaedia; **enzyklopädisch** Adj. encyclopaedic
Epen s. Epos
Epidemie die; ~, ~n epidemic
Epilepsie die; ~, ~n (Med.) epilepsy no art.; **Epileptiker** der; ~s, ~: epileptic; **epileptisch** Adj. epileptic
episch Adj. epic
Episode die; ~, ~n episode
Epoche die; ~, ~n epoch
Epos ['e:pɔs] das; ~, **Epen** epic [poem]; epos
er Personalpron. 3. Pers. Sg. Nom. Mask. he; (betont) him; (bei Dingen/Tieren) it; s. auch ihm; ihn; seiner

erachten *tr. V. (geh.)* consider; etw. **als** *od.* **für seine Pflicht** ~: consider sth. [to be] one's duty

erarbeiten *tr. V.* work for

Erb·anlage die hereditary disposition

erbarmen *refl. V. (geh.)* take pity ⟨Gen. on⟩; **Erbarmen das;** ~s pity; **erbärmlich 1.** *Adj.* a) *(elend)* wretched; b) *(unzulänglich)* pathetic; c) *(abwertend: gemein)* mean; wretched; d) *(sehr groß)* terrible ⟨hunger, fear, etc.⟩; **2.** *adv.* terribly

erbauen 1. *tr. V.* a) build; b) *(geh.: erheben)* uplift; **2.** *refl. V.* **sich an etw.** *(Dat.)* ~: be uplifted by sth.; **Erbauer der;** ~s, ~: architect

¹Erbe das; ~s a) inheritance; b) *(Vermächtnis)* legacy; **²Erbe der;** ~n, ~n heir; **erben** *tr. (auch itr.) V.* inherit

erbetteln *tr. V.* get by begging

erbeuten *tr. V.* carry off, get away with ⟨valuables, prey, etc.⟩; capture ⟨enemy plane, tank, etc.⟩

Erb-: ~**folge die** succession; ~**gut das** *(Biol.)* genetic make-up

Erbin die; ~, ~**nen** heiress

erbitten *unr. tr. V. (geh.)* request

erbittern *tr. V.* enrage; **erbittert 1.** *Adj.* bitter; **2.** *adv.* ~ **kämpfen** wage a bitter struggle

erblassen *itr. V.; mit sein (geh.)* turn pale; blanch *(literary)*

erbleichen *itr. V.; mit sein (geh.)* s. **erblassen**

erblich *Adj.* hereditary ⟨title, disease⟩

erblicken *tr. V. (geh.)* catch sight of; *(fig.)* see

erblinden *itr. V.; mit sein* lose one's sight

erblühen *itr. V.; mit sein (geh.)* bloom; blossom

Erb·masse die *(Biol.)* genetic make-up

erbost *Adj.* furious

erbrechen 1. *unr. tr. V.* bring up ⟨food⟩; **2.** *unr. itr., refl. V.* vomit; **Erbrechen das;** ~s vomiting

erbringen *unr. tr. V.* produce

Erbschaft die; ~, ~**en** inheritance; **Erbschaft[s]·steuer die** estate *or* death duties *pl.*

Erbse die; ~, ~**n** pea

Erb-: ~**stück das** heirloom; ~**sünde die** original sin; ~**teil das** share of an/the inheritance

Erd-: ~**achse die** earth's axis; ~**apfel der** *(bes. österr.) s.* Kartoffel; ~**beben das** earthquake; ~**beere die** strawberry; ~**boden der** ground; earth;

etw. dem ~**boden gleichmachen** raze sth. to the ground

Erde die; ~, ~**n** a) *(Erdreich)* soil; earth; b) *o. Pl. (fester Boden)* ground; c) *o. Pl. (Welt)* earth; world; d) *o. Pl. (Planet)* Earth

erdenklich *Adj.* conceivable

Erd-: ~**gas das** natural gas; ~**geschoß das** ground floor; first floor *(Amer.)*; ~**kunde die** geography; ~**nuß die** peanut; ~**oberfläche die** earth's surface; ~**öl das** oil

erdöl-, Erdöl-: ~**exportierend** *Adj.* oil-exporting ⟨country⟩; ~**gewinnung die** oil production; ~**leitung die** oil pipeline

erdrosseln *tr. V.* strangle

erdrücken *tr. V.* a) crush; b) *(fig.: belasten)* overwhelm; **erdrückend** *Adj.* overwhelming; oppressive ⟨heat, silence⟩

Erd-: ~**rutsch der** landslide; ~**teil der** continent

erdulden *tr. V.* endure ⟨sorrow, misfortune⟩; tolerate ⟨insults⟩; *(über sich ergehen lassen)* undergo

ereifern *refl. V.* get excited

ereignen *refl. V.* happen; ⟨accident, mishap⟩ occur; **Ereignis das;** ~**ses,** ~**se** event; occurrence

Eremit der; ~**en,** ~**en** hermit

ererbt *Adj.* inherited

¹erfahren *unr. tr. V.* a) find out; learn; *(hören)* hear; b) *(geh.: erleben)* experience; *(erleiden)* suffer; **²erfahren** *Adj.* experienced; **Erfahrung die;** ~, ~**en** experience; ~**en sammeln** gain experience *sing.*; **etw. in** ~ **bringen** discover sth.; **erfahrungs·gemäß** *Adv.* in our/my experience

erfassen *tr. V.* a) *(mitreißen)* catch; b) *(begreifen)* grasp ⟨situation, etc.⟩; c) *(registrieren)* record; **Erfassung die** registration

erfinden *unr. tr. V.* invent; **das ist alles erfunden** it is pure fabrication; **Erfinder der;** ~s, ~ a) inventor; b) *(Urheber)* creator; **erfinderisch** *Adj.* inventive; *(schlau)* resourceful; **Erfindung die;** ~, ~**en** invention

erflehen *tr. V. (geh.)* beg

Erfolg der; ~**[e]s,** ~**e** success; **keinen** ~ **haben** be unsuccessful

erfolgen *itr. V.; mit sein* take place; occur; **es erfolgte keine Reaktion** there was no reaction

erfolg-: ~**los 1.** *Adj.* unsuccessful; **2.** *adv.* unsuccessfully; ~**reich 1.** *Adj.* successful; **2.** *adv.* successfully

Erfolgs·erlebnis das feeling of achievement

erfolg·versprechend *Adj.* promising

erforderlich *Adj.* required; necessary; **erfordern** *tr. V.* require; demand

erforschen *tr. V.* discover 〈*facts, causes, etc.*〉; explore 〈*country*〉; **Erforschung die** research (+ *Gen.* into); (*eines Landes usw.*) exploration

erfreuen 1. *tr. V.* please; **2.** *refl. V.* **sich an etw.** *(Dat.)* ~: take pleasure in sth.; **erfreulich** *Adj.* pleasant

erfrieren 1. *unr. itr. V.; mit sein* freeze to death; 〈*plant, harvest, etc.*〉 be damaged by frost; **2.** *unr. refl. V.* **sich** *(Dat.)* **die Finger** ~: get frostbite in one's fingers

erfrischen 1. *tr. (auch itr.)* *V.* refresh; **2.** *refl. V.* freshen oneself up; **erfrischend** *(auch fig.)* *Adj.* refreshing; **Erfrischung die;** ~, ~en *(auch fig.)* refreshment; **Erfrischungs·raum der** refreshment room

erfüllen 1. *tr. V.* grant 〈*wish, request*〉; fulfil 〈*contract*〉; carry out 〈*duty*〉; meet 〈*condition*〉; **2.** *refl. V.* 〈*wish*〉 come true; **Erfüllung die: in** ~ **gehen** come true

erfunden *Adj.* fictional 〈*story*〉

ergänzen *tr. V.* **a)** *(vervollständigen)* complete; *(erweitern)* add to; **b)** *(hinzufügen)* add 〈*remark*〉; **Ergänzung die;** ~, ~en **a)** *(Vervollständigung)* completion; *(Erweiterung)* enlargement; **b)** *(Zusatz)* addition; *(zu einem Gesetz)* amendment

ergattern *tr. V. (ugs.)* manage to grab

ergaunern *tr. V.* get by underhand means

¹**ergeben 1.** *unr. refl. V.* **a) sich in etw.** *(Akk.)* ~: submit to sth.; **b)** *(kapitulieren)* surrender 〈*Dat.* to〉; **c)** *(folgen, entstehen)* arise (*aus* from); **2.** *unr. tr. V.* result in; ²**ergeben** *Adj.* **a)** *(zugeneigt)* devoted; **b)** *(resignierend)* **mit** ~**er Miene** with an expression of resignation; **Ergebnis das;** ~ses, ~se result; **ergebnis·los** *Adj.* fruitless

ergehen *unr. refl. V.* **sich in etw.** *(Dat.)* ~: indulge in sth.

ergiebig *Adj.* rich 〈*deposits, resources*〉; fertile 〈*topic*〉

ergötzen *(geh.)* **1.** *tr. V.* enthrall; **2.** *refl. V.* **sich an etw.** *(Dat.)* ~: be delighted by sth.

ergrauen *itr. V.; mit sein* go grey

ergreifen *unr. tr. V.* **a)** *(greifen)* grab;

b) *(festnehmen)* catch 〈*thief etc.*〉; **c)** *(fig.: erfassen)* seize; **d)** *(fig.: aufnehmen)* take up 〈*career*〉; take 〈*initiative, opportunity*〉; **e)** *(fig.: bewegen)* move; **ergreifend** *Adj.* moving; **ergriffen** *Adj.* moved

ergründen *tr. V.* ascertain; discover 〈*cause*〉

erhaben *Adj.* solemn 〈*moment*〉; awe-inspiring 〈*sight*〉; sublime 〈*beauty*〉; **über etw.** *(Akk.)* ~ **sein** be above sth.

Erhalt der; ~[e]s *(Amtsdt.)* receipt; **erhalten** *unr. tr. V.* **a)** receive 〈*letter, news, gift*〉; be given 〈*order*〉; get 〈*good mark, impression*〉; **b)** *(bewahren)* preserve 〈*town, building*〉 **erhältlich** *Adj.* obtainable; **Erhaltung die;** ~: preservation; *(des Friedens)* maintenance

erhängen *tr. V.* hang

erhärten *tr. V.* strengthen 〈*suspicion, assumption*〉; substantiate 〈*claim*〉

erheben 1. *unr. tr. V.* **a)** raise **b)** *(verlangen)* levy 〈*tax*〉; charge 〈*fee*〉; **2.** *unr. refl. V.* **a)** rise; **b)** *(rebellieren)* rise up 〈*gegen* against〉; **erhebend** *Adj.* uplifting; **erheblich 1.** *Adj.* considerable; **2.** *adv.* considerably

erheitern *tr. V.* **jmdn.** ~: cheer sb. up

erhellen *tr. V.* light up

erhitzen 1. *tr. V.* heat 〈*liquid*〉; **jmdn.** ~: make sb. hot; **2.** *refl. V.* heat up; 〈*person*〉 become hot

erhoffen *tr. V.* **sich** *(Dat.)* **viel/wenig von etw.** ~: expect a lot/little from sth.

erhöhen 1. *tr. V.* increase 〈*prices, productivity, etc.*〉; **2.** *refl. V.* 〈*rent, prices*〉 rise; **Erhöhung die;** ~, ~en increase 〈*Gen.* in〉

erholen *refl. V. (auch fig.)* recover (*von* from); *(sich ausruhen)* have a rest; **erholsam** *Adj.* restful; **Erholung die;** ~: **s. erholen:** recovery; rest; ~ **brauchen** need a rest; **erholungs·bedürftig** *Adj.* in need of a rest *postpos.*

erhören *tr. V. (geh.)* hear

Erika die; ~, ~s *od.* **Eriken** *(Bot.)* erica

erinnern 1. *refl. V.* **sich an jmdn./etw.** ~: remember sb./sth.; **sich [daran]** ~, **daß** ...: remember *or* recall that ...; **2.** *tr. V.* **jmdn. an etw./jmdn.** ~: remind sb. of sth./sb.; **Erinnerung die;** ~, ~en memory 〈*an* + *Akk.* of〉; **etw. [noch gut] in** ~ **haben** [still] remember sth. [well]; **zur** ~ **an jmdn./etw.** in memory of sb./sth.

erjagen *tr. V.* **a)** catch; **b)** *(gewinnen)* win 〈*fame*〉; make 〈*money, fortune*〉

erkalten *tr. V.; mit sein* cool; **erkäl-**

ten *refl. V.* catch cold; **Erkältung
die;** ~, ~en cold

erkämpfen *tr. V.* win; **den Sieg** ~:
gain a victory

erkaufen *tr. V.* a) *(durch Opfer)* win;
b) *(durch Geld)* buy

erkennbar *Adj.* recognizable; *(sichtbar)* visible; **erkennen** *unr. tr. V.* a)
recognize; b) *(deutlich sehen)* make
out; **erkenntlich** *Adj.* a) sich [für
etw.] ~ zeigen show one's appreciation
for sth.; b) *s.* erkennbar; **Erkenntnis
die;** ~, ~se discovery; **zu der ~ kommen, daß ...** : come to the realization
that ...

Erker der; ~s, ~: bay window; **Erker·fenster das** bay window

erklärbar *Adj.* explicable; **erklären
1.** *tr. V.* a) explain; b) *(mitteilen)* state;
declare; c) **jmdn. für tot ~** : pronounce
someone dead; **jmdn. zu etw. ~** : name
sb. as sth; **2.** *refl. V.* sich
einverstanden/bereit ~: declare oneself [to be] in agreement/willing; **erklärlich** *Adj.* understandable; **erklärt** *Adj.* declared; **Erklärung die;**
~, ~en a) *(Darlegung)* explanation; b)
(Mitteilung) statement

erklimmen *unr. tr. V. (geh.)* climb

erklingen *unr. itr. V.; mit sein* ring out

erkranken *itr. V.; mit sein* become ill
(an + *Dat.* with); **schwer erkrankt sein**
be seriously ill; **Erkrankung die;** ~,
~en illness; *(eines Körperteils)* disease

erkunden *tr. V.* reconnoitre *(terrain)*;
erkundigen *refl. V.* **sich nach jmdm./
etw. ~** : ask after sb./enquire about
sth.; **Erkundigung die;** ~, ~en enquiry

erlahmen *itr. V.; mit sein* tire;
(strength) flag

erlangen *tr. V.* gain; obtain *(credit,
visa)*; reach *(age)*

Erlaß der; Erlasses, Erlasse decree;
erlassen *unr. tr. V.* a) enact *(law)*;
declare *(amnesty)*; issue *(warrant)*; b)
(verzichten auf) remit *(sentence)*

erlauben 1. *tr. V.* a) allow; b) *(ermöglichen)* permit; **2.** *refl. V.* sich *(Dat.)*
etw. ~: permit oneself sth.; **Erlaubnis die;** ~, ~se permission;
(Schriftstück) permit

erläutern *tr. V.* explain; comment on
(picture etc.); annotate *(text)*; **Erläuterung die** the explanation

Erle die; ~, ~n alder

erleben *tr. V.* experience; **etwas
Schreckliches ~** : have a terrible experience; **er wird das nächste Jahr**

nicht mehr ~ : he won't see next year;
du kannst was ~ ! *(ugs.)* you won't
know what's hit you!; **Erlebnis das;**
~ses, ~se experience

erledigen 1. *tr. V.* deal with *(task)*;
settle *(matter)*; **ich muß noch einige
Dinge erledigen** I must see to a few
things; **sie hat alles pünktlich erledigt**
she got everything done on time; **2.**
refl. V. *(matter, problem)* resolve itself;
vieles erledigt sich von selbst a lot of
things sort them'selves out; **erledigt**
Adj. closed *(case)*; *(ugs.)* worn out
(person)

erlegen *tr. V.* shoot *(animal)*

erleichtern *tr. V.* a) make easier; b)
(befreien) relieve; **Erleichterung
die;** ~, ~en a) zur ~ der Arbeit to
make the work easier; b) *(Befreiung)*
relief; c) *(Verbesserung, Milderung)* alleviation

erleiden *unr. tr. V.* suffer

erlernbar *Adj.* learnable; **erlernen**
tr. V. learn

erlesen *Adj.* superior *(wine)*; choice
(dish)

erleuchten *tr. V.* a) light; b) *(geh.: mit
Klarheit erfüllen)* inspire; **Erleuchtung die;** ~, ~en inspiration

erliegen *unr. itr. V.; mit sein* succumb
(Dat. to); **einem Irrtum ~** : be misled;
einer Krankheit *(Dat.)* ~: die from an
illness

erlogen *Adj.* made up

Erlös der; ~es, ~e proceeds *pl.*

erlöschen *unr. itr. V.; mit sein* *(fire)*
go out; **ein erloschener Vulkan** an extinct volcano

erlösen *tr. V.* save, rescue *(von* from);
Erlöser der; ~s, ~ a) saviour; b)
(christl. Rel.) redeemer; **Erlösung die**
release *(von* from)

ermächtigen *tr. V.* authorize; **Ermächtigung die;** ~, ~en authorization

ermahnen *tr. V.* admonish; tell
(coll.); *(warnen)* warn; **Ermahnung
die** admonition; *(Warnung)* warning

Ermang[e]lung die; ~: in ~
(+ *Gen.*) *(geh.)* in the absence of

ermäßigen *tr. V.* reduce; **Ermäßigung die** reduction

ermatten *(geh.)* **1.** *itr. V.; mit sein*
become exhausted; **2.** *tr. V.* exhaust,
tire

ermessen *unr. tr. V.* estimate, gauge;
Ermessen das; ~s estimation

ermitteln 1. *tr. V.* ascertain *(facts)*;
discover *(culprit, address)*; establish

⟨*identity, origin*⟩; decide ⟨*winner*⟩; calculate ⟨*quota, rates, data*⟩; **2.** *itr. V. (Rechtsw.)* investigate; **Ermittlung die; ~, ~en** *a)* ⟨*das Ermitteln*⟩ s. **ermitteln a:** ascertainment; discovery; *b)* ⟨*Untersuchung*⟩ investigation

ermöglichen *tr. V.* enable

ermorden *tr. V.* murder; **Ermordung die; ~, ~en** murder

ermüden 1. *itr. V.; mit sein* tire; **2.** *tr. V.* tire; make tired; **ermüdend** *Adj.* tiring; **Ermüdung die; ~, ~en** tiredness

ermuntern *tr. V.* encourage; **ermunternd** *Adj.* encouraging

ermutigen *tr. V.* encourage; **Ermutigung die; ~, ~en** encouragement

ernähren 1. *tr. V. a)* feed ⟨*young, child*⟩; *b)* ⟨*unterhalten*⟩ keep ⟨*family, wife*⟩; **2.** *refl. V.* feed oneself; **Ernährer der; ~s, ~, Ernährerin die; ~, ~nen** breadwinner; **Ernährung die; ~:** feeding; *(Nahrung)* diet

ernennen *unr. tr. V.* appoint; **Ernennung die** appointment ⟨zu as⟩

erneuern *tr. V. a)* replace; *b)* ⟨*wiederherstellen*⟩ renovate ⟨*roof, building*⟩; *(fig.)* thoroughly reform ⟨*system*⟩; **Erneuerung die** *a)* replacement; *b)* *(Wiederherstellung)* renovation; **erneut 1.** *Adj.* renewed; **2.** *adv.* once again

erniedrigen *tr. V.* humiliate; **Erniedrigung die; ~, ~en** humiliation

ernst 1. *Adj. a)* serious; *b)* ⟨*aufrichtig*⟩ genuine ⟨*intention, offer*⟩; *c)* ⟨*gefahrvoll*⟩ serious ⟨*injury*⟩; grave ⟨*situation*⟩; **2.** *adv.* seriously; **Ernst der; ~[e]s** *a)* seriousness; **das ist mein [voller] ~:** I mean that [quite] seriously; *b)* *(Wirklichkeit)* **daraus wurde [blutiger/bitterer] ~:** it became [deadly] serious; **der ~ des Lebens** the serious side of life

ernst-, Ernst-: ~fall der: im ~: when the real thing happens; **~gemeint** *Adj. (präd. getrennt geschrieben)* serious; sincere ⟨*wish*⟩; **~haft 1.** *Adj.* serious; **2.** *adv.* seriously; **~haftigkeit die; ~:** seriousness

ernstlich 1. *Adj. a)* serious; *b)* ⟨*aufrichtig*⟩ genuine ⟨*wish*⟩; **2.** *adv. a)* seriously; *b)* ⟨*aufrichtig*⟩ genuinely ⟨*sorry, repentant*⟩

Ernte die; ~, ~n *a)* harvest; *b)* *(Ertrag)* crop; **die ~ einbringen** bring in the harvest; **Ernte·dank·fest das** harvest festival; **ernten** *tr. V.* harvest

ernüchtern *tr. V.* sober up; *(fig.)* bring down to earth; **~d** sobering; **Ernüchterung die; ~, ~en** *(fig.)* disillusionment

Eroberer der; ~s, ~, Eroberin die; ~, ~nen conqueror; **erobern** *tr. V. a)* conquer; take ⟨*town, fortress*⟩; seize ⟨*power*⟩; **Eroberung die; ~, ~en** conquest; *(einer Stadt, Festung)* taking

eröffnen *tr. V. a)* open; start ⟨*business, practice*⟩; *b)* ⟨*mitteilen*⟩ **jmdm. etw. ~:** reveal sth. to sb.; *c)* **ein Testament ~:** read a will; **Eröffnung die** *a)* opening; *(einer Sitzung)* start; *b)* *(Mitteilung)* revelation; *c)* *(Testaments~)* reading

erörtern *tr. V.* discuss; **Erörterung die; ~, ~en** discussion

Erotik die; ~: eroticism; **erotisch** *Adj.* erotic

Erpel der; ~s, ~: drake

erpicht *Adj.* **in auf etw. (Akk.) ~ sein** be keen on sth.

erpressen *tr. V. a)* *(nötigen)* blackmail; *b)* *(erlangen)* extort ⟨*money etc.*⟩; **Erpresser der; ~s, ~:** blackmailer; **Erpressung die** blackmail *no indef. art.;* *(von Geld, Geständnis)* extortion

erproben *tr. V.* test ⟨*medicine*⟩ ⟨an + Akk. on⟩

erraten *unr. tr. V.* guess

errechnen *tr. V.* calculate

erregen 1. *tr. V. a)* annoy; *b)* *(sexuell)* arouse; *c)* *(verursachen)* arouse; **2.** *refl. V.* get excited; **erregend** *Adj.* exciting; *(sexuell)* arousing; **Erreger der; ~s, ~** *(Med.)* pathogen; **erregt** *Adj.* excited; *(sexuell)* aroused; **Erregung die** excitement

erreichbar *Adj. a)* within reach *postpos.;* *b)* **der Ort ist mit dem Zug ~:** the place can be reached by train; **erreichen** *tr. V. a)* reach; **den Zug ~:** catch the train; **er ist telefonisch zu ~:** he can be contacted by telephone; *b)* *(durchsetzen)* achieve ⟨*goal, aim*⟩

errichten *tr. V. a)* build ⟨*house, bridge, etc.*⟩; *b)* *(aufstellen)* erect

erringen *unr. tr. V.* gain ⟨*victory*⟩; reach ⟨*first etc. place*⟩

erröten *itr. V.; mit sein* blush

Errungenschaft die; ~, ~en achievement

Ersatz der; ~es *a)* replacement; *b)* *(Entschädigung)* compensation

Ersatz-: ~kasse die private health insurance company; **~mann der;** *Pl.* **~männer, ~leute** replacement; *(Sport)*

substitute; ~**rad** das spare wheel; ~**reifen** der spare tyre; ~**teil** das *(bes. Technik)* spare part; spare *(Brit.)*

ersaufen *unr. itr. V.; mit sein (salopp)* drown; **ersäufen** *tr. V.* drown

erschaffen *unr. tr. V.* create; **Erschaffung** die creation

erscheinen *unr. itr. V.; mit sein (book)* be published; **Erscheinung** die; ~, ~en a) *(Vorgang)* phenomenon; b) *(äußere Gestalt)* appearance; c) *(Vision)* apparition; **eine ~ haben** see a vision

Erscheinungs-: ~**bild** das appearance; ~**form** die manifestation

erschießen *unr. tr. V.* shoot dead; **Erschießung** die; ~, ~en shooting

erschlaffen *itr. V.; mit sein (muscle, limb)* become limp; *(skin)* grow slack

¹**erschlagen** *unr. tr. V.* strike dead; kill; ²**erschlagen** *Adj. (ugs.)* a) *(erschöpft)* worn out; b) *(verblüfft)* **wie ~ sein** be flabbergasted *(coll.)* or thunderstruck

erschließen *unr. tr. V.* develop *(area, building land)*; tap *(resources)*

erschöpfen *tr. V.* exhaust; **erschöpfend** *Adj.* exhaustive; **erschöpft** *Adj.* exhausted; **Erschöpfung** die exhaustion

¹**erschrecken** *unr. itr. V.; mit sein* be startled; **vor etw.** *(Dat.)* od. **über etw.** *(Akk.)* ~: be startled by sth.; ²**erschrecken** *tr. V.* frighten; scare; ³**erschrecken** *unr. od. regelm. refl. V.* get a fright; **erschreckend** *Adj.* alarming; **erschrocken** 1. 2. *Part. v.* ¹erschrecken; 2. *Adj.* frightened

erschüttern *tr. V. (auch fig.)* shake; **erschütternd** *Adj.* deeply distressing; deeply shocking *(conditions)*; **Erschütterung** die; ~, ~en a) vibration; *(der Erde)* tremor; b) *(Ergriffenheit)* shock; *(Trauer)* distress

erschweren *tr. V.* **etw.** ~: make sth. more difficult; **erschwerend** 1. *Adj.* complicating *(factor)*; 2. *adv.* **es kommt ~ hinzu, daß er ...:** to make matters worse he ...

erschwinglich *Adj.* reasonable

ersehen *unr. tr. V.* see; **aus etw. zu ~ sein** be evident from sth.

ersetzen *tr. V.* a) replace *(durch by)*; b) *(erstatten)* reimburse *(expenses)*; **jmdm. einen Schaden** ~: compensate sb. for damages

ersichtlich *Adj.* apparent

erspähen *tr. V. (geh.)* espy *(literary)*; catch sight of

ersparen *tr. V.* save; **Ersparnis** die; ~, ~se saving

ersprießlich *Adj. (geh.)* fruitful *(contacts, collaboration)*

erst 1. *Adv.* a) *(zu~)* first; ~ **einmal** first [of all]; b) *(nicht eher als)* **eben** ~: only just; ~ **nächste Woche** not until next week; **er war ~ zufrieden, als ...:** he was not satisfied until ...; c) *(nicht mehr als)* only; 2. *Partikel* **so was lese ich gar nicht ~:** I dont even start reading that sort of stuff

erst... *Ordinalz.* a) first; **etw. das ~e Mal tun** do sth. for the first time; **am Ersten [des Monats]** on the first [of the month]; **als ~er/~e etw. tun** be the first to do sth.; b) *(best...)* **das ~e Hotel** the best hotel; **der/die Erste [der Klasse]** the top boy/girl [of the class]

erstarren *itr. V.; mit sein (jelly, plaster)* set; *(limbs, fingers)* grow stiff

erstatten *tr. V.* a) reimburse *(expenses)*; b) **Anzeige gegen jmdn.** ~: report sb. [to the police]; **Erstattung** die; ~, ~en *(von Kosten)* reimbursement

Erst·aufführung die première

erstaunen *tr. V.* astonish; **Erstaunen** das; ~s astonishment; **erstaunlich** 1. *Adj.* astonishing; 2. *adv.* astonishingly

Erst·ausgabe die first edition

erstechen *unr. tr. V.* stab [to death]

erstehen *(geh.)* 1. *unr. tr. V. (kaufen)* purchase; 2. *unr. itr. V.; mit sein (difficulties, problems)* arise

ersteigen *unr. tr. V.* climb

ersteigern *tr. V.* buy [at an auction]

erstellen *tr. V. (Papierdt.)* a) *(bauen)* build; b) *(anfertigen)* make *(assessment)*; draw up *(plan, report, list)*

erste·mal *Adv.* **das ~:** for the first time; **ersten·mal** *Adv.* **zum ~:** for the first time; **beim ~:** the first time

erstens *Adv.* firstly; in the first place; **erster...** *Adj.* the former

erst·geboren *Adj.* first-born

ersticken 1. *itr. V.; mit sein* suffocate; *(sich verschlucken)* choke; 2. *tr. V.* a) *(töten)* suffocate; b) smother *(flames)*

erstklassig 1. *Adj.* first-class; 2. *adv.* superbly; **erstmals** *Adv.* for the first time; **erstrangig** *Adj.* a) first-class; b) *(vordringlich)* of top priority *postpos.*

erstreben *tr. V.* strive for; **erstrebens·wert** *Adj. (ideals etc.)* worth striving for; desirable *(situation)*

erstrecken *refl. V.* a) *(sich ausdeh-*

nen) stretch; **b)** *(dauern)* sich über 10 Jahre ~: carry on for 10 years

erstürmen *tr. V.* take by storm

ersuchen *tr. V. (geh.)* ask; jmdn. ~, etw. zu tun request sb. to do sth.

ertappen *tr. V.* catch *⟨thief, burglar⟩*

erteilen *tr. V.* give *⟨advice, information⟩*; give, grant *⟨permission⟩*; **Erteilung die** giving; *(einer Genehmigung)* granting

ertönen *itr. V.; mit sein* sound

Ertrag der; ~[e]s, Erträge **a)** yield; **b)** *(Gewinn)* return

ertragen *unr. tr. V.* bear; **erträglich** *Adj.* tolerable; bearable *⟨pain⟩*

ertrag·reich *Adj.* lucrative *⟨business⟩*; productive *⟨land, soil⟩*

ertränken *tr. V.* drown; **ertrinken** *unr. itr. V.; mit sein* be drowned; drown

erübrigen 1. *tr. V.* spare *⟨money, time⟩*; **2.** *refl. V.* be unnecessary

erwachen *itr. V.; mit sein (geh.)* awake

Erwachen das; ~s *(auch fig.)* awakening

¹**erwachsen** *unr. itr. V.; mit sein* **a)** grow *(aus out of)*; *⟨rumour⟩* spread; **b)** *(sich ergeben)* *⟨difficulties, tasks⟩* arise; ²**erwachsen** *Adj.* grown-up *attrib.*; ~ sein be grown up; **Erwachsene der/die;** *adj. Dekl.* adult; grown-up

erwägen *unr. tr. V.* consider; **Erwägung die;** ~, ~en consideration; etw. in ~ ziehen take sth. into consideration

erwählen *tr. V. (geh.)* choose

erwähnen *tr. V.* mention; **erwähnens·wert** *Adj.* worth mentioning *postpos.*; **Erwähnung die;** ~, ~en mention

erwärmen 1. *tr. V.* heat; **2.** *refl. V.* *(warm werden)* *⟨air, water⟩* warm up

erwarten *tr. V.* expect; jmdn. am Bahnhof ~: wait for sb. at the station; **Erwartung die;** ~, ~en expectation

erwartungs·: ~gemäß *Adv.* as expected; **~voll** *Adj.* expectant

erwecken *tr. V.* **a)** *(auf~)* wake; **b)** *(erregen)* arouse *⟨longing, pity⟩*

erweichen *tr. V.* soften

erweisen 1. *tr. V.* **a)** prove; **b)** *(bezeigen)* jmdm. Achtung ~: show respect to sb.; **2.** *unr. refl. V.* sich als etw. ~: prove to be sth.

erweitern 1. *tr. V.* widen *⟨river, road⟩*; expand *⟨library, business⟩*; enlarge *⟨collection⟩*; dilate *⟨pupil, blood vessel⟩*; **2.** *refl. V.* *⟨road, river⟩* widen;

⟨pupil, blood vessel⟩ dilate; **Erweiterung die;** ~, ~en *s.* erweitern: widening; expansion; enlargement; dilation

Erwerb der; ~[e]s **a)** *(Aneignung)* acquisition; **b)** *(Kauf)* purchase; **erwerben** *unr. tr. V.* **a)** *(verdienen)* earn; **b)** *(sich aneignen)* gain; **c)** *(kaufen)* acquire

erwerbs·: ~los *Adj.: s.* arbeitslos; **~tätig** *Adj.* gainfully employed; **~unfähig** *Adj.* incapable of gainful employment *postpos.*; unable to work *postpos.*

Erwerbung die acquisition; *(Gekauftes)* purchase

erwidern *tr. V.* **a)** reply; **b)** *(reagieren auf)* return *⟨greeting, visit⟩*; reciprocate *⟨sb.'s feelings⟩*; **Erwiderung die;** ~, ~en **a)** reply *(auf + Akk.* to); **b)** *s.* erwidern **b)**: return; reciprocation

erwiesen *Adj.* proved; proven *⟨fact⟩*; **erwiesener·maßen** *Adv.* as has been proved

erwirken *tr. V.* obtain

erwirtschaften *tr. V.* etw. ~: obtain sth. by careful management

erwischen *tr. V. (ugs.)* **a)** catch *⟨culprit, train, bus⟩*; **b)** *(greifen)* grab; **c)** *(bekommen)* manage to get; **d)** *(unpers.)* es hat ihn erwischt *(ugs.)* *(er ist tot)* he's bought it *(sl.)*; *(er ist krank)* he's got it; *(er ist verletzt)* he's been hurt; *(scherzh.: er ist verliebt)* he's got it bad *(coll.)*

erwünscht *Adj.* wanted

erwürgen *tr. V.* strangle

Erz [ɛrts *od.* eːɐ̯ts] **das;** ~es, ~e ore

erzählen *tr. V. (auch itr.)* tell *⟨joke, story⟩*; jmdm. etw. ~: tell sb. sth.; **Erzähler der** story-teller; *(Autor)* writer [of stories]; narrative writer; **Erzählung die;** ~, ~en **a)** narration; *(Bericht)* account; *(Literaturw.)* story

Erz·: ~bischof der archbishop; **~bistum das, ~diözese die** archbishopric; archdiocese; **~engel der** archangel

erzeugen *tr. V.* produce; generate *⟨electricity⟩*; **Erzeuger der;** ~s, ~ *(Vater)* father; **Erzeugnis das** product; **Erzeugung die** *(von Lebensmitteln usw.)* production; *(von Industriewaren)* manufacture; *(Strom~)* generation

Erz·feind der arch enemy

erziehen *unr. tr. V.* bring up; *(in der Schule)* educate; ein Kind zu Sauberkeit und Ordnung ~: bring a child up to be clean and tidy; **Erzieher** der; ~s, ~, **Erzieherin** die; ~, ~nen educator; *(Pädagoge)* educationalist; *(Lehrer)* teacher; **Erziehung** die; o. Pl. upbringing; *(Schul~)* education; **Erziehungs·berechtigte** der/die; adj. Dekl. parent or [legal] guardian

erzielen tr. V. reach ⟨agreement, compromise, speed⟩; achieve ⟨result, effect⟩; make ⟨profit⟩; obtain ⟨price⟩

erzürnen *(geh.)* tr. V. anger; *(stärker)* incense

erzwingen unr. tr. V. force

es Personalpron.; 3. Pers. Sg. Nom. u. Akk. Neutr. **a)** *(s. auch Gen. seiner; Dat. ihm)* *(Sache)* it; *(weibliche Person)* she/her; *(männliche Person)* he/him; **b)** ohne Bezug auf ein bestimmtes Subst., mit unpers. konstruierten Verben, als formales Satzglied it; **ich bin es it's me; wir sind traurig, ihr seid es auch** we are sad, and so are you; **es sei denn, [daß] ...:** unless ...; **es ist genug!** that's enough; **es hat geklopft** there was a knock; **es klingelt** someone is ringing; **es wird schöner** the weather is improving; **es geht ihm gut/schlecht** he is well/unwell; **es wird gelacht** there is laughter; **es läßt sich aushalten** it is bearable; **er hat es gut** he has it good; **er meinte es gut** he meant well

Esche die; ~, ~n *(Bot.)* ash

Esel der; ~s, ~ **a)** donkey; ass; **b)** *(ugs.: Dummkopf)* ass *(coll.)*

Esels-: **~brücke** die *(ugs.)* mnemonic; **~ohr** das *(ugs.: umgeknickte Stelle)* dog-ear

Eskalation die; ~, ~en escalation

Eskimo der; ~[s], ~[s] Eskimo

Eskorte die; ~, ~n escort; **eskortieren** tr. V. escort

Espe die; ~, ~n aspen

eßbar Adj. edible; **nicht ~:** inedible; **essen** unr. tr., itr. V. eat; **etw. gern ~:** like sth.; **sich satt ~:** eat one's fill; **gut ~:** have a good meal; *(immer)* eat well; **~ gehen** go out for a meal; **Essen** das; ~s, ~ *(Mahlzeit)* meal; *(Speise)* food; **[das] ~ machen/kochen** get/cook the meal

Essen[s]-: **~marke** die meal-ticket; **~zeit** die mealtime

Essenz die; ~, ~en essence

Esser der; ~s, ~: **er ist ein schlechter ~:** he has a poor appetite

Essig der; ~s, ~e vinegar; **Essiggurke** die pickled gherkin

Eß-: **~kastanie** die sweet chestnut; **~löffel** der *(Suppenlöffel)* soup-

spoon; *(für Nach-, Vorspeise)* dessert-spoon; **~stäbchen** das chopstick; **~teller** der dinner plate; **~tisch** der dining-table; **~waren** Pl. food sing.; **~zimmer** das dining-room

Establishment [ɪsˈtɛblɪʃmənt] das; ~s, ~s Establishment

Este der; ~n, ~n Estonian; **Est·land** (das); ~s Estonia

Estragon [ˈɛstragɔn] der; ~s tarragon

Estrich [ˈɛstrɪç] der; ~s, ~e composition floor

etablieren tr. V. establish; set up; **etabliert** Adj. established

Etage [eˈtaːʒə] die; ~, ~n floor; storey

Etappe die; ~, ~n stage

Etat [eˈtaː] der; ~s, ~s budget

etepetete [eːtəpeˈteːtə] Adj. *(ugs.)* fussy; finicky

Ethik die; ~, ~en **a)** ethics sing.; **b)** o. Pl. *(sittliche Normen)* ethics pl.; **ethisch** Adj. ethical

Etikett das; ~[e]s, ~en od. ~e od. ~s label; **Etikette** die; ~, ~n etiquette; **etikettieren** tr. V. label

etlich... Indefinitpron. u. unbest. Zahlwort: Sg. quite a lot of; Pl. quite a few

Etüde die; ~, ~n *(Musik)* étude

Etui [ɛtˈviː] das; ~s, ~s case

etwa 1. Adv. **a)** *(ungefähr)* about; **~ so groß wie ...:** about as large as ...; **~ so** roughly like this; **b)** *(beispielsweise)* for example; 2. Partikel **störe ich ~?** am I disturbing you at all?; **etwaig...** [ˈɛtva(ː)ɪg...] Adj. possible

etwas Indefinitpron. **a)** something; *(fragend, verneinend)* anything; **irgend ~:** something; **b)** *(Bedeutsames)* **aus ihm wird ~:** he'll make something of himself; **c)** *(ein Teil)* some; *(fragend, verneinend)* any; **~ von dem Geld** some of the money; **d)** *(ein wenig)* a little; **~ lauter/besser** a little louder/better

Etymologie die; ~, ~n etymology

euch 1. Dat. u. Akk. Pl. des Personalpron. ihr you; 2. Dat. u. Akk. Pl. des Reflexivpron. der 2. Pers. Pl. yourselves

¹euer Possessivpron. your; **Grüße von Eu[e]rer Helga/Eu[e]rem Hans** Best wishes, Yours, Helga/Hans; **²euer** Gen. des Personalpron. ihr *(geh.)* **wir werden ~ gedenken** we will remember you

Eule die; ~, ~n owl; **~n nach Athen tragen** carry coals to Newcastle

Eunuch der; ~en, ~en eunuch

Euphorie die; ~, ~n *(bes. Med., Psych.)* euphoria

eure *s.* ¹euer; **eurer·seits** *s.* deinerseits; **euret·wegen** *Adv. s.* deinetwegen

Eurocheque ['ɔyroʃɛk] der; ~s, ~s Eurocheque

Europa (das); ~s Europe

Europäer der; ~s, ~, **Europäerin** die; ~, ~nen European; **europäisch** *Adj.* European; **die Europäische Gemeinschaft** the European Community

Europa-: ~**meister** der *(Sport)* European champion; ~**meisterschaft** die *(Sport)* a) *(Wettbewerb)* European Championship; b) *(Sieg)* European title; ~**parlament** das; *o. Pl.* European Parliament; ~**pokal** der *(Sport)* European cup; ~**rat** der; *o. Pl.* Council of Europe; ~**straße** die European long-distance road

Euro·scheck der *s.* Eurocheque

Euter das *od.* der; ~s, ~: udder

e.V., E. V. *Abk.* eingetragener Verein

ev. *Abk.* evangelisch ev.

evakuieren [evaku'iːrən] *tr. V.* evacuate; **Evakuierung** die; ~, ~en evacuation

evangelisch [evaŋ'geːlɪʃ] *Adj.* Protestant; **Evangelium** das; ~s, Evangelien a) *(auch fig.)* gospel; b) *(christl. Rel.)* Gospel

eventuell [evɛn'tu̯ɛl] 1. *Adj.* possible; 2. *adv.* possibly; perhaps

Evolution [evolu'tsi̯oːn] die; ~, ~en evolution

evtl. *Abk.* eventuell

EWG [eːveː'geː] die; ~: EEC

ewig 1. *Adj.* eternal; *(abwertend)* never-ending; 2. *adv.* eternally; for ever; **Ewigkeit** die; ~, ~en a) eternity; b) *(ugs.)* es dauert eine ~: it takes ages *(coll.)*

ex *Adv. (ugs.)* etw. ex trinken drink sth. down in one *(coll.)*; **Ex-** *(vor Personenbez.: vormalig)* ex-

exakt *Adj.* exact; precise

Examen das; ~s, ~ *od.* Examina examination

Exekution die; ~, ~en execution; **Exekutive** die; ~, ~n *(Rechtsw., Politik)* executive

Exempel das; ~s, ~: example; **Exemplar** das; ~s, ~e specimen; *(Buch, Zeitung usw.)* copy

exerzieren *tr., itr. V.* drill

Exil das; ~s, ~e exile

Existenz die; ~, ~en a) existence; b) *(Lebensgrundlage)* livelihood; c) *(Mensch)* character

Existenz-: ~**grundlage** die basis of one's livelihood; ~**minimum** das subsistence level

existieren *itr. V.* exist

Exitus der; ~ *(Med.)* death

exkl. *Abk.* exklusive| excl.

exklusiv 1. *Adj.* exclusive; 2. *adv.* exclusively; **exklusive** *Präp. + Gen.* exclusive of

Ex·kommunikation die excommunication

Exkursion die; ~, ~en study trip

exotisch 1. *Adj.* exotic; 2. *adv.* exotically

expandieren *tr., itr. V.* expand; **Expansion** die; ~, ~en expansion

Expedition die; ~, ~en expedition

Experiment das; ~[e]s, ~e experiment; **experimentell** 1. *Adj.* experimental; 2. *adv.* experimentally; **experimentieren** *itr. V.* experiment

Experte der; ~n, ~n, **Expertin** die; ~, ~nen expert (für in)

explodieren *itr. V.; mit sein (auch fig.)* explode; ⟨costs⟩ rocket; **Explosion** die; ~, ~en explosion; **explosiv** 1. *Adj. (auch fig.)* explosive; 2. *adv.* explosively

Exponent der; ~en, ~en *(Math.)* exponent; **exponiert** *Adj.* exposed

Export der; ~[e]s, ~e export

Export-: ~**artikel** der export; ~**bier** das export beer

Exporteur [ɛkspɔr'tøːɐ̯] der; ~s, ~e *(Wirtsch.)* exporter

Export-: ~**firma** die exporter; ~**handel** der export trade

exportieren *tr., itr. V.* export

Expreß·gut das express freight

Expressionismus der; ~: expressionism *no art.;* **expressionistisch** *Adj.* expressionist

extra *Adv.* a) *(gesondert)* ⟨pay⟩ separately; b) *(zusätzlich, besonders)* extra; c) *(eigens)* especially; **Extra** das; ~s, ~s extra; **Extra·blatt** das special edition

Extrakt der; ~[e]s, ~e extract

extravagant [-va'gant] *Adj.* flamboyant; flamboyantly furnished *(flat)*

extrem *Adj.* extreme; **Extrem** das; ~s, ~e extreme; **Extrem·fall** der extreme case; **Extremismus** der; ~: extremism; **Extremist** der; ~en, ~en extremist; **extremistisch** *Adj.* extremist

Exzellenz die; ~, ~en Excellency

exzentrisch 1. *Adj.* eccentric; 2. *adv.* eccentrically

Exzeß der; Exzesses, Exzesse excess

F

f, F [εf] **das;** ~, ~ **a)** *(Buchstabe)* f/F; **b)** *(Musik)* [key of] F

f. *Abk.* **folgend** f.

Fa. *Abk.* **Firma**

Fabel die; ~, ~n fable; *(Kern einer Handlung)* plot

fabelhaft 1. *Adj.* *(ugs.: großartig)* fantastic *(coll.)*; **2.** *adv.* *(ugs.)* fantastically *(coll.)*

Fabrik die; ~, ~en factory

Fabrikant der; ~en, ~en manufacturer; **Fabrikat das;** ~[e]s, ~e product; *(Marke)* make; **Fabrikation die;** ~: production

Fabrik-: ~**besitzer der** factoryowner; ~**direktor der** works manager

fabrizieren *tr. V.* *(ugs. abwertend)* knock together *(coll.)*

Fach das; ~[e]s, **Fächer a)** compartment; *(für Post)* pigeon-hole; **b)** *(Studien~, Unterrichts~)* subject; *(Wissensgebiet)* field; *(Berufszweig)* trade; **ein Mann vom** ~: an expert

Fach-: ~**arbeiter der** skilled worker; ~**arzt der** specialist (**für** in); ~**geschäft das** specialist shop

fachlich *Adj.* specialist *(knowledge, work)*; technical *(problem, explanation, experience)*

Fach-: ~**mann der** expert; ~**werk das** *o. Pl. (Bauweise)* half-timbered construction; ~**werk·haus das** half-timbered house

Fackel die; ~, ~n torch

fade *Adj.* insipid

Faden der; ~s, **Fäden** thread; **ein** ~: a piece of thread

faden·scheinig *Adj.* threadbare; flimsy *(excuse)*

Fagott das; ~[e]s, ~e bassoon

fähig *Adj.* **a)** *(begabt)* able; capable; **b) zu etw.** ~ **sein** be capable of sth.; **Fähigkeit die;** ~, ~en **a)** *meist Pl.* ability; capability; **geistige** ~en intellectual faculties; **b)** *o. Pl. (Imstandesein)* ability (**zu** to)

fahl *Adj.* pale; pallid; wan *(light)*

fahnden *itr. V.* search (**nach** for)

Fahne die; ~, ~n flag

Fahr·bahn die carriageway

Fähre die; ~, ~n ferry

fahren 1. *unr. itr. V.; mit sein* **a)** *(als Fahrzeuglenker)* drive; *(mit dem Fahrrad, Motorrad usw.)* ride; **b)** *(als Mitfahrer; mit öffentlichem Verkehrsmittel)* go (**mit** by); *(mit dem Aufzug/der Rolltreppe/der Seilbahn)* take the lift *(Brit.)* or *(Amer.)* elevator/escalator/cable-car; *(per Anhalter)* hitch-hike; **c)** *(reisen)* go; **in Urlaub** ~: go on holiday; **d)** *(los~)* go; leave; **e)** *(motor vehicle, train, lift, cable-car)* go; *(ship)* sail; **mein Auto fährt nicht** my car won't go; **f)** *(verkehren)* *(train etc.)* run; **2.** *unr. tr. V.* **a)** *(fortbewegen)* drive *(car, lorry, train, etc.)*; ride *(bicycle, motor cycle)*; **b) 50/80 km/h** ~: do 50/80 k.p.h.; **hier muß man 50 km/h** ~: you've got to keep to 50 k.p.h. here; sail *(boat)*; **Auto** ~: drive [a car]; **Kahn** *od.* **Boot/Kanu** ~: go boating/canoeing; **Ski** ~: ski; **U-Bahn** ~: ride on the underground *(Brit.)* or *(Amer.)* subway; **c)** *(befördern)* take

Fahrenheit *o. Art.* **70 Grad** ~: 70 degrees Fahrenheit

fahren|lassen *unr. tr. V.* let go; **Fahrer der;** ~s, ~: driver; **Fahrerflucht die:** ~ **begehen** fail to stop after [being involved in] an accident; **Fahrerin die;** ~, ~nen driver

Fahr-: ~**gast der** passenger; ~**geld das** fare

fahrig *Adj.* nervous

fahr-, Fahr-: ~**karte die** ticket; ~**karten·automat der** ticket machine; ~**karten·schalter der** ticket window; ~**lässig 1.** *Adj.* negligent *(behaviour)*; ~**e Tötung/Körperverletzung** *(Rechtsw.)* causing death/injury through [culpable] negligence; **2.** *adv.* negligently; ~**lehrer der** driving instructor

Fähr·mann der ferryman

Fahr-: ~**plan der** timetable; schedule *(Amer.)*; ~**preis der** fare; ~**prüfung die** driving test; ~**rad das** bicycle; cycle; **mit dem** ~ **fahren** cycle; ride a bicycle; ~**rad·ständer der** bicycle rack; ~**schein der** ticket; ~**schein·automat der** ticket machine; ~**schein·entwerter der** ticket cancelling machine; ~**schule die** driving school; ~**spur die** traffic-lane

fährst *2. Pers. Sg. Präsens v.* **fahren**

Fahr-: ~**stuhl der** lift *(Brit.);* elevator *(Amer.); (für Lasten)* hoist; ~**stunde die** driving lesson

Fahrt die; ~, ~**en a)** journey; **freie** ~ **haben** have a clear run; *(Schiffsreise)* voyage; *(kurze Reise, Ausflug)* trip; **b)** *o. Pl. (Geschwindigkeit)* **in voller** ~: at full speed; **fährt** *3. Pers. Sg. Präsens v.* **fahren**

Fährte die trail; jmds. ~ **verfolgen** track sb.

Fahrt·kosten *Pl. (für öffentliche Verkehrsmittel)* fare/fares; *(für Autoreisen)* travel costs; **Fahr·treppe die** escalator; **Fahrt·richtung die** direction; **in** ~ **parken** park in the direction of the traffic; **die** ~ **ändern** change direction; **fahr·tüchtig** *Adj. (driver)* fit to drive; *(vehicle)* roadworthy

Fahrt-: ~**wind der** airflow; ~**ziel das** destination

Fahr-: ~**werk das** *(Flugw.)* undercarriage; ~**zeit die** travelling time; ~**zeug das** vehicle; *(Luft~)* aircraft; *(Wasser~)* vessel

fair [fɛːɐ̯] **1.** *Adj.* fair **(gegen** to); **2.** *adv.* fairly

Fakten *s.* **Faktum**; **faktisch 1.** *Adj.* real; actual; **2.** *adv.* **das bedeutet** ~ ...: it means in effect ...

Faktor der; ~**s,** ~**en** *(auch Math.)* factor

Faktum das; ~**s, Fakten** fact

Fakultät die; ~, ~**en** *(Hochschulw.)* faculty

Falke der; ~**n,** ~**n** *(auch Politik fig.)* hawk

Fall der; ~**|e|s, Fälle a)** *(Sturz)* fall; **zu** ~ **kommen** have a fall; **jmdn. zu** ~ **bringen** *(fig.)* bring about sb.'s downfall; **b)** *(das Fallen)* descent; **der freie** ~: free fall; **c)** *(Ereignis; Rechtsw., Med., Grammatik)* case; *(zu erwartender Umstand)* eventuality; **es ist [nicht] der** ~: it is [not] the case; **gesetzt den** ~: assuming; **auf jeden** ~, **in jedem** ~, **auf alle Fälle** in any case; **auf keinen** ~: on no account; **Falle die;** ~, ~**n** *(auch fig.)* trap; **fallen** *unr. itr. V.; mit sein* **a)** fall; etw. ~ **lassen** drop sth.; **b)** *(hin~, stürzen)* fall [over]; **über einen Stein** ~: trip over a stone; **c)** *(prices, light, glance, choise)* fall; *(temperature, water level)* fall, drop; *(fever)* subside; *(shot)* be fired; **d)** *(im Kampf sterben)* die; fall *(literary)*; **fällen** *tr. V.* **a)** fell *(tree, timber)*; **b)** **ein Urteil** ~ *(judge)* pass sentence; *(jury)* return a verdict; **fällig** *Adj.* due; **falls** *(Konj.)*

a) *(wenn)* if; **b)** *(für den Fall, daß)* in case; **Fall·schirm der** parachute; **mit dem** ~ **abspringen** *(im Notfall)* parachute out; *(als Sport)* make a [parachute] jump

falsch 1. *Adj.* **a)** *(unecht, imitiert)* false *(teeth, plait)*; imitation *(jewellery)*; **b)** *(gefälscht)* forged; assumed *(name)*; **c)** *(irrig, fehlerhaft)* wrong; **2.** *adv.* wrongly; **die Uhr geht** ~: the clock is wrong; **fälschen** *tr. V.* forge; **Fälscher der;** ~**s,** ~**forger; Falschgeld das** counterfeit money; **fälschlich 1.** *Adj.* false; **2.** *adv.* falsely; **Falsch·meldung die** false report; **Fälschung die;** ~, ~**en** fake

Falt·blatt das leaflet; *(in Zeitungen, Zeitschriften, Büchern)* insert; **Falte die;** ~, ~**n a)** crease; **b)** *(im Stoff)* fold; *(mit scharfer Kante)* pleat; **c)** *(Haut~)* wrinkle; **falten 1.** *tr. V.* fold; **die Hände** ~: fold one's hands; **2.** *refl. V. (auch Geol.)* fold; *(skin)* become wrinkled; **Falten·rock der** pleated skirt; **Falter der;** ~**s,** ~ *(Nacht~)* moth; *(Tag~)* butterfly; **faltig a)** *Adj.* *(clothes)* gathered [in folds]; wrinkled *(skin, hands)*; **b)** *(zerknittert)* creased **·fältig** *Adj., adv. -fold*

familiär *Adj.* **a)** family *(problems, worries)*; **b)** *(zwanglos)* familiar; informal; **Familie** [fa'mi:li̯ə] **die;** ~, ~**n** family; ~ **Meyer** the Meyer family

Familien-: ~**angehörige der/die;** *adj. Dekl.* member of the family; ~**feier die** family party; ~**leben das;** *o. Pl.* family life; ~**name der** surname; ~**planung die;** *o. Pl.* family planning *no art.;* ~**stand der** marital status; ~**vater der:** ~**vater sein** be the father of a family; **ein guter** ~**vater** be a good husband and father

Fan [fɛn] **der;** ~**s,** ~**s fan**

Fanatiker der; ~**s,** ~: fanatic; *(religiös)* fanatic; zealot; **fanatisch 1.** *Adj.* fanatical; **2.** *adv.* fanatically

fand *1. u. 3. Pers. Sg. Prät. v.* **finden**

Fanfare die; ~, ~**n** *(Signal)* fanfare

Fang der; ~**|e|s, Fänge a)** *(Tier~)* trapping; *(von Fischen)* catching; **b)** *(Beute)* bag; *(von Fischen)* catch; **fangen 1.** *unr. tr. V.* catch; capture *(fugitive etc.);* **2.** *unr. refl. V.* **a)** *(in eine Falle geraten)* be caught; **b)** *(wieder in die normale Lage kommen)* **sich [gerade] noch** ~: [just] manage to steady oneself;

Fang·frage die catch question

Farb-: ~**bild das** *(Foto)* colour photo; ~**dia das** colour slide

Farbe die; ~, ~n a) colour; b) *(für Textilien)* dye; *(zum Malen, Anstreichen)* paint; ~n **mischen/auftragen** mix/apply paint; **farb·echt** *Adj.* colour-fast; **färben** 1. *tr. V.* dye; 2. *refl. V.* change colour; **sich schwarz/rot** *usw.* ~: turn black/red *etc*; 3. *itr. V.* *(ugs.: ab~)* ⟨material, blouse etc.⟩ run; **-far-ben** *Adj.* coloured

färben-: ~**blind** *Adj.* colour-blind; ~**froh** *Adj.* colourful; ~**prächtig** *Adj.* vibrant with colour *postpos.*

Farb-: ~**fernsehen** das colour television; ~**fernseher** der *(ugs.)* colour telly *(coll.)* or television; ~**film** der colour film; ~**foto** das colour photo

farbig 1. *Adj.* a) coloured; b) *(bunt, auch fig.)* colourful; 2. *adv.* colourfully; **-farbig** *Adj.* -coloured; **Farbige** der/die; *adj. Dekl.* coloured man/woman; *Pl.* coloured people

farblich 1. *Adj.* in colour *postpos.*; as regards colour *postpos*; 2. *adv.* etw. ~ abstimmen match sth. in colour

farb-, Farb-: ~**los** *Adj. (auch fig.)* colourless; clear ⟨varnish⟩; neutral ⟨shoe polish⟩; ~**stift** der coloured pencil; ~**stoff** der a) *(Med., Biol.)* pigment; b) *(für Textilien)* dye; c) *(für Lebensmittel)* colouring; ~**ton** der shade

Färbung die; ~, ~en colouring

Farn der; ~[e]s, ~e, **Farn·kraut** das fern

Fasan der; ~[e]s, ~e[n] pheasant

Fasching der; ~s, ~e *od.* ~s [pre-Lent] carnival

Faschismus der; ~: fascism *no art.* **Faschist** der; ~en, ~en fascist; **faschistisch** *Adj.* fascist

faseln *itr. V.* *(ugs. abwertend)* drivel

Faser die; ~, ~n fibre; **fasern** *itr. V.* fray

Faß das; **Fasses, Fässer** barrel; *(Öl~)* drum; *(kleines Bier~)* keg; *(kleines Sherry~ usw.)* cask; **Bier vom** ~: draught beer; **ein** ~ **ohne Boden** an endless drain on sb.'s resources

Fassade die; ~, ~n façade

faßbar *Adj.* a) tangible ⟨results⟩; b) *(verständlich)* comprehensible

Faß·bier das draught beer; beer on draught

fassen 1. *tr. V.* a) *(greifen)* grasp; take hold of; b) *(festnehmen)* catch ⟨thief, culprit⟩; c) *(aufnehmen können)* ⟨hall, tank⟩ hold; d) *(begreifen)* **ich kann es nicht** ~: I cannot take it in; e) **einen Entschluß** ~: make *or* take a decision; 2. *itr. V.* a) *(greifen)* **nach etw.** ~: reach

for sth.; **in etw.** *(Akk.)* ~: put one's hand in sth.; **faßlich** *Adj.* comprehensible

Fasson [fa'sõ:] die; ~, ~s style; shape

Fassung die; ~, ~en a) *(Form)* version; b) *o. Pl.* *(Selbstbeherrschung)* composure; **die** ~ **bewahren** keep one's composure; **die** ~ **verlieren** lose one's self-control; **jmdn. aus der** ~ **bringen** upset sb.; c) *(für Glühlampen)* holder; **fassungs·los** *Adj.* stunned

fast *Adv.* almost; nearly; ~ **nie** hardly ever

fasten *itr. V.* fast; **Fast·nacht** die carnival

faszinieren *tr. V.* fascinate

fatal *Adj.* a) *(peinlich, mißlich)* awkward; b) *(verhängnisvoll)* fatal

fauchen *itr. V.* ⟨cat⟩ hiss; ⟨tiger, person⟩ snarl

faul *Adj.* a) *(verdorben)* rotten; bad ⟨food, tooth⟩; foul ⟨water, air⟩; b) *(träge)* lazy; **Fäule** die; ~: foulness; **faulen** *itr. V.; meist mit sein* rot; ⟨water⟩ go foul; ⟨meat, fish⟩ go off

faulenzen *itr. V.* laze about; loaf about *(derog.)*; **Faulenzer** der; ~s, ~: idler; lazy-bones *sing.* *(coll.)*

Faulheit die; ~: laziness; **faulig** *Adj.* stagnating ⟨water⟩; ~ **schmecken/riechen** taste/smell off; **Fäulnis** die; ~: rottenness

Faul-: ~**pelz** der *(fam.)* lazy-bones *sing.* *(coll.)*; ~**tier** das a) *(Zool.)* sloth; b) *(ugs.: Faulenzer)* s. ~**pelz**

Faust die; ~, **Fäuste** fist; **eine** ~ **machen** clench one's fist; **das paßt wie die** ~ **aufs Auge** *(ugs.)* *(paßt nicht)* that clashes horribly; *(paßt)* that matches perfectly; **auf eigene** ~: on one's own initiative; **Fäustchen** das; ~s, ~: **sich** *(Dat.)* **ins** ~ **lachen** laugh up one's sleeve; **faust·dick** *Adj.* as thick as a man's fist *postpos.*; *(fig.)* barge-faced ⟨lie⟩; **Fäustling** der; ~s, ~e mitten; **Faust·regel** die rule of thumb

Favorit [favo'ri:t] der; ~en, ~en favourite

Fax das; ~, ~[e] fax; **faxen** *tr. V.* fax

Faxen *Pl.* *(ugs.)* fooling around

Fazit ['fa:tsɪt] das; ~s, ~s *od.* ~e result

Februar der; ~[s], ~e February

fechten *unr. itr. V.* fence; **Fechter** der; ~s, ~: fencer

Feder die; ~, ~n a) *(Vogel~)* feather; b) *(zum Schreiben)* nib; c) *(Technik)* spring

feder-, Feder-: ~**ball** der a) *(Spiel)* badminton; b) *(Ball)* shuttlecock;

~**bett** das duvet *(Brit.)*; stuffed quilt *(Amer.)*; ~**führend** *Adj.* in charge *postpos.*; ~**halter** der fountain-pen; ~**leicht** *Adj.* ⟨person⟩ as light as a feather; featherweight ⟨object⟩; ~**lesen** das: nicht viel ~**lesen|s|** mit jmdm./etw. machen give sb./sth. short shrift

federn 1. *itr. V.* ⟨springboard, floor, etc.⟩ be springy; 2. *tr. V. (mit einer Federung versehen)* spring; **das Bett ist gut gefedert** the bed is well-sprung; **Federung** die; ~, ~**en** *(Kfz-W.)* suspension

Fee die; ~, ~**n** fairy

Fege·feuer das purgatory; **fegen** 1. *tr. V.* a) *(bes. nordd.: säubern)* sweep; b) *(schnell entfernen)* brush; 2. *itr. V.* sweep up

fehl *Adv.* ~ **am Platz|e|** sein be out of place; **Fehl·anzeige** die: ~! *(ugs.)* no chance! *(coll.)*; **fehlen** *itr. V.* a) *(nicht vorhanden sein)* **ihm fehlt das Geld** he has no money; b) *(ausbleiben)* be absent; c) *(verschwunden sein)* be missing; **in der Kasse fehlt Geld** money is missing from the till; d) *(vermißt werden)* **er/das wird mir ~ :** I shall miss him/that; e) *(erforderlich sein)* be needed; **ihm ~ noch zwei Punkte zum Sieg** he needs only two points to win; **es fehlte nicht viel, und ich wäre eingeschlafen** I all but fell asleep; f) *unpers. (mangeln)* **es fehlt an Lehrern** there is a lack of teachers; g) *(krank sein)* **was fehlt Ihnen?** what seems to be the matter?; **fehlt dir etwas?** is there something wrong?; **Fehler** der; ~**s,** ~ a) *(Irrtum)* mistake; error; *(Sport)* fault; b) *(schlechte Eigenschaft)* fault; **fehler·frei** *Adj.* faultless; **fehlerhaft** *Adj.* faulty; defective; imperfect *(pronunciation)*; **Fehler·quelle** die source of error

fehl-, Fehl-: ~**geburt** die miscarriage; ~**schlag** der failure; ~**schlagen** *unr. itr. V.; mit sein* fail; ~**start** der *(Leichtathletik)* false start; ~**tritt** der *(fig. geh.)* slip; ~**zündung** die *(Technik)* misfire

Feier die; ~, ~**n** a) *(Veranstaltung)* party; *(aus festlichem Anlaß)* celebration; b) *(Zeremonie)* ceremony; **Feier·abend** der *(Arbeitsschluß)* finishing time; **nach ~ :** after work; ~ **machen** finish work; **feierlich** 1. *Adj.* ceremonial ⟨act etc.⟩; solemn ⟨silence⟩; 2. *adv.* solemnly; ceremoniously; **Feierlichkeit** die; ~, ~**en** a) o.

Pl. solemnity; b) *meist Pl. (Veranstaltung)* celebration; **feiern** 1. *tr. V.* a) celebrate ⟨birthday, wedding, etc.⟩; b) acclaim ⟨artist, sportsman, etc.⟩; 2. *itr. V.* celebrate

Feier·tag der holiday; **ein gesetzlicher/kirchlicher ~** a public holiday/religious festival

feig[e] 1. *Adj.* cowardly; 2. *adv.* in a cowardly way

Feige die; ~, ~**n** fig

Feigheit die; ~: cowardice; **Feigling** der; ~**s,** ~**e** coward

Feile die; ~, ~**n** file; **feilen** *tr., itr. V.* file

feilschen *itr. V.* haggle **(um over)**

fein 1. *Adj.* a) fine; finely-ground ⟨flour⟩; finely-granulated ⟨sugar⟩; b) *(hochwertig)* high-quality ⟨fruit, soap, etc.⟩; fine ⟨silver, gold, etc.⟩; fancy ⟨cakes, pastries, etc.⟩; c) *(ugs.: erfreulich)* great *(coll.)*; 2. *adv.* ~ **|he|raussein** *(ugs.)* be sitting pretty *(coll.)*

Feind der; ~**|e|s,** ~**e** enemy; **feindlich** 1. *Adj.* a) hostile; b) *(Milit.)* enemy ⟨attack, activity⟩; 2. *adv.* in a hostile manner; **Feindschaft** die; ~, ~**en** enmity; **feind·selig** *Adj.* hostile

Feinheit die; ~, ~**en** a) fineness; delicacy; b) *(Nuance)* subtlety

fein-, Fein-: ~**kost·geschäft** das delicatessen; ~**machen** *refl. V.* *(ugs.)* dress up; ~**schmecker** der; ~**s,** ~ gourmet; ~**sinnig** *Adj.* sensitive and subtle; ~**waschmittel** das mild detergent

feist *Adj. (meist abwertend)* fat

Feld das; ~**|e|s,** ~**er** a) field; b) *(Sport: Spiel~)* pitch; field; c) *(auf Formularen)* box; space; *(auf Brettspielen)* space; *(auf dem Schachbrett)* square; d) o. *Pl. (Tätigkeitsbereich)* field; sphere

Feld-: ~**herr** der *(veralt.)* commander; ~**marschall** der Field Marshal; ~**salat** der corn salad; ~**stecher** der binoculars *pl.;* ~**webel** der; ~**s,** ~ *(Milit.)* sergeant; ~**weg** der path; track; ~**zug** der *(Milit., fig.)* campaign

Felge die; ~, ~**n** [wheel] rim

Fell das; ~**|e|s,** ~**e** a) *(Haarkleid)* fur; *(Pferde-, Hunde-, Katzen~)* coat; *(Schaf~)* fleece; b) *(Material)* fur; c) *(abgezogen)* hide; **ein dickes ~ haben** *(ugs.)* be thick-skinned

Fels der; ~**en,** ~**en** rock; **Felsen** der; ~**s,** ~: rock; *(an der Steilküste)* cliff; **felsen·fest** *Adj.* firm; unshakeable

⟨*opinion, belief*⟩; **fẹlsig** *Adj.* rocky; **Fẹls·wand** die rock face

feminịn *Adj.* feminine; **Feminịsmus** der; ~ feminism *no art.*; **Feminịstin** die; ~, ~**nen** feminist

Fẹnchel der; ~s fennel

Fẹnster das; ~s, ~: window

Fẹnster-: ~**bank** die window-sill; ~**laden** der [window] shutter; ~**leder** das wash-leather; ~**platz** der window-seat; ~**putzer** der windowcleaner; ~**rahmen** der windowframe; ~**scheibe** die window-pane

Ferien ['fe:riən] *Pl.* **a)** holiday[s *pl.*] *(Brit.)*; vacation *(Amer.)*; **in die** ~ **fahren** go on holiday/vacation; ~ **haben** have a *or* be on holiday/vacation; **Ferien·haus** das holiday/vacation house

Fẹrkel das; ~s, ~: piglet

fẹrn 1. *Adj.* distant; **2.** *adv.* ~ **von der Heimat** far from home; **3.** *Präp. mit Dat.* (*geh.*) far [away] from; **fẹrn|bleiben** *unr. itr. V.; mit sein* (*geh.*) stay away; **Fẹrne** die; ~, ~**n** distance; **fẹrner** *Adv.* furthermore

fẹrn-, Fẹrn-: ~**fahrer** der long-distance lorry-driver *(Brit.)* or *(Amer.)* trucker; ~**gespräch** das long-distance call; ~**glas** das binoculars *pl.*; ~|**halten** *unr. tr., refl. V.* keep away; ~**heizung** die district heating system; ~**licht** das *(Kfz-W.)* full beam; ~**melde·amt** das telephone exchange; ~**ọst** *o. Art.* Far East; ~**rohr** das telescope; ~**ruf** der telephone number; ~**schreiben** das telex [message]; ~**schreiber** der telex [machine]

Fẹrnseh-: ~**antenne** die television aerial *(Brit.)* or *(Amer.)* antenna; ~**apparat** der television [set]

fẹrn|sehen *unr. itr. V.* watch television; **Fẹrn·sehen** das; ~s television; **im** ~: on television; **Fẹrn·seher** der; ~s, ~ (*ugs.*) telly *(Brit. coll.)*; TV

Fẹrnseh-: ~**gebühren** *Pl.* television licence fee; ~**gerät** das television [set]; ~**programm** das **a)** *(Sendungen)* television programmes *pl.*; **b)** *(Kanal)* television channel; **c)** *(Blatt, Programmheft)* television [programme] guide; ~**sendung** die television programme; ~**spiel** das television play; ~**zuschauer** der television viewer

Fẹrn·sprecher der telephone

Fẹrnsprech-: ~**gebühren** *Pl.* telephone charges; ~**teilnehmer** der telephone subscriber; telephone customer *(Amer.)*

Fẹrn-: ~**steuerung** die *(Technik)* remote control; ~**straße** die major road; ~**verkehr** der long-distance traffic; ~**zug** der long-distance train

Fẹrse die; ~, ~**n** heel

fẹrtig *Adj.* **a)** finished ⟨*manuscript, picture, etc.*⟩; **das Essen ist** ~: lunch/dinner *etc.* is ready; **|mit etw.|** ~ **sein/werden** have finished/finish [sth.]; **b)** *(bereit, verfügbar)* ready (**zu, für** for); **c)** *(ugs.: erschöpft)* shattered *(coll.)*

fẹrtig-, Fẹrtig-: ~**bau** der; *Pl.* ~**ten** prefabricated building; ~**bauweise** die prefabricated construction; prefabrication ~|**bringen** *unr. tr. V.* manage

fẹrtigen *tr. V.* make

Fẹrtig-: ~**gericht** das ready-to-serve meal; ~**haus** das prefabricated house; prefab *(coll.)*

Fẹrtigkeit die; ~, ~**en** skill

fẹrtig-, Fẹrtig-: ~|**machen** *tr. V.* (*ugs.*) finish ⟨*task, job, etc.*⟩; get ⟨*meals, beds*⟩ ready; **jmdn.** ~ **machen** *(erschöpfen)* wear sb. out; *(durch Schikanen)* wear sb. down; *(deprimieren)* get sb. down; ~|**stellen** *tr. V.* complete; ~**stellung** die completion

Fẹssel die; ~, ~**n** fetter; shackle; ⟨*Kette*⟩ chain; **fẹsseln** *tr. V.* **a)** tie up; **b)** *(faszinieren)* ⟨*book*⟩ grip; ⟨*work, person*⟩ fascinate

fẹst 1. *Adj.* **a)** *(nicht flüssig od. gasförmig)* solid; **b)** firm ⟨*bandage*⟩; sound ⟨*sleep*⟩; sturdy ⟨*shoes*⟩; strong ⟨*fabric*⟩; solid ⟨*house, shell*⟩; steady ⟨*voice*⟩; **der** ~**en Überzeugung sein, daß** ...: be of the firm opinion that ...; **c)** *(dauernd)* permanent ⟨*address*⟩; fixed ⟨*income*⟩; **2.** *adv.* **a)** ⟨*tie, grip*⟩ tight[ly]; **b)** *(ugs. auch* ~**e**) ⟨*work*⟩ with a will; ⟨*eat*⟩ heartily; ⟨*sleep*⟩ soundly; **c)** ⟨*believe, be convinced*⟩ firmly; **sich auf jmdn./etw.** ~ **verlassen** rely one hundred per cent on sb./sth.; **d)** *(endgültig)* firmly; **etw.** ~ **vereinbaren** come to a firm arrangement about sth.; **e)** *(auf Dauer)* permanently; ~ **befreundet sein** be close friends; *(als Paar)* be going steady

Fẹst das; ~[e]s, ~e **a)** celebration; *(Party)* party; **b)** *(Feiertag)* festival; **frohes** ~! happy Christmas/Easter!

fẹst-: ~|**binden** *unr. tr. V.* tie [up]; ~|**bleiben** *unr. itr. V.; mit sein* stand firm; ~|**fahren** *unr. itr., refl. V.* (*itr. V.*

mit sein) get stuck; *(fig.)* get bogged down; ~|halten 1. *unr. tr. V.* a) *(halten, packen)* hold on to; b) *(nicht weiterleiten)* withhold ⟨*letter, parcel, etc.*⟩; c) *(verhaftet haben)* hold, detain ⟨*suspect*⟩; 2. *unr. refl. V.* sich an jmdm./ etw. ~halten hold on to sb./sth.

festigen 1. *tr. V.* strengthen; consolidate ⟨*position*⟩; 2. *refl. V.* ⟨*friendship, ties*⟩ become stronger

Festival ['fɛstivəl] *das*; ~s, ~s festival

fest-, Fest-: ~|kleben *tr., itr. V.; mit sein* stick (an + *Dat.* to); ~land *das*; *o. Pl.* ⟨*Kontinent*⟩ continent; *(im Gegensatz zu den Inseln)* mainland; ~legen *tr. V.* a) fix ⟨*time, deadline, price*⟩; arrange ⟨*programme*⟩; b) *(verpflichten)* sich [auf etw. *(Akk.)*] ~legen [lassen] commit oneself [to sth.]; jmdn. [auf etw. *(Akk.)*] ~legen tie sb. down [to sth.]

festlich 1. *Adj.* festive ⟨*atmosphere*⟩; formal ⟨*dress*⟩; 2. *adv.* festively; formally

fest-: ~|machen *tr. V.* a) *(befestigen)* fix; b) *(fest vereinbaren)* arrange ⟨*meeting etc.*⟩; ~|nageln *tr. V.* a) *(befestigen)* nail (an + *Dat.* to); b) *(ugs.: festlegen)* jmdn. [auf etw. *(Akk.)*] ~nageln tie sb. down [to sth.]; ~|nehmen *unr. tr. V.* arrest

Fest·rede die speech

fest-, Fest-: |schnallen *tr. V.* tie (an + *Dat.* to); ~|sitzen *unr. itr. V.* be stuck; ~|stehen *unr. itr. V.* ⟨*order, appointment, etc.*⟩ have been fixed; ⟨*decision*⟩ be definite; ⟨*fact*⟩ be certain; ~|stellen *tr. V.* a) establish ⟨*identity, age, facts*⟩; b) *(wahrnehmen)* detect; diagnose ⟨*illness*⟩; ~stellung die a) establishment; b) *(Wahrnehmung)* realization; die ~stellung machen, daß ...: realize that ...

Fest·tag der holiday; *(Ehrentag)* special day

Festung die; ~, ~en fortress

Fest·zelt das marquee

fest|ziehen *unr. tr. V.* pull tight

Fete die; ~, ~n *(ugs.)* party

fett 1. *Adj.* a) fatty ⟨*food*⟩; ~er Speck fat bacon; b) *(sehr dick)* fat; 2. *adv.* ~ essen eat fatty foods; **Fett** das; ~[e]s, ~e fat; ~ ansetzen ⟨*animal*⟩ fatten up; ⟨*person*⟩ put on weight

fett-, Fett-: ~arm *Adj.* low-fat ⟨*food*⟩; low in fat *pred.*; ~auge das speck of fat; ~fleck[en] der grease mark; ~gedruckt *Adj. (präd. getrennt geschrieben)* bold

fettig *Adj.* greasy

fett-, Fett-: ~leibig *Adj.* obese; ~leibigkeit die; ~: obesity; ~näpfchen das: ins ~näpfchen treten *(scherzh.)* put one's foot in it; ~reich *Adj.* high-fat

Fetzen der; ~s, ~: scrap

feucht *Adj.* damp; humid ⟨*climate*⟩; **feucht·fröhlich** *Adj. (ugs. scherzh.)* merry ⟨*company*⟩; boozy *(coll.)* ⟨*evening*⟩; **Feuchtigkeit** die moisture

feucht-: ~kalt *Adj.* cold and damp; ~warm *Adj.* muggy

feudal *Adj.* a) feudal ⟨*system*⟩; b) aristocratic ⟨*regiment etc.*⟩; c) *(ugs.: vornehm)* plush ⟨*hotel etc.*⟩

Feuer das; ~s, ~ a) fire; jmdm. ~ geben give sb. a light; b) *(Brand)* fire; blaze; ~! fire!; c) *o. Pl. (Milit.)* das ~ einstellen cease fire

feuer-, Feuer-: ~eifer der enthusiasm; zest; ~fest *Adj.* heat-resistant ⟨*dish, plate*⟩; fire-proof ⟨*material*⟩; ~gefährlich *Adj.* [in]flammable; ~holz das; *o. Pl.* firewood; ~leiter die *(bei Häusern)* fire escape; *(beim ~wehrauto)* [fireman's] ladder; ~löscher der; ~s, ~: fire extinguisher; ~melder der fire alarm

feuern 1. *tr. V.* a) *(ugs.: entlassen)* fire *(coll.)*; sack *(coll.)*; b) *(ugs.: schleudern, werfen)* fling; 2. *itr. V. (Milit.)* fire (auf + *Akk.* at)

feuer-, Feuer-: ~rot *Adj.* fiery red; ~schlucker der fire-eater; ~sirene die fire siren; ~stein der flint; ~versicherung die fire insurance; ~waffe die firearm; ~wehr die; ~, ~en fire service; ~wehr·auto das fire engine; ~wehr·mann der; *Pl.* ~männer od. ~leute fireman; ~werk das firework display; *(~werkskörper)* fireworks *pl.*; ~werks·körper der firework; ~zeug das lighter

Feuilleton [fœjə'tõː] das; ~s, ~s arts section

feurig *Adj.* fiery

ff. *Abk.* folgende [Seiten] ff.

Ffm. *Abk.* Frankfurt am Main

Fiaker ['fiakɐ] der; ~s, ~ *(österr.)* cab

Fiasko das; ~s, ~s fiasco

Fibel die; ~, ~n reader; primer

ficht [fiçt] *Imperativ Sg. u. 3. Pers. Sg. Präsens v.* fechten

Fichte die; ~, ~n spruce

ficken *tr., itr. V. (vulg.)* fuck *(coarse)*

fidel *Adj. (ugs.)* jolly

Fieber das; ~s [high] temperature; *(über 38 °C)* fever; ~ haben have a

[high] temperature/a fever; **bei jmdm. ~ messen** take sb's temperature; **fieber·frei** *Adj.* ⟨*person*⟩ free from fever; **fieberhaft** *Adj.* feverish; **fieberig** *Adj.* feverish; **fiebern** *itr. V.* have a temperature; **Fieber·thermometer das** [clinical] thermometer; **fiebrig** *Adj.* feverish

Fiedel die; ~, ~n *(veralt., scherzh.)* fiddle

fiel *1. u. 3. Pers. Sg. Prät. v.* **fallen**

fiepen *itr. V.* ⟨*dog*⟩ whimper; ⟨*bird*⟩ cheep

fies 1. *Adj.* *(ugs.)* nasty ⟨*person, character*⟩; **2.** *adv.* in a nasty way

Figur die; ~, ~en a) *(einer Frau)* figure; *(eines Mannes)* physique; b) *(Bildwerk)* figure; c) *(geometrisches Gebilde)* shape

fiktiv *Adj.* fictitious

Filet [fi'le:] *das;* ~s, ~s fillet

Filiale die; ~, ~n branch

Filigran das; ~s, ~e filigree

Film der; ~[e]s, ~e a) *(Fot.)* film; b) *(Kino~)* film; movie *(Amer. coll.)*; **fil-men** *tr., itr. V.* film

Film-: ~kamera die film camera; *(Schmalfilmkamera)* cine-camera; **~produzent der** film producer; **~regisseur der** film director; **~schau·spieler der** film actor

Filter der, ~s, ~: filter; **filtern** *tr. V.* filter

Filter-: ~papier das filter paper; **~zigarette die** [filter-]tipped cigarette

Filz der; ~es, ~e felt

Fimmel der; ~s, ~: **einen ~ für etw. haben** *(ugs. abwertend)* have a thing about sth. *(coll.)*

Finale das; ~s, ~[s] a) *(Sport)* final; b) finale

Finanz die; ~: finance *no art.*

Finanz-: ~amt das a) *(Behörde)* ≈ Inland Revenue; b) *(Gebäude)* tax office; **~beamte der** tax officer

Finanzen *Pl.* finances; **finanziell** [finan'tsiɛl] *Adj.* financial; **finanzieren** *tr. V.* finance; **Finanzierung die;** ~, ~en financing

Finanz-: ~minister der minister of finance; **~politik die** *(des Staates, eines Unternehmens)* financial policy; *(allgemeine)* politics of finance

Findel·kind das foundling

finden *unr. tr. V.* find; **Freunde ~:** make friends; **Finder der;** ~s, ~: finder; *s. auch* **ehrlich 1 a; Finder·lohn der** reward [for finding sth.]; **findig** *Adj.* resourceful; **Findling der;** ~s,

~e a) *(Findelkind)* foundling; b) *(Geol.)* erratic block

fing *1. u. 3. Pers. Sg. Prät. v.* **fangen**

Finger der; ~s, ~: finger; **lange ~ machen** *(ugs.)* get itchy fingers

Finger-: ~abdruck der fingerprint; **~fertigkeit die;** *o. Pl.* dexterity; **~hut der** thimble

fingern *itr. V.* fiddle; **an etw.** *(Dat.)* **~:** fiddle with sth.; **nach etw. ~:** fumble [around] for sth.

Finger-: ~nagel der fingernail; **~spitze die** fingertip; **~spitzen·gefühl das;** *o. Pl.* feeling

fingieren *tr. V.* fake; **ein fingierter Name** a false name

Fink der; ~en, ~en finch

Finne der; ~n, ~n, **Finnin die;** ~, ~nen Finn; **finnisch** *Adj.* Finnish; **Finnland (das)** ~ Finland

finster 1. *Adj.* dark; dimly-lit ⟨*pub, district*⟩; **2.** *adv.* **jmdn. ~ ansehen** give sb. a black look; **Finsternis die;** ~, ~se darkness; *(auch bibl., fig.)* dark

Finte die; ~, ~n trick; **jmdn. durch eine ~ täuschen** deceive sb. by trickery

firm *Adj.* **in etw.** *(Dat.)* **~ sein** be well up in sth.

Firma die; ~, **Firmen** firm; company

Firmen-: ~inhaber der owner of the/a company; **~schild das** company's name plate; **~zeichen das** trademark

Firmung die; ~, ~en confirmation

First der; ~[e]s, ~e ridge

Fisch der; ~[e]s, ~e a) fish; **[fünf] ~e fangen** catch [five] fish; **kleine ~e** *(fig.)* small fry; b) *(Astrol.)* **die ~e** Pisces; **er ist [ein] ~:** he is a Piscean; **fischen 1.** *tr. V.* a) fish for; b) *(ugs.)* etw. aus etw. ~: fish sth. out of sth.; **2.** *itr. V.* fish; **nach etw. ~:** fish for sth.; **Fischer der;** ~s, ~ fisherman

Fischer·boot das fishing boat

Fischerei die; ~: fishing

Fisch-: ~fang der; *o. Pl.* **vom ~ leben** make a/one's living by fishing; **auf ~ gehen** go fishing; **~geschäft das** fishmonger's [shop] *(Brit.)*; fish store *(Amer.)*; **~grät[en]·muster das** *(Textilw.)* herringbone pattern; **~konserve die** canned fish; **~kutter der** fishing trawler; **~stäbchen das** *(Kochk.)* fish finger

Fiskus der; ~, **Fisken** od. **~se** Government *(as managing the State finances)*

Fittich der; ~[e]s, ~e *(dichter.)* wing

fix 1. *Adj.* *(ugs.)* quick; **ein ~er Bursche** a bright lad; **~ und fertig** quite finished; *(völlig erschöpft)* completely shattered *(coll.)*; **2.** *adv. (ugs.)* quickly; **mach ~!** hurry up!

fixen *itr. V. (Drogenjargon)* fix *(sl.)*; **Fixer der;** ~s, ~ *(Drogenjargon)* fixer

fixieren *tr. V.* **a)** fix one's gaze on; **jmdn. scharf ~:** gaze sharply at sb.; **b)** *(geh.: schriftlich niederlegen)* take down

Fix·stern der *(Astron.)* fixed star

Fjord [fjɔrt] **der;** ~[e]s, ~e fiord

FKK [ɛf kaː ˈkaː] *Abk.* Freikörperkultur nudism *no art.;* naturism *no art.;* **FKK-Strand der** nudist beach

flach *Adj.* **a)** flat; **b)** *(niedrig)* low; **c)** *(nicht tief)* shallow ⟨water, dish⟩; **Flä·che die;** ~, ~n **a)** area; **b)** *(Ober~)* surface; **c)** *(Geom.)* area; *(einer dreidimensionalen Figur)* side

Flächen-: ~inhalt *der* area; ~maß *das* unit of square measure

flach|fallen *itr. V.; mit sein (ugs.)* ⟨trip⟩ fall through; ⟨event⟩ be cancelled; **Flach·land das;** *o. Pl.* lowland

Flachs der; ~es flax

flachsen *itr. V.* mit jmdm. ~ *(ugs.)* joke with sb.

flackern *itr. V.* flicker

Fladen der; ~s, ~ *flat, round unleavened cake made with oat or barley flour*

Flagge die; ~, ~n flag; **flaggen** *itr. V.* put out the flags

flambieren *tr. V. (Kochk.)* flambé

Flamme die; ~, ~n **a)** flame; **b)** *(Brennstelle)* burner

Flanell der; ~s, ~e flannel

flanieren *itr. V.; mit Richtungsangabe mit sein* stroll

Flanke die; ~, ~n **a)** *(Weiche)* flank; **b)** *(Ballspiele: Vorlage)* centre; **c)** *(Teil des Spielfeldes)* wing

Flasche die; ~, ~n bottle; **eine ~ Wein** a bottle of wine; **dem Kind die ~ geben** feed the baby

Flaschen-: ~bier *das* bottled beer; ~öffner *der* bottle-opener; ~zug *der* block and tackle

flatterhaft *Adj.* fickle; **flattern** *itr. V. mit Richtungsangabe mit sein* flutter

flau *Adj.* **a)** slack ⟨breeze⟩; **b)** *(leicht übel)* queasy ⟨feeling⟩

Flaum der; ~[e]s fuzz

Flausch der; ~[e]s, ~e brushed wool; **flauschig** *Adj.* fluffy

Flause die; ~, ~n; *meist Pl. (ugs.)* **er hat nur ~n im Kopf** he can never think of anything sensible

Flaute die; ~, ~n a) *(Seemannsspr.)* calm; **b)** *(Kaufmannsspr.)* fall[-off] in trade

Flechte die; ~, ~n a) *(Bot.)* lichen; **b)** *(Med.)* eczema

flechten *unr. tr. V.* plait ⟨hair⟩; weave ⟨basket, mat⟩

Fleck der; ~[e]s, ~e a) stain; *(andersfarbige Stelle)* patch; **flecken** *itr. V.* stain; **flecken·los 1.** *Adj.* spotless; **2.** *adv.* spotlessly

Fleck·entferner der stain *or* spot remover

fleckig *Adj.* stained; blotchy ⟨face, skin⟩

Fleder·maus die bat

Flegel der; ~s, ~ *(abwertend)* lout; **flegelhaft** *Adj. (abwertend)* loutish

flehen ['fleːən] *itr. V.* plead (**um** for)

Fleisch das; ~[e]s a) flesh; **b)** *(Nahrungsmittel)* meat; **Fleisch·brühe die** bouillon; consommé; **Fleischer der;** ~s, ~: butcher; **Fleischerei die;** ~, ~en butcher's shop

fleischig *Adj.* plump ⟨hands, face⟩; fleshy ⟨leaf, fruit⟩

Fleisch-: ~käse *der* meat loaf; ~klößchen *das* small meat ball; ~pastete *die (Kochk.)* pâté; ~salat *der (Kochk.)* meat salad; ~vergiftung *die* food poisoning [from meat]; ~waren *Pl.* meat products; ~wolf *der* mincer; ~wunde *die* fleshwound; ~wurst *die* pork sausage

Fleiß der; ~es hard work; *(Eigenschaft)* diligence; **fleißig 1.** *Adj.* hard-working; **2.** *adv.* hard; ~ **lernen** learn as much as one can

flennen *itr. V. (ugs.)* blubber

fletschen *tr., itr. V.* **die Zähne** *od.* **mit den Zähnen ~:** bare one's teeth

Fleurop ⓦ ['flɔyrɔp] **die** Interflora (P)

flexibel 1. *Adj.* flexible; **2.** *adv.* flexibly

flicht *Imperativ Sg. u. 3. Pers. Sg. Präsens v.* flechten

flicken *tr. V.* mend; repair ⟨engine, cable⟩; **Flicken der;** ~s, ~: patch

Flick-: ~werk *das; o. Pl. (abwertend)* botched-up job; ~zeug *das* repair kit

Flieder der; ~s, ~: lilac

Fliege die; ~, ~n a) fly; **b)** *(Schleife)* bow-tie; **fliegen 1.** *unr. itr. V.; mit sein* **a)** fly; **b)** *(ugs.: fallen)* vom Pferd/ Fahrrad ~: fall off a/the horse/bicycle; **c)** *(ugs.: entlassen werden)* get the sack *(coll.)*; von der Schule ~: be chucked out [of the school] *(coll.)*; **2.** *unr. tr. V.* fly

Fliegen-: ~**fenster** das wire-mesh window; ~**gewicht** das *(Schwerathletik)* flyweight; ~**pilz** der fly agaric; **Flieger** der; ~s, ~ pilot; **Flieger-alarm** der air-raid warning; **fliegerisch** Adj. aeronautical

fliehen ['fli:ən] unr. itr. V.; mit sein flee (vor + Dat. from); *(aus dem Gefängnis usw.)* escape (aus from); **ins Ausland/über die Grenze** ~: flee the country/escape over the border

Flieh·kraft die *(Physik)* centrifugal force

Fliese die; ~, ~n tile

Fließ·band das conveyor belt; **am** ~**band arbeiten** od. *(ugs.)* **stehen** work on the assembly line

fließen unr. itr. V.; mit sein flow; ~**des Wasser** running water; **eine Sprache** ~**d sprechen** speak a language fluently

flimmern itr. V.; mit Richtungsangabe mit sein shimmer

flink 1. Adj. nimble ⟨fingers⟩; sharp ⟨eyes⟩; quick ⟨hands⟩; 2. adv. quickly

Flinte die; ~, ~n shotgun; **die** ~ **ins Korn werfen** *(fig.)* throw in the towel

Flirt der; ~s, ~s flirtation; **flirten** itr. V. flirt

Flitter der; ~s frippery; trumpery

Flitter·wochen Pl. honeymoon sing.

flitzen itr. V.; mit sein *(ugs.)* shoot; dart; **Flitzer** der; ~s, ~ *(ugs.)* sporty job (coll.)

floaten ['flovtn] tr., itr. V. *(Wirtsch.)* float

flocht 1. u. 3. Pers. Sg. Prät. v. **flechten**

Flocke die; ~, ~n a) flake; b) *(Staub~)* piece of fluff; **flockig** Adj. fluffy

flog 1. u. 3. Pers. Sg. Prät. v. **fliegen**

floh 1. u. 3. Pers. Sg. Prät. v. **fliehen**

Floh der; ~[e]s, **Flöhe** flea

Floh-: ~**markt** der flea market; ~**zirkus** der flea-circus

Flora die; ~, **Floren** flora

Florett das; ~[e]s, ~e foil

florieren itr. V. flourish

Florist der; ~en, ~en, **Floristin** die; ~, ~nen [qualified] flower-arranger

Floskel die; ~, ~n cliché

floß 1. u. 3. Pers. Sg. Prät. v. **fließen**

Floß das; ~es, **Flöße** raft

Flosse die; ~, ~n a) *(Zool., Flugw.)* fin; b) *(zum Tauchen)* flipper

flößen tr., itr. V. float

Flößer der; ~s, ~ raftsman

Flöte die; ~, ~n flute; *(Block~)* recorder; **flöten** 1. itr. V. ⟨bird⟩ flute; 2. tr. V. whistle; **flöten|gehen** unr. itr.

V.; mit sein *(ugs.)* ⟨money⟩ go down the drain; ⟨time⟩ be wasted

flott 1. Adj. a) *(schwungvoll)* lively; b) *(schick)* smart; 2. adv. ⟨work⟩ quickly; ⟨dance, write⟩ in a lively manner; ⟨be dressed⟩ smartly

Flotte die; ~, ~n fleet

flott|machen tr. V. refloat ⟨ship⟩; get ⟨car⟩ back on the road

Flöz das; ~es, ~e *(Bergbau)* seam

Fluch der; ~[e]s, **Flüche** curse; oath; **fluchen** itr. V. curse; swear

Flucht die; ~: flight; **flucht·artig** 1. Adj. hurried; hasty; 2. adv. hurriedly; hastily; **flüchten** 1. itr. V.; mit sein vor jmdm./etw. ~: flee from sb./sth.; **vor der Polizei** ~: run away from the police; 2. refl. V. take refuge; **flüchtig** 1. Adj. a) fugitive; b) cursory; superficial ⟨insight⟩; 2. adv. a) *(oberflächlich)* cursorily; b) *(eilig)* hurriedly; **Flüchtigkeit** die; ~, ~en cursoriness;

Flüchtigkeits·fehler der slip; **Flüchtling** der; ~s, ~e refugee; **Flucht·weg** der escape route

Flug der; ~[e]s, **Flüge** flight

Flug-: ~**bahn** die trajectory; ~**blatt** das pamphlet; leaflet

Flügel der; ~s, ~ a) wing; b) *(Klavier)* grand piano

Flug·gast der [air] passenger

flügge Adj. fully-fledged

Flug-: ~**gesellschaft** die airline; ~**hafen** der airport; ~**linie** die a) *(Strecke)* air route; b) *(Gesellschaft)* airline; ~**lotse** der air traffic controller; ~**platz** der airfield; ~**schein** der air ticket; ~**verkehr** der air traffic

Flug·zeug das; ~[e]s, ~e aeroplane *(Brit.)*; airplane *(Amer.)*; aircraft

Flugzeug-: ~**absturz** der plane crash; ~**entführer** der [aircraft] hijacker; ~**entführung** die [aircraft] hijack[ing]; ~**träger** der aircraft carrier

Flunder die; ~, ~n flounder

flunkern itr. V. tell stories

Fluor das; ~s *(Chemie)* fluorine

¹Flur der; ~[e]s, ~e *(Korridor)* corridor; *(Diele)* [entrance] hall; **im/auf dem** ~: in the corridor/hall

²Flur die; ~, ~en farmland no indef. art.

Fluß der; **Flusses**, **Flüsse** river; *(fließende Bewegung)* flow

fluß-, Fluß-: ~**ab[wärts]** Adv. downstream; ~**auf[wärts]** Adv. upstream; ~**bett** das river bed

Flüßchen das; ~s, ~: small river
flüssig 1. *Adj.* a) liquid; b) *(fließend, geläufig)* fluent; 2. *adv.* (*write, speak*) fluently; **Flüssigkeit** die; ~, ~en a) liquid; *(auch Gas)* fluid; b) *(Geläufigkeit)* fluency; **flüssig|machen** *tr. V.* make available (*money, funds*)
Fluß·pferd das hippopotamus
flüstern *itr., tr. V.* whisper
Flut die; ~, ~en a) *o. Pl.* tide; b) *meist Pl.* (*geh.: Wassermasse*) flood; **fluten** *itr. V.; mit sein* (*geh.*) flood; **Flut·licht** das; *o. Pl.* floodlight
focht *1. u. 3. Pers. Sg. Prät. v.* fechten
Föderalismus der; ~: federalism *no art.;* **föderalistisch** *Adj.* federalist
Fohlen das; ~s, ~: foal
Föhn der; ~[e]s, ~e föhn
Folge die; ~, ~n a) *(Auswirkung)* consequence; *(Ergebnis)* consequence; result; b) *(Aufeinander~)* succession; *(zusammengehörend)* sequence; c) *(Fortsetzung)* (*einer Sendung*) episode; *(eines Romans)* instalment; **Folge·erscheinung** die consequence; **folgen** *itr. V.; mit sein* follow; **jmdm. im Amt/in der Regierung** ~: succeed sb. in office/in government; **auf etw.** *(Akk.)* ~: follow sth.; **aus etw.** ~: follow from sth.; **folgend** *Adj.* der/die/das ~e the next in order; **im** ~en *od.* **in** ~em in [the course of] the following discussion/passage *etc.;* **folgendermaßen** *Adv.* as follows; *(so)* in the following way; **folge·richtig** 1. *Adj.* logical; consistent (*behaviour, action*); 2. *adv.* logically; (*act, behave*) consistently; **folgern** 1. *tr. V.* etw. aus etw. ~: infer sth. from sth.; 2. *itr. V.* richtig ~: draw a/the correct conclusion; **Folgerung** die; ~, ~en conclusion
folglich *Adv.* consequently; **folgsam** 1. *Adj.* obedient; 2. *adv.* obediently
Folie ['fo:liə] die; ~, ~n *(Metall~)* foil; *(Plastik~)* film
Folklore die; ~ a) folklore; b) *(Musik)* folk-music
Folter die; ~, ~n torture; **foltern** *tr. V.* torture; *(fig.)* torment; **Folterung** die; ~, ~en torture
Fön Ⓦ der; ~[e]s, ~e hair-drier
Fond [fõ:] der; ~s, ~s *(geh.)* back
Fonds [fõ:] der; ~ [fõ:(s)], ~ [fõ:s] fund
Fondue [fõ'dy:] die; ~, ~s *od.* das; ~s, ~s *(Kochk.)* fondue
fönen *tr. V.* blow-dry
Fontäne die; ~, ~n jet; *(Springbrunnen)* fountain

forcieren [fɔr'si:rən] *tr. V.* step up (*production*); intensify (*efforts*); push forward (*developments*)
Förderer der; ~s, ~: patron
fordern *tr. V.* a) demand; b) *(in Anspruch nehmen)* make demands on
fördern *tr. V.* a) promote; patronize, support (*artist, art*); further (*investigation*); foster (*talent, tendency*); improve (*appetite*); aid (*digestion, sleep*); b) *(Bergbau, Technik)* mine (*coal, ore*); extract (*oil*)
Forderung die; ~, ~en a) demand; b) *(Kaufmannsspr.)* claim (**an** + *Akk.* against)
Förderung die; ~, ~en a) *o. Pl. s.* fördern a) promotion; patronage; support; furthering; fostering; improvement; aiding; b) *(Bergbau, Technik)* output; *(das Fördern)* mining; *(von Erdöl)* extraction
Forelle die; ~, ~n trout
Form die; ~, ~en a) shape; **in** ~ **von Tabletten** in the form of tablets; b) *(bes. Sport: Verfassung)* form; **in** ~ **sein** be on form; c) *(vorgeformtes Modell)* mould; *(Back~)* baking tin; d) *(Darstellungs~, Umgangs~)* form
formal 1. *Adj.* formal; 2. *adv.* formally; **formalisieren** *tr. V.* formalize
Formalität die; ~, ~en formality
Format das; ~[e]s, ~e a) size; *(Buch~, Papier~, Bild~)* format; b) *o. Pl. (Persönlichkeit)* stature
formbar *Adj.* malleable
Formel die; ~, ~n formula
formell *Adj.* formal
formen *tr. V.* a) *(gestalten)* form; shape; b) *(bilden, prägen)* mould, form (*character, personality*);
Form·fehler der irregularity
formieren *tr., refl. V.* form
förmlich 1. *Adj.* a) formal; b) *(regelrecht)* positive; 2. *adv.* a) formally; b) *(geradezu)* **sich** ~ **fürchten** be really afraid
form·los *Adj.* a) informal; b) *(gestaltlos)* shapeles
Form·sache die formality
Formular das; ~s, ~e form; **formulieren** *tr. V.* formulate; **Formulierung** die; ~, ~en a) *o. Pl. (das Formulieren)* formulation; *(eines Entwurfes, Gesetzes)* drafting; b) *(formulierter Text)* formulation
form·vollendet 1. *Adj.* perfectly executed (*pirouette, bow, etc.*); (*poem*) perfect in form; 2. *adv.* faultlessly
forsch *Adj.* forceful

forschen *itr. V.* a) **nach jmdm./etw. ~:** search *or* look for sb./sth.; b) *(als Wissenschaftler)* research; **Forscher der; ~s, Forscherin die; ~, ~nen** researcher; **Forschung die; ~, ~en** research; **Forschungs·reisende der/die** explorer

Forst der; ~|e|s, ~e|n| forest; **Förster der; ~s, ~:** forest warden

Forst·wirtschaft die forestry

Forsythie [for'zy:tsiə] **die; ~, ~n** forsythia

fort *Adv.* a) *s.* weg; b) *(weiter)* **und so ~:** and so on

fort-, Fort-: **~an** [-'-] *Adv.* from now/then on; **~bestand der;** *o. Pl.* continuation; *(eines Staates)* continued existence; **~bewegen 1.** *tr. V.* move; shift; **2.** *refl. V.* move [along]; **~bleiben** *unr. itr. V.; mit sein* fail to come; **~bringen** *unr. tr. V.:* s. wegbringen; **~dauern** *itr. V.* continue; **~fahren 1.** *unr. V.* a) *mit sein* leave; b) *auch mit sein (weitermachen)* continue; go on; **2.** *unr. tr. V.* drive away; **~führen** *tr. V.* a) lead away; b) *(fortsetzen)* continue; **~gang der;** *o. Pl.* a) departure **(aus** from); b) *(Weiterentwicklung)* progress; **~gehen** *unr. itr. V.; mit sein* leave; **geh ~!** go away!; **~geschritten** *Adj.* advanced; **~geschrittene der/die; adj. Dekl.** advanced student/player; **~|kommen** *unr. itr. V.; mit sein* s. wegkommen a, b; **~|laufen** *unr. itr. V.; mit sein* a) *s.* weglaufen; b) *(sich ~setzen)* continue; **~laufend 1.** *Adj.* continuous; **2.** *adv.* continuously; **~|pflanzen** *refl. V.* a) reproduce [oneself/itself]; b) *(sich verbreiten)* ⟨idea, mood⟩ spread; ⟨sound, light⟩ travel; **~pflanzung die** reproduction; **~|schaffen** *tr. V.* take away; **~|schreiten** *unr. itr. V.; mit sein (process)* continue; ⟨time⟩ move on; **~schritt der** progress; **~schritte** progress *sing.;* **ein ~schritt** a step forward; **~schrittlich 1.** *Adj.* progressive; **2.** *adv.* progressively; **~schrittlichkeit die; ~:** progressiveness; **~|setzen 1.** *tr. V.* continue; **2.** *refl. V.* continue; **~setzung die; ~, ~en** a) *(das ~setzen)* continuation; b) *(anschließender Teil)* instalment; **~während 1.** *Adj.; nicht präd.* continual; **2.** *adv.* continually; **~werfen** *unr. tr. V.:* s. wegwerfen

Foto das; ~s, ~s photo; **~s machen** take photos

Foto-: **~album das** photo album; **~apparat der** camera

fotogen *Adj.* photogenic **Foto·graf der; ~en, ~en** photographer; **Fotografie die; ~, ~n** a) *o. Pl.* photography *no art.;* b) *(Lichtbild)* photograph; **fotografieren** *tr. V.* photograph; take a photograph/photographs of; **Fotografin die; ~, ~nen** photographer

foto-, Foto-: **~kopie die** photocopy; **~kopieren** *tr., itr. V.* photocopy; **~kopierer der** photocopier; **~labor das** photographic laboratory; **~modell das** photographic model

Foul [faul] **das; ~s, ~s** *(Sport)* foul (**an** + *Dat.* on)

Foyer [foa'je:] **das; ~s, ~s** foyer

FPÖ *Abk.* Freiheitliche Partei Österreichs

Fr. *Abk.* a) Franken SFr.; b) Frau; c) Freitag Fri.

Fracht die; ~, ~en *(Schiffs~, Luft~)* cargo; freight; *(Bahn~, LKW~)* goods *pl.;* freight; **Fracht·brief der** consignment note; waybill; **Frachter der; ~s, ~:** freighter

Fracht-: **~gut das** slow freight; slow goods *pl.;* **~schiff das** cargo ship

Frack der; ~|e|s, Fräcke tails *pl.;* evening dress

Frage die; ~, ~n question; *(Angelegenheit)* issue; **in ~ kommen** be possible; **das kommt nicht in ~** *(ugs.)* that is out of the question; **Fragebogen der** questionnaire; *(Formular)* form; **fragen 1.** *tr., itr. V.* a) ask; b) *(sich erkundigen)* **nach etw. ~:** ask *or* inquire about sth.; c) *(nachfragen)* ask for; **2.** *refl. V.* **sich ~, ob ...:** wonder whether ...; **Frage·zeichen das** question mark; **fraglich** *Adj.* a) doubtful; b) *nicht präd. (betreffend)* in question *postpos.;* relevant

Fragment das; ~|e|s, ~e fragment

frag·würdig *Adj.* a) questionable; b) *(zwielichtig)* dubious

Fraktion die; ~, ~en parliamentary party; *(mit zwei Parteien)* parliamentary coalition

Fraktions- *(Parl.):* **~führer der** leader of the parliamentary party/coalition; **~zwang der** obligation to vote in accordance with party policy

frank *Adv.* **~ und frei** frankly and openly; openly and honestly

Franken der; ~s ~: [Swiss] franc

Frankfurter die; ~, ~ *(Wurst)* frankfurter

frankieren *tr. V.* frank

Frank·reich (das); ~s France

Franse die; ~, ~n strand [of a/the fringe]

Franzose der; ~n, ~n Frenchman; **er ist ~:** he is French; **die ~n** the French; **Französin** die; ~, ~nen Frenchwoman; **französisch** *Adj.* French; **Französisch** das; ~[s] French

Fräse die; ~, ~n *(für Holz)* moulding machine; *(für Metall)* milling machine

fraß *1. u. 3. Pers. Sg. Prät. v.* fressen; **Fraß** der; ~es *(derb)* muck

Fratze die; ~, ~n a) hideous face; b) *(ugs.: Grimasse)* grimace

Frau die; ~, ~en a) woman; b) *(Ehe-)* wife; c) *(Titel, Anrede)* ~ Schulze Mrs Schulze; *(in Briefen)* **Sehr geehrte ~ Schulze** Dear Madam; *(bei persönlicher Bekanntschaft)* Dear Mrs/Miss/ Ms Schulze

Frauen-: ~arzt der, ~ärztin die gynaecologist; ~bewegung die o. Pl. women's movement; ~rechtlerin die; ~, ~nen feminist; Women's Libber *(coll.)*

Fräulein das; ~s, ~ *(ugs. ~s)* a) *(junges ~)* young lady; *(ältliches ~)* spinster; b) *(Titel, Anrede)* ~ Mayer/ Schulte Miss Mayer/Schulte

fraulich *1. Adj.* feminine; *2. adv.* in a feminine way

frech *1. Adj.* a) impertinent; cheeky; bare-faced ⟨lie⟩; b) *(keck, keß)* saucy; *2. adv.* impertinently; cheekily; **Frechheit** die; ~, ~en a) o. Pl. impertinence; cheek; b) *(Äußerung)* impertinent *or* cheeky remark

frei *1. Adj.* a) *(unabhängig)* free; b) *(nicht angestellt)* free-lance; c) *(ungezwungen)* free and easy; d) *(nicht mehr in Haft)* free; e) *(offen)* open; f) *(unbesetzt)* vacant; free; g) *(kostenlos)* free ⟨food, admission⟩; h) *(verfügbar)* spare; free ⟨time⟩; *2. adv.* freely

frei-, Frei-: ~bad das open-air swimming-pool; ~bekommen 1. *unr. itr. V. (ugs.)* get time off; 2. *unr. tr. V.* jmdn./etw. ~bekommen get sb./ sth. released; ~beruflich 1. *Adj.* self-employed; free-lance; ⟨*doctor, lawyer*⟩ in private practice; 2. *adv.* ~be**ruflich tätig sein/arbeiten** work free-lance/practise privately; ~betrag der *(Steuerw.)* [tax] allowance

Freier der; ~s, ~ *(veralt.)* suitor

frei-, Frei-: ~exemplar das *(Buch)* free copy; *(Zeitung)* free issue; ~geben *unr. tr. V.* release; ~gebig *Adj.*

generous; open-handed; ~gehege das outdoor enclosure; ~gepäck das baggage allowance; ~hafen der free port; ~halten *unr. tr. V.* a) treat; b) *(offenhalten)* keep ⟨*entrance, roadway*⟩ clear; **Einfahrt ~halten!** no parking in front of entrance; ~handels·zone die free-trade zone; ~händig *adv.* ⟨*cycle*⟩ without holding on

Freiheit die; ~, ~en a) freedom; ~, Gleichheit, Brüderlichkeit Liberty, Equality, Fraternity; b) *(Vorrecht)* freedom; privilege; **freiheitlich** 1. *Adj.* liberal ⟨*philosophy, conscience*⟩; ~ **und demokratisch** free and democratic; 2. *adv.* liberally

Freiheits-: ~beraubung die *(jur.)* wrongful detention; ~strafe die term of imprisonment

frei-, Frei-: ~herr der baron; ~karte die complimentary ticket; ~kaufen *tr. V.* ransom ⟨*hostage*⟩; buy the freedom of ⟨*slave*⟩; ~kommen *unr. itr. V.* **aus dem Gefängnis ~kommen** be released from prison; ~körper·kultur die; o. Pl. nudism *no art.*; naturism *no art.*; ~lassen *unr. tr. V.* set free; release; ~legen *tr. V.* uncover

freilich *Adv.* of course

Frei·licht-: ~bühne die, ~theater das open-air theatre

frei-, Frei-: ~machen 1. *refl. V. (ugs.: frei nehmen)* take time off; 2. *tr. V. (Postw.)* frank; **etw. mit 0,50 DM ~machen** put a 50-pfennig stamp on sth.; ~marke die postage stamp; ~mütig 1. *Adj.* frank; 2. *adv.* frankly; ~schaffend *Adj.* free-lance; ~schwimmen *unr. refl. V.* **sich ~schwimmen** pass the 15-minute swimming test; ~sprechen *unr. tr. V.* a) *(Rechtsw.)* acquit; b) *(für unschuldig erklären)* exonerate ⟨*von* from⟩; ~spruch der *(Rechtsw.)* acquittal; ~stellen *tr. V.* a) jmdm. etw. ~stellen leave sth. up to sb.; b) *(befreien)* release ⟨*person*⟩; jmdn. vom Wehrdienst ~stellen exempt sb. from military service; ~stoß der *(Fußball)* free kick

Frei·tag der Friday; *s. auch* Dienstag, Dienstag-; **freitags** *Adv.* on Friday[s]; *s. auch* dienstags

frei-, Frei-: ~tod der *(verhüll.)* suicide *no art.*; ~treppe die [flight of] steps; ~übung die; *meist Pl. (Sport)* keep-fit exercise; ~wild das fair game; ~willig 1. *Adj.* voluntary

⟨*decision*⟩; optional ⟨*subject*⟩; **2.** *adv.* voluntarily; **sich ~willig melden** volunteer; **~zeichen das** ringing tone; **~zeit die** *o. Pl.* spare time; **~zügig** *Adj.* a) generous; b) ⟨*gewagt, unmoralisch*⟩ risqué ⟨*remark, film, dress*⟩; **~zügigkeit die** generosity

fremd *Adj.* a) foreign; b) ⟨*nicht eigen*⟩ other people's; of others *postpos.*; c) ⟨*unbekannt*⟩ strange

fremd·artig *Adj.* strange

¹**Fremde der/die**; *adj. Dekl.* a) stranger; b) ⟨*Ausländer*⟩ foreigner; ²**Fremde die**; ~ ⟨*geh.*⟩ **die ~:** foreign parts *pl.*

Fremden-: **~führer der** tourist guide; **~verkehr der** tourism *no art.*; **~zimmer das** room

fremd-, Fremd-: **~|gehen** *unr. itr. V.*; *mit sein* (ugs.) be unfaithful; **~herrschaft die** foreign domination; **~ländisch** *Adj.* foreign; ⟨*exotisch*⟩ exotic

Fremdling der; ~s, ~e ⟨*veralt.*⟩ stranger

fremd-, Fremd-: **~sprache die** foreign language; **~sprachig** *Adj.* bilingual/multilingual ⟨*staff, secretary*⟩; foreign ⟨*literature*⟩; foreign-language ⟨*edition, teaching*⟩; **~sprachlich** *Adj.* foreign-language ⟨*teaching*⟩; foreign ⟨*word*⟩; **~wort das**; *Pl.* **~wörter** foreign word

frenetisch **1.** *Adj.* frenetic; **2.** *adv.* frenetically

Frequenz die; ~, ~en ⟨*Physik*⟩ frequency; ⟨*Med.: Puls~*⟩ rate

Fresse die; ~, ~n ⟨*derb*⟩ a) ⟨*Mund*⟩ gob (sl.); b) ⟨*Gesicht*⟩ mug (sl.); **fressen 1.** *unr. tr. V.* a) ⟨*animal*⟩ eat; ⟨*sich ernähren von*⟩ feed on; b) (ugs.: verschlingen) swallow up ⟨*money, time, distance*⟩; drink ⟨*petrol*⟩; c) ⟨*zerstören*⟩ eat away; d) ⟨*derb: von Menschen*⟩ guzzle; **2.** *unr. itr. V.* ⟨*von Tieren*⟩ feed; ⟨*derb: von Menschen*⟩ stuff one's face (sl.); **Fressen das**; ~s a) ⟨*für Hunde, Katzen usw.*⟩ food; ⟨*für Vieh*⟩ feed; b) ⟨*derb: Essen*⟩ grub (sl.); **Fresserei die**; ~, ~en ⟨*derb*⟩ guzzling

Freude die; ~, ~n joy; ⟨*Vergnügen*⟩ pleasure; **~ an etw.** (Dat.) **haben** take pleasure in sth.

Freuden-: **~haus das** house of pleasure; **~tag der** happy day; **freudestrahlend** *Adj.* beaming with joy; **freudig** *Adj.* joyful; joyous ⟨*heart*⟩; delightful ⟨*surprise*⟩; **freud·los** *Adj.* joyless; **freuen 1.** *refl. V.* be glad

⟨*über* + *Akk.* about⟩; ⟨*froh sein*⟩ be happy; **sich auf etw.** (Akk.) **~:** look forward to sth.; **2.** *tr. V.* please

Freund der; ~es, ~e a) friend; b) ⟨*Verehrer, Geliebter*⟩ boy-friend; **Freundin die**; ~, ~nen a) friend; b) ⟨*Geliebte*⟩ girl-friend; ⟨*älter*⟩ lady-friend; **freundlich 1.** *Adj.* a) kind ⟨*face*⟩; friendly ⟨*reception*⟩; b) ⟨*angenehm*⟩ pleasant; c) ⟨*freundschaftlich*⟩ friendly; **2.** *adv.* **jmdm. ~ danken** thank sb. kindly; **Freundlichkeit die**; ~: kindness; **Freundschaft die**; ~, ~en friendship; **mit jmdm. ~ schließen** make friends with sb.; **freundschaftlich 1.** *Adj.* friendly; **2.** *adv.* in a friendly way

Frevel ['fre:fl] **der**; ~s, ~ ⟨*geh., veralt.*⟩ crime; outrage

Friede der; ~ns, ~n ⟨*älter, geh.*⟩ s. **Frieden**; **Frieden der**; ~s, ~: peace

Friedens-: **~forschung die** peace studies *pl.*, *no art.*; **~konferenz die** peace conference; **~nobelpreis der** Nobel Peace Prize; **~pfeife die** pipe of peace; **~richter der** lay magistrate dealing with minor offences; ≈ Justice of the Peace; **~taube die** dove of peace; **~verhandlungen** *Pl.* peace negotiations; **~vertrag der** peace treaty

fried·fertig *Adj.* peaceable ⟨*person, character*⟩; **Fried·hof der** cemetery; ⟨*Kirchhof*⟩ graveyard; **friedlich 1.** *Adj.* peaceful; **2.** *adv.* peacefully; **fried·liebend** *Adj.* peace-loving

frieren *unr. itr. V.* a) be or feel cold; b) *mit sein* ⟨*ge~*⟩ freeze

Frikadelle die; ~, ~n rissole

frisch 1. *Adj.* fresh; new-laid ⟨*egg*⟩; clean ⟨*linen, underwear*⟩; wet ⟨*paint*⟩; **2.** *adv.* freshly; **Frische die**; ~ freshness; **geistige ~:** mental alertness; **körperliche ~:** physical fitness; **Frisch·halte·beutel der** airtight bag

Friseur [fri'zø:ɐ] **der**; ~s, ~e, **Friseuse** [fri'zø:zə] **die**; ~, ~n hairdresser; **frisieren** *tr. V.* **jmdn./sich ~:** do sb.'s/one's hair; **sich ~ lassen** have one's hair done

friß *Imperativ Sg. v.* **fressen**

frißt *2. u. 3. Pers. Sg. Präsens v.* **fressen**

Frist die; ~, ~en a) time; period; **die ~ verlängern** extend the deadline; b) ⟨*begrenzter Aufschub*⟩ extension

frist-: **~gemäß, ~gerecht** *Adj.*, *adv.* within the specified time *postpos.*; ⟨*bei Anmeldung usw.*⟩ before the

closing date *postpos.*; **~los 1.** *Adj.* instant; **2.** *adv.* without notice
Frisur die; ~, ~en hairstyle
fritieren *tr. V.* deep-fry
frivol [fri'vo:l] *Adj.* **a)** *(schamlos)* suggestive *(remark, picture, etc.)*; risqué *(joke)*; earthy *(man)*; flighty *(woman)*; **b)** *(leichtfertig)* frivolous
froh *Adj.* **a)** happy; cheerful *(person, mood)*; good *(news)*; **b)** *(ugs.: erleichtert)* pleased, glad **(über** + *Akk.* about)
fröhlich *Adj.* cheerful; happy
Fröhlichkeit die; ~: cheerfulness; *(eines Festes, einer Feier)* gaiety
Froh·sinn der; *o. Pl.* cheerfulness; gaiety
fromm; ~er *od.* **frömmer, ~st...** *od.* **frömmst... 1.** *Adj.* pious, devout *(person)*; devout *(Christian)*; **2.** *adv.* piously; **Frömmigkeit** die; ~: piety; devoutness
Fron·leichnam [fro:n-] *o. Art.* [the feast of] Corpus Christi
Front die; ~, ~en **a)** *(Gebäude~)* front; façade; **b)** *(Kampfgebiet)* front [line]; **frontal 1.** *Adj.* head-on *(collision)*; frontal *(attack)*; **2.** *adv.* *(collide)* head-on; *(attack)* from the front; **Front·an·trieb** der *(Kfz-W.)* front-wheel drive
fror *1. u. 3. Pers. Sg. Prät. v.* **frieren**
Frosch der; ~[e]s, **Frösche** frog
Frosch-: ~mann der; *Pl.* **~männer** frogman; **~perspektive** die worm's-eye view; **~schenkel** der frog's leg
Frost der; ~[e]s, **Fröste** frost; **Frost·beule** die chilblain; **fröstELN** *itr. V.* feel chilly; **frostig 1.** *Adj.* cold *(fig.)* frosty; **2.** *adv.* frostily; **Frost·schutz·mittel** das **a)** frost protection agent; **b)** *(Kfz-W.)* antifreeze
Frottee das u. der; ~s, ~s terry towelling; **Frottee·handtuch** das terry towel; **frottieren** *tr. V.* rub; towel
frotzeln 1. *tr. V.* tease; **2.** *itr. V.* **über** *jmdn./etw.* ~: make fun of sb./sth.
Frucht die; ~, **Früchte** fruit; **fruchtbar** *Adj.* fertile; fruitful *(work, idea, etc.)*; **Fruchtbarkeit** die; ~: fertility; fruitfulness **Frucht·becher** der fruit sundae; **fruchten** *tr. V.* **nichts** ~: be no use; **fruchtig** *Adj.* fruity; **frucht·los** *Adj.* fruitless, vain *(efforts)*; **Frucht·saft** der fruit juice
früh 1. *Adj.* **a)** early; **b)** *(vorzeitig)* premature; **2.** *adv.* early; **heute** ~: this

morning; **früh·auf: von ~auf** from early childhood on[wards]; **Frühaufsteher** die; ~s, ~: early riser; **Frühe** die; ~: **in aller** ~: at the crack of dawn; **früher** ['fry:ɐ] **1.** *Adj., nicht präd.* **a)** *(vergangen)* earlier; former; **b)** *(ehemalig)* former *(owner, occupant, friend)*; **2.** *adv.* formerly; ~ **war er ganz anders** he used to be quite different; **Früh·erkennung** die *(Med.)* early recognition
frühestens *Adv.* at the earliest; **Früh·geburt** die **a)** premature birth; **b)** *(Kind)* premature baby
Früh·jahr das spring; **Frühjahrsmüdigkeit** die springtime tiredness
Frühling der; ~s, ~e spring; **Frühlings·anfang** der first day of spring
früh-, Früh-: ~reif *Adj.* precocious *(child)*; **~schoppen** der morning drink; *(um Mittag)* lunchtime drink; **~sport** der early-morning exercise
Früh·stück das; ~s, ~e breakfast; **frühstücken** *itr. V.* have breakfast; **Frühstücks·pause** die morning break; coffee break
früh·zeitig 1. *Adj.* early; *(vorzeitig)* premature; **2.** *adv.* early; *(vorzeitig)* prematurely
Frustration die; ~, ~en *(Psych.)* frustration; **frustrieren** *tr. V.* frustrate
Fuchs der; ~es, **Füchse** fox; **fuchsen** *tr. V.* annoy; vex; **fuchs·teufelswild** *Adj.* *(ugs.)* livid *(coll.)*
Fuchtel die; ~: **unter jmds.** ~ *(ugs.)* under sb.'s thumb; **fuchteln** *itr. V.* *(ugs.)* **mit etw.** ~: wave sth. about
Fuder das; ~s, ~: cart-load
¹Fuge die; ~, ~n joint; *(Zwischenraum)* gap; **²Fuge** die; ~, ~n *(Musik)* fugue
fügen 1. *tr. V.* place; set; **etw zu etw.** ~ *(fig.)* add sth. to sth.; **2.** *refl. V.* **a)** *(sich ein~)* **sich in etw.** *(Akk.)* ~: fit into sth.; **b)** *(gehorchen)* **sich** ~: fall into line; **fügsam** *Adj.* obedient
fühlbar *Adj.* noticeable; **fühlen 1.** *tr., itr. V.* feel; **2.** *refl. V.* **sich krank** ~: feel sick; **Fühler** der; ~s, ~: feeler; antenna; **Fühlungnahme** die; ~: initial contact
fuhr *1. u. 3. Pers. Sg. Prät. v.* **fahren**
Fuhre die; ~, ~n load
führen 1. *tr. V.* **a)** lead; **b)** *(verkaufen)* stock, sell *(goods)*; **c)** *(durch~)* **Gespräche/Verhandlungen** ~: hold conversations/negotiations; **eine glückliche Ehe** ~: be happily married; **d)** *(leiten)* manage, run *(company, business,*

pub, etc.⟩; lead ⟨party, country⟩; command ⟨regiment⟩; e) ⟨Amtsspr.⟩ drive ⟨train, motor, vehicle⟩; f) ⟨als Kennzeichnung, Bezeichnung haben⟩ bear; einen Titel/Künstlernamen ~: have a title/use a stage name; g) ⟨angelegt haben⟩ keep ⟨diary, list, file⟩; h) ⟨registrieren⟩ jmdn. in einer Liste/Kartei ~: have sb. on a list/on file; i) ⟨tragen⟩ etw. bei od. mit sich ~: have sth. on one; eine Waffe/einen Ausweis bei sich ~: carry a weapon/a pass; 2. itr. V. a) lead; b) ⟨an der Spitze liegen⟩ lead; be ahead; **führend** Adj. leading; high-ranking ⟨official⟩; prominent ⟨position⟩

Führer der; ~s, ~ a) ⟨Leiter⟩ leader; b) ⟨Fremden~⟩ guide; **Führerin** die; ~, ~nen s. Führer; **führer·los** 1. Adj. leaderless; ⟨ohne Lenker⟩ driverless ⟨car⟩; 2. adv.: s. 1; without a leader; without a driver; **Führer·schein** der driving licence (Brit.); driver's license (Amer.); **Führung** die; ~, ~en a) o. Pl. s. führen 1d: management; running; leadership; command; b) ⟨Fremden~⟩ guided tour; c) o. Pl. ⟨führende Position⟩ lead

Führungs-: ~**kraft** die manager; ~**spitze** die ⟨Politik⟩ top leadership; ⟨im Betrieb⟩ top management; ~**zeugnis** das document issued by police certifying that holder has no criminal record

Fuhr-: ~**unternehmer** der haulage contractor; ~**werk** das cart

Fülle die; ~ a) wealth; abundance; b) ⟨Körper~⟩ corpulence; **füllen** 1. tr. V. fill; ⟨Kochk.⟩ stuff; b) ⟨fig.⟩ fill in ⟨gap, time⟩; 2. refl. V. ⟨voll werden⟩ fill [up]; **Füller** der; ~s, ~ ⟨ugs.⟩ [fountain-]pen; **Füll·federhalter** der fountain-pen; **füllig** Adj. corpulent, portly ⟨person⟩; ample ⟨figure, bosom⟩; **Füllung** die; ~, ~en stuffing; ⟨Kochk.; Zahnmed.⟩ filling; ⟨in Schokolade⟩ centre

fummeln itr. V. ⟨ugs.⟩ a) ⟨fingern⟩ fiddle; b) ⟨erotisch⟩ pet

Fund der; ~[e]s, ~e ⟨auch Archäol.⟩ find

Fundament das; ~[e]s, ~e a) ⟨Bauw.⟩ foundations pl.; b) ⟨Basis⟩ base; basis; **fundamental** Adj. fundamental

Fund-: ~**büro** das lost property office (Brit.); lost and found office (Amer.); ~**grube** die treasure-house

fundieren tr. V. underpin

fündig Adj. ~ sein yield something; ~ werden make a find; ⟨bei Bohrungen⟩ make a strike

Fund·ort der place or site where sth. is/was found

fünf Kardinalz. five; **Fünf** die; ~, ~en five; ⟨Schulnote⟩ E

fünf-, Fünf-: ~**eck** das; ~s, ~e pentagon; ~**fach** Vervielfältigungsz. fivefold; ~**fache** das; adj. Dekl. five times as much; ~**hundert** Kardinalz. five hundred; ~**kampf** der ⟨Sport⟩ pentathlon

Fünfling der; ~s, ~e quintuplet; quin ⟨coll.⟩

fünf-: ~**mal** Adv. five times; ~**stellig** Adj. five-figure

fünft... Ordinalz. fifth; **Fünf·tagewoche** die five-day [working] week; **fünf·tausend** Kardinalz. five thousand

fünftel Bruchz. fifth; **Fünftel** das ⟨schweiz. meist der⟩; ~s, ~ fifth; **fünftens** Adv. fifthly; **fünf·zehn** Kardinalz. fifteen; **fünfzig** Kardinalz. fifty; **Fünfzig** die; ~, ~: fifty; **fünfziger** indekl. Adj.; nicht präd. die ~ Jahre the fifties; **Fünfziger** der; ~s, ~ a) ⟨ugs.⟩ fifty-pfennig piece; b) ⟨50jähriger⟩ fifty-year-old; **fünfzigst...** Ordinalz. fiftieth

fungieren itr. V. als etw. ~ ⟨person⟩ act as sth.; ⟨word etc.⟩ function as sth.

Funk der; ~s radio; **Funk·ausstellung** die radio and television exhibition

Funke der; ~ns, ~n ⟨auch fig.⟩ spark

funkeln itr. V. ⟨light, star⟩ twinkle; ⟨gold, diamonds⟩ glitter; ⟨eyes⟩ blaze

funken tr. V. radio; ⟨transmitter⟩ broadcast; **Funker** der; ~s, ~ radio operator

Funk-: ~**gerät** das radio set; ⟨tragbar⟩ walkie-talkie; ~**haus** das broadcasting centre; ~**kolleg** das radio-based ⟨adult education⟩ course; ~**sprech·gerät** das radiophone; ⟨tragbar⟩ walkie-talkie; ~**spruch** der radio signal; ⟨Nachricht⟩ radio message; ~**stille** die radio silence; ~**streife** die [police] radio patrol; ~**taxi** das radio taxi

Funktion die; ~, ~en function; **Funktionär** der; ~s, ~e official; functionary; **funktionieren** itr. V. work; function; **funktions·tüchtig** Adj. working; sound ⟨organ⟩

Funk-: ~**turm** der radio tower; ~**verbindung** die radio contact

Funzel die; ~, ~n *(ugs.)* useless light
für 1. *Präp. mit Akk.* for; etw. ~ **ungültig** erklären declare sth. invalid *s. auch* was 1
Furche die; ~, ~n a) furrow; b) *(Wagenspur)* rut
Furcht die; ~ : fear; ~ vor jmdm./etw. haben fear sb./sth.; **furchtbar** 1. *Adj.* a) dreadful; b) *(ugs.: unangenehm)* terrible *(coll.);* 2. *adv. (ugs.)* terribly *(coll.);* **fürchten** 1. *refl. V.* sich [vor jmdm./etw.] ~ : be afraid *or* frightened [of sb./sth.]; 2. *tr. V.* be afraid of; ich fürchte, [daß] ...: I'm afraid [that] ...; **fürchterlich** *Adj. s.* furchtbar; **furcht·los** 1. *Adj.* fearless; 2. *adv.* fearlessly; **furchtsam** 1. *Adj.* timid; 2. *adv.* timidly
für·einander *Adv.* for one another; for each other
Furie ['fu:riə] die; ~, ~n Fury
Furnier das; ~s, ~e veneer
Für·sorge die; ~ a) care; b) *(veralt.: Sozialhilfe)* welfare; c) *(veralt.: Sozialamt)* social services *pl.;* **für·sorglich** 1. *Adj.* considerate; 2. *adv.* considerately
Für·sprache die support; **Für·sprecher** der advocate
Fürst der; ~en, ~en prince; **Fürstentum** das; ~s, Fürstentümer principality; **fürstlich** 1. *Adj.* a) royal; b) *(fig.: üppig)* lavish; 2. *adv.* lavishly
Furt die; ~, ~en ford
Furunkel der *od.* das; ~s, ~ : boil; furuncle
Für·wort das; *Pl.* -wörter pronoun
Fusion die; ~, ~en amalgamation; *(von Konzernen)* merger; **fusionieren** *itr. V.* merge
Fuß der; ~es, Füße foot; *(einer Lampe, Säule)* base; *(von Möbeln)* leg; zu ~ gehen go on foot; walk; bei ~! heel!; *(fig.)* auf freiem ~ sein be at large; auf großem ~ leben live in great style
Fuß·ball der a) *o. Pl. (Ballspiel)* [Association] football; b) *(Ball)* football; **Fußballer** der; ~s, ~ : footballer
Fußball-: ~platz der football ground; *(Spielfeld)* football pitch; ~spiel das a) football match; b) *o. Pl. (Sportart)* football *no art.;* ~spieler der football player
Fuß·boden der floor; **fußen** *itr. V.* auf etw. *(Dat.)* ~ : be based on sth.; **Fuß·ende** das foot; **Fußgänger** der; ~s, ~, **Fußgängerin** die; ~, ~nen pedestrian

Fußgänger-: ~brücke die footbridge; ~übergang der, ~überweg der pedestrian crossing; ~unterführung die pedestrian subway; ~zone die pedestrian precinct
Fuß-: ~nagel der toe-nail; ~note die footnote; ~stapfen der; ~s, ~ : footprint; ~tritt der the kick; ~volk das a) *(hist.)* footmen *pl.;* b) *(abwertend: Untergeordnete)* lower ranks *pl.;* ~weg der footpath
futsch *Adj. (salopp)* ~ sein have gone for a burton *(Brit. sl.)*
'**Futter** das; ~s *(Tiernahrung)* feed; *(für Pferde, Kühe)* fodder
²**Futter** das; ~s *(von Kleidungsstücken)* lining
Futteral das; ~s, ~e case
'**füttern** *tr. V.* feed
²**füttern** *tr. V.* (mit ²Futter ausstatten) line
Fütterung die; ~, ~en feeding
Futur das; ~s, ~e *(Sprachw.)* future [tense]

G

g, G [ge:] das; ~, ~ a) *(Buchstabe)* g/G; b) *(Musik)* [key of] G
g *Abk.* a) Gramm g; b) Groschen
gab *1. u. 3. Pers. Sg. Prät. v.* geben
Gabe die; ~, ~n a) *(geh.: Geschenk, Talent)* gift; *(Almosen, Spende)* alms *pl.*
Gabel die; ~, ~n fork; *(Telefon-)* cradle; **gabeln** *refl. V.* fork; **Gabel·stapler** der; ~s, ~ : fork-lift truck; **Gabelung** die; ~, ~en fork
Gaben·tisch der gift table
gackern *itr. V.* a) cluck; b) *(ugs.: lachen)* cackle
gaffen *itr. V. (abwertend)* gape; gawp *(coll.)*
Gag [gɛk] der; ~s, ~s a) *(Theater, Film)* gag; b) *(Besonderheit)* gimmick
Gage ['ga:ʒə] die; ~, ~n salary; *(für einzelnen Auftritt)* fee
gähnen *itr. V. (auch fig.)* yawn
Gala ['ga:la, *auch* 'gala] die; ~ : formal dress

galant 1. *Adj.* gallant; *(amourös)* amorous; **2.** *adv.* gallantly

Gala·vorstellung die gala performance

Galeere die; ~, ~n galley

Galerie die; ~, ~n gallery

Galgen der gallows *sing.*

Galgen-: ~**frist die** reprieve; ~**humor der** gallows humour

Galle die; ~, ~n a) *(Gallenblase)* gall[-bladder]; b) *(Sekret) (bei Tieren)* gall; *(bei Menschen)* bile

Galopp der; ~s, ~s *od.* ~e gallop; **galoppieren** *itr. V.; meist mit sein* gallop

galt *1. u. 3. Pers. Sg. Prät. v.* gelten

galvanisch [gal'va:nɪʃ] *Adj.* galvanic

Gamasche die; ~, ~n gaiter; *(bis zum Knöchel reichend)* spat

Gambe die; ~, ~n *(Musik)* viola da gamba

Gamma·strahlen *Pl. (Physik, Med.)* gamma rays

gammelig *Adj. (ugs.)* a) bad; rotten; b) *(unordentlich)* scruffy; **gammeln** *itr. V.* a) *(ugs.)* go off; b) *(nichts tun)* loaf around; bum around *(Amer. coll.)*; **Gammler der**; ~s, ~ *(ugs.)* drop-out *(coll.)*

gang: ~ **und gäbe sein** be quite usual

Gang der; ~[e]s, Gänge a) walk; gait; b) *(Besorgung)* errand; c) *o. Pl. (Verlauf)* course; d) *(Technik)* gear; e) *(Flur) (in Zügen, Gebäuden usw.)* corridor; *(Verbindungs-)* passage[-way]; *(im Theater, Kino, Flugzeug)* aisle; f) *(Kochk.)* course; **gangbar** *Adj.* passable; *(fig.)* practicable

Gängel·band das *in* jmdn. am ~ führen keep sb. in leading-reins; **gängeln** *tr. V. (ugs.)* jmdn. ~: boss sb. around

gängig *Adj.* a) *(üblich)* common; *(aktuell)* current; b) *(leicht verkäuflich)* popular

Gang·schaltung die *(Technik)* gear system; *(Art)* gear-change

Gangway ['gæŋweɪ] **die**; ~, ~s gangway

Ganove [ga'no:və] **der**; ~n, ~n *(ugs. abwertend)* crook *(coll.)*

Gans die; ~, Gänse goose

Gänse-: ~**blümchen das** daisy; ~**braten der** roast goose; ~**füßchen das**; *meist Pl. (ugs.) s.* Anführungszeichen; ~**haut die** *(fig.)* goose-flesh; goose pimples *pl.*; ~**marsch** *in* im ~marsch in single *or* Indian file

Gänserich der; ~s, ~e gander

ganz 1. *Adj.* a) *(gesamt)* whole; entire; den ~en Tag/das ~e Jahr all day/year; b) *(ugs.: alle)* die ~en Kinder/Leute/ Gläser usw. all the children/people/ glasses *etc.*; c) *(vollständig)* whole; d) *(ugs.: ziemlich [viel])* eine ~e Menge/ ein ~er Haufen quite a lot/quite a pile; e) *(ugs.: unversehrt)* intact; etw. wieder ~ machen mend sth.; **2.** *adv.* quite; **Ganze das**; *adj. Dekl.* a) whole; b) *(alles)* das ~: the whole thing; **gänzlich** *Adv.* entirely

ganz-: ~**tägig** 1. *Adj.* all-day; eine ~tägige Arbeit a full-time job; **2.** *adv.* all day; ~**tags** *Adv.* ~ arbeiten work full-time

¹**gar** *Adj.* cooked; done *pred.*

²**gar** *Partikel* a) *(überhaupt)* ~ nicht [wahr] not [true] at all; ~ nichts nothing at all; ~ niemand *od.* keiner nobody at all; ~ keines not a single one; ~ kein Geld no money at all; b) *(südd., österr., schweiz.: verstärkend)* ~ zu only too; c) *(geh.: sogar)* even

Garage [ga'ra:ʒə] **die**; ~, ~n garage

Garant der; ~en, ~en guarantor; **Garantie die**; ~, ~n guarantee; **garantieren** 1. *tr. V.* guarantee; **2.** *itr. V.* für etw. ~: guarantee sth.; **garantiert** *Adv. (ugs.)* wir kommen ~ zu spät we're dead certain to arrive late *(coll.)*; **Garantie·schein der** guarantee [certificate]

Garaus ['ga:ʔlaʊs] jmdm. den ~ machen do sb. in *(coll.)*

Garbe die; ~, ~n a) sheaf; b) *(Geschoß~)* burst of fire

Garde die; ~, ~n guard

Garderobe die; ~, ~n a) *o. Pl.* wardrobe; clothes *pl.*; b) *(Flur~)* coatrack; c) *(im Theater o. ä.)* cloakroom; checkroom *(Amer.)*; **Garderoben- frau die** cloakroom *or (Amer.)* checkroom attendant

Gardine die; ~, ~n a) net curtain; b) *(landsch., veralt.)* curtain

Gardinen-: ~**predigt die** *(ugs.)* telling-off *(coll.); (einer Ehefrau zu ihrem Mann)* curtain lecture; ~**stange die** curtain rail

gären *tr., itr. V.* cook

gären *regelm. (auch unr.) itr. V.* ferment; *(fig.)* seethe

Garn das; ~[e]s, ~e a) thread; *(Näh~)* cotton; b) *(Seew.)* yarn

Garnele die; ~, ~n shrimp

garnieren *tr. V.* a) decorate; b) *(Gastr.)* garnish

Garnison die; ~, ~en garrison

Garnitur die; ~, ~en a) set; (Wäsche) set of [matching] underwear; (Möbel) suite; b) (ugs.) die erste/zweite ~: the first/second-rate people pl.

garstig Adj. a) nasty; bad (behaviour) no indef. art.; b) (ugs.) die erste/zweite ~: the first/second-rate people pl.

Gärtchen das; ~s, ~: little garden; **Garten** der; ~s, Gärten garden

Garten-: ~arbeit die gardening; ~bau der; o. Pl. horticulture; ~fest das garden party; ~haus das summer-house; ~laube die summer-house; garden house; ~lokal das beer garden; (Restaurant) open-air café; ~schau die horticultural show; ~zwerg der a) garden gnome; b) (salopp abwertend) little runt

Gärtner der; ~s, ~: gardener; **Gärtnerei** die; ~, ~en nursery; **Gärtnerin** die; ~, ~nen gardener

Gärung die; ~, ~en fermentation

Gas das; ~es, ~e a) gas; b) (Treibstoff) petrol (Brit.); gasoline (Amer.); gas (Amer. coll.); ~ wegnehmen take one's foot off the accelerator; ~ geben accelerate; put one's foot down (coll.)

gas-, Gas-: ~flasche die gas-cylinder; (für einen Herd, Ofen) gas bottle; ~förmig Adj. gaseous; ~hahn der gas tap; ~herd der gas cooker; ~leitung die gas pipe; (Hauptrohr) gas main; ~maske die gas mask; ~pedal das accelerator [pedal]; gas pedal (Amer.); ~pistole die pistol that fires gas cartridges

Gasse die; ~, ~n lane; (österr.) street; **Gassen·junge** der (abwertend) street urchin

Gast der; ~[e]s, Gäste a) guest; b) (Besucher eines Lokals) patron; c) (Besucher) visitor; **Gast·arbeiter** der immigrant or guest worker

Gäste-: ~buch das guest book; ~zimmer das (privat) guest room; spare room; (im Hotel) room

gast-, Gast-: ~freundlich Adj. hospitable; ~freundschaft die hospitality; ~geber der host; ~geberin, die hostess; ~haus das, ~hof der the inn

gastieren itr. V. give a guest performance

gastlich Adj. hospitable; **Gastlichkeit** die; ~: hospitality

Gastronom der; ~en, ~en restaurateur; **Gastronomie** die; ~: catering no art.; (Gaststättengewerbe) restaurant trade

Gast-: ~spiel das guest performance; ~stätte die public house; (Speiselokal) restaurant; ~wirt der publican;

landlord; (eines Restaurants) [restaurant] proprietor; (Pächter) restaurant manager; ~wirtschaft die s. ~stätte

Gas-: ~vergiftung die gas-poisoning no indef. art.; ~versorgung die gas supply; ~werk das gasworks sing.; ~zähler der gas meter

Gatte der; ~n, ~n husband

Gatter das; ~s, ~ a) (Zaun) fence; (Lattenzaun) fence; paling; b) (Tor) gate;

Gattin die; ~, ~nen (geh.) wife

Gattung die; ~, ~en a) kind; sort; (Kunst~) genre; form; b) (Biol.) genus

Gaudi das; ~s (bayr., österr.) die; ~ (ugs.) bit of fun

Gaukler der; ~s, ~ a) (veralt.: Taschenspieler) itinerant entertainer; b) (geh.: Betrüger) charlatan

Gaul der; ~[e]s, Gäule nag (derog.)

Gaumen der; ~s, ~: palate

Gauner der; ~s, ~ (abwertend) crook (coll.); rogue; (ugs.) swindle; **Gauner·sprache** die thieves' cant or Latin

Gaze ['gaːzə] die; ~, ~n gauze

geachtet Adj. respected

Geäst das; ~[e]s branches pl.

geb. Abk. a) geboren; b) geborene

Gebäck das; ~[e]s, ~e cakes and pastries pl.; (Kekse) biscuits pl.; (Törtchen) tarts pl.

gebacken 2. Part. v. backen

Gebälk das; ~[e]s, ~e beams pl.; (Dach~) rafters pl.

gebar 1. u. 3. Pers. Sg. Prät. v. gebären

Gebärde die; ~, ~n gesture; **gebärden** refl. V. behave

gebären unr. tr. V. bear; give birth to; s. auch geboren

Gebäude das; ~s, ~ a) building; b) (Gefüge) structure

gebaut Adj. gut ~ sein have a good figure

Gebein das; ~[e]s, ~e bones pl.; (sterbliche Reste) [mortal] remains

Gebell das; ~[e]s barking; (der Jagdhunde) baying

geben 1. unr. tr. V. give; jmdm. die Hand ~: shake sb.'s hand; ~ Sie mir bitte Herrn N. please put me through to Mr N.; Unterricht ~: teach; eins plus eins gibt zwei one and one is or makes two; etw. von sich ~: utter sth.; 2. unr. V. (unpers.) es gibt there is/are; (coll.); heute gibt's Fisch we're having fish today; morgen gibt es Schnee it'll snow tomorrow; 3. unr. itr.

V. **a)** *(Karten austeilen)* deal; **b)** *(Sport: aufschlagen)* serve; **4.** *unr. refl. V.* **a)** sich [natürlich/steif] ~: act *or* behave [naturally/stiffly]; **b)** das gibt sich noch it will get better

Gebet das; ~|e|s, ~e prayer

gebeten *2. Part. v.* bitten

Gebets-: ~mühle die prayer wheel; ~teppich der *(islam. Rel.)* prayer mat

gebiert *3. Pers. Sg. Präsens v.* gebären

Gebiet das; ~|e|s, ~e region; area; *(Staats~)* territory; *(Bereich, Fach)* field

gebieten *(geh.)* **a)** command; order; **b)** *(erfordern)* demand; **Gebieter** der; ~s, ~ *(veralt.)* master; **gebieterisch** *(geh.) Adj.* imperious; *(herrisch)* domineering; peremptory ⟨tone⟩

Gebilde das; ~s, ~: object; *(Bauwerk)* structure

gebildet *Adj.* educated

Gebirge das; ~s, ~: mountain range; im ~: in the mountains; **gebirgig** *Adj.* mountainous

Gebiß das; Gebisses, Gebisse *pl.* set of teeth; teeth *pl.*; **b)** *(Zahnersatz)* denture; plate *(coll.)*; *(für beide Kiefer)* dentures *pl.*; **gebissen** *2. Part. v.* beißen

geblasen *2. Part. v.* blasen

geblichen *2. Part. v.* bleichen

geblümt *Adj.* flowered

Geblüt das; ~|e|s *(geh.)* blood

gebogen *2. Part. v.* biegen

geboren **1.** *2. Part. v.* gebären; **2.** *Adj.* blind/taub ~ sein be born blind/deaf; Frau Anna Schmitz ~e Meyer Mrs Anna Schmitz née Meyer

geborgen **1.** *2. Part. v.* bergen; **2.** *Adj.* safe; secure; **Geborgenheit** die; ~: security

geborsten *2. Part. v.* bersten

gebot *1. u. 3. Pers. Sg. Prät. v.* gebieten; **Gebot** das; ~|e|s, ~e **a)** *(Grundsatz)* precept; die Zehn ~e *(Rel.)* the Ten Commandments; **b)** *(Vorschrift)* regulation; **geboten 1.** *2. Part. v.* bieten, gebieten; **2.** *Adj. (ratsam)* advisable; *(notwendig)* necessary

Gebr. *Abk.* Gebrüder Bros.

gebracht *2. Part. v.* bringen

gebrannt *2. Part. v.* brennen

gebraten *2. Part. v.* braten

Gebrauch der **a)** *o. Pl.* use; **b)** *meist Pl. (Brauch)* custom; **gebrauchen** *tr. V.* use; **gebräuchlich** *Adj.* **a)** normal; customary; **b)** *(häufig)* common

gebrauchs-, Gebrauchs-: ~an-

weisung die instructions *pl.* [for use]; ~fertig *Adj.* ready for use *pred.*; ~gegenstand der item of practical use

gebraucht *Adj.* second-hand; used ⟨car⟩ **Gebraucht·wagen** der used car

Gebrechen das; ~s, ~ *(geh.)* affliction; **gebrechlich** *Adj.* infirm; **Gebrechlichkeit** die; ~: infirmity

gebrochen 1. *2. Part. v.* brechen; **2.** *Adj.* ~es Englisch/Deutsch broken English/German; **3.** *adv.* ~ Deutsch sprechen speak broken German

Gebrüder *Pl.*: die ~ Meyer Meyer Brothers

Gebrüll das; ~|e|s roaring

Gebrumm das; ~|e|s *(von Bären)* growling; *(von Flugzeugen, Bienen)* droning; *(von Insekten)* buzz[ing]

gebückt *Adj.* in ~er Haltung bending forward

Gebühr die; ~, ~en charge; *(Maut)* toll; *(Anwalts~)* fee

gebühren *(geh.) itr. V.* jmdm. gebührt Achtung usw. sb. deserves respect *etc.*; **gebührend 1.** *Adj.* fitting; **2.** *adv.* fittingly

gebühren-, Gebühren-: ~ermäßigung die: reduction of charges/fees; ~frei **1.** *Adj.* free of charge *pred.*; **2.** *adv.* free of charge; ~pflichtig *Adj.* eine ~pflichtige Verwarnung a fine and a caution

gebunden 1. *2. Part. v.* binden; **2.** *Adj. (verpflichtet)* bound

Geburt die; ~, ~en birth; **Geburtenkontrolle** die; ~: birth control; **gebürtig** *Adj.* ein ~er Schwabe a Swabian by birth

Geburts-: ~anzeige die birth announcement; ~datum das date of birth; ~helfer der *(Arzt)* obstetrician; ~ort der place of birth; ~tag der birthday; jmdm. zum ~ gratulieren wish sb. many happy returns of the day; ~urkunde die birth certificate

Gebüsch das; ~|e|s, ~e bushes *pl.*

gedacht *2. Part. v.* denken, gedenken

Gedächtnis das; ~ses, ~se **a)** memory; **b)** *(Andenken)* memory

Gedächtnis-: ~lücke die gap in one's memory; ~schwund der loss of memory

gedämpft *Adj.* subdued ⟨mood⟩; subdued, soft ⟨light⟩; muffled ⟨sound⟩

Gedanke der; ~ns, ~n **a)** thought; der ~ an etw. *(Akk.)* the thought of sth.; **b)** *Pl. (Meinung)* ideas; **c)** *(Einfall)* idea

gedạnken-, Gedạnken-: ~**gang** der train of thought; ~**los 1.** *Adj.* unconsidered; *(zerstreut)* absent-minded; **2.** *adv.* without thinking; *(zerstreut)* absent-mindedly; ~**losigkeit** die *(Zerstreutheit)* absent-mindedness; *(Unüberlegtheit)* lack of thought; ~**strich** der dash; ~**verloren** *Adv.* lost in thought; ~**voll 1.** *Adj.* pensive; **2.** *adv.* pensively

gedạnklich 1. *Adj.* intellectual; **2.** *adv.* intellectually

Gedạ̈rm das; ~|e|s, ~e intestines *pl.*; bowels *pl.*, *(eines Tieres)* entrails *pl.*

Gedẹck das; ~|e|s, ~e **a)** place setting; cover; **b)** *(Menü)* set meal; **c)** *(Getränk)* drink [with a cover charge]

gedeihen *unr. itr. V.; mit sein* **a)** thrive; **b)** *(fortschreiten)* progress

gedẹnken *unr. itr. V.* **a)** jmds./einer Sache ~ *(geh.)* remember sb./sth.; *(in einer Feier)* commemorate sb./sth.; **b)** etw. zu tun ~: intend to do or doing sth.

Gedẹnk·stätte die memorial

Gedịcht das; ~|e|s, ~e poem

gediegen 1. *Adj.* solid *(furniture)*; sound *(piece of work)*; **2.** *adv.* ~ gebaut/verarbeitet solidly built/made

gediẹh *1. u. 3. Pers. Sg. Prät. v.* gedeihen; **gediehen** *2. Part. v.* gedeihen

Gedrạ̈nge das; ~s pushing and shoving; *(Menge)* crush; crowd

gedrọschen *2. Part. v.* dreschen

gedrụngen 1. *2. Part. v.* dringen; **2.** *Adj.* stocky; thick-set

Gedụld die; ~: patience; **gedụlden** *refl. V.* be patient; **gedụldig 1.** *Adj.* patient; **2.** *adv.* patiently; **Gedụldsspiel** das puzzle

gedụrft *2. Part. v.* dürfen

geeignet *Adj.* suitable; *(richtig)* right

Gefahr die; ~, ~en **a)** danger; *(Bedrohung)* danger; threat (für to); **bei** ~: in case of emergency; **b)** *(Risiko)* risk; **auf eigene** ~: at one's own risk; **gefährden** *tr. V.* endanger; jeopardize *(enterprise, success, position, etc.)*

gefahren *2. Part. v.* fahren

gefährlich 1. *Adj.* dangerous; *(gewagt)* risky; **2.** *adv.* dangerously

gefahr·los 1. *Adj.* safe; **2.** *adv.* safely

Gefährt das; ~|e|s, ~e vehicle

Gefährte der; ~n, ~n, **Gefährtin** die; ~, ~nen *(geh.)* companion; *(Ehemann/Ehefrau)* partner in life

Gefälle das; ~s, ~: slope; incline; *(einer Straße)* gradient

¹**gefạllen** *unr. itr. V.* **a)** das gefällt mir

|gut| I like it [a lot]; **b)** sich *(Dat.)* etw. ~ lassen put up with sth.

²**gefạllen** *2. Part. v.* fallen, gefallen

¹**Gefạllen** der; ~s, ~: favour

²**Gefạllen** das; ~s pleasure

Gefạllene der; *adj. Dekl.* soldier killed in action; **die** ~**n** the fallen

gefạ̈llig 1. *Adj.* **a)** obliging; helpful; **b)** *(anziehend)* pleasing; agreeable *(programme, behaviour)*; **2.** *adv.* pleasingly; agreeably; **Gefạ̈lligkeit** die; ~, ~en favour; **gefạ̈lligst** *Adv. (ugs.)* kindly

gefạngen *2. Part. v.* fangen; **Gefạngene** der/die; *adj. Dekl.* prisoner

gefạngen-: ~**|halten** *unr. tr. V.* jmdn./ein Tier ~**halten** hold sb. prisoner/keep an animal in captivity; ~**|nehmen** *unr. tr. V.* jmdn. ~**nehmen** take sb. prisoner

Gefạngenschaft die; ~, ~en captivity

Gefạ̈ngnis das; ~ses, ~se **a)** prison; gaol; **b)** *(Strafe)* imprisonment

Gefạ̈ngnis-: ~**strafe** die prison sentence; ~**wärter** der [prison] warder

Gefạsel das; ~s *(ugs. abwertend)* twaddle *(coll.)*; drivel *(derog.)*

Gefạ̈ß das; ~es, ~e **a)** vessel; container; **b)** *(Anat.)* vessel

gefạßt *Adj.* **a)** calm; composed; **b)** *in* **auf etw.** *(Akk.)* **|nicht|** ~ **sein** [not] be prepared for sth.

Gefẹcht das; ~|e|s, ~e battle

Gefieder das; ~s, ~: plumage; feathers *pl.*; **gefiedert** *Adj.* feathered

geflịssentlich 1. *Adj.* deliberate; **2.** *adv.* deliberately

geflọchten *2. Part. v.* flechten

geflọgen *2. Part. v.* fliegen

geflọhen *2. Part. v.* fliehen

geflọssen *2. Part. v.* fließen

Geflügel das; ~s *(ugs. abwertend)* poultry

gefọchten *2. Part. v.* fechten

Gefọlge das; ~s, ~: entourage

gefrạgt *Adj.* in great demand *post-pos.*; sought-after

gefräßig *Adj. (abwertend)* greedy

Gefreite der; *adj. Dekl. (Milit.)* lance-corporal *(Brit.)*; private first class *(Amer.)*; *(Marine)* able seaman; *(Luftw.)* aircraftman first class *(Brit.)*; airman third class *(Amer.)*

gefrẹssen *2. Part. v.* fressen

gefrieren *unr. itr. V.; mit sein* freeze

Gefrier-, Gefrier-: ~**fach** das freezing compartment; ~**punkt** der freezing-point; ~**schrank** der freezer;

~|**trocknen** *tr. V.; meist im Inf. u. 2. Part.* freeze-dry

gefroren *2. Part. v.* frieren, gefrieren

Gefüge das; ~s, ~: structure; **gefügig** *Adj.* compliant; docile ⟨animal⟩

Gefühl das; ~s, ~e a) sensation; feeling; b) *(Gemütsverfassung)* feeling; **gefühl·los** *Adj.* a) numb; b) *(herzlos, kalt)* unfeeling

gefühls-, Gefühls-: ~**betont** *Adj.* emotional; ~**duselei** die; ~ *(ugs. abwertend)* mawkishness; ~**mäßig** *Adj.* emotional ⟨reaction⟩; ⟨action⟩ based on emotion

gefühl·voll **1.** *Adj.* sensitive; *(ausdrucksvoll)* expressive; **2.** *adv.* sensitively; expressively

gefüllt *2. Part. v.* füllen

gefunden *2. Part. v.* finden; *s. auch* Fressen b

gegangen *2. Part. v.* gehen

gegeben *2. Part. v.* geben

gegen *Präp. mit Akk.* a) against; ~ etw. stoßen knock into sth.; **ein Mittel ~ Krebs** a cure for cancer; ~ **die Abmachung** contrary to the agreement; b) ~ **Abend/Morgen** towards evening/dawn; ~ **vier Uhr** around 4 o'clock; c) *(im Vergleich zu)* compared with; d) *(im Ausgleich für)* for; ~ **Quittung** against a receipt

Gegen-: ~**angriff** der counterattack; ~**argument** das counterargument; ~**besuch** der return visit

Gegend die; ~, ~en a) area; b) *(Körperregion)* region

Gegen-: ~**darstellung** die: **eine** ~**darstellung |der Sache|** an account [of the matter] from an opposing point of view; ~**druck** der counterpressure

gegen·einander *Adv.* against each other *or* one another

Gegen-: ~**gewicht** das counterweight; **ein** ~**gewicht zu** *od.* **gegen etw. bilden** *(fig.)* counterbalance sth.; ~**leistung** die service in return; ~**mittel** das *(gegen Gift)* antidote; *(gegen Krankheit)* remedy; ~**probe** die cross-check; ~**satz** der a) *(Gegenteil)* opposite; b) *(Widerspruch)* conflict; ~**sätzlich** *Adj.* conflicting; ~**seitig** **1.** *Adj.* *(wechselseitig)* mutual; **2.** *adv.* **sich** ~**seitig helfen/überbieten** help/outdo each other *or* one another; ~**seitigkeit** die reciprocity; **auf** ~**seitigkeit** *(Dat.)* **beruhen** be mutual; ~**spieler** der opponent; *(Sport)* opposite number

Gegen·stand der object; *(Thema)* subject; topic; **gegenständlich** *Adj.* *(Kunst)* representational; *(Philos.)* objective; **gegenstands·los** *Adj.* a) *(hinfällig)* invalid; b) *(grundlos, unbegründet)* unfounded ⟨accusation, complaint, jealousy⟩; baseless ⟨fear⟩

gegen-, Gegen-: ~**stimme** die vote against; **ohne** ~**stimme** unanimously; ~**stück** das companion piece; *(fig.)* counterpart; ~**teil** das opposite; **im** ~**teil** on the contrary; ~**teilig** *Adj.* opposite; contrary

gegen·über *Präp. mit Dat.* a) opposite; b) *(in bezug auf)* ~ **jmdm.** *od.* **jmdm.** ~ **freundlich sein** be kind to sb.; c) *(im Vergleich zu)* compared with

gegenüber-, Gegenüber-: ~**stehen** *unr. itr. V.* a) **jmdm./einer Sache** ~**stehen** stand facing sb./sth.; *(fig.)* face sb./sth.; b) **jmdm./einer Sache feindlich/wohlwollend** ~**stehen** be ill/well disposed towards sb./sth.; ~|**stellen** *tr. V.* confront; ~**stellung** die confrontation; b) *(Vergleich)* comparison; ~|**treten** *unr. itr. V.; mit sein* **jmdm./einer Sache treten** *(auch fig.)* face sb./sth.

Gegen·verkehr der oncoming traffic

Gegenwart die; ~ a) present; b) *(Anwesenheit)* presence; c) *(Grammatik)* present [tense]; **gegenwärtig** **1.** *Adj.* present; **2.** *adv.* at present; at the moment

Gegen-: ~**wehr** die; *o. Pl.* resistance; ~**wind** der head wind; ~**zug** der *(Brettspiele, fig.)* countermove

gegessen *2. Part. v.* essen

geglichen *2. Part. v.* gleichen

geglitten *2. Part. v.* gleiten

Gegner der; ~s, ~ a) adversary; opponent; b) *(Sport)* opponent; **gegnerisch** *Adj.* opposing; opponents' ⟨goal⟩

gegolten *2. Part. v.* gelten

gegoren *2. Part. v.* gären

gegossen *2. Part. v.* gießen

gegriffen *2. Part. v.* greifen

gehabt *2. Part. v.* haben

¹**Gehalt** der; ~|e|s, ~e a) meaning; *(Anteil)* content

²**Gehalt** das, *österr. auch:* der; ~|e|s, Gehälter salary

gehalten *2. Part. v.* halten

Gehalts-: ~**empfänger** der salary earner; ~**erhöhung** die salary increase

gehalt·voll *Adj.* nutritious ⟨food⟩; ⟨novel, speech⟩ rich in substance

gehässig *Adj. (abwertend)* spiteful; **Gehässigkeit** die; ~, ~en a) *(Wesen)* spitefulness; b) *(Äußerung)* spiteful remark

gehauen *2. Part. v.* hauen

gehäuft *Adj.* ein ~er Teelöffel/Eßlöffel a heaped teaspoon/tablespoon

Gehäuse das; ~s, ~ *(einer Maschine)* casing; housing; *(einer Kamera, Uhr)* case

geh·behindert *Adj.* able to walk only with difficulty *postpos.*; disabled

Gehege das; ~s, ~ a) *(Jägerspr.)* preserve; b) *(im Zoo)* enclosure

geheim 1. *Adj.* a) secret; b) *(mysteriös)* mysterious; 2. *adv.* ~ abstimmen vote by secret ballot

geheim-, Geheim-: ~agent der secret agent; ~dienst der secret service; ~|halten *unr. tr. V.* keep secret **Geheimnis** das; ~ses, ~se secret; **Geheimnis·tuerei** die; ~ *(ugs.)* secretiveness; **geheimnis·voll** *Adj.* mysterious

Geheiß das: auf jmds. ~ *(geh.)* at sb.'s behest

gehen *unr. itr. V.; mit* sein a) walk; go; über die Straße ~: cross the street; b) *(sich irgendwohin begeben)* go; c) *(regelmäßig besuchen)* attend; d) *(weg~)* go; leave; e) *(in Funktion sein)* work; meine Uhr geht falsch my watch is wrong; f) *(möglich sein)* ja, das geht yes, I/we can manage that; das geht nicht that can't be done; g) *(ugs.: gerade noch angehen)* Hast du gut geschlafen? – Es geht Did you sleep well? – Not too bad; h) *(sich entwickeln)* der Laden/das Geschäft geht gut/gar nicht the shop/business is doing well/not doing well at all; i) *(unpers.)* wie geht es dir? How are you?; jmdm. geht es gut/schlecht *(gesundheitlich)* sb. is well/not well; *(geschäftlich)* sb. is doing well/badly; j) *(unpers.) (sich um etw. handeln)* ; worum geht es hier? what is this all about?; 2. *unr. tr. V. (zurücklegen)* 10 km ~: walk 10 km.

gehen|lassen *unr. refl. V. (sich nicht beherrschen)* lose control of oneself; *(sich vernachlässigen)* let oneself go

geheuer *Adj.* a) in diesem Gebäude ist es nicht ~: this building is eerie; b) ihr war doch nicht |ganz| ~: she felt |a little| uneasy; c) die Sache ist |mir| nicht ganz ~: |I feel| there's something odd about this business

Gehilfe der; ~n, ~n assistant

Gehirn das; ~|e|s, ~e brain

Gehirn-: ~erschütterung die concussion; ~schlag der stroke; ~wäsche die brainwashing *no indef. art.*

gehoben 1. *2. Part. v.* heben; 2. *Adj.* a) higher; senior ⟨position⟩; b) *(gewählt)* elevated, refined

geholfen *2. Part. v.* helfen

Gehör das; ~|e|s |sense of| hearing

gehorchen *itr. V.* jmdm. ~: obey sb.

gehören 1. *itr. V.* a) jmdm.: belong to sb.; b) *(Teil eines Ganzen sein)* zu jmds. Freunden/Aufgaben ~: be one of sb.'s friends/part of sb.'s duties; c) *(passend sein)* dein Roller gehört nicht in die Küche! your scooter does not belong in the kitchen!; d) *(nötig sein)* es hat viel Fleiß dazu gehört it took a lot of hard work; dazu gehört sehr viel that takes a lot; 2. *refl. V. (sich schikken)* be fitting; es gehört sich |nicht|, ... zu ...: it is |not| good manners to ...; **gehörig** 1. *Adj.* a) proper; b) *(ugs.: beträchtlich)* ein ~er Schrecken/eine ~e Portion Mut a good fright/a good deal of courage; 2. *adv. (ugs.: beträchtlich)* ~ essen/trinken eat/drink heartily

gehorsam *Adj.* obedient; **Gehorsam** der; ~s obedience

Geh·steig der pavement *(Brit.)*; sidewalk *(Amer.)*

Geier der; ~s, ~: vulture

Geige die; ~, ~n violin

Geiger·zähler der *(Physik)* Geiger counter

geil *Adj. (oft abwertend: sexuell erregt)* randy; horny *(sl.)*; *(lüstern)* lecherous

Geisel die; ~, ~n hostage

Geißel die; ~, ~n *(hist., auch fig.)* scourge

Geist der; ~|e|s, ~er a) *o. Pl. (Verstand)* mind; b) *o. Pl. (Scharfsinn)* wit; c) *o. Pl. (innere Einstellung)* spirit; d) *(denkender Mensch)* mind; intellect; ein großer/kleiner ~: a great mind/a person of limited intellect; e) *(überirdisches Wesen)* spirit; der Heilige ~ *(christl. Rel.)* the Holy Ghost or Spirit; f) *(Gespenst)* ghost; **Geisterfahrer** der *person driving on the wrong side of the road or the wrong carriageway;* **geisterhaft** *Adj.* ghostly; eerie *⟨atmosphere⟩*

geistes-, Geistes-: ~abwesend 1. *Adj.* absent-minded; 2. *adv.* absentmindedly; ~blitz der *(ugs.)* brainwave; ~gegenwart die presence of mind; ~gegenwärtig 1. *Adj.* quickwitted; 2. *adv.* with great presence of

mind; **~krank** *Adj.* mentally ill;
~wissenschaften *Pl.* arts; humanities; **~zustand** der; *o. Pl.* mental state

geistig 1. *Adj.* **a)** intellectual; *(Psych.)* mental; **b)** alcoholic *⟨drinks⟩*; **2.** *adv.* intellectually; *(Psych.)* mentally;
geistlich *Adj.* sacred *⟨song, music⟩*; religious *⟨order, book, writings⟩*; **Geistliche** der; *adj. Dekl.* clergyman
geist-: **~los** *Adj.* dim-witted; *(trivial)* trivial; **~reich 1.** *Adj.* witty; *(klug)* clever; **2.** *adv.:* wittily; cleverly

Geiz der; **~es** meanness; *(Knauserigkeit)* miserliness; **geizen** *itr. V.* be mean; **Geiz·hals** der *(abwertend)* skinflint; **geizig** *Adj.* mean; *(knauserig)* miserly

gekannt *2. Part. v.* kennen
Gekicher das; **~s** giggling
geklungen *2. Part. v.* klingen
geknickt *Adj. (ugs.)* dejected
gekniffen *2. Part. v.* kneifen
gekommen *2. Part. v.* kommen
gekonnt 1. *2. Part. v.* können; **2.** *Adj.* accomplished; *(hervorragend ausgeführt)* masterly
gekrochen *2. Part. v.* kriechen
gekünstelt 1. *Adj.* artificial; **2.** *adv.* **er lächelte ~:** he gave a forced smile
Gelächter das; **~s,** **~:** laughter
geladen *2. Part. v.* laden
Gelände das; **~s,** **~** **a)** *(Landschaft)* ground; terrain; **b)** *(Grundstück)* site; *(von Schule, Krankenhaus usw.)* grounds *pl.*
Geländer das; **~s,** **~:** banisters *pl.*; handrail; *(am Balkon, an einer Brücke)* railing[s *pl.*]; *(aus Stein)* parapet
gelang *3. Pers. Sg. Prät. v.* gelingen
gelangen *itr. V.;* **mit sein an etw.** *(Akk.)/***zu etw. ~:** reach sth.; *(fig.)* **zu Ansehen ~** gain esteem
gelassen 1. *2. Part. v.* lassen; **2.** *Adj.* calm; *(gefaßt)* composed; **Gelassenheit** die; **~:** calmness; *(Gefaßtheit)* composure
Gelatine [ʒelaˈtiːnə] die; **~:** gelatine
gelaufen *2. Part. v.* laufen
geläufig *Adj.* *(vertraut)* common *⟨expression, concept⟩*
gelaunt gut/schlecht ~ sein be in a good/bad mood
gelb *Adj.* yellow; **Gelb** das; **~s, ~** *od.* *(ugs.)* **~s** yellow; **gelblich** *Adj.* yellowish; yellowed *⟨paper⟩*; sallow *⟨skin⟩*; **Gelb·sucht** die; *o. Pl. (Med.)* jaundice

Geld das; **~es, ~er** money; **großes ~:** large denominations *pl.*; **kleines/bares ~:** change/cash
geld-, Geld-: **~automat** der cash dispenser **~beutel** der *(bes. südd.)* purse; **~börse** die purse; **~gier** die avarice; **~gierig** *Adj.* avaricious; **~mittel** *Pl.* financial resources; **~schein** der banknote; bill *(Amer.)*; **~schrank** der safe; **~strafe** die fine; **~stück** das coin; **~wechsel** der exchanging of money; „**~wechsel**" 'bureau de change'
Gelee [ʒeˈleː] der *od.* das; **~s, ~s** jelly
gelegen 1. *2. Part. v.* liegen; **2.** *Adj.* **a)** *(passend)* convenient; **Gelegenheit** die; **~, ~en** opportunity; *(Anlaß)* occasion
Gelegenheits-: **~arbeit** die casual work; **~kauf** der bargain
gelegentlich 1. *Adj.* occasional; **2.** *adv.* occasionally
gelehrig *Adj.* *⟨child⟩* who is quick to learn; *⟨animal⟩* that is quick to learn; **gelehrt** *Adj.* learned; **Gelehrte** der/ die; *adj. Dekl.* scholar
Geleit das; **~[e]s, ~e** *(geh.)* **sie bot uns ihr ~ an** she offered to accompany us; **geleiten** *tr. V. (geh.)* escort; **Geleit·schutz** der *(Milit.)* escort
Gelenk das; **~[e]s, ~e** joint; **gelenkig 1.** *Adj.* agile *⟨person⟩*; supple *⟨limb⟩*; **2.** *adv.* agilely; **Gelenkigkeit** die; **~:** agility; *(von Gliedmaßen)* suppleness
gelernt *Adj.* qualified
gelesen *2. Part. v.* lesen
Geliebte der/die; *adj. Dekl.* lover/ mistress
geliefert *Adj.:* **~ sein** *(salopp)* have had it *(coll.)*
geliehen *2. Part. v.* leihen
gelind[e] 1. *Adj.* mild; **2.** *adv.* mildly; **~e gesagt** to put it mildly
gelingen *unr. itr. V.; mit sein* succeed; **Gelingen** das; **~s** success
gelitten *2. Part. v.* leiden
gellen *itr. V.* **a)** *(hell schallen)* ring out; **b)** *(nachhallen)* ring
geloben *tr. V. (geh.)* vow; **das Gelobte Land** the Promised Land
gelogen *2. Part. v.* lügen
gelöst *Adj.* relaxed
gelten 1. *unr. itr. V.* **a)** *(gültig sein)* be valid; *⟨banknote, coin⟩* be legal tender; *⟨law etc.⟩* be in force; **b)** *(angesehen werden)* **als etw. ~:** be regarded as sth.; **c)** *(+ Dat.) (bestimmt sein für)* be directed at; **2.** *unr. tr. V.* **a)** *(wert sein)* **sein Wort gilt viel/wenig** his word car-

ries a lot of/little weight; **b)** *unpers.* es gilt, etw. **zu tun** it is essential to do sth.; **geltend: etw. ~ machen** assert sth.; **Geltung die; ~ a)** validity; **für jmdn. ~ haben** apply to sb.; **b)** *(Wirkung)* recognition; **zur ~ kommen** show to [its best] advantage; **Geltungs·bedürfnis das** need for recognition

gelungen 1. *2. Part. v.* gelingen; **2.** *Adj.* **a)** *(ugs.: spaßig)* priceless; **b)** *(ansprechend)* inspired

gemächlich [gə'mε(:)çlıç] **1.** *Adj.* leisurely; **2.** *adv.* in a leisurely manner

gemacht *in* ein **~er Mann sein** *(ugs.)* be a made man

Gemahl der; ~s, ~e *(geh.)* consort; husband; **Gemahlin die; ~, ~nen** *(geh.)* consort; wife

Gemälde das; ~s, ~: painting

gemäß *Präp. + Dat.* in accordance with

gemäßigt *Adj.* moderate; qualified *⟨optimism⟩*; temperate *⟨climate⟩*

gemein 1. *Adj.* **a)** vulgar *⟨joke, expression⟩*; nasty *⟨person⟩*; **b)** *(niederträchtig)* mean; dirty *⟨lie⟩*; mean *⟨trick⟩*; **2.** *adv.* in a mean *or* nasty way

Gemeinde die; ~, ~n a) municipality; *(Bewohner)* community; **b)** *(Pfarr~)* parish; **c)** *(versammelte Gottesdienstteilnahme)* congregation

Gemeinde-: ~rat der a) *(Gremium)* local council; **b)** *(Mitglied)* local councillor; **~schwester die** district nurse; **~verwaltung die** local administration

gemein·gefährlich *Adj.* dangerous to the public; **Gemein·gut das;** *o. Pl. (geh.)* common property

Gemeinheit die; ~, ~en a) *o. Pl.* meanness; **b)** *(Handlung)* mean trick

gemein·nützig *Adj.* serving the public good *postpos., not pred.;(wohltätig)* charitable

gemeinsam 1. *Adj.* **a)** common *⟨interests, characteristics⟩*; mutual *⟨acquaintance, friend⟩*; joint *⟨property, account⟩*; shared *⟨experience⟩*; **b)** *(miteinander unternommen)* joint; **2.** *adv.* together; **Gemeinsamkeit die; ~, ~en** common feature

Gemeinschaft die; ~, ~en a) community; **b)** *o. Pl. (Verbundenheit)* coexistence; **gemeinschaftlich** *s.* gemeinsam

gemein·verständlich *Adj.* generally comprehensible; **Gemein·wohl das** public good

gemessen 1. *2. Part. v.* messen; **2.** *Adj. (würdevoll)* measured *⟨steps, tones, language⟩*; deliberate *⟨words, manner of speaking⟩*

Gemetzel das; ~s, ~: massacre

gemieden *2. Part. v.* meiden

Gemisch das; ~[e]s, ~e mixture **(aus, von o)**

gemocht *2. Part. v.* mögen

gemolken *2. Part. v.* melken

Gemse die; ~, ~n chamois

Gemurmel das; ~s murmuring

Gemüse das; ~s, ~: vegetables *pl.*

gemußt *2. Part. v.* müssen

Gemüt das; ~[e]s, ~er a) nature; **b)** *(Empfindungsvermögen)* heart; **c)** *(Mensch)* soul

gemütlich 1. *Adj.* snug; cosy; *(bequem)* comfortable; *(ungezwungen)* informal; **2.** *adv.* cosily; *(bequem)* comfortably; **~ beisammensitzen** sit pleasantly together; **Gemütlichkeit die; ~:** snugness; *(Zwanglosigkeit)* informality

gemüts·krank *Adj.* *(Med., Psych.)* emotionally disturbed; **Gemüts·mensch der** *(ugs.)* even-tempered person; **gemüt·voll** *Adj.* warm-hearted; *(empfindsam)* sentimental

Gen das; ~s, ~e *(Biol.)* gene

genannt *2. Part. v.* nennen

genas *1. u. 3. Pers. Sg. Prät. v.* genesen

genau 1. *Adj.* **a)** *(exakt)* exact; precise; **b)** *(sorgfältig, gründlich)* meticulous, *⟨person⟩*; careful *⟨study⟩*; **2.** *adv.* **a)** exactly; precisely; **~ um 8⁰⁰** at 8 o'clock precisely; **b)** *(gerade, eben)* just; **c)** *(als Verstärkung)* just; **d)** *(als Zustimmung)* exactly; precisely; **e)** *(sorgfältig)* **~ arbeiten/etw. ~ durchdenken** work/think sth. out meticulously

genau·genommen *Adv.* strictly speaking

Genauigkeit die; ~a) *(Exaktheit)* exactness; precision; *(einer Waage)* accuracy; **b)** *(Sorgfalt)* meticulousness; **genau·so** *Adv.* **a)** *mit Adjektiven* just as; **b)** *mit Verben* in exactly the same way; *(in demselben Maße)* just as much

genehm *Adj. in* jmdm. **~ sein** *(geh.)* *(jmdm. passen)* be convenient to sb.; *(jmdm. angenehm sein)* be acceptable to sb.

genehmigen *tr. V.* approve *⟨plan, alterations, application⟩*; authorize *⟨stay⟩*; grant *⟨request⟩*; give permission for ⟨*demonstration*⟩; **sich** *(Dat.)* etw. ~ *(ugs.)* treat oneself to sth.; **Genehmigung** die; ~, ~en *a)* s. **genehmigen**; approval; authorization; granting; permission (*Gen.* for); *b)* *(Schriftstück)* permit; *(Lizenz)* licence **geneigt** *Adj.* in ~ sein, etw. zu tun be inclined to do sth.

General der; ~s, ~e od. **Generäle** general

General-: ~**direktor** der chairman; president *(Amer.)*; ~**probe** die *(auch fig.)* dress rehearsal; ~**streik** der general strike; ~**vertreter** der general representative

Generation die; ~, ~en generation; **Generations·konflikt** der generation gap

Generator der; ~s, ~en generator

generell 1. *Adj.* general; 2. *adv.* generally

genesen *unr. itr. V.; mit sein (geh.)* recover; **Genesung** die; ~, ~en *(geh.)* recovery

genetisch *(Biol.) Adj.* genetic

Genf (das); ~s Geneva; **Genfer** 1. der; ~s, ~: Genevese; 2. *Adj.* Genevese; **der ~** See Lake Geneva

genial *Adj.* brilliant; **Genialität** die; ~: genius

Genick das; ~[e]s, ~e back or nape of the neck

Genie [ʒe'ni:] das; ~s, ~s genius

genieren [ʒe'ni:rən] *refl. V.* be embarrassed

genießbar *Adj. (eßbar)* edible; *(trinkbar)* drinkable; **genießen** *unr. tr. V.* enjoy; **Genießer** der; ~s, ~: **er ist ein richtiger ~**: he is a regular 'bon viveur'

Genitale das; ~s, **Genitalien** [geni'ta:liən], **Genital·organ** das genital organ

Genitiv der; ~s, ~e *(Sprachw.)* genitive [case]

genommen 2. *Part. v.* nehmen

genoß 1. u. 3. *Pers. Sg. Prät. v.* genießen

Genosse der; ~n, ~n comrade

genossen 2. *Part. v.* genießen

Genossenschaft die; ~, ~en cooperative; **Genossin** die; ~, ~nen comrade

genug *Adv.* enough

genügen *itr. V.* a) be enough; b) einer **Sache** *(Dat.)* ~: satisfy sth.; **genügend** 1. *Adj.* a) enough; b) *(befriedigend)* satisfactory; 2. *adv.* enough; **genügsam** *Adj.* modest

Genugtuung [-tu:ʊŋ] die; ~, ~en satisfaction

Genus das; ~, **Genera** *(Sprachw.)* gender

Genuß der; **Genusses**, **Genüsse** a) o. *Pl.* consumption; b) *(Wohlbehagen)* etw. mit ~ essen/lesen eat sth. with relish/enjoy reading sth.

genüßlich *Adv.* ⟨*eat, drink*⟩ with relish

Geograph der; ~en, ~en geographer; **Geographie** die; ~: geography *no art.*; **geographisch** *Adj.* geographic[al]

Geologe der; ~n, ~n geologist; **Geologie** die; ~: geology *no art.*; **geologisch** *Adj.* geological

Geometrie die; ~: geometry *no art.*; **geometrisch** *Adj.* geometric[al]

Gepäck das; ~[e]s luggage *(Brit.)*; baggage *(Amer.)*; *(am Flughafen)* baggage

Gepäck-: ~**annahme** die a) checking in the luggage/baggage; b) *(Schalter)* [in-counter of the] luggage office *(Brit.)* or baggage office *(Amer.)*; *(zur Aufbewahrung)* [in-counter of the] left-luggage office *(Brit.)* or checkroom *(Amer.)*; *(am Flughafen)* baggage check-in; ~**aufbewahrung** die left-luggage office *(Brit.)*; checkroom *(Amer.)*; *(Schließfächer)* luggage lockers *(Brit.)*; baggage lockers *(Amer.)*; ~**ausgabe** die [out-counter of the] luggage office *(Brit.)* or *(Amer.)* baggage office; *(zur Aufbewahrung)* [out-counter of the] left-luggage office *(Brit.)* or *(Amer.)* checkroom; *(am Flughafen)* baggage reclaim; ~**kontrolle** die baggage check; ~**netz** das luggage rack *(Brit.)*; baggage rack *(Amer.)* ~**schalter** der s. ~**annahme** b; ~**schein** der luggage ticket *(Brit.)*; baggage check *(Amer.)*; ~**träger** der a) porter; b) *(am Fahrrad)* carrier; rack

gepfeffert *Adj. (ugs.)* steep *(coll.)* ⟨*price, rent, etc.*⟩

gepfiffen 2. *Part. v.* pfeifen

gepflegt *Adj.* a) well-groomed spruce ⟨*appearance*⟩; neat ⟨*clothing*⟩; b) *(hochwertig)* choice ⟨*food, drink*⟩

Gepflogenheit die; ~, ~en *(geh.)* custom; *(Gewohnheit)* habit

gepriesen 2. *Part. v.* preisen

gequält *Adj.* forced ⟨*smile, gaiety*⟩; pained ⟨*expression*⟩

gequollen 2. *Part. v.* quellen

gerade, *(ugs.)* **grade** 1. *Adj.* a)

straight; b) *(nicht schief)* upright; c) *(aufrichtig)* forthright; direct; d) *(Math.)* even *(number)*; 2. *Adv.* just; *(direkt)* right; **Gerade die; ~n, ~n** *(Geom.)* straight line

gerade-: ~aus *Adv.* straight ahead; **~|biegen** *unr. tr. V.* a) bend straight; straighten [out]; b) *(ugs.: bereinigen)* straighten out; **~heraus** [----'-] *(ugs.) Adv.* etw. **~heraus sagen** say sth. straight out; **~so** *Adv.* **~so groß/lang wie ...:** just as big/long as ...; **~|stehen** *unr. itr. V.* a) stand up straight; b) *(fig.: einstehen)* **für etw. ~stehen** accept responsibility for sth.; **~zu** *Adv.* really; *(beinahe)* almost

Geranie [geˈraːni̯ə] **die; ~, ~n** geranium

gerann *3. Pers. Sg. Prät. v.* gerinnen

gerannt *2. Part. v.* rennen

gerät *3. Pers. Sg. Präsens v.* geraten

Gerät das; ~|e|s, ~e a) piece of equipment; *(Fernseher, Radio)* set; *(Garten~)* tool; b) *(Turnen)* piece of apparatus

¹geraten *unr. itr. V.; mit sein* a) *(gelangen)* get; b) *(werden)* turn out; **(gut~)** turn out well

²geraten 1. *2. Part. v.* raten; **¹geraten;** 2. *Adj.* advisable

Geratewohl: aufs ~ *(ugs.)* ⟨select⟩ at random; **wir fuhren aufs ~ los** *(ugs.)* we went for a drive just to see where we ended up

gerät *3. Pers. Sg. Präsens v.* **¹geraten**

geraum *Adj. (geh.)* considerable

geräumig *Adj.* spacious ⟨room⟩; roomy ⟨cupboard etc.⟩

Geräusch das; ~|e|s, ~e sound; *(unerwünscht)* noise

geräusch-: ~arm 1. *Adj.* quiet; 2. *adv.* quietly **~los** 1. *Adj.* silent; 2. *adv.* a) silently; b) *(fig. ugs.)* without [any] fuss; **~voll** *Adj.* noisy

gerben *tr. V.* tan ⟨hides, skins⟩

gerecht 1. *Adj.* just *(unparteiisch)* fair; 2. *adv.* justly

gerechtfertigt *Adj.* justified

Gerechtigkeit die; ~: justice; **Gerechtigkeits · sinn der** sense of justice

Gerede das; ~s *(abwertend)* a) *(ugs.)* talk; b) *(Klatsch)* gossip

geregelt *Adj.* regular, steady ⟨job⟩

gereizt *Adj.* irritable

¹Gericht das; ~|e|s, ~e court; *(Richter)* bench; *(Gebäude)* court[-house]; **das Jüngste ~** *(Rel.)* the Last Judgement

²Gericht das; ~|e|s, ~e dish

gerichtlich 1. *Adj.* judicial; legal ⟨proceedings⟩; 2. *adv.* **jmdn. ~ verfolgen** take sb. to court

Gerichts-: ~hof der Court of Justice; **~kosten** *Pl.* legal costs; **~saal der** courtroom; **~verfahren das** legal proceedings *pl.;* **~vollzieher der; ~s, ~:** bailiff

gerieben *2. Part. v.* reiben

gering *Adj.* a) low; little ⟨value⟩; small ⟨quantity, amount⟩; short ⟨distance, time⟩; b) *(unbedeutend)* slight; minor ⟨role⟩

geringfügig 1. *Adj.* slight; minor ⟨alteration, injury⟩; trivial ⟨amount, detail⟩; 2. *adv.* slightly; **Geringfügigkeit die; ~, ~en** triviality; **gering|-schätzen** *tr. V.* think very little of ⟨person, achievement⟩; set little store by ⟨success, riches⟩; **geringschätzig** *Adj.* disdainful; disparaging ⟨remark⟩

gerinnen *unr. itr. V.; mit sein* ⟨blood⟩ clot; ⟨milk⟩ curdle

Gerippe das; ~s, ~: skeleton

gerippt *Adj.* ribbed; fluted ⟨glass, column⟩

gerissen 1. *2. Part. v.* reißen; 2. *Adj.* *(ugs.)* crafty

geritten *2. Part. v.* reiten

Germane der; ~n, ~n *(hist.)* ancient German; Teuton; **germanisch** *Adj.* *(auch fig.)* Germanic; Teutonic; **Germanistik die; ~:** German studies *pl., no art.*

gern[e] *Adj.* **lieber, am liebsten** *Adv.* a) etw. **~ tun** like or enjoy doing sth.; **er spielt lieber Tennis als Golf** he prefers playing tennis to golf; **etw. ~/am liebsten essen** like sth./like sth. best; **ja, ~/aber ~:** yes, of course; certainly!; b) *(durchaus)* **das glaube ich ~:** I can well believe that

gerochen *2. Part. v.* riechen

Geröll das; ~s, ~e debris; *(größer)* boulders *pl.*

geronnen *2. Part. v.* rinnen, gerinnen

Gerste die; ~: barley; **Gersten-korn das** *(Med.)* sty

Gerte die; ~, ~n switch

Geruch der; ~|e|s, Gerüche smell; *(von Blumen)* scent

Gerücht das; ~|e|s, ~e rumour

gerufen *2. Part. v.* rufen

geruhsam 1. *Adj.* peaceful; leisurely ⟨stroll⟩; 2. *adv.* leisurely; quietly

Gerümpel das; ~s junk

gerungen *2. Part. v.* ringen

Gerüst das; ~|e|s, ~e scaffolding *no pl., no indef. art.*

gesamt *Adj.*whole; entire; **gesamt-deutsch** *Adj.* all-German; **Gesamt·eindruck** der general impression; **Gesamtheit die**: die ~ der Bevölkerung the entire population

Gesamt-: **~schule die** comprehensive [school]; **~werk das** œuvre; *(Bücher)* complete works *pl.*

gesandt 2. *Part. v.* senden

Gesandte der/die; *adj. Dekl.* envoy; **Gesandtschaft die**; ~, ~en legation

Gesang der; ~|e|s, Gesänge a) singing; b) *(Lied)* song

Gesang-: **~buch das** hymn-book; **~verein der** choral society

Gesäß das; ~es, ~e backside; buttocks *pl.*

geschaffen 2. *Part. v.* schaffen 1

Geschäft das; ~|e|s, ~e a) business; *(Transaktion)* [business] deal; **ein gutes ~ machen** make a good profit; b) *(Laden)* shop; store *(Amer.)*

Geschäfte·macher der *(abwertend)* profit-seeker

geschäftig *Adj.* bustling

geschäftlich 1. *Adj.* business *attrib.*; 2. *adv.* on business

geschäfts-, Geschäfts-: **~freund** der business associate; **~führer** der manager; *(Vereinswesen)* secretary; **~führung die**; *o. Pl.* management; **~inhaber** der owner of the/a business; **~jahr das** financial year; **~kosten** *Pl.* **auf ~kosten** on expenses; **~lage die** [business] position; **~leitung die** *s.* **~führung**; **~leute** *s.* **~mann; ~mann** der; *Pl.* **~leute** businessman; **~ordnung die** standing orders *pl.*; *(im Parlament)* [rules *pl.* of] procedure; **~partner** der business partner; **~reise die** business trip; **~schluß der** closing-time; **~stelle die** branch; *(einer Partei, eines Vereins)* office; **~straße die** shopping-street; **~tüchtig** *Adj.* able, *(businessman, landlord, etc.)*; **~viertel das** business quarter; *(Einkaufszentrum)* shopping district; **~wagen der** company car; **~zeit die** business hours *pl.*; *(im Büro)* office hours *pl.*

geschah 3. *Pers. Sg. Prät. v.* geschehen

geschehen *unr. itr. V.; mit sein* happen; occur; *(ausgeführt werden)* be done; **jmdm. geschieht etw.** sth. happens to sb.

gescheit *Adj.* a) *(intelligent)* clever; b) *(ugs.: vernünftig)* sensible

Geschenk das; ~|e|s, ~e present; gift

Geschenk-: **~artikel** der gift; **~packung die** gift pack

Geschichte die; ~, ~n a) history; b) *(Erzählung)* story; **geschichtlich** *Adj.* a) historical; b) *(bedeutungsvoll)* historic

¹**Geschick das**; ~|e|s, ~e *(geh.)* fate

²**Geschick das**; ~|e|s skill; **Geschicklichkeit die**; ~: skilfulness; skill; **geschickt** 1. *Adj.* a) skilful; b) *(klug)* clever; adroit; 2. *adv.* a) *(gewandt)* skilfully; b) *(klug)* cleverly; adroitly

geschieden 2. *Part. v.* scheiden

geschienen 2. *Part. v.* scheinen

Geschirr das; ~|e|s, ~e a) crockery; *(benutzt)* dishes *pl.*; b) *(für Zugtier)* harness

Geschirr-: **~spül·maschine die** dishwasher; **~tuch das**; *Pl.* **-tücher** tea-towel; dish towel *(Amer.)*

geschissen 2. *Part. v.* scheißen

geschlafen 2. *Part. v.* schlafen

geschlagen 2. *Part. v.* schlagen

Geschlecht das; ~|e|s, ~er a) sex; b) *(Generation)* generation; c) *(Sippe)* family; d) *(Sprachw.)* gender; **geschlechtlich** *Adj.* sexual

geschlechts-, Geschlechts-: **~krank** *Adj. (person)* suffering from VD; **~krankheit die** venereal disease; **~teil das** genitals *pl.*; **~verkehr** der sexual intercourse; **~wort das** *s.* Artikel a

geschlichen 2. *Part. v.* schleichen

geschliffen 1. 2. *Part. v.* schleifen; 2. *Adj.* polished

geschlossen 1. 2. *Part. v.* schließen; 2. *Adj.* united *(action, front)*; unified *(procedure)*; **eine ~e Ortschaft** a built-up area

geschlungen 2. *Part. v.* schlingen

Geschmack der; ~|e|s, Geschmäcke taste; **geschmacklos** 1. *Adj.* tasteless; 2. *adv.* tastelessly; **Geschmacklosigkeit die**; ~, ~en lack of [good] taste; bad taste; *(Äußerung)* tasteless remark; **Geschmack[s]·sache die** *in* **das ist ~**: that is a question *or* matter of taste **geschmack·voll** 1. *Adj.* tasteful. 2. *adv.* tastefully

Geschmeide das; ~s, ~ *(geh.)* jewellery *no pl.*

geschmeidig 1. *Adj.* a) sleek *(hair, fur)*; soft *(leather, boots, skin)*; b) *(gelenkig)* supple *(fingers)*; lithe *(body, movement, person)*; 2. *adv. (gelenkig)* agilely

geschmissen 2. *Part. v.* **schmeißen**

geschmolzen 2. *Part. v.* **schmelzen**

Geschnetzelte das; *adj. Dekl.: small, thin slices of meat [cooked in sauce]*

geschnitten 2. *Part. v.* **schneiden**

geschoben 2. *Part. v.* **schieben**

geschollen 2. *Part. v.* **schallen**

gescholten 2. *Part. v.* **schelten**

Geschöpf das; ~[e]s, ~e creature

geschoren 2. *Part. v.* **scheren**

¹**Geschoß** das; Geschosses, Geschosse projectile; *(Kugel)* bullet; *(Rakete)* missile

²**Geschoß** das; Geschosses, Geschosse floor; storey

geschossen 2. *Part. v.* **schießen**

geschraubt *Adj. (ugs.)* stilted

Geschrei das; ~s a) shouting; *(von Verletzten, Tieren)* screaming; screams *pl.; (ugs. fig.)* fuss

geschrieben 2. *Part. v.* **schreiben**

geschrie[e]n 2. *Part. v.* **schreien**

geschritten 2. *Part. v.* **schreiten**

geschunden 2. *Part. v.* **schinden**

Geschütz das; ~es, ~e [big] gun; **Geschütz·feuer** das artillery-fire; shell-fire

geschützt *Adj.* sheltered

Geschwader das; ~s, ~ *(Marine)* squadron; *(Luftwaffe)* wing *(Brit.)*; group *(Amer.)*

Geschwätz das; ~es *(ugs. abwertend)* prattling; *(Klatsch)* gossip; **geschwätzig** *Adj. (abwertend)* talkative

geschwiegen 2. *Part. v.* **schweigen**

geschwind *(bes. südd.)* 1. *Adj.* swift; quick; 2. *adv.* swiftly; quickly

Geschwindigkeit die; ~, ~en speed **Geschwindigkeits·: ~begrenzung** die, **~beschränkung** die speed limit

Geschwister *Pl.* brothers and sisters

geschwollen 1. 2. *Part. v.* **schwellen**; 2. *Adj.* a) swollen; b) *(fig. abwertend)* pompous; 3. *adv.* pompously

geschwommen 2. *Part. v.* **schwimmen**

geschworen 2. *Part. v.* **schwören**; **Geschworene** der/die; *adj. Dekl.* juror

Geschwulst die; ~, Geschwülste tumour

geschwunden 2. *Part. v.* **schwinden**

geschwungen 1. 2. *Part. v.* **schwingen**; 2. *Adj.* curved

Geschwür das; ~s, ~e ulcer; *(Furunkel)* boil

gesehen 2. *Part v.* **sehen**

Geselle der; ~n, ~n journeyman; *(Kerl)* fellow; **gesellen** *refl. V.* sich zu jmdm. ~: join sb.; **gesellig** *Adj.* sociable; ein ~er Abend/~es Beisammensein a convivial evening/a friendly get-together; **Geselligkeit** die; ~: die ~ lieben enjoy [good] company

Gesellschaft die; ~, ~en a) society; b) *(Veranstaltung)* party; c) *(Kreis von Menschen)* group of people; d) *(Wirtschaft)* company; **Gesellschafter** der; ~s, ~ a) ein guter ~ sein be good company; b) *(Wirtsch.)* partner; *(Teilhaber)* shareholder; **Gesellschafterin** die; ~, ~nen a) [lady] companion; b) *(Wirtsch.)* partner; *(Teilhaber)* shareholder; **gesellschaftlich** *Adj.* social

gesellschafts-, Gesellschafts-: ~fähig *Adj. (auch fig.)* socially acceptable; **~ordnung** die social order; **~reise** die group tour; **~schicht** die stratum of society; **~spiel** das party game

gesessen 2. *Part. v.* **sitzen**

Gesetz das; ~es, ~e a) law; *(geschrieben)* statute; b) *(Regel)* rule

Gesetz-: ~buch das statute-book; **~geber** der legislator; *(Organ)* legislature; **~gebung** die; ~: legislation

gesetzlich 1. *Adj.* a) legal; statutory ⟨holiday⟩; lawful ⟨heir, claim⟩; 2. *adv.* legally; **gesetz·mäßig** 1. *Adj.* a) law-governed; ~ sein be governed by or obey a [natural] law/[natural] laws; b) *(gesetzlich)* legal; *(rechtmäßig)* lawful; 2. *adv.* in accordance with a [natural] law/[natural] laws; **Gesetz·mäßigkeit** die a) conformity to a [natural] law/[natural] laws; b) *(Gesetzlichkeit)* legality; *(Rechtmäßigkeit)* lawfulness

gesetzt *Adj.* staid

gesetz·widrig *Adj.* illegal; unlawful

Gesicht das; ~[e]s, ~er face; *(fig.)* das ~ einer Stadt the appearance of a town

Gesichts-: ~ausdruck der expression; look; **~creme** die face-cream; **~punkt** der point of view; **~wasser** das face-lotion; **~züge** *Pl.* features

Gesindel das; ~s *(abwertend)* rabble

gesinnt *Adj.* christlich/sozial ~ [sein] [be] Christian-minded/public-spirited; jmdm. freundlich ~ sein be well-disposed towards sb.; **Gesinnung** die; ~, ~en [basic] convictions *pl.;* [fundamental] beliefs *pl.;* **gesin-**

nungs·los *(abwertend) Adj.* unprincipled; **Gesinnungs·wandel** der change of attitude

gesittet 1. *Adj.* well-behaved; well-mannered

gesogen 2. *Part. v.* saugen

gesondert 1. *Adj.* separate; 2. *adv.* separately

gesonnen *Adj.* ~ sein, etw. zu tun feel disposed to do sth.

gesotten 2. *Part. v.* sieden

Gespann das; ~[e]s, ~e a) *(Zugtiere)* team; b) *(Wagen)* horse and carriage; c) *(Menschen)* couple; pair

gespannt *Adj.* a) eager; rapt *(attention)*; ~ zuhören listen with rapt attention; b) tense *(situation, atmosphere)*; strained *(relationships)*

Gespenst das; ~[e]s, ~er a) ghost; b) *(geh.: Gefahr)* spectre

gespenstig, gespenstisch *Adj.* ghostly; eerie *(building, atmosphere)*

gespie[e]n 2. *Part. v.* speien

gesponnen 2. *Part. v.* spinnen

Gespött das; ~[e]s mockery; ridicule

Gespräch das; ~[e]s, ~e conversation; *(Diskussion)* discussion; *(Telefon~)* call (mit to); **gesprächig** *Adj.* talkative

Gesprächs-: ~**partner** der: mein heutiger ~partner wird X sein today I shall be talking to X; ~**stoff** der topics *pl.* of conversation; ~**thema** das topic of conversation

gesprochen 2. *Part. v.* sprechen

gesprossen 2. *Part. v.* sprießen

gesprungen 2. *Part. v.* springen

Gespür das; ~s feel

gest. *Abk.* gestorben d.

Gestalt die; ~, ~en a) build; b) *(Mensch, Persönlichkeit)* figure; c) *(in der Dichtung)* character; d) *(Form)* form; **gestalten** *tr. V.* fashion; lay out *(public gardens)*; shape *(character, personality)*; arrange *(party, conference, etc.)*; **Gestaltung** die; ~, ~en s. **gestalten:** fashioning; laying out; arranging

gestand 1. u. 3. Pers. Sg. Prät. v. gestehen

gestanden 2. *Part. v.* stehen, gestehen

geständig *Adj.:* ~ sein have confessed; **Geständnis** das; ~ses, ~se confession

Gestank der; ~[e]s *(abwertend)* stench; stink

gestatten 1. *tr., itr. V.* permit; allow; ~ Sie, daß ich ...: may I ...?; 2. *refl. V.* sich *(Dat.)* etw. ~: allow oneself sth.

Geste ['gɛstə, 'geːstə] die; ~, ~n *(auch fig.)* gesture

Gesteck das; ~[e]s, ~e flower arrangement

gestehen *tr., itr. V.* confess

Gestein das; ~[e]s, ~e rock

Gestell das; ~[e]s, ~e a) *(für Weinflaschen)* rack; *(zum Wäschetrocknen)* horse; b) *(Unterbau)* frame

gestern *Adv.* yesterday

gestiegen 2. *Part. v.* steigen

gestikulieren *itr. V.* gesticulate

Gestirn das; ~[e]s, ~e star

gestochen 1. 2. *Part. v.* stechen; 2. *Adj.* extremely neat *(handwriting)*

gestohlen 2. *Part. v.* stehlen

gestorben 2. *Part. v.* sterben

gestoßen 2. *Part. v.* stoßen

Gesträuch das; ~[e]s, ~e shrubbery; bushes *pl.*

gestreift *Adj.* striped

gestrichen 1. 2. *Part. v.* streichen; 2. *Adj.* level *(measure)*

gestrig *Adj.* yesterday's

gestritten 2. *Part. v.* streiten

Gestrüpp das; ~[e]s, ~e undergrowth

gestunken 2. *Part. v.* stinken

Gestüt das; ~[e]s, ~e stud[-farm]

Gesuch das; ~[e]s, ~e request (um for); *(Antrag)* application (um for); **gesucht** *Adj.* a) [much] sought-after; b) *(gekünstelt)* laboured

gesund; gesünder, *seltener:* ~er, **gesündest...,** *seltener:* ~est... *Adj.* healthy; **wieder** ~ **werden** get better; **bleib** ~! look after yourself!; **Gesundheit** die; ~: health; ~! *(ugs.)* bless you!; **gesundheitlich** 1. *Adj.: nicht präd.* ~e Betreuung health care; **sein** ~er Zustand [the state of] his health; 2. *adv.* wie geht es Ihnen ~? how are you?

gesundheits-, Gesundheits-: ~**amt** das [local] public health department; ~**schädlich** *Adj.* detrimental to [one's] health *postpos.;* ~**zeugnis** das certificate of health; ~**zustand** der state of health

gesungen 2. *Part. v.* singen

gesunken 2. *Part. v.* sinken

getan 2. *Part. v.* tun

Getier das; ~[e]s *(geh.)* animals *pl.*

Getöse das; ~s [thundery] roar; *(von vielen Menschen)* din

getragen 2. *Part. v.* tragen

Getränk das; ~[e]s, ~e drink; beverage *(formal)*

getrauen *refl. V.* dare

Getreide das; ~s grain

Getreide-: ~**anbau** der growing of cereals; ~**handel** der corn-trade

getrennt 1. *Adj.* separate; **2.** *adv.* ⟨*pay*⟩ separately; ⟨*sleep*⟩ in separate rooms

getreten *2. Part. v.* **treten**

getreu 1. *Adj. (geh.)* exact; faithful ⟨*image*⟩; **2.** *adv. (geh.)* ⟨*report, describe*⟩ faithfully

Getriebe das; ~s, ~ gears *pl.; (in einer Maschine)* gear system; **getrieben** *2. Part. v.* **treiben**

getroffen *2. Part. v.* **treffen, triefen**

getrogen *2. Part. v.* **trügen**

getrost 1. *Adj.* confident; **2.** *adv.* confidently; **du kannst es mir ~ glauben** you can take my word for it

getrunken *2. Part. v.* **trinken**

Getto das; ~s, ~s ghetto

Getue das; ~s *(ugs. abwertend)* fuss (um about)

Getümmel das; ~s tumult

geübt *Adj.* accomplished; practised ⟨*eye, ear*⟩

Gewächs das; ~es, ~e plant; **gewachsen 1.** *2. Part. v.* **wachsen; 2.** in **jmdm./einer Sache ~ sein** be a match for sb./be equal to sth.

gewagt *Adj.* daring; *(gefährlich)* risky; *(fast anstößig)* risqué ⟨*joke etc.*⟩

gewählt *Adj.* refined; **2.** *adv.* in a refined manner

Gewähr die; ~: guarantee; **keine ~ übernehmen** be unable to guarantee sth.; **gewähren** *tr. V.* **a)** grant; give ⟨*pleasure, joy*⟩; **gewähr·leisten** *tr. V.* guarantee

Gewahrsam der; ~s **a)** *(Obhut)* safekeeping; **b)** *(Haft)* custody

Gewährs·mann der; *Pl.* ~männer *od.* ~leute informant; source

Gewalt die; ~, ~en **a)** power; **b)** *o. Pl. (Willkür)* force; **c)** *o. Pl. (körperliche Kraft)* force; violence; **Gewalt·anwendung** die use of force *or* violence; **Gewalten·teilung** die separation of powers; **gewaltig 1.** *Adj.* **a)** *(immens)* huge; **b)** *(imponierend)* mighty, huge, massive ⟨*building etc*⟩; monumental ⟨*literary work etc.*⟩; **2.** *adv. (ugs.)* very much; **gewalt·los 1.** *Adj.* non-violent; **2.** *adv.* without violence; **Gewalt·losigkeit** die; ~: non-violence; **gewaltsam 1.** *Adj.* forcible ⟨*expulsion*⟩; enforced ⟨*separation*⟩; violent ⟨*death*⟩; **2.** *adv.* forcibly; **gewalt·tätig** *Adj.* violent

Gewand das; ~⟨e⟩s, **Gewänder** *(geh.)* robe; gown

gewandt 1. *2. Part. v.* **wenden; 2.** *Adj.* skilful; *(körperlich)* agile; **3.** *adv.* skilfully; *(körperlich)* agilely; **Gewandtheit** die; ~: s. **gewandt 2:** skill; skilfulness; agility

gewann *1. u. 3. Pers. Sg. Prät. v.* **gewinnen**

gewaschen *2. Part. v.* **waschen**

Gewässer das; ~s, ~: stretch of water

Gewebe das; ~s, ~ **a)** *(Stoff)* fabric; **b)** *(Med., Biol.)* tissue

Gewehr das; ~⟨e⟩s, ~e rifle; *(Schrot~)* shotgun

Geweih das; ~⟨e⟩s, ~e antlers *pl.*

Gewerbe das; ~s, ~: business; *(Handel, Handwerk)* trade

Gewerbe-: ~**freiheit** die right to carry on a business *or* trade; ~**ordnung** die laws *pl.* governing trade and industry; ~**schein** der licence to carry on a business *or* trade; ~**treibende** der/die; *adj. Dekl.* tradesman/tradeswoman; ~**zweig** der branch of trade

gewerblich 1. *Adj.* commercial; business *attrib.; (industriell)* industrial; **2.** *adv.* ~ **tätig sein** work; **gewerbs·mäßig** *Adj.* professional

Gewerkschaft die; ~, ~en trade union; **Gewerkschaft⟨l⟩er** der; ~s, ~: trade unionist; **gewerkschaftlich 1.** *Adj.* [trade] union *attrib.;* **2.** *adv.:* ~ **organisiert sein** belong to a [trade] union; **Gewerkschaftsfunktionär** der [trade] union official

gewesen *2. Part. v.* ¹**sein**

gewichen *2. Part. v.* **weichen**

Gewicht das; ~⟨e⟩s, ~e *(auch fig.)* weight; **[nicht] ins ~ fallen** be of [no] consequence; **Gewicht·heben** das; ~s weight-lifting; **gewichtig** *Adj.* weighty; **Gewichts·klasse** die *(Sport)* weight [division *or* class]

gewieft *Adj. (ugs.)* cunning

gewiesen *2. Part. v.* **weisen**

gewillt *Adj.* **in ~ [nicht] ~ sein, etw. zu tun** be [un]willing to do sth.

Gewimmel das; ~s throng; *(von Insekten)* teeming mass

Gewinde das; ~s, ~ *(Technik)* thread

Gewinn der; ~⟨e⟩s, ~e **a)** profit; **b)** *(Preis einer Lotterie)* prize; *(beim Spiel)* winnings *pl.;* **c)** *(Sieg)* win; **Gewinn·beteiligung** die *(Wirtsch.)* profit-sharing; *(Betrag)* profit-sharing bonus; **gewinn·bringend** *Adj.* lucrative

gewinnen 1. *unr. tr. V.* win; gain

⟨time, influence, validity, etc.⟩; 2. *unr. itr. V.* win (**bei** at); **gewinnend** *Adj.* winning; **Gewinner der; ~s, ~**: winner

Gewinn-: **~spanne** die profit margin; **~sucht** die greed for profit; **~zahl** die winning number

Gewirr das; **~[e]s** a) tangle; b) *(Durcheinander)* ein **~** von Ästen a maze of branches

gewiß 1. *Adj.* certain; 2. *adv.* certainly

Gewissen das; **~s, ~**: conscience; **gewissenhaft** 1. *Adj.* conscientious; 2. *adv.* conscientiously; **gewissen·los** *Adj.* unscrupulous; **Gewissens·bisse** *Pl.* pangs of conscience

gewissermaßen *Adv. (sozusagen)* as it were; *(in gewissem Sinne)* to a certain extent; **Gewißheit die; ~, ~en** certainty

Gewitter das; **~s, ~**: thunderstorm; **Gewitter·wolke** die thundercloud; **gewittrig** *Adj.* thundery

gewitzt *Adj.* shrewd

gewoben 2. *Part. v.* weben

gewogen 1. 2. *Part. v.* wiegen; 2. *Adj. (geh.)* well disposed (+ *Dat.* towards)

gewöhnen 1. *tr. V.* jmdn. an jmdn./ etw. **~**: get sb. used to sb./sth.; accustom sb. to sb./sth.; 2. *refl. V.* sich an jmdn./etw. **~**: get used *or* get *or* become accustomed to sb./sth.; accustom oneself to sb./sth.; **Gewöhnheit die; ~, ~en** habit; **gewohnheits·mäßig** 1. *Adj.* habitual ⟨drinker etc.⟩; automatic ⟨reaction etc.⟩; 2. *adv. (regelmäßig)* habitually; **gewöhnlich** 1. *Adj.* a) normal; ordinary; b) *(gewohnt, üblich)* usual; c) *(abwertend: ordinär)* common; 2. *adv.* a) |für| **~**: usually; wie **~**: as usual; b) *(abwertend: ordinär)* in a common way

gewohnt *Adj.* a) usual; b) etw. *(Akk.)* **~** sein be used to sth.

Gewölbe das; **~s, ~**: vault

gewonnen 2. *Part. v.* gewinnen

geworben 2. *Part. v.* werben

geworfen 2. *Part. v.* werfen

gewrungen 2. *Part. v.* wringen

Gewühl das; **~[e]s** milling crowd

gewunden 2. *Part. v.* winden

Gewürz das; **~es, ~e** spice; *(würzende Zutat)* seasoning

Gewürz-: **~gurke** die pickled gherkin; **~nelke** die clove

gewußt 2. *Part. v.* wissen

gez. *Abk.* gezeichnet sgd.

Gezeiten *Pl.* tides

gezielt 1. *Adj.* specific ⟨questions, measures, etc.⟩; deliberate ⟨insult, indiscretion⟩; well-directed ⟨advertising campaign⟩; 2. *adv.* ⟨proceed, act⟩ purposefully

geziemen *(geh. veralt.)* 1. *itr. V.* jmdm. |nicht| **~**: [ill] befit sb; 2. *refl. V.* be proper; sich für jmdn. **~**: befit sb.

geziert 1. *Adj. (abwertend)* affected; 2. *adv. (abwertend)* affectedly

gezogen 2. *Part. v.* ziehen

Gezwitscher das; **~s** twittering

gezwungen 1. 2. *Part. v.* zwingen; 2. *Adj.* forced; **gezwungenermaßen** *Adv.* of necessity

gib *Imperativ Sg. Präsens v.* geben; **gibst** 2. *Pers. Sg. Präsens v.* geben; **gibt** 3. *Pers. Sg. Präsens v.* geben

Gicht die; **~**: gout

Giebel der; **~s, ~**: gable

Gier die; **~**: greed (**nach** for); **gierig** 1. *Adj.* greedy; 2. *adv.* greedily

gießen 1. *unr. tr. V.* a) pour (**in** + *Akk.* into, **über** + *Akk.* over); b) *(verschütten)* spill (**über** + *Akk.* over); c) *(begießen)* water; 2. *(unpers., ugs.)* pour [with rain]

Gießer der; **~s, ~**: caster; **Gießerei** die; **~, ~en** foundry

Gift das; **~[e]s, ~e** a) poison; *(Schlangen~)* venom; **gift·grün** *Adj.* garish green; **giftig** *Adj.* poisonous; venomous ⟨snake⟩; toxic, poisonous ⟨substance, gas, chemical⟩; *(fig.)* venomous

Gift-: **~müll** der toxic waste; **~schlange** die venomous snake; **~zahn** der poison fang

Gigant der; **~en, ~en** giant; **gigantisch** *Adj.* gigantic

Gilde die; **~, ~n** *(hist.)* guild

gilt 3. *Pers. Sg. Präsens v.* gelten

Gimpel der; **~s, ~**: bullfinch

Gin [dʒɪn] der; **~s** gin

ging 1. u. 3. *Pers. Sg. Prät. v.* gehen

Ginster der; **~s, ~**: broom

Gipfel der; **~s, ~**: peak; *(höchster Punkt des Berges)* summit; *(fig.)* height; **Gipfel·konferenz** die summit conference; **gipfeln** *itr. V.* in etw. *(Dat.)* **~**: culminate in sth.

Gips der; **~es, ~e** plaster; gypsum *(Chem.)*; **Gips·abdruck** der plaster cast; **gipsen** *tr. V.* plaster; put ⟨leg, arm, etc.⟩ in plaster; **Gips·verband** der plaster cast

Giraffe die; **~, ~n** giraffe

Girlande die; ~, ~n festoon

Giro ['ʒiːro] das; ~s, ~s, österr. auch **Giri** (Finanzw.) giro; **Giro·konto** das (Finanzw.) current account

gis, Gis das; ~, ~ (Musik) G sharp

Gischt der; ~[e]s, ~e od. die; ~, ~en spray

Gitarre die; ~, ~n guitar

Gitter das; ~s, ~: bars pl.; (vor Fenster-, Türöffnungen) grille; (in der Straßendecke, im Fußboden) grating; (Geländer) railing[s pl.]; **Gitter·fenster** das barred window

Glacé·hand·schuh [glaˈseː...] der kid glove

Gladiole die; ~, ~n gladiolus

Glanz der; ~es a) (von Licht, Sternen, Augen) brightness; (von Haar, Metall, Perlen, Leder usw.) lustre; sheen; b) (der Jugend, Schönheit) radiance; (des Adels usw.) splendour; **glänzen** itr. V. a) (Glanz ausstrahlen) shine; ⟨hair, metal, etc.⟩ gleam; ⟨elbows, trousers, etc.⟩ be shiny; b) (Bewunderung erregen) shine (bei at); **glänzend** (ugs.) 1. Adj. a) shining; gleaming ⟨hair, metal, etc.⟩; shiny ⟨elbows, trousers, etc.⟩; b) (bewundernswert) brilliant; splendid ⟨references, marks, results, etc.⟩; 2. adv. ~ mit jmdm. auskommen get on very well with sb.; **es geht mir/uns** ~ I am/we are very well

glanz-, Glanz-: ~**leistung** die (auch iron.) brilliant performance; ~**los** Adj. dull; lacklustre; ~**nummer die** star turn; ~**voll** 1. Adj. brilliant; sparkling ⟨variety number⟩; 2. adv. brilliantly

Glas das; ~es, Gläser a) o. Pl. glass; b) (Trinkgefäß) glass; zwei ~ od. Gläser Wein two glasses of wine; c) (Behälter) jar; **Glas·bläser der** glassblower; **Gläschen** ['glɛːsçən] das; ~s, ~ a) [little] glass; b) (kleines Gefäß) [little] [glass] jar; **Glaser der**; ~s, ~: glazier; **gläsern** Adj. glass; **Glas·faser** die; meist Pl. glass fibre; **glasieren** tr. V. a) glaze; b) (Kochk.) ice; glaze ⟨meat⟩; **glasig** Adj. a) glassy; b) (Kochk.) transparent; **Glas·malerei** die stained glass; **Glasur** die; ~, ~en a) glaze; b) (Kochk.) icing; (auf Fleisch) glaze

glatt 1. Adj. a) smooth; (rutschig) slippery; b) (ugs.: offensichtlich) downright ⟨lie⟩; outright ⟨deception, fraud⟩; flat ⟨refusal⟩; 2. adv. a) smoothly; b) (ugs.: rückhaltlos) jmdm. etw. ~ ins Gesicht sagen tell sb. sth. straight to

his/her face ⟨reject, deny⟩ flatly; **Glätte** die; ~: smoothness; (Rutschigkeit) slipperiness; **Glatt·eis** das glaze; ice; (auf der Straße) black ice; **glätten** tr. V. smooth out ⟨piece of paper, etc.⟩; smooth [down] ⟨feathers, fur, etc.⟩; plane ⟨wood etc.⟩

glatt-: ~**gehen** unr. itr. V.; mit sein (ugs.) go smoothly; ~**weg** Adv. (ugs.) etw. ~weg ablehnen/ignorieren turn sth. down flat/simply ignore sth.; **das ist** ~**weg erlogen/erfunden** that's a downright lie/that's pure invention

Glatze die; ~, ~n bald head

Glaube der; ~ns faith (an + Akk. in); (Überzeugung, Meinung) belief (an + Akk. in); **glauben** 1. tr. V. (meinen) think; 2. itr. V. believe (an + Akk. in)

Glaubens-: ~**bekenntnis** das creed; ~**freiheit** die; o. Pl. religious freedom

glaubhaft 1. Adj. credible; 2. adv. convincingly; **gläubig** 1. Adj. devout; (vertrauensvoll) trusting; 2. adv. devoutly; (vertrauensvoll) trustingly; **Gläubige** der/die; adj. Dekl. believer; **Gläubiger der**; ~s, ~ creditor

glaub·würdig 1. Adj. credible; 2. adv. convincingly

gleich 1. Adj. a) (identisch, von derselben Art) same; ⟨~berechtigt, ~wertig, Math.⟩; b) (ugs.: gleichgültig) es ist mir völlig od. ganz ~: I couldn't care less (coll.); ganz ~, wer anruft, ...: no matter who calls, ...; 2. adv. a) (übereinstimmend) ~ groß/alt usw. sein be the same height/age etc.; ~ gut/schlecht usw. equally good/bad etc.; b) (in derselben Weise) ~ aufgebaut/gekleidet having the same structure/wearing identical clothes; c) (sofort) at once; straight away; (bald) in a moment; d) (räumlich) right; just; ~ rechts/links immediately on the right/left

gleich-, Gleich-: ~**alt[e]rig** [~alt[ə]rɪç] Adj. of the same age (mit as); ~**artig** 1. Adj. of the same kind postpos. (+ Dat. as); (sehr ähnlich) very similar (+ Dat. to); 2. adv. in the same way; ~**berechtigt** Adj. having equal rights postpos.; ~**berechtigte Partner** equal partners; ~**berechtigung** die equal rights pl.; ~**bleiben** unr. itr. V.; mit sein remain the same; ⟨speed, temperature, etc.⟩ remain constant; ~**bleibend** Adj. constant; steady ⟨temperature, speed, etc.⟩;

gleichen unr. itr. V. jmdm./einer Sache ~: be like *or* resemble sb./sth.; **gleichermaßen** *Adv.* equally

gleich-, Gleich-: ~falls *Adv. (auch)* also; *(ebenfalls)* likewise; **danke ~falls!** thank you, [and] the same to you; ~förmig 1. *Adj.* a) *(einheitlich)* uniform; b) *(monoton)* monotonous; 2. *adv.* a) *(einheitlich)* uniformly; b) *(monoton)* monotonously; ~ge-schlechtlich *Adj.* homosexual; ~gewicht das; *o. Pl.* balance; ~ge-wichts·störung die disturbance of one's sense of balance; ~gültig 1. *Adj.* indifferent (**gegenüber** towards); *(belanglos)* trivial; **das ist mir [vollkommen] ~:** it's a matter of [complete] indifference to me; 2. *adv.* indifferently; ~gültigkeit die indifference (**gegenüber** towards)

Gleichheit die; ~, ~en a) identity; *(Ähnlichkeit)* similarity; b) *o. Pl. (gleiche Rechte)* equality; **Gleichheits-zeichen das** equals sign

gleich-, Gleich-: ~|kommen *unr. itr. V.; mit sein* a) *(entsprechen)* be tantamount to; b) *(die gleiche Leistung erreichen)* **jmdm./einer Sache [an etw. (Dat.)]** ~kommen equal sb./sth. [in sth.]; ~|machen *tr. V.* make equal; ~mäßig 1. *Adj.* regular *(interval, rhythm)*; uniform *(acceleration, distribution)*; even *(heat)*; 2. *adv.* regularly; **etw. ~mäßig verteilen/auftragen** distribute sth. equally/apply sth. evenly; ~mut der equanimity

Gleichnis das; ~ses, ~se *(Allegorie)* allegory; *(Parabel)* parable; **gleichsam** *Adv. (geh.)* as it were

gleich-, Gleich-: ~|schalten *tr. V.* force into line; ~schenk[e]lig *Adj.* (*Math.*) isosceles; ~schritt der; *o. Pl.* marching in step; ~seitig *Adj.* (*Math.*) equilateral; ~|setzen *tr. V.* equate; ~|stellen *tr. V.* equate; ~strom der *(Elektrot.)* direct current

Gleichung die; ~, ~en equation

gleich-: ~wertig *Adj.* of the same value *postpos.;* ~wohl *[-'- od. '--] Adv.* nevertheless; ~zeitig 1. *Adj.* simultaneous; 2. *adv.* at the same time

Gleis das; ~es, ~e track *fig.;* *(Bahnsteig)* platform; *(einzelne Schiene)* rail

gleiten *unr. itr. V.; mit sein* glide; *(hand)* slide; **Gleit·flug** der glide

Gletscher der; ~s, ~: glacier; **Gletscher·spalte** die crevasse

glich *1. u. 3. Pers. Sg. Prät. v.* gleichen

Glied das; ~[e]s, ~er a) limb; *(Finger~, Zehen~)* joint; b) *(Ketten~, auch fig.)*

link; c) *(Teil eines Ganzen)* section; *(Mitglied)* member; **gliedern** 1. *tr. V.* structure; organize *(thoughts)*; 2. *refl. V.* **sich in Gruppen/Abschnitte** *usw.* ~: be divided into groups/sections *etc.;* **Gliederung** die; ~, ~en structure

Glied-: ~maße [-ma:sə] die; ~, ~n limb; ~satz der *(Sprachw.)* subordinate clause

glimmen *unr. od. regelm. itr. V.* glow; **Glimm·stengel** der *(ugs. scherzh.)* fag *(sl.);* ciggy *(coll.)*

glimpflich 1. *Adj.* a) **der Unfall nahm ein ~es Ende** the accident turned out not to be too serious; b) *(mild)* lenient *(sentence, punishment);* 2. *adv.* a) *(ohne Schaden)* ~ **davonkommen** get off lightly; b) *(mild)* leniently

glitschig *Adj. (ugs.)* slippery

glitt *1. u. 3. Pers. Sg. Prät. v.* gleiten

glitzern *itr. V. (star)* twinkle; *(diamond, decorations)* sparkle; *(snow, eyes, tears)* glisten

global 1. *Adj.* a) *(global;* world-wide; b) *(umfassend)* all-round *(education);* overall *(control, planning, etc.);* c) *(allgemein)* general; 2. *adv.* a) world-wide; b) *(umfassend)* in overall terms; c) *(allgemein)* in general terms; **Globen** s. Globus

Globetrotter der; ~s, ~: globetrotter

Globus der; ~ *od.* ~ses, **Globen** globe

Glöckchen das; ~s, ~: [little] bell; **Glocke** die; ~, ~n bell

Glocken-: ~blume die *(Bot.)* campanula; ~rock der widely flared skirt; ~spiel das a) carillon; *(mit einer Uhr gekoppelt auch)* chimes *pl.;* b) *(Instrument)* glockenspiel

glomm *1. u. 3. Pers. Sg. Prät. v.* glimmen

Glorien·schein der glory; *(um den Kopf, fig.)* halo; **glorifizieren** *tr. V.* glorify; **Glorifizierung** die; ~, ~en glorification; **glor·reich** 1. *Adj.* glorious; 2. *adv.* gloriously

Glossar das; ~s, ~e glossary

Glosse die; ~, ~n commentary; *(spöttische Bemerkung)* sneering comment

glotzen *itr. V. (abwertend)* goggle; gawp *(coll.)*

Glück das; ~[e]s a) luck; **[es ist] ein ~, daß...:** it's lucky that ...; **[kein] ~ haben** be [un]lucky; **viel ~!** [the] best of luck!; b) happiness

Glucke die; ~, ~n brood-hen

glücken *tr. V.; mit sein* succeed; **etw. glückt jmdm.** sb. is successful with sth.

gluckern *itr. V.* gurgle; glug

glücklich 1. *Adj.* **a)** happy (über + *Akk.* about); **b)** *(erfolgreich)* lucky *⟨winner⟩;* successful *⟨outcome⟩;* safe *⟨journey⟩;* **c)** *(vorteilhaft)* fortunate; **2.** *adv.* **a)** *(erfolgreich)* successfully; **b)** *(vorteilhaft, zufrieden)* happily *⟨chosen, married⟩;* **glücklicher·weise** *Adv.* fortunately; luckily; **glück·selig 1.** *Adj.* blissfully happy; **2.** *adv.* blissfully; **Glück·selig·keit** die; ~: bliss

glucksen *itr. V.* **a)** *s.* gluckern; **b)** *(lachen)* chuckle

Glücks-: **~klee** der four-leaf clover; **~pfennig** der lucky penny; **~pilz** der *(ugs.)* lucky devil *(coll.)*

Glück[s]·sache die: das ist ~: it's a matter of luck; **Glücks·spiel** das game of chance; **glück·strahlend** *Adj.* radiantly happy; **Glücks·zahl** die lucky number; **Glück·wunsch** der congratulations *pl.;* herzlichen ~ zum Geburtstag! happy birthday!

Glüh·birne die light-bulb; **glühen** *itr. V.* glow; **glühend 1.** *Adj.* red-hot *⟨metal etc.⟩;* blazing *⟨heat⟩;* ardent *⟨admirer etc.⟩;* passionate *⟨words, letter, etc.⟩;* **2.** *adv.* *⟨love⟩* passionately; *⟨admire⟩* ardently; ~ heiß blazing hot; **Glüh·wein** der mulled wine

Glut die; ~, ~en **a)** embers *pl.;* **b)** *(geh.) Leidenschaft)* passion; **glut·rot** *Adj.* fiery red

Glyzerin das; ~s glycerine

GmbH *Abk.* **Gesellschaft mit beschränkter Haftung** ≈ p.l.c.

Gnade die; ~, ~n *(Gunst)* favour; *(Rel.)* grace; *(Milde)* mercy

gnaden-, Gnaden-: **~brot** das: jmdm./einem Tier das ~brot geben keep sb./an animal in his/ her/its old age; **~frist** die reprieve; **~gesuch** das plea for clemency; **~los** *(auch fig.)* **1.** *Adj.* merciless; **2.** *adv.* mercilessly; **~schuß** der coup de grâce *(by shooting)*

gnädig *Adj.* gracious; *(glimpflich)* lenient *⟨sentence etc.⟩*

Gnom der; ~en, ~en gnome

Gockel der; ~s, ~ *(bes. südd., sonst ugs. scherzh.)* cock

Gold das; ~[e]s gold; **Gold·barren** der gold bar; **golden 1.** *Adj.* *(aus Gold)* gold; *(herrlich)* golden *⟨days, memories, etc.⟩;* **2.** *adv.* like gold

Gold-: **~grube** die *(auch fig.)* goldmine; **~hamster** der golden hamster

goldig *Adj.* sweet

gold-, Gold-: **~richtig** *(ugs.) Adj.*

absolutely right; **~schmied** der goldsmith; **~schnitt** der gilt; **~währung,** die *(Wirtsch.)* currency tied to the gold standard

¹Golf der; ~[e]s, ~e gulf

²Golf das; ~s *(Sport)* golf

Golf-: **~platz** der golf-course; **~schläger** der golf club; **~spieler** der, **~spielerin** die golfer; **~strom** der Gulf Stream

Gondel die; ~, ~n gondola; **gondeln** *itr. V.;* mit sein *(ugs.)* **a)** *(mit einem Boot)* cruise; **b)** *(reisen)* travel around; **c)** *(herumfahren)* cruise around

Gong der; ~s, ~s gong; **gongen** *itr. V.* es hat gegongt the gong has sounded

gönnen *tr. V.* jmdm. etw. ~: not begrudge sb. sth.; sich/jmdm. etw. ~: allow oneself/sb. sth.; **Gönner** der; ~s, ~: patron; **gönnerhaft** *(abwertend) Adj.* patronizing

gor *3. Pers. Sg. Prät. v.* gären

Göre die; ~, ~n *(nordd., oft abwertend)* kid *(coll.)*

Gorilla der; ~s, ~s gorilla

goß *1. u. 3. Pers. Sg. Prät. v.* gießen

Gosse die; ~, ~n gutter

Gotik die; ~ *(Stil)* Gothic [style]; *(Epoche)* Gothic period; **gotisch** *Adj.* Gothic

Gott der; ~es, Götter **a)** *o. Pl.; o. Art.* God; grüß |dich| ~! *(landsch.)* hello!; um ~es Willen *(bei Erschrecken)* for God's sake; *(bei einer Bitte)* for heaven's sake; **b)** *(übermenschliches Wesen)* god

Gottes-: **~dienst** der service; **~haus** das *(geh.)* house of God; **~lästerung** die blasphemy

Gottheit die; ~, ~en deity; **Göttin** die; ~, ~nen goddess; **göttlich 1.** *Adj.* *(auch fig.)* divine; **2.** *adv.* divinely

gott-, Gott-: **~lob** *adv.* thank goodness; **~los 1.** *Adj.* **a)** ungodly *(life etc.);* impious *⟨words, speech, etc.⟩;* **b)** *(Gott leugnend)* godless *⟨theory etc.⟩;* **2.** *adv. (verwerflich)* irreverently; **~vater** der God the Father; **~vertrauen** das trust in God

Götze der; ~n, ~n *(auch fig.)* idol; **Götzen-:** **~bild** das idol; **~diener** der idolater

Gouverneur [guvɛrˈnøːɐ̯] der; ~s, ~e governor

Grab das; ~[e]s, Gräber grave; das Heilige ~: the Holy Sepulchre; das ~

des Unbekannten Soldaten the tomb of the Unknown Warrior; **graben** unr. tr., itr. V. dig; **Graben der**; ~s, **Gräben** ditch; (Schützen~) trench; (Festungs~) moat

Grab-: ~**kammer die** burial chamber; ~**mal das**; Pl. ~mäler, geh. ~male monument; ~**stein der** gravestone

gräbst 2. Pers. Sg. Präsens v. **graben**; **gräbt** 3. Pers. Sg. Präsens v. **graben**

Gracht die; ~, ~en canal

Grad der; ~[e]s, ~e degree; (Milit.) rank; **Grad·messer der** gauge, yardstick (für of)

graduell 1. Adj. gradual; slight ⟨difference etc.⟩; 2. adv. gradually; ⟨different⟩ in degree; **graduiert** Adj. graduate; **ein** ~**er Ingenieur** an engineering graduate

Graf der; ~en, ~en count; (britischer ~) earl

Grafik usw. s. **Graphik** usw.

Gräfin die; ~, ~nen countess; **Grafschaft die**; ~, ~en a) count's land; (in Großbritannien) earldom; b) (Verwaltungsbezirk) county

Gram der; ~[e]s (geh.) grief; sorrow; **grämen** 1. tr. V. grieve; 2. refl. V. grieve (über + Akk., um over)

Gramm das; ~s, ~e gram

Grammatik die; ~, ~en grammar; **grammatisch** 1. Adj. grammatical; 2. adv. grammatically

Grammophon ⓦ **das**; ~s, ~e gramophone; phonograph (Amer.)

Granat der; ~[e]s, ~e (Schmuckstein) garnet; **Granat·apfel der** pomegranate

Granate die; ~, ~n shell; (Hand~) grenade

grandios 1. Adj. magnificent; 2. adv. magnificently

Granit der; ~s, ~e granite

grantig (südd., österr. ugs.) 1. Adj. bad-tempered; 2. adv. bad-temperedly

Graphik die; ~, ~en graphic art[s pl.]; (Kunstwerk) graphic; (Druck) print; **Graphiker der**; ~s, ~, **Graphikerin die**; ~, ~nen [graphic] designer; (Künstler[in]) graphic artist; **graphisch** 1. Adj. graphic; 2. adv. graphically

Gras das; ~es, Gräser grass; **über etw.** (Akk.) ~ **wachsen lassen** (ugs.) let the dust settle on sth.; **grasen** itr. V. graze; **Gras·halm der** the blade of grass

gräßlich 1. Adj. a) (abscheulich) horrible; terrible ⟨accident⟩; b) (ugs.: un-

angenehm) dreadful (coll.); c) (ugs.: sehr stark) terrible (coll.); 2. adv. a) (abscheulich) horribly; terribly; b) (ugs.: unangenehm) terribly (coll.); c) (ugs.: sehr) terribly (coll.)

Grat der; ~[e]s, ~e ridge

Gräte die; ~, ~n [fish-]bone

Gratifikation die; ~, ~en bonus

gratis Adv. free [of charge]; gratis

Grätsche die; ~, ~n (Turnen) straddle; (Sprung) straddle-vault

Gratulant der; ~en, ~en, **Gratulantin die**; ~, ~nen well-wisher; **Gratulation die**; ~, ~en congratulations pl.; **gratulieren** itr. V. jmdm. ~: congratulate sb.; **jmdm. zum Geburtstag** ~: wish sb. many happy returns [of the day]

grau Adj. grey; (trostlos) dreary; drab

¹**grauen** itr. V. (geh.) **der Morgen/der Tag graut** morning/day is breaking

²**grauen** itr. V. (unpers.) **ihm graut [es] davor/vor ihr** he dreads [the thought of] it/he's terrified of her; **Grauen das**; ~s, ~: horror (vor + Dat. of); **grauen·haft** 1. Adj. horrifying; (ugs.: sehr unangenehm) terrible (coll.); 2. adv. horrifyingly; (ugs.: sehr unangenehm) terribly (coll.)

grau-: ~**haarig** Adj. grey-haired; ~**meliert** Adj. (präd. getrennt geschrieben) greying ⟨hair⟩

Graupe die; ~, ~n a) grain of pearl barley; b) Pl. (Gericht) pearl barley sing.

graupeln itr. V. (unpers.) **es graupelt** there's soft hail falling

grausam 1. Adj. a) cruel; b) (furchtbar) terrible; dreadful; 2. adv. a) cruelly; b) (furchtbar) terribly, dreadfully; **Grausamkeit die**; ~, ~en a) o. Pl. cruelty; b) (Handlung) act of cruelty

grausen 1. tr., itr. V. (unpers.) **es grauste ihm od. ihn davor/vor ihr** he dreaded it/he was terrified of her; 2. refl. V. **sich vor etw./jmdm.** ~: dread sth./be terrified of sb.; **Grausen das**; ~s horror; **grausig** s. **grauenhaft**

gravieren tr. V. engrave; **gravierend** Adj. serious, grave; **Gravierung die**; ~, ~en engraving

Gravitation die; ~ (Physik, Astron.) gravitation

Gravur [gra'vuːɐ] **die**; ~, ~en engraving

Grazie ['graːtsi̯ə] **die**; ~, ~n a) o. Pl. (Anmut) gracefulness; b) Pl. (Myth.) Graces

greifen 1. *unr. tr. V.* a) *(er~)* take hold of; grasp; *(rasch ~)* seize; b) *(fangen)* catch; 2. *unr. itr. V.* a) in/unter/hinter etw./sich *(Akk.)* ~: reach into/under/behind sth./one; **nach etw.** ~: reach for sth.; *(hastig)* make a grab for sth.; b) *(Technik)* grip

Greis der; ~es, ~e old man; **Greisin** die; ~, ~nen old woman

grell 1. *Adj.* a) *(hell)* glaring, ⟨light, sun, etc.⟩; b) *(auffallend)* garish ⟨colour etc.⟩; loud ⟨dress, pattern, etc.⟩; c) *(schrill)* shrill, ⟨cry, voice, etc.⟩; 2. *adv.* a) *(hell)* with glaring brightness; b) *(auffallend)* **gegen od. von etw.** ~ **abstechen** contrast sharply with sth.; c) *(schrill)* shrilly

Gremium das; ~s, Gremien committee

Grenze die; ~, ~n a) boundary; *(Staats~)* border; *(gedachte Trennungslinie)* borderline; b) *(fig.)* limit; **grenzen** *itr. V.* **an etw.** *(Akk.)* ~: border [on] sth.; **grenzen·los** 1. *Adj.* boundless; *(fig.)* boundless, unbounded ⟨joy, wonder, jealousy, grief, etc.⟩; unlimited ⟨wealth, power⟩; limitless ⟨patience, ambition⟩; extreme ⟨tiredness, anger, foolishness⟩; 2. *adv.* endlessly; *(fig.)* beyond all measure; **Grenzen·losigkeit** die; ~: boundlessness

Grenz-: ~**übergang** der border crossing-point; ~**verkehr** der [cross-]border traffic

Greuel der; ~s, ~ a) etw./jmd. ist jmdm. ein ~: sb. loathes *or* detests sth./sb.; b) *meist Pl.* *(fig.)* *(~tat)* atrocity; **Greuel·tat** die atrocity; **greulich** 1. *Adj.* a) *(horrifying)* b) *(unangenehm)* awful; 2. *adv.* a) horrifyingly; b) *(unangenehm)* terribly

Grieche der; ~n, ~n Greek; **Griechen·land** (das); ~s Greece; **griechisch** 1. *Adj.* Greek; 2. *adv.* ⟨speak, write⟩ in Greek; **Griechisch** das; ~|s| Greek *no art.*

griesgrämig 1. *Adj.* grumpy; 2. *adv.* in a grumpy manner

Grieß der; ~es, ~e semolina; **Grieß·brei** der semolina

griff 1 *u.* 3. *Pers. Sg. Prät. v.* greifen; **Griff** der; ~|e|s, ~e a) grip; grasp; b) *(Knauf, Henkel)* handle; **griff·bereit** *Adj.* ready to hand *postpos.*

Griffel der; ~s, ~: slate-pencil

griffig *Adj.* a) *(handlich)* handy; b) *(gut greifend)* that grips well *postpos., not pred.*; non-slip ⟨surface, floor⟩

Grill der; ~s, ~s grill; *(Rost)* barbecue

Grille die; ~, ~n a) cricket; b) *(sonderbarer Einfall)* whim

grillen 1. *tr. V.* grill; 2. *itr. V.* **im Garten** ~: have a barbecue in the garden

Grimasse die; ~, ~n grimace

grimmig 1. *Adj.* furious ⟨person⟩; grim ⟨expression⟩; 2. *adv.* grimly

grinsen *itr. V.* grin; *(höhnisch)* smirk

Grippe die; ~, ~n a) influenza; flu *(coll.)*; b) *(volkst.: Erkältung)* cold

Grips der; ~es brains *pl.*

grob 1. *Adj.* a) *(coarse; thick ⟨wire⟩;* rough ⟨work⟩; b) *(ungefähr)* rough; c) *(schwerwiegend)* gross; flagrant ⟨lie⟩; d) *(barsch)* rude; 2. *adv.* a) coarsely; b) *(ungefähr)* roughly; c) *(schwerwiegend)* grossly; d) *(barsch)* rudely; **Grobheit** die; ~, ~en a) *o. Pl.* rudeness; b) *(Äußerung)* rude remark

Grobian der; ~|e|s, ~e lout

Grog der; ~s, ~s grog

grölen 1. *tr. V.* *(ugs. abwertend)* bawl [out]; roar, howl ⟨approval⟩; 2. *itr. V.* bawl

Groll der; ~|e|s *(geh.)* rancour; **grollen** *itr. V.* *(geh.)* a) **|mit| jmdm.** ~: bear a grudge against sb.; b) ⟨thunder⟩ rumble

Grönland (das); ~s Greenland

Gros [gro:] das; ~ [gro:s], ~ [gro:s] bulk

Groschen der; ~s, ~ a) *(österreichische Münze)* groschen; b) *(ugs.: Zehnpfennigstück)* ten-pfennig piece; *(fig.)* penny; cent *(Amer.)*

groß; größer, größt... 1. *Adj.* a) big, large; great ⟨length, width, height⟩; tall ⟨person⟩; wide ⟨selection⟩; 1 m² ~: 1 m² in area; **im ~en und ganzen** by and large; b) *(älter)* big ⟨brother, sister⟩; *(erwachsen)* grown-up; c) *(lange dauernd)* long, lengthy; d) *(intense)* ⟨heat, cold⟩; high ⟨speed⟩; great, major ⟨event, artist, work⟩; 2. *adv.* **ein Wort ~ schreiben** write a word with a capital; *(ugs.: besonders)* greatly; **groß·artig** 1. *Adj.* magnificent; 2. *adv.* magnificently

Großbritannien (das); ~s the United Kingdom; [Great] Britain

Groß·buchstabe der capital [letter]

Größe die; ~, ~n size; *(Höhe, Körper~)* height; *(fig.)* greatness; **die ~ der Katastrophe** the [full] extent of the catastrophe

Groß·eltern *Pl.* grandparents; **Größen·wahn** der delusions *pl.* of grandeur; **größer** *s.* groß

Groß-: ~**fahndung** die large-scale

search; ~handel der wholesale trade; ~händler der wholesaler; ~industrielle der/die; adj. Dekl. big industrialist

Grossist der; ~en, ~en (Kaufmannsspr.) wholesaler

groß-, Groß-: ~macht die great power; ~maul das (ugs. abwertend) big-mouth (coll.); ~mut die; o. Pl.: generosity; ~mütig Adj. generous; ~mutter die grandmother; ~reinemachen das (ugs.) thorough cleaning; ~|schreiben unr. tr. V. (ugs.) in ~geschrieben werden be stressed; s. auch groß 2; ~spurig (abwertend) 1. Adj. boastful; (hochtrabend) pretentious; 2. adv. boastfully; (hochtrabend) pretentiously; ~stadt die city; large town; ~städter der city-dweller

größt... s. groß; Groß·teil der a) (Hauptteil) major part; b) (nicht unerheblicher Teil) large part; größtenteils Adv. for the most part; größt·möglich Adj. greatest possible

groß-, Groß-: ~|tun unr. itr. V. boast; ~vater der grandfather; ~|ziehen unr. tr. V. bring up; raise, rear (animal); ~zügig 1. Adj. generous; grand and spacious (building, garden, etc.); 2. adv. a) generously; b) (weiträumig) on a grand scale; ~zügigkeit die generosity

grotesk 1. Adj. grotesque; 2. adv. grotesquely

Grotte die; ~, ~n grotto

grub 1. u. 3. Pers. Sg. Prät. v. graben; Grübchen das; ~s, ~: dimple; Grube die; ~, ~n pit; (Bergbau) mine

grübeln itr. V. ponder (über + Dat. on, over)

Gruben·arbeiter der miner; mineworker

grüezi Adv. (schweiz.) hallo

Gruft die; ~, Grüfte vault; (in einer Kirche) crypt

grün Adj. green; Grün das; ~s, ~ od. (ugs.) ~s a) green; b) o. Pl. (Pflanzen) greenery; Grün·anlage die green space; (Park) park

Grund der; ~[e]s, Gründe a) ground; (eines Gewässers) bottom; b) (Ursache, Veranlassung) reason

Grund-: ~besitz der a) (Eigentum an Land) ownership of land; b) (Land) land; ~buch das land register

gründen 1. tr. V. a) found; set up, establish (business); start [up] (club); b) (aufbauen) base (plan, theory, etc.)

(auf + Akk. on); 2. itr. V. auf od. in etw. (Dat.) ~: be based on sth. 3. refl. V. sich auf etw. (Akk.) ~: be based on sth.; Gründer der; ~s, ~, Gründerin die; ~, ~nen: founder

grundieren tr. V. prime

grund-, Grund-: ~gesetz das Basic Law; ~kenntnis die; meist Pl. basic knowledge no pl. (in + Dat. of); ~lage die basis; foundation; ~legend 1. Adj. fundamental, basic (für to); seminal (idea, work); 2. adv. fundamentally

gründlich 1. Adj. thorough; 2. adv. thoroughly; Gründlichkeit die; ~: thoroughness

grund·los 1. Adj. groundless; 2. adv. sich ~los aufregen/ängstigen be needlessly agitated/alarmed; Grundnahrungs·mittel das basic food[stuff]

Grün·donnerstag der Maundy Thursday

Grund-: ~prinzip das fundamental principle; ~recht das basic or constitutional right; ~riß der a) (Bauw.) [ground-] plan; b) (Leitfaden) outline; ~satz der principle

grund·sätzlich 1. Adj. a) fundamental (difference, question, etc.); b) (aus Prinzip) (opponent etc.) on principle; c) (allgemein) (agreement etc.) in principle; 2. adv. a) fundamentally; b) (aus Prinzip) on principle; c) (allgemein) in principle

Grund-: ~schule die primary school; ~stein der foundation-stone; ~stück das plot [of land]

Gründung die; ~, ~en s. gründen 1 a: foundation; setting up; establishing; starting [up]

Grund-: ~wasser das (Geol.) ground water; ~zug der essential feature

Grüne das; adj. Dekl. green; im ~n/ins ~: [out] in/into the country

Grün-: ~fläche die green space; (im Park) lawn; ~span der verdigris; ~streifen der central reservation (grassed and often with trees and bushes)

grunzen tr., itr. V. grunt

Gruppe die; ~, ~n a) group; b) (Klassifizierung) class; category

Gruppen-: ~reise die (Touristik) group travel no pl., no art.; ~sieg der (Sport) top place in the group

gruppieren 1. tr. V. arrange; 2. refl. V. form a group/groups; Gruppierung die; ~, ~en grouping

gruselig *Adj.* eerie; creepy; **gruseln 1.** *tr.*, *itr. V. (unpers.)* es gruselt jmdn. *od.* jmdm. sb.'s flesh creeps; **2.** *refl. V.* be frightened

Gruß der; ~es, Grüße **a)** greeting; *(Milit.)* salute; **b)** *(im Brief)* **mit herzlichen Grüßen** [with] best wishes; **mit bestem ~/freundlichen Grüßen** yours sincerely; **grüßen 1.** *tr. V.* **a)** greet; *(Milit.)* salute; **b)** *(Grüße senden)* **grüße deine Eltern** [ganz herzlich] **von mir** please give your parents my [kindest] regards; **2.** *itr. V.* say hello; *(Milit.)* salute

Grütze die; ~, ~n groats *pl.*; **rote ~:** red fruit pudding *(made with fruit juice, fruit and cornflour, etc.)*

gucken *itr. V. (ugs.)* **a)** look; *(heimlich)* peep; **b)** *(hervorsehen)* stick out; **c)** *(dreinschauen)* look; **Guck·loch** das spy-hole

Guerilla [ge'rɪlja] die; ~, ~s guerrilla war; *(Einheit)* guerrilla unit

Gulasch ['gʊlaʃ, 'gu:laʃ] das *od.* der; ~[e]s, ~ *od.* ~s goulash

Gulden der; ~s, ~ guilder

gültig *Adj.* valid; current *(note, coin)*; **Gültigkeit** die; ~: validity; ~ **haben/ erlangen** be/become valid

Gummi der *od.* das; ~s, ~[s] rubber

Gummi-: **~band** das; *Pl.* ~bänder rubber *or* elastic band; *(in Kleidung)* elastic *no indef. art.*; **~bärchen** das jelly baby; **~baum** der rubber plant **gummieren** *tr. V.* gum

Gummi-: **~handschuh** der rubber glove; **~knüppel** der [rubber] truncheon; **~sohle** die rubber sole; **~stiefel** der rubber boot; *(für Regenwetter)* wellington [boot] *(Brit.)*

Gunst die; ~: favour; goodwill; **günstig 1.** *Adj.* favourable; propitious *(sign)*; auspicious *(moment)*; beneficial *(influence)*; good; **2.** *adv.* favourably; **~ beeinflussen** have *or* exert a beneficial influence on sth.

Gurgel die; ~, ~n throat; jmdm. **die ~ zudrücken** throttle sb.; **gurgeln** *itr. V.* gargle

Gurke die; ~, ~n cucumber; *(eingelegt)* gherkin

gurren *itr. V. (auch fig.)* coo

Gurt der; ~[e]s, ~e strap; *(im Auto, Flugzeug)* [seat-]belt; **Gürtel** der; ~s, ~: belt

Gürtel-: **~linie** die waist[line]; **~reifen** der radial[-ply] tyre

GUS [ge:u:'ɛs] *Abk.* Gemeinschaft Unabhängiger Staaten CIS

Guß der; Gusses, Güsse **a)** *(das Gießen)* casting; **b)** *(ugs.: Regenschauer)* downpour

Guß·eisen das cast iron; **guß·eisern** *Adj.* cast-iron

gut; besser, best... 1. *Adj.* good; fine *(wine)*; **ein ~es neues Jahr** a happy new year; **mir ist nicht ~:** I'm not feeling well; **~en Appetit!** enjoy your lunch/dinner *etc.!*; **eine ~e Stunde** [von hier] a good hour [from here]; **2.** *adv.* **a)** well; **b)** *(mühelos)* easily; *s. auch* **besser, best...**

Gut das; ~[e]s, Güter **a)** property; *(Besitztum, auch fig.)* possession; **b)** *(landwirtschaftlicher Grundbesitz)* estate; **c)** *(Fracht~, Ware)* item; **Güter** goods; *(Fracht~)* freight *sing.*; goods *(Brit.)*;

gut-, Gut-: **~achten** das; ~s, ~: [expert's] report; **~artig** *Adj.* **a)** good-natured; **b)** *(nicht gefährlich)* benign; **~aussehend** *Adj.* good-looking; **~bürgerlich** *Adj.* good middle-class; **~bürgerliche Küche** good plain cooking; **~dünken** das; ~s discretion

Güte die; ~: goodness; kindness; *(Qualität)* quality

Güter-: **~abfertigung** die **a)** *(Abfertigung von Waren)* dispatch of freight *or* *(Brit.)* goods; **b)** *(Annahmestelle)* freight *or* *(Brit.)* goods office; **~bahnhof** der freight depot; goods station *(Brit.)*; **~wagen** der goods wagon *(Brit.)*; freight car *(Amer.)*; **~zug** der goods train *(Brit.)*; freight train *(Amer.)*

gut-, Gut-: **~gehen** *unr. itr. V.*; mit sein **a)** *(unpers.)* es geht jmdm. **gut** sb. is well; **b)** *(~ ausgehen)* turn out well; **~gelaunt** *Adj. (präd. getrennt geschrieben)* cheerful; **~gemeint** *Adj. (präd. getrennt geschrieben)* well-meant; **~gläubig** *Adj.* innocently trusting; **~haben** das; ~s, ~: credit balance; **~heißen** *unr. tr. V.* approve of; **~herzig** *Adj.* kind-hearted

gütig 1. *Adj.* kindly; **2.** *adv.* ~ **lächeln** give a kindly smile; **gütlich** *Adj.* amicable

gut-, Gut-: **~machen** *tr. V.* make good *(damage)*; put right *(omission, mistake, etc.)*; **~mütig** *Adj.* good-natured; **~mütigkeit** die; ~: good nature

Guts·besitzer der owner of a/the estate; landowner

gut-, Gut-: **~schein** der voucher,

coupon (für, auf + *Akk.* for); ~|-schreiben *unr. tr. V.* credit; ~schrift die credit

Guts·hof der estate; manor

gut-: ~|tun *unr. itr. V.* do good; ~willig 1. *Adj.* willing; *(entgegen-kommend)* obliging; 2. *adv.* etw. ~willig herausgeben/versprechen hand sth. over voluntarily/promise sth. willingly

Gymnasium das; ~s, Gymnasien ≈ grammar school

Gymnastik die; ~: physical exercises *pl.; (Turnen)* gymnastics *sing.*

Gynäkologe der; ~n, ~n gynaecologist

H

———

h, H [ha:] das; ~, ~ a) *(Buchstabe)* h/H; b) *(Musik)* [key of] B

h *Abk.* a) Uhr hrs; b) Stunde hr[s]

H *Abk.* a) Herren; b) Haltestelle

¹ha [ha(:)] *Interj.* a) *(Überraschung)* ah; b) *(Triumph)* aha

²ha *Abk.* Hektar ha

Haar das; ~|e|s, ~e hair; blonde ~e od. blondes ~ haben have fair hair; *(fig.)* ~e auf den Zähnen haben *(ugs. scherzh.)* be a tough customer; um ein ~ *(ugs.)* very nearly

Haar-: ~ausfall der hair loss; ~bürste die hairbrush; ~büschel das tuft of hair

haaren *itr. V.* moult; Haares·breite die *in* um ~: by a hair's breadth; Haar·festiger der setting lotion; haar·genau *(ugs.)* 1. *Adj.* exact; 2. *adv.* exactly; haarig *Adj.* hairy

haar-, Haar-: ~klemme die hairgrip; ~nadel die hairpin; ~nadel·kurve die hairpin bend; ~schnitt der haircut; *(modisch)* hairstyle; ~spange die hair-slide; ~sträubend *Adj.* a) *(grauenhaft)* hair-raising; b) *(empörend)* outrageous; shocking; ~teil das hairpiece; ~wasch·mittel das shampoo; ~wasser das; *Pl.* ~wässer hair lotion

Habe die; ~ *(geh.)* possessions *pl.;* haben 1. *unr. tr. V.* have; have got; heute ~ wir schönes Wetter the weather is fine today; es gut/schlecht/schwer ~: have it good *(coll.)*/have a bad time [of it]/have a difficult time; du hast zu gehorchen you must obey; das Jahr hat 12 Monate there are 12 months in a year; 2. *refl. V. (ugs.: sich aufregen)* make a fuss; 3. *Hilfsverb* have; **ich habe/hatte ihn eben gesehen** I've/I'd just seen him; **er hat es gewußt** he knew it; 4. *mod. V.* du hast zu gehorchen you must obey; **er hat sich nicht einzumischen** he's not to interfere; **Haben das;** ~s, ~ *(Kaufmannsspr.)* credit; **Habe·nichts der;** ~, ~e pauper; **Hab·gier die** *(abwertend)* greed; **hab·gierig 1.** *Adj. (abwertend)* greedy; 2. *adv.* greedily

Habicht der; ~s, ~e hawk

Hab-: ~seligkeiten *Pl.* [meagre] belongings; ~sucht die; ~ *(abwertend)* greed; avarice

Hachse die; ~, ~n *(südd.)* knuckle

Hack das; ~s *(ugs., bes. nordd.)* mince; Hack·braten der meat loaf

¹Hacke die; ~, ~n hoe; *(Pickel)* pick[axe]

²Hacke die; ~, ~n *(bes. nordd. u. md.)* heel

hacken 1. *itr. V.* a) hoe; b) *(picken)* peck; 2. *tr. V.* a) hoe *(garden, flower-bed, etc.);* b) *(zerkleinern)* chop; chop [up] *(meat, vegetables, etc.)*

Hack·fleisch das minced meat; mince

Häcksel der *od.* das; ~s *(Landw.)* chaff

hadern *itr. V. (geh.)* mit etw. ~: be at odds with sth.

Hafen der; ~s, Häfen harbour; port

Hafen-: ~arbeiter der dock-worker; docker; ~kneipe die dockland pub *(Brit. coll.)* or *(Amer.)* bar; ~rundfahrt die trip round the harbour; ~stadt die port; ~viertel das dock area

Hafer der; ~s oats *pl.*

Hafer-: ~brei der porridge; ~flocken *Pl.* porridge oats

Haff das; ~|e|s, ~s *od.* ~e lagoon

Haft die; ~ a) *(Gewahrsam)* custody; *(aus politischen Gründen)* detention; b) *(Freiheitsstrafe)* imprisonment -haft *Adj., adv.* -like

haftbar *Adj. (bes. Rechtsspr.)* für etw. ~ sein be liable for sth.; Haft·befehl der *(Rechtsw.)* warrant [of arrest]

¹haften *itr. V.* stick; *(sich festsetzen)* *(smell, dirt, etc.)* cling (**an** + *Dat.* to)

²haften *itr. V.* für jmdn./etw. ~: be responsible for sb./liable for sth.; *(Rechtsw., Wirtsch.)* be liable

haften|bleiben *unr. itr. V.; mit sein* stick (**an/auf** + *Dat.* to); *(smell, smoke)* cling (**an/auf** + *Dat.* to); *(ugs.: im Gedächtnis bleiben)* stick

Häftling der; ~s, ~e prisoner

Haft·pflicht die liability (**für** for); **Haftpflicht·versicherung** die personal liability insurance; *(für Autofahrer)* third party insurance

Haft·schale die contact lens

Haftung die; ~, ~en liability; Gesellschaft mit |un|beschränkter ~: [un]limited [liability] company

Hagebutte die; ~, ~n a) *(Frucht)* rose-hip; b) *(ugs.: Heckenrose)* dog-rose

Hagel der; ~s, ~ *(auch fig.)* hail; **ha·geln** *itr., tr. V. (unpers.)* hail

hager *Adj.* gaunt

haha [ha'ha(:)] *Interj.* ha ha

Häher der; ~s, ~: jay

¹Hahn der; ~|e|s, Hähne cock; *(Wetter~)* weathercock

²Hahn der; ~|e|s, Hähne, *fachspr.:* ~en a) tap; faucet *(Amer.)*; b) *(bei Waffen)* hammer

Hähnchen das; ~s, ~: chicken; **Hah·nen·fuß** der buttercup

Hai der; ~s, ~e shark

Häkchen das; ~s, ~ a) [small] hook; b) *(Zeichen)* mark; *(beim Abhaken)* tick; **häkeln** *tr., itr. V.* crochet; **Häkel·nadel** die crochet-hook

haken 1. *tr. V.* hook (**an** + *Akk.* on to); 2. *itr. V. (klemmen)* be stuck; **Haken** der; ~s, ~ a) hook; b) *(Zeichen)* tick; c) *(ugs.: Schwierigkeit)* catch; d) *(Boxen)* hook; **Haken·kreuz** das swastika

halb 1. *Adj. u. Bruchz.* half; eine ~e Stunde/ein ~er Meter half an hour/a metre; zum ~en Preis [at] half price; ~ Europa/die ~e Welt half of Europe/half the world; es ist ~ eins it's half past twelve; die ~e Wahrheit half [of] the truth; |noch| ein ~es Kind sein be hardly more than a child; 2. *adv.* ~ voll/leer half-full/-empty; ~ angezogen half dressed; **Halb·dunkel** das semi-darkness; **Halbe** der *od.* die *od.* das; *adj. Dekl. (ugs.)* half litre *(of beer etc.)*; **Halb·edelstein** der *(veralt.)* semi-precious stone

halber *Präp. mit Gen.; nachgestellt*

(wegen) on account of; *(um ... willen)* for the sake of

halb-, Halb-: ~**finale** das *(Sport)* semi-final; ~**gar** *Adj.* half-cooked; ~**gefror[e]ne** das; *adj. Dekl.* soft ice cream

halbieren *tr. V.* cut/tear *(object)* in half; halve *(amount, number)*

halb-, Halb-: ~**insel** die peninsula; ~**jahr** das six months *pl.;* half year; ~**jährlich** 1. *Adj.* six-monthly; 2. *adv.* every six months; ~**kreis** der semicircle; ~**kugel** die hemisphere; ~**lang** *Adj.* mid-length *(hair);* mid-calf length *(coat, dress, etc.);* ~**links** [-'-] *Adv. (Fußball) (play)* [at] inside left; ~**mast** *Adv.* at half-mast; ~**mond** der a) *(Mond)* half-moon; b) *(Figur)* crescent; ~**offen** *Adj. (präd. getrennt geschrieben)* half-open; ~**pension** die half-board; ~**rechts** [-'-] *Adv. (Fußball) (play)* [at] inside right; ~**schuh** der shoe; ~**starke** der; *adj. Dekl. (abwertend)* [young] hooligan; ~**tags** *Adv. (work)* part-time; *(morgens/nachmittags) (work)* [in the] mornings/afternoons; ~**voll** *Adj. (präd. getrennt geschrieben)* half-full; ~**wegs** *Adv.* to some extent; ~**wüchsig** [-vy:ksıç] *Adj.* adolescent; ~**wüchsige** der/die; *adj. Dekl.* adolescent; ~**zeit** die *(bes. Fußball)* a) half; b) *(Pause)* half-time

Halde die; ~, ~n *(Bergbau)* slag-heap

half 1. u. 3. Pers. Sg. Prät. v. **helfen**

Hälfte die; ~, ~n a) half; b) *(ugs.: Teil)* part

¹Halfter der *od.* das; ~s, ~: halter

²Halfter die; ~, ~n; *auch das*; ~s, ~: holster

Hall der; ~|e|s, ~e a) *(geh.)* reverberation; b) *(Echo)* echo

Halle die; ~, ~n hall; *(Fabrik~)* shed; *(Hotel~, Theater~)* foyer

hallen *itr. V.* a) reverberate; *(shot, bell, cry)* ring out; b) *(widerhallen)* echo

Hallen- indoor *(swimming-pool, handball)*

Hallig die; ~, ~en small low island *(particularly one of those off Schleswig-Holstein)*

hallo *Interj.* hello; **Hallo** das; ~s, ~s cheering

Halluzination die; ~, ~en hallucination

Halm der; ~|e|s, ~e stalk; stem

Hals der; ~es, Hälse *(Kehle)* throat; über Kopf *(ugs.)* in a rush

Hals-: ~**ab·schneider** der *(ugs. ab-*

wertend) shark; **~band** das; *Pl.* **~bänder** *(für Tiere)* collar; **~bruch** der *s.* **~~ und Beinbruch; ~entzündung** die inflammation of the throat; **~~Nasen-Ohren-Arzt** der ear, nose, and throat specialist; **~schlagader** die carotid [artery]; **~schmerzen** *Pl.* sore throat *sing.;* **~starrig** [~ʃtarıç] *Adj. (abwertend)* stubborn; obstinate; **~tuch** die cravat; **~~ und Beinbruch** *Interj. (scherzh.)* good luck; **~weh** das *(ugs.) s.* **~schmerzen**

halt *Interj.* stop; **Halt** der; **~|e|s, ~e** hold

haltbar *Adj.* **a)** ~ sein *(food)* keep [well]; **~ bis 5. 3.** use by 5 March; **b)** *(nicht verschleißend)* hard-wearing *(material, clothes);* **c)** *(aufrechtzuerhalten)* tenable *(hypothesis etc.);* **Haltbarkeit** die; **~** *(Strapazierfähigkeit)* durability

halten 1. *unr. tr. V.* **a)** *(auch Milit.)* hold; **die Hand vor den Mund ~:** put one's hand in front of one's mouth; **b)** *(Ballspiele)* save *(shot, penalty, etc.);* **c)** *(bewahren)* keep; *(beibehalten, aufrechterhalten)* keep up *(speed etc.);* maintain *(temperature, equilibrium);* **d)** *(erfüllen)* keep; **sein Wort/ein Versprechen ~:** keep one's word/a promise; **e)** *(besitzen, beschäftigen, beziehen)* keep *(chickens etc.);* take *(newspaper, magazine, etc.);* **f)** *(einschätzen)* **jmdn. für reich/ehrlich ~:** think sb. is rich/honest; **viel von jmdm.~:** think a lot of sb.; **g)** *(ab~, veranstalten)* give, *(speech, lecture);* **2.** *unr. itr. V.* **a)** *(stehenbleiben)* stop; **b)** *(unverändert, an seinem Platz bleiben)* last; **c)** *(Sport)* save; **d)** *(beistehen)* zu **jmdm. ~:** stand by sb.; **3.** *unr. refl. V.* **a)** *(sich durchsetzen, behaupten)* **wir werden uns/die Stadt wird sich nicht länger ~ können** we/the town won't be able to hold out much longer; **b)** *(sich bewähren)* **sich gut ~:** do well; **c)** *(unverändert bleiben) (weather, flowers, etc.)* last; *(milk, meat, etc.)* keep; **d)** *(Körperhaltung haben)* **sich schlecht/gerade ~:** hold oneself badly/straight; **e)** *(bleiben)* **sich auf den Beinen/im Sattel ~:** stay on one's feet/in the saddle; **sich links/rechts ~:** keep [to the] left/right; **sich an etw.** *(Akk.)* **~:** keep to sth.

Halter der; **~s, ~** **a)** *(Fahrzeug~)* keeper; **b)** *(Tier~)* owner; **c)** *(Vorrichtung)* holder; **Halterung** die; **~, ~en** support

Halte-: ~stelle die stop; **~verbot** das **a)** „**~verbot**" 'no stopping'; **hier ist ~verbot** this is a no-stopping zone; **b)** *(Stelle)* no-stopping zone; **~verbots·schild** das no-stopping sign

-haltig, *(österr.)* **-hältig:** vit**amin~/silber~** *usw.* containing vitamins/silver *etc. postpos., not pred.;* **vitamin~ sein** contain vitamins

halt-: ~los *Adj.* **a)** *(labil)* **~los sein** be a weak character; **ein ~loser Mensch** a weak character; **b)** *(unbegründet)* unfounded; **~|machen** *itr. V.* stop

Haltung die; **~, ~en a)** *(Körper~)* posture; **b)** *(Pose)* manner; **c)** *(Einstellung)* attitude; **d)** *(Fassung)* composure

Halunke der; **~n, ~n** scoundrel; villain

Hamburger der; **~s, ~** *od.* **~s** *(Frikadelle)* hamburger

hämisch 1. *Adj.* malicious; **2.** *adv.* maliciously

Hammel der; **~s, ~** **a)** wether; **b)** *(Fleisch)* mutton; **Hammel·fleisch** das mutton

Hammer der; **~s, Hämmer a)** hammer; *(Holz~)* mallet; **~ und Sichel** hammer and sickle; **b)** *(Technik)* ram; **hämmern** *itr., tr. V.* hammer

Hämorrhoiden [hɛmɔroˈiːdn] *Pl. (Med.)* haemorrhoids; piles

Hampel·mann der; **~|e|s, Hampelmänner a)** jumping jack; **b)** *(ugs. abwertend)* puppet

hampeln *itr. V. (ugs.)* jump about

Hamster der; **~s, ~:** hamster

hamstern *tr., itr. V.* **a)** *(horten)* hoard; **b)** *(Lebensmittel tauschen)* barter goods for [food]

Hand die; **~, Hände hand; jmdm. die ~ geben** shake sb.'s hand; **~ und Fuß/ weder ~ noch Fuß haben** *(ugs.)* make sense/no sense; **alle** *od.* **beide Hände damit voll haben, etw. zu tun** *(ugs.)* have one's hands full doing sth.; **die Hände in den Schoß legen** sit back and do nothing; **etw. aus der ~ geben** let sth. out of one's hands; **~ in ~ arbeiten** work hand in hand; **etw. zur ~ haben** have sth. handy; **zu Händen |von|** Herrn Müller attention Herr Müller

Hand-: ~arbeit die a) handicraft; **etw. in ~arbeit herstellen** make sth. by hand; **b)** *(Gegenstand)* handmade article; **c)** *(Nadelarbeit)* [piece of] needlework; **~ball** der handball; **~besen** der brush; **~betrieb** der; *o. Pl.* manual operation; **~bewegung** die **a)**

movement of the hand; b) *(Geste)* gesture; **~bremse** die handbrake; **~buch** das handbook; *(technisches ~buch)* manual

Händchen das; ~s, ~: [little] hand; **Hände** *s.* Hand

Hände-: **~druck** der; *Pl.* **~drücke** handshake; **~klatschen** das; ~s clapping

Handel der; ~s trade; **handeln** 1. *itr. V.* a) trade; deal; b) *(feilschen)* haggle; c) *(agieren)* act; d) *(sich verhalten)* behave; e) **von etw.** *od.* **über etw.** *(Akk.)* ~ *(book, film, etc.)* be about *or* deal with sth.; 2. *refl. V. (unpers.)* **es handelt sich um ...:** it is a matter of ...; *(es dreht sich um)* it's about ...

handels-, Handels-: **~abkommen** das trade agreement; **~bank** die merchant bank; **~bilanz** die a) *(eines Betriebes)* balance-sheet; b) *(eines Staates)* balance of trade; **~einig, ~eins** in mit jmdm. **~einig** *od.* **~eins werden/sein** agree/have agreed terms with sb.; **~flotte** die merchant fleet; **~gesellschaft** die company; **~klasse** die grade; **~marine** die merchant navy; **~partner** der trading partner; **~register** das register of companies; **~schiff** das merchant ship; **~schule** die commercial college; **~straße** die *(hist.)* trade route; **~üblich** *Adj.* **~übliche Praktiken/Größen** standard business practices/standard [commercial] sizes; **~unternehmen** das trading concern; **~vertreter** der [sales] representative; travelling salesman/ saleswoman; **~vertretung** die trade mission; **~zentrum** das trading centre

hände·ringend *Adv. (ugs.: dringend)* *(need)* urgently; *(search for sb./sth.)* desperately

hand-, Hand-: **~feger** der brush; **~fest** *Adj.* robust; sturdy; substantial *(meal etc.)*; c) solid *(proof)*; concrete *(suggestion)*; complete *(lie)*; well-founded *(argument)*; **~fläche** die palm [of one's/the hand]; flat of one's/the hand; **~gas** das *(Kfz-W.)* hand throttle; **~gearbeitet** *Adj.* hand-made; **~gelenk** das wrist; **~gemenge** das fight; **~gepäck** das hand-baggage; **~geschrieben** *Adj.* handwritten; **~granate** die hand-grenade; **~greiflich** *Adj.* a) *(tätlich)* **~greiflich werden** start using one's fists; b) tangible *(success, advantage, proof, etc.)*; palpable *(contradiction,*

error); obvious *(fact)*; **~griff** der a) mit einem **~griff/wenigen ~griffen** in one movement/without much trouble; *(schnell)* in no time at all/next to no time; b) *(am Koffer, an einem Werkzeug)* handle; **~habe die;** ~, ~n: eine [rechtliche] **~habe** [gegen jmdn.] a legal handle [against sb.]; **~haben** *tr. V.* a) handle; operate *(device, machine)*; b) *(praktizieren)* implement *(law etc.)*; **~habung die;** ~, **~en a)** handling; *(eines Gerätes, einer Maschine)* operation; b) *(Durchführung)* implementation

Handikap ['hεndikεp] das; ~s, ~s *(auch Sport)* handicap; **handikapen** ['hεndikεpn] *tr. V.* handicap

Händ-: **~käse der** *(landsch.)* small, hand-formed curd cheese; **~koffer** der [small] suitcase; **~kuß der** kiss on sb.'s hand; **~langer der;** ~s, ~ *(ungelernter Arbeiter)* labourer; *(abwertend)* lackey; **~lauf der** handrail

Händler der; ~s, ~: trader

handlich *Adj.* handy; easily carried *(parcel, suitcase)*; easily portable *(television, camera)*

Handlung die; ~, **~en a)** *(Vorgehen)* action; *(Tat)* act; b) *(Fabel)* plot

handlungs-, Handlungs-: **~fähig** *Adj.* able to act *pred.*; working *attrib.* *(majority)*; **~freiheit die;** o. *Pl.* freedom of action; **~reisende der/die s.** Handelsvertreter; **~weise die** conduct

hand-, Hand-: **puppe die** glove *or* hand puppet; **~schelle die** handcuff; **~schlag der** handshake; **~schrift die** handwriting; **~schriftlich** 1. *Adj.* hand-written; 2. *adv.* by hand; **~schuh der** glove; **~schuhfach das** glove compartment; **~signiert** *Adj.* signed; **~spiegel der** hand-mirror; **~stand der** *(Turnen)* handstand; **~tasche die** handbag; **~tuch das;** *Pl.* -tücher towel; **~umdrehen:** im **~umdrehen** in no time at all; **~voll die;** ~ *(auch fig.)* handful

Hand·werk das craft; *(als Beruf)* trade; **sein ~ kennen** *od.* **verstehen/beherrschen** know one's job; **Handwerker** der; ~s, ~: tradesman; **handwerklich** *Adj.* ein ~er Beruf a [skilled] trade; **Handwerks·zeug das** tools *pl.*

Hand·zeichen das sign [with one's hand]; *(eines Autofahrers)* hand signal; *(Abstimmung)* show of hands

Hanf der; ~[e]s hemp

Hang der; ~|e|s, **Hänge** slope; *(Neigung)* tendency

Hänge-: ~**brücke** die suspension bridge; ~**lampe** die pendant-light; ~**matte** die hammock

¹**hängen** unr. itr. V.; südd., österr., schweiz. mit sein hang (an + Dat. from); *(an einem Fahrzeug)* be hitched (an + Dat. to); ²**hängen** 1. tr. V. a) hang (in/über + (Akk.) in/over; an/ auf + Akk. on); *(befestigen)* hitch up (an + Akk. to); couple on *(railway carriage, etc.)* (an + Akk. to); 2. refl. V. a) sich an etw. *(Akk.)* ~: hang on to sth.; b) *(sich festsetzen)* cling (an + Akk. to); **hängen|bleiben** unr. itr. V.; mit sein *(ugs.)* a) *(festgehalten werden)* [mit dem Ärmel usw.] an/in etw. *(Dat.)* ~: get one's sleeve etc. caught on/in sth.; b) *(verweilen)* get stuck *(coll.)*; c) *(haften)* **an/auf etw.** *(Dat.)* ~: stick to sth.; **hängend** Adj. hanging; **Hänge·schrank** der wall-cupboard

hänseln tr. V. tease

Hanse·stadt die Hanseatic city

Hantel die; ~, ~n *(Sport)(kurz)* dumbbell; *(lang)* barbell

hantieren itr. V. be busy

Häppchen das; ~s, ~ a) [small] morsel; b) *(Appetithappen)* canapé

Happen der; ~s, ~: morsel

happig Adj. *(ugs.)* ~e **Preise** fancy prices *(coll.)*

Happy-End ['hɛpi'|ɛnt] das; ~|s|, ~s happy ending

Harfe die; ~, ~n harp

Harke die; ~, ~n rake; **harken** tr. V. rake

harm·los 1. Adj. a) *(ungefährlich)* harmless; slight *(injury, cold, etc.)*; mild *(illness)*; safe *(medicine, bend, road, etc.)*; b) *(arglos)* innocent; harmless *(fun, pastime, etc.)*; 2. adv. a) *(ungefährlich)* harmlessly; b) *(arglos)* innocently; **Harmlosigkeit** die; ~ a) *(Ungefährlichkeit)* harmlessness; *(einer Krankheit)* mildness; *(eines Medikamentes)* safety; b) *(Arglosigkeit, harmloses Verhalten)* innocence

Harmonie die; ~, ~n *(auch fig.)* harmony; **harmonieren** itr. V. a) harmonize; b) *(miteinander auskommen)* get on well

Harmonika die; ~, ~s od. **Harmoniken** harmonica

harmonisch 1. Adj. harmonious; *(Musik)* harmonic; 2. adv. harmoniously; *(Musik)* harmonically

Harmonium das; ~s, **Harmonien** harmonium

Harn der; ~|e|s, ~e *(Med.)* urine; **Harn·blase** die bladder

Harnisch der; ~s, ~e armour

Harpune die; ~, ~n harpoon

harren itr. V. *(geh.)* jmds./einer Sache od. auf jmdn./etw. ~: await sb./sth.

harsch 1. Adj. a) *(vereist)* crusted; b) *(barsch)* harsh; 2. adv. harshly; **Harsch** der; ~|e|s crusted snow

hart; **härter**, **härtest...** 1. Adj. a) hard; b) tough *(situation, job)*; harsh *(reality, truth)*; c) *(streng)* harsh *(penalty, punishment, judgement)*; tough *(measure, law, course)*; d) *(rauh)* rough *(game, opponent)*; 2. adv. hard chair; a) *(mühevoll)* *(work)* hard; b) *(streng)* harshly; c) *(nahe)* close (an + Dat. to); **Härte** die; ~, ~n a) *(auch Physik)* hardness; b) *(Widerstandsfähigkeit)* toughness; c) *(schwere Belastung)* hardship; d) *(Strenge)* harshness; e) *(Heftigkeit)* *(eines Aufpralls usw.)* force; *(eines Streits)* violence; f) *(Rauheit)* roughness; **Härte·fall** der a) case of hardship; b) *(ugs.: Person)* hardship case; **härten** tr., itr. V. harden; **härter** s. hart; **härtest...** s. hart

hart-, Hart-: ~**gekocht** Adj. hard-boiled *(egg)*; ~**geld** das coins pl.; ~**herzig** 1. Adj. hard-hearted; 2. adv. hard-heartedly; ~**herzigkeit** die; ~: hard-heartedness; ~**näckig** 1. Adj. a) *(eigensinnig)* obstinate; stubborn; b) *(ausdauernd)* dogged; 2. adv. a) *(eigensinnig)* obstinately; stubbornly; b) *(ausdauernd)* doggedly; ~**näckigkeit** die; ~ a) *(Eigensinn)* obstinacy; stubbornness; b) *(Ausdauer)* doggedness; ~**wurst** die dry sausage

Harz das; ~es, ~e resin

Harzer Käse der; ~ ~s, ~ ~: Harz [Mountain] cheese

Haschee *(Kochk.)* das; ~s, ~s hash; ¹**haschen** tr. V. *(veralt.)* catch; ²**haschen** itr. V. *(ugs.)* smoke [hash] *(coll.)*

Häschen ['hɛːsçən] das; ~, ~: bunny

Haschisch das od. der; ~|s| hashish

Hase der; ~n, ~n a) hare; b) *(landsch.)* s. Kaninchen

Hasel·nuß die hazel-nut

Hasen-: ~**fuß** der *(spöttisch abwertend)* coward; chicken *(sl.)*; ~**scharte** die *(Med.)* harelip

Haspel die; ~, ~n *(Technik)* *(für Garn)* reel; *(für ein Seil, Kabel)* drum

Haß der; **Hasses** hatred (auf + *Akk.*, gegen of, for); **hassen** *tr., itr. V.* hate; **haß·erfüllt** *Adj.* filled with hatred *postpos.*

häßlich 1. *Adj.* a) ugly; b) *(gemein)* nasty; c) *(unangenehm)* awful ⟨*weather, cold, situation, etc.*⟩; 2. *adv.* a) ⟨*dress*⟩ unattractively; b) *(gemein)* nastily; **Häßlichkeit** die; ~, ~en a) *o. Pl. (Aussehen)* ugliness; b) *o. Pl. (Gesinnung)* nastiness

hast 2. *Pers. Sg. Präsens v.* **haben**

Hast die; ~: haste; **hasten** *itr. V.; mit sein* hurry; **hastig** 1. *Adj.* hasty; hurried; 2. *adv.* hastily; hurriedly

hat 3. *Pers. Sg. Präsens v.* **haben**

hätscheln *tr. V.* caress

hatschi *Interj.* atishoo

hatte 1. u. 3. *Pers. Sg. Prät. v.* **haben**; **hätte** 1. u. 3. *Pers. Sg. Konjunktiv II v.* **haben**

Haube die; ~, ~n a) bonnet; *(einer Krankenschwester)* cap; b) *(Kfz-W.)* bonnet *(Brit.);* hood *(Amer.)*

Hauch der; ~[e]s, ~e *(geh.)* a) *(Atem, auch fig.)* breath; b) *(Luftzug)* breath of wind; c) *(leichter Duft)* delicate smell; d) *(dünne Schicht)* [gossamer-]thin layer; **hauch·dünn** *Adj.* gossamer-thin ⟨*material, dress*⟩; wafer-thin ⟨*layer, slice, majority*⟩; **hauchen** *itr. V.* breathe **(gegen, auf + Akk. on)**

Haue die; ~, ~n a) *(südd., österr.: Hakke)* hoe; b) *(ugs.: Prügel)* a hiding *(coll.);* **hauen** 1. *unr. tr. V.* a) *(ugs.: schlagen)* belt; clobber *(coll.);* b) *(ugs.: auf einen Körperteil)* hit; c) *(herstellen)* carve ⟨*figure, statue, etc.*⟩ **(in + Akk.** in); 2. *unr. itr. V.* a) *(ugs.: prügeln)* er **haut immer gleich** he's quick to hit out; b) *(auf einen Körperteil)* belt *(coll.);* hit; c) *(ugs.: auf/gegen etw. schlagen)* thump; 3. *unr. refl. V.* *(ugs.: sich prügeln)* have a punch-up *(coll.)*

Haufen der; ~s, ~: heap; pile; *(Gruppe)* bunch *(coll.);* **häufen** 1. *tr. V.* heap, pile **(auf + Akk.** on to); *(aufheben)* hoard ⟨*money, supplies*⟩; 2. *refl. V. (sich mehren)* pile up

häufig 1. *Adj.* frequent; 2. *adv.* frequently; often; **Häufigkeit** die; ~, ~en frequency; **Häufung** die; ~, ~en increasing frequency

Haupt das; ~[e]s, **Häupter** *(geh., auch fig.)* head

haupt-, Haupt-: ~**bahnhof** der main station; ~**beruflich** 1. *Adj.* sei-

ne ~**berufliche Tätigkeit** his main occupation; 2. *adv.* er ist ~**beruflich als Elektriker tätig** his main occupation is that of electrician; ~**darsteller** der *(Theater, Film)* male lead; ~**darstellerin** die *(Theater, Film)* female lead; ~**eingang** der main entrance; ~**fach** das major; ~**figur** die main character; ~**film** der main feature; ~**gebäude** das main building; ~**gericht** das main course; ~**gewinn** der first prize

Häuptling der; ~s, ~e chief[tain]

haupt-, Haupt-: ~**mahlzeit** die main meal; ~**mann** der; *Pl.* ~**leute** *(Milit.)* captain; ~**person** die central figure; ~**postamt** das main post office; ~**quartier** das *(Milit., auch fig.)* headquarters *sing. or pl.;* ~**rolle** die main role; lead; ~**sache** die main thing; ~**sächlich** 1. *Adv.* mainly; principally; 2. *Adj.; nicht präd.* main; principal; ~**saison** die high season; ~**satz** der main clause; *(alleinstehend)* sentence; ~**schlagader** die aorta; ~**schul·abschluß** der ≈ secondary school leaving certificate; ~**schule** die ≈ secondary modern school; ~**stadt** die capital [city]; ~**städtisch** *Adj.* metropolitan; ~**straße** die main street; ~**verkehr** der bulk of the traffic

Hauptverkehrs-: ~**straße** die main road; ~**zeit** die rush hour

Haupt-: ~**wache** die main police station; ~**wort** das *(Sprachw.)* noun

hau ruck *Interj.* heave[-ho]

Haus das; ~es, **Häuser** house; *(Amts-, Firmengebäude usw.)* building; *(Heim)* home; **nach** ~**e** home; **zu** ~**e** at home; **das erste** ~ **am Platze** the best hotel in the town

haus-, Haus-: ~**angestellte** der/die domestic servant; ~**apotheke** die medicine cabinet; ~**arbeit** die housework; *(Schulw.)* homework; ~**arrest** der house arrest; ~**arzt** der family doctor; ~**aufgabe** die homework; ~**backen** 1. *Adj.* plain; unadventurous *(clothes);* 2. *adv.* ⟨*dress*⟩ unadventurously; ~**besetzer** der squatter; ~**besitzer** der house-owner; *(Vermieter)* landlord; ~**besitzerin** die house-owner; *(Vermieterin)* landlady; ~**besuch** der house-call; ~**boot** das houseboat

Häuschen ['hɔysçən] das; ~s, ~: small house; **aus dem** ~ **sein** *(ugs.)* be over the moon *(coll.);* **hausen** *itr. V.*

(ugs. abwertend) live; **b)** *(Verwüstungen anrichten)* [**furchtbar**] ~: wreak havoc; **Häuser·block der** block [of houses]

haus-, Haus-: ~**flur der** hall[way]; *(im Obergeschoß)* landing; ~**frau die** housewife; **freund der a)** friend of the family; *(verhüll.: Liebhaber)* manfriend *(euphem.);* ~**friedensbruch der** *(Rechtsw.)* trespass; ~**gebrauch der** domestic use; **das reicht für den** ~**gebrauch** *(ugs.)* it's good enough to get by *(coll.);* ~**gehilfin die** [home] help; ~**gemacht** *Adj.* home-made

Haus·halt der a) household; **b)** *(Arbeit im ~)* housekeeping; **jmdm. den** ~ **führen** keep house for sb.; **c)** *(Politik)* budget; **haus|halten** *unr. itr. V.* be economical *(mit* with); **Haushälterin die; ~, ~nen** housekeeper

Haushalts-: ~**debatte, die** *(Politik)* budget debate; ~**geld das;** *o. Pl.* housekeeping money; ~**jahr das** financial year; ~**kasse die** housekeeping money; ~**plan der** budget; ~**waren** *Pl.* household goods

Haus·herr der a) *(Familienoberhaupt)* head of the household; **b)** *(als Gastgeber)* host; **c)** *(Rechtsspr.) (Eigentümer)* owner; *(Mieter)* occupier; **haushoch 1.** *Adj.* as high as a house; *(fig.)* overwhelming; **2.** *adv. (fig.)* ~ **gewinnen** win hands down

hausieren *itr. V.* |mit etw.| ~: hawk [sth.]; peddle [sth.]; „**Hausieren verboten**" 'no hawkers'; **Hausierer der; ~s, ~:** pedlar; hawker

häuslich *Adj.* **a)** domestic; **b)** *(das Zuhause liebend)* home-loving

Hausmacher·art die: nach ~: homemade-style *attrib.*

Hausmacher·kost die plain cooking

Haus-: ~**marke die a)** house wine; **b)** *(ugs.: bevorzugtes Getränk)* favourite tipple *(coll.);* ~**meister der,** ~**meisterin die** caretaker; ~**mittel das** household remedy; ~**musik die** music at home; ~**nummer die** house number; ~**ordnung die** house rules *pl.;* ~**putz der** spring-clean; *(regelmäßig)* clean-out; ~**rat der** household goods *pl.;* ~**schlüssel der** front-door key; house-key; ~**schuh der** slipper

Haussuchung die; ~, ~en house search; **Haussuchungs·befehl der** search warrant

Haus-: ~**tier das a)** pet; **b)** *(Nutztier)* domestic animal; ~**tür die** front door; ~**verbot das** ban on entering the

house/pub/restaurant *etc.;* ~**verwalter der** manager [of the block]; ~**wirt der** landlord; ~**wirtin die** landlady; ~**wirtschaft die;** *o. Pl.* domestic science and home economics

Haut die; ~, Häute skin; **aus der ~ fahren** *(ugs.)* go up the wall *(coll.);* **Haut·arzt der** skin specialist; **häuten 1.** *tr. V.* skin; flay; **2.** *refl. V.* shed its skin/their skins

haut-, Haut-: ~**eng** *Adj.* skin-tight; ~**farbe die** [skin] colour; ~**krankheit die** skin disease

Haxe die; ~, ~n *s.* **Hachse**

he *Interj. (ugs.)* hey

Heb·amme die midwife

Hebel der; ~s, ~: lever

heben *unr. itr. V.* **a)** lift; raise ⟨baton, camera, glass⟩; **b)** *(verbessern)* raise ⟨standard, level⟩; increase ⟨turnover, self-confidence⟩; improve ⟨mood⟩; enhance ⟨standing⟩; boost ⟨morale⟩

¹**hecheln** *itr. V. (ugs. abwertend)* gossip

²**hecheln** *itr. V.* pant [for breath]

Hecht der; ~|e|s, ~e pike; **Hecht·sprung der a)** *(Turnen)* Hecht vault; **b)** *(Schwimmen)* racing dive; *(vom Sprungturm)* pike-dive

Heck das; ~|e|s, ~e *od.* ~**s** stern; *(Flugzeug~)* tail; *(Auto~)* rear

Hecke die; ~, ~n a) hedge; **b)** *(wildwachsend)* thicket

Hecken-: ~**rose die** dogrose; ~**schütze der** sniper

Heck·scheibe die rear window

Heer das; ~|e|s, ~e armed forces *pl.;* *(für den Landkrieg, fig.)* army

Hefe die; ~, ~n yeast

¹**Heft das; ~|e|s, ~e** *(geh.)* haft; handle

²**Heft das; ~|e|s, ~e a)** *(bes. Schule)* exercise-book; **b)** *(Nummer einer Zeitschrift)* issue; **Heftchen das; ~s, ~:** book [of tickets/stamps *etc.*]; **heften 1.** *tr. V.* **a)** *(mit einer Nadel)* pin; *(mit einer Klammer)* clip; *(mit Klebstoff)* stick; **b)** *(Schneiderei)* tack; **c)** *(Buchbinderei)* stitch; *(mit Klammern)* staple; **2.** *refl. V.* **sich an jmds. Fersen** *(Akk.)* ~: stick hard on sb.'s heels

heftig 1. *Adj.* violent; heavy ⟨rain, shower, blow⟩; severe ⟨pain⟩; ⟨person⟩ with a violent temper; **2.** *adv.* ⟨rain, snow, breathe⟩ heavily; ⟨hit⟩ hard; ⟨quarrel⟩ violently

Heft-: ~**klammer die** staple; ~**pflaster das** sticking plaster; ~**zwecke die** *s.* **Reißzwecke**

hegen *tr. V.* **a)** *(bes. Forstw., Jagdw.)*

look after, tend; b) ⟨geh.: *umsorgen*⟩ look after; c) ⟨fig.⟩ feel ⟨contempt, hatred, mistrust⟩; cherish ⟨hope, wish, desire⟩; harbour ⟨grudge, suspicion⟩

Hehl der od. das: kein|en| ~ aus etw. machen make no secret of sth.; **Hehler** der; ~s, ~: receiver [of stolen goods]; **Hehlerei** die; ~, ~en ⟨Rechtsw.⟩ receiving [stolen goods] no art.

¹Heide der; ~n, ~n heathen

²Heide die; ~, ~n a) heath; ⟨~landschaft⟩ heathland; **Heide·kraut** das; o. Pl. heather

Heidel·beere die bilberry

heidnisch Adj. heathen

heikel Adj. a) ⟨schwierig⟩ delicate, ticklish ⟨matter, subject⟩; ticklish tricky ⟨problem, question, situation⟩; b) ⟨wählerisch⟩ fussy (**in bezug auf** + Akk. about)

heil Adj. ⟨nicht entzwei⟩ in one piece; **wieder ~ sein** ⟨injured part⟩ have healed [up]; **Heil** das; ~s a) ⟨Wohlergehen⟩ benefit; b) ⟨Rel.⟩ salvation; **Heiland** der; ~|e|s, ~e Saviour

Heil·anstalt die ⟨Anstalt für Kranke od. Süchtige⟩ sanatorium; ⟨psychiatrische Klinik⟩ mental hospital; **heilbar** Adj. curable

Heil·butt der halibut

heilen 1. tr. V. cure; heal ⟨wound⟩; 2. itr. V.; mit sein ⟨wound⟩ heal [up]; ⟨fracture⟩ mend

heil·froh Adj. very glad

heilig Adj. a) holy; **die Heilige Schrift** the Holy Scriptures pl.; **der Heilige Abend** Christmas Eve b) ⟨geh.: unantastbar⟩ sacred ⟨right, tradition, cause, etc.⟩; **Heilig·abend** der Christmas Eve; **Heilige** der/die; adj. Dekl. saint; **heiligen** tr. V. keep ⟨tradition, Sabbath, etc.⟩; **der Zweck heiligt die Mittel** the end justifies the means; **Heiligen·schein** der gloriole; ⟨um den Kopf⟩ halo; **Heiligkeit** die; ~: holiness; **Heiligtum** das; ~s, Heiligtümer shrine

Heil-: ~**kraut** das medicinal herb; ~**mittel** das ⟨auch fig.⟩ remedy (**gegen** for); ⟨Medikament⟩ medicament; ~**praktiker** der non-medical practitioner

heilsam Adj. salutary; **Heils·armee** die Salvation Army; **Heilung** die; ~, ~en ⟨einer Wunde⟩ healing; ⟨von Krankheit, Kranken⟩ curing

Heim das; ~|e|s, ~e a) ⟨Zuhause⟩ home; b) ⟨Anstalt, Alters~⟩ home; ⟨für

Obdachlose⟩ hostel; **Heim·arbeit** die outwork

Heimat die; ~, ~en a) ⟨~ort⟩ home; home town/village; ⟨~land⟩ home; homeland; b) ⟨Ursprungsland⟩ natural habitat

Heimat-: ~**kunde** die local history, geography, and natural history; ~**land** das native land; ⟨fig.⟩ home

heimatlich Adj. native ⟨dialect⟩; nostalgic ⟨emotions⟩

heimat-, Heimat-: ~**los** Adj. homeless; ~**museum** das museum of local history; ~**ort** der home town/village; ~**vertriebene** der/die; adj. Dekl. expellee [from his/her homeland]

heim-, Heim-: ~|**bringen** unr. tr. V. a) jmdn. ~: take or. see sb. home; b) bring home; ~|**fahren** 1. unr. itr. V.; mit sein drive home; 2. unr. tr. V. drive home; ~**fahrt** die journey home; ⟨mit dem Auto⟩ drive home; ~|**gehen** unr. itr. V.; mit sein go home

heimisch Adj. ⟨einheimisch⟩ indigenous, native ⟨plants, animals, etc.⟩ (**in** + Dat. to); domestic ⟨industry⟩; **sich ~ fühlen** feel at home; ~ **werden** [**in** (+ Dat.)] settle in[to]

heim-, Heim-: ~**kehr** die; ~: return home; homecoming; ~|**kehren** itr. V.; mit sein return home (**aus** from); ~|**kommen** unr. itr. V.; mit sein come home

heimlich 1. Adj. secret; 2. adv. secretly; **Heimlichkeit** die; ~, ~en; meist Pl. secret

heim-, Heim-: ~**reise** die journey home; ~|**suchen** itr. V. ⟨storm, earthquake, epidemic⟩ strike; ⟨disease⟩ afflict; ⟨nightmares, doubts⟩ plague; ~**tückisch** 1. Adj. ⟨bösartig⟩ malicious; ⟨fig.⟩ insidious ⟨disease⟩; 2. adv. maliciously; ~**wärts** Adv. ⟨nach Hause zu⟩ home; ⟨in Richtung Heimat⟩ homeward[s]; ~**weg** der way home-; ~**weh** das homesickness; ~**weh haben** be homesick (**nach** for); ~|**zahlen** tr. V. jmdm. etw. ~**zahlen** pay sb. back for sth.

Heinzel·männchen das brownie

Heirat die; ~, ~en marriage; **heiraten** 1. itr. V. get married; 2. tr. V. marry

Heirats-: ~**antrag** der: jmdm. einen ~**antrag machen** propose to sb.; ~**anzeige** die announcement of a/the forthcoming marriage; ~**schwindler** der person who makes a spurious offer of marriage for purposes of fraud

heiser 1. *Adj.* hoarse; 2. *adv.* in a hoarse voice; **Heiserkeit die;** ~ *s.* heiser: hoarseness

heiß 1. *Adj.* hot; jmdm. ist ~: sb. feels hot; etw. ~ **machen** heat sth. up; heated ⟨*debate, argument*⟩; fierce ⟨*fight, battle*⟩; ardent ⟨*wish, love*⟩; ein ~es Thema a controversial subject; 2. *adv.* ⟨*fight*⟩ fiercely; ⟨*love*⟩ dearly; ⟨*long*⟩ fervently

heißen *unr. itr. V.* ⟨*den Namen tragen*⟩ be called; ⟨*bedeuten*⟩ mean; ⟨*lauten*⟩ ⟨*saying*⟩ go; ⟨*unpers.*⟩ es heißt, daß ...: they say that ...; in dem Artikel heißt es ...: in the article it says that ...

heiter *Adj.* cheerful; fine ⟨*weather, day*⟩; **Heiterkeit die;** ~ a) ⟨*Frohsinn*⟩ cheerfulness; b) ⟨*Belustigung*⟩ merriment

heizbar *Adj.* heated; **Heiz·decke die** electric blanket; **heizen** 1. *itr. V.* have the heating on; 2. *tr. V.* heat ⟨*room etc.*⟩; **Heizer der;** ~s, ~ ⟨*einer Lokomotive*⟩ fireman; ⟨*eines Schiffes*⟩ stoker

Heiz-: ~**kissen das** heating pad; ~**körper der** radiator; ~**ofen der** stove; heater; ~**platte die** hotplate

Heizung die; ~, ~en a) [central] heating no pl., no indef. art.; b) ⟨*ugs.: Heizkörper*⟩ radiator

Hektar das od. der; ~s, ~e hectare

Hektik die; ~: hectic rush; ⟨*des Lebens*⟩ hectic pace; **hektisch** *Adj.* hectic

Held der; ~en, ~en hero; **heldenhaft** 1. *Adj.* heroic; 2. *adv.* heroically; **Heldentum das;** ~s heroism; **Heldin die;** ~, ~nen heroine

helfen *unr. itr. V.* help; jmdm. [bei etw.] ~ help sb. [with sth.]; ⟨*unpers.*⟩ es hilft nichts it's no use or good; **Helfer der;** ~s, ~ helper; ⟨*Mitarbeiter*⟩ assistant; ⟨*eines Verbrechens*⟩ accomplice

Helikopter der; ~s, ~ helicopter

hell 1. *Adj.* a) ⟨*von Licht erfüllt*⟩ light; well-lit ⟨*stairs*⟩; b) ⟨*klar*⟩ bright ⟨*day, sky, etc.*⟩; c) ⟨*viel Licht spendend*⟩ bright ⟨*light, lamp, star, etc.*⟩; d) ⟨*blaß*⟩ light ⟨*colour*⟩; fair ⟨*skin, hair*⟩; light-coloured ⟨*clothes*⟩; e) ⟨*akustisch*⟩ high, clear ⟨*sound, voice*⟩; ringing ⟨*laugh*⟩; f) ⟨*klug*⟩ bright; g) ⟨*ugs.: absolut*⟩ sheer, utter ⟨*madness, foolishness, despair*⟩; 2. *adv.* brightly

hell-: ~**blau** *Adj.* light blue; ~**blond** *Adj.* very fair; light blonde

Helle das; *adj. Dekl.* ≈ lager

Heller der; ~s, ~: heller; bis auf den letzten ~/bis auf ~ und Pfennig ⟨*ugs.*⟩ down to the last penny or ⟨*Amer.*⟩ cent

hell-: ~**grün** *Adj.* light green; ~**häutig** *Adj.* fair-skinned

Helligkeit die; ~, ~en ⟨*auch Physik*⟩ brightness

hell-, Hell-: ~**rot** *Adj.* light red; ~**sehen** *unr. itr. V.; nur im Inf.* ~sehen können have second sight; ~**seher der** clairvoyant; ~**wach** *Adj.* wide awake

Helm der; ~[e]s, ~e helmet

Hemd das; ~[e]s, ~en shirt; ⟨*Unterhemd*⟩ [under]vest; undershirt; **Hemds·ärmel der** shirt-sleeve

hemmen *tr. V.* a) ⟨*verlangsamen*⟩ slow [down]; b) ⟨*aufhalten*⟩ check; stem ⟨*flow*⟩; c) ⟨*beeinträchtigen*⟩ hinder; **Hemmung die;** ~, ~en a) ⟨*Gehemmtheit*⟩ inhibition; b) ⟨*Bedenken*⟩ scruple; **hemmungs·los** 1. *Adj.* unrestrained; 2. *adv.* unrestrainedly

Hendl das; ~s, ~[n] ⟨*bayr., österr.*⟩ chicken; ⟨*Brathähnchen*⟩ [roast] chicken

Hengst der; ~[e]s, ~e ⟨*Pferd*⟩ stallion

Henkel der; ~s, ~: handle

Henker der; ~s, ~: hangman; ⟨*Scharfrichter, auch fig.*⟩ executioner

Henne die; ~, ~n hen

her [he:ɐ̯] *Adv.* ~ **damit** give it to me; give it here ⟨*coll.*⟩; vom Fenster ~: from the window; von ihrer Kindheit ~: since childhood; von der Konzeption ~: as far as the basic design is concerned

herab *Adv.* down; von oben ~ ⟨*fig.*⟩ condescendingly

herab-: ~|**hängen** *unr. itr. V.* hang [down] ⟨*von from*⟩; ~**hängende Schultern** drooping shoulders; ~|**lassen** 1. *unr. tr. V.* let down; lower; 2. *unr. refl. V.* ⟨*iron.: bereit sein*⟩ sich ~lassen, etw. zu tun condescend to do sth.; ~**lassend** 1. *Adj.* condescending; patronizing ⟨*zu towards*⟩; 2. *adv.* condescendingly; patronizingly; ~|**sehen** *unr. itr. V.* auf jmdn. ~sehen look down on sb.; ~|**setzen** *tr. V.* a) reduce; b) ⟨*abwerten*⟩ belittle

heran *Adv.* an etw. ⟨*Akk.*⟩ ~: right up to sth.

heran-, Heran-: ~|**bilden** *tr. V.* train [up]; ⟨*auf der Schule, Universität*⟩ educate; ~|**bringen** *unr. V.* a) bring [up] ⟨*an + Akk., zu* to); b) ⟨*vertraut machen*⟩ jmdn. an etw. ⟨*Akk.*⟩ ~bringen introduce sb. to sth.; ~|**fahren**

unr. itr. V.; mit sein drive up (**an** + *Akk.* to); ~|**kommen** *unr. itr. V.; mit sein an etw. (Akk.)* ~**kommen** come near to sth.; *(erreichen)* reach sth.; *(erwerben)* obtain sth.; ~|**reifen** *itr. V.; mit sein (fruit, crops)* ripen; **zur Frau** ~**reifen** mature into a woman; ~|**treten** *unr. itr. V.; mit sein (sich wenden)* **an jmdn.** ~**treten** approach sb.; ~|**wachsen** *unr. itr. V.; mit sein* grow up; ~**wachsende der/die;** *adj. Dekl.* young person; ~|**ziehen** *unr. tr. V.* pull over; pull up ⟨*chair*⟩; **etw. zu sich** ~**ziehen** pull sth. towards one

herauf *Adv.* up

herauf-: ~|**beschwören** *tr. V.* a) *(verursachen)* cause ⟨*disaster, war, crisis*⟩; b) *(erinnern)* evoke ⟨*memories etc.*⟩; ~|**kommen** *unr. itr. V.; mit sein (nach oben kommen)* come up; ~|**setzen** *tr. V.* increase, put up ⟨*prices, rents, interest rates, etc.*⟩

heraus *Adv.* ~ **aus den Federn!/dem Bett!** rise and shine!/out of bed!

heraus-: ~|**bekommen** *unr. tr. V.* a) *(entfernen)* get out (**aus** of); b) *(ugs.: lösen)* work out ⟨*problem, answer, etc.*⟩; solve ⟨*puzzle*⟩; c) *(ermitteln)* find out; d) *(als Wechselgeld bekommen)* **5 DM** ~**bekommen** get back 5 marks change; **ich bekomme noch 5 DM** ~: I still have 5 marks [change] to come; ~|**bringen** *unr. tr. V.* a) *(nach außen bringen)* bring out (**aus** of); b) *(nach draußen begleiten)* show out; c) *(veröffentlichen)* bring out; *(aufführen)* put on, stage ⟨*play*⟩; screen ⟨*film*⟩; d) *(auf den Markt bringen)* bring out; e) *(populär machen)* make widely known; ~|**fahren 1.** *unr. itr. V.; mit sein* a) *(nach außen fahren)* **aus etw.** ~**fahren** drive/ride out of sth.; b) *(fahrend* ~**kommen)** *unr. itr. V.* **den Wagen [aus dem Hof]** ~**fahren** drive the car out [of the yard]; **jmdn.** ~**fahren** drive sb. out (**zu** to); ~|**finden 1.** *unr. tr. V.* find out; trace ⟨*fault*⟩; **2.** *unr. itr. V.* find one's way out (**aus** of); ~|**fordern 1.** *tr. V.* a) *(auch Sport)* challenge; b) *(heraufbeschwören)* provoke ⟨*person, resistance, etc.*⟩; invite ⟨*criticism*⟩; court ⟨*danger*⟩; **2.** *itr. V.* **zu etw.** ~**fordern** provoke sth.; ~**forderung die** *(auch Sport)* challenge; *(Provokation)* provocation; ~|**geben 1.** *unr. tr. V.* a) *(aushändigen)* hand over ⟨*property, person, hostage, etc.*⟩; *(zurückgeben)* give back; b) *(als Wechselgeld zurückgeben)* **5 DM/zuviel** ~**ge-**

ben give 5 marks/too much change; c) *(veröffentlichen)* publish; d) *(issue* ⟨*stamp, coin, etc.*⟩; **2.** *itr. V.* give change; ~**geber der** publisher; *(Redakteur)* editor; ~|**gehen** *unr. itr. V.; mit sein* a) go out (**aus** of); b) *(sich entfernen lassen)* ⟨*stain etc.*⟩ come out; ~|**halten** *unr. refl. V.* keep out; ~|**hängen** *tr. V.* hang out (**aus** of); ~|**helfen** *unr. itr. V.* **jmdm.** ~**helfen** *(auch fig.)* help sb. out (**aus** of); ~|**holen** *tr. V.* a) *(nach außen holen)* bring out; b) *(ugs.: erwirken)* win ⟨*wage increase, advantage, etc.*⟩; ~|**kommen** *unr. itr. V.; mit sein* a) come out (**aus** of); b) *(erscheinen; ugs.: auf den Markt kommen, bekannt werden)* come out; ~|**nehmen** *unr. tr. V.* a) take out (**aus** of); b) *(ugs.: entfernen)* take out ⟨*appendix, tonsils, tooth, etc.*⟩; ~|**reden** *refl. V. (ugs.)* talk one's way out (**aus** of); ~|**reißen** *unr. tr. V.* a) tear out (**aus** of); pull up ⟨*plant*⟩; ~|**rutschen** *itr. V.; mit sein (ugs.)* ⟨*remark etc.*⟩ slip out; ~|**stellen** *refl. V.* **es stellte sich** ~, **daß** ...: it turned out that ...; ~|**suchen** *tr. V.* pick out; look out ⟨*file*⟩

herb *Adj.* [slightly] sharp ⟨*taste*⟩; dry ⟨*wine*⟩; [slightly] sharp ⟨*smell, perfume*⟩; bitter ⟨*disappointment*⟩; severe ⟨*face, features*⟩; austere ⟨*beauty*⟩; harsh ⟨*words, criticism*⟩

herbei-: ~|**eilen** *itr. V.; mit sein* hurry over; ~|**laufen** *unr. itr. V.; mit sein* come running up

Herberge die; ~, ~**n** *(veralt.: Gasthaus)* inn

her|**bringen** *unr. tr. V.* **etw.** ~: bring sth. [here]

Herbst der; ~|**e**|**s**, ~**e** autumn; fall *(Amer.)*; s. auch **Frühling**; **Herbstanfang der** beginning of autumn; **herbstlich** *Adj.* autumn *attrib.*; autumnal

Herd der; ~|**e**|**s**, ~**e** cooker; *(fig.)* centre *(of disturbance/rebellion)*

Herde die; ~, ~**n** herd

herein-: ~|**bitten** *unr. tr. V.* **jmdn.** ~**bitten** ask or invite sb. in; ~|**brechen** *unr. itr. V.; mit sein (geh.)* ⟨*night, evening, dusk*⟩ fall; ⟨*winter*⟩ set in; ⟨*storm*⟩ strike, break; ~|**bringen** *unr. tr. V.* bring in; ~|**fallen** *unr. itr. V.; mit sein (ugs.)* be taken for a ride *(coll.)*; be done *(coll.)*; ~|**kommen** *unr. itr. V.; mit sein* come in; ~|**lassen** *unr. tr. V.* let in; ~|**legen** *tr. V. (ugs.)* **jmdn.** ~**legen** take sb. for a ride *(coll.)* (**mit, bei** with); ~|**platzen** *itr.*

V.; mit sein (ugs.) burst in; ~|**schnei-en** *unr. itr. V.; mit sein (ugs.)* turn up out of the blue *(coll.)*

her-, Her-: ~**fahrt** die journey here; ~|**fallen** *unr. itr. V.; mit sein* über jmdn. ~**fallen** attack sb.; *(gierig zu essen beginnen)* über etw. *(Akk.)* ~**fallen** fall upon sth.; ~**gang** der: der ~**gang** der Ereignisse the sequence of events; ~|**geben** *unr. tr. V.* hand over; *(weggeben)* give away; ~|**gehen** *unr. itr. V.; mit sein* neben/vor/hinter jmdm. ~**gehen** walk along beside/in front of/behind sb.; ~|**haben** *unr. tr. V. (ugs.)* wo hat er/sie das ~? where did he/she get that from?; ~|**halten** *unr. itr. V.* ~**halten müssen** [für jmdn./etw.] be the one to suffer [for sb./sth.]; ~|**hören** *itr. V.* listen

Hering der; ~s, ~e a) herring; b) *(Zeltpflock)* peg

her-: ~|**kommen** *unr. itr. V.; mit sein* come here; ~**kömmlich** *Adj.* conventional; traditional *⟨custom⟩*

Herkunft die; ~, **Herkünfte** origin

her-: ~|**laufen** *unr. itr. V.; mit sein* vor/hinter/neben jmdm. ~**laufen** run [along] in front of/behind/alongside sb.; *(nachlaufen)* hinter jmdm. ~**laufen** run after sb.; *(fig.)* chase sb. up; ~|**leiten** *tr., refl. V.* derive *(aus, von* from); ~|**machen** *(ugs.) refl. V.* sich über etw. *(Akk.)* ~**machen** get stuck into sth. *(coll.)*

Hermelin der; ~s, ~e *(Pelz)* ermine

hermetisch 1. *Adj.* hermetic; 2. *adv.* hermetically

Heroin das; ~s heroin

Herr der; ~n, ~en a) *(Mann)* gentleman; b) *(Titel, Anrede)* ~ Schulze Mr Schulze; **Sehr geehrter** ~ **Schulze!** Dear Sir; *(bei persönlicher Bekanntschaft)* Dear Mr Schulze; **meine** ~**en** gentlemen; c) *(Gebieter)* master

herren-, Herren-: ~**ausstatter** der [gentle]men's outfitter; ~**los** *Adj.* abandoned *⟨car, luggage⟩*; stray *⟨dog, cat⟩*; ~**salon** der men's hairdressing salon; ~**schuh** der man's shoe; ~**schuhe** men's shoes; ~**toilette** die [gentle]men's toilet

Herr·gott der; ~s: der |**liebe/unser** ~: the Lord [God]; God; **Herrgottsfrühe** die *in* in aller ~: at the crack of dawn

her·richten *tr. V. (bereitmachen)* get *⟨room, refreshments, etc.⟩* ready; arrange *⟨table⟩*; *(in Ordnung bringen)* renovate

Herrin die; ~, ~en mistress; **herrisch** 1. *Adj.* overbearing; imperious; 2. *adv.* imperiously; **herrlich** 1. *Adj.* marvellous; magnificent *⟨view, clothes⟩*; 2. *adv.* marvellously; **Herrlichkeit** die; ~, ~en a) *o. Pl. (Schönheit)* magnificence; splendour; b) *meist Pl. (herrliche Sache)* marvellous thing; **Herrschaft** die; ~, ~en a) *o. Pl.* rule; *(Macht)* power; b) *Pl. (Damen u. Herren)* ladies and gentlemen; **herrschen** *itr. V.* rule; *⟨monarch⟩* reign, rule; **draußen** ~ 30° **Kälte** it's 30° below outside; **Herrscher** der; ~s, ~: ruler; **herrsch·süchtig** *Adj.* domineering

her-: ~|**rühren** *itr. V.* von jmdm./etw. ~**rühren** come from sb./stem from sth.; ~|**sein** *unr. itr. V.; mit sein* einen Monat/lange ~**sein** be a month/a long time ago; **es ist lange** ~, **daß wir ...:** it is a long time since we ...; **von Köln** ~**sein** be from Cologne; **hinter jmdm.** *(ugs.)*/etw. ~**sein** be after sb./sth.; ~|**stellen** *tr. V.* produce

Her·steller der; ~s, ~: producer; **Her·stellung** die production

herüber *Adv.* over

herum *Adv.* um ... ~ *(Richtung)* round; *(Anordnung)* around; **um Weihnachten** ~: around Christmas

herum-: ~|**ärgern** *refl. V. (ugs.)* sich mit jmdm./etw. ~**ärgern** keep getting annoyed with sb./sth.; ~|**drehen** 1. *tr. V. (ugs.)* turn *⟨key⟩*; turn over *⟨coin, mattress, hand, etc.⟩*; 2. *refl. V.* turn [a]round; ~|**fahren** *(ugs.)* 1. *unr. itr. V.; mit sein (sich plötzlich herumdrehen)* spin round; 2. *unr. tr. V.* jmdn. |**in der Stadt**| ~**fahren** drive sb. around the town; ~|**führen** 1. *tr. V.* jmdn. |**in der Stadt**| ~**führen** show sb. around the town; 2. *itr. V.* um etw. ~**führen** *⟨road etc.⟩* go round sth.; ~|**gehen** *unr. itr. V.; mit sein (vergehen)* pass; um etw. ~**gehen** go round the town; etw. ~**gehen lassen** circulate sth.; pass; ~|**kommen** *unr. itr. V.; mit sein (ugs.)* a) *(vermeiden können)* um etw. |**nicht**| ~**kommen** [not] be able to get out of sth.; b) *(viel reisen)* get around or about; **in der Welt** ~**kommen** see a lot of the world; ~|**laufen** *unr. itr. V.; mit sein* a) walk/*(schneller)* run around or about; um etw. ~**laufen** go round sth.; b) *(gekleidet sein)* wie ein Hippie ~**laufen** go about looking like a hippie; ~|**lungern** *itr. V. (salopp)* loaf around; ~|**schlagen** *unr. refl. V.*

(ugs.) **sich mit Problemen/Einwänden ~schlagen** grapple with problems/ battle against objections; **~|sein** *unr. itr. V.; mit sein; Zusammenschreibung nur im Inf. und Part. (ugs.) (vergangen sein)* have passed; **~|sitzen** *unr. itr. V. (ugs.)* sit around *or* about; **~|sprechen** *unr. refl. V.* get around *or* about; **~|stöbern** *itr. V. (ugs.)* keep rummaging around *or* about (**in** + *Dat.* in); **~|treiben** *unr. refl. V. (ugs. abwertend)* **sich auf den Straßen/in Discos ~treiben** hang around the streets/in discos; **sich in der Welt ~treiben** roam about the world

herunter *Adv.* a) *(nach unten)* down; b) *(fort)* off; **~ vom Sofa!** [get] off the sofa!

herunter-: **~|bringen** *unr. tr. V.* bring down; **~|fallen** *unr. itr. V.; mit sein* fall down; **vom Tisch/Stuhl ~fallen** fall off the table/chair; **~|gehen** *unr. itr. V.; mit sein* a) come down; b) *(niedriger werden) (temperature)* drop; *(prices)* come down, fall; **~gekommen** 1. 2. *Part. v.* **~kommen;** 2. *Adj.* poor *(health);* dilapidated *(building);* run-down *(area);* down and out *(person);* **~|handeln** *tr. V. (ugs.)* **einen Preis ~handeln** beat down a price; **~|hängen** *unr. itr. V.* hang down; **~|hauen** *unr. tr. V. (ugs.)* **jmdm. eine ~hauen** give sb. a clout round the ear *(coll.);* **~|kommen** *unr. itr. V.; mit sein* a) come down; b) *(ugs.: verfallen)* go to the dogs *(coll.);* **~|lassen** *unr. tr. V.* lower; **~|schlucken** *tr. V.* swallow; **~|sein** *unr. itr. V.; mit sein; Zusammenschreibung nur im Inf. und Part. (ugs.)* be down; *(körperlich)* **~sein** be in poor health; **~|spielen** *tr. V. (ugs.)* play down *(coll.)*

hervor *Adv.* **aus ... ~:** out of

hervor-: **~|heben** *unr. tr. V.* stress; **~ragend** 1. *Adj.* outstanding[ly good]; 2. *adv.* **~ragend** geschult outstandingly well trained; **~ragend spielen/arbeiten** play/work outstandingly well; **~|tun** *unr. refl. V.* distinguish oneself; *(wichtig tun)* show off

Herz das; **~ens, ~en** a) heart; *(Kartenspiel)* hearts *pl.;* **von ~en kommen** come from the heart; **ein ~ für die Armen haben** feel for the poor; **ein ~ für Kinder haben** have a love of children; **schweren ~ens** with a heavy heart; **etw. auf dem ~en haben** have sth. on one's mind; **es nicht übers ~ bringen, etw. zu tun** not have the heart to do sth.; **sich**

(Dat.) **etw. zu ~en nehmen** take sth. to heart; **Herz·anfall der** heart attack; **herzens·gut** ['--'] *Adj.* kindhearted; **Herzens·lust die: nach ~:** to one's heart's content; **herz·haft** 1. *Adj.* hearty *(meal);* (von kräftigem Geschmack) tasty; 2. *adv.* heartily; *(nahrhaft)* **er ißt gern ~:** he likes to have a hearty meal

her|ziehen *unr. itr. V.; mit sein od. haben (ugs.)* **über jmdn./etw. ~:** run sb./ sth. down

herzig 1. *Adj.* sweet; delightful; 2. *adv.* sweetly; delightfully

herz-, Herz-: **~infarkt der** heart attack; **~klopfen das; ~s:** jmd. **hat ~klopfen** sb.'s heart is pounding; **~krank** *Adj.* *(person)* with a heart condition

herzlich 1. *Adj.* warm *(smile, reception);* kind *(words, regards);* (ehrlich gemeint) sincere; **~en Dank** many thanks; 2. *adv.* warmly; *(ehrlich gemeint)* sincerely; *(congratulate)* heartily; **~ wenig** very *or (coll.)* precious little; **Herzlichkeit die** warmth; kindness; *(Aufrichtigkeit)* sincerity; **herz·los** 1. *Adj.* heartless; 2. *adv.* heartlessly

Herzog der; **~s, Herzöge** duke; **Herzogin die;** **~, ~nen** duchess

herz-, Herz-: **~schlag der** heartbeat; *(Herzversagen)* heart failure; **~schmerz der;** *meist Pl.* pain in the region of the heart; **~transplantation die** *(Med.)* heart transplantation; **~zerreißend** 1. *Adj.* heart-rending; 2. *adv.* heart-rendingly

Hessen (das); **~s** Hesse

Hetze die; ~ a) [mad] rush; b) *o. Pl. (abwertend)* smear campaign; **hetzen** 1. *tr. V.* a) hunt; b) *(antreiben)* rush; 2. *itr. V.* a) *(in großer Eile sein)* rush; b) *mit sein (hasten)* rush; *(rennen)* dash; race; **Hetz·rede die** *(abwertend)* inflammatory speech

Heu das; **~[e]s** hay

Heuchelei die; **~:** hypocrisy; **heucheln** 1. *itr. V.* be a hypocrite; 2. *tr. V.* feign; **Heuchler der;** **~s, ~:** hypocrite; **heuchlerisch** 1. *Adj.* hypocritical; 2. *adv.* hypocritically

heuer *Adv. (südd., österr., schweiz.)* this year

Heuer die; **~, ~n** *(Seemannsspr.)* pay; wages *pl.*

Heu·ernte die a) hay harvest; b) *(Ertrag)* hay crop

heulen itr. V. a) howl; ⟨siren etc.⟩ wail; b) (ugs.: weinen) howl; bawl

Heurige der; adj. Dekl. (bes. österr.) a) (Wein) new wine; b) (Weinlokal) inn with new wine on tap

Heu-: ~**schnupfen** der hay fever; ~**schrecke** die grasshopper

heute Adv. today; ~ **früh** early this morning; ~ **morgen/abend** this morning/evening; ~ **mittag** [at] midday today; ~ **nacht** tonight; (letzte Nacht) last night; ~ **in einer Woche** a week [from] today; today week; ~ **vor einer Woche** a week ago today; **heutig** Adj. a) (von diesem Tag) today's; der ~**e** Tag today; b) (gegenwärtig) today's; of today postpos.; **in der ~en** Zeit nowadays; **heut·zu·tage** Adv. nowadays

Hexe die; ~, ~n witch; **hexen** itr. V. work magic

Hexen·schuß der; o. Pl. lumbago no indef. art.; **Hexerei** die; ~, ~en witchcraft; (von Kunststücken usw.) magic

hieb 1. u. 3. Pers. Sg. Prät. v. hauen; **Hieb** der; ~[e]s, ~e a) (Schlag) blow; (mit der Peitsche) lash; b) Pl. (ugs.: Prügel) hiding sing.; **hieb·fest** Adj. **hieb- und stichfest** watertight; cast-iron

hielt 1. u. 3. Pers. Sg. Prät. v. halten

hier Adv. a) here; |von| ~ **oben/unten** [from] up/down here; b) (jetzt) now; **von** ~ **an** from now on

hieran Adv. here; **sich** ~ **festhalten** hold on to this; (fig.) **im Anschluß** ~: immediately after this

Hierarchie [hierar'çi:] die; ~, ~n hierarchy

hierauf Adv. a) on here; (darauf) on this; **wir werden** ~ **zurückkommen** we'll come back to this; b) (danach) after that; then; c) (infolgedessen) whereupon; **hieraus** Adv. out of here; (aus dieser Tatsache, Quelle) from this

hier-: ~|**behalten** unr. tr. V. jmdn./ etw. ~: keep sb./sth. here; ~**bei** Adv. a) (bei dieser Gelegenheit) Diese Übung ist sehr schwierig. Man kann sich ~ leicht verletzen. This exercise is very difficult. You can easily injure yourself doing it; b) (bei der erwähnten Sache) here; ~|**bleiben** unr. itr. V.; mit sein stay here; ~**durch** Adv. through here; (auf Grund dieser Sache) because of this; ~**für** Adv. for this

hier·her Adv. here; **ich gehe bis** ~ **und nicht weiter** I'm going this far and no further

hierher-: ~|**gehören** itr. V. belong here; (hierfür wichtig sein) be relevant [here]; ~|**kommen** unr. itr. V.; mit sein come here

hier·hin Adv. here; **bis** ~: up to here

hier-: ~**in** Adv. a) (räumlich) in here; b) in this; ~|**lassen** unr. tr. V. etw. ~: leave sth. here; ~**mit** Adv. with this/ these; ~**mit ist der Fall erledigt** that puts an end to the matter; ~**nach** Adv. (anschließend) after that

Hieroglyphe die; ~, ~n hieroglyph

hier-: ~**sein** unr. itr. V.; mit sein; Zusammenschreibung nur im Inf. und Part. be here; ~**über** Adv. a) (über dem Erwähnten) above here; (über das Erwähnte) over here; b) (das Erwähnte betreffend) about this/these; ~**von** Adv. of this/these; ~**zu** Adv. with this; (hinsichtlich dieser Sache) about this; ~**zu gehört/gehören** ...: this includes/these include; ~**zu reicht mein Geld nicht** I haven't got enough money for that; ~**zu·lande** Adv. [here] in this country

hiesig Adj.; nicht präd. local

hieß 1. u. 3. Pers. Sg. Prät. v. heißen

Hi-Fi-Anlage ['haifi-] die hi-fi system

Hilfe die; ~, ~n a) help; (für Notleidende) aid; relief; **zu** ~! help!; b) (Hilfskraft) help; (im Geschäft) assistant

Hilfe-: ~**leistung** die help; ~**ruf** der cry for help; ~**stellung** die (Turnen) jmdm. ~**stellung geben** act as spotter for sb.

hilflos 1. Adj. helpless; 2. adv. helplessly; **Hilflosigkeit** die; ~ helplessness

hilfs-, Hilfs-: ~**bedürftig** Adj. a) (schwach) in need of help postpos.; b) (notleidend) in need; needy; ~**bereit** Adj. helpful; ~**bereitschaft** die helpfulness; ~**kraft** die assistant; ~**mittel** das aid; ~**zeit·wort** das (Sprachw.) auxiliary [verb]

Himalaja der; ~[s]: der/im ~: the/in the Himalayas pl.

Him·beere die raspberry

Himmel der; ~s, ~ sky; (Rel.) heaven; ~ **noch [ein]mal!** for Heaven's sake!

Himmel·bett das four-poster bed; **himmel·blau** Adj. sky-blue; clear blue ⟨eyes⟩

Himmels-: ~**richtung** die point of the compass; ~**schlüsselchen** das cowslip

himmel·weit *Adj.* enormous, vast ⟨*difference*⟩; **himmlisch** *Adj. (auch fig.)* heavenly

hin *Adv.* a) *(räumlich)* zur Straße ~ liegen face the road; b) *(zeitlich)* gegen Mittag ~: towards midday; c) *(in Verbindungen)* nach außen ~: outwardly; **auf meinen Rat** ~: on my advice; **auf seine Bitte** ~: at his request; d) *(in Wortpaaren)* ~ **und zurück** there and back; **einmal Köln** ~ **und zurück** a return [ticket] to Cologne; ~ **und her** to and fro; back and forth; ~ **und wieder** [every] now and then

hinab *Adv. s.* hinunter

hinab|- *s.* hinunter|-

hinauf *Adv.* up; bis ~ zu up to

hinauf-: ~|**fahren** *unr. itr. V.; mit sein* go up; *(im Auto)* drive up; *(mit einem Motorrad)* ride up; ~|**gehen** *unr. itr. V.; mit sein (nach oben gehen)* go up; b) *(nach oben führen)* lead up; c) *(ugs.: steigen)* ⟨*prices, taxes, etc.*⟩ go up; rise; ~|**klettern** *itr. V.; mit sein* climb up; ~|**steigen** *unr. itr. V.; mit sein* climb up; ~|**ziehen** 1. *unr. tr. V.* pull up; 2. *unr. itr. V.; mit sein* move up; 3. *unr. refl. V. (sich erstrecken)* stretch up

hinaus *Adv.* a) *(räumlich)* out; b) *(zeitlich)* **auf Jahre** ~: for years to come; c) *(etw. überschreitend)* **über etw.** *(Akk.)* ~: in addition to sth.

hinaus-: ~|**bringen** *unr. tr. V.* jmdn./etw. ~bringen see sb. out/take sth. out *(aus of)*; ~|**fahren** 1. *unr. itr. V.; mit sein* **aus etw.** ~fahren *(mit dem Auto)* drive out of sth.; *(mit dem Zweirad)* ride out of sth.; ⟨*car, bus*⟩ go out of sth.; ⟨*train*⟩ pull out of sth.; **zum Flugplatz** ~fahren drive out to the airport; 2. *unr. tr. V.* jmdn./etw. ~fahren drive sb./take sth. out; ~|**fallen** *unr. itr. V.; mit sein* fall out *(aus of)*; ~|**finden** *unr. itr. V.* find one's way out *(aus of)*; ~|**gehen** *unr. itr. V.; mit sein* a) go out *(aus of)*; b) *(gerichtet sein)* das Zimmer geht zum Garten/nach Westen ~: the room looks out on to the garden/faces west; ~|**kommen** *unr. itr. V.; mit sein* come out *(aus of)*; ~|**laufen** *unr. itr. V.; mit sein* a) run out *(aus of)*; b) *(als Ergebnis haben)* **auf etw.** *(Akk.)* ~laufen lead to sth.; ~|**sehen** *unr. itr. V.* look out; **zum Fenster** ~sehen look out of the window; ~|**sein** *unr. itr. V.; mit sein* **über etw.** *(Akk.)* ~sein be past sth.; ~|**tragen** *unr. tr. V.* jmdn./etw. ~tragen carry

sb./sth. out; ~|**werfen** *unr. tr. V. (auch ugs. fig.)* throw out *(aus of)*; ~|**ziehen** 1. *unr. tr. V.* a) *(nach draußen ziehen)* jmdn./etw. ~ziehen pull sb./sth. out *(aus of)*; tow ⟨*ship*⟩ out; b) *(verzögern)* put off; delay; 2. *unr. refl. V.* be delayed; ~|**zögern** 1. *tr. V.* delay; 2. *refl. V.* be delayed

hin-, Hin-: ~|**blick der** *in od.* ~blick auf etw. *(Akk.) (wegen)* in view of; *(hinsichtlich)* with regard to; ~|**bringen** *unr. tr. V.* jmdn./etw. ~bringen take sb./sth. [there]; ~|**denken** *unr. itr. V.* wo denkst du hin? *(ugs.)* whatever are you thinking of?

hinderlich *Adj.* ~ sein get in the way; **hindern** *tr. V.* a) *(abhalten)* jmdn. ~: stop sb. (an + *Dat.* from); b) *(behindern)* hinder; **Hindernis** das *(~ses, ~se* obstacle

hin|deuten *itr. V.* a) **auf jmdn./etw.** *od.* **zu jmdm./etw.** ~: point to sb./sth.; b) **auf etw.** *(Akk.)* ~ *(fig.)* point to sth.

hin·durch *Adv.* a) *(räumlich)* durch den Wald ~: through the wood; b) *(zeitlich)* das ganze Jahr ~: throughout the year

hinein *Adv.* a) *(räumlich)* in; **in etw.** *(Akk.)* ~: into sth.; b) *(zeitlich)* bis in den Morgen/tief in die Nacht ~: till morning/far into the night

hinein-: ~|**bringen** *unr. tr. V.* take in; ~|**fahren** *(mit dem Auto)* drive in; *(mit dem Zweirad)* ride in; **in etw.** *(Akk.)* ~fahren drive/ride into sth.; ~|**fallen** *unr. itr. V.; mit sein* fall in; **in etw.** *(Akk.)* ~fallen fall into sth.; ~|**gehen** *unr. itr. V.; mit sein* go in; **in etw.** *(Akk.)* ~gehen go into sth.; ~|**gucken** *itr. V. (ugs.)* look in; **in etw.** *(Akk.)* ~gucken look in[to] sth.; ~|**kommen** *unr. itr. V.; mit sein* a) come in; **in etw.** *(Akk.)* ~kommen come into sth.; b) *(gelangen, auch fig.)* get in; **in etw.** *(Akk.)* ~kommen get into sth.; ~|**reden** *itr. V.* jmdm. in seine Angelegenheiten/Entscheidungen usw. ~reden interfere in sb.'s affairs/decisions *etc.*; ~|**sehen** *unr. itr. V.* look in; **in etw.** *(Akk.)* ~sehen look into sth.; ~|**versetzen** *refl. V.* sich in jmdn. *od.* jmds. Lage ~versetzen put oneself in sb.'s position

hin-, Hin-: ~|**fahren** 1. *unr. itr. V.; mit sein* go there; 2. *unr. tr. V.* drive sb. there; ~|**fahrt die** journey there; *(Seereise)* voyage out; ~|**fallen** *unr. itr. V.; mit sein* a) fall over; b) jmdm. fällt etw. ~: sb. drops sth.; **etw. ~fallen lassen** drop sth.; **~fällig** *Adj.* **a)** infirm; frail; **b)** *(ungültig)* invalid; ~**fliegen** *unr. itr. V.;* **mit sein** fly there; **~flug der** outward flight

hing *1. u. 3. Pers. Sg. Prät. v.* hängen

Hin·gabe die; ~: devotion; *(Eifer)* dedication; **Hingebung die;** ~: devotion; **hingebungs·voll 1.** *Adj.* devoted; **2.** *adv.* devotedly; with devotion; *(listen)* with rapt attention; ⟨dance, play⟩ with abandon

hin·gegen *Konj., Adv. (jedoch)* however; *(andererseits)* on the other hand

hin-: ~|**gehen** *unr. itr. V.;* **mit sein a)** go [there]; **zu jmdm./etw. ~gehen** go to sb./sth.; **b)** *(verstreichen)* go by; ~|**halten** *unr. tr. V.* **a)** hold out; **b)** *(warten lassen)* **jmdn. ~halten** keep sb. waiting; ~|**hören** *itr. V.* listen

hinken ['hɪŋkn̩] *itr. V.* **a)** walk with a limp; **b)** *mit sein (hinkend gehen)* limp

hin-: ~|**kommen** *unr. itr. V.;* **mit sein a)** get there; **b)** *(an einen Ort gehören)* go; belong; **c)** *(ugs.: stimmen)* be right; ~|**länglich 1.** *Adj.* sufficient; *(angemessen)* adequate; **2.** *adv.* sufficiently; *(angemessen)* adequately; ~|**legen 1.** *tr. V.* put; *(weglegen)* put down; **2.** *refl. V.* lie down; ~|**reichend 1.** *Adj.* sufficient; *(angemessen)* adequate; **2.** *adv.* sufficiently; *(angemessen)* adequately; ~**reise die** journey there; *(mit dem Schiff)* voyage out; ~**reißend** *Adj.* enchanting ⟨*person, picture, view*⟩; captivating ⟨*speaker, play*⟩; ~|**richten** *tr. V.* execute; ~|**richtung die** execution

Hinrichtungs·kommando das firing-squad

hin-, Hin-: ~|**sehen** *unr. itr. V.* look; ~|**sein** *unr. itr. V.; mit sein (nur im Inf. u. Part. zusammengeschrieben) (ugs.)* **a)** *(verloren sein)* be gone; **b)** *(nicht mehr brauchbar sein)* have had it *(coll.)*; *(car)* be a write-off; **c)** *(salopp: tot sein)* have snuffed it *(sl.)*; **d)** *(ugs.: hingerissen sein)* **von jmdm./etw. ganz ~sein** be mad about sb./bowled over by sth.; ~|**setzen 1.** *tr. V.* put; **2.** *refl. V.* sit down; ~**sicht die**; *o. Pl.* **in gewisser ~sicht** in a way/in some respect or ways; **in jeder ~sicht** in every respect; **in finanzieller ~sicht** financially; ~**sichtlich** *Präp. mit Gen. (Amtsspr.)* with regard to; *(in Anbetracht)* in view of; ~|**stellen 1.** *tr. V.* put; put up ⟨building⟩; *(absetzen)* put down; **2.** *refl. V.* stand

hinten *Adv.* at the back; **sich ~ anstellen** join the back of the queue (*Brit.*) or (*Amer.*) line; **weiter ~:** further back; *(in einem Buch)* further on; **die Adresse steht ~ auf dem Brief** the address is on the back of the envelope; **nach ~ hinaus liegen/gehen** be at the back; **die anderen sind ganz weit ~:** the others are a long way back

hinter 1. *Präp. mit Dat.* behind; *(nach)* after; **3 km ~ der Grenze** 3 km beyond the frontier; **eine Prüfung ~ sich haben** *(fig.)* have got an examination over [and done] with; **viele Enttäuschungen/eine Krankheit ~ sich haben** have experienced many disappointments/have got over an illness; **2.** *Präp. mit Akk.* behind

hinter... *Adj.; nicht präd.* back

hinter-, Hinter-: ~|**einander** *Adv.* **a)** *(räumlich)* one behind the other; **b)** *(zeitlich)* one after another or the other; ~**gedanke der** ulterior motive; ~**gehen** [--'-] *unr. tr. V.* deceive; ~**grund der** background; ~**gründig 1.** *Adj.* enigmatic; **2.** *adv.* enigmatically; ~**halt der** ambush; ~**hältig 1.** *Adj.* underhand; **2.** *adv.* in an underhand manner; ~**her** *Adv. (räumlich)* behind; *(nachher)* afterwards; ~**hof der** courtyard; ~**land das** hinterland; *(Milit.)* back area; ~**lassen** [--'-] *unr. tr. V.* leave; ~**legen** [--'-] *tr. V.* deposit (bei with); ~**list die** guile; deceit; ~**listig** *Adj.* deceitful; ~**mann der**; *Pl.* ~**männer a)** person behind; **b)** *(Gewährsmann)* [secret] informant

Hintern der; ~s, ~ *(ugs.)* backside; bottom

hinter-, Hinter-: ~**rad das** rear wheel; ~**teil das** backside; behind; ~**treffen das** *(ugs.)* **in ins ~treffen geraten** *od.* **kommen** fall behind; ~**treiben** [--'-] *unr. tr. V.* foil ⟨plan⟩; prevent ⟨marriage, promotion⟩; block ⟨law, investigation, reform⟩; ~**treppe die** back stairs *pl.;* ~**tür die** back door; ~**wäldler** [~vɛltlɐ] **der;** ~s, ~ *(spött.)* backwoodsman

hinüber *Adv.* over; across

Hin- und Rück·fahrt die journey there and back; round trip (*Amer.*)

hinunter *Adv.* down

hinunter-: ~|**fahren 1.** *unr. itr. V.; mit sein* go down; *(mit dem Auto)* drive down; *(mit dem Fahrrad)* ride down; **2.** *unr. tr. V.* **jmdn./ein Auto/eine Ladung ~fahren** drive sb. down/

drive a car down/take a load down; **~|gehen** *unr. itr. V.; mit sein* go down; ⟨*aircraft*⟩ descend; **~|reichen** 1. *tr. V.* hand down; 2. *itr. V.* (*sich bis hinunter erstrecken*) reach down (bis auf + *Akk.* to)

Hin·weg der way there

hin·weg *Adv.* a) (geh.) ~ mit dir! away with you!; b) über etw. ~: over sth.

hinweg-: **~|gehen** *unr. itr. V.; mit sein* über etw. (*Akk.*) ~gehen pass over sth.; **~|kommen** *unr. itr. V.; mit sein* über etw. (*Akk.*) ~kommen get over sth.; **~|setzen** *refl. V.* sich über etw. (*Akk.*) ~setzen ignore sth.

Hinweis ['hɪnvaɪs] *der; ~es, ~e* hint; **unter ~ auf** (+ *Akk.*) with reference to

hin-: **~|weisen** 1. *unr. itr. V.* auf jmdn./etw. ~weisen point to sb./sth.; 2. *unr. tr. V.* jmdn. auf etw. (*Akk.*) ~weisen point sth. out to sb.; **~weisend** *Adj.* (Grammatik) demonstrative; **~|werfen** *unr. tr. V.* throw down; **~|ziehen** 1. *unr. tr. V.* pull, draw (**zu** to, towards); 2. *unr. itr. V.; mit sein* a) (*umziehen*) move there; wo ist sie ~gezogen? where did she move to?; 3. *unr. refl. V.* a) (*sich erstrecken*) drag on (über + *Akk.* for); b) (*sich verzögern*) be delayed

hinzu-: **~|fügen** *tr. V.* add; **~|kommen** *unr. itr. V.; mit sein* a) (*kommt gleich mit*) come along; b) (*hinzugefügt werden*) zu etw. ~kommen be added to sth.; **es kommt noch ~, daß ...** (*fig.*) there is also the fact that ...; **~|tun** *unr. tr. V.* (*ugs.*) add

Hirn das; ~|e|s, ~e a) brain; b) (*Speise; ugs.: Verstand*) brains *pl.*

Hirsch der; ~|e|s, ~e deer; (*Rothirsch*) red deer; (*männlicher Rothirsch*) stag; (*Speise*) venison

Hirse die; ~, ~n millet

Hirt der; ~en, ~en, **Hirte** der; ~n, ~n herdsman; (*Schaf~*) shepherd

hissen *tr. V.* hoist

historisch *Adj.* a) historical; b) (*geschichtlich bedeutungsvoll*) historic

Hit der; ~|s|, ~s (*ugs.*) hit

Hitze die; ~: heat

hitze-, Hitze-: **~beständig** *Adj.* heat-resistant; **~frei** *Adj.* ~frei haben have the rest of the day off [school/ work] because of excessively hot weather; **~welle** die heat wave

hitzig *Adj.* a) hot-tempered; b) (*erregt*) heated ⟨*discussion etc.*⟩

hitz-, Hitz-: **~kopf** der hothead; **~köpfig** *Adj.* hot-headed; **~schlag** der heat-stroke

hl *Abk.* Hektoliter hl

hob *1.* u. *3. Pers. Sg. Prät. v.* heben

Hobby das; ~s, ~s hobby

Hobel der; ~s, ~ a) plane; b) (*Küchengerät*) [vegetable] slicer; **Hobel·bank** die woodworker's bench; **hobeln** *tr., itr. V.* a) plane; b) (*schneiden*) slice

hoch; höher, höchst ... 1. *Adj.* high; tall ⟨*tree, mast*⟩; long ⟨*grass*⟩; deep ⟨*snow, water*⟩; heavy ⟨*fine*⟩; large ⟨*sum, amount*⟩; severe, extensive ⟨*damage*⟩; senior ⟨*official, officer, post*⟩; high-level ⟨*diplomacy, politics*⟩; **höchste Gefahr** extreme danger; **es ist höchste Zeit, daß ...**: it is high time that ...; **das hohe C** top C; **vier ~ zwei** (*Math.*) four to the power [of] two; four squared; 2. *adv.* (*in großer Höhe*) high; (*nach oben*) up; (*zahlenmäßig viel, sehr*) highly; **~ verschuldet/versichert** heavily in debt/insured for a large sum [of money]; **etw. ~ und heilig versprechen** promise sth. faithfully; **Hoch** das; ~s, ~s a) (*Hochruf*) ein |dreifaches| ~ **auf jmdn. ausbringen** give three cheers for sb.; b) (*Met.*) high

Hoch·achtung die great respect; **hochachtungs·voll** *Adv.* (*Briefschluß*) yours faithfully

hoch-, Hoch-: **~aktuell** *Adj.* highly topical; **~amt** das (*kath. Rel.*) high mass; **~|arbeiten** *refl. V.* work one's way up; **~begabt** *Adj.* (*präd. getrennt geschrieben*) highly gifted; **~betagt** *Adj.* aged; **~betrieb** der; o. Pl. (*ugs.*) **es herrschte ~ betrieb** im Geschäft the shop was at its busiest; **~blüte** die golden age; **~burg** die stronghold; **~deutsch** *Adj.* High German; **~deutsch** das, **~deutsche** das High German; **~druck** der (*Physik, Met.*) high pressure; **~empfindlich** *Adj.* highly sensitive ⟨*instrument, device, material, etc.*⟩; fast ⟨*film*⟩; extremely delicate ⟨*fabric*⟩; **~|fahren** *unr. itr. V.; mit sein* a) (*ugs.*) go up; (*mit dem Auto*) drive up; (*mit dem Fahrrad, Motorrad*) ride up; b) (*auffahren*) start up; **aus dem Sessel ~fahren** start [up] from one's chair; c) (*aufbrausen*) flare up; **~finanz** die high finance; **~fliegend** *Adj.* ambitious; **~form** die top form; **~gebirge** das [high] mountains *pl.*; **~gefühl** das [feeling of] elation; **~|gehen** *unr. itr.*

V.; mit sein (ugs.) go up; (zornig werden) blow one's top (coll.); explode;
(explodieren) ⟨bomb, mine⟩ go off;
~genuß der in ein ~genuß sein to be a
real delight; ~geschlossen Adj.
high-necked ⟨dress⟩; ~gestellt Adj.:
nicht präd. ⟨person⟩ in a high position;
important ⟨person⟩; ~glanz der: etw.
auf ~glanz bringen give sth. a high
polish; (fig.) make sth. spick and
span; ~gradig 1. Adj. extreme; 2.
adv. extremely; ~|halten unr. tr. V.
hold up; ~haus das high-rise-build-
ing; ~|heben unr. tr. V. lift up; raise
⟨arm, leg, hand⟩; ~interessant Adj.
extremely interesting; ~kant Adv.
(ugs.) in jmdn. ~kant hinauswerfen
chuck sb. out (sl.); throw sb. out on
his/her ear (coll.); ~|kommen unr.
itr. V.; mit sein (ugs.) come up; (vor-
wärtskommen) get on; ~|krempeln
tr. V. roll up; ~|leben itr. V. in jmdn./
etw. ~leben lassen cheer sb./sth.; er le-
be ~! three cheers for him; ~lei-
stungs·sport der top-level sport;
~modern Adj. ultra-modern; ~mut
der arrogance; ~mütig Adj. arrogant; ~näsig Adj. (abwertend) stuck-
up; ~|nehmen unr. tr. V. (ugs.: ver-
spotten) jmdn. ~nehmen pull sb.'s leg;
~ofen der blast furnace; ~prozen-
tig Adj. high-proof ⟨spirits⟩; ~rech-
nung die (Statistik) projection; ~ruf
der cheer; ~saison die high season;
~|schlagen 1. unr. tr. V. turn up ⟨col-
lar, brim⟩; 2. unr. itr. V.; mit sein ⟨wa-
ter, waves⟩ surge up; ⟨flames⟩ leap up;
~schule die college; (Universität)
university

Hochsee·fischerei die deep-sea
fishing no art.

hoch-, Hoch-: ~sitz der (Jagdw.)
raised hide; ~sommer der high summer; ~spannung die (Elektrot.) high
voltage; ~spielen tr. V. blow up

höchst [høːçst] Adv. extremely; most;
höchst... s. hoch

Hoch·stapler [~ʃtaːplɐ] der; ~s, ~
confidence trickster; con-man (coll.);
(Aufschneider) fraud

höchstens Adv. at most; (bestenfalls)
at best

Höchst-: ~fall der in im ~fall at [the]
most; ~form die (bes. Sport) peak
form; ~geschwindigkeit die top
speed; (Geschwindigkeitsbegrenzung)
speed limit

Hoch·stimmung die high spirits pl.

höchst-, Höchst-: ~leistung die

supreme performance; (Ergebnis) supreme achievement; ~maß das: ein
~maß an etw. (Dat.) a very high degree of sth.; ~wahrscheinlich Adv.
very probably

hoch-, Hoch-: ~tour die: auf ~tou-
ren laufen run at full speed; (intensiv
betrieben werden) be in full swing;
~trabend (abwertend) 1. Adj. high-
flown; 2. adv. in a high-flown man-
ner; ~|treiben unr. tr. V. force up
⟨prices etc.⟩; ~verrat der high
treason; ~wasser das (Flut) high
tide; (Überschwemmung) flood;
~wertig Adj. high-quality ⟨goods⟩;
highly nutritious ⟨food⟩; ~würden o.
Art.; ~|s| (veralt.) Reverend Father

Hochzeit die; ~, ~en wedding

Hochzeits-: ~feier die wedding;
~nacht die wedding night; ~reise
die honeymoon [trip]

Hocke die; ~, ~n a) (Körperhaltung)
squat; crouch; b) (Turnen) squat
vault; **hocken** 1. itr. V. a) mit haben
od. (südd.) sein squat; crouch; b) mit
haben od. (südd.) sein (ugs.: sich aufhalten) sit around; 2. refl. V. crouch
down; **Hocker** der; ~s, ~: stool

Höcker der; ~s, ~: hump; (auf der
Nase) bump; (auf dem Schnabel)
knob

Hockey ['hɔki] das; ~s hockey

Hoden der; ~s, ~: testicle

Hof der; ~[e]s, Höfe a) courtyard;
(Schul-) playground; (Gefängnis-)
[prison] yard; b) (Bauern-) farm; c)
(Herrscher, Hofstaat) court

Hof·dame die lady of the court; (Begleiterin der Königin) lady-in-waiting;
hof·fähig Adj. presentable at court
pred.

hoffen 1. tr. V. hope; 2. itr. V. hope;
auf etw. (Akk.) ~: hope for sth.; (Vertrauen setzen auf) auf jmdn./etw. ~:
put one's faith in sb./sth.; **hoffentlich** Adv. hopefully; ~! let's hope so;
Hoffnung die; ~, ~en hope

hoffnungs-, Hoffnungs-: ~los 1.
Adj. hopeless; despairing ⟨person⟩; 2.
adv. hopelessly; ~losigkeit die; ~:
despair; (der Lage) hopelessness;
~voll 1. Adj. a) hopeful; full of hope
pred.; b) (erfolgversprechend) promising; 2. adv. a) full of hope; b) (erfolgversprechend) promisingly

höflich 1. Adj. polite; 2. adv. politely;
Höflichkeit die; ~: politeness

hohe ['hoːə] s. hoch; **Höhe** ['høːə] die;
~, ~n height; etw. in die ~ heben

lift sth. up; **das ist ja die ~!** *(fig. ugs.)* that's the limit

Hoheit die; ~, ~en sovereignty (über + *Akk.* over); **Seine/Ihre ~:** His/ Your Highness

Hoheits-: ~**gebiet** das [sovereign] territory; ~**gewässer** das; *meist Pl.* territorial waters

Höhen-: ~**flug** der *(fig.)* flight; ~**lage** die altitude; ~**luft** die; *o. Pl.* mountain air; ~**messer** der altimeter; ~**sonne** die *(Med.)* sun lamp; ~**unterschied** der difference in altitude

Höhepunkt der high point; *(einer Veranstaltung)* high spot; *(einer Laufbahn, des Ruhms)* pinnacle; *(Orgasmus)* climax

höher ['hø:ɐ] *s.* hoch

hohl *Adj.* hollow; **Höhle** die; ~, ~n a) cave; *(größer)* cavern; b) *(Tierbau)* lair

Hohl-: ~**maß** das measure of capacity; ~**raum** der cavity; [hollow] space; ~**spiegel** der concave mirror

Hohn der; ~[e]s scorn; derision; **höhnen** *(geh.) itr. V.* jeer; **höhnisch** 1. *Adj.* scornful; 2. *adv.* scornfully

Hokuspokus der; ~: hocus-pocus; *(abwertend: Drum und Dran)* fuss

hold *Adj. (dichter. veralt.)* fair; lovely; lovely ⟨*sight, smile*⟩

holen 1. *tr. V.* a) fetch; get; b) *(ab~)* fetch; c) *(ugs.: erlangen)* get ⟨*prize etc.*⟩; carry off ⟨*medal, trophy, etc.*⟩; 2. *refl. V. (ugs.: sich zuziehen)* catch; **sich** ⟨*Dat.*⟩ **[beim Baden] einen Schnupfen ~:** catch a cold [swimming]

Holland (das); ~s Holland; **Holländer** der; ~s, ~: Dutchman; **holländisch** *Adj.* Dutch

Hölle die; ~, ~n hell *no art.;* **Höllenlärm** der *(ugs.)* diabolical noise or row *(coll.);* **höllisch** 1. *Adj.* a) infernal; ⟨*spirits, torments*⟩ of hell; b) *(ugs.: sehr groß)* tremendous *(coll.);* 2. *adv. (ugs.: sehr)* hellishly *(coll.)*

Holm der; ~[e]s, ~e a) *(Turnen)* bar

holpern *itr. V.* mit sein *(fahren)* jolt; bump; **holprig** *Adj.* a) bumpy; rough; b) *(stockend)* halting ⟨*speech*⟩; clumsy ⟨*verses, style, language, etc.*⟩

Holunder der; ~s, ~: elder

Holz das; ~es, Hölzer wood; *(Bau~, Tischler~)* timber; wood; **Holz·bein** das wooden leg; **hölzern** *Adj. (auch fig.)* wooden; **Holz·fäller** der woodcutter; lumberjack *(Amer.);* **holzfrei** *Adj.* wood-free ⟨*paper*⟩; **holzig** *Adj.* woody

Holz-: ~**klotz** der block of wood; *(als Spielzeug)* wooden block; ~**kohle** die charcoal; ~**kopf** der *(salopp abwertend)* blockhead; ~**pantoffel** der clog; ~**scheit** das piece of wood; *(Brenn~)* piece of firewood; ~**schnitt** der a) *o. Pl.* woodcutting *no art.;* b) *(Blatt)* woodcut; ~**schuh** der clog; ~**stoß** der pile of wood; ~**weg** der: **auf dem ~weg sein** be on the wrong track *(fig.);* ~**wolle** die; *o. Pl.* wood-wool; ~**wurm** der woodworm

homogen *Adj.* homogeneous

homöopathisch *Adj.* homoeopathic

Homo·sexualität die; ~: homosexuality; **homo·sexuell** 1. *Adj.* homosexual; 2. *adv.* ~ **veranlagt sein** have homosexual tendencies

Honig der; ~s, ~e honey; **Honig·kuchen** der honey cake; **Honig·wabe** die honeycomb

Honorar das; ~s, ~e fee; *(Autoren~)* royalty; **Honoratioren** [honora-ˈtsi̯oːrən] *Pl.* notabilities; **honorieren** *tr. V.* a) jmdn. ~: pay sb. [a/his/her fee]; b) *(würdigen)* appreciate; *(belohnen)* reward

Hopfen der; ~s, ~: hop

hopp *Interj.* quick; look sharp; **hoppeln** *itr. V.;* mit sein hop; (über + *Akk.* across, over); **hoppla** *Interj.* oops; whoops; **hopsen** *itr. V.; mit sein (ugs.) (springen)* jump; *(hüpfen)* ⟨*animal*⟩ hop; ⟨*child*⟩ skip; ⟨*ball*⟩ bounce; **Hopser** der; ~s, ~ *(ugs.)* [little] jump

Hör·apparat der hearing-aid; **hörbar** 1. *Adj.* audible; 2. *adv.* audibly; *(geräuschvoll)* noisily; **horchen** *itr. V.* listen (**auf** + *Akk.* to); *(heimlich zuhören)* eavesdrop

Horde die; ~, ~n horde; *(von Halbstarken)* mob

hören 1. *tr. V.* hear; *(anhören)* listen to; 2. *itr. V.* hear; *(zuhören)* listen; **auf jmdn./jmds. Rat ~:** listen to sb./sb.'s advice; **Hören·sagen** das: **vom ~:** from hearsay; **Hörer** der; ~s, ~ a) listener; b) *(Telefon~)* receiver

Hör-: ~**fehler** der a) das war ein ~**fehler** he/she *etc.* misheard; b) *(Schwerhörigkeit)* hearing defect; ~**funk** der radio; **im ~funk** on the radio; ~**gerät** das hearing-aid

hörig *Adj.:* jmdm. ~ **sein** be submissively dependent on sb.; *(sexuell)* be sexually enslaved to sb.

Horizont der; ~[e]s, ~e *(auch Geol., fig.)* horizon; **horizontal** 1. *Adj.*

horizontal; 2. *adv.* horizontally; **Ho-rizontale die**: ~, ~n a) (*Linie*) horizontal line; b) *o. Pl.* (*Lage*) **die** ~: the horizontal

Hormon das; ~s, ~e hormone

Horn das; ~[e]s, **Hörner** horn; **Hörnchen das**, ~s, ~ (*Gebäck*) croissant; **Horn·haut die** a) (*Hautschwiele*) callus; hard skin *no indef. art.*; b) (*am Auge*) cornea

Hornisse die; ~, ~n hornet

Horoskop das; ~s, ~e horoscope

Hör·rohr das stethoscope

Horror der; ~s horror

Hör-: ~**saal** der the lecture theatre *or* hall; ~**spiel** das radio play

Horst der; ~[e]s, ~e eyrie

Hort der; ~[e]s, ~e *s.* **Kinderhort**; **horten** *tr. V.* hoard; stockpile ⟨*raw materials*⟩

Hortensie die; ~, ~n hydrangea

Hör·weite die: in/außer ~weite in/out of earshot

Höschen ['høːsçən] **das**; ~s, ~: trousers *pl.*; pair of trousers; (*kurzes* ~) shorts *pl.*; pair of shorts; **Hose die**; ~, ~n a) (*lang*) trousers *pl.*; pants *pl.* (*Amer.*); (*Unter-*) pants *pl.*; (*Freizeit~*) slacks *pl.*; (*Bund~*) breeches *pl.*; (*Reit~*) riding breeches *pl.*; **eine** ~: a pair of trousers/pants/slacks *etc.*

Hosen-: ~**an·zug** der the trouser suit (*Brit.*); pant suit; ~**matz** der (*ugs. scherzh.*) toddler; ~**rock** der culottes *pl.*; ~**tasche** die trouser-pocket; pants pocket (*Amer.*); ~**träger** *Pl.* braces; suspenders (*Amer.*); pair of braces/suspenders

Hospital das; ~s, ~e *od.* **Hospitäler** hospital

Hostie ['hɔstiə] **die**; ~, ~n (*christl. Rel.*) host

Hotel das; ~s, ~s hotel; **Hotel·bar die** hotel bar; **Hotel garni** [~ gar'ni:] **das**; ~ ~, ~s ~s bed-and-breakfast hotel; **Hotelier** [hotelie:] **der**; ~s, ~s hotelier

hüben *Adv.* over here

hübsch 1. *Adj.* pretty; nice ⟨*area, flat, voice, tune, etc.*⟩; nice-looking ⟨*boy, person*⟩; **ein** ~**es Sümmchen** (*ugs.*) a tidy sum (*coll.*); a nice little sum; **das ist eine** ~**e Geschichte** (*ugs. iron.*) this is a fine *or* pretty kettle of fish (*coll.*); 2. *adv.* prettily; (*ugs.: sehr*) ~ **kalt** perishing cold

Hub·schrauber der; ~s, ~: helicopter

huckepack *Adv.* jmdn. ~ **tragen** (*ugs.*) give sb. a piggyback

hudeln *itr. V.* (*bes. südd., österr.*) be sloppy (**bei** in)

Huf der; ~[e]s, ~e hoof

Huf-: ~**eisen** das horseshoe; ~**schmied** der farrier

Hüfte die; ~, ~n hip

Hüft-: ~**gelenk** das (*Anat.*) hip-joint; ~**gürtel** der girdle

Hügel der; ~s, ~ hill; **hügelig** *Adj.* hilly

Huhn das; ~[e]s, **Hühner** a) chicken; (*Henne*) chicken; hen; **Hühnchen das**; ~s, ~: small chicken; **mit jmdm.** [**noch**] **ein** ~ **zu rupfen haben** (*ugs.*) [still] have a bone to pick with sb.

Hühner-: ~**auge** das (*am Fuß*) corn; ~**brühe** die chicken broth

hui [huɪ] *Interj.* whoosh

huldigen *itr. V.* jmdm. ~: pay tribute to sb.; **Huldigung die**; ~, ~en tribute

Hülle die; ~, ~n cover; **hüllen** *tr. V.* (*geh.*) wrap

Hülse die; ~, ~n a) case; b) (*Bot.*) pod

human *Adj.* humane; **Humanismus der**; ~: humanism; (*Epoche*) Humanism *no art.*; **humanitär** *Adj.* humanitarian

Humbug ['humbuk] **der**; ~s (*ugs.*) humbug

Hummel die; ~, ~n bumble-bee

Hummer der; ~s, ~: lobster

Humor der; ~s humour; (*Sinn für* ~) sense of humour; **den** ~ **nicht verlieren** remain good-humoured; **Humorist der**; ~en, ~en a) (*Autor*) humorist; b) (*Vortragskünstler*) comedian; **humoristisch** *Adj.* humorous

humor-: ~**los** *Adj.* humourless; ~**voll** *Adj.* humorous

humpeln *itr. V.* a) *auch mit sein* walk with a limp; b) *mit sein* (*sich* ~*d fortbewegen*) limp

Hund der; ~[e]s, ~e a) dog; **auf den** ~ **kommen** (*ugs.*) go to the dogs (*coll.*); **vor die** ~**e gehen** (*ugs.*) go to the dogs (*coll.*); (*sterben*) kick the bucket (*sl.*); b) (*abwertend*) bastard (*coll.*)

hunde-, Hunde-: ~**elend** *Adj.; nicht attr.* (*ugs.*) [really] wretched *or* awful; ~**hütte** die [dog-]kennel; ~**kuchen** der dog-biscuit; ~**müde** *Adj.; nicht attr.* (*ugs.*) dog-tired; ~**rasse** die breed of dog

hundert *Kardinalz.* a) a *or* one hundred; b) (*ugs.: viele*) hundreds of; ¹**Hundert das**; ~s, ~e hundred; ²**Hundert die**; ~, ~en hundred; **Hunderter der**; ~s, ~ (*ugs.*) hundred-mark/-dollar *etc.* note; **hun-**

dert·mal *Adv.* a hundred times; **auch wenn du dich ~ beschwerst** *(ugs.)* however much you complain

Hundert-: **~mark·schein** der hundred-mark note; **~meter·lauf** der *(Leichtathletik)* hundred metres *sing.*

hundert·prozentig 1. *Adj.* **a)** *(von 100 %)* [one-]hundred per cent *attrib.*; **b)** *(ugs.: völlig)* a hundred per cent; **c)** *(ugs.: ganz sicher)* absolutely reliable; **2.** *adv.* *(ugs.)* **ich bin nicht ~ sicher** I'm not a hundred per cent sure; **hundertst...** ['hʊndɐtst...] *Ordinalz.* hundredth; **hundertstel** ['hʊndɐtstḷ] *Bruchz.* hundredth; **Hundertstel das** *(schweiz. meist* der*)*; **~s, ~:** hundredth; **hundert·tausend** *Kardinalz.* a or one hundred thousand

Hüne der; **~n, ~n** giant; **Hünen·grab das** megalithic tomb; *(Hügelgrab)* barrow

Hunger der; **~s a)** ~ **bekommen/haben** get/be hungry; **b)** *(geh.: Verlangen)* hunger; *(nach Ruhm, Macht)* craving; **Hunger·kur die** starvation diet; **hungern** *itr. V.* go hungry; starve; **nach etw. ~:** *(fig.)* hunger for sth.; **Hungers·not die** famine; **Hunger·streik** der hunger-strike; **hungrig** *Adj.* *(auch geh. fig.)* hungry *(nach* for*)*

Hupe die; ~, ~n horn; **hupen** *itr. V.* sound one's horn; **dreimal ~:** hoot three times

hüpfen *itr. V.; mit sein* hop; *(ball)* bounce

Hürde die; ~, ~n hurdle; **Hürden·lauf** der *(Leichtathletik)* hurdling; *(Wettbewerb)* hurdles *pl.*

Hure die; ~, ~n *(abwertend)* whore; **huren** *itr. V.* *(abwertend)* whore

hurra *Interj.* hurray; hurrah; **~ schreien** cheer; **Hurra das; ~s, ~s** cheer

hurtig 1. *Adj.* rapid; **2.** *adv.* quickly

huschen *itr. V.; mit sein* *(lautlos u. leichtfüßig)* *(person)* steal; *(lautlos u. schnell)* dart; *(mouse, lizard, etc.)* dart; *(smile)* flit; *(light)* flash; *(shadow)* slide quickly

hüsteln *itr. V.* give a slight cough; **husten 1.** *itr. V.* cough; *(Husten haben)* have a cough; **2.** *tr. V.* cough up *(blood, phlegm)*; **Husten der; ~s, ~:** cough

Husten-: **~bonbon das** cough-drop; **~tropfen** *Pl.* cough-drops

¹Hut der; **~es, Hüte** hat; *(fig.)* **da geht einem/mir der ~ hoch** *(ugs.)* it makes you/me mad *(coll.)*; **das kann er sich**

(Dat.) **an den ~ stecken** *(ugs. abwertend)* he can keep it *(coll.)*

²Hut die; ~ *(geh.)* keeping; care; **auf der ~ sein** be on one's guard; **hüten 1.** *tr. V.* look after; tend *(sheep, cattle, etc.)*; **2.** *refl. V.* be on one's guard

Hut·schnur die in das geht mir über die ~ *(ugs.)* that's going too far

Hütte die; ~, ~n a) hut; *(ärmliches Haus)* shack; hut; **b)** *(Eisen~)* iron [and steel] works *sing. or pl.*; **c)** *(Jagd~)* [hunting-]lodge

Hütten-: **~käse** der cottage cheese; **~schuh** der slipper-sock

Hyäne die; ~, ~n hyena

Hyazinthe die; ~, ~n hyacinth

Hydrant der; ~en, ~en hydrant; **Hydraulik die; ~** *(Technik)* **a)** *(Theorie)* hydraulics *sing., no art.*; **b)** *(Vorrichtungen)* hydraulics *pl.*; **hydraulisch** *(Technik)* **1.** *Adj.* hydraulic; **2.** *adv.* hydraulically; **Hydro·kultur die; ~, ~en** *(Gartenbau)* hydroponics *sing.*

Hygiene die; ~ a) *(Gesundheitspflege)* health care; **b)** *(Sauberkeit)* hygiene; **hygienisch 1.** *Adj.* hygienic; **2.** *adv.* hygienically

Hymne ['hʏmnə] **die; ~, ~n** hymn; *(National~)* national anthem

Hypnose die; ~, ~n hypnosis; **hypnotisieren** *tr. V.* hypnotize

Hypochonder [hypo'xɔndɐ] **der; ~s, ~:** hypochondriac

Hypotenuse die; ~, ~n *(Math.)* hypotenuse

Hypothek die; ~, ~en *(Bankw.)* mortgage; *(fig.)* burden

Hypothese die; ~, ~n hypothesis; **hypothetisch 1.** *Adj.* hypothetical; **2.** *adv.* hypothetically

Hysterie die; ~, ~n hysteria; **hysterisch 1.** *Adj.* hysterical; **2.** *adv.* hysterically

I

i, I das; ~, ~: i/I; **das Tüpfelchen auf dem i** *(fig.)* the final touch

i *Interj.* ugh; **i bewahre, i wo** *(ugs.)* [good] heavens, no!

i. A. *Abk.* im Auftrag|e| p.p.
IC *Abk.* Intercity IC
ich *Personalpron.; 1. Pers. Sg. Nom.* I;
immer ~ *(ugs.)* [it's] always me; ~
nicht not me; **Menschen wie du und** ~:
people like you and me; *s. auch (Gen.)*
meiner, *(Dat.)* mir, *(Akk.)* mich
ich das; ~|s|, ~|s| a) self; b) *(Psych.)*
ego
Ich-Form die; *o. Pl.* first person
ideal 1. *Adj.* ideal; **2.** *adv.* ideally;
Ideal das; ~s, ~e ideal
Ideal-: ~**bild das** ideal; ~**fall der**
ideal case; ~**gewicht das** ideal
weight
idealisieren *tr. V.* idealize; **Idealis-**
mus der; ~ *(auch Philos.)* idealism;
Idealist der; ~en, ~en idealist;
idealistisch *(auch Philos.)* **1.** *Adj.*
idealistic; **2.** *adv.* idealistically; **Idee**
die; ~, ~n a) idea; b) *(ein bißchen)* eine ~: a shade; **eine** ~ **[Salz/Pfeffer]** a
touch [of salt/pepper]; **ideell** *Adj.*
non-material; *(geistig-seelisch)* spiritual; **ideen·los** *Adj.* [completely]
lacking in ideas *postpos.*
Identifikation [identifika'tsio:n] **die;**
~, ~en *(auch Psych.)* identification;
identifizieren 1. *tr. V.* identify; **2.**
refl. V. (auch Psych.) sich mit jmdm./
etw. ~: identify with sb./sth.; **iden-**
tisch *Adj.* identical; **Identität die;** ~,
~: identity
Ideologe der; ~n, ~n ideologue;
Ideologie die; ~, ~n [-i:ən] ideology;
ideologisch 1. *Adj.* ideological; **2.**
adv. ideologically
Idiot der; ~en, ~en *(auch ugs. abwer-*
tend) idiot; **Idioten·hügel der** *(ugs.*
scherzh.) nursery slope; **Idiotie die;**
~, ~n [-i:ən] a) idiocy; b) *(ugs. abwer-*
tend: Dummheit) madness; **Idiotin**
die; ~, ~nen *(auch ugs. abwertend)*
idiotisch **1.** *Adj.* a) *(Psych.)* severely
subnormal; b) *(ugs. abwertend)* idiotic; **2.** *adv. (auch ugs. abwertend)*
idiotically
Idol das; ~s, ~e *(auch bild. Kunst)* idol
Idyll das; ~s, ~e idyll; **Idylle die;** ~,
~n idyll; **idyllisch** *Adj.* idyllic
Igel der; ~s, ~: hedgehog
Iglu der od. das; ~s, ~s igloo
Ignoranz [igno'rants] **die;** ~: ignorance; **ignorieren** *tr. V.* ignore
ihm *Dat. von* er, es: *(bei männlichen*
Personen) him; *(bei weiblichen Perso-*
nen) her; *(bei Dingen, Tieren)* it; **gib es**
~: give it to him; give it to him; **Freunde**
von ~: friends of his

ihn *Akk. von* er *(bei männlichen Perso-*
nen) him; *(bei Dingen, Tieren)* it
ihnen *Dat. von* sie, *Pl.* them; **gib es** ~:
give it to them; give them it; **Freunde**
von ~: friends of theirs
Ihnen *Dat. von* Sie you; **ich habe es** ~
gegeben I gave it to you; **Freunde von**
~: friends of yours
¹ihr [i:ɐ̯] *Dat. von* sie, *Sg. (bei Personen)*
her; *(bei Dingen, Tieren)* it
²ihr, *(in Briefen)* **Ihr** *Personalpron.; 2.*
Pers. Pl. Nom. you
³ihr *Possessivpron.* a) *Sg. (einer Person)*
her; *(eines Tieres, einer Sache)* its; b)
Pl. their
Ihr *Possessivpron. (Anrede)* your; ~
Hans Meier *(Briefschluß)* yours, Hans
Meier; **welcher Mantel ist** ~**er?** which
coat is yours?
ihrer a) *Gen. von* sie, *Sg. (geh.)* **wir ge-**
dachten ~: we remembered her; b)
Gen. von sie, *Pl. (geh.)* **wir werden** ~
gedenken we will remember them; **es**
waren ~ **zwölf** there were twelve of
them
Ihrer *Gen. von* Sie *(geh.)* **wir werden** ~
gedenken we will remember you
ihrerseits *Adv.* for her/their part;
(von ihr/ihnen) on her/their part
Ihrerseits *Adv. s.* deinerseits
ihresgleichen *indekl. Pron.* people
pl. like her/them; *(abwertend)* the
likes of her/them
Ihresgleichen *indekl. Pron.* people
pl. like you; *(abwertend)* the likes of
you
ihretwegen *Adv.: s.* meinetwegen:
because of her/them; for her/their
sake; about her/them; as far as she is/
they are concerned
Ihretwegen *Adv.: s.* deinetwegen
Ikone die; ~, ~n icon
illegal 1. *Adj.* illegal; **2.** *adv.* illegally;
Illegalität die; ~, ~en illegality; **ille-**
gitim ['ɪlegiti:m] *Adj. (geh.)* illegitimate
illuminieren *tr. V.* illuminate
Illusion die; ~, ~en illusion; **illuso-**
risch *Adj.* illusory; *(zwecklos)* pointless
Illustration [ɪlʊstra'tsio:n] **die;** ~, ~en
illustration; **illustrieren** *tr. V.* illustrate; **Illustrierte die;** *adj. Dekl.* magazine
Iltis der; ~ses, ~se polecat; *(Pelz)* fitch
im *Präp. + Art.* a) = in dem; b) *(räum-*
lich) in the; **im Theater** at the theatre;
im Fernsehen on television; **im Bett** in
bed; c) *(zeitlich)* **im Mai** in May; **im**

letzten **Jahr** last year; **im Alter von ...** at the age of ...; d) *(Verlauf)* etw. **im Sitzen tun** do sth. [while] sitting down; **im Gehen sein** be going

Image ['ɪmɪtʃ] das; ~[s], ~s ['ɪmɪtʃs] image; **imaginär** *Adj. (geh., Math.)* imaginary

Imbiß der; **Imbisses, Imbisse** a) *(kleine Mahlzeit)* snack; b) s. **Imbißstube**; **Imbiß·stube** die café

Imitation die; ~, ~en imitation; **imitieren** *tr. V.* imitate

Imker der; ~s, ~: bee-keeper

Immatrikulation [ɪmatrikula'tsi̯oːn] die; ~, ~en *(Hochschulw.)* registration; **immatrikulieren** *tr., refl. V. (Hochschulw.)* register

immer *Adv.* a) always; **schon** ~: always; ~ **wieder** time and time again; ~, **wenn** every time that; b) ~ + *Komp.* ~ **dunkler** darker and darker; ~ **mehr** more and more; *(ugs.: jeweils)* ~ **drei Stufen auf einmal** three steps at a time; d) *(auch)* **wo/wer/wann/wie [auch]** ~: wherever/whoever/whenever/however; e) *(verstärkend)* ~ **noch, noch** ~: still; f) *(ugs.: bei Aufforderung)* ~ **geradeaus!** keep [going] straight on

immer-, Immer-: ~**fort** *Adv.* all the time; ~**grün** *Adj.* evergreen; ~**grün** das periwinkle; ~**hin** *Adv.* a) *(wenigstens)* at any rate; b) *(trotz allem)* all the same; c) *(schließlich)* after all; ~**zu** *Adv. (ugs.)* the whole time

Immigrant der; ~en, ~en immigrant; **Immigration** [ɪmigra'tsi̯oːn] die; ~, ~en immigration; **immigrieren** *itr. V.; mit sein* immigrate

Immobilien *Pl.* property *sing.*; real estate *sing.*

immun a) *(Med., fig.)* immune (**gegen** to); b) *(Rechtsspr.)* ~ **sein** have immunity; **Immunität** die; ~, ~en a) *(Med.)* immunity (**gegen** to); b) *(Rechtsspr.)* immunity (**gegen** from)

Imperativ der; ~s, ~e a) *(Sprachw.)* imperative; b) *(Philos.)* **[kategorischer]** ~: [categorical] imperative

Imperfekt das; ~s, ~e *(Sprachw.)* imperfect [tense]

Imperialismus der; ~: imperialism *no art.;* **imperialistisch** *Adj.* imperialistic

Imperium das; ~s, **Imperien** *(hist., fig.)* empire

impfen *tr. V.* vaccinate; inoculate

Impf-: ~**paß** der vaccination certificate; ~**stoff** der vaccine

Impfung die; ~, ~en vaccination

implantieren *tr. V. (Med.)* implant

imponieren *itr. V.* impress; **imponierend 1.** *Adj.* impressive; **2.** *adv.* impressively

Import der; ~[e]s, ~e import; **Importeur** [ɪmpɔr'tøːɐ̯] der; ~s, ~e importer; **importieren** *tr., itr. V.* import

imposant 1. *Adj.* imposing; impressive ⟨*achievement*⟩; **2.** *adv.* imposingly

impotent *Adj.* impotent; **Impotenz** die; ~: impotence

imprägnieren *tr. V.* impregnate; *(wasserdicht machen)* waterproof

Improvisation die; ~, ~en improvisation; **improvisieren** *tr., itr. V.* improvise

Impuls der; ~es, ~e stimulus; *(innere Regung)* impulse; **impulsiv 1.** *Adj.* impulsive; **2.** *adv.* impulsively

imstande *Adj.* ~ **sein, etw. zu tun** be able to do sth.

in 1. *Präp. mit Dat.* a) *(auf die Frage: wo?/wann?/wie?)* in; **er hat** ~ **Tübingen studiert** he studied at Tübingen; *s. auch* **im; 2.** *Präp. mit Akk. (auf die Frage: wohin?)* into; *s. auch* **ins**

In·anspruchnahme die; ~, ~n *(starke Belastung)* demands *pl.*

In·begriff der quintessence; **inbegriffen** *Adj.* included

In·betriebnahme die; ~, ~n, **In·betriebsetzung** die; ~, ~en *(Amtsspr.)* opening; *(von Maschinen)* bringing into service

In·brunst die; ~ *(geh.)* fervour; *(der Liebe)* ardour; **in·brünstig** *(geh.)* **1.** *Adj.* fervent; ardent ⟨*love*⟩; **2.** *adv.* fervently; ⟨*love*⟩ ardently

in·dem *Konj.* a) *(während)* while; *(gerade als)* as; b) *(dadurch, daß)* ~ **man etw. tut** by doing sth.

Inder ['ɪndɐ] der; ~s, ~: Indian

in·dessen 1. *Konj. (geh.)* a) *(während)* while; b) *(wohingegen)* whereas; **2.** *Adv.* a) *(inzwischen)* meanwhile; in the mean time; b) *(jedoch)* however

Index der; ~ *od.* ~es, ~e *od.* **Indizes** *Pl.* ~e *od.* **Indizes** *(Register)* index; b) *Pl.* ~e *od.* **Indizes** *(kath. Kirche)* Index

Indianer der; ~s, ~: [American] Indian; **Indianer·häuptling** der Indian chief

Indien ['ɪndi̯ən] (das) India

in·different *Adj.* indifferent

Indikativ der; ~s, ~e [-iːvə] *(Sprachw.)* indicative [mood]

in·direkt 1. *Adj.; nicht präd.* indirect; **2.** *adv.* indirectly

indisch *Adj.* Indian

in·diskret *Adj.* indiscreet; **In·diskretion die**; ~, ~en indiscretion

Individualist der; ~en, ~en *(geh.)* individualist; **Individualität die**; ~, ~en *(geh.)* **a)** *o. Pl.* individuality; **b)** *(Persönlichkeit)* personality; **individuell 1.** *Adj.* individual; private *(property, vehicle, etc.)*; **2.** *adv.* individually; **Individuum das**; ~s, **Individuen** *(auch Chemie, Biol.)* individual

Indiz das; ~es, ~ien **a)** *(Rechtsw.)* piece of circumstantial evidence; ~ien circumstantial evidence *sing.*; **b)** *(Anzeichen)* sign *(für of)*

indoktrinieren *tr. V.* indoctrinate

Indonesien [indo'ne:zjən] **(das)** Indonesia; **Indonesier der**; ~s, ~Indonesian; **indonesisch** *Adj.* Indonesian

industrialisieren *tr. V.* industrialize; **Industrialisierung die**; ~: industrialization; **Industrie die**; ~, ~n industry

Industrie-: ~**betrieb der** industrial firm; ~**gebiet das** industrial area; ~**kaufmann der** *person with three years' business training employed on the business side of an industrial company*

industriell 1. *Adj.* industrial; **2.** *adv.* industrially; **Industrielle der/die**; *adj. Dekl.* industrialist

Industrie-: ~**staat der** industrial nation; ~**stadt die** industrial town; ~**zweig der** branch of industry

in·einander *Adv.* ~ verliebt sein be in love with each other *or* one another; ~ verschlungene Ornamente intertwined decorations; **ineinander|greifen** *unr. itr. V.* mesh together *(lit. or fig.)*

infam 1. *Adj.* disgraceful; **2.** *adv.* disgracefully

Infanterie die; ~, ~n *(Milit.)* infantry

Infarkt der; ~[e]s, ~e *(Med.)* infarction

Infekt der; ~[e]s, ~e *(Med.)* infection

Infektion [ɪnfɛk'tsjo:n] **die**; ~, ~en *(Med.)* **a)** *(Ansteckung)* infection; **b)** *(ugs.: Entzündung)* inflammation

Infektions-: ~**gefahr die** *(Med.)* risk of infection; ~**herd der** *(Med.)* seat of the/an infection; ~**krankheit die** *(Med.)* infectious disease

Inferno das; ~s *(geh.)* inferno

Infinitiv der; ~s, ~e *(Sprachw.)* infinitive

infizieren 1. *tr. V.* infect; **2.** *refl. V.* become infected; **sich bei jmdm.** ~: be infected by sb.

in flagranti *Adv. (geh.)* in flagrante [delicto]

Inflation die; ~, ~en *(Wirtsch.)* inflation; *(Zeit der* ~*)* period of inflation

in·folge 1. *Präp. + Gen.* as a result of; **2.** *Adv.* ~ **von etw.** *(Dat.)* as a result of sth.

infolge·dessen *Adv.* consequently

Informatik die; ~: computer science *no art.*; **Information die**; ~, ~en **a)** information *no pl., no indef. art.* (über + Akk. about, on); eine ~: [a piece of] information; **b)** *(Büro)* information bureau; *(Stand)* information desk

Informations-: ~**material das** informational literature; ~**quelle die** source of information

informativ *Adj.* informative; **informieren 1.** *tr. V.* inform (über + Akk. about); **2.** *refl. V.* inform oneself, find out (über + Akk. about)

Infra·rot das; ~s *(Physik)* infra-red radiation; **Infra·struktur die** infrastructure

Infusion die; ~, ~en *(Med.)* infusion

Ing. *Abk.* Ingenieur; **Ingenieur** [ɪnʒe'niø:ɐ̯] der; ~s, ~e [qualified] engineer

Ingwer der; ~s, ~ ginger

Inhaber der; ~s, ~ **a)** holder; **b)** *(Besitzer)* owner

inhaftieren *tr. V.* take into custody; detain; **Inhaftierung die**; ~, ~en detention

inhalieren *tr. V.* inhale

In·halt der; ~[e]s, ~e **a)** contents *pl.*; **b)** *(einer Geschichte usw.)* content; **c)** *(bes. Math.)* *(Flächen~)* area; *(Raum~)* volume

Inhalts-: ~**angabe die** summary [of contents]; synopsis; *(eines Films, Dramas)* synopsis; ~**verzeichnis das** table of contents; *(auf einem Paket)* list of contents

Initiale die; ~, ~n initial [letter]

Initiative die; ~, ~n initiative; **Initiator** [ini'tsja:tor] der; ~s, ~en initiator; *(einer Organisation)* founder

Injektion die; ~, ~en *(Med.)* injection; **injizieren** *tr. V. (Med.)* inject

inkl. *Abk.* inklusive incl.

inklusive [ɪnklu'zi:və] **1.** *Präp. + Gen. (bes. Kaufmannsspr.)* including; **2.** *Adv.* inclusive

inkognito *Adv. (geh.)* incognito

in·kompetent Adj. incompetent; **In·kompetenz** die incompetence

in·konsequent 1. Adj. inconsistent; 2. adv. die inconsistently; **In·konsequenz** die inconsistency

in·korrekt 1. Adj. incorrect; 2. adv. incorrectly

In·kraft·treten das; ~s: **mit [dem] ~ des Gesetzes** when the law comes/came into force

In·land das; ~[e]s a) **im ~**: at home; b) (Binnenland) interior; inland; **im/ins ~**: inland; **inländisch** Adj. domestic; home-produced (goods)

Inlands-: ~**markt** der domestic market; ~**porto** das inland postage

in·mitten 1. Präp. + Gen. (geh.) in the midst of; 2. Adv. **~ von** in the midst of

inne|haben unr. tr. V. hold, occupy (position); hold (office)

innen Adv. inside; (auf/an der Innenseite) on the inside

innen-, Innen-: ~**architekt** der interior designer; ~**aufnahme** die (Fot.) indoor photo[graph]; (Film) interior shot; ~**einrichtung** die furnishings pl.; home-produced (goods); ~**hof** der inner courtyard; ~**leben** das; o. Pl. a) (inner) thoughts and feelings pl.; b) (oft scherzh.: Ausstattung) inside; ~**minister** der Minister of the Interior; ≈ Home Secretary (Brit.); ≈ Secretary of the Interior (Amer.); ~**politik** die (eines Staates) home affairs pl.; (einer Regierung) domestic policy/policies pl.; ~**politisch** s. ~**politik**: 1. Adj. ~**politische Fragen** matters of domestic policy; 2. adv. as regards home affairs/domestic policy; ~**stadt** die town centre; downtown (Amer.); (einer Großstadt) city centre

inner... Adj. inner; (inländisch; Med.) internal; inside (pocket, lane); **Innere** das; adj. Dekl.; o. Pl. inside; (eines Gebäudes, Wagens, Schiffes) interior; inside; (eines Landes) interior; **Innereien** Pl. entrails; (Kochk.) offal sing.; **inner·halb** 1. Präp. + Gen. a) within; **~ der Familie/Partei** (fig.) within the family/party; b) (binnen) within; **~ einer Woche** within a week; 2. Adv. a) **~ von** within; b) (im Verlauf) **~ von zwei Jahren** within two years; **innerlich** 1. Adj. inner; 2. adv. inwardly; **innerst...** Adj. innermost; **Innerste** das; adj. Dekl.; o. Pl. innermost being

inne|wohnen itr. V. (geh.) **etw. wohnt**

jmdm./einer Sache ~: sb./sth. possesses sth.

innig 1. Adj. deep (affection, sympathy); fervent (wish); intimate (friendship); **mein ~ster Dank** my sincerest thanks; 2. adv. (love) with all one's heart; **Innigkeit** die; ~: depth; (einer Beziehung) intimacy

Innung ['ɪnʊŋ] die; ~, ~en [trade] guild

in·offiziell 1. Adj. unofficial; 2. adv. unofficially

in puncto as regards

ins Präp. + Art. = **in das**

Insasse der; ~n, ~n a) (Fahrgast) passenger; b) (Bewohner) inmate

ins·besond[e]re Adv. particularly; in particular

In·schrift die inscription

Insekt [ɪn'zɛkt] das; ~s, ~en insect

Insel die; ~, ~n island

Inserat das; ~[e]s, ~e advertisement (in a newspaper); **Inserent** der; ~en, ~en advertiser; **inserieren** itr. V. advertise

ins·geheim Adv. secretly

ins·gesamt Adv. in all; altogether; (alles in allem) all in all

insofern 1. Adv. [ɪn'zo:fɛrn] (in dieser Hinsicht) to this extent; 2. Konj. [ɪnzo'fɛrn] (falls) provided [that]

insoweit [ɪn'zo:vait/ɪnzo'vait] Adv./Konj. s. insofern

in spe [ɪn 'spe:] future attrib.; **mein Schwiegersohn ~ ~**: my future son-in-law

Inspektion [ɪnspɛk'tsi̯o:n] die; ~, ~en inspection; (Kfz-W.) service

Inspiration [ɪnspira'tsi̯o:n] die; ~, ~en inspiration; **inspirieren** tr. V. inspire

inspizieren tr. V. inspect

Installateur [ɪnstala'tø:ɐ̯] der; ~s, ~e plumber; (Gas~) [gas-]fitter; (Heizungs~) heating engineer; (Elektro~) electrician; **Installation** [ɪnstala'tsi̯o:n] die; ~, ~en installation; (Rohre) plumbing no pl.; **installieren** tr. V. install

in·stand Adv. **etw. ist gut/schlecht ~**: sth. is in good/poor condition; **etw. ~ halten** keep sth. in good condition; **etw. ~ setzen/bringen** repair sth.; **In·stand·haltung** die maintenance

in·ständig 1. Adj. urgent; 2. adv. urgently

Instanz [ɪn'stants] die; ~, ~en a) authority; b) (Rechtsw.) **[die] erste/zweite/dritte ~**: the court of original jurisdiction/the appeal court/the court of final appeal; **durch alle ~en gehen** go through all the courts

Instinkt [ɪn'stɪŋkt] der; ~[e]s, ~e instinct; **instinktiv** 1. *Adj.* instinctive; 2. *adv.* instinctively

Institut das; ~[e]s, ~e a) institute; **Institution** [ɪnstitu'tsi̯oːn] die; ~, ~en *(auch fig.)* institution

Instruktion [ɪnstrʊk'tsi̯oːn] die; ~, ~en instruction

Instrument [ɪnstru'mɛnt] das; ~[e]s, ~e instrument; **instrumental** *(Musik)* 1. *Adj.* instrumental; 2. *adv.* instrumentally

Insulin das; ~s insulin

inszenieren *tr. V.* stage; put on; *(Regie führen bei)* direct; *(fig.) (einfädeln)* engineer; *(organisieren)* stage; **Inszenierung** die; ~, ~en staging; *(Regie)* direction; *(Aufführung)* production

intakt *Adj.* a) *(unbeschädigt)* intact; b) *(funktionsfähig)* in [proper] working order *postpos.*; healthy ⟨*economy*⟩

integer *Adj.* **eine integre Persönlichkeit** a person of integrity; **~ sein** be a person of integrity

Integral das; ~s, ~s *(Math.)* integral

integrieren *tr. V.* integrate

Intellekt der; ~[e]s intellect; **intellektuell** *Adj.* intellectual; **Intellektuelle der/die;** *adj. Dekl.* intellectual; **intelligent** 1. *Adj.* intelligent; 2. *adv.* intelligently; **Intelligenz** die; ~, ~a) intelligence; b) *(Gesamtheit der Intellektuellen)* intelligentsia; **Intelligenz·quotient** der intelligence quotient

Intendant der; ~en, ~en *(Theater)* manager and artistic director; *(Fernseh~, Rundfunk~)* director-general

Intensität die; ~: intensity

intensiv 1. *Adj. (gründlich)* intensive *(kräftig)* intense; 2. *adv.* intensively; **intensivieren** *tr. V.* intensify; increase ⟨*exports*⟩; strengthen ⟨*connections*⟩; **Intensiv·station** die intensive-care unit

Intercity-Zug der inter-city train

interessant 1. *Adj.* interesting; 2. *adv.* **~ schreiben** write in an interesting way; **interessanterweise** *Adv.* interestingly enough; **Interesse** das; ~s, ~n interest; **~ an jmdm./etw. haben** be interested in sb./sth.; **interesse·halber** *Adv.* out of interest; **Interessen·gebiet** das field of interest; **Interessent** der; ~en, ~en interested person; *(möglicher Käufer)* potential buyer; **Interessen·ver-**

band der [organized] interest group; **Interessen·vertretung** die a) representation; b) *(Vertreter von Interessen)* representative body; **interessieren** 1. *refl. V.* **sich für jmdn./etw. ~:** be interested in sb./sth. 2. *tr. V.* interest; **das interessiert mich nicht** I'm not interested [in it]; **interessiert** *Adj.* interested (**an** + *Dat.* in)

Interjektion [ɪntɛrjɛk'tsi̯oːn] die; ~, ~en *(Sprachw.)* interjection

Interkontinental·rakete die *(Milit.)* intercontinental ballistic missile

intern 1. *Adj.* internal; 2. *adv.* internally

Internat das; ~[e]s, ~e boarding-school

inter·national 1. *Adj.* international; 2. *adv.* internationally; **Inter·nationale** die; ~, ~n a) International; Internationale; b) *(Lied)* Internationale

Internats-: ~schüler der, **~schülerin** die boarding-school pupil; boarder

internieren *tr. V. (Milit.)* intern; **Internierung** die; ~, ~en internment

Internist der; ~en, ~en *(Med.)* internist

Interpol die; ~: Interpol *no art.*

interpret der; ~en, ~en interpreter *(of music, text, events, etc.)*; **Interpretation** [ɪntɛrpreta'tsi̯oːn] die; ~, ~en interpretation *(of music, text, events, etc.)*; **interpretieren** *tr. V.* interpret *(music, texts, events, etc.)*; **Interpretin** die; ~, ~nen *s.* Interpret

Interpunktion [ɪntɛrpʊnk'tsi̯oːn] die; ~ *(Sprachw.)* punctuation

Intervall [ɪntɛr'val] das; ~s, ~e *(Musik, Math.)* interval

intervenieren *itr. V. (geh., Politik)* intervene; **Intervention** [ɪntɛrvɛn'tsi̯oːn] die; ~, ~en *(geh., Politik)* intervention; *(Protest)* representations *pl.*

Interview [ɪntɐ'vjuː] das; ~s, ~s interview; **interviewen** [ɪntɐ'vjuːən] *tr. V.* interview

intim 1. *Adj.* intimate; 2. *adv.* **~ befreundet sein** be intimate friends; **Intimität** [ɪntimi'tɛːt] die; ~, ~en intimacy; **Intim·sphäre** die private life

in·tolerant *Adj.* intolerant

intransitiv 1. *Adj. (Sprachw.)* intransitive; 2. *adv.* intransitively

Intrige [ɪn'triːgə] die; ~, ~n intrigue

Intuition [ɪntui'tsi̯oːn] die; ~, ~en intuition; **intuitiv** 1. *Adj.* intuitive; 2. *adv.* intuitively

intus ['ɪntʊs] *in etw. ~ haben (ugs.) (begriffen haben)* have got sth. into one's head; *(gegessen od. getrunken haben)* have put sth. away *(coll.)*

Invalide der; *adj. Dekl.* invalid

Invasion die; ~, ~en invasion

Inventar das; ~s, ~e *(einer Firma)* fittings and equipment *pl.*; *(eines Hauses, Büros)* furnishings and fittings *pl.*; **Inventur** die; ~, ~en stocktaking

investieren tr., itr. V. *(auch fig.)* invest (**in** + *Akk.* in); **Investition** [ɪnvɛsti'tsjo:n] die; ~, ~en investment; **Investitions·güter** Pl. *(Wirtsch.)* capital goods; **Investor** [ɪn'vɛstɔr] der; ~s, ~en [-'to:rən] *(Wirtsch.)* investor

in·wie·fern Adv. in what way; *(bis zu welchem Grade)* to what extent; **in·wie·weit** Adv. to what extent

Inzest der; ~[e]s, ~e incest; **In·zucht** die; ~: inbreeding

in·zwischen Adv. a) *(seither)* in the meantime; since [then]; b) *(bis zu einem Zeitpunkt)* *(in der Gegenwart)* by now; *(in der Vergangenheit/Zukunft)* by then; c) *(währenddessen)* meanwhile

IOK [i:o:'ka:] das; ~[s] Internationales Olympisches Komitee IOC

Ion das; ~s, ~en *(Physik, Chemie)* ion

Irak (das); ~s od. der; ~[s] Iraq; **Iraker** der; ~s, ~Iraqi; **irakisch** Iraqi

Iran (das); ~s od. der; ~[s] Iran; **Iraner** der; ~s, ~; **iranisch** Adj. Iranian

irden Adj. earthen[ware]; **irdisch** Adj. a) earthly; worldly ⟨goods, pleasures, possessions⟩; b) *(zur Erde gehörig)* terrestrial; das ~e Leben life on earth

Ire der; ~n, ~n Irishman

irgend Adv. a) ~ jemand someone; somebody; *(fragend, verneinend)* anyone; anybody; ~ etwas something; *(fragend, verneinend)* anything; ~ so etwas something like that; b) *(irgendwie)* wenn ~ möglich if at all possible

irgend-: ~ein Indefinitpron. a) *(attr.)* some; *(fragend, verneinend)* any; b) *(subst.)* ~einer/~eine someone; somebody; *(fragend, verneinend)* anyone; anybody; ~eines od. *(ugs.)* ~eins any one; ~einmal Adv. sometime; ~wann Adv. [at] some time [or other]; *(zu jeder beliebigen Zeit)* [at] any time; ~was Indefinitpron. *(ugs.)* something [or other]; *(fragend, verneinend)* anything; ~welch Indefinitpron. some; *(fragend, verneinend)* any; ~wer Indefinitpron. *(ugs.)* somebody or other *(coll.)*; *(fragend, verneinend)* anyone; anybody; ~wie Adv. somehow; ~wo Adv. somewhere; *(fragend, verneinend)* anywhere; ~woher Adv. from somewhere; *(fragend, verneinend)* from anywhere; ~wohin Adv. somewhere; *(fragend, verneinend)* anywhere

Irin die; ~, ~nen Irishwoman

Iris die; ~, ~ *(Bot., Anat.)* iris

irisch Adj. Irish; **Irland (das);** ~s Ireland

Ironie die; ~, ~n irony; **ironisch 1.** Adj. ironic; ironical; **2.** adv. ironically

irre 1. Adj. insane; **2.** adv. *(salopp)* terribly *(coll.)*; **Irre** der/die; adj. Dekl. madman/madwoman; lunatic; *(fig.)* lunatic

irre|führen tr. V. mislead; *(täuschen)* deceive; **Irreführung die: eine bewußte ~führung** a deliberate attempt to mislead; **~führung der Öffentlichkeit** misleading the public

irrelevant ['ɪrelevant] Adj. irrelevant (für to)

irre|machen tr. V. disconcert; put off; **irren 1.** refl. V. be mistaken; **Sie haben sich in der Nummer geirrt** you've got the wrong number; **2.** itr. V. a) **da ~** Sie you are wrong there; b) *mit sein (ziellos umherstreifen)* wander

Irren-: ~anstalt die *(veralt. abwertend)* mental home; ~haus das *(abwertend)* [lunatic] asylum

Irr·fahrt die wandering; **irriger·weise** Adv. mistakenly

irritieren tr., itr. V. a) *(verwirren)* put off; b) *(stören)* disturb

Irr-, Irr-: ~licht das will o' the wisp; ~sinn der; o. Pl. a) insanity; madness; b) *(ugs. abwertend)* lunacy; ~sinnig 1. Adj. a) *(geistig gestört)* insane; mad; *(absurd)* idiotic; b) *(ugs.: extrem)* terrible *(coll.)*; terrific *(coll.)* ⟨speed, heat, cold⟩; 2. adv. *(ugs.)* terribly *(coll.)*

Irrtum der; ~s, Irrtümer mistake; ~! wrong!; **im** ~ **sein** be wrong or mistaken; **irrtümlich 1.** Adj. incorrect; **2.** adv. by mistake

Ischias ['ɪʃias] der od. das od. Med. die; ~: sciatica

Islam [ɪs'la:m od. 'ɪslam] der; ~[s]: der ~: Islam; **islamisch** Adj. Islamic

Island (das); ~s Iceland; **Isländer** der; ~s, ~ Icelander; **isländisch** Adj. Icelandic

Isolation die; ~, ~en s. Isolierung; **Isolator** der; ~s, ~en insulator; **Isolier·band** das; Pl. ~bänder insulating tape; **isolieren** tr. V. a) isolate; b) (Technik) insulate ⟨wiring, wall, etc.⟩; lag ⟨boilers, pipes, etc.⟩; **Isolier·station** die (Med.) isolation ward; **Isolierung** die; ~, ~en a) isolation; b) (Technik) s. isolieren b: insulation; lagging

Isotop das; ~s, ~e isotope

Israel ['israe:l] (das); ~s Israel; **Israeli** der; ~|s|, ~|s|/die; ~, ~|s| Israeli; **israelisch** Adj. Israeli; **Israelit** der; ~en, ~en Israelite; **israelitisch** Adj. Israelite

iß Imperativ Sg. v. essen

ißt 2. u. 3. Pers. Sg. Präsens v. essen

ist 3. Pers. Sg. Präsens v. sein

Italien [i'ta:li̯ən] (das); ~s Italy; **Italiener** [ita'li̯e:nɐ] der; ~s, ~: Italian; **italienisch** Adj. Italian

I-Tüpfel|chen| das; ~s, ~: final touch; **bis aufs |letzte|** ~: down to the last detail

i. V. [iː'faʊ] Abk. in Vertretung

J

j, J [jɔt, österr.: je:] das; ~, ~: j/J

ja 1. Interj. yes; (nachgestellt: nicht wahr?) won't you/doesn't it etc.?; 2. Partikel Sie wissen **ja**, daß ...: you know, of course, that ...; **da seid ihr ja!** there you are!; **Ja** das; ~|s|, ~|s| yes; **mit** ~ **stimmen** vote yes

Jacht die; ~, ~en yacht

Jacke die; ~, ~n jacket; (gestrickt) cardigan; **Jacken·kleid** das dress and jacket combination; **Jacket·krone** ['dʒɛkɪt-] die (Zahnmed.) jacket crown; **Jackett** [ʒa'kɛt] das; ~s, ~s jacket

Jade die; ~: jade

Jagd die; ~, ~en a) o. Pl. die ~: shooting; hunting; **auf die** ~ **gehen** go hunting/shooting; b) (Veranstaltung)

shoot; (Hetzjagd) hunt; c) (Verfolgung) hunt; (Verfolgungsjagd) chase; **auf jmdn./etw.** ~ **machen** hunt for sb./sth.

Jagd-: ~**beute** die bag; kill; ~**bomber** der (Luftwaffe) fighter-bomber; ~**flieger** der (Luftwaffe) fighter pilot; ~**flugzeug** das (Luftwaffe) fighter aircraft; ~**gewehr** das sporting gun; ~**horn** das hunting-horn; ~**hund** der gun-dog; ~**hütte** die shooting box; ~**revier** das preserve; shoot; ~**schein** der game licence; ~**wurst** die chasseur sausage; ~**zeit** die open season

jagen 1. tr. V. a) hunt ⟨game, fugitive, criminal, etc.⟩; shoot ⟨game, game birds⟩; (hetzen) chase ⟨fugitive, criminal, etc.⟩; b) (treiben) drive; **jmdn. aus dem Haus** ~: throw sb. out of the house; 2. itr. V. (die Jagd ausüben) go shooting or hunting; **Jäger** der; ~s, ~: a) hunter; b) (Milit.) rifleman; c) (Soldatenspr.: Jagdflugzeug) fighter; **Jäger·hut** der huntsman's hat

Jäger-: ~**latein** das (scherzh.) [hunter's] tall story/stories; **das ist das reinste** ~**latein** that's all wild exaggeration; ~**rock** der hunting jacket; ~**schnitzel** das (Kochk.) escalope chasseur

Jaguar der; ~s, ~e jaguar

jäh [je:] 1. Adj. (geh.) a) sudden; abrupt ⟨change, movement, stop⟩; sudden, sharp ⟨pain⟩; b) (steil) steep; precipitous; 2. adv. a) ⟨change⟩ abruptly; b) ⟨fall, drop⟩ steeply; **jählings** Adv. (geh.) a) (plötzlich) ⟨change, end, stop⟩ suddenly, abruptly; ⟨die⟩ suddenly; b) (steil) steeply

Jahr das; ~|es|, ~e year; **ein halbes** ~: six months; **im** ~|e| **1908** in [the year] 1908; **er ist zwanzig** ~ **alt** he is twenty years old; **Kinder bis zu zwölf** ~**en** children up to the age of twelve; **zwischen den** ~**en** between Christmas and the New Year; **jahr·aus** Adv. ~, **jahrein** year in, year out; **jahre·lang** 1. Adj.; nicht präd. [many] years of; long-standing ⟨feud, friendship⟩; 2. adv. for [many] years

jähren refl. V. **heute jährt sich zum zehntenmal, daß ...:** it is ten years ago today that ...

Jahres-: ~**bilanz** die (Wirtsch., Kaufmannsspr.) annual balance [of accounts]; (Dokument) annual balance sheet; ~**einkommen** das annual income; ~**ende** das end of the year;

~**frist**; *o. Art.*; *o. Pl.* in *od.* innerhalb *od.* binnen ~**frist** within [a period of] a *or* one year; ~**hälfte die: die erste/zweite ~hälfte** the first/secound half *or* six months of the year; ~**karte die** yearly season ticket; ~**tag der** anniversary; ~**urlaub der** annual holiday *or (formal)* leave *or (Amer.)* vacation; ~**wechsel der** turn of the year; **zum ~wechsel die besten Wünsche** best wishes for the New Year; ~**zahl die** date; ~**zeit die** season

Jahr·gang der a) *(Altersklasse)* year; **der ~ 1900** those born in 1900; b) *(eines Weines)* vintage; c) *(einer Zeitschrift)* set [of issues] for a/the year; **Jahr·hundert das** century; **Jahr·hundert·wende die** turn of the century; -**jährig** a) *(... Jahre alt)* **ein elfjähriges Kind** an eleven-year-old child; b) *(... Jahre dauernd)* ...year's/years'; **nach vierjähriger Vorbereitung** after four years' preparation; **mit dreijähriger Verspätung** three years late; **jährlich 1.** *Adj.*; *nicht präd.* annual; yearly; **2.** *adv.* annually; yearly; **zweimal ~:** twice a year

Jahr-: ~**markt der** fair; fun-fair; ~**tausend das** thousand years; millennium; ~**zehnt das** decade

jahrzehnte·lang 1. *Adj.*; *nicht präd.* decades of 〈practice, experience, etc.〉; **2.** *adv.* for decades

Jäh·zorn der violent anger; **jäh·zornig 1.** *Adj.* violent-tempered; **2.** *adv.* in a blind rage

ja·ja *Part. (ugs.)* a) *(seufzend)* ~|, **so ist das Leben|** o well|, [that's life]; b) *(ungeduldig)* ~|, **ich komme schon|**! all right, all right|, I'm coming!]

Jalousie [ʒaluˈziː] **die;** ~, ~**n** Venetian blind

Jamaika (das); -s Jamaica; **Jamaikaner der;** ~**s,** ~Jamaican

Jammer der; ~**s** [mournful] wailing; *(Elend)* misery; **jämmerlich 1.** *Adj.* pitiful; b) wretched 〈appearance, existence, etc.〉; paltry, meagre 〈quantity〉; **2.** *adv.* pitifully; **jammern** *itr. V.* wail; *(sich beklagen)* moan; **jammer·schade** *Adj.*; *nicht attr. (ugs.)* **es ist ~schade, daß ...:** it's a crying shame that ...; **es ist ~schade um ihn** it's a great pity about him

Janker der; ~**s,** ~ *(südd., österr.)* Alpine jacket

Januar der; ~|s|, ~**e** January

Japan (das); ~s Japan; **Japaner der;**

~**s,** ~Japanese; **japanisch** *Adj.* Japanese

japsen *itr. V. (ugs.)* pant

Jargon [jarˈgõː] **der;** ~**s,** ~**s** jargon

Jasmin der; ~**s,** ~**e** jasmine

Ja·stimme die yes-vote

jäten *tr., itr. V.* weed; **Unkraut ~:** weed

Jauche die; ~, ~**n** liquid manure; **Jauche·grube die** liquid-manure reservoir

jauchzen *itr. V.* cheer; **vor Freude ~:** shout for joy; **Jauchzer der;** ~**s,** ~: cry of delight

jaulen *itr. V.* howl

Jause die; ~, ~**n** *(österr.)* a) snack; **eine ~ machen** have a snack; b) *(Nachmittagskaffee)* [afternoon] tea

ja·wohl *Part.* certainly; **Ja·wort das** consent; **jmdm. das ~ geben** consent to marry sb.

Jazz [dʒæz *od.* dʒɛs *od.* jats] **der;** ~: jazz; **Jazz·keller der** jazz cellar

¹**je 1.** *Adv.* a) *(jemals)* ever; **mehr/besser denn je** more/better than ever; b) *(jeweils)* **je zehn Personen** ten people at a time; **sie kosten je 30 DM** they cost 30 DM each; c) *(entsprechend)* **je nach Gewicht** according to weight; **2.** *Präp. mit Akk.* per; for each; **3.** *Konj.* **je länger, je lieber** the longer the better; **je nachdem** it all depends

²**je** *Interj.* **ach je, wie schade!** oh dear, what a shame!

Jeans [dʒiːnz] *Pl. od.* **die;** ~, ~: jeans *pl.;* denims *pl.*

jede *s.* **jeder; jeden·falls** *Adv.* a) in any case; b) *(zumindest)* at any rate; **jeder, jede, jedes** *Indefinitpron. u. unbest. Zahlwort* **1.** *attr.* a) *(alle)* every; b) *(alle einzeln)* each; c) *(jeglicher)* all; **2.** *alleinstehend* a) *(alle)* everyone; everybody; b) *(alle einzeln)* **jedes der Kinder** each of the children

jeder-: ~**mann** *Indefinitpron. u. unbest. Zahlwort; nur alleinstehend* everyone; everybody; ~**zeit** *Adv.* [at] any time

jedes *s.* **jeder; jedes·mal** *Adv.* every time

je·doch *Konj., Adv.* however

je·her [od. '-'-] *Adv.* **seit** *od.* **von ~:** always; since time immemorial

jemals *Adv.* ever

jemand *Indefinitpron.* someone; somebody; *(fragend, verneinend)* anyone; anybody

Jemen (das); ~**s** *od.* **der;** ~|s| Yemen

jener, jene, jenes *Demonstrativpron.*

(geh.) **1.** *attr.* that; *(im Pl.)* those; **2.** *alleinstehend* that one; *(im Pl.)* those

jenseits 1. *Präp. mit Gen.* on the other side of; *(in größerer Entfernung)* beyond; **2.** *Adv.* on the other side; ~ **vom Rhein** on the other side of the Rhine; **Jenseits das;** ~: hereafter; beyond

¹Jersey [ˈdʒɔːɐzi] **der;** ~[s], ~s *(Textilind.)* jersey

²Jersey das; ~s, ~s *(Sport: Trikot)* jersey

Jesus (der); Jesu Jesus

Jet [dʒɛt] **der;** ~[s], ~s jet; **mit einem** ~ **fliegen/reisen** fly/travel by jet

jetzig *Adj.; nicht präd.* current

jetzt *Adv.* **a)** just now; **bis** ~: up to now; **bis** ~ **noch nicht** not yet; **von** ~ **an** *od.* **ab** from now on[wards]; **erst** ~ *od.* ~ **erst** only just; **schon** ~: already; **b)** *(heutzutage)* now; nowadays

jeweilig *Adj.; nicht präd.* **a)** *(in einem bestimmten Fall)* particular; **b)** *(zu einer bestimmten Zeit)* current; of the time *postpos., not pred.;* **c)** *(zugehörig, zugewiesen)* respective; **jeweils** *Adv.* **a)** *(jedesmal)* ~ **am ersten/letzten Mittwoch des Monats** on the first/last Wednesday of each month; **b)** *(zur Zeit)* at the time

Jg. *Abk.* Jahrgang

Jh. *Abk.* Jahrhundert c.

jiddisch [ˈjɪdɪʃ] *Adj.* Yiddish

Job [dʒɔp] **der;** ~s, ~s *(ugs.; auch DV)* job; **jobben** [dʒɔbn̩] *itr. V. (ugs.)* do a job/jobs

Joch das; ~[e]s, ~e yoke

Jockei, Jockey [ˈdʒɔke *od.* ˈdʒɔki] **der;** ~s, ~s jockey

Jod [joːt] **das;** ~[e]s iodine

jodeln *itr., tr. V.* yodel

jod·haltig *Adj.* iodiferous

Joga der *od.* **das;** ~[s] yoga

joggen [ˈdʒɔgn̩] *itr. V.; mit Richtungsangabe mit sein* jog

Joghurt [ˈjoːgʊrt] **der** *od.* **das;** ~[s], ~[s] yoghurt; **Joghurt·becher der** yoghurt pot *(Brit.)* *or (Amer.)* container

Johannis·beere die currant; **rote/weiße/schwarze** ~**n** redcurrants/white currants/blackcurrants

johlen *itr. V.* yell; *(vor Wut)* howl

Joint [dʒɔɪnt] **der;** ~s, ~s *(ugs.)* joint *(sl.)*

Jolle die; ~, ~n keel-centre-board yawl

Jongleur [ʒɔŋˈloːɐ] **der;** ~s, ~e juggler; **jonglieren** *tr., itr. V.* juggle

Joppe die; ~, ~n heavy jacket

Jordanien (das) ~s Jordan; **Jorda-**

nier der; ~s, ~: Jordanian; **jordanisch** *Adj.* Jordanian

Jot das; ~, ~: j, J

Journalismus der; ~: journalism *no art.;* **Journalist der;** ~en, ~en journalist; **journalistisch 1.** *Adj.; nicht präd.* journalistic; **eine** ~**e Ausbildung** a training in journalism; **2.** *adv.* journalistically; ~ **tätig sein** be a journalist

jr. *Abk.* junior Jr.

Jubel der; ~s rejoicing; jubilation; *(laut)* cheering; **jubeln** *itr. V.* cheer; **über etw.** *(Akk.)* ~: rejoice over sth.; **Jubilar der;** ~s, ~e man celebrating his anniversary/birthday; **Jubiläum das;** ~s, Jubiläen anniversary; *(eines Monarchen)* jubilee; **jubilieren** *itr. V. (geh.)* jubilate *(literary);* rejoice

juchzen [ˈjʊxtsn̩] *itr. V. (ugs.)* shout with glee

jucken 1. *tr., itr. V.* **a) mir juckt die Haut** I itch; **es juckt mich hier** I've got an itch here; **b)** *(Juckreiz verursachen)* irritate; **2.** *tr. V. (reizen, verlocken)* **es juckt mich, das zu tun** I am itching to do it; **3.** *refl. V. (ugs.: sich kratzen)* scratch; **Juck·reiz der** itch

Jude der; ~n, ~n Jew; **Juden·stern der** *(ns.)* Star of David; **Judentum das;** ~s **a)** *(Volk)* Jewry; Jews *pl.;* **b)** *(Kultur u. Religion)* Judaism; **Jüdin die;** ~, ~nen Jewess; **jüdisch** *Adj.* Jewish

Judo [ˈjuːdo] **das;** ~[s] judo *no art.*

Jugend die; ~ **a)** youth; **b)** *(Jugendliche)* young people

jugend-, Jugend-: ~**amt das** youth office *(agency responsible for education and welfare of young people);* ~**arrest der** detention in a community home; ~**bewegung die** *(hist.)* [German] youth Movement; ~**buch das** book for young people; ~**frei** *Adj. ⟨film, book, etc.⟩* suitable for persons under 18; **nicht** ~**frei** *⟨film⟩* not U-certificate *pred.;* ~**gefährdend** *Adj.* liable to have an undesirable influence on the moral development of young people *postpos.;* ~**heim das** youth centre; ~**herberge die** youth hostel; ~**kriminalität die** juvenile delinquency

jugendlich 1. *Adj.* **a)** *nicht präd.* young *⟨offender, customer, etc.⟩;* **b)** *(für Jugendliche charakteristisch)* youthful; **Jugendliche der/die;** *adj. Dekl.* young person; **die** ~**n** the young people

Jugend-: ~**liebe die** sweetheart of one's youth; ~**schutz der** protection of young people; ~**schutz·gesetz das** laws *pl.* protecting young people; ~**sprache die** young people's language *no art.*; ~**stil der** art nouveau; *(in Deutschland)* Jugendstil; ~**strafe die** youth custody sentence; ~**sünde die** youthful folly; ~**zeit die** youth; ~**zentrum das** youth centre

Jugo·slawe der Yugoslav; **Jugo·slawien (das);** ~**s** Yugoslavia; **jugo·slawisch** *Adj.* Yugoslav[ian]

Julei der; ~|s|, ~s *s.* Juli

Juli der; ~|s|, ~s July; *s. auch* April

jung *Adj.*: jünger, jüngst... a) young; new *(project, undertaking, sport, marriage, etc.)*; b) *(letzt...)* recent; **in jüngster Zeit** recently

¹**Junge der;** ~n, ~n *od. (ugs.)* Jung[en]s boy; ²**Junge das;** *adj. Dekl.* **ein** ~**s** one of the young; ~ **kriegen** give birth to young; **jungen** *itr. V.* give birth; ⟨cat⟩ have kittens; ⟨dog⟩ have pups; **jungenhaft** *Adj.* boyish; **jünger** *Adj.* youngish; **sie ist noch** ~: she is still quite young; *s. auch* jung; **Jünger der;** ~**s**, ~: follower; **Jungfer die;** ~, ~**n** *(abwertend: ältere ledige Frau)* spinster; **Jungfern·fahrt die** maiden voyage; **Jungfern·häutchen das** hymen; **Jung·frau die a)** virgin; b) *(Astrol.)* Virgo; **jung·fräulich** *Adj. (geh., auch fig.)* virgin; **Jung·geselle der** bachelor; **Jung·gesellin die;** ~, ~**nen** bachelor girl

Jüngling der; ~**s**, ~**e** *(geh., spött.)* youth; boy; **jüngst** *Adv. (geh.)* recently; **jüngst...** *s.* jung; **Jüngste der/die;** *adj. Dekl.* youngest [one]

Jung-: ~**verheiratete der/die;** *adj. Dekl.,* young married man/woman; **die** ~**verheirateten** the newly-weds; ~**wähler der** first-time voter

Juni der; ~|s|, ~s June; *s. auch* April

junior *indekl. Adj.; nach Personennamen* junior; **Junior der;** ~**s**, ~**en a)** *(oft scherzh.)* junior *(joc.);* b) *(Kaufmannsspr.)* junior partner; **Junior·chef der** owner's *or (coll.)* boss's son

Juno der; ~|s|, ~s *s.* Juni

Junta ['xʊnta] **die;** ~, ~**ten** junta

Jura *o. Art., o. Pl.* law; ~ **studieren** read Law; **Jurist der;** ~**en**, ~**en**, **Juristin die;** ~, ~**nen** lawyer; jurist; **juristisch** *Adj.* legal

Jury [ʒy'ri:] **die;** ~, ~**s a)** *(Preisrichter)* panel [of judges]; jury; b) *(Sachverständige)* panel [of experts]

Justiz die; ~: justice; *(Behörden)* judiciary

Justiz-: ~**irrtum der** miscarriage of justice; ~**minister der** Minister of Justice; ~**vollzugs·anstalt die** *(Amtsspr.)* penal institution *(formal);* prison

Jute ['ju:tə] **die;** ~: jute

Juwel das *od.* **der;** ~**s**, ~**en** piece of jewellery; *(Edelstein)* jewel; **Juwelier** [juvə'li:ɐ̯] **der;** ~**s** jeweller; **Juwelier·geschäft das** jeweller's shop

Jux der; ~**es**, ~**e** *(ugs.)* joke

K

k, K [ka:] **das;** ~, ~: k/K

Kabarett das; ~**s**, ~**s** *od.* ~**e a)** satirical revue; b) *(Ensemble)* cabaret act; **Kabarettist der;** ~**en**, ~**en** revue performer

kabbeln *refl. V. (ugs.)* bicker (**mit** with)

Kabel das; ~**s**, ~: cable; *(für kleineres Gerät)* flex

Kabeljau der; ~**s**, ~**e** *od.* ~**s** cod

kabeln *tr., itr. V. (veralt.)* cable

Kabine die; ~, ~**n a)** cabin; b) *(Umkleideraum, abgeteilter Raum)* cubicle; c) *(einer Seilbahn)* [cable-]car; **Kabinett das;** ~**s**, ~**e** Cabinet

Kabrio das; ~**s**, ~**s**, **Kabriolett das;** ~**s**, ~**s** convertible

Kachel die; ~, ~**n** [glazed] tile; **kacheln** *tr. V.* tile

Kadaver der; ~**s**, ~: carcass

Kader der *od. (schweiz.)* **das;** ~**s**, ~ cadre; b) *(Sport)* squad

Käfer der; ~**s**, ~: beetle

Kaff das; ~**s**, ~**s** *od.* **Käffer** *(ugs. abwertend)* dump *(coll.)*

Kaffee ['kafe *od. (österr.)* ka'fe:] **der;** ~**s**, ~**s a)** coffee; b) *(Nachmittags~)* afternoon coffee; ~ **trinken** have afternoon coffee

Kaffee-: ~**kanne die** coffee-pot; ~**kränzchen das** *(veralt.)* a) *(Zusammentreffen)* coffee afternoon; b) *(Gruppe)* coffee circle; ~**maschine**

die coffee-maker; **~mühle** die coffee-grinder; **~satz** der coffee-grounds *pl.;* **~tante** die *(ugs. scherzh.)* coffee addict

Käfig der; ~s, ~e cage

kahl *Adj.* **a)** *(ohne Haare)* bald; **b)** *(ohne Grün, schmucklos)* bare

kahl-, Kahl-: ~|**fressen** *unr. tr. V.* etw. ~fressen strip sth. bare; **~köpfig** *Adj.* bald[-headed]; **~|scheren** *unr. tr. V.* jmdn. ~scheren shave sb.'s head; **~schlag** der **a)** clear-felling *no indef. art.;* **b)** *(Waldfläche)* clear-felled area

Kahn der; ~|e|s, **Kähne a)** *(Ruder~)* rowing-boat; *(Stech~)* punt; **b)** *(Lastschiff)* barge

Kai der; ~s, ~s quay

Kaiser der; ~s, ~: emperor; **Kaiserin** die; ~, ~nen empress

Kaiser-: **~krone** die imperial crown; **~reich** das empire; **~schnitt** der Caesarean section

Kajüte die; ~, ~n *(Seemannsspr.)* cabin

Kakao [ka'kaʊ] der; ~s, ~s cocoa

Kakerlak der; ~s *od.* ~en, ~en cockroach

Kaktus der; ~, **Kakteen** cactus

Kalauer der; ~s, ~: corny joke *(coll.);* *(Wortspiel)* atrocious *or* *(coll.)* corny pun

Kalb das; ~|e|s, **Kälber a)** calf; **b)** *(ugs.: ~fleisch)* veal; **kalben** *itr. V.* calve; **Kalb·fleisch** das veal

Kalbs-: **~braten** der *(Kochk.)* roast veal *no indef. art.;* *(Gericht)* roast of veal; **~leder** das calfskin; **~schnitzel** das veal cutlet

Kalender der; ~s, ~: calendar; *(Taschen~)* diary; **Kalender·jahr** das calendar year

Kalesche die; ~, ~n *(hist.)* barouche

Kali das; ~s, ~s potash

Kaliber das; ~s, ~: a) *(Technik, Waffenkunde)* calibre; b) *(ugs., oft abwertend)* sort; kind

Kalifornien [kali'fɔrniən] *(das)* ~s California

Kalium *(Chemie)* das; ~s potassium

Kalk der; ~|e|s, ~e calcium carbonate; *(Baustoff)* lime; quicklime; **kalken** *tr. V.* whitewash

Kalk-: **~mangel** der; *o. Pl.* calcium deficiency; **~stein** der limestone

Kalkül das *od. der;* ~s, ~e *(geh.)* calculation; **Kalkulation** die; ~, ~en *(auch Wirtsch.)* calculation; **kalkulieren** *tr. V.* calculate ⟨cost, price⟩; cost ⟨product, article⟩

Kalorie die; ~, ~n calorie; **kalorien-arm 1.** *Adj.* low-calorie *attrib.;* **~arm sein** be low in calories; **2.** *adv.* **~arm kochen** cook low-calorie meals

kalt; **kälter, kältest...** **1.** *Adj.* cold; frosty ⟨atmosphere, smile⟩; **2.** *adv.* a) ~ duschen have a cold shower **Getränke/Sekt ~ stellen** cool drinks/chill champagne; **b)** *(nüchtern)* coldly; **c)** *(abweisend, unfreundlich)* frostily

kalt-, Kalt-: ~|**bleiben** *unr. itr. V.;* mit sein remain unmoved; **~blütig 1.** *Adj.* **a)** cool-headed; **b)** *(abwertend: skrupellos)* cold-blooded; **2.** *adv.* **a)** coolly; **b)** *(abwertend: skrupellos)* cold-bloodedly; **~blütigkeit** die; ~: *s.* **~blütig a, b:** cool-headedness; cold-bloodedness

Kälte die; ~ cold; *(fig.)* coldness

Kälte-: **~einbruch** der *(Met.)* sudden onset of cold weather; **~grad** der degree of frost

kälter *s.* kalt; **kältest...** *s.* kalt; **Kälte·welle** die cold spell

kalt-, Kalt-: **~herzig** *Adj.* cold-hearted; **~lächelnd** *Adv.* *(ugs. abwertend)* etw. ~lächelnd tun take callous pleasure in doing sth.; ~|**lassen** *unr. tr. V.* *(ugs.)* jmdn. ~lassen leave sb. unmoved; *(nicht interessieren)* leave sb. cold *(coll.);* ~|**machen** *tr. V.* *(salopp)* jmdn. ~machen do sb. in *(sl.);* **~miete** die rent exclusive of heating; **~schale** die cold sweet soup made with fruit, beer, wine, or milk; **~schnäuzig** [~ʃnɔytsɪç] *(ugs.)* **1.** *Adj.* cold and insensitive; *(frech)* insolent; **2.** *adv.* coldly and insensitively; *(frech)* insolently; ~|**stellen** *tr. V.* *(ugs.)* jmdn. ~stellen put sb. out of the way *(coll. joc.)*

kam *1. u. 3. Pers. Prät. v.* kommen

Kambodscha [kam'bɔdʒa] *(das)*; ~s Cambodia

käme *1. u. 3. Pers. Konjunktiv II v.* kommen

Kamel das; ~s, ~e camel

Kamera die; ~, ~s camera

Kamerad der; ~en, ~en companion; *(Freund)* friend; *(Mitschüler)* mate; *(Soldat)* comrade; *(Sport)* team-mate; **Kameradschaft** die; ~: comradeship; **kameradschaftlich 1.** *Adj.* comradely; **2.** *adv.* in a comradely way

Kamera·mann der *Pl.* ~männer *od.* ~leute cameraman

Kamerun ['kaməru:n] *(das)*; ~s Cameroon; the Cameroons *pl.*

Kamille die; ~, ~n camomile

Kamin der, *schweiz.*: das; ~s, ~e fireplace; **Kamin·feger** der *(bes. südd.)* s. **Schornsteinfeger**

Kamm der; ~[e]s, **Kämme a)** comb; **b)** *(bei Hühnern usw.)* comb; **c)** *(Gebirgs~)* ridge; **kämmen** tr. V. comb

Kammer die; ~, ~n **a)** store-room; **b)** *(Biol., Med., Technik, Waffenkunde)* chamber; **c)** *(Parl.)* chamber

Kammer-: ~**diener** der *(veralt.)* valet; ~**jäger** der pest controller; ~**musik** die, *o. Pl.* chamber music; ~**sänger** der *title awarded to singer of outstanding merit;* ~**zofe** die *(veralt.)* lady's maid

Kamm·garn das worsted

Kampagne [kam'panjə] die; ~, ~n campaign

Kampf der; ~[e]s, **Kämpfe a)** *(militärisch)* battle (**um** for); **b)** *(zwischen persönlichen Gegnern)* fight; *(fig.)* struggle; **c)** *(Wett~)* contest; *(Boxen)* contest; bout; **d)** *(Einsatz aller Mittel)* fight (**um, für** for; **gegen** against); **kampf·bereit** Adj. ready to fight *postpos.; (army, troops)* ready for battle; **kämpfen** itr. V. **a)** fight; **b)** *(Sport: sich messen)* ⟨team⟩ play; ⟨wrestler, boxer⟩ fight

Kämpfer der; ~s camphor

Kämpfer der; ~s, ~, **Kämpferin** die; ~, ~nen fighter

kampf-, Kampf-: ~**fähig** Adj. ⟨troops⟩ fit for action; ⟨boxer etc.⟩ fit to fight; ~**handlungen** Pl. fighting *sing.;* ~**richter** der *(Sport)* judge; ~**unfähig** Adj. ⟨troops⟩ unfit for action; ⟨boxer etc.⟩ unfit to fight

kampieren itr. V. camp

Kanada (das); ~s Canada; **Kanadier** [ka'na:diɐ] der; ~s, ~ Canadian; **kanadisch** Adj. Canadian

Kanal der; ~s, **Kanäle a)** canal; **b)** *(Geogr.)* der ~: the [English] Channel; **c)** *(für Abwässer)* sewer; **d)** *(zur Entwässerung, Bewässerung)* channel; *(Graben)* ditch; **e)** *(Rundf., Ferns., Weg der Information)* channel; **Kanalisation** die; ~, ~en sewerage system; sewers *pl.;* **kanalisieren** tr. V. **a)** *(lenken)* channel ⟨energies, goods, etc.⟩; **b)** *(schiffbar machen)* canalize

Kanaren Pl. Canaries; **Kanarien·vogel** [ka'na:riən-] der canary; **Kanarische Inseln** Pl. Canary Islands

Kandare die; ~, ~n curb bit; **jmdn. an die ~ nehmen** *(fig.)* take sb. in hand

Kandidat der; ~en, ~en **a)** candidate; **b)** *(beim Quiz usw.)* contestant; **Kandidatur** die; ~, ~en candidature (**auf** + *Akk.* for); **kandidieren** itr. V. stand [as a candidate] (**für** for)

kandieren tr. V. candy; **kandiert** crystallized ⟨orange, petal⟩; glacé ⟨cherry, pear⟩; candied ⟨peel⟩; **Kandis** der; ~, **Kandis·zucker** der rock candy

Känguruh ['kɛŋguru] das; ~s, ~s kangaroo

Kaninchen das; ~s, ~: rabbit

Kanister der; ~s, ~: can; [metal/plastic] container

kann 1. u. 3. Pers. Sg. Präsens v. **können**

Kännchen das; ~s, ~: [small] pot; *(für Milch)* [small] jug; **Kanne** die; ~, ~n **a)** pot; *(für Milch, Wein, Wasser)* jug; **b)** *(Henkel~)* can; *(für Milch)* pail; *(beim Melken)* churn

kannst 2. Pers. Sg. Präsens v. **können**

kannte 1. u. 3. Pers. Sg. Prät. v. **kennen**

Kanon der; ~s, ~s canon

Kanone die; ~, ~n cannon; *(fig. ugs.: Könner)* ace

Kantate die; ~, ~n *(Musik)* cantata

Kante die; ~, ~n edge; **kantig** Adj. square-cut ⟨timber, stone⟩; roughedged ⟨rock⟩; angular ⟨face⟩; square ⟨chin⟩

Kantine die; ~, ~n canteen

Kanton der; ~s, ~e canton

Kantor der; ~s, ~en choirmaster and organist

Kanu das; ~s, ~s canoe

Kanüle die; ~, ~n *(Med.)* cannula

Kanzel die; ~, ~n **a)** pulpit; **b)** *(Flugw.)* cockpit

Kanzlei die; ~, ~en *(veralt.: Büro)* office; **b)** *(Anwalts~)* chambers *pl. (of barrister);* office *of lawyer)*

Kanzler der; ~s, ~ chancellor

Kap das; ~s, ~s cape

Kapazität die; ~, ~en **a)** capacity; **b)** *(Experte)* expert

Kapelle die; ~, ~n **a)** *(Archit.)* chapel; **b)** *(Musik~)* band; [light] orchestra; **Kapell·meister** der bandmaster; *(im Orchester)* conductor; *(im Theater usw.)* musical director

Kaper die; ~, ~n caper *usu. in pl.*

kapern tr. V. **a)** *(hist.)* capture; **b)** *(ugs.)* jmdn. [für etw.] ~: rope sb. in[to sth.]

kapieren *(ugs.)* **1.** tr. V. *(ugs.)* get *(coll.);* **2.** itr. V. **kapiert?** got it? *(coll.)*

Kapital das; ~s, ~e od. ~ien a) capital; b) (fig.) asset; **Kapitalismus** der; ~: capitalism no art.; **Kapitalist** der; ~en, ~en capitalist; **kapitalistisch** Adj. capitalistic

Kapital·verbrechen das serious offence; (mit Todesstrafe bedroht) capital offence

Kapitän der; ~s, ~e (Seew.) captain

Kapitel das; ~s, ~: chapter

Kapitulation die; ~, ~en surrender; capitulation; **seine ~ erklären** admit defeat; **kapitulieren** itr. V. a) surrender; capitulate; b) (fig.: aufgeben) give up; **vor etw.** (Dat.) ~: give up in the face of sth.

Kaplan der; ~s, **Kapläne** (kath. Kirche) chaplain; (Hilfsgeistlicher) curate

Kappe die; ~, ~n cap

kappen tr. V. a) (Seemannsspr.) cut; b) (beschneiden) cut back (hedge etc.); (abschneiden) cut off (branches etc.)

Käppi das; ~s, ~s garrison cap

Kapsel die; ~, ~n capsule

Kapstadt (das) Cape Town

kaputt Adj. a) broken; **das Telefon ist ~**: the phone is not working; b) (ugs.: erschöpft) shattered (coll.)

kaputt-: ~|**gehen** unr. itr. V.; mit sein (ugs.) (entzweigehen) break; (machine) break down, (sl.) pack up; (light-bulb) go; (zerbrechen) be smashed; ~|**lachen** refl. V. (ugs.) kill oneself [laughing] (coll.); ~|**machen** (ugs.) 1. tr. V. break; spoil (sth. made with effort); ruin (clothes, furniture, etc.); finish (person) off; 2. refl. V. wear oneself out

Kapuze die; ~, ~n hood; (bei Mönchen) cowl; hood; **Kapuziner** der; ~s, ~: Capuchin [friar]

Karabiner der; ~s, ~: carbine

Karaffe die; ~, ~n carafe; (mit Glasstöpsel) decanter

Karambolage [karambo'la:ʒə] die; ~, ~n (ugs.) crash; collision

Karamel der (schweiz.: das); ~s caramel; **Karamel·bonbon** der od. das caramel [toffee]

Karat das; ~[e]s, ~e carat

Karate das; ~[s] karate

Karawane die; ~, ~n caravan

Kardinal der; ~s, **Kardinäle** (kath. Kirche) cardinal

Kardinal-: ~**tugend** die; meist Pl. cardinal virtue; ~**zahl** die cardinal [number]

Karenz die; ~, ~en, **Karenz·zeit** die waiting period

Kar·freitag der Good Friday

karg 1. Adj. meagre (wages etc.); frugal (meal etc.); poor (light, accommodation); (wenig fruchtbar) barren; 2. adv. ~ **bemessen sein** (helping) be mingy (Brit. coll.); (supply) be scanty; ~ **leben** live frugally; **kärglich** 1. Adj. meagre, poor (wages etc.); poor (light); frugal (meal); scanty (supply); 2. adv. poorly (lit, paid, rewarded)

karibisch Adj. Caribbean

kariert Adj. check, checked (material, pattern); check (jacket etc.); squared (paper)

Karies ['ka:riɛs] die; ~: caries

Karikatur die; ~, ~en cartoon; (Porträt) caricature; **Karikaturist** der; ~en, ~en cartoonist; (Porträtist) caricaturist; **karikieren** tr. V. caricature

karitativ Adj. charitable

Karl [karl] (der) Charles; ~ **der Große** Charlemagne

Karneval ['karnəval] der; ~s, ~e od. ~s carnival; ~ **feiern** join in the carnival festivities

Karnickel das; ~s, ~ (landsch.) rabbit

Kärnten (das); ~s Carinthia

Karo das; ~s, ~s a) square; (auf der Spitze stehend) diamond; b) o. Pl. (~muster) check; c) o. Art.; o. Pl. (Kartenspiel: Farbe) diamonds pl.; d) (Kartenspiel: Karte) diamond; **Karo·as** das ace of diamonds

Karosse die; ~, ~n [state-]coach; **Karosserie** die; ~, ~n bodywork

Karotte die; ~, ~n small carrot

Karpaten Pl. Carpathians; Carpathian Mountains

Karpfen der; ~s, ~: carp

Karre die; ~, ~n (bes. nordd.) a) s. **Karren**; b) (abwertend: Fahrzeug) [old] heap (coll.)

Karree das; ~s, ~s: **ums ~ gehen/fahren** walk/drive round the block

karren tr. V. a) cart; b) (salopp: mit einem Auto) run (coll.); **Karren** der; ~s, ~ (bes. südd., österr.) cart; (zweirädrig) barrow

Karriere [ka'rjɛːrə] die; ~, ~n career; ~ **machen** make a [successful] career for oneself

Kar·samstag der Easter Saturday

Karte die; ~, ~n card; (Speise~) menu; (Fahr~, Flug~, Eintritts~) ticket; (Land~) map; **alles auf eine ~ setzen** stake everything on one chance; **Kartei** die; ~, ~en card file

Kartei-: ~**karte** die file card; ~**kasten** der file-card box

Kartell das; ~s, ~e *(Wirtsch., Politik)* cartel

Kartell-: ~**amt** das *government body concerned with the control and supervision of cartels;* ≈ Monopolies and Mergers Commission *(Brit.);* ~**gesetz** das law relating to cartels; ≈ monopolies law *(Brit.)*

Karten-: ~**haus** das house of cards; ~**spiel** das a) *(Spiel mit Karten)* card-game; **b)** *(Satz Spielkarten)* pack or *(Amer.)* deck [of cards]; ~**vor·ver·kauf** der; *o. Pl.* advance booking

Kartoffel die; ~, ~n potato

Kartoffel-: ~**brei** der mashed potatoes *pl.;* mash *(coll.);* ~**chips** Pl. [potato] crisps *(Brit.)* or *(Amer.)* chips; ~**käfer** der Colorado beetle; ~**kloß** der potato dumpling; ~**puffer** der potato pancake *(made from grated raw potatoes);* ~**püree** das; *s.* ~**brei**

Karton [kar'tɔŋ] der; ~s, ~s a) *(Pappe)* card[board]; **b)** *(Schachtel)* cardboard box

Karussell das; ~s, ~s od. ~e merry-go-round; carousel *(Amer.);* *(kleineres)* roundabout

Kar·woche die Holy Week

Karzinom das; ~s, ~e *(Med.)* carcinoma

kaschieren tr. V. conceal; hide; disguise *(fault)*

¹**Kaschmir** (das); ~s Kashmir; ²**Kaschmir** der; ~s, ~e *(Textilw.)* cashmere

Käse der; ~s, ~: cheese; *(ugs. abwertend: Unsinn)* rubbish

Käse-: ~**blatt** das *(salopp abwertend)* rag; ~**glocke** die cheese dome

Kaserne die; ~, ~n barracks *sing. or pl.*

käse·weiß Adj. *(ugs.)* [as] white as a sheet; **käsig** Adj. *(ugs.)* pasty; pale

Kasino das; ~s, ~s a) *(Spiel~)* casino; **b)** *(Offiziers~)* [officers'] mess; **c)** *(Speiseraum)* canteen

Kasko·versicherung die *(Voll~)* comprehensive insurance; *(Teil~)* insurance against theft, fire, or act of God

Kasper der; ~s, ~: ≈ Punch; *(fig. ugs.)* clown; **Kasperl** das; ~s, ~[n] *(österr.)* **Kasperle** das od. der; ~s, ~: *s.* Kasper

Kasper-: ~**puppe** die ≈ Punch and Judy puppet; ~**theater** das ≈ Punch and Judy show; *(Puppenbühne)* ≈ Punch and Judy theatre

Kasse die; ~, ~n a) cash-box; *(Regi-*

strier~) till; **b)** *(Ort zum Bezahlen)* cash desk; *(im Supermarkt)* checkout; *(in einer Bank)* counter; **c)** *(Kassenraum)* cashier's office; **d)** *(Theater~, Kino~)* box-office

Kasseler das; ~s smoked loin of pork

Kassen-: ~**arzt** der doctor who treats members of health insurance schemes; ~**bon** der sales slip; receipt; ~**patient** der patient who is a member of a health insurance scheme; ~**zettel** der s. ~**bon**

Kassette die; ~, ~n a) box; case; **b)** *(mit Büchern, Schallplatten)* boxed set; *(Tonband~, Film~)* cassette; **Kassetten·recorder** der cassette recorder

kassieren 1. tr. V. a) collect; **b)** *(ugs.: wegnehmen)* confiscate; take away *(driving licence);* 2. itr. V. a) **bei jmdm. ~**: give sb. his/her bill or *(Amer.)* check; *(ohne Rechnung)* settle up with sb.; **darf ich bei Ihnen ~?** would you like your bill?/can I settle up with you?; **Kassierer** der; ~s, ~, **Kassiererin** die; ~, ~nen cashier; *(bei einem Verein)* treasurer

Kastanie [kas'taːnjə] die; ~, ~n chestnut; **kastanien·braun** Adj. chestnut

Kästchen das; ~s, ~ a) small box; **b)** *(vorgedrucktes Quadrat)* square; *(auf Fragebögen)* box

Kaste die; ~, ~n caste

kasteien refl. V. a) *(als Bußübung)* chastise oneself; **b)** *(sich Entbehrungen auferlegen)* deny oneself; **Kasteiung** die; ~, ~en a) *(als Bußübung)* self-chastisement; **b)** *(Auferlegung von Entbehrungen)* self-denial

Kastell das; ~s, ~e *(hist.: röm. Lager)* fort; **b)** *(Burg)* castle

Kasten der; ~s, **Kästen** a) box; *(für Flaschen)* crate; **b)** *(ugs.: Briefkasten)* post-box; **c)** *(ugs. abwertend) (Gebäude)* barracks sing. or pl.; *(Auto)* heap *(coll.); (fig. ugs.)* etw. auf dem ~ haben have got it up top *(coll.);* **Kastenbrot** das tin[-loaf]

Kastration [kastra'tsĭoːn] die; ~, ~en castration; **kastrieren** tr. V. castrate

Katalog der; ~[e]s, ~e *(auch fig.)* catalogue; **katalogisieren** tr. V. catalogue

Katalysator der; ~s, ~en [-za'toːrən] *(Chemie, fig.)* catalyst; *(Kfz-W.)* catalytic converter

katapultieren tr. V. *(auch fig.)* catapult; eject *(pilot)*

Katarrh [ka'tar] der; ~s, ~e (Med.) catarrh

katastrophal [katastro'fa:l] 1. Adj. disastrous; (stärker) catastrophic; 2. adv. disastrously; (stärker) catastrophically; **Katastrophe** [katas'tro:fə] die; ~, ~n (Unglück) disaster; (stärker, auch Literaturw.) catastrophe

Katastrophen-: ~alarm der disaster alert; **~gebiet das** disaster area; **~schutz** der (Organisation) emergency services pl.; (Maßnahmen) disaster procedures pl.

Kategorie die; ~, ~n category; **kategorisch** 1. Adj. categorical; 2. adv. categorically

Kater der; ~s, ~ a) tom-cat; b) (ugs.) hangover

Kathedrale die; ~, ~n cathedral

Katholik der; ~en, ~en, **Katholikin** die; ~, ~nen [Roman] Catholic; **katholisch** Adj. [Roman] Catholic; **Katholizismus** der; ~: [Roman] Catholicism no art.

Kätzchen das; ~s, ~ a) little cat; pussy; (junge Katze) kitten; b) meist Pl. catkin; **Katze** die; ~, ~n cat

katzen-, Katzen-: ~auge das reflector; Cat's-eye (P); **~jammer** der a) (Kater) hangover; b) (fig.) mood of depression; **~musik** die (ugs. abwertend) terrible row (coll.); **~sprung** der stone's throw; **~wäsche** die (ugs.) **~wäsche machen** have a lick and a promise (coll.)

Kauderwelsch das; ~[s] gibberish no indef. art.

kauen tr., itr. V. chew; [die] Nägel ~: bite one's nails

kauern 1. itr., refl. V. crouch [down]; (ängstlich) cower

Kauf der; ~[e]s, Käufe a) (das Kaufen) buying; purchasing (formal); b) (das Gekaufte) purchase; **kaufen** 1. tr. V. buy; purchase; 2. itr. V. (einkaufen) shop; **Käufer** der; ~s, ~: buyer; purchaser (formal)

Kauf-: ~haus das department store; **~kraft** die (Wirtsch.) a) (Wert des Geldes) purchasing power; b) (Zahlungsfähigkeit) spending power

käuflich 1. Adj. a) for sale postpos.; b) (bestechlich) venal; ~ sein be easily bought; 2. adv. etw. ~ erwerben/erstehen purchase sth.; **Kauf-mann** der; Pl. **Kaufleute** a) (Geschäftsmann) businessman; (Händler) trader; b) (Besitzer) shopkeeper; (eines Lebens-

mittelladens) grocer; **kaufmännisch** Adj. commercial; business attrib.; **Kauf-preis** der the purchase price

Kau-gummi der od. das; ~s, ~s chewing gum

Kaukasus der; ~: the Caucasus

Kaulquappe die; ~, ~n tadpole

kaum Adv. hardly; scarcely; ~ hatte er Platz genommen, als ...: no sooner had he sat down than ...

kausal Adj. (geh., Sprachw.) causal

Kau-tabak der chewing tobacco

Kaution [kau'tsio:n] die; ~, ~en a) (bei Freilassung eines Gefangenen) bail; b) (beim Mieten einer Wohnung) deposit

Kautschuk der; ~s, ~e rubber

Kauz der; ~es, Käuze a) (Wald~) tawny owl; (Stein~) little owl; b) (Sonderling) strange fellow; oddball (coll.)

Kavalier [kava'li:ɐ̯] der; ~s, ~e gentleman; **Kavaliers·delikt** das trifling offence

Kavallerie die; ~, ~n (Milit. hist.) cavalry; **Kavallerist** der; ~en, ~en cavalryman

Kaviar ['ka:vjar] der; ~s, ~e caviare

kcal Abk. Kilo|gramm|kalorie kcal

keck 1. Adj. a) cheeky; saucy (Brit.); b) (veralt.: verwegen) bold; c) (flott) jaunty, pert ⟨hat etc.⟩; 2. adv. a) cheekily; saucily (Brit.); b) (veralt.: verwegen) boldly; c) (flott) jauntily; **Keckheit** die; ~, ~en a) cheek; sauce (Brit.); b) (veralt.: Kühnheit) boldness

Kegel der; ~s, ~ a) cone; b) (Spielfigur) skittle; (beim Bowling) pin; **Kegel·bahn** die skittle alley; **kegelförmig** Adj. conical; **kegeln** 1. itr. V. play skittles or ninepins; 2. tr. V. eine Partie ~: play a game of skittles or ninepins; eine Neun ~: score a nine

Kehle die; ~, ~n throat; **Kehl·kopf** der (Anat.) larynx

Kehre die; ~, ~n sharp bend; **¹kehren** 1. tr. V. turn; 2. refl. V. turn

²kehren 1. itr. V. (bes. südd.) sweep; do the sweeping; 2. tr. V. sweep; (mit einem Handfeger) brush; **Kehricht** der od. das; ~s (schweiz.: Müll) refuse; garbage (Amer.)

Kehr-seite die a) back; (einer Münze, Medaille) reverse; (scherzh.) (Gesäß) backside; b) (nachteiliger Aspekt) drawback; disadvantage; **kehrt|machen** itr. V. (ugs.) turn [round and go] back

keifen itr. V. (abwertend) nag

Keil der; ~[e]s, ~e a) *(zum Spalten)* wedge; b) *(zum Festklemmen)* chock; *(unter einer Tür)* wedge; **keilen** *refl. V.* (ugs.: sich prügeln) fight; scrap; **Keiler** der; ~s, ~ *(Jägerspr.)* wild boar; **Keilerei** die; ~, ~en *(ugs.)* punch-up *(coll.)*; fight

Keil-: ~**riemen** der *(Technik)* V-belt; ~**schrift** die cuneiform script

Keim der; ~[e]s, ~e *(Bot.)* shoot; *(Biol.)* embryo; **keimen** *itr. V.* germinate; *(fig.)* (hope) stir; **keim·frei** *Adj.* germ-free; sterile; **Keim·zelle** die nucleus

kein *Indefinitpron.* a) no; b) (ugs.: nicht ganz, nicht einmal) less than; **kein...** *Indefinitpron.* ~er/~e nobody; no one; ~s von beiden neither [of them]; **keinerlei** *indekl. unbest. Gattungsz.* no ... what[so]ever

keines-: ~**falls** *Adv.* on no account; ~**wegs** *Adv.* by no means

kein·mal *Adv.* not [even] once

Keks der; ~ od. ~es, ~ od. ~e biscuit *(Brit.)*; cookie *(Amer.)*

Kelch der; ~[e]s, ~e goblet; *(Rel.)* chalice

Kelle die; ~, ~n a) ladle; b) *(Signalstab)* signalling disc; c) *(Maurer~)* trowel

Keller der; ~s, ~: cellar; *(~geschoß)* basement; **Keller·assel** die woodlouse; **Kellerei** die; ~, ~en winery; *(Kellerräume)* [wine] cellars *pl.*; **Keller·geschoß** das basement

Kellner der; ~s, ~: waiter; **kellnern** *itr. V.* (ugs.) work as a waiter/waitress

Kelte der; ~n, ~n Celt

Kelter die; ~, ~n winepress; **keltern** *tr. V.* press (grapes etc.)

keltisch *Adj.* Celtic

Kenia (das); ~s Kenya; **Kenianer** der; ~s, ~: Kenyan

kennen *unr. tr. V.* a) know; b) *(bekannt sein mit)* know; **kennen·lernen** *tr. V.* get to know; *(erstmals begegnen)* meet; *(in Berührung gebracht werden mit)* come to know; **Kenner** der; ~s, ~: expert (+ Gen. on); *(von Wein, Speisen)* connoisseur; **Kennerblick** der expert eye; mit ~: with an expert eye; **Kenn·marke** die [police] identification badge; ≈ [police] warrant card *or* (Amer.) ID card; **kenntlich** *Adj.*: ~ sein to be recognizable (an by); etw./jmdn. ~ machen mark sth./make sb. [easily] identifiable; **Kenntnis** die; ~, ~se knowledge

kenn-, Kenn-: ~**wort** das; *Pl.* ~wörter code-word; *(Parole)* password; code-word; ~**zahl** die index; ~**zeichen** das a) sign; b) *(Erkennungszeichen)* badge; *(auf einem Behälter, einer Ware usw.)* label; *(am Fahrzeug)* registration number; ~**zeichnen** *tr. V.* a) mark; label; mark (way); b) *(charakterisieren)* characterize; ~**zeichnend** *Adj.* typical, characteristic (für of)

kentern *itr. V. mit sein* capsize

Keramik die; ~, ~en o. *Pl.* ceramics *pl.*; pottery; *(~gegenstand)* piece of pottery

Kerbe die; ~, ~n notch

Kerbel der; ~s chervil

Kerb·holz das: etwas auf dem ~holz haben *(ugs.)* have done a job *(sl.)*

Kerker der; ~s, ~ *(hist.)* dungeons *pl.*; *(einzelne Zelle)* dungeon

Kerl der; ~s, ~e *(nordd., md. auch:* ~s*)* *(ugs.)* fellow *(coll.)*; bloke *(Brit. sl.)*

Kern der; ~[e]s, ~e pip; *(von Steinobst)* stone; *(von Nüssen usw.)* kernel; *(Atom~)* nucleus; *(fig.)* der ~ einer Sache the heart of a matter; der harte ~: the hard core

kern-, Kern-: ~**energie** die nuclear energy *no art.*; ~**gehäuse** das core; ~**gesund** *Adj.* fit as a fiddle *pred.*

kernig *Adj.* earthy (language); forceful (speech); pithy (saying)

kern-, Kern-: ~**kraft** die nuclear power; ~**kraftwerk** das nuclear power station *or* plant; ~**los** *Adj.* seedless; ~**obst** das pomaceous fruit; ~**physik** die nuclear physics *sing., no art.*; ~**reaktor** der nuclear reactor; ~**seife** die washing soap; ~**spaltung** die *(Physik)* nuclear fission *no art.*; ~**waffe** die; *meist Pl.* nuclear weapon

Kerze die; ~, ~n candle

kerzen-, Kerzen-: ~**gerade**, *(ugs.)* ~**grade** 1. *Adj.* dead straight; 2. *adv.* bolt upright; ~**halter** der candleholder; ~**leuchter** der candlestick

keß I. *Adj.* a) pert; jaunty (hat, dress, etc.); b) *(frech)* cheeky; 2. *adv.* a) *(flott)* jauntily; b) *(frech)* cheekily

Kessel der; ~s, ~ a) kettle; *(zum Kochen)* pot; *(Wasch~)* copper; b) *(Berg~)* basin-shaped valley; c) *(Milit.)* encircled area

Kessel-: ~**stein** der; o. *Pl.* scale; ~**treiben** das *(Hetzkampagne)* witchhunt

Kette die; ~, ~n chain; *(Hals~)* necklace; *(von Ereignissen)* string; **ketten** *tr. V.* chain (**an** + Akk. to)

Ketten-: ~**hund** der guard-dog *(kept on a chain)*; ~**raucher** der chain-smoker

Ketzer der; ~s, ~ *(auch fig.)* heretic; **Ketzerei** die; ~, ~en *(auch fig.)* heresy

keuchen *itr. V.* gasp for breath; **Keuch·husten** der whooping cough *no art.*

Keule die; ~, ~n a) club; b) *(Kochk.)* leg

keusch 1. *Adj.* chaste; 2. *adv.* ~ leben lead a chaste life; **Keuschheit** die; ~ chastity

Kfz [ka:lɛfˈtsɛt] *Abk.* Kraftfahrzeug

kg *Abk.* Kilogramm kg

KG *Abk.* Kommanditgesellschaft

kichern *itr. V.* giggle

kicken *(ugs.)* 1. *itr. V.* play football; 2. *tr. V.* kick

kidnappen [ˈkɪtnɛpn̩] *tr. V.* kidnap; **Kidnapper** der; ~s, ~: kidnapper

Kiebitz der; ~es, ~e lapwing; peewit

¹**Kiefer** der; ~s, ~: jaw; *(~knochen)* jaw-bone

²**Kiefer** die; ~, ~n pine[tree]

Kiefer·höhle die *(Anat.)* maxillary sinus

Kiefern·holz das pine[-wood]

Kiel der; ~[e]s, ~e keel; **kiel·holen** *tr. V. (Seemannsspr.)* keel-haul *(person)*; **Kiel·wasser** das wake

Kieme die; ~, ~n; *meist Pl.* gill

Kien der; ~[e]s resinous wood

Kies der; ~es, ~e gravel; *(auf dem Strand)* shingle; **Kiesel** der; ~s, ~: pebble; **Kiesel·stein** der pebble

Kies-: ~**grube** die gravel pit; ~**weg** der gravel path

kiffen *itr. V. (ugs.)* smoke pot *(sl.)* or grass *(sl.)*; **Kiffer** der; ~s, ~ *(ugs.)* pot-head *(sl.)*

kikeriki [kikariˈki:] *Interj. (Kinderspr.)* cock-a-doodle-doo

Killer der; ~s, ~ *(salopp)* killer; *(gegen Bezahlung)* hit man *(sl.)*

Kilo das; ~s, ~[s] kilo; **Kilo·gramm** das kilogram; **Kilometer** der; ~s, ~: kilometre; **kilometer·lang** 1. *Adj.* miles long *pred.*; 2. *adv.* for miles [and miles]; **Kilometer·stand** der mileage reading

Kimme die; ~, ~n sighting notch

Kimono der; ~s, ~s kimono

Kind das; ~[e]s, ~er a) child; ein ~ erwarten be expecting; [~er,] ~er! my goodness!

Kinder-: ~**arzt** der paediatrician; ~**bett** das cot; *(für größeres Kind)* child's bed; ~**dorf** das children's village

Kinderei die; ~, ~en childishness *no indef. art., no pl.*

kinder-, Kinder-: ~**feindlich** *Adj.* hostile to children *pred.*; ~**freundlich** *Adj.* fond of children *pred.*; *(town, resort)* which caters for children; *(planning, policy)* which caters for the needs of children; ~**garten** der nursery school; ~**gärtnerin** die nusery-school teacher; ~**heilkunde** die paediatrics *sing., no art.*; ~**hort** der day-home for schoolchildren; ~**lähmung** die poliomyelitis; ~**leicht** *(ugs.) Adj.* childishly simple; dead easy; das ist ~**leicht** it's kid's stuff *(coll.)*; it's child's play *(coll.)*; ~**lieb** *Adj.* fond of children *pred.*; ~**los** *Adj.* childless; ~**reich** *Adj.* with many children *postpos., not pred.*; ~**sterblichkeit** die child mortality; ~**stube** die; *o. Pl.* eine gute/schlechte ~**stube** gehabt haben have been well/badly brought up; ~**teller** der *(auf der Speisekarte)* children's menu; ~**wagen** der pram *(Brit.)*; baby carriage *(Amer.)*; *(Sportwagen)* push-chair *(Brit.)*; stroller *(Amer.)*

Kindes-: ~**alter** das; *o. Pl.* childhood; ~**mißhandlung** die *(Rechtsw.)* child abuse

Kindheit die; ~: childhood; **kindisch** 1. *Adj.* childish, infantile; naïve *(ideas)*; 2. *adv.* childishly; **kindlich** 1. *Adj.* childlike; 2. *adv. (behave)* in a childlike way

Kinkerlitzchen *Pl. (ugs.)* trifles

Kinn das; ~[e]s, ~e chin

Kinn-: ~**haken** der hook to the chin; ~**lade** die jaw

Kino das; ~s, ~s cinema *(Brit.)*; movie theater *(Amer.)*; **Kino·karte** die cinema ticket *(Brit.)*; movie ticket *(Amer.)*

Kiosk der; ~[e]s, ~e kiosk

¹**Kippe** die; ~, ~n *(ugs.)* cigarette end; dog-end *(sl.)*

²**Kippe** die; ~, ~n a) *(Bergmannsspr.)* slag-heap; etw. steht auf der ~ *(fig.)* it's touch and go with sth.; *(etw. ist noch nicht entschieden)* sth. hangs in the balance; **kippen** 1. *tr. V.* a) tip [up]; b) *(ausschütten)* tip [out]; 2. *itr. V.; mit sein* tip over; *(top-heavy object)* topple over; *(person)* topple; *(boat)* overturn; *(car)* roll over

Kipp-: ~**fenster** das horizontally pivoted window; ~**schalter** der tumbler switch

Kirche die; ~, ~n church; **in die** ~ **gehen** go to church

Kirchen-: ~**fest** das church festival; ~**lied** das hymn; ~**musik** die church music; ~**steuer** die church tax

Kirch·hof der (veralt.) churchyard; **kirchlich** 1. Adj. ecclesiastical; church attrib. ⟨wedding, funeral⟩; 2. adv. ~ **getraut/begraben werden** have a church wedding/funeral

Kirch-: ~**turm** der [church] steeple; (ohne Turmspitze) church tower; ~**weih** die; ~, ~en fair (held on the anniversary of the consecration of a church)

Kirmes die; ~, **Kirmessen** (bes. md., niederd.) s. Kirchweih

Kirsch·baum der cherry[-tree]; **Kirsche** die; ~, ~n cherry

Kirsch-: ~**torte** die cherry gateau; (mit Tortenboden) cherry flan; ~**wasser** das kirsch

Kissen das; ~s, ~: cushion; (Kopf~) pillow

Kiste die; ~, ~n box; (Truhe) chest; (Latten~) crate

Kitsch der; ~[e]s kitsch; **kitschig** Adj. kitschy

Kitt der; ~[e]s, ~e putty; (für Porzellan, Kacheln usw.) cement

Kittchen das; ~s, ~ (ugs.) clink (sl.)

Kittel der; ~s, ~ a) overall; (eines Arztes usw.) white coat; b) (hemdartige Bluse) smock

kitten tr. V. cement [together]

Kitz das; ~es, ~e (Reh~) fawn; (Ziegen~, Gemsen~) kid

kitzeln tr.. itr. V. tickle; **kitzlig** Adj. (auch fig.) ticklish

KKW [ka:ka:ʹveː] Abk. Kernkraftwerk

Klacks der; ~es, ~e (ugs.) dollop (coll.); (~ Senf) dab

Kladde die; ~, ~n rough book

Kladderadatsch der; ~[e]s, ~e (ugs.) unholy mess (coll.)

klaffen itr. V. yawn; ⟨hole, wound⟩ gape; **kläffen** itr. V. (abwertend) yap

Klafter [ʹklaftɐ] der od. das; ~s, ~ (Raummaß für Holz) cord

Klage die; ~, ~n a) (Äußerung der Trauer) lament; b) (Beschwerde) complaint; c) (Rechtsw.) action; (im Strafrecht) charge; **klagen** 1. itr. V. a) (geh.: jammern) wail; (stöhnend) moan; b) (sich beschweren) complain (über + Akk. about); c) (bei Gericht)

take legal action; 2. tr. V. **jmdm. sein Leid/seine Not** ~: pour out one's sorrows pl./troubles pl.; **Kläger** der; ~s, ~, **Klägerin** die; ~, ~nen (im Zivilrecht) plaintiff; (im Strafrecht) prosecuting party; (bei einer Scheidung) petitioner; **kläglich** Adj. a) (mitleiderregend) pitiful; b) (minderwertig) pathetic; c) (erbärmlich) despicable ⟨behaviour, role, compromise⟩; pathetic ⟨result, defeat⟩

Klamauk der; ~s (ugs. abwertend) fuss; (Lärm, Krach) row (coll.)

klamm Adj. a) (feucht) cold and damp; b) (steif) numb; **Klammer** die; ~, ~n (Wäsche~) peg; (Haar~) [hair-]grip; (Zahn~) brace; (Büro~) paper-clip; (Heft~) staple; (Schriftzeichen) bracket; **klammern** 1. refl. V. **sich an jmdn./etw.** ~ (auch fig.) cling to sb./sth.; 2. tr. V. a) **eine Wunde** ~: close a wound with a clip/clips; b) (mit einer Büroklammer) clip; (mit einer Heftmaschine) staple; (mit Wäscheklammern) peg

Klamotten Pl. (salopp) (Kleidung) gear sing. (sl.); (Kram) stuff sing.

Klampfe die; ~, ~n (volkst.: Gitarre) guitar

klang 1. u. 3. Pers. Sg. Prät. v. klingen

Klang der; ~[e]s, **Klänge** a) (Ton) sound; b) (~farbe) tone

Klapp·bett das folding bed; **Klappe** die; ~, ~n a) [hinged] lid; (am LKW) tail-gate; (seitlich) side-gate; (am Kombiwagen) back; (am Ofen) [drop-]door; b) (an Musikinstrumenten) key; (an einer Trompete) valve; c) (Filmjargon) clapper-board; d) (salopp: Mund) trap (sl.); **klappen** 1. tr. V. **nach oben/unten** ~: turn up/down ⟨collar, hat-brim⟩; lift up/put down ⟨lid⟩; **nach vorne/hinten** ~: tilt forward/back ⟨seat⟩; 2. itr. V. a) ⟨door, shutter⟩ bang; b) (stoßen) bang; c) (ugs.: gelingen) work out all right; **klapperig** Adj. rickety; **klappern** itr. V. a) rattle; b) (ein Klappern erzeugen) make a clatter; **Klapperschlange** die rattlesnake; **klapprig** Adj. rickety

Klapp-: ~**sitz** der tip-up seat; ~**stuhl** der folding chair

Klaps der; ~es, ~e (ugs.) smack; slap; **Klaps·mühle** die (salopp) loony-bin (sl.)

klar 1. Adj. a) clear; straight ⟨question, answer⟩; **sich** (Dat.) **über etw.** (Akk.) **im** ~**en sein** realize sth.; b) nicht attr.

(fertig) ready; **2.** *adv.* clearly; **Klär-anlage** die sewage treatment plant; **Klare** der; **~n**, **~n** schnapps; **klären 1.** *tr. V.* **a)** settle 〈*question, issue, matter*〉; clarify 〈*situation*〉; clear up 〈*case, affair, misunderstanding*〉; **b)** *(reinigen)* purify; treat 〈*effluent, sewage*〉; **2. refl.** *V.* **a)** 〈*situation*〉 become clear; 〈*question, issue, matter*〉 be settled; **b)** *(rein werden)* 〈*liquid, sky*〉 clear; 〈*weather*〉 clear [up]; **klar|gehen** *unr. itr. V.; mit sein (ugs.)* go OK *(coll.)*; **Klarheit** die; **~**: clarity; **sich** *(Dat.)* **über etw.** *(Akk.)* **~ verschaffen** clarify sth.

Klarinette die; **~**, **~n** clarinet

klar-: **~|machen** *tr. V.* **a)** *(ugs.)* make clear; **b)** *(Seemannsspr.)* get ready; **~|sehen** *unr. itr. V.* understand the matter

Klarsicht·folie die transparent film; **klar|stellen** *tr. V.* clear up; clarify; **Klar·text** der *(auch DV)* clear text; **im ~text** *(fig.)* in plain language; **Klä-rung** die; **~**, **~en** **a)** clarification; **b)** *(Reinigung)* purification; *(von Abwässern)* treatment; **klar|werden** *unr. V.; mit sein; nur im Inf. und Part. zu-sammengeschrieben* **1.** *refl.* *V.* **sich** *(Dat.)* **über etw.** *(Akk.)* **~**: realize sth.; **2.** *itr. V.* **jmdm. wird etw. klar** sth. becomes clear to sb.

klasse *(ugs.)* **1.** *indekl. Adj.* great *(coll.)*; **2.** *adv.* marvellously; **Klasse** die; **~**, **~n a)** *(Schul~)* class; *(Raum)* class-room; *(Stufe)* year; grade *(Amer.)*; **b)** *(Sport)* league; *(Boxen)* division; **c)** *(Fahrzeug~, Boots~, Qualitätsstufe)* class

klassen-, Klassen-: **~arbeit** die *(Schulw.)* [written] class test; **~ge-sellschaft** die *(Soziol.)* class society; **~kampf** der *(marx.)* class struggle; **~lehrer** der, **~lehrerin** die*(Schulw.)* class teacher; **~los** *Adj.* *(Soziol.)* classless; **~sprecher** der, **~spre-cherin** die *(Schulw.)* class spokes-man; **~treffen** das *(Schulw.)* class re-union; **~ziel** das *(Schulw.)* required standard *(for pupils in a particular class)*; **~zimmer** das *(Schulw.)* class-room

klassifizieren *tr. V.* classify (**als** as); **Klassifizierung** die; **~**, **~en** classi-fication; **Klassik** die; **~ a)** *(Antike)* classical antiquity *no art.*; **b)** *(Zeit kul-tureller Höchstleistung)* classical period

Klassiker der; **~s**, **~:** classical writer/composer; **klassisch** *Adj.* classical; *(vollendet, zeitlos; auch iron.)* classic; **Klassizismus** der; **~:** classicism

Klatsch der; **~[e]s**, **~e a)** *o. Pl. (ugs. abwertend)* gossip; **b)** *(Geräusch)* smack; **Klatsch·base** die *(ugs. ab-wertend)* gossip; **klatschen** *itr. V.* **a)** *auch mit sein* 〈*waves, wet sails*〉 slap; **b)** *(mit den Händen; applaudieren)* clap; **c)** *(schlagen)* slap; **d)** *(ugs. abwertend: reden)* gossip (**über** + *Akk.* about); **klatschhaft** *Adj.* gossipy; fond of gossip *pred.*; **Klatsch·mohn** der corn-poppy; **klatsch·naß** *Adj.* *(ugs.)* sopping wet; dripping wet 〈*hair*〉

Klaue die; **~**, **~n a)** claw; *(von Raubvö-geln)* talon; *(salopp: Hand)* mitt *(sl.)*; **b)** *o. Pl. (salopp abwertend: Schrift)* scrawl; **klauen** *(ugs.)* **1.** *tr. V.* pinch *(sl.)*; **jmdm. etw. ~** pinch sth. from sb.; **2.** *itr. V.* pinch *(sl.)* things

Klause die; **~**, **~n** hermitage; *(Kloster-zelle)* cell; **Klausel** die; **~**, **~n** clause; *(Bedingung)* condition; *(Vorbehalt)* proviso

Klavier [kla'vi:ɐ] das; **~s**, **~e** piano **Klebe·folie** die adhesive film; **kle-ben 1.** *itr. V.* **a)** stick (**an** + *Dat.* to); **b)** *(ugs.: klebrig sein)* be sticky (**von**, **vor** + *Dat.* with); **2.** *tr. V.* **a)** *(befesti-gen)* stick; *(mit Klebstoff)* glue; **jmdm. eine ~** *(salopp)* belt sb. one *(coll.)*; **b)** *(reparieren)* stick or glue 〈*vase etc.*〉 back together; **Kleber** der; **~s**, **~:** ad-hesive; glue; **klebrig** *Adj.* sticky

Kleb-: **~stoff** der adhesive; glue; **~streifen** der adhesive or sticky tape

kleckern *(ugs.)* itr. V. make a mess; **Klecks** der; **~es**, **~e a)** stain; *(nicht aufgesogen)* blob; *(Tintenfleck)* [ink-]blot; **b)** *(ugs.: kleine Menge)* spot; *(von Senf, Mayonnaise)* dab; **klecksen** *itr. V.* **a)** make a stain/stains; *(mit Tin-te)* make a blot/blots; *(pen)* blot; **b)** *(ugs. abwertend: schlecht malen)* daub

Klee der; **~s** clover; **Klee·blatt** das clover-leaf

Kleid das; **~es**, **~er a)** dress; **b)** *Pl.* *(Kleidung)* clothes; **kleiden 1.** *refl. V.* dress; **2.** *tr. V.* **a)** dress; **b)** *(jmdm. ste-hen)* suit

Kleider-: **~bügel** der clothes-hanger; coat-hanger; **~bürste** die clothes-brush; **~haken** der coat-hook; **~schrank** der wardrobe; **~ständer** der coat-stand

kleidsam *Adj.* becoming; **Kleidung** die; **~:** clothes *pl.*

Kleidungs·stück das garment
klein 1. *Adj.* a) little; small; **er ist ~er
als ich** he is shorter than me; b) *(jung)*
little; **von ~ auf** from an early age; c)
(von kurzer Dauer) little, short *‹while›*;
short *‹walk, break, holiday›*; brief
‹moment›; d) *(von geringer Menge)*
small; low *‹price›*; **~es Geld haben**
have some [small] change; e) *(von geringem Ausmaß)* small *‹party, gift›*;
scant *‹attention›*; slight *‹cold, indisposition, mistake, irregularity›*; minor
‹event, error›; f) *(unbedeutend)* lowly
‹employee›; minor *‹official›*; ~ **anfangen** *(ugs.)* start off in a small way; 2.
adv. **die Heizung ~/~er einstellen** turn
the heating down low/lower; **ein Wort
~ schreiben** write a word with a small
initial letter
klein-, Klein-: ~anzeige die *(Zeitungsw.)* small *or* classified advertisement; **~asien (das)** Asia Minor;
~bürgerlich *Adj.* a) *(das Kleinbür-
gertum betreffend)* lower middle-
class; b) *(abwertend: spießbürgerlich)*
petit bourgeois
¹**Kleine der**; *adj. Dekl.* a) *(kleiner Junge)* little boy; b) *(ugs. Anrede)* little
man; ²**Kleine die**; *adj. Dekl.* a) *(kleines Mädchen)* little girl; b) *(ugs. Anrede)* love; *(abwertend)* little madam
klein-, Klein-: ~familie die *(Soziol.)*
nuclear family; **~geld das**; *o. Pl.*
[small] change; **~gläubig** sceptical
Kleinigkeit die; **~, ~en** small thing;
(Einzelheit) [small] detail; **ich habe
noch eine ~ zu erledigen** I still have a
small matter to attend to; **eine ~ essen**
have a [small] bite to eat; **eine ~ für
jmdn. sein** be no trouble for sb.
klein-, Klein-: ~kind das small
child; **~kram der** *(ugs.)* odds and
ends *pl.*; *(unbedeutende Dinge)* trivial
matters *pl.*; **~kriegen** *tr. V.* *(ugs.)* a)
(zerkleinern) crush [to pieces]; b) *(zerstören)* smash; break; c) *(aufbrauchen)* get through; d) **jmdn. ~kriegen**
get sb. down *(coll.)*; *(durch Drohun-
gen)* intimidate sb.; *(gefügig machen)*
bring sb. into line; **~laut** 1. *Adj.* subdued; *(verlegen)* sheepish; 2. *adv.* in a
subdued fashion; *(verlegen)* sheep-
ishly
kleinlich *(abwertend)* 1. *Adj.* pernick-
ety; *(ohne Großzügigkeit)* mean; *(engstirnig)* small-minded; petty; 2. *adv.*
meticulously
Kleinod das; **~[e]s, ~e od. ~ien** *(geh.)*
a) *(Schmuckstück)* piece of jewellery;

(Edelstein) jewel; b) *(Kostbarkeit)*
gem
klein-, Klein-: ~|schneiden *unr. tr.
V.* cut into small pieces; chop up *‹onion›* [small]; **~stadt die** small town;
~städter der small-town dweller
Kleinste der/die/das; *adj. Dekl.*
youngest boy/girl/child
klein|stellen *tr. V.* turn down [low]
Kleister der; **~s, ~:** paste
Klementine die; **~, ~n** clementine
Klemme die; **~, ~n** clip; **in der ~ sein
od. sitzen** *(ugs.)* be in a fix *(coll.)*;
klemmen 1. *tr. V.* a) *(befestigen)*
tuck; stick *(coll.)*; b) *(quetschen)* **sich
(Dat.) den Fuß/die Hand ~:** get one's
foot/hand caught or trapped; 2. *refl.
V.* **sich hinter etw. (Akk.) ~** *(fig. ugs.)*
put some hard work into sth.; 3. *itr. V.*
‹door, drawer, etc.› stick
Klempner der; **~s, ~:** tinsmith; *(~
und Installateur)* plumber
Kleptomanie die; **~** *(Psych.)* kleptomania *no art.*
klerikal *Adj.* *(auch abwertend)* clerical; church *‹property›*; **Klerus der;
~:** clergy
Klette die; **~, ~n** bur; *(Pflanze)* bur-
dock
klettern *itr. V.; mit sein (auch fig.)*
climb; **auf einen Baum ~:** climb up a
tree; **Kletter·pflanze die** creeper;
(Bot.) climbing plant; climber
klicken *itr. V.* click
Klient der; **~en, ~en, Klientin die**; **~,
~nen** client
Klima das; **~s, ~s** od. **Klimate** climate; **Klima·an·lage die** air-condi-
tioning *no indef. art.;* **klimatisch**
Adj. climatic; **klimatisieren** *tr. V.*
air-condition; **Klima·wechsel der**
change of climate
Klimm·zug der *(Turnen)* pull-up
klimpern 1. *itr. V.* jingle; 2. *tr. V.* *(ugs.
abwertend)* plunk out *‹tune etc.›*
Klinge die; **~, ~n** blade
Klingel die; **~, ~n** bell
Klingel-: ~beutel der offertory-bag;
collection-bag; **~knopf der** bell-push
klingeln *itr. V.* ring; *‹alarm clock›* go
off; **es klingelt** *(an der Tür)* there is a
ring at the door; *(Telefon)* the telephone is ringing
klingen *unr. itr. V.* sound; **die Glok-
ken klangen** the bells were ringing
Klinik die; **~, ~en** hospital; *(speziali-
siert)* clinic
Klinke die; **~, ~n** door-handle
Klinker der; **~s, ~:** [Dutch] clinker

klipp *Adv.:* ~ **und klar** *(ugs.)* quite plainly

Klippe die; ~, ~n rock

klirren *itr. V.* clink; ⟨*weapons in fight*⟩ clash; ⟨*window-pane*⟩ rattle; ⟨*chains, spurs*⟩ rattle; ⟨*harness*⟩ jingle

Klischee das; ~s, ~s cliché

klitsch·naß *Adj. (ugs.)* sopping wet; *(tropfnaß)* dripping wet

klitze·klein *Adj. (ugs.)* teeny[-weeny] *(coll.)*

Klo das; ~s, ~s *(ugs.)* loo *(Brit. coll.)*; john *(Amer. coll.)*

Kloake die; ~, ~n cesspit; *(Kanal)* sewer

klobig *Adj.* heavy and clumsy [-looking] ⟨*shoes, furniture*⟩; bulky ⟨*figure*⟩; *(plump)* clumsy

Klo·papier das *(ugs.)* loo-paper *(Brit. coll.)*; toilet-paper

klopfen 1. *itr. V.* a) *(schlagen)* knock; b) *(pulsieren)* ⟨*heart*⟩ beat; ⟨*pulse*⟩ throb; 2. *tr. V.* beat ⟨*carpet*⟩

Klöppel der; ~s, ~ ⟨*Glocken*~⟩ clapper; **klöppeln** *tr., itr. V.* [etw.] ~: make [sth. in] pillow-lace

Klops der; ~es, ~e *(nordostd.)* meat ball

Klosett das; ~s, ~s *od.* ~e lavatory

Kloß der; ~es, **Klöße** dumpling; *(Fleisch*~*)* meat ball

Kloster das; ~s, **Klöster** ⟨*Mönchs*~⟩ monastery; ⟨*Nonnen*~⟩ convent

Klotz der; ~es, **Klötze** block [of wood]; *(Stück eines Baumstamms)* log

Klub der; ~s, ~s club; **Klub·sessel** der club chair

¹**Kluft** die; ~, ~en *(ugs.)* gear *(coll.)*; *(Uniform)* garb

²**Kluft** die; ~, **Klüfte** *(veralt.) (Spalte)* cleft; *(im Gletscher)* crevasse; *(Abgrund)* chasm; *(fig.)* gulf

klug *klüger, klügst...* Adj. clever; bright ⟨*child, pupil*⟩; intelligent ⟨*eyes*⟩; *(vernünftig)* wise; sound ⟨*advice*⟩; *(geschickt)* shrewd ⟨*politician, negotiator, question*⟩; astute ⟨*businessman*⟩; **klüger** *s.* klug; **Klugheit** die; ~ *s.* klug: cleverness; brightness; intelligence; wisdom; soundness; shrewdness; astuteness; **klügst...** *s.* klug

klumpen *itr. V.* go lumpy; **Klumpen** der; ~s, ~: lump; **ein** ~ **Gold** a gold nugget

km *Abk.* Kilometer km.

knabbern 1. *tr. V.* nibble; 2. *itr. V. an* etw. *(Dat.)* ~: nibble [at] sth.

Knabe der; ~n, ~n *(geh. veralt./ südd., österr., schweiz.)* boy; *(ugs.: Bursche)*

chap *(coll.)*; **knabenhaft** 1. *Adj.* boyish; 2. *adv.* boyishly

Knäcke·brot das crispbread; *(Scheibe)* slice of crispbread; **knacken** 1. *itr. V.* a) ⟨*bed, floor, etc.*⟩ creak; b) *mit sein (ugs.: zerbrechen)* snap; ⟨*window*⟩ crack; 2. *tr. V.* a) crack ⟨*nut, shell*⟩; *(salopp: aufbrechen)* crack ⟨*safe*⟩ [open]; break into ⟨*car, bank, etc.*⟩; **knackig** *Adj.* a) crisp; b) *(ugs.: attraktiv)* delectable; **Knacks** der; ~es, ~e *(ugs.)* crack; *(fig.: Defekt)* **einen** ~ **bekommen** ⟨*person*⟩ have a breakdown; ⟨*health*⟩ suffer

Knall der; ~[e]s, ~e bang; **knallen** 1. *itr. V.* a) ⟨*shot*⟩ ring out; ⟨*firework*⟩ go bang; ⟨*cork*⟩ pop; ⟨*door*⟩ slam; ⟨*whip, rifle*⟩ crack; **mit der Tür** ~: slam the door; b) *(ugs.: schießen)* shoot, fire *(auf* + *Akk.* at); c) *(Ballspiele)* **aufs Tor** ~: belt the ball/puck at the goal *(coll.)*; 2. *tr. V.* a) *(ugs.)* slam down; *(werfen)* sling *(coll.)*; b) *(ugs.: schlagen)* **jmdm. eine** ~ *(salopp)* belt sb. one *(coll.)*

knall-: ~**hart** *(ugs.)* 1. *Adj.* very tough ⟨*demands, measures, etc.*⟩; ⟨*person*⟩ as hard as nails; 2. *adv.* brutally; **gegen** etw. ~**hart vorgehen** take very tough action against sth.; ~**rot** *Adj.* bright *or* vivid red; **sie wurde** ~**rot** she turned as red as a beetroot

knapp 1. *Adj.* a) meagre; narrow ⟨*victory, lead*⟩; narrow, bare ⟨*majority*⟩; **die Vorräte wurden** ~: supplies ran short; **vor einer** ~**en Stunde** just under an hour ago; b) *(eng)* tight-fitting ⟨*garment*⟩; *(zu eng)* tight ⟨*garment*⟩; c) *(kurz)* terse ⟨*reply, greeting*⟩; succinct ⟨*description, account, report*⟩; 2. *adv.* a) ~ **bemessen sein** be meagre, ⟨*time*⟩ be limited; ~ **gewinnen/verlieren** win/ lose narrowly; **er ist** ~ **fünfzig** he is just this side of fifty; b) *(eng)* ~ **sitzen** fit tightly; *(zu eng)* be a tight fit; c) *(kurz)* ⟨*reply*⟩ tersely; ⟨*describe, summarize*⟩ succinctly; **Knappheit** die; ~ a) *(Mangel)* shortage *(an* + *Dat.* of); b) *(Kürze) (einer Antwort, eines Grußes)* terseness; *(einer Beschreibung, eines Berichts)* succinctness

knarren *itr. V.* creak

Knast der; ~[e]s, **Knäste** *od.* ~e *(ugs.)* a) *o. Pl. (Strafe)* bird *(sl.)*; time; b) *(Gefängnis)* clink *(sl.)*; prison

knattern *itr. V.* clatter; ⟨*sail*⟩ flap; ⟨*radio*⟩ crackle

Knäuel der *od.* das; ~s, ~ ball; *(wirres* ~*)* tangle

Knauf der; ~[e]s, **Knäufe** knob; *(eines Schwertes, Dolches)* pommel

knauserig *Adj. (ugs. abwertend)* stingy; tight-fisted; **knausern** *itr. V. (ugs. abwertend)* be stingy; skimp

knautschen *(ugs.)* 1. *tr. V.* crumple; crease ⟨*dress*⟩; 2. *itr. V.* ⟨*dress, material*⟩ crease

Knebel der; ~s, ~ a) gag; b) *(Griff)* toggle; **knebeln** *tr. V.* gag

Knecht der; ~[e]s, ~e farm-labourer; **knechten** *tr. V. (geh.)* reduce to slavery; enslave; *(unterdrücken)* oppress; **Knechtschaft** die; ~, ~en *(geh.)* bondage; slavery

kneifen 1. *unr. tr., itr. V.* pinch; 2. *unr. itr. V.* a) ⟨*clothes*⟩ be too tight; b) *(ugs.: sich drücken)* chicken (*sl.*) out (vor + *Dat.* of); **Kneif·zange** die pincers *pl.*

Kneipe die; ~, ~n *(ugs.)* pub *(Brit. coll.)*; bar *(Amer.)*

kneippen *itr. V. (ugs.)* take a Kneipp cure; **Kneipp·kur** die Kneipp cure

kneten *tr. V.* a) *(bearbeiten)* knead ⟨*dough, muscles*⟩; work ⟨*clay*⟩; b) *(formen)* model ⟨*figure*⟩; **Knet·masse** die Plasticine (P)

Knick der; ~[e]s, ~e sharp bend; *(Falz)* crease; **knicken** 1. *tr. V.* a) *(brechen)* snap; b) *(falten)* crease ⟨*page, paper, etc.*⟩; 2. *itr. V.; mit sein* snap

Knicks der; ~es, ~e curtsy; **knicksen** *itr. V.* curtsy (vor + *Dat.* to)

Knie das; ~s, ~ [ˈkniː(ə)] a) knee; b) *(Biegung)* sharp bend

knie-, Knie-: ~**beuge** die kneebend; ~**fall** der: einen ~fall tun od. machen *(auch fig.)* go down on one's knees (vor + *Dat.* before); ~**kehle** die hollow of the knee

knien [ˈkniː(ə)n] 1. *itr. V.* kneel; 2. *refl. V.* kneel [down]

Knie-: ~**scheibe** die kneecap; ~**strumpf** der knee-length sock

Kniff der; ~es, ~e a) pinch; b) *(Falte)* crease; c) *(Kunstgriff)* trick

knipsen *tr. V.* a) *(entwerten)* clip; punch; b) *(fotografieren)* take a snap[shot] of

Knirps der; ~es, ~e a) (Wz Taschenschirm) telescopic umbrella; b) *(ugs.: Junge)* nipper *(coll.)*

knirschen *itr. V.* crunch; **mit den Zähnen ~:** grind one's teeth

knistern *itr. V.* rustle; ⟨*wood, fire*⟩ crackle

knittern *tr., itr. V.* crease; crumple

knobeln *itr. V. (mit Würfeln)* play dice

Knob·lauch der garlic; **Knob·lauch·zehe** die clove of garlic

Knöchel der; ~s, ~: ankle; *(am Finger)* knuckle; **Knochen** der; ~s, ~: bone

knochen-, Knochen-: ~**bau** der; o. *Pl.* bone structure; ~**bruch** der fracture; ~**hart** *Adj. (ugs.)* rock-hard; ~**mark** das bone marrow

knochig *Adj.* bony

Knödel der; ~s, ~ *(bes. südd., österr.)* dumpling

Knolle die; ~, ~n tuber

Knopf der; ~[e]s, **Knöpfe** button; *(Knauf)* knob; **knöpfen** *tr. V.* button [up]; **Knopf·loch** das buttonhole

Knorpel der; ~s, ~ *(Anat.)* cartilage; *(im Steak o. ä.)* gristle

knorrig *Adj.* gnarled

Knospe die; ~, ~n bud; **knospen** *itr. V.* bud

knoten *tr. V.* knot; **Knoten** der; ~s, ~: knot; *(Haartracht)* bun; knot; *(Med.)* lump; **Knoten·punkt** der junction; intersection

knuffen *tr. V.* poke

Knüller der; ~s, ~ *(ugs.)* sensation; *(Angebot, Verkaufsartikel)* sensational offer

knüpfen *tr. V.* a) tie (an + *Akk.* to); Bedingungen an etw. ⟨*Akk.*⟩ ~: attach conditions to sth.; b) *(durch Knoten herstellen)* knot; make ⟨*net*⟩

Knüppel der; ~s, ~ cudgel; *(Polizei~)* truncheon; **knüppel·dick** *Adv. (ugs.)* es kam ~dick it was one disaster after the other; **Knüppel·schaltung** die *(Kfz-W.)* floor[-type] gearchange

knurren 1. *itr. V.* a) ⟨*animal*⟩ growl; *(wütend)* snarl; *(fig.)* ⟨*stomach*⟩ rumble; b) *(murren)* grumble (über + *Akk.* about)

knusprig *Adj.* crisp; crusty ⟨*bread, roll*⟩

knutschen *(ugs.)* 1. *tr. V.* smooch with *(coll.)*; *(sexuell berühren)* pet; **sich ~:** smooch *(coll.)*/pet; 2. *itr. V.* smooch *(coll.)*; *(sich sexuell berühren)* pet

k. o. [kaˈʔoː] *Adj.; nicht attr.* a) *(Boxen)* jmdn. k. o. schlagen knock sb. out; b) *(ugs.: übermüdet)* all in *(coll.)*

koalieren *itr. V. (Politik)* form a coalition (mit with); **Koalition** die; ~, ~en coalition

Kobalt das; ~s *(Chemie)* cobalt

Kobold der; ~[e]s, ~e goblin

Kobra die; ~, ~s cobra

Koch der; ~|e|s, Köche cook; *(Küchenchef)* chef; **Koch·buch** das cookery book *(Brit.);* cookbook *(Amer.);* **kochen** 1. *tr. V.* a) boil; *(zubereiten)* cook *(meal);* make *(purée, jam);* Tee ~: make some tea; b) *(waschen)* boil; 2. *itr. V.* a) *(Speisen zubereiten)* cook; b) *(sieden) (water, milk, etc.)* boil; **Kocher** der; ~s, ~ [small] stove; *(Kochplatte)* hotplate

Köcher der; ~s, ~ *(für Pfeile)* quiver

Köchin die; ~, ~nen cook

Koch-: ~löffel der wooden spoon; ~nische die kitchenette; ~topf der [cooking] pot

Köder der; ~s, ~: bait; **ködern** *tr. V.* lure

Koffein das; ~s caffeine; **koffeinfrei** *Adj.* decaffeinated

Koffer der; ~s, ~: [suit]case

Koffer-: ~kuli der luggage trolley; ~radio das portable radio; ~raum der boot *(Brit.);* trunk *(Amer.)*

Kognak ['kɔnjak] der; ~s, ~s brandy; s. auch Cognac

Kohl der; ~|e|s a) cabbage; b) *(ugs. abwertend: Unsinn)* rubbish; rot *(sl.)*

Kohl·dampf der; *o. Pl. (salopp)* |einen| ~ haben be ravenously hungry

Kohle die; ~, ~n coal; ¹**kohlen** *itr. V.* smoulder; *(wick)* smoke

²**kohlen** *itr. V. (fam.) (lügen)* tell fibs; *(übertreiben)* exaggerate

Kohlen-: ~grube die coal-mine; ~händler der coal merchant ~monoxyd [--'---] das *(Chemie)* carbon monoxide; ~säure die carbonic acid; ~stoff der; *o. Pl.* carbon

Kohle·papier das carbon paper

Köhler der; ~s, ~: charcoal burner

Kohl-: ~kopf der [head of] cabbage; ~rübe die swede

Koitus, **Koitus** *(geh.)* sexual intercourse; coitus *(formal)*

Koje die; ~, ~n a) *(Seemannsspr.)* bunk; berth; b) *(Ausstellungsstand)* stand

Kokain das; ~s cocaine

kokett 1. *Adj.* coquettish; 2. *adv.* coquettishly

Kokos·nuß die coconut

Koks der; ~es coke

Kolben der; ~s, ~ a) *(Technik)* piston; b) *(Chemie: Glas~)* flask; c) *(Teil des Gewehrs)* butt

Kolchose [kɔl'ço:zə] die; ~, ~n kolkhoz; Soviet collective farm

Kolibri der; ~s, ~s humming-bird

Kolik die; ~, ~en colic

Kollaborateur [kɔlabora'tø:ɐ̯] der; ~s, ~e collaborator

Kollaps der; ~es, ~e collapse

Kolleg das; ~s, ~s lecture

Kollege der; ~n, ~n colleague; **kollegial** 1. *Adj.* helpful and considerate; 2. *adv. (act etc.)* like a good colleague/good colleagues; **Kollegium** das; ~s, Kollegien a) *(Gruppe)* group; *(unmittelbar zusammenarbeitend)* team; b) *(Lehrkörper)* [teaching] staff

Kollekte die; ~, ~n collection; **Kollektion** [kɔlɛk'tsio:n] die; ~, ~en collection; *(Sortiment)* range; **kollektiv** 1. *Adj.* collective; 2. *adv.* collectively

kollidieren *itr. V.* a) *mit sein* collide; b) *(fig.)* conflict

Kollier [kɔ'lie:] das; ~s, ~s necklace

Kollision die; ~, ~en collision

Köln (das) ~s Cologne; **Kölner** 1. *indekl. Adj.* Cologne attrib.; *(in Köln)* in Cologne postpos., *not pred;* ⟨suburb, archbishop, mayor, speciality⟩ of Cologne; 2. der; ~s, ~: inhabitant of Cologne; *(von Geburt)* native of Cologne; **Kölnerin** die; ~, ~nen s. Kölner 2

Kolonialismus der; ~: colonialism *no art.;* **Kolonie** die; ~, ~n colony; **kolonisieren** *tr. V.* colonize

Kolonne die; ~, ~n column

Koloß der; Kolosses, Kolosse *(auch fig. ugs.)* giant; **kolossal** 1. *Adj.* a) colossal; gigantic; b) *(ugs.: sehr groß)* tremendous *(coll.);* incredible *(coll.)* ⟨rubbish, nonsense⟩; 2. *adv. (ugs.)* tremendously *(coll.)*

Kolumbianer der; ~s, ~: Colombian; **Kolumbien** [ko'lʊmbjən] (das); ~s Colombia

Kombination die; ~, ~en a) combination; b) *(gedankliche Verknüpfung)* deduction; piece of reasoning; c) *(Kleidungsstücke)* ensemble; suit; *(Herren~)* suit; **kombinieren** 1. *tr. V.* combine; 2. *itr. V.* deduce; reason

Kombi-: ~wagen der estate [car]; station wagon *(Amer.);* ~zange die combination pliers pl.

Komet der; ~en, ~en comet

Komfort der; ~s comfort; **komfortabel** 1. *Adj.* comfortable; 2. *adv.* comfortably

Komik die; ~: comic effect; *(komisches Element)* comic element; **Komiker** der; ~s, ~ a) *(Vortragskünstler)* comedian; b) *(Darsteller)* comic actor; **komisch** *Adj.* a) comical; funny; b) *(seltsam)* funny

Komitee das; ~s, ~s committee

Komma das; ~s, ~s od. ~ta comma; *(Math.)* decimal point; **zwei ~ acht** two point eight

Kommandant der; ~en, ~en *(Milit.)* commanding officer; **Kommandeur** [kɔman'døːɐ̯] der; ~s, ~e *(Milit.)* s. **Kommandant; kommandieren** 1. *tr. V.* a) command; be in command of; order ⟨retreat, advance⟩; b) *(ugs.)* **jmdn. ~:** boss sb. about *(coll.)*; 2. *itr. V. (ugs.)* boss people about *(coll.)*

Kommandit·gesellschaft die *(Wirtsch.)* limited partnership

Kommando das; ~s, ~s command

kommen *unr. itr. V.; mit sein* a) come; **angelaufen ~:** come running along; *(auf jmdn. zu)* come running up; b) *(gelangen, geraten)* get; **unter ein Auto ~:** be knocked down by a car; **wie kommst du darauf?** what gives you that idea?; c) **~ lassen** *(bestellen)* order ⟨taxi⟩; **den Arzt/die Polizei ~ lassen** send for a doctor/the police; d) *(aufgenommen werden)* **zur Schule/ aufs Gymnasium ~:** start school/ grammar school; e) *(auftauchen)* ⟨seeds, plants⟩ come up; ⟨buds, flowers⟩ come out; ⟨teeth⟩ come through; f) *(seinen festen Platz haben)* go; belong; **in die Schublade~:** *(sich ereignen)* come about; **wie kommt es, daß ...:** how is it that ...; **how come that ...** *(coll.)*; i) *(etw. erlangen)* **zu Geld ~:** become wealthy; **zu Erfolg/Ruhm** *usw.* **~:** gain success/ fame *etc.*

kommend *Adj.* a) *(folgend)* next; b) *(mit großer Zukunft)* der **~e Mann/ Meister** the coming man/future champion

Kommentar der; ~s, ~e commentary; *(Stellungnahme)* comment; **kein ~!** no comment!; **Kommentator** der; ~s, ~e commentator; **kommentieren** *tr. V.* a) *(erläutern)* furnish with a commentary ⟨text, work⟩; b) *(Stellung nehmen zu)* comment on

kommerziell 1. *Adj.* commercial; 2. *adv.* commercially

Kommiß der; **Kommisses** *(Soldatenspr.)* army; **Kommissar** der; ~s, ~e a) *(Beamter der Polizei)* detective superintendent; b) *(staatlicher Beauf-*

trager) commissioner; **Kommission** die; ~, ~en a) *(Gremium)* committee; *(Prüfungs~)* commission; b) **etw. in ~ nehmen/haben/geben** *(Wirtsch.)* take/have sth. on commission/give sth. to a dealer for sale on commission

Kommode die; ~, ~n chest of drawers

kommunal *Adj.* local; *(bei einer städtischen Gemeinde)* municipal; local; **Kommunal·wahl** die local [government] elections *pl.;* **Kommunikation** [ˈkɔmunikaˈtsi̯oːn] die; ~, ~en *(Sprachw., Soziol.)* communication; **Kommunion** die; ~, ~en *(kath. Kirche)* [Holy] Communion; **Kommuniqué** [kɔmyni'keː] das; ~s, ~s communiqué; **Kommunismus** der; ~: communism; **Kommunist** der; ~en, ~en communist; **kommunistisch** 1. *Adj.* communist; 2. *adv.* Communist ⟨influenced, led, ruled, etc.⟩; **kommunizieren** *itr. V.* a) *(geh.)* communicate; b) *(kath. Kirche)* receive [Holy] Communion

Komödiant der; ~en, ~en *(veralt.)* actor; player; *(abwertend: Heuchler)* play-actor; **Komödie** [ko'møːdi̯ə] die; ~, ~n comedy; *(Theater)* comedy theatre

Kompagnon [kɔmpan'jõː] der; ~s, ~s *(Wirtsch.)* partner; associate

kompakt *Adj.* solid

Kompanie die; ~, ~n company

Komparativ der; ~s, ~e *(Sprachw.)* comparative

Kompaß der; **Kompasses, Kompasse** compass

kompensieren *tr. V.* etw. mit etw. od. durch etw. ~: compensate for sth. by sth.

kompetent *Adj.* competent; **Kompetenz** die; ~, ~en competence; *(bes. Rechtsw.)* authority

komplett 1. *Adj.* complete; 2. *adv.* fully ⟨furnished, equipped⟩; *(ugs.: ganz und gar)* completely

Komplex der; ~es, ~e *(auch Psych.)* complex

Komplikation [kɔmplikaˈtsi̯oːn] die; ~, ~en *(auch Med.)* complication

Kompliment das; ~[e]s, ~e compliment

Komplize der; ~n, ~n *(abwertend)* accomplice

komplizieren *tr. V.* complicate; **kompliziert** 1. *Adj.* complicated; 2. *adv.* ~ **aufgebaut sein** have a complicated *or* complex structure

Komplott das; ~|e|s, ~e plot; conspiracy

komponieren tr., itr. V. compose; **Komponist** der; ~en, ~en composer; **Komposition** [kɔmpozi-'tsioːn] die; ~, ~en composition; **Kompost** der; ~|e|s, ~e compost; **Kompott** das; ~|e|s, ~e stewed fruit; compote

Kompresse die; ~, ~n (Med.) a) (Umschlag) [wet] compress; b) (Mull) [gauze] pad; **Kompressor** der; ~s, ~en (Technik) compressor

Kompromiß der; Kompromisses, Kompromisse compromise

kompromiß-, Kompromiß-: ~bereit Adj. willing to compromise pred.; ~los 1. Adj. uncompromising; 2. adv. uncompromisingly; ~vorschlag der compromise proposal

kompromittieren tr. V. compromise

Kondensation [kɔndɛnza'tsioːn] die; ~, ~en (Physik, Chemie) condensation; **Kondensator** der; ~s, ~en (Elektrot.) capacitor; **kondensieren** tr., itr. V. (itr. auch mit sein) (Physik, Chemie) condense

Kondens-: ~milch die condensed milk; ~streifen der the condensation trail; ~wasser das condensation

Kondition [kɔndi'tsioːn] die; ~, ~en condition; **Konditional·satz** der (Sprachw.) conditional clause; **Konditions·training** das fitness training **Konditor** der; ~s, ~en pastry-cook; **Konditorei** die; ~, ~en cake-shop; (Lokal) café

kondolieren itr. V. offer one's condolences; jmdm. |zu jmds. Tod| ~: offer one's condolences to sb. |on sb.'s death|

Kondom das od. der; ~s, ~e condom **Konfekt** das; ~|e|s a) confectionery; sweets pl. (Brit.); candies pl. (Amer.); b) (bes. südd., österr., schweiz.: Teegebäck) [small] fancy biscuits pl. (Brit.) or (Amer.) cookies pl.

Konfektion die; ~, ~en ready-made garments pl.

Konferenz die; ~, ~en conference; (Besprechung) meeting; **konferieren** 1. itr. V. confer (über + Akk. on, about)

Konfession die; ~, ~en denomination; **konfessionell** 1. Adj.; nicht präd. denominational; 2. adv. as regards denomination; ~ |un|gebunden sein have [no] denominational ties **Konfetti** das; ~|s| confetti

Konfirmand der; ~en, ~en (ev. Rel.) confirmand; **Konfirmation** [kɔnfirma'tsioːn] die; ~, ~en (ev. Rel.) confirmation; **konfirmieren** tr. V. (ev. Rel.) confirm

konfiszieren tr. V. (bes. Rechtsw.) confiscate

Konfitüre die; ~, ~n jam

Konflikt der; ~|e|s, ~e conflict

Konföderation die; ~, ~en confederation

konform Adj. concurring attrib.; ~ gehen be in agreement; **Konformist** der; ~en, ~en conformist

Konfrontation die; ~, ~en confrontation; **konfrontieren** tr. V. confront

konfus 1. Adj. confused; 2. adv. in a confused fashion

¹**Kongo** der; ~|s| (Fluß) Congo; ²**Kongo** (das) ~s od. der; ~|s| (Staat) the Congo

Kongreß der; Kongresses, Kongresse congress; conference; der ~ (USA): Congress; **Kongreß·halle** die conference hall

König der; ~s, ~e king; **Königin** die; ~, ~nen queen; **königlich** 1. Adj. a) royal; b) (vornehm) regal; c) (reichlich) princely (gift, salary, wage); 2. adv. (pay) handsomely; (ugs.: außerordentlich) (enjoy oneself) immensely (coll.); **König·reich** das kingdom; **Königs·haus** das royal house; **Königtum** das; ~s, Königtümer a) o. Pl. (Monarchie) monarchy; b) (veralt.: Reich) kingdom

Konjugation [kɔnjuga'tsioːn] die; ~, ~en (Sprachw.) conjugation; **konjugieren** tr. V. (Sprachw.) conjugate; **Konjunktion** [kɔnjʊŋk'tsioːn] die; ~, ~en (Sprachw.) conjunction; **Konjunktiv** der; ~s, ~e (Sprachw.) subjunctive; **Konjunktur** die; ~, ~en (Wirtsch.) a) (wirtschaftliche Lage) [level of] economic activity; economy; (Tendenz) economic trend; b) (Hoch~) boom; (Aufschwung) upturn [in the economy]; **konjunkturell** Adj. economic; **Konjunktur·politik** die (Wirtsch.) measures pl. aimed at avoiding violent fluctuations in the economy

konkav (Optik) 1. Adj. concave; 2. adv. concavely

konkret 1. Adj. concrete; 2. adv. in concrete terms

Konkurrent der; ~en, ~en, **Konkurrentin** die; ~, ~nen (Sport, Wirtsch.)

competitor; **Konkurrẹnz** die; ~, ~en *(Sport, Wirtsch.)* competition; **konkurrẹnz·fähig** *Adj.* competitive; **Konkurrẹnz·kampf** der competition; *(zwischen zwei Menschen)* rivalry; **konkurrieren** *itr. V.* compete; **Konkụrs** der; ~es, ~e a) *(Bankrott)* bankruptcy; b) *(gerichtliches Verfahren)* bankruptcy proceedings *pl.*

können 1. *unr. Modalverb; 2. Part.* ~ a) be able to; **er kann gut reden/tanzen** he is a good talker/dancer; **ich kann nicht schlafen** I cannot *or (coll.)* can't sleep; **kann das explodieren?** could it explode?; **man kann nie wissen** you never know; **es kann sein, daß ...:** it could be that ...; **kann ich Ihnen helfen?** can I help you?; b) *(Grund haben)* **du kannst ganz ruhig sein** you don't have to worry; **das kann man wohl sagen!** you could well say that; c) *(dürfen)* **kann ich gehen?** can I go?; ~ **wir mit|kommen|?** can we come too?; 2. *unr. tr. V. (beherrschen)* know ⟨language⟩; be able to play ⟨game⟩; **sie kann das** |gut| she can do that [well]; **etw./nichts für etw.~:** be/not be responsible for sth.; 3. *unr. itr. V.* a) *(fähig sein)* **er kann nicht anders** there's nothing else he can do; *(es ist seine Art)* he can't help it *(coll.)*; b) *(Zeit haben)* **ich kann heute nicht** I can't today *(coll.)*; c) *(ugs.: Kraft haben)* **kannst du noch |weiter|?** can you go on?; d) *(ugs.: umgehen* ~ |gut| **mit jmdm.** ~ : get on [well] with sb.; **Kọ̈nnen** das; ~s ability; **Kọ̈nner** der; ~s, ~: expert; **kọnnte** *1. u. 3. Pers. Sg. Prät. v.* **können; kọ̈nnte** *1. u. 3. Pers. Sg. Konjunktiv II v.* können

konsequẹnt 1. *Adj.* consistent; *(folgerichtig)* logical; 2. *adv.* consistently; *(folgerichtig)* logically; **Konsequẹnz** die; ~, ~en a) *(Folge)* consequence; b) *o. Pl. (Unbeirrbarkeit)* determination

konservatịv 1. *Adj.* conservative; 2. *adv.* conservatively; **Konservative** der/die; *adj. Dekl.* conservative; **Konservatọrium** das; ~s, Konservatọrien conservatoire; conservatory *(Amer.)*; **Konsẹrve** die; ~, ~n a) *(Büchse)* can; tin *(Brit.)*; b) *(konservierte Lebensmittel)* preserved food; *(in Dosen)* canned *or (Brit.)* tinned food

Konsẹrven-: ~**büchse** die, ~**dose** die can; tin *(Brit.)*

konservieren *tr. V.* preserve; conserve ⟨work of art⟩; **Konservierung** die; ~, ~en preservation; **Konservierungs·mittel** das preservative

konsolidieren *tr. V.* consolidate

Konsonạnt der; ~en, ~en consonant

Konsọrtium [kɔn'zɔrtsiʊm] das; ~s, Konsọrtien *(Wirtsch.)* consortium

konspiratịv [kɔnspira'tiːf] *Adj.* conspiratorial

konstạnt [kɔn'stant] 1. *Adj.* a) constant; b) *(beharrlich)* persistent; 2. *adv.* a) constantly; b) *(beharrlich)* persistently

Konstellation [kɔnstɛla'tsi̯oːn] die; ~, ~en a) *(von Parteien usw.)* grouping; *(von Umständen)* combination; b) *(Astron., Astrol.)* constellation

konstituieren [kɔnstitu'iːrən] 1. *tr. V. (gründen)* constitute; set up; 2. *refl. V.* be constituted; **Konstitution** [kɔnstitu'tsi̯oːn] die; ~, ~en constitution

konstruieren [kɔnstru'iːrən] *tr. V.* a) *(entwerfen)* design; b) *(aufbauen, Geom., Sprachw.)* construct; c) *(abwertend)* fabricate; **Konstrukteur** [kɔnstrʊk'tøːɐ̯] der; ~s, ~e designer; design engineer; **Konstruktion** [kɔnstrʊk'tsi̯oːn] die; ~, ~en a) *(Aufbau, Geom., Sprachw.)* construction; *(das Entwerfen)* designing; b) *(Entwurf)* design; *(Bau)* construction; **konstruktịv** 1. *Adj.* constructive; 2. *adv.* constructively

Kọnsul der; ~s, ~n *(Dipl., hist.)* consul; **Konsulạt** das; ~|e|s, ~e *(Dipl., hist.)* consulate; **konsultieren** *tr. V. (auch fig.)* consult

Konsụm der; ~s consumption; **Konsumẹnt** der; ~en, ~en consumer; **Konsụm·gesellschaft** die consumer society; **konsumieren** *tr. V.* consume

Kontạkt der; ~|e|s, ~e contact; **mit** *od.* **zu jmdm.** ~ **haben/halten** be/remain in contact with sb.

Kontạkt-: ~**linse** die contact lens; ~**mann** der; *Pl.:* ~**männer** *od.* ~**leute** *(Agent)* contact

Kọnten *s.* Konto

kọntern *tr., itr. V. (Boxen, auch fig.)* counter; *(Ballspiele)* counter-attack; **Kọnter·revolution** die counter-revolution

Kontinẹnt der; ~|e|s, ~e continent; **kontinentạl** *Adj.* continental

Kontingẹnt das; ~|e|s, ~e quota

kontinuierlich 1. *Adj.* steady; 2. *adv.* steadily; **Kontinuität** die; ~: continuity

Kọnto das; ~s, Kọnten *od.* Kọnti account; **ein laufendes ~:** a current account

Konto-: **~aus·zug** der *(Bankw.)* [bank] statement; **~nummer** die account number

Kontor das; ~s, ~e branch; *(einer Reederei)* office

Konto·stand der *(Bankw.)* balance; state of an/one's account

kontra 1. *Präp. mit Akk. (Rechtsspr., auch fig.)* versus; 2. *Adv.* against

Kontra das; ~s, ~s *(Kartenspiele)* double; **jmdm.** ~ **geben** *(fig. ugs.)* flatly contradict sb.

Kontrahent der; ~en, ~en adversary; opponent

konträr *Adj.* contrary; opposite; **Kontrast** der; ~[e]s, ~e contrast

Kontroll·abschnitt der stub; **Kontrolle** die; ~, ~n a) *(Überwachung)* surveillance; b) *(Überprüfung)* check; *(bei Waren, bei Lebensmitteln)* inspection; c) *(Herrschaft)* control; **die ~ über etw.** *(Akk.)* **verlieren** lose control of sth.; **Kontrolleur** [kɔntrɔ'løːɐ̯] der; ~s, ~e inspector; **Kontrollgang** der tour of inspection; *(eines Nachtwächters)* round; *(eines Polizisten)* patrol; **kontrollieren** *tr. V.* a) *(überwachen)* check; monitor; b) *(überprüfen)* check; inspect *(goods, food)*; c) *(beherrschen)* control; **Kontrollturm** der control tower

Kontroverse [kɔntro'vɛr] die; ~, ~n controversy (**um, über** + *Akk.* about)

Kontur die; ~, ~en; *meist Pl.* contour; outline

Konvention [kɔnvɛn'tsi̯oːn] die; ~, ~en convention; **konventionell** 1. *Adj.* a) *(konventionell)* b) *(förmlich)* formal; 2. *adv.* a) conventionally; b) *(förmlich)* formally

Konversation [kɔnvɛrza'tsi̯oːn] die; ~, ~en conversation; **Konversations·lexikon** das encyclopaedia

konvertieren [kɔnvɛr'tiːrən] *itr. V.; auch mit sein (Rel.)* be converted

konvex [kɔn'vɛks] *(Optik)* 1. *Adj.* convex; 2. *adv.* convexly

Konvoi [kɔn'vɔy] der; ~s, ~s *(bes. Milit.)* convoy

Konzentration [kɔntsɛntra'tsi̯oːn] die; ~, ~en concentration

Konzentrations-: **~fähigkeit** die; *o. Pl.* ability to concentrate; **~lager** das *(bes. ns.)* concentration camp

konzentrieren 1. *refl., tr. V.* concentrate; **sich auf etw.** *(Akk.)* ~: concentrate on sth.; **konzentriert** 1. *Adj.*

concentrated; 2. *adv.* with concentration

Konzept das; ~[e]s, ~e a) [rough] draft; b) *(Programm)* programme; *(Plan)* plan

Konzern der; ~[e]s, ~e *(Wirtsch.)* group [of companies]

Konzert das; ~[e]s, ~e a) *(Komposition)* concerto; b) *(Veranstaltung)* concert; **Konzert·saal** der concert-hall

Konzession die; ~, ~en a) *(Amtsspr.)* licence; b) *(Zugeständnis)* concession

Konzil das; ~s, ~e od. ~ien *(kath. Kirche)* council

konzipieren *tr. V.* draft; design *(device, car, etc.)*

kooperativ 1. *Adj.* co-operative; 2. *adv.* co-operatively; **kooperieren** *tr. V.* co-operate

Koordinate die; ~, ~n coordinate; **Koordinaten·system** das *(Math.)* system of coordinates; **koordinieren** *tr. V.* coordinate

Kopenhagen *(das)*; ~s Copenhagen

Kopf der; ~[e]s, Köpfe a) head; **ein ~ Salat** a lettuce; ~ **an ~:** shoulder to shoulder; *(im Wettlauf)* neck and neck; *(fig.)* **nicht wissen, wo einem der ~ steht** not know whether one is coming or going; ~ **hoch!** chin up!; **den ~ hängen lassen** become disheartened; b) *(Person)* person; **ein kluger/fähiger ~ sein** be a clever/able man/woman; **pro ~:** per head; **die führenden Köpfe der Wirtschaft** the leading minds in the field of economics; c) *(Wille)* **seinen ~ durchsetzen** make sb. do what one wants; d) *(Verstand)* mind; **sich** *(Dat.)* **den ~ zerbrechen** *(ugs.)* rack one's brains (**über** + *Akk.* over)

Kopf-: **~bahn·hof** der terminal station; **~bedeckung** die headgear; **ohne ~bedeckung** without anything on one's head

Köpfchen das; ~s, ~: brains *pl.*; **muß man haben** you've got to have it up here *(coll.)*; **köpfen** *tr. V.* a) decapitate; *(hinrichten)* behead; b) *(Fußball)* head

Kopf-: **~ende** das head end; **~haut** die [skin of] scalp; **~hörer** der headphones *pl.*; **~kissen** das pillow; **~lastig** *Adj.* down by the head *pred.*; **~los** 1. *Adj.* rash; *(in Panik)* panic-stricken; 2. *adv.* rashly; **~los davonrennen** flee in panic; **~rechnen** *itr. V.*; *nur im Inf. gebr.* do mental arithmetic; **~rechnen** das mental arithmetic; **~salat** der the head lettuce;

~**schmerz** der; *meist Pl.* headache; ~**schmerzen haben** have a headache *sing.;* ~**sprung der** header; ~**stand** der headstand; ~|**stehen** *unr. itr. V. (ugs.: überrascht sein)* be bowled over; ~**stein · pflaster** das cobblestones *pl.;* ~**tuch** das headscarf; ~**weh** das; *o. Pl. (ugs.)* headache; ~**weh haben** have a headache; ~**zerbrechen** das; ~**s:** etw. bereitet *od.* macht jmdm. ~**zerbrechen** sb. has to rack his/her brains about sth.; *(etw. macht jmdm. Sorgen)* sth. is a worry to sb.

Kopie die; ~, ~n *copy; (Durchschrift)* carbon copy; *(Fotokopie)* photocopy; *(Fot., Film)* print; **kopieren** *tr. V.* copy; *(fotokopieren)* photocopy; *(Fot., Film)* print; **Kopier · gerät** das photocopier

¹**Koppel** das; ~s, ~, *österr.:* die; ~, ~n *(Gürtel)* [leather] belt *(as part of a uniform);* ²**Koppel** die; ~, ~n paddock

koppeln *tr. V.* couple (**an** + *Akk.* to); dock ⟨*spacecraft*⟩

Koppelung *s.* Kopplung; **Kopplung** die; ~, ~en coupling; *(Raumf.)* docking

kopulieren *itr. V.* copulate

Koralle die; ~, ~n coral

Koran der; ~s, ~e Koran

Korb der; ~es, Körbe a) basket; b) jmdm. einen ~ geben turn sb. down; **Korb · ball** der; *o. Pl.* netball

Kord der; ~[e]s a) corduroy; cord; b) *s.* Kordsamt

Kordel die; ~, ~n cord

Kord · samt der cord velvet

Korea (das); ~s Korea; **Koreaner** der; ~s, ~: Korean; **koreanisch** *Adj.* Korean

Korinthe die; ~, ~n currant

Kork der; ~s, ~e cork; **Korken** der; ~s, ~: cork; **Korken · zieher** der corkscrew

¹**Korn** das; ~[e]s, Körner a) *(Frucht)* grain; *(Getreide~)* grain [of corn]; *(Pfeffer~)* corn; b) *o. Pl. (Getreide)* corn; grain; c) *(Salz~, Sand~)* grain; *(Hagel~)* stone; ²**Korn** der; ~[e]s, ~ *(ugs.)* corn schnapps; corn liquor *(Amer.);* **Korn · blume** die cornflower; **Körnchen** das; ~s, ~: tiny grain; *(von Sand usw.)* [tiny] grain; granule; **Körner** *s.* Korn; **Korn · feld** das cornfield; **körnig** *Adj.* granular

Korona die; ~, Koronen crowd *(coll.)*

Körper der; ~s, ~: body

körper-, Körper-: ~**bau** der; *o. Pl.* physique; ~**behindert** *Adj.* physic-

ally handicapped; ~**behinderte** der/die physically handicapped person; ~**behinderte** *Pl.* physically handicapped people; ~**geruch** der body odour; BO *(coll.);* ~**größe** die height

körperlich 1. *Adj.* physical; 2. *adv.* physically

Körper-: ~**pflege** die body care *no art.;* ~**spray** der *od.* das deodorant spray; ~**teil** der part of the/one's body; ~**verletzung** die *(Rechtsw.)* bodily harm *no indef. art.*

Korps [ko:ɐ] das; ~ [ko:ɐ(s)], ~ [ko:ɐs] a) *(Milit.)* corps; b) *(Studentenverbindung)* student duelling society

korpulent *Adj.* corpulent

korrekt 1. *Adj.* correct; 2. *adv.* correctly; **korrekter · weise** *Adv.* to be [strictly] correct; **Korrektheit** die; ~: correctness; **Korrektor** der; ~s, ~en ['to:rən] proof-reader; **Korrektur** die; ~, ~en correction

Korrespondent der; ~en, ~en correspondent; **Korrespondenz** die; ~, ~en correspondence; **korrespondieren** *itr. V.* correspond (**mit** with)

Korridor der; ~s, ~e corridor

korrigieren *tr. V.* correct; revise ⟨*opinion, view*⟩

korrupt *Adj.* corrupt; **Korruption** [kɔrʊp'tsio:n] die; ~, ~en corruption

Korsett das; ~s, ~s *od.* ~e corset

Korsika (das); ~s Corsica

koscher *Adj.* kosher

Kose-: ~**form** die familiar form; ~**name** der pet name

Kosinus der; ~, ~ *od.* ~se *(Math.)* cosine

Kosmetik die; ~ a) beauty culture *no art.;* b) *(fig.)* cosmetic procedures *pl.;* **Kosmetikerin** die; ~, ~nen cosmetician; beautician; **kosmetisch** 1. *Adj. (auch fig.)* cosmetic; 2. *adv.* jmdn. ~ **beraten** give sb. advice on beauty care; **sich** ~ **behandeln lassen** have beauty treatment

kosmisch *Adj.* cosmic ⟨*ray, dust, etc.*⟩; space ⟨*age, station, research, etc.*⟩; meteoric ⟨*iron*⟩; **Kosmos** der; ~: cosmos

Kost die; ~: food; ~ **und Logis** board and lodging

kostbar 1. *Adj.* valuable; precious ⟨*time*⟩; 2. *adv.* expensively ⟨*dressed*⟩; luxuriously ⟨*decorated*⟩; **Kostbarkeit** die; ~, ~en a) *(Sache)* treasure; b) *o. Pl. (Eigenschaft)* value

¹**kosten** 1. *tr. V.* a) taste; try; 2. *itr. V. (probieren)* have a taste

²kosten tr. V. a) cost; b) (erfordern) take; cost (lives); **Kosten** Pl. cost sing.; costs; (Auslagen) expenses; (Rechtsw.) costs

kosten-, Kosten-: **~deckend** Adj. that covers/cover [one's] costs postpos., not pred.; **~erstattung** die reimbursement of costs; **~los** 1. Adj. free; 2. adv. free of charge; **~pflichtig** (Rechtsw.) 1. Adj. eine ~pflichtige Verwarnung a fine and a caution; 2. adv. eine Klage ~pflichtig abweisen dismiss a case with costs; ein Auto ~pflichtig abschleppen tow a car away at the owner's expense; **~voran·schlag** der estimate

Kost·geld das payment for [one's] board

köstlich 1. Adj. delicious; (unterhaltsam) delightful; 2. adv. (taste) deliciously; **sich ~ amüsieren/unterhalten** enjoy oneself enormously (coll.); **Köstlichkeit** die; ~, ~en (Sache) delicacy

Kost·probe die; ~, ~n taste

kost·spielig Adj. costly

Kostüm das; ~s, ~e a) suit; b) (Theater~, Verkleidung) costume; **kostümieren** tr. V. dress up

Kot der; ~[e]s, ~e excrement

Kotangens der; ~, ~ (Math.) cotangent

Kotelett [kɔt'lɛt] das; ~s, ~s chop; (vom Nacken) cutlet; **Koteletten** Pl. side-whiskers

Köter der; ~s, ~ (abwertend) cur

Kot·flügel der (Kfz-W.) wing

kotzen itr. V. (derb) puke (coarse)

KP [ka:'pe:] Abk. Kommunistische Partei CP

Krabbe die; ~, ~n a) (Zool.) crab; b) (ugs.: Garnele) shrimp; (größer) prawn; **krabbeln** 1. itr. V.; mit sein crawl; 2. tr. V. (ugs.: kraulen) tickle

Krach der; ~[e]s, Kräche a) o. Pl. (Lärm) noise; tony wait... (lautes Geräusch) crash; c) (ugs.: Streit) row; **krachen** 1. itr. V. a) (Krach auslösen) (thunder) crash; (shot) ring out; b) mit sein (ugs.: bersten) (ice) crack; (bed) collapse; c) mit sein (ugs.: mit Krach auftreffen) crash; 2. refl. V. (ugs.) row (coll.); **krächzen** itr. V. (raven, crow) caw; (parrot) squawk; (person) croak

kraft (Präp. + Gen. (Amtsspr.) ~ [meines] Amtes by virtue of my office; ~ Gesetzes by law; **Kraft** die; ~, Kräfte strength; (Wirksamkeit) power; (Physik) force; (Arbeits~) employee; mit

letzter ~: with one's last ounce of strength; **aus eigener ~:** by one's own efforts; **mit vereinten Kräften werden wir ...:** if we join forces or combine our efforts we will ...; **außer ~ setzen** repeal (law); countermand (order); **außer ~ sein/treten** no longer be/cease to be in force; **in ~ treten/sein/bleiben** come into/be in/remain in force

Kraft-: **~aufwand** der effort; **~brühe** die strong meat broth; **~fahrer** der driver; motorist; **~fahrzeug** das motor vehicle

Kraftfahrzeug-: **~brief** der vehicle registration document; log-book (Brit.); **~schein** der vehicle registration document; **~steuer** die vehicle tax

kräftig 1. Adj. strong; vigorous (plant, shoot); powerful, hefty (blow, kick, etc.); nourishing (soup, bread, meal, etc.); 2. adv. powerfully (built); (rain, snow) heavily; (eat) heartily; **kräftigen** tr. V. (holiday, air, etc.) invigorate; (food etc.) fortify

kraft-, Kraft-: **~meier** der; ~s, ~ (ugs.: abwertend) muscleman; **~probe** die trial of strength; **~rad** das (Amtsspr.) motorcycle; **~stoff** der (Kfz-W.) fuel; **~stoff·verbrauch** der fuel consumption; **~voll** 1. Adj. powerful; 2. adv. powerfully; **~wagen** der motor vehicle; **~werk** das power station

Kragen der; ~s, ~, südd., österr. u. schweiz. auch: Krägen collar; **Kragen·weite** die collar size

Krähe ['krɛːə] die; ~, ~n crow; **krähen** itr. V. (auch fig.) crow; **Krähen·füße** Pl. (ugs.) crow's feet

krakeelen itr. V. (ugs.) kick up a row (coll.)

krakeln tr., itr. V. (ugs.) scrawl; **kraklig** Adj. (ugs. abwertend) scrawly

Kralle die; ~, ~n claw; **krallen** 1. refl. V. sich an etw. (Akk.) ~ (cat) dig its claws into sth.; (person) clutch sth. [tightly]; 2. tr. V. (fest greifen) die Finger in/um etw. (Akk.) ~: dig one's fingers into sth./clutch sth. [tightly] with one's fingers

Kram der; ~[e]s (ugs.) a) stuff; (Gerümpel) junk; b) (Angelegenheit) affair; **kramen** 1. itr. V. in etw. (Dat.) ~: rummage about in sth.; 2. tr. V. (ugs.) etw. aus etw. ~: fish (coll.) sth. out of sth.; **Krämer** der; ~s, ~: grocer; **Kram·laden** der (ugs. abwertend) junk shop

Krampf der; ~|e|s, **Krämpfe a)** cramp; *(Zuckung)* spasm; **b)** *o. Pl.* painful strain; *(sinnloses Tun)* senseless waste of effort; **Krampf·ader die** varicose vein; **krampfhaft 1.** *Adj.* convulsive; *(verbissen)* desperate; **2.** *adv.* convulsively; *(verbissen)* desperately

Kran der; ~|e|s, **Kräne a)** crane; **b)** *(südwestd.: Wasserhahn)* tap; faucet *(Amer.)*

Kranich der; ~s, ~e crane

krank; kränker, kränkst... *Adj.* ill *usu. pred.*; sick; bad ⟨*leg, tooth*⟩; diseased ⟨*plant, organ*⟩; *(fig.)* ailing ⟨*economy, business*⟩; ~ **werden** be taken ill; jmdn. ~ **schreiben** give a medical certificate; **Kranke der/die**; *adj. Dekl.* sick man/woman; *(Patient)* patient; **kränkeln** *itr. V.* be in poor health; **kränken** *tr. V.* jmdn. ~: hurt sb. *or* sb.'s feelings

Kranken-: ~**geld** das sickness benefit; ~**haus das** hospital; ~**kasse die** health insurance scheme; *(Körperschaft)* health insurance institution; *(privat)* health insurance company; ~**pfleger** der male nurse; ~**schein** der health insurance certificate; ~**schwester die** nurse; ~**versicherung die a)** *(Versicherung)* health insurance; **b)** *(Unternehmen)* health insurance company; ~**wagen der** ambulance

krank|feiern *itr. V. (ugs.)* skive off work *(sl.)* [pretending to be ill]; **kränker** s. **krank**; **krankhaft 1.** *Adj.* pathological; morbid ⟨*growth, state, swelling, etc.*⟩; **2.** *adv.* pathologically; morbidly ⟨*swollen, sensitive*⟩; **Krankheit die;** ~, ~**en a)** illness; *(bestimmte Art, von Pflanzen, Organen)* disease; **b)** *o. Pl. (Zeit des Krankseins)* illness; **Krankheits·erreger der** pathogen; **kränklich** *Adj.* ailing; **kränkst...** s. **krank**; **Kränkung die;** ~, ~**en**: eine ~: an injury to one's/sb.'s feelings

Kranz der; ~es, **Kränze** wreath; garland; *(auf einem Grab usw.)* wreath; **Kränzchen das;** ~s, ~: coffee circle; coffee klatch *(Amer.)*

Krapfen der; ~s, ~: doughnut

kraß 1. *Adj.* blatant ⟨*case*⟩; flagrant ⟨*injustice*⟩; stark ⟨*contrast*⟩; complete ⟨*contradiction*⟩; sharp ⟨*difference*⟩; out-and-out ⟨*egoist*⟩; **2.** *adv.* sich ~ **ausdrücken** put sth. bluntly; **sich von etw.** ~ **unterscheiden** be in stark contrast to sth.

Krater der; ~s, ~: crater

Kratz·bürste die *(ugs. scherzh.)* prickly so-and-so; **kratzen 1.** *tr. V.* scratch; *(entfernen)* scrape; **2.** *itr. V.* **a)** scratch; **b)** *(jucken)* itch; **Kratzer** der; ~s, ~ *(ugs.)* scratch; **kratzig** *Adj.* itchy ⟨*material*⟩

Kraul das; ~s *(Sport)* crawl; [1]**kraulen 1.** *itr. V.* do the crawl; **2.** *tr. V.; auch mit sein* **eine Strecke** ~: cover a distance using the crawl

[2]**kraulen** *tr. V.* jmdm. das Kinn ~: tickle sb. under the chin; jmdn. in den Haaren ~: run one's fingers through sb.'s hair

kraus *Adj.* creased ⟨*skirt etc.*⟩; frizzy ⟨*hair*⟩; **Krause die;** ~, ~n *(Kragen)* ruff; *(am Ärmel)* ruffle

kräuseln 1. *tr. V.* ruffle ⟨*water, surface*⟩; gather ⟨*material etc.*⟩; frizz ⟨*hair*⟩; **2.** *refl. V.* ⟨*hair*⟩ go frizzy; ⟨*water*⟩ ripple; ⟨*smoke*⟩ curl up

Kraut das; ~|e|s, **Kräuter a)** herb; **b)** *o. Pl. (bes. südd., österr.: Kohl)* cabbage

Krawall der; ~s, ~e **a)** riot; **b)** *o. Pl. (ugs.: Lärm)* row *(coll.)*

Krawatte die; ~, ~n tie

kreativ 1. *Adj.* creative; **2.** *adv.* ~ **veranlagt sein** have a creative bent

Kreatur die; ~, ~en creature

Krebs der; ~es, ~e **a)** crustacean; *(Fluß~)* crayfish; *(Krabbe)* crab; **b)** *(Krankheit)* cancer

krebs-, Krebs-: ~**erregend,** ~**erzeugend** *Adj.* carcinogenic; ~**krank** *Adj.* ~**krank sein** have cancer; ~**rot** *Adj.* as red as a lobster *postpos.*

Kredit der; ~|e|s, ~e credit; *(Darlehen)* loan; **Kredit·karte die** credit card; **mit** ~**karte bezahlen** pay by credit card; **kredit·würdig** *Adj.* *(Finanzw.)* credit-worthy

Kreide die; ~, ~n chalk; **kreide-bleich** *Adj.* as white as a sheet *postpos.*; **Kreide·felsen der** chalk cliff

kreieren [kre'i:rən] *tr. V.* create

Kreis der; ~es, ~e circle *(Verwaltungsbezirk)* district; *(Wahl~)* ward; **Kreis·bahn die** orbit

kreischen *itr. V.* screech; ⟨*door*⟩ creak

Kreisel der; ~s, ~ *(Kinderspielzeug)* top; *(ugs.: Kreisverkehr)* roundabout; **kreisen** *itr. V.; auch mit sein* ⟨*planet*⟩ revolve **(um** around); ⟨*satellite etc.*⟩ orbit; ⟨*aircraft, bird*⟩ circle

kreis-, Kreis-: ~**förmig** *Adj.* circular; ~**lauf** der *(Physiol.)* circulation; *(der Natur, des Lebens usw.)* cycle;

~lauf·störungen Pl. (Med.) circulatory trouble sing.; ~rund Adj. [perfectly] round; ~säge die circular saw
Kreiß·saal der (Med.) delivery room
Kreis-: ~stadt die chief town of a/the district; ~verkehr der the roundabout
Krem die; ~, ~s s. Creme
Krematorium das; ~s, Krematorien crematorium
kremig s. cremig
Krempe die; ~, ~n brim
Krempel der; ~s (ugs. abwertend) stuff; (Gerümpel) junk
krepieren itr. V.; mit sein (salopp) ⟨person⟩ snuff it (sl.)
Krepp der; ~s, ~s od. ~e crêpe
Kresse die; ~, ~n (Bot.) cress
Kreta (das) ~s Crete
Kreuz das; ~es, ~e a) cross; (Kreuzzeichen) sign of the cross; b) (Teil des Rückens) small of the back; jmdn. aufs ~ legen (salopp) take sb. for a ride (sl.); c) o. Art., o. Pl. (Kartenspiel) (Farbe) clubs pl.; (Karte) club; d) (Autobahn) interchange; e) (Musik) sharp; **kreuzen** 1. tr. V. (auch Biol.) cross; 2. refl. V. a) (überschneiden) cross; b) (zuwiderlaufen) clash (mit with); 3. itr. V.; mit haben od. sein (fahren) cruise
Kreuz-: ~fahrer der (hist.) crusader; ~fahrt die cruise; ~feuer das (Milit., auch fig.) cross-fire; ~gang der cloister
kreuzigen tr. V. crucify; **Kreuzigung** die; ~, ~en crucifixion
Kreuz-: ~otter die adder; [common] viper; ~ritter der (hist.) crusader; ~schmerzen Pl. pain sing. in the small of the back
Kreuzung die; ~, ~en a) crossroads sing.; b) (Biol.) crossing; cross-breeding; (Ergebnis) cross
kreuz-, Kreuz-: ~verhör das cross-examination; ~weise crosswise; ~wort·rätsel das crossword [puzzle]; ~zug der (hist., fig.) crusade
kribbelig Adj. (ugs.) (vor Ungeduld) fidgety; (nervös) edgy; **kribbeln** itr. V. (jucken) tickle; (prickeln) tingle
kriechen unr. itr. V. a) mit sein ⟨insect, baby⟩ crawl; ⟨plant⟩ creep; ⟨person, animal⟩ creep, crawl; b) auch mit sein (fig. abwertend) crawl (vor + Dat. to); **Kriecher** der; ~s, ~ (abwertend) crawler; **Kriech·spur** die (Verkehrsw.) crawler lane
Krieg der; ~[e]s, ~e war
kriegen tr. V. (ugs.) get; (erreichen) catch ⟨train, bus, etc.⟩

Krieger der; ~s, ~: warrior; **kriegerisch** Adj. a) (kampflustig) warlike; b) (militärisch) military; **eine ~e Auseinandersetzung** an armed conflict
kriegs-, Kriegs-: ~beil das tomahawk; das ~beil begraben (scherzh.) bury the hatchet; ~bemalung die (Völkerk.) war-paint; ~beschädigt Adj. war-disabled; ~beschädigte der/die war invalid; ~dienst der a) (im Krieg) active service; b) (Wehrdienst) military service; den ~dienst verweigern be a conscientious objector; ~dienst·verweigerer der conscientious objector; ~erklärung die declaration of war; ~gefangene der prisoner of war; POW; ~gefangenschaft die captivity; ~schiff das warship; ~verbrechen das (Rechtsw.) war crime
Krimi der; ~[s], ~[s] (ugs.) crime thriller; **Kriminal·beamte** der [plain-clothes] detective; **Kriminalität** die; ~: crime no art.
Kriminal-: ~polizei die criminal investigation department; ~roman der crime novel; (mit Detektiv als Held) detective novel
kriminell 1. Adj. criminal; 2. adv. ~ veranlagt sein have criminal tendencies; ~ handeln act illegally; **Kriminelle** der/die; adj. Dekl. criminal
Krimskrams der; ~[es] (ugs.) stuff
Kringel der; ~s, ~ (Kreis) [small] ring; (Kritzelei) round squiggle; (Gebäck) [ring-shaped] biscuit; **kringeln** refl. V. curl [up]; ⟨hair⟩ go curly; sich ~ [vor Lachen] (ugs.) kill oneself [laughing] (coll.)
Kripo die; ~ (ugs.) die ~: ≈ the CID
Krippe die; ~, ~n a) (Futtertrog) manger; crib; b) (Weihnachts~) model of a nativity scene; c) (Kinder~) crèche
Krise die; ~, ~n (auch Med.) crisis; **kriseln** itr. V. (unpers.) es kriselt in ihrer Ehe/in der Partei their marriage is in trouble/the party is in a state of crisis; **Krisen·herd** der trouble spot
¹**Kristall** der; ~s, ~e crystal; ²**Kristall** das; ~s crystal no indef. art.
Kriterium das; ~s, Kriterien criterion
Kritik die; ~, ~en a) criticism no indef. art. (an + Dat. of); an jmdm./etw. ~ üben criticize sb./sth.); b) (Besprechung) review; **Kritiker** der; ~s, ~: critic; **kritik·los** 1. Adj. uncritical; 2. adv. uncritically; **kritisch** 1. Adj. critical; 2. adv. critically; **kritisieren**

tr. V. criticize; review ⟨*book, play, etc.*⟩

kritzeln 1. *itr. V. (schreiben)* scribble; *(zeichnen)* doodle; **2.** *tr. V.* scribble

Kroatien [kroˈaːt͡si̯ən] (das); ~s Croatia; **kroatisch** *Adj.* Croatian

kroch *1. u. 3. Pers. Sg. Prät. v.* **kriechen**

Krokant der; ~s praline

Krokette die; ~, ~n *(Kochk.)* croquette

Krokodil das; ~s, ~e crocodile; **Krokodils·tränen** *Pl. (ugs.)* crocodile tears

Krokus der; ~, ~ *od.* ~se crocus

Krone die; ~, ~n crown; (eines Baumes) top; crown; *(einer Welle)* crest; **die ~ der Schöpfung** the pride of creation; **krönen** *tr. V. (auch fig.)* crown; **Kronen·korken der** crown cork

Kron-: ~**juwel das** *od.* **der;** *meist Pl.* **die** ~**juwelen** the crown jewels; ~**leuchter der** chandelier; ~**prinz der** crown prince

Krönung die; ~, ~en coronation; *(fig.)* culmination; **Kron·zeuge der** *(Rechtsw.)* person who turns Queen's/King's evidence; **als** ~ **auftreten** turn Queen's/King's evidence

Kropf der; ~[e]s, **Kröpfe** *(Med.)* goitre

Kröte die; ~, ~n a) toad; b) *Pl. (salopp: Geld)* **ein paar/eine ganze Menge** ~n **verdienen** earn a few bob *(Brit. sl.)*/a fair old whack *(sl.)*

Krücke die; ~, ~n crutch; **Krück·stock der** walking-stick

Krug der; ~[e]s, **Krüge** jug; *(größer)* pitcher; *(Bier~)* mug

Krume die; ~, ~n crumb; **Krümel der;** ~s, ~ : crumb; **krümeln** *itr. V.* a) crumble; b) *(Krümel machen)* make crumbs

krumm 1. *Adj.* a) bent ⟨*nail, back*⟩; crooked ⟨*stick, branch, etc.*⟩; bandy ⟨*legs*⟩; b) *nicht präd. (ugs.: unrechtmäßig)* crooked; **2.** *adv.* crookedly; **krümmen 1.** *tr. V.* bend; **2.** *refl. V.* a) *(sich winden)* writhe; b) *(krumm verlaufen)* ⟨*road, path, river*⟩ bend

krumm-: ~**lachen** *refl. V. (ugs.)* **sich über etw.** *(Akk.)* ~**lachen** fall about laughing over sth.; ~**nehmen** *unr. tr. V. (ugs.)* **etw.** ~**nehmen** take sth. the wrong way

Krümmung die; ~, ~en bend

Krüppel der; ~s, ~ : cripple

Kruste die; ~, ~n crust; *(vom Braten)* crisp

Kruzifix das; ~es, ~e crucifix

Krypta die; ~, **Krypten** *(Archit.)* crypt

Kuba (das); ~s Cuba; **Kubaner der;** ~s, ~ : Cuban

Kübel der; ~s, ~ : pail

Kubik- cubic ⟨*metre, foot, etc.*⟩

Küche die; ~, ~n kitchen; *(Einrichtung)* kitchen furniture *no indef. art.*; *(Kochk.)* cooking; cuisine; **kalte/warme** ~: cold/hot food

Kuchen der; ~s, ~ : cake; *(Obst~)* flan; *(Torte)* gateau

Kuchen-: ~**form die** cake-tin; ~**gabel die** pastry-fork

Küchen·gerät das kitchen utensil; *(als Kollektivum)* kitchen utensils *pl.*

Kuckuck der; ~s, ~e a) cuckoo; **zum** ~ **[noch mal]!** *(salopp)* for crying out loud! *(coll.)*; b) *(scherzh.: Pfandsiegel)* bailiff's seal *(placed on distrained goods)*; **Kuckucks·uhr die** cuckoo clock

Kufe die; ~, ~n runner; *(von Flugzeugen, Hubschraubern)* skid

Kugel die; ~, ~n a) ball; *(Geom.)* sphere; *(Kegeln)* bowl; *(beim Kugelstoßen)* shot; b) *(ugs.: Geschoß)* bullet; **Kugel·lager das** *(Technik)* ball-bearing; **kugeln** *itr. V.* roll; **2.** *refl. V.* **sich [vor Lachen]** ~ *(ugs.)* double *or* roll up [laughing]

kugel-, Kugel-: ~**rund** [-ʹ-] *Adj.* round as a ball *postpos.*; *(scherzh.: dick)* rotund; tubby; ~**schreiber der** ball-pen; Biro (P); ~**sicher** *Adj.* bullet-proof; ~**stoßen das;** ~s shot[-put]; *(Disziplin)* putting the shot *no art.*

Kuh die; ~, **Kühe** cow

Kuh-: ~**fladen der** cow-pat; ~**haut die: das geht auf keine** ~**haut** *(fig. salopp)* it's absolutely staggering

kühl 1. *Adj.* cool; etw. ~ **lagern** keep sth. in a cool place; **2.** *adv.* coolly

Kühle die; ~, ~n *(ugs.)* hollow

Kühle die; ~ : coolness

kühlen *tr. V.* cool; chill ⟨*wine*⟩; refrigerate ⟨*food*⟩; **2.** *itr. V.* ⟨*cold compress, ointment, breeze, etc.*⟩ have a cooling effect; **Kühler der;** ~s, ~ a) *(am Auto)* radiator; *(~haube)* bonnet *(Brit.)*; hood *(Amer.)*; b) *(Sekt~)* ice-bucket; **Kühler·haube die** bonnet *(Brit.)*; hood *(Amer.)*

Kühl-: ~**schrank der** refrigerator; fridge *(Brit. coll.)*; icebox *(Amer.)*; ~**truhe die** [chest] freezer; *(im Lebensmittelgeschäft)* freezer [cabinet]

Kühlung die; ~, ~en cooling; *(Vor-*

richtung) cooling system; *(für Lebensmittel)* refrigeration system; **Kühl·wasser das** cooling water

kühn 1. *Adj.* bold; *(dreist)* audacious; **2.** *adv.* boldly; *(gewagt)* daringly; *(dreist)* audaciously; **Kühnheit die;** ~: boldness; *(Gewagtheit)* daringness; *(Dreistigkeit)* audacity

Kuh·stall der cowshed

Küken das; ~s, ~: chick

kulant *Adj.* obliging; fair *(terms)*; **Kulanz die;** ~: willingness to oblige

Kuli der; ~s, ~s **a)** coolie; **b)** *(ugs.)* ball-point; Biro **(P)**

kulinarisch *Adj.* culinary

Kulisse die; ~, ~n piece of scenery; flat; *(Hintergrund)* backdrop; **die ~n** the scenery *sing.*

kullern *(ugs.)* *itr. V.* mit sein roll

Kult der; ~|e|s, ~e *(auch fig.)* cult; **kultivieren** *tr. V.* *(auch fig.)* cultivate; **kultiviert 1.** *Adj.* cultured; *(vornehm)* refined; **2.** *adv.* in a cultured manner; *(vornehm)* in a refined manner; **Kultur die;** ~, ~en **a)** *o. Pl.* culture; *(kultivierte Lebensart)* refinement; **ein Mensch von** ~: a cultured person; **b)** *(Zivilisation, Lebensform)* civilization

Kultur-: ~**abkommen das** cultural agreement; ~**austausch der** cultural exchange; ~**beutel der** sponge-bag *(Brit.);* toilet-bag

kulturell 1. *Adj.* cultural; **2.** *adv.* culturally

Kultur-: ~**film der** documentary film; ~**geschichte die a)** *o. Pl.* history of civilization; *(einer bestimmten Kultur)* cultural history; ~**politik die** cultural and educational policy

Kultus·minister der minister for education and cultural affairs

Kümmel der; ~s, ~: caraway [seed]; *(Branntwein)* kümmel

Kummer der; ~s sorrow; grief; *(Ärger, Sorgen)* trouble; ~ **um** *od.* **über jmdn.** grief for sb.; **jmdm.** ~ **machen** give sb. trouble; **kümmerlich** *Adj.* **a)** *(schwächlich)* puny; stunted *(vegetation, plants);* **b)** *(ärmlich)* wretched; miserable; **c)** *(abwertend: gering)* miserable; meagre *(knowledge, left-overs);* **kümmern 1.** *refl. V.* **a)** sich um jmdn./etw. ~: take care of sb./sth.; **b)** *(sich befassen mit)* sich nicht um Politik ~: not be interested in politics; **2.** *tr. V.* concern

Kumpan der; ~s, ~e *(ugs.)* **a)** pal *(coll.);* buddy *(coll.);* **b)** *(abwertend:*

Mittäter) accomplice; **Kumpel der;** ~s, ~ **a)** *(Bergmannsspr.)* miner; **b)** *(salopp: Kamerad)* pal *(coll.);* buddy *(coll.)*

kündbar *Adj.* terminable *(contract);* redeemable *(loan, mortgage);* **¹Kunde der;** ~n, ~n customer; *(eines Architekten-, Anwaltbüros, einer Versicherung usw.)* client

²Kunde die; ~ *(geh.)* tidings *pl. (literary);* **Kunden·dienst der** *o. Pl.* service to customers; *(Wartung)* after-sales service; **Kundgebung die;** ~, ~en rally; **kundig** *Adj.* (kenntnisreich) knowledgeable; *(sachverständig)* expert; **kündigen 1.** *tr. V.* cancel *(subscription, membership);* terminate *(contract, agreement);* **seine Stellung** ~: hand in one's notice **(bei** to); **2.** *unr. itr. V.* **a)** *(ein Mietverhältnis beenden)* *(tenant)* give notice; **jmdm.** ~ *(landlord)* give sb. notice to quit; **zum 1. Juli** ~: give notice for 1 July; **b)** *(ein Arbeitsverhältnis beenden)* *(employee)* hand in one's notice **(bei** to); **jmdm.** ~ *(employer)* give sb. his/her notice; **Kündigung die;** ~, ~en **a)** *(der Mitgliedschaft, eines Abonnements)* cancellation; *(eines Vertrags)* termination; **b)** *(eines Arbeitsverhältnisses)* **jmdm. die** ~ **aussprechen** give sb. his/her notice; **Kundin die;** ~, ~nen customer/client; **Kundschaft die;** ~, ~en *o. Pl.; s.* **¹Kunde a:** customers *pl.;* clientele; **Kundschafter der;** ~s, ~: scout; **kund|tun** *(geh.)* *unr. tr. V.* announce

künftig 1. *Adj.* future; **2.** *adv.* in future

Kunst die; ~, **Künste a)** art; **b)** *(das Können)* skill; **die ärztliche** ~: medical skill; **das ist keine** ~! *(ugs.)* there's nothing to it

kunst-, Kunst-: ~**aus·stellung die** art exhibition; ~**buch das** art book; ~**erzieher der,** ~**erzieherin die** art teacher; ~**faser die** synthetic fibre; ~**führer der** guide to cultural and artistic monuments [of an/the area]; ~**genuß der** enjoyment of art; *(Ereignis)* artistic treat; ~**gerecht 1.** *Adj.* expert; **2.** *adv.* expertly; ~**geschichte die** *o. Pl.* art history; ~**geschichtlich 1.** *Adj.* art historical *(studies, evidence, expertise);* *(work)* on art history; **2.** *adv.* ~**geschichtlich interessiert/versiert** interested/well versed in art history; ~**gewerbe das** arts and crafts *pl.;* ~**griff der** trick; dodge;

~**halle** die art gallery; ~**händler** der [fine-]art dealer; ~**handwerk das** craftwork; ~**kritiker** der art critic; ~**leder** imitation leather

Künstler der; ~s, ~, **Künstlerin** die; ~, ~**nen a)** artist; *(Zirkus~, Varieté~)* artiste; b) *(Könner)* genius (**in** + *Dat.* at); **künstlerisch 1.** *Adj.* artistic; **2.** *adv.* artistically; **Künstler · name** der stage-name; **künstlich 1.** *Adj.* a) artificial; b) *(gezwungen)* forced 〈*laugh, cheerfulness, etc.*〉; **2.** *adv.* artificially

kunst-, Kunst-: ~**los** *Adj.* plain; ~**post · karte** die art postcard; ~**sammler** der art collector; ~**sammlung** die art collection; ~**stoff** der synthetic material; plastic; ~**stück** das trick; **das ist kein** ~**stück** *(ugs.)* it's no great feat; ~**turnen** das gymnastics *sing.;* ~**voll 1.** *Adj.* ornate and artistic; *(kompliziert)* elaborate; **2.** *adv.* a) ornately or elaborately and artistically; b) *(geschickt)* skilfully; ~**werk** das work of art

kunter · bunt 1. *Adj.* multi-coloured; *(abwechslungsreich)* varied; *(ungeordnet)* jumbled 〈*confusion, muddle, etc.*〉; **2.** *adv.* 〈*painted, printed*〉 in many colours; ~ **durcheinander sein** be higgledy-piggledy

Kupfer das; ~s **a)** copper; b) *(~geschirr)* copperware; *(~geld)* coppers *pl.*

Kupfer-: ~**geld** das coppers *pl.;* ~**stich** der a) *o. Pl.* copperplate engraving *no art.;* b) *(Blatt)* copperplate print *or* engraving

Kuppe die; ~, ~**n a)** [rounded] hilltop; b) *(Finger~)* tip; end

Kuppel die; ~, ~**n** dome; *(kleiner)* cupola

kuppeln die; ~: procuring; **kuppeln** *itr. V.* operate the clutch; **Kuppelung** *s.* Kupplung; **Kuppler** der; ~s, ~: procurer; **Kupplerin** die; ~, ~**nen** procuress; **Kupplung** die; ~, ~**en a)** *(Kfz-W.)* clutch; b) *(Technik: Vorrichtung zum Verbinden)* coupling

Kur die; ~, ~**en** [health] cure; *(ohne Aufenthalt im Badeort)* course of treatment

Kür die; ~, ~**en** *(Eiskunstlauf)* free programme; *(Turnen)* optional exercises *pl.*

Kurbel die; ~, ~**n** crank [handle]; *(an Spieldosen, Grammophonen)* winder; *(an einem Brunnen)* [winding-]handle; **kurbeln** *tr. V.* etw. nach oben/unten

~: wind sth. up/down; **Kurbel · welle** die *(Technik)* crankshaft

Kürbis der; ~ses, ~se pumpkin

Kurde der; ~**n**, ~**n** Kurd

Kur-: ~**fürst** der *(hist.)* Elector; ~**gast** der visitor to a/the spa; *(Patient)* patient at a/the spa

Kurier der; ~s, ~e courier

kurieren *tr. V. (auch fig.)* cure (**von** of)

kurios 1. *Adj.* curious; **2.** *adv.* curiously; strangely; oddly; **Kuriosität** die; ~, ~**en a)** *o. Pl.* strangeness; b) *(Gegenstand)* curiosity; curio

Kur-: ~**konzert** das concert [at a spa]; ~**ort** der spa; ~**pfuscher** der *(ugs. abwertend)* quack

Kurs der; ~es, ~e **a)** *(Richtung)* course; **ein harter/weicher** ~ *(fig.)* hard/soft line; b) *(von Wertpapieren)* price; *(von Devisen)* exchange rate; **der** ~ **des Dollars** the dollar rate; c) *(Lehrgang)* course; *(Teilnehmer)* class

Kürschner der; ~s, ~: furrier

kursieren *itr. V.; auch mit sein* circulate; **Kurs · teilnehmer** der course participant; **Kursus** der; ~, Kurse *s.* Kurs; **Kurs · wagen** der *(Eisenb.)* through carriage

Kur · taxe die visitors' tax *(at a spa)*

Kurve die; ~, ~**n a)** *(einer Straße)* bend; b) *(Geom.)* curve; c) *(in der Statistik, Temperatur~ usw.)* graph; **kurven** *itr. V.; mit sein* a) 〈*aircraft*〉 circle; 〈*tanks etc.*〉 circle [round]; b) *(ugs.: fahren)* drive around; **kurven · reich** *Adj.* winding; twisting

kurz; kürzer, kürzest... 1. *Adj.* short; *(zeitlich; knapp)* short, brief; quick 〈*look*〉; **2.** *adv.* a) *(zeitlich)* briefly; *(knapp)* ~ **gesagt** in a word; b) *(wenig)* just; ~ **vor/hinter der Kreuzung** just before/past the crossroads; ~ **vor/nach Pfingsten** just before/after Whitsun; **Kurz · arbeit** die short-time working; **kurz · ärm[e]lig** *Adj.* short-sleeved; **Kürze** die; ~ a) shortness; b) *(geringe Dauer)* shortness; brevity; **in** ~: shortly; c) *(Knappheit)* brevity; **Kürzel** das; ~s, ~: shorthand symbol; **kürzen** *tr. V.* shorten; abridge 〈*article, book*〉; cut 〈*pension, budget*〉; **kürzer** *s.* kurz; **kürzerhand** *Adv.* without more ado; **kürzest... ** *s.* kurz

kurz-, Kurz-: ~**fristig 1.** *Adj.* a) 〈*refusal, resignation, etc.*〉 at short notice; b) *(für kurze Zeit)* short-term; **2.** *adv.* a) at short notice; b) *(für kurze Zeit)* for a short time; *(auf kurze Sicht)* in the short term; *(in kurzer Zeit)* without delay; **~geschichte** die short story; **~lebig** *Adj. (auch fig.)* short-lived

kürzlich *Adv.* recently; not long ago

kurz-, Kurz-: ~parker der short-stay *(Brit.) or* short-term parker; **~schluß** der *(Elektrot.)* short-circuit; **~sichtig** *(auch fig.)* 1. *Adj.* short-sighted; 2. *adv.* short-sightedly

Kürzung die; ~, ~en cut

kurz-, Kurz-: ~waren *Pl.* haberdashery *sing. (Brit.);* notions *(Amer.);* **~welle** die *(Physik, Rundf.)* short wave; **~zeitig** 1. *Adj.* brief; 2. *adv.* briefly

kuscheln *refl. V.* sich an jmdn. ~: snuggle up to sb.

kuschen *itr. V.* knuckle under (vor + *Dat.* to)

Kusine die; ~, ~n s. Cousine

Kuß der; Kusses, Küsse kiss; **kußecht** *Adj.* kissproof; **küssen** *tr., itr. V.* kiss; **Kuß·hand** die: jmdm. eine ~ zuwerfen blow sb. a kiss; **mit ~** *(ugs.)* gladly

Küste die; ~, ~n coast; **Küsten·wache** die coastguard [service]

Küster der; ~s, ~: sexton

Kutsche die; ~, ~n coach; **Kutscher** der; ~s, ~: coach-driver; **kutschieren** *itr. V.; mit sein* drive, ride [in a coach]; 2. *tr. V.* jmdn. ~: drive sb. [in a coach]

Kutte die; ~, ~n [monk's/nun's] habit

Kutter der; ~s, ~: cutter

Kuvert [ku've:ɐ̯] das; ~s, ~s envelope; *(geh.: Gedeck)* cover

Kuwait [ku'vait] (das); ~s Kuwait

Kybernetik die; ~: cybernetics *sing.*

L

l, L [ɛl] das; ~, ~: l/L

l *Abk.* Liter l.

laben *(geh.)* 1. *tr. V.* jmdn. ~: give sb. refreshment; 2. *refl. V.* refresh oneself (an + *Dat.*, mit with)

labil *Adj.* a) *(Med.)* delicate *(constitution, health)*; poor *(circulation)*; b)

(auch Psych.) unstable *(person, character, situation, etc.)*

Labor das; ~s, ~s, *auch:* ~e laboratory; **Laboratorium** das; ~s, Laboratorien laboratory

Labyrinth das; ~[e]s, ~e maze; labyrinth

¹Lache die; ~, ~n *(ugs.)* laugh

²Lache ['la(:)xə] die; ~, ~n puddle; *(von Blut, Öl)* pool

lächeln *itr. V.* smile (über + *Akk.* at); **Lächeln** das; ~s smile; **lachen** 1. *itr. V.* laugh (über + *Akk.* at); 2. *tr. V.* was gibt es denn zu ~? what's so funny?; **Lachen** das; ~s laughter; **ein lautes ~**: a loud laugh; **lächerlich** 1. *Adj.* ridiculous; ludicrous *(argument, statement)*; 2. *adv.* ridiculously; **Lächerlichkeit** die; ~: ridiculousness; *(von Argumenten, Behauptungen usw.)* ludicrousness; **lachhaft** *Adj.* ridiculous

Lachs der; ~es, ~e salmon

Lack der; ~[e]s, ~e a) varnish; *(für Metall, Lackarbeiten)* lacquer; **lackieren** *tr. V.* varnish; spray *(car)*; **Lack·leder** das patent leather

Lade die; ~, ~n *(landsch.)* drawer; **Lade·hemmung** die jam; **¹laden** 1. *unr. tr. V.* load; *(Physik)* charge; 2. *unr. itr. V.* load [up]

²laden *unr. tr. V.* a) *(Rechtsspr.)* summon; b) *(geh.: ein~)* invite

Laden der; ~s, Läden a) shop; store *(Amer.);* der ~ läuft *(ugs.)* business is good; b) *(Fenster~)* shutter

Laden-: ~diebstahl der shop-lifting; **~schluß** der shop *or (Amer.)* store closing-time; **~tisch** der [shop-] counter

Lade-: ~rampe die loading ramp; **~raum** der *(beim Auto)* luggage-space; *(beim Flugzeug, Schiff)* hold; *(bei LKWs)* payload space

lädieren *tr. V.* damage

lädst 2. *Pers. Sg. Präsens v.* laden; **lädt** 3. *Pers. Sg. Präsens v.* laden

Ladung die; ~, ~en a) *(Schiffs~, Flugzeug~)* cargo; *(LKW~)* load; b) *(beim Sprengen, Schießen; Physik)* charge; c) *(Rechtsspr.: Vor~)* summons *sing.*

lag 1. u. 3. *Pers. Sg. Prät. v.* liegen; **Lage** die; ~, ~n a) situation; **eine gute ~ haben** be well situated; b) *(Art des Liegens)* position; c) *(Situation)* situation; **Lage·plan** der map of the area; **Lager** das; ~s, ~ a) camp; b) store-room; *(in Geschäften, Betrieben)* stock-room; c) *(Warenbestand)* stock

Lager-: ~**feuer** das camp-fire; ~**halle** die warehouse

lagern 1. *tr. V.* **a)** store; **b)** *(hinlegen)* lay down; **2.** *itr. V.* **a)** camp; **b)** *(liegen)* lie; *(foodstuffs, medicines, etc.)* be kept

Lager-: ~**platz** der campsite; ~**raum** store-room; *(im Geschäft, Betrieb)* stock-room

Lagerung die; ~, ~en storage

Lagune die; ~, ~n lagoon

lahm *Adj.* **a)** *(gelähmt)* lame; *(ugs.: unbeweglich)* stiff; **b)** *(ugs.: unzureichend)* lame *(excuse, explanation, etc.)*; **c)** *(ugs. abwertend: matt)* dreary; **lahmen** *itr. V.* be lame; **lähmen** *tr. V.* paralyse; *(fig.)* paralyse *(economy, industry)*; bring *(traffic)* to a standstill; **Lähmung** die; ~, ~en paralysis; *(fig.) (der Wirtschaft, Industrie)* paralysis; **zu einer ~ des Verkehrs führen** bring traffic to a standstill

Laib der; ~[e]s, ~e loaf; **ein [halber] ~ Brot** [half] a loaf of bread

Laich der; ~[e]s, ~e spawn; **laichen** *itr. V.* spawn

Laie der; ~n, ~n *(Mann)* layman; *(Frau)* laywoman

Lakai der; ~en, ~en lackey; liveried footman

Lake die; ~, ~n brine

Laken das; ~s, ~ *(bes. nordd.)* sheet

Lakritze die; ~, ~n liquorice

lallen *tr., itr. V.* *(baby)* babble; *(drunk/drowsy person)* mumble

Lamelle die; ~, ~n *(einer Jalousie)* slat; *(eines Heizkörpers)* rib

lamentieren *itr. V.* *(ugs.)* moan *(über + Akk.* about)

Lametta das; ~s lametta

Lamm das; ~[e]s, **Lämmer** lamb

lamm-, Lamm-: ~**fell** das lambskin; ~**fleisch** das lamb; ~**fromm 1.** *Adj.* *(person)* as meek as a [little] lamb; **2.** *adv.* *(answer)* like a lamb

Lampe die; ~, ~n light; *(Tisch~, Öl~, Signal~)* lamp

Lampen~: ~**fieber** das stage fright; ~**schirm** der [lamp]shade

Lampion [lamˈpiɔŋ] der; ~s, ~s Chinese lantern

Land das; ~[e]s, **Länder** *od. (veralt.)* ~e **a)** *o. Pl.* land *no indef. art.*; *(dörfliche Gegend)* country *no indef. art.*; **an ~:** ashore; **auf dem ~ wohnen** live in the country; **b)** *(Staat)* country; **c)** *(Bundesland)* Land; state; *(österr.)* province; **Land·bevölkerung** die rural population

Lande-: ~**an·flug** der *(Flugw.)* [landing] approach; ~**bahn** die *(Flugw.)* [landing] runway

landen 1. *itr. V.; mit sein* **a)** land; *(ankommen)* arrive; **b)** *(ugs.: gelangen)* land up; **2.** *tr. V.* **a)** land *(aircraft, troops, passengers, fish, etc.)*; **b)** *(ugs.: zustande bringen)* pull off *(victory, coup)*; have *(smash hit)*

Ländereien Pl. estates

Länder-: ~**kampf** der *(Sport)* international match; ~**spiel** das *(Sport)* international [match]

Landes-: ~**innere** das interior [of the country]; ~**kunde** die; *o. Pl.* regional studies *pl., no art.*; ~**regierung** die government of a/the Land/province; ~**sprache** die language of the country; ~**tracht** die national costume *or* dress; ~**verrat** der *(Rechtsw.)* treason; ~**währung** die currency of a/the country

land-, Land-: ~**flucht** die migration from the countryside [to the towns]; ~**gewinnung** die reclamation of land; ~**haus** das country house; ~**karte** die map; ~**kreis** der district; ~**läufig** *Adj.* widely accepted

ländlich *Adj.* rural; country *attrib.* *(life)*

Land-: ~**plage** die *(fig.)* pest; nuisance; ~**ratte** die *(ugs.)* landlubber

Landschaft die; ~, ~en landscape; *(ländliche Gegend)* countryside; **landschaftlich 1.** *Adj.* regional; **2.** *adv.* ~ **herrlich gelegen sein** be in a glorious natural setting

Lands·mann der; Pl. ~**leute** fellow-countryman; compatriot

Land-: ~**straße** die country road; *(im Gegensatz zur Autobahn)* ordinary road; ~**streicher** der tramp; ~**strich** der area; ~**tag** der Landtag; state parliament; *(österr.)* provincial parliament; **Landung** die; ~, ~en landing; **Landungs·brücke** die [floating] landing-stage

land-, Land-: ~**weg** der overland route; **auf dem ~weg** overland; ~**wirt** der farmer; ~**wirtschaft** die *o. Pl.* agriculture *no art.*; farming *no art.*; ~**wirtschaftlich 1.** *Adj.* agricultural; **2.** *adv.* ~ **genutzt werden** be used for agricultural purposes; ~**zunge** die *(Geogr.)* tongue of land

lang; länger, längst... 1. *Adj.* long; *(ugs.: groß)* tall; **2.** *adv.* [for] a long time; **eine Sekunde/mehrere Stunden ~:** for a second/several hours

lang-: ~**ärm[e]lig** *Adj.* long-sleeved; ~**atmig** 1. *Adj.* long-winded; 2. *adv.* long-windedly; ⟨*relate*⟩ at great length

lange; **länger, am längsten** *Adv.* a) a long time; **bist du schon ~ hier?** have you been here long?; **b)** *(bei weitem)* **ich bin noch ~ nicht fertig** I'm nowhere near finished; **hier is es ~ nicht so schön** it isn't nearly as nice here; **Länge die;** ~, ~**n** length; *(Geogr.)* longitude

langen *(ugs.)* 1. *itr. V.* **a)** be enough; **b)** *(greifen)* reach (**in** + *Akk.* into; **auf** + *Akk.* on to; **nach** for); 2. *tr. V.* **jmdm. eine** ~ *(ugs.)* give sb. a clout [around the ear] *(coll.)*

Längen·grad der *(Geogr.)* degree of longitude

länger 1. *s.* lang, lange; 2. *Adj.* **seit ~er Zeit** for quite some time

Lange·weile die; ~ *od.* **Langenweile** boredom; ~ **haben** be bored

lang-, Lang-: ~**fristig** 1. *Adj.* long-term; long-dated ⟨*loan*⟩; 2. *adv.* on a long-term basis; ~**jährig** *Adj.* ⟨*customer, friend*⟩ of many years' standing; long-standing ⟨*friendship*⟩; ~**jährige Erfahrung** many years of experience; ~**lauf der** *(Skisport)* cross-country

länglich *Adj.* oblong; **längs** 1. *Präp.* + *Gen. od.* (*selten*) *Dat.* along; 2. *adv.* lengthways; **Längs·achse die** the longitudinal axis

langsam 1. *Adj.* slow; 2. *adv.* **a)** slowly; ~, **aber sicher** *(ugs.)* slowly but surely; **b)** *(allmählich)* gradually

Lang-: ~**schläfer der** late riser; ~**spiel·platte die** long-playing record; LP

Längs·schnitt der longitudinal section

längst *Adv.* **a)** *(schon lange)* a long time ago; **b)** *(bei weitem)* **hier ist es ~ nicht so schön** it isn't nearly as nice here; **längst...** *s.* lang; **längstens** *Adv.* ⟨*höchstens*⟩ at [the] most; *(spätestens)* at the latest

Languste die; ~, ~**n** spiny lobster

lang-, Lang-: ~**weilen** 1. *tr. V.* bore; 2. *refl. V.* be bored; ~**weilig** 1. *Adj.* boring; dull ⟨*place*⟩; 2. *adv.* boringly; ~**welle die** *(Physik, Rundf.)* long wave; ~**wierig** *Adj.* lengthy; prolonged ⟨*search*⟩

Lanze die; ~, ~**n** lance; *(zum Werfen)* spear

Laos ['laːɔs] **(das); Laos'** Laos; **Laote** [la'oːtə] **der;** ~**n,** ~**n** Laotian

lapidar 1. *Adj.* *(kurz, aber wirkungsvoll)* succinct; *(knapp)* terse; 2. *adv.* succinctly/tersely

Lappalie die; ~, ~**n** trifle

Lapp der; ~**n,** ~**n** Lapp

Lappen der; ~**s,** ~: cloth; *(Fetzen)* rag; *(Wasch~)* flannel

läppisch *Adj.* silly

Lapp·land (das) Lapland

Lärche die; ~, ~**n** larch

Lärm der; ~**[e]s** noise; *(Krach)* din; row *(coll.)*; **Lärm·belästigung die** disturbance caused by noise; **lärmen** *itr. V.* make a noise *or* *(coll.)* row

Larve die; ~, ~**n** grub; larva

las *1. u. 3. Pers. Sg. Prät. v.* lesen

lasch 1. *Adj.* limp ⟨*handshake*⟩; feeble ⟨*action, measure*⟩; lax ⟨*upbringing*⟩; 2. *adv. s. Adj.:* limply; feebly; laxly

Lasche die; ~, ~**n** ⟨*Gürtel~*⟩ loop; *(eines Briefumschlags)* flap; *(Schuh~)* tongue

Laser ['leːzɐ] **der;** ~**s,** ~ *(Physik)* laser

laß *Imperativ Sg. v.* lassen; **lassen** 1. *unr. tr. V.* **a)** *mit Inf.* + *Akk.* *(2. Part.* ~*)* *(veranlassen)* **etw. tun/machen/bauen/waschen** ~: have *or* get sth. done/made/built/washed; **jmdn. warten** ~: keep sb. waiting; **jmdn. grüßen** ~: send one's regards to sb.; **jmdn. kommen/rufen** ~: send for sb.; **b)** *mit Inf.* + *Akk.* *(2. Part.* ~*)* *(erlauben)* **jmdn. etw. tun** ~: let sb. do sth.; allow sb. to do sth.; **c)** *(belassen)* **jmdn. in Frieden** ~: leave sb. in peace; **d)** *(hinein~/heraus~)* let *or* allow (**in** + *Akk.* into, **aus** out of); **e)** *(unterlassen)* stop; **f)** *(zurück~; bleiben* ~*)* leave; **g)** *(überlassen)* **jmdn. etw.** ~: let sb. have sth.; **h)** *(als Aufforderung)* **laß/laßt uns gehen/fahren!** let's go!; **i)** *(verlieren)* lose; *(ausgeben)* spend; 2. *unr. refl. V.* **die Tür läßt sich leicht öffnen** the door opens easily; **das läßt sich nicht beweisen** it can't be proved; 3. *unr. itr. V.* **a)** *(ugs.)* **Laß mal. Ich mache das schon** Leave it. I'll do it; **b)** *(veranlassen)* **ich lasse bitten** would you ask him/her/them to come in

lässig 1. *Adj.* casual; 2. *adv.* casually

läßt *3. Pers. Sg. Präsens v.* lassen

Last die; ~, ~**en** load; *(Gewicht)* weight; *(Bürde)* burden; **lasten** *itr. V.* be a burden; **auf jmdm./etw.** ~: weigh heavily [up]on sb./sth.; ¹**Laster der;** ~**s,** ~ *(ugs.: Lkw)* truck; lorry *(Brit.)*

²**Laster das;** ~**s,** ~: vice; **lasterhaft** *Adj. (abwertend)* depraved; **lästern**

1. *itr. V. (abwertend)* über jmdn./etw. ~: make malicious remarks about sb./sth.; **2.** *tr. V. (veralt.)* blaspheme against

lästig *Adj.* tiresome; troublesome ⟨*illness, cough, etc.*⟩

Last-: ~schrift die debit; ~wagen der truck; lorry *(Brit.)*

Lasur die; ~, ~en varnish; *(farbig)* glaze

Latein das; ~s Latin; **Latein·amerika (das)** Latin America; **lateinisch** *Adj.* Latin

latent *Adj.* latent

Laterne die; ~, ~n **a)** *(Leuchte)* lamp; lantern *(Naut.)*; **b)** *(Straßen~)* street light; **Laternen·pfahl** der lamppost

Latrine die; ~, ~n latrine

latschen *itr. V.; mit sein (salopp)* trudge; *(schlurfend)* slouch; **Latschen** der; ~s, ~ *(ugs.)* old worn-out shoe/slipper

Latte die; ~, ~n **a)** lath; *(Zaun~)* pale; **b)** *(Sport: Quer~ des Tores)* [cross]bar; **c)** *(Leichtathletik)* bar; **Latten·zaun** der paling fence

Latz der; ~es, Lätze bib; **Lätzchen** das; ~s, ~: bib

lau *Adj.* tepid, lukewarm ⟨*water etc.*⟩; mild ⟨*wind, air, evening, etc.*⟩

Laub das; ~[e]s leaves *pl.*; dichtes ~: thick foliage; **Laub·baum** der broad-leaved tree

Laube die; ~, ~n summer-house; *(überdeckter Sitzplatz)* bower; arbour

Laub-: ~frosch der tree frog; ~säge die fretsaw; ~wald der deciduous wood/forest

Lauch der; ~[e]s *(Porree)* leek

Lauer die; ~: auf der ~ liegen *od.* sein *(ugs.)* *(jmdm. auflauern)* lie in wait; **lauern** *itr. V. (auch fig.)* lurk

Lauf der; ~[e]s, Läufe **a)** *o. Pl.* running; **b)** *(Sport: Wettrennen)* heat; **c)** *o. Pl. (Ver~)* course; im ~[e] der Zeit in the course of time; im ~[e] der Jahre/des Tages over the years/during the day; **d)** *(von Schußwaffen)* barrel; **Lauf·bahn** die **a)** *(Werdegang)* career; **b)** *(Leichtathletik)* running-track; **laufen 1.** *unr. itr. V.; mit sein* **a)** run; *(beim Eislauf)* skate; *(beim Ski~)* ski; *(gehen)* go; *(zu Fuß gehen)* walk; in *(Akk.)*/gegen etw. ~: walk into sth.; **dauernd zum Arzt ~** *(ugs.)* keep running to the doctor; **b)** *(im Gang sein)* ⟨*machine*⟩ be running; *(radio, television, etc.)* be on; *(funktionie-*

ren) ⟨*machine*⟩ run; ⟨*radio, television, etc.*⟩ work; **c)** *(gelten)* ⟨*contract, agreement, engagement, etc.*⟩ run; **d)** *(gespielt werden)* ⟨*programme, play, etc.*⟩ be on; **2.** *unr. tr. u. itr. V.* **a)** *mit sein (zurücklegen)* ⟨*zu Fuß*⟩ walk; *(rennen)* run; **b)** *mit sein (erzielen)* einen Rekord ~: set up a record; **c)** *mit haben od. sein* Ski/Schlittschuh/Rollschuh ~: ski/skate/roller-skate; **laufend 1.** *Adj.* **a)** *(ständig)* regular ⟨*interest, income*⟩; recurring ⟨*costs*⟩; **b)** *(gegenwärtig)* current ⟨*issue, year, month, etc.*⟩; **2.** *adv.* constantly; ⟨*increase*⟩ steadily; **Läufer** der; ~s, ~ **a)** *(Sport)* runner; *(Handball; Fußball veralt.)* half-back; **b)** *(Teppich) (long narrow)* carpet; **Lauf·feuer** das brush fire; wie ein ~: like wildfire

Lauf-: ~masche die ladder; ~paß der: er hat seiner Freundin den ~paß gegeben *(ugs.)* he finished with his girl-friend *(coll.)*; ~schritt der: im ~schritt, marsch, marsch! at the double, quick march!

läufst *2. Pers. Sg. Präsens v.* laufen; **Lauf·stall** der playpen; **läuft** *3. Pers. Sg. Präsens v.* laufen

Lauge die; ~, ~n **a)** soapy water; **b)** *(Chemie)* alkaline solution; **Laugen·brezel** die *(südd.)* pretzel

Laune die; ~, ~n mood; **launenhaft** *Adj.* temperamental; *(unberechenbar)* capricious; **launig** witty; **launisch** *Adj.: s.* launenhaft

Laus die; ~, Läuse louse

Laus·bub der little rascal

lauschen *itr. V.* **a)** *(horchen)* listen; **b)** *(zuhören)* listen [attentively]; **Lauscher** der; ~s, ~: eavesdropper; **lauschig** *Adj.* cosy, snug ⟨*corner*⟩

lausig 1. *Adj. (ugs.)* **a)** *(abwertend: unangenehm, schäbig)* lousy *(sl.)*; rotten *(coll.)*; **b)** *(sehr groß)* perishing *(Brit. sl.)*, freezing ⟨*cold*⟩; terrible *(coll.)* ⟨*heat*⟩; **2.** *adv.* terribly *(coll.)*

¹laut 1. *Adj.* loud; *(geräuschvoll)* noisy; **2.** *adv.* loudly; *(geräuschvoll)* noisily

²laut *Präp.* + *Gen. od. Dat. (Amtsspr.)* according to

Laut der; ~[e]s, ~e sound

Laute die; ~, ~n lute

lauten *itr. V.* ⟨*answer, instruction, slogan*⟩ be, run; ⟨*letter, passage, etc.*⟩ read, go; ⟨*law*⟩ state; **läuten 1.** *tr., itr. V.* ring; ⟨*alarm clock*⟩ go off; **2.** *itr. V. (bes. südd.: klingeln)* ring; **es läutete** the bell rang *or* went *(zu for)*

¹**lauter** *Adj.* (geh.) honourable ⟨person, intentions, etc.⟩; honest ⟨truth⟩

²**lauter** *indekl. Adj.* nothing but; sheer ⟨nonsense, joy, etc.⟩

läutern *tr. V.* (geh.) reform ⟨character⟩; purify ⟨soul⟩; **Läuterung** die ~, ~en (geh.) reformation; (der Seele) purification

laut·hals *Adv.* at the top of one's voice; ~ **lachen** roar with laughter

lautlich 1. *Adj.* phonetic; 2. *adv.* phonetically

laut-, Laut-: ~**los** 1. *Adj.* silent; soundless; (wortlos) silent; 2. *adv.* silently; soundlessly; ~**schrift** die (Phon.) phonetic alphabet; (Umschrift) phonetic transcription; ~**sprecher** der loudspeaker; (einer Stereoanlage usw.) speaker; ~**stark** 1. *Adj.* loud; vociferous, loud ⟨protest⟩; 2. *adv.* loudly ⟨protest⟩ vociferously; ~**stärke** die volume

lau·warm *Adj.* lukewarm

Lava die; ~, **Laven** (Geol.) lava

Lavendel der; ~s, ~: lavender

Lawine die; ~, ~n (auch fig.) avalanche; eine ~ von Protesten (fig.) a storm of protest; **Lawinen·gefahr** die danger of avalanches

lax 1. *Adj.* lax; 2. *adv.* laxly

Lazarett das; ~[e]s, ~e military hospital

leben *itr. V.* live; (lebendig sein) be alive; leb[e] wohl! farewell!; von seiner Rente/seinem Gehalt ~ : live on one's pension/salary; **Leben** das; ~s, ~ a) life; das ~ : life; sich (Dat.) das ~ nehmen take one's [own] life; am ~ sein/bleiben be/stay alive; ums ~ kommen lose one's life; b) (Betriebsamkeit) auf dem Markt herrschte ein reges ~ : the market was bustling with activity; das ~ auf der Straße the comings and goings in the street; **lebend** *Adj.* living; live ⟨animal⟩; **lebendig** 1. *Adj.* living; (lebhaft) lively; 2. *adv.* (lebhaft) in a lively way

lebens-, Lebens-: ~**abend** der (geh.) evening of one's life (literary); ~**art** die a) way of life; b) o. Pl. (Umgangsformen) manners pl.; ~**aufgabe** die life's work; ~**bejahend** *Adj.* ⟨person⟩ with a positive attitude to life; ~**bereich** der area of life; ~**dauer** die life-span; ~**ende** das end [of one's life]; ~**erinnerungen** Pl. memories of one's life; (aufgezeichnet) memoirs; ~**erwartung** die life expectancy; ~**fähig** *Adj.* (auch fig.)

viable; ~**freude** die; o. Pl. zest for life; ~**froh** *Adj.* full of zest for life postpos.; ~**gefahr** die mortal danger; „Achtung, ~**gefahr!**" 'danger'; ~**gefährlich** 1. *Adj.* highly dangerous; critical ⟨injury⟩; 2. *adv.* critically ⟨injured, ill⟩; ~**geister** Pl. jmds. ~**geister** [wieder] wecken put new life into sb.; ~**groß** *Adj.* life-size; ~**größe** die: eine Statue in ~**größe** a life-size statue

Lebenshaltungs·kosten Pl. cost of living sing.

lebens-, Lebens-: ~**jahr** das year of [one's] life; ~**kraft** die vitality; ~**künstler** der: ein [echter/wahrer] ~**künstler** a person who always knows how to make the best of things; ~**lage** die situation [in life]; ~**länglich** 1. *Adj.* ~**länglicher** Freiheitsentzug life imprisonment; 2. *adv.* jmdn. ~**länglich** gefangenhalten keep sb. imprisoned for life; ~**lauf** der curriculum vitae; c.v.; ~**lustig** *Adj.* ⟨person⟩ full of the joys of life

Lebens·mittel das; meist Pl. food[stuff]; ~ Pl. food sing.; **Lebensmittel·geschäft** das food shop

lebens-: ~**müde** *Adj.* weary of life pred.; ~**notwendig** *Adj.* essential; ~**raum** der a) (Umkreis) lebensraum; b) (Biol.) s. Biotop; ~**retter** der rescuer; ~**standard** der standard of living; ~**unterhalt** der: seinen ~**unterhalt** verdienen/bestreiten earn one's living/support oneself; ~**versicherung** die life insurance; ~**wandel** der way of life; ~**weg** der [journey through] life; ~**weise** die way of life; ~**zeichen** das sign of life; ~**zeit** die life[-span]; auf ~**zeit** for life

Leber die; ~, ~n liver

Leber-: ~**fleck** der liver spot; ~**käse** der; o. Pl. meat loaf made with mincemeat, [minced liver,] eggs, and spices; ~**tran** der fish-liver oil; (des Kabeljaus) cod-liver oil; ~**wurst** die liver sausage

Lebe-: ~**wesen** das living being; ~**wohl** [--'-] das; ~[e]s, ~ od. ~e (geh.) farewell

lebhaft 1. *Adj.* a) lively; busy ⟨traffic⟩; brisk ⟨business⟩; b) (deutlich) vivid ⟨idea, picture, etc.⟩; c) (kräftig) bright ⟨colour⟩; vigorous ⟨applause, opposition⟩. 2. *adv.* a) in a lively way; b) (deutlich) vividly; c) (kräftig) brightly ⟨coloured⟩

leb-, Leb-: ~kuchen der ≈ ginger-
bread; ~los Adj. lifeless; ~zeiten
Pl. bei od. ~zeiten during
sb.'s lifetime

lechzen itr. V. (geh.) nach einem
Trunk ~: long for a drink; nach Rache
usw. ~: thirst for revenge etc.

leck Adj. leaky; ~ sein leak; Leck
das; ~le|s, ~s leak

¹lecken 1. tr. V. lick; 2. itr. V. an etw.
(Dat.) ~: lick sth.

²lecken itr. V. (leck sein) leak

lecker Adj. tasty ⟨meal⟩; delicious
⟨cake etc.⟩; good ⟨smell, taste⟩; Lek-
ker·bissen der delicacy; Leckerei
die; ~, ~en (ugs.) dainty; (Süßigkeit)
sweet [meat]

led. Abk. ledig

Leder das; ~s, ~: leather; Leder-
waren Pl. leather goods

ledig Adj. single; eine ~e Mutter an
unmarried mother; Ledige der/die;
adj. Dekl. single person; lediglich
Adj. merely

leer Adj. empty; clean ⟨sheet of paper⟩;
Leere die; ~ (auch fig.) emptiness;
leeren tr., refl. V. empty

leer-, Leer-: ~gefegt Adj. deserted
⟨street, town⟩; wie ~gefegt deserted;
~lauf der; o. Pl. im ~lauf den Berg
hinunterfahren ⟨driver⟩ coast down the
hill in neutral; ⟨cyclist⟩ freewheel
down the hill; ~stehend Adj. empty,
unoccupied; ~taste die space-bar

Leerung die; ~, ~en emptying; (von
Briefkästen) collection

Lefze die; ~, ~n lip

legal 1. Adj. legal; 2. adv. legally; legalisieren tr. V. legalize; Legalität
die; ~: legality

legen 1. tr. V. a) lay [down]; b) (verlegen) lay ⟨pipe, cable, carpet, tiles,
etc.⟩; 2. tr., itr. V. ⟨hen⟩ lay; 3. refl. V.
a) lie down; b) (nachlassen) die down;
abate; ⟨enthusiasm⟩ wear off, subside

legendär Adj. legendary

Legende die; ~, ~n legend

leger [le'ʒe:ɐ̯] 1. Adj. casual; 2. adv.
casually

legieren tr. V. alloy; Legierung die;
~, ~en alloy

Legislative die; ~, ~n (Politik) legislature; Legislatur·periode die
legislative period; legitim Adj. legitimate; Legitimation [legitima-
'tsio:n] die; ~, ~en a) legitimation; b)
(Ausweis) proof of identity; legiti-
mieren 1. tr. V. a) (rechtfertigen) justify; b) (bevollmächtigen) authorize; c)

(für legitim erklären) legitimize ⟨child,
relationship⟩; 2. refl. V. show proof of
one's identity

Lehm der; ~s loam; (Ton) clay

Lehne die; ~, ~n (Rücken~) back;
(Arm~) arm; lehnen 1. tr., refl. V.
lean ⟨an + Akk., gegen against⟩; 2. itr.
V. be leaning ⟨an + Dat. against⟩;
Lehn·stuhl der armchair

Lehr·buch das textbook

Lehre die; ~, ~n a) apprenticeship; b)
(Weltanschauung) doctrine; c) (Theorie, Wissenschaft) theory; d) (Erfahrung) lesson; lehren tr., itr. V. teach;
Lehrer der; ~s, ~ (auch fig.) teacher;
(Ausbilder) instructor; Lehrerin die;
~, ~nen teacher

Lehr-: ~gang der course (für, in +
Dat. in); ~jahr das year as an apprentice; ~körper der (Amtsspr.)
teaching staff; faculty (Amer.)

Lehrling der; ~s, ~e apprentice; (in
kaufmännischen Berufen) trainee

lehr-, Lehr-: ~reich Adj. informative; ~stelle die apprenticeship; (in
kaufmännischen Berufen) trainee
post; ~stoff der (Schulw.) syllabus

Leib der; ~le|s, ~er (geh.) body;
Leib·gericht das favourite dish;
leibhaftig Adj. in person postpos.;
(echt) real; leiblich Adj. physical
⟨well-being⟩; (blutsverwandt) real

Leib-: ~schmerzen Pl. abdominal
pain sing.; ~wächter der bodyguard

Leiche die; ~, ~n [dead] body;
corpse; leichen·blaß Adj. deathly
pale; Leichnam der; ~s, ~e (geh.)
body

leicht 1. Adj. light; lightweight ⟨suit,
material⟩; easy ⟨task, question, job,
etc.⟩; slight ⟨accent, illness, wound,
doubt, etc.⟩; mild ⟨cigar, cigarette⟩; 2.
adv. lightly ⟨built⟩; (einfach, schnell,
spielend) easily; (geringfügig) slightly

leicht-, Leicht-: ~athletik die
[track and field] athletics sing.; ~fal-
len unr. itr. V.; mit sein be easy; das
fällt mir ~: its easy for me; ~fertig 1.
Adj. careless ⟨behaviour, person⟩; rash
⟨promise⟩; ill-considered, slapdash
⟨plan⟩; 2. adv. carelessly; ~gläubig
Adj. gullible

Leichtigkeit die; ~ (geringes Gewicht) lightness; (Mühelosigkeit) ease

leicht-, Leicht-: ~|machen tr. V.
jmdm./sich etw. ~machen make sth.
easy for sb./oneself; ~|nehmen unr.
tr. V. etw. ~nehmen make light of sth.;
~sinn der; o. Pl. carelessness no in-

def. art.; (mit Gefahr verbunden) recklessness *no indef. art.;* ~**sinnig 1.** *Adj.* careless; *(sich, andere gefährdend)* reckless; *(fahrlässig)* negligent; **2.** *adv.* carelessly; *(gefährlich)* recklessly; *(promise)* rashly; ~**verletzt** *Adj.; präd.* getrennt geschrieben slightly injured

leid *Adj.; nicht attr.* **a)** es tut mir ~ [, daß ...] I'm sorry [that ...]; **er tut mir ~:** I feel sorry for him; **b)** *(überdrüssig)* etw./jmdn. ~ sein/werden *(ugs.)* be/get fed up with sth./sb. *(coll.);* **Leid** das; ~[e]s **a)** *(Schmerz)* suffering; *(Kummer)* grief; sorrow; **b)** *(Böses)* harm; wrong; **leiden 1.** *unr. itr. V.* suffer **(an, unter** + *Dat.* from); **2.** *unr. tr. V.* **a)** jmdn. [gut] ~ können *od.* mögen like sb.; **b)** *(geh.: ertragen müssen)* suffer *(hunger, thirst, etc.);* **Leiden** das; ~s, ~ **a)** *(Krankheit)* illness; *(Gebrechen)* complaint; **b)** *(Qual)* suffering; **leidend** *Adj.* **a)** *(krank)* ailing; **b)** *(schmerzvoll)* strained *(voice);* martyred *(expression)*

Leidenschaft die; ~, ~en passion **(zu, für** for); **leidenschaftlich 1.** *Adj.* passionate; vehement *(protest);* **2.** *adv.* passionately; *(eifrig)* dedicatedly; **etw.** ~ gern tun adore doing sth.

leider *Adv.* unfortunately; **leidig** *Adj.* tiresome; **leidlich** *Adj.* reasonable

Leier die; ~, ~n lyre

leihen *unr. tr. V.* **a)** jmdm. etw. ~: lend sb. sth.; **b)** *(entleihen)* borrow

Leih-: ~**gebühr** die hire *or (Amer.)* rental charge; *(bei Büchern)* borrowing fee; ~**haus** das pawnbroker's; pawnshop; ~**mutter** die surrogate mother; ~**wagen** der hire *or (Amer.)* rental car

Leim der; ~[e]s glue; **leimen** *tr. V.* glue **(an** + *Akk.* to)

Leine die; ~, ~n rope; *(Wäsche~, Angel~)* line; *(Hunde~)* lead *(esp. Brit.);* leash; **Leinen** das; ~s **a)** *(Gewebe)* linen; **b)** *(Buchw.)* cloth; **Lein·wand** die **a)** *o. Pl.* linen; *(grob)* canvas; **b)** *(des Malers)* canvas; **c)** *(für Filme und Dias)* screen

leise 1. *Adj.* **a)** quiet; soft *(steps, music, etc.);* **b)** *(leicht)* faint; slight; slight, gentle *(touch);* **2.** *adv.* **a)** quietly; **b)** *(leicht; kaum merklich)* slightly; *(touch, rain)* gently

Leiste die; ~, ~n strip; *(Holz~)* batten; *(profiliert)* moulding

leisten 1. *tr. V.* do *(work);* *(schaffen)* achieve *(a lot, nothing);* **jmdm.** Hilfe ~: help sb.; **2.** *refl. V. (ugs.)* sich *(Dat.)* etw. ~: treat oneself to sth.; sich *(Dat.)* etw. [nicht] ~ können [not] be able to afford sth.; **Leistung** die; ~, ~en **a)** *o. Pl. (Qualität bzw. Quantität der Arbeit)* performance; **b)** *(Errungenschaft)* achievement; *(im Sport)* performance; **c)** *o. Pl. (Leistungsvermögen, Physik: Arbeits~)* power; **d)** *(Zahlung, Zuwendung)* payment; *(Versicherungsw.)* benefit; **e)** *(Dienst~)* service

leistungs-, Leistungs-: ~**fähig** *Adj.* capable *(person);* *(körperlich)* able-bodied; ~**gesellschaft** die competitive society; ~**prinzip** das; *o. Pl.* competitive principle; ~**sport** der competitive sport *no art.*

Leit·artikel der *(Zeitungsw.)* leading article; **leiten** *tr. V.* **a)** *(anführen)* lead; head; be head of *(school);* *(verantwortlich sein für)* be in charge of *(project, expedition, etc.);* manage *(factory, enterprise);* *(den Vorsitz führen bei)* chair; conduct *(orchestra, choir);* ~**der Angestellter** manager; **b)** *(begleiten, führen)* lead; **c)** *(lenken)* direct; route *(traffic);* *(um~)* divert; **¹Leiter** der; ~s, ~: leader; *(einer Abteilung)* head; *(eines Instituts)* director; *(einer Schule)* head teacher; headmaster *(Brit.);* principal *(esp. Amer.);* *(Vorsitzender)* chair[man]

²Leiter die; ~, ~n ladder

Leiterin die; ~, ~nen s. ¹**Leiter;** *(einer Schule)* head teacher; headmistress *(Brit.);* principal *(esp. Amer.)*

Leit·planke die crash barrier; guardrail *(Amer.)*

Leitung die; ~, ~en **a)** *o. Pl. s.* leiten **a:** leading; heading; being in charge of; management; chairing; **b)** *o. Pl. (einer Expedition usw.)* leadership; *(Verantwortung)* responsibility *(Gen.* for); *(eines Betriebes, Unternehmens)* management; *(einer Sitzung, Diskussion)* chairmanship; **c)** *(leitende Personen)* management; *(einer Schule)* head and senior staff; **d)** *(Rohr~)* pipe; *(Haupt~)* main; **e)** *(Draht, Kabel)* cable; *(für ein Gerät)* lead; **f)** *(Telefon~)* line

Leitungs·wasser das tap-water

Lektion [lɛkˈtsi̯oːn] die; ~, ~en lesson; **Lektüre** die; ~, ~en **a)** *o. Pl.* reading; **b)** *(Lesestoff)* reading [matter]

Lende die; ~, ~n loin

lenken tr. V. **a)** auch itr. steer; be at the controls of ⟨aircraft⟩; guide ⟨missile⟩; ⟨fahren⟩ drive ⟨car etc.⟩; **b)** direct ⟨thoughts etc.⟩ (**auf** + Akk. to); turn ⟨attention⟩ (**auf** + Akk. to); **c)** ⟨kontrollieren⟩ control ⟨person, press, economy⟩; govern ⟨state⟩; **Lenker** der; ~s, ~ **a)** handlebars pl.; **b)** (Fahrer) driver

Lenk-: ~**rad** das steering-wheel; ~**stange** die handlebars pl.

Lenz der; ~es, ~e (dichter. veralt.) spring

Leopard der; ~en, ~en leopard

Lepra die; ~: leprosy no art.

Lerche die; ~, ~n lark

lernen 1. itr. V. study; (als Lehrling) train; **2.** tr. V. learn (**aus** from)

lesbar Adj. legible; (klar) lucid ⟨style⟩; (verständlich) comprehensible

Lesbe die; ~, ~n (ugs.) Lesbian; **Lesbierin** ['lɛsbjərin] die; ~, ~nen Lesbian; **lesbisch** Adj. Lesbian

Lese·buch das reader; ¹**lesen** unr. tr., itr. V. read; ²**lesen** unr. tr. V. **a)** pick ⟨grapes, berries, fruit⟩; gather ⟨firewood⟩; **Ähren** ~: glean [ears of corn]; **b)** (aussondern) pick over; **Leser** der; ~s, ~, **Leserin** die; ~, ~nen reader; **leserlich 1.** Adj. legible; **2.** adv. legibly; **Lese·zeichen** das bookmark; **Lesung** die; ~, ~en reading

Lette der; ~n, ~n, **Lettin** die; ~, ~nen Latvian; **lettisch** Adj. Latvian; Lettish ⟨language⟩; **Lett·land** (das); ~s Latvia

Letzt: zu guter ~: in the end; **letzt...** Adj. last; ~**en Endes** in the end; (äußerst...) ultimate; (neuest...) latest ⟨news⟩; **letzte·mal: das** ~: [the] last time; **letzten·mal: beim** ~: last time; **zum** ~: for the last time; **letzter...** Adj. latter; **letztlich** Adv. ultimately; in the end

Leuchte die; ~, ~n light; **leuchten** itr. V. **a)** ⟨moon, sun, star, etc.⟩ be shining; ⟨fire, face⟩ glow; **b)** shine a/the light; **jmdm.** ~: light the way for sb.; **leuchtend** Adj. **a)** shining ⟨eyes⟩; brilliant ⟨colours⟩; bright ⟨blue, red, etc.⟩; **b)** (großartig) shining ⟨example⟩; **Leuchter** der; ~s, ~: candelabrum; (für eine Kerze) candlestick

Leucht-: ~**reklame** die neon sign; ~**turm** der lighthouse; ~**zifferblatt** das luminous dial

leugnen 1. tr. V. deny; **2.** itr. V. deny it

Leukämie die; ~, ~n (Med.) leukaemia

Leumund der; ~[e]s (geh.) reputation

Leute Pl. people; **die reichen/alten** ~: the rich/the old

Leutnant der; ~s, ~s second lieutenant (Milit.)

leut·selig 1. Adj. affable; **2.** adv. affably

Lexikon das; ~s, **Lexika** od. **Lexiken** encyclopaedia (Gen., für of)

Libanese der; ~n, ~n, **Libanesin** die; ~, ~nen Lebanese; **Libanon** (das) od. der; ~s Lebanon

Libelle die; ~, ~n dragon-fly

liberal 1. Adj. liberal; **2.** adv. liberally; **Liberale** die/der; adj. Dekl. liberal; **liberalisieren** tr. V. liberalize; relax ⟨import controls⟩

Libero der; ~s, ~s (Fußball) sweeper

Libyen (das); ~s Libya; **libysch** Adj. Libyan

licht Adj. **a)** light; **b)** (dünn bewachsen) sparse; thin; **Licht** das; ~[e]s, ~er **a)** o. Pl. light; **b)** (elektrisches ~) light; **c)** Pl. auch ~**e** ⟨Kerze⟩ candle; **Licht·bild** das [small] photograph (for passport etc.); **licht·empfindlich** Adj. sensitive to light; ¹**lichten 1.** tr. V. thin out ⟨trees etc.⟩; **2.** refl. V. ⟨trees⟩ thin out; ⟨hair⟩ grow thin; ⟨fog, mist⟩ lift

²**lichten** tr. V. (Seemannsspr.) **den/die Anker** ~: weigh anchor

lichterloh 1. Adj. blazing ⟨fire⟩; leaping ⟨flames⟩; **2.** adv. ~ **brennen** be blazing fiercely

Licht-: ~**hupe** die headlight flasher; ~**reklame** die neon sign; ~**schalter** der light-switch

Lichtung die; ~, ~en clearing

Lid das; ~[e]s, ~er eyelid

lieb 1. Adj. **a)** (liebevoll) kind ⟨words, gesture⟩; **b)** (liebenswert) likeable; nice; (stärker) lovable ⟨child, girl, pet⟩; ~ **aussehen** look sweet or (Amer.) cute; **c)** (artig) good ⟨child, dog⟩; **d)** (geschätzt) dear; **sein liebstes Spielzeug** his favourite toy; ~**er Hans/~e Else!** (am Briefanfang) dear Hans/Else; **e)** (angenehm) welcome; **es wäre mir ~/~er, wenn ...:** I should be glad/should prefer it if ...; **2.** adv. **a)** (liebenswert) kindly; **b)** (artig) nicely; **Liebe** die; ~, ~**n a)** o. Pl. love; ~ **zu jmdm./zu etw.** love for sb./of sth.; **aus** ~ [**zu jmdm.**] for love [of sb.]; **tu mir die** ~ **und ...:** do me a favour and ...; **mit** ~: lovingly; with loving care; **b)** (ugs.:

geliebter Mensch) love; **Liebelei** die; ~, ~en flirtation; **lieben** 1. *tr. V.* a) **jmdn.** ~: love sb.; *(sexuell)* make love to sb.; **sich** ~: be in love; *(sexuell)* make love; b) **etw.** ~: be fond of sth.; *(stärker)* love sth.; 2. *itr. V.* be in love; **liebend** *Adv.* etw. ~ **gern tun** [simply] love doing sth.; **liebens·würdig** *Adj.* kind; charming *(smile)*; **lieber** *Adv.* a) *s.* **gern**; b) better; **laß das** ~: better not do that

Liebes-: ~**brief** der love-letter; ~**paar** das courting couple; ~**roman** der romantic novel

liebe·voll 1. *Adj.* loving *attrib. (care)*; affectionate *(embrace, gesture, person)*; 2. *adv.* lovingly; affectionately; *(mit Sorgfalt)* lovingly; **lieb|haben** *unr. tr. V.* love; *(gern haben)* be fond of; **Liebhaber** der; ~s, ~ a) lover; b) *(Interessierter, Anhänger)* enthusiast *(Gen.* for); *(Sammler)* collector; **lieblich** 1. *Adj.* a) charming; *(angenehm)* sweet *(scent, sound)*; 2. *adv.* sweetly; *(angenehm)* pleasingly; **Liebling** der; ~s, ~e *(bes. als Anrede)* darling; *(bevorzugte Person)* favourite; **Lieblings-** favourite; **lieb·los** 1. *Adj.* loveless. 2. *adv.* a) without affection; *(ohne Sorgfalt)* without proper care; **liebsten: am** ~: *s.* **gern**

Liechtenstein (das); ~s Liechtenstein

Lied das; ~[e]s, ~er song

liederlich *Adj.* slovenly; messy *(hairstyle, person)*

Lieder-: ~**macher** der; ~s, ~, ~**macherin** der; ~, ~nen singer-songwriter

lief *1. u. 3. Pers. Sg. Prät. v.* **laufen**

Lieferant der; ~en, ~en supplier; **lieferbar** *Adj.* available; *(vorrätig)* in stock; **liefern** *tr. V.* a) *(bringen)* deliver **(an** + Akk. to); *(zur Verfügung stellen)* supply; b) *(hervorbringen)* produce; provide *(eggs, honey, examples, raw material, etc.)*

Liefer-: ~**schein** der delivery note; ~**termin** der delivery date

Lieferung die; ~, ~en delivery

Liefer-: ~**wagen** der [delivery] van; ~**zeit** die delivery time

Liege die; ~, ~n day-bed; *(zum Ausklappen)* bed-settee; *(als Gartenmöbel)* sun-lounger; **liegen** *unr. itr. V.* lie; *(person)* be lying down; *(sich befinden)* be; *(object)* be [lying]; *(town, house, etc.)* be [situated]; **im Bett** ~:

lie in bed; **das liegt an ihm** *od.* **bei ihm** it is up to him; *(ist seine Schuld)* it is his fault; **es liegt mir nicht** it doesn't suit me; *(es spricht mich nicht an)* it doesn't appeal to me; *(ich mag es nicht)* I don't like it; **daran liegt ihm viel/wenig/nichts** he sets great/little/ no store by that

liegen-: ~**|bleiben** *unr. itr. V.; mit sein* a) stay [lying]; **[im Bett]** ~: stay in bed; b) *(things)* stay, be left; *(vergessen werden)* be left behind; *(nicht erledigt werden)* be left undone; ~**|lassen** *unr. tr. V.* a) leave; *(vergessen)* leave [behind]; b) *(unerledigt lassen)* leave *(work)* undone; leave *(letters)* unposted/unopened

Liege-: ~**stuhl** der deck-chair; ~**wagen** der couchette car

lieh *1. u. 3. Pers. Sg. Prät. v.* **leihen**

lies *Imperativ Sg. v.* **lesen**

ließ *1. u. 3. Pers. Sg. Prät. v.* **lassen**

liest *3. Pers. Sg. Präsens v.* **lesen**

Lift der; ~[e]s, ~e *od.* ~s a) lift *(Brit.)*; elevator *(Amer.)*; b) *Pl.:* ~e *(Ski-, Sessel~)* lift

Liga die; ~, **Ligen** league; *(Sport)* division

Likör der; ~s, ~e liqueur

lila *indekl. Adj.* mauve; *(dunkel~)* purple; **Lila** das; ~s *od. (ugs.)* ~s mauve; *(Dunkel~)* purple

Lilie ['li:liə] die; ~, ~n lily

Liliputaner der; ~s, ~: dwarf

Limit das; ~s, ~s limit

Limo die, *auch:* das; ~, ~[s] *(ugs.)* fizzy drink; **Limonade** die; ~, ~n fizzy drink; *(Zitronen~)* lemonade

Linde die; ~, ~n lime[-tree]

lindern *tr. V.* relieve *(suffering, pain)*; slake *(thirst)*

Lineal das; ~s, ~e ruler

Linie ['li:niə] die; ~, ~n line; *(Verkehrsstrecke)* route; **die** ~ **12** *(Verkehrsw.)* the number 12; **auf die [schlanke]** ~ **achten** *(ugs. scherzh.)* watch one's figure; **auf der ganzen** ~ *(fig.)* all along the line

linien-, Linien-: ~**bus** der regular bus; ~**flug** der scheduled flight; ~**richter** der *(Fußball usw.)* linesman; *(Tennis)* line judge; *(Rugby)* touch judge; ~**treu** 1. *Adj.* loyal to the party line *postpos.;* 2. *adv. (act)* in accordance with the party line

linieren, liniieren *tr. V.* rule

link... *Adj.* a) left; b) *(innen, nicht sichtbar)* wrong, reverse *(side)*; c) *(in der Politik)* left-wing; **linkisch** 1.

Adj. awkward; **2.** *adv.* awkwardly; **links** *Adv.* on the left; *(Politik)* on the left wing

links-, Links-: ~**abbieger** der *(Verkehrsw.)* motorist/cyclist/car etc. turning left; ~**außen** der; ~, ~ *(Ballspiele)* left wing; outside left; ~**händer** der; ~s, ~: left-hander; ~**kurve** die left-hand bend; ~**verkehr** der driving *no art.* on the left

Linoleum das; ~s linoleum; lino

Linse die; ~, ~n **a)** *(Bot., Kochk.)* lentil; **b)** *(Med., Optik)* lens

Lippe die; ~, ~n lip; **Lippen·stift** der lipstick

liquid *Adj.* *(Wirtsch.)* liquid *(funds, resources);* solvent *(business);* **liquidieren** *(verhüll.: töten; Wirtsch.)* liquidate

lispeln *itr. V.* lisp

Lissabon (das); ~s Lisbon

List die; ~, ~en **a)** [cunning] trick; **b)** *(listige Art)* o. *Pl.* cunning

Liste die; ~, ~n list; **schwarze ~:** blacklist

listig 1. *Adj.* cunning; crafty; **2.** *adv.* cunningly; craftily

Litauen (das); ~s Lithuania; **Litauer** der; ~s, ~: Lithuanian; **litauisch** *Adj.* Lithuanian

Liter der, *auch:* das; ~s, ~: litre

literarisch *Adj.* literary; **Literatur** die; ~, ~en literature

Litfaß·säule die advertising column

Lithographie die; ~, ~n *(Druck)* lithograph

litt *1. u. 3. Pers. Sg. Prät. v.* leiden

Litze die; ~, ~n braid

Lizenz die; ~, ~en licence

Lkw, LKW [εlka:'ve:] der; ~[s], ~[s] *Abk.* Lastkraftwagen truck; lorry *(Brit.)*

Lob das; ~[e]s, ~e praise *no indef. art.*

Lobby ['lɔbi] die; ~, ~s *od.* Lobbies lobby

loben *tr.V.* praise; **löblich** *Adj.* commendable; **Lob·lied** das song of praise

Loch das; ~[e]s, Löcher hole; **lochen** *tr. V.* punch holes/a hole in; punch *(ticket);* **Locher** der; ~s, ~: punch; **löcherig** *Adj.* full of holes *pred.*

Locke die; ~, ~n curl

locken *tr. V.* **a)** lure; **b)** *(reizen)* tempt **Locken·wickler** der [hair] curler

locker 1. *Adj.* loose; *(entspannt)* relaxed *(position, muscles);* slack *(rope, rein);* **2.** *adv.* ~ sitzen *(tooth, screw, nail)* be loose; *(entspannt, ungezwun-*

gen) loosely; **locker|lassen** *unr. itr. V. (ugs.)* **nicht** ~: not give up; **lockern 1.** *tr. V.* loosen; slacken [off] *(rope etc.);* relax *(muscles, limbs);* **2.** *refl. V. (brick, tooth, etc.)* work itself loose; *(person)* loosen up

lockig *Adj.* curly

Lock·vogel der decoy

Loden·mantel der loden coat

Löffel der; ~s, ~: spoon; *(als Maßangabe)* spoonful; *(Jägerspr.)* ear; **löffeln** *tr. V.* spoon [up]

log *1. u. 3. Pers. Sg. Prät. v.* lügen

Logarithmus der; ~, Logarithmen *(Math.)* logarithm; log

Loge ['lo:ʒə] die; ~, ~n box; **logieren** *itr. V. (veralt.)* stay

Logik die; ~: logic; **logisch 1.** *Adj.* logical; **2.** *adv.* logically

Lohn der; ~[e]s, Löhne **a)** wage[s *pl.*]; pay *no indef. art., no pl.;* **b)** o. *Pl. (Belohnung)* reward; **Lohn·büro** das payroll office

lohnen 1. *refl., itr. V.* be worth it; **2.** *tr. V.* be worth; **lohnend** *Adj.* rewarding

Lohn·steuer die income tax; **Lohnsteuer·karte** die income-tax card; **Lohn·tüte** die pay-packet *(Brit.);* wage packet

Lokal das; ~s, ~e pub *(Brit. coll.);* bar *(Amer.);* *(Speise~)* restaurant; **Lokalität** die; ~, ~en locality

Lokal-: ~**blatt** das local paper; ~**termin** der *(Rechtsspr.)* visit to the scene [of the crime]

Lokomotive [lokomo'ti:və] die; ~, ~n locomotive; **Lokomotiv·führer** der engine-driver *(Brit.);* engineer *(Amer.)*

Lokus der; ~ *od.* ~ses, ~ *od.* ~se *(salopp)* loo *(Brit. coll.);* john *(Amer. coll.)*

London (das); ~s London; **Londoner 1.** *indekl. Adj.* London; **2.** der; ~s, ~: Londoner

Lorbeer der; ~s, ~en **a)** laurel; **b)** *(Gewürz)* bay-leaf

Lore die; ~, ~n car; *(kleiner)* tub

los 1. *Adj.* **a)** *(gelöst, ab)* off; **b)** es ist etwas ~: there is something going on; **c)** jmdn./etw. ~ sein be rid of sb./sth.; **2.** *Adv.* *(als Aufforderung)* come on!

Los das; ~es, ~e **a)** lot; **b)** *(Lotterie~)* ticket

Lösch·blatt das piece of blotting-paper; **löschen** *tr. V.* **a)** put out; extinguish; **seinen Durst ~** *(fig.)* quench one's thirst; **b)** *(tilgen)* delete *(entry);* erase *(recording, memory, etc.);* **Lösch·papier** das blotting paper

lose 1. *Adj.* loose; 2. *adv.* loosely

Lose·geld das ransom

losen *itr. V.* draw lots **(um for)**

lösen 1. *tr. V.* **a)** remove ⟨*stamp, wall-paper*⟩; **etw. von etw. ~:** remove sth. from sth.; **b)** (*lockern*) undo ⟨*screw, belt, tie*⟩; **c)** (*klären*) solve; resolve ⟨*contradiction, conflict*⟩; **d)** (*annullieren*) break of ⟨*engagement*⟩; cancel ⟨*contract*⟩; sever ⟨*relationship*⟩; **e)** (*kaufen*) buy, obtain ⟨*ticket*⟩; 2. *refl. V.* **a)** (*lose werden*) come off; (*sich lockern*) ⟨*wallpaper, plaster*⟩ come off; ⟨*packing, screw*⟩ come loose; **b)** (*sich klären*) ⟨*puzzle, problem*⟩ be solved; **c)** (*sich auflösen*) dissolve

los-: **~fahren** *unr. itr. V.*; *mit sein* set off; (*wegfahren*) move off; **~gehen** *unr. itr. V.*; *mit sein* **a)** (*aufbrechen*) set off; **b)** (*ugs.: beginnen*) start; **c)** (*ugs.: abgehen*) ⟨*button, handle, etc.*⟩ come off; **~kommen** *unr. itr. V.*; *mit sein* (*ugs.*) **a)** get away; **b)** (*freikommen*) get free; **~lassen** *unr. tr. V.* **a)** (*nicht festhalten*) let go of; **b)** (*freilassen*) let ⟨*person, animal*⟩ go; **~legen** *itr. V.* (*ugs.*) get going

löslich *Adj.* soluble

los-: **~machen** 1. *tr. V.* (*ugs.*) let ⟨*animal*⟩ loose; untie ⟨*string, line, rope*⟩; unhitch ⟨*trailer*⟩; **~reißen** *unr. V.* break free *or* loose; **~sagen** *refl. V.* **sich von jmdm./etw. ~sagen** break with sb./sth.; **~schlagen** *unr. itr. V.* (*bes. Milit.*) attack; launch one's attack

Losung die; ~, ~en slogan; (*Milit.: Kennwort*) password

Lösung die; ~, ~en **a)** solution ⟨*Gen., für* to⟩; **b)** *s.* lösen 1 d: breaking off; cancellation; severing

los|werden *unr. tr. V.*; *mit sein* get rid of

Lot das; ~[e]s, ~e plumb[-bob] **[nicht] im ~ sein** be [out of] plumb

löten *tr. V.* solder

Lotion [lo'tsjo:n] die; ~, ~en lotion

Lotse der; ~n, ~n (*Seew.*) pilot; **lotsen** *tr. V.* guide

Lotterie die; ~, ~n lottery; **Lotto** das; ~s, ~s national lottery

Lotto-: **~schein** der national-lottery coupon; **~zahlen** *Pl.* winning national-lottery numbers

Löwe der; ~n, ~n **a)** lion; **b)** (*Astrol.*) Leo; the Lion

Löwen-: **~anteil** der lion's share, **~mäulchen** das snapdragon; **~zahn** der dandelion

Löwin die; ~, ~nen lioness

loyal [loa'ja:l] 1. *Adj.* loyal; 2. *adv.* loyally; **Loyalität** die; ~: loyalty

LP [el'pe:] die; ~, ~[s] *Abk.* Langspielplatte LP

Luchs der; ~es, ~e lynx

Lücke die; ~, ~n gap; **Lücken·büßer** der; ~s, ~ (*ugs.*) stopgap; **lückenhaft** *Adj.* sketchy; **lückenlos** *Adj.* complete

lud 1. *u.* 3. *Pers. Sg. Prät. v.* laden

Luft die; ~, Lüfte air; **an die frische ~ gehen** get out in[to] the fresh air; **die ~ anhalten** hold one's breath; **tief ~ holen** take a deep breath; **in die ~ gehen** (*fig. ugs.*) blow one's top (*coll.*)

luft-, Luft-: **~ballon** der balloon; **~brücke** die airlift; **~dicht** *Adj.* airtight; **~druck** der **a)** (*Physik*) air pressure; **b)** (*Druckwelle*) blast

lüften 1. *tr. V.* **a)** air ⟨*room, clothes, etc.*⟩; **b)** raise ⟨*hat*⟩; **c)** disclose ⟨*secret*⟩; 2. *itr. V.* air the room/house etc.

luft-, Luft-: **~fahrt** die; *o. Pl.* aviation *no art.*; **~feuchtigkeit** die [atmospheric] humidity; **~gekühlt** *Adj.* air-cooled; **~gewehr** das air rifle; airgun

luftig *Adj.* airy ⟨*room, building, etc.*⟩; light ⟨*clothes*⟩

Luftkissen·boot das hovercraft

luft-, Luft-: **~leer** *Adj.* **ein ~leerer Raum** a vacuum; **~linie** die *o. Pl.* **1 000 km ~linie** 1,000 km. as the crow flies; **~loch** das air-hole; **~matratze** die air-bed; air mattress; Lilo (*P*); **~pirat** der [aircraft] hijacker; **~post** die airmail; **etw. per** *od.* **mit ~post schicken** send sth. [by] airmail; **~pumpe** die air pump; (*für Fahrrad*) [bicycle-]pump; **~röhre** die (*Anat.*) windpipe; **~schiff** das airship; **~schloß** das castle in the air; **~schutz** der air-raid protection *no art.*; **~schutz·keller** der air-raid shelter; **~verschmutzung** die air pollution; **~waffe** die air force

Lüge die; ~, ~n lie; **lügen** 1. *itr., tr. V.* lie; **das ist gelogen!** that's a lie!; **Lügner** der; ~s, ~: liar

Luke die; ~, ~n (*Dach~*) skylight; (*bei Schiffen*) hatch; (*Keller~*) trap-door

lukrativ 1. *Adj.* lucrative; 2. *adv.* lucratively

Lümmel der; ~s, ~: lout; (*ugs., fam.: Bengel*) rascal

Lump der; ~en, ~en scoundrel; **lumpen** (*ugs.*) *tr. V.* **sich nicht ~ lassen** splash out (*coll.*); **Lumpen** der; ~s,

~: rag; **Lumpen·sammler** der rag-and-bone man

Lunge die; ~, ~n lungs *pl.*

Lungen-: ~**entzündung** die pneumonia *no indef. art.*; ~**krebs** der lung cancer; ~**zug** der inhalation

Lunte die; ~, ~n fuse; match

Lupe die; ~, ~n magnifying glass

Lurch der; ~|e|s, ~e amphibian

Lust die; ~ a) ~ **haben**, etw. zu tun feel like doing sth.; b) *(Vergnügen)* pleasure; joy; **lustig 1.** *Adj.* a) merry; jolly; enjoyable ⟨*time*⟩; b) *(komisch)* funny; 2. *adv.* a) merrily; b) *(komisch)* funnily

lust-, Lust-: ~**los 1.** *Adj.* listless; 2. *adv.* listlessly; ~**spiel** das comedy

lutherisch *Adj.* Lutheran

lutschen 1. *tr. V.* suck; 2. *itr. V.* suck; **an** etw. *(Dat.)* ~: suck sth.

Luxemburg (das); ~s Luxembourg

luxuriös 1. *Adj.* luxurious; 2. *adv.* luxuriously; **Luxus** der; ~: luxury

Lymph·knoten der lymph node

lynchen *tr. V.* lynch

Lyrik die; ~: lyric poetry; **lyrisch** *Adj.* lyrical; lyric ⟨*poetry*⟩

Lyzeum das; ~s, Lyzeen girls' high school

M

m, M [ɛm] das; ~, ~: m/M

m *Abk.* Meter m

machen 1. *tr. V.* a) make; **aus Plastik/ Holz** *usw.* **gemacht** made of plastic/ wood *etc.*; **sich** *(Dat.)* **etw.** ~ **lassen** have sth. made; **etw. aus jmdm.** ~: make sb. into sth.; **jmdn. zum Präsidenten** *usw.* ~: make sb. president *etc.*; **jmdm./sich |einen| Kaffee** ~: make [some] coffee for sb./oneself; b) *(verursachen)* **jmdm. Arbeit** ~: make [extra] work for sb.; **das macht das Wetter** that's [because of] the weather; c) *(ausführen)* do ⟨*job, repair, etc.*⟩; **einen Spaziergang** ~: go for a walk; **eine Reise** ~: go on a journey; **einen Besuch |bei jmdm.|** ~: pay [sb.] a visit; d) *(tun)* do; **was machst du da?**

what are you doing?; **so etwas macht man nicht** that [just] isn't done; e) **was macht ...?** *(wie ist es um ... bestellt?)* how is ...?; **was macht die Gesundheit/ Arbeit?** how are you keeping/ how ist the job [getting on]?; f) *(ergeben) (beim Rechnen)* be; *(bei Geldbeträgen)* come to; **zwei mal zwei macht vier** two times two is four; **das macht 12 DM** that is 12 marks; *(Endsumme)* that comes to 12 marks; g) *(schaden)* **was macht das schon?** what does it matter?; **macht nichts!** *(ugs.)* it doesn't matter; h) *(teilnehmen an)* **einen Kursus** od. **Lehrgang** ~: take a course; i) **mach's gut!** *(ugs.)* look after yourself!; *(auf Wiedersehen)* so long!; 2. *refl. V.* a) **sich an** etw. *(Akk.)* ~: get down to sth.; b) *(ugs.: sich entwickeln)* do well; c) **mach dir nichts daraus!** *(ugs.)* don't let it bother you; 3. *itr. V.* a) **mach schon!** *(ugs.)* get a move on! *(coll.)*; b) **das macht hungrig/durstig** it makes you hungry/thirsty; **das macht dick** it's fattening; **Machenschaften** *Pl.* *(abwertend)* wheeling and dealing *sing.*

Macht die; ~, Mächte power; **an die** ~ **kommen** come to power; **Macht·haber** der; ~s, ~: ruler; **mächtig 1.** *Adj.* a) powerful; b) *(beeindruckend groß)* mighty; 2. *adv.* *(ugs.)* terribly *(coll.)*

macht-, Macht-: ~**kampf** der power struggle; ~**los** *Adj.* powerless; **gegen etw.** ~ **los sein** be powerless in the face of sth.; ~**probe** die trial of strength

Mädchen das; ~s, ~ a) girl; b) *(Haus~)* maid; **mädchenhaft** *Adj.* girlish; **Mädchen·name** der a) girl's name; b) *(Name vor der Ehe)* maiden name

Made die; ~, ~n maggot; **madig** *Adj.* maggoty; **jmdn./etw.** ~ **machen** *(ugs.)* run sb./sth. down

Madonna die; ~, Madonnen madonna

mag *1. u. 3. Pers. Sg. Präsens v.* mögen

Magazin das; ~s, ~e a) *(Lager)* store; *(für Waren)* stock-room; b) *(für Patronen, Dias, Film usw.; Zeitschrift)* magazine

Magen der; ~s, Mägen od. ~: stomach

magen-, Magen-: ~**bitter** der; ~s, ~: bitters *pl.*; ~**schmerzen** *Pl.* stomach-ache *sing.*

mager *Adj.* a) thin; b) *(fettarm)* low-fat; low in fat *pred.*; lean ⟨*meat*⟩; c) *(fig.)* poor ⟨*soil, harvest*⟩; meagre ⟨*profit, increase, success, report, etc.*⟩; thin ⟨*programme*⟩

Mager-: ~milch die skim[med] milk; **~quark** der low-fat curd cheese

Magie die; ~: magic; **Magier** ['ma:gi̯ɐ] der; ~s, ~ *(auch fig.)* magician; **magisch** Adj. magic ⟨*powers*⟩; *(geheimnisvoll)* magical

Magistrat der; ~[e]s, ~e City Council

Magnet der; ~en od. ~[e]s, ~e magnet; **magnetisch 1.** Adj. magnetic; **2.** adv. magnetically; **Magnetismus** der; ~: magnetism; **Magnet·nadel** die [compass] needle

Mahagoni das; ~s mahogany

Mäh·drescher der combine harvester; **mähen 1.** tr. V. mow; cut ⟨*corn*⟩; **2.** itr. V. mow; *(Getreide ~)* reap

Mahl das; ~[e]s, Mähler *(geh.)* meal; repast *(formal)*

mahlen unr. tr., itr. V. grind

Mahl·zeit die meal

Mähne die; ~, ~n mane

mahnen tr. V. urge; remind ⟨*debtor*⟩

Mahn-: ~mal das memorial *(erected as a warning to future generations)*; **~schreiben** das reminder

Mahnung die; ~, ~en a) exhortation; *(Warnung)* admonition; b) s. Mahnschreiben

Mai der; ~[e]s od. ~: May

Mai~: ~baum der maypole; **~glöckchen** das lily of the valley; **~käfer** der May-bug

Mais der; ~es maize; corn *(esp. Amer.)*; *(als Gericht)* sweet corn; **Mais·kolben** der corn-cob; *(als Gericht)* corn on the cob

Majestät die; ~, ~en a) *(Titel)* Majesty; **Eure ~:** Your Majesty; b) o. Pl. *(geh.)* majesty; **majestätisch 1.** Adj. majestic; **2.** adv. majestically

Major der; ~s, ~e *(Milit.)* major

Majoran der; ~s, ~e marjoram

makaber Adj. macabre

Makedonien [make'do:ni̯ən] **(das)**; ~s Macedonia

Makel der; ~s, ~ *(geh.)* a) *(Schmach)* stigma; b) *(Fehler)* blemish; **makel·los 1.** Adj. flawless; spotless ⟨*white, cleanness*⟩; **2.** adv. immaculately; spotlessly ⟨*clean*⟩

Make-up [me:k'lap] das; ~s, ~s make-up

Makkaroni Pl. macaroni sing.

Makler der; ~s, ~: estate agent *(Brit.)*; realtor *(Amer.)*

Makrele die; ~, ~n mackerel

Makrone die; ~, ~n macaroon

mal 1. Adv. times; *(bei Flächen)* by; **2.** Partikel **komm ~ her!** come here!; **¹Mal** das; ~[e]s, ~e time; **mit einem ~[e]** all at once; **²Mal** das; ~[e]s, ~e od. Mäler *(Muttermal)* birthmark; *(braun)* mole

Malaie der; ~n, ~n Malay; **Malaysia (das)**; ~s Malaysia

Mal·buch das colouring-book; **malen** tr., itr. V. paint; decorate ⟨*flat, room, walls*⟩; **Maler** der; ~s, ~: painter; **Malerei** die; ~, ~en painting; **malerisch 1.** Adj. picturesque; **2.** adv. picturesquely

mal|nehmen unr. tr., itr. V. multiply *(mit by)*

Malz·bier das malt beer

Mama die; ~, ~s *(fam.)* mamma; **Mami** die; ~, ~s *(fam.)* mummy *(Brit. coll.)*; mommy *(Amer. coll.)*

Mammut das; ~s, ~e od. ~s mammoth

man Indefinitpron. im Nom. one; you *2nd person;* *(irgend jemand)* somebody; *(die Behörden; die Leute dort)* they pl.; *(die Menschen im allgemeinen)* people pl; **~ hat mir gesagt ...:** I was told ...

Management ['mænɪdʒmənt] das; ~s, ~s management; **managen** ['mɛnɪdʒn] tr. V. a) *(ugs.)* fix; organize; b) *(betreuen)* manage ⟨*singer, artist, player*⟩; **Manager** ['mɛnɪdʒɐ] der; ~s, ~: manager; *(eines Fußballvereins)* club secretary

manch Indefinitpron. a) attr. many a; **in** [**so**] **~er** Beziehung in many respects; b) alleinstehend ~er many a person/man; ~e Pl. some; *(viele)* many; [**so**] **~es** a number of things; *(allerhand Verschiedenes)* all kinds of things; **mancherlei** unbest. Gattungsz. a) attr. various; a number of; b) alleinstehend various things; **manch·mal** Adv. sometimes

Mandant der; ~en, ~en client

Mandarine die; ~, ~n mandarin [orange]

Mandel die; ~, ~n a) almond; b) *(Anat.)* tonsil; **Mandel·entzündung** die tonsillitis no indef. art.

Manege [ma'ne:ʒə] die; ~, ~n *(im Zirkus)* ring; *(in der Reitschule)* arena

¹Mangel der; ~s, Mängel a) o. Pl. *(Fehlen)* lack **(an** + Dat. of); *(Knappheit)* shortage, lack **(an** + Dat. of); b) *(Fehler)* defect

²Mangel die; ~, ~n [large] mangle

mangelhaft 1. *Adj.* faulty ⟨*goods, German, English, etc.*⟩; *(unzulänglich)* inadequate ⟨*knowledge, lighting*⟩; *(Schulw.)* **die Note „~"** the mark 'unsatisfactory'; *(bei Prüfungen)* the fail mark; **2.** *adv.* faultily; *(unzulänglich)* inadequately; **¹mangeln** *itr. V.*; *unpers.* **es mangelt an etw.** *(Dat.) (etw. fehlt)* there is a lack of sth.; *(etw. ist unzureichend vorhanden)* there is a shortage of sth.; **jmdm./einer Sache mangelt es an etw.** *(Dat.)* sb./sth. lacks sth.

²mangeln *tr. V.* mangle

mangels *Präp. mit Gen.* in the absence of

Manie die; ~, ~n mania

Manier die; ~, ~en a) manner; b) *Pl.* *(Umgangsformen)* manners; **manierlich 1.** *Adj.* a) *(fam.)* well-mannered; well-behaved ⟨*child*⟩; b) *(ugs.: einigermaßen gut)* decent; **2.** *adv.* a) *(fam.)* nicely; b) *(ugs.: einigermaßen gut)* **ganz/recht ~:** quite/really nicely

Manifest das; ~[e]s, ~e manifesto

Maniküre die; ~: manicure; **maniküren** *tr. V.* manicure

manipulieren *tr. V.* manipulate; rig ⟨*election result etc.*⟩

Manko das; ~s, ~s shortcoming; deficiency

Mann der; ~[e]s, **Männer** a) man; b) *(Ehemann)* husband; **Männchen** das; ~s, ~ a) little man; b) *(Tier~)* male; **~ machen** ⟨*animal*⟩ sit up and beg

Mannequin ['manəkɛ̃] das; ~s, ~s mannequin; [fashion] model

mannig·fach *Adj.* multifarious

männlich 1. *Adj.* a) male; b) *s.* **maskulin 1**; **2.** *adv.* in a masculine way; **Mannschaft** die; ~, ~en *(Sport, auch fig.)* team; *(Schiffs-, Flugzeugbesatzung)* crew; *(Milit.)* unit

Manöver das; ~s, ~ a) *(Milit.)* exercise; ~ *Pl.* manœuvres; b) *(Bewegung; fig. abwertend: Trick)* manœuvre; **manövrieren** *itr. V., tr. V.* manœuvre

Mansarde die; ~, ~n attic; *(Zimmer)* attic room

Manschette die; ~, ~n cuff; **Manschetten·knopf** der cuff-link

Mantel der; ~s, **Mäntel** coat

Manuskript das; ~[e]s, ~e a) manuscript; *(Typoskript)* typescript; b) *(Notizen)* notes *pl.*

Mappe die; ~, ~n a) folder; b) *(Aktentasche)* briefcase; *(Schul~)* schoolbag

Marathon·lauf [...tɔn...] der marathon

Märchen das; ~s, ~: fairy story; fairy-tale; *(ugs.: Lüge)* [tall] story *(coll.)*; **Märchen·buch** das book of fairy stories; **märchenhaft 1.** *Adj.* magical; **2.** *adv.* magically; *(ugs.)* fantastically *(coll.)*

Margarine die; ~: margarine

Margerite die; ~, ~n ox-eye daisy

Maria (die); ~s *od. (Rel.)* **Mariä** Mary; **Marien·käfer** der ladybird

Marihuana das; ~s marijuana

Marinade die; ~, ~n *(Kochk.)* marinade; *(Salatsauce)* [marinade] dressing

Marine die; ~, ~n fleet; *(Kriegs~)* navy

Marionette die; ~, ~n puppet; marionette; **Marionetten·theater** das puppet theatre

¹Mark die; ~, ~: mark; **Deutsche ~:** Deutschmark

²Mark das; ~[e]s a) *(Knochen~)* marrow; b) *(Frucht~)* pulp

markant *Adj.* striking; prominent ⟨*figure, nose, chin*⟩; clear-cut ⟨*features, profile*⟩

Marke die; ~, ~n a) *(Waren~)* brand; *(Fabrikat)* make; b) *(Brief~, Rabatt~, Beitrags~)* stamp; c) *(Essen~)* meal-ticket; d) *(Erkennungs~)* [identification] disc; *(Dienst~)* [police] identification badge; ≈ warrant card *(Brit.)* or *(Amer.)* ID card

Marken-: **~artikel** der proprietary or *(Brit.)* branded article; **~zeichen** das trade mark

markieren *tr. V.* a) mark; b) *(ugs.: vortäuschen)* sham ⟨*illness, breakdown, etc.*⟩; **2.** *itr. V. (ugs.: simulieren)* put it on *(coll.)*; **Markierung** die; ~, ~en marking

Markt der; ~[e]s, **Märkte** market; *(~platz)* market-place or -square; **freitags ist ~:** Friday is market-day

Markt-: **~forschung** die market research *no def. art.*; **~frau** die market-woman; **~halle** die covered market; **~lücke** die gap in the market; **~platz** der market-place; **~stand** der market stall; **~wirtschaft** die market economy

Marmelade die; ~, ~n jam; *(Orangen~)* marmalade

Marmor der; ~s marble

Marokkaner der; ~s, ~: Moroccan; **marokkanisch** *Adj.* Moroccan; **Marokko (das);** ~s Morocco

Marone die; ~, ~n [sweet] chestnut

Mars der; ~: Mars *no def. art.*

Marsch der; ~[e]s, **Märsche** march; *(Wanderung)* [long] walk; **marschieren** *itr. V.; mit sein* march; *(wandern)* walk

Mars·mensch der Martian

Marter die; ~, ~n *(geh.)* torture; *(seelisch)* torment; **martern** *tr. V.* (geh.) torture

Märtyrer der; ~s, ~: martyr; **Martyrium** das; ~s, Martyrien martyrdom

Marxismus der; ~: Marxism *no art.;* **Marxist** der; ~en, ~en Marxist; **marxistisch** *Adj.* Marxist

März der; ~[es] March

Marzipan das ~s marzipan

Masche die; ~, ~n stitch; *(Lauf~)* run; ladder *(Brit.);* *(beim Netz)* mesh; **Maschen·draht** der wire netting

Maschine die; ~, ~n a) *(auch ugs.: Motorrad)* machine; b) *(ugs.: Automotor)* engine; c) *(Flugzeug)* [aero]plane; d) *(Schreib~)* typewriter; **maschine·geschrieben** *Adj.* typewritten; **maschinell** 1. *Adj.* machine *attrib.;* by machine *postpos.;* 2. *adv.* by machine; ~ hergestellt machine-made

Maschinen-: ~**gewehr** das machine-gun; ~**pistole** die sub-machine-gun

maschine|schreiben *unr. itr. V.; nur im Inf. u. Part.* type

Masern *Pl.* measles *sing. or pl.*

Maserung die; ~, ~en *(wavy)* grain

Maske die; ~, ~n mask; **Masken·ball** der the masked ball; **Maskerade** die; ~, ~n [fancy-dress] costume; **maskieren** 1. *tr. V.* mask; 2. *refl. V.* put on a mask/masks

Maskottchen das; ~s, ~: [lucky] mascot

maskulin *[auch '---]* 1. *Adj. (auch Sprachw.)* masculine; 2. *adv.* in a masculine way

maß *1. u. 3. Pers. Sg. Prät. v.* messen

¹**Maß** das; ~es, ~e a) measure *(für of);* *(fig.)* das ~ ist voll enough is enough; b) *(Größe)* measurement; c) *(Grad)* degree (an + *Dat.* of); in großem/gewissem ~e to a great/certain extent; ²**Maß** die; ~, ~[e] *(bayr., österr.)* litre [of beer]

Massage [ma'sa:ʒə] die; ~, ~n massage

Massaker das; ~s, ~: massacre

Maß-: ~**anzug** der made-to-measure suit; ~**arbeit** die a) custom-made item; *(Kleidungsstück)* made-to-

measure item; b) *(genaue Arbeit)* neat work

Masse die; ~, ~n a) mass; b) *(Gemisch)* mixture

Maß·einheit die unit of measurement

Massen·grab das mass grave; **massenhaft** 1. *Adj.; nicht präd.* in huge numbers *postpos.;* 2. *adv.* on a huge scale

massen-, Massen-: ~**karambolage** die multiple crash; ~**medium** das mass medium; ~**mörder** der mass murderer; ~**produktion** die mass production; ~**weise** *Adv.* in huge numbers

Masseur [ma'sø:ɐ̯] der; ~s, ~e masseur; **Masseurin** die; ~, ~nen, **Masseuse** [ma'sø:zə] die; ~, ~n masseuse

maß·gebend, maß·geblich 1. *Adj.* authoritative *(book, expert, opinion);* definitive *(text);* influential *(person, circles, etc.);* decisive *(factor, influence, etc.);* 2. *adv. (influence)* to a considerable extent; *(entscheidend)* decisively; **maß|halten** *unr. itr. V.* exercise moderation

massieren *tr. V.* massage

mäßig 1. *Adj.* moderate; *(mittel~)* mediocre; 2. *adv.* in moderation; moderately *(gifted, talented);* *(mittel~)* indifferently; **mäßigen** *refl. V.* (geh.) a) practise or exercise moderation; b) *(sich beherrschen)* control or restrain oneself; **Mäßigkeit** die; ~: moderation; **Mäßigung** die; ~: moderation

massiv 1. *Adj.* a) solid; b) *(heftig)* massive *(demand);* crude *(accusation, threat);* strong *(attack, criticism, pressure);* 2. *adv. (attack)* strongly; *(accuse, threaten)* crudely

maß-, Maß-; ~**krug** der *(südd., österr.)* litre beer-mug; *(aus Steingut)* stein; ~**los** 1. *Adj.* extreme; gross *(exaggeration, insult);* excessive *(demand, claim);* boundless *(ambition, greed, sorrow, joy);* 2. *adv.* extremely; *(exaggerate)* grossly; ~**nahme** die; ~, ~n measure; ~**regel** die regulation; *(Maßnahme)* measure; ~**regeln** *tr. V. (zurechtweisen)* reprimand; *(bestrafen)* discipline; ~**stab** der a) standard; b) *(einer Karte, eines Modells usw.)* scale; ~**voll** 1. *Adj.* moderate; 2. *adv.* in moderation

Mast der; ~[e]s, ~en, *auch:* ~e *(Schiffs~, Antennen~)* mast; *(Stange,*

Fahnen~) pole; *(Hochspannungs~)* pylon

mästen *tr. V.* fatten

masturbieren *itr., tr. V.* masturbate

Match [mɛtʃ] *das od. der;* ~[e]s, ~s *od.* ~e match

Material *das;* ~s, ~ien material; *(Bau~; Hilfsmittel)* materials *pl.;* **Materialismus** *der;* ~: materialism; **Materialist** *der;* ~en, ~en materialist; **materialistisch** 1. *Adj.* materialistic; 2. *adv.* materialistically; **Materie** *die;* ~, ~n a) matter; b) *(geh.: Thema, Gegenstand)* subject-matter; **materiell** 1. *Adj. (finanziell)* financial; 2. *adv.* materially; *(finanziell)* financially

Mathematik *die;* ~: mathematics *sing., no art.;* **mathematisch** 1. *Adj.* mathematical; 2. *adv.* mathematically

Matjes *der;* ~, ~: matie [herring]

Matratze *die;* ~, ~n mattress

Matrose *der;* ~n, ~n sailor; seaman

Matsch *der;* ~[e]s *(ugs.)* mud; *(breiiger Schmutz)* sludge; *(Schnee~)* slush; **matschig** *Adj. (ugs.)* a) muddy; slushy *⟨snow⟩;* b) *(weich)* mushy; squashy *⟨fruit⟩*

matt 1. *Adj.* a) weak; feeble *⟨applause, reaction⟩;* b) *(glanzlos)* matt; dull *⟨metal, mirror, etc.⟩;* c) *(undurchsichtig)* frosted *⟨glass⟩;* pearl *⟨light-bulb⟩;* d) subdued; *(Schach)* checkmated; ~! checkmate!; 2. *adv.* a) *(kraftlos)* weakly; b) *(mäßig) ⟨protest, contradict⟩* feebly

Matte *die;* ~, ~n mat

Matt·scheibe *die (ugs.)* telly *(Brit. coll.);* box *(coll.)*

Mätzchen *das;* ~s, ~: ~ machen *(ugs.)* fod about *or* around

Mauer *die;* ~, ~n wall; **mauern** 1. *tr. V.* build; 2. *itr. V.* lay bricks; **Mauer·werk** *das* a) masonry; *(aus Ziegeln)* brickwork; b) *(Mauern)* walls *pl.*

Maul *das;* ~[e]s, Mäuler *(von Tieren)* mouth; *(derb: Mund)* gob *(sl.)*

Maul-: ~esel *der* mule; ~korb *der (auch fig.)* muzzle; ~tier *das* mule; ~wurf *der* mole

Maurer *der;* ~s, ~: bricklayer

Maus *die;* ~, Mäuse mouse

Mauschelei *die;* ~, ~en *(ugs. abwertend)* shady wheeling and dealing *no indef. art.;* **mauscheln** *itr. V. (ugs. abwertend)* engage in shady wheeling and dealing

Mäuschen *das;* ~s, ~: little mouse;

mäuschen·still *Adj.* ~ sein be as quiet as a mouse; **Mause·falle** *die* mousetrap

Maut *die;* ~, ~en toll

maximal 1. *Adj.* maximum; 2. *adv.* ~ zulässige Geschwindigkeit maximum permitted speed; **Maxime** *die;* ~, ~n maxim; **Maximum** *das;* ~s, Maxima maximum *(an + Dat. of)*

Mayonnaise [majɔˈnɛːzə] *die;* ~, ~n mayonnaise

Mäzen *der;* ~s, ~e *(geh.)* patron

MdB, M.d.B. *Abk.* Mitglied des Bundestages Member of the Bundestag

m.E. *Abk.* meines Erachtens in my opinion *or* view

Mechanik *die;* ~: mechanics *sing., no art.;* **Mechaniker** *der;* ~s, ~: mechanic; **mechanisch** 1. *Adj.* mechanical; power *attrib. ⟨loom, press⟩;* 2. *adv.* mechanically; **Mechanismus** *der;* ~, Mechanismen mechanism

meckern *itr. V.* a) *(auch fig.)* bleat; b) *(ugs.: nörgeln)* grumble; moan

Mecklenburg-Vorpommern (das); ~s Mecklenburg-Western Pomerania

Medaille [meˈdaljə] *die;* ~, ~n medal; **Medaillon** [medalˈjõː] *das;* ~s, ~s a) locket; b) *(Kochk., bild. Kunst)* medallion

Medikament *das;* ~[e]s, ~e medicine; *(Droge)* drug

meditieren *itr. V.* meditate *(über + Akk.* [up]on)

Medium *das;* ~s, Medien medium

Medizin *die;* ~, ~en medicine; **Mediziner** *der;* ~s, ~: doctor; *(Student)* medical student; **medizinisch** 1. *Adj.* medical; medicinal *⟨bath etc.⟩;* medicated *⟨toothpaste, soap, etc.⟩;* 2. *adv.* medically

Meer *das;* ~[e]s, ~e *(auch fig.)* sea; am ~: by the sea; **Meer·enge** *die* straits *pl.;* strait

Meeres-: ~bucht *die* bay; ~früchte *Pl. (Kochk.)* seafood *sing.;* ~spiegel *der* sea-level

Meer-: ~jungfrau *die* mermaid; ~rettich *der* horse-radish; ~schweinchen *das* guinea-pig

Megaphon *das;* ~s, ~e megaphone; loud hailer

Mehl *das;* ~[e]s flour; **mehlig** *Adj.* a) floury; b) mealy *⟨potato, apple, etc.⟩*

mehr 1. *Indefinitpron.* more; 2. *adv.* a) more; b) nicht ~: not ... any more; no longer; es war niemand ~ da there was no one left; das wird nie ~ vorkommen it will never happen again; da ist

nichts ~ zu machen there is nothing more to be done

mehr-: ~bändig *Adj.* in several volumes *postpos.;* **~deutig 1.** *Adj.* ambiguous; **2.** *adv.* ambiguously

mehren *(geh.) refl. V.* increase; **mehrer...** *Indefinitpron. u. unbest. Zahlwort* a) *attr.* several; b) *alleinstehend* ~e several people; ~es several things *pl.;* **mehr·fach 1.** *Adj.* multiple; *(wiederholt)* repeated; **2.** *adv.* several times; *(wiederholt)* repeatedly; **Mehrheit die; ~, ~en** majority

mehr-, Mehr-: ~jährig *Adj.* lasting several years *postpos.;* **~malig** *Adj.* *nicht präd.* repeated; **~mals** *Adv.* several times; *(wiederholt)* repeatedly; **~sprachig** *Adj.* multilingual; **~stimmig** *(Musik)* **1.** *Adj.* for several voices *postpos.;* **ein ~stimmiges Lied** a part-song; **2.** *adv.* **~stimmig singen** sing in harmony; **~teilig** *Adj.* in several parts *postpos.;* **~wert der** *(Wirtsch.)* surplus value; **~wertsteuer die** *(Wirtsch.)* value added tax *(Brit.);* VAT *(Brit.);* sales tax *(Amer.);* **~zahl die;** *o. Pl.* a) *(Sprachw.)* plural; b) *(Mehrheit)* majority

meiden *unr. tr. V. (geh.)* avoid

Meile die; ~, ~n mile

mein *Possessivpron.* my; **~e Damen und Herren** ladies and gentlemen; **das Buch dort, ist das ~[e]s?** that book over there, is it mine?

Mein·eid der perjury *no indef. art.;* **einen ~ schwören** commit perjury

meinen 1. *itr. V.* think; **2.** *tr. V.* a) *(sagen wollen, im Sinn haben)* mean; b) *(beabsichtigen)* mean; intend; **es gut mit jmdm. ~:** mean well by sb.; d) *(sagen)* say

meiner *Gen. von ich (geh.)* **gedenkt ~:** remember me; **erbarme dich ~:** have mercy upon me; **meinerseits** *Adv.* for my part; **ganz ~:** the pleasure is [all] mine; **meinetwegen** *Adv.* a) *(wegen mir)* because of me; *(mir zuliebe)* for my sake; *(um mich)* about me; b) *[auch ·-'-]* *(von mir aus)* as far as I'm concerned; **~!** if you like

Meinung die; ~, ~en opinion (zu on, über + *Akk.* about); **meiner ~ nach** in my opinion; **ganz meine ~:** I agree entirely; **einer ~ sein** be of the same opinion

Meinungs-: ~forschung die opinion research; **~freiheit die** freedom to form and express one's own opinions; *(Redefreiheit)* freedom of

speech; **~umfrage die** [public] opinion poll; **~verschiedenheit die** difference of opinion

Meise die; ~, ~n tit[mouse]

Meißel der; ~s, ~: chisel; **meißeln** *tr. V.* chisel; carve *(statue, sculpture)* with a chisel

meist *Adv.* mostly; **meist...** *Indefinitpron. u. unbest. Zahlw.* most; **die ~en Leute ...:** most people ...; **am ~en** most; **meistens** *Adv. s.* meist

Meister der; ~s, ~ a) master; b) *(Werk~, Polier)* foreman; c) *(Sport)* champion; **meisterhaft 1.** *Adj.* masterly; **2.** *adv.* in a masterly manner; **meistern** *tr. V.* master; **Meisterschaft die; ~, ~en** a) *o. Pl.* mastery; b) *(Sport)* championship

Meister-: ~stück das masterpiece **(an +** *Dat.* of); **~titel der** *(Sport)* championship [title]; **~werk das** masterpiece **(an +** *Dat.* of)

Melancholie [melaŋko'li:] **die; ~** *(Gemütszustand)* melancholy; *(Psych.)* melancholia; **melancholisch 1.** *Adj.* melancholy; melancholic, melancholic *(person, temperament);* **2.** *adv.* melancholically

melden 1. *tr. V.* report; *(registrieren lassen)* register *(birth, death, etc.)* *(Dat.* with); **2.** *refl. V.* a) report; *(am Telefon)* answer; b) *(ums Wort bitten)* put one's hand up; c) *(von sich hören lassen)* get in touch *(bei* with); **Meldung die; ~, ~en** a) report; *(Nachricht)* piece of news; b) *(Wort~)* request to speak

meliert *Adj.* mottled; **[grau]~es Haar** hair streaked with grey

melken *regelm. (auch unr.) tr. V.* milk

Melodie die; ~, ~n melody; *(Weise)* tune; **melodisch 1.** *Adj.* melodic; **2.** *adv.* melodically

Melone die; ~, ~n a) melon; b) *(ugs. Hut)* bowler [hat]

Membran die; ~, ~en a) *(Technik)* diaphragm; b) *(Biol., Chemie)* membrane

Memoiren [me'moa:rən] *Pl.* memoirs

Menge die; ~, ~n a) quantity; amount; b) *(große ~)* lot *(coll.);* **eine ~** *(ugs.)* lots [of it/them] *(coll.);* c) *(Menschen~)* crowd; d) *(Math.)* set

Mengen-: ~lehre die; *o. Pl.* set theory *no art.;* **~rabatt der** bulk discount

Mensa die; ~, ~s od. Mensen refectory *(of university, college)*

Mensch der; ~en, ~en a) *(Gattung)*

der ~: man; **die ~en** man *sing.;* human beings; mankind *sing.;* b) *(Person)* person; man/woman; **~en** people

menschen-, Menschen-: ~affe der anthropoid [ape]; **~auflauf** der crowd [of people]; **~feind** der misanthropist; **~fresser** der *(ugs.)* cannibal; **~freund** der philanthropist; **~handel** der trade *or* traffic in human beings; **~kenner** der judge of human nature; **~kenntnis** die; *o. Pl.* ability to judge human nature; **~leben** das life; **~leer** Adj. deserted; **~menge** die crowd [of people]; **~recht** das human right; **~schlag** der breed [of people]; **~seele** die: **keine ~seele** not a [living] soul

Menschens·kind: ~! *(salopp) (erstaunt)* good heavens; good grief; *(vorwurfsvoll)* for heaven's sake

menschen·unwürdig 1. *Adj. (accommodation)* unfit for human habitation; *(conditions)* unfit for human beings; *(behaviour)* unworthy of a human being; **2.** *adv. (treat)* in a degrading and inhumane way; *(live, be housed)* in conditions unfit for human beings; **Menschen·verstand** der human intellect; **Menschheit** die; ~: mankind *no art.;* humanity *no art.;* human race; **menschlich 1.** Adj. a) human; b) *(annehmbar)* civilized; c) *(human)* humane *(person, treatment, etc.);* **2.** adv. a) **er ist mir ~ sympathisch** I like him as a person; b) *(human)* humanely; **Menschlichkeit** die humanity *no art.*

Mensen *s.* Mensa

Mentalität die; ~, **~en** mentality

Menü die; ~s, **~s** *(auch DV)* menu

merkbar 1. Adj. noticeable; **2.** adv. noticeably; **Merk·blatt** leaflet; **merken 1.** *tr. V.* notice; **2.** *refl. V.* **sich** *(Dat.)* **etw. ~:** remember sth.; **merklich** *s.* merkbar; **Merkmal** das; ~s, **~e** feature

Merkur der; ~s Mercury

merkwürdig 1. Adj. strange; odd; **2.** adv. strangely; oddly

meßbar Adj. measurable

¹Messe die; ~, **~n** *(Gottesdienst, Musik)* mass

²Messe die; ~, **~n** *(Ausstellung)* [trade] fair

messen 1. *unr. tr. V.* a) *auch itr.* measure; b) *(beurteilen)* judge (**nach** by); **2.** *unr. refl. V. (geh.)* compete (**mit** with)

Messer das; ~s, ~: knife

messer-, Messer-: ~scharf 1. Adj. razor-sharp; *(fig.)* incisive *(logic);* razor-sharp *(wit, intellect);* **2.** adv. *(fig. ugs.) (argue)* incisively; **~stich** der knife-thrust; *(Wunde)* knife-wound

Messias der; ~, **~se** Messiah

Messing das; ~s brass

Messung die; ~, **~en** measurement

Metall das; ~s, **~e** metal; **Metall·industrie** die metal-processing and metal-working industries *pl.;* **metallisch** Adj. metallic; metal *attrib.,* metallic *(conductor)*

Metapher die; ~, **~n** metaphor

Meta·physik die; ~: metaphysics *sing., no art.*

Meteor der; ~s, **~e** meteor; **Meteorit** der; **~en** *od.* ~s, **~e[n]** meteorite

Meteorologe der; **~n,** **~n** meteorologist; **Meteorologie** die; ~: meteorology *no art.*

Meter der *od.* das; ~s, ~: metre

meter-, Meter-: ~dick Adj. *(sehr dick)* metres thick *postpos.;* **~hoch** Adj. metres high *postpos.;* *(snow)* metres deep; **~maß** das tapemeasure; *(Stab)* [metre] rule

Methode die; ~, **~n** method; **methodisch 1.** Adj. methodological; *(nach einer Methode vorgehend)* methodical; **2.** adv. methodologically; *(nach einer Methode)* methodically

Metier [me'tie:] das; ~s, **~s** profession

Metrik die; ~, **~en** metrics

Metropole die; ~, **~n** metropolis

Mett·wurst die soft smoked sausage made of minced pork and beef

Metzger der; ~s, ~ *(bes. westmd., südd., schweiz.)* butcher; **Metzgerei** die; ~, **~en** *(bes. westmd., südd., schweiz.)* butcher's [shop]

Meute die; ~, **~n a)** *(Jägerspr.)* pack; b) *(ugs. abwertend)* mob; **Meuterei** die; ~, **~en** mutiny; **meutern** *itr. V.* a) mutiny; *(prisoners)* riot; b) *(ugs.: Unwillen äußern)* moan

Mexikaner der; ~s, ~: Mexican; **mexikanisch** Adj. Mexican; **Mexiko** (das); ~s Mexico

MEZ *Abk.* mitteleuropäische Zeit CET

mg *Abk.* Milligramm mg

MG [em'ge:] das; ~s, **~s** *Abk.* Maschinengewehr

Mi. *Abk.* Mittwoch Wed.

miau *Interj.* miaow; **miauen** *itr. V.* miaow

mich 1. Akk. von ich me; **2.** Akk. des Reflexivpron. der 1.Pers. Sg. myself

mick[e]rig *Adj. (ugs.)* miserable; measly *(sl.)*; puny ⟨person⟩

mied *1. u. 3. Pers. Sg. Prät. v.* meiden

Mieder·waren *Pl.* corsetry *sing.*

Miene die; ~, ~n expression

mies *(ugs.)* **1.** *Adj.* lousy *(sl.)*; **2.** *adv.* lousily *(sl.)*

Mies·muschel die [common] mussel

Miete die; ~, ~n rent; *(für ein Auto, Boot)* hire charge; **zur ~ wohnen** live in rented accommodation; **mieten** *tr. V.* rent; *(für kürzere Zeit)* hire; **Mieter** der; ~s, ~: tenant; **Miets·haus** das block of rented flats *(Brit.)* or *(Amer.)* apartments

Miet-: ~**vertrag** der tenancy agreement; ~**wagen** der hire-car

Migräne die; ~, ~n migraine

mikro-, Mikro- micro-

Mikrobe die; ~, ~n microbe

mikro-, Mikro-: ~**film** der microfilm; ~**phon** [--'-] das; ~s, ~e microphone; ~**skop** [--'-] das; ~s, ~e microscope; ~**skopisch** --'--] **1.** *Adj.* microscopic; **2.** *adv.* microscopically

Milbe die; ~, ~n mite

Milch die; ~: milk; **Milch·flasche** die milk-bottle; **milchig 1.** *Adj.* milky; **2.** *adv.* ~ **weiß** milky-white

Milch-: ~**kaffee** der coffee with plenty of milk; ~**kännchen** das milk-jug; ~**reis** der rice pudding; ~**straße** die Milky Way; Galaxy

mild, milde 1. *Adj.* mild; lenient ⟨judge, judgement⟩; soft ⟨light⟩; smooth ⟨brandy⟩; **2.** *adv.* ⟨gütig⟩ leniently; *(gelinde)* mildly; **Milde** die; ~: mildness; *(Güte)* leniency; **mildern** *tr. V.* moderate; mitigate ⟨punishment⟩; **Milderung** die; ~: s. mildern: moderation; mitigation

Milieu [mi'ljø:] das; ~s, ~s environment

militant *Adj.* militant; ¹**Militär** das; ~s armed forces *pl.*; military; *(Soldaten)* soldiers *pl.*; ²**Militär** der; ~s, ~s [high-ranking military] officer

Militär-: ~**dienst** der military service; ~**diktatur** die military dictatorship

militärisch *Adj.* military; **militarisieren** *tr. V.* militarize; **Military** ['mɪlɪtərɪ] die; ~, ~s *(Reiten)* three-day event; **Miliz** die; ~, ~en militia; *(Polizei)* police

Mill. *Abk.* Million m.

milli- Milli- milli-

Milliarde die; ~, ~n billion

Milli-: ~**gramm** das milligram;

~**meter** der *od.* das millimetre; ~**meter·papier** das [graph] paper ruled in millimetre squares

Million die; ~, ~en million; **Millionär** der; ~s, ~e millionaire

Millionen-: ~**schaden** der damage *no pl., no indef. art.* running into millions; ~**stadt** die town with over a million inhabitants

millionst... *Ordinalz.* millionth

Milz die; ~: spleen

Mimik die; ~: gestures and facial expressions *pl.*

Mimose die; ~, ~n a) mimosa; b) *(fig.)* over-sensitive person

minder *Adv. (geh.)* less; **minder...** *Adj.* inferior ⟨goods, brand⟩; **minder·bemittelt** *Adj.* without much money *postpos., not pred.;* ~**bemittelt sein** not have much money; **geistig** ~**bemittelt** *(fig. salopp abwertend)* not all that bright *(coll.)*; **Minderheit** die; ~, ~en minority

minder·jährig *Adj.* ⟨child etc.⟩ who is/was a minor; **Minder·jährige** der/die; *adj. Dekl.* minor; **mindern** *tr. V. (geh.)* reduce; **Minderung** die; ~, ~en reduction *(Gen.* in); **minderwertig** *Adj.* inferior; **mindest...** *Adj.* least; *(geringst...)* slightest; **das ist das** ~**e, was du tun kannst** it is the least you can do; **mindestens** *Adv.* at least

Mine die; ~, ~n a) *(Bergwerk, Sprengkörper)* mine; b) *(Bleistift~)* lead; *(Kugelschreiber~, Filzschreiber~)* refill

Mineral das; ~s, ~e *od.* **Mineralien** mineral; **Mineralogie** die; ~: mineralogy *no art.*

Mineral-: ~**öl** das mineral oil; ~**wasser** das mineral water

Mini die; ~s, ~s *(Mode)* mini *(coll.)*; **Mini-** mini-; **Miniatur** die; ~, ~en miniature

minimal 1. *Adj.* minimal; marginal ⟨advantage, lead⟩; very slight ⟨benefit, profit⟩; **2.** *adv.* minimally; **Minimum** das; ~s, **Minima** minimum **(an +** Dat. of)

Minister der; ~s, ~: minister **(für** for); *(eines britischen Hauptministeriums)* Secretary of State **(für** for); *(eines amerikanischen Hauptministeriums)* Secretary **(für** of); **Ministerium** das; ~s, **Ministerien** Ministry; Department *(Amer.)*; **Minister·präsident** der a) *(eines deutschen Bundeslandes)* minister-president; b) *(Pre-*

mierminister) Prime Minister; **Ministrant** der; ~en, ~en *(kath. Kirche)* server

Minorität die; ~, ~en s. **Minderheit**

minus *Konj., Adv. (bes. Math.)* minus; **Minus** das; ~: deficit; **Minus·zeichen** das minus sign

Minute die; ~, ~n minute; **minuten·lang** 1. *Adj.* lasting [for] several minutes *postpos.*; 2. *adv.* for several minutes; **Minuten·zeiger** der minute-hand

Mio. *Abk.* Million[en] m.

mir 1. *Dat. von* **ich** to me; *(nach Präpositionen)* me; **Freunde von ~**: friends of mine; **gehen wir zu ~**: let's got to my place; **von ~ aus** as far as I'm concerned; 2. *Dat. des Reflexivpron. der 1. Pers. Sg.* myself

Mirabelle die; ~, ~n mirabelle

Misch-: ~**brot** das bread made from wheat and rye flour; ~**ehe** die mixed marriage

mischen 1. *tr. V.* mix; 2. *refl. V.* a) *(sich ver~)* mix (mit with); *⟨smell, scent⟩* blend (mit with); b) *(sich ein~)* **sich in etw.** *(Akk.)* **~**: interfere in sth.; **Misch·farbe** die non-primary colour; **Mischling** der; ~s, ~e half-caste; **Mischmasch** der; ~[e]s, ~e *(ugs., meist abwertend)* hotchpotch; mishmash; **Mischung** die; ~, ~en mixture; *(Tee~, Kaffee~, Tabak~)* blend; *(Pralinen~)* assortment; **Misch·wald** der mixed [deciduous and coniferous] forest

miserabel *(ugs.)* 1. *Adj.* dreadful *(coll.)*; 2. *adv.* dreadfully *(coll.)*; **ihm geht es gesundheitlich ~**: he's in a bad way; **Misere** die; ~, ~n *(geh.)* wretched *or* dreadful state; *(Elend)* misery; *(Not)* distress

miß *Imperativ Sg. v.* **messen**

miß·achten *tr. V.* a) *(ignorieren)* disregard; ignore; b) *(geringschätzen)* be contemptuous of

miß·billigen *tr. V.* disapprove of; **Miß·billigung** die disapproval

Miß·brauch der s. **mißbrauchen**: abuse; misuse; **miß·brauchen** *tr. V.* abuse; misuse; abuse *⟨trust⟩*

missen *tr. V. (geh.)* **jmdn./etw. nicht ~** mögen not want to be without sb./sth.

Miß·erfolg der failure

Misse·tat die *(geh. veralt.)* misdeed

miß·fallen *unr. itr. V.* **etw. mißfällt jmdm.** sb. dislikes sth.; **Mißfallen** das; ~s displeasure; *(Mißbilligung)* disapproval

Miß·geschick das mishap

miß·glücken *itr. V.; mit sein* fail

miß·gönnen *tr. V.* **jmdm. etw. ~**: begrudge sb. sth.

Miß·griff der error of judgement

miß·handeln *tr. V.* maltreat; **Miß·handlung** die maltreatment

Mission die; ~, ~en mission; **Missionar** der; ~s, ~e, missionary

Miß·kredit der **in jmdn./etw. in ~** **bringen** bring sb./sth. into discredit

mißlang *1. u. 3. Pers. Sg. Prät. v.* **mißlingen**

mißliebig *Adj.* unpopular

mißlingen *unr. itr. V.; mit sein* fail; **Mißlingen** das; ~s failure; **mißlungen** 2. *Part. v.* **mißlingen**

Miß·mut der ill humour *no indef. art.*; **miß·mutig** 1. *Adj.* bad-tempered; sullen *⟨face⟩*; 2. *adv.* bad-temperedly

Miß·stand der deplorable state of affairs *no pl.*

mißt *2. u. 3. Pers. Sg. Präsens v.* **messen**

miß·trauen *itr. V.* **jmdn./einer Sache** **~**: mistrust *or* distrust sb./sth.; **Miß·trauen** das; ~s mistrust, distrust (**gegen** of); **mißtrauisch** 1. *Adj.* mistrustful; distrustful; 2. *adv.* mistrustfully; distrustfully

miß·verständlich 1. *Adj.* unclear; *⟨formulation, concept, etc.⟩* that could be misunderstood; 2. *adv.* *⟨express oneself, describe⟩* in a way that could be misunderstood; **Miß·verständnis** das misunderstanding; **miß·verstehen**[1] *unr. tr. V.* misunderstand

Mist der; ~[e]s a) dung; *(Dünger)* manure; *(mit Stroh usw. gemischt)* muck; b) *(~haufen)* dung/manure/muck heap; c) *(ugs. abwertend)* *(Unsinn)* rubbish *no indef. art.*; *(Minderwertiges)* junk *no indef. art.*

Mistel die; ~, ~n mistletoe

Mist·haufen der dung/manure/muck heap

mit 1. *Präp. mit Dat.* with; **ein Zimmer** **~ Frühstück** a room with breakfast included; **~ 50 [km/h] fahren** drive at 50 [k.p.h]; **~ der Bahn/dem Auto fahren** go by train/car; **~ 20 [Jahren]** at [the age of] twenty; 2. *Adv.* a) too; as well; b) **seine Arbeit war ~ am besten** *(ugs.)* his work was among the best

Mit·arbeit die; *o. Pl.* collaboration

---

[1] *ich mißverstehe, mißverstanden, mißzuverstehen*

(bei/an + *Dat.* on); *(Mithilfe)* assistance **(bei, in** + *Dat.* in); *(Beteiligung)* participation **(in** + *Dat.* in); **mit|arbeiten** *itr. V.* collaborate **(bei/an** + *Dat.* on) *(sich beteiligen)* participate **(in** + *Dat.* in); **Mit·arbeiter der a)** collaborator; **freier** ~: free-lance worker; **b)** *(Angestellter)* employee

mit|bekommen *unr. tr. V.* **a) etw.** ~: be given sth. to take with one; **b)** *(wahrnehmen)* be aware of; *(durch Hören, Sehen)* hear/see

mit|bestimmen 1. *itr. V.* have a say; **2.** *tr. V.* have an influence on; **Mitbestimmung die;** *o. Pl.* participation **(bei** in); *(der Arbeitnehmer)* codetermination

mit|bringen *unr. tr. V.* **a) etw.** ~: bring sth. with one; **jmdm./sich etw.** ~: bring sth. with one for sb./bring sth. back for oneself; **b)** *(haben)* have *(ability, gift, etc.);* **Mitbringsel das;** **~s,** ~: [small] present; *(Andenken)* [small] souvenir

mit·einander *Adv.* **a)** with each other *or* one another; ~ **sprechen** talk to each other *or* one another; **b)** *(gemeinsam)* together

mit|erleben *tr. V.* **a)** witness *(events etc.);* **b)** *(mitmachen)* be alive during

mit|fahren *unr. itr. V.; mit sein* **bei jmdm. [im Auto]** ~: go/travel with sb. [in his/her car]; *(mitgenommen werden)* get a lift with sb. [in his/her car]

mit·fühlend 1. *Adj.* sympathetic; **2.** *adv.* sympathetically

mit|führen *tr. V.* **a)** *(Amtsspr.: bei sich tragen)* **etw.** ~: carry sth. [with one]; **b)** *(transportieren)* *(river, stream)* carry along

mit|geben *unr. tr. V.* **jmdm. etw.** ~: give sb. sth. to take with him/her; *(fig.)* provide sb. with sth.

Mit·gefühl das; *o. Pl.* sympathy

mit|gehen *unr. itr. V.; mit sein* **a)** go too; **mit jmdm.** ~: go with sb.; **b)** *(sich mitreißen lassen)* **begeistert** ~: respond enthusiastically

Mit·gift die; ~, **~en** *(veralt.)* dowry

Mit·glied das member *(Gen.,* in + *Dat.* of)

mit|halten *unr. itr. V.* keep up **(bei** in, **mit** with)

Mit·hilfe die; *o. Pl.* help; assistance

mit|hören 1. *tr. V.* listen to; *(zufällig)* overhear *(conversation, argument, etc.);* *(abhören)* listen in on; **2.** *itr. V.* listen; *(zufällig)* overhear

mit|kommen *unr. tr. V.; mit sein* **a)** come too; **kommst du mit?** are you coming [with me/us]?; **b)** *(Schritt halten)* keep up

Mit·läufer der *(abwertend)* [mere] supporter

Mit·laut der consonant

Mit·leid das pity, compassion **(mit** for); *(Mitgefühl)* sympathy **(mit** for); **Mit·leidenschaft die: jmdn./etw. in** ~ **ziehen** affect sb./sth.; **mit·leidig 1.** *Adj.* compassionate; *(mitfühlend)* sympathetic; **2.** *adv.* compassionately; *(mitfühlend)* sympathetically

mit|machen 1. *tr. V.* **a)** *(teilnehmen an)* go on *(trip);* join in *(joke);* follow *(fashion);* fight in *(war);* do *(course, seminar);* **das mache ich nicht mit** *(ugs.)* I can't go along with it; **b)** *(ugs.: erleiden)* **zwei Weltkriege/viele Bombenangriffe mitgemacht haben** have been through two world wars/many bomb attacks; **2.** *itr. V.* **a)** *(sich beteiligen)* join in; **b)** *(ugs.: funktionieren)* **mein Herz/Kreislauf macht nicht mit** my heart/circulation can't take it

Mit·mensch der fellow human being

mit|nehmen *unr. tr. V.* **a) jmdn.** ~: take sb. with one; **etw.** ~: take sth. with one; *(verhüll.: stehlen)* walk off with sth. *(coll.); (kaufen)* take sth.; **Essen/Getränke zum Mitnehmen** food/drinks to take away *or* (Amer.) to go; **b)** *(in Mitleidenschaft ziehen)* **jmdn.** ~: take it out of sb.

mit|reden *itr. V.* **a)** join in the conversation; **b)** *(mitbestimmen)* have a say

Mit·reisende der/die fellow passenger

mit|reißen *unr. tr. V.* **die Begeisterung/seine Rede hat alle Zuhörer mitgerissen** the audience was carried away with enthusiasm/by his speech

mit·samt *Präp. mit Dat.* together with

Mit·schuld die share of the blame *or* responsibility **(an** + *Dat.* for)

Mit·schüler der, Mit·schülerin die schoolfellow

mit|spielen *itr. V.* **a)** join in the game; **b)** in einem Film ~: be in a film; **in einem Orchester/in** *od.* **bei einem Fußballverein** ~: play in an orchestra/for a football club; **Mit·spieler der, Mit·spielerin die** player; *(in derselben Mannschaft)* team-mate

mittag *Adv.* **heute/Montag** ~: at midday today/on Monday; **Mittag der;** ~**s,** ~**e a)** midday *no art.;* **gegen** ~: around midday; **zu** ~ **essen** have lunch; **b)** *o. Pl. (ugs.: Mittagspause)* lunch-hour; **Mittag·essen das** lunch; **Mittags** *Adv.* at midday; **12 Uhr ~:** 12 noon

Mittags-: **~pause die** lunch-hour; **~ruhe** the period of quiet after lunch; **~zeit die a)** *o. Pl. (Zeit gegen 12 Uhr)* lunch-time *no art.;* **b)** *(~pause)* lunch-hour

Mitte die; ~, ~n middle; *(eines Kreises, einer Kugel, Stadt)* centre; ~ **des Monats/Jahres** in the middle of the month/year

mit|teilen *tr. V.* **jmdm. etw. ~:** tell sb. sth.; *(informieren)* inform sb. of sth.; **mitteilsam** *Adj.* communicative; *(gesprächig)* talkative; **Mit·teilung die** communication; *(Bekanntgabe)* announcement

Mittel das; ~**s,** ~ **a)** means; *(Methode)* way; method; *(Werbe~, Propaganda~ usw.)* device *(Gen.* for); **mit allen ~n versuchen,** etw. **zu tun** try by every means to do sth.; **b)** *(Arznei)* **ein ~ gegen Husten** *usw.* a cure for coughs *etc.;* **c)** *Pl. (Geld~)* funds; *(Privat~)* means

Mittel·alter das; *o. Pl.* Middle Ages *pl.;* **mittel·alterlich** *Adj.* medieval

mittelbar 1. *Adj.* indirect; **2.** *adv.* indirectly

mittel-, Mittel-: **~ding das;** *o. Pl.* **ein ~ding sein** be something in between; **~europa (das)** Central Europe; **~finger der** middle finger; **~gebirge das** low mountains *pl.;* **~linie die** centre line; *(Fußball)* halfway line; **~los** *Adj.* without means *postpos.;* **~mäßig** *Adj.* mediocre; **~meer das** Mediterranean [Sea]; **~punkt der a)** *(Geom.)* centre; *(einer Strecke)* midpoint; **b)** *(Mensch/Sache im Zentrum)* centre of attention; **~scheitel der** centre parting; **~schule die** *s.* Realschule; **~stand der;** *o. Pl.* middle class; **~weg der** middle course; **~welle die** *(Physik, Rundf.)* medium wave

mitten *Adv.* ~ **an/auf etw.** *(Akk./Dat.)* in the middle of sth.; ~ **durch die Stadt** right through the town

mitten-: **~drin** *Adv.* [right] in the middle; **~durch** *Adv.* [right] through the middle

Mitter·nacht die; *o. Pl.* midnight *no art.;* **Mitternachts·sonne die** midnight sun

mittler... *Adj.* middle; moderate *(speed);* medium-sized *(company,*

town); medium *(quality, size);* *(durchschnittlich)* average

mittler·weile *Adv.* since then; *(bis jetzt)* by now; *(unterdessen)* in the meantime

Mittwoch der; ~**|e|s,** ~**e** Wednesday; **mittwochs** *Adv.* on Wednesday[s]

mit·unter *Adv.* from time to time

mit·wirken *itr. V.* **an etw.** *(Dat.)***/bei etw. ~:** collaborate on/be involved in sth.; **in einem Orchester/Theaterstück ~:** play in an orchestra/act or appear in a play; **Mitwirkende der/die** *adj. Dekl. (an einer Sendung)* participant; *(in einer Show)* performer; *(in einem Theaterstück)* actor

Mit·wisser der; ~**s** ~: ~ **einer Sache** *(Gen.)* **sein** be an accessory to sth.

mixen *tr. V.* mix; **sich** *(Dat.)* **einen Drink ~:** fix oneself a drink; **Mixer der;** ~**s,** ~ **a)** *(Bar~)* barman; bartender *(Amer.);* **b)** *(Gerät)* blender and liquidizer

mm *Abk.* Millimeter mm.

Mo. *Abk.* Montag Mon.

Mob der; ~**s** *(abwertend)* mob

Möbel das; ~**s,** ~ **a)** *Pl.* furniture *sing., no indef. art.;* **b)** piece of furniture; **Möbel·wagen der** furniture van; removal van; **mobil** *Adj.* **a)** mobile; ~ **machen** mobilize; **b)** *(ugs.) (lebendig)* lively; **Mobiliar das;** ~**s** furnishings *pl.;* **mobilisieren** *tr. V.* **a)** *(Milit., fig.)* mobilize; **b)** *(aktivieren)* activate; **Mobilmachung die;** ~, ~**en** mobilization; **Mobil·telefon das** cellular phone; **möblieren** *tr. V.* furnish

mochte *1. u. 3. Pers. Sg. Prät. v.* **mögen; möchte** *1. u. 3. Pers. Sg. Konjunktiv II v.* **mögen**

Mode die; ~, ~**n** fashion; **Mode·farbe die** fashionable colour

Modell das; ~**s,** ~**e** *(auch fig.)* model; **jmdm.** ~ **sitzen** *od.* **stehen** sit for sb.; **modellieren** *tr. V.* model, mould *(figures, objects);* mould *(clay, wax);* **Modell·kleid das** model dress

Moden·schau die fashion show

Moder der; ~**s** mould; *(~geruch)* mustiness

Moderation die; ~, ~**en** *(Rundf., Ferns.)* presentation; **Moderator der;** ~**s,** ~**en,** **Moderatorin die;** ~, ~**nen** *(Rundf., Ferns.)* presenter; **moderieren** *tr. V. (Rundf., Ferns.)* present *(programme)*

¹modern *itr. V.; auch mit sein* go mouldy

²modern 1. *Adj.* modern; *(modisch)* fashionable; **2.** *adv.* in a modern manner; *(modisch)* fashionably; **modernisieren** *tr. V.* modernize

Mode-: ~**schöpfer** der couturier; ~**schöpferin** die couturière; ~**wort** das; *Pl.* ~**wörter** vogue-word; ~**zeitschrift** die fashion magazine

modifizieren *tr. V. (geh.)* modify

modisch 1. *Adj.* fashionable; **2.** *adv.* fashionably

Mofa das; ~**s**, ~**s** [low-powered] moped

Mogelei die; ~, ~**en** *(ugs.)* cheating *no pl.*; **mogeln** *itr. V.* cheat

mögen 1. *unr. Modalverb;* **2.** *Part.* ~: **a)** *(wollen)* want to; **das hätte ich sehen** ~: I would have liked to see that; **b)** *(geh.: sollen)* **das mag genügen** that should be enough; **c)** *(Vermutung, Möglichkeit)* **sie mag/mochte vierzig sein** she must be/must have been [about] forty; **[das] mag sein** maybe; **d)** *Konjunktiv II (den Wunsch haben)* **ich/sie möchte gern wissen ...**: I would/she would like to know ...; **2.** *unr. tr. V.* like; **sie mag keine Rosen** she does not like roses; **sie** ~ **sich** they're fond of one another; **möchten Sie ein Glas Wein?** would you like a glass of wine?; **ich möchte lieber Tee** I would prefer tea; **3.** *unr. itr. V.* **a)** *(es wollen)* like to; **b)** **ich möchte nach Hause** I want to go home; **er möchte zu Herrn A** he would like to see Mr A

möglich *Adj.* possible; **es war ihm nicht** ~ **[zu kommen]** he was unable [to come]; **alles** ~**e** *(ugs.)* all sorts of things; **[das ist doch] nicht** ~! impossible!; **sein** ~**stes tun** do one's utmost; **möglicherweise** *Adv.* possibly; **Möglichkeit** die; ~, ~**en a)** possibility; *(Methode)* way; **es besteht die** ~, **daß ...**: there is a possibility that ...; **b)** *(Gelegenheit)* opportunity; chance; **möglichst** *Adv.* **a)** if [at all] possible; **b)** ~ **schnell** as fast as possible

Mohammed (der) Muhammad; **Mohammedaner** der; ~**s**, ~: Muslim; Muhammadan; **mohammedanisch** *Adj.* Muslim; Muhammadan

Mohn der; ~**s** poppy; *(Samen)* poppy seed; *(auf Brot, Kuchen)* poppy seeds *pl.*

Mohn-: ~**blume** die poppy; ~**brötchen** das poppy-seed roll; ~**kuchen** der poppy-seed cake

Möhre die; ~, ~**n** carrot

Mohren·kopf der chocolate marshmallow

Mohr·rübe die carrot

mokieren *refl. V. (geh.)* **sich über etw.** *(Akk.)* ~: scoff at sth.; **sich über jmdn.** ~: mock sb.

Mokka der; ~**s** strong black coffee

Molch der; ~**[e]s**, ~**e** newt

Mole die; ~, ~**n** [harbour] mole

Molekül das; ~**s**, ~**e** molecule

molk *1. u. 3. Pers. Sg. Prät. v.* **melken**; **Molkerei** die; ~, ~**en** dairy

Moll das; ~ *(Musik)* minor [key]

mollig 1. *Adj.* **a)** *(rundlich)* plump; **b)** *(warm)* snug; **2.** *adv.* snugly; ~ **warm** warm and snug

¹Moment der; ~**[e]s**, ~**e** moment; **jeden** ~ *(ugs.)* [at] any moment; **im** ~: at the moment; **²Moment** das; ~**[e]s**, ~**e** factor, element **(für** in); **momentan 1.** *Adj.* **a)** present; **b)** *(vorübergehend)* temporary; *(flüchtig)* momentary; **2.** *adv.* **a)** at present; **b)** *(vorübergehend)* temporarily

Monaco (das); ~**s** Monaco

Monarch der; ~**en**, ~**en** monarch; **Monarchie** die; ~, ~**n** monarchy; **Monarchin** die; ~, ~**nen** monarch

Monat der; ~**s**, ~**e** month; **im** ~ **April** in the month of April; **monatelang 1.** *Adj.* lasting for months *postpos., not pred.*; **2.** *adv.* for months [on end]; **monatlich 1.** *Adj.* monthly; **2.** *adv.* every month; *(pro Monat)* per month

Monats-: ~**erste** der first [day] of the month; ~**hälfte** die half of the month; ~**karte** die monthly season-ticket; ~**letzte** der last day of the month

Mönch der; ~**[e]s**, ~**e** monk

Mond der; ~**[e]s**, ~**e** moon; **auf od. hinter dem** ~ **leben** *(fig. ugs.)* be a bit behind the times *(coll.)*; **nach dem** ~ **gehen** *(ugs.)* ⟨clock, watch⟩ be hopelessly wrong

Mond-: ~**finsternis** die eclipse of the moon; ~**landung** die moon landing

Mongole der; ~**n**, ~**n a)** Mongol; **b)** *(Bewohner der Mongolei)* Mongolian; **Mongolei** die; ~: Mongolia

Monitor der; ~**s**, ~**en** monitor

Mono·gramm das; ~**s**, ~**e** monogram; **Monographie** die; ~, ~**n** monograph

Monolog der; ~**s**, ~**e** monologue

Monopol das; ~**s**, ~**e** monopoly **(auf** + *Akk.*, **für** in, of)

monoton 1. *Adj.* monotonous; **2.** *adv.*

monotonously; **Monotonie** die; ~, ~n monotony

Monster das; ~s, ~: monster; *(häßlich)* [hideous] brute; **Monstren** Monstrum; **monströs** Adj. monstrous; **Monstrum** das; ~s, Monstren a) monster; b) *(Sache)* hulking great thing *(coll.)*

Mon·tag der Monday

Montage [mɔn'taːʒə] die; ~, ~n a) *(Zusammenbau)* assembly; *(Einbau)* installation; *(Aufstellen)* erection; *(Anbringen)* fitting (**an** + Akk. od. Dat. to); mounting (**auf** + Akk. od. Dat. on); b) *(Film. bild. Kunst, Literaturw.)* montage

montags Adv. on Monday[s]

montieren tr. V. a) *(zusammenbauen)* assemble *(aus* from); erect *(building)*; b) *(anbringen)* fit (**an** + Akk. od. Dat. to; **auf** + Akk. od. Dat. on); *(einbauen)* install (**in** + Akk. in); *(befestigen)* fix (**an** + Akk. od. Dat. to)

Monument das; ~[e]s, ~e monument; **monumental** Adj. monumental

Moor das; ~[e]s, ~e bog; *(Bruch)* marsh

Moos das; ~es, ~e moss

Moped ['moːpɛt] das; ~s, ~s moped

Mops der; ~es, Möpse pug [dog]; *(salopp: dicke Person)* podge *(coll.)*

Moral die; ~ a) *(Norm)* morality; b) *(Sittlichkeit)* morals pl.; c) *(Selbstvertrauen)* morale; d) *(Lehre)* moral; **moralisch** 1. Adj. a) moral; b) *(tugendhaft)* virtuous; 2. adv. a) morally; b) *(tugendhaft)* virtuously; **moralisieren** itr. V. *(geh.)* moralize; **Moralist** der; ~en, ~en moralist

Morast der; ~[e]s, ~e od. Moräste a) bog; swamp; b) o. Pl. *(Schlamm)* mud

Mord der; ~[e]s, ~e murder (**an** + Dat. of); *(durch ein Attentat)* assassination; **einen ~ begehen** commit murder; **morden** tr., itr. V. murder; **Mörder** der; ~s, ~: murderer *(esp. Law)*; killer; *(politischer ~)* assassin; **Mörderin** die; ~, ~nen murderer; murderess; *(politische ~)* assassin; **mörderisch** 1. Adj. a) murderous; 2. adv. *(ugs.)* dreadfully *(coll.)*; **Mordfall** der murder case; **mords-, Mords-** *(ugs.)* terrific *(coll.)*

Mord-: ~**verdacht** der suspicion of murder; ~**versuch** der attempted murder; *(Attentat)* assassination attempt; ~**waffe** die murder weapon

morgen Adv. a) tomorrow; ~ **in einer Woche** tomorrow week; a week to-

morrow; ~ **um diese Zeit** this time tomorrow; **bis ~!** until tomorrow!; **see you tomorrow!**; b) *(am Morgen)* **heute ~:** this morning; **[am] Sonntag ~:** on Sunday morning; **Morgen** der; ~s, ~: morning; **am ~:** in the morning; **am folgenden** od. **nächsten ~:** next morning; **früh am ~, am frühen ~:** early in the morning; **morgendlich** Adj. morning

Morgen-: ~**grauen** das daybreak; ~**mantel** der dressing-gown; ~**rot** das *(geh.)* rosy dawn

morgens Adv. in the morning; *(jeden Morgen)* every morning; **Dienstag** od. **dienstags ~:** on Tuesday morning[s]; **von ~ bis abends** from morning to evening; **morgig** Adj. tomorrow's

Morphium das; ~s: morphine; **morphium·süchtig** Adj. addicted to morphine pred.

morsch Adj. *(auch fig.)* rotten

Mörser der; ~s, ~ *(Gefäß, Geschütz)* mortar

Mörtel der; ~s mortar

Mosaik das; ~s, ~en od. ~e mosaic

Mosambik (das); ~s Mozambique

Moschee die; ~, ~n mosque

Moschus der; ~: musk

Mosel die; ~: Moselle; **Mosel·wein** der Moselle [wine]

Moskau (das); ~s Moscow; **Moskauer** 1. indekl. Adj. Moscow attrib.; 2. der; ~s, ~: Muscovite

Moskito der; ~s, ~s mosquito

Moslem der; ~s, ~s Muslim; **moslemisch** Adj. Muslim

Most der; ~[e]s, ~e a) [cloudy fermented] fruit-juice; b) *(landsch.: neuer Wein)* new wine; **Mostrich** der; ~s *(nordostd.)* mustard

Motel das; ~s, ~s motel

Motiv das; ~s, ~e a) motive; b) *(fachspr.: Thema)* motif; theme; *(bild. Kunst)* subject

Motor der; ~s, ~en engine; *(Elektro~)* motor; **Motor·haube** die *(Kfz-W.)* bonnet *(Brit.)*; hood *(Amer.)*; **motorisieren** tr. V. motorize; **Motor·rad** das motor cycle; **Motor·rad·fahrer** der motor-cyclist

Motor-: ~**roller** der motor scooter; ~**schaden** der engine trouble no indef. art.

Motte die; ~, ~n moth; **Motten·kugel** die moth-ball

Motto das; ~s, ~s motto; *(Schlagwort)* slogan

Möwe die; ~, ~n gull

Mrd. *Abk.* Milliarde bn.

Mücke die; ~, ~n midge; *(größer)* mosquito; **Mücken·stich** der midge/mosquito bite

Mucks der; ~es, ~e *(ugs.)* murmur [of protest]; **keinen ~ sagen** not utter a [single] word

müde 1. *Adj.* tired; *(ermattet)* weary; *(schläfrig)* sleepy; **jmdn./etw.** *od.* **jmds./einer Sache ~ sein** *(geh.)* be tired of sb./sth.; 2. *adv.* wearily; *(schläfrig)* sleepily; **Müdigkeit** die; ~: tiredness

muffelig *(ugs.)* 1. *Adj.* grumpy; 2. *adv.* grumpily

muffig *Adj.* musty

Mühe die; ~, ~n trouble; **sich** *(Dat.)* **mit jmdm./etw. ~ geben** take [great] pains over sb./sth.; **mit Müh und Not** with great difficulty; **mühelos** 1. *Adj.* effortless; 2. *adv.* effortlessly; **mühe·voll** *Adj.* laborious; painstaking *(work)*

Mühle die; ~, ~n a) mill; *(Kaffee~)* [coffee-] grinder; b) *(Spiel)* o. *Art.*, o. *Pl.* nine men's morris

Mühsal die; ~, ~e *(geh.)* tribulation; *(Strapaze)* hardship; **mühsam** 1. *Adj.* laborious; 2. *adv.* laboriously; **müh·selig** *(geh.)* 1. *Adj.* laborious; arduous *(journey, life)*; 2. *adv.* with [great] difficulty

Mulde die; ~, ~n hollow

Mull der; ~[e]s *(Stoff)* mull; *(Verband~)* gauze

Müll der; ~s refuse; rubbish; garbage *(Amer.)*; trash *(Amer.)*; *(Industrie~)* [industrial] waste

Mull·binde die gauze bandage

Müller der; ~s, ~: miller

Müll-: ~**halde** die refuse dump; ~**mann** der; *Pl.* ~**männer** *(ugs.)* dustman *(Brit.)*; garbage man *(Amer.)*; ~**sack** der refuse bag; ~**schlucker** der rubbish *or (Amer.)* garbage chute; ~**tonne** die dustbin *(Brit.)*; garbage *or* trash can *(Amer.)*; ~**wagen** der dust-cart *(Brit.)*; garbage truck *(Amer.)*

mulmig *Adj. (ugs.)* uneasy

Multiplikation die; ~, ~en *(Math.)* multiplication; **multiplizieren** *tr. V.* multiply *(mit by)*

Mumie ['mu:mi̯ə] die; ~, ~n mummy

Mumm der; ~s *(ugs.) (Mut)* guts *pl. (coll.)*; *(Tatkraft)* drive; zap *(sl.)*; *(Kraft)* muscle-power

Mumps der *od.* die; ~: mumps *sing.*

München *(das)*; ~s Munich;

Münch[e]ner 1. *indekl. Adj.* Munich *attrib*; 2. der; ~s, ~: inhabitant/native of Munich

Mund der; ~[e]s, **Münder** mouth; **er küßte sie auf den ~:** he kissed her on the lips; **mit vollem ~ sprechen** speak with one's mouth full; **den ~ nicht aufmachen** *(fig. ugs.)* not say anything; **den** *od.* **seinen ~ halten** *(ugs.) (zu sprechen aufhören)* shut up *(coll.)*; *(nichts sagen)* not say anything; *(nichts verraten)* keep quiet *(über + Akk.* about); **sie ist nicht auf den ~ gefallen** *(fig. ugs.)* she's never at a loss for words; **Mund·art** die dialect

münden *itr. V.; mit sein* **in etw.** *Akk.* ~: *(river)* flow into sth.; *(corridor, street)* lead into sth.

mund-, Mund-: ~**faul** *Adj. (ugs.)* uncommunicative; ~**gerecht** *Adj.* bite-sized; ~**geruch** der bad breath *no indef. art.*; ~**harmonika** die mouth-organ

mündig *Adj.* of age *pred.*; ~ **werden** come of age

mündlich 1. *Adj.* oral; 2. *adv.* orally; **Mund·stück** das mouthpiece; *(bei Zigaretten)* tip; **mund·tot** *Adj.* **jmdn. ~ machen** silence sb.; **Mündung** die; ~, ~en a) mouth; *(größere Trichter~)* estuary; b) *(bei Feuerwaffen)* muzzle

Mund-zu-Mund-Beatmung die mouth-to-mouth resuscitation

Munition die; ~: ammunition

munkeln *tr., itr. V. (ugs.)* **man munkelt, daß ...:** there is a rumour that ...

Münster das; ~s, ~: minster; *(Dom)* cathedral

munter 1. *Adj.* a) cheerful; *(lebhaft)* lively *(eyes, game)*; b) *(wach)* awake; 2. *adv.* cheerfully; **Munterkeit** die; ~: cheerfulness

Münz·automat der slot-machine; **Münze** die; ~, ~n coin

Münz-: ~**fernsprecher** der payphone; pay station *(Amer.)*; ~**tankstelle** die coin-in-the-slot petrol *(Brit.)* or *(Amer.)* gas station; ~**wechsler** der change machine

mürbe *Adj.* crumbly *(biscuit, cake, etc.)*; tender *(meat)*; soft *(fruit)*; **jmdn. ~ machen** *(fig.)* wear sb. down

Murmel die; ~, ~n marble

murmeln *tr., itr. V.* mumble; mutter; *(sehr leise)* murmur

Murmel·tier das marmot

murren *itr. V.* grumble; **mürrisch** 1. *Adj.* grumpy; 2. *adv.* grumpily

Mus das *od.* der; ~es, ~e purée
Muschel die; ~, ~n a) mussel; *(Schale)* [mussel-]shell; b) *(am Telefon) (Hör~)* ear-piece; *(Sprech~)* mouthpiece
Muse die; ~, ~n muse
Museum das; ~s, Museen museum
Musik die; ~, ~en music; **musikalisch** 1. *Adj.* musical; 2. *adv.* musically; **Musikant** der; ~en, ~en musician; **Musik·box** die juke-box; **Musiker** der; ~s, ~, **Musikerin** die; ~, ~nen musician
Musik-: ~hochschule die college of music; ~instrument das musical instrument; ~stunde die music-lesson
musisch 1. *Adj.* artistic; *(education)* in the arts; 2. *adv.* artistically; **musizieren** *itr. V.* play music; *(bes. unter Laien)* make music
Muskat der; ~[e]s, ~e nutmeg; **Muskat·nuß** die nutmeg
Muskel der; ~s, ~n muscle
Muskel-: ~kater der stiff muscles *pl.;* ~protz der *(ugs.)* muscleman
Muskulatur die; ~, ~en musculature; muscular system; **muskulös** *Adj.* muscular
Müsli das; ~s, ~s muesli
muß *1. u. 3. Pers. Sg. Präsens v.* müssen; **Muß** das; ~: necessity; must *(coll.)*
Muße die; ~: leisure
müssen 1. *unr. Modalverb;* 2. *Part.* ~ a) have to; **er muß es tun** he must do it; he has to *or (coll.)* has got to do it; **das muß 1968 gewesen sein** it must have been in 1968; **er muß gleich hier sein** he will be here at any moment; b) *Konjunktiv II* **es müßte doch möglich sein** it ought to be possible; **reich müßte man sein!** how nice it would be to be rich!; 2. *unr. itr. V.* **ich muß nach Hause** I have to *or* must go home; **ich muß mal** *(fam.)* I need to spend a penny *(Brit. coll.)* or *(Amer. coll.)* go to the john
müßig 1. *Adj.* idle *(person)*; *(hours, weeks, life)* of leisure; 2. *adv.* idly; **Müßig·gang** der *o. Pl.* leisure; *(Untätigkeit)* idleness
mußte *1. u. 3. Pers. Sg. Prät. v.* müssen
Muster das; ~s, ~ a) *(Vorlage)* pattern; b) *(Vorbild)* model (**an** + *Dat.* of); c) *(Verzierung)* pattern; d) *(Warenprobe)* sample; **muster·gültig** 1. *Adj.* exemplary; impeccable *(order)*; 2. *adv.* in an exemplary fashion
mustern *tr. V.* a) eye; b) *(Milit.: ärzt-*

lich untersuchen) jmdn. ~: give sb. his medical; **Musterung** die; ~, ~en a) scrutiny; b) *(Milit.: von Wehrpflichtigen)* medical examination; medical
Mut der; ~[e]s courage; **mutig** 1. *Adj.* brave; 2. *adv.* bravely; **mut·los** *Adj.* dejected; *(entmutigt)* disheartened; **Mut·losigkeit** die; ~: dejection
mutmaßlich *Adj.* supposed; suspected *(murderer etc.)*
Mut·probe die test of courage
¹**Mutter** die; ~, Mütter mother;
²**Mutter** die; ~, ~n nut; **mütterlich** 1. *Adj.* a) maternal *(line, love, instincts, etc.)*; b) *(fürsorglich)* motherly *(woman, care)*; 2. *adv.* in a motherly way; **mütterlicher·seits** *Adv.* on the/his/her *etc.* mother's side
Mutter-: ~liebe die motherly love *no art.;* ~mal das; *Pl.* ~male birthmark
Mutterschaft die; ~: motherhood
mutter-, Mutter-: ~seelen·allein *Adj.* all alone; ~söhnchen das mummy's *or (Amer.)* mama's boy; ~sprache die mother tongue; ~tag der; *o. Pl.* Mother's Day *no def. art.*
Mutti die; ~, ~s mummy *(Brit. coll.);* mum *(Brit. coll.);* mommy *(Amer. coll.);* mom *(Amer. coll.)*
mut·willig 1. *Adj.* wilful; wanton *(destruction)*; 2. *adv.* wilfully
Mütze die; ~, ~n cap
MW *Abk. (Rundf.)* Mittelwelle MW
Mw.-St., MwSt. *Abk.* Mehrwertsteuer VAT
mysteriös 1. *Adj.* mysterious; 2. *adv.* mysteriously; **Mystik** die; ~: mysticism
Mythologie die; ~, ~n mythology; **Mythos** der; ~, Mythen myth

N

n, N [ɛn] das; ~, ~: n/N
N *Abk.* Nord[en] N
na *Interj. (ugs.)* well; **na so [et]was!** well I never!; **na und?** *(wennschon)* so what?; *(beschwichtigend)* **na, na, na!** now, now, come along; *(triumphierend)* **na also!** there you are!; *(unsi-*

cher) **na, ich weiß nicht** hmm, I'm not sure; *(ärgerlich)* **na, was soll das denn?** now what's all this about?; *(drohend)* **na warte!** just [you] wait!

Nabel der; ~s, ~: navel; **Nabelschnur** die umbilical cord

nach 1. *Präp. mit Dat.* a) *(räumlich)* to; **der Zug ~ München** the train for Munich *or* the Munich train; **~ Hause gehen** go home; **~ Osten [zu]** eastwards; [towards] the east); b) *(zeitlich)* after; **zehn [Minuten] ~ zwei** ten [minutes] past two; c) *(mit bestimmten Verben, bezeichnet das Ziel der Handlung)* for; d) *(bezeichnet [räumliche und zeitliche] Reihenfolge)* after; **~ Ihnen/dir!** after you; e) *(gemäß)* according to; **~ meiner Ansicht** *od.* **Meinung, meiner Ansicht** *od.* **Meinung ~:** in my view *or* opinion; **der neusten Mode gekleidet** dressed in [accordance with] the latest fashion; **dem Gesetz ~:** in accordance with the law; by law; **etw. schmecken/riechen** taste/smell of sth.; **2.** *Adv.* a) *(räumlich)* **[alle] mir ~!** [everybody] follow me!; b) *(zeitlich)* **und ~:** little by little; gradually; **~ wie vor** still

nach|ahmen *tr. V.* imitate; **Nachahmung** die; ~, ~en imitation

Nachbar der; ~n , ~n neighbour; **Nachbar·haus** das house next door; **Nachbarin** die; ~, ~nen neighbour; **Nachbarschaft** die; ~ a) *(Beziehungen)* **gute ~:** good neighbourliness; c) *(Gegend)* neighbourhood; *(Nähe)* vicinity

nach|bestellen *tr. V.* [noch] etw. ~: order more of sth.; *(shop)* reorder sth.

Nach·bildung die a) *o. Pl.* copying; b) *(Gegenstand)* copy

nach|blicken *tr. V. (geh.)* jmdm./einer Sache ~: gaze after sb./sth.

nach|datieren *tr. V.* backdate

nach·dem *Konj.* a) after; b) *s.* ¹je 3 b

nach|denken *unr. itr. V.* think; **denk mal [gut** *od.* **scharf] nach** have a [good] think; **Nach·denken** das thought; **nachdenklich 1.** *Adj.* thoughtful; **2.** *adv.* thoughtfully

Nach·druck der; *Pl.* ~e a) *o. Pl.* mit ~: emphatically; b) *(Druckw.)* reprint; **nachdrücklich 1.** *Adj.* emphatic; **2.** *adv.* emphatically

nach|eifern *tr. V.* jmdm. ~: emulate sb.

nach·einander *Adv.* one after the other

nach|empfinden *unr. tr. V.* empathize with *(feeling)*; share *(delight, sorrow)*

Nach·erzählung die retelling [of a story]; *(Schulw.)* reproduction

Nachfahr der; ~en , ~en *(geh.)* descendant

Nach·folge die succession; **Nachfolger** der; ~s, ~, **Nachfolgerin** die; ~, ~nen successor

Nach·forschung die investigation

Nach·frage die demand *(nach* for)

nach|fühlen *tr. V.* empathize with

nach|füllen *tr. V.* top up; **Salz/Wein ~:** put [some] more salt/wine in

nach|geben *unr. itr. V.* give way

Nach·gebühr die excess postage

nach|gehen *unr. itr. V.; mit sein* a) jmdm./einer Sache ~: follow sb./sth.; einer Sache ~ *(fig.)* look into a matter; **einem Beruf ~:** practise a profession; b) *(nicht aus dem Kopf gehen)* jmdm. ~: remain on sb.'s mind; c) *(clock, watch)* be slow; [um] **eine Stunde ~:** be an hour slow

Nach·geschmack der after-taste

nach·giebig *Adj.* indulgent; **Nachgiebigkeit** die; ~: indulgence

nach·haltig 1. *Adj.* lasting; **2.** *adv. (auf längere Zeit)* for a long time

Nach·hause·weg der way home

nach|helfen *unr. itr. V.* help

nach·her *[auch:* '--] *Adv.* afterwards; *(später)* later [on]; **bis ~!** see you later!

Nachhilfe·unterricht der coaching

nach|holen *tr. V. (nachträglich erledigen)* catch up on *(work, sleep)*; make up for *(working hours missed)*

Nachkomme der; ~n, ~n descendant; **nach|kommen** *unr. itr. V.; mit sein* follow [later]; come [on] later; **Nachkommenschaft** die; ~: descendants *pl.*; **Nachkömmling** der; ~s, ~e much younger child *(than the rest)*

Nach·kriegs- post-war *(generation, period, etc.)*

Nach·laß der; Nachlasses, Nachlasse *od.* Nachlässe a) *o. Pl.* estate; b) *(Kaufmannsspr.: Rabatt)* discount; **nach|lassen 1.** *unr. itr. V.* let up; *(pain, stress, pressure)* ease; *(effect)* wear off; *(interest, enthusiasm, strength, courage)* wane; *(health, hearing, memory)* deteriorate; *(business)* drop off; **2.** *unr. tr. V. (Kaufmannsspr.)* give a discount of sth.; **nach·lässig 1.** *Adj.* careless; **2.** *adv.* carelessly; **Nachlässigkeit** die; ~, ~en carelessness

nach|laufen *unr. itr. V.; mit sein* jmdm./einer Sache ~: run after sb./ sth.

nach|lesen *unr. tr. V.* look up

nach|lösen 1. *tr. V.* eine Fahrkarte ~: buy a ticket [on the train, bus, etc.]; 2. *itr. V.* pay the excess [fare]

nach|machen *tr. V. (auch tun)* copy; *(imitieren)* imitate; *(genauso herstellen)* reproduce *(period furniture etc.);* forge *(signature)*

nach · mittag *Adv.* heute ~: this afternoon; |am| Sonntag ~: on Sunday afternoon; **Nach · mittag** der afternoon; am ~: in the afternoon; am späten ~: late in the afternoon; **nachmittags** *Adv.* in the afternoon; dienstags od. Dienstag ~: on Tuesday afternoons; um vier Uhr ~: at four in the afternoon; at 4 p.m.

Nachnahme die; ~, ~n: per ~: cash on delivery; COD

Nach · name der surname

nachprüfbar *Adj.* verifiable; **nach|prüfen** *tr., itr. V.* check

nach|rechnen *tr. V.* check *(figures)*

Nach · rede die: üble ~: malicious gossip; *(Rechtsw.)* defamation [of character]

Nachricht die; ~, ~en a) news *no pl.;* eine ~ hinterlassen leave a message; b) *Pl. (Ferns., Rundf.)* news *sing.;* ~en hören listen to the news

Nachrichten-: ~sprecher der, ~sprecherin die news-reader

nach|rücken *itr. V.; mit sein* move up

Nach · ruf der; ~|e|s, ~e obituary (auf + Akk. of); **nach|rufen** *unr. tr., itr. V.* jmdm. |etw.| ~: call [sth.] after sb.

nach|sagen *tr. V.* a) *(wiederholen)* repeat; b) man sagt ihm nach, er sei ...: he is said to be ...; jmdm. Schlechtes ~: speak ill of sb.

Nach · saison die late season

nach|schicken *tr. V.* a) *(durch die Post o. ä.)* forward; b) jmdm. jmdn. ~: send sb. after sb.

nach|schlagen 1. *unr. tr. V.* look up; 2. *unr. itr. V.* im Lexikon/Wörterbuch ~: consult the encyclopaedia/dictionary; **Nachschlage · werk** das work of reference

Nach · schlüssel der duplicate key

Nach · schub der *(Milit.)* a) supply (an + Dat. of); b) *(~material)* supplies pl. (an + Dat. of)

nach|sehen 1. *unr. itr. V.* a) jmdm./einer Sache ~: gaze after sb./sth.; b) *(kontrollieren)* check; c) *(nachschla-*

gen) have a look; 2. *unr. tr. V.* a) *(nachlesen)* look up; b) *(überprüfen)* check [over]

nach|senden *unr. od. regelm. tr. V.* forward

Nach · sicht die leniency; **nachsichtig** 1. *Adj.* lenient (gegen, mit towards); 2. *adv.* leniently

nach|sitzen *unr. itr. V.* be in detention; |eine Stunde| ~ müssen have [an hour's] detention

Nach · speise die dessert; sweet

Nach · spiel das: die Sache wird noch ein ~ haben this affair will have repercussions; ein gerichtliches ~ haben result in court proceedings

nach|sprechen *unr. tr. V.* |jmdm.| etw. ~: repeat sth. [after sb.]

nächst... 1. *Sup. zu* nahe; 2. *Adj.* next; *(kürzest)* shortest *(way);* am ~en Tag the next day; beim ~en Mal, das ~e Mal the next time; der ~e bitte! next [one], please; wer kommt als ~er dran? whose turn is it next?; **Nächste** der; ~n, ~n *(geh.)* neighbour; **Nächsten · liebe** die charity [to one's neighbour]; **nächstens** *Adv.* a) shortly; b) *(ugs.: wenn es so weitergeht)* if it goes on like this

nächst-: ~liegend *Adj.; nicht präd.* first, immediate *(problem);* [most] obvious *(explanation etc.);* ~möglich *Adj.* earliest possible

nach|suchen *itr. V. (geh.)* um etw. ~: request sth.; *(bes. schriftlich)* apply for sth.

nacht *Adv.* gestern/morgen/Dienstag ~: last night/tomorrow night/on Tuesday night; heute ~: tonight; **Nacht** die; ~, Nächte night; bei ~, in der ~: at night[-time]; über ~ bleiben stay overnight

Nacht-: ~arbeit die; *o. Pl.* night work *no art.;* ~dienst der night duty; ~dienst haben be on night duty; *(chemist's shop)* be open late

Nach · teil der disadvantage; **nachteilig** 1. *Adj.* detrimental; harmful; 2. *adv.* detrimentally; harmfully

Nacht-: ~essen das *(bes. südd., schweiz.)* s. Abendessen; ~hemd das night-shirt

Nachtigall die; ~, ~en nightingale

Nach · tisch der; *o. Pl.* dessert; sweet

nächtlich *Adj.* nocturnal; night *(sky);* *(darkness, stillness)* of the night; **Nacht · lokal** das night-spot *(coll.)*

nach|tragen *unr. tr. V. (schriftlich ergänzen)* insert; add; **nach · tragend**

Adj. unforgiving; *(rachsüchtig)* vindictive; **nachträglich 1.** *Adj.* later; subsequent *(apology)*; *(verspätet)* belated *(greetings, apology)*; **2.** *adv.* afterwards; subsequently; *(verspätet)* belatedly

nachtrauern *itr. V.* jmdm./einer Sache ~: bemoan the passing of sb./sth.

Nacht·ruhe die night's sleep; **nachts** *Adv.* at night; **Montag** *od.* **montags** ~: on Monday nights; **um 3 Uhr** ~: at 3 o'clock in the morning

Nacht-: ~**schicht** die night-shift; ~**schwester** die night nurse; ~**tisch** der bedside table; ~**tischlampe** die bedside light; ~**topf** der chamber-pot; ~**wächter** der nightwatchman

Nach·untersuchung die follow-up examination; check-up

nachvollziehen *unr. tr. V.* reconstruct; *(begreifen)* comprehend

nachwachsen *unr. itr. V.*; *mit sein* |wieder| ~: grow again

Nach·wehen *Pl.* *(Med.)* afterpains; *(fig. geh.)* unpleasant after-effects

Nachweis der; ~es, ~e proof *no indef. art.* *(Gen., über* + *Akk.* of); *(Zeugnis)* certificate *(über* + *Akk.* of); **nachweisbar 1.** *Adj.* demonstrable *(fact, truth, error, defect, guilt)*; detectable *(substance, chemical)*; **2.** *adv.* demonstrably; **nachweisen** *unr. tr. V.* prove; **nachweislich** *Adv.* as can be proved

nachwinken *itr. V.* jmdm./einer Sache ~: wave after sb./sth.

Nach·wirkung die after-effect

Nach·wort das; *Pl.* ~worte afterword

Nach·wuchs der; *o. Pl* a) *(fam.: Kind[er])* offspring; *(fig.: junge Kräfte)* new blood; *(für eine Branche usw.)* new recruits *pl.*; *(in der Ausbildung)* trainees *pl.*

nachzahlen *tr., itr. V.* a) pay later; b) *(zusätzlich zahlen)* **25 DM** ~: pay another 25 marks

nachzählen *tr., itr. V.* [re]count

Nach·zahlung die additional payment

Nachzügler der straggler; *(spät Ankommender)* latecomer

Nackedei der; ~s, ~s *(fam. scherzh.)* |kleiner| ~: naked little thing

Nacken der; ~s, ~: back *or* nape of the neck; *(Hals)* neck

nackt *Adj.* naked; bare *(feet, legs, arms, skin, fists)*; *(fig.)* plain *(truth, fact)*; bare *(existence)*; **Nackt·ba-**

de·strand der nudist beach; **Nackte** der/die; *adj. Dekl.* naked man/ woman; **Nackt·foto** das nude photo

Nadel die; ~, ~n needle; *(Steck~, Hut~, Haar~)* pin

Nadel-: ~**baum** der conifer; coniferous tree; ~**wald** der coniferous forest

Nagel der; ~s, Nägel nail; **den** ~ **auf den Kopf treffen** *(fig. ugs.)* hit the nail on the head *(coll.)*

Nagel-: ~**bürste** die nailbrush; ~**feile** die nail-file; ~**lack** der nail varnish *(Brit.)*; nail polish

nageln *tr. V.* nail **(an** + *Akk.* to, **auf** + *Akk.* on); *(Med.)* pin; **nagel·neu** *Adj.* *(ugs.)* brand-new; **Nagel·schere** die nail-scissors *pl.*

nagen 1. *itr. V.* gnaw; **an etw.** *(Dat.)* ~: gnaw [at] sth.; **2.** *tr. V.* gnaw off; **ein Loch ins Holz** ~: gnaw a hole in the wood

nah *s.* nahe

Nah·aufnahme die *(Fot.)* close-up [photograph]

nahe ['na:ə]; **näher** ['nɛːɐ], **nächst...** **1.** *Adj.* a) *(räumlich)* near *pred.*; close *pred.*; nearby *attrib.*; b) *(zeitlich)* imminent; near *pred.*; c) *(eng)* close *(relationship etc.)*; **2.** *adv.* a) *(räumlich)* ~ **an** (+ *Dat./Akk.*), ~ **bei** close to; ~ **gelegen** nearby; **von** ~**m** from close up; b) *(zeitlich)* ~ **an die achtzig** *(ugs.)* pushing eighty *(coll.)*; c) *(eng)* closely; **3.** *Präp. mit Dat.* *(geh.)* near; close to; **Nähe** die; ~: closeness

nahe-: ~**bei** *Adv.* nearby; close by; ~**gehen** *unr. itr. V.*; *mit sein* jmdm. ~**gehen** affect sb. deeply; ~**kommen** *unr. itr. V.*; *mit sein* einer Sache *(Dat.)* ~**kommen** come close to sth.; *(amount)* approximate to sth.; jmdm./ **sich** |menschlich| ~**kommen** get to know sb./one another well; ~**legen** *tr. V.* suggest; give rise to *(suspicion, supposition, thought)*; ~**liegen** *unr. itr. V.* *(thought)* suggest itself; *(suspicion, question)* arise; ~**liegend** *Adj.* obvious *(reason, solution)*

nähen 1. *itr. V.* sew; *(Kleider machen)* make clothes; **2.** *tr. V.* a) sew *(seam, hem)*; make *(dress etc.)*; b) *(Med.)* stitch

näher 1. *Komp. zu* nahe; **2.** *Adj.* a) *(kürzer)* shorter *(way, road)*; b) *(genauer)* more precise *(information)*; closer *(investigation, inspection)*; **3.** *adv.* a) **bitte treten Sie** ~! please come in/nearer/this way; b) *(genauer)* more closely; *(im einzelnen)* in [more] detail

näher|kommen unr. itr. V.; mit sein jmdm. |menschlich| **~kommen** get on closer terms with sb.; **nähern** refl. V. approach; sich jmdm./einer Sache ~: approach sb./sth.

nahe-: ~|**stehen** unr. itr. V. jmdm. ~**stehen** be on intimate terms with sb.; ~**zu** Adv. almost; nearly; (mit Zahlenangabe) close on

Näh-: ~**garn** das [sewing] cotton; ~**kasten** der sewing-box

nahm 1. u. 3. Pers. Sg. Prät. v. nehmen

Näh-: ~**maschine** die sewing-machine; ~**nadel** die sewing-needle

nähren 1. tr. V. feed (mit on); 2. refl. V. (geh.) sich von etw. ~: live on sth.; ⟨animal⟩ feed on sth.; **nahrhaft** Adj. nourishing; **Nahrung** die; ~: food; **Nahrungs·mittel** das food [item]; ~**mittel** Pl. foodstuffs; **Nähr·wert** der nutritional value

Näh·seide die sewing silk

Naht die; ~, Nähte seam

Näh-: ~**verkehr** der local traffic; ~**verkehrs·zug** der local train

Näh·zeug das sewing things pl.

naiv 1. Adj. naïve; 2. adv. naïvely; **Naivität** die; ~: naïvety

Name der; ~ns, ~n name; **namens** Adv. by the name of

Namens-: ~**schild** das a) (an Türen usw.) name-plate; b) (zum Anstecken) name-badge; ~**tag** der name-day

namentlich 1. Adj. by name postpos.; 2. adv. by name; 3. Adv. (besonders) particularly; **namhaft** Adj. a) (berühmt) noted; b) (ansehnlich) noteworthy ⟨sum, difference⟩; notable ⟨contribution, opportunity⟩; **nämlich** Adv. a) er kann nicht kommen, er ist ~ krank he cannot come, as he is ill; b) (und zwar) namely

nannte 1. u. 3. Pers. Sg. Prät. v. nennen

nanu Interj. ~, was machst du denn hier? hello, what are you doing here?; ~, Sie gehen schon? what, you're going already?

Napf der; ~|e|s, Näpfe bowl (esp. for animal's food)

Narbe die; ~, ~n scar; **narbig** Adj. scarred

Narkose die; ~, ~n (Med.) narcosis

Narr der; ~en, ~en fool; **Narren·freiheit** die freedom to do as one pleases; **Närrin** die; ~, ~nen fool; **närrisch** 1. Adj. crazy; carnival-crazy ⟨season⟩; 2. adv. crazily

Narzisse die; ~, ~n narcissus

naschen 1. itr. V. (Süßes essen) eat sweet things; (heimlich essen) have a nibble; 2. tr. V. eat ⟨sweets, chocolate, etc.⟩; er hat Milch genascht he has been at the milk; **naschhaft** Adj. sweet-toothed; ~ sein have a sweet tooth

Nase die; ~, ~n nose; die ~ voll haben (ugs.) have had enough

Nasen-: ~**bluten** das; ~s bleeding from the nose; ~**loch** das nostril; ~**tropfen** Pl. nose-drops

nase·weis 1. Adj. precocious; pert ⟨remark, reply⟩; 2. adv. precociously; **Nas·horn** das rhinoceros

naß; nasser od. nässer, nassest... od. nässest...: Adj. wet; sich/das Bett ~ machen wet oneself/one's bed; **Nässe** die; ~: wetness; **naß·kalt** Adj. cold and wet; **Naß·rasur** die wet shaving no art.

Nation die; ~, ~en nation; **national** 1. Adj. a) national; 2. adv. nationally

National-: ~**elf** die (Fußball) national side; ~**hymne** die national anthem

Nationalismus der; ~ nationalism usu. no art.; **nationalistisch** 1. Adj. nationalist; nationalistic; 2. adv. nationalistically; **Nationalität** die; ~, ~en nationality

national-, National-: ~**mannschaft** die national team; ~**sozialismus** der National Socialism; ~**sozialist** der National Socialist; ~**sozialistisch** Adj. National Socialist

NATO, Nato die; ~: NATO, Nato no art.

Natron das; ~s |doppeltkohlensaures| ~: sodium bicarbonate; |kohlensaures| ~: sodium carbonate

Natter die; ~, ~n colubrid

Natur die; ~, ~en nature; die freie ~: [the] open countryside; **Naturalien** [natu'ra:ljən] Pl. natural produce sing. (used as payment); in ~ (Dat.) bezahlen pay in kind; **Naturalismus** der; ~: naturalism; **naturalistisch** 1. Adj. naturalistic; 2. adv. naturalistically; **Naturell** das; ~s, ~e temperament

natur-, Natur-: ~**erscheinung** die natural phenomenon; ~**farben** Adj. natural-coloured; ~**freund** der nature-lover; ~**gemäß** Adv. naturally; ~**geschichte** die; o. Pl. natural history; ~**gesetz** das law of nature; ~**getreu** 1. Adj. lifelike ⟨portrait, imitation⟩; faithful ⟨reproduction⟩; 2. adv. ⟨draw⟩ true to life; ⟨reproduce⟩

faithfully; ~**heilkunde** die naturo-
pathy *no art.;* ~**katastrophe** die
natural disaster

natürlich 1. *Adj.* natural; 2. *adv.*
⟨*laugh, behave*⟩ naturally; 3. *Adv.* a)
⟨*selbstverständlich, wie erwartet*⟩
naturally; of course; b) ⟨*zwar*⟩ of
course; **Natürlichkeit** die; ~: naturalness

Natur-: ~**park** der ≈ national park;
~**produkt** das natural product;
~**schutz** der [nature] conservation;
~**schutz·gebiet** das nature reserve;
~**verbunden** *Adj.* ⟨*person*⟩ in tune
with nature; ~**volk** das primitive
people; ~**wissenschaft** die natural
science *no art.;* ~**wissenschaftler**
der [natural] scientist; ~**wissenschaftlich** 1. *Adj.* scientific; 2. *adv.*
scientifically; ~**wunder** das miracle
or wonder of nature

Navigation die; ~: navigation *no art.*
n. Chr. *Abk.* nach Christus AD
Neandertaler der; ~s, ~: Neander-
thal man

Nebel der; ~s, ~: fog; *(weniger dicht)*
mist; **nebelig** *s.* neblig

Nebel-: ~**scheinwerfer** der fog-
lamp; ~**wand** die wall of fog

neben 1. *Präp. mit Dat.* a) *(Lage)* next
to; beside; b) *(außer)* apart from;
aside from *(Amer.);* c) *(verglichen mit)*
beside; 2. *Präp. mit Akk. (Richtung)*
next to; beside; **neben·an** *Adv.* next
door; **neben·bei** *Adv.* a) ⟨*work*⟩ on
the side; *(zusätzlich)* as well; b) *(beiläufig)* ⟨*remark, ask*⟩ by the way;
⟨*mention*⟩ in passing

neben-, Neben-: ~**beruf** der second
job; sideline; ~**beruflich** 1. *Adj.* eine
~berufliche Tätigkeit a second job; 2.
adv. on the side; er arbeitet ~beruf-
lich als Übersetzer he translates as a
sideline; ~**beschäftigung** die second job; sideline; ~**buhler** der,
~**buhlerin** die rival

neben·einander *Adv.* a) next to each
other; *(fig.: zusammen)* ⟨*live, exist*⟩
side by side; ~ wohnen live next door
to each other; b) *(gleichzeitig)*
together

nebeneinander-: ~**legen** *tr. V.* lay
or place ⟨*objects*⟩ side by side; ~**setzen** *tr. V.* put *or* place ⟨*persons, objects*⟩ next to each other; ~**sitzen**
unr. itr. V. sit next to each other;
~**stellen** *tr. V.* put *or* place ⟨*tables,
chairs, etc.*⟩ next to each other

Neben·erwerb der secondary oc-

cupation; ~**fach** das subsidiary subject; minor *(Amer.);* ~**fluß** der tributary; ~**gebäude** das a) annexe; out-
building; b) *(Nachbargebäude)* neighbouring building; ~**geräusch** das
background noise; ~**haus** das house
next door

neben·her *Adv. s.* nebenbei

nebenher-: ~**fahren** *unr. itr. V.; mit
sein* drive/ride alongside; ~**gehen**
unr. itr. V.; mit sein walk alongside

neben-, Neben-: ~**kosten** *Pl.* a) additional costs; b) *(bei Mieten)* heating,
lighting, and services; ~**produkt** das
by-product; ~**rolle** die supporting
role; ~**sache** die minor matter; ~**sachen** inessentials; ~**sächlich** *Adj.* of
minor importance *postpos.;* unimportant; minor ⟨*detail*⟩; ~**satz** der
(Sprachw.) subordinate clause;
~**straße** die side street; ~**tätigkeit**
die second job; sideline; ~**tisch** der
next table; ~**verdienst** der additional income; ~**wirkung** die side-
effect; ~**zimmer** das next room

neblig *Adj.* foggy; *(weniger dicht)*
misty

Necessaire [nesɛˈsɛːɐ̯] das; ~s, ~s
sponge-bag *(Brit.);* toilet bag *(Amer.)*

necken *tr. V.* tease; **Neckerei** die;
~: teasing

nee *(ugs.)* no; nope *(Amer. coll.)*

Neffe der; ~n, ~n nephew

negativ 1. *Adj.* negative; 2. *adv.* ⟨*answer*⟩ in the negative; **Negativ** das;
~s, ~e *(Fot.)* negative

Neger der; ~s, ~: Negro; **Negerin**
die; ~, ~nen Negress

Neid der; ~[e]s envy; jealousy;
neiden *tr. V. (geh.)* jmdm. etw. ~:
envy sb. [for] sth.; **neidisch** 1. *Adj.*
envious; 2. *adv.* enviously

neigen 1. *tr. V.* tip; tilt; incline ⟨*head,
upper part of body*⟩; 2. *refl. V.:* ⟨*person*⟩ lean; ⟨*ship*⟩ heel over, list;
⟨*scales*⟩ tip; 3. *itr. V.* a) zu Erkältun-
gen/Krankheiten ~: be prone to
colds/illnesses; b) *(tendieren)* tend;
Neigung die; ~, ~en a) *(Vorliebe)* inclination; b) *o. Pl. (Tendenz)* tendency

nein *Interj.* no; **Nein** das; ~[s], ~[s]
no; **Nein·stimme** die no-vote

Nektar der; ~s, ~e *(Bot.)* nectar; **Nektarine** die; ~, ~n nectarine

Nelke die; ~, ~n **a)** pink; *(Dianthus caryophyllus)* carnation; **b)** *(Gewürz)* clove

nennen 1. *unr. tr. V.* **a)** call; **b)** *(angeben)* give ⟨name, date of birth, address, reason, price, etc.⟩; **c)** *(anführen)* give ⟨example⟩; *(erwähnen)* mention ⟨person, name⟩; **2.** *unr. refl. V.* ⟨person, thing⟩ be called

neo-, Neo-: neo-
Neon das; ~s neon
Neon-: ~**licht** das neon light; ~**röhre** die neon tube
Nepal (das); ~s Nepal
Nepp der; ~s *(ugs. abwertend)* daylight robbery *no art.*; rip-off *(sl.)*; **Nepp·lokal** das *(ugs. abwertend)* clip-joint *(sl.)*

Nerv der; ~s, ~en nerve; **die ~en verlieren** lose control [of oneself]; **jmdm. auf die ~en gehen** *od.* **fallen** get on sb.'s nerves

nerven-, Nerven-: ~**aufreibend** *Adj.* nerve-racking; ~**bündel** das *(ugs.)* bundle of nerves *(coll.)*; ~**gift** das neurotoxin; ~**heilanstalt** die *(veralt.)* psychiatric hospital; ~**krank** *Adj.* ⟨person⟩ suffering from a nervous disease; ~**probe** die mental trial; ~**säge** die *(salopp)* pain in the neck *(coll.)*; ~**zusammenbruch** der nervous breakdown

nervlich *Adj.* nervous ⟨strain⟩; **nervös 1.** *Adj. (auch Med.)* nervous; jittery ⟨person⟩; **2.** *adv.* nervously; **Nervosität** die; ~ nervousness; **nervtötend** *Adj.* nerve-racking ⟨wait⟩; soul-destroying ⟨activity, work⟩

Nerz der; ~es, ~e mink; **Nerz·mantel** der mink coat

Nessel die; ~, ~n nettle

Nest das; ~[e]s, ~er **a)** nest; **b)** *(fam.: Bett)* bed; **c)** *(ugs. abwertend: kleiner Ort)* little place

nett 1. *Adj.* nice; *(freundlich)* kind; **2.** *adv.* nicely; *(freundlich)* nicely; kindly; **netter·weise** *Adv.* kindly

netto *Adv.* ⟨weigh, earn, etc.⟩ net

Netto-: ~**einkommen** das net income; ~**gehalt** das net salary

Netz das; ~es, ~e **a)** net; *(Einkaufs~)* string bag; *(Gepäck~)* [luggage-]rack; **b)** *(Spinnen~)* web; **c)** *(Verteiler~, Verkehrs~ usw.)* network; *(für Strom, Wasser, Gas)* mains *pl.*; **Netz·haut** die *(Anat.)* retina

neu 1. *Adj.* new; **die ~este Mode** the latest fashion; **das ist mir ~:** that is news to me; **der/die Neue** the new man/woman/boy/girl; **2.** *adv.* **a)** ~ **tapeziert/gestrichen** repapered/repainted; **sich ~ einrichten** refurnish one's home; **b)** *(gerade erst)* **diese Ware ist ~ eingetroffen** this item has just come in; **neu·artig** *Adj.* new; **Neu·bau** der; *Pl.* **Neubauten** new house/building; **Neubau·wohnung** die flat *(Brit.)* or *(Amer.)* apartment in a new block/house

neuerdings *Adv.* **er trägt ~ eine Brille** he has recently started wearing glasses; **neu·eröffnet** *Adj.* **a)** newly-opened; **b)** *(wiedereröffnet)* reopened; **Neu·eröffnung** die **a)** opening; **b)** *(Wiedereröffnung)* reopening; **Neuerung** die; ~, ~en innovation; **neu·geboren** *Adj.* newborn; **Neu·gier, Neugierde** die; ~ curiosity; *(Wißbegierde)* inquisitiveness; **neu·gierig 1.** *Adj.* curious; an inquisitive; inquisitive ⟨person⟩; **ich bin ~, was er dazu sagt** I'm curious to know what he'll say about it; **2.** *adv.* ⟨ask⟩ inquisitively; ⟨peer⟩ nosily *(coll. derog.)*; **Neuheit** die; ~, ~en **a)** o. *Pl.* novelty; **b)** *(Neues)* new product/gadget/article *etc.*; **Neuigkeit** die; ~, ~en piece of news; ~**en** news *sing.*; **Neu·jahr** das New Year's Day; **Neu·land** das *(fig.)* new ground; **neulich** *Adv.* recently; ~ **morgens** the other morning; **Neuling** der; ~s, ~e newcomer; *(auf einem Gebiet)* novice; **Neu·mond** der new moon

neun *Kardinalz.* nine; **Neun** die; ~, ~en nine

neun-: ~**hundert** *Kardinalz.* nine hundred; ~**jährig** *Adj. (9 Jahre alt)* nine-year-old *attrib.*; *(9 Jahre dauernd)* nine-year *attrib.*; ~**mal** *Adv.* nine times

neunt... *Ordinalz.* ninth

neun·tausend *Kardinalz.* nine thousand; **Neuntel** das *(schweiz. meist* der)*; ~s, ~: ninth; **neuntens** *Adv.* ninthly; **neun·zehn** *Kardinalz.* nineteen; **neunzig** *Kardinalz.* ninety; **neunziger** *indekl. Adj.*; *nicht präd.* **die ~ Jahre** the nineties; **neunzigst...** *Ordinalz.* ninetieth

neu·reich *Adj.* nouveau riche

Neurose die; ~, ~n neurosis; **neurotisch** *Adj.* neurotic

Neu·see·land (das); ~s New Zealand; **Neuseeländer** der; ~s, ~: New Zealander

neutral 1. *Adj.* neutral; 2. *adv.* sich ~ verhalten remain neutral; **Neutralität** die; ~, ~en neutrality; **Neutron** das; ~s, ~en neutron; **Neutrum** das; ~s, **Neutra** (österr. nur so) od. **Neutren** (Sprachw.) neuter

neu-, Neu-: ~**wert** der value when new; ~**wertig** *Adj.* as new; ~**zeit** die; o, *Pl.* modern age; ~**zeitlich** *Adj.* modern

nicht *Adv.* a) not; ~! [no,] don't!; ~|wahr|? isn't it/he/she *etc.*; don't you/we/they *etc.*; du magst das, ~|wahr|? you like that, don't you?; was du ~ sagst! you don't say!

nicht-, Nicht-: non-

Nicht·angriffs·pakt der non-aggression pact

Nichte die; ~, ~n niece

nichtig *Adj.* a) (geh.) vain (things, pleasures, etc.); trivial (reason); b) (Rechtsspr.) void; **Nicht·raucher** der non-smoker; „~raucher" 'no smoking'; **nicht·rostend** *Adj.* non-rusting (blade); stainless (steel); **nichts** *Indefinitpron.* nothing; ich möchte ~: I don't want anything

nichts-, Nichts-: ~**nutz** der; ~es, ~e (veralt.) good-for-nothing; ~**nutzig** *Adj.* (veralt.) good-for-nothing attrib.; worthless (existence); ~**sagend** 1. *Adj.* empty; (fig.: ausdruckslos) expressionless (face); 2. *adv.* meaninglessly (formulated); ~**tun** das idleness no art.

Nickel das; ~s nickel

nicken *itr. V.* nod

nie *Adv.* never

nieder 1. *Adj.; nicht präd.* lower (class, intelligence); minor (official); lowly (family, origins, birth); menial (task); 2. *Adv.* down

nieder-, Nieder-: ~**gang** der fall; decline; ~**gehen** *unr. itr. V.; mit sein* (plane etc., rain, avalanche) come down; ~**geschlagen** *Adj.* dejected; ~**geschlagenheit** die; ~: dejection; ~**lage** die defeat

Nieder·lande *Pl.*: die ~: the Netherlands; **Niederländer** der; ~, ~: Dutchman; **Niederländerin** die; ~, ~nen Dutchwoman; **niederländisch** *Adj.* Dutch; Netherlands attrib. (government, embassy, etc.)

nieder-, Nieder-: ~|**lassen** *unr. refl. V.* a) set up in business; (doctor, lawyer) set up in practice; b) (seinen Wohnsitz nehmen) settle; ~**lassung** die; ~, ~en (Wirtsch.) branch; ~|**le-**

gen *tr. V.* a) (geh.: hinlegen) lay or put down; lay (wreath); b) (fig.) resign [from] (office); relinquish (command)

Nieder·sachsen (das) Lower Saxony

nieder-, Nieder-: ~**schlag** der precipitation; ~|**schlagen** *unr. tr. V.* a) jmdn. ~schlagen knock sb. down; b) (beenden) suppress, put down (revolt, uprising, etc.); c) (senken) lower (eyes, eyelids); ~**trächtig** 1. *Adj.* malicious (person, slander, lie, etc.); (verachtenswert) despicable (person); base (misrepresentation, slander, lie); 2. *adv.* (betray, lie, treat) in a despicable way; ~**trächtigkeit** die; ~, ~en a) o. Pl. s. ~**trächtig** 1: maliciousness; despicableness; baseness; b) (gemeine Handlung) despicable act

Niederung die; ~, ~en low-lying area; (an Flußläufen, Küsten) flats pl.; (Tal) valley

niedlich 1. *Adj.* sweet; cute (Amer. coll.); 2. *adv.* sweetly

niedrig 1. *Adj.* low; lowly (origins, birth); base (instinct, desire, emotion); vile (motive); 2. *adv.* (hang, fly) low

niemals *Adv.* never; **niemand** *Indefinitpron.* nobody; no one

Niere die; ~, ~n kidney

Nieren-: ~**entzündung** die nephritis; ~**stein** der kidney stone

Niesel·regen der drizzle

niesen *itr. V.* sneeze

¹**Niete** die; ~, ~n a) (Los) blank; b) (ugs.: Mensch) dead loss (coll.) (in + Dat. at)

²**Niete** die; ~, ~n rivet; **nieten** *tr. V.* rivet

Nikolaus·tag der St Nicholas' Day

Nikotin das; ~s nicotine; **nikotinarm** *Adj.* low-nicotine attrib.; low in nicotine pred.

Nil der; ~|s| Nile; **Nil·pferd** das hippopotamus

nimm *Imperativ Sg. v.* nehmen

nippen *itr. V.* sip

nirgends, nirgend·wo *Adv.* nowhere

Nische die; ~, ~n niche; (Erweiterung eines Raumes) recess

nisten *itr. V.* nest

Nitrat das; ~|e|s, ~e nitrate

Niveau [ni'vo:] das; ~s, ~s level; (Qualitäts~) standard

Nixe die; ~, ~n nixie; (mit Fischschwanz) mermaid

nobel *Adj.* a) (geh.) noble;

noble[-minded] ⟨*person*⟩; b) *(oft spött.: luxuriös)* elegant; posh *(coll.)*

Nobel·preis der Nobel prize

noch 1. *Adv.* a) *([wie] bisher)* still; ~ **nicht** not yet; **sie sind immer ~ nicht da** they're still not here; **ich habe Großva- ter ~ gekannt** I'm old enough to have known grandfather; **er hat ~ Glück gehabt he was lucky; das geht ~:** that's [still] all right; b) *(als Rest einer Menge)* **ich habe [nur] ~ zehn Mark** I've [only] ten marks left; **es sind ~ 10 km bis zur Grenze** it's another 10 km. to the border; c) *(bevor etw. anderes geschieht)* just; **ich will ~ [schnell] du- schen** I just want to have a [quick] shower; d) *(irgendwann einmal)* some time; one day; **er wird ~ anrufen/kom- men** he will still call/come; e) *(womög- lich)* if you're/he's *etc.* not careful; **du kommst ~ zu spät!** you'll be late if you're not careful; f) *(drückt eine ge- ringe zeitliche Distanz aus)* only; *ge- stern* **habe ich ihn ~ gesehen** I saw him only yesterday; g) *(nicht später als)* ~ **am selben Abend** the [very] same eve- ning; h) *(außerdem, zusätzlich)* **wer war ~ da?** who else was there?; ~ **etwas Kaffee?** [would you like] some more coffee?; **Geld/Kleider** *usw.* ~ **und ~** heaps and heaps of money/clothes *etc. (coll.);* i) **er ist ~ größer [als Karl]** he is even taller [than Karl]; **er will ~ mehr haben** he wants even more; **jeder ~ so dumme Mensch versteht das** anyone, however stupid, can under- stand that; j) **wie heißt sie [doch] ~?** [now] what's her name again?; 2. *Partikel* **das ist ~ Qualität!** that's what I call quality; **der wird sich ~ wundern** *(ugs.)* he's in for a surprise; **er kann ~ nicht einmal lesen** he can't even read; 3. *Konj. (und auch nicht)* nor; **weder ... noch** neither ... nor; **noch·mals** *Adv.* again

Nominativ der; ~s, ~e *(Sprachw.)* nominative [case]

Nonne die; ~, ~n nun

Nord *o. Art.; o. Pl. (bes. Seemannsspr., Met.) s.* Norden

nord-, Nord-: ~**afrika** (das) North Africa; ~**amerika** (das) North America; ~**deutsch** *Adj.* North Ger- man

Norden der; ~s north; **der ~:** the North; **nach ~:** northwards; **Nord· irland** (das) Northern Ireland; **nor- disch** *Adj.* Nordic; **Nord·kap** das North Cape; **nördlich** 1. *Adj.* a) *(im*

Norden gelegen) northern; b) *(nach, aus dem Norden)* northerly; c) *(aus dem Norden kommend, für den Norden typisch)* Northern; 2. *adv.* north- wards; ~ **von ...:** [to the] north of ...; 3. *Präp. mit Gen.* [to the] north of; **Nord·pol** ['--] der North Pole; **Nord·rhein-Westfalen** (das); ~s North Rhine-Westphalia; **Nord·see** die; *o. Pl.* North Sea; **nord·wärts** *Adv.* northwards; **Nord·wind** der northerly wind

Nörgelei die; ~ *(abwertend) o. Pl.* grumbling; **nörgeln** *itr. V. (abwer- tend)* moan, grumble **(an** + *Dat.* about)

Norm die; ~, ~**en** a) norm; b) *(gefor- derte Arbeitsleistung)* quota; c) *(Sport)* qualifying standard; d) *(technische, in- dustrielle ~)* standard; **normal** 1. *Adj.* normal; 2. *adv.* normally; **Nor- mal·benzin** das ≈ two-star petrol *(Brit.);* regular *(Amer.);* **normaler- weise** *Adv.* normally; **normali- sieren** 1. *tr. V.* normalize; 2. *refl. V.* return to normal

Normandie die; ~: Normandy

normen *tr. V.,* **normieren** *tr. V.* standardize

Norwegen (das); ~s Norway; **Nor- weger** der; ~s, ~, **Norwegerin** die; ~, ~**nen** Norwegian; **norwegisch** *Adj.* Norwegian

Nostalgie die; ~: nostalgia

Not die; ~, **Nöte** a) *(Gefahr)* **in ~ sein** be in desperate straits; b) *o. Pl. (Man- gel, Armut)* need; poverty [and hard- ship]; ~ **leiden** suffer poverty [and hardship]; **in ~ geraten/sein** en- counter hard times/be suffering want [and deprivation]; c) *o. Pl. (Verzwei- flung)* distress; d) *(Sorge, Mühe)* trouble; **mit knapper ~:** by the skin of one's teeth; f) *o. Pl. (veralt.: Notwen- digkeit)* necessity; **zur ~:** if need be

Notar der; ~s, ~e notary; **Notariat** das; ~[e]s, ~e a) *(Amt)* notaryship; b) *(Kanzlei)* notary's office

not-, Not-: ~**arzt** der doctor on [emergency] call; ~**ausgang** der emergency exit; ~**bremse** die emer- gency brake; ~**dienst** der *s.* Bereit- schaftsdienst; ~**dürftig** 1. *Adj.* make- shift ⟨*shelter, repair*⟩; scanty ⟨*cover, clothing*⟩; 2. *adv.* scantily ⟨*clothed*⟩

Note die; ~, ~**n** a) *(Zeichen)* note; b) *Pl. (Text)* music *sing.;* c) *(Schul~)* mark; d) *(Eislauf, Turnen)* score

not-, Not-: ~**fall** der a) emergency; b)

im ~fall *(nötigenfalls)* if need be;
~falls *Adv.* if need be; **~gedrungen**
Adv. of necessity
notieren 1. *tr. V.* [sich *(Dat.)*] etw. ~:
make a note of sth.; 2. *itr. V. (Börsenw., Wirtsch.)* be quoted (mit at)
nötig 1. *Adj.* necessary; etw./jmdn. ~
haben need sth./sb.; 2. *adv.* er braucht
~ Hilfe he is in urgent need of help;
nötigen *tr. V.* compel; force;
(Rechtsspr.) coerce
Notiz die; ~, ~en note; *(Zeitungs~)*
brief report; **von jmdm./etw. [keine] ~**
nehmen take [no] notice of sb./sth.
Notiz-: ~**block** der; *Pl.* ~**blocks,**
schweiz.: ~**blöcke** notepad; ~**buch**
das notebook
not-, Not-: ~**lage** die serious difficulties *pl.;* ~**landen**[1] *itr. V.; mit sein*
do an emergency landing; ~**landung**
die emergency landing; ~**leidend**
Adj. needy; ~**lösung die** stopgap;
~**lüge die** evasive lie; *(aus Rücksichtnahme)* white lie
notorisch 1. *Adj.* notorious; 2. *adv.*
notoriously
Not-: ~**ruf der a)** *(Hilferuf)* emergency
call; *(eines Schiffes)* Mayday call; **b)**
(Nummer) emergency number;
~**ruf·nummer die** emergency number; ~**ruf·säule die** emergency telephone *(mounted in a pillar);* ~**stand**
der crisis; *(Staatsrecht)* state of emergency; ~**unterkunft die** emergency
accommodation *no pl., no indef. art.;*
~**wehr die** self-defence
not·wendig *Adj.* necessary; **Notwendigkeit die;** ~, ~en necessity
Nougat ['nuːgat] **der;** *auch das;* ~s
nougat
Novelle die; ~, ~n *(Literaturw.)*
novella
November der; ~[s], ~: November
Nr. *Abk.* Nummer No
Nu der: im Nu in no time
Nuance ['nʸãːsə] **die;** ~, ~n nuance;
(Grad) shade
nüchtern 1. *Adj. (nicht betrunken;
realistisch)* sober; *(ungeschminkt)*
bare, plain *(fact);* **der Patient muß ~**
sein the patient's stomach must be
empty; 2. *adv.* soberly
nuckeln *(ugs.) itr. V.* suck (**an** + *Dat.*
at)
Nudel die; ~, ~n piece of spaghetti/
vermicelli/tortellini *etc.; (als Suppen-*

einlage) noodle; ~**n** *(Teigwaren)* pasta
sing.; (als Suppeneinlage) noodles
nuklear 1. *Adj.* nuclear; 2. *adv.* ~ **an-**
getrieben nuclear-powered
null Kardinalz. nought; ~ **Komma**
sechs [nought] point six; **gegen ~ Uhr**
around twelve midnight; **Null die;** ~,
~**en a)** nought; zero; **in ~ Komma**
nichts *(ugs.)* in less than no time;
gleich ~ sein *(fig.)* be practically zero;
auf ~ stehen ⟨*indicator, needle, etc.*⟩ be
at zero; **b)** *(ugs.: Versager)* failure;
dead loss *(coll.);* **Null·punkt der**
zero
numerieren *tr. V.* number; **Numerierung die;** ~, ~en numbering;
Nummer die; ~, ~**n a)** number; **ein**
Wagen mit [einer] Münchner ~: a car
with a Munich registration; **ich bin**
unter der ~ 24 26 79 zu erreichen I can
be reached on 24 26 79; **b)** *(Ausgabe)*
issue; **c)** *(Größe)* size; **Nummern·schild das** number-plate;
license plate *(Amer.)*
nun 1. *Adv.* now; 2. *Partikel* now; **das**
hast du ~ davon! it serves you right!;
kommst du ~ mit oder nicht? now are
you coming or not?; ~ **gut** [well], all
right; ~, ~! now, come on; ~ **ja** ...:
well, yes ...
nur 1. *Adv.* **a)** *(nicht mehr als)* only;
just; **b)** *(ausschließlich)* only; **nicht**
~ ..., sondern auch ...: not only ..., but
also ...; ~ **so zum Spaß** just for fun; 2.
Konj. but; **ich kann dir das Buch leihen, ~ nicht heute** I can lend you the
book, only not today; 3. *Partikel* **wenn**
er ~ hier wäre if only he were here; ~
zu! go ahead; **laß dich ~ nicht erwischen** just don't let me/them *etc.* catch
you; **was sollen wir ~ tun?** what on
earth are we going to do?; **so schnell**
er ~ konnte just as fast as he could
Nürnberg (das) ~s Nuremberg
Nuß die; ~, Nüsse **a)** nut; **Nuß·baum**
der walnut-tree; **Nuß·knacker der**
nutcrackers *pl.*
Nutte die; ~, ~n *(derb)* tart *(sl.);*
hooker *(Amer. sl.)*
nutz-: ~**bar** *Adj.* usable; exploitable,
utilizable ⟨*mineral resources, invention*⟩; cultivatable ⟨*land, soil*⟩; ~**bringend** 1. *Adj.* useful; *(gewinnbringend)* profitable; 2. *adv.* profitably
nutzen 1. *tr. V.* **a)** use; exploit, utilize
⟨*natural resources*⟩; cultivate ⟨*land,
soil*⟩; harness ⟨*energy source*⟩; exploit
⟨*advantage*⟩; **b)** *(be~, aus~)* use;
make use of; 2. *itr. V. s.* **nützen** 1;

---

[1] *ich notlande, notgelandet, notzulanden*

Nutzen der; ~s a) benefit; [jmdm.] von ~ sein be of use [to sb.]; b) (Profit) profit; **nützen** 1. itr. V. be of use (Dat. to); **nichts** ~: be no use; 2. tr. V. s. **nutzen** 1; **nützlich** Adj. useful; **nutzlos** 1. Adj. useless; (vergeblich) vain attrib.; in vain pred.; 2. adv. uselessly; (vergeblich) in vain; **Nutz·losigkeit** die; ~: uselessness; (Vergeblichkeit) futility; **Nutznießer** der; ~s, ~, **Nutznießerin** die; ~, ~nen beneficiary; **Nutzung** die; ~, ~ en use; (des Landes, des Bodens) cultivation; (von Bodenschätzen) exploitation; utilization; (einer Energiequelle) harnessing

Nylon Ⓦ ['nailɔn] das; ~s nylon

Nymphe die; ~, ~n (Myth., Zool.) nymph

Nymphomanin die; ~, ~nen (Psych.) nymphomaniac

O

o, O das; ~, ~: o/O

O Abk. Ost[en] E

ö, Ö das; ~, ~: o/O umlaut

o. ä. Abk. oder ähnlich[es] or similar

Oase die; ~, ~n (auch fig.) oasis

ob Konj. a) whether; b) **und ob!** of course!

OB Abk. Oberbürgermeister

Obacht die; ~ (bes. südd.) caution; ~ **auf jmdn./etw. geben** take care of sb./ sth.; (aufmerksam sein) pay attention to sb./sth.

Obdach das; ~[e]s (geh.) shelter; **obdach·los** Adj. homeless; **Obdachlose** der/die; adj. Dekl. homeless person/man/woman; **die** ~n the homeless

Obduktion die; ~, ~en (Med., Rechtsw.) post-mortem [examination]; autopsy

O-Beine Pl. bandy legs; bow-legs

oben Adv. a) **hier/dort** ~: up here/ there; **weiter** ~: further up; **nach** ~: upwards; **von** ~: from above; **von** ~ **herab** (fig.) condescendingly; b) (im Gebäude) upstairs; **nach** ~: upstairs;

c) (am oberen Ende, zum oberen Ende hin) at the top; **nach** ~ [hin] towards the top; **von** ~: from the top; c) (an der Oberseite) on top; d) (in einer Hierarchie, Rangfolge) at the top; e) ([weiter] vorn im Text) above; **oben·genannt** Adj. above-mentioned

ober... Adj. upper attrib.; top attrib.

Ober der; ~s, ~: waiter; **Herr** ~! waiter!

Ober-: ~**arm** der upper arm; ~**bekleidung** die outer clothing; ~**bürgermeister** der mayor

Ober·fläche die surface; (Flächeninhalt) surface area; **oberflächlich** 1. Adj. superficial; 2. adv. superficially

ober·halb 1. Adv. above; ~ **von** above; 2. Präp. mit Gen. above

Ober-: ~**haupt** das head; (einer Verschwörung) leader; ~**hemd** das shirt; ~**kiefer** der upper jaw; ~**körper** der upper part of the body; ~**schenkel** der thigh; ~**schicht** die (Soziol.) upper class; ~**schule** die secondary school; ~**seite** die top

oberst... s. ober...

Ober·teil das od. der top [part]; (eines Bikinis, Anzugs, Kleids usw.) top [half]

ob·gleich Konj. s. obwohl

obig Adj. above

Objekt das; ~s, ~e object; (Kaufmannsspr.: Immobilie) property; **objektiv** 1. Adj. objective; 2. adv. objectively; **Objektiv** das; ~s, ~e lens; **Objektivität** die; ~: objectivity

Obrigkeit die; ~, ~en authorities pl.

ob·schon Konj. (geh.) although

Obst das; ~[e]s fruit

Obst-: ~**baum** der fruit-tree; ~**garten** der orchard; ~**kuchen** der fruit flan; ~**saft** der fruit juice

obszön 1. Adj. obscene; 2. adv. obscenely; **Obszönität** die; ~, ~en obscenity

ob·wohl Konj. although; though

Ochse ['ɔksə] der; ~n, ~n a) ox; bullock; b) (salopp) numskull (coll.); **Ochsen·schwanz·suppe** die oxtail soup

od. Abk. oder

öde Adj. a) deserted; desolate ⟨area, landscape⟩; b) (unfruchtbar) barren; c) (langweilig) tedious; dreary ⟨life, time, existence⟩; **Öde** die; ~: s. öde a–c: desertedness; desolateness; barrenness; tediousness; dreariness

oder Konj. or; (in Fragen) **er ist doch hier,** ~? he is here, isn't he? (zweifelnd) he is here – or isn't he?

OEZ *Abk.* osteuropäische Zeit EET

Ofen der; ~s, **Öfen** heater; *(Kohle~)* stove; *(Back~)* oven; *(Brenn~, Trocken~)* kiln; **Ofen·rohr** das [stove] flue

offen 1. *Adj.* a) open; **ein ~es Hemd** a shirt with the collar unfastened; ~ **haben** *od.* **sein** be open; **~es Licht** a naked light; b) *(frei)* vacant *(job, post);* c) *(ungewiß, ungeklärt)* open *(question);* uncertain *(result);* d) *(noch nicht bezahlt)* outstanding *(bill);* e) *(freimütig, aufrichtig)* frank [and open] *(person);* frank, candid *(look, opinion, reply);* **2.** *adv.* openly; ~ **gesagt** frankly; to be frank; **offen·bar 1.** *Adj.* obvious; **2.** *adv.* obviously; **Offenbarung** die; ~, ~en revelation; **offen|bleiben** *unr. itr. V.;* **mit sein** a) stay open; b) *(ungeklärt bleiben)* remain open; *(decision)* be left open; **Offen·heit** die; ~: *s.* **offen e:** frankness [and openness]; candour

offen-: ~kundig 1. *Adj.* obvious; **2.** *adv.* obviously; **~lassen** *unr. tr. V.* etw. ~lassen leave sth. open; **~sichtlich 1.** *Adj.* obvious; **2.** *adv.* obviously

offensiv 1. *Adj.* a) offensive; b) *(Sport)* attacking; **2.** *adv.* a) offensively; b) *(Sport)* ~ **spielen** play an attacking game; **Offensive** die; ~, ~n *(auch Sport)* offensive

offen|stehen *unr. itr. V.* be open

öffentlich 1. *Adj.* public; state *attrib.,* [state-] maintained *(school);* **der ~e Dienst** the civil service; **2.** *adv.* publicly; *(perform, appear)* in public; **Öffentlichkeit** die; ~: public

offiziell 1. *Adj.* official; **2.** *adv.* officially

Offizier der; ~s, ~e officer

öffnen 1. *tr. V.* open; turn on *(tap);* undo *(coat, blouse, button, zip);* **2.** *itr. V.* a) *[jmdm.]* ~: open the door [to sb.]; b) *(geöffnet werden) (shop, bank, etc.)* open; **3.** *refl. V.* open; **Öffner** der; ~s, ~: opener; **Öffnung** die; ~, ~en opening; **Öffnungs·zeiten** *Pl.* opening times

oft *Adv.* öfter, am öftesten often; **wie oft soll ich dir noch sagen, daß ...?** how many [more] times do I have to tell you that ...?; **öfter** *Adv.* now and then; **oftmals** *Adv.* often; frequently

OG *Abk.* Obergeschoß

ohne 1. *Präp. mit Akk.* without; ~ **mich!** [you can] count me out!; ~ **weiteres** *(leicht, einfach)* easily; *(ohne Ein-*

wand) readily; **2.** *Konj.* ~ **zu zögern** without hesitation; **ohne·hin** *Adv.* anyway

Ohnmacht die; ~, ~en a) faint; **in ~ fallen** faint; b) *(Machtlosigkeit)* powerlessness; impotence; **ohnmächtig 1.** *Adj.* a) unconscious; ~ **werden** faint; ~ **sein** have fainted; b) *(machtlos)* powerless; impotent; **2.** *adv.* impotently; ~ **zusehen** watch helplessly

Ohr das; ~[e]s, ~en ear; **gute/schlechte ~en haben** have good/poor hearing *sing.;* **jmdn. übers ~ hauen** *(fig. ugs.)* put one over on sb. *(coll.);* **Öhr** das, ~[e]s, ~e eye; **Ohren·schmerz** der earache; **~schmerzen haben** have [an] earache *sing.*

ohr-, Ohr-: ~feige die box on the ears; **~feigen** *tr. V.* jmdn. **~feigen** box sb.'s ears; **ich könnte mich ~feigen!** *(ugs.)* I could kick myself!; **~läppchen** das ear-lobe; **~ring** der ear-ring

okay [o'ke] *(ugs.) Interj., Adj., adv.* OK *(coll.);* okay *(coll.)*

öko-, Öko-: eco-

Ökologie die; ~: ecology; **ökologisch 1.** *Adj.* ecological; **2.** *adv.* ecologically

ökonomisch 1. *Adj.* a) economic; b) *(sparsam)* economical; **2.** *adv.* economically

Oktober der; ~[s], ~: October

Öl das; ~[e]s, ~e oil; **in Öl malen** paint in oils; **ölen** *tr. V.* oil; **Öl·farbe** die a) oil-based paint; b) *(zum Malen)* oil-paint; **ölig** *Adj.* oily

Olive die; ~, ~n olive

Öl-: ~ofen der oil heater; **~sardine** die sardine in oil; **eine Dose ~n** a tin of sardines; **~wechsel** der *(bes. Kfz-W.)* oil-change

Olympiade die; ~, ~n Olympic Games *pl.;* Olympics *pl.;* **Olympia-stadion** das Olympic stadium; **olympisch** *Adj.* Olympic; **die Olympischen Spiele** the Olympic Games; the Olympics

Oma die; ~, ~s *(fam.)* granny *(coll./ child lang.)*

Omelett [ɔm[ə]'lɛt] das; ~[e]s, ~e *od.* ~s omelette

Omnibus der; ~ses, ~se omnibus *(formal); (Privat- und Reisebus auch)* coach

Onkel der; ~s, ~ *od. (ugs.)* ~s uncle

OP [o:'pe:] der; ~[s], ~[s] *Abk.* Operationssaal

Opa der; ~s, ~s *(fam.)* grandad *(coll./ child lang.)*

Opal der; ~s, ~e opal

OPEC ['o:pɛk] die; ~ *Abk.* OPEC

Oper die; ~, ~n opera; *(Opernhaus)* Opera; opera-house

Operation die; ~, ~en operation; **Operations·saal** der operating-theatre *(Brit.)* or -room

Operette die; ~, ~n operetta

operieren 1. *tr. V.* operate on *(patient)*; 2. *itr. V.* operate

Opern·glas das opera-glass[es *pl.*]

Opfer das; ~s, ~: a) sacrifice; b) *(Geschädigter)* victim; **opfern** *tr. V. (auch fig.)* sacrifice; offer up *(fruit, produce, etc.)*

Opium das; ~s opium

opponieren *itr. V.* gegen jmdn./etw. ~: oppose sth./sb.; **Opposition** die; ~, ~en opposition; **oppositionell** *Adj.* opposition *attrib. (group, movement, etc.); (newspaper, writer, artist, etc.)* opposed to the government

Optik die; ~: optics *sing., no art.*; **Optiker** der; ~s, ~: optician

optimal 1. *Adj.* optimal; optimum *attrib.*; 2. *adv.* jmdn. ~ beraten give sb. the best possible advice; **Optimismus** der; ~: optimism; **Optimist** der; ~en, ~en, **Optimistin** die; ~, ~nen optimist; **optimistisch** 1. *Adj.* optimistic; 2. *adv.* optimistically

optisch 1. *Adj.* optical; visual *(impression); eine ~ Täuschung* an optical illusion; 2. *adv.* optically; visually *(impressive, effective)*

orange [o'rãːʒ(ə)] *indekl. Adj.* orange; **Orange** die; ~, ~n orange; **Orangen-:** ~marmelade die orange marmalade; ~saft der orange-juice

Orchester [ɔr'kɛstɐ] das; ~s, ~: orchestra

Orden der; ~s, ~: a) order; b) *(Ehrenzeichen)* decoration

ordentlich 1. *Adj.* a) [neat and] tidy; neat *(handwriting, clothes);* b) *(anständig)* respectable; proper *(manners);* c) *(planmäßig)* ordinary *(meeting); ~es Mitglied* full member; d) *(ugs.: richtig)* proper; real; *ein ~es Stück Kuchen* a nice big piece of cake; e) *(ugs.: recht gut)* decent *(wine, flat, marks, etc.); ganz ~:* pretty good; 2. *adv.* a) tidily; neatly; *(write)* neatly; b) *(anständig)* properly; c) *(ugs.: gehörig) ~ feiern* have a real good celebration *(coll.);* d) *(ugs.: recht gut) (ski, speak, etc.)* really well

Ordinal·zahl die ordinal [number]; **ordinär** 1. *Adj.* vulgar; 2. *adv.* vulgarly; **Ordinate** die; ~, ~n *(Math.)* ordinate

ordnen *tr. V.* arrange; **sein Leben/seine Finanzen ~:** straighten out one's life/put one's finances in order; **Ordner** der; ~s, ~: file; **Ordnung** die; ~, ~en order; *(geregelter Ablauf)* routine; **~ halten** keep things tidy; **in ~ sein** *(ugs.)* be OK *(coll.)* or all right; **hier ist etw. nicht in ~:** there's something wrong here; **sie ist in ~** *(ugs.)* she's OK *(coll.);* **in ~!** *(ugs.)* OK! *(coll.);* all right!

ordnungs-, Ordnungs-: ~gemäß 1. *Adj. (conduct etc.)* in accordance with the regulations; 2. *adv.* in accordance with the regulations; ~halber *Adv.* as a matter of form; ~widrig *(Rechtsw.)* 1. *Adj. (actions, behaviour, etc.)* contravening the regulations; illegal *(parking);* 2. *adv.* ~widrig parken park illegally; ~zahl die ordinal [number]

Organ das; ~s, ~e organ; *(ugs.: Stimme)* voice; **Organisation** die; ~, ~en organization; **Organisator** der; ~s, ~en organizer; **organisatorisch** *Adj.* organizational; **organisch** 1. *Adj.* organic; 2. *adv.* organically; **organisieren** 1. *tr. V.* organize; 2. *itr. V.* gut ~ können be a good organizer; 3. *refl. V.* organize; **Organismus** der; Organismen organism

Organist der; ~en, ~en, **Organistin** die; ~, ~nen organist

Orgasmus der; ~, Orgasmen orgasm

Orgel die; ~, ~n organ

Orgie ['ɔrgiə] die; ~, ~n *(auch fig.)* orgy

Orient ['o:riɛnt] der; ~s Middle East and south-western Asia *(including Afghanistan and Nepal); der Vordere ~:* the Middle East; **orientalisch** *Adj.* oriental; **orientieren** 1. *refl. V.* a) get one's bearings; b) sich über etw. *(Akk.)* ~ *(fig.)* inform oneself about sth.; c) sich an etw. *(Dat.)* ~ *(fig.)* be oriented towards sth.; *(policy, advertising)* be geared towards sth; 2. *tr. V. (unterrichten)* inform (über + *Akk.* about); **Orientierung** die; ~: a) die ~ verlieren lose one's bearings; b) *(Unterrichtung)* zu Ihrer ~: for your information; **Orientierungs·sinn** der sense of direction

original 1. *Adj.* original; 2. *adv.* ~ italienischer Espresso genuine Italian espresso coffee; **etw. ~ übertragen** broadcast sth. live; **Original das; ~s, ~e** original; **Original·fassung die** original version; **Originalität die; ~:** originality; **originell 1.** *Adj.* original; **2.** *adv.* with originality

Orkan der; ~|e|s, ~e hurricane

Ornament das; ~|e|s, ~e ornament

¹Ort der; ~|e|s, ~e place; *(Dorf)* village; *(Stadt)* town; **an ~ und Stelle** there and then; **²Ort: vor ~** *(fig.)* on the spot

Orthographie die; ~; ~n orthography; **orthographisch 1.** *Adj.* orthographic; **~e Fehler** spelling mistakes; **2.** *adv.* orthographically; **Orthopäde der; ~n, ~n** orthopaedic specialist; **orthopädisch 1.** *Adj.* orthopaedic; **2.** *adv.* orthopaedically

örtlich 1. *Adj. (auch Med.)* local; **2.** *adv. (auch Med.)* locally; **~ betäubt werden** be given a local anaesthetic; **Ortschaft die; ~, ~en** *(Dorf)* village; *(Stadt)* town

Orts-: ~gespräch das *(Fernspr.)* local call; **~name der** place-name; **~netz·kennzahl die** *(Fernspr.)* dialling code; area code *(Amer.)*

Öse die; ~, ~n eye

Ossi der; ~s, ~s *(salopp)* East German

Ost *o. Art.; o. Pl. (bes. Seemannsspr., Met.)* s. **Osten**

ost-, Ost-: ~block der; *o. Pl.* Eastern bloc; **~deutsch** *Adj.* Eastern German; *(hist.: auf die DDR bezogen)* East German; **~deutschland (das)** Eastern Germany; *(hist.: DDR)* East Germany

Osten der; ~s east; **der ~:** the East; **der Ferne ~:** the Far East; **der Nahe ~:** the Middle East

Oster-: ~ei das Easter egg; **~glocke die** daffodil; **~hase der** Easter hare *(said to bring children their Easter Eggs)*

Ostern das; ~, ~: Easter; **Frohe** *od.* **Fröhliche ~:** Happy Easter!; **zu ~:** at Easter

Österreich (das); ~s Austria; **Österreicher der; ~s, Österreicherin die ~, ~nen** Austrian; **österreichisch** *Adj.* Austrian

Ost·europa (das) Eastern Europe; **östlich 1.** *Adj.* **a)** *(im Osten gelegen)* eastern; **b)** *(nach, aus dem Osten)* easterly; **c)** *(aus dem Osten kommend, für den Osten typisch; Politik)* Eastern; *(influence, policies)* of the East; **2.** *adv.* eastwards; **~ von ...:** [to the] east of ...;

3. *Präp. mit Gen.* [to the] east of; **Ost·see die;** *o. Pl.* Baltic [Sea]; **ost·wärts** *Adv.* eastwards; **Ost·wind der** easterly wind

¹Otter der; ~s, ~ *(Fisch~)* otter

²Otter die; ~, ~n *(Viper)* adder; viper

Otto·motor der Otto engine

Ouvertüre [uver'ty:rə] **die; ~, ~n** *(auch fig.)* overture *(Gen. to)*

oval *Adj.* oval

Ozean der; ~s, ~e ocean; **Ozean·dampfer der** ocean liner

Ozon der *od.* **das; ~s** ozone

P

p, P [pe] **das; ~, ~:** p/P

paar *indekl.* Indefinitpron. **ein ~ ...:** a few ...; *(zwei od. drei)* a couple of ...; **Paar das; ~|e|s, ~e** pair; *(Mann und Frau)* couple; **ein ~ Würstchen** two sausages; **paaren** *refl. V. ⟨animals⟩* mate; *⟨people⟩* couple; **Paar·lauf der** pairs *pl.;* **paar·mal** *Adv.* **ein ~mal** a few times; *(zwei- oder dreimal)* a couple of times; **paar·weise** *Adv.* in pairs

Pacht die; ~, ~en a) lease; **etw. in ~ nehmen** lease sth.; **etw. in ~ haben** have sth. on lease; **etw. in ~ geben** lease sth.; **pachten** *tr. V.* lease; **Pächter der; ~s, ~, Pächterin die; ~, ~nen** leaseholder; *(eines Hofes)* tenant

¹Pack der; ~|e|s, ~e *od.* **Päcke a)** pack; **b)** s. **Packen;** **²Pack das; ~|e|s** *(ugs. abwertend)* rabble; **Päckchen das; ~s, ~ a)** package; *(auch Postw.)* small parcel; *(Bündel)* packet; **b)** s. **Packung a;** **packen 1.** *tr. V.* **a)** pack; **b)** *(fassen)* grab [hold of]; *(fig.)* Furcht packte ihn/er wurde von Furcht gepackt he was seized with fear; **2.** *itr. V. (Koffer usw. ~)* pack; **Packen der; ~s, ~:** pile; *(zusammengeschnürt)* bundle; *(von Geldscheinen)* wad; **Pack·papier das** [stout] wrapping-paper; **Packung die; ~, ~en a)** packet; pack *(esp. Amer.);* **b)** *(Med., Kosmetik)* pack

Pädagoge der; ~n, ~n *(Erzieher, Lehrer)* teacher; *(Wissenschaftler)* educationalist; **pädagogisch** 1. *Adj.* educational; **seine** ~en **Fähigkeiten** his teaching ability *sing.;* 2. *adv.* educationally *(sound, wrong)*

Paddel das; ~s, ~: paddle; **Paddel·boot** das canoe; **paddeln** *itr. V.; mit sein* paddle; *(als Sport)* canoe

paffen 1. *tr. V.* puff at *(pipe etc.);* 2. *itr. V.* puff away

Page ['paːʒə] der; ~n, ~n bellboy

Paket das; ~[e]s, ~e pile; *(zusammengeschnürt)* bundle; *(Eingepacktes, Post~)* parcel; *(Packung)* packet; pack *(esp. Amer.)*

Paket-: ~**karte** die parcel dispatch form; ~**schalter** der parcels counter

Pakistan (das); ~s Pakistan; **Pakistaner** der; ~s, ~, **Pakistani** der; ~[s], ~[s] Pakistani; **pakistanisch** *Adj.* Pakistani

Pakt der; ~[e]s, ~e pact; **paktieren** *itr. V.* make *or* do a deal/deals

Palast der; ~[e]s, **Paläste** palace

Palästina (das); ~s Palestine; **Palästinenser** der; ~s, ~: Palestinian; **palästinensisch** *Adj.* Palestinian

Palette die; ~, ~n palette

Palme die; ~, ~n palm[-tree]

Pampelmuse die; ~, ~n grapefruit

Panama (das); ~s Panama; **Panama·kanal** der; *o. Pl.* Panama Canal

panieren *tr. V.* bread; coat *(sth.)* with breadcrumbs; **Panier·mehl** das breadcrumbs *pl.*

Panik die; ~, ~en panic; **panisch** *Adj.* panic attrib. *(fear, terror);* panic-stricken *(flight);*

Panne die; ~, ~n a) breakdown; *(Reifen~)* puncture; flat [tyre]; b) *(Mißgeschick)* mishap; **Pannen·dienst** der breakdown service

Panorama das; ~s, **Panoramen** panorama

Panther der; ~s, ~: panther

Pantoffel der; ~s, ~n backless slipper

Pantomime die; ~, ~n mime

Panzer der; ~s, ~ a) *(Milit.)* tank; b) *(Zool.)* armour *no indef. art.; (von Schildkröten, Krebsen)* shell

Panzer-: ~**glas** das bullet-proof glass; ~**schrank** der safe

Papa der; ~s, ~s *(ugs.)* daddy *(coll.)*

Papagei der; ~en *od.* ~s, ~e[n] parrot

Papi der; ~s, ~s *(ugs.)* daddy *(coll.)*

Papier das; ~s, ~e a) paper; b) *Pl. (Ausweis[e])* [identity] papers; c) *(Finanzw.: Wert~)* security

Papier-: ~**geld** das paper money; ~**korb** der waste-paper basket

Pappe die; ~, ~n cardboard

Pappel die; ~, ~n poplar

päppeln *tr. V.* feed up

Papp·karton der cardboard box

Paprika der; ~s, ~[s] a) pepper; b) *o. Pl. (Gewürz)* paprika

Papst der; ~[e]s, **Päpste** pope; **päpstlich** *Adj.* papal

Parabel die; ~, ~n a) *(bes. Literaturw.)* parable; b) *(Math.)* parabola

Parade die; ~, ~n parade

Paradies das; ~es, ~e paradise; **paradiesisch** *Adj.* paradisical; *(herrlich)* heavenly

paradox *Adj.* paradoxical

Paragraph der; ~en, ~en section; *(in Vertrag)* clause

parallel 1. *Adj.* parallel; 2. *adv.* ~ **verlaufen** run parallel *(mit, zu* to); **Parallele** die; ~, ~n parallel; **Parallelogramm** das; ~s, ~e parallelogram; **Parallel·straße** die street running parallel *(Gen.* to)

Para·nuß die Brazil-nut

Parasit der; ~en, ~en *(auch fig.)* parasite

parat *Adj.* ready

Parfum [par'fœ:], **Parfüm** das; ~s, ~s perfume; **Parfümerie** die; ~, ~en perfumery; **parfümieren** *tr. V.* perfume

Pariser 1. *indekl. Adj.* Parisian; Paris *attrib.;* 2. der; ~s, ~ Parisian; **Pariserin** die; ~, ~nen Parisian

Parität die; ~, ~en parity

Park der; ~s, ~s park; *(Schloß~ usw.)* grounds *pl.*

Parka der; ~s, ~s parka

parken *tr., itr. V.* park; „**Parken verboten!**" 'No Parking'

Parkett das; ~[e]s, ~e a) parquet floor; b) *(Theater)* [front] stalls *pl.;* parquet *(Amer.)*

Park-: ~**gebühr** die parking-fee; ~**haus** das multi-storey car-park; ~**lücke** die parking-space; ~**platz** der car-park; parking lot *(Amer.); (für ein einzelnes Fahrzeug)* parking-space; ~**scheibe** die parking-disc; ~**schein** der car-park ticket; ~**uhr** die parking-meter; ~**verbot** das ban on parking; **im** ~**verbot stehen** be parked illegally; ~**verbots·schild** das no-parking sign

Parlament das; ~[e]s, ~e parliament; **Parlamentarier** der; ~s, ~, **Parlamentarierin** die; ~, ~nen member of

parliament; **parlamentạrisch** *Adj.*
parliamentary

Parodie die; ~, ~n parody (**auf** +
Akk. of)

Parọle die; ~, ~n a) *(Wahlspruch)*
motto; *(Schlagwort)* slogan; b) *(bes.
Milit.: Kennwort)* password

Partei die; ~, ~en a) *(Politik,
Rechtsw.)* party; b) *(Gruppe, Mannschaft)* side; **für jmdn. ~ ergreifen** *od.*
nehmen side with sb.; **parteiisch 1.**
Adj. biased; **2.** *adv.* in a biased manner; **partei·los** *Adj. (Politik)* independent *(MP)*; **Partei·tag** der party
conference *or (Amer.)* convention

Parterre das; ~s, ~s ground floor;
first floor *(Amer.)*

Partie die; ~, ~n a) part; b) *(Spiel,
Sport: Runde)* game; *(Golf)* round; c)
eine gute ~ [für jmdn.] sein be a good
match [for sb.]

Partisan der; ~s *od.* ~en, ~en, **Partisanin** die, ~, ~nen guerrilla; *(gegen
Besatzungstruppen im Krieg)* partisan

Partitur die; ~, ~en *(Musik)* score

Partizip das; ~s, ~ien [-'tsi:pi̯ən]
(Sprachw.) participle

Partner der; ~s, ~, **Partnerin** die; ~,
~nen partner; **Partnerschaft** die; ~,
~en partnership; **partnerschaft-
lich 1.** *Adj. (co-operation etc.)* on a
partnership basis; **2.** *adv.* in a spirit of
partnership; **Partner·stadt** die twin
town *(Brit.)*; sister city *or* town
(Amer.)

Party ['pa:ɐ̯ti] die; ~, ~s *od.* **Parties**
party

Parzelle die; ~, ~n [small] plot [of
land]

Paß der; **Passes, Pässe a)** *(Reise~)*
passport; **b)** *(Gebirgs~; Ballspiele)*
pass

passạbel 1. *Adj.* reasonable; presentable *(appearance)*; **2.** *adv.* reasonably
well

Passage [pa'sa:ʒə] die; ~, ~n a) [shop-
ping] arcade; b) *(Abschnitt)* passage;
Passagier [pasa'ʒiːɐ̯] der; ~s, ~e
passenger; **blinder ~**: stowaway

Passagier-: **~dampfer** der passenger steamer; **~flugzeug** das passenger aircraft; **~liste** die passenger
list

Paß·amt das passport office

Passạnt der; ~en, ~en, **Passạntin**
die; ~, ~nen passer-by

Paß·bild das passport photograph

Pässe s. Paß

passen *itr. V.* a) *(die richtige Größe/*
Form haben) fit; b) *(geeignet sein)* be
suitable (**auf** + *Akk.*, **zu** for); *(harmonieren) (colour etc.)* match; **zu etw./
jmdm. ~**: go well with sth./be well
suited to sb.; **zueinander ~** *(things)* go
well together; *(two people)* be suited to
each other; c) *(genehm sein)* **jmdm. ~**
(time) suit sb.; d) *(Kartenspiel)* pass;
passend *Adj.* a) *(geeignet)* suitable
(dress, present, etc.); right *(words, expression, moment)*; b) *(harmonierend)*
matching *(shoes etc.)*

Paß·foto das *s.* Paßbild

passierbar *Adj.* passable *(road)*; nav-
igable *(river)*; negotiable *(path)*; **passieren 1.** *tr. V.* pass; **die Grenze ~**:
cross the border; **2.** *itr. V.*; *mit sein*
happen

Passion die; ~, ~en a) passion; b)
(christl. Rel.) Passion

passioniert *Adj.* passionate *(collector, card-player, huntsman)*

passiv 1. *Adj.* passive; **2.** *adv.* pass-
ively; **Passiv** das; ~s, ~e *(Sprachw.)*
passive; **Passivität** die; ~: passivity

Paß-: **~kontrolle** die passport
check; **~zwang** der obligation to
carry a passport

Paste die; ~, ~n paste

Pastell das; ~[e]s, ~e a) *(Farbton)* pastel shade; b) *o. Pl. (Maltechnik)* pastel
no art.

Pastell-: **~farbe** die pastel colour;
~ton der pastel shade

Pastete die; ~, ~n a) *(gefüllte ~)* vol-
au-vent; b) *(in einer Schüssel o. ä. ge-
gart)* pâté; *(in einer Hülle aus Teig gebacken)* pie

pasteurisieren [pastøri'ziːrən] *tr. V.*
pasteurize

Pastịlle die; ~, ~n pastille

Pạstor der; ~s, ~en, **Pastorin** die; ~,
~nen pastor

Pate der; ~n, ~n godfather; *(männlich
od. weiblich)* godparent

Paten-: **~kind** das godchild; **~onkel**
der godfather; **~stadt** die *s.* Partnerstadt

patẹnt *(ugs.)* **1.** *Adj.* a) *(tüchtig)* capable; b) *(zweckmäßig)* ingenious; **2.**
adv. ingeniously; neatly *(solved)*; **Patẹnt** das; ~[e]s, ~e a) *(Schutz)* patent;
etw. zum *od.* **als ~ anmelden** apply for
a patent for sth.; b) *(Erfindung)* [pa-
tented] invention

Pạten·tante die godmother

patentieren *tr. V.* patent; **Patẹnt-
lösung** die patent remedy (**für, zu**
for)

Pater der; ~s, ~ *od.* **Patres** *(kath. Kirche)* Father; **Paternoster** der; ~s, ~ *(Aufzug)* paternoster [lift]

pathetisch 1. *Adj.* emotional *(speech, manner)*; melodramatic *(gesture)*; pompous *(voice)*; **2.** *adv.* emotionally; *(dramatisch)* [melo]dramatically; **Pathos** das; ~: emotionalism

Patient [pa'tsiɛnt] der; ~en, ~en, **Patientin** die; ~, ~nen patient

Patin die; ~, ~nen godmother

Patres *s.* **Pater**

Patriot der; ~en, ~en, **Patriotin** die; ~, ~nen patriot; **patriotisch 1.** *Adj.* patriotic; **2.** *adv.* patriotically; **Patriotismus** der; ~: patriotism

Patrone die; ~, ~n cartridge

Patrouille [pa'trʊljə] die; ~, ~n patrol; **patrouillieren** [patrʊl'jiːrən] *itr. V.; auch mit sein* be on patrol

Patsche die; ~, ~n *(ugs.) s.* **Klemme**; **patschen** *itr. V., mit sein (ugs.)* splash; **patsch·naß** *Adj. (ugs.)* sopping wet

patzig *(ugs.)* **1.** *Adj.* snotty *(coll.)*; *(frech)* cheeky; **2.** *adv.* snottily *(coll.)*; *(frech)* cheekily

Pauke die; ~, ~n kettledrum; **auf die ~ hauen** *(ugs.) (feiern)* paint the town red *(sl.)*; *(sich lautstark äußern)* come right out with it

pausbäckig *Adj.* chubby-faced; chubby *(face)*

pauschal 1. *Adj.* **a)** all-inclusive *(price, settlement)*; **b)** *(verallgemeinernd)* sweeping *(judgement, criticism, statement)*; indiscriminate *(prejudice)*; wholesale *(discrimination)*; **2.** *adv.* **a)** *(cost)* all in all; *(pay)* in a lump sum; **b)** *(ohne zu differenzieren)* wholesale

Pauschale die; ~, ~n flat-rate payment

Pauschal-: ~**preis** der flat rate; *(Inklusivpreis)* all-in price; ~**reise** die package holiday; *(mit mehreren Reisezielen)* package tour

Pause die; ~, ~n break; *(Ruhe~)* rest; *(Theater)* interval *(Brit.)*; intermission *(Amer.)*

pausen *tr. V.* trace; *(eine Lichtpause machen)* Photostat *(Brit.* P*)*

pausen·los 1. *Adj.;* incessant *(noise, moaning, questioning)*; continous *(work, operation)*; **2.** *adv.* incessantly; *(work)* non-stop

Pavian ['paːvjaːn] der; ~s, ~e baboon

Pavillon ['paviljɔn] der; ~s, ~s pavilion

Pazifik der; ~s Pacific; **pazifisch** *Adj.* Pacific *(area)*; **der Pazifische Ozean** the Pacific Ocean

Pech das; ~[e]s, ~e **a)** pitch; **b)** *o. Pl. (Mißgeschick)* bad luck; **pechschwarz** *Adj. (ugs.)* jet-black

Pedal das; ~s, ~e pedal

Pediküre die; ~, ~n pedicure; **pediküren** *tr. V.* pedicure

Pegel der; ~s, ~ **a)** water-level indicator; *(Tide~)* tide-gauge; **b)** *(Wasserstand)* water-level

peilen *tr. V.* take a bearing on *(transmitter, fixed point)*

Pein die; ~ *(geh.)* torment; **peinigen** *tr. V. (geh.)* torment; *(foltern)* torture;

peinlich 1. *Adj.* **a)** embarrassing; awkward *(question, position, pause)*; **es ist mir sehr ~:** I feel very bad *(coll.)* or embarrassed about it; **b)** *(äußerst genau)* meticulous; **2.** *adv.* **a)** unpleasantly *(surprised)*; **b)** *(überaus [genau])* meticulously; **Peinlichkeit** die; ~, ~en **a)** *o. Pl.* embarrassment; **die ~ der Situation** the awkwardness of the situation; **b)** *o. Pl. (Genauigkeit)* meticulousness; **c)** *(peinliche Situation)* embarrassing situation

Peitsche die; ~, ~n whip; **peitschen** *tr. V.* whip; *(fig.) (storm, waves, rain)* lash

Pelikan der; ~s, ~e pelican

Pelle die; ~, ~n *(bes. nordd.)* skin; *(abgeschält)* peel; **pellen** *(bes. nordd.) tr., refl. V.* peel; **Pell·kartoffel** die potato boiled in its skin

Pelz der; ~es, ~e **a)** fur; coat; *(des toten Tieres)* skin; pelt; **b)** *o. Pl. (Material)* fur; *(~mantel)* fur coat; **Pelz·mantel** der fur coat

Pendel das; ~s, ~: pendulum

pendeln *itr. V.* **a)** swing [to and fro]; *(mit weniger Bewegung)* dangle; **b)** *mit sein (bus, ferry, etc.)* operate a shuttle service; *(person)* commute

penetrant 1. *Adj.* **a)** penetrating *(smell, taste)*; overpowering *(stink, perfume)*; **b)** *(aufdringlich)* pushing, *(coll.)* pushy *(person)*; overbearing *(tone, manner)*; aggressive *(question)*; **2.** *adv.* **a)** overpoweringly; **b)** *(aufdringlich)* overbearingly

penibel 1. *Adj.* over-meticulous *(person)*; *(pedantisch)* pedantic; **2.** *adv.* painstakingly; over-meticulously *(dressed)*

Penis der; ~, ~se penis

Penner der; ~s, ~*(salopp)* tramp *(Brit.)*; hobo *(Amer.)*

Pensen s. Pensum
Pension [pã'zịo:n] die; ~, ~en a) o. Pl. (Ruhestand) in ~ gehen retire; in ~ sein be retired; b) (Ruhegehalt) [retirement] pension; c) (Haus für [Ferien]gäste) guest-house; d) o. Pl. (Unterkunft u. Verpflegung) board; **Pensionär** [pãzịo'nɛ:ɐ̯] der; ~s, ~e, **Pensionärin** die; ~, ~nen retired civil servant; **pensionieren** tr. V. pension off; retire; **sich |vorzeitig| ~ lassen** take [early] retirement; **Pensionierung** die; ~, ~en retirement
Pensum das; ~s, **Pensen** work quota
per Präp. mit Akk. a) (mittels) by; ~ **Adresse X** care of X; c/o X; b) (Kaufmannsspr.: [bis] zum) by; (am) on; c) (Kaufmannsspr.: pro) per
perfekt 1. Adj. a) perfect ⟨crime, host⟩; faultless ⟨English, French, etc.⟩; b) ~ **sein** (ugs.: abgeschlossen, fertig sein) be finalized; 2. adv. perfectly; **Perfekt** das; ~s (Sprachw.) perfect
Pergament·papier das grease-proof paper
Periode die; ~, ~n period
Perle die; ~, ~ **a)** (auch fig.) pearl; b) (aus Holz, Glas o. ä.) bead; **Perlmutt** das; ~s mother-of-pearl
Perlon Ⓦ das; ~s ≈ nylon
Perser der; ~s, ~ **a)** Persian; b) s. **Perserteppich**; **Perserin** die; ~, ~nen Persian; **Perser·teppich** der Persian carpet; **Persianer** der; ~s, ~ (~mantel) Persian lamb coat; **Persien** (das); ~s Persia; **persisch** Adj. Persian
Person die; ~, ~en person; (in der Dichtung, im Film) character; **Personal** das; ~s (in einem Betrieb o. ä.) staff; (im Haushalt) domestic staff pl.; **Personal·ausweis** der identity card; **Personalien** Pl. personal particulars; **Personal·pronomen** das (Sprachw.) personal pronoun
Personen-: ~**kraftwagen der** (bes. Amtsspr.) private car or (Amer.) automobile; ~**name der** personal name; ~**wagen der** (Auto) [private] car; automobile (Amer.); (im Unterschied zum Lastwagen) passenger car or (Amer.) automobile; ~**zug der** stopping train
persönlich 1. Adj. personal; ~ **werden** get personal; 2. adv. personally; (auf Briefen) 'private [and confidential]'; **Persönlichkeit** die; ~, ~en **a)** personality; b) (Mensch) person of character; **eine ~ sein** have a strong

personality; ~**en des öffentlichen Lebens** public figures
Perspektive die; ~, ~n perspective; (Blickwinkel) angle; (Zukunftsaussicht) prospect
Peru (das); ~s Peru; **Peruaner** der; ~s, ~: Peruvian; **peruanisch** Adj. Peruvian
Perücke die; ~, ~n wig
pervers Adj. perverted
Pessimismus der; ~: pessimism; **Pessimist** der; ~en, ~en, **Pessimistin** die; ~, ~nen pessimist; **pessimistisch** 1. Adj. pessimistic; 2. adv. pessimistically
Pest die; ~: plague
Petersilie [petɐ'zi:lịə] die; ~: parsley
Petroleum [pe'tro:leʊm] das; ~s paraffin (Brit.); kerosene (Amer.)
Petrus (der); **Petri** (christl. Rel.: Apostel) St Peter
Pf Abk. **Pfennig**
Pfad der; ~|e|s, ~e path
Pfad-: ~**finder der** Scout; ~**finderin die;** ~, ~nen Guide (Brit.); girl scout (Amer.)
Pfaffe der; ~n, ~n (abwertend) cleric; Holy Joe (derog.)
Pfahl der; ~|e|s, Pfähle post; stake
Pfand das; ~|e|s, Pfänder **a)** security; pledge (esp. fig.); b) (für Flaschen usw.) deposit (auf + Dat. on); **pfänden** tr. V. seize [under distress] (Law) ⟨goods, chattels⟩; attach ⟨wages etc.⟩ (Law); **Pfänder** s. **Pfand**; **Pfändung** die; ~, ~en seizure; distraint (Law); (von Geldsummen, Vermögensrechten) attachment (Law)
Pfanne die; ~, ~n [frying-]pan; **Pfann·kuchen der a)** pancake; b) (Berliner ~) doughnut
Pfarrei die; ~, ~en **a)** (Bezirk) parish; b) (Dienststelle) parish office; c) s. **Pfarrhaus; Pfarrer** der; ~s, ~: pastor; (anglikanisch) vicar; (von Freikirchen) minister; **Pfarrerin** die; ~, ~nen [woman] pastor; (in Freikirchen) [woman] minister; **Pfarr·haus das** vicarage; (katholisch) presbytery; (in Schottland) manse
Pfau der; ~|e|s, ~en peacock; **Pfauen·auge das** peacock butterfly
Pfd. Abk. Pfund lb.
Pfeffer der; ~s, ~: pepper; **Pfeffer·kuchen der** ≈ gingerbread; **Pfefferminz** o. Art., indekl. peppermint; **Pfeffer·minze** die peppermint [plant]; **Pfefferminz·tee der** peppermint tea

pfeffern *tr. V.* season with pepper
Pfeife die; ~, ~n pipe; *(Triller~)* whistle; **pfeifen 1.** *unr. itr. V.* whistle; ⟨*bird*⟩ sing; *(auf einer Triller-pfeife o. ä.)* ⟨*policeman, referee, etc.*⟩ blow one's whistle; **auf jmdn./etw. ~** *(ugs.)* not give a damn about sb./sth.; **2.** *unr. tr. V.* whistle ⟨*tune etc.*⟩; ⟨*bird*⟩ sing ⟨*song*⟩; *(auf einer Pfeife)* pipe, play ⟨*tune etc.*⟩
Pfeil der; ~[e]s, ~e arrow
Pfeiler der; ~s, ~: pillar; *(Brücken~)* pier
Pfennig der; ~s, ~e pfennig; **es kostet 20 ~:** it costs 20 pfennig[s]
pferchen *tr. V.* cram; pack
Pferd das; ~[e]s, ~e horse; *(Schachfigur)* knight; **mit ihr kann man ~e stehlen** *(ugs.)* she's game for anything
Pferde-: **~rennen** das horse-race; *(Sportart)* horse-racing; **~schwanz** der *(Frisur)* pony-tail; **~stall** der stable
pfiff *1. u. 3. Pers. Sg. Prät. v. pfeifen*
Pfiff der; ~[e]s, ~e a) whistle; b) *(ugs.: besonderer Reiz)* style
Pfifferling der; ~s, ~e chanterelle; **keinen** *od.* **nicht einen ~ wert sein** *(ugs.)* be not worth a bean *(sl.)*
pfiffig 1. *Adj.* smart; bright ⟨*idea*⟩; artful ⟨*smile, expression*⟩; **2.** *adv.* artfully
Pfingsten das; ~, ~: Whitsun
Pfingst-: **~montag** der Whit Monday *no def. art.;* **~sonntag** der Whit Sunday *no def. art.*
Pfirsich der; ~s, ~e peach
Pflanze die; ~, ~n plant; **pflanzen** *tr. V.* plant; **Pflanzen·öl** das vegetable oil; **pflanzlich** *Adj.* plant *attrib.* ⟨*life, motif*⟩; vegetable ⟨*dye, fat*⟩
Pflaster das; ~s, ~ a) *(Straßen~)* road surface; *(auf dem Gehsteig)* pavement; **ein teures/gefährliches ~** *(ugs.)* an expensive/dangerous place *or* spot to be; b) *(Wund~)* sticking-plaster; **pflastern** *tr. (auch itr.) V.* surface; *(mit Kopfsteinpflaster, Steinplatten)* pave; **Pflaster·stein** der paving-stone; *(Kopfstein)* cobble-stone
Pflaume die; ~, ~n plum; **getrocknete ~n** [dried] prunes
Pflege die; ~: care; *(Maschinen~, Fahrzeug~)* maintenance; *(fig.: von Beziehungen, Kunst, Sprache)* cultivation; **jmdn./etw. in ~ (Akk.) nehmen** look after sb./sth.
pflege-, Pflege-: **~eltern** *Pl.* foster-parents; **~fall** der: **ein ~ sein** be in [permanent] need of nursing; **~kind** das foster-child; **~leicht** *Adj.* easy-care *attrib.* ⟨*textiles, flooring*⟩
pflegen 1. *tr. V.* look after; care for; take care of ⟨*skin, teeth, floor*⟩; look after ⟨*bicycle, car, machine*⟩; look after, tend ⟨*garden, plants*⟩; cultivate ⟨*relations, arts, interests*⟩; foster ⟨*contacts, co-operation*⟩; pursue ⟨*hobby*⟩; **2.** *mod. V.* **etw. zu tun ~:** usually do sth.; **Pfleger** der; ~s, ~ a) *(Kranken~)* [male] nurse; b) *(Tier~)* keeper; **Pflegerin** die; ~, ~nen a) *(Kranken~)* nurse; b) *(Tier~)* keeper
Pflicht die; ~, ~en duty
pflicht-, Pflicht-: **~bewußt 1.** *Adj.* conscientious; **2.** *adv.* with a sense of duty; **~bewußtsein** das, **~gefühl** das; *o. Pl.* sense of duty; **~übung** die *(fig.)* ritual exercise
Pflock der; ~[e]s, Pflöcke peg
pflücken *tr. V.* pick
Pflug der; ~[e]s, Pflüge plough; **pflügen** *tr., itr. V.* plough
Pforte die; ~, ~n *(Tor)* gate; *(Tür)* door; *(Eingang)* entrance; **Pförtner** der; ~s, ~ porter; *(eines Wohnblocks, Büros)* door-keeper; *(am Tor)* gate-keeper
Pfosten der; ~s, ~ post
Pfote die; ~, ~n paw
Pfropf der; ~[e]s, ~e blockage; **pfropfen** *tr. V. (ugs.)* cram; stuff; **gepfropft voll** crammed [full]; packed; **Pfropfen** der stopper; *(Korken)* cork; *(für Fässer)* bung
pfui *Interj.* ugh; ~ rufen boo
Pfund das; ~[e]s, ~e pound
Pfütze die; ~, ~n puddle
Phänomen das; ~s, ~e phenomenon
Phantasie die; ~, ~n a) *o. Pl.* imagination; b) *meist Pl. (Produkt der ~)* fantasy; **phantasie·los 1.** *Adj.* unimaginative; **2.** *adv.* unimaginatively; **phantasie·voll 1.** *Adj.* imaginative; **2.** *adv.* imaginatively; **phantastisch 1.** *Adj.* a) fantastic; ⟨*idea*⟩ divorced from reality; b) *(ugs.: großartig)* fantastic *(coll.);* **2.** *adv. (ugs.)* fantastically *(coll.)*
Phase die; ~, ~n phase
Philosoph der; ~en, ~en philosopher; **Philosophie** die; ~, ~n philosophy; **philosophieren** *itr. (auch tr.) V.* philosophize; **philosophisch 1.** *Adj.* philosophical; ⟨*dictionary, principles*⟩ of philosophy; **2.** *adv.* philosophically

Photo 652

Photo das; ~s, ~s s. Foto
Phrase die; ~, ~n *(abwertend)* [empty] phrase; cliché
Physik die; ~: physics *sing.*, *no art.;* **physikalisch** *Adj.* physics *attrib.* ⟨*experiment, formula, research, institute*⟩; physical ⟨*map, process*⟩; **Physiker** der; ~s, ~ physicist; **physisch** 1. *Adj.* physical; 2. *adv.* physically
Pianist der; ~en, ~en, **Pianistin** die; ~, ~nen pianist
Pickel der; ~s, ~: pimple
picken 1. *itr. V.* peck (nach at; **an** + *Akk.*, **gegen** on, against); 2. *tr. V.* ⟨*bird*⟩ peck; *(ugs.)* ⟨*person*⟩ pick
Picknick das; ~s, ~e *od.* ~s picnic
piep[s]en *itr. V. (ugs.)* squeak; ⟨*small bird*⟩ cheep
Pietät [pie'tɛ:t] die; ~: respect; *(Ehrfurcht)* reverence
Pik das; ~[s], ~[s] *(Kartenspiel)* a) *(Farbe)* spades *pl.;* b) *(Karte)* spade
pikant 1. *Adj.* a) piquant; b) *(fig.: witzig)* ironical; c) *(verhüll.: schlüpfrig)* racy ⟨*joke, story*⟩; 2. *adv.* piquantly ⟨*seasoned*⟩
pikiert 1. *Adj.* piqued; 2. *adv.* ⟨*reply, say*⟩ in an aggrieved tone
Pilger der; ~s, ~: pilgrim; **pilgern** *itr. V.* go on a pilgrimage
Pille die; ~, ~n pill
Pilot der; ~en, ~en pilot
Pils das; ~, ~: Pils
Pilz der; ~es, ~e fungus; *(Speise~, auch fig.)* mushroom
Pinguin der; ~s, ~e penguin
Pinie ['pi:niə] die; ~, ~n [stone- or umbrella] pine
pinkeln *itr. V. (salopp)* pee *(coll.)*
Pinsel der; ~s, ~: brush; *(Mal~)* paintbrush
Pinzette die; ~, ~n tweezers *pl.*
Pionier der; ~s, ~e *(Milit.)* sapper; *(fig.: Wegbereiter)* pioneer
Pirat der; ~en, ~en pirate
pissen *itr. V. (derb)* piss *(coarse)*
Pistazie [pɪs'ta:tsiə] die; ~, ~n pistachio
Piste die; ~, ~n *(Ski~)* piste; *(Renn~)* course; *(Flugw.)* runway
Pistole die; ~, ~n pistol
Pizza die; ~, ~s *od.* ~zen pizza
Pkw, PKW ['pe:ka:ve:] der; ~[s], ~[s] [private] car; automobile *(Amer.)*
plädieren *itr. V. (Rechtsw.)* plead (**auf** + *Akk.* for); *(fig.)* argue; **Plädoyer** [plɛdoa'je:] das; ~s, ~s *(Rechtsw.)* summing up *(for the defence/prosecution); (fig.)* plea

Plage die; ~, ~n a) nuisance; b) *(ugs.: Mühe)* bother; trouble; **plagen** 1. *tr. V.* a) torment; b) *(ugs.: bedrängen)* harass; *(mit Bitten, Fragen)* pester; 2. *refl. V.* a) *(sich abmühen)* slave away; b) *(leiden)* **sich mit etw.** ~: be bothered by sth.
Plakat das; ~[e]s, ~e poster; **Plakette** die; ~, ~n badge
Plan der; ~[e]s, Pläne a) plan; b) *(Karte)* map; plan
Plane die; ~, ~n tarpaulin
planen *tr., itr. V.* plan
Planet der; ~en, ~en planet
planieren *tr. V.* level; grade; **Planier·raupe** die bulldozer
Planke die; ~, ~n plank
plan-: ~**los** 1. *Adj.* aimless; *(ohne System)* unsystematic; 2. *adv. s.* 1: aimlessly; unsystematically; ~**mäßig** 1. *Adj.* a) scheduled ⟨*service, steamer*⟩; ~**mäßige Ankunft/Abfahrt** scheduled time of arrival/departure; b) *(systematisch)* systematic; 2. *adv.* a) *(wie geplant)* according to plan; *(pünktlich)* on schedule; b) *(systematisch)* systematically
Plansch·becken das paddling-pool; **planschen** *itr. V.* splash [about]
Plantage [plan'ta:ʒə] die; ~, ~n plantation
Planung die; ~, ~en planning; **Plan·wirtschaft** die planned economy
¹Plastik die; ~, ~en sculpture; **²Plastik** das; ~s *(ugs.)* plastic
Plastik-: ~**beutel** der, ~**tüte** die plastic bag
Platane die; ~, ~n plane-tree
Platin das; ~s platinum
plätschern *itr. V.* a) splash; b) *mit sein (~d auftreffen)* splash (**an** + *Akk.*, **gegen** against); **plätschern** *itr. V.* a) splash; ⟨*rain*⟩ patter; ⟨*stream*⟩ burble; b) *mit sein* ⟨*stream*⟩ burble along
platt *Adj.* flat; **ein Platter** *(ugs.)* a flat *(coll.)*
platt·deutsch *Adj.* Low German
Platte die; ~, ~n a) *(Stein~)* slab; *(Metall~)* plate; sheet; *(Span~, Hartfaser~ usw.)* board; *(Tisch~)* [table-]top; *(Grab~)* [memorial] slab; b) *(Koch~)* hotplate; c) *(Schall~)* [gramophone] record; d) *(Teller)* plate; *(zum Servieren, aus Metall)* dish; **kalte** ~: selection of cold meats [and cheese]; **Platten·spieler** der record-player; **Platt·fuß** der a) flat foot; b) *(ugs.: Reifenpanne)* flat *(coll.)*

Platz der; ~es, Plätze a) square; b) *(Sport~)* ground; *(Spielfeld)* field; *(Tennis~, Volleyball~ usw.)* court; *(Golf~)* course; c) *(Stelle, wo jmd., etw. hingehört)* place; **nicht** *od.* **fehl am ~|e| sein** *(fig.)* be out of place; d) *(Sitz~)* seat; *(am Tisch, Steh~ usw.)* place; ~ **nehmen** sit down; e) *(bes. Sport: Plazierung)* place; f) *(Ort)* place; **am ~:** in the town/village; g) *o. Pl. (Raum)* space; room; ~ **machen** make room *(Dat.* for); **Plätzchen** **das; ~s, ~** a) little place; b) *(Keks)* biscuit *(Brit.);* cookie *(Amer.)*

platzen *itr. V.; mit sein* a) burst; *(explodieren)* explode; b) *(ugs.: scheitern)* fall through; **der Wechsel/das Treffen ist geplatzt** the bill has bounced *(sl.)*/the meeting is off; c) **in eine Versammlung ~** *(ugs.)* burst into a meeting

Platz-: **~karte** die reserved-seat ticket; **~konzert** das open-air concert *(by a military or brass band);* **~mangel** der lack of space; **~regen** der cloudburst; **~wunde** die lacerated wound

plaudern *itr. V.* chat

plausibel *Adj.* plausible

pleite *(ugs.)* ~ **sein** *(person)* be broke *(coll.);* *(company)* have gone bust *(coll.);* ~ **gehen** go bust *(coll.);* **Pleite** **die; ~, ~n** *(ugs.)* a) *(Bankrott)* bankruptcy *no def. art.;* ~ **machen** go bust *(coll.);* b) *(Mißerfolg)* wash-out *(sl.)*

Plissee das; ~s, ~s accordion pleats *pl.*

Plombe die; ~, ~n a) *(Siegel)* [lead] seal; b) *(veralt.: Zahnfüllung)* filling; **plombieren** *tr. V.* a) *(versiegeln)* seal; b) *(veralt.)* fill *(tooth)*

plötzlich 1. *Adj.* sudden; 2. *adv.* suddenly

plump 1. *Adj.* a) *(dick)* plump; *(unförmig)* ungainly *(shape);* *(rundlich)* bulbous; b) *(schwerfällig)* clumsy *(movements, style);* c) *(fig.)* *(dreist)* crude *(lie, deception, trick);* *(leicht durchschaubar)* blatantly obvious; *(unbeholfen)* clumsy *(excuse, advances);* crude *(joke, forgery);* 2. *adv.* a) *(schwerfällig)* clumsily; b) *(fig.)* in a blatantly obvious manner

plündern *itr., tr. V.* a) *(loot)* plunder *(town);* b) *(scherzh.)* raid *(larder, fridge, account)*

Plural der; ~s, ~e plural

plus *Konj., Adv.* plus; **Plus** das; ~: surplus; *(Vorteil)* advantage

Plüsch der; ~|e|s, ~e plush

Plusquam·perfekt das pluperfect [tense]

PLZ *Abk.* Postleitzahl

Po der; ~s, ~s *(ugs.)* bottom

Pöbel der; ~s rabble

pochen *itr. V. (klopfen)* knock *(gegen/an* + *Akk.* at, on); *(geh.: pulsieren)* *(heart)* pound

Pocken *Pl.* smallpox *sing.*

Podest das *od.* der; ~|e|s, ~e rostrum; **Podium** das; ~s, **Podien** *(Plattform)* platform; *(Bühne)* stage; *(trittartige Erhöhung)* rostrum

Poesie die; ~: poetry; **Poet** der; ~en, ~en *(veralt.)* poet; bard *(literary);* **poetisch** 1. *Adj.* poetic[al]; 2. *adv.* poetically

Pointe ['poɛ̃:tə] die; ~, ~n *(eines Witzes)* punch line; *(einer Geschichte)* point; *(eines Sketches)* curtain line

Pokal der; ~s, ~e a) *(Trinkgefäß)* goblet; b) *(Siegestrophäe, ~wettbewerb)* cup

Pökel·fleisch das salt meat; **pökeln** *tr. V.* salt

Poker das *od.* der; ~s poker; **pokern** *itr. V.* play poker

Pol der; ~s, ~e pole

Pole der; ~n, ~n Pole

polemisch 1. *Adj.* polemic[al]; 2. *adv.* polemically

Polen das; ~s Poland

Police [po'li:sə] die; ~, ~n *(Versicherungsw.)* policy

polieren *tr. V.* polish

Poli·klinik die out-patients' clinic

Polin die; ~, ~nen Pole

Politik die; ~, ~en a) *o. Pl.* politics *sing., no art.;* b) *(eine spezielle ~)* policy; **Politiker** der; ~s, ~, **Politikerin** die; ~, ~nen politician; **politisch** 1. *Adj.* political; 2. *adv.* politically; **politisieren** 1. *itr. V.* talk politics; 2. *tr. V.* make politically active

Politur die; ~, ~en polish

Polizei die; ~, ~en police *pl.*

Polizei-: **~auto** das police car; **~beamte** der police officer; **~kontrolle** die police check

polizeilich 1. *Adj.* police; ~e Meldepflicht obligation to register with the police; 2. *adv.* by the police

Polizei-: **~präsidium** das police headquarters *sing. or pl.;* **~revier** das police station; **~streife** die police patrol; **~stunde** die closing time; **~wache** die police station

Polizist der; ~en, ~en policeman

polnisch *Adj.* Polish
Polster das; ~s, ~: upholstery *no pl., no indef. art.;* **Polster·möbel** *Pl.* upholstered furniture *sing.;* **polstern** *tr. V.* upholster *(furniture)*
poltern *itr. V.* **a)** crash about; **b)** *mit sein* der Karren polterte über das Pflaster the cart clattered over the cobblestones
Polyp der; ~en, ~en *(Zool., Med.)* polyp
Pommern (das); ~s Pomerania
Pommes frites [pom'frit] *Pl.* chips *(Brit.);* French fries *(Amer.)*
pompös 1. *Adj.* grandiose; 2. *adv.* grandiosely
¹**Pony** ['poni] das; ~s, ~s pony; ²**Pony** der; ~s, ~s *(Frisur)* fringe
Popeline·mantel der poplin coat
populär 1. *Adj.* popular (bei with); 2. *adv.* popularly; **Popularität** die; ~: popularity
Pore die; ~, ~n pore
Pornographie die; ~: pornography
Porree der; ~s leek
Portal das; ~s, ~e portal
Portemonnaie [portmo'ne:] das; ~s, ~s purse
Porti *Pl. s.* Porto
Portier [por'tje:] der; ~s, ~s, *österr.:* [por'ti:ɐ] der; ~s, ~e porter
Portion [por'tsjo:n] die; ~, ~en **a)** *(beim Essen)* portion; helping; **b)** *(ugs.: Anteil)* amount
Porto das; ~s, ~s *od.* Porti postage (für on, for)
Portugal (das); ~s Portugal; **Portugiese** der; ~n, ~n Portuguese; **portugiesisch** *Adj.* Portuguese
Portwein der port
Porzellan das; ~s porcelain; china
Posaune die; ~, ~n trombone
Position [pozi'tsjo:n] die; ~, ~en position; **positiv** 1. *Adj.* positive; 2. *adv.* positively; **Positiv** das; ~s, ~e *(Fot.)* positive
Possessiv·pronomen das *(Sprachw.)* possessive pronoun
Post die; ~, ~en **a)** post *(Brit.);* mail; etw. mit der *od.* per ~ schicken send sth. by post *or* mail; **b)** *(~amt)* post office
Post-: ~amt das post office; ~anweisung die postal remittance form; ~auto das mail van; ~bote der *(ugs.)* postman *(Brit.);* mailman *(Amer.)*
Posten der; ~s, ~ **a)** post; **b)** *(bes. Milit.: Wachmann)* sentry

post-, Post-: ~fach das post-office or PO box; *(im Büro, Hotel o. ä.)* pigeon-hole; ~karte die postcard; ~lagernd *Adj., adv.* poste restante; general delivery *(Amer.);* ~leitzahl die postcode; Zip code *(Amer.);* ~stempel der *(Abdruck)* postmark; ~wendend *Adv.* by return [of post]
potent *Adj.* potent; **Potenz** die; ~, ~en **a)** *o. Pl.* potency; **b)** *(Math.)* power; **potenzieren** *tr. V. (Math.)* mit 5 ~: raise to the power [of] 5
Pracht die; ~: splendour; **prächtig, pracht·voll** 1. *Adj.* splendid; 2. *adv.* splendidly
prädestiniert *Adj.* predestined
Prädikat das; ~[e]s, ~e **a)** *(Auszeichnung)* rating; **b)** *(Sprachw.)* predicate
Prag (das); ~s Prague
prägen *tr. V.* **a)** emboss; **b)** mint *(coin);* **c)** *(fig.: beeinflussen)* shape
prägnant 1. *Adj.* concise; succinct; 2. *adv.* concisely; succinctly
Prägung die; ~, ~en embossing; *(von Münzen)* minting
prahlen *itr. V.* boast, brag (mit about)
Praktik die; ~, ~en practice; **Praktika** *s.* Praktikum; **Praktikant** der; ~en, ~en, **Praktikantin** die; ~, ~nen **a)** *(in einem Betrieb)* student trainee; **b)** *(an der Hochschule)* physics/chemistry student *(doing a period of practical training);* **Praktikum** das; ~s, **Praktika** period of practical training; **praktisch** 1. *Adj.* practical; ~er Arzt general practitioner; 2. *adv.* practically; *(auf die Praxis bezogen; wirklich)* in practice; **praktizieren** *tr. V.* practise
Praline die; ~, ~n [filled] chocolate
prall *Adj.* **a)** hard *(ball);* bulging *(sack, wallet, bag);* big strong *attrib.* *(thighs, muscles, calves);* well-rounded *(breasts);* **b)** *(intensiv)* blazing *(sun);* **prallen** *itr. V.; mit sein* crash (gegen/auf/an + Akk. into); collide (gegen/auf/an + Akk. with)
Prämie ['prɛ:mjə] die; ~, ~n **a)** *(Leistungs~; Wirtschaft)* bonus; *(Belohnung)* reward; *(Spar~, Versicherungs~)* premium; **b)** *(einer Lotterie)* [extra] prize; **prämieren** *tr. V.* award a prize to *(person, film);* give an award for *(best essay etc.)*
Pranger der; ~s, ~ *(hist.)* pillory
Pranke die; ~, ~n paw
Präparat das; ~[e]s, ~e preparation
Präposition die; ~, ~en *(Sprachw.)* preposition

Prärie die; ~, ~n prairie

Präsens ['prɛːzɛns] das; ~ *(Sprachw.)* present [tense]; **präsentieren** tr. V. present

Präservativ das; ~s, ~e condom

Präsident der; ~en, ~en; **Präsidentin** die; ~, ~nen president; **Präsidium** das; ~s, Präsidien a) committee; b) *(Vorsitz)* chairmanship; c) *(Polizei~)* police headquarters *sing. or pl.*

prasseln itr. V. pelt down; ⟨shots⟩ clatter; ⟨fire⟩ crackle

prassen itr. V. live extravagantly; *(schlemmen)* feast

Präteritum das; ~s *(Sprachw.)* preterite [tense]

Praxis die; ~, Praxen a) o. Pl. *(im Unterschied zur Theorie)* practice *no art.*; *(Erfahrung)* [practical] experience; b) *(eines Arztes, Anwalts usw.)* practice; *(~räume) (eines Arztes)* surgery *(Brit.);* office *(Amer.); (eines Anwalts usw.)* office

präzise 1. *Adj.* precise; 2. *adv.* precisely; **Präzision** die; ~: precision

predigen 1. itr. V. deliver a/the sermon; 2. tr. V. preach; **Prediger** der; ~s, ~: preacher; **Predigt** die; ~, ~en sermon

Preis der; ~es, ~e a) *(Kauf~)* price **(für** of); b) *(Belohnung)* prize; **Preis·aus·schreiben** das [prize] competition

Preisel·beere die cowberry; cranberry *(Gastr.)*

preisen unr. tr. V. *(geh.)* praise

preis-, Preis-: ~günstig 1. *Adj.* ⟨goods⟩ available at unusually low prices; **das ist [sehr] ~günstig** that is [very] good value; 2. *adv.* at a low price; **~nachlaß** der price reduction; **~schild** das price-tag; **~steigerung** die increase in prices; **~träger** der prizewinner; **~verleihung** die presentation [of prizes/awards]; **~wert** 1. *Adj.* good value *pred.*; 2. *adv.* ⟨eat⟩ at a reasonable price; **dort kann man ~wert einkaufen** you get good value for money there

Prellung die; ~, ~en bruise

Premiere [prəˈmi̯eːrə] die; ~, ~n opening night

Presse die; ~, ~n a) press; *(Zitronen~)* squeezer; b) o. Pl. *(Zeitungen)* press

Presse-: ~freiheit die freedom of the press; **~meldung** die press report

pressen tr. V. press

Preß·luft-: ~bohrer der pneumatic

drill; **~hammer** der pneumatic hammer

Prestige [prɛsˈtiːʒə] das; ~s prestige

prickeln itr. V. tingle

pries 1. u. 3. Pers. Sg. Prät. v. **preisen**

Priester der; ~s, ~: priest; **Priesterin** die; ~, ~nen priestess

prima *(ugs.)* 1. *indekl. Adj.* great *(coll.);* 2. *adv.* ⟨taste⟩ great *(coll.);* ⟨sleep⟩ fantastically well *(coll.)*

primär 1. *Adj.* primary; 2. *adv.* primarily

Primel die; ~, ~n primula; *(Schlüsselblume)* cowslip

primitiv 1. *Adj.* primitive; *(einfach, schlicht)* simple; 2. *adv.* primitively; *(einfach, schlicht)* in a simple manner

Prinz der; ~en, ~en prince; **Prinzessin** die; ~, ~nen princess

Prinzip das; ~s, ~ien [-ˈtsiːpi̯ən] principle; **aus** ~: on principle; **prinzipiell** 1. *Adj.* in principle *postpos., not pred.*; ⟨rejection⟩ on principle; 2. *adv.* *(im Prinzip)* in principle; *(aus Prinzip)* on principle

Prise die; ~, ~n pinch

privat 1. *Adj.* private; *(persönlich)* personal; 2. *adv.* privately

Privat-: ~adresse die private *or* home address; **~angelegenheit** die private matter; **~besitz** der private property; **~eigentum** das private property; **~leben** das; o. Pl. private life; **~lehrer** der private tutor; **~patient** der private patient; **~unterricht** der private tuition

pro *Präp. mit Akk.* per; ~ **Stück** each; **a** piece

pro-: pro-; **~westlich/~kommunistisch** pro-western/pro-communist

Probe die; ~, ~n a) test; b) *(Muster, Teststück)* sample; c) *(Theater~, Orchester~)* rehearsal

Probe-: ~fahrt die trial run; *(vor dem Kauf, nach einer Reparatur)* test drive; **~jahr** das probationary year

proben tr., itr. V. rehearse; **probeweise** *Adv.* ⟨employ⟩ on a trial basis; **Probe·zeit** die probationary period; **probieren** 1. tr. V. a) try; have a go at; b) *(kosten)* taste; try; c) *(aus~)* try out; *(an~)* try on ⟨clothes, shoes⟩; 2. itr. V. a) *(versuchen)* try; b) *(kosten)* have a taste

Problem das; ~s, ~e problem; **problematisch** *Adj.* problematic[al]; **problem·los** 1. *Adj.* problem-free; 2. *adv.* without any problems

Produkt das; ~[e]s, ~e *(auch Math.,*

fig.) product; **Produktion** die; ~, ~en production; **produktiv** 1. productive; prolific *(writer, artist, etc.)*; 2. *adv.* *(work, co-operate)* productively; **Produktivität** die; ~: productivity; **Produzent** der; ~en, ~en producer; **produzieren** *tr. V.* produce

Prof. *Abk.* Professor Prof.; **professionell** 1. *Adj.* professional; 2. *adv.* professionally; **Professor** der; ~s, ~en; **Professorin** die; ~, ~nen professor; **Profi** der; ~s, ~s *(ugs.)* pro *(coll.)*

Profil das; ~s, ~e a) *(Seitenansicht)* profile; **im** ~: in profile; b) *(von Reifen, Schuhsohlen)* tread

Profit der; ~[e]s, ~e profit; **profitieren** *itr. V.* profit (von, bei by)

Prognose die; ~, ~n prognosis; *(Wetter~, Wirtschafts~)* forecast

Programm das; ~s, ~e a) programme; program *(Amer., Computing)*; *(Ferns.: Sender)* channel

Programm-: ~heft das programme; ~hinweis der programme announcement

programmieren *tr. V.* a) *(DV)* program; b) *(auf etw. festlegen)* programme

Programm-: ~vorschau die *(im Fernsehen)* preview [of the week's/evening's *etc.* viewing]; *(im Kino)* trailers *pl.;* ~zeitschrift die radio and television magazine

progressiv 1. *Adj.* progressive; 2. *adv.* progressively

Projekt das; ~[e]s, ~e project; **Projektor** der; ~s, ~en projector; **projizieren** *tr. V. (Optik)* project

proklamieren *tr. V.* proclaim

Prolet der; ~en, ~en *(abwertend)* peasant; **Proletariat** das; ~[e]s proletariat; **Proletarier** [proleˈtaːri̯ɐ] der; ~s, ~: proletarian; **proletarisch** *Adj.* proletarian

Promenade die; ~, ~n promenade

Promille das; ~s, ~: [part] per thousand; **er fährt nur ohne** ~ *(ugs.)* he never drinks and drives; **er hatte 1,8** ~: he had a blood alcohol level of 1.8 per thousand; **Promille·grenze** die *(ugs.)* legal [alcohol] limit

prominent *Adj.* prominent; **Prominenz** die; ~: prominent figures *pl.*

prompt 1. *Adj.* prompt; 2. *adv.* a) promptly; b) *(ugs., meist iron.: wie erwartet)* [and] sure enough

Pronomen das; ~s, ~ *od.* **Pronomina** *(Sprachw.)* pronoun

Propaganda die; ~: propaganda; **propagieren** *tr. V.* propagate

Propan·gas das; *o. Pl.* propane

Propeller der; ~s, ~ propeller

Prophet der; ~en, ~en prophet; **prophezeien** *tr. V.* prophesy *(Dat.* for); predict *(result, weather)*

Proportion die; ~, ~en proportion

Prosa die; ~: prose

prosit *Interj.* your [very good] health; ~ **Neujahr!** happy New Year!

Prospekt der *od. (bes. österr.)* das ~[e]s, ~e *(Werbeschrift)* brochure; *(Werbezettel)* leaflet

prost *Interj. (ugs.)* cheers *(Brit. coll.)*

Prostituierte die/der; *adj. Dekl.* prostitute; **Prostitution** die; ~: prostitution *no art.*

Protest der; ~[e]s, ~e protest; **Protestant** der; ~en, ~en, **Protestantin** die; ~, ~nen Protestant; **protestantisch** *Adj.* Protestant; **protestieren** *itr. V.* protest, make a protest (gegen against, about); **Protest·kundgebung** die protest rally

Prothese die; ~, ~n artificial limb; prosthesis *(Med.)*; *(Zahn~)* set of dentures; dentures *pl.*

Protokoll das; ~s, ~e a) *(wörtlich mitgeschrieben)* transcript; *(Ergebnis~)* minutes *pl.; (bei Gericht)* record; **etw. zu** ~ **geben** make a statement about sth.; b) *(diplomatisches Zeremoniell)* protocol; **protokollieren** 1. *tr. V.* take down; take the minutes of *(meeting)*; minute *(remark)*; 2. *itr. V.* take the minutes; *(bei Gericht)* keep the record

Proviant der; ~s, ~e provisions *pl.*

Provinz die; ~, ~en province; **provinziell** 1. *Adj.* provincial; 2. *adv.* provincially

Provision die; ~, ~en *(Kaufmannsspr.)* commission; **provisorisch** 1. *Adj.* provisional; temporary; 2. *adv.* temporarily

Provokation die; ~, ~en provocation; **provozieren** *tr. V.* provoke

Prozedur die; ~, ~en procedure

Prozent das; ~[e]s, ~e a) *nach Zahlenangaben Pl.* ungebeugt per cent *sing.;* **fünf** ~: five per cent; b) *Pl. (ugs.: Gewinnanteil)* share *sing.* of the profits; *(Rabatt)* discount *sing.;* **auf etw.** *(Akk.)* ~ **bekommen** get a discount on sth.; -**prozentig** *adj.* -per-cent

Prozent-: ~rechnung die percentage calculation; ~satz der percentage

prozentual 1. *Adj.* percentage; **2.** *adv.* ~ **am Gewinn beteiligt sein** have a percentage share in the profits

Prozeß der; Prozesses, Prozesse a) trial; *(Fall)* [court] case; **einen ~ gewinnen/verlieren** win/lose a case; **b)** *(Vorgang)* process; **prozessieren** *itr. V.* go to court; **gegen jmdn. ~:** bring an action against sb.; **Prozeß·kosten** *Pl.* legal costs

prüde *(abwertend)* **1.** *Adj.* prudish; **2.** prudishly

prüfen *tr. V.* **a)** *auch itr.* examine *(pupil, student, etc.)*; **mündlich/schriftlich geprüft werden** have an oral/a written examination; **b)** *(untersuchen)* examine *(auch + Akk.* for); check *(device, machine, calculation)* *(auf + Akk.* for); investigate *(complaint); (testen)* test *(auch + Akk.* for); **c)** *(kontrollieren)* check; examine *(accounts, books);* **d)** *(vor einer Entscheidung)* check *(price);* examine *(offer);* consider *(application);* **Prüfer der;** ~s, ~, **Prüferin die;** ~, ~**nen a)** inspector; *(Buch~)* auditor; **b)** *(im Examen)* examiner; **Prüfung die;** ~, ~**en a)** examination; exam *(coll.);* **eine ~ machen od. ablegen** take an examination; **b)** *s.* **prüfen b–d:** examination; check; investigation; test; consideration

Prügel *Pl.* *(Schläge)* beating *sing.; (als Strafe für Kinder)* hiding *(coll.);* **prügeln 1.** *tr. (auch itr.)* *V.* beat; **2.** *refl. V.* **sich ~:** fight; **sich mit jmdm. [um etw.] ~:** fight sb. [over *or* for sth.]

Prunk der; ~[e]s splendour; magnificence

PS [pe:'ɛs] *das;* ~, ~: *Abk.* **Pferdestärke** h.p.

Psalm der; ~s, ~**en** psalm

Psychiater der; ~s, ~: psychiatrist; **Psychiatrie die;** ~ psychiatry *no art.;* **psychisch 1.** *Adj.* psychological; mental *(process, illness);* **2.** *adv.* psychologically; ~ **gesund/krank sein** be mentally fit/ill

psycho-, Psycho- [psy:ço-]: ~**loge der;** ~n, ~n psychologist; ~**logie die;** ~: psychology; ~**login die** psychologist; ~**logisch 1.** *Adj.* psychological; **2.** *adv.* psychologically

Pubertät die; ~: puberty

Publikum das; ~s **a)** *(Zuschauer, Zuhörer)* audience; *(bei Sportveranstaltungen)* crowd; **b)** *(Kreis von Interessierten)* public; *(eines Schriftstellers)* readership; **c)** *(Besucher)* clientele; **publizieren** *tr. (auch itr.) V.* publish

Pudding der; ~s, ~e *od.* ~s thick, *usually flavoured, milk-based dessert;* ≈ blancmange

Pudel der; ~s, ~ poodle

Puder der; ~s, ~: powder; **Puder·dose die** powder compact; **pudern** *tr. V.* powder; **Puder·zucker der** icing sugar *(Brit.);* confectioners' sugar *(Amer.)*

¹**Puff der;** ~[e]s, **Püffe** *(ugs.)* **a)** *(Stoß)* thump; *(leichter/kräftiger Stoß mit dem Ellenbogen)* nudge/dig; **b)** *(Knall)* bang; ²**Puff der** *od. das;* ~s, ~s *(salopp: Bordell)* knocking-shop *(Brit. sl.);* brothel; **puffen** *(ugs.) tr. V.: s.* ¹**Puff a:** thump; nudge; dig

Pulli der; ~s, ~s *(ugs.),* **Pullover der;** ~s, ~: pullover; sweater; **Pullunder der;** ~s, ~: slipover

Puls der; ~es, ~e pulse; **Puls·ader die** artery

Pult das; ~[e]s, ~e desk; *(Lese~)* lectern

Pulver das; ~s, ~ powder

pumm[e]lig *Adj. (ugs.)* chubby

Pumpe die; ~, ~n pump; **pumpen** *tr., itr. V.* **a)** *(auch fig.)* pump; **b)** *(salopp) s.* **leihen a, b**

Punkt der; ~[e]s, ~e **a)** *(Tupfen)* dot; *(größer)* spot; **b)** *(Satzzeichen)* full stop; **c)** *(I-Punkt)* dot; **d)** *(Stelle)* point; **ein schwacher/wunder ~** *(fig.)* a weak/sore point; **e)** *(Gegenstand, Thema, Abschnitt)* point; *(einer Tagesordnung)* item; **f)** *(Bewertungs~)* point; *(bei einer Prüfung)* mark

pünktlich 1. *Adj.* punctual; **2.** *adv.* punctually; on time; **Pünktlichkeit die;** ~: punctuality

Punsch der; ~[e]s, ~e *od.* **Pünsche** punch

Pupille die; ~, ~n pupil

Puppe die; ~, ~n **a)** doll[y]; **b)** *(Marionette)* puppet; marionette

Puppen-: ~**stube die** doll's house; dollhouse *(Amer.);* ~**wagen der** doll's pram

pur *Adj.* **a)** *(rein)* pure; **b)** *(unvermischt)* neat *(whisky etc.);* straight

Püree die; ~s, ~s **a)** purée; **b)** *s.* **Kartoffelbrei**

Purpur der; ~s crimson

Puste die; ~ *(salopp)* puff; breath

Pustel die; ~, ~n pimple; pustule *(Med.)*

pusten *(ugs.) tr., itr. V.* blow

Pute die; ~, ~n turkey hen; *(als Braten)* turkey; **Puter der;** ~s, ~: turkeycock; *(als Braten)* turkey

Putsch der; ~[e]s, ~e putsch; coup [d'état]; **putschen** itr. V. organize a putsch or coup

Putz der; ~es plaster; *(für Außenmauern)* rendering; **putzen** tr. V. **a)** *(blank reiben)* polish; **b)** *(säubern)* clean; groom ⟨horse⟩; [sich *(Dat.)*] die Zähne/die Nase ~: clean or brush one's teeth/blow one's nose; **c)** auch itr. *(saubermachen)* clean ⟨room, shop, etc.⟩; ~ gehen work as a cleaner; **d)** *(vorbereiten)* wash and prepare ⟨vegetables⟩; **Putz·frau** die cleaner

Puzzle ['paz]] das; ~s, ~s, **Puzzle-spiel** das jigsaw [puzzle]

Pyjama [py'dʒa:ma] der *(österr., schweiz. auch: das)*; ~s, ~s pyjamas pl.

Pyramide die; ~, ~n pyramid

Q

q, Q [ku:] das; ~, ~: q, Q

Quadrat das; ~[e]s, ~e square; **quadratisch** Adj. square; **Quadratmeter** der od. das square metre

quaken itr. V. ⟨duck⟩ quack; ⟨frog⟩ croak

Qual die; ~, ~en a) o. Pl. torment; b) meist Pl. *(Schmerzen)* agony; ~en pain sing.; agony sing.; *(seelisch)* torment sing.; **quälen** tr. V. **a)** torment ⟨person, animal⟩; be cruel to ⟨animal⟩; *(foltern)* torture; **b)** *(plagen)* ⟨cough etc.⟩ plague; *(belästigen)* pester; **Quälerei** die; ~, ~en **a)** torment; *(Folter)* torture; *(Grausamkeit)* cruelty; **b)** *(das Belästigen)* pestering

Qualifikation die; ~, ~en **a)** *(Ausbildung)* qualifications pl.; **b)** *(Sport)* qualification; **qualifizieren** refl. V. **a)** gain qualifications **b)** *(Sport)* qualify

Qualität die; ~, ~en quality; **qualitativ 1.** Adj. qualitative; ⟨difference, change⟩ in quality; **2.** adv. with regard to quality; **Qualitäts·erzeugnis** das quality product

Qualle die; ~, ~n jellyfish

Qualm der; ~[e]s [thick] smoke; **qual-men** itr. V. **a)** give off clouds of [thick] smoke; **b)** *(ugs.: rauchen)* puff away

qual·voll 1. Adj. agonizing; **2.** adv. agonizingly

Quantität die; ~, ~en quantity; **Quantum** das; ~s, Quanten quota (an + Dat. of); *(Dosis)* dose

Quarantäne [karan'tɛ:nə] die; ~, ~n quarantine

Quark der; ~s quark

Quartal das; ~s, ~e quarter [of the year]

Quartett das; ~[e]s, ~e **a)** quartet; **b)** *(Spiel)* ≈ Happy Families; *(Satz von vier Karten)* set [of four]

Quartier das; ~s, ~e accommodation no indef. art.; accommodations pl. *(Amer.)*; place to stay; *(Mil.)* quarters pl.

Quarz der; ~es, ~e quartz

quasi Adv. |so| ~: more or less; *(so gut wie)* as good as

Quaste die; ~, ~n tassel

Quatsch der; ~[e]s *(ugs.)* **a)** *(Äußerung)* rubbish; **b)** *(Handlung)* nonsense; *(Unfug)* messing about; laß den ~: stop that nonsense

Queck·silber das mercury

Quelle die; ~, ~n spring; *(eines Flusses; fig.)* source; **quellen** unr. itr. V.; mit sein **a)** ⟨liquid⟩ gush, stream; *(aus der Erde)* well up; ⟨smoke⟩ billow; **b)** *(sich ausdehnen)* swell [up]

quer Adv. sideways; *(schräg)* diagonally; *(rechtwinklig)* at right angles; ~ durch/über (+ Akk.) straight through/across

quer-, Quer-: ~achse die transverse axis; **~schnitt** der *(auch fig.)* cross-section; **~schnitt[s]·gelähmt** Adj. *(Med.)* paraplegic; **~straße** die intersecting road

quetschen tr. V. crush; sich *(Dat.)* die Hand ~: get one's hand caught

quietschen itr. V. squeak; ⟨brakes, tyres⟩ squeal, screech; *(ugs.) ⟨person⟩* squeal, shriek

Quirl der; ~[e]s, ~e long-handled blender with a star-shaped head

quitt Adj. *(ugs.)* quits

Quitte die; ~, ~n quince

quittieren tr. V. **a)** auch itr. acknowledge, confirm ⟨receipt, condition⟩; give a receipt for ⟨sum, invoice⟩; **b)** etw. mit etw. ~: react or respond to sth. with sth.; **Quittung** die; ~, ~en **a)** receipt; **b)** *(fig.)* come-uppance *(coll.)*

Quiz [kvɪs] **das; ~, ~:** quiz

quoll *1. u. 3. Pers. Sg. Prät. v.* **quellen**

Quote die; ~, ~n proportion; **Quoten·regelung die** *requirement that women should be adequately represented*

R
_____

r, R [ɛr] **das; ~, ~:** r, R

Rabatt der; ~|e|s, ~e discount

Rabatte die; ~, ~n border

Rabe der; ~n, ~n raven

rabiat 1. *Adj.* violent; brutal; ruthless ⟨*methods*⟩; **2.** *adv. (gewalttätig)* violently; brutally

Rache die; ~: revenge; **|an jmdm.| ~ nehmen** take revenge [on sb.]

Rachen der; ~s, ~ a) *(Schlund)* pharynx *(Anat.)*; **b)** *(Maul)* mouth; maw *(literary)*; *(fig.)* jaws *pl.*

rächen 1. *tr. V.* avenge ⟨*person, crime*⟩; take revenge for ⟨*insult, crime*⟩; **2.** *refl. V.* **a)** take one's revenge; **b)** ⟨*mistake etc.*⟩ take its/their toll

Rachitis die; ~ *(Med.)* rickets *sing.*

Rach·sucht die; *o. Pl. (geh.)* lust for revenge; **rach·süchtig** *(geh.)* **1.** *Adj.* vengeful; **2.** *adv.* vengefully

Rad das; ~es, Räder ['rɛ:dɐ] **a)** wheel; **das fünfte ~ am Wagen sein** *(fig. ugs.)* be superfluous; **b)** *(Fahr~)* bicycle; bike *(coll.)*

Radar [ra'da:ɐ] *der od.* **das; ~s** radar

Radar: ~falle die *(ugs.)* [radar] speed trap; **~kontrolle die** [radar] speed check

rad-, Rad-: dampfer der paddle-steamer; **~|fahren** *unr. itr. V. ; mit sein* cycle; ride a bicycle *or (coll.)* bike *(coll.)*

Radien *s.* **Radius**

radieren *tr. (auch itr.) V.* erase; **Radier·gummi der** rubber [eraser]

Radieschen das; ~s, ~: radish

radikal 1. *Adj.* radical; drastic ⟨*measure, method, cure*⟩; **2.** *adv.* radically; *(vollständig)* totally; **Radikalismus der; ~:** radicalism

Radio das *(südd., schweiz. auch:* **der)**; **~s, ~s** radio; **~ hören** listen to the radio; **Radio·wecker der** radio alarm clock

Radius der; ~, Radien radius

Rad·kappe die hub-cap

Radler der; ~s, ~: cyclist

Rad-: ~rennbahn die cycle-racing track; **~rennen das** cycle race; *(Sport)* cycle-racing; **~sport der** cycling *no def. art.*; **~tour die** cycling tour; **~weg der** cycle-path *or* -track

raffen *tr. V.* **a)** snatch; rake in *(coll.)* ⟨*money*⟩; **etw. |an sich| ~:** seize sth.; *(eilig)* snatch sth.; **b)** gather ⟨*material, curtain*⟩

Raffinerie die; ~, ~n refinery; **Raffinesse die; ~, ~n a)** *o. Pl. (Schlauheit)* guile; ingenuity; **b)** *meist Pl. (Finesse)* refinement; **raffiniert 1.** *Adj.* **a)** ingenious ⟨*plan, design*⟩; *(verfeinert)* refined, subtle ⟨*colour, scheme, effect*⟩; sophisticated ⟨*dish, cut of clothes*⟩; **b)** *(gerissen)* cunning ⟨*person, trick*⟩; **2.** *adv.* **a)** ingeniously; *(verfeinert)* with great refinement/ sophistication; **b)** *(gerissen)* cunningly

Rage ['ra:ʒə] **die; ~** *(ugs.)* fury

ragen *itr. V.* **a)** *(vertikal)* rise [up]; ⟨*mountains*⟩ tower up; **b)** *(horizontal)* project, stick out (**in** + *Akk.* into; **über** + *Akk.* over)

Ragout [ra'gu:] **das; ~s, ~s** ragout

Rahm der; ~|e|s cream

rahmen *tr. V.* frame; **Rahmen der; ~s, ~ a)** frame; *(Fahrgestell)* chassis; **b)** *(fig.)* framework

Rakete die; ~, ~n rocket; *(Lenkflugkörper)* missile

rammen *tr. V.* ram

Rampe die; ~, ~n a) *(Lade~)* [loading] platform; **b)** *(schiefe Fläche)* ramp; **Rampen·licht das: im ~ |der Öffentlichkeit| stehen** be in the limelight

Ramsch der; ~|e|s, ~e *(ugs.)* **a)** *(Ware)* trashy goods *pl.*; **b)** *(Kram)* junk

ran *Adv. (ugs.)* **a)** *s.* **heran; b)** *(fang|t| an)* off you go; *(fangen wir an)* let's go; **c)** *(greif|t| an)* go at him/them!

Rand der; ~|e|s, Ränder a) edge; *(Einfassung)* border; *(Hut~)* brim; *(Brillen~, Gefäß~, Krater~)* rim; *(eines Abgrunds)* brink; *(auf einem Schriftstück)* margin; *(Weg~)* verge; *(Stadt~)* outskirts *pl.*; **b)** *(Schmutz~)* mark; *(rund)* ring

randalieren *itr. V.* riot

Rạnd·bemerkung die marginal note or comment

rang 1. u. 3. Pers. Sg. Prät. v. **ringen**

Rạng der; ~[e]s, **Rạnge a)** rank; (in der Gesellschaft) status; b) (im Theater) circle; **erster** ~: dress circle; **zweiter** ~: upper circle; **dritter** ~: gallery

rangieren [raŋ'ʒiːrən] tr. V. shunt ⟨trucks etc.⟩; switch ⟨cars⟩ (Amer.)

Rạng·ordnung die order of precedence; (Verhaltensf.) pecking order

Rạnke die; ~, ~n (Bot.) tendril; **rạnken** refl. V. climb, grow (**an** + Dat. up, **über** + Akk. over)

rạnn 1. u. 3. Pers. Sg. Prät. v. **rinnen**

rạnnte 1. u. 3. Pers. Sg. Prät. v. **rennen**

Rạnzen der; ~s, ~: satchel

rạnzig Adj. rancid

Rạppe der; ~n, ~n black horse

Rạppen der; ~s, ~: [Swiss] centime

Rạps der; ~es (Bot.) rape

rạr Adj. scarce; (selten) rare; **Rarität** die; ~, ~en rarity

rasạnt (ugs.) 1. Adj. tremendously fast (coll.) ⟨car, horse, etc.⟩; 2. adv. at terrific speed (coll.)

rạsch 1. Adj. quick; speedy, swift ⟨end, action, decision, progress⟩; 2. adv. quickly; ⟨decide, end, proceed⟩ swiftly, rapidly

rạscheln itr. V. rustle; ⟨mouse etc.⟩ make a rustling noise

rạsen itr. V. a) mit sein (ugs.: eilen) dash or rush [along]; (fahren) tear or race along; (fig.) ⟨pulse⟩ race; b) (toben) ⟨person⟩ rage

Rạsen der; ~s, ~: grass no indef. art.; (gepflegte ~fläche) lawn

rạsend 1. Adj. a) (sehr schnell) breakneck attrib. ⟨speed⟩; b) (tobend) raging; c) (heftig) violent; 2. adv. (ugs.) incredibly (coll.)

Rạsen·mäher der; ~s, ~: lawnmower

Raserei die; ~, ~en (ugs.) tearing along no art.

Rasier·apparat der [safety] razor; (elektrisch) electric shaver; **rasieren** tr. V. shave; **sich** ~: shave; **sich naß/trocken/elektrisch** ~: have a wet shave/ have a dry shave/use an electric shaver

Rasier-: ~**klinge** die razor-blade; ~**wasser** das aftershave; (vor der Rasur) pre-shave lotion

Rạsse die; ~, ~n **a)** breed; b) (Menschen~) race

Rạssel die; ~, ~n rattle; **rạsseln** itr. V. rattle

Rạssen-: ~**haß** der racial hatred no art.; ~**trennung** die; o. Pl. racial segregation no art.

Rassịsmus der; ~: racism; racialism; **Rassịst** der; ~en, ~en racist; racialist

Rạst die; ~, ~en rest; ~ **machen** stop for a break; **rạsten** itr. V. rest; take a rest or break

Rạst-: ~**haus** das roadside café; (an der Autobahn) motorway restaurant; ~**platz** der **a)** place to rest; b) (an Autobahnen) parking place (with benches and WCs); picnic area; ~**stätte** die service area

Rasụr die; ~, ~en shave

Rạt der; ~[e]s, **Rạte a)** o. Pl. advice; **ein** ~: a word of advice; b) (Gremium) council

rạt 3. Pers. Sg. Präsens v. **raten**

Rạte die; ~, ~n **a)** (Teilbetrag) instalment; **etw. auf** ~**n kaufen** buy sth. by instalments or (Brit.) on hire purchase or (Amer.) on the installment plan; b) (Statistik) rate

rạten 1. unr. itr. V. **a)** jmdm. ~: advise sb.; b) (schätzen) guess; 2. tr. V. **a)** jmdm. ~, **etw. zu tun** advise sb. to do sth.; b) (er~) guess

Raten·zahlung die payment by instalments

Rạt·haus das town hall

Ration die; ~, ~en ration; **rational** Adj. rational; **rationalisieren** tr., itr. V. rationalize

rationẹll 1. Adj. efficient; (wirtschaftlich) economic; 2. adv. efficiently; (wirtschaftlich) economically; **rationieren** tr. V. ration

rat·los 1. Adj. baffled; helpless ⟨look⟩; 2. adv. helplessly; **Rat·losigkeit** die; ~: helplessness; **ratsam** Adj.; nicht attr. advisable; **Rat·schlag** der [piece of] advice

Rätsel das; ~s, ~ **a)** riddle; (Bilder~, Kreuzwort~ usw.) puzzle; b) (Geheimnis) mystery; **rätselhaft** 1. Adj. mysterious; (unergründlich) enigmatic; 2. adv. mysteriously; (unergründlich) enigmatically

Rạtte die; ~, ~n (auch fig.) rat

Raub der; ~[e]s **a)** robbery; b) (Beute) stolen goods pl.; **rauben** tr. V. steal; kidnap ⟨person⟩; **jmdm. etw.** ~: rob sb. of sth.; (geh.: wegnehmen) deprive sb. of sth.; **Räuber** der; ~s, ~: robber

Raub-: ~**fisch** der predatory fish; ~**mord** der (Rechtsw.) murder (**an** + Dat. of) in the course of a robbery or with robbery as motive; ~**tier** das predator; **~überfall** der robbery (**auf** + *Akk.* of); **~vogel** der bird of prey

Rauch der; **~|e|s** smoke; **rauchen 1.** *itr. V.* smoke; **2.** *tr. (auch itr.) V.* smoke ⟨*cigarette, pipe, etc.*⟩; „Rauchen verboten" 'No smoking'; **Raucher** der; **~s, ~**: smoker; **Raucher·abteil** das smoking-compartment; smoker; **Raucherin** die; **~, ~nen** smoker; **räuchern** *tr. V.* smoke ⟨*meat, fish*⟩; **rauchig** *Adj.* smoky; husky ⟨*voice*⟩; **Rauch·verbot** das ban on smoking

räudig *Adj.* mangy

rauf *Adv. (ugs.)* up; **~ mit euch!** up you go!; *s. auch* **herauf; hinauf**

raufen 1. *itr., refl. V.* fight; **2.** *tr. V.* **sich** ⟨*Dat.*⟩ **die Haare/den Bart ~:** tear one's hair/at one's beard

rauh 1. *Adj.* **a)** *(nicht glatt)* rough; **b)** *(nicht mild)* harsh ⟨*climate, winter*⟩; raw ⟨*wind*⟩; **c)** *(kratzig)* husky, hoarse ⟨*voice*⟩; **d)** *(entzündet)* sore ⟨*throat*⟩; **e)** *(grob, nicht feinfühlig)* rough; harsh ⟨*words, tone*⟩; **2.** *adv.* **a)** *(kratzig)* ⟨*speak etc.*⟩ huskily, hoarsely; **b)** *(grob, nicht feinfühlig)* roughly

Rauh-: ~faser·tapete die woodchip wallpaper; **~reif** der hoar-frost

Raum der; **~|e|s, Räume** *(Wohn~, Nutz~)* room; **b)** *(Gebiet)* area; region; **c)** *o. Pl. (Platz)* room; space; **räumen** *tr. V.* **a)** clear [away]; clear ⟨*snow*⟩; **b)** *(an einen Ort)* clear; move; **c)** *(frei machen)* clear ⟨*street, building, warehouse, stocks, etc.*⟩; **d)** *(verlassen)* vacate; **Raum·fahrt** die; **~**: space travel; **räumlich 1.** *Adj.* **a)** spatial; **aus ~en Gründen** for reasons of space; **b)** *(dreidimensional)* three-dimensional; stereoscopic ⟨*vision*⟩; **2.** *adv.* **a)** spatially; **b)** *(dreidimensional)* three-dimensionally; **Raum·schiff** das spaceship; **Räumung** die; **~, ~en a)** clearing; **b)** *(das Verlassen)* vacation; vacating; **c)** *(wegen Gefahr)* evacuation; **d)** *(eines Lagers)* clearance

raunen *tr., itr. V. (geh.)* whisper

Raupe die; **~, ~n** caterpillar

raus *Adv. (ugs.)* out; **~ mit euch!** out you go!; *s. auch* **heraus; hinaus**

Rausch der; **~|e|s, Räusche a)** state of drunkenness; **b)** *(starkes Gefühl)* transport; **der ~ der Geschwindigkeit** the exhilaration *or* thrill of speed; **rauschen** *itr. V.* ⟨*water, wind, torrent*⟩ rush; ⟨*trees, leaves*⟩ rustle; ⟨*skirt, curtains, silk*⟩ swish; ⟨*waterfall, strong wind*⟩ roar; ⟨*rain*⟩ pour down;

Rausch·gift das drug; narcotic; **~ nehmen** take drugs; be on drugs

räuspern *refl. V.* clear one's throat

raus|schmeißen *unr. tr. V. (ugs.)* chuck *(coll.)* ⟨*objects*⟩ out *or* away; give ⟨*employee*⟩ the push *(coll.)* or sack *(coll.)*; chuck *(coll.)* or throw ⟨*customer, drunk, tenant*⟩ out (**aus** of)

Raute die; **~, ~n** *(Geom.)* rhombus

Razzia die; **~, Razzien** raid

reagieren *itr. V.* react (**auf** + *Akk.* to); **Reaktion** die; **~, ~en** reaction (**auf** + *Akk.* to); **reaktionär** *Adj.* reactionary; **Reaktionär** der; **~s, ~e** reactionary; **Reaktor** der; **~s, ~en** [-'to:rən] reactor

real 1. *Adj.* real; **2.** *adv.* actually; **realisieren** *tr. V. (geh.)* realize; **Realismus** der; **~**: realism; **Realist** der; **~en, ~en** realist; **realistisch 1.** *Adj.* realistic; **2.** *adv.* realistically; **Realität** die; **~, ~en** reality

Rebe die; **~, ~n a)** vine shoot; **b)** *(Weinstock)* [grape] vine

Rebell der; **~en, ~en** rebel; **rebellieren** *itr. V.* rebel (**gegen** against); **Rebellion** die; **~, ~en** rebellion; **rebellisch** *Adj.* rebellious

Reb-: ~huhn das partridge; **~stock** der vine

rechen *tr. V. (bes. südd.)* rake; **Rechen** der; **~s, ~** *(bes. südd.)* rake

Rechen-: ~fehler der arithmetical error; **~maschine** die calculator

Rechenschaft die; **~**: account; **jmdn. für etw. zur ~ ziehen** call *or* bring sb. to account for sth.

rechnen 1. *tr. V.* **a)** **eine Aufgabe ~:** work out a problem; **b)** *(veranschlagen)* reckon; estimate; **gut/rund gerechnet** at a generous/rough estimate; **c)** *(berücksichtigen)* take into account; **d)** *(einbeziehen)* count; **2.** *itr. V.* **a)** do *or* make a calculation/calculations; **gut/schlecht ~ können** be good/bad at figures; **b)** *(zählen)* reckon; **c)** *(ugs.: berechnen)* calculate; estimate; **d)** *(wirtschaften)* budget carefully; **e)** **auf jmdn./etw.** *od.* **mit jmdm./etw. ~:** count on sb./sth.; **f) mit etw. ~** *(etw. einkalkulieren)* reckon with sth.; *(etw. erwarten)* expect sth.; **Rechnen** das; **~s** arithmetic; **Rechner** der; **~s, ~**: calculator; *(Computer)* computer; **rechnerisch** *Adj.* arithmetical; **Rechnung** die; **~, ~en a)** calculation; **b)** *(schriftliche Kosten~)* bill; invoice *(Commerc.)*; **|jmdn.|** **etw. in ~ stellen** charge [sb.] for sth.

recht 1. *Adj.* a) *(geeignet, richtig)* right; b) *(gesetzmäßig, anständig)* right; proper; ~ **und billig** right and proper; c) *(wunschgemäß)* jmdm. ~ **sein** be all right with sb.; d) *(wirklich, echt)* real; 2. *adv.* a) *(geeignet)* **du kommst gerade** ~: you are just in time; b) *(richtig)* correctly; c) *(gesetzmäßig, anständig)* properly; d) *(wunschgemäß)* **es** jmdm. ~ **machen** please sb.; e) *(wirklich, echt)* really; f) *(ziemlich)* quite; rather; *s. auch* **Recht d**; **recht...** *Adj.* a) right; right[-hand] *⟨edge⟩*; b) *(außen, sichtbar)* right *⟨side⟩*; c) *(in der Politik)* right-wing; **Recht** das; ~[e]s, ~e a) *(Rechtsordnung)* law; b) *(Rechtsanspruch)* right; **sein** ~ **fordern** *od.* **verlangen** demand one's rights; c) *o. Pl. (Berechtigung)* right **(auf** + *Akk.* to); **gleiches** ~ **für alle!** equal rights for all!; **im** ~ **sein** be in the right; **zu** ~: rightly; d) **recht haben** be right; jmdm. **recht geben** admit that sb. is right

recht·fertigen *tr. V.* justify (**vor** + *Dat.* to); **Recht·fertigung** die justification

rechtlich 1. *Adj.* legal; 2. *adv.* legally; **recht·los** *Adj.* without rights *postpos.*; **rechtmäßig** 1. *Adj.* lawful; rightful; legitimate *⟨claim⟩*; 2. *adv.* lawfully; rightfully; **Rechtmäßigkeit** die; ~: legality; *(eines Anspruchs)* legitimacy

rechts *Adv.* a) on the right; **von** ~: from the right; b) *(Politik)* on the right wing

Rechts-: ~**abbieger** der *(Verkehrsw.)* motorist/cyclist/car *etc.* turning right; ~**anwalt** der, ~**anwältin** die lawyer; solicitor *(Brit.)*; attorney *(Amer.)*; *(vor Gericht)* barrister *(Brit.)*; attorney[-at-law] *(Amer.)*; advocate *(Scot.)*; ~**außen** der [-'--] der; ~, ~ *(Ballspiele)* right wing; outside right

recht-, Recht-: ~**schaffen** 1. *Adj.* honest; 2. *adv.* honestly; ~**schreibfehler** der spelling mistake; ~**schreibung** die orthography

rechts-, Rechts-: ~**händer** der; ~s, ~: right-hander; ~**kräftig** *(Rechtsw.)* 1. *Adj.* final [and absolute] *⟨decision, verdict, etc.⟩*; 2. *adv.* jmdn. ~**kräftig verurteilen** pass a final sentence on sb.; ~**kurve** die right-hand bend

Recht·sprechung die; ~, ~en administration of justice; *(eines Gerichts)* jurisdiction

rechts-, Rechts-: ~**staat** der [constitutional] state founded on the rule of law; ~**staatlich** *Adj.* founded on the rule of law *postpos.*; ~**verkehr** der driving *no art.* on the right; ~**widrig** 1. *Adj.* unlawful; 2. *adv.* unlawfully

recht-: ~**wink[e]lig** *Adj.* right-angled; ~**zeitig** 1. *Adj.* timely; *(pünktlich)* punctual; 2. *adv.* in time; *(pünktlich)* on time

Reck das; ~[e]s, ~e *od.* ~s horizontal bar

recken 1. *tr. V.* stretch; 2. *refl. V.* stretch oneself

Redakteur [redak'tø:ɐ̯] der; ~s, ~e, **Redakteurin** die; ~, ~nen editor; **Redaktion** die; ~, ~en a) *(Redakteure)* editorial staff; b) *(Büro)* editorial department *or* office/offices *pl.*

Rede die; ~, ~n a) *(Ansprache)* address; speech; **eine** ~ **halten** give *or* make a speech; b) *o. Pl. (Vortrag)* rhetoric; c) *(Äußerung, Ansicht)* **nicht der** ~ **wert sein** be not worth mentioning; jmdn. **zur** ~ **stellen** make someone explain himself/herself; **reden** 1. *tr. V.* talk; **Unsinn** ~: talk nonsense; **kein Wort** ~: not say *or* speak a word; 2. *itr. V.* a) *(sprechen)* talk; speak; **viel/wenig** ~: talk a lot *(coll.)*/not talk much; b) *(sich äußern, eine Rede halten)* speak; **gut** ~ **können** be a good speaker; c) *(sich unterhalten)* talk; **mit** jmdm./**über** jmdn. ~: talk to/about sb.; **Redens·art** die a) expression; *(Sprichwort)* saying; b) *Pl. (Phrase)* empty *or* meaningless words

Rede·wendung die *(Sprachw.)* idiom

redlich 1. *Adj.* honest; 2. *adv.* honestly; **Redlichkeit** die; ~: honesty

Redner der; ~s, ~, **Rednerin** die ~, ~nen a) speaker; b) *(Rhetoriker)* orator; **red·selig** *Adj.* talkative

reduzieren 1. *tr. V.* reduce (**auf** + *Akk.* to); 2. *refl. V.* decrease; diminish

Reeder der; ~s, ~: shipowner; **Reederei** die; ~, ~en shipping firm

reell 1. *Adj.* honest, straight *⟨person, deal, etc.⟩*; sound, solid *⟨business, firm, etc.⟩*; straight *⟨offer⟩*; 2. *adv.* honestly

Reet das; ~s *(nordd.)* reeds *pl.*

Referat das; ~[e]s, ~e a) paper; b) *(kurzer schriftlicher Bericht)* report; **referieren** *itr. V.* **über etw.** *(Akk.)* ~: present a paper on sth.; *(zusammenfassend)* give a report on sth.

reflektieren *tr. V.* reflect
Reflex der; ~es, ~e reflex; **Refle-xiv·pronomen** das *(Sprachw.)* reflexive pronoun
Reform die; ~, ~en reform; **Reform·haus** das health-food shop; **reformieren** *tr. V.* reform
Refrain [rə'frɛ̃:] der; ~s, ~s chorus
Regal das; ~s, ~e [set *sing.* of] shelves *pl.*
rege 1. *Adj.* a) *(betriebsam)* busy *(traffic)*; brisk *(demand, trade, business, etc.)*; b) *(lebhaft)* lively; keen *(interest)*; 2. *adv.* a) *(betriebsam)* actively; b) *(lebhaft)* actively
Regel die; ~, ~n a) rule; **nach allen ~n der Kunst** *(fig.)* well and truly; b) rule; custom; **die ~ sein** be the rule; **in der** *od.* **aller ~:** as a rule; c) *(Menstruation)* period; **regel·mäßig** 1. *Adj.* regular; 2. *adv.* regularly; **Regel·mäßigkeit** die regularity; **regeln** 1. *tr. V.* settle *(matter, question, etc.)*; put *(finances, affairs, etc.)* in order; b) *(einstellen, regulieren)* regulate; *(steuern)* control; 2. *refl. V.* take care of itself; **Regelung** die; ~, ~en a) *o. Pl. s.* **regeln** 1 a, b: settlement; putting in order; regulation; control; b) *(Vorschrift)* regulation
regen 1. *tr. V.* *(geh.)* move; 2. *refl. V.* a) *(sich bewegen)* move; b) *(geh.)* *(hope, doubt, desire, conscience)* stir
Regen der; ~s, ~ a) rain; **vom** *od.* **aus dem ~ in die Traufe kommen** *(fig.)* jump out of the frying-pan into the fire; b) *(fig.)* shower
Regen-: ~**bogen** der rainbow; ~**mantel** der raincoat; mackintosh; ~**schirm** der umbrella; ~**tag** der rainy day; ~**wetter** das; *o. Pl.* wet weather; ~**wolke** die rain cloud; ~**wurm** der earthworm
Regie [re'ʒi:] die; ~ a) *(Theater, Film, Ferns., Rundf.)* direction; b) *(Leitung, Verwaltung)* management
regieren 1. *itr. V.* rule (über + *Akk.* over); *(party, administration)* govern; 2. *tr. V.* rule; govern; *(monarch)* reign over; **Regierung** die; ~, ~en a) *o. Pl.* *(Herrschaft)* rule; *(eines Monarchen)* reign; b) *(Kabinett)* government; **Regierungs·sitz** der seat of government
Regiment das; ~[e]s, ~e *od.* ~er a) *Pl.* ~e *(Herrschaft)* rule; b) *Pl.* ~er *(Milit.)* regiment
Region die; ~, ~en region; **regional** 1. *Adj.* regional; 2. *adv.* regionally

Regisseur [reʒi'søːɐ̯] der; ~s, ~e, **Regisseurin** die; ~, ~nen director
Register das; ~s, ~ a) index; b) *(amtliche Liste)* register; c) *(Musik)* *(bei Instrumenten)* register; *(Orgel~)* stop; **registrieren** *tr. V.* a) register; b) *(bewußt wahrnehmen)* note; register
Regler der; ~s, ~ *(Technik)* regulator; *(Kybernetik)* control
reg·los *Adj.* motionless
regnen 1. *itr., tr. V.* *(unpers.)* rain; **es regnet** it is raining; 2. *itr. V.*; **mit sein** *(fig.)* rain down; **regnerisch** *Adj.* rainy
regulär *Adj.* a) proper; normal *(working hours)*; b) *(normal, üblich)* normal; **regulieren** *tr. V.* regulate; **Regulierung** die; ~, ~en regulation
Regung die; ~, ~en *(geh.: Gefühl)* stirring; **regungs·los** *Adj.* motionless
Reh das; ~[e]s, ~e roe-deer
Reh-: ~**bock** der roebuck; ~**kitz** das fawn [of a/the roe-deer]
Reibe die; ~, ~n, **Reib·eisen** das grater; **reiben** 1. *unr. tr. V.* a) rub; b) *(zerkleinern)* grate; 2. *unr. itr. V.* rub (an + *Dat.* on); **Reibung** die; ~, ~en *(Physik, fig.)* friction; **reibungs·los** 1. *Adj.* smooth; 2. *adv.* smoothly
reich 1. *Adj.* a) *(vermögend)* rich; b) *(prächtig)* costly *(goods, gifts)*; rich *(décor, finery)*; c) *(üppig)* rich; abundant *(harvest)*; abundant *(mineral resources)*; ~ **an etw.** *(Dat.)* **sein** be rich in sth.; d) *(vielfältig)* rich *(collection, possibilities)*; wide, large *(selection, choice)*; wide *(knowledge, experience)*; 2. *adv.* richly
Reich das; ~[e]s, ~e a) empire; *(König~)* kingdom; realm; **das [Deutsche] ~** *(hist.)* the German Reich *or* Empire; **das Dritte ~** *(hist.)* the Third Reich; b) *(fig.)* realm
reichen 1. *itr. V.* a) *(aus~)* be enough; **das Geld reicht nicht** I/we *etc.* haven't got enough money; **jetzt reicht's mir aber!** now I've had enough!; **danke, es reicht** that's enough, thank you; b) *(sich erstrecken)* reach *(forest, fields, etc.)* extend; 2. *tr. V.* a) pass; hand; **jmdm. die Hand ~:** hold out one's hand to sb.; **sich** *(Dat.)* **die Hand ~:** shake hands; b) *(servieren)* serve *(food, drink)*
reich·haltig *Adj.* extensive; varied *(programme)*; substantial *(meal)*; **reichlich** 1. *Adj.* large; ample *(space, time)*; good *(hour, year)*; 2. *adv.* a) amply; b) *(mehr als)* over; more than;

c) *(ugs.: ziemlich, sehr)* a bit too ⟨*cheeky, dear, late*⟩; **Reichtum der;** ~**s, Reichtümer a)** *o. Pl.* wealth **(an** + *Dat.* of); **b)** *Pl. (Vermögenswerte)* riches

Reich·weite die reach; *(eines Geschützes, Senders, Flugzeugs)* range

reif *Adj.* **a)** ripe ⟨*fruit, grain, cheese*⟩; mature ⟨*brandy, cheese*⟩; ~ **für etw. sein** *(ugs.)* be ready for sth.; **b)** *(erwachsen, ausgewogen)* mature

¹**Reif der;** ~[e]s hoar-frost

²**Reif der;** ~[e]s, ~e *(geh.)* ring; *(Arm~)* bracelet; *(Diadem)* circlet

Reife die; ~ **a)** ripeness; *(von Menschen, Gedanken, Produkten)* maturity; **b)** *(Reifung)* ripening; **reifen 1.** *itr. V.; mit sein* **a)** ⟨*fruit, cereal, cheese*⟩ ripen; **b)** *(geh.: älter, reifer werden)* mature ⟨zu into⟩; **c)** ⟨*idea, plan, decision*⟩ mature; **2.** *tr. V.* ripen ⟨*fruit, cereal*⟩;

Reifen der; ~**s,** ~ **a)** hoop; **b)** *(Gummi~)* tyre; **c)** *s.* ²**Reif**

Reifen-: ~**panne die** puncture; ~**wechsel der** tyre change

reiflich 1. *Adj.* [very] careful; **2.** *adv.* [very] carefully

Reigen der; ~**s,** ~ **a)** round dance; **b)** *(fig.)* **den** ~ **eröffnen** start off

Reihe die; ~, ~**n a)** row; **in Reih und Glied** *(Milit.)* in rank and file; **aus der** ~ **tanzen** *(fig. ugs.)* be different; **b)** *o. Pl. (Reihenfolge)* series; **er/sie usw. ist an der** ~: it's his/her *etc.* turn; **der** ~ **nach, nach der** ~: in turn; **c)** *(größere Anzahl)* number; **reihen** *(geh.)* *tr. V.* string; threed

Reihen-: ~**folge die** order; ~**haus das** terraced house

Reiher der; ~**s,** ~: heron

Reim der; ~[e]s, ~e rhyme; **reimen 1.** *itr. V.* make up rhymes; **2.** *tr., refl. V.* rhyme **(auf** + *Akk.* with)

¹**rein** *Adv.* *(ugs.)* ~ **mit dir!** in you go/come!

²**rein 1.** *Adj.* **a)** *(unvermischt)* pure; **b)** *(nichts anderes als)* pure; sheer; plain, unvarnished ⟨*truth*⟩; **c)** *(frisch, sauber)* clean; fresh ⟨*clothes, sheet of paper, etc.*⟩; pure, clean ⟨*water, air*⟩; clear ⟨*complexion*⟩; **etw. ins** ~**e schreiben** make a fair copy of sth.; **etw. ins** ~**e bringen** clear sth. up; **2.** *Adv.* purely; ~ **gar nichts** *(ugs.)* absolutely nothing

Rein·fall der *(ugs.)* let-down

Rein·gewinn der net profit

Reinheit die; ~ **a)** purity; **b)** *(Sauberkeit)* cleanness; *(des Wassers, der*

Luft) purity; *(der Haut)* clearness; **reinigen** *tr. V.* clean; purify ⟨*effluents, air, water, etc.*⟩; **Kleider** [chemisch] ~ **lassen** have clothes [dry-] cleaned; **Reinigung die;** ~, ~**en a)** *s.* reinigen: cleaning; purification; drycleaning; **b)** *(Betrieb)* [dry-]cleaner's;

reinlich *Adj.* cleanly; **Reinlichkeit die;** ~: cleanliness

rein·rassig *Adj.* thoroughbred ⟨*animal*⟩; **Rein·schrift die** fair copy

Reis der; ~es rice

Reise die; ~, ~**n** journey; *(kürzere Fahrt, Geschäfts~)* trip; *(Ausflug)* outing; trip; *(Schiffs~)* voyage; **eine** ~ **machen** go on a trip/an outing; **auf** ~**n sein** travel; *(nicht zu Hause sein)* be away; **glückliche** *od.* **gute** ~! have a good journey

Reise-: ~**an·denken das** souvenir; ~**büro das** travel agent's; travel agency; ~**bus der** coach; ~**führer der a)** *(~leiter)* courier; **b)** *(Buch)* guidebook; ~**führerin die** courier; ~**gepäck das** luggage *(Brit.)*; baggage *(Amer.)*; *(am Flughafen)* baggage; ~**gesellschaft die a)** *(~gruppe)* party of tourists; **b)** *(ugs.: ~veranstalter)* tour operator; ~**kosten** *Pl.* travel expenses; ~**leiter der,** ~**leiterin die** courier

reisen *itr. V.; mit sein* **a)** travel; **b)** *(ab~)* leave; set off; **Reisende der/die;** *adj. Dekl.* traveller; *(Fahrgast)* passenger

Reise-: ~**paß der** passport; ~**scheck der** traveller's cheque; ~**tasche die** hold-all; ~**verkehr der** holiday traffic; ~**ziel das** destination

Reisig das; ~s brushwood

Reiß·brett das drawing-board

reißen 1. *unr. tr. V.* **a)** tear; *(in Stücke)* tear up; **b)** *(ziehen an)* pull; *(heftig)* yank *(coll.)*; **c)** *(werfen, ziehen)* break; snap; ⟨*film*⟩ break; ⟨*muscle*⟩ tear; **b)** *(ziehen)* **an etw.** *(Dat.)* ~: pull at sth.; **3.** *unr. refl. V.* *(ugs.: sich bemühen um)* **sie** ~ **sich um die Eintrittskarten** they are fighting each other to get tickets; **reißend** *Adj.* rapacious ⟨*animal*⟩; raging ⟨*torrent*⟩; ~**en Absatz finden** sell like hot cakes

Reiß-: ~**leine die** *(Flugw.)* rip-cord;

~nagel der s. ~zwecke; **~verschluß** der zip [fastener]; **~zwecke** die drawing-pin *(Brit.)*; thumbtack *(Amer.)*

reiten 1. *unr. itr. V.; meist mit sein* ride; **2.** *unr. tr. V.; auch mit sein* ride; **Schritt/Trab/Galopp** ~: ride at a walk/trot/gallop; **Reiten** das; ~s ~s riding *no art.;* **Reiter** der; ~s, ~, **Reiterin** die; ~, ~nen rider

Reit-: **~hose** die riding breeches *pl.;* **~pferd** das saddle-horse; **~stiefel** der riding boot

Reiz der; ~es, ~e a) *(Physiol.)* stimulus; b) *(Anziehungskraft)* attraction; appeal *no pl.; (des Verbotenen, der Ferne usw.)* lure; c) *(Zauber)* charm; **reizbar** Adj. irritable; **Reizbarkeit** die; ~: irritability; **reizen 1.** tr. V. a) annoy; tease *(animal); (herausfordern, provozieren)* provoke; s. auch gereizt; b) *(Physiol.)* irritate; c) *(Interesse erregen bei)* jmdn. ~: attract sb.; appeal to sb.; d) *(Kartenspiele)* bid; **2.** itr. V. *(Kartenspiele)* bid; **reizend 1.** Adj. charming; delightful, lovely ⟨child⟩; **2.** adv. charmingly; **reizlos** Adj. unattractive; ⟨landscape, scenery⟩ lacking in charm; **reizvoll** Adj. a) *(hübsch)* charming; b) *(interessant)* attractive

rekeln refl. V. *(ugs.)* stretch

Reklamation [reklama'tsĭo:n] die; ~, ~en complaint *(wegen about);* **Reklame** die; ~, ~n a) advertising *no indef. art.;* ~ für jmdn./etw. machen promote sb./advertise *or* promote sth.; b) *(ugs.: Werbemittel)* advert *(Brit. coll.);* ad *(coll.); (im Fernsehen, Radio usw)* commercial; **reklamieren 1.** itr. V. complain; **2.** tr. V. a) complain about *(bei to, wegen on account of);* b) *(beanspruchen)* claim

rekonstruieren tr. V. reconstruct

Rekord der; ~[e]s, ~e record

Rekrut der; ~en, ~en *(Milit.)* recruit

Rektor der; ~s, ~en a) *(einer Schule)* head[master]; b) *(Universitäts~)* Rector; ≈ Vice-Chancellor *(Brit.); (einer Fachhochschule)* principal; **Rektorin** die; ~, ~nen a) *(einer Schule)* head[mistress]; b) s. Rektor b

Relation die; ~, ~en relation; **relativ 1.** Adj. relative; **2.** adv. relatively

Relativ-: **~pronomen** das *(Sprachw.)* relative pronoun; **~satz** der *(Sprachw.)* relative clause

Relief das; ~s, ~s od. ~e relief

Religion die; ~, ~en religion; **religi-**

ös 1. Adj. religious; **2.** adv. in a religious manner

Relikt das; ~[e], ~e relic

Reling die; ~, ~s od. ~e [deck-]rail

Reliquie die; ~, ~n relic

Remis das; ~ [rə'mi:(s)], ~ [rə'mi:s] *(bes. Schach)* draw

Ren das; ~s, ~s od. ~e reindeer

Rendezvous [rãde'vu:] das; ~ [...'vu:(s)], ~ ['rãde'vu:s] rendezvous

Renn-bahn die *(Sport)* race-track; *(für Pferde)* racecourse; **rennen** unr. itr. V.; mit sein run; **an/gegen** jmdn./etw. ~: run *or* bang into sb./sth.; **Rennen** das; ~s, ~: running; *(Pferde~, Auto~)* racing; *(Wettbewerb)* race

Renn-: **~fahrer** der racing driver; **~pferd** das racehorse; **~rad** das racing cycle; **~wagen** der racing car

renommiert Adj. renowned

renovieren tr. V. renovate; redecorate ⟨room, flat⟩; **Renovierung** die; ~, ~en renovation; *(eines Zimmers, einer Wohnung)* redecoration

rentabel 1. Adj. profitable; **2.** adv. profitably

Rente die; ~, ~n a) pension; b) *(Kapitalertrag)* annuity

Ren-tier das reindeer

rentieren refl. V. be profitable; ⟨equipment, machinery⟩ pay its way

Rentner der; ~s, ~, **Rentnerin** die; ~, ~nen pensioner

Reparatur die; ~, ~en repair (an + Dat. to)

Reparatur-werkstatt die repair [work]shop; *(für Autos)* garage

reparieren tr. V. repair; mend

Repertoire [repɛr'tŏa:ɐ] das; ~s, ~s repertoire

Report der; ~[e]s, ~e, **Reportage** [repɔr'ta:ʒə] die; ~, ~n report; **Reporter** der; ~s, ~, **Reporterin** die; ~, ~nen reporter

Repräsentant der; ~en, ~en, **Repräsentantin** die; ~, ~nen representative; **repräsentativ** Adj. representative; **repräsentieren** tr. V. represent

Repressalie die; ~, ~n repressive measure

Reproduktion die reproduction; **reproduzieren** tr. V. reproduce

Reptil das; ~s, ~ien reptile

Republik die; ~, ~en republic; **republikanisch** Adj. republican

Reservat das; ~[e]s, ~e a) reservation; b) *(Naturschutzgebiet)* reserve;

Reserve die; ~, ~n reserve

Reserve-: ~rad das spare wheel; ~reifen der spare tyre

reservieren tr. V. reserve; **Reservoir** [rezεr'voaːɐ̯] das; ~s, ~e (auch fig.) reservoir (**an** + Dat. of)

Residenz die; ~, ~en a) residence; b) (Hauptstadt) [royal] capital

Resignation die; ~, ~en resignation; **resignieren** itr. V. give up

resolut 1. Adj. resolute; 2. adv. resolutely; **Resolution** die; ~, ~en resolution

Resonanz die; ~, ~en resonance

Respekt der; ~[e]s a) (Achtung) respect (**vor** + Dat. for); b) (Furcht) jmdm. ~ **einflößen** intimidate sb.; **respektieren** tr. V. respect; **respekt·los** 1. Adj. disrespectful; 2. adv. disrespectfully; **Respektlosigkeit** die; ~: disrespectfulness; **respekt·voll** 1. Adj. respectful; 2. adv. respectfully

Ressort [rε'soːɐ̯] das; ~s, ~s area of responsibility; (Abteilung) department

Rest der; ~[e]s, ~e a) rest; **ein ~ von** a little bit of; b) (Endstück) remnant; c) (Math.) remainder

Restaurant [rεsto'rãː] das; ~s, ~s restaurant; **restaurieren** tr. V. restore

restlich Adj. remaining; **rest·los** 1. Adj. complete; 2. adv. completely

Resultat das; ~[e]s, ~e result

Retorte die; ~, ~n retort

retten 1. tr. V. save; (vor Gefahr) save; rescue; (befreien) rescue; **jmdm. das Leben ~:** save sb.'s life; 2. refl. V. (fliehen) escape (**aus** from); **Retter** der; ~s, ~, **Retterin** die; ~, ~nen rescuer

Rettich der; ~s, ~e radish

Rettung die rescue; (vor Zerstörung) saving

rettungs-, Rettungs-: ~boot das lifeboat; ~hubschrauber der rescue helicopter; ~los 1. Adj. hopeless; inevitable ⟨disaster⟩; 2. adv. hopelessly; ~ring der lifebelt

Reue die; ~: remorse (**über** + Akk. for); (Rel.) repentance; **reuen** tr. V. **etw. reut jmdn.** sb. regrets sth.; **reu·mütig** Adj. remorseful; repentant ⟨sinner⟩

Reuse die; ~, ~n fish-trap

Revanche [re'vãːʃ(ə)] die; ~, ~n revenge; (Sport) return match/fight/game; **revanchieren** refl. V. a) get one's revenge, (coll.) get one's own back (**bei** on); b) **sich bei jmdm. für eine Einladung ~** (ugs.) return sb.'s invitation

Revers [rə'veːɐ̯] das od. (österr.) der; ~ [rə'veːɐ̯(s)], ~ [rə'veːɐ̯s] lapel

Revier das; ~s, ~e a) (Aufgabenbereich) province; b) (Zool.) territory; c) (Polizei~) (Dienststelle) [police] station; (Bereich) district; (des einzelnen Polizisten) beat

Revision die; ~, ~en a) revision; (Änderung) amendment; b) (Rechtsw.) appeal [on a point/points of law]; ~ **einlegen, in die ~ gehen** lodge an appeal [on a point/points of law]

Revolte die; ~, ~n revolt; **Revolution** die; ~, ~en (auch fig.) revolution; **revolutionär** 1. Adj. revolutionary; 2. adv. in a revolutionary way; **Revolutionär** der; ~s, ~e, **Revolutionärin** die; ~, ~nen revolutionary

Revolver der; ~s, ~: revolver

Rezept das; ~[e]s, ~e a) (Med.) prescription; b) (Anleitung) recipe; **Rezeption** die; ~, ~en reception no art.; **rezept·pflichtig** Adj. ⟨drug etc.⟩ obtainable only on prescription

R-Gespräch ['εr-] das reverse-charge call (Brit.); collect call (Amer.)

Rhabarber der; ~s rhubarb

Rhein der; ~[e]s Rhine; **rheinisch** Adj. Rhenish; (speciality etc.) of the Rhine region; **Rhein·land** das; ~[e]s Rhineland; **Rheinland-Pfalz** (die); ~': the Rhineland-Palatinate

Rhetorik die; ~, ~en rhetoric

Rheuma das; ~s (ugs.) rheumatism; **rheumatisch** (Med.) 1. Adj. rheumatic; 2. adv. rheumatically; **Rheumatismus** der; ~, **Rheumatismen** (Med.) rheumatism

Rhinozeros das; ~[ses], ~se rhinoceros; rhino (coll.)

Rhododendron der od. das; ~s, Rhododendren rhododendron

rhythmisch 1. Adj. rhythmical; rhythmic; 2. adv. rhythmically; **Rhythmus** der; ~, **Rhythmen** (auch fig.) rhythm

richten 1. tr. V. a) direct ⟨gaze⟩ (**auf** + Akk. at, towards); turn ⟨eyes, gaze⟩ (**auf** + Akk. towards); point ⟨torch, telescope, gun⟩ (**auf** + Akk. at); aim ⟨gun, missile, telescope, searchlight⟩ (**auf** + Akk. on); (fig.) direct ⟨activity, attention⟩ (**auf** + Akk. towards); address ⟨letter, remarks, words⟩ (**an** + Akk. to); level ⟨criticism⟩ (**an** + Akk. at); b) (gerade~) straighten ⟨beams⟩; c) (aburteilen) judge; (verurteilen) condemn; s. auch **zugrunde** a; 2. refl. V. a) (sich hinwenden) **sich auf jmdn./etw. ~**

(auch fig.) be directed towards sb./ sth.; **b)** **sich an jmdn./etw. ~** *⟨person⟩* turn on sb./sth.; *⟨appeal, explanation⟩* be directed at sb./sth.; **sich gegen jmdn./etw. ~** *⟨person⟩* criticize sb./ sth.; *⟨criticism, accusations, etc.⟩* be aimed *or* levelled at sb./sth.; **c)** *⟨sich orientieren⟩* **sich nach jmdm./jmds. Wünschen ~**: fit in with sb./sb.'s wishes; **d)** *⟨abhängen⟩* **sich nach jmdm./etw. ~**: depend on sb./sth.; **3.** *itr. V. ⟨urteilen⟩* judge; **Richter** der; **~s, ~, Richterin** die; **~, ~nen** judge
Richt·geschwindigkeit die recommended maximum speed
richtig 1. *Adj.* **a)** right; *⟨zutreffend⟩* right; correct; accurate *⟨prophecy, premonition⟩*; **b)** *⟨ordentlich⟩* proper; **c)** *⟨wirklich, echt⟩* real; **2.** *adv.* **a)** right; correctly; **b)** *⟨ordentlich⟩* properly; **c)** *⟨richtiggehend⟩* really
richtig|stellen *tr. V.* correct
Richt-: ~linie die guideline; **~schnur** die; *Pl.* **~schnuren** *(fig.)* guiding principle
Richtung die; **~, ~en a)** direction; **b)** *(fig.: Tendenz)* movement; trend
rieb *1. u. 3. Pers. Sg. Prät. v.* reiben
riechen 1. *unr. tr. V.* **a)** smell; **b)** *(wittern) ⟨dog etc.⟩* pick up the scent of; **2.** *unr. itr. V.* **a)** smell; **an jmdm./etw. ~**: smell sb./sth.; **b)** *(einen Geruch haben)* smell *(nach* of)
rief *1. u. 3. Pers. Sg. Prät. v.* rufen
Riegel der; **~s, ~ a)** bolt; **b)** **ein ~ Schokolade** a bar of chocolate
Riemen der; **~s, ~ a)** strap; *(Treib~, Gürtel)* belt; **sich am ~ reißen** *(ugs.)* pull oneself together; get a grip on oneself; **b)** *(Ruder)* [long] oar
Riese der; **~n, ~n** giant
rieseln *itr. V.; mit Richtungsangabe mit sein* trickle [down]; *⟨snow⟩* fall gently
Riesen- giant; enormous *⟨selection, profit, portion⟩*; tremendous *(coll.) ⟨effort, rejoicing, success⟩*; terrific *(coll.)*; terrible *(coll.) ⟨stupidity, scandal, fuss⟩*
riesen·groß *Adj.* enormous; huge; terrific *(coll.) ⟨surprise⟩*; **Riesenschritt** der giant stride; **riesig 1.** *Adj.* enormous; huge; vast *⟨country⟩*; tremendous *⟨effort, progress⟩*; **2.** *adv. (ugs.)* tremendously *(coll.)*; terribly *(coll.)*
Riesling der; **~s, ~e** Riesling
riet *1. u. 3. Pers. Sg. Prät. v.* raten
Riff das; **~[e]s, ~e** reef
Rille die; **~, ~n** groove

Rind das; **~[e]s, ~er a)** cow; *(Stier)* bull; **~er cattle** *pl.*; **b)** *(~fleisch)* beef
Rinde die; **~, ~n a)** *(Baum~)* bark; **b)** *(Brot~)* crust; *(Käse~)* rind
Rinder·braten der roast beef *no indef. art.; (roh)* roasting beef *no indef. art.*
Rind-: ~fleisch das beef; **~vieh** das cattle *pl.*
Ring der; **~[e]s, ~e** ring; **Ringel·natter** die ring-snake
ringen 1. *unr. tr. V. (Sport, fig.)* wrestle; *(fig.: kämpfen)* struggle, fight *(um* for; *gegen, mit* with); **nach Luft ~**: struggle for breath; **2.** *unr. tr. V.* **die Hände ~**: wring one's hands; **Ringen** das; **~s** *(Sport)* wrestling *no art.*
Ring-: ~finger der ring-finger; **~kampf** der **a)** [stand-up] fight; **b)** *(Sport)* wrestling bout
rings *Adv.* all around; **rings·herum** *Adv.* all around [it/them *etc.*]
Ring·straße die ring road
rings-: ~um, ~umher *Adv.* all around
Rinne die; **~, ~n** channel; *(Dach~, Rinnstein)* gutter; *(Abfluß)* drainpipe; **rinnen** *unr. itr. V.; mit sein* run; **Rinn·stein** der gutter
Rippchen das; **~s, ~** *(Kochk. südd.)* rib [of pork]; **Rippe** die; **~, ~n** rib
Risiko das; **~s, Risiken** risk; **riskant 1.** *Adj.* risky; **2.** *adv.* riskily; **riskieren** *tr. V.* risk
riß *1. u. 3. Pers. Sg. Prät. v.* reißen
Riß der; **Risses, Risse** tear; *(Spalt, Sprung)* crack; **rissig** *Adj.* cracked; chapped *⟨lips⟩*
ritt *1. u. 3. Pers. Sg. Prät. v.* reiten
Ritt der; **~[e]s, ~e** ride; **Ritter** der; **~s, ~**: knight; **Ritter·sporn** der delphinium; **rittlings** *Adv.* astride
Ritze die; **~, ~n** crack; [narrow] gap; **ritzen** *tr. V.* scratch
Rivale der; **~n, ~n, Rivalin** die; **~, ~nen** rival; **Rivalität** die; **~, ~en** rivalry *no indef. art.*
Robbe die; **~, ~n** seal
Robe die; **~, ~n** robe; *(schwarz)* gown
Roboter der; **~s, ~**: robot
robust *Adj.* robust
roch *1. u. 3. Pers. Sg. Prät. v.* riechen
Rochade die; **~, ~n** *(Schach)* castling
röcheln *itr. V. ⟨dying person⟩* give the death-rattle
Rock der; **~[e]s, Röcke** skirt
Rodel·bahn die toboggan-run; *(Sport)* luge-run; **rodeln** *itr. V.; mit sein* sledge; toboggan

roden *tr. V.* clear ⟨*wood, land*⟩; *(ausgraben)* grub up ⟨*tree*⟩

Rogen der; ~s, ~: roe

Roggen der; ~s rye

Roggen-: ~**brot** das rye bread; **ein** ~brot a loaf of rye bread; ~**brötchen** das rye-bread roll

roh 1. *Adj.* **a)** raw ⟨*food*⟩; unboiled ⟨*milk*⟩; unfinished ⟨*wood*⟩; **b)** *(ungenau)* rough; **c)** *(brutal)* brutish; brute *attrib.* ⟨*force*⟩; 2. *adv.* **a)** *(ungenau)* roughly; **b)** *(brutal)* brutishly; *(grausam)* callously; *(grob)* coarsely

Roh-: ~**bau** der shell [of a/the building]; ~**kost** die raw fruit and vegetables *pl.*; ~**material** das raw material; ~**öl** das crude oil

Rohr das; ~[e]s, ~e **a)** *(Leitungs~)* pipe; *(als Bauteil)* tube; **b)** *o. Pl.* *(Röhricht)* reeds *pl.*; **c)** *(Werkstoff)* reed; **Röhre** die; ~, ~n tube; *(Elektronen~)* valve *(Brit.);* tube *(Amer.)*

Roh·stoff der raw material

Rokoko das; ~[s] rococo

Rolladen der; ~s, **Rolläden** [roller] shutter; **Roll·bahn** die *(Flugw.)* taxiway; **Rolle** die; ~, ~n **a)** *(Spule)* reel; **b)** *(zylindrischer [Hohl]körper; Zusammengerolltes)* roll; **c)** *(Walze)* roll; **d)** *(Rad)* [small] wheel; *(an Möbeln usw.)* castor; *(für Gardine, Schiebetür usw.)* runner; **e)** *(Turnen, Kunstflug)* roll; **f)** *(Theater, Film usw., fig.)* role; part; *(Soziol.)* role; **es spielt keine** ~: it is of no importance; *(es macht nichts aus)* it doesn't matter; **rollen** 1. *tr. V.* roll; 2. *itr. V.* **a)** *mit sein* ⟨*ball, wheel, etc.*⟩ roll; ⟨*vehicle*⟩ move; ⟨*aircraft*⟩ taxi; **Roller** der; ~s, ~: scooter

Roll-: ~**feld** das runway[s] and taxiway[s]; ~**kragen** der polo-neck; ~**laden** der s. Rolladen; ~**mops** der rollmops; ~**schuh** der roller-skate; ~**schuh laufen** roller-skate; ~**splitt** der loose chippings *pl.*; ~**stuhl** der wheelchair; ~**treppe** die escalator

Rom *(das)*; ~s Rome

Roman der; ~s, ~e novel

Romantik die; ~: romanticism; **die** ~: Romanticism; **romantisch** 1. *Adj.* romantic; 2. *adv.* romantically

Romanze die; ~, ~n romance

Römer der; ~s, ~: Roman

römisch-katholisch *Adj.* Roman Catholic

röntgen *tr. V.* X-ray

Röntgen-: ~**aufnahme** die, ~**bild** das X-ray [image/photograph *or* picture]; ~**strahlen** *Pl.* X-rays

rosa 1. *indekl. Adj.* pink; 2. *adv.* pink; **Rosa** das; ~s, ~ *od.* ~s pink; **Rose** die; ~, ~n rose

rosé 1. *indekl. Adj.* pale pink; **Rosé** der; ~s, ~s rosé [wine]

Rosen-: ~**kohl** der; *o. Pl.* [Brussels] sprouts *pl.*; ~**kranz** der *(kath. Kirche)* rosary; **einen** ~**kranz beten** say a rosary; ~**montag** der the day before Shrove Tuesday

rosig *Adj.* **a)** rosy; pink ⟨*piglet etc.*⟩; **b)** *(fig.)* rosy; optimistic ⟨*mood*⟩

Rosine die; ~, ~n raisin

Rosmarin der; ~s rosemary

Roß das; **Rosses, Rosse** *od.* **Rösser** horse; steed *(poet./joc.);* **hoch zu** ~: on horseback; **auf dem** *od.* **seinem hohen** ~ **sitzen** *(fig.)* be on one's high horse

¹Rost der; ~[e]s, ~e **a)** *(Gitter)* grating; *(eines Ofens, einer Feuerstelle)* grate; *(Brat~)* grill; **b)** *(Bett~)* base

²Rost der; ~[e]s rust

Rost-: ~**braten** der grilled steak; ~**bratwurst** die grilled sausage

rosten *itr. V.; auch mit sein* rust

rösten ['rœstn̩, 'rø:stn̩] *tr. V.* roast; toast ⟨*bread*⟩

rost·frei *Adj.* stainless ⟨*steel*⟩

Rösti die; ~ *(schweiz. Kochk.)* thinly sliced fried potatoes *pl.*

rostig *Adj.* rusty

rot 1. *Adj.* red; ~ **werden** turn red; ⟨*person*⟩ blush; ⟨*traffic-light*⟩ change to red; 2. *adv.* red; **Rot** das; ~s, ~ *od.* ~s red; **Rot·barsch** der rose-fish; **Röte** die; ~: red[ness]; **röten** 1. *tr. V.* redden; 2. *refl. V.* go *or* turn red; **rot·haarig** *Adj.* red-haired; **Rot·hirsch** der red deer

rotieren *itr. V.* **a)** rotate; **b)** *(ugs.: hektisch sein)* get into a flap *(coll.)*

Rot-: ~**käppchen** (das) Little Red Riding Hood; ~**kehlchen** das; ~s, ~: robin [redbreast]; ~**kohl** der, *(bes. südd., österr.)* ~**kraut** das red cabbage

rötlich *Adj.* reddish; **Rot·stift** der red pencil; **Rötung** die; ~, ~en reddening; **Rot·wein** der red wine

Rotz der; ~es *(salopp)* snot *(sl.)*

Rouge [ru:ʒ] das; ~s, ~s rouge

Roulade [ru:la:də] die; ~, ~n *(Kochk.)* [beef/veal/pork] olive

Route ['ru:tə] die; ~, ~n route; **Routine** [ru'ti:nə] die; ~ **a)** *(Erfahrung)* experience; *(Übung)* practice; **b)** *(Gewohnheit)* routine *no def. art.*

Rübe die; ~, ~n turnip; **rote** ~: beetroot; **gelbe** ~ *(südd.)* carrot

rüber *Adv. (ugs.)* over

Rubin der; ~s, ~e ruby

Rubrik die; ~, ~en column; *(fig.: Kategorie)* category

Ruck der; ~|e|s, ~e jerk

Rück·blick der look back (**auf** + *Akk.* at); retrospective view (**auf** + *Akk.* of)

rücken *itr., tr. V.* move

Rückender; ~s, ~:back;*(Buch~)*spine

Rücken-: **~deckung die a)** *(bes. Milit.)* rear cover; **b)** *(fig.)* backing; **~lehne** die [chair/seat] back; **~mark** das *(Anat.)* spinal cord; **~schmerzen** *Pl.* backache *sing.;* **~schwimmen** das backstroke; **~wind** der tail wind

rück-, Rück-: **~|erstatten** *tr. V.; nur im Inf. u. 2. Part.* repay; **~erstattung die** repayment; **~fahrkarte die, ~fahrschein der** return [ticket]; **~fahrt die** return journey; **~fall der** *(Med., auch fig.)* relapse; **~fällig** *Adj. (Med., auch fig.)* relapsed *(patient, alcoholic, etc.);* **~fällig werden** have a relapse; *(alcoholic etc.)* go back to one's old ways; *(criminal)* commit a second offence; **~flug der** return flight; **~frage die** query; **~gabe die** return; **~gang der** drop, fall *(Gen.* in); **~gängig** *Adj.* **~gängig machen** cancel *(agreement, decision, etc.);* **~grat das** spine; *(bes. fig.)* backbone; **~halt** der support; backing; **~halt·los 1.** *Adj.* unreserved, unqualified *(support);* **2.** *adv.* unreservedly; **~kehr die** return; **~lage die** savings *pl.;* **~läufig** *Adj.* decreasing *(number);* declining *(economic growth etc.);* falling *(rate, production, etc.);* **~licht das** rear- *or* tail-light

rücklings *Adv.* on one's back

Rück-: **~nahme die** taking back; **~reise die** return journey; **~ruf der** *(Fernspr.)* return call

Ruck·sack der rucksack; *(Touren~)* back-pack

rück-, Rück-: **~schlag der** set-back; **~schritt der** retrograde step; **~seite die** back; *(einer Münze usw.)* reverse; far side; **~sicht die** consideration; **~sicht auf jmdn. nehmen** show consideration for *or* towards sb.; **~sicht·nahme die, ~:** consideration; **~sichts·los 1.** *Adj.* inconsiderate; thoughtless; *(verantwortungslos)* reckless *(driver);* *(schonungslos)* ruthless; **2.** *adv. s. Adj.:* inconsiderately;

recklessly; ruthlessly; **~sichts·losigkeit die; ~, ~en** *s.* rücksichtslos : lack of consideration; recklessness; ruthlessness; **~sichts·voll 1.** *Adj.* considerate; **2.** *adv.* considerately; **~sitz** der back seat; **~spiegel** der rear-view mirror; **~sprache die** consultation; **~stand** der a) *(Rest)* residue; b) *(ausstehende Zahlung)* arrears *pl.;* c) *(Zurückbleiben hinter dem gesetzten Ziel)* backlog; *(bes. Sport: hinter dem Gegner)* deficit; |mit etw.| **im ~stand sein/in ~stand** *(Akk.)* geraten be/get behind [with sth.]; **~ständig** *Adj.* a) backward; *(schon länger fällig)* outstanding *(payment, amount);* *(wages)* still owing; **~strahler** der reflector; **~tritt** der resignation *(von* from); *(von einer Kandidatur, einem Vertrag usw.)* withdrawal *(von* from)

rückwärts *Adv.* backwards; **Rückwärts·gang** der *(Kfz-W.)* reverse [gear]

rück-, Rück-: **~weg** der return journey; **~wirkend 1.** *Adj.* retrospective; backdated *(pay increase);* **2.** retrospectively; **~zahlung die** repayment; **~zug** der retreat

Rüde der; ~n, ~n [male] dog

Rudel das; ~s, ~: herd; *(von Wölfen, Hunden)* pack

Ruder das; ~s, ~ a) *(Riemen)* oar; b) *(Steuer~)* rudder; **Ruder·boot das** row-boat; rowing-boat *(Brit.);* **rudern 1.** *itr. V.; mit sein* row; **2.** *tr. V.* row

Ruf der; ~|e|s, ~e a) call; *(Schrei)* shout; cry; *(Tierlaut)* call; b) *o. Pl. (fig.: Forderung)* call *(nach* for); c) *o. Pl. (Telefonnummer)* telephone [number]; d) *(Leumund)* reputation; **rufen 1.** *unr. itr. V.* call *(nach* for); *(schreien)* shout *(nach* for); *(animal)* call; **2.** *unr. tr. V.* a) *(aus~)* call; *(schreien)* shout; b) *(herbei~, an~)* jmdn. ~: call sb.; **jmdn. zu Hilfe ~:** call to sb. to help

Ruf-: **~name** der first name *(by which one is generally known);* **~nummer die** telephone number

Rüge die; ~, ~n reprimand; **rügen** *tr. V.* reprimand *(person);* censure *(carelessness etc.)*

Ruhe die; ~ a) *(Stille)* silence; ~ [bitte]! quiet *or* silence [please]!; b) *(Ungestörtheit)* peace; **jmdn. mit etw. in ~ lassen** stop bothering sb. with sth.; c) *(Unbewegtheit)* rest; d) *(Erholung)* rest *no def. art.;* e) *(Gelassenheit)*

calm[ness]; composure; |die| ~ **bewah-ren/die** ~ **verlieren** keep calm/lose one's composure; **in |aller| ~:** [really] calmly; **ruhe·los 1.** *Adj.* restless; **2.** *adv.* restlessly; **ruhen** *itr. V.* **a)** *(aus~)* rest; **b)** *(geh.: schlafen)* sleep; **c)** *(stillstehen)* ⟨*work, business*⟩ have stopped; ⟨*production, firm*⟩ be at a standstill

Ruhe-: ~**pause** die break; ~**stand** der; *o. Pl.* retirement; ~**störung** die disturbance; *(Rechtsw.)* disturbance of the peace; ~**tag** der closing day; „**Dienstag ~tag"** 'closed on Tuesdays'

ruhig 1. *Adj.* **a)** *(still, leise)* quiet; **b)** *(friedlich, ungestört)* peaceful ⟨*times, life, valley, etc.*⟩; quiet ⟨*talk, reflection, life*⟩; **c)** *(unbewegt)* calm ⟨*sea, weather*⟩; still ⟨*air*⟩; *(fig.)* peaceful ⟨*melody*⟩; *(gleichmäßig)* steady ⟨*breathing, hand, steps*⟩; smooth ⟨*flight, crossing*⟩; **d)** *(gelassen)* calm ⟨*voice etc.*⟩; quiet, calm ⟨*person*⟩; **2.** *adv.* **a)** *(still, leise)* quietly; **sich ~ ver-halten** keep quiet; **b)** *(friedlich, ohne Störungen)* peacefully; *(ohne Zwischenfälle)* uneventfully ⟨*work, think*⟩ in peace; **c)** *(unbewegt)* ⟨*sit, lie, stand*⟩ still; *(gleichmäßig)* ⟨*burn, breathe*⟩ steadily ⟨*run, fly*⟩ smoothly; **d)** *(gelassen)* ⟨*speak, watch, sit*⟩ calmly; **3.** *Adv.* by all means

Ruhm der; ~|e|s fame; **rühmen 1.** *tr. V.* praise; **2.** *refl. V.* boast (+ *Gen.* about); **ruhm·reich** *Adj.* glorious ⟨*victory, history*⟩; celebrated ⟨*general, army, victory*⟩

Ruhr die; ~, ~en dysentery *no art.*

Rühr·ei das scrambled egg[s *pl.*]; **rüh-ren 1.** *tr. V.* **a)** *(um~)* stir; *(ein~)* stir ⟨*egg, powder, etc.*⟩ **(an, in + Akk.** into); **b)** *(bewegen)* move ⟨*limb, fin-gers, etc.*⟩; **c)** *(fig.)* move; touch; **2.** *itr. V.* **a)** *(um~)* stir; **b)** *(geh.: her~)* das **rührt daher, daß ...:** that stems from the fact that ...; **3.** *refl. V.* **a)** *(sich bewe-gen)* move; **b)** *(Milit.)* **rührt euch!** at ease!; **rührend 1.** *Adj.* touching; **2.** *adv.* touchingly; **rühr·selig 1.** *Adj.* **a)** emotional ⟨*person*⟩; **b)** *(allzu gefühl-voll)* over-sentimental; **2.** *adv.* in an over-sentimental manner; **Rührung** die; ~: emotion

Ruine die; ~, ~n ruin; **ruinieren** *tr. V.* ruin

rülpsen *itr. V. (ugs.)* burp

rum *Adv. (ugs.) s.* **herum**

Rum der; ~s, ~s rum

Rumäne der; ~n, ~n Romanian; **Ru-**

mänien (das); ~s Romania; **rumä-nisch** *Adj.* Romanian

Rummel der; ~s *(ugs.)* **a)** commotion; *(Aufhebens)* fuss (um about); **b)** *(Jahr-markt)* fair

Rumpf der; ~|e|s, Rümpfe **a)** trunk [of the body]; **b)** *(beim Schiff)* hull; **c)** *(beim Flugzeug)* fuselage

rümpfen *tr. V.* die **Nase |bei etw.| ~:** wrinkle one's nose [at sth.]; **über jmdn./etw. die Nase rümpfen** *(fig.)* look down one's nose at sb./turn up one's nose at sth

rund 1. *Adj.* **a)** round; **b)** *(dicklich)* plump ⟨*arms etc.*⟩; chubby ⟨*cheeks*⟩; fat ⟨*stomach*⟩; **c)** *(ugs.: ganz)* round ⟨*dozen, number, etc.*⟩; **2.** *Adv.* **a)** *(ugs.: etwa)* about; **b)** ~ **um jmdn./etw.** [all] around sb./sth.; **Rund·blick** der panorama; view in all directions; **Runde** die; ~, ~n **a)** *(Sport: Strecke)* lap; **b)** *(Sport: Durchgang usw.)* round; **über die ~n kommen** *(fig. ugs.)* get by; manage; **c)** *(Personenkreis)* circle; *(Gesellschaft)* company; **d)** *(Rundgang)* round; **e)** *(Lage)* round

rund-, Rund-: ~**erneuern** *tr. V. (Kfz-W.)* remould; ~**fahrt** die tour (durch of); ~**funk** der **a)** radio; **b)** *(Einrichtung, Gebäude)* radio station

Rundfunk-: ~**anstalt** die broadcast-ing corporation; ~**gerät** das radio set; ~**sendung** die radio pro-gramme; ~**sprecher** der radio an-nouncer

rund-, Rund-: ~**gang** der round (durch of); ~**herum** *Adv.* **a)** *(ringsum)* all around; **b)** *(völlig)* completely

rundlich *Adj.* **a)** roundish; **b)** *(mollig)* plump

Rund-: ~**reise** die [circular] tour (durch of); ~**weg** der circular path *or* walk

runter *Adv. (ugs.)* ~ **|da|!** get off [there]; *s. auch* **herunter; hinunter**

Runzel die; ~, ~n wrinkle; **runz[e]lig** *Adj.* wrinkled; **runzeln** *tr. V.* die **Stirn/die Brauen ~:** wrinkle one's brow/knit one's brows; *(ärger-lich)* frown

rupfen *tr. V.* **a)** pluck ⟨*goose, hen, etc.*⟩; **b)** *(abreißen)* pull up ⟨*weeds, grass*⟩; pull off ⟨*leaves etc.*⟩

Rüsche die; ~, ~n ruche; frill

Ruß der; ~es soot

Russe der; ~n, ~n Russian

Rüssel der; ~s, ~ *(des Elefanten)* trunk; *(des Schweins)* snout; *(bei In-sekten u. ä.)* proboscis

rußen *itr. V.* give off sooty smoke

Russin die; ~, ~nen Russian; **russisch 1.** *Adj.* Russian; **2.** *adv. (auf~)* in Russian; **Russisch das**; ~|s| Russian; **Ruß·land (das)**; ~s Russia

rüsten *itr. V.* arm

rüstig 1. *Adj.* sprightly; active

rustikal 1. *Adj.* country-style ⟨*food, inn, clothes, etc.*⟩; rustic ⟨*furniture*⟩; **2.** *adv.* in [a] country style

Rüstung die; ~, ~en **a)** armament *no art.*; ⟨*Waffen*⟩ arms *pl.*; weapons *pl.*; **b)** *(hist.)* suit of armour

Rüstungs-: ~industrie die armaments *or* arms industry; **~kontrolle die** arms control; **~stopp der** arms freeze

Rute die; ~, ~n switch; ⟨*Birken~, Angel~, Wünschel~*⟩ rod

Rutsch·bahn die slide; **rutschen** *itr. V.; mit sein* slide; ⟨*clutch, carpet*⟩ slip; **rutschig** *Adj.* slippery

rütteln *tr., itr. V.* shake

S

s, S [ɛs] *das*; ~, ~: s, S

s *Abk.* Sekunde sec.; s.

S *Abk.* **a)** Süden S.; **b)** *(österr.)* Schilling Sch.

s. *Abk.* siehe

S. *Abk.* Seite p.

Sa. *Abk.* Samstag Sat.

Saal der; ~|e|s, Säle **a)** hall; ⟨*Ball~*⟩ ballroom; **b)** *(Publikum)* audience

Saar·land das; ~|e|s Saarland; Saar *(esp. Hist.)*

Saat die; ~, ~en **a)** *(das Gesäte)* [young] crops *pl.*; **b)** *o. Pl. (das Säen)* sowing; **c)** *(Samenkörner)* seed[s *pl.*]

Säbel der; ~s, ~ sabre

Sabotage [zabo'ta:ʒə] *die*; ~, ~n sabotage *no art.*; **sabotieren** *tr. V.* sabotage

sach·dienlich *Adj.* useful; **Sache die**; ~, ~n **a)** *Pl.* things; **b)** *(Angelegenheit)* matter; business *(esp. derog.)*; **zur ~ kommen** come to the point; **c)** *(Rechts~)* case; **d)** *o. Pl. (Anliegen)* cause

sach-, Sach-: ~gemäß, ~gerecht 1. *Adj.* proper; correct; **2.** *adv.* properly; correctly; **~kenntnis die** expertise; **~kundig 1.** *Adj.* with a knowledge of the subject *postpos., not pred.;* **2.** *adv.* expertly

sachlich 1. *Adj.* **a)** *(objektiv)* objective; *(nüchtern)* functional ⟨*building, style, etc.*⟩; matter-of-fact ⟨*letter etc.*⟩; **b)** *nicht präd. (sachbezogen)* factual ⟨*error*⟩; **2.** *adv. (objektiv)* objectively; ⟨*state*⟩ as a matter of fact; *(nüchtern)* ⟨*furnished*⟩ in a functional style; ⟨*written*⟩ in a matter-of-fact way; **b)** *(sachbezogen)* factually ⟨*wrong*⟩; **sächlich** *Adj. (Sprachw.)* neuter; **Sach·schaden der** damage [to property] *no indef. art.*

Sachse der; ~n, ~n Saxon; **Sachsen-Anhalt (das)**; ~s Saxony-Anhalt

sacht, sachte 1. *Adj.* **a)** *(behutsam)* gentle; **b)** *(leise)* quiet; **2.** *adv.* **a)** gently; **b)** *(leise)* quietly

Sach-: ~verhalt der; ~|e|s, ~e facts *pl.* [of the matter]; **~verstand der** expertise; grasp of the subject

Sack der; ~|e|s, Säcke sack; *(aus Papier, Kunststoff)* bag

Sack-: ~gasse die cul-de-sac; **~hüpfen das** ~s sack race

Sadismus der; ~: sadism *no art.*; **Sadist der**; ~en, ~en, **Sadistin die**; ~, ~nen sadist; **sadistisch 1.** *Adj.* sadistic; **2.** *adv.* sadistically

säen *tr. (auch itr.) V.* sow

Saft der; ~|e|s, Säfte **a)** juice; **b)** *(in Pflanzen)* sap; **saftig** *Adj.* **a)** juicy; sappy ⟨*stem*⟩; lush ⟨*meadow, green*⟩; **b)** *(ugs.)* hefty ⟨*slap, blow*⟩; steep *(coll.)* ⟨*prices, bill*⟩; crude ⟨*joke, song, etc.*⟩; strongly-worded ⟨*letter etc.*⟩

Sage die; ~, ~n legend; *(bes. nordische)* saga

Säge die; ~, ~n saw

sagen 1. *tr. V.* **a)** say; **was ich noch ~ wollte** [oh] by the way; **unter uns gesagt** between you and me; **b)** *(mitteilen)* **jmdm. etw. ~:** say sth. to sb.; *(zur Information)* tell sb. sth.; **c)** *(nennen)* **zu jmdm./etw. X ~:** call sb./sth. X; **d)** *(anordnen, befehlen)* tell; **2.** *refl. V.* **sich** *(Dat.)* **etw. ~:** say sth. to oneself

sägen *tr., itr. V.* saw

sah *1. u. 3. Pers. Sg. Prät. v. sehen*

Sahne die; ~: cream

Saison [zɛ'zõ:] *die*; ~, ~s season

Saite die; ~, ~n string; **Saiten·instrument das** stringed instrument

Sakko der od. das; ~s, ~s jacket

Sakrament das; ~[e]s, ~e sacrament; **Sakristei** die; ~, ~en sacristy

Salami die; ~, ~[s] salami

Salat der; ~[e]s, ~e a) salad; b) o. Pl. |grüner| ~: lettuce; ein Kopf ~: a [head of] lettuce

Salat-: ~besteck das salad-servers pl.; ~soße die salad-dressing

Salbe die; ~, ~n ointment

Salbei der od. die; ~: sage

Saldo der; ~s, ~s od. **Saldi** (Buchf., Finanzw.) balance

Säle s. Saal

Salmiak der od. das; ~: sal ammoniac

Salon [za'lõ:] der; ~s, ~s a) (Raum) drawing-room; b) (Geschäft) [hairetc.] salon

salopp 1. Adj. casual ⟨clothes⟩; informal ⟨behaviour⟩; 2. adv. ⟨dress⟩ casually

Salto der; ~s, ~s od. **Salti** somersault; (beim Turnen auch) salto

salutieren itr. V. (bes. Milit.) salute

Salve die; ~, ~n (Milit.) salvo; (aus Gewehren) salvo

Salz das; ~es, ~e salt; **salzen** tr. V. salt; **salzig** Adj. salty

Salz-: ~kartoffel die; meist Pl. boiled potato; ~säure die; o. Pl. (Chemie) hydrochloric acid; ~stange die salt stick; ~streuer der; ~s, ~: salt-sprinkler; salt-shaker (Amer.); ~wasser das; Pl. ~wässer a) o. Pl. (zum Kochen) salted water; b) (Meerwasser) salt water

Sambia (das); ~s Zambia

Samen der; ~s, ~ a) (~korn) seed; b) o. Pl. (~körner) seed[s pl.]; c) o. Pl. (Sperma) sperm; semen

sammeln 1. tr. (auch itr.) V. a) collect; gather ⟨honey, firewood, fig.: experiences, impressions, etc.⟩; gather, pick ⟨berries etc.⟩; b) (zusammenkommen lassen) gather ⟨people⟩ [together]; assemble ⟨people⟩; cause ⟨light rays⟩ to converge; 2. refl. V. gather [together]; **Sammler** der; ~s, ~: collector; **Sammlung** die; ~, ~en collection; b) |innere| ~: composure

Samstag der; ~[e]s, ~e Saturday; s. auch Dienstag; Dienstag-; **samstags** Adv. on Saturdays

samt 1. Präp. mit Dat. together with; 2. Adv. ~ und sonders one and all

Samt der; ~[e]s, ~e velvet

sämtlich Indefinitpron. u. unbest. Zahlwort all the

Sand der; ~[e]s sand

Sandale die; ~, ~n sandal

sandig Adj. sandy

Sand-: ~kasten der [child's] sand-pit; sand-box (Amer.); ~kuchen der Madeira cake; ~mann der, ~männchen das; o. Pl. sandman; ~stein der sandstone; ~strand der sandy beach

sandte 1. u. 3. Pers. Sg. Prät. v. senden

sanft 1. Adj. gentle; (leise) soft; (friedlich) peaceful; 2. adv. gently; (leise) softly; (friedlich) peacefully

sang 1. u. 3. Pers. Sg. Prät. v. singen; **Sänger** der; ~s, ~, **Sängerin** die; ~, ~nen singer

sanieren 1. tr. V. a) redevelop ⟨area⟩; rehabilitate ⟨building⟩; (renovieren) renovate [and improve] ⟨flat etc.⟩; b) (Wirtsch.) restore ⟨firm⟩ to profitability; 2. refl. V. ⟨company etc.⟩ restore itself to profitability; ⟨person⟩ get oneself out of the red; **Sanierung** die; ~, ~en a) s. sanieren a: redevelopment; rehabilitation; renovation; b) restoration to profitability; **sanitär** Adj. sanitary; **Sanitäter** der; ~s, ~: first-aid man; (im Krankenwagen) ambulance man

sank 1. u. 3. Pers. Sg. Prät. v. sinken

sann 1. u. 3. Pers. Sg. Prät. v. sinnen

Saphir der; ~s, ~e sapphire

Sardelle die; ~, ~n anchovy

Sardine die; ~, ~n sardine

Sarg der; ~[e]s, Särge coffin

saß 1. u. 3. Pers. Sg. Prät. v. sitzen

Satan der (bibl.) Satan no def. art.

Satellit der; ~en, ~en satellite

Satire die; ~, ~n satire

satt Adj. a) full [up] pred.; well-fed; sich ~ essen/trinken eat/drink as much as one wants; eat/drink one's fill; b) jmdn./etw. ~ haben (ugs.) be fed up with sb./sth. (coll.)

Sattel der; ~s, Sättel a) saddle; **satteln** 1. tr. V. saddle; 2. itr. V. saddle the/one's horse

sättigen itr. V. be filling

Sattler der; ~s, ~: saddler; (allgemein) leather-worker

Satz der; ~es, Sätze a) (sprachliche Einheit) sentence; b) (Musik) movement; c) (Tennis, Volleyball) set; (Tischtennis, Badminton) game; d) (Sprung) leap; jump; e) (Amtsspr.: Tarif) rate; f) (Set) set; g) (Boden~) sediment; (von Kaffee) grounds pl.

Satzung die; ~, ~en articles of association pl.; statutes pl.

Satz·zeichen das punctuation mark

Sau die; ~, **Säue** a) *(weibliches Schwein)* sow; b) *(bes. südd.: Schwein)* pig

sauber 1. *Adj.* a) clean; b) *(sorgfältig)* neat; 2. *adv.* a) *(sorgfältig)* neatly; b) *(fehlerlos)* |sehr| ~: [quite] perfectly; **Sauberkeit** die; ~: cleanness; **sauber·machen** 1. *tr. V.* clean; 2. *itr. V.* clean; do the cleaning; **säubern** *tr. V.* clean; **Säuberung** die; ~, ~en cleaning

Sauce s. Soße

Saudi [zaudi] der; ~s, ~s Saudi; **Saudi-Arabien** (das) Saudi Arabia

sauer 1. *Adj.* a) sour; pickled ⟨herring, gherkin, etc.⟩; acid[ic] ⟨wine, vinegar⟩; saurer Regen acid rain; b) *(ugs.: verärgert)* cross, annoyed **(auf** + *Akk.* with); 2. *adv.* in vinegar; **Sauer·braten** der braised beef marinated in vinegar and herbs; sauerbraten *(Amer.)*; **Sauerei** die; ~, ~en a) *(salopp abwertend)* a) *(Unflätigkeit)* obscenity b) *(Gemeinheit)* bloody scandal *(sl.)*; **Sauer-:** ~**kirsche** die the sour cherry; ~**kraut** das *o. Pl.* sauerkraut

säuerlich *Adj.* |leicht| ~: slightly sour; slightly sharp ⟨sauce⟩

Sauer-: ~**stoff** der; *o. Pl.* oxygen; ~**stoffgerät** das oxygen apparatus; ~**stoffmangel** der *o. Pl.* lack of oxygen; ~**teig** der leaven

saufen 1. *unr. itr. V.* *(salopp: trinken)* drink; swig *(coll.)*; ⟨Alkohol trinken⟩ drink; booze *(coll.)*; 2. *unr. tr. V.* *(salopp: trinken)* drink; **Säufer** der; ~s, ~ *(salopp)* boozer *(coll.)*; **säuft** 3. *Pers. Sg. Präsens v.* saufen

saugen 1. *tr. V.* a) *auch unr.* suck; b) *auch itr.* *(staub~)* vacuum; hoover *(coll.)*; 2. *regelm. (auch unr.) itr. V.* an etw. *(Dat.)* ~: suck [at] sth.; 3. *unr. (auch regelm.) refl. V.* sich voll etw. ~: become soaked with sth.; **säugen** *tr. V.* suckle; **Säuge·tier** das *(Zool.)* mammal; **Säugling** der; ~s, ~e baby; **Säuglings·pflege** die baby care

Säule die; ~, ~n column; *(nur als Stütze, auch fig.)* pillar

Saum der; ~|e|s, **Säume** hem; **säumen** *tr. V.* hem; *(fig. geh.)* line

säumig *(geh.) Adj.* tardy

Sauna die; ~, ~s *od.* **Saunen** sauna

Säure die; ~, ~n a) *o. Pl. (von Früchten)* sourness; *(von Wein, Essig)* acidity; *(von Soßen)* sharpness; b) *(Chemie)* acid; **Saure·gurken·zeit** die *(ugs.)* silly season *(Brit.)*

Saus: in ~ und Braus leben live the high life

säuseln 1. *itr. V.* ⟨leaves, branches, etc.⟩ rustle; ⟨wind⟩ murmur; 2. *tr. V.* *(iron.: sagen)* whisper; **sausen** *itr. V.* a) ⟨wind⟩ whistle; ⟨storm⟩ roar; ⟨head, ears⟩ buzz; b) *mit sein* ⟨person⟩ rush; ⟨vehicle⟩ roar; c) *mit sein* ⟨whip, bullet, etc.⟩ whistle

Savanne [za'vanə] die; ~, ~n savannah

Saxophon das; ~s, ~e saxophone

S-Bahn ['ɛs-] die city and suburban railway

SB- [ɛs'beː-] self-service *(attrib.)*

Schabe die; ~, ~n cockroach

schaben *tr.. itr. V.* scrape; **Schaber** der; ~s, ~: scraper

schäbig 1. *Adj.* a) *(abgenutzt)* shabby; b) *(jämmerlich, gering)* pathetic; c) *(gemein)* shabby; 2. *adv.* a) *(abgenutzt)* shabbily; b) *(jämmerlich)* miserably; c) *(gemein)* meanly

Schach das; ~s, ~s a) *(Spiel)* chess; b) *(Stellung)* check; **jmdn./etw. in ~ halten** *(ugs. fig.)* keep sb./sth. in check

Schach-: ~**brett** das chessboard; ~**figur** die chess piece; ~**spiel** das *o. Pl. (Spiel)* chess; *(das Spielen)* chess-playing; b) *(Brett und Figuren)* chess set

Schacht der; ~|e|s, **Schächte** shaft

Schachtel die; ~, ~n a) box; **eine ~ Zigaretten** a packet *or (Amer.)* pack of cigarettes; b) **alte ~** *(salopp abwertend)* old bag *(sl.)*

schade *Adj.* |ach, wie| ~! [what a] pity or shame; |es ist| ~ um jmdn./etw. it's a pity or shame about sb./sth.; **für jmdn./für** *od.* **zu etw. zu** ~ **sein** be too good for sb./sth.

Schädel der; ~s, ~: skull; *(Kopf)* head; **Schädel·bruch** der *(Med.)* skull fracture

schaden *itr. V.* **jmdm./einer Sache** ~: damage or harm sb./sth.; **Schaden** der; ~s, **Schäden** a) damage no pl., no indef. art.; **ein kleiner/großer** ~: little/ major damage; b) *(Nachteil)* disadvantage

schaden-, Schaden-: ~**ersatz** der *(Rechtsw.)* damages pl.; ~**freude** die *o. Pl.* malicious pleasure; ~**froh** 1. *Adj.* gloating; ⟨grin⟩ gleeful; 2. *adv.* with malicious pleasure

schadhaft *Adj.* defective; **schädigen** *tr. V.* damage ⟨health, reputation, interests⟩; harm, hurt ⟨person⟩; cause losses to ⟨*firm, industry, etc.*⟩; **Schä-digung** die; ~, ~en damage *no pl., no indef. art. (Gen. to)*; **schädlich** *Adj.* harmful; **Schädling** der; ~s, ~e pest

Schaf das; ~|e|s, ~e a) sheep; b) *(ugs.: Dummkopf)* twit *(Brit. sl.)*; **Schaf·bock** der the ram; **Schäfchen** das; ~s, ~: [little] sheep; *(Lamm)* lamb; **Schäfer** der; ~s, ~: shepherd; **Schäfer·hund** der sheep-dog; |deutscher| ~: Alsatian; **Schaf·fell** das sheepskin

schaffen 1. *unr. tr. V.* a) create; b) *auch regelm. (herstellen)* create ⟨*conditions, jobs, situation, etc.*⟩; make ⟨*room, space, fortune*⟩; 2. *tr. V.* a) *(bewältigen)* manage; es ~, etw. zu tun manage to do sth.; b) *(ugs.: erschöpfen)* wear out; c) etw. aus etw./in etw. *(Akk.)* ~: get sth. out of/into sth.; 3. *itr. V.* a) *(südd.: arbeiten)* work; b) sich *(Dat.)* zu ~ machen busy oneself; jmdm. zu ~ machen cause sb. trouble

Schaffner der; ~s ~ *(im Bus)* conductor; *(im Zug)* guard *(Brit.)*; conductor *(Amer.)*; **Schaffnerin** die; ~, ~nen *(im Bus)* conductress *(Brit.)*; *(im Zug)* guard *(Brit.)*; conductress *(Amer.)*

Schaffung die; ~: creation

Schafott das; ~|e|s, ~e scaffold

Schafs·käse der sheep's milk cheese; **Schaf·wolle** die sheep's wool

Schakal der; ~s, ~e jackal

schal *Adj.* stale ⟨*drink, taste, smell, joke*⟩; empty ⟨*words, feeling*⟩

Schal der; ~s, ~s od. ~e scarf

Schale die; ~, ~n a) *(Obst~)* skin; *(abgeschälte ~)* peel *no pl.*; b) *(Nuß~, Eier~)* shell; c) *(Schüssel)* bowl; *(flacher)* dish; d) sich in ~ werfen od. schmeißen *(ugs.)* get dressed [up] to the nines; **schälen** 1. *tr. V.* peel ⟨*fruit, vegetable*⟩; shell ⟨*egg, nut, pea*⟩; 2. *refl. V.* peel

Schall der; ~|e|s, ~e od. Schälle sound; **Schall·dämpfer** der a) silencer; b) *(Musik)* mute; **schalldicht** *Adj.* sound-proof; **schallen** *regelm. (auch unr.) itr. V.* ring out; ~des Gelächter ringing laughter

Schall-: ~geschwindigkeit die speed *or* velocity of sound; ~platte die record

Schalotte die; ~, ~n shallot

schalt *1. u. 3. Pers. Sg. Prät. v.* schelten

schalten 1. *tr. V.* switch; 2. *itr. V.* a) *(Schalter betätigen)* switch, turn (auf + Akk. to); b) ⟨*machine*⟩ switch (auf + Akk. to); c) *(im Auto)* change [gear]; d) ~ und walten manage one's affairs; e) *(ugs.: begreifen)* twig *(coll.)*; catch on *(coll.)*; **Schalter** der; ~s, ~ a) switch; b) *(Post~, Bank~ usw.)* counter

Schalter-: ~beamte der counter clerk; *(im Bahnhof)* ticket clerk; ~halle die hall; *(im Bahnhof)* booking-hall *(Brit.)*; ticket office

Schaltjahr das leap year; **Schaltung** die; ~, ~en *(Elektrot.)* circuit; wiring system

Scham die; ~: shame; **schämen** *refl. V.* be ashamed ⟨*Gen., für, wegen* of⟩; **Scham·gefühl** das; *o. Pl.* sense of shame; **schamhaft** 1. *Adj.* bashful; 2. *adv.* bashfully; **scham·los** 1. *Adj.* a) *(skrupellos, dreist)* shameless; b) *(unanständig)* indecent; shameless ⟨*person*⟩; 2. *adv.* a) *(skrupellos, dreist)* shamelessly; b) *(unanständig)* indecently

Schande die; ~: disgrace; **schändlich** 1. *Adj.* disgraceful; 2. *adv.* disgracefully

Schar die; ~, ~en crowd; horde; **scharen·weise** *Adv.* in swarms *or* hordes

scharf; schärfer, schärfst... 1. *Adj.* a) sharp; b) *(stark gewürzt, brennend, stechend)* hot; strong ⟨*drink, vinegar, etc.*⟩; caustic ⟨*chemical*⟩; pungent ⟨*smell*⟩; c) *(durchdringend)* shrill; *(hell)* harsh; *(kalt)* biting ⟨*cold, wind, etc.*⟩; sharp ⟨*frost*⟩; d) *(deutlich wahrnehmend)* keen; e) *(schnell)* fast; hard ⟨*ride, gallop, etc.*⟩; f) *(explosiv)* live; ⟨*Ballspiele*⟩ powerful ⟨*shot*⟩; g) das ~e S *(bes. österr.)* the German letter 'ß'; h) ~ auf jmdn./etw. sein *(ugs.)* really fancy sb. *(coll.)*/be really keen on sth; 2. *adv.* a) ~ würzen/abschmecken season/flavour highly; ~ riechen smell pungent; b) *(durchdringend)* shrilly; *(hell)* harshly; *(kalt)* bitingly; c) *(deutlich wahrnehmend)* ⟨*listen, watch, etc.*⟩ closely, intently; ⟨*think, consider, etc.*⟩ hard; d) *(deutlich hervortretend)* sharply; e) *(schonungslos)* ⟨*attack, criticize, etc.*⟩ sharply, strongly; ⟨*watch, observe, etc.*⟩ closely; f) *(schnell)* fast; ~ bremsen brake hard *or* sharply; **Schärfe** die; ~ a) sharpness; b) *(von Geschmack)* hotness; *(von Chemikalien)* causticity; *(von Geruch)* pungency; c) *(Intensität)* shrillness; *(des*

Frostes) sharpness; **schärfen 1.** *tr. V. (auch fig.)* sharpen; **2.** *refl. V.* become sharper *or* keener

scharf-: ~**kantig** *Adj.* sharp-edged; ~**sichtig** *Adj.* sharp-sighted; perspicacious; ~**sinnig 1.** *Adj.* astute; **2.** *adv.* astutely

Scharlach der; ~s *(Med.)* scarlet fever

Scharnier das; ~s, ~e hinge

scharren *itr. V.* a) scrape; b) *(wühlen)* scratch; **2.** *tr. V.* scrape, scratch out ⟨hole, hollow, etc.⟩

Schaschlik der *od.* das; ~s, ~s *(Kochk.)* shashlik

Schatten der; ~s, ~ a) shadow; b) *o. Pl. (schattige Stelle)* shade; **schattig** *Adj.* shady

Schatz der; ~es, Schätze treasure *no indef. art.;* **schätzen 1.** *tr. V.* a) estimate; **sich glücklich** ~: deem oneself lucky; b) *(ugs.: annehmen)* reckon; c) *(würdigen, hochachten)* **jmdn.** ~: hold sb. in high esteem; **2.** *itr. V.* guess; **Schätzung** die; ~, ~en estimate

Schau die; ~, ~en a) *(Ausstellung)* exhibition; b) *(Vorführung)* show; c) **zur** ~ **stellen** *(ausstellen)* exhibit; display; *(offen zeigen)* display

Schauder der; ~s, ~: shiver; **schauderhaft 1.** *Adj.* terrible; **2.** *adv.* terribly; **schaudern** *itr. V.* a) *(vor Kälte)* shiver; b) *(vor Angst)* shudder

schauen *(bes. südd., österr., schweiz.)* **1.** *itr. V.* a) look; b) *(sich kümmern um)* **nach jmdm./etw.** ~: take *or* have a look at sb./sth.; c) *(achten)* **auf etw.** *(Akk.)* ~: set store by sth.; d) *(ugs.: sich bemühen)* **schau, daß du ...:** see *or* mind that you ...; e) *(nachsehen)* have a look; **2.** *tr. V.* **Fernsehen** ~: watch television

Schauer der; ~s, ~: shower

Schauer·geschichte die horror story; **schauerlich 1.** *Adj.* a) horrifying; b) *(ugs.: fürchterlich)* terrible *(coll.);* **2.** *(ugs.: fürchterlich)* terribly *(coll.)*

Schaufel die; ~, ~n shovel; *(Kehr~)* dustpan; **schaufeln** *tr. V.* shovel; *(graben)* dig

Schau·fenster das shop-window; **Schaufenster·bummel** der: **einen** ~ **machen** go window-shopping

Schaukel die; ~, ~n a) swing; b) *(Wippe)* see-saw; **schaukeln 1.** *itr. V.* a) swing; *(im Schaukelstuhl)* rock; b)

(sich hin und her bewegen) sway [to and fro]; *(sich auf und ab bewegen)* ⟨ship, boat⟩ pitch and toss; ⟨vehicle⟩ bump [up and down]; **2.** *tr. V.* rock

Schaukel-: ~**pferd** das rocking-horse; ~**stuhl** der rocking-chair

Schau·lustige der/die; *adj. Dekl.* curious onlooker

Schaum der; ~s, Schäume a) foam; *(von Seife usw.)* lather; *(von Getränken, Suppen usw.)* froth; b) *(Geifer)* foam; froth; **schäumen** *itr. V.* foam; froth; ⟨soap etc.⟩ lather; ⟨beer, fizzy drink, etc.⟩ froth [up]

Schaum-: ~**gummi** der foam rubber; ~**wein** der sparkling wine

Schau-: ~**spiel** das a) *o. Pl. (Drama)* drama *no art.;* b) *(ernstes Stück)* play; c) *(geh.: Anblick)* spectacle; ~**spieler** der actor; ~**spielerin** die actress; ~**steller** der; ~s, ~: showman

Scheck der; ~s, ~s cheque; **Scheckheft** das cheque-book; **Scheck·karte** die cheque card

scheel *(ugs.)* **1.** *Adj.* disapproving; *(neidisch)* envious; jealous; **2.** *adv.* disapprovingly; *(neidisch)* enviously; jealously

Scheibe die; ~, ~n a) disc; b) *(abgeschnittene* ~*)* slice; c) *(Glas~)* pane [of glass]; *(Fenster~)* [window-]pane; **Scheiben·wischer** der windscreen-wiper

Scheide die; ~, ~n a) sheath; b) *(Anat.)* vagina

scheiden *unr. tr. V.* dissolve ⟨marriage⟩; divorce ⟨married couple⟩; **sich** ~ **lassen** get divorced *or* get a divorce; **Scheidung** die; ~, ~en divorce

Schein der; ~|e|s, ~e a) *o. Pl. (Licht~)* light; b) *o. Pl. (An~)* appearances *pl., no art.;* *(Täuschung)* pretence; **etw. nur zum** ~ **tun** [only] pretend to do sth.; make a show of doing sth.; c) *(Geld~)* note; **scheinbar 1.** *Adj.* apparent; seeming; **2.** *adv.* seemingly; **scheinen** *unr. itr. V.* a) shine; b) *(den Eindruck erwecken)* seem; appear; **mir scheint, [daß]** ...: it seems *or* appears to me that ...

schein-, Schein-: ~**heilig 1.** *Adj.* hypocritical; b) *adv.* hypocritically; ~**werfer** der floodlight; *(am Auto)* headlight

Scheiße die; ~ *(derb)* shit *(coarse);* crap *(coarse);* **scheißen** *unr. itr. V. (derb)* [have *or* *(Amer.)* take a] shit *(coarse);* crap *(coarse);* have a crap *(coarse)*

Scheitel der; ~s, ~: parting; **scheiteln** tr. V. part ⟨hair⟩

scheitern itr. V.; mit sein fail; ⟨talks, marriage⟩ break down; ⟨plan, project⟩ fail, fall through

Schelle die; ~, ~n bell; **schellen** itr. V. (westd.) s. **klingeln**

Schell·fisch der the haddock

Schelm der; ~[e]s, ~e rascal; rogue; **schelmisch** 1. Adj. roguish; 2. adv. roguishly

Schelte die; ~, ~n (geh.) scolding; **schelten** (südd., geh.) 1. unr. itr. V. auf od. über jmdn./etw. ~: moan about sb./sth.; 2. unr. tr. V. scold

Schema das; ~s, ~s od. ~ta od. **Schemen** pattern; **schematisch** 1. Adj. a) diagrammatic; b) (mechanisch) mechanical; 2. adv. a) in diagram form; b) (mechanisch) mechanically

Schemel der; ~s, ~ stool; b) (südd.: Fußbank) footstool

Schenkel der; ~s, ~: thigh

schenken tr. V. a) give; jmdm. etw. [zum Geburtstag] ~: give sb. sth. or sth. to sb. [as a birthday present or for his/her birthday]; b) (ugs.: erlassen) jmdm./sich etw. ~: spare sb./oneself sth.

Scherbe die; ~, ~n fragment

Schere die; ~, ~n a) scissors pl.; eine ~: a pair of scissors; b) (Zool.) claw; ¹**scheren** unr. tr. V. crop; (von Haar befreien) shear, clip ⟨sheep⟩

²**scheren** tr., refl. V. sich um jmdn./ etw. nicht ~: not care about sb./sth.; **Schereien** Pl. (ugs.) trouble no pl.

Scherz der; ~es, ~e joke; **scherzen** itr. V. joke; **scherzhaft** 1. Adj. jocular; 2. adv. jocularly

scheu 1. Adj. shy; timid ⟨animal⟩; (ehrfürchtig) awed; 2. adv. a) shyly; b) (von Tieren) timidly; **Scheu** die; ~ a) shyness; (Ehrfurcht) awe; b) (von Tieren) timidity

scheuchen tr. V. shoo; drive

scheuen 1. tr. V. shrink from; shun ⟨people, light, company, etc.⟩; 2. refl. V. sich vor etw. (Dat.) ~: be afraid of or shrink from sth. 3. itr. V. ⟨horse⟩ shy (vor + Dat. at)

scheuern 1. tr., itr. V. a) (reinigen) scour; scrub; b) (reiben) rub; chafe; 2. tr. V. (reiben an) rub

Scheuer-: ~**pulver** das scouring powder; ~**tuch** das; Pl. ~**tücher** scouring cloth

Scheune die; ~, ~n barn

Scheusal das; ~s, ~e monster;

scheußlich 1. Adj. a) dreadful; b) (ugs.: äußerst unangenehm) dreadful (coll.); ghastly (coll.) ⟨weather, taste, smell⟩; 2. adv. a) dreadfully; b) (ugs.: sehr) dreadfully (coll.)

Schi usw. s. **Ski** usw.

Schicht die; ~, ~en a) (Lage) layer; (Geol.) stratum; (von Farbe) coat; (sehr dünn) film; b) (Gesellschafts~) stratum; c) (Arbeits~) shift; ~ **arbeiten** work shifts; be on shift work; **schichten** tr. V. stack

schick 1. Adj. a) stylish; chic ⟨clothes, fashions⟩; smart ⟨woman, girl, man⟩; b) (ugs.: großartig, toll) great (coll.); fantastic (coll.); 2. adv. a) stylishly; smartly ⟨furnished, decorated⟩

schicken 1. tr. V. send; jmdm. etw. ~, etw. an jmdn. ~: send sth. to sb.; send sb. sth.; 2. itr. V. nach jmdm. ~: send for sb; 3. refl. V. (veralt.: sich ziemen) be proper or fitting

Schicksal das; ~s, ~e [das] ~: fate; destiny; (schweres Los) fate; **Schicksals·schlag** der stroke of fate

Schiebe·dach das sunroof; **schieben** 1. unr. tr. V. a) push; b) (stecken) put; c) etw. auf jmdn./etw. ~: blame sb./sth. for sth.; 2. unr. refl. V. sich durch die Menge ~: push one's way through the crowd; 3. unr. itr. V. push; (heftig) shove; **Schiebe·tür** die sliding door; **Schiebung** die; ~, ~en (ugs.) a) shady deal; b) (o. Pl.: Begünstigung) pulling strings

schied 1. u. 3. Pers. Sg. Prät. v. **scheiden**

Schieds·richter der referee; (Tennis, Hockey, Kricket) umpire

schief 1. Adj. a) (schräg) leaning ⟨wall, fence, post⟩; (nicht parallel) crooked; sloping ⟨surface⟩; worn[-down] ⟨heels⟩; b) (fig.: verzerrt) distorted ⟨picture, presentation, view, impression⟩; false ⟨comparison⟩; 2. adv. a) (schräg) das Bild hängt/der Teppich liegt ~: the picture/carpet is crooked; der Tisch steht ~: the table isn't level; b) (fig.: verzerrt) etw. ~ darstellen give a distorted account of sth.

Schiefer der; ~s (Gestein) slate

schief-: ~**gehen**, ~**laufen** unr. itr. V.; mit sein (ugs.) go wrong

schielen itr. V. a) squint; auf dem rechten Auge ~: have a squint in one's right eye; b) (ugs.: blicken) look out of the corner of one's eye

schien 1. u. 3. Pers. Sg. Prät. v. **scheinen**

Schien·bein das shinbone; **Schiene** die; ~, ~n a) rail; b) *(Gleit~)* runner; c) *(Med.: Stütze)* splint; **schienen** *tr. V.* jmds. Arm/ Bein ~: put sb.'s arm/leg in a splint/ splints

schießen 1. *unr. itr. V.* a) shoot; **auf** jmdn./etw. ~: shoot/fire at sb./sth.); b) *mit sein (fließen, heraus~)* gush; *(spritzen)* spurt; c) *mit sein (schnell wachsen)* shoot up; **2.** *unr. tr. V.* a) shoot; fire *(bullet, missile, rocket)*; b) *(Fußball)* score *(goal)*; c) *(ugs.: fotografieren)* **einige Aufnahmen** ~: take a few snaps; **Schießerei** die; ~, ~en a) shooting *no indef. art., no pl.;* b) *(Schußwechsel)* gun-battle

Schiff das; ~|e|s, ~e a) ship; **mit dem** ~: by ship *or* sea; b) *(Archit.: Kirchen~)* *(Mittel~)* nave; *(Quer~)* transept; *(Seiten~)* aisle; **Schiffahrt** die; *o. Pl.* shipping *no indef. art.; (Schifffahrtskunde)* navigation

Schiff-: ~bruch der *(veralt.)* shipwreck; **~brüchige** der/die; *adj. Dekl.* shipwrecked man/woman

Schiffer der; ~s, ~: boatman; *(eines Lastkahns)* bargee; *(Kapitän)* skipper

Schiffs-: ~arzt der ship's doctor; **~brücke** die pontoon bridge; **~junge** der ship's boy; **~reise** die voyage; *(Vergnügungsreise)* cruise; **~verkehr** der shipping traffic

Schikane die; ~, ~n a) harassment *no indef. art.;* b) **mit allen** ~n *(ugs.) (kitchen, house)* with all mod cons *(Brit. coll.); (car, bicycle, stereo)* with all the extras; **schikanieren** *tr. V.* jmdn. ~: harass sb.

¹**Schild** der; ~|e|s, ~e shield; ²**Schild** das; ~|e|s, ~er sign; *(Nummern~)* number-plate; *(Namens~)* name-plate; *(auf Denkmälern, Gebäuden usw.)* plaque; *(Etikett)* label; **schildern** *tr. V.* describe; **Schild·kröte** die tortoise; *(Seeschildkröte)* turtle

Schilf das; ~|e|s a) reed; b) *o. Pl. (Röhricht)* reeds *pl.*

schillern *itr. V.* shimmer

Schilling der; ~s, ~e schilling

schilt *3. Pers. Sg. Präsens v.* schelten

Schimmel der; ~s, ~ a) *o. Pl.* mould; *(auf Leder, Papier)* mildew; b) *(Pferd)* white horse; **schimmelig** *Adj.* mouldy; mildewy *(paper, leather)*; **schimmeln** *itr. V.; auch mit sein* go mouldy; *(leather, paper)* get covered with mildew

Schimmer der; ~s *(Schein)* gleam;

(von Seide) shimmer; sheen; **keinen ~ |von etw.| haben** *(ugs.)* not have the faintest idea [about sth.] *(coll.);* **schimmern** *itr. V.* gleam; *(water, sea)* glisten, shimmer; *(metal)* glint, gleam; *(silk etc.)* shimmer

schimmlig *s.* schimmelig

Schimpanse der; ~n, ~n chimpanzee

schimpfen 1. *itr. V.* a) carry on *(coll.)* *(auf, über + Akk.* about); *(meckern)* grumble, moan *(auf, über + Akk.* at); b) **mit jmdm.** ~: tell sb. off; scold sb.; **2.** *tr. V.* jmdn. ~: tell sb. off; **Schimpf·wort** das *(Beleidigung)* insult; *(derbes Wort)* swear-word

schinden *unr. tr. V.* maltreat; ill-treat; **Zeit** ~ *(ugs.)* play for time

Schinken der; ~s, ~ ham; **Schinken·speck** der bacon

Schippe die; ~, ~n *(Schaufel)* shovel

Schirm der; ~|e|s, ~e umbrella; brolly *(Brit. coll.); (Sonnen~)* sunshade

Schirm-: ~herr der patron; ~**herrin** die patroness; **~herrschaft** die patronage; **~ständer** der umbrella stand

schiß *1. u. 3. Pers. Sg. Prät. v.* scheißen

Schlacht die; ~, ~en battle; **schlachten** *tr. (auch itr.) V.* slaughter; kill *(rabbit, chicken, etc.);* **Schlachter** der; ~s, ~ *(nordd.)* butcher; **Schlachterei** die; ~, ~en *(nordd.)* butcher's [shop]

Schlacht-: ~hof der abattoir; **~vieh** das animals *pl.* kept for meat; *(kurz vor der Schlachtung)* animals *pl.* for slaughter

Schlacke die; ~, ~n cinders *pl.;* *(Hochofen~)* slag

Schlaf der; ~|e|s sleep; **einen leichten/ festen/gesunden** ~ **haben** be a light/ heavy/good sleeper; **Schlaf·an·zug** der pyjamas *pl.;* **Schläfchen** das; ~s, ~ nap; snooze *(coll.)*

Schläfe die; ~, ~n temple

schlafen *unr. itr. V.* a) *(auch fig.)* sleep; **tief** *od.* **fest** ~: be sound asleep; **lange** ~: sleep for a long time; *(am Morgen)* sleep in; ~ **gehen** go to bed; b) *(ugs.: nicht aufpassen)* be asleep; **Schläfer** der; ~s, ~: sleeper

schlaff 1. *Adj.* a) slack; flabby *(stomach, muscles)*; b) *(schlapp, matt)* limp *(body, hand, handshake)*; shaky *(knees)*; **2.** *adv.* a) slackly; b) *(schlapp, matt)* limply

Schlaf-: ~gelegenheit die place to sleep; **~mittel** das sleep-inducing drug

schläfrig 1. *Adj.* sleepy; **2.** *adv.* sleepily

Schlaf-: ~**saal** der dormitory; ~**sack** sleeping-bag

schläft *3. Pers. Sg. Präsens v.* **schlafen**

Schlaf-: ~**tablette** die sleeping-pill; ~**wagen** der sleeping-car; sleeper; ~**zimmer** das bedroom

Schlag der; ~|e|s, **Schläge** a) blow; *(Faust~)* punch; *(Klaps)* slap; *(Tennis~, Golf~)* stroke; shot; ~ **auf** ~ *(fig.)* in quick succession; b) *(Auf~, Aufprall)* bang; *(dumpf)* thud; *(Klopfen)* knock; c) o. *Pl.* *(des Herzens, Pulses)* beating; *(eines Pendels)* swinging; d) *(einzelne rhythmische Bewegung* *(Herz~, Puls~, Takt~)* beat; *(eines Pendels)* swing; e) o. *Pl.* *(Töne)* *(einer Uhr)* striking; *(einer Glocke)* ringing; f) *(einzelner Ton)* *(Stunden~)* stroke; *(Glocken~)* ring; ~ **acht** Uhr on the stroke of eight

schlag-, Schlag-: ~**ader** die artery; ~**anfall** der stroke; ~**artig 1.** *Adj.* very sudden; **2.** *adv.* quite suddenly; ~**baum** der barrier

schlagen 1. *unr. tr. V.* a) hit; beat; strike; *(mit der Faust)* punch; hit; *(mit der flachen Hand)* slap; b) *(mit Richtungsangabe)* hit *(ball)*; **einen Nagel in etw.** *(Akk.)* ~: knock a nail into sth.; c) *(rühren)* beat *(mixture)*; whip *(cream)*; *(mit einem Schneebesen)* whisk; d) *(läuten)* *(clock)* strike; *(bell)* ring; e) *(legen)* throw; f) *(einwickeln)* wrap **(in** + *Akk.* in); g) *(besiegen, übertreffen)* beat; **2.** *unr. itr. V.* a) **er schlug mit der Faust auf den Tisch** he beat the table with his fist; b) **mit den Flügeln** ~ *(bird)* beat or flap its wings; c) *mit sein* *(prallen)* bang; **mit dem Kopf auf etw.** *(Akk.)/gegen etw.* ~: bang one's head on/against sth.; d) *mit sein* **jmdm. auf den Magen** ~: affect sb.'s stomach; e) *(pulsieren)* *(heart, pulse)* beat; *(heftig)* *(heart)* pound; *(pulse)* throb; f) *(läuten)* *(clock)* strike; *(bell)* ring; **3.** *unr. refl. V.* fight; **sich mit jmdm.** ~: fight with sb.; **Schläger** der; ~s, ~ **a)** pop song; b) *(Erfolg)* *(Buch)* best seller; *(Ware)* best-selling line; *(Film, Stück, Lied)* hit

Schläger der; ~s, ~ **a)** *(Raufbold)* tough; thug; b) *(Tennis~, Federball~, Squash~)* racket; *(Tischtennis~, Kriket~)* bat; *(Eishockey~, Polo~)* stick; *(Golf~)* club; **Schlägerei** die; ~, ~**en** brawl; fight

Schlager·sänger der pop singer

schlag-, Schlag-: ~**fertig** *Adj.* quick-witted *(reply)*; *(person)* who is quick at repartee; ~**fertigkeit** die o. *Pl.* quickness at repartee; ~**loch** das pothole; ~**obers** das; ~ *(österr.)*, ~**rahm** der *(bes. südd., österr., schweiz.)*, ~**sahne** die whipping cream; *(geschlagen)* whipped cream; ~**zeile** die headline; ~**zeug** das drums *pl.*

schlaksig *(ugs.)* *Adj.* gangling; lanky

Schlamassel der od. das; ~s *(ugs.)* mess

Schlamm der; ~|e|s, ~**e** od. **Schlämme** a) mud; b) *(Schlick)* sludge; **schlammig** *Adj.* a) muddy; b) *(schlickig)* sludgy; muddy

Schlamperei die; ~, ~**en** *(ugs. abwertend)* sloppiness; **schlampig** *(ugs. abwertend)* **1.** *Adj.* a) *(liederlich)* slovenly; b) *(nachlässig)* sloppy; slipshod *(work)*; **2.** *adv.* a) *(liederlich)* in a slovenly way; b) *(nachlässig)* sloppily

schlang *1. u. 3. Pers. Sg. Prät. v.* **schlingen**; **Schlange** die; ~, ~**n** a) snake; b) *(Menschen~)* queue; line *(Amer.)*; ~ **stehen** queue; stand in line *(Amer.)*; c) *(Auto~)* tailback *(Brit.)*; backup *(Amer.)*; **schlängeln** *refl. V.* *(snake)* wind [its way]; *(road)* wind; snake [its way]; **Schlangen·linie** die wavy line

schlank *Adj.* slim *(person)*; slim, slender *(build, figure)*; **Schlankheits·kur** die slimming diet

schlapp *Adj.* a) worn out; tired out; *(wegen Schwüle)* listless; *(wegen Krankheit)* run-down; b) *(ugs.: ohne Schwung)* wet *(sl.)*; feeble; c) slack *(rope, cable)*; loose *(skin)*; flabby *(stomach, muscles)*; **Schlappe** die; ~, ~**n** setback; **schlapp|machen** itr. V. *(ugs.)* flag; *(zusammenbrechen)* flake out *(coll.)*; *(aufgeben)* give up

schlau 1. *Adj.* a) shrewd; astute; *(gerissen)* wily; crafty; cunning; b) *(ugs.: gescheit)* clever; bright; smart; **aus jmdm. nicht ~ werden** *(ugs.)* not be able to make sb. out; **2.** *adv.* shrewdly; astutely; *(gerissen)* craftily; cunningly

Schlauch der; ~|e|s, **Schläuche** a) hose; b) *(Fahrrad~, Auto~)* tube; **Schlauch·boot** das rubber dinghy; inflatable [dinghy]; **schlauchen** *(ugs.)* tr., auch itr. V. **jmdn.** ~: take it out of sb.; **schlauch·los** *Adj.* tubeless *(tyre)*

Schläue die; ~: shrewdness; astuteness; *(Gerissenheit)* wiliness; craftiness; cunning

Schlaufe die; ~, ~n loop

schlecht 1. *Adj.* a) bad; poor, bad *(food, quality, style, harvest, health, circulation)*; poor *(salary, eater, appetite)*; poor-quality *(goods)*; bad, weak *(eyes)*; **um jmdn./mit etw. steht es ~:** sb./sth. is in a bad way; b) *(böse)* bad; wicked; c) *nicht attr. (ungenießbar)* off; **das Fleisch ist ~ geworden** meat has gone off; 2. *adv.* a) badly; **er sieht/hört ~:** his sight is poor/he has poor hearing; **über jmdn.** *od.* **von jmdm. ~ sprechen** speak ill of sb.; b) *(schwer)* **heute geht es ~:** today is difficult; c) **~ und recht, mehr ~ als recht** after a fashion

schlecht-: ~**bezahlt** *Adj. (präd. getrennt geschrieben)* badly *or* poorly paid; ~|**gehen** *unr. itr. V.; unpers.; mit sein* **es geht ihr/mir ~:** she is/I am doing badly; *(gesundheitlich)* she is/I am ill *or* unwell *or* poorly; ~**gelaunt** *Adj. (präd. getrennt geschrieben)* bad-tempered; ~**machen** *tr. V.* jmdn. ~**machen** run sb. down; disparage sb.

schlecken *(bes. südd., österr.) tr. V.* lap up

schleichen 1. *unr. itr. V.; mit sein* creep; *(heimlich)* creep; sneak; *(cat* slink, creep; *(langsam fahren)* crawl along; 2. *unr. refl. V.* creep; sneak; *(cat)* slink, creep; **schleichend** *Adj.* insidious *(disease)*; slow[-acting] *(poison)*; creeping *(inflation)*; gradual *(crisis)*

Schleier der; ~s, ~: veil; **schleierhaft** *Adj.* jmdm. ~haft sein/bleiben be/remain a mystery to sb.

Schleife die; ~, ~n a) bow; *(Fliege)* bow-tie; b) *(starke Biegung)* loop

¹**schleifen** *unr. tr. V.* grind; cut *(diamond, glass)*; *(mit Schleifpapier usw.)* sand; *(schärfen)* sharpen

²**schleifen** 1. *tr. V.* a) *(auch fig.)* drag; b) *(niederreißen)* raze *(sth.)* [to the ground]; 2. *itr. V.; auch mit sein* drag; **die Kupplung ~ lassen** *(Kfz-W.)* slip the clutch

Schleim der; ~|e|s, ~e mucus; *(im Hals)* phlegm; *(von Schnecken)* slime; **schleimig** *Adj. (auch fig.)* slimy; *(Physiol., Zool.)* mucous

schlemmen *itr. V.* have a · feast; **Schlemmer** der; ~s, ~: gourmet

schlendern *itr. V.; mit sein* stroll

Schlenker der; ~s, ~ *(ugs.)* swerve; **einen ~ machen** swerve

schlenkern *tr., itr. V.* swing; **mit den Armen ~:** swing one's arms

Schleppe die; ~, ~n train; **schleppen** 1. *tr. V.* a) *(ziehen)* tow *(vehicle, ship)*; b) *(tragen)* carry; lug; c) *(ugs.: mitnehmen)* drag; 2. *refl. V.* drag *or* haul oneself; **Schlepper** der; ~s, ~ a) *(Schiff)* tug; b) *(Traktor)* tractor

Schlepp-: ~**lift** der T-bar [lift]; ~**tau** das tow-line

Schleuder die; ~, ~n sling; *(mit Gummiband)* catapult *(Brit.)*; slingshot *(Amer.)*; **schleudern** 1. *tr. V.* hurl; 2. *itr. V.; mit sein (vehicle)* skid

schleunigst *Adv.* a) *(auf der Stelle)* at once; immediately; straight away; b) *(eilends)* hastily; with all haste

Schleuse die; ~, ~n a) sluice[-gate]; b) *(Schiffs~)* lock

schlich *1. u. 3. Pers. Sg. Prät. v.* **schleichen**

schlicht 1. *Adj.* a) simple; plain *(pattern, furniture)*; b) *(unkompliziert)* simple, unsophisticated *(person, view, etc.)*; 2. *adv.* simply; simply, plainly *(dressed, furnished)*

schlichten 1. *tr. V.* settle *(argument etc.)*; settle *(industrial dispute etc.)* by mediation; 2. *itr. V.* mediate

Schlick der; ~|e|s, ~e silt

schlief *1. u. 3. Pers. Sg. Prät. v.* **schlafen**

Schließe die; ~, ~n clasp; *(Schnalle)* buckle; **schließen** 1. *unr. tr. V.* a) close; shut; turn off *(tap)*; fasten *(belt, bracelet)*; do up *(button, zip)*; close *(street, route, border, electrical circuit)*; fill, close *(gap)*; b) *(außer Betrieb setzen)* close [down] *(shop, school)*; c) *(ein~)* etw./jmdn./sich in etw. *(Akk.)* ~: lock sth./sb./oneself in sth.; d) *(beenden)* close *(meeting, proceedings, debate)*; end, conclude *(letter, speech, lecture)*; e) *(eingehen, vereinbaren)* conclude *(treaty, pact, cease-fire, agreement)*; reach *(settlement, compromise)*; enter into *(contract)*; f) *(folgern)* infer *(aus* from); 2. *unr. itr. V.* a) close, shut; b) *(enden)* end; conclude; c) |aus etw.| auf etw. *(Akk.)* ~: infer sth. [from sth.]; 3. *unr. refl. V. (door, window)* close, shut; *(wound, circle)* close; **Schließ·fach** das locker; *(bei der Post)* PO box; *(bei der Bank)* safe-deposit box; **schließlich** *Adv.* a) finally; in the end; b) *(immerhin, doch)* after all

schliff *1. u. 3. Pers. Sg. Prät. v.* **schleifen**

Schliff der; ~[e]s, ~e a) *o. Pl.* cutting; *(von Messern, Sensen usw.)* sharpening; b) *(Art, wie etw. geschliffen wird)* cut; *(von Messern, Scheren usw.)* edge; c) *o. Pl.* **einem Brief/Text** *usw.* **den letzten ~ geben** put the finishing touches *pl.* to a letter/text *etc.*

schlimm 1. *Adj.* a) grave, serious *(error, mistake, accusation, offence)*; bad, serious *(error, mistake)*; b) *(übel)* bad; nasty, bad *(experience)*; **[das ist alles] halb so ~**: it's not as bad as all that; **ist nicht ~!** [it] doesn't matter; **2.** *adv.* ~ **d[a]ran sein** be in a bad way; *(in einer ~en Situation)* be in dire straits; **schlimmsten·falls** *Adv.* if the worst comes to the worst

Schlinge die; ~, ~n a) loop; *(für den Arm)* sling; *(zum Aufhängen)* noose; b) *(Fanggerät)* snare

schlingen 1. *unr. tr. V.* **etw. um etw. ~**: loop sth. round sth.; **2.** *unr. refl. V.* **sich um etw. ~**: wind itself round sth; **3.** *unr. itr. V.* bolt one's food

schlingern *itr. V.; mit sein* ⟨ship, boat⟩ roll; ⟨train, vehicle⟩ lurch from side to side

Schlips der; ~es, ~e tie

Schlitten der; ~s, ~: sledge; sled; *(Pferde~)* sleigh; *(Rodel~)* toboggan; **~ fahren** go tobogganing

schlittern *itr. V.* slide

Schlitt-: **~schuh** der [ice-]skate; **~schuh laufen** *od.* **fahren** [ice-]skate; **~schuh·laufen** das [ice-]skating *no art.*; **~schuh·läufer** der [ice-]skater

Schlitz der; ~es, ~e a) slit; *(Briefkasten-, Automaten~)* slot; b) *(Hosen~)* flies *pl.*; fly

schloß *1. u. 3. Pers. Sg. Prät. v.* **schließen**

Schloß das; Schlosses, Schlösser a) lock; *(Vorhänge~)* padlock; **hinter ~ und Riegel** *(ugs.)* behind bars; b) *(Verschluß)* clasp; c) *(Wohngebäude)* castle; *(Palast)* palace; *(Herrschaftshaus)* mansion

Schlosser der; ~s, ~: metalworker; *(Maschinen~)* fitter; *(für Schlösser)* locksmith; *(Auto~)* mechanic

Schlot der; ~[e]s, ~e *od.* **Schlöte** chimney[-stack]; *(eines Schiffes)* funnel

schlottern *itr. V.* a) shake; b) ⟨clothes⟩ hang loose

Schlucht die; ~, ~en ravine

schluchzen *itr. V.* sob

Schluck der; ~[e]s, ~e *od.* **Schlücke** swallow; mouthful; *(großer ~)* gulp; *(kleiner ~)* sip; **Schluck·auf** der; ~s

hiccups *pl.*; **Schlückchen** das; ~s, ~: sip; **schlucken 1.** *tr. V.* swallow; *etw. hastig* ~: gulp sth. down; **2.** *itr. V.* swallow; **Schlucker** der; ~s, ~: **armer ~** *(ugs.)* poor devil *or (Brit. coll.)* blighter

schludrig *s.* schludrig; **schludern** *itr. V. (ugs.)* work sloppily; **schludrig** *(ugs.)* **1.** *Adj.* a) slipshod ⟨work, examination⟩; botched ⟨job⟩; slapdash ⟨person, work⟩; b) *(schlampig [aussehend])* scruffy; **2.** *adv.* a) in a slipshod or slapdash way; b) *(schlampig)* scruffily

schlug *1. u. 3. Pers. Sg. Prät. v.* **schlagen**

Schlummer der; ~s *(geh.)* slumber *(poet./rhet.)*; **schlummern** *itr. V. (geh.)* slumber *(poet./rhet.)*

Schlund der; ~[e]s, Schlünde [back of the] throat; pharynx *(Anat.)*

schlüpfen *itr. V.; mit sein* slip; *[aus dem Ei]* ~: ⟨chick⟩ hatch out

Schlüpfer der; ~s, ~ *(für Damen)* knickers *pl. (Brit.)*; panties *pl.*; *(für Herren)* [under]pants *pl. or* trunks *pl.*

schlüpfrig *Adj.* a) slippery; b) *(anstößig)* lewd

schlurfen *itr. V.; mit sein* shuffle

schlürfen 1. *tr. V.* slurp [up] *(coll.)*; **2.** *itr. V.* slurp *(coll.)*

Schluß der; Schlusses, Schlüsse a) end; *(eines Vortrags o. ä.)* conclusion; *(eines Buchs, Schauspiels usw.)* ending; **am** *od.* **zum** ~: at the end; *(schließlich)* in the end; b) *(Folgerung)* conclusion

Schlüssel der; ~s, ~: key

Schlüssel-: **~bein** das collar-bone; clavicle *(Anat.)*; **~blume** die cowslip; *(Primel)* primula; **~bund** der *od.* das bunch of keys; **~loch** das keyhole

schlüssig 1. *Adj.* a) conclusive ⟨proof, evidence⟩; convincing, logical ⟨argument, conclusion⟩; b) **sich** *(Dat.)* ~ **werden** make up one's mind; **2.** *adv.* conclusively

Schluß-: **~licht** das; *Pl.* ~lichter tailor rear-light; **~strich** der [bottom] line; **~verkauf** der [end-of-season] sale[s *pl.*]

schmächtig *Adj.* slight

schmackhaft *Adj.* tasty

schmal; ~er *od.* schmäler, ~st... *od.* schmälst.... *Adj.* narrow; slim ⟨hips, hands, figure, etc.⟩; thin ⟨lips, face, nose, etc.⟩; **schmälern** *tr. V.* diminish; restrict ⟨rights⟩

¹**Schmalz** das; ~es dripping; *(Schwei-*

ne~) lard; **²Schmalz** der; **~es** *(abwertend)* schmaltz *(coll.);* **Schmalz·brot** das slice of bread and dripping; **schmalzig** *(abwertend)* 1. *Adj.* schmaltzy *(coll.);* 2. *adv.* with slushy sentimentality

schmarotzen *itr. V. (fig.)* sponge; free-load *(sl.)*

Schmarren der; **~s**, ~ *(österr., auch südd.)* pancake broken up with a fork after frying

schmatzen *itr. V.* smack one's lips; *(geräuschvoll essen)* eat noisily

Schmaus der; **~es**, **Schmäuse** *(veralt., scherzh.)* [good] spread *(coll.)*

schmecken 1. *itr. V.* taste **(nach** of); |gut| ~ : taste good; **schmeckt es |dir|?** are you enjoying it or your meal?; 2. *tr. V.* taste *(kosten)* sample

schmeicheln *itr. V.* jmdm. ~ : flatter sb.; **Schmeichler** der; **~s**, ~ : flatterer

schmeißen *(ugs.)* 1. *unr. tr. V.* chuck *(coll.);* sling *(coll.); (schleudern)* fling; hurl; 2. *unr. refl. V.* throw oneself; *(mit Wucht)* hurl oneself; 3. *unr. itr. V.* **mit etw. |nach jmdm.| ~ :** chuck sth. [at sb.] *(coll.)*

Schmeiß·fliege die blowfly; *(blaue ~)* bluebottle

schmelzen 1. *unr. itr. V.; mit sein* melt; *(fig.)(doubts, apprehension, etc.)* dissolve, fade away; 2. *unr. tr. V.* melt; smelt *(ore);* render *(fat);* **Schmelz·käse** der processed cheese

Schmerz der; **~es**, **~en** a) *(physisch)* pain; *(dumpf u. anhaltend)* ache; **wo haben Sie ~en?** where does it hurt?; **~en haben** be in pain; b) *(psychisch)* pain; *(Kummer)* grief; **schmerz-empfindlich** *Adj.* sensitive to pain *pred.;* **schmerzen** 1. *tr. V.* jmdn. ~ : hurt sb.; *(jmdm. Kummer bereiten)* grieve sb.; cause sb. sorrow; 2. *itr. V.* hurt; **schmerzhaft** *Adj.* painful; **schmerzlich** 1. *Adj.* painful; distressing; 2. *adv.* painfully

schmerz-, Schmerz-: **~los** 1. *Adj.* painless; 2. *adv.* painlessly; **~stillend** *Adj.* pain-killing; **~tablette** die pain-killing tablet

Schmetterling der; **~s**, **~e** butterfly

schmettern 1. *tr. V.* a) hurl **(an** + *Akk.* at, **gegen** against); b) *(laut spielen, singen usw.)* blare out *(march, music); (person)* sing lustily *(song);* c) *(Tennis usw.)* smash *(ball);* 2. *itr. V.* *(trumpet, music, etc.)* blare out

Schmied der; **~|e|s**, **~e** blacksmith; **Schmiede** die; ~, **~en** smithy; forge; **schmieden** *tr. V. (auch fig.)* forge

schmiegen 1. *refl. V.* snuggle, nestle **(in** + *Akk.* in); **sich an jmdn.** ~ : snuggle [close] up to sb.; 2. *tr. V.* press **(an** + *Akk.* against)

schmieren 1. *tr. V.* a) lubricate; b) *(streichen)* spread *(butter, jam, etc.)* **(auf** + *Akk.* on); **Brote** ~ : spread slices of bread; 2. *itr. V.* a) *(oil, grease)* lubricate; b) *(ugs: unsauber schreiben) (person)* scrawl, scribble; *(pen, ink)* smudge, make smudges; **schmierig** *Adj.* greasy; **Schmier-seife** die soft soap

schmilzt 2. u. 3. Pers. Sg. Präsens v. **schmelzen**

Schminke die; ~, **~n** make-up; **schminken** 1. *tr. V.* make up *(face, eyes);* 2. *refl. V.* make oneself up

Schmirgel·papier das emery-paper; *(Sandpapier)* sandpaper

schmiß 1. u. 3. Pers. Sg. Prät. v. **schmeißen**

Schmöker der; **~s**, ~ *(ugs.)* light-weight adventure story/romance; **schmökern** *(ugs.)* 1. *itr. V.* bury oneself in a book; 2. *tr. V.* bury oneself in *(book)*

schmollen *itr. V.* sulk; **Schmoll-mund** der pouting mouth

schmolz 1. u. 3. Pers. Sg. Prät. v. **schmelzen**

Schmor·braten der braised beef; **schmoren** 1. *tr. V.* braise; 2. *itr. V.* a) braise; b) *(ugs.: schwitzen)* swelter

Schmuck *Adj.* attractive

Schmuck der; **~|e|s** a) *(~stücke)* jewelry, jewellery *(esp. Brit.);* b) s. **~stück;** c) *(Zierde)* decoration

schmücken *tr. V.* decorate; embellish *(writings, speech)*

schmuck-, Schmuck-: **~käst-chen** das, **~kasten** der jewelry or *(esp. Brit.)* jewellery box; **~los** *Adj.* plain; bare *(room);* **~stück** das piece of jewelry or *(esp. Brit.)* jewellery

schmuddelig *Adj.* *(ugs.)* grubby; mucky *(coll.); (schmutzig u. unordentlich)* messy; grotty *(Brit. sl.)*

Schmuggel der; **~s** smuggling *no art.;* **schmuggeln** *tr., itr. V.* smuggle **(in** + *Akk.* into; **aus** out of); **Schmuggler** der; **~s**, ~ : smuggler

schmunzeln *itr. V.* smile to oneself

schmusen *itr. V. (ugs.)* cuddle; *(couple)* kiss and cuddle

Schmutz der; ~es dirt; *(Schlamm)* mud; **schmutzen** *itr. V.* get dirty; **schmutzig** *Adj.* dirty

Schnabel der; ~s, Schnäbel **a)** beak; **b)** *(ugs.: Mund)* gob *(sl.)*

Schnake die; ~, ~n **a)** daddy-long-legs; **b)** *(bes. südd.: Stechmücke)* mosquito

Schnalle die; ~, ~n *(Gürtel~)* buckle; **schnallen** *tr. V.* **a)** *(mit einer Schnalle festziehen)* buckle ⟨shoe, belt⟩; fasten ⟨strap⟩; **b)** *(mit Riemen/Gurten befestigen)* strap **(auf** + *Akk.* on to)

schnalzen *itr. V.* [mit der Zunge/den Fingern] ~: click one's tongue/snap one's fingers

schnappen 1. *itr. V.* **nach jmdm./etw.** ~ *⟨animal⟩* snap at sb./sth.; **nach Luft** ~: gasp for breath; **2.** *tr. V.* ⟨dog, bird, etc.⟩ snatch; **[sich** *(Dat.)*] **jmdn./etw.** ~ *(ugs.) ⟨person⟩* grab sb./sth.; *(mit raschem Zugriff)* snatch sb./sth.; **Schnapp·schuß** der snapshot

Schnaps der; ~es, Schnäpse **a)** spirit; *(Klarer)* schnapps; **b)** *o. Pl. (Spirituosen)* spirits *pl.*

schnarchen *itr. V.* snore

schnattern *itr. V.* **a)** ⟨goose etc.⟩ cackle, gaggle; **b)** *(ugs.: eifrig schwatzen)* jabber [away]; chatter

schnauben *itr. V.* snort **(vor** with)

schnaufen *itr. V.* puff **(vor** with)

Schnauze die; ~, ~n **a)** *(von Tieren)* muzzle; *(der Maus usw.)* snout; *(Maul)* mouth; **b)** *(derb: Mund)* gob *(sl.);* **[halt die]** ~! shut your trap! *(sl.);* **schnauzen** *tr., itr. V. (ugs.)* bark; *(ärgerlich)* snap; snarl

Schnecke die snail; *(Nackt~)* slug; **Schnecken·haus** das snail-shell

Schnee der; ~s snow

Schnee-: ~ball der snowball; ~besen der whisk; ~flocke die snowflake; ~gestöber das snow flurry; ~glöckchen das snowdrop; ~kette die snow-chain; ~matsch der slush; ~pflug der snow-plough; ~sturm der snowstorm

Schneewittchen (das) Snow White

Schneide die; ~, ~n *[cutting]* edge; **schneiden 1.** *unr. itr. V.* cut **(in** + *Akk.* into); **2.** *unr. tr. V.* **a)** cut; *(in Scheiben)* slice ⟨bread, sausage, etc.⟩; *(klein* ~) cut up, chop ⟨wood, vegetables⟩; *(stutzen)* prune ⟨tree, bush⟩; trim ⟨beard⟩; cut, mow ⟨grass⟩; **sich** *(Dat.)* **die Haare** ~ **lassen** have one's hair cut; **b)** **eine Kurve** ~: cut a corner **Schneider** der; ~s, ~: tailor; *(Da-*

men~) dressmaker; **Schneiderei** die; ~, ~en tailor's shop; *(Damen~)* dressmaker's shop; **Schneiderin** die; ~, ~nen *s.* Schneider; **schneidern** *tr. V.* make; make, tailor *(suit)*

Schneide·zahn der incisor

schneien 1. *itr., tr. V. (unpers.)* snow; **es schneit** it is snowing; **2.** *itr. V.; mit sein (fig.)* rain down; fall like snow

Schneise die; ~, ~n *(Wald~)* aisle; *(als Feuerschutz)* firebreak

schnell 1. *Adj.* quick ⟨journey, decision, service, etc.⟩; fast ⟨car, skis, road, track, etc.⟩; quick, swift ⟨progress, movement, blow, action⟩; **2.** *adv.* quickly; ⟨drive, move, etc.⟩ fast, quickly; ⟨spread⟩ quickly, rapidly; *(bald)* soon ⟨sold, past, etc.⟩; **mach** ~! *(ugs.)* move it! *(coll.);* **schnellen** *itr. V.; mit sein* shoot **(aus** + *Dat.* out of; **in** + *Akk.* into); **Schnelligkeit** die; ~, ~en speed; **Schnell·imbiß** der snack-bar; **schnellstens** *Adv.* as quickly as possible

Schnell-: ~straße die expressway; ~zug der express [train]

Schnepfe die; ~, ~n snipe

schneuzen 1. *tr. V.* **sich** *(Dat.)* **/einem Kind die Nase** ~: blow one's/a child's nose; **2.** *refl. V.* blow one's nose

schnippeln *(ugs.)* **1.** *itr. V.* snip [away] **(an** + *Dat.* at); **2.** *tr. V.* shred ⟨vegetables⟩; chop ⟨beans etc.⟩ [finely]

schnippen 1. *itr. V.* snap one's fingers **(nach** at); **2.** *tr. V.* flick **(von** off, from)

schnippisch 1. *Adj.* pert ⟨reply, tone, etc.⟩; **2.** *adv.* pertly

Schnipsel der *od.* das; ~s, ~: scrap; *(Papier~, Stoff~)* snippet; shred

schnipseln *s.* schnippeln

schnitt 1. u. 3. Pers. Sg. Prät. v. schneiden

Schnitt der; ~[e]s, ~e **a)** cut; **b)** *(das Mähen) (von Gras)* mowing; *(von Getreide)* harvest

Schnitt-: ~blume die cut flower; ~bohne die French bean

Schnitte die; ~, ~n slice; **eine** ~ [Brot] a slice of bread; **schnittig 1.** *Adj.* stylish, smart ⟨suit, appearance, etc.⟩; *(sportlich)* racy ⟨car, yacht, etc.⟩; **2.** *adv.* stylishly; *(sportlich)* racily

Schnitt-: ~lauch der chives *pl.;* ~wunde die cut; *(lang u. tief)* gash

Schnitzel das; ~s, ~ **a)** *(Fleisch)* [veal/pork] escalope; **b)** *(von Papier)* scrap; *(von Holz)* shaving; **schnitzeln** *tr. V.*

chop up ⟨*vegetables*⟩ [into small pieces]; shred ⟨*cabbage*⟩; **schnitzen** *tr., itr. V.* carve

schnodderig (*ugs.*) **1.** *Adj.* brash; **2.** *adv.* brashly

schnöde (*geh.*) **1.** *Adj.* **a)** (*verachtenswert*) contemptible; **b)** (*gemein*) contemptuous, scornful ⟨*glance, reply, etc.*⟩. **2.** *adv.* (*gemein*) contemptuously; ⟨*exploit, misuse*⟩ flagrantly

Schnörkel *der*; ~s, ~: scroll; ⟨*der Handschrift, in der Rede*⟩ flourish

schnorren *tr., itr. V.* (*ugs.*) scrounge (*coll.*) ⟨**bei,** *von* + *Dat.* off⟩; **Schnorrer** *der*; ~s, ~ (*ugs.*) scrounger (*coll.*)

schnüffeln *itr. V.* **a)** sniff; **b)** (*ugs.: spionieren*) snoop [about] (*coll.*); **Schnüffler** *der*; ~s, ~ (*ugs.*) Nosey Parker; ⟨*Spion*⟩ snooper (*coll.*)

schnupfen 1. *tr. V.* sniff; **Tabak** ~: take snuff; **2.** *itr. V.* take snuff; **Schnupfen** *der*; ~s, ~: [head] cold; **Schnupf·tabak** *der* snuff

schnuppe: das/er ist mir ~/mir völlig ~ (*ugs.*) I don't care/I couldn't care less about it/him (*coll.*)

schnuppern *itr. V.* sniff; **an etw.** (*Dat.*) ~ sniff sth.

Schnur *die*; ~, **Schnüre a)** (*Bindfaden*) piece of string; (*Kordel*) piece of cord; **b)** (*ugs.: Kabel*) flex (*Brit.*); lead; cord (*Amer.*); **schnüren** *tr. V.* tie ⟨*bundle, string, etc.*⟩; tie, lace up ⟨*shoe, corset, etc.*⟩

Schnurr·bart *der* moustache; **schnurren** *itr. V.* ⟨*cat*⟩ purr; ⟨*machine*⟩ hum

Schnür-: ~schuh *der* lace-up shoe; **~senkel** *der*; ~s, ~ (*bes. nordd.*) [shoe-]lace; ⟨*für Stiefel*⟩ bootlace

schob *1. u. 3. Pers. Prät. v.* schieben

Schock *der*; ~[e]s, ~s shock; **schockieren** *tr. V.* shock; **über etw.** (*Akk.*) **schockiert sein** be shocked at sth.

Schöffe *der*; ~n, ~n lay judge (*acting together with another lay judge and a professional judge*); **Schöffen·gericht** *das court presided over by a professional judge and two lay judges*

Schokolade *die*; ~, ~n **a)** chocolate; **b)** (*Getränk*) [drinking] chocolate

Schokolade[n]-: ~eis *das* chocolate ice-cream; **~guß** *der* chocolate icing; **~pudding** *der* chocolate blancmange; **~torte** *die* chocolate cake *or* gateau

scholl *1. u. 3. Pers. Sg. Prät. v.* schallen

Scholle *die*; ~, ~n **a)** (*Erd~*) clod [of

earth]; **b)** (*Eis~*) [ice-]floe; **c)** (*Fisch*) plaice

schön 1. *Adv.* **a)** (*bereits*) (*oft nicht übersetzt*) already; (*in Fragen*) yet; **wie lange bist du ~ hier?** how long have you been here?; **b)** (*fast gleichzeitig*) then and there; **c)** (*jetzt*) ~ |**mal**| now; (*inzwischen*) meanwhile; **d)** (*selbst, sogar*) even; (*nur*) only; **e)** (*ohne Ergänzung, ohne weiteren Zusatz*) on its own; |**allein**| ~ **der Gedanke daran** the mere thought of it; ~ **deshalb** for this reason alone; **f)** (*wohl*) really; **Lust hätte ich ~, aber ...:** I'd certainly like to, but ...; **2. Partikel a)** (*ugs. ungeduldig: endlich*) **nun komm ~!** come on!; hurry up!; **b)** (*beruhigend: bestimmt*) all right; **c)** (*durchaus*) **das ist ~ möglich** that is quite possible

schön 1. *Adj.* **a)** beautiful; handsome ⟨*youth, man*⟩; **b)** (*angenehm*) pleasant, nice ⟨*day, holiday, dream, relaxation, etc.*⟩; fine ⟨*weather*⟩; (*nett*) nice; **das war eine ~e Zeit** those were wonderful days; **c)** (*gut*) good; **d)** (*in Höflichkeitsformeln*) ~e **Grüße** best wishes; **recht ~en Dank für ...:** thank you very much for ...; **e)** ~! (*ugs.: einverstanden*) OK (*coll.*); all right; **f)** (*iron.: leer*) ~e **Worte** fine[-sounding] words; (*schmeichlerisch*) honeyed words; **g)** (*ugs.: beträchtlich*) handsome, (*coll.*) tidy ⟨*sum, fortune, profit*⟩; considerable ⟨*quantity, distance*⟩; pretty good ⟨*pension*⟩; **h)** (*iron.: unerfreulich*) nice (*coll. iron.*); **das sind ja ~e Aussichten!** this is a fine look-out *sing.* (*iron.*); **2.** *adv.* **a)** beautifully; **b)** (*angenehm, erfreulich*) nicely; ~ **warm/weich/langsam** nice and warm/soft/slow; **c)** (*gut*) well; **d)** (*in Höflichkeitsformeln*) **bitte** ~, **können Sie mir sagen, ...:** excuse me, could you tell me ...; **e)** (*iron.: viel*) **es so ~ heißt, wie man so ~ sagt** as they say; **f)** (*ugs.: beträchtlich*) really; (*vor einem Adjektiv*) pretty; **ganz ~ arbeiten müssen** have to work jolly hard (*Brit. coll.*); **3. Partikel** (*ugs.*) **bleib ~ liegen!** lie there and be good

schonen 1. *tr. V.* treat ⟨*clothes, books, furniture, etc.*⟩ with care; (*schützen*) protect ⟨*hands, furniture*⟩; (*nicht strapazieren*) spare ⟨*voice, eyes, etc.*⟩; conserve ⟨*strength*⟩; **2.** *refl. V.* take things easy

Schönheit *die*; ~, ~en beauty

Schönheits-: ~chirurgie *die* cosmetic surgery *no art.*; **~pflege** *die* beauty care *no art.*

Schon·kost die light food

schön|machen (ugs.) 1. tr. V. smarten ⟨person, thing⟩ up; make ⟨person, thing⟩ look nice; 2. refl. V. smarten oneself up

schonungs|los 1. Adj. unsparing, ruthless ⟨criticism etc.⟩; blunt ⟨frankness⟩; 2. adv. unsparingly; ⟨say⟩ without mincing one's words

Schopf der; ~[e]s, Schöpfe shock of hair

schöpfen tr. V. a) scoop [up] ⟨water, liquid⟩; ⟨mit einer Kelle⟩ ladle ⟨soup⟩; b) (geh.: einatmen) draw, take ⟨breath⟩

Schöpfer der; ~s, ~: creator; ⟨Gott⟩ Creator; **schöpferisch** 1. Adj. creative; 2. adv. creatively

Schöpf-: ~kelle die, ~löffel der ladle

Schöpfung die; ~, ~en (geh.) creation; die ~ (die Welt) Creation

Schoppen der; ~s, ~: [quarter-litre/half-litre] glass of wine/beer

schor 1. u. 3. Pers. Sg. Prät. v. scheren

Schorf der; ~[e]s, ~e scab

Schorn·stein der chimney; (Lokomotiv~, Schiffs~) funnel; **Schornstein·feger** der; ~s, ~: chimney-sweep

schoß 1. u. 3. Pers. Sg. Prät. v. schießen

Schoß der; ~es, Schöße lap

Schote die; ~, ~n pod

Schotte der; ~n, ~n Scot; Scotsman; die ~n the Scots; the Scottish; **Schotten·rock** der tartan skirt; (Kilt) kilt; **Schottin** die; ~, ~nen Scot; Scotswoman; **schottisch** Adj. Scottish; ~er Whisky Scotch whisky; **Schottland** (das); ~s Scotland

schräg 1. Adj. diagonal ⟨line, beam, cut, etc.⟩; sloping ⟨surface, roof, wall, side, etc.⟩; slanting, slanted ⟨writing, eyes, etc.⟩; tilted ⟨position of the head etc., axis⟩; 2. adv. at an angle; ⟨diagonal⟩ diagonally; **Schräge** die; ~, ~n a) (schräge Fläche) sloping surface; b) (Neigung) slope

schrak 1. u. 3. Pers. Sg. Prät. v. schrecken

Schramme die; ~, ~n scratch; **schrammen** tr. V. scratch

Schrank der; ~[e]s, Schränke cupboard; closet (Amer.); (Glas~; kleiner Wand~) cabinet; (Kleider~) wardrobe; (Bücher~) bookcase; **Schränkchen** das; ~s, ~: cabinet

Schranke die; ~, ~n a) (auch fig.) barrier; b) (fig.: Grenze) limit

Schraube die; ~, ~n bolt; (Holz~, Blech~) screw; **schrauben** tr. V. a) s. Schraube: bolt/screw ⟨an, auf + Akk. on to⟩; b) (drehen) screw ⟨nut, hook, light-bulb, etc.⟩ ⟨auf + Akk. on to; in + Akk. into⟩

Schrauben-: ~schlüssel der spanner; ~zieher der; ~s, ~: screwdriver

Schraub·verschluß der screw-top

Schreber·garten der ≈ allotment (cultivated primarily as a garden)

Schreck der; ~[e]s, ~e fright; scare; (Schock) shock; jmdm. einen ~ einjagen give sb. a fright; **schrecken** regelm. (auch unr.) itr. V. start [up]; aus dem Schlaf ~: awake with a start; start from one's sleep; **Schrecken** der; ~s, ~: fright; scare; (Entsetzen) horror; (große Angst) terror; jmdm. einen ~ einjagen give sb. a fright; **schreckhaft** Adj. easily scared; **schrecklich** 1. Adj. terrible; 2. adv. terribly

Schrei der; ~[e]s, ~e cry; (lauter Ruf) shout; (durchdringend) yell; (gellend) scream; (kreischend) shriek

Schreib·block der; Pl. ~blocks od. ~blöcke writing-pad

schreiben 1. unr. itr. V. write; (mit der Schreibmaschine) type; an einem Roman usw. ~: be writing a novel etc.; jmdm. od. an jmdn. ~: write to sb.; 2. unr. tr. V. a) write; (mit der Schreibmaschine) type; wie schreibt man dieses Wort? how is this word spelt?; 3. unr. refl. V. be spelt; **Schreiben** das; ~s, ~ a) o. Pl. writing no def. art.; b) (Brief) letter; **Schreiber** der; ~s, ~: writer; (Verfasser) author; **Schreiberin** die; ~, ~en writer; (Verfasserin) authoress

Schreib-: ~maschine die typewriter; ~maschinen·papier das typing paper; ~papier das writing-paper; ~tisch der desk

Schreibung die; ~, ~en spelling

Schreib-: ~waren Pl. stationery sing.; ~waren·geschäft das stationer's

schreien unr. itr. V. ⟨person⟩ cry [out]; (laut rufen/sprechen) shout; (durchdringend) yell; (gellend) scream; ⟨baby⟩ yell, bawl; zum Schreien sein (ugs.) be a scream (sl.)

Schreiner der; ~s, ~ (bes. südd.) s. Tischler

schreiten unr. itr. V.; mit sein (geh.) walk; (mit großen Schritten) stride

schrickst 2. Pers. Sg. Präsens v.

schrecken; schrickt 3. Pers. Sg. Präsens v. **schrecken**
schrie 1. u. 3. Pers. Sg. Prät. v. **schrei-
en**
schrieb 1. u. 3. Pers. Sg. Prät. v.
schreiben; Schrieb der; ~[e]s, ~e
(ugs.) missive (coll.)
Schrift die; ~, ~en a) (System) script;
(Alphabet) alphabet; b) (Hand~)
[hand]writing; c) (Werk) work;
schriftlich 1. Adj. written; 2. adv. in
writing
Schrift-: ~steller der; ~s, ~: writer;
~**stück** das [official] document;
~**wechsel** der correspondence
schrill 1. Adj. shrill; 2. adv. shrilly;
schrillen itr. V. shrill; sound shrilly
schritt 1. u. 3. Pers. Sg. Prät. v. **schreiten; Schritt** der; ~[e]s, ~e a) step; einen ~ machen od. tun take a step; b)
Pl. (Geräusch) footsteps; c) (Entfernung) pace; d) (Gleich~) aus dem ~
kommen get out of step; e) o. Pl.
(Gangart) walk; seinen ~ verlang-
samen/beschleunigen slow/quicken
one's pace; [mit jmdm./etw.] ~ halten
(auch fig.) keep up or keep pace [with
sb./sth.]; f) (~geschwindigkeit) walking pace; „~ fahren" 'dead slow'; g)
(fig.: Maßnahme) step; measure;
Schritt·geschwindigkeit die
walking pace
schroff 1. Adj. a) precipitous (rock
etc.); b) (plötzlich) sudden (transition,
change); (kraß) stark (contrast); c)
(barsch) curt (refusal, manner);
brusque (manner, behaviour, tone); 2.
adv. a) (rise, drop) sheer; (fall away)
precipitously; b) (plötzlich, unvermit-
telt) suddenly; c) (barsch) curtly; (interrupt) abruptly; (treat) brusquely
schröpfen tr. V. (ugs.) fleece
Schrot der od. das; ~[e]s, ~e a) coarse
meal; (aus Getreide) whole meal
(Brit.); whole grain; b) (Munition)
shot; **schroten** tr. V. grind (grain
etc.) [coarsely]; crush (malt) [coarsely]
Schrot-: ~flinte die shotgun; ~**kugel** die pellet
Schrott der; ~[e]s, ~e a) scrap
[-metal]; ein Auto zu ~ fahren (ugs.)
write a car off; b) o. Pl. (salopp fig.)
rubbish; **schrott·reif** Adj. ready for
the scrap-heap postpos.
schrubben tr. (auch itr.) V. scrub;
Schrubber der; ~s, ~: [long-
handled] scrubbing-brush
Schrulle die; ~, ~n cranky idea; (Marotte) quirk

schrumpelig Adj. (ugs.) wrinkly;
schrumpeln itr. V.; mit sein (ugs.)
(skin) go wrinkled; (apple etc.) shrivel
schrumpfen itr. V.; mit sein shrink;
(metal, rock) contract; (apple etc.)
shrivel; (skin) go wrinkled; (abnehmen) decrease; (supplies, capital,
hopes) dwindle
Schub der; ~[e]s, Schübe a) (Physik:
~kraft) thrust; b) (Med.: Phase)
phase; stage; c) (Gruppe, Anzahl)
batch
Schuber der; ~s, ~: slip-case
Schub-: ~karre die, ~**karren** der
wheelbarrow; ~**lade** die drawer
Schubs der; ~es, ~e (ugs.) shove;
schubsen tr. (auch itr.) V. (ugs.)
push; shove
schüchtern 1. Adj. a) shy (person,
smile, etc.); shy, timid (voice, knock,
etc.); b) (fig.: zaghaft) tentative, cautious (attempt, beginnings, etc.); 2.
adv. shyly; (knock, ask, etc.) timidly;
Schüchternheit die; ~: shyness
Schuft der; ~[e]s, ~e scoundrel
schuften (ugs.) itr. V. slave away
Schuh der; ~[e]s, ~e shoe; (hoher ~,
Stiefel) boot; jmdm. etw. in die ~e
schieben (fig. ugs.) pin the blame for
sth. on sb.
Schuh-: ~creme die shoe-polish;
~**größe** die shoe size; welche ~**größe
hast du?** what size shoe[s] do you
take?; ~**macher** der; ~s, ~: shoemaker; ~**sohle** die sole [of a/one's
shoe]
Schul-: ~abschluß der school-
leaving qualification; ~**buch** das
school-book; ~**bus** der school bus
schuld s. Schuld b; **Schuld** die; ~,
~en a) o. Pl. guilt; er ist sich (Dat.)
keiner ~ bewußt he is not conscious of
having done any wrong; b) o. Pl. (Ver-
antwortlichkeit) blame; es ist [nicht]
seine ~: it is [not] his fault; [an etw.
(Dat.)] schuld haben od. sein be to
blame [for sth.]; c) (Verpflichtung zur
Rückzahlung) debt; 5000 Mark ~en
haben have debts of 5,000 marks, owe
5,000 marks; **schuld·bewußt** 1.
Adj. guilty (look, face, etc.); 2. adv.
guiltily; **schulden** tr. V. owe; was
schulde ich Ihnen? how much do I owe
you?; **Schuld·gefühl** das feeling of
guilt; **schuldig** Adj. a) guilty; der [an
dem Unfall] ~e Autofahrer the driver
to blame [for the accident]; b) jmdm.
etw. ~ sein/bleiben owe sb. sth.; c) (gebührend) due; proper; **Schuldige**

der/die; ~ adj. Dekl. guilty person; (im Strafprozeß) guilty party; **schuld·los** Adj. innocent (an + Dat. of); **Schuld·spruch** der verdict of guilty

Schule die; ~, ~n a) school; zur od. in die ~ gehen, die ~ besuchen go to school; auf od. in der ~: at school; **schulen** tr. V. train; **Schüler** der; ~s, ~: pupil; (Schuljunge) schoolboy; **Schülerin** die; ~, ~nen pupil; (Schulmädchen) schoolgirl

schul-, Schul-: ~**ferien** Pl. school holidays or (Amer.) vacation sing.; ~**frei** Adj. (day) off school; ~**hof** der school yard; ~**jahr** das a) school year; b) (Klasse) year; ~**junge** der schoolboy; ~**kind** das schoolchild; ~**klasse** die [school] class; ~**mädchen** das schoolgirl; ~**ranzen** der [school] satchel; ~**tag** der school day; ~**tasche** die school-bag; (Ranzen) [school] satchel

Schulter die; ~, ~n shoulder; jmdm. auf die ~ klopfen pat sb. on the shoulder or (fig.) back; **Schulterblatt** das (Anat.) shoulder-blade; **schultern** tr. V. shoulder; **das Gewehr ~:** shoulder arms

Schul-: ~**weg** der way to school; ~**zeit** die school-days pl.

schummerig Adj. dim (light etc.); dimly lit (room etc.)

Schund der; ~[e]s trash

Schuppe die; ~, ~n a) scale; b) Pl. (auf dem Kopf) dandruff sing.; (auf der Haut) flaking skin sing.; **schuppen** 1. tr. V. scale (fish); 2. refl. V. (skin) flake; (person) have flaking skin

Schuppen der; ~s, ~ a) shed; b) (ugs.: Lokal) joint (sl.)

schüren tr. V. a) poke (fire); b) (fig.) stir up (hatred, envy, etc.)

schürfen 1. itr. V. scrape; 2. tr. V. a) sich (Dat.) das Knie usw. ~: graze one's knee etc.; b) (Bergbau) mine (ore etc.) open-cast or (Amer.) opencut; **Schürf·wunde** die graze; abrasion

Schurke der; ~n, ~n rogue

Schur·wolle die new wool

Schürze die; ~, ~n apron; (Frauen~, Latz~) pinafore

Schuß der; Schusses, Schüsse a) shot (auf + Akk. at); weit od. weitab vom ~ (fig. ugs.) well away from the action; b) (Menge Munition/Schießpulver) round; drei ~ Munition three rounds of ammunition; c) (~wunde) gunshot

wound; d) (kleine Menge) dash; e) (Drogenjargon) shot; fix (sl.); f) (Ski-sport) schuss; ~ fahren schuss; g) (ugs.) etw. in ~ bringen/halten get sth. into/keep sth. in [good] shape

Schüssel die; ~, ~n bowl; (flacher) dish

schusselig (ugs.) 1. Adj. scatterbrained; 2. adv. in a scatter-brained way

Schuß-: ~**linie** die line of fire; in die/ jmds. ~**linie** geraten od. kommen (auch fig.) come under fire/come under fire from sb.; ~**verletzung** die gunshot wound; ~**waffe** die weapon (firing a projectile); (Gewehr usw.) firearm

Schuster der; ~s, ~ (ugs.) shoemaker; (Flick~) shoe-repairer

Schutt der; ~[e]s rubble; „~ abladen verboten" 'no tipping'; 'no dumping'

Schüttel·frost der [violent] shivering fit

schütteln 1. tr. V. a) shake; den Kopf [über etw. (Akk.)] ~ shake one's head [over sth.]; jmdm. die Hand ~: shake sb.'s hand; shake sb. by the hand; b) (unpers.) es schüttelte ihn [vor Kälte] he was shaking [with or from cold]; 2. refl. V. shake oneself/itself; 3. itr. V. mit dem Kopf ~: shake one's head

schütten 1. tr. V. pour (liquid, flour, etc.); (unabsichtlich) spill (liquid, flour, etc.); tip (rubbish, coal, etc.); 2. itr. V. (unpers.) (ugs.: regnen) pour [down]

schütter Adj. sparse; thin

Schutz der; ~es protection (vor + Dat., gegen against); (Zuflucht) refuge

schutz-, Schutz-: ~**bedürftig** Adj. in need of protection postpos.; ~**blech** das mudguard; ~**brief** der (Kfz-W.) travel insurance; (Dokument) travel insurance certificate

Schütze der; ~n, ~n a) marksman; b) (Fußball usw.: Tor~) scorer; c) (Milit.: einfacher Soldat) private; d) (Astrol.) Sagittarius

schützen 1. tr. V. protect (vor + Dat. from, gegen against); safeguard (interest, property, etc.) (vor + Dat. from); gesetzlich geschützt registered [as a trade-mark]; 2. itr. V. provide or give protection (vor + Dat. from, gegen against); (vor Wind, Regen) give shelter (vor + Dat. from)

Schützen·fest das shooting competition with fair

Schutz·engel der guardian angel

Schützen-: ~**graben** der trench; ~**panzer** der armoured personnel carrier; ~**verein** der rifle club

Schutz-: ~**helm** der helmet; *(bei Motorradfahrern usw.)* crash-helmet; *(bei Bauarbeitern usw.)* safety helmet; ~**hütte** die a) *(Unterstand)* shelter; b) *(Berghütte)* mountain hut; ~**impfung** die vaccination

Schützling der; ~s, ~e protégé; *(Anvertrauter)* charge

schutz-, Schutz-: ~**los** *Adj.* defenceless; ~**mann** der; *Pl.* ~**männer** *od.* ~**leute** *(ugs. veralt.)* [police] constable; copper *(Brit. coll.)*; ~**patron** der patron saint; ~**suchend** *Adj.* seeking protection *postpos.*; ~**umschlag** der dust-jacket

schwabbelig *Adj.* flabby *(stomach, person, etc.)*; wobbly *(jelly etc.)*; **schwabbeln** *itr. V.* *(ugs.)* wobble

Schwabe der; ~n, ~n Swabian; **Schwaben** (das); ~s Swabia; **Schwäbin** die; ~, ~nen Swabian; **schwäbisch** *Adj.* Swabian

schwach; schwächer, schwächst... 1. *Adj.* a) weak; weak, delicate *(child, woman)*; frail *(invalid, old person)*; low-powered *(engine, bulb, amplifier, etc.)*; weak, poor *(eyesight, memory, etc.)*; poor *(hearing)*; delicate *(health, constitution)*; ~ werden grow weak; *(fig.: schwanken)* weaken; *(fig.: nachgeben)* give in; b) *(nicht gut)* poor *(pupil, player, performance, result, etc.)*; weak *(argument, opponent, play, film, etc.)*; c) *(gering, niedrig)* poor, low *(attendance etc.)*; slight *(effect, resistance, gradient, etc.)*; light *(wind, rain, current)*; faint *(voice, pressure, hope, smile, smell)*; weak, faint *(pulse)*; faint, dim *(light)*; pale *(colour)*; d) *(wenig konzentriert)* weak *(solution, coffee, poison, etc.)*; e) *(Sprachw.)* weak; 2. *adv.* a) weakly; b) *(nicht gut)* poorly; c) *(in geringem Maße)* poorly *(attended, developed)*; slightly *(poisonous, sweetened, inclined)*; *(rain)* slightly; *(remember, glow, smile)* faintly; d) *(Sprachw.)* ~ gebeugt weak; **Schwäche** die; ~, ~n weakness; eine ~ für jmdn./etw. haben have a soft spot for sb./a weakness for sth.; **Schwäche·anfall** der sudden feeling of faintness; **schwächen** *tr. V.* weaken; **schwächlich** *Adj.* weakly *(person)*; frail *(old person, constitution)*; **Schwächling** der; ~s, ~e weakling

schwach-, Schwach-: ~**sinn** der; *o. Pl.* a) *(Med.)* mental deficiency; b) *(ugs.)* [idiotic *(coll.)*] rubbish; ~**sinnig** 1. *Adj.* a) *(Med.)* mentally deficient; b) *(ugs.)* idiotic *(coll.)*, nonsensical *(measure, policy, etc.)*; rubbishy *(film etc.)*; 2. *adv.* *(ugs.)* idiotically *(coll.)*; stupidly

schwafeln *(ugs.)* 1. *itr. V.* rabbit on *(Brit. sl.)*, waffle *(von* about); 2. *tr. V.* blether *(nonsense)*

Schwager der; ~s, **Schwäger** brother-in-law; **Schwägerin** die; ~, ~nen sister-in-law

Schwalbe die; ~, ~n swallow

Schwall der; ~[e]s, ~e torrent

schwamm *1. u. 3. Pers. Sg. Prät. v.* schwimmen

Schwamm der; ~[e]s, **Schwämme** a) sponge; ~ **drüber!** *(ugs.)* [let's] forget it; b) *(südd., österr.: Pilz)* mushroom; **Schwammerl** das; ~s, ~[n] *(bayr., österr.)* mushroom; **schwammig** 1. *Adj.* a) spongy; b) *(aufgedunsen)* flabby, bloated *(face, body, etc.)*; 2. *adv.* *(unpräzise)* vaguely

Schwan der; ~[e]s, **Schwäne** swan

schwand *1. u. 3. Pers. Sg. Prät. v.* schwinden

schwang *1. u. 3. Pers. Sg. Prät. v.* schwingen

schwanger *Adj.* pregnant *(von* by); **Schwangere** die; *adj. Dekl.* expectant mother; pregnant woman; **schwängern** *tr. V.* make *(woman)* pregnant; **Schwangerschaft** die; ~, ~en pregnancy

Schwank der; ~[e]s, **Schwänke** comic tale; *(auf der Bühne)* farce

schwanken *itr. V.*; mit Richtungsangabe mit sein a) sway; *(boat)* rock; *(heftiger)* roll; *(ground, floor)* shake; b) *(fig.: unbeständig sein)* *(prices, temperature, etc.)* fluctuate; *(number, usage, etc.)* vary; c) *(fig.: unentschieden sein)* waver; *(zögern)* hesitate

Schwanz der; ~es, **Schwänze** a) tail; b) *(salopp: Penis)* prick *(coarse)*; cock *(coarse)*

schwänzeln *itr. V.* wag its tail/their tails

schwänzen *tr., itr. V.* *(ugs.)* skip, cut *(lesson etc.)*; **[die Schule]** ~: play truant *or (Amer.)* hookey

schwappen *itr. V.* slosh

Schwarm der; ~[e]s, **Schwärme** a) swarm; b) *(fam.: Angebete[r])* idol; heart-throb; **schwärmen** *itr. V.* a) mit Richtungsangabe mit sein swarm;

b) *(begeistert sein)* für jmdn./etw. ~:
be mad about *or* really keen on sb./
sth.; von etw. ~: go into raptures
about sth.; **schwärmerisch 1.** *Adj.*
rapturous; **2.** *adv.* rapturously

Schwarte die; ~, ~n **a)** rind; **b)** *(ugs.:
dickes Buch)* tome

schwarz; schwärzer, schwärzest... 1.
Adj. **a)** black; Black *(person)*;
filthy[-black] *(hands, finger-nails,
etc.)*; mir wurde ~ vor den Augen
everything went black; der ~e Erdteil
od. Kontinent the Dark Continent;
das Schwarze Meer the Black Sea; ins
Schwarze treffen *(fig.)* hit the nail on
the head; *(illegal)* illicit *(deal, exchange, etc.)*; der ~e Markt the black
market; **2.** *adv.* *(illegal)* illegally;
Schwarz das; ~[es], ~: black

Schwarz·brot das black bread

Schwarze der/die; *adj. Dekl.* Black;
schwärzen *tr. V.* blacken

schwarz-, Schwarz-: ~|fahren
unr. itr. V.; mit sein dodge paying the
fare; ~**fahrer** der fare-dodger;
~**haarig** *Adj.* black-haired; ~**handel** der black market (mit in); *(Tätigkeit)* black marketeering (mit in);
~**markt** der black market; ~**sehen**
unr. itr. V. **a)** *(pessimistisch sein)* look
on the black side; be pessimistic (**für**
about); **b)** *(schwarz fernsehen)* watch
television without a licence; ~**seher**
der **a)** *(ugs.)* pessimist; **b)** *(jmd, der
schwarz fernsieht)* [television] licence
dodger; ~**wald** der; ~[es] Black
Forest; **schwarz·weiß** *Adj.* black
and white; **Schwarzweiß·foto** das
black and white photo; **Schwarz-
wurzel** die black salsify

schwatzen, *(bes. südd.)* **schwätzen**
1. *itr. V.* chat; *(über belanglose Dinge)*
chatter; natter *(coll.)*; **2.** *tr. V.* say; talk
(nonsense, rubbish); **Schwätzer** der;
~s, ~: chatterbox; *(klatschhafter
Mensch)* gossip; **schwatzhaft** *Adj.*
talkative; *(klatschhaft)* gossipy

Schwebe die; in der ~ sein/bleiben
(fig.)/remain in the balance

Schwebe-: ~**bahn** die cableway;
~**balken** der *(Turnen)* [balance] beam

schweben *itr. V.* **a)** *(bird, balloon,
etc.)* hover; *(cloud, balloon, mist)*
hang; in Gefahr ~ *(fig.)* be in danger;
b) *mit sein (durch die Luft)* float

Schwede der; ~n, **Schweden**
(das); ~s Sweden; **Schwedin**
die; ~, ~nen Swede;
schwedisch *Adj.* Swedish

Schwefel der; ~s sulphur

Schweif der; ~[e]s, ~e tail;
schweifen *itr. V.; mit sein (geh.;
auch fig.)* wander

Schweige·geld das hush money

schweigen *unr. itr. V.* remain *or* stay
silent; say nothing; ganz zu ~ von ...:
not to mention ...; **Schweigen** das;
~s silence; **schweigsam** *Adj.* silent;
quiet

Schwein das; ~[e]s, ~e **a)** pig; **b)** *o. Pl.
(Fleisch)* pork; **c)** *(salopp: gemeiner
Mensch)* swine; *(Schmutzfink)* mucky
devil *(coll.)*; mucky pig *(coll.)*; **d)** *(salopp: Mensch)* ein armes ~: a poor
devil; kein ~ war da there wasn't a
bloody *(Brit. sl.) or (coll.)* damn soul
there; **e)** *(ugs.: Glück)* |großes| ~ haben
have a [big] stroke of luck; *(davonkommen)* get away with it *(coll.)*

Schweine-: ~**braten** der roast pork
no indef. art.; ~**fleisch** das pork;
~**kotelett** das *(Kochk.)* pork chop

Schweinerei die; ~, ~en *(ugs.)* **a)**
(Schmutz) mess; **b)** *(Gemeinheit)*
mean *or* dirty trick

Schweine-: ~**schnitzel** das escalope of pork; ~**stall** der *(auch fig.)*
pigsty; pigpen *(Amer.)*

schweinisch *(ugs.) Adj.* **a)** *(schmutzig)* filthy; **b)** *(unanständig)* dirty;
smutty

Schweins·leder das pigskin

Schweiß der; ~es sweat; mir brach
der ~ aus I broke out in a sweat;
Schweiß·brenner der welding
torch; **schweißen** *tr., itr. V.* weld;
Schweißer der; ~s, ~: welder

Schweiß-: ~**fuß** der sweaty foot; ~**perle** die bead of sweat

Schweiz die; ~: Switzerland *no art.;*
Schweizer der; ~s, ~: Swiss;
schweizer·deutsch *Adj.* Swiss
German; **Schweizerin** die; ~, ~nen
Swiss; **schweizerisch** *Adj.* Swiss

schwelen *(auch fig.)* smoulder

schwelgen *itr. V.* feast

Schwelle die; ~, ~n **a)** threshold; **b)**
(Eisenbahn~) sleeper *(Brit.)*; [cross-]
tie *(Amer.)*

schwellen *unr. itr. V.; mit sein* swell;
(limb, face, cheek, etc.), swell [up];
Schwellung die; ~, ~en swelling

Schwemme die; ~, ~n glut (**an** +
Dat. of)

Schwengel der; ~s, ~ **a)** *(Glocken~)*
clapper; **b)** *(Pumpen~)* handle

schwenken 1. *tr. V.* **a)** swing; wave
(flag, handkerchief); **b)** *(spülen)* rinse;

2. *itr. V.; mit sein* 〈*marching column*〉 swing, wheel; 〈*camera*〉 pan; 〈*path, road, car*〉 swing

schwer 1. *Adj.* **a)** heavy; **2** Kilo ~ sein weigh two kilos; **b)** *(mühevoll)* heavy 〈*work*〉; hard, tough 〈*job*〉; hard 〈*day*〉; difficult 〈*birth*〉; es ~/nicht ~ haben have it hard/easy; **c)** *(schlimm)* severe 〈*shock, disappointment, strain, storm*〉; serious, grave 〈*wrong, injustice, error, illness, blow, reservation*〉; serious 〈*accident, injury*〉; heavy 〈*punishment, strain, loss, blow*〉; **2.** *adv.* **a)** heavily 〈*built, laden, armed*〉; ~ tragen be carrying sth. heavy [with difficulty]; **b)** 〈*work*〉 hard; 〈*breathe*〉 heavily; ~ hören be hard of hearing; **c)** *(schwierig)* with difficulty; **d)** *(sehr)* seriously 〈*injured*〉; greatly, deeply 〈*disappointed*〉; 〈*punish*〉 severely, heavily; ~ verunglücken have a serious accident

Schwer-: ~arbeiter der worker engaged in heavy physical work; ~behinderte der/die severely handicapped person; *(körperlich auch)* severely disabled person; die ~behinderten the severely handicapped/disabled; ~beschädigte der/die; *adj. Dekl.* severely disabled person

Schwere die; ~ **a)** weight; **b)** *(Schwerkraft)* gravity; **c)** *s.* schwer 1 c: severity; seriousness; gravity; heaviness; **schwere·los** *Adj.* weightless; **Schwerelosigkeit die;** ~: weightlessness

schwer-, Schwer-: ~fallen *unr. itr. V.; mit sein* jmdm. fällt etw. ~: sb. finds sth. difficult; ~fällig **1.** *Adj.* *(auch fig.)* ponderous; cumbersome 〈*bureaucracy, procedure*〉; **2.** *adv.* ponderously; ~gewicht das **a)** *(Sport)* heavyweight; **b)** *o. Pl. (Schwerpunkt)* main focus; ~hörig *Adj.* hard of hearing *pred.*; ~industrie die heavy industry; ~kraft die; *o. Pl.* gravity; ~krank *Adj.; präd. getrennt geschrieben* seriously ill

schwerlich *Adv.* hardly

schwer-, Schwer-: ~|machen *unr. V.* jmdm./sich etw. ~machen make sth. difficult for sb./oneself; ~metall das heavy metal; ~mütig **1.** *Adj.* melancholic; **2.** *adv.* melancholically; ~|nehmen *unr. tr. V.* take 〈*sth.*〉 seriously; ~punkt der centre of gravity; *(fig.)* main focus; *(Hauptgewicht)* main stress

Schwert das; ~|e|s, ~er sword; **Schwert·lilie die** iris

schwer-, Schwer-: ~|tun *unr. refl. V. (ugs.)* sich mit od. bei etw. ~tun *(ugs.)* have trouble with sth.; ~verbrecher der serious offender; ~verdaulich *Adj.; präd. getrennt geschrieben (auch fig.)* hard to digest *pred.*; ~verletzt *Adj.; präd. getrennt geschrieben* seriously injured; ~wiegend *Adj.* serious; momentous 〈*decision*〉

Schwester die; ~, ~n **a)** sister; **b)** *(Kranken~)* nurse; **schwesterlich 1.** *Adj.* sisterly; **2.** *adv.* ~ handeln act in a sisterly way

schwieg *1. u. 3. Pers. Prät. v.* schweigen

Schwieger-: ~eltern *Pl.* parents-in-law; ~mutter die mother-in-law; ~sohn der son-in-law; ~tochter die daughter-in-law; ~vater der father-in-law

Schwiele die; ~, ~n callus; ~n an den Händen horny hands

schwierig *Adj.* difficult; **Schwierigkeit die;** ~, ~en difficulty

Schwimm-: ~bad das swimming-baths *pl. (Brit.);* swimming-pool; ~becken das swimming-pool

schwimmen 1. *unr. itr. V.* **a)** meist mit sein swim; **b)** meist mit sein *(treiben, nicht untergehen)* float; **c)** *(ugs.: unsicher sein)* be all at sea; ins Schwimmen geraten start to flounder; **2.** *unr. tr. V.; auch mit sein* swim; **Schwimmen das;** ~: swimming *no art.;* **Schwimmer der;** ~s, ~ **a)** swimmer; **b)** *(Technik)* float

Schwimm-: ~flosse die flipper; ~lehrer der swimming instructor; ~weste die life-jacket

Schwindel der; ~s **a)** dizziness; giddiness; **b)** *(Betrug)* swindle; *(Lüge)* lie; **schwindel·frei** *Adj.* ~ sein have a head for heights; **schwindelig** *s.* schwindlig; **schwindeln** *itr. V.* **a)** *(unpers.)* mich od. mir schwindelt I feel dizzy *or* giddy; **b)** *(lügen)* tell fibs

schwinden *unr. itr. V.; mit sein* fade; 〈*supplies, money*〉 run out; 〈*effect*〉 wear off; 〈*fear, mistrust*〉 lessen; 〈*powers, influence*〉 wane

Schwindler der; ~s, ~ *(Lügner)* liar; *(Betrüger)* swindler; *(Hochstapler)* con man *(coll.)*

schwindlig *Adj.* dizzy; giddy; jmdm. wird es ~: sb. gets dizzy *or* giddy

schwingen 1. *unr. itr. V.* **a)** mit sein swing; **b)** *(vibrieren)* vibrate; **2.** *unr. tr. V.* swing; wave 〈*flag, wand*〉; brandish ⟨*sword, axe, etc.*⟩; **3.** *unr. refl. V.* **sich aufs Pferd/Fahrrad ~**: leap on to one's horse/bicycle; **Schwingung die; ~, ~en a)** swinging; *(Vibration)* vibration; **b)** *(Physik)* oscillation

Schwips der; **~es, ~e** *(ugs.)* **einen ~ haben** be tipsy

schwirren *itr. V.* **mit sein** ⟨*arrow, bullet, etc.*⟩ whiz; ⟨*bird*⟩ whirl; ⟨*insect*⟩ buzz

schwitzen *itr. V. (auch fig.)* sweat

schwor *1. u. 3. Pers. Sg. Prät. v.* **schwören; schwören 1.** *unr. tr., itr. V.* swear ⟨*fidelity, friendship*⟩; swear, take ⟨*oath*⟩; **2.** *unr. itr. V.* swear an/the oath

schwul *Adj. (ugs.)* gay *(coll.)*

schwül *Adj.* sultry; close

Schwule der; *adj. Dekl. (ugs.)* gay *(coll.); (abwertend)* queer *(sl.)*

Schwüle die; **~:** sultriness

schwülstig 1. *Adj.* bombastic; pompous; over-ornate ⟨*art, architecture*⟩; **2.** *adv.* bombastically; pompously

Schwund der; **~[e]s** decrease, drop *(Gen.* in*); (an Interesse)* waning; falling off

Schwung der; **~[e]s, Schwünge a)** *(Bewegung)* swing; **b)** *(Linie)* sweep; **c)** *o. Pl. (Geschwindigkeit)* momentum; **~ holen** build *or* get up momentum; **d)** *o. Pl. (Antrieb)* drive; energy; **e)** *o. Pl. (mitreißende Wirkung)* sparkle; **schwung·haft** *Adj.* thriving; brisk, flourishing ⟨*trade, business*⟩; **schwung·voll a)** lively; **b)** *(kraftvoll)* vigorous; sweeping ⟨*movement, gesture*⟩; bold ⟨*handwriting, line, stroke*⟩; **2.** *adv.* spiritedly; *(kraftvoll)* with great vigour

Schwur der; **~[e]s, Schwüre a)** *(Gelöbnis)* vow; **b)** *(Eid)* oath; **Schwur·ge·richt das** *court with a jury*

sechs *Kardinalz.* six; **Sechs** die; **~, ~en** six

sechs-, Sechs-: ~eck das hexagon; **~eckig** *Adj.* hexagonal; **~fach** *Vervielfältigungsz.* sixfold; **~hundert** *Kardinalz.* six hundred; **~mal** *Adv.* six times

sechst... *Ordinalz.* sixth

sechs·tausend *Kardinalz.* six thousand

sechstel *Bruchz.* sixth; **Sechstel das,** *schweiz. meist* der; **~s, ~:** sixth; **sechstens** *Adv.* sixthly; **sechzehn** *Kardinalz.* sixteen; **sechzig** *Kardinalz.* sixty; **sechzigst...** *Ordinalz.* sixtieth

SED [ɛs|eː'deː] die; **~:** *Abk. (ehem. DDR)* **Sozialistische Einheitspartei Deutschlands** Socialist Unity Party of Germany

¹See der; **~s, ~n** lake; **²See** die; **~:** die **~:** the sea; **an die ~ fahren** go to the seaside; **auf hoher ~:** on the high seas

See-: ~bad das seaside health resort; **~fahrt** die *o. Pl.* seafaring *no art.;* sea travel *no art.;* **~gang** der; *o. Pl.* leichter/starker *od.* hoher *od.* schwerer **~gang** light/heavy *or* rough sea; **~hund** der [common] seal; *(Pelz)* seal[skin]; **~igel** der sea-urchin; **~krank** *Adj.* seasick; **~krankheit die;** *o. Pl.* seasickness; **~lachs der** pollack

Seele die; **~, ~n** soul; *(Psyche)* mind; **seelen·ruhig 1.** *Adj.* calm; **2.** *adv.* calmly; **seelisch 1.** *Adj.* psychological ⟨*cause, damage, tension*⟩; mental ⟨*equilibrium, breakdown, illness, health*⟩; **2.** *adv.* **~ bedingt** sein have psychological causes; **~ krank** mentally ill; **Seel·sorge** die; *o. Pl.* pastoral care; **Seelsorger** der; **~s, ~:** pastoral worker; *(Geistlicher)* pastor

See-: ~macht die sea power; **~mann** der; *Pl.* **~leute** seaman; sailor; **~meile** die nautical mile; **~not** die; *o. Pl.* distress [at sea]; **in ~ geraten** get into difficulties *pl.;* **~pferd[chen] das** sea-horse; **~räuber** der pirate; **~reise** die voyage; *(Kreuzfahrt)* cruise; **~rose** die waterlily; **~stern** der starfish; **~tüchtig** *Adj.* seaworthy; **~zunge** die sole

Segel das; ~s, ~: sail

Segel-: ~boot das sailing-boat; **~flieger** der glider pilot; **~flugzeug das** glider

segeln *itr. V.; mit sein* sail

Segel-: ~schiff das sailing ship; **~tuch das** sailcloth

Segen der; **~s, ~:** blessing; *(Gebet in der Messe)* benediction

Segler der; **~s, ~:** yachtsman

segnen *tr. V.* bless

sehen 1. *unr. itr. V.* **a)** see; **schlecht/gut ~:** have bad/good eyesight; **mal ~, wir wollen** *od.* **werden ~** *(ugs.)* we'll see; **siehst!** *(ugs.)* there, you see!; **b)** *(hin~)* look **(auf** + *Akk.* at); **sieh mal** *od.* **doch!** look!; **siehe da!** lo and behold!; **2.** *unr. tr. V.* **a)** *(auch fig.)* see; **jmdn./etw. [nicht] zu ~ bekommen** [not] get to see sb./sth.; **ich habe ihn kommen** *|gel~|:* I saw him coming; **b)** *(an~)* watch ⟨*television programme*⟩;

sehens·wert *Adj.* worth seeing *postpos.*; **Sehens·würdigkeit die;** ~, ~en sight; **Seher der;** ~s, ~: seer; prophet; **Seh·fehler der** sight defect
Sehne die; ~, ~n a) tendon; b) *(Bogen~)* string
sehnen *refl. V.* sich nach jmdm./etw. ~: long *or* yearn for sb./sth.
sehnig *Adj.* a) stringy *(meat)*; b) *(kräftig)* sinewy *(figure, legs, etc.)*
sehnlichst 1. *Adj.* das ist mein ~es Verlangen/mein ~er Wunsch that's what I long for most/that's my dearest wish; 2. *adv.* etw. ~ herbeiwünschen look forward longingly to sth.; **Sehn·sucht die** longing; ~ nach jmdm. haben long to see sb.; **sehn·süchtig** *Adj.* longing *attrib.*, yearning *attrib.* *(desire, look, gaze, etc.)*
sehr *Adv.* a) mit *Adj. u. Adv.* very; ~ viel a great deal; jmdn. ~ gern haben like sb. a lot *(coll.)* *or* a great deal; b) mit *Verben* very much; greatly; danke ~! thank you *or* thanks [very much]; bitte ~, Ihr Steak! here's your steak, sir/madam
Seh·test der eye test
sei *1. u. 3. Pers. Sg. Präsens Konjunktiv u. Imperativ Sg. v.* sein
seicht 1. *Adj.* *(auch fig.)* shallow; 2. *adv.* *(fig.)* shallowly
seid *2. Pers. Pl. Präsens u. Imperativ Pl. v.* sein
Seide die; ~, ~n silk
Seidel das; ~s, ~: beer-mug
seiden *Adj.; nicht präd.* silk; **Seiden·papier das** tissue paper; **seidig** 1. *Adj.* silky; 2. *adv.* silkily
Seife die; ~, ~n soap
Seifen-: ~blase die soap bubble; ~schale die soap-dish; ~schaum der; *o. Pl.* lather
Seil das; ~s, ~e rope; *(Draht~)* cable
Seil-: ~bahn die cableway; ~tänzer der tightrope-walker; ~winde die cable winch
¹sein *unr. itr. V.* be; *(existieren)* be; exist; *(sich ereignen)* be; happen; wie dem auch sei be that as it may; ist Schwede/Lehrer he is Swedish *or* a Swede/a teacher; bist du es? is that you?; mir ist kalt/besser I am *or* feel cold/better; mir ist schlecht I feel sick; drei und vier ist *od.* (ugs.) sind sieben three and four is *or* makes seven; es ist drei Uhr/Mai/Winter it is three o'clock/May/winter; er ist aus Berlin he is *or* comes from Berlin; was

darf es ~? *(im Geschäft)* what can I get you?; es war einmal ein Prinz once upon a time there was a prince; 2. *mod. V.* *(in der Funktion von* können/ müssen + *Passiv)* es ist niemand zu sehen there's no one to be seen; das war zu erwarten that was to be expected; die Schmerzen sind kaum zu ertragen the pain is hardly bearable; die Richtlinien sind strengstens zu beachten the guidelines are to be strictly followed; 3. *Hilfsverb* a) *(zur Bildung des Perfekts usw. im Aktiv)* have; er ist gestorben he has died; b) *(zur Bildung des Perfekts usw. im Passiv und des Zustandspassivs)* be; wir sind gerettet worden/wir waren gerettet we were saved
²sein *Possessivpron.* *(einer männlichen Person)* his; *(einer weiblichen Person)* her; *(einer Sache, eines Tiers)* its; *(nach* man*)* one's; his *(Amer.)*
seiner *(geh.)* *Gen. von* er: sich ~ erbarmen have pity on him; ~ gedenken remember him
seiner-: ~seits *Adv.* for his part; *(von ihm)* on his part; ~zeit *Adv.* at that time
seines·gleichen *indekl. Pron.* his own kind
seinet·wegen *Adv. s.* meinetwegen: because of him; for his sake; about him; as far as he is concerned
Seismo·graph der; ~en, ~en seismograph
seit 1. *Präp. mit Dat.* *(Zeitpunkt)* since; *(Zeitspanne)* for; ich bin ~ zwei Wochen hier I've been here [for] two weeks; 2. *Konj.* since; ~ du hier wohnst since you have been living here; seit·dem 1. *Adv.* since then; 2. *Konj. s.* seit 2
Seite die; ~, ~n a) side; zur *od.* auf die ~ gehen move aside *or* to one side; ~ an ~: side by side; jmdm. zur ~ stehen stand by sb.; von allen ~n *(auch fig.)* from all sides; nach allen ~n in all directions; *(fig.)* on all sides; b) *(Buch-, Zeitungs~)* page
Seiten-: ~ansicht die side view; ~hieb der *(fig.)* side-swipe *(auf +* Akk. at); ~ruder das *(Flugw.)* rudder
seitens *Präp. mit Gen.* *(Papierdt.)* on the part of
Seiten-: ~sprung der infidelity; ~straße die side-street; ~wind der; *o. Pl.* side wind; cross-wind; ~zahl die a) page number; b) *(Anzahl der Seiten)* number of pages

seit·her *Adv.* since then

seitlich 1. *Adj.* at the side *(postpos.)*; 2. *adv. (an der Seite)* at the side; *(von der Seite)* from the side; *(nach der Seite)* to the side; **seit·wärts** *Adv.* sideways

Sekretär der; ~s, ~e a) secretary; b) *(Schreibschrank)* bureau *(Brit.)*; **Sekretariat** das; ~[e]s, ~e [secretary's/secretaries'] office; **Sekretärin** die; ~, ~nen secretary

Sekt der; ~[e]s, ~e high-quality sparkling wine; ≈ champagne

Sekte die; ~, ~n sect

sekundär 1. *Adj.* secondary; 2. *adv.* secondarily; **Sekunde** die; ~, ~n a) *(auch Math., Musik)* second; b) *(ugs.: Augenblick)* second; moment; **Sekunden·zeiger** der second hand

selb... *Demonstrativpron.* same; **selber** *indekl. Demonstrativpron. s.* **selbst** 1; **selbst** 1. *indekl. Demonstrativpron.* myself / yourself / himself / herself / itself / ourselves / yourselves / themselves; **von ~:** automatically; 2. *Adv.* even

Selbst·achtung die self-respect

selb·ständig 1. *Adj.* independent; self-employed *(business man, tradesman, etc.)*; **sich ~ machen** set up on one's own; 2. *adv.* independently; ~ **denken** think for oneself; **Selbständigkeit** die; ~: independence

selbst-, Selbst-: ~**auslöser** der *(Fot.)* delayed-action shutter release; ~**bedienung** die self-service *no art.*; ~**befriedigung** die masturbation *no art.*; ~**beherrschung** die self-control *no art.*; ~**bewußt** 1. *Adj.* self-confident; 2. *adv.* self-confidently; ~**bewußtsein** das self-confidence *no art.*; ~**erkenntnis** die; *o. Pl.* self-knowledge *no art.*; ~**gefällig** 1. *Adj.* self-satisfied; smug; 2. *adv.* smugly; ~**gefälligkeit** die; *o. Pl.* self-satisfaction; smugness; ~**gemacht** *Adj.* home-made; ~**gespräch** das conversation with oneself; ~**los** 1. *Adj.* selfless; 2. *adv.* selflessly; unselfishly; ~**mord** der suicide *no art.*; ~**mörder** der suicide; ~**sicher** 1. *Adj.* self-confident; 2. *adv.* in a self-confident manner; ~**süchtig** 1. *Adj.* selfish; 2. *adv.* selfishly; ~**tätig** 1. *Adj.* automatic; 2. *adv.* automatically; ~**verständlich** 1. *Adj.* natural; **etw. für ~verständlich halten** regard sth. as a matter of course; *(für gegeben hinnehmen)* take sth. for granted; 2. *adv.*

naturally; of course; ~**vertrauen** das self-confidence; ~**verwaltung** die self-government *no art.*; ~**zweck** der; *o. Pl.* end in itself

selig 1. *Adj.* a) *(Rel.)* blessed; b) *(tot)* late [lamented]; c) *(glücklich)* blissful *(idleness, slumber, etc.)*; blissfully happy *(person)*; 2. *adv.* blissfully; **Seligkeit** die; ~, ~en bliss *no pl.*; [blissful] happiness *no pl.*

Sellerie der; ~s, ~[s] *od.* die; ~, ~: celeriac; *(Stangen~)* celery

selten 1. *Adj.* rare; infrequent *(visit, visitor)*; 2. *adv.* a) rarely; b) *(sehr)* exceptionally; uncommonly; **Seltenheit** die; ~, ~en rarity; **Seltenheits·wert** der; ~[e]s rarity value

Selters·wasser das seltzer [water]

seltsam 1. *Adj.* strange; odd; 2. *adv.* strangely

Semester das; ~s, ~: semester

Semikolon das; ~s, ~s semicolon

Seminar das; ~s, ~e a) seminar *(über + Akk.* on); b) *(Institut)* department

Semmel die; ~, ~n *(bes. österr., bayr., ostmd.)* [bread] roll; **Semmel·knödel** der *(bayr., österr.)* bread dumpling

Senat der; ~[e]s, ~e senate; **Senator** der; ~s, ~en

¹**senden** *unr. (auch regelm.) tr. V. (geh.)* send

²**senden** *regelm. (schweiz. unr.) tr., itr. V.* broadcast *(programme, play, etc.)*; transmit *(signals, Morse, etc.)*; **Sender** der; ~s, ~: [broadcasting] station; *(Anlage)* transmitter

Sende-: ~**reihe** die series [of programmes]; ~**schluß** der close-down

Sendung die; ~, ~en a) consignment; b) *(Rundf., Ferns.)* programme

Senf der; ~[e]s, ~e mustard

senior *indekl. Adj.; nach Personennamen* senior; **Senior** der; ~s, ~en a) *(Kaufmannsspr.)* senior partner; b) *(Sport)* senior [player]; c) *(Rentner)* senior citizen; **Senioren·heim** das home for the elderly

Senke die; ~, ~n hollow; **senken** 1. *tr. V.* lower; 2. *refl. V. (curtain, barrier, etc.)* fall, come down; *(ground, building, road)* subside, sink; *(water-level)* fall, sink

senk-, Senk-: ~**fuß** der flat foot; ~**recht** 1. *Adj.* vertical; ~ **zu etw.** perpendicular to sth.; 2. *adv.* vertically; ~**rechte** die vertical; *(Geom.: Gerade)* perpendicular

Sensation die; ~, ~en sensation;

sensationell 1. *Adj.* sensational; 2. *adv.* sensationally

Sense die; ~, ~n scythe

sensibel 1. *Adj.* sensitive; 2. *adv.* sensitively; **Sensibilität** die; ~: sensitivity

sentimental 1. *Adj.* sentimental; 2. *adv.* sentimentally; **Sentimentalität** die; ~, ~en sentimentality

separat 1. *Adj.* separate; self-contained *(flat etc.)*; 2. *adv.* separately

September der; ~[s], ~: September

Serbe der; ~n, ~n Serb; Serbian; **Serbien (das)**; ~s Serbia; **serbisch** *Adj.* Serbian

Serenade die; ~, ~n serenade

Serie die; ~, ~n series; **serien·mä·ßig** 1. *Adj.* standard *(product, model, etc.)*; 2. *adv.* a) ~ gefertigt *od.* gebaut produced in series; b) *(nicht als Sonderausstattung)* *(fitted, supplied, etc.)* as standard

seriös *Adj.* respectable *(person, hotel, etc.)*; trustworthy *(firm, partner, etc.)*; serious *(offer, applicant, artist, etc.)*

Serpentine die; ~, ~n hairpin bend

Serum das; ~s, **Seren** serum

¹Service [zɛr'viːs] das; ~, ~: [dinner etc.] service; **²Service** ['zøːɐvis] der; ~, ~s ['zøːɐvisis] *(Bedienung, Kundendienst)* service; **servieren** *tr. V.* serve; **Serviererin** die; ~, ~nen waitress; **Serviette** [zɛr'vi̯ɛt̯ə] die; ~, ~n napkin; serviette *(Brit.)*

Servo·lenkung die power [-assisted] steering *no indef. art.*

Sesam der; ~s sesame seeds *pl.*

Sessel der; ~s, ~ a) armchair; b) *(österr.: Stuhl)* chair; **Sessel·lift** der chair-lift

seßhaft *Adj.* settled; ~ werden settle down

setzen 1. *refl. V.* a) sit [down]; setzen Sie sich sit down; take a seat; sich aufs Sofa *usw.* ~: sit on the sofa *etc.*; b) *(coffee, froth, etc.)* settle; *(sediment, etc.)* sink to the bottom; 2. *tr. V.* a) put; b) *(einpflanzen)* plant *(tomatoes, potatoes, etc.)*; c) *(aufziehen)* hoist *(flag etc.)*; set *(sails, navigation lights)*; d) *(Druckw.)* set *(manuscript etc.)*; 3. *itr. V.* a) *meist mit sein (springen)* leap, jump; b) über einen Fluß ~ *(mit einer Fähre o. ä.)* cross a river; c) *(beim Wetten)* bet; auf ein Pferd/auf Rot ~: back a horse/put one's money on red;

Setzer der; ~s, ~, **Setzerin** die; ~, ~nen *(Druckw.)* [type]setter; **Setzling** der; ~s, ~e seedling

Seuche die; ~, ~n epidemic

seufzen *itr., tr. V.* sigh; **Seufzer** der; ~s, ~: sigh

Sex der; ~[es] sex *no art.*; **Sexualität** die; ~: sexuality *no art.*; **sexuell** 1. *Adj.* sexual; 2. *adv.* sexually

sezieren *tr. V.* dissect *(corpse)*

sfr., *(schweiz. nur:)* **sFr.** *Abk.* Schweizer Franken

Shampoo [ʃam'puː], **Shampoon** [ʃam'poːn] das; ~s, ~s shampoo

Sherry ['ʃɛri] der; ~s, ~s sherry

Show [ʃoʊ] die; ~, ~s show

siamesisch *Adj.* Siamese; **Si·am·katze** die Siamese cat

Sibirien (das); ~s Siberia

sich *Reflexivpron. der 3. Pers. Sg. und Pl. Akk. und Dat.* a) himself/herself/itself/themselves; *(auf man bezogen)* oneself; *(auf das Anredepronomen Sie bezogen)* yourself/yourselves; ~ **freuen/wundern/schämen/täuschen** be pleased/surprised/ashamed/mistaken; ~ **sorgen** worry; b) *(reziprok)* one another, each other

Sichel die; ~, ~n sickle

sicher 1. *Adj.* a) safe *(road, procedure, etc.)*; secure *(job, investment, etc.)*; b) reliable *(evidence, source)*; certain *(proof)*; reliable, sure *(judgment, taste, etc.)*; c) *(selbstbewußt)* assured *(person, manner)*; d) *(gewiß)* certain; sure; 2. *adv.* a) safely; b) *(zuverlässig)* reliably; ~ [Auto] fahren be a safe driver; c) *(selbstbewußt)* [self-]confidently; 3. *Adv.* certainly; **sicher|gehen** *unr. itr. V.; mit sein* play safe; **Sicherheit** die; ~, ~en a) *o. Pl.* safety; *(der Öffentlichkeit)* security; jmdn./etw. in ~ *[vor etw. (Dat.)]* bringen save *or* rescue sb./sth. [from sth.]; b) *o. Pl. (Gewißheit)* certainty; c) *(Wirtsch.: Bürgschaft)* security

sicherheits-, Sicherheits-: ~**abstand** der *(Verkehrsw.)* safe distance between vehicles; ~**gurt** der seat-belt; ~**halber** *Adv.* to be on the safe side; ~**nadel** die safety-pin; ~**schloß** das safety lock

sicherlich *Adv.* certainly; **sichern** *tr. V.* make *(door etc.)* secure; *(garantieren)* safeguard *(rights, peace)*; *(schützen)* protect *(rights etc.)*; sich *(Dat.)* etw. ~: secure sth.; **sicher|stellen** *tr. V.* a) impound *(goods, vehicle)*; b) guarantee ⟨supply, freedom, etc.⟩; **Sicherung die**; ~, ~en a) o. Pl. safeguarding; ⟨das Schützen⟩ protection; b) (Elektrot.) fuse; c) (techn. Vorrichtung) safety-catch

Sicht die; ~: view ⟨auf + Akk., in + Akk. of⟩; gute od. klare/schlechte ~: good/poor visibility; **sichtbar 1.** Adj. visible; (fig.) apparent ⟨reason⟩; 2. adv. visibly; **sichten** tr. V. sight; **sichtlich 1.** Adj. obvious; evident; 2. adv. obviously; evidently; visibly ⟨impressed⟩

Sicht-: ~verhältnisse Pl. visibility sing.; ~vermerk der visa; ~weite die visibility no art.; außer/in ~weite sein be out of/in sight

sickern itr. V.; mit sein seep; (spärlich fließen) trickle

sie 1. Personalpron.; 3. Pers. Sg. Nom. Fem. she; (betont) her; (bei Dingen, Tieren) it; s. auch ¹ihr; ihrer a.; 2. Personalpron.; 3. Pers. Pl. Nom. they; (betont) them; s. auch ihnen; ihrer b; 3. Akk. von sie 1 her; (bei Dingen, Tieren) it; 4. Akk. von sie 2 a them

Sie Personalpron.; 3. Pers. Pl. Nom. u. Akk; Anrede an eine od. mehrere Personen you; s. auch Ihnen; Ihrer

Sieb das; ~[e]s, ~e sieve; (für Tee) strainer; ¹**sieben** tr. V. a) sieve ⟨flour etc.⟩; riddle ⟨sand, gravel, etc.⟩; b) (auswählen) screen ⟨candidates⟩

²**sieben** Kardinalz. seven; **Sieben die**; ~, ~ od. ~en

sieben-, Sieben-: ~fach Vervielfältigungsz. sevenfold; ~mal Adj. seven times; ~sachen Pl. (ugs.) meine/deine usw. ~sachen my/your etc. belongings or (coll.) bits and pieces

siebt... Ordinalz. seventh; **siebtel** Bruchz. seventh; **Siebtel das**, schweiz. meist der; ~s, ~: seventh; **siebtens** Adv. seventh; **siebzehn** Kardinalz. seventeen; **siebzig** Kardinalz. seventy; **siebzigst...** Ordinalz. seventieth

siedeln itr. V. settle

sieden unr. od. regelm. itr. V. boil; **Siede·punkt** der (auch fig.) boilingpoint

Siedler der; ~s, ~: settler; **Siedlung die**; ~, ~en a) (Wohngebiet) [housing] estate; b) (Niederlassung) settlement

Sieg der; ~[e]s, ~e victory, (bes. Sport) win ⟨über + Akk. over⟩

Siegel das; ~s, ~: seal; (von Behörden) stamp

siegen itr. V. win; über jmdn. ~: gain or win a victory over sb.; (bes. Sport) win against sb.; beat sb.; **Sieger der**; ~s, ~: winner; (Mannschaft) winners pl.; (einer Schlacht) victor; **Siegerehrung die** presentation ceremony; awards ceremony; **sieges·sicher 1.** Adj. confident of victory pred.; 2. adv. confident of victory; **siegreich** Adj. victorious; winning ⟨team⟩; successful ⟨campaign⟩

sieh, siehe Imperativ Sg. v. sehen; **siehst** 2. Pers. Sg. Präsens v. sehen; **sieht** 3. Pers. Sg. Präsens v. sehen

Signal das; ~, ~e signal; **signalisieren** tr. V. indicate ⟨danger, change, etc.⟩

Signatur die; ~, ~en a) initials pl.; (Kürzel) abbreviated signature; (des Künstlers) autograph; b) (Unterschrift) signature; c) (in einer Bibliothek) shelf-mark; **signieren** tr. V. sign; autograph ⟨one's own work⟩

Silbe die; ~, ~n syllable

Silber das; ~s a) silver; b) (silbernes Gerät) silver[ware]; **Silber·medaille die** silver medal; **silbern 1.** Adj. silver; silvery ⟨moonlight, shade, gleam, etc.⟩; 2. adv. ⟨shine, shimmer, etc.⟩ with a silvery lustre; **Silber·papier das** silver paper

Silhouette [zi'lu̯ɛtə] die; ~, ~n silhouette

Silo der od. das; ~s, ~s silo

Silvester der od. das; ~s, ~: New Year's Eve

Simbabwe (das); ~s Zimbabwe

simpel Adj. a) simple ⟨question, task⟩; b) (beschränkt) simple-minded ⟨person⟩; simple ⟨mind⟩; 2. adv. a) simply; b) (beschränkt) in a simpleminded manner; **Simpel der**; ~s, ~ (bes. südd. ugs.) simpleton; fool

Sims der od. das; ~es, ~e ledge; sill; (Kamin~) mantelpiece

Simulant der; ~en, ~en malingerer; **simulieren 1.** tr. V. feign, sham (illness, emotion, etc.); simulate ⟨situation, condition, etc.⟩; 2. itr. V. feign illness

simultan 1. Adj. simultaneous; 2. adv. simultaneously

sind 1. u. 3. Pers. Pl. Präsens v. ¹sein

Sinfonie die; ~, ~n symphony; **Sinfonie·orchester das** symphony orchestra

singen unr. tr., itr. V. sing

Singular der; ~s singular

Sing·vogel der songbird

sinken unr. itr. V.; mit sein a) ⟨ship,

sun) sink, go down; *(plane, balloon)* descend, go down; **b)** *(nieder~)* fall; **c)** *(niedriger werden)* ⟨*temperature, level*⟩ fall, drop; **d)** *(an Wert verlieren; nachlassen; abnehmen)* fall, go down

Sinn der; ~|e|s, ~e **a)** sense; **b)** *Pl. (geh.: Bewußtsein)* senses; mind *sing.*; **nicht bei ~en** sein be out of one's senses *or* mind; **c)** *o. Pl. (Gefühl, Verständnis)* feeling; **d)** *o. Pl. (~gehalt, Bedeutung)* meaning; **e)** *(Ziel u. Zweck)* point; **Sinn·bild** das symbol

Sinnes-: ~**organ** das sense-organ; sensory organ; ~**täuschung** die trick of the senses

sinn·gemäß 1. *Adj.* **eine ~e** Übersetzung a translation which conveys the general sense; **2.** *adv.* **etw.** ~ **übersetzen/wiedergeben** translate the general sense of sth./give the gist of sth.; **sinnlich** *Adj.* sensory *(impression, perception, stimulus)*; sensual *(love, mouth)*; sensuous *(pleasure, passion)*; **Sinnlichkeit** die; ~: sensuality; **sinn·los 1.** *Adj.* **a)** senseless; **b)** *(zwecklos)* pointless; **2.** *adv.* **a)** senselessly; **b)** *(zwecklos)* pointlessly; **Sinnlosigkeit** die; ~ **a)** senselessness; **b)** *(Zwecklosigkeit)* pointlessness; **sinn·voll 1.** *Adj.* **a)** *(vernünftig)* sensible; **b)** *(einen Sinn ergebend)* meaningful; **2.** *adv.* **a)** *(vernünftig)* sensibly; **b)** *(einen Sinn ergebend)* meaningfully

Sint·flut die Flood; Deluge; **sint·flut·artig 1.** *Adj.* torrential; **2.** *adv.* in torrents

Sippe die; ~, ~n **a)** *(Völkerk.)* sib; **b)** *(ugs.: Verwandtschaft)* clan; **Sippschaft** die; ~, ~en *(ugs.)* s. Sippe b

Sirene die; ~, ~n siren

Sirup der; ~s, ~e syrup

Sitte die; ~, ~n **a)** *(Brauch)* custom; tradition; **b)** *(moralische Norm)* common decency; **c)** *Pl. (Benehmen)* manners; **sittlich 1.** *Adj.* moral; **2.** *adv.* morally; **Sittlichkeit** die; *o. Pl.* morality

Sittlichkeits-: ~**verbrechen** das sexual crime; ~**verbrecher** der sex offender

Situation die; ~, ~en situation

Sitz der; ~es, ~e **a)** seat; **b)** *(Verwaltungs~)* headquarters *sing. or pl.*; **c)** *(von Kleidungsstücken)* fit

sitzen unr. itr. V.; *südd., österr., schweiz. mit* sein **a)** sit; **b)** *(sein)* be; **c)** *([gut] passen)* fit

sitzen-: ~|**bleiben** unr. itr. V. *(ugs.)*

a) *(nicht versetzt werden)* stay down [a year]; **b)** *(unverheiratet bleiben)* be left on the shelf; **c)** **auf etw.** *(Dat.)* ~|**bleiben** *(für etw. keinen Käufer finden)* be left *or (coll.)* stuck with sth.; ~|**lassen** unr. tr. V. *(ugs.)* **a)** *(nicht heiraten)* jilt; **b)** *(im Stich lassen)* leave in the lurch; **c) etw. nicht auf sich** *(Dat.)* ~**lassen** not take sth.

Sitzplatz der seat; **Sitzung** die; ~, ~en meeting; *(Parlaments~)* sitting; session; **Sitzungs·saal** der conference hall

Skala die; ~, Skalen scale

Skalp der; ~s, ~e scalp

Skalpell das; ~s, ~e scalpel

skalpieren tr. V. scalp

Skandal der; ~s, ~e scandal; **skandalös** *Adj.* scandalous

Skandinavien *(das)*; ~s Scandinavia; **Skandinavier** der; ~s, ~: Scandinavian; **skandinavisch** *Adj.* Scandinavian

Skat der; ~|e|s, ~e *od.* ~s skat

Skelett das; ~|e|s, ~e skeleton

Skepsis die; ~: scepticism; **skeptisch 1.** *Adj.* sceptical; **2.** *adv.* sceptically

Ski [ʃiː] der; ~s, ~er *od.* ~: ski; ~ **laufen** *od.* **fahren** ski

Ski-: ~**läufer** der skier; ~**lehrer** der ski-instructor; ~**lift** der ski-lift; ~**springen** das; ~s ski-jumping *no art.*

Skizze die; ~, ~n sketch; **Skizzen·block** der sketch-pad; **skizzieren** tr. V. sketch

Sklave der; ~n, ~n slave; **Sklaven·händler** der slave-trader; **Sklaverei** die; ~: slavery *no art.*; **Sklavin** die; ~, ~nen slave; **sklavisch 1.** *Adj.* slavish; **2.** *adv.* slavishly

Skonto der *od.* das; ~s, ~s *(Kaufmannsspr.)* [cash] discount

Skorbut der; ~|e|s scurvy *no art.*

Skorpion der; ~s, ~e scorpion

Skrupel der; ~s, ~: scruple; **skrupel·los 1.** *Adj.* unscrupulous; **2.** *adv.* unscrupulously; **Skrupellosigkeit** die; ~: unscrupulousness

Skulptur die; ~, ~en sculpture

Slalom der; ~s, ~s slalom

Slawe der; ~n, ~n Slav; **slawisch** *Adj.* Slav[ic]; Slavonic

Slip der; ~s, ~s briefs *pl.*

Slowake der; ~n, ~n Slovak; **Slowakei** die; ~: Slovakia *no art.*

Smaragd der; ~|e|s, ~e emerald

Smoking der; ~s, ~s dinner-jacket or (Amer.) tuxedo and dark trousers

so 1. *Adv.* a) *(auf diese Weise; in, von dieser Art)* like this/that; this/that way; **weiter so!** carry on in the same way!; b) *(dermaßen, überaus)* so; c) *(genauso)* as; **so gut ich konnte** as best I could; d) *(ugs.: solch)* such; **so ein Idiot!** what an idiot!; **so einer/eine/ eins** one like that; e) *betont (eine Zäsur ausdrückend)* right; OK *(coll.)*; g) *(ugs.: schätzungsweise)* about; 2. *Konj.* **so daß** ... *(damit)* so that ...; *(und deshalb)* and so ...; 3. *Partikel* a) *just*; **ach, das hab' ich nur so gesagt** oh, I didn't mean anything by that; b) *(in Aufforderungssätzen verstärkend)* **so komm doch** come on now

So. *Abk.* Sonntag Sun.

s. o. *Abk.* siehe oben

sobald *Konj.* as soon as

Socke die; ~, ~n sock

Sockel der; ~s, ~ a) *(einer Säule, Statue)* plinth; b) *(unterer Teil eines Hauses, Schrankes)* base

Soda·wasser das; *Pl.* Sodawässer soda; soda-water

Sod·brennen das; ~s heartburn

so·eben *Adv.* just

Sofa das; ~s, ~s sofa; settee

so·fern *Konj.* provided [that]

soff 1. u. 3. Pers. Sg. Prät. v. saufen

so·fort *Adv.* immediately; at once; **sofortig** *Adj. (unmittelbar)* immediate

sog 1. u. 3. Pers. Sg. Prät. v. saugen; **Sog** der; ~[e]s, ~e suction; *(bei Schiffen)* wake; *(bei Fahr-, Flugzeugen)* slip-stream; *(von Wasser, auch fig.)* current

so·gar *Adv.* even

so·genannt *Adj.* so-called

so·gleich *Adv.* immediately; at once

Sohle die; ~, ~n a) *(Schuh~)* sole; *(Einlege~)* insole; b) *(Fuß~)* sole [of the foot]

Sohn der; ~es, Söhne son

Soja-: **~bohne** die soy[a] bean; **~so-ße** die soy[a] sauce

so·lang[e] *Konj.* so or as long as

Solarium das; ~s, Solarien solarium

solch *Demonstrativpron.* a) *attr.* such; **das macht ~en Spaß** it's so much fun!; b) *alleinstehend* **~e wie die** people like that

Sold der; ~[e]s, ~e [military] pay

Soldat der; ~en, ~en soldier; **Solda-ten·friedhof** der military or war cemetery; **Soldatin** die; ~, ~nen [fe-male or woman] soldier; **soldatisch** 1. *Adj.* military *(discipline, expression, etc.)*; soldierly *(figure, virtue)*; 2. *adv.* in a military manner

Söldner der; ~s, ~: mercenary

solidarisch 1. *Adj.* ~es Verhalten zeigen show one's solidarity; 2. *adv.* ~ **handeln/sich ~ verhalten** act in/show solidarity; **solidarisieren** *refl. V.* show [one's] solidarity; **Solidarität** die; ~: solidarity

solide 1. *Adj.* a) solid; sturdy *(shoes, material)*; [good-]quality *(goods)*; b) *(gut fundiert)* sound *(work, education, knowledge)*; solid *(firm)*; c) *(anstän-dig)* respectable *(person, life, pro-fession)*; 2. *adv.* a) solidly *(built)*; sturdily *(made)*; b) *(gut fundiert)* soundly *(educated, constructed)*; c) *(anständig)* *(live)* respectably, steadily

Solist der; ~en, ~en soloist

Soll das; ~[s], ~[s] a) *(Bankw.)* debit; b) *(Arbeits~)* quota; **sein ~ erfüllen** od. **erreichen** achieve one's target

sollen 1. *unr. Modalverb;* 2. *Part.* ~ a) *(bei Aufforderung, Anweisung, Auf-trag)* **was soll ich als nächstes tun?** what should I do next?; |**sagen Sie ihm,| er soll bald hereinkommen** tell him to come in; b) *(bei Wunsch, Absicht, Vor-haben)* **das sollte ein Witz sein** that was meant to be a joke; **was soll denn das heißen?** what is that supposed to mean?; c) *(bei Ratlosigkeit)* **was soll ich nur machen?** what am I to do?; d) *(Notwendigkeit ausdrückend)* **man soll so etwas nicht unterschätzen** it shouldn't be taken so lightly; e) *häu-fig im Konjunktiv II (Erwartung, Wün-schenswertes ausdrückend)* **du solltest dich schämen** you ought to be ashamed of yourself; **das hättest du besser nicht tun ~:** it would have been better if you hadn't done that; f) *(jmdm. beschieden sein)* **er sollte seine Heimat nicht wiedersehen** he was never to see his homeland again; g) *im Konjunktiv II (eine Möglichkeit aus-drückend)* **wenn du ihn sehen solltest, sage ihm bitte ...:** if you should see him, please tell him ...; h) *im Präsens (sich für die Wahrheit nicht verbür-gend)* **das Restaurant soll sehr teuer sein** the restaurant is supposed or said to be very expensive; i) *im Konjunktiv II (Zweifel ausdrückend)* **sollte das sein Ernst sein?** is he really being ser-ious?; j) *(können)* **mir soll es gleich sein** it's all the same to me; 2. *tr., itr.*

V. **was soll das?** what's the idea?; **was soll ich dort?** what would I do there?

Solo das; ~s, ~s *od.* **Soli** solo

so·mit [auch: '--] *Adv.* consequently; therefore

Sommer der; ~s, ~: summer

Sommer·ferien *Pl.* summer holidays; **sommerlich** 1. *Adj.* summer; summery ⟨*warmth, weather*⟩; summer's *attrib.* ⟨*day, evening*⟩; 2. *adv.* es **war** ~ **warm** it was as warm as summer

sommer-, Sommer-: **~reifen** der standard tyre; **~schluß·verkauf** der summer sale/sales; **~sprosse** die freckle; **~sprossig** *Adj.* freckled; **~zeit** die ⟨*Uhrzeit*⟩ summer time

Sonate die; ~, **~n** ⟨*Musik*⟩ sonata

Sonde die; ~, **~n** probe; ⟨*zur Ernährung*⟩ tube

Sonder·angebot das special offer; **sonderbar** 1. *Adj.* strange; odd; 2. *adv.* strangely; oddly; **Sonder·fall** der special case

sonder·gleichen *Adv.*, *nachgestellt* **eine Frechheit/Unverschämtheit ~:** the height of cheek/impudence

sonderlich *Adv.* particularly; **Sonderling** der; ~s, **~e** strange *or* odd person; **Sonder·müll** der hazardous waste

¹**sondern** *tr. V.* ⟨*geh.*⟩ separate ⟨*von* from⟩

²**sondern** *Konj.* but; **nicht nur ..., ~ [auch] ...:** not only ... but also ...

Sonder-: **~schule** die special school; **~zug** der special train

sondieren *tr. V.* sound out

Sonett das; ~[e]s, **~e** sonnet

Sonn·abend der ⟨*bes. nordd.*⟩ Saturday; **sonn·abends** *Adv.* on Saturday[s]

Sonne die; ~, **~n** sun; ⟨*Licht der* ~⟩ sun[light]; **sonnen** *refl. V.* sun oneself

sonnen-, Sonnen-: **~aufgang** der sunrise; **~baden** *itr. V.* sunbathe; **~blume** die sunflower; **~brand** der sunburn *no indef. art.*; **~brille** die sun-glasses *pl.*; **~energie** die solar energy; **~finsternis** die solar eclipse; **~hut** der sun-hat; **~licht** das sunlight; **~öl** das sun-oil; **~schein** der *o. Pl.* sunshine; **~schirm** der sunshade; **~stich** der sunstroke *no indef. art.*; **~strahl** der the ray of sun[shine]; **~uhr** die sundial; **~untergang** der sunset

sonnig *Adj.* sunny

Sonn·tag der Sunday; **sonn·täg-lich** 1. *Adj.* Sunday *attrib.*; 2. *adv.* **~ gekleidet** dressed in one's Sunday best; **sonntags** *Adv.* on Sunday[s]

sonst *Adv.* a) der ~ **so freundliche Mann ...:** the man, who is/was usually so friendly, ...; **alles war wie ~:** everything was [the same] as usual; ~ **noch was?** ⟨*ugs., auch iron.*⟩ anything else?; **wer/was/wie/wo [denn] ~?** who/what/how/where else?; b) ⟨*andernfalls*⟩ otherwise; or; **sonstig...** *Adj.*; *nicht präd.* other; further

sonst-: **~was** *Indefinitpron.* ⟨*ugs.*⟩ anything else; **~wer** *Indefinitpron.* ⟨*ugs.*⟩ somebody else; ⟨*fragend, verneinend*⟩ anybody else; **~wo** *Adv.* ⟨*ugs.*⟩ somewhere else; ⟨*fragend, verneinend*⟩ anywhere else

so·oft *Konj.* whenever

Sopran der; ~s, **~e** ⟨*Musik*⟩ soprano ⟨*im Chor*⟩ sopranos *pl.*; **Sopranistin** die; ~, **~nen** soprano

Sorge die; ~, **~n** worry; **keine ~!** don't [you] worry!; **sorgen** 1. *refl. V.* worry ⟨**um** about⟩; 2. *itr. V.* **für jmdn./ etw. ~:** take care of sb./sth.

sorgen-, Sorgen-: **~frei** 1. *Adj.* carefree; 2. *adv.* **~frei leben** live in a carefree manner; **~kind** das ⟨*auch fig.*⟩ problem child; **~voll** 1. *Adj.* worried; 2. *adv.* worriedly

Sorg·falt die; ~: care; **sorg·fältig** 1. *Adj.* careful; 2. *adv.* carefully

sorg·los 1. *Adj.* a) ⟨*ohne Sorgfalt*⟩ careless; b) ⟨*unbekümmert*⟩ carefree; 2. *adv.* **~ mit etw. umgehen** treat sth. carelessly; **Sorglosigkeit** die; ~ a) ⟨*Mangel an Sorgfalt*⟩ carelessness; b) ⟨*Unbekümmertheit*⟩ carefreeness; **sorgsam** 1. *Adj.* careful; 2. *adv.* carefully

Sorte die; ~, **~n** a) sort; type; kind; b) *Pl.* ⟨*Devisen*⟩ foreign currency *sing.*

sortieren *tr. V.* sort [out] ⟨*pictures, letters, washing, etc.*⟩; grade ⟨*goods etc.*⟩

Sortiment das; ~[e]s, **~e** range ⟨**an** + *Dat.* of⟩

so·sehr *Konj.* however much

Soße die; ~, **~n** sauce; ⟨*Braten~*⟩ gravy; sauce; ⟨*Salat~*⟩ dressing

sott *1. u. 3. Pers. Sg. Prät. v.* sieden

Souffleur [zu'flø:ɐ̯] der; ~s, **~e**, **Souffleuse** [zu'flø:zə] die; ~, **~n** prompter; **soufflieren** [zu'fli:rən] *tr. V.* prompt

Souvenir [suvə'ni:ɐ̯] das; ~s, **~s** souvenir

souverän [zuvə'rɛ:n] *Adj.* sovereign; **Souveränität** die; ~: sovereignty

so·viel 1. *Konj.* as *or* so far as; 2. *Indefinitpron.* ~ *wie od.* **als** as much as; **halb/doppelt** ~: half/twice as much

so·weit 1. *Konj.* a) as *or* so far as; b) *(in dem Maße, wie)* [in] so far as; 2. *Adv.* by and large; *(bis jetzt)* up to now; ~ **sein** *(ugs.)* be ready

so·wenig *Indefinitpron.* ~ *wie od.* **als** möglich as little as possible

so·wie *Konj.* a) *(und)* as well as; b) *(sobald)* as soon as

so·wie·so *Adv.* anyway

sowjetisch *Adj.* Soviet

Sowjet·union die *(1922–1991)* Soviet Union

so·wohl *Konj.* ~ ... **als** *od.* **wie** [auch]...: both ... and ...; ... as well as ...

sozial 1. *Adj.* social; 2. *adv.* socially

sozial-, Sozial-: ~**abgaben** *Pl.* social welfare contributions; ~**arbeiter der** social worker; ~**demokrat der** Social Democrat; ~**demokratisch** *Adj.* social democratic; ~**hilfe die** social welfare

Sozialismus der; ~: socialism *no art.*; **Sozialist der;** ~en, ~en, **Sozialistin die;** ~, ~nen socialist; **sozialistisch** 1. *Adj.* socialist; 2. ~ **regierte** Länder countries with socialist governments

Sozial-: ~**politik die** social policy; ~**produkt das** *(Wirtsch.)* national product; ~**staat der** welfare state

Soziologe der; ~n, ~n sociologist; **Soziologie die;** ~: sociology; **soziologisch** 1. *Adj.* sociological; 2. *adv.* sociologically

Sozius der; ~, ~se a) *Pl. auch:* **Sozii** *(Wirtsch.: Teilhaber)* partner; b) *(beim Motorrad)* pillion

so·zu·sagen *Adv.* as it were

Spachtel der; ~s, ~ *od.* **die;** ~, ~n putty-knife; *(zum Malen)* palette-knife; **spachteln** *tr. V.* a) stop, fill *(hole, crack, etc.)*; smooth over *(wall, panel, surface, etc.)*; b) *(ugs.: essen)* put away *(coll.)* *(food, meal)*

Spagat der *od.* **das;** ~[e]s, ~e splits *pl.*

Spaghetti *Pl.* spaghetti *sing.*

spähen *itr. V.* peer; *(durch ein Loch, eine Ritze usw.)* peep; **Späher der;** ~s, ~ *(Milit.)* scout; *(Posten)* lookout; *(Spitzel)* informer

Spalier das; ~s, ~e a) trellis; b) *(Ehren~)* guard of honour; ~ **stehen** line the route; *(soldiers)* form a guard of honour

Spalt der; ~[e]s, ~e opening; *(im Fels)* fissure; crevice; *(zwischen Vorhängen)*

chink; gap; *(langer Riß)* crack; **Spalte die;** ~, ~n a) crack; *(Fels~)* crevice b) *(Druckw.)* column; **spalten** *unr.* *(auch regelm.)* *tr., refl. V.* split

Span der; ~[e]s, **Späne** *(Hobel~)* shaving

Span·ferkel das sucking pig

Spange die; ~, ~n clasp; *(Haar~)* hair-slide *(Brit.)*; barrette *(Amer.)*; *(Arm~)* bracelet; bangle

Spaniel ['ʃpa:njəl] der; ~s, ~s spaniel

Spanien ['ʃpa:njən] *(das)*; ~s Spain; **Spanier der;** ~s, ~: Spaniard; **spanisch** *Adj.* Spanish

Spann·korb der chip basket; chip

spann *1. u. 3. P. Sing. Prät. v.* spinnen

spannen 1. *tr. V.* a) tighten *(violin string, violin bow, etc.)*; draw *(bow)*; tension *(spring, tennis net, drumhead, saw-blade)*; stretch *(fabric, shoe, etc.)*; draw *or* pull *(line)* tight *or* taut; flex *(muscle)*; cock *(gun, camera shutter)*; b) *(befestigen)* put up *(washing-line)*; stretch *(net, wire, tarpaulin, etc.)* *(über* + *Akk.* over); c) *(schirren)* harness *(vor, an* + *Akk.* to); 2. *refl. V.* a) become *or* go taut; *(muscles)* tense; b) *(geh.: sich wölben)* **sich über** etw. *(Akk.)*: span sth.; 3. *itr. V.* *(clothing)* be [too] tight; *(skin)* be taut; **spannend** 1. *Adj.* exciting; *(stärker)* thrilling; 2. *adv.* excitingly; *(stärker)* thrillingly; **Spannung die;** ~, ~en a) *o. Pl.* excitement; *(Neugier)* suspense; b) *o. Pl.* *(eines Romans, Films usw.)* suspense; c) *(Zwistigkeit, Nervosität)* tension; d) *(Elektrot.)* voltage; **Spann·weite die** [wing-]span

Spar·buch das savings book

sparen 1. *tr. V.* save; 2. *itr. V.* a) save; **für** *od.* **auf** etw. *(Akk.)* ~: save up for sth.; b) *(sparsam wirtschaften)* economize *(mit* on); **an** etw. *(Dat.)* ~: be sparing with sth.; *(beim Einkauf)* economize on sth.; **Sparer der;** ~s, ~: saver

Spargel der; ~s, ~, *schweiz. auch* **die;** ~, ~n asparagus *no pl., no indef. art.*

Spar-: ~**groschen der** *(ugs.)* nest-egg; savings *pl.*; ~**kasse die** savings bank; ~**konto das** savings *or* deposit account

spärlich 1. *Adj.* sparse *(vegetation, beard, growth)*; thin *(hair, applause)*; scanty *(left-overs, knowledge, news, evidence, clothing)*; poor *(lighting)*; 2. *adv.* sparsely, thinly *(populated, covered)*; poorly *(lit, attended)*; scantily *(dressed)*

sparsam 1. *Adj.* thrifty ⟨*person*⟩; *(wirtschaftlich)* economical; **mit etw. ~ sein** be economical with sth.; 2. *adv.* ~ **mit der Butter/dem Papier umgehen** use butter/paper sparingly; economize on butter/paper; **Sparsamkeit** die; ~: thrift[iness]; *(Wirtschaftlichkeit)* economicalness

Sparte die; ~, ~n a) *(Teilbereich)* area; *(eines Geschäfts)* line [of business]; b) *(Rubrik)* section

Spaß der; ~es, **Späße a)** o. Pl. *(Vergnügen)* fun; ~ **an etw.** *(Dat.)* **haben** enjoy sth.; [**jmdm.**] ~ **machen** be fun [for sb.]; **viel ~!** have a good time!; b) *(Scherz)* joke; *(Streich)* prank; **er macht nur ~:** he's only joking; ~ **beiseite!** joking aside; ~ **muß sein!** there's no harm in a joke; ~ **verstehen** be able to take a joke; **im** *od.* **zum** *od.* **aus ~:** as a joke; for fun; **Späße machen** joke; b) **er läßt nicht mit sich ~:** he won't stand for any nonsense; **mit ihm/damit ist nicht zu ~:** he/it is not to be trifled with; **spaßes·halber** *Adv.* for the fun of it; for fun; **spaßig** *Adj.* funny; comical; amusing

spät 1. *Adj.* late; **wie ~ ist es?** what time is it?; 2. *adv.* late; ~ **am Abend** late in the evening

Spaten der; ~s, ~: spade

später 1. *Adj.* a) later ⟨*years, generations, etc.*⟩; b) *(zukünftig)* future ⟨*owner, wife, etc.*⟩; 2. *Adv.* later; **spätestens** *Adv.* at the latest

Spatz der; ~en, ~en a) sparrow; b) *(fam.: Liebling)* pet

Spätzle *Pl.* spaetzle; *kind of noodles*

spazieren *itr. V.*; **mit sein** stroll

spazieren-: ~**fahren** 1. *unr. itr. V.*; **mit sein** go for a ride; 2. *tr. V.* **ein Kind** [**im Kinderwagen**] ~**fahren** take a baby for a walk [in a pram]; ~|**gehen** *unr. itr. V.*; **mit sein** go for a walk

Spazier-: ~**gang** der walk; ~**gänger** der; ~s, ~: person out for a walk

SPD [espe:'de:] die; ~ *Abk.* Sozialdemokratische Partei Deutschlands SPD

Specht der; ~[e]s, ~e woodpecker

Speck der; ~[e]s, ~e a) bacon fat; *(Schinken~)* bacon; b) *(ugs. scherzh.: Fettpolster)* fat; flab *(sl.)*; **speckig** *Adj.* greasy

Spediteur [ʃpedi'tøːɐ̯] der; ~s, ~e carrier; haulage contractor; *(Möbel~)* furniture-remover

Speer der; ~[e]s, ~e a) spear; b) *(Sportgerät)* javelin

Speichel der; ~s saliva

Speicher der; ~s, ~ a) storehouse; *(Lagerhaus)* warehouse; b) *(südd.: Dachboden)* loft; c) *(Elektronik)* memory; **speichern** *tr. V.* store

speien *(geh.) unr. tr., itr. V.* spit

Speise die; ~, ~n a) *(Gericht)* dish; b) *o. Pl. (geh.: Nahrung)* food

Speise-: ~**gaststätte** die restaurant; ~**kammer** die larder; ~**karte** die menu; ~**lokal** das restaurant

speisen *(geh.)* 1. *itr. V.* eat; *(dinieren)* dine; 2. *tr. V.* eat; *(dinieren)* dine on

Speise-: ~**saal** der dining-hall; *(im Hotel, in einer Villa usw.)* dining-room; ~**wagen** der the restaurant car *(Brit.)*; ~**zettel** der menu

Spektakel der; ~s, ~ *(ugs.) (Lärm)* row *(coll.)*; rumpus *(coll.)*; **spektakulär** 1. *Adj.* spectacular; 2. *adv.* spectacularly

Spekulation die; ~, ~en speculation; **spekulieren** *itr. V.* a) *(ugs.)* **darauf ~, etw. tun zu können** count on being able to do sth.; b) *(Wirtsch.)* speculate *(mit in)*

Spelunke die; ~, ~n *(ugs. abwertend)* dive *(coll.)*

Spelze die; ~, ~n *(des Getreidekorns)* husk

Spende die; ~, ~n donation; contribution; **spenden** *tr., itr. V.* a) donate; give; b) *(fig. geh.)* give ⟨*light*⟩; afford, give ⟨*shade*⟩; give off ⟨*heat*⟩; **Spender** der; ~s, ~, **Spenderin** die; ~, ~nen donor; donator; **spendieren** *tr. V. (ugs.)* get, buy ⟨*drink, meal, etc.*⟩; stand ⟨*round*⟩

Spengler der; ~s, ~ *(südd., österr., schweiz.)* s. Klempner

Sperling der; ~s, ~e sparrow

Sperma das; ~s, **Spermen** sperm; semen

sperr·angel·weit *Adv. (ugs.)* ~ **offen** *od.* **geöffnet** wide open

Sperre die; ~, ~n a) barrier; *(Straßen~)* road-block; *(Milit.)* obstacle; b) *(fig.)* ban; *(Handels~)* embargo; *(Import~, Export~)* blockade; *(Nachrichten~)* [news] black-out; **sperren** 1. *tr. V.* a) close; close off ⟨*area*⟩; block ⟨*entrance, access, etc.*⟩; lock ⟨*mechanism etc.*⟩; b) cut off ⟨*water, gas, electricity, etc.*⟩; c) *(Bankw.)* stop ⟨*cheque, overdraft facility*⟩; freeze ⟨*bank account*⟩; d) *(ein~)* **ein Tier/jmdn. in etw.** *(Akk.)* ~ **:** shut an animal/sb. in sth.; e) *(Sport: von der Teilnahme ausschließen)* ban; f) *(Druckw.: spationieren)* print ⟨*word,* *text*⟩ with the letters spaced; **2.** *refl. V.* **sich [gegen etw.]** ~: balk [at sth.]; **Sperr·holz das** plywood; **sperrig** *Adj.* unwieldy

Sperr-: ~**müll** *der* bulky refuse *(for which there is a separate collection service);* ~**sitz** *der (im Kino)* seat in the back stalls; *(im Zirkus)* front seat; *(im Theater)* seat in the front stalls; ~**stunde** die closing time

Spesen *Pl.* expenses; **auf** ~: on expenses

Spezi *der*; ~**s,** ~[**s]** *(südd., österr., schweiz. ugs.)* [bosom] pal *(coll.);* chum *(coll.)*

spezialisieren *refl. V.* specialize *(auf* + *Akk.* in); **Spezialist** *der*; ~**en,** ~**en** specialist; **Spezialität** *die*; ~, ~**en** speciality; **speziell 1.** *Adj.* special; specific ⟨*question, problem, etc.*⟩; **2.** *Adv.* especially; *(eigens)* specially; **spezifisch 1.** *Adj.* specific; characteristic ⟨*smell, style*⟩; **2.** *adv.* specifically

spicken *tr. V.* lard

spie *1. u. 3. Pers. Sg. Prät. v.* **speien**

Spiegel *der*; ~**s,** ~ **a)** mirror; **b)** *(Wasser~, fig.: Konzentration)* level

spiegel-, Spiegel-: ~**bild** *das* reflection; ~**blank** *Adj.* shining; ~**ei** *das* fried egg; ~**glatt** *Adj.* like glass *postpos.;* as smooth as glass *postpos.*

spiegeln 1. *itr. V.* **a)** *(glänzen)* shine; gleam; **b)** *(als Spiegel wirken)* reflect the light; **2.** *tr. V.* reflect; mirror; **3.** *refl. V.* be mirrored *or* reflected

Spiegel·reflex·kamera die reflex camera

Spiel *das*; ~[**e]s,** ~**e a)** play; **b)** *(Glücks~; Gesellschafts~)* game; *(Wett~)* game; match; **auf dem** ~ **stehen** be at stake; **etw. aufs** ~ **setzen** put sth. at stake; risk sth.; **Spiel·bank** die; *Pl.* ...**banken** casino; **spielen 1.** *itr. V.* **a)** play; **auf der Gitarre** ~: play the guitar; **um Geld** ~: play for money; **b)** *(als Schauspieler)* act; perform; **c) der Roman/Film spielt im 17. Jahrhundert/in Berlin** the novel/film is set in the 17th century/in Berlin; **d)** *(fig.)* **das Blau spielt ins Violette** the blue is tinged with purple; **2.** *tr. V.* **a)** play; **Cowboy** ~: play at being a cowboy; **Geige** *usw.* ~: play the violin *etc.;* **b)** *(aufführen, vorführen)* put on ⟨*play*⟩; show ⟨*film*⟩; perform ⟨*piece of music*⟩; play ⟨*record*⟩; **den Beleidigten/Unschuldigen** ~ *(fig.)* act offended/play the innocent; **spielend**

Adv. easily; **Spieler** *der*; ~**s,** ~: player; *(Glücks~)* gambler; **Spielerei** *die*; ~, ~**en a)** *o. Pl.* playing *no art.; (im Glücksspiel)* gambling *no art.;* **b) eine** ~ **mit Worten/Zahlen** playing [around] with words/numbers; **Spielerin** *die*; ~, ~**nen** *s.* **Spieler**

Spiel-: ~**feld** *das* field; pitch *(Brit.); (Tennis, Squash, Volleyball usw.)* court; ~**film** *der* feature film; ~**kamerad** *der* playmate; ~**karte** die playing-card; ~**plan** *der* programme; ~**platz** *der* playground; ~**raum** *der* room to move *(fig.);* scope; latitude; ~**sachen** *Pl.* toys; ~**verderber** *der*; ~**s,** ~: spoil-sport; ~**waren** *Pl.* toys; ~**zeug** *das* **a)** toy; *(fig.)* toy; plaything; **b)** *o. Pl. (~sachen, ~waren)* toys *pl.*

Spieß *der*; ~**es,** ~**e a)** *(Waffe)* spear; **den** ~ **umdrehen** *od.* **umkehren** *(ugs.)* turn the tables; **b)** *(Brat~)* spit; **c)** *(Fleisch~)* kebab; **d)** *(Soldatenspr.)* [company] sergeant-major

Spießer *der*; ~**s,** ~ *(abwertend)* [petit] bourgeois; **spießig** *(abwertend)* **1.** *Adj.* [petit] bourgeois; **2.** *adv.* ⟨*think, behave, etc.*⟩ in a [petit] bourgeois way

Spinat *der*; ~[**e]s,** ~**e** spinach

Spind *der od. das;* ~[**e]s,** ~**e** locker

Spindel *die*; ~, ~**n** spindle

Spinne *die*; ~, ~**n** spider; **spinnen 1.** *unr. tr. V.* **a)** spin *(fig.);* plot ⟨*intrigue*⟩; think up ⟨*idea*⟩; hatch ⟨*plot*⟩; **2.** *unr. itr. V.* **a)** spin; **b)** *(ugs.: verrückt sein)* be crazy *or (sl.)* nuts; **Spinnen·netz** *das* spider's web; **Spinner** *der*; ~**s,** ~ **a)** *(Beruf)* spinner; **b)** *(ugs. abwertend)* nut-case *(sl.);* idiot; **Spinnerei** *die*; ~, ~**en** spinning mill; **Spinnerin** *die*; ~, ~**nen** *s.* **Spinner**

Spinn-: ~**rad** *das* spinning-wheel; ~**webe** *die*; ~, ~**n** cobweb

Spion *der*; ~**s,** ~**e a)** spy; **b)** *(Guckloch)* spyhole; **Spionage** [ʃpio'na:ʒə] *die*; ~: spying; espionage; **spionieren** *itr. V.* spy; **Spionin** *die*; ~, ~**nen** spy

Spirale *die*; ~, ~**n** spiral

Spiral·feder die coil spring

Spirituose *die*; ~, ~**n** spirit *usu. in pl.*

Spiritus *der*; ~, ~**se** spirit; ethyl alcohol

Spiritus·kocher der spirit stove

Spital *das*; ~**s,** **Spitäler** *(bes. österr., schweiz.)* hospital

spitz 1. *Adj.* **a)** pointed; sharp ⟨*pencil, needle, stone, etc.*⟩; fine ⟨*pen nib*⟩; *(Geom.)* acute ⟨*angle*⟩; **b)** *(schrill)* shrill

⟨cry etc.⟩; c) (boshaft) cutting ⟨remark etc.⟩; 2. adv. a) ~ **zulaufen** taper to a point; ~ **zulaufend** pointed; b) (boshaft) cuttingly

Spitz der; ~es, ~e spitz

spitz-, Spitz-: ~**bart** der goatee; ~**bube** der (scherzh.: Schlingel) rascal; ~**bübisch** 1. Adj. mischievous; 2. adv. mischievously

spitze indekl. Adj. (ugs.) s. klasse; **Spitze** die; ~, ~n a) point; (Pfeil~, Horn~ usw.) tip; b) (Turm~, Baum~, Mast~ usw.) top; (eines Berges) summit; c) (Zigarren~, Haar~, Zweig~) end; (Schuh~) toe; (Finger~, Nasen~) tip; d) (vorderes Ende) front; **an der** ~ **liegen** (Sport) be in the lead or in front; e) (führende Position) top; f) (einer Firma, Organisation usw.) head; (einer Hierarchie) top; (leitende Gruppe) management; g) (Höchstwert) maximum; peak; h) |absolute/einsame| ~ **sein** (ugs.) be [absolutely] great ⟨coll.⟩; i) (fig.: Angriff) dig ⟨gegen at⟩; j) (Textilwesen) lace

Spitzel der; ~s, ~: informer

spitzen tr. V. sharpen ⟨pencil⟩; purse ⟨lips, mouth⟩; prick up ⟨ears⟩

Spitzen-: ~**erzeugnis** das top-quality product; ~**klasse** die top class; ~**qualität** die top quality; ~**sportler** top sportsman

spitz-, Spitz-: ~**findig** Adj. hairsplitting; ~**hacke** die pick; ~|**kriegen** tr. V. (ugs.) tumble to ⟨coll.⟩; ~**name** der nickname

Spleen [ʃpliːn] der; ~s, ~e od. ~s strange habit; eccentricity

Splitt der; ~|e|s, ~e [stone] chippings pl.; (zum Streuen) grit

Splitter der; ~s, ~: splinter; (Granat~, Bomben~) splinter; **splittern** itr. V. **a)** (Splitter bilden) splinter; **b)** mit sein (in Splitter zerbrechen) ⟨glass, windscreen, etc.⟩ shatter; **splitternackt** Adj. (ugs.) stark naked; starkers pred. (Brit. sl.); **Splitter--partei** die splinter party

sponsern tr. V. sponsor; **Sponsor** der; ~s, ~en sponsor

spontan 1. Adj. spontaneous; 2. adv. spontaneously

sporadisch 1. Adj. sporadic; 2. adv. sporadically

Spore die; ~, ~n spore

Sporn der; ~|e|s, Sporen (des Reiters) spur; **einem Pferd die Sporen geben** spur a horse

Sport der; ~|e|s **a)** sport; (als Unter-

richtsfach) sport; PE; ~ **treiben** do sport; **b)** (Hobby, Zeitvertreib) hobby; pastime

Sport-: ~**fest** das sports festival; (einer Schule) sports day; ~**flugzeug** das sports plane; ~**geist** der; o. Pl. sportsmanship; ~**journalist** der sports journalist; ~**kleidung** die sportswear

Sportler der; ~s, ~: sportsman; **Sportlerin** die; ~, ~nen sportswoman; **sportlich** 1. Adj. **a)** sporting attrib.; **b)** (fair) sportsmanlike; sporting; c) (fig.: flott, rasant) sporty ⟨car, driving, etc.⟩; **d)** (zu sportlicher Leistung fähig) sporty, athletic ⟨person⟩; e) (jugendlich wirkend) sporty, smart but casual ⟨clothes⟩; smart but practical ⟨hair-style⟩; 2. adv. **a)** as far as sport is concerned; **b)** (fair) sportingly; c) (fig.: flott, rasant) in a sporty manner

Sport-: ~**platz** der sports field; (einer Schule) playing field/fields pl.; ~**schuh** der sports shoe; ~**stadion** das [sports] stadium; ~**verein** der sports club; ~**wagen** der **a)** (Auto) sports car; **b)** (Kinderwagen) pushchair (Brit.); stroller (Amer.)

Spott der; ~|e|s mockery; (höhnischer) ridicule; derision; **spott·billig** Adj., adv. (ugs.) dirt cheap; **spötteln** itr. V. mock [gently]; poke or make [gentle] fun; **spotten** itr. V. **a)** mock; poke or make fun; (höhnischer) ridicule; be derisive; **b)** einer Sache (Gen.) ~: be contemptuous of or scorn sth.; **Spötter** der; ~s, ~: mocker; **spöttisch** 1. Adj. mocking; (höhnischer) derisive; 2. adv. mockingly; **Spott·preis** der (ugs.) ridiculously low price

sprach 1. u. 3. Pers. Sg. Prät. v. sprechen; **Sprache** die; ~, ~n **a)** language; **in englischer** ~: in English; **b)** (Sprechweise) way of speaking; speech; (Stil) style; c) etw. zur ~ **bringen** bring sth. up; raise sth.; **heraus mit der** ~! come on, out with it!; **Sprachen·schule** die language school

Sprach-: ~**fehler** der speech impediment or defect; ~**führer** der phrasebook; ~**kenntnisse** Pl. knowledge sing. of a language/languages; ~**kurs** der language course

sprachlich 1. Adj. linguistic; 2. adv. linguistically

sprach-, Sprach-: ~**los** Adj. (über-

rascht) speechless; **~rohr** das *(Repräsentant)* spokesman; *(Propagandist)* mouthpiece; **~unterricht** der language teaching

sprang *1. u. 3. Pers. Sg. Prät. v.* **springen**

Spray [ʃpre:] das *od.* der; ~s, ~s spray; **Spray·dose** die aerosol [can]; **sprayen** *tr., itr. V.* spray

Sprech-: **~anlage** die intercom *(coll.);* **~chor** der chorus

sprechen *1. unr. itr. V.* speak (über + Akk. about; von about, of); *(sich unterhalten, sich besprechen auch)* talk (über + Akk., von about); *(parrot etc.)* talk; **deutsch/flüsternd ~:** speak German/in a whisper; **für/gegen etw. ~:** speak in favour of/against sth.; **mit jmdm. ~:** speak *or* talk with *or* to sb.; **mit wem spreche ich?** who is speaking please?; *2. unr. tr. V.* **a)** speak *(language, dialect);* say *(word, sentence);* „**Hier spricht man Deutsch**" 'German spoken'; **b)** *(rezitieren)* say, recite *(poem, text);* say *(prayer);* **c)** *(aus)* pronounce *(name, word, etc.);* **Sprecher** der; ~s, ~ **a)** spokesman; **b)** *(Ansager)* announcer; *(Nachrichten~)* newscaster; news-reader; **c)** *(Kommentator, Erzähler)* narrator

sprech-, Sprech-: **~funk·gerät** das radio-telephone; *(Walkie-talkie)* walkie-talkie; **~stunde** die consultation hours *pl.; (eines Arztes)* surgery; **~stunden·hilfe** die *(eines Arztes)* receptionist; *(eines Zahnarztes)* assistant; **~zimmer** das consulting-room

spreizen *tr. V.* spread *(fingers, toes, etc.);* **die Beine ~:** spread one's legs apart; open one's legs

Spreiz·fuß der *(Med.)* spread foot

sprengen *tr. V.* **a)** blow up; blast *(rock);* **etw. in die Luft ~:** blow sth. up; **b)** *(gewaltsam öffnen, aufbrechen)* force [open] *(door);* force *(lock);* burst, break *(bonds, chains); (fig.)* break up *(meeting, demonstration);* **c)** *(be~)* water *(flower-bed, lawn);* sprinkle *(street, washing)* with water; *(verspritzen)* sprinkle; *(mit dem Schlauch)* spray

Sprenkel der; ~s, ~: spot; dot; speckle; **sprenkeln** *tr. V.* sprinkle spots of *(colour);* sprinkle *(water)*

Spreu die; ~: chaff

sprich *Imperativ Sg. v.* **sprechen;** **sprichst** *2. Pers. Sg. Präsens v.* **sprechen;** **spricht** *3. Pers. Sg. Präsens v.*

sprechen; **Sprich·wort** das; *Pl.* Sprichwörter proverb

sprießen *unr. itr. V.; mit sein (leaf, bud)* shoot, sprout; *(seedlings)* come *or* spring up; *(beard)* sprout

Spring·brunnen der fountain; **springen** *1. unr. itr. V.* **a)** *mit sein (auch Sport)* jump; *(mit Schwung)* leap; spring; jump; *(frog, flea)* hop, jump; *(sich in Sprüngen fortbewegen)* bound; **b)** *mit sein (fig.) (pointer, milometer, etc.)* jump (auf + Akk. to); *(traffic-lights)* change (auf + Akk. to); *(spark)* leap; *(ball)* bounce; **c)** *mit sein (string, glass, porcelain, etc.)* break; *(Risse, Sprünge bekommen)* crack; *2. unr. tr. V.; auch mit sein (Sport)* perform *(somersault, twist dive, etc.)*

Springer der; ~s, ~ **a)** *(Sport)* jumper; **b)** *(Schachfigur)* knight

spring·lebendig *Adj.* extremely lively; full of beans *pred. (coll.)*

Spring·reiten das show-jumping *no art.*

sprinten *itr. (auch tr.) V.; mit sein* sprint; **Sprinter** der; ~s, ~, **Sprinterin** die; ~, **~nen** *(Sport)* sprinter

Sprit der; **~[e]s, ~e a)** *(ugs.: Treibstoff)* gas *(Amer. coll.);* juice *(sl.);* petrol *(Brit.);* **b)** *(ugs.: Schnaps)* shorts *pl.*

Spritze die; ~, **~n a)** syringe; **b)** *(Injektion)* injection; **c)** *(Feuer~)* hose; *(Löschfahrzeug)* fire engine

spritzen *1. tr. V.* **a)** *(versprühen)* spray; *(ver~)* splash; *(in Form eines Strahls)* spray, squirt *(water, foam, etc.);* pipe *(cream etc.);* **b)** *(be~, besprühen)* water *(lawn, tennis-court);* water, spray *(street, yard);* spray *(plants, crops, etc.); (mit Lack)* spray *(car etc.);* **jmdn. naß ~:** splash sb.; *(mit Wasserpistole, Schlauch)* spray sb.; **c)** *(injizieren)* inject *(drug etc.); (ugs.: einer Injektion unterziehen)* **jmdn./sich ~:** give sb. an injection/inject oneself; *2. itr. V.; mit Richtungsangabe mit sein (hot fat)* spit; *(mud etc.)* spatter, splash; *(blood, water)* spurt; **Spritzer** der; ~s, ~ *(kleiner Tropfen)* splash; *(von Farbe)* splash; spot; **spritzig** *1. Adj.* **a)** sparkling *(wine);* tangy *(fragrance, perfume);* **b)** lively *(show, music, article);* sparkling *(performance);* racy *(style);* nippy *(coll.);* zippy *(car, engine);* agile *(person);* *2. adv.* sparklingly *(produced, performed, etc.);* racily *(written);* **Spritz·tour** die *(ugs.)* spin

spröd, spröde Adj. **a)** brittle ⟨glass, plastic, etc.⟩; dry ⟨hair, lips, etc.⟩; ⟨rissig⟩ chapped ⟨lips, skin⟩; ⟨rauh⟩ rough ⟨skin⟩; **b)** ⟨fig.: abweisend⟩ aloof ⟨person, manner, nature⟩

sproß 1. u. 3. Pers. Sg. Prät. v. sprießen; **Sproß** der; Sprosses, Sprosse ⟨Bot.⟩ shoot

Sprosse die; ~, ~n **a)** ⟨auch fig.⟩ rung; **b)** ⟨eines Fensters⟩ glazing bar

Sprößling der; ~s, ~e ⟨ugs. scherzh.⟩ offspring; **seine** ~e his offspring pl.

Sprotte die; ~, ~n sprat

Spruch der; ~⟨e⟩s, Sprüche ⟨Wahl~⟩ motto; ⟨Sinn~⟩ maxim; ⟨Aus~⟩ saying; aphorism; ⟨Zitat⟩ quotation

spruch·reif Adj. **das ist noch nicht ~**: that's not definite, so people mustn't start talking about it yet

Sprudel der; ~s, ~ **a)** sparkling mineral water; **b)** ⟨österr.⟩ fizzy drink;

sprudeln itr. V.; mit sein bubble; ⟨lemonade, champagne, etc.⟩ effervesce; **Sprudel·wasser** das; Pl. -wässer sparkling mineral water

Sprüh·dose die aerosol [can]; **sprühen** 1. tr. V. spray; 2. itr. V.; mit Richtungsangabe mit sein ⟨sparks, spray⟩ fly; ⟨fig.⟩ ⟨eyes⟩ sparkle ⟨vor + Dat. with⟩; ⟨intellect, wit⟩ sparkle

Sprüh·regen das drizzle; fine rain

Sprung der; ~⟨e⟩s, Sprünge **a)** ⟨auch Sport⟩ jump; ⟨schwungvoll⟩ leap; ⟨Satz⟩ bound; ⟨fig.⟩ jump; **keine großen Sprünge machen können** ⟨fig. ugs.⟩ not be able to afford many luxuries; **auf dem** ~⟨e⟩ **sein** ⟨fig. ugs.⟩ be in a rush; **b)** ⟨ugs.: kurze Entfernung⟩ stone's throw; **c)** ⟨Riß⟩ crack

Sprung·brett das ⟨auch fig.⟩ springboard; **sprunghaft** 1. Adj. **a)** erratic ⟨person, character, manner⟩; disjointed ⟨conversation, thoughts⟩; **b)** ⟨unvermittelt⟩ sudden; **c)** ⟨ruckartig⟩ rapid ⟨change⟩; sharp ⟨increase⟩; 2. adv.; s. 1 b–c: disjointedly; suddenly; rapidly; sharply

Spucke die; ~: spit; **spucken** 1. itr. V. spit; **in die Hände** ~ ⟨fig.: an die Arbeit gehen⟩ go to work with a will; 2. tr. V. spit; cough up ⟨blood, phlegm⟩

Spuk der; ~⟨e⟩s, ~e ⟨ghostly or supernatural⟩ manifestation; **spuken** itr. V.; unpers. **hier/in dem Haus spukt es** this place/the house is haunted

Spule die; ~, ~n spool ⟨für Tonband, Film⟩ spool; reel

Spüle die; ~, ~n sink unit; ⟨Becken⟩ sink

spulen tr., itr. V. spool; ⟨am Tonbandgerät⟩ wind

spülen 1. tr. V. **a)** rinse; bathe ⟨wound⟩; **b)** ⟨landsch.: abwaschen⟩ wash up ⟨dishes, glasses, etc.⟩; **Geschirr** ~: wash up; 2. itr. V. **a)** ⟨beim WC⟩ flush [the toilet]; **b)** ⟨den Mund ausspülen⟩ rinse out [one's mouth]; **c)** ⟨landsch.⟩ s. abwaschen 2

Spül-: ~maschine die dishwasher; ~mittel das washing-up liquid

Spur die; ~, ~en **a)** ⟨Abdruck im Boden⟩ track; ⟨Folge von Abdrücken⟩ tracks pl.; **eine heiße** ~ ⟨fig.⟩ a hot trail; **jmdm./einer Sache auf der** ~ **sein** be on to the track or trail of sb./sth.; **b)** ⟨Anzeichen⟩ trace; ⟨eines Verbrechens⟩ clue ⟨Gen. to⟩; **c)** ⟨sehr kleine Menge; auch fig.⟩ trace; **d)** ⟨Verkehrsw.: Fahr~⟩ lane; **die** ~ **wechseln** change lanes

spürbar 1. Adj. noticeable; distinct, perceptible ⟨improvement⟩; evident ⟨relief, embarrassment⟩; 2. adv. noticeably; perceptibly; ⟨sichtlich⟩ clearly ⟨relieved, on edge⟩; **spüren** tr. V. feel; ⟨instinktiv⟩ sense

spur·los 1. Adj. total, complete ⟨disappearance⟩; 2. adv. ⟨disappear⟩ completely or without trace

Spür·sinn der; o. Pl. ⟨feiner Instinkt⟩ intuition

Spurt der; ~⟨e⟩s, ~s od. ~e spurt; **spurten** itr. V. **a)** mit Richtungsangabe mit sein spurt; **b)** mit sein ⟨ugs.: schnell laufen⟩ sprint

sputen refl. V. ⟨veralt.⟩ make haste

St. Abk. **a)** Sankt St.; **b)** Stück

Staat der; ~⟨e⟩s, ~en state; **staatlich** 1. Adj. state attrib.;⟨power, unity, etc.⟩ of the state; state-owned ⟨factory etc.⟩; 2. adv. by the state; ~ **anerkannt/geprüft** state-approved/-certified

staats-, Staats-: ~angehörige der/die national; ~angehörigkeit die nationality; ~anwalt der public prosecutor; ~bürger der citizen; **er ist deutscher** ~bürger he is a German citizen or national; ~bürgerlich Adj. civil ⟨rights⟩; civic ⟨duties, loyalty⟩; ⟨education, attitude⟩ as a citizen; ~bürgerschaft die s. ~angehörigkeit; ~grenze die state frontier or border; ~mann der; Pl. -männer statesman; ~oberhaupt das head of state; ~präsident der [state] president

Stab der; ~⟨e⟩s, Stäbe **a)** rod; ⟨länger⟩

pole; *(eines Käfigs, Gitters, Geländers)* bar; b) *(Milit.)* staff; c) *(Team)* team

stabil 1. *Adj.* sturdy *(chair, cupboard)*; robust, sound *(health)*; stable *(prices, government, economy, etc.)*; 2. *adv.* ~ **gebaut** solidly built; **stabilisieren** 1. *tr. V.* stabilize; 2. *refl. V.* a) stabilize; b) *(health, circulation, etc.)* become stronger

Stab·lampe die torch *(Brit.)*; flashlight *(Amer.)*

Stabs·arzt der *(Milit.)* medical officer, MO *(with the rank of captain)*

stach 1. u. 3. Pers. Sg. Prät. v. **stechen**

Stachel der; ~s, ~n a) spine; *(Dorn)* thorn; b) *(Gift~)* sting; c) *(spitzes Metallstück)* spike; *(an ~draht)* barb

Stachel-: ~**beere** die gooseberry; ~**draht** der barbed wire

stachelig *Adj.* prickly

Stadion das; ~s, **Stadien** stadium

Stadium das; ~s, **Stadien** stage

Stadt die; ~, **Städte** a) town; *(Groß~)* city; die ~ **Basel** the city of Basel; **in die ~ gehen** go into town; go downtown *(Amer.)*; b) *(Verwaltung)* town council; *(in der Großstadt)* city council; city hall *no art. (Amer.)*

Stadt-: ~**bahn** die urban railway; ~**bummel** der *(ugs.)* **einen** ~**bummel machen** take a stroll through the town/city centre

Städter der; ~s, ~, **Städterin** die; ~, ~**nen** a) town-dweller; *(Großstädter, -städterin)* city-dweller; b) *(Stadtmensch)* townie *(coll.)*

Stadt-: ~**führer** der town/city guidebook; ~**gespräch** das: ~**gespräch sein** be the talk of the town

städtisch 1. *Adj.* a) *(kommunal)* municipal; b) *(urban)* urban *(life, way of life, etc.)*; 2. *adv.* a) *(kommunal)* municipally

Stadt-: ~**mauer** die town/city wall; ~**mitte** die town centre; *(einer Großstadt)* city centre; downtown *(Amer.)*; ~**park** der municipal park; ~**plan** der [town/city] street plan *or* map; ~**rand** der outskirts *pl.* of the town/city; **am** ~: on the outskirts of the town/city; ~**rundfahrt** die sightseeing tour round a/the town/city; ~**teil** der district; part [of a/the town]; ~**tor** das town/city gate; ~**viertel** das district

Staffel die; ~, ~**n** a) *(Sport: Mannschaft)* relay team; b) *(Sport: ~lauf)* relay race; c) *(Luftwaffe: Einheit)* flight; d) *(Eskorte)* escort formation

Staffelei die; ~, ~**en** easel

stahl 1. u. 3. Pers. Sg. Prät. v. **stehlen**

Stahl der; ~[e]s, **Stähle** *od.* ~e steel

Stahl-: ~**beton** der reinforced concrete; ~**blech** das sheet steel

stählern *Adj.; nicht präd.* steel

stak 1. u. 3. Pers. Sg. Prät. v. **stecken**

Stall der; ~[e]s, **Ställe** *(Pferde~, Renn~)* stable; *(Kuh~)* cowshed; *(Hühner~)* [chicken-]coop; *(Schweine~)* [pig]sty; *(für Kaninchen, Kleintiere)* hutch; *(für Schafe)* pen; **Stallung** die; ~, ~**en** *(Pferdestall)* stable; *(Kuhstall)* cow-shed; *(Schweinestall)* [pig]sty

Stamm der; ~[e]s, **Stämme** a) *(Baum~)* trunk; b) *(Volks~)* tribe; **Stamm·baum** der family tree; *(eines Tieres)* pedigree

stammeln tr., itr. V. stammer

stammen itr. V. come (**aus, von** from); *(datieren)* date (**aus, von** from)

Stamm-: ~**gast** der *(im Lokal/Hotel)* regular customer/visitor; regular *(coll.)*; ~**tisch** der a) *(Tisch)* regulars' table *(coll.)*; b) *(~tischrunde)* group of regulars *(coll.)*; c) *(Treffen)* gettogether with the regulars *(coll.)*

stampfen 1. itr. V. a) *(laut auftreten)* stamp; b) *mit sein (sich fortbewegen)* tramp; *(mit schweren Schritten)* trudge; 2. tr. V. a) **mit den Füßen den Rhythmus** ~: tap the rhythm with one's feet; b) *(fest~)* compress; c) *(zerkleinern)* mash *(potatoes)*

stand 1. u. 3. Pers. Sg. Prät. v. **stehen**; **Stand** der; ~[e]s, **Stände** a) o. Pl. *(das Stehen)* standing position; **[bei jmdm. *od.* gegen jmdn.] einen schweren** ~ **haben** *(fig.)* have a tough time [of it] [with sb.]; b) *(~ort)* position; c) *(Verkaufs-; Box für ein Pferd)* stall; *(Messe-, Informations~)* stand; *(Zeitungs~)* [newspaper] kiosk; d) o. Pl. *(erreichte Stufe; Zustand)* state; **etw. auf den neu[e]sten** ~ **bringen** bring sth. up to date; e) *(des Wassers, Flusses)* level; *(des Thermometers, Zählers, Barometers)* reading; *(der Kasse, Finanzen)* state; *(eines Himmelskörpers)* position; f) o. Pl. *(Familien~)* status; g) *(Gesellschaftsschicht)* class; *(Berufs~)* trade; *(Ärzte, Rechtsanwälte)* [professional] group

Standard der; ~s, ~s standard

Ständchen das; ~s, ~: serenade; **jmdm. ein** ~ **bringen** serenade sb.

Ständer der; ~s, ~: stand; *(Kleider~)* coat-stand; *(Wäsche~)* clothes-horse

standes-, Standes-: ~amt das registry office; ~amtlich 1. *Adj.; nicht präd.* registry office *⟨wedding, document⟩;* 2. *adv.* ~amtlich heiraten get married in a registry office; ~beamte der registrar

stand-, Stand-: ~fest *Adj.* steady; stable; strong *⟨stalk, stem⟩;* ~haft 1. *Adj.* steadfast; 2. *adv.* steadfastly; ~haftigkeit die; ~: steadfastness; ~|halten *unr. itr. V.* stand firm; einer Sache *(Dat.)* ~halten withstand sth.

ständig 1. *Adj.* constant *⟨noise, worry, pressure, etc.⟩;* permanent *⟨residence, correspondent, staff, member, etc.⟩;* standing *⟨committee⟩;* regular *⟨income⟩;* 2. *adv.* constantly

Stand-: ~licht das *(Kfz-W.)* sidelights *pl.;* ~ort der; *Pl.* ~orte a) position; *⟨eines Betriebes o.ä.⟩* location; site; b) *(Milit.: Garnison)* garrison; base; ~punkt der *(fig.)* point of view; viewpoint; auf dem ~punkt stehen, daß ...: take the view that ...; ~spur die *(Verkehrsw.)* hard shoulder; ~uhr die grandfather clock

Stange die; ~, ~n pole; *(aus Metall)* bar; *(dünner)* rod; *(Kleider~)* rail; *(Vogel~)* perch; im Anzug von der ~ *(ugs.)* an off-the-peg-suit

Stangen-: ~brot das French bread; ~spargel der asparagus spears *pl.*

stank 1. *u.* 3. *Pers. Sg. Prät. v.* stinken

Stapel der; ~s, ~: pile; ein ~ Holz a pile or stack of wood; **stapeln** 1. *tr. V.* pile up; stack; 2. *refl. V.* pile up

stapfen *itr. V.; mit sein* tramp

¹**Star** der; ~|e|s, ~e *od. (schweiz.)* ~en *(Vogel)* starling

²**Star** der; ~s, ~s *(berühmte Persönlichkeit)* star

³**Star** der; ~|e|s *(Med.)* grauer ~: cataract; grüner ~: glaucoma

starb 1. *u.* 3. *Pers. Sg. Prät. v.* sterben

stark; stärker, stärkst... 1. *Adj.* a) strong; potent *⟨drink, medicine, etc.⟩;* powerful *⟨engine, lens, voice, etc.⟩; (ausgezeichnet)* excellent; *s. auch* Stück c; b) *(dick)* thick; stout *⟨rope, string⟩; (verhüll.: korpulent)* well-built *(euphem.);* c) *(zahlenmäßig groß, umfangreich)* sizeable, large; big *(de-mand⟩;* eine 100 Mann ~e Truppe a 100-strong unit; d) *(heftig, intensiv)* heavy; severe *⟨frost, pain⟩;* strong *⟨impression, current, resistance, dislike⟩;* grave *⟨doubt, reservations⟩;* great *⟨exaggeration, interest⟩;* loud *⟨applause⟩;* e) *(Jugendspr.: großartig)* great *(coll.);*

fantastic *(coll.);* 2. *adv.* a) *(sehr, überaus, intensiv) (mit Adj.)* very; heavily *⟨indebted, stressed⟩;* greatly *⟨increased, reduced, enlarged⟩;* strongly *⟨emphasized, characterized⟩;* badly *⟨damaged, worn, affected⟩; (mit Verb;* heavily; *⟨exaggerate, impress⟩* greatly; *⟨enlarge, reduce, increase⟩* considerably; *⟨support, oppose, suspect⟩* strongly; *⟨remind⟩* very much; ~ erkältet sein have a heavy or bad cold; b) *(Jugendspr.: großartig)* fantastically *(coll.);* **Stark bier** das strong beer; **Stärke** die; ~, ~n a) *o. Pl.* strength; *⟨eines Motors⟩* power; *(einer Glühbirne)* wattage; b) *(Dicke)* thickness; *(Technik)* gauge; c) *o. Pl. (zahlenmäßige Größe)* strength; d) *(besondere Fähigkeit, Vorteil)* strength; jmds. ~/nicht jmds. ~ sein be sb.'s forte/not be sb.'s strong point; e) *(Intensität)* strength; *(von Sturm, Schmerzen, Abneigung)* intensity; *(von Frost)* severity; *(von Lärm, Verkehr)* volume; f) *(organischer Stoff)* starch; **stärken** 1. *tr. V.* a) strengthen; boost *⟨power, prestige⟩; ⟨drink, food, etc.⟩* fortify *⟨person⟩;* b) *(steif machen)* starch *⟨washing etc.⟩;* 2. *refl. V.* refresh oneself; **Stärkung** die; ~, ~en a) *o. Pl.* strengthening; b) *(Erfrischung)* refreshment

starr 1. *Adj.* a) rigid *(steif)* stiff (vor + *Dat.* with); fixed *⟨expression, smile, stare⟩;* b) *(nicht abwandelbar)* inflexible, rigid *⟨law, rule, principle⟩;* c) *(unnachgiebig)* inflexible *⟨person, attitude, etc.⟩;* 2. *adv.* rigidly; *(steif)* stiffly

starren *itr. V.* a) stare (in + *Akk.* into, auf, an, gegen + *Akk.* at); jmdm. ins Gesicht ~: stare sb. in the face; b) vor/von Schmutz ~: be filthy

Starr·sinn der; *o. Pl.* pig-headedness

starr·sinnig *Adj.* pig-headed

Start der; ~|e|s, ~s start; *(eines Flugzeugs)* take-off; *(einer Rakete)* launch; **Start·bahn** die [take-off] runway; **start·bereit** *Adj.* ready to start *postpos.; ⟨aircraft⟩* ready for take-off; **starten** 1. *itr. V.; mit sein* a) start; *⟨aircraft⟩* take off; *⟨rocket⟩* blast off, be launched; b) *(den Motor anlassen)* start the engine; 2. *tr. V.* start; launch *⟨rocket, satellite, attack⟩;* start [up] *⟨engine, machine, car⟩*

Station die; ~, ~en a) station; b) *(Haltestelle)* stop; c) *(Zwischen~, Aufenthalt)* stopover; ~ machen stop over or

off; **d)** *(Kranken~)* ward; **stationär**
1. *Adj. (Med.)* ⟨treatment⟩ in hospital,
as an in-patient; **2.** *adv. (Med.)* in hospital; **jmdn. ~ behandeln** treat sb. as
an in-patient; **stationieren** *tr. V.*
station ⟨troops⟩; deploy ⟨weapons,
bombers, etc.⟩

Stations-: **~arzt** der ward doctor;
~schwester die ward sister; **~taste**
die *(Rundf.)* preset [tuning] button;
preset

Statistik die; **~:** statistics *sing., no
art.*

statt 1. *Präp. mit Gen.* instead of; **~**
dessen instead [of this]; **2.** *Konj.:* **s. an-**
statt

statt-: **~|finden** *unr. itr. V.* take
place; ⟨process, development⟩ occur;
~haft *Adj.* permissible

stattlich 1. a) well-built; imposing
⟨figure, stature, building, etc.⟩; fine
⟨farm, estate⟩; impressive ⟨trousseau,
collection⟩; **b)** *(beträchtlich)* considerable; **2.** *adv.* impressively

Statue die; **~,** **~n** statue

Statur die; **~,** **~en** build

Status der; **~,** **~** [ˈʃtaːtuːs] status

Statut das; **~|e|s,** **~en** statute

Stau der; **~|e|s,** **~s** *od.* **~e a)** build-up;
b) *(von Fahrzeugen)* tailback *(Brit.)*;
backup *(Amer.)*

Staub der; **~|e|s** dust; **~ wischen** dust;
~ saugen vacuum *or (Brit. coll.)*
hoover; **sich aus dem ~|e| machen** *(fig.
ugs.)* make oneself scarce *(coll.)*;
stauben *itr. V.* cause dust; **staubig**
Adj. dusty

staub-, Staub-: **~saugen** *itr., tr. V.*
vacuum, *(Brit. coll.)* hoover; **~sau-**
ger der vacuum cleaner; Hoover
(Brit. P); **~tuch** das; *Pl.* **~tücher**
duster

Staude die; **~,** **~n** *(Bot.)* herbaceous
perennial

stauen 1. *tr. V.* dam [up] ⟨stream,
river⟩; staunch ⟨blood⟩; **2.** *refl. V.* ⟨wa-
ter, blood, etc.⟩ accumulate, build up;
⟨people⟩ form a crowd; ⟨traffic⟩ form a
tailback/tailbacks *(Brit.)* or *(Amer.)*
backup/backups

staunen *itr. V.* be amazed or as-
tonished (**über** + *Akk.* at); *(beeindruckt sein)* marvel (**über** + *Akk.* at);
~d with or in amazement; **Staunen**
das; **~s** amazement (**über** + *Akk.* at);
(Bewunderung) wonderment

Stauung die; **~,** **~en a)** *(eines Bachs,
Flusses)* damming; *(des Blutes, Wassers)* stemming the flow; *(das Sich-*

stauen) build-up; **b)** *(Verkehrsstau)*
tailback *(Brit.)*; backup *(Amer.)*; jam

Std. *Abk.* Stunde hr.

stechen 1. *unr. itr. V.* **a)** prick; ⟨wasp,
bee⟩ sting; ⟨mosquito⟩ bite; **b)** *(hin-
ein~)* **mit etw. in etw.** *(Akk.)* **~:** stick
or jab sth. into sth.; **2.** *unr. tr. V. (mit
dem Messer, Schwert)* stab; *(mit der
Nadel, mit einem Dorn usw.)* prick;
⟨bee, wasp⟩ sting; ⟨mosquito⟩ bite; **sich
in den Finger ~:** prick one's finger

Stech-: **~mücke** die mosquito; gnat;
~uhr die time clock

Steck-: **~brief** der description [of
a/the wanted person]; *(Plakat)*
'wanted' poster; **~dose** die socket;
power point

stecken 1. *tr. V.* **a)** put; **b)** *(mit Na-
deln)* pin ⟨hem, lining, etc.⟩; pin [on]
⟨badge⟩; pin up ⟨hair⟩; **2.** *itr. V.* be; **wo
steckt meine Brille?** *(ugs.)* where have
my glasses got to or gone?; **hinter etw.**
(Dat.) **~** *(fig. ugs.)* be behind sth.

stecken-, Stecken-: **~|bleiben**
unr. itr. V.; mit sein get stuck; **~|las-**
sen *unr. tr. V.* leave; **~pferd** das **a)**
(Spielzeug) hobby-horse; **b)** *(Liebha-
berei)* hobby

Stecker der; **~s,** **~:** plug; **Steck·na-**
del die pin

Steg der; **~|e|s,** **~e** *(Brücke)* [narrow]
bridge; *(Laufbrett)* gangplank;
(Boots~) landing-stage

Steg·reif der: **aus dem ~:** impromptu

stehen *unr. itr. V.; südd., österr.,
schweiz. mit sein* **a)** stand; **b)** *(sich befinden)* be; ⟨upright object, building⟩
stand; **c)** *(einen bestimmten Stand haben)* **auf etw.** *(Dat.)* **~** ⟨needle, hand⟩
point to sth.; **das Barometer steht tief/
auf Regen** the barometer is reading
low/indicating rain; **das Spiel/es steht
1:1** *(Sport)* the score is one all; **die Sache steht gut/schlecht** things are going
well/badly; **d)** *(einen bestimmten
Kurs, Wert haben)* ⟨currency⟩ stand
(**bei** at); **wie steht das Pfund?** what is
the rate for the pound?; **e)** *(nicht in
Bewegung sein)* be stationary; ⟨machi-
ne etc.⟩ be at a standstill; **meine Uhr
steht** my watch has stopped; **f)** *(geschrieben, gedruckt sein)* be; **in der
Zeitung steht, daß ...:** it says in the
paper that ...; **g)** *(Sprachw.: gebraucht
werden)* ⟨subjunctive etc.⟩ occur; be
found; **h) jmdm. |gut| ~** ⟨dress etc.⟩ suit
sb. [well]

stehen-: **~|bleiben** *unr. itr. V.; mit
sein* **a)** stop; ⟨traffic⟩ come to a stand-

still; **b)** *(stehengelassen werden)* stay; be left; *(zurückgelassen werden)* be left behind; *(der Zerstörung entgehen)* ⟨*building*⟩ be left standing; ~|**lassen** *unr. tr. V.* **a)** leave; **b)** *(vergessen)* leave [behind]

Steh·lampe die standard lamp *(Brit.)*; floor lamp *(Amer.)*

stehlen *unr. tr., itr. V.* steal; *s. auch* **gestohlen 2**

Steh·platz der *(im Theater usw.)* standing place; *(im Bus)* space to stand

Steiermark die; ~: Styria *no art.*

steif 1. *Adj.* stiff; *(förmlich)* stiff; formal; **2.** *adv.* stiffly

steigen 1. *unr. itr. V.; mit sein* **a)** climb; ⟨*mist, smoke, sun*⟩ rise; ⟨*balloon*⟩ climb, rise; **auf die Leiter ~:** get on to the ladder; **in den/aus dem Bus/ Zug ~:** board *or* get on/get off *or* out of the bus/train; **b)** *(ansteigen, zunehmen)* rise; ⟨*price, cost, salary, output*⟩ increase, rise; ⟨*debts, tension*⟩ increase, mount; ⟨*chances*⟩ improve; **2.** *unr. tr. V.; mit sein* climb ⟨*stairs, steps*⟩ climb; **Steiger** der; ~s, ~ *(Bergbau)* overman

steigern 1. *tr. V.* **a)** increase ⟨*speed, value, sales, consumption, etc.*⟩ (auf + Akk. to); step up ⟨*demands, production, etc.*⟩; raise ⟨*standards, requirements*⟩; *(verstärken)* intensify ⟨*fear, tension*⟩; heighten ⟨*effect*⟩; **b)** *(Sprachw.)* compare ⟨*adjective*⟩; **2.** *refl. V.* ⟨*confusion, speed, profit, etc.*⟩ increase; ⟨*pain, excitement, tension, etc.*⟩ become more intense; ⟨*costs*⟩ escalate; ⟨*effect*⟩ be heightened; **Steigerung** die; ~, ~en **a)** increase *(Gen.* in); *(Verstärkung)* intensification; *(einer Wirkung)* heightening; *(Verbesserung)* improvement *(Gen.* in); *(bes. Sport: Leistungs~)* improvement [in performance]; **b)** *(Sprachw.)* comparison

Steigung die; ~, ~en gradient

steil 1. *Adj.* steep; meteoric ⟨*career*⟩; rapid ⟨*rise*⟩; **2.** *adv.* steeply; **Steil·hang** der steep escarpment

Stein der; ~|e|s, ~e stone; *(Fels)* rock; *(Bau~)* [stone]block; **mir fällt ein ~ vom Herzen** that's a weight off my mind; **Stein·bock** der **a)** ibex; **b)** *(Astrol.)* Capricorn; the Goat; **steinern** *Adj.* stone; **Stein·gut** das earthenware; **stein·hart** *Adj.* rock-hard; **steinig** *Adj.* stony

Stein-: ~**kohle** die [hard] coal;

~**metz** der; ~en, ~en stonemason; ~**obst** das stone-fruit; ~**pilz** der cep; ~**schlag** der rock fall; „**Achtung** ~**schlag**" 'beware falling rocks'; ~**zeit** die Stone Age; *(fig.)* stone age

Steiß·bein das *(Anat.)* coccyx

Stelle die; ~, ~n **a)** place; **an jmds.** ~ **treten** take sb.'s place; **ich an deiner** ~ ...: ... if I were you; **an achter** ~ **liegen** be in eighth place; **die erste** ~ **hinter** *od.* **nach dem Komma** *(Math.)* the first decimal place; **an** ~ (+ *Gen.*) instead of; **auf der** ~: immediately; **b)** *(begrenzter Bereich)* patch; *(am Körper)* spot; **c)** *(Passage)* passage; *(Punkt im Ablauf einer Rede usw.)* point; **d)** *(Arbeits~)* job; post; **eine freie** ~: a vacancy; **e)** *(Dienst~)* office; *(Behörde)* authority; **stellen 1.** *tr. V.* **a)** put; *(mit Sorgfalt)* place; *(aufrecht hin~)* stand; **b)** *(ein~)* set ⟨*points, clock, scales*⟩; **den Wecker auf 6 Uhr ~:** set the alarm for 6 o'clock; **die Heizung höher/niedriger ~:** turn the heating up/down; **c)** *(bereit~)* provide; **d)** **jmdn. besser ~:** ⟨*firm*⟩ improve sb.'s pay; **gut/schlecht/besser gestellt** comfortably/badly/better off; **e)** *verblaßt* put ⟨*question*⟩; set ⟨*task, topic, condition*⟩; make ⟨*application, demand, request*⟩; **jmdm. eine Frage ~:** ask sb. a question; **2.** *refl. V.* **a)** place oneself; **sich auf die Zehenspitzen ~:** stand on tiptoe; **b)** **sich schlafend/taub/tot usw. ~:** feign sleep/ deafness/death *etc.*; pretend to be asleep/deaf/dead *etc.*

stellen-, Stellen-: ~**angebot** das offer of a job; *(Inserat)* job advertisement; „~**angebote**" 'situations vacant'; ~**gesuch** das 'situation wanted' advertisement; ~**weise** *Adv.* in places

Stellung die; ~, ~en position; **zu etw.** ~ **nehmen** express one's opinion on sth.; **Stellungnahme** die; ~, ~n opinion; *(kurze Äußerung)* statement; **Stell·vertreter** der deputy

Stelze die; ~, ~n stilt; **stelzen** *itr. V.; mit sein* strut; stalk

stemmen 1. *tr. V.* **a)** *(hoch~)* lift [above one's head]; **b)** *(drücken)* brace ⟨*feet, knees*⟩ (gegen against); **2.** *refl. V.* **sich gegen etw.** ~: brace oneself against sth.

Stempel der; ~s, ~: stamp; *(Post~)* postmark; **stempeln** *tr. V.* stamp ⟨*passport, form*⟩; postmark ⟨*letter*⟩; cancel ⟨*postage stamp*⟩

Stengel der; ~s, ~: stem; stalk

steno-, Steno-: ~**gramm** das shorthand text; ~**graph** der; ~en, ~en stenographer; ~**graphie** die; ~, ~n stenography no art.; shorthand no art.; ~**graphieren** itr. V. do shorthand; ~**typistin** die shorthand typist

Stepp·decke die quilt

Steppe die; ~, ~n steppe

steppen tr. (auch itr.) V. backstitch

sterben unr. itr. V.; mit sein die; **im Sterben liegen** lie dying; **ster-bens·krank** Adj. mortally ill; **sterblich** Adj. mortal

stereo Adv. in stereo; **Stereo** das; ~s stereo; **Stereo·anlage** die stereo [system]

steril Adj. sterile

Sterling ['stɛːlɪŋ]: **Pfund ~:** pound/ pounds sterling

Stern der; ~[e]s, ~e star; **Sternchen** das; ~s, ~ (Druckw.) asterisk; **Stern·schnuppe** die; ~, ~n shooting star

Stethoskop [ʃteto'skoːp] das; ~s, ~e (Med.) stethoscope

¹**Steuer** das; ~s, ~: [steering-]wheel; (von Schiffen) helm; ²**Steuer** die; ~, ~n tax

steuer-, Steuer-: ~**berater** der tax consultant or adviser; ~**bord** das od. österr. der; o. Pl. (Seew., Flugw.) starboard; ~**erklärung** die tax return; ~**frei** Adj. tax-free; ~**mann** der; Pl. ~leute od. ~männer (Rudersport) cox

steuern 1. tr. V. (fahren) steer; (fliegen) pilot, fly ⟨aircraft⟩; fly ⟨course⟩; 2. itr. V. **a)** be at the wheel; (auf dem Schiff) be at the helm; **b)** mit sein (Kurs nehmen, ugs.: sich hinbewegen; auch fig.) head; **Steuerung** die; ~, ~en a) ⟨System⟩ controls pl.; **b)** o. Pl. s. steuern 1: steering; piloting; flying

Steward ['stjuːɐt] der; ~s, ~s steward; **Stewardeß** ['stjuːɐdɛs] die; ~, ~, Stewardessen stewardess

stich Imper. Sg. v. stechen

Stich der; ~[e]s, ~e **a)** (mit einer Waffe) stab; **b)** (Dornen~, Nadel~) prick; (von Wespe, Biene usw.) sting; (Mük-ken~ usw.) bite; **c)** (~wunde) stab wound; **d)** (beim Nähen) stitch; **e)** (Schmerz) stabbing or shooting pain; **f)** (Kartenspiel) trick; **g)** jmdn./etw. im ~ lassen leave sb. in the lurch/abandon sth.; **sticheln** itr. V. make snide remarks (coll.) (gegen about)

stich-, Stich-: ~**flamme** die tongue of flame; ~**haltig** Adj. sound ⟨argu-

ment, reason⟩; valid ⟨assertion, reply⟩; conclusive ⟨evidence⟩; ~**probe die** [random] sample; (bei Kontrollen) spot check

stichst 2. Pers. Sg. Präsens v. stechen; **sticht** 3. Pers. Sg. Präsens v. stechen

Stich-: ~**tag** der set date; deadline; ~**wunde** die stab wound

sticken 1. itr. V. do embroidery; 2. tr. V. embroider; **Stickerei** die; ~, ~en embroidery no pl.; (gestickte Arbeit) piece of embroidery; **Stick·garn** das embroidery thread

stickig Adj. stuffy; stale ⟨air⟩; **Stick·stoff** der nitrogen

Stief- step ⟨brother, child, mother, etc.⟩

Stiefel der; ~s, ~ boot

Stief·mütterchen das (Bot.) pansy; **stief·mütterlich** 1. Adj. poor, shabby ⟨treatment⟩; 2. adv. ~ behandeln treat ⟨person⟩ poorly or shabbily; neglect ⟨pet, flowers, doll, problem⟩

stieg 1. u. 3. Pers. Sg. Prät. v. steigen

Stieglitz der; ~es, ~e goldfinch

stiehl Imp. Sg. v. stehlen; **stiehlst** 2. Pers. Sg. Präsens v. stehlen; **stiehlt** 3. Pers. Sg. Präsens v. stehlen

Stiel der; ~[e]s, ~e (Griff) handle; (Besen~) [broom-]stick; (für Süßigkeiten) stick; (bei Gläsern) stem; (bei Blumen) stem; (an Obst usw.) stalk

Stier der; ~[e]s, ~e bull

stieren itr. V. stare [vacantly] (auf + Akk. at)

Stier·kampf der bullfight

stieß 1. u. 3. Pers. Sg. Prät. v. stoßen

Stift der; ~[e]s, ~e **a)** (aus Metall) pin; (aus Holz) peg; **b)** (Blei~) pencil; (Mal~) crayon; (Schreib~) pen

stiften tr. V. **a)** found, establish ⟨monastery, hospital, etc.⟩; endow ⟨prize, scholarship⟩; (als Spende) donate, give (für to); **b)** (herbeiführen) cause, create ⟨unrest, confusion, strife, etc.⟩; bring about ⟨peace, order, etc.⟩; arrange ⟨marriage⟩; **Stifter** der; ~s, ~: founder; (Spender) donor

Stift·zahn der (Zahnmed.) post crown

Stil der; ~[e]s, ~e style; **stilistisch** 1. Adj. stylistic; 2. adv. stylistically

still 1. Adj. quiet; (ohne Geräusche) silent; still; (reglos) still; (wortlos) silent; (heimlich) secret; **der Stille Ozean** the Pacific [Ocean]; 2. adv. quietly; (geräuschlos) silently; (wortlos) in silence; **Stille** die; ~: quiet; (Geräuschlosigkeit) silence; stillness; **stillegen** tr. V. close or shut down;

close ⟨*railway line*⟩; **stillen** 1. *tr. V.* a) **ein Kind ~**: breast-feed a baby; b) (*befriedigen*) satisfy; quench ⟨*thirst*⟩; c) (*eindämmen*) stop ⟨*bleeding, tears, pain*⟩; 2. *itr. V.* breast-feed

still-, **Still**-: ~**|halten** *unr. itr. V.* keep *or* stay still; ~**|legen** *s.* **stillegen**; ~**|schweigen das schweigen bewahren** maintain silence; keep silent; ~**schweigend** 1. *Adj.* silent; (*ohne Abmachung*) tacit ⟨*assumption, agreement*⟩; 2. *adv.* in silence; (*ohne Abmachung*) tacitly; ~**|sitzen** *unr. itr. V.* sit still; ~**stand der**; *o. Pl.* standstill; ~**|stehen** *unr. itr. V.* a) ⟨*factory, machine*⟩ stand idle; ⟨*traffic*⟩ be at a standstill; ⟨*heart etc.*⟩ stop; b) (*Milit.*) stand to attention

Stimm·bruch der: er ist im ~: his voice is breaking; **Stimme die; ~, ~n** a) voice; b) (*bei Wahlen*) vote

stimmen 1. *itr. V.* a) be right *or* correct; **stimmt es, daß ...?** is it true that ...?; b) (*seine Stimme geben*) vote; **mit Ja ~**: vote yes *or* in favour; 2. *tr. V.* a) (*in eine Stimmung versetzen*) make; b) (*Musik*) tune ⟨*instrument*⟩

Stimm-: ~**enthaltung die** abstention; ~**recht das** right to vote

Stimmung die; ~, ~en a) mood; b) (*Atmosphäre*) atmosphere

Stink·bombe die stink-bomb; **stinken** *unr. itr. V.* stink (**nach** of); **stinkig** *Adj.* (*salopp abwertend*) stinking; smelly

stirb *Imp. Sg. v.* **sterben**; **stirbst** 2. *Pers. Sg. Präsens v.* **sterben**; **stirbt** 3. *Pers. Sg. Präsens v.* **sterben**

Stirn die; ~, ~en forehead; brow

stöbern *itr. V.* (*ugs.*) rummage

stochern *itr. V.* poke

¹**Stock der;** ~**|e|s, Stöcke** a) stick; (*Zeige~*) pointer; stick; (*Takt~*) baton; (*Ski~*) pole; stick; b) (*Pflanze*) (*Rosen~*) [rose-]bush; (*Reb~*) vine; ²**Stock der;** ~**|e|s, ~** (*Etage*) floor; storey; **in welchem ~?** on which floor?; **stock·dunkel** *Adj.* (*ugs.*) pitch-dark; **stocken** *itr. V.* a) (*traffic*) be held up; ⟨*conversation, production*⟩ stop; ⟨*business*⟩ slacken; ⟨*journey*⟩ be interrupted; b) (*innehalten*) falter; **stock·finster** *Adj.* (*ugs.*) pitch-dark

-**stöckig** -storey *attr.*; -storeyed

Stockung die; ~, ~en hold-up (*Gen.* in); **Stockwerk das** floor; storey

Stoff der; ~**|e|s, ~e** a) material; fabric; b) (*Materie*) substance; c) *o. Pl.* (*Phi-*

los.) matter; d) (*Thema*) subject[-matter]; (*Gesprächsthema*) topic; **Stoffwechsel der**; *o. Pl.* metabolism

stöhnen *itr. V.* moan; (*vor Schmerz*) groan

Stola die; ~, Stolen shawl; (*Pelz~*) stole

Stollen der; ~**s, ~** a) (*Kuchen*) Stollen; b) (*Bergbau*) gallery; c) (*bei Sportschuhen*) stud

stolpern *itr. V.; mit sein* stumble; trip

stolz 1. *Adj.* proud (**auf** + *Akk.* of); **eine ~e Summe** (*ugs.*) a tidy sum; 2. *adv.* proudly; **Stolz der;** ~**es** pride (**auf** + *Akk.* in); **stolzieren** *itr. V.; mit sein* strut

stop *Interj.* stop; (*Verkehrsw.*) halt

stopfen *tr. V.* a) darn; b) (*hineintun*) stuff; c) (*füllen*) stuff ⟨*cushion, quilt, etc.*⟩; fill ⟨*pipe*⟩; plug, stop [up] ⟨*hole, leak*⟩

Stopf-: ~**garn das** darning-cotton; ~**nadel die** darning-needle

Stopp der; ~**s, ~s** stop; (*Einstellung*) freeze (*Gen.* on)

Stoppel die; ~, ~n stubble *no pl.*; **stoppelig** *Adj.* stubbly

stoppen *tr., itr. V.* stop

Stopp-: ~**licht das;** *Pl.* ~**er** stoplight; ~**schild das** stop sign; ~**uhr die** stop-watch

Stöpsel der; ~**s, ~** plug

Stör der; ~**s, ~e** sturgeon

Storch der; ~**|e|s, Störche** stork

stören 1. *tr. V.* a) disturb; disrupt ⟨*court proceedings, lecture, church service, etc.*⟩; interfere with ⟨*transmitter, reception*⟩; b) (*mißfallen*) bother; 2. *itr. V.* a) disturb; b) (*Unruhe stiften*) make *or* cause trouble; 3. *refl. V.* **sich an jmdm./etw. ~**: take exception to sb./sth.; **Störenfried der;** ~**|e|s, ~e** trouble-maker

störrisch 1. *Adj.* stubborn; 2. *adv.* stubbornly

Störung die; ~, ~en a) disturbance; (*einer Gerichtsverhandlung, Vorlesung, eines Gottesdienstes usw.*) disruption; **bitte entschuldigen Sie die ~ aber ...**: I'm sorry to bother you, but ...; b) **eine technische ~**: a technical fault

Stoß der; ~**es, Stöße** a) (*mit der Faust*) punch; (*mit dem Fuß*) kick; (*mit dem Kopf, den Hörnern*) butt; (*mit dem Ellbogen*) dig; b) (*mit einer Waffe*) ⟨*Stich*⟩ thrust; (*Schlag*) blow; c) (*beim Schwimmen, Rudern*) stroke; d) (*Stapel*) pile; stack; **stoßen** 1. *unr. tr. V.* a) *auch itr.* (*mit der Faust*) punch; (*mit* *dem Fuß)* kick; *(mit dem Kopf, den Hörnern)* butt; *(mit dem Ellbogen)* dig; **b)** *(hineintreiben)* plunge, thrust ⟨*dagger, knife*⟩; push ⟨*stick, pole*⟩; **c)** *(schleudern)* push; **die Kugel ~:** put the shot; **2.** *itr. V.* **a)** *mit sein (auftreffen)* bump *(gegen* into); **mit dem Kopf gegen etw. ~:** bump one's head on sth.; **b)** *mit sein (fig.)* **auf etw.** *(Akk.)* **~** *(etw. entdecken)* come upon sth.; **auf Ablehnung ~** *(abgelehnt werden)* meet with disapproval; **c)** *(grenzen)* **an etw.** *(Akk.)* **~** ⟨*room, property, etc.*⟩ be [right] next to sth.; **3.** *unr. refl. V.* bump or knock oneself; **sich an etw.** *(Dat.)* **~** *(fig.)* object to sth.

Stoß-: ~seufzer der heartfelt groan; **~stange** die bumper

stößt *3. Pers. Sg. Präsens v.* stoßen; **stoß·weise** *Adv.* **a)** spasmodically; **b)** *(in Stapeln)* by the pile; in piles

Stotterer der; ~s, ~: stutterer; **stottern 1.** *itr. V.* stutter; **2.** *tr. V.* stutter [out]

Str. *Abk.* Straße St./Rd.

stracks *Adv.* **a)** *(direkt)* straight; **b)** *(sofort)* straight away

straf·bar *Adj.* punishable; **Strafe** die; ~, ~n punishment; *(Rechtsspr.)* penalty; *(Freiheits~)* sentence; *(Geld~)* fine; **strafen** *tr. V.* punish

straff 1. *Adj.* **a)** tight, taut ⟨*rope, lines, etc.*⟩; firm ⟨*breasts, skin*⟩; **b)** *(energisch)* tight ⟨*organization, planning, etc.*⟩; strict ⟨*discipline, leadership, etc.*⟩; **2.** *adv.* **a)** *[zu]* **~** sitzen ⟨*clothes*⟩ be [too] tight; **b)** *(energisch)* tightly, strictly

straf·fällig *Adj.* **~ werden** commit a criminal offence

straffen *tr. V.* **a)** tighten; firm ⟨*skin*⟩; **b)** *(fig.)* tighten up ⟨*text, procedure, organization, etc.*⟩

straf-, Straf-: ~frei *Adj.* **~frei ausgehen** go unpunished; **~gefangene** der/die prisoner; **~gesetz·buch** das penal code

sträflich 1. *Adj.* criminal; **2.** *adv.* criminally; **Sträfling** der; ~s, ~e prisoner

straf-, Straf-: ~los *Adj.* unpunished; **~tat** die criminal offence; **~täter** der offender; **~zettel** der *(ugs.)* [parking-, speeding-, *etc.*] ticket

Strahl der; ~[e]s, ~en *(auch Phys., Math., fig.)* ray; *(von Scheinwerfern, Taschenlampen)* beam; *(von Flüssigkeit)* jet; **strahlen** *itr. V.* **a)** shine; **bei ~dem Wetter/Sonnenschein** in glori-

ous sunny weather/in glorious sunshine; **~d weiß** sparkling white; **b)** *(glänzen)* sparkle; **c)** *(lächeln)* beam *(vor + Dat.* with); **Strahler** der; ~s, ~ a) radiator; **b)** *(Heiz~)* radiant heater; **Strahlung** die; ~, ~en radiation

Strähne die; ~, ~n strand; **eine graue ~:** a grey streak; **strähnig 1.** *Adj.* straggly ⟨*hair*⟩; **2.** *adv.* in strands

stramm 1. *Adj.* **a)** *(straff)* tight, taut ⟨*rope, line, etc.*⟩; tight ⟨*clothes*⟩; **b)** *(kräftig)* strapping ⟨*girl, boy*⟩; sturdy ⟨*legs, body*⟩; **c)** *(gerade)* upright, erect ⟨*posture, etc.*⟩; **2.** *adv.* **a)** *(straff)* tightly; **b)** *(kräftig)* sturdily ⟨*built*⟩

strampeln *itr. V.* ⟨*baby*⟩ kick [his/her feet]

Strand der; ~[e]s, Strände beach; **am ~:** on the beach; **Strand·bad** das bathing beach *(on river, lake)*; **stranden** *itr. V.; mit sein* ⟨*ship*⟩ run aground; **Strand·korb** der basket chair

Strang der; ~[e]s, Stränge rope

Strapaze die; ~, ~n strain *no pl.*; **strapazieren** *tr. V.* be a strain on ⟨*person, nerves*⟩; **strapazier·fähig** *Adj.* hard-wearing ⟨*clothes, shoes*⟩; durable ⟨*material*⟩

Straße die; ~, ~n *(in Ortschaften)* street; road; *(außerhalb)* road; **Straßen-: ~bahn** die tram *(Brit.)*; streetcar *(Amer.)*; **~ecke** die street corner; **~feger** der *(bes. nordd.)* road-sweeper; **~graben** der ditch [at the side of the road]; **~karte** die road-map; **~sperre** die road-block

sträuben 1. *tr. V.* ruffle [up] ⟨*feathers*⟩; bristle ⟨*fur, hair*⟩; **2.** *refl. V.* ⟨*hair, fur*⟩ bristle, stand on end; ⟨*feathers*⟩ become ruffled; **b)** *(sich widersetzen)* resist

Strauch der; ~[e]s, Sträucher shrub; **straucheln** *itr. V.; mit sein (geh.)* stumble

¹Strauß der; ~es, Sträuße bunch of flowers; bouquet [of flowers]

²Strauß der; ~es, ~e *(Vogel)* ostrich; **Sträußchen** das; ~s, ~: posy

streben *itr. V.* **a)** *mit sein* make one's way briskly; **b)** *(trachten)* strive *(nach* for); **Streber** der; ~s; ~ *(abwertend)* pushy person *(coll.)*; *(in der Schule)* swot *(Brit. sl.)*; grind *(Amer. sl.)*; **strebsam** *Adj.* ambitious and industrious

Strecke die; ~, ~n distance; *(Abschnitt, Route)* route; *(Eisenbahn~)*

line; **strecken 1.** *tr. V. (gerade machen)* stretch ⟨*arms, legs*⟩; *(dehnen)* stretch [out] ⟨*arms, legs, etc.*⟩; **den Kopf aus dem Fenster ~:** stick one's head out of the window *(coll.)*; **2.** *refl. V.* stretch out; **strecken·weise** *Adv.* in places; *(fig.: zeitweise)* at times

Streich der; ~|e|s, ~e trick; prank; **jmdm. einen ~ spielen** play a trick on sb.; **streicheln** *tr. V.* stroke; **streichen 1.** *unr. tr. V.* **a)** stroke; **b)** *(an~)* paint; „**frisch gestrichen**" 'wet paint'; **c)** *(aufstragen)* spread ⟨*butter, jam, ointment, etc.*⟩; *(be~)* **ein Brötchen mit Butter/mit Honig ~:** butter a roll/spread honey on a roll; **d)** *(aus~, tilgen)* delete; cancel ⟨*train, flight*⟩; **2.** *unr. itr. V.* **a)** stroke; **jmdm. über den Kopf ~:** stroke sb.'s head; **b)** *(an~)* paint

Streich-: **~holz** das match; **~instrument** das string[ed] instrument; **~käse** der cheese spread; **~wurst** die [soft] sausage for spreading; ≈ meat spread

Streife die; ~, ~n **a)** *(Personen)* patrol; **b)** *(Streifengang)* patrol; **streifen 1.** *tr. V.* **a)** *(leicht berühren)* touch; ⟨*shot*⟩ graze; **b)** *(kurz behandeln)* touch ⟨*problem, subject, etc.*⟩; **c) den Ring vom Finger ~:** slip the ring off one's finger; **die Ärmel nach oben ~:** pull/push up one's sleeves; **2.** *itr. V. mit sein* roam; **Streifen** der; ~s, ~ **a)** stripe; **b)** *(Stück, Abschnitt)* strip; **Streifen·wagen** der patrol car; **streifig** *Adj.* streaky

Streik der; ~|e|s, ~s strike; **Streik·brecher** der strike-breaker; blackleg *(derog.)*; **streiken** *itr. V.* **a)** strike; be on strike; *(in den Streik treten)* come out or go on strike; strike; **b)** *(ugs.: nicht mitmachen)* go on strike; *(ugs.: nicht funktionieren)* pack up *(coll.)*; **Streikende** der/die; *adj. Dekl.* striker; **Streik·posten** der picket

Streit der; ~|e|s, ~e *(Zank)* quarrel; *(Auseinandersetzung)* dispute; argument; **streiten** *unr. itr., refl. V.* quarrel; argue; *(sich zanken)* quarrel; **Streiterei** die; ~, ~en arguing *no pl., no indef. art.*; *(Gezänk)* quarrelling *no pl.*; **Streitigkeit** die; ~, ~en *meist Pl.* **a)** quarrel; argument; **b)** *(Streitfall)* dispute

streng 1. *Adj.* **a)** strict; severe *(punish-*

ment); stringent, strict ⟨*rule, regulation, etc.*⟩; stringent ⟨*measure*⟩; rigorous ⟨*examination, check, test, etc.*⟩; stern ⟨*reprimand, look*⟩; absolute ⟨*discretion*⟩; complete ⟨*rest*⟩; **b)** *(schmucklos, herb)* austere, severe ⟨*cut, collar, style, etc.*⟩; severe ⟨*face, features, hairstyle, etc.*⟩; **c)** *(durchdringend)* pungent, sharp ⟨*taste, smell*⟩; **d)** *(rauh)* severe ⟨*winter*⟩; sharp, severe ⟨*frost*⟩; **2.** *adv.* ⟨*mark, judge, etc.*⟩ strictly, severely; ⟨*punish*⟩ severely; ⟨*look, reprimand*⟩ sternly; ⟨*smell*⟩ strongly; **Strenge** die; ~ **a)** s. **streng a:** strictness; severity; stringency; rigour; sternness; **b)** *(von [Gesichts]zügen)* severity; **c)** *(von Geruch, Geschmack)* pungency; sharpness; **d)** *s.* **streng d:** severity; sharpness; **strengstens** *Adv.* [most] strictly

Streß der; **Stresses** stress

Streu die; ~, ~en straw; **streuen** *tr. V.* **a)** spread ⟨*manure, sand, grit*⟩; sprinkle ⟨*salt, herbs, etc.*⟩; strew, scatter ⟨*flowers*⟩; **b)** *auch itr.* **die Straßen |mit Sand/Salz| ~:** grit/salt the roads

streunen *itr. V.; meist mit sein* wander or roam about or around; **~de Katzen/Hunde** stray cats/dogs

Streusel·kuchen der streusel cake

strich *1. u. 3. Pers. Sg. Prät. v.* **streichen**

Strich der; ~|e|s, ~e *(Linie)* line; *(Gedanken~)* dash; *(Schräg~)* diagonal; *(Binde-, Trennungs~)* hyphen; **auf den ~ gehen** *(salopp)* walk the streets; **stricheln** *tr. V.* **a)** sketch in [with short lines]; **b)** *(schraffieren)* hatch

Strich-: **~junge** der *(salopp)* [young] male prostitute; **~mädchen** das *(salopp)* street-walker; hooker *(Amer. sl.)*; **~punkt** der semicolon

Strick der; ~|e|s, ~e cord; *(Seil)* rope; **stricken** *tr., itr. V.* knit

Strick-: **~jacke** die cardigan; **~nadel** die knitting-needle; **~zeug** das knitting

striegeln *tr. V.* groom ⟨*horse*⟩

strikt 1. *Adj.* strict; **2.** *adv.* strictly

Strippe die; ~, ~n *(ugs.)* string; **an der ~ hängen** *(fig.)* be on the phone *(coll.)*; *(dauernd)* hog the phone *(coll.)*

Stripperin die; ~, ~nen *(ugs.)* stripper

stritt *1. u. 3. Pers. Sg. Prät. v.* **streiten**

strittig *Adj.* contentious ⟨*point, problem*⟩; disputed ⟨*territory*⟩; ⟨*question*⟩ in dispute, at issue

Stroh das; ~|e|s straw

Stroh-: ~**blume die a)** *(Immortelle)* immortelle; **b)** *(Korbblütler)* straw-flower; ~**halm der** straw; ~**witwe die** *(ugs. scherzh.)* grass widow; ~**witwer der** *(ugs. scherzh.)* grass widower

Strolch der; ~|e|s, ~e *(fam. scherzh.: Junge)* rascal

Strom der; ~|e|s, Ströme river; *(fig.)* stream; *(Strömung; Elektrizität)* current; *(~versorgung)* electricity; **unter** ~ **stehen** be live

strom-: ~**abwärts** *Adv.* down-stream; ~**auf[wärts]** *Adv.* upstream

strömen *itr. V.; mit sein* stream; **Strömung die;** ~, ~en current; *(Met.)* airstream; *(fig.)* trend

Strophe die; ~, ~n verse; *(einer Ode)* strophe

strotzen *itr. V.* von *od.* vor etw. *(Dat.)* ~: be full of sth.; **von** *od.* **vor Gesundheit** ~: be bursting with health

strubbelig *Adj.* tousled

Strudel der; ~s, ~ **a)** whirlpool; **b)** *(bes. südd., österr.: Gebäck)* strudel

Strumpf der; ~|e|s, Strümpfe stocking; *(Socke, Knie~)* sock

Strumpf-: ~**band das** garter; *(Straps)* suspender *(Brit.)*; garter *(Amer.)*; ~**hose die** tights *pl. (Brit.)*; pantyhose *(esp. Amer.)*

Strunk der; ~|e|s, Strünke stem; stalk; *(Baum~)* stump

struppig *Adj.* shaggy; tangled, tousled *(hair)*

Stube die; ~, ~n **a)** *(veralt.: Wohnraum)* [living-]room; parlour *(dated)*; **b)** *Milit.* [barrack-]room; **Stubenfliege die** [common] house-fly

Stück das; ~|e|s, ~e **a)** piece; *(kleines)* bit; *(Teil, Abschnitt)* part; **ein** ~ **Kuchen** a piece *or* slice of cake; **ein** ~ **Zucker/Seife** a lump of sugar/ a piece *or* bar of soap; **im** *od.* **am** ~: unsliced *(sausage, cheese, etc.)*; **b)** *(Einzel~)* item; *(Exemplar)* specimen; **ich nehme 5** ~: I'll take five [of them]; **30 Pfennig das** ~: thirty pfennigs each; ~ **für** ~: piece by piece; *(eins nach dem andern)* one by one; **das ist ja ein starkes** ~ *(ugs.)* that's a bit much; **ein faules/freches** ~ *(salopp)* a lazy/cheeky thing *or* devil; **c)** *(Bühnen~)* play; *(Musik~)* piece; **Stückchen das;** ~s, ~ [little] piece; bit; **stückeln** *tr. V.* put together *(sleeve, curtain)* with patches

Student der; ~en, ~en, **Studentin die;** ~, ~nen **a)** student; **b)** *(österr.: Schüler)* [secondary-school] pupil; **Studie** ['ʃtu:diə] **die;** ~, ~n study

Studien-: ~**aufenthalt der** study visit (**in** + *Dat.* to); ~**freund der** university/college friend; ~**reise die** study trip

studieren *tr., itr. V.* study; **Studierende der/die;** *adj. Dekl.* student; **Studio das;** ~s, ~s studio; **Studium das;** ~s, Studien study; *(Studiengang)* course of study

Stufe die; ~, ~n **a)** step; *(einer Treppe)* stair; „**Vorsicht,** ~!" 'mind the step'; **b)** *(Raketen~, Geol., fig.: Stadium)* stage; *(Niveau)* level; *(Steigerungs~, Grad)* degree; *(Rang)* grade

Stuhl der; ~|e|s, Stühle chair

Stuhl-: ~**gang der;** *o. Pl.* bowel movement[s]; *(Kot)* stool; ~**lehne die** *(Rückenlehne)* chair-back; *(Armlehne)* chair-arm

stülpen *tr. V.* etw. auf *od.* über etw. *(Akk.)* ~: pull/put sth. on to *or* over sth.

stumm *Adj.* dumb 〈*person*〉; *(schweigsam)* silent; *(wortlos)* wordless; mute 〈*glance, gesture*〉; **Stumme der/die;** *adj. Dekl.* mute; **die** ~**n** the dumb

Stummel der; ~s, ~: stump; *(Bleistift~)* stub; *(Zigaretten~/Zigarren~)* [cigarette-/cigar-]butt

Stümper der; ~s, ~: botcher; bungler; **stümperhaft 1.** *Adj.* incompetent; botched 〈*job*〉; *(laienhaft)* amateurish 〈*attempt, drawing*〉; **2.** *adv.* incompetently; *(laienhaft)* amateurishly; **stümpern** *itr. V.* work incompetently; *(pfuschen)* bungle

stumpf *Adj.* **a)** blunt 〈*pin, needle, knife, etc.*〉; **b)** *(glanzlos, matt)* dull 〈*paint, hair, metal, colour, etc.*〉; **Stumpf der;** ~|e|s, Stümpfe stump

Stumpf·sinn der; *o. Pl.* **a)** apathy; *(Monotonie)* monotony; tedium; **stumpf·sinnig 1.** *Adj.* **a)** apathetic; vacant 〈*look*〉; **b)** *(monoton)* tedious; souldestroying 〈*job, work*〉; **2.** *adv.* **a)** apathetically; 〈*stare*〉 vacantly; **b)** *(monoton)* tediously

Stunde die; ~, ~n hour; *(Unterrichts~)* lesson; **eine** ~ **Aufenthalt/Pause** an hour's stop/break; a stop/break of an hour

stünde *1. u. 3. Pers. Sg. Konjunktiv II v.* stehen

stunden *tr. V.* jmdm. einen Betrag *usw.* ~: allow sb. to defer payment of a sum *etc.*

stunden-, Stunden-: ~**kilometer der** kilometre per hour; k.p.h.; ~**lang 1.** *Adj.* lasting hours *postpos.*; **2.** *adv.*

for hours; ~**lohn** der hourly wage; ~**plan** der timetable; ~**zeiger** der hour-hand

-stündig adj. -hour; **-stündlich** adj. -hourly; **zwei~/halb~:** two-hourly/half-hourly; adv. every two hours/half an hour; **stündlich** Adj., adv. hourly

Stups der; ~es, ~e (ugs.) push; shove; (leicht) nudge; **stupsen** tr. V. (ugs.) push; shove; (leicht) nudge; **Stups·nase** die snub nose

stur (ugs.) **1.** Adj. **a)** obstinate; dogged (insistence); (phlegmatisch) dour; **b)** (unbeirrbar) dogged; persistent; **c)** (stumpfsinnig) tedious; **2.** adv. **a)** obstinately; **b)** (unbeirrbar) doggedly; **c)** (stumpfsinnig) tediously (learn, copy) mechanically

stürbe 1. u. 3. Pers. Sg. Konjunktiv II v. sterben

Sturheit die; ~ (ugs.) **a)** obstinacy; (phlegmatisches Wesen) dourness; **b)** (Stumpfsinnigkeit) deadly monotony

Sturm der; ~|e|s, Stürme **a)** storm; (heftiger Wind) gale; **b)** (Milit.) assault (**auf** + Akk. on); ~ **klingeln** ring the [door]bell like mad; **stürmen 1.** itr. V. **a)** unpers. es stürmt [heftig] it's blowing a gale; **b)** mit sein (rennen) rush; (verärgert) storm; **2.** tr. V. (Milit.) storm (town, position, etc.); (fig.) besiege (booking-office, shop, etc.); **Stürmer** der; ~s, ~ (Sport) striker; forward; **stürmisch 1.** Adj. **a)** stormy; (fig.) tempestuous, turbulent; **b)** (ungestüm) tumultuous (applause, welcome, reception); wild (enthusiasm); passionate (lover, embrace, temperament); vehement (protest); **2.** adv. (protest) vehemently; (embrace) impetuously, passionately; (demand) clamorously; (applaud) wildly

Sturz der; -es, Stürze **a)** fall; (Unfall) accident; **b)** (fig.: von Preis, Temperatur usw.) [sharp] fall, drop (Gen. in); **c)** (Verlust des Amtes, der Macht) fall; (Absetzung) overthrow; (Amtsenthebung) removal from office; **stürzen 1.** itr. V.; mit sein **a)** fall; (fig.) (temperature, exchange rate, etc.) drop [sharply]; (prices) tumble; (government) fall, collapse; **b)** (laufen) rush; dash; **c)** (fließen) stream; pour; **2.** refl. V. sich auf jmdn./etw. ~ pounce on sb./sth.; sich in etw. ~: throw oneself into sth.; **3.** tr. V. **a)** throw; (mit Wucht) hurl; **b)** (umdrehen) upturn (mould); turn out (pud-

ding, cake, etc.); **c)** (des Amtes entheben) oust (person) [from office]; (gewaltsam) overthrow (leader, government); **Sturz·helm** der crash-helmet

Stute die; ~, ~n mare

Stütze die; ~, ~n (auch fig.) support

¹**stutzen** itr. V. stop short

²**stutzen** tr. V. trim; dock (tail); clip (ear, hedge, wing); prune (tree, bush)

stützen 1. tr. V. support; (mit Pfosten o. ä.) prop up; (aufstützen) rest (head, hands, arms, etc.); **2.** refl. V. sich auf jmdn./etw. ~: lean or support oneself on sb./sth.

stutzig Adj. ~ werden begin to wonder; jmdn. ~ machen make sb. wonder

s.u. Abk. siehe unten see below

Subjekt das; ~|e|s, ~e **a)** subject; **b)** (abwertend: Mensch) creature; **subjektiv 1.** Adj. subjective; **2.** adv. subjectively; **Subjektivität** die; ~: subjectivity

Substantiv das; ~s, ~e (Sprachw.) noun; **Substanz** die; ~, ~en **a)** (auch fig.) substance; **b)** (Grundbestand) die ~: the reserves pl.

sub·tropisch Adj. subtropical

Suche die; ~, ~n search (nach for); **auf der** ~ |**nach jmdm./etw.|** sein be looking/(intensiver) searching [for sb./sth.]; **suchen 1.** tr. V. **a)** look for; (intensiver) search for; „Leerzimmer gesucht" 'unfurnished room wanted'; **b)** (bedacht sein auf, sich wünschen) seek (protection, advice, company, warmth, etc.); look for (adventure); **2.** itr. V. search; nach jmdm./etw. ~: look/search for sb./sth.

Sucht die; ~, Süchte od. ~en **a)** addiction (nach to); |**bei jmdm.|** zur ~ werden (auch fig.) become addictive [in sb.'s case]; **b)** Pl. Süchte (übermäßiges Verlangen) craving (nach for); **süchtig** Adj. **a)** addicted; **b)** (fig.) nach etw. ~ sein be obsessed with sth.

Süd o. Art.; o. Pl. (bes. Seemannsspr., Met.) s. Süden

Süd-: ~**afrika (das)** South Africa; ~**amerika (das)** South America

Sudan (das); ~s od. der; ~s Sudan

Süden der; ~s south; der ~: the South; **Süd·frucht** die tropical [or sub-tropical] fruit; **Südländer** der; ~s, ~: Southern European; **südländisch** Adj. Southern [European]; Latin (temperament); ~ **aussehen** have Latin looks; **südlich 1.** Adj. **a)** southern; **b)** (nach, von Süden) southerly; **c)** (aus dem Süden) Southern; **2.** adv.

southwards; **3.** *Präp. mit Gen.* [to the] south of

süd-, Süd-: ~**pol** der South Pole; ~**see die;** ~**: die** ~**:** the South Seas *pl.;* ~**see·insel** die South Sea island; ~**tirol** (das) South Tirol ~**wärts** *Adv.* southwards; ~**wind** der south *or* southerly wind

Sues·kanal ['zu:ɛs-] der; ~s Suez Canal

Sühne die; ~, ~**n** *(geh.)* atonement; expiation; **sühnen** *tr., itr. V.* [für] etw. ~: atone for *or* pay the penalty for sth.

Sultanine die; ~, ~**n** sultana

Sülze die; ~, ~**n** **a)** diced meat/fish in aspic; *(vom Schweinskopf)* brawn; **b)** *(Aspik)* aspic

Summe die; ~, ~**n** sum

summen 1. *itr. V.* hum; *(lauter, heller)* buzz; **2.** *tr. V.* hum ⟨tune, song, etc.⟩

summieren *refl. V.* add up **(auf +** *Akk.* to)

Sumpf der; ~[e]s, **Sümpfe** marsh; *(bes. in den Tropen)* swamp; **sumpfig** *Adj.* marshy

Sund der; ~[e]s, ~**e** *(Geogr.)* sound

Sünde die; ~, ~**n** sin; *(fig.)* misdeed; transgression; **Sünden·bock** der *(ugs.)* scapegoat; **Sünder** der; ~s, ~, **Sünderin** die; ~, ~**nen** sinner; **sündigen** *itr. V.* sin

Super das; ~s, ~: four star *(Brit.);* premium *(Amer.);* **super-** ultra-⟨long, high, fast, modern, masculine, etc.⟩; **Super-** super-⟨hero, figure, car, group, etc.⟩; terrific *(coll.),* tremendous *(coll.)* ⟨success, offer, chance, idea, etc.⟩; **Superlativ** ['zu:pɐlati:f] der; ~s, ~**e** *(Sprachw.)* superlative; **Super·markt** der supermarket

Suppe die; ~; ~**n** soup; **Suppen·löffel** der soup-spoon

Surf·brett ['sɔ:f-] das surf-board; **surfen** ['sɔ:fn̩] *itr. V.* surf; **Surfer** ['sɔ:fɐ] der; ~s, ~: surfer

surren *itr. V.* **a)** *(summen)* hum; ⟨camera, fan⟩ whirr; **b)** *mit sein (schwirren)* whirr

suspekt 1. *Adj.* suspicious; jmdm. ~ sein arouse sb.'s suspicions; **2.** *adv.* suspiciously

süß 1. *Adj.* sweet; **2.** *adv.* sweetly; **süßen** *tr. V.* sweeten; **Süßigkeit** die; ~, ~**en** sweet *(Brit.);* candy *(Amer.);* ~**en** sweets *(Brit.);* candy *sing. (Amer.); (als Ware)* confectionery *sing.;* **süßlich 1.** *Adj.* **a)** [slightly] sweet; on the sweet side *pred.;* **b)** *(sen-*

timental) sickly mawkish; **2.** *adv.* ⟨write, paint⟩ mawkishly

süß-, Süß-: ~**most** der unfermented fruit juice; ~**sauer 1.** *Adj.* sweet-and-sour; *(fig.)* wry ⟨smile, face⟩; **2.** *adv.* **a)** etw. ~**sauer** zubereiten give sth. a sweet-and-sour flavour; **b)** *(fig.)* ⟨smile⟩ wryly; ~**speise** die sweet; dessert; ~**stoff** der sweetener; ~**wasser** das; *Pl.* ~**wasser** fresh water

svw. *Abk.* soviel wie

Symbol das; ~s, ~**e** symbol; **symbolisch 1.** *Adj.* symbolic; **2.** *adv.* symbolically

Sympathie [zympa'ti:] die; ~, ~**n** sympathy (für with); **sympathisch 1.** *Adj.* congenial, likeable ⟨person, manner⟩; appealing ⟨voice, appearance, material⟩; **2.** *adv.* in an appealing way; *(angenehm)* agreeably

Symphonie usw. s. Sinfonie usw.

Synagoge die; ~, ~**n** synagogue

Syrer der; ~s, ~, **Syrerin** die; ~, ~**nen** Syrian; **Syrien** ['zy:riən] (das); ~s Syria; **syrisch** *Adj.* Syrian

System das; ~s, ~**e** system; **systematisch 1.** *Adj.* systematic; **2.** *adv.* systematically

Szene ['stse:nə] die; ~, ~**n** *(auch fig.)* scene

T

t, T [te:] das; ~, ~: t, T

t *Abk.* Tonne t

Tab. *Abk.* Tabelle

Tabak ['ta(:)bak] der; ~s, ~**e** tobacco; **Tabaks·pfeife** die [tobacco-]pipe

Tabelle die; ~, ~**n** table

Tabernakel das *od.* der; ~s, ~: tabernacle

Tablett das; ~[e]s, ~s *od.* ~**e** tray; **Tablette** die; ~, ~**n** tablet

tabu *Adj.* taboo; **Tabu** das; ~s, ~**s** taboo

Tacho der; ~s, ~**s** *(ugs.)* speedo *(coll.);* **Tacho·meter** der *od.* das speedometer

Tadel der; ~s, ~ **a)** censure; **b)** *(im*

Klassenbuch) black mark; **tadel·los**
1. *Adj.* impeccable; immaculate *(hair,
clothing, suit, etc.);* perfect *(condition,
teeth, pronunciation, German, etc.);* 2.
adv. (dress) impeccably; *(fit, speak,
etc.)* perfectly; *(live, behave, etc.)* irre-
proachably; **tadeln** *tr. V.* jmdn. |für
od. wegen etw.| ~: rebuke sb. [for sth.]

Tafel die; ~, ~n a) *(Schiefer~)* slate;
(Wand~) blackboard; b) *(plattenför-
miges Stück)* slab; **eine ~ Schokolade**
a bar of chocolate; c) *(Gedenk~)*
plaque; d) *(geh.: festlicher Tisch)*
table; **Täfelchen** das; ~s, ~ : s. **Tafel
b**: [small] slab; [small] bar; **tafeln** *itr.
V. (geh.)* feast; **täfeln** *tr V.* panel
Tafel-: ~**spitz** der *(österr.)* boiled fillet of beef; ~**wasser** das; *Pl.* ~wäs-
ser [bottled] mineral water; ~**wein**
der table wine

Taft der; ~|e|s, ~e taffeta

Tag der; ~|e|s, ~e day; **am** ~|e| during
the day[time]; **guten** ~! hello; *(bei Vorstellung)* how do you do?; **an diesem**
~: on this day; **dreimal am** ~: three
times a day; **am folgenden** ~: the next
day; **eines** ~es one day; some day;
tag·aus *Adv.* ~, tagein day in, day
out; day after day; **Tage·buch das**
diary; **tag·ein** *Adv. s.* tagaus; **ta-
ge·lang** 1. *Adj.* lasting for days *postpos.;* **nach** ~em **Regen** after days of
rain; 2. *adv.* for days [on end]; **tagen**
itr. V. meet; day breaks; **das Gericht/Parlament**
tagt the court/parliament is in session

Tages-: ~**karte** die a) *(Gastron.)*
menu of the day; b) *(Fahr-, Eintrittskarte)* day ticket; ~**kasse** die a) box-
office *(open during the day);* b) *(~ein-
nahme)* day's takings *pl.;* ~**licht** das;
o. Pl. daylight; ~**zeit** die time of day;
~**zeitung** die daily newspaper
-tägig a) *(... Tage alt)* **ein sechstägiges**
Küken a six-day-old chick; b) *(... Tage
dauernd)* **nach dreitägiger Vorbereitung** after three days' preparation;
täglich 1. *Adj.* daily; 2. *adv.* every
day; **zweimal** ~: twice a day; ~ **drei**
Tabletten einnehmen take three tablets
daily; **tags** *Adv.* a) by day; in the
daytime; b) **zuvor/davor** the day before; ~ **darauf** the next *or* following
day; the day after; **tags·über** *Adv.*
during the day; **tag·täglich** 1. *Adj.*
day-to-day; daily; 2. *adv.* every single
day; **Tagung** die; ~, ~en conference
Taifun der; ~s, ~e typhoon
Taille ['taljə] die; ~, ~n waist
Taiwan (das); ~s Taiwan

Takt der; ~|e|s, ~e a) *(Musik)* time;
(Einheit) bar; measure *(Amer.);* **aus
dem ~ kommen** lose the beat; b)
o. Pl. (rhythmischer Bewegungsablauf)
rhythm; c) *o. Pl. (Feingefühl)* tact
Taktik die; ~, ~en: |eine| ~: tactics *pl.;*
taktisch 1. *Adj.* tactical; 2. *adv.* tac-
tically
takt-: ~**los** 1. *Adj.* tactless; 2. *adv.*
tactlessly; ~**voll** 1. *Adj.* tactful; 2.
adv. tactfully
Tal das; ~|e|s, **Täler** valley
Talent das; ~|e|s, ~e talent **(zu,** für **for)**;
(Mensch) talented person
Talg der; ~|e|s, ~e suet; *(zur Herstel-
lung von Seife, Kerzen usw.)* tallow
Talisman der; ~s, ~e talisman
Tampon der; ~s, ~s tampon
Tamtam das; ~s *(ugs. abwertend)*
|großes| ~: [a big] fuss
Tang der; ~|e|s, ~e seaweed
Tangente die; ~, ~n *(Math.)* tangent
Tank der; ~s, ~s tank; **tanken** *tr., itr.
V.* fill up; **Öl** ~: fill up with oil
Tank-: ~**säule** die petrol-pump
(Brit.); gasoline pump *(Amer.);*
~**stelle** die petrol station *(Brit.);* gas
station *(Amer.);* ~**wart** der; ~s, ~e
petrol-pump attendant *(Brit.)*
Tanne die; ~, ~n fir|-tree|
Tannen-: ~**baum** der *(ugs.)* fir-tree;
(Weihnachtsbaum) Christmas tree;
~**grün** das; *o. Pl.* fir sprigs *pl.;*
~**zweig** der fir branch
Tansania [tanˈzaːni̯a] **(das)**; ~s Tanza-
nia
Tante die; ~, ~n a) aunt; b) *(Kinderspr.: Frau)* lady; c) *(ugs.: Frau)*
woman
Tanz der; ~es, **Tänze** dance
Tanz-: ~**abend** der evening dance;
~**bar** die night-spot *(coll.)* with dancing; ~**café** das coffee-house with
dancing
tanzen *itr., tr. V.* dance; **Tänzer** der;
~s, ~; **Tänzerin** die; ~, ~nen dancer;
(Ballett~) ballet-dancer
Tanz-: ~**fläche** die dance-floor; ~**lokal** das café/restaurant with dancing;
~**orchester** das dance band;
~**stunde** die a) *(~kurs)* dancing-
class; b) *(einzelne Stunde)* dancing
lesson
Tapete die; ~, ~n wallpaper; **tapezieren** *tr. V.* [wall]paper
tapfer 1. *Adj.* brave; 2. *adv.* bravely;
Tapferkeit die; ~: courage; bravery
tappen *itr. V.* a) *mit sein (patter;* b) *(tastend greifen)* grope **(nach** for); **Taps**

Tarif 716

der; ~es, ~e *(ugs. abwertend)* clumsy
oaf

Tarif der; ~s, ~e charge; *(Post~, Wasser~)* rate; *(Verkehrs~)* fares *pl.*;
(Zoll~) tariff; *(Lohn~)* [wage] rate;
(Gehalts~) [salary] scale

tarnen 1. *tr., itr. V.* camouflage; 2.
refl. V. camouflage oneself

Tasche die; ~, ~n bag; *(in Kleidung, Rucksack usw.)* pocket; **jmdm. auf der
~ liegen** *(fig. ugs.)* live off sb.

Taschen-: ~**buch** das paperback;
~**lampe** die [pocket] torch *(Brit.)* or
(Amer.) flashlight; ~**messer** das
penknife; ~**rechner** der pocket calculator; ~**tuch** das; *Pl.* ~**tücher**
handkerchief; ~**uhr** die pocket-watch

Tasse die; ~, ~n cup

Taste die; ~, ~n a) *(eines Musikinstruments, einer Schreibmaschine)* key; b)
(Fuß~) pedal [key]; c) *(am Telefon, Radio, Fernsehgerät, Taschenrechner usw.)* button; **tasten** 1. *itr. V. (fühlend suchen)* grope, feel **(nach** for); 2.
refl. V. (sich tastend bewegen) grope or
feel one's way; **Tasten·telefon** das
push-button telephone

tat *1. u. 3. Pers. Sg. Prät. v.* **tun;** **Tat**
die; ~, ~en act; *(das Tun)* action; **eine
gute ~** a good deed; **in der ~** *(verstärkend)* actually; *(zustimmend)* indeed

Tatar das; ~[s] steak tartare

Täter der; ~s, ~, **Täterin** die; ~, ~nen
culprit; **tätig** *Adj.* a) ~ **sein** work; b)
(rührig, aktiv) active; **tätigen** *tr. V.
(Kaufmannsspr., Papierdt.)* transact
(business, deal, etc.); **Tätigkeit** die;
~, ~en activity; *(Arbeit)* job; **Tatkraft** die energy; drive; **tat·kräftig**
1. *Adj.* energetic *(person)*; 2. *adv.*
energetically

tätowieren *tr. V.* tattoo; **Tätowierung** die; ~, ~en tattoo

Tat·sache die fact; **tatsächlich** 1.
Adj. actual; real; 2. *adv.* actually;
really

tätscheln *tr. V.* pat

Tatze die; ~, ~n paw

¹**Tau** der; ~[e]s dew

²**Tau** das; ~[e]s, ~e *(Seil)* rope

taub *Adj.* a) deaf; b) *(wie abgestorben)*
numb; c) *(leer, unbefruchtet usw.)*
empty *(nut)*; dead *(rock)*

¹**Taube** die; ~, ~n pigeon; *(Turtel~;
auch Politik fig.)* dove

²**Taube** der/die; *adj. Dekl.* deaf person; deaf man/woman; **die ~n** the
deaf; **Taubheit** die; ~: deafness;
taub·stumm *Adj.* deaf and dumb;

Taub·stumme der/die; *adj. Dekl.*
deaf mute

tauchen 1. *itr. V.* a) *auch mit* sein dive
(nach for); b) *mit* sein *(ein~)* dive;
(auf~) rise; emerge; 2. *tr. V.* a) *(ein~)*
dip; b) *(unter~)* duck; **Taucher** der;
~s, ~, **Taucherin** die; ~, ~nen diver;
(mit Flossen und Atemgerät) skindiver; **Tauch·sieder** der; ~s, ~:
portable immersion heater

tauen 1. *itr. V.* a) *unpers.* **es taut** it's
thawing; b) *mit* sein *(schmelzen)* melt;
2. *tr. V.* melt; thaw

Taufe die; ~, ~n *(christl. Rel.)* a) *o. Pl.
(Sakrament)* baptism; b) *(Zeremonie)*
christening; baptism; **taufen** *tr. V.* a)
baptize; b) *(einen Namen geben)*
christen

taugen *itr. V.* **nichts/nicht viel/etwas
~:** be no/not much/some good or use;
tauglich *Adj.* [nicht] ~: [un]suitable;
(für Militärdienst) fit [for service]

Taumel der; ~s a) *[feeling of]* dizziness; b) *(Rausch)* frenzy; fever;
taumelig *Adj.* dizzy; giddy;
taumeln *itr. V.* a) *auch mit* sein *(wanken)* reel, sway **(vor** + *Dat.* with); b)
mit sein *(sich ~d bewegen)* stagger

Tausch der; ~[e]s, ~e exchange; **ein
guter/schlechter ~** a good/bad deal;
tauschen 1. *tr. V.* exchange **(gegen**
for); **sie tauschten die Plätze** they
changed places; 2. *itr. V.* **mit jmdm. ~**
(fig.) change places with sb.

täuschen 1. *tr. V.* deceive; **wenn mich
nicht alles täuscht** unless I'm completely mistaken; 2. *itr. V.* be deceptive; 3. *refl. V.* be wrong or mistaken
(in + *Dat.* about); **täuschend** 1.
Adj. remarkable, striking *(similarity,
imitation)*; 2. *adv.* remarkably;
Täuschung die; ~, ~en deception;
(Selbst~) delusion

tausend *Kardinalz.* a) a or one thousand; b) *(ugs.: sehr viele)* thousands
of; ~ **Dank/Küsse** a thousand thanks/
kisses; **Tausend** das; ~s, ~e od. ~ a)
nicht in Verbindung mit Kardinalzahlen; Pl.: ~ thousand; b) *Pl. (eine unbestimmte große Zahl)* thousands;
tausend·ein[s] *Kardinalz.* a or one
thousand and one; **Tausender** der;
~s, ~ *(ugs.) (Tausendmarkschein usw.)*
thousand-mark/-dollar etc. note; *(Betrag)* thousand marks/dollars etc.;
tausenderlei *Gattungsz.; indekl.*
(ugs.) a thousand and one different
(answers, kinds, etc.); **tausend·mal**
Adv. a thousand times; **Tausend-**

mark·schein der thousand-mark note; **tausendst...** Ordinalz. thousandth; s. auch **acht...**; **tausendstel** Bruchz. thousandth; **Tausendstel** das (schweiz. meist der); ~s, ~: thousandth

Tau·wetter das thaw

Taxi das; ~s, ~s taxi; **Taxi·fahrer** der taxi-driver

Tb, Tbc [te:'be:, te:be:'tse:] die; ~ Abk. Tuberkulose TB

Technik die; ~, ~en a) o. Pl. technology; (Studienfach) engineering no art.; b) o. Pl. (technische Ausrüstung) equipment; c) (Arbeitsweise, Verfahren) technique; **Techniker** der; ~s, ~, **Technikerin** die; ~, ~nen technical expert; **technisch** ['tɛçnɪʃ] 1. Adj. technical; technological (progress, age); 2. adv. technically; technologically (advanced); **Technologie** die; ~, ~n technology

TEE [te:|e:'|e:] der; ~|s|, ~|s| Abk. Trans-Europ-Express TEE

Tee der; ~s, ~s tea

Tee-: ~beutel der tea-bag; ~kanne die teapot; ~löffel der teaspoon; ~sieb das tea-strainer; ~tasse die teacup

Teich der; ~|e|s, ~e pond

Teig der; ~|e|s, ~e dough; (Kuchen~, Biskuit~) pastry; (Pfannkuchen~, Waffel~) batter; **Teig·waren** Pl. pasta sing.

Teil a) der; ~|e|s, ~e part; fünfter ~: fifth; b) der od. das; ~|e|s, ~e (Anteil; Beitrag) share; c) der; ~|e|s, ~e (beteiligte Person|en|; Rechtsw.: Partei) party; d) das; ~|e|s, ~e (Einzel~) part; **teil·bar** Adj. divisible (durch by); **Teilchen** das; ~s, ~ a) (kleines Stück) [small] part; b) (Partikel) particle; **teilen** 1. tr. V. a) divide (durch by); b) (auf~; teilhaben |lassen| an) share (unter + Dat. among); 2. refl. V. sich (Dat.) etw. |mit jmdm.| ~ share sth. [with sb.]; **teil|haben** unr. itr. V. share (an + Dat. in); **Teil·kaskoversicherung** die insurance giving limited cover

Teilnahme die; ~, ~n a) participation (an + Dat. in); ~ an einem Kurs attendance at a course; b) (Interesse) interest (an + Dat. in); c) (geh.: Mitgefühl) sympathy; **teilnahms·los** Adj. indifferent; **Teilnahmslosigkeit** die indifference; **teilnahms·voll** 1. Adj. compassionate; 2. adv. compassionately; **teil|nehmen** unr. itr. V.

|an etw. (Dat.)| ~: take part |in sth.|; |an einem Lehrgang| ~: attend |a course|; **Teilnehmer** der; ~s, ~ a) participant (Gen., an + Dat. in); (bei Wettbewerb auch) competitor, contestant (an + Dat. in); b) (Fernspr.) subscriber

teils Adv. partly; **Teilung** die; ~, ~en division; **teil·weise** 1. Adv. partly; 2. adj. partial; **Teilzeit·arbeit** die part-time work no indef. art.

Teint [tɛ̃:] der; ~s, ~s complexion

Telefon ['te:lefo:n, auch tele'fo:n] das; ~s, ~e telephone; phone (coll.); ans ~ gehen answer the [tele]phone

Telefon-: ~anruf der [tele]phone call; ~anschluß der telephone; line; ~apparat der telephone

Telefonat das; ~|e|s, ~e telephone call

Telefon-: ~buch das [tele]phone book or directory; ~gespräch das telephone conversation

telefonieren itr. V. make a [tele]phone call; mit jmdm. ~: talk to sb. [on the telephone]; **telefonisch** 1. Adj. telephone; 2. adv. by telephone; **Telefonist** der; ~en, ~en, **Telefonistin** die; ~, ~nen telephonist; (in einer Firma) switchboard operator

Telefon-: ~nummer die [tele]phone number; ~verzeichnis das telephone list; ~zelle die [tele]phonebooth or (Brit.) -box; call-box (Brit.)

Telegraf der; ~en, ~en telegraph; **Telegrafie** die; ~: telegraphy no art.; **telegrafieren** itr., tr. V. telegraph; **telegrafisch** 1. Adj. telegraphic; 2. adv. by telegraph or telegram

Telegramm das telegram

Tele·objektiv das (Fot.) telephoto lens

Teller der; ~s, ~: plate

Temperament das; ~|e|s, ~e a) (Wesensart) temperament; b) o. Pl. (Schwung) eine Frau mit ~: a woman with spirit; das ~ geht oft mit mir durch I often lose my temper; **temperament·voll** Adj. spirited (person, speech, dance, etc.)

Temperatur die; ~, ~en temperature

Temperatur-: ~anstieg der rise in temperature; ~rückgang der drop or fall in temperature

Tempo das; ~s, ~s od. Tempi a) Pl. ~s speed; b) (Musik) tempo; time

Tempus das; ~, Tempora (Sprachw.) tense

Tendenz die; ~, ~en trend; **tendieren** itr. V. tend (**zu** towards)
Teneriffa (das); ~s Tenerife
Tennis das; ~: tennis no art.
Tennis-: ~**ball** der tennis-ball; ~**platz** der tennis-court; ~**schläger** der tennis-racket; ~**spieler** der tennis-player
Tenor der; ~s, Tenöre, (österr. auch:) ~e (Musik) tenor; (im Chor) tenors pl.; tenor voices pl.
Teppich der; ~s, ~e carpet; (kleiner) rug; **Teppich·boden** der fitted carpet
Termin der; ~s, ~e date; (Anmeldung) appointment; (Verabredung) engagement; (Rechtsw.) hearing; **Terminal** ['tø:gmɪnəl] das; ~s, ~s terminal; **Termin·kalender** der appointments book
Terpentin das, (österr. meist:) der; ~s a) (Harz) turpentine; b) (ugs.: Terpentinöl) turps sing. (coll.); **Terpentin·öl** das oil of turpentine
Terrain [tɛ'rɛ:] das; ~s, ~s terrain
Terrasse die; ~, ~n terrace
Terrier ['tɛrɪɐ] der; ~s, ~: terrier
Terrine die; ~, ~n tureen
Territorium das; ~s, Territorien territory
Terror der; ~s terrorism no art.; **terrorisieren** tr. V. a) terrorize; b) (ugs.: belästigen) pester; **Terrorist** der; ~en, ~en terrorist
Terz die; ~, ~en (Musik) third
Test der; ~[e]s, ~s od. ~e test
Testament das; ~[e]s, ~e a) will; b) (christl. Rel.) Testament
testen tr. V. test (**auf** + Akk. for)
teuer 1. Adj. expensive; dear usu. pred.; **wie ~ war das?** how much did that cost?; 2. adv. expensively; dearly; **etw. ~ kaufen/verkaufen** pay a great deal for sth./sell sth. at a high price; **Teuerung** die; ~, ~en rise in prices
Teufel der; ~s, ~: devil; **teuflisch** 1. Adj. a) devilish, fiendish (plan, trick, etc.); diabolical (laughter, pleasure, etc.); b) (ugs.: groß, intensiv) terrible (coll.); dreadful (coll.); 2. adv. a) diabolically; b) (ugs.) terribly (coll.)
Text der; ~[e]s, ~e text; (Wortlaut) wording; (eines Theaterstücks) script; (einer Oper) libretto; (eines Liedes, Chansons usw.) words pl.; (eines Schlagers) words pl.; lyrics pl.; (zu einer Abbildung) caption; **texten** tr. V. write (song, advertisement, etc.)

Textilien Pl. a) textiles; b) (Fertigwaren) textile goods
Thailand (das); ~s Thailand
Theater das; ~s, ~ a) theatre; **ins ~ gehen** go to the theatre; **im ~:** at the theatre; ~ **spielen** act; (fig.) play-act; pretend; b) o. Pl. (fig. ugs.) fuss
Theater-: ~**abonnement** das theatre subscription [ticket]; ~**stück** das [stage] play
Theke die; ~, ~n a) (Schanktisch) bar; b) (Ladentisch) counter
Thema das; ~s, Themen subject; topic; (einer Abhandlung) subject; theme; (Leitgedanke) theme
Themse die; ~: Thames
Theologe der; ~n, ~n theologian; **Theologie** die; ~, ~n theology no art.; **theologisch** 1. Adj. theological; 2. adv. theologically
Theorie die; ~, ~n theory
Therapeut der; ~en, ~en, **Therapeutin** die; ~, ~nen therapist; therapeutist; **therapeutisch** 1. Adj. therapeutic; 2. adv. therapeutically
Therapie die; ~, ~n therapy (**gegen** for)
Thermo·meter das (österr. u. schweiz. der od. das) thermometer; **Thermos·flasche** ⓦ die Thermos flask (P); vacuum flask; **Thermostat** der; ~[e]s od. ~en, ~e od. ~en thermostat
Thron der; ~[e]s, ~e throne
Thun·fisch der tuna
Thüringen (das); ~s Thuringia; **Thüringer Wald** der Thuringian Forest
Thymian der; ~s, ~e thyme
ticken itr. V. tick
tief 1. Adj. (auch fig.) deep; (niedrig) low; low (neckline, bow); deep; intense (pain, suffering); 2. adv. deep; (niedrig) low; (intensiv) deeply; (stoop, bow) low; (breathe, inhale) deeply; **Tief** das; ~s, ~s (Met.) low
tief-, Tief-: ~**bewegt** Adj. (präd. getrennt geschrieben) deeply moved; ~**blau** Adj. deep blue; ~**druck** der; o. Pl. (Met.) low pressure
Tiefe die; ~, ~n depth; **in die ~ stürzen** plunge into the depths
tief-, Tief-: ~**garage** die underground car park; ~**greifend;** tiefer greifend, am tiefsten greifend od. tiefstgreifend 1. Adj. profound; profound, deep (crisis); far-reaching (improvement); 2. adv. profoundly; ~**gründig** Adj. profound; ~**kühlen** tr. V. [deep-]freeze

Tief·kühl-: ~fach das freezer [compartment]; ~kost die frozen food

tief-, Tief-: ~punkt der low [point]; ~see die *(Geogr.)* deep sea; ~sinnig 1. *Adj.* profound; 2. *adv.* profoundly

Tiegel der; ~s, ~ *(zum Kochen)* pan; *(Schmelz~)* crucible; *(Behälter)* pot

Tier das; ~[e]s, ~e animal

Tier-: ~arzt der veterinary surgeon; vet; ~garten der zoo; zoological garden; ~heim das animal home

tierisch 1. *Adj.* a) animal *attrib.;* savage *(cruelty, crime)*; b) *(ugs.: unerträglich groß)* terrible *(coll.);* ~er Ernst deadly seriousness; 2. *adv.* a) *(roar)* like an animal; savagely *(cruel)*; b) *(ugs.: unerträglich)* terribly *(coll.)*.

tier-, Tier-: ~kreis der ~s, o. *Pl. (Astron., Astrol.)* zodiac; ~kreis·zeichen das *(Astron., Astrol.)* sign of the zodiac; ~lieb *Adj.* animal-loving *attrib.;* fond of animals *postpos.;* ~park der zoo; ~pfleger der animal-keeper; ~quälerei [---'-] die cruelty to animals; ~reich das; o. *Pl.* animal kingdom

Tiger der; ~s, ~: tiger

tilgen *tr. V.* a) *(geh.)* delete *(word, letter, error)*; erase *(record, endorsement)*; *(fig.)* wipe out *(shame, guilt, traces)*; b) *(Wirtsch., Bankw.)* repay; pay off

Tilsiter der; ~s, ~: Tilsit [cheese]

Tinte die; ~, ~n ink; **in der ~ sitzen** *(ugs.)* be in the soup *(coll.);* **Tinten·fisch der** cuttlefish *(Krake)* octopus

Tip der; ~s, ~s a) *(ugs.)* tip; b) *(bei Toto, Lotto usw.)* [row of] numbers; **tippen** 1. *itr. V.* a) an/gegen etw. *(Akk.)* ~: tap sth.; b) *(ugs.: maschineschreiben)* type; c) *(wetten)* do the pools/lottery *etc.;* **im Lotto ~:** do the lottery; 2. *tr. V.* a) tap sth; b) *(ugs.: mit der Maschine schreiben)* type; c) *(setzen auf)* choose; **sechs Richtige ~:** make six correct selections

tipp·topp *(ugs.)* 1. *Adj. (tadellos)* immaculate; *(erstklassig)* tip-top; 2. *adv.* immaculately

Tirol (das); ~s [the] Tyrol; **Tiroler der;** ~s, ~, **Tirolerin die;** ~, ~nen Tyrolese; Tyrolean

Tisch der; ~[e]s, ~e table; **reinen ~ machen** *(ugs.)* sort things out

Tisch-: ~dame die dinner partner; ~decke die table-cloth; ~gebet das grace; ~herr der dinner partner; ~lampe die table-lamp

Tischler der; ~s, ~: joiner; *(bes. Kunst~)* cabinet-maker; **Tischlerei die;** ~, ~en a) *(Werkstatt)* joiner's/ cabinet-maker's [workshop]; b) *o. Pl. (Handwerk)* joinery/cabinet-making

Tisch-: ~nachbar der person next to one [at table]; ~platte die table-top; ~tennis das table tennis; ~tuch das; *Pl.* ~tücher table-cloth; ~wäsche die table-linen; ~wein der table wine; ~zeit die lunch-time

Titel der; ~s, ~ a) title; b) *(ugs.: Musikstück, Song usw.)* number

Titel-: ~bild das cover picture; ~blatt das title-page; ~rolle die title-role; ~seite die a) *(einer Zeitung, Zeitschrift)* [front] cover; b) *(eines Buchs)* title-page

titulieren *tr. V.* call

tja [tja(:)] *Interj.* [yes] well; *(Resignation ausdrückend)* oh, well

Toast [to:st] **der;** ~[e]s, ~e od. ~s toast; **Toast·brot das;** *o. Pl.* [sliced white] bread for toasting; **toasten** *tr. V.* toast; **Toaster der;** ~s, ~: toaster

toben *itr. V.* a) go wild **(vor** + *Dat.* with); *(fig.) (storm, sea, battle)* rage; b) *(tollen)* romp or charge about; c) mit sein *(laufen)* charge

Tochter die; ~, **Töchter** daughter

Tod der; ~[e]s, ~e death; **eines natürlichen/gewaltsamen ~es sterben** die a natural/violent death; **jmdn. zum ~e verurteilen** sentence sb. to death; **tod·ernst** 1. *Adj.* deadly serious; 2. *adv.* deadly seriously

Todes-: ~anzeige die a) *(in einer Zeitung)* death notice; b) *(Karte)* card announcing a person's death; ~fall der death; *(in der Familie)* bereavement; ~nachricht die news of his/her/their *etc.* death; ~opfer das death; fatality; ~strafe die death penalty; ~ursache die cause of death; ~urteil das death sentence

Tod·feind der deadly enemy; **todkrank** *Adj.* critically ill; **tödlich** 1. *Adj.* a) fatal *(accident, illness, outcome, etc.)*; lethal, deadly *(poison, bite, shot, trap, etc.)*; lethal *(dose)*; b) *(sehr groß, ausgeprägt)* deadly *(hatred, seriousness, certainty, boredom)*; 2. *adv.* a) fatally; b) *(sehr)* terribly *(coll.)*

tod-, Tod-: ~müde *Adj.* dead tired; ~sicher *(ugs.)* 1. *Adj.* sure-fire *(coll.)*; 2. *adv.* for certain or sure; ~sünde die *(auch fig.)* deadly or mortal sin; ~unglücklich *Adj. (ugs.)* extremely or desperately unhappy

Toilette [toa'lɛtə] die; ~, ~n toilet
Toiletten·papier das toilet paper
toi, toi, toi ['tɔy 'tɔy 'tɔy] Interj. good luck!; ⟨unberufen!⟩ touch wood!
Tokio (das); ~s Tokyo
tolerant 1. Adj. tolerant (gegen of); 2. adv. tolerantly; **Toleranz** die; ~: tolerance; **tolerieren** tr. V. tolerate
toll 1. Adj. a) ⟨ugs.⟩ ⟨großartig⟩ great ⟨coll.⟩; fantastic ⟨coll.⟩; ⟨erstaunlich⟩ amazing; ⟨heftig, groß⟩ enormous ⟨respect⟩; terrific ⟨coll.⟩ ⟨noise, storm⟩; b) ⟨wild⟩ wild; 2. adv. a) ⟨ugs.: großartig⟩ terrifically well ⟨coll.⟩; b) ⟨ugs.: heftig⟩ ⟨rain, snow⟩ like billy-o ⟨coll.⟩; c) ⟨wild⟩ bei dem Fest ging es ~ zu it was a wild party; **tollen** itr. V. a) romp about; b) mit sein romp
toll-, Toll-: ~kühn 1. Adj. daredevil attrib.; daring; 2. adv. daringly; **~wut** die rabies sing.; **~wütig** Adj. rabid
Tolpatsch der; ~[e]s, ~e ⟨ugs.⟩ clumsy or awkward creature; **tolpatschig** ⟨ugs.⟩ 1. Adj. clumsy; awkward; 2. adv. clumsily; awkwardly
Tölpel der; ~s, ~: fool; **tölpelhaft** 1. Adj. foolish; 2. adv. foolishly
Tomate die; ~, ~n tomato; **Tomaten·mark** das tomato purée
Tombola die; ~, ~s raffle
¹Ton der; ~[e]s, ~e clay
²Ton der; ~[e]s, **Töne** a) ⟨auch Physik, Musik; beim Telefon⟩ tone; ⟨Klang⟩ note; b) ⟨Film, Ferns. usw., ~wiedergabe⟩ sound; c) ⟨ugs.: Äußerung⟩ word; d) ⟨Farb~⟩ shade; e) ⟨Akzent⟩ stress
ton-, Ton-: ~angebend Adj. predominant; **~art** die a) ⟨Musik⟩ key; b) ⟨fig.⟩ tone; **~band** das; Pl. **~bänder** tape
Ton·band·gerät das tape recorder
tönen 1. itr. V. ⟨geh.⟩ sound; ⟨bell⟩ sound, ring; ⟨schallen, widerhallen⟩ resound; 2. tr. V. ⟨färben⟩ tint
Ton·fall der tone; ⟨Intonation⟩ intonation
Tonne die; ~, ~n a) ⟨Behälter⟩ drum; ⟨Müll~⟩ bin; ⟨Regen~⟩ water-butt; b) ⟨Gewicht⟩ tonne; **tonnen·weise** Adv., adj. by the ton
Tönung die; ~, ~en tint; shade
Topf der; ~es, **Töpfe** a) pot; ⟨Braten-, Schmor~⟩ casserole; ⟨Stielkasserolle⟩ saucepan; b) ⟨zur Aufbewahrung⟩ pot; c) ⟨Krug⟩ jug; d) ⟨Nacht~⟩ chamber pot; ⟨für Kinder⟩ potty ⟨Brit. coll.⟩; e) ⟨Blumen~⟩ [flower]pot; **Topf·blume** die [flowering] pot plant

Töpfchen das; ~s, ~: potty ⟨Brit. coll.⟩; **Töpfer** der; ~s, ~: potter; **Töpferei** die; ~, ~en a) o. Pl. ⟨Handwerk⟩ pottery no art.; b) ⟨Werkstatt⟩ pottery; potter's workshop; c) ⟨Erzeugnis⟩ piece of pottery; **~en** pottery sing.
Topf-: ~lappen der oven cloth; **~pflanze** die pot plant
Tor das; ~[e]s, ~e a) gate; ⟨einer Garage, Scheune⟩ door; ⟨fig.⟩ gateway; b) ⟨Ballspiele⟩ goal; c) ⟨Ski⟩ gate
Torf der; ~[e]s, ~e peat
Torheit die; ~, ~en ⟨geh.⟩ a) o. Pl. foolishness; b) ⟨Handlung⟩ foolish act
Tor·hüter der ⟨Ballspiele⟩ goalkeeper
töricht ⟨geh.⟩ 1. Adj. foolish; 2. adv. foolishly
torkeln itr. V.; mit sein stagger
Tor·mann der; Pl. **~männer** od. **~leute** ⟨Ballspiele⟩ goalkeeper
Tornister [tɔr'nɪstɐ] der; ~s, ~: knapsack; ⟨Schulranzen⟩ satchel
torpedieren tr. V. ⟨Milit., fig.⟩ torpedo; **Torpedo** der; ~s, ~s torpedo
Törtchen das; ~s, ~: tartlet; **Torte** die; ~, ~n ⟨Creme-, Sahne~⟩ gateau; ⟨Obst~⟩ [fruit] flan
Torten-: ~boden der flan case; ⟨ohne Rand⟩ flan base; **~guß** der glaze; **~heber** der cake-slice
Tortur die; ~, ~en a) ordeal; b) ⟨veralt.: Folter⟩ torture
Tor-: ~wart der; ~[e]s, ~e ⟨Ballspiele⟩ goalkeeper; **~weg** der gateway
tosen itr. V. roar; ⟨storm⟩ rage
tot Adj. dead; **~ umfallen** drop dead
total 1. Adj. total; 2. adv. totally; **totalitär** ⟨Politik⟩ 1. Adj. totalitarian; 2. adv. in a totalitarian way; ⟨organized, run⟩ along totalitarian lines; **Total·schaden** der ⟨Versicherungsw.⟩ an beiden Fahrzeugen entstand ~: both vehicles were a write-off
tot·ärgern refl. V. ⟨ugs.⟩ get livid ⟨coll.⟩; **Tote** der/die; adj. Dekl. dead person; **die ~n** the dead; **töten** tr., itr. V. kill; deaden ⟨nerve etc.⟩
toten-, Toten-: ~blaß, ~bleich Adj. deathly pale; **~gräber** der grave-digger; **~kopf** der a) skull; b) ⟨als Symbol⟩ death's head; ⟨mit gekreuzten Knochen⟩ skull and crossbones; **~schädel** der skull; **~still** Adj. deathly quiet; **~stille** die deathly silence; **~wache** die vigil by the body
tot-, Tot-: ~|fahren unr. tr. V. [run over and] kill; **~geboren** Adj. ⟨präd.

getrennt geschrieben) stillborn; **~ge-burt die** still birth; **~|lachen** refl. V. (ugs.) kill oneself laughing; **zum Tot-lachen sein** be killing (coll.)

Toto das od. **der;** ~s, ~s **a)** (Pferde~) tote (sl.); **im** ~: on the tote; **b)** (Fuß-ball~) [football] pools pl.; **|im|** ~ spielen do the pools; **Toto·schein der** pools coupon/(sl.) tote ticket

tot-, Tot-: ~|**schießen** unr. tr. V. (ugs.) jmdn. ~schießen shoot sb. dead; **~schlag der** (Rechtsw.) man-slaughter no indef. art.; ~|**schlagen** unr. tr. V. beat to death; ~|**stellen** refl. V. pretend to be dead; play dead; ~|**treten** unr. tr. V. trample (person) to death; step on and kill (insect)

Tötung die; ~, ~en killing; **fahrlässige** ~ (Rechtsspr.) manslaughter by culpable negligence

Toupet [tu'pe:] **das;** ~s, ~s toupee; **toupieren** [tu'pi:rən] tr. V. back-comb

Tour [tu:ɐ̯] **die;** ~, ~en tour (**durch** of); (kürzere Fahrt, Ausflug) trip; (mit dem Auto) drive; (mit dem Fahrrad) ride; (feste Strecke) route; **in einer** ~ (ugs.) the whole time; **Tourismus** [tu'rɪs-mʊs] **der;** ~: tourism no art.; **Tourist der;** ~en, ~en tourist; **Touristen-klasse die** tourist class; **Touristin die;** ~, ~nen tourist

Tournee [tʊr'ne:] **die;** ~, ~s od. ~n [tʊr'ne:ən] tour; **auf** ~ **sein/gehen** be/go on tour

Trab der; ~[e]s trot; **im** ~: at a trot; **im** ~ **reiten** trot; **traben** itr. V.; mit sein (auch ugs.: laufen) trot

Tracht die; ~, ~en **a)** (Volks~) na-tional costume; (Berufs~) uniform; **b)** **eine** ~ **Prügel** a thrashing; (als Strafe) a hiding

trachten itr. V. (geh.) strive (**nach** for, after)

Tradition die; ~, ~en tradition; **tra-ditionell** 1. Adj. traditional; 2. adv. traditionally

traf 1. u. 3. Pers. Sg. Prät. v. **treffen**; **träfe** 1. u. 3. Pers. Sg. Konjunktiv II v. **treffen**

Trafik die; ~, ~en (österr.) tobaccon-ist's [shop]

Trag·bahre die stretcher; **tragbar** Adj. **a)** portable; **b)** wearable (clothes); **c)** (finanziell) supportable (cost, debt, etc.); **d)** (erträglich) bear-able; tolerable

träge 1. Adj. **a)** sluggish; 2. adv. sluggishly

tragen 1. unr. tr. V. **a)** carry; **b)** (brin-gen) take; **c)** (ertragen) bear (fate, des-tiny); bear, endure (suffering); **d)** (hal-ten) hold; **einen/den linken Arm in der Schlinge** ~: have one's arm/one's left arm in a sling; **e)** (von unten stützen) support; **f)** (belastbar sein durch) be able to carry or take (weight); **g)** (übernehmen, aufkommen für) bear, carry (costs etc.); take (blame, responsi-bility, consequences); **h)** (am Körper) wear (clothes, wig, glasses, jewellery, etc.); have (false teeth, beard, etc.); **j)** (hervorbringen) (tree) bear (fruit); (field) produce (crops); 2. unr. tr. V. **a)** carry; **b)** (am Körper) **man trägt |wieder| kurz/lang** short/long skirts are in fashion [again]; **c) der Baum trägt gut** the tree produces a good crop; **tragend** Adj. (Stabilität gebend) load-bearing; supporting (wall, col-umn, function, etc.)

Träger der; ~s, ~ **a)** porter; **b)** (Zei-tungs~) paper boy/girl; delivery boy/girl; **c)** (Bauw.) girder; [supporting] beam; **d)** (an Kleidung) strap; (Ho-sen~) braces pl.; **e)** (Inhaber) (eines Amts) holder; (eines Namens, Titels) bearer; (eines Preises) winner; **Trä-gerin die;** ~, ~nen s. **Träger a, b, e**

Trage·tasche die carrier-bag

Trag-: ~**fähigkeit die** load-bearing capacity; ~**fläche die** wing; ~**flü-gel·boot das** hydrofoil

Trägheit die; ~, ~en sluggishness

Tragik die; ~: tragedy; **tragi·ko-misch** 1. Adj. tragicomic; 2. adv. tragicomically; **tragisch** 1. Adj. tragic; **das ist nicht |so|** ~ (ugs.) it's not the end of the world (coll.); 2. adv. tragically; **Tragödie die;** ~, ~n tra-gedy

Trag·weite die; o. Pl. consequences pl.

Trainer ['trɛ:nɐ] **der;** ~s, ~: coach; trainer; (einer Fußballmannschaft) manager; **trainieren** 1. tr. V. **a)** train; coach (swimmer, tennis-player); manage (football team); exercise (muscles etc.); **b)** (üben, einüben) prac-tise (exercise, jump, etc.); **Fußball** ~: do football training; 2. itr. V. train; **Training** ['trɛ:nɪŋ] **das;** ~s, ~s train-ing no indef. art.

Trainings-: ~**anzug der** track suit; ~**hose die** track-suit bottoms pl.

Trakt der; ~[e]s, ~e section; (Flügel) wing; **Traktor der;** ~s, ~en tractor

trällern *itr., tr. V.* warble

trampeln 1. *itr. V.* a) |mit den Füßen| ~: stamp one's feet; b) *mit sein (treten)* trample (**auf** + *Akk.* on); 2. *tr. V.* trample; **Trampel·pfad der** [beaten] path

trampen ['trɛmpn̩] *itr. V. mit sein* hitch-hike

Tramway ['tramve] **die**; ~, ~s *(österr.)* tram *(Brit.);* streetcar *(Amer.)*

Tran der; ~|e|s train-oil

tranchieren [trã'ʃiːrən] *tr. V.* carve

Träne die; ~, ~n tear; ~n lachen laugh till one cries; **tränen** *itr. V. ⟨eyes⟩* water

tranig *Adj. (ugs. abwertend: langsam)* sluggish; slow

trank *1. u. 3. Pers. Sg. Prät. v.* trinken; **Tränke die**; ~, ~n watering-place; **tränken** *tr. V.* a) water; b) *(sich vollsaugen lassen)* soak

Transfer der; ~s, ~s *(bes. Wirtsch., Sport)* transfer

Trans·formator der; ~s, ~en transformer

Transistor der; ~s, ~en transistor

Transit [tran'ziːt, *auch:* 'tranzɪt] **das**; ~s, ~s transit visa; **transitiv** *(Sprachw.)* 1. *Adj.* transitive; 2. *adv.* transitively; **Transit·verkehr der** transit traffic

transparent *Adj.* transparent; *(Licht durchlassend)* translucent; **Transparent das**; ~|e|s, ~e *(Spruchband)* banner; *(Bild)* transparency; **Transparenz die**; ~ transparency

Transport der; ~|e|s, ~e a) transportation; b) *(beförderte Lebewesen od. Sachen) (mit dem Zug)* train-load; *(mit mehreren Fahrzeugen)* convoy; *(Fracht)* consignment; **transportabel** *Adj.* transportable; *(tragbar)* portable; **Transporteur der** [...'tøːɐ] **der**; ~s, ~e carrier; **transport·fähig** *Adj.* moveable; **transportieren** *tr. V.* transport *⟨goods, people⟩;* move *⟨patient⟩;* **Transport·kosten** *Pl.* carriage *sing.;* transport costs

Transvestit der; ~en, ~en transvestite

Trapez das; ~es, ~e a) *(Geom.)* trapezium *(Brit.);* trapezoid *(Amer.);* b) *(im Zirkus o. ä.)* trapeze

trappeln *itr. V.; mit sein* patter [along]; *⟨feet⟩* patter; *⟨hoofs⟩* go clip-clop

Trara das; ~s *(ugs.)* razzmatazz *(coll.)*

trat *1. u. 3. Pers. Sg. Prät. v.* treten

Tratsch der; ~|e|s *(ugs.)* gossip; tittle-

tattle; **tratschen** *itr. V. (ugs.)* gossip; *(schwatzen)* chatter

Traube die; ~, ~n a) *(Beeren)* bunch; *(von Johannisbeeren o. ä.)* cluster; b) *(Wein~)* grape; c) *(Menschenmenge)* bunch; cluster

trauen 1. *itr. V.* jmdm./einer Sache ~: trust sb./sth.; 2. *refl. V.* dare; 3. *tr. V. (verheiraten) ⟨vicar, registrar, etc.⟩* marry

Trauer die; ~ a) grief (über + *Akk.* over); *(um einen Toten)* mourning (um + *Akk.* for); b) *(~zeit)* [period of] mourning; c) ~ **tragen** be in mourning

Trauer-: ~**fall der** bereavement; ~**feier die** memorial ceremony; *(beim Begräbnis)* funeral ceremony; ~**karte die** [pre-printed] card of condolence; ~**kleidung die** mourning clothes *pl.*

trauern *itr. V.* mourn; um jmdn. ~: mourn for sb.

Trauer-: ~**spiel das** tragedy; *(fig. ugs.)* deplorable business; ~**weide die** weeping willow

träufeln *tr. V.* [let] trickle (**in** + *Akk.* into); drip *⟨ear-drops etc.⟩*

Traum der; ~|e|s, Träume ['trɔymə] dream; **träumen** 1. *itr. V.* dream (von of, about); *(unaufmerksam sein)* [day]-dream; 2. *tr. V.* dream; **Träumer der**; ~s, ~, **Träumerin die**; ~, ~nen dreamer; **träumerisch** 1. *Adj.* dreamy; 2. *adv.* dreamily; **traumhaft** *(ugs.)* 1. *Adj.* marvellous; fabulous *(coll.);* 2. *adv.* fabulously *(coll.)*

traurig 1. *Adj.* a) sad; unhappy *⟨childhood, youth⟩;* painful *⟨duty⟩;* b) *(kümmerlich)* sorry *⟨state etc.⟩;* miserable *⟨result⟩;* 2. *adv.* sadly; **Traurigkeit die**; ~: sadness; sorrow

Trau-: ~**ring der** wedding-ring; ~**schein der** marriage certificate

Trauung die; ~, ~en wedding [ceremony]; **Trau·zeuge der** witness *(at wedding ceremony)*

Trecker der; ~s, ~: tractor

Treff der; ~s, ~s *(ugs.)* rendezvous; *(Ort)* meeting-place; **treffen** 1. *unr. tr. V.* a) hit; *⟨punch, blow, object⟩* strike; **ihn trifft keine Schuld** he is in no way to blame; b) *(erschüttern)* affect [deeply]; *(verletzen)* hurt; c) *(begegnen)* meet; d) *(vorfinden)* come upon, find *⟨anomalies etc.⟩;* **es gut/schlecht ~**: be *or* strike lucky/be unlucky; e) *(als Funktionsverb)* make *⟨arrangements, choice, preparations, de-*

cision, etc.); **2.** *unr. itr. V.* **a)** ⟨*person, shot, etc.*⟩ hit the target; **nicht ~:** miss [the target]; **b)** *mit sein auf etw. (Akk.)* **~:** come upon sth.; **auf Widerstand/Ablehnung/Schwierigkeiten ~:** meet with resistance/rejection/difficulties; **3.** *unr. refl. V.* **a)** sich mit jmdm. **~:** meet sb.; **b)** *unpers.* es trifft sich gut/schlecht it is convenient/inconvenient; **Treffen** *das;* ~s, ~: meeting; **treffend 1.** *Adj.* apt; **2.** *adv.* aptly; **Treffer** *der;* ~s, ~ **a)** *(Milit., Boxen, Fechten usw.)* hit; *(Schlag)* blow; *(Ballspiele)* goal; **b)** *(Gewinn)* win; *(Los)* winner; **trefflich** *(geh.)* **1.** *Adj.* excellent; splendid ⟨*person*⟩; **2.** *adv.* excellently; splendidly

treff-, Treff-: ~punkt *der* meeting-place; **~sicher 1.** *Adj.* accurate ⟨*language, mode of expression*⟩; unerring ⟨*judgement*⟩; **2.** *adv.* accurately; **~sicherheit** *die; o. Pl.* accuracy

Treib·eis *das* drift-ice

treiben 1. *unr. tr. V.* **a)** drive; **b)** *(sich beschäftigen mit)* go in for ⟨*farming, cattle-breeding, etc.*⟩; study ⟨*French etc.*⟩; carry on, pursue ⟨*studies, trade, craft*⟩; **viel Sport ~:** do a lot of sport; **es wüst/übel/toll ~** *(ugs.)* lead a dissolute/bad life/live it up; **2.** *unr. itr. V.* *meist, mit Richtungsangabe nur, mit sein* drift; **Treiben** *das;* ~s **a)** *(Durcheinander)* bustle; **b)** *(Tun)* activities *pl.;* doings *pl.*

Treib-: ~haus *das* hothouse; **~hauseffekt** *der* greenhouse effect; **~stoff** *der* fuel

Trenchcoat ['trɛntʃkoʊt] *der;* ~[s], ~s trench coat

Trend *der;* ~s, ~s trend ⟨zu + *Dat.* towards⟩; *(Mode)* vogue

trennen 1. *tr. V.* **a)** separate ⟨von from⟩; sever ⟨*head, arm*⟩; **b)** *(auf-)* unpick ⟨*dress, seam*⟩; **c)** *(teilen)* divide ⟨*word, parts of a room etc., fig.: people*⟩; **2.** *refl. V.* **a)** *(voneinander weggehen)* part [company]; **b)** *(eine Partnerschaft auflösen)* ⟨*couple, partners*⟩ split up; **c)** sich von etw. **~:** part with sth.; **Trennung** *die;* ~, ~en *(von Menschen)* separation ⟨von from⟩; *(von Gegenständen)* parting; *(von Wörtern)* division

trepp-, Trepp-: ~ab *Adv.* down the stairs; **~auf** *Adv.* up the stairs

Treppe *die;* ~, ~n staircase; [flight *sing.* of] stairs *pl.;* *(im Freien, auf der Bühne)* [flight *sing.* of] steps *pl.*

Treppen-: ~absatz *der* half-landing;

~geländer *das* banisters *pl.;* **~haus** *das* stair-well; **~stufe** *die* stair; *(im Freien)* step

Tresen *der;* ~s, ~ *(bes. nordd.)* bar; *(Ladentisch)* counter

Tresor *der;* ~s, ~e safe

Tret·boot *das* pedalo; **treten 1.** *unr. itr. V.* **a)** *mit sein* step ⟨in + *Akk.* into, auf + *Akk.* on to⟩; **b)** *(seinen Fuß setzen)* auf etw. *(Akk.)* **~:** tread on sth.; **c)** *(ausschlagen)* kick; **2.** *unr. tr. V.* **a)** *(Tritt versetzen)* kick ⟨*person, ball, etc.*⟩; **b)** *(trampeln)* trample ⟨*path*⟩; **c)** *(mit dem Fuß niederdrücken)* step on ⟨*brake, pedal*⟩; operate ⟨*bellows, clutch*⟩

treu 1. *Adj.* faithful; loyal; faithful ⟨*husband, wife*⟩; loyal ⟨*ally, subject*⟩; **jmdm. ~ sein** be true to sb.; **sich selbst** *(Dat.)*/**seinem Glauben ~ bleiben** be true to oneself/one's faith; **2.** *adv.* faithfully; loyally; **Treue** *die;* ~ **a)** loyalty; *(von [Ehe]partnern)* fidelity; **b)** *(Genauigkeit)* accuracy

treu-, Treu-: ~hand[anstalt] *die o. Pl. (Wirtschaft)* German privatization agency; **~herzig 1.** *Adj.* ingenuous; *(naiv)* naïve; *(unschuldig)* innocent; **2.** *adv.* ingenuously; *(naiv)* naïvely; *(unschuldig)* innocently; **~los 1.** *Adj.* disloyal, faithless ⟨*friend, person*⟩; unfaithful ⟨*husband, wife, lover*⟩; **2.** *adv.* faithlessly

Tribunal *das;* ~s, ~e tribunal; **Tribüne** *die;* ~, ~n [grand]stand

Trichter *der;* ~s, ~ funnel

Trick *der;* ~s, ~s trick; *(fig.: List)* ploy

trieb 1. u. 3. Pers. Sg. Prät. v. treiben; **Trieb** *der;* ~[e]s, ~e **a)** *(innerer Antrieb)* impulse; *(Drang)* urge; *(Verlangen)* [compulsive] desire; **b)** *(Sproß)* shoot

trieb-, Trieb-: ~feder *die* mainspring; *(fig.)* driving or motivating force; **~haft 1.** *Adj.* compulsive; carnal ⟨*sensuality*⟩; **2.** *adv.* compulsively; **~wagen** *der (Eisenb.)* railcar

triefen *unr. od. regelm. itr. V.* **a)** *mit sein (fließen)* ⟨*in Tropfen*⟩ drip; *(in kleinen Rinnsalen)* trickle; **b)** *(naß sein)* be dripping wet; ⟨*nose*⟩ run

triff *Imperativ Sg. v.* **treffen;** **trifft** *3. Pers. Sg. Präsens v.* **treffen**

triftig *Adj.* good ⟨*reason, excuse*⟩; valid, convincing ⟨*reason, argument*⟩

¹Trikot [tri'ko] *der od. das;* ~s, ~s *(Stoff)* cotton jersey; **²Trikot** *das;* ~s, ~ *(ärmellos)* singlet; *(eines Tänzers)* leotard; *(eines Fußballspielers)* shirt

Triller der; ~s, ~: trill; **trillern** 1. *itr. V.* trill; 2. *tr. V.* warble ⟨*song*⟩; **Triller·pfeife** die police/referee's whistle

Trimm-dich-Pfad der keep-fit trail; **trimmen** *tr. V. (durch Sport)* get ⟨*person*⟩ into shape

trinken 1. *unr. itr. V.* drink; **auf jmdn./ etw.** ~: drink to sb./sth.; 2. *unr. tr. V.* drink; **einen Kaffee/ein Bier** ~: have a coffee/beer; **Trinker** der; ~s, ~: alcoholic; **Trinkerei** die; ~, ~en drinking *no art.*

Trink-: ~**geld** das tip; ~**wasser** das; *Pl.* ~**wässer** drinking-water; „**kein** ~**wasser**'' 'not for drinking'

Trio das; ~s, ~s *(Musik, fig.)* trio

trippeln *itr. V.; mit sein* trip; ⟨*child*⟩ patter

trist *Adj.* dreary; dismal

tritt *Imperativ Sg. u. 3. Pers. Sg. Präsens v.* treten; **Tritt** der; ~[e]s, ~e *(Schritt; Trittbrett)* step; *(Fuß*~*)* kick; **Tritt·brett** das step

Triumph der; ~[e]s, ~e triumph; **triumphieren** *(itr. V.* a) exult; b) *(siegen)* be triumphant; triumph *(lit. or fig.)* (**über** + *Akk.* over)

trivial 1. *Adj.* a) *(platt)* banal; trite; *(unbedeutend)* trivial; b) *(alltäglich)* humdrum *(life, career)*; 2. *adv. (platt)* banally; *(say etc.)* tritely

trocken 1. *Adj. (auch fig.)* dry; 2. *adv.* drily; **Trocken·haube** die [hood-type] hair-drier; **Trockenheit** die; ~, ~en *a)* o. *Pl.* dryness; b) *(Dürreperiode)* drought

trocken-, Trocken-: ~**legen** *tr. V.* a) **ein Baby** ~**legen** change a baby's nappies *(Brit.)* or *(Amer.)* diapers; b) *(entwässern)* drain ⟨*marsh, pond, etc.*⟩; ~**milch** die dried milk; ~**reiben** *unr. tr. V.* rub ⟨*hair, child, etc.*⟩ dry; wipe ⟨*crockery, window, etc.*⟩ dry

trocknen 1. *itr. V.; meist mit sein* dry; 2. *tr. V.* dry

Troddel die; ~, ~n tassel

Trödel der; ~s *(ugs.)* junk; *(für den Flohmarkt)* jumble; **trödeln** *itr. V.* a) *(ugs.)* dawdle (mit over); b) *mit sein (ugs.: schlendern)* saunter; **Trödler** der; ~s, ~ *(ugs.)* junk-dealer

troff *1. u. 3. Pers. Sg. Prät. v.* triefen

trog *1. u. 3. Pers. Sg. Prät. v.* trügen

Trog der; ~[e]s, **Tröge** trough

trollen *(ugs.) refl. V.* push off *(coll.)*

Trommel die; ~, ~n drum; **trommeln** 1. *itr. V.* a) beat the drum; *(als Beruf, Hobby usw.)* play the drums; b)

(auf etw.) schlagen, auftreffen) drum (**auf** + *Akk.* on, **an** + *Akk.* against); **Trommel·wirbel** der drum-roll; **Trommler** der; ~s, ~drummer

Trompete die; ~, ~n trumpet; **trompeten** 1. *itr. V.* play the trumpet; *(fig.) (elephant)* trumpet; 2. *tr. V.* play *(piece)* on the trumpet; **Trompeter** der; ~s, ~trumpeter

Tropen *Pl.* tropics; **Tropen-** tropical; **Tropen·helm** der sun-helmet

Tropf der; ~[e]s, ~e *(Med.)* drip; **Tröpfchen** das; ~s, ~: droplet; *(kleine Menge)* drop; **tröpfeln** 1. *itr. V.* a) *mit sein* drip (**auf** + *Akk.* on to, **aus**, **von** from); b) *unpers. (ugs.: leicht regnen)* es tröpfelt it's spitting [with rain]; 2. *tr. V.* let ⟨*sth.*⟩ drip (**in** + *Akk.* into, **auf** + *Akk.* on to); **tropfen** 1. *itr. V.*; *mit Richtungsangabe mit sein* drip; ⟨*tears*⟩ fall; *unpers.* **es tropft [vom Dach usw.]** water is dripping from the roof *etc.*; 2. *tr. V.* let ⟨*sth.*⟩ drip (**in** + *Akk.* into, **auf** + *Akk.* on to); **Tropfen** der; ~s, ~ drop; **ein guter/edler** ~: a good/fine vintage; **Tropf·stein·höhle** die limestone cave with stalactites and/or stalagmites

Trophäe die; ~, ~n *(hist., Jagd, Sport)* trophy

tropisch *Adj.* tropical

Troß der; **Trosses, Trosse** a) *(Milit.)* baggage train; b) *(Gefolge)* retinue; *(fig.: Zug)* procession [of hangers-on]

Trost der; ~[e]s consolation; *(bes. geistlich)* comfort; **nicht [ganz** *od.* **recht] bei** ~ **sein** *(ugs.)* be out of one's mind; **trösten** 1. *tr. V.* comfort, console (mit with); 2. *refl. V.* console oneself; **tröstlich** *Adj.* comforting; **trost·los** *Adj.* a) hopeless; *(verzweifelt)* in despair *postpos.*; b) *(deprimierend, öde)* miserable; dreary; hopeless *(situation)*; **Trost·preis** der consolation prize

Trott der; ~[e]s, ~e trot; *(fig.)* routine

Trottel der; ~s, ~ *(ugs.)* fool; **trottelig** *(ugs.)* 1. *Adj.* doddery; 2. *adv.* in a feeble-minded way

trotten *itr. V.*; *mit sein* trot [along]

trotz *Präp. mit Gen., seltener mit Dat.* in spite of; despite; **Trotz** der; ~es defiance; **trotz·dem** *[auch: '-'-]* *Adv.* nevertheless; **trotzen** *itr. V.* a) *(geh.: widerstehen)* jmdm./einer Sache *(auch fig.)* defy sb./sth.; b) *(trotzig sein)* be contrary; **trotzig** 1. *Adj.* defiant; *(widerspenstig)* contrary; difficult ⟨*child*⟩; 2. *adv.* defiantly

trüb[e] 1. *Adj.* **a)** *(nicht klar)* murky ⟨*stream, water*⟩; cloudy ⟨*liquid, wine, juice*⟩; *(schlammig)* muddy ⟨*puddle*⟩; *(schmutzig)* dirty ⟨*glass, window-pane*⟩; dull ⟨*eyes*⟩; **b)** *(nicht hell)* dim ⟨*light*⟩; dull, dismal ⟨*day, weather*⟩; grey, overcast ⟨*sky*⟩; **2.** *adv.* ⟨*shine, light*⟩ dimly

Trubel der; ~s [hustle and] bustle

trüben 1. *tr. V.* **a)** make ⟨*liquid*⟩ cloudy; cloud ⟨*liquid*⟩; **b)** *(beeinträchtigen)* dampen ⟨*mood*⟩; mar ⟨*relationship*⟩; cloud ⟨*judgement*⟩; **2.** *refl. V.* ⟨*liquid*⟩ become cloudy; ⟨*eyes*⟩ become dull; ⟨*sky*⟩ darken; **Trübsal die;** ~, ~e *(geh.)* **a)** *(Leiden)* affliction; **b)** *o. Pl. (Kummer)* grief; ~ **blasen** *(ugs.)* mope ⟨wegen over, about⟩

trüb-, Trüb-: ~**selig 1.** *Adj.* **a)** *(öde)* dreary, depressing ⟨*place, area, colour*⟩; **b)** *(traurig)* gloomy; **2.** *adv. (traurig)* gloomily; ~**sinn der;** *o. Pl.* melancholy; ~**sinnig 1.** *Adj.* melancholy;

Trübung die; ~, ~en **a)** clouding; *(des Auges)* dimming; **b)** *(Beeinträchtigung)* deterioration; *(der Stimmung)* dampening

trudeln *itr. V. mit sein* roll

Trüffel die; ~, ~n truffle

trug *1. u. 3. Pers. Prät. v.* **tragen; trüge** *1. u. 3. Pers. Sg. Konjunktiv II v.* **tragen**

trügen 1. *unr. tr. V.* deceive; **2.** *unr. itr. V.* be deceptive; ⟨*feeling, deception*⟩ be a delusion; **trügerisch 1.** *Adj.* deceptive; false ⟨*hope, sign, etc.*⟩; treacherous ⟨*ice*⟩; **2.** *adv.* deceptively

Truhe die; ~, ~n chest

Trümmer *Pl. (eines Gebäudes)* rubble *sing.; (Ruinen)* ruins; *(eines Flugzeugs usw.)* wreckage *sing.; (kleinere Teile)* debris *sing.;* **Trümmer·haufen der** pile *or* heap of rubble

Trumpf der; ~[e]s, **Trümpfe** *(auch fig.)* trump [card]; *(Farbe)* trumps *pl.;* ~ **sein** *(fig.: Mode sein)* be the in thing; **trumpfen** *itr. V.* play a trump

Trunk der; ~[e]s, **Trünke** *(geh.) (Getränk)* drink; beverage *(formal);* **Trunkenheit die;** ~: drunkenness; ~ **am Steuer** drunken driving; **Trunk·sucht die;** *o. Pl.* alcoholism *no art.*

Trupp der; ~s, ~s troop; *(von Arbeitern, Gefangenen)* gang; *(von Soldaten, Polizisten)* squad; **Truppe die;** ~, ~n **a)** *(Einheit der Streitkräfte)* unit; **b)** *Pl. (Soldaten)* troops; **c)** *o. Pl. (Streit-*

kräfte) [armed] forces *pl.; (Heer)* army; **d)** *(Gruppe von Schauspielern, Artisten)* troupe; *(von Sportlern)* squad

Trut·hahn der turkey [cock]

tschau *Interj. (ugs.)* ciao *(coll.)*

Tscheche der; ~n, ~n Czech; **tschechisch** *Adj.* Czech; **Tschechoslowakei die;** ~: Czechoslovakia *no art.;* **tschechoslowakisch** *Adj.* Czechoslovak[ian]

Tsd. *Abk.* Tausend

T-Shirt ['tiːʃɔːt] **das;** ~s, ~s T-shirt

Tube die; ~, ~n tube

Tuberkulose die; ~, ~n *(Med.)* tuberculosis *no art.*

Tuch das; ~[e]s, **Tücher** *od.* ~e **a)** *Pl.* Tücher cloth; *(Kopf~, Hals~)* scarf; **b)** *Pl.* ~e *(Gewebe)* cloth

tüchtig 1. *Adj.* **a)** efficient; *(fähig)* capable, competent **(in +** *Dat.* at**); b)** *(ugs.: beträchtlich)* sizeable ⟨*piece, portion*⟩; big ⟨*gulp*⟩; hearty ⟨*eater, appetite*⟩; **2.** *adv.* **a)** efficiently; *(fähig)* competently; **b)** *(ugs.: sehr)* really ⟨*cold, warm*⟩; ⟨*snow, rain*⟩ good and proper *(coll.);* ⟨*eat*⟩ heartily; **Tüchtigkeit die;** ~: efficiency; *(Fähigkeit)* ability; competence; *(Fleiß)* industry

Tücke die; ~, ~n **a)** *o. Pl. (Hinterhältigkeit)* deceit[fulness]; *(List)* guile; **b)** *meist Pl. ([verborgene] Gefahr/Schwierigkeit)* [hidden] danger/difficulty

tuckern *itr. V.; mit Richtungsangabe mit sein* chug

tückisch 1. *Adj.* **a)** *(hinterhältig)* wily; *(betrügerisch)* deceitful; **b)** *(gefährlich)* treacherous ⟨*bend, slope, spot, etc.*⟩; **2.** *adv.* craftily

tüfteln *itr. V. (ugs.)* fiddle **(an +** *Dat.* with**);** do finicky work **(an +** *Dat.* on**);** *(geistig)* rack one's brains **(an +** *Dat.* over**)**

Tugend die; ~, ~en virtue; **tugendhaft 1.** *Adj.* virtuous; **2.** *adv.* virtuously

Tüll der; ~s, ~e tulle

Tülle die; ~, ~n *(bes. nordd.)* spout

Tulpe die; ~, ~n tulip

tummeln *refl. V.* romp [about]; **Tummel·platz der** *(auch fig.)* playground

Tumor der; ~s, ~en *(Med.)* tumour

Tümpel der; ~s, ~: pond

Tumult der; ~[e]s, ~e tumult; commotion; *(Protest)* uproar

tun 1. *unr. tr. V.* **a)** do; **so etwas tut man nicht** that is just not done; [etwas] mit etw./jmdm. zu ~ **haben** be concerned with sth./have dealings with sb.; **b)** *als Funktionsverb* make ⟨*remark, catch, etc.*⟩; take ⟨*step, jump*⟩; do ⟨*deed*⟩; **c)** *(bewirken)* work, perform ⟨*miracle*⟩; **d)** *(an~)* jmdm. etw. ~: do sth. to sb.; **e) es** ~ *(ugs.: genügen)* be good enough; **f)** *(ugs.: irgendwohin bringen)* put; **2.** *unr. itr. V.* **a)** *(ugs.: funktionieren)* work; **b)** **freundlich/geheimnisvoll** ~: pretend to be *or* (coll.) act friendly/ act mysteriously; **3.** *unr. refl. V.;* *unpers.* **es hat sich einiges getan** quite a bit has happened

Tünche die; ~, ~n distemper; wash; |weiße| ~: whitewash; **tünchen** *tr. (auch itr.) V.* distemper; **weiß** ~: whitewash

Tunell das; ~s, ~s *(südd., österr., schweiz.)* s. **Tunnel**

Tunesien [tu'ne:zi̯ən] **(das)**; ~s Tunisia; **tunesisch** *Adj.* Tunisian

Tunke die; ~, ~n *(bes. ostmd.)* sauce; *(Bratensoße)* gravy; **tunken** *tr. V. (bes. ostmd.)* dip

Tunnel der; ~s, ~ *od.* ~s tunnel

tupfen *tr. V.* **a)** dab; **b)** *(mit Tupfen versehen)* dot; **Tupfen** der; ~s, ~: dot; *(größer)* spot; **Tupfer** der; ~s, ~ *(Med.)* swab

Tür die; ~, ~en door; *(Garten~)* gate; **an die** ~ **gehen** *(öffnen)* [go and] answer the door; **vor die** ~ **gehen** go outside

Turban der; ~s, ~e turban

Turbine die; ~, ~n turbine

turbulent 1. *Adj. (auch fachspr.)* turbulent; **2.** *adv. (auch fachspr.)* turbulently

Tür·griff der door-handle

Türke der; ~n, ~n Turk; **Türkei** die; ~: Turkey *no art.*

türkis *indekl. Adj.* turquoise; **Türkis** der; ~es, ~e turquoise

türkisch *Adj.* Turkish

Tür·klinke die door-handle

Turm der; ~|e|s, Türme **a)** tower; *(spitzer Kirch~)* spire; steeple; **b)** *(Schach)* rook; **c)** *(Sprung~)* diving-platform; **Türmchen** das; ~s, ~: turret; **¹türmen** **1.** *tr. V. (stapeln)* stack up; *(häufen)* pile up; **2.** *refl. V.* be piled up; ⟨*clouds*⟩ gather

²türmen *itr. V.; mit sein (salopp)* scarper *(Brit. sl.)*

Turm·falke der kestrel

turnen 1. *itr. V.* do gymnastics; *(Schulw.)* do gym; **2.** *tr. V.* do, perform ⟨*exercise, routine*⟩; **Turnen** das; ~s gymnastics *sing., no art.; (Schulw.)*

gym *no art.;* PE *no art.;* **Turner** der; ~s, ~, **Turnerin** die; ~, ~nen gymnast

Turn-: ~**halle** die gymnasium; ~**hemd** das [gym] singlet; ~**hose** die gym shorts *pl.*

Turnier das; ~s, ~e *(auch hist.)* tournament; *(Reit~)* show; *(Tanz~)* competition

Turn·schuh der gym shoe

Turnus der; ~, ~se regular cycle

Turn·verein der gymnastics club

Tusch der; ~|e|s, ~e fanfare

Tusche die; ~, ~n Indian *(Brit.)* or *(Amer.)* India ink

tuscheln *itr., tr. V.* whisper

Tüte die; ~, ~n bag

tuten *itr. V.* hoot; ⟨*siren, [fog-]horn*⟩ sound

Typ der; ~s, ~en **a)** type; **b)** *Gen. auch* ~**en** *(ugs.: Mann)* bloke *(Brit. sl.);* **Type** die; ~, ~n *(Druck~, Schreibmaschinen~)* type

Typhus der; ~ typhoid *[fever]*

typisch 1. *Adj.* typical *(für of);* **2.** *adv.* typically

Tyrann der; ~en, ~en *(auch fig.)* tyrant; **Tyrannei** die; ~, ~en *(auch fig.)* tyranny; **tyrannisch 1.** *Adj.* tyrannical; **2.** *adv.* tyrannically; **tyrannisieren** *tr. V.* tyrannize

U

___

u, U [u:] das; ~, ~: u, U

ü, Ü [y:] das; ~, ~: u umlaut

u. *Abk.* und

u. a. *Abk.* unter anderem

U-Bahn die underground *(Brit.);* subway *(Amer.); (bes. in London)* tube; **U-Bahn-Station** die underground station *(Brit.);* subway station *(Amer.); (bes. in London)* tube station

übel *Adj.* **a)** foul, nasty ⟨*smell, weather*⟩; bad, nasty ⟨*headache, cold, taste*⟩; nasty ⟨*consequences, situation*⟩; sorry ⟨*state, affair*⟩; foul, *(coll.)* filthy ⟨*mood*⟩; **nicht** ~ *(ugs.)* not bad at all; **b)** *(unwohl)* jmdm. **ist/wird** ~: sb. feels sick; **c)** *(verwerflich)* bad;

wicked; nasty, dirty ⟨trick⟩. **Übel** das; ~s, ~ evil; **Übelkeit** die; ~, ~en nausea

übel|nehmen unr. tr. V. jmdm. etw. ~: hold sth. against sb.; etw. ~: take offence at sth.; **Übel·täter** der wrongdoer

üben tr. V. **a)** (auch itr.) practise; rehearse ⟨scene, play⟩; practise on ⟨musical instrument⟩; **b)** (trainieren, schulen) exercise ⟨fingers⟩; train ⟨memory⟩

über 1. Präp. mit Dat. **a)** (Lage, Standort) over; above; (in einer Rangfolge) above; ~ jmdm. wohnen live above sb.; **zehn Grad ~ Null** ten degrees above zero; **sie trug eine Jacke ~ dem Kleid** she wore a jacket over her dress; **b)** (während) during; ~ **dem Lesen/der Arbeit einschlafen** fall asleep over one's book/magazine etc./over one's work; 2. Präp. mit Akk. **a)** (Richtung) over; (quer hinüber) across; ~ **Ulm nach Stuttgart** via Ulm to Stuttgart; **b)** (während) over; (für die Dauer von) for; **c)** (betreffend) about; ~ **etw. reden/schreiben** talk/write about sth.; **ein Scheck/eine Rechnung ~ 1000 Mark** a cheque/bill for 1,000 marks; **d)** Kinder ~ **10 Jahre** children over ten [years of age]; 3. Adv. **a)** (mehr als) over; **b)** ~ **und** ~: all over

über·all [od. --'-] Adv. **a)** everywhere; **b)** (bei jeder Gelegenheit) always

über·anstrengen tr. V. overtax ⟨person, energy⟩; strain ⟨eyes, nerves, heart⟩; **sich** ~: over-exert oneself

über·arbeiten 1. tr. V. rework; revise ⟨text, edition⟩; 2. refl. V. overwork

über·aus Adv. (geh.) extremely

über·backen unr. tr. V. etw. mit Käse usw. ~: top sth. with cheese etc. and brown it lightly [under the grill/in a hot oven]

überbelichten[1] tr. V. (Fot.) overexpose

über·bieten unr. tr. V. **a)** outbid (um by); **b)** (übertreffen) surpass; outdo ⟨rival⟩; break ⟨record⟩ (um by); exceed ⟨target⟩ (um by)

Über·blick der **a)** view; **einen guten ~ über etw.** (Akk.) **haben** have a good view over sth.; **b)** (Abriß) survey; **c)** o. Pl. (Einblick) overall view; **über·blicken** tr. V. s. übersehen a, b

über·bringen unr. tr. V. deliver; convey ⟨greetings, congratulations⟩

über·brücken tr. V. bridge ⟨gap, gulf⟩; reconcile ⟨difference⟩; **Über·brückung** die; ~, ~en (fig.) bridging; (von Gegensätzen) reconciliation

überdacht Adj. covered ⟨terrace, station platform, etc.⟩

über·dauern tr. V. survive ⟨war, separation, hardship⟩

über·dies Adv. moreover

Über·druck der; Pl. ~drücke excess pressure

Überdruß der; **Überdrusses** surfeit (**an** + Dat. of); **überdrüssig** Adj. jmds./einer Sache ~ sein/werden be/grow tired of sb./sth.

über·eilen tr. V. rush; **übereilt** over-hasty

über·einander Adv. **a)** one on top of the other; **b)** ⟨talk etc.⟩ about each other

übereinander-: ~**legen** tr. V. Holzscheite usw. ~**legen** lay pieces of wood etc. one on top of the other; ~**schlagen** unr. tr. V. **die Arme/Beine** ~**schlagen** fold one's arms/cross one's legs

überein|kommen unr. itr. V.; mit sein agree; come to an agreement; **Überein·kommen** das; ~s, ~, **Übereinkunft** die; ~, **Übereinkünfte** agreement

überein|stimmen itr. V. **a)** (einer Meinung sein) agree (**in** + Dat. on); **b)** (sich gleichen) ⟨colours, styles⟩ match; ⟨figures, statements, reports, results⟩ tally, agree; ⟨views, opinions⟩ coincide; **Überein·stimmung** die **a)** agreement (**in** + Dat. on; Gen. between)

über·empfindlich 1. Adj. oversensitive (**gegen** to); (Med.) hypersensitive (**gegen** to). 2. adv. oversensitively; (Med.) hypersensitively

'über|fahren 1. unr. tr. V. jmdm. ~: ferry or take sb. over; 2. unr. itr. V.; mit sein cross over; **²über·fahren** unr. tr. V. **a)** run over; **b)** (hinwegfahren über) cross; go over ⟨crossroads⟩; **Über·fahrt** die crossing (**über** + Akk. of)

Über·fall der attack (**auf** + Akk. on); (aus dem Hinterhalt) ambush (**auf** + Akk. on); (mit vorgehaltener Waffe) hold-up; (auf eine Bank o. ä.) raid (**auf** + Akk. on); **über·fallen** unr. tr. V. **a)** attack; raid ⟨bank, enemy position, village, etc.⟩; (hinterrücks) ambush; (mit vorgehaltener Waffe) hold up; b) *(überkommen)* ⟨*tiredness, home-sickness, fear*⟩ come over; **über·fäl·lig** *Adj.* overdue

über·fliegen *unr. tr. V.* a) fly over; overfly *(formal)*; b) *(flüchtig lesen)* skim [through]

über·flügeln *tr. V.* outshine; outstrip

Über·fluß der; *o. Pl.* abundance **(an** + *Dat.* of); *(Wohlstand)* affluence; **über·flüssig** *Adj.* superfluous; unnecessary *(purchase, words, work)*

über·fluten *tr. V. (auch fig.)* flood

über·fordern *tr. V.* jmdn. [mit etw.] ~: overtax sb. [with sth.]; ask *or* demand too much of sb. [with sth.]

¹über|führen *tr. V.* transfer; **²über·führen** *tr. V.* a) *s.* **¹überführen;** b) jmdn. [eines Verbrechens] ~: find sb. guilty [of a crime]; convict sb. [of a crime]; **Über·führung die** a) transfer; b) *(eines Verdächtigen)* conviction; c) *(Brücke)* bridge; *(Hochstraße)* overpass; *(Fußgänger~)* [foot-]bridge

über·füllt *Adj.* crammed full **(von** with); *(mit Menschen)* overcrowded **(von** with); over-subscribed *(course)*

Über·gabe die a) handing over **(an** + *Akk.* to); *(von Macht)* handing over; b) *(Auslieferung an den Gegner)* surrender **(an** + *Akk.* to)

Über·gang der a) crossing; b) *(Stelle zum Überqueren)* crossing; *(Bahn~)* level crossing *(Brit.)*; grade crossing *(Amer.)*; *(Grenz~)* crossing-point; c) *(Wechsel, Überleitung)* transition **(zu, auf** + *Akk.* to)

über·geben 1. *unr. tr. V.* a) hand over; pass *(baton)*; b) *(übereignen)* transfer, make over *(Dat.* to); c) *(ausliefern)* surrender *(Dat., an* + *Akk.* to); d) eine Straße dem Verkehr ~: open a road to traffic; **2.** *unr. refl. V.* *(sich erbrechen)* vomit

¹über|gehen *unr. itr. V.; mit sein* a) pass; b) **zu etw.** ~: go over to sth.; **c) in etw.** *(Akk.)* ~ *(zu etw. werden)* turn into sth.

²über·gehen *unr. tr. V.* a) *(nicht beachten)* ignore; b) *(auslassen, überspringen)* skip [over]; c) *(nicht berücksichtigen)* pass over

über·geordnet *Adj.* higher *(court, authority, position)*; greater *(significance)*; superordinate *(concept)*

Über·gewicht das a) excess weight; *(von Person)* overweight; b) *(fig.)* predominance

über·glücklich *Adj.* blissfully happy; *(hoch erfreut)* overjoyed

über|greifen *unr. itr. V.* **auf etw.** *(Akk.)* ~: spread to sth.

Über·griff der *(unrechtmäßiger Eingriff)* encroachment **(auf** + *Akk.* on); infringement **(auf** + *Akk.* of); *(Angriff)* attack **(auf** + *Akk.* on)

Über·größe die outsize

überhand|nehmen *unr. itr. V.* get out of hand; *(attacks, muggings, etc.)* increase alarmingly; *(weeds)* run riot

über|hängen *tr. V.* sich *(Dat.)* eine Jacke ~: put a jacket round one's shoulders; sich *(Dat.)* das Gewehr/die Tasche ~: hang the rifle/bag over one's shoulder

über·häufen *tr. V.* jmdn. mit etw. ~: heap *or* shower sth. on sb.

überhaupt *Adv.* a) in general; b) ~ **nicht** not at all; ~ **keine Zeit haben** have no time at all; ~ **nichts** nothing at all

überheblich 1. *Adj.* arrogant; supercilious *(grin)*; **2.** *adv.* arrogantly; *(grin)* superciliously

Überheblichkeit die; ~: arrogance

über·holen 1. *tr. V.* a) overtake *(esp. Brit.)*; pass *(esp. Amer.)*; b) *(übertreffen)* outstrip; c) *(wieder instand setzen)* overhaul; **2.** *itr. V.* overtake *(esp. Brit.)*; pass *(esp. Amer.)*; **Überhol·spur die** overtaking lane *(esp. Brit.)*; pass lane *(esp. Amer.)*; **überholt** *Adj.* *(veraltet)* outdated; **Überholung die;** ~, ~en overhaul

Überhol·verbot das prohibition of overtaking

über·hören *tr. V.* not hear

über·irdisch 1. *Adj.* celestial; heavenly; *(übernatürlich)* supernatural; **2.** *adv.* celestially; *(übernatürlich)* supernaturally

über|kochen *itr. V.; mit sein (auch fig. ugs.)* boil over

über·kommen *unr. tr. V.* Mitleid/Ekel/Furcht überkam mich I was overcome by pity/revulsion/fear

über·laden *unr. tr. V. (auch fig.)* overload

über·lassen *unr. tr. V.* a) jmdm. etw. ~: let sb. have sth.; b) sich *(Dat.)* selbst ~ sein be left to one's own devices; c) etw. jmdm. ~ *(etw. jmdn. entscheiden/tun lassen)* leave sth. to sb.

über·lasten *tr. V.* overload; overtax *(person)*; *(mit Arbeit)* overwork *(person)*

Über·lauf der overflow; **¹über|laufen** *unr. itr. V.; mit sein* a) overflow; b) *(auf die gegnerische Seite überwech-*

seln) defect; *⟨partisan⟩* go over to the other side; **²über·laufen** *unr. tr. V.* seize; **ein Frösteln/Schauer überlief mich, es überlief mich [eis]kalt** a cold shiver ran down my spine; **²über·laufen** *Adj.* overcrowded; **Über·läufer der** *(auch fig.)* defector

über·leben *tr. V.* survive; **Über·lebende der/die;** *adj. Dekl.* survivor

¹über·legen *tr. V.* jmdm. etw. ~: put sth. over sb.; **²über·legen 1.** *tr. V.* consider; think about; **es sich anders ~:** change one's mind; **2.** *itr. V.* think; **³überlegen 1.** *Adj.* **a)** superior; clear, convincing *⟨win, victory⟩;* **jmdm. ~ sein** be superior to sb. **(an + Dat.** in); **b)** *(herablassend)* supercilious; **2.** *adv.* **a)** in a superior manner; *⟨play⟩* much the better: *⟨win, argue⟩* convincingly; **b)** *(herablassend)* superciliously; **Überlegenheit die;** ~ superiority; **überlegt 1.** *Adj.* carefully considered; **2.** *adv.* in a carefully considered way; **Überlegung die;** ~, ~en) *o. Pl.* thought; **b)** *(Gedanke)* idea; ~en *(Gedankengang)* thoughts

über·liefern *tr. V.* hand down; **Über·lieferung die** tradition

überlisten *tr. V.* outwit

überm *Präp. + Art.* = über dem

Über·macht die; *o. Pl.* superior strength; *(zahlenmäßig)* superior numbers *pl.*

über·mannen *tr. V.* overcome

Über·maß das; *o. Pl.* excessive amount, excess **(an + Dat.** of); **über·mäßig 1.** *Adj.* excessive; **2.** *adv.* excessively

über·menschlich *Adj.* superhuman

über·mitteln *tr. V.* send; *(als Mittler weitergeben)* pass on, convey *⟨greetings, regards, etc.⟩*

über·morgen *Adv.* the day after tomorrow

Übermüdung die; ~: overtiredness

Über·mut der high spirits *pl.;* **übermütig 1.** *Adj.* high-spirited; **2.** *adv.* high-spiritedly

über·nächst... Adj. im ~en Jahr, ~es Jahr the year after next; **am ~en Tag** two days later

über·nachten *itr. V.* stay overnight; **übernächtigt** *Adj.* *⟨person⟩* tired or worn out *[through lack of sleep];* tired *⟨face, look, etc.⟩;* **Übernachtung die;** ~, ~en overnight stay; **~ und Frühstück** bed and breakfast

Übernahme die; ~ *(von Waren, einer Sendung)* taking delivery *no art.;* (ei-

ner Idee usw.) adoption, taking over *no indef. art.;* *(der Macht, einer Praxis usw.)* take over

über·natürlich *Adj.* supernatural

über·nehmen 1. *unr. tr. V.* take delivery of *⟨goods, consignment⟩;* take over *⟨power, practice, business, etc.⟩;* take on *⟨job, position, etc.⟩;* undertake to pay *⟨costs⟩;* **b)** *(sich zu eigen machen)* adopt *⟨ideas, methods, subject, etc.⟩* **(von** from); borrow *⟨word, phrase⟩* **(von** from); **2.** *tr. refl. V.* overdo things or it; **sich mit etw. ~:** take on too much with sth.

über·prüfen *tr. V.* check **(auf + Akk.** for); review *⟨issue, situation, results⟩;* **Über·prüfung die a)** *o. Pl.* checking *no indef. art.* **(auf + Akk.** for); **b)** *(Kontrolle)* check; *(einer Lage, Frage usw.)* review

über·queren *tr. V.* cross

über·ragen *tr. V.* **a)** jmdn./etw. ~: tower above sb./sth.; **b)** *(übertreffen)* jmdn. an etw. **(Dat.)** ~: be head and shoulders above sb. in sth.; **überragend 1.** *Adj.* outstanding; **2.** *adv.* outstandingly

überraschen *tr. V.* surprise; **Überraschung die;** ~, ~en surprise

über·reden *tr. V.* persuade

über·reichen *tr. V.* [jmdm.] etw. ~: present sth. [to sb.]

über·rumpeln *tr. V.* jmdn. ~: take sb. by surprise

über·runden *tr. V.* **a)** *(Sport)* lap; **b)** *(übertreffen)* outstrip

übers *Präp. + Art.* = über das

Überschall-: ~flugzeug das supersonic aircraft; ~geschwindigkeit die supersonic speed

über·schätzen *tr. V.* overestimate; overrate *⟨artist, talent, etc.⟩*

überschaubar *Adj.* eine ~e Menge/Zahl a manageable quantity/number

Über·schlag der a) rough calculation or estimate; **b)** *(Turnen)* handspring; **c)** *s.* Looping; **¹über·schlagen 1.** *unr. tr. V.* **die Beine ~:** cross one's legs; **2.** *unr. V.;* mit sein *⟨wave⟩* break; **²über·schlagen 1.** *unr. tr. V.* **a)** skip *⟨chapter, page, etc.⟩;* **b)** *(ungefähr berechnen)* calculate or estimate roughly; **2.** *unr. refl. V.* go head over heels; *⟨car⟩* turn over

über·schnappen *itr. V.;* mit sein *(ugs.)* go crazy

über·schneiden *unr. refl. V.* cross, intersect; *(fig.)* overlap

über·schreiben *unr. tr. V.* **a)** entitle;

head ⟨*chapter, section*⟩; **b)** etw. jmdm. *od.* auf jmdn. ~: transfer sth. to sb.

über·schreiten *unr. itr. V.* cross; *(fig.)* exceed

Über·schrift die heading; *(in einer Zeitung)* headline; *(Titel)* title

Über·schuß der surplus (**an** + *Dat.* of); **überschüssig** *Adj.* surplus

über·schütten *tr. V.* cover

Überschwang der; ~[e]s exuberance

über·schwemmen *tr. V. (auch fig.)* flood; **Überschwemmung** die; ~, ~en flood; *(das Überschwemmen)* flooding *no pl.*

überschwenglich 1. *Adj.* effusive ⟨*words etc.*⟩; wild ⟨*joy, enthusiasm*⟩; **2.** *adv.* effusively

Über·see *o. Art.* aus *od.* von ~: from overseas; **in/nach** ~: overseas

über·sehen *unr. tr. V.* **a)** look out over; **b)** *(abschätzen)* assess ⟨*damage, situation, consequences, etc.*⟩; **c)** *(nicht sehen)* overlook; miss ⟨*turning, signpost*⟩; **d)** *(ignorieren)* ignore

über·senden *unr. (auch regelm.) tr. V.* send

¹**über|setzen 1.** *tr. V.* ferry over; **2.** *itr. V.; auch mit sein* cross [over]; ²**über·setzen** *tr., itr. V. (auch fig.)* translate; **Über·setzer** der, **Übersetzerin** die; ~, ~nen translator; **Überset·zung** die; ~, ~en translation

Über·sicht die **a)** *o. Pl.* overall view, overview (**über** + *Akk.* of); **b)** *(Darstellung)* survey; *(Tabelle)* summary; **über·sichtlich 1.** *Adj.* clear; ⟨*crossroads*⟩ which allows a clear view; **2.** *adv.* clearly

¹**über|siedeln,** ²**über·siedeln** *itr. V.; mit sein* move (**nach** to)

über·spielen *tr. V.* **a)** *(hinweggehen über)* cover up; smooth over ⟨*difficult situation*⟩; **b)** *(aufnehmen)* [auf ein Tonband] ~: transfer ⟨*record*⟩ to tape; put ⟨*record*⟩ on tape

über·spitzen *tr. V.* etw. ~: push *or* carry sth. too far

über·springen *unr. tr. V.* **a)** jump ⟨*obstacle*⟩; **b)** *(auslassen)* miss out

¹**über|stehen** *tr. V.; südd., österr., schweiz. mit sein* jut out

²**über·stehen** *unr. tr. V.* come through ⟨*danger, war, operation*⟩; get over ⟨*illness*⟩

über·steigen *unr. tr. V.* **a)** climb over; **b)** *(fig.)* exceed

über·stimmen *tr. V.* outvote

Über·stunde die; ~n machen do overtime

über·stürzen 1. *tr. V.* rush; **2.** *refl. V.* rush; *(rasch aufeinanderfolgen)* ⟨*events, news, etc.*⟩ come thick and fast; **überstürzt 1.** *Adj.* hurried ⟨*escape, departure*⟩; over-hasty ⟨*decision*⟩; **2.** *adv. (decide, act)* over-hastily; ⟨*depart*⟩ hurriedly

übertölpeln *tr. V.* dupe; con *(coll.)*

über·tönen *tr. V.* drown out

Übertrag der; ~[e]s, **Überträge** *(bes. Buchf.)* carry-over; **über·tragbar** *Adj.* transferable (**auf** + *Akk.* to); *(auf etw. anderes anwendbar)* applicable (**auf** + *Akk.* to); *(übersetzbar)* translatable; *(ansteckend)* infectious ⟨*disease*⟩; **über·tragen** *unr. tr. V.* **a)** transfer (**auf** + *Akk.* to); transmit ⟨*power, torque, etc.*⟩ (**auf** + *Akk.* to); communicate ⟨*disease, illness*⟩ (**auf** + *Akk.* to); carry over ⟨*subtotal*⟩; *(auf etw. anderes anwenden)* apply (**auf** + *Akk.* to); *(übersetzen)* translate; **b)** *(senden)* broadcast ⟨*concert, event, match, etc.*⟩; *(im Fernsehen)* televise; **c)** *(geben)* jmdm. Aufgaben/Pflichten usw. ~: hand over tasks/duties *etc.* to sb.; *(anvertrauen)* entrust sb. with tasks/duties *etc.*; **Übertragung** die; ~, ~en **a)** *s.* übertragen **a:** transference; transmission; communication; carrying over; application; translation; **b)** *(das Senden)* broadcasting; *(Sendung)* broadcast; *(im Fernsehen)* televising/television broadcast

über·treffen *unr. tr. V.* **a)** surpass, outdo (**an** + *Dat.* in); break ⟨*record*⟩; **b)** *(übersteigen)* exceed

über·treiben *unr. tr. V.* **a)** auch itr. exaggerate; **b)** *(zu weit treiben)* overdo; **Übertreibung** die; ~, ~en exaggeration

¹**über|treten** *unr. itr. V.; mit sein* change sides; **zum Katholizismus/Islam** ~: convert to Catholicism/Islam; ²**über·treten** *unr. tr. V.* contravene ⟨*law*⟩; violate ⟨*regulation, prohibition*⟩; **Übertretung** die; ~, ~en **a)** *s.* ²übertreten: contravention; violation; **b)** *(Vergehen)* misdemeanour

übertrieben *Adj.* **1.** exaggerated; *(übermäßig)* excessive ⟨*care, thrift, etc.*⟩; **2.** *adv.* excessively

Über·tritt der change of allegiance, switch (**zu** to); *(Rel.)* conversion (**zu** to)

über·trumpfen *tr. V.* outdo

über·vor·teilen *tr. V.* cheat

über·wachen *tr. V.* keep under surveillance ⟨suspect, agent, area, etc.⟩; supervise ⟨factory, workers, process⟩; control ⟨traffic⟩; monitor ⟨progress, production process, experiment, patient⟩; **Überwachung die**; ~, ~en s. **überwachen**: surveillance; supervision; controlling; monitoring

überwältigen tr. V. **a)** overpower; **b)** (fig.) ⟨sleep, emotion, fear, etc.⟩ overcome; ⟨sight, impressions, beauty, etc.⟩ overwhelm; **überwältigend 1.** Adj. overwhelming ⟨sight, impression, victory, majority, etc.⟩; overpowering ⟨smell⟩; stunning ⟨beauty⟩; **2.** adv. stunningly ⟨beautiful⟩

über·weisen unr. tr. V. **a)** transfer ⟨money⟩ (an, auf + Akk. to); **b)** refer ⟨patient⟩ (an + Akk. to); **Überweisung die a)** o. Pl. transfer (an, auf + Akk. to); **b)** (Summe) remittance; **c)** (eines Patienten) referral (an + Akk. to)

überwiegend 1. [auch --'--] Adj. overwhelming; **2.** adv. mainly

über·winden 1. unr. tr. V. overcome; get past ⟨stage⟩; **2.** unr. refl. V. overcome one's reluctance; **sich [dazu] ~, etw. zu tun** bring oneself to do sth.; **Über·windung die a)** s. **überwinden 1**: overcoming; getting past; **b)** (das Sichüberwinden) **es war eine große ~** für ihn it cost him a great effort

Über·zahl die; o. Pl. majority; **über·zählig** Adj. surplus

überzeugen 1. tr. V. convince; **2.** itr. V. be convincing; **überzeugend 1.** Adj. convincing; **2.** adv. convincingly; **überzeugt** Adj. convinced; **Über·zeugung die** (feste Meinung) conviction

¹über|ziehen unr. tr. V. pull on; **²über·ziehen** unr. tr. V. **a)** etw. mit etw. ~: cover sth. with sth.; **b)** overdraw ⟨account⟩ (um by); **Überzug der a)** (Beschichtung) coating; **b)** (Bezug) cover

üblich Adj. usual; (normal) normal; (gebräuchlich) customary

U-Boot das submarine; sub (coll.)

übrig Adj. remaining attrib.; (ander...) other; **alle ~en Gäste ...**: all the other guests ...; **im ~en** besides; **es ist etwas ~**: there is some left; **übrig|bleiben** unr. itr. V.; mit sein be left; ⟨food, drink⟩ be left over; **übrigens** Adv. by the way; **übrig|lassen** unr. tr. V. leave; leave ⟨food, drink⟩ over

Übung die; ~, ~en **a)** exercise; **b)** o. Pl. (das Üben, Geübtsein) practice

UdSSR [u:de:|ɛs|ɛs|'ɛr] Abk. die; ~ (1922–1991) Union der Sozialistischen Sowjetrepubliken USSR

Ufer das; ~s, ~: bank; (des Meers) shore

UG Abk. Untergeschoß

Uganda (das); ~s Uganda

Uhr die; ~, ~en **a)** clock; (Armband~, Taschen~) watch; (Wasser~, Gas~) meter; (an Meßinstrumenten) dial; gauge; **auf die** od. **nach der ~ sehen** look at the time; **rund um die ~** (ugs.) round the clock; **b)** o. Pl. **acht ~**: eight o'clock; **wieviel ~ ist es?** what's the time?; **what time is it?**

Uhr-: ~**armband das** watch-strap; ~**kette die** watch-chain; ~**macher der** watchmaker/clockmaker; ~**werk das** clock/watch mechanism; ~**zeiger der** clock-/watch-hand; ~**zeiger·sinn der:** im/entgegen dem ~**zeigersinn** clockwise/anticlockwise; ~**zeit die** time; **jmdn. nach der ~zeit fragen** ask sb. the time

Uhu der; ~s, ~s eagle owl

Ukraine die; ~: Ukraine; **Ukrainer der**; ~s, ~, **Ukrainerin die**; ~, ~nen Ukrainian

UKW [u:ka:'ve:] o. Art.; Abk. Ultrakurzwelle VHF; **UKW-Sender der** VHF station; ≈ FM station

Ulk der; ~s, ~e lark (coll.); (Streich) trick; [practical] joke; **ulkig** (ugs.) **1.** Adj. funny; **2.** adv. in a funny way

Ulme die; ~, ~n elm

Ultimatum das; ~s, **Ultimaten** ultimatum

Ultra·kurz·welle die ultra-short wave; (Rundf.: Wellenbereich) very high frequency; VHF

Ultra·schall der (Physik, Med.) ultrasound; **ultra·violett** Adj. ultraviolet

um 1. Präp. mit Akk. **a)** (räumlich) [a]round; **um die Ecke** round the corner; **b)** (zeitlich) (genau) at; (etwa) around [about]; **c)** **Tag um Tag/Stunde um Stunde** day after day/hour after hour; **d)** (bei Maß- u. Mengenangaben) by; **2.** Adv. around; about; **um [die] 10 Mark/50 Personen [herum]** around or about ten marks/50 people ...; **3.** Konj. **a)** (final) **um ... zu** [in order] to; **b)** (konsekutiv) **er ist groß genug/ist noch zu klein, um ... zu ...:** he is big enough/is still too young to ...; **c)** **je ... um so the ..., the**; **um so besser/schlimmer!** all the better/worse!

um|ändern tr. V. change; revise ⟨text, novel⟩; alter ⟨garment⟩

umarmen *tr. V.* embrace; *(an sich drücken)* hug; **Umarmung die; ~, ~en** embrace; hug

Um·bau der; ~[e]s, ~ten *s.* umbauen: rebuilding; alteration; conversion; *(fig.)* reorganization; **um|bauen** *tr., auch itr. V.* rebuild; *(leicht ändern)* alter; *(zu etw. anderem)* convert (**zu** into); *(fig.)* reorganize ⟨*system, administration, etc.*⟩

um|benennen *unr. tr. V.* change the name of; rename

um|biegen 1. *unr. tr. V.* bend; **2.** *unr. itr. V.; mit sein* turn

um|binden *unr. tr. V.* put on

um|blättern 1. *tr. V.* turn [over]; **2.** *itr. V.* turn the page/pages

um|blicken *refl. V.* **a)** look around; **b)** *(zurückblicken)* [turn to] look back (**nach** at)

um|bringen *unr. tr. V.* kill

Um·bruch der a) radical change; *(Umwälzung)* upheaval; **b)** *o. Pl. (Druckw.)* make-up; *(Ergebnis)* page proofs *pl.*

um|buchen 1. *tr. V.* change (**auf +** *Akk.* to); **2.** *itr. V.* change one's booking (**auf +** *Akk.* to)

um|drehen 1. *tr. V.* turn round; turn over ⟨*coin, hand, etc.*⟩; turn ⟨*key*⟩; **2.** *refl. V.* turn round; *(den Kopf wenden)* turn one's head; **3.** *itr. V.; auch mit sein (ugs.: umkehren)* turn back; *(ugs.: wenden)* turn round; **Um·drehung die;** *(eines Motors usw.)* revolution; rev *(coll.)*

um·einander *Adv.* **sich ~ kümmern/sorgen** take care of/worry about each other *or* one another

¹um|fahren *unr. tr. V.* knock down; **²um·fahren** *unr. tr. V.* go round; make a detour round ⟨*obstruction etc.*⟩; *(im Auto)* drive round; *(im Schiff)* sail round; *(auf einer Umgehungsstraße)* bypass ⟨*town, village, etc.*⟩

um|fallen *unr. itr. V.; mit sein* **a)** fall over; **b)** *(zusammenbrechen)* collapse; **tot ~:** fall down dead

Um·fang der a) circumference; *(eines Quadrats usw.)* perimeter; *(eines Baums, Menschen usw.)* girth; **b)** *(Größe)* size; **c)** *(Ausmaß)* extent; **um·fang·reich** *Adj.* extensive; substantial ⟨*book*⟩

um·fassen *tr. V.* **a)** grasp; *(umarmen)* embrace; **b)** *(enthalten)* contain; *(einschließen)* include; span, cover ⟨*period*⟩; **umfassend 1.** *Adj.* full ⟨reply, information, survey, confession⟩; extensive, wide ⟨*knowledge, powers*⟩; **2.** *adv.* ⟨*inform*⟩ fully

um|formen *tr. V.* reshape; revise ⟨*poem, novel*⟩; transform ⟨*person*⟩

Um·frage die survey; *(Politik)* opinion poll

um|füllen *tr. V.* **etw. in etw.** *(Akk.)* **~:** transfer sth. into sth.

Um·gang der; o. Pl.* **a) *(gesellschaftlicher Verkehr)* contact; **b)** *(das Umgehen)* **den ~ mit Pferden lernen** learn how to handle horses; **umgänglich** *Adj.* affable; *(gesellig)* sociable

Umgangs-: **~form die gute/schlechte/keine ~formen haben** have good/bad/no manners; **~sprache die** colloquial language

um·geben *unr. tr. V.* **a)** surround; ⟨*hedge, fence, wall, etc.*⟩ enclose; **b)** **etw. mit etw. ~:** surround sth. with sth.; *(einfrieden)* enclose sth. with sth.; **Umgebung die; ~, ~en** surroundings *pl.; (Nachbarschaft)* neighbourhood; *(eines Ortes)* surrounding area

¹um|gehen *unr. itr. V.; mit sein* **a)** *(im Umlauf sein)* ⟨*list, rumour, etc.*⟩ go round, circulate; ⟨*illness, infection*⟩ go round; **b)** *(spuken)* **hier geht ein Gespenst um** this place is haunted; **c)** *(behandeln)* **mit jmdm. freundlich/liebevoll usw. ~:** treat sb. kindly/lovingly etc.; **er kann mit Geld nicht ~:** he can't handle money

²um·gehen *unr. tr. V.* **a)** go round; make a detour round; *(auf einer Umgehungsstraße)* bypass ⟨*town etc.*⟩; **b)** *(vermeiden)* avoid; evade ⟨*question, issue*⟩; **c)** *(nicht befolgen)* circumvent ⟨*law, restriction, etc.*⟩; evade ⟨*obligation, duty*⟩; **umgehend 1.** *Adj.* immediate; **2.** *adv.* immediately; **Umgehung die; ~, ~en a) durch ~ der Innenstadt** by bypassing *or* avoiding the town centre; **b)** *s.* **²umgehen c:** circumvention; evasion; **Umgehungs·straße die** bypass

umgekehrt 1. *Adj.* inverse ⟨*ratio, proportion*⟩; reverse ⟨*order*⟩; opposite ⟨*sign*⟩; **2.** *adv.* inversely ⟨*proportional*⟩

um|graben *unr. tr. V.* dig over

Um·hang der cape; **um|hängen** *tr. V.* **a)** etw. **~:** hang sth. somewhere else; **b)** **jmdm./sich einen Mantel/eine Decke ~:** drape a coat/blanket round sb.'s/one's shoulders

um|hauen *unr. tr. V.* fell; *(fig.)* knock down

um·her *Adv.* around

umher-: *s.* herum-

um|hören *refl. V.* keep one's ears open; *(direkt fragen)* ask around

um|jubeln *tr. V.* cheer

um|kehren 1. *itr. V.; mit sein* turn back; **2.** *tr. V.* turn upside down; turn over ⟨*sheet of paper*⟩; *(nach links drehen)* turn ⟨*garment etc.*⟩ inside out; *(nach rechts drehen)* turn ⟨*garment etc.*⟩ right side out

um|kippen 1. *itr. V.; mit sein* **a)** fall over; ⟨*boat*⟩ capsize, turn over; ⟨*vehicle*⟩ overturn; **b)** *(ugs.: ohnmächtig werden)* keel over; **2.** *tr. V.* tip over; knock over ⟨*lamp, vase, glass, cup*⟩; capsize ⟨*boat*⟩; turn ⟨*boat*⟩ over; overturn ⟨*vehicle*⟩

um|klappen *tr. V.* fold down

Umkleide·kabine die changing-cubicle

um|knicken *itr. V.; mit sein* [mit dem Fuß] ~: go over on one's ankle; **b)** bend; ⟨*branch*⟩ bend and snap

um|kommen *unr. itr. V.; mit sein* die; *(bei einem Unglück, durch Gewalt)* get killed; die; ⟨*food*⟩ go off

Um·kreis der *o. Pl.* surrounding area; **im ~ von 5 km** within a radius of 5 km.; **um·kreisen** *tr. V.* circle; ⟨*spacecraft, satellite*⟩ orbit; ⟨*planet*⟩ revolve [a]round

Um·lauf der a) *(von Planeten)* revolution; **b)** *o. Pl. (Zirkulation)* circulation; **in od. im ~ sein** be circulating; ⟨*coin, banknote*⟩ be in circulation; **in ~ bringen** circulate; bring ⟨*coin, banknote*⟩ into circulation; **Umlaufbahn die** *(Astron., Raumf.)* orbit

Um·laut der *(Sprachw.)* umlaut

um|legen *tr. V.* **a)** *(um einen Körperteil)* put on; **b)** *(verlegen)* transfer ⟨*patient, telephone call*⟩; **c)** *(salopp: ermorden)* jmdn. ~: bump sb. off *(sl.)*

um|leiten *tr. V.* divert; **Um·leitung die** diversion

umliegend *Adj.* surrounding ⟨*area*⟩; *(nahe)* nearby ⟨*building*⟩

um|räumen 1. *tr. V.* rearrange; **2.** *itr. V.* rearrange things

um|rechnen *tr. V.* convert **(in +** *Akk.* **into)**

¹um|reißen *unr. tr. V.* pull ⟨*mast, tree*⟩ down; knock ⟨*person*⟩ down; ⟨*wind*⟩ tear ⟨*tent etc.*⟩ down

²um·reißen *unr. tr. V.* outline; summarize ⟨*subject, problem, situation*⟩

um|rennen *unr. tr. V.* [run into and] knock down

um·ringen *tr. V.* surround

Um·riß der *(auch fig.)* outline

um|rühren *tr. V. (auch itr.)* stir

um|rüsten *tr. V. (Technik)* convert **(auf +** *Akk.* **to, zu into)**

ums [ʊms] *Präp. + Art.* **a)** = **um das; b)** ~ **Leben kommen** lose one's life

um|satteln *itr. V. (ugs.)* change jobs; ⟨*student*⟩ change courses

Um·satz der turnover; *(Verkauf)* sales *pl.* **(an +** *Dat.* of); ~ **machen** *(ugs.)* make money

um|säumen *tr. V.* hem

um|schalten 1. *tr. V. (auch fig.)* switch [over] **(auf +** *Akk.* to); move ⟨*lever*⟩; **2.** *itr. V.* switch *or* change over **(auf +** *Akk.* to)

Um·schlag der a) cover; **b)** *(Brief~)* envelope; **c)** *(Schutz~)* jacket; *(einer Broschüre, eines Heftes)* cover; **d)** *(Med.: Wickel)* compress; *(warm)* poultice; **um|schlagen 1.** *unr. tr. V.* **a)** turn up ⟨*sleeve, collar, trousers*⟩; turn over ⟨*page*⟩; **b)** *(umladen, verladen)* turn round, trans-ship ⟨*goods*⟩; **2.** *unr. itr. V.; mit sein* change **(in +** *Akk.* into); ⟨*wind*⟩ veer [round]

¹um·schreiben *unr. tr. V.* rewrite; **²um·schreiben** *unr. tr. V.* **a)** *(in Worte fassen)* describe; *(definieren)* define ⟨*meaning, sb.'s task, etc.*⟩; *(paraphrasieren)* paraphrase ⟨*word, expression*⟩; **b)** *(Sprachw.)* construct **(mit** with); **Um·schreibung die** description; *(Definition)* definition; *(Verhüllung)* circumlocution **(**Gen. **for)**

Um·schrift die *(Sprachw.)* transcription

um|schulen 1. *tr. V. (beruflich)* retrain; **2.** *itr. V.* retrain **(auf +** *Akk.* as)

um|schütten *tr. V.* **a)** pour [into another container]; decant ⟨*liquid*⟩; **b)** *(verschütten)* spill

Um·schwung der complete change; *(in der Politik usw.)* U-turn

um|sehen *unr. refl. V.* **a)** look; **sich im Zimmer ~:** look [a]round the room; **b)** *(zurücksehen)* look round *or* back

umseitig *Adj., adv.* overleaf

um|setzen *tr. V.* **a)** move; *(auf anderen Posten usw.)* move, transfer **(in +** *Akk.* to); *(umpflanzen)* transplant; *(in anderen Topf)* repot; **b)** *(verwirklichen)* implement ⟨*plan*⟩; translate ⟨*plan, intention, etc.*⟩ into action *or* reality; realize ⟨*ideas*⟩; **c)** *(Wirtsch.)* turn over, have a turnover of ⟨*x marks etc.*⟩; sell ⟨*shares, goods*⟩

Um·sicht die; *o. Pl.* circumspection;

um·sichtig 1. *Adj.* circumspect; **2.** *adv.* circumspectly

um|siedeln 1. *tr. V.* resettle; **2.** *itr. V.; mit sein* move (**in** + *Akk.,* **nach** to)

um·sonst *Adv.* **a)** *(unentgeltlich)* free; for nothing; **b)** *(vergebens)* in vain

Um·stand der a) *(Gegebenheit)* circumstance; *(Tatsache)* fact; **unter Umständen** possibly; **b)** *(Aufwand)* business; **macht keine |großen| Umstände** please don't go to any bother

umständlich 1. *Adj.* involved, elaborate *(procedure, method, description, explanation, etc.)*; elaborate, laborious *(preparation, check, etc.)*; awkward, difficult *(journey, job)*; *(weitschweifig)* long-winded; *(Umstände machend)* awkward *(person)*; **2.** *adv.* in an involved *or* roundabout way; *(weitschweifig)* at great length

Umstands·kleid *das* maternity dress

umstehend *Adj.* standing round *postpos.*

um|steigen *unr. itr. V.* change (**in** + *Akk.* [on] to)

¹um|stellen 1. *tr. V.* **a)** rearrange, change round *(furniture, books, etc.)*; reorder *(words etc.)*; transpose *(two words)*; **b)** *(anders einstellen)* reset *(lever, switch, points, clock)*; **c)** *(ändern)* change *or* switch over (**auf** + *Akk.* to); **2.** *refl. V.* adjust (**auf** + *Akk.* to);
²um·stellen *tr. V.* surround

um|stimmen *tr. V.* win *(person)* round

um|stoßen *unr. tr. V.* **a)** knock over; **b)** *(rückgängig machen)* change *(plan, decision)*; *(zunichte machen)* upset, wreck *(plan, theory)*

umstritten *Adj.* disputed; controversial *(book, author, policy, etc.)*

Um·sturz der coup; **um|stürzen 1.** *tr. V.* overturn; *(fig.)* topple, overthrow *(political system, government)*; **2.** *itr. V.* overturn; *(wall, building, chimney)* fall down; **umstürzlerisch** *Adj.* subversive

Um·tausch der exchange; **um|tauschen** *tr. V.* exchange *(goods, article)* (**gegen** for); change *(dollars, pounds, etc.)* (**in** + *Akk.* into)

Um·trunk der communal drink

um|tun *unr. refl. V.* *(ugs.)* look [a]round; **sich nach etw.** ~**:** be on the look-out for sth.

um|wandeln *tr. V.* convert *(substance, building, etc.)* (**in** + *Akk.* into); *(ändern)* change; alter

Um·weg der detour

Um·welt die a) environment; **b)** *(Menschen)* people *pl.* around sb.

umwelt-, Umwelt-: ~**bedingt** *Adj.* caused by the *or* one's environment *postpos.*; ~**freundlich 1.** *Adj.* environment-friendly; **2.** *adv.* in an ecologically desirable way; ~**schutz der** environmental protection *no art.*; ~**schützer der** environmentalist; conservationist; ~**verschmutzung die** pollution [of the environment]

um|wenden *regelm. (auch unr.) tr. V.* **a)** turn over *(page, joint, etc.)*; **b)** turn round *(vehicle, horse)*

um|werfen *unr. tr. V.* **a)** knock over; knock *(person)* down *or* over; *(fig. ugs.: aus der Fassung bringen)* bowl *(person)* over; stun *(person)*; **b)** *(fig. ugs.: umstoßen)* knock *(plan)* on the head *(coll.)*; **umwerfend** *(ugs.)* **1.** *Adj.* fantastic *(coll.)*; stunning *(coll.)*; **2.** *adv.* fantastically [well] *(coll.)*; brilliantly

um·wickeln *tr. V.* wrap; bind; *(mit einem Verband)* bandage

Umzäunung *die* ~, ~**en** fence, fencing *(Gen.* round)

um|ziehen 1. *unr. itr. V.; mit sein* move (**an** + *Akk.,* **in** + *Akk.,* **nach** to); **2.** *unr. tr. V.* **jmdn.** ~**:** change sb. *or* get sb. changed; **sich** ~**:** change *or* get changed

um·zingeln *tr. V.* surround; encircle

Um·zug der a) move; *(von Möbeln)* removal; **b)** *(Festzug)* procession

UN [u:ʔɛn] *Pl.* UN *sing.*

unabänderlich 1. *Adj.* unalterable; irrevocable *(decision)*; **2.** *adv.* irrevocably

unabhängig 1. *Adj.* independent (**von** of); *(unbeeinflußt)* unaffected (**von** by); **2.** *adv.* independently (**von** of); ~ **davon, ob .../was .../wo ...** *usw.* irrespective *or* regardless of whether .../what .../where ... *etc.*; **Unabhängigkeit die** independence

unabkömmlich *Adj.* indispensable; **sie ist im Moment** ~**:** she is otherwise engaged

unablässig 1. *Adj.* incessant; **2.** *adv.* incessantly

unabsichtlich 1. *Adj.* unintentional; **2.** *adv.* unintentionally

unabwendbar *Adj.* inevitable

unachtsam 1. *Adj.* **a)** inattentive; **b)** *(nicht sorgfältig)* careless; **2.** *adv.* *(ohne Sorgfalt)* carelessly; **Unachtsamkeit die;** ~ **a)** inattentiveness; **b)** *(mangelnde Sorgfalt)* carelessness

unangebracht *Adj.* inappropriate

unangefochten *Adj.* unchallenged; *(Rechtsw.)* uncontested ⟨*verdict, will, etc.*⟩

unangenehm 1. *Adj.* unpleasant (*Dat.* for); *(peinlich)* embarrassing ⟨*question, situation*⟩; **2.** *adv.* unpleasantly

unannehmbar *Adj.* unacceptable; **Unannehmlichkeit die** trouble

unansehnlich *Adj.* unprepossessing; plain ⟨*girl*⟩

unanständig 1. *Adj.* improper; *(anstößig)* indecent; dirty ⟨*joke*⟩; rude ⟨*word, song*⟩; **2.** *adv.* improperly; **Unanständigkeit die** impropriety; indecency; *(Obszönität)* obscenity

unappetitlich 1. *Adj.* unappetizing; *(fig.)* unsavoury ⟨*joke*⟩; disgusting ⟨*wash-basin, nails, etc.*⟩; **2.** *adv.* unappetizingly

Unart die bad habit; **unartig** *Adj.* naughty

unästhetisch *Adj.* unpleasant ⟨*sight etc.*⟩; ugly ⟨*building etc.*⟩

unauffällig *Adj.* inconspicuous; unobtrusive ⟨*scar, defect, skill, behaviour, surveillance, etc.*⟩; discreet ⟨*signal, elegance*⟩; **2.** *adv.* inconspicuously; unobtrusively

unaufgefordert *Adv.* without being asked

unaufhaltsam 1. *Adj.* inexorable; **2.** *adv.* inexorably

unaufmerksam *Adj.* inattentive (**gegenüber** to); careless ⟨*driver*⟩

unaufrichtig *Adj.* insincere; **Unaufrichtigkeit die** insincerity

unausbleiblich *Adj.* inevitable

unbändig 1. *Adj.* **a)** boisterous; **b)** *(überaus groß/stark)* unbridled; **2.** *adv.* **a)** wildly; **b)** *(sehr, äußerst)* unrestrainedly; tremendously *(coll.)*

unbarmherzig *Adj.* merciless

unbeabsichtigt 1. *Adj.* unintentional; **2.** *adv.* unintentionally

unbeachtet *Adj.* unnoticed

unbedenklich *adv.* without second thoughts

unbedeutend 1. *Adj.* insignificant; minor ⟨*artist, poet*⟩; slight, minor ⟨*improvement, change, error*⟩; **2.** *adv.* slightly

unbedingt 1. *Adj.* absolute; **2.** *adv.* absolutely; **3.** *Adv. (auf jeden Fall)* whatever happens

unbefangen *Adj.* **a)** *(ungehemmt)* uninhibited; **b)** *(unvoreingenommen)* impartial

unbefristet 1. *Adj.* for an indefinite period *postpos.*; indefinite ⟨*strike*⟩; unlimited ⟨*visa*⟩; **2.** *adv.* for an indefinite period

unbefugt 1. *Adj.* unauthorized; **2.** *adv.* without authorization

unbegreiflich *Adj.* incomprehensible (*Dat.*, **für** to); incredible ⟨*love, goodness, stupidity, carelessness, etc.*⟩

unbegrenzt 1. *Adj.* unlimited; **2.** *adv.* ⟨*stay, keep, etc.*⟩ indefinitely

Unbehagen das uneasiness, disquiet; *(Sorge)* concern (**an** + *Dat.* about);

unbehaglich 1. *Adj.* uneasy ⟨*feeling, atmosphere*⟩; uncomfortable ⟨*thought, room*⟩; **2.** *adv.* uneasily

unbeholfen 1. *Adj.* clumsy; **2.** *adv.* clumsily

unbekannt *Adj.* **a)** unknown; *(nicht vertraut)* unfamiliar; unidentified ⟨*caller, donor*⟩; „**Empfänger ~**" 'not known at this address'; **b)** *(nicht vielen bekannt)* little known; obscure ⟨*poet, painter, etc.*⟩; ¹**Unbekannte der/die**; *adj. Dekl.* unknown *or* unidentified man/woman; *(Fremde[r])* stranger; ²**Unbekannte die**; *adj. Dekl. (Math.; auch fig.)* unknown

unbekleidet *Adj.* without any clothes on *postpos.*; bare ⟨*torso etc.*⟩; naked ⟨*corpse*⟩

unbekümmert 1. *Adj.* carefree; *(ohne Bedenken, lässig)* casual; **2.** *adv.* **a)** in a carefree way; **b)** *(ohne Bedenken)* without caring or worrying

unbeleuchtet *Adj.* unlit ⟨*street, corridor, etc.*⟩; ⟨*vehicle*⟩ without [any] lights

unbeliebt *Adj.* unpopular (**bei** with)

unbemannt *Adj.* unmanned

unbemerkt *Adj., adv.* unnoticed

unbenutzt *Adj.* unused

unbequem 1. *Adj.* **a)** uncomfortable; **b)** *(lästig)* awkward, embarrassing ⟨*question, opinion*⟩; troublesome ⟨*politician etc.*⟩; unpleasant ⟨*criticism, truth, etc.*⟩; **2.** *adv.* uncomfortably

unberechenbar 1. *Adj.* unpredictable; **2.** *adv.* unpredictably

unberechtigt 1. *Adj.* **a)** *(ungerechtfertigt)* unjustified; **b)** *(unbefugt)* unauthorized

unberührt *Adj.* untouched; **sie ist noch ~**: she is still a virgin

unbeschrankt *Adj.* ⟨*crossing*⟩ without gates, with no gates

unbeschreiblich 1. *Adj.* indescribable; unimaginable ⟨*fear, beauty*⟩; ⟨*fear, beauty*⟩ beyond description; **2.**

adv. indescribably ⟨*beautiful*⟩; unbelievably ⟨*busy*⟩

unbesorgt *Adj.* unconcerned; **seien Sie ~**: don't [you] worry

unbeständig *Adj.* changeable ⟨*weather*⟩; fickle ⟨*lover etc.*⟩

unbestimmt 1. *Adj.* a) indefinite; indeterminate ⟨*age, number*⟩; *(ungewiß)* uncertain; b) *(ungenau)* vague; c) *(Sprachw.)* indefinite ⟨*article, pronoun*⟩; 2. *adv. (ungenau)* vaguely

unbewacht *Adj.* unsupervised; unattended ⟨*car-park*⟩

unbewaffnet *Adj.* unarmed

unbeweglich *Adj.* motionless; still ⟨*air, water*⟩; fixed ⟨*gaze, expression*⟩

unbewußt *Adj.* unconscious

unbrauchbar *Adj.* unusable; *(untauglich)* useless ⟨*method, person*⟩

und *Konj.* and; *(folglich)* [and] so; **ich ~ tanzen?** what, me dance?; **sei so gut ~ mach das Fenster zu** be so good as to shut the window

Undank der ingratitude; **undankbar** *Adj.* ungrateful ⟨*person, behaviour*⟩

undeutlich 1. *Adj.* unclear; indistinct; *(ungenau)* vague ⟨*idea, memory, etc.*⟩; 2. *adv.* indistinctly; *(ungenau)* vaguely

undicht *Adj.* leaky; leaking; **~e Fenster** windows which do not fit tightly

undurchführbar *Adj.* impracticable

undurchlässig *Adj.* impermeable; *(wasserdicht)* watertight; waterproof; *(luftdicht)* airtight

unehelich *Adj.* illegitimate ⟨*child*⟩; unmarried ⟨*mother*⟩

unehrlich 1. *Adj.* dishonest; 2. *adv.* dishonestly; by dishonest means

uneigennützig *Adj.* unselfish

uneinig *Adj.* ⟨*party*⟩ divided by disagreement; **[sich *(Dat.)*] ~ sein** disagree; **Uneinigkeit** die disagreement (in + *Dat.* on); **uneins** *Adj.*; *nicht attr.* **~ sein** be divided (in + *Dat.* on); ⟨*persons*⟩ be at variance *or* at cross purposes (in + *Dat.* over)

unempfindlich *Adj.* a) insensitive (gegen to); b) *(immun)* immune (gegen to, against); c) *(strapazierfähig)* hardwearing

unendlich 1. *Adj.* infinite; boundless; *(zeitlich)* endless; *(Math.)* infinite; 2. *adv.* infinitely ⟨*lovable, sad*⟩; immeasurably ⟨*happy*⟩; ⟨*happy*⟩ beyond measure

unentbehrlich *Adj.* indispensable (*Dat.*, für to)

unentgeltlich [*od.* '----] 1. *Adj.* free;

2. *adv.* free of charge; ⟨*work*⟩ for nothing, without pay

unentschieden 1. *Adj.* unsettled; undecided ⟨*question*⟩; *(Sport, Schach)* drawn; 2. *adv.* **~ spielen** draw

unentwegt [*od.* --'-] 1. *Adj.* a) *(beharrlich)* persistent ⟨*fighter, champion, efforts*⟩; b) *(unaufhörlich)* constant; incessant; 2. *adv.* a) *(beharrlich)* persistently; b) *(unaufhörlich)* constantly; incessantly

unerbittlich 1. *Adj. (auch fig.)* inexorable; unsparing ⟨*critic*⟩; relentless ⟨*battle, struggle*⟩; implacable ⟨*hate, enemy*⟩; 2. *adv. (auch fig.)* inexorably

unerfahren *Adj.* inexperienced

unerfreulich 1. *Adj.* unpleasant; bad ⟨*news*⟩; 2. *adv.* unpleasantly

unerheblich *Adj.* insignificant

unerhört 1. *Adj. (empörend)* outrageous; 2. *adv.* outrageously

unerlaubt 1. *Adj.* unauthorized; 2. *adv.* without authorization

unermüdlich 1. *Adj.* tireless, untiring (bei, in + *Dat.* in); 2. *adv.* tirelessly

unerreichbar *Adj.* inaccessible; *(fig.)* unattainable; **unerreicht** *Adj.* unequalled

unerschöpflich *Adj.* inexhaustible

unersetzlich *Adj.* irreplaceable

unerträglich [*od.* '----] *Adj.* unbearable; intolerable ⟨*situation, conditions, etc.*⟩

unerwartet 1. *Adj.* unexpected; **es kam für alle ~**: it came as a surprise to everybody; 2. *adv.* unexpectedly

unerwünscht *Adj.* unwanted; unwelcome ⟨*interruption, visit, visitor*⟩; undesirable ⟨*side-effects*⟩

unfähig *Adj.* a) **~ sein, etw. zu tun** *(ständig)* be incapable of doing sth.; *(momentan)* be unable to do sth.; b) *(inkompetent)* incompetent

unfair 1. *Adj.* unfair (gegen to); 2. *adv.* unfairly

Un·fall der accident

Unfall-: **~arzt** der casualty doctor; **~stelle** die scene of an/the accident; **~versicherung** die accident insurance

unförmig *Adj.* shapeless; huge ⟨*legs, hands, body*⟩; bulky, ungainly ⟨*shape, shoes, etc.*⟩

unfrei *Adj.* not free *pred.*; subject, dependent ⟨*people*⟩; ⟨*life*⟩ of bondage;

unfreiwillig *Adj.* involuntary; *(erzwungen)* enforced ⟨*stay*⟩; *(nicht beabsichtigt)* unintended ⟨*publicity, joke, humour*⟩; 2. *adv.* involuntarily; without wanting to; *(unbeabsichtigt)* unintentionally

unfreundlich 1. *Adj.* unfriendly **(zu, gegen)**; unkind ⟨*words, remark*⟩; 2. *adv.* in an unfriendly way

unfrisiert *Adj.* ungroomed ⟨*hair*⟩

unfruchtbar *Adj.* infertile; *(fig.)* unproductive; **Unfruchtbarkeit die** infertility; *(fig.)* unproductiveness

Unfug der; ~|e|s **a)** [piece of] mischief; grober ~: public nuisance; **b)** *(Unsinn)* nonsense

Ungar der; ~n, ~n Hungarian; **ungarisch** *Adj.* Hungarian; **Ungarn (das);** ~s Hungary

ungeachtet *Präp. mit Gen. (geh.)* notwithstanding; despite

ungebildet *Adj.* uneducated

ungebräuchlich *Adj.* uncommon; rare; rarely used ⟨*method, process*⟩

ungedeckt *Adj.* uncovered ⟨*cheque*⟩

Ungeduld die impatience; **ungeduldig** 1. *Adj.* impatient; 2. *adv.* impatiently

ungeeignet *Adj.* unsuitable; *(für eine Aufgabe)* unsuited **(für, zu** to, for)

ungefähr 1. *Adj.* approximate; rough ⟨*idea, outline*⟩; 2. *adv.* approximately; roughly

ungefährlich *Adj.* safe; harmless ⟨*animal, person, illness, etc.*⟩

ungeheizt *Adj.* unheated

ungeheuer 1. *Adj.* enormous; tremendous ⟨*strength, energy, effort, enthusiasm, fear, success, pressure, etc.*⟩; vast, immense ⟨*fortune, knowledge*⟩; *(schrecklich)* terrible *(coll.)*, terrific *(coll.)* ⟨*pain, rage*⟩; 2. *adv.* tremendously; terribly *(coll.)* ⟨*difficult, clever*⟩; **Ungeheuer das;** ~s, ~ *(auch fig.)* monster

ungehindert *Adj.* unimpeded

ungehörig 1. *Adj.* improper; *(frech)* impertinent; 2. *adv.* improperly; *(frech)* impertinently

ungehorsam *Adj.* disobedient **(gegenüber** to); **Ungehorsam der** disobedience **(gegenüber** to)

ungekürzt *Adj.* unabridged ⟨*edition, book*⟩; uncut ⟨*film, speech*⟩

ungelegen 1. *Adj.* **das kommt mir sehr** ~/**nicht** ~ : that is very inconvenient *or* awkward/quite convenient for me; 2. *adv.* inconveniently

ungelernt *Adj.* unskilled

ungemütlich 1. *Adj.* uninviting, cheerless ⟨*room, flat*⟩; uncomfortable, unfriendly ⟨*atmosphere*⟩; 2. *adv.* uncomfortably ⟨*furnished*⟩

ungenau 1. *Adj.* inaccurate; imprecise, inexact ⟨*definition, formulation, etc.*⟩; *(undeutlich)* vague ⟨*memory, idea, impression*⟩; 2. *adv.* inaccurately; ⟨*define*⟩ imprecisely, inexactly; *(remember)* vaguely

ungeniert [ˈʊnʒeniːɐ̯t] 1. *Adj.* free and easy; uninhibited; 2. *adv.* openly; ⟨*yawn*⟩ unconcernedly; ⟨*undress etc.*⟩ without any embarrassment

ungenießbar *Adj. (nicht eßbar)* inedible; *(nicht trinkbar)* undrinkable; *(fig. ugs.)* unbearable

ungenügend 1. *Adj.* inadequate; **die Note ,,** ~ **"/ein Ungenügend** *(Schulw.)* the/an 'unsatisfactory' [mark]; 2. *adv.* inadequately

ungepflegt *Adj.* neglected ⟨*garden, park, car, etc.*⟩; unkempt ⟨*person, appearance, hair*⟩; uncared-for ⟨*hands*⟩

ungerade *Adj.* odd ⟨*number*⟩

ungerecht 1. *Adj.* unjust, unfair **(gegen, zu, gegenüber** to); 2. *adv.* unjustly; unfairly; **Ungerechtigkeit die;** ~, ~en injustice

ungern *Adv.* reluctantly; **etw.** ~ **tun** not like *or* dislike doing sth.

ungeschält *Adj.* unpeeled ⟨*fruit*⟩

ungeschickt 1. *Adj.* clumsy; awkward; 2. *adv.* clumsily; awkwardly

ungesetzlich 1. *Adj.* unlawful; illegal; 2. *adv.* unlawfully; illegally

ungestempelt *Adj.* uncancelled ⟨*stamp*⟩

ungestört *Adj.* undisturbed; uninterrupted ⟨*development*⟩

ungesund *Adj. (auch fig.)* unhealthy

Ungetüm das; ~s, ~e monster

ungewiß *Adj.* uncertain; **über etw.** *(Akk.)* **im ungewissen sein** be uncertain *or* unsure about sth.; **Ungewißheit die** uncertainty

ungewöhnlich 1. *Adj.* **a)** unusual; **b)** *(sehr groß)* exceptional ⟨*strength, beauty, ability, etc.*⟩; outstanding ⟨*achievement, success*⟩; 2. *adv.* **a)** ⟨*behave*⟩ abnormally, strangely; **b)** *(enorm)* exceptionally

ungewohnt 1. *Adj.* unaccustomed; *(nicht vertraut)* unfamiliar ⟨*method, work, surroundings, etc.*⟩; 2. *adv.* unusually

Ungeziefer das; ~s vermin *pl.*

ungezogen 1. *Adj.* naughty; badly behaved; bad ⟨*behaviour*⟩; *(frech)* cheeky; 2. *adv.* naughtily; *(behave)* badly

ungläubig 1. *Adj.* **a)** disbelieving; **b)** *(Rel.)* unbelieving; 2. *adv.* in disbelief; **unglaublich 1.** *Adj.* incredible; **2.** *adv.* *(ugs.:* äußerst*)* incredibly *(coll.)*; **unglaubwürdig** *Adj.* implausible; untrustworthy, unreliable ⟨*witness etc.*⟩

ungleich 1. *Adj.* unequal; odd, unmatching ⟨*socks, gloves, etc.*⟩; *(unähnlich)* dissimilar; **2.** *adv.* **a)** unequally; **b)** *(ungleichmäßig)* unevenly

Unglück das; ~[e]s, ~e **a)** *(Unfall)* accident; *(Flugzeug~, Zug~)* crash; accident; **b)** *o. Pl. (Not)* misfortune; *(Leid)* suffering; **c)** *(Pech)* bad luck; ~ **haben** be unlucky; **das bringt** ~: that's unlucky; **d)** *(Schicksalsschlag)* misfortune; **unglücklich 1.** *Adj.* **a)** unhappy; **b)** *(nicht vom Glück begünstigt)* unfortunate ⟨*person*⟩; *(bedauernswert, arm)* hapless ⟨*person, animal*⟩; **c)** *(ungünstig, ungeschickt)* unfortunate ⟨*moment, combination, meeting, etc.*⟩; unhappy ⟨*end, choice, solution*⟩; **2.** *adv.* **a)** unhappily; **b)** *(ungünstig)* unfortunately; *(ungeschickt)* unhappily, clumsily ⟨*translated, expressed*⟩; **unglücklicherweise** *adv.* unfortunately; **Unglücks·fall** der accident

ungültig *Adj.* invalid; void *(esp. Law)*; spoilt ⟨*vote, ballot-paper*⟩; disallowed ⟨*goal*⟩

ungünstig 1. *Adj.* **a)** unfavourable; unfortunate, bad ⟨*shape, layout*⟩; **b)** *(unpassend)* inconvenient ⟨*time*⟩; *(ungeeignet)* inappropriate, inconvenient ⟨*time, place*⟩; **2.** *adv.* **a)** unfavourably; badly ⟨*designed, laid out*⟩; **b)** *(unpassend)* inconveniently

Unheil das disaster; **unheilbar 1.** *Adj.* incurable; **2.** *adv.* incurably; **unheil·voll** *Adj.* disastrous; *(verhängnisvoll)* fateful

unheimlich 1. *Adj.* **a)** eerie; **b)** *(ugs.) (schrecklich)* terrible *(coll.)* ⟨*hunger, headache, etc.*⟩; terrific *(coll.)* ⟨*fun etc.*⟩; **2.** *adv.* **a)** eerily; **b)** *(ugs.: äußerst)* terribly *(coll.)*; incredibly *(coll.)* ⟨*quick, long*⟩

unhöflich 1. *Adj.* impolite; **2.** *adv.* impolitely; **Unhöflichkeit** die impoliteness

unhygienisch 1. *Adj.* unhygienic; **2.** *adv.* unhygienically

Uniform die; ~, ~en uniform

uninteressant *Adj.* uninteresting; *(nicht von Belang)* of no interest *postpos.*; unimportant

Union [u'njo:n] die; ~, ~en union

Universität die; ~, ~en university

Universum das; ~s universe

Unkenntnis die; *o. Pl.* ignorance

unklar *Adj.* unclear; **sich** *(Dat.)* **über etw.** *(Akk.)* **im** ~**en sein** be unclear or unsure about sth.

Unkosten *Pl.* **a)** [extra] expense *sing.*; expenses; **b)** *(ugs.: Ausgaben)* costs; expenditure *sing.*

Unkraut das weeds *pl.*

unleserlich 1. *Adj.* illegible; **2.** *adv.* illegibly

unmäßig 1. *Adj.* immoderate; excessive; **2.** *adv.* excessively; ⟨*eat, drink*⟩ to excess

Unmensch der brute; **unmenschlich 1.** *Adj.* **a)** inhuman; brutal; appalling ⟨*conditions*⟩; **b)** *(entsetzlich)* appalling; **2.** *adv.* **a)** in an inhuman way; **b)** *(entsetzlich)* appallingly *(coll.)*

unmißverständlich 1. *Adj.* **a)** *(eindeutig)* unambiguous; **b)** *(offen, direkt)* blunt ⟨*answer, refusal*⟩; unequivocal ⟨*language*⟩; **2.** *adv.* **a)** *(eindeutig)* unambiguously; **b)** *(offen, direkt)* bluntly; unequivocally

unmittelbar 1. *Adj.* immediate; direct ⟨*contact, connection, influence, etc.*⟩; **2.** *adv.* immediately; directly

unmöbliert *Adj.* unfurnished

unmodern 1. *Adj.* old-fashioned; *(nicht modisch)* unfashionable; **2.** *adv.* in an old-fashioned way; *(nicht modisch)* unfashionably

unmöglich 1. *Adj.* impossible; *(ugs.: seltsam)* incredible; **2.** *adv. (ugs.)* ⟨*behave*⟩ impossibly; ⟨*dress*⟩ ridiculously; **3.** *Adv. (ugs.)* **ich/es usw. kann** ~ ...: I/it *etc.* can't possibly ...

unmoralisch 1. *Adj.* immoral; **2.** *adv.* immorally

unmündig *Adj.* under-age

unnatürlich 1. *Adj.* unnatural; forced ⟨*laugh*⟩; **2.** *adv.* unnaturally; ⟨*laugh*⟩ in a forced way; ⟨*speak*⟩ affectedly

unnötig 1. *Adj.* unnecessary; **2.** *adv.* unnecessarily

UNO ['u:no] die; ~: UN

unordentlich 1. *Adj.* **a)** untidy; **b)** *(ungeregelt)* disorderly ⟨*life*⟩; **2.** *adv.* untidily; ⟨*tie, treat, etc.*⟩ carelessly; **Unordnung** die disorder; mess

unparteiisch 1. *Adj.* impartial; **2.** *adv.* impartially

unpassend 1. *Adj.* inappropriate; unsuitable ⟨*dress etc.*⟩; **2.** *adv.* inappropriately; unsuitably ⟨*dressed etc.*⟩

unpersönlich 1. *Adj.* impersonal; distant, aloof ⟨*person*⟩; **2.** *adv.* impersonally; ⟨*answer, write*⟩ in impersonal terms

unpraktisch 1. *Adj.* unpractical; **2.** *adv.* in an unpractical way

unpünktlich 1. *Adj.* unpunctual ⟨*person*⟩; late, unpunctual ⟨*payment*⟩; **2.** *adv.* late

Unrecht *das; o. Pl.* wrong; **zu ~:** wrongly; **unrecht haben** be wrong; **jmdm. unrecht tun** do sb. an injustice; **unrechtmäßig 1.** *Adj.* unlawful; **2.** *adv.* unlawfully

unregelmäßig 1. *Adj.* irregular; **2.** *adv.* irregularly

unreif *Adj.* a) unripe; b) *(nicht erwachsen)* immature

Unruhe *die (auch fig.)* unrest; *(Lärm)* noise; *(Unrast)* restlessness; *(Besorgnis)* anxiety; **unruhig 1.** *Adj.* a) restless; *(besorgt)* anxious; unsettled, troubled ⟨*time*⟩; b) *(laut)* noisy; c) *(ungleichmäßig)* uneven ⟨*breathing, pulse, etc.*⟩; fitful ⟨*sleep*⟩; disturbed ⟨*night*⟩; **2.** *adv.* a) restlessly; *(besorgt)* anxiously; b) *(ungleichmäßig)* unevenly; ⟨*sleep*⟩ fitfully

uns 1. a) *Akk. von* **wir** us; b) *Dat. von* **wir; gib es ~:** give it to us; **bei ~:** at our home *or* (coll.) place; **2.** *Reflexivpron. der 1. Pers. Pl.* a) *refl.* ourselves; b) *reziprok* one another

unsachlich 1. *Adj.* unobjective; **2.** *adv.* without objectivity

unsauber 1. *Adj.* a) dirty; b) *(nachlässig)* untidy; sloppy; **2.** *adv. (nachlässig)* untidily

unschädlich *Adj.* harmless

unscharf *Adj.* blurred ⟨*photo, picture*⟩

unscheinbar *Adj.* inconspicuous

Unschuld *die; o. Pl.* innocence; **unschuldig 1.** *Adj.* innocent; **2.** *adv.* innocently

unselbständig *Adj.* dependent [on other people]

¹unser *Possessivpron. der 1. Pers. Pl.* our; **das ist ~s** that is ours; **²unser** *Gen. von* **wir** *(geh.)* of us; **in ~ aller/ beider Interesse** in the interest of all/ both of us; **unser·einer, unser·eins** *Indefinitpron.* (*ugs.*) the likes of us *pl.;* our sort (coll.); **unser·er·seits** *Adv.* for our part; *(von uns)* on our part; **unser[e]s·gleichen** *indekl. Indefinitpron.* people *pl.* like us; **unsert·wegen** *Adv., s.* **meinetwegen:** because of us; for our sake; about us; as far as we are concerned

unsicher 1. *Adj.* uncertain; *(nicht selbstsicher)* insecure; **2.** *adv.* ⟨*walk, stand, etc.*⟩ unsteadily; *(nicht selbstsicher)* ⟨*smile, look*⟩ diffidently

unsichtbar *Adj.* invisible **(für** to)

Unsinn *der* nonsense; **~ machen** mess *or* fool about; **unsinnig** *Adj.* nonsensical ⟨*statement, talk, etc.*⟩; absurd, ridiculous ⟨*demand etc.*⟩

Unsitte *die* bad habit; **unsittlich 1.** *Adj.* indecent; **2.** *adv.* indecently

unsr... *s.* **¹unser**

unsterblich *Adj.* immortal

unsympathisch *Adj.* uncongenial, disagreeable ⟨*person*⟩; unpleasant ⟨*characteristic, nature, voice*⟩

Untat *die* misdeed; evil deed

untauglich *Adj.* unsuitable; *(für Militärdienst)* unfit [for service] *postpos.*

unten *Adv.* a) down; **hier/da ~:** down here/there; **von ~:** from below; b) *(in Gebäuden)* downstairs; **nach ~:** downstairs; c) *(am unteren Ende, zum unteren Ende hin)* at the bottom; **~ [links] auf der Seite/im Schrank** at the bottom [left] of the page/cupboard; d) *(an der Unterseite)* underneath; e) *(im Text)* below; **unten·genannt** *Adj.* undermentioned *(Brit.)*; mentioned below *postpos.*

unter 1. *Präp. mit Dat. (Lage, Standort)* under; *(zwischen)* among[st]; **Mengen ~ 100 Stück** quantities of less than 100; **~ Angst/Tränen** in or out of fear/in tears; **2.** *Präp. mit Akk.* under; *(zwischen)* among[st]; **~ Null sinken** drop below zero; **3.** *Adv.* less than; **~ 30 [Jahre alt] sein** be under 30 [years of age]

unter... *Adj.* lower; bottom; *(ganz unten)* bottom; *(in der Rangfolge o. ä.)* lower

Unter·arm *der* forearm; **unterbelichten¹** *tr. V. (Fot.)* underexpose

unter·bleiben *unr. itr. V.; mit sein* **etw. unterbleibt** sth. does not occur *or* happen; **unter·brechen** *unr. tr. V.* interrupt; break ⟨*journey, silence*⟩; **Unter·brechung** *die s.* **unterbrechen:** interruption; break (*Gen.* in)

unter|bringen *unr. tr. V.* a) put; b) *(beherbergen)* put up; **Unterbringung** *die;* **~, ~en** accommodation *no indef. art.*

unter·der·hand *Adv.* on the quiet

unter·dessen *s.* inzwischen; **unter·drücken** *tr. V.* suppress; hold back ⟨*comment, question, answer, criticism, etc.*⟩; oppress ⟨*minority etc.*⟩; **Unter·drückung** *die;* **~, ~en** a) *(das Unter-*

---

¹ ich unterbelichte, unterbelichtet, unterzubelichten

drücken) suppression; **b)** (das Unter-
drücktwerden, -sein) oppression

unter·ein·ander Adv. **a)** (räumlich)
one below the other; **b)** (miteinander)
among[st] ourselves/themselves etc.

unter·ernährt Adj. undernourished;
Unter·ernährung die malnutrition

Unter·führung die underpass; (für
Fußgänger) subway (Brit.); [ped-
estrian] underpass (Amer.)

unter-, Unter-: ~gang der **a)** (Son-
nen-, Mond- usw.): setting; **b)** (von
Schiffen) sinking; **c)** (das Zugrundege-
hen) decline; ~|gehen unr. itr. V.; mit
sein **a)** (sun, star, etc.) set; (ship) sink,
go down; (person) drown, go under;
b) (zugrunde gehen) come to an end;
~geordnet Adj. secondary (role, importance, etc.); subordinate (position,
post, etc.); ~gewicht das; o. Pl.
underweight; ~grund der o. Pl. (bes.
Politik) underground

Untergrund·bahn die underground
[railway] (Brit.); subway (Amer.)

unter-, Unter-: ~|haken tr. V. (ugs.)
jmdn. ~haken take sb.'s arm; ~halb
1. Adv. below; ~halb von below; **2.**
Präp. mit Gen. below; ~halt der; o.
Pl. **a)** living; **b)** (~haltszahlung)
maintenance; **c)** (Instandhaltung[skosten])
upkeep; ~halten **1.** unr. tr. V. **a)** support; **b)** (instand halten) maintain
(building); **c)** (betreiben) run, keep
(car, hotel); **d)** (pflegen) maintain,
keep up (contact, correspondence); **e)**
entertain (guest, audience); **2.** unr.
refl. V. **a)** talk; converse; **b)** (sich vergnügen) enjoy oneself; ~haltsam
Adj. entertaining; ~haltung die **a)** o.
Pl. (Versorgung) support; **b)** o. Pl. (Instandhaltung) maintenance; **c)** (Gespräch) conversation; **e)** (Zeitvertreib)
entertainment; ~händler der (bes.
Politik) negotiator; ~hemd das vest
(Brit.); undershirt (Amer.); ~hose die
(Herren~) briefs pl.; [under]pants pl.
(Damen~) panties; knickers (Brit.);
~irdisch **1.** Adj. underground; **2.**
adv. underground; ~kiefer der lower
jaw; ~|kommen unr. itr. V.; mit sein
find accommodation

unter·kühlt Adj. ~ sein be suffering
from hypothermia or exposure

Unter-: ~kunft die; ~, ~künfte accommodation no indef. art. or pl.;
lodging no indef. art.; ~kunft und Frühstück
bed and breakfast; ~kunft und Verpflegung board and lodging; ~lage
die **a)** (Schreib~) pad; (für eine

Schreibmaschine usw.) mat; **b)** Pl.
documents; papers

unter-: ~|lassen unr. tr. V. refrain
from [doing]; ~|laufen unr. itr. V.; mit
sein occur; jmdm. ist ein Fehler/Irr-
tum ~: sb. made a mistake; ~|legen
Adj. inferior; jmdm. ~ sein be inferior
to sb. (an + Dat. in)

unter·leib der lower abdomen

unter·liegen unr. itr. V. **a)** mit sein
(besiegt werden) lose; be beaten or defeated; **b)** (unterworfen sein) be subject to

unterm Präp. + Art. = unter dem

unter·mauern tr. V. (mit Argumenten, Fakten absichern) back up

Unter-: ~miete die subtenancy; sub-
lease; ~mieter der subtenant; lodger

untern (ugs.) Präp. + Art. = unter den

unter-, Unter-: ~|nehmen unr. tr. V.
a) (durchführen) undertake; make;
take (steps); **b)** etwas ~nehmen do
something; ~nehmen das; ~mens,
~nehmen **a)** (Vorhaben) enterprise; **b)** (Firma) concern; ~nehmer
der; ~nehmers, ~nehmer employer;
~nehmungs·lustig Adj. active; sie
ist sehr ~nehmungslustig she is always
out doing things

Unter·offizier der **a)** non-commissioned officer; **b)** (Dienstgrad) corporal

unter·ordnen 1. tr. V. subordinate;
2. refl. V. accept a subordinate role

Unterredung die; ~, ~en discussion

Unterricht der; ~[e]s, ~e instruction;
(Schul~) teaching; (Schulstunden)
classes pl.; **unterrichten 1.** tr. V. **a)**
teach; **b)** (informieren) inform (über
+ Akk. of, about); **2.** itr. V. (Unterricht geben) teach; **3.** refl. V. (sich informieren) inform oneself (über +
Akk. about); **Unterrichts·stunde**
die lesson; period

Unter·rock der [half] slip

unter·rühren tr. V. stir in

unters Präp. + Art. = unter das

unter·sagen tr. V. forbid; prohibit

Unter·satz der s. Untersetzer

unter-, Unter-: ~schätzen tr. V.
underestimate (amount, effect, etc.);
underrate (talent, ability, etc.);
~scheiden **1.** unr. tr. V. distinguish;
2. unr. refl. V. differ (durch in, von
from); ~scheidung die (Vorgang)
differentiation; (Resultat) distinction

Unter-: ~schenkel der shank; lower
leg; ~schicht die (Soziol.) lower
class

Unter·schied der; ~[e]s, ~e difference; **unterschiedlich 1.** Adj. different; (uneinheitlich) variable; varying; **2.** adv. [sehr/ganz] ~: in [very/quite] different ways; **unterschieds·los 1.** Adj. uniform; equal ⟨treatment⟩; **2.** adv. ⟨treat⟩ equally; (ohne Benachteiligung) without discrimination

unter·schlagen unr. tr. V. embezzle ⟨money, funds, etc.⟩; (unterdrücken) intercept ⟨letter⟩; withhold ⟨fact, news, information, etc.⟩

Unter·schlupf der; ~[e]s, ~e shelter; (Versteck) hiding-place; hide-out; **unter|schlüpfen** itr. V.; mit sein (ugs.) hide out

unter·schreiben unr. itr., tr. V. sign; **Unter·schrift** die signature; (Bild~) caption

Unter-: ~see·boot das submarine; **~setzer** der mat; (für Gläser) coaster **untersetzt** Adj. stocky

Unter·stand der (Schutzbunker) dugout; (Unterschlupf) shelter **unter|stehen 1.** unr. itr. V. jmdm. ~: be subordinate or answerable to sb.; **2.** unr. refl. V. dare

¹**unter|stellen 1.** tr. V. (zur Aufbewahrung) keep; store ⟨furniture⟩; **2.** refl. V. take shelter

²**unter·stellen** tr. V. a) jmdm. eine Abteilung ~: put sb. in charge of a department; **die Behörde ist dem Ministerium unterstellt** the office is under the ministry; **b)** (unterschieben) jmdm. böse Absichten usw. ~: insinuate that sb.'s intentions etc. are bad; **Unter·stellung** die (falsche Behauptung) insinuation

unter·streichen unr. tr. V. a) underline; b) (hervorheben) emphasize **unter·stützen** tr. V. support; **Unter·stützung** die a) support; b) (finanzielle Hilfe) allowance; (für Arbeitslose) [unemployment] benefit no art.

unter·suchen tr. V. examine; (überprüfen) test (auf + Akk. for); (aufzuklären suchen) investigate; (durchsuchen) search (auf + Akk., nach for); **Untersuchung** die; ~, ~en a) s. untersuchen: examination; test; investigation; search; b) (wissenschaftliche Arbeit) study; **Untersuchungs·haft** die imprisonment or detention while awaiting trial

Unter·tasse die saucer **unter|tauchen 1.** itr. V.; mit sein a)

(im Wasser) dive [under]; b) (verschwinden) disappear; **2.** tr. V. duck **Unter·teil** das od. der bottom part; **unter·teilen** tr. V. divide; (gliedern) subdivide

unter·treiben unr. itr. V. play things down

Unter·wäsche die underwear **unterwegs** Adv. on the way; (nicht zu Hause) out [and about]

unter·weisen unr. tr. V. (geh.) instruct

Unter·welt die; ~: underworld **unter·werfen 1.** unr. tr. V. a) subjugate ⟨people, country⟩; b) (unterziehen) subject (Dat. to); **2.** unr. refl. V. sich [jmdm./einer Sache] ~: submit [to sb./sth.]; **unterwürfig 1.** Adj. obsequious; **2.** adv. obsequiously **unter·zeichnen** tr. V. sign **unter·ziehen 1.** unr. tr. V. etw. einer Untersuchung/Überprüfung (Dat.) ~: examine/check sth.; **2.** unr. refl. V. sich einer Operation (Dat.) ~: undergo or have an operation

untragbar Adj. unbearable **untreu** Adj. disloyal; (in der Ehe, Liebe) unfaithful; **Untreue** die disloyalty; (in der Ehe, Liebe) unfaithfulness **untröstlich** Adj. inconsolable **Untugend** die bad habit

unüberlegt 1. Adj. rash; **2.** adv. rashly

unübersehbar 1. Adj. a) (offenkundig) conspicuous; b) (sehr groß) enormous; **2.** adv. (sehr) extremely **unübersichtlich 1.** Adj. unclear; confusing ⟨arrangement⟩; blind ⟨bend⟩; broken ⟨country etc.⟩; **2.** adv. unclearly; confusingly ⟨arranged⟩ **unübertrefflich 1.** Adj. superb; **2.** adv. superbly; **unübertroffen** Adj. unsurpassed

unumgänglich Adj. [absolutely] necessary

unumwunden 1. Adj. frank; **2.** adv. frankly; openly

ununterbrochen 1. Adj. incessant; **2.** adv. incessantly

unveränderlich Adj. unchangeable **unverantwortlich 1.** Adj. irresponsible; **2.** adv. irresponsibly

unverbesserlich Adj. incorrigible **unverbindlich 1.** Adj. a) not binding pred.; without obligation postpos; b) (reserviert) non-committal ⟨answer, words⟩; impersonal ⟨attitude, person⟩; **2.** adv. ⟨send, reserve⟩ without obligation

unverblümt 1. *Adj.* blunt; 2. *adv.* bluntly

unverbraucht *Adj.* untouched; unspent ⟨energy⟩; fresh ⟨air⟩

unverdaut *Adj.* undigested

unverdorben *Adj.* unspoilt

unverfroren *Adj.* insolent; impudent

unvergänglich *Adj.* immortal ⟨fame⟩; unchanging ⟨beauty⟩; abiding ⟨recollection⟩

unvergeßlich *Adj.* unforgettable

unvergleichlich 1. *Adj.* incomparable; 2. *adv.* incomparably

unverheiratet *Adj.* unmarried

unverhofft 1. *Adj.* unexpected; 2. *adv.* unexpectedly

unverkäuflich *Adj.* diese Vase ist ~: this vase is not for sale; ⟨nicht absetzbar⟩ unsaleable

unvermeidlich *Adj.* unavoidable; ⟨sich als Folge ergebend⟩ inevitable

Unvermögen das lack of ability

unvermutet 1. *Adj.* unexpected; 2. *adv.* unexpectedly

unvernünftig *Adj.* stupid; foolish

unverrichtet *Adj.* ~er Dinge without having achieved anything

unverschämt 1. *Adj.* a) impertinent ⟨person, manner, words, etc.⟩; barefaced ⟨lie⟩; b) ⟨ugs.: sehr groß⟩ outrageous ⟨price, luck, etc.⟩; 2. *adv.* impertinently; ⟨lie⟩ barefacedly; blatantly; **Unverschämtheit** die ~, ~en impertinence

unversehens *Adv.* suddenly

unversehrt *Adj.* unscathed; ⟨unbeschädigt⟩ undamaged

unverständlich *Adj.* incomprehensible; **Unverständnis** das lack of understanding

unverträglich *Adj.* a) quarrelsome; b) incompatible ⟨blood groups, medicines, transplant tissue⟩

unverwechselbar *Adj.* unmistakable; distinctive

unverwüstlich *Adj.* indestructible

unverzeihlich *Adj.* unforgivable

unverzüglich 1. *Adj.* prompt; 2. *adv.* promptly

unvollkommen 1. *Adj.* a) imperfect; b) ⟨unvollständig⟩ incomplete; 2. *adv.* a) imperfectly; b) ⟨unvollständig⟩ incompletely; **Unvollkommenheit** die a) imperfectness; b) ⟨Unvollständigkeit⟩ incompleteness

unvollständig *Adj.* incomplete; **Unvollständigkeit** die incompleteness

unvorhergesehen *Adj.* unforeseen; unexpected ⟨visit⟩

unvorsichtig 1. *Adj.* careless; ⟨unüberlegt⟩ rash; 2. *adv.* carelessly; ⟨unüberlegt⟩ rashly

unvorstellbar 1. *Adj.* inconceivable; 2. *adv.* unimaginably

unvorteilhaft *Adj.* a) unattractive ⟨figure, appearance⟩; b) ⟨ohne Vorteil⟩ unfavourable, poor ⟨purchase, exchange⟩; unprofitable ⟨business⟩

Unwahrheit die a) o. Pl. untruthfulness; b) ⟨Äußerung⟩ untruth; **unwahrscheinlich** 1. *Adj.* a) improbable; unlikely; b) ⟨ugs.: sehr viel⟩ incredible ⟨coll.⟩; 2. *adv.* ⟨ugs.: sehr⟩ incredibly ⟨coll.⟩

unweiblich *Adj.* unfeminine

unweigerlich 1. *Adj.* inevitable; 2. *adv.* inevitably

Unwetter das [thunder]storm

unwichtig *Adj.* unimportant

unwiderruflich 1. *Adj.* irrevocable; 2. *adv.* irrevocably

unwiderstehlich *Adj.* irresistible

Unwille[n] der; o. Pl. displeasure

unwillig 1. *Adj.* indignant; ⟨widerwillig⟩ unwilling; 2. *adv.* indignantly; ⟨widerwillig⟩ unwillingly

unwillkürlich 1. *Adj.* a) spontaneous ⟨cry, sigh⟩; instinctive ⟨reaction, movement, etc.⟩; b) ⟨Physiol.⟩ involuntary ⟨movement etc.⟩; 2. *adv.* a) ⟨shout etc.⟩ spontaneously; ⟨react, move, etc.⟩ instinctively; b) ⟨Physiol.⟩⟨move etc.⟩ involuntarily

unwirklich ⟨geh.⟩ *Adj.* unreal

unwirsch 1. *Adj.* surly; ill-natured; 2. *adv.* ill-naturedly

unwirtschaftlich 1. *Adj.* uneconomic ⟨procedure etc.⟩; ⟨nicht sparsam⟩ uneconomical ⟨driving etc.⟩; 2. *adv.* ⟨work, drive, etc.⟩ uneconomically

Unwissenheit die; ~: ignorance;
unwissentlich 1. *Adj.* unconscious; 2. *adv.* unknowingly; unwittingly

unwohl *Adv.* unwell; mir ist ~: I don't feel well; **Unwohlsein** das; ~s indisposition

unwürdig *Adj.* a) undignified ⟨person, behaviour⟩; degrading ⟨treatment⟩; b) ⟨unangemessen⟩ unworthy

unzählig *Adj.* innumerable; countless

Unze die; ~, ~n ounce

unzeitgemäß *Adj.* anachronistic

unzerbrechlich *Adj.* unbreakable

unzertrennlich *Adj.* inseparable

Unzucht die; ~ treiben fornicate; gewerbsmäßige ~: prostitution; **unzüchtig** 1. *Adj.* obscene ⟨letter, ges-

ture⟩; **2.** *adv.* ⟨*touch, approach, etc.*⟩ indecently; ⟨*speak*⟩ obscenely

unzufrieden *Adj.* dissatisfied; *(stärker)* unhappy; **Unzufriedenheit die** dissatisfaction; *(stärker)* unhappiness

unzugänglich *Adj.* inaccessible ⟨*area, building, etc.*⟩; unapproachable ⟨*character, person, etc.*⟩

unzulänglich *(geh.)* **1.** *Adj.* insufficient; **2.** *adv.* insufficiently

unzumutbar *Adj.* unreasonable

unzurechnungsfähig *Adj.* not responsible for one's actions *pred.*; *(geistesgestört)* of unsound mind *postpos.*

unzustellbar *Adj. (Postw.)* „~“: 'not known [at this address]'

unzutreffend *Adj.* inappropriate; *(falsch)* incorrect

unzuverlässig *Adj.* unreliable; **Unzuverlässigkeit die** unreliability

unzweckmäßig 1. *Adj.* unsuitable; *(unpraktisch)* impractical; **2.** *adv.* unsuitably; *(unpraktisch)* impractically

üppig 1. *Adj.* lush ⟨*vegetation*⟩; thick ⟨*hair, beard*⟩; full ⟨*bosom, lips*⟩; voluptuous ⟨*figure, woman*⟩; *(fig.)* sumptuous, opulent ⟨*meal*⟩; **2.** *adv.* luxuriantly; *(fig.)* sumptuously

Ur·abstimmung die [*esp.* strike] ballot

Ural der; ~[s] Urals *pl.*; Ural Mountains *pl.*

ur·alt *Adj.* very old; ancient

Uran das; ~s uranium

urbar *Adj.* **ein Stück Land ~ machen** cultivate a piece of land

Ur·einwohner der native inhabitant; **Ur·enkel der** great-grandson; **Ur·groß·eltern** *Pl.* great-grandparents

Ur·heber der; ~s, ~ originator; initiator; *(bes. Rechtsspr.: Verfasser, Autor)* author

urig *Adj.* natural ⟨*person*⟩; real ⟨*beer*⟩; cosy ⟨*pub*⟩

Urin der; ~s, ~e *(Med.)* urine; **urinieren** *itr. V.* urinate

Ur·kunde die; ~, ~n document; *(Bescheinigung, Sieger~, Diplom~ usw.)* certificate

Urlaub der; ~[e]s, ~e holiday[s] *(Brit.)*; vacation; *(bes. Milit.)* leave

Urlaubs-: ~**reise die** holiday [trip]; ~**zeit die** holiday period *or* season

Urne die; ~, ~n urn; *(Wahl~)* [ballot-]box

Ur·sache die cause

Ur·sprung der origin; **ur·sprünglich 1.** *Adj.* **a)** original ⟨*plan, price, form, material, etc.*⟩; **b)** *(natürlich)*

natural; **2.** *adv.* **a)** originally; **b)** *(natürlich)* naturally

Urteil das; ~s, ~e judgement; *(Strafe)* sentence; *(Gerichts~)* verdict; **urteilen** *itr. V.* form an opinion; judge; **über etw./jmdn. ~:** judge sth./sb.; **Urteils·vermögen das;** *o. Pl.* competence to judge

Ur·wald der primeval forest; *(tropisch)* jungle

USA [uː|ɛs|'aː] *Pl.* USA

usw. *Abk.* und so weiter etc.

Utensil das; ~s, ~ien [... jən] piece of equipment; ~ien equipment *sing.*

Utopie die; ~, ~n utopian dream; **utopisch** *Adj.* utopian

UV *Abk.* Ultraviolett UV

V

v, V [vau] *das;* ~, ~: v, V

v. *Abk.* von

vage 1. *Adj.* vague; **2.** *adv.* vaguely

vakuum·verpackt *Adj.* vacuum-packed

Vanille [va'nɪljə] *die;* ~: vanilla; **Vanille·zucker der** vanilla sugar

variabel 1. *Adj.* variable; **2.** *adv.* variably

variieren *tr., itr. V.* vary

Vase ['vaːzə] *die;* ~, ~n vase

Vater der; ~s, Väter father; **Gott ~:** God the Father; **Vater·land das;** *Pl.* ~länder fatherland; **väterlich 1.** *Adj.* **a)** paternal ⟨*line, love, instincts, etc.*⟩; **b)** *(fürsorglich)* fatherly; **2.** *adv.* in a fatherly way; **väterlicherseits** *Adv.* on the/his/her *etc.* father's side; **Vaterschaft die;** ~, ~en fatherhood; **Vaterunser das;** ~s, ~: Lord's Prayer; **Vati der;** ~s, ~s *(fam.)* dad[dy] *(coll.)*

Vatikan [vati'kaːn] *der;* ~s Vatican

v. Chr. *Abk.* vor Christus BC

Vegetarier [vege'taːrɪɐ] *der;* ~s, ~: vegetarian; **vegetarisch 1.** *Adj.* vegetarian; **2.** *adv.* **er ißt** *od.* **lebt ~:** he is a vegetarian; **Vegetation die;** ~, ~en vegetation *no indef. art.;* **vegetieren** *itr. V.* vegetate

Veilchen das; ~s, ~: violet
Vene ['ve:nə] die; ~, ~n vein
Venedig [ve'ne:dɪç] (das); ~s Venice
Venezolaner [venetso'la:nɐ] der; ~s, ~: Venezuelan; **venezolanisch** Adj. Venezuelan; **Venezuela** (das); ~s Venezuela
Ventil [vɛn'ti:l] das; ~s, ~e valve; **Ventilator** [vɛnti'la:tor] der; ~s, ~en ventilator
Venus ['ve:nʊs] die; ~: Venus no def. art.

verabreden 1. tr. V. arrange; 2. refl. V. sich im Park/zum Tennis/für den folgenden Abend ~: arrange to meet in the park/for tennis/next evening; **Verabredung** die; ~, ~en a) arrangement; b) (verabredete Zusammenkunft) appointment; **eine ~ absagen** call off a meeting
verabscheuen tr. V. detest; loathe
verabschieden 1. tr. V. a) say goodbye to; b) (aus dem Dienst) retire ⟨general, civil servant, etc.⟩; 2. refl. V. sich [von jmdm.] ~: say goodbye [to sb.]; **Verabschiedung** die; ~, ~en a) leave-taking; b) (aus dem Dienst) retirement
verachten tr. V. despise; **verächtlich** 1. Adj. a) contemptuous; b) (verachtenswürdig) contemptible; 2. adv. contemptuously; **Verachtung** die; ~: contempt
verallgemeinern tr., itr. V. generalize; **Verallgemeinerung** die; ~, ~en generalization
veralten itr. V.; mit sein become obsolete
Veranda [ve'randa] die; ~, Veranden veranda; porch
veränderlich Adj. changeable; **verändern** tr., refl. V. change; **Veränderung** die change (Gen. in)
verängstigen tr. V. frighten; scare
verankern tr. V. fix ⟨tent, mast, pole, etc.⟩; (mit einem Anker) anchor
veranlagen tr.V. (Steuerw.) assess (mit at); **veranlagt** Adj. künstlerisch/praktisch ~ sein have an artistic bent/be practically minded; **Veranlagung** die; ~, ~en [pre]disposition
veranlassen tr. V. cause; induce; ~, daß ... see to it that ... **Veranlassung** die; ~, ~en reason
veranschaulichen tr. V. illustrate
veranschlagen tr. V. estimate (mit at)
veranstalten tr. V. organize; hold,

give ⟨party⟩; hold ⟨auction⟩; do ⟨survey⟩; **Veranstalter** der; ~s, ~ organizer; **Veranstaltung** die; ~, ~en a) (das Veranstalten) organizing; organization; b) (etw., was veranstaltet wird) event
verantworten 1. tr. V. etw. ~: take responsibility for sth.; 2. refl. V. sich für etw. ~: answer for sth.; sich vor jmdm. ~: answer to sb.; **verantwortlich** Adj. responsible; **Verantwortung** die; ~, ~en responsibility (für for)
verantwortungs-: **~bewußt** Adj. responsible; **~los** Adj. irresponsible; **~voll** Adj. responsible
verarbeiten tr. V. use; etw. zu etw. ~: make sth. into sth.; (geistig bewältigen) assimilate ⟨film, experience, impressions⟩
verärgern tr. V. annoy
verarzten tr. V. (ugs.) patch up (coll.) ⟨person⟩; fix (coll.) ⟨wound etc.⟩
veräußern tr. V. dispose of ⟨property⟩
Verb [vɛrp] das; ~s, ~en verb
Verband der a) (Binde) bandage; dressing; b) (von Vereinen, Clubs o.ä.) association
Verband[s]-: **~kasten** der first-aid-box; **~material** das dressing materials pl.
Verband·zeug das first-aid things pl.
Verbannung die; ~, ~en banishment
verbergen unr. tr. V. hide; conceal
verbessern 1. tr. V. a) improve; reform ⟨schooling, world⟩; b) (korrigieren) correct; 2. refl. V. a) improve; b) [beruflich] aufsteigen) better oneself; **Verbesserung** die a) improvement; b) (Korrektur) correction
verbeugen refl. V. bow (vor + Dat. to); **Verbeugung** die; ~, ~en bow
verbieten unr. tr. V. a) forbid; jmdm. etw.~: forbid sb. sth.; „Betreten des Rasens/Rauchen verboten" 'keep off the grass'/'no smoking'; b) (für unzulässig erklären) ban
verbinden 1. unr. tr. V. a) (bandagieren) bandage; dress; b) (zubinden) bind; jmdm. die Augen ~: blindfold sb.; c) (zusammenfügen) join; d) (in Beziehung bringen) connect (durch by); link ⟨towns, lakes, etc.⟩ (durch by); e) (verknüpfen) combine ⟨abilities, qualities, etc.⟩; f) auch itr. (telefonisch) jmdn. [mit jmdm.] ~: put sb. through [to sb.]; 2. unr. refl. V. a) (auch Chemie) combine (mit with); b) (sich zusammentun) join [together]; join

forces; **verbindlich 1.** *Adj.* **a)** friendly; **b)** *(bindend)* obligatory; compulsory; binding ⟨*agreement, decision, etc.*⟩; **2.** *adv.* **a)** *(freundlich)* in a friendly manner; **b)** ~ **zusagen** definitely agree; **jmdm. etw. ~ zusagen** make sb. a firm offer of sth.; **Verbindung die a)** *(das Verknüpfen)* linking; **b)** *(Zusammenhalt)* join; connection; **c)** *(verknüpfende Strecke)* link; **d)** *(durch Telefon, Funk, Verkehrs~)* connection (**nach** to); **e)** *(Kombination)* combination; **in ~ mit etw.** in conjunction with sth.; **f)** *(Kontakt)* contact; **sich mit jmdm. in ~ setzen** get in touch *or* contact with sb.; **g)** *(Zusammenhang)* connection

verbissen 1. *Adj.* dogged; doggedly determined; **2.** *adv.* doggedly

verbitten *unr. refl. V.* **sich** *(Dat.)* **etw. ~:** refuse to tolerate sth.

verbittern *tr. V.* embitter

verblassen *itr. V.; mit sein (auch fig. geh.)* fade

Verbleib der; ~**[e]s** *(geh.)* whereabouts *pl.*; **verbleiben** *unr. itr. V.; mit sein* remain; **wie seid ihr verblieben?** what did you arrange?

Verblendung die; ~, ~**en** blindness

verblüffen *tr. (auch itr.) V.* amaze; **verblüffend 1.** *Adj.* amazing; **2.** *adv.* amazingly

verblühen *itr. V.; mit sein (auch fig.)* fade

verbluten *itr. (auch refl.) V.; mit sein* bleed to death

verbohrt *Adj.* pigheaded

verborgen *Adj. (abgelegen)* secluded; *(nicht sichtbar)* hidden

Verbot das; ~**[e]s,** ~**e** ban ⟨*Gen.*, **von** on⟩; **Verbots·schild das;** *Pl.* ~**schilder** sign *(prohibiting sth.)*; *(Verkehrsw.)* prohibitive sign

Verbrauch der; ~**[e]s** consumption; (**von, an** + *Dat.* of); **verbrauchen** *tr. V.* use; consume ⟨*food, drink*⟩; spend ⟨*provisions*⟩; spend ⟨*money*⟩; consume, use ⟨*fuel*⟩; *(fig.)* use up ⟨*strength, energy*⟩; **Verbraucher der;** ~**s,** ~: consumer

Verbrechen das; ~**s,** ~: crime (**an** + *Dat.*, **gegen** against); **Verbrecher der;** ~**s,** ~: criminal; **verbrecherisch** *Adj.* criminal

verbreiten 1. *tr. V.* spread; radiate ⟨*optimism, calm, etc.*⟩; **2.** *refl. V.* spread; **Verbreitung die;** ~, ~**en a)** *s.* **verbreiten 1:** spreading; radiation; **b)** *(Ausbreitung)* spread

verbrennen 1. *unr. itr. V.; mit sein* burn; **2.** *tr. V.* burn; cremate ⟨*dead person*⟩; **sich** *(Dat.)* **den Mund ~** *(fig.)* say too much; **Verbrennung die;** ~, ~**en a)** *s.* **verbrennen 2:** burning; cremation; **b)** *(Wunde)* burn

verbringen *unr. tr. V.* spend

verbummeln *tr. V. (ugs.)* **a)** waste ⟨*time*⟩; **b)** *(vergessen)* forget [all] about; clean forget; *(verlieren)* lose

verbünden *refl. V.* form an alliance; **Verbündete der/die;** *adj. Dekl.* ally

verbüßen *tr. V.* serve ⟨*sentence*⟩

Verdacht der; ~**[e]s,** ~**e** *od.* **Verdächte** suspicion; **verdächtig 1.** *Adj.* suspicious; **2.** *adv.* suspiciously; **Verdächtige der/die;** *adj. Dekl.* suspect; **verdächtigen** *tr. V.* suspect

verdammen *tr. V.* condemn; *(Rel.)* damn ⟨*sinner*⟩

verdampfen 1. *itr. V.; mit sein* evaporate; **2.** *tr. V.* evaporate

verdanken *tr. V.* **jmdm./einer Sache etw. ~:** owe sth. to sb./sth.

verdarb *1. u. 3. Pers. Sg. Prät. v.* **verderben**

verdattert *(ugs.) Adj.* flabbergasted; *(verwirrt)* dazed; stunned

verdauen 1. *tr. V. (auch fig.)* digest; **2.** *itr. V.* digest ⟨one's food⟩; **verdaulich** *Adj.* digestible; **Verdauung die;** ~: digestion

Verdeck das; ~**[e]s,** ~**e** top; hood *(Brit.)*; *(bei Kinderwagen)* hood; **verdecken** *tr. V.* hide; cover

verderben 1. *unr. itr. V.; mit sein* go bad *or* off, spoil; **2.** *unr. tr. V.* spoil; *(stärker)* ruin; spoil ⟨*appetite, enjoyment, fun, etc.*⟩; **3.** *unr. refl. V.* **sich** *(Dat.)* **den Magen/die Augen ~:** give oneself an upset stomach/ruin one's eyesight; **Verderben das;** ~**s** ruin; **verderblich** *Adj.* perishable ⟨*food*⟩; pernicious ⟨*influence, effect, etc.*⟩

verdeutlichen *tr. V.* **etw. ~:** make sth. clear; *(erklären)* explain sth.

verdichten *refl. V.* ⟨*fog, smoke*⟩ thicken, become thicker; *(fig.)* ⟨*suspicion, rumour*⟩ grow; ⟨*feeling*⟩ intensify

verdienen 1. *tr. V.* **a)** earn; **b)** *(wert sein)* deserve; **2.** *itr. V.* **beide Eheleute ~:** husband and wife are both earning; **Verdiener der;** ~**s,** ~: wage-earner; **¹Verdienst der** income; earnings *pl.*; **²Verdienst das;** ~**[e]s,** ~**e** merit

verdienst·voll 1. *Adj.* commendable; ⟨*person*⟩ of outstanding merit; **2.** *adv.* commendably; **verdient** *Adj.*

⟨person⟩ of outstanding merit; **sich um etw. ~ machen** render outstanding services to sth.

verdoppeln 1. *tr. V.* double; *(fig.)* double, redouble ⟨efforts etc.⟩; 2. *refl. V.* double

verdorben 2. *Part. v.* verderben

verdorren *itr. V.; mit sein* wither [and die]; ⟨meadow⟩ scorch

verdrängen *tr. V.* **a)** drive out ⟨inhabitants⟩; *(fig.: ersetzen)* displace; **b)** *(Psych.)* repress; *(bewußt)* suppress

verdrehen *tr. V.* **a)** twist ⟨joint⟩; roll ⟨eyes⟩; **b)** *(ugs. abwertend: entstellen)* twist ⟨words, facts, etc.⟩

verdrießen *unr. tr. V. (geh.)* irritate; annoy; **verdrießlich** 1. *Adj.* morose; 2. *adv.* morosely; **verdroß** *1. u. 3. Pers. Sg. Prät. v. verdrießen;* **verdrossen** 1. *Adj. (mißmutig)* morose; *(mißmutig und lustlos)* sullen; 2. *adv. (mißmutig)* morosely; *(mißmutig und lustlos)* sullenly; **Verdruß der;** **Verdrusses, Verdrusse** annoyance

verdunkeln *tr. V.* darken; *(vollständig)* black out ⟨room, house, etc.⟩

Verdunk[e]lung die; ~, ~**en** darkening; *(vollständig)* black-out

verdünnen *tr. V.* dilute

verdunsten *itr. V.; mit sein* evaporate; **Verdunstung die;** ~: evaporation

verdursten *itr. V.; mit sein* die of thirst

verdutzt *Adj.* taken aback *pred.;* nonplussed; *(verwirrt)* baffled

verehren *tr. V.* **a)** venerate; **b)** *(geh.: bewundern)* admire; *(ehrerbietig lieben)* worship; **Verehrer der;** ~**s,** ~, **Verehrerin die;** ~, ~**en** admirer; **Verehrung die;** *o. Pl.* **a)** veneration; **b)** *(Bewunderung)* admiration

vereidigen *tr. V.* swear in; **Vereidigung die;** ~, ~**en** swearing in

Verein der; ~**s,** ~**e** organization; *(der Kunstfreunde usw.)* association; society; *(Sport~)* club; **vereinbar** *Adj.; nicht attr.* compatible; **vereinbaren** *tr. V.* agree; arrange ⟨meeting etc.⟩; **Vereinbarung die;** ~, ~**en a)** agreeing; *(eines Termins usw.)* arranging; **b)** *(Abmachung)* agreement

vereinfachen *tr. V.* simplify

vereinheitlichen *tr. V.* standardize

vereinigen *tr., refl. V.* unite; *(in der Wirtschaft)* merge; **vereinigt** *Adj.* united; **Vereinigung die a)** organization; **b)** *(das Vereinigen)* uniting; *(von Unternehmen)* merging

vereinzelt 1. *Adj.; nicht präd.* occasional; 2. *adv. (zeitlich)* occasionally; *(örtlich)* here and there

vereisen *itr. V.; mit sein* freeze or ice over; ⟨wing⟩ ice up; ⟨lock⟩ freeze up

vereiteln *tr. V.* thwart

vereitern *itr. V.; mit sein* go septic

verenden *itr. V.; mit sein* perish; die

verengen *refl. V.* narrow; ⟨pupils⟩ contract

vererben *tr. V.* leave, bequeath ⟨property⟩ *(Dat.,* **an** + *Akk.* to)

Vererbung die; ~, ~**en** heredity *no art.*

verfahren 1. *unr. refl. V.* lose one's way; 2. *unr. itr. V.; mit sein* proceed; **Verfahren das;** ~**s,** ~ **a)** procedure; *(Technik)* process; *(Methode)* method; **b)** *(Rechtsw.)* proceedings *pl.*

Verfall der; *o. Pl.* **a)** decay; *(fig.: der Preise, einer Währung)* collapse; **b)** *(Auflösung)* decline; **verfallen** *unr. itr. V.; mit sein* **a)** *(baufällig werden)* fall into disrepair; **b)** *(körperlich)* ⟨strength⟩ decline; **c)** *(untergehen)* ⟨empire⟩ decline; *(morals, morale)* deteriorate; **d)** *(ungültig werden)* expire

verfassen *tr. V.* write; draw up ⟨resolution⟩; **Verfasser der;** ~**s,** ~, **Verfasserin die;** ~, ~**nen** writer; *(eines Buchs, Artikels usw.)* author; writer; **Verfassung die a)** *(Politik)* constitution; **b)** *o. Pl. (Zustand)* state [of health/mind]; **in guter/schlechter ~ sein** be in good/poor shape

verfaulen *itr. V.; mit sein* rot

verfehlen *tr. V.* miss; **Verfehlung die;** ~, ~**en** misdemeanour; *(Rel.: Sünde)* transgression

verfeinden *refl. V.* **sich ~ mit** make an enemy of

verfeinern *tr. V.* improve; refine ⟨method, procedure⟩

verfertigen *tr. V.* produce

verfilmen *tr. V.* film; make a film of; **Verfilmung die;** ~, ~**en a)** *(das Verfilmen)* filming; **b)** *(Film)* film [version]

verflixt *(ugs.)* 1. *Adj.* **a)** *(ärgerlich)* awkward, unpleasant ⟨situation, business, etc.⟩; **b)** *(verdammt)* blasted *(Brit.);* blessed; confounded; **~ [noch mal]!** [damn and] blast! *(Brit. coll.);* **c)** *nicht präd. (sehr groß)* er **hat ~es Glück gehabt** he was damned lucky *(coll.);* 2. *adv. (sehr)* damned *(coll.)*

verflossen *Adj. (ugs.)* former

verfluchen *tr. V.* curse; **verflucht** 1.

Adj. (salopp) damned *(coll.);* bloody *(Brit. sl.);* ~ |**noch mal**|! damn [it]! *(coll.);* **2.** *adv. (sehr)* damned *(coll.)*

verfolgen *tr. V.* pursue; hunt, track ⟨*animal*⟩; *etw.* |**strafrechtlich**| ~: prosecute sth.; **Verfolgung die;** ~, ~**en** pursuit; *(eines Ziels, Plans usw.)* pursuance

verfressen *Adj. (salopp)* greedy

verfügen 1. *tr. V. (anordnen)* order; *(dekretieren)* decree; **2.** *itr. V.* über etw. *(Akk.)* |**frei**| ~ können be free to decide what to do with sth.; über etw. *(Akk.)* ~ *(etw. haben)* have sth. at one's disposal; **Verfügung die;** ~, ~**en a)** *(Anordnung)* order; *(Dekret)* decree; **b)** *o. Pl. (Disposition)* etw. zur ~ haben have sth. at one's disposal; jmdm. etw. zur ~ **stellen** put sth. at sb.'s disposal

verführen *tr. V.* **a)** *(verleiten)* tempt; **b)** *(sexuell)* seduce; **Verführer der** seducer; **verführerisch 1.** *Adj.* **a)** *(verlockend)* tempting; **b)** *(aufreizend)* seductive; **2.** *adv.* **a)** *(verlockend)* temptingly; **b)** *(aufreizend)* seductively; **Verführung die a)** temptation; **b)** *(sexuell)* seduction

vergangen 1. *Adj.* **a)** *(vorüber, vorbei)* bygone, former ⟨*times, years, etc.*⟩; **b)** *(letzt...)* last ⟨*year, week, etc.*⟩; **Vergangenheit die;** ~ **a)** past; **b)** *(Grammatik: Präteritum)* past tense; **vergänglich** *Adj.* transient; transitory; ephemeral; **Vergänglichkeit die;** ~: transience

Vergaser der; ~**s,** ~: carburettor

vergaß *1. u. 3. Pers. Sg. Prät. v.* vergessen

vergeben *unr. tr. V.* **a)** *auch itr. (geh.: verzeihen)* forgive; jmdm. etw. ~: forgive sb. [for] sth.; **b)** throw away ⟨*chance, goal, etc.*⟩; **c)** *(geben)* place ⟨*order*⟩ (an + *Akk.* with); award ⟨*grant, prize*⟩ (an + *Akk.* to); **vergebens 1.** *Adv.* in vain; vainly; **2.** *adj.* es war ~: it was *of* or to no avail; **vergeblich 1.** *Adj.* futile; vain, futile ⟨*attempt, efforts*⟩; **2.** *adv.* in vain; **Vergebung die;** ~, ~**en** *(geh.)* forgiveness

vergehen *unr. itr. V.; mit sein (time)* pass [by], go by; *(pain)* wear off, pass; *(pleasure)* fade; **Vergehen das;** ~**s,** ~: crime; *(Rechtsspr.)* offence

vergelten *unr. tr. V.* repay

vergessen 1. *unr. tr. (auch itr.) V.* forget; **Vergessenheit die;** ~: oblivion; **vergeßlich** *Adj.* forgetful

vergeuden *tr. V.* waste; **Vergeudung die;** ~, ~**en** waste

vergewaltigen *tr. V.* rape; **Vergewaltigung die;** ~, ~**en** rape

vergewissern *refl. V.* make sure *(Gen.* of)

vergießen *unr. tr. V.* spill; **Tränen** ~: shed tears

vergiften *tr. V. (auch fig.)* poison; **Vergiftung die;** ~, ~**en** poisoning

vergiß *Imper. Sg. v.* vergessen; **Vergiß∙mein∙nicht das;** ~|e|s, ~|e| forget-me-not; **vergißt** *2. u. 3. Pers. Sg. Präs. v.* vergessen

Vergleich der; ~|e|s, ~**e** a) comparison; **b)** *(Rechtsw.)* settlement; **vergleichbar** *Adj.* comparable; **vergleichen** *tr. V.* compare; **Vergleichs∙form die** *(Sprachw.)* comparative/superlative form

vergnügen *refl. V.* enjoy oneself; have a good time; **Vergnügen das;** ~**s,** ~: pleasure; *(Spaß)* fun; **viel** ~! *(auch iron.)* have fun!; **vergnügt 1.** *Adj.* cheerful; **2.** *adv.* cheerfully; **Vergnügungs∙viertel das** pleasure district

vergolden *tr. V.* gold-plate ⟨*jewellery etc.*⟩; *(mit Blattgold)* gild

vergraben *unr. tr. V.* bury

vergrämt *Adj.* care-worn

vergreifen *unr. refl. V.* sich an jmdm. ~: assault sb.; **vergriffen** *Adj.* out of print *pred.*

vergrößern 1. *tr. V.* **a)** *(erweitern)* extend ⟨*room, area, building, etc.*⟩; **b)** *(vermehren)* increase; **c)** *(größer reproduzieren)* enlarge ⟨*photograph etc.*⟩; **2.** *refl. V.* **a)** *(größer werden)* ⟨*firm, business, etc.*⟩ expand; **b)** *(zunehmen)* increase; **3.** *itr. V.* ⟨*lens etc.*⟩ magnify; **Vergrößerung die;** ~, ~**en a)** *s.* vergrößern 1, 2: extension; increase; enlargement; expansion; **b)** *(Foto)* enlargement; **Vergrößerungs∙glas das** magnifying glass

Vergünstigung die; ~, ~**en** privilege

vergüten *tr. V.* **a)** *(erstatten)* jmdm. etw. ~: reimburse sb. for sth.; **b)** *(bes. Papierdt.: bezahlen)* remunerate, pay for ⟨*work, services*⟩; **Vergütung die;** ~, ~**en a)** *(Rückerstattung)* reimbursement; **b)** *(Geldsumme)* remuneration

verhaften *tr. V.* arrest; **Sie sind verhaftet** you are under arrest; **Verhaftung die;** ~, ~**en** arrest

verhalten *unr. refl. V.* **a)** behave; *(reagieren)* react; **b)** *(beschaffen sein)* be; **Verhalten das;** ~**s** behaviour

Verhaltens·weise die behaviour; **Verhältnis** das; ~ses, ~se a) ein ~ von drei zu eins a ratio of three to one; b) *(persönliche Beziehung)* relationship **(zu** with); **mit jdm. ein ~ haben** *(ugs.)* have an affair with sb.; c) *Pl. (Umstände)* conditions; **verhältnis·mäßig** *Adv.* relatively; comparatively; **Verhältnis·wort** das; *Pl. ~wörter (Sprachw.)* preposition

verhandeln 1. *itr. V.* a) negotiate (über + *Akk.* about); b) *(strafrechtlich)* try a case; *(zivilrechtlich)* hear a case; **2.** *tr. V.* a) etw. ~: negotiate over sth.; b) *(strafrechtlich)* try *(case)*; *(zivilrechtlich)* hear *(case)*; **Verhandlung** die a) ~en negotiations; b) *(strafrechtlich)* hearing; *(zivilrechtlich)* hearing; **die ~ gegen X** the trial of X

verhängen tr. V. impose *(fine, punishment)* (über + *Akk.* on); declare *(state of emergency, state of siege)*; *(Sport)* award, give *(penalty etc.)*; **Verhängnis** das; ~ses, ~se undoing; **verhängnis·voll** *Adj.* disastrous

verharmlosen tr. V. play down

verharren itr. V. *(geh.)* remain

verhärten 1. tr. V. harden; make *(person)* hard; **2.** refl. V. *(tissue)* become hardened

verhaßt *Adj.* hated; detested

verhätscheln tr. V. *(ugs.)* pamper

verhauen *(ugs.)* unr. tr. V. beat up; *(als Strafe)* beat

verheben unr. refl. V. do oneself an injury [while lifting sth.]

verheeren tr. V. devastate; lay waste [to]; **verheerend** *Adj.* a) devastating; b) *(ugs.: scheußlich)* ghastly *(coll.)*

verhehlen tr. V. *(geh.)* conceal (*Dat.* from)

verheilen itr. V.; mit sein *(wound)* heal [up]

verheimlichen tr. V. [jdm.] etw. ~: keep sth. secret [from sb.]

verheiraten refl. V. get married; sich mit jdm. ~: marry sb.; get married to sb.; **Verheiratete** der/die; *adj. Dekl.* married person; married man/ woman; **Verheiratung** die; ~, ~en marriage

verhelfen unr. itr. V. jdm./einer Sache zu etw. ~: help sb./sth. to get/ achieve sth.

verherrlichen tr. V. glorify

verheult *Adj.* *(ugs.)* *(eyes)* red from crying; *(face)* puffy or swollen from crying

verhexen tr. V. *(auch fig.)* bewitch

verhindern tr. V. prevent; **Verhinderung** die; ~, ~en prevention

verhöhnen tr. V. mock

Verhör das; ~[e]s, ~e interrogation; questioning; *(bei Gericht)* examination; **verhören 1.** tr. V. interrogate; question; *(bei Gericht)* examine; **2.** refl. V. mishear

verhüllen tr. V. cover; *(fig.)* disguise

verhungern itr. V.; mit sein die of starvation; starve [to death]

verhüten tr. V. prevent; **Verhütung** die; ~, ~en prevention; *(Empfängnis~)* contraception; **Verhütungsmittel** das contraceptive

verirren refl. V. a) get lost; lose one's way; *(animal)* stray; b) *(irgendwohin gelangen)* stray **(in, an** + *Akk.* into)

verjagen tr. V. chase away

verkalken itr. V.; mit sein a) *(tissue)* calcify; *(arteries)* become hardened; b) *(ugs.: senil werden)* become senile

Verkauf der sale; **verkaufen** tr. V. *(auch fig.)* sell (*Dat.,* an + *Akk.* to); **"zu ~"** 'for sale'; **Verkäufer** der, **Verkäuferin** die a) seller; vendor *(formal)*; b) *(Berufsbez.)* sales or shop assistant; *(im Außendienst)* salesman/ saleswoman; **verkäuflich** *Adj.* (zum Verkauf geeignet) saleable; *(zum Verkauf bestimmt)* for sale postpos.; **verkaufs·offen** *Adj.* der ~e Samstag Saturday on which the shops are open all day; **Verkaufs·preis** der retail price

Verkehr der; ~s a) traffic; b) *(Kontakt)* contact; communication; c) *(Geschlechts~)* intercourse; **verkehren** itr. V. a) auch mit sein *(fahren)* run; *(aircraft)* fly; b) *(in Kontakt stehen)* **mit jdm. ~:** associate with sb.; c) *(zu Gast sein)* **bei jdm. ~:** visit sb. regularly

Verkehrs-: ~ampel die traffic lights *pl.*; **~aufkommen** das volume of traffic; **~hindernis** das obstruction to traffic; **~knotenpunkt** der [traffic] junction; **~kontrolle** die traffic check; **~meldung** die traffic announcement; **~mittel** das means of transport; **die öffentlichen ~mittel** public transport *sing.*; **~schild** das; *Pl. ~schilder* traffic sign; road sign; **~teilnehmer** der road-user; **~unfall** der road accident; **~zeichen** das traffic sign; road sign

verkehrt 1. *Adj.* wrong; **2.** *adv.* wrongly; **alles ~ machen** do everything wrong

verkennen *unr. tr. V.* fail to recognize; misjudge *(situation)*

verklagen *tr. V.* sue; take to court; **eine Firma auf Schadenersatz ~:** sue a company for damages

verkleben 1. *itr. V.; mit sein* stick together; 2. *tr. V. (zukleben)* seal up *(hole)*; *(festkleben)* stick [down] *(floorcovering etc.)*

verkleiden *tr. V.* disguise; *(kostümieren)* dress up; **sich ~:** disguise oneself/dress [oneself] up; **Verkleidung die** a) *o. Pl.* disguising; *(das Kostümieren)* dressing up; b) *(Kleidung)* disguise; *(bei einer Party)* fancy dress

verkleinern 1. *tr. V.* a) make smaller; b) *(verringern)* reduce *(size, number, etc.)*; c) *(kleiner reproduzieren)* reduce *(photograph etc.)*; 2. *refl. V.* become smaller; *(number)* decrease; **Verkleinerungs·form die** *(Sprachw.)* diminutive form

verknoten *tr. V.* tie; knot

verknüpfen *tr. V.* a) *(knoten)* tie; knot; b) *(in Beziehung setzen)* link

verkochen *tr. V.; mit sein* boil away

verkohlen *itr. V.* char

¹**verkommen** *unr. itr. V.; mit sein* go to the dogs; *(moralisch, sittlich)* go to the bad; ²**verkommen** *Adj.* depraved

verkösten *tr. V.* feed; provide with meals

verkraften *tr. V.* cope with

verkrampfen *refl. V. (muscle)* become cramped; *(person)* tense up; **Verkrampfung die; ~, ~en** tenseness; tension

verkriechen *unr. refl. V. (animal)* creep [away]; *(person)* hide [oneself away]

verkrümmt *Adj.* bent *(person)*; crooked *(finger)*; curved *(spine)*; **Verkrümmung die** crookedness

verkrüppeln *tr. V.* cripple

verkümmern *itr. V.; mit sein (person, animal)* go into a decline; *(plant etc.)* become stunted; *(talent, emotional life, etc.)* wither away

verkünden *tr. V.* announce; pronounce *(judgement)*; promulgate *(law, decree)*; **verkündigen** *tr. V. (geh.)* announce; proclaim; **Verkündigung die** announcement; proclamation

verkürzen *tr. V.* a) *(verringern)* reduce; *(abkürzen)* shorten; b) *(abbrechen)* cut short *(stay, life)*; put an end to, end *(suffering)*

verladen *unr. tr. V.* load

Verlag der; ~|e|s, ~e publishing house or firm; publisher's

verlagern *tr. V.* shift; *(an einen anderen Ort)* move; *(fig.)* transfer; shift *(emphasis)*

verlangen *tr. V.* demand; *(nötig haben) (task etc.)* require, call for *(patience, knowledge, experience, skill, etc.)*; *(berechnen)* charge; *(sehen/sprechen wollen)* ask for; **du wirst am Telefon verlangt** you're wanted on the phone *(coll.)*; **Verlangen das; ~s, ~** a) desire *(nach* for); b) **auf ~:** on request

verlängern *tr. V.* extend; lengthen, make longer *(skirt, sleeve, etc.)*; renew *(passport, driving-licence, etc.)*; **Verlängerung die; ~, ~en** *s.* **verlängern:** extension; lengthening; renewal

verlangsamen *tr. V.* **das Tempo/seine Schritte ~:** reduce speed/slacken one's pace; slow down

¹**verlassen** 1. *unr. refl. V.* rely, depend *(auf + Akk.* on); 2. *unr. tr. V.* leave; ²**verlassen** *Adj.* deserted *(street etc.)*; empty *(house)*; *(öd)* desolate *(region etc.)*

verläßlich 1. *Adj.* reliable; 2. *adv.* reliably

Verlauf der; ~|e|s, Verläufe course; **verlaufen** 1. *unr. itr. V.; mit sein* a) *(sich erstrecken)* run; b) *(ablaufen) (test, rehearsal, etc.)* go; *(party etc.)* go off; 2. *unr. refl. V.* get lost; lose one's way; **Verlaufs·form die** *(Sprachw.)* progressive *or* continuous form

verlautbaren *tr. V.* announce [officially]; **verlauten** *itr. V.; mit sein* be reported; **wie verlautet** according to reports

verleben *tr. V.* spend; **verlebt** *Adj.* dissipated

¹**verlegen** *tr. V.* a) mislay; b) *(verschieben)* postpone *(auf + Akk.* until); *(vor~)* bring forward *(auf + Akk.* to); **einen Termin ~:** alter an appointment; c) *(verlagern)* move; transfer *(patient)*; d) *(legen)* lay *(cable, pipe, carpet, etc.)*; ²**verlegen** 1. *Adj.* embarrassed; 2. *adv.* in embarrassment; **Verlegenheit die; ~, ~en** a) *o. Pl. (Befangenheit)* embarrassment; **jmdn. in ~ bringen** embarrass sb.; b) *(Unannehmlichkeit)* embarrassing situation

Verleger der; ~s, ~, Verlegerin die; ~, ~nen publisher

Verleih der; ~|e|s, ~e a) *o. Pl.* hiring out; *(von Autos)* renting *or* hiring out;

b) *(Unternehmen)* hire firm; *(Film~)* distribution company; *(Video~)* video library; *(Auto~)* rental or hire firm; **verleihen** *unr. tr. V.* **a)** hire out; rent or hire out *⟨car⟩; (umsonst)* lend [out]; **b)** *(überreichen)* award; confer *⟨award, honour⟩*

Verleihung die; ~, ~en a) *s.* **verleihen a:** hiring out; renting out; lending [out]; **b)** *s.* **verleihen b:** awarding; conferring; *(Zeremonie)* award; conferment

verleiten *tr. V.* jmdn. dazu ~, etw. zu tun lead or induce sb. to do sth.

verlernen *tr. V.* forget

verlesen 1. *unr. tr. V.* read out; **2.** *unr. refl. V. (falsch lesen)* make a mistake/ mistakes in reading

verletzen *tr. V.* **a)** injure; *(durch Schuß, Stich)* wound; **b)** *(kränken)* hurt *⟨person, feelings⟩;* **c)** *(verstoßen gegen)* violate; infringe *⟨regulation⟩;* break *⟨agreement, law⟩;* **verletzlich** *Adj.* vulnerable; **Verletzte der/die;** *adj. Dekl.* casualty; *(durch Schuß, Stich)* wounded person; **Verletzung die; ~, ~en a)** *(Wunde)* injury; **b)** *(Kränkung)* hurting; **c)** *s.* **verletzen c:** violation; infringement; breaking

verleugnen *tr. V.* deny; disown *⟨friend, relation⟩*

verleumden *tr. V.* slander; *(schriftlich)* libel; **Verleumdung die; ~, ~en** slander; *(in Schriftform)* libel

verlieben *refl. V.* fall in love (**in** + *Akk.* with); **Verliebte der/die;** *adj. Dekl.* lover

verlieren *unr. tr., itr. V.* lose; **Verlierer der; ~s, ~:** loser

verloben *refl. V.* get engaged; **verlobt sein** be engaged; **Verlobte der/die;** *adj. Dekl.* fiancé/fiancée

verlockend *Adj.* tempting; **Verlockung die** temptation

verlogen *Adj.* lying, mendacious *⟨person⟩;* false *⟨morality etc.⟩*

verlor *1. u. 3. Pers. Sg. Prät. v.* **verlieren;** **verloren** *2. Part. v.* **verlieren;** **verloren|gehen** *unr. itr. V.; mit sein* get lost

verlosen *tr. V.* raffle; **Verlosung die; ~, ~en** raffle; draw

verlottern *itr. V.; mit sein (person)* go to seed

Verlust der; ~[e]s, ~e loss (**an** + *Dat.* of)

vermachen *tr. V.* jmdm. etw. ~: leave or bequeath sth. to sb.; *(fig.: schenken, überlassen)* give sth. to sb.

vermählen *refl. V.* *(geh.)* sich [jmdm. od. mit jmdm.] ~ : marry or wed [sb.]; **Vermählung die; ~, ~en** *(geh.)* **a)** marriage; **b)** *(Fest)* wedding ceremony

vermehren 1. *tr. V.* increase (**um** by); **2.** *refl. V.* **a)** increase; **b)** *(sich fortpflanzen)* reproduce; **Vermehrung die; ~, ~en a)** increase *(Gen.* in); **b)** *(Fortpflanzung)* reproduction

vermeiden *unr. tr. V.* avoid

vermeintlich *Adj.* supposed

vermengen *tr. V.* mix (**miteinander** together)

Vermerk der; ~[e]s, ~e note; *(amtlich)* remark; **vermerken** *tr. V.* make a note of; note [down]; *(in Akten, Wachbuch usw.)* record

¹**vermessen** *unr. tr. V.* measure; survey *⟨land, site⟩;* ²**vermessen** *Adj.* *(geh.)* presumptuous

vermieten *tr. V.* *(auch itr.)* V. rent [out], let [out] (**an** + *Akk.* to); hire [out] *⟨boat, car, etc.⟩;* „Zimmer zu ~" 'room to let'; **Vermieter der** landlord; **Vermieterin die** landlady

vermindern 1. *tr. V.* reduce; decrease; reduce, lessen *⟨danger, stress⟩;* lower *⟨resistance⟩;* reduce *⟨debt⟩;* **2.** *refl. V.* decrease; *⟨resistance⟩* diminish

vermischen 1. *tr. V.* mix (**miteinander** together); blend *⟨teas, tobaccos, etc.⟩;* **2.** *refl. V.* mix; *(fig.)* mingle *⟨races, animals⟩* interbreed; **Vermischung die** *s.* **vermischen:** mixing; blending; *(fig.)* mingling

vermissen *tr. V.* **a)** miss; **b)** *(nicht haben)* ich vermisse meinen Ausweis my identity card is missing; **Vermißte der/die;** *adj. Dekl.* missing person

vermitteln 1. *tr. V.* mediate, act as [a] mediator (**in** + *Dat.* in); **2.** *tr. V.* **a)** *(herbeiführen)* arrange; negotiate *⟨transaction, cease-fire, compromise⟩;* **b)** *(besorgen)* jmdm. eine Stelle ~: find sb. a job; **c)** *(weitergeben)* impart *⟨knowledge, insight, values, etc.⟩;* communicate, *⟨message, information, etc.⟩;* convey *⟨feeling⟩;* pass on *⟨experience⟩;* **Vermittler der; ~s, ~ a)** *(Mittler)* mediator; **b)** *s.* **vermitteln 2 c:** imparter; communicator; conveyer; **c)** *(von Berufs wegen)* agent; **Vermittlung die; ~, ~en a)** *(Schlichtung)* mediation; **b)** *s.* **vermitteln 2 a:** arrangement; negotiation; **c)** *s.* **vermitteln 2 c:** imparting; communicating; conveying; **d)** *(Telefonzentrale)* exchange; *(in einer Firma)* switchboard

vermögen *(geh.) unr. tr. V.* etw. zu tun ~: be able to do sth.; be capable of doing sth.; **Vermögen** *das;* ~s, ~ a) *o. Pl. (geh.: Fähigkeit)* ability; b) *(Besitz)* fortune; **er hat** ~: he has money; **vermögend** *Adj.* wealthy; well-off; **Vermögen[s]·steuer die** wealth tax

vermummen *tr. V.* wrap up [warmly]; *(verbergen)* disguise

vermuten *tr. V.* suspect; **das ist zu** ~: that is what one would suppose *or* expect; we may assume that; **vermutlich** 1. *Adj.* probable; 2. *Adv.* presumably; *(wahrscheinlich)* probably; **Vermutung die;** ~, ~en supposition

vernachlässigen *tr. V.* neglect; *(unberücksichtigt lassen)* ignore; disregard; **Vernachlässigung die;** ~, ~en neglect

vernarben *itr. V.; mit sein* [form a] scar; heal *(lit. or fig.)*

vernehmbar *Adj. (geh.)* audible; **vernehmen** *unr. tr. V.* a) *(geh.: hören, erfahren)* hear; b) *(verhören)* question; **vernehmlich** 1. *Adj.* [clearly] audible; 2. *adv.* audibly; **Vernehmung die;** ~, ~en questioning

verneigen *refl. V. (geh.)* bow *(vor + Dat.* to, *(literary)* before)

verneinen *tr. V. (auch itr.) V.* a) say 'no' to *(question)*; answer *(question)* in the negative; b) *(Sprachw.)* negate; **Verneinung die;** ~, ~en *(Sprachw.)* negation

vernichten *tr. V.* destroy; exterminate *(pests, vermin)*; **Vernichtung die;** ~, ~en destruction; *(von Schädlingen)* extermination

Vernunft die; ~: reason; **vernünftig** 1. *Adj.* a) sensible; b) *(ugs.: ordentlich, richtig)* decent; 2. *adv.* a) sensibly; b) *(ugs.: ordentlich, richtig)* *(talk, eat)* properly; *(dress)* sensibly

veröffentlichen *tr. V.* publish; **Veröffentlichung die;** ~, ~en publication

verordnen *tr. V.* [jmdm. etw.] ~: prescribe [sth. for sb.]; **Verordnung die** prescribing

verpachten *tr. V.* lease

verpacken *tr. V.* pack; wrap up *(present, parcel)*; **Verpackung die** a) *o.Pl.* packing; b) *(Umhüllung)* packaging *no pl.*; wrapping

verpassen *tr. V.* miss

verpflanzen *tr. V. (auch Med.)* transplant; graft *(skin)*

verpflegen *tr. V.* cater for; feed; **Verpflegung die;** ~, ~en a) *o.Pl.* catering *no indef. art.* *(Gen.* for); b) *(Nahrung)* food; **Unterkunft und** ~: board and lodging

verpflichten 1. *tr. V.* a) oblige; commit; *(festlegen, binden)* bind; b) *(einstellen, engagieren)* engage *(manager, actor, etc.)*; 2. *refl. V.* undertake; promise; **sich vertraglich** ~: sign a contract; **Verpflichtung die;** ~, ~en a) obligation; commitment; b) *(Engagement)* engaging; engagement

verprügeln *tr. V.* beat up; *(zur Strafe)* thrash

Verputz der plaster; *(auf Außenwänden)* rendering; **verputzen** *tr. V.* plaster; render *(outside wall)*

verquollen *Adj.* swollen

Verrat der; ~[e]s betrayal *(an + Dat.* of); **verraten** *unr. tr. V.* a) betray *(an + Akk.* to); b) *(ugs.: mitteilen)* jmdm. den Grund *usw.* ~: tell sb. the reason *etc.*; c) *(erkennen lassen)* show, betray *(feelings, surprise, fear, etc.)*; show *(influence, talent)*; **Verräter der;** ~s, ~: traitor; **Verräterin die;** ~, ~en traitress; **verräterisch** *Adj.* treacherous *(plan, purpose, act, etc.)*

verrechnen 1. *tr. V.* include *(amount etc.)*; *(gutschreiben)* credit *(cheque etc.)* to another account; 2. *refl. V.* miscalculate; **Verrechnungs·scheck der** crossed cheque

verregnen *itr. V.; mit sein* be spoilt *or* ruined by rain

verreiben *unr. tr. V.* rub in

verreisen *itr. V.; mit sein* go away

verrenken *tr. V.* dislocate; **Verrenkung die;** ~, ~en dislocation

verrichten *tr. V.* perform

verriegeln *tr. V.* bolt

verringern 1. *tr. V.* reduce; 2. *refl. V.* decrease; **Verringerung die;** ~: reduction; decrease *(Gen.,* von in)

verrosten *itr. V.; mit sein* rust; **verrostet** rusty

verrückt *(ugs.)* 1. *Adj.* a) mad; ~ werden go mad *or* insane; b) *(überspannt, ausgefallen)* crazy *(idea, fashion, prank, day, etc.)*; 2. *adv.* crazily; *(behave)* crazily *or* like a madman; *(dress etc.)* in a mad *or* crazy way; **Verrückte der/die;** *adj. Dekl. (ugs.)* madman/madwoman; lunatic

verrühren *tr. V.* stir together; mix

verrutschen *itr. V.* slip

Vers der; ~es, ~e verse

versagen *itr. V.* fail; *(machine, en-*

gine) stop [working]; **menschliches Versagen** human error; **Versager der; ~s, ~:** failure

versalzen *unr. tr. V.* put too much salt in/on; *(fig. ugs.)* spoil

versammeln *tr., refl. V.* assemble; **Versammlung die a)** meeting; **b)** *(Gremium)* assembly

versäumen *tr. V.* **a)** *(verpassen)* miss; lose ⟨*time, sleep*⟩; **b)** *(vernachlässigen, unterlassen)* neglect ⟨*duty, task*⟩

verschaffen *tr. V.* **jmdm. etw. ~:** provide sb. with sth.; get sb. sth.; **sich** *(Dat.)* **etw. ~:** get hold of sth.; obtain sth.

verschämt [fɛɐ̯ˈʃɛːmt] **1.** *Adj.* bashful; **2.** *adv.* bashfully

verschenken *tr. V.* give away

verscheuchen *tr. V.* chase away

verschicken *tr. V. s.* **versenden**

verschieben **1.** *unr. tr. V.* **a)** shift; move; **b)** *(aufschieben)* put off, postpone ⟨*auf* + *Akk.* till⟩; **2.** *unr. refl. V.* be postponed ⟨*um* for⟩; ⟨*start*⟩ be put back *or* delayed ⟨*um* by⟩; **Verschiebung die** postponement

verschieden **1.** *Adj.* **a)** different ⟨*von* from⟩; **b)** *(vielfältig)* various; **die ~sten...:** all sorts of ...; **die ~en...:** the various ...; **c) ~es** various things *pl.*; **2.** *adv.* differently; **verschieden·artig 1.** *Adj.* different in kind *pred.*; *(mehr als zwei)* diverse; **2.** *adv.* diversely; **Verschiedenheit die; ~, ~en** difference; *(unter mehreren)* diversity; **verschiedentlich** *Adv.* on various occasions

verschimmeln *itr. V.; mit sein* go mouldy; **verschimmelt** mouldy

¹**verschlafen** **1.** *unr. itr. (auch refl.)V.* oversleep; **2.** *unr. tr. V.* **a)** *(schlafend verbringen)* sleep through ⟨*morning, journey, etc.*⟩; **b)** *(versäumen)* not wake up in time for ⟨*appointment*⟩; not wake up in time to catch ⟨*train, bus*⟩; **c)** *(ugs.: vergessen)* forget about ⟨*appointment etc.*⟩; ²**verschlafen** *Adj.* half-asleep; *(fig.)* sleepy ⟨*town*⟩

Verschlag der shed

¹**verschlagen** *unr. tr. V.* **die Seite ~:** lose one's place *or* page; **jmdm. die Sprache ~:** leave sb. speechless; ²**verschlagen 1.** *Adj.* sly; shifty; **2.** *adv.* slyly; shiftily

verschlechtern 1. *tr. V.* make worse; **2.** *refl. V.* get worse; deteriorate; **Verschlechterung die; ~, ~en** worsening, deterioration *(Gen.* in)

Verschleiß der; ~es, ~e wear *no*

indef. art.; **b)** *(Verbrauch)* consumption ⟨*an* + *Dat.* of⟩; **verschleißen 1.** *unr. itr. V.; mit sein* wear out; **2.** *unr. tr. V.* wear out; *(fig.)* run down, ruin ⟨*one's nerves, one's health*⟩; use up ⟨*energy, ability, etc.*⟩

verschleppen *tr. V.* **a)** carry off; take away ⟨*person*⟩; **b)** *(weiterverbreiten)* carry, spread ⟨*disease, bacteria, mud, etc.*⟩; **c)** *(verzögern)* delay; *(in die Länge ziehen)* draw out; let ⟨*illness*⟩ drag on [and get worse]

verschleudern *tr. V.* **a)** sell dirt cheap; *(mit Verlust)* sell at a loss; **b)** *(verschwenden)* squander

verschließbar *Adj.* closable; lockable ⟨*suitcase, drawer, etc.*⟩; |**luftdicht**| **~:** sealable ⟨*container etc.*⟩; **verschließen** *unr. tr. V.* **a)** close; stop, *(mit einem Korken)* cork ⟨*bottle*⟩; **b)** *(abschließen)* lock; lock up ⟨*house etc.*⟩; **c)** *(wegschließen)* lock away ⟨*in* + *Dat. od. Akk.* in⟩

verschlimmern 1. *tr. V.* make worse; **2.** *refl. V.* get worse; ⟨*position, conditions*⟩ deteriorate, worsen

verschlingen *unr. tr. V.* **a)** [inter]twine ⟨*threads etc.*⟩ ⟨*zu* into⟩; **b)** *(essen, fressen)* devour ⟨*food*⟩; *(fig.)* devour ⟨*novel, money, etc.*⟩

verschlissen 2. *Part. v.* **verschleißen 2**

verschlossen *Adj. (wortkarg)* taciturn; *(zurückhaltend)* reserved

verschlucken 1. *tr. V.* swallow; **2.** *refl. V.* choke

Verschluß der *(am BH, an Schmuck usw.)* fastener; fastening; *(an Taschen, Schmuck)* clasp; *(an Schuhen, Gürteln)* buckle; *(am Schrank, Fenster, Koffer usw.)* catch; *(an Flaschen)* top; *(Stöpsel)* stopper

verschmähen *tr. V. (geh.)* spurn

verschmerzen *tr. V.* get over

verschmieren *tr. V.* smear ⟨*window etc.*⟩; *(beim Schreiben)* mess up ⟨*paper*⟩; scrawl all over ⟨*page*⟩; smudge ⟨*ink*⟩

verschmitzt 1. *Adj.* mischievous; **2.** *adv.* mischievously

verschmutzen 1. *itr. V.; mit sein* get dirty; ⟨*river etc.*⟩ become polluted; **2.** *tr. V.* dirty; soil; pollute ⟨*air, water, etc.*⟩; **Verschmutzung die; ~, ~en** *(der Umwelt)* pollution; *(von Stoffen, Teppichen usw.)* soiling

verschnaufen *itr. (auch refl.) V.* have *or* take a breather

verschneit *Adj.* snow-covered *attrib.*; covered with snow *postpos.*

verschnörkelt *Adj.* ornate
verschnüren *tr. V.* tie up
verschollen *Adj.* missing
verschonen *tr. V.* spare; **jmdn. mit etw. ~:** spare sb. sth.
verschränken *tr. V.* fold ⟨arms⟩; cross ⟨legs⟩; clasp ⟨hands⟩
verschreiben 1. *unr. tr. V. (Med.: verordnen)* prescribe; 2. *unr. refl. V.* **a)** make a slip of the pen; **b) sich einer Sache** *(Dat.)* **~:** devote oneself to sth.; **verschreibungs·pflichtig** *Adj.* available only on prescription *postpos.*
verschrie[e]n *Adj.* notorious **(wegen** for)
verschulden 1. *tr. V.* be to blame for ⟨accident, death, etc.⟩; 2. *refl. V.* get into debt; **Verschulden das; ~s** guilt; **durch eigenes ~:** through one's own fault; **verschuldet** *Adj.* in debt *postpos.* **(bei** to); **hoch ~:** deeply in debt
verschütten *tr. V.* **a)** spill; **b)** *(begraben)* bury ⟨person⟩ [alive]
verschwägert *Adj.* related by marriage *postpos.*
verschweigen *unr. tr. V.* conceal (*Dat.* from)
verschwenden *tr. V.* waste **(an +** *Akk.* on); **Verschwender der; ~s, ~** *(von Geld)* spendthrift; *(von Dingen)* wasteful person; **verschwenderisch** 1. *Adj.* wasteful ⟨person⟩; ⟨life⟩ of extravagance; 2. *adv.* wastefully; **Verschwendung die; ~, ~en** wastefulness; extravagance
verschwiegen *Adj.* discreet; *(still, einsam)* secluded; **Verschwiegenheit die; ~:** secrecy; *(Diskretion)* discretion
verschwimmen *unr. itr. V.; mit sein* blur
verschwinden *unr. itr. V.; mit sein* disappear; vanish; **verschwinde [hier]** off with you!; go away!; hop it! *(sl.)*; **ich muß mal ~** *(ugs. verhüll.)* I have to pay a visit *(coll.)* or *(Brit. coll.)* spend a penny
verschwommen 1. *Adj.* blurred ⟨photograph, vision⟩; blurred, hazy ⟨outline⟩; vague, woolly ⟨idea, concept, formulation, etc.⟩; 2. *adv.* vaguely; ⟨remember⟩ hazily
versehen 1. *unr. tr. V.* **a)** *(ausstatten)* provide; equip ⟨car, factory, machine, etc.⟩; **b)** *(ausüben, besorgen)* perform ⟨duty etc.⟩; 2. *unr. refl. V.* make a slip; slip up; **Versehen das; ~s, ~:** over-

sight; slip; **aus ~:** by mistake; inadvertently; **versehentlich** 1. *Adv.* by mistake; inadvertently; 2. *adj.; nicht präd.* inadvertent
Versehrte der/die; *adj. Dekl.* disabled person; **die ~n** the disabled
versenden *unr. (auch regelm.) tr. V.* send ⟨letter, parcel⟩; send out ⟨invitations⟩; dispatch ⟨goods⟩
versetzen 1. *tr. V.* **a)** move; transfer, move ⟨employee⟩; *(in die nächsthöhere Klasse)* move ⟨pupil⟩ up, *(Amer.)* promote ⟨pupil⟩ **(in +** *Akk.* to); *(umpflanzen)* transplant, move ⟨plant⟩; *(fig.)* transport **(in +** *Akk.* to); **b)** *(nicht geradlinig anordnen)* stagger; **c)** *(verpfänden)* pawn; **d)** *(verkaufen)* sell; **e)** *(ugs.: vergeblich warten lassen)* stand ⟨person⟩ up *(coll.)*; **f)** *(vermischen)* mix; **g)** *(erwidern)* retort; **h)** etw. **in Bewegung/Tätigkeit ~:** set sth. in motion/operation; **jmdn. in die Lage ~,** etw. zu tun put sb. in a position to do sth.; **jmdm.** einen Stoß/Fußtritt/Schlag *usw.* **~:** give sb. a push/kick/deal sb. a blow *etc.*; 2. *refl. V.* **sich in jmds. Lage** *(Akk.)* **~:** put oneself in sb.'s position or place; **Versetzung die; ~, ~en** ⟨eines Schülers⟩ moving up, *(Amer.)* promotion **(in +** *Akk.* to); ⟨eines Angestellten⟩ transfer
verseuchen *tr. V. (auch fig.)* contaminate; **radioaktiv ~:** contaminate with radioactivity
versichern *tr. V.* **a)** assert ⟨sth.⟩; **b)** *(vertraglich schützen)* insure **(bei** with); **Versicherte der/die;** *adj. Dekl.* insured [person]; **Versicherung die; ~** *(Beteuerung)* assurance; **b)** *(Schutz durch Vertrag)* insurance; *(Vertrag)* insurance [policy] **(über +** *Akk.* for); *(Gesellschaft)* insurance [company]
Versicherungs-: ~beitrag der insurance premium; **~gesellschaft die** insurance company; **~police die** insurance policy
versickern *itr. V.; mit sein* ⟨river etc.⟩ drain or seep away
versiegeln *tr. V.* seal
versiegen *tr. V.; mit sein (geh.)* dry up; run dry
versinken *unr. itr. V.; mit sein* sink; **im Schlamm ~:** sink into the mud
versöhnen 1. *refl. V.* **sich [miteinander] ~:** become reconciled; **sich mit jmdm. ~:** make it up with sb.; 2. *tr. V.* reconcile; **Versöhnung die; ~, ~en** reconciliation

versonnen 1. *Adj.* dreamy; **2.** *adv.* dreamily

versorgen *tr. V.* **a)** supply; **b)** *(unterhalten, ernähren)* provide for *(children, family)*; **c)** *(sorgen für)* look after; **jmdn. ärztlich ~:** give sb. medical care; *(kurzzeitig)* give sb. medical attention; **Versorger der;** ~s, ~, **Versorgerin die;** ~, ~nen breadwinner; **Versorgung die;** ~, ~en a) *o. Pl.* supply[ing]; **b)** *(Unterhaltung, Ernährung)* support[ing]; **c)** *(Bedienung, Pflege)* care; **ärztliche ~:** medical care *or* treatment; *(kurzzeitig)* medical attention

Verspannung die *(Med.: der Muskulatur)* tension

verspäten *refl. V.* be late; **verspätet** *Adj.* late ⟨*arrival etc.*⟩; belated ⟨*greetings, thanks*⟩; **~ eintreffen** arrive late; **Verspätung die;** ~, ~en lateness; *(verspätetes Eintreffen)* late arrival; **[fünf Minuten] ~ haben** be [five minutes] late

versperren *tr. V.* block; obstruct ⟨*view*⟩

verspielen *tr. V.* gamble away; *(fig.)* squander, throw away ⟨*opportunity, chance*⟩; forfeit ⟨*right, credibility, etc*⟩; **verspielt 1.** *Adj. (auch fig.)* playful; fanciful, fantastic ⟨*form, design, etc.*⟩; **2.** *adv.* playfully *(lit. or fig.)*; ⟨*dress, designed*⟩ fancifully, fantastically

verspotten *tr. V.* mock; ridicule

versprechen 1. *unr. tr. V.* promise; **sich** *(Dat.)* **etw. von etw./jmdm. ~:** hope for sth. *or* to get sth. from sth./ sb.; **2.** *unr. refl. V.* make a slip/slips of the tongue; **Versprechen das;** ~s, ~, **Versprechung die;** ~, ~en promise

versprühen *tr. V.* spray

verspüren *tr. V.* feel

Verstand der; ~[e]s *(Fähigkeit zu denken)* reason *no art.; (Fähigkeit, Begriffe zu bilden)* mind; *(Vernunft)* [common] sense *no art.;* **hast du denn den ~ verloren?** *(ugs.)* have you taken leave of your senses?; **verständig 1.** *Adj.* sensible; **2.** *adv.* sensibly

verständigen 1. *tr. V.* notify, inform **(von, über** + *Akk.* of); **2.** *refl. V.* **a)** make oneself understood; **sich mit jmdm. ~:** communicate with sb.; **b)** *(sich einigen)* **sich [mit jmdm.] über/auf etw.** *(Akk.)* **~:** come to an understanding [with sb.] about *or.* on sth.; **Verständigkeit die;** ~: understanding; intelligence; **Verständigung die;** ~,

~en **a)** notification; **b)** *(das Sichverständlichmachen)* communication *no art.;* **c)** *(Einigung)* understanding; **Verständigungs·schwierigkeit die** difficulty of communication; **verständlich 1.** *Adj.* **a)** comprehensible; *(deutlich)* clear *(pronunciation, presentation, etc.)*; **sich ~ machen** make oneself understood; **jmdm. etw. ~ machen** make sth. clear to sb.; **b)** *(begreiflich, verzeihlich)* understandable; **2.** *adv.* comprehensibly; *(deutlich)* ⟨*speak, express oneself, present*⟩ clearly; **verständlicher·weise** *Adv.* understandably; **Verständlichkeit die;** ~: comprehensibility; clarity; **Verständnis das;** ~ses, ~se understanding; **ich habe volles ~ dafür, daß ...:** I fully understand that ...; **für die Unannehmlichkeiten bitten wir um [Ihr] ~:** we apologize for the inconvenience caused

verständnis-: ~los **1.** *Adj.* uncomprehending; **2.** *adv.* uncomprehendingly; ~voll **1.** *Adj.* understanding; **2.** *adv.* understandingly

verstärken 1. *tr. V.* **a)** strengthen; **b)** *(zahlenmäßig)* reinforce ⟨*troops etc.*⟩ **(um** by); enlarge ⟨*orchestra, choir*⟩ **(um** by); **c)** *(intensiver machen)* intensify, increase ⟨*effort, contrast*⟩; strengthen, increase ⟨*impression, suspicion*⟩; *(größer machen)* increase ⟨*pressure, voltage, effect, etc.*⟩; *(lauter machen)* amplify ⟨*signal, sound, guitar, etc.*⟩; **2.** *refl. V.* increase; **Verstärker der;** ~s, ~: amplifier; **Verstärkung die;** ~, ~en **a)** strengthening; **b)** *(zahlenmäßig)* reinforcement *(esp. Mil.)*; **c)** *(Zunahme)* increase *(Gen.* in); *(der Lautstärke)* amplification; **d)** *(zusätzliche Person[en])* reinforcements *pl.*

verstauben *itr. V.; mit sein* get dusty; gather dust *(lit. or fig.)*

verstauchen *tr. V.* sprain; **sich** *(Dat.)* **den Fuß/die Hand ~:** sprain one's ankle/wrist; **Verstauchung die;** ~, ~en sprain

verstauen *tr. V.* pack **(in** + *Dat. od. Akk.* in[to]); *(bes. im Boot/Auto)* stow **(in** + *Dat. od. Akk.* in)

Versteck das; ~[e]s, ~e hiding-place: **~ spielen** play hide-and-seek; **verstecken 1.** *tr. V.* hide **(vor** + *Dat.* from); **2.** *refl. V.* **sich [vor jmdm./etw.] ~:** hide [from sb./sth.]; **versteckt** *Adj.* hidden; *(heimlich)* secret ⟨*malice, activity, etc.*⟩; disguised ⟨*foul*⟩

verstehen 1. *unr. tr. V.* understand;

wie soll ich das ~? how am I to interpret that?; **jmdn./etw. falsch ~:** misunderstand sb./sth.; 2. *unr. refl. V.* **sich mit jmdm. ~:** get on with sb.; **das versteht sich [von selbst]** that goes without saying

versteigern *tr. V.* auction; **etw. ~ lassen** put sth. up for auction; **Versteigerung die** auction

verstellbar *Adj.* adjustable; **verstellen 1.** *tr. V.* **a)** *(falsch plazieren)* misplace; **b)** *(anders einstellen)* adjust ⟨*seat etc.*⟩; alter [the adjustment of] ⟨*mirror etc.*⟩; reset ⟨*alarm clock, points, etc.*⟩; **c)** *(versperren)* block, obstruct; **d)** *(zur Täuschung verändern)* disguise ⟨*voice, handwriting*⟩; 2. *refl. V.* pretend; **Verstellung die** pretence; *(der Stimme, Schrift)* disguising

verstimmen *tr. V.* put ⟨*person*⟩ in a bad mood; *(verärgern)* annoy; **verstimmt** *Adj.* **a)** *(Musik)* out of tune *pred.;* **b)** *(verärgert)* put out, peeved, disgruntled (über + *Akk.* by, about); **ein ~er Magen** an upset stomach; **Verstimmung die** bad mood

verstohlen 1. *Adj.* furtive; 2. *adv.* furtively

verstopfen 1. *tr. V.* block; **verstopft sein** *(pipe, drain, jet, nose, etc.)* be blocked (durch, von with); 2. *itr. V.;* **mit sein** become blocked; **Verstopfung die;** ~, ~en *(Med.)* constipation

verstorben *Adj.* late; **Verstorbene der/die;** *adj. Dekl. (geh.)* deceased

verstören *tr. V.* distress; **verstört** *Adj.* distraught

Verstoß der violation (gegen of); **verstoßen 1.** *unr. tr. V.* disown; 2. *unr. itr. V.* **gegen etw. ~:** infringe sth.

verstreichen 1. *unr. tr. V.* apply, put on ⟨*paint*⟩; spread ⟨*butter etc.*⟩; 2. *unr. itr. V.; mit sein (geh.)* ⟨*time*⟩ pass [by]

verstreuen *tr. V.* scatter; put down ⟨*bird food, salt*⟩; *(versehentlich)* spill

verstricken 1. *tr. V.* **jmdn. in etw.** *(Akk.)* ~: involve sb. in sth.; draw sb. into sth.; 2. *refl. V.* **sich in etw.** *(Akk.)* ~: become entangled *or* caught up in sth.

verstümmeln *tr. V.* mutilate; *(fig.)* garble ⟨*report*⟩; chop, mutilate ⟨*text*⟩

verstummen *itr. V.; mit sein (geh.)* fall silent; ⟨*music, noise, conversation*⟩ cease

Versuch der; ~[e]s, ~e attempt; *(Experiment)* experiment (an + *Dat.* on); *(Probe)* test; **versuchen** *tr. V.* **a)** try; attempt; **b)** *(probieren)* try ⟨*cake etc.*⟩

versündigen *refl. V.* **sich an jmdm./ etw. ~:** sin against sb./sth.

versüßen *tr. V.* **jmdm./sich etw. ~** *(fig.)* make sth. more pleasant for sb./ oneself

vertauschen *tr. V.* exchange; switch; reverse ⟨*roles, poles*⟩; **etw. mit od. gegen etw. ~:** exchange sth. for sth

verteidigen *tr. V.* defend; **Verteidiger der;** ~s, ~, **Verteidigerin, die;** ~, ~nen *(auch Sport)* defender; *(Rechtsw.)* defence counsel; **Verteidigung die;** ~, ~en defence; **Verteidigungs·minister der** minister of defence

verteilen *tr. V.* distribute, hand out ⟨*leaflets, prizes, etc.*⟩ (an + *Akk.* to, unter + *Akk.* among); share [out], distribute ⟨*money, food*⟩ (an + *Akk.* to, unter + *Akk.* among); allocate ⟨*work*⟩; distribute ⟨*weight etc.*⟩ (auf + *Akk.* over); spread ⟨*cost*⟩ (auf + *Akk.* among); distribute, spread ⟨*butter, seed, dirt, etc.*⟩; **Verteilung die** distribution; *(der Rollen, der Arbeit)* allocation

verteuern 1. *tr. V.* make ⟨*goods*⟩ more expensive; 2. *refl. V.* become more expensive

verteufeln *tr. V.* condemn; denigrate

vertiefen 1. *tr. V. (auch fig.)* deepen (um by); 2. *refl. V.* **sich ~ in** (+ *Akk.*) bury oneself in ⟨*book, work, etc.*⟩; **in etw.** *(Akk.)* **vertieft sein** be engrossed in sth.; **Vertiefung die;** ~, ~en *(Mulde)* depression; hollow

vertikal 1. *Adj.* vertical; 2. *adv.* vertically; **Vertikale die;** ~; ~n *s.* Senkrechte

vertilgen *tr. V.* **a)** *(vernichten)* exterminate ⟨*vermin*⟩; kill off ⟨*weeds*⟩; **b)** *(ugs.: verzehren)* devour, *(joc.)* demolish ⟨*food*⟩

vertonen *tr. V.* set ⟨*text, poem*⟩ to music; **Vertonung die;** ~, ~en setting

Vertrag der; ~[e]s, **Verträge** contract; *(zwischen Staaten)* treaty; **vertragen 1.** *unr. tr. V.* endure; tolerate *(esp. Med.);* *(aushalten, leiden können)* stand; bear; **ich vertrage keinen Kaffee** coffee disagrees with me; 2. *unr. refl. V.* **sich mit jmdm. ~:** get on *or* along with sb.; *(passen)* **sich mit etw. ~:** go with sth.; **verträglich 1.** *Adj.* contractual; 2. *adv.* contractually; by contract; **verträglich** *Adj.* **a)** digestible ⟨*food*⟩; **b)** *(umgänglich)* good-natured; easy to get on with *pred.*

vertrauen itr. V. jmdn./einer Sache
~: trust sb./sth.; **auf etw.** (Akk.) ~:
[put one's] trust in sth.; **Vertrauen
das**; ~s trust; confidence; **jmdn. ins ~
ziehen** take sb. into one's confidence;
vertrauen·erweckend Adj. inspiring
vertrauens-, Vertrauens-:~bruch
der breach of trust; **~person** die person in a position of trust; **~sache** die
matter or question of trust; **~selig**
Adj. all too trusting; **~voll** 1. Adj.
trusting ⟨relationship⟩; ⟨collaboration,
co-operation⟩ based on trust; (zuversichtlich) confident; 2. adv. trustingly;
(zuversichtlich) confidently; **~wür-
dig** Adj. trustworthy
vertraulich 1. Adj. a) confidential; b)
(freundschaftlich, intim) familiar
⟨manner, tone, etc.⟩; intimate ⟨conver-
sation⟩; 2. adv. a) confidentially; b)
(freundschaftlich, intim) in a familiar
way; **Vertraulichkeit die**; ~, ~en a)
o. Pl. confidentiality; b) (vertrauliche
Information) confidence; c) o. Pl. (di-
stanzloses Verhalten) familiarity; (Intimität) intimacy; **vertraut** Adj. a)
close ⟨friend etc.⟩; intimate ⟨circle,
conversation, etc.⟩; b) (bekannt) familiar; **jmdn./sich mit etw. ~ machen** familiarize sb./oneself with sth.; **Ver-
traute der/die**; adj. Dekl. close
friend
vertreiben unr. tr. V. a) drive out (aus
of); drive away ⟨animal, smoke,
clouds⟩ (aus from); fight off ⟨tired-
ness, troubles⟩; b) (verkaufen) sell
vertreten 1. unr. tr. V. a) stand in or
deputize for ⟨colleague etc.⟩; ⟨teacher⟩
cover for ⟨colleague⟩; b) (eintreten für,
repräsentieren) represent ⟨person,
firm, interests, constituency, country,
etc.⟩; (Rechtsw.) act for ⟨person, pro-
secution, etc.⟩; ~ sein be represented;
c) (einstehen für, verfechten) support
⟨point of view, principle⟩; hold ⟨opin-
ion⟩; advocate ⟨thesis etc.⟩; 2. unr.
refl. V. sich (Dat.) die Füße od. Beine
~ (ugs.) stretch one's legs; **Vertreter
der**; ~s, ~ a) (Stell~) deputy; stand-
in; b) (Interessen~, Repräsentant)
representative; (Handels~) sales representative; commercial traveller; c)
(Verfechter, Anhänger) supporter; advocate; **Vertretung die**; ~, ~en deputy; (Delegierte[r]) representative;
(Delegation) delegation (Handels~)
[sales] agency; **eine diplomatische ~:** a
diplomatic mission

Vertriebene der/die; adj. Dekl. expellee [from his/her homeland]
vertrocknen itr. V.; mit sein dry up
vertrödeln tr. V. (ugs. abwertend)
dawdle away, waste ⟨time⟩
vertrösten tr. V. put ⟨person⟩ off (auf
+ Akk. until)
vertun 1. unr. tr. V. waste; 2. unr. refl.
V. (ugs.) make a slip
vertuschen tr. V. hush up ⟨scandal
etc.⟩; keep ⟨truth etc.⟩ secret
verübeln tr. V. jmdm. eine Äußerung
usw. ~: take sb.'s remark etc. amiss
verüben tr. V. commit ⟨crime etc.⟩
verunglücken itr. V.; mit sein have
an accident; ⟨car etc.⟩ be involved in
an accident; **mit dem Auto/Flugzeug
~:** be in a car/an air accident or
crash; **Verunglückte der/die**; adj.
Dekl. accident victim; casualty
verunreinigen tr. V. pollute; contaminate ⟨water, milk, flour, oil⟩
verunsichern tr. V. jmdn. ~: make
sb. feel unsure or uncertain
verunstalten tr. V. disfigure
verursachen tr. V. cause
verurteilen tr. V. pass sentence on;
sentence; (fig.) condemn ⟨behaviour,
action⟩; **jmdn. zum Tode ~:** sentence
or condemn sb. to death; **Verurteil-
te der/die**; adj. Dekl. convicted man/
woman; **Verurteilung die**; ~, ~en
sentencing; (fig.) condemnation
vervollkommnen tr. V. perfect
vervollständigen tr. V. complete
verwachsen Adj. deformed
verwählen refl. V. misdial
verwahren 1. tr. V. keep [safe]; 2. refl.
V. protest; **verwahrlosen** itr. V.; mit
sein get in a bad state; ⟨house, build-
ing⟩ fall into disrepair; ⟨garden,
hedge⟩ become overgrown; ⟨person⟩
let oneself go; **verwahrlost** neglected;
overgrown ⟨hedge, garden⟩; dilapidated ⟨house, building⟩; unkempt ⟨per-
son, appearance, etc.⟩; (in der Kleidung) ragged ⟨person⟩; **Verwahrlo-
sung die**; ~: (eines Gebäudes) di-
lapidation; (einer Person) advancing
decrepitude
verwaisen itr. V. be orphaned
verwalten tr. V. a) administer ⟨estate,
property⟩; run ⟨house⟩; hold ⟨money⟩
in trust; b) (leiten) run, manage ⟨hos-
tel, kindergarten, etc.⟩; (regieren) administer ⟨area, colony, etc.⟩; govern
⟨country⟩; **Verwalter der**; ~s, ~,
Verwalterin die; ~, ~nen administrator; (eines Amts usw.) manager; (ei-

nes Nachlasses) trustee; **Verwaltung die; ~, ~en a)** administration; *(eines Landes)* government; *(eines Amtes)* tenure; *(einer Aufgabe)* performance; **b)** *(Organ)* administration

verwandeln 1. *tr. V.* convert (**in** + *Akk.,* **zu** into); *(völlig verändern)* transform (**in** + *Akk.,* **zu** into); **2.** *refl. V.* **sich in etw.** *(Akk.)* od. **zu etw. ~:** turn *or* change into sth.; *(bei chemischen Vorgängen usw.)* be converted into sth.; **Verwandlung die; ~, ~en** conversion (**in** + *Akk.,* **zu** into); *(völlige Veränderung, das Sichverwandeln)* transformation (**in** + *Akk.,* **zu** into)

¹verwandt *2. Part. v.* verwenden

²verwandt *Adj.* related (**mit** to); *(fig.)* similar ⟨views, ideas, forms⟩; **Verwandte der/die;** *adj. Dekl.* relative; relation; **Verwandtschaft die; ~, ~en a)** relationship (**mit** to); *(fig.)* affinity; **b)** *o. Pl. (Verwandte)* relatives *pl.;* relations *pl.;* **die ganze ~:** all one's relatives; **verwandtschaftlich** *Adj.* family ⟨ties, relationships, etc.⟩

verwarnen *tr. V.* warn, caution (**wegen** for); **Verwarnung die; ~, ~en** warning; caution

verwechseln *tr. V.* **a)** |miteinander| **~:** confuse ⟨two things/people⟩; **etw. mit etw./jmdn. mit jmdm. ~:** mistake sth. for sth./sb. for sb.; confuse sth. with sth./sb. with sb.; **b)** *(vertauschen)* mix up; **Verwechslung die; ~, ~en a)** |case of| confusion; **b)** *(Vertauschung)* mixing up; **eine ~:** a mix-up

verwegen 1. *Adj.* daring *(auch fig.)*; audacious; **2.** *adv. (auch fig.)* audaciously; **Verwegenheit die; ~:** daring; *(auch fig.)* audacity

verwehren *tr. V.* **jmdm. etw. ~:** refuse *or* deny sb. sth.

Verwehung die; ~, ~en |snow|drift

verweigern *tr. V.* refuse; **Verweigerung die; ~, ~en** refusal

Verweis der; ~es, ~e a) reference (**auf** + *Akk.* to); *(Quer~)* cross-reference; **b)** *(Tadel)* reprimand; **verweisen** *unr. tr. V.* **a) jmdn./einen Fall** *usw.* **an jmdn./etw. ~** *(auch Rechtsspr.)* refer sb./a case *etc.* to sb./sth.; **b)** *(wegschicken)* **jmdn. von der Schule/aus dem Saal ~:** expel sb. from the school/ send sb. out of the room; **einen Spieler vom Platz ~:** send a player off [the field]; **c)** *auch itr. (hinweisen)* |**jmdn.**| **auf etw.** *(Akk.)* **~:** refer [sb.] to sth.

verwelken *itr. V.; mit sein* wilt

verwendbar *Adj.* usable; **Verwend-**

barkeit die; ~: usability; **verwenden** *unr. od. regelm. tr. V.* **a)** use (**zu**, **für** for); **b)** *(aufwenden)* spend ⟨time⟩ (**auf** + *Akk.* on); **Verwendung die; ~:** use

verwerfen *unr. tr. V.* reject; dismiss ⟨thought⟩; **verwerflich** *(geh.)* **1.** *Adj.* reprehensible; **2.** *adv.* reprehensibly

verwertbar *Adj.* utilizable; usable; **verwerten** *tr. V.* utilize, use (**zu** for); make use of ⟨suggestion, experience, knowledge, etc.⟩

verwesen *itr. V.; mit sein* decompose; **Verwesung die; ~:** decomposition

verwickeln 1. *refl. V.* get tangled up *or* entangled; **sich in etw.** *(Akk. od. Dat.)* **~:** get caught [up] in sth.; **2.** *tr. V.* involve; **Verwicklung die; ~, ~en** complication

verwildern *itr. V.* ⟨garden⟩ become overgrown; ⟨domestic animal⟩ return to the wild

verwirklichen 1. *tr. V.* realize ⟨dream⟩; realize, put into practice ⟨plan, proposal, idea, etc.⟩; carry out ⟨project, intention⟩; **2.** *refl. V.* ⟨hope, dream⟩ be realized; **Verwirklichung die; ~, ~en** realization; *(eines Wunsches, einer Hoffnung)* fulfilment

verwirren *tr. (auch itr.) V.* confuse; verwirrt confused; **~d** bewildering; **Verwirrung die; ~, ~en** confusion

verwischen *tr. V.* smudge ⟨signature, writing, etc.⟩; smear ⟨paint⟩; *(fig.)* cover up ⟨tracks⟩

verwitwet *Adj.* widowed

verwöhnen *tr. V.* spoil; **verwöhnt** *Adj.* spoilt; *(anspruchsvoll)* discriminating; ⟨taste, palate⟩ of a gourmet

verworren *Adj.* confused, muddled ⟨ideas, situation, etc.⟩

verwunden *tr. V.* wound; injure; **Verwundete der/die;** *adj. Dekl.* casualty; **die ~n** the wounded; **Verwundung die; ~, ~en** wound

verwünschen *tr. V.* curse

verwüsten *tr. V.* devastate; **Verwüstung die; ~, ~en** devastation

verzählen *refl. V.* miscount

verzaubern *tr. V.* cast a spell on; bewitch; *(fig.)* enchant; **jmdn. in etw.** *(Akk.)* **~:** transform sb. into sth.

Verzehr der; ~|e|s consumption; **verzehren** *tr. V.* consume

Verzeichnis das; ~ses, ~se list; *(Register)* index

verzeihen *unr. tr., itr. V.* forgive; *(entschuldigen)* excuse ⟨behaviour, re-*

mark, etc.*)*; ~ **Sie [bitte], können Sie mir sagen ...?** excuse me, could you tell me ...?; **Verzeihung** die; ~: forgiveness; ~! sorry!; **jmdn. um ~ bitten** apologize to sb.

verzerren 1. tr. V. **a)** contort *(face etc.)* (zu into); **b)** *(akustisch, optisch)* distort *(sound, image)*; etw. verzerrt darstellen *(fig.)* present a distorted account or picture of sth.

Verzicht der; ~[e]s, ~e **a)** renunciation (auf + Akk. of); **b)** *(auf Reichtum, ein Amt usw.)* relinquishment (auf + Akk. of); **verzichten** itr. V. do without; ~ **auf** (+ Akk.) do without; *(sich enthalten)* refrain from; *(aufgeben)* give up *(share, smoking, job, etc.)*; renounce *(inheritance)*; relinquish *(right, privilege)*; *(opfern)* sacrifice *(holiday, salary)*

¹**verziehen 2.** Part. v. **verzeihen**

²**verziehen 1.** unr. tr. V. **a)** screw up *(face, mouth, etc.)*; **b)** *(schlecht erziehen)* spoil; **2.** unr. refl. V. **a)** *(aus der Form geraten)* go out of shape; *(wood)* warp; **b)** *(wegziehen)* *(clouds, storm)* move away, pass over; *(fog, mist)* disperse; **c)** *(ugs.: weggehen)* take oneself off; **3.** unr. itr. V.; mit sein move [away]; „**Empfänger [unbekannt] verzogen**" 'no longer at this address'

verzieren tr. V. decorate; **Verzierung** die; ~, ~en decoration

verzögern 1. tr. V. **a)** delay (um by); **b)** *(verlangsamen)* slow down; **2.** refl. V. be delayed (um by); **Verzögerung** die; ~, ~en delay *(Gen. in)*; *(Verlangsamung)* slowing down

Verzug der; ~[e]s delay; **im ~ sein/in ~ kommen** be/fall behind

verzweifeln itr. V.; mit sein despair; **über etw./jmdn. ~:** despair at sth./of sb.; **verzweifelt 1.** Adj. despairing *(person)*; desperate *(situation, attempt, effort, struggle, etc)*; ~ **sein** be in despair; **2.** adv. desperately; **Verzweiflung** die; ~ despair

verzweigen refl. V. branch [out]

Veteran [vete'ra:n] der; ~en, ~en *(auch fig.)* veteran

Vetter der; ~s, ~n cousin

vgl. Abk. vergleiche cf.

v.H. Abk. vom Hundert per cent

via ['vi:a] Präp. via

Viadukt [via'dʊkt] das od. der; ~[e]s, ~e viaduct

vibrieren [vi'bri:rən] itr. V. vibrate

video-, Video- ['vi:do-]: video; **Video** das; ~s, ~s *(ugs.)* video

Vieh das; ~[e]s *(Nutztiere)* livestock sing. or pl.; **b)** *(Rind~)* cattle pl.; **Vieh·zucht** die; o. Pl. [live]stock/cattle breeding no art.

viel 1. Indefinitpron. u. unbest. Zahlw. **a)** Sg. a great deal of; a lot of *(coll.)*; **wie/nicht/zu ~:** how/not/too much; ~[es] *(vielerlei)* much; **der ~e Regen** all the rain; **um ~es jünger** a great deal younger; **b)** Pl. many; **gleich ~[e]** the same number of; **die ~en Menschen** all the people; **2.** Adv. **a)** *(oft, lange)* a great deal; a lot *(coll.)*; **b)** *(wesentlich)* much; a great deal; a lot *(coll.)*; ~ **zu klein** much too small; **vielerlei** indekl. unbest. Gattungsz. **a)** attr. many different; all kinds or sorts of; **b)** subst. all kinds of things

viel-, Viel-: ~**fach 1.** Adj. **a)** multiple; **die ~fache Menge** many times the amount; **b)** *(vielfältig)* many kinds of; **2.** adv. many times; ~**falt** die; ~: diversity; ~**fältig 1.** Adj. many and diverse; **2.** adv. in many different ways

vielleicht Adv. perhaps; maybe

viel-: ~**mals** Adv. **ich bitte ~mals um Entschuldigung** I'm very sorry; **danke ~mals** thank you very much; ~**mehr** [od. -'-] Konj. u. Adv. rather; ~**sagend 1.** Adj. meaningful; **2.** adv. meaningfully; ~**seitig** Adj. versatile *(person)*; ~**versprechend 1.** Adj. [very] promising; **2.** adv. [very] promisingly

vier Kardinalz. four; **Vier** die; ~, ~en four; **eine ~ schreiben/bekommen** *(Schulw.)* get a D

vier-, Vier-: *(s. auch* **acht-, Acht-**); ~**beiner** der; ~s, ~ *(ugs.)* four-legged friend; ~**beinig** Adj. four-legged; ~**eck** das quadrilateral; *(Rechteck)* rectangle; *(Quadrat)* square; ~**eckig** Adj. quadrilateral; *(rechteckig)* rectangular; ~**fach** Vervielfältigungsz. fourfold; quadruple; ~**fache** das; adj. Dekl. **um das ~fache:** fourfold; by four times the amount; ~**hundert** Kardinalz. four hundred

Vierling der; ~s, ~e quadruplet

vier-, Vier-: ~**mal** Adv. four times; ~**spurig** Adj. four-lane *(road, motorway)*; ~**spurig sein** have four lanes; ~**stellig** Adj. four-figure attrib.; ~**sterne·hotel** [-'----] das four-star hotel

viert... Ordinalz. fourth; **vier·tausend** Kardinalz. four thousand; **viertel** ['fɪrtl] Bruchz. quarter; **ein ~**

Pfund a quarter of a pound; **Viertel** ['fɪrtl] das (schweiz. meist der); ~s, ~ a) quarter; ~ vor/nach eins [a] quarter to/ past one; **drei** ~: three-quarters; b) (Stadtteil) quarter; district

viertel-, Viertel-: ~**finale das** (Sport) quarter-final; ~**jahr das** three months pl.; ~**jährlich** 1. Adj. quarterly; 2. adv. quarterly; ~**liter der** quarter of a litre; ~**note die** (Musik) crotchet (Brit.); quarter note (Amer.); ~**pfund das** quarter [of a] pound; ~**stunde die** quarter of an hour; ~**stündig** Adj. quarter-of-an-hour; ~**stündlich** 1. Adj. every quarter of an hour postpos.; 2. adv. every quarter of an hour

viertens Adv. fourthly; **viertürig** Adj. four-door attrib.; ~ **sein** have four doors

Vierwaldstätter See, (schweiz.:) **Vierwaldstättersee der** Lake Lucerne

vier- ['fiːr-]: ~**zehn** Kardinalz. fourteen; ~**zehn·tägig** Adj. two-week; ~**zehn·täglich** 1. Adj. fortnightly; 2. adv. fortnightly

vierzig ['fɪrtsɪç] Kardinalz. forty; s. auch achtzig; **vierzigst** ... Ordinalz. fortieth; s. auch acht ...

Vikar der; ~s, ~e a) (kath. Kirche) locum tenens; b) (ev. Kirche) ≈ [trainee] curate

Villa ['vɪla] die; ~, **Villen** villa; **Villen·viertel das** exclusive residential district

violett [vjo'lɛt] purple; violet; **Violett das;** ~s, ~ od. ugs. ~s purple; violet; (im Spektrum) violet

Violine [vjo'liːnə] die; ~, ~n (Musik) violin

Viper ['viːpɐ] die; ~, ~n viper; adder

Viren s. Virus

Virtuose [vɪr'tuoːzə] der; ~n, ~n virtuoso; **Virtuosität die;** ~: virtuosity

Virus ['viːrʊs] das; ~, **Viren** virus

Visa s. Visum; **Visen** s. Visum

Visier [vi'ziːɐ] das; ~s, ~e (am Helm) visor; (an der Waffe) backsight

Vision [vi'zioːn] die; ~, ~en vision

Visite [vi'ziːtə] die; ~, ~n round; ~ **machen** do one's round; **Visiten·karte die** visiting-card

Visum ['viːzʊm] das; ~s, **Visa** od. **Visen** visa

Vitamin [vita'miːn] das; ~s, ~e vitamin

vitamin-, Vitamin-: ~**arm** Adj. low in vitamins postpos.; ~**mangel der;**

o. Pl. vitamin deficiency; ~**reich** Adj. rich in vitamins postpos.

Vitrine [vi'triːnə] die; ~, ~n display case; (Möbel) display cabinet

Vize- vice-

Vogel der; ~s, **Vögel** bird; **einen** ~ **haben** (salopp) be off one's rocker (sl.)

Vogel-: ~**käfig der** birdcage; ~**nest das** bird's nest; ~**perspektive die** bird's eye view; ~**scheuche die;** ~, ~n scarecrow

Vokabel [vo'kaːbl] die; ~, ~n word; ~n vocabulary sing.

Vokal [vo'kaːl] der; ~s, ~e (Sprachw.) vowel

Volk das; ~[e]s, **Völker** people

volks-, Volks-: ~**abstimmung die** plebiscite; ~**eigen** Adj. (ehem. DDR) publicly or nationally owned; ~**entscheid der** (Politik) referendum; ~**fest das** public festival; (Jahrmarkt) fair; ~**hochschule die** adult education centre; ~**kunde die** folklore; ~**lied das** folk-song; ~**musik die** folk-music; ~**polizei die;** o. Pl. (ehem. DDR) People's Police; ~**republik die** People's Republic; ~**stamm der** tribe; ~**tanz der** folk-dance; ~**tracht die** traditional costume; (eines Landes) national costume

volkstümlich 1. Adj. popular; 2. adv. ~ **schreiben** write in terms readily comprehensible to the layman; **Volks·wirtschaft die** national economy; (Fach) economics sing., no art.; **volks·wirtschaftlich** 1. Adj. economic; 2. adv. economically

voll 1. Adj. full; ample ⟨bosom⟩; (salopp: betrunken) plastered (sl.); ~ **von** od. **mit etw. sein** be full of sth.; **jmdn. nicht für** ~ **nehmen** not take sb. seriously; 2. adv. fully; ~ **und ganz** completely; **voll·auf** [od. '--] Adv. completely; **vollaufen** unr. itr. V., trennbar fill up; **etw.** ~ **lassen** fill sth. [up]

voll-, Voll-: ~**automatisch** 1. Adj. fully automatic; 2. adv. fully automatically; ~**bad das** bath; ~**bart der** full beard; ~**bringen** [-'--] unr. tr. V. (geh.) accomplish; achieve

voll·enden tr. V. complete; **voll·endet** 1. Adj. accomplished ⟨performance⟩; perfect ⟨gentleman, host, manners, reproduction⟩; 2. adv. ⟨play⟩ in an accomplished manner; **vollends** Adv. completely; **Voll·endung die** completion; **voller** indekl. Adj. full of; ~ **Flecken** covered with stains

Volley·ball ['vɔlibal] der volleyball

voll-, Voll-: ~**führen** [-'--] *tr. V.* perform; ~**füllen** *tr. V.* fill up; ~**gas das;** *o. Pl.* ~**gas geben** put one's foot down; **mit** ~**gas** at full throttle; ~**gießen** *unr. tr. V.* fill [up]

völlig 1. *Adj.* complete; total; **2.** *adv.* completely; totally; **du hast** ~ **recht** you are absolutely right

voll-, Voll-: ~**jährig** *Adj.* of age *pred.;* ~**jährig werden** come of age; ~**jährigkeit die;** ~: majority *no art.;* ~**kasko·versicherung die** fully comprehensive insurance

voll·kommen 1. *Adj.* **a)** [-'-- *od.* '---] *(vollendet)* perfect; **b)** ['---] *(vollständig)* complete; total; **2.** ['---] *adv.* completely; totally

voll-, Voll-: ~**korn·brot das** wholemeal *(Brit.)* or *(Amer.)* wholewheat bread; ~**laufen** *s.* vollaufen; ~**machen** *tr. V.* fill up; [**sich** *(Dat.)*] **die Hosen/Windeln** ~**machen** *(ugs.)* mess one's pants/nappy; ~**macht die;** ~, ~**en** **a)** authority; **b)** *(Urkunde)* power of attorney; ~**milch die** full-cream milk; ~**milch·schokolade die** full-cream milk chocolate; ~**mond der;** *o. Pl.* full moon; ~**pension die;** *meist o. Art.; o. Pl.* full board *no art.;* ~**ständig 1.** *Adj.* complete; full ⟨*text, address, etc.*⟩; **2.** *adv.* completely; ⟨*list*⟩ in full; ~**ständigkeit die;** ~: completeness; ~**strecken** [-'--] *tr. V.* enforce ⟨*penalty, fine, law*⟩; carry out ⟨*sentence*⟩ (**an** + *Dat.* on); ~**tanken** *tr. (auch itr.) V.* fill up; **bitte** ~**tanken** fill it up, please; ~**treffer der** direct hit; **ein** ~**treffer sein** *(fig.)* hit the bull's eye; ~**zählig** *Adj.* complete

voll·ziehen *unr. tr. V.* carry out (**an** + *Dat.* on); execute, carry out ⟨*order*⟩; perform ⟨*sacrifice, ceremony, sexual intercourse*⟩; **Voll·zug der** *s.* vollziehen: carrying out; execution; performance

Volt [vɔlt] **das;** ~ *od.* ~[e]s, ~: *(Physik, Elektrot.)* volt

Volumen [vo'lu:mən] **das;** ~s, ~: volume

vom *Präp.* + *Art.* **a)** = von dem; **b)** *(räumlich)* from the; **links/rechts** ~ **Eingang** to the left/right of the entrance; ~ **Stuhl aufspringen** jump up out of one's chair; **c)** *(zeitlich)* ~ **Morgen bis zum Abend** from morning till night; ~ **ersten Januar an** [as] from the first of January; **d)** *(zur Angabe der Ursache)* **das kommt** ~ **Rauchen/Alko-**

hol that comes from smoking/drinking alcohol; **jmdn.** ~ **Sehen kennen** know sb. by sight; **von** *Präp. mit Dat.* **a)** *(räumlich)* from; **nördlich/südlich** ~ **Mannheim** to the north/south of Mannheim; **rechts/links** ~ **mir** on my right/left; ~ **hier an** *od. (ugs.)* **ab** from here on[ward]; ~ **Mannheim aus** from Mannheim; **b)** *(zeitlich)* from; ~**jetzt an** *od. (ugs.)* **ab** from now on; ~ **heute/morgen an** [as] from today/tomorrow; starting today/tomorrow; **in der Nacht** ~ **Freitag auf** *od.* **zu Samstag** during Friday night; **das Brot ist** ~ **gestern** it's yesterday's bread; **c)** *(anstelle eines Genitivs)* of; **acht** ~ **hundert/zehn** eight out of a hundred/ten; **d)** *(zur Angabe des Urhebers, der Ursache, beim Passiv)* by; **der Roman ist** ~ **Fontane** the novel is by Fontane; **müde** ~ **der Arbeit sein** be tired from work[ing]; **sie hat ein Kind** ~ **ihm** she has a child by him; **e)** *(zur Angabe von Eigenschaften)* of; **eine Fahrt** ~ **drei Stunden** a three-hour drive; **von·einander** *Adv.* from each other *or* one another; **vonstatten** *Adv.* ~ **gehen** proceed

vor 1. *Präp. mit Dat.* **a)** *(räumlich)* in front of; *(weiter vorn)* ahead of; in front of; *(nicht ganz so weit wie)* before; *(außerhalb)* outside; **kurz** ~ **der Abzweigung** just before the turn-off; ~ **der Stadt** outside the town; **etw.** ~ **sich haben** *(fig.)* have sth. before one; **das liegt noch** ~ **mir** *(fig.)* I still have that to come *or* have that ahead of me; **b)** *(zeitlich)* before; **es ist fünf |Minuten|** ~ **sieben** it is five [minutes] to seven; **c)** *(bei Reihenfolge, Rangordnung)* before; **knapp** ~ **jmdm. siegen** win just ahead *or* in front of sb.; **d)** *(auf Grund von)* with; ~ **Freude strahlen** beam with joy; ~ **Hunger/Durst umkommen** *(ugs.)* die of hunger/thirst; **e)** ~ **fünf Minuten/10 Jahren/Wochen** *usw.* five minutes/ten years/weeks ago; **heute** ~ **einer Woche** a week ago today; **2.** *Präp. mit Akk.* in front of; ~ **sich hin** to oneself

Vor·abend der evening before; *(fig.)* eve

vor·an *Adv.* forward[s] ahead; first

voran-: ~**gehen** *unr. itr. V.;* **mit sein** **a)** go first; **b)** *(Fortschritte machen)* make progress; ~**kommen** *unr. itr. V.;* **mit sein** **a)** make headway; **b)** *(Fortschritte machen)* make progress

Vor·arbeiter der foreman

vor·aus 1. [-'-] *Präp. mit Dat., nachge-**

stellt in front; *jmdm./seiner Zeit* ~ *sein (fig.)* be ahead of sb./one's time; **2.** *Adv.* **im** ~ ['--] in advance

voraus-, Voraus-: ~|**gehen** *unr. itr. V.; mit sein* **a)** go [on] ahead; **b)** *(zeitlich)* **einem Ereignis** ~**gehen** precede an event; ~**sage die** *s.* **Vorhersage;** ~|**sagen** *tr. V.* predict; ~|**sehen** *unr. tr. V.* foresee; ~|**setzen** *tr. V.* **a)** *(als gegeben ansehen)* assume; ~**gesetzt,** |**daß**| ...: provided [that] ...; **b)** *(erfordern)* require *⟨skill, experience, etc.⟩*; presuppose *⟨good organization, planning, etc.⟩*; ~**setzung die** ~, ~**en a)** *(Annahme)* assumption; *(Prämisse)* premiss; **b)** *(Vorbedingung)* prerequisite; **unter der** ~**setzung, daß** ...: on condition *or* on the pre-condition that ...; ~**sichtlich 1.** *Adj.* anticipated; **2.** *adv.* probably

Vor·bau der; *Pl.* ~**ten** porch

Vorbehalt der; ~|**e|s,** ~**e** reservation; **unter dem** ~, **daß** ...: with the reservation that ...; **vor**|**behalten** *unr. tr. V.* **sich** *(Dat.)* **etw.** ~: reserve oneself sth. „**Änderungen** ~" 'subject to alterations'

vor·bei *Adv.* **a)** *(räumlich)* past; by; **an etw.** *(Dat.)* ~: past sth.; **b)** *(zeitlich)* past; over; *(beendet)* finished; over; **es ist acht Uhr** ~ *(ugs.)* it is past *or* gone eight o'clock

vorbei-: ~|**fahren** *unr. itr. V.; mit sein* **a)** drive/ride past; pass; **an jmdm.** ~**fahren** drive/ride past *or* pass sb.; **b)** *(ugs.: einen kurzen Besuch machen)* |**bei jmdm./der Post**| ~**fahren** drop in *(coll.)* [at sb.'s/at the post office]; ~|**gehen** *unr. itr. V.; mit sein* **a)** pass; go past; **an jmdm./etw.** ~**gehen** pass *or* go past sb./sth.; **der Schuß ist** ~**gegangen** the shot missed; **b)** *(ugs.: einen kurzen Besuch machen)* |**bei jmdm./der Post**| ~**gehen** drop in *(coll.)* [at sb.'s/at the post office]; **c)** *(vergehen)* pass; ~|**kommen** *unr. itr. V.; mit sein* pass; **an etw.** *(Dat.)* ~**kommen** pass sth.; ~|**reden** *itr. V.* **an etw.** *(Dat.)* ~**reden** talk round sth. without getting to the point; **aneinander** ~**reden** talk at cross purposes; ~|**schießen** *unr. itr. V.* miss

vor|**bereiten** *tr. V.* prepare; **jmdn./sich auf** *od.* **für etw.** ~: prepare sb./oneself for sth.; **Vor·bereitung die;** ~, ~**en** preparation; ~**en** |**für etw.**| **treffen** make preparations for sth.

vor|**bestellen** *tr. V.* order in advance; **Vor·bestellung die** advance order

vor·bestraft *Adj.* with a previous conviction/previous convictions *postpos., not pred.*

vor|**beugen 1.** *tr. V.* bend *⟨head, upper body⟩* forward; **sich** ~: lean forward; **2.** *itr. V.* **einer Sache** *(Dat.)* *od.* **gegen etw.** ~: prevent sth.; **Vor·beugung die** prevention **(gegen** of); **zur** ~: as a preventive

Vor·bild das model; **jmdm. ein gutes** ~ **sein** be a good example to sb.; **vorbildlich 1.** *Adj.* exemplary; **2.** *adv.* in an exemplary way

vor|**bringen** *unr. tr. V.* say; **eine Forderung/ein Anliegen** ~: make a demand/express a desire; **Argumente** ~: present arguments

vor·christlich *Adj.* pre-Christian

vor|**datieren** *tr. V.* postdate

vorder... *Adj.* front; **der Vordere Orient** the Middle East

Vorder-: ~**grund der** foreground; **im** ~**grund stehen** *(fig.)* be prominent *or* to the fore; ~**mann der;** *Pl.* ~**männer** person in front; **jmdn. auf** ~**mann bringen** *(ugs.)* lick sb. into shape

vor|**drängen** *refl. V.* push [one's way] forward *or* to the front; *(fig.)* push oneself forward

vor|**dringen** *unr. itr. V.; mit sein* push forward; advance

vor·dringlich 1. *Adj.* **a)** priority *attrib.* *⟨treatment⟩*; **b)** *(dringlich)* urgent; **2.** *adv.* **a)** as a matter of priority; **b)** *(dringlich)* as a matter of urgency

Vor·druck der; *Pl.* **Vordrucke** form

vor·eilig 1. *Adj.* rash; **2.** *adv.* rashly

vor·einander *Adv.* **a)** one in front of the other; **b)** *(einer dem anderen gegenüber)* opposite each other; face to face; **c)** **Angst** ~ **haben** be afraid of each other

vor·eingenommen *Adj.* prejudiced; biased; **für/gegen jmdn.** ~ **sein** be prejudiced in sb.'s favour/against sb.

vorenthalten[1] *unr. tr. V.* **jmdm. etw.** ~: withhold sth. from sb.

vor·erst [*od.* -'-] *Adv.* for the present

Vorfahr der; ~**en , ** ~**en** forefather; **vor**|**fahren** *unr. itr. V.; mit sein* **a)** *(ankommen)* drive/ride up; **b)** *(weiter nach vorn fahren)* *⟨person⟩* drive *or* move forward; *⟨car⟩* move forward; **c)** *(vorausfahren)* drive *or* go on ahead; **Vor·fahrt die;** *o. Pl.* right of way; „~ **beachten/gewähren"** 'give way'

---

[1] *ich enthalte vor (od. seltener: vorenthalte), vorenthalten, vorzuenthalten*

Vorfahrt[s]-: ~**schild** das right-of-way sign; ~**straße** die main road

Vor·fall der incident; occurrence; **vor|fallen** unr. itr. V.; mit sein a) (sich ereignen) happen; occur; b) (nach vorn fallen) fall forward

vor|finden unr. tr. V. find

Vor·freude die anticipation

vor|führen tr. V. show ⟨film, slides, etc.⟩; present ⟨circus act, programme⟩; perform ⟨play, trick, routine⟩; (demonstrieren) demonstrate; **jmdn. dem Richter ~:** bring sb. before the judge; **Vor·führung** die show; (eines Theaterstücks) performance

Vor·gang der occurrence; (Amtsspr.) file; **Vorgänger** der; ~s, ~, **Vorgängerin** die; ~, ~**nen** predecessor

Vor·garten der front garden

vor|geben unr. tr. V. pretend

Vor·gebirge das promontory

vor·gefaßt Adj. preconceived

vor|gehen unr. itr. V.; mit sein a) (ugs.: nach vorn gehen) go forward; b) (vorausgehen) go on ahead; **jmdn. ~ lassen** let sb. go first; c) ⟨clock⟩ be fast; d) (einschreiten) **gegen jmdn./etw. ~:** take action against sb./sth.; e) (verfahren) proceed; f) (sich abspielen) happen; go on; g) (Vorrang haben) have priority; come first

Vor·geschmack der; o. Pl. foretaste

Vor·gesetzte der/die; adj. Dekl. superior

vor·gestern Adv. the day before yesterday

vor|greifen unr. itr. V. **jmdm. ~:** anticipate sb. or jump in ahead of sb.

vor|haben unr. tr. V. intend; (geplant haben) plan; **Vor·haben** das; ~s, ~: plan; (Projekt) project

Vor·halle die entrance hall; (eines Theaters, Hotels) foyer

vor|halten unr. itr. V. a) hold up; **mit vorgehaltener Schußwaffe** at gunpoint; b) (zum Vorwurf machen) **jmdm. etw. ~:** reproach sb. for sth.; **Vorhaltungen** Pl. **jmdm. [wegen etw.] ~ machen** reproach sb. [for sth.]

vorhanden Adj. existing; (verfügbar) available; ~ **sein** exist or be in existence/be available

Vor·hang der (auch Theater) curtain; **Vorhänge·schloß** das padlock

Vor·haut die foreskin

vor·her [od. -'-] beforehand; (davor) before; **vorher|gehen** unr. itr. V.; mit sein **in den ~den Wochen** in the preceding weeks

Vor·herrschaft die supremacy; **vor|herrschen** itr. V. predominate

vorher-, Vorher-: ~**sage** die prediction; (des Wetters) forecast; ~**sagen** tr. V. predict; forecast ⟨weather⟩; ~**sehen** unr. tr. V. s. **voraussehen**

vor·hin [od. -'-] Adv. a short time or while ago

vorig... Adj. last

Vor·jahr das previous year; **vor·jährig** Adj. of the previous year

Vor·kämpfer der pioneer

Vorkehrungen Pl. precautions

Vor·kenntnis die background knowledge

vor|kommen unr. itr. V.; mit sein a) (sich ereignen) happen; b) (vorhanden sein) occur; c) (erscheinen) seem; **das Lied kommt mir bekannt vor** I seem to know the song; **Vorkommnis** das; ~**ses, ~se** incident; occurrence

vor|laden unr. tr. V. summon; **Vor·ladung** die summons

Vor·lage die a) o. Pl.; s. **vorlegen:** presentation; showing; production; submission; tabling; b) (Entwurf) draft; c) (Muster) pattern; (Modell) model

Vor·läufer der precursor; forerunner; **vor·läufig** 1. Adj. temporary; provisional; interim ⟨order, agreement⟩; 2. adv. for the time being

vor·laut 1. Adj. forward; 2. adv. forwardly

vor|legen tr. V. present; show; produce ⟨certificate, identity card, etc.⟩; show ⟨sample⟩; submit ⟨evidence⟩; table ⟨parliamentary bill⟩

vor|lesen unr. tr., itr. V. read aloud or out; read ⟨story, poem, etc.⟩ aloud; **jmdm. [etw.] ~:** read [sth.] to sb.; **Vor·lesung** die lecture; (~sreihe) series or course of lectures

vor·letzt... Adj. last but one; penultimate ⟨page, episode, etc.⟩

Vor·liebe die preference; **vor·lieb|nehmen** unr. itr. V. **mit jmdm./etw. ~:** put up with sb./sth.; (sich begnügen) make do with sb./sth.

vor|liegen unr. itr. V. **jmdm. ~:** be with sb.; **die Ergebnisse liegen uns noch nicht vor** we do not have the results yet; **im ~den Fall** in the present case

vorm Präp. + Art. a) = vor dem; b) (räumlich) in front of the; c) (zeitlich, bei Reihenfolge) before the

vor|machen tr. V. (ugs.) **jmdm. etw. ~:** show sb. sth.; (vortäuschen) kid (coll.) or fool sb.

vormalig *Adj.* former; **vormals** *Adv.* formerly

Vor·marsch der *(auch fig.)* advance

vor|merken *tr. V.* make a note of; **ich habe Sie für den Kurs vorgemerkt** I've put you down for the course

vor·mittag *Adv.* **heute/morgen/Freitag** ~: this/tomorrow/Friday morning; **Vor·mittag** der morning; **vormittags** *Adv.* in the morning

Vor·mund der; *Pl.* **Vormunde** *od.* **Vormünder** guardian

vorn[e] *Adv.* at the front; **nach** ~: to the front; **von** ~: from the front; **noch einmal von** ~ **anfangen** start afresh; **von** ~ **bis hinten** *(ugs.)* from beginning to end

vornehm 1. *Adj.* *(nobel; adelig)* noble; *(kultiviert)* distinguished; *(elegant)* exclusive *(district, hotel, restaurant, resort)*; elegant *(villa, clothes)*; 2. *adv.* nobly; *(elegant)* elegantly

vor|nehmen *unr. refl. V.* **sich** *(Dat.)* **etw.** ~: plan sth.; **sich** *(Dat.)* ~, **mit dem Rauchen aufzuhören** resolve to give up smoking

vorn-: ~**herein** *in* **von** ~**herein** from the outset; ~**über** *Adv.* forwards

Vor·ort der suburb

Vor·rang der; *o. Pl.* **a)** priority (vor + *Dat.* over); **b)** *(bes. österr.: Vorfahrt)* right of way

Vor·rat der supply, stock (**an** + *Dat.* of); **vorrätig** *Adj.* in stock *postpos.*

Vor·recht das privilege

Vor·richtung die device

vor|rücken 1. *tr. V.* move forward; advance *(chess piece)*; 2. *itr. V.; mit sein* move forward; **auf den 5. Platz** ~: move up to fifth place

Vor·ruhestand der early retirement

vors *Präp.* + *Art.* = vor das

vor|sagen *unr. tr. V.* **a)** *auch itr.* **jmdm. [die Antwort]** ~: tell sb. the answer; *(flüsternd)* whisper the answer to sb.) **b)** *(aufsagen)* recite

Vor·saison die start of the season; early [part of the] season

Vor·satz der intention; **vorsätzlich** 1. *Adj.* intentional; wilful *(murder, arson, etc.)*; 2. *adv.* intentionally

Vor·schau die preview

Vor·schein der: **zum** ~ **kommen** appear; *(entdeckt werden)* come to light

vor|schieben *unr. tr. V.* **a)** push *(bolt)* across; **b)** *(nach vorn schieben)* push forward

vor|schießen *unr. tr. V.* **jmdm. Geld** ~: advance sb. money

Vor·schlag der suggestion; proposal; **vor|schlagen** *unr. tr. V.* **jmdm.] etw.** ~: suggest *or* propose sth. [to sb.]

vor·schreiben *unr. tr. V.* stipulate, set *(conditions)*; lay down *(rules)*; prescribe *(dose)*; **Vor·schrift** die instruction; order; *(gesetzliche od. amtliche Bestimmung)* regulation; **vorschrifts·mäßig** 1. *Adj.* correct; proper; 2. *adv.* correctly; properly

Vor·schuß der advance

vor|sehen 1. *unr. tr. V.* **a)** plan; etw. **für/als etw.** ~: intend sth. for/as sth.) **b)** *(law, plan, contract, etc.)* provide for; 2. *unr. refl. V.* **sich [vor jmdm./ etw.]** ~: be careful [of sb./sth.]

vor|setzen *tr. V.* **jmdm. etw.** ~: serve sb. sth.; *(fig.)* serve *or* dish sb. up sth.

Vor·sicht die; *o. Pl.* care; *(bei Risiko, Gefahr)* caution; **zur** ~: as a precaution; ~! be careful!; „~, **Stufe!"** 'mind the step!'; **vorsichtig** 1. *Adj.* careful; *(bei Risiko, Gefahr)* cautious; **sei** ~! be careful!; take care!; 2. *adv.* carefully; with care; **vorsichts·halber** *Adv.* as a precaution; to be on the safe side; **Vorsichts·maßnahme** die precautionary measure; precaution

Vor·silbe die [monosyllabic] prefix

vor|singen *unr. tr. V.* **jmdm.] etw.** ~: sing sth. [to sb.]

Vor·sitz der chairmanship; **Vorsitzende** der/die; *adj. Dekl.* chair[person]; *(bes. Mann)* chairman; *(Frau auch)* chairwoman

Vor·sorge die; *o. Pl.* precautions *pl.*; *(für den Todesfall, Krankheit, Alter)* provisions *pl.*; **vor|sorgen** *itr. V.* **für etw.** ~: make provisions for sth.; provide for sth.; **Vorsorge·untersuchung** die *(Med.)* medical check-up; **vorsorglich** *adv.* as a precaution

Vor·spann der *(Film, Ferns.)* opening credits *pl.*

Vor·speise die starter; hors d'œuvre

Vor·spiel das *(Theater)* prologue; *(Musik)* prelude; **vor|spielen** *tr. V.* **a)** play *(piece of music)* (*Dat.* to, for); act out, perform *(scene)* (*Dat.* for, in front of) **b)** *(vorspiegeln)* **jmdm. etw.** ~: feign sth. to sb.

vor|sprechen 1. *unr. tr. V.* **a)** *(zum Nachsprechen)* **jmdm. etw.** ~: pronounce *or* say sth. first for sb.; **b)** *(zur Prüfung)* recite; 2. *unr. itr. V.* audition

Vor·sprung der lead (vor + *Dat.* over)

Vor·stadt die suburb

Vor·stand der *(einer Firma)* board [of directors]; *(eines Vereins, einer Gesellschaft)* executive committee; *(einer Partei)* executive

vor|stehen *unr. itr. V.* a) project, jut out; ⟨*teeth, chin*⟩ stick out; **~de Zähne** buck-teeth; projecting teeth; b) *(geh.: leiten)* **einer Institution ~**: be the head of an institution

vor|stellen 1. *tr. V.* **jmdn./sich jmdm. ~**: introduce sb./oneself to sb.; *(bei Bewerbung)* **sich ~**: come/go for [an] interview; **die Uhr |um eine Stunde| ~**: put the clock forward [one hour]; 2. *refl. V.* **sich** *(Dat.)* **etw. ~**: imagine sth.; **Vor·stellung** die a) *(Begriff)* idea; b) *o. Pl. (Phantasie)* imagination; c) *(Aufführung)* performance; *(im Kino)* showing

Vor·stoß der advance; **vor|stoßen** *unr. itr. V.; mit sein* advance; push forward

Vor·strafe die previous conviction

vor|strecken *tr. V.* stretch ⟨*arm, hand*⟩ out; advance ⟨*money, sum*⟩

Vor·tag der day before

vor|täuschen *tr. V.* feign; simulate ⟨*reality etc.*⟩; fake ⟨*crime*⟩

Vor·teil [od. 'fortail] der advantage; **vorteilhaft** 1. *Adj.* advantageous; 2. *adv.* advantageously

Vortrag der; **~|e|s, Vorträge** talk; *(wissenschaftlich)* lecture; **einen ~ halten** give a talk/lecture; **vor|tragen** *unr. tr. V.* a) sing ⟨*song*⟩; perform, play ⟨*piece of music*⟩; recite ⟨*poem*⟩; b) *(darlegen)* present ⟨*case, matter, request, demands*⟩; lodge, make ⟨*complaint*⟩; express ⟨*wish, desire*⟩

vor·trefflich 1. *Adj.* excellent; 2. *adv.* excellently

vorüber *Adv.* over; *(räumlich)* past; **vorüber|gehen** *unr. itr. V.; mit sein* a) go or walk past; pass by; **an jmdm./ etw. ~**: go past sb./sth.; pass sb./sth.; *(achtlos)* pass sb./sth. by; b) *(vergehen)* pass; ⟨*pain*⟩ go; **vorüber- gehend** 1. *Adj.* temporary; passing ⟨*interest, infatuation*⟩; brief ⟨*illness, stay*⟩; 2. *adv.* temporarily; *(für kurze Zeit)* for a short time; briefly

Vor·urteil das bias; *(voreilige Schluß- folgerung)* prejudice

Vor·vergangenheit die *(Sprachw.)* pluperfect

Vor·verkauf der advance sale of tickets

vor|verlegen *tr. V. (zeitlich)* bring forward **(auf** + *Akk.* to; **um** by)

Vorwahl die, **Vorwähl·nummer** die *(Fernspr.)* dialling code

Vorwand der; **~|e|s, Vorwände** pretext; *(Ausrede)* excuse

vor·wärts *Adv.* forwards; *(weiter)* onwards; **vorwärts|kommen** *unr. itr. V.; mit sein* make progress; *(im Beruf, Leben)* get on; get ahead

vor·weg *Adv.* beforehand; **vor- weg|nehmen** *unr. tr. V.* anticipate

vor|weisen *unr. tr. V.* produce

vor|werfen *unr. tr. V.* **jmdm. etw. ~**: reproach sb. with sth.; *(beschuldigen)* accuse sb. of sth.

vor·wiegend *Adv.* mainly

vor·witzig *Adj.* bumptious; pert ⟨*child*⟩

Vor·wort das; *Pl.* **~e** foreword

Vor·wurf der reproach; *(Beschuldigung)* accusation; **vorwurfs·voll** 1. *Adj.* reproachful; 2. *adv.* reproachfully

Vor·zeichen das a) *(Omen)* omen; b) *(Math.)* [algebraic] sign

vor|zeigen *tr. V.* produce; show

Vor·zeit die prehistory; **vorzeitig** 1. *Adj.* premature; early ⟨*retirement*⟩; 2. *adv.* prematurely

vor|ziehen *unr. tr. V.* prefer

Vor·zimmer das outer office

Vor·zug der a) *o. Pl.* preference (gegenüber over); b) *(gute Eigenschaft)* good quality; merit; **vorzüglich** 1. *Adj.* excellent; first-rate; 2. *adv.* excellently

vulgär 1. *Adj.* vulgar; 2. *adv.* in a vulgar way

Vulkan [vʊl'ka:n] der; **~s, ~e** volcano; **vulkanisch** *Adj.* volcanic; **vulkani- sieren** *tr. V.* vulcanize

v. u. Z. *Abk.* vor unserer Zeit|rechnung| BC

W

w, W [ve:] das; **~s, ~**: w, W

W *Abk.* a) West, Westen W.; b) Watt W.

Waage die; **~, ~n** [pair *sing.* of] scales *pl.*; **waage·recht** 1. *Adj.* horizontal;

2. *adv.* horizontally; **Waage · rech · te** die horizontal; **Waag · schale** die scale pan

Wabe die; ~, ~n honeycomb

wach 1. *Adj.* awake; 2. *adv.* alertly; attentively; **Wache** die; ~, ~n a) *(Milit.)* guard *or* sentry duty; *(Seew.)* watch [duty]; b) *(Wächter, Milit.)* guard; *(Seew.)* watch; c) *(Polizei~)* police station; **wachen** *itr. V. (geh.)* be awake; **bei jmdm. ~:** stay up at sb.'s bedside; sit up with sb.; **Wach · hund** der guard-dog

Wacholder der; ~s, ~: juniper

Wach · posten der *(Milit.)* guard

Wachs das; ~es, ~e wax

wachsam *Adj.* watchful; vigilant

¹**wachsen** *unr. itr. V.; mit sein* grow

²**wachsen** *tr. V.* wax

Wachs · figur die waxwork; **~fi · guren · kabinett** das waxworks *sing. or pl.;* waxworks museum

wächst 2. u. 3. *Pers. Sg. Präsens v.* wachsen; **Wachstum** das; ~s growth

Wachtel die; ~, ~n quail

Wächter der; ~s, ~: guard; *(Nacht~, Turm~)* watchman; *(Park~)* [park-] keeper; **Wach[t] · turm** der watch-tower

wackelig *Adj.* a) wobbly ⟨chair, table, etc.⟩; loose ⟨tooth⟩; b) *(ugs.: kraftlos, schwach)* frail; **Wackel · kontakt** der *(Elektrot.)* loose connection; **wackeln** *itr. V.* wobble ⟨tooth etc.⟩ be loose; ⟨house, window, etc.⟩ shake; **mit dem Kopf/den Ohren ~:** waggle one's head/ears

wacker *(veralt.)* 1. *Adj.* upright; 2. *adv.* valiantly; **sich ~ halten** put up a good show

Wade die; ~, ~n *(Anat.)* calf; **Wa · den · krampf** der cramp in one's calf

Waffe die; ~, ~n weapon

Waffel die; ~, ~n waffle; *(dünne ~, Eis~)* wafer; *(Eistüte)* cone

Waffen · : ~gewalt die; *o. Pl.* **mit ~gewalt** by force of arms; **~handel** der arms trade; **~händler** der arms dealer; **~schein** der firearms licence; **~stillstand** der armistice

Wage · mut der daring; **wage · mu · tig** *Adj.* daring; **wagen** 1. *tr. V.* risk; **[es] ~, etw. zu tun** dare to do sth.; 2. *refl. V.* **sich irgendwohin/nicht irgend · wohin ~:** venture somewhere/not dare to go somewhere

Wagen der; ~s, ~: *(PKW)* car; *(Pferde~)* cart; *(Eisenbahn~)* coach; *(Güter~)* truck; *(Straßen-*

bahn~) car; *(Kinder~, Puppen~)* pram *(Brit.);* baby carriage *(Amer.);* *(Sport~)* push-chair *(Brit.);* stroller *(Amer.);* **Wagen · heber** der jack; **Waggon** [va'gɔŋ, *südd., österr.:* va-'goːn] der; ~s, ~s, *südd., österr.:* ~s, ~e wagon; truck *(Brit.);* car *(Amer.)*

waghalsig 1. *Adj.* daring; *(leichtsinnig)* reckless; 2. *adv.* daringly; *(speculate)* riskily; *(leichtsinnig)* recklessly; **Wagnis** das; ~ses, ~se daring exploit *or* feat; *(Risiko)* risk

Wahl die; ~, ~en a) *o. Pl.* choice; **eine/ seine ~ treffen** make a/one's choice; b) *(in ein Gremium, Amt usw.)* election; **geheime ~:** secret ballot; **wahl · berechtigt** *Adj.* eligible *or* entitled to vote postpos.; **Wahl · be · teiligung** die turn-out; **wählen** 1. *tr. V.* a) choose; *(aus~)* select; b) *(Fernspr.)* dial ⟨number⟩; c) *(durch Stimmabgabe)* elect; d) *(stimmen für)* vote for ⟨party, candidate⟩; 2. *itr. V.* a) choose; b) *(Fernspr.)* dial; c) *(stimmen)* vote; **Wähler** der; ~s, ~: voter; **Wahl · ergebnis** das election result; **Wählerin** die; ~, ~nen voter; **wäh · lerisch** *Adj.* choosy; particular (**in** + *Dat.* about)

wahl-, Wahl-: ~gang der ballot; **~geheimnis** das secrecy of the ballot; **~kabine** die polling-booth; **~kampf** der election campaign; **~kreis** der constituency; **~lokal** das polling-station; **~los** 1. *Adj.* indiscriminate; 2. *adv.* indiscriminately; **~recht** das *o. Pl.* right to vote

Wähl · scheibe die *(Fernspr.)* dial

Wahl-: ~sieg der election victory; **~spruch** der motto; **~urne** die ballot-box

Wahn der; ~[e]s mania delusion; **Wahn · sinn** der; *o. Pl.* a) *(Irresein)* insanity; madness; b) *(ugs.: Unvernunft)* madness; lunacy; **wahnsinnig** 1. *Adj.* a) *(geistesgestört)* insane; mad; b) *(ugs.: ganz unvernünftig)* mad; crazy; c) *(ugs.: groß, heftig, intensiv)* terrific *(coll.)* ⟨effort, speed, etc.⟩; terrible *(coll.)* ⟨fright, job, pain⟩; 2. *adv. (ugs.)* incredibly *(coll.);* terribly *(coll.)*

wahr *Adj.* a) true; **nicht ~?** *translation depends on preceding verb-form;* **du hast Hunger, nicht ~?** you're hungry, aren't you?; **nicht ~, er weiß es doch?** he does know, doesn't he?; b) *(wirklich)* real ⟨reason, motive, feelings, joy, etc.⟩; actual ⟨culprit⟩; *(echt)* true, real ⟨friend, friendship, love, art⟩

wahren tr. V. (geh.) preserve ⟨balance, equality, neutrality, etc.⟩; maintain ⟨authority, right⟩; (verteidigen) defend
währen itr. V. (geh.) last; **während** 1. Konj. a) (zeitlich) while; b) (adversativ) whereas; 2. Präp. mit Gen. during; (über einen Zeitraum von) for
wahr|haben unr. tr. V. in etw. nicht ~ wollen not want to admit sth.; **wahrhaft** (geh.) 1. Adj. true; 2. adv. truly; **wahrhaftig** 1. Adj. (geh.) truthful ⟨person⟩; 2. adv. really; genuinely; **Wahrheit** die; ~, ~en truth; **wahrheitsgetreu** 1. Adj. truthful; faithful ⟨account⟩; 2. adv. truthfully; (portray) faithfully
wahr|nehmen unr. tr. V. a) (mit den Sinnen erfassen) perceive; (spüren) feel; detect ⟨sound, smell⟩; (bemerken) notice; (erkennen, ausmachen) make out; b) (nutzen) take advantage of ⟨opportunity⟩; exploit ⟨advantage⟩; exercise ⟨right⟩; c) (vertreten) look after ⟨sb.'s interests, affairs⟩; d) (erfüllen, ausführen) carry out, perform ⟨function, task, duty⟩; fulfil ⟨responsibility⟩; **Wahrnehmung** die; ~, ~en a) perception; (eines Sachverhalts) awareness; (eines Geruchs, eines Tons) detection; b) (Nutzung) (eines Rechts) exercise; (einer Gelegenheit, eines Vorteils) exploitation; (Vertretung) representation; d) (einer Funktion, Aufgabe, Pflicht) performance; execution; (einer Verantwortung) fulfilment
wahr·sagen 1. itr. V. tell fortunes; 2. tr. V. predict, foretell ⟨future⟩; **Wahrsager** der; ~s, ~, **Wahrsagerin** die; ~, ~nen fortune-teller
wahrscheinlich 1. Adj. probable; likely; 2. adv. probably; **Wahrscheinlichkeit** die; ~, ~en probability; likelihood
Währung die; ~, ~en currency; **Währungs·reform** die currency reform
Wahr·zeichen das symbol; (einer Stadt, einer Landschaft) [most famous] landmark
Waise die; ~, ~n orphan; **Waisen·haus** das orphanage
Wal der; ~[e]s, ~e whale
Wald der; ~[e]s, **Wälder** wood; (größer) forest; **Wald·brand** der forest fire; **Wäldchen** das copse; **Wald·meister** der; o. pl. (Bot.) woodruff
Waliser der; ~s, ~: Welshman; **Waliserin** die; ~, ~nen Welshwoman; **walisisch** Adj. Welsh

Wall der; ~[e]s, **Wälle** earthwork; embankment; rampart (esp. Mil.)
Wall-: ~**fahrer** der pilgrim; ~**fahrt** die pilgrimage
Wal·nuß die walnut
Wal·roß das; Pl. -rosse walrus
walten itr. V. (geh.) ⟨good sense, good spirit⟩ prevail; ⟨peace, silence, harmony, etc.⟩ reign
Walze die; ~, ~n roller; (Straßen~) [road-]roller; (Schreib~) platen; **walzen** tr. V. roll ⟨field, road, steel, etc.⟩; **wälzen** 1. tr. V. roll; heave ⟨heavy object⟩; (fig.) shove ⟨blame, responsibility⟩ (auf + Akk. on); etw. in Mehl usw. ~ (Kochk.) toss sth. in flour etc.; Probleme ~ (fig. ugs.) mull over problems; 2. refl. V. roll; (auf der Stelle) roll about or around; (im Krampf, vor Schmerzen) writhe around; **Walzer** der; ~s, ~: waltz
wand 1. u. 3. Pers. Sg. Prät. v. winden
Wand die; ~, **Wände** wall; (Trenn~) partition; (bewegliche Trenn~) screen; (eines Behälters, Schiffs) side
Wandel der; ~s change; **wandeln** refl., tr. V. change (in + Akk. into)
Wanderer der; ~s, ~: rambler; hiker; **Wander·karte** die rambler's [path] map; **wandern** itr. V.; mit sein a) hike; ramble; b) (ugs.: gehen; fig.) wander (lit. or fig.); c) (ziehen, reisen) travel; (ziellos) roam; ⟨exhibition, circus, theatre⟩ tour, travel; ⟨animal, people, tribe⟩ migrate
Wanderung die; ~, ~en a) hike; walking tour; eine ~ machen go on a hike/tour/trek; b) (Zool., Soziol.) migration
Wander·weg der footpath (constructed for ramblers)
Wandlung die; ~, ~en change; (grundlegend) transformation
Wand-: ~**malerei** die (Bild) mural; ~**schrank** der wall cupboard or (Amer.) closet
wandte 1. u. 3. Pers. Prät. v. wenden
Wange die; ~, ~n (geh.) cheek
wankelmütig Adj. (geh.) vacillating; **wanken** itr. V. a) sway; ⟨person⟩ totter; (unter einer Last) stagger; b) mit sein (unsicher gehen) stagger; totter
wann Adv. when; seit ~ wohnst du dort? how long have you been living there?
Wanne die; ~, ~n bath[tub]
Wanze die; ~, ~n bug (coll.)
Wappen das; ~s, ~: coat of arms
war 1. u. 3. Pers. Sg. Prät. v. sein

warb *1. u. 3. Pers. Sg. Prät. v.* **werben**

ward *(geh.) 1. u. 3. Pers. Sg. Prät. v.* **werden**

Ware die; ~, ~n a) ~[n] goods *pl.;* b) *(einzelne* ~*)* article; commodity *(Econ., fig.); (Erzeugnis)* product

Waren-: ~**haus das** department store; ~**lager das** *(einer Fabrik o.ä.)* stores *pl.; (eines Geschäftes)* stockroom; *(größer)* warehouse; ~**muster das,** ~**probe die** sample; ~**zeichen das** trade mark

warf *1. u. 3. Pers. Sg. Prät. v.* **werfen**

warm; wärmer, wärmst ... 1. *Adj. (auch fig.)* warm; hot *(meal, food, bath, spring);* das Essen ~ **machen** heat up the food; „~" *(auf Wasserhahn)* 'hot'; keen, lively *(interest);* 2. *adv.* warmly; ~ **essen/duschen** have a hot meal/shower; **Wärme die;** ~: warmth; *(Hitze; auch Physik)* heat; **wärmen 1.** *tr. V.* warm; *(aufwärmen)* warm up *(food, drink);* 2. *itr. V.* be warm; *(warm halten)* keep one warm; **Wärm·flasche die** hot-water bottle

Warm·wasser-: ~**bereiter der;** ~**s,** ~: water-heater; ~**heizung die** hot-water heating

Warn-: ~**blinkanlage die** *(Kfz-W.)* hazard warning lights *pl.;* ~**dreieck das** *(Kfz-W.)* hazard warning triangle

warnen *tr. (auch itr.) V.* warn *(vor + Dat.* of, about); **jmdn. |davor|, ~, etw. zu tun** warn sb. against doing sth.

Warn-: ~**schild das** warning sign; ~**schuß der** warning shot; ~**signal das** warning signal; ~**streik der** token strike

Warnung die; ~, ~en warning *(vor + Dat.* of, about)

Warschau (das); ~s Warsaw

Warte-: ~**halle die** waiting room; *(Flugw.)* departure lounge; ~**liste die** waiting list

warten 1. *itr. V.* wait *(auf + Akk.* for); 2. *tr. V.* service *(car etc.)*

Wärter der; ~**s,** ~: attendant; *(Tier~, Zoo~, Leuchtturm~)* keeper; *(Kranken~)* orderly; *(Gefängnis~)* warder

Warte-: ~**saal der** waiting-room; ~**zimmer das** waiting-room

Wartung die; ~, ~en service; *(das Warten)* servicing; *(Instandhaltung)* maintenance

warum *Adv.* why

Warze die; ~, ~n wart; *(Brust~)* nipple

was 1. *Interrogativpron. Nom. u. Akk. u. (nach Präp.) Dat. Neutr.;* ~ kostet **das?** what *or* how much does that cost?; **ach** ~! *(ugs.)* oh, come on!; ~ **für ein .../~ für ...:** what sort *or* kind of ...; **2.** *Relativpron. Nom. u. Akk. u. (nach Präp.) Dat. Neutr.;* |**das,**| ~: what; **alles,** ~ ...: everything *or* all that ...; **vieles/nichts/etwas,** ~ ...: much/nothing/something that ...; **mich betrifft, |so| ...:** as far as I'm concerned, ...; **3.** *Indefinitpron. Nom. u. Akk. u. (nach Präp.) Dat. Neutr. (ugs.)* s. **etwas; 4.** *Adv. (ugs.) (warum, wozu)* why; what ... for

Wasch-: ~**anlage die** car-wash; ~**automat der** washing-machine; ~**becken das** wash-basin

Wäsche die; ~, ~n a) *o. Pl. (zu waschende Textilien)* washing; *(für die Wäscherei)* laundry; b) *o. Pl. (Unter~)* underwear; c) *(das Waschen)* washing *no pl.; (einmalig)* wash; **in der** ~ **sein** be in the wash; **wasch·echt** *Adj.* a) colour-fast *(textile, clothes);* fast *(colour);* b) *(fig.)* genuine

Wäsche-: ~**klammer die** clothespeg *(Brit.);* clothes-pin *(Amer.);* ~**korb der** laundry-basket; ~**leine die** clothes-line

waschen 1. *unr. tr.V.* wash; **sich** ~: wash [oneself]; have a wash; **Wäsche** ~: do the/some washing; **2.** *unr. itr. V.* do the washing; **Wäscherei die;** ~, ~**en** laundry

Wäsche-: ~**schleuder die** spin-drier; ~**trockner der a)** *(Maschine)* tumble-drier; b) *(Gestell)* clothes-airer

Wasch-: ~**gelegenheit die** washing facilities *pl.;* ~**küche die** laundry-room; ~**lappen der** [face] flannel; washcloth *(Amer.);* ~**maschine die** washing-machine; ~**mittel das** detergent; ~**pulver das** washing-powder; ~**straße die** [automatic] car-wash

wäscht *3. Pers. Sg. Präsens v.* **waschen**

Wasser das; ~**s,** ~/**Wässer a)** *o. Pl.* water; b) *(Mineral~, Tafel~)* mineral water; *(Heil~)* water; c) *o. Pl. (Gewässer)* **ein fließendes/stehendes** ~: a moving/stagnant stretch of water; d) *o. Pl. (Urin)* water; urine; ~ **lassen** pass water

wasser-, Wasser-: ~**ball der a)** *o. Pl. (Spiel)* water polo; ~**dicht** *Adj.* waterproof *(clothing, watch, etc.);* watertight *(container, seal, etc.);* ~**fall der** waterfall; ~**farbe die** water-colour; ~**hahn der** water-tap; faucet *(Amer.)*

wässerig *s.* **wäßrig**

Wạsser-: ~**kessel** der kettle; ~**lei-tung** die water-pipe; *(Hauptleitung)* water-main

wạssern *itr. V.; mit sein* land [on the water]; **wạssern** *tr. V.* soak; *(Phot.)* wash *(negative, print)*

wạsser-, Wạsser-: ~**pflanze** die aquatic plant; ~**rohr** das water-pipe; ~**schlauch** der [water-]hose; ~**schutz·polizei** die river/lake police; **¹**~**ski** der water-ski; ~ **fahren** water-ski; **²**~**ski** das; ~s water-skiing *no art.;* ~**spiegel** der a) *(Oberfläche)* surface [of the water]; b) *(Niveau)* water-level; ~**sport** der water-sport *no art.;* ~**spülung** die flush

Wạsser·stoff der; *o. Pl.* hydrogen; **Wạsser·stoff·bombe** die hydrogen bomb

Wạsser-: ~**strahl** der jet of water; ~**straße** die waterway; ~**tempera-tur** die water-temperature; ~**tiefe** die depth of the water; ~**tropfen** der drop of water; ~**turm** der water-tower; ~**werfer** der water-cannon; ~**werk** das waterworks *sing.;* ~**zei-chen** das watermark

wäßrig *Adj.* watery

wạten *itr. V.; mit sein* wade

wạtscheln *itr. V.; mit sein* waddle

¹Wạtt das; ~[e]s, ~en mud-flats *pl.*

²Wạtt das; ~s, ~ *(Technik, Physik)* watt

Wạtte die; ~, ~n cotton wool; **Wạt-te·bausch** der wad of cotton wool

Wạtten·meer das tidal shallows *pl.*

wattiert *Adj.* quilted; padded *(shoulder etc., envelope)*

WC [ve:'tse:] das; ~[s], ~[s] toilet; WC

wẹben *tr., itr. V.* weave; **Wẹber** der; ~s, ~: weaver; **Wẹb·stuhl** der loom

Wẹchsel der; ~s, ~ a) *(das Auswech-seln)* change; *(Geld~)* exchange; b) *(Aufeinanderfolge)* alternation; **im** ~: alternately; *(bei mehr als zwei)* in rotation; c) *(das Überwechseln)* move; *(Sport)* transfer; d) *(Bankw.)* bill of exchange (**über** + Akk. for)

wẹchsel-, Wẹchsel-: ~**geld** das; *o. Pl.* change; ~**haft** *Adj.* changeable; ~**jahre** *Pl.* change of life *sing.;* menopause *sing.;* ~**kurs** der exchange rate

wẹchseln 1. *tr. V.* a) change; **das Hemd** ~: change one's shirt; **die Woh-nung** ~: move home; b) *([aus]tau-schen)* exchange *(letters, glances, etc.);* c) *(um~)* change *(money, note, etc.)* (**in** + Akk. into); 2. *itr. V.* change

wẹchsel-, Wẹchsel-: ~**seitig** 1. *Adj.* mutual; 2. *adv.* mutually; ~**strom** der *(Elektrot.)* alternating current; ~**stube** die bureau de change; ~**wirkung** die interaction

wẹcken *tr. V.* jmdn. [aus dem Schlaf] ~: wake sb. [up]; *(fig.: hervorrufen)* arouse *(interest, curiosity, anger);* **Wẹcker** der; ~s, ~ alarm clock

wẹdeln *itr. V.* *(tail)* wag; **[mit dem Schwanz]** ~ *(dog)* wag its tail

wẹder *Konj.* ~ **A noch B** neither A nor B

wẹg *Adv.* away; *(verschwunden, ~ge-gangen)* gone; **er ist schon seit einer Stunde** ~: he left an hour ago; **weit** ~: far away; a long way away

Wẹg der; ~[e]s, ~e a) *(Fuß~)* path; *(Feld~)* track; b) *(Zugang)* way; *(Pas-sage, Durchgang)* passage; **sich** *(Dat.)* **einen** ~ **durch etw. bahnen** clear a path or way through sth.; c) *(Route, Verbin-dung)* way; route; d) *(Strecke, Entfer-nung)* distance; *(Gang)* walk; *(Reise)* journey; **auf dem kürzesten** ~: by the shortest route; **auf halbem** ~[e] *(auch fig.)* half-way; **sich auf den** ~ **machen** set off; **etw. in die** ~e **leiten** get sth. under way; e) *(ugs.: Besorgung)* er-rand; f) *(Methode)* way; *(Mittel)* means

wẹg-: ~**bleiben** *unr. itr. V.; mit sein (nicht kommen)* stay away; *(nicht nach Hause kommen)* stay out; ~**bringen** *unr. tr. V.* take away; *(zur Reparatur, Wartung usw.)* take in

wẹgen *Präp. mit Gen.* a) because of; ~ **Umbau[s]** geschlossen closed for al-terations; b) *(um ... willen)* for the sake of; ~ **der Kinder**/*(ugs.)* **dir** for the chil-dren's/your sake; c) *(bezüglich)* about; regarding

wẹg-: ~**fahren** 1. *unr. itr. V.; mit sein* a) leave; *(im Auto)* drive off; *(losfah-ren)* set off; b) *(irgendwohin fahren)* go away; 2. *unr. tr. V.* drive away; *(mit dem Handwagen usw.)* take away; ~**fallen** *unr. itr. V.; mit sein* be dis-continued; *(nicht mehr zutreffen)* no longer apply; ~**fliegen** *unr. itr. V.; mit sein* fly away; *(~geblasen werden)* fly off; ~**gehen** *unr. itr. V. A* leave; *(ugs.: ausgehen)* go out; *(ugs.: ~zie-hen)* move away; b) *(verschwinden)* *(spot, fog, etc.)* go away; c) *(sich entfer-nen lassen)* *(stain)* come out; ~**jagen** *tr. V.* chase away; ~**kommen** *unr. itr. V.; mit sein* a) get away; b) *(abhan-den kommen)* go missing; c) **gut/**

schlecht *usw.* [bei etw.] ~**kommen** *(ugs.)* come off well/badly *etc.* [in sth.]; ~|**kriegen** *tr. V.* get rid of *(cold, pain, etc.)*; get out, get rid of *(stain)*; ~|**lassen** *unr. tr. V.* **a)** jmdn. ~**lassen** let sb. go; *(ausgehen lassen)* let sb. go out; **b)** *(auslassen)* leave out; omit; ~|**laufen** *unr. itr. V.*; *mit sein* run away **(von, vor** + *Dat.* from); ~|**legen** *tr. V.* put aside; *(an seinen Platz legen)* put away; ~|**nehmen** *unr. tr. V.* **a)** take away; move ⟨head, arm⟩; **b)** jmdm. etw. ~**nehmen** take sth. away from sb.; ~|**schicken** *tr. V.* **a)** send off ⟨letter, parcel⟩; **b)** send ⟨person⟩ away; ~|**schmeißen** *unr. tr. V. (coll.)* chuck away *(coll.)*; ~|**schütten** *unr. tr. V.* pour away; ~|**sehen** *unr. itr. V.* look away; ~|**stellen** *tr. V.* put away; *(beiseite stellen)* put aside; ~|**stoßen** *unr. tr. V.* push or shove away; ~|**tragen** *unr. tr. V.* carry away

Wegweiser der; ~s, ~ signpost

weg-: ~|**werfen** *unr. tr. V. (auch fig.)* throw away; ~**werfend** *Adj.* dismissive ⟨gesture, remark⟩; ~|**wischen** *tr. V.* wipe away; ~|**ziehen 1.** *unr. tr. V.* pull away; draw back ⟨curtain⟩; pull off ⟨blanket⟩; **2.** *unr. itr. V.*; *mit sein* **a)** *(umziehen)* move away; **b)** *(wandern)* ⟨animals, nomads, etc.⟩ leave [on their migration]

weh *(ugs.)* **1.** *Adj.* sore; **2.** *adv.* ~ **tun** hurt; **mir tut der Magen/Kopf** ~; my stomach/head is aching *or* hurts; **jmdm./sich** ~ **tun** hurt sb./oneself; **Wehe** die; ~, ~n: ~n haben have contractions; **in den** ~**n liegen** be in labour

wehen *itr. V.* **a)** *(blasen)* blow; **b)** *(flattern)* flutter

weh-, Weh-: ~**leidig** *(abwertend)* **1.** *Adj.* *(überempfindlich)* soft; *(weinerlich)* whining *attrib.*; **2.** *adv.* selfpityingly; *(weinerlich)* whiningly; ~**mut** die; ~ *(geh.)* wistful nostalgia; ~**mütig** *Adj.* wistfully nostalgic

¹**Wehr** die; ~, ~en sich [gegen jmdn./etw.] zur ~ **setzen** make a stand [against sb./sth.]; resist [sb./sth.];

²**Wehr** das; ~[e]s, ~e weir

Wehr·dienst der; *o. Pl.* military service *no art.*; **seinen** ~ **ableisten** do one's military service

Wehr·dienst-: ~**verweigerer** der; ~s, ~: conscientious objector; ~**verweigerung** die conscientious objection

wehren *refl. V.* defend oneself

wehr-, Wehr-: ~**los** *Adj.* defenceless; ~**pflicht** die; *o. Pl.* military service; **die allgemeine** ~**pflicht** compulsory military service; ~**pflichtig** *Adj.* liable for military service *postpos.*

Weib das; ~[e]s, ~er **a)** *(veralt., ugs.)* woman; female *(derog.)*; **Weibchen** das; ~s, ~ female; **weiblich 1.** *Adj.* **a)** female; **b)** *(für die Frau typisch; Sprachw.)* feminine; **2.** *adv.* femininely

weich 1. *Adj. (auch fig.)* soft; **ein** ~**es** Ei a soft-boiled egg; **2.** *adv.* softly

¹**Weiche** die; ~, ~n *(Flanke)* flank

²**Weiche** die; ~, ~n points *pl. (Brit.)*; switch *(Amer.)*

weichen *unr. itr. V.*; *mit sein* move; **vor jmdm./einer Sache** ~: give way to sb./sth.

weich·gekocht *Adj. (präd. getrennt geschrieben)* soft-boiled ⟨egg⟩; **weichlich 1.** *Adj.* soft; *(ohne innere Festigkeit)* weak; **2.** *adv.* softly

¹**Weide** die; ~, ~n willow

²**Weide** die; ~, ~n pasture; **weiden** *itr., tr. V.* graze

Weiden·kätzchen das willow catkin

weigern *refl. V.* refuse; **Weigerung** die; ~, ~en refusal

Weih·bischof der *(kath. Kirche)* suffragan bishop; **Weihe** die; ~, ~n *(Rel.)* consecration; *(kath. Kirche: Priester~, Bischofs~)* ordination; **weihen** *tr. V.* **a)** *(Rel.)* consecrate; *(zueignen)* dedicate *(Dat.* to); **b)** *(kath. Kirche: ordinieren)* ordain

Weiher der; ~s, ~: [small] pond

Weihnachten das; ~, ~: Christmas; **frohe** *od.* **fröhliche** *od.* **gesegnete** ~! Merry *or* Happy Christmas!; **weihnachtlich** *Adj.* Christmassy

Weihnachts-: ~**baum** der Christmas tree; ~**feiertag** der: der erste/zweite ~**feiertag** Christmas Day/Boxing Day; ~**fest** das Christmas; ~**geschenk** das Christmas present *or* gift; ~**lied** das Christmas carol; ~**mann** der; *Pl.* ~**männer** Father Christmas; Santa Claus; ~**markt** der Christmas fair; ~**zeit** die Christmas time

Weih-: ~**rauch** der incense; ~**wasser** das *(kath. Kirche)* holy water

weil *Konj.* because

Weile die; ~: while; **weilen** *itr. V. (geh.)* *(ver~)* stay; *(sein)* be

Wein der; ~[e]s, ~e wine

Wein-: ~**berg** der vineyard; ~**brand** der brandy

weinen *itr. V.* cry (über + *Akk.* over, about); *(aus Trauer, Kummer)* cry, weep (**um** for); **weinerlich** 1. *Adj.* tearful; weepy; 2. *adv.* tearfully

wein-, Wein-: ~**essig** der wine vinegar; ~**flasche** winebottle; ~**glas** das wineglass; ~**handlung** die winemerchant's; ~**karte** die wine-list; ~**lokal** das wine bar; ~**probe** die wine-tasting [session]; ~**rot** *Adj.* wine-red; ~**stube** die wine bar; ~**traube** die grape

weise 1. *Adj.* wise; 2. *adv.* wisely

Weise die; ~, ~**n** a) *(Art, Verfahren)* way; b) *(Melodie)* tune; melody

weisen 1. *unr. tr. V. (geh.: zeigen)* show; **jmdn. aus dem Zimmer** ~: send sb. out of the room; 2. *unr. itr. V. (irgendwohin zeigen)* point

Weisheit die; ~, ~**en** a) o. Pl. wisdom; b) *(Erkenntnis)* wise insight; *(Spruch)* wise saying; **Weisheits·zahn** der wisdom tooth; **weis|machen** *tr. V. (ugs.)* **das kannst du mir nicht** ~! you can't expect me to swallow that!

¹**weiß** 1. u. 3. Pers. Sg. Präsens v. wissen

²**weiß** *Adj.* white; **Weiß** das; ~|e|s, ~: white

weis·sagen *tr. V.* prophesy; **Weissagung** die; ~, ~**en** prophecy

Weiß-: ~**bier** das weiss beer; ~**brot** das white bread; ~**dorn** der hawthorn

Weiße der/die; *adj. Dekl.* white; white man/woman; **weißen** *tr. V.* paint white; *(tünchen)* whitewash

weiß-, Weiß-: ~**gold** das white gold; ~**herbst** der ≈ rosé wine; ~**kohl** der, *(bes. südd., österr.)* ~**kraut** das white cabbage

weißlich *Adj.* whitish

weißt 2. Pers. Sg. Präsens v. wissen

Weiß-: ~**wein** der white wine; ~**wurst** die veal sausage

Weisung die; ~, ~**en** *(geh., sonst Amtsspr.)* instruction; *(Direktive)* directive

weit 1. *Adj.* wide; long ⟨way⟩; **jmdm. zu** ~ **sein** ⟨clothes⟩ be too loose on sb.; 2. *adv.* a) *(räumlich ausgedehnt)* ~ ge-öffnet wide open; ~ **und breit war niemand zu sehen** there was no one to be seen anywhere; b) *(lang)* far; ~**er** further; farther; **am** ~**esten** [the] furthest *or* farthest; ~ |**entfernt** *od.* **weg**| **wohnen** live a long way away *or* off; live far away; **von** ~**em** from a distance; **das geht zu** ~ *(fig.)* that is going too

far; c) *(zeitlich entfernt)* ~ **nach Mitternacht** well past midnight; d) *(in der Entwicklung)* far; **Weit·blick** der; *o. Pl.* far-sightedness; **Weite** die; ~, ~**n** a) *(räumliche Ausdehnung)* expanse; b) *(bes. Sport: Entfernung)* distance; c) *(eines Kleidungsstückes)* width; **weiten** 1. *tr. V.* widen; 2. *refl. V.* widen; ⟨pupil⟩ dilate; **weiter** *Adv.* a) s. **weit** 2; b) **und so** ~: and so on; c) *(~hin, anschließend)* then; d) *(außerdem, sonst)* ~ **nichts** nothing more *or* else; **weiter...** *Adj.* further; **bis auf** ~**es** for the time being; s. *auch* **ohne**

weiter-, Weiter-: ~|**bringen** *unr. tr. V.* **die Diskussion brachte uns nicht** ~: the discussion did not get us any further [forward]; ~|**erzählen** *tr. V.* a) continue telling; *itr.* **erzähl weiter!** do carry *or* go on; b) *(~sagen)* pass on; ~|**fahren** *unr. itr. V.; mit sein* continue [on one's way]; *(~ reisen)* travel on; ~|**führen** *tr., itr. V.* continue; ~|**geben** *unr. tr. V.* pass on; ~|**gehen** *unr. itr. V.; mit sein* go on; **bitte** ~**gehen!** please move along *or* keep moving!; ~**hin** *Adv.* a) *(immer noch)* still; b) *(künftig)* in future; c) *(außerdem)* in addition; ~|**kommen** *unr. itr. V.; mit sein* a) get further; b) *(Fortschritte machen)* make progress; **im Beruf** ~**kommen** get on in one's career; ~|**machen** *(ugs.) itr. V.* carry on; go on; ~|**reichen** *tr. V.* pass on; ~|**sagen** *tr. V.* pass on; ~|**sehen** *unr. itr. V.* see; ~|**verarbeiten** *tr. V.* process; ~**verarbeitung** die processing

weit-, Weit-: ~**gehend** 1. *Adj.* extensive, wide, sweeping ⟨powers⟩; far-reaching ⟨support, concessions, etc.⟩; wide ⟨support, agreement, etc.⟩; general ⟨renunciation⟩; 2. *adv.* to a large *or* great extent; ~**gereist** *Adj.* widely travelled; ~**hin** *Adv.* for miles around; ~**läufig** 1. *Adj.* a) *(ausgedehnt)* extensive; *(geräumig)* spacious; b) *(entfernt)* distant; 2. *adv.* a) *(ausgedehnt)* spaciously; b) *(entfernt)* distantly; ~**räumig** 1. *Adj.* spacious ⟨room, area, etc.⟩; wide ⟨gap, space⟩; 2. *adv.* spaciously; ~**reichend** 1. *Adj. (fig.)* far-reaching ⟨importance, consequences⟩; sweeping ⟨changes, powers⟩; extensive ⟨relations, influence⟩; 2. *adv.* extensively; ~**sichtig** *Adj.* long-sighted; ~**sichtigkeit** die ~ long-sightedness; ~**sprung** der *(Sport)* long jump *(Brit.)*; broad jump *(Amer.)*; ~**verbreitet** *Adj.* widespread; common; common ⟨*plant, animal*⟩; **~winkel·objektiv das** wide-angle lens

Weizen der; ~s wheat

welch 1. *Interrogativpron. (bei Wahl aus einer unbegrenzten Menge)* what; *(bei Wahl aus einer begrenzten Menge) (adj.)* which; *(subst.)* which one; 2. *Relativpron. (bei Menschen)* who; *(bei Sachen)* which; 3. *Indefinitpron.* some; *(in Fragen)* any

welk *Adj.* withered ⟨*skin, hands, etc.*⟩; wilted ⟨*leaves, flower*⟩; limp ⟨*lettuce*⟩; **welken** *itr. V.; mit sein* ⟨*plant, flower*⟩ wilt

Well·blech das corrugated iron; **Welle die; ~, ~n a)** *(auch fig.)* wave; *(Rundf.: ~nlänge)* wavelength; b) *(Technik)* shaft

wellen-, Wellen-: **~bad das** artificial wave pool; **~brecher der** breakwater; **~gang der**; o. Pl. swell; **bei starkem ~gang** in heavy seas; **~länge die** wavelength; **~sittich der** budgerigar

Well·fleisch das boiled belly pork; **wellig** *Adj.* wavy ⟨*hair*⟩; undulating ⟨*scenery, hills, etc.*⟩; uneven ⟨*surface, track, etc.*⟩; **Well·pappe die** corrugated cardboard

Welt die; ~, ~en a) o. Pl. world; **auf der ~:** in the world; **die Alte/Neue ~:** the Old/New World; **die dritte/vierte ~** the Third/Fourth World; **auf die od. zur ~ kommen** be born; **alle ~** *(fig. ugs.)* the whole world; everybody; **(~all)** universe

welt-, Welt-: **~all das** universe; **~anschauung die** world-view; **~ausstellung die** world fair; **~berühmt** *Adj.* world-famous

Welten·bummler der; ~s, ~ globetrotter

welt-, Welt-: **~fremd** 1. *Adj.* unworldly; 2. *adv.* unrealistically; **~frieden der** world peace; **~karte die** map of the world; **~krieg der** world war; **der erste/zweite ~krieg** the First/Second World War

weltlich *Adj.* a) worldly; b) *(nicht geistlich)* secular

welt-, Welt-: **~literatur die** world literature *no art.*; **~macht die** world power; **~markt der** *(Wirtsch.)* world market; **~meister der** world champion; **~meisterschaft die** world championship; **~raum der** space *no art.*; **~reise die** world tour; **~rekord der** world record; **~stadt die** cosmopolitan city; **~weit** 1. *Adj.* worldwide; 2. *adv.* throughout the world; **~wirtschaft die** world economy

wem *Dat. von* wer 1. *Interrogativpron.* to whom; who ... to; **mit/von/zu ~:** with/from/to whom; who ... with/from/to; 2. *Relativpron.* the person to whom ...; the person who ... to; 3. *Indefinitpron. (ugs.: jemandem)* to somebody or someone; *(fragend od. verneint)* to anybody or anyone

wen *Akk. von* wer 1. *Interrogativpron.* whom; who *(coll.)*; **an/für ~:** to/for whom ...; who ... to/for; 2. *Relativpron.* the person whom; 3. *Indefinitpron. (ugs.: jemanden)* somebody; someone; *(fragend od. verneint)* anybody; anyone

Wende die; ~, ~n change (zu for); **Wende·kreis der a)** *(Geogr.)* tropic; b) *(Kfz-W.)* turning circle; **Wendel·treppe die** spiral staircase; **¹wenden** 1. *tr., auch itr. V. (auf die andere Seite)* turn [over]; *(in die entgegengesetzte Richtung)* turn [round]; **bitte ~!** please turn over; 2. *itr. V.* turn [round]; 3. *refl. V.* **sich zum Besseren/Schlechteren ~:** take a turn for the better/worse; **²wenden** 1. *unr. (auch regelm.) tr. V.* turn; 2. *unr. (auch regelm.) refl. V.* a) *(person)* turn; b) *(sich richten)* **sich an jmdn.** turn to sb. [for advice]; **wendig** 1. *Adj.* a) agile; manœuvrable ⟨*vehicle, boat, etc.*⟩; b) *(gewandt)* astute; 2. *adv.* a) *(beweglich)* agilely; b) *(gewandt)* astutely; **Wendung die; ~, ~en a)** *(Änderung der Richtung)* turn; b) *(Veränderung)* change

wenig 1. *Indefinitpron. u. unbest. Zahlw.* a) *Sing.* little; **das ist ~:** that isn't much; **zu ~ Zeit/Geld haben** not have enough time/money; **ein Exemplar/50 Mark zu ~:** one copy too few/ 50 marks too little; b) *Pl.* a few; **mit ~en Worten** in a few words; 2. *Adv.* little; **~ mehr** not much more; **weniger** 1. *Komp. von* wenig; *Indefinitpron. u. unbest. Zahlw.* (+ *Sg.*) less; (+ *Pl.*) fewer; **immer ~:** less and less; 2. *Komp. von* wenig; *Adv.* less; **das ist ~ angenehm/erfreulich/schön** that is not very pleasant/pleasing/nice; *s. auch* mehr 1; 3. *Konj.* less; **fünf ~ drei** five, take away three; **wenigst...** *Sup. von* wenig; **wenigst...** *Sup. von* wenig; 1. *Indefinitpron. u. unbest. Zahlw.* least; **am ~en** least; 2. *Sup. von* wenig; **am ~en** the least; **wenigstens** *Adv.* at least

wenn *Konj.* **a)** *(konditional)* if; **außer**
~: unless; ~ **es nicht anders geht** if
there's no other way; **b)** *(temporal)*
when; **jedesmal,** *od.* **immer,** ~: whenever; **c)** *(konzessiv)* **wenn ... auch** even
though; **d)** *(in Wunschsätzen)* if only
wer *Nom. Mask. u. Fem.; s. auch*
(Gen.) **wessen;** *(Dat.)* **wem;** *(Akk.)* **wen**
1. *Interrogativpron.* who; ~ **von ...:**
which of; **2.** *Relativpron.* the person
who; *(jeder, der)* anyone *or* anybody
who; **3.** *Indefinitpron. (ugs.: jemand)*
someone; *(in Fragen, Konditionalsät-*
zen) anyone; anybody

Werbe-: ~**agentur die** advertising
agency; ~**fernsehen das** television
commercials *pl.;* ~**funk der** radio
commercials *pl.*
werben 1. *unr. itr. V.* advertise; **für**
etw. ~: advertise sth.; **2.** *unr. tr. V.* attract *(readers, customers, etc.);* recruit
(soldiers, members, etc.); **Werbung**
die; ~: advertising; **für etw.** ~ **machen**
advertise sth.
Werde·gang der career; **werden 1.**
unr. itr. V.; mit sein become; get; **älter**
~: get *or* grow old[er]; **wahnsinnig** *od.*
verrückt ~: go mad; **das muß anders**
~: things have to change; **wach** ~:
wake up; **rot** ~: go *or* turn red; **Arzt/**
Professor ~: become a doctor/pro-
fessor; **zu etw.** ~: become sth.; **es wird**
[höchste] Zeit it is [high] time; **es wird**
10 Uhr it is nearly 10 o'clock; **es wird**
Herbst autumn is coming; **sind die Fo-**
tos [etwas] geworden? *(ugs.)* have the
photos turned out [well]?; **2.** *Hilfs-*
verb; 2. Part. **worden a)** *(zur Bildung*
des Futurs) **wir** ~ **uns um ihn kümmern**
we will take care of him; **es wird gleich**
regnen it is going to rain any minute;
es wird um die 80 Mark kosten *(ich ver-*
mute, es kostet um die 80 Mark) it will
cost around 80 marks; **b)** *(zur Bildung*
des Passivs) **du wirst gerufen** you are
being called; **er wurde gebeten** he was
asked
werfen 1. *unr. tr. V.* throw; drop
(bombs); **2.** *unr. itr. V.* **a)** throw; **mit**
etw. ~: throw sth.; **b)** *(Junge kriegen)*
give birth; *(dog, cat)* litter; **3.** *unr. refl.*
V. throw oneself; **sich vor einen Zug**
~: throw oneself under a train
Werft die; ~, ~**en** shipyard
Werk das; ~[e]s, ~**e a)** work; **b)** *(Be-*
trieb, Fabrik) factory; works *sing. or*
pl.; **ab** ~: ex works
Werk·bank die; *Pl.* ~**bänke** work-
bench

Werk[s]-: ~**angehörige der/die**
factory *or* works employee; ~**arzt der**
factory *or* works doctor
werk-, Werk-: ~**statt die,** ~**statt,**
~**stätten** workshop; *(Kfz-W.)* garage;
~**stoff der** material; ~**tag der** working day; workday; ~**tags** *Adv.* on
weekdays; ~**tätig** *Adj.* working;
~**tätige der/die;** *adj. Dekl.* worker;
~**zeug das;** *Pl.* ~**zeuge** *(auch fig.)* tool
Werkzeug·kasten der tool-box
Wermut der; ~[e]s, ~**s a)** *(Pflanze)*
wormwood; **b)** *(Wein)* vermouth
wert *Adj. (geh.)* esteemed; *(als Anre-*
de) my dear ...; **etw./nichts** ~ **sein** be
worth sth./be worthless; **Wert der;**
~[e]s, ~**e** value; **im** ~[e] **von ...:**
worth ...; ~ **auf etw.** *(Akk.)* **legen** set
great store by *or* on sth.; **wert·be-**
ständig *Adj.* of lasting value *post-*
pos.; **werten** *tr., itr. V.* judge; assess
wert-, Wert-: ~**gegenstand der**
valuable object; ~**gegenstände** valuables; ~**los** *Adj.* worthless; valueless;
~**papier das** *(Wirtsch.)* security;
~**sache die** valuable item; ~**sachen**
valuables; ~**sendung die** *(Postw.)*
registered item
Wertung die; ~, ~**en** judgement;
wert·voll *Adj.* valuable; *(moralisch)*
estimable
Wesen das; ~s nature; **wesentlich**
1. *Adj.* fundamental (**für** to); **im** ~**en**
essentially; **2.** *adv. (erheblich)* considerably; much
wes·halb *Adv. s.* **warum**
Wespe die; ~, ~**n** wasp
wessen *Interrogativpron.* **a)** *Gen. von*
wer whose; **b)** *Gen. von* **was:** ~ **wird er**
beschuldigt? what is he accused of?
Wessi der; ~**s,** ~**s** *(salopp)* West German
West *o. Art.; o. Pl. (bes. Seemannsspr.,*
Met.) s. **Westen; west·deutsch**
Adj. Western German; *(hist.: auf die*
alte BRD bezogen) West German;
West·deutschland (das) Western
Germany; *(hist.: alte BRD)* West Germany
Weste die; ~, ~**n** waistcoat *(Brit.);*
vest *(Amer.)*
Westen der; ~s west; **der** ~: the
West; **Western der;** ~[s], ~: west-
ern; **West·europa (das)** Western
Europe; **Westfalen (das);** ~s West-
phalia; **westfälisch** *Adj.* Westpha-
lian; **West·indien (das)** the West
Indies *pl.;* **westlich 1.** *Adj.* **a)** west-
ern; **b)** *(nach Westen)* westerly; **c)** *(aus*

dem Westen) Western; **2.** *adv.* westwards; **3.** *Präp. mit Gen.* [to the] west of; **west·wärts** *Adv.* [to the] west; **West·wind** *der* west[erly] wind

wes·wegen *Adv. s.* **warum**

Wett·bewerb *der;* ~[e]s, ~e **a)** competition; **b)** *o. Pl. (Wirtsch.)* competition *no indef. art.;* **Wette** *die;* ~, ~n bet; **eine** ~ [mit jmdm.] **abschließen** make a bet [with sb.]; **mit jmdm. um die** ~ **laufen** race; **wett·eifern** *itr. V.* **mit jmdm.** [um etw.] ~: compete with sb. [for sth.]; **wetten** *itr. V.* bet; **mit jmdm.** ~: have a bet with sb.; **mit jmdm. um etw.** ~: bet sb. sth.

Wetter *das;* ~s weather

Wetter-: **~aussichten** *Pl.* weather outlook *sing.;* **~bericht** *der* weather report; *(Vorhersage)* weather forecast; **~karte** *die* weather-chart; weathermap; **~lage** *die* weather situation; **~vorhersage** *die* weather forecast; **~warte** *die* weather station

wett-, Wett-: **~kampf** *der* competition; **~lauf** *der* race; **~|machen** *tr. V.* make up for (**durch** with); **~rennen** *das* race; **~rüsten** *das;* ~s arms race; **~streit** *der* the contest

wetzen *tr. V.* sharpen; whet

WEZ *Abk.* **Westeuropäische Zeit** GMT

Whiskey ['vɪskɪ] *der;* ~s ~s whiskey; **Whisky** ['vɪskɪ] *der;* ~s, ~s whisky

wich *1. u. 3. Pers. Sg. Prät. v.* **weichen**

wichtig *Adj.* important; **Wichtigkeit** *die;* ~ importance

Wicke *die;* ~, ~n vetch; *(im Garten)* sweet pea

Wickel *der;* ~s, ~: compress; **wickeln** *tr. V.* wind; *(ein~)* wrap (**in** + *Akk. in); (aus~)* unwrap (**aus** + *Dat.* from); *(ab~)* unwind (**von** from); **ein Kind** ~: change a baby's nappy

Widder *der;* ~s, ~: **a)** ram; **b)** *(Astrol.)* Aries

wider *Präp. mit Akk. (geh.)* against

wider-: **~fahren** *unr. itr. V.; mit sein (geh.)* etw. ~fährt jmdm. sth. happens to sb.; **~|legen** *tr. V.* etw. ~legen refute sth.; **jmdm.** ~legen prove sb. wrong

widerlich 1. *Adj.* revolting; repulsive *(person, behaviour, etc.);* awful *(headache etc.);* **2.** *adv.* revoltingly; *(behave)* in a repugnant *or* repulsive manner; awfully *(cold, sweet, etc.)*

wider-, Wider-: **~rede** *die* keine ~rede! don't argue!; **~ruf** *der* retraction; **[bis] auf** ~**ruf** until revoked; **~rufen** [--'--] *unr. tr., auch itr. V.* re-

tract *(statement, claim, confession, etc.);* **~setzen** [--'--] *refl. V.* sich jmdm./einer Sache ~setzen oppose sb./sth.; **~spenstig 1.** *Adj.* unruly; stubborn *(horse, mule, etc.);* **2.** *adv.* wilfully; **~|spiegeln, ~spiegeln** [--'--] **1.** *tr. V.* mirror; *(fig.)* reflect; **2.** *refl. V.* be mirrored; *(fig.)* be reflected; **~sprechen** [--'--] *unr. itr. V.* contradict; **~spruch** *der* **a)** *o. Pl. (Widerrede, Protest)* opposition; protest; **b)** *(etw. Unvereinbares)* contradiction; **~sprüchlich** *Adj.* contradictory *(news, statements, etc.);* inconsistent *(behaviour, attitude, etc.)*

Wider·stand *der* **a)** resistance (**gegen** to); **b)** *(Hindernis)* opposition

widerstands-: **~fähig** *Adj.* robust; resistant *(material etc.);* hardy *(animal, plant);* **~los** *Adj., adv.* without resistance *postpos.*

wider-: **~stehen** [--'--] *unr. itr. V.* **a)** *(nicht nachgeben)* jmdm./einer Sache ~stehen resist [sb./sth.]; **b)** *(standhalten)* jmdm./einer Sache ~stehen withstand sb./sth.; **~streben** [--'--] *itr. V.* etw. ~strebt jmdm. sb. dislikes or detests sth.; **~wärtig 1.** *Adj.* revolting, repugnant *(smell, taste, etc.);* offensive *(person, behaviour, etc.);* **2.** *adv.* *(behave etc.)* in an offensive manner; **~wille** *der* aversion (**gegen** to); **~willig** *adv.* reluctantly; unwillingly

widmen 1. *tr. V.* **a)** dedicate; **b)** *(verwenden für/auf)* devote; **2.** *refl. V.* sich jmdm./einer Sache ~: attend to sb./sth.; *(ausschließlich)* devote oneself to sb./sth.; **Widmung** *die;* ~, ~en dedication (**an** + *Akk.* to)

widrig *Adj.* unfavourable; adverse

wie 1. *Interrogativadv.* how; ~ [**bitte**]? [I beg your] pardon?; ~ **spät ist es?** what time is it?; **2.** *Relativadv.* ~ **er es tut** the way or manner in which he does it; **3.** *Konj.* **a)** *Vergleichspartikel* as; [**so**] ... ~ ...: as ... as ...; **ich fühlte mich** ~ ...: I felt as if I were ...; „**N**" ~ „**Nordpol**" N for November; **b)** *(zum Beispiel)* like; such as; **c)** *(und, sowie)* as well as; both

wieder *Adv.* again; **alles ist** ~ **beim alten** everything is back as it was before; **ich bin gleich** ~ **da** I'll be right back *(coll.)*

wieder-, Wieder-: **~|bekommen** *unr. tr. V.* get back; **~beleben** *tr. V.* revive, resuscitate *(person);* **~belebungs·versuch** *der* attempt at resuscitation; **~|erkennen** *unr. tr. V.*

recognize; ~|**finden** *unr. tr. V.* find again; ~**gabe** die *(Bericht)* report; *(Übersetzung)* rendering; *(Reproduktion)* reproduction; ~|**geben** *unr. tr. V.* **a)** *(zurückgeben)* give back; **b)** *(berichten)* report; *(wiederholen)* repeat

wieder·gut|machen *tr. V.* make good; put right; **den Schaden ~** *(bezahlen)* pay for the damage

wieder|haben *untr. tr. V. (auch fig.)* have back

wieder-: ~**her|stellen** *tr. V.* **a)** reestablish ⟨contact, peace⟩; **b)** *(reparieren)* restore ⟨building⟩; ~**holen 1.** *tr. V.* repeat; *(repetieren)* revise ⟨lesson, vocabulary, etc.⟩; **2.** *refl. V.* **a)** *(wieder dasselbe sagen)* repeat oneself; **b)** *(erneut geschehen)* happen again; **c)** *(wiederkehren)* be repeated; recur

wieder|holen *tr. V.* fetch *or* get back
wiederholt 1. *Adj.* repeated; **2.** *adv.* repeatedly; **Wiederholung** die; ~, ~**en** repetition; *(eines Fußballspiels usw.)* replay; *(einer Sendung)* repeat; *(einer Aufführung)* repeat performance; *(von Lernstoff)* revision

Wieder·hören das: |**auf|** ~! goodbye! *(at end of telephone call)*

wieder-, Wieder-: ~**kehr** die; ~ *(geh.)* return; ~|**kehren** *itr. V.; mit sein (geh.)* return; ~|**kommen** *unr. itr. V.; mit sein* **a)** *(zurückkommen)* return; come back; **b)** *(noch einmal kommen)* come back *or* again; **c)** *(sich noch einmal ereignen)* ⟨opportunity, past⟩ come again; ~|**kriegen** *tr. V. (ugs.)* get back; ~**schauen** das: |**auf|** ~**schauen!** *(südd., österr.)* goodbye!; ~|**sehen** *unr. tr. V.* see again; ~**sehen** das; ~**s**, ~: reunion; |**auf|** ~**sehen!** goodbye!; ~**um** *Adv.* **a)** *(erneut)* again; **b)** *(andererseits)* on the other hand; ~**wahl** die re-election; ~|**wählen** *tr. V.* re-elect

Wiege die; ~, ~**n** *(auch fig.)* cradle
¹**wiegen** *unr. itr., tr. V.* weigh;
²**wiegen** *tr. V.* rock; shake ⟨head⟩
Wiegen·lied das lullaby; cradle-song
wiehern *itr. V.* whinny; *(lauter)* neigh
Wien (das); ~s Vienna; ¹**Wiener** der; ~s, ~: Viennese; ²**Wiener** *Adj.* Viennese; *s. auch* Würstchen; **Wienerin** die; ~, ~**nen** Viennese; **wienerisch** *Adj.* Viennese

wies *1. u. 3. Pers. Sg. Prät. v.* weisen
Wiese die; ~, ~**n** meadow; *(Rasen)* lawn

wie·so *Interrogativadv.* why
wie·viel [*od.* '--] *Interrogativpron.*

(+ Sg.) how much; *(+ Pl.)* how many; ~ **Uhr ist es?** what time is it?

wie·viel·mal [*od.* -'--] *Interrogativadv.* how many times

wievielt... [*od.* '--] *Interrogativadj.* **der ~e Band?** which number volume?; **der Wievielte ist heute?** what is the date today?

wie·weit *Interrogativadv.* to what extent; how far

wild 1. *Adj. (auch fig.)* wild; *(wütend)* furious ⟨cursing, shouting, etc.⟩; ~**es Parken** illegal parking; ~**er Streik** wildcat strike; ~ **auf etw./jmdn. sein** *(ugs.)* be mad *or* crazy about sth./sb. *(coll.)*; ~ **werden** be furious; **jmdn.** ~ **machen** infuriate sb.; **2.** *adv.* **a)** wildly; **wie** ~ *(ugs.)* like mad *(coll.)*; **b)** *(ordnungswidrig)* illegally; **Wild** das; ~|**es a)** *(Tiere, Fleisch)* game; **b)** *(einzelnes Tier)* [wild] animal; **Wild·bret** [~bret] das; ~**s** *(geh.)* game; **Wilde** der/die; *adj. Dekl.* savage; **Wilderer** der; ~**s**, ~: poacher; **wild·fremd** *Adj.* completely strange; ~**e Leute** complete strangers; **Wildheit** die; ~: wildness; **Wild·leder** das suede; **Wildnis** die; ~, ~**se** wilderness

Wild-: ~**schwein** das wild boar; ~**wechsel** der *o. Pl.* game crossing; ~**west·film** der western

will [vɪl] *1. u. 3. Pers. Sg. Präsens v.* wollen

Wille der; ~**ns** will; *(Wunsch)* wish

willen *Präp. mit Gen.* **um jmds./einer Sache ~:** for sb.'s/sth.'s sake; **Willen** der; ~**s** *s.* Wille; **willen·los 1.** *Adj.* will-less; **2.** *adv.* will-lessly; **willens** *Adj.* ~ **sein, etw. zu tun** *(geh.)* be willing to do sth.; **willens·stark** *Adj.* strong-willed; **willentlich 1.** *Adj.* deliberate; **2.** *adv.* deliberately; on purpose; **willig 1.** *Adj.* willing; **2.** *adv.* willingly

will·kommen *Adj.* welcome; **jmdn.** ~ **heißen** welcome sb.

Will·kür die; ~: arbitrary use of power; *(Handlung o. ä.)* arbitrariness; **willkürlich 1.** *Adj.* arbitrary; *(vom Willen gesteuert)* voluntary ⟨muscle, movement, etc.⟩; **2.** *adv.* arbitrarily; *(vom Willen gesteuert)* voluntarily

wimmeln *itr. V.* **von Fehlern** ~: be teeming with mistakes

wimmern *itr. V.* whimper

Wimpel der; ~**s**, ~: pennant

Wimper die; ~, ~**n** [eye]lash

Wind der; ~|**es**, ~**e** wind; **Wind·beutel** der cream puff

Winde die; ~, ~n winch

Windel die; ~, ~n nappy *(Brit.)*; diaper *(Amer.)*; **Windel·höschen** das nappy pants *pl.*

winden 1. *unr. tr. V. (geh.)* make ⟨*wreath, garland*⟩; **etw. um etw. ~**: wind sth. around sth.; **2.** *unr. refl. V.* ⟨*plant, tendrils*⟩ wind (**um** around); ⟨*snake*⟩ coil [itself], wind itself (**um** around); **sich vor Schmerzen ~**: writhe in pain

Windes·eile die: **in ~**: in next to no time; **Wind·hund** der greyhound; **windig** *Adj.* windy

Wind-: **~mühle** die windmill; **~pocken** *Pl.* chicken-pox *sing.*; **~schutz·scheibe** die windscreen *(Brit.)*; windshield *(Amer.)*; **~stärke** die: **~stärke 7/9** *usw.* wind force 7/9 *etc.*; **~still** *Adj.* windless; still; **~stoß** der gust of wind; **~surfing** das windsurfing *no art.*

Windung die; ~, ~en a) bend; b) *(spiralförmiger Verlauf)* spiral; *(einer Spule o.ä.)* winding

Wink der; ~[e]s, ~e sign; *(Hinweis)* hint; *(Ratschlag)* tip; hint

Winkel der; ~s, ~ a) *(Math.)* angle; **toter ~**: blind spot; b) *(Ecke; auch fig.)* corner; **winkelig** *Adj.* twisty ⟨*streets*⟩

winken 1. *itr. V. a)* wave; **mit etw. ~**: wave sth.; b) *(auffordern heranzukommen)* jmdm. **~**: beckon sb. over; **einem Taxi ~**: hail a taxi; **2.** *tr. V.* beckon; **jmdm. zu sich ~**: beckon sb. over [to one]

winklig *Adj. s.* winkelig

winseln *itr. V.* ⟨*dog*⟩ whimper

Winter der; ~s, ~: winter; **Winter·anfang** der beginning of winter; **winterlich 1.** *Adj.* wintry; winter *attrib.* ⟨*clothing, break*⟩; **2.** *adv.* **~ kalt** cold and wintry

Winter-: **~reifen** der winter tyre; **~schlußverkauf** der winter sale[s *pl.*]; **~sport** der winter sports *pl.*; **~zeit** die; *o. Pl.* winter-time

Winzer der; ~s, ~winegrower

winzig 1. *Adj.* tiny; **2.** *adv.* **~ klein** tiny; minute

Wipfel der; ~s, ~: tree-top

Wippe die; ~, ~n see-saw; **wippen** *itr. V.* bob up and down; *(hin und her)* bob about; *(auf einer Wippe)* see-saw

wir *Personalpron.; 1. Pers. Pl. Nom.* we; *s. auch (Gen.)* unser; *(Dat.)* uns; *(Akk.)* uns

wirb *Imperativ Sg. v.* werben

Wirbel der; ~s, ~ a) *(kreisende Bewegung)* *(im Wasser)* whirlpool; *(in der Luft)* whirlwind; *(kleiner)* eddy; *(von Rauch, beim Tanz)* whirl; b) *(Trubel)* hurly-burly; c) *(Aufsehen)* fuss; d) *(Anat.)* vertebra; **wirbeln 1.** *itr. V.* **mit sein** whirl; ⟨*water, snowflakes*⟩ swirl; **2.** *tr. V.* swirl ⟨*leaves, dust*⟩; whirl ⟨*dancer*⟩

Wirbel-: **~säule** die spinal column; **~sturm** der cyclone

wirbt *3. Pers. Sg. Präsens v.* werben

wird *3. Pers. Sg. Präsens v.* werden

wirf *Imperativ Sg. v.* werfen; **wirft** *3. Pers. Sg. Präsens v.* werfen

wirken *itr. V. a) (eine Wirkung haben)* have an effect; **gegen etw. ~**: be effective against sth.; b) *(erscheinen)* seem; appear

wirklich 1. *Adj.* real; **2.** *Adv.* really; **Wirklichkeit** die; ~, ~en reality

wirksam 1. *Adj.* effective; **2.** *adv.* effectively; **Wirksamkeit** die; ~: effectiveness; **Wirk·stoff** der active agent; **Wirkung** die; ~, ~en effect (**auf** + *Akk.* on); **mit ~ vom 1. Juli** *(Amtsspr.)* with effect from 1 July

wirkungs-: **~los 1.** *Adj.* ineffective; **2.** *adv.* ineffectively; **~voll 1.** *Adj.* effective; **2.** *adv.* effectively

wirr *Adj. (unordentlich)* tousled ⟨*hair, beard*⟩; tangled ⟨*ropes, roots*⟩; *(unklar, verwirrt)* confused; **Wirren** *Pl.* turmoil *sing.*; **Wirrwarr** der; ~s chaos; *(von Stimmen)* clamour

Wirsing der; ~s, **Wirsingkohl** der savoy [cabbage]

Wirt der; ~[e]s, ~e landlord; **Wirtin** die; ~, ~nen landlady

Wirtschaft die; ~, ~en a) economy; *(Geschäftsleben)* commerce and industry; b) *(Gast~)* public house; pub *(Brit. coll.)*; bar *(Amer.)*; c) *(Haushalt)* household; d) *o. Pl. (ugs. abwertend: Unordnung)* mess; shambles *sing.*; **wirtschaften** *itr. V.* **mit dem Geld gut ~**: manage one's money well; **mit Verlust/Gewinn ~**: run at a loss/ profit; **wirtschaftlich 1.** *Adj.* a) economic; b) *(finanziell)* financial; c) *(sparsam, rentabel)* economical; **2.** *adv.; s. Adj.:* economically; financially; **Wirtschaftlichkeit** die; ~: economic viability

Wirtschafts-: **~hilfe** die economic aid *no indef. art.*; **~krise** die economic crisis; **~minister** der minister for economic affairs; **~politik** die economic policy

Wirts: ~haus das pub *(Brit. coll.)*; **~leute** *Pl.* landlord and landlady
Wisch der; **~[e]s, ~e** *(salopp)* piece or bit of paper; **wischen** *itr., tr. V.* wipe; **Staub ~:** do the dusting; dust
wispern *itr., tr. V.* whisper
wiß-, Wiß-: ~begier, ~begierde die; *o. Pl.* thirst for knowledge; **~begierig** *Adj.* eager for knowledge; *(child)* eager to learn
wissen 1. *unr. tr. V.* know; **von jmdm./ etw. nichts [mehr] ~ wollen** want to have nothing [more] to do with sb./ sth.; **2.** *unr. itr. V.* **von etw./um etw. ~:** know about sth.; **Wissen** das; **~s** knowledge; **meines/unseres ~s** to my/ our knowledge; **Wissenschaft die; ~, ~en** science; **Wissenschaftler der; ~s ~, Wissenschaftlerin die; ~, ~nen** academic; *(Natur~)* scientist; **wissenschaftlich 1.** *Adj.* scholarly; *(natur~)* scientific; **2.** *adv.* in a scholarly manner; *(natur~)* scientifically; **wissens·wert** *Adj.* ~ sein be worth knowing; **wissentlich 1.** *Adj.* deliberate; **2.** *adv.* knowingly; deliberately
wittern 1. *itr. V.* sniff the air; **2.** *tr. V.* get wind of; *(fig.: ahnen)* sense; **Witterung die; ~, ~en a)** *(Wetter)* weather *no indef. art;* **b)** *(Jägerspr.) (Geruchssinn)* sense of smell; *(Geruch)* scent
Witwe die; ~, ~n widow; ~ **werden** be widowed; **Witwer der; ~s, ~:** widower
Witz der; **~es, ~e** joke
Witz-: ~blatt das humorous magazine; **~bold der; ~es, ~e** joker
witzig 1. *Adj.* funny; **2.** *adv.* amusingly; **witz·los** *Adj.* **a)** dull; **b)** *(ugs.: sinnlos)* pointless
wo 1. *Adv.* where; **2.** *Konj.* **a)** *(da, weil)* seeing that; **b)** *(obwohl)* although; when; **wo·anders** *Adv.* somewhere else; **wo·bei** *Adv.* **a)** *(interrogativ)* ~ **hast du sie ertappt?** what did you catch her doing?; **b)** *(relativisch)* **er gab sechs Schüsse ab, ~ einer der Täter getötet wurde** he fired six shots - one of the criminals was killed
Woche die; ~, ~n week; **in dieser/der nächsten/der letzten ~:** this/next/last week; **heute in/vor einer ~:** a week today/a week ago today
wochen-, Wochen-: ~bett das: im **~bett liegen** be lying in; **~ende** das weekend; **~lang 1.** *Adj.* lasting weeks *postpos;* **2.** *adv.* for weeks [on end];

~tag der weekday *(including Saturday);* **~tags** *Adv.* on weekdays [and Saturdays]
wöchentlich *Adj., adv.* weekly; **Wochen·zeitung** die weekly newspaper; **-wöchig a)** *(... Wochen alt)* ... -week-old; **b)** *(... Wochen dauernd)* ... week's/weeks'; ...-week; **Wöchnerin die; ~, ~nen** woman who has just given birth
Wodka der; **~s, ~s** vodka
wo·durch *Adv.* **a)** *(interrogativ)* how; **b)** *(relativisch)* as a result of which; **wo·für** *Adv.* **a)** *(interrogativ)* for what; **b)** *(relativisch)* for which
wog *1. u. 3. Pers. Sg. Prät. v.* **wiegen**
Woge die; ~, ~n wave
wo·gegen 1. *Adv.* **a)** *(interrogativ)* against what; what ... against; **b)** *(relativisch)* against which; which ... against; **2.** *Konj.* whereas
wogen *itr. V. (geh.) (sea)* surge; *(fig.) (corn)* wave
wo·her *Adv.* **a)** *(interrogativ)* where ... from; ~ **weißt du das?** how do you know that?; **b)** *(relativisch)* where ... from; **wo·hin** *Adv.* **a)** *(interrogativ)* where [... to]; **b)** *(relativisch)* where; **wo·hingegen** *Konj.* whereas
wohl I. *Adv.* **a)** well; **jmdm. ist nicht ~, jmd. fühlt sich nicht ~:** sb. does not feel well; **b)** *(behaglich)* at ease; happy; **leb ~!/leben Sie ~!** farewell!; **c)** *(durchaus)* well; **d)** *(ungefähr)* about; **2.** *Partikel* probably; ~ **kaum** hardly; **Wohl das; ~[e]s** welfare; **auf** jmds. ~ **trinken** drink sb.'s health; **zum** ~! cheers!
wohl-, Wohl-: ~auf [-'-] *Adj.(geh.)* **~auf sein** be well; **~befinden** das well-being; **~behagen** das sense of well-being; **~behalten** *Adj.* safe and well *(person);* undamaged *(thing);* **~fahrts·staat** der welfare state; **~gefallen** das pleasure; **~gemerkt** *Adv.* please note; **~habend** *Adj.* prosperous
wohlig 1. *Adj.* pleasant; agreeable; **2.** *adv.* *(sigh, purr, etc.)* with pleasure
wohl, Wohl-: ~klang der *(geh.)* melodious sound; **~schmeckend** *Adj. (geh.)* delicious; **~stand** der; *o. Pl.* prosperity; **~stands·gesellschaft** die *o. Pl.* affluent society; **~tat die a)** *(gute Tat)* good deed; *(Gefallen)* favour; **b)** *o. Pl. (Genuß)* blissful relief; **~tätig** *Adj.* charitable; **~tuend** *Adj.* agreeable; **~[e]s·tun** *unr. itr. V.* **etw. tut** jmdm. ~: sth. does sb. good; **~ver**

dient *Adj.* well-earned; **~weislich** *Adv.* deliberately; **~wollen das; ~s** goodwill; **~wollend 1.** *Adj.* benevolent; favourable ⟨*judgement, opinion*⟩; **2.** *adv.* benevolently; ⟨*judge, consider*⟩ favourably

Wohn·anhänger der caravan; trailer *(Amer.);* **wohnen** *itr. V.* live; *(kurzfristig)* stay

wohn-, Wohn-: ~gemeinschaft die group sharing a flat *(Brit.)* or *(Amer.)* apartment/house; **~haft** *Adj.* resident **(in** + *Dat.* in); **~heim das** *(für Alte, Behinderte)* home; *(für Obdachlose, Lehrlinge)* hostel; *(für Studenten)* hall of residence

wohnlich *Adj.* homely

Wohn-: ~mobil das; ~s, ~e motor home; **~ort der;** *Pl.* ~e place of residence; **~sitz der** place of residence; **ohne festen ~sitz** of no fixed abode

Wohnung die **~, ~en** a) flat *(Brit.);* apartment *(Amer.);* b) *o. Pl. (Unterkunft)* lodging

Wohn-: ~verhältnisse *Pl.* living conditions; **~wagen** der caravan; trailer *(Amer.);* **~zimmer das** living-room

wölben 1. *tr. V.* curve; vault, arch ⟨*roof, ceiling*⟩; **2.** *refl. V.* curve; ⟨*bridge, ceiling*⟩ arch; **Wölbung die; ~, ~en** curve; *(einer Decke)* arch; vault

Wolf der; **~[e]s, Wölfe** wolf

Wolke die; **~, ~n** cloud

wolken-, Wolken-: ~bruch der; *Pl.* **~brüche** cloudburst; **~bruch·artig** *Adj.* torrential; **~kratzer** der skyscraper; **~los** *Adj.* cloudless

wolkig *Adj.* cloudy

Wolle die; **~, ~n** wool; **¹wollen** *Adj.* woollen

²wollen 1. *unr. Modalverb;* **2.** *Part.* ~ etw. tun ~ *(den Wunsch haben, etw. zu tun)* want to do sth.; *(die Absicht haben, etw. zu tun)* be going to do sth.; **die Wunde will nicht heilen** the wound [just] won't heal; **2.** *unr. itr. V.* **du mußt nur ~, dann ...** you only have to want to enough, then ... **ganz wie du willst** just as you like; *(ugs.)* **ich will nach Hause** I want to go home; **zu wem ~ Sie?** whom do you want to see?; **3.** *unr. tr. V.* want; **das habe ich nicht gewollt** I never meant that to happen

wo·mit *Adv.* a) *(interrogativ)* ~ schreibst du? what do you write with?; b) *(relativisch)* ~ du schreibst

which *or* that you write with; *(more formal)* with which you write; **womöglich** *Adv.* possibly; **wo·nach** *Adv.* a) *(interrogativ)* after what; what ... after; ~ suchst du? what are you looking for?; b) *(relativisch)* after which; which ... after

Wonne die; **~, ~n** *(geh.)* bliss *no pl.;* ecstasy; *(etw., was Freude macht)* joy; **wonnig** *Adj.* sweet

woran *Adv.* a) *(interrogativ)* ~ denkst du? what are you thinking of?; b) *(relativisch)* nichts, ~ man sich anlehnen könnte nothing one could lean against; **worauf** *Adv.* a) *(interrogativ)* ~ wartest du? what are you waiting for?; b) *(relativisch)* etwas, ~ man sich verlassen kann something one can rely on; c) *(relativisch:* woraufhin) whereupon

woraus *Adv.* a) *(interrogativ)* ~ schließt du das? what do you infer that from?; b) *(relativisch)* es gab nichts, ~ wir den Wein hätten trinken können there was nothing for us to drink the wine out of

worden *2. Part. v.* werden 2

worin *Adv.* a) *(interrogativ)* in what; what ... in; b) *(relativisch)* in which; which ... in

Wort das; **~[e]s, Wörter/~e** a) *Pl.* **Wörter,** *(auch:)* ~e word; ~ für ~: word for word; **DM 1000 (in ~en: tausend)** DM 1,000 (in words: one thousand); b) *Pl.* ~e *(Äußerung)* word; **mir fehlen die ~e** I'm lost for words; **Dr. Meyer hat das ~:** it's Dr Meyer's turn to speak; c) *Pl.* ~e *(Spruch)* saying; *(Zitat)* quotation; d) *Pl.* ~e *(geh.: Text)* words *pl.;* **in ~ und Bild** in words and pictures; e) *Pl.* ~e *(Versprechen)* word; **[sein] ~ halten** keep one's word; **wort·brüchig** *Adj.* ~ werden break one's word; **Wörter·buch das** dictionary

wort-, Wort-: ~getreu *Adj.* word-for-word; **~karg 1.** *Adj.* taciturn ⟨*person*⟩; **2.** *adv.* taciturnly; **~laut** der wording; **im [vollen] ~laut** verbatim

wörtlich 1. *Adj.* a) word-for-word; b) *(der eigentlichen Bedeutung entsprechend)* literal; **2.** *adv.: s. Adj.:* word for word; literally

wort-, Wort-: ~los 1. *Adj.* silent; wordless; **2.** *adv.* without saying a word; **~spiel das** play on words; pun; **~wechsel** der exchange of words; **~wörtlich** *Adj.* word-for-word

worüber *Adv.* **a)** *(interrogativ)* over what ...; what ... over; **b)** *(relativisch)* over which; which ... over; **worum** *Adv.* **a)** *(interrogativ)* around what; what ... around; **b)** *(relativisch)* around which; which ... around; **worunter** *Adv.* **a)** *(interrogativ)* under what; what ... under; **b)** *(relativisch)* under which; which ... under; **wo·von** *Adv.* **a)** *(interrogativ)* from where; where ... from; **b)** *(relativisch)* from which; which ... from; **wo·vor** *Adv.* **a)** *(interrogativ)* in front of what; what ... in front of; **b)** *(relativisch)* in front of which; which ... in front of; **wo·zu** *Adv.* **a)** *(interrogativ)* to what; what ... to; *(wofür)* what ... for; **b)** *(relativisch)* ~ **du dich auch entschließt** whatever you decide on

Wrack das; ~|e|s, ~s od. ~e wreck

wrang *1. und 3. Pers. Sg. Prät. v.* **wringen; wringen** *unr. tr. V. (bes. nordd.)* wring

Wucher der; ~s profiteering; *(beim Verleihen von Geld)* usury; **wuchern** *itr. V.* **a)** *auch mit sein* ⟨plants, weeds, etc.⟩ proliferate, run wild; **b)** *(Wucher treiben)* |mit etw.| ~: profiteer [on sth.]; *(beim Verleihen von Geld)* lend [sth.] at extortionate interest rates; **Wucherung** die; ~, ~en growth

wuchs *1. u. 3. Pers. Sg. Prät. v.* **wachsen; Wuchs** der; ~es *(Gestalt)* stature

Wucht die; ~ force; *(von Schlägen)* power; weight; **wuchtig 1.** *Adj.* **a)** *(voller Wucht)* powerful; mighty; **b)** *(schwer, massig)* massive; **2.** *adv.* powerfully

wühlen 1. *itr. V.* **a)** dig; *(mit der Schnauze, dem Schnabel)* root (**nach** for); *(mole)* tunnel, burrow; **b)** *(ugs.: suchen)* rummage [around] (**nach** for); **2.** *tr. V.* burrow; tunnel out ⟨burrow⟩

wulstig *Adj.* bulging

wund *Adj.* sore; **Wunde** die; ~, ~n wound

wunder *Adv.* (ugs.) **er denkt, er sei** ~ **wer** he thinks he's really something; **Wunder** das; ~s, ~ **a)** miracle; ~ **wirken** *(fig. ugs.)* work wonders; **ein/kein** ~ **sein** (ugs.) be a/no wonder; **b)** *(etw. Erstaunliches)* wonder; **wunderbar 1.** *Adj.* **a)** miraculous; **b)** *(sehr schön, herrlich)* wonderful; marvellous; **2.** *adv. (sehr schön, herrlich)* wonderfully; marvellously; **b)** (ugs.: sehr) wonderfully

Wunder-: ~**kerze die** sparkler; ~**kind das** child prodigy

wunderlich 1. *Adj.* strange; odd; **2.** *adv.* strangely; oddly; **wundern 1.** *tr. V.* surprise; **mich wundert** od. **es wundert mich, daß ...:** I'm surprised that ...; **2.** *refl. V.* **sich über jmdn./etw.** ~: be surprised at sb./sth.

wunder-: ~**schön 1.** *Adj.* simply beautiful; *(herrlich)* simply wonderful; **2.** *adv.* quite beautifully; ~**voll 1.** *Adj.* wonderful; **2.** *adv.* wonderfully

wund|liegen *unr. refl. V.* get bedsores (**an** + *Dat.* on); **Wund·starr·krampf** der *(Med.)* tetanus

Wunsch der; ~|e|s, **Wünsche** wish (**nach** to have); *(Sehnen)* desire (**nach** for); **haben Sie |sonst| noch einen** ~? will there be anything else?; **auf jmds.** ~: at sb.'s wish; **mit den besten/herzlichsten Wünschen** with best/warmest wishes; **wünschen** *tr. V.* **a)** **sich** *(Dat.)* **etw.** ~: want sth.; *(im stillen)* wish for sth.; **b)** *(in formelhaften Wünschen)* wish; **jmdm. alles Gute/frohe Ostern** ~: wish sb. all the best/a happy Easter; **c)** *auch itr. V. (begehren)* want; **was** ~ **Sie?, Sie** ~? *(im Lokal)* what would you like?; *(in einem Geschäft)* can I help you?

Wunsch-: ~**kind das** wanted child; ~**konzert das** request concert; *(im Rundfunk)* request programme; ~**zettel der** *(zum Geburtstag o. ä.)* list of presents one would like

wurde *1. u. 3. Pers. Sg. Prät. v.* **werden; würde** *1. u. 3. Pers. Sg. Konjunktiv II v.* **werden**

Würde die; ~ dignity; **würde·los 1.** *Adj.* undignified; *(schimpflich)* disgraceful; **2.** *adv.* in an undignified way; *(schimpflich)* disgracefully; **Würden·träger der** dignitary; **würde·voll 1.** *Adj.* dignified; **2.** *adv.* with dignity; **würdig 1.** *Adj.* **a)** dignified; **b)** *(wert)* worthy; **2.** *adv.* **a)** with dignity; **b)** *(angemessen)* worthily; **würdigen** *tr. V.* **a)** *(anerkennen, beachten)* recognize; *(schätzen)* appreciate; *(lobend hervorheben)* acknowledge; **b)** *(für wert halten)* **jmdn. keines Blickes/keiner Antwort** ~: not deign to look at/answer sb.

Wurf der; ~|e|s, **Würfe a)** throw; *(beim Kegeln)* bowl; **b)** *o. Pl. (das Werfen)* throwing/pitching/bowling; **c)** *(Zool.)* litter

Würfel der; ~s, ~ cube; *(Spiel~)* dice; die *(formal)*; **Würfel·becher der** dice-cup; **würfeln 1.** *itr. V.* throw the dice; **um etw.** ~: play dice for sth.; **2.**

tr. V. **a)** throw; **b)** *(in Würfel schneiden)* dice
Würfel-: ~**spiel** das dice; *(Brettspiel)*
dice game; ~**zucker** der; *o. Pl.* cube
sugar
würgen 1. *tr. V.* strangle; throttle; **2.**
itr. V. (Brechreiz haben) retch
Wurm der; ~|e|s, **Würmer** worm; *(Ma-
de)* maggot; **wurmig** *Adj.,* **wurmstichig** *Adj.* worm-eaten; *(madig)*
maggoty
Wurst die; ~, **Würste** sausage; **es geht
um die** ~ *(fig. ugs.)* the crunch has
come; **jmdm. ist jmd./etw.** ~ *(ugs.)* sb.
doesn't care about sb./sth.; **Würstchen** das; ~s, ~ **a)** [small] sausage;
Frankfurter/Wiener ~: frankfurter/
wienerwurst; **b)** *(fig. ugs.)* nobody;
(hilfloser Mensch) poor soul; **Würst-
chen·bude** die sausage-stand
Würze die; ~, ~n spice; seasoning
Wurzel die; ~, ~n *(auch fig.)* root;
wurzeln *itr. V.* take root
würzen *tr. V.* season; **würzig** *Adj.*
tasty; full-flavoured *(beer, wine)*; aromatic *(fragrance)*; tangy *(air)*
wusch *1. u. 3. Pers. Sg. Prät. v. waschen*
wußte *1. und 3. Pers. Sg. Prät. v. wissen;* **wüßte** *1. und 3. Pers. Sg. Konjunktiv II v. wissen*
wüst 1. *Adj.* **a)** *(öde)* desolate; **b)** *(unordentlich)* chaotic; **c)** *(ungezügelt)*
wild; *(unanständig)* rude; **2.** *adv.* **a)**
(unordentlich) chaotically; **b)** *(ungezügelt)* wildly
Wüste die; ~, ~n desert
Wut die; ~: rage; fury; **wüten** *itr. V.*
(auch fig.) rage; *(zerstören)* wreak
havoc; **wütend 1.** *Adj.* furious;
angry *(voice, mob)*; **2.** *adv.* furiously;
in a fury

X

¹**x, X** [ɪks] das; ~, ~: x, X
²**x** *unbest. Zahlwort (ugs.)* umpteen
(coll.)
x-Achse die *(Math.)* x-axis
X-Beine *Pl.* knock-knees

x-beliebig *Adj. (ugs.)* irgendein ~er/
irgendeine ~e/irgendein ~es any old
(coll. attrib.); jeder ~e Ort any old
place *(coll.)*
x-fach 1. *Vervielfältigungsz.* die ~e
Menge *(Math.)* x times the amount;
(ugs.) umpteen times the amount
(coll.); **2.** *adv. (ugs.)* ~ erprobt sein
(tested etc.) umpteen times *(coll.)*;
x-mal *Adv. (ugs.)* umpteen times
(coll.)
x-t... *Ordinalz. (ugs.)* umpteenth *(coll.)*

Y

y, Y [ˈʏpsilɔn] das; ~, ~: y, Y
y-Achse die *(Math.)* y-axis
Yacht *s.* Jacht
Yoga *s.* Joga
Ypsilon das; ~|s|, ~s y, Y; *(im griechi-
schen Alphabet)* upsilon

Z

z, Z [tsɛt] das; ~, ~: z, Z
Zacke die; ~, ~n point; peak; *(einer
Säge, eines Kamms)* tooth; *(einer Gabel, Harke)* prong; **Zacken** der; ~s,
~ *s.* Zacke
zaghaft 1. *Adj.* timid; *(zögernd)*
hesitant; **2.** *adv.* timidly; *(zögernd)*
hesitantly; **Zaghaftigkeit** die; ~:
timidity; *(Zögern)* hesitancy
zäh 1. *Adj.* **a)** tough *(dough,
soil)*; *(dickflüssig)* glutinous; viscous
(oil); **b)** *(widerstandsfähig)* tough *(person)*; **c)** *(beharrlich)* tenacious; tough
(negotiations); dogged *(resistance)*; **2.**
adv. (beharrlich) tenaciously; *(resist)*
doggedly; **Zähigkeit** die; ~ **a)** *(Widerstandsfähigkeit)* toughness; **b)** *(Be-*

harrlichkeit) tenacity; **mit** ~: tenaciously

Zahl die; ~, ~en number; *(Ziffer)* numeral; *(Zahlenangabe, Geldmenge)* figure; **in den roten/schwarzen** ~en in the red/black; **zahlbar** *Adj. (Kaufmannsspr.)* payable; **zahlen** 1. *tr. V.* pay **(an** + *Akk.* to); 2. *itr. V.* pay; ~ **bitte!** *(im Lokal)* [can I/we have] the bill, please!; **zählen** 1. *itr. V.* **a)** count; **zu einer Gruppe** *usw.* ~: be one of *or* belong to a group *etc.;* **b)** **auf jmdn./etw.** ~: count on sb./sth; 2. *tr. V.* count; **jmdn. zu seinen Freunden** ~: count sb. among one's friends

zahl-, Zahl-: ~**karte** die *(Postw.)* paying-in slip; ~**los** *Adj.* countless; ~**reich** *Adj.* numerous

Zahlung die; ~, ~en payment; **Zählung** die; ~, ~en counting; **eine** ~: a count; **Zahlungs·mittel das** means of payment; **Zahl·wort das;** *Pl.* ~**wörter** *(Sprachw.)* numeral

zahm 1. *Adj.* tame; 2. *adv.* tamely; **zähmen** *tr. V. (auch fig.)* tame

Zahn der; ~[e]s, **Zähne** tooth; *(Raubtier~)* fang; *(an einer Briefmarke usw.)* serration

Zahn-: ~**arzt** der dentist; *(mit chirurgischer Ausbildung)* dental surgeon; ~**bürste** die toothbrush

zahnen *itr. V. (baby)* be teething

zahn-, Zahn-: ~**fleisch das** gum; *(als Ganzes)* gums *pl.;* ~**los** *Adj.* toothless; ~**lücke** die gap in one's teeth; ~**pasta** die; ~, ~**pasten** toothpaste; ~**prothese** die dentures *pl.;* [set *sing.* of] false teeth *pl.;* ~**schmerzen** *Pl.* toothache *sing.;* ~**stocher** der; ~s, ~: toothpick; ~**weh das;** *o. Pl. (ugs.)* toothache

Zange die; ~, ~n a) *(Werkzeug)* pliers *pl.; (Eiswürfel~, Zucker~)* tongs *pl.; (Geburts~)* forceps *pl.; (Knei/~)* pincers *pl.;* **eine** ~: a pair of pliers/tongs/forceps/pincers *pl.;* **b)** *(bei Tieren)* pincer

Zank der; ~[e]s squabble; row; **zanken** *refl. (auch itr.) V.* squabble, bicker **(um** *od.* **über** + *Akk.* over); **zänkisch** *Adj.* quarrelsome

Zäpfchen das; ~s, ~ suppository; **zapfen** *tr. V.* tap, draw *(beer, wine);* **Zapfen** der; ~s, ~ **a)** *(Bot.)* cone; **b)** *(Stöpsel)* bung; **Zapf·säule** die petrol-pump *(Brit.);* gasoline pump *(Amer.)*

zappeln *itr. V.* wriggle; *(child)* fidget **Zar** der; ~en, ~en *(hist.)* Tsar; **Zarin** die; ~, ~nen *(hist.)* Tsarina

zart 1. *Adj. (auch fig.)* delicate; soft *(skin);* tender *(bud, shoot; meat, vegetables);* fine *(biscuits);* gentle *(kiss, touch);* soft *(pastel colours);* 2. *adv. (empfindlich)* delicately; *(kiss, touch)* gently; **zärtlich** 1. *Adj.* tender; 2. *adv.* tenderly; **Zärtlichkeit** die; ~, ~en a) *o. Pl. (Zuneigung)* tenderness; affection; **b)** *meist Pl. (Liebkosung)* caress

Zauber der; ~s, ~ a) *(auch fig.)* magic; *(Bann)* [magic] spell; **b)** *o. Pl. (ugs. abwertend: Aufheben)* fuss; **Zauberei** die; ~, ~en a) *o. Pl. (das Zaubern)* magic; **b)** *(Zaubertrick)* magic trick; **Zauberer** der; ~s, ~: magician; **zauber·haft** 1. *Adj.* enchanting; 2. *adv.* enchantingly; **Zauberin** die; ~, ~nen a) sorceress; **b)** *(Zauberkünstlerin)* conjurer; **Zauber·künstler** der conjurer; magician; **zaubern** 1. *itr. V.* **a)** do magic; **b)** *(Zaubertricks ausführen)* do conjuring tricks; 2. *tr. V. (auch fig.)* conjure

zaudern *itr. V. (geh.)* delay

Zaum der; ~[e]s, **Zäume** bridle; **zäumen** *tr. V.* bridle; **Zaum·zeug das** bridle

Zaun der; ~[e]s, **Zäune** fence; **Zaun·könig** der wren

z. B. *Abk.* zum Beispiel e.g.

ZDF [tset|de:'|ɛf] das; ~ *Abk.* Zweites Deutsches Fernsehen Second German Television Channel

Zebra das; ~s, ~s zebra; **Zebra·streifen** der zebra crossing *(Brit.);* pedestrian crossing

Zeche die; ~, ~n a) *(Rechnung)* bill *(Brit.);* check *(Amer.);* **b)** *(Bergwerk)* pit; mine; **zechen** *itr. V. (veralt., scherzh.)* tipple

Zeh der; ~s, ~en, **Zehe** die; ~, ~n a) toe; **b)** *(Knoblauch~)* clove; **Zehen·spitze** die: **auf** ~n on tiptoe

zehn *Kardinalz.* ten; **Zehn** die; ~, ~en ten; **Zehner** der; ~s, ~ a) *(ugs.: Geldschein, Münze)* ten; **b)** *(ugs.: Autobus)* number ten; **c)** *(Math.)* ten; **zehn·fach** Vervielfältigungsz. tenfold; **Zehnfache das** *adj. Dekl.* das ~: ten times as much

zehn-, Zehn-: ~**kampf** der *(Sport)* decathlon; ~**mal** *Adv.* ten times; ~**mark·schein** der ten-mark note; ~**pfennig·[brief]marke** die ten-pfennig stamp; ~**pfennig·stück** das ten-pfennig piece

zehnt... *Ordinalz.* tenth; **zehn·tausend** *Kardinalz.* ten thousand;

zehntel *Bruchz.* tenth; **Zehntel das** (*schweiz. meist* der); **~s, ~:** tenth; **zehntens** *Adv.* tenthly

zehren *itr. V.* **von etw. ~:** live on or off sth.

Zeichen das; ~s, ~ sign; (*Markierung*) mark; (*Chemie, Math., auf Landkarten usw.*) symbol; **jmdm. ein ~ geben** signal to sb.

Zeichen-: ~setzung die punctuation; **~sprache die** sign language

zeichnen 1. *tr. V.* draw; (*fig.*) portray ⟨*character*⟩; **2.** *itr. V.* draw; **Zeichner der; ~s, ~, Zeichnerin die; ~, ~nen** graphic artist; (*Technik*) draughtsman/-woman; **Zeichnung die; ~, ~en** drawing

Zeige·finger der index finger; forefinger; **zeigen 1.** *itr. V.* point; **2.** *tr. V.* show; **3.** *refl. V.* **a)** (*sich sehen lassen*) appear; **b)** (*sich erweisen*) prove to be; **es wird sich ~, ...:** time will tell ...; **Zeiger der; ~s, ~:** pointer; (*Uhr~*) hand

Zeile die; ~, ~n line; (*Reihe*) row

zeit *Präp. mit Gen.* **~ meines** usw./**unseres** usw. **Lebens** all my *etc.* life/our *etc.* lives; **Zeit die; ~, ~en a)** o. Pl. time *no art.*; **mit der ~:** with or in time; (*allmählich*) gradually; **b)** (*~punkt*) time; **zur ~:** at the moment; **c)** (*~abschnitt, Lebensabschnitt*) time; period; (*Geschichtsabschnitt*) age; period; **d)** (*Sprachw.*) tense

zeit-, Zeit-: ~alter das age; era; **~gemäß** *Adj.* (*modern*) up-to-date; (*aktuell*) topical ⟨*theme*⟩; contemporary ⟨*views*⟩; **; ~genosse der, ~genossin die** contemporary; **~genössisch** *Adj.* contemporary; **~geschehen das: das** [aktuelle] **~geschehen** current events *pl.*

zeitig *Adj., adv.* early

Zeit·lang die: eine ~: for a while; **zeit·lebens** *Adv.* all one's life; **zeitlich 1.** *Adj.* ⟨*length, interval*⟩ in time; chronological ⟨*order, sequence*⟩; **2.** *adv.* with regard to time

zeit-, Zeit-: ~los 1. *Adj.* timeless; classic ⟨*fashion, shape*⟩; **2.** *adv.* timelessly; **~lupe die;** o. Pl. slow motion; **~punkt der** moment; **~raubend** *Adj.* time-consuming; **~raum der** period; **~schrift die** magazine; (*bes. wissenschaftlich*) journal; periodical; **~spanne die** period

Zeitung die; ~, ~en [news]paper; **Zeitungs·notiz die** newspaper item

zeit-, Zeit-: ~verschwendung

die waste of time; **~vertreib der; ~[e]s, ~e** pastime; **zum ~vertreib** to pass the time; **~weilig 1.** *Adj.* temporary; **2.** *adv.* temporarily; **~weise** *Adv.* (*gelegentlich*) occasionally; (*von Zeit zu Zeit*) from time to time; **~wort das; Pl. ~wörter** (*Sprachw.*) verb

Zelle die; ~, ~n cell

Zelluloid [tsɛluˈlɔyt] **das; ~[e]s** celluloid

Zelt das; ~[e]s, ~e tent; (*Fest~*) marquee; (*Zirkus~*) big top; **zelten** *itr. V.* camp

Zelt-: ~lager das camp; **~plane die** tarpaulin

Zement der; ~[e]s, ~e cement

Zensur die; ~, ~en mark; grade (*Amer.*)

Zenti- [tsɛnti-]: **~meter der,** *auch:* **das** centimetre; **~meter·maß das** [centimetre] measuring-tape

Zentner der; ~s, ~ a) metric hundredweight; **b)** (*österr., schweiz.*) s. Doppelzentner

zentral 1. *Adj.* central; **2.** *adv.* centrally; **Zentrale die; ~, ~n a)** (*zentrale Stelle*) head or central office; (*der Polizei, einer Partei*) headquarters *sing.* or *pl.;* (*Funk~*) control centre; **b)** (*Telefon~*) [telephone] exchange; (*eines Hotels, einer Firma o. ä.*) switchboard; **Zentral·heizung die** central heating

Zentren s. Zentrum

Zentrifugal·kraft die (*Physik*) centrifugal force; **Zentrifuge die; ~, ~n** centrifuge

Zentrum das; ~s, Zentren centre; **im ~:** at the centre; (*im Stadt~*) in the town/city centre

Zeppelin der; ~s, ~e Zeppelin

Zepter das, *auch:* **der; ~s, ~:** sceptre

zerbeißen *unr. itr. V.* bite in two

zerbersten *unr. itr. V.; mit sein* burst apart

zerbrechen 1. *unr. itr. V.; mit sein* break [into pieces]; smash [to pieces]; ⟨*glass*⟩ shatter; (*fig.*) ⟨*marriage, relationship*⟩ break up; **2.** *unr. tr. V.* break; smash; shatter ⟨*dishes, glass*⟩; **zerbrechlich** *Adj.* fragile; (*fig.*) frail

zerbröckeln 1. *itr. V.; mit sein* crumble away; **2.** *tr. V.* break into small pieces

zerdrücken *tr. V.* mash

Zeremonie die; ~, ~n ceremony; (*fig.*) ritual; **Zeremoniell das; ~s, ~e** ceremonial

zerfallen *unr. itr. V.; mit sein* **a)** (*auch*

fig.) disintegrate (**in** + *Akk.*, **zu** into); ⟨*building*⟩ fall into ruin, decay; ⟨*corpse*⟩ decompose, decay

zerfetzen *tr. V.* rip or tear to pieces; (*fig.*) tear apart ⟨*body, limb*⟩

zerfleischen *tr. V.* tear ⟨*person, animal*⟩ limb from limb

zerfressen *unr. tr. V.* **a)** eat away; ⟨*moth etc.*⟩ eat holes in; **b)** *(zersetzen)* corrode ⟨*metal*⟩; eat away ⟨*bone*⟩

zergehen *unr. itr. V.; mit sein* melt; *(in Wasser, im Mund)* ⟨*tablet etc.*⟩ dissolve

zerhacken *tr. V.* chop up (**zu** into)

zerhauen *unr. tr. V.* chop up

zerkleinern *tr. V.* chop up *(zermahlen)* ⟨*rock etc.*⟩

zerknautschen *tr. V. (ugs.)* crumple

zerknirscht **1.** *Adj.* remorseful; **2.** *adv.* remorsefully

zerknittern *tr. V.* crease; crumple

zerknüllen *tr. V.* crumple up [into a ball]

zerkratzen *tr. V.* scratch

zerkrümeln *tr. V.* crumble up

zerlegen *tr. V.* **a)** dismantle; take to pieces; **b)** *(zerschneiden)* cut up ⟨*animal, meat*⟩; carve ⟨*joint*⟩

zerplatzen *itr. V.; mit sein* burst

Zerr·bild das distorted image

zerreiben *unr. tr. V.* crush

zerreißen **1.** *unr. tr. V.* **a)** tear up; *(in kleine Stücke)* tear to pieces; break ⟨*thread*⟩; **b)** *(beschädigen)* tear ⟨*stocking, trousers, etc.*⟩ (**an** + *Dat.* on); **2.** *unr. itr. V.; mit sein* ⟨*thread, string, rope*⟩ break; ⟨*paper, cloth, etc.*⟩ tear

zerren **1.** *tr. V.* **a)** drag; **b)** **sich** *(Dat.)* **einen Muskel/eine Sehne ~:** pull a muscle/tendon; **2.** *itr. V.* **an etw.** *(Dat.) ~ :* tug or pull at sth.; **Zerrung** die; ~, ~**en** pulled muscle/tendon

zerrütten *tr. V.* ruin; shatter ⟨*nerves*⟩

zerschellen *itr. V.; mit sein* be dashed or smashed to pieces

zerschlagen **1.** *unr. tr. V.* smash ⟨*plate, windscreen, etc.*⟩; smash up ⟨*furniture*⟩; (*fig.*) smash ⟨*spy ring etc.*⟩; **2.** *unr. refl. V.* ⟨*plan, deal*⟩ fall through

zerschmettern *tr. V.* smash; shatter ⟨*glass, leg, bone*⟩

zerschneiden *unr. tr. V.* cut; *(in Stücke)* cut up; *(in zwei Teile)* cut in two

zersetzen *tr. V.* corrode ⟨*metal*⟩; decompose ⟨*organism*⟩

zersplittern *itr. V.; mit sein* ⟨*wood, bone*⟩ splinter; ⟨*glass*⟩ shatter

zerspringen *itr. V.; mit sein* shatter; *(Sprünge bekommen)* crack

zerstäuben *tr. V.* spray

zerstören *tr. V.* destroy; ⟨*hooligan*⟩ smash up, vandalize; (*fig.*) ruin ⟨*health, life*⟩; **Zerstörung** die *s.* **zerstören:** destruction; smashing up; vandalization; (*fig.*) ruin[ation]

zerstreuen **1.** *tr. V.* scatter; disperse ⟨*crowd*⟩; **jmdn./sich ~** *(ablenken)* take sb.'s/one's mind off things; **2.** *refl. V.* disperse; *(schneller)* scatter; **zerstreut 1.** *Adj.* distracted; *(vergeßlich)* absent-minded; **2.** *adv.* absentmindedly; **Zerstreuung** die; ~, ~**en** *(Ablenkung)* diversion

zerstückeln *tr. V.* break ⟨*sth.*⟩ up into small pieces; *(zerschneiden)* cut or chop ⟨*sth.*⟩ up into small pieces; dismember ⟨*corpse*⟩

zerteilen *tr. V.* divide into pieces; *(zerschneiden)* cut into pieces; cut up

Zertifikat das; ~[e]s, ~e certificate

zertrampeln *tr. V.* trample all over ⟨*flower-bed etc.*⟩; trample ⟨*child etc.*⟩ underfoot

zertreten *unr. tr. V.* stamp on; stamp out ⟨*cigarette, match*⟩

zertrümmern *tr. V.* smash; smash, shatter ⟨*glass*⟩; smash up ⟨*furniture*⟩; wreck ⟨*car, boat*⟩; reduce ⟨*building*⟩ to ruins

Zerwürfnis das; ~ses, ~se *(geh.)* quarrel; dispute; *(Bruch)* rift

zerzausen *tr. V.* ruffle; **zerzaust aussehen** look dishevelled

zetern *itr. V.* scold [shrilly]; *(sich beklagen)* moan (**über** + *Akk.* about)

Zettel der; ~s, ~: slip or piece of paper; *(mit einigen Zeilen)* note; *(Bekanntmachung)* notice; *(Formular)* form; *(Kassen~)* receipt; *(Hand~)* leaflet

Zeug das; ~[e]s, ~e **a)** *o. Pl. (ugs.)* **dummes ~:** nonsense: rubbish; **b)** *(Kleidung)* things *pl.*; **Zeuge** der; ~**n**, ~**n** witness

zeugen *tr. V.* procreate; ⟨*man*⟩ father ⟨*child*⟩

Zeugen·aussage die testimony; **Zeugin** die; ~, ~**nen** witness; **Zeugnis** das; ~ses, ~se **a)** *(Schulw.)* report; **b)** *(Arbeits~)* reference; testimonial; **c)** *(Gutachten)* certificate

Zeugung die; ~, ~**en** procreation; *(eines Kindes)* fathering; **zeugungsfähig** *Adj.* fertile

z. Hd. *Abk.* **zu Händen** attn.

Zickzack der; ~[e]s, ~e zigzag

Ziege die; ~, ~**n** goat; *(Schimpfwort: Frau)* cow *(sl. derog.)*

Ziegel der; ~s, ~ brick; *(Dach~)* tile; **Ziegel·stein** der brick

Ziegen-: ~**bock** der he- *or* billy-goat; ~**käse** der goat's cheese

ziehen 1. *unr. tr. V.* **a)** pull; *(sanfter)* draw; *(zerren)* tug; *(schleppen)* drag; **etw. nach sich ~** *(fig.)* result in sth.; entail sth.; **b)** *(heraus~)* extract *(tooth)*; take out, remove *(stitches)*; draw *(cord, sword, pistol)*; **den Hut ~:** raise one's hat; **die [Quadrat]wurzel ~** *(Math.)* extract the square root; **c)** *(dehnen)* stretch *(elastic etc.)*; stretch out *(sheets etc.)*; **d)** *(Gesichtspartien bewegen)* make *(face, grimace)*; **e)** *(bei Brettspielen)* move *(chess-man etc.)*; **f)** *(zeichnen)* draw *(line etc.)*; **g)** *(anlegen)* dig *(trench)*; build *(wall)*; erect *(fence)*; put up *(washing-line)*; run, lay *(cable, wires)*; draw *(frontier)*; **h)** *(auf~)* grow *(plants, flowers)*; breed *(animals)*; 2. *unr. itr. V.* **a)** *(reißen)* pull; **an etw.** *(Dat.)* ~: pull on sth.; **b)** *(funktionieren)* *(stove, pipe, chimney)* draw; **c)** *mit sein (um~)* move *(nach, in + Akk.* to); **d)** *mit sein (gehen)* go; *(marschieren)* march; *(umherstreifen)* roam; *(weggehen)* go away; leave; *(fog, clouds)* drift; **e)** *(saugen)* draw; **an einer Zigarette/Pfeife ~:** draw on a cigarette/pipe; **f)** *(tea, coffee)* draw; **g)** *(Kochk.)* simmer; **h)** *unpers.* es zieht there's a draught; 3. *unr. refl. V.* *(road)* run, stretch; *(frontier)* run; **Zieh·harmonika** die piano accordion; **Ziehung** die; ~, ~en draw

Ziel das; ~[e]s, ~e **a)** destination; **b)** *(Sport)* finish; *(~linie)* finishing-line; *(Pferderennen)* finishing-post; **c)** *(~scheibe; auch Milit.)* target; **d)** *(Zweck)* aim; goal; **sein ~ erreichen** achieve one's objective *or* aim; **ziel·bewußt** 1. *Adj.* determined; 2. *adv.* determinedly; **zielen** *itr. V.* aim **(auf + Akk.,** at); *(fig.)* **auf jmdn./etw. ~** *(reproach, efforts, etc.)* be aimed at sb./sth.

ziel-, Ziel-: ~**los** 1. *Adj.* aimless; 2. *adv.* aimlessly; ~**scheibe** die *(auch fig.)* target *(Gen.* for); ~**strebig** 1. *Adj.* **a)** purposeful; **b)** *(energisch)* single-minded *(person)*; 2. *adv.* **a)** purposefully; **b)** *(energisch)* single-mindedly

ziemlich 1. *Adj.* *(ugs.)* fair, sizeable *(quantity, number)*; 2. *adv.* **a)** quite; fairly; **b)** *(ugs.: fast)* pretty well

Zierde die; ~, ~n *(auch fig.)* ornament; **zieren** *refl. V.* be coy; **zierlich**

1. *Adj.* dainty; petite, dainty *(woman, figure)*; 2. *adv.* daintily

Ziffer die; ~, ~n numeral; *(in einer mehrstelligen Zahl)* digit; figure; **Ziffer·blatt** das dial; face

-**zig, zig** *unbest. Zahlwort (ugs.)* umpteen *(coll.)*

Zigarette die; ~, ~n cigarette; **Zigarillo** der *od.* das; ~, ~s cigarillo; small cigar; **Zigarre** die; ~, ~n cigar

Zigeuner der; ~s, ~, **Zigeunerin** die; ~, ~nen gypsy

zig·mal *Adv. (ugs.)* umpteen times *(coll.)*; **zig·tausend** *unbest. Zahlwort (ugs.)* umpteen thousand *(coll.)*

Zimmer das; ~s, ~: room; **Zimmermädchen** das chambermaid

zimmern *tr. V.* make *(shelves etc.)*; **Zimmer·suche** die room-hunt

zimperlich 1. *Adj.* timid; *(leicht angeekelt)* squeamish; *(prüde)* prissy; 2. *adv.: s. Adj.:* timidly; squeamishly; prissily

Zimt der; ~[e]s, ~e cinnamon

Zink das; ~[e]s zinc

Zinke die; ~, ~n prong; *(eines Kammes)* tooth

Zinn das; ~[e]s tin; *(Gegenstände)* pewter[ware]

Zins der; ~es, ~en interest; **Zinses·zins** der compound interest

zins·los 1. *Adj.* interest-free; 2. *adv.* free of interest; **Zins·satz** der interest rate

Zipfel der; ~s, ~ *(einer Decke, eines Tisch-, Handtuchs usw.)* corner; *(Wurst~, eines Halstuchs)* [tail-]end; **Zipfel·mütze** die [long-]pointed cap

zirka *Adv.* about; approximately

Zirkulation die; ~, ~en circulation; **zirkulieren** *itr. V.; auch mit sein* circulate

Zirkus der; ~, ~se **a)** circus; **b)** *(ugs.) o. Pl. (Trubel)* hustle and bustle; *(Krach)* to-do

zirpen *itr. V.* chirp

zischeln *tr. V.* whisper angrily

zischen *itr. V.* **a)** hiss; *(hot fat)* sizzle; **b)** *mit sein* hiss

Zitat das; ~[e]s, ~e quotation *(aus* from)

zitieren *tr., itr. V.* **a)** quote; *(Rechtsspr.)* cite; **b)** *(rufen)* summon

Zitronat das; ~[e]s candied lemon-peel; **Zitrone** die; ~, ~n lemon

Zitronen-: ~**limonade** die lemonade; ~**presse** die lemon-squeezer; ~**saft** der lemon-juice

Zitrus·frucht die citrus fruit

zittern itr. V. tremble (**vor** + Dat. with); (vor Kälte) shiver; (beben) ⟨walls, windows⟩ shake; **vor jmdm./ etw. ~**: be terrified of sb./sth.; **zittrig** Adj. shaky; doddery ⟨old man⟩

Zitze die; ~, ~n teat

zivil 1. Adj. **a)** civilian; non-military ⟨purposes⟩; civil ⟨aviation, marriage, law, defence⟩; **b)** (annehmbar) decent; 2. adv. (annehmbar) decently; **Zivil** das; ~s civilian clothes pl.; **Zivil·bevölkerung** die civilian population; **Zivilisation** [tsiviliza'tsio:n] die; ~, ~en civilization; **zivilisieren** tr. V. civilize; **zivilisiert** 1. Adj. civilized; 2. adv. in a civilized way; **Zivilist** der; ~en, ~en civilian; **Zivil·kleidung** die civilian clothes pl.

Zofe die; ~, ~n (hist.) lady's maid

zog 1. u. 3. Pers. Sg. Prät. v. ziehen

zögern itr. V. hesitate; **ohne zu ~**: without hesitation

Zoll der; ~[e]s, Zölle Adj.) [customs] duty; **b)** o. Pl. (Behörde) customs pl.

zoll-, Zoll-: **~amt** das customs house or office; **~beamte** der customs officer; **~frei** 1. Adj. duty-free; free of duty ⟨pred.⟩; 2. adv. free of duty; **~kontrolle** die customs examination or check; **~stock** der folding rule

Zone die; ~, ~n zone

Zoo der; ~s, ~s zoo; **Zoologe** der; ~n, ~n zoologist; **Zoologie** die; ~: zoology no art.; **zoologisch** Adj. zoological; **~er Garten** zoological gardens pl.

Zoom das; ~s, ~s (Film, Fot.: Objektiv) zoom; **Zoom·objektiv** das (Film, Fot.) zoom lens

Zopf der; ~[e]s, Zöpfe plait; (am Hinterkopf) pigtail

Zorn der; ~[e]s anger; (stärker) wrath; fury; **zornig** 1. Adj. furious; 2. adv. furiously

Zote die; ~, ~n dirty joke; **zotig** 1. Adj. smutty; dirty ⟨joke⟩; 2. adv. smuttily

zottig Adj. shaggy

zu 1. Präp. mit Dat. **a)** (Richtung) to; **zu ... hin** towards ...; **b)** (zusammen mit) with; **zu dem Käse gab es Wein** there was wine with the cheese; **c)** (Lage) at; **zu beiden Seiten** on both sides; **d)** (zeitlich) at; **zu Weihnachten** at Christmas; **e)** (Art u. Weise) **zu meiner Zufriedenheit/Überraschung** to my satisfaction/surprise; (bei Mengenangaben o. ä) **zu Dutzenden/zweien** by the dozen/in twos; **f)** (ein Zahlen-

verhältnis ausdrückend) **ein Verhältnis von 3 zu 1** a ratio of 3 to 1; **g)** (einen Preis zuordnend) at; for; **h)** (Zweck) for; **i)** (Ziel, Ergebnis) into; **zu etw. werden** turn into sth.; **j)** (über) about; on; **sich zu etw. äußern** comment on sth.; **k)** (gegenüber) freundlich/häßlich **zu jmdm. sein** be friendly/nasty to sb.; s. auch **zum**; **zur**; 2. Adv. **a)** (allzu) too; **zu sehr** too much; **b)** (nachgestellt) (Richtung) towards; 3. Konj. **a)** (mit Infinitiv) to; **was gibt's da zu lachen?** what is there to laugh about?; **b)** (mit 1. Part.) **die zu erledigende Post** the letters pl. to be dealt with

Zubehör das; ~[e]s, ~e od. schweiz. ~den accessories pl.; (eines Staubsaugers, Mixers o. ä.) attachments pl.; (Ausstattung) equipment

zu|bereiten tr. V. prepare ⟨meal etc.⟩; make up ⟨medicine, ointment⟩; (kochen) cook ⟨fish, meat, etc.⟩

zu|billigen tr. V. **jmdm. etw. ~**: grant or allow sb. sth.

zu|binden unr. tr. V. tie [up]

zu|blinzeln itr. V. **jmdm. ~**: wink at sb.

zu|bringen unr. tr. V. spend; **Zubringer** der; ~s, ~ **a)** (Straße) access road; **b)** (Verkehrsmittel) shuttle

Zucht die; ~, ~en **a)** breeding; (von Pflanzen) cultivation; **ein Pferd aus deutscher ~**: a German-bred horse; **b)** o. Pl. (geh.: Disziplin) discipline; **züchten** tr. V. (auch fig.) breed; cultivate ⟨plants⟩; culture ⟨bacteria, pearls⟩; **Züchter** der; ~s, ~, **Züchterin** die; ~, ~nen breeder; (von Pflanzen) grower [of new varieties]; **Züchtung** die; ~, ~en **a)** breeding; (von Pflanzen) cultivation; **b)** (Zuchtergebnis) strain

zucken itr. V.; mit Richtungsangabe mit sein twitch; ⟨body, arm, leg, etc.⟩ jerk; (vor Schreck) start; ⟨flames⟩ flicker; **mit den Achseln/Schultern ~**: shrug one's shoulders; **zücken** tr. V. draw ⟨sword, dagger, knife⟩

Zucker der; ~s, ~ **a)** sugar; **b)** o. Pl. (ugs.: ~krankheit) diabetes; **~ haben** be a diabetic

zucker-, Zucker-: **~dose** die sugar bowl; **~hut** der sugar loaf; **~krank** Adj. diabetic

zuckern tr. V. sugar

Zuckung die; ~, ~en twitch

zu|decken tr. V. cover up; cover [over] ⟨well, ditch⟩; **jmdn./sich ~**: tuck sb./oneself up

zu|drehen *tr. V.* **a)** *(abdrehen)* turn off; **b)** *(zuwenden)* **jmdm. den Rücken ~:** turn one's back on sb.

zu|dringlich 1. *Adj.* pushy *(coll.)*, pushing *(person, manner)*; *(sexuell)* importunate *(person, manner)*; *(prying (glance)*; **2.** *adv.* importunately; **Zu|dringlichkeit die** ~, ~en **a)** *o. Pl.* pushiness *(coll.)*; *(in sexueller Hinsicht)* importunate manner; **b)** *(Handlung)* ~en insistent advances *or* attentions

zu|drücken *tr. V.* press shut; push *(door)* shut; **jmdm. die Kehle ~:** choke *or* throttle sb.

zu·einander *Adv.* to one another

zu·erst *Adv.* **a)** first; **b)** *(anfangs)* at first; to start with; **c)** *(erstmals)* first

Zu|fahrt die a) *o. Pl.* access [for vehicles]; **b)** *(Straße, Weg)* access road; *(zum Haus)* driveway; **Zu|fahrts·straße die** access road

Zu·fall der chance; *(zufälliges Zusammentreffen von Ereignissen)* coincidence; **durch ~:** by chance; **zu|fallen** *unr. itr. V.; mit sein* ⟨*door etc.*⟩ slam shut; *(zum Haus)* close; **b)** *(zukommen)* **jmdm. ~** *⟨task⟩* fall to sb.; *⟨prize, inheritance⟩* go to sb.; **zu·fällig 1.** *Adj.* accidental; chance *attrib.* ⟨*meeting, acquaintance*⟩; random ⟨*selection*⟩; **2.** *adv.* by chance; **wissen Sie ~, wie spät es ist?** *(ugs.)* do you by any chance know the time?; **Zufalls·treffer der** fluke

zu|fassen *itr. V.* make a snatch *or* grab

zu|fliegen *unr. itr. V.; mit sein (ugs.)* ⟨*door, window, etc.*⟩ slam shut

Zu·flucht die refuge (**vor** + *Dat.* from); *(vor Unwetter o. ä.)* shelter (**vor** + *Dat.* from); **Zuflucht·ort der** place of refuge; sanctuary

Zu·fluß der a) *o. Pl. (das Zufließen)* inflow; supply; *(fig.)* influx; **b)** *(Gewässer)* feeder stream/river

zu|flüstern *tr. V.* **jmdm. etw. ~:** whisper sth. to sb.

zu·folge *Präp. mit Dat.; nachgestellt* according to

zu·frieden 1. *Adj.* contented; *(befriedigt)* satisfied; **mit etw. ~ sein** be satisfied with sth.; **2.** *adv.* contentedly; **zufrieden|geben** *unr. refl. V.* be satisfied; **Zufriedenheit die** ~: contentment; *(Befriedigung)* satisfaction; **zufrieden|stellen** *tr. V.* satisfy; **zu|friedenstellend 1.** *Adj.* satisfactory; **2.** *adv.* satisfactorily

zu|frieren *unr. itr. V.; mit sein* freeze over

zu|fügen *tr. V.* **jmdm. etw. ~:** inflict sth. on sb.; **jmdm. Schaden/[ein] Unrecht ~:** do sb. harm/an injustice

Zufuhr die ~: supply; *(Material)* supplies *pl.*; **zu|führen 1.** *itr. V.* **auf etw.** *(Akk.)* **~:** lead towards sth.; **2.** *tr. V.* **a)** *(zuleiten)* **einer Sache** *(Dat.)* **etw. ~:** supply sth. to sth.; **b)** *(bringen)* **einer Partei Mitglieder ~:** bring new members to a party

Zug der; ~[e]s, Züge **a)** *(Bahn)* train; **b)** *(Kolonne)* column; *(Umzug)* procession; *(Demonstrations~)* march; **c)** *(das Ziehen)* pull; traction *(Phys.)*; **d)** *(Vorrichtung)* pull; **e)** *(Wanderung)* migration; **f)** *(beim Brettspiel)* move; **g)** *(Schluck)* swig *(coll.)*; mouthful; *(großer Schluck)* gulp; **das Glas auf einen ~ leeren** empty the glass at one go; **h)** *(beim Rauchen)* pull; drag *(coll.)*; **i)** *(Atem~)* breath; **j)** *o. Pl. (Zugluft; beim Ofen)* draught; **k)** *(Gesichts~)* feature; *(Wesens~)* characteristic; trait

Zu·gabe die a) *(Geschenk)* [free] gift; **b)** *(im Konzert, Theater)* encore

Zu·gang der a) *(Weg, auch fig.)* access; *(Eingang)* entrance; **b)** *o. Pl. (das Hinzukommen) (von Personen)* intake; *(von Patienten)* admission; *(Zuwachs)* increase (von in); **zu·gange: ~ sein** *(ugs.)* be busy *or* occupied; **zugänglich** *Adj.* **a)** accessible; *(geöffnet)* open; *(zur Verfügung stehend)* available *(Dat., für* to); *(verständlich)* accessible *(Dat.,* für to); **c)** *(aufgeschlossen)* approachable *(person)*

zu·geben *unr. tr. V.* admit; admit to ⟨*deed, crime*⟩

zu·gegen *Adj.* **~ sein** be present

zu|gehen *unr. itr. V.; mit sein* **a) auf jmdn./etw. ~:** approach sb./sth.; **b) jmdm. ~** *(zugeschickt werden)* be sent to sb.; **c)** *(ugs.: sich schließen)* close; shut; **die Tür geht nicht zu** the door will not shut

Zügel der; ~s, ~: rein; **zügel·los** *(fig.)* **1.** *Adj.* unrestrained; unbridled ⟨*rage, passion*⟩; **2.** *adv.* without restraint; **zügeln** *tr. V.* rein [in] ⟨*horse*⟩; *(fig.)* curb, restrain ⟨*desire etc.*⟩

zu|gesellen *refl. V.* **sich jmdm./einer Sache ~:** join sb./sth.

Zu·geständnis das concession; **zu·gestehen** *unr. tr. V.* admit; concede

zu·getan *Adj.* **jmdm. [herzlich] ~ sein** *(geh.)* be [very] attached to sb.

zugig *Adj.* draughty, *(im Freien)* windy ⟨*corner etc.*⟩

zügig 1. *Adj.* speedy; rapid; 2. *adv.* speedily; rapidly

zu·gleich *Adv.* at the same time

Zug·luft die *o. Pl.* draught

zu|greifen *unr. itr. V.* a) take hold; b) *(sich bedienen)* help oneself; c) *(fleißig arbeiten)* ⟨*hart od.* kräftig⟩ ~: [really] knuckle down to it; **Zu·griff** der *(Zugang)* access ⟨**auf** + *Akk.* to⟩

zu·grunde *Adv.* a) ~ **gehen** *(sterben)* die ⟨**an** + *Dat.* of⟩; *(zerstört werden)* be destroyed ⟨**an** + *Dat.* by⟩; ~ **richten** destroy; *(finanziell)* ruin ⟨*company, person*⟩; b) etw. **einer Sache** *(Dat.)* ~ **legen** base sth. on sth.; etw. **liegt einer Sache** ~: sth. is based on sth.

zu|gucken *itr. V.* (ugs.) ~ **zusehen**

zu·gunsten 1. *Präp. mit Gen.* in favour of; 2. *Adv.* ~ **von** in favour of

zu·gute *Adv.* **jdm. seine Unerfahrenheit** *usw.* ~ **halten** *(geh.)* make allowances for sb.'s inexperience *etc.*; **sich** *(Dat.)* **viel auf etw.** *(Akk.)* ~ **tun** *od.* **halten** *(geh.)* be proud/very proud of sth.; **jdm./einer Sache** ~ **kommen** stand sb./sth. in good stead

zu|haben *unr. itr. V.* (ugs.) ⟨*shop, office*⟩ be shut *or* closed

zu|halten *unr. itr. V.* hold closed; *(nicht öffnen)* keep closed

zu|hängen *tr. V.* cover ⟨*window, cage*⟩

zu|hauen (ugs.) 1. *unr. itr. V.* bang *or* slam ⟨*door, window*⟩ shut; 2. *unr. itr. V.* hit *or* strike out

Zu·hause das; ~s home

zu|hören *itr. V.* **jdm./einer Sache** ~: listen to sb./sth.; **Zu·hörer** der, **Zu·hörerin** die listener

zu|kleben *tr. V.* seal ⟨*letter, envelope*⟩

zu|knallen (ugs.) 1. *tr. V.* slam; 2. *itr. V.; mit sein* slam

zu|knöpfen *tr. V.* button up

zu|kommen *itr. V.; mit sein* **auf jdm.** ~: approach sb.

Zukunft die; ~: future

Zulage die extra pay *no indef. art.*; additional allowance *no indef. art.*

zu|lassen *unr. itr. V.* a) allow; permit; b) *(teilnehmen lassen)* admit; c) *(mit einer Lizenz usw. versehen)* **jdm. als Arzt** ~: register sb. as a doctor; d) *(Kfz-W.)* register ⟨*vehicle*⟩; e) *(geschlossen lassen)* leave closed *or* shut ⟨*door, window, etc.*⟩; **zu·lässig** *Adj.* permissible; admissible ⟨*appeal*⟩; **Zu·lassung** die; ~, ~**en** registration

Zu·lauf der *o. Pl.* ~ **haben** ⟨*shop, restaurant, etc.*⟩ enjoy a large clientele; ⟨*doctor, lawyer*⟩ have a large practice; **zu|laufen** *unr. itr. V.; mit sein* a) **auf jdm./etw.** ~ *(auch fig.)* run towards sb./sth.; b) **jdm.** ~ ⟨*cat, dog, etc.*⟩ adopt sb. as a new owner

zu|legen *refl. V.* **sich** *(Dat.)* **etw.** ~: get oneself sth.

zu·letzt *Adv.* a) last [of all]; b) *(als letzter/letzte/letztes)* last; c) *(fig.: am wenigsten)* least of all; d) *(schließlich, am Ende)* in the end; **bis** ~: [right up] to *or* until the end

zum *Präp.* + *Art.* a) = **zu dem**; b) *(räumlich: Richtung)* to the; c) *(räumlich: Lage)* **etw.** ~ **Fenster hinauswerfen** throw sth. out of the window; d) *(Hinzufügung)* **Milch** ~ **Tee nehmen** take milk with [one's] tea e) *(zeitlich)* at the; **spätestens** ~ **15. April** by 15 April at the latest; f) *(Zweck)* ~ **Spaß/Vergnügen** for fun/pleasure; g) *(Folge)* ~ **Ärger seines Vaters** to the annoyance of his father

zu|machen *tr. V.* close; fasten, do up ⟨*dress*⟩; seal ⟨*envelope, letter*⟩; turn off ⟨*tap*⟩; put the top on ⟨*bottle*⟩; *(stillegen)* close *or* shut down ⟨*factory, mine, etc.*⟩

zu·mal 1. *Adv.* especially; particularly; 2. *Konj.* especially *or* particularly since

zumindest *Adv.* at least

zu·mute *Adj.* **jdm. ist unbehaglich** *usw.* ~: sb. feels uncomfortable *etc.*; **mir war nicht danach** ~: I didn't feel like it *or* in the mood

zu|muten *tr. V.* **jdm. etw.** ~ *(abverlangen)* expect *or* ask sth. of sb.; *(antun)* expect sb. to put up with sth.; **Zumutung** die; ~, ~**en** unreasonable demand; **eine** ~ **sein** be unreasonable

zu·nächst *Adv.* a) *(als erstes)* first; *(anfangs)* at first; b) *(im Moment, vorläufig)* for the moment

Zunahme die; ~, ~**n** increase ⟨*Gen.*, **an** + *Dat.* in⟩

Zu·name der surname; last name

zünden 1. *tr. V.* ignite ⟨*gas, fuel, etc.*⟩; detonate ⟨*bomb, explosive device, etc.*⟩; let off ⟨*fireworks*⟩; fire ⟨*rocket*⟩; 2. *itr. V.* ⟨*rocket, engine*⟩ fire; ⟨*lighter, match*⟩ light; ⟨*gas, fuel, explosive*⟩ ignite

Zünd-: ~**holz** das *(bes. südd., österr.)* match; ~**schlüssel** der *(Kfz-W.)* ignition key

Zündung die; ~, ~**en** a) *s.* **zünden** 1:

ignition; detonation; letting off; firing; b) (Kfz-W.: Anlage) ignition

zu|**nehmen** unr. itr. V. a) increase (**an** + Dat. in); ⟨moon⟩ wax; b) (schwerer werden) put on or gain weight

Zu·neigung die; ~, ~en affection

Zunge die; ~, ~n tongue; [jmdm.] die ~ herausstrecken put one's tongue out [at sb.]

zu·nichte Adj. etw. ~ **machen** ruin sth.

zu·oberst Adv. [right] on [the] top

zupfen 1. itr. V. **an** etw. (Dat.) ~: pluck or pull at sth.; 2. tr. V. a) etw. **aus/von** usw. etw. ~: pull sth. out of/ from etc. sth.; b) (auszupfen) pull out; pluck ⟨eyebrows⟩; c) pluck ⟨string, guitar, tune⟩; d) jmdn. am Ärmel ~: pull or tug [at] sb.'s sleeve

zur Präp. + Art. a) = zu der; b) (räumlich, fig.: Richtung) to the; ~ Schule/ Arbeit gehen go to school/work; c) (räumlich: Lage) ~ Tür hereinkommen come [in] through the door; d) (Zusammengehörigkeit, Hinzufügung) with; e) (zeitlich) at the; ~ Zeit at the moment; at present; f) (Zweck) ~ Entschuldigung by way of [an] excuse; g) (Folge) ~ vollen Zufriedenheit to the complete satisfaction

zurechnungs·fähig Adj. sound of mind pred.

zurecht-: ~|**finden** unr. refl. V. find one's way [around]; ~|**kommen** unr. itr. V.; mit sein get on (**mit** with); ~|**legen** tr. V. lay out [ready]; jmdm. etw. ~**legen** lay sth. out ready for sb.; ~|**machen** tr. V. (ugs.) a) (vorbereiten) get ready; b) (herrichten) do up; c) jmdn./sich ~: get sb. ready/get [oneself] ready; ⟨schminken⟩ make sb. up/put on one's make-up; ~|**weisen** unr. tr. V. rebuke; reprimand ⟨pupil, subordinate, etc.⟩

zu|**reden** itr. V. jmdm. ~: persuade sb.; (ermutigen) encourage sb.

Zürich (das) ~s Zurich

zu·rück Adv. back; (weiter hinten) behind; **einen Schritt** ~: a step backwards; ~! get or go back!

zurück·, Zurück-: ~|**behalten** unr. tr. V. a) keep [back]; retain; b) be left with ⟨scar, heart defect, etc.⟩; ~|**bekommen** unr. tr. V. get back; **Sie bekommen 10 Mark** ~: you get 10 marks change; ~|**bleiben** unr. itr. V.; mit sein a) remain; b) (nicht mithalten) fall behind; (fig.) fall behind; (bleiben) remain; ~|**erstatten** tr. V. refund;

jmdm. etw. ~**erstatten** refund sth. to sb.; ~|**fahren** unr. itr. V.; mit sein a) go back; return; b) (nach hinten fahren) go back[wards]; ~|**fallen** unr. itr. V.; mit sein a) (in Rückstand geraten) fall behind; b) (auf einen niedrigen Rang) drop (**auf** + Akk. to); c) **an** jmdn.** ~fallen** ⟨property⟩ revert to sb.; d) **auf** jmdn.** ~fallen** ⟨actions, behaviour⟩ reflect [up]on sb.; ~|**fliegen** unr. itr. V.; mit sein fly back; ~|**führen** tr. V. etw. auf etw. (Akk.) ~**führen** attribute sth. to sth.; ~|**geben** unr. tr. V. give back; return; take back ⟨defective goods⟩; ~|**gehen** unr. itr. V.; mit sein a) go back; return; b) (nach hinten) go back; c) (verschwinden) disappear; ⟨swelling, inflammation⟩ go down; ⟨pain⟩ subside; d) (sich verringern) decrease; ⟨fever⟩ abate; ⟨flood⟩ subside; ⟨business⟩ fall off; e) (zurückgeschickt werden) be returned or sent back; ~|**greifen** unr. itr. V. **auf** jmdn./etw.** ~greifen** fall back on sb./sth.; ~|**halten** 1. unr. tr. V. a) jmdn.** ~halten** hold sb. back; (von etw. abhalten) stop sb.; b) (am Vordringen hindern) keep back ⟨crowd, mob, etc.⟩; c) (behalten) withhold ⟨news, letter, etc.⟩; d) (nicht austreten lassen) hold back ⟨tears etc.⟩; 2. unr. refl. V. restrain or control oneself; **sich in einer Diskussion** ~**halten** keep in the background in a discussion; ~**haltend** 1. Adj. a) reserved; b) (kühl, reserviert) cool, restrained ⟨reception, response⟩; c) (Wirtsch.: schwach) slack ⟨demand⟩; 2. adv. (behave) with reserve or restraint; (kühl, reserviert) coolly; ~**haltung** die; o. Pl. reserve; (Kühle, Reserviertheit) coolness; (Wirtsch.) caution; ~|**kehren** itr. V.; mit sein return; come back; ~|**kommen** unr. itr. V.; mit sein come back; return; (zurückgelangen) get back; ~**kommen auf** (+ Akk.) come back to ⟨subject, question, point, etc.⟩; ~|**kriegen** tr. V. s. ~bekommen; ~|**lassen** unr. tr. V. leave; ~|**legen** tr. V. a) put back; b) (reservieren) put aside, keep ⟨Dat., für for⟩; c) (sparen) put away; d) (hinter sich bringen) cover ⟨distance⟩; ~|**lehnen** refl. V. lean back; ~|**nehmen** unr. tr. V. (auch fig. widerrufen) take back; ~|**rufen** unr. tr. V. a) call back; recall ⟨ambassador⟩; b) auch itr. (telefonisch) call or (Brit.) ring back; ~|**schicken** tr. V. send back ~|**schrecken** regelm., veralt. unr. itr.

V.; mit sein vor etw. (Dat.) ~**schrecken** *(fig.)* shrink from sth.; **er schreckt vor nichts** ~: he will stop at nothing; ~|**senden** *unr. od. regelm. tr. V. (geh.) s.* ~**schicken;** ~|**treten** *unr. itr. V.; mit sein* step back; *(von einem Amt)* resign; step down; *(government)* resign; *(von einem Vertrag usw.)* withdraw (von from); back out (von of); *(fig.: in den Hintergrund treten)* become less important; ~|**weisen** *unr. tr. V.* reject *(proposal, question, demand, application, etc.)*; turn down, refuse *(offer, request, help, etc.)*; turn away *(petitioner, unwelcome guest)*; repudiate *(accusation, claim, etc.)*; ~|**werfen** *unr. tr. V.* throw back; reflect *(light, sound)*; repulse *(enemy)*; *(fig.: in einer Entwicklung)* set back; ~|**zahlen** *tr. V.* pay back; ~|**ziehen** **1.** *unr. tr. V.* **a)** pull back; draw back *(bolt, curtains, one's hand, etc.)*; **b)** *(abziehen, zurückbeordern)* withdraw *(troops)*; recall *(ambassador)* **c)** *(rückgängig machen)* withdraw; cancel *(order, instruction)*; **2.** *unr. refl. V.* withdraw

Zu·ruf *der* shout; **zu|rufen** *unr. tr. V. jmdm. etw.* ~: shout sth. to sb.

Zu·sage *die* **a)** *(auf eine Einladung hin)* acceptance; *(auf eine Stellenbewerbung hin)* offer; **b)** *(Versprechen)* promise; undertaking; **zu|sagen** **1.** *itr. V.* **a)** accept; **b)** *jmdm.* ~ *(gefallen)* appeal to sb.; **2.** *tr. V.* promise

zusammen *Adv.* together

zusammen-, Zusammen-: ~|**arbeiten** *itr. V.* co-operate; ~|**binden** *unr. tr. V.* tie together; ~|**brechen** *unr. itr. V.; mit sein* collapse; *(fig.)(order, communications, system, telephone network)* break down; *(traffic)* come to a standstill; ~**bruch** der collapse; *(fig., auch psychisch, nervlich)* breakdown; ~|**drücken** *tr. V.* press together; ~|**fahren** *unr. itr. V.; mit sein (~zucken)* start; jump; ~|**fallen** *unr. itr. V.; mit sein* **a)** collapse; **b)** [zeitlich] ~**fallen** coincide; ~|**fassen** *tr. V.* summarize; ~**fassung** die summary; ~|**fegen** *tr. V. (bes. nordd.)* sweep together; ~|**fließen** *unr. itr. V.; mit sein (rivers, streams)* flow into each other; ~**fluß** der confluence; ~|**fügen** *tr. V.* fit together; ~|**führen** *tr. V.* bring together; ~|**gehören** *itr. V.* belong together; ~**gehörig** *Adj.* [closely] related *or* connected *(subjects, problems, etc.)*; matching *attrib.*

(pieces of tea service, cutlery, etc.); ~**gehörigkeit** die; ~: **ein starkes Gefühl der** ~**gehörigkeit** a strong sense of belonging together; ~**hang** der connection; *(einer Geschichte, Rede)* coherence; *(Kontext)* context; ~|**hängen** *unr. itr. V.* **a)** be joined [together]; **b)** *mit etw.* ~**hängen** *(fig.)* be related to sth.; *(durch etw. [mit] verursacht sein)* be the result of sth.; ~|**kehren** *tr. V. (bes. südd.) s.* ~**fegen;** ~**klappbar** *Adj.* folding; ~|**klappen** *tr. V.* fold up; ~|**kommen** *unr. itr. V.; mit sein* meet; **mit jmdm.** ~**kommen** meet sb.; **b)** *(zueinanderkommen; auch fig.)* get together; *(gleichzeitig auftreten)* occur *or* happen together; ~**kunft** die; ~, ~**künfte** meeting; ~|**laufen** *unr. itr. V.; mit sein* **a)** *(people, crowd)* gather, congregate; **b)** *(rivers, streams)* flow into each other, join up; ~|**leben** *itr. V.* live together; ~**leben** das; *o. Pl.* living together *no art.;* ~|**legen** **1.** *tr. V.* **a)** put *or* gather together; **b)** *(zusammenfalten)* fold [up]; **c)** *(miteinander verbinden)* amalgamate, merge *(classes, departments, etc.)*; combine *(events)*; **d)** put *(patients, guests, etc.)* together [in the same room]; **2.** *itr. V.* club together; ~|**nehmen** **1.** *unr. tr. V.* **a)** summon up *(courage, strength, understanding)*; **2.** *unr. refl. V.* get *or* take a grip on oneself; **nimm dich** ~**!** pull yourself together!; ~|**passen** *intr. V.* go together; *(persons)* be suited to each other; ~**prall** der; ~|e|s, ~e collision; ~|**prallen** *itr. V.; mit sein* collide (mit with); ~|**sein** *unr. itr. V.; mit sein; Zusschr. nur im Inf. u. Part.* **a)** be together; **b)** *(zusammenleben)* be *or* live together; ~|**setzen** **1.** *tr. V.* put together; **2.** *refl. V.* **a)** sich aus etw. ~**setzen** be made up *or* composed of sth.; **b)** *(sich zueinander setzen)* sit together; *(zu einem Gespräch)* get together; ~|**stehen** *unr. itr. V.* stand together; ~|**stellen** *tr. V.* put together; draw up *(list)*; ~**stoß** der collision; *(fig.)* clash (mit with); ~|**stoßen** *unr. itr. V.; mit sein* collide (mit with); ~|**treffen** *unr. itr. V.; mit sein* meet; **mit jmdm.** ~**treffen** meet sb.; *(zeitlich)* coincide; ~|**zählen** *tr. V.* add up; ~|**zucken** *itr. V.; mit sein* start; jump

Zu·satz der addition; *(Zugesetztes, Additiv)* additive; **zusätzlich 1.** *Adj.* additional; **2.** *adv.* in addition

zu|schauen *itr. V. (südd., österr., schweiz.) s.* zusehen; **Zu·schauer der, Zu·schauerin die;** ~, ~**nen** spectator; *(im Theater, Kino)* member of the audience; *(an einer Unfallstelle)* onlooker; *(Fernseh~)* viewer; **die** ~: *(im Theater, Kino)* the audience *sing.*

zu|schicken *tr. V.* send

zu|schieben *unr. tr. V.* **a)** push ⟨drawer, door⟩ shut; **b)** *(fig.)* jmdm. die Schuld ~: lay the blame on sb.

Zu·schlag der a) additional *or* extra charge; *(für Nacht-, Feiertagsarbeit usw.)* additional *or* extra payment; **b)** *(Eisenb.)* supplement ticket; **zu|schlagen 1.** *unr. tr. V.* bang *or* slam ⟨door, window, etc.⟩ shut; close ⟨book⟩; *(heftig)* slam ⟨book⟩ shut; **2.** *unr. itr. V.* **a)** mit sein ⟨door, trap⟩ slam *or* bang shut; **b)** *(einen Schlag führen)* throw a blow/blows; *(losschlagen)* hit *or* strike out; *(fig.)* ⟨army, police, murderer⟩ strike

zu|schließen 1. *unr. tr. V.* lock; **2.** *unr. itr. V.* lock up

zu|schnüren *tr. V.* tie up

zu|schrauben *tr. V.* screw the lid *or* top on ⟨jar, flask⟩; screw ⟨lid, top⟩ on

Zu·schrift die letter; *(auf eine Anzeige)* reply

Zu·schuß der contribution **(zu** towards**)**

zu|sehen *unr. itr. V.* **a)** watch; jmdm. [beim Arbeiten *usw.*] ~: watch sb. [working *etc.*]; **b)** *(dafür sorgen)* make sure; see to it

zu|senden *unr. od. regelm. tr. V.: s.* zuschicken; **Zu·sendung die** sending

zu|spitzen *refl. V.* become aggravated

zu|sprechen 1. *unr. tr. V.* **a)** er sprach ihr Trost/Mut zu his words gave her comfort/courage; **b)** jmdm. ein Erbe *usw.* ~: award sb. an inheritance *etc.*; **2.** *unr. itr. V.* jmdm. ermutigend/tröstend *usw.* ~: speak encouragingly/comfortingly to sb.

Zu·stand der a) condition; *(bes. abwertend)* state; **b)** *(Stand der Dinge)* state of affairs; **zu·stande Adv.** etw. ~ bringen [manage to] bring about sth.; ~ kommen come into being; *(geschehen)* take place; **zu·ständig Adj.** appropriate relevant ⟨authority, office, etc.⟩; **[für etw.] ~ sein** *(verantwortlich)* be responsible [for sth.]

zu|stehen *unr. itr. V.* etw. steht jmdm. zu sb. is entitled to the

zu|steigen *unr. itr. V.; mit sein* get on;

ist noch jemand zugestiegen? *(im Bus)* ≈ any more fares, please?; *(im Zug)* ≈ tickets, please!

zu|stellen *tr. V.* deliver ⟨letter, parcel, etc.⟩

zu|stimmen *itr. V.* agree; jmdm. [in einem Punkt] ~: agree with sb. [on a point]; einer Sache *(Dat.)* ~: agree to sth.; **Zu·stimmung die** *(Billigung)* approval **(zu** of**)**; *(Einverständnis)* agreement **(zu** to, with**)**

zu|stoßen *unr. itr. V.; mit sein* jmdm. ~: happen to sb.

Zu·tat die ingredient

zu·teil Adv. jmdm./einer Sache ~ werden *(geh.)* be granted to sb./sth.; **zu|teilen** *tr. V.* jmdm./etw. ~: allot *or* assign sth./sth. to sb.; jmdm. seine Portion ~: mete out his/her share to sb.

zu|tragen *unr. refl. V. (geh.)* occur; **zuträglich Adj.** healthy ⟨climate⟩; jmdm./einer Sache ~ sein be good for sb./sth.; be beneficial to sb./sth.

zu|trauen *tr. V.* jmdm. etw. ~: believe sb. [is] capable of [doing] sth.; sich *(Dat.)* etw. ~: think one can do *or* is capable of doing sth.; **Zutrauen das;** ~s confidence, trust **(zu** in**)**; **zutraulich 1. Adj.** trusting; **2. adv.** trustingly; **Zutraulichkeit die;** ~: trust[fulness]

zu|treffen *unr. itr. V.* **a)** be correct; **b)** auf etw. für jmdn./etw. ~: apply to sb./sth.; **zutreffend 1. Adj.** **a)** correct; **b)** *(geltend)* applicable; relevant; **2. adv.** correctly

zu|trinken *unr. itr. V.* jmdm. ~: raise one's glass and drink to sb.

Zu·tritt der entry; admittance; „kein ~", „~ verboten" 'no entry'; 'no admittance'; ~ [zu etw.] haben have access [to sth.]

zu·unterst Adv. right at the bottom

zuverlässig 1. Adj. reliable; *(verläßlich)* dependable ⟨person⟩; **2. adv.** reliably; **Zuverlässigkeit die;** ~: reliability; *(Verläßlichkeit)* dependability

zuversichtlich 1. Adj. confident; **2. adv.** confidently

zuviel 1. indekl. Indefinitpron. too much; *(ugs.: zu viele)* too many; **2. adv.** too much

zu·vor Adv. before

zuvor|kommen *unr. itr. V.; mit sein* **a)** jmdm. ~: beat sb. to it; **b)** einer Sache *(Dat.)* ~: anticipate sth.; **zuvorkommend 1. Adj.** obliging; *(höflich)* courteous; **2.** *adv.* obligingly; *(höflich)* courteously

zu·weilen *Adv. (geh.)* now and again

zu|weisen *unr. tr. V.* jmdm. etw. ~: allocate *or* allot sb. sth.

zu|wenden *unr. od. regelm. refl. V.* sich jmdm./einer Sache ~ *(auch fig.)* turn to sb./sth.

zu·wenig 1. *indekl. Indefinitpron.* too little; *(ugs.: zu wenige)* too few; **2.** *adv.* too little

zuwider *Adj.* jmdm. ~ sein be repugnant to sb.

zu|winken *itr. V.* jmdm./einander ~: wave to sb./one another

zu|zahlen *tr. V.* pay ⟨five marks etc.⟩ extra

zu|ziehen 1. *unr. tr. V.* pull ⟨door⟩ shut; draw ⟨curtain⟩; do up ⟨zip⟩; **2.** *unr. refl. V.* sich ⟨Dat.⟩ eine Krankheit ~: catch an illness; **3.** *unr. itr. V.; mit sein* move into the area

zuzüglich *Präp. mit Gen.* plus

zwang *1. u. 3. Pers. Sg. Prät. v.* zwingen; **Zwang** der; ~[e]s, Zwänge **a)** (compulsion); **b)** *(unwiderstehlicher Drang)* irresistible urge; **zwängen** 1. *tr. V.* squeeze; **2.** *refl. V.* squeeze [oneself]; **zwanglos** 1. *Adj.* **a)** informal; casual ⟨behaviour⟩; **b)** *(unregelmäßig)* haphazard ⟨arrangement⟩; **2.** *adv.* **a)** informally; **b)** *(unregelmäßig)* haphazardly ⟨arranged⟩; **Zwangs·lage** die predicament; **zwangs·läufig** 1. *Adj.* inevitable; **2.** *adv.* inevitably

zwanzig *Kardinalz.* twenty; *s. auch* achtzig; **zwanziger** *indekl. Adj.; nicht präd.* die ~ Jahre the twenties; **Zwanzig·mark·schein** der twenty-mark note; **zwanzigst ...** *Ordinalz.* twentieth

zwar *Adv.* **a)** admittedly; **b)** und ~: to be precise

Zweck der; ~[e]s, ~e purpose; *(Sinn)* point; es hat keinen ~: it's pointless; es hat keinen ~, das zu tun there is no point in doing that

zweck-, Zweck-: ~los *Adj.* pointless; ~mäßig 1. *Adj.* appropriate; expedient ⟨behaviour, action⟩; functional ⟨building, fittings, furniture⟩; **2.** *adv.* appropriately ⟨arranged, clothed⟩; ⟨act⟩ expediently; ⟨equip, furnish⟩ functionally; ~mäßigkeit die appropriateness; *(einer Handlung)* expediency; *(eines Gebäudes)* functionalism

zwecks *Präp. mit Gen. (Papierdt.)* for the purpose of

zwei *Kardinalz.* two; *s. auch* ¹acht; **Zwei** die; ~, ~en **a)** *(Zahl)* two; **b)** *(Schulnote)* B

zwei-, Zwei-: ~bettzimmer das twin-bedded room; ~deutig 1. *Adj.* ambiguous; *(fig.: schlüpfrig)* suggestive ⟨remark, joke⟩; **2.** *adv.* ambiguously; *(fig.)* suggestively; ~deutigkeit die; ~, ~en ambiguity; *(fig.)* suggestiveness; ~dimensional 1. *Adj.* two-dimensional; **2.** *adv.* two-dimensionally; ~einhalb *Bruchz.* two and a half

zweierlei *Gattungsz.; indekl.* **a)** *attr.* two sorts *or* kinds of; two different ⟨sizes, kinds, etc.⟩; odd ⟨socks, gloves⟩; **b)** *(alleinstehend)* two [different] things; **zweifach** *Vervielfältigungsz.* double; *(~mal)* twice; **Zweifache** das; *adj. Dekl.* das ~: twice as much

Zweifel der; ~s, ~: doubt (an + *Dat.* about); etw. in ~ ziehen question sth.; **zweifelhaft** *Adj.* **a)** doubtful; **b)** *(fragwürdig)* dubious; *(suspekt)* suspicious; **zweifel·los** *Adv.* undoubtedly; **zweifeln** *itr. V.* doubt; an jmdm./etw. ~: doubt sb./sth.; have doubts about sb./sth.

Zweig der; ~[e]s, ~e [small] branch; *(meist ohne Blätter)* twig

zwei-, Zwei-: ~hundert *Kardinalz.* two hundred; ~mal *Adv.* twice; ~mark·stück das two-mark piece; ~pfennig·stück das two-pfennig piece; ~reiher der double-breasted suit/coat/jacket; ~schneidig *Adj.* double-edged; ~sprachig 1. *Adj.* bilingual; ⟨sign⟩ in two languages; **2.** *adv.* bilingually; ⟨written⟩ in two languages; ⟨published⟩ in a bilingual edition; ~spurig *Adj.* **a)** two-lane ⟨road⟩; **b)** two-track ⟨vehicle⟩; **c)** two- *or* twin-track ⟨recording⟩; ~stellig *Adj.* two-figure attrib. ⟨number, sum⟩; ~stöckig *Adj.* two-storey attrib.; ~stöckig sein have two storeys

zweit ... *Ordinalz.* second; jeder ~e every other one; *s. auch* erst ...

zwei·tägig *Adj.* (2 Tage alt) two-day-old attrib.; (2 Tage dauernd) two-day attrib.; **zweit·ältest ...** *Adj.* second oldest; **zwei·tausend** *Kardinalz.* two thousand; **zweit·best ...** *Adj.* second best

zweite·mal *Adv.* das ~: for the second time; **zweiten·mal** *Adv.* zum ~: for the second time; beim ~: the second time [round]; **zweitens** *Adv.*

secondly; in the second place; **Zweite[r]-Klasse-Abteil das** second-class compartment; **zweit·rangig** *Adj.* of secondary importance *postpos.; (~klassig)* second-rate; **zweitürig** *Adj.* two-door *(car)*

Zweit-: ~**wagen der** second car; ~**wohnung die** second home

Zwei·zimmerwohnung die two-room flat *(Brit.)* or *(Amer.)* apartment

Zwerg der; ~**|e|s,** ~**e** dwarf; *(Garten~)* gnome

Zwetsche die; ~, ~**n** damson plum

Zwieback der; ~**|e|s,** ~**e** od. **Zwiebäcke** rusk; *(unzählbar)* rusks *pl.*

Zwiebel die; ~, ~**n** onion; *(Blumen~)* bulb

zwie-, Zwie-: ~**gespräch das** *(geh.)* dialogue; ~**spalt der;** ~**|e|s,** ~**e** od. ~**spälte** [inner] conflict; ~**spältig** *Adj.* conflicting *(mood, feelings)*; discordant *(impression)*; *(widersprüchlich)* contradictory *(nature, attitude, person, etc.)*

Zwilling der; ~**s,** ~**e** twin

Zwillings-: ~**bruder der** twin brother; ~**paar das** pair of twins; ~**schwester die** twin sister

zwingen 1. *unr. tr. V.* force; **jmdn. zu etw.** ~, **jmdn. |dazu|** ~, **etw. zu tun** force *or* compel sb. to do sth.; **zwingend** *Adj.* compelling *(reason, logic)*; conclusive *(proof, argument)*; imperative *(necessity)*

zwinkern *itr. V.* |mit den Augen| ~: blink; *(als Zeichen)* wink

Zwirn der; ~**|e|s,** ~**e** [strong] thread *or* yarn

zwischen *Präp. mit Dat./Akk.* between; *(mitten unter)* among[st]

zwischen-, Zwischen-: ~**durch** [·'·] *Adv.* a) *(zeitlich)* between times;

(zwischen zwei Zeitpunkten) in between; *(von Zeit zu Zeit)* from time to time; ~**fall der** incident; ~**landen** *itr. V.; mit sein* in X ~**landen** land in X on the way; ~**mahlzeit die** snack [between meals]; ~**menschlich** 1. *Adj.* interpersonal *(relations)*; *(contacts)* between people; 2. *adv.* on a personal level; ~**raum der** space; gap; *(Lücke)* gap; ~**zeit die** interim

Zwist der; ~**|e|s,** ~**e** *(geh.)* strife *no indef. art.; (Fehde)* feud; dispute; **Zwistigkeit die;** ~, ~**en** *(geh.)* dispute

zwitschern *itr. V. (auch tr.) V.* chirp

Zwitter der; ~**s,** ~ *(Biol.)* hermaphrodite

zwo *Kardinalz. (ugs.; bes. zur Verdeutlichung)* two

zwölf *Kardinalz.* twelve; ~ **Uhr mittags/nachts** [twelve o'clock] midday/midnight; *s. auch* **¹acht; zwölft...** *Ordinalz.* twelfth; *s. auch* **acht...;** **zwölftel** *Bruchz.* twelfth; *s. auch* **achtel;** **Zwölftel das** *(schweiz. meist der)* ~**s,** ~: twelfth

zwot... *Ordinalz. (ugs.; bes. bei Datumsangaben)* second; **zwotens** *Adv. (ugs.)* secondly

Zylinder [tsi'lɪndɐ] **der;** ~**s,** ~ **a)** cylinder; **b)** *(Hut)* top hat; **zylindrisch** 1. *Adj.* cylindrical; 2. *adv.* cylindrically

zynisch 1. *Adj.* cynical; 2. *adv.* cynically

Zynismus der; ~: cynicism

Zypern (das) ~**s** Cyprus; **Zyprer der;** ~**s,** ~, **Zyprerin die;** ~, ~**nen** Cypriot

Zypresse die; ~, ~**n** cypress

Zypriot der; ~**en,** ~**en,** **Zypriotin die;** ~, ~**nen** Cypriot; **zypriotisch, zyprisch** *Adj.* Cypriot

Zyste die; ~, ~**n** *(Med.)* cyst

Englische unregelmäßige Verben

Ein Sternchen (*) weist darauf hin, daß die korrekte Form von der jeweiligen Bedeutung abhängt.

Infinitive	Past Tense	Past Participle	Infinitive	Past Tense	Past Participle
Infinitiv	*Präteritum*	*2. Partizip*	*Infinitiv*	*Präteritum*	*2. Partizip*
arise	arose	arisen	flee	fled	fled
awake	awoke	awoken	fling	flung	flung
be	was *sing.*,	been	floodlight	floodlit	floodlit
	were *pl.*		fly	flew	flown
bear	bore	borne	forbid	forbade,	forbidden
beat	beat	beaten		forbad	
become	became	become	forecast	forecast,	forecast,
begin	began	begun		forecasted	forecasted
bend	bent	bent	foretell	foretold	foretold
bet	bet, betted	bet, betted	forget	forgot	forgotten
bid	*bade, bid	*bidden, bid	forgive	forgave	forgiven
bind	bound	bound	forsake	forsook	forsaken
bite	bit	bitten	freeze	froze	frozen
bleed	bled	bled	get	got	got, *(Amer.)*
blow	blew	blown			gotten
break	broke	broken	give	gave	given
breed	bred	bred	go	went	gone
bring	brought	brought	grind	ground	ground
broadcast	broadcast	broadcast	grow	grew	grown
build	built	built	hang	*hung,	*hung,
burn	burnt, burned	burnt, burned		hanged	hanged
burst	burst	burst	have	had	had
bust	bust, busted	bust, busted	hear	heard	heard
buy	bought	bought	hew	hewed	hewn, hewed
cast	cast	cast	hide	hid	hidden
catch	caught	caught	hit	hit	hit
choose	chose	chosen	hold	held	held
cling	clung	clung	hurt	hurt	hurt
come	came	come	keep	kept	kept
cost	*cost, costed	*cost, costed	kneel	knelt,	knelt,
creep	crept	crept		*(esp. Amer.)*	*(esp. Amer.)*
cut	cut	cut		kneeled	kneeled
deal	dealt	dealt	know	knew	known
dig	dug	dug	lay	laid	laid
dive	dived,	dived	lead	led	led
	(Amer.) dove		lean	leaned,	leaned,
do	did	done		*(Brit.)* leant	*(Brit.)* leant
draw	drew	drawn	leap	leapt, leaped	leapt, leaped
dream	dreamt,	dreamt,	learn	learnt,	learnt,
	dreamed	dreamed		learned	learned
drink	drank	drunk	leave	left	left
drive	drove	driven	lend	lent	lent
dwell	dwelt	dwelt	let	let	let
eat	ate	eaten	²lie	lay	lain
fall	fell	fallen	light	lit, lighted	lit, lighted
feed	fed	fed	lose	lost	lost
feel	felt	felt	make	made	made
fight	fought	fought	mean	meant	meant
find	found	found	meet	met	met

Infinitive	Past Tense	Past Participle	Infinitive	Past Tense	Past Participle
Infinitiv	*Präteritum*	*2. Partizip*	*Infinitiv*	*Präteritum*	*2. Partizip*
mow	mowed	mown, mowed	spend	spent	spent
			spill	spilt, spilled	spilt, spilled
overhang	overhung	overhung	spin	spun	spun
pay	paid	paid	spit	spat, spit	spat, spit
prove	proved	proved, proven	split	split	split
			spoil	spoilt, spoiled	spoilt, spoiled
put	put	put			
quit	quitted, *(Amer.)* quit	quitted, *(Amer.)* quit	spread	spread	spread
			spring	sprang, *(Amer.)* sprung	sprung
read [ri:d]	read [red]	read [red]			
rid	rid	rid			
ride	rode	ridden	stand	stood	stood
²ring	rang	rung	steal	stole	stolen
rise	rose	risen	stick	stuck	stuck
run	ran	run	sting	stung	stung
saw	sawed	sawn, sawed	stink	stank, stunk	stunk
say	said	said	strew	strewed	strewed, strewn
see	saw	seen			
seek	sought	sought	stride	strode	stridden
sell	sold	sold	strike	struck	struck
send	sent	sent	string	strung	strung
set	set	set	strive	strove	striven
sew	sewed	sewn, sewed	sublet	sublet	sublet
shake	shook	shaken	swear	swore	sworn
shear	sheared	shorn, sheared	sweep	swept	swept
			swell	swelled	swollen, swelled
shed	shed	shed			
shine	shone	shone	swim	swam	swum
shit	shitted, shit	shitted, shit	swing	swung	swung
shoe	shod	shod	take	took	taken
shoot	shot	shot	teach	taught	taught
show	showed	shown	tear	tore	torn
shrink	shrank	shrunk	tell	told	told
shut	shut	shut	think	thought	thought
sing	sang	sung	thrive	thrived, throve	thrived, thriven
sink	sank, sunk	sunk			
sit	sat	sat	throw	threw	thrown
slay	slew	slain	thrust	thrust	thrust
sleep	slept	slept	tread	trod	trodden, trod
slide	slid	slid	understand	understood	understood
sling	slung	slung	undo	undid	undone
slink	slunk	slunk	wake	woke	woken
slit	slit	slit	wear	wore	worn
smell	smelt, smelled	smelt, smelled	¹weave	wove	woven
			weep	wept	wept
sow	sowed	sown, sowed	wet	wet, wetted	wet, wetted
speak	spoke	spoken	win	won	won
speed	*sped, speeded	*sped, speeded	²wind [waɪnd]	wound [waʊnd]	wound [waʊnd]
spell	spelled, *(Brit.)* spelt	spelled, *(Brit.)* spelt	wring	wrung	wrung
			write	wrote	written

German irregular verbs

Irregular and partly irregular verbs are listed alphabetically by infinitive. 1st, 2nd, and 3rd person present and imperative forms are given after the infinitive, and preterite subjunctive forms after the preterite indicative, where they take an umlaut, change *e* to *i*, etc.

Verbs with a raised number in the German-English section of the Dictionary have the same number in this list.

Compound verbs (including verbs with prefixes) are only given if a) they do not take the same forms as the corresponding simple verb, e.g. *befehlen*, or b) there is no corresponding simple verb, e.g. *bewegen*.

An asterisk (*) indicates a verb which is also conjugated regularly.

Infinitive *Infinitiv*	Preterite *Präteritum*	Past Participle *2. Partizip*
abwägen	wog (wöge) ab	abgewogen
backen (du bäckst, er bäckt; *auch:* du backst, er backt)	backte, *älter:* buk (büke)	gebacken
befehlen (du befiehlst, er befiehlt; befiehl!)	befahl (beföhle, befähle)	befohlen
beginnen	begann (begänne, *seltener:* begönne)	begonnen
beißen	biß	gebissen
bergen (du birgst, er birgt; birg!)	barg (bärge)	geborgen
bersten (du birst, er birst; birst!)	barst (bärste)	geborsten
besinnen	besann (besänne)	besonnen
²bewegen	bewog (bewöge)	bewogen
biegen	bog (böge)	gebogen
bieten	bot (böte)	geboten
binden	band (bände)	gebunden
bitten	bat (bäte)	gebeten
blasen (du bläst, er bläst)	blies	geblasen
bleiben	blieb	geblieben
bleichen*	blich	geblichen
braten (du brätst, er brät)	briet	gebraten
brechen (du brichst, er bricht; brich!)	brach (bräche)	gebrochen
brennen	brannte (brennte)	gebrannt
bringen	brachte (brächte)	gebracht
denken	dachte (dächte)	gedacht
dreschen (du drischst, er drischt; drisch!)	drosch (drösche)	gedroschen
dringen	drang (dränge)	gedrungen
dürfen (ich darf, du darfst, er darf)	durfte (dürfte)	gedurft
empfehlen (du empfiehlst, er empfiehlt, empfiehl!)	empfahl (empföhle, *seltener:* empfähle)	empfohlen
erklimmen	erklomm (erklömme)	erklommen
erlöschen (du erlischst, er erlischt; erlisch!)	erlosch (erlösche)	erloschen
erschallen*	erscholl (erschölle)	erschollen
¹,³erschrecken (du erschrickst, er erschrickt; erschrick!)	erschrak (erschräke)	erschrocken
erwägen	erwog (erwöge)	erwogen

Infinitive *Infinitiv*	Preterite *Präteritum*	Past Participle *2. Partizip*
essen (du ißt, er ißt; iß!)	aß (äße)	gegessen
fahren (du fährst, er fährt)	fuhr (führe)	gefahren
fallen (du fällst, er fällt)	fiel	gefallen
fangen (du fängst, er fängt)	fing	gefangen
fechten (du fichtst, er ficht; ficht!)	focht (föchte)	gefochten
finden	fand (fände)	gefunden
flechten (du flichtst, er flicht; flicht!)	flocht (flöchte)	geflochten
fliegen	flog (flöge)	geflogen
fliehen	floh (flöhe)	geflohen
fließen	floß (flösse)	geflossen
fressen (du frißt, er frißt; friß!)	fraß (fräße)	gefressen
frieren*	fror (fröre)	gefroren
gären*	gor (göre)	gegoren
gebären (*geh.:* du gebierst, sie gebiert; gebier!)	gebar (gebäre)	geboren
geben (du gibst, er gibt; gib!)	gab (gäbe)	gegeben
gedeihen	gedieh	gediehen
gehen	ging	gegangen
gelingen	gelang (gelänge)	gelungen
gelten (du giltst, er gilt; gilt!)	galt (gölte, gälte)	gegolten
genesen	genas (genäse)	genesen
genießen	genoß (genösse)	genossen
geschehen (es geschieht)	geschah (geschähe)	geschehen
gewinnen	gewann (gewönne, gewänne)	gewonnen
gießen	goß (gösse)	gegossen
gleichen	glich	geglichen
gleiten	glitt	geglitten
glimmen	glomm (glömme)	geglommen
graben (du gräbst, er gräbt)	grub (grübe)	gegraben
greifen	griff	gegriffen
haben (du hast, er hat)	hatte (hätte)	gehabt
halten (du hältst, er hält)	hielt	gehalten
[1]hängen	hing	gehangen
hauen	haute, *geh.:* hieb	gehauen
heben	hob (höbe)	gehoben
heißen	hieß	geheißen
helfen (du hilfst, er hilft; hilf!)	half (hülfe, *selten:* hälfe)	geholfen
kennen	kannte (kennte)	gekannt
klingen	klang (klänge)	geklungen
kneifen	kniff	gekniffen
kommen	kam (käme)	gekommen
können (ich kann, du kannst, er kann)	konnte (könnte)	gekonnt
kriechen	kroch (kröche)	gekrochen
[1,2]laden (du lädst, er lädt)	lud (lüde)	geladen
lassen (du läßt, er läßt)	ließ	gelassen
laufen (du läufst, er läuft)	lief	gelaufen
leiden	litt	gelitten
leihen	lieh	geliehen
[1,2]lesen (du liest, er liest; lies!)	las (läse)	gelesen
liegen	lag (läge)	gelegen
lügen	log (löge)	gelogen
mahlen	mahlte	gemahlen
meiden	mied	gemieden

Infinitive *Infinitiv*	Preterite *Präteritum*	Past Participle *2. Partizip*
melken* (du milkst, er milkt; milk!; du melkst, er melkt; melke!)	molk (mölke)	gemolken
messen (du mißt, er mißt; miß!)	maß (mäße)	gemessen
mißlingen	mißlang (mißlänge)	mißlungen
mögen (ich mag, du magst, er mag)	mochte (möchte)	gemocht
müssen (ich muß, du mußt, er muß)	mußte (müßte)	gemußt
nehmen (du nimmst, er nimmt; nimm!)	nahm (nähme)	genommen
nennen	nannte (nennte)	genannt
pfeifen	pfiff	gepfiffen
preisen	pries	gepriesen
quellen (du quillst, er quillt; quill!)	quoll (quölle)	gequollen
raten (du rätst, er rät)	riet	geraten
reiben	rieb	gerieben
reißen	riß	gerissen
reiten	ritt	geritten
rennen	rannte (rennte)	gerannt
riechen	roch (röche)	gerochen
ringen	rang (ränge)	gerungen
rinnen	rann (ränne, *seltener:* rönne)	geronnen
rufen	rief	gerufen
salzen*	salzte	gesalzen
saufen (du säufst, er säuft)	soff (söffe)	gesoffen
saugen*	sog (söge)	gesogen
schaffen*	schuf (schüfe)	geschaffen
schallen*	scholl (schölle)	geschallt
scheiden	schied	geschieden
scheinen	schien	geschienen
scheißen	schiß	geschissen
schelten (du schiltst, er schilt; schilt!)	schalt (schölte)	gescholten
¹scheren	schor (schöre)	geschoren
schieben	schob (schöbe)	geschoben
schießen	schoß (schösse)	geschossen
schinden	schindete	geschunden
schlafen (du schläfst, er schläft)	schlief	geschlafen
schlagen (du schlägst, er schlägt)	schlug (schlüge)	geschlagen
schleichen	schlich	geschlichen
¹schleifen	schliff	geschliffen
schließen	schloß (schlösse)	geschlossen
schlingen	schlang (schlänge)	geschlungen
schmeißen	schmiß	geschmissen
schmelzen (du schmilzt, er schmilzt; schmilz!)	schmolz	geschmolzen
schneiden	schnitt	geschnitten
schrecken* (du schrickst, er schrickt; schrick!)	schrak (schräke)	geschreckt
schreiben	schrieb	geschrieben
schreien	schrie	geschrie[e]n
schreiten	schritt	geschritten
schweigen	schwieg	geschwiegen
schwellen (du schwillst, er schwillt; schwill!)	schwoll (schwölle)	geschwollen
schwimmen	schwamm (schwömme, *seltener:* schwämme)	geschwommen

Infinitive *Infinitiv*	Preterite *Präteritum*	Past Participle *2. Partizip*
schwinden	schwand (schwände)	geschwunden
schwingen	schwang (schwänge)	geschwungen
schwören	schwor (schwüre)	geschworen
sehen (du siehst, er sieht; sieh[e]!)	sah (sähe)	gesehen
sein (ich bin, du bist, er ist, wir sind, ihr seid, sie sind; sei!)	war (wäre)	gewesen
senden*	sandte (sendete)	gesandt
sieden*	sott (sötte)	gesotten
singen	sang (sänge)	gesungen
sinken	sank (sänke)	gesunken
sitzen	saß (säße)	gesessen
sollen (ich soll, du sollst, er soll)	sollte	gesollt
spalten*	spaltete	gespalten
speien	spie	gespie[e]n
spinnen	spann (spönne, spänne)	gesponnen
sprechen (du sprichst, er spricht; sprich!)	sprach (spräche)	gesprochen
sprießen	sproß (sprösse)	gesprossen
springen	sprang	gesprungen
stechen (du stichst, er sticht; stich!)	stach (stäche)	gestochen
stehen	stand (stünde, *auch:* stände)	gestanden
stehlen (du stiehlst, er stiehlt; stiehl!)	stahl (stähle, *seltener:* stöhle)	gestohlen
steigen	stieg	gestiegen
sterben (du stirbst, er stirbt; stirb!)	starb (stürbe)	gestorben
stinken	stank (stänke)	gestunken
stoßen (du stößt, er stößt)	stieß	gestoßen
streichen	strich	gestrichen
streiten	stritt	gestritten
tragen (du trägst, er trägt)	trug (trüge)	getragen
treffen (du triffst; er trifft; triff!)	traf (träfe)	getroffen
treiben	trieb	getrieben
treten (du trittst, er tritt; tritt!)	trat (träte)	getreten
triefen*	troff (tröffe)	getroffen
trinken	trank (tränke)	getrunken
trügen	trog (tröge)	getrogen
tun	tat (täte)	getan
verderben (du verdirbst, er verdirbt; verdirb!)	verdarb (verdürbe)	verdorben
verdrießen	verdroß (verdrösse)	verdrossen
vergessen (du vergißt, er vergißt, vergiß!)	vergaß (vergäße)	vergessen
verlieren	verlor (verlöre)	verloren
verschleißen*	verschliß	verschlissen
verzeihen	verzieh	verziehen
¹wachsen (du wächst, er wächst)	wuchs (wüchse)	gewachsen
waschen (du wäschst, er wäscht)	wusch (wüsche)	gewaschen
weichen	wich	gewichen
weisen	wies	gewiesen
²wenden*	wandte (wendete)	gewandt
werben (du wirbst, er wirbt; wirb!)	warb (würbe)	geworben
werden (du wirst, er wird; werde!)	wurde, *dichter.:* ward (würde)	geworden; *als Hilfsv.:* worden
werfen (du wirfst, er wirft; wirf!)	warf (würfe)	geworfen
¹wiegen	wog (wöge)	gewogen

Infinitive *Infinitiv*	Preterite *Präteritum*	Past Participle *2. Partizip*
winden	wand (wände)	gewunden
wissen (ich weiß, du weißt, er weiß)	wußte (wüßte)	gewußt
wollen (ich will, du willst, er will)	wollte	gewollt
wringen	wrang (wränge)	gewrungen
ziehen	zog (zöge)	gezogen
zwingen	zwang (zwänge)	gezwungen

Weights and Measures / Maße und Gewichte

Weight / Gewichte

1,000 milligrams (mg) *1 000 Milligramm (mg)*	= 1 gram (g) = *1 Gramm (g)*	= 15.43 grains
1,000 grams *1 000 Gramm*	= 1 kilogram (kg) = *1 Kilogramm (kg)*	= 2.205 pounds
1,000 kilograms *1 000 Kilogramm*	= 1 tonne (t) = *1 Tonne (t)*	= 19.684 hun- dredweight
	1 grain (gr.)	= 0.065 g
437½ grains	= 1 ounce (oz.)	= 28.35 g
16 ounces	= 1 pound (lb.)	= 0.454 kg
14 pounds	= 1 stone (st.)	= 6.35 kg
112 pounds	= 1 hundredweight	= 50.8 kg
20 hundredweight	= 1 ton (t.)	= 1,016.05 kg

Length / Längenmaße

10 millimetres (mm) *10 Millimeter (mm)*	= 1 centimetre (cm) = *1 Zentimeter (cm)*	= 0.394 inch
100 centimetres *100 Zentimeter*	= 1 metre (m) = *1 Meter (m)*	= 39.4 inches / 1.094 yards
1,000 metres *1 000 Meter*	= 1 kilometre (km) = *1 Kilometer (km)*	= 0.6214 mile ≈ ⅝ mile
	1 inch (in.)	= 25.4 mm
12 inches	= 1 foot (ft.)	= 30.48 cm
3 feet	= 1 yard (yd.)	= 0.914 m
220 yards	= 1 furlong	= 201.17 m
8 furlongs	= 1 mile (m.)	= 1.609 km
1,760 yards	= 1 mile	= 1.609 km

Square measure / Flächenmaße

100 square metres (sq. m)	= 1 are	
100 Quadratmeter (m²)	*= 1 Ar (a)*	= 0.025 acre
100 ares	= 1 hectare (ha)	
100 Ar	*= 1 Hektar (ha)*	= 2.471 acres
100 hectares	= 1 square kilometre (sq. km)	
100 Hektar	*= 1 Quadratkilometer (km²)*	= 0.386 square miles
	1 square inch	= 6.452 cm²
144 square inches	= 1 square foot	= 929.03 cm²
9 square feet	= 1 square yard	= 0.836 m²
4,840 square yards	= 1 acre	= 0.405 ha
640 acres	= 1 square mile	= 2.59 k² / 259 ha

Cubic measure / Raummaße

1 cubic centimetre (cc)		= 0.06 cubic inches
1 Kubikzentimeter (cm³)		
1,000,000 cubic centimetres	= 1 cubic metre (cu. m)	= 35.714 cubic feet /
1 000 000 Kubikzentimeter	*= 1 Kubikmeter (m³)*	1.307 cubic yards
	1 cubic inch	= 16.4 cm³
1,728 cubic inches	= 1 cubic foot	= 0.028 m³
27 cubic feet	= 1 cubic yard	= 0.764 m³

Capacity / Hohlmaße

10 millilitres (ml)	= 1 centilitre (cl)	
10 Milliliter (ml)	*= 1 Zentiliter (cl)*	
100 centilitres	= 1 litre (l)	= 1.76 pints (2.1 US pints) / 0.22 gallons (0.264 US gallons)
100 Zentiliter	*= 1 Liter (l)*	
4 gills	= 1 pint (pt.) (1.201 US pints)	= 0.568 l
2 pints	= 1 quart (qt.) (1.201 US quarts)	= 1.136 l
4 quarts	= 1 gallon (gal.) (1.201 US gallons)	= 4.546 l